to the House of the God of Jacob and He will teach us
n shall go forth the Law and the word of the lord from
lem

ENCYCLOPAEDIA JUDAICA

[redacted]

VOLUME 4

B

ENCYCLOPAEDIA JUDAICA

[redacted]

ENCYCLOPAEDIA JUDAICA JERUSALEM

Library of Congress Catalog Card Number: 72–90254

Second printing, 1973

Produced and printed in Jerusalem, Israel

A Clal Project

GLOSSARY

Asterisked terms have separate entries in the Encyclopaedia.

Actions Committee, early name of the Zionist General Council, the supreme institution of the World Zionist Organization in the interim between Congresses. The Zionist Executive's name was then the "Small Actions Committee."

***Adar,** twelfth month of the Jewish religious year, sixth of the civil, approximating to February-March.

***Aggadah,** name given to those sections of Talmud and Midrash containing homiletic expositions of the Bible, stories, legends, folklore, anecdotes, or maxims. In contradistinction to **halakhah*.

***Agunah,** woman unable to remarry according to Jewish law, because of desertion by her husband or inability to accept presumption of death.

***Aḥaronim,** later rabbinic authorities. In contradistinction to **rishonim* ("early ones").

Ahavah, liturgical poem inserted in the second benediction of the morning prayer *(*Ahavah Rabbah)* of the festivals and/or special Sabbaths.

Aktion (Ger.), operation involving the mass assembly, deportation, and murder of Jews by the Nazis during the *Holocaust.

***Aliyah,** (1) being called to Reading of the Law in synagogue; (2) immigration to Ereẓ Israel; (3) one of the waves of immigration to Ereẓ Israel from the early 1880s.

***Amidah,** main prayer recited at all services; also known as *Shemoneh Esreh* and *Tefillah*.

***Amora** (pl. **amoraim**), title given to the Jewish scholars in Ereẓ Israel and Babylonia in the third to sixth centuries who were responsible for the **Gemara*.

Aravah, the *willow; one of the *Four Species used on *Sukkot ("festival of Tabernacles") together with the **etrog, hadas,* and **lulav*.

***Arvit,** evening prayer.

Asarah be-Tevet, fast on the 10th of Tevet commemorating the commencement of the siege of Jerusalem by Nebuchadnezzar.

Asefat ha-Nivḥarim, representative assembly elected by Jews in Palestine during the period of the British Mandate (1920–48).

***Ashkenaz,** name applied generally in medieval rabbinical literature to Germany.

***Ashkenazi** (pl. **Ashkenazim**), German or West-, Central-, or East-European Jew(s), as contrasted with *Sephardi(m).

***Av,** fifth month of the Jewish religious year, eleventh of the civil, approximating to July-August.

***Av bet din,** vice-president of the supreme court *(bet din ha-gadol)* in Jerusalem during the Second Temple period; later, title given to communal rabbis as heads of the religious courts (see **bet din*).

***Badḥan,** jester, particularly at traditional Jewish weddings in Eastern Europe.

***Bakkashah** (Heb. "supplication"), type of petitionary prayer, mainly recited in the Sephardi rite on Rosh Ha-Shanah and the Day of Atonement.

Bar, "son of . . ."; frequently appearing in personal names.

***Baraita** (pl. **beraitot**), statement of **tanna* not found in *Mishnah.

***Bar mitzvah,** ceremony marking the initiation of a boy at the age of 13 into the Jewish religious community.

Ben, "son of . . ."; frequently appearing in personal names.

Berakhah (pl. **berakhot**), *benediction, blessing; formula of praise and thanksgiving.

***Bet din** (pl. **battei din**), rabbinic court of law.

***Bet ha-midrash,** school for higher rabbinic learning; often attached to or serving as a synagogue.

***Bilu,** first modern movement for pioneering and agricultural settlement in Ereẓ Israel, founded in 1882 at Kharkov, Russia.

***Bund,** Jewish socialist party founded in Vilna in 1897, supporting Jewish national rights; Yiddishist, and anti-Zionist.

Cohen (pl. **Cohanim**), see Kohen.

***Conservative Judaism,** trend in Judaism developed in the United States in the 20th century which, while opposing extreme changes in traditional observances, permits certain modifications of *halakhah* in response to the changing needs of the Jewish people.

***Consistory** (Fr. *consistoire*), governing body of a Jewish communal district in France and certain other countries.

***Converso(s),** term applied in Spain and Portugal to converted Jew(s), and sometimes more loosely to their descendants.

***Crypto-Jew,** term applied to a person who although observing outwardly Christianity (or some other religion) was at heart a Jew and maintained Jewish observances as far as possible (see Converso; Marrano; Neofiti; New Christian; Jadīd al-Islām).

***Dayyan,** member of rabbinic court.

Decisor, equivalent to the Hebrew *posek* (pl. **posekim*), the rabbi who gives the decision (*halakhah*) in Jewish law or practice.

***Devekut,** "devotion"; attachment or adhesion to God; communion with God.

***Diaspora,** Jews living in the "dispersion" outside Ereẓ Israel; area of Jewish settlement outside Ereẓ Israel.

Din, a law (both secular and religious), legal decision, or lawsuit.

Divan, diwan, collection of poems, especially in Hebrew, Arabic, or Persian.

Dunam, unit of land area (1,000 sq. m., c. 1/4 acre), used in Israel.

Einsatzgruppen, mobile units of Nazi S.S. and S.D.; in U.S.S.R. and Serbia, mobile killing units.

***Ein-Sof,** "without end"; "the infinite"; hidden, impersonal aspect of God; also used as a Divine Name.

***Elul,** sixth month of the Jewish religious calendar, 12th of the civil, precedes the High Holiday season in the fall.

Endloesung, see *Final Solution.

***Ereẓ Israel,** Land of Israel; Palestine.

***Eruv,** technical term for rabbinical provision permitting the alleviation of certain restrictions.

***Etrog,** citron; one of the *Four Species used on *Sukkot together with the **lulav, hadas,* and *aravah*.

Even ha-Ezer, see Shulḥan Arukh.

***Exilarch,** lay head of Jewish community in Babylonia (see also *resh galuta*), and elsewhere.

***Final Solution** (Ger. *Endloesung*), in Nazi terminology, the Nazi-planned mass murder and total annihilation of the Jews.

***Gabbai,** official of a Jewish congregation; originally a charity collector.

***Galut,** "exile"; the condition of the Jewish people in dispersion.
***Gaon** (pl. **geonim**), head of academy in post-talmudic period, especially in Babylonia.
Gaonate, office of *gaon.
***Gemara,** traditions, discussions, and rulings of the **amoraim*, commenting on and supplementing the *Mishnah, and forming part of the Babylonian and Palestinian Talmuds (see Talmud).
***Gematria,** interpretation of Hebrew word according to the numerical value of its letters.
General Government, territory in Poland administered by a German civilian governor–general with headquarters in Cracow after the German occupation in World War II.
***Genizah,** depository for sacred books. The best known was discovered in the synagogue of Fostat (old Cairo).
Get, bill of *divorce.
***Ge'ullah,** hymn inserted after the **Shema* into the benediction of the morning prayer of the festivals and special Sabbaths.
***Gilgul,** metempsychosis; transmigration of souls.
***Golem,** automaton, especially in human form, created by magical means and endowed with life.
***Ḥabad,** initials of *ḥokhmah, binah, da'at*: "wisdom, understanding, knowledge"; ḥasidic movement founded in Belorussia by *Shneur Zalman of Lyady.
Hadas, *myrtle; one of the *Four Species used on Sukkot together with the **etrog*, **lulav*, and *aravah*.
***Haftarah** (pl. **haftarot**), designation of the portion from the prophetical books of the Bible recited after the synagogue reading from the Pentateuch on Sabbaths and holidays.
***Haganah,** clandestine Jewish organization for armed self-defense in Ereẓ Israel under the British Mandate, which eventually evolved into a people's militia and became the basis for the Israel army.
***Haggadah,** ritual recited in the home on *Passover eve at *seder* table.
Haham, title of chief rabbi of the Spanish and Portuguese congregations in London, England.
***Ḥakham,** title of rabbi of *Sephardi congregation.
***Ḥakham bashi,** title in the 15th century and modern times of the chief rabbi in the Ottoman Empire, residing in Constantinople (Istanbul), also applied to principal rabbis in provincial towns.
Hakhsharah ("preparation"), organized training in the Diaspora of pioneers for agricultural settlement in Ereẓ Israel.
***Halakhah** (pl. **halakhot**), an accepted decision in rabbinic law. Also refers to those parts of the *Talmud concerned with legal matters. In contradistinction to **aggadah*.
Ḥaliẓah, biblically prescribed ceremony (Deut. 25:9–10) performed when a man refuses to marry his brother's childless widow, enabling her to remarry.
***Hallel,** term referring to Psalms 113–18 in liturgical use.
***Ḥalukkah,** system of financing the maintenance of Jewish communities in the holy cities of Ereẓ Israel by collections made abroad, mainly in the pre-Zionist era (see *kolel*).
Ḥalutz (pl. **ḥalutzim**), pioneer, especially in agriculture, in Ereẓ Israel.
Ḥalutziyyut, pioneering.
***Ḥanukkah,** eight-day celebration commemorating the victory of *Judah Maccabee over the Syrian king *Antiochus Epiphanes and the subsequent rededication of the Temple.
Ḥasid, adherent of *Ḥasidism.
***Ḥasidei Ashkenaz,** medieval pietist movement among the Jews of Germany.
***Ḥasidism,** (1) religious revivalist movement of popular mysticism among Jews of Germany in the Middle Ages; (2) religious movement founded by *Israel ben Eliezer Ba'al Shem Tov in the first half of the 18th century.
***Haskalah,** "Enlightenment"; movement for spreading modern European culture among Jews c. 1750–1880. See *maskil*.
***Havdalah,** ceremony marking the end of Sabbath or festival.
***Ḥazzan,** precentor who intones the liturgy and leads the prayers in synagogue; in earlier times a synagogue official.
***Ḥeder** (lit. "room"), school for teaching children Jewish religious observance.
Heikhalot, "palaces"; tradition in Jewish mysticism centering on mystical journeys through the heavenly spheres and palaces to the Divine Chariot (see Merkabah).
***Ḥerem,** excommunication, imposed by rabbinical authorities for purposes of religious and/or communal discipline; originally, in biblical times, that which is separated from common use either because it was an abomination or because it was consecrated to God.
Ḥeshvan, see Marḥeshvan.
***Ḥevra kaddisha,** title applied to charitable confraternity (**ḥevrah*), now generally limited to associations for burial of the dead.
***Ḥibbat Zion,** see Ḥovevei Zion.
***Histadrut** (abbr. for Heb. **Ha-Histadrut ha-Kelalit shel ha-Ovedim ha-Ivriyyim be-Ereẓ Israel**). Ereẓ Israel Jewish Labor Federation, founded in 1920; subsequently renamed Histadrut ha-Ovedim be-Ereẓ Israel.
***Holocaust,** the organized mass persecution and annihilation of European Jewry by the Nazis (1933–1945).
***Hoshana Rabba,** the seventh day of *Sukkot on which special observances are held.
Ḥoshen Mishpat, see Shulḥan Arukh.
Ḥovevei Zion, federation of *Ḥibbat Zion, early (pre-*Herzl) Zionist movement in Russia.
Illui, outstanding scholar or genius, especially a young prodigy in talmudic learning.
***Iyyar,** second month of the Jewish religious year, eighth of the civil, approximating to April-May.
I.Ẓ.L. (initials of Heb. ***Irgun Ẓeva'i Le'ummi;** "National Military Organization"), underground Jewish organization in Ereẓ Israel founded in 1931, which engaged from 1937 in retaliatory acts against Arab attacks and later against the British mandatory authorities.
***Jadīd al-Islām** (Ar.), a person practicing the Jewish religion in secret although outwardly observing Islam.
***Jewish Legion,** Jewish units in British army during World War I.
***Jihād** (Ar.), in Muslim religious law, holy war waged against infidels.
***Judenrat** (Ger. "Jewish council"), council set up in Jewish communities and ghettos under the Nazis to execute their instructions.
***Judenrein** (Ger. "clean of Jews"), in Nazi terminology the condition of a locality from which all Jews had been eliminated.
***Kabbalah,** the Jewish mystical tradition:
Kabbalah iyyunit, speculative Kabbalah;
Kabbalah ma'asit, practical Kabbalah;
Kabbalah nevu'it, prophetic Kabbalah.
Kabbalist, student of Kabbalah.
***Kaddish,** liturgical doxology.
Kahal, Jewish congregation; among Ashkenazim, *kehillah*.
***Kalām** (Ar.), science of Muslim theology; adherents of the Kalām are called *mutakallimūn*.
***Karaite,** member of a Jewish sect originating in the eighth century which rejected rabbinic (*Rabbanite) Judaism and claimed to accept only Scripture as authoritative.
***Kasher,** ritually permissible food.
Kashrut, Jewish *dietary laws.
***Kavvanah,** "intention"; term denoting the spiritual concentration accompanying prayer and the performance of ritual or of a commandment.
***Kedushah,** main addition to the third blessing in the reader's repetition of the *Amidah* in which the public responds to the precentor's introduction.
Kefar, village; first part of name of many settlements in Israel.
Kehillah, congregation; see *kahal*.
Kelippah (pl. **kelippot**), "husk(s)"; mystical term denoting force(s) of evil.
***Keneset Yisrael,** comprehensive communal organization of the Jews in Palestine during the British Mandate.
Keri, variants in the masoretic (*masorah) text of the Bible between the spelling (*ketiv*) and its pronunciation (*keri*).
***Kerovah** (collective plural (corrupted) from **kerovez**), poem(s) incorporated into the **Amidah*.
Ketiv, see *keri*.
***Ketubbah,** marriage contract, stipulating husband's obligations to wife.
Kevuẓah, small commune of pioneers constituting an agricultural settlement in Ereẓ Israel (evolved later into *kibbutz).
***Kibbutz** (pl. **kibbutzim**), larger-size commune constituting a settlement in Ereẓ Israel based mainly on agriculture but engaging also in industry.
***Kiddush,** prayer of sanctification, recited over wine or bread on eve of Sabbaths and festivals.
***Kiddush ha-Shem,** term connoting martyrdom or act of strict integrity in support of Judaic principles.

***Kinah** (pl. **kinot**), lamentation dirge(s) for the Ninth of Av and other fast days.

***Kislev,** ninth month of the Jewish religious year, third of the civil, approximating to November-December.

Klaus, name given in Central and Eastern Europe to an institution, usually with synagogue attached, where *Talmud was studied perpetually by adults; applied by Ḥasidim to their synagogue (*"kloyz"*).

***Knesset,** parliament of the State of Israel.

K(c)ohen (pl. **K(c)ohanim**), Jew(s) of priestly (Aaronide) descent.

***Kolel,** (1) community in Ereẓ Israel of persons from a particular country or locality, often supported by their fellow countrymen in the Diaspora; (2) institution for higher Torah study.

Kosher, see *kasher*.

***Kristallnacht** (Ger. "crystal night," meaning "night of broken glass"), organized destruction of synagogues, Jewish houses, and shops, accompanied by mass arrests of Jews, which took place in Germany and Austria under the Nazis on the night of Nov. 9–10, 1938.

***Lag ba-Omer,** 33rd (Heb. **lag**) day of the **Omer* period falling on the 18th of *Iyyar; a semi-holiday.

Leḥi (abbr. for Heb. ***Loḥamei Ḥerut Israel,** "Fighters for the Freedom of Israel"), radically anti-British armed underground organization in Palestine, founded in 1940 by dissidents from *I.Ẓ.L.

Levir, husband's brother.

***Levirate marriage** (Heb. *yibbum*), marriage of childless widow *(yevamah)* by brother *(yavam)* of the deceased husband (in accordance with Deut. 25:5); release from such an obligation is effected through *ḥaliẓah*.

LḤY, see Leḥi.

***Lulav,** palm branch; one of the *Four Species used on *Sukkot together with the **etrog, hadas,* and *aravah*.

***Ma'aravot,** hymns inserted into the evening prayer of the three festivals, Passover, Shavuot, and Sukkot.

Ma'ariv, evening prayer; also called **arvit*.

***Ma'barah,** transition camp; temporary settlement for newcomers in Israel during the period of mass immigration following 1948.

***Maftir,** reader of the concluding portion of the Pentateuchal section on Sabbaths and holidays in synagogue; reader of the portion of the prophetical books of the Bible (**haftarah*).

***Maggid,** popular preacher.

***Maḥzor** (pl. **maḥzorim**), festival prayer book.

***Mamzer,** bastard; according to Jewish law, the offspring of an incestuous relationship.

***Mandate, Palestine,** responsibility for the administration of Palestine conferred on Britain by the League of Nations in 1922; mandatory government: the British administration of Palestine.

***Maqāma** (Ar., pl. **maqamāt**), poetic form (rhymed prose) which, in its classical arrangement, has rigid rules of form and content.

***Marḥeshvan,** popularly called Ḥeshvan; eighth month of the Jewish religious year, second of the civil, approximating to October-November.

***Marrano(s),** descendant(s) of Jew(s) in Spain and Portugal whose ancestors had been converted to Christianity under pressure but who secretly observed Jewish rituals.

Maskil (pl. **maskilim**), adherent of *Haskalah ("Enlightenment") movement.

***Masorah,** body of traditions regarding the correct spelling, writing, and reading of the Hebrew Bible.

Masorete, scholar of the masoretic tradition.

Masoretic, in accordance with the masorah.

Meliẓah, in Middle Ages, elegant style; modern usage, florid style using biblical or talmudic phraseology.

Mellah, *Jewish quarter in North African towns.

***Menorah,** candelabrum; seven-branched oil lamp used in the Tabernacle and Temple; also eight-branched candelabrum used on *Ḥanukkah.

Me'orah, hymn inserted into the first benediction of the morning prayer (*Yoẓer ha-Me'orot*).

***Merkabah,** *merkavah,* "chariot"; mystical discipline associated with Ezekiel's vision of the Divine Throne-Chariot (Ezek. 1).

Meshullaḥ, emissary sent to conduct propaganda or raise funds for rabbinical academies or charitable institutions.

***Mezuzah** (pl. **mezuzot**), parchment scroll with selected Torah verses placed in container and affixed to gates and doorposts of houses occupied by Jews.

***Midrash,** method of interpreting Scripture to elucidate legal points (*Midrash Halakhah*) or to bring out lessons by stories or homiletics (*Midrash Aggadah*). Also the name for a collection of such rabbinic interpretations.

***Mikveh,** ritual bath.

***Minhag** (pl. **minhagim**), ritual custom(s); synagogal rite(s); especially of a specific sector of Jewry.

***Minḥah,** afternoon prayer; originally meal offering in Temple.

***Minyan,** group of ten male adult Jews, the minimum required for communal prayer.

***Mishnah,** earliest codification of Jewish Oral Law.

Mishnah (pl. mishnayot), subdivision of tractates of the Mishnah.

Mitnagged (pl. ***Mitnaggedim**), originally, opponents of *Ḥasidism in Eastern Europe.

***Mitzvah,** biblical or rabbinic injunction; applied also to good or charitable deeds.

Mohel, official performing circumcisions.

***Moshav,** smallholders' cooperative agricultural settlement in Israel, see moshav ovedim.

Moshavah, earliest type of Jewish village in modern Ereẓ Israel in which farming is conducted on individual farms mostly on privately owned land.

Moshav ovedim ("workers' moshav"), agricultural village in Israel whose inhabitants possess individual homes and holdings but cooperate in the purchase of equipment, sale of produce, mutual aid, etc.

***Moshav shittufi** ("collective moshav"), agricultural village in Israel whose members possess individual homesteads but where the agriculture and economy are conducted as a collective unit.

Mostegab (Ar.), poem with biblical verse at beginning of each stanza.

***Muqaddam** (Ar., pl. **muqaddamūn**), "leader," "head of the community."

***Musaf,** additional service on Sabbath and festivals; originally the additional sacrifice offered in the Temple.

Musar, traditional ethical literature.

***Musar movement,** ethical movement developing in the latter part of the 19th century among Orthodox Jewish groups in Lithuania; founded by R. Israel *Lipkin (Salanter).

***Nagid** (pl. **negidim**), title applied in Muslim (and some Christian) countries in the Middle Ages to a leader recognized by the state as head of the Jewish community.

Nakdan (pl. **nakdanim**), "punctuator"; scholar of the 9th to 14th centuries who provided biblical manuscripts with masoretic apparatus, vowels, and accents.

***Nasi** (pl. **nesi'im**), talmudic term for president of the Sanhedrin, who was also the spiritual head and, later, political representative of the Jewish people; from second century a descendant of Hillel recognized by the Roman authorities as patriarch of the Jews. Now applied to the president of the State of Israel.

***Negev,** the southern, mostly arid, area of Israel.

***Ne'ilah,** concluding service on the *Day of Atonement.

Neofiti, term applied in southern Italy to converts to Christianity from Judaism and their descendants who were suspected of maintaining secret allegiance to Judaism.

***Neology; Neolog; Neologism,** trend of *Reform Judaism in Hungary forming separate congregations after 1868.

***Nevelah** (lit. "carcass"), meat forbidden by the *dietary laws on account of the absence of, or defect in, the act of **sheḥitah* (ritual slaughter).

***New Christians,** term applied especially in Spain and Portugal to converts from Judaism (and from Islam) and their descendants; "Half New Christian" designated a person one of whose parents was of full Jewish blood.

***Niddah** ("menstruous woman"), woman during the period of menstruation.

***Nisan,** first month of the Jewish religious year, seventh of the civil, approximating to March-April.

Niẓoẓot, "sparks"; mystical term for sparks of the holy light imprisoned in all matter.

Nosaḥ (nusaḥ), "version"; (1) textual variant; (2) term applied to distinguish the various prayer rites, e.g., *nosaḥ Ashkenaz;* (3) the accepted tradition of synagogue melody.

***Notarikon,** method of abbreviating Hebrew words or phrases by acronym.

Novella(e) (Heb. **ḥiddush(im)*), commentary on talmudic and later rabbinic subjects that derives new facts or principles from the implications of the text.

***Nuremberg Laws,** Nazi laws excluding Jews from German citizenship, and imposing other restrictions.

Ofan, hymns inserted into a passage of the morning prayer.

***Omer,** first sheaf cut during the barley harvest, offered in the Temple on the second day of Passover.

Omer, Counting of (Heb. *Sefirat ha-Omer*), 49 days counted from the day on which the *omer* was first offered in the Temple (according to the rabbis the 16th of Nisan, i.e., the second day of Passover) until the festival of Shavuot; now a period of semi-mourning.

Oraḥ Ḥayyim, see Shulḥan Arukh.

***Orthodoxy** (Orthodox Judaism), modern term for the strictly traditional sector of Jewry.

***Pale of Settlement,** 25 provinces of czarist Russia where Jews were permitted permanent residence.

***Palmaḥ** (abbr. for Heb. *peluggot maḥaẓ;* "shock companies"), striking arm of the *Haganah.

***Pardes,** medieval biblical exegesis giving the literal, allegorical, homiletical, and esoteric interpretations.

***Parnas,** chief synagogue functionary, originally vested with both religious and administrative functions; subsequently an elected lay leader.

Partition plan(s), proposals for dividing Ereẓ Israel into autonomous areas.

Paytan, composer of **piyyut* (liturgical poetry).

***Peel Commission,** British Royal Commission appointed by the British government in 1936 to inquire into the Palestine problem and make recommendations for its solution.

Pesaḥ, *Passover.

***Pilpul,** in talmudic and rabbinic literature, a sharp dialectic used particularly by talmudists in Poland from the 16th century.

***Pinkas,** community register or minute-book.

***Piyyut** (pl. **piyyutim**), Hebrew liturgical poetry.

***Pizmon,** poem with refrain.

Posek (pl. ***posekim**), decisor; codifier or rabbinic scholar who pronounces decisions in disputes and on questions of Jewish law.

***Prosbul,** legal method of overcoming the cancelation of debts with the advent of the *sabbatical year.

***Purim,** festival held on Adar 14 or 15 in commemoration of the delivery of the Jews of Persia in the time of *Esther.

Rabban, honorific title higher than that of rabbi, applied to heads of the *Sanhedrin in mishnaic times.

***Rabbanite,** adherent of rabbinic Judaism. In contradistinction to *Karaite.

Reb, rebbe, Yiddish form for rabbi, applied generally to a teacher or ḥasidic rabbi.

***Reconstructionism,** trend in Jewish thought originating in the United States.

***Reform Judaism,** trend in Judaism advocating modification of *Orthodoxy in conformity with the exigencies of contemporary life and thought.

Resh galuta, lay head of Babylonian Jewry (see exilarch).

Responsum (pl. ***responsa**), written opinion (*teshuvah*) given to question (*she'elah*) on aspects of Jewish law by qualified authorities; pl. collection of such queries and opinions in book form *(she'elot u-teshuvot)*.

***Rishonim,** older rabbinical authorities. Distinguished from later authorities (**aḥaronim*).

***Rishon le-Zion,** title given to Sephardi chief rabbi of Ereẓ Israel.

***Rosh Ha-Shanah,** two-day holiday (one day in biblical and early mishnaic times) at the beginning of the month of *Tishri (September-October), traditionally the New Year.

Rosh Ḥodesh, *New Moon, marking the beginning of the Hebrew month.

Rosh Yeshivah, see *Yeshivah.

***R.S.H.A.** (initials of Ger. *Reichssicherheitshauptamt*: "Reich Security Main Office"), the central security department of the German Reich, formed in 1939, and combining the security police (Gestapo and Kripo) and the S.D.

***Sanhedrin,** the assembly of ordained scholars which functioned both as a supreme court and as a legislature before 70 C.E. In modern times the name was given to the body of representative Jews convoked by Napoleon in 1807.

***Savora** (pl. **savoraim**), name given to the Babylonian scholars of the period between the **amoraim* and the **geonim*, approximately 500–700 C.E.

S.D. (initials of Ger. *Sicherheitsdienst*: "security service"), security service of the *S.S. formed in 1932 as the sole intelligence organization of the Nazi party.

Seder, ceremony observed in the Jewish home on the first night of Passover (outside Ereẓ Israel first two nights), when the **Haggadah* is recited.

***Sefer Torah,** manuscript scroll of the Pentateuch for public reading in synagogue.

***Sefirot, the ten,** the ten "Numbers"; mystical term denoting the ten spheres or emanations through which the Divine manifests itself; elements of the world; dimensions, primordial numbers.

Selektion (Ger.), (1) in ghettos and other Jewish settlements, the drawing up by Nazis of lists of deportees; (2) separation of incoming victims to concentration camps into two categories—those destined for immediate killing and those to be sent for forced labor.

Seliḥah (pl. ***seliḥot**), penitential prayer.

***Semikhah,** ordination conferring the title "rabbi" and permission to give decisions in matters of ritual and law.

Sephardi (pl. ***Sephardim**), Jew(s) of Spain and Portugal and their descendants, wherever resident, as contrasted with *Ashkenazi(m).

Shabbatean, adherent of the pseudo-messiah *Shabbetai Ẓevi (17th century).

Shaddai, name of God found frequently in the Bible and commonly translated "Almighty."

***Shaḥarit,** morning service.

Shali'aḥ (pl. **sheliḥim**), in Jewish law, messenger, agent; in modern times, an emissary from Ereẓ Israel to Jewish communities or organizations abroad for the purpose of fund-raising, organizing pioneer immigrants, education, etc.

Shalmonit, poetic meter introduced by the liturgical poet *Solomon ha-Bavli.

***Shammash,** synagogue beadle.

***Shavuot,** Pentecost; Festival of Weeks; second of the three annual pilgrim festivals, commemorating the receiving of the Torah at Mt. Sinai.

***Sheḥitah,** ritual slaughtering of animals.

***Shekhinah,** Divine Presence.

Shelishit, poem with three-line stanzas.

***Sheluḥei Erez Israel** (or **shadarim**), emissaries from Ereẓ Israel.

***Shema** ([Yisrael]; "hear . . . [O Israel]," Deut. 6:4), Judaism's confession of faith, proclaiming the absolute unity of God.

Shemini Aẓeret, final festal day (in the Diaspora, final two days) at the conclusion of *Sukkot.

Shemittah, *Sabbatical year.

Sheniyyah, poem with two-line stanzas.

***Shephelah,** southern part of the coastal plain of Ereẓ Israel.

***Shevat,** eleventh month of the Jewish religious year, fifth of the civil, approximating to January-February.

***Shi'ur Komah,** Hebrew mystical work (c. eighth century) containing a physical description of God's dimensions; term denoting enormous spacial measurement used in speculations concerning the body of the **Shekhinah*.

Shivah, the "seven days" of *mourning following burial of a relative.

***Shofar,** horn of the ram (or any other ritually clean animal excepting the cow) sounded for the memorial blowing on *Rosh Ha-Shanah, and other occasions.

Shoḥet, person qualified to perform **sheḥitah*.

Shomer, *Ha-Shomer, organization of Jewish workers in Ereẓ Israel founded in 1909 to defend Jewish settlements.

***Shtadlan,** Jewish representative or negotiator with access to dignitaries of state, active at royal courts, etc.

***Shtetl,** Jewish small-town community in Eastern Europe.

***Shulḥan Arukh,** Joseph *Caro's code of Jewish law in four parts:
Oraḥ Ḥayyim, laws relating to prayers, Sabbath, festivals, and fasts;
Yoreh De'ah, dietary laws, etc;
Even ha-Ezer, laws dealing with women, marriage, etc;
Ḥoshen Mishpat, civil, criminal law, court procedure, etc.

Siddur, among Ashkenazim, the volume containing the daily prayers (in distinction to the **maḥzor* containing those for the festivals).

***Simḥat Torah,** holiday marking the completion in the synagogue of the annual cycle of reading the Pentateuch; in Ereẓ Israel observed on Shemini Aẓeret (outside Ereẓ Israel on the following day).

***Sinai Campaign,** brief campaign in October-November 1956 when Israel army reacted to Egyptian terrorist attacks and blockade by occupying the Sinai peninsula.

Sitra aḥra, "the other side" (of God); left side; the demoniac and satanic powers.

***Sivan,** third month of the Jewish religious year, ninth of the civil, approximating to May-June.

***Six-Day War,** rapid war in June 1967 when Israel reacted to Arab threats and blockade by defeating the Egyptian, Jordanian, and Syrian armies.

***S.S.** (initials of Ger. *Schutzstaffel*: "protection detachment"), Nazi formation established in 1925 which later became the "elite" organization of the Nazi Party and carried out central tasks in the "Final Solution."

***Status quo ante** community, community in Hungary retaining the status it had held before the convention of the General Jewish Congress there in 1868 and the resultant split in Hungarian Jewry.

***Sukkah,** booth or tabernacle erected for *Sukkot when, for seven days, religious Jews "dwell" or at least eat in the *sukkah* (Lev. 23:42).

***Sukkot,** festival of Tabernacles; last of the three pilgrim festivals, beginning on the 15th of Tishri.

Sūra (Ar.), chapter of the Koran.

Ta'anit Esther (Fast of *Esther), fast on the 13th of Adar, the day preceding Purim.

Takkanah (pl. ***takkanot**), regulation supplementing the law of the Torah; regulations governing the internal life of communities and congregations.

***Tallit (gadol),** four-cornered prayer shawl with fringes *(ẓiẓit)* at each corner.

***Tallit katan,** garment with fringes *(ẓiẓit)* appended, worn by observant male Jews under their outer garments.

***Talmud,** "teaching"; compendium of discussions on the Mishnah by generations of scholars and jurists in many academies over a period of several centuries. The Jerusalem (or Palestinian) Talmud mainly contains the discussions of the Palestinian sages. The Babylonian Talmud incorporates the parallel discussion in the Babylonian academies.

Talmud torah, term generally applied to Jewish religious (and ultimately to talmudic) study; also to traditional Jewish religious public schools.

***Tammuz,** fourth month of the Jewish religious year, tenth of the civil, approximating to June-July.

Tanna (pl. ***tannaim**), rabbinic teacher of mishnaic period.

***Targum,** Aramaic translation of the Bible.

***Tefillin,** phylacteries, small leather cases containing passages from Scripture and affixed on the forehead and arm by male Jews during the recital of morning prayers.

Tell (Ar. "mound," "hillock"), ancient mound in the Middle East composed of remains of successive settlements.

***Terefah,** food that is not **kasher*, owing to a defect in the animal.

***Territorialism,** 20th century movement supporting the creation of an autonomous territory for Jewish mass-settlement outside Ereẓ Israel.

***Tevet,** tenth month of the Jewish religious year, fourth of the civil, approximating to December-January.

Tikkun ("restitution," "reintegration"), (1) order of service for certain occasions, mostly recited at night; (2) mystical term denoting restoration of the right order and true unity after the spiritual "catastrophe" which occurred in the cosmos.

Tishah be-Av, Ninth of *Av, fast day commemorating the destruction of the First and Second Temples.

***Tishri,** seventh month of the Jewish religious year, first of the civil, approximating to September-October.

Tokheḥah, reproof sections of the Pentateuch (Lev. 26 and Deut. 28); poem of reproof.

***Torah,** Pentateuch or the Pentateuchal scroll for reading in synagogue; entire body of traditional Jewish teaching and literature.

Tosafist, talmudic glossator, mainly French (12th–14th centuries), bringing additions to the commentary by *Rashi.

***Tosafot,** glosses supplied by tosafist.

***Tosefta,** a collection of teachings and traditions of the *tannaim*, closely related to the Mishnah.

Tradent, person who hands down a talmudic statement in the name of his teacher or other earlier authority.

***Tu bi-Shevat,** the 15th day of Shevat, the New Year for Trees; date marking a dividing line for fruit tithing; in modern Israel celebrated as arbor day.

***Uganda Scheme,** plan suggested by the British government in 1903 to establish an autonomous Jewish settlement area in East Africa.

***Va'ad Le'ummi,** national council of the Jewish community in Ereẓ Israel during the period of the British *Mandate.

***Wannsee Conference,** Nazi conference held on Jan. 20, 1942, at which the planned annihilation of European Jewry was endorsed.

Waqf (Ar.), (1) a Muslim charitable pious foundation; (2) state lands and other property passed to the Muslim community for public welfare.

***War of Independence,** war of 1947–49 when the Jews of Israel fought off Arab invading armies and ensured the establishment of the new State.

***White Paper(s),** report(s) issued by British government, frequently statements of policy, as issued in connection with Palestine during the *Mandate period.

***Wissenschaft des Judentums** (Ger. "Science of Judaism"), movement in Europe beginning in the 19th century for scientific study of Jewish history, religion, and literature.

***Yad Vashem,** Israel official authority for commemorating the *Holocaust in the Nazi era and Jewish resistance and heroism at that time.

Yeshivah (pl. ***yeshivot**), Jewish traditional academy devoted primarily to study of rabbinic literature; *rosh yeshivah*, head of the yeshivah.

YHWH, the letters of the holy name of God, the Tetragrammaton.

Yibbum, see levirate marriage.

Yiḥud, "union"; mystical term for intention which causes the union of God with the **Shekhinah*.

Yishuv, settlement; more specifically, the Jewish community of Ereẓ Israel in the pre-State period. The pre-Zionist community is generally designated the "old yishuv" and the community evolving from 1880, the "new yishuv."

Yom Kippur, Yom ha-Kippurim, *Day of Atonement, solemn fast day observed on the 10th of Tishri.

Yoreh De'ah, see Shulḥan Arukh.

Yoẓer, hymns inserted in the first benediction *(Yoẓer Or)* of the morning **Shema*.

***Ẓaddik,** person outstanding for his faith and piety; especially a ḥasidic rabbi or leader.

Ẓimẓum, "contraction"; mystical term denoting the process whereby God withdraws or contracts within Himself so leaving a primordial vacuum in which creation can take place; primordial exile or self-limitation of God.

***Zionist Commission (1918),** commission appointed in 1918 by the British government to advise the British military authorities in Palestine on the implementation of the *Balfour Declaration.

Ẓiyyonei Zion, the organized opposition to Herzl in connection with the *Uganda Scheme.

***Ẓiẓit,** fringes attached to the **tallit* and **tallit katan*.

***Zohar,** mystical commentary on the Pentateuch; main textbook of *Kabbalah.

Zulat, hymn inserted after the **Shema* in the morning service.

The illuminated letter "B" at the beginning of the Psalms in *Extracts from Gregory the Great* shows King David playing his harp and the young David killing Goliath. N. France, 12th century. Douai, Bibliothèque Municipale, ms. 315A, vol. I, fol. 5.

BAALAH (Heb. בַּעֲלָה), name of several biblical localities, evidently associated with the worship of Baal. (1) Mount Baalah is mentioned as one of the demarcation points on the northwestern boundary of the territory of Judah, between Shikkeron and Jabneel in the vicinity of Ekron (Josh. 15:11). Its location is dependent on the identification of *Ekron, but the prevailing opinion is the ridge of Mughār, near Wadi Qaṭra. (2) A city of Baalah is listed in the Negev district of Judah (Josh. 15:29). It is also among the settlements of Simeon as Balah (Josh. 19:3) or Bilhah (I Chron. 4:29). Its identification is unknown. (3) Baalah is mentioned as another name for *Kiriath-Jearim (Josh. 15:9–10); in I Chronicles 13:6 it is called Baalath (Heb. version). (4) A city of Baalath appears in the list of Danite settlements (Josh. 19:44) after Eltekeh and Gibbethon; this is perhaps identical with the Baalath fortified by Solomon (I Kings 9:18). It has been identified with the mound Mughār or of Qatra; in this case it would be identical with (1).

Bibliography: (1) Kallai, in: BIES, 17 (1952), 63; Aharoni, in: PEQ, 90 (1958), 28–30; Mazar, in: IEJ, 10 (1960), 70; (2) Abel, Geog, 2 (1938), 258; (3) Mazar, in: *Sefer Dinaburg* (1949), 317; EM, s.v.; Aharoni, Land, index.

[M.A.-Y.]

BAAL-BERITH (Heb. בַּעַל בְּרִית; "Lord of Covenant"), the name of the deity worshiped in the earliest Israelite period at the Temple of Shechem (Judg. 9:4). That temple was destroyed in the 12th century B.C.E. by *Abimelech, the half-Shechemite son of the great judge Gideon (Jerubbaal), after his suppression of a counterrevolt. Abimelech himself had come to power as "king" with the aid of funds from the Baal-Berith temple. As Abimelech's revenge moved apace, the terrified populace sought refuge in the "stronghold of El-Berith" (9:46), where they died en masse. The polemic of the narrative is directed against Abimelech and the conspirators who had profaned the great Shechem temple; it was never again rebuilt, except as a granary, as archaeological work has shown. Critics have suggested that the narrative of Abimelech seems to be an old pre-Deuteronomic account later inserted into the historical work because it explicated a brief Deuteronomic reference to an early particularist tendency in 8:33–35. In that place it is asserted that Israel's whoring after the Baalim consisted of making Baal-Berith their god and forgetting YHWH when they betrayed the family of YHWH's charismatic deliverer. In later circles the original significance of the "house of Baal-Berith" had long been lost, and the element "baal" in such a combination could only smack of the repudiated fertility cult. Something of its earliest significance can be glimpsed, however, in patriarchal stories connecting Abraham, Jacob, and Joseph with the site in various ways and in the archaeology of Shechem. The Baal-Berith temple was preceded on the same site by a Middle Bronze Age fortress-temple, which in turn perpetuated a piece of ground considered holy since the first half of the 18th century B.C.E. Genesis 34:2 personifies Shechem as one of the sons of Hamor ("ass"), reminiscent of Amorite treaty terminology at Mari, where "killing an ass" is a technical term for concluding a covenant. That Joshua-Judges contains no developed conquest tradition for the Shechem area is largely due, according to some scholars, to the influence of the Baal-Berith sanctuary (Josh. 24). According to tradition, such a situation had been anticipated by the strategists (Deut. 27; Josh. 8:30–35).

The Hebrew term Baal-Berit is also applied to the father of the child at a *circumcision *(berit)* ceremony, and in modern Hebrew the term means ally.

Bibliography: G. E. Wright, *Shechem: Biography of a Biblical City* (1965), 80–138. [R.G.B.]

BAAL-GAD (Heb. בַּעַל גָּד), biblical locality below Mount Hermon that was apparently sacred to *Gad, the god of fortune. Baal-Gad is described as the northernmost point conquered by Joshua (Josh. 11:17; 12:7) and, accordingly, the "land that yet remaineth" (i.e., that the tribes did not conquer), extends ". . . from Baal-Gad under Mount Hermon unto the entrance of Hamath" (Josh. 13:5) or, as in a parallel passage " . . . from Mount Baal-Hermon unto the entrance of Hamath" (Judg. 3:3). The exact location of Baal-Gad is not known, but the sources clearly indicate that it must be situated in the southern part of the Lebanon Valley, at the foot of Mount Hermon, not far from Dan. It has been proposed to identify it with Ḥaṣbayyā on the Ḥasbani River.

Bibliography: Maisler (Mazar), in: BJPES, 12 (1946), 91ff.; Abel, Geog, 2 (1938), 258ff.; Aharoni, Land, index. [Yo.A.]

BA'AL HA-BAYIT (Heb. בַּעַל הַבַּיִת, pl. *Ba'alei Battim*, "Head of the household"; in Yid., pronounced *"Balebos"*), head of a family. The term is often also associated with the notion of wealth and is used to describe a man of wealth and secure economic position, e.g., a landlord. The Yiddish adjective *balebatish*, in the sense of bourgeois, is derived from this term. *Ba'al ha-bayit* was also applied to married and taxpaying members of the congregation, as opposed to **bahur* ("young man"). The feminine form is *ba'alat bayit*, in Yiddish *baleboste*, denoting a housewife, often in the sense of a good housekeeper. [Ed.]

Initial letter *bet* showing the *ba'al ha-bayit* (master of the house) presiding at the *seder*. Woodcut from an Amsterdam *Haggadah*, 1712. Jerusalem, J.N.U.L.

BAAL-HAZOR (Heb. בַּעַל חָצוֹר), biblical locality "which is beside Ephraim" (II Sam. 13:23; a Greek version reads Tophraim, i.e., Ophrah?) where *Absalom had *Amnon killed to avenge his sister Tamar at the feast of sheepshearing. It may be identical with the *Hazor mentioned in the territory of Benjamin in the post-Exilic period (Neh. 11:33). The identification of Baal-Hazor with the highest point in the central range of Mount Ephraim, Jebel al-ʿAṣūr, a mountain 3,293 ft. (1,003 m.) high, north of Beth-El and near Ophrah (al-Ṭayba), has been strengthened by the mention of Ramath-Hazor as a high observation point in the *Genesis Apocryphon* found among the Dead Sea Scrolls. Baal-Hazor is possibly the "mountain of Azor," a proposed emendation of Azotus, which is found in I Maccabees 9:15 in the account of the battle of Eleasa, but the version is doubtful.

Bibliography: EM, s.v.; N. Avigad and Y. Yadin, *Genesis Apocryphon* (1956), 28; Alt, in: PJB, 24 (1928), 12ff.; 25 (1929), 11ff.; Abel, in: RB, 23, p. 386–7. [M.A.-Y.]

BAALIS (Heb. בַּעֲלִיס), king of Ammon during the first half of the sixth century B.C.E. The name appears to be composed of the theophoric root "Baal" and a suffix of unclear meaning; it is ancient and appears in *Ugaritic documents in alphabetic writing as *Bʿls* and in syllabic writing as *Baʿala-si*. The Bible mentions Baalis only once (Jer. 40:14), in connection with the murder of *Gedaliah, who had been appointed by the Babylonian king as governor of the Judean cities after the conquest of Jerusalem in 586 B.C.E. Johanan son of Kareah and some army officers warned Gedaliah that Baalis had dispatched Ishmael son of Nethaniah to murder him. For his motives, see *Ammonites and *Ishmael.

Bibliography: Bright, Hist, 310; Ginsberg, in: *A. Marx Jubilee Volume* (1950), 366ff.; Yeivin, in: *Tarbiz*, 12 (1940/41), 261–2, 265–6; W. Rudolph, *Jeremia* (Ger., 1947), 685ff. [B.O.]

BAAL-MAKHSHOVES (pen name of **Israel Isidor Elyashev**; 1873–1924), Yiddish literary critic, pioneer, and creator of Yiddish literary criticism as an art form. Born in Kovno, Baal-Makhshoves was educated at a Courland yeshivah which combined the moral severity of the *Musar movement with a modern curriculum which included mathematics, geography, and German. The influence of the Musar movement intensified his skepticism, melancholy, and analytic sagacity. After completing his studies at a Swiss high school, he studied medicine at Heidelberg and Berlin. Although he practiced medicine in Kovno, Vilna, Riga, Warsaw, and St. Petersburg, his main interest was in belles lettres. In 1896 he began to write in German and Russian and in 1901 he published his first Yiddish critical reviews in *Der Yud*. Influenced by the writer I. L. *Peretz, Baal-Makhshoves continued to write in Yiddish. In a brilliant essay, *"Tsvey Shprakhn—Eyneyntsike Literatur"* ("Two Languages—One Literature"), he stressed the unity of Jewish literature despite its linguistic duality. In another famous essay, *"Dray Shtetlakh"* ("Three Townlets"), he called attention to the three different interpretations of shtetl culture in the works of Peretz, Sholem Asch, and I. M. Vaisenberg. An early admirer of Theodor Herzl, he translated *Altneuland* into Yiddish and participated in the Fifth and Twelfth Zionist Congresses. His war years were spent as a medical officer in the Russian Army. As Yiddish editor of *Klal-verlag* (Berlin, 1922–23), he had another burst of literary activity cut short by his illness and subsequent death. Baal-Makhshoves introduced European aesthetic standards and norms into his interpretation of Yiddish literature. He discovered new talents and encouraged H. *Leivick, David *Bergelson, and the postrevolutionary Kiev Group. He held that both Hebrew and Yiddish should be recognized as Jewish national languages, the former because it linked the Jewish people with its historic past and the latter because it united Jews in the Diaspora. He saw himself fulfilling a role in Yiddish literature similar to that of critics like Byelinski and Lessing in Russian and German literature, and as heralding a Jewish literary renaissance whose pioneers were *Mendele Mokher Seforim, *Shalom Aleichem, I. L. Peretz, Sholem *Asch, and Ḥ. N. *Bialik, to each of whom he devoted a penetrating essay. He accepted Taine's theory that historical, geographical, and ethnic environment determined the character of literary creativity, and formulated the view that true creativity led from regionalism to national culture, illustrating it in his essay on the impact of South Russian Jewish life on Yiddish literature. Less well-known but no less valuable are his *Ironishe Mayselekh* ("Ironic Tales") written after 1910, in which he expressed his increasing pessimism and disillusionment. His selected works appeared in five volumes (1915, 1923[2], 1929[3]) and in a single volume in 1953.

Bibliography: Rejzen, Leksikon, 2 (1927), 744–66; S. Niger, *Lezer, Dikhter un Kritiker* (1928), 495–565; Eliashev, in: *Lite,* 1 (1951), 1313–72; N. B. Minkoff, *Zeks Yidishe Kritiker* (1954), 227–90; LNYL, 1 (1956), 359–66; S. Niger, *Kritik un Kritiker* (1959), 360–82. [S.K./Sh.B.]

BAAL-MEON (Heb. בַּעַל מְעוֹן), city in Transjordan also called Beth-Baal-Meon (Josh. 13:17), Beth-Meon (Jer. 48:23), and apparently Beon (Num. 32:3). It was allotted to the tribe of Reuben (Num. 32:37–38; Josh. 13:17) and remained in Israelite hands until the revolt of Mesha, king of Moab (mid-ninth century B.C.E.). According to Mesha's stele (1.9), he captured the city from Israel and rebuilt it, constructing a pool or water channel there *(ashu'aḥ).* Baal-Meon is listed among the cities of Moab by Jeremiah (48:23) and Ezekiel (25:9). Its identification with the modern village of Maīn, 4½ mi. (7 km.) southwest of Madeba, coincides with Eusebius (Onom. 44:21; 46:2), who identified Beelmaus with a large village nine miles from Heshbon near the hot springs of Ba'aru. The village is built on ancient remains, and the most important find there has been the mosaic pavement of a church on which a number of churches of the Holy Land are depicted. The Tosefta (Shev. 7:11) contains a reference to Baal-Meon in the Shephelah of Transjordan.

Bibliography: Conder, Survey, 176–7; A. Musil, *Arabia Petraea,* 1 (1907), 397–9; Abel, Geog, 2 (1938), 259; Press, Ereẓ, s.v.

[M.A.-Y.]

BAAL-PERAZIM (Heb. בַּעַל פְּרָצִים), locality (perhaps an old Canaanite sanctuary) near Jerusalem, where David defeated the Philistines in their attempt to conquer Jerusalem from the Israelites (II Sam. 5:20 and I Chron. 14:11, where the name is explained etiologically; called Mount Perazim in Isa. 28:21, where the same victory is referred to). Proposals for the identification of the site include the mountain of Sharafāt, the mountain of Ramat Raḥel, and Deir Abu Tor; the latter two are supported by the mention of the valley of Rephaim in the same context.

Bibliography: EM, s.v.; Noth, Hist Isr, 187–8; Abel, Geog, 2 (1938), 259. [M.A.-Y.]

BA'AL SHEM (Heb. בַּעַל שֵׁם, "Master of the Divine Name"; lit. "Possessor of the Name"), title given in popular usage and in Jewish literature, especially kabbalistic and ḥasidic works, from the Middle Ages onward, to one who possessed the secret knowledge of the Tetragrammaton and the other "Holy Names," and who knew how to work miracles by the power of these names. The designation *ba'al shem* did not originate with the kabbalists, for it was

The 18th-century "*ba'al shem* of London," Samuel Jacob Ḥayyim Falk. Cecil Roth Collection.

already known to the last Babylonian *geonim.* In a responsum, Hai Gaon stated: "They testified that they saw a certain man, one of the well-known *ba'alei shem,* on the eve of the Sabbath in one place, and that at the same time he was seen in another place, several days' journey distant." It was in this sense that *Judah Halevi criticized the activities of the *ba'alei shem* (*Kuzari,* 3:53). In medieval German ḥasidic tradition this title was accorded to several liturgical poets, e.g., Shephatiah and his son Amittai of southern Italy (in *Abraham b. Azriel, *Arugat ha-Bosem,* 2 (1947), 181). The Spanish kabbalists used the expression *ba'alei shemot* from the middle of the 13th century onward. Some even said that there were different methods used by the *ba'alei sefirot,* the theoretical kabbalists, and the *ba'alei shemot,* the magicians, in their kabbalistic teachings. *Isaac b. Jacob ha-Kohen, Todros ha-Levi *Abulafia, and *Moses de Leon all mentioned this tendency among the kabbalists without disapproval, whereas Abraham *Abulafia wrote disparagingly of the *ba'alei shem.* From the end of the 13th century, the term *ba'al shem* was also used for writers of amulets based on Holy Names (*Oẓar Neḥmad,* vol. 2, p. 133). There were large numbers of *ba'alei shem,* particularly in Germany and Poland, from the 16th century onward. Some were important rabbis and talmudic scholars, such as Elijah *Loans of Frankfort and Worms, Elijah Ba'al Shem of Chelm, and Sekel Isaac Loeb *Wormser (the *ba'al shem* of Michelstadt). Others were scholars who devoted themselves entirely to the study of Kabbalah, such as Joel Ba'al Shem of Zamosc and Elhanan "Ba'al ha-Kabbalah" of Vienna (both 17th century), Benjamin Beinisch ha-Kohen of Krotoszyn (beginning of the 18th century), and Samuel Essingen. In the 17th and 18th centuries the number of *ba'alei shem* who were not at all talmudic scholars increased. But they attracted a following by their real or imaginary powers of healing the sick. Such a *ba'al shem* was often a combination of practical kabbalist, who performed his cures by means of prayers, amulets, and incantations, and a popular healer familiar with *segullot* ("remedies") concocted from animal, vegetable, and mineral matter. The literature of that period teems with stories and testimonies about *ba'alei shem* of this kind, some of which, however, were written in criticism of their characters and deeds. It was generally thought that the *ba'alei shem* were at their most efficacious in the treatment of mental disorders and in the exorcism of evil spirits (see *Dibbuk). There is a variation to the title *ba'al shem,* known as *"ba'al shem tov."* The founder of modern *Ḥasidism, *Israel b. Eliezer Ba'al Shem Tov, usually referred to by the initials "BeShT," is the most famous and practically unique bearer of this title. The title *"ba'al shem tov"* existed before the Ḥasid, but it did not designate a special quality or a distinction between bearers of this title and *ba'alei shem.* For example, Elhanan Ba'al Shem Tov, who died in 1651; Benjamin Krotoschin, who so styled himself in his book *Shem Tov Katan* (Sulzbach, 1706); and Joel Ba'al Shem I, who actually signed himself *"BeShT,"* in common with the founder of Ḥasidism. In the 18th century, Samuel Jacob Ḥayyim *Falk, the "*ba'al shem* of London," achieved considerable prominence. He was called "Doctor Falk" by Christians. The theory propounded by several scholars that these wandering *ba'alei shem* were responsible for spreading Shabbateanism has not been proved. Several books by these *ba'alei shem* have been published concerning practical Kabbalah, *segullot* ("remedies"), and *refu'ot* ("healing"). These include: *Toledot Adam* (1720) and *Mifalot Elohim* (1727), edited by Joel Ba'al Shem and based on the works of his grandfather Joel Ba'al Shem I, *Shem Tov Katan* (1706) and *Amtaḥat Binyamin* (1716). The deeds of the *ba'alei shem* became legendary. Fictitious characters of the same type were sometimes invented, such as Adam Ba'al Shem of Bingen, the hero of a series of miraculous stories in Yiddish which were printed as early as the 17th century. Ḥasidic legend subsequently created an imaginary connection between this character and Israel Ba'al Shem Tov. The leaders of the Haskalah generally regarded the *ba'alei shem* as charlatans and adventurers.

Bibliography: N. Prilutski, *Zamelbikher far Yidischen Folklor,* 2 (1917), 40-42; J. Guenzig, *Die "Wundermaenner" im juedischen Volke* (1921); B. Segel, in: *Globus,* 62 (1892); Adler, in: JHSET, 5 (1908), 148–73; G. Scholem, in: *Zion,* 20 (1955), 80. [G.SCH.]

BAAL WORSHIP.

Name and Etymology. The word *baʿl,* common Semitic for "owner, master, husband," became the usual designation of the great weather-god of the Western Semites. In spite of the fact that the word is used as the theophorous element in personal names, such as Eshbaal, Merib-Baal, Jerub Baal, it was long believed that the term remained an appellation and did not become a proper name, except in the case of the Mesopotamian Bel and in late theological speculation. The basis for this view was the fact that in biblical usage the plural of the term, with the article, "the Baalim," appears to designate minor local gods (Judg. 2:11; 3:7; 8:33) while the singular of the word in combination with other terms apparently designated minor or local gods, such as Baal-Berith, Baal-Gad, Baal-Hamon, Baal-Hazor, Baal-Hermon, or, in the feminine form, a goddess, Baalat-Beer, Baalat-Gebal. Further, in biblical usage when applied to the great weather-god, the singular regularly has the article, "the Baal," which suggests that the word was not regarded as a proper name. Nevertheless, despite the biblical tendency to avoid the use of the word as a proper name, it is now quite clear that by pre-Israelite times the term had become the usual name of the weather-god of Syria-Palestine. In the Tell El-Amarna letters the logogram for the weather-god is conventionally read *Addu,* but that it is sometimes to be read *Baʿlu* is indicated by the addition of the phonetic complement *-lu,* as well as by the names like *Mut* ^{d}*Im* written syllabically as *mu-ut-ba-aḫ-lum.* In the Tell

Figure 1. The "Baal of the lightning," a stele from Ras Shamra (Ugarit), showing the god holding a lance in the form of lightning in his left hand. Height 4 ft. 8 in. (1.42 m.). Paris, Louvre, Ao 15775.

El-Amarna letters Canaanite clients addressed the Egyptian king as "My Baal, my Addu." In the Ugaritic mythological texts Baʿlu *(bʿl)* is the name of the god which is used more than twice as often as his next most frequent name, Haddu *(hd).* The latter name (Amarna, Addu) is to be related to Arabic *hadda* ("break," "crash") with reference to thunder. The variant form Hadad *(hdd)* is attested only once in Ugaritic.

That there were minor Baalim also at Ugarit is indicated by a god list in Akkadian (see *Ugaritica,* 5, p. 44 ll. 4–10; reconstructed text) which presents after the great "Weather-god, Lord of Mount Ḫazi" presents six other "weather-gods," numbered two through seven. In the parallel Ugaritic list, which is unfortunately very fragmentary, the "Weather-god, Lord of Mount Ḫazi" apparently corresponds to Baal Ṣapān while those following are termed simply Baalim *(bʿlm).* It may be, however, that these extra Baalim are Baal's attendants, mentioned as the seven or eight lads whom Baal is ordered to take with him in his descent into the netherworld.

Other titles and epithets. Besides the names Baal and Haddu, the Ugaritic texts furnish a variety of other titles, such as "Mighty Baal" *(ʾaliyn bʿl)* and "Prince, Lord of Earth" *(Zbl bʿl arṣ)*. The latter title has a biblical echo in the corrupted form Baal-Zebub (II Kings 1:2 ff.), from an original Baal-Zebul, which is preserved in this form in the New Testament (Matt. 10:25; 12:24; Mark 3:22; Luke 11:15, 18). A frequent epithet is "Cloud Rider" *(rkb ʿrpt)* which has an almost identical parallel in Psalms 68:5. A vivid description of theophany in a thunderstorm is found in Psalms 18:7–15 (=II Sam. 22:8–16). Of special interest is the designation *ʿAliy(ʿly)* which is twice applied to Baal in the Krt Epic:

To the earth Baal rained,
To the field rained ʿAliy.
Sweet to the earth was Baal's rain
To the field the rain of ʿAliy.

Before the discovery and recognition of this name in Ugaritic, H. S. Nyberg had restored it in Deuteronomy 33:12; I Samuel 2:10; II Samuel 23:1; Isaiah 59:18; 63:7 and Hosea 7:16. Since the Ugaritic verified the antiquity and authenticity of this divine name, additional instances have been alleged in the Psalter and in Job.

A common designation of Baal in the Ugaritic myths is *bn-dgn* "son of Dagān"; but Baal is also considered the son of El who is called "Bull El his [i.e., Baal's] father; El King who begot him[Baal]" *(Tr il abh; il mlk dyknnh)*. Since El and Dagān are distinct deities, this seeming confusion over Baal's paternity needs explanation. A solution has been supplied by a tradition ascribed to the ancient Phoenician priest Sakkunyaton (Greek Sanchuniathōn) that when El-Kronos defeated Ouranos, he captured in the battle Ouranos' pregnant concubine and gave her to Dagān. The divine child was named Demarous, one of the cognomens of Zeus-Baal-Hadad. The Semitic original of this name has been recognized in one of Baal's names in Ugaritic:

Then said Mighty Baal:
Foes of Hadd why haste ye?
Why haste ye opponents of Dmrn?

(The name is to be connected with the root ‡*ḏmr*, "be strong, brave," and is probably the same as that of Abraham's son Zimrān (‡*ḏamarān*), the *-n* afformative being preserved in the genitive case of the Greek form Demarountos). Thus, according to Sakkunyaton, Baal's natural father was Ouranos and Dagān became his foster-father, while El-Kronos effected the transfer. That Baal appears to be a relative newcomer in the Ugaritic pantheon has been generally recognized, and it may be that Sakkhunyaton's story about Baal's paternity reflects a mythologizing of the process by which Baal was integrated into the family of El.

Baal's Residence. Baal's abode was Mount Ṣapān, identified as Jebel el-Aqraʿ ("Mount Baldy") some 30 miles north of Ugarit. A god Baal Ṣapān was known from Egyptian and Akkadian sources before the discovery of the Ugaritic documents. In an Akkadian catalogue of Ugaritic deities Baal Ṣapān is listed as *ᵈIM be-el ḫuršān ḫa-zi*, "Storm-God, Lord of Mount Ḫazi" (see above; Ḫaz [z] i being the Hurrian name of Mount Ṣapān which survives in the Greek and Latin Kasios/Casius as the name of the storied mountain of the gods). Isaiah 14:13 alludes to this divine abode as "the Mount of Assembly in the recesses of *ẓafon*," *(har moʿed be-yarkete ẓafon)*, the latter phrase being the equivalent of Ugaritic *mrym ṣpn* or *ṣrrt ṣpn*, the height or fastness of Ṣapan). The cosmic character of *ẓafon* leads to its use as a synonym for "sky"in Job 26:7: "who stretched out *ẓafon* on emptiness who suspended earth on naught." That *ẓafon* designated the "north" in Hebrew is presumably due to the fact that Mount Casius lies directly north of Palestine. In Psalms 89:13 *ẓafon* and *yamin*, in parellelism with Tabor and Hermon, hardly designate the directions north and south; *yamin* is almost certainly a corruption of Amana, the southern portion of the Taurus mountains, the alteration of *ʾamanah* to *yamin* being occasioned by the misunderstanding of *ẓafon* as the direction rather than the name of the holy mountain. In Psalms 48:2–3, Mount Zion is equated with "the recesses of *ẓafon*" (the phrase quoted above from Isa. 14:13). The association of the name Baal-Zephon with Israel's exit from Egypt (Ex. 14:2, 9; Num. 33:7) has been made the basis of intriguing speculation by Eissfeldt.

Baal in the Ugaritic Myths. The bulk of the Ugaritic mythological texts is concerned with the activities of Baal. In correlating the sequence of events, Baal's victory over the sea-god, Yamm, is probably to be placed near the beginning of the action, since it was presumably this exploit which gained him the dominant position among the gods, just as *Marduk achieved preeminence by defeating the sea-monster Tiamat. With the help of wonder weapons supplied and blessed by the versatile Koshar (the craftsman god), Baal was able to defeat and rout the sea-god. It has been suggested that this clash was indirectly a conflict between Baal and El, with Yamm serving as champion for the venerable El, as the Titans fought on behalf of Kronos in the Greek version of the myth and the stone colossus Ulikummi for Kumarbi in the Hurrian-Hittite version which is roughly contemporary with the Ugaritic texts.

The biblical allusions to YHWH's victory over the sea preserve echoes of the older exploit of Baal (cf. Isa. 27:1; 30:7; 51:9–10; Ezek. 29:3–5; 32:2–6; Nah. 1:4; Hab. 3:8; Ps. 74:13–14; 89:9–10; 93:1ff.; Job 3:8; 7:12; 9:13; 26:12–13; 38:8–11; 40:25). YHWH's victory over the waters is connected either with the rescue of Israel at the Exodus (Ps. 114) or with eschatological victory (Isa. 27:1). The eschatological traits were taken over with the Canaanite myths. The triumph of Baal recounted in the myths and perhaps reenacted in ritual drama gave assurance of help in the present and the future as in the past. The prize of the victory was kingship over the gods and the enthronement ritual guaranteed the natural order of life and the welfare of the society. The motifs of these myths were adopted and adapted in Jewish and Christian eschatology.

The longest of the texts deals with the construction of Baal's house on top of Mount Ṣapān. A complaint is made to Bull El, father of the gods, that Baal has no house like other gods. Apparently in anticipation of developments the artisan god Koshar had cast furnishings of gold and silver. Asherah, mother of the gods, was prevailed upon to intercede with El to gain permission for the building. El is praised for his wisdom in granting the request since now it is insured that Baal will give his rain in season. The building materials, gold, silver, and lapis lazuli, were procured and the architect-builder Koshar was invited to dinner and consultation. Koshar twice recommended that a window be installed and Baal twice vetoed the suggestion, although Koshar insisted that Baal would have to reconsider. Baal's objection to the window somehow concerned his three daughters and the sea-god (Yamm), but the text is broken at this point. (The suggestion that Jer. 9:20 presents a parallel is mistaken since the Ugaritic text mentions the sea-god and not Death (Mot) in connection with the window.) Baal's house was constructed in an extraordinary fashion. For seven days a fire burned inside the building and when it subsided the house was plated with gold, silver, and lapis lazuli. Baal rejoiced and celebrated with a banquet. After a sortie against the sea-god, Baal returned to his house and ordered Koshar to install a window; Koshar laughed, reminded Baal of the debate, and complied. Through the window, a cleft in the clouds, Baal gave forth his holy voice which convulsed the earth and sent his enemies scurrying to the hills and woods. Issuing a challenge to his enemy Mot (death), who presumed to rule gods and men, Baal dispatched his messengers to Mot's infernal, filthy abode, warning them not to get close to Mot's rapacious jaws.

The sequel to this action is furnished by the group of texts which recount Baal's confrontations with Mot. In the first encounter, Baal is invited to a banquet at which he is to be both guest and main course. Baal's response to Mot's invitation to come and be devoured is abject surrender: "Thy slave am I, thine eternal." Before descending to the realm of death, Baal copulates with a heifer and begets a male offspring. After a textual gap, there is a report that Baal's corpse has been found. El and Anath mourn violently, mutilating their faces and bodies. With the help of the sun-goddess Shapsh, Anath locates the dead Baal, carries him to the height of Ṣapān, and weeping buries him with funerary sacrifices. Ashtar the Awful *(ʿṯtr ʿrẓ)* was then nominated to replace Baal, but when he ascended the throne his feet did not reach the footstool nor his head the top and so he declined to reign on the heights of Ṣapān and descended from Baal's throne, but ruled over all El's earth. Since the root *ʿṯr* in Arabic is connected with artificial irrigation, it is apparent that Ashtar's failure to measure up to Baal represents the inadequacy of irrigation as a substitute for natural rainfall.

Baal's sister-consort Anath demanded that Mot release her brother. Mot refused and boasted how he had mangled Baal. Anath then dismembered Mot, scattered and burned the pieces, and gave them to the birds. Baal's resurrection followed Mot's demise, the good news being transmitted through a dream of El:

In a dream of Beneficent El Benign,
A vision of the Creator of Creatures,
The skies rained oil,
The wadies flowed honey.
So I knew that Mighty Baal lives,
The Prince, Lord of Earth, exists.

The fields were still parched from the drought and again Anath and Shapsh set out to find Baal. Next both Mot and Baal appear reconstituted and reactivated and again in conflict. They clash violently till both are prostrate and the Sun-goddess warns Mot not to fight with Baal lest El hear and overthrow him. This time, Baal puts up a fight and holds Mot off in battle. Thus it is clear that Baal, representing the life-giving rains, fluctuates in his ability to withstand the power of Mot, who represents drought, sterility, and death.

YHWH Versus Baal. The worship of Baal in Syria-Palestine was inextricably bound to the economy of the land which depends on the regularity and adequacy of the rains. Unlike Egypt and Mesopotamia, which depend on irrigation, the Promised Land drinks water from the rain of heaven (Deut. 11:10–11). During the summer months the rains cease, but the temporary drought is no threat unless it is abnormally prolonged. Figs and grapes ripen during the dry season and the grain harvest also takes place before the rains resume. In a normal good year, when the rains come in due season, there is no hiatus in productivity, for the land yields its increase, the trees produce their fruit, the threshing overlaps, the vintage overlaps the sowing, and there is food aplenty, prosperity, and peace (Lev. 26:4–6). But not all years are good, and in a bad year, or a series of bad years, when the rains fail, the skies become like iron, the land like brass, and man's toil is futile for the earth will not yield its increase (Lev. 26:19–20). A series of bad years, which were apparently believed to come in seven year cycles (cf. Gen. 41; II Sam. 1:21), would be catastrophic. Thus in any year anxiety about the rainfall would be a continuing concern of the inhabitants which would suffice to give rise to rites to ensure the coming of the rains. Thus the basis of the Baal cult was the utter dependence of life on the rains which were regarded as Baal's bounty.

The allure of Baal worship seduced the Israelites even before they reached the Promised Land. At Shittim they attached themselves to Baal-Peor, ate sacrifices for the dead, and indulged in sacred sexual orgies (Num. 25:1–11; Ps. 106:28). Settlement in a land dependent on rainfall enhanced the appeal of the Baal cult

Figure 2. One of the Ugaritic tablets of the Baal myths, c. 15th–14th century B.C.E. It deals with a message from Baal to his sister-consort, Anath.

and its pervasive influence persisted through the centuries, as the unrelenting protests of the prophets and the sporadic efforts at reform attest. The horrendous and repulsive aspects of the worship—sexual excesses and perversions (Isa. 57:3–10), perhaps including copulation with animals (Hos. 13:2) such as Baal himself performed in the Ugaritic myth—are indicted in the prophetic tirades. Virtually all reference to Baal's consort, the violent virgin Anath—with whom Baal copulates by the thousand in one of the Ugaritic mythological fragments—has been excluded from the Bible, but the goddesses Ashtart (Judg. 2:13) and *Asherah (Judg. 6:30; II Kings 16:32–33) are associated with him.

The conflict of Yahwism and Baalism reached a crisis with Elijah's challenge to Baal's prophets to settle the question whether it was Baal or YHWH who really supplied the rain (I Kings 18). The spectacular victory for Yahwism did not have a lasting effect. Extra-biblical evidence for the flourishing Baal cult at Samaria in the ninth and eighth centuries B.C.E. was furnished by Harvard University excavations in the form of personal names containing Baal as the theophorous element, such as *'byb'l*, "Baal is my father," *b'l zmr*, "Baal sings" or "Baal is strong," *b'l zkr*, "Baal remembers," *b'l m'ny*, "Baal is my answer," etc. Jehu's massacre of the Baal worshipers (II Kings 10:18–28) did not eradicate bull worship (II Kings 10:31). In Judah the murder of the queen mother, *Athaliah, and of Mattan, priest of Baal, and the smashing of the altars and cult images in the Baal temple (II Kings 11:18) did not wipe out the cult (II Kings 12:3–4). Ahaz fostered Baal worship (II Chron. 28:2); Hezekiah attempted to eliminate it; Manasseh his son again gave it royal support (II Kings 21:3); and Josiah in his turn purged the Temple of YHWH of the utensils made for Baal and Asherah (II Kings 23:4).

The contest on Mount Carmel was reported as demonstrating that Baal was an impotent nonentity and that the rain came only from YHWH. This viewpoint was developed as the basic and final argument against Baalism. With Baal's functions accredited to YHWH, it was natural and fitting that some of Baal's titles would also be taken over. Portions of ancient Baal liturgy were adapted to the praise of Israel's God, as the Ugaritic poems have shown. To accommodate Baal ideology to Yahwism required some radical transformations. The summer drought did not mean that YHWH had died (like Baal), nor did the return of the rains signal the resurrection. The rains were fully controlled by YHWH who called them from the sea and poured them out on the surface of the earth (Amos 5:8b; 9:6b). He could, and did, withhold the rain from one city and lavish it on another (Amos 4:7). None of the foolish practices of the heathen could bring the rains; only YHWH could and did (Jer. 10:11–13; 14:22). If the rains failed and drought and death came upon the land and people, it was not because Mot had mangled Baal and made the glowing sun-goddess destructive; it was rather YHWH's way of meting out merited punishment to a faithless and sinful people (Deut. 11:17; I Kings 8:35–36; Jer. 3:2–3). The continued worship of Baal was given as one of the causes for the destruction of Judah (Jer. 19:5ff.). Payment of the full tithe to the food stores of the Temple, some thought, would guarantee that YHWH would open the windows of heaven and pour down overflowing blessings (Mal. 3:10; cf. Avot 5:11 on the connection between tithing and rain). The prophet Haggai attributed the drought and scarcity in his day to the failure to rebuild the Temple (Hag. 1:7–11).

When the rain failed, it was inevitable that some would question YHWH's power and resort to Baal. In distress some would naturally revert to the old ways of reviving or reactivating the rain-god—prayer, mourning, self-laceration, dancing, and water-pouring (I Kings 18:26–28; Hos. 7:14–16). The right remedy, according to Israel's prophets, was to repudiate Baal completely and to seek and return to Israel's true God (Isa. 55:6–13; Jer. 4:1–2; Hos. 14:2).

Bibliography: O. Eissfeldt, *Beitraege zur Religionsgeschichte des Altertums I* (1932); H. L. Ginsberg, *Kitvei Ugarit* (1936); J. Oberman, *Ugaritic Mythology* (1948); A. S. Kapelrud, *Baal in the Ras Shamra Texts* (1952); M. Dahood, in: *Studi Semitici*, 1 (1958), 75–78; N. Habel, *Yahweh Versus Baal: A Conflict of Religious Cultures* (1964); J. Gray, *The Legacy of Canaan* (rev. ed., 1965); H. B. Huffmon, *Amorite Personal Names in the Mari Texts* (1965), 174; W. F. Albright, *Yahweh and the Gods of Canaan* (1968); Albright, Arch Rel; S. M. Paul, in: *Biblica*, 49 (1968), 343–6; U. Oldenburg, *The Conflict Between El and Ba'l in Canaanite Religion* (1969).

[Ma.Po.]

BAAL-ZEPHON (Heb. בַּעַל צְפֹן), a sanctuary in Egypt which the Israelites passed during the *Exodus from Egypt (Ex. 14:2, 9; Num. 33:7). Scholars disagree as to the site of Baal-Zephon and locate it according to their view of the route followed by the Israelites when they departed from Egypt. Those who assume a southern passage was taken suggest Jebel Abu Ḥasan, 8 mi. (13 km.) N. of Suez, which is identified with a Migdal Baal-Zephon mentioned in a papyrus from the Hellenistic period (Cairo papyrus 31169). Others who prefer a northern route identify Baal-Zephon with the sanctuary of Zeus Casius, which is known of from the fifth century B.C.E. onward in the vicinity of the Serbonic Lake (Baḥr al-Bardawīl, the "Reed Sea," according to this theory). Since another mountain called Mons Casius (Jebel Aqra on the Syrian coast) was known in earlier times as Baal-Zephon, it is consequently assumed that the southern Baal-Zephon was also called Casius. The site is identified with a hillock on the western extremity of the lake called *Maḥmūdiyya.* W. F. Albright has identified Baal-Zephon with the Egyptian port Taḥpanḥes (Daphne). A survey in 1967 directed by M. Dothan has identified Baal-Zephon with Ras Kasrun near the Serbonic Lake; the survey also identified it as the site of the Hellenistic-Roman city of Casius.

Bibliography: O. Eissfeldt, *Baal Zaphon...* (Ger., 1932); Bourdon, in: RB, 41 (1932), 541ff.; Albright, in: BASOR, 118 (1950), 17; EM, 2 (1965), 291–2; Aharoni, Land, 179; M. Dothan, in: *Eretz-Israel,* 9 (1969), 48–59. [M.A.-Y.]

BAASHA (or **Baasa;** Heb. בַּעְשָׁא), son of Ahijah of the tribe of Issachar, king of Israel (906–883 B.C.E.). Baasha, perhaps an officer under King *Nadab, who was besieging *Gibbethon, then held by the Philistines, assassinated him there and proclaimed himself king. He massacred all the members of the House of Jeroboam I, which he had supported. By this act he overthrew the hegemony of Ephraim over the other tribes. Like his predecessor, he resided at Tirzah (I Kings 15:27ff.). After ensuring by alliance the friendship and neutrality of his northern neighbors—the Arameans of Damascus—he turned to the south. According to I Kings 15:16, 32 he was at war with King *Asa of Judah throughout his reign. He succeeded in occupying Ramah, a dominating height north of Jerusalem, and began to fortify it, threatening the Davidic capital. Asa, in turn, bribed Ben-Hadad, king of *Aram, to break his alliance with Baasha and invade Israel (*ibid.* 17–21; II Chron. 16:1–5), and Baasha was forced to withdraw from Ramah. It has been suggested that he fell in battle while fighting the Arameans, but the biblical report suggests a peaceful death at home (I Kings 16:16). Like Jeroboam before him, Baasha seems to have been sponsored by the prophet Jehu son of Hanani, who gave him the charismatic title *nagid,* and like Jeroboam he disappointed his sponsor (*ibid.* 16:1–4, 7).

According to rabbinic legend (Mid. Ag. to Num. 30:15), it was Baasha who murdered the prophet *Shemaiah.

Bibliography: Noth, Hist Isr, 228, 230, 233, 239; Bright, Hist, index; EM, 2 (1965), 303–4 (incl. bibl.). [H.Re.]

BAAZOV, HERZL (1904–1945), Georgian writer. Born several weeks after Theodor *Herzl's death and named after him, Baazov grew up in Kutaisi in the house of his father, David Baazov, which was the first Zionist, Hebrew-speaking home in Georgia. Baazov became a well-known Georgian playwright and poet, and most of his writings were dedicated to Georgian Jewish life. At the age of 19, he translated the Song of Songs into Georgian. His first play, about the life and death of Itzko (Abraham Isaac) Rizhinashvili—a young Jewish revolutionary who was killed during the upheaval of 1905 in a fight with Czarist gendarmes—was staged at the Tbilisi (Tiflis) State Theater. Another of his plays, "The Dumb Opened Their Mouths," dealt with the social changes in the life of the Tat-speaking *Mountain Jews after the Russian Revolution. He also wrote poetry, including the well-known poem "Cain." In the 1930s he began to write a trilogy about the changes in Jewish life in Georgia after the revolution. In spite of his positive attitude to the revolution as a social phenomenon, he was suddenly arrested and deported in 1937, after the publication of the first part of the trilogy. No indictment against him was ever published, but it is assumed that he was accused of "Jewish bourgeois nationalism." In 1945 he died in exile, somewhere in the Soviet far north. An indirect rehabilitation of his name occurred in 1964, when the official Georgian Writers' Union celebrated his 60th birthday. Several of his writings were republished, but were not translated into Russian. The Georgian writer G. Tsitsishvili published a book on Baazov's life and work (1964) that, inter alia, mentions his close relations with S. *Mikhoels, P. *Markish, and other Soviet Jewish writers and artists.

His younger brother, Meir Baazov (1915–1970), an engineer, was also a Hebrew scholar and served in the 1940s as director of the Hebrew section of the Georgian National Library in Tbilisi. [Mo.N.]

BAB, JULIUS (1880–1955), German drama critic and literary historian. Born in Berlin, where he studied literature and philosophy, Bab was a critic of the Berlin theater for more than three decades. He was also lecturer and adviser to the Berlin people's theater, the *Volksbuehne.* In June 1933, in an attempt to maintain cultural life among the Jews after the rise of Nazism, Bab founded the *Juedischer Kulturbund,* which had its own theater. In 1940 he fled to the U.S., where he became the dramatic critic of the *New York Staatszeitung.* Bab's collected reviews of the Berlin theater, *Die Chronik des deutschen Dramas* (1921–22), are an important source for the history of modern German drama. His other works include monographs on Shakespeare, Shaw, Dehmel, and Albert Bassermann and a volume of essays, *Am Rande der Zeit* (1915). A book of verse, *Ausgewaehlte Gedichte...* (1930), includes the poem "Der Jude."

Bibliography: L. Rauschenbusch, in: *Quarterly Journal of Speech,* 2 (1946), 33–40; H. Bergholz, in: *Books Abroad,* 25 (1951), 26f. [R.K.]

BABAD, a family of rabbis. The founder of the family was Isaac of Cracow, son of Issachar Berish, a *parnas* of the Council of Four Lands, and grandson of Heschel, *av bet din* of Cracow. He served as rabbi of Brzezany and then of Brody, where he died in 1704. His children added the word Babad (an acronym of Benei Av Bet Din, "children of the *av bet din*") to their signatures, and it eventually became their surname. Members of the family included:

Joshua Heschel b. Isaac Babad (1754–1838), grandson of the communal leader, Jacob Jekel Babad of Brody, who served as rabbi of Budzanow and, from 1801, of Tarnopol. He was one of the opponents, in 1813, of the teaching system in the school founded by Joseph *Perl, where secular studies were also taught. After a short stay in Lublin (1828), he was compelled to leave the city because of his dispute with the *Mitnaggedim* there, and he returned to Tarnapol, where he died. Joshua's responsa on the four parts of the Shulḥan Arukh, *Sefer Yehoshu'a* (Zolkiew, 1829), was considered a basic halakhic work, upon which contemporary rabbis relied for their rulings.

Menachem Munish b. Joshua Heschel Babad (1865–1938), a well-known personality in Galician Jewry and a halakhic authority of note. He was born in Brody where he was educated by his father and afterward by his father-in-law. He succeeded his father as *av bet din* of Strzyzow in 1892, and in 1894, after the death of his father-in-law, he accepted a call to serve as rabbi of Jaworow, a post which he occupied until 1911. The rest of his life was spent in Tarnopol. Menahem participated in rabbinical conferences of 1925 and 1927 in Cracow and Lvov. His method of study, resembling that of the Lithuanian yeshivot, was characterized by a logical analysis of the words of the sages, a comprehensive review of every aspect of the subject under discussion, and a summation of all the relevant views. His many responsa were collected in *Ḥavaẓẓelet ha-Sharon* (1931–38), covering all four parts of the Shulḥan Arukh.

Bibliography: I. J. Eisenstadt and S. Wiener, *Da'at Kedoshim* (1898), 104, 128 (first pagination); Cohen-Zedek, in: *Dor Yesharim*, 30—supplement to: *Ha-Goren*, 1 (1898); S. B. Nissenbaum, *Le-Korot ha-Yehudim be-Lublin* (1899), 96–97; Z. Horowitz, *Kitvei ha-Ge'onim* (1928), 35, 39; A. Polisiuk, *Tehillah le-David* (1937); Halpern, Pinkas, index; Friedmann, in: *YIVO Bleter*, 31–32 (1948), 170 n91; EG, 3 (1955), 262–6.

[J.Ho.]

BABAD, JOSEPH BEN MOSES (1800–1874/5), Polish rabbi and author. Little is known about him. His father was *av bet din* at Przeworsk. Babad served as rabbi at Bohorodezany, Zabariz, Sniatyn, and Tarnopol. Babad's best-known work is his *Minḥat Ḥinnukh*, consisting of expositions of the *Sefer* **ha-Ḥinnukh* ("The Book of Education") ascribed to Aaron ha-Levi of Barcelona (1869, frequently republished; the 1952 edition containing 26 addenda (commentaries, novellae, notes, and emendations) to *Sefer ha-Ḥinnukh* and *Minḥat Ḥinnukh* by various authors). The publisher, Reuben Kohen Rappaport, stated in the introduction that he had long tried to persuade the author to publish it, but in his modesty he had refused and finally agreed only after the theft of a manuscript containing his novellae on the Torah. As Babad himself states, the arrangement of his work is based on that of *Sefer ha-Ḥinnukh*. On each *halakhah* he quotes commentators and halakhic authorities. *Minḥat Ḥinnukh* together with *Sefer ha-Ḥinnukh* cover all the principles, laws, and customs concerning the commandments, from talmudic times to the *aḥaronim*. In his novellae and legal statements, Babad arrives at no final conclusion, but instead poses questions and problems, stimulating the reader to new ideas and further research. The many supplementary comments and novellae on *Minḥat Ḥinnukh* have created an entire literature around these two works.

ספר
מנחת חינוך
חלק ראשון
לעמבערג
Minchas Chinoch
Eigenthum · Druck und Verlag des U. W. Salat Lemberg 1889
Nachdruck verboten

Title page of part one of *Minḥat Ḥinnukh*, Joseph Babad's commentary on *Sefer ha-Ḥinnukh*, second edition, Lemberg, 1889. Jerusalem, J.N.U.L.

There are extant two responsa addressed to Babad by his grandfather Joshua Hoeschel Babad, two from Joseph Joel Deutsch to Babad when he was *av bet din* at Zabariz and Sniatyn, and one responsum of Babad, dated 1850 (*Koveẓ Teshuvot*, Supplement to *Minḥat Ḥinnukh* (1952), 120ff.). His son Simeon Babad, who served as rabbi at Tarnopol until 1909, wrote glosses to *Minḥat Ḥinnukh*. He was succeeded in turn by his son Joshua Hoeschel who occupied the position until his death in 1919.

Bibliography: Z. Horowitz, *Kitvei ha-Ge'onim* (1928), 39; H. Tchernowitz, *Toledot ha-Posekim* 2 (1947), 98, 105; J. Lewinstein, *Dor va-Dor ve-Doreshav* (1949²), 77, no. 1544; B. Wachstein, *Zur Bibliographie der Gedaechtnis- und Trauervortraege in der hebraeischen Literatur*, 1 (1922), 24; 2 (1927), 20; EG, 3 (1955), 262–3; *Sefer ha-Hashlamah le-Minḥat Ḥinnukh ha-Shalem*, 2 (1952), end.

[Y.Ho.]

BABAI IBN LUṬF (17th century), poet and chronicler. He was born in Kashan (Persia) where he began in 1656 to compose his chronicle in Judeo-Persian entitled *Kitāb Anusi* ("The Book of the Events of the Forced Conversions of Persian Jewry to Islam"), a description of the religious persecution and martyrdom of Persian Jews under Shah *Abbas I (1588–1629). The chronicle, composed in the Persian language and written in Hebrew characters, is divided into 83 chapters. In language and form, in arrangement of facts, in symbolism and in metaphor, it is typically Persian and shows the extent to which the form and patterns of Persian classical poetry, as well as the Judeo-Persian poetry of *Shāhin and ʿImrānī, influenced Babai ibn Luṭf. His grandson Babai ibn Farḥād, also of Kashan and like his grandfather an eyewitness and victim of the events he described, continued the chronicle. Adopting the same language, form, and symbolism, he depicts the suffering and persecution of Persian Jews under Shah *Abbas II (1642–1666), and the troubled times experienced by the Jewish communities during the Persian-Afghan wars until 1725. The chronicles supply important details about the life of the Jewish communities in Persia under the Safavids. Above all the martyrology of the Persian Jews and their life as crypto-Jews (see *Anusim; *Jadid al Islam) are depicted.

Bibliography: W. Bacher, in: REJ, 51 (1906), 265–79; 52 (1906), 234–71; M. Seligsohn, in: REJ, 44 (1902), 87–103, 244–59; W. J. Fischel, in: *Zion*, 2 (1937), 273–93; C. Levy, *Taʾrīkh-i Yahūd Iran*, 3 (1960); H. Mizraḥi, *Toledot Yehudei Paras u-Meshorereihem* (1966), 93–110.

[W.J.F.]

BĀB AL-ABWĀB ("Gate of the Gates"; Persian **Darband;** modern ***Derbent**), a pass and town at the eastern end of the Caucasus range, where the road narrows between the mountains and the Caspian Sea. Bāb al-Abwāb is mentioned in both the "Letter of Ḥasdai" and the

"Reply of King Joseph" (see *Khazars), in the latter specifically as marking the southern limit of the Khazar domain. This agrees in general with the accounts of the Arabic geographers and historians. The latter described Bāb al-Abwāb as guarding one of the two main passes of the Caucasus through which the Khazars invaded the lands of Islam. Extensive arrangements for the defense of Bāb al-Abwāb are reported by the geographer al-Iṣṭakhrī (tenth century). Previously, the town had more than once been overrun from the north, though the successful Khazar attack against Ardabil (apparently in 730), referred to in the "Reply of King Joseph," was made via Dariel (now Daryal).

Bibliography: Dunlop, Khazars, index; Dunlop, in: EIS[2] (incl. bibl.); al-Iṣṭakhrī, *Kitāb al-Masālik wa-al-Mamālik* (1961), 109–10; M. Artamonov, *Istoriya Khazar* (1962), index.

[D.M.D.]

BABA RABBAH (or **Baba ha-Gadol,** "the Great Baba," 4th cent. C.E.), Samaritan high priest, eldest son of the high priest Nethanel (300-332 C.E.). According to the dating of the Samaritan chronicles, Baba Rabbah lived in the middle of the fourth century C.E. He is regarded as the most outstanding Samaritan political leader and reformer. His epithet "the Great" distinguishes him from other high priests called Baba, before and after his time. All information about Baba Rabbah is derived solely from the Samaritan chronicles: the *Tolidah,* the Samaritan *Book of Joshua,* the *Kitāb al-Ta'rīkh* of *Abu al-Fat, and the *New Chronicle* (see *Samaritans, Literature). The last three embellish their narrative with much legendary material. Of special interest is the legend of the Roman agent Jarman or Jarmūn related in the Samaritan *Book of Joshua.* By the emperor's decree, the Roman had been posted at the high priest Nethanel's door to prevent him from circumcising his eldest son Baba Rabbah; but Jarman was a God-fearing man who preferred to obey the law of the Eternal King rather than the earthly ruler. In gratitude, the Samaritans continue to bless his name at every circumcision ceremony at the conclusion of a poem composed by Markah in glorification of this act. According to the other two chronicles, however, the high priest in this story is Akbon, Baba's brother, who succeeded him in office.

Baba Rabbah lived in an age of great political and religious upheaval; pagan Rome had been succeeded by the Byzantine Empire. This turning point, when the foreign rulers were preoccupied with their own affairs, provided a brief respite for the oppressed Samaritan community. Baba Rabbah achieved numerous victories over the Romans and some neighboring states and time and again succeeded in driving the enemy out of Samaritan territory. To secure the safety of his country, he maintained an army of 3,000 men on constant alert. After he led his people for 40 years, the Byzantine emperor invited him to Constantinople to conclude a peace treaty. On his arrival he was received with princely honors but was held as a prisoner until his death.

During his rule, Baba Rabbah divided the country into 12 administrative districts, each under the leadership of a layman and a priest. The list of these districts indicates that at this time Samaritan communities existed in all parts of the Holy Land. Baba founded a legislative council of three priests and four laymen and conferred upon each member the title *ḥakham.* They constituted, after Baba Rabbah himself, the highest authority in the community. One of their tasks was to tour the country at regular intervals to ensure that people were instructed in the laws of the Torah and to decide on difficult halakhic matters. In conjunction with his administrative reforms, Baba Rabbah made efforts to promote a revival of religion and literature. He reopened all the synagogues and schools that the Romans had closed and founded many new ones, building one of the nine new synagogues at the foot of Mt. Gerizim. He had a cistern installed at this holy place for the purification of the people who came to pray there. Many old manuscripts of the law were then collected and preserved. It was probably also at this time that the foundations of the *Defter,* the Samaritan common prayer book, were laid by *Amram Darah and his son Markah, who composed liturgical and midrashic poems in Aramaic.

Bibliography: J. A. Montgomery, *The Samaritans* (1907, repr. 1968), 101-4; J. Macdonald, *Theology of the Samaritans* (1964), index; A. E. Cowley, *Samaritan Liturgy,* 2 (1909), xx–xxii; M. Gaster, *Samaritans* (1925), 39; I. Ben-Zvi, *Sefer ha-Shomeronim* (1935), 24; M. Avi-Yonah, in: *Eretz Israel,* 4 (1956), 127-32; R. Tsadaqa, *Aggadot Am Shomeroniyyot* (1965), 22-35; H. G. Kippenberg, *Garizim und Synagoge* (1971, index), TEXTS: E. Vilmar (ed.) *Abulfathi, Annales Samaritani* (1865), 125–47 (Arabic with Latin notes and introduction); T. G. J. Juynboll (ed.), *Chronicon Samaritanum, Liber Josuae* (1848), lii–lv (Arabic text); J. Bowman, *Transcript of the Original Text of the Samaritan Chronicle Tolidah* (1957), 16a–17b. (Heb. with Eng. notes); E. N. Adler and M. Seligsohn (eds.), *Une Nouvelle Chronique Samaritaine* (1903), 51-61.

[AY.L.]

BABEL, ISAAC EMMANUILOVICH (1894–1941?), Russian writer. He was born in Odessa, then the center of Yiddish as well as Hebrew literature (both Mendele and Bialik lived there), of Jewish communal and political life (Odessa was, simultaneously, the center of Zionist and Socialist movements), a cosmopolitan port with a strong Western European orientation. Although Russian was not, strictly speaking, Babel's native or even second language (he grew up in a Yiddish-speaking milieu, and his first literary efforts were written in French), he is now generally acknowledged as one of the truly great Russian stylists, and probably the most sophisticated Russian prose writer to emerge so far in this century. At the same time Babel is a profoundly Jewish writer not only in his choice of settings and of subject matter, but also in a more profound sense. His imagination is nourished primarily by the tension between his Jewish ethos and the non-Jewish environment and by his inability to conquer within himself traces of residual Jewishness, particularly those of a moral character.

Babel was not a prolific writer. His renown rests chiefly on two collections of short stories, *Red Cavalry* (*Konarmiya,* 1926) and *Odessa Tales* (1927). Together with two plays, *The Sunset* (1928) and *Maria* (1935), several tales and a few film scripts, these constitute his entire literary legacy.

The incongruities and paradoxes that are so characteristic of Babel's work are also, by a strange coincidence, to be found in Babel's biography. He fought for the Communist cause in the ranks of Cossack horsemen, those traditional archenemies of Jewish shopkeepers, whose role in the anti-Semitic pogroms Babel knew from personal experience and had, in fact, described in sharp outline in "The History of My Dovecote." A peaceful intellectual, he sought acceptance by fierce warriors. Only recently emancipated from a religious orthodoxy, he desperately tried to embrace a secular faith that was even more rigid. The author of a book that made an army immortal, he was denounced by that army's commander, Semyon Budyonnyi, as a slanderer. A fighter for the Soviet regime, he is thought to have died in a Soviet concentration camp.

A disciple of Flaubert and Maupassant, Babel excelled in the highly polished conte, often an extended anecdote related by the protagonist in his own language—be it a peasant dialect, soldier slang, or the strongly Yiddish-accented Russian of Odessa slums. Few writers could equal Babel in the ability to portray a character by means of a few

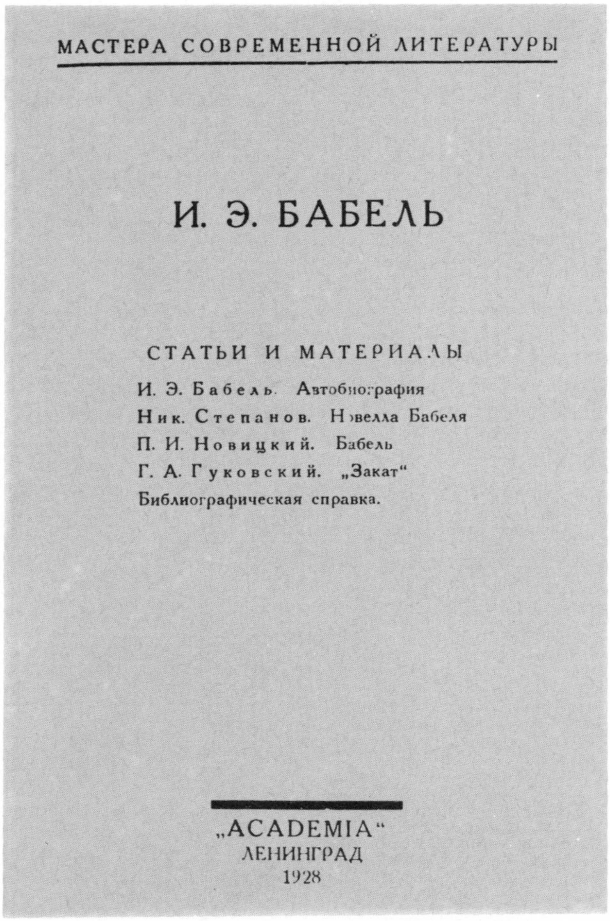
МАСТЕРА СОВРЕМЕННОЙ ЛИТЕРАТУРЫ

И. Э. БАБЕЛЬ

СТАТЬИ И МАТЕРИАЛЫ

И. Э. Бабель. Автобиография
Ник. Степанов. Новелла Бабеля
П. И. Новицкий. Бабель
Г. А. Гуковский. „Закат"
Библиографическая справка.

„ACADEMIA"
ЛЕНИНГРАД
1928

Figure 1. Title page of the volume on Isaac Babel, the second in the series *Masters of Contemporary Literature*, Leningrad, 1928. It contains an autobiographical essay and critical studies of his work. Jerusalem, J.N.U.L.

malapropisms, a partiality for a single "fancy" foreign word, or a slightly irregular syntactical construction.

In the neo-Romantic Babel the traditional motif of infatuation with a "noble savage" is found often and in many different forms. Babel, however, posits the problem somewhat differently. Where other writers—from Rousseau to Tolstoy—saw a confrontation between an intellectual and the natural man, Babel sees a Jew aspiring to the status of a pagan, yet destined to remain frustrated in his desire by the restraints of the Jewish ethic. Try as he may, he will never learn the ways of violence and will, therefore, never gain acceptance into the gentile world: in one of his tales the narrator vainly implores Providence to grant him "the simplest of all proficiencies, the ability to kill fellow men." He loses his best friend, Afonka Bida (to an ear attuned to Yiddish, "the Russian Misfortune") because he would not shoot a wounded comrade. To be admitted into a circle of Cossacks, he must first hideously kill a goose—but then, that night, he must wrestle with his Jewish conscience which abhors murder. Babel's Jewish narrator envies his non-Jewish protagonists' ability to kill one's own father, trample to death a former master, or shoot a black marketeer masquerading as a helpless mother. His Jewishness and hence his alienations have numerous attributes—he wears glasses, he cannot learn to swim, he is a poor horseman, he carries with him books.

It is this envy of what he saw as gentile physical strength and absence of moral restraints that caused Babel to create a gallery of Jewish protagonists who bore little resemblance to pathetic Jews described in certain Yiddish literature or to the Zionist dreamers and visionaries in certain modern Hebrew novels. Babel's Odessa Jews who "bubble like cheap red wine" include an imposing amazon, who presides over a den of thieves and a brothel, dignified beggars with patriarchal beards who oversee Jewish cemeteries and discourse on the vanity of human existence, and the legendary Benya Krik ("Bennie the Howl"), a colorful gangster, the terror of Odessa's merchants and policemen. Babel's scenes of resplendent Jewish wedding feasts and magnificent funeral processions are reminiscent of the lush canvases of a Breughel.

The picturesque world of Polish Ḥasidim and Odessa cart drivers, of waterfront philosophers and ritual slaughterers was disappearing before Babel's eyes, a victim of secularism, pogroms, and the Revolution. Its death was recorded in some of Babel's best tales. A few of these relate only an amusing or a paradoxical incident—e.g., an old-age home receives a new lease on life as a funeral cooperative, but only for as long as it continues the swindle of not burying the corpse together with the only coffin it owns; the first honest funeral arranged by it will also spell its doom. Other stories have moral overtones of varying degrees of significance. An infant is named Karl by its Communist atheist parents in honor of Marx; but the grandparents conspire to have it secretly circumcised and the infant emerges with the hybrid name Karl-Yankel (i.e., Jacob). A rabbi's son joins the Communist Party but, for the time being, continues to live with his parents because he does not want to leave his mother. Just as Babel, long after ceasing to believe in God, could not shed the commandment "thou shalt not kill," so the rabbi's son remains faithful to another commandment which makes it incumbent upon us to honor our parents. In another story, the rabbi's son ultimately leaves his parental home to fight and then to die for the Revolution, but the break with his past is tortured and incomplete: among the killed soldier's belongings his comrades find a portrait of Lenin and another of

Figure 2. Isaac Babel. Drawing from the volume on him in *Masters of Contemporary Literature*, Leningrad, 1928. Jerusalem, J.N.U.L.

Maimonides, Communist Party resolutions with Hebrew verse written in their margins, the text of the *Song of Songs*, and some empty cartridges.

The inability to shift one's allegiances completely was most poignantly illustrated in the short story "Gedali." The protagonist, an old Jew, the owner of a Dickensian curiosity shop, is puzzled because murder and looting are his town's lot no matter whether its current masters are Communist or anti-Communist: how then, he asks, can one tell which is the Revolution and which the counter-revolution? Old Gedali cannot agree to the proposition that ends justify means. He is troubled because the Revolution demands that all of the old values, the good as well as the bad, be discarded: "To the Revolution we say 'yes,' but can we say 'no' to the Sabbath?" And he tells his Communist visitor that what the world really needs is not more politics, but an International of Good Men, in which all men could live in peace and harmony, and in which "every soul would get first category rations."

After some twenty years of disgrace, Babel—or, more precisely, his memory—was cleared by the Soviet authorities of the false charges which caused his arrest and death. His best known works were reprinted in the 1950s and in 1966 but subsequently he was again ignored. [M.F.]

His Life. Until the age of 16, Babel was provided, by private tutors, with a thorough Jewish education, including Hebrew, Bible, and Talmud. At the same time he attended a Russian commercial school in Odessa. During his student years he seems to have been active in Zionist youth circles. In 1915, after graduating from the Kiev Institute of Financial and Business Studies, he went to Petrograd, where he had to avoid the police because as a Jew he had no residence permit. It was in prerevolutionary Petrograd that his first two stories were published in Maxim Gorki's *Letopris* (November 1916; in English in *The Lonely Years*, 1964). After the revolution, he served on the Rumanian front in 1918 and contracted malaria. According to his autobiographical note, the details of which are sometimes contested, he subsequently served the new regime in various functions, as, e.g., in the Cheka (security police), the Commissariat of Education, in "expeditions for provisions" (i.e., confiscating agricultural products in the villages), in the northern army against the White counterrevolutionaries, etc. During his service on the Polish front in Budyonny's 1st Cavalry Army, he developed asthma, and while convalescing in Odessa and the Caucasus, between 1921 and 1924, he wrote and published most of his Jewish *Odessa Tales*.

In 1931, while reporting on the collectivization in the Ukraine, Babel conceived a full novel or a cycle of stories on the collectivization. One chapter appeared in *Novy Mir* (October 1931), but it did not meet ideological requirements and the publication was stopped. Only one other chapter was found and published posthumously (both are in *The Lonely Years*). A fragmentary story called *The Jewess* (published for the first time in the New York Russian magazine *Novy Zhurnal*, June 1968, and in English in *You Must Know Everything*) also seems to have originated in the same period as the beginning of a full-fledged novel. In 1928 and 1932 he was allowed to visit his wife and daughter, who had emigrated to Paris. Babel was sent abroad for the last time as a member of the Soviet writers' delegation to a left-wing congress in Paris in 1935, but in the meantime he virtually stopped publishing. The literary authoritarianism inaugurated in 1934 with the establishment of the Soviet Writers Union induced him to become "a master of silence." He continued writing incessantly but evaded publishing by finding various excuses. "With the death of Gorki" (1936), says his daughter, Natalie, "Babel lost not only a friend but a powerful protector. The ground crumbled under him." Babel was arrested and disappeared in 1939, and all his manuscripts, except those which were deposited with personal friends, were probably destroyed by the secret police. The reason for his arrest is unknown, though Ilya *Ehrenburg indicated in a speech in 1964 that it was somehow connected with his frequent visits to the house of the head of the secret police (NKVD), Nikolai Yezhov, whose wife Babel had known for a long time. Since Yezhov was deposed and executed in 1938, there might be something to this theory. Officially the date of his death was subsequently given as 1941, but after his arrest he was never seen in a camp or in exile, and it is therefore possible that he was shot at once.

Babel's ties with Judaism never ceased. Six of his stories appeared in 1926 in Hebrew translation, "edited by the author," in the only issue of ***Bereshit***, a Hebrew literary almanac in the U.S.S.R. In 1937 he was given the task of preparing the jubilee edition of *Sholem Aleichem's works. He reported for a newspaper on the new Jewish agricultural settlements established in 1928. Though not religious, he went to synagogue on the Day of Atonement, celebrated with his friends the Passover *seder*, and in his letters always reminded his family of approaching festivals. Jewish themes were constantly on his mind as a writer, from the folkloric *Shabbos Nahamu* (intended as the first story in a cycle centered on the figure of Hershele Ostropoler) to the Judaic concept of a "revolution of good people" in the *Red Cavalry* story "Gedali."

The first English edition of *Red Cavalry* appeared in 1929 and the *Collected Stories* (with introduction by Lionel Trilling) in 1955. His other writings became known in the West only in the 1960s, when his daughter, Nathalie, edited and published in English *The Lonely Years, 1925–1939* (1964) containing unpublished stories and private correspondence and *You Must Know Everything* (1969), which also includes a biographical introduction and speeches and reminiscences by I. Ehrenburg, Konstantin Paustovsky, and others. [Ed.]

Bibliography: J. Stova-Sander, *Isaac Babel', 1894–1941: l'homme et l'oeuvre* (1968); A. B. Murphy, in: *Slavonic and East European Review*, 44 (1966), 361–80; I. Ehrenburg, *Memoirs, 1921–1941* (1963), 108–18 and index; R. Rosenthal, in: *Commentary*, 3 (1947), 126–31; *Russkiye Sovetskiye Pisateli: Prosaiki*, 1 (1959), 103–18 (incl. bibl.).

BABEL, TOWER OF, the edifice whose building is portrayed in Genesis 11:1–9 as the direct cause of the diversity of languages in the world and the dispersion of mankind over all the earth. According to the preceding narrative, mankind after the flood was descended from one common ancestor, *Noah. The story of Babel thus explains how the descendants of this one man came to be so widely scattered and divided into separate nations speaking so many different languages.

The story relates how, at the time when all men still spoke one language, there was a migration from the East to the plain of *Shinar (Babylonia). At this site it was decided to build a "city and a tower with its top in the sky" so that the builders would be able to make a name for themselves and avoid being scattered over the entire world. However, their building project was frustrated by the Lord who confounded their language. As a result, mankind was distributed over the face of the earth. The unfinished tower was called Babel, a name which was explained by its resemblance to the Hebrew verb *bll* ("to confuse"), since here the Lord "confounded the speech of the whole earth."

Figure 1. The Tower of Babel as depicted in a mosaic in the basilica of San Marco, Venice, c. 1220. Photo Alinari, Florence.

Scholars agree that the edifice referred to in Genesis 11 is clearly a *ziqqurat*, or Mesopotamian temple tower. The *ziqqurat* (from Akk. *zaqāru*, "to raise up," "elevate") was the central feature of the great temples which were built in all important Mesopotamian cities. Rising in progressively smaller, steplike levels from a massive base, these towers ranged from three or four stories to as many as seven and were ordinarily constructed of crude sun-dried bricks covered with kiln-fired bricks. Clearly, the writer of the account in Genesis 11 was familiar with the building techniques of Mesopotamia, since he is at pains to point out that bricks and bitumen were used in the construction; that is in contrast to the stone and clay which were the common building materials in Canaan.

The particular *ziqqurat* described here was formerly identified with the tower of Ezida, the temple of the god Nebo (Nabû) in Borsippa, a city southwest of Babylon. However, the discovery at the end of the 19th century of Esagila, the great temple of *Marduk in *Babylon, has led most scholars to agree that it is the tower of this temple which inspired the writer of Genesis 11. This *ziqqurat*, which was called *E-temen-an-ki*, "house of the foundations of heaven and earth," rose to a height of about 300 feet, and contained two sanctuaries: one at its base, which was 300 feet square, and one at its summit. The tower was probably constructed at the time of *Hammurapi, but was damaged or destroyed several times and repaired by Esarhaddon (seventh century B.C.E.) and Nebuchadnezzar II (sixth century B.C.E.), among others. It is interesting to note that the Babylonians believed that Esagila was built by the gods, thus making the statement in Genesis 11:5 "... which the sons of men had built," particularly meaningful, since it may be understood as a polemic against this belief. This tower, which was the object of such pride among the Babylonians, was the product of strictly human endeavor which can be quickly and easily destroyed in accordance with the Divine Will. In fact, it is quite likely that it was the sight of the ruins of Esagila (which was destroyed in the mid-16th century B.C.E., with the destruction of Babylon by the Hittites) which inspired the creator of the Tower of Babel narrative.

Although it is clear from the story that the work on the city and tower displeased the Lord, the specific sin of the builders is nowhere mentioned. Many scholars believe that it was the presumption of these men in thinking that they could build a tower with "its top in the sky," and their conceit in wanting "to make a name" for themselves, which incurred the wrath of the Lord. Others believe that their goal was to storm the heavens and that it was for this sin that mankind was punished.

Modern scholars (already anticipated by R. *Samuel ben Meir) have pointed out that the desire to remain together in one place was in direct conflict with the divine purpose as is expressed to Noah and his sons after the flood: "Be fertile and increase and fill up the earth" (Gen. 9:7) and was, therefore, an affront to God and so necessarily doomed to failure. It is hardly likely that the expressed wish to "make a name for ourselves" could be construed as sinful, since a similar phrase is used in connection with the divine promises to Abraham (Gen. 12:2). Further, Babylonian temple inscriptions frequently refer to the "making great" of the name of the king under whom the particular temple was built or repaired, thereby demonstrating that this formula was commonly used in such instances and need not be understood as expressing an inordinate desire for fame. As for the phrase "with its top in the sky," it has been noted that there are several examples of Babylonian temple inscriptions which describe buildings as reaching to heaven so that the phrase should be understood not as an expression of the presumption of these people or of their desire to ascend to heaven, but rather as a borrowing by the biblical writer from the technical terminology of Mesopotamian temple inscriptions with which he was evidently familiar. According to this interpretation the sin of these

Figure 2. The building of the Tower of Babel is depicted in the upper left-hand panel of a page from the *Golden Haggadah*, Spain, 14th century. London, British Museum, Add. Ms. 27210, fol. 3R.

people was, therefore, not presumption or a desire to reach heaven and gain fame, but rather an attempt to change the divinely ordained plan for mankind.

A new link to an ultimate cuneiform background of the Tower of Babel narrative has been provided by a Sumerian literary work, no doubt composed during the third Dynasty of Ur, which states that originally mankind spoke the same language, until Enki, the Sumerian god of wisdom, confounded their speech. Though the reason for the confusion of tongues is not stated, Kramer has suggested that it may have been inspired by Enki's jealousy of another god, Enlil. Hence, in the Sumerian version it was a case of the rivalry between two gods, whereas in the Bible the rivalry was between God and man (see below "The Meaning of the Story").

The etymology of the name Babel given in this narrative is a contrived one, used ironically. The Babylonians understood it to mean "the gate of the god" *(bāb-ilim),* thereby endowing the city with additional honor and importance. By a play on words, the Bible has given it a pejorative sense, making the pride in this city seem almost ludicrous.

The Tower of Babel narrative is a turning point in history, as understood by the Bible, in that it signals the end of the era of universal monotheism which had existed since the beginning of time. Since the divine election of Abraham and his descendants immediately follows, it must be tacitly assumed that the incident led to the introduction of idolatry into the world. [My.S.]

The Meaning of the Story. The bridge which some modern writers have constructed between the single short clause "and fill the earth" in Genesis 1:28 (or 9:7) and the account of the vain attempt of an early generation of men to avoid dispersal in Genesis 11:1–9, is superior homiletics but (quite apart from the finding of source analysis that the one belongs to document P and the other to document J) unsound exegesis. Genesis 1:28 reads as follows: "God blessed them [namely, the human beings, male and female, whose creation has just been narrated in the preceding verse] and God said to them, 'Be fertile and increase, fill the earth and master it; and rule the fish of the sea, the birds of the sky, and all the living things that move about on earth.'" This purports to be, and is, not a command but a blessing; moreover "and fill the earth" is preceded by "be fertile and increase." It is absurd to read into it a wish of God that the human species shall spread over the earth otherwise than as, with increasing numbers, its own interests may dictate. And in 11:1–9 there is nothing to suggest that the human population has already attained such a figure that there is a need for a migration of colonists to realms beyond the confines of the plain of Shinar; and neither is there a word in 11:1–9 about that being the Deity's motive in bringing about the dispersal. Instead, there is an explicit declaration of an entirely different motive by no less an authority than the Lord himself, who explains to the divine beings, verses 6–7; "If this is what, as one people with one language common to all, they have been able to do as a beginning, nothing they may propose to do will be beyond their reach. Come, let us go down, etc." It takes a willful shutting of the mind to avoid hearing the same anxiety lest man should wrest complete equality with the divine beings (or worse) in these words as in the Lord's earlier explanation to the same audience, in 3:22, of his motive in driving man out of the Garden of Eden: "Now that man has become like one of us in knowing good and bad [i.e., in being intellectually mature, the first evidence of which was his newfound modesty], what if he should stretch out his hand and take also from the tree of life and eat, and live forever!" Once, to obviate the danger of further baleful results from cooperation between man and snake, the Lord set up a barrier of enmity between them (3:15); now, in order to eliminate the threat of disastrous consequences from the cooperation of men with each other, he is erecting among them barriers of language and distance. [H.L.G.]

In the Aggadah: The biblical account of the Tower of Babel is singularly brief and vague (Gen. R. 38). The prevailing opinion of the rabbis is that it was designed to serve the purposes of idolatry and constituted an act of rebellion against God (Sanh. 109a; Gen. R. 38:6; et al.), for which reason they also associated Nimrod ("the rebel") with its building (Ḥul. 89a). Many additional reasons are also suggested, among them the fear of a recurrence of the flood and the need to guard against such a recurrence by supporting the heavens or by splitting them so that waters would drain away slowly from the earth's surface (*Ma'asim al Aseret ha-Dibberot;* cf. Sanh. 109a). According to Josephus they were trying to dwell higher than the water level of the flood (Ant., I, IV). In this way the builders thought they would be spared, believing as they did that God had power over water alone (PdRE 24). At the same time the rabbis laud the unity and love of peace that prevailed among them (Gen. R. 38), as a result of which they were given an opportunity to repent, but they failed, however, to seize it *(ibid.).* Various opinions are expressed as to the punishment which the builders incurred (Tanḥ. B., 23). According to the Mishnah (Sanh. 10:3), they were excluded from a share in the world to come. In the view of one *amora,* their punishment varied with the differing aims that inspired them; those who thought to dwell in heaven being dispersed throughout the world, those who sought to wage war against God being transformed into apes and demons, and those bent on idol worship being caught up in a confusion of tongues (Sanh. 109a). One-third of the tower was destroyed by fire, one-third subsided into the earth, and one-third is still standing. It is so high that to anyone ascending and looking down from the top, palm trees look like locusts *(ibid.).* This *aggadah* testifies to the existence of ruins at that time, which were popularly believed as being of the Tower of Babel. *Aggadot* about the tower are also to be found in Josephus and in the apocrypha (cf. Jub. 10:18–28), while several of its motifs are much discussed in Hellenistic Jewish literature.

[I.T.-S.]

In The Arts. The biblical story of the tower of Babel appears repeatedly in medieval and Renaissance literature, treated as an historical incident with strong moral overtones. Some examples are the *Chronicon* of Isidore of Seville (c. 560–636 C.E.), the *Weltchronik* of Rudolf von Ems (1200–1254), and the *Speculum humanae salvationis* (c. 1324), a Dominican manual of devotion which was frequently copied. Giovanni *Boccaccio wrote on the subject in his *De casibus virorum illustrium* (1355–60), as did an anonymous poet of Lyons in *Le Triumphe de Haulte Folie* (c. 1550). Two 17th-century Spanish works were entitled *Torre de Babilonia:* one was an *auto sacramentale* by the eminent dramatist Pedro Calderón de la Barca, the other by the Marrano author Antonio Enríquez *Gómez. Modern treatments include *Tower of Babel* (1874) by the English poet Alfred Austin and *Babel* (1952), an apocalyptic work by the French poet Pierre Emmanuel (1916–).

The subject appealed to medieval artists, appearing in 12th-century mosaics at Palermo and Monreale in Sicily and in the 13th-century Cathedral of St. Mark, Venice. There are representations in illuminated manuscripts from the 12th to the 14th centuries, including the German *Hortus Deliciarum* ("Garden of Delights") and the Sarajevo *Haggadah.* Two 15th-century painters who used the theme were the Frenchman Jean Fouquet and the Italian Benozzo Gozzoli, who painted the fresco of Campo Santo, Pisa, now destroyed. With its landscape setting and the opportunities it offered for fantasy and close observation of the

Figure 3. "The Tower of Babel" by Pieter Brueghel the Elder, 1563. Vienna, Kunsthistorisches Museum.

daily scene, the Tower was of considerable interest to the early Flemish painters. It was generally depicted either as a multistory structure, diminishing in size as it rose or, more often, as a square or circular building surrounded by a ramp. Some artists illustrated contemporary building methods, a fine example occurring in the Book of Hours of the Duke of Bedford (Paris, c. 1423), where the construction of the Tower proceeds at night under the stars. In Pieter Brueghel's *Tower of Babel* (1563), the building—leaning slightly—is shown in a vast landscape near the banks of a river, with a king arriving to inspect the progress of the work.

Although the Babel story might appear to be a temptation to composers, since the confusion of tongues can be expressed most effectively in music, very few works have in fact been written on the theme. These are mainly oratorios including César Franck's *La Tour de Babel* (1865) and Anton Rubinstein's markedly unsuccessful *Der Turm zu Babel* (1858; revised as an opera, 1872). Two 20th-century works are *La Tour de Babel* (1932) by René Barbier and Igor Stravinsky's *Babel*, a cantata for narrator, men's chorus, and orchestra (1944, published in 1952). [Ed.]

Bibliography: In the Bible: Abraham Ibn Ezra, Commentary to Gen. 11:1–9; M. D. Cassuto, *Mi-No'aḥ ad Avraham* (1959[3]), 154–69; S. R. Driver, *The Book of Genesis* (1904[2]), 132–7; Kaufmann Y., Toledot, 2 (1960), 412–5; N. M. Sarna, *Understanding Genesis* (1967), 63–80 (incl. bibl.); J. Skinner, *The Book of Genesis* (ICC, 1930), 223–31; S. N. Kramer, in: JAOS, 88 (1968), 108–11. In the Aggadah: Ginzberg, Legends, index; U. Cassuto, *Commentary on the Book of Genesis*, 2 (1964), 225–49; J. Gutmann, in: *Oz le-David [Ben Gurion]* (1964), 584–94. In the Arts: H. Minkowski, *Aus dem Nebel der Vergangenheit steigt der Turm zu Babel: Bilder aus 1000 Jahren* (1960); L. Réau, *Iconographie de l'art chrétien*, 2 pt. 1 (1957), 120–3, incl. bibl.; T. Ehrenstein, *Das Alte Testament im Bilde* (1923), 125–32; H. Gressmann, *Tower of Babel* (1928), 1–19.

BABI YAR, a ravine on the outskirts of *Kiev which has come to symbolize Jewish martyrdom at the hands of the Nazis in the Soviet Union. On Sept. 29–30, 1941, 33,771 Jews were machine-gunned there, according to an official German report. The carnage was performed by a special *SS unit *(Sonderkommando)* supported by Ukrainian militia men. At the end of 778 days of Nazi rule in Kiev, the ravine had become a mass grave for over 100,000 persons, the majority of them being Jews. A note of the Soviet government to the Allies about German war crimes, dated Jan. 6, 1942 and signed by V. M. Molotov, gives a vivid description of the massacre, pointing out that the victims

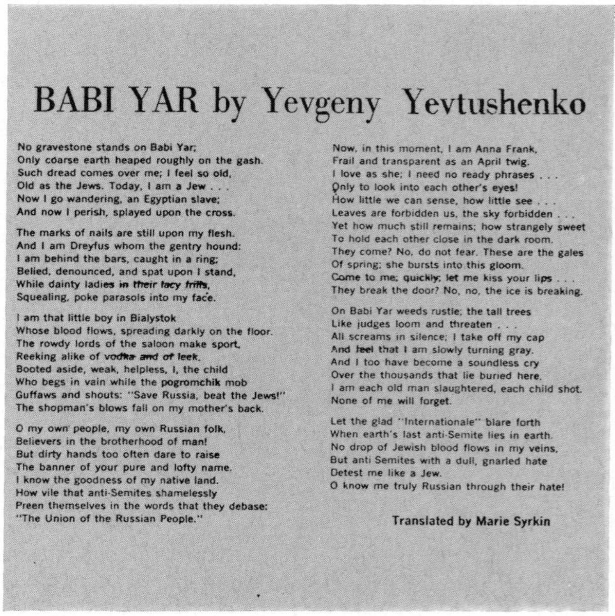

BABI YAR by Yevgeny Yevtushenko

No gravestone stands on Babi Yar;
Only coarse earth heaped roughly on the gash.
Such dread comes over me; I feel so old,
Old as the Jews. Today, I am a Jew . . .
Now I go wandering, an Egyptian slave;
And now I perish, splayed upon the cross.

The marks of nails are still upon my flesh.
And I am Dreyfus whom the gentry hound:
I am behind the bars, caught in a ring;
Belied, denounced, and spat upon I stand,
While dainty ladies in their lacy frills,
Squealing, poke parasols into my face.

I am that little boy in Bialystok
Whose blood flows, spreading darkly on the floor.
The rowdy lords of the saloon make sport,
Reeking alike of vodka and of leek.
Booted aside, weak, helpless, I, the child
Who begs in vain while the pogromchik mob
Guffaws and shouts: "Save Russia, beat the Jews!"
The shopman's blows fall on my mother's back.

O my own people, my own Russian folk,
Believers in the brotherhood of man!
But dirty hands too often dare to raise
The banner of your pure and lofty name.
I know the goodness of my native land.
How vile that anti-Semites shamelessly
Preen themselves in the words that they debase:
"The Union of the Russian People."

Now, in this moment, I am Anna Frank,
Frail and transparent as an April twig.
I love as she; I need no ready phrases . . .
Only to look into each other's eyes!
How little we can sense, how little see . . .
Leaves are forbidden us, the sky forbidden . . .
Yet how much still remains; how strangely sweet
To hold each other close in the dark room.
They come? No, do not fear. These are the gales
Of spring; she bursts into this gloom.
Come to me; quickly; let me kiss your lips . . .
They break the door? No, no, the ice is breaking.

On Babi Yar weeds rustle; the tall trees
Like judges loom and threaten . . .
All screams in silence; I take off my cap
And feel that I am slowly turning gray.
And I too have become a soundless cry
Over the thousands that lie buried here.
I am each old man slaughtered, each child shot.
None of me will forget.

Let the glad "Internationale" blare forth
When earth's last anti-Semite lies in earth.
No drop of Jewish blood flows in my veins,
But anti Semites with a dull, gnarled hate
Detest me like a Jew.
O know me truly Russian through their hate!

Translated by Marie Syrkin

Figure 1. A translation of Yevtushenko's *Babi Yar* by Marie Syrkin, Hadassah Magazine, March 1967.

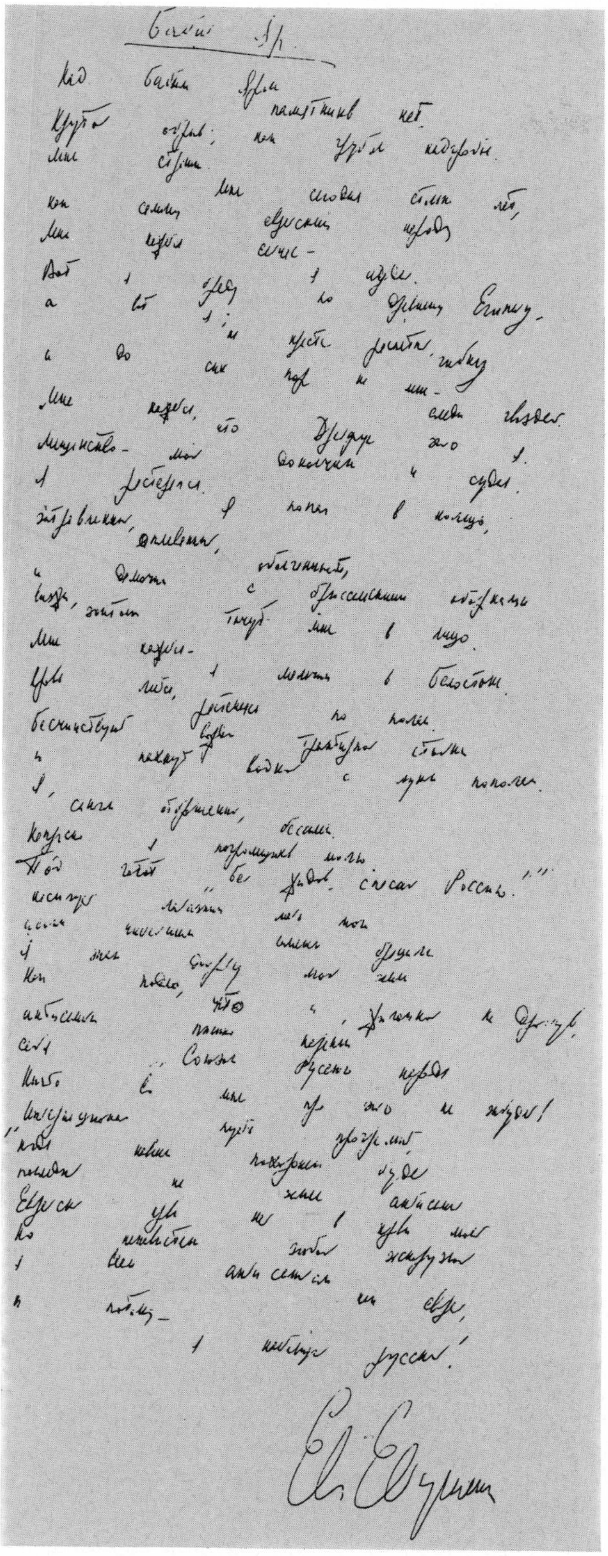

Figure 2. Beginning and end of the manuscript of the poem *Babi Yar* by Yevgeni Yevtushenko, Jerusalem, J.N.U.L. Schwadron Collection.

were "a great number of Jews, including women and children of all ages." In spite of German efforts in August 1943 to erase all traces of the mass burial through massive incineration, the evidence could not be suppressed and after the war the Soviet public at large learned of the martyrdom through newspaper accounts, official reports, and belles lettres. In 1947 I. Ehrenburg in his novel *Burya* ("The Storm") described dramatically the mass killing of the Jews of Kiev in Babi Yar. Preparations were made for a monument at Babi Yar as a memorial to the victims of Nazi genocide. The architect A. V. Vlasov had designed a memorial and the artist B. Ovchinnikov had produced the necessary sketches.

But since the anti-*"cosmopolitan" campaign of 1948–49, an effort was made to eliminate all references to Babi Yar. This policy had as an objective the removal from Jewish consciousness of those martyrological elements that might sustain it. Even after the death of Stalin, Babi Yar remained lost in the "memory hole" of history. Intellectuals, however, refused to be silent. On Oct. 10, 1959, the novelist Viktor Nekrasov cried out in the pages of *Literaturnaya Gazeta* for a memorial at Babi Yar, and against the official intention to transform the ravine into a sports stadium. Far more impressive was the poem *Babi Yar* written by Yevgeni *Yevtushenko published in the same journal on Sept. 19, 1961. With its open attack upon anti-Semitism and its implied denunciation of those who rejected Jewish martyrdom, the poem exerted a profound impact on Soviet youth as well as upon world public opinion. Dmitri Shostakovich set the lines to music in his 13th Symphony, performed for the first time in December 1962.

Russian ultranationalism struck back almost immediately. Yevtushenko was sharply criticized by a number of literary apologists of the regime and then publicly denounced by Premier Nikita Khrushchev in *Pravda* on March 8, 1963. The theme of a specific Jewish martyrdom was condemned. But Babi Yar would not remain suppressed. It again surfaced during the summer of 1966 in a documentary novel written by Anatoly Kuznetsov published in *Yunost* (Eng. tr. 1967). Earlier that year the Ukrainian Architects Club in Kiev held a public exhibit of more than 200 projects and some 30 large-scale detailed plans for a memorial to Babi Yar. None of the inscriptions in the proposed plans mentioned Jewish martyrdom.

Bibliography: Y. Yevtushenko, *A Precocious Autobiography* (London, 1963); W. Korey, in: *New Republic* (Jan. 8, 1962); idem, in: *Saturday Review* (Feb. 3, 1968); S. M. Schwarz, *Yevrei v Sovetskom Soyuze 1939–1965* (1966), 359–71.

[W.K.]

BABOVICH (Bobovitch), SIMḤAH BEN SOLOMON (1790–1855), *Karaite *ḥakham* in the Crimea. Babovich mainly devoted himself to obtaining more rights for the Karaites in Russia. In 1827, in conjunction with the Karaite scholar Joseph Solomon *Luzki, he obtained release of the Karaites from the law regarding military service for Jews. The Karaites in Eupatoria commemorated this event in an annual prayer. When in 1837 the Russian government granted religious autonomy to the Karaites, Babovich was appointed their spiritual head, although he was not distinguished as a scholar. In 1839 Babovich was instructed by the government to provide exact information on the origin, nature, and history of the Karaites. Babovich turned to A. *Firkovich, who then proceeded to produce a series of documents, some partly falsified.

Bibliography: J. M. Jost, *Geschichte des Judentums und seiner Sekten*, 2 (1858), 374; Isaac b. Solomon, *Pinnat Yikrat*, (1834, with letters from Jost and their Tatar translation); J. Fuerst, Karaeertum, 3 (1869), 137; A. Firkovich, *Iggeret Teshu'at Yisrael* (1840, with Judeo-Tatar translation); idem, *Avnei Zikkaron* (1872), 2, 5, 18ff.; A. Harkavy, *Altjuedische Denkmaeler aus der Krim* (1876), 270ff.; E. Deinard, *Massa Krim* (1878), 20–40.

[I.M./Ed.]

BABYLON (Heb. בָּבֶל), ancient city located on the eastern bank of the Euphrates River, about 20.4 mi. (34 km.) S. of Baghdad, near the modern village of Hillah. Akkadian scribes derived the name from the words *bāb-ili(m)* ("gate of god"), whereas in Genesis 11:9 the name is explained as a derivation from the root *bll* ("to confuse"). Biblical

Figure 1. An impression of the walled city of Babylon as rebuilt in the Neo-Babylonian period (seventh–sixth centuries B.C.E.), with the temple of Marduk on its seven-storied base on the left and the palace complex on the right. From *Nineveh and Babylon* by André Parrot, 1961.

tradition associates Babylon with Erech and Akkad (Gen. 10:10), implying that it was one of the earliest cities in Babylonia. This view of the antiquity of Babylon was also current in Babylon itself in the period after *Hammurapi. The antiquity of Babylon is stressed by the theory of B. Landsberger of the heritage of the earliest, pre-Sumerian settlers of Mesopotamia. The name "Babel" is part of this heritage and it has no factual Sumerian or Semitic etymology.

The first certain mention of Babylon in cuneiform texts is from the time of the Third Dynasty of *Ur (c. 2113–2006 B.C.E.), when it served as a provincial capital and seat of a governor (cf. Yale Oriental Series, IV/2 pp. 15ff.; W. W. Hallo, *Journal of Cuneiform Studies*, vol. 14, p. 95). During the Isin-Larsa period (c. 2017–1794) it became the capital of a small independent kingdom under an Amorite dynasty. The city gained greater strength during the time of Hammurapi (1792–1749 B.C.E.), when it extended its influence over most of southern Mesopotamia. Under Hammurapi's son, however, the southern part of the kingdom was lost to the kings of the "Dynasty of the Sea land" (see *Mesopotamia). During the Cassite and Middle Babylonian periods Babylon maintained precariously its basic position as a capital city in southern Mesopotamia. As Assyria rose, it aspired to rule over Babylon. During the reign of the Assyrian king Tukulti-Ninurta I (1244–1208), Babylon was partially destroyed, but it recovered from its misfortune shortly afterward. When Tiglath-Pileser III (745–727) took Babylon he gave it the status of an independent kingdom united to Assyria only by a personal union. In Babylon he reigned under another name, Pulu, which happens to have found its way into the Bible (II Kings 15:19). Shalmaneser V (726–722) continued the practice of employing another name in Babylon. The Chaldean Merodach-Baladan proclaimed an independent kingdom on Shalmaneser's death, but Sargon II (722–705) overthrew him in 710; and, though he did not adopt a different throne name in Babylon, he made it his residence for the years 710, 709, and 708 and added "the king of Akkad, viceroy of Babylon" to his title. On his death Merodach-Baladan returned and Babylon became a center of resistance, allowing *Sennacherib no other alternative but to destroy the city in 689. *Esarhaddon (680–669) rebuilt the city and toward the end of his life he divided his kingdom between his two sons, making Shamash-shum-ukin his heir in Babylon and Ashurbanipal in Assyria. The latter had to besiege and reconquer Babylon, when Shamash-shum-ukin tried to establish the independence of southern Mesopotamia. In 626 Nabopolassar, like Merodach-Baladan, a Chaldean, made himself king of Akkad at Babylon and he and his successor Nebuchadnezzar III proceeded to build the Neo-Babylonian empire at the expense of the Assyrian Empire, which was completely liquidated in 609. As the capital of the Neo-Babylonian Empire, to which Judah was annexed in 586, Babylon underwent a vast program of public building and fortification. After the fall of the Neo-Babylonian Empire to the Persians, Babylon maintained its dominant position. With the fall of the Persian Empire to Alexander the Great, Babylon offered no resistance and was made the capital of his new empire. Seleucus I (Nicator), Alexander's successor, founded *Seleucia not far away on the Tigris, and the inhabitants of Babylon slowly moved to Seleucia, deserting Babylon. About the city plan of Babylon much can be learned from cuneiform sources (apart from the later classical references of Herodotus), the majority of which were collected by E. Unger (see bibl.) and from the excavations.

Figure 2. The Ishtar Gate of the Neo-Babylonian palace built on the north side of the city, reconstructed in the British Museum, London. It was decorated with 575 dragons and bulls and 120 lions on a background of lapis-lazuli glazed bricks. Photo from A. Parrot, *Nineveh and Babylon*.

Figure 3. Detail of the decorated façade of the Neo-Babylonian palace in the British Museum. Photo from A. Parrot, *Nineveh and Babylon.*

Major excavations were conducted on the site by the German architect R. Koldewey from 1899 to 1917. These excavations revealed data for all levels of occupation from Old Babylonian (c. 1894–1595 B.C.E.) to Parthian (c. 539–331 B.C.E.), but their main importance lay in the extensive evidence for the Neo-Babylonian period (c. 625–539 B.C.E.). Koldewey uncovered two palaces of *Nebuchadnezzar and the ancient fortress that adjoined the interior wall of the city (Herodotus, 1:181). The royal palace (1046 ft. × 617 ft.; 322 × 190 m.), containing the throne room (169 ft. × 55 ft.; 52 × 17 m.), was found around one of the courtyards. The façade of the palace was made of enamel-covered bricks, decorated with pillars and capitals in various colors on a blue background. The royal throne was located in an alcove in the wall opposite the entrance. To the northeast stood a thick-walled building which contained a corridor and rows of vaulted rooms. It is assumed that this was the location of the Hanging Gardens referred to by the Greek authors and considered in their time one of the wonders of the world. In this building were discovered clay tablets upon which were inscribed allocations of food—i.e., the king's allowance for those who ate at his board—including lists of the daily portions given to *Jehoiachin, king of Judah.

To the east of the palaces passed the main road, which was used for processions on the *akītu* festival, the Babylonian New Year celebration. At the road's northern end the processions passed into the inner city by way of the "Ishtar Gate," which was decorated on the outside with reliefs of wild bulls, fanciful animals with serpentine limbs and lion's feet, and wild birds, and the inside with reliefs of lions. South of Nebuchadnezzar's palace, at the end of the parade road, was a large temple of *Marduk, Esagila, whose walls were made of trees from Lebanon decorated with gold, marble, and precious stones. North of it stood the *ziqqurat* (see Tower of *Babel), a pyramidal structure, built in successive stepped-back stages on a square base. Each of its sides was 295 ft. (91 m.) long. The highest tower, according to Herodotus' description (1:181), contained a "great temple." The city and suburbs, which also extended to the west of the Euphrates, were connected by a drawbridge. The city itself, traversed by straight streets, contained many three- and four-story buildings (1:180). The greatness of Babylon left its mark in biblical sources (see Isa. 13:19). Jeremiah mentions several times "the walls of Babylon," well known from the "city plan" and other inscriptions. Babylon's city-god, Marduk, became the state god under the Cassites perhaps when Nebuchadnezzar I recovered Marduk's statue from Elam—and was represented in *Enuma Elish* as having had supremacy over the entire pantheon conferred on him by the gods. In later times, the god was mostly called Bel. Both names are known in the Bible.

For later periods see *Babylonia.

Bibliography: R. Koldewey, *The Excavations at Babylon* (1914); E. Unger, *Babylon, die heilige Stadt . . .* (1931); B. Landsberger, *Die Serie anaittišu* (1937); S. A. Pallis, *Early Exploration in Mesopotamia* (1954); I. J. Gelb, in: *Journal of the Institute of Asian Studies*, 1 (1955), 1–4; A. Parrot, *Babylon and the Old Testament* (1958); S. N. Kramer, *The Sumerians* (1963), 40–41; EM, 2 (1965), 10–27 (incl. extensive bibl.); C. J. Gadd, in: CAH², 1 (1965), ch. 22; H. W. F. Saggs, in: D. W. Thomas (ed.), *Archaeology and Old Testament Study* (1967), 39–56; idem, *The Greatness that was Babylon* (1962). [ED.]

BABYLONIA, ancient country in Western Asia between the Tigris and the Euphrates; corresponding approximately to the modern *Iraq.

Introduction. The area was settled by the Sumerians in the third millennium B.C.E. Sargon I (24th century B.C.E.) founded the *Akkadian dynasty which dominated the area for 200 years. At a later period (c. 1850 B.C.E.) the *Amorites ruled over northern Babylonia. The city gained greater strength during the time of *Hammurapi (1792–1749 B.C.E.) when it extended its influence over most of southern Mesopotamia. Later rulers of the area were the *Hittites and the Assyrians. The Assyrian kingdom was overthrown in 612 B.C.E. and succeeded by the neo-Chaldean kingdom of which the outstanding figure was *Nebuchadnezzar. However, 25 years after his death the country was captured by *Cyrus, king of Persia, and ceased to exist as an independent kingdom.

For a full description of this period up to Cyrus see *Mesopotamia.

Achaemenid Period. A turning point in Near Eastern history was heralded by the Medes' conquest of the Assyrian capital, Nineveh, in 612 B.C.E., and arrived when Babylon fell to the Achaemenid Persians in 538. After two millennia of Semitic rule in the ancient Near East, an age was beginning in which Iranians and then others would dominate; but the new masters of the area would continue to draw heavily on the older cultural heritage.

The first important Achaemenid, Cyrus, conquered Media in 549, Lydia in 546, and Babylon in 538; next, *Cambyses took Egypt in 525; then *Darius extended the empire into northern India by some time before 513. This conquest ranks in its speed and its scale with the later exploits of Alexander (for whom it may have served as a model) and with the initial spread of Islam. While Persepolis, in an upland valley of what is today southwestern Iran, remained the Achaemenids' ceremonial capital, much of the business of the extended empire was handled from Susa, at the edge of the Mesopotamian plain.

Babylon, further to the west, became a more local administrative center.

Organized into a score of satrapies or provinces and held together by an effective system of roads, communications, and standardized coinage, the empire introduced a largely new conception of legitimacy or imperial ideology to the area. The ancient Near Eastern empires had often ruled by the forcible displacement of local institutions or had placed them in subservient vassal relationships by treaty. The Achaemenids, though still relying on the universal language of force, sought to exercise it by posing as heirs of local dynastic traditions and by following wherever expedient the local idiom. Thus in Egypt the Persian kings ruled as pharaohs, and in Babylon as kings of Babylon; and Isaiah 45 provides evidence that Jews in Babylonia on the eve of the Persian conquest expected Cyrus to be the anointed of the Lord. On taking Babylon, Cyrus did not in fact promulgate the Judean cult but restored a variety of local cults. He relates in a cylinder inscription (Pritchard, Texts, 315) that he restored to their localities the divine images which Nabonidus, the last Babylonian king, had carried off to Babylon. Later, Darius reprimanded his satrap Gadatas in Asia Minor for abuse of local shrine property (text in A.T. Olmstead, *History of the Persian Empire,* 156). The policy seems to have been one of religious tolerance provided that subject populations were politically docile (Ezra 1 and 4–7); Xerxes' inscription in which he tells of suppressing the worship of *daevas,* gods false by Zoroastrian standards (text *ibid.,* 232) could be interpreted either as a case of political rebellion or of heresy in the Iranian heartland, to which the lenient policy of more westerly regions was inapplicable. In any event, diversity of religion under imperial patronage appears to have replaced the Near East's earlier close association of palace and temple wherever Jews were concerned.

Exiled from Judea by the Babylonians in 597 and 586 B.C.E., a small community of leading Judeans whose experience was to be adopted as the spiritual heritage of all Israel had been settled along the canals of Babylon (Ps. 137:1), such as the Chebar (Ezek. 1:1) and in ruined sites, such as Tel-Abib (Ezek. 3:15), Tel-Melah, and Tel-Harsha (Ezra 2:59; Neh. 7:61), which they were apparently expected to rebuild and cultivate (cf. Jer. 29:4–5). The initial feeling in this "foreign land" was one of intense yearning for Jerusalem (Ps. 137). Some not clearly datable biblical materials may describe this experience, such as the Tower of Babel account (Gen. 11, commonly regarded as much earlier), which associates the problem of linguistic diversity with the locality of Babylon; but Ezekiel provides the clearest contemporary evidence for conditions at the start of the Exile.

Following the Achaemenids' permission to return to Palestine and restore the Judean cult, there is virtually no specific evidence concerning the status of the Jewish community of Babylon. That such a community remained there is evident from its mention, for example, as the home of Ezra, and from its existence in post-Achaemenid times. Later tradition emphasizes the continuity of the Babylonian community; the *Seder Olam Zuta* sets forth a line of exilarchs back to the deported Jehoiachin (Jeconiah), the next to last of the kings of Judah—evidence at least that the idea of exiles who did not return was credible later on. Scholars have sought to document Jewish business success in Babylonia on the basis of personal names in cuneiform texts of the family of Murashu in Nippur from the reign of Artaxerxes I, an attempt which while plausible puts severe strain on the linguistic evidence. That, in the course of time, Jews attained positions of privilege and responsibility is inferred from Nehemiah's service as cupbearer at the Achaemenid court. Some may not have been trusted; Eusebius (*Eusebius Werke,* ed. by R. Helm 7 (1956), 112–3) relates Artaxerxes III's deportation of Jews to Hyrcania, on the Caspian Sea, as the result of a revolt around 350 B.C.E.

Seleucid Period. Alexander led a Macedonian army in the conquest of Babylon in 331 B.C.E. and died there after his Bactrian and Indian campaigns in 323. His generals thereupon dismembered his empire in a struggle for control of it. The dynasty of Seleucus, which was to rule Mesopotamia for two centuries, was heir to a domain without a stable ethnic base or heartland. Whereas Persians had been rulers of "Iran and non-Iran," as later usage put it, the Macedonian Seleucids were rulers only of non-Macedonia. Seleucid imperial policy, therefore, began as a colonial policy throughout all the realm: it called for the founding of new cities, populated by immigrant Macedonian and Greek garrisons, administrators, and merchants, strategically situated and fortified along the principal roads and rivers. Seleucia on the Tigris, founded by Seleucus I, was one of these, and it tended to flourish at Babylon's expense. Antiochus I transferred a considerable Semitic population to Seleucia from Babylon in 275 B.C.E., a policy of centralization causing a decline in Babylon's material fortunes which is documented in cuneiform literature.

The initial Hellenization of Babylonia was followed in time by a more complex interaction between Seleucid institutions and those of the indigenous populations. In the name of royal if not divine prerogative, Antiochus III began to tap temple treasuries to pay the indemnity he owed after losing to the Romans, but encountered stiff resistance and was killed during one such attempt at a temple in Elam in 187. Antiochus IV sought to strengthen a shaky empire by extending Greek communities and institutions in the older centers of the empire, including a refurbishing of Babylon. But it was a desperate and futile attempt to stem the tide of history, and amounted to a Greek veneer on Semitic Babylon; the old local institutions survived, and individuals bore double, Greek-Babylonian, names. The Babylonia which came under Parthian rule in 129 B.C.E. was still ethnically and culturally heterogeneous.

With the Greeks as a ruling minority in Babylonia, the Jews as a subject minority appear to have prospered by trusting and being trusted. Josephus reports that Alexander reaffirmed the privileges which the Persians had accorded them (Ant., 11:338). Jews served in the Greek armies: Josephus (Apion, 1:192) mentions Alexander's excusing Jewish soldiers on grounds of religious scruples from the army's work on the temple of Bel in Babylon; and a Jewish contingent (in c. 220 B.C.E.) aided in the defense of Babylonia against a Galatian invasion (II Macc. 8:20). Antiochus III sent 2,000 Jewish families, about 210 B.C.E., as settlers to assist in an effort to control Asia Minor (Jos., Ant., 12:147–53).

The extent to which during the second century B.C.E. the declining fortunes of the Seleucids undermined any common interest between the Jews of the Babylonian Diaspora and the imperial government is difficult to judge, again owing to the scarcity of sources; but Babylonian silence during the Maccabean uprising in Palestine suggests that to the end of Seleucid rule, loyalties were determined with reference primarily to local rather than distant conditions. A mark of Seleucid times which lasted when others passed was the Babylonian Jews' use of the Seleucid era (counting the years from 312 B.C.E.) as the basis of dating under Parthian and Sassanian rule down to the time of the *geonim.* [W.G.O.]

Parthian Period. The Parthians, an Iranian people, were originally a nomadic tribe called the Parni. They had settled in the region east and north of the Caspian, called Parthia, and so came to be called by the name of that territory. The Arsacid dynasty was founded about 240 B.C.E. by Arsaces, and all subsequent rulers bore that name. The expansion of the Parthian territory began with the annexation of Hyrcania, but moved slowly until the Seleucid Empire had been weakened elsewhere. Then the Parthians rapidly inherited the portions of the empire east of the Euphrates. Mithridates I, the real founder of the Parthian Empire, ascended the throne in 171, reached Media in 155, and Seleucia on the Tigris in 141. For the next 20 years, Babylonia was contested by Parthians, Seleucids, and the Hellenistic state of Characene. By 120, however, Mithridates II had permanently established his rule on the Euphrates' frontier. Since the Parthians were fundamentally a military aristocracy, they were concerned with fostering local support among indigenous populations. They made little effort to win over the conquered peoples to their culture and religion. They preserved Greek legal forms and allowed the Jews to continue their usual way of life. The Greek colonies in the region accepted Parthian rule, which promised free access to, and preserved the security of, the trade routes of Central Asia. The Seleucids' attitude to the Jews was favorable, and the Jews allied themselves with their regime.

From around 120 B.C.E. to their fall in 224 C.E., the Parthians treated the Jewish settlements well. Palestinian Jewry under the Hasmoneans and Arsacid Parthia had a common interest in the destruction of Seleucid power. In 140/39, a circular from Rome informed the various countries of the civilized world, including Parthia, of Roman friendship for the Jews (I Macc. 15:16–24; Jos., Ant., 14:145–7). In 129 B.C.E. Hyrcanus was forced to accompany the Seleucid Antiochus VII in a Parthian campaign. As soon as he could, he returned to Palestine and reestablished his independence of the Seleucids. According to tannaitic tradition (TJ, Ber. 7:2, 11b; Naz. 5:5, 54b; Eccles. R. 7:12) a Parthian embassy was sent to the court of Alexander Yannai (104–78 B.C.E.). It may be that the embassy was intended to arrange joint opposition to the rise of the Armenian Tigranes, who invaded both Palestine and Parthian Babylonia around 87 B.C.E., and exiled Palestinian Jews to his empire. After their great victory over Rome at Carrhae, in 53 B.C.E., the Parthians for more than a decade became the dominant power in the Middle East, and attempted to contest Roman rule in Palestine. In 40–39 B.C.E., they deposed Herod, the ally of Rome, and put in his place as ruler of Judea Antigonus, nephew of Hyrcanus the Hasmonean. Elsewhere in the Middle East they replaced pro-Roman with pro-Parthian dynasties. The Parthian general, Pacorus, was killed in a brief engagement in 38 B.C.E., whereupon the Parthians withdrew across the Euphrates. Rome quickly reestablished her hegemony, which was never again seriously threatened by the Parthians. For the next century, domestic instability paralyzed the Parthian government.

Information on Babylonian Jewry under Parthian rule is not abundant. There is information on a Babylonian Jew, *Zamaris (Zimri), who emigrated to Palestine during Herod's reign. He went with his feudal retinue (Jos., Ant., 17:23ff.). All the information about him points to him as a Babylonian Jewish noble, who had fully mastered the arts of war as practiced by the Parthians. In later times, we hear of Babylonian Jews called Arda, Arta, and Pyl-y Barish; Arda/Arta would be the equivalent of the Hebrew Barukh, justified or blessed. Pyl-y Barish, meaning elephant rider, is also an Iranian name. These Jews (referred to in Git. 14b; TJ, Kid. 3:4, 64a) were dressed like Parthian nobles, in the tall *bashlyk* ("high hat") characteristic of the nobility. They were, moreover, well acquainted with the common law, for they insisted that rabbinical collectors of funds for the Palestinian schools supply them with a quit-claim for a silver cup being transported to Palestine. The Palestinians reported that the nobles had great power: "If they give an order to arrest you, you are arrested; to kill you, you are killed." They enjoyed the usual retinue of horses and mules. It may therefore be inferred that among the Jews in Babylonia was an upper class of "assimilated" nobility, familiar with Parthian culture and possessing considerable legal learning, as well as authority in the Jewish community. About the traditions and culture of the mass of Jews, who were farmers and tradesmen, nothing is known. It may be supposed that they revered the Scriptures, Jerusalem, and the Temple cult. There are many references to Babylonian pilgrimage before 70 C.E. The Babylonian Jews accepted the Jewish calendar from the Jerusalem authorities. Traditions on Hillel and Nahum "the Median" are confused, enigmatic, and in no way probative. What sects or groups existed is not known. About 40 C.E., the royal family of *Adiabene, situated between two tributaries of the Tigris, converted to Judaism. Josephus reports (Ant., 18:314ff.) that two Jewish brothers, *Anilaeus and Asinaeus (Ḥanilai, Ḥasinai) established a "Jewish state" in Babylonia, which lasted from about 20 to about 35 C.E.

Babylonian Jewry did little, if anything, to support the war against Rome. Its chief interest lay in the Temple cult. When the Temple was destroyed, the Romans quickly employed Josephus to absolve them of war-guilt, and he addressed himself specifically to "our brethren across the Euphrates." Similarly, the Bar Kokhba Revolt of 132–135 attracted no perceptible support from the Babylonian Jews. By contrast, when *Trajan invaded the Parthian Empire, in around 114 to 117, a great rebellion broke out behind his lines in the Jewish-occupied territories he had taken. The Jews in Cyprus, Egypt, and Cyrenaica also revolted. The chronology of Trajan's campaign is difficult to establish. It is not known for sure when the Jewish rebellions took place, or whether they were coordinated. The Babylonian one, however, seems clearly related to the Parthian cause.

The Jews normally profited from their position on both sides of the contested frontier between Rome and Parthia. The exilarch and patriarch, moreover, cooperated in the silk trade, one of the chief commodities of international commerce. Silk was imported to Babylonia from the Far East, transshipped for reweaving according to Roman taste from the coarse, thick fabric of China to the preferable sheer weave desired in Rome, and then manufactured into garments. The textile factories of Syria and Palestine thus depended upon a steady supply of silk. Ḥiyya, Simeon the son of Judah ha-Nasi, and Rabban Simeon b. Gamaliel together traded in silks at Tyre (Gen. R. 77:2) and Judah b. Bathyra of Nisibis and Abba b. Abba, father of Samuel, similarly were in the silk trade (Mid., Sam I. 10:3). Other evidences of Jewish participation in the silk trade are found in Christian Syriac sources (W. Cureton, *Ancient Syriac Documents,* 14). Silk merchants were, indeed, among the chief transmitters of Pharisaic Judaism and Christianity in the Orient. The earliest Christian apostles to Edessa and elsewhere in the Parthian Empire were originally Jewish silk merchants. Any effort to rearrange the trading routes of the Middle East thus would adversely affect the Jewish merchants of Babylonia and Palestine. Jewish opposition to Trajan may well have been motivated by considerations of international trade. But even without that the memory of the Roman destruction of the Temple would certainly have supplied a sufficient cause for opposition. Whether a messianic impulse motivated still others is not proved one way or the other. Further unrest in Palestine in the time of

Parthian-Roman struggles, specifically in 161–165 and 193–197, suggests that some Jews regarded Parthian success as the harbinger of the Messiah. This is made quite explicit by Simeon b. Yoḥai, who said that if a man saw a Persian (Parthian) horse tethered to a gravestone in Palestine, he should listen for the footsteps of the Messiah.

Pharisaic Judaism exercised little influence in Babylonian Jewry before the destruction of the Temple. Only two Pharisaic authorities resident in the Parthian empire are known. One was Judah b. Bathyra, who was stationed at Nisibis, and was in charge of collecting and transmitting the contributions of the Jews of Mesopotamia to the Temple in Jerusalem. The other collection center was at Nehardea, in Babylonia, where lived Nehemiah of Bet Deli, about whom little more is known than that he lived in Babylonia before 70 C.E. and was originally a Palestinian Pharisee (Yev. 16:7). The first rabbinical academies were established in Parthian territory as a direct consequence of the Bar Kokhba Revolt. During the war and the consequent repressions, the students of Ishmael fled from Palestine to Huzal, in central Babylonia, and some of those of Akiva went to Nisibis. The latter, however, soon returned while those of Ishmael remained. There they educated the first native-born and -bred rabbis of Babylonia, in particular Aḥai the son of Josiah, and Issi b. Judah; other Babylonian *tannaim* included the group from Kifri, Ḥiyya, Rav, Rabbah b. Ḥana; and among the later figures were Ḥanina b. Ḥama, and the Nehardeans Abba b. Abba, father of Samuel, and Levi b. Sisi.

Nathan, son of the exilarch, was sent by his father to Palestine for studies with Akiva. The exilarch probably extended a warm welcome to Palestinian refugees, and certainly made use of the graduates of their academies in his courts and administration. Among Babylonian Jewry was a class of native-born aristocrats, who probably acted, like other Parthian nobles, as local strongmen. In attempting to create a central administration for the Jewish community, the exilarch found useful the well-trained lawyers coming out of the Pharisaic-rabbinic schools, who were eager to enforce "the Torah" as they had learned it in Pharisaic traditions, and, unlike the Jewish nobility, were dependent solely upon the exilarch for whatever power they might exercise. For his part, the exilarch made use of the rabbinical bureaucrats to circumvent the power of the local Jewish nobility. Their claim to exposit "the whole Torah" as revealed to Moses at Sinai would have won for themselves and their patron considerable popular attention and support. The Palestinian schools after 140 were anxious to retain control of the new academies in Babylonia. When, therefore, in about 145 C.E. Hananiah, a nephew of R. Joshua b. Hananiah, presumed to proclaim the Jewish calendar in Babylonia, the Palestinians sent two sages, one of them the grandson of the last high priest in Jerusalem, to rebuke him (Ber. 63a; TJ, Sanh. 1:2, 19a; Ned. 6:13, 40a).

Sasanian Period. The change of dynasty from Arsacids to Sasanians represented more than the mere exchange of one Iranian royal family for another. The Parthians had, as stated, few, if any, cultural pretensions. They bore no special fealty to a particular divinity or cult. They ruled their vast empire mostly through local satraps or (as in the Jewish instance) ethnic-religious figures, dependent upon them for legitimation, but bound mainly by ties of feudal loyalty. Throughout the whole period of their rule, they had made extensive use of the Jews, in particular, as allies in international politics and trade. When Artapan V fell, Rav lamented, "The bond is parted" (Av. Zar. 10b–11a), and rightly so, for the ancient alliance between Iran and Israel in Babylonia had come to an end.

The Sasanians on the other hand sought not merely to reign but to rule. They originated as a priestly family in a temple in Staxr, in Fārs (Persia), and never neglected the divinities who, they believed, had favored them with a royal throne and empire. They moreover determined to rule directly, not merely through feudal powers, and so established great bureaus of administration in the capital Ctesiphon. They claimed the Achaemenids as their ancestors, and intended to recreate the glorious empire of their alleged forebears, including its religion. Unlike the Arsacids, they had had no experience in ruling a heterogeneous population. While the Arsacid Empire had gradually expanded from northeastern Iran so that they slowly gained experience in governing Hellenes, Jews, Syrians, Babylonians, and other Semites, not to mention other Iranian peoples, the Sasanians came to power suddenly. They emerged in a few years from the obscurity of a provincial temple to the authority of the whole Iranian Empire. They supposed, therefore, that they might quickly convert everyone to the worship of Ohrmazd, Anahita, and other divinities held sacred in Persia proper, and they founded a "state-church," hierarchically organized just like the secular bureaucracy, to achieve just that end. As a result the situation for Jewry suddenly deteriorated.

The Sasanian administration used the Mazdean religion to strengthen its hold on Iran proper, including Babylonia, as well as on Armenia, Georgia, Adiabene, and other regions. The Jews probably suffered, but certainly not alone. The times of Ardashir (224–41) proved difficult. There are, however, few unequivocal accounts of "persecutions of the Jews" or of Judaism. Two important talmudic stories show that the status of the Jewish community had changed radically. First, the Babylonian Talmud, *Bava Kamma* 117a contains the story of the execution of capital punishment in a Babylonian Jewish court by R. Kahana. Rav thereupon said, "Until now, the Greeks [= Parthians], who did not punish bloodshed were here, but now the Persians, who do punish bloodshed are here." R. Kahana was advised to flee to Palestine. Second, R. Shila administered lashes to a man who had intercourse with a gentile woman. The man informed against the Jewish judge, who successfuly hoodwinked the Persian agent *(frestak)* who had come to investigate the execution of judgment without proper government authorization *(hermana)*. These stories prove that the status of the Jewish government required renegotiation. Apparently at the outset the Jews supposed they could continue as before. The Sasanian regime quickly made it clear that they could not. There are, moreover, some references to "decrees against Judaism." The Babylonian Talmud, *Yevamot* 63b, records that the Mazdean Mobads "decreed concerning meat . . . the baths . . . and they exhumed the dead." Use of fire on Mazdean festivals was restricted; Rav was asked whether one may move a Ḥanukkah lamp "on account of the Magi" on the Sabbath (Shab. 45a). An equivocal reference suggests that "the Persians destroyed synagogues" (Yoma 10a). In any event, Jews clearly at this time preferred the rule of Rome, as is clear from Rav's statement (Shab. 11a).

When *Shapur I came to power in 242, however, he extended freedom of religious and cultural life to all the disparate peoples of the Iranian Empire, hoping eventually to unify the disparate empire, possibly through the syncretistic teaching of Mani, who included in his pantheon Jesus, Zoroaster, and Buddha (though not Moses). Further, since the Persians planned to renew war with the West, it was to Shapur's advantage to reconcile the peoples of the Tigris-Euphrates Valley, whose brethren lived on the other side of the frontier. Shapur's success with Babylonian Jewry was complete. During his raid into Asia Minor in 260, he besieged Caesarea-Mazaca, the greatest city in Cappadocia.

The Talmud (MK 26a) reports that when the amora Samuel heard Shapur had slain 12,000 Jews there, "he did not rend his clothes." The same account reports that Shapur told Samuel he had never killed a Jew in his life, "but the Jews of Caesarea-Mazaca had brought it on themselves." In the west, however, Shapur's armies pillaged, burned, and killed; they were out not to build a new empire in the Roman Orient, but to destroy an old one. So the Jews, among other peoples behind the Roman lines, fought for their lives and for Rome. A far greater threat to Babylonian Jewry came from the transient Palmyrene Empire, created by Odenathus (Papa b. Nezar of talmudic sources), who in 262–263 conducted a quick invasion of central Babylonia and devastated Jewish settlements there. Since Jewish and Palmyrene merchants competed with one another, an economic motivation may have played some part in the attacks on the Jews. The Palmyrene siege of Ctesiphon was raised by Shapur, but not before Nehardea was destroyed. The Jews of both Palestine and Babylonia applauded the fall of Odenathus' wife and successor, Zenobia.

Since the chief threat to Jewry lay in the cessation of the right to self-government, it was important to Samuel and to the exilarch whom he served to regain autonomous government. The early Sasanian regime, as noted, insisted upon supervising the Jewish court system. The best way to end that supervision was to agree at the outset that "the law of the land is law." This Samuel decreed (see **Dina de-Malkhuta Dina*). The saying specifically applied to rules of land acquisition and tenure, collection of taxes, and similar matters of interest to the state. It was a strictly temporary and narrowly political agreement, which did not affect the religious or cultural policies of the Persians. The rabbis continued to work through prayer and study of Torah to hasten the coming of the Messiah, who would end the rule of all pagan kings and put into power the King of the king of kings.

Shapur I was succeeded by Hormizd I (272–73), Bahram I (273–76), Bahram II (276–92), and Bahram III (292). In the time of the Bahrams, Kartir, a leading Mazdean religious official, became a powerful influence in state policy. Calling himself "Soul-savior of Bahram," Kartir first saw to the martydom of Mani and the banishment of Manichaeans. He then turned to the extirpation of other non-Mazdean religions; in his famous inscription, he refers to his "opposition" to Jews, Brahmans, Nazoreans, Christians, and Manichaeans, among others. Shapur's policy of religious toleration, not to mention syncretism, was thus effectively reversed. There is little evidence in rabbinical sources to verify Kartir's claim to have given the Jews much trouble. The Babylonian Talmud, Gittin 16b–17a, tells the story that a Magus came and removed a lamp from the room of the ailing master, Rabbah b. Bar Ḥana, who thereupon exclaimed, "Merciful Lord! Either in your shadow or in the shadow of the son of Esau!" *Judah b. Ezekiel further refers to the exclusion of Jews from the offices of canal supervisor and chiliarch (Ta'an. 20a). But the Jews seem to have suffered less than did the Manichaeans, who were martyred and banished, and the Christians, whose churches were destroyed. No rabbi is known to have enjoyed the attentions of the king of kings, but possibly the rabbis simply did not preserve stories of what contacts did take place, presumably because exilarchic agents and not they were involved in the negotiations. In the time of Narseh (293–301), whatever persecutions earlier took place were brought to an end. Narseh renewed the tolerant policy of his father, Shapur. The reference of *Seder Olam Zuta* to a persecution of Jews in 313 is unverified by any earlier, more reliable source. Shapur II (309–79), crowned king at his birth, was then four years old; the Sasanian government was weak, and the empire was in a state of disorder. Perhaps a local Mobad or government authority somewhere made trouble for the Jews. In 331, Rabbah b. Naḥamani, head of the academy of Pumbedita, was arrested because he was accused of assisting Jews to evade taxes. According to a legendary account the heavenly court required Rabbah's traditions on a matter of ritual cleanness, so he was called to heaven (BM 86a), but one can hardly base upon that a general persecution of the Jews. The Talmud contains stories about the friendship for the Jews of Shapur's mother, Ifra Hormizd, who is otherwise unknown (BB 8a, 10b; Ta'an. 24b; Nid. 20b, Zev. 116b). In any event, during the reign of Shapur II, the Jewish community was unmolested. That is an important fact, for in the same period, particularly after Shapur II unsuccessfully besieged Nisibis in 339, the Christian community was devastated. Priests and bishops were put to death and monks and nuns tortured and forced to violate their vows. Ordinary Christians were pressured to apostatize. In 363, *Julian "the Apostate" invaded the Iranian Empire, and besieged Ctesiphon. Among the many towns and villages he destroyed was one Jewish town, Birta, specifically referred to by Ammianus Marcellinus and Sozomen (3,20). Piruz Shapur, with its large Jewish population, and probably Maḥoza, the Jewish suburb of Ctesiphon, were also destroyed. After Julian had proclaimed his intention of rebuilding a Jewish temple in Jerusalem, a local Babylonian pseudo-messiah called upon Maḥozan Jewry to follow him to Palestine. The Persian government massacred those who did so. The fortunes of war, rather than a specific Jewish policy, thus caused considerable hardship between 360 and 370. In his Armenian campaigns after 363, Shapur II deported from Armenia to Isfahan and other parts of the Persian Empire large numbers of Armenian Jews and Christians, with the intention of strengthening the economy of the territories sheltered from Rome by the Zagros mountains, including Fārs proper.

The Babylonian Talmud contains references to Yezdegerd I (397–417), who supposedly had some contacts with leading rabbis as well as with the exilarch. The persecution of Christians, renewed in 414, was not marked by similar treatment of the Jewish communities. Bahram V (420–38) is not referred to in Jewish sources. Yezdegerd II (438–57) in 456 decreed that the Jews might not observe the Sabbath. He was, according to Jewish sources, shortly thereafter swallowed by a serpent, in answer to the prayer of the heads of the academies Mar b. R. Ashi and R. Zoma. Firuz (459–86) persisted in his father's anti-Jewish policy. The Jews of Isfahan were accused of having flayed alive two Magi. Half of the Jewish population was slaughtered and their children given to Mazdeans. Firuz "the wicked" also killed the exilarch, Huna Mari, son of Mar Zutra I. The year 468 is called in the Talmud "the year of the destruction of the world," and from that date to 474, synagogues were destroyed, study of Torah was prohibited, children were forcibly delivered to the Mazdean priesthood, and, possibly, Sura was destroyed. The next significant trouble took place in the time of Kovad I (488–531), when Mazdak arose as a prophet of the doctrine of community of property and women. Kovad accepted the doctrine and, among other groups, the Jews were persecuted when they rejected Mazdakism. The exilarch Mar Zutra II gathered an armed force and defended the Jewish community for seven years. He was captured and killed in 520, in Maḥoza. Nevertheless a number of Jews then served in the Persian armies fighting the Byzantines. Information on the century between Kovad's death and the Arab conquest (640) is slight. Chosroes (531–78) was well liked by Iranian and Arab historians. The Jews were apparently well treated. The

Christian Nestorians in his day found refuge in Persia from Christian Byzantine persecution. Apparently some persecutions of Jews recurred under Hormizd IV (579–80), and Pumbeditan rabbis took shelter in Firuz Shapur, near Nehardea, then under Arab rule. Under Chosroes Parwez (590–628) Jewish life returned to normal. When the Persians invaded Palestine and took Jerusalem in 624, they were enthusiastically welcomed by local Jewry.

For the continuation of Jewish history in this area see *Iraq. See also *Academies; *Exilarch; Babylonian *Talmud. [JA.N.]

Bibliography: ACHAEMENID AND SELEUCID PERIODS: A. Berliner, *Beitraege zur Geographie und Ethnographie Babyloniens im Talmud und Midrasch* (1883); S. Daiches, *The Jews in Babylonia in the Time of Ezra and Nehemiah according to Babylonian Inscriptions* (1910); Juster, Juifs, 1 (1914); A. T. Olmstead, *History of the Persian Empire* (1948); Taubenschlag, in: *Journal of Juristic Papyrology*, 7–8 (1953–54), 169–85; S. K. Eddy, *The King is Dead, Studies in the Near Eastern Resistance to Hellenism* (1961). PARTHIAN AND SASANIAN PERIODS: Neusner, Babylonia, 4 vols. (1965–69); S. Funk, *Die Juden in Babylonien*, 2 vols. (1902–08); J. Obermeyer, *Die Landschaft Babylonien im Zeitalter des Talmuds und des Gaonats* (1929); A. Christensen, *L'Iran sous les Sassanides* (1944²); M. Beer, *Ma'amadam ha-Kalkali ve-ha-Ḥevrati shel Amora ei Bavel* (1962); R. N. Frye, *The Heritage of Persia* (1962).

BACAU (Rum. **Bacău**), city in Moldavia, Rumania. A Jewish community is attested there in the 18th century. A *ḥevra kaddisha* was established in 1774. In 1820 there were 55 Jewish taxpaying heads of families in Bacau. The Jewish population numbered 3,819 in 1859 and 7,902 (48.3% of the total) in 1899. From 1803 to 1859 Isaac of Botosani, who acquired renown as a miracle worker *(ba'al mofet)*, was rabbi there. A *talmud torah* was founded in 1828, the Po'alei Ẓedek Tailors' Association in 1832, a Ḥevrat Gomelei Ḥasadim (mutual aid society; their minute books are in the YIVO Archives) in 1836, and a Ḥevrat Mishnayot in 1851. When the Jewish autonomous organization lost its official status in Rumania at the beginning of the 1860s, communal activity in Bacau also disintegrated. After 1866 Bacau became one of the centers of anti-Jewish agitation in Rumania, and the community suffered frequent persecution. During the last quarter of the 19th century secular education began to spread among the Jews of Bacau and at the end of the 1870s and beginning of the 1880s one-third of the pupils in general schools in Bacau were Jewish. The main occupations of the Jews in Bacau were commerce and crafts: of the commercial enterprises in the town in 1899, 563 (85.6%) were Jewish, and there were 573 (66.6%) Jewish artisans in 1901. The Jewish population numbered 9,593 (30.8% of the total) in 1930, of whom 50.8% declared Yiddish as their mother tongue. By this time the community had a well-organized communal framework. It maintained a kindergarten, two primary schools (for boys and girls), a hospital, an old age home, an orphanage, and a *mikveh*, as well as 30 synagogues. [EL.F.]

Holocaust Period. With *Antonescu's rise to power, the Jews of Bacau were subjected to repression: their property and shops were confiscated and a part of the Jewish cemetery was adapted for agriculture. When war against the Soviet Union broke out (June 1941), the Jews from towns and villages in the district were driven from their homes and sent to Bacau, whose Jewish community did its best to help. The community kitchen dispensed 1,000 meals a day, and 1,000 families received financial aid. The men were sent to Transylvania and Bessarabia on forced labor. In the spring of 1944, when the front was drawing near, the Jews were forced to dig defense trenches. Under Soviet occupation in the summer of 1944, all the local officials fled and the Jewish community took over municipal affairs, keeping law and order, burying the non-Jewish dead, running the municipal hospital, and paying the salaries of the municipal employees. Most of the survivors of the Holocaust settled in Israel. In 1969 there were 600 families and two synagogues in Bacau. [TH.L.]

Bibliography: Edmond (E. Schwarzfeld), *Radu Porumbaru şi isprăvile lui la fabrica de hârtie din Bacău* (1885); A. D. Birnberg, *Comunitatea Bacău*, 1888 (Mss. in YIVO Archives, New York); A. Lachower, in: YIVOA, 10 (1955), 300–13; E. Feldman, in: *Papers of the Fourth World Congress of Jewish Studies*, 2 (1968), 219–22 (Heb.). HOLOCAUST PERIOD: PK Romanyah, 10–17; M. Carp, *Cartea Neagră* 1 (1946), 66, 118; C. Cristian, *Patru ani de urgie* (1945), index; W. Filderman, in: *Sliha*, no. 3 (Rum., Tel Aviv, 1956).

°**BACCHIDES** (second century B.C.E.), Syrian general and governor of Seleucid territories west of the Euphrates. A friend of Demetrius I, Bacchides was given the task of installing Alcimus as high priest. To this end he was assigned a large body of troops, for it was evident that opposition would be forthcoming from Judah Maccabee and the other leaders of the Hasmonean uprising. The pious **ḥasidim*, rejoicing at the sight of a priest from the tribe of Aaron assuming the office of high priest, were inclined to accept the peaceful overtures of Bacchides. However, he disregarded his oath and immediately slew 60 of the *Ḥasidim*, thus reuniting the bulk of the Jewish population behind Judah. Leaving an army with Alcimus, Bacchides handed the country over to him and returned to Syria. Meanwhile, Judah decisively defeated another Syrian general, Nicanor (13 Adar, 161 B.C.E.). Within two months Bacchides returned to Judea, accompanied by a force of 20,000 foot soldiers and 2,000 horsemen. Judah's army, camped near Elasa, dwindled from 3,000 to 800, and in the fierce battle which ensued Judah was killed. Bacchides again entrusted the administration of Judea to the Hellenists, while the rebels, led by Jonathan and Simeon, dispersed and fled south and beyond the Jordan. Bacchides succeeded in tracking Jonathan down, but waited until the Sabbath to attack the Jewish army, thinking that they would not fight. However, Jonathan fought back and the Syrian general suffered many casualties in an indecisive battle. Bacchides retreated to Jerusalem and fortified the citadel there. He also fortified many places around Jerusalem in order to strengthen the Seleucid hold on the city. Believing that the royalist rule was secure, Bacchides returned to Syria and remained there for two years (until 158). His last expedition to Judea, at the request of the Hellenists, was virtually a disaster. By that time Bacchides had become dissatisfied with those Jews who repeatedly urged him to attack the Hasmonean brothers. Sensing this, Jonathan proposed peace and a release of prisoners. Bacchides agreed, considering this the most dignified way of withdrawing, and returned for the last time to Syria.

Bibliography: I Macc., 7:8–20; 9; Jos., Ant., 12:393–7, 420–34; 13:4–33; Schuerer, Gesch, 1 (1901⁴), 216ff.; Klausner, Bayit Sheni, 3 (1959²), 40–41, 46–53. [I.G.]

BACHARACH (Bacherach), town in the Rhine Valley, West Germany. Jews were living in Bacharach in the first part of the 12th century and were engaged in moneylending. While the troops were assembling there in preparation for the Second *Crusade, several families left the town and took refuge in the nearby castle of Stahleck. Three householders who went on royal orders to collect their debts were martyred by the crusaders on the eve of Pentecost, 1147. In 1283, 26 Jews were massacred as the result of a *blood libel. Heinrich

The Rabbi of Bacharach. Woodcut by Joseph Budko for Heinrich Heine's *Der Rabbi von Bacherach*, Euphorion edition, Berlin, 1921.

Heine's incomplete epic, *Der Rabbi von Bacherach*, was based on a massacre in 1287 following a blood libel in Oberwesel. The Jews in Bacharach were attacked by the *Armleder in 1338–39, and others lost their lives in the *Black Death persecutions, 1348–49. A document dated 1510 shows that the Jewish community had by then been reestablished. There were 34 Jews living in the town in 1924 and 200 in the area in 1932. The five Jews who remained in Bacharach were deported by July 26, 1942 by the Nazis. A number of noted Jewish families derived their name from Bacharach (see next entry).

Bibliography: Germ Jud, 1 (1963), 17; 2 (1968), 44; AWJD (June 9, 1967), 17; Kahlenberg, in: *Zwischen Rhein und Mosel*. . . . 17 (1967), 643ff.

[Z.Av./Ed.]

BACHARACH (Bachrach; also spelled **Bacherach, Bachrich),** name of several families originally from *Bacharach on the Rhine. Gottschalk of Bacharach is mentioned in Frankfort in 1391 and Ephraim Gumbrecht Bacharach in 1457. Menahem (Man) Bacharach was rabbi in Worms from 1506 to 1520. Two *dayyanim* named Bacharach are mentioned in 15th-century Mainz. There were two branches of the family living in Frankfort in the 16th and 17th centuries. Israel and Tobias ben Joseph Solomon were martyred in *Ruzhany on Sept. 19, 1659, following a *blood libel. Tobias' descendants lived at Tiktin and include the talmudist Judah b. Joshua Ezekiel *Bachrach and Jacob b. Moses *Bachrach, author of a history of the Hebrew script. The first Bacharach known in Vienna is Judah Loeb ben Aaron (d. 1657). His grandson Jacob found refuge in Třebíč, Moravia, in 1670 and became a leader of the community there. His descendants are found in Konice and Třešt (both in Moravia). Two Bacharachs are mentioned in a list of Nikolsburg (Mikulov) Jews of 1765. The best-known line, founded in Bohemia, is represented first by Abraham Samuel ben Isaac Bacharach (1575–1615), who was rabbi in Worms. His wife Eva (Ḥavvah; 1580–1651) had a wide knowledge of Hebrew and rabbinical literature rarely found among women in her day. She died in Sofia on her way to Ereẓ Israel. Their son was Moses Samson *Bacharach and their grandson was Jair Ḥayyim *Bacharach. Common in Bohemia was the abbreviation Bacher. Others of the family in Hungary include the Hebrew poet Simon *Bacher and his son the scholar Wilhelm *Bacher.

Bibliography: I. T. Eisenstadt and S. Wiener, *Da'at Kedoshim* (1897–98), 32–41, 213–4 (first pagination); Flesch, in: *Zeitschrift fuer die Geschichte der Juden in der Tschechoslowakei*, 2 (1931), 229–35.

[Ed.]

BACHARACH, family of business, political, and communal leaders in Atlantic City, New Jersey. Benjamin (1865–1936) was a local merchant and banker. Born in Philadelphia, he and his brothers Isaac and Harry were brought to Atlantic City in 1881 by their parents. Benjamin served as president of the Beth Israel Synagogue of Atlantic City, in which the entire family was active. Isaac (1870–1956) was a businessman and banker who pursued a political career. After serving on the Atlantic City Council (1907–13), Isaac, a Republican, was elected to the State Assembly in 1911 and in 1915 to Congress, where he represented the Second District of New Jersey until 1936. A member of the House Ways and Means Committee, Bacharach wrote the 1931 act providing for emergency loans based on the value of insurance policies. Harry (1873–1947), a Republican, was appointed postmaster by President McKinley (1901) and was reappointed by President Roosevelt in 1905 and 1909. He won elections as mayor of Atlantic City in 1911, 1916, and 1932. He served for many years as member and chairman of the New Jersey Public Utilities Commission and as a member of the Water Policy Commission. He was also active in local banking, real estate, and civic affairs, and was a founder of the Jewish Community Center of Atlantic City (1924–25). The Betty Bacharach Home for Afflicted Children (Longport, N.J.) was founded by the Bacharach brothers and two sisters in 1924 in memory of their mother.

Bibliography: *Biographical Directory of the American Congress* (1961); Philip R. Goldstein, *Centers In My Life* (1964), 76, 159.

[J.Bra.]

BACHARACH, ALFRED LOUIS (1891–1966), British chemist and writer on musical subjects. Bacharach was an innovator in the fortification of baby milks with vitamin D, which brought about the almost complete eradication of rickets in the northern cities of Britain. He was born in London, and graduated at Cambridge. After five years in the Wellcome Research Laboratory, he joined the Glaxo Laboratories in 1920. He pioneered in the development of biological assay methods for vitamins, and also microbiological assay procedures. He wrote *Science and Nutrition* (1938), and edited *The Nation's Food* (1946), *Evaluation of Drug Activities: Pharmacometrics* (in two volumes, with D. R. Laurence, 1964), *Exploration Medicine* (with O. G. Edholm, 1965), and *The Physiology of Human Survival* (1965). Bacharach, an accomplished pianist, edited *The Musical Companion* (1934; new edition, 1957), *Lives of the Great Composers* (1935), *British Music of Our Time* (1946), and *The Music Masters* (1957).

Bibliography: *Chemistry in Britain*, 3 (1967), 395. [S.A.M.]

BACHARACH, JAIR ḤAYYIM BEN MOSES SAMSON (1638–1702), German talmudic scholar, with an extensive knowledge in the general sciences. Bacharach was the son of

R. Moses Samson b. Abraham Samuel *Bacharach. Born in Leipnik, where his father officiated as rabbi, Bacharach, in his childhood, accompanied his father to Prague where the latter functioned as preacher, and then to Worms, where his father assumed the position of rabbi of the community. In 1653 Bacharach married Sarlan, the daughter of R. Sussmann Brilin of Fulda. He spent six years at the house of R. Sussmann, acquiring a profound knowledge of the Talmud and its commentaries, with special emphasis on Alfasi and Asher b. Jehiel. Deeply immersed in kabbalistic studies, he, like his father, became very much interested in the Shabbatean movement. He accumulated an impressive library of writings connected with Shabbetai Ẓevi's messianic pretensions. Moreover, a group of 13 talmudic scholars obligated themselves to meet daily under his leadership for purposes of study and self-sanctification in preparation of the impending redemption. Even decades later, after he recognized Shabbetai Ẓevi as a pseudo-Messiah, he always referred to him as "Rabbenu Shabbatai Ẓevi." His stepbrother, Tobias b. Moses *Cohn, in his *Ma'aseh Tuviyyah,* wrote apparently alluding to him: "Even many of the sages of the land and the great renowned rabbis, whom I would not want to mention publicly, accepted him as master and king over them."

In 1666, Jair was appointed rabbi and *rosh bet din* ("head of rabbinic court") at Coblenz. This was a position that carried prestige and comfort with it. Suddenly, in 1669, he was compelled to leave his office. This must have been the result of partisan intrigue. His character is shown by the fact that he did not record the names of the offenders. The same year he again settled at Worms. When his father died in 1670, Bacharach temporarily functioned in his place as rabbi of Worms. However, he was disappointed in his hope of assuming the rabbinate of Worms, the pretext being that it was against the rule to appoint a resident of the city as rabbi. His resentment at being passed over in favor of R. Aaron Teomim, whom he deemed far inferior in scholarship, appears to have found a measure of satisfaction in his work *Matteh Aharon,* left in manuscript, in which he severely criticized the scholarly methods of the elected rabbi who had just published a commentary on the Passover *Haggadah* under the same title. After the latter had suffered a violent death, Bacharach placed parentheses around the sharper expressions, solemnly instructing any future publisher to soften the more offending passages. The work was finally published by Jellinek in *Bikkurim* (1865), 4–26; and again in *Ha-Misderonah* (1887), 348–64.

Title page of the first part of Jair Bacharach's collection of responsa, *Ḥavvat Yair,* Frankfort, 1699. Jerusalem, J.N.U.L.

In 1689 when Worms was occupied by the French armies of Louis XIV, Bacharach fled to Metz with his family. In March 1690 he left for Frankfort by himself in an unsuccessful attempt to collect some debts, and at this time his family was in such dire straits that his wife, with his consent, sold his extensive library for 250 Reichsthaler. During the next few years he was often forced to change his domicile, residing in various cities in the Rhineland. At Frankfort in 1699 he published his monumental collection of 238 responsa under the name *Ḥavvat Yair.* The title comes from Numbers 32:41, and means "The Tent-Villages of Jair," implying that his decisions were but modest expressions of his opinions in contrast to former respondents whose works were like fortified towns. In the German pronunciation the title becomes "Ḥaves Yoir," meaning also "the Jair of Ḥavvah," and thus constituting a tribute to his erudite grandmother, Ḥavvah or Eva, the granddaughter of *Judah Loew b. Bezalel and the female founder of the Bacharach house. This epoch-making work, which has gone through many editions, demonstrates not only Bacharach's exhaustive knowledge of all branches of traditional rabbinic learning, but also the whole extent of his knowledge of the general sciences, such as mathematics, astronomy, and music, and shows also his opposition to the distorted type of *pilpul* current in his day. It contains some writings of his father and his grandfather.

Other printed works of Bacharach include: *Ḥut ha-Shani* ("Scarlet Thread," 1679) containing responsa of his father and grandfather, as well as 17 refutations of R. Samuel ben David's *Naḥalat Shivah* (1677) and notes on Alfasi published in the Vilna edition. Altogether he is said to have left 46 volumes of manuscripts (some of these being excerpts or collections of the works of others). The more important of these are: *Eẓ Ḥayyim,* a compendium on the Jewish religion; glosses to Maimonides' *Guide;* a commentary on the *Shulḥan Arukh;* chronological tables and genealogical lists.

In 1699, the reestablished Jewish community of Worms finally chose Bacharach, now deaf, old, and sick, as their rabbi. He had been granted his dearest wish: the satisfaction of being elected by this historic congregation to succeed his father and grandfather. He lived three more years. Bacharach's method was one of strict logic. He manifested his independence vis-à-vis his father, citing the precedent of Maimonides. Thus, he says in one passage, vindicating his right to disagree with earlier authorities: "The spirit of God has made me, as it has made them" (Responsum no. 155). He was strict with respect to the obligatoriness of established religious custom. While he was a believer in the Kabbalah and busied himself with *gematria,* he warned against giving oneself over to the study of Kabbalah or philosophy—placing great value on simple faith.

Bibliography: D. Kaufmann, *R. Jair Chajjim Bacharach* (Ger., 1894); idem, in: JQR 3 (1891), 292–313, 485–536 (earlier English outline of previous work); Marx, in: *Essays . . . J. H. Hertz* (1942), 307–11; S. Freehof, *Responsa Literature* (1955), 84–87; idem, *Treasury of Responsa* (1963), 171–5.

[J.H.]

BACHARACH, MOSES SAMSON BEN ABRAHAM SAMUEL (1607–1670), rabbi and author. Bacharach was born in Pohořelice, Moravia, where his father Abraham Samuel (a prominent scholar in rabbinics and in other fields) was then rabbi. His mother Ḥavvah, the daughter of Isaac Katz, son-in-law of R. Judah Loew ben Bezalel of Prague, was also distinguished for her learning and even wrote comments on Midrash and Targum. At the age of eight, upon the death of his father, Bacharach was taken to Prague, where he was educated under the tutelage of his two uncles, R. Ḥayyim and R. Naphtali ha-Kohen, both distinguished scholars. In 1627 he married a daughter of R. Isaac b. Phoebus, chief rabbi of Moravia. His father-in-law was taken prisoner, and the payment of a 10,000 gulden ransom left Moses impoverished, forcing him to accept the rabbinate of Hodonin (Moravian Slovakia) in 1629. In 1632 he became rabbi and head of the yeshivah at Leipnik. He experienced the travails of the Jews in the Thirty-Years' War, to which he gave expression in a *seliḥah* which the Jewish community of Leipnik recited annually on the 17th of Tammuz. Subsequently, on the foundation of a charitable religious association (the *Barukh she-Amar* society), he composed a joyous song of thanks for deliverance from danger during the war, which was recited every year on Simḥat Torah. In 1650 he was chosen rabbi of the community of Worms—perhaps the most influential position in German Jewry. He was in that office 20 years until his death. Some of his writings were included in the published works of his son, the famed R. Jair Ḥayyim *Bacharach.

Bibliography: D. Kaufmann, *R. Jair Chajjim Bacharach . . .* (Ger., 1894), 23–28, 45, 53–54, 129–30; F. Hillel, *Leipniker Rabbiner* (1928), 16–43; A. E. Franklin, *Records of Franklin Family* (1935²) 4, 45.

[J.H.]

BACHARACH, NAPHTALI BEN JACOB ELHANAN, kabbalist who lived in the first half of the 17th century. The dates of his birth and death are unknown. Bacharach was born in Frankfort, but also spent some years in Poland with the kabbalists before he returned to his home town, and in 1648 he published his comprehensive book *Emek ha-Melekh* ("The King's Valley"), one of the most important kabbalistic works. The book contains a wide and systematic presentation of theology according to the Lurianic Kabbalah. It was based on many authorities, but relied mainly on Israel *Sarug's version presented in his book *Limmudei Aẓilut* (1897), which Bacharach included almost in its entirety into his own book with hardly an acknowledgment of the fact. Bacharach's claims that he brought back the sources of Luria's Kabbalah with him from Ereẓ Israel, where he supposedly lived for some time, do not deserve credit. He also accused Joseph Solomon *Delmedigo who he claimed had been his pupil, of transcribing kabbalistic manuscripts which were in Bacharach's possession, and then publishing them, with noticeable distortions, in his books *Ta'alumot Ḥokhmah* (1629) and *Novelot Ḥokhmah* (1631). However, the contrary seems much more likely; that it was Bacharach who culled from Delmedigo's work as well as from many other sources without acknowledging them. While Delmedigo's interest lay in the abstract philosophical aspect of Kabbalah, which he attempted to explain to himself, Bacharach appears as an enthusiastic and fanatical kabbalist, with a special flair for the mystical and non-philosophical traits of Kabbalah—in Isaac Luria's Kabbalah as well as in the Kabbalah of the early kabbalists. This accounts for the strong emphasis given to such elements as the doctrine of the *Sitra Aḥra* ("Other Side"—the Evil) and demonology. He wove the old kabbalistic themes together with the later ones in an elaborately detailed style. Without referring to Sarug, who is his most important source, Bacharach claims to derive his teachings from the books of Ḥayyim *Vital, although important chapters of his doctrine, such as his version of the doctrine of *Ẓimẓum* ("Withdrawal") and all it entails, are completely foreign to Vital's writings. The merger of both these traditions characterizes this book, written with talent and clarity. Bacharach also borrowed liberally from certain parts of the book *Shefa Tal* by R. Shabbetai Sheftel *Horowitz (1612). His style is pervaded by messianic tension. The book *Emek ha-Melekh* had a great impact on the development of the late Kabbalah. It was widely recognized as an authoritative source on the doctrine of Isaac Luria and kabbalists from many countries, especially Ashkenazim, the great Ḥabad Ḥasidim, and the school of the Gaon *Elijah b. Solomon Zalman of Vilna, quoted him extensively. His influence is also noticeable in Shabbatean literature, in Moses Ḥayyim *Luzzatto's system of Kabbalah, and in the book *Kelaḥ* [138] *Pitḥei Ḥokhmah.* On the other hand, strong criticism of the book was soon expressed. Already in 1655, Ḥayyim ha-Kohen of Aleppo, a disciple of Ḥayyim Vital, in the introduction to his book *Mekor Ḥayyim* (1655), protested against Bacharach's claim of being the true interpreter of Luria's doctrine. The protests of Benjamin ha-Levi in his approbation to *Zot Ḥukkat ha-Torah* by Abraham *Ḥazkuni (1659), and of the preacher Berechiah Berach, in his introduction to *Zera Berakh* (2nd part, 1662), against misrepresentations of Luria's Kabbalah were also intended for Bacharach. Moses *Ḥagiz says in *Shever Poshe'im* (1714) that *Emek ha-Melekh* is called *Emek ha-Bakha* ("Valley of Weeping"). Isaiah Bassan complains to M. Ḥ. Luzzatto about the numerous translations of chapters from *Emek ha-Melekh* in Latin referring to the *Kabbalah Denudata* by *Knorr von Rosenroth "which were among the important causes of prolonging our exile" (*Iggerot Shadal,* 29). Ḥ. J. D. *Azulai also wrote: "I have heard that no genuine writings got into his (Bacharach's) hands . . . therefore the initiated refrain from reading either it or the *Novelot Ḥokhmah.*" In *Emek ha-Melekh* there is a reference to many other books by Bacharach concerning aspects of the kabbalist doctrine. Of these only a part of the *Gan ha-Melekh* on the Zohar is extant in an Oxford manuscript.

Bibliography: Azulai, 2 (1852), 114 no. 406; G. Scholem, in: KS, 30 (1954/55), 413; Scholem, Shabbetai Ẓevi, 54–56; M. Horovitz, *Frankfurter Rabbinen,* 2 (1883), 41–45.

[G.Sch.]

BACHE, U.S. family of investment bankers and art collectors. Bache, Jules Semon (1862–1944) was born in New York. After some years with his father's trading firm he became a cashier in 1880 for Leopold Cahn and Co., investment bankers. Twelve years later he became head of the firm, which he renamed J. S. Bache and Co. Under his leadership the company became prominent in investment banking and securities trading, with interests in railroads, mining, manufacturing, trading, and insurance. Bache's philanthropy included donations to hospitals and scientific research, civic institutions, and the arts. He gave his outstanding collection of paintings, sculptures, tapestries, enamels, furniture, and porcelains to the State of New York for the Metropolitan Museum of Art. [J.O.R.]

BACHER, EDUARD (1846–1908), Austrian journalist; editor in chief from 1879 of the liberal Vienna daily *Neue Freie Presse,* and from 1888 its publisher. He first practiced as a lawyer after graduating at Vienna, then entered the employ of the *Neue Freie Presse* as parliamentary reporter in 1872. He was politically active in the German Liberal Party in Austria, but opposed the Zionism of Theodor

*Herzl, and though Herzl was then on his staff, allowed no reports to appear in his newspaper on the Zionist movement or the Zionist Congresses.

Bibliography: T. Herzl, *Complete Diaries*, ed. by R. Patai, 5 vols. (1960), index. [Ed.]

BACHER, SIMON (1823–1891), poet and Hebrew translator. Bacher was born in Szent Miklos, Hungary, and was the father of the Orientalist Wilhelm *Bacher and a descendant of Jair Ḥayyim *Bacharach. When writing in Hebrew, he used the latter's surname. In 1867 he moved to Budapest, where he was employed as a bookkeeper. From 1874 until his death he served as the treasurer of the Jewish community. Bacher wrote poetry in the flowery syle of the Haskalah and also translated German and Hungarian poetry into Hebrew. He was a regular contributor to the Hebrew periodicals *Ha-Ḥavaẓẓelet* and *Kokhevei Yiẓḥak*. In 1865 his Hebrew translation of Lessing's *Nathan der Weise* appeared in Vienna, and in 1868 he published *Zemirot ha-Arez* ("Songs of the Land"), an anthology of translations from Hungarian poetry. His selected works *Sha'ar Shimon* (3 vols., 1894), were published posthumously by his son.

Bibliography: W. Bacher, in: *Sha'ar Shimon*, 1 (1894), 9–36; J. Patai, *Mi-Sefunei ha-Shirah* (1939), 31–35. [G.El.]

BACHER, WILHELM (1850–1913), Hungarian Semitic scholar. Bacher was born in Liptó-Szent-Miklós (now Liptovsky Svätý Mikuláš, Czechoslovakia), the son of the Hebrew poet Simon *Bacher. In 1876 he was ordained and appointed rabbi of Szeged, Hungary, and the following year professor at the newly founded rabbinical seminary in Budapest, where he taught biblical exegesis, Midrash, homiletics, and Hebrew poetry and grammar. From 1907 until the end of his life he was head of the seminary. In 1884 with Joseph Banoczi he founded the Hungarian Jewish monthly *Magyar Zsidó Szemle*. In 1894 he helped found a Jewish-Hungarian literary society, Izraelita Magyar Irodalmi Társulat, and was the editor of its yearbook until 1899; this society instituted the publication of a Hungarian translation of the Bible (1898–1907). At the same time Bacher served as a consulting editor for the *Jewish Encyclopedia* (1901–06) and wrote a number of monographs for it. Bacher's fields of study included biblical exegesis, Hebrew philology, *aggadah* and Midrash, and Judeo-Persian literature. Many of his works were translated into Hebrew by A. Z. *Rabinovitz. In his works on *aggadah* he

Wilhelm Bacher, Hungarian Semitic scholar. Jerusalem, J.N.U.L.

classified aggadic sayings by author determining the contribution of each *tanna* and *amora*. These works include *Die Agada der Babylonischen Amoräer* (1878, also in Hg., 1913²); *Die Agada der Tannaiten* (2 vols., 1884–90); *Die Agada der Palaestinischen Amoräer* (3 vols., 1892–99; repr. 1965; *Die Prooemien der Alten juedischen Homilie* (1913); *Rabbanan, Beitrag zur Geschichte der anonymen Agada* (1914); and *Tradition und Tradenten in den Schulen Palaestinas und Babyloniens* (1914). In the last work Bacher discusses the manner in which the *amoraim* in Babylonia and Palestine transmitted the teachings of the early scholars, especially the *tannaim* of the *beraitot*. Of particular significance from the standpoint of content and style is Bacher's *Exegetische Terminologie der juedischen Traditionsliteratur* (2 parts, 1899, 1905, repr. 1965). In the first part of this work Bacher arranged the Hebrew and Aramaic terms used by the *tannaim* in their exegesis in alphabetical order and in the second part, those of the Palestinian and Babylonian *amoraim*. He also dealt with the terms used by the *amoraim* to explain the terminology of the *tannaim*. Bacher dealt extensively with medieval Jewish biblical exegesis. In addition to *Die Juedische Bibelexegese vom Anfange des Zehnten bis zum Ende des Fuenfzehnten Jahrhunderts* (1892), he wrote detailed studies on Abraham ibn Ezra's works, Saadiah's Arabic translation of the Book of Job (in: Derenbourg, *Oeuvres Complètes de R. Saadiah*, 1899), Moses ha-Kohen ibn *Gikatilla's work on the same book, and on *Samuel b. Hophni. He published a study in German and Hungarian on the biblical exegesis of Jewish religious philosophers before Maimonides, *Die Bibelexegese der Juedischen Religionsphilosophen des Mittelalters vor Maimûni* (1892), and on the exegetical methods of Maimonides, *Die Bibelexeges Moses Maimûnis* (1896). He wrote two works on the biblical commentaries of Ibn Janaḥ, *Leben und Werke des Abulwaîd Merwân ibn Ganâh* (1885), and a detailed study of the biblical exegesis of the Zohar. Bacher dealt extensively with the development of Hebrew during the Middle Ages, including the masorah, the beginning of the study of Hebrew grammar (*Die Anfaenge der hebraeischen Grammatik*, 1895), and the pioneering work of Judah ibn *Ḥayyuj in the field of Hebrew grammar (*Die Grammatische Terminologie des Jehuda b. Dawid Hajjug*, 1882). Bacher was the only Jewish scholar of his generation to deal with Judeo-Persian literature. His continuous flow of publications, based on the collection of Judeo-Persian manuscripts of Elkan Nathan *Adler, made him the undisputed authority in this field. Among his many works on Judeo-Persian literature are *Hebraeisch-Persisches Woerterbuch aus dem vierzehnten Jahrhundert* (1900) by Solomon b. Samuel of Turkestan; "Ein persischer Kommentar zum Buche Samuel" (in ZDMG, 51 (1897), 329–425); *Zwei juedisch-persische Dichter, Schahin und Imrani* (1907–08); and "Juedisch-Persisches aus Buchârâ" (in ZDMG, 55 (1901), 244–57; 56 (1902), 729–59). Bacher helped lay the foundations for the study of Hebrew grammar from the talmudic period to the end of the Middle Ages; he was the first scholar to deal with the Hebrew and Arabic poetry of Yemen. Above all, he was one of the first scholars to engage in the scientific study of *aggadah* and Midrash.

Bibliography: S. Kraus, in: *Ha-Shilo'aḥ*, 30 (1914), 168–78, 384–92, 487–97; *Magyar Zsidó Szemle*, 27 (1910), 1–81, articles honoring Bacher, including bibliography of his works; L. Blau, *Bibliographie der Schriften Wilhelm Bachers* (1910), completed by D. Friedmann, *Nachtrag zu L. Blau's Bibliographie der Schriften Wilhelm Bachers* (1928); M. Liber, in: REJ, 67 (1914), 161–9; B. Heller, in: *Zsidó Plutarchos* (1928), 9–38 (Hg.); W. J. Fischel, in: L. Finkelstein (ed.), *The Jews, Their History, Culture and Religion*, 2 (1960), 1149–1190 (with bibliography); J. I. Dienstag, in: *Sinai*, 55 (1964), 65–82.

[M.N.Z./Ed.]

BACHI, ARMANDO (1883–1943), Italian soldier. Born in Verona, Bachi went into the artillery where he was commissioned in 1902, and remained in this branch of the Army for most of his career. In World War I he became deputy chief of staff of the 48th and 30th divisions, and was awarded the Military Cross. After the war he was a lecturer in artillery at the Turin Military Academy and in 1934 was given command of an artillery corps. By 1938 he had become a lieutenant general in command of a motorized army corps, but when the racial laws were enacted in that year he was forced to resign his commission. In 1943 he and his family were arrested and died in Auschwitz. [Mo.K.]

BACHI, RICCARDO (1875–1951), Italian economist and statistician. Bachi was born in Turin and studied in Venice. He laid the foundations for the scientific study of price fluctuations and wrote on the economic history of the Risorgimento. From 1904 to 1908 Bachi edited the Italian Labor Department bulletin on employment, and from 1909 to 1921 issued *L'Italia Economica*, an annual publication which he founded. From 1915, he taught statistics and economics at the universities of Macerata, Parma, and Genoa, and in 1926 was appointed to the chair of political economy at the Royal Institute of Economic Sciences in Rome. After the enactment of the anti-Jewish laws in Italy in 1938, he went to Palestine, where from 1940 to 1946, he lectured at the Tel Aviv branch of the Hebrew University.

Riccardo Bachi, Italian economist and statistician. Photo Ricarda Schwerin. Jerusalem.

In 1946 he returned to the University of Rome. Interested in Zionism from the 1920s, he investigated the economic history of Jews, in particular the economic relations between Jews and non-Jews in the Diaspora. Noteworthy among Bachi's writings are his *Principi di scienza economica*, 2 vols. (1937–40), *Israele disperso e ricostruito* (1952), and his introduction to the Hebrew translation of Simḥah Luzzatto's "On the Jews of Venice" *(Ma'amar al Yehudei Veneẓyah* 1950).

Bibliography: L. Einaudi, *Riforma Sociale* (1931), 416ff.; RMI, 16 (1950), 14–216; A. M. Ratti, *Vita e opere di Riccardo Bachi* (1961), 69–100 (bibliography).

[J.B.S.]

BACHI, ROBERTO (1909–), statistician. Born in Rome, he was the son of Riccardo *Bachi. He taught statistics at the Italian universities before settling in Palestine in 1938. He organized the department of statistics at the Hebrew University in Jerusalem, where he was appointed professor of statistics and demography in 1947. He served as dean of the faculty of social sciences in 1953, and was prorector of

Roberto Bachi, Israel statistician. Photo Ricarda Schwerin. Jerusalem.

the university in 1959–60. From 1949 he served as statistician to the Israel government and directed its Central Bureau of Statistics in which capacity he planned and directed all government censuses. He was a member of the Israel Academy of Science and Humanities. Bachi published several books on demography and statistics, his principal work being *Graphical Rational Patterns* (1968). He also headed the department of Jewish demography in the Institute of Contemporary Jewry at the Hebrew University. In this capacity he stimulated Jewish communities in many parts of the world to collect scientific statistical data.

[J.B.S.]

BACHMANN, JACOB (1846–1905), Russian *ḥazzan* and composer of synagogue music. Bachmann served as a boy-singer with the *ḥazzan* of his native town of Berdichev. He developed a phenomenal voice and was admitted to the Petrograd Conservatoire in 1864. Anton *Rubinstein became his teacher and later took him on his concert tours as a solo singer. Bachmann, nevertheless, decided to be a *ḥazzan* and established his reputation at the synagogues of Berdichev, Rostov, and Constantinople. During his stay at Lemberg until 1884, Bachmann founded a mixed choir and took up composition. As successor to Osias *Abrass at Odessa (1884–85) he was acclaimed by the public. He later settled in Budapest. Bachmann's voice is said to have covered the entire range from dramatic tenor to powerful bass, highlighted by an extraordinary echo-falsetto. His compositions are influenced by Rubinstein, the "Westerner" in Russian music. Bachmann was eager to show command of contemporary musical devices (*Schirath Jacob*, pp. 54, 79, 89, 95, 96), including reminiscences of Bach (*ibid.*, p. 188) or Meyerbeer (*ibid.*, p. 89), and was able to write striking, though rather conventional, choral settings (*ibid.*, pp. 18–19). However, Bachmann has to be judged by his improvisations in traditional *ḥazzanut*, a small part of which is included in his printed works. Bachmann's cantorial recitative was at its best at the sublime moments of the High Holy Days' liturgy (*ibid.*, 159–64. Works: *Cantata* (Ps. 45) for the silver jubilee of Francis I (1879); *Schirath Jacob* (1884); *Uwaschofor godol* (1889); and *Attah Zokher* (after 1905). Unpublished works are in manuscripts in David Putterman Library, N.Y.

See also G. Ephros, *Cantorial Anthology*, 2 (1929), 117–9.

Bibliography: Wininger, Biog, 1 (1925), 214–5; E. Zaludkowski, *Kultur-Treger fun der Yidisher Liturgye* . . . (1930), 191–2; Sendrey, Music, indexes; Minkowski, in: *Reshumot*, 5 (1927), 145–60.

[H.Av.]

BACHRACH, JACOB BEN MOSES (also called **Ba'al ha-Ma'amarim** or **Jacob ha-Bachri;** 1824–1896), rabbi and grammarian. Bachrach, a descendant of Jair *Bacharach,

Jacob Bachrach, Hebrew grammarian and a founder of the Ḥovevei Zion movement. Jerusalem, Schwadron Collection, J.N.U.L.

was born in Sejny in the district of Suwalki; he studied with his grandfather Judah *Bachrach. In addition to being an accomplished talmudist he was versed in secular knowledge. For many years he was superintendent of the Hebrew department of a printing establishment in Koenigsberg. In 1858 he published in that press his *Mazref ha-Avodah,* which deals with the controversy over Ḥasidism between Benjamin Wolf of Slonim, a disciple of *Elijah b. Solomon Zalman the Gaon of Vilna and Joseph of Nemirov, a disciple of *Levi Isaac of Berdichev. Later editions of this book carry the title *Vikkuḥa Rabbah* ("Great Debate"). In 1858 he also published the *Sefer Yuḥasin* of Abraham *Zacuto with corrections and comments. Between 1861 and 1864 he published Jacob b. Asher's *Turim* with his own annotations. From Koenigsberg he moved to Sebastopol. There, while managing a refinery, he began to take an interest in the literature of the *Karaites and engage in polemics with them. In 1893 his book *Me-ha-Ibbur u-Minyan ha-Shanim* ("Concerning Intercalation and the Calendar") appeared in Warsaw. In it he attempted to prove the antiquity of the Hebrew *calendar, in opposition to the Karaite theory on one side and to the opinion of Ḥ. Z. Slonimṣky on the other side. From there he moved to Bialystok, where he played an important role in founding the Ḥovevei Zion movement and was sent to Ereẓ Israel in 1882. His findings during his visit there are contained in his *Sefer ha-Massa le-Ereẓ Yisrael* (Warsaw, 1884), one of the earliest propaganda books of the Ḥovevei Zion. For a short time, he was also private secretary to Samuel *Mohilever. Bachrach also engaged in scientific study of the Hebrew language. Among other things, he tried to prove the antiquity of the Hebrew vowels and accents, in opposition to the opinion of Elijah *Levita who had held that these were not introduced until after the conclusion of the Talmud. These studies appeared in *Sefer ha-Yaḥas li-Khetav Ashuri ve-Toledot ha-Nekuddot ve-ha-Te'amim* ("History of the Assyrian Script, Vowels, and Accents," Warsaw, 1854) and *Hishtaddelut im Shadal* ("Engagement with Samuel David Luzzatto," Warsaw, 1897), a kind of extension to his earlier work. Despite the great acumen shown in his works, they did not meet with the general approval of the scholars of his time.

Bibliography: E. Atlas, in: *Ha-Asif,* 1 (1884), 246ff.; S. Wiener, *Kohelet Moshe* (1893–1918), nos. 3311, 4521, 4723; *Lu'aḥ Aḥi'asaf,* 5 (1898), 326; EZD, 1 (1958), 291–3; Kressel, Leksikon, 1 (1965), 241–2.

[A.D.]

BACHRACH, JUDAH BEN JOSHUA EZEKIEL (1775–1846), Lithuanian rabbi and author. Judah succeeded Isaac Avigdor as *av bet din* of Sejny (near Suwalki in Poland) where he remained until his death. After his death, his novellae and glosses to the Talmud and to Alfasi were published in the Vilna (Romm) edition under the title *Nimmukei ha-Grib* (=**Ha-G**aon **R**abbi **J**udah **B**achrach). His glosses to Maimonides' *Mishneh Torah* are also known. Bachrach is particularly important because of his ties with *Elijah b. Solomon Zalman Gaon of Vilna, who was a relative of his father-in-law, Israel Burlioner. Bachrach possessed a number of tractates of the Talmud which had been used by Elijah Gaon and which contained manuscript glosses by him, differing from those published in the Vienna edition of the Talmud of 1826–31. These volumes were purchased by the Romm publishers from Bachrach's children and the glosses were published in the Vilna edition of 1880–86.

Bibliography: I. T. Eisenstadt and S. Wiener, *Da'at Kedoshim* (1897–98), 68; R. N. N. Rabinowicz, *Ma'amar al Hadpasat ha-Talmud,* ed. by A. M. Habermann (1952), 129, 176.

[Y.Ho.]

BACHRACH, MOSES BEN ISAIAH MENAHEM (also known as **Moses Mendels;** 1574–1641), talmudic scholar. Bachrach was *av bet din* in Szydlow, Wlodzimierz, Cracow, and Frankfort from before 1605 until after 1614. Apparently he then went to serve in a similar capacity in the district of Cracow since Meir of *Lublin mentions him in one of his responsa of that period as being there. He carried on a halakhic correspondence with Benjamin Aaron *Slonik in 1619, at which time he was in Vladimir. In 1636 he was succeeded by R. Yom Tov Lipmann *Heller as *av bet din* in Prague, moving from there to Posen, where he succeeded Simeon Wolf b. David Auerbach as *av bet din,* and where he remained for the rest of his life. He participated in the sessions of the Council of the Four Lands in Yaroslav (1614) and in Lublin (1639). Jacob *Reischer in his *Shevut Ya'akov* refers to him as an outstanding talmudic scholar. *Moshel ba-Elyonim Attah Yadata,* a *seliḥah* he wrote during an epidemic, is still extant. It is included in the *Seliḥot* of Posen, Cracow, Prague, Worms, and Alsace. One of his responsa is included in the responsa *Ḥinnukh Beit Yehudah* of Judah Leib b. Ḥanokh (Amsterdam, 1708, no. 76). His son Israel wrote *Sefer Marot ha-Ẓedek* and an index to the *Shelah* of Isaiah *Horowitz (Amsterdam, 1682). His daughter, Edel, translated an abridged version of *Josippon into Yiddish (Cracow, 1770).

Bibliography: M. Horovitz, *Frankfurter Rabbinen* (1969²), 38, 47, 62, 280–1; Dembitzer, in: *Oẓar ha-Sifrut,* 4 (1892), 230–1;

Wettsein, in: *Ha-Eshkol*, 5 (1905), 253; Halpern, Pinkas, 61, 490; Davidson, Oẓar, 3 (1930), 107 no. 834; D. Avron (ed.), *Pinkas ha-Kesherim shel Kehillat Pozna* (1966), 72, 120.

[Ed.]

BACK, SAMUEL (1841–1899), rabbi and scholar. Back, who was born in Galgocz (Hlohovec, Czechoslovakia), served as rabbi in Prague-Smichov from 1872. He wrote on philosophical, historical, and talmudical subjects. His published works include: *Josef Albos Bedeutung in der Geschichte der juedischen Religionsphilosophie* (1869); *Das Synhedrion unter Napoleon I* (1879); *R. Meir ben Baruch aus Rothenburg* (1895); *Entstehungsgeschichte der portugiesischen Gemeinde in Amsterdam und Rabbi Menasse ben Israel* (1883); *Elischa ben Abuja-Acher* (1891); and "Die Fabel in Talmud und Midrash" (in MGWJ, vols. 25, 29, 30, 33). Back also published sermons and eulogies as well as articles in learned periodicals.

[Ed.]

BACKER, GEORGE (1902–), U.S. publisher, politician, and communal leader. Backer was born in New York. He worked briefly in the family's real estate firm, but devoted himself mainly to politics and the arts. In 1937 and 1938 Backer ran unsuccessfully for Congress as an American Labor Party candidate, and served on the New York City Council. From World War II he was a leader of the reform wing of New York Democrats, and was closely associated, as friend and political adviser, with W. Averell Harriman. In 1939 Backer purchased the *New York Post*, became its publisher and editor, and imbued it with a strong liberal outlook. His former wife, Dorothy *Schiff, assumed control of the newspaper after their divorce in 1942. Backer had a deep interest in music and drama, sponsoring theatrical productions and writing plays. His novel *Appearance of a Man* was published in 1966. Backer's Jewish activities date from the early 1930s when he became alarmed at the rise of Nazism. He visited Germany and Poland in 1933, 1934, and 1936, urging Jews to emigrate, and was active in American organizations aiding refugees. Among the Jewish groups with which he was affiliated are the American Jewish Joint Distribution Committee, American ORT, Jewish Telegraphic Agency, and American Jewish Committee.

Bibliography: *New York Times* (July 20, 1966).

[Mo.Ro.]

°**BACON, ROGER** (c. 1214–1294), English philosopher and Hebraist. Bacon studied at Oxford (probably) and—from 1236 at the latest—Paris. He learned Hebrew, and his transliterations, reflecting Sephardi pronunciation, imply Jewish assistance. Bacon's advanced criticisms of scientific and theological methodology led Bonaventura, general of the Franciscans, to stop his teaching at Paris; after Stephen Tempier's Paris condemnation (1277) of the 219 propositions and of magical instruction, he was allegedly imprisoned for 14 years by Jerome de Ascoli, later Pope Nicholas IV. Meanwhile, in 1266, Clement IV (Guy du Foulques) had directed him to disregard his order's instructions and to write up, *in extenso*, his scholarship and views on ecclesiastical abuses. Bacon's resultant writings contain frequent references to Hebrew as the fountainhead of all philosophical knowledge and as indispensable for Bible study, all Latin versions being corrupt. While criticizing *Andrew of Saint Victor for his addiction to Jewish exegesis and deprecating contemporary acknowledgment of Andrew as authoritative, Bacon commended the former's resort to the original Hebrew text. He extolled Robert *Grosseteste's endeavors to promote Hebrew studies, and a certain *"homo sapientissimus"* (probably William of Mara) for pursuing them.

Besides substantial competence in biblical Hebrew, Bacon evinced interest in the Jewish calendar and a grasp of linguistic science; he appreciated the affinity of Hebrew, Aramaic, and Arabic as comparable to that of the Romance languages. He contemplated writing a Hebrew grammar, and a fragment—the earliest known Hebrew grammar by a named gentile scholar in the West—survives (Cambridge Ms. Ff. 6. 13; appended to Bacon's *Greek Grammar*, ed. E. Nolan, 1902). Hirsch, who assembled and translated the relevant passages in Bacon's works, tentatively connected some correspondence (Ms. Toulouse 402) regarding Hebrew grammar and the calendar with Bacon (S. Berger, *Quam Notitiam* . . . (1893), 37–38).

Bibliography: S. A. Hirsch, in: JQR, 12 (1899/1900), 34–35; B. Smalley, *The Study of the Bible in the Middle Ages* (1952^2), index; A. G. Little, *Roger Bacon* (1928).

[Ra.L.]

BACRI, Algerian family.

Joseph Coen Bacri (1740?–1817), banker, trader, and communal leader. Born in Algiers, he founded the Bacri Frères firm which played a significant role in Algerian politics for fifty years. The firm was an important wheat supplier to France during the Napoleonic period. In 1811, after the execution on a charge of treason of his son David, who had been active manager of the firm for several years, Joseph reassumed the management of the firm's affairs and was appointed leader of the Algerian Jewish community by the dey. However, in 1816, the dey confiscated his possessions and banished him from Algiers. Bacri died in poverty in Leghorn.

David Coen Bacri (1770–1811), son of Joseph, financier and communal leader. David had widespread shipping and trading interests and served as the financial agent for many European firms and governments. In 1797 he married Aziza, a niece of Naphtali *Busnach. Busnach, a statesman who was able to manipulate the Algerian Regency for his own purposes, became a partner in the firm. Under David's management, the firm of Bacri Busnach became so powerful and its operations so extensive that it was able to defy the British government and buy captured allied vessels from French privateers.

Acting on the advice of Bacri Busnach, the dey authorized a five-million franc loan to the French Directory. The credit for the loan was later transferred to the firm. The subsequent 30-year-long dispute over the settlement of the loan was one of the factors which exacerbated relations between Algiers and France, and led eventually to the French occupation of Algeria. After Naphtali's assassination by a soldier of the dey's palace guard in June 1805, Bacri Busnach became insolvent. David was imprisoned for allegedly owing the government five million francs. The European governments who had profited by David's business activities put pressure on the Algerian Regency and secured his release. These same governments then helped David set up the firm "Bacri" in payment for his past services to them. In 1806 the dey named him head of the Jewish community. Subsequently, his enemy, David Duran, who wanted the leadership for himself, denounced Bacri to the authorities and he was executed for treason.

Jacob Coen Bacri (1763–1836), financier. Bacri served as French consul in Algiers under the restored Bourbon monarchy. In 1827, he represented Charles X in negotiations with Dey Hassan in regard to a French claim. Hassan, angered by Bacri's impassioned defense of French interests, insulted him. The French government regarded the dey's action as a national insult and as an immediate excuse to declare war. The war resulted in the French conquest of Algiers in 1830 and the banishment of the dey.

Bacri, who left Algiers at the outbreak of the war, settled in Paris. During the last years of his life, he was continually importuned by creditors because of his inability to collect a 35-million-franc debt from the Spanish government.

Bibliography: M. Eisenbeth, in: *Revue Africaine,* 96 (1952), 372–83; Hirschberg, Afrikah, index (includes bibliographies).

[J.O.R.]

BADAJOZ, city in Castile, western Spain, near the Portuguese frontier. Jewish settlement evidently began to develop in the 11th century, when Jewish artisans and merchants engaged in international trade are mentioned. After the Christian reconquest the Jews of Badajoz were ordered to pay the *oncena* in addition to other taxes for which they were liable (1258). In the 15th century the Badajoz community claimed that it had been exempted from all taxes and imposts and was required to produce evidence at the synod of *Valladolid. The tax assessment for Castilian Jewry of 1474 required the Badajoz and Almendral communities to pay the sum of 7,500 *maravedis.* The enactment ordering the segregation of Jews from Christians was implemented in Badajoz during the 1480s, and many Jews were turned out of their homes. After the edict of expulsion of the Jews from Spain in 1492, large numbers of the exiles passed through Badajoz on their way to Portugal. Badajoz remained an important Converso center. Between 1493 and 1499 the local inquisitional tribunal punished no fewer than 231 New Christians. David *Reuveni was burned at an auto-da-fé in Badajoz in 1535 after a long imprisonment there. In 1635 a large group of Portuguese Marranos was discovered in Badajoz and was relentlessly pursued by the Inquisition.

Bibliography: M. Ramón Martínez, *Historia del reino de Badajoz durante la dominación española* (1905), 80–81; J. Lucio d'Azevedo, *Evolução do Sebastianismo* (1918), 194ff.; H. C. Lea, *History of the Inquisition of Spain* (1922), index; Suárez Fernández, Documentos, index; Rodríguez-Moñino, in: REJ, 115 (1956), 73–86; Baer, Urkunden, index; A. Z. Aescoly, *Ha-Tenu'ot ha-Meshiḥiyyot be-Yisrael* (1956), 372; Ashtor, Korot, 2 (1966), 128–366. [H.B.]

°**BADÈ, WILLIAM FREDERIC** (1871–1936), biblical archaeologist. Born in Carver, Minnesota, Badè taught Old Testament literature at Moravian Theological Seminary, Bethlehem, Pennsylvania, from 1898 to 1902; from 1902 to 1936 he was professor of Old Testament literature and Semitic languages at the Pacific School of Religion, Berkeley, California. He excavated Tell al-Naṣba (Mizpah?), north of Jerusalem, in five campaigns between 1926 and 1935, clearing the mound almost completely. Badè published *Old Testament in the Light of Today* (1915), *A Manual of Excavations in the Near East* (1934), and *Excavations at Tell al-Naṣba, 1926 and 1927: A Preliminary Report* (1928).

Bibliography: Albright, in: BASOR, 62 (1936), 4–5; idem, in: JAOS, 52 (1932), 52–53.

[M.A.-Y.]

BADEN, part of the *Land* of Baden-Wuerttemberg, West Germany. The former grand duchy was created in 1806 from parts of various territories (including the Palatinate), where until then the Jews had formed no united community or shared a common history. The earliest records of the presence of Jews in these territories relate to Gruensfeld (1218), Ueberlingen (1226), *Freiburg (c. 1230), Lauda and *Tauberbischofsheim (1235), *Constance (1241), and Sinsheim (early 13th century). The Jews had been expelled from several of these areas at various times: the Palatinate in 1391, the margravate of Baden in 1470, Austrian Breisgau in 1573, and the diocese of Basle in 1581. Until 1806 the history of the Jews in the margravate of Baden, which subsequently formed the nucleus of the state of Baden, may be summarized briefly. After the *Black Death, 1348–49, few Jews lived there but even these were expelled in 1470, as a result of the blood libel of *Endingen (South Baden). Jews were allowed to return to Baden at the beginning of the 16th century. In 1535 the margravate of Baden was divided into Baden-Baden and Baden-Durlach, to be united again in 1771. The Jews were expelled from Baden-Baden in 1614, but readmitted during the Thirty Years' War (1618–48). According to the first legislation concerning the status of the Jews in Baden-Baden in 1714, the territorial organization of the Jewry was headed by two lay officers (*Schultheisse*) and a rabbi. In Baden-Durlach Jews were first tolerated officially in 1537, but were expelled during the Thirty Years' War and readmitted in 1666. The Jewish population numbered 24 families in 1709, increasing to 160 families by 1738.

After the grand duchy of Baden was created, the position of its *Schutzjuden* ("protected Jews") improved. In the first constitutional edict of May 14, 1807, Judaism was recognized as a tolerated religion; a year later, the sixth edict afforded the Jews irrevocable civil rights and abolished the marriage restrictions imposed on them (see *Familiants' Laws). The ninth edict (the so-called *"Judenedikt"* of Jan. 13, 1809) granted the Jews an officially recognized state organization, required them to adopt permanent family names, and determined their as yet very curtailed civil status. The struggle for emancipation continued until 1862 when they achieved full civic equality. Anti-Jewish outrages occurred in Baden in 1819 (*Hep-Hep), 1848, and 1862. In 1862 the last of Baden's cities to exclude Jews (Baden-Baden, Freiburg, Constance, and Offenburg), finally allowed them to settle there. Nevertheless, animosity toward the Jews continued to be expressed in Baden, where Adolph *Stoecker's anti-Semitic Christian Social Party found numbers of adherents. After the Baden Army Corps was incorporated into the Prussian army, no Jew was promoted to the position of reserve officer or

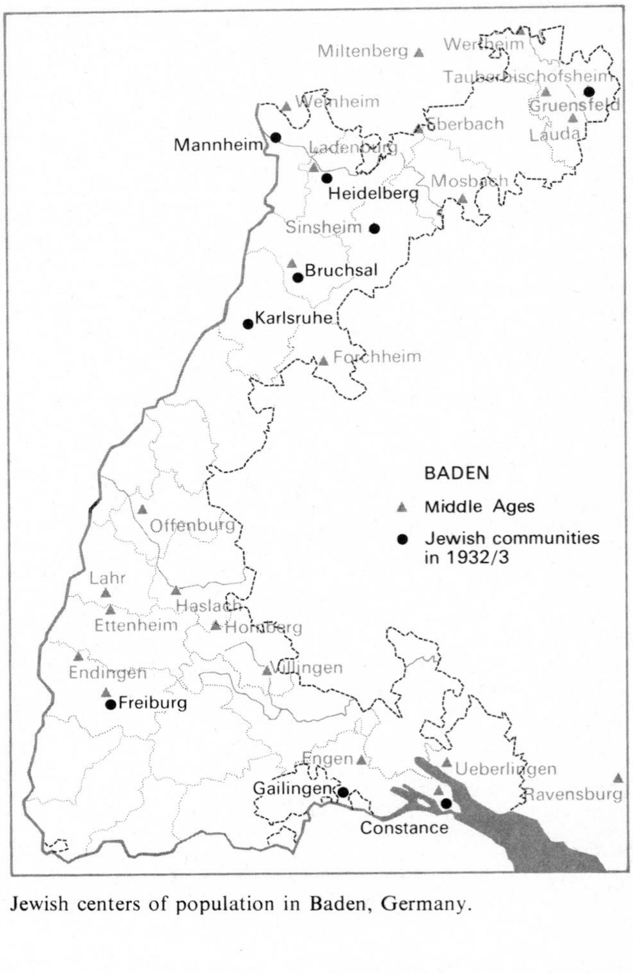

Jewish centers of population in Baden, Germany.

medical officer. Professorships too were granted almost exclusively to baptized Jews.

In 1868 Grand Duke Frederick I appointed the Durlach lawyer, Moritz *Ellstaetter, his minister of finance, making him the first German Jew to hold a ministerial position. Theodor *Herzl tried to interest the German emperor in Zionism through the intervention of the grand duke. The Jews of Baden also participated in its political life. In 1862 the lawyer R. Kusel was elected to represent Karlsruhe in the second chamber, and Ludwig Frank of Mannheim was elected to the Landtag and later to the Reichstag as Social Democratic member. He was among the 589 Baden Jews who fell in World War I. Two Jews were in the first postwar cabinet of Baden, L. Marum (minister of justice, murdered by the Nazis in 1933) and Ludwig *Haas (minister of the interior), who was also active in Jewish affairs.

In the Middle Ages Baden Jewry engaged in moneylending, later in livestock-dealing (which was the main source of income for the Jews in the countryside) and retail trading. In the 19th century occupational difficulties resulted in Jewish emigration to America, although at this time it was possible for Jews to engage in industry also. Baden Jewry was one of the earliest German Jewish Territorial Organizations to establish a state-recognized central organization (1809)—the Oberrat ("supreme council")—which in conjunction with the Synod (established in 1895) represented and directed the affairs of the community. Until its reorganization on May 14, 1923, the Oberrat was under state control. Religious controversy between the Orthodox and *Reform factions began in the early 19th century, the Reform later tending to predominate with the decline of the rural communities. When the *Karlsruhe community included an organ in its new synagogue (1868) and introduced reforms into the services, the Orthodox Jews, led by B. H. Wormser, established a separatist congregation there, the only one in Baden, which was given state recognition.

In 1806 Baden had a Jewish population of about 12,000, which had risen to 24,099 by 1862. As the result of emigration after the rise of Nazism it decreased from 20,617 in 1933 to 8,725 by 1939. The Jews of Baden were among the first to be deported from Germany. On Oct. 22, 1940, some 5,600 Baden Jews, along with others from the Palatinate and the Saar, were transported to *Gurs concentration camp (southern France), from where they were further deported to Poland from 1942 onward. Approximately 500 Jews from Baden survived in France. The Oberrat was reestablished after the war. In 1962 the cemetery in Gurs was leased to the Baden Oberrat for 99 years. The community of Baden numbered 1094 in 1969; in 1969 there were six communities in Baden (66 Jews in Baden-Baden, 248 in Freiburg, 135 in *Heidelberg, 260 in Karlsruhe, 387 in *Mannheim and Constance), with N. P. Levinson as chief rabbi.

Bibliography: B. Rosenthal, *Heimatgeschichte der badischen Juden* (1927), includes bibl.; *Gedenkbuch zum 125-jaehrigen Bestehen des Oberrats der Israeliten Badens* (1934); A. Lewin, *Geschichte der badischen Juden 1738–1909* (1909); R. Ruerup, in: *Zeitschrift fuer die Geschichte des Oberrheins*, 114 (1966), 241–300; N. Stein, in: YLBI, 1 (1956), 177–90; P. Sauer, *Dokumente ueber die Verfolgung der juedischen Buerger in Baden-Wuerttemberg . . .*, 2 pts. (1966); H. Schnee, *Die Hoffinanz und der moderne Staat*, 2 (1963), 43–86; idem, *Die Schicksale der juedischen Buerger Baden-Wuerttembergs 1933–45* (1969); F. Hundsnurscher and G. Taddey, *Die juedischen Gemeinden in Baden* (1968); Germ Jud, 2 (1968), 45–47; *Die Opfer der National-sozialistischen Judenverfolgung in Baden-Wuerttemberg* (1969).

[B.Br.]

BADEN BEI WIEN, spa in N.E. Austria. During the later Middle Ages Jews doing business there lived in nearby Tribuswinkel. In 1805 Isaac Schischa of Mattersdorf was granted permission to settle in the town, opened a Jewish restaurant, and established a prayer room. From around 1800 there was a *Judenbad*, a bath frequented by Jews in Baden, but Jews were not granted the right of residence in the city until 1861. A synagogue for 500 was built in 1873, and the community of 80 members was officially recognized in 1878. The first rabbi, W. Reich, installed in 1880, brought about a compromise between Orthodox and Liberal elements and was active in the foundation of the Agudat Israel orphan home. The community increased mainly by settlers from Hungary. By 1928 it numbered 1,500 (6.7% of the total population), and was the third largest in Austria, but in 1934 there were only 1,108 Jewish inhabitants. On Nov. 10, 1938, the synagogue and all community buildings were blown up, and the Jewish population was arrested to "make room" for Aryans. In 1946 the congregation was reconstituted, with a prayer room; in 1968 it had 30 members.

Bibliography: W. Reich (ed.), *Festschrift zum 40-jaehrigen Jubileum der Chewra Kadische zu Baden bei Wien* (1914); *Juedisches Jahrbuch fuer Oesterreich* (1932); L. Moses, *Die Juden in Niederoesterreich* (1935), 203; Rosenkranz, in: *Yad Vashem Bulletin*, no. 14 (1964), 35–41.

[H.W.]

BADER, GERSHOM (Gustav; 1868–1953), Hebrew and Yiddish journalist and writer. Bader, who was born in Cracow, taught there after attending rabbinical seminaries outside Galicia. From 1893 until 1912 he lived in Lvov, where in 1904 he founded the first Yiddish daily in Galicia, the *Togblat* (from 1906, *Nayes Lemberger Togblat*), and contributed regularly to *Ha-Maggid* and other Hebrew papers. From 1896 to 1912 he published and edited the *Yidisher Folkskalender*, a popular Galician literary almanac. He translated Genesis into Polish and published Hebrew language textbooks. His anthologies, *Leket Peraḥim* and *Zer Peraḥim* (1895–96), helped to popularize Hebrew literature and in 1896 he edited the fifth volume of the literary miscellany *Oẓar ha-Sifrut*. From 1896 to 1912 he produced the *Lukhes* annuals in Yiddish, and in 1903–04 a parallel Hebrew annual miscellany, *Ḥermon*. In 1912 Bader settled in New York, where he contributed to the *Togblat* and the *Jewish Morning Journal*. Of his Yiddish plays, the most successful was *Dem Rebens Nign* ("The Rabbi's Melody"), produced in 1919. His writings include: *Ḥelkat Meḥokek*, a life of Jesus (1889); *Medinah va-Ḥakhameha*, a lexicon of Galician Jewish cultural figures (1934); and *Mafte'aḥ le-Rashei Tevot . . .*, a dictionary of talmudic abbreviations (1951); *Jewish Spiritual Heroes* (3 vols., in English 1940); and his memoirs, *Mayne Zikhroynes* (1953).

Bibliography: G. Bader, *Medinah va-Ḥakhameha* (1934), autobiographical preface; idem, in: *Genazim*, 1 (1960), 82–90 (autobiography); Rabbi Binyamin, *Mishpeḥot Soferim* (1959), 134–5.

[G.K.]

BADGE, JEWISH, distinctive sign compulsorily worn by Jews.

Muslim World. The introduction of a mark to distinguish persons not belonging to the religious faith of the majority did not originate in Christendom, where it was later radically imposed, but in Islam. It seems that Caliph Omar II (717–20), not Omar I, as is sometimes stated, was the first ruler to order that every non-Muslim, the *dhimmī*, should wear vestimentary distinctions (called *giyār*, i.e., distinguishing marks) of a different color for each minority group. The ordinance was unequally observed, but it was reissued and reinforced by Caliph al-Mutawakkil (847–61). Subsequently it remained in force over the centuries, with a few variations. Thus in Sicily the Saracen governor in

Figure 1. A bearded Jew wearing the "Tablets of the Law" badge on his outer garment, as decreed by King Henry III of England in 1217 and reenforced in 1253. This figure is the corbel supporting the 13th-century statue of the *synagoga* in Lincoln Cathedral.

Figure 2. The "Tablets of the Law" badge is depicted in this English caricature of the Jew "Aaron son of the devil," dated 1277. Aaron is wearing the typical Jewish hood. London, Public Record Office.

887/8 compelled the Christians to wear on their garments and put on their doors a piece of cloth in the form of a swine, and the Jews to affix a similar sign in the form of a donkey. In addition, the Jews were compelled to wear yellow belts and special hats.

Christendom. Although written documentary testimony concerning distinctive signs worn by Jews from the 12th century is still lacking, pictorial representations of this period, especially in the Germanic countries, introduce the pointed hat. This is subsequently referred to as the "Jewish hat," worn by Jews or depicted in allegorical representations of Judaism ("Synagoga"). It would seem, however, that this distinction was instituted by the Jews themselves. There are some ambiguous references to the compulsory imposition of distinctive Jewish clothing in documents from the beginning of the 13th century (Charter of Alais, 1200: Synodal rules of Odo, bishop of Paris, c. 1200). The consistent record, however, can be traced back only to canon 68 of the Fourth *Lateran Council (1215): "In several provinces, a difference in vestment distinguishes the Jews or the Saracens from the Christians; but in others, the confusion has reached such proportions that a difference can no longer be perceived. Hence, at times it has occurred that Christians have had sexual intercourse in error with Jewish or Saracen women and Jews or Saracens with Christian women. That the crime of such a sinful mixture shall no longer find evasion or cover under the pretext of error, we order that they [Jews and Saracens] of both sexes, in all Christian lands and at all times, shall be publicly differentiated from the rest of the population by the quality of their garment, especially since that this is ordained by Moses. . . ." Both the allusion to biblical law (Lev. 19), and the inclusion of the canon among a series of others regulating the Jewish position, indicate that the decree was directed especially against the Jews.

Implementation of the council's decision varied in the countries of the West in both the form of the distinctive sign and the date of its application.

ENGLAND. In England papal influence was at this time particularly strong. The recommendations of the Lateran Council were repeated in an order of March 30, 1218. However, before long the wealthier Jews, and later on entire communities, paid to be exempted, notwithstanding the reiteration of the order by the diocesan council of Oxford in 1222. In 1253, however, the obligation to wear the badge was renewed in the period of general reaction, by Henry III, who ordered the *tabula* to be worn in a prominent position. In the *statutum de Judeismo* of 1275, Edward I stipulated the color of the badge and increased the size. A piece of yellow taffeta, six fingers long and three broad, was to be worn above the heart by every Jew over the age of seven years. In England, the badge took the form of the Tablets of the Law, considered to symbolize the Old Testament, in which form it is to be seen in various caricatures and portraits of medieval English Jews.

Figure 3. The typical pointed hat worn by Jews in France, from a historiated initial letter "V" showing the prophet Joel. *Stavordale Bible,* N. France, 12th century. London, British Museum, Add. ms. 28106-7.

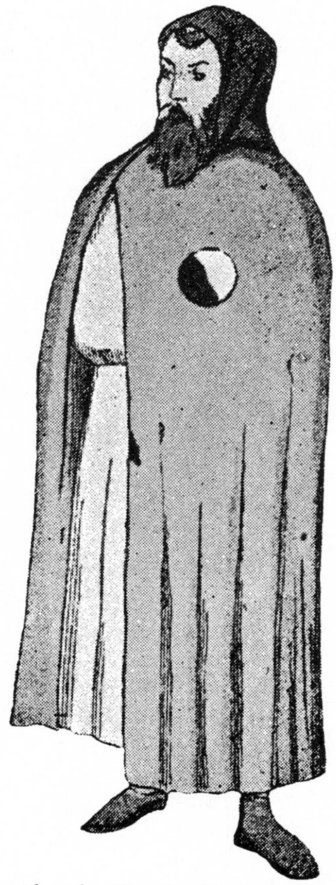

Figure 4. A red and white circular badge worn by French Jews in the 13th and 14th centuries. A drawing after a French 14th-century miniature. Paris, Bibliothèque Nationale, ms. Français 820, fol. 192.

FRANCE. In 1217, the papal legate in southern France ordered that the Jews should wear a *rota* ("wheel") on their outer garment but shortly afterward the order was rescinded. However, in 1219 King Philip Augustus ordered the Jews to wear the badge, apparently in the same form. Discussions regarding the permissibility of wearing the badge on the Sabbath when not attached to the garment are reported by *Isaac b. Moses of Vienna, author of the *Or Zaru'a,* who was in France about 1217–18. Numerous church councils (Narbonne 1227, Rouen 1231, Arles 1234, Béziers 1246, Albi 1254, etc.) reiterated the instructions for wearing the badge, and a general edict for the whole of France was issued by Louis IX (Saint Louis) on June 19, 1269. This edict was endorsed by Philip the Bold, Philip the Fair, Louis X, Philip V, and others, and by the councils of Pont-Audemer (1279), Nîmes (1284), etc. The circular badge was normally to be worn on the breast; some regulations also required that a second sign should be worn on the back. At times, it was placed on the bonnet or at the level of the belt. The badge was yellow in color, or of two shades, white and red. Wearing it was compulsory from the age of either seven or thirteen years. Any Jew found without the badge forfeited his garment to his denunciator. In cases of a second offense a severe fine was imposed. When traveling, the Jew was exempted from wearing the badge. Philip the Fair extracted fiscal benefits from the compulsory wearing of the badge, by annual distribution of the badges by the royal tax collectors at a fixed price.

SPAIN. The obligation to wear the Badge of Shame was reenacted by the secular authorities in Spain shortly after the promulgation of the decrees of the Lateran Council, and in 1218 Pope Honorius III instructed the archbishop of Toledo to see that it was rigorously enforced. The Spanish Jews did not submit to this passively, and some of them threatened to leave the country for the area under Muslim rule. In consequence, the pope authorized the enforcement of the regulation to be suspended. The obligation was indeed reenacted sporadically (e.g., in Aragon 1228, Navarre 1234, Portugal 1325). However, it was not consistently enforced, and Jews who had influence at court would often secure special exemption. Alfonso X the Wise of Castile in his *Siete Partidas* (1263) imposed a fine or lashing as the penalty for a Jew who neglected the order. In 1268 James I of Aragon exempted the Jews from wearing the badge, requiring them on the other hand to wear a round cape *(capa rotunda).* In Castile, Henry III (1390–1406) yielded in 1405 to the demand of the Cortes and required even his Jewish courtiers to wear the badge. As a result of Vicente *Ferrer's agitation, the Jews were ordered in 1412 to wear distinctive clothing and a red badge, and they were further required to let their hair and beards grow long. The successors of Henry III renewed the

Figure 5. A typical hat worn by Jews in Spain. A panel from a page of *Las Cantigas de Santa Maria,* composed by Alfonso X of Castile (1252–1284). Madrid, Escorial Library, ms. T-I-1, Cant. 34.

Figure 6. Circular badge worn by an Italian Jewish bridegroom. Bottom half of an initial word panel from the *Hamburg Halakhah Miscellany,* Padua, 1477. Hamburg, Staats- und Universitäts-bibliothek, Cod. Heb. 337 (Scrin 132) fol. 75v.

Figure 7. The circular badge worn by Italian Jews. Detail from a 15th-century painting by an unknown Italian artist of the Madonna and Child. The four Jewish figures are Daniel Norsa and his family. Mantua, Church of Sant' Andrea. Photo Alinari, Florence.

Figure 8. The German Jewish pointed hat as depicted in the *Regensburg Pentateuch*, a Hebrew illuminated manuscript, Germany, 1300. Jerusalem, Israel Museum, ms. 180/52, fol. 154v.

decrees concerning the badge. In Aragon, John I, in 1393, prescribed special clothing for the Jews. In 1397, Queen Maria (the consort of King Martin) ordered all the Jews in Barcelona, both residents and visitors, to wear on their chests a circular patch of yellow cloth, a span in diameter, with a red "bull's eye" in the center. They were to dress only in clothing of pale green color—as a sign of mourning for the ruin of their Temple, which they suffered because they had turned their backs upon Jesus—and their hats were to be high and wide with a short, wide *cuculla*. Violators were to be fined ten *libras* and stripped of their clothes wherever caught. When in 1400 King Martin granted the Jews of Lérida a charter of privileges, he required them, nevertheless, to wear the customary badge. In 1474, the burghers of Cervera sought to impose upon the local Jews a round badge of other than the customary form. In the period before the expulsion of the Jews from Spain in 1492, the wearing of the Jewish badge was almost universally enforced, and some persons demanded that it should be extended also to Conversos.

ITALY. Presumably the order of the Lateran Council was reenacted in Rome very soon after its promulgation in 1215, but it was certainly not consistently enforced. In 1221–22 the "enlightened" emperor Frederick II Hohenstaufen ordered all the Jews of the Kingdom of Sicily to wear a distinguishing badge of bluish color in the shape of the Greek letter τ and also to grow beards in order to be more easily distinguishable from non-Jews. In the same year the badge was imposed in Pisa and probably elsewhere. In the Papal States the obligation was first specifically imposed so far as is known by Alexander IV in 1257: there is extant a moving penitential poem written on this occasion by Benjamin b. Abraham *Anav expressing the passionate indignation of the Roman Jews on this occasion. The badge here took the form of a circular yellow patch a handspan in diameter to be worn on a prominent place on the outer garment: for the women, two blue stripes on the veil. In 1360 an ordinance of the city of Rome required all male Jews, with the exception of physicians, to wear a coarse red cape, and all women to wear a red apron, and inspectors were appointed to enforce the regulation. Noncompliance was punished by a fine of 11 scudi; informers who pointed out offenders were entitled to half the fine. The ordinance was revised in 1402, eliminating the reward for informing, and exempting the Jews from wearing the special garb inside the ghetto. In Sicily, there was from an early period a *custos rotulae* whose function it was to ensure that the obligation was not neglected. Elsewhere in Italy, however, the enforcement was sporadic, although it was constantly being demanded by fanatical preachers and sometimes temporarily enacted. The turning point came with the bull *Cum nimis absurdum* of Pope *Paul IV in 1555, which inaugurated the ghetto system. This enforced the wearing of the badge (called by the Italian Jews *scimanno*, from Heb. *siman*) for the Papal States, later to be imitated throughout Italy (except in Leghorn), and enforced until the period of the French Revolution. In Rome, as well as in the Papal States in the south of France, it took the form of a yellow hat for men, a yellow kerchief for women. In the Venetian dominions the color was red. In Candia (Crete), then under Venetian rule, Jewish shops had to be distinguished by the badge. David d'Ascoli, who published in 1559 a Latin protest against the degrading regulation, was severely punished and his work was destroyed.

GERMANY. In Germany and the other lands of the Holy Roman Empire, the pointed hat was first in use as a distinctive sign. It was not officially imposed until the second half of the 13th century (*Schwabenspiegel*, art. 214,

Figure 9. A German Jew and Jewess from Worms, 16th century, in typical Jewish dress with circular badges on their garments. Worms, Stadtarchiv.

Figure 10. A decree issued in Vienna, 1551, by Ferdinand I, Archduke of Austria, requiring Jews to wear a distinguishing mark "... namely on the outer coat or dress over the left breast a yellow ring, circumference and diameter of the circle as herein prescribed and not narrower nor smaller, made of yellow cloth...." Freiburg, Stadtarchiv, XII[c].

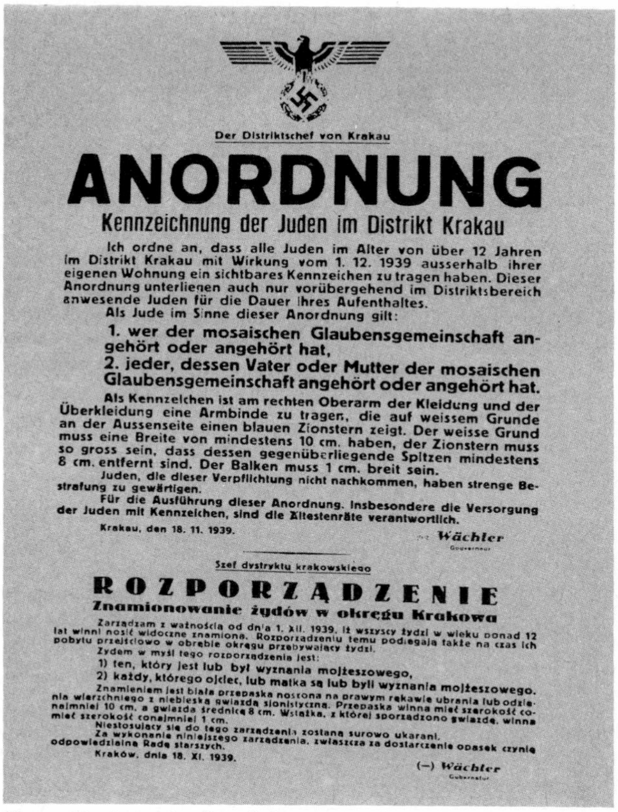

Der Distriktschef von Krakau

ANORDNUNG

Kennzeichnung der Juden im Distrikt Krakau

Ich ordne an, dass alle Juden im Alter von über 12 Jahren im Distrikt Krakau mit Wirkung vom 1. 12. 1939 ausserhalb ihrer eigenen Wohnung ein sichtbares Kennzeichen zu tragen haben. Dieser Anordnung unterliegen auch nur vorübergehend im Distriktsbereich anwesende Juden für die Dauer ihres Aufenthaltes.

Als Jude im Sinne dieser Anordnung gilt:

1. wer der mosaischen Glaubensgemeinschaft angehört oder angehört hat,

2. jeder, dessen Vater oder Mutter der mosaischen Glaubensgemeinschaft angehört oder angehört hat.

Als Kennzeichen ist am rechten Oberarm der Kleidung und der Überkleidung eine Armbinde zu tragen, die auf weissem Grunde an der Aussenseite einen blauen Zionstern zeigt. Der weisse Grund muss eine Breite von mindestens 10 cm. haben, der Zionstern muss so gross sein, dass dessen gegenüberliegende Spitzen mindestens 8 cm. entfernt sind. Der Balken muss 1 cm. breit sein.

Juden, die dieser Verpflichtung nicht nachkommen, haben strenge Bestrafung zu gewärtigen.

Für die Ausführung dieser Anordnung. Insbesondere die Versorgung der Juden mit Kennzeichen, sind die Ältestenräte verantwortlich.

Krakau, den 18. 11. 1939.

Wächler
Gouverneur

Szef dystryktu krakowskiego

ROZPORZĄDZENIE

Znamionowanie żydów w okręgu Krakowa

Zarządzam z ważnością od dnia 1. XII. 1939, iż wszyscy żydzi w wieku ponad 12 lat winni nosić widoczne znamiona. Rozporządzeniu temu podlegają także na czas ich pobytu przejściowo w obrębie okręgu przebywający żydzi.

Żydem w myśl tego rozporządzenia jest:

1) ten, który jest lub był wyznania mojżeszowego,

2) każdy, którego ojciec, lub matka są lub byli wyznania mojżeszowego.

Znamieniem jest biała przepaska noszona na prawym rękawie ubrania lub odzienia wierzchniego z niebieską gwiazdą sjonistyczną. Przepaska winna mieć szerokość conajmniej 10 cm, a gwiazda średnicę 8 cm. Wstążka, z której sporządzono gwiazdę, winna mieć szerokość conajmniej 1 cm.

Niestosujący się do tego zarządzenia zostaną surowo ukarani.

Za wykonanie niniejszego zarządzenia, zwłaszcza za dostarczenie opasek czynię odpowiedzialną Radę starszych.

Kraków, dnia 18. XI. 1939.

(—) Wächler
Gubernator

Figure 11. An order for all Jews over 12 years of age to wear a white armband with a blue star of David, issued by the German governor of Cracow on November 18, 1939. Jerusalem, Yad Vashem Archives.

c. 1275; *Weichbild-Vulgata,* art. 139, second half of 13th century; cf. Council of Breslau, 1267; Vienna, 1267; Olmuetz, 1342; Prague, 1355, etc.). The church councils of Breslau and Vienna, both held in 1267, required the Jews of Silesia, Poland, and Austria to wear not a badge but the pointed hat characteristic of Jewish garb (the *pileum cornutum*). A church council held in Ofen (Budapest) in 1279 decreed that the Jews were to wear on the chest a round patch in the form of a wheel. The badge was imposed for the first time in Augsburg in 1434, and its general enforcement was demanded by Nicolaus of *Cusa and John of *Capistrano. In 1530, the ordinance was applied to the whole of Germany (*Reichspolizeiordnung,* art. 22). In the course of the 15th century, a Jewish badge, in addition to the Jewish hat, was introduced in various forms into Germany. A church council which met in Salzburg in 1418 ordered Jewish women to attach bells to their dresses so that their approach might be heard from a distance. In Augsburg in 1434 the Jewish men were ordered to attach yellow circles to their clothes, in front, and the women were ordered to wear yellow pointed veils. Jews on a visit to Nuremberg were required to wear a type of long, wide hood falling over the back, by which they would be distinguished from the local Jews. The obligation to wear the yellow badge was imposed upon all the Jews in Germany in 1530 and in Austria in 1551. As late as in the reign of Maria Theresa (1740–80) the Jews of Prague were required to wear yellow collars over their coats.

Discontinuance. In the new communities which became established in Western Europe (and later America) from the close of the 16th century under somewhat more free conditions the wearing of the Jewish badge was never imposed, though sometimes suggested by fanatics. In Poland, partly probably because the Jews constituted a distinct ethnic element, it was likewise virtually unknown except in some major cities under German influence. Similarly the Court Jews of Germany were unable to perform their function unless dressed like other people. In the course of the 18th century, although there was no official modification of the established policy, the wearing of the Jewish badge came to be neglected over a good part of Europe. In Venice the red hat continued to be worn by elderly persons and rabbis through sheer conservatism.

From the 17th century, there were some regional suspensions of the distinctive sign in Germany, as also for the Jews of Vienna in 1624, and for those of Mannheim in 1691. It was abrogated at the end of the 18th century with

Figure 12. A Dutch Jewish woman wearing the yellow badge, 1942. Jerusalem, Yad Vashem Archives.

Jewish emancipation. Thus on Sept. 7, 1781, the yellow "wheel" was abolished by Emperor Joseph II in all the territories of the Austrian crown. In the Papal States in France the yellow hat was abolished in 1791 after the French Revolution reached the area, although some persons retained it until forbidden to do so by official proclamation. In the Papal States in Italy, on the other hand, the obligation was reimposed as late as 1793. When in 1796–97 the armies of the French Revolution entered Italy and the ghettos were abolished, the obligation to wear the Jewish badge disappeared. Its reimposition was threatened but not carried out during the reactionary period after the fall of Napoleon, and it then seemed that the Badge of Shame was only an evil memory of the past.

It was to commemorate the yellow badge or hat that Theodor Herzl chose this color for the cover of the first Zionist periodical *Die Welt.* It was in the same spirit that the *Juedische Rundschau,* the organ of the Zionist Organization in Germany, wrote on the morrow of the Nazi rise to power: "Wear it with pride, this yellow badge" (no. 27, April 4, 1933). [B.Bl.]

Yellow Badge in the Nazi Period. In 1938 the Nazis compelled Jewish shopkeepers to display the words "Jewish business" in their windows but did not introduce distinctive signs to be worn by Jews until after the occupation of Poland. The first to issue an order on his own initiative, without awaiting instructions from the central authority, was the town Kommandant of Wloclawek, S.S. Oberfuehrer Cramer, who, on Oct. 24, 1939, ordered that every Jew in Wloclawek was to wear a distinctive sign on the back in the form of a yellow triangle at least 15 cm. in size. The order was published in the *Leslauer Bote* (Oct. 25, 1939). The order applied to all Jews, without distinction of age or sex. This device was rapidly adopted by other commanders in the occupied regions in the East and received official approval, in consideration of the anti-Semitic sentiments prevailing among the local Polish public, which received the new German measure with enthusiasm. The dates of application of the measure varied. There were regions where the instructions were applied even before they were issued in the General-Government, such as in Cracow, where the Jews were compelled to wear the sign from Nov. 18, 1939, whereas the date throughout the General-Gouvernment was Dec. 1, 1939. In Lvov, the order was applied as from July 15, 1941, and in eastern Galicia from Sept. 15, 1941. On the other hand, in certain places the instruction is known to have been applied only after publication of the general order, as for example in Warsaw on Dec. 12, 1939, and not on Dec. 1, 1939, even though Warsaw was included in the General-Government. In the smaller communities, the official German instructions were replaced by an announcement of the *Judenrat.

Figure 13. A replica of the Dutch Jewish badge printed and distributed by the Dutch underground in 1942. The text reads: "Jews and non-Jews stand united in their struggle." Amsterdam, Jewish Historical Museum.

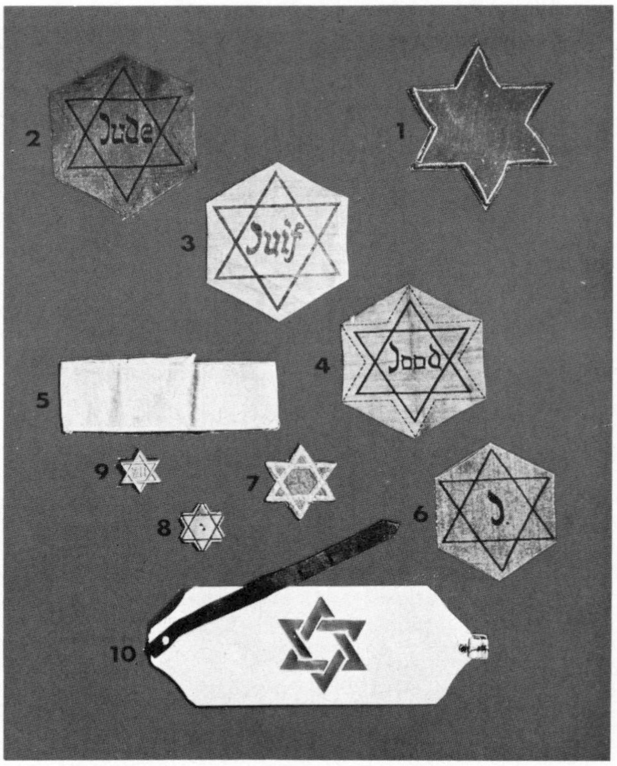

Figure 14. Jewish badges decreed by the Nazis during their occupation of Europe in World War II. 1. Bulgaria, Poland (part), Lithuania, Hungary, Greece (part) (yellow star). 2. Germany, Alsace, Bohemia-Moravia (black on yellow). 3. France (black on yellow). 4. Holland (black on yellow). 5. Greece (part), Serbia, Belgrade, Sofia (yellow armband). 6. Belgium (black on yellow). 7. Slovakia (blue star on yellow background). 8. Bulgaria (black on yellow). 9. Slovakia (yellow star). 10. Poland (part), East and Upper Silesia (blue star on white armband). Jerusalem, Yad Vashem Archives.

In the West, the situation was totally different. In the *Reichsgebiet* (the territory of the Reich proper, as opposed to the occupied territories), the order was issued on Sept. 1, 1941. It was published in the *Reichsgesetzblatt* and was applied as from Sept. 19, 1941. This date was also valid for the Jews of Bohemia, Moravia, and Slovakia. The age from which the wearing of the sign was compulsory was six years for Germany and Western Europe and ten years for Eastern Europe. In certain places the age differed. In Holland, the order was applied as from May 1942, while in Belgium and France the Jews were compelled to wear the distinctive sign from June 1942. A meeting had been held in Paris in March 1942 to coordinate the application of the order in these three countries. In Bulgaria, the order was applied from September 1942, in Greece from February 1943, and in Hungary from April 1944. The type of distinctive sign varied, the following being the principal forms: a yellow Shield (Star) of David inscribed with *J* or *Jude,* etc.; a white armband with a blue Shield of David on it; a Shield of David, with or without inscription and in various colors; a yellow armband with or without inscription; a yellow button in the form of a Shield of David; a metal tag inscribed with the letter *J;* a yellow triangle; a yellow circle. This general use of the Shield of David as the Jewish badge was unknown in the Middle Ages. The inscriptions appearing on the badges were specially chosen to resemble Hebrew characters. After the Jews were compelled to reside in ghettos, they were also forced to wear the distinctive sign in conformity with the order applying to the region in which the ghetto was located. In the concentration camps they wore the sign which designated political prisoners on which was sewn a triangle or a yellow stripe to distinguish them from non-Jewish prisoners. In the *Reichsgebiet,* as well as in several of the occupied countries, the Germans introduced distinctive signs on Jewish business premises, passports, and ration cards, where the letter *J* was overprinted in a most conspicuous manner.

Reactions. Jews reacted with dignity to the order and wore the sign as if it were a decoration. However, they did not realize the danger which lay in wearing a distinctive sign. Non-Jews, especially in Eastern Europe, generally accepted this anti-Jewish measure with enthusiasm and saw in it an opportunity to remove the Jews from commercial, economic, and public life. In the West, reactions varied. The Jews could often rely on the hatred of the Germans by the public, and this even brought active support to the Jews. The Dutch wore the badge out of solidarity with the Jewish citizens. Three-hundred thousand replicas of the badge were produced and distributed throughout Holland bearing the inscription: "Jews and non-Jews stand united in their struggle!" In Denmark the badge was never introduced as a result of the courageous resistance of King Christian X, who was said to have threatened to wear it himself.

Consequences. The principal objective in introducing distinctive signs for the Jews was to erect a barrier between them and non-Jews and to restrict their movements. The Germans achieved this objective to a large extent, despite the various reactions which rendered application of the order difficult. The Jews increasingly concentrated in closed districts even before the establishment of the ghettos by the Nazis for fear of being arrested and deported to concentration camps. A Jew had the choice of concealing the sign and thus becoming an offender liable to a deportation sentence to the concentration camps, or of wearing the sign and becoming an easy prey to his enemies. The distinctive signs were thus an effective means in the hands of the Germans to facilitate their plan to exterminate the Jews.

For special articles of clothing worn compulsorily or voluntarily by Jews, see *Dress.

[B.M.A.]

Bibliography: G. Rezasco, *Segno degli ebrei* (1889); U. Robert, *Signes d'Infamie...* (1891); F. Singermann, *Kennzeichnung der Juden im Mittelalter* (1915); Kisch, in: HJ, 19 (1957), 89ff.; Lichtenstadter, *ibid.*, 5 (1943), 35ff.; Strauss, in: JSOS, 4 (1942), 59; A. Cohen, *Anglo-Jewish Scrapbook* (1943), 249–59; Aronstein, in: *Zion,* 13–14 (1948–49), 33ff.; B. Blumenkranz, *Le Juif médiéval au miroir de l'art chrétien* (1966); S. Grayzel, *Church and the Jews in the XIIIth Century* (1966), index; Baron, Social[2], 11 (1967), 96–106; A. Rubens, *History of Jewish Costume* (1967), index. Nazi Period: L. Poliakov, *L'Etoile jaune* (1949); G. Reitlinger, *The Final Solution* (1953), index s.v. *Judenstern.*

BADḤAN (Heb. בַּדְחָן; "entertainer"), merrymaker, rhymester who entertained guests, especially at weddings. The Talmud mentions professional jesters who cheered the melancholy (Ta'an. 22a) or who amused bride and groom (Ket. 17a; Ber. 30b–31a). Jewish itinerant singers, called *badḥanim* or *leiẓanim* ("jesters") are mentioned in medieval rabbinical literature (e.g., R. Elijah b. Isaac of Carcassonne's *Asufot*); they seem to have appeared as professional entertainers at weddings and at Ḥanukkah and Purim celebrations, much after the pattern of the troubadours and ballad singers. The merrymaking of these *badḥanim,* who were also the forerunners of Jewish theatrical art, consisted not only of folksongs and comic stories but also of skillful puns on scriptural verses and talmudical passages, which required a certain amount of Jewish learning. As a result, the rabbinical authorities protested against the *badḥanim* who parodied the *Kaddish* at wedding festivities or who committed the near-blasphemy of "amusing the guests with jests on scriptural verses and holy words. Happy the man who abstains from such" (R. David ha-Levi, in *Turei Zahav* to Sh. Ar., OḤ 560:5).

Figure 1. A Galician *badḥan* brings tears to the eyes of the wedding party as he sings the bride's praises. An early 20th-century Polish postcard. Jerusalem, Israel Museum Archives.

In Eastern Europe the *badḥan* (or *marshalik,* from Ger. *marschalc,* in the sense of "master of ceremonies," and not from Heb. *mashal,* "proverb"), acted as the professional wedding jester. The *Chmielnicki persecutions (1648–49), and the rabbinical opposition to unbridled merrymaking, even at weddings (based upon Sot. 9:14), led the *badḥanim* to introduce a new style of entertainment—the *forshpil*—in which the *badḥan* addressed the bride with a rhymed penitential exhortation while the women performed the ceremony of *bedeken,* i.e., covering the bride with the veil before proceeding to the *ḥuppah* (see *Marriage Customs). In the case of orphans, the *badḥan's* rhymes invoked the memory of the departed parents and injected a sorrowful note. Later, at the wedding feast, the *badḥan* entertained the guests with music and with jests that contained personal allusions to the important guests and

Figure 2. A *badḥan* dancing at a Galician wedding. A postcard from Cracow, 1902. Jerusalem, Israel Museum Archives.

participants. In the course of time the literary style of the *badḥan* developed into a sort of Hebrew and Yiddish folk-poetry, the most renowned exponent of which was Eliakum *Zunser of Vilna, who composed over 600 songs of this kind. A fine portrayal of the *badḥan* is the character of Breckeloff in I. *Zangwill's *Children of the Ghetto.* In recent times the institution of the *badḥan* has been replaced by more modern forms of entertainment.

Bibliography: A. Berliner, *Aus dem Leben der deutschen Juden im Mittelalter* (1900), 57, 58; I. Abrahams, *Jewish Life in the Middle Ages* (1932²), 213–4; Hirsch, in: JQR, 13 (1901), 601–2; Lifschitz, in: *Arkhiv far di Geshikhte fun Yidishen Teater un Drame,* 1 (1930), 38–74; Eisenstein, Yisrael, 2 (1908), 302–3.

[M.Y.]

BADHAV, ISAAC BEN MICHAEL (1859–1947), Jerusalem rabbi and scholar. Badhav was born in Jerusalem, and was the maternal grandson of Isaac *Covo. In his youth he studied in the *bet ha-midrash* Doresh Zion and in the yeshivah Shevet Aḥim. He engaged to a considerable extent in communal matters, and in 1886 was one of the founders of the Jerusalem Ḥevrat Shomerei Mitzvah u-Malbishei Arumim. In 1887 he was sent on a mission to Tripoli by the Beth El congregation, returning in 1889. In 1901 he was appointed teacher in the *bet ha-midrash* of Ḥayyim Hezekiah *Medini, Sedei Ḥemed in Hebron, but he remained there for a short time only, returning to Jerusalem. He lived in poverty all his life. Badhav devoted himself to collecting old Hebrew books and manuscripts and assembled a large library containing exceptionally important documentary archives which included ancient and valuable documents and records. These he obtained from members of the old Jerusalem families by persuading them to furnish him with their personal accounts of Israel and Jerusalem. They are a valuable source for research, particularly into Jerusalem.

קובץ
מעשה נסים
בו יבואו מעשיות וספורים שנעשו
לישראל בשנים קדמונית בדרך נס
ויוצאים לאור על ידי
יצחק בכ"ר מיכאל בדאהב
הי"ו ס"ט
הירושלמי
שנת ה"א תר"ץ 5690
פעה"ק ירושלם תובב"א
דפוס חיים בר"ש הלוי ז"ל צוקרמן

Title page of Isaac Badhav's *Ma'aseh Nissim,* stories of the deliverance of Jewish communities from danger which gave rise to local Purim celebrations. Jerusalem, 1930. Cecil Roth Collection.

In 1900 he published a catalog of his manuscripts entitled *Ginzei Ẓiyyon vi-Yrushalayim.* A second catalog, *Pardes ha-Torah ve-ha-Ḥokhmah,* was published in 1910. These manuscripts which contain materials dealing with the fields of *halakhah, aggadah,* philosophy, grammar, Kabbalah, geonica, medieval literature, history, poetry, and folklore are of great importance, because some of them are unique. Badhav also published many pamphlets containing laws and customs, poems and parables, amulets, prayers, petitions and memoirs, as well as responsa of early authorities, including some of the responsa of Maimonides. He translated into Ladino various historical studies. Because of his lack of means the pamphlets were issued in an irregular and haphazard manner. His two most important books are still in manuscript form: *Sefer ha-Gittin,* containing formulae of bills of divorce of the different communities, particularly those from Oriental countries—a book of importance not only for practical purposes but also for the purposes of research into Jewish history and folklore; and *Shem ha-Gedolim ha-Kelali,* an encyclopedia of great Jewish scholars and their works, both those which have been published and those which are extant in manuscript form.

Bibliography: M. D. Gaon, *Yehudei ha-Mizraḥ be-Ereẓ Yisrael,* 2 (1937), 128–30; Benayahu, in: *Hed ha-Mizraḥ* (March 29, 1946), 6–7; idem, in: *Yerushalayim,* 1 (1948), 58–60.

[A.D.]

BADIḤI, YAḤYA BEN JUDAH (c. 1810–1887), Yemenite author of works on the Pentateuch and *halakhah.* Badiḥi belonged to one of the distinguished wealthy families of San'a, members of which were skilled goldsmiths by trade and served as minters to the Imams. This was a responsible but dangerous task for Jews since false accusations were frequently brought against them by the authorities. This was the case when Badiḥi and his father were imprisoned by the reigning Imam El-Mahdi (1815–1835). The father regained his freedom by paying a high ransom, but Badiḥi, faced with the choice between death or apostasy, succeeded in escaping to Karokaban, where the ruler treated the Jews with greater tolerance. Here he served as head of the local *bet din.* When Jacob *Saphir visited Yemen in 1859, he met Badiḥi, whom he described as one of the leading and most God-fearing scholars of Yemen Jewry. Badiḥi wrote three works which are still in manuscript: *Ḥen Tov,* a collection of rabbinic commentaries on the Pentateuch to which he added his original explanations with an appendix of 52 of his own responsa; *Zivḥei Shelamim;* and *Leḥem Todah* (based on the *Zevaḥ Todah* of Yaḥya Ṣalaḥ) both on the laws of *sheḥitah* and *terefot.* This latter work, a resume of the laws of *sheḥitah* and *terefot* according to Yemenite customs, was written both to supply exact information for *shoḥetim* in the villages and to stimulate Torah study, which had declined considerably because of various decrees issued against the Jews and because of their many wanderings.

Bibliography: J. Saphir, *Massa Teiman,* ed. by A. Yaari (1951), 137–8, 186; Y. Ratzaby, in: KS, 28 (1952/53), 265, 270, and suppl. 34 (1958/59), 110–1.

[Y.R.]

BADT, HERMANN (1887–1946), German civil servant and constitutional lawyer, active in the Zionist movement. He was the son of the classical scholar Benno Badt. Born in Breslau, he maintained Orthodox traditions and joined the *Mizrachi Party. In 1919, he was the first Jew in Prussia to be admitted to the civil service after the revolution of 1918. From 1922 to 1926 he was a Social Democratic member of the Prussian Diet and then became the highest-ranking Jewish civil servant in Germany, the Ministerialdirektor in the Prussian Ministry of the Interior in charge of constitutional affairs. In 1932 he represented Prussia before the Staatsgerichtshof (State Court) of the German Reich in its unsuccessful legal action against Chancellor von Papen, who had deposed the legal government and instituted himself as a dictatorial "Reichskommissar" (Reich Commissioner) in Prussia. Badt visited Palestine several times before settling there in 1933; in 1931 he flew over it in a zeppelin. Among other enterprises, he founded the Kinneret company to promote middle-class settlement on the land where kibbutz Ein Gev was founded.

Bibliography: E. Hamburger, in: YLBI, 14 (1969), 54; A. Brecht, *Mit der Kraft des Geistes* (1967), index; O. Braun, *Von Weimar zu Hitler* (1940); *Handbuch fuer den Preussischen Landtag* (1925).

[E.H.]

BAECK, LEO (1873–1956), German rabbi and religious thinker, leader of Progressive Judaism. Baeck was born in Lissa (now Leszno, Poland) the son of Rabbi Samuel *Baeck. Leo Baeck first studied at the Conservative Jewish Theological Seminary of Breslau and from 1894 at the Liberal *Hochschule fuer die Wissenschaft des Judentums in Berlin. At the same time he also studied philosophy at the University of Breslau under J. *Freudenthal and at the University of Berlin under the philosopher Wilhelm Dilthey. Baeck served as rabbi in Oppeln (1897–1907), Duesseldorf (1907–12), and Berlin (from 1912 on), and as an army chaplain in World War I. He began lecturing on midrashic literature and homiletics at the Hochschule in 1912.

Leo Baeck, leader of Progressive Judaism.

Baeck was a member of the committee of the *Central-Verein deutscher Staatsbuerger juedischen Glaubens and published numerous articles in its journal, *C.V. Zeitung*, and periodical, *Der Morgen*. Baeck was a non-Zionist member of the Jewish Agency and occasionally contributed to the German Zionist weekly **Juedische Rundschau*. From 1933, when he declared that the "thousand-year" history of the German Jews had come to an end, he was president of the Reichsvertretung, the representative body of German Jews, and devoted himself to defending the rights remaining for Jews under the Nazis. He refused all invitations to serve as a rabbi or professor abroad, declaring that he would remain with the last *minyan* (prayer quorum) of Jews in Germany as long as possible. At *Theresienstadt concentration camp, to which he was deported in 1943, he was named honorary president of the Aeltestenrat and continued the work of encouraging his people. Thus, he became a "witness of his faith," a theme that had long occupied a central position in his writings. After the war, in July 1945, he moved to London, where he became president of the Council of Jews from Germany and chairman of the World Union for Progressive Judaism. From 1948 until his death he taught intermittently in the United States as professor of the history of religion at Hebrew Union College in Cincinnati.

Thought and works. Baeck was a philosophical-theological thinker of wide general knowledge, a preacher, and a historian of religion. In 1901 he published a polemic article against *Wesen des Christentums* by the Protestant theologian Adolf von Harnack (MGWJ, vol. 45). Four years later Baeck published his main work *Wesen des Judentums* (1905; *The Essence of Judaism*, 1936). Ten more German editions and printings of it were published, as well as English (1948[3]), Japanese, and Hebrew (1968) translations. The apologetic character that dominated the first edition was considerably modified in the second and the extreme rationalism was eliminated. This transformation was the result of the influences of mysticism and Jewish nationalism. Baeck had always viewed the essence of Judaism as a dialectical polarity between "mystery" and "command." The commands, according to Baeck, do not necessarily form a system of commandments like the established *halakhah*, which imposes a required and fixed way of life; rather, they appear from time to time in the form of instructions for action like flashes of lightning that break through the cloud covering the divine "mystery." Baeck adhered to Hermann *Cohen's interpretation of Judaism as "ethical monotheism." He believed that piety is achieved by the fulfillment of the duties between man and man and that even ritual observances are directed toward this ethical aim. In this respect Baeck was a liberal Jew, but he was far from spiritual assimilation, because he maintained that ethics must be supported by faith in God.

Baeck sharply rejected Christianity and had a sympathetic, although critical, attitude toward Zionism. In Christianity he saw a "romantic" religion of the abstract spirit longing for redemption (in *Festschrift zum 50-jaehrigen Bestehen der Hochschule fuer die Wissenschaft des Judentums* (1922), 1–48), as distinguished from Judaism, the "classical" religion of the concrete spirit working for the improvement of this world. In 1897, although not a political Zionist, he opposed the protest that most German rabbis joined against holding the first Zionist Congress in Munich. He thought that the building of Palestine was a valuable prospect for embodying the spirit of Judaism, but not a guarantee that it would be realized. This, according to him, could succeed wherever there is a Jewish community that truly desires it.

Other works of Baeck include *Wege im Judentum* (1933), a collection of essays and speeches; *Aus drei Jahrtausenden* (1938), a collection of scholarly papers destroyed by the Nazis and reprinted in 1958; *Die Pharisaeer* (1934; *The Pharisees and other Essays*, 1947); *Maimonides, der Mann, sein Werke und seine Wirkung* (1954); *Dieses Volk* (2 vols., 1955–57; *This People Israel*, 1965); *Judaism and Christianity* (1958). In 1954 the *Leo Baeck Institute for the study of the history of the Jews from German-speaking countries was established in his name, and he served as its first president.

Bibliography: T. Wiener, in: SBB, 1 no. 3 (1954), bibliography of L. Baeck's writings; *Essays Presented to Leo Baeck on the Occasion of his Eightieth Birthday* (1954); E. Simon, *Geheimnis und Gebot, Die Neuen Wege* (1948); idem, in: L. Baeck, *Mahut ha-Yahadut* (1968), 7–44; E. H. Boehm, *We Survived* (1949), 284–98; A. H. Friedlander, *Leo Baeck, Teacher of Theresienstadt* (1968); H. Liebeschuetz, in: YLBI, 2 (1957), 1–44; 11 (1966), 3–27; K. J. Ball-Kaduri, in: *Yad Vashem Studies*, 6 (1967), 121–34; F. Bamberger, in: *Studies of the Leo Baeck Institute* (1967), 1–15 (with remarks by E. Simon); L. Baeck, *Judaism and Christianity* (1958), 3–19 (introduction); K. Stendhal, introd. to *The Pharisees and other essays* (1966[2]).

[A.E.S.]

BAECK, SAMUEL (1834–1912), German rabbi and scholar. Baeck, who was born in Kromau (Moravia), the son and grandson of rabbis, served as rabbi of Leipa (Bohemia) and Lissa (Lezno, Poland) and was active in German-Jewish communal affairs. He successfully advocated the teaching of Jewish religion in Prussian high schools, for which he wrote some textbooks. His *Geschichte des juedischen Volkes und seiner Literatur . . .* (1888) went into three editions. To J. Winter and A. Wuensche (eds.) *Die juedische Literatur* (1894–96) Baeck contributed the sections on the halakhic, homiletic, and other literature from the 15th to the 18th centuries (also separately printed, 1893). Leo *Baeck was his son.

[Ed.]

BAENA, JUAN ALFONSO DE (c. 1445), Spanish poet and scribe to Juan II of Castile. The *Cancionero de Baena,* an anthology of 14th- and 15th-century poetry which he compiled and presented to the king in 1445, deals with the social and political life of the period and includes many references to Jews and conversos. Hostility toward the conversos is expressed in several poems by Alfonso Alvarez de Villasandino (nos. 140–2, 183). Two *decires,* or poetic compositions, of the monk Diego de Valencia (probably a converted Jew himself) deal with conversos; the text of the first (no. 501) contains a number of Hebrew words. The *Cancionero* also includes poems celebrating the birth in 1405 of the future King Juan II. One of these (no. 230), the composition of a certain Don Mossé (described as surgeon to Henry III), indicates the part played by the Jews in Spanish cultural life. It is probable that Baena himself was a converted Jew. Another Juan de Baena (also known as Juan de Pineda) rose from obscurity as a tailor in Córdoba to eminence at the court of Toledo. A converso, he was brought to trial and condemned to death in 1486.

Bibliography: J. M. Azaceta (ed.), *Cancionero de Juan de Baena* (1966); A. Millares Carlo, *Literatura española hasta fines del siglo XV* (1950), 185–91; J. Amador de los Ríos, *Estudios . . . Judíos de España* (1848), 406–27; Baer, Spain, 2 (1966), 347ff.

[K.R.S.]

BAER, ABRAHAM (1834–1894), cantor. Baer was born in Wielen (Filehne), Poznan (Poland). He was a teacher and *ḥazzan* in various towns in western Prussia and in Posen, before becoming assistant cantor in Goteborg, Sweden, in 1857 and chief cantor in 1860. Collaborating with the organist of the synagogue, Joseph Czapek, he published a two-volume collection of hymns (principally those of *Sulzer) for choir, with organ accompaniment, *Musik till sângerna vid Gudstjensten* (2 vols., 1872). Five years later came his great work *Baal T'fillah,* a collection of melodies and recitatives according to the Polish, German, and Sephardi rituals, which became the basic manual for European cantors. The fruit of 15 years' work, it contains about 1,500 melodies which cover the liturgy of the year. Among them are several melodies of Sulzer, *Naumburg, and *Lewandowski, and some of his own. The collection went through five editions between 1877 and 1930.

Bibliography: A. Baer, *Baal T'fillah oder der praktische Vorbeter* (1883[2]), xiii–xxviii; J. Schoenberg, *Die traditionellen Gesaenge des israelitischen Gottesdienstes in Deutschland* (1926); Sendrey, Music, indexes.

[H.B.-D.]

BAER, MAXIMILIAN ADELBERT (Max; 1909–1959), U.S. prizefighter, world heavyweight champion in 1934–35. Born in Omaha, Nebraska, Baer was raised on a ranch in California. He began to box in 1929, and recorded a major victory in 1933 when he knocked out Germany's Max Schmeling, a former world champion. On June 14, 1934, Baer won the world title with an 11th-round knockout of Italy's Primo Carnera. He lost the championship the following year to James J. Braddock on a 15-round decision, and was defeated again in 1935 by Joe Louis. Baer retired in 1941 with a record of 65 victories (50 by knockouts), 13 defeats and one no-decision. Baer wore a *Magen David* on his boxing trunks and claimed "Jewish blood" on his father's side. However, many boxing experts maintained that Baer's claim was a publicity stunt. After Baer retired, he became an actor and appeared on stage, screen, radio, and television.

Max Baer, U.S. prizefighter and world heavyweight champion in 1934.

Buddy (1915–), a brother, also boxed in the heavyweight division. He fought for the championship in 1941 and 1942, and lost to Joe Louis on both occasions.

Bibliography: B. Postal et al. (eds.), *Encyclopaedia of Jews in Sports* (1965), 146.

[J.H.S.]

BAER, SELIGMAN ISAAC (1825–1897), Hebrew grammarian, masorah scholar, and liturgist. Born at Mosbach (Baden, Germany), Baer was a pupil of Wolf *Heidenheim, who left him many of his manuscripts. At the age of 19 he turned to masoretic studies. Franz *Delitzsch was impressed by Baer's scholarly approach and together they published the Psalms with masorah (1860) followed by most of the other books of the Bible with masorah texts. Delitzsch prefaced each book with a Latin introduction (except the last two which appeared after his death, i.e., Jeremiah in 1890 and Kings in 1895). These masoretic editions were compiled by Baer from manuscripts representing the variants of the masorah of *Ben Asher, *Ben Naphtali, and other masorah texts. All his life, Baer remained in the humble position of a teacher in the Jewish community school at Biebrich (Rhineland), but on the initiative of Delitzsch he was awarded an honorary Ph.D. by the University of Leipzig (1876). Baer's masoretic Bible edition was generally regarded as a genuine rendition of the traditional masorah text although it also evoked some criticism, notably by C. D. *Ginsburg and E. *Kautzsch. Baer's masorah text was printed in the widely accepted Vilna edition of the rabbinic Bible *(Mikra'ot Gedolot).* He also wrote a book on the cantillation in the poetical books of the Bible (*Torat Emet,* 1852) and on the secondary accent, the *meteg* (*Die Methegsetzung,* 1867); and published Ben Asher's *Dikdukei Te'amim* (together with H. L. Strack, 1879) and *Zwei alte Thorarollen aus Arabien* (1870).

Baer's greatest achievement lay in the field of liturgy. His many editions of liturgical texts, in which he followed the example and standards set by Heidenheim, were not only a scholarly feat but added dignity and decorum to Orthodox synagogue services throughout Western Europe, where his editions gained great popularity. The most important of these is his *Avodat Yisrael* prayer book with a scholarly commentary *Yakhin Lashon* (1868, several times reprinted, the latest in 1937) which has been accepted as the standard prayer book text by most subsequent editions of the *siddur*. Besides this major work, Baer edited: *Seliḥot, Kinot, Seder ha-Berakhot* (1858), a handbook for mourners, cemetery use, etc., in three versions (*Toẓe'ot Ḥayyim*, 1862; *Sefer Gemilut Ḥasadim*, 1880; *Derekh la-Ḥayyim*, 1926); *Tikkun ha-Sofer ve-ha-Kore*, a handbook for scribes and readers of the Torah (1875); a prayer book *Tefillat Yesharim* (1876[5], with prayers in German at the end; these also appeared separately as *Kol Bat Ziyyon*, 1875[3]); *Piyyutim* (1874); *Divrei ha-Berit*, circumcision service (1874). Most of these texts are accompanied by a German translation, and some are in two versions for the western and eastern Ashkenazi rites. These handsome little books ran into several editions and were reprinted after World War II.

עבדו את ה׳ ביראה
סדר
עבודת ישראל
כולל
התפלות לכל השנה
על נכון מסודרות והיטב מבוארות.
רעדעלהיים
בשנת תרכ״ח לפ״ק.

Title page of Seligman Baer's *Avodat Yisrael*, Roedelheim, 1868, which became the standard prayer book for Ashkenazi communities in Germany. Jerusalem, J.N.U.L.

Baer's only venture into the realm of practical *halakhah*, a handbook for *shoḥatim* (*Zivḥei Ẓedek*, 1857, with a Yiddish translation; 1862 with a German one), was severely criticized by S. B. *Bamberger, chiefly on the grounds that Baer was not an ordained rabbi. Baer also edited *Sefer Yesod ha-Yirah* (*Kobeẓ al Jad*, 11 (1895), 1–29).

Bibliography: A. Berliner, in: AZDJ, 59 (1902), 467; JC (March 12, 1897); ADB; H. Gullanz, *Shekel ha-Kodesh* (1919), with *Yesod ha-Yirah*.

[I.M./Ed.]

BAER, YITZHAK (Fritz; 1888–), historian. Born in Halberstadt, where he obtained a thorough Jewish education, Baer studied philosophy, classical philology, and history (the latter under Heinrich Finke) at the universities of Berlin, Strasbourg, and Freiburg. From 1919 Baer was

Yitzhak Baer, Israel historian.

research associate of the Akademie fuer die Wissenschaft des Judentums in Berlin, under whose auspices he went twice to Spain (1925–26) to collect archival source material on the history of the Jews in Christian Spain. In 1928 he was appointed lecturer and in 1930 professor of medieval Jewish history at the Hebrew University in Jerusalem. From 1932 to 1945 he was professor of general medieval history, and served from 1930 to 1959 as head of the university's department of Jewish history. Baer was one of the founders and editors of the Jewish historical review *Zion*. A coeditor of the "Historiographical Library" and *Sefer ha-Yishuv*, he took a leading part in the Israel Historical Society and was one of the 20 founding members of the Israel Academy of Sciences. He also contributed important articles to the German *Encyclopaedia Judaica* and its Hebrew counterpart *(Eshkol)*. Baer's first extensive research was into the history of the Jews of Christian Spain. On this subject he wrote his dissertation *Studien zur Geschichte der Juden im Koenigreich Aragonien waehrend des 13. und 14. Jahrhunderts* (Berlin, 1913); *Untersuchungen ueber Quellen und Komposition des Schebet Jehuda* (Berlin, 1923; second printing 1936); *Probleme der juedisch-spanischen Geschichte* (in KAWJ, 6 (1925), 5–25); articles on Abner of Burgos (in *Tarbiz*, 11 (1939/40), 188–206), on the disputations of Paris, Barcelona, and Tortosa, on Isaac Abrabanel (in *Tarbiz*, 8 (1936/37), 241–59); *Die Juden im christlichen Spanien* (1929, 1936), an important two-volume collection of unpublished documents on Spain, which served as the basis for his *History of the Jews in Christian Spain* (Heb., 1945, 1959[2], repr. 1965; Eng. ed., 2 vols., 1961–66), which is regarded as the standard work on the subject. Baer's work is remarkable for its broad historical outlook, accuracy in detail, and scholarly synthesis. These qualities have enabled him to throw new light on the economic, social, legal, political, as well as the religious and cultural condition of Spanish Jewry. His works are a model of historiography. Especially important among his studies of the development and history of the Jewish communal organization are his *Das Protokollbuch der Landjudenschaft des Herzogtums Kleve*, 1 (1922, repr. 1936), and his article on the beginnings and fundaments of Jewish communal organization in the Middle Ages (*Zion*, 15 (1949/50, 1–41). His method seeks to bring to light the internal forces that fashioned the Jewish communities within the framework of general history and local conditions. Baer believed that the essential features of Jewish communal organization were already set during the early generations of the Second Temple period and that these forms of organization were a product of the religious and national experiences of the people, and not that the Diaspora gave birth to them, although there were changes reflecting special conditions of time and place. Baer also investigated the spiritual and religious world of the Jewish people from the Second Temple period and the Middle Ages. Among his studies in this area are a series of articles in *Zion* written between 1932 and 1961 dealing with the theology of the *Sefer Ḥasidim* (see also Baer's contribution to *G. Scholem . . . Festschrift,* 1968) and the *Ḥasidei Ashkenaz* in general; with the historical basis of *halakhah;* with the relations between Jews, the early Christian Church, and the Roman Empire until Constantine; as well as his book *Galut* (Ger. 1936; Eng. 1947, Port. 1952), and *Yisrael ba-Ammim* (1955), and "Social Ideals of the Second Commonwealth" (in *Cahiers d'Histoire Mondiale,* 11 (1967/68), 69–91). From all these emerges an original view of the entire course of Jewish history. According to Baer the driving force of Jewish history lies in the continuing socioreligious activity of groups of pious and practical men of faith who aimed at perfecting the world. They succeeded in influencing the active elements among the people, with their beliefs and teachings, maintaining close ties with the non-Jewish world, and participating in its religiocultural and socioethical development. Baer reveals keen understanding of hellenistic and Christian culture and society. From this vantage point he examined the history of the Jews in the days of the Second Temple. His conclusions may be evaluated from his above-mentioned works, as well as from articles in *Molad* (21 (1963), 308ff.), *Zion* (23–24 (1958–59), nos. 3–4), and on *Serekh ha-Yaḥad* ("The Manual of Discipline," *Zion,* 29, 1964), which he sees as a Judeo-Christian document of the beginning of the second century C.E. He also dealt with the image of Judaism in the synoptic gospels (*Zion,* 31, 1966) and came to the conclusion that the polemics reflect conditions of the period following the destruction of the Temple. Baer is recognized as one of the most fruitful students and teachers of Jewish history of modern times. A jubilee volume was published in his honor in 1961 on the occasion of his 70th birthday (including his bibliography up to 1959).

Bibliography: I. Sonne, in: JSOS, 9 (1947), 61–80; L. Yahil, in: *Molad,* 21 (1963), 549–3; H. H. Ben-Sasson, in: *Religion and Society, Lectures of the Historical Society of Israel* (Heb., 1964), 23–40; J. M. Millás, in: KS, 9 (1932/33), 464–5; C. Roth, *ibid.,* 15 (1938/39), 200–1; F. Cantera, in: *Sefarad,* 1 (1941), 232–3; 26 (1966), 346–52; J. M. Millás, *ibid.,* 5 (1945), 417–40; 6 (1946), 163–88; 22 (1962), 178–80.

[B.D.]

BAERWALD, ALEX (1878–1930), one of the first Jewish architects in Ereẓ Israel. He was born in Berlin, and studied architecture at Charlottenburg. In 1910, he was invited by the Hilfsverein to plan the Technion buildings and the Reali school in Haifa. In these buildings, Baerwald tried to create a Jewish style of architecture, based on Muslim architecture.

The Central Jezreel Valley Hospital in Afulah, designed by Alex Baerwald, was opened in 1930.

Baerwald settled in Palestine in 1925, when he was appointed a lecturer at the Technion (which had been opened in 1924), and founded its Faculty of Architecture. He built many buildings in Haifa, Tel Aviv and elsewhere in Palestine, in the same style that he developed in the Technion buildings (Bet Struck, the Anglo-Palestine Bank in Haifa). In spite of the quality of these buildings and their high architectural standard their influence on the development of architecture in Jewish Palestine was very limited. Baerwald himself designed a number of buildings in the contemporary modern European style. These include the Central Jezreel Valley Hospital and the Electricity Company's power stations at Haifa and Tiberias.

[A.E.]

BAERWALD, MORITZ (1860–1919), German lawyer and politician. Baerwald was born in Thorn, West Prussia, and founded a law firm in Bromberg, Posen, where Jewish business and professional men constituted the nucleus of the urban bourgeoisie and enjoyed privileges not easily available to them elsewhere in Germany. Baerwald was elected to the board of attorneys, to the Bromberg city government, and to the Prussian Diet in 1912. In 1919 he was elected to the German National Assembly but, like all the other deputies from Posen, resigned when Posen was reincorporated in Poland. Baerwald was vice-president of the assembly of representatives of the Jewish community of Bromberg.

Bibliography: *Handbuch der Verfassunggebenden deutschen Nationalversammlung* (1919).

[E.HA.]

BAERWALD, PAUL (1871–1961), banker and philanthropist. Baerwald, born in Frankfort, was the scion of a family of German bankers. He began his career with a banking firm in Frankfort. In 1896 he emigrated to the U.S. and in

Paul Baerwald, U.S. banker and philanthropist.

1907 became a partner in Lazard Frères of New York City. In subsequent years Baerwald held directorships in a number of corporations. Baerwald's Jewish communal work began in 1917 when he was asked to become associate treasurer of the *American Jewish Joint Distribution Committee (JDC) by his close friend, Felix M. *Warburg. He became treasurer (1920) and later chairman (1932). Baerwald's chairmanship of the JDC coincided with the Nazi period. During that time the JDC aided most of the European Jews who found haven in overseas countries. In 1938 Baerwald joined President Roosevelt's Advisory Committee on Political Refugees, which tried to find means to aid Nazi victims. He supervised the rescue work of the JDC during World War II and, risking its credit, sent money to Europe which had to be borrowed from New York banks. A high percentage of the President's War Refugee Board funds (1944–45) came from the JDC under

Baerwald's direction. This financial policy was carried on in the postwar years when the JDC aided more than 500,000 refugees to reach Israel. In 1957 the American Jewish Joint Distribution Committee, the *Hebrew University of Jerusalem, and the Israel Ministry of Social Welfare founded the Paul Baerwald School of Social Work at the Hebrew University.

[Ye.B.]

°BAETHGEN, FRIEDRICH WILHELM ADOLPH (1849–1905), German Bible critic and semitic scholar, son of a Lutheran pastor in Lachem. After Baethgen completed his studies at Goettingen and Kiel, he was appointed lecturer in biblical studies at Kiel in 1878, and six years later became assistant professor of theology there. During this period he did pioneering work in the fields of biblical Hebrew poetry, Syriac grammar, and Peshitta on Psalms (*Die Psalmen,* 1897², 1904³). In 1888, the year in which his *Beitraege zur semitischen Religionsgeschichte* first appeared, he went to Halle as assistant professor of theology. In the following year he became professor of theology at Greifswald, where he was also an influential member of the Pomeranian consistory. From 1895 until his death he was professor of theology in Berlin.

[Ed.]

BAEYER, ADOLF VON (1835–1917), German organic chemist and Nobel prize winner. Baeyer was born in Berlin. His mother was the daughter of J. E. *Hitzig, literature historian and authority on criminal law and his father, Johann Jacob Baeyer, a non-Jewish scientist. Adolf Baeyer

Adolf von Baeyer, organic chemist and Nobel prize winner.

made his first chemical discovery—a double carbonate of copper and sodium—when he was 12. He went to Heidelberg, where he came under the influence of his lifelong friend, August Kekulé, the German chemist, with whom he went to Ghent in 1858. In 1860 he returned to Berlin, and was appointed professor of organic chemistry at the Gewerbeinstitut (later the Charlottenburg Technische Hochschule). There he worked on the study of uric acid, and began 20 years of research on indigo. This was the basis of synthetic indigo, which eventually completely displaced the natural product, and was the foundation of the German dyestuffs industry. His work on alizarin also led to alizarin dyes, driving the natural pigment off the market. His field also extended into physiological chemistry. In 1872 Baeyer became professor at Strasbourg and in 1875 in Munich, where he continued to teach and experiment until he was 80. His work covered many fields, including acetylenic compounds, strain within chemical molecules, the structure of benzene, the constitution of terpenes, oxygen compounds with quadrivalent oxygen, carbonium compounds, and the relationship between color and chemical constitution. His many papers in chemical journals helped to lay the foundations for the new science of organic chemistry. He was awarded the Nobel prize in 1905 for "the advancement of organic chemistry and the chemical industry, through his work on organic dyes and hydroaromatic compounds." His numerous other awards included the Davy Medal of the British Royal Society in 1881, and a German patent of nobility in 1885.

Bibliography: K. Schmorl, *Adolf von Baeyer, 1835–1917* (Ger. 1952), incl. bibl.; T. Levitan, *The Laureates (1960), 27*–29; Henrich, in: American Chemical Society, *Journal of Chemical Education,* 7 (1930), 1231–48; Perkin, in: Chemical Society (London), *Journal of the Chemical Society,* 123 (1923), 1520–46; G. Bugge, *Buch der grossen Chemiker,* 2 (1930), 321–35, index.

[S.A.M.]

BAGHDAD, capital city of *Iraq. Baghdad was the capital of the Abbasid dynasty from its foundation in 762. From then a Jewish community existed there which eventually became the largest Jewish community of Iraq, and the seat of the exilarch. During the geonic period the Jews lived in a special quarter, Dār al-Yahūd ("Jewish Quarter"). The bridge in the western section of the town, which led to the Karkh quarter, was named Qanṭarat al-Yahūd ("Bridge of the Jews"). A tomb situated in this quarter was until recently the site of prayer gatherings. The local Jews believed it to be the tomb of Joshua son of Jehozadak, the high priest. By the end of the ninth century the famous yeshivot of Sura and Pumbedita were established in Baghdad. The Karaites also played an important part in the life of the city.

Early and Early Modern History. During the tenth century there were two distinguished Jewish families in Baghdad, *Netira and *Aaron. They were both influential in the royal court and they showed concern for the welfare of the community. At the end of the tenth century R. Isaac b. Moses ibn Sakrī of Spain was the *rosh yeshivah.* He had traveled to Iraq and "had been ordained as *gaon* in order to fill the position of Rav Hai, of saintly memory." During the 12th century, beginning with the reign of Caliph al-Muktafī, the situation of the Jews in Baghdad greatly improved. A short while before 1170 Benjamin of Tudela, the traveler, found approximately 40,000 Jews living peacefully in Baghdad, among them scholars and exceedingly wealthy people. He noted that there were 28 synagogues and ten yeshivot. During the reigns of Caliph al-Muktafī and his successors, the rights and the authority of the exilarch were increased and with it the prestige of the Baghdad community also grew. In that period the exilarch *Daniel b. Ḥasdai was referred to by the Arabs as "Our lord, the son of David." The Baghdad community reached the height of its prosperity during the term of office of *rosh yeshivah* *Samuel b. Ali ha-Levi (c. 1164–94), an opponent of Maimonides, who raised Torah study in Baghdad to a high level.

During the late 12th century through the middle 13th century, some prominent poets, as well as the great scholars and the *rashei yeshivot* appointed by the caliphs, lived in Baghdad. The most important were R. Eleazar b. Jacob ha-Bavli and R. Isaac b. Israel, whom Judah *Al-Ḥarizi, the poet and traveler, referred to as the greatest Iraqi poet. Isaac b. Israel headed the Baghdad yeshivah from 1221 to 1247. There were many physicians, perfumers, shopkeepers, goldsmiths, and moneychangers among the Jews of Baghdad; however, Judah Al-Ḥarizi considered this period as one of decline in view of the past importance of the community.

In 1258 Baghdad was conquered by the Mongols and the Jews were not maltreated, as was the case with the Muslims. Arghūm Khān (1284–91) appointed the Jew *Saʿd al-Dawla, who had previously been the sultan's physician, director of financial administration of Iraq. During the few years he held office, Saʿd al-Dawla developed the economic importance of Baghdad and as a result of this he was appointed chief vizier of the Mongol Empire in 1289. After

Figure 1. Opening pages of a *Haggadah* written and illuminated in Baghdad in 1868 by Ezekiel b. Sassoon Ezekiel Ya'uda. Letchworth, Sassoon Collection, Ms. 363, pp. 1–2.

the death of Arghūn, Saʿd al-Dawla was executed on the pretext that he had not given the khān the appropriate medical care. After their final conversion to Islam in the early 14th century, the Īl-Khānids reinstated decrees which they formerly had abolished, concerning the discriminatory dress of the Jews and Christians and the special taxes which applied to all "unbelievers" under Muslim rule. When Baghdad was conquered for a second time in 1393 by Tamerlane, many Jews fled to Kurdistan and Syria, leaving almost no Jews in Baghdad until the end of the 15th century.

During the struggle between the Ottomans and the Persian kings of the Safavid dynasty for the domination of Iraq, the political situation of the Jews of Baghdad underwent many changes. Generally, the Jews were oppressed by the Persians, who were fanatical Shiʿites and haters of non-Muslims; on the other hand they enjoyed fair treatment under the Ottomans. The conquest of Baghdad in 1514 by Shah Ismāʿīl I did not worsen the situation of the Jews, but with the beginning of the reign of his son Ṭahmāsp I (1524–76), they suffered greatly from the hostile attitude of the Persian authorities. During the first part of the Ottoman rule, which lasted from 1534 to 1623, there was again an improvement in the situation for the Jews. Their economic position improved; their trade with foreign countries increased; and there were several wealthy merchants among them. In the early 17th century Pedro *Teixeria, the Portuguese Marrano explorer, found 25,000 houses in Baghdad, of which 250 belonged to Jews. In 1623 the Persians again conquered Baghdad, and during their rule, which lasted until 1638, there was a new deterioration in the situation of the Jews. Because of this, they gave their support to Sultan Murād IV, who conquered Baghdad in 1638. The day of the conquest, Tevet 16, 5399, was fixed as a *yom nes* ("day of miracle"). Additional evidence of the sympathy of the Jews toward the Ottomans is the custom fixing 11 Av, 5493 (1733), the day that the Persians were defeated trying to reoccupy Baghdad, as a *yom nes*. Carsten Niebuhr, a Danish traveler and scholar who visited Iraq some 30 years later, relates that there was a large Jewish community in Baghdad and that its influence was felt in the economic life of the city.

During the second half of the 18th century and the early 19th century Turkish rule deteriorated in efficiency and the attitude of the government toward the Jews became harsh. Even so, some Jewish bankers were involved in the affairs of the governing circles, especially in the attempted rebellion of the governors.

During the reign of Sultan Mahmud II, the banker Ezekiel *Gabbai supported the removal of the governor of Baghdad, who had rebelled against the sultan in 1811. The last Mamluk governor, Dā'ūd Pasha (1817–31), who had also tried to rebel against the sultan, oppressed the Jews of Baghdad, and many of the wealthier ones fled to Persia, India, and other countries. Among them was David S. *Sassoon, a member of the distinguished Baghdad family.

The number of Jews at that time was still considerable. R. *David D'Beth Hillel, who visited the city in 1828, found 6,000 Jewish families there led by a pasha, also known as "king of the Jews," who was also responsible for the judicial affairs of the community. The English traveler Wellsted, who visited Baghdad in 1831, praised the remarkable moral conduct of the Jews, which he attributed to their religious upbringing. Wellsted made special note of the feeling of mutual responsibility among the Jews of Baghdad. According to him, there were no poor among them because anyone who lost his means of livelihood was assisted by his companions. R. Jehiel Kestelmann, an emissary from Safed, claims to have found 20,000 Jews in Baghdad in 1860. With the opening of the Suez Canal in 1869 and the improvement of the city's economic situation, the economic status of the Jews also improved. Many Jews from other localities settled in the city. According to the traveler Ephraim *Neumark, the Baghdad community numbered 30,000 in 1884; 50,000 in the early 20th century; and 100,000 in the 1930s.

Community Leaders. In the 18th and 19th centuries important changes in cultural and religious life occurred, because of the activities of outstanding rabbis in the community. A notable improvement took place with the arrival of R. Ẓedakah *Ḥozin from Aleppo in 1743. Ḥozin improved the educational system of the city and the Jewish religious education improved. During the 18th century Palestinian emissaries visited the Baghdad community, strengthening its ties with the Palestinian population and reinforcing religious values within the community. Besides collecting funds for the communities of Jerusalem, Safed, and Hebron, these emissaries also delivered sermons and resolved halakhic problems. The most prominent of Baghdad's rabbis during the 19th century was R. ʿAbdallah *Somekh, who is considered the greatest Iraqi rabbi of the last generations. In 1840 he founded a rabbinical college, Beit Zilkha, whose graduates filled rabbinical positions in many different localities. Among the Jews of Baghdad in the 19th century were still some writers of *piyyutim*, such as R. Sasson b. Israel (1820–1885). In the same century there were wealthy philanthropists who contributed generously to the community projects, especially to educational and religious institutions. The most prominent of them were Jacob Ẓemaḥ (d. 1847), Ezekiel b. Reuben Manasseh (d. 1851), Joseph Gurji (d. 1894), Eliezer *Kadoorie (1867–1944), and Menaḥem *Daniel (1846–1940).

Until 1849 the community of Baghdad was led by a *nasi*, who was appointed by the vilayet governor, and who also acted as his banker (*ṣarrāf bāshī*). The first of these leaders claimed to be descendants of the house of David and their positions were inherited by members of their families. Later, however, the position was purchased. The most renowned of these leaders were Sassoon b. R. Ẓalaḥ (1781–1817), the father of the *Sassoon family, and Ezra b. Joseph Gabbai (1817–24). From 1849 the community was led by the *ḥakham bashi* who represented the Jews to the Turkish authorities. The first one was R. Raphael Kaẓin. The *nasi*, and later the *ḥakham bashi*, were assisted by a council of 10 and later 12, delegates, which included three rabbis and nine laymen drawn from the wealthier members of the community. The council collected the taxes and dealt with community affairs. The collection of the *ʿaskarlī* ("military service ransom tax"), which replaced the *jizya* (poll tax), was sometimes the cause of violent conflicts within the community.

World War I and After. Until the British conquest of Baghdad in March 1917, the Jews were oppressed by the vilayet governor and the police commissioner who attempted to extort money from them and to recruit their youth for the Turkish army. Hundreds of young men were recruited and the majority were sent to the Caucasus where many died of starvation and cold. Wealthy Jews were tortured and killed after being accused of devaluating the Turkish pound. The Jews naturally rejoiced when the British occupied Baghdad. The day of their entry was fixed as a *yom nes* (17 Adar, 5677, or February 3, 1917). From the conquest until 1929, the Jews of Baghdad enjoyed complete freedom. Many of them were employed in the civil service, while others were even appointed to important government positions. Zionist activities also prospered for some time. However, in 1929, when the British decided to grant independence to Iraq, many Jewish officials were dismissed from government services, Zionist activity was prohibited, and, in general, there was an increase of anti-Semitism. This was especially so after Dr. A. Grobbe, the German ambassador in Baghdad, began to propagandize in 1932.

In 1934 there were large-scale dismissals of Jewish civil servants, and from 1936 murders of Jews and bombing of their institutions were added to even more dismissals. These attacks reached a climax on Shavuot 5701 (June 1–2, 1941) with Rashīd Ali's pro-Axis revolution against the British. During those two days savage mobs massacred Jews and looted their property with the passive support of army and police officers. Neither the regent ʿAbd al-Ilāh, who had arrived in the city before the beginning of the riots, nor the British troops, who were stationed outside the city, made any effort to intervene. According to various sources 120 to 180 Jews, including women, elderly people, and children, were killed and 800 injured during some 30 hours. This was accompanied by cases of rape and abduction of women. The value of the looted property was estimated at 1,000,000 dinars (or 1,000,000 pounds sterling—then 4,000,000 dollars). Thousands of Jews left the city, most of them for India and Palestine. However, many of them returned before the end of the year after failing to integrate themselves in these countries and having heard that the situation in Baghdad had improved. A period of prosperity

Figure 2. Hanging lamp from Baghdad, brass, 18th century. It is shaped like a *Magen David* and ornamented with the hand-shaped amulet, the *ḥamsa*. 36½×19½ in. (93×50 cm.). Jerusalem, Sir Isaac and Lady Wolfson Museum in Hechal Shlomo. Photo David Harris, Jerusalem.

ensued and continued until 1945; even though the decrees concerning their employment in government service and their admission to public schools had not been repealed, the Jews lived in Baghdad at ease and without fear.

After 1945 there were frequent demonstrations against the Jews and especially against Zionism. With the proclamation of the partition of Palestine, November 1947, even greater danger threatened the Jews of Baghdad. There was fear of a massacre, and the Jewish underground defense, organized with help of Palestinian Jews, was in a state of preparedness; the catastrophe was averted when martial law was proclaimed by the government. Nonetheless, many Jews were brought before military courts and fines were levied on the majority of them.

There were 77,000 Jews in Baghdad in 1947. After the mass exodus to Israel in 1950–51, approximately 5,000 Jews were left. Jews continued to leave Baghdad so that only about 2,000 remained in 1968. Immediately after the establishment of the State of Israel, hundreds of Baghdadi Jews were arrested. Many of the detainees were accused of communist or Zionist activities. A few hundred Jewish youth had joined these clandestine movements, especially after 1948. Two communist and two Zionist leaders were hanged publicly in Baghdad. During the government of ʿAbd Al-Karīm Qassem (July 1958–February 1963) the attitude toward the Jews was more favorable. Even so, there were severe periodical restrictions on departure from Iraq, property confiscation, and a strengthening of economic pressure on the community.

Fourteen Iraqis, including nine Jews, were hanged publicly in Baghdad on January 27, 1969, after being convicted on charges of spying for Israel. [A.B.-Y.]

Institutions and Community Life—1917–1970. During the British administration and after World War II, the number of Jewish educational institutions, especially the secondary ones, increased. In spite of the restrictions on the number of Jews admitted to government secondary schools, the number of Jews in these institutions was higher in 1950 than in 1920; but, because of lack of data, only the number in Jewish educational institutions will be mentioned.

During this period there were also important social changes within the Baghdad community. The majority of women removed the gown (Arabic, *ʿabā*ʾ) and the veil (Persian, *pūshī*), which they formerly wore in the street. The number of girls engaged in teaching and in clerical work increased and some of them received a university education. There was also a change in the occupations of the Jews. Whereas in 1920 they were engaged in trade, banking, labor, and public services, in 1950 thousands earned their livelihood by clerical work or in the professions such as law. Immediately after the British conquest, the Jews began to leave their quarter to settle in all parts of the city. In the 1930s the Battāwīn and Karrāda quarters were established and inhabited by the wealthy. The attitude toward religion also underwent a change. During the first years after the British conquest there were only a few Jews who profaned the Sabbath or ate non-kasher food, whereas at the end of this period the number of Sabbath observers decreased.

From the end of the Ottoman period until 1931 the Jews of Baghdad had a "General Council" of 80 members, which included 20 rabbis and was led by the chief rabbi. The General Council elected a council for religious matters and a council for material welfare. The former dealt with ritual slaughter, burials, and the rabbinical courts, while the latter was responsible for the schools, hospitals, and charitable trusts. In 1926, however, a group of intellectuals gained the upper hand in the latter council and attempted to remove the chief rabbi, Ezra *Dangoor. After a stormy period, in

Figure 3. The Great Synagogue of Baghdad, the oldest in the city, last reconstructed in 1855. Standing in the archway is Ezra Dangoor, chief rabbi of Baghdad 1923–8. Cecil Roth Photo Collection.

1931, the community passed the "Law of the Jewish Community." It deprived the rabbis of the community's leadership and made it possible for a nonreligious person to assume leadership. In spite of this in February 1933 R. Sasson *Kadoorie was elected chairman of the community. His position was, however, a secular one, while a rabbi without any community authority was elected to the position of chief rabbi. Just before the mass emigration of 1951, there were about 20 Jewish educational institutions in Baghdad; 16 were under supervision of the community committee, the rest were privately run. In 1950 about 12,000 pupils attended these institutions while many others attended government and foreign schools; approximately another 400 students were enrolled in Baghdad colleges of medicine, law, economy, pharmacy, and engineering. All but two of the Jewish educational institutions closed in 1952. These two had approximately 900 pupils in 1960, while about 50 Jewish pupils attended government schools. The Baghdad community also had a school for the blind, founded in 1930, which was the only one of its kind in Iraq. It closed in 1951.

Year	Talmud Torah	Kindergartens and Elementary Schools	Secondary Schools	Total
1920	2,500	3,350	150	6,000
1950	1,880	8,970	2,626	14,476

Pupils in Jewish educational institutions in Baghdad in 1920 and just before the mass exodus of 1950–51.

The Jews of Baghdad had two hospitals; one, a general hospital named for Meir Elias, founded in 1910, and the second, an eye hospital named for Rima Kadoorie, founded in 1924. At both these hospitals, Jews received treatment, and operations were performed for the needy for little or no payment. Every school in town had a clinic. The community also had several philanthropic societies to provide dowries for girls without means, help to mothers, maintenance of yeshivah students, and for the vocational training of poor children. All these institutions, including the hospitals, closed. Afterward, the community committee arranged for the sick to be admitted to various hospitals in the town.

Only seven synagogues remained in 1960 of the 60 synagogues of Baghdad in 1950. The community committee had subcommittees for religious affairs and administration.

These two subcommittees were elected by the general committee, elected in turn by men of the community every four years. In November 1949, Sasson Kadoorie was forced to resign, when local Jewry blamed him for not acting to free the numerous young Jews arrested on charges of Zionism. He was replaced by Ezekiel Shemtob, who served until 1953, when Kadoorie again became president of the community. Kadoorie still presided in 1970. In accordance with an Iraqi law of 1954, a council elected every two years and supervised by the Ministry of Justice worked with the president. The subcommittees were abolished and a government law in December 1951 also abolished the rabbinical court in Baghdad. [H.J.C.]

Hebrew Printing. The first Hebrew (lithographic) printing press in Baghdad was founded by Moses Baruch Mizraḥi in 1863. The press printed a Hebrew newspaper named *Ha-Dover* ("The Speaker") or *Dover Mesharin* ("Upright Speaker") until 1870 and three small books. A second printing press with movable characters was founded in Baghdad in 1868 by Raḥamim b. Reuben, a resident of Baghdad, who had previously gained printing experience in Bombay. The brothers Moses and Aaron Fetaya later formed a partnership with Raḥamim, and after his death they continued his work until 1882. Fifty-five books were printed on this printing press.

In 1888 a new press was founded in Baghdad by Solomon Bekhor Ḥuẓin (1843–1892), a scholar, poet, author, journalist, bookseller, and communal worker. He brought his printing letters from Leghorn, Italy. Besides prayer books, he also printed many books which he considered useful to the members of his community. These included tales and works by Baghdad scholars which had been in manuscript until then. After his death, the printing press was taken over by his son, Joshua Ḥuẓin, and operated until 1913. Seventy-five books were printed on it.

In 1904 a new press was founded in Baghdad by R. Ezra Reuben Dangoor (1848–1930), who was also *ḥakham bashi* of Baghdad. This printing press was in existence until 1921 and over 100 books were printed on it. For the greater part they were books of prayers and *piyyutim* according to the custom of the Baghdad Jews, but there were also some popular books in the Judeo-Arabic jargon and a Hebrew weekly, *Yeshurun*, of which five issues were published in 1920. This was a second and last attempt at Hebrew journalism in Baghdad. During the British Mandate in Iraq, two small Hebrew printing presses were founded in Baghdad: the al-Waṭaniyya al-Isrāʾīliyya (The Israel Homeland) press, which printed about 20 books between 1922 and 1927; and the Elisha Shoḥet press, which printed more than 40 books between 1924 and 1937. When the British Mandate ended, these printing presses declined and finally ceased operation altogether.

[A.Ya.]

Bibliography: Ben-Jacob, in: *Zion*, 15 (1951), 56–69; idem, *Toledot ha-Rav Abbdaʿala Somekh* (1949); idem, in: *Hed ha-Mizraḥ*, 2 (1943/44), no. 8, 13–14; idem, in: *Sinai*, 54 (1964), 95–101; idem, *Yehudei Bavel* (1965); A. S. Yahuda, *Bagdadische Sprichwoerter* (1906); S. Poznański, *Babylonische Geonim*... (1914); J. Obermeyer, *Die Landschaft Babylonien* (1929); D. S. Sassoon, *A History of the Jews in Baghdad* (1949); Yaari, Sheluḥei, index; Cohen, in: *Middle Eastern Studies* (Oct. 1966), 2–17; H. Y. Cohen, *Ha-Pe'ilut ha-Ẓiyyonit be-Irak* (1969). Hebrew Printing: A. Yaari, *Ha-Defus ha-Ivri be-Arẓot ha-Mizraḥ*, 2 (1940), 100–59; idem, in: KS, 24 (1947/48), 71–72; A. Ben-Jacob, *ibid.*, 22 (1945/46), 82–83.

BAGINSKY, ADOLF ARON (1843–1918), German physician and founder of modern pediatrics. Baginsky was born in Silesia and in 1881 joined the faculty of Berlin University, being appointed associate professor in 1892. In 1890, with the assistance of Virchow, he founded the children's hospital, Kaiser und Kaiserin Friedrich Kinderkrankenhaus, of which he became director. His main contributions to pediatrics were in the fields of infectious diseases, the study of milk, and hygiene. Baginsky was a leader in the movement for the promotion of child welfare and his services in this field won him orders and decorations from many governments. He was founder and editor of the pediatric journal, *Archiv fur Kinderheilkunde* (1879). His works included *Lehrbuch der Kinderheilkunde* (1882; "Textbook of Pediatrics"; translated into a number of

Adolf Baginsky, father of modern pediatrics.

languages), *Handbuch der Schulhygiene* ("Manual on School Hygiene," 1877), and *Praktische Beitraege zur Kinderheilkunde* ("Practical Contributions to Pediatrics" 1880–84), as well as many articles on physiological and chemical subjects.

Baginsky was an active member of the Jewish community in Berlin and of the movement to check anti-Semitism in Germany. He also wrote an interesting essay on the significance of hygiene in Mosaic legislation in which he expresses his admiration for the hygienic laws in the Bible.

Bibliography: S. R. Kagan: *Jews in Medicine* (1952), 357–8.

[S.M.]

BAGOHI (Gr. Βαγώας), governor of the Persian satrapy Yehud (Judea) in the time of Darius II and Artaxerxes II. Among the *Elephantine papyri there was found a letter sent in 408 B.C.E. by the Jews of Elephantine-Yeb to "Bagohi, governor of Judah," in which it is written that a similar letter had been sent to "Delaiah and Shelemiah, sons of Sanballat, governor of Samaria." In this letter they appeal for assistance in the reconstruction of their temple, which had been destroyed by the priests of the Egyptian god Khnub. This letter reveals that a similar appeal had been made three years earlier to "Bagohi, governor of Judah," to Johanan, the high priest in Jerusalem, to Ostanes the brother of Anani, and to the nobles of the Jews, but no reply had been received. It is probable that the reason for the failure of the high priest to reply was his negative attitude toward this temple, but it may also have been the tense relations existing between the Persian governor and the high priest. Josephus (Ant. 11:297–301) relates that when Johanan the high priest murdered his brother Joshua in the Temple (probably at the beginning of the fourth century B.C.E.), Bagohi forced his way into the Temple, declaring to the priests who opposed his entry (since he was a Gentile) that his defilement of the Temple was less than that of a person guilty of fratricide. The discovery of the Elephantine documents has disposed of the attempts of Wilrich and Wellhausen to dismiss the story as a legend on the grounds that no person of this name was known.

Bibliography: E. Meyer, *Der Papyrusfund von Elephantine* (1912^3); Cowley, Aramaic, 108ff., no. 30; A. Schalit, in *Sefer Yoḥanan Lewy* (1949), 252–72.

[A.Sch.]

BAGRIT, SIR LEON (1902–), British industrialist and automation pioneer. Bagrit was born in Kiev, Russia, but his family arrived in England as refugees from Belgium at the beginning of World War I. He studied engineering at London University, helping to support himself at college by playing the violin in a philharmonic orchestra. He was employed for several years by engineering companies for which he designed machinery but in 1935, in order to be free to use his patents, he established his own firm. In 1937 this was taken over by Elliott Brothers, Bagrit becoming managing director. In 1962, as chairman of the company, now renamed Elliott-Automation, he turned to the development of automated control systems for nuclear, aeronautical, and industrial purposes. The company was the first in Europe devoted to automation. In 1967 Elliott-Automation was taken over by the English Electric Company, with Bagrit as deputy chairman.

He was a member of the Council for Scientific and Industrial Research (1963–65) and the Advisory Council on Technology (1964–). A director of the Royal Opera House, he founded the Friends of Covent Garden. He became a consultant on automation to the Israel government. He was knighted in 1962. [M.M.B.]

BAGRITSKI, EDUARD GEORGIYEVICH, pseudonym of **E. G. Dzyuba** (1895–1934), Soviet Russian poet. Bagritski, who was born into a middle-class Odessa family and had a traditional Jewish upbringing, was a dedicated communist. His verse, at first complex and influenced by Symbolism, gradually became simpler and more graceful, earning him a place among the leading Russian poets of the 20th century. Like his fellow writers from Odessa, *Babel, Olesha, *Ilf, and the Katayev brothers, Bagritski successfully combined literary sophistication with romantic naïveté in his perception and salutation of reality. This combination of highly polished craftsmanship and childlike wonder constitutes the most endearing quality of his lyric verse. It also accounts for the success even of his propagandist poems. Bagritski's most important work was the poem *Duma pro Opanasa* (1926; "The Lay of Opanas"), a blend of lyric and narrative verse which contains elements of Ukrainian folk poetry and of the old Slavic epic. "The Lay of Opanas" describes a Ukrainian peasant who deserts from a Red Army unit commanded by a Jew named Kogan, joins an anarchist band, captures his former commander, but later offers to release him. Kogan, a devoted Communist, proudly refuses, and is thereupon shot by Opanas, who is himself subsequently executed by the Reds. Bagritski's is one of the most successful treatments of the revolutionary theme in Soviet literature. Some of Bagritski's best poetry appeared in the collection *Yugo-zapad* ("South-West," 1928). He was also known for his Russian translations of English, French, Yiddish, and Ukrainian verse.

Bibliography: G. Struve, *Soviet Russian Literature 1917–1950* (1951). [M.F.]

BAHIA, the first region to be settled in *Brazil, today a state in the federal republic; situated in the N. E. part of the country. The presence of Portuguese *New Christians (*Marranos) is closely related to the discovery, conquest, and colonization of Brazil. When the tribunal of the *Inquisition was established in Portugal (1536), the emigration of Marranos to the Brazilian colony grew considerably, and many of them arrived in Bahia with the first governors. Despite the laws prohibiting the emigration of Marranos to the colony and discriminatory legislation in Portugal, local conditions and the type of colonization adopted in Brazil favored the establishment of a New Christian settlement. One of the first Marrano colonists to arrive in Bahia (1538) was Felipe Guilhem, who held important functions in Thomé de Sousa's government (1549–53) and was considered one of the pioneers of the exploration of the country.

In the second half of the 16th century, Bahia absorbed a relatively large number of New Christians who greatly contributed to the establishment of the first villages, to the struggle against the Indians, to the finance of and participation in the expeditions to the interior, and to cultivation of the land and of sugar cane in particular. Production and trade in sugar cane became the chief source of wealth in the second half of the 16th and in the 17th centuries. News of the Marranos' prosperity, increasing numbers, and only slight attachment to Catholicism led the inquisitors to set up a board of inquiry in Bahia to locate suspects. Their sessions, known as visitations or inspections, were held in 1591–93, 1618, and later. At this time many New Christians were denounced as heretics, and they were punished (some were sent to the inquisitional prisons in Lisbon and others were burned). An important investigation, known as the 1646 Inquiry, was made in Bahia in the 17th century, at the Jesuit seminary. With the aid of various testimonies, this inquiry revealed the role that the Portuguese of Jewish descent played in the political, economic, and administrative life in Bahia. The 1646 Inquiry had a lasting impact on local Jews. In the 18th century many members of Brazilian families were still prevented from assuming public office because they were descendants of those denounced in 1646. During the Dutch invasion of 1624, Marranos took an active part in the city's defense and in political, financial, and military affairs. The New Christians continued to hold important positions in Bahia society until the end of the 18th century. At this time the Marranos' communal life was never really separated from that of the other Christians. However, they represented a force in opposition to the church, which was skeptical and critical of their practices of Jewish origin.

In spite of their continual contacts with Europe, very few New Christians left Bahia. The persistent immigration during the Colonial Period, as well as uninterrupted persecution by the Inquisition against the New Christians, kept the "New Christians' conflict" a live issue in Bahia until the mid-18th century, when Marquess de Pombal's decree eliminated discrimination against them (1773). Consequently the New Christians were absorbed into the wider society, their descendants being among the most prominent and ancient families of Bahia.

Contemporary Period. In the late 1960s, approximately 200 Jewish families lived in Bahia state, 180 of whom lived in the capital Salvador. Other families were scattered in Ilhéus and Itabuana. The present community was founded in 1912 by immigrants from Eastern Europe, mainly from Bessarabia. After World War I the community grew and founded its main societies: Sociedad Beneficiente Israelito (1922) and Sociedade Ezra da Bahia (1930). Both societies, philanthropic in character, aid new immigrants. In 1924 a Jewish school was founded in which all Jewish children receive their education. The central Jewish body of Salvador, the Sociedade Israelita da Bahia, established in 1949, serves as a focal point for local Jewry.

Bibliography: A. Novinsky, in: *Proceedings of the 5th World Congress of Jewish Studies, 1969;* idem, in: *Comentário,* 4 (1963), 231–42; idem, in: *Revista de História,* 36 (1968), 417–23; Roth, Marranos (1966), 157, 284. [A.No.]

BAHIR, SEFER HA- (Heb. סֵפֶר הַבָּהִיר; "Book of Bahir"), earliest work of kabbalistic literature, i.e., of that literature which adopts the specific approach and the symbolic structure characteristic of kabbalistic teaching.

Title page of an edition of *Sefer ha-Bahir,* Berlin, 1706. Jerusalem, J.N.U.L.

Titles. Among the medieval Spanish kabbalists *Sefer ha-Bahir* was known by two names, each based on the opening sentences of the book: (1) *Midrash R. *Neḥunya ben ha-Kanah* ("R. Neḥunya b. ha-Kanah said," which is the opening phrase of the first section); and (2) *Sefer ha-Bahir,* based on the statement: "One verse says: 'And now men see not the light which is bright (*bahir*) in the skies'" (Job 37:21). Although the second title is the older, the first became popular because of its use by Naḥmanides in his commentary on the *Pentateuch. Although the kabbalists came to ascribe the book to the *tanna* R. *Neḥunya there is no evidence for this in the book itself. The book is a *Midrash in the strict literary connotation of the word: an anthology of various statements, most of them brief, attributed to different *tannaim* and *amoraim.* The main characters in the book are called "R. Amora" (or "Amorai"), and "R. Raḥamai" (or "Reḥumai"). The first name is fictitious, while the second appears to have been coined in imitation of the *amora,* Raḥumi. There are also statements attributed to R. Berechiah, R. Johanan, R. Bun, and others who are known from midrashic literature. However, only very few of these statements actually come from these sources, and all of them were attributed to rabbis mentioned in the later Midrashim, who were themselves accustomed to ascribe aggadic sayings to earlier rabbis (e.g., **Pirkei de-R. Eliezer, Otiyyot de-R. Akiva,* and similar works). There are also in *Sefer ha-Bahir* several chapters in which no names are mentioned at all.

Contents. Ideas and traditions on many subjects are transmitted in the form of explanations of biblical verses, short discussions between different speakers, or statements devoid of any literary support. In addition to familiar aggadic sayings (which are few in number), there are commentaries on the mystical significance of particular verses; on the shapes of several letters of the alphabet; on the vocalization and cantillation signs; on statements in the *Sefer *Yeẓirah* ("Book of Creation"), and on sacred names and their use in magic. The interpretation of some verses contains explanations of the esoteric meanings of some of the commandments of the Pentateuch (e.g., **tefillin, *ẓiẓit, *terumot, shillu'aḥ ha-ken* (see Deut. 22:6, 7), **lulav, *etrog,* and others). There is apparently no definite order in the book. Sometimes one can detect a certain train of thought in the arrangement of the various chapters, but the thread is soon broken, and the sense of the book often leaps inexplicably from one subject to another. Alternatively, statements are strung together because of some extraneous association, without any definite sequence of thought. All this gives *Sefer ha-Bahir* the appearance of a Midrash, or a collection of sayings taken from various sources. Nevertheless, it is possible to distinguish certain sections which seem to have a literary unity. These are chiefly: (1) the string of statements which are based on the *Sefer Yeẓirah,* and which develop the contents of that book in a new vein; and (2) the orderly list which is given, although with frequent interruptions, of the ten *Sefirot* ("Divine Emanations"), called here the ten *ma'amarot* ("sayings"), by which the world was created.

Ideas. The book, as it has survived, confirms the tradition of the 13th-century kabbalists that *Sefer ha-Bahir* was handed down to them in extremely mutilated form, as remnants of scrolls, booklets, and traditions. It contains sections which break off in the middle of a sentence and are not connected at all with what follows. There are discussions which are begun and not completed. Additional material interrupting the sequence of the argument is found in greater proportion in those very sections which seem to have an inner consistency. In its present form the book is very short, containing about 12,000 words. The structure of the book is extremely loose. It is simply a collection of material brought together within a certain framework without any literary or editorial skill. The language of the book is a mixture of Hebrew and Aramaic. The style is frequently very difficult, and, even apart from the numerous errors in the printed edition, the book is still hard to understand, and linguistically unclear. Nevertheless, it has in some parts a certain spiritual exaltation and even a beauty of description. There are numerous parables, sometimes embodying the very essence of an idea which cannot be expressed in any other form, or serving as replies to questions posed by speakers. Some of these sayings are mere adaptations of statements from earlier talmudic and midrashic sources, but most of them are without parallel there.

The prime importance of *Sefer ha-Bahir* lies in its use of symbolic language. It is the earliest source that deals with the realm of the divine attributes (*Sefirot; "logoi,"* "beautiful vessels," "kings," "voices," and "crowns"), and that interprets a large part of Scripture as if it was concerned not with what happened in the created world alone, but also with events in the divine realm, and with the action of God's attributes. These attributes are for the first time given symbolic names, derived from the vocabulary of the interpreted verses. The principles on which the symbolic system of the book is based are nowhere explained in an orderly manner, and the speakers use them as if they could be taken for granted. Only in the aforesaid list of the ten *ma'amarot* a few symbolic names, given to each *ma'amar,* are listed.

The *Sefirot,* first mentioned in the *Sefer Yeẓirah* as corresponding to the ten basic numbers, became in *Sefer ha-Bahir* divine attributes, lights, and powers, each one of which fulfills a particular function in the work of creation. This divine realm, which can be described only in highly symbolic language, is the fundamental core of the book. Even the *ta'amei ha-mitzvot* (reasons for the *mitzvot*) are related to this supernal realm: the fulfillment of a certain commandment signifying the activity of a *Sefirah* or of a divine attribute (or the combined activity of several of them).

Sefer ha-Bahir adopts the view of the *Sefer Yeẓirah* that there are ten *Sefirot*, and it goes on to the general conclusion that each attribute or *Sefirah* is alluded to either in Scripture or in rabbinic writings by a very large number of names and symbols which give some idea of its nature. The descriptions of the domain of these attributes are sometimes couched only in allusive terms, which are often described in the pictorial style that gives to *Sefer ha-Bahir* a striking mythological character. The divine powers constitute "the secret tree" from which the souls blossom forth. But these powers are also the sum of the "holy forms" which are joined together in the likeness of supernal man. Everything in the lower world, particularly everything that has sanctity, contains a reference to something in the world of the divine attributes. God is Master of all the powers, and His glorious, unique nature can be discerned in several places. Nevertheless, there is some doubt as to whether those who drew up the list of the ten *ma'amarot* distinguished Him from the first *Sefirah* (*keter elyon*, "the supreme crown"), or whether they considered the *keter elyon* itself to be God. The book emphasizes the concept of the "thought" of God in place of the "will" of God. The technical term **Ein-Sof* ("The Infinite") as an epithet for God does not yet appear in the book.

Place in Kabbalah. Generally speaking, *Sefer ha-Bahir* represents a stage in the development of the *Kabbalah, displaying great variations in detail from the material usually found in later works. This also makes comprehension of the work more difficult. A great distance separates *Sefer ha-Bahir* from the Kabbalah of *Isaac the Blind, to whom *Sefer ha-Bahir* was attributed by some later scholars. *Sefer ha-Bahir* is of the utmost importance as the only evidence of its kind for the state of the Kabbalah as it was when it came to the notice of a wider public, and for the early stages of its development before its dissemination among a wider public. There is a striking affinity between the symbolism of *Sefer ha-Bahir*, on the one hand, and the speculations of the Gnostics, and the theory of the "aeons," on the other. The fundamental problem in the study of the book is: is this affinity based on an as yet unknown historical link between the gnosticism of the mishnaic and talmudic era and the sources from which the material in *Sefer ha-Bahir* is derived? Or should it possibly be seen as a purely psychological phenomenon, i.e., as a spontaneous upsurge from the depths of the soul's imagination, without any historical continuity?

Sefer ha-Bahir appeared at the end of the 12th century in southern France, but the circumstances of its appearance are unknown. There are several reasons to support the theory that the book was actually compiled about this time. Some of the statements in the book show quite clearly the influence of the writings of *Abraham b. Ḥiyya. Did the compilers have before them older manuscripts containing fragments, written in Hebrew, of a gnostic character, which inspired them to elaborate the new symbolic arrangement that appears in *Sefer ha-Bahir?* Was the whole book, in its present form, or in a fuller form, composed only just before its appearance, and actually in southern France? These questions had remained largely unanswered until in recent times it was proved that at least part of *Sefer ha-Bahir* was merely a literary adaptation of a much earlier book, the *Sefer *Raza Rabba*, which is mentioned in the responsa of the *geonim* (see *Gaon), but which is lost, although important fragments appear in one of the books of the Ashkenazi Ḥasidim. A comparison of the parallel texts in the *Raza Rabba* and *Sefer ha-Bahir* demonstrates the link between them. But the elaboration in *Sefer ha-Bahir* adds fundamental elements of a gnostic character, which are not found in the original source. Consequently, one must presume that if there is an historical link between the symbolism of *Sefer ha-Bahir* and gnosticism, then this link was established through additional sources which are not known today. The widespread tradition among the kabbalists that parts of *Sefer ha-Bahir* came to them from Germany was strengthened considerably by the discovery of fragments of the *Raza Rabbah*. But the problem as to whether this is a collective work, the creation of a circle of 12th-century mystics, or whether it is a new compilation of much earlier material, has not yet been sufficiently clarified. The complete absence of any attempt to justify opinions which contradict the accepted Jewish traditions can be explained more easily by adopting the second theory. There is no indication at all in the book that the idea of transmigration of souls which it supports had been rejected by every Jewish philosopher up to the appearance of *Sefer ha-Bahir*. All the mystical interpretations and the elucidation of the reasons for the commandments appear without any note of apology. It is difficult to suppose that the book was compiled or composed in completely nonscholarly circles, who were unconcerned with the ideas current in contemporary literature and wrote absolutely independently. An analysis of the book's sources does not support this theory, and so the literary enigma of the earliest work of kabbalistic writing remains unsolved.

Influence. In Spanish kabbalist circles *Sefer ha-Bahir* was accepted as an ancient and authoritative source, "composed by the mystic sages of the Talmud" (*Jacob b. Jacob ha-Kohen). It had great influence on the development of their teaching. The absence of any clear ideological formulation in the book meant that men of completely opposing views could find support in it. From this point of view it had no parallel until the appearance of the *Zohar. On the other hand, the book was not accepted without protest from those who were opposed to Kabbalah. *Meir b. Simeon of Narbonne wrote very harshly about it and regarded it as an heretical book attributed to Neḥunya b. ha-Kanah. However, the latter was "a righteous man who did not stumble therein, and is not to be numbered with the sinners" (c. 1240).

Editions and Commentaries. Among the many manuscripts of the book there is one version which is superior to the printed edition in a large number of details, but it does not contain any new material. In 1331 Meir b. Solomon Abi-*Sahula, a pupil of Solomon b. Abraham Adret, wrote a commentary on *Sefer ha-Bahir* which was published anonymously in Vilna and in Jerusalem, under the title *Or ha-Ganuz* ("The Hidden Light"). Fragments of a philosophical commentary by *Elijah b. Eliezer of Candia are extant in manuscript (Vatican Ms. 431). David Ḥavillo (d. 1661; Gaster Ms. 966) and Meir *Poppers (in Jerusalem) both of whom were followers of the Lurianic Kabbalah, wrote commentaries on *Sefer ha-Bahir* which have been preserved. It is noteworthy that the various editions of the book differ in the way the book is divided into sections.

The first edition of *Sefer ha-Bahir* was printed in Amsterdam in 1651 (by an anonymous Christian scholar). The latest edition, prepared by R. Margoliot with the addition of notes and parallel material, was published in Jerusalem in 1951. The book has been translated into German by G. Scholem.

Bibliography: G. Scholem, *Ursprung und Anfaenge der Kabbalah* (1962), 33–174; Scholem, Mysticism, index; idem, in: EJ, 3 (1929), 979, includes bibliography; L. Baeck, *Aus drei Jahrtausenden* (1939), 398–415; S. Shahar, Catharism and the Beginnings of the Kabbalah in Languedoc (Elements Common to the Catharic Scriptures and the Book *Bahir*), [in Hebrew], Tarbiz, 40 (1971), 483–507. [G.SCH.]

BAHLUL, family of rabbis in Meknès, Morocco. DANIEL BEN JUDAH (second half of 17th century) was a halakhist, kabbalist, and preacher. He wrote copious notes on *Yazeh Yakar,* a work by Abraham Galanté on the Zohar to Exodus (Jerusalem National Library Ms.), and a volume of sermons which is frequently quoted in the work of his son Eleazar. His other sons were Samuel and Joseph.

Title page of Eleazar Bahlul's manuscript of *Sefer Mareh Einayim,* Fez, Morocco, 1712. Jerusalem, J.N.U.L., Ms. 8° 2062.

SAMUEL was also a rabbi of Meknès. His signature occurs on the halakhic rulings of the community, one of which is dated 1732. ELEAZAR was one of the important scholars of Meknès. His signature appears on the decisions given in 1726 and 1730. Of his many works, which are extant in manuscript, the most important is *Sefer Mareh Einayim* (Jerusalem National Library), composed in Fez between 1710 and 1712, a collection of sermons by Castilian exiles and Moroccan rabbis from the 16th century, as well as sermons which Eleazar had heard from Ereẓ Israel emissaries. He also wrote *Pekuddat Elazar* on Proverbs, and a commentary on rabbinic maxims. In 1718 he edited and adapted *Refu'ot u-Segullot* and *Tivei Asavim* of Jacob Katan of Fez. JOSEPH was the secretary to the *bet din* of Meknès in 1834 and was later appointed *dayyan.*

Bibliography: J. M. Toledano, *Ner ha-Ma'arav* (1911), 145; J. Ben-Naim, *Malkhei Rabbanan* (1931), 22b, 29a, 61b, 94a, 126a; G. Scholem, *Kitvei Yad be-Kabbalah* (1937), 102–4. [ED.]

BAHREIN, territory extending along the Arabian shore of the Persian Gulf southward from Basra including many small islands. Talmudic references to ports and islands on the Persian Gulf indicate that Jews were already settled in this region. The Jews in the capital of Bahrein, Hajar, are recorded in Arabic sources as having refused to accept Islam when Muhammad sent a force to occupy the territory in 630. In the 12th century *Benjamin of Tudela refers to 500 Jews living in Qays and to a Jewish population of 5,000 in al-Qaṭīfa (undoubtedly an exaggeration) who were said to control the pearl fishery. In the 19th century, Jewish merchants from Iraq, Persia, and India went to Bahrein, and there was a small Jewish colony. It has dwindled as a consequence of the political situation. In 1968 only some 100 Jews remained in the capital city of Manama.

Bibliography: A. T. Wilson, *The Persian Gulf* (1954), 83–91; Fischel, in: *Alexander Marx Jubilee Volume* (Eng., 1950), 203–8; Gustinsky, in: *Edot,* 1 (1946), 238–40.

[W.J.F.]

BAḤUR (Heb. בָּחוּר). In the Bible *baḥur* is first used to mean "selected for military fitness," and applied especially to handpicked warriors (I Sam. 26:2; II Sam. 10:9; Judg. 20:15; I Chron. 19:10; et al.). Later, *ne'arim* was used for "youngsters," and *baḥur* came to mean young men in the prime of their life; cf. "The glory of young men is their strength" (Prov. 20:29). In many cases it is mentioned with *betulah* meaning virgin (Deut. 32:25) and Jeremiah contrasts *baḥur–betulah* with old-man–boy and with man–woman (51:22). Later the term was used for an unmarried man (Ket. 7a). The Talmud uses it also in the sense of an innocent young man who has not "tasted sin" (Pes. 87a), and eventually as student at a talmudical school (yeshivah). In Yiddish, pronounced *boḥer,* it is also the term for an unmarried young man. In modern Hebrew it means a young man and the feminine *baḥurah,* an unmarried girl.

[ED.]

BAHURIM (Heb. בַּחוּרִים, בַּחֻרִים), a biblical locality southeast of Jerusalem to which *Paltiel accompanied Saul's daughter Michal when he was forced to return her to her former husband, David (I Sam. 25:44; II Sam. 3:16). On his flight from Absalom, David passed Bahurim after ascending the western slope of the Mount of Olives. He was cursed there by Shimei, son of Gera, a native of the place (II Sam. 16:5ff.; I Kings 2:28). Jonathan and Ahimaaz, who acted as intermediaries between David and his secret supporters in Jerusalem, hid there in a well when they fell under suspicion (II Sam. 17:18ff.). Its accepted identification is with Ra's al-Tamīm on the eastern slope of the Mount of Olives, where Iron Age pottery has been found.

Bibliography: Voigt, in: AASOR, 5 (1925), 67ff.; EM, s.v.; Press, Ereẓ, 1 (1951), 65; Elliger, in: PJB, 31 (1935), 49ff., 70ff.

[M.A.-Y.]

BAḤUẒIM (probably from the Hebrew בַּחוּץ, "outside"), name given by the Jews to the apparently Jewish tribes living in the 15th and 16th centuries along the Algerian-Tunisian border in the regions of Kabylia and Constantine in Algeria and of Le Kef in Tunisia, whom the Arabs named Yahūd al-ʿArab ("Arab Jews"). These seminomadic tribes were agriculturists in Tunisia, and peddlers and jewelers in Algeria. Completely illiterate, the Baḥuẓim observed the Sabbath and swore by *Sidna Musa* ("our Master Moses"). They had their sons circumcised by the rabbi of the nearest town, who also officiated at their marriages and funeral rites. The theory brought forward by N. *Slouschz that these tribes were originally Berbers who had adopted Judaism was followed by several authors; hence they used the term "Judaized Berbers." However, Ḥ.Z. *Hirschberg asserted that they were really marginal elements of the Jewish community living outside the Jewish centers. Their existence as such during the 16th century and their ignorance of the Berber language seem to confirm the latter's theory.

In 1852 there were about 1,500 Baḥuẓim in Algeria, and in 1912 there were still about a hundred Baḥuẓim tents in Tunisia. After the end of World War I these tribes steadily disappeared. Some of them converted to Islam, while others settled in the surrounding Jewish communities, which willingly accepted them.

Bibliography: Netter, in: *Univers Israélite*, 7 (1852), 341–6; idem, in: MGWJ, 1 (1852), 377–82; J. Cohen-Ganouna, *Le Judaïsme Tunisien* (1912), 59–60; Bugéja, in: *Bulletin de la Société des Conférences Juives d'Alger*, 3 (1928/29), 101–25; Slouschz, in: *Keneset . . . le-Zekher Bialik*, 1 (1936), 443–64; Hirschberg, Afrikah, 2 (1965), 29–30. [R.At.]

BAHYA (Pseudo), name given to the author of the Neoplatonic work *Kitāb Maʿanī al-Nafs* ("On the Essence of the Soul," Ar. version ed. by I. Goldziher, 1902; translated into Heb. by I. D. Broydé, 1896), at one time attributed to *Baḥya ibn Paquda. Nothing is known of the author. It appears that Pseudo-Baḥya wrote this work sometime between the middle of the 11th and the middle of the 12th centuries, since he cites *Avicenna and *Nissim ben Jacob who lived in the first half of the 11th century, but gives no indication that he was influenced by the late 12th-century developments in Islamic and Jewish philosophy.

On the Essence of the Soul presents the structure of the universe as a hierarchy of ten emanations created by God. These emanations are the active intellect, soul of the universe, nature, matter, bodies of the spheres, stars, fire, air, water, and earth. Each emanation is dependent on its predecessor for the divine power necessary to activate it. From the ten emanations are formed the composite substances of the sensual world to which the soul must descend. Criticizing the naturalist position that the soul is an accident of the body, the author maintains that the rational soul is spiritual, a product of the soul of the universe. While passing through each emanation in its descent, the soul acquires "outer garments" of impurities until it finally reaches earth and is embodied in man. Different degrees of impurity depending on the length of the soul's stay in each of the emanations through which it descends provide the differences between souls, which, however, are all similar in essence. Once it inheres in a body, the rational soul unites with the lower vegetative and animal souls, and it loses its original suprasensual knowledge. In order to reverse this process and ascend to the spiritual source from which it derived, the rational soul must purify itself by cultivating virtue and by governing the lower souls.

The author bases the immortality of the soul after death on the fact that all things composed of elements return back to their elements. Hence the soul returns to its origin, which is the spiritual soul of the universe, by means of an ascent which the soul can make once it has attained moral and intellectual perfection. Souls possessing only moral perfection can rise to an earthly paradise where they can acquire the knowledge necessary for their ascent to the suprasensual world. Souls possessing only intellectual perfection or no perfection at all are doomed to their earthly surroundings. As a part of their punishment these souls strive unsuccessfully to ascend to the suprasensual world. There is no direct evidence of the work having had any influence in medieval Jewish philosophy and it is not cited by other critics.

Bibliography: A. Borrisov, in: *Bulletin of the Academy of Sciences of URSS, Class of Humanities* (Rus., 1929), 785–99; 41 (1897), 241–56; Husik, Philosophy, 106–13; Guttmann, Philosophies, 124–7. [M.D.G.]

BAHYA BEN ASHER BEN HLAVA (13th century), exegete, preacher, and kabbalist. His great commentary on the Pentateuch (Naples, 1492) was written in 1291. According to tradition, he lived in Saragossa and served there as *dayyan* and preacher. He was a disciple of Solomon b. Abraham Adret, whom he called "my master," whenever he quoted from his commentaries. Curiously enough, Baḥya mentions neither his teacher's kabbalistic sayings nor his commentaries on the mystical teachings of Naḥmanides as did Solomon b. Adret's other disciples. There are also kabbalistic matters quoted anonymously by Baḥya which are attributed to Solomon b. Adret by other authors. This might confirm the assumption of J. Reifmann (*Alummah*, 1 (1936), 82) that Baḥya was not Solomon b. Adret's disciple in Kabbalah. It is also possible that he did not have his teacher's permission to quote him in kabbalistic matters. Isaac b. Todros of Barcelona, the commentator on Naḥmanides' esoteric teachings, is quoted by Baḥya only once, without the attribute "my teacher."

His Writings. Following *Botarel and for various reasons, spurious works (as well as writings whose authors are unknown) have been attributed to Baḥya. J. Reifmann's assumption that Baḥya wrote *Ha-Emunah ve-ha-Bittaḥon* (Korets, 1785), *Ma'arekhet ha-Elohut* (Mantua, 1558), and *Ma'amar ha-Sekhel* (Cremona, 1557), does not stand up to critical examination. Béla Bernstein has pointed out that a commentary on Job published in Baḥya's name was really a compilation made from two of his books: *Kad ha-Kemaḥ* (Constantinople, 1515) and *Shulḥan shel Arba* (Mantua, 1514). There was also the opinion that Baḥya's mention of *Ḥoshen Mishpat* was simply a printing error.

The clarity of Baḥya's style and his easy exposition have made his books (which draw their material from a variety of sources) popular with the public, particularly his commen-

Page from Baḥya b. Asher's commentary on the Pentateuch, Naples, 1492. It is the opening page of the exegesis on Exodus. Jerusalem, J.N.U.L.

tary on the Pentateuch which has been published frequently from 1492 (with explanations and references, 2 vols., 1966–67). Additional testimony to its popularity are the numerous quotations from it in the book **Ẓe'enah u-Re'enah*. In his work Baḥya interprets the Pentateuch in four ways: literal, homiletical, rational, and according to the Kabbalah. He uses many different sources, beginning with talmudic and midrashic literature, exegetic and philosophic literature, and ending with kabbalistic literature. The way of *sekhel* ("reason") does not always mean philosophic-rationalistic interpretation. According to Baḥya, all that is outside the divine world, including demonological matters, belongs to "the way of reason," insofar as it is necessary to explain the verses or the *mitzvot* according to the subject. Baḥya is considered of great importance in Kabbalah and is one of the main sources through which the kabbalistic sayings of Naḥmanides' contemporaries have been preserved. As a rule, Baḥya does not divulge his kabbalistic sources. With the exception of the *Sefer ha-*Bahir,* which he considers an authentic Midrash, and Naḥmanides, who is his guide in Kabbalah, he rarely mentions other kabbalists, although he uses extensively the writings of Jacob b. Sheshet *Gerondi, *Asher b. David, Joseph *Gikatilla, and others. He treats the Zohar in a similar manner. Parts of the Zohar were known to him, and he copied from them. However, he mentions it only twice (as "Midrash Rabbi Simeon b. Yoḥai"). *Kad ha-Kemaḥ* contains alphabetically arranged clarifications on the foundations of faith and had a wide circulation. The best edition is that of Breit which contains a commentary (1880–92). A critical edition of *Kad ha-Kemaḥ, Shulḥan shel Arba,* and Baḥya's commentary to *Pirkei Avot* was published by C. B. Chavel (*Kitvei Rabbenu Baḥya,* 1970).

Bibliography: J. Reifmann, in: *Alummah,* 1 (1936), 69–101; B. Bernstein, *Die Schrifterklaerung des Bachja B. Asher* (1891); Gottlieb, in: *Tarbiz,* 33 (1963/64), 287–313; idem, in: *Bar-Ilan Sefer ha-Shanah,* 2 (1964), 215–50 (Heb.), 27 (Eng. summary); 3 (1965), 139–85; 4–5 (1967), 306–23 (Heb.), 61 (Eng. summary); idem, *Ha-Kabbalah be-Khitvei R. Baḥya ben Asher* (1970).

[E.G.]

BAḤYA (Baḥye) BEN JOSEPH IBN PAQUDA (second half of 11th century), moral philosopher. Little is known about the particulars of Baḥya's life beyond the fact that he lived in Muslim Spain, probably at Saragossa. Baḥya was also known as a *paytan* and some of his *piyyutim* are metered. Twenty *piyyutim,* either published or in manuscript, signed with the name Baḥya are assumed to be his. Baḥya's major work, *Kitāb al-Hidāya ilā Farā'iḍ al-Qulūb* (ed. A. S. Yahuda, 1912), was written around 1080. It was translated into Hebrew by Judah ibn *Tibbon in 1161 under the title *Ḥovot ha-Levavot* ("Duties of the Hearts"), and in this version it became popular and had a profound influence on all subsequent Jewish pietistic literature. Joseph *Kimḥi also translated portions of it, but his version gained no circulation and is still in manuscript. Several abridgments were made of the Hebrew translation, and the work was translated into Arabic, Spanish, Portuguese, Italian, and Yiddish. In more recent times it has been translated into English (*Duties of the Heart,* text and translation by M. Hyamson, 1962), German (*Choboth ha-L'baboth. Lehrbuch der Herzenspflichten,* tr. by M. Stern, 1856), and French *Introduction aux devoirs des coeurs,* tr. by A. Chouraqui, 1950). In his *Ḥovot ha-Levavot* Baḥya drew a great deal upon non-Jewish sources, borrowing from Muslim mysticism, Arabic Neoplatonism, and perhaps also from the *Hermetic writings. From Muslim authors he borrowed the basic structure of the book as well as definitions, aphorisms, and examples to illustrate his

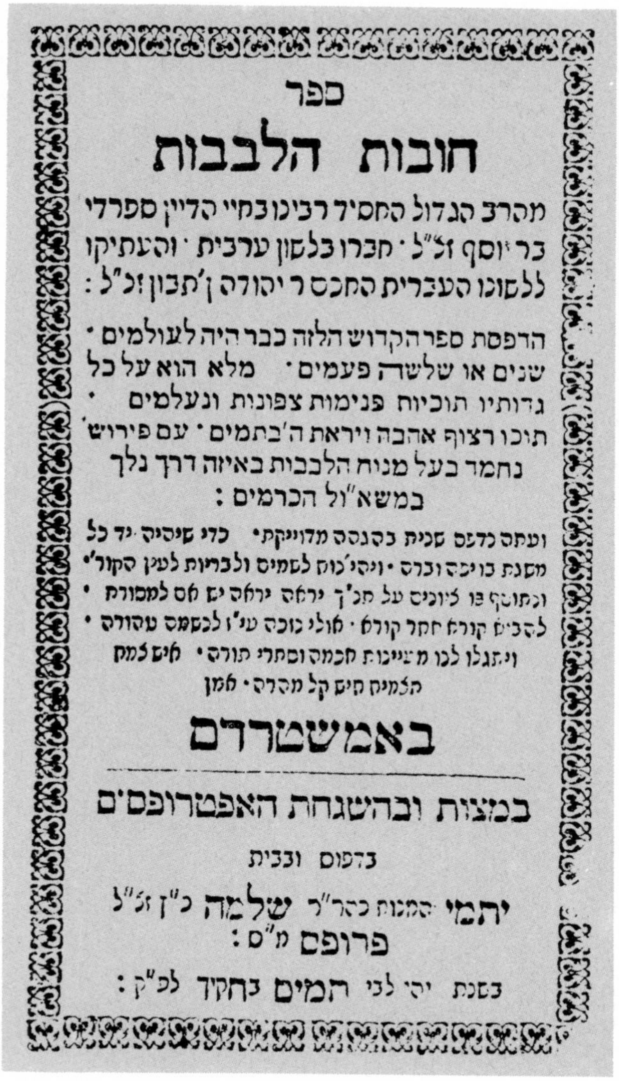
ספר
חובות הלבבות
מהרב הגדול החסיד רבינו בחיי הדיין ספרדי
בר יוסף ז"ל · חברו בלשון ערבית · והעתיקו
ללשונו העברית החכם ר יהודה ן' תבון ז"ל :
הדפסת ספר הקדוש הלזה כבר היה לעולמים ·
שנים או שלשה פעמים · מלא הוא על כל
גדותיו תוכיות פנימות צפונות ונעלמים ·
תוכו רצוף אהבה ויראת ה' בתמים · עם פירוש
נחמד בעל מנות הלבבות באיזה דרך נלך
במשא"ול הכרמים :
באמשטרדם
במצות ובהשגחת האפטרופס"ים
בדפוס ובבית
יתמי המנוח כהר"ר שלמה כ"ץ ז"ל
פרופס מ"ס :
בשנת יהי לבי תמים בחקיך לפ"ק :

Title page of Baḥya ibn Paquda's *Ḥovot ha-Levavot,* Amsterdam, 1737. Jerusalem, J.N.U.L.

doctrines. In most cases his immediate sources cannot be identified, and the theory that he was influenced by Al-*Ghazali does not seem to be well-founded.

Despite the fact that Baḥya borrowed so liberally from non-Jewish sources, *Ḥovot ha-Levavot* remains an essentially Jewish book. In the introduction to this work Baḥya divides the obligations incumbent upon the religious man into duties of the members of the body *(ḥovot ha-evarim),* those obligations which involve overt actions; and duties of the hearts *(ḥovot ha-levavot),* those obligations which involve not man's actions, but his inner life. The first division includes the various ritual and ethical observances commanded by the Torah, e.g., the observance of the Sabbath, prayer, and the giving of charity, while the second consists of beliefs, e.g., the belief in the existence and unity of God, and attitudes or spiritual traits, e.g., trust in God, love and fear of Him, and repentance. The prohibitions against bearing a grudge and taking revenge are also examples of duties of the hearts. Baḥya explains that he wrote this work because the duties of man's inner life had been sorely neglected by his predecessors and contemporaries whose writings had concentrated on religious observances, that is, the duties of the members of the body. To remedy this deficiency Baḥya wrote his work, which may be considered a kind of counterpart to the halakhic compendia of his predecessors and contemporaries. Just as their halakhic compendia contained directions for the actions of the religious man, so Baḥya's work contained directions for his inner life. *Ḥovot ha-Levavot* is modeled after the works of Muslim mysticism, which attempt to lead the reader through various ascending stages of man's inner life, toward spiritual perfection and finally union (or at least communion) with God. In similar fashion *Ḥovot ha-Levavot* is divided into ten "gates" (chapters), each of which is devoted to a particular duty of the heart, which the Jew must observe if he is to attain spiritual perfection. The ten chapters deal with the affirmation of the unity of God *(yiḥud),* the nature of the world disclosing the workings of God *(beḥinat ha-olam),* divine worship *(avodat ha-Elohim),* trust in God *(bittaḥon),* sincerity of purpose *(yiḥud ha-ma'aseh),* humility *(keni'ah),* repentance *(teshuvah),* self-examination *(ḥeshbon ha-nefesh),* asceticism *(perishut),* and the love of God *(ahavat ha-Shem).*

In accordance with Platonic teachings (probably influenced partially by the Epistles of the Sincere Brethren), he maintains that man's soul, which is celestial in origin, is placed, by divine decree, within the body, where it runs the risk of forgetting its nature and mission. The human soul receives aid from the intellect and the revealed Law in achieving its goal. To elucidate this point Baḥya makes use of the Muʿtazilite (see *Kalām) distinction between rational and traditional commandments. He holds that the duties of the members of the body may be divided into rational commandments and traditional (religious) commandments, while the duties of the hearts are all rooted in the intellect. With the aid of reason and the revealed Law the soul can triumph over its enemy, the evil inclination *(yeẓer),* which attacks it incessantly in an effort to beguile it into erroneous beliefs and to enslave it to bodily appetites. Since the basis of religion is the belief in the existence of God, the first chapter of the work is devoted to a philosophical and theological explication of the existence and unity of God and a discussion of His attributes. In the second chapter Baḥya examines the order in the universe and the extraordinary structure of man, the microcosm. Such an examination leads to a knowledge of God, and to a sense of gratitude towards Him as creator. In the third chapter he discusses divine worship which is the expression of man's gratitude to God. To fulfill his duties to God without faltering and to achieve his true goal, man must diligently practice a number of virtues. One of these is trust in God, which is based on the belief that God is good, and that he has a knowledge of what is best for man, and the power to protect him. To trust in God does not mean that one should neglect one's work, leaving everything to Him, but rather that one should conscientiously attempt to carry out one's duties, trusting that God will remove any obstacles which lie in the way of their fulfillment. While man has the freedom to will and choose, the realization of his actions is dependent on God's will. Further, a sound spiritual life requires sincerity, a perfect correspondence between man's conscience and behavior. Man's intentions must coincide with his actions in aiming toward the service of God. Humility, repentance, and self-examination are also essential. Another virtue is asceticism or temperance. Baḥya considers total asceticism, involving the breaking of all social ties, an ideal rarely attained in the biblical past and hardly to be recommended in the present. Actually, he recommends the pursuit of the middle way prescribed by the revealed Law, defining the genuine ascetic as one who directs all his actions to the service of God, while at the same time fulfilling his functions within society. The observance of these virtues leads to the highest stage of the spiritual life, the love of God. True love of God is the ardor of the soul for union with the Divine Light, a concept of a distinctly mystic character. Baḥya does not, however, develop this concept in all its implications. The love of God, in his view, is a synthesis of the degrees of perfection described above, but does not go beyond them. The lover of God, such as described by him, keeps at a distance from his loved one. Despite Baḥya's dependence upon Muslim mysticism, which is here more pronounced than elsewhere in the work, his teaching remains in the line of Jewish tradition, and he cannot be called a mystic in the strict sense of the term. It has been definitely established that the Judeo-Arabic Neoplatonic tract, *Kitāb Maʿanī al Nafs* (ed. by I Goldziher, 1907; translated into Hebrew by I. Broydé as *Sefer Torat ha-Nefesh,* 1896) at one time attributed to Baḥya, was not written by him (see *Baḥya (Pseudo)).

Bibliography: Husik, Philosophy, 80–105; Guttmann, Philosophies, 104–10; Kokowzoff, in: *Sefer Zikkaron . . . S. Poznański* (1927), 13–21; G. Vajda, *La théologie ascétique de Baḥya ibn Paquda* (1947); idem, in: REJ, 102 (1937), 93–104; M. Sister, in: *Bericht der Lehranstalt fuer die Wissenschaft des Judentums,* 50 (1936), 33–75; idem, in: MGWJ, 81 (1937), 86–93; D. Kaufmann, *Meḥkarim be-Sifrut Yemei ha-Beinayim* (1962), 11–77; Kaufmann, Schriften, 2 (1910), 1–98; D. H. Baneth, in: *Sefer Magnes* (1938), 23–30; Ramos Gil, in: *Archivo de Filologia Aragonesa,* 3 (1950), 129–80; idem, in: *Sefarad,* 11 (1951), 305–38; idem, in: *ME'AH,* 1 (1952), 85–148; J. H. Schirmann, *Shirim Ḥadashim min ha-Genizah* (1966), 203–8; Davidson Oẓar, 4 (1933), 370. [G.V.]

BAIA-MARE (Hg. Nagybánya), mining and industrial town in Transylvania, Rumania, within Hungary until 1918 and between 1940 and 1945. The prohibition against Jewish settlement in Hungarian mining towns (issued in 1693) was abolished in 1848. In 1850 Jewish artisans, businessmen, and farmers began to settle in Baia-Mare. Subsequently Jews did much to develop local commerce and industry. A community was organized in 1860, and a burial society founded in 1862. The first synagogue was opened in 1887. During the *Tisza-Eszlar blood libel case in 1882, a mob attacked the synagogue and pillaged it. The community always remained Orthodox, and Satmar Ḥasidism (see *Teitelbaum) had a strong following. There was also a flourishing Zionist movement. The Jewish population numbered 701 in 1890 (out of a total of 9,838); 1,402 in 1910 (out of 12,877); 2,030 in 1930 (out of 13,904); and 3,623 in 1941 (out of 21,404).

Most of the Jews were deported to death camps during the *Holocaust. A ghetto was established in Baia-Mare from which Jews from the surrounding areas were sent to the death camps. The Hungarian military headquarters in charge of the conscription of the Jews of northern Transylvania for forced labor was located in Baia-Mare. Its commander during the most difficult years, 1943–44, was Lieut. Col. Imre Reviczky, and he did much to assist the Jews who arrived in the depot and joined the local rabbi, Moses Aaron Krausz (1886–1944), in rescue action. Reviczky's memory has been perpetuated in the Martyrs' Forest

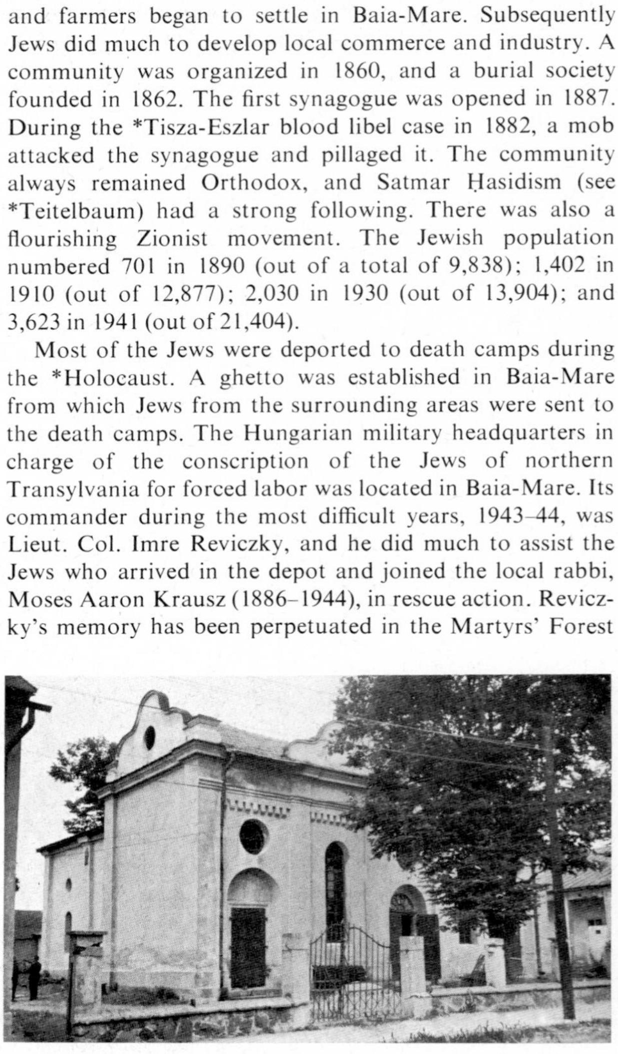

A synagogue in Baia-Mare, Rumania.

near Jerusalem by those whom he saved. The survivors who returned from the camps after the war reestablished the communal institutions. The Jewish population in Baia-Mare numbered 950 in 1947. Subsequent emigration reduced the community considerably; in 1969 it numbered 120 families.

Bibliography: *Magyar Zsidé Lexikon* (1929), 626. [Y.M.]

BAIERSDORF, village in Bavaria, West Germany, formerly the summer residence of the margraves of Kulmbach-Bayreuth. Tombstones in the Jewish cemetery indicate the presence of Jews in Baiersdorf at the end of the 14th century, although the first document in which they are mentioned dates from 1473. In 1632 they numbered 12 families. The synagogue, established before 1530, was

The Baiersdorf synagogue, built in 1711, destroyed in 1938. Baiersdorf Municipality.

rebuilt in 1651. After persecutions in 1680, the margrave issued an order in 1695 granting the Jews freedom of trade. In 1699 a "Jewish pharmacy" was opened in Baiersdorf. The community increased to 40 families (300 persons) in 1713 and 83 families in 1771. The Bavarian restrictions limiting Jewish households (*Matrikel-Gesetz*) led many of the younger sons to emigrate to England and America (for instance, the *Seligman family), and by about 1900 only 12 Jewish families remained. The synagogue built in 1711 was destroyed under the Nazi regime in November 1938; only three Jews remained in Baiersdorf at the time.

Bibliography: ZGJD, 2 (1888), 95–96; A. Eckstein, *Geschichte der Juden im Markgrafentum Bayreuth* (1907); *Baiersdorf, Entwicklungsgeschichte einer fraenkischen Kleinstadt* (1953), 98–105, 143, 179. [Z.F.]

BAIERSDORF, SAMSON SOLOMON (d. 1712), son of Judah Selke, court agent of the margrave of Brandenburg-Bayreuth. Baiersdorf entered the margrave's service in 1670. He influenced him to issue a decree in 1695 granting the Jews in the margravate freedom of trade. In 1698 he bought real estate from the margrave. Although later involved in a court intrigue, Baiersdorf managed to retain his position. He donated the money for the synagogue of *Bayreuth, consecrated in 1711. Baiersdorf's daughter married Moses, the son of *Glueckel of Hameln, who became rabbi of *Baiersdorf in 1700. His sons, Veit and Solomon, known by the family name of Samson, and his son-in-law and brother also became court agents; the latter was permitted to retain an armed guard.

Bibliography: H. Schnee, *Die Hoffinanz und der moderne Staat*, 3 (1955), 222–3; 4 (1963), 33; S. Stern, *The Court Jew* (1950), 100, 198, 251; Glueckel von Hameln, *Memoirs* (1932), 204–8, 220f., 232–5. [Ed.]

BAIGNEUX-LES-JUIFS, village northwest of *Dijon. Jews settled in the commune at its establishment in the middle of the 13th century, giving the locality its name. They were expelled with the other Jews in the duchy of Burgundy in 1306. The inventory made of their debts and property indicates that the community was fairly numerous and prosperous. Green and red wax, parchment, ink, and paint were taken from a Jew referred to as Rebi or Rabi—most probably the scribe of the community. The medieval synagogue was located on the present Rue Vergier-au-Duc.

Bibliography: J. Garnier and E. Champeux, *Chartes de Communes . . . Bourgogne* (1898), 161f.; Gauthier, in: *Mémoires de la société d'émulation du Jura*, 3 (1914), 78, 225–32. [B.Bl.]

°**BAIL, CHARLES-JOSEPH** (1777–1827), French soldier, publicist, and civil servant. Bail was in charge of the administration of the Bonapartist kingdom of *Westphalia, and thus had close contacts with the heads of the Jewish *Consistoire there. After the fall of Napoleon, he continued to defend the basic principles of the revolution. In this spirit he published a pamphlet on "The Jews in the 19th Century or Considerations of their Civil and Political Status in Europe" (*Les Juifs au XIXe siècle . . .* Paris, 1816). He here

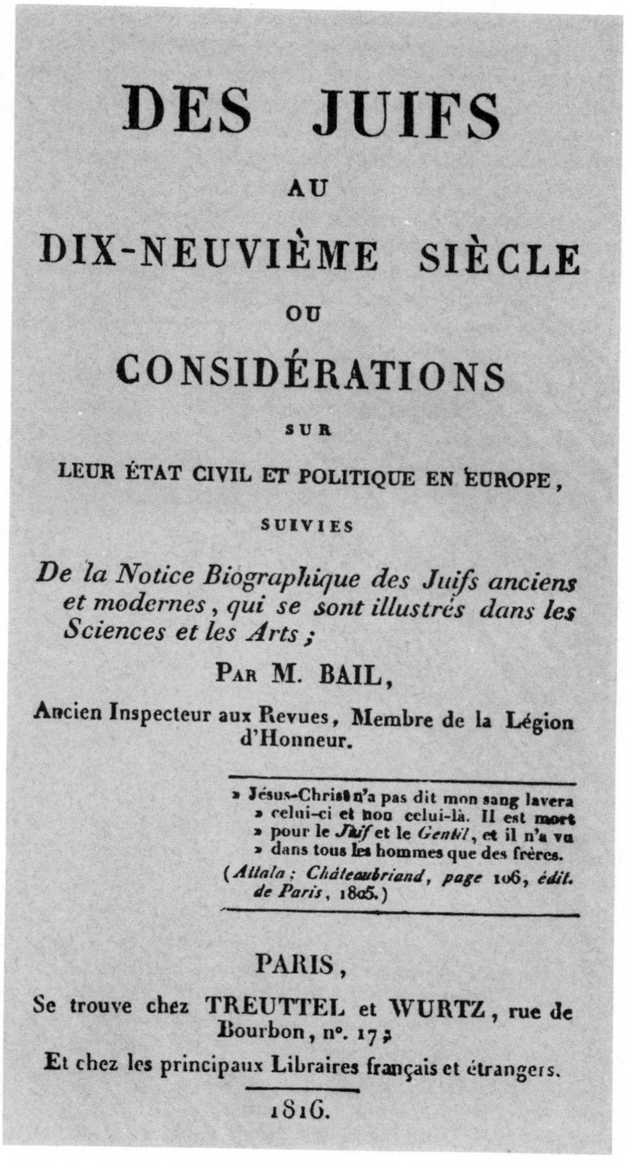

DES JUIFS
AU
DIX-NEUVIÈME SIÈCLE
OU
CONSIDÉRATIONS
SUR
LEUR ÉTAT CIVIL ET POLITIQUE EN EUROPE,
SUIVIES
De la Notice Biographique des Juifs anciens et modernes, qui se sont illustrés dans les Sciences et les Arts;
PAR M. BAIL,
Ancien Inspecteur aux Revues, Membre de la Légion d'Honneur.

» Jésus-Christ n'a pas dit mon sang lavera
» celui-ci et non celui-là. Il est mort
» pour le *Juif* et le *Gentil*, et il n'a vu
» dans tous les hommes que des frères.
(*Atala; Châteaubriand, page* 106, *édit. de Paris*, 1805.)

PARIS,
Se trouve chez TREUTTEL et WURTZ, rue de Bourbon, n°. 17;
Et chez les principaux Libraires français et étrangers.
1816.

Title page of Charles-Joseph Bail's pamphlet in defense of the Jews, 1816.

defended the basic principles of equality, ascribing the separatist characteristics of the Jews to their depressed civil and political status. The same year, following criticism from the Catholic Romantic side, Bail published a second edition in which he imputed some of the separatist characteristics of the Jews to their religion and form of society, although in the main still defending his original thesis. Bail took part in a competition held by the Académie des Inscriptions et Belles-Lettres on the history of the Jews in Europe in the Middle Ages. Although unsuccessful, Bail subsequently published his work "The Situation of the Jews in France, Spain and Italy" (*Etat des Juifs en France . . .* Paris, 1823).

Bibliography: S. de Sacy, *Lettre à MXXX, relativement à l'ouvrage intitulé: Des Juifs au 19e siècle* (Paris, 1817); A. T. d'Esquiron de St. Agnan, *Considérations sur l'existence civile et politique des Israélites—suivies de quelques idées sur l'ouvrage de M. Bail . . . et trois lettres de M. de Cologna, grand rabbin du consistoire Israélite de Paris* (n.d.); *Dictionnaire de Bibliographie Française*, 4 (1948), s.v.; *Nouvelle Biographie Universelle*, 4 (1853), s.v. [B.M.]

BAITOS (Boethus) BEN ZONIN (beginning of second century), respected and wealthy resident of Lydda, whose home was a meeting place for scholars. It is related that the rabbis, headed by Rabban *Gamaliel of Jabneh, "reclined in the home of Baitos b. Zonin in Lydda and discussed Passover *halakhot* the whole of that night [of the *Passover Seder] until cockcrow" (Tosef., Pes. 10:12). He also discussed halakhic problems with the rabbis (TJ, Pes. 2:end of 4, 29c; Pes. 37a). Baitos conducted his life in accordance with the teachings of the rabbis, particularly *Eleazar b. Azariah (Meg. 27b; BM 63a; BB 13b), and his conduct is cited in tannaitic sources as evidence for the *halakhah* in both ritual and monetary matters (BM 5:3; Av. Zar. 5:2).

Bibliography: Hyman, Toledot, 270. [Z.K.]

BAIZERMAN, family of U.S. artists. SAUL BAIZERMAN (1899–1957) was born in Vitebsk and went to America in 1910. Baizerman, who worked in hammered copper, represented the classic style in modern American sculpture. His reliefs express abstract thought by means of the movements of the nude human body. Being concave as well as convex, they are made to be seen from both sides. Some of his best known works are "The March of the Innocents," "Exuberance," "Crescendo," and "Eroica." Baizerman for some years conducted his own school. His wife EUGENIE (1899–1949), painter and forerunner of abstract impressionism, was born in Poland and went to New York at the age of 14. In the 1930s she developed a personal form of neo-impressionism in which, using jagged brushstrokes, human figures merged with pastoral settings till their contours almost disappeared. Twelve years after her death a retrospective exhibition was held which established her reputation.

"A Quiet Scene" by Eugenie Baizerman, 1947, oil on canvas, 78×54 in. (198×137 cm.). New York, Whitney Museum of American Art.

Bibliography: R. Goodenough, in: *Art News* (March 1952), 40–43. [ED.]

BAJA, county town on the Danube, in southern Hungary. Jews settled there about 1725. In 1753 there were ten families, mainly merchants in wool, leather, and tobacco. The community numbered 16 families in 1773 when it received permission to build a synagogue and appoint a rabbi. In March 1840 the communal buildings were devastated and the community nearly ruined in a general conflagration. A new synagogue was dedicated in 1845, a secondary school was opened in 1878, and the hospital was rebuilt in 1882. The Jewish population increased from 516 in the 1830s (3.7% of the total) to 600 in 1850 (4%), and 4,325 in 1908 (19.5%). Meir *Ash (Eisenstadt) officiated as rabbi in Baja from 1805 to 1815. His successor Schwerin Goetz Kohn directed a yeshivah there. The development of new lines of communication, however, proved disadvantageous to Baja and by 1920 the Jewish population had diminished to 2,400 (12%).

The synagogue in Baja, Hungary, dedicated in 1845.

On April 14, 1944, German military detachments deported 150 men from the Jewish community. Those who did not perish in *Auschwitz were later taken to *Bergen-Belsen and Stettin (now Szczecin) where the rabbi of Baja, Joseph Klein, was beaten to death by German guards. The first hostages were followed two months later by the mass deportation of almost the entire Jewish community of Baja to Auschwitz. Fifteen to 20 families lived to see the liberation of their city. There were only 70 Jews in Baja in 1964.

Bibliography: G. Dudás, *Bács bodrog vármegye monographiája*, 2 (1896), 254–15, 309–10; M. Pollák, *A bajai zsidó hitközség iskoláinak története* (1896); S. Kohn, *Kohn Schwerin Götz* (Hung. 1899).

[L.H.]

BAK (also **Pak**), a family of Jewish printers of Ashkenazi origin, who lived first in Venice and later in Prague. According to Zunz, the name represents the initials of *Benei Kedoshim* (Children of the Martyrs).

GERSON, the progenitor of the family, lived in Italy in the early 16th century, where his son JACOB followed the printing trade. Jacob printed the *Midrash Tanḥuma* in Verona (1595) and in Venice *Tanna de-Vei Eliyahu* (1598), and *Tiferet Yisrael* by *Judah Loew (the Maharal) of Prague in 1599. Apparently his connections with the latter brought him to Prague. From 1605 until his death in 1618 he printed numerous Hebrew and Judeo-German books. He was succeeded by his sons JOSEPH and JUDAH, who in 1623 set up a new printing house called "Jacob Bak's Sons." Their output was considerable, despite the temporary slowing down during the Thirty Years' War and the persecutions of 1648/49 and 1656. In about 1660 Joseph left the printing business, and Judah carried on alone. A libel action brought against the press led to its closing down in 1669. Judah died in 1671, and two years later his sons, JACOB (1630–1688) and JOSEPH (d. 1696), were authorized to resume printing books, as "Judah Bak's sons," but a special permit was required for each book. In 1680 Joseph completed a *maḥzor* at nearby Weckelsdorf—the only Hebrew work ever printed there. Between 1680 and 1683 Joseph apparently continued alone in Prague, while Jacob

Figure 1. Title page of the *Midrash Tanḥuma* printed by Jacob Bak, founder of the Bak printing house, in Verona in 1595, Jerusalem, J.N.U.L.

Figure 2. Title page of the *maḥzor* printed by the brothers Jacob and Joseph Bak at Weckelsdorf in 1680. The frame specifies the festivals for which the prayer book is designed. Jerusalem, J.N.U.L.

worked under the name "Judah Bak's Sons" (1682–88). Joseph was joined by Jacob's son MOSES (d. 1712), in 1686. From 1697 Moses ran the firm with his cousin, Joseph's son (later "The Bak Press"). Moses' son JUDAH (d. 1767/68), who was a compositor, managed the press from 1735 to 1756. In 1757 Judah's brother YOM TOV LIPMANN joined as his partner, and the firm became "Moses Bak's Sons." The firm later became "The Bak and Katz Press" (1784–89), and afterwards passed into other hands entirely. The Bak family were pioneers in the field of Jewish printing, while also making an important contribution to the Jewish community of the time. Israel *Bak, the printer of Safed and Jerusalem, does not seem to have any connection with this Bak family.

Bibliography: Zunz, Gesch, 264–6, 282–303; S. Hock, *Mishpeḥot K. K. Prag* (1892), 46–48; H. D. Friedberg, *Toledot ha-Defus ha-Ivri be-Arim . . . she-be-Eiropah ha-Tikhonah* (1937), 19–26; A. Tauber, *Meḥkarim Bibliografiyyim* (1932), 9–14; A. Yaari, *Ha-Defus ha-Ivri be-Arẓot ha-Mizraḥ* (1937), 14–15.

[A.M.H.]

BAK, printers and pioneers in Ereẓ Israel. ISRAEL BAK (1797–1874) was born in Berdichev, Ukraine, into a family of printers. Later he owned a Jewish press in Berdichev, printing about 30 books between 1815 and 1821 when the press closed down. In 1831, after various unsuccessful efforts to reopen the works, he emigrated to Palestine and settled in Safed. There he renewed the tradition of printing Hebrew works, which had come to an end in the last third of the 17th century. During the peasant revolt against

Printer's mark of Israel Bak. The woodcut of Jerusalem depicts the Western Wall, the Temple Mount and the Mount of Olives. Jerusalem, J.N.U.L.

Muhammad Ali in 1834 his printing press was destroyed and he was wounded. Later he reopened his press, and also began to work the land on Mount Yarmak (Meron), overlooking Safed. His was the first Jewish farm in Ereẓ Israel in modern times. After the Safed earthquake in 1837 and the Druze revolt in 1838, during which his farm and printing press were destroyed, he moved to Jerusalem. In 1841 he established the first—and for 22 years, the only—Jewish printing press in Jerusalem. One hundred and thirty books were printed on it, making it an important cultural factor in Jerusalem. Bak also published and edited the second Hebrew newspaper in Ereẓ Israel, *Ḥavaẓẓelet* (1863). After a short time its publication stopped and was renewed only in 1870 by his son-in-law I. D. *Frumkin and others. Israel Bak was a leader of the ḥasidic community; as a result of his efforts and those of his son Nisan, a central synagogue for the Ḥasidim, called Tiferet Israel (after R. Israel of Ruzhin), came into being. In Jerusalem it was also known as "Nisan Bak's synagogue." It was destroyed in 1948 during the War of Independence.

NISAN (1815–1889), only son of Israel, was born in Berdichev and emigrated to Palestine with his father in 1831. Nisan managed the printing press after the death of his father until 1883, when he sold the business; thereafter he devoted himself exclusively to communal affairs in Jerusalem. He was an active worker in the ḥasidic community and the representative of the Ruzhin-Sadagura dynasty in Jerusalem. Through his contacts with the Turkish government he did much to modify decrees aimed against the *yishuv.* He initiated and executed several building projects in Jerusalem, such as the Kiryah Ne'emanah quarter, first named Oholei Moshe vi-Yhudit, but better known as Battei Nisan Bak. He and his brother-in-law I. D. Frumkin were pioneers of the Haskalah in Jerusalem; they also opposed the methods of **ḥalukkah* distribution. In 1884 Nisan and others founded the Ezrat Niddaḥim Society, which fought the missions and established the Yemenite quarter in Jerusalem.

Bibliography: G. Kressel (ed.), *Mivḥar Kitvei I. D. Frumkin* (1954), index; A. Yaari, *Ha-Defus ha-Ivri be-Arẓot ha-Mizraḥ* (1937), 20–22 (list of books printed by Israel Bak in Safed); S. Halevi, *Ha-Sefarim ha-Ivriyyim she-Nidpesu be-Yrushalayim* (1963), index; G. Kressel, *Toledot ha-Ittonut ha-Ivrit be-Ereẓ Yisrael* (1964), index; Tidhar, 1 (1947), 64f.; M. Benayahu, in: *Aresheth,* 4 (1966), 271–95.
[G.K.]

BAKER, EDWARD MAX (1875–1957), U.S. investment broker and communal leader. Baker was born in Erie, Pennsylvania. His maternal grandfather was Rabbi David *Einhorn, and his uncles were Rabbis Emil G. *Hirsch and Kaufmann *Kohler, leaders of Reform Judaism. In 1901 Baker entered the brokerage business in Cleveland. He became resident manager of a national brokerage firm in 1911 and served as president of the Cleveland Stock Exchange for 14 years. Baker was a founder of the Cleveland Federation of Jewish Charities (1903), serving as its president (1923–27) and as a trustee for more than five decades. He was also a member of the national board of the American Jewish Committee and of other major Jewish institutions. Equally active in Cleveland civic affairs, Baker served as chairman of the Republican County Committee (1907–08). He was a founder of the Cleveland Legal Aid Society; a founder and president of the Cleveland City Club, a community forum; and member of the first Board of Trustees of the Associated Charities of Cleveland.
[JU.R.]

BAKHCHISARAI, town in Crimea, Ukrainian S.S.R. From the 16th to the 18th centuries it was the capital of the khans of Crimea. A settlement of Rabbanite Jews (Krimchaks) as well as of Karaites evidently existed in Bakhchisarai in the second half of the 18th century. In the 1870s the Karaites abandoned *Chufut-Kale, approximately $1\frac{1}{4}$ mi. (about 2 km.) to the east, and moved to Bakhchisarai. A Jewish traveler in the 1870s found about 20 families of Rabbanite Jews and some 70 Karaite families there: in 1897 there were 210 Rabbanites and 967 Karaites. The Hebrew poet Saul *Tchernichowsky wrote several poems about Bakhchisarai. The community decreased after World War I. The remaining Jews were nearly all murdered during the German occupation in World War II.

Bibliography: E. Deinard, *Massa ba-Ḥaẓi ha-I Krim* (1878), 104.
[Y.S./EL.F.]

BAKI (Heb. בָּקִי; "expert"), person possessing expertise in a particular field of ritual law, e.g., in divorce law *("Baki be-tiv Gittin")* or in dietary laws *("Baki bi-terefot");* also a person well versed in Talmud and rabbinic literature is called *"Baki be-Shas u-Fosekim."*
[ED.]

BAKKASHAH (pl. **bakkashot;** Heb. בַּקָּשׁוֹת, בַּקָּשָׁה, "Supplication(s)"), liturgical compositions of the same type as **seliḥot.* The word denotes a wide range of prayers in prose or verse, petitionary and abstract in content, mainly for recitation throughout the year. A number of *bakkashot* found at the beginning of the Sephardi prayer books from the 17th century onward are meant to be recited by congregants before dawn while waiting for the regular service to begin. Groups of Sephardim in Jerusalem called *Omerei Bakkashot* ("Sayers of Supplications") continue this practice every Sabbath from midnight until sunrise. At first these *bakkashot* had been said daily, but later, as a result of reduced attendance, they were confined to the Sabbath except during the month of Elul. The custom apparently originated in Safed among the followers of Isaac *Luria, and from there spread to other communities. It is first mentioned in a letter of Solomon Shlumal dated 1603 (S. Assaf, in: *Kobez al Jad,* 3 (1939), 123). This practice is not to be confused with Ashkenazi societies of Shomerim la-Boker ("Morning Watchers"), which recite hymns on Monday and Thursday mornings before dawn. The term was, however, often applied arbitrarily to certain hymns included in the service. *Saadiah Gaon's two *bakkashot,* that of *Baḥya ibn Paquda, and Solomon ibn *Gabirol's *Keter ha-Malkhut* (Venice, 1572) are examples. The term also refers to some of the short hymns by such poets as Abraham and Moses *ibn Ezra and *Judah Halevi. Different collections of *bakkashot* exist, and all of them include the poem *Yedid Nefesh* by Eleazar *Azikri. Each composition concludes with a collection of scriptural verses beginning with "And Hannah prayed . . ." (I Sam. 2:1). Recently, different collections have appeared, such as the volume of hymns published by Mordecai Ḥayyim Elijah Levi (1929) and the *Tehillat Yesharim ha-Shalem* (ed. by Z. J. Manẓur, 1954). [E.D.G.]

Musical Tradition. Although the singing of *bakkashot* is traditional in many communities, it evolved into an organized form of semireligious activity only in Syria (Aleppo and Damascus) and Morocco. The melodies are extremely varied and include sophisticated and popular idioms, the latest innovations, and traditional tunes which have disappeared from contemporary cultures. The musical factor is prominent and often tends to overshadow the basically religious purpose of the meeting. The singing of *bakkashot* may thus be considered as half religious concert and half prayer meeting, attended equally for religious, aesthetic, and social reasons. After the establishment of an important community of Aleppo Jews in Jerusalem at the beginning of the 20th century, Aleppo *bakkashot* became a model for other Middle Eastern communities, but were themselves much modified by the participation of non-Aleppo singers. The result was the generalized *bakkashot* style now common to several ethnic groups. In contrast, the wider distribution of Moroccan settlement, especially after 1948, in homogeneous immigrants' villages, helped to preserve the purity of the Moroccan *bakkashot* tradition. The Aleppo *bakkashot* consist of certain fixed *piyyutim* and optional ones which are selected for the occasion according to circumstances and the character of the audience. Each *bakkashah* is performed antiphonally by two groups. Between one *bakkashah* and the next, a soloist or smaller group takes turns in singing the so-called *petiḥah* (opening), which may be a psalm or the last verse of the preceding *piyyut*. The melodies are improvised, highly melismatic, and constructed so as to establish a modulation from the **maqām* (melodic pattern) of the preceding to that of the following song. The concluding *bakkashah, Yedid Nefesh*, is sung in the *maqām* of the current Sabbath. In the Moroccan *bakkashot* the repertoire is fixed and arranged in sets of different *piyyutim*—except for three or four recurring ones—for each *bakkashah* night, which also has its own dominant *maqām*. Each set takes the form of the "Andalusian" *nuba* of Moroccan art music, which is a kind of vocal and instrumental suite. Since instruments are not permitted, the singers add their own vocal imitations of instrumental passages. The Moroccan *bakkashot*, however, are also sung at celebrations outside the synagogue, and then the appropriate instruments are used.

See also *Aleppo, Musical Tradition. [AM.SH.]

Bibliography: *Oẓar ha-Tefillot* (Ashkenazi rite, 1923), 56–63; Idelsohn, Liturgy, 157; Elbogen, Gottesdienst, 74, 229, 324; I. Davidson et al. (eds.), *Siddur Sa'adiah Ga'on* (1941), 47–81; R. Katz, in: *Acta Musicologica*, 40 (1968), 65–85 (Eng.).

BAKST, LEON (born **Lev Samuilovich Rosenberg;** 1867–1924), Russian artist. Born in St. Petersburg, he took the name Leon Bakst to honor his maternal grandfather. In his youth he was baptized but later returned to Judaism. At the age of 15, on the advice of the sculptor *Antokolski, he enrolled in the Academy of Fine Arts. In 1890 he met Alexander Benois, a Russian artist who introduced Bakst to the Mir Iskusstva ("World of Art") group that tried to overcome the prevailing provincialism of Russian art and to link Russia to the West. The impresario Serge Diaghilev was a member and he employed Bakst as chief designer of costumes and décors for his ballets. From its start in Paris, in 1909, until his death, Bakst was associated with Diaghilev's Ballets Russes. The subjects for the ballets were usually taken from Russian folklore, or from Oriental tales. Bakst, with his vivid imagination and his predilection for bright color, provided an atmosphere that carried the audience into a fairyland. While his creations are no longer in use on the stage, his sketches in pencil, pen-and-ink, crayon, watercolor, gouaches, or mixed media often appear in exhibitions of Russian art. They have become particularly appreciated since the recent revival of interest in *art nouveau*. As a teacher at the Svanseva School in St. Petersburg, Bakst had a strong influence on the young Marc *Chagall.

Bibliography: A. Levinson, *Bakst* (Fr., 1924); R. Lister, *The Moscovite Peacock; a Study of the Art of L. Bakst* (1954). [A.W.]

Costume design by Leon Bakst for the ballet "Scheherazade," 1921. Jerusalem, Dr. J. Leron Collection.

BAKST, NICOLAI (Noah) IGNATYEVICH (1843–1904), Russian scientist, writer, and public figure. Born in Mir, Belorussia, Bakst studied at the rabbinical seminary in Zhitomir, where his father Isaac Moses taught Talmud, and thereafter at the University of St. Petersburg. After graduating he was sent to Germany by the Russian Ministry of Public Instruction. There he continued his studies under the noted physiologist Hermann Helmholtz and others. In 1867 he was appointed lecturer in physiology at the University of St. Petersburg, specializing in study of the nervous system. He wrote a number of works in German and Russian on physiology and the nervous system.

The emergence of anti-Semitism in Germany and the pogroms in Russia of 1881 awakened Bakst's interest in the Jewish question. For him the solution was to grant full civil rights to the Jews in Russia and improve their material and moral condition. Bakst became a highly esteemed public figure in Russian Jewry; he was one of the initiators of

*ORT and active in its management. He served as an expert on the Pahlen Commission (1883–88), set up to examine the laws regulating Jewish life. This prompted Bakst to publish a series of articles on different aspects of Jewish life and thought in Jewish and non-Jewish journals.

Bibliography: S. A. Wengeroff, *Kritiko-biograficheskiy slovar*, 3 (1892), 73–75; Galpern, in: *Voskhod*, 24 no. 27 (1904), 5–8; YE, 4 (c. 1910), 698–701. [Ed.]

BAKU, port on the western shore of the Caspian Sea, capital of Azerbaijan S.S.R. from 1920. A community of Persian Jews existed in Baku in the 18th century. The inhabitants, who were Muslims, harrassed the Jews there and in 1814 threatened their lives following a blood libel. Although the Russian authorities offered them their protection, the Jews left and took refuge in *Kuba, also in the province of Baku, where there was a large community of *Caucasian Mountain Jews. Later, however, some returned to Baku.

A new chapter in the history of the community began in the 1870s with the development of the oil industry in Baku and its surrroundings. Although restrictions were imposed to discourage Jews coming from European Russia, and on Jewish participation in the industry, the number of Jewish concessionaires and professional and skilled workers increased. Jews took a large share in initiating new enterprises and providing capital, in exploiting oil wells and setting up refineries, in developing transport facilities, and in marketing oil and oil products within Russia and abroad. Among pioneer industrial companies owned by Jews was that of Dembo and Kagan, founded by A. Dembo of Kovno and Ḥayyim Cohen of Brest-Litovsk. Also active in this sphere were the Dembot brothers, in collaboration with Baron H. Guenzburg, Bikhowsky, Leites, Ickowich, and A. M. Feigel. A central position in oil exploitation, transportation, and marketing was occupied by the *Rothschilds, who founded the Caspian-Black Sea Company and by the end of the 19th century headed a syndicate of many of the large oil companies. Another large company was Polak and Sons, owned by Grigori Polak and his sons Saveli (Shevaḥ) and Michael. Prominent in the field of technology was the chemical engineer Arkadi Beilin, who worked in a number of companies, including those of the Rothschilds, and after marrying the daughter of Grigori Polak joined Polak and Sons. In 1913–14 the share of the Jewish companies in kerosene production in Baku reached 44% while the proportion of Jews occupied in oil products marketing was even greater.

Jewish communal and Zionist institutions followed in the wake of the economic development. According to the 1897 census there were 2,341 Jews in Baku, of whom the majority were Caucasian with some from European Russia. The Jewish population continued to increase after the 1917 revolution through the influx of Mountain Jews who, deprived of their traditional livelihoods in the villages, moved to the towns. In 1926 the Jewish population numbered 21,995 (19,583 of European origin, 1,985 Caucasian Jews, and 427 Georgian Jews). According to the 1959 census it numbered 29,179 (3% of the total) in Baku and its vicinity. In 1970 the Jewish population was estimated at 80,000 (60,000 of European origin, the rest Tati, Georgian, and Bukharan). Most of the non-European Jews reside in the old part of the city. The European, Tati, and Georgian communities each have their synagogue. The Tati synagogue is the oldest and largest. While *matzot* can be obtained on Passover, ritually slaughtered meat is not available. Two local rabbis signed *Izvestia's* denunciation of the Sinai Campaign (on November 29, 1956). It appears that since that time the European Jewish community has been deprived of its rabbis who have not been replaced.

A conference in Baku of Zionists from the Caucasus, 1917. Tel Aviv, Raphaeli Collection.

Bibliography: J. J. Chorny, *Sefer ha-Massa'ot* (1884); H. Landau, in: *YIVO Bleter*, 14 (1939), 269–85. [S.K.]

°**BAKUNIN, MIKHAIL ALEKSANDROVICH** (1814–1876), Russian revolutionary, one of the founders and theoreticians of Anarchism. While he was imprisoned in the Petropavlovsk fortress in St. Petersburg (1851) he wrote his "Confession" *(Ispoved)*, in which he reproached the Polish independence leaders Adam *Mickiewicz and Joachim Lelewel for their favorable attitude to Jews. Through his conflict with *Marx, *Hess, and other Jewish Socialists at the end of the 1860s, Bakunin's hatred of the Jews grew beyond bounds. In his answer to a letter of Moses Hess in the review *Le réveil* (Oct. 20, 1869), he referred to the Jews as a nation of exploiters, entirely opposed to the interests of the proletariat. At another time he stated that the Jews were more dangerous than the Jesuits and constituted a real power in Europe: they reigned despotically over commerce and banking, and had taken over three-quarters of German journalism as well as a large portion of the press in other countries. Bakunin considered Marx as the modern Moses, a typical representative of the Jewish people.

Bibliography: Yu.M. Steklov (pseud.), *Mikhail Aleksandrovich Bakunin*, 3 (Rus., 1927), 346–50, 388–404; Silberner, in: HJ, 14 (1952), 93–106; W. Polonski (ed.), *Materialy dlya biografii M. Bakunina* ... 1 (1923). [Ed.]

°**BAKY, LÁSZLÓ** (1898–1946), Hungarian anti-Semitic politician. Baky was a leading member first of the Hungarian National Socialist Party and later of *Szálasi's *Arrow-Cross Party, which he left temporarily in 1941. In March 1944 he became undersecretary of state in the Ministry of the Interior, in charge of Jewish affairs. He presided at the secret meeting of April 4, 1944, where the arrangement for the deportations of Jews was drawn up, and was one of those who directed the setting-up of ghettos and the deportations. On June 29–30, 1944, Baky attempted an unsuccessful fascist coup against Horthy. Nevertheless, he retained his position until September 5. Later he was one of the founders of a group of right-wing deputies who sought to give a legal framework to the Szálasi regime. Baky was sentenced to death by a Budapest People's Court and executed in 1946.

Bibliography: J. Lévai, *Black Book on the Martyrdom of Hungarian Jewry* (1948), passim; A. Geyer, *A magyarországi fasizmus zsidóüldözésének bibliográfiája, 1945–1958* (1958), index. [B.V.]

BALAAM (Heb. בִּלְעָם), son of Beor, soothsayer from *Aram invited by *Balak, king of Moab, to curse Israel who were then encamped in the steppes of Moab across the Jordan from Jericho before entering the Promised Land (Num. 22:1–24:25).

Biblical Account. Before summoning Balaam, Balak expressed his fears of Israel to the Midianites: "Now this horde will lick clean all that is about us as an ox licks up the grass of the field." Although warned by God in a vision that he should not accede to Balak's request, after further urging by Balak's emissaries, with God's permission to proceed, Balaam set off for Moab riding on his she-ass. The Bible relates that as he was riding, an angel sent by the Lord stood in the way with his sword drawn in his hand. The ass perceived him and three times swerved aside, refusing to continue even though Balaam beat her with his stick; finally granted the gift of speech, she reproached Balaam for his ill-treatment. Balaam's eyes were opened, he saw the angel, and affirmed his obedience to God's will. On Balaam's arrival at Ir-Moab, Balak met him and reproached him for his reluctance to come. Balaam, however, told him that he had not the power to speak freely but could utter only the words that God put into his mouth. Balak took Balaam up to a high place, Bamoth-Baal, from where he had a view of the people of Israel. On Balaam's instructions seven altars were prepared, and a bull and a ram were offered up on each altar. However, to Balak's surprise, Balaam pronounced a blessing on Israel instead of a curse. The same procedure was twice repeated (at Sadeh-Zophim on the summit of Pisgah, and at the peak of Peor), but each time Balaam's words took the form of an ever-more commendatory blessing, culminating on the third occasion with the famous description,

How fair are your tents, O Jacob,
Your dwellings, O Israel!
Like palm groves that stretch out,
Like gardens beside a river,
Like aloes planted by the Lord,
Like cedars beside the water . . .

which foretold the subsequent triumph of Israel over its enemies.

On Balak's expressions of anger at Balaam's words, Balaam delivered a further oracle which told that "A star rises from Jacob," and of the victory over Moab and Edom. To this he added predictions of the downfall of Amalek and the Kenites, and eventually of Asshur (Assyria) and Eber.

Balaam then returned home. He was later slain in a battle between Israel and the Midianites (see below). The episode impressed itself deeply on the memory of Israel, as signifying an act of God's grace toward the people. It is referred to in Deut. 23:4–5; Josh. 13:12; 24:9–10; Neh. 13:2; Micah 6:5) and in later literature. [Ed.]

Critical View. Balaam is one of the most enigmatic characters in the Bible. That the tradition about him is both ancient and reliable is suggested by the preservation of his Oracles, which are archaic in language and content. As in the case of the poem in Exodus 15 and the prose narrative in Exodus 14, or the poem in Judges 5, and the prose in Judges 4, there is much preserved in the prose narratives on Balaam which does not appear in the poems. Most scholars have divided the Balaam chapters between the J and E documents, but it is now increasingly clear that Numbers 31, which also deals with the history of Transjordan and is usually attributed to the P document, may go back to the same stratum of oral tradition. The inconsistencies which exist in the prose narrative may well go back to real or apparent contradictions in the original body of tradition. As noted by O. Eissfeldt, the references to the elders of Midian in Numbers 22:4, 7 confirm other evidence in Numbers 25:17–18 and Numbers 31, that Moab was at that time under a Midianite protectorate of some kind; which ties in well with Genesis 36:35. In view of the confirmation of many details of the Balaam narrative and Oracles by evidence from archaeological sources, there is no longer room for the former skepticism. Balaam's name is of a

Balaam, on his way to curse the Israelites, confronted by the angel of the Lord. Miniature from a Byzantine Octateuch, 11th century. Rome, Vatican Library, Vat. Gk. 747.

well-attested Northwest-Semitic type and is identical with the name of the Canaanite town of Bileam (I Chron. 6:55) or Ibleam (Josh. 17:11, Judg. 1:27) in western Manasseh. The original form of the name was *Yabil-ʿammu,* probably meaning "May the clan lead," similar in formation to *Yabil-Werra* and to *Bildad* for *Yabil-Dadda* (W. F. Albright, 1927). His home is given in the prose tradition (Num. 22:5) as "Pethor, on the River [in] the land of the people *[bene]* of *ʿAmmô,*" which should be corrected to *ʿAmau* (Albright, 1950). *ʿAmaw* appears in a late 15th-century Egyptian inscription as the name of a land which supplied wood from the forests of Nahren (Aram Naharaim) for the royal chariot. It is also mentioned twice in the Idrimi stele of the same period in the genitive *(māt Amae)* as the name of a district of Alalakh in northern Syria. A. S. Yahuda's identification with Egyptian *ʿ3mw* ("Semitic nomads") is impossible. As pointed out by S. Daiches the role played by Balaam as a professional diviner reminds one strongly of the Old Babylonian *bārûm.* It is interesting to note that a cuneiform seal of a West-Semitic *bārûm,* named *Manum,* was found in a 13th-century level at Beth-Shean. The Mari texts provide much earlier information about the role of the *bārûm* in warfare; he was expected to forecast the military future, and for this purpose one or more members of the guild accompanied an army. An interesting new illustration has recently been pointed out: in an official cuneiform letter of about 1400 B.C.E. from Gezer (unrecognized until 1943) seven "oxen" are mentioned in connection with a military expedition; they are clearly to be explained as a sacrifice similar in function to the three sacrifices of seven bullocks and seven rams in the prose narrative of Balaam. The name of Balaam's father, Beor, is almost certainly a shortened (hypocoristic) form of a name like *Baʿal-ram* ("Baal is exalted"). This name was common in that general period and there are various other shortened forms of it, such as *Baʿalraya* (late 13th century B.C.E.) and *Baʿraʾ* (eighth cent. B.C.E.).

To judge from the texts of the Oracles, which were probably delivered, at least in part, by Balaam and remembered by word of mouth, Balaam was for some time a convert to Israel's faith during Moses' later life in Transjordan, and this temporary conversion is reflected by the content of the Oracles. Ultimately, however, Balaam defected from Yahwism, worked against it, and was finally slain in a battle between Israel and the Midianites (Num. 31:8, 16). Since he had been induced to lend his prestige to the Midianite-Moabite coalition against Israel (Num. 22:5ff.), his end was poetic justice. The Oracles of Balaam show, when the masoretic and Samaritan recensions are carefully compared and with the aid of older versions of the masoretic text, that in the original written text there was a strong tendency to omit all vowel letters, as in Canaanite (Ugaritic and linear alphabetic) and later Phoenician. Final vowel letters, which came into use in Israel about the ninth century, are often lacking in the Hebrew and especially in the Samaritan text of the Oracles, even where poetic rhythm requires a long vowel. These and other facts indicate a date for the oldest written form of the Oracles about the time of David (Albright, 1944). The oral composition of the Oracles may now be dated much earlier. While the Balaam Oracles are not in the earliest style of the Mosaic period (Albright, 1968), the evidence of style and grammar points to a date between the Song of Moses in Exodus 15 and the Song of Deborah, on the one hand, and the 11th century B.C.E. on the other. The fact that the style of Balaam is rather later than that of both Miriam and Deborah is perhaps to be explained by the background of the guild of *bārū,* where Mesopotamian models were more familiar than Canaanite traditions. The triumphal epic form of the other two poems was also quite different from the oracular form of Balaam. In no case can one separate such passages as Numbers 24:24 from the irruption of the Sea Peoples in the late 13th century B.C.E. (or possibly the beginning of the 12th). The text has hitherto been misunderstood because the introductory colon of the verse is missing in Hebrew and is preserved only in Greek, where we must probably read "Gog" instead of "Og," especially in view of the fact that the strange Hebrew "Agag" in Numbers 24:7 appears as "Gog" in the Greek text. There is no longer any doubt that Gog is the same word for "barbarian" which appears as *Gagaya* in Amarna and as *Ggy* in Ugaritic. This is only one out of many illustrations of the significance of the Oracles of Balaam for the origin of much of the eschatological terminology of Ezekiel 38:39. In later eschatology the influence of the Balaam Oracles is well-known. [W.F.A.]

In the Aggadah. Some rabbis inflated the importance of Balaam. They saw in him one of "The seven prophets who prophesied to the peoples of the world" (BB 15b; "God raised up Moses for Israel and Balaam for the peoples of the world"—Num. R., 20:1; Tanḥ., Balak, 1), and believed that in many respects he was greater than Moses: "No prophet like Moses had risen in Israel, but such a one has risen among the peoples of the world. Who is he? Balaam the son of Beor. But there is a difference between the prophecy of Moses and that of Balaam. Moses did not know who spoke with him but Balaam knew. . . . Moses did not know when [God] would speak with him till he was addressed by Him, whereas Balaam knew. . . . Moses did not speak with Him till he had stood up . . . whereas Balaam spoke with Him as he was falling" (Sif. Deut. end). They explained Balaam's power to curse by the fact that he could ascertain the exact hour of God's anger (Av. Zar. 4a–b; Sanh. 105b). Others, however, identified him with Elihu the son of Barachel the Buzite (Job 32:2) for Barachel means "God has blessed"; the epithet "Buzite" is derived from *"buz"* ("contempt"), hence it teaches that Balaam's prophecy was of a low order and contemptible (T.J. Sot. 5:8, 20d). Some rabbis saw in him an immoral figure: "An evil eye, a haughty spirit and a proud soul" are the marks of the disciples of "Balaam the Wicked" (Avot, 5:19). Balaam was one of Pharaoh's counselors and it was he who advised that the male children should be cast into the Nile (Sanh. 106a); and in the end he wished "to uproot an entire people for naught and for no reason" (Num. R. 20:1; Tanḥ. Balak, 1) and counseled Balak how to destroy them. It was this act which caused the departure of the holy spirit from the gentile peoples (*ibid.*), and since then prophecy was preserved in Israel alone. There is no basis for the theory put forward by some scholars that Balaam in the *aggadah* represents Jesus (but see *Jesus in Talmud and Aggadah). [Y.M.G.]

In Islam. Balaam is not mentioned by name in the Koran, and it is not even clear that he is intended by the inference in Sura 7 (lines 174–5), as read by several interpreters of the Koran, historians, and authors of *Legends of the Prophets (Qiṣaṣ al-Anbiyā).* The verses read: "Relate to them of him to whom we gave our signs, and who turned away from them; and Satan followed him, and he was of those who were led astray. But had it been our will, we would have exalted him through our signs, but he clung unto the earth, and followed his desire. He is like the dog who puts forth his tongue whether you chase him away or let him alone. That is the parable of the people who deny our signs. Tell them this history, that they may consider it."

It is the general opinion that the inference is to Balaam who acquiesced to the request of Balak, king of Moab (Num. 22–24), as related in the Bible and Jewish legend, and who was responsible for the going astray of the children of Israel with the daughters of Moab (*ibid.* 25). However, some interpret Muhammad's words as referring to *Umayya ibn Abī al-Salt, Muhammad's contemporary and competitor as a prophet who was sent to the Arabs. Others maintain that the inference is to Luqmān, an Eastern sage, to whom Muhammad dedicated Sura 31. Nevertheless, B. Heller presents a number of convincing arguments against this identification. [H.Z.H.]

In the Arts. Balaam is regarded with general disfavor in Hebrew literature, and it was exclusively in Christian literature that he was accorded any importance—mainly because he was alleged to have predicted the advent of Jesus (Num. 24:17). By the Middle Ages, however, Balaam had become a figure of fun, and it is in this spirit that he is portrayed in such medieval miracle plays as the *Ordo Prophetarum,* the Chester and Stonyhurst cycles, and the *Mistère du Viel Testament.* Such treatment destroyed Balaam's literary standing, although the 16th-century French Christian kabbalist Guillaume Postel resurrected the "prophet of the Gentiles" in some of his patriotic visionary works. One rare later treatment is the dramatic poem *Balaam* (1787) by C. Davy.

Among artists, portrayal of the subject was largely influenced by Christian theological interpretation of Balaam's prophecy, that "a star rises from Jacob," which was seen as a prefiguration of the star of Bethlehem that according to the Gospels appeared to the Magi. Balaam is represented as a bearded figure wearing an antique tunic and mantle and a Phrygian cap or oriental turban. Such early representations are found in third and fourth century catacombs. The figure of Balaam is sometimes placed next to the Madonna and Child and often appears on sarcophagi. In Byzantine art, Balaam is depicted as one of the foretellers of Jesus in a fresco on Mount Athos. There are similar treatments in the West, such as the 12th-century "Tree of Jesse" window at Chartres and the 14th-century ceiling of St. Michael's at Hildesheim. Balaam appears with his ass in a late 12th-century bronze door at Monreale and a 14th-century facade at Orvieto. There are other representations in illuminated manuscripts and incunabula, such as the Luebeck Bible (1494). Artists who painted the subject include Taddeo Zuccari (1529–66), Luca Giordano (1632–1705), and Rembrandt. There are also cycles covering Balak's command, his sacrifice, and Balaam and Balak on Mount Peor; a notable example of this is the illuminated Bible of San Paolo Fuori le Mura (c. 850). Others occur in later baroque Bible illustrations. [Ed.]

Bibliography: Daiches, in: *Hilprecht Anniversary Volume* (1909), 60–70 (reprinted in *Bible Studies* (1950), 110–9); W. F. Albright, *Yahweh and the Gods of Canaan* (1968), index; idem, in: JAOS, 35 (1915), 386ff.; idem, in: AJSLL, 44 (1927), 31–32; idem, in: JBL, 63 (1944), 207ff.; idem, in: BASOR, 118 (1950), 15–16, 20;

Yahuda, in: JBL, 64 (1945), 547ff.; R. T. O'Callaghan, Aram Naharaim (1948), 119ff.; Eissfeldt, in: JBL, 87 (1968), 383ff.; T. H. Gaster, *Myth, Legend, and Custom in the Old Testament* (1969), 303–10; Ginzberg, Legends, 3 (1947), 354–82, 410–1; 6 (1946), 123–5; Y. Kaufmann, Toledot, 1 (1954^2), index; Urbach, in: *Tarbiz*, 25 (1955/56), 272–89; M. Z. Segal, *Mevo ha-Mikra*, 1 (1967), 115–6; IN ISLAM: Ṭabarī, *Tafsīr*, 9 (1337 H), 83–84; Nīsābūrī, *ibid.*, 76ff.; Tabarī, *Ta'rikh*, 1 (1357 H), 308, 310; Thalabī, *Qiṣaṣ* (1356 H), 139–202; I. Eisenberg (ed.), Kisā'ī, *Qiṣaṣ* (1922), 227–9; A. Geiger, *Was hat Mohammed aus dem Judenthume aufgenomanen?* (1833), 176–7; Heller, *Shorter Encyclopaedia of Islam*, s.v. *Luqmān;* Vajda, in: EIS[3].

BALABAN, BARNEY (1887–1971), U.S. motion picture executive. Balaban was born in Chicago and worked at the age of 12 as a messenger for Western Union. In 1908, he formed a company which developed a chain of cinemas, introducing raked floors, comfortable seats, balconies, and air-conditioning. Paramount Pictures bought a two-third interest in the business and in 1936 Balban was elected president of Paramount Pictures. Under his guidance it invested in television and pioneered the wide screen. Balaban was active in Jewish affairs. [L.G.]

BALABAN, MEIR (Majer; 1877–1942), historian of Polish Jewry. The Balaban family had been active in Lemberg and Zolkiew (Zholkva) as Hebrew printers from 1830 to 1914. After studying law at the university of his native Lemberg, Balaban taught for seven years in Galician towns in schools founded by Baron de Hirsch. He later returned to the university, devoting himself to the study of history. In those years he was active in the Zionist movement and served on the editorial staff of the Zionist weekly *Wschód* ("The East"). After graduating, Balaban continued teaching religion in various secondary schools. During World War I he served as a military chaplain in Lublin and as an official of Jewish affairs for the Austrian occupation authorities in Poland. From 1918 to 1920 he was head of the Jewish High School in Częstochowa. From 1920 to 1930 he directed the rabbinical seminary Taḥkemoni in Warsaw, and from 1928 lectured on Jewish history at the University of Warsaw, becoming associate professor in 1936. He was one of the founders of the Institute for Jewish Studies in Warsaw (1927) and served as its director for several years.

Meir Balaban, founder of Polish-Jewish historiography.

Balaban published about 70 historical studies and about 200 short papers and reviews in various periodicals. He was justly considered the founder of the historiography of Polish Jewry, especially of its communal life. His studies were based on a wealth of source material found in government and municipal archives, as well as in the archives of the Jewish communities. His first book, *Zydzi lwówscy na przełomie XVI–XVII wieku* ("The Jews of Lvov [Lemberg] at the Turn of the 17th Century," 1906), received a prize from the University of Lemberg. In this work he displayed a thorough grasp of his subject, scholarly meticulousness, and a capacity for presenting lucidly the various aspects of life in great detail. These characteristics also mark his second monumental work *Dzieje żydów w Krakowie i na Kazimierzu, 1304–1868* ("A History of the Jews of Cracow," 2 vols., 1931–36). His book on the Jews of Lublin, *Die Judenstadt von Lublin* (Berlin, 1919), is a vivid survey of history of the Jews in that city. A series of articles on the organization of the Jewish communities in old Poland reflect his vast legal knowledge. These papers first appeared in Russian, but were later revised and published again in Polish in the monthly publication of the Jewish community of Warsaw (1937–39). To the 11th volume of *Istoriya yevreiskogo naroda* ("A History of the Jewish People," 1914), of which he was a coeditor, Balaban contributed an exhaustive study of the Council of the Four Lands. Collections of his articles and treatises, containing the biographies of rabbis, doctors, and communal leaders, and the history of printing houses, blood accusations, and the Karaites in Poland, were published in German, Polish, and Yiddish. Balaban contributed over 150 articles to the Russian-Jewish Encyclopedia *Yevreyskaya Entsiklopediya.* Particularly significant are his studies on the Shabbatean and Frankist movements, summarized in his *Le-Toledot ha-Tenu'ah ha-Frankit* ("History of the Frankist Movement," 2 vols., 1934–35). He also wrote a book on the synagogues and other antiquities of the Jews in Poland, *Zabytki historyczne Żydów w Polsce* ("Jewish Antiquities in Poland," 1929). A summary of the history of the Jews in Poland until the end of the 18th century is contained in the second and third volumes of a textbook entitled *Historja i literatura żydowska* ("The History of the Jewish People and its Literature," 1925; first of 3 vols. also in Hebrew, 1931); most of the historical chapters are included in *Beit Yisrael be-Polin* (vol. 1, 1928). His studies of the history of the Jews in 19th-century Poland are confined to Galicia. From the outset of his scholarly career Balaban applied himself to collecting a bibliography on the history of the Jews in Poland; his first prizewinning publication in this field appeared in Polish in 1903. The first part of his own bibliography for the years 1900–30 appeared in 1939. When the Nazis overran Poland, Balaban refused to flee. He died in Warsaw in November 1942 before the liquidation of the ghetto and was thus vouchsafed burial in the Jewish cemetery.

Bibliography: N. M. Gelber, in: *Gazit*, 5 nos. 9–10 (1943), 7–10; R. Mahler, in: *Yidishe Kultur*, nos. 8–9 (1943), 56–59; H. Zeidman, in: S. K. Mirsky (ed.), *Ishim u-Demuyyot be-Ḥokhmat Yisrael* (1959), 223–74, includes bibliography. [R.MA.]

BALAGUER, town in Aragon, northeastern Spain. At the time of the Christian reconquest at the end of the 11th century, several Jews already owned houses and land there. In 1280 Pedro III ordered an inquiry regarding violations of the interest laws by the local Jews. Efforts by the counts of Urgel to restore the community after the *Black Death and the anti-Jewish disorders accompanying it in 1348–49 were apparently successful. During the persecutions of 1391 the Jews in Balaguer took refuge in the citadel, but were forced to leave by King John I. In 1416 Alfonso V, after suppressing a revolt, imposed a fine of 45 pounds of silver upon the Jews of the town, notwithstanding the fact that the community had become impoverished through migration to the estates of the nobility and the conversions to Christianity at the time of the *Tortosa disputation. New settlers were not granted exemption from taxes. The community existed until the expulsion of the Jews from Spain in 1492.

Bibliography: J. M. Pou y Martí, *Historia de la ciudad Balaguer* (1913), 47ff.; 62, 116, 330; Baer, Urkunden, 1 pt. 1 (1929), index; Vendrell, in: *Sefarad,* 3 (1943), 137ff.; Piles, *ibid.,* 10 (1950), 179; Baer, Spain, 1 (1961), 115, 212. [H.B.]

BALAK (Heb. בָּלָק), son of Zippor; the first king of Moab whose name is known. Balak's memory survived only because of his ill-fated association with *Balaam, whom he had hired to curse Israel after the latter's victories over the

Balak, king of Moab, before one of the series of seven altars built at the direction of Balaam (Num. 23). Balaam is seen on the left. Miniature in a 12th-century Byzantine Octateuch. Rome, Vatican Library, Vat. Gk. 746.

Amorites (Num. 22–24; et al.). In Joshua 24:9 (cf. Judg. 11:25) he is described as having fought Israel. Micah 6:5 refers to the frustration of Balak's design as exemplifying God's kindness to Israel. No satisfactory explanation of the name has so far been advanced.

For bibliography, see *Balaam. [Ed.]

BALANCE (Heb. פֶּלֶס, *peles;* Isa. 40:12; Prov. 16:11; cf. *pilles* "make straight, level," Isa. 26:7; Ps. 78:50; synonomous by synecdoche with pair of scales, *moznayim* —Lev. 19:36; Isa. 40:12; Jer. 32:10; et al.—and with balance beam קָנֶה, *kaneh;* Isa. 46:6). The equal arm balance of the ancient Near East (as distinguished from the unequal arm balance with counterpoise introduced by the Romans) consisted of a horizontal beam moving freely on a central fulcrum, with the object to be weighed and standard weights suspended at opposite ends in pans or on hooks. In its earliest form the beam was suspended at its center by a cord held in the hand, and equilibrium was estimated visually. Under the eighteenth dynasty in Egypt larger balances were developed, supported by an upright frame resting on the ground. From the frame was suspended a weighing plummet (Heb. *mishkolet,* II Kings 21:13; Isa. 28:17) which could be compared with a pointer extending downward at right angles from the pivotal point of the beam.

The principle of the balance was probably derived from the yoke of the burden bearer (Isa. 9:3), with its two equalized loads. The earliest mechanical balances were small, and were used only for objects of high value in relation to their size, e.g., gold, silver, jewels, spices, etc. The oldest known example is a stone balance beam from the pre-dynastic Gerzean civilization in Egypt. Weights from the Sumerian and Indus civilizations show that the balance was in use there in the third millennium. Hand balances and large standing balances are illustrated in many Egyptian reliefs and wall paintings, the former also on a Hittite relief from Carchemish and the latter on one from 9th century Assyria. From ancient Israel a crude sketch of a man holding a pair of scales, incised on the base of a scale-weight of the seventh–sixth centuries B.C.E., is extant (unpublished). Biblical references to the balance are both literal (Lev. 19:36; Jer. 32:10; Ezek. 45:10; et al.) and figurative (Isa. 40:12; Ps. 62:10; Job 6:2; et al.). Fraudulent weighing is repeatedly denounced in the Bible, i.e., substandard weights (Amos 8:5), different sets of weights for buying and selling (Deut. 25:13), and false balances (Hos. 12:8; Prov. 11:1). An effort to standardize weights by marking them with an official shekel sign, attributable on archaeological grounds to Josiah, may have been accompanied by regulations for the construction and operation of balances. In later times the levites were made custodians of "all measures of quantity and size" (I Chron. 23:29).

See also *Weights and Measures.

Bibliography: A. B. Kisch, *Seals and Weights* (1965), 26–78; F. G. Skinner, *Weights and Measures* (1967); EM, 4 (1962), 540–3 (incl. bibl.). [R.B.Y.S.]

BALANJAR, town of the *Khazars located between *Bāb al-Abwāb and *Samandar in the north Caucasus region. It was formerly identified by Artamonov (see bibliography) with the ruins of Endere near Andreyeva, or as the site of present-day Buinaksk, but is now placed by him south of Makhachkala, where the remains of a town have been found (communication of November 1964). Balanjar is mentioned in Arabic sources as existing in the seventh and eighth centuries. Originally the name appears to have been an ethnic designation. A Pehlevi source cited by the historian al-Ṭabarī (vol. I, 895–6) states that in the time of the Sassanid ruler Khusraw Anūshirwān (531–79) a tribal group within the West Turkish empire was called Balanjar. According to the historian al-Masʿūdī (*al-Tanbīh,* 62), Balanjar was formerly the Khazar capital. It was the principal objective of the Arabs after they reached the Caucasus in 641 or 642. In 652 the Muslims attempted unsuccessfully to besiege Balanjar, then a fortified town, and were heavily defeated nearby. In 723, during the second Arab-Khazar war, it was captured by al-Jarrāḥ ibn Abdallah al-Ḥakamī, and is occasionally mentioned later.

Bibliography: Dunlop, Khazars, index; M. I. Artamonov, *Istoriya Khazar* (1962), index. [D.M.D.]

BALASSAGYARMAT, city in northern Hungary. Jews were living there, probably in an organized community, before 1663. The poll of 1725 mentions only one Jewish family, in 1746 there were 19 families, and by 1778, 47 families. The synagogue, destroyed in a fire in 1776, was rebuilt, and in 1769 a burial society (*ḥevra kaddisha*) was established. In 1840 construction of a synagogue was begun on the former site. Completed in 1868, it was an impressive building. The Jewish population numbered 839 in 1825, 2,401 in 1920, and 1,720 (13.9%) in 1941, remaining approximately the same in 1944. Rabbis of Balassagyarmat include Judah Leb Engel (from 1730); Benjamin Ze'ev Wolf *Boskowitz; Mordecai and Ezekiel *Banet; and successive members of the Deutsch family (Aaron David, Joseph Israel, and David) from 1851 to 1944. After the outbreak of World War II the Jews in Balassagyarmat were segregated in a ghetto and subsequently sent to forced labor camps. Following the German invasion (1944) they were deported to *Auschwitz, where about 1,500 Jews from Balassagyarmat perished. Only 220 survivors returned in 1945. Many subsequently moved away or emigrated, mainly after 1956. In 1968 the former Orthodox congregation, which had included the congregations of Nógrádpatak and Dejtar, numbered approximately 70 persons. The Great Synagogue, heavily damaged in the war, was sold in 1953; one remains in use, although the congregation has no rabbi.

Bibliography: M. Stein, *Magyar Rabbik*, 2 (1906), 7–8; 4 (1908), 3–4; 5 (1909), 5–6; M. Ladányi, *Nógrád és Hont vármegye* (1934), 139; MHJ, 5, pt. 1 (1959), 510. [L.H.]

BALÁZS, BÉLA (1884–1949), Hungarian author and motion picture critic. Balázs was born in Szeged and studied at Budapest. After the revolution in 1918–19 he moved to Vienna and Berlin and finally settled in the U.S.S.R., where he lectured at the Moscow Film Academy. He returned to Hungary after World War II and taught at the Budapest Academy of Dramatic Art. Balázs' interest in philosophy is evident in all his writing. His books include *Halálesztétika* ("Aesthetics of Death," 1907), *A tragédiának metafizikus teóriája* ("Metaphysical Theory of Tragedy," 1908), and *Dialógus a dialógusról* ("Dialogue about the Dialogue," 1913). He also wrote poems and several plays, of which, *A kékszakállu herceg vára* ("Duke Bluebeard's Castle," 1912), provided the libretto for an opera by Béla Bartók. Bartók also set to music Balázs' fairy-tale ballet, *A fából faragott királyfi* ("Wooden Prince," 1912). Balázs was a pioneer of motion picture criticism, and wrote two books on film technique (1952, 1961). The Hungarian communist regime established a prize in his name for work in cinema art.

Bibliography: E. Gyertyán, *Balázs Béla és a film* (1958); A. Komlós, in: B. Balázs, *Az én utam* (1960), introd. [J.Z.]

BALBO, MICHAEL BEN SHABBETAI COHEN (1411–after 1484), rabbi and poet in Candia (Crete). Although Candia was his permanent home, he is occasionally mentioned in nearby Canea and three sermons which he preached there in 1471, 1475, and 1477, are extant (Vatican Ms. 305). Moses *Capsali in a responsum of 1458 refers to him as one of the communal leaders. Balbo's signature is found on many ordinances enacted in Candia between the years 1468 and 1479. He wrote letters and poems to many contemporary scholars, one poem dealing with the capture of Constantinople by the Turks in 1453. Balbo took issue with scholars on various topics; in his polemic against Moses Ashkenazi (who was known by the curious name of *Esrim ve-Arba*—"Twenty-Four") he vigorously attacked Ashkenazi for his rejection of the doctrine of metempsychosis. Balbo also wrote on behalf of the Candia community on such topical subjects as the ransoming of captives and *agunot*. These writings are valuable material for the history of his time. In a colophon at the end of a manuscript of the *Sefer Mitzvot Katan*, which he copied, he refers to the deaths of his son Isaiah and of Isaiah's son Michael in 1484.

Bibliography: Freimann in: *Zion*, 1 (1936), 185–207; E. S. Artom and M. D. Cassuto (eds.), *Takkanot Kandyah*, 1 (1943), index; Urbach, in: KS, 34 (1958/59), 101; Malachi, in: KS, 41 (1965/66), 392f.

[Y.Ho.]

BALCON, SIR MICHAEL (1896–), British film producer. He began film-making in 1920 and during the next 40 years was responsible for many outstanding British films which opened new avenues in realism and humor. Among them were *The Captive Heart, It Always Rains on Sunday, Passport to Pimlico, Kind Hearts and Coronets, The Lavender Hill Mob, Whisky Galore, The Cruel Sea, Dunkirk,* and *The Long and the Short and the Tall.* His book *Michael Balcon Presents . . . A Lifetime of Films* was published in 1969. He was knighted for his services to the industry in 1948. Balcon was born and educated in Birmingham. He founded Gainsborough Pictures Ltd. in 1928, was director of production for Gaumont-British, director and producer at Ealing Studios, and chairman of British Lion Films.

[Ed.]

°**BALFOUR, ARTHUR JAMES, EARL OF** (1848–1930), British statesman, signatory of the *Balfour Declaration. In 1902, he became prime minister, but was defeated in the general election of 1905. He returned to Asquith's coalition as first lord of the admiralty in 1915 and served as foreign secretary in Lloyd George's coalition government, formed in December 1916. Balfour began to take an interest in the Jewish question in 1902–03, when *Herzl conducted negotiations with Joseph *Chamberlain, the British colonial secretary, and with Lord Lansdowne, the foreign secretary, regarding Jewish settlement in areas adjoining Palestine, such as the Sinai Peninsula. In 1906 he met Chaim *Weizmann in Manchester and was impressed by his personality. Balfour's interest in Zionism revived and grew more intense during World War I, when he became foreign secretary, in which capacity he signed the Balfour Declaration of Nov. 2, 1917. He was enthusiastically welcomed by the Jewish population when he visited Palestine in 1925 to attend the dedication ceremony of the Hebrew University in Jerusalem, at which he delivered the opening address. His anthology, *Speeches on Zionism* (1928), was translated into Hebrew. The motivation behind Balfour's attraction to Zionism has been the subject of conjecture. Being a rationalist it is doubtful whether religious tradition was a factor although his biographer Blanche *Dugdale introduces his Scottish ancestry with its Old Testament tradition. A more likely theory is that of Leonard Stein, who points out that Balfour had spoken out against the persecution of the Jews saying "The treatment of the race has been a disgrace to Christendom" and he saw the establishment of a Jewish state as an historic act of amends. Streets were named after him in Jerusalem, Tel Aviv, and Haifa. There is also a Balfour Forest at Ginnegar, and a moshav, *Balfouriyyah, founded in 1922 in the Jezreel Valley. The Balfour family continued the

Lord Balfour with Chaim Weizmann during his visit to Palestine in 1925.

tradition of interest in the Zionist movement. Robert Arthur Lytton 3rd Earl of Balfour (1902–1969), his nephew, supported *Youth Alivah. In 1939 he offered the family estate and home, Whittingham, to a Jewish committee as a training school for refugee boys and girls from Germany. Balfour's niece and biographer Blanche Dugdale worked in the political department of the Jewish Agency in London as a close collaborator of Chaim Weizmann.

Bibliography: B. Dugdale, *A. J. Balfour*, 2 vols. (1939); K. Young, *A. J. Balfour* (1963); L. Stein, *Balfour Declaration* (1961).

[EH/ED]

BALFOUR DECLARATION, British declaration of sympathy with Zionist aspirations. The declaration was communicated to Lord Rothschild by Arthur James *Balfour, in his capacity as foreign secretary, in the following letter, dated November 2, 1917, and made public a week later:

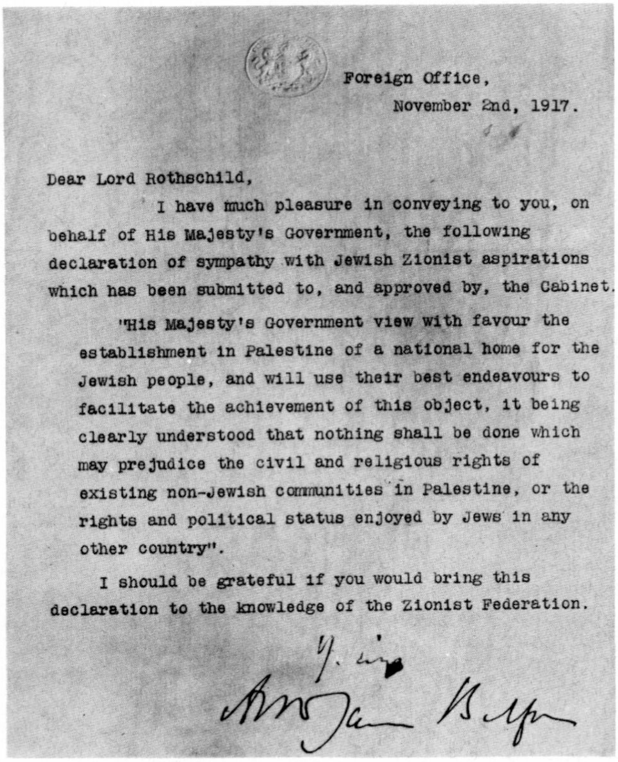

Foreign Office,
November 2nd, 1917.

Dear Lord Rothschild,

I have much pleasure in conveying to you, on behalf of His Majesty's Government, the following declaration of sympathy with Jewish Zionist aspirations which has been submitted to, and approved by, the Cabinet.

"His Majesty's Government view with favour the establishment in Palestine of a national home for the Jewish people, and will use their best endeavours to facilitate the achievement of this object, it being clearly understood that nothing shall be done which may prejudice the civil and religious rights of existing non-Jewish communities in Palestine, or the rights and political status enjoyed by Jews in any other country".

I should be grateful if you would bring this declaration to the knowledge of the Zionist Federation.

Figure 1. The Balfour Declaration, now in the British Museum, London.

Balfour's name has been associated with the Declaration, as he warmly advocated it; but the final decision rested with the war cabinet, which gave its approval as a considered act of policy.

Alone of the Great Powers, Great Britain had before World War I shown in a practical form a sympathetic interest in the Zionist movement. This was evidenced by the consideration given in 1902 to Herzl's request for facilities for Jewish colonization in the Sinai Peninsula (*El Arish), and by the offer, in 1903, of a tract of land for an autonomous Jewish settlement, under Zionist auspices, in British East Africa (*Uganda Scheme). Though nothing came of these projects, British contacts with the Zionist Organization before the war form part of the background to the Balfour Declaration. At the outbreak of war in 1914, one of the members of Asquith's cabinet was Herbert *Samuel. Though he had never made it known, he was in sympathy with the Zionist movement. When Turkey entered the war on the side of the Central Powers, Samuel at once began advocating the idea that Great Britain and the Jews had a common interest in the detachment of Palestine from the Turkish Empire, and that Britain should encourage Zionist aspirations. The foreign secretary Sir Edward Grey showed some interest in Samuel's ideas, which, from the outset, had a strong appeal to another leading member of the Asquith government, *Lloyd George.

Very early in the war, Chaim *Weizmann, already a prominent, though not yet a commanding, figure in the World Zionist Movement, had begun what he described as a political reconnaissance. Starting from the same premises as Samuel, he likewise became convinced that Great Britain and the Zionists were natural allies. In September 1914 he engaged the interest of C. P. *Scott, the influential editor of the *Manchester Guardian* and a close personal friend of Lloyd George. Through Scott, Weizmann was brought into contact with Samuel in December 1914 and discovered that Samuel's views were substantially identical with his own. In January 1915 Samuel arranged for him to meet Lloyd George. Weizmann was further encouraged by receiving an assurance of sympathy with the Zionist cause from the ex-prime minister Balfour, on whom he had made a lasting impression in an interview in 1906. Weizmann's scientific gifts enabled him to render important services to the Admiralty and the Ministry of Munitions; these brought him to the notice of Lloyd George, who became minister of munitions in the spring of 1915. They also kept him in contact with Balfour who, about the same time, joined the Asquith cabinet as first lord of the admiralty. In 1915–16 Weizmann interested leading public figures, among them Lord Robert Cecil, in Zionist associations. In his talks with them he laid the foundation of opinion favorable to the Zionist cause when it was later brought into the sphere of practical politics. At the end of 1914 Weizmann's efforts had been strengthened by the arrival in London of Nahum *Sokolow who, unlike Weizmann, had the status and authority of a member of the Zionist executive. In 1917 Sokolow played a prominent part in the events leading to the Balfour Declaration, exercising during that decisive year an important influence in contacts and negotiations and undertaking missions to Paris and Rome, where his diplomatic talents were used to the marked advantage of the Zionist cause.

The Zionists gained an important supporter early in 1916, when Samuel attracted the interest of Sir Mark Sykes, one of the government's most influential advisers on eastern affairs. Sykes' education in Zionism was continued by his contacts with Moses *Gaster and, later in 1916, with Aaron *Aaronsohn. He believed that it was essential for Great Britain to establish a firm foothold in Palestine and that an understanding with the Zionists could help to strengthen Great Britain's position as a partner in the Anglo-French condominium in Palestine envisaged by the *Sykes-Picot Agreement of May 1916. From other quarters the government had been advised that an appeal to Zionist sentiment might be an effective means of enlisting the sympathy of American Jews, who, mainly because of their antipathy for Czarist Russia, were inclined, on the whole, to look coldly on the Allied cause. In the spring of 1916 Grey had gone so far as to suggest to the French and Russian governments, but without success, that the Allies should jointly issue a declaration pledging them to take Zionist aspirations in Palestine into account in the postwar settlement.

By the end of 1916 the combined efforts of Weizmann and Samuel, energetically seconded by C. P. Scott, resulted in the emergence in the inner circle of policy makers of an influential body of opinion among the circle favorably

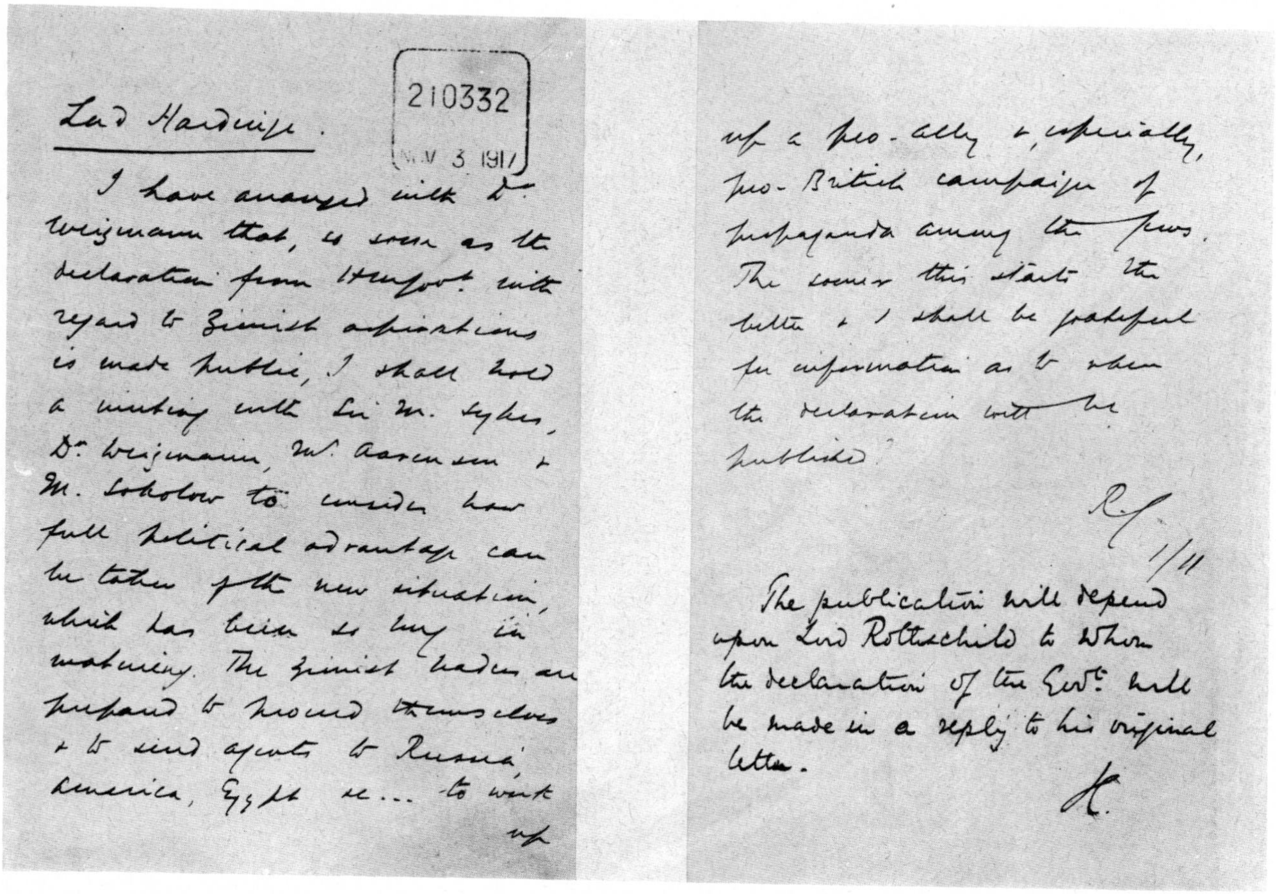
210332
NOV 3 1917

Lord Hardinge.

I have arranged with Dr. Weizmann that, as soon as the declaration from Balfour with regard to Zionist aspirations is made public, I shall hold a meeting with Sir M. Sykes, Dr. Weizmann, Mr. Aaronsohn & Mr. Sokolow to consider how full political advantage can be taken of the new situation, which has been so long in maturing. The Zionist leaders are prepared to proceed themselves & to send agents to Russia, America, Egypt &c... to work up a pro-ally &, especially, pro-British campaign of propaganda among the Jews. The sooner this starts the better & I shall be grateful for information as to when the declaration will be published?

R.G. 1/11

The publication will depend upon Lord Rothschild to whom the declaration of the Govt. will be made in a reply to his original letter.

H.

Figure 2. Memo from Sir Ronald Graham, head of the Eastern department of the British Foreign Office to Lord Hardinge of Penshurst, the permanent undersecretary, November 1, 1917, inquiring about the date of publication of the Balfour Declaration. Lord Hardinge's reply says: "The publication will depend upon Lord Rothschild to whom the declaration of the Govt. will be made in a reply to his original letter." London, Public Record Office.

disposed to the idea of some link between Great Britain and the Zionists. This, however, had not crystallized into a decision or a British pledge to the Zionists. The change of government in December 1916, with Lloyd George becoming prime minister and Balfour foreign secretary, and the decision taken about the same time in favor of a British invasion of Palestine, told strongly in favor of the Zionists. Lord Milner, an important member of Lloyd George's war cabinet, became a strong supporter of a pro-Zionist policy. Through James Malcolm, the London representative of the Armenian liberation movement, Weizmann met Sykes at the end of January 1917. At a meeting with Zionist leaders immediately afterward (February 7, 1917), attended also by Herbert Samuel, Sykes opened the negotiations which were to lead to the Balfour Declaration.

Two months later the British government began to display an active interest in the idea of a Jewish National Home or, as it was sometimes phrased, a Jewish Commonwealth in Palestine, under British protection. They were actuated, apart from sentiment, by the idea that by expressing a strong desire for British control of Palestine, the Jews could in some measure strengthen the British case for abandoning the Anglo-French condominium projected in the Sykes-Picot Agreement and for substituting, instead, some form of British control. To this was added, after the March revolution in Russia, the hope that an appeal to Zionist sentiment among the Russian Jews might win their sympathy to the Allied cause and thus help to stem the pacifist tide to sweep revolutionary Russia out of the war. The influential body of Anglo-Jewish opinion represented by the Conjoint Foreign Committee, composed of representatives of the *Board of Deputies of British Jews and the *Anglo-Jewish Association, was strongly anti-Zionist. But when, in June 1917, an adverse vote at the Board of Deputies discredited the committee, the way was opened for invitation by Balfour to Weizmann to arrange for the drafting of a pro-Zionist declaration for consideration by the British government. Sokolow prepared the document, but not until early in September did the matter come before the war cabinet. Because a pro-Zionist policy was vehemently opposed by Edwin *Montagu, a Jewish member of the government, it was decided to delay a decision and in the meantime, to consult President Wilson. The American reply was noncommittal, and the whole question was shelved. As a result, however, of Weizmann's personal appeal to Lloyd George, it was restored to the agenda and reconsidered early in October. Once more the war cabinet temporized, deciding to consult President Wilson again and also to invite the views of representative Jews, both Zionists and anti-Zionists. This time Wilson did not discourage the proposal; influenced, it would seem, by the representations of the American Zionist leader, Louis *Brandeis, he now agreed to the proposed declaration.

By this time the arguments in favor of a pro-Zionist pronouncement had been strengthened in three respects. The situation in Russia was rapidly deteriorating, and the British government hoped that, if the Russian Jews were convinced that an Allied victory would open the way for the fulfillment of Zionist aspirations, they would exert themselves to keep Russia in the war or, should this be impossible, would try to prevent Russian resources, especially the produce of the Ukraine, from being exploited by the Germans. Though the war cabinet was thinking first and foremost of Russia, it also believed that a pro-Zionist

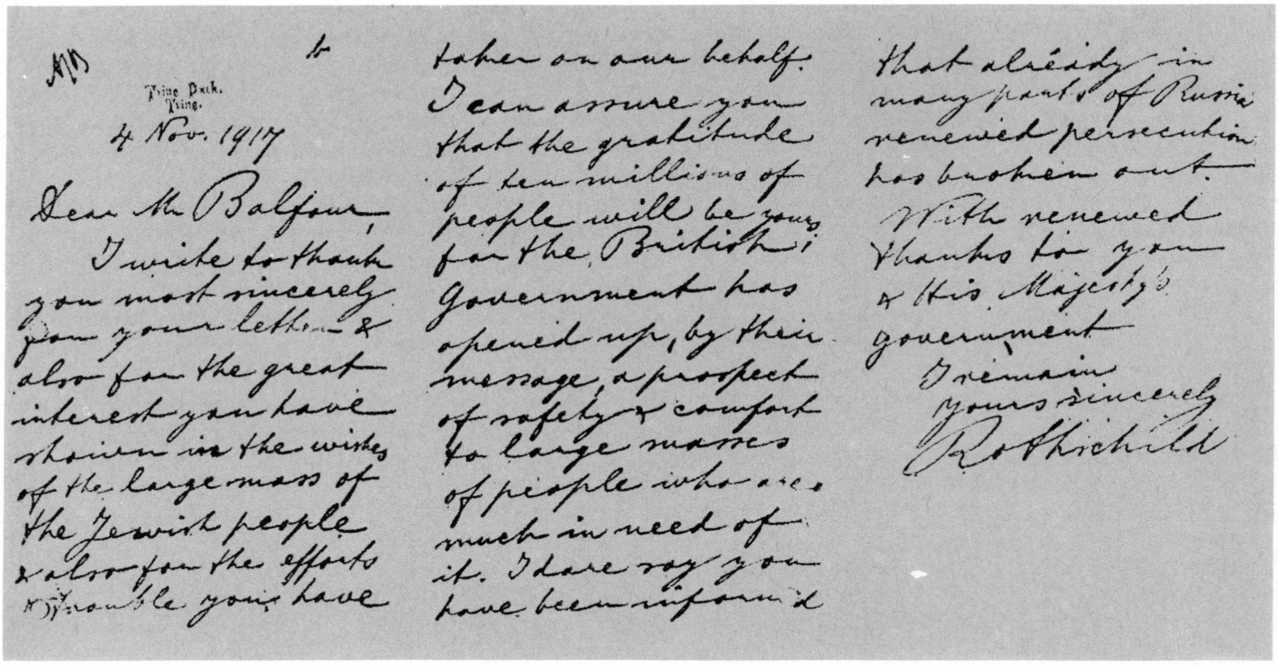

Tring Park. Tring.

4 Nov. 1917

Dear Mr Balfour,

I write to thank you most sincerely for your letter & also for the great interest you have shown in the wishes of the large mass of the Jewish people & also for the efforts & trouble you have taken on our behalf. I can assure you that the gratitude of ten millions of people will be yours, for the British Government has opened up, by their message, a prospect of safety & comfort to large masses of people who are so much in need of it. I dare say you have been informed that already in many parts of Russia renewed persecution has broken out. With renewed thanks to you & His Majesty's government I remain yours sincerely Rothschild

Figure 3. Lord Rothschild's reply to Balfour, November 4, 1917, following his receipt of the Balfour Declaration. It reads: "Dear Mr. Balfour, I write to thank you most sincerely for your letter and also for the great interest you have shown in the wishes of the large mass of the Jewish people and also for the efforts and trouble you have taken on our behalf. I can assure you that the gratitude of ten millions of people will be yours, for the British Government has opened up, by their message, a prospect of safety and comfort to large masses of people who are in need of it. I dare say you have been informed that already in many parts of Russia renewed persecution has broken out. With renewed thanks to you and His Majesty's Government, I remain, Yours sincerely, Rothschild."

pronouncement might have a good effect in the United States, where a large section of the Jewish population was reported to be apathetic about the war. Last, there were rumors that the Germans were courting the Zionists and might come out first with a pro-Zionist declaration, if the British government failed to act promptly. Thus, the question which the British government considered in the autumn of 1917 was not whether it should work, in the eventual peace settlement, for the fulfillment of Zionist aspirations, but the narrower question whether it should there and then make a public pledge to the Zionists. It is, therefore, not surprising that the propaganda value of the Declaration was strongly emphasized by Balfour in commending it to the war cabinet and securing final approval by that body on October 31, 1917. But though the decision to authorize the Declaration was reached strictly on grounds of expediency, other motives and ideas were involved. Speaking in London in 1949, Field Marshal Smuts, who had been a member of the war cabinet at the time of the Declaration, said that a powerful argument in its favor had been that "it would rally Jewry on a worldwide scale to the Allied cause." But, he continued, moral and religious motives reinforced the political considerations.

The Declaration was approved on April 24, 1920, at the Allies' conference at *San Remo and incorporated in the Mandate on Palestine conferred upon Britain by the League of Nations on July 24, 1922. The struggle over its practical implementation lasted throughout the entire 30 years of British rule in Palestine.

Bibliography: L. Stein, *Balfour Declaration* (1961); B. E. C. Dugdale, *Balfour Declaration* (1940); A. J. Balfour, *Opinions and Arguments* (1928[2]), section 5; K. Young, *A. J. Balfour* (1963), ch. 17; C. Weizmann, *Trial and Error* (1950), chs. 15, 18, and index; C. Sykes, *Crossroads to Israel* (1965); Parzen, in: *Herzl Year Book*, 5 (1963), 309–50; Barzilai, in: *Zion* 33, no. 3–4 (1968), 190–202, with Eng. summary; Goldblatt, in: AJHSQ, A. T. Mason, *Brandeis, A Free Man's Worship* (1946), ch. 29 (for the American involvement).

[L.J.S.]

BALFOURIYYAH (Heb. בַּלְפוּרִיָּה), moshav in the Jezreel Valley, Israel. The settlement was founded on Nov. 2, 1922, north of Afulah, on land owned by the American Zionist Commonwealth Federation. Some of the founders were immigrants from the United States, the others from Eastern Europe. In 1968 Balfouriyyah's economy was based on field and garden crops, cattle, and poultry. The moshav's name refers to the date of its founding which was the fifth anniversary of the *Balfour Declaration.

[E.O.]

BALI, ABRAHAM BEN JACOB (second half of the 15th to the beginning of the 16th century), Karaite author and physician living in Turkey. Bali was a pupil of the Rabbanite R. Shabbetai b. Malchiel ha-Kohen. Although disagreeing with the Rabbanites, Bali refers with respect to the contemporary Rabbanite scholars Mordecai *Comtino, Moses ha-Yevani Capuzato, and Solomon "Sharvit ha-Zahav" in his works. They include *Iggeret Issur Ner Shabbat*, upholding the Karaite prohibition against burning lights on the Sabbath; *Iggeret ha-Kohanim*, on the status of Rabbanites of priestly descent who become Karaites; *Perush Inyan Sheḥitah*, a commentary on the chapter dealing with ritual slaughter in *Aaron b. Elijah of Nicomedia's *Gan Eden;* a commentary on al-*Ghazālī's *Maqāṣid al-Falāsifa*, in which Bali used a Hebrew translation of it and followed the commentary of Moses Narboni, which he much admired; and *Perush al Ḥamishah Perakim min ha-Haysharah le-Abu Nasr*, a commentary on the first five chapters of al-*Fārābī's *Logic*, translated into Hebrew under the title *Iggeret le-Petiḥat Sifrei ha-Higgayon*.

Bibliography: Mann, Texts, 2 (1935), 1420; Danon, in: JQR, 15 (1924/25), 312–3; Steinschneider, in: HB, 20 (1880), 96–97; A. Neubauer, *Beitraege und Documente Zur Geschichte des*

Karaeertums (1866); J. Gurland, *Ginzei Yisrael* (St. Petersburg, 1886). [I.M./Ed.]

BALI, MOSES BEN ABRAHAM, Karaite poet, physician, and *ḥakham* in Cairo in the late 15th and early 16th centuries. Two volumes of his liturgical poems have been preserved in the *Firkovich collection in Leningrad: the first, *Sefer Zeraḥ,* completed in 1489, consists of 224 *piyyutim* arranged in the order of the weekly lessons; the second, *Taḥkemoni,* contains 237 *piyyutim* for Sabbaths and festivals.

Bibliography: Fuerst, Karaeertum, 2 (1865), 294; Geiger, in: WZJT, 3 (1837), 443, no. 9–10. [I.M./Ed.]

BALIDEH (al-Balideh), MOSES (15th century), Yemenite scholar. Balideh was the author of more than ten works on diverse subjects, mostly in the form of commentaries and expositions of rabbinic sayings. With the exception of his Midrash on the last chapter of Proverbs, *Sharḥ Eshet Ḥayil,* all his works are in manuscript in the British Museum (Margoliouth, Cat, no. 1101). Although he enjoyed a distinguished reputation, his works did not achieve wide circulation among Yemenite Jewry and were therefore almost unknown to succeeding generations. They include a commentary on the *Midrash Yelammedenu,* a commentary bearing a marked resemblance to the *Midrash ha-Gadol* in respect to sources, arrangement, and tenor. Balideh wrote a commentary concerning the ten items recounted as having been created on the (first) Sabbath at twilight (Avot 5:6) in addition to commentaries on some works of Maimonides.

Bibliography: Ratzaby, in: KS, 28 (1952/53), 260, 263, 268, 277–8; Y. L. Naḥum, *Mi-Ẓefunot Yehudei Teiman* (1962), 206–22. [Y.R.]

BALINT, MICHAEL (1896–), psychoanalyst. Born in Hungary, Balint, in constant partnership with his wife, devoted a lifetime of research and practice to the development of psychoanalysis as a science. Entering the field while it was still young and taking on form, Balint spent much time studying psychoanalytic technique, as well as the patient's response to various forms of therapy. This work is discussed in his *The Doctor, His Patient, and the Illness* (1957), and *Psychotherapeutic Techniques in Medicine* (1961).

Balint also devoted much research to understanding the mechanisms of human sexuality, concentrating in large part on sexual perversions and their relation to neurotic and psychotic symptoms. In addition to writing *Problems of Human Pleasure and Behavior* (1957), he edited many anthologies on the subject of sexuality. [Ed.]

BALKH, town in northern Afghanistan (within medieval Khurasan). Balkh was formerly the stronghold of Jewish settlements in Afghanistan. According to Persian and Muslim traditions, it was founded after the destruction of Jerusalem by Nebuchadnezzar (586 B.C.E.), who is said to have settled the exiled Jews there. It was to Balkh, according to Muslim tradition, that the prophet Jeremiah fled, and where the prophet Ezekiel was buried. According to the Muslim historian al-Ṭabarī, another Jewish prophet with the unidentifiable name of *SMY* conducted religious disputations with Zoroaster in Balkh. Reference by Arab geographers to a *Bāb al-Yahūd* ("Gate of Jews") in Balkh, and to *"al-Yahūdiyya"* ("Jewish territory" or "Jewish town") provide additional evidence that a large Jewish settlement existed there. The name *al-Yahūdiyya* or *al-Yahūdān-al Kubrā* ("the Great Jewry") was, however, later euphemistically changed to *al-Maymana* ("the 'auspicious' town") since the term *"al-Yahūdiyya"* was rejected by the Muslims. It was at Balkh that the sectarian *Ḥiwi al-Balkhī was born in the ninth century. The Jews of Balkh were forced to maintain a public garden. Maḥmūd of Ghazna (1034) imposed special taxes on the Jews of the town, stipulating, however, that not more than 500 *dirham* should be accepted from them. The Jewish community continued well into the 13th century, when a Jewish merchant from Balkh named Khawāja Rashīd al-Dīn al-Ḥakīm went from Khurasan to India. However, the community was evidently destroyed during the Mongol invasions.

Bibliography: Frye, in: EIS[2], 1 (1960), 1000–02 (includes bibliography). [W.J.F.]

BALLAGI (formerly **Bloch**), **MÓR** (1815–1891), linguist and theologian. Born in Inocz, Hungary, he attended yeshivot and studied mathematics at Pest, continuing in Paris and Tuebingen. In 1843 he became a Protestant. During the Hungarian revolution in 1848, Ballagi served as secretary to General Görgey. He taught Hebrew, Greek, and biblical exegesis at the theological academy of the Reformed Church at Kecskemét from 1851, and in Pest from 1855 to 1877. While still a Jew Ballagi published a monograph, *A zsidókról* (1840), advocating the emancipation of Hungarian Jewry and the establishment of a rabbinical college. He translated into Hungarian the Hebrew prayer book (1841), the Pentateuch (1840–41), and the Book of Joshua (1842), and wrote a primer of the Hebrew language, *A héber nyelv elemi tankönyve* (1856; 2nd edition revised by Ignaz Goldziher in 1872), *Renaniana* (Hg., 1864), and biblical studies (*Bibliai tanulmányok,* 2 vols., 1865). Ballagi also compiled a dictionary of the Hungarian language, and published a Hungarian-German, German-Hungarian dictionary.

Bibliography: S. Imre, *Emlékbeszéd Ballagi Mór rendes tagról* (1893); S. Csekey, *Budapesti Református Theológiai Akadémia története* (1955); Scheiber, in: *Református Egyház,* 7 (1955), 520. [Al.Sch.]

BALLARAT, country town in Central Victoria, Australia. After the gold rush in 1851 a number of Jews went to Ballarat and in 1853 there was a *minyan* on the gold fields on the High Holidays and in 1859 there were 347 male Jews in the town. A Jew, Charles Dyte, took a leading part in the diggers' revolt in 1854 (known as the Eureka Stockade) against unjust government licensing. Later he became mayor of Ballarat. In 1855 a small synagogue was dedicated, the congregational president being Henry Harris. D. Isaacs was first minister, *shoḥet,* and teacher, followed in 1864 by S. Herman, I. M. Goldreich (1868), B. Lenzer (1905), M. Rosenthal (1922), L. Goren (1926), and Z. Mandelbaum (the last resident rabbi of Ballarat who ministered until 1942). A more commodious building, including rooms for a minister's residence and a Hebrew day school, was erected on land granted by the government in 1861. A *mikveh* was built and a burial plot consecrated. A Philanthropic Society, founded in 1857, was affiliated with the *Anglo-Jewish Association. In 1908 the congregation separated into two factions and the Central Hebrew Congregation was formed, with M. Levy as minister, but lasted only four years. In these early days Ballarat was regarded as the center of Orthodox Judaism in Australia.

Two Ballarat Jews achieved distinction in the arts: Nathan Spielvogel, a well-known short-story writer, and Abbey Alston, an artist whose works are found in most Australian national galleries. With the drift to Melbourne, the Ballarat community declined. In 1969 the Jewish population had dwindled to about 10–15 families.

Bibliography: N. F. Spielvogel, in: *Australian Jewish Historical Society,* 1, pt. 3 (1940), 92–94; 1, pt. 6 (1941), 206–7; 2, pt. 6 (1946),

350–8; L. E. Fredman, *ibid.*, 4, pt. 5 (1956), 279–80; L. M. Goldman, *ibid.*, 4 pts. 7 and 8 (1958), 440–1, 452–3, 459–60, 465–6, 477–8; D. J. Benjamin, *ibid.*, 4, pt. 3 (1960), 134.

[SH.G.]

BALLIN, ALBERT (1857–1918), German shipping magnate and politician. He was the 13th child of a Danish Jew who settled about 1830 in Hamburg, where he opened a wool dyeing shop. Later his father established a passenger shipping business, which young Ballin expanded after his father's death. During the large-scale emigration of the 1880s, Ballin, as chief passenger agent for the English Carr Line, adapted the company's vessels for the transportation of steerage passengers. After keen competition with Hapag (the Hamburg-America Line), Germany's leading shipping line, the two companies merged in 1886; Ballin became head of the passenger department. Hapag rapidly grew into one of the world's foremost shipping lines. This success was due mainly to Ballin's foresight and his setting

The West German postage stamp commemorating the centenary of Albert Ballin's birth.

of new standards of speed and comfort. His capacity for negotiation and compromise enabled him to form the first trans-Atlantic shipping conference, called the North-Atlantic Steamship Lines Association. In 1901 he established the International Mercantile Marine Company, in cooperation with Morgan's shipping interests. Kaiser William II frequently turned to him for counsel on economic matters, and he undertook the organization of food supplies for the blockaded Reich and set up its central purchasing agency. He had failed before the war in his effort, together with Sir Ernest *Cassel, to create a basis for a German-British agreement on naval armaments. During World War I, Ballin was the only member of the Kaiser's circle who remained unbaptized. Ballin advocated a speedy termination of hostilities, even without territorial gains. These views conflicted with those of the military and reduced his influence with the Kaiser. In 1918 Ballin was entrusted with negotiations for an armistice and peace preparations. On Nov. 9, revolution broke out in Germany. Kaiser William II fled the country and Ballin committed suicide.

Bibliography: P. F. Stubmann, *Mein Feld ist die Welt* (1960[2]); Kaiser Wilhelm II, *Ereignisse und Gestalten aus den Jahren 1878–1918* (1922), 122–8; L. Cecil, *Albert Ballin: Business and Politics in Imperial Germany 1888–1918* (1967); E. Rosenbaum, in: YLBI, 3 (1958), 257–99.

[J.O.R.]

BALLIN, JOEL (1822–1885), Danish engraver and painter. He was born at Vejle, Jutland, and studied painting in Copenhagen, and engraving at Leipzig and Paris. His first painting was exhibited in 1841. Ballin lived from 1846 in Paris and London where he produced a series of reproductions of the paintings of Ostade and Protais and of some English and French artists. In 1861 he was awarded the gold medal of the Paris Salon. On his return to Denmark in 1883 Ballin was commissioned to engrave the works of prominent Danish artists. His "Procession on Simḥat Torah in the Synagogue of Copenhagen" is owned by the Copenhagen Jewish community.

Bibliography: *Dansk Biografisk Leksikon*, 2 (1933), 54–55.

[JU.M.]

BALLIN, SAMUEL JACOB (1802–1866), Danish physician, best known for his efforts to combat Asiatic cholera. Born and educated in Copenhagen, he was early recognized as an expert in the treatment of Asiatic cholera and in 1831–32 traveled abroad by royal order to study the disease further. His published findings became a valuable source of information concerning the disease. During the great cholera epidemic in Copenhagen (1853) he was appointed chief physician of the cholera hospital and a member of the Board of Health. In honor of his achievements, he was appointed a member of the Royal Medical Society and given a professorship. Ballin was an active member of the National Liberal Party and an enthusiastic supporter of a Scandinavian union. Ballin was physician of the Jewish community for a number of years. [N.Ko.]

BALLY, DAVICION (1809–1884), merchant and banker, a leader of the Sephardi community of Bucharest and its president for some time. Bally, who was self-educated, promoted *Haskalah among Sephardi Jewry in Rumania, tending to favor assimilation into Rumanian culture. In 1836 he was appointed treasurer of the police, a position which he held on an honorary basis for ten years; at the same time he was sympathetic to the national revolutionary movement in Walachia. He used his connections with the government circles to prevent the arrest of the would-be revolutionaries in 1848, and after its outbreak, sided openly with the abortive revolution. Bally called for administrative reforms in the Sephardi community and for new methods of educating Jewish youth. He emphasized the study of Rumanian in the community school and also proposed the establishment of an educational framework for girls. However his proposals and reforms encountered strong opposition; some were not accepted at all, while the remainder were short-lived. Bally fought against anti-Semitism and published articles in defense of the Jews in the press; as a result of his intervention the governor *(Caimacam)* of Walachia withdrew a sharply anti-Jewish work from circulation in 1858. When anti-Jewish policy was enforced after 1866 by the government led by the former revolutionaries of 1848, Bally unsuccessfully attempted to influence them to abandon it. In 1882 Bally went to Ereẓ Israel to spend his last years there.

Bibliography: M. Schwarzfeld, in: *Anuar pentru Israeliţi*, 9 (1886), 1–29.

[EL.F.]

BALMES, ABRAHAM BEN MEIR DE (c. 1440–1523), physician, philosopher, translator, and grammarian. His grandfather, also called Abraham de Balmes (d. 1489), mentioned repeatedly in the royal records between 1463 and 1480, was court physician to King Ferdinand I of Naples (1472). Balmes was born in Lecce, southern Italy, and obtained doctorates in medicine and philosophy at the University of Naples in 1492 by special permission of Pope Innocent VIII. In 1510 when the Jews were expelled from Naples, Balmes appears to have gone to northern Italy. Later he became personal physician to Cardinal Domenico Grimani, who was deeply interested in Hebrew literature. Under Grimani's auspices, Balmes translated the works of a number of medieval Arabic authors from their Hebrew

A page on Hebrew script from Abraham de Balmes' grammar, *Mikneh Avram*, Venice, 1523.

versions into Latin. These included the *Liber de Mundo* (On the Quadrant) of Ibn al-Hayham (11th century), the *Epistola expeditionis* based on a philosophical work by Avempace, Geminus' work on astronomy under the title "Introduction to Ptolemy's Almagest," *Averroes' "Epitome of Aristotle's Organon," "Middle Commentary on the Topics," and on "Sophistical Refutation," part of *De Substantia Orbis*, and logical questions by Averroes and other Arabic authors. The translation of the "Long Commentary on Aristotle's Posterior Analytics" published in Venice about 1520 seems to have been part of a more ambitious project which was to have included, besides other versions, an original philosophical work of his own *(Liber de demonstratione Abrami de Balmes)*, no longer extant. Balmes' Averroistic materials were incorporated in the standard 16th-century edition of Aristotle, published in Venice in 1560. The Christian printer Daniel *Bomberg urged Balmes to write his famous Hebrew grammar *Mikneh Avram*. This appeared together with a Latin translation entitled *Peculium Abramae* in Venice at the end of 1523, some months after the author's death. The final chapter (on biblical accent marks) was completed by a fellow physician, Kalonymus b. David. In this work Balmes relied upon the grammarians *Ibn Janaḥ and Profiat *Duran. He mentioned Plato's *Cratylus* (which deals with semantics)—an indication of his interest in the philological conceptions of the Greek philosophers. His grammatical teachings lean too heavily on the theory of logic, and because of this and his attempt to use Latin philology to explain various aspects of Hebrew grammar, he exerted only limited influence upon Hebrew grammatical literature. Balmes' attempt to codify the Hebrew syntax, to which he devoted a special section of his book *(Sha'ar ha-Harkavah ve-ha-Shimmush)* is, however, of some significance. The work was greatly used by Christian Hebraists of the ensuing period. According to Gedaliah *ibn Yaḥya, who was present at Balmes' funeral, he had taught officially at the University of Padua, and many of his gentile students followed his bier.

Bibliography: D. Amram, *Makers of Hebrew Books in Italy* (1909), 169–172; Gedaliah b. Joseph Yaḥya, *Shalshelet ha-Kabbalah* (Amsterdam, 1697), 49b–50a; C. Roth, *Jews in the Renaissance* (1959), 76; F. Secret, *Les Kabbalists chrétiens de la Renaissance* (1964), 107; N. Ferorelli, *Abramo de Balmes ebreo di Lecce e i suoi parenti* (offprint from *Archivio Storico per le Province Napoletane*, 31 (1906), 632–54); Steinschneider, Uebersetzungen, 972–3 and index s.v. *Abraham de Balmes*.

[Jo.H./Ed.]

BALOGH, THOMAS, BARON (1905–), British economist whose main interest lay in planning, development, and labor economics. Born in Budapest, he worked as a Rockefeller Fellow at Harvard University, 1928–30. In 1931 he joined the economic staff of the League of Nations and settled in London, working as an economist until 1939, when he became associated with the Oxford University Institute of Statistics. From 1955 to 1960 he taught in England and in the United States. Balogh served as a consultant to various United Nations agencies and foreign governments, including India, Malta, Greece, Peru, and Turkey. In 1964 he became an economic adviser to the British Labor government under Harold Wilson. He received a life peerage in 1968. Balogh's publications include: *Dollar Crisis* (1949), *Unequal Partners* (1963), *Planning for Progress* (1963), and *Economics of Poverty* (1966).

[J.O.R.]

BALSAM, spice designated in the Bible by various names: בֹּשֶׂם *(bosem)*, בֶּשֶׂם *(besem)*, צֳרִי *(ẓori)*, נָטָף *(nataf)*, and in rabbinic literature as קְטָף *(kataf)*, בַּלְסָם *(balsam)*, אפּוֹבַּלְסָמוֹן *(appobalsamon)*, אֲפַרְסְמוֹן *(afarsemon)*; *afarsemon* occurs most frequently in the Talmud and Midrash, designating the perfume extracted from the sap of the *Commiphora opobalsamum*. It was the only tropical, and the most expensive, spice grown in Ereẓ Israel. According to Josephus (Ant., 8:174–5), balsam was originally brought to Ereẓ Israel by the Queen of Sheba as one of the gifts included in the "hundred and twenty talents of gold, and of spices very great store, and precious stones; there came no more such abundance of *bosem*" (I Kings 10:10). Generally, in the Bible, *bosem* signifies spices of all kinds. Yet in the Song of Songs, in the verses "I have gathered my myrrh with my *bosem*" (5:1) and "the beds of *bosem*" (5:13; 6:2), the reference is to balsam alone. At present the tree grows wild in the valley of Mecca where it is called *beshem*. Many strains of this species are found, some in Somalia and Yemen. As a perfume it is hardly used today. It serves in the Orient as a healing agent for wounds and as an antidote to snakebite and the sting of scorpions. Apparently, the *ẓori* of the Bible also signifies some remedy compounded of balsam sap and other ingredients. The "balm *(ẓori)* of Gilead" is mentioned as having healing properties. *Nataf* was one of the elements constituting the incense burned in the Tabernacle (Ex. 30:34) and is identified as *ẓori* in an early *baraita* dating back to the Second Temple (Ker. 6a). The word in another context designates balsam oil (Shab. 25b–26a), and this identification appears to be correct (see also *Storax). Balsam oil was most highly regarded in rabbinic literature and by Greek and Roman writers. Among the latter, Theophrastus, Strabo, Diodorus, and Pliny the Younger lavished high praise on the balsam grown in orchards near the Dead Sea.

Pliny's remarks are especially enlightening. In their struggle against the Romans, the Jews strove desperately to destroy the balsam orchards and prevent them from falling into the hands of the enemy. The Romans, however, captured them and, in his triumphal march in Rome, Titus displayed

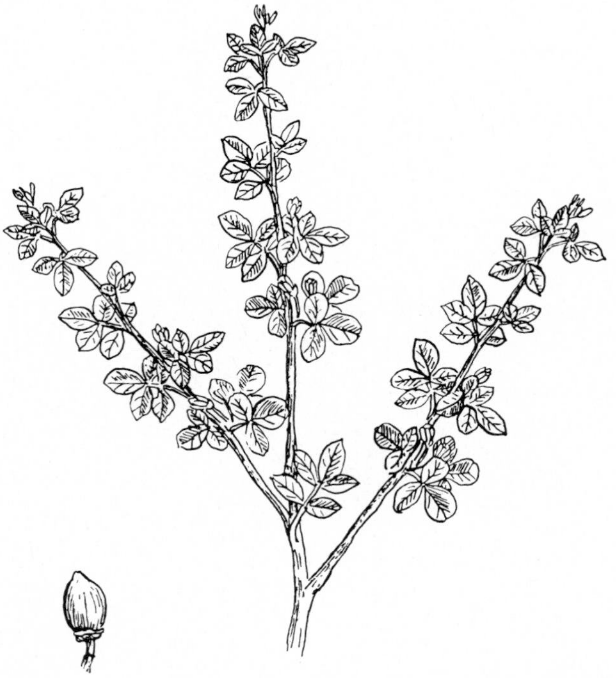

A branch of the balsam tree and the fruit on the left. Jerusalem, J. Feliks Collection.

balsam trees brought from Judea. The orchards in Jericho and En-Gedi henceforth provided the Romans with an important source of revenue (*Historia Naturalis*, 12:25). Admiration was expressed in the Talmud for the balsam "of Rabbi (Judah ha-Nasi's) household and the household of the emperor." It was the best and most expensive spice of ancient times, and accordingly Rav, the Babylonian *amora*, composed for it a special blessing: "Who creates the oil of our land" (Ber. 43a). The perfume has a pungent odor and the Midrash cites it as one of the enticements of the sinful daughters of Zion: "She would place the balsam between her heel and her shoe and, when she saw a band of young men, she pressed upon it so that the perfume seeped through them like snake poison" (Lam. R. 4:18). Tradition has it that, after King Josiah hid away the "holy oil" with which the kings of Judah were anointed, balsam oil was used in its stead (Ker. 5b). In the messianic era, the righteous will "bathe in 13 rivers of balsam" (TJ, Av. Zar. 3:1, 42c). Remains of the terraces in the hills of En-Gedi, where balsam trees once grew, can still be seen. Excavations in the vicinity have uncovered a workshop complete with its ovens and its vessels. From his investigations in the Arabian Peninsula, the German botanist Schweinfurth has reconstructed the process of balsam production. The bark of the tree was split and the sap soaked up in cotton wool. The sap was then squeezed into oil which absorbed the pungent odor. The tree is a thorn bush with trifoliate leaves, and belongs to the genus *Commiphora* which includes several species, among them myrrh.

Bibliography: Pauly-Wissowa, 4 (1896), 2836–39; O. Warburg, *Pflanzenwelt*, 2 (1916), 282ff.; Loew, Flora, 1 (1926), 299–304; J. Feliks, *Olam ha-Ẓome'aḥ ha-Mikra'i* (1968[2]), 246–8, 256–8.

[J.F.]

BALTA, city in Odessa oblast, Ukrainian S.S.R. At the beginning of the 16th century, when Balta lay on the border between Poland and Turkey, there were Jews living in both sectors of the city (in the Józefgrod quarter on the Polish side). Many of the Jewish inhabitants together with refugees who had fled there from other districts were massacred by the *Haidamacks in 1768. The city was incorporated in Russia in 1791. Balta's importance as a commercial center increased after the construction of the Odessa–Kiev railroad in 1866. The Jewish population, which numbered 8,413 in 1863, mainly engaged in wholesale and retail grain dealing, the processing of agricultural products, tobacco and soap, tanning, flourmilling, and liquor distilling. A pogrom broke out in 1882 in which over 1,200 Jewish houses and shops were pillaged; an attempt to organize Jewish *self-defense was suppressed by the police. Balta subsequently became the center of the Zionist movement in Podolia, Volhynia, and Bessarabia. The Zionist leader M. *Sheinkin served there as a government-appointed rabbi *(rav mi-ta'am)* in 1901–1904. Pogroms again broke out in the wake of the October revolution of 1905. The community was severely affected during the civil war of 1919, in which Balta repeatedly changed hands between the Bolsheviks and the troops of *Petlyura, the Ukrainian nationalist leader. Threatened by general pillage and massacre, many Jews fled to Odessa. The Jewish population, which numbered 13,234 in 1897 (57% of the total), had decreased to 9,116 by 1926 (39.6%). In 1938 they formed half of the total population of 23,000.

During World War II Balta was incorporated in the Rumanian-occupied zone of *Transnistria. The Jews who remained in Balta were confined in a ghetto, and a number were later executed. About 3,000 remained after the liberation in 1944. Fourteen hundred Jews were listed in Balta in the 1959 census. A number of small Jewish communities formerly existed in the vicinity of Balta, of which the largest were Bogopol, Krivoye Ozero, and Golovanevsk.

Bibliography: Dubnow, Hist Russ, 2 (1918), 299–304, 314–7; S. Bernfeld, *Sefer ha-Dema'ot*, 2 (1920), 296–7; M. Altman, in: *He-Avar*, 3 (1955), 60–85; 10 (1963), 83–105; *Judenpogrome in Russland*, 2 (1909), 420–4.

[Y.S.]

BALTAZAR, CAMIL (pseudonym of **Leopold Goldstein**; 1902–), Rumanian poet. Baltazar's first poems appeared in 1921 in *Sburătorul Literar*, a review edited by the Rumanian critic Eugen Lovinescu, and his contributions were published thereafter in many of the leading literary periodicals. Baltazar's poetry was written mainly before

Camil Baltazar, Rumanian poet, from a drawing by Marcel Janco.

World War II. His first collection, *Vecernii* ("Vespers"), appeared in 1923. This was followed by *Flaute de mătase* ("Silken Flutes," 1924), *Reculegeri în nemurirea ta* ("Meditation on a Friend's Immortality," 1925), *Biblice*

("Poems from the Bible," 1926), *Strigări trupești pe lîngă glesne* ("Poems on Amorous Yearnings," 1927), and *Cina cea de taină* ("The Last Supper," 1929). In his themes and mode of expression, Baltazar was, from the outset, hailed as an innovator. Though his sensitivity led to a preoccupation with human suffering, he was widely known as "the poet of light" because of the serenity with which he transfigured the most somber themes. During the early 1930s, Baltazar published an anthology of Russian prose (1930) and translations from such German writers as Thomas Mann, Franz *Werfel, and Jakob *Wassermann. His completion of this work was marked by the verse collection *Intoarcerea poetului la uneltele sale* ("The Poet's Return to his Tools," 1934). *Tărîm transcendent* ("Transcendental Realm") appeared five years later. After World War II, Baltazar became a contributor to the Rumanian Jewish newspaper *Revista Cultului Mozaic* and published further collections of his poems. Owing to the artistic dictates of the new (Communist) regime, Baltazar's "socialist" verse was largely devoid of literary value.

Bibliography: E. Lovinescu, in: *Critice*, 7 (1922), 165; 9 (1924); idem, *Istoria literaturii romîne contemporane* (1927), 415–24; G. Călinescu, *Istoria Literaturii Romîne dela Origini pînă în prezent* (1941), 753–6.

[D.L.A.Fe.]

BALTIMORE, largest city in the state of Maryland, U.S. Some 106,000 Jews lived there in 1968. Founded in 1729, Baltimore attracted only a few Jews during its first century.

Synagogues. The first synagogue was established in 1830 by some 20 members of German and Dutch extraction. With greater religious toleration and economic expansion, the Jewish population grew from about 125 in 1825 to approximately 1,000 in 1840, and to over 8,000 in 1860. By then, Baltimore had become the battleground of conflicting Jewish religious ideologies: Orthodoxy championed by Abraham *Rice, who arrived in 1840; radical Reform represented by David *Einhorn, who went to Baltimore in 1855 to serve the 13-year-old Har Sinai Congregation; and a moderate traditional religious ideology expounded by Benjamin *Szold, who settled in the city in 1859. New congregations were constantly created by ideological differences, population movements within the city, and the great influx of East European Jews, who founded numerous *landsmanshaft* synagogues. In the 1940s many small synagogues began to amalgamate and by the late 1960s there were 50 large and small synagogues. About 12,000 of the community's 21,000 families hold membership in a congregation.

Charities. The Hebrew Benevolent Society, the city's first Jewish charity organization, was founded in 1834. In 1906 most of the charity organizations and institutions sponsored by the German Jews united to form the Federated Jewish Charities. A year later the charity organizations sponsored by the East European Jews amalgamated to form the United Hebrew Charities. In 1921 the two combined into the Associated Jewish Charities. The Associated, supported in the 1960s by over 21,000 contributors, was concerned with every phase of Jewish philanthropy, as well as recreational and educational activities. Seventy percent of those served by the Associated's Sinai Hospital are non-Jews. The Jewish Community Center is one of the largest in the country. The city's Jewish Welfare Fund provides, primarily, for overseas needs, especially Israel.

Education. The first Hebrew school was opened in 1842. Ten years later a society was formed to provide education for poor and orphan children. For a long time all Hebrew schools were under synagogal auspices, but a trend toward community-operated schools started in the early 1900s. In the 1940s this trend was reversed, and by 1950 virtually all schools were again congregational. Samson *Benderly, the father of modern Jewish education in America, was the most important influence upon the advancement of Hebrew education in the city. He started his revolutionary experiments in 1900 in Baltimore and continued them there until 1910. The advancement of Jewish education in Baltimore continued under the leadership of Louis L. *Kaplan, who served as the director of the Board of Jewish Education. Over 90% of Jewish school age children in Baltimore attend Jewish schools. In addition to afternoon and Sunday schools, Baltimore has three Jewish day schools with over 1,500 students, comprising 15% of all Jewish school students, a considerably higher percentage than the national average of about 10%. The two institutions of higher Jewish learning in the city are the

Baltimore's Lloyd Street Synagogue, the oldest synagogue building in Maryland, built in 1845.

Baltimore Hebrew College, founded in 1919 by Israel *Efros, and the Ner Israel Rabbinical College, founded by Rabbi Jacob I. Ruderman in 1933. The Hebrew College has approximately 800 students in its regular and extension courses. Ner Israel has an enrollment of about 500 students from 11 countries.

In the 1850s Baltimore Jewry had a number of literary associations, as well as the first YMHA in the country, all of which were active in providing informal education for adults. The influx of East European Jews brought an increase in this type of educational activity. In the 1960s thousands of adults were attending various courses offered by the Baltimore Hebrew College and all the major synagogues in the city. The Jewish Historical Society of Maryland, founded in 1960, collects and publishes documents pertaining to Baltimore Jewish history. In 1964 the Society restored the Lloyd Street Synagogue, which was built in 1845. The synagogue was officially proclaimed a historic site by the city authorities.

Publications. Beginning with Einhorn's monthly *Sinai* in 1856, many Jewish newspapers and magazines were published in Baltimore in English, German, and Yiddish. The first American Hebrew weekly *Ha-Pisgah* appeared in Baltimore from 1891 to 1893. The weekly *Jewish Times* has appeared since 1919.

Zionism. Baltimore is an important center of Zionist activity. As early as 1847, funds were being collected for Palestine. One of America's first *Ḥibbat Zion groups was organized in the city in 1884. The only American delegate to the First Zionist Congress was a Baltimorean, Rabbi Shepsel Schaffer, and the renowned Baltimore ophthalmologist, Harry *Friedenwald, was the second president of the American Zionist Federation. Henrietta *Szold, a native Baltimorean, also began her Zionist activities in this city. In 1905 the founding convention of the Po'alei Zion in the

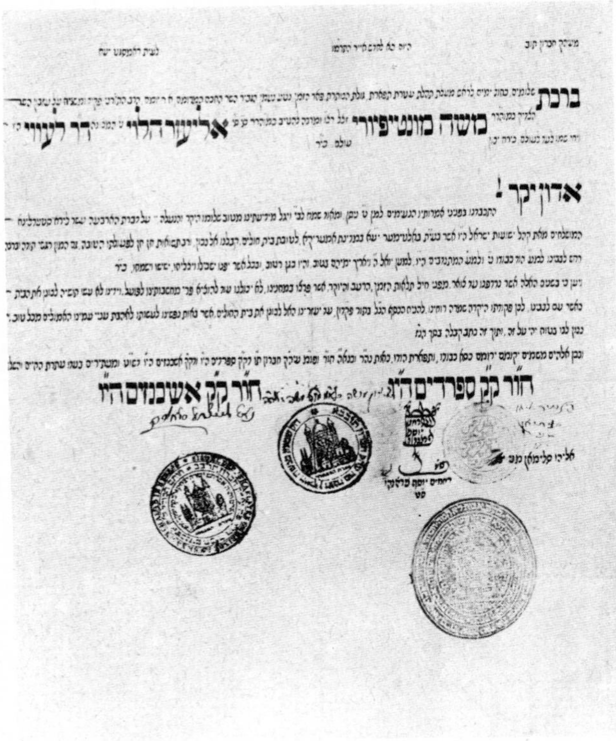

Figure 2. A letter sent in 1886 to Eliezer Levi, administrator of Sir Moses Montefiore's funds in Ereẓ Israel, by the Sephardi and Ashkenazi communities of Hebron, thanking him for a gift of 14 pounds sterling from the Baltimore community toward the building of a hospital. It explains that because of the dire conditions in Hebron, the money has been used for the relief of starvation. Cecil Roth Collection.

United States took place in Baltimore, where a strong Labor Zionist group came into being. All Zionist groups in the city are extremely active, and the largest single Jewish organization is Hadassah, with over 6,300 members.

Economics. There were only two wealthy families, the Ettings and the Cohens, among the early 19th-century Jewish settlers. While they were bankers and railroad magnates, the rest of the city's Jews were poor peddlers and small storekeepers. The German-Jewish immigrants who went to Baltimore before the 1870s were primarily from Bavaria. Most of them were poor and their main occupation was peddling. In time, many of them became leading merchants and garment manufacturers. Many of their descendants are still leaders in these enterprises, though the younger generation tends to concentrate in the professions. The East European Jews met with greater difficulties. The local immigration officers were known, even in Europe, for their unfriendly attitude to newcomers, and many immigrants were sent back. The German Jews did all they could to stop the influx of the East European Jews, and even supplied funds for those willing to return to Europe. Despite this, the recurrent waves of immigration continued unabated. While Baltimore had about 10,000 Jews in 1880, the estimate for 1924 was already 65,000. Most of the Russian immigrants became workers in the garment sweatshops owned by German Jews. Thus, the German Jews were the benefactors of the Russian Jews through the charities they controlled, at the same time that they employed them under harsh conditions. There were strikes and lockouts, including a nine-month strike in 1909 to force the manufacturers to provide workers with sewing machines so that the immigrants would not have to carry their own to the shops. Strikes eventually led to the organization of the needle trade unions. The Sonneborn firm, one of the largest men's clothing factories in the country, employing 4,000 workers, was a pioneer in 1914 in accepting collective bargaining. The immigrants lived in filthy, overcrowded houses in East Baltimore, but the ghetto was rich in cultural activities. The Zionists, the Bundists, and the Anarchists, as well as the Orthodox and the *maskilim,* all tried to enrich the immigrant's cultural life with the classes, concerts, and lectures that they sponsored. The "Russian Night School," established in 1889 by Henrietta Szold, became the prototype of night schools in the country. The Jewish Educational Alliance, established in 1913, became, with its manifold activities, a second home for thousands of newcomers. Many workers left the workshops to set up small enterprises of their own. Some of these gradually grew into large-scale businesses. Jacob Epstein, who came to Baltimore in 1881 as a poor immigrant boy, built a multi-million dollar mail-order business. He became a leading philanthropist and patron of art and contributed richly to Jewish as well as general causes.

Areas of Residence. East Baltimore, the original area of German-Jewish residence, later became the area of settlement for East European Jews. Eventually, the East European Jews moved out to better areas of the city, but at all times, Jews lived in concentrated districts. During the 1960s they resided in the northwestern part of the city and the adjoining suburbs.

General Cultural Life. Baltimore Jews have played an important role in the city's general educational and cultural life. The sculptor Ephraim Kaiser, the painter Saul Bernstein, the miniaturist Louis Rosenthal, the writer Gertrude *Stein, and the poet Karl *Shapiro are only a few of the Baltimore Jews who have won distinction in the arts.

Politics. Since 1826, when Etting and Cohen were elected to the City Council, many Baltimore Jews have served at all levels of the city, state, and federal government. Isidor Rayner served as U.S. senator from 1904 to 1912. Philip *Perlman was appointed solicitor general of the U.S. in 1947, the first Jew to hold this office. In 1954 Simon E. *Sobeloff, also from Baltimore, was appointed to the same office.

Armed Forces. In the Mexican War, Baltimore Jews formed a special unit, the "First Hebrew Guards of Baltimore." During the Civil War, Jews were as divided as the rest of the population. The antislavery group was led by Rabbi Einhorn; Rabbi Bernhard *Illowy defended the status quo; while Rabbi Szold spoke for Jewish neutrality in the struggle. Leopold *Blumenberg distinguished himself on the battlefield with the Union forces and was elevated to the rank of major general.

Jews and Non-Jews. Relations between Jews and non-Jews in Baltimore were generally amicable, but old prejudices lingered on. In the 1850s, the German anti-Semitic cry "Hep, Hep" was heard in Baltimore and

Figure 3. Temple Oheb Shalom, Baltimore, designed by Walter Gropius, 1960. Photo Sussman—Ochs, Baltimore.

Jews lived in fear when the city was under the rule of the anti-immigrant "Know Nothings." Anti-Semitism revived in the 1920s and increased again with the rise of Nazism. This led to the formation of a Jewish community council to fight discrimination. Despite the occasional defacement of synagogues with swastikas, anti-Semitism and discrimination were of relatively minor importance in the 1960s.

Bibliography: I. Blum, *Jews of Baltimore* (1910); A. Guttmacher, *History of the Baltimore Hebrew Congregation, Nidhei Isroel: 1830–1905* (1905); L. F. Cahn, *History of Oheb Shalom: 1853–1953* (1953); I. M. Fein, in: *The Jewish Experience in America*, 3 (1969), 323–52; A. Shusterman, *Legacy of a Liberal* (1967). [I.M.F.]

BAMBERG, city in Bavaria, West Germany. There were Jews living in Bamberg before the First Crusade (1096), when they were forcibly baptized but later allowed to return

The synagogue in Bamberg, Germany, built in 1910 and destroyed by the Nazis in 1938.

to Judaism. Establishments in the medieval "Jewish Lane" (today Pfahlplaetzchen) included a dance hall for weddings, a hostel *(hekdesh)* for the needy sick and transients, a *mikveh*, and a synagogue. 135 Jews were martyred in Bamberg during the *Rindfleisch massacres in 1298. During the persecution following the outbreak of the *Black Death in 1348 the Jews there set fire to their homes and perished in flames. Between the 14th and 17th centuries Jews repeatedly attempted to settle in Bamberg, paying high "protection" taxes, only to be later attacked and expelled. In 1633 they numbered ten families, whose right of residence was recognized in 1644. An annual "plum fast" *(Zwetschgen Taanit)* was observed by the Bamberg community, to commemorate the preservation of the Jews there in 1699 by one of their number who averted a massacre by pouring plums over the mob. The community increased from 287 in 1810 to 1,270 in 1880 (4.3% of the total population), subsequently declining to 862 in 1933 (1.6%) and 418 in May 1939.

Prominent members of the community included the talmudist and *paytan* Samuel b. Baruch *Bamberg (13th century). Notable rabbis were Moses *Mintz who served there from c. 1469 to 1474; Samuel Meseritz (c. 1661–65), author of *Naḥalat Shivah;* and Joseph Kobak (1862–82), editor of *Jeschurun*. A. Eckstein, rabbi of Bamberg (1888–1935), wrote a number of studies on the history of the Jewish communities in Bavaria.

During the Nazi regime, the synagogue was burned down on Nov. 10, 1938, and 30 to 40 Torah scrolls were destroyed. The Jews were concentrated in a ghetto, which was liquidated on Sept. 9, 1942, and about 300 of them were deported. After the war many displaced persons assembled in Bamberg (14,000 in 1947), but only 17 of the former Jewish citizens remained. In 1965 the cemetery was desecrated. The community then numbered 70.

Bibliography: PK; Germ Jud 1 (1963), 18–22; 2 (1968), 49–51; H. F. Brettinger, *Juden in Bamberg* (1963); A. Eckstein, *Geschichte der Juden im ehemaligen Fuerstbistum Bamberg* (1898); idem, in: *Festschrift zur Einweihung der neuen Synagoge in Bamberg* (1910); idem, *Die israelitische Kultusgemeinde Bamberg, 1803–53* (1910); *Bilder aus der Vergangenheit der israelitischen Gemeinde Bamberg* (1933); R. M. Kloos, in: *Bericht des historischen Vereins Bamberg*, 103 (1967), 341–86. Part of the communal archives are in the Jewish Historical General Archives in Jerusalem. [Z.F.]

BAMBERG, SAMUEL BEN BARUCH (first half of the 13th century), rabbi and *paytan*. Samuel was born in Metz, but lived in Bamberg, after which he was called. He studied under his father, *Baruch b. Samuel of Mainz, and *Eliezer b. Samuel of Metz. He corresponded on halakhic problems with *Eliezer b. Joel ha-Levi, *Simḥah b. Samuel of Speyer, and *Isaac b. Moses of Vienna, and was highly esteemed by leading contemporary scholars. Like his father, he was a talented poet, and fragments of his prayer book have survived. The name is mentioned in the *Memorbuch* of Nuremberg, but it is difficult to assume that he was one of the martyrs there. *Meir b. Baruch of Rothenberg was his pupil. For a time Samuel was regarded as the author of *Likkutei ha-Pardes* (Venice, 1519), but this view is no longer accepted. Of his works no more than excerpts and fragments of his responsa remain. His decisions are of a very independent nature, though his style is modest and austere.

Bibliography: Michael, Or, nos. 1203, 1205; Urbach, Tosafot, 354–6, passim; A. Eckstein, *Geschichte der Juden im ehemaligen Fuerstbistum Bamberg* (1898), 140, 297–8. [Y.AL.]

BAMBERGER, BERNARD JACOB (1904–), U.S. Reform rabbi, scholar, and author. Bamberger was born in Baltimore, Maryland and ordained at Hebrew Union College (1926). After serving as rabbi of Temple Israel in Lafayette, Indiana (1926–29), Bamberger moved to Congregation Beth Emeth in Albany, where he remained until 1944. From then he served as rabbi of Congregation Shaarey Tefila in New York City. Bamberger wrote several scholarly and popular books. They include *Proselytism in*

Bernard J. Bamberger, U.S. rabbi.

the Talmudic Period (1968^2); *Fallen Angels* (1952), a study of Jewish demonology and its influence on Christian thought; *The Bible: A Modern Jewish Approach* (1955); and *Story of Judaism* (1957). He served as president of the

Synagogue Council of America (1950–51), and of the Central Conference of American Rabbis (1959–61). He was a member of the Jewish Publication Society's Bible translation committee. [H.H.]

BAMBERGER, EDOUARD-ADRIEN (1825–1910), French politician and physician. Born in Strasbourg, he moved in 1858 to Metz where he became vice-president of the Metz Education League. He strenuously opposed the policies of Napoleon III and campaigned to bring about the anti-Empire majority in Metz in 1870. Elected as a Republican deputy in the National Assembly, Bamberger considerably influenced the votes on Napoleon III's responsibility for France's debacle and the subsequent deposition of the emperor. He voted against the treaty ceding his native Alsace to Germany and led the deputies from the annexed province out of the Assembly when the treaty was accepted. Recalled by Thiers following the 1871 insurrection, Bamberger resumed his seat at Versailles and voted regularly for the Republican majority. He was defeated in the 1881 elections, retired from politics, and became assistant librarian in the Museum of Natural History. During the parliamentary debates on the law concerning child labor, he moved an amendment—which was rejected—demanding that Jewish apprentices be exempt from working on Saturday.

Bibliography: *Biographie complète des 534 députés . . .* (1876).

[Ed.]

BAMBERGER, EUGEN (1857–1932), German chemist; a pioneer in the field of semi-microtechniques. Bamberger studied at Berlin University and in 1883 became an assistant to Baeyer in Munich, where he was appointed professor in 1891. From 1893 he was professor of general chemistry at the Zurich Polytechnic. From 1905 he was semi-paralyzed but continued his experimental work. Bamberger was meticulous in his work, and inculcated clean and safe experimental techniques in his assistants. He insisted on following up not only the main product of any reaction under study, but also the minor products. He was entirely the "pure" chemist, his vast output covering most of the contemporary aspects of organic chemistry. His contributions were notable in the field of constitutions of natural products.

Bibliography: *Berichte der deutschen chemischen Gesellschaft*, 66 (1933), 32; *Helvetica Chimica Acta*, 16 (1933), 644ff. [S.A.M.]

BAMBERGER, FRITZ (1902–), philosophical scholar and author. Born in Frankfort, Bamberger from 1926 to 1933 was a research fellow of the *Akademie fuer die Wissenschaft des Judentums and until 1938 occupied various teaching posts in Berlin. Emigrating to the United

Fritz Bamberger, writer on Jewish philosophy.

States, he became professor of philosophy at the College for Jewish Studies, Chicago, from 1939 to 1942, and was on the staff and later editor in chief of *Coronet* magazine from 1942 to 1961. He was a founder of the Society of Jewish Bibliophiles. From 1962 Bamberger was professor of intellectual history and assistant to the president of the Hebrew Union College-Jewish Institute of Religion in New York. His collection of Spinoziana is considered to be the finest private collection of its kind.

Bamberger's main interest in the field of Jewish philosophy centered on Moses *Mendelssohn (*Moses Mendelssohns geistige Gestalt* (1929); "Moses Mendelssohns Begriff vom Judentum" in: *Wissenschaft des Judentums im deutschen Sprachbereich*, ed. by K. Wilhelm (1967), 521ff.), and he edited three volumes of the bicentenary edition of Mendelssohn's writings (1929–32; cf. also *Denkmal der Freundschaft* (1929), and *Living Legacy* (1963), 86ff.). Other philosophers to whom he devoted studies were Spinoza (SBB, 5 (1961), 9ff.); Maimonides (*Das System des Maimonides*, 1935); Julius Guttmann (*Philosopher of Judaism*, 1960; also in German in: *Deutsches Judentum, Aufstieg und Krise* (1963), 85–119); and Leo Baeck (*The Man and the Idea*, 1958). Bamberger edited *Die Lehren des Judentums* (3 vols., 1928–30, together with S. Bernfeld); *Juedische Gestalten und ihre Zeit* (1936); *Das Buch Zunz* (1931; cf. also Zunz's *Conception of History* in PAAJR, 1941); and an anthology of ancient Jewish aphorisms (*Books are the Best Things*, 1962).

[Ed.]

BAMBERGER, HEINRICH VON (1822–1888), Austrian physician and teacher. Bamberger was born in Prague and studied medicine there. In 1854 he was appointed special professor of pathology at Wuerzburg University, where he remained until 1872, when he became professor at the University of Vienna. Bamberger became famous for his brilliant lectures and for his diagnostic techniques. He is especially known for his textbook on cardiac diseases and for his diagnoses of symptoms of cardiac diseases. His name

Heinrich von Bamberger, Austrian physician. Bildarchiv d. Ost. National-Bibliotek.

was given to Bamberger's disease, Bamberger's bulbar pulse, and Bamberger's sign for pericardial effusion. He advocated the use of albuminous mercuric solution in the therapy of syphilis and reported albuminuria during the latter period of severe anemia. He also described muscular atrophy and hypertrophy. During the last two years of his life Bamberger was president of the Vienna Medical Association.

Bibliography: S. R. Kagan, *Jewish Medicine* (1952), 292. [S.M.]

BAMBERGER, LOUIS (1855–1944), U.S. merchant and philanthropist. Bamberger was born in Baltimore, Maryland. As a boy he began work in a dry goods store, but while still a young man he moved to New York to engage in wholesale merchandising. In 1892 he and his brother-in-law, Felix Fuld, founded L. Bamberger and Co., a small department store, in Newark, New Jersey. Adopting advanced methods of merchandising and the latest techniques of publicity, Bamberger's grew into one of the largest and most profitable American establishments. In 1929 R. H. Macy of New York took over the Bamberger firm but Louis Bamberger continued to serve as president of the Newark store until 1939. He gave his employees a cooperative interest in the firm, established a pension program for them, and marked his own retirement by distributing cash gifts and annuities to workers who had been employed for a minimum of 15 years. Another of

Louis Bamberger, U.S. merchant and philanthropist.

Bamberger's successful enterprises was the Newark radio station WOR, which he built in the 1920s. Bamberger's philanthropies covered a wide range of interests. He gave generously to Newark's hospitals and Community Chest, and to the furtherance of the arts and sciences. The long list of Jewish causes and institutions to which he contributed included the *Jewish Theological Seminary of America. A charter member of the Newark Museum, and later its honorary president, he provided the funds for the new building, opened in 1926, and donated a vast quantity of art, archaeological, scientific, and industrial objects. Bamberger's greatest benefaction, which he shared with his sister, Mrs. Felix Fuld, was a gift of $5,000,000 for the establishment of the Institute for Advanced Study at Princeton. He and his sister also contributed to the Fuld House at Princeton, which provided quarters for the Institute.

Bibliography: Newark Museum Association, *Louis Bamberger . . . a Tribute . . .* (1944); T. Mahoney, *Great Merchants* (1955), 167–70, 194. [M.M.B.]

BAMBERGER, LUDWIG (1823–1899), German banker, politician, and economist; leading advocate of a gold standard for German currency. He studied law at Heidelberg and practiced as an attorney in his native city of Mainz. He joined the revolutionary movement of 1848 and edited the republican newspaper *Mainzer Zeitung* which advocated the unification of Germany and democratic government. He took part in the insurrection of 1849, fled to Switzerland, and was condemned to death in absentia. When, in 1866, a general amnesty was declared, Bamberger returned to Germany, and entered politics as a liberal,

Ludwig Bamberger, one of Bismarck's financial advisers, 1871.

sitting in the German Reichstag from 1871 to 1893. During the years of his exile in London and in Paris he had entered the family firm of *Bischoffsheim where he acquired considerable knowledge of finance. He became one of Bismarck's principal advisers on indemnification after the Franco-Prussian war of 1870. Later, Bamberger disagreed with Bismarck's policy of protective tariffs which he considered reactionary and in 1884 he and other followers seceded and formed the more liberal Freisinnige Partei. Though in opposition, he continued to exercise great influence on legislation of economic or financial character. He was an enthusiastic advocate of the gold standard and a champion of free trade and founded an association for its promotion. Bamberger was not a practicing Jew but in his memoirs he deplores German anti-Semitism. Stung by the anti-Semitic attacks of the German historian, Heinrich von Trietschke, he published a pamphlet *"Deutschtum und Judentum"* which was a vigorous rejoinder. He made numerous contributions to political and economic literature and his articles in the weekly *Die Nation* were published in book form under separate titles: *Wandlungen und Wanderungen in der Sozialpolitik* (1898); *Bismarck Posthumus* (1899). He also published his collected writings in five volumes (1894–98), and his memoirs appeared posthumously (1899).

Bibliography: O. Hartwig, *Ludwig Bamberger* (Ger., 1900); W. Kelsch, *Ludwig Bamberger als Politiker* (1933); YLBI, 13 (1968). [J.O.R.]

BAMBERGER, SELIGMANN BAER (Isaac Dov ha-Levi; 1807–1878), rabbinical scholar and leader of German Orthodoxy. Born in the Bavarian village of Wiesenbronn,

Bamberger studied at the yeshivah of Fuerth and in his native village. Bamberger opposed the proponents of Reform at a meeting of Jewish communities of Lower Franconia in 1834, and at an assembly of notables called by the Bavarian government in 1836 where he represented A. *Bing, the district rabbi of Wuerzburg. In 1840 he was elected to succeed Bing in the face of fierce opposition from the Reformers. Bamberger continued the local yeshivah, founded an elementary school in 1855, and a teachers' training college in 1864. In 1872 he signed a declaration by German and Austrian rabbis demanding that Orthodox Jews leave the Reform-dominated, state-established congregations in accordance with the recently passed Secession Law. However, five years later he was induced by opponents of Secession in Frankfort to approve continued membership in congregations which provided for the needs of the Orthodox, thus lending his authority to the establishment of the so-called Communal Orthodoxy. This led to a heated controversy with S.R. *Hirsch, the father of Secessionist Orthodoxy. In contrast to Hirsch and E. Hildesheimer, who spoke for the urban, middle-class *ba'alei-battim*, Bamberger represented (and typified) the unsophisticated, tradition-minded *Landsjude* of the small town and rural communities of southern Germany.

The "Wuerzburger Rav," as he was called, was one of the last great German-style talmudists, and his literary work was chiefly devoted to subjects of practical *halakhah; Melekhet Shamayim* (on the writing of Torah Scrolls etc., 1860[2]); *Amirah le-Veit Ya'akov* (laws of interest to women, originally German in Hebrew characters, 1858); *Moreh la-Zoveḥim* (handbooks for *shoḥatim*, 1864[2]); *Naḥalei Devash* (on the law of *ḥalizah*, 1867). Bamberger also wrote a commentary on Isaac ibn Ghayyat's halakhic compendium (*Sha'arei Simḥah*, 2 pts., 1861–62) and a treatise on the *Al Tikrei* formula in Talmud and Midrash (*Korei be-Emet*, 2 pts., 1871–78). His responsa appeared posthumously in *Zekher Simḥah* (1925), *Neti'ah shel Simḥah* (1928), and *Yad ha-Levi* (1965), all published by one or another of his descendants. Together with A. Adler and M. Lehmann, Bamberger published a German translation of the Pentateuch (1873, 1913[7]) on behalf of the Orthodox-Israelitische Bibelanstalt to counter L. Philippson's Bible translation, against which he had published a polemical pamphlet (1860).

Descendants. Bamberger became the founder of a widespread rabbinical family. Five of his six sons became rabbis, and his three daughters all married rabbis. His son SIMON SIMḤAH (1832–1897) was rabbi at Fischach and Aschaffenburg (Bavaria). He published *Ḥinnukh la-Ne'arim* (on the laws of *ẓiẓit* and *tefillin;* with Yiddish translation, 1882[3]); *Pekuddat ha-Levi'im* (Aaron b. Joseph of Barcelona's commentary on Alfasi, *Berakhot* and *Ta'anit*, with notes, 1874); *Avodat ha-Levi'im* (Jonathan b. David of Lunel's commentary on Alfasi, *Ḥullin*, 1871). SOLOMON (1835–1918) was rabbi at Lengnau, Niederlangenthal, and Sennheim (the latter two in Alsace). His talmudic researches dealt mainly with Nathan b. Jehiel's *Arukh* (*Limmud Arukh* on various talmudic tractates, 1868–97; *Hegyon Shelomo*, 1878). MOSES LOEB (1838–1899) was district rabbi at Kissingen, Bavaria. SECKEL ISAAC (1839–1885) was *dayyan* at Frankfort. NATHAN (1842–1919) succeeded his father as rabbi and seminary principal at Wuerzburg. He published *Likkutei ha-Levi*, on the religious customs of Wuerzburg (1907), and collaborated with his brother Simon Simḥah on *Pekuddat ha Levi'im*. He also wrote a memoir of his father (1897).

In the third generation: SECKEL (1863–1934), son of Simon Simḥah and district rabbi at Kissingen, wrote a halakhic tract on the immersion of vessels (*Tevilat Kelim*, with German translation, 1887); an edition of the *Midrash Lekaḥ Tov* on the Song of Songs and Ruth (1887); and a translation with commentary of *Avot* (1897, 1935[3]). MOSES LOEB (II; 1869–1924), also a son of Simon Simḥah, was rabbi at Schoenlanke (Pomerania, now Trzcianka, Poland); edited J. Ettlinger's essays and addresses (1899) and Joseph ibn Naḥmias' commentary on Esther (1891–93), Proverbs (1911), and Jeremiah (1913). He also wrote on book censorship in the duchy of Baden (1902), on the history of the Jews of Wuerzburg (1905), and of Schoenlanke (1912). SELIG (1872–1936), son of Solomon and rabbi of the Hamburg *klaus*, edited and translated into German a large number of halakhic, aggadic, and liturgical texts. He also edited Maimonides' commentary on tractate *Ḥallah* (1895). SOLOMON MENAḤEM (1869–1920), son of Seckel Isaac, was rabbi at Bingen, Burgpreppach, and Hanau. He was a cofounder of the *Juedisch-Literarische Gesellschaft. SIMON SIMḤAH (II; 1871–1961), son of Nathan and rabbi at Aschaffenburg (Bavaria), wrote on circumcision (*Beschneidungsakt*, 1913) and the creation (*Die Schoepfungsurkunde*, 1903).

The next generation included SIMON SIMḤAH (III; 1899–1957), son of Seckel Isaac, rabbi at Stuttgart and later in Israel, and his brother MOSES LOEB (III; 1902–1960), rabbi in Mainz and Nottingham and founder-principal of the Jewish Boarding School in Gateshead, England. Erich *Fromm, the social psychologist, and Saul Esh, the historian, were also descendants of S. B. Bamberger, as was the bookseller-publisher Nathan Wolf Bamberger (1888–1948), who in 1934 cofounded in Jerusalem the firm of Bamberger and Wahrmann which specialized in rare Jewish books.

Bibliography: S. Esh (ed.), *Bamberger Family* (1964, with bibliographies); N. Bamberger, *Seligmann Baer Bamberger* (Ger., 1897); M. Auerbach, in: *Jeschurun*, 15 (1928), 524–38; H. Schwab, *History of Orthodox Jewry in Germany* (1951), 73–81; idem, *Chachme Ashkenaz* (Eng., 1964), 19–23; S. Bamberger, *Zekher ... Yiẓḥak Dov Bamberger* (1958); M. L. Bamberger, in: L. Jung (ed.), *Jewish Leaders* (1964), 179–95.

[ED.]

BAMBERGER, SIMON (1846–1926), U.S. mining industrialist, railroad builder, and governor of Utah. Born in Germany, Bamberger went to the United States when he was 14. He worked first in the store of his elder brother, Herman, in Wilmington, Ohio, and later the brothers became clothing manufacturers in St. Louis, Missouri. In pursuit of a debtor, Simon Bamberger found himself at Piedmont, Wyoming, a Union Pacific Railroad work camp. He stayed there, put up shacks and tents which he rented to workers on the new railroad and cashed their paychecks at a discount. He then moved on to Ogden, Utah, where he bought an interest in a hotel, and in 1869 settled in Salt Lake City. He was joined there by his brothers and they tended to his business interests, leaving him free to seek his fortune in gold mining. He found it in the lucrative Centennial Eureka Mines. Subsequently he built a railroad to a coalfield in southern Utah and after a struggle lasting 17 years against competing interests and harassing litigation, the Bamberger Railroad was put into operation between Salt Lake City and Ogden, with Simon Bamberger as director and treasurer.

In 1898, Bamberger entered public service as a member of Salt Lake City's Board of Education, where he devoted himself to improving teachers' conditions. From 1903 to 1907 he sat in the State Senate and was elected governor of Utah, 1916–20, the first Democrat and non-Mormon to become governor. During his administration Bamberger sponsored legislation for the control and supervision of public utilities, improved public health services, guaranteed full-year salaries for teachers, the right of workers to voluntary association, benefits for farmers, and other liberal measures.

Simon Bamberger, first non-Mormon Governor of Utah.

Bamberger was one of the founders of Utah's first Jewish congregation, Bnai Israel, and was later its president. He supported the Utah colonization fund established by the Jewish Agricultural Society which attempted to settle 140 Jews from New York and Philadelphia in the Clarion Colony. He was also prominent in several Jewish philanthropic and communal institutions.

Bibliography: AJYB, 19 (1917/18), 249f.; N. Warrum, *Utah Since Statehood* (1919); L. L. Watters, *Pioneer Jews of Utah* (1952), 9f., 30f., 163–9; B. Postal and L. Koppman, *A Jewish Tourist's Guide to the U.S.* (1954), 608ff.

[M.M.B.]

BAMBUS, WILLY (1863–1904), one of the first German Jews to join *Ḥibbat Zion. He propagated the organization's ideas in the periodical *Serubabel,* edited by him in

Willy Bambus, German Zionist. Jerusalem, Schwadron Collection, J.N.U.L.

Berlin (1887–88). Bambus became a leading member of *Esra, a society founded in 1883 for the advancement of Jewish agricultural settlement in Palestine and Syria. Later, together with Hirsch *Hildesheimer, Emile *Meyerson, and Isaac Turoff, he established the central committee of Ḥovevei Zion in Paris, with branches in many countries. His intention was to transform the movement into a world organization. Herzl's creation of the Zionist Organization led him to abandon his idea and for a time he became a political Zionist. However, disagreeing with Herzl's rejection of the so-called "infiltration," i.e., small-scale settlement in Palestine without prior international agreement, he became strongly opposed to political Zionism. He expressed this primarily in the periodical *Zion* which he edited from 1895. In 1901 he was instrumental in the creation of the *Hilfsverein der deutschen Juden of which he became the first general secretary. After the Kishinev pogrom (1903) he worked in the defense organization against anti-Semitism (Komitee zur Abwehr antisemitischer Angriffe) in Berlin, and endeavored, unsuccessfully, to establish a bank for Jewish emigrants. His works included *Palaestina, Land und Leute* (1898), *Die Kriminalitaet der Juden* (1896), *Die Juden als Soldaten* (1897), and several works on Jewish settlement in Ereẓ Israel.

Bibliography: A. Bein, *Theodor Herzl* (1962²), 215–8, 227, 241; R. Lichtheim, *Geschichte des deutschen Zionismus* (1954), index; G. Herlitz, in: *Davar* (Nov. 8, 1954); I. Turoff-Berlin, in: *Die Welt,* no. 47 (1904), 3–4; H. Loewe, *ibid.*, no. 49 (1904), 6–8.

[O.K.R.]

BA-MEH MADLIKIN (Heb. בַּמֶּה מַדְלִיקִין; "with what may one kindle?"), opening words of the second chapter of the Mishnah tractate *Shabbat* which deals with the oils and wicks proper to be used for the Sabbath lights, and with what must be done on Fridays before the commencement of the Sabbath. This chapter, which consists of seven paragraphs, is recited, according to traditional practice, during the Friday evening service either before the start of the *Arvit* prayer (Sephardi and Ashkenazi ritual in Ereẓ Israel) or at the end of it (Ashkenazi ritual). Some ḥasidic rites do not recite it at all. The reading of the chapter of the Mishnah was instituted in the geonic period as a reminder of the duty of kindling the Sabbath lights, as a precaution against any unintentional desecration of the Sabbath caused by adjusting the lamp, and as a safeguard for latecomers to the synagogue (the recital of this chapter by the congregation made it possible for latecomers to finish their prayers with the other congregants and to leave for home together without fear of injury in the dark). *Ba-Meh Madlikin* is not recited on a Sabbath falling on or immediately following a holiday because latecomers to the service would be few.

Bibliography: Eisenstein, Yisrael, 3 (1909), 95; Eisenstein, Dinim, 46ff.; Baer S., Seder, 192; Elbogen, Gottesdienst, 11ff.

[Ed.]

BAND, MAX (Mordecai; 1900–), Lithuanian-born U.S. painter, best known for his portraits of the Holocaust survivors, particularly the Jewish children. He studied painting in Berlin, moved to Paris in 1925, and settled in California in 1940.

Drawing by Max Band. Jerusalem, J. Leron Collection.

The essence of his paintings lies in their portrayal of the thoughts of people enveloped in loneliness. At the same time, Band's paintings also proclaim faith in man and in life. Among the best known of Band's works are "The Accused" (1938), "Blood, Sweat and Tears" (1941), and portraits of President Roosevelt, Bialik, and Martin Buber. He also compiled and illustrated *Themes from the Bible* (1964), a book consisting of biblical texts.

Bibliography: W. George, *Max Band* (Fr., 1932); P. Fierens, *Max Band* (Fr., 1935); A. Millier, *The Art of Max Band* (1945).

[P.N.]

BANET (Baneth, Benet, Panet, Benedict, Binet, Bineter), family of Moravian rabbis and scholars. Its first known member, MORDECAI BEN YOM TOV, approved a *mahzor* following the Polish ritual in Nikolsburg (Mikulov) in 1716. ABER (Aberl; d. 1758), possibly Mordecai's son, was *dayyan* in Nikolsburg. A responsum (*Noda bi-Yhudah, Mahadurah Tinyana* ḤM no. 12) was addressed by Ezekiel *Landau to JOHANAN BANET, a *dayyan* in Alt-Ofen (Budapest). Johanan's son JACOB (d. 1812) was *dayyan* in Alt-Ofen. One of Jacob's four sons was Ezekiel b. Jacob *Baneth. FRADL, a daughter of Aber, married Abraham Bia of Csurgo (Hungary). Their son Mordecai *Banet, who took his mother's family name, became head of the Nikolsburg branch of the family. In the 19th and 20th centuries members of the family distinguished themselves in various fields of modern Jewish scholarship (see Eduard Ezekiel *Baneth; David Hartwig *Baneth; Moritz *Benedikt; Friedrich Adolf *Paneth).

Bibliography: EJ, 4 (1929), s.v. *Benet* (with genealogy).

[H.BRO./ED.]

BANET (Benet), MORDECAI BEN ABRAHAM (1753–1829), Moravian rabbi, one of the leading talmudists of his time. Banet was born in Csurgo, Hungary. He studied at the yeshivah of Fuerth under Joseph Steinhardt, author of the responsa *Zikhron Yosef.* In 1784 he was appointed *dayyan* in Nikolsburg, Moravia. In 1787 and 1788 he served as rabbi of Lundenburg, Moravia, and subsequently of Sasvar, Hungary, and from 1789 as rabbi and head of the yeshivah of Nikolsburg, and district rabbi of Moravia. Banet's yeshivah attracted students from near and far, and during the 40 years that he headed it several thousands of students passed through. Banet fought vigorously against the Reform movement, particularly against Aaron *Chorin, and vehemently opposed the founding of the Reform Temple in Hamburg. At the same time he displayed a certain understanding of the spiritual needs of his contemporaries. At the request of the government, he prepared two courses of study for students for the rabbinate which included secular studies. His proposals were published in the *Toledot Mordekhai Banet* (1832) of his son Jacob Abraham. Under Banet's influence, his son Naphtali *Banet compiled a handbook (in Hebrew and German) on the fundamentals of the Jewish religion. Because of his great influence on his community, his talented leadership, and the support of the government, Banet succeeded in postponing the disintegration of Moravian Jewry for at least one generation later than that of the breakup of Bohemian Jewry. He was one of the chief opponents of Saul *Berlin in the controversy over his work *Besamim Rosh* (Berlin, 1793).

Of Banet's works, only *Be'ur Mordekhai* (2 vols. Vienna, 1805–13), novellae to the *Mordekhai* of Mordecai b. Hillel, was published during his lifetime. After his death the following were published: *Magen Avot* (Zolkiew, 1835; 1903²; with notes by Shalom Mordecai ha-Kohen), on the main categories of work forbidden on the Sabbath; *Har*

ספר

מחשבת מרדכי

והוא חיבור נחמד על התורה מאת כבוד הרב הגאון
הגדול בענקים, חכם חרשים ונבון לחשים, לו זרוע
עם גבורה, ארי שבחבורה, רועה ישראל מאור הגולה,
כקש״ת מרן מו״ה מרדכי בנעט זצללה״ה שהי׳ אב״ד
דק״ק נ״ש וכל מדינת מעהרין יע״א. בעה״מ ס׳ ביאור
מרדכי, וס׳ מגן אבות, וספר שו״ת הר המור וספר שו״ת
פרשת מרדכי, וספר תכלת מרדכי:

ועלה לרצון על מזבח הדפוס ע״י הרבני האברך
מו״ה מנחם שמואל פריעדמאן נ״י מקאלוב

אחת שאלתי מי אשר אשלח לידו את הספר ימחול
לשלוח מחירו תומ״י למען אוכל להוציא לאור עולם גם
יתר כתבי י״ק מהגאון הקדוש הנ״ל דברי הלכה:

ואדרעססע שלי:
Manó Friedman, Nagy-Kálló
Com. Szabolcs.

מונקאטש,
בדפוס המשובח של השותפים קאהן & פריעד
שנת תרס״ב לפ״ק.

Druck von Kahn & Fried, Munkacs.

Title page of *Maḥashevet Mordekhai*, Mordecai Banet's aggadic homilies and talmudic novellae, Munkacs, Hungary, 1902. Jerusalem, J.N.U.L.

ha-Mor (Prague, 1861), responsa, published together with the *Hokhmat Shelomo* of Solomon Kwetsch, his pupil; *Parashat Mordekhai* (1889), responsa on the Shulḥan Arukh, together with notes by the publisher, Abraham Isaac Glueck; *Tekhelet Mordekhai* (1892), aggadic homilies and talmudic novellae, also containing a biography of the author; *Maḥashevet Mordekhai* (1902), aggadic novellae to the Pentateuch; *Sefer Maharam Banet* (also called *Divrei Mordekhai;* 1906), novellae on aspects of the dietary laws with notes by the publisher Abraham Jungreisz.

Bibliography: R. Ferber, *Pe'er Mordekhai* (1951); R. Kestenberg-Gladstein, *Neuere Geschichte der Juden in den boehmischen Laendern,* 1 (1969), index s.v. *Benet;* B. Mevorakh, in: *Ẓion,* 34 (1969), 208ff.

[M.N.Z.]

BANET (Benet), NAPHTALI BEN MORDECAI (1789–1857), Moravian rabbi and author, third son of Mordecai *Banet. Banet officiated as rabbi and principal of the yeshivah in Safov (Schaffa, Moravia) from 1836 to 1857. He enjoined a fast and a penitential prayer to be recited on the 24th of Sivan in memory of the great conflagration of 1822 which almost destroyed the entire Jewish quarter of Schaffa; the custom was adhered to by the community until the Holocaust. Banet's writings include *Berit Melaḥ* on *meliḥah* (salting) laws (Prague, 1816); *Emunat Yisrael,* a catechism of the fundamentals of Judaism for Jewish youth, in Hebrew and German (*ibid.,* 1832); *Torat Dat Moshe ve-Yisrael,* on the principles of Judaism, in Hebrew and German (*ibid.,* 1826). The latter were intended to serve as a substitute for Herz Homberg's catechism *Benei Ẓiyyon* and expressed a conservative point of view.

Bibliography: A. Walden, *Sefer Shem ha-Gedolim he-Ḥadash* (1870), pt. 2, 8a, no. 97; D. Feuchtwang, in: *Festschrift Adolf Schwarz* (1917), 550; E. Faerber, *Pe'er Mordekhai* (1951), 55–58; B. Mevorakh, in: *Zion*, 34 (1969), 208ff.

[M.N.Z.]

BANETH, family of scholars. EDUARD EZEKIEL BANETH (1855–1930), talmudic scholar, was a descendant of the well-known *Banet family of rabbis and scholars. He was born in Liptó-Szent-Miklós (Slovakia). From 1882 to 1895 he served as rabbi at Krotoszyn (near Poznan) and then as lecturer of Talmud at the Lehranstalt fuer die Wissenschaft des Judentums in Berlin. In 1919 the Prussian Ministry of Education awarded him the title of professor. Baneth's work was devoted mainly to talmudic and rabbinic literature, the development of *halakhah*, and the Jewish calendar. Among his published works are *Ursprung der Sadokaeer und Boethosaeer* (1882); *Maimunis Neumondberechnung* (4 vols., 1898–1903); *Der Sederabend* (1904); *Avot mit Maimunis arabischem Kommentar* (1905); *Maimonides als Chronologe und Astronom* (1914); *Soziale Motive in der rabbinischen Rechtspflege* (1922); *Bilder talmudischer Ethik* (1926); and *Der juedische und buergerliche Kalender* (1928). Baneth also contributed to the Samter-Hoffmann German translation and commentary of the Mishnah (order of *Mo'ed*, 1927[2]).

His son DAVID HARTWIG (ZVI; 1893–) was an Arabist. Born in Krotoszyn, from 1920 to 1924 he was an assistant at the Akademie fuer die Wissenschaft des Judentums. He then went to Palestine where he was a lecturer at the Hebrew University on Arabic philosophy, language, and literature. From 1946 he was professor of Arabic language and literature. In his earlier years David made important contributions to ancient Aramaic and Canaanite studies, but his life work consisted in the study of Jewish thought as expressed in Arabic, in Arabic as used by Jews, and in medieval Hebrew. He wrote on the enigmatic Jewish rationalist *Ibn Kammuna (MGWJ, vol. 69, 1925), on the relationship between *Judah Halevi and the Muslim theologian *Ghazali (*Korrespondenzblatt*, vol. 5, 1929; see also *Keneset*, vol. 7, 1942), and on the use made by both Ghazali and the Jewish pietist Baḥya ibn Paquda of a passage in a book of a Christian author (*Magnes Jubilee Volume*, 1938).

Baneth was at his best in the editing and criticism of texts, such as his edition of Maimonides' letters (*Iggerot ha-Rambam*, 1946), his revisions of Maimonides' *Terminology of Logic* (edited by L. Roth, 1935) and of the *Book of Beatitude*, ascribed to Maimonides (prepared for edition by H. S. Davidowitz, 1939), as well as his discussion of the Hebrew translations of Maimonides' treatise on resurrection (*Tarbiz*, vol. 11, 1939/40, and vol. 13, 1941/42) and of Maimonides' Hebrew usage (*Tarbiz*, vol. 6, 1934/35 and vol. 23, 1951/52). He published many detailed reviews of Judeo-Arabic works in *Kirjath Sepher*. Of particular importance are Baneth's studies of the language and contents of the Cairo *Genizah* documents (cf. S. Shaked, *A Tentative Bibliography of Geniza Documents* (1964), 268–9). Most of the Arabic *Genizah* texts published by S. *Assaf were prepared for edition and translated into Hebrew by Baneth. By emphasizing that most deviations from classical Arabic grammar in the *Genizah* documents were not "mistakes," but represented the living language of the period, Baneth pointed the way for a sound approach to the understanding of those medieval writings.

[M.D.H./S.D.G./S.M.S.]

BANETH (Benet, Paneth), EZEKIEL BEN JACOB (1773–1854), rabbi, born in Alt-Ofen (Budapest), Hungary. In 1810 Ezekiel was appointed rabbi of Szecseny. He became rabbi of *Paks in 1825 and subsequently of *Balassagyarmat, and from 1847 officiated at Nyitra. He corresponded on halakhic matters with Moses Sofer, Judah Aszód, and other rabbis. His yeshivah was attended by pupils from various parts of the country. One of his most talented students was his youngest son Jerachmeel Bernhard (1815–1871), rabbi of Liptoszentmiklos (Liptovsky Svaty Mikulas). Ezekiel was also an eloquent preacher. Recognized by his contemporaries as a halakhic authority, he left no written work, having destroyed his commentary on the Tosefta before his death. His grandson was Eduard Ezekiel *Baneth.

Bibliography: M. Stein (ed.), *Magyar rabbik*, 4 (1908), 36, 74; D. Feuchtwang, in: *Festschrift Adolf Schwarz* (1917), 539–56.

[J.Z.]

BANIAS, ruined city at the foot of Mount Hermon on the Hermon Brook, one of the sources of the River Jordan. It was called by the Jews *Dan or Mivẓar Dan ("the Fort of Dan"; a suggested identification with the biblical Beth-Rehob is uncertain). It stood over a cliff with a grotto dedicated to the Greek god Pan and the nymphs, and hence was named Paneas (Banias being an Arabic corruption). In 198 B.C.E., Antiochus III conquered Palestine from the Ptolemies by his victory near this place. Later the city belonged to the Itureans, from whom it was transferred by Augustus to Herod who named it Caesarea in honor of Augustus and to whom he erected a temple there. Philip the Tetrarch (*Herod Philip), Herod's son, developed the city, resided there, and struck coins with images of its buildings. It was generally known as Caesarea Philippi ("of Philip") to distinguish it from the better-known Caesarea-by-the-Sea. As such it is mentioned in the New Testament (Matt. 16:13; Mark 8:27) in connection with Jesus' visit to the area. In 61 C.E. *Agrippa II renamed it Neronias in honor of the emperor Nero, but it kept this name only until 68. In 70 *Titus held games there to celebrate his victory and many Jewish captives were put to death. In the Talmud, Caesarea is called Keissariyyon or Little Caesarea; the Mishnah also mentions the cave of Pamias referring to the same place. Caesarea's territory extended as far as Hadar and the Phiale Lake; the Ḥuleh Valley also belonged to it. A statue of Hadrian which stood there was regarded by the early Christians as representing Jesus healing a woman. The Talmud refers to the emperor Diocletian's oppression of the people of Paneas (Lieberman, in JQR, 36 (1946), 350ff.; TJ,

The grotto at Banias dedicated to the Greek god Pan. Photo Zev Radovan, Jerusalem.

Shev. 9:2, 38d). In Roman-Byzantine times Caesarea belonged to Phoenicia; its bishops took part in church councils from 325 to 451. In Crusader times it was called Belinas and a powerful castle (Qalʿāt al-Subayba) was erected above it. [M.A.-Y.]

Since Banias was situated on the main road from Palestine to Damascus it served in the Middle Ages as an administrative center to a district with the same name. During the 11th century there was a relatively large Jewish community, whose members were called the Baniasites. They were frequently mentioned in *genizah* documents. A document of 1056 shows that the Banias community was well organized and had a *bet din*.

Since Babylonian Jews had settled in Banias the community was split into two sections, the Palestinians and the Babylonians, who differed in their versions of prayers. These two sections existed to the beginning of the 12th century. A Karaite pseudo-messiah is reported in 1102. *Benjamin of Tudela mentions no community in Banias in 1170 and it is possible that it ceased to exist during the Crusades. Later, Banias was reinhabited by Jews. Even during the early Ottoman period, Jews still lived at Banias, as attested by a document from 1624 which mentions the murder of a Jewish physician, by the name of Elijah ha-Kohen of Banias, by an Arab sheik (Ben Zvi, in *Tarbiz*, 3 (1932), 442). From 1948 to 1967 Banias served the Syrians as a base for attacks on *Dan. In June 1967 it was occupied by the Israel Defense Forces. [Ed.]

Bibliography: E. Orni and E. Efrat, *Geography of Israel* (1964), 74; Mann, Egypt, 2 (1922), 203; J. Braslavski, in: BJPES, 5 (1938), 128–31; Assaf, *ibid.*, 6 (1939), 16–19; Schuerer, Gesch, 2 (1906), 204ff.; M. Avi-Yonah, Geog, 150–2; Kuk, in: *Ha-Tor*, 6 (1926), no. 35, 8–10; no. 36, 8–9.

BANISHMENT, a form of punishment widely imposed throughout the ancient world. India, the Greek cities, the Roman republic, and the Teutonic peoples all used this practice to rid themselves of undesirables, ranging from criminals to political agitators who threatened the safety of the state and the authority of its rulers. Bereft of his property and prohibited from ever returning home, the victim was reduced to the level of an outcast, a permanent stranger or wanderer in foreign lands. The custom seems to have been known in Canaan, as attested by the *Ugarit texts (*Aqhat*, 1:152–5; T. H. Gaster, *Thespis* (1961), 365–6; cf. 366n.). In ancient Israel, too, banishment was not unknown, although it appears almost exclusively as a form of divine punishment. Thus Adam was expelled from the Garden of Eden (Gen. 3:23–24) and Cain was doomed to be a wanderer, hidden from the presence of God (4:14–16). Two notable cases in the Bible are the banishment by Solomon of Abiathar the high priest to his family estate in Anathoth (I Kings 2:26; cf. Jer. 1:1) and the banishment of Amos from the Northern Kingdom of Amaziah the priest (Amos 7:12). Collective banishment, or exile, was considered the ultimate punishment that could be meted out to the entire people for acts of defiance against God (cf. Deut. 28:64 ff.), which were variously interpreted in different times (see *Galut). **Karet* was an extreme form of this divine punishment, involving the actual "cutting off" of the individual from life on earth (Lev. 20:2–6; cf. Zimmerli in bibl.). The only form of banishment still in existence in biblical society was that imposed on a man guilty of manslaughter or involuntary homicide, for whom *Cities of Refuge were provided (cf. Num. 35:10 ff.; Deut. 4:41–43; 19:1 ff.; Josh. 20). It has been conjectured that banishment was not otherwise sanctioned as a punishment because residence abroad was viewed as something that cut the victim off entirely from God (Hos. 9:3–5; cf. Gen. 4:14; Ezek. 11:15) and even forced him to worship idols (Deut. 4:27–28; I Sam. 26:19; Jer. 16:13). For this reason too, exile was dreaded (cf. Deut. 28:65; Ezek. 37:11) and deemed to have horrendous consequences. In later centuries, milder forms of banishment from the religious community were resorted to by means of excommunication, though, contrary to the view of some scholars, there does not seem to be any definite evidence of this practice in the Bible (cf. Greenberg in bibl.). [D.L.L.]

Second Temple and Talmud Periods. Banishment was resorted to by the Romans as part of their repressive policies. Thus *Archelaus the son of Herod I was banished by the Romans to Vienne in Gaul and probably remained there until he died. It is possibly to these administrative acts that *Avtalyon refers in his statement, "Ye sages, be heedful of your words lest ye incur the penalty of banishment *[galut]* and be banished to a place of evil waters" (Avot 1:11). Nevertheless the Pharisees seem also to have exercised this power. Josephus (Wars, 1:111) states that when they were in power they banished and brought back whomsoever they chose. The gravity of the punishment was not only that the victims would be exiled "to a place of evil waters and the disciples who come after you will drink thereof and die" (see above) but that they were also banished from the Divine Presence. On the verse, "For they have driven me out this day that I should not cleave to the inheritance of the Lord" (I Sam. 26:19), the Talmud comments that "he who lives outside the Land of Israel is regarded as worshiping idols" (Ket. 110b), and this sentiment is reflected in the words of the *Musaf* prayer for festivals: "But on account of our sins we were banished from our land and removed far from our country, and we are unable to appear and prostrate ourselves before Thee and to fulfill our obligations." [L.I.R.]

Middle Ages to 18th century. In the Middle Ages banishment continued to be one of the punishments imposed on offenders in communities having a measure of criminal jurisdiction over their members (see Judicial *Autonomy) or able to withhold or withdraw domiciliary rights *(ḥezkat ha-yishuv)*. Hence it was imposed most frequently in Spain and Poland and Lithuania, although also occasionally elsewhere. A distinction was drawn between banishment of the offender from the city and from the realm, as also banishment for a limited period and for life. The Spanish kingdoms, especially at the height of Jewish autonomy in the 13th century, recognized the right of the communal organizations to banish recalcitrants or exclude new members. James I of Aragon (1213–76) gave the communities the right to punish offenders by fine, ban, flagellation, or expulsion. Privileges accorded to the Barcelona community in 1241 and 1272 empowered the communal elders "to eject or expel [recalcitrant members] from the Jewish quarter or the entire city." A similar ordinance for Calatayud Jewry empowered the community in 1229 to expel two individuals of bad repute. In the 1280s the *kahal* of Alagon banished six butchers from the city for four years and excommunicated all members who ate meat purchased from them. James II of Aragon, on a complaint from the Valencia community in 1294, instructed the local prefect and judge to prevent influential Christians from concealing offenders condemned by the community to deportation. In 1280 Pedro III of Aragon, in a basic privilege granted to all Catalonian communities, empowered their elders to punish with incarceration and exile all crimes of assault and battery, libel, and the like, in accordance with Jewish law and their own judgment. The same privilege, granted by John I of Aragon to the Huesca community in 1390, provided that the elders could summarily sentence offenders to death, mutilation, flogging, or exile, without appeal. Offenses for which banishment was imposed included murder for which there was only one witness (Solomon b. Jehiel Luria, *Yam shel Shelomo le-Bava Kamma,* 8, no. 7), or for which no witness was available but where hearsay was convincing (Resp. Judah b. Asher, no. 58), and attack on a victim who dies after a lapse of a certain time (Resp. sent to Salamanca by Isaac b. Sheshet, no. 251). In Spain in particular banishment was meted out to delators and informers (communal statutes of the delegates of Castile, 1432). R. Menahem of Merseburg (early 14th century) banished a man for two or three years for viciously beating his wife (*Nimmukei Maharar Menaḥem me-Resburk* at the end of Resp. Jacob Weill, Venice, 1549). Prostitution and adultery were punished by life banishment by *takkanot* of Prague of 1612. There is even a report of a man who was excommunicated and "run out" of Ereẓ Israel by the Safed rabbis in 1548 for indulging in unnatural practices with his wife (Eleazar Azikri, *Sefer Ḥaredim* (1601), part 3, ch. 2). Forfeiture of domiciliary rights throughout Lithuania was applied by the Council of Lithuania to thieves, receivers, and forgers, and could be broadened also to any persons engaged in suspicious or prohibited dealings, infringing ethics, or disturbing the peace of the community. Since the whole community was liable to make good a claim by a gentile for money he had lent to a defaulting Jewish debtor, in Lithuania the Jew wishing to borrow from a gentile had first to obtain permission from the *av bet din.* A borrower who failed to do so could be banished, and his right of domicile forfeited (*Pinkas ha-Va'ad,* paras. 163 and 637). The Lithuanian Council also withdrew the right of domicile from and imposed banishment on a person provoking a gentile by quarrels or blows (idem, para. 21). Its regulations of 1623, when itinerant beggary and unlicensed behavior was widespread, lay down expulsion for a beggar, if necessary with the assistance of gentile officers. In 1628 the Lithuanian Council withheld the right of domicile from any Jew absent ten years from his community of origin who had failed to pay his fiscal contribution. Banishment was frequently applied in the Sephardi community of *Hamburg, its governing body *(*mahamad)* being empowered by the Hamburg senate to expel from the community any of its members infringing morals or engaged in dishonest business dealings, among other offenses. The offender thus sentenced was served with a writ from the beadle *(shamash).* If he proved unable to travel for lack of funds, the *mahamad* lent his relatives money to defray the expenses of the journey. Sometimes the offender was sent abroad, mainly to Amsterdam, and if his conduct subsequently improved was permitted to return. This punishment was also meted out to juvenile offenders. [ED.]

Bibliography: IN BIBLE: Mak. 2:6; Sif. Num. 60; Jos., Ant., 4:172–3; Philo, Spec., 3:123; F. Rundgren, in: VT, 7 (1957), 400–4; W. Zimmerli, in: ZAW, 66 (1954), 10–19; M. Greenberg, in: JBL, 78 (1959), 125–23. MIDDLE AGES: S. Assaf, *Ha-Onashin Aḥarei Ḥatimat ha-Talmud* (1922), 35–38; Baron, Community, index; Baer, Spain, 1 (1961), 430.

BANJA LUKA (Banya Luka), city in northwestern Yugoslavia. The earliest reference to a Jewish community dates from 1713, when Jewish merchants of Banja Luka appealed to the French government to appoint one of them French mercantile consul in the town. The community had both a Sephardi and an Ashkenazi synagogue and numbered 226 persons in 1875, 336 in 1895, and 457 in 1927. The Palestinian parachutists Hannah *Szenes and Yoel Palgi were dropped in Banja Luka on March 13, 1944, en route to Hungary. The community was exterminated by the Nazis and no trace remains.

Bibliography: *Jevrejski Almanah,* 1–2 (1926–27), index.

[S.MAR.]

BANKING AND BANKERS

Antiquity. There is little likelihood that financial transactions played a prominent role in the pre-Exilic epoch in Ereẓ Israel; according to the ethos of Jewish society, then founded on a pronounced agrarian structure, lending was part of the assistance a man owed to his neighbor or brother in need (cf. Deut. 23:21). During the Babylonian era Jews had greater opportunities to come into contact with a highly developed banking tradition and to participate in credit operations. After the Exile, commerce and credit certainly had a place in Ereẓ Israel. Though the society remained predominantly agrarian, Jerusalem had a number of wealthy families, including tax agents and landowners, who speculated and deposited their gains in the Temple, which had in some ways the function of a national bank (see *Heliodorus). Organized banking probably arose in connection with *Ma'aserot* ("tithes"), in particular *Ma'aser sheni,* and the pilgrimages to Jerusalem, through the activities of the *moneychangers. The use of Greek terms indicates a strong Hellenistic influence on the establishment of banking. Meanwhile, the Jewish communities forming in the Diaspora, the most important at first being that of *Babylonia, were given an impulse toward a new way of life by the long-standing traditions of a capitalist type of economy existing around them (see *Nippur and *Murashu's sons). In Babylonia, Jews engaged in financial transactions: some were farmers of taxes and customs, and the wealthiest of them were landowners; among the latter were *Huna, the head of the academy of Sura, and Rav *Ashi. However, talmudic references show that the standards of an agrarian economy were still dominant and therefore gamblers and usurers were not thought trustworthy witnesses (see e.g., Sanh. 3:3).

Another important Jewish colony was to be found at *Alexandria, center of the trade between the Mediterranean and the Arabian and Indian world, where Jews were engaged not only in commerce and international trade but in moneylending too. According to *Josephus, a Jewish tax agent was able to make a loan of 3,000 talents. The

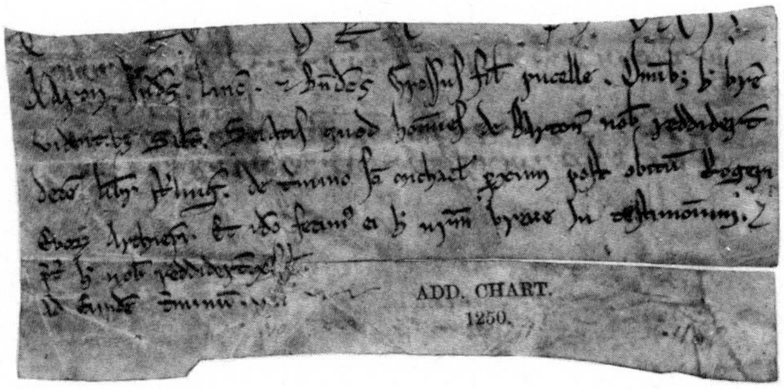

Figure 1. A receipt, written in Latin, by the 12th-century English financier, Aaron of Lincoln. "Aaron, the Jew of Lincoln, and Benedict Grossus, son of Pucella, send their greetings to all who may see this note. Know that the men of Barton [upon Humber] returned ten pounds sterling to us last Michaelmas [September 29], after the death of Roger, Archbishop of York [d. 26 November 1181]. And therefore we have drawn up this, our brief, as proof of it, and besides this, they returned ten shillings to us on the same date." London, British Museum, Add. Ch. 1250r.

*alabarch Alexander Lysimachus, who loaned King *Agrippa I 200,000 drachmas (Jos., Ant., 18:159–160), was also the steward of Antonia, mother of Emperor Claudius. Another Alexandrian Jew was treasurer to Candace, queen of Ethiopia.

Middle Ages. THE CALIPHATE. With the rapid development of city life and commerce in the caliphate of Baghdad from the late eighth century and the transition of the majority of Jews under caliphate rule from agriculture and a village environment to the cities, banking became one of the occupations of some upper-class Jews, especially in Baghdad and later under the Fatimids (from 968) in Egypt. This *Jahbadhiyya,* as it was called, was a form of banking based on the savings and economic activities of the whole Jewish merchant class and not only on the fortunes of the very rich: the bankers loaned to the state and its officers money deposited with them as well as from their own fortunes. The vast sums at the disposal of these Jewish bankers and their relative immunity from confiscation by the autocratic authorities both tend to confirm that these Jewish "court bankers" from the beginning of the tenth century onward were well-known to their Muslim debtors as a kind of "deposit banker" for Jewish merchants. Under the Fatimid caliph al-Mustanṣir the brothers *Abu Saʿd al-Tustarī and Abu Naṣr Ḥesed b. Sahl al-Tustarī (both died in 1048) were influential in the finances of Egypt. With the rise of *Saladin and the foundation of the Ayyubid dynasty in Egypt (1169), the position of the Jews deteriorated but they were able to continue their moneychanging activities at least. Toward the end of the Mamluk period (1517), Samuel, a moneychanger in Cairo, must have possessed considerable wealth, for the Arab chronicler Ibn Iyās tells that the sultan extorted from him more than 500,000 dinars. During the Muslim rule on the Iberian peninsula, Córdoba Jews were active in the financial administration in the tenth and eleventh centuries. The responsa of this period show a highly developed money economy existing before the First and Second Crusades.

EARLY MERCHANTS IN EUROPE. Persecution, such as occurred in Alexandria in 414 or the oppressive measures promulgated in the Byzantine Empire beginning with *Constantine and intensified under *Justinian, may have contributed to the fact that from the fifth century Jewish merchants followed their Greek and Syrian counterparts to Gaul and not only traded in luxury goods but also loaned money.

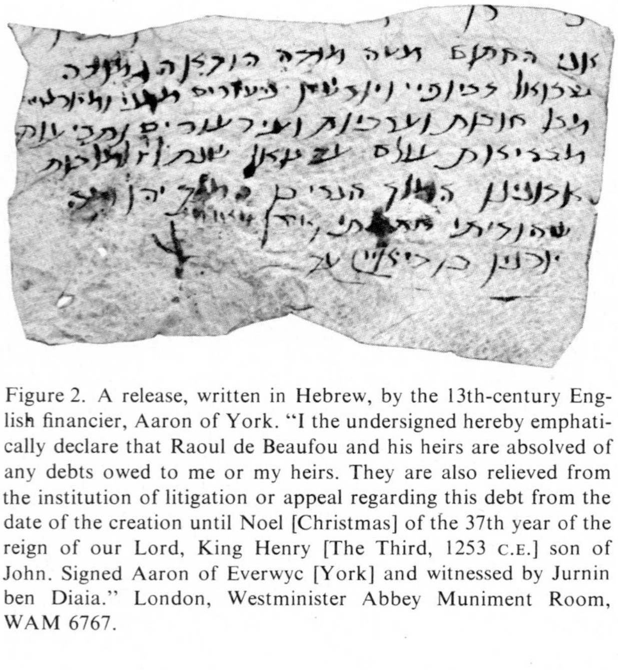

Figure 2. A release, written in Hebrew, by the 13th-century English financier, Aaron of York. "I the undersigned hereby emphatically declare that Raoul de Beaufou and his heirs are absolved of any debts owed to me or my heirs. They are also relieved from the institution of litigation or appeal regarding this debt from the date of the creation until Noel [Christmas] of the 37th year of the reign of our Lord, King Henry [The Third, 1253 C.E.] son of John. Signed Aaron of Everwyc [York] and witnessed by Jurnin ben Diaia." London, Westmінister Abbey Muniment Room, WAM 6767.

With the disappearance of the Syrians and Greeks from Europe in the seventh century, the Jewish merchants were able to expand. Within the administration of the Merovingian kings (from 481) Jews possibly farmed taxes or advanced money on revenues to high officials; according to Gregory of Tours (c. 538–94), the count of Tours and his vicar were indebted to the Jew Armentarius. During the Carolingian period (from the mid-eighth century), Jews settled in the Rhineland again as they had done during the Roman Empire—some of them lending money on pledges or giving money to merchants in a kind of commenda partnership. Archbishop Anno of Cologne (d. 1075), as well as Emperor Henry IV (1056–1106), borrowed money from Jews.

THE MONEYLENDERS IN EUROPE. After the First Crusade (1096) the Jewish merchant, in his necessarily long journeys, no longer enjoyed even minimal physical security. In Western and Central Europe, especially in *Spain, the crystallization of the essentially Christian nature of the rising city communes combined with this insecurity to drive out the Jews from commerce and prohibit them from engaging in crafts. In France, England (up to 1290), Germany, Austria, Bohemia, Moravia, and northern and central Italy, Jews had to turn to loan-banking on a larger or smaller scale in order to make a living. The canonical prohibition against taking interest by Christians, which was stressed in successive *Church councils (especially the Fourth Lateran Council of 1215), and the vast opportunities for capital investment in land and sea trade open to the wealthy Christian made lending on interest for consumer and emergency needs virtually a Jewish monopoly in Western and Central Europe between the 12th and 15th centuries. By the 13th century the notion that the *Wucherer* ("usurer") was a Jew was already current, for example, in the writings of *Berthold of Regensburg, Walther von der Vogelweide, and Ulrich von Lichtenstein. The word *judaizare* became identical with "taking interest." Testimony from the 12th century shows that moneylending was then becoming the main occupation of the Jews; this was the case of those of Bacharach (1146) and of Muenzenberg (1188). However, there is little data to suggest that Jewish banking transactions were on a large scale even in the 13th century, but there is evidence that the bishop of Basle had debts with Basle Jews and that various monasteries had Jewish creditors.

The transition from a natural economy to a money economy in the course of the "commercial revolution," and the stabilization of territorial principalities opened new possibilities for Jewish banking activity, especially in the Rhineland and in southern Germany. Jews from Siegburg, Trier, Mainz, Speyer, Strasbourg, and Basle as well as from Ulm and Nuremberg appear as sources of credit. The most important banking transaction in the first half of the 14th century went through the hands of Vivelin the Red, who transmitted 61,000 florins in gold which King Edward III of England paid to Baldwin of Trier for becoming allied with him against France. Margrave Rudolf III of Baden was indebted to David the Elder, called Watch, and to Jekelin of Strasbourg and his partners. Muskin and Jacob Daniels served the archbishop of Trier in the administration of his finances; during the first half of the 14th century, Daniels was probably the most important Jewish banker of the Rhineland. He was followed in the service of the archbishop by his son-in-law Michael. At the same time Abraham von Kreuznach at Bingen had a similar position with the archbishop of Mainz. Gottschalk von Recklinghausen and his company was another group on the lower Rhine. Such banking activity is recorded in other parts of Central Europe as far as Silesia.

Moneychanging and coinage privileges were often combined with moneylending, and Jews were frequently the sole agents arranging loans. From the first half of the 12th century moneychanging as a special form of banking is supported by documentary evidence. To spread the risk, partnerships of between two and ten persons were formed. As security, custom at first recognized mainly pledges, but from the middle of the 13th century the letter of credit came into use, though princes still preferred to pledge jewels. Often, instead of a pawn, bail was given by several persons. In western Germany hypothecation of real estate was preferred, and in this way Jews acquired in pledge houses, vineyards, farms, villages, castles, towns, and even seigneuries. Interest rates do not seem to have exceeded 36% but in the case of deferred payment they could rise to 100% or beyond. From the 12th century popes and princes exploited the financial capacity of the Jews by frequent remission of debts or forced loans. The *Black Death and consequent persecutions of Jews gave rulers an opportunity forcibly to seize property and to restore pawns and letters of credit to debtors. The liquidation of Jewish debts by King *Wenceslaus IV of Bohemia around the end of the 14th century is a well-known example of such royal rapacity. With these and other measures and the rise of the merchant class, who gradually took over the function of loan-bankers to the princes and even to emperors during the 15th and early 16th centuries, the Jews were deprived of imperial protection and forced to leave the towns. They retired to the small seigneuries or migrated to Eastern Europe, where a less-developed economy offered them possibilities of making a livelihood. In Bohemia, Hungary, and in Poland and Lithuania both princes and nobility made use of their financial help. As the Eastern European kingdoms developed with the colonization of the forests, Jews played an increasing part in commerce and especially in the *arenda*. In the larger towns some engaged in moneylending and banking activities.

In 12th-century France moneylending was an important Jewish business, but in the 13th century they came up against the superior competition of the Lombards, a rivalry even more intense in the Netherlands. In England, where *Aaron of Lincoln and *Aaron of York were powerful bankers, a special *Exchequer of the Jews was set up to centralize Jewish transactions. However in the 13th century the crown began to rely on the greater resources of the Cahorsins and Italian bankers and in 1290 the Jews were expelled. In Italy Jewish bankers could expand their sphere of activity under the silent protection of the popes, despite resistance on the part of the Christian burghers (see *Popes and the Jews). From the second half of the 13th century they spread throughout central Italy and gradually expanded toward the north, migrating at first to the smaller and medium-sized towns. In Pisa and then in Florence the Da *Pisa family became important loan-bankers; in Florence in 1437 Cosimo de' Medici permitted a Jewish group to establish four loan-banks; in Venice in 1366 Jews, probably of German origin, obtained the right to lend on pledges. Here as in other places in northern Italy, Jewish loan-bankers from the south came into competition with Jews migrating from Germany or southern France. Finally only few towns, such as Milan and Genoa, refused to admit Jewish loan-bankers. However, their activities were seriously challenged when the anti-Jewish preaching of the *Franciscans resulted in the establishment of branches of the *Monti di Pietà* toward the middle of the 15th century.

The Iberian Peninsula after the Christian reconquest offers many examples of large-scale credit activities and tax farming by Jews. It is known that they provided money for armaments against the Moors. El Cid borrowed from Raquel and

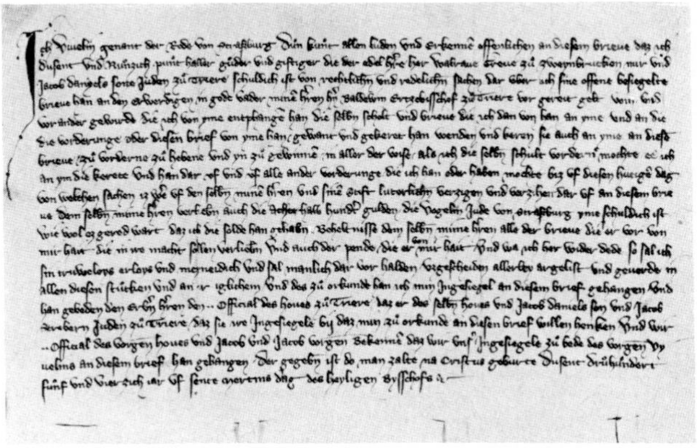

Figure 3. A document, dated 11 November, 1345, recording that the promissory note of Count Welrav of Zweibruecken for a loan of 1090 "pfund heller" from Jacob Daniels, a Jew of Trier, is being given to Baldwin, the Archbishop of Trier, by Vivelin the Red of Strasbourg. It also mentions that the archbishop is holding a sum of 750 gulden owed by Vogelin, a Strasbourg Jew. Two of the signatories of the deed are Jacob Daniels and another Trier Jew, Jacob Strebern. Coblenz, State Archives, Department 1A, No. 5238.

Vidas, Jews of Burgos, for his expedition against Valencia. King Alfonso VI of Castile (1072–1109) also obtained loans from Jews for his military expeditions. His successors employed Jews in the financial administration, especially as *almoxarifes* (revenue collectors), an activity combined with moneylending. Thus, Judah Ibn Ezra was in the service of Alfonso VII, Joseph Ibn Shoshan of Alfonso VIII, and Solomon *ibn Zadok (Don Çulema) and his son Çag de la Maleha were *almoxarifes* in the service of Alfonso X, while Meir ibn Shoshan served as his treasurer. When Sancho IV (1258–95) came to the throne, *Abraham el-Barchilon was prominent in the financial administration, supervising the farming of the taxes. Generally, in Castile the Jews abstained from farming the direct taxes, which from 1288 the Cortes opposed. The Jews therefore tended to prefer the administration of the customs and other rights belonging to the office of *almoxarife*. The court of Aragon relied on Jewish financial administrators in a similar fashion. King James I employed *Benveniste de Porta as a banker, probably giving him as security for his advances the office of bailiff of Barcelona and Gerona. Judah de la *Cavalleria, the most powerful Jew in the Aragonese administration, had control over all the bailiffs of the kingdom. Under Pedro III the family of *Ravaya were most influential. Though during the 14th century the Jews in Aragon and Navarre were subjected to increasing pressures, Judah Ha-Levi and Abraham Aben-Josef of Estella were general farmers of the rents under Charles II and Charles III of Navarre. In Castile—in spite of the Cortes' opposition—Jews such as the *Abrabanel family in Seville continued to be active as *almoxarifes*. The young Alfonso XI appointed Joseph de *Écija as his *almoxarife mayor* (c. 1322); Pedro the Cruel (1350–69) made Samuel b. Meir ha-Levi *Abulafia of Toledo, known as the richest Jew of his time, his chief treasurer, and Henry of Trastamara had Joseph *Picho as his financial officer *(contador mayor)* despite his promise to remove all Jews from royal office (1367).

THE CONVERSOS. The persecutions of 1391 and the mass conversions which followed brought an important change. Some of the Conversos were able to use the act of baptism to climb to high positions in the financial administration: examples are Luis de la *Cavalleria, chief treasurer under John II of Aragon, Luis *Sánchez, royal bailiff of the kingdom of Aragon (c. 1490), and his brother Gabriel *Sánchez, who was treasurer-general. Under Henry IV of

Castile (1454–74) Diego Arias de Avila was the king's secretary and auditor of the royal accounts; in spite of Diego's unpopularity his son Pedro succeeded him. Even Isabella the Catholic depended on the financial advice of the Jew Abraham *Senior, from 1476 chief tax gatherer in Castile, and Isaac *Abrabanel, who after having been banker of Alfonso V of Portugal served as the queen's private financial agent and loaned her a considerable sum for the war against Granada. The Converso Luis de *Santangel, chancellor and comptroller of the royal household and great-grandson of the Jew Noah Chinillo, loaned Isabella money to finance Columbus' expedition to America. Though some men like Isaac Abrabanel, who went to Naples, remained faithful to Judaism, a number of Jews of Spanish origin stayed in Portugal and, after accepting baptism, rose to financial influence there, especially in combination with the East Indian spice trade. Prominent among them were Francisco and Diogo *Mendes. The latter, who took up residence in Antwerp, became one of the most important merchant bankers there, lending money to the king of Portugal, the emperor, and Henry VIII of England. The firm "Herdeiros de Francisco e Diogo Mendes" was administered for some time after Diogo's death (1543) by Francisco's widow, Doña Beatrice de Luna (Gracia *Nasi) and her nephew João Miques (Joseph *Nasi). They subsequently emigrated to Turkey, where the latter combined commercial and banking activity with political influence. Another to rise to high position was Alvaro Mendes from Tavira, Portugal, who in Constantinople took the name Solomon *Abenaes. Jewish moneychangers and tax farmers were to be found in many places of the Ottoman Empire. After the union between Spain and Portugal (1580), a number of influential Conversos took the opportunity to invest their capital in financing the various ventures of the crown, provisioning the army in Flanders and in the East Indies, and supplying contracts for Africa. Their activities expanded especially after the financial crisis of 1626 and continued until the Portuguese revolt of 1640 which restored independent sovereignty to the country. After this all members of the *gente de nação* (as Conversos were called) living in Spain became suspect. The last important financial venture by *New Christians in Portugal

Jch bitt euch jud leicht mir zů hand/
Bar gelt auff bürgen oder pfand/
Was eüch gebürt gebt mir verstand/

Figure 4. Woodcut of a Jewish moneylender, Augsburg, Germany, 1531. The borrower is saying: "Please, Jew, give me cash against a promissory note or security, let me know what I owe you."

was the financing of the Brazil Company established in 1649. However, Jewish involvement in banking proper really begins with the activities of those Conversos who, fleeing the Inquisition in Portugal and Spain, settled in *Antwerp, *Hamburg, and *Amsterdam, some remaining nominally Christian and some openly returning to Judaism. In Antwerp the Ximenes and Rodrigues d'Evora families were outstanding among an important group of merchant bankers who had commercial relations extending as far as the East Indies and Brazil. While they remained Catholics (like the Mendes de Brito group in Portugal), those who emigrated to Hamburg and Amsterdam formed Sephardi communities. In Hamburg they participated in the founding of the bank in 1619; 30 (by 1623, 46) local Jews were among its first shareholders, and some of them were financial agents for various North European courts, especially those of Denmark and Schleswig-Holstein. Most famous in Antwerp were Diego *Teixeira de Sampaio (Abraham Senior), consul and paymaster general for the Spanish government, and his son Manuel (Isaac Ḥayyim Senior), who succeeded him as financial agent of Christina of Sweden. Manuel Teixeira was an outstanding member of the Hamburg exchange and participated actively in the transfer of Western European subsidies to the German or Scandinavian courts.

At Amsterdam at first only a few Jews were shareholders in the bank founded in 1609 and of the East India Company. One hundred and six Portuguese had accounts in 1620. Generally their resources were not sufficiently great to add any special weight to the formative stage of Amsterdam capitalism. Through Holland's developing overseas trade, especially with Brazil (until 1654) and then with the West Indies, as well as through the growth of the Amsterdam capital market and the transfer of subsidies and provisioning of armies through Amsterdam, Jewish financiers rose to importance in the exchange market, and were especially active in trading company shares. Outstanding were the *Pinto family and Antonio (Isaac) Lopez *Suasso (Baron d'Avernas le Gras); nevertheless the wealth of the Sephardi families remained far below that of their Christian counterparts. In the second half of the 18th century the Pinto family remained prominent, and another influential financier of Sephardi origin was David *Bueno de Mesquita.

Partly as a consequence of the marriage between Charles II of England and Catherine of Braganza (1662), and especially after William and Mary became joint sovereigns of England (1689), London, too, became a center of Sephardi banking, leading figures being Anthony (Moses) da *Costa, Solomon de *Medina, and Isaac *Pereira. In the reign of Queen Anne (1702–14), Manasseh *Lopes was a leading banker; during the 18th century Samson *Gideon, Francis and Joseph *Salvador, and the *Goldsmid brothers, leading members of the Ashkenazi community, were outstanding. In the middle of the 18th century Jacob Henriques claimed that his father had planned the establishment of the Bank of England (1694).

THE HOLY ROMAN EMPIRE. Only a few Jewish financiers, such as Joseph zum goldenen Schwan at Frankfort or *Michel Jud, were active in the German principalities in the 16th century. In the early 17th century the Hapsburgs employed the services of Jacob *Bassevi of Treuenberg of Prague, Joseph Pincherle of Gorizia, and Moses and Jacob Marburger of Gradisca. The rise of the absolute monarchies in Central Europe brought numbers of Jews, mostly of Ashkenazi origin, into the position of negotiating loans for the various courts, giving rise to the phenomenon of *Court Jews. The most famous and most active of them in financial affairs were, in the second half of

Figure 5. A Jewish pawnbroker, as depicted by the 15th-century Italian artist, Paolo Uccello. A panel from the series "The Profanation of the Host." Urbino, Galleria Nazionale delle Marche.

the 17th and the beginning of the 18th century, Leffmann *Behrends in Hanover, Behrend *Lehmann in Halberstadt, Bendix Goldschmidt in Hamburg, Aaron Beer in Frankfort, and Samuel *Oppenheimer and Samson *Wertheimer in Vienna. Later Diego d'*Aguilar, and the *Arnstein and *Eskeles families became prominent. In the early 18th century Joseph Suess *Oppenheimer was the outstanding figure in southern Germany; his financial influence was widespread, especially in Wuerttemberg, until his fall and execution in 1738. Important court bankers around the end of the 18th century were Israel *Jacobson in Brunswick, the *Bleichroeder family in Berlin, Simon Baruch and Solomon *Oppenheimer in Bonn, the *Rothschilds in Frankfort, the Reutlinger, Seligmann, and *Haber families in Karlsruhe, the Kaulla family in Stuttgart, and Aron Elias Seligmann, later baron of Eichthal, in Munich.

Italy. In the 15th and beginning of the 16th century the Italian loan-bankers reached their greatest eminence, including the Pisa, *Volterra, Norsa, Del Banco, *Rieti, and Tivoli families. In their wealth and style of life these men belonged to the Renaissance milieu as much as the artists and men of letters. However, with the expansion of the institution of the *Monte di Pietà* and the restrictive policy of the popes of the Counterreformation, their influence declined. The Da Pisa disappeared from Florence in 1570. However there were still between 60 and 70 loan-bankers operating in Rome toward the end of the 16th century and a century later about 20 were still in existence. In the first half of the 16th century about 500 loan-bankers were active throughout Italy; toward the end of the century about 280 remained in 131 places. Abraham del Banco was involved in the establishment of the famous Venetian Banco Giro in 1619.

19th and 20th centuries. Jewish banking in the 19th century begins with the rise of the house of *Rothschild in Frankfort, a city which became the new banking center of Europe as a result of the political upheaval caused by the French Revolution and the Napoleonic Wars. The founder of the house (which became the symbol of the 19th-century type of merchant banking), Meyer Amschel Rothschild started as a banker to the elector of Hesse-Kassel. His sons rose to prominence as the major European bankers Amschel Meyer in Frankfort, Solomon Meyer in Vienna, Carl Meyer in Naples, James Meyer in Paris, and Nathan Meyer in London. After the death of Abraham Goldsmid and Francis Baring in 1810, Nathan Rothschild became the dominant figure in the London money market. The majority of the English financial dealings with the continent went through the Rothschilds' offices. After the Congress of Vienna (1815) the Rothschilds extended their business into most European states, specializing in the liquidation of inflated paper currencies and in the foundation of floating public debts. In 1818 they made loans to European governments, beginning with Prussia and following with issues to England, Austria, Naples, Russia, and other states, partly in collaboration with Baring, Reid, Irving and Company. Between 1815 and 1828 the total capital of the Rothschilds rose from 3,332,000 to 118,400,000 francs.

The Merchant Bankers. Prominent merchant bankers in Germany besides the Rothschilds were Joseph *Mendelssohn and Samuel *Bleichroeder. Mendelssohn founded his firm in Berlin in 1795, and was joined by his brother Abraham *Mendelssohn in 1804; they issued state loans for industrial development to several foreign countries, particularly Russia. Samuel Bleichroeder, Berlin correspondent of the Rothschilds, established his own business in 1803. His son Gerson Bleichroeder became a confidant of Bismarck and served as his agent for financing the war of 1866 and for the transfer of the French war indemnity in 1871. The Bleichroeder bank also made loans to foreign states. After the death of Gerson Bleichroeder in 1893 his partner Paul Schwabach continued the business. The brothers Moses, Marcus, and Gerson *Warburg founded a bank in Hamburg in 1798. Its main business was concerned with the Hamburg overseas trade, especially transactions with England and the United States. Paul M. *Warburg, a brother of Max M. *Warburg, head of the Hamburg bank before World War I, established a branch office in New York. Toward the end of the 18th century J. M. *Speyer, through his bank's provisioning of armies and exchange business, had a capital of 420,000 florins, the largest Jewish fortune in Frankfort at that time. In 1809 G. J. Elissen opened a banking house which took the name of J. L. Speyer-Elissen in 1818 and Lazard Speyer-Elissen in 1838. Philipp Speyer and Co., the U.S. branch, negotiated the American credit during the Civil War, participated in the development of the railroads in America, and conducted transactions in Mexico and Cuba, partly in association with the Deutsche Bank. In 1928 Speyer amalgamated with C. Schlesinger, Trier, and Company to form Lazard Speyer-Elissen K. a. A., Frankfort and Berlin. The bank established by Solomon *Oppenheim in Bonn in 1789 acquired a leading position; at the beginning of the 19th century Solomon moved to Cologne, where his son Abraham became one of the most influential bankers in the Rhineland, financing insurance associations, railroad construction, and industrial investment.

Jewish bankers played an important part in the development of joint stock banks. Ludwig *Bamberger and Hermann Markuse were among the founders of the Deutsche Bank (1870), which was active in financing German foreign trade. The Disconto-Gesellschaft, established by David Hansemann in 1851, which amalgamated with the Deutsche Bank in 1929, had several Jewish partners. Eugen *Gutmann was the main founder of the Dresdner Bank, and Abraham Oppenheim was one of

Figure 6. The Amsterdam home of the Pinto banking family. Engraving by Romeyn de Hooghe (1645–1708). Amsterdam, Portuguese Jewish community.

the founders of the Bank fuer Handel und Industrie (Darmstaedter Bank; 1853). The leading personality in the Berliner Handelsgesellschaft (established in 1856) was Carl *Fuerstenberg. Richard Witting, brother of Maximilian Harden, was one of the directors of the Nationalbank fuer Deutschland; when it merged with the Darmstaedter Bank in 1921, Jacob *Goldschmidt, then director of the latter, took control of the new enterprise. In 1932 the two other most important banks in Germany, the Deutsche Bank and the Dresdener Bank, were directed by Oskar *Wassermann and Herbert Gutman respectively.

In England, banks were established by Sir David *Salomons (London and Westminster Bank, 1832), the Stern brothers (1833), Samuel *Montagu (1853), Emile Erlanger (1859), the Speyer brothers, *Seligman brothers, and S. Japhet and Co., many of them immigrants from Frankfort; the Speyer bank negotiated loans on behalf of Greece, Bulgaria, and Hungary, as well as for Latin American states. David *Sassoon and Company, established in Bombay in 1832, had branches throughout the Orient, handling extensive transactions. Sir Ernest *Cassel, partly in association with Sir Carl Meyer, established banks in Egypt and Turkey. Industrial banks were organized by Sir Moses *Montefiore and the Anglo-American Corporation, which was connected with the diamond and finance corporation of A. Dunkelsbueler, established by Sir Ernest *Oppenheimer. In South Africa the General Mining and Finance Corporation was set up by Hamilton Ehrlich and Turk, and one of the most important enterprises in South African financing was the Barnato brothers' company.

In France Achille *Fould, a competitor of the Rothschilds, was a supporter of Napoleon III and later his finance minister. Together with his brother Benoit he inherited the Paris firm of Fould, Oppenheimer et Cie., which had been established by his father. Meanwhile the brothers Emile and Isaac *Péreire, who moved to Paris from Marseilles in 1822, financed railway construction in France and Spain. Through the Crédit Mobilier, organized in 1852, they mobilized credit for various investment projects, but ran into difficulties in 1867. Among the other important Jewish banks was the Banque de Paris et des Pays-Bas (1872), with Henri Bamberger as one of the directors. The leading position among the private banks was held by Rothschild; from 1889 to 1901 all loans to Russia from Paris were issued through the Rothschild bank. Baron Maurice de *Hirsch from Munich, son-in-law of the Brussels banker Raphael Jonathan *Bischoffsheim, invested successfully in railroad construction. Other Jewish banks were those of Louis Dreyfus and *Lazard Frères. In Italy, where Luigi *Luzzatti's agricultural associations were largely philanthropic, Jewish bankers played a leading part in the foundation of the Banca Commerciale Italiana and the Credito Italiano. The Rothschilds, Sterns, and Goldsmids also invested money in Spain and Portugal.

Russia and Eastern Europe. A number of Jewish banks were established in Vienna during the 19th century, the most influential of which was Arnstein and Eskeles. This bank however was declared bankrupt in 1859. Weikersheim and Company and from 1821 Salomon Rothschild also established banks in Vienna. Jews participated in the foundation of the Niederoesterreichische Eskomptgessellschaft (1853) and the Kreditanstalt (1855), which made an essential contribution to the development of the Vienna stock exchange and extended international loan facilities, also investing in industry and railroads. Leading private banks in Hungary were of Jewish origin, such as the Ungarische Allgemeine Kreditbank (Hungarian General Credit Bank; established in 1867) with Siegmund Kornfeld as a general director, the Pester Ungarische Kommerzialbank (Hungarian Commercial Bank at Pest), established in 1841 by Moritz Ullmann, and the Ungarische Hypothekenbank (Hungarian Hypothecary Credit Bank; 1869) with Nándor (Ferdinand) Beck de Madarassy as its general director. In Prague the *Petschek family established a bank in 1920; in Galicia, under the Austrian regime, Brody (Nathanson, Kallir) and Lemberg had Jewish banks. Between the end of the 18th century and the beginning of the 19th Jewish banks of some importance rose in Russia. In St. Petersburg Nicolai and Ludwig *Stieglitz, immigrants from Germany, opened a bank in 1803, which under Ludwig (who with his brother was converted to Christianity in 1812) became one of the leading financial institutions in Russia. Otherwise Jewish banking activity was limited to southern Russia, especially to Berdichev and Odessa. In 1860 Yozel (Yerzel) *Guenzburg, originally a tax farmer, established the St. Petersburg bank J. Y. Guenzburg, and later the discount and credit bank there, managed by his son Horace; Guenzburg also established banks in Kiev and Odessa. Lazar (Eliezer) *Poliakoff opened a bank at Moscow in 1860 and participated in the foundation of the Moskowsky Zemelny Bank and other Moscow banks. Poliakoff and his two brothers also founded banks in southern Russia. Abram *Zak was director of the Petersburg Discount and Credit Bank (1871–93), and Soloveitchik established the Siberian Trade Bank. At the beginning of the 20th century private banks of some importance were those of H. *Wawelberg in St. Petersburg, and O. Chayes and R. Sonschein and Company in Odessa.

Toward the end of the 18th century several bankers such as Koenigsberger, Levy, and Simon Simoni emigrated from the west to Poland. Jacob *Epstein, court purveyor to King Stanislas II Augustus, founded an important dynasty of bankers. The Polish revolt of 1863 caused the bankruptcy of many Jewish banks. The bank of Wilhelm Landauer in Warsaw, established in 1857, closed in that year. However, Landauer returned to Warsaw some years later and opened a joint stock company in 1913. Mieczyslaw Epstein founded the Warsaw Discount Bank in 1871. Leopold *Kronenberg took part in the foundation of the Warsaw Credit Union in 1869 and the following year established the first joint stock bank in Poland, Bank Handlowy at Warsaw. The Natanson family bank was in operation between 1866 and 1932. In Rumania, Maurice *Blank (d. 1921) established the house Marmorosch, Blank and Company, which his son, Aristide, directed after him.

Scandinavia and the Netherlands. The Goeteborgs

Bank in 1848 was established in Sweden through the agency of L. E. Magnes, Morris Jacobsson, Edward Magnus, and others. Theodor *Mannheimer was the first managing director of Scandinaviska Kreditakteibolaget, and Louis *Fraenkel managed Stockholm's Handelsbank from 1893 to 1911. The Danish merchant financiers Joseph *Hambro and his son Carl Joachim *Hambro settled in London in 1832 and founded Hambro's Bank there. A leading Danish banker was Isaac *Glückstadt, who managed the Landsmans-Bank at Copenhagen from 1872 until his death in 1910; he was succeeded by his son Emil. A. Levy Martin was finance minister in 1870 and from 1873 till 1897 director of the Copenhagen Handelsbank. From 1913 until his death in 1923, Markus Rubin was director of the Danish Notenbank. In Holland the firm of Lissa and Kann was established in 1805. Another Dutch firm of the same era was Wertheimer and Gompertz, later known as the Bankassociatie. In 1859 the firm of Lippman, Rosenthal and Company was established as a subsidiary of the International Bank of Luxembourg. Its international activities were widespread, especially through Netherlands state loans. The bank of Elzbacher in Amsterdam later merged with the Amsterdamsche Bank. In Rotterdam Rothschild was represented by Moses Ezechiels en Zonen (liquidated in 1888). The bank of Benjamin Marx (established in 1869), later Marx and Company, was in existence until 1922. In Belgium Jacques Errera, Joseph Oppenheim, and Isaac Stern, all from Brussels, and the brothers Sulzbach and J. May from Frankfort participated in the foundation of the Banque de Bruxelles in 1871. Private banks were those of F. M. Philippson and Company, the Societé Henri Lambert and Cassel and Company. Moving from Alsace to Switzerland in 1812, Isaac Dreyfus established a bank in Basle; after 1849 the firm was known as Isaac Dreyfus Soehne. It participated in the foundation of the Basler Handelsbank as well as the Basler Bankverein. The Hitler regime spelled the end of Jewish banking in the greater part of Europe; all Jewish banks in Germany were liquidated or transferred to a non-Jewish company (Solomon Oppenheim Jr. and Company in Cologne, for example, was changed into the firm of Pferdmenges and Company).

The United States. Already in early colonial times individual Jews were active in America as money brokers,

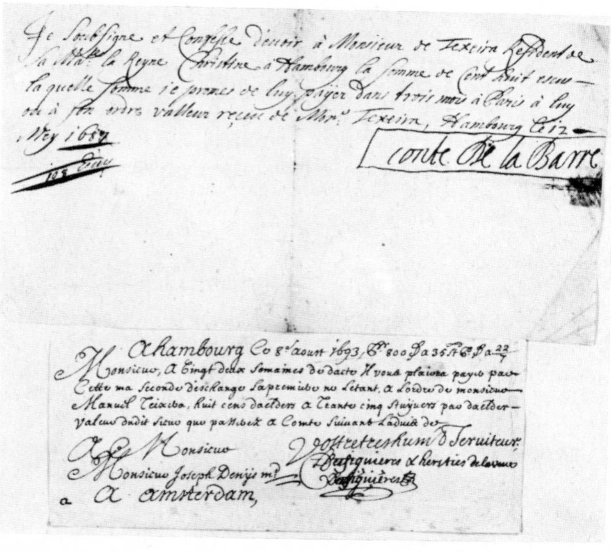
Je soubsigne et confesse devoir à Monsieur de Texeira Resident de
sa Ma[te]. la Reyne Christine à Hambourg la somme de cent huit escus
la quelle somme je promes de luy payer dans trois mois à Paris à luy
ou à son ordre valleur receue de Mon[r]. Texeira, Hambourg le 12
May 1687
108 Escus
Conte de la Barre

A Hambourg Ce 8e aoust 1693
Monsieur, A vingt deux semaines de dacte il vous plaira payer par
cette ma seconde d'eschange la premiere ne l'etant, a l'ordre de monsieur
Manuel Teixeira, huit cens daelders a trente cinq stuijvers par daelder
valeur dudit sieur que passerez a compte suivant l'advis de
A Monsieur
Monsieur Joseph Denijs
a Amsterdam,

Figure 7. Two documents of the 17th-century Hamburg banker, Manuel Teixeira. Above: a promissory note from Count De la Barre, 12 May, 1687. Below: A bill of exchange to the order of Teixeira addressed to Joseph Denys in Amsterdam, 8 August, 1693.

such as Asser *Levy, who functioned in New York City during the second half of the 17th century. Often such figures were helped by their extensive family or fellow-Jewish contacts overseas, as was the case with David *Franks, who was instrumental in raising money for the British army during the French and Indian War with the aid of his brother Moses, a London financier. The best known Jewish financier of the times was the legendary patriot Haym *Salomon, an immigrant from Poland who succeeded under extremely trying conditions in raising large amounts of desperately needed cash for the American Revolution by negotiating bills of exchange with France and the Netherlands. Yet another figure who helped finance the war for American independence was Isaac *Moses, later among the founders of the Bank of New York. It was not until the middle of the 19th century, however, with the arrival in America of a large German-Jewish immigration, that Jewish banking houses on the European model came to exist in the United States. Some of the founders of these firms, like Philip and Gustav *Speyer of Speyer & Co., went to the United States as American representatives of already established European concerns; others, like August *Belmont, crossed the Atlantic with a degree of previously acquired banking experence; still others, like the *Lehman brothers, Meyer and Emanuel, were essentially self-made men. Among other Jewish banking houses started by immigrants from Germany that developed into financial powers during the years 1840–1880 were Kuhn, Loeb Co., Lazard Frères, J. W. Seligman Co., Goldman, Sachs & Co., and Ladenburg, Thalman & Co. All of these firms functioned essentially as investment bankers—the more established field of commercial banking offered relatively few opportunities to the German-Jewish immigrant—a capacity in which they helped to finance large numbers of American utilities and corporations whose rapid growth throughout the latter half of the 19th century created an insatiable demand for capital. To raise such funds these Jewish houses not only freely utilized their widespread European connections, particularly in France, England, and Germany, but created a chain of interlocking associations and directorates among themselves which enabled them quickly to mobilize sums many times larger than their individual holdings and to compete successfully with gentile firms several times their size. Not only was it common for the children and relatives of a given firm to marry each other, but marital alliances frequently occurred as well among different Jewish banking families, as was the case with the *Loebs, the *Kuhns, the *Schiffs, and the *Warburgs. Frequently too the children of such families married into families of large German-Jewish companies in a variety of other fields and the latter would then proceed to raise capital through the banking houses which they had joined. Socially, the result of such commercial and kinship ties was the creation of a German-Jewish banking and business aristocracy based in New York City whose descendants continued for over a century to play a dominant role in the financial, cultural, and political life of the American Jewish community, and to a lesser extent, of the nation at large. The contribution of such Jewish banking houses to the process of capital formation in the United States in the late 19th and early 20th century was considerable by any standard. Several of them, such as Speyer & Co., August Belmont & Co., and J. & W. Seligman, raised large sums for the federal government both during and after the Civil War (the Jewish house of Erlanger Co., on the other hand, obtained sizeable loans for the Confederacy); others, such as Kuhn, Loeb, were particularly active in the westward expansion of the railroads. In the late 19th century Seligman Co. alone was capitalized at an estimated $10,000,000, while during the Russo-Japanese War of 1905 Jacob *Schiff of Kuhn, Loeb was able on short notice to float a bond issue of $200,000,000 on behalf of the Japanese government. Although the total assets of such Jewish firms were nevertheless small when compared to those of the American banking system as a whole, their clannishness and ability to coordinate their actions made them the focus of anti-Semitic agitation from the 1890s on, when caricatures of ruthless Jewish oligarchs at the head of an international Jewish money conspiracy began to abound in the ranks of the Populist movement. In reality, however, the fiscal policies of the German-Jewish firms tended to be highly conservative and their owners exercised their fortunes with an unusual degree of social as well as fiscal responsibility. Although a number of the great 19th-century Jewish banking houses such as Lazard Frères and Kuhn, Loeb have survived into the present, none has continued as a family or even exclusively Jewish concern and even the most prosperous of them have lost their former importance as a result of the steady trend in the American financial market toward the predominance of ever larger and more impersonal corporations. At the same time, the general field of commercial banking in the United States has remained relatively closed to Jewish participation despite heavy Jewish involvement in such related fields as stock brokerage, investment analysis, and corporate management. A study undertaken by B'nai B'rith in 1939 revealed that out of 93,000 bankers in the United States only 0.6% were Jewish, and that even in New York City Jews formed only 6% of banking executives as compared to 28% of the general population. Similar statistics for a later period are unavailable, but reports of discrimination against Jews in major banks throughout the country persist and in 1968 the American Jewish Committee publicly filed a complaint before the Human Rights Commission of New York City charging the banking system with job bias against Jews.

Assessment of the Role of Jewish Bankers. As shown above, Jewish activity, in particular in the late Middle Ages and in the 18th and 19th centuries, often played an important, sometimes a central, constructive role in the economy and social life of various countries, sometimes even internationally. However, banking always remained a subsidiary Jewish economic activity. Frequently, when Jews appeared to command large assets, they gave this impression because they mostly owned mobile property. The wealthy Jews always formed a small group, particularly in comparison with the wealthy nobles or Christian merchants. It was

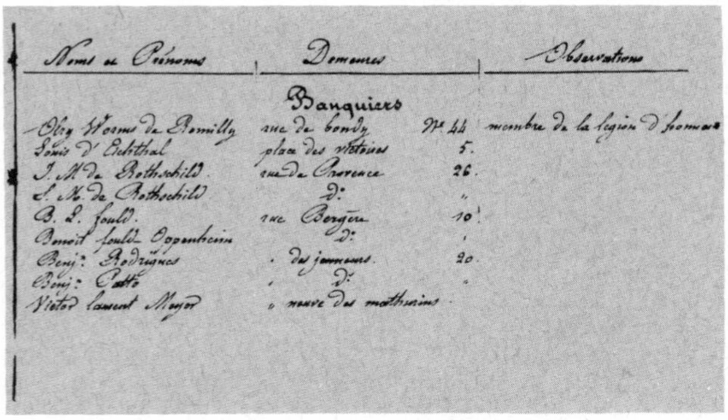

Figure 8. List of Jewish bankers living in the Seine department of France, 1817. They are Olry Worms de Romilly, member of the Legion of Honor, Louis d'Eichtal, J. M. de Rothschild, S. M. de Rothschild, B. L. Fould, Benoit Fould-Oppenheim, Benjamin Rodrigues, Benjamin Catto, and Victor Laurent Meyer. Jerusalem, C.A.H.J.P.

Figure 9. The Rothschild advertisement in the London *Jewish Chronicle*, 25 September, 1970.

really only in the 19th century that Jewish financiers achieved remarkable wealth, largely resulting from the activities of some European courts in consequence of the upheavals brought about by the French Revolution and the Napoleonic Wars. With the growth of joint stock banks and of central banks in the middle of the 19th century the field of private banking became limited. Around the beginning of the 20th century, Jewish influence in finance and banking had reached its zenith; afterward it declined at an accelerating rate.

See also *Israel; Economic Affairs.

Bibliography: Antiquity: Baron, Social[2], index s.v. *Banking and bankers;* L. Herzfeld, *Handelsgeschichte der Juden des Alterthums* (1894[2]); V. Tcherikover, *Hellenistic Civilization and the Jews* (1959), 333–43. Middle Ages–18th Century: I. Schipper, *Toledot ha-Kalkalah ha-Yehudit,* 2 vols. (1935–36); W. Sombart, *Jews and Modern Capitalism* (1951); J. Guttmann, *Die Juden und das Wirtschaftsleben* (1913), review of W. Sombart; M. Hoffmann, *Geldhandel der deutschen Juden waehrend des Mittelalters* (1910); G. Caro, *Sozial- und Wirtschaftsgeschichte der Juden,* 2 vols. (1908–20), index s.v. *Bankiers;* H. Waetjen, *Das Judentum und die Anfaenge der modernen Kolonisation* (1914); H. Schnee, *Hoffinanz und der Moderne Staat,* 6 vols. (1953–67); S. D. Goitein, *A Mediterranean Society,* 1 (1967); L. Poliakov, *Les Banchieri juifs et le Saint-Siège du XIIIè au XVIIè siècle* (1965). 19th and 20th Centuries: P. Emden, *Money Powers of Europe . . .* (1938); M. Lévy-Leboyer, *Les banques européennes . . .* (1964); J. Wechsberg, *Merchant Bankers* (1966); J. Riesser, *German Great Banks* (1911[3]); A. Marcus, *Die Wirtschaftliche Krise der deutschen Juden* (1931); idem, in: YIVOA, 7 (1952), 175–203; Goldberg, in: *Yivo Ekonomishe Shriftn,* 2 (1932), 56–92; S. Birmingham, *Our Crowd* (1967); K. Zielenziger, *Juden in der deutschen Wirtschaft* (1930); B. E. Supple, in: *Business History Review,* 31 no. 2 (1957); E. O. Eisenberg, in: *The National Jewish Monthly,* 53 no. 6 (Feb., 1939); Milano, in: JQR, 30 (1939/40), 149–86; Giuseppi, in: JHSEM, 6 (1962), 143–74; G. Myers, *History of the Great American Fortunes* (1910, 1937[2]); D. S. Landes, *Bankers and Pashas . . . in Egypt* (1958); K. Grunwald, *Hamizraḥ ha-Ḥadash: Ha-Banka'im ha-Yehudim be-Iraq,* 1 (1960), 160–5; H.-D. Kircholtes, *Juedische Privatbanken in Frankfurt/M.* (1969). See also bibliographies in articles on individual countries and families.

[H.Ke./Ed.]

BANNER, a recognized symbol shared by a large group of people: a family, tribe, military unit, or nation. In the Bible, banner is denoted by the word *nes.* Although scholars differ concerning the exact meaning of another term, *degel,* this term apparently designates a military unit (perhaps originally the emblem of the group). The *nes* was composed of two parts: a long pole with a symbol, the *ʾot,* carved or drawn on it. Isaiah 30:17 gives a clear description of the pole: "Till you are left like a flagstaff on the top of a mountain, like a signal *[nes]* on a hill." Numbers 21:8 distinguished the *nes* from the symbol that it bears: "Make a *seraf* [fiery] figure and mount it on a standard *[nes]* . . . " The *nes* (and the *ʾot* which was on it) was positioned so that the community to whom it belonged could see it from a distance and converge around it. During the period of Israel's wandering in the desert, the special design of each tribe's *nes* and *ʾot* enabled each of them to recognize and gather around its own standard and unit (Num. 2:2). The motif drawn on the *ʾot* was apparently related to the tradition of the community, or was significantly associated with it, in a manner similar to the totem in use among certain present-day tribal societies. The term *nes* is also used symbolically in the Bible to denote a sign which can be seen from a distance and can serve as a summons not only for a tribe or the nation of Israel but also for the entire world (Isa. 5:26). When the people of Israel went into exile, this concept came to be the symbol for the gathering of the exiles scattered over the face of the earth, and for the redemption of Israel in general (Jer. 4:6). The verb derived from this noun, *nss,* serves as a metaphoric description for divine inspiration in the soul of man (Isa. 59:19). With a meaning closer to that of the word *nzz,* this verb also describes the landscape in which precious stones are scattered (Zech. 9:16). Many Egyptian monuments from all periods depict standards or flags attached to poles which are carried by men. The symbols which appear on these standards or flags include illustrations of gods, cartouches, and other religious symbols. Some of the standards consist of a shield of metal or some other material mounted on a pole, with a group of ribbons attached to the join of the symbol and pole. Two different types of standards are depicted on Assyrian monuments from Nineveh. The first type, consisting of a pole bearing a ring to which streamers were attached, was placed on the side of a chariot, toward the rear, in a special place designated for it. The second, consisting of a pole with an opening at the top into which the symbol, probably of metal, was inserted, was carried by the charioteer. There are two recurring symbols on these monuments: one depicts two animals, and the other, a king or god standing on a bull. As is the case with other practical objects, these banners also served ritual needs. This type of ritual banner was found at Hazor (Stratum Ib). It consists of a silver-coated bronze tablet of approximately four in. (ten cm.). The snake goddess, surrounded by various other symbols, is depicted on it in relief. The base of the banner from Hazor was designed to be joined to the top of a pole as were the large banners.

See also *Flag.

Knights holding banners with the emblems of the four major tribes of Israel. Full page initial word panel for the Book of Numbers from the *Duke of Sussex Pentateuch,* S. Germany, c. 1300. The emblems are (top) the lion of Judah, (left) the serpent of Dan, (right) the eagle of Reuben, and (bottom) the bull of Ephraim. London, British Museum, Add. Ms. 15282, fol. 179 v.

Bibliography: N. De G. Davies, *The Rock Tombs of El-Amarna,* 1 (1903), pls. xv, xx, 2 (1905), pl. xvii; J. G. Wilkinson, *The Manners and Customs of the Ancient Egyptians,* 1 (1878), 195; A. H. Layard, *The Monuments of Nineveh,* 1 (1853), pls. 10, 11, 19, 22, 27; Y. Yadin et al. (eds.), *Hazor* 2 (1959), 109–110; Y. Aharoni, in: *Qadmoniot,* 1 (1968), 101.

[Z.Y.]

BÁNÓCZI, Hungarian literary family. (1) József (1849–1926), Hungarian literary historian, philologist, and Jewish educator. József was born in Szentgál, abandoned his rabbinical studies for a university education, and graduated from Leipzig. In 1878 he became a lecturer in philosophy at Budapest University, and later an associate professor. From 1879 József was a corresponding member of the Hungarian Academy of Sciences. He was appointed principal of the Budapest Jewish Teachers' College in 1887 and held the post until his death. József distinguished himself mainly by his research into the history of the Hungarian language and literature. He also helped to create Hungarian terminology for philosophical expressions. He wrote biographies of Miklós Révai, the first Hungarian philologist (1879), and of the poet Károly Kisfaludy (1882–83). József encouraged Jewish studies and founded the *Izraelita Magyar Irodalmi Társulat* (the Hungarian-Jewish Society for Literature), whose annual he edited. József, together with Wilhelm *Bacher and Samuel *Krauss; published a Jewish-sponsored Hungarian translation of the Bible. (2) László (1884–1945), son of József Bánóczi, Hungarian playwright, author and translator. László graduated from the university of his native Budapest. He was responsible for the establishment of the Thália theater, which catered to working-class audiences and was its first director. László was prominent in the Hungarian Social Democratic Party, which he represented on the Budapest Municipal Council. His books on the drama included *Shakespeare a mai szinpadon* ("Shakespeare on the Contemporary Stage," 1910). During World War II, László was active in the theater fostered by the O.M.I.K.E., a Jewish association for popular education, and it was mainly due to his efforts that Hungarian-Jewish cultural life was maintained in a wide field of activities.

Bibliography: *Magyar Zsidó Lexikon* (1929), 84–85; *Irodalmi Lexikon* (1927), 96; *Magyar Irodalmi Lexikon,* 1 (1963), 97.

[Al.Sch.]

BANSKA BYSTRICA (Hg. **Besztercebánya;** Ger. **Neusohl**), town in Slovakia, Czechoslovakia. Jews were not admitted there until 1848. The first to settle came from the surrounding villages and Galicia, and developed the manufacture of wood and leather products, and alcoholic beverages. A *Neolog congregation was established, which maintained an old-age home and a primary school. The Orthodox community was concentrated in the village suburb of Radvan, numbering about 250 persons, under the supervision of the *Lučenec rabbinate. A Zionist group was founded immediately after the First Zionist Congress was held in 1897. The Jewish population numbered 1,204 in 1930 (about 9% of the total). During World War II two-thirds of their number perished in death camps. Many were murdered after suppression of the partisan revolt on Oct. 28, 1944, of which Banska Bystrica was the center. The woman parachutist and resistance fighter Ḥavivah *Reik was born in Banka Bystrica. A small community was reestablished after World War II.

Bibliography: H. Iltis (ed.), *Die aussaeen unter Traenen...* (1959), 139–40; A. Nir, *Shevilim be-Ma'gal ha-Esh* (1967), 55; M. Lányi and H. Propper, *A szlovenszkói zsidó hitközégek története* (1933), 276–7.

[EL.SH.]

BANUS (first cent. C.E.), ascetic who according to Josephus "dwelt in the wilderness, wearing only such clothing as trees provided, feeding on such things as grew of themselves, and using frequent ablutions of cold water, by day and night, for purity's sake" (Jos., Life, 11–12). In his youth, Josephus claims to have been a devoted disciple of Banus, living with him for three years (c. 54–56 C.E.) before returning to the city to lead the life of a Pharisee. It is probable that Banus was an adherent of one of the many sects which were spread over the whole country, especially in the wilderness of Judea, not necessarily an *Essene or a member of the *Qumran sect. He may have been a hemerobaptist.

[I.G.]

BANUŞ, MARIA (1914–), Rumanian poet. Born in Bucharest, her first poems were published in 1928. She gained fame with her first collection of verse, *Tara fetelor* ("The Maidens' Land," 1937), a lyrical description of the awakening sensuality of adolescence. Maria Banuş came to

Maria Banuş, Rumanian poet.

be regarded as Rumania's outstanding poet on feminine themes. Despite her early detachment from Judaism, she adopted a more positive attitude toward Jewish life in the *shtetel* as a result of her experiences during the Holocaust. *Bucurie* ("Joy," 1949) includes some important poems about Jewish suffering during the Hitler era. After World War II, Maria Banuş regarded the Communist Party as the savior of mankind. Social and humanitarian themes dominate her *Torentul* ("The Torrent," 1959) and *Magnet* ("The Lodestone," 1962), in which the poet denounces war and calls on mothers everywhere to join in the effort to secure lasting peace.

Maria Banuş' collections of verse include *Fiilor mei* ("To my Sons," 1949); *Versuri alese* ("Selected Poems," 1953); *Despre pămînt* ("About the Earth," 1954); and *Se arată lumea* ("The World Shows Up," 1956). She also wrote two social dramas, *Ziua cea mare* ("The Great Day," 1951) and *Indrăgostiţii* ("The Lovers," 1954), and published translations of Goethe, Pushkin, Rilke, and Shakespeare. Many of her poems have been translated into English, Russian, and Chinese. She published *Din poezia de dragoste a lumii* ("Love Poetry in World Literature," 1965) including poems by Hebrew and Yiddish poets.

Bibliography: G. Călinescu, *Istoria literaturii romîne* (1941), 847, 925; C. Baltazar, *Scriitor şi om* (1946), 15–27; Popescu, in: *Contemporanul* (July 4 and 11, 1958); Damian, in: *Gazeta literară* (Aug. 13, 1959); Călinescu, in: *Contemporanul* (March 6, 1959); Georgescu, in: *Viaţa romînească* (Oct. 1964), 125–7.

[D.L.]

BAPTISM, FORCED. The nature of the Christian sacrament of baptism created special problems when it was carried out compulsorily, which differentiated it sharply from forced conversion to Islam (see *Anusim; *Jadid al-Islam). There is evidence that when Christianity established itself as the dominant religion in the Roman Empire, from the fourth century, large numbers of Jews were forcibly baptized: a detailed account is extant of the process in the island of *Minorca in 418. In due course, the church doctrine regarding this matter crystallized. From the time of Pope *Gregory I, it was generally agreed that by its very nature baptism should be accepted willingly and not imposed by force. Various problems however still remained. It was difficult to define what baptism by force actually implied, apart from sheer physical immersion: did it cover also "willing" acceptance of conversion under menace of death, or under a remoter anticipation of violence, or with the alternative of expulsion? Moreover, when baptism was illegally imposed, did it remain valid, or was the victim at liberty to return to his former faith unmolested? This last was a peculiarly complicated problem in the context of medieval Christianity, for if baptism was valid however conferred, the backsliding was an act of heresy, punishable by death according to the code later elaborated by the Inquisition. In any case, the conception of forcible baptism did not apply in the case of the children or grandchildren of the unwilling converts, who were frequently taken by their parents to church for baptism as a matter of routine when they were born (see *Conversos, *Marranos). Another problem presented itself in the case of infants: at what age could they be presumed to have minds of their own and to accept baptism "willingly" and not passively, or in return for some trivial temptation? On the whole, it may be said that whereas the church doctrine on the matter of forced baptism, which it theoretically condemned, remained unchanged, its attitude as regards *ex post facto* problems hardened through the centuries.

In the seventh century a wave of forced conversions spread over Europe, sparked off when in 614 Emperor *Heraclius forbade the practice of Judaism in the Byzantine Empire. He is said to have summoned his fellow sovereigns to follow his example; and similar steps were taken in Gaul in 626 by King Dagobert; in Italy in 661 by the Lombard sovereign Perctarit; and in Spain from

616 under successive Visigothic rulers. In the Byzantine possessions, including southern Italy, Heraclius' example was imitated in 873–4 under *Basil I. It is difficult however in most such cases to determine how effectively, and for how long a period, the edicts were put into execution; while on the other hand it is debatable how far baptism with the alternative of exile can be strictly considered in the category of "forced conversion." Moreover the mob sometimes took matters into its own hands and imposed baptism on the steadfast believers who had prepared themselves for the heroic alternative. This is what seems to have happened for example at the time of the campaign of the Byzantine emperor *Romanus I Lecapenus in 932–36 to suppress Judaism in his dominions, when a number of Jewish leaders died rather than submit.

Apart from such cases of mass baptism to escape expulsion as mentioned above, the earliest recorded instance of forced baptism in the more restricted sense seems to have been shortly after 820 in Lyons, where as part of his campaign to convert the Jews (described in his *Epistola de baptismo Judaicorum*), Archbishop *Agobard of Lyons assembled the children who had not been sent into safety by their parents and baptized all those who to his mind appeared to show some desire for conversion. When about 938 the archbishop of Mainz asked Leo VII whether he should force the Jews of his diocese to be baptized or expel them, the pope advised on the latter course. Many Jews, especially in the Rhineland, were baptized literally by force during the first and subsequent *Crusades, and the antipope *Clement III protested violently against their being permitted subsequently to revert to Judaism. On the other hand, after Benedict, the leader of the Jews of York was forcibly baptized on the day of Richard I's coronation (Sept. 3, 1189), the archbishop of Canterbury declared that if he desired to return to worship the devil he should be given free choice. One of the clauses in the *Constitutio pro Judaeis* issued by successive popes (including some of those least favorable to Jews) from the beginning of the 12th down to the close of the 15th century (see *Popes) declared categorically that no Christian should use violence to force Jews to be baptized so long as they were unwilling—though without specifying what was to happen if the illegal process actually took place. Indeed, Pope *Innocent III, in a letter of 1201 to the archbishop of Arles, considered that a Jew who submitted to baptism under threat of force expressed a conditional willingness to accept the sacrament, with the corollary that he was not at liberty to renounce it. On the other hand, Innocent IV in 1246 categorically forbade the forced baptism of children, the same presumably applying a fortiori to adults. However, in the last decades of the 13th century the strength of the Jewish communities of the Kingdom of Naples was broken by a wave of forced baptisms, sparked off by an apostate from Trani named Manuforte: the descendants of the victims, known as neofiti (see *Crypto-Jews), long remained a recognizable group, suspected of secret fidelity to their ancestral religion.

The events in the Kingdom of Naples in a way set the example for the wholesale wave of compulsory baptisms which swept Spain in and after 1391. This left in its train the phenomenon of the Marranos, which continued to be a problem in the Iberian Peninsula for centuries to come. It may be noted that a very large number, perhaps the majority, of these insincere conversions, especially after the initial episodes, were not the immediate result of actual violence, but were ostensibly quasi-spontaneous in anticipation of it or as the result of moral rather than physical pressure. This did not however apply to the large-scale happenings in Portugal in 1496/97, when practically the whole of the considerable Jewish community of that

ÉDIT DU Sᵀ. OFFICE.

NOUS FRERE JEAN-BAPTISTE MABIL, DOCTEUR EN SAINTE THÉOLOGIE, DE L'ORDRE DES FRERES PRECHEURS, INQUISITEUR-GÉNERAL DE LA FOI DANS AVIGNON ET TOUT LE COMTAT VENAISSIN.

EN exécution des ordres ſuprêmes de Notre Saint Pere le Pape PIE VI, heureuſement regnant, & au nom de la Sacrée Congrégation du Saint Office de Rome, à nous adreſſés par Lettre de ſon Eminence Monſeigneur le Cardinal TORRIGIANI, en date de Rome du ſixieme préſent Mars. Ordonnons être faites très-expreſſes inhibitions & défenſes par criée publique & ſon de trompette précédent, & par affiche publique des Copies des Préſentes, aux Places & Lieux accoutumés de la préſente Ville D'Avignon, & de toutes les Villes, Villages & Bourgs du Comtat Venaiſſin, & même aux Places & Portes des Carrieres & Sinagogues des Juifs de la préſente Ville, & des Villes de Carpentras, Cavaillon & Liſle, A tous les Habitans de la préſente Ville, deſdites Villes, Villages & Bourgs tant Chrétiens, que Juifs, de baptiſer les enfans Juifs, ni ſe jacter, ou menacer de les baptiſer ou menacer de dire de les avoir baptiſés; Et en outre a fait inhibitions & defenſes à toutes perſonnes, de quelque état, & qualité qu'elles ſoient, d'enlever de leurs Parens les enfans Juifs, ſous prétexte de Baptême, ou ſur la déclaration, que quelqu'un pourroit avoir fait de les avoir baptiſés, & ſous prétexte de les faire élever dans la Religion Catholique, ſous peines corporelles, même de la Galere pour les hommes, & du foüet par les Rues publiques pour les femmes, encourables ſans aucune remiſſion par tous ceux qui oſeront baptiſer leſdits enfans Juifs, ou ſe vanter, ou menacer de les baptiſer, ou menacer de dire de les avoir baptiſés. Voulant & ordonnant, que telle Publication & Affiche publique ſervent de perſonnelle intimation. DONNÉ à Avignon dans le Palais du Saint Office, le vingtieme Mars mille ſept cens ſoixante & ſeize.

F. JEAN-BAPTISTE MABIL, *Inquiſiteur-Général.*
Vû JOSEPH RIGAUD, *Avocat Fiſcal.*
PONCET, *Secrétaire du Saint Office.*

A Avignon, chez BONNET Freres, Imprimeurs du St. Office, vis-à-vis le Puits des Bœufs.

An edict issued at Avignon in 1776 by the order of Pope Pius VI prohibiting the forced baptism of Jewish children. The text reads: "Edict of the Holy Office. We, Brother Jean Baptiste Mabil, Doctor of Theology of the Order of the Preaching Friars, inquisitor-general of the faith in Avignon and the whole Comtat Venaissin. In execution of the supreme orders of our holy father Pope Pius VI, happily reigning, and in the name of the sacred congregation of the Holy Office of Rome, addressed to us in a letter from his Eminence Monseigneur Cardinal Torrigiani, dated Rome, the sixth of the present month of March. We order the absolute prohibition and interdiction, by public proclamation preceded by trumpet calls, and by public posters in the usual places in this town of Avignon and in all the towns, villages and boroughs of Comtat Venaissin, and also in public squares and entrances to business premises and Jewish synagogues in this town and in the towns of Carpentras, Cavaillon, and Lisle, for all the inhabitants of this town and the towns, villages and boroughs aforesaid, Christians as well as Jews, of baptizing Jewish children, and of speaking of or threatening baptism, and of threatening to say that they have been baptized; and in addition the prohibition and interdiction of all persons, whatever their rank and quality, from taking Jewish children away from their parents under the pretext of baptism, or on the declaration that someone may have had them baptized, and under the pretext of having them brought up in the Catholic religion, on pain of corporal punishment, including the galleys for men, and whipping through the public streets for women, to be incurred without any remission by all those who dare to baptize the said Jewish children, or who boast, or threaten to baptize them, or threaten to say that they have had them baptized. Requiring and ordering that such publication and public posting serve as personal notification. Given at Avignon in the palace of the Holy Office, the twentieth of March 1776. F. Jean-Baptiste Mabil, inquisitor-general, witnessed by Joseph Rigaud, financial counsel, Poncet, secretary of the Holy Office."

country were hounded into Christianity by actual violence or were baptized forcibly notwithstanding their protests. This explains the greater tenacity of Marranism in that country in subsequent generations, and down to the present day.

Pope *Martin V categorically forbade (c. 1419) the baptism of Jewish infants below the age of 12 without the parents' permission, to counteract an abuse which was at this time becoming widespread. But a new chapter in the history of forcible baptism began with the institution in Rome in 1543 of the House of *Catechumens (Casa dei Catecumeni), speedily followed in other cities. To justify their existence these institutions had to elaborate a system of propagating the faith, in which ultimately it became difficult to differentiate force from persuasion. Any person who could be imagined by whatever casuistry as having shown an inclination toward Christianity, or who could be considered to be under the authority of a person already converted, could be immured in the House of Catechumens in order to "explore his intention," meanwhile being submitted to unremitting pressure. In 1635 it was decided that the baptism of the head of a household could entail, if he expressed the desire, that of all those members of his family who were under age or dependent upon him, and this was subsequently extended to cover even more remote cases. There had moreover grown up a popular superstition that any person who secured the baptism of an unbeliever was assured of paradise, this leading to a spate of such ceremonies, verging on parody in execution though not in their tragic outcome, throughout the Catholic world.

At Reggio Emilia, during the plague of 1630, a barber summarily christened after his own style 17 or 18 Jewish children in the pest-house that had been set up—the survivors being thereafter brought up as Christians. In 1747 Pope *Benedict XIV decided that once baptized, even against the prescriptions of canon law, a child was to be considered a Christian and educated under church influence. In 1762, the son of the rabbi of Carpentras was pounced on and baptized in ditch water by a callous ruffian and thereafter lost to his family. The kidnapping for baptism of Terracina children in 1783, at the request of a remote relative, caused a veritable revolt in the Roman ghetto. Similar abuses took place in the Catholic lands of Central Europe and in Poland, where the *Jesuits were said to be the principal culprits in the mid-18th century. After the Napoleonic wars, the abuse in its worst form was restricted to those areas in Italy where the popes, now driven by circumstances into reaction, still wielded temporal power. The best-known instance was the *Mortara Case (1858) in Bologna; but it was neither the worst nor the last. In the Russian Empire in the second quarter of the 19th century the institution of the *Cantonists—involving the virtual kidnapping for military service of Jewish male children from the age of 12, or even 8—was introduced in the expressed hope of compelling them to abandon Judaism. The number of forced or virtually forced baptisms which resulted probably exceeded all similar cases in other lands throughout history. During the Nazi persecutions in Central and Eastern Europe in 1940–45, many Jewish children were baptized by well-meaning Christians in order to help in saving their lives, or when contact with their parents was lost.

Bibliography: B. Blumenkranz, *Juifs et Chrétiens dans le monde occidental* (1960), index s.v. *baptême;* S. Grayzel, *The Church and the Jews in the XIIIth Century* (1966²), index s.v. *Baptism, involuntary* and *Conversion, of Jews;* J. Parkes, *Conflict of the Church and the Synagogue* (1934), index; Roth, Italy, index; idem, *Personalities and Events in Jewish History* (1953), 256–74; idem, *Gleanings* (1967), 240–63.

[C.R.]

BĀQĀ AL-GHARBIYYA; BĀQĀ AL SHARQIYYA (باقا الغربية باقا الشرقية), two Muslim-Arab villages in central Israel, east of Ḥaderah. The first became part of Israel following the 1949 armistice agreement with Jordan. The village's economy was developed by the introduction of new farming methods and the establishment of workshops and preserves-industry enterprises. It serves as an administrative center for the Arab villages of the vicinity and is the seat of the Muslim Shariʿa Court for central Israel. In 1968 it had a population of 6,400. Bāqā al-Sharqiyya, which remained on the Jordanian side of the border in 1949, was occupied by Israel during the Six-Day War of 1967. In contrast to Bāqā al-Gharbiyya, its layout and economic and social structure remained largely traditional. Its population in 1967 was 1,205. [E.O.]

BAʿQŪBA, town c. 25 mi. (40 km.) N. of Baghdad. Under the Abbasid caliphate, Baʿqūba was a district center, with a prosperous Jewish community. At the end of the eighth century, Manasseh b. R. Joseph of Baʿqūba, was head of the academy of *Pumbedita. Even later, many Jews lived in the town. In the early 12th century, a self-styled herald of the messiah, Ibn Shadad, appeared in Baʿqūba and began a movement which was suppressed by the Muslim authorities. The community existed into the 19th century.

Bibliography: J. Obermeyer, *Landschaft Babylonien* (1929), 144f.; Goitein, in: JJS, 4 (1953), 79; Mann, in: REJ, 71 (1920), 90f.; A. Ben-Jacob, *Yehudei Bavel* (1965), 13f., 222.

[E.A.]

BAR, town in Vinnitsa oblast, Ukrainian S.S.R. It passed to Russia at the second partition of Poland in 1793, and from 1796 to the 1917 Russian Revolution was a district capital in the province (government) of Podolia. The Bar community was one of the oldest in the Ukraine. Jews are first mentioned there in 1542. By an agreement concluded in 1556 with the citizens of Bar the Jews were permitted to own buildings and had the same rights and duties as the other residents; they were permitted to visit other towns in the district for business purposes but were forbidden to provide lodging for Jewish visitors in the city. The agreement was formally ratified the same year by the Polish king Sigismund II. The community grew during the second half of the 16th and the first half of the 17th century, and Jews from Bar engaged in trade in places as far away as Moldavia. According to a contemporary chronicler the Bar community in 1648 numbered some 600 Jewish families, "men of wealth and standing." During the *Chmielnicki uprising in that year, many of the Jews in Bar were massacred. There was a further slaughter of the Jewish inhabitants by Cossacks and Tatars in 1651. There were 17 houses (out of 107) in Jewish ownership in Bar in 1565, 23 in 1570–71, and approximately 20 in 1661. In 1717, authorization to erect a synagogue in Bar was granted by the bishop. After 1793, under Russian rule, the community also developed. The Jewish population numbered 4,442 in 1847, 5,773 in 1897 (58% of the total), and 10,450 (46%) in 1910. Twenty Jews in Bar lost their lives during a pogrom in the summer of 1919. Religious and communal life came to an end with the establishment of the Soviet government. The Jewish population totaled 5,270 in 1926 (55%).

After the German and Rumanian invasion in World War II Bar was included in the district of *Transnistria, administered by Rumania. Many Jews expelled from Rumania were deported to Bar which itself was under

German administration. In October 1942, 12,000 Jews from the area, both local residents and expellees, were murdered.

Bibliography: *Bulletin of Rescue Committee of Jewish Agency for Palestine* (May 1946), 6–8; M. Carp, *Cartea Neagră*, 3 (1947), index; idem, *Transnistria, Lebn, Leidn un Umkum* (1950), 263.

[Y.S.]

BARAITA, BERAITOT (Aram. בָּרַיְתָא (בְּרַיְיתָא) pl. בָּרַיְתוֹת (בְּרַיְיתוֹת)), the Aramaic for the Hebrew *ḥiẓonah* ("outside"; *ḥiẓonah* occurs in Num. R. 18:17; et al.). A *baraita* is thus a Mishnah *ḥiẓonah* ("an outside Mishnah"). This term covers every *halakhah*, halakhic Midrash, and historical or aggadic tradition, which is "outside" (i.e., not included in) *Judah ha-Nasi's *Mishnah; some directly connected with a Mishnah and others independent of the Mishnah. The expression *baraita* is employed in the Babylonian Talmud (it occurs only once in the Jerusalem Talmud TJ, Nid. 3:3, 50d) mainly to emphasize a view opposed to that of the Mishnah. The author of a *baraita* is called *tanna bara* ("an outside *tanna*") as against *tanna didan* ("our *tanna* of the Mishnah"). An anonymous *baraita* is generally referred to as a *mishnah* or *matnita*, the latter term being however applied in the Jerusalem Talmud to both a *mishnah* and a *baraita*. On the basis of the talmudic expression, "Go and teach it outside" (*le-bara*), it has been suggested that a *baraita* refers to a *halakhah* taught outside the regular "tannaitic" schools, a suggestion rejected by H. Albeck (*Meḥkarim ba-Baraita u-va-Tosefta* (1944), 3) on the grounds that talmudic sources indicate no connection between the two.

Some *beraitot* are no longer extant, and of those that are, not all are quoted in the two Talmuds. The *amoraim* apparently derived them either from those who made a special study of them, or directly from compilations of *beraitot* (see *Tannaim). The redaction of these compilations is undoubtedly post-mishnaic, since they refer to many *tannaim* of later generations and of the transitional period between the *tannaim* and the *amoraim*.

Date. The *beraitot* did not originate in a specific period. They include early traditions which either served as a basis for the formulation of the Mishnah, or are analogous to it and on occasion embody more original versions. Others contain large sections of tannaitic *mishnayot* not incorporated in the Mishnah. Some very early traditions date from the Second Temple period (e.g., on R. Joshua b. Peraḥyah and R. Ḥilafta b. Kevina: Tosef., Makhsh. 3:3–4; the dispute between Hillel and Benei *Bathyra: TJ, Pes. 6:1, 33a; and parallel passages). Other *beraitot* are explicable only as having been based on the Mishnah in general and on that of Judah ha-Nasi in particular. In referring to their completion, I. Halevy (Dorot, 2 (1923), ch. 28) had in mind only the later *beraitot* which, dependent on the Mishnah, originated in the days of the *amoraim*.

Mishnah-Baraita. The *amoraim* used all the extensive material excluded from Judah ha-Nasi's Mishnah but contained in the *beraitot* for supplementary, comparative, corroborative, or critical purposes, or for solving a problem newly raised in the school. Sometimes a *baraita* was preferred to a *mishnah* (Er. 36b; Suk. 19b; TJ, Ḥag. 1:1, 75d; et al.), but generally the latter is the more authoritative. Where they conflicted with or contradicted each other, it was preferable to declare the *baraita* a faulty tradition (Shab. 121b; Pes. 99b) rather than to emend the Mishnah. The *amoraim* were not always acquainted with *beraitot*, and hence the occasional remark: "He does not know the *matnita*" (Shab. 19b; Er. 19b), or "If it has been taught, it has been taught" (i.e., do not try to change the meaning; Shab. 115b). In post-talmudic times this influenced the method of arriving at a legal decision, since a disputed *baraita* does not represent the *halakhah* (*Iggeret Sherira Ga'on*, ed. B. M. Lewin (1921), 36; *Seder Tanna'im ve-Amora'im*, ed. by A. Marx, in *Festschrift I. Lewy* (1911)).

The Place of Origin of the Beraitot. Like the Mishnah, the *beraitot* originated in Ereẓ Israel, and hence at times the question: "What is the position in Babylonia?" (BB 12a), or the statement "Nowadays" (Meg. 31a). It is generally agreed, however, that in tannaitic times there were centers of learning in Babylonia (Nisibis is explicitly mentioned) in which traditions and *halakhot* were preserved, and *halakhot* and halakhic Midrashim originated. Some Babylonian *tannaim* studied and taught in Babylonia, or having studied in Ereẓ Israel, principally in the school of R. Ishmael, brought their knowledge back to Babylonia where they further developed it. According to Sherira Gaon (op. cit. 90), before the time of Judah ha-Nasi, the Babylonian sages had *mishnayot*, for example, those of R. Nathan. Z. H. Chajes (*Kol Sifrei Z. H. Chajes*, 2 (1958), 521) has drawn attention to *beraitot* of Babylonian origin, these being indicated in the Jerusalem Talmud by the words *tannayyei tamman* תנויי תמן ("there"; i.e., in Babylonia, "it has been taught") and in the Babylonian by *ve-khan* ("and here:" Git. 15a; et al.). There are further indications of the Babylonian origin of *beraitot;* such as when the Babylonian Talmud says of two contradictory *beraitot*, "The one refers to us, the other to them" (Suk. 36a, et al.); when *beraitot* contain the names of Babylonian *tannaim*, such as R. Aḥa, R. Zutra, R. Nathan (Ber. 2, 13b, 48b, et al.), or are quoted from the compilations of Babylonian *tannaim*, such as "The school of Rav, or of Samuel, taught," or are reported by Babylonian *amoraim*, such as "R. Joseph taught," and possibly most of those introduced by *be-matnita tanei* ("in the *matnita [baraita]* it was taught"). It is doubtful, as some contend, whether the halakhic Midrashim of the school of R. Ishmael, in which only Babylonian *tannaim* are quoted, originated in Babylonia, since these compilations were also known in Ereẓ Israel. Furthermore, the Babylonian *geonim* refer to the **Mekhilta* of the school of R. Ishmael as a *Mekhilta* of Ereẓ Israel (*Teshuvot ha-Ge'onim*, ed. by A. Harkavy, 4 (1887), no. 229).

Types of Beraitot. The *beraitot* belonging to the transitional and amoraic periods constitute a special type. Some of these "emanated from the mouth of the company [of sages]," or were formulated after "they [the *amoraim*] took a vote and decided" on them. These expressions frequently were used by the earlier *amoraim* (Shab. 3a; Yev. 92b, et al.). In the transitional period, new rulings, cast in mishnaic language, were promulgated as can be seen from the statement (TJ, Beẓah 1:4, 60c) that after his son Judah had given a wrong decision, Ḥiyya publicly taught through a *tanna*, the correct *halakhah*. In the amoraic period two types of *halakhah* made their appearance. One, called *memrot* ("statements") was clearly indicated as either new *halakhot* or interpretations of the *amoraim*. The other occurred as *beraitot* transmitted by *tannaim* or by *amoraim* such as R. Joseph or R. Sheshet.

A different attitude can be sensed on the part of the *amoraim* to *beraitot* of this type, usually quoted in the name of a *tanna*, of an *amora*, or as the compilation of a school. Aware that these traditions contained tannaitic or amoraic additions or adaptations, the *amoraim* often controverted them with the remark, "Go and teach it outside *[le-bara]*, it is not a *mishnah*," or "Repudiate it." But sometimes they endorsed them by adding, "So indeed it has been taught" (Er. 86a; Suk. 26a), indicative of the generally ambivalent approach of the *amoraim* to these *beraitot*, undoubtedly because of their mode of study and their attitude to the *tannaim*. To this type of *beraitot* belong many introduced by the expression "A *tanna* taught a *baraita* in the presence of

R . . . ," or "In the *matnita* it is taught," in addition to those quoted from amoraic compilations such as those of the school of Samuel, of Bar Kappara, or of R. Ishmael. Common to all these *beraitot* is that they seldom present conflicting views or the names of *tannaim*, and are anonymous. To this category also largely belong *beraitot* introduced by "R. Ḥiyya taught" or "R. Oshaya taught." These two sages of the transitional period enjoyed a special status, as is apparent from the comment (Ḥul. 141a–b) that "Every *matnita* which has not been taught in the school of R. Ḥiyya or of R. Oshaya is not authentic." It can be inferred from *Sanhedrin* 33a that these *beraitot*, which H. Albeck (op. cit., 29) has stated refer to anonymous ones taught in the school of Ḥiyya and Oshaya, are compared to Judah ha-Nasi's Mishnah. Most scholars agree that these *beraitot* of Ḥiyya and Oshaya are not identical with the "larger *mishnayot*" mentioned in the Palestinian sources together with the Mishnah of Bar Kappara (TJ, Hor. 3:9, 48c; Eccl. R. 6:2, no. 1; Song R. 8:2, no. 1). These were in the nature of a parallel Mishnah to that of Judah ha-Nasi, containing apparently additions, variant readings, a different tradition regarding controversies, and different halakhic rulings. Since Ḥiyya's Mishnah was dependent on and parallel to Judah ha-Nasi's, the *amoraim* declared: "If R. Judah ha-Nasi has not taught it, whence could R. Ḥiyya have known it?" (Er. 92a, et al.), and "The Mishnah needs R. Ḥiyya's *matnita*, and R. Ḥiyya's *matnita* needs the Mishnah" (TJ, Shab. 1:1, 3a).

There were likewise *beraitot* "of the school of Judah ha-Nasi," which occur in the Jerusalem Talmud and sometimes also in the Babylonian Talmud (Er. 75b.; Ned. 39b). They are contrasted in the former with Judah ha-Nasi's Mishnah in the expression, "We have learnt in a *mishnah*—the school of Judah ha-Nasi taught." Z. Frankel regards these as a different version of Judah ha-Nasi's Mishnah, and likewise other scholars, such as I. H. Weiss, contend that some pupils of Judah ha-Nasi were opposed to his Mishnah and the form it took. Other scholars again (see, for example, Epstein, Mishnah, 75) maintain that these were actual *beraitot* which, proposing variant readings to, or interpreting and complementing, the Mishnah, emanated from the school of Judah ha-Nasi or from him personally. Scholars are divided on the question as to whether the *beraitot* were committed to writing at the time, a question which applies equally to the Mishnah. However, if there is clear and explicit evidence of the existence of written notes and compilations, this refers to *beraitot*, such as the secret scroll which Rav found in the home of Ḥiyya (Shab. 6b, et al.), the notebook of R. Ilfa (Men. 70a; TJ, Ma'as. 2:4, 49d), and the statement "Levi inserted this passage in his *baraita*" (Yev. 10a, acc. to the Arukh), "I saw the list of forbidden relatives of the second degree of Mar bar Rabbana and sixteen were written down" (*ibid.*, 21b), "he did not show me the *baraita*, he told it to me verbally" (TJ Dem. 2:2, 22d), etc. Similarly it is possible to prove that *beraitot* were altered in a manner which can be explained only on the assumption that the alterations or omissions could have been made only in a written text (see *Tarbiz* 28 (1959), 162–4). It is evident from this, therefore, that the teachers of the *beraitot* made use of written material when they delivered their discourses to their *amoraim* in the *bet ha-midrash*.

Terms Used to Indicate a Baraita. *Beraitot* which are not in the name of their redactors or of *tannaim-amoraim* are quoted in the Babylonian Talmud after the expressions *tyuvta* ("refutation"), *rumya* ("objection"), *tanya* ("it is stated in the *baraita*"), *tannu rabbanan* ("the rabbis have taught"), and *tanna* ("it is taught"). These different expressions may refer to different types of *beraitot*. Contrary to Sherira Gaon's view that the statement *tannu rabbanan* introduces *beraitot* of Ḥiyya and Oshaya taught in the schools, rather than those of other compilations, a careful examination of the relevant passages shows that this introductory expression is also used for *beraitot* the text of which was not established in the schools (see, for example, Beẓah 26a–b), for historical traditions, *aggadot*, halakhic matter, and halakhic Midrashim quoted from various compilations. H. Albeck's (*op. cit.*, 10) suggestion therefore that all these terms are merely a matter of style can be accepted. In tractate *Nedarim*, for example, *tannu rabbanan* is not used at all (apart from one passage in a manuscript) and in certain tractates the word *"tanna"* is limited to minor additions to a *mishnah* or *baraita*. Weiss (Dor, 2 (1904) 149, 151, 212) establishes the principle that *tanya* occurs before *beraitot* beginning with the name of a sage, *tannu rabbanan* before anonymous *beraitot*, which are however also introduced by *tanya* when quoted within an argument as justification, objection, or confirmation. The differences may also be explained as follows: *tannu rabbanan* introduces a *halakhah* that comprises a complete subject, *tanya* a fragmentary *halakhah*, and *tanna* additions to a *mishnah* or *baraita*. In certain tractates such as *Nedarim*, *Nazir*, *Temurah*, *Me'ilah*, and *Keritot*, a somewhat different system is employed.

Where two *beraitot* contradict each other the formula in the Jerusalem Talmud is אית תנא . . . ואית תנא (*it tana . . . ve-it tana;* "one *tanna* reads . . . another *tanna* reads), while in the Babylonian Talmud the formula is תנו רבנן or תניא or תנן . . . תניא אידך (*tannu rabbanan* or *tanya* or *tannan* or *tanya idakh;* "our rabbis taught or a *tanna* taught or we teach . . . the other *tanna* taught"). *Beraitot* are also introduced by *ika de'amrei* ("some say"), *ve-amrei lah* ("others state"), *lishna aḥarina* ("another version reads"), *tanei bi midrasha* ("a *baraita* was taught in the school"), while a type of *memra* that is apparently a tannaitic tradition is introduced by *shonin* ("they taught"). Sometimes a *memra* is followed by *ve-tana tuna* ("the *tanna* is a confirmation," i.e., confirms what I say), after which there comes a *mishnah* or *baraita* to confirm or provide a basis for the *memra*.

Beraitot are also quoted without a characteristic introductory phrase (e.g., Yev. 98b; Ḥag. 6a; Yoma 30a; et al.), these being at times in a paraphrased or Aramaic version (Shab. 81a). In the Talmuds stories about the *tannaim* which have their source in *beraitot* are in colloquial Aramaic (see, e.g., BB 3b; Ber. 27b; Av. Zar. 17b; TJ, Ḥag. 2:2, 77d). Generally however *beraitot* are in rabbinic Hebrew, although they also contain proverbs in Aramaic (e.g., Er. 41a; MK 18b). The language is likewise used for the original part of *Megillat Ta'anit*, for spells against sorcery, the statements of earlier figures, such as Simeon the Just and Jonathan the high priest (Tosef., Sot. 13:5–10), and for sages' verbal testaments (*ibid.*, 13:4).

Baraita and Memra ("statement"). The dividing line between these two is somewhat blurred, particularly as regards *halakhot* of the transitional period. *Memrot* of this type are introduced by *itmar* ("it was stated"; see, e.g., Yev. 32b) and *be'i minnei* ("he asked of"; see, e.g., Zev. 30b), and are transmitted by *amoraim* in the name of *tannaim* (see Git. 5b, 26b; Yev. 4a). Apparently, therefore, a considerable amount of tannaitic material was communicated orally by *tannaim* to *amoraim* without being given a definitive tannaitic form, and this probably explains why *amoraim* frequently quote *halakhot* and interpretations which, the Talmud subsequently declares, occur in *beraitot*.

Compilations. In the talmudic period there were many compilations of *beraitot*, some of these, such as the *Tosefta, being companion works to the Mishnah. Of the compilations, not all of which have been preserved, the best known are those of the schools of Ḥiyya, Oshaya, and Bar Kappara; those on specific subjects, such as *Ribbit de-R. Ḥiyya* ("Usury of R. Ḥiyya"), **Seder Olam*, and **Megillat Ta'anit;* and those comprising halakhic Midrashim, such as *Mekhilta de-R. Ishmael, *Mekhilta de-R. Shimon bar Yoḥai, *Sifra, *Sifrei.*

On compilations of *beraitot,* see the respective articles. See also *Aggadah, *Hermeneutics.

Bibliography: B. M. Lewin (ed.), *Iggeret R. Sherira Ga'on* (1921), 6, 27, 34–47; Malachi b. Jacob, *Yad Malakhi* (1856[2]); N. Krochmal, *Moreh Nevukhei ha-Zeman* (1928), ch. 73; idem, in: *He-Ḥalutz,* 3 (1856), 110–31; Weiss, Dor, vol. 2, 239–58; Halevy, Dorot, 2 (1923), 114–52, 162–216; Ch. Albeck, *Meḥkarim ba-Baraita* . . . (1944); M. Higger, *Oẓar ha-Beraitot* (1948), 9–134; Epstein, Mishnah (1948), 30–63, 171–4, 673–706, 726–803, 1291; Bacher, in: *Yerushalayim,* 10 (1913), 59–82; Bacher, Trad; E. Z. Melamed, in: *Sefer ha-Zikkaron M. Z. Ilan* (1959), 71–84; Neusner, in: PAAJR, 30 (1962), 79–127.

[B.D.-V.]

BARAITA DE-MELEKHET HA-MISHKAN ("On the Building of the Tabernacle"), ancient collection containing 14 chapters, giving a description of the building of the Tabernacle. The *baraita* is quoted by early authorities, including Hai Gaon, Rashi, the tosafists, and Naḥmanides, under the name *Baraita de-Melekhet ha-Mishkan* or *Mishnat Melekhet ha-Mishkan.* It is written in mishnaic Hebrew and contains practically no later additions. The sages quoted in it are *tannaim,* the latest of them being Judah ha-Nasi and his contemporaries. Extracts from it are cited in the amoraic literature. It was therefore evidently compiled at the same time as the other *beraitot,* i.e., after the close of the Mishnah but before that of the Babylonian Talmud. The chapter arrangement is as follows: chapter 1—the dimensions of the Tabernacle, its boards, their appearance and arrangement; 2—the curtains of *tekhelet* ("blue"), their preparation and the manner in which they were placed over the Tabernacle; 3—the curtains of goats' skins and the other covers of the Tabernacle—the rams' skins dyed red and the *taḥash* (unidentified animal mentioned in the Bible) skins; 4—the weaving of the veil and the screen at the entrance; 5—the court of the Tabernacle; 6 and 7—the ark of the covenant and the tablets which it contained; 8—the table and the showbread; 9 and 10—the candelabrum, its construction and manner of kindling; 11—the altar of incense and the altar of burnt offerings; 12—the laver; 13—the work of the levites in the Tabernacle and the Israelite encampments in the wilderness; 14—the clouds of glory. The priestly garments are not treated at all. Extracts from *Baraita de-Melekhet ha-Mishkan* are included in the *Baraita of 49 Rules.* Some are even of the opinion that the last two chapters, in which the aggadic element is considerable, originally belonged to the *Baraita of 49 Rules* (L. Gruenhut, *Sefer ha-Likkutim,* 2 (1898), 11–13). The *baraita* was first published in Venice in 1602, and a critical edition was published in 1908 by Meir Ish Shalom (Friedmann), on the basis of various manuscripts and editions, together with an introduction.

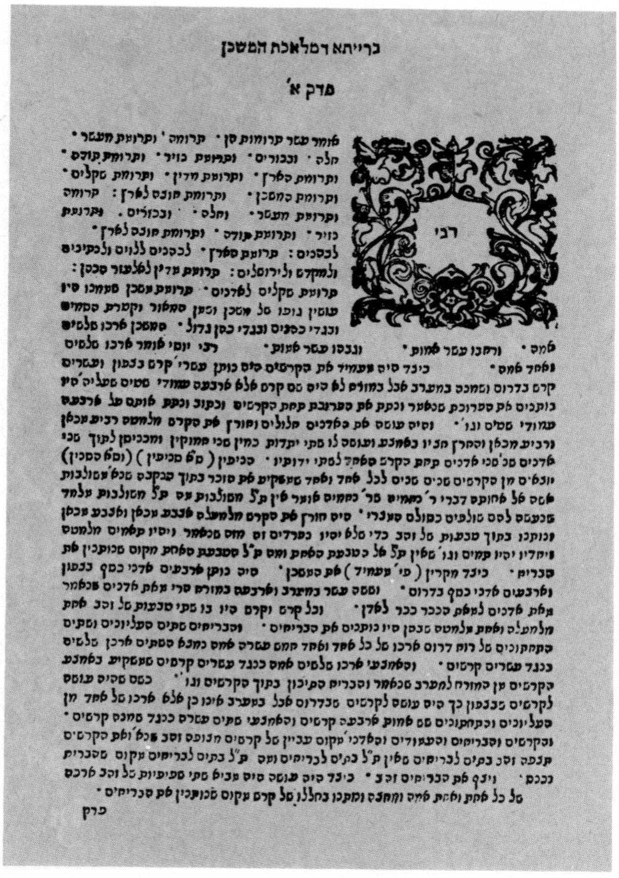
ברייתא דמלאכת המשכן

פרק א'

Opening page of the first edition of *Baraita de-Melekhet ha-Mishkan,* Venice, 1602. It formed the second part of a volume mainly devoted to the *Mishpatei Shevuot* of R. Hai Gaon. Jerusalem, J.N.U.L.

Bibliography: A. Jellinek (ed.), *Beit ha-Midrash,* 3 (1938[2]), xxix–xxx; S. Buber, *Yeri'ot Shelomo* (1896), 15–16; L. Ginzberg (ed.), *Ginzei Schechter,* 1 (1928), 374–83.

[Y.D.G.]

BARAITA DE-NIDDAH, ancient work on ritual purity, first mentioned by Naḥmanides and probably known to the *geonim* and the German-French talmudists of the 13th century. It was published in 1890 by C. M. Horowitz. The *baraita* consists of *aggadah* and *halakhah* concerning the biblical and post-biblical laws of the menstruant woman (*niddah*; Lev. 15:19–33). There is no mention of any Babylonian scholars and the chronology of *tannaim* and *amoraim* is ignored. The tendency of the *baraita* is to oppose the lenient rulings of the school of *Hillel and of R. *Akiva. The account in the Talmud (Er. 13b; TJ, Ber. 1:7, 3b) of a heavenly voice deciding in favor of the Hillelites is rendered in the *baraita* as follows: "Blessed be the strict. Both [Hillel and Shammai] speak the words of the living God; but we must regulate ourselves according to the teachings of the School of Shammai" (Horowitz, p. 21).

The *baraita* lays special stress on the laws of ritual cleanness, particularly with regard to food. B. M. Lewin (*Metivot* (1933), 108–12) points out that the stringencies referred to have no basis in the Talmud, but did exist among Jews in Ereẓ Israel. S. Lieberman, however, maintains that although some of the passages are difficult to understand and were not accepted as *halakhah,* a talmudic basis can be found for them (*ibid.,* addition to paragraph 78, p. 115–8). He is of the opinion that the laws concerning ritual cleanness and uncleanness contained in the *baraita* come from a rabbinic source in Ereẓ Israel and not from the Samaritans or the Sadducees. There appears to have been a section of the community in Ereẓ Israel that laid great stress on the laws of cleanness, as is reflected in Samaritan literature. It is possible that this *baraita* originated within such a framework.

See also *Niddah.

Bibliography: C. M. Horowitz, *Tosefata Attikata,* 4 and 5 (1890).

[M.J.G.]

BARAITA OF 32 RULES, *baraita* giving 32 hermeneutic rules to be used in the aggadic interpretation of Scripture. Rashi makes frequent use of the *Baraita of 32 Rules* in his commentaries on the Bible and Talmud, referring to it by this name or as the *baraita* of Yose b. Eleazar, the Galilean.

Until the 19th century it was known only from being quoted in the 14th century *Sefer Keritot,* the methodological work of *Samson b. Isaac of Chinon.

The *baraita* now appears at the beginning of the *Midrash Mishnat R. Eli'ezer* (discovered and published by H. G. Enelow (1933), 10ff.); and at the beginning of *Midrash ha-Gadol* to Genesis (ed. by M. Margaliot (1947), 22ff.). Although ascribed to Yose b. Eleazar, who lived about 150 C.E., many examples of the application of its rules are attributed to later *tannaim* and even to the *amoraim* Johanan, and Yose b. Ḥanina. It is therefore probable that the original *baraita* merely listed the rules, the examples being added later as a kind of *Gemara.* The *Midrash ha-Gadol* version contains the introductory statement, "These are the rules whereby the *aggadah* is to be understood," clearly indicating that these rules were to be applied only to the *aggadah* and not to the *halakhah.* The *baraita* deals mainly with the syntax, style, and subject matter of Scripture, and after each rule gives one or more examples of its application. Although the 13 halakhic rules of R. Ishmael (see *Hermeneutics) are included in the *baraita,* all the examples given are taken from aggadic passages, even Ishmael's rules being applied with less rigor. Under *ribbui* ("addition") for instance, the example given is that the word "and" in Genesis (Gen. 21:1) teaches that all the barren women in the world were blessed with children at the same time as Sarah. The word "also" in "I also saw in my dreams" (Gen. 40:16) teaches that in addition to his own dream the chief baker saw in his dream the interpretation of the chief butler's dream. Some of the rules are almost word games. Number 29 is *gematria* computing the numerical value of words. The numerical value of Eliezer, servant of Abraham, for instance, is 318. Hence, it is inferred that when Abraham went to war with 318 men to save Lot (Gen. 14:14) the reference is to Eliezer only. Number 30 is *atbash,* the substitution of the last letter of the alphabet for the first, of the penultimate letter for the second, etc. Thus לֵב קָמָי (Lev-Kamai; Jer. 51:1) becomes כַּשְׂדִּים (*Kasdim;* Chaldees). Number 31 is *notarikon,* the interpretation of each letter of a word or its breaking up as an anagram or acrostic. Thus אַבְרֵךְ (*avrekh;* "Abrech") applied to Joseph (Gen. 41:43) becomes the two words *av* ("father," in wisdom), and *rakh* ("tender" in years), describing the qualities of Joseph. Lieberman points out that some of these eccentric methods of interpreting texts were common literary devices among the Greeks, and were also used by them and by the rabbis in the interpretation of dreams. Being current literary devices, they were well-known and used by the rabbis both in aggadic interpretation and in finding some support in the biblical text for a decision. They were never used however, to derive halakhic decisions from the text. Lieberman finds support for this view in an anonymous Midrash, appended to the *Baraita of 32 Rules* in the *Midrash ha-Gadol.* Commenting on "For a dream cometh through a multitude of business" (Eccles., 5:2), the author says, "If the contents of dreams, which have no effect, may yield a multitude of interpretations, how much more then should the important contents of the Torah imply many interpretations in every case."

Bibliography: Zunz, Vortraege, 90; Bacher, Tann, 2 (1890), 293–8; H. L. Strack, *Introduction to the Talmud and Midrash* (1945), 95–98, 289–96; S. Lieberman, *Hellenism in Jewish Palestine* (1950), 68–78.

[B.D.K.]

BARAK (Heb. בָּרָק; "lightning"), Israelite military commander during the period of the Judges (Judg. 4–5), son of Abinoam, from Kedesh in Naphtali. It appears that Barak was well-known as a capable military leader before the prophet *Deborah encouraged him to go to battle against King *Jabin of Hazor. For this purpose Barak succeeded in organizing people mainly from his own tribe of Naphtali, along with warriors from the tribe of Zebulun. After mustering his forces on Mount Tabor, he advanced toward the vicinity of the Wadi Kishon, where the battle was waged under his command; in the ensuing battle, the army led by *Sisera, Jabin's military commander, was utterly routed.

There is no biblical datum available as to the nature and activities of Barak either before or after the aforementioned war. He is neither portrayed as endowed with the spirit of the Lord nor described as a judge. Due to a possible similarity in meaning between his name, Barak, and that of Deborah's husband, Lappidoth, some of the medieval commentators identified the two (David Kimḥi and Levi b. Gershom; cf. *Midrash Yalkut Shofetim,* 42). However, this is not borne out by the context.

Bibliography: EM, 2 (1965), 363–4 (incl. bibl.). For further bibliography see *Deborah.

[Y.M.G.]

BARANGA, AUREL (1913–), Rumanian playwright and poet. Born in Bucharest, Baranga qualified as a physician and first published poems in the avant-garde review *Unu* (1928–32). In 1930–31 he edited *Alge,* a journal that cultivated the absurd. Later he wrote for the left-wing press. After World War II Baranga devoted himself entirely to writing: he became a reporter and wrote poems. When Rumanian Nazis were put on trial in Bucharest in 1945, he was among the first to make the Rumanian public aware of the full extent of Nazi barbarism. His articles on the deportation of Rumanian Jews to the Transnistria concentration camps were collected in *Ninge peste Ucraina* ("Snow Falls over the Ukraine," 1945, 1946[2]).

Aurel Baranga, Rumanian playwright. Photo Litani, Tel Aviv.

It was, however, in the theater that Baranga increasingly displayed his creative talents. From 1947 he wrote many stage successes, some of which were translated into English, French, Russian, and Chinese. Among them are *Iarbă rea* ("The Herb," 1949), *Mielul turbat* ("The Rabid Lamb," 1953), *Reţeta fericirii* ("Recipe for Happiness," 1957), *Sfîntul Milică Blajinul* (1965), *Opiniă publică* (1967; *Public Opinion,* 1968), *Simfonia patetică* (1969), *Travesti* and *Farsa infernală* (1969). These advocate a society based on the author's ethic of humanistic socialism and satirize Rumanian inertia, bureaucracy, and old-fashioned ideas. *Opiniă publică,* which ran for a year in Bucharest, satirized "socialist realism" and parodied the Communist political trial. Twice the winner of Rumania's state prize for literature, Baranga was assistant director of the Bucharest National Theater, and coeditor of the periodical *Viaţa Romînească.* In 1968 he published the verse collection *Poezii.*

Bibliography: *Teatrul romînesc în contemporaneitate* (1964); D. Săraru, *Teatrulromînesc şi interpreţi contemporani* (1966); Jaffe, in: *Al ha-Mishmar* (July 19, 1968); H. Kamm, in: *New York Times* (May 3, 1968).

[D.L.]

BARANOVICHI (Pol., **Baranowicze**), capital of Baranovichi oblast, Belorussian S.S.R. (from 1921–39 in Poland). After Baranovichi became a railroad junction at the end of the 19th century, Jews from the surroundings began to settle there without official permission (see *Russia). In 1897 the Jewish community of Baranovichi, then still a village, numbered 24. Jewish domicile was authorized in 1903 and the community rapidly expanded. In 1921 there were 6,605 Jews (57.5% of the total population).

After World War I Baranovichi became the center of residence of the *admorim* ("ḥasidic rabbis") of the *Koidanovo and *Slonim dynasties. Educational institutions included Hebrew and Yiddish schools and two large yeshivot. Six Yiddish weeklies were published in Baranovichi between 1928 and 1939, and a kibbutz training center "Shaḥariyyah" of the He-Ḥalutz movement was established near the city. Jewish communal and cultural activities ceased when Baranovichi became part of the U.S.S.R. in 1939. [Y.S.]

Holocaust Period. On the eve of the Holocaust, 12,000 Jews lived in Baranovichi. Under Soviet rule (1939–41), Jewish community organizations were disbanded and any kind of political or youth activity was forbidden. Some youth groups organized flight to Vilna, which was then part of Lithuania, and from there reached Palestine. The Hebrew Tarbut school became a Russian institution. A Jewish high school did continue to function, however. In the summer of 1940 Jewish refugees from western Poland who had found refuge in Baranovichi after September 1939 were deported to the Soviet interior. When Germans captured the city on June 27, 1941, 400 Jews were kidnapped, leaving no trace. A *Judenrat was set up, headed by Joshua Izikzon. The community was forced to pay a fine of five kg. of gold, ten kg. of silver, and 1,000,000 rubles. The ghetto was fenced off from the outside on Dec. 12, 1941. The ghetto inhabitants suffered great hardship that winter, although efforts were made to alleviate the hunger. The Jewish doctors and their assistants fought to contain the epidemics. On March 4, 1942, the ghetto was surrounded. In a *Selektion* carried out by the Nazis to separate the "productive" from the "nonproductive," over 3,000 elderly persons, widows, orphans, etc., were taken to trenches prepared in advance and murdered. Resistance groups, organized in the ghetto as early as the spring of 1942, collected arms and sabotaged their places of work. Plans for rebellion were laid, but the uprising never came to pass, partly due to German subterfuge. In the second German *Aktion* on Sept. 22, 1942, about 3,000 persons were murdered. On Dec. 17, 1942, another *Aktion* was carried out, in which more than 3,000 persons were killed near Grabowce. Baranovichi was now declared **judenrein.* At the end of 1942 Jews were already fighting in groups among the partisans. A few survivors from the ghetto were still in some of the forced labor camps in the district, but most of them were liquidated in 1943. On July 8, 1944, when the city was taken by the Soviet forces, about 150 Jews reappeared from hiding in the forests. Later a few score more returned from the U.S.S.R. [Ar.W.]

Postwar Period. In 1954 a monument was erected in the city as a memorial to the Jews murdered by the Nazis. Later it was destroyed and in its place a public latrine was built. The big synagogue was confiscated by the authorities, leaving a small one for the 3,000 Jews (1969 estimate). Societies of emigrants from Baranovichi function in Israel, the U.S.A., Argentina, Chile, and South Africa. [Ed.]

Bibliography: *Bulletin of the Joint Rescue Committee of the Jewish Agency for Palestine* (April, 1945), 13–22; *Baranoviz: Sefer Zikkaron* (Heb. and Yid., 1953); *Baranovich in Umkum un Vidershtand,* 1 (1964); Ben-Mordekhai, in: S.K. Mirsky (ed.), *Mosdot Torah be-Eiropah be-Vinyanam u-ve-Ḥurbanam* (1956), 329–35.

BARANOWICZ, DAVID ELIEZER (1859–1915), Hebraist. Baranowicz, who was born in Vilna, lived in great poverty. He wrote several books on Hebrew grammar which were well received and ran into several editions. He wrote the following books: *Oraḥ Selulah le-Dikduk Sefat*

ארח סלולה
לדקדוק שפת עבר
בדרך קצרה ומובנת, וכוללת כל הדינים
הנחוצים, ישנים גם חדשים.
חלק הנקוד
כתוב בשפת זשארגאן עם הערות יקרות
ומועילות בשפת קדש
מאתי דוד אליעזר בּאראנאוויץ מתושבי ווילנא
יוסף בן אחרן
זאנאוויטץ.
ווילנא
יהודה ליב ב"ר אליעזר ליפמאן מ"ץ נ"י.
בשנת וארח ישרים סללה לפ"ק
ОРАХЪ СЛУЛО.
Правила Еврейскаго языка. Составилъ
Д. Л. Барановичъ.

Title page of *Orah Selulah le-Dikduk Sefat Ever,* a Hebrew grammar by David Baranowicz, Vilna, 1883. Jerusalem, J.N.U.L.

Ever (1883) on Hebrew grammar with an appendix in Yiddish on vocalization; *Luḥot ha-Pe'alim* (1889); *Kunteres Yefalles Nativ* (1909), which is an abridgment of his major unpublished work by the same name containing a critique of the Hebrew grammarian Koestlin's *Sefer ha-Maslul* ("Book of the Path") and of the methods of the ancient Hebrew grammarians; *Derekh Ḥadashah le-Ve'ur Kitvei ha-Kodesh* ("A New Way to Explain the Holy Scripture," 1910), a commentary on the Scriptures based upon a grammatical approach. His best-known works are *Messibbot ha-Shem* ("Rules of the Noun") and *Messibbot ha-Po'al* ("Rules of the Verb") which contain analyses of the Hebrew nouns and verbs (last edition, 1945). He also edited several books of Hebrew grammar. His autobiography was printed in *Ha-Toren* 3 (1915), 226–7.

Bibliography: Kressel, Leksikon, 1 (1965), 365. [Ed.]

BÁRÁNY, ROBERT (1876–1936), Austrian otologist and Nobel Prize winner. Bárány qualified at the University of Vienna in 1900, and for the next five years did research in hospitals in Frankfort, Heidelberg, and Freiburg, returning to Vienna in 1905. By 1914 his research encompassed all aspects of the physiology and pathology of the inner ear. His greatest innovation in the clinical study of ear diseases was the discovery of a method of examination of each of the two labyrinths separately, using cold and hot water. He was also the first to describe a practical operative procedure for otosclerosis ("hardening of the ear") cases. During World War I Bárány served as a surgeon in the Austrian Army. He was captured by the Russians in 1915. They released him after it became known that he had been awarded the Nobel Prize for medicine in 1914. Bárány was not made a full professor at Vienna because he was a Jew. However, in 1917 he was appointed professor of otology at the University of Uppsala, Sweden. Bárány only began to display interest in Judaism and Jewish questions toward the end of his life, when the Nazis came to power. In his will he left his valuable library to the National Library in Jerusalem. His major works are *Der primaere Wundnaht bei Schussverletzungen des Gehirns* (in: *Wiener klinische Wochenschrift*, 21 (1916)); and *Die Radikaloperation des Ohres ohne Gehoergangplastik bei chronischen Mittelohreiterungen* (1923).

Bibliography: E. Wodak, *Der Báránysche Zeigeversuch* (1927); NDB, 1 (1953), 581.

[Y.G.G.]

BARASCH, JULIUS (Judah; 1815–1863), physician, author, and communal leader in Walachia, often called the "Mendelssohn of Rumania." Barasch, who was born in Brody, settled in Bucharest in 1841 and practiced medicine.

Julius Barasch, leader of Walachian Jewry.

From 1843 he served as a government physician, at first in Calarasi and Craiova and from 1850 in Bucharest. In addition he taught science in several colleges, being the first teacher of the subject in Walachia. Barasch did much to popularize science by organizing lectures and courses for the public and publishing textbooks and periodicals on popular topics. His *Minunile Naturii* ("Natural Wonders," 1 vol., 1850, 1852²) and *Isis sau Natura* ("Isis or Nature," 4 vols., 1856–59) were the first of their kind in Rumania. In these publications Barasch attempted to formulate a scientific terminology in Rumanian. He played a decisive role in spreading Enlightenment (*Haskalah) among Bucharest Jewry, in the modernization of Jewish education, and in the introduction of religious reform in Walachia. He initiated the establishment of the first secular Jewish school in Walachia, which opened in Bucharest in 1851. For a time he served as its principal. He also initiated the plan to establish a modern temple in Bucharest and worked toward its realization. Barasch encouraged the founding of the Societatea de Cultură Israelită ("Association for Jewish Culture") in 1862, which he directed. It promoted the spread of Haskalah among Bucharest Jewry. He also led the struggle for civil rights by Walachian Jewry after the Congress of Paris in 1856. In 1857 he helped to found the first Jewish periodical in Walachia, *Israelitul Român*, which appeared in Rumanian and in French and was established principally to further the cause of Jewish emancipation in Walachia.

In 1861 Barasch published anonymously in France a brochure entitled *L'Emancipation Israélite en Roumanie* which was the first work on the subject. Barasch was one of the early advocates of the revival of the Jewish people in its homeland. In his youth, while studying in Berlin, he joined a student organization founded there by Moritz *Steinschneider which envisioned a Jewish state in Ereẓ Israel. He saw Hebrew as the unifying bond of the Jewish people and did much to develop Hebrew literature. He conceived the idea of publishing a scientific encyclopedia in Hebrew, but only one volume, on philosophy, was published (*Oẓar Hokhmah*, 1856). Barasch wrote on Jewish subjects in German, describing Jewish communities in countries and localities he visited. The accounts are an important source of knowledge of Jewish life in the mid-19th century in the communities concerned and particularly of the history of the Jews in Rumania.

Bibliography: Klausner, Sifrut, 4, 1 (1963³), 134–6; Zaltzman, in: *Iyyun*, 3 (1952), 151–68; M. Schwarzfeld, *Dr. Iuliu Barasch* (Rum., 1919), incl. bibliography; N. M. Gelber, *Zur Vorgeschichte des Zionismus* (1927), 209, 307–8.

[El.F.]

BARASH, ASHER (1889–1952), Hebrew writer. Born in Lopatin, Eastern Galicia, at an early age he was already well acquainted with modern Hebrew literature; however, most of his juvenilia was written in Yiddish, the rest in German and Polish. At the age of 16, Barash left home and wandered all over Galicia, returning from time to time to Lvov. This period is reflected in several of his more important works: *Pirkei Rudorfer* ("Rudorfer's Episodes," 1920–27), *Sippurei Rudorfer* ("Rudorfer's Stories," 1936–44), and other autobiographical stories. At that time, Barash began to publish his literary efforts, first in Yiddish and then in Hebrew, the latter in 1910 with a number of Hebrew poems in the second *Me'assef Sifruti*, edited by David Frischmann, and in *Shallekhet*, edited by Gershon Shofman. His first long story, *"Min ha-Migrash"* (1910) also appeared in *Shallekhet*. In 1914, Barash moved to Ereẓ Israel, where he taught, first at the Herzlia secondary school in Tel Aviv and, after World War I, at the Reali high school in Haifa. This period is described in his work *Ke-Ir Neẓurah* ("As a Besieged City," 1944).

After World War II he composed his best works in poetry and prose, wrote criticism, and edited several works. In conjunction with Ya'akov *Rabinowitz, he edited the prose volumes *Hedim,* the *Miẓpeh Almanac,* and *Atidot,* a youth journal. He was also active in the organizational

Asher Barash, Hebrew novelist.

work of the Association of Hebrew Writers, and established the bio-bibliographical institute, Genazim, which now bears his name. Barash's works were collected in three volumes (*Kol Kitvei Asher Barash,* 1961[2]). In 1931, he wrote *Torat ha-Sifrut* ("Theory of Literature," in two volumes) which was the first attempt in modern Hebrew literature to present the Hebrew reader with a systematic theory of literature.

It is, however, as an author of fiction that Barash left his impact. His works mainly highlight the world he left behind. His description, often touched by nostalgia, is at the same time indicative of the author's awareness that this world must inevitably disintegrate. Barash was also sentient to the new life evolving in Ereẓ Israel, and this consciousness he conveyed in three works, *Ke-Ir Neẓurah, Ish u-Veito Nimḥu* ("The Man and His Home Perished," 1933–34), and *Gannanim* ("Gardeners," 1937–38). Among his historical fiction are two stories, *"Mul Sha'ar ha-Shamayim"* ("Facing the Gates of Heaven," 1924) and *"Ha-Nishar be-Toledo"* (1944, "Last in Toledo," in *Israel Argosy,* 8 (1962), 144–71).

Barash's literary works are characterized by a rather personal style, precise language, and a quiet tone tending to simplicity and clear and unsentimental description. He rejected both the traditional style of the school of *Mendele Mokher Seforim and the extreme impressionistic and psychological style of some modernists. These stylistic qualities rapidly won him the title of a cool realist, uninvolved in the world he creates.

Barash's affection for the "good people," who are mostly marginal characters in his stories, was interpreted as an "objective" description of the pleasanter aspects of life. This simplistic and superficial approach to his works, however, ignores the cracks in his seemingly tranquil world through which can be glimpsed the hidden abyss that he keenly sensed. In his essay on Barash (in *Arai va-Keva* (1942), 147–58) Halkin dwells on this hidden but basic aspect in Barash's writing. He points to the strange but consistent contrast between the seemingly realistic tranquility and the knowledge (which Barash may have tried to conceal from himself) that this pleasant existence is but a thin shell protecting man from the chaos which threatens to erupt at any moment and engulf him.

The early story *"Aḥim"* ("Brothers," 1911) describes two brothers, one anchored in the full life of a traditional Jewish family, and the other living in debauchery and poverty. When engaged on a mission of mercy to his brother's family, the rich brother finds himself strangely jealous of the other's way of life. In his early book, *Temunot mi-Beit Mivshal ha-Shekhar* ("Sketches from the Brewery," 1915–28), considered his best, the theme of the story of "The Burning Bed" sharply offsets the peaceful enterprise at the brewery and hints at the inevitable destruction of this idyllic setting.

In *Ammud ha-Esh* ("The Pillar of Fire," 1936) Barash depicts the contrast between a good, stable, and humdrum provincial life, with its lovable yet ridiculous Zionist activity, and the explosion of the oil well, a pillar of fire. The burning oil well transforms the small town and its industrious life into a hell, simultaneously attractive and repelling, which threatens the sanity of the people. The thematic juxtaposition, found in almost all of Barash's stories, lends them depth and ambiguity. The same is evident in his method of characterization. Some of his characters appear to serve his "healthy" realistic tendencies, while others result from his romantic affinity for the strange, the rare, and the threatening.

Structurally, Barash's stories and novels follow a conservative, ordered, and clear pattern that seems to avoid confusion. Each story opens with a systematic exposition that acquaints the reader with the significance of events and characters. At times, the author introduces an omniscient narrator who defines the characters clearly. The dramatis personae, however, do not conform to this characterization. In the denouement of the plot and events, their deeds and behavior, whether openly or secretly, contradict the authoritative evaluation of the narrator. What at first seemed a simple structure is actually a literary device through which the complexity of the characters, originally imagined to be much more artless, is revealed. Barash tends toward short and limited narratives. This is clearly evident even in his more extensive works which are comprised of more or less independent "sketches" or "episodes." *Ke-Ir Neẓurah* is a collection of random contemporary historical fiction, narratives, and personal experiences which are organically disconnected. These portrayals may provide the main outlines of characters and events for a full-length novel, but they cannot sustain its necessary unity and complexity.

The novel *Ahavah Zarah* ("Alien Love," 1930–38) poignantly describes events and experiences characteristic of the problematic coexistence of Jews and non-Jews in a small Galician town. The "grandmother" is undoubtedly one of Barash's best-drawn satirical characters. Barash's simplistic solution to the love conflict of a Jew for a non-Jewish girl introduces a foreign tendentious element into the novel which reduces its tragic significance. Barash thus presents, but does not resolve, the problems in the sphere of human emotions. The girl marries a policeman who is an anti-Semite; the boy recognizes the evil that is rooted in the non-Jew, even in his own beloved. The solution is ideological and logical, stultifying the human elements in the story and the humanity in the characters.

In *Torat ha-Sifrut,* Barash attempts to guide the "novice poet" and the teacher of literature. His normative approach was undoubtedly useful and served as a guide to the teacher and the student of literature in the technique of writing. Today, however, Barash's dogmatic statements seem old-fashioned and at times even incorrect: they often unnecessarily limit literary concepts and terms. The anthology of Hebrew poetry edited by Barash, *Mivḥar ha-Shirah ha-Ivrit ha-Ḥadashah* (1938), attests to good taste and knowledgeable choice of material and is still a faithful and discerning reflection of the best of Hebrew poetry. In 1969, *Selected Stories of Asher Barash* appeared.

A list of his works translated into English appears in Goell, Bibliography, index.

Bibliography: Halkin, in: *Arai va-Keva* (1942), 147–58; D. Sadan, *Bein Din le-Ḥeshbon* (1963), 226–33; Even, in: *Moznayim*, 22 (1966), 215–20; Kressel, Leksikon, 1 (1965), 383–6; S. Lachower, *Asher Barash, Bibliografyah, 1906–52* (1953); Waxman, Literature, 4 (1960²), 173–4. [Yo.E.]

BARASH, EPHRAIM (1892–1943), head of the Judenrat in Bialystok. Barash, who was born in Volkovysk (then Russian Poland), was active from his youth in communal life, in Jewish self-defense, and the Zionist movement. During World War I he was a refugee in Russia. After the war he formed the municipal council of Volkovysk where he became president of the Jewish Trade Bank, a member of the community council, chairman of the local Zionist organization, and honorary chairman of He-Ḥalutz. In 1934 he settled in Bialystok and became general manager of the Jewish community council. When the Germans captured the town at the end of June 1941, Barash was appointed vice-chairman of the Judenrat of which he was the guiding spirit. He organized ghetto life, established industrial enterprises, and although well aware of German plans concerning the Jews, believed that the Jews would be spared if they could be employed in work essential to the German war effort. Barash actively collaborated with the local Jewish fighting organization (led by Mordecai *Tenenbaum), and helped them financially and by providing material for manufacturing arms. He was in personal contact with some of the Germans, and believed that they would give him ample warning of their intention to liquidate the ghetto, at which time he intended to join the partisans. However, when the ghetto was liquidated in the latter half of August 1943, Barash and his wife were sent to Majdanek extermination camp, where he was killed.

Bibliography: M. Einhorn (ed.), *Volkovyzker Yisker-Bukh*, 2 vols. (1949); N. Blumental, *Darko shel Yudenrat* (1962). [N.B.]

BARATZ, HERMANN (Hirsch; 1835–1922), jurist and historian born in Dubno, Volhynia. He graduated from the government rabbinical seminary in Zhitomir (1859) and from the law faculty of the University of Kiev (1869), and in 1863 was appointed adviser on Jewish affairs to the governor general of Kiev; from 1871 to 1901 he served as censor of Hebrew books. In 1881, with Max *Mandelstamm, he represented the Jews in the province of Kiev before the commission to investigate the causes of the pogroms in southern Russia. Baratz, who contributed to the Russian Jewish press from its beginnings in 1860, was one of the founders in 1904 of the Kiev branch of the *Society for the Promotion of Culture among the Jews in Russia. He wrote on the history of the Jews in Kiev, and published studies on the history of ancient Russian law; his chief work concerned the influence of the Bible and talmudic sources on ancient Russian literature. Three volumes of his studies were published posthumously by his sons, the first dealing with the Jewish sources of the ancient Russian chronicle *Povest vremyonnykh let* (1922), and the second and third with the Jewish element in ancient Russian literature (1926, 1927).

Bibliography: KS, 2 (1925/26), 19–20. [Y.S.]

BARATZ, JOSEPH (1890–1968), Zionist labor leader; a founder of the collective settlement movement in Ereẓ Israel. Baratz was born in Kamenets, Ukraine. In Ereẓ Israel, where he settled in 1906, he worked as a laborer. In 1910, he became one of the founders of the first kevuẓah, *Deganyah. He was a leading figure in the *Ha-Po'el ha-Ẓa'ir Party (and later in *Mapai), and opened the founding conference of the *Histadrut in Haifa in 1920. During World War II and the Israel War of Independence, Baratz devoted himself to the welfare needs of the Jewish soldiers in Ereẓ Israel, becoming chairman of the Israel Soldiers' Aid Committee in 1948. The Soldiers' House (Beit ha-Ḥayyal) in Tel Aviv is named for him. He was a member

Joseph Baratz, a founder of the kibbutz movement.

of the First Knesset. His books include *A Village by the Jordan: the Story of Degania* (1954), which appeared in 13 languages; and *Im Ḥayyaleinu* ("With Our Soldiers," 1945). His wife, Miriam (née Ostrovsky), was one of the first settlers of the Second Aliyah, living and working in Deganyah from its founding.

Bibliography: Tidhar, 3 (1958), 1402; B. Shohetman, *Divrei J. Baratz* (1950), incl. bibl.; D. Lazar, *Rashim be-Yisrael*, 2 (1955), 233–7. [A.A.]

BARAZANI, ASENATH BAT SAMUEL (1590?–1670?), Kurdish head of yeshivah and poet. Asenath was taught by her father Samuel *Barazani and married her cousin Jacob b. Abraham, one of Kurdistan's noted scholars and her father's successor. She describes her upbringing in a letter to the community of Amadiya: "Never in my life did I step outside my home. I was the daughter of the king of Israel . . . I was raised by scholars; I was pampered by my late father. He taught me no art or craft other than heavenly matters . . . " Barazani was poor all her life. When her husband died, she succeeded him as the chief teacher of Torah in Kurdistan. Expert in Jewish literature, she headed the Mosul yeshivah which attracted pupils from many communities. She wrote letters of instruction and exhortation to communities, as well as letters requesting aid for her yeshivah. Phinehas Hariri, one of Kurdistan's scholars and kabbalists, addressed a letter to her (1664) in the manner reserved for great and famous rabbis. Barazani was called *"tanna'it"* (lady *tanna*), and tales were told of her greatness and of the miracles she wrought. She is reputed to have studied Kabbalah and to have written a commentary to Proverbs. She died in Mosul. Her son, Samuel, assisted her in the yeshivah and later became rabbi in Baghdad. David Barazani, one of Asenath's descendants, was one of the outstanding Kurdistani scholars of the 18th century. He traveled among the communities, instructing them in *halakhah*. His center, apparently, was Mosul. Scholars of Ereẓ Israel and Baghdad corresponded with him on halakhic matters and his responsa, sermons, and novellae are extant in manuscript (Jewish Theological Seminary, New York). David was also a *paytan*, and one of his *piyyutim* for Sukkot is regularly recited by Kurdistani Jews.

Bibliography: Mann, Texts, 1 (1931), 481–5, 507–19; Ben-Zvi, in: *Sinai*, 28 (1951), 91, 99; A. Ben-Jacob, *Kehillot Yehudei Kurdistan* (1961), 35–40, 157, 164ff., 198, 205ff.; Benayahu, in: *Sefunot*, 9 (1965), 27ff., 35ff. [Ed.]

BARAZANI, SAMUEL BEN NETHANEL HA-LEVI (1560?–1630?), rabbi and kabbalist. His name derives from the town Barazan in Kurdistan, where he was probably born. His numerous wanderings were apparently the result of the political situation. He maintained yeshivot in Barazan, Akrah, Mosul, and Amadiyah. During his last years, he was the most distinguished scholar of Kurdistan and the acknowledged leader of Kurdistan Jewry. His authority was absolute though he held no official position. He revived the Jewish community of Kurdistan, where his disciples filled positions in many of the important communities. Barazani sent letters of rebuke and of comfort to the communities with the aim of preventing the prevalent religious laxity. He lived in great poverty and want. He was regarded as a saint, and his grave in Amadiyah became a place of pilgrimage. Barazani's books, many of which have been lost, are permeated with kabbalistic themes, and reflect an acquaintance with philosophy. Some of his *piyyutim*, festival prayers, and *reshuyyot* are included in the liturgy of Kurdistan, and some have been published. Among Barazani's works extant in manuscript are *Avnei Zikkaron* of which many copies exist, on the laws of ritual slaughter, *Sefer ha-Iyyun, Sefer Derashot,* and fragments of *Sefer Ḥaruzot*. His daughter was Asenath *Barazani. The Barazani family included many rabbis of Mosul, other Kurdish towns, and until recently, Baghdad.

Bibliography: Benayahu, in: *Sefunot*, 9 (1965), 21–125; A. Ben-Jacob, *Kehillot Yehudei Kurdistan* (1961), 33–38; idem, *Yehudei Bavel* (1965), 86.

[ED.]

BARBADOS, island in British West Indies. The first known Jewish settlers were ex-Marranos who had escaped from *Brazil after its reconquest from the Dutch by the Portuguese. In 1655 Abraham de Mercado, formerly an elder of the Recife community, and his son David Raphael, both physicians, were allowed to settle there. Jews were granted protection in 1656 and a community, K. K. Nidhe Israel, was established in Bridgetown; in due course a subsidiary community, K. K. Semah David, was formed at Speightstown on the other side of the island. By 1679 about 300 Jews lived in Barbados, a conversionist movement of little consequence being launched among them by the Quaker George Fox in 1685. During the 18th century the settlement grew very prosperous, though the Speightstown community came to an end. Raphael Ḥayyim Isaac *Carigal of Hebron served as rabbi of Bridgetown from 1774 until his death in 1777; in 1792 the community had 147 male members. In 1802 all political disabilities were repealed by the local legislature (confirmed by the British Parliament in 1820). With the island's economic decline, the community rapidly dwindled. At the beginning of the 20th century there were fewer than 20 persons left, and in 1925 the last of them died. The former synagogue is now used as the law library. A few Jews have settled in the island in recent years. In 1968 there were about 80 Jews out of a total population of 251,000.

Bibliography: Roth, Mag Bibl, index; W. S. Samuel, *Review of the Jewish Colonists in Barbados in the Year 1680* (1936 = JHSET, 13 (1936), 1-111); idem, in: JHSET, 14 (1940), 44ff.; E. M. Shilstone, *Monumental Inscriptions in the Burial Ground of the Jewish Synagogue at Bridgetown, Barbados* (1956); Cadbury, in: *Bulletin of Friends' Historical Association*, 29 (1940), 97–106; A. M. Hyamson, *Sephardim of England* (1951), 151–4.

[C.R.]

BARBARIANS, people of the Germanic linguistic group (Vandals, Franks, Goths, Burgundians, Lombards, Angles, and Saxons), of the Indo-Iranian group (Alans and Sarmatians), and the Hunnic peoples who were recruited

Barbarians and Romans in battle as depicted on a Roman sarcophagus. Rome, National Museum, Ludovisi Collection.

by, allied to, or invaded the Roman Empire during the fourth, fifth, and sixth centuries C.E. Most of the barbarians were pagans when they entered the empire but were eventually converted to orthodox Christianity. One important exception were the Goths who, when they settled in Italy, Gaul, and Spain were Arian Christians. Even these were eventually converted to orthodox Christianity. During the barbarian invasions the Jews, mostly city dwellers who were outwardly assimilated to their neighbors, no doubt suffered together with the rest of the population. Although no factual record survives, it may be assumed that this contributed to the numerical decline of the once prosperous Jewish communities of the Roman Empire. On the sack of Rome in 455, the Vandals carried off to Africa the spoils of the Temple brought back from Jerusalem by Titus.

When the barbarians entered the Roman Empire, they were profoundly influenced by the Christian-Roman population. In general it can be said that, while the barbarians were pagans, they treated the Jews well, probably better than the vanquished Christians who posed a threat to their power, since a community of interest existed between Jews and barbarians as a result of the opprobrium with which they both were regarded by the orthodox population. The same favorable attitude existed when they adopted Arian Christianity. Once, however, the barbarians became members of the orthodox church, the position of the Jews rapidly deteriorated. Restrictions were placed upon them, they were persecuted, and they were ultimately faced, especially in Spain, with the choice of conversion, exile, or death. General expulsions were decreed in Gaul in 626, in Burgundy about the same time, and in Lombardy in 661. More is known of the long attempt of the *Visigothic kings of Spain to suppress Judaism from 613 onward. In this the Jews suffered equally with all those minorities who were not orthodox Christians.

Bibliography: J. B. Bury, *The Invasion of Europe by the Barbarians* (1928); S. Katz, *The Jews in the Visigothic and Frankish Kingdoms of Spain and Gaul* (1937); B. Blumenkranz, *Juifs et chrétiens dans le monde occidental, 430–1096* (1960); J. M. Wallace-Hadrill, *The Barbarian West* (1962); J. Parkes, *Conflict of Church and Synagogue* (1934).

[ED.]

BARBASH, SAMUEL (c. 1850–1921), banker, leader of Ḥovevei Zion and of political Zionism in Russia. Barbash was born in Podolia. In the early 1880s he moved to Odessa, where he established a large bank, heading it until the Russian Revolution of 1917. He was one of the two guarantors to the Russian government for the legalization of the *Odessa Committee, the center of the Ḥovevei Zion movement, and served as its treasurer throughout the committee's existence. He was a member of the board of directors of the *Jewish Colonial Trust in its first years and its representative in Russia. He was active in many economic spheres affecting Zionism. Throughout his life he supported Hebrew cultural and literary projects.

Bibliography: M. Kleinmann (ed.), *Enẓiklopedyah le-Ẓiyyonut*, 1 (1947), 176–7; M. b. H. Ha-Kohen, *Sefer Shemot* (1938), 81–82.

[G.K.]

BARBASTRO, city in northern Aragon, Spain. Ramón Berenguer IV, count of Barcelona, conferred an estate upon a Jew named Zecri of Barbastro in 1144 as a reward for his services. In 1179 the bishop of Huesca granted Benjamin Abenbitals and Joseph b. Solomon permission to erect shops near the cathedral. Toward the middle of the 13th century the Jews occupied the citadel of Barbastro, which became the Jewish quarter. The charter of privileges granted to them in 1273 allowed them to request the bailiff to execute informers *(malshinim)* and prosecute Jews of dissolute morals.

In 1285 Pedro II endorsed new communal tax regulations. The Jews of Barbastro paid for the right to maintain a bureau in which the promissory notes for loans were drawn up. In 1330 Alfonso IV acceded to the request of the community to abrogate his instruction that a Christian burgher should be appointed to administer Jewish communal affairs, and endorsed the continuation of the former administrative system. The circumstances of the community were so straitened at this period that a special levy imposed by the king did not amount to more than 20 Jaca *sólidos*. In 1363, however, a levy of 500 Jaca *sólidos* was imposed by Pedro IV to meet the cost of the war with Castile. In 1383 the king renewed the privilege of the Barbastro community prohibiting apostates from entering the Jewish quarter and preaching missionary sermons there, while Jews could not be compelled to enter into religious disputations with Christians.

During the massacres of 1391 the Jews of Barbastro took refuge in the citadel, which was subjected to a regular siege: on August 18, King John I instructed the local authorities to take measures against the culprits. The community evidently ceased to exist after the disputation of *Tortosa, and as a result of the pressure exerted by the Dominican preacher Vicente *Ferrer. In 1415 Benedict XIII ordered the synagogue to be converted into a church because all the Jews in the city had become baptized and left the faith. It remained, however, a *Converso center.

Bibliography: Baer, Studien, 146; Baer, Urkunden, 1 pt. 1 (1929), index; Baer, Spain, 1 (1961), 55, 142, 426; Neuman, Spain, 1 (1942), index; del Arco, in: *Sefarad*, 7 (1947), 273, 280–1, 329; Rius, *ibid.*, 12 (1952), 339–40, 348–9; Cabezudo, *ibid.*, 23 (1963), 265–84.

[H.B.]

BARBY, MEIR BEN SAUL (1729?–1789), rabbi of Pressburg. Barby took his name from his birthplace, Barby, a small town near Halberstadt. He studied under Ẓevi Hirsch b. Naphtali Herz Bialeh (Ḥarif) of Halberstadt and Jacob Poppers, rabbi of Frankfort. On his return from Frankfort, he was appointed *dayyan* of Halberstadt, was rabbi of Halle for a year, and was then appointed rabbi of Pressburg in 1763. In Pressburg he established a large yeshivah. Barby issued many community *takkanot*, some of them designed to prevent laxity in Jewish life—such as frequenting the theater and card playing. A vehement opponent of the *Shabbateans, he excommunicated one of their adherents, Nathan Erholz, and dismissed him from the post of rabbi of Stampen. In 1771 he was a candidate for the vacant post of rabbi of Frankfort, but was not elected. He was in halakhic correspondence with many prominent scholars, including Ezekiel *Landau, Isaiah *Berlin, and Meir Posner, and he gave approbations to many works. Aside from his Torah erudition, Barby had a good

מהר״ם ברבי

נדפס פה פראג

Gegenwärtiges Buch, Mahram Barbi betitelt, enthaltend Erklärungen über die Talmudische Traktate Joma, Sukka, Schvuos &c. welche der bey der jüdischen Nazion in der Gelehrsamkeit berühmte verstorbene Presburger Rabbiner Mayer Barbi, verfasset hat, habe durchgelesen, und in selben nichts anstößiges wahrgenommen. Urkund dessen meine amtliche Fertigung und beigedrucktes gewöhnliches Sigill. Prag den 14. August 1792.

Karl Fischer,
k. k. Zensor, Revisor und Translator im hebräischen Fache.

L. S.

Title page of part two of *Ḥiddushei Hilkhot Maharam Barby* by Meir Barby, Prague, 1792. Jerusalem, J.N.U.L.

knowledge of medicine and music. Though he opposed the publication of his responsa, many of his novellae are cited in the works of his contemporaries. His only published work is *Ḥiddushei Hilkhot Maharam Barby* (2 vols., Dyhrenfurth-Prague, 1786–92).

Bibliography: *Arim ve-Immahot be-Yisrael*, 7 (1960), 41–45.

[Y.AL.]

BARCELONA, Mediterranean port in Catalonia, northeast Spain, seat of one of the oldest Jewish communities in the country. *Amram Gaon sent his version of the prayer book to "the scholars of Barcelona." In 876/7 a Jew named Judah (Judacot) was the intermediary between the city and the emperor Charles the Bald. Tenth- and eleventh-century sources mention Jews owning land in and around the city. The prominence of Jews in Barcelona is suggested by the statement of an Arabic chronicler that there were as many Jews as Christians in the city, but a list of 1079 records only 60 Jewish names. The book of *Usatges* ("Custumal") of Barcelona (1053–71) defines the Jewish legal status. Jewish ownership of real estate continued: the site of the ancient Jewish cemetery is still known as Montjuich. A number of Jewish tombstones have been preserved. From the end of the 11th century the Jews lived in a special quarter in the heart of the old city, near the main gate and not far from the harbor. The main street of the quarter is still called Calle del Cal ("The Quarter of the *Kahal*"). Bacelona Jews were subject to the jurisdiction of the counts of Barcelona. The forms of contract used by Jews here from an early date formed the basis of the *Sefer ha-Shetarot* of *Judah b. Barzillai al-Bargeloni, written at the beginning of the 12th century.

In the first half of the 11th century, some Barcelona Jews

were minters, and coins have been found bearing the name of the Jewish goldsmith who minted them. In 1104, four Jews of Barcelona received the monopoly to repatriate Muslim prisoners of war to southern Spain. Shortly afterward, *Abraham b. Ḥiyya was using his mathematical knowledge in the service of the king of Aragon and the counts of Barcelona, possibly assisting them to apportion territories conquered from the Muslims. From the beginning of the 13th century, the Jewish community provided beds for the royal retinues on their visits to Barcelona and looked after the lions in the royal menagerie. The Jews were mainly occupied as artisans and merchants, some of them engaging in overseas trade.

Communal Life. Documents of the second half of the 11th century contain the first mention of *nesi'im* ("princes"; see **nasi*) of the house of Sheshet (see Sheshet b. Isaac *Benveniste), who served the counts as suppliers of capital, advisers on Muslim affairs, Arab secretaries, and negotiators. From the middle of the 12th century the counts would frequently appoint Jews also as bailiffs *(baile)* of the treasury; some of these were also members of the Sheshet family. Christian anti-Jewish propaganda in Barcelona meanwhile increased. In 1263 a public *disputation was held at Barcelona in which *Naḥmanides confronted Pablo *Christiani in the presence of James I of Aragon. The bailiff and mintmaster of Barcelona at the time was Benveniste de Porta, the last Jew to hold this office. The Jews were subsequently replaced by Christian burghers; Jews from families whose ancestors had formerly acquired wealth in the service of the counts now turned to commerce and moneylending. However, learned Jews such as Judah *Bonsenyor continued to perform literary services for the sovereign.

By the beginning of the 13th century, a number of Jewish merchants and financiers had become sufficiently influential to displace the *nesi'im* in the conduct of communal affairs. In 1241, James I granted the Barcelona community a constitution to be administered by a group of *ne'emanim* (*secretarii*, or "administrative officers")—all drawn from among the wealthy, who were empowered to enforce discipline in religious and social matters and to try monetary suits. James further extended the powers of these officials in 1272. Solomon b. Abraham *Adret was now rabbi in Barcelona, an office which he held for about 50 years. Under his guidance, the Barcelona Jewish community became foremost in Spain in scholarship, wealth, and public esteem. He and his sons were among the seven *ne'emanim*, and he must have favored the new constitution. The *ne'emanim* did not admit to their number either intellectuals whose beliefs were suspect or shopkeepers and artisans. When the controversy over the study of philosophy was renewed at the end of Adret's life, the intellectuals of Barcelona did not therefore dare to voice their opinions. In 1305, Adret prohibited the youth from studying philosophy under penalty of excommunication: this provision was also signed by the *ne'emanim* and some 30 prominent members of the community.

A third constitution was adopted in 1327, by which time the community had been augmented, in 1306, by 60 families of French exiles. The privileges, such as exemption from taxes, enjoyed by Jews close to the court were now abolished, and, alongside the body of *ne'emanim*, legal status was accorded to the "Council of Thirty," an institution that had begun to develop early in the 14th century. The new regulations helped to strengthen the governing body. Several Spanish communities used this constitution as a model. *Berurei averot* ("magistrates for misdemeanors") were appointed for the first time in 1338 to punish offenders against religion and the accepted code of conduct. In the following year *berurei tevi'ot* ("magistrates for claims") were elected to try monetary suits. The communal jurisdiction of Barcelona, which at times acted on behalf of all the communities of Catalonia and Aragon, extended to several communities, both small and large, including that of Tarragona.

In the 14th century the monarchy yielded to the demands of the Christian merchants of Barcelona and restricted Jewish trade with Egypt and Syria. In addition, the community suffered severely during the *Black Death of 1348. Most of the "thirty" and the *ne'emanim* perished in the plague, and the Jewish quarter was attacked by the mob. Despite protection extended by the municipality, several Jews were killed. In December 1354, delegates for the communities of Catalonia and the province of Valencia convened in Barcelona with the intention of establishing a national roof organization for the Jewish communities of the kingdom in order to rehabilitate them after the devastations of the plague. In the second half of the century R. Nissim *Gerondi restored the yeshivah of Barcelona to its former preeminence. Among his disciples were R. *Isaac b. Sheshet and R. Ḥasdai *Crescas, both members of old, esteemed Barcelona families who took part in the community administration after the late 1360s.

The Decline. Around 1367 the Jews were charged with desecrating the *Host, several community leaders being among the accused. Three Jews were put to death, and for three days the entire community, men, women, and children, were detained in the synagogue without food. Since they did not confess, the king ordered their release. However, Nissim Gerondi, Isaac b. Sheshet, Ḥasdai Crescas, and several other dignitaries were imprisoned for a brief period.

The community gradually recovered after these misfortunes. Jewish goldsmiths, physicians, and merchants were again employed at court. After Isaac b. Sheshet's departure from Barcelona and Nissim Gerondi's death, Ḥasdai Crescas was almost the sole remaining notable; he led the community for about 20 years. The main element in the

Figure 1. Relic of the Barcelona ghetto wall, forming part of a building on Calle del Cal. Photo M. Ninio, Jerusalem.

Figure 2. Stone on a house in Barcelona bearing a Hebrew inscription indicating that it marked a *hekdesh*—gift donated in charity—by Rabbi Samuel of Cerdagne (believed to have lived c. 14th century). The inscription reads: "Hekdesh of Rabbi Samuel of Cerdagne, may his soul rest in peace." The Spanish plaque below mistranslates the Hebrew and adds the information that the stone was found with other remains from the time when Jews lived in the house, which was rebuilt in 1820. The house is on the corner of Arco de San Ramon del Cal and Calle de Marlet. Photo M. Ninio, Jerusalem.

Barcelona community was now the artisans—weavers, dyers, tailors, shoemakers, carpenters, blacksmiths, and coral-workers. These were organized into guilds, and demanded their share in the communal administration. After the long period in which the ruling oligarchy had been exercising their authority to their own advantage, the 1327 charter was abolished by royal edict in 1386. A new charter was approved by which representatives of the two lower estates, the merchants and artisans, shared in the administration.

During the persecutions of 1391, the city fathers and even the artisans of Barcelona tried to protect the Jews of the city, but without success. The violence in Barcelona was instigated by a band of Castilians, who had taken part in the massacres in Seville and Valencia and arrived in Barcelona by boat. News of the onslaught on the Jewish quarter in Majorca set off the attack on Saturday, August 5. About 100 Jews were killed and a similar number sought refuge in the "New Castle" in the Jewish quarter. The gate of the *judería* and the notarial archives were set on fire and looting continued throughout that day and night. The Castilians were arrested and ten were sentenced to the gallows. The following Monday, however, the "little people" *(populus minutus)*, mostly dock workers and fishermen, broke down the prison doors and stormed the castle. Many Jews were killed. At the same time, serfs from the surrounding countryside attacked the city, burned the court records of the bailiff, seized the fortress of the royal vicar, and gave the Jews who had taken refuge there the alternative of death or conversion. The plundering and looting continued throughout that week. Altogether about 400 Jews were killed; the rest were converted. Only a few of them (including Ḥasdai Crescas, whose son was among the martyrs) escaped to the territories owned by the nobility or to North Africa. At the end of the year John I condemned 26 of the rioters to death, but acquitted the rest. In 1393 John took measures to rehabilitate the Jewish community in Barcelona. He allotted the Jews a new residential quarter and ordered the return of the old cemetery. All their former privileges were restored and a tax exemption was granted for a certain period, as well as a moratorium on debts. Ḥasdai was authorized to transfer Jews from other places to resettle Barcelona, but only a few were willing to move. Reestablishment of a Jewish community in Barcelona was finally prohibited in 1401 by Martin I in response to the request of the burghers.

The Conversos. The renewed prosperity of Barcelona during the 15th century should be credited in part to the Conversos, who developed wide-ranging commercial and industrial activities. Despite protests by the city fathers, in 1486 Ferdinand decided to introduce the Inquisition on the Castilian model in Barcelona. At the outset of the discussions on procedure the Conversos began to withdraw their deposits from the municipal bank and to leave the city. The most prosperous merchants fled, credit and commerce declined, the artisans also suffered, and economic disaster threatened. The inquisitors entered Barcelona in July 1487. Some ships with refugees on board were detained in the harbor. Subsequently several high-ranking officials of Converso descent were charged with observing Jewish religious rites and put to death. In 1492 many of the Jews expelled from Aragon embarked from Barcelona on their way abroad.

20th Century. At the beginning of the 20th century a few Jewish peddlers from Morocco and Turkey settled in Barcelona. After the conquest of Salonika by the Greeks in 1912 and the announcement by the Spanish government of its willingness to encourage settlement of Spanish Jews on its territory (1931), Jews from Greece and from other Balkan countries migrated to Barcelona. Other Jews arrived from Poland during World War I, followed by immigrants from North Africa, and by artisans—tailors, cobblers, and hatmakers—from Poland and Rumania. There were over 100 Jews in Barcelona in 1918, while in 1932 the figure had risen to more than 3,000, mostly of Sephardi origin. After 1933 some German Jews established ribbon, leather, and

Figure 3. One of the pair of ceramic candlesticks flanking the ark in the Casa Sefardita synagogue in Barcelona. They are believed to be of Indian origin. Photo M. Ninio, Jerusalem.

candy industries. By 1935 Barcelona Jewry numbered over 5,000, the Sephardim by now being a minority. During the Spanish Civil War (1936–39), many left for France and Palestine. Some of the German Jews left the city after the Republican defeat in 1939, but during and after World War II Barcelona served as a center for refugees, maintained by the *American Jewish Joint Distribution Committee, and others returned to resettle.

The Barcelona community, consisting of approximately 3,000 people in 1968, is the best organized in Spain. The communal organization unites both Sephardi and Ashkenazi synagogues. There is also a community center, which includes a rabbinical office and cultural center. The community runs Jewish Sunday schools for children attending secular schools, and has a *talmud torah*. Youth activities include summer camps and a growing Maccabi movement. An old-age home supported by Jewish agencies outside Spain is maintained. The University of Barcelona offers courses in Jewish studies. Together with leaders of the Madrid community, Barcelona community heads were received in 1965 by General Franco, the first meeting between a Spanish head of state and Jewish leaders since 1492.

Bibliography: J. Fiter Ingles, *Expulsíon de los judíos de Barcelona* (1876); Loeb, in: REJ, 4 (1882), 57–77; F. de Bofarull y Sans, *Los judíos en el territorio de Barcelona* (1910); J. Miret y Sans and M. Schwab, *Documents de juifs Catalans des XIe, XIIe et XIIe siécles* (1915), 191; idem, in: *Boletín de la Real Academia de la Historia,* 69 (1916), 569–82; Baer, Urkunden, 1 pt. 1 (1929), index; Prevosti, in: *Sefarad,* 10 (1951), 75–90; A. López de Meneses, in: *Estudios de Edad Media de la Corona de Aragón,* 5 (1952), 677; idem, in: *Sefarad,* 19 (1959), 97–106, 323ff.; Madurell y Marimón, *ibid.*, 16 (1956), 369–98; 17 (1957), 73–102; 18 (1958), 60–82; 21 (1961), 300–38; 22 (1962), 345–72; 23 (1963), 74–104; 25 (1965), 247–82; 27 (1967), 290–8; Baron, Social², 4 (1957), 34, 249, notes 37f.; Cardoner, in: *Sefarad,* 22 (1962), 373–5; Suárez Fernández, Documentos, index; Baer, Spain, index; Millás Vallicrosa, in: *Sefarad,* 27 (1967), 64–70.

[Z.Av./H.B.]

BARCELONA, DISPUTATION OF, religious disputation between Jews and Christians in 1263. The apostate Pablo *Christiani proposed to King James I of Aragon that a formal public religious disputation on the fundamentals of faith should be held between him and R. Moses b. Naḥman (*Naḥmanides) whom he had already encountered in *Gerona. The disputation took place with the support of the ecclesiastical authorities and the generals of the Dominican and Franciscan orders, while the king presided over a number of sessions and took an active part in the disputation. The Dominicans *Raymond de Peñaforte, Raymond *Martini, and Arnold de Segarra, and the general of the Franciscan order in the kingdom, Peter de Janua, were among the Christian disputants. The single representative for the Jewish side was Naḥmanides. The four sessions of the disputation took place on July 20, 27, 30, and 31, 1263 (according to another calculation, July 20, 23, 26, and 27). Naḥmanides was guaranteed complete freedom of speech in the debate; he took full advantage of the opportunity thus afforded and spoke with remarkable frankness.

Basing himself on the Talmud as a whole, and in particular on the aggadic and homiletical passages, the Christian contestant sought to prove three points: that the Messiah had already appeared; that he was "both human and divine," and had died to atone for the sins of mankind; and that, in consequence, the precepts of Judaism had lost their validity. Against this Naḥmanides argued that the literal meaning of the passages quoted from the Talmud do not admit this christological interpretation. On the question of *aggadah,* he held, against his innermost convictions, that

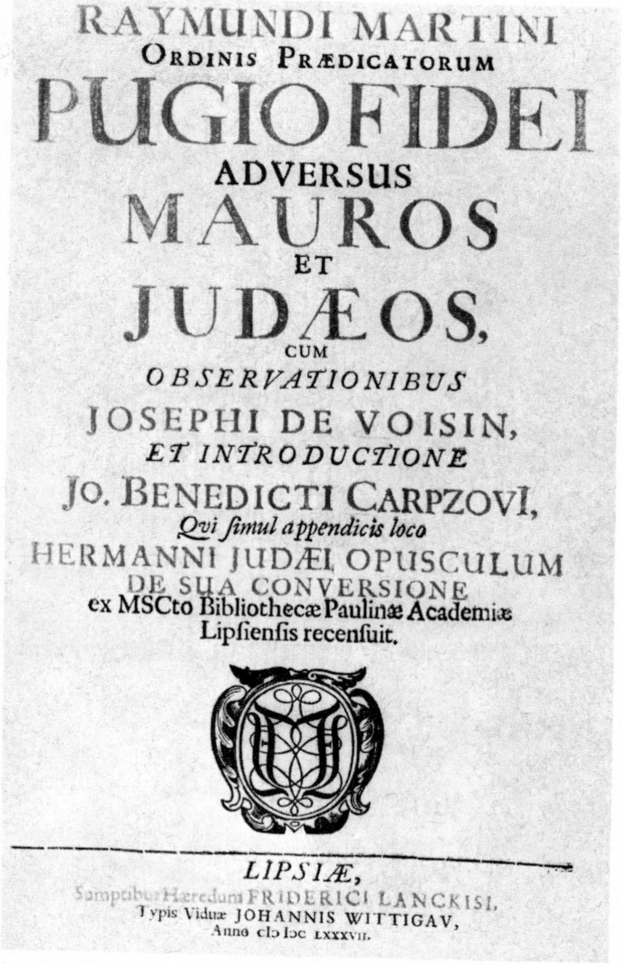
RAYMUNDI MARTINI
ORDINIS PRÆDICATORUM
PUGIO FIDEI
ADVERSUS
MAUROS
ET
JUDÆOS,
CUM
OBSERVATIONIBUS
JOSEPHI DE VOISIN,
ET INTRODUCTIONE
JO. BENEDICTI CARPZOVI,
Qui simul appendicis loco
HERMANNI JUDÆI OPUSCULUM
DE SUA CONVERSIONE
ex MSCto Bibliothecæ Paulinæ Academiæ
Lipsiensis recensuit.

LIPSIÆ,
Sumptibus Hæredum FRIDERICI LANCKISI,
Typis Viduæ JOHANNIS WITTIGAV,
Anno cIↃ IↃc LXXXVII.

Figure 1. Title page of *Pugio Fidei,* written by Raymond Martini as a result of the Disputation of Barcelona. Leipzig, 1687. Jerusalem, J.N.U.L.

acceptance of the homiletical passages in the Talmud is not obligatory for Jews, and that the main issue between Judaism and Christianity does not depend on belief in the Messiah. Naḥmanides even went on to attack the illogicality in Christian dogma concerning the nature of the Divinity. Some of his utterances hint at the future destruction of Christendom. He referred slightingly to the fate of Jesus, who was persecuted in his own lifetime and hid from his pursuers. Rome, which had been a mighty empire before Jesus lived, declined after adopting Christianity, "and now the servants of Muhammad have a greater realm than they." Naḥmanides also made the point that "from the time of Jesus until the present the world has been filled with violence and injustice, and the Christians have shed more blood than all other peoples." He similarly attacked the whole concept of the combination of human and divine attributes in Jesus.

A number of ecclesiastics who saw the turn the disputation was taking urged that it should be ended as speedily as possible. It was, therefore, never formally concluded, but interrupted. According to the Latin record of the proceedings, the disputation ended because Naḥmanides fled prematurely from the city. In fact, however, he stayed on in Barcelona for over a week after the disputation had been suspended in order to be present in the synagogue on the following Sabbath when a conversionist sermon was to be delivered. The king himself attended the synagogue in state and gave an address, an event without medieval precedent. Naḥmanides was permitted to reply on this occasion. The following day, after receipt of a gift of 300 *sólidos* from the king, he returned home.

Figure 2. Frontispiece of the 1687 edition of *Pugio Fidei*, designed to show the book's power to refute Judaism and Islam. Jerusalem, J.N.U.L.

The disputation had far-reaching consequences. It prompted the Dominican Raymond Martini to devise a better method of providing christological interpretations to the *aggadah*. In 1280 Martini concluded his book *Pugio Fidei* (Paris, 1651), and henceforward it was used indiscriminately by every Christian controversialist wishing to invalidate Judaism. The king cooperated with missionary activities throughout the realm and the Jews were forced to listen to the sermons preached by the Dominican friars. An order was issued by the latter between August 26 and 29 directing the Jews to erase from their copies of the Talmud any passages vilifying Jesus and Mary. Failure to do so was punishable by a fine, and books which had not been censored as required would be burned. The *Mishneh Torah* of *Maimonides was also condemned to be burned because of the references to Jesus in the chapter on the laws of kingship at the end of the work. Subsequently, the bishop of Gerona obtained a copy of Naḥmanides' own account of the disputation. Perhaps through his agency, proceedings were then instituted against Naḥmanides in 1265 before the court of the Inquisition on the charge that he had blasphemed Jesus. James's intention to sentence him to two years' banishment, and to condemn his work on the disputation to be burned, evidently did not satisfy the Dominicans. He thereupon ordered the case to be tried before him personally, intending to adjourn it until the fanaticism had abated. The militant Christian religious mendicant orders acted as the instrument of the church in its war on Judaism. It was at the request of the friars that Pope Clement IV ordered the archbishop of Tarragona to collect all the Jewish books in the kingdom of Aragon and surrender them to the Dominicans and Franciscans for examination; Pablo Christiani was recommended as a trustworthy and able assistant for this task. The bull *Turbato Corde*, also issued by Clement, became the basis of the Inquisition policy for prosecuting suspected Judaizers (see papal *bulls), and may also be regarded as an outcome of the disputation. The inference drawn by Naḥmanides is self-evident: he left Spain for Ereẓ Israel, arriving there in 1267.

Bibliography: Baer, Spain, 1 (1961), 150–62; idem, in: *Tarbiz*, 2 (1930/31), 172–87; C. Roth, *Gleanings* (1967), 34–61; M. A. Cohen, in: HUCA, 35 (1964), 157–92; Ben-Sasson, in: *Molad*, 1 (1967), 363–5. [H.B.]

BARD, BASIL JOSEPH ASHER (1914–), English lawyer and chemist. Bard studied chemistry at the Royal College of Science and also became a barrister. During World War II he worked in the legal departments of various government ministries dealing with the production and supply of explosives and aircraft. In 1950 he entered the government National Research Development Corporation and was successively commercial manager, technical director, executive director, and finally chief executive. Bard became the first chairman of the British branch of the Licensing Executives Society and served on a number of government committees. Bard was actively interested in Jewish communal and Zionist affairs. [S.A.M.]

BARDACH, ISRAEL (Isaac ben Ḥayyim Moses; c. late 18th century), Hebrew grammarian. Bardach, who lived in Lithuania, is known as the author of *Ta'amei Torah* (Vilna, 1822), a book on the accents (cantillations) of the Torah

ספר
טעמי תורה
חלק שני
מדקדוק הלשון
כולל ביאור כל מדרגות הטעמים ושמושיהם
והנחותיהם כמשפטיהם במקראי קודש ·
בביאור יותר נאות · מאשר נתבארו בספרי
המדקדקים, שהיו מלפנים ומקדם · ונוסף עליהם עוד
חדשות והוא ביאור כל מדריגות הטעמים · ושמושיהם
והנחותיהם בכתבי קודש איוב משלי תהלים הנקראים
טעמי אמת אשר עדיין לא נתבארו בספריהם כלל ·
ומחבר זה התבונן בהם · עד שעמד עליהם
ועל דרכיהם · בעזר הצור וישעתו · הוא הרב החריף
המא"הג והבקי סיני ועוקר הרים בנפ"ת · והמקובל
האלהי · והמליץ · והמדקדק הגדול · והאמיתי · החסיד
המפורסם מוה' ישראל יצחק במוה' חיים משה
ברד"ח · נ"י מ"ץ ור"ץ · דק"ק לאדמור יצ"ו · מנוע
ב"ח וט"ז ומוהרש"א :
הובא
טעם עליון
וא"ק ואבי"ע
הטעמים :
ווילנא
בדפוס
טוב טעם ודעת

Title page of *Ta'amei Torah* by Israel Bardach, Vilna, 1822. Jerusalem, J.N.U.L.

which was published by his brother Meir Bardach. The second part of this work contains a treatise on Hebrew grammar. In the introduction to *Ta'amei Torah*, Bardach mentions that he had also written commentaries on the *Idra Rabba* (of the *Zohar), on the Babylonian and Jerusalem Talmuds, and on the Shulḥan Arukh. However, the existence of all of these is unknown.

Bibliography: Benjacob, Oẓar, 211, no. 122. [Ed.]

BARDAKI, ISAIAH BEN ISSACHAR BER (1790–1862), Polish rabbi and later head of the Jerusalem community. Bardaki was born in Pinsk and settled in Ereẓ Israel in 1810, after the death of his first wife. In 1823 he married the daughter of R. *Israel b. Samuel of Shklov who mentions Bardaki with great affection. This marriage assured him of a leading position in the growing Ashkenazi community of Jerusalem. Upon the death of his father-in-law, he became head of the community. Wherever he went he was accompanied by his own interpreter and his personal attendant. Bardaki greatly strengthened the community, although he was opposed to all modern trends. Several buildings adjoining the Or ha-Ḥayyim Yeshivah were constructed under his auspices and the compound was named after him Ḥaẓar Rabbi Yeshayahu. He was a vice-consul of Austria (a post of great importance in the *capitulations regime prevailing in Jerusalem), and received the title of *ḥakham bashi* ("chief rabbi"). Several of his works are extant in manuscript.

Bibliography: A. M. Luncz, in: *Yerushalayim*, 5 (1898), 232–4; Y. Yellin, *Zikhronot le-Ven Yerushalayim* (1924), 8–10; Frumkin-Rivlin, 3 (1929), 227–9; A. Yaari, *The Goodly Heritage* (1958), 46, 53–4; J. Rimon and J. Z. Wassermann, *Yerushalayim ha-Attikah* (1958), 150–2.

[Y.Al.]

BARDEJOV (Hg. **Bártfa**; Ger. **Bartfeldt**), town in Slovakia, Czechoslovakia, on the Polish border. Jews, mainly from Galicia, settled in Bardejov in the 18th century. Jewish residence in Bardejov was formally authorized around the beginning of the 19th century. The synagogue was built in 1808. A main Jewish occupation was export of wine to Poland, and Jewish enterprise helped to develop Bardejov as a fashionable health resort in the early 19th century. The Jewish population numbered approximately 300 in Bardejov and its surroundings in 1848, 181 in the town itself in 1851, 480 in 1862, 1,710 in 1900 (of whom, in 1901, 220 owned businesses, 24 kept taverns, and 89 worked as artisans), and 2,264 in 1930. In 1940, during World War II, the Jewish houses were raided by Germans. Jews from eastern Slovakia were assembled in Bardejov for transportation to the death camps (2,411 by 1942). About 1,500 Jews were deported from Bardejov and the vicinity. Only one-tenth of the community survived the Holocaust.

After the war Bardejov became a rehabilitation center for Jewish survivors from the concentration camps and a transit center for "illegal" emigration to Palestine (see *Beriḥah). Anti-Semitism was still rife and Jews were attacked in June 1947 without being protected by the police. Of the few Jews, mainly physicians, who tried to resettle there, only one family remained by 1965. Ritual objects from Bardejov are preserved in the Divrei Ḥayyim synagogue in Jerusalem, named in honor of R. Ḥayyim *Halberstamm, whose descendants were rabbis in Bardejov.

The synagogue at Bardejov. Photo World Federation of Hungarian Jews.

Bibliography: *Magyar Zsidó Lexikon* (1929), 92; M. Atlas, in: *Zeitschrift fuer Geschichte der Juden* (1966), 151–70; L. Rotkirchen, *Ḥurban Yahadut Slovakyah* (1961); P. Meyer et al., *Jews in the Soviet Satellites* (1953), 637; M. Lányi and H. Propper, *A szlovenszkói zsidó hitközségek története* (1933), 142.

[Ed.]

BAREKHI NAFSHI (Heb. בָּרְכִי נַפְשִׁי; "Bless the Lord, O my soul"), initial words of Psalm 104. The central theme of this psalm is the glorification of God as the Creator of the universe, the majesty and beauty of which testify to the wisdom of the Master of all creatures. This psalm is regarded as one of the loftiest and most beautiful examples of ancient Hebrew poetry and a magnificent expression of monotheism. According to traditional Ashkenazi custom, this psalm is recited in private, on the afternoons of the Sabbaths between Sukkot and Passover, together with the 15 "Psalms of Ascent" (120–134). The reason for this custom may well be the analogy of this psalm with the account of creation given in Genesis and read on the Sabbath following the Sukkot festival *(Shabbat Bereshit)*. After Passover the recitation of *Pirkei *Avot* replaces that of the Psalms. The praise of the Creator and the creation is also the reason why Psalm 104 is recited on New Moons after the morning service (and in the Sephardi rite also before the evening service).

Bibliography: Baer S., Seder, 266 ff.; Eisenstein, Dinim, 56.

[Ed.]

BAREKHU (Heb. בָּרְכוּ), opening word of the call to worship by the *sheli'aḥ ẓibbur* at the formal beginning of the daily morning and evening services. The full invocation is *Barekhu et Adonai ha-mevorakh* ("Bless ye the Lord who is [to be] blessed"). The congregation responds *Barukh Adonai ha-mevorakh le-olam va-ed* ("Blessed be the Lord who is [to be] blessed for ever and ever"). "Bless," in this context, is the equivalent of "praise." *Barekhu* is also recited by the person who is called up to the Torah reading and is followed by the same congregational response. In the morning and evening services *Barekhu* also serves to introduce the reading of the *Shema;* this accounts for the absence of *Barekhu* before the **Minḥah* service which lacks the *Shema. Barekhu* is considered to be one of the *devarim she-bi-kedushah* (lit. "holy things") and may only be recited in the presence of a quorum of at least ten grown male Jews (*minyan*; Sof. 10:7; Sh. Ar. OḤ 55:1). The invocation *Barekhu* possibly originated in the time of Ezra, as might have the practice of standing at *Barekhu;* compare with Nehemiah (9:5) "Then the Levites . . . said, 'Stand up [cf. the practice of standing at *Barekhu*] and bless the Lord your God from everlasting to everlasting and let them say: Blessed be Thy glorious Name, that is exalted above all blessing and praise.'" A shorter formula, *Barekhu et Adonai,* occurs in Psalms 134:1–2 and 135:19. In the opinion of R. Akiva, the liturgical invocation, in

The word *Barekhu* handwritten in a decorated frame at the beginning of the *Ma'ariv* service for the first night of Passover. From a Frankfort *maḥzor,* 1816. Jerusalem, J.N.U.L.

accordance with scriptural precedent, should consist simply of *Barekhu et Adonai,* whereas the formula *Barekhu et Adonai ha-mevorakh* was advocated by his contemporary, R. Ishmael (Ber. 7:3). The latter formula was preferred by most of the *amoraim* (Ber. 50a; TJ, Ber. 7:4, 11c), and became standard. There is evidence that in the early period *Barukh Adonai ha-mevorakh* . . . was the response to *Barekhu* only in the Torah reading, while different responses were used for *Barekhu* as the invocation to worship. These were *Barukh Shem kevod malkhuto le-olam va-ed* ("Blessed be His Name, whose glorious kingdom is for ever and ever"), the standard response when the Divine Name was mentioned in the Temple of Jerusalem; and *Yehe Shemeih rabba mevarakh le-alam u-le-almei almayya* ("Let His great Name be blessed for ever and to all eternity"; Sif. Deut. 306, ed. by M. Friedmann (1864), 132b). In the course of time, however, *Barukh Shem kevod* . . . became the response to the *Shema* only: *Yehe Shemeih rabba* . . . was reserved for the *Kaddish;* and *Barukh Adonai ha-mevorakh* . . . became the exclusive response to *Barekhu.* At one time *Barekhu* was also used as a summons to recite Grace after Meals, but in the amoraic period, it was felt that this second-person form of address removed the leader from group participation and the invitation was standardized to *Nevarekh* ("Let us bless"; Ber. 7:3 and 49b–50a; TJ, Ber. 7:2–3, 11b–c; Tosef. Ber. 5:18). This objection, however, did not apply to *Barekhu* in the synagogue. The Reader may employ the "you" form but only when inviting the congregation to join him in prayer. Even then, he repeats the congregational response, thus associating himself with the praise of God. The Sephardi rite, as well as some ḥasidic congregations, retained the paradoxical practice (Sof. 10:7) of reciting *Barekhu* at the conclusion of the daily morning and evening services when there is no Torah reading. The custom accommodates worshipers who arrive too late to hear *Barekhu* at the opening of the services.

Bibliography: Liebreich, in: HUCA, 32 (1961), 227–37; M. Kadushin, *Worship and Ethics* (1964), 135–41; J. Heinemann, *Ha-Tefillah bi-Tekufat ha-Tanna'im ve-ha-Amora'im* (1966²), English abstract, v–vi, and index, s.v. [H.Ki.]

BARENBOIM, DANIEL (1942–), pianist and conductor. Barenboim, who was born in Buenos Aires, studied the piano with his father, Enrique (1912–), who had taught at the Vienna Music Academy. Daniel Barenboim gave his first public recital at the age of seven, graduated at the Santa Cecilia Academy, Rome, in 1956, and thereafter toured widely. He gained a reputation as an outstanding conductor, on occasion doubling in the roles of pianist and conductor. Barenboim settled in Israel in 1952. In 1967 he married the cellist Jacqueline du Pré, who subsequently often appeared with him. [H.Sh.]

BARGAS, ABRAHAM DE (c. 1740), Spanish Marrano author and physician. After escaping from Spain, Bargas settled first in France, where he was personal physician to the duke of Gramont, and later in Italy, where he became physician to the Leghorn Jewish community. There he composed a volume of ethical discourses on the Bible, *Pensamientos sagrados y educaciones morales* . . . (Florence, 1749). He also wrote an account of the earthquake of 1742, *Fiel relación de los terremotos* . . . (Leghorn, 1742), and translated into Spanish the order of service for the fast-day instituted to commemorate that event: *Traducción de la oración del ayuno y de los temblores de tierra* . . . (Pisa, 1746). He wrote some occasional poems, among them *El Casto Niceto* (Leghorn, n.d.).

Bibliography: Kayserling, Bibl, 15–16; A. S. Toaff, *Cenni storici sulla communità ebraica e sulla sinagoga di Livorno* (1955). [C.R.]

BAR GIORA, SIMEON, Jewish military leader in the war against Rome (66–70 C.E.). Simeon was born, according to Josephus, in *Gerasa, a large Hellenistic city in Transjordan, where the Jews lived in peace with the city's non-Jewish population. Some scholars, however, identify his birthplace with the village of Jerash in the neighborhood of Hartuv (Press, Ereẓ, 1 (1951²), 174, s.v. *Geresh*), others with Kefar Jorish near Shechem on the grounds that Simeon's activity began in its vicinity, i.e., in the province of Acrabatene. Since the word *giora* means proselyte in Aramaic, many scholars hold that his father was a convert to Judaism. The main source of information about Simeon is Josephus who is to be treated with circumspection, especially where an appraisal of the man and his activities are concerned, since Josephus entertained feelings of intense animosity toward him.

Simeon, already apparently known as a partisan leader, first distinguished himself in the battle at Beth-Horon against *Cestius Gallus (66 C.E.), in which the Jews inflicted a crushing defeat on the Roman army. Despite this achievement, however, Simeon was relegated to the background, since in Jerusalem the moderate party in control was disposed to come to terms with Rome. Simeon gathered around him a band of ardent patriots and, according to Josephus, engaged in brigandage. It is obvious, however, even from Josephus' own biased account, that these acts of "brigandage" were military operations conducted by the rebels under the leadership of Simeon against their internal enemies, opponents of the revolt, and sympathizers with Rome. In retaliation for these operations, the forces of the moderate government in Jerusalem compelled Simeon to take refuge among the

*Sicarii who, under the command of *Eleazar b. Jair, had captured *Masada. For a time Simeon remained with them, taking part in their raids. Subsequently leaving them, he parted company, and "terrorized" the southern part of Ereẓ Israel. Although growing increasingly stronger, he was unable to capture Jerusalem. The Zealots in Jerusalem, who were fearful of him, seized his wife but released her because of his threats. In addition to his continuous war against the party in control in Jerusalem, Simeon also fought against the Idumeans and succeeded in occupying Idumea with the help of supporters among the Idumeans themselves. Hebron, too, fell into his hands. In April 69 C.E. he entered Jerusalem, the gates of the city having been opened to him by the enemies of *John of Giscala, who had called on Simeon to come to their aid. Simeon thus gained control of the larger part of Jerusalem, both of the Upper and a considerable section of the Lower City.

The struggle between Simeon and John of Giscala continued. Constant hostilities were waged between them in the city, and came to an end only when Titus' forces reached the outskirts of Jerusalem (April 70 C.E.). Although all the rebels joined together during the siege to fight against the Romans and performed deeds of astounding bravery, the advantage enjoyed by the Roman army proved decisive. The Temple was burned and the devastated city captured by the enemy. Simeon and several of his most loyal friends hid in an underground passage among the ruins, but, unable to escape, Simeon finally surrendered to the Romans and was taken prisoner. The circumstances of his surrender were extremely strange. Josephus relates that Simeon suddenly appeared among the Temple ruins, as though out of the bowels of the earth, dressed in white and covered with a purple mantle. At the sight of him the Romans were terrified, but after recovering from their fear, bound him in chains. His strange appearance was probably connected with messianic expectations on his part; or by submitting to the victorious enemy he may have deliberately invited martyrdom.

Simeon was led as a prisoner in the triumphal procession held in Rome by Vespasian and his sons to celebrate their victory over the Jews. Scourged all the way, he was taken to the Mamertine prison, at the northeast end of the Forum, and executed at the moment of the culmination of the triumph. That he and not John of Giscala played this part in the triumphal procession shows that the Romans regarded him as the most important leader in Jerusalem and as the rebel commander. This is evident from other extant information as well. His army was far larger than that of his rivals, having numbered about 15,000 at the beginning of the siege of Jerusalem. His soldiers were also the best organized and disciplined. The fact that he was invited to Jerusalem by the priests and the people may have provided him with some legal basis for his leadership, although not all the patriot elements recognized his authority. Since information about them is very sparse, it is difficult to comprehend and explain the basis of the conflict between their different parties. At times it is even difficult to distinguish between the parties themselves. Nevertheless, from extant information it would appear that Simeon b. Giora was the leader of a clear eschatological trend in the movement of rebellion against Rome, and possibly filled the role of "king messiah" within the complex of eschatological beliefs held by his followers. His exceptional bravery and daring, mentioned by Josephus, undoubtedly attracted many to him, and won him preeminence among the rebel leaders. In contrast to the bitter hostility that existed between him and John of Giscala, there was a measure of understanding between him and the Sicarii at Masada.

Conspicuous among Simeon's characteristics was the enmity he bore toward the rich and the sympathy he showed to the poor, even to the extent of freeing slaves. This approach of his doubtless had its origin in his party's social outlook, opposed as it was to the existing order also in regard to the economic system and social justice.

Bibliography: J. Klausner, *Ke-she-Ummah Nilḥemet al Ḥerutah* (1955[9]), 151–86; M. Hengel, *Die Zeloten* (1961), 303–4, 381–2; M. Stern, in: *Ha-Ishiyyut ve-Dorah* (1963), 70–78; O. Michel, in: *New Testament Studies*, 14 (1967/68), 402–8 (Ger.); C. Roth, in: *Commentary*, 29 (1960), 52–58.

[U.R.]

°**BAR HEBRAEUS** (or **Bar ʿEbhrāyā** or **Ibn al-ʿIbrī**), **JOHANAN** (later: **Gregorius** or **Abu al Faraj;** 1226–1286), the last of the important writers in Syriac. He was the son of an apostate Jewish physician, Aaron (hence the appellation Son of the Hebrew), and knew Hebrew. Born in Malaṭīya (in Asia Minor) he went with his father to Antioch, where he became a monk. He also pursued secular studies, at first under his father's tutelage and later with a Nestorian scholar in Tripoli (Syria). In 1246 he was ordained Jacobite (Monophysite) bishop of Gubos (near Mulafryn) and assumed the name Gregorius. In 1252 he was appointed Maphriyan (archbishop) of Mesopotamia and Persia. Bar Hebraeus traveled widely, supervising the congregations of his church. He died at Maghāra in Azerbaijan.

Bar Hebraeus was a prolific writer. His commentary *Oẓar Razei* ("Treasury of Secret Wisdom") on the Old and New Testaments, reveals the influence of traditional Jewish exegesis. In addition to theological works such as *Ḥokhmat Ḥokhmeta,* which contains a systematic exposition of Aristotle's teaching, he also wrote on Syriac grammar and composed a Syriac *Chronicle,* a history of the world from creation to his own time, in two parts: ecclesiastical history and secular history. It was translated into English by E. A. W. Budge in 1932, and became widely known. Bar Hebraeus also wrote many poems and compiled a collection of entertaining stories (English translation, *Oriental Wit and Wisdom, or the Laughable Stories,* 1889). In addition, he translated Arabic works into Syriac (including the philosophical work of Avicenna, *Kitāb al-Ishārāt*), and also wrote works in Arabic, including an abridgment of the secular portion of his *Chronicle* with some revisions and addenda, and an epitome of the large work of al-Ghāfikī on medications (part published in the original with an English translation, with a commentary by M. Meyerhof and G. P. Sohby, 1932).

Bibliography: A. Baumstark, *Geschichte der syrischen Literatur* (1922), 312–20; G. Graf, *Geschichte der christlichen arabischen Literatur,* 2 (1947), 272–81; Brockelmann, Arab Lit, 1 (1898), 349–50, 591; W. Wright, *Short History of Syriac Literature* (1894), 265–81.

[E.A.]

BAR HEDYA (fl. first half of the fourth century), Babylonian scholar. Bar Hedya was one of the *neḥutei, amoraim* who moved between Babylonia and Ereẓ Israel, transmitting the rabbinical traditions of both countries. He testified, among other things, that in Ereẓ Israel care was taken to ensure that Hoshana Rabba (the 7th day of Tabernacles) did not fall on a Sabbath (Suk. 43b). Known for his interpretations of dreams, *Abbaye and *Rava turned to him in this connection. Abbaye, who paid him, received favorable dream interpretations; Rava, who did not pay him, received unfavorable interpretations. Upon the materialization of Bar Hedya's predictions, Rava also began to pay him, whereupon his dreams were then favorably interpreted. It finally became clear to Rava that the secret of Bar Hedya's ability lay in the fact that "all dreams follow the mouth" (of the interpreter) (Ber. 56a).

Bibliography: Hyman, Toledot, 285; Levy, Neuhebr Tal, 1 (1924[2]), 258, no.2.

[Y.D.G.]

BAR-HILLEL, YEHOSHUA (1915–), philosopher and theoretical linguist. Bar-Hillel was born in Vienna, educated in Germany, and after 1933, at the Hebrew University. He served in World War II, and lost an eye fighting in the Israel War of Independence. At the end of the war, he returned to the Hebrew University. He became a professor in 1961, a member of the Israel Academy of Arts and Sciences in 1963, and president of the International Union of History and Philosophy of Science in 1967. Bar-Hillel's early writings were concerned with the philosophy of mathematics, and culminated in the publication of his book with A. H. *Fraenkel, *Foundations of Set Theory* (1958). This sets out the major foundational approaches to mathematics and emphasizes their connection with broader philosophical issues. As distinct from Fraenkel's Platonism, Bar-Hillel's contributions stress that mathematical entities have only a pseudo-existence. Bar-Hillel's writings deal with the philosophy of language, philosophy of science, inductive logic, machine translation, mechanization of information retrieval, algebraic linguistics, and the semantics of natural languages. Some of these latter topics form the subject of his *Language and Information* (1964), which is concerned with the development of a science of language. [A.S.]

BARI, Adriatic port in southern Italy. Bari was one of the flourishing Jewish centers of *Apulia which according to tradition were founded by captives brought to Italy by *Titus. However, no inscriptions have survived to show that the community may be traced back to the Roman period, as is the case in neighboring towns. The community in Bari evidently rose to importance somewhat later. In the ninth century the miracle-worker *Aaron of Baghdad visited Bari. The names of scholars who taught at the local rabbinical academy in the tenth and eleventh centuries are recorded, including Moses Calfo, who is mentioned in the *Arukh* of *Nathan b. Jehiel. Legend talks of "four rabbis," who sailed from Bari in 972, were captured at sea by Saracen raiders, and sold into slavery in Spain and North Africa; after being ransomed, they founded famous talmudic academies (see *Moses b. Enoch). The legend at least indicates that Bari was known as a center of talmudic learning. This is confirmed by the adage cited by Rabbenu *Tam in the 12th century: "From Bari shall go forth the Law and the word of the Lord from Otranto" (a paraphrase of Isa. 2:3). The theological teaching of the Bari schools evidently attained a wide influence: Andrea, archbishop of Bari (d. 1078), actually became converted to Judaism (see *Obadiah the Proselyte).

The Jews of Bari underwent a number of vicissitudes. They were included in the edicts of forced conversion issued by the Byzantine emperors in the ninth and tenth centuries (see **anusim*). In about 932, the Jewish quarter was destroyed by mob violence and several Jews were killed. Between 1068 and 1465 the Jews in Bari suffered from the rival claims of the king and the archbishop on taxes levied on the Jews in the city. The Jews in Bari were also victims of the campaign to convert Jews to Christianity initiated by Charles of Anjou in 1290; in 1294, 72 families were forced to adopt Christianity, but continued to live in Bari as *neofiti* (see *Crypto Jews).

There followed a century and a half of tranquility until the Jewish quarter was again attacked in 1463; in 1495 Jewish property worth 10,000 ducats was pillaged. The expulsion of the Jews from the kingdom of Naples in 1510–11 sealed the fate of those in Bari: a small number was readmitted in 1520 and was finally forced to leave in 1540–41. The Via della Sinagoga in Bari remains to attest the existence of the former community, and several early medieval tombstones are in the Museo Provinciale. Jewish communal life was briefly resumed during World War II, when in 1943 many Jews from other parts of Italy and from Yugoslavia took refuge in Bari from Nazi-occupied territories. Toward the end of the war a refugee camp was established at Bari. The beginning of the "illegal" immigration to Palestine movement in Italy was situated in the area around Bari. During this period Jewish soldiers, mainly from Palestine, were active in aiding and organizing the refugees.

Bibliography: N. Ferorelli, *Gli Ebrei nell' Italia meridionale* (1915); E. Munkácsi, *Der Jude von Neapel* (1939); U. Cassuto, in: *Festschrift . . . Hermann Cohen* (1912), 389–404 (It.); G. Summo, *Gli Ebrei in Puglia dall' XI al XVI secolo* (1939); Milano, Italia, index; Roth, Dark Ages, index; Roth, Italy, index. [A.Mil.]

BAR-ILAN (Berlin), MEIR (1880–1949), leader of religious Zionism. Bar-Ilan was born in Volozhin, Russia, the son of R. Naphtali Ẓevi Judah *Berlin. He completed his studies in yeshivot at Volozhin, Telz, Brisk (Brest-Litovsk), and Novogrudok. As a young man he joined the *Mizrachi movement, representing it at the Seventh Zionist Congress (1905), at which, unlike the majority of Mizrachi delegates, he voted against the *Uganda Scheme. In 1911 he was appointed secretary of the world Mizrachi movement, working in Berlin, and he coined the Mizrachi slogan *"Ereẓ Yisrael le-Am Yisrael al Pi Torat Yisrael"* ("The land of Israel for the people of Israel according to the Torah of Israel"). He moved to the United States in 1915, served as president of the U.S. Mizrachi, and from 1925 was a

Meir Bar-Ilan, central figure in the Zionist religious movement.

member of the Board of Directors of the *Jewish National Fund. In 1926 Bar-Ilan settled in Jerusalem where he served as president of the World Mizrachi center and as the Mizrachi representative in Zionist and *yishuv* institutions, including clandestine committees for defense. Between 1929 and 1931 he was a member of the Zionist Executive. A leading opponent of the Palestine partition plan in 1937, and of the British White Paper of 1939, he advocated civil disobedience and complete noncooperation of the Jewish population toward the British government. After the establishment of the State of Israel, he organized a committee of scholars to examine the legal problems of the new state in the light of Jewish law, and was an initiator of the National Religious Front, the group of religious parties that presented a united platform in the first Knesset elections. A central figure in the Zionist religious movement, Bar-Ilan founded and edited a religious Zionist weekly, *Ha-Ivri* ("The Hebrew"), which was published in Berlin from 1910 to 1914 and in New York from 1916 to 1921. Between 1938 and 1949 he was editor in chief of the Mizrachi daily, *Ha-Ẓofeh,* in Tel Aviv. Some of his articles were collected in his books *Bi-Shevilei ha-Teḥiyyah* ("In the Paths of Renaissance," 1940) and *Kitvei Rabbi Meir Bar-Ilan* (1950). His memoirs, *Mi-Volozhin ad Yerushalayim*

("From Volozhin to Jerusalem," 1939–40), were originally published in Yiddish. He also wrote a book about his father, entitled *Rabban shel Yisrael* "Rabbi of Israel" (1943). He initiated and organized the publishing of the Talmudic Encyclopaedia, begun in 1947. He also founded the institute for the publication of a new complete edition of the Talmud. Bar-Ilan University near Tel Aviv, founded by the American Mizrachi movement, is named in his honor, as is the Meir Forest in the Hebron hills, and the moshav Bet Meir near Jerusalem.

Bibliography: I. Avigur, *Ilan ve-Nofo* (1952); M. Krone, *Ha-Rav Meir Bar-Ilan* (1954); EZD, 1 (1958), 334–47; A. Hertzberg, *The Zionist Idea* (1960), 546–54.

[Z.K.]

BAR-ILAN UNIVERSITY, Orthodox university in Israel, founded in 1955. The university's purpose is to advance knowledge in both Jewish studies and general science and research in accordance with the ideology of *Torah im Derekh Ereẓ* ("Torah with general knowledge"), which led to the foundation of similar institutions in the Diaspora, such as Yeshiva University in New York. In the late 1940s a plan evolved to establish a religious university in Ereẓ Israel was supported by the *Mizrachi movement in the United States. The idea received further impetus under Pinkhos *Churgin's leadership in the U.S. Located on a site east of Ramat Gan, the university was named for Meir *Bar-Ilan. At the outset, the Bar-Ilan project received little encouragement in Israel. The government doubted the need for a university in addition to the Hebrew University in Jerusalem. *Agudat Israel and similar Orthodox groups were fearful of imperiling certain types of religious education, particularly the yeshivot. However, it gradually became clear that there was a need for extending and diversifying higher education in Israel. The first president of the university was Pinkhos Churgin (1955–57), its founder. In 1957 Joseph *Lookstein was appointed chancellor. Under Lookstein's leadership the university grew rapidly and received a charter from the state of New York. The first academic year began with 80 students and 19 lecturers. In 1969–70 the University had over 4,500 students and almost 600 lecturers, with more than 800 foreign students. Bar-Ilan is modeled on the American university pattern, which follows a credits system. The compulsory basic study of Jewish subjects includes Bible and Talmud. University studies are divided into three stages: the B.A. in humanities and B.S. in sciences, which require a four-year study period, as against three years in other institutions in Israel; the M.A. or M.S.; and the Ph.D. Instruction and research are carried out within separate faculties for Jewish studies, languages and literature, humanities and social studies, and science and mathematics. The university also has a criminology institute and a school of social work, whose students receive a B.S.W. at the end of their course. There are also university extension courses at Ashkelon (begun in 1965) and Safed (begun in 1968). The university campus covers 270 dunams, with 20 buildings. Dormitories provide housing for 300 students, with an additional 500 units planned. The university published the *Bar-Ilan Annual, Studies in Judaica and the Humanities*. It is administered by a senate, comprised of the deans and representatives of the professors, and lecturers, and the Board of Trustees, which includes religious and civic leaders and scholars from Israel and the Diaspora.

Bibliography: A. Ben-Yosef, in: *Sefer ha-Shanah shel Bar-Ilan*, 4–5 (1967), 12–29.

[Ed.]

BARIT, JACOB (1797–1883), Russian talmudist and communal leader. Born in Simno, Suvalki province, he left in 1822 for Vilna, where he kept a distillery. Attracted by the ideas of the *Haskalah, he studied foreign languages, mathematics, and astronomy. In 1850 he became principal of the yeshivah founded by R. Ḥayyim Naḥman Parnas, a position he held for 25 years. By the end of 1840 he was the acknowledged leader of the Vilna community. When Sir Moses *Montefiore visited Vilna in 1846 Barit advised him on his petition to Nicholas I. He was a member of the delegation sent to St. Petersburg in 1852 in connection with the oppressive new conscription law. On several rabbinical committees summoned by the Ministry of the Interior, Barit was eloquent in advocating Jewish rights. In 1871 when the governor general of Vilna formed a committee to investigate the accusations made against the Jews by the apostate Jacob *Brafmann, Barit successfully convinced the committee of their falsehood.

Bibliography: M. I. Barit, *Toledot Ya'akov* (1883); S. P. Rabbinovitz, *Kneset Israel*, 2 (1887), 157–62; H. N. Maggid-Steinschneider, *Ir Vilna* (1900), 62–67; Dinur, in: *He-Avar*, 15 (1968), 254–8.

[Ed.]

BARKAI (Heb. בַּרְקַאי; "first morning light"), kibbutz in central Israel, at the western entrance of the Iron Valley, affiliated with Kibbutz Arẓi ha-Shomer ha-Ẓa'ir. It was founded on May 10, 1949, by pioneers from North America, joined later by newcomers from Rumania and from English-speaking and other countries. Farming branches include citrus and banana plantations, tobacco, field crops, and livestock.

[E.O.]

Bar-Ilan University, 1969. Photo Nat Suffrin, Tel Aviv.

BAR KAPPARA (beginning of third century C.E.), Palestinian scholar in the transition period between the *tannaim* and the *amoraim.* He was called Bar Kappara because his first name was the same as that of his father, *Eleazar ha-Kappar (Tosef., Beẓah, 1:7, et al.). Bar Kappara was a disciple of *Judah ha-Nasi and like his contemporaries, *Ḥiyya bar Abba and *Oshaya Rabbah, was the author of a compilation of *halakhot.* These were called "The Mishnah of Bar Kappara" or "The Great Mishnayot of Bar Kappara" (BB 154b; Eccles. R. 6:2). This collection, a supplement to the Mishnah of Judah ha-Nasi, was used to explain obscure passages in the standard Mishnah and brought to the knowledge of the *amoraim* various traditions and opinions that differed from the Mishnah of Judah ha-Nasi.

The academy of Bar Kappara was in the "south" (TJ, Nid. 3:2, 50c), seemingly in Caesarea or in nearby Parod (Av. Zar. 31a). It is possible, however, that it was in Lydda (Lieberman, p. 123). It is also very probable that Bar Kappara was the final compiler of *Sifrei Zuta* (*ibid.*, p. 122). Among his associates were some of the outstanding scholars of the generation, such as *Oshaya and *Joshua b. Levi, who transmitted his *halakhah* and *aggadah* (Ker. 8a; Ber. 34a, et al.). It is related that once when walking on the shore of Caesarea Bar Kappara came upon the survivor of a shipwreck who proved to be a Roman proconsul. Bar Kappara took the destitute man home, fed and clothed him, and provided him with a substantial sum of money. Some time later, when Bar Kappara appeared before this same proconsul on behalf of some captive Jews, the official, remembering the sage's former kindness to him, had the captives promptly released.

Bar Kappara was distinguished for his original views, and he greatly valued the study of the natural sciences. It is reported in his name: "Whosoever can calculate the movements of the solstices and planets, but fails to do so, to him is applied the verse [Isa. 5:12] 'But they regard not the work of the Lord; neither have they considered the operation of His hands'" (Shab. 75a). He also looked favorably upon the use of Greek, even recommending it to his disciples: "Let the words of Torah be uttered in the language of Japheth [Greek] in the tents of Shem" (Gen. R. 36:8, in reference to Gen. 9:27). On the other hand he was averse to metaphysical speculation, apparently as a result of his opposition to the Gnostic teachings that were widespread at that time. Commenting on the verse, "For ask now of the days past, which were before thee, since the day that God created man upon the earth, and from one end of heaven unto the other" (Deut. 4:32), Bar Kappara stated: "You may speculate upon what came after creation and not upon what came before it. You may investigate from one end of heaven unto the other, but not what is beyond it." His opposition to asceticism is seen in the statement (though possibly it is his father's), "to what does Scripture refer when it says [of the Nazirite, Num. 6:11], 'Make atonement for him, for that he sinned by reason of the soul?' Against which soul did he sin? Against his own soul, in that he denied himself wine. And if one who denied himself only wine is termed a sinner, how much more so he who denies himself the enjoyment of all permitted things" (Ta'an. 11a, and parallel passages).

Bar Kappara showed great talent as a poet, and as an author of fables and epigrams. The Jerusalem Talmud (Ber. 1:8, 3d) quotes a beautiful prayer which he composed and which he used to recite during the repetition of the Thanksgiving blessing in the *Amidah.* It is related that during the marriage feast of Simeon, son of Judah I (or of his son, see Lev. R. 28:2), Bar Kappara told 300 *fox fables, and so intently did the guests listen that they completely ignored the fact that their food was becoming cold. Despite his closeness with Bar Kappara, Judah ha-Nasi did not ordain him, because of his satirical remarks about the *nasi* and his household: "On one occasion, Simeon, son of Judah, and Bar Kappara were studying together when a difficulty arose about a certain *halakhah.* Simeon said to Bar Kappara, 'Only my father, Rabbi Judah, can explain this.' Bar Kappara retorted, 'There is no rabbi in the world who understands it' [Rashi to MK 16a]. Simeon told his father, who was vexed, and when Bar Kappara next presented himself, Judah said to him, 'I have never known you'" (MK 16a), thus disowning him. On another occasion, Bar Kappara and Ben Elasah, the rich but ignorant son-in-law of Judah, were in the *nasi's* house at a gathering of scholars who were engaged in learned discourse. Bar Kappara proposed to Ben Elasah that he too take part in the discussion, and to this end composed for him a poetic riddle to present to his father-in-law as a genuine problem. The riddle was in fact a criticism of the conduct of Judah's household and of the fear which he inspired. The *nasi,* realizing from the smile upon Bar Kappara's face that he was the author of the riddle, exclaimed, "I do not recognize you as an elder" (i.e., "I do not wish to grant you recognition"), and Bar Kappara understood that he would not be ordained (TJ, MK 3:1, 81c). In spite of everything, however, Bar Kappara was closely attached to Judah. It was he who stood the deathwatch and who was the first to inform the sages, in moving words, of the *nasi's* death: "Mortals and angels have been wrestling for the holy ark; the angels have won and the ark has been taken captive."

Bibliography: Y. M. Kahana, in: *Ha-Asif,* 3 (1886), 330–33; Graetz, Hist, 2 (1949), 455–6, 470; Bacher, Tann; Hyman, Toledot, 288–92; Alon, Toledot, 2 (1961), 145–7; S. Lieberman, *Sifrei Zuta al Sefer ba-Midbar* (1968), 104–24.

[Y.D.G.]

BAR KOCHBA ASSOCIATION, an organization of Jewish university students in Prague. It was founded in 1893 by students of the Prague German University and subsequently became a focal point of Zionist intellectual activities. Among the members who later played prominent roles in the Zionist movement were Shmuel Hugo *Bergman, Oskar Epstein, Hugo Hermann, Leo *Hermann, Hans Kohn, and Robert *Weltsch. The members of Bar Kochba contributed much to the deepening of Zionist ideology, particularly in the years preceding World War I. They were largely influenced by Martin Buber who, between 1909 and 1911, delivered his *Drei Reden ueber das Judentum* before this group. The Zionist outlook of these young men found expression in the weekly *Selbstwehr,* which they edited for a time, and in *Vom Judentum,* a collection of essays on the problems of Zionism and Judaism in general (1913). There were small-scale attempts at renewing the activities of Bar Kochba after World War I, including the publication of *Juedische Jugendblaetter* (jointly with *Blau-Weiss). Its functions were taken over by its sister society, Theodor Herzl, which consisted of Czech-speaking Jewish university students in Prague.

Bibliography: H. Yachil, *Devarim al ha-Ẓiyyonut ha-Czekhoslovakit* (1967), 8–11; Y. Borman, in: *Gesher,* 15, no. 2–3 (1969), 243–50; *Semestralberichte des Vereins Bar-Kochba in Prag* (1910–13); F. Weltsch (ed.), *Prague vi-Yrushalayim* (1954), 77–121; H. Kohn, *Living in a World Revolution* (1965), 47–55.

[O.K.R.]

BAR KOKHBA (d. 135 C.E.), leader of the revolt in Judea against Rome (132–135 C.E.).

The Man and the Leader. Bar Kokhba is known in talmudic sources as Ben Kozevah, Bar Kozevah, or Ben Koziva (Heb. בן כוזבה, בר כוסבא, בן כזיבא; Sanh. 93b; BK

Figure 1a. Coin of the Bar Kokhba revolt, with date palm and inscription *Shimon Nesi Yisrael* ("Simeon prince of Israel"). Jerusalem, Israel Department of Antiquities and Museums.

97b; TJ, Ta'an 4:8, 68d), and in Christian sources as Βαρχωχεβας (Eusebius, *Historia Ecclesiastica,* 4:6, 2). In the recently discovered contemporary letters addressed to or originating from him, he is referred to as Simeon bar Kosevah, Bar or Ben Koseva (שמעון בר כוסבה, בר כוסבא, בן כוסבא, the last form being found also in a contemporary Greek letter). The name שמעון (or its abbreviation שמע), which appears on coins of the revolt, undoubtedly refers to him. His original name was probably Bar Koseva, and it is doubtful whether it was derived from a settlement in the Judean mountains or whether it indicates his father's name or a general family name. The appellation Bar Kokhba was apparently given to him during the revolt on the basis of the homiletical interpretation, in a reference to messianic expectations, of the verse (Num. 24:17): "There shall step forth a star [כּוֹכָב, *kokhav*] out of Jacob." Bar Kokhba was general midrashic designation for the "king messiah" (see *Messiah), and customarily used before the destruction of *Jerusalem. Thus, in the verse "a star out of Jacob . . . a scepter . . . out of Israel" *(ibid.)*, Onkelos renders "star" as *malka* ("king") and "scepter" as *meshiḥa* ("messiah"), a midrashic interpretation current among the *Zealots who joined in the war against the Romans. While this appellation became the popular one, his original name was retained in documents and letters. The disappointment that followed in the wake of the defeat (and perhaps even at the height of the revolt) may have led the people to give a derogatory turn to his original name of Bar Koseva by altering it to Bar Kozivah (בר כוזיבה) in a punning allusion to "a lie" *(kazav)*. Even the homiletical interpretation of "a star out of Jacob" quoted by R. *Akiva was from then on interpreted ambiguously, as evidenced by R. *Simeon b. Yoḥai's statement: "'There shall step forth a star out of Jacob'—Kozeva stepped forth out of Jacob" (TJ, *loc cit.*). Similarly, in talmudic sources Bar Kokhba coins are referred to specifically as those of Ben Koziva. "A coin of one who rebelled, such as Ben Koziva," or "Koziva coins" (BK 97b; TJ, Ma'as. Sh. 1:1, 52d; Tosef., *ibid.*, 1:6).

Bar Kokhba's personality does not emerge clearly from the scant and obscure sources available, some of which, like those in the Talmud and Midrash, have legendary overtones, while later ones, such as the sparse references in the Church Father Eusebius, are tendentious. The few traits of his personality that emerge from the administrative and economic documents found in the Judean Desert do not contradict the main features of his character as incidentally portrayed in the literary sources. He may be described as a leader who, in charge of both the economy and the army, ruled imperiously, concerned himself even with minor details, and did not refrain from threatening senior officers of his army with punishment or even from inflicting deterrent punishment.

Bar Kokhba's title in documents is נשיא ישראל or הנסי על ישראל ("*nasi* of Israel"), the former occurring also on coins of the revolt. According to the Talmud, Akiva said: "This is the king messiah" whereupon Johanan b. Torta answered him derisively: "Akiva, grass will grow in your cheeks and the son of David will still not have come" (TJ, Ta'an. 4:8; Lam. R. 2:2, no. 4). Eusebius states that Bar Kokhba regarded himself as the savior who had come down to the Jews like a star from heaven, to deliver them from their somber troubles. Some adduce proof of Bar Kokhba's messiahship from the *Vision of Peter,* a Christian work written a few years after the revolt, which refers to a deceiver who falsely represented himself as a messiah and was—according to this tendentious account—nothing but a murderer. But these are simply expressions of the Christian authors' hatred which distorted their outlook, and are devoid of real historical value. Nevertheless, the messianic hopes which were cherished by the nation centered around Bar Kokhba. As might be expected from such a powerful, dominant personality, he himself probably had pretentions to being a redeemer and fostered these hopes. That the very appellation Bar Kokhba expresses a messianic belief in the "star out of Jacob" as an ideal ruler can be seen from apocryphal literature (Test. Patr., Levi 18:3; and Judah 24:1; and cf. Rev. 22:16; *The Damascus Document,* 7:19–20; and *War of the Sons of Light with the Sons of Darkness,* 7:5, 1). *The Damascus Document* states that the "star out of Jacob" will be "the *nasi* of the entire community" and accordingly it might be contended that Bar Kokhba's title of *nasi* had a messianic allusion. But the documents contain no hint of a messianic reference, and the sway of the *nasi* applied to wholly mundane affairs such as the army, administration, and the economy. According to coins struck during the revolt, the *nasi* may have assigned in a compromise matters relating to worship and faith to Eleazar ha-Kohen (perhaps on the basis of the division between the *nasi* and the priesthood, as described in Ezek. 44–46). The basically authentic statement about a Sanhedrin at Bethar (Sanh. 17b) suggests that at a certain time a *bet din* participated in Bar Kokhba's rule. Therefore, the title *nasi* may itself have indicated a more restricted role than that regarded as implicit in "king messiah."

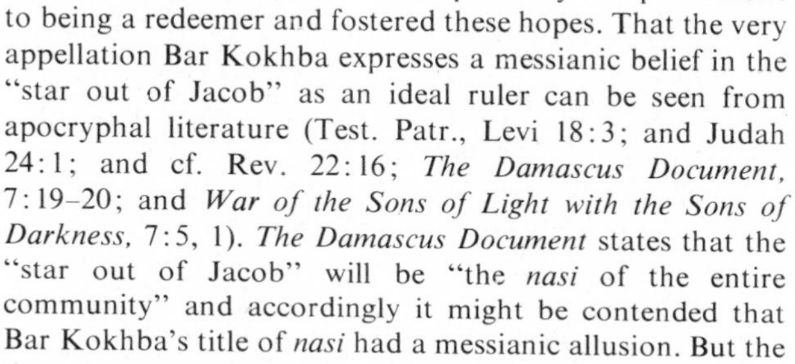

Figure 1b. Two coins of the Bar Kokhba revolt. The one on the right is inscribed *shanah aḥat li-ge'ulat Yisrael* ("Year one of the redemption of Israel"), the one on the left *shblḥr Israel,* a contraction for "Year two of the freedom of Israel." Jerusalem, Israel Department of Antiquities and Museums.

The *aggadah* which relates how Bar Kokhba's men were selected—by having a finger cut off or by uprooting a cedar tree (TJ, *loc cit.;* Lam. R. 2:2 no. 4)—reflects the exclusiveness of an elite rebel army and the harshness and even cruelty of its leader. The controversies between him and the sages, and his reliance on his own powers rather than on help from Heaven, are depicted in the *aggadah* as self-aggrandizement against God: "When he went forth to battle, he said 'Neither assist nor discourage us.'" To decide precisely the historical kernel that has been preserved in this tradition is difficult, but Bar Kokhba's letters to his subordinates (such as to Jeshua b. Galgolah or Jonathan and Masbelah) confirm that he was a stern leader who vigorously insisted on his views and with a firm hand controlled not only the population but also his senior officers. In contrast to the situation during the Jewish War (66–70/73 C.E.), the nation was now united under the leadership of a single commander in chief. This is evident from documents indicating that even in the final stages of the revolt he still exercised unlimited authority over his men. Presumably the unity of the nation in this war derived not only from the *nasi's* powerful personality, but also from the memory of past sufferings and the yearning for liberation. Geography, too, may have been a factor in this unity, for while the revolt spread to Galilee and Transjordan, it was mainly although not exclusively centered in Judea, making it both possible and practicable to exercise effective control.

Figure 1c. Two undated coins attributed to the third year of the Bar Kokhba revolt. The one on the left is inscribed "For the freedom of Jerusalem," the one on the right, "Jerusalem." Jerusalem, Israel Department of Antiquities and Museums.

Such was the background to the acceptance of a strong leader's authority, unopposed apparently by the soldiers. This unanimity of the nation can be inferred from Eusebius (as from the *Book of Revelation*) where Bar Kokhba is described as a murderer and bandit who deceived the people. Even in later generations, despite the disappointment engendered by his defeat, his image persisted as the embodiment of messianic hopes. This is evident from Maimonides who, in referring to the "king messiah," states: "Rabbi Akiva, the greatest of the sages of the Mishnah, was a supporter of King Ben Koziva, saying of him that he was the king messiah. He and all the contemporary sages regarded him as the king messiah, until he was killed for sins which he had committed" (Maim. Yad, Melakhim, 11:3).

The Bar Kokhba Revolt. Only sparse and fragmentary information exists, some of it late, on the Bar Kokhba revolt, its origins, course, and outcome. The main source consists of the scant statements of the Roman historian Dio Cassius in the 69th part of his history of Rome, written between 194 and 216 C.E. As for Bar Kokhba's documents, they contain nothing specific about the war itself or about its political and military significance, being mainly economic and administrative records. The revolt most probably broke out in 132 C.E. Dio Cassius states that before it began Hadrian had established a new city in Jerusalem, called Aelia Capitolina (after his own name Aelius and in honor of Jupiter Capitolinus). He built a

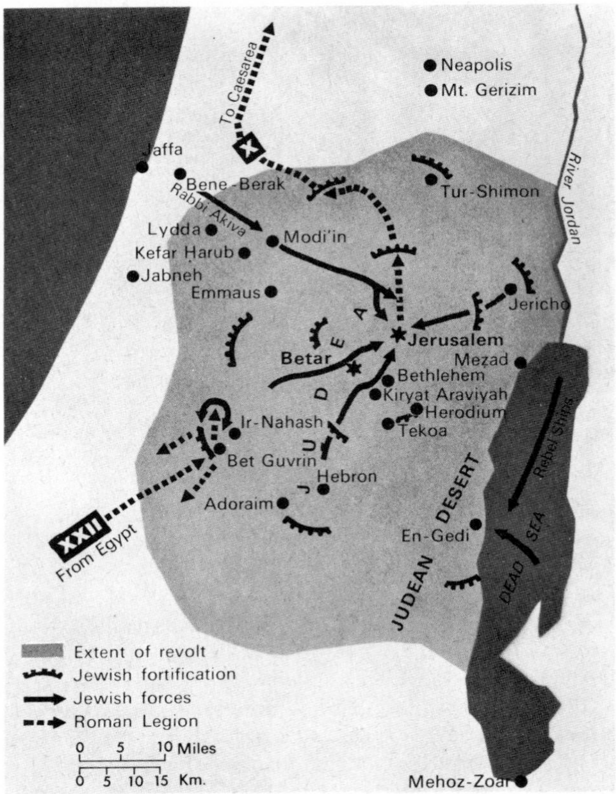

Map 1. Extent of the Bar Kokhba revolt in its first year, 132 C.E. After Y. Aharoni, Carta's "Atlas of the Bible," Heb. ed., 1966.

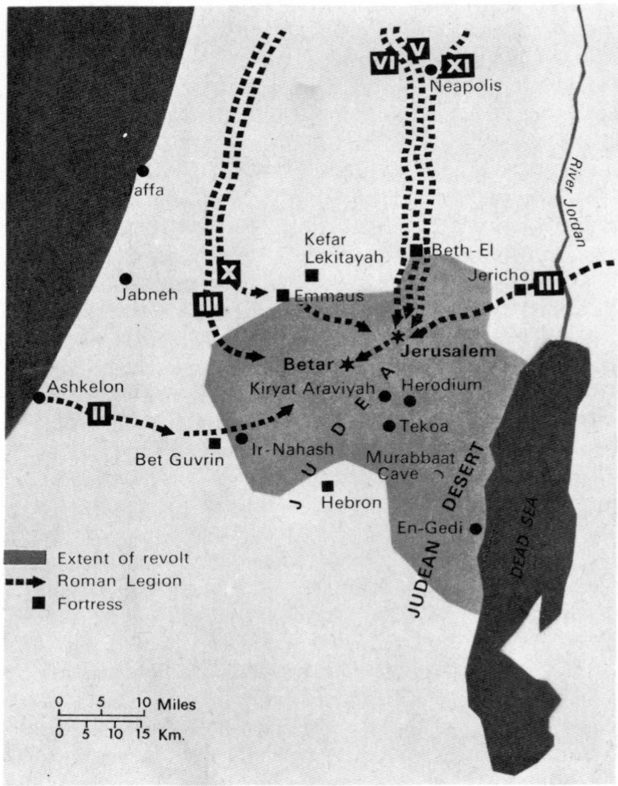

Map 2. Extent of the Bar Kokhba revolt in its third and fourth years. After Y. Aharoni, Carta's "Atlas of the Bible," Heb. ed., 1966.

temple to Jupiter in the new city, thereby infuriating the Jews and provoking "a fierce and protracted war." On the other hand, Eusebius declares that Aelia Capitolina was established after the revolt. Hadrian probably began to build Aelia Capitolina before the revolt, and its non-Jewish character inflamed the Jews against Rome, but the work was not completed until after the war (see *Hadrian for a contrary view). During 129–132 C.E. Hadrian stayed in Ereẓ Israel and its neighborhood, and his departure for Greece in the summer of 132 was the signal for the outbreak of the revolt. There were other factors that aggravated the situation, e.g., the harsh rule of *Tinneius Rufus, the new Roman governor of Judea; and the disillusionment of the Jews who had hoped that Hadrian would restore the ruins of Jerusalem, when rumors that he was rebuilding the Temple fostered messianic expectations. Their hopes, speedily shattered, were replaced by profound resentment. Agitation against Rome had, it seems, existed in Judea many years before the outbreak of the revolt, and the sages may have tried to mitigate it, as may be inferred from the account of the assembly in the valley of Rimmon at which *Joshua b. Hananiah calmed the turbulent mood of the people (Gen. 64:10). Ultimately, however, the revolt was a continuation of the uprisings of the Jews of the Diaspora against Rome in 115–117 C.E., which included "the war of *Quietus" ending in 117. Even if Hadrian intended no particular enmity against the Jews, and behaved in Judea with the same degree of cultural universalism that he adopted in other places, nonetheless his innovations, bearing as they did a Hellenistic-Roman stamp, provoked the vehement opposition of the Jews both against non-Jewish culture and more especially against emperor-worship.

Dio Cassius gives a brief account of the course of the revolt. Accumulating arms by deceiving the Roman authorities, the Jews awaited a suitable opportunity, and when Hadrian left they openly rebelled. At first the Jews did not fight pitched battles. Instead they seized towns which they fortified with walls and subterranean passages. In an increasing number of clashes the rebels inflicted losses on the Romans. Hadrian was compelled to hurriedly send for one of his ablest generals, *Julius Severus, who specially came from Britain to Judea. Due to the large number of the rebels and their desperate fury, Severus refrained from waging open war, and preferred to surround their fortresses and hem them in to prevent food from reaching them. Gradually he succeeded in wearing down the Judean fighters, on whom he inflicted heavy blows without respite until he reduced them to a state of complete submission. Dio Cassius relates that the Romans demolished 50 fortresses, destroyed 985 villages, and killed 580,000 people in addition to those who died of hunger, disease, and fire. He adds that many Romans perished as well, and when Hadrian informed the Senate of his victory he did not begin with the usual formula: "I and my army are well." Dio Cassius states that the insurrection, which was prepared in detail, spread until "the whole of Judea was in revolt" (he referred apparently to most of Ereẓ Israel, including Galilee and Golan). He further states that the Jews "throughout the world" supported the rising as did non-Jews, too, and it was "as though the whole world raged." In its scope and vehemence, the revolt assumed the dimensions of a war which constituted a threat to the empire. As usual with Roman historians, Dio Cassius cites a supernatural omen, to show that the destruction of Judea was predestined, when he states that the "sanctified" tomb of Solomon had fallen down of itself.

Greek and Roman inscriptions mention the participation in the war of detachments of legions brought from all parts

Figure 2. The stamp of the Roman Tenth Legion, originally brought to Jerusalem for the suppression of the Bar Kokhba revolt. It reads "Leg[io] X Fr[etensis]," and is used here on a roof-tile, third century C.E. Jerusalem, Israel Museum.

of the empire, from Egypt and as far away as Britain—the Tenth "Fretensis," the Third "Cyrenaica," the Fourth "Scythica," the Second "Trajana," the Twenty-Second "Diotrajana" legions, and perhaps also the Sixth "Ferrata" legion. The Syrian navy also presumably took part in the war. Although exact figures cannot be computed since these were auxiliary troops and detachments of legions, the magnitude of the Roman army indicates the dimensions of the war. Isolated evidence—an inscription on a tomb, third-century talmudic references to the destruction of Galilee (BK 80a; TJ, Pe'ah 7:1, 20a), the remarks of Sulpicius Severus (fourth century C.E.) on the rebellion of the Jews in Syria and Palestine in the days of Hadrian—shows the revolt spread to the north of Ereẓ Israel, to Beth-Shean and Galilee. However, the main conflict took place in Judea, the Shephelah, the mountains, and finally in the Judean Desert.

The war apparently lasted about three and a half years, during which Jerusalem was taken by the rebels, as evident both from the inscription לחרות ירושלים on coins of the revolt and perhaps also from the Judean Desert documents. Appian, a contemporary of the revolt, Eusebius, in his *De Theophania,* and Jerome (fifth century C.E.), in his commentary on Jeremiah 31:15, all state that Jerusalem was destroyed in the days of Hadrian. It would therefore appear that Bar Kokhba captured the city and only after his military defeat did Hadrian regain control and destroy it. There may be an allusion to this in Midrashim which tell of Hadrian's entry into Jerusalem and his desecration of the Temple Mount (Tanḥ. B., Ex. 128; Ex. R. 5:5, Deut. R. 3:13). Some maintain that the design on coins of the revolt, depicting a four-columned building surmounted by a star, symbolizes the Temple, and if the undated coins bearing the inscription לחרות ירושלים or simply ירושלים are indeed to be assigned to the third year of the revolt, Jerusalem was still in Bar Kokhba's hands toward the end of the revolt in the third year of the war, that is, in Tishri 134 C.E. This is confirmed by one of the Judean Desert documents which is dated (שנ)ת` תלת לחרות ירו(ו)שלים ("the third year of the freedom of Jerusalem"). This scant evidence shows that during the Bar Kokhba revolt Jerusalem not only symbolized the yearning for freedom but also served the

Figure 3. A passage under the fortress of Herodium, south of Jerusalem, used during the Bar Kokhba revolt. Similar passages have been found in other subterranean hideouts used by the rebels in the Hebron hills. Photo Government Press Office, Tel Aviv.

political expression of the consolidation of the revolt and of its sway in Judea. There is, however, no evidence that the Temple was rebuilt at that time, nor is there any proof that Bar Kokhba was about to rebuild the Temple. However, an altar may have been erected for sacred worship.

Bar Kokhba made a final stand at *Bethar in the Judean Hills, but from the finds in the Judean Desert it would appear that after the fall of the last stronghold the flame of revolt continued to flicker in the desert and in the vicinity of the Dead Sea. Nevertheless, in talmudic and midrashic sources Bethar represents the fortress in which the rebels found refuge, and its fall, along with the defeat of Bar Kokhba who met his death there, symbolizes the end of the revolt. The place was apparently chosen as the rebels' main stronghold because of its strategic situation on the edge of a mountain overlooking the Valley of Sorek and dominating the important Jerusalem-Bet Guvrin road, and possibly also because of its fertile soil. Since it was not adequately fortified, Jerusalem could not serve as a stronghold. At that time Bethar was considered a large city (*kerakh;* TJ, Ta'an 4:8, 69a; Lam. R. 2:2 no. 4; cf. Mid. Hag. to Deut. 28:52), perhaps because numerous inhabitants from the entire neighborhood had gathered there, as attested by Jerome (in his commentary on Zech. 8:19) who mentions that many thousands of Jews found refuge in it—*Bether ad quam multa milia confugerant Judaeorum* (and cf. the midrashic references to 400 synagogues in Bethar).

The actual siege of Bethar began apparently after the recapture of Jerusalem. Whether Bar Kokhba's men had intended it from the outset to be their principal fortress or were driven there by the force of circumstances cannot be known. Even during the siege those in Bethar maintained contact with camps of fighters in the Judean Desert. One of the documents states: "Near the well of Ben Koseva, Nasi of Israel, in the camp," referring probably to the camp of Bethar, which is not mentioned, however, in the Dead Sea documents. Severus' strategy was to intensify the siege on the fortress, and a siege wall *(circumvallatio)* was built for this purpose. It was attacked by the besieged in desperate sallies, while the blockade grew tighter. A clear reminder of the Roman armies' presence in Bethar itself was preserved in a Latin inscription which was engraved on a rock near the well of Bethar and mentions detachments of the Fifth "Macedonica" and the Eleventh "Claudia" legions. The inscription is now illegible.

Eusebius states that Bethar was besieged in the 18th year of Hadrian's reign, that is, in 134 C.E., about two years after the outbreak of the revolt, and that its fall was caused by hunger and thirst. According to the talmudic account (TJ, Ta'an 4:8, 68d; Lam. R. 2:2, no. 4), Hadrian unsuccessfully laid siege to Bethar for three and a half years, until a Samaritan pretended that *Eleazar of Modi'in (ha-Moda'i) had conspired with him to surrender the city to the Romans. Incensed at this, Bar Kokhba killed Eleazar. "Immediately Bethar was captured and Ben Koziva met his death." Presumably great importance was attached in besieged Bethar to sages such as Eleazar of Modi'in, one of the leading rabbis of his generation, but whether he is identical with the Eleazar whose name appears on coins of the revolt cannot be determined. (In one of his letters, Bar Kokhba mentions a רבנו בטניה בר מיסה, whom he regarded as a great man.) These circumstances suggest that eventually a dispute broke out between the sages and the commander in chief, and spread among the besieged. In any event these reports, like the statement of Eusebius, indicate that the capture of Bethar was difficult and was achieved under unusual circumstances.

The death of Bar Kokhba is enveloped in a legendary halo. The accounts of the massacre perpetrated in Bethar attest to the ferocity of the struggle (Git. 56a–b; Song. R. 2:17; cf. ARN 138, 115: "Not a soul escaped"). The sages state that on Av 15th the burial of the slain was permitted (Ta'an. 31a). Tradition has it that Bethar was taken on the Ninth of Av (*ibid.*, 29a), and Jerome *(loc. cit.)* also says that it occurred in August: *in hoc mense* (scil. *Augusto*). On the basis of the latest date—the fourth year of the liberation of Israel—mentioned in one of the documents, Bar Kokhba's rule lasted more than three years. In Jewish tradition the fall of Bethar was a disaster equal to the destruction of the First and Second Temples.

The Jewish population of Judea was largely exterminated in the period of repression which followed the fall of

Figure 4. Stones rounded for use as weapons during the Bar Kokhba revolt. They were found in the stronghold of Herodium. Photo Government Press Office, Tel Aviv.

Bethar. The subjugation was associated with massacres and religious persecution, the sale of Jews into slavery, and uprooting of the people from the soil. The Jewish center of gravity now moved northward, chiefly to Galilee. Thus ended the final and perhaps greatest war of liberation of the Jews in ancient times. The independence of Judea had come to an end.

The Judean Desert Documents. The finds, dating from the days of Bar Kokhba and brought to light in the Judean Desert in 1952–61, contain additional facts of great importance for an understanding of the social and economic conditions prevailing during the Bar Kokhba war in 132–135 C.E. The first documents were found in 1952 in Wadi Muraba'at about 11 mi. (18 km.) southwest of *Qumran. Among them are commercial contracts, letters of divorce, two letters from Bar Kokhba, and one from the administrators of the community addressed to Jeshua b. Galgolah. An archaeological expedition undertaken in the Judean Desert south of En-Gedi in 1960–61 uncovered, alongside material finds such as skeletons, linen, remnants of clothes, metal and glass vessels, and remains of food, many documents of the time of the Bar Kokhba war, chiefly in one of the caves in Naḥal Ḥever, now named "The Cave of the Letters." The letters and economic documents in Hebrew, Aramaic, and Greek uncovered in the cave testify to the economic position in southern Judea on the eve of the revolt and at the height of the war (on the documents, their language, literary form, and historical significance see *Dead Sea Scrolls).

The letters, written apparently in Bar Kokhba's name but not personally by him, deal with everday matters. Some of them are not entirely clear. The dates mentioned in them range from the second to the fourth year of the liberation of Israel (132–134 C.E.). The letters open with an almost identical formula:

משמעון בן כוסבה לישע בן גלגולה לאנשי הכרך שלו. משמעון לישוע בן גלגולה שלום; שמעון בר כוסבה הנסי על ישראל ליהונתן ולמסבלה סלם; משמעון בר כוסבא לאנשי עינגדי למסבלא (ו)ליהו(נ)תן ב(ר) בעין שלום; שמעון ליהודה בר מנשה לקרית ערביה.

"From Simeon ben Kosevah to Jeshua ben Galgolah and the men of his fortress!"; "From Simeon to Jeshua ben Galgolah, peace!"; "Simeon bar Kosevah the *nasi* ["prince"] of Israel to Jonathan and Masbela, peace!"; "From Simeon bar Koseva to the men of En-Gedi to Masbela (and) to Jonathan B(ar) Ba'ayan peace!" "Simeon to Judah bar Manasseh to Kiryat Araviyah." In a letter to Jeshua b. Galgolah, one of his army commanders, Bar Kokhba refers to the **גלילאים** *(gll'ym),* who are to be protected and, sternly reminding his men of this, threatens them with irons: "I call Heaven to witness against me . . . that I shall put your feet in irons." The actual occasion and the identity of the **גלילאים** are not clear from the letter. In another

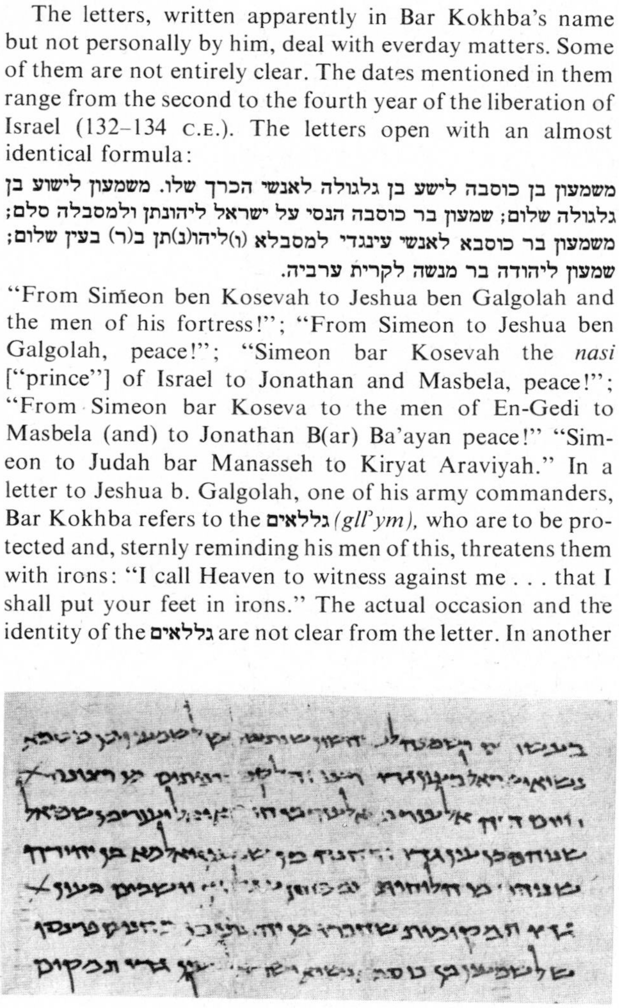

Figure 5. A land-lease found in the Cave of the Letters at Naḥal Ḥever in the Judean Desert. Written in Hebrew on papyrus, it deals with lands leased from the Bar Kokhba administration. Jerusalem, Israel Museum, Shrine of the Book.

Figure 6a. Domestic objects found in the Cave of Letters, from 135 C.E. They include bronze jugs, door keys and a basket woven from palm leaves. Jerusalem, Israel Museum, Shrine of the Book. Photo David Harris, Jerusalem.

letter to Jeshua, Bar Kokhba orders him to offer hospitality on the Sabbath to men who were bringing wheat to the camp and to provide them with accommodation until "after the Sabbath."

In other letters found in Naḥal Ḥever, the *nasi* writes to Masbelah b. Simeon and Jonathan b. Bayahu, who were apparently in command of the En-Gedi front, about the wheat supply, the grain harvest, the confiscation of property, the supervision of the men, and the mobilization of the men of *Tekoa on the border of the Judean Desert. His language is harsh, and he frequently threatens them with punishment if they fail to carry out his orders ("and if you will not do this, you will be punished"). In a Hebrew letter to Jonathan and Masbelah of En-Gedi, Bar Kokhba orders them to attend to the loading of a boat anchored in the harbor there. To the commanders in the rear and the population of the inhabited area of the desert, with whom he was incensed for having failed to supply food as commanded by the *nasi,* and who had neglected their duty, Bar Kokhba uses stern language: "You are living well, eating and drinking off the property of the house of Israel, and care nothing about your brethren."

In an Aramaic letter to Judah b. Manasseh of Kiryat Araviyah, Bar Kokhba orders Judah to supply him with the *Four Species for Tabernacles and apparently reminds him about separating the tithe: **ותקן יתהן** ("and give the dues from them"). Such references, made incidentally or hinted at in the letters, may indicate that Bar Kokhba's men, even under danger, strictly and quite naturally kept the commandments of Judaism, such as the sanctity of the Sabbath, the laws of the priestly and levitical dues, and the fullest observance of festivals. The letters and other documents uncovered in the Judean Desert contain nothing specific about the attitude of the sages toward the rule of Bar Kokhba nor is there any mention in them of Bethar and of the war there. Nevertheless it is possible to comprehend from them explicitly and at first hand about Bar Kokhba's aggressive personality and his status, the economic straits in which the fighters of Judea found themselves, and the geographic extent of the revolt. The *nasi* was concerned about supply problems, food for his camp, and matters pertaining to real estate. The economic documents found in Wadi Muraba'at show that leases were made in the name and with the sanction of Bar Kokhba: "On the instructions of Simeon b. Koseva." Apparently the land belonged nominally to the *nasi,* it being clearly stated in a lease, "You have leased the ground from Simeon, the Nasi of Israel." In his name the lessors laid down the quota of grain that was to be given to them. As was to be expected in a time of war, the authorities insisted on the cultivation of the fields and confiscated the lands of those who neglected to till them. They "were dispossessed of the land and lost everything." In effect, Bar Kokhba regarded himself as holding the authority of the Roman emperor and transferred the lands of liberated Judea to his own possession. His orders concerning leases, sales, and confiscations were grounded on a juridical succession to the Roman rule, by virtue of which he was empowered to exercise control over the lands of Judea and confiscate property for the public good. Contracts found in Naḥal Ḥever indicate that Bar Kokhba wished to prevent the concentration of the lands of En-Gedi in the hands of a few owners in order to increase the supply of food in a time of stress.

From the names of the settlements mentioned in these documents, Bar Kokhba's men apparently controlled extensive areas, in the frontier regions of the Judean mountains, in the neighborhood of Bet Guvrin (Ir-Nahash), and in the Judean Desert, and maintained contact, it seems, with regions east and south of the Dead Sea, such as Ma'aleh ha-Luḥit in the district of Eglatin in Moab and *Zoar in the Aravah. Herodium, the town of Herod about 6 mi. (10 km.) southeast of Jerusalem and mentioned in the documents, became an economic center, in which the *nasi's* representatives were stationed; En-Gedi was an important supply harbor for the rebels. The settlements of Tekoa and Kiryat Araviyah in the vicinity of Bethlehem are mentioned in the documents. According to the reconstruction of ב . . . שלים as Jerusalem, proposed by J. T. Milik who made a study of the Wadi Muraba'at documents, that city is referred to in two of them, one dating from the second, and the other from the fourth year "of the liberation of Israel" (Elul, 133 and Tishri, 134, respectively). After the defeat, the fugitives from the war in Judea gathered in the Judean Desert, which then became the rebel center. The remains of Roman military camps found above the caves in Naḥal Ḥever show that the legions besieged the remnants of the fighters who, together with their families, had taken refuge in these hiding places. Surrounded by the Romans, there they met their death.

Figure 6b. Objects for women's use found in the Cave of Letters. They include a skein and balls of wool, a copper hand-mirror in a wooden frame, and buttons and beads. Jerusalem, Israel Museum, Shrine of the Book. Photo David Harris, Jerusalem.

Bibliography: S. Abramsky, *Bar Kokhva, Nesi Yisrael* (1961), contains bibliography; S. Yeivin, *Milḥemet Bar Kokhva* (1952^{2}); Allon, Toledot, 1 (1958^{3}), 290–354; 2 (1961^{2}), 1–83; BIES, 25 (1960/61), 5–108; Schuerer, Hist. 278, 299–304; Y. Yadin, *The Finds from the Bar Kokhba Period in the Cave of Letters* (1963); Y. Aharoni and B. Rothenburg, *Be-Ikkevot Melakhim u-Moredim* (1964^{3}); P. Benoit et al., *Les grottes de Muraba'at* (1961).

[Sh.Ab.]

BARLAD (Birlad), town in Moldavia, E. Rumania. The Jewish community there is first attested in 1738 when the prince of Moldavia, Gregor Ghica, appointed Marco (Mordecai) as leader *(starosty)* of the Jews of Barlad "according to ancient custom." "A row of Jewish stores" is mentioned in 1767 and a "Jewish street" in 1819; 53 Jewish households were recorded in 1803. In 1838 the Jews were accused of desecrating Christian holy objects, and 23 notables of the community, including three women, were imprisoned. They were released only after payment of a heavy fine. In December 1867, there was an outbreak of violence when the Jews were accused of murdering an anti-Semitic priest. The community numbered 2,000 in 1859; 5,883 (24% of the total) in 1899, about one-third of the merchants and artisans in the city being Jews; and 3,727 in 1930 (14% of the total), mainly occupied in commerce (many as clerks) and as artisans. There were then in Barlad a Jewish kindergarten and two Jewish schools, for boys and for girls.

[El.F.]

Holocaust Period and After. In 1941 there were 3,063 Jews living in Barlad. *Antonescu's rise to power in September 1940 marked the beginning of their economic repression, including the confiscation of property. All the Jewish men, including professionals, were sent on forced labor; but the latter were released when their Rumanian colleagues rallied to their side and threatened to join them on forced labor. On the outbreak of war against the Soviet Union in June 1941 all the Jews from the villages and towns in the district were expelled and sent to Barlad. Sources of livelihood were scarce, and the community had to take care of the unemployed; 200 families were subsidized in 1940 and by 1943 their number had grown to 600. The community also opened its own secondary school for the Jewish children who had been dismissed from the public secondary schools. Four men who had been deported to *Transnistria eventually returned to Barlad.

In 1969, 100 Jewish families lived in Barlad where there was one synagogue. [T.L.]

Bibliography: M. Carp, *Cartea Neagră,* 1 (1946), 115, 158; Filderman, in: *Sliha,* 1 no. 4 (1956).

BAR-LE-DUC, capital of the Meuse department, northeastern France; former capital of the Duchy of Bar. The 12th-century Jewish community in Bar-le-Duc was reputedly expelled by the count of Bar, but Jews are again found there from 1220. They were expelled in 1309 but were allowed to return to the county in 1321, and settled in 30 localities. In 1322 the Jews were again expelled, but had returned by 1328 to be banished again in 1477. They resided in Bar-le-Duc in the Rue des Juifs, the present Rue de la Couronne. After the French Revolution Jews again settled in Bar-le-Duc. From 1808 the community was affiliated to the Consistory of Nancy and administered by the rabbinate of Verdun. It numbered 170 in 1892. During World War II 18 Jews living in Bar-le-Duc were deported or shot. In 1968, 40 Jews lived there.

Bibliography: Weill, in: REJ, 125 (1966), 287ff.

[G.We.]

BAR-LEV (originally **Brotzlewsky**), **HAIM** (1924–), Israel military commander; eighth chief of staff of the Israel army. Born in Vienna, Austria, he came from Yugoslavia to Palestine in 1939, and in 1942 was graduated from the Mikveh Israel agricultural school. Bar-Lev belongs to the *Palmaḥ tradition in the Israel Army. In 1946, during the struggle against the British regime, he was in charge of blowing up Allenby Bridge near Jericho. During the War of Independence in 1948–49 he served successively as commander of the Eighth Battalion in the Negev Brigade, commander of a

General Haim Bar-Lev, eighth chief of staff of the Israel Defense Forces. Tel Aviv, Government Press Office.

mechanized battalion, and brigade operations officer. In 1956, after attending the Senior Officers' School in England, he became director of training at G.H.Q. During the Sinai Campaign of 1956 he commanded an armored brigade. From 1957 to 1961 he was commanding officer of the Armored Corps. He then studied administration and economics at Columbia University, and in 1964 was appointed head of General Staff Branch at G.H.Q. In May 1966 he went to Paris to continue his studies, but was recalled a year later and appointed deputy chief of staff on the eve of the Six-Day War. In 1968–71 he was chief of staff of the Israel Defense Forces. In 1972 he was appointed minister of commerce and industry. [J.WA.]

BARLEY (Heb. שְׂעוֹרָה; *se'orah*), one of the *seven species with which Ereẓ Israel was blessed (Deut. 8:8). In biblical times barley bread was a staple food and was extensively cultivated, especially as it grows even in poor soil and in areas with a low rainfall. The fact that barley was so widely sown accounts for the biblical ruling that the value of a field is to be estimated on the basis of the amount of barley required to sow it (Lev. 27:16). In the days of the Judges the farmer in Ereẓ Israel sustained himself mainly on barley, a cake of barley bread symbolizing the agricultural Israelites (in contrast to the nomadic Midianites) in the dream of the Midianite soldier (Judg. 7:13). It formed part of the diet of David's army (II Sam. 17:28) as also of the hewers of the timber in Lebanon for the Temple of Solomon (II Chron. 2:9).

In mishnaic times wheat largely replaced barley as human food, and barley was used mainly as animal fodder (it is referred to in this connection only once in the Bible (I Kings 5:8)) and the rabbis, therefore, in a homiletical view, give as the reason for the offering of barley meal in the ordeal of a woman suspected of adultery (Lev. 5:15) "that she had behaved like an animal" (Num. 5:15; cf. Sot. 9a). It became principally the poor man's food; hence the proverb, "Why do you eat barley bread?—Because I have no wheaten bread" (Sif. Num. 49). In the Bible the price of barley flour is given as half that of fine wheaten flour (II Kings 7:1), which was also the ratio of their prices in mishnaic times (Tosef., BM 9:10), the nutritive value of the former being regarded as half that of the latter (Pe'ah 8:5). The Karaite Anan held that for fulfilling the commandment on Passover unleavened bread made of barley was to be used, this being in his view, "the bread of affliction" and poverty. Of the cereals, barley ripens first (Ex. 9:31) and "the barley harvest season" is the designation of the spring (Ruth 1:22). On the second day of Passover, the *omer* ("sheaf"), the first fruit of the harvest, was reaped (Lev. 23:9–15), and although there is no specific reference to its being barley, the rabbinic tradition to that effect is undoubtedly correct (Men. 84b) as the barley harvest begins at Passover time. One kind of beer was brewed from barley (BB 96b), another from a mixture of barley, figs, and blackberries (Pes. 107a), and yet another, called "Egyptian *zythos*" from a third part of barley, a third part of safflower, and a third part of salt (*ibid.*, 42b). The brewing of beer has a long tradition in Egypt; it is depicted in ancient Egyptian drawings. *Se'orah*, the Hebrew name for barley, derives from the long hairs (Heb. *se'ar*, "hair") of its ears, and the cereal is designated by cognate words in almost all Semitic languages. The Greeks regarded barley as the very earliest crop grown in the world. In Ereẓ Israel there are at present cultivated species of two- and six-rowed barley (*Five Species). These species have been found in Egyptian tombs. A wild barley *(Hordeum spontaneum)* which grows in Ereẓ Israel is thought to be the origin of two-rowed barley. In excavations at Gezer four-rowed barley has been uncovered, and in the caves of En-Gedi and of the Judean Desert, two- and four-rowed barley of the mishnaic and talmudic periods have been found.

Bibliography: Loew, Flora, 1 (1926), 707–23; J. Feliks, *Olam ha-Ẓome'aḥ ha-Mikra'i* (1957), 146–8, 318; idem, *Ha-Ḥakla'ut be-Ereẓ-Yisrael . . .* , (1963), 362 (index); idem, *Kilei Zera'im . . .* (1967), 23–27.

[J.F.]

Coin of Agrippa I, king of Judea 41–44 C.E., depicting three ears of barley. Haifa, Dagon Museum.

BARLIN, FREDERICK WILLIAM (fl. early 19th century), English portrait painter. Barlin, who worked in London, was the son of Berliner, the *ḥazzan* of the Chatham synagogue. Barlin exhibited at the Royal Academy in 1802

Haham Raphael Meldola, portrait by the painter Frederick W. Barlin. London, Spanish and Portuguese Congregation.

and 1807. Two of his portraits are of particular significance: that of Solomon *Herschel, chief rabbi of the Ashkenazi Jews in England, and that of the Sephardi haham Raphael *Meldola. The latter was painted wearing a three-cornered hat in a courtly, elegant, and typically English manner. This portrait was later engraved and published by Joshua Lopez.

Bibliography: Roth, Art, 533; A. Rubens, *Anglo-Jewish Portraits* (1935), 53–55, 80.

[Ed.]

BAR MITZVAH, BAT MITZVAH (Heb. masc. בַּר מִצְוָה fem. בַּת מִצְוָה lit. "son/daughter of the commandment," i.e., a person under obligation, responsible), term denoting both the attainment of religious and legal maturity as well as the occasion at which this status is formally assumed for boys at the age of 13 plus one day, for girls at 12 plus one day (Maim. Yad, Ishut, 2:9–10). Upon reaching this age a Jew is obliged to fulfill all the *commandments (Avot 5:1; cf. Yoma 82a). Although the term occurs in the Talmud for one who is subject to the law (BM 96a), its usage to denote the occasion of assuming religious and legal obligations does not appear before the 15th century (*Sefer Ẓiyyoni* of R. Menahem Ẓiyyoni to Gen. 1:5). A special celebration for a girl, the bat mitzvah, is not found mentioned before *Ben Ish Ḥai,* the legal code by Joseph Ḥayyim b. Elijah (19th cent.).

While the occasion of becoming bar/bat mitzvah was thus formalized only in later times, it is obvious from various sources that the status of obligation for boys of 13 was assumed in early times. According to Eleazar b. Simeon (second century C.E.), a father was responsible for the deeds of his son until the age of 13. For example the vows of a boy 13 and a day old are considered valid vows (Nid. 5:6). From then on a person can perform acts having legal implications, such as being a member of a *bet din,* being reckoned as part of a *minyan,* and buying and selling property. Yet there are notable exceptions, e.g., the testimony of a 13-year-old is not valid regarding real estate because he is "not knowledgeable about buying and selling" (Maim. Yad, Edut, 9:8).

Jewish law fixed 13 as the age of responsibility considering this the time of physical maturity for boys (and 12 for girls; Kid. 16b). At this age young people are thought to be able to control their desires (ARN² 16, 62–63). Rashi claims that bar mitzvah as a status of obligation was "in the category of biblical laws, as it was given to Moses at Sinai" (comment. to Avot 5:1). Midrashic literature gives many references for 13 as the turning point in the life of a young person, e.g., Abraham rejected the idols of his father at this age (PdRE 26), and at 13 Jacob and Esau went their separate ways, the former to study Torah, the latter to idol-worship (Gen. R. 63:10). Until 13 a son receives the merit of his father and is also liable to suffer for his parent's sin; after that each one bears his own sin (Yal. Ruth 600). This is also the time of transition from elementary school to the *bet ha-midrash (ibid.).* A tradition recorded in talmudic literature (Sof. 18:7, ed. M. Higger 1937) alludes to the fact that in Jerusalem during the period of the Second Temple, it was customary for the sages to bless a child who had succeeded in completing his first fast day at 12 or 13.

Being Called to the Torah. The calling up to the reading of the Torah is a symbol of a boy's attaining maturity. He is called up on the first occasion that the Torah is read following his 13th birthday according to the Jewish calendar. This is the first public demonstration of his new role as a full member of the community and, in modern times, it is to this occasion that the term bar mitzvah usually refers. When the boy's father is called to the Torah, he recites the benediction, "Blessed is He who has now freed me from the responsibility of this one" (Gen. R. *loc. cit.*). Among observant Jews in Eastern Europe the boy was usually called up to the Torah on the Monday or the Thursday following his birthday. In Western Europe, the occasion took on a more ceremonial importance, and it was customary for the bar mitzvah boy to be called up to the Torah to read the *maftir* portions and the *haftarah* on the first Sabbath after his birthday. For this task he had previously been prepared. According to an old Ashkenazi custom in Lithuania, Ereẓ Israel, etc., the boy recited the *maftir* on the Sabbath just before becoming fully 13, and immediately upon coming of age he received an ordinary *aliyah.* In the 17th and 18th centuries the custom was

Figure 1. A silver book cover given to a boy on his bar mitzvah by his father, Central Europe, 18th century. The *menorah* below the inscription is flanked by figures of Moses and Aaron. The back cover depicts Jacob's dream and the sacrifice of Isaac. Jerusalem, Sir Isaac and Lady Wolfson Museum in Hechal Shlomo. Photo David Harris, Jerusalem.

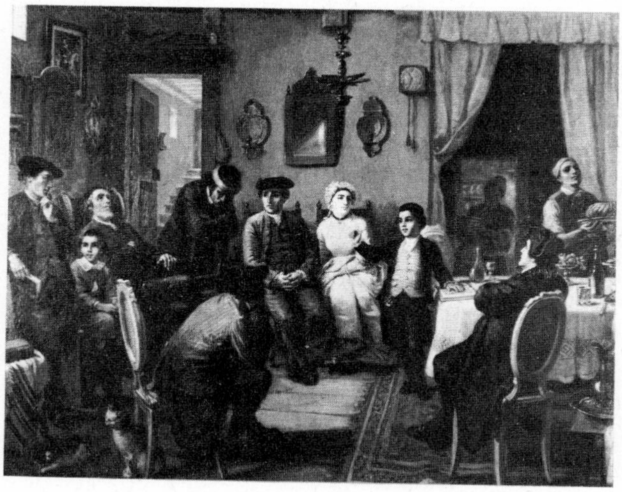

Figure 2. "The Bar Mitzvah Speech" by Moritz Oppenheim. The scene is typical of a 19th-century German Jewish household. New York, Oscar Gruss Collection.

recorded in Worms, Germany, that those boys who were able and had pleasing voices conducted parts or all of the service. In some communities it was and still is customary for the young man to read the whole portion of the week. On a Sabbath when a bar mitzvah is celebrated, the morning service assumes a more festive atmosphere. Members of the boy's family are also called up to the reading of the Torah, and a special sermon is frequently delivered by the rabbi, stressing the boy's new responsibilities and privileges. In many modern synagogues, the rabbi ends his sermon by invoking the *Priestly Blessing or other blessing, and the bar mitzvah boy is given a gift from the congregation. After the service, a festive *Kiddush* is often held, with a banquet on the same or the following day. Some authorities ruled that parents must arrange a banquet when their son became bar mitzvah just as they do on the day of his wedding (see Magen Avraham on Sh. Ar., O. Ḥ. 225:2). Among the Jews of Morocco a special *piyyut* is recited when a bar mitzvah boy is called up to the Torah and, in most synagogues, a special **Mi she-Berakh* blessing is made at the end of the reading for the boy and his family.

Putting on Tefillin. The major ritual innovation obligatory on a boy reaching bar mitzvah is that henceforth he is required to put on *tefillin* for the morning prayer. He is usually coached in the forms of the rite some time before the bar mitzvah. The Sephardim and some of the Ḥasidim, interpreting the Kabbalah very exactly, insist that *tefillin* cannot be worn one day before bar mitzvah. Only when the boy has become fully 13 and one day does he keep this commandment. For the Sephardim the first occasion of putting on the *tefillin* was part of the celebration of the bar mitzvah itself. At that time a scholar or elder was honored with aiding the young man in donning the *tefillin*. Ḥasidim of the *Ḥabad* school taught that boys began putting on *tefillin* two months prior to the actual bar mitzvah, the first month without pronouncing the blessing, and the second month saying it.

The Bar Mitzvah Derashah. Solomon Luria (16th century) states that the bar mitzvah celebration was customary among Ashkenazim and that the boy was tutored to deliver a *derashah* ("talmudic discourse") during the banquet (*Yam shel Shelomo* BK 7:37). It usually dealt with some aspect of the rite; Sephardim call it the *"tefillin derashah."* The discourse frequently serves as an occasion for the boy to thank his parents for their love and care, and the guests for their participation in his celebration. The custom is still observed today, with sons of traditional families giving a talmudic discourse, and others a more general talk. In Conservative, Reform, and some Orthodox synagogues a prayer before the ark is sometimes said by the bar mitzvah boy in place of the *derashah*.

Most congregational Hebrew schools have special classes for the preparation of bar/bat mitzvah students. In some congregations (notably the United Synagogue of Great Britain) the boy is not allowed to celebrate his bar mitzvah until after he passes an examination in Hebrew and the fundamentals of the Jewish religion.

Since 1967, some boys from Israel and abroad celebrate their bar mitzvah at the Western Wall. Some Jews from outside Israel make a special pilgrimage to celebrate their son's bar mitzvah there.

Confirmation. Reform congregations have instituted what is known as a Confirmation ceremony. This was originally in 19th century German Reform a substitution for bar mitzvah. The ceremony was held at a later age—16 or 17—on the grounds that before that age a young person cannot really understand the implications of the rituals. In modern times, especially in the U.S., confirmation has been adopted as a ceremony additional to bar mitzvah which is celebrated in a more traditional manner. The main intention of confirmation was to prolong the period of a child's Jewish education, and as such it is usually a ceremony with a "class" of young people being confirmed at the same time. The ceremony is usually held on or about Shavuot. The confirmands recite various sections from Scriptures and publicly declare their devotion to Judaism. The boys and girls frequently receive a special certificate, testifying their acceptance into the Jewish community.

Bat Mitzvah. Bat mitzvah was officially introduced in France and Italy and widely adopted in other countries. Forms of the ceremony differ widely, ranging from having the girl recite the *haftarah* and conduct certain specific prayers in the synagogue service, to confining the entire celebration to the home or school. In many congregations a collective bat mitzvah ceremony similar to the confirmation ceremony is held for girls. In most Israel synagogues the bat mitzvah is celebrated by calling the girl's father and brothers to the Torah, a special sermon is preached, and the girl is presented with a gift. In recent times, bat mitzvah has become customary among Jewish circles, often not as a religious ceremony but more as a birthday celebration and family occasion.

Bibliography: L. Loew, *Lebensalter* (1875), 210–22, 410ff.; I. Rivkind, *Le-Ot u-le-Zikkaron. Toledot Bar Mitzvah* (1942), incl.

Figure 3. A bar mitzvah at Masada, the ancient fortress in the Judean desert, 1968. Tel Aviv, Government Press Office.

bibl.; Assaf, Mekorot, 4 (1943), 108, 114, 127; Sadan (Stock), in: *Dat u-Medinah* (1949), 59ff.; ET, 4 (1952), 165–8; M. Z. Levinsohn-Lavi, in: *Sefer ha-Yovel shel Hadoar* (1952), 42–46; C. Roth, in: A. I. Katsh (ed.), *Bar Mitzvah* (1955), 15–22; J. Nacht, in: *Yeda-Am*, 17–18 (1955), 106–11; Joseph Manspach, *Minhag Bar Mizvah*, ed. by A. M. Habermann (1958); B. Yashar, *Le-Vat Yisrael be-Hagiyah le-Mitzvot* (1963); S. B. Freehot, *Current Reform Responsa* (1969), index.

[Z.K./Ed.]

BARNACLE GOOSE MYTHS. The barnacle goose is a migratory bird, whose winter habitat is the Arctic region, when it is seldom seen outside the Arctic circle. In summer, however, large flocks are found on the western shores of the British Isles and other parts of the temperate zone. According to a popular medieval fable, the barnacle goose was produced out of the fruit of a tree, or grew upon the tree attached by its bill (hence called the tree goose), or was produced out of a shell. This fable—the origin of which is obscure—was taken quite literally by both Jews and non-Jews, and in consequence it was a matter of doubt whether it was to be regarded as bird, fish, or a completely distinct species. *Isaac b. Moses of Vienna (*Or Zaru'a*) quotes R. Tam—who was the first to deal with the subject—as ruling that it may be eaten after ritual slaughtering like poultry. This decision was in opposition to the views of contemporary famous scholars who permitted it to be eaten in the same way as fruit. Samuel he-Ḥasid and his son *Judah he-Ḥasid of Regensburg agreed with R. Tam. R. *Isaac b. Joseph of Corbeil forbade it (*Sefer Mitzvot Katan* no. 210), as he regarded it as a species of shellfish. The Zohar (3:156) states that R. Abba saw a tree from whose branches grew geese. The Shulḥan Arukh (YD 84:15) rules that birds that grow on trees are forbidden since they are regarded as creeping things. The fable was disputed, however, by various scholars but as late as 1862 R. Bernard Issachar Dov *Illowy in New Orleans quoted a conflict of authorities whether it might be eaten, and vigorously denounced those who would permit it. He too referred to the belief of many early naturalists that it grows on trees.

Bibliography: J. G. T. Graesse, *Beitraege zur Literatur und Sage des Mittelalters* (1850), 80; Lewysohn, Zool, 362f., no. 515; Ginzberg, Legends, 1 (1909), 32; 5 (1925), 50f.; Zimmels, in: *Minḥat Bikkurim . . . Arje Schwarz* (1926), 1–9.

[H.Fr.]

BARNATO, BARNEY (Barnett Isaacs; 1852–1897), South African financier and mining magnate. Born in London, Barnato was educated at the Jews' Free School and went to Kimberley, South Africa, in 1873, during the diamond rush. He joined his brother Henry and they began buying diamonds as well as claims which were becoming unworkable as separate units. Within a short time the mines

Barney Barnato, South African mining magnate. Johannesburg, Africana Museum.

were bringing in an income of $9,000 a week. In 1881 the Barnato brothers formed the Barnato Diamond Mining Company, with a capital of over $500,000. It soon rivaled the De Beers Mining Company of Cecil J. Rhodes, who was aiming at control of the diamond fields. The struggle between Rhodes and Barnato ended in 1888 with the amalgamation of the two companies into the De Beers Consolidated Mining Company, in which Barnato became a life governor. In the same year he was elected to the legislative assembly of Cape Colony. With the discovery of the Witwatersrand gold fields, Barnato acquired large holdings in Johannesburg, where the Barnato group eventually became one of the big mining units. In 1895, his optimism and business acumen saved the Rand from a serious slump. He denounced the Jameson Raid of that year which was aimed at overthrowing the government of Paul Kruger, but interceded with Kruger to reduce the offenders' sentences. Barnato was a colorful figure who loved to act in Shakespeare and sport fancy waistcoats. His wealth, financial shrewdness, and mode of living made him almost legendary. His vast interests, however, imposed a considerable strain on him and on a voyage to England in 1897, apparently emotionally disturbed, he jumped overboard and was drowned.

Bibliography: H. Raymond, *B. I. Barnato* (1897); L. Herrman, *History of the Jews in South Africa* (1935), 228ff.; R. Lewinsohn, *Barney Barnato* (1937); S. Jackson, *The Great Barnato* (1970).

[L.S.]

BARNAY, LUDWIG (1842–1924), German actor. Barnay achieved his first success at the age of 20 in Budapest, where his father was secretary of the Hebrew congregation. From 1875 to 1880, he was the leading actor-manager of Hamburg, worked in Berlin from 1884 to 1890, and toured the U.S. in 1883 and 1888. He distinguished himself in heroic roles in Schiller and Shakespeare, winning particular acclaim as William Tell and Mark Antony. Banished for a time from the German stage after a quarrel in 1894, when he was director of the Berliner Theater, he was reinstated ten years later as director of the Berlin Schauspielhaus. The union of professional actors, which he founded in 1871,

Ludwig Barnay, German actor. An engraving, after a photograph. Jerusalem, Schwadron Collection, J.N.U.L.

remained an influential body until it was dissolved by the Nazis in 1933. Barnay published his memoirs, *Erinnerungen*, in 1903.

[Ed.]

BARNERT, NATHAN (1838–1927), U.S. businessman, public figure, and philanthropist. Barnert was born in Santomischel near Posen, Prussia, and was taken to the U.S. in 1849. After adventuring in California during the

Statue of Nathan Barnert at City Hall, Paterson, N.J.

gold rush, Barnert moved to Paterson, New Jersey, at 20, and opened a clothing establishment. During the Civil War, he filled large contracts for Union Army uniforms, using his profits for business expansion and acquisition of real estate holdings. Barnert retired from mercantile life at the age of 40 to devote all his attention to his profitable real estate interests. He used his capital to create a new industry in Paterson, the furnishing of supplies for paper mills. He also had great success in building large, modern textile mills as speculative projects. A Democrat in a normally Republican city, Barnert was elected to the Paterson Board of Aldermen in 1876 and 1879. He was elected mayor of Paterson in 1883 and 1889, and pursued a reform administration. An observant Jew, Barnert never appeared at City Hall on the Sabbath or festivals. He was a devoted worshiper at Congregation B'nai Jeshurun, to which, in 1889, he donated the land and assumed construction costs for a new synagogue building, whose dedication was attended by President William McKinley. Barnert built a Hebrew school (1904), and a nonsectarian hospital and nurses' home. Among his other benefactions were a synagogue building for the Jewish community of Santomischel, and an orphan asylum in Jerusalem. A statue of Nathan Barnert was dedicated in Paterson's City Hall Square in 1925.

Bibliography: M. Baum, *Biography of Nathan Barnert* (1914).

[D.H.P.]

BARNETT, LIONEL DAVID (1871–1960), British orientalist. Barnett, who was born in Liverpool, was keeper of the department of oriental printed books and manuscripts at the British Museum from 1908 to 1936. He was an authority on Indian literature, and lectured in Indian history at the London University School of Oriental and African Studies until 1946. He wrote *Antiquities of India* (1913) and *Hindu Gods and Heroes* (1922), and his translations included *A History of Greek Drama* (1900) and, from the Sanskrit, *Brahma-Knowledge* (1907). Barnett was an elder of the Spanish and Portuguese congregation in London, and in 1931 published *El libro de los acuerdos*, an English translation from the earliest records of the congregation, for the years 1663 to 1681. He also edited the Bevis Marks records of the contributions made to history by the congregation (2 vols., 1940–49).

Lionel Barnett's son, Richard David Barnett (1909–), like his father, made his career at the British Museum. Born in London, he began in 1932 as assistant keeper in the department of Egyptian and Assyrian antiquities and in 1955 was appointed head of the newly established department of Western Asiatic antiquities. From 1933 to 1935 he was secretary of the British School in Athens. Richard Barnett's research extended to Assyriology, the cultures of Syria, Phoenicia, and Asia Minor, as well as biblical archaeology. In 1956 he organized the special exhibition at the Victoria and Albert Museum in London commemorating the tercentenary of the resettlement of Jews in the British Isles, and his catalog of the exhibition was one of his most distinguished publications. He was president of the Jewish Historical Society of England (1959–61) and contributed several important papers on the history of the Sephardim in England to its transactions. His publications include: *Carchemish: Report on the Excavations at Djerabis* (vol. 3 (with Sir L. Woolley, 1952)); *Catalogue of the Nimrod Ivories in the British Museum* (1957); *Assyrian Palace Reliefs and their influence on the Sculptures of Babylonia and Persia* (1960); *The Sculptures of Aššur-naṣir apli II* . . . (1962); and *Illustrations of Old Testament History* (1966).

[P.P.K.]

BARNETT, SIR LOUIS EDWARD (1865–1946), New Zealand surgeon and professor. Barnett was born in Wellington, New Zealand, and in 1895 received a permanent lectureship in surgery at Otago University,

Sir Louis Barnett, New Zealand surgeon.

where from 1905 to 1924 he was professor. He served with the rank of lieutenant-colonel in the Royal Australian and New Zealand Medical Corps (1915–1917) and was knighted for his overseas war service. Barnett was one of the founders of the Radium Insitute in Dunedin and a pioneer in X-ray and radium research at Otago University. Most of his work was in the fields of cancer and hydatids research, and as a result of his efforts the incidence of hydatids in New Zealand was considerably reduced.

[M.S.P.]

BARNETT, ZERAH (1843–1935), pioneer of the modern Ereẓ Israel settlement and one of the founders of Petaḥ Tikvah. Barnett, who was born in Tytuvênai, Lithuania, settled in London in 1864 as a fur manufacturer and trader. There he organized communal life for the East European immigrants who remained outside the Anglo-Jewish community. After acquiring British nationality in 1871, he went to Ereẓ Israel for the first time and helped establish the Me'ah She'arim quarter outside the walls of Old Jerusalem. Having spent all his savings, Barnett returned to London to earn money and then went back to Ereẓ Israel—a process which he repeated 15 times. Wherever he went, he advocated Jewish settlement in Ereẓ Israel. In 1878 Barnett joined the group that established Petaḥ Tikvah. As London Ḥovevei Zion delegate to the *Katowice Conference (1884), he described the experiences and hardships of the new settlers from first-hand knowledge. Early in the 1890s Barnett settled in Jaffa, where, in order to improve living conditions, he built the Neveh Shalom quarter, and moved there with his family. He helped build the Sha'arei Torah school, introducing Hebrew as the language of instruction. He also founded the Or Zore'aḥ Yeshivah in Jaffa. Barnett published his memoirs, *Zikhronot,* in 1929. He died in Jaffa and was buried in Jerusalem.

Zerah Barnett, one of the founders of Petaḥ Tikvah. Jerusalem, Schwadron Collection, J.N.U.L.

Bibliography: H. Trager, *Pioneers in Palestine* (1923); A. Yaari, *Goodly Heritage* (1958), 80, 89–93; Y. Churgin (ed.), *Sifriyyat Rishonim,* 1 no. 9 (1943); G. Kressel, *Em ha-Moshavot Petaḥ Tikvah* (1953), 56f.

[G.K./Y.S.]

BARON, BERNHARD (1850–1929), industrialist and philanthropist. Born in Rostov-on-Don, Russia, Baron immigrated to the United States as a boy and worked in a Maryland cigar factory. In 1890 he began manufacturing cigarettes by hand, to be sold at a cheap price. He opened a factory in Baltimore in 1894 and two years later perfected his own cigarette-making machine. In 1896 he took his invention to London, where he set up a company for manufacturing cigarettes. Seven years later he purchased Carreras, one of the oldest tobacco companies in England, and as a result of an extensive advertising campaign expanded it into one of the largest cigarette companies in the world. Within 20 years Baron had accumulated a fortune with over 20 million dollars, much of which he proceeded to give away on an unprecedented scale. He set up two charitable trusts in his name, which distributed over a million pounds to hospitals and children's homes, and made substantial gifts to the Jewish National Fund, the Keren Hayesod, and the Hebrew University of Jerusalem. He also made possible the erection of a new building for St. George's Jewish welfare settlement in the East End of London. Despite his enormous wealth, Baron remained simple in his tastes and despised opulence. He refused a title but after his death his son, Louis Bernhard Baron (1876–1934), was made a baronet.

Bibliography: P. H. Emden, *Jews of Britain* (1943), 491–5; DNB, *Concise Dictionary,* pt. 2 (1961), s.v.

[Ed.]

BARON, DEVORAH (1887–1956), Hebrew author. Daughter of a rabbi, she was born in Ozdah, Belorussia, and published her first Hebrew stories in Eastern European periodicals (*Ha-Meliẓ and *Ha-Ẓefirah). In 1911 she settled in Ereẓ Israel and later married Yosef *Aharonovitz, a prominent Labor Zionist leader and the editor of **Ha-Po'el ha-Ẓa'ir,* for which she was the literary editor.

She published *Sippurim,* her first volume of short stories in 1927, and in 1934, when the Bialik Prize was instituted, she was its first recipient. Following her husband's death in 1937, she edited his collected works together with Eliezer Shoḥat. She received awards for *Le-Et Attah* (1943), a volume of short stories drawn from her experiences as an exile in Egypt during World War I, and for her collected short stories *Parshiyyot* (1951). Childhood reminiscences and Jewish life in Eastern Europe are major themes in Devorah Baron's fiction. Her style, influenced by 19th-century European fiction, combines realism with impressionism. She writes movingly of her parents' home and her mother is often her favorite heroine. She is first described in *"Bereshit"* ("In the Beginning"), in *"Meẓulah"* ("Depths"), and in other stories, frequently portrayed as an unfortunate widow, struggling to maintain her orphaned children. Devorah Baron's Jewish town is permeated by a deep sense of loneliness experienced in the midst of an alien

Devorah Baron, writer of Hebrew short stories.

world and of the insecurity caused by poverty and anti-Jewish prejudice. At the same time, until the Holocaust, the Jewish town throbbed with a life which drew upon the inner resources of a deep faith. Its spirit was nurtured by a remarkable historical memory; its physical existence was safeguarded by the fertility of its families. The story *"Mishpaḥah"* ("Family") for example, describes how an attempt to force divorce upon a childless couple is prevented, and ends with a miracle of triumphant motherhood. *Me-Emesh* ("Since Last Night," 1956), the last volume to be published during the writer's lifetime, contains four stories, which describe Ereẓ Israel during World War II, the volunteers who joined the British Army, and an encounter with remnants of European Jewry. The short story of one bereaved mother epitomizes the fate of the Jewish town and of all Eastern European Jewry, from the period of the slaughter of the defenseless in "normal" times to the "final solution" under the Nazis.

In her later years, while confined to her sickbed, Devorah Baron composed a group of stories depicting the world as seen through the window of an "invalid's room" (*"Be-Lev ha-Kerakh,"* in *Parashiyyot*). Her perception remained sharp to the end, and her stories are animated by a deep empathy for the weak and the innocent. No other woman writer in Israel was as familiar with the sources of Judaism as Devorah Baron. Every human experience in her stories finds an echo in the age-old heritage of her people and in its literature. The rhythm of almost every period of Hebrew prose is clearly felt in the flow of her narrative. She is a true poet of the lost world of the Jewish town. A selection of her stories translated into English appeared in 1969 under the title *The Thorny Path.* A list of her works translated into English appears in Goell, Bibliography, 62. Bibliographical information and 118 letters appear in the posthumously published *Aggav Orḥa* (1960).

Bibliography: J. Fichmann, *Benei Dor* (1952), 254–87; Y. Keshet, *Maskiyyot* (1953), 82–100; Y. Zmora, *Sifrut al Parashat Dorot,* 3 (1950), 113–30; R. Wallenrod, *The Literature of Modern Israel* (1956), index; R. Katznelson-Shazar, *Al Admat ha-Ivrit* (1966).

[R.K.S.]

BARON, JOSEPH LOUIS (1894–1960), U.S. Reform rabbi. Baron was born in Vilna. He immigrated to the United States in 1907 and studied rabbinics at the Rabbi Isaac Elhanan Yeshiva, Jewish Theological Seminary, and Hebrew Union College, receiving his ordination from the last (1920). He served as rabbi in Davenport, Iowa, from 1920 to 1926, then moved to Temple Emanu-el in Milwaukee, Wisconsin. In addition to his post there, Baron helped found a number of Reform congregations in Madison, Waukesha, and Janesville, Wisconsin. He taught philosophy at Milwaukee State Teachers' College. A collection of his sermons, *In Quest of Integrity,* was published in 1936. Baron also published several papers and monographs, and compiled *A Treasury of Jewish Quotations* (1956).

[Ed.]

BARON, SALO (Shalom) WITTMAYER (1895–), historian. Baron was born in Tarnow (Galicia) and taken to Vienna early in World War I. He studied at the university there and received doctorates in philosophy (1917), political science (1922), and law (1923); he was ordained by the Jewish Theological Seminary in Vienna in 1920. Baron taught history at the Jewish Teachers College (Juedisches Paedagogium) in Vienna during the years 1919–26. He went to the United States at the invitation of Stephen S. Wise to teach at the Jewish Institute of Religion in New York and remained at the Institute from 1927 till 1930. From 1930 to 1963 he taught at Columbia University, and served as director of the Center of Israel and Jewish Studies at Columbia from 1950 to 1968. From 1957 he also taught at the Jewish Theological Seminary. Baron was the first member of an American history faculty to teach Jewish studies. The many such chairs that now exist owe much to his example, and a substantial number of his former students are among their occupants.

Among Baron's many involvements in public and academic affairs were his presidency of the American Academy for Jewish Research (1940–43, 1958–66, and 1968 on); his presidency of the Conference on Jewish Social Studies (1941–54, 1963–67), and honorary presidency (1955–62 and 1967 on); his presidency of the American

Salo W. Baron, Jewish historian.

Jewish Historical Society (1953–55); his founding and presidency of Jewish Cultural Reconstruction, which after World War II worked in identifying and reclaiming the libraries and other cultural treasures despoiled by the Nazis; and his trusteeship of Tel Aviv University from 1967. From 1952 he was a corresponding member of the International Commission for a Scientific and Cultural History of Mankind. Baron's first major work, *Judenfrage auf dem Wiener Kongress* (1920), dealt with the Jewish question at the Congress of Vienna. He began to write articles as a youth and subsequently wrote many hundreds. Using his exceptional range of talents in many languages and disciplines, Baron undertook the largest synthetic work of Jewish history in the contemporary period, *A Social and Religious History of the Jews* (3 vols., 1937; 2nd ed., vols. 1–14, 1952–69; index to vols. 1–8, 1960). His emphasis has been on the social history of the people, rather than on the achievements of individual figures; on elements and areas of cross-fertilization between Jews and their environment, rather than on pogroms and suffering; and on the Jewish Diaspora and Ereẓ Israel as the two centers of Jewish creativity, contrary to the views both of a Diaspora-oriented historian, such as Simon *Dubnow, and the new school of Israel-centered scholars, such as Ben Zion *Dinur. A bibliography that covers his works to 1955 appears in a Festschrift in his honor (*Essays on Jewish Life and Thought,* 1959). In addition to the works mentioned above, Baron's major publications are *Bibliography of Jewish Social Studies 1938–39* (1941); *The Jewish Community* (3 vols., 1942); *Modern Nationalism and Religion* (1947); *Jews of the United States, 1790–1840; A Documentary History* (edited with J. L. Blaú) 3 vols., 1963; *Russian Jews Under Tsars and Soviets* (1964); and *History and Jewish Historians* (1964). Baron edited *Essays on Maimonides* (1941), *Judaism, Postbiblical and Talmudic Periods* (1954), coedited *Freedom and Reason* (1951), a Festschrift in memory of Morris Raphael Cohen, and wrote the introductory essay for *Jerusalem: City Holy and Eternal* (1954). He has also been one of the editors of the quarterly *Jewish Social Studies* since it appeared in 1939, and a consulting editor of the *Encyclopaedia Judaica.*

[Ar.H.]

BARON DE HIRSCH FUND, fund established by Baron Maurice de *Hirsch, the financier and philanthropist who dedicated his fortune to the welfare of East European Jews at a time when worsening conditions in Russia made mass emigration a stark necessity. Convinced that modern secular education could ameliorate the lot of his oppressed brethren, De Hirsch hoped to regenerate them into a class of independent farmers and handicraftsmen in the New World. In 1889, on the advice of Oscar S. *Straus and Michael *Heilprin, De Hirsch allocated the proceeds of a $2,400,000 fund toward agricultural colonies and trade schools in the United States. With the cooperation of Jacob Schiff and other American Jewish leaders, the Baron de Hirsch Fund was incorporated in New York in 1891. Judge Myer S. Isaacs became president; Schiff, vice-president; and the trustees included Straus, Mayer Sulzberger, and William Hackenburg. A subsidized rural community, Woodbine, was established in southern New Jersey, with an agricultural school which functioned until 1917. In New York the Baron de Hirsch Trade School continued to serve a generation of immigrants. Significant also was the fund's support of the Jewish Agricultural Society and of classes in English, legal aid, and other services to integrate newcomers in America.

Bibliography: S. Joseph, *History of the Baron de Hirsch Fund* (1935).

[J.Br.]

BARONDESS, JOSEPH (1867–1928), U.S. labor and communal leader. Barondess was born in Kamenets-Podolsk, Ukraine. He immigrated to the U.S. in 1888, working in New York City as a cloakmaker. Soon after, he joined the United Hebrew Trades and became a labor organizer in the garment industry, helping to lead the first great cloakmakers' strike in 1890. Indicted in 1891 on an extortion charge brought against him by the cloak manufacturers, Barondess was sentenced to a 21-month prison term but was released in a few weeks, after widespread protests and petitions for his pardon. His career as an organizer ended when he led an unsuccessful strike in 1894, but he remained active in the Socialist Labor Party, joining its moderate wing in 1898 in the battle against Daniel *De Leon, which led to the founding of the Socialist Party in 1901. By then, however, Barondess had retired from socialist politics and was devoting himself largely to an insurance business that he had started. In his new role as a successful businessman, Barondess accepted appointment to the National Civic Foundation in 1900 and to the New York City Board of Education in 1910. Partly as a reaction to the Russian pogroms of 1903, Barondess became active in the Zionist movement and during the last years of his life served as an honorary vice-president of the Zionist Organization of America. He was also among the founders of the American Jewish Congress and a member of the American-Jewish delegation to the Versailles peace talks in 1919. His career typified that of many immigrants, whose process of integration in the U.S. was marked by initial disillusionment with American society, socialism, a higher economic status, and finally a retreat from radical political activity and a return to the Jewish fold.

Joseph Barondess (front row, sixth from right) with other members of the Jewish delegation to the Versailles Peace Conference, 1919. Photo Jewish Agency Archives, Jerusalem.

Bibliography: *New York Times* (June 20, 1928), 25; B. Weinstein, *Di Yidishe Yunions in Amerike* (1929), 116, 319–36.

[Ed.]

BAROU, NOAH (1889–1955), economist. Born in Poltava, Russia, Barou became involved in revolutionary activities as a student and was exiled. After studying in Germany, he returned to Russia in 1913 and was general secretary of the central committee of the illegal left-wing Zionist organization, *Po'alei Zion. After the 1917 Revolution he was one of the three secretaries of the Ukrainian Trade Union Congress. In 1922 he left Russia and eventually settled in England, where he served from 1923 to 1936 as general secretary of the Po'alei Zion World Federation. He was one of the founders of the *World Jewish Congress and an active member of the *Board of Deputies of British Jews. In the early 1950s, Barou made the first contacts with representatives of the West German Federal Republic that led to the meeting of Nahum *Goldmann, president of the Jewish Material Claims Conference, with Chancellor Konrad Adenauer. This meeting laid the foundations for the *reparations eventually made to Jews for material losses at the hands of the Nazis. An authority on cooperative finance, Barou published numerous monographs in English. They include *Cooperative Banking* (1932), *Cooperation in the Soviet Union* (1946), and *British Trade Unions* (1947). He edited *The Cooperative Movement in Labour Britain* (1948).

Noah Barou, economist, and a founder of the World Jewish Congress.

Bibliography: H. F. Infield (ed.), *Essays . . . in Memory of Dr. Noah Barou 1889–1955* (1962), includes bibliography.

[C.R.]

BARRASSA, JACOB (17th century), Marrano physician and writer. Born as Diego de Barros, probably in Portugal, he studied science, medicine, and astronomy in Spain, and published an annual "prognostication and calendar," *Prognóstico e lunario* (e.g. Seville, 1630 and 1635), based in part on Semitic sources. He embraced Judaism in Amsterdam shortly afterward and wrote a polemical work (still unpublished) on the ostensibly difficult passages of Scripture. He was one of the "Parnasim de Talmud Torah" in 1642, and a warden of the community in 1651.

Bibliography: C. Roth, *Life of Menasseh ben Israel* (1934), 122–3.

[C.R.]

BARRENNESS AND FERTILITY, the inability or ability of man and woman to procreate. Procreation is considered a blessing in the Bible and it is a commandment (Gen. 1:28; 9:7; Rashi, *ibid.*) applicable to all. The world was created to be inhabited (Isa. 45:18) and God's blessings bestowed on Israel always included fecundity (Lev. 26:9; Deut. 28:11) and the absence of barrenness (Ex. 23:26; Deut. 7:14). *Children are seen as the greatest blessing: "a heritage of the Lord" (Ps. 127:3–5); "Thy wife shall be as a fruitful vine . . . thy children like olive plants . . ." (*ibid.*, 128:3–4). The prodigious fertility of the Israelites in Egypt antagonized the Egyptians (Ex. 1:7, 12) and is interpreted by the Midrash (Tanḥ. and Rashi ad loc.) to imply that the women bore "six (children) at once." Procreation is one of the main purposes of marriage, and in later times an offspring (especially a male offspring) was also prized because it meant that *Kaddish* would be recited in one's memory; hence the popular phrase "to have a *Kaddish*" for a (male) child. Barrenness was a curse and a punishment (Lev. 20:20–21; Jer. 22:30, and MK 27b); Abimelech and his wives were punished, though only temporarily, with barrenness (Gen. 20:17–18), and so was Michal, Saul's daughter and David's wife (II Sam. 6:23). Sarah, Rebekah, Rachel, Samson's mother, Hannah, and the Shunamite woman were all barren at first, but God, who holds the key to fecundity (Ta'an. 2a; cf. Men. 98a), granted their and their husbands' prayers (cf. Ps. 113:9). Rachel preferred death to childlessness (Gen. 30:1), which prompted the comment of the *amora* Joshua b. Levi that to be without children is death (Ned. 64b). A childless scholar is not eligible to sit on the Sanhedrin (San. 36b). Isaiah called Zion in her distress "a barren woman that has not borne" (Isa. 54:1). However, for the eunuch who exclaimed "I am a dry tree," he has a word of comfort saying "I shall give them in my house and within my walls a monument and a memorial better than sons and daughters . . ." (Isa. 56:3–5; cf. Wisd. 3:13–15). Teaching Torah to the son of another person is equivalent to having fathered him (Sanh. 19b, 99b). Ben Sira said that it was better to die childless than to have children who were without the fear of the Lord (Ecclus. 16:1–4). According to a rabbinic story, King Hezekiah had refrained from procreation because he had foreseen that his children would be sinners but was rebuked

Figure 1. *Duda'im* (mandrakes), which Leah gave to Jacob (Gen. 30:14–17). An illustration from *La république des hébreux* by Basnage, Amsterdam, 1713. Jerusalem, J.N.U.L.

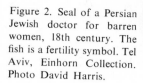

Figure 2. Seal of a Persian Jewish doctor for barren women, 18th century. The fish is a fertility symbol. Tel Aviv, Einhorn Collection. Photo David Harris.

by the prophet Isaiah, "What have you to do with the secrets of the All Merciful? you have to do your duty and let God do what it pleases Him" (Ber. 10a). The cause of sterility may lie as much with the husband as with the wife; this is suggested by Abraham (Gen. 15:2) and by the Talmud for both Abraham and Isaac (Yev. 64a; cf. Num. R. 10:5). A husband should divorce his wife after ten years of childless marriage; though she may marry again (Yev. 6:6; Sh. Ar., EH 154:6). Distinction ought to be made between accidental sterility and congenital or self-inflicted impotence or barrenness. Deuteronomy 23:2 prohibits an impotent man to marry a free-born Israelite (see Yev. 8:2) when the impotence is self-inflicted (*ibid.*, 75b; cf. Jos., Ant., 4:290). A priest who "hath his stones crushed" is unfit for Temple service (Lev. 21:20). The Talmud defines an *eilonit* ("ram-like, barren") as a woman who by the age of 18 or 20 is without the symptoms of feminity (ET, 1 (1947), 243–46 and ref.). According to some authorities, marriage to an *eilonit*, when contracted in ignorance of her condition, is invalid. Impotence and sterility may be only temporary, due to undernourishment (Ket. 10b). Certain foods, such as eggs, fish, garlic, wine, milk, cheese, and fat meat increase sexual potency (Ber. 40a; Sot. 11b; Yoma 18a–b, BK 82a), while salt, egg-barley, sleeping on the ground, bloodletting, and crying are detrimental to it (Git. 70a–b; ARN[1] 41:132). The *duda'im* (mandrakes, "love-flowers"), which Reuben brought to his mother Leah, who gave them to her sister Rachel (Gen. 30:14ff.), have been interpreted to be an aphrodisiac flower, though this is far from certain (see B. Jacob, Genesis, ad. loc.). The Talmud suggests that the suppression of the urge to urinate is a cause of sterility in men, and many pupils of the *amora* Huna (third century) became sterile on account of his over long lectures (Yev. 64b). See also *Birth Control; *Castration; *Vital Statistics.

Bibliography: J. Preuss, *Biblisch-talmudische Medizin* (1923[3]), 477–80, 538ff.

[A.C.]

°**BARRÈS, AUGUSTE MAURICE** (1862–1923), French writer and politician. His extreme individualism and nationalism greatly influenced his generation. He contributed regularly to the nationalist anti-Semitic daily *La Cocarde* (founded in 1888), which he edited for a while, and there propounded many of the views on blood purity, the state, and the individual which were later developed and put into practice in Germany. He also expressed these opinions in his novels. Like Charles *Maurras, Barrès was influenced by H. A. Taine, who emphasized race and environment as the determinant factors in history, and by *Proudhon, who identified capitalists with bankers and bankers with Jews. With Maurras, Barrès laid the ideological foundations of the *Action Française, a forerunner of the Fascist movement. At the time of the *Dreyfus case, Barrès was among the most vehement of Dreyfus' accusers. During World War I, however, he became an ideologist of the "Union sacrée," and temporarily setting aside his prejudices accepted the Jews as members of the "spiritual family" of France.

Bibliography: P. de Boisdeffre, *Maurice Barrès* (Fr., 1962), incl. bibl.; M. R. Curtis, *Three Against the Third Republic* (1959), incl. bibl.

[Ed.]

BARRIOS, DANIEL LEVI (Miguel) DE (1635–1701), Spanish poet and playwright. Barrios was born in Montilla, of a Portuguese Marrano family, and was one of the most eminent exiles who contributed to Spanish literature. Following the execution in 1655 of a relative, Marco (Isaac) de Almeyda *Bernal, Barrios' family left Spain, his parents

Daniel Levi de Barrios and his family in an allegorical portrayal of harmony on earth under the rule of God. Engraving by Chr. v. Hagen after a painting by Aaron De Chaves (d. 1705) illustrating Barrios' poem, *Imperio de Dios en la harmonia del mundo,* Brussels, 1673(?).

settling in Algiers and he in Italy. After a sojourn at Nice and Leghorn (where he reverted to Judaism), he sailed with his first wife, Debora Váez, to Tobago, where she soon died. Barrios then moved to the Netherlands and in 1662 married Abigail de Pina in Amsterdam. At about the same time he took a commission as a captain in the Spanish Netherlands, and for the next 12 years lived outwardly as a Christian in Brussels, while simultaneously maintaining a connection with the Jewish community in Amsterdam. In 1674, Barrios renounced his military commission and thereafter lived openly as a professing Jew in Amsterdam. A follower of Shabbetai Ẓevi, Barrios had mystical delusions and often fasted for long periods. This so alarmed his wife that she hurried to R. Jacob *Sasportas on the first day of Passover, 1675, and pleaded for his assistance. Sasportas found Barrios prepared for the Messiah's advent before the New Year and convinced that the Christians, headed by the Dutch monarch, would convert to Judaism. As he dryly records in his *Ẓiẓat Novel Ẓevi* (1737), Sasportas found it necessary to remind the deluded poet of his immediate family obligations and of the perilous state of his health.

Barrios' work can be divided into two periods, before and after 1674. In Brussels, he emphasized classical and pagan allusions and in Amsterdam stressed his Jewishness, while retaining a great admiration for the Spanish poet Luis de Góngora. His first work, *Flor de Apolo* (Brussels, 1665), is a collection of poetry on varied themes; in the same volume he published three plays, *Pedir favor al contrario, El canto junto al encanto* and *El Español de Orán,* which were typical of the contemporary Spanish theater. An allegorical drama, *Contra la verdad no hay fuerza* (Amsterdam, undated, but before 1672), glorified the memory of three martyrs who died in an auto-da-fé in Cordoba in June while *Coro de las Musas* (Brussels and Amsterdam, 1672) contains poetic eulogies of the Spanish provinces and of famous people and cities, preceded by a panegyric on Charles II of England.

The works of Barrios' Amsterdam period constitute five major collections. *Sol de la vida* (Antwerp, 1679) contains the *Libre albedrío,* a defense of the doctrine of free will. His *Triumpho del govierno popular y de la antigüedad holandesa* (Amsterdam, 1683), of which at least seven versions exist, includes sections on the history of the Amsterdam Sephardi community and its organizations. Some copies contain two religious poems: *La mayor perfección de Ley santisima* and *Triumpho canta la inmortalidad del Pueblo de Israel.* The undated treatise, *Relación de los poetas y escritores españoles de la Nación judaica amstelodama* (republished by M. Kayserling in REJ, 18 (1889), 276–89), is a rich, though sometimes highly romanticized, source of information on Sephardi literary figures. *Alegrías o pinturas lucientes de himeneo* (Amsterdam, 1686), a collection of wedding poems and panegyrics, commemorates some eminent Sephardi families. The most notable compositions in *Estrella de Jacob sobre Flores de Lis* (Amsterdam, 1686) are *"La Memoria renueva el dolor,"* on the death of the poet's wife, and two religious compositions, *"Providencia de Dios sobre Israel"* and *"Días penitenciales." Metros nobles* (Amsterdam, 1675?) contains the religious poems also found in the (presumably earlier) *Triumpho del govierno popular.* Outstanding among Barrios' many other writings is his *Imperio de Dios en la harmonía del mundo* (Brussels, 1673?), the first part of a grandiose work intended as a poetic version of the Pentateuch. Barrios' literary output is uneven in quality, since he wrote to gain patronage in order to provide for himself and his family. As the poet laureate of Amsterdam Jewry he was a facile versifier, but some of his religious poems, thanks to their sincerity of feeling and elegance of expression, deserve wider recognition. Their general themes are the permanence and excellence of the Jewish faith, belief in free will, the author's repentance for the sin of posing as a Christian, and the harmony of Creation. Barrios glorified Sephardi culture (and its prime center, the Jewish community of Amsterdam), and perpetuated the memory of notable victims of the Inquisition. There is some evidence that Rembrandt's painting, "The Jewish Bride" (c. 1665) was a portrait of Barrios and his second wife.

Bibliography: W. C. Pieterse, Daniel Levi de Barrios als geschiedschrijver ... (1968); K. R. Scholberg, *Poesía religiosa Miguel de Barrios* (1962); idem, in: JQR, 53 (1962/63), 120–59; J. Amador de los Ríos, *Estudios históricos* (1848), 608–19; Kayserling, Bibl, 16–26; J. A. C. Zwarts, *Significance of Rembrandt's "The Jewish Bride"* (1929); H. V. Besso, *Dramatic Literature of the Sephardic Jews of Amsterdam* (1947), 73–84; J. Sasportas, *Ẓiẓat Novel Ẓevi,* ed. by J. Tishby (1954), 363ff.; Scholem, Shabbetai Ẓevi, 2 (1957), 446f.

[K.R.S.]

BARRON, JENNIE LOITMAN (1891–1969), U.S. jurist. She was born in Boston. In 1934, after 20 years of private law practice, Jennie Loitman Barron was appointed assistant attorney general of Massachusetts, thereby becoming the first woman ever to prosecute a major criminal case in that state. In 1937 she was named associate justice of the Boston Municipal Court, and in 1959 associate justice of the State Superior Court (the first woman to be appointed to a Superior Court in the state). A lecturer on crime and juvenile delinquency, she was also

Jennie Loitman Barron, U.S. jurist.

director of the Home Owners' Cooperative Bank, chairman of the League of Women Voters, and honorary president of the Boston Women's Division of the American Jewish Congress.

[E.GR.]

BARROS BASTO, ARTURO CARLOS DE (1887–1961), leader of *Marrano revival in Portugal. Born at Amarante near Oporto, of a New Christian family, he was introduced to the secret practices of the Marranos by his grandfather, entered a military career, and in the revolution in 1910

Arturo Barros Basto, leader of an attempted Marrano revival in Portugal.

hoisted the Republican flag on the town hall of Oporto. On returning from World War I, he studied Hebrew, entered Judaism officially, and threw himself into the work of Marrano regeneration. He organized a community at Oporto, secured foreign support for the construction of a monumental synagogue, set up a rudimentary seminary in connection with it, and went on missionary journeys through the Marrano centers of northern Portugal. Barros Basto established a Portuguese periodical, *Ha-Lappid* ("The Torch"), to spread Jewish ideas among the Marranos. He also edited various handbooks of religious guidance and wrote a history of the Jews of Oporto. Largely owing to the change of the religious atmosphere in Portugal, but partly to his over-ambitious plans and certain faults of character, the project had only a limited success, notwithstanding its promising beginning. He died, almost blind, a disappointed man.

Bibliography: Portuguese Marranos Committee, London, *Marranos in Portugal* (1938); C. Roth, *L'Apôtre des Marranes* (1929); *Jewish Guardian* (June 6, 1930); Roth, Marranos, 370–5; Friedenberg, in: *Midstream* (Spring, 1960), 2–4, 105–7.

[C.R.]

°**BARRUEL, AUGUSTIN** (1741–1820), French Jesuit and anti-revolutionary polemicist. Barruel specialized in propagating fantastic stories about the part played by Freemasonry and secret societies in the Revolution. In 1807 Barruel alerted the French Government to an alleged world Jewish conspiracy. A mysterious Italian called Simonini (whose existence is doubtful) had delivered to Barruel the "plans of world Jewry" to become "masters of the world, turning the churches into as many synagogues, and reducing Christians to utter serfdom." Barruel's fantasies received the endorsement of Pope *Pius VII and were possibly the cause of *Napoleon's sudden decision to dissolve the French *Sanhedrin. In the longer perspective it was to have graver consequences, for the "Jewish plot" theme has served as a prototype for other deliberate fabrications, last but not least the Protocols of the *Elders of Zion.

Bibliography: L. Poliakov, *Histoire de l'antisémitisme*, 3 (1968), index; DHGE, 6 (1932), 937; N. Cohn, *Warrant for Genocide; the Myth of the Jewish World Conspiracy and the Protocols of the Elders of Zion* (1967), 25–32, passim.

[ED.]

BARSIMSON, JACOB, regarded as the earliest Jewish resident of New Amsterdam (later New York). Barsimson probably arrived there on July 8, 1654, aboard the ship *Peartree*, from Holland, thus preceding the 23 Jews who arrived in September of that year from Brazil. A man of small means, he was taxed below the majority of other New Amsterdam residents. In November 1655 Barsimson joined with Asser *Levy in petitioning for the right held by other inhabitants to stand guard and thus avoid payment of a special tax. The Dutch West India Company overruled Governor Peter Stuyvesant, who had rejected the petition. Barsimson may have returned to Amsterdam in 1659.

Bibliography: Oppenheim, in: A. J. Karp (ed.), *The Jewish Experience in America*, 1 (1969), 37–50.

[L.HE.]

BARTH, JACOB (1851–1914), Semitic linguist. Barth was born in Flehingen, Baden. Among his teachers in Talmud was his future father-in-law, Azriel *Hildesheimer. He studied Semitic philology at the universities of Berlin, Leipzig (under H. L. Fleischer), and Strasbourg (under Th. Noeldeke). From 1874 until his death he taught Hebrew, biblical exegesis, and Jewish philosophy at the Orthodox

Jacob Barth, German Semitic linguist. Lithograph by Hermann Struck. Jerusalem, J.N.U.L.

Rabbinical Seminary founded by Hildesheimer at Berlin. In 1876 he was appointed lecturer in Semitic philology at the University of Berlin, and in 1880 associate professor. Being a Jew he was not appointed full professor, but he received the title of Geheimer Regierungsrat. Barth was one of the most important Semitic linguists of his time, and at least two of his works are still standard reference books: *Die Nominalbildung in den semitischen Sprachen* (1894), and *Die Pronominalbildung in den semitischen Sprachen* (1918). Despite Barth's tendency to adopt odd etymologies and to excessive schematization, these works, as well as others, show his genius in discerning linguistic analogies. Barth was also one of the outstanding Arabic scholars of his time. He edited grammatical, poetical, and historical texts, as well as the commentary of Maimonides to Mishnah *Makkot* (1880). His contributions to the study of Hebrew include both linguistics and lexicography (especially his *Etymologische Studien zum semitischen, inbesonders zum hebraeischen und aramaeischen Lexikon* (1902). Being strictly Orthodox, he avoided higher criticism. but accepted the separate authorship of Isaiah 40ff., which, in his view, was supported by the Talmud. Similarly, he usually refrained from emendation of the Bible text, although he had a natural tendency to text corrections (as exhibited in his Arabic studies). His commentary on almost all the books of the Bible, which originated in his lectures at the Hildesheimer Seminary, has not been published.

[J.Bl.]

His son, Aharon (1890–1957), was an Israel banker and Zionist leader. Born in Berlin, as a young man he became an active leader in the Mizrachi movement in Germany, representing it at most of the Zionist Congresses after 1920. From 1921 to 1938 he served as attorney for the Zionist Congress court, and from 1946 as its chairman. He settled in Palestine in 1933 and was appointed director-general of the Anglo-Palestine Bank (later Bank Leumi le-Israel) in 1947, retaining this post until his death. Of his articles and brochures on various Zionist and religious topics, the most important is *Dorenu mul She'elot ha-Neẓaḥ* published in 1954 and republished in 1955 (Eng. tr. *The Modern Jew Faces Eternal Problems,* Jerusalem 1956). In it, he summarized his views on traditional and modern aspects of Judaism. He is noted for his modern religious interpretation of Orthodoxy, stressing the contemporary relevance of Orthodox Jewish practice. He wrote the brochure *Letter to an English Friend* (1948), in which he propounds the religious basis for the Jewish claim to Palestine, and *The Mitzvoth: Their Aim and Purpose* (1949).

Eliezer (Lazar) (1880–1949), Aharon's elder brother, was a leader and central figure in the religious Zionist movement in Germany. Born in Berlin, he became a leader of the Zionist Organization of Germany, participated in most Zionist Congresses after 1903, and served as a member of the Zionist General Council. During 1929–31 he represented Mizrachi on the Zionist Executive in London. He published numerous articles on Zionist topics.

[B.J.]

Bibliography: Rabbiner-Seminar zu Berlin, *Bericht ueber die ersten 25 Jahre* (1898), 9, 57; Eppenstein, in: *Jahresbericht des Rabbiner Seminars zu Berlin fuer 1914–5* (1915), 91–99; C.H. Becker, *Der Islam* (1916), 200–2; J. Fueck, *Die arabischen Studien in Europa* (1955), 242–3; EJ, 3 (1929), 1100–01; J. Blau, in: *Ḥokhmat Yisrael be-Ma'arav Eiropah,* ed. by S. Federbush (1959), 47–52; EẒD, 1 (1958), 227–33; S. Daniel, in: *Gevilin be-Maḥashavah Datit Le'ummit* (July 1957), 58–72.

°**BARTH, KARL** (1886–1968), Swiss Protestant theologian. From 1922, he served as professor of theology in various German universities. With the Nazi rise to power in Germany and the consequent split in German Protestantism, Barth helped to found the Confessing Church (Bekennende Kirche) which opposed Hitler and the National-Socialist ideology as incompatible with Christian commitment to the teaching and kingship of Jesus. In 1934, he drafted the theological declaration of Barmen, whereby the German Lutherans and Reformed united to define and defend their position against the totalitarian claims of the state. Expelled from Germany in 1935, he returned to his native Basle, where he was appointed professor of dogmatics.

His principal theological work, the monumental *Kirchliche Dogmatik,* which remained incomplete at his death, was published between 1932–53. While Barth took a courageous stand against anti-Semitism, seeing in hatred and persecution of the Jews an attack on the very foundations of the Christian message, his work evinces no understanding of actual Judaism. Throughout Barth's writings Judaism appears as a theoretical construction, a kind of figment of theological imagination, whose purpose it is to serve as a foil to the message of the gospel.

While not hostile in its intention, Barth's representation of Judaism is a complete caricature and falsification of Jewish reality. According to Barth, Israel is God's Chosen People and in spite of its obstinacy in assimilating to other peoples, the Divine election remains valid. Since the crucifixion of Jesus, there simply cannot be any normal existence for the Jewish people, for the Jew represents man as such, sinner, called by God's grace and rejecting this grace. In this exemplary role of man, the Jew necessarily irritates the nations of the world by acting as a kind of mirror in which the nations see their sinful humanity reflected. The Nazis sought to destroy the Jews, the people of Jesus, in order to liberate themselves from the rule of God and to break, as it were, the mirror in which fallen man sees himself reflected. Beside his numerous theological, literary, and political writings, Barth also wrote some works on the church in the Third Reich, and on the existence of Christians in the countries under communist rule.

Bibliography: W. Pauck, *Karl Barth* (Eng., 1931); Taubes, in: JR, 34 (1954), 14, 231–43; R. Niebuhr, *Essays in Applied Christianity* (1959); F.W. Marquardt, *Die Entdeckung des Judentums fuer die christliche Theologie—Israel im Denken Karl Barths* (1967).

[Ed.]

BARTHOLDY, JACOB (1779–1825), Prussian diplomat and art connoisseur. Bartholdy, uncle of the composer Felix *Mendelssohn, was one of the group of gifted apostate Jews whose services were enlisted by von Hardenberg, the Prussian chancellor. Born in Berlin into a prosperous Jewish family, Bartholdy studied law and philosophy, traveled extensively in Western Europe before becoming an officer in the Austrian army in the 1809 war against France. After entering the Prussian diplomatic service, he was appointed Prussian consul-general in Rome and took part in the conference of Aix-la-Chapelle (1818). In the same year he became Prussian chargé d'affaires at the court of Tuscany with the title of privy councillor of legation. Bartholdy was an enthusiastic art patron and his home was decorated with frescoes by contemporary German artists. After his death, these were bought by the Prussian government who also acquired his important collection of Etruscan vases, bronze, and ivory.

Bibliography: A. Kohut, *Beruehmte israelitische Maenner und Frauen . . . ,* 2 (1901), 301; *Genealogical Tables of Moses Mendelssohn and Frommet Guggenheim,* in the Archives of the Leo Baeck Institute, New York.

[E.Ha.]

°**BARTOLOCCI, GIULIO** (1613–1687), Italian Christian Hebraist and bibliographer. Bartolocci was taught Hebrew by the convert Giovanni Battista Jonah Galileo (formerly Judah Jonah of Safed), and in 1651 became professor of Hebrew language and rabbinic literature at the Collegium Neophytorum (for Jewish converts) in Rome; at the same time he served as *scriptor hebraicus* in the Vatican Library. He is remembered above all for his *Bibliotheca Magna Rabbinica . . . de scriptoribus et scriptis hebraicis, ordine alphabetico hebraice et latine digestis* (Heb. title *Kiryat Sefer*), a comprehensive bibliography of Jewish books (Rome, 4 vols., 1675–93). The last volume was edited by Bartolocci's student Carlo Giuseppe Imbonati, who added a fifth volume, *Bibliotheca Latina-Hebraica* (1694; all 5 vols. repr. 1969), containing a bibliography of Latin works by Christian authors on the Jews or on Judaism. Bartolocci's work is the first systematic, all-inclusive bibliography of Jewish literature. It served as the basis for Wolf's *Bibliotheca Hebraea* and for subsequent works in the field. Some of the works which Bartolocci regarded as most important he presents in full, in the Hebrew (or Aramaic) original and in Latin translation. Among these are the *Antiochus Scroll, Alphabet of Ben Sira,* and *Otiyyot de-Rabbi Akiva.* Occasionally, he gives biographies of important writers. His biographies of biblical commentators such as Rashi, Ibn Ezra, David Kimḥi, Gersonides, and Abrabanel were published also in A. Reland's *Analecta Rabbinica* (Utrecht, 1702). His work still retains some importance. Other works by Bartolocci remain in manuscript.

Bibliography: G. M. Mazzuccheli, *Gli Scrittori d'Italia,* 2 (1763), 468; Roth, Italy, 394; Milano, Italia, 681; Steinschneider, in: ZHB, 2 (1897), 51 no. 99.

[C.R.]

BARTOV, HANOCH (1926–), Israel novelist. Bartov, who was born in Petaḥ Tikvah, served in the Jewish Brigade during World War II and during the War of Independence served in the Israel Army. Bartov was a member of kibbutz Ein ha-Ḥoresh, and a reporter for the daily *La-Merḥav.* He

Hanoch Bartov, Israel novelist. Photo Marlin-Yaron, Tel Aviv.

served as cultural attaché at the Israel Embassy, London in 1966–68. Bartov's writings include stories, novels, plays, and journalism. In *Ha-Ḥeshbon ve-ha-Nefesh* ("The Reckoning and the Soul," 1953), he discusses the ideological disillusionment of Israel youth when they returned to civilian life after the War of Independence. Problems of new immigrants are treated in the novel *Shesh Kenafayim le-Eḥad* ("Each has Six Wings," 1954), which he later adapted for the stage. A visit to the U.S. is vividly recorded in the travel-book *Arba'ah Yisre'elim ve-Khol Amerikah* ("Four Israelis and All The U.S.A.," 1961). The subject of *Piẓei Bagrut* (1965; *The Brigade,* 1968) is the Jewish Brigade during World War II and the conflict between Jewish mores and the wish to revenge the Holocaust. His other works include: *Ha-Shuk ha-Katan* ("The Small Market," 1957); *Sa ha-Bayta, Yonatan* ("Go Home, Jonathan," 1962); *Shel Mi Attah Yeled* ("Whose Child Are You," 1970). His short story "The Stranger and I" appears in *Hebrew Short Stories* (vol. 2, 1965), 226–32.

[G.Av.]

BARUCH (Heb. בָּרוּךְ; "blessed"), son of Neriah son of Mahseiah, scribe and trusted companion of the prophet *Jeremiah, who set down in writing all the latter's prophecies and may have composed the biographical narrative about Jeremiah (Jer. 36:4). Baruch's brother Seraiah was the quartermaster of Zedekiah (51:59), the last king of Judah. In the fourth year (or possibly the fifth) of the reign of *Jehoiakim, Baruch wrote down, at Jeremiah's dictation, all of the prophet's oracles, and read them in the temple court before the entire community, which had assembled for a fast day proclaimed in Kislev of that year. Baruch then read them before the king's ministers (36:4ff.). When the king was informed of these events, he ordered the scroll to be read before him. When he heard the prophet's message forecasting doom, Jehoiakim tore the scroll, cast it into the fire, and ordered Jeremiah and Baruch to be placed under arrest; they, however, succeeded in hiding from him. Then Jeremiah redictated the contents of the destroyed scroll and added to it (36:32). As a reward for Baruch's loyalty, Jeremiah declared that he would be saved (45:1ff.).

In the tenth year of Zedekiah's reign, when Jerusalem was under siege by the Babylonians, Jeremiah bought a field from Hanamel, his uncle's son. He entrusted the deeds of purchase to Baruch, asking him to place them in an earthenware vessel for safekeeping "that they may last for a long time" (32:1–16). The Babylonian commanders released Baruch together with Jeremiah, and did not force him to go into exile to Babylon (40:1–7). Baruch apparently exerted a great influence over Jeremiah. When *Gedaliah son of Ahikam was killed and the remnant of the population that had escaped exile, fearing the vengeance of Nebuchadnezzar, asked Jeremiah whether they should stay in the country or go down to Egypt, he advised them to remain. But they suspected him of acting under Baruch's instigation, thinking that Baruch, out of hatred for them, planned to place them at the mercy of the Babylonian king. Baruch was then taken along with Jeremiah and the remnant of the population to Egypt.

In the Aggadah. Baruch is held to be a priest as well as a prophet and one of the descendants of Rahab (Meg. 14b; SOR, 20). He is identified with Ebed-Melech the Ethiopian, who saved Jeremiah from the dungeon (Sif. Num., on 12:1). Five years after the destruction of the Temple, Baruch (with Jeremiah) was taken from Egypt to Babylon, where he died (Meg. 16b; SOR 26:1; cf. Jos. Ant., 10:181–2). He is also said to have prophesied there in the second year of the reign of Darius, but was unable to return to Judah because of his advanced age. According to this tradition, Ezra was his pupil (Song. R. 5:5; Meg. 16b).

In the Middle Ages the Iraqi Jews possessed several legends about Baruch's grave, which was said to be near that of Ezekiel in Mushid ʾAli. A certain Arab ruler in Baghdad—at the time of the exilarch Solomon—wished to see the graves of Ezekiel and Baruch. When the grave was opened, Baruch's body was found in a marble coffin, looking as if alive. It was decided to transport him some distance from Ezekiel's grave, but, after a mile-long journey, the cart stopped and would not move, and he was buried at that spot (*Travels of R. Petachia of Ratisbonne . . .*, ed. and tr. by A. Benisch (1856), 21, 23, 49, 51). Jewish tradition extolled Baruch's piety and several apocalypses were attributed to him as well as an apocryphal letter (see Apocalypse of *Baruch (Syriac); Book of *Baruch; Greek Apocalypse of *Baruch; Rest of the Words of *Baruch).

Baruch came to have considerable importance in the apocryphal literature where a number of books were attributed to him. Moreover, there are apparently fragments of Baruch and Jeremiatic apocryphal literature among the Dead Sea Scrolls. According to the apocryphal books he received many visions and revelations of an apocalyptic nature. In II Baruch his assumption is foretold (II Bar. 25.1, 76:1).

Bibliography: S. Yeivin, in: *Tarbiz,* 12 (1940/41), 260; de Vaux, Anc. Isr, 49, 120, 168; Noth, Personennamen, 183; EM, 2 (1965), 337–8 (includes bibliography); Ginzberg, Legends, index.

[Y.M.G.]

BARUCH, name of several kabbalists. Baruch Sheli'aḥ-Ẓibbur Togarmi, as is suggested by his cognomen Togarmi, was a cantor of eastern origin. He wrote a treatise, extant in several manuscripts (Paris, Oxford, New York), called *Maftehot ha-Kabbalah* ("The Keys to Kabbalah"), which contains a short, factually complete commentary on the *Sefer *Yeẓirah,* identical with the one described by Abraham *Abulafia in his *Oẓar Eden Ganuz* as being by his master, Baruch (no surname). In the early 14th century, *Isaac b. Samuel of Acre quotes a Baruch Togarmi in *Me'irat Einayim* in such a way as to suggest a scholar who lived at least one generation earlier. He says, "I saw written in the name of Baruch Togarmi" and ends with the eulogy for the dead. The three quotations display the same characteristic of short allusions to kabbalistic secrets through wordplay as the above-mentioned treatise, *Maftehot.* This is significant for the early history of the Abulafian current in the Kabbalah. The author already knows a distinct group of such kabbalists who are occupied with the (mystical) knowledge of the name of God. From his statements, it is to be understood that he belonged to a circle whose members believed themselves able to discover "by the three ways of the Kabbalah," i.e., *gematria* ("numerical value of words"), *notarikon* ("interpretation of each letter in a word as abbreviation of other words"), and *temurah* ("interchange of letters according to certain systematic rules") particularly profound mysteries of the mystic cosmology and theology. However, according to his testimony, he was not allowed either to divulge in public or even merely to set down in writing most of it. The treatise is full of obscure wordplay and peculiar *gematriot.* For example, the word "body" here means the evil principle, through the equation גוף רע (*guf ra,* "evil body"—359) equals שטן (*satan*—359). The work originates clearly from the same circle as the book *Sod ha-Levanah* (ed. by J. Klausner, in *Madda'ei ha-Yahadut,* 2 (1927), 240–1), which has survived in the name of Jacob Cohen (c. 1260–70, that is at the time of R. Baruch). According to this, Baruch would have lived in Spain. Thus, it is a plausible assumption that it was through him that Abulafia, during his stay in Barcelona in 1270–73, was introduced to the Kabbalah of this circle.

Baruch the Kabbalist was author of the book *Mafte'aḥ ha-Kabbalah* ("Key to Kabbalah") which was in Carmoly's possession (Cod. 249 of the Kirchheim Catalogue of Carmoly's Mss. of 1876). This book has no connection with the work of the above-mentioned Baruch Sheli'aḥ-Ẓibbur Togarmi. It belongs to an entirely different literary environment and it dates from the 14th century. This author already quotes the *Zohar and the **tikkunim,* and is familiar with the homily on Jeremiah 9:22 from the end of the 13th century and possibly later (preserved in the Berlin Hebr. Ms. 193, fol. 79–98 and dated by Steinschneider not before 1350; cf. also HB, 18 (1877), 20). He also copied several passages from Shem Tov *ibn Gaon's work *Baddei ha-Aron,* which was completed in 1325. That is the origin of all the passages which are common to Baruch the Kabbalist's work, and that of Shem Tov's *Sefer ha-Emunot.* Since Baruch undoubtedly knew Shem Tov ibn Gaon's works, there is nothing to uphold Carmoly's assumption that Baruch's book was the one used in the *Emunot. Mafte'aḥ ha-Kabbalah* was not a comprehensive work (Carmoly's manuscript, which is incomplete, contains only 28 folios) and did not add anything novel to the doctrines of Kabbalah, only excerpts from other sources in defense of the Kabbalistic tradition. Moses Botarel relied apparently on this book when he quoted in length from a spurious work *Ḥoshen ha-Mishpat* in his *Yeẓirah* commentary (to ch. 4, mishnah 4). It is possible, however, that Botarel had in mind Baruch Togarmi as the author of a *Yeẓirah* commentary. Botarel also named Baruch among the authorities who dealt with the technique of *She'elat Ḥalom* ("Dream Queries") and, as a matter of fact, Baruch's exposition is still extant in manuscripts (Gaster 603, fol. 9 and in other manuscripts). Apart from this, an older kabbalist named Baruch, who could not have lived after 1400 since he is already mentioned in manuscripts from that period, is mentioned occasionally in manuscripts dealing with practical Kabbalah. In the old Paris manuscript no. 602, he is described as the "father-in-law of the kabbalist Menahem," who is himself unknown. In the Gaster manuscript no. 720, the theurgic use of the so-called *shem ha-kanaf,* i.e., of the mystic "name" *Ẓemarkad,* was transmitted "from the tradition of Baruch." In a work of similar character such as his *Yeẓirah* commentary (which is partly preserved in a Jerusalem manuscript), Botarel attributes a commentary on the *Ḥagigah* talmudic tract, particularly its second chapter, to a kabbalist called Baruch of Narbonne. It is to be assumed that he means by this the same person, who therefore belongs to the second half of the 14th century. S. Sachs, who mistakes this Baruch for the one mentioned above, ascribes *Ma'amar ha-Sekhel* (Cremona, 1557), which gives the 613 commandments a kabbalistic explanation, to him.

Baruch Ashkenazi, who is called by Shem Tov *Attia, in the introduction to his commentary on the Psalms, an "old kabbalist," is, as clearly shown by his surname, a third person. There are no further details about him.

Bibliography: Scholem, Mysticism, 127. [G.Sch.]

BARUCH, prominent U.S. family. Simon (1840–1921) emigrated from his native Posen, Prussia, to America in 1855. He settled in South Carolina, where his first employers, impressed with his talents, assisted him to study at the medical colleges of South Carolina and Virginia. Baruch received his degree in 1862 and became a surgeon in Lee's Confederate Army, serving at the front for three years. Captured and interned at Fort McHenry, he wrote a book on military surgery, *Two Penetrating Wounds of the Chest,* which remained a standard work through World War I. In 1864, he was sent to Thomasville, North Carolina, to prepare hospital facilities for Confederate troops pursuing Sherman. After the war he lived in South Carolina, where he was elected president of the State Medical Association (1874) and chairman of the State Health Board (1880). In 1881 he moved to New York to escape the turbulence of Reconstruction, occupying the chair of hydrotherapy at Columbia University's College of Physicians and Surgeons. Credited with being the first doctor to successfully diagnose and remove a ruptured appendix, he also contributed to the treatment of malaria, childhood diseases, and typhoid fever. He edited the

Journal of Balneology, the *Dietetic and Hygienic Gazette*, and *Gailland's Medical Journal*.

Simon's wife, the former ISOBEL WOLFE of Winnsboro, South Carolina, was a descendant of Isaac Rodriguez Marques, an early colonial settler. The couple had four

Bernard Baruch, U.S. public figure, photographed on his 90th birthday.

sons, Hartwig, Bernard Mannes, Herman Benjamin, and Sailing Wolfe (1874–1962). HARTWIG (1868–1953), the eldest, became a Broadway actor. HERMAN (1872–1953) received a medical degree from the College of Physicians and Surgeons in 1895. He practiced medicine until 1903, when he joined his brother Bernard's Wall Street firm and became a member of the New York Stock Exchange. In 1918 Herman became a lifetime partner in H. Hentz and Company. He entered public service in 1943 when he participated in a Brazil conference sponsored by the board of Economic Warfare. After World War II Herman served as U.S. ambassador to Portugal (1945–47) and as ambassador to the Netherlands (1947–49).

BERNARD BARUCH (1870–1965), stock analyst, self-styled "speculator" and statesman, was born in Camden, South Carolina. He received a B.A. from the City College of New York, and in 1889 he joined the Wall Street firm of Arthur A. Housman. Bernard became a partner in 1896, and a member of the New York Stock Exchange. By 1902, by means of his financial wizardry and careful market research into raw materials such as gold, copper, sulfur, and rubber, he had amassed a fortune of over three million dollars.

Bernard first entered public life in 1916. Then, as a result of his keen knowledge of the raw materials market, President Wilson appointed him to the advisory commission of the Council of National Defense and made him chairman of the Commission on Raw Materials, Minerals, and Metals. During World War I he served as chairman of the War Industries Board with power to virtually mobilize the American wartime economy. At the war's end he served on the Supreme Economic Council at the Conference of Versailles, where he was President Wilson's personal economic adviser, and from that time on his advisory services were sought by every president of the United States. During World War II President Franklin Roosevelt named him chairman of a committee to report on the rubber shortage and to plan a solution. In 1943 he became adviser to War Mobilization Director James Byrnes, and in 1946 he was named the U.S. representative to the United Nations Atomic Energy Commission. In 1939, Bernard advocated a "United States of Africa" in Uganda, as a refuge for Jews and all victims of persecution. The founding of Israel he saw as only a part way solution. No Zionist, he opposed the establishment of any state on the basis of religion, and looked upon himself always as first an American and then a Jew. Bernard was the formal author of the first official United States policy on the control of atomic energy, which he proposed before the United Nations on June 14, 1946. His plan called for the creation of an International Atomic Development Authority, empowered to universally control all dangerous uses of atomic energy and to inspect all atomic installations. It did not prohibit atomic weapons outright, which the Russians demanded, although they rejected inspection. It was vetoed by the USSR in 1948 and it was never adopted. Bernard wrote *American Industry in the War* (1941), *My Own Story* (1957), and a sequel, *Public Years* (1960).

Bibliography: SIMON: DAB; J. R. Marcus (ed.), *Memoirs of American Jews, 1775–1865*, 3 (1956), 269–81; H. Simonhoff, *Saga of American Jewry, 1865–1914* (1959), 125–9; BERNARD: C. Field, *Bernard Baruch* (1944); M. L. Coit, *Mr. Baruch* (1957), incl. bibl.

[M.L.C.]

BARUCH, APOCALYPSE OF (Syriac) (abbr. II Bar.), an apocalyptic work ascribed to Jeremiah's scribe Baruch and purportedly containing the visions of Baruch on the eve of and subsequent to the destruction of Jerusalem. The work has been preserved partly in Greek and all of it in Syriac.

Contents. Chapters 1–4: In the 25th year of Jeconiah, king of Judah, Baruch is commanded to leave Jerusalem as its hour of destruction has come, and as long as he and his righteous companions are in the city, God is unable to destroy it. Baruch is informed in a vision that the destruction will be temporary, affecting only the earthly Jerusalem, the reflection of the heavenly and eternal Jerusalem. Chapters 5–8: The following day Baruch sees four angels with torches setting fire to the city at its four corners, while a fifth angel descends and stores away the sacred vessels of the Temple until the end of days. Chapters 9–12: After seven days Baruch is commanded to beg Jeremiah to accompany the exiles to Babylonia, but he himself is to remain with the ruined Temple. Baruch laments that Zion is destroyed whereas Babylonia is preserved. Chapters 13–20: Seven days later a mysterious voice informs Baruch that he will survive until the end of days. Chapters 21–30: After Baruch has fasted for seven

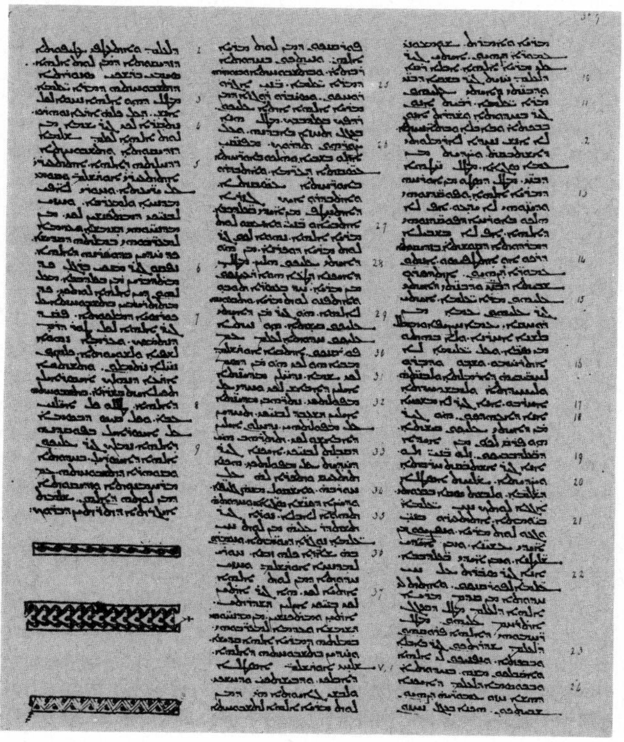

Last page of the Apocalypse of Baruch, from the facsimile edition of the Syriac version, published together with the Latin translation of A. M. Ceriani, Milan, 1876. Jerusalem, J.N.U.L.

days, the voice answers his question: "When will the messianic age come?" He is told that it will come in due time, but not before all the souls destined to be born will have been created. Chapters 31–34: Baruch prophesies to the people that the Temple will be rebuilt, destroyed again, and once more rebuilt for all eternity. Chapters 35–41: While Baruch sits on the ruins of the Temple, a vision is revealed to him. He sees a forest planted in a valley and surrounded by mountains. Opposite the forest is a vine, below which flows a spring. Rising to a mighty stream, the spring overturns the forest, leaving only a cedar standing, but it, too, is soon swept away by the waters of the spring. The interpretation of the vision is: The mountains and the forest are four future kingdoms, the forest being the fourth one; the spring represents the messianic age; the vine is the Messiah; and the cedar is the last ruler of the wicked kingdom (Rome). Chapters 42–52: Baruch goes to Hebron and after he fasts there for seven days, he is informed by the voice that the righteous will be resurrected at the end of days and exalted above the angels. Chapters 53–74: In a final vision, which the angel Ramiel explains to him, Baruch sees a cloud rising from the sea and shedding 12 times alternately dark and bright waters. Lightning, flashing above the black cloud, restores the places destroyed by the dark waters. Twelve rivers arise, but submit to the lightning. The interpretation of the vision is as follows: The six dark waters refer to the sins of man (those of Adam, the Egyptians, the Canaanites, Jeroboam, Manasseh, and the Babylonians), while the six bright waters represent the elect of the nation (Abraham and his progeny; Moses, Aaron, Joshua, and Caleb; David and Solomon; Hezekiah; Josiah; the restoration of Jerusalem in the Second Temple era). The last dark waters refer to the interval between the Second Temple and the advent of the Messiah, a period of causeless hatred and social revolutions, the final flash of lightning being the messianic kingdom. Chapters 75–87: Baruch thanks God for the revelations he has received and writes two letters, one to the ten tribes and the other to the two and a half tribes. Only the contents of the former are given. In this letter, carried by an eagle to the captives in Babylonia, Baruch promises a speedy redemption, if they make full repentance.

The Apocalypse of Baruch and Talmudic Literature. There are many parallels between the Apocalypse of Baruch and *aggadot* in the Talmud and Midrash. According to the *aggadah* (PR 26:131) God likewise commands Jeremiah to leave Jerusalem on the eve of its destruction (II Bar. 2:1); angels set fire to the city (*ibid.*, chs. 6–8); the priests hand over the keys of the Temple to Heaven (Ta'an. 29a; Lev. R. 19:6; PR *ibid.*; ARN^1 4, 12; II Bar. 10:18); Baruch enters Paradise alive (II Bar. 13:3–4; cf. Sif. Num. 99). There are several other features common to the Apocalypse of Baruch and the *aggadah*, such as that Manasseh made an idol with five faces (II Bar. 64:3; Sanh. 103b; Deut. R. 2:13 (20)); that he was burnt to death by the Assyrians (II Bar. 64:7; PdRK 162); that some sacred articles of the Temple (missing subsequently in the Second Temple) were swallowed up by the earth (II Bar. 6:7–8; Yoma 21b; Num. R. 15:10); that the patriarchs knew the Torah (Yoma 28b); and that Abraham, when eating secular meals, observed the rules of levitical cleanness required for sacred food (BM 87a).

There are further parallels between the Apocalypse of Baruch and the *aggadah:* The Heavenly Jerusalem (the counterpart of the earthly Temple), revealed to Adam (II Bar. 4:3; Sif. Deut. 37) and to Abraham in "the covenant between the pieces" (Gen. R. 44:21; 56:10; II Bar. 4:4); the souls in the "treasury" (II Bar. 30:2; Yev. 62a; Sif. Num. 139; ARN ch. 12; Shab. 152b); and the abundance and fertility that would be in time to come (Ket. 100a–b). The language of many ancient prayers is very similar to that of Baruch (cf. 11:4 "those that sleep in the dust"; 54:13—which resembles the language in the **Nishmat* prayer).

In form and purpose the Apocalypse of Baruch is close to IV *Ezra, but it is impossible to determine which was composed first. In any event the Apocalypse of Baruch was written shortly after the destruction of the Second Temple (see II Bar. 20:2–4) and before the Bar Kokhba revolt. The Syriac version, which is derived from the Greek translation, was published in 1861 in Latin by A. M. Ceriani (*Monumenta sacra et profana*, t. 1^2, I–IV, 73–98), as well as in facsimile (1876–83). The work was undoubtedly written originally in Hebrew (see II Bar. 21:14; see Greek Apocalypse of *Baruch; Rest of the Words of *Baruch).

Bibliography: F. Rosenthal, *Vier apocryphische Buecher aus der Zeit und Schule R. Akibas* (1885); Ryssel, in: Kautzsch, *Apokryphen und Pseudepigraphen*, 2 (1900), 404ff.; M. Kmosko, *Patriologia Syriaca*, 2 (1907); Schuerer, Gesch, 3 (1909^4), 305–15; Charles, Apocrypha, 2 (1913), 470–526; Perles, in: REJ, 73 (1921), 182–3; B. Violet, *Die Apokalypsen des Esra und des Baruch* (1924); P. Riessler, *Altjuedisches Schrifttum ausserhalb der Bibel* (1928), 55–113; A. Kahana, (ed.), *Ha-Sefarim ha-Ḥizonim*, 1 (1936), 362–407; J. Klausner, *Ha-Ra'yon ha-Meshiḥi be-Yisrael* (1950^3); Klausner, Bayit Sheni, 5 (1951^2), 291–4.

[J.M.G.]

BARUCH, BOOK OF (abbr. I Bar.), an apocryphal book which together with the Epistle of *Jeremiah is associated in the Septuagint with the writings attributed to the prophet Jeremiah and is regarded as canonical in both the Eastern and Latin churches. It purports to be a letter sent by *Baruch, Jeremiah's amanuensis, from Babylonia to Palestine after the destruction of the First Temple (1:1–4). It contains five chapters which fall into two or three sections. The first (1:1–3:8) opens with Baruch's reading of the book to the people assembled in Babylonia on the banks of the river Soud (LXX Σοῦδ, Syriac *ṣwr;* cf. 4QpJer *swr*) and the assembled multitude's repentance and mourning (1:1–14). This is followed by a penitential prayer which comprises the remainder of the prose section. The first part of this prayer strongly resembles the prayer in Daniel 9:4–19 and a comparison leads to the conclusion that the prayer in Baruch is based on that in Daniel. The continuation of the prayer (2:20–3:8) is composed of a mosaic of biblical verses and some original sections. Prayers of repentance associated with public fasts and lamentation are mentioned in the literature of the period (cf. I Macc. 3:46–54; Judith 4:8ff.; and Ta'an 2:1). In form, the prayers in Baruch and Daniel show a strong resemblance to the liturgical texts from Qumran called *Divrei ha-Me'orot* (Baillet, in RB, 58 (1961), 195–250). The second section (3:9–44) is sapiential in character. It is addressed to Israel (3:9) and in part reproaches Israel for abandoning wisdom and in part praises wisdom. This poem contrasts the true wisdom known to Israel with that of the peoples of the East, famed for their wisdom. The passage, in common with Ben Sira and later wisdom writing, identifies true wisdom with that revealed to Israel, i.e., with the Torah. The final section of the book is composed of two poems of lamentation and comfort. The first (4:9–29) is a message of solace addressed to Israel by a personified Jerusalem, seen as a mother bewailing her children (4:10, 12, etc.). In 4:30 the speaker changes and Jerusalem is herself comforted with the message of the eventual redemption of Israel. The book is extant in Greek, Syriac, Syro-Hexaplar, three Old Latin versions, as well as Armenian, Arabic, Ethiopic, and Coptic. It has been suggested that the translation of the first section into Greek was the work of the translator of the second part of Septuagint Jeremiah (Thackeray, in: JTS, 4 (1903), 261–6). The question of the original language is intimately related to that of the literary unity of the work. A number of scholars have proposed that the book is a compilation of two or three original documents: the prayers of confession, the wisdom poem, and the laments. In general, all agree that the first section (1:1–3:8) was written in Hebrew, and most scholars who accept the documentary theory consider the third section (4:9–5:9) to be originally

Greek and dependent on Wisdom of Solomon II (Charles, Apocrypha, 1 (1913), 572–3). This stance, modified by a vigorous defense of the coherence of the present form of the book as the work of a single "author-redactor" has been supported by Wambacq (*Biblica,* 47 (1966), 574–6), while A. Cahana in his Hebrew edition maintained the theory of literary unity and original Hebrew (*Ha-Sefarim ha-Ḥiẓonim,* 1 (1936), 350ff.). The book has been dated variously between the late Hasmonean period (*ante quem non*—dependence on Daniel) and the destruction of the Second Temple (the historical framework of the book). The existence of further Baruch-Jeremiah apocrypha at Qumran weakens this latter argument considerably.

Bibliography: Charles, Apocrypha, 1 (1913), 569–95; J. J. Kneucker, *Das Buch Baruch* (1879); R. Harwell, *The Principal Versions of Baruch* (1915); B. N. Wambacq, in: *Sacra Pagina,* 1 (1959), 455–60; idem, in: *Biblica,* 40 (1959), 463–75; O. Eissfeldt, *The Old Testament, an Introduction* (1965), 592–4 (includes bibliography).

[M.E.S.]

BARUCH, GREEK APOCALYPSE OF (abbr. III Bar.), an apocalypse describing the journey of *Baruch through the heavens. Baruch, Jeremiah's scribe, weeps over the destruction of Jerusalem and questions God's righteousness. He is granted this heavenly journey in order to subdue his anger and console him in his grief. In the introduction, the angel of the Lord offers to show the mourning Baruch the secrets of God. He takes him to the First Heaven where they see men in monstrous form who are identified as the people who built the Tower of Babel. The angel also explains certain measurements of the First Heaven. In the Second Heaven they meet doglike human monsters who initiated the building of the tower. In the Third Heaven, the angel shows Baruch the dragon in Hades; he also tells him how it came about that God permitted Noah to plant the cursed vine which had been the cause of Adam and Eve's sin (the vine being identified with the forbidden fruit of the Garden of Eden—cf. Ber. 40a; Gen. R. 19:5). God promises him to change the curse into a blessing; the angel, however, warns against overindulgence in wine, for the most awful sins result from it. In this heaven Baruch also observes the coming and going of the sun and the moon. The sun's chariot is driven by four angels; other angels are busy purifying the sun's crown, defiled by men's daily sins. The phoenix absorbs with his wings most of the fiery rays of the sun, so as to prevent life on earth from burning up. Baruch is frightened by this spectacle and by the accompanying thunder. Next, the angel and Baruch pass the dwelling place of the righteous souls. In the Fifth Heaven, Baruch sees the archangel Michael weighing the good deeds of people, brought by the angel appointed over each individual, and sending them their reward. The angels who could not bring any good deeds from their protégés are ordered to attend upon the sinners until they repent, and if they do not, to inflict upon them all the prophesied evils. Baruch then returns to the earth and is instructed to reveal to the sons of men those of God's secrets which he has seen and heard.

In the present form the Greek Apocalypse of Baruch is the work of a Christian writer: the Christological interpretation of the vine in chapter 4; the citation from the New Testament in chapter 15; and the technical terms deriving from a Christian background, namely ἐκκλησία ("church") and πνευματικοὶ πατέρες ("spiritual fathers") in chapter 13 are organic parts of the present story and cannot possibly be explained as mere interpolations. It is obvious however that this is not the original form of the book. The ultimate aim of the traveler through the heavens is to see the Glory of God, an aim usually attained in the Seventh Heaven (cf. Slavonic Enoch, ch. 9ff.; Test. Patr. Levi 3:8; Ḥag. 12b. etc.). Indeed, twice in the book (III Bar. 7:2; 11:2) the guiding angel assures Baruch, "Wait and you shall see the Glory of God," a promise which is never fulfilled, for Baruch reaches no further than the Fifth Heaven. This reinforces the probability that the present work is a later version of an apocalypse of Baruch which in an earlier version, mentioned by *Origen (*De principiis* 2:3, 6), included the Seven Heavens.

The main issues dealt with in the Greek Apocalypse of Baruch are the heavenly mechanisms of, and causes behind, cosmological matters, and man's just reward for his deeds. The latter brings it into the realm of the testament- and Adam-literature; it is in the light of this genre and not in that of direct New Testament influence (as M. R. James avers) that the lists of sins (III Bar. 4:7; 8:5; 13:4) should be understood. The uranological traditions of the Greek Apocalypse of Baruch are closely related to the Enoch books (cf. Ethiopic Enoch chs. 72, 73; Slavonic Enoch chs. 3–9, esp. 6); some stories have parallels in aggadic literature (see Ginzberg, and Artom's notes in Kahana); the theme that the souls of the righteous dwell as birds around a lake (ch. 10) might well be of Egyptian origin (in the hieroglyphics the bird designates the heavenly soul).

The Apocalypse is written in a very simple Koine-Greek of late antiquity; there is no evidence that it was translated from a Semitic language. Two Slavonic versions (see Picard, pp. 70–71 and Turdeanu) mainly follow the Greek text.

Bibliography: S. Novaković, in: *Starine,* 18 (1886), 203–9; M. I. Sokolov, in: *Drevnosti,* no.4, 201–58; M. R. James, *Apocrypha Anecdota,* 2 (1897), li-lxxi, 83–102; V. Ryssel, in: E. Kautzsch (ed.), *Die Apocryphen und Pseudepigraphen,* 2 (1900), 446–57; L. Ginzberg, in: JE, 2 (1902), 549–51; W. Luedtke, in: ZAW, 31 (1911), 219–22; H. M. Hughes, in: Charles, Apocrypha, 2 (1913), 527–41; E. S. Artom, *Ha-Sefarim ha-Ḥiẓonim, Ḥazon Barukh 2* (1967); idem, in: A. Kahana (ed.), *Ha-Sefarim ha-Ḥiẓonim,* 1 (1936), 408–25; E. Turdeanu, in: RHR, 138 (1950), 177–81; J.-C. Picard (ed.). *Apocalypse Baruchi graece* (1967), 61–96.

[YA.G.]

BARUCH, JACOB BEN MOSES ḤAYYIM (late 18th century), author and editor, born in Leghorn. Baruch is especially known for his *Shivḥei Yerushalayim* ("The Praises of Jerusalem") or *Shabbeḥi Yerushalayim* ("Praise, O Jerusalem"), an anthology of excerpts from various authors containing extracts from the following works: *Ẓaḥ ve-Adom* by Raphael Treves, on the holy places in Jerusalem; *Imrei Kadosh* from the *Sha'ar ha-Gilgulim* of Samuel b. Ḥayyim Vital; and an Ereẓ Israel travelog, whose author remained unidentified for a long time and it was unknown whether Baruch's text constituted the whole of his work or merely extracts from it. Another manuscript was published in a scholarly edition by Izhak Ben-Zvi (1938), who identified the traveler as Moses Bassola, a conclusion which had been reached earlier by Azariah de' Rossi on his examination of the manuscript (*Me'or Einayim,* ch. 56; ed. D. Cassel (1866), 450), which Ben-Zvi has shown was the one used by Baruch. *Shivḥei* (or *Shabbeḥi*) *Yerushalayim* (first published at Leghorn in 1785) enjoyed great popularity, particularly because of its lively description of the holy sites visited, and it appeared in more than ten editions. In 1790 Baruch edited *Sha'ar ha-Ḥeshek* ("The Portal of Delight"), which comprises a large part of the introduction to Johanan *Allemanno's *Ḥeshek Shelomo* on Song of Songs, an elaboration on King Solomon's wisdom.

Bibliography: I. Ben-Zvi, *She'ar Yashuv* (1927), 17–79; idem (ed.), *Masot Ereẓ Yisrael le-R. Moshe Basola* (1938); A. Yaari, *Masot Ereẓ Yisrael* (1946), 125–65.

[Y.AL.]

ספר
שבח"י ירושלים
לידע ולהודיע איפה הם רועים גדולים צדיקים
במיתתן שלמים וכן רבים מישיני אדמת
עפר חלקם בחיים · הולדות הם של צדיקים כיוצא
בהם ונונה להם מי מרד זכיותם וצדקתם מהאי
שופרא דבלי בארעא יחסיתא דצדיקייא במיתתן
קרויים חיים · הא לכם זרע קדש דברי פי חכם חן
אשר לא היה לעולמים מה שכתב רבינו מוהרד"ו
זצוק"ל ממה שקבל מרבינו האר"י זצוק"ל בלשונו
לשון הזהב אות באות אשר חדשות הוא מגיד
ומגלה מסתגרין ראשונים כמלאכים השמוני' בארץ
החיים · ועוד זאת יתירה פרשת אלה מסעי מאיש
נבון וחכם לא נודע שמו אשר היה בשנת רפ"ב לפ"ק
הששי וילך סובב בכל א"י לדעת דבר דבור על
אופניו אנבי העירותיהו לזכות את הרבים וימצאו
הכל כשלחן ערוך אשר כל מוצאו ימצא חיים :
מידי היתה זאת לכם הצעיר וזעיר יעקב ברוך
נר"ו והמחזיקים בידי ישאו ברכה מאת
ה' פטון ושמחה ישיגו כל הימים אשר כס חיים · כיר"א
פה ליוורנו יע"א
מנת וכחל ה' את יהודה חלקו על אדמת הקדש
ובחר עוד בירושלים לפ"ק ·
בדפוס השותפים
החכם כמהר"ר אברהם יצחק קאשטילו י"ץ
והמשכיל כמהר"ר אליעזר סעדון י"ץ

Title page of the first edition of Jacob b. Moses Ḥayyim Baruch's anthology, *Shivḥei Yerushalayim,* Leghorn, Italy, 1785. Jerusalem, J.N.U.L.

BARUCH, JOSEPH MARCOU (1872–1899), early Zionist propagandist in Western Europe and Mediterranean countries. Baruch, born in Constantinople, conducted an anti-assimilation campaign among Jewish students in Berne and was wounded in a duel with a non-Jewish student over an anti-Semitic remark. In 1893 Baruch went to Vienna and joined the student circle of the Zionist Kadimah association. In 1894, in Algeria, he edited the newspaper *Le Juge,* in which, despite the opposition of local Jewish leaders, he tried to awaken the national consciousness of Algerian Jewry. Registered with the police as an anarchist, Baruch was compelled to leave the country. In 1895, after returning to Vienna, he went to Bulgaria and established a Zionist group in Sofia. In Philippopolis (Plovdiv) he published a French-language newspaper with a Ladino supplement, called *Carmel,* and helped establish Zionist associations in various Bulgarian towns, until he was imprisoned. He was released under the protection of Prince Konstantinov, and in 1896 left Bulgaria for Egypt where he continued his Zionist activity in Port Said, Alexandria, and Cairo. Some of his ideas later reached Herzl, particularly his criticism of "infiltration" (i.e., small-scale settlement in Palestine without prior political guarantees), and his advocacy of the foundation of an internationally recognized Jewish state. Toward this end he proposed war with Turkey, even joining the group called Garibaldi's army, which eventually fought for the liberation of Crete from Turkish rule. When Herzl appeared on the Zionist scene, Baruch was among his supporters. He attended the Second and Third Zionist Congresses (1898, 1899), and went on Zionist propaganda tours. Herzl's feelings for Baruch alternated between sympathy and dislike, as a result of the latter's eccentric personality, and Herzl was even afraid he might make an attempt on his life. Baruch's last days were spent in Italy, where he published his book *Le Juif à l'Ile du Diable,* a defense of Alfred Dreyfus. He committed suicide in Florence.

Bibliography: Y. Weinschal, *Marcou Baruch, Nevi Milḥemet ha-Shiḥrur* (1949); T. Herzl, *Complete Diaries,* ed. by R. Patai, 5 (1960), index; Molcho, in: *Haolam,* 33 (1946), 16–18; M. D. Gaon, *Yehudei ha-Mizraḥ be-Ereẓ Yisrael be-Avar u-va-Hoveh,* 2 (1938), 172–5.

[G.K.]

BARUCH, REST OF THE WORDS OF, apocryphal book, also called *Paralipomena Jeremiae* (Chronicles of Jeremiah) in its present form, a Christian reworking of a patently Jewish source. It is connected with the wider Baruch and Jeremiah literature represented also by the Syriac and Greek Apocalypses of *Baruch, the Greek Book of *Baruch, the Epistle of *Jeremiah, as well as fragments from Qumran Cave 4.

Its story opens with the destruction of the Temple, which is announced by God to Jeremiah. At God's orders, Jeremiah buries the Temple vessels beneath the Temple, where they are to remain until the coming of the Messiah. He also enquires what is to be done with the slave Abimelech (Ebedmelech of Jer. 38, and one Armenian recension) and is instructed to send him to Agrippa's vineyard where he would be hidden until the return from exile. Jeremiah was to go with the exiles of Babylon (cf. Jer. 43, but see SOR 26), while Baruch was to remain in Jerusalem.

The role played by Abimelech is unique to this book. He arrives in Agrippa's vineyard to pick some figs and, it being midday, lies down to rest and awakens only after 66 years. He examines his figs and finds them fresh. Going to Jerusalem, he does not recognize the city and, in his confusion, accosts an old man who tells him of what has happened while he slept. He is led to Baruch by an angel and they rejoice over the miracle of the figs in which they see a sign of redemption. Baruch prays for guidance in sending a letter to Jeremiah and the following morning a miraculous eagle appears and carries Baruch's letter and some of the figs to Jeremiah. To prove its genuineness, the eagle alights on the body of a dead man and he is restored to life. Jeremiah then reads the letter to the people in Babylon; they repent and weep, and the exiles set forth for Jerusalem. Before they depart, however, Jeremiah examines them to ensure that there are no uncircumcised among them and none married to foreign women. Those who are thus disqualified desire to return to Babylon, but are not permitted to do so by the Babylonians, and so they build themselves the city of Samaria. The story concludes with the offering of sacrifices in Jerusalem and Jeremiah's death in the Temple. The sequel is Christian and, as generally agreed, not part of the original work. This story is extant in Greek, various Slavonic, Ethiopic, Coptic (P. Morgan Ms. 601), and three different Armenian recensions. The problem of textual history and the relationship between the various text forms have not been adequately studied. Klausner (EIV, s.v.) defends the primacy of the Ethiopic but, like most previous students of the work, he was not familiar with the Armenian recensions. The Jewish nature of the original is apparent from many distinctive features. Thus the approval of sacrifice, the rejection of foreign women, and the attitude to circumcision, to mention the most prominent, clearly disprove the theory of a Christian original.

It is probable that the book was composed after the

destruction of the Second Temple, and some would even suggest that the hatred displayed toward the Samaritans indicates a date in the reign of the emperor Hadrian. It depends at many points on the Syriac Apocalypse of *Baruch. Recent studies have emphasized the prominence of Jewish religious ideas and terminology in this work.

Bibliography: A. Dillmann, *Chrestomathia Aethiopica* (1866), 1–15; J. R. Harris, *The Rest of the Words of Baruch* (1889); J. Issaverdens, *Uncanonical Writings of the Old Testament* (1900); E. Kautzsch, *Apokryphen und Pseudepigraphen des Alten Testaments*, 2 (1900), 402ff.; DBI, suppl. 1 (1928), 454f. (incl. bibl.); J. Klausner, *Meḥkarim Ḥadashim u-Mekorot Attikim* (1957), 90–117; J. Licht, in: *Bar Ilan, Sefer ha-Shanah*, 1 (1963), 66–80; G. Delling, *Juedische Lehre und Froemmigkeit in den Paralipomena Jeremiae* (1967); W. Baars, in: VT, 17 (1967), 487ff.

[M.E.S.]

BARUCH BEN DAVID YAVAN (18th cent.), *Court Jew of the Polish king August III, financier of his minister Count Bruehl. He was a leader in the *Council of Four Lands and as **shtadlan* for the Council used his influence at court for furthering Jewish causes. Baruch received a talmudic education under R. Jacob Joshua *Falk and knew several languages. He was prominent in combating the remnants of *Shabbateanism and the *Frankists. In the controversy over Jonathan *Eybeschuetz' adherence to Shabbateanism he upheld Jacob *Emden (who was related to him by their children's marriage) in his condemnation of Eybeschuetz. Baruch did not hesitate to effect the removal of Ḥayyim b. Abraham, an adherent of Eybeschuetz, from his post of rabbi of Lublin and his imprisonment in 1751. Baruch took a leading role in Jewish diplomatic efforts to counter the Frankists. When the disputation between the talmudists and Frankists became in 1757 the occasion for an ecclesiastical order to burn the Talmud, Baruch, aided by the *shtadlan* Mordecai Merkil, sought the help of Count Bruehl. He obtained access to the papal nuncio and succeeded in saving many talmudic works. Baruch also persuaded Count Bruehl to use his influence at the papal curia to thwart the *blood libel instigated by Frank. In 1764 he frustrated Frank's intrigues with Russia, using his connections with the Russian nobility to convince the synodal authorities of the Russian Orthodox Church that Frank's application for acceptance into their faith was insincere.

Bibliography: H. Graetz, *Frank und die Frankisten* (1868); A. Kraushar, *Frank i Frankiści* (1895); M. Balaban, *Le-Toledot ha-Tenu'ah ha-Frankit* (1934).

[N.M.G.]

BARUCH BEN ISAAC OF ALEPPO (c. 1050–c. 1125), scholar. Baruch appears to have been born in Spain, where he studied together with his younger kinsman *Baruch b. Samuel of Aleppo. From there he went to Aleppo where he was the head of a large yeshivah. From 1085 his signature appears on various documents, among them a letter of recommendation on behalf of Obadiah the Proselyte of Normandy. He wrote a commentary on the order *Kodashim*, of the Babylonian Talmud, which was highly recommended by *Joseph Rosh ha-Seder, who considered it equal to the commentaries of *Hananel b. Ḥushi'el on the orders *Mo'ed*, *Nashim*, and *Nezikin* and of *Isaac b. Melchizedek on *Zera'im* and *Tohorot*. He also wrote commentaries on other tractates, including *Shabbat* (quoted by Isaiah di Trani in his commentary on this tractate) and *Bava Meẓia* (see *Ginzei Kedem*, 5 (1934), 131–4). S. Assaf was of the opinion that the commentary on tractate *Zevaḥim* (Jerusalem, 1942), attributed to Hananel, was by Baruch, but this identification does not appear to be correct.

Bibliography: Mann, in: *Ha-Tekufah*, 24 (1928), 337, 352–4; Epstein, in: *Tarbiz*, 16 (1944/45), 49–53; Assaf, *ibid.*, 19 (1947/48), 105–8.

[I.T.-S.]

BARUCH BEN ISAAC OF REGENSBURG (second half of 12th century), talmudic scholar. He was a member of the *bet din* of Regensburg, together with *Isaac b. Jacob Ha-Lavan of Prague, Abraham ben Moses of Regensburg, and *Judah he-Ḥasid b. Samuel (*Sefer Ḥasidim*, ed. by J. Wistinetzki (1924[2]), 390). Baruch was one of the teachers of *Abraham b. Azriel, the author of *Arugat ha-Bosem*. There is record of a question addressed to Baruch and his two fellow judges by R. *Joel ben Isaac ha-Levi (*Sefer Ravyah*, no. 1031). Baruch engaged in disputations with his older contemporary *Eliezer b. Nathan of Mainz, who esteemed him highly, and with *Isaac b. Samuel ha-Zaken of Dampierre. Some scholars have incorrectly identified him with *Baruch b. Isaac of Worms, author of the *Sefer ha-Terumah*.

Bibliography: H. Gross, in: MGWJ, 34 (1885), 558–60; idem, in: ZHB, 11 (1907), 179; J. Wellesz, in: MGWJ, 48 (1904), 442; V. Aptowitzer *Mavo le-Sefer Ravyah* (1938), 174, 326–9; Urbach, Tosafot, 286ff., 299, 334; idem, *Arugat ha-Bosem* (1963), index; idem, in: *Tarbiz*, 10 (1938/39), 86ff.

[M.N.Z./ED.]

BARUCH BEN ISAAC OF WORMS (late 12th–early 13th century), German tosafist. Although Baruch lived in Worms, he probably came from France and is sometimes referred to as **Ha-Ẓarefati** ("the Frenchman"). Baruch was a pupil of *Isaac b. Samuel the Elder, of Dampierre, and after his teacher's death, spent a considerable amount of time in France with Judah of Paris. Baruch emigrated to Ereẓ Israel (1237?). It seems certain that he is not to be identified with *Baruch b. Isaac of Regensburg.

He is renowned as the author of *Sefer ha-Terumah* (written shortly before 1202; first published Venice, 1523), which comprises a summary of the established *halakhot* on several subjects, including the laws pertaining to Ereẓ Israel, combined and arranged according to the chapters of the relevant tractates of the Talmud. The whole work reflects the teachings of Isaac b. Samuel. In it Baruch mentions *Samuel b. Meir (Rashbam) and *Isaac b. Meir, as well as statements of Rabbi Jacob *Tam and his pupils; however, very few German scholars are referred to. By virtue of its wealth of material and its terse, easy style, well adapted to its purpose of leading, through discussion, to the practical *halakhah*, the book spread through France, Germany, Italy, and Spain, and was widely quoted by many later authorities among them, *Eliezer of Worms, *Isaac b. Moses Or Zarua, *Moses b. Jacob of Coucy, Zedekiah *Anav, *Aaron b. Jacob of Lunel, and *Naḥmanides. Entire halakhic passages from the work were inserted by copyists into the **Maḥzor Vitry*. Numerous manuscripts of *Sefer ha-Terumah* and some manuscripts of an anonymous abridgment are extant. Baruch also wrote *tosafot* to several tractates of the Talmud, but only those on *Zevaḥim* have been preserved and they are printed in the standard editions of the Talmud. A. Epstein held that the anonymous commentary on *Tamid* atrributed to Abraham b. David (Prague, 1725) should be ascribed to Baruch, but—despite a measure of similarity between the commentary and a number of quotations in Baruch's name which are known—this is unlikely. E. E. Urbach has maintained that the commentary on the *Sifra* ascribed to Abraham b. David was written by Baruch, but this too is uncertain.

Bibliography: A. Epstein, *Das talmudische Lexikon "Yiḥusei Tanna'im ve-Amora'im"* (1895); Urbach, Tosafot, 263, 286–99, 511–2; V. Aptowitzer, *Mavo le-Sefer Ravyah* (1938), 327–8.

[I.T-S.]

BARUCH BEN JEHIEL OF MEDZIBEZH (1757–1810), ḥasidic *ẓaddik;* grandson of *Israel b. Eliezer the Baal Shem Tov, the founder of modern *Ḥasidism. Baruch, who studied under Phinehas Shapira of Korets, officiated from 1780 as rabbi in Tulchin, but encountered opposition and returned to Medzibezh in 1788. He attributed great importance to his descent and regarded himself as the heir to the Ba'al Shem Tov's leadership. He held that the *ẓaddik* could save and lead the whole world; the duty of the common man was only "to destroy the evil impulses and abandon his desires." Regarding himself the leader of Ḥasidism by hereditary right, he held "court" in Medzibezh in a highly autocratic and luxurious fashion, though preaching asceticism to others. He kept a "court jester," Hershele Ostropoler. His behavior aroused opposition from other ḥasidic leaders. In 1808 he met Shneur Zalman of Lyady in an effort to settle their differences. Baruch attached mystical importance to the custom practiced by Ḥasidim of giving presents to the rabbis *(pidyonot).* He encouraged Ḥasidim to emigrate to Ereẓ Israel. He took part in the assembly of ḥasidic rabbis at Berdichev (1802–03) which discussed the government's prohibition of Jewish settlement in the villages among other matters. His writings include *Amarot Tehorot* (1865; first published in his brother's (*Moses Ḥayyim Ephraim) *Degel Maḥaneh Ephraim,* Zhitomir, 1850), and *Buẓina di-Nehora,* 1880).

Bibliography: M. Bodek, *Seder ha-Dorot he-Ḥadash* (1865), 23; Horodezky, Ḥasidut, 3 (1953[4]), 12–17; Dubnow, Ḥasidut, 1 (1930), 205–8; M. Buber, *Tales of the Ḥasidim,* 1 (1947), 87–97; M. E. Gutman, *Mi-Gibborei ha-Ḥasidut,* 3 (1928). [N.A.]

BARUCH BEN SAMUEL (d. 1834), adventurer and physician. Baruch was born in Pinsk, and emigrated to Safed in 1819. The reports of a messenger who traveled from Safed to Yemen and back in 1825 gave rise to wondrous tales about a Jew from the tribe of Dan whom he allegedly met in Yemen and of stories about the "Sons of Moses" and the Ten Tribes. The community of Safed decided to send a messenger to these remote Jews to come to the aid of their brethren in Palestine. They chose Baruch who, in their opinion, possessed the qualities necessary for such a bold undertaking. They gave him a letter addressed to the Ten Tribes and made him swear to devote himself wholly to this task.

Baruch started his journey in 1831. His travels took him to Damascus, Aleppo, Kurdistan, Mesopotamia, Baghdad, Basra, Bushire, Muscat, and Aden. Toward the end of 1833 Baruch reached Yemen. The rabbis of San'a received him cordially and one of the members of the community (*dayyan* Māri Yiḥye al-Abyat) accompanied him to Ḥaydān at the northern extremity of Yemen, where, according to the rumor, the tribe of Dan lived. Baruch and his companion made their way into the desert where they met a shepherd, who appeared to them like a Danite. They gave him the letter and he promised to deliver the answer to them in Ḥaydān. Then Baruch and his companion hurried back to San'a for the autumn Holidays. The Jews of Ḥaydān promised to forward the anticipated answer to San'a, but it never came.

When Baruch returned to San'a, he offered to cure the sickly imam of Yemen, al-Mahdi. He hoped thereby to enlist the imam's aid in the completion of his mission. After his recovery, the imam appointed Baruch his court physician. Baruch began to behave haughtily toward the Muslims, and thus aroused their enmity and jealousy. In 1834 Ibrahim Pasha of Egypt attacked Yemen and captured Mocha. Baruch assured the imam that if he would give him an army, he would drive out the conqueror on condition that afterward he himself be appointed the ruler of that city. This proposal served Baruch's enemies as a pretext for charging him with spying for Egypt. The imam believed this false accusation and in February, 1834, during his daily walk in the garden with Baruch, the imam shot his physician. The dying Baruch predicted that the Imam and his family would lose their kingdom. His prediction came true in less than a year.

Bibliography: J. Saphir, *Even Sappir,* 1 (1866), 83–86; E. Brauer, *Ethnologie der jemenitischen Juden* (1934), 42–44; Yaari, Sheluḥei, 147ff. [Y.R.]

BARUCH BEN SAMUEL OF ALEPPO (also called **Baruch of Greece,** or the Sephardi; 1070/80–1130/40), talmudic commentator. It is surmised that he was either from southern Italy or Spain. He emigrated to Ereẓ Israel and then to Aleppo, from where he sent questions to Samuel b. Ali, head of the Baghdad yeshivah. His commentaries are frequently quoted by the scholars of Germany, Italy, Provence, and Spain, among them *Isaac b. Moses of Vienna, author of *Or Zaru'a* and *Isaiah b. Mali di Trani. He is mostly quoted by Zechariah *Agmati in his commentary on *Bava Kamma, Bava Meẓia* and *Bava Batra.* Baruch relied mainly on *Hananel's commentary and *Perushei Magenza* (Mainz) attributed to *Gershom b. Judah. He followed the method of giving a precis of the talmudic text and interweaving his own commentary. Like *Nissim b. Jacob and Hananel b. Ḥushiel he referred to the talmudic sources, *Sifra, Sifrei,* and Tosefta, and was meticulous with regard to variant readings. He also wrote *Ḥibbur Tohorot,* which is mentioned by Isaiah di Trani, and a book of halakhic decisions. Only his commentary to *Horayot* has survived and is printed in the Romm editions of the Talmud, although erroneously ascribed to Hananel.

Bibliography: S. Assaf, in: *Tarbiz,* 1 no. 1 (1930), 126; Epstein, *ibid.,* 1 no. 4 (1930), 27–62; 16 (1944/45), 49–53. [J.Ho.]

BARUCH BEN SAMUEL OF MAINZ (c. 1150–1221), scholar and *paytan.* Baruch was a pupil of Moses b. Solomon ha-Kohen, whom he succeeded as a member of the *bet din* of Mainz. There is no basis for Aptowitzer's statement that a dispute for the position between him and his kinsman, *Eliezer b. Samuel of Metz, took place. Baruch also studied under *Judah b. Kalonymus b. Meir of Speyer, and possibly *Ephraim b. Isaac of Regensburg. He was in halakhic correspondence with many contemporary scholars, including *Judah he-Ḥasid.

Baruch is best known for his *Sefer ha-Ḥokhmah,* a comprehensive work (now lost) covering the subject matter of *Nashim* and *Nezikin,* as well as the laws of *Issur ve-Hetter;* it also included his responsa. The work was still extant in the 16th century when Solomon *Luria and Bezalel *Ashkenazi used it. It is extensively quoted by the *rishonim,* particularly by *Mordecai b. Hillel and by *Meir b. Baruch of Rothenburg, sometimes being referred to as "The Book of Baruch of Mainz." Baruch is not mentioned at all by name in *tosafot,* although some ascribe to him the authorship of the printed *tosafot* to *Sotah.* Of Baruch's *piyyutim,* 33 of which have been preserved (published by Habermann—see bibl.), some deal with the persecutions in *Blois (1171), *Speyer and *Boppard (1196), and Wuerzburg (before 1221), and are a valuable historical source. One *piyyut* is devoted to the talmudic discussion *"ilan de-Ulla"* ("the tree of Ulla," BB 26b–27a), a rare phenomenon in *piyyut.* These *piyyutim,* some of which are rhymed, excel in their variety and their style—biblical language being interspersed with the language of rabbinical and early mystical literature. Baruch revised a number of his *piyyutim* in order to bring them up to date, as in the *seliḥot, Be-Terem Noledu Harim* and *Be-Terem Har* *ve-Givah.* Highly popular among congregants, his *seliḥot* were affectionately termed *"berukhah," "mevorekhet,"* and *"mevorakh"* ("blessed," a play on words from his name). His son, R. SAMUEL OF BAMBERG, the teacher of R. *Meir b. Baruch of Rothenburg, was also noted as an halakhic scholar and as a *paytan.*

Bibliography: Urbach, Tosafot, 134–6, 352–4; Habermann, in: YMḤSI, 6 (1945), 47ff.; Epstein, in: *Tarbiz,* 12 (1940/41), 190–6; idem, in: MGWJ, 83 (1939, 1963²), 346–55; Davidson, Oẓar 4 (1933), 373; Germ Jud, 1 (1934), 201; V. Aptowitzer (ed.), *Mavo le-Sefer Ravyah* (1938), 313–4, 329–30.

[I.T.-S./ED.]

BARUCH (ben Abraham) OF KOSOV (c. 1725/30–1795), kabbalist. He was a disciple of *Menahem Mendel of Vitebsk and also studied with *Menahem Mendel of Przemyslany for a short while. Baruch became *maggid* in Kosov. In his sermons he tried to make the kabbalist doctrine, as taught mainly by Isaac *Luria and Ḥayyim *Vital, easily comprehensible by the use of explanatory metaphors. According to Baruch, Luria was the highest authority on Kabbalah. Therefore, he advised all who wished to study the *Zohar, first to read Luria and Vital. Baruch interpreted (as did Joseph *Ergas) Luria's doctrine of *"*ẓimẓum*" (i.e., God's self-willed withdrawal), as a metaphor and not as an actual fact. On this point he argued against the realistic interpretation of Immanuel Ḥai *Ricchi. Baruch taught that the true life of every material entity was conditioned by its spiritual aspect. He therefore contended that full surrender and complete attachment to God was possible because this was an intellectual discipline originating in a love which knows no limits. He maintained that it was possible to attain a concept of things, first through the senses, then on a higher level, through the imagination, and finally, at the highest stage, through wisdom. It was only through wisdom that one could perceive the spiritual quality inherent in every material being. Only wisdom had the capacity to feel the pain which the soul inevitably felt when man committed a sin. Baruch conceded that the questions of predestination and free will were so difficult as to be unanswerable. Nevertheless he believed in both, and counseled unconditional belief in them (*Ammud ha-Avodah,* 54–55, 107; *Yesod ha-Emmunah,* 76–99). Baruch was totally and aggressively against the followers of *Shabbetai Ẓevi and Jacob *Frank. In 1760 his antagonism to the latter apparently motivated him to begin writing the above books with the aim of refuting the anthropomorphism applied by Frankists to the basic concepts of Kabbalah. From 1761 he had started to collect from learned authorities their written commentaries on the manuscripts of his books. However, it was only in 1854 that they were actually printed in Czernowitz: (1) *Yesod ha-Emunah,* on the Pentateuch and miscellanies; (2) *Ammud ha-Avodah,* on the basic questions of Kabbalah, including "a lengthy introduction to explain the essence of the spiritual entities."

Bibliography: A. Yaari, *Meḥkerei Sefer* (1958), 453–4; I. Tishby, in: *Zion,* 32 (1967), 24–29.

[SH.A.H./ED.]

BARUK, HENRI (1897–), French psychiatrist. In 1931 he was appointed chief physician at the Charenton mental institution, and in 1946 became professor at the Sorbonne. His early scientific studies concentrated on psychiatric disorders caused by tumors on the brain. He succeeded in creating, by artificial means, aggression psychoses in animals. This led him to study the connections between psychiatric illness and defective moral awareness in human beings, and he subsequently displayed a tendency to extend psychiatry into the area of general anthropology. In 1957 he became chairman of the French Neurological Society.

Henri Baruk, French neurologist. Portrait by Benn. St. Maurice, H. Baruk Collection.

Baruk compared biblical medicine with that of Greece and wrote studies on religious belief and medical ethics. He opposed scientific experiments on the human body and all methods of psychiatric treatment which suppress or diminish the personality. Baruk was active in Jewish affairs in France, as chairman of the Society for the History of Hebrew Medicine in Paris and of the French Friends of the Hebrew University of Jerusalem. His works include: *Hebraic Civilization and the Science of Man,* 1961 (originally a lecture in Edinburgh in 1960); *Le Test Tzedek, le jugement moral et la délinquance* (1950); *Psychiatrie morale, expérimentale, individuelle et sociale; Psychoses et néuroses* (1965).

[J.O.L.]

BARUKH (Heb. בָּרוּךְ), initial word of the *berakhah* pattern of prayer. *Barukh* is conventionally translated "blessed," but the etymology is disputed. The root (ברך) seems to have meant originally "bend (or fall) upon the knees (*berekh* = knee)" in prayerful obeisance (Ps. 95:6; Isa. 45:23). Cassuto maintains, however, that it meant originally "bestow a gift" (Gen. 24:1, 35; 33:11, et al.). *Barukh* is a homonym expressing a reciprocal relationship: man can address God as *barukh* by expressing feelings of thanksgiving, reverence, love, and praise, while he is *barukh* by God who bestows His material and spiritual gifts. The person upon whom the divine blessing rests is called *berukh Adonai* "blessed of the Lord" (Gen. 24:31, 26:29). *Barukh Adonai,* in the sense of man blessing God, occurs 24 times in the Bible.

The pattern *barukh Attah Adonai* ("blessed art Thou, Lord") occurs only twice in biblical literature (Ps. 119:12; I Chron. 29:10). This second person form attained currency no earlier than about the fourth century B.C.E. There is, however, no substantive difference between the second and third person forms. As applied to God "blessed" is identical with "praised" and the formula of blessing viz. benediction is, in fact, one of praise.

The prototype of the classical *berakhah* is to be found in the biblical formula, *barukh Adonai . . . asher . . .* (e.g., Gen.

Initial word *Barukh,* in a decorated panel and repeated as the opening of five more marriage benedictions. From the *Rothschild Miscellany,* fol. 24, N. Italy, c. 1740, Jerusalem, Israel Museum, Ms. 180/51.

24:27; Ex. 18:10), in which he who has experienced the marvelous or miraculous expresses adoration and awe. This pattern persisted for centuries and was eventually adapted for liturgical use as the Jew's response to "the miracles of every day." But the insertion of the pronoun *Attah* ("Thou") was slow in gaining exclusive acceptance. Some of the variant forms of the *berakhah* persisted until the third century C.E. when the standard pattern was fully established (Ber. 40b). In third-century Babylonia, Rav and Samuel were still debating whether *Attah* was required in the formula (TJ, Ber. 9:1, 12d). Rav's pattern, *barukh Attah Adonai,* became the standard opening phrase; but the old biblical formula in which *barukh (Attah) Adonai* was followed by the characteristic phrase, *asher* ("who", i.e., "performed some beneficent act") remained in use. This juxtaposition of direct address to God and a sequel in the third person created a syntactical paradox which has exercised commentators and theologians down to the present. Many commentators explain the juxtaposition of second and third person homiletically as indicating both God's nearness and transcendence. The second person address is referred to in traditional sources as *nigleh* ("revealed") and the third person as *nistar* ("hidden").

See *Benedictions, *Prayer.

Bibliography: Blank, in: HUCA, 32 (1961), 87–90; Bamberger, in: *Judaism,* 5 (1956), 167–8; M. Kadushin, *The Rabbinic Mind* (1965²), 266–70 (theological aspect); J. Heinemann, *Ha-Tefillah bi-Tekufat ha-Tanna'im ve-ha-Amora'im* (1966²), 29–77 (textual criticism).

[H.Kı.]

BARUKH SHE-AMAR (Heb. בָּרוּךְ שֶׁאָמַר; "Blessed be He who spoke"), benediction opening the section of **Shaḥarit* called "passages of song," i.e., the morning psalms (*Pesukei de-Zimra* or *Zemirot*). In the Ashkenazi rite the benediction is placed at the beginning of the whole section, while in the Sephardi and other rites some verses and psalms are recited before *Barukh she-Amar.* In the original Sephardi prayer books (Leghorn, Amsterdam, and Vienna) there is a longer version, with additions for Sabbath. In the Eastern Sephardi rites—according to the Kabbalah—there is a shorter version of 87 words, which is similar to the Ashkenazi rite with slight variations. In its present form it is a combination of two separate prayers of which only the second part can be considered a benediction. The first part is a hymn praising God, the Creator and Redeemer. In spite of numerous variations and later accretions, the prayer may be of talmudic origin. It is first mentioned by Moses Gaon (c. 820) and is found in the prayer book of Amram Gaon (also ninth century), where the prayer is introduced as follows: "When Jews enter the synagogue to pray, the *ḥazzan* of the congregation rises and begins . . . " Nathan ha-Bavli reports a century later that at the ceremony of the installation of the exilarch *Barukh she-Amar* was sung antiphonically, and hence some scholars have suggested that the response *Barukh Hu* ("blessed be He"), was repeated as a refrain after every clause, and not only for the first one as in the present text. According to Saadiah's *Siddur* it was recited only on Sabbaths. The style of the hymn is midrashic and most of the phrases used are found in various passages of Talmud and Midrash (see S. Baer, *Siddur* (1868), 58). Eleazer b. Judah of Worms of the 12th–13th centuries, quoting from the *Heikhalot* texts of the early mystics, refers to the esoteric significance of the 87 words contained in *Barukh she-Amar* (at least in the Ashkenazi rite (Rokeaḥ 320)); the extant texts of the *Heikhalot* do not, however, have this passage. D. *Hoffmann has interpreted the first part of the prayer as an exposition of the various meanings of the Tetragrammaton. In Prague a Barukh she-Amar Society was active from the 16th century until World War II. The members rose early in order to be in the synagogue before the reciting of *Barukh she-Amar.*

Bibliography: Abrahams, Companion, 31ff.; Elbogen, Gottesdienst, 82ff.; Idelsohn, Liturgy, 80f.; D. Hoffmann, *Das Buch Leviticus,* 1 (1905), 95ff.

[Ed.]

BARUKH SHEM KEVOD MALKHUTO LE-OLAM VA-ED (Heb. בָּרוּךְ שֵׁם כְּבוֹד מַלְכוּתוֹ לְעוֹלָם וָעֶד; "Blessed be His name, whose glorious kingdom is forever and ever" (Singer, Prayer, and *Union Prayer Book*) or "Blessed be His glorious kingdom for ever and ever" (*Rabbinical Assembly Prayerbook*)), a doxology of ancient origin, based upon Nehemiah 9:5 "Stand up and bless the Lord your God from everlasting to everlasting; and let them say: Blessed be Thy glorious Name, that is exalted above all blessing and praise." Talmudic sources state that in the Temple it was not customary to respond "Amen" after blessings pronounced by the priests (Tosef., Ber. 7:22), but rather the aforesaid *Barukh Shem Kevod Malkhuto le-Olam va-Ed.* This was also the custom after the high priest pronounced the Holy Name (the Tetragrammaton) in his public confessions on the Day of Atonement (Yoma 35b, 39a, 66a; Ta'an. 16b; Tosef., Ta'an. 1:12; Sif. Deut. 306; see **Avodah*). This formula is pronounced in the daily prayers after the first verse of the *Shema* before continuing with the verses of Deuteronomy 6:4–9. In the Orthodox ritual, however, this formula is pronounced in a whisper, either because it is not biblical as is the rest of the *Shema* (Pes. 56a; Gen. R. 98:3) or because it is recited by the angels in heaven, corresponding to the people of Israel's reciting of the *Shema* (Deut. R. 2:36). It has also been suggested that precisely because the phrase was recited aloud in the

Temple (Ta'an. 16b), it should be whispered after its destruction. For the second reason, this doxology is pronounced aloud in Orthodox synagogues only on the Day of Atonement, since on this day "Israel is as pure as the angels" (Deut. R. 2:36). Another explanation for uttering this formula in a whisper is that martyrs used to pronounce the *Shema* as they met their death while their relatives, out of fear of the oppressors, responded quietly. But on the Day of Atonement, when all are ready for martyrdom, it is pronounced aloud (see M.A. Mirkin's commentary to Deut. R. 98:3). In the Ashkenazi rite, at the close of the *Ne'ilah* service on the Day of Atonement, this formula is pronounced aloud three times as a solemn affirmation of the Jewish faith and in anticipation of the day when this belief will be realized by all mankind.

Bibliography: J. Heinemann, *Ha-Tefillah bi-Tekufat ha-Tanna'im ve-ha-Amora'im* (1966[2]), 79, 84; E. Munk, *World of Prayer* (1961), 114; Werner, in: HUCA, 19 (1945–46), 282–9.

[Ed.]

BARUKH SHE-PETARANI (Heb. בָּרוּךְ שֶׁפְּטָרַנִי; "Blessed be He who has relieved me," i.e., from the responsibility for my son's conduct), benediction pronounced by the father at his son's *bar mitzvah (see: Isserles, to Sh. Ar., OḤ 225:1; Maim. Yad, Teshuvah, 6:1). This benediction is based upon the Midrash: R. Eleazar said, "A man is bound to occupy himself with his son until the age of 13, thereafter he should say; Blessed be He who has released me from the responsibility (literally 'punishment') for my son's conduct" (Gen. R. 63:10), because from now on the boy assumed responsibility for his actions as a member of the community. At bar mitzvah ceremonies in Reform congregations, the *She-Heḥeyanu* blessing has been substituted for *Barukh she-Petarani* since they objected to the idea that parents are accountable for the religious transgressions of their offspring. In Yiddish *barukh she-petarani* became a familiar expression after getting rid of any annoying thing or person.

[Ed.]

BAR-YEHUDAH (Idelson), ISRAEL (1895–1965), Israel labor leader, born in Konotop, Ukraine. He studied mining engineering and joined the Ẓe'irei Zion movement. After he became secretary of its left wing (Ẓiyyonim Soẓialistim) in 1921, he was arrested by the Soviet authorities and exiled to the Arctic region. Released in 1923 Bar-Yehudah left for Berlin. There he served, with Berl *Locker, as secretary of the World Union of *Po'alei Zion. In 1926, upon settling in Palestine, he became secretary of the Petaḥ Tikvah Workers' Council and was imprisoned for leading a picket group which demanded the introduction of Jewish labor in the local citrus groves. After joining kibbutz *Yagur in 1930 he became a leading member of Ha-Kibbutz ha-Me'uḥad,

Israel Bar Yehudah, Israel labor leader and cabinet minister (right) with the actress Hanna Rovina and Zalman Aranne, then minister of Education and Culture (second from left).

mainly as coordinator of its defense committee. As a member of the *Mapai faction Bar-Yehudah was active in the central institutions of the *Histadrut, the *yishuv*, and the Zionist organizations. When Mapai split, in 1944, he joined *Aḥdut ha-Avodah and became one of its leaders and a member of its Knesset faction. During his term as minister of interior (1955–59) the question of "Who is a Jew" according to Israel law became a public issue in connection with identity-card registration. From 1962 until his death Bar-Yehudah served as minister of transport. During 1960–62 he was his party's secretary-general.

Bibliography: D. Lazar, *Rashim be-Yisrael*, 1 (1953), 107–11.

[A.A.]

BAR-YOSEF (Zenwirth), YEHOSHUA (1911–), Israel novelist and playwright. Bar-Yosef was born in Safed and studied in yeshivot in Transylvania and Jerusalem. Bar-Yosef realistically describes the world of the old *yishuv*, the pre-Zionist Jewish settlers in Ereẓ Israel. His trilogy *Ir

Yehoshua Bar-Yosef, Israel novelist and playwright.

Kesumah* ("Enchanted City," 1949) is set in Safed. Bar-Yosef views life as a constant battle between the spiritual and the temporal, the Will to Evil and the Will to Good, the sacred and the profane. Bar-Yosef's plays *Be-Simta'ot Yerushalayim* ("In the Alleys of Jerusalem") and *Shomerei ha-Ḥomot* ("Guardians of the City Walls") were produced at the Ohel Theater. While his early work is graphically realistic, he later showed a tendency to symbolism. His son Yosef (1933–) has written short stories, a novel entitled *Ḥayyav u-Moto shel Yonatan Argaman* ("The Life and Death of Jonathan Argaman," 1959), and a play entitled *Tura* (1963), which dealt with problems of an Oriental family's integration into Israel society.

Bibliography: S. Kremer, *Ḥillufei Mishmarot* (1959), 218–22.

[Y.T.]

BARZILAI, Italian family. Giuseppe (1824–1902), orientalist. Born in Gradisca (Goerz), Giuseppe studied at Padua and was at one time secretary of the Trieste Jewish community. His work on the relations between the Semitic and Indo-Germanic languages (1885) won a prize from the *Académie Française*. He also translated the Song of Songs and Lamentations into Italian verse (1865 and 1867).

Salvatore (1860–1939), son of Giuseppe, Italian politician, played no part in Jewish life. An ardent supporter of the Italian claim to Trieste, at the age of 18 he was found guilty of treason against Austria, but was acquitted on appeal after a year of imprisonment. Salvatore studied law at Bologna, and began to practice in 1882 specializing in criminal law. Later he became recognized as an eminent legal authority. He was foreign editor of *La Tribuna* of Rome from 1883 to 1891, and entered the Chamber of Deputies in 1890 as an extreme left republican advocating Italy's withdrawal from the Triple Alliance. His irredentism was so great that he became known as "the Deputy from Trieste." He strongly supported Italy's declaration of war against Germany and Austria in 1915, and was later appointed minister for the liberated territories. Salvatore was an Italian delegate at the peace conference in 1919, and became a senator in 1920. Among his writings are *La criminalità in Italia* (1885); *La recidiva* (1883); *Il nuovo Codice Penale* (1889). [Ed.]

BARZILLAI (Heb. בַּרְזִלַּי), name of two biblical persons. (1) Barzillai the Gileadite (Heb. הַגִּלְעָדִי), a wealthy man of Rogelim. When David and his men fled to Mahanaim in Gilead because of *Absalom's rebellion, he, like two other prominent Transjordanians, Machir son of Ammiel of Lo-Debar and Shobi son of Nahash, the Ammonite, welcomed them with food. Barzillai also sustained David throughout his stay in Mahanaim. On David's return to Jerusalem, Barzillai accompanied him as far as the west bank of the Jordan; however, owing to his advanced age, Barzillai did not accept David's invitation to come to Jerusalem and reside at the royal court (II Sam. 17:27; 19:32–41). Instead, he sent his son Chimham (or Chimhan) with David and from this time Chimham and his family lived at the king's court (I Kings 2:7). It seems that a quarter near Bethlehem was set aside for Chimham and his relatives and was therefore called "Chimhan's (*keri; ketiv:* "Chemoham") Residence" (Geruth Chimham, Jer. 41:17). In post-Exilic Judah two priestly families, Habaiah and Hakkoz—which claimed descent from Barzillai—were disqualified from the priesthood. The sons of Hakkoz were readmitted in the same generation (Ezra 2:61; Neh. 7:63). (2) Barzillai of Abel-Meholah (a city in Transjordan), the father of *Adriel, the husband of *Merab, the daughter of King Saul (II Sam. 21:8, where it reads Michal instead of Merab, cf. I Sam. 18:19). It has also been suggested that Barzillai from Meholah was Barzillai the Gileadite.

Bibliography: de Vaux, Anc Isr, 121–2; B. Maisler (Mazar), in: *Tarbiz*, 12 (1940/41), 120; EM, 2 (1965), 342–3 (incl. bibl.).

[Y.M.G.]

BASCH, VICTOR GUILLAUME (1863–1944), French philosopher and a defender of human rights. Basch was born in Budapest and studied German at the Sorbonne. He served as a professor at the universities of Nancy, Rennes, and Paris. In 1918 he held the newly established chair of aesthetics at the Sorbonne. Basch became well-known when

Victor Basch, French philosopher. Jerusalem, Schwadron Collection, J.N.U.L.

he championed Alfred Dreyfus. He was a founder of the League for the Rights of Man and its president in 1926. Basch was a socialist supporter of the left-wing coalition known as the Popular Front and a leader of the Alliance Israélite Universelle. During World War II, Basch was a member of the central committee of the French underground. He and his wife were executed by the Vichy government.

His writings include *Essai critique sur l'esthétique de Kant* (1896); *La guerre de 1914 et le droit* (1915); *Les doctrines politiques des philosophes classiques de l'Allemagne* (1927), and *Essais d'esthétique de philosophie et de littérature* (1934), as well as other works on literature, philosophy, and political issues. [Z.S.]

BASCHKO, ẒEVI HIRSCH BEN BENJAMIN (1740–1807), rabbi and halakhist. Baschko was the last to occupy the position of rabbi (which he held from 1802) of the

ספר
תפארת צבי
על
שאלות ותשובות
נדפס פה לבוב
Gedruckt in Lemberg bey Herz Grosman 1816

Title page of part one of *Tiferet Ẓevi*, responsa on the Shulḥan Arukh by Ẓevi Hirsch Baschko, nominally printed at Lvov (Lemberg), 1816. Jerusalem, J.N.U.L.

joint communities of Altona, Hamburg, and Wandsbek (the "Three Communities") before the union was dissolved. Born in Zamosc, Poland, of a distinguished family, he was rabbi first of Tischwitz (Tyszowce), then from 1771 of Brody, and from 1788 of Glogau, where he established an important yeshivah. He was one of the greatest rabbis of his day; among those who addressed halakhic questions to him were Isaiah Berlin, Solomon Zalman Fuerth, Phinehas Horowitz of Frankfort, and Meir Posner, while Ezekiel Landau and Akiva Eger referred to him in unusually high terms of esteem. He wrote *Tiferet Ẓevi*, responsa on the Shulḥan Arukh in two parts, the first on *Oraḥ Ḥayyim* and *Yoreh De'ah* (Warsaw, 1816(?)) and the second on *Even ha-Ezer* (Jozsefov, 1867). His responsa also appear in the works of contemporary rabbis. Some of his commentaries and homilies are still in manuscript. He died in Ottensen, near Altona, and was buried at Altona, his tombstone bearing the inscription, "There arose none, nor will there ever be another, like him." His sons were also rabbis: Moses at Tomaszow, and Judah Loeb at Komarno.

Bibliography: E. Duckesz, *Ivvah le-Moshav* (1903), xxvii (Ger. pt.), 77–83 (Heb. pt.); I. Wolfsberg, in: *Arim ve-Immahot be-Yisrael*, 2 (1948), 33f.; N. M. Gelber, *ibid.*, 6 (1955), 59. [Y.AL.]

BASEVI, Italian family of German origin, especially associated with Verona. In Hebrew, they called themselves Bath-Sheba and in abbreviation, Bash (ב״ש). The name Naphtali was common in the family, and therefore some of its members took a deer's head as their crest and became known as "Basevi Cervetto" (Italian: "little deer"), in accordance with the Blessing of Jacob (Gen. 49:21). Others took a boat as their crest, in accordance with the Blessing of Moses (Deut. 33:23), and became known as "Basevi della Gondola." It is not clear what precise relationship existed between this family and the Bassevi family of Prague (see *Bassevi, Jacob von Treuenberg). The brothers ABRAHAM and JOSEPH, sons of Sabbatai Mattathias Bath-Sheba, were printers in Salonika (1594–1605). Abraham subsequently became a printer in Damascus (1605–06), while his brother had been a proofreader in the Verona press, a Midrash *Tanḥuma* appearing with his name (1595).

GIOACCHINO (1780–1867) was one of the earliest Italian Jews to attain distinction as a lawyer. He defended the Tyrolese hero Andreas Hofer in his trial for armed rebellion against Napoleon. ABRAMO (1818–1885), although a qualified physician, devoted himself to music, composed some operas, launched the publication of musical texts, and organized popular orchestral concerts. His writings (e.g.,

Figure 1. George Basevi, English architect. The bust is attributed to T. I. Mazzotti. Cambridge, Fitzwilliam Museum.

Figure 2. Jacob Basevi Cervetto by Johann Zoffany. London, Edward Croft-Murray Collection.

Della Certezza, 1842) anticipated the theories of the American programists.

In the 18th century some of the Basevi family emigrated to England. NATHAN OR NAPHTALI (1738–1808), of Verona, settled in London in 1762 and was an early president of the *Board of Deputies of British Jews. His daughter, Maria, was the mother of Benjamin *Disraeli. The conversion of the Disraeli children in 1817 was followed by that of the family of JOSHUA, Maria's brother. A Lloyds underwriter, he moved to Brighton, where he was chairman of the magistrates from 1838 to 1843 and also a deputy lieutenant of the County of Sussex.

Joshua's son, NATHANIEL (1792–1869), was the first Jewish-born barrister to practice in England. Another son, GEORGE (1794–1845), an architect and a nephew of Maria d'Israeli, and himself a convert to Christianity, was articled to Sir John Soane, the most original British architect of his time. In 1816–19 Basevi traveled in Italy and Greece and his first buildings reveal the influences of classical architecture. These include St. Mary's Church, Greenwich, England, designed in 1823, when Basevi was 29 years old. His best-known building, the Fitzwilliam Museum, Cambridge, England, begun in 1836, already reveals a trend to more dramatic, baroque treatment which is fully evident in the famous building of the Conservative Club (now the Bath Club) of 1843, in St. James's Street, London, designed with Sydney Smirke. Earlier in his career Basevi designed several country houses and the main part of Belgrave Square, the largest and most elegant of early 19th-century London thoroughfares. Basevi died as a result of a fall from the spire of Ely Cathedral, of which he was resident architect. Casts of a plaster bust of Basevi, attributed to T. I. Mazzotti, are in the Fitzwilliam Museum, Cambridge, the Soane Museum, London, and the Royal Institute of British Architects, London. Other members of the family include: JAMES PALLADIO (1832–1871), Anglo-Indian surveyor and explorer; JACOB BASEVI CERVETTO (1682–1783), generally known as James Cervetto, musician, who introduced the playing of the cello into England, and his illegitimate son, JAMES CERVETTO (1746–1837), also a musician and one of the best cellists of his time. Both father and son composed various musical works, especially for the cello. Most of the members of this family were not professing Jews.

Josef Basewi (b. 1840) founded the Giuseppe Basewi sugar firm in Trieste, which attained considerable importance in opening oriental markets to Austrian export.

Bibliography: A. M. Hyamson, *Sephardim of England* (1951), index; R. Blake, *Disraeli* (1966), index; Jamilly, in: JHSET, 18 (1953–55), 133–4; Roth, in: *Juedische Familien-Forschung*, 4 (1928), 57–60; G. Bedarida, *Ebrei d'Italia* (1950), index. George Basevi: Roth, Art; Victoria and Albert Museum, *Anglo-Jewish Art and History (catalogue)* (1956); *The Penguin Dictionary of Architecture* (1966); N. Pevsner, *The Buildings of England*.

[V.D.L.]

BASHAN (Heb. בָּשָׁן, הַבָּשָׁן), a region north of the Yarmuk River and east of the Jordan and lakes Ḥuleh and Kinneret. In biblical times, the city of *Salchah (Salcah) was at the eastern extremity of Bashan (Deut. 3:10; Josh. 13:11) and the city of Dan at its western (Deut. 33:22). Most of its area, some 4,334 sq. mi. (11,200 sq. km.) is covered with basalt as a result of lava eruptions occurring during the Pleistocene period or later. In some parts of Bashan, the volcanic material has eroded into fertile soil, but others are still covered with rocks.

The meaning of the name is not clear; by analogy with the Arabic word *batan* it may mean a rockless plain. Targum Onkelos and the Palestine Targum translate Bashan as *Matnan* (a possible variant of Batnan) and the Syriac Peshitta as *Matnin*. The Palestine Targum has *Butnaya* as a variant (Deut. 33:22) as does the Jerusalem Talmud, probably through Greek influence (cf. Ma'as 4:6, 51b, et al.).

With its sufficient rainfall in normal years and lava soil, Bashan is a very fertile region. Once possessing forests and pastures, it is praised in the Bible for its lofty trees (Isa. 2:13; Ezek. 27:6; Zech. 11:2), its cattle and sheep (Deut. 32:14; Amos 4:1; Ps. 22:13), and, with the Carmel, it is mentioned as an area of outstanding fertility (Isa. 33:9; Jer. 50:19; Nah. 1:4). Although its forests disappeared many generations ago, good pasture is still found in Upper *Golan and on Jebel Druze. The Plain of Bashan is noted for its hardy, superior wheat, but years of drought occur there more often than on the western side of the Jordan, with the exception of the Negev. The ancient "King's Highway" from Elath to Damascus passed through Bashan (Num. 20:17), merging with a branch of the Via Maris that

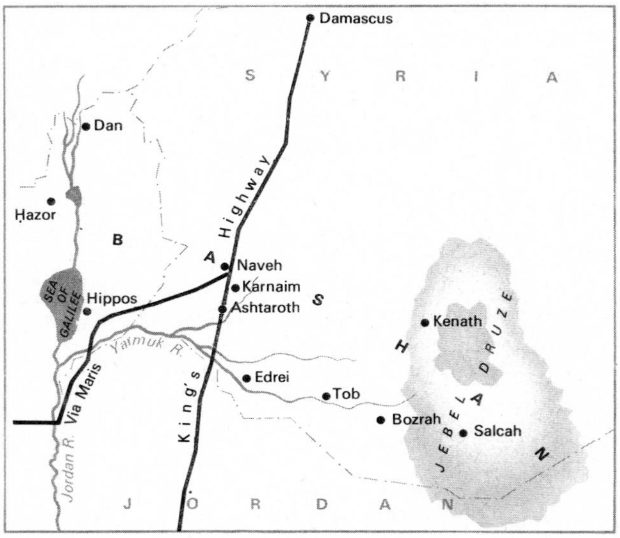

Map of the Bashan area in ancient times.

crossed the Jordan near the Sea of Galilee; a second branch led to Damascus by way of Dan and Banias. Today Bashan is crossed by a highway that follows the same route and, in the east, also by the Hejaz railroad.

The ancient inhabitants of Bashan were the *Rephaim, one of whom was *Og, king of Bashan (Deut. 2:11; 3:11), whose 60 fortified cities were proverbial (Deut. 3:4; I Kings 4:13, etc.). Some of Bashan's important cities are mentioned in Egyptian documents from the Middle and New Kingdoms: Ashtaroth, Bozrah, Zer, Kenath, Tob, etc. Ashtaroth and *Edrei were the main cities of Og (Josh. 12:4–5), whom Moses defeated at Edrei (Num. 21:33). He allotted his land to the half-tribe of Manasseh (Num. 32:33–42), but most of the original inhabitants remained there (Num. 32:17). Foreign enclaves, such as those of the Geshurites east of the Sea of Galilee, and the Maacathites in Upper Golan south of Mt. Hermon survived into the early days of the monarchy (Josh. 13:13; II Sam. 10:6–8; 13:37). In the period of the First Temple, Damascus attacked Bashan and *Gilead and, from time to time, imposed its rule on them (I Kings 22:3). *Joash and his son *Jeroboam II were the last Israelite kings to hold Bashan (II Kings 13:25; 14:25). In 732 B.C.E. it was conquered by Tiglath-Pileser III who exiled many of its inhabitants (II Kings 15:29; cf. Isa. 8:23) and established two Assyrian provinces there—Karnini (Karnaim) and Hawrina (Hauran)—that evidently existed through Babylonian and Persian rule.

Under the Ptolemies, Bashan was divided into three provinces: Gaulanitis, Batanea, and Trachonitis. The Seleucids consolidated the whole of Transjordan north of the Arnon into a single unit called Galaditis (Gilead). In 164 B.C.E. *Judah Maccabee went to the aid of the persecuted Jews of Bashan, defeated their enemies led by a certain Timotheus, and evacuated the Jews from Transjordan (I Macc. 5:9ff.; Jos., Ant., 12:330ff.). Alexander *Yannai in 85 B.C.E. wrested Golan from the Nabateans, who, by the latter part of the second century, had spread out from their settlements in Edom and reached as far as Damascus. Some 20 years later, however, Pompey conquered Golan from the Jews and gave it to the Itureans, who controlled most of Bashan. He granted autonomy to the Greek cities Hippos (Susita) in Lower Golan and Raphana and Kanatha in the Plain of Bashan and included them in the *Decapolis. From 30 to 20 B.C.E. Herod gradually received all of Bashan from Emperor Augustus, and it remained the domain of his heirs Herod Philip and Agrippa I and II until about 100 C.E. In the days of Herod, Jews from Western Palestine and Babylonia were settled there. His army commander *Zamaris (Zimra), a Babylonian Jew, cleared Trachonitis (al-Lijā) of marauders and the area was later named for him—Terakhona de-Zimra, or Terakona. For halakhic purposes this region was considered part of Ereẓ Israel (Tosef., Shev. 4:11). In 106 C.E. Bashan was annexed to the Provincia Arabia, the capital of which was Bozrah.

In Byzantine times the al-Jafna dynasty of the Ghasān tribe ruled Bashan; its capital was Jabiyya, northwest of Nawe. Chosroes II, king of Persia, penetrated into Bashan in 614 and defeated the Byzantines near Edrei (Darʿā). The Muslims invaded in 634 and after the battle of the Yarmuk (Aug. 20, 636) Golan was included in Jund al-Urdun (Jordan Province), the capital of which was Tiberias. The rest of Bashan apparently became part of the district of Damascus—capital of the caliphate from 660 to 750. Because of its proximity to the centers of power and of Muslim culture, Bashan flourished under the Umayyad dynasty; thereafter it declined rapidly until, in Turkish times, it was inhabited by Bedouins, who plundered its few remaining villages. In 1711 Druze from Mt. Lebanon began to settle on Mt. Bashan, which was later renamed for them (Jebel Druze). Their number increased considerably there in 1860, when many Druze fled from Mt. Lebanon. Far from submitting to the Bedouin, the Druze established their authority over many tribes. The attempts of the Egyptians (from 1832 to 1840) and of the Turks (from 1840 to 1918) to extend their sovereignty over Jebel Druze were only partly successful. In 1925 the Druze rebelled against the French, who subdued the revolt, and subsequently granted the Bashan Druze area broad autonomy. Until the end of the British Mandate, Bashan was the most tranquil part of Syria; after 1944, it became part of the Republic of Syria. Attempts by the Damascus government to treat it like other provinces met with constant opposition and periodic rebellions.

On the Bashan Plain and in Golan, Turkish rule succeeded in enforcing its sovereignty over the inhabitants in the late 19th century. To strengthen its authority in these districts, the Turkish government settled Circassian refugees there in 1880–84. At the end of the 19th century, a French company laid a railroad line in Bashan from Damascus to al-Muzayyīb, north of the Yarmuk, to expedite the export of its wheat. In 1907 the Hejaz railway was built parallel to the French line as far as Edrei (Darʿā), and then branching off to cross the Yarmuk, thus connecting Bashan with Haifa. The French tracks were removed by the Turks during World War I. Good roads were constructed during the French Mandate, linking up with the road networks of Syria, Transjordan, and Palestine. During the 1890s, Baron Edmond de Rothschild purchased thousands of acres on both sides of Nahr al-ʿAllān and founded a Jewish settlement, but the pasha of Damascus expelled the settlers in 1899. A small private settlement called Benei Yehudah was founded in 1886 by Jews from Tiberias and Safed in the Golan, east of Lake Kinneret, but it was abandoned in 1920 as a result of the Arab riots and attacks after contact was broken between the two banks of the Jordan.

See also *Golan.

Bibliography: Avi-Yonah, Land, index; Glueck, in: D. W. Thomas (ed.), *Archaeology and Old Testament Study* (1967), 450ff.; EM, s.v. (incl. bibl.).

[A.J.Br.]

BASHEVIS SINGER, ISAAC (1904–), Yiddish novelist, critic, and journalist. The younger brother of the novelist I. J. *Singer, Bashevis was born into a rabbinical family in Leoncin, Poland. He grew up in Warsaw, where he made his career until his emigration to America in 1935. His education was traditional, although the rabbinical seminary he attended also taught secular subjects and modern Hebrew. More than three years of his adolescence he spent in his grandfather's village, Bilgoraj. His home on poor and teeming Krochmalna Street where his father held a *bet din;* the old-world tradition and way of life of Bilgoraj where he steeped himself in the Kabbalah; and his brother's example as a secular Yiddish writer were all of the greatest importance to Bashevis' artistic and moral development.

Bashevis' Pseudonyms. Prolific and versatile, Bashevis' multiple talents group themselves behind his various pseudonyms. He made his debut in the literary world with *"Oyf der Elter"* (in *Literarishe Bleter,* no. 60, 1925) which he signed *"Tse"* (**צא**). In the same journal that year (no. 80), his story *"Vayber"* was published under the pseudonym "Isaac Bashevis," (a derivative of his mother's first name, Bas-Sheva (Yid. for Bath-Sheba)), which he used only for his serious literary creations. Its adoption was prompted by the desire to avoid confusion with his famous brother, Israel Joshua Singer. For his more or less serious journalism

Isaac Bashevis Singer (right) with Dr. Issachar Joel at the Jewish National and University Library, Jerusalem, 1969.

Bashevis adopted the name Y. Varshavski, and for his feuilletons and lighter pieces, that of D. Segal. However, his pseudonyms are not inflexible: with shaping and reordering, Varshavski's memoirs became Bashevis' *Mayn Tatn's Beys-Din Shtub.*

Imagistic Portrayals of Inner Forces. Bashevis was recognized early in his literary career. His first major fictional work, *Sotn in Goray* (1935; *Satan in Goray,* 1955) had been preceded by short stories in such respected journals as *Varshever Shriftn* (1926–27) and the Warsaw *Globus,* where *Sotn in Goray* and its antecedent *"Der Yid fun Bovl"* first appeared. The kabbalist protagonist of the latter, after a life-long traffic with the occult, is finally claimed by the satanic host, despite his conscious will to resist. Here we see the implacable workings of dark inner forces which Bashevis projects in images derived from folklore. The typical Bashevis hero is virtually helpless before his passion: he is "possessed." The village of Goray in *Sotn in Goray* is "possessed" by the false messianism which in 17th-century Poland wrought havoc on Jewish life. "Let none attempt to force the Lord" is the moral of this parable for all times. This "anti-Prometheanism" (a term used by Shlomo *Bickel in his criticism on Bashevis) is a dominant note in Bashevis' work.

U.S. Publications in English Translation. In the United States, Bashevis' stories and serialized novels became a regular feature of the New York Yiddish daily *Forward,* and in the 1950s his stories began to appear in translation in serious magazines. His first *Forward* serial, *Di Familye Mushkat* (1950; *The Family Moskat,* 1950), is a realistic epical novel of pre-World War II Warsaw. *Satan in Goray* initiated the U.S. acclaim of Bashevis as the artist of the grotesque and demoniac who generated more interest than the realistic chronicler of the more recent Polish Jewish past. Of the volumes that Bashevis published in English from 1955, only three appeared in book form in Yiddish; two of these, five to six years after their English translation. Bashevis was thus in the curious position of writing for two very distinct audiences: the sophisticated public that read him in translation in *Commentary* and in the *New Yorker,* and the *Jewish Daily Forward* Yiddish readership, less sophisticated, but with wider Jewish knowledge. Bashevis declared that "Nothing can spoil a writer more than writing for the translator" (*Commentary,* vol. 36, no. 5, 1963); yet the suspicion that he himself did persists.

Motifs and Styles of his Works. Bashevis is above all a marvelous and interesting storyteller, no matter where he may be leading his expectant, and often puzzled, reader. If his demons, imps, and spirits are regarded as a shorthand ("a kind of spiritual stenography" Bashevis called it) for complex human behavior, then one need not be distressed by the author's professed belief in their substantive reality. Bashevis' fictional writings tend to center around the sexual and the sacred, especially their interrelationship: "In my stories it is just one step from the study house to sexuality and back again. Both phases of human existence have continued to interest me" (*In My Father's Court*, p. 175). Though eroticism has been present in Yiddish literature for over half a century, many Yiddish readers, preferring a "balanced view" of Jewish life and of man in general, find the sexual motif in Bashevis overworked and exaggerated.

Bashevis' serious fiction falls into three groups: his realistic novels, his short romances or novellas, and his short stories. To these may be added his belletristic memoirs (Yid., *Mayn Tatn's Beys-Din Shtub*, 1950; *In My Father's Court*, 1966), a work which is both art and documentary. Bashevis is at home in a variety of styles, modes, and subjects; he moves freely from the medieval to the contemporary, from the naturalistic to the fantastic, from psychological illumination to parapsychological mystification. His typical pose is one of ironic detachment.

Realistic Novels. *The Manor* (1967; written 1953–55), first serialized in the *Forward* under the title *Der Hoyf* of which it constitutes part 1, is a realistic family chronicle of late 19th-century Polish Jewish life. Similar in style to *The Family Moskat*, it suffers from the same loose structure but is largely redeemed by the same vividness. A continuation was called *The Estate* (1970).

Set in 19th-century Poland, *The Magician of Lublin* (1960) has for its protagonist a Jewish magician-acrobat Don Juan whose Faustian striving eventuates in penitential self-incarceration. *The Slave* (1962; Yid., *Der Knekht*, 1967), a universalistic parable set in 17th-century Poland after the *Chmielnicki massacres, portrays an enslaved Jew who falls in love with the daughter of his peasant master; the gulf between them is bridged by the unifying and transcendent power of love. The miracle at the end of *The Slave* disturbs readers who look amiss at interference, whether authorial or supernatural.

Shorter Fictional Works. It is in the shorter forms of fiction that Bashevis excels, and some of his stories (e.g., "Gimpel the Fool") are among the finest in any language. *Gimpel the Fool and Other Stories* (1957; Yid., *Gimpl Tam un Andere Dertseylungen*, 1963), *The Spinoza of Market Street* (1961), and *Short Friday* (1964) are quite varied collections of short stories written over a period of many years. Their typical setting is the *shtetl*, often visited by Satan's emissaries. The demoniac tales, rich in grotesquerie and often narrated by devils and imps, range from studies in pathology to parables of the arbitrariness of the evil in life. Typically, it is through the weakness of the flesh that Satan conquers.

Free of demons and asserting the freedom to behave irrationally, *The Spinoza of Market Street* concerns an ineffectual philosopher who achieves salvation through the flesh. The irrational expresses itself in a context of "normalcy," where soup and sympathy come to acquire magical properties. "Gimpel the Fool" is in the great divine-fool tradition and recalls *Peretz's "Bontshe Shvayg." Its theme is the ambiguous nature of sublunary truth and reality: "No doubt," says Gimpel, "the world is entirely an imaginary world, but it is only once removed from the true world. . . . Whatever may be there, it will be real, without complication, without ridicule, without deception. God be praised: there even Gimpel cannot be deceived."

Bashevis' Place in Yiddish and World Literature. The leading exponent of Yiddish imaginative prose, Bashevis is also an important figure in contemporary world literature. Enjoying a somewhat ambiguous place among Yiddish writers, he is nonetheless firmly rooted in Jewish tradition. Like Yiddish literature itself, Bashevis' art is a unique amalgam of the indigenous and the naturalized, of specifically Jewish and general world culture.

Bibliography: I. H. Buchen, *I. B. Singer and the Eternal Past* (1968); M. Allentuck (ed.), *The Achievements of Isaac Bashevis Singer* (1969); Fixler, in: *Kenyon Review* (Spring 1964), 371–86; I. Howe, in: *Commentary*, 30 (1960), 350–3; 36 (1963), 364–72; Dan Jacobson, *ibid.*, 39 (1966), 48–52; I. B. Singer, *Selected Stories* (1966), v–xxiv; S. E. Hyman, in: *The New Leader* (July 28, 1962); Eisenberg, in: *Judaism*, 11 (1962), 345–56; S. Bickel, *Shrayber fun Mayn Dor*, 1 (1958), 358–65; Gross-Zimmermann, in: *Goldene Keyt*, 60 (1967), 190–4; Y. Y. Trunk, *Di Yidishe Proze in Poyln* (1949), 136–49.

[L.P.]

BASHIRI, YAḤYA (Yaḥya b. Abraham b. Sa'adiah al-Bashiri; Heb. name **Abner bar Ner ha-Sharoni;** 17th century), Yemenite kabbalist and scribe. His extant work is characterized by accuracy and beauty. Later Yemenite scholars, particularly Yaḥya *Ṣaliḥ, refer to Bashiri in their writings; while popular legends extol his piety and the miracles he performed by virtue of his knowledge of practical Kabbalah. His two extant works, still in manuscript, are: *Ḥavaẓẓelet ha-Sharon*, a kabbalistic work on the letters of the Hebrew alphabet, and *Bashiri*, a pentateuchal commentary based on *gematria*. He is known to have written other works, which have not survived: two commentaries on the *Ein Ya'akov* of Jacob ibn Ḥabib and *Amirat ha-Emunot*, the contents of which are unknown. The numerous quotations from Bashiri in the *Ḥelek ha-Dikduk* of Ṣaliḥ reveal the *variae lectiones* collected by Bashiri in the course of copying the books of the Pentateuch, on which he may even have compiled a distinct work. His love of books is evidenced by his written vow (appearing in a colophon to the *Midrash ha-Gadol*, on Deuteronomy) never to sell a book "in his lifetime or thereafter," i.e., even if this be necessary to provide funds for his burial shroud.

Bibliography: A. Elnadaf, *Seridei Teiman* (1928), 7a, 9b; Y. Ratzhaby, in: KS, 28 (1952/53), 260, 264, 268, 405; A. Koraḥ, *Sa'arat Teiman* (1954), 2.

[Y.R.]

°BASHUYSEN, HEINRICH JACOB VAN (1679–1750), Calvinist theologian and Hebraist of Dutch origin. Bashuysen was born in Hanau (Germany), where he taught Hebrew at the high school (1701); later he was principal of the high school in Zerbst (1716). In 1708 he established, at his own expense, a Hebrew printing press in Hanau which published over 100 books, many written by himself. He had a special interest in rabbinical literature which he tried to impart to his students. In 1712 he published the Psalms in Hebrew with excerpts in Latin, from rabbinical commentaries. In 1714 he published *Moses b. Daniel of Rohatin's rabbinical work *Sugyot ha-Talmud* with a Latin translation (in *Clavis Talmudica*). The fact that this work appeared only a few years after the publication of the original (in Zolkiew, 1693) testifies to Bashuysen's constant contacts with Jewish scholars. He also translated (into Latin) and published parts of *Maimonides' *Mishneh Torah* (1705–1708) and Isaac *Abrabanel's commentary on the Pentateuch, restoring sections omitted in the Venice edition (1712), but his plan to publish all the works of Abrabanel did not materialize. Bashuysen had a particular interest in

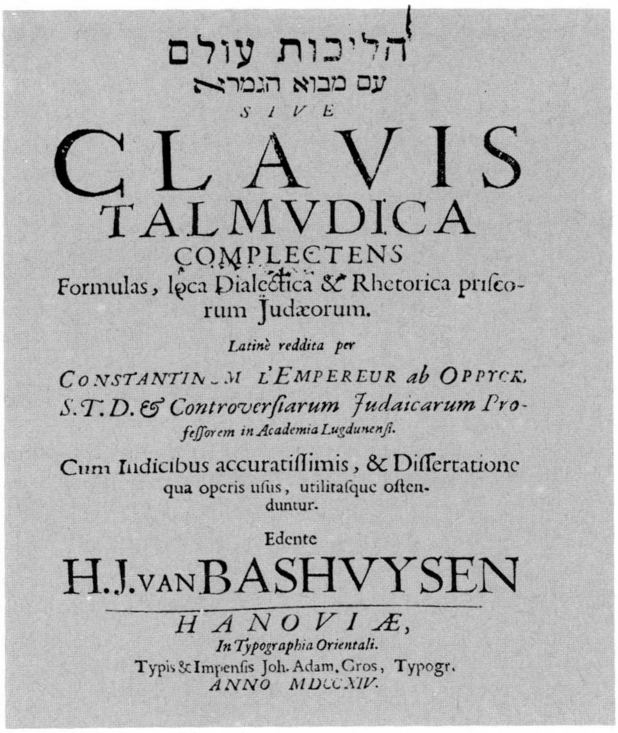
הליכות עולם
עם מבוא הגמרא
SIVE
CLAVIS
TALMVDICA
COMPLECTENS
Formulas, loca Dialectica & Rhetorica priscorum Judæorum.
Latinè reddita per
CONSTANTINUM L'EMPEREUR ab OPPYCK,
S.T.D. & Controversiarum Judaicarum Professorem in Academia Lugdunensi.
Cum Indicibus accuratissimis, & Dissertatione qua operis usus, utilitasque ostenduntur.
Edente
H.J. VAN BASHVYSEN
HANOVIÆ,
In Typographia Orientali.
Typis & Impensis Joh. Adam. Gros, Typogr.
ANNO MDCCXIV.

Title page of *Clavis Talmudica*, a Latin translation of *Halikhot Olam im Mevo ha-Gemara*, edited by Heinrich van Bashuysen, Hanover, 1714. This "Key to the Talmud" contains "the formulas and passages on dialectic and rhetoric of ancient Jews." Jerusalem, J.N.U.L.

the Hebrew language and wrote several books on this subject, including *Panegyricus hebraicus de lingua hebraica eiusque autoritate cum versione latina* (Hanover, 1706) and *Exercitatio paradoxa de novo et faciliore methodo discendi per Rabbinos linguam Hebraicam* (Zerbst, 1720).

Bibliography: ADB, 2 (1875), 124ff; Steinschneider, Cat Bod, nos. 4521, 9338; idem, in: ZHB, 2 (1897), 51ff.; Zunz, Gesch, 15.

[Ed.]

BASHYAZI (Heb. בשיצי; traditional Rabbanite transcription for the Turkish name Bashyatchi), family of Karaite scholars in Adrianople and Constantinople. Although the family moved to Constantinople in 1455, they retained the cognomen "Adrianopolitans" even in later generations. The Karaite school of Adrianople tended toward liberalism. The Bashyazi family, its leading exponents, advocated the kindling of Sabbath lights contrary to the prevalent Karaite custom of spending Sabbath in darkness. Menahem b. Joseph Bashyazi first permitted this practice around 1440. His grandson Elijah found support for this ruling in liberal Karaite halakhic sources and through his influence it was accepted in the Karaite communities of Turkey, Crimea, Poland, and Lithuania, although in Egypt, Syria, and Ereẓ Israel the Karaites continued to refrain from kindling lights on the Sabbath. Menahem also abolished the Karaite custom of starting the weekly Torah readings from the beginning of the Pentateuch in the month of Nisan and directed that the cycle should start in Tishri, conforming to Rabbanite practice. The more conservative Karaites opposed the change.

His grandson Elijah b. Moses (c. 1420–1490) was the ideologist of the Karaite rapprochement with Rabbanism and a codifier of Karaite law. Elijah, in addition to upholding the rulings of his grandfather Menahem and father Moses, provided them with a theoretical basis and expanded them (e.g., concerning intercalation). He remains the supreme Karaite authority. Elijah is reported to have begun the compilation of his great code *Adderet Eliyahu* in about 1480, but the section on the calendar refers to the year 1457. After his death his pupil and son-in-law Caleb *Afendopolo attempted to complete the work. The *Adderet* was distributed chapter by chapter and its contents were recognized as binding even during the author's lifetime. It was also one of the first Karaite works to appear in print (Constantinople, 1530–31; Eupatoria, 1835; Odessa, 1870). Its Sabbath laws became the subject of much Karaite polemical literature. Other sections, especially those dealing with the sanctification of the new moon (Elijah was the first to draw up an official calendar for this), the ten principles of faith (new and final formulation of the Karaite credo), and the laws of *sheḥitah* and incest were submitted to a series of adaptations, abridgments, and interpretations by Karaite religious leaders in different countries. In addition to reflecting the various schools of late medieval Karaite thought, the *Adderet* attests to Bashyazi's knowledge of both general and Jewish subjects.

Particularly noteworthy is Elijah's use of Rabbanite techniques and sources, even where they were antagonistic to Karaism. Elijah interpreted their hostility as a device to achieve publicity so as to cover their actual sympathy toward Karaism. However, he sharply attacked several Rabbanite scholars, including Mordecai *Comtino. While one of his three polemical works, *Iggeret ha-Yerushah* (published in the Eupatoria edition of *Adderet*), is directed against the Rabbanites, his *Iggeret ha-Ẓom* and *Iggeret Gid ha-Nasheh* are written to refute his Karaite opponents. Elijah's correspondence with Karaite leaders in Lithuania shows that his reputation had spread to the northern Karaite communities. He introduced the Lithuanian Karaites to his liberalization of Karaite *halakhah* and customs, recommending the establishment of a *bet din* of three in *Troki on the model of that in Constantinople, and the institution of kindling the Sabbath lights. His pupils included the Rabbanite *Moses of Kiev, well-known among Lithuanian Karaites. The Karaite prayerbook contains several prayers and hymns composed by Elijah, including *Meliẓat ha-Mitzvot,* recited on Shavuot.

Moses (first half of 16th century), great-grandson of Elijah, died relatively young. He renewed the connections with the Arabic-speaking Karaite communities. He also traveled to the East, returning with ancient Karaite manuscripts in Arabic and isolated pages of *Sefer ha-Mitzvot* by *Anan b. David in Aramaic on which he based his *Zevaḥ Pesaḥ* and *Sefer Re'uven* (in manuscript). His explanation of the laws of incest, *Sefer Yehudah,* was published by I. Markon, and an important part of his *Matteh Elohim,* on the history of the Karaite schism, was incorporated into *Mordecai b. Nisan's *Sefer David Mordekhai.*

Bibliography: S. Poznański, *Karaite Literary Opponents of Saadiah Gaon* (1908), 82–85; idem, in: *Zekher Ẓaddikim* (1920), 33–34; R. Mahler, *Ha-Kara'im* (1949), 286–7; Danon, in: JQR, 15 (1926/27), 305–7, 311–2; 17 (1924/25) 168–9; Mann, Texts, 2 (1935), index s.v. *Elyah ben Moses Bashiatzi;* L. Nemoy (ed.), *Karaite Anthology* (1952), 236–70; Ankori, in: PAAJR, 24 (1955), 11; idem, in: *Tarbiz,* 25 (1955/56), 44–65, 183–201; idem, *Karaites in Byzantium* (1959), index; idem, *Beit Bashyazi ve-Takkanotav* (1966).

[Ed.]

°**BASIL I,** Byzantine emperor 867–886. Basil first attempted to achieve the conversion of the Jews by persuasion and invited rabbis to a *disputation to defend their faith, vainly offering them material benefits if they would confess defeat. When this attempt failed he issued in 874 an edict ordering all his Jewish subjects to become converted to Christianity. The decree was also connected with his policy to propagate orthodox Christianity among the Bulgars, Russians, and other peoples, and forcible conversion of nonorthodox sects, notably the Paulicians, whom he probably associated with iconoclasm. His attempt to convert by force the Jewish communities in southern Italy then under Byzantine rule is recorded in the 11th-century Hebrew chronicle of *Ahimaaz b. Paltiel, which portrays Basil as a cruel and persistent enemy of the Jews and Judaism. Despite his decree, the legal status of the Jews remained unchanged and there was no curtailment of their existing rights. The decree, whether formally rescinded or not, eventually fell into disuse under Basil's son and successor Leo VI.

Bibliography: J. Starr, *Jews in the Byzantine Empire* (1939), 4–6, 127ff.; A. A. Vasiliev, *History of the Byzantine Empire*, 1 (1964), 332–3; Baron, Social[2], 3 (1957), 180ff.; B. Klar (ed.), *Megillat Aḥima'aẓ* (1944), 20–23; A. Sharf, in: Roth, Dark Ages, 57ff.; A. Vogt, *Basile I empereur de Byzance, et la civilisation byzantine à la fin du IX siècle* (1908); Neubauer, Chronicles, 2 (1895), 111–24.

[An. Sh.]

BASILEA, SOLOMON AVIAD SAR-SHALOM (c. 1680–1749), rabbi and kabbalist in Mantua, Italy. Solomon received instruction from the most learned scholars in the city, including his father, Menahem Samson Basilea, Judah b. Eliezer *Briel (Bariel), Moses *Zacuto, and *Benjamin b. Eliezer Ha-Cohen Vitale of Reggio. He also studied geometry and astronomy. Solomon became rabbi of Mantua in 1729. At the age of 44 he began a methodical study of Kabbalah according to the system of Isaac *Luria. In 1733 he was accused by the Inquisition of having mocked Catholicism and of retaining unexpurgated Hebrew works, and was imprisoned for a year. He was subsequently confined to his house and finally to the ghetto bounds. He courageously supported Moses Ḥayyim *Luzzatto against his accusers in the controversy over the latter's kabbalistic practices. Solomon Basilea's main work *Emunat Ḥakhamim* (Mantua, 1730) was intended to emphasize the continuity in Jewish tradition of the mystic significance of the Torah and the error of scholars opposing that interpretation. To support his thesis, Solomon reviewed not only the whole of Hebrew literature but also Greek, Arabic, and Renaissance philosophy. Basilea did not believe that the Zohar was written by Simeon b. Yoḥai, but that it nevertheless contained his esoteric doctrines as handed down to his disciples. Basilea also rejected the views which ascribed the authorship of the Zohar to *Moses b. Shem Tov de Leon. The book was very well received by the kabbalists, but opponents of the Kabbalah were critical of it. Jacob *Emden wrote a refutation of the *Emunat Ḥakhamim* in *Mitpaḥat Sefarim*, 2 (1768). Some rabbinical decisions of Solomon Basilea are included in the collections of his fellow student Isaac *Lampronti and others. He also wrote on the calendar and a commentary on Euclid's *Elements* as well as notes on the 1715 edition of *Tofteh Arukh* by Moses Zacuto. In his collections, he includes the responsa of his father Menahem Samson ben Solomon (d. 1693), rabbi in Alessandria and from 1630 in Mantua. Menahem's responsa also appear in collections of his contemporaries, Moses Zacuto and Nethanel b. Aaron *Segrè.

Bibliography: Ghirondi-Neppi, 36–39; S. Wiener, *Mazkeret Rabbanei Italyah* (1898), 37–40 (third pagination); Milano, Italia, 667; M. Mortara, *Catalogo dei manoscritti ebraici . . . di Mantova* (1878), 45–47; S. Simonsohn, *Toledot ha-Yehudim be-Dukkasut Mantovah* (1964), index.

[A. Mil.]

BASILICA (Greek *βασιλική*, talmudic בָּסִילְקִי), elongated rectangular building divided by colonnades. During the Roman period this term was broadened from the narrow

The nave of the basilica of the Church of the Nativity in Bethlehem, view toward the high altar. The church was originally built by the emperor Justinian, in the sixth century. Photo David Harris, Jerusalem.

meaning of a meeting place for merchants to any assembly hall. In particular the term referred to a hall used in the philosophers' schools and in wealthy homes for reading and lectures. In these basilicas, the apse was the area set aside for the lecturer or teacher. The entire hall was oriented toward the podium set in the apse, which had a concave roof serving as an acoustical ceiling. This type of basilica was the prototype for the early synagogues and churches. Talmudic sources refer to three types of basilicas, which served as palaces, bathhouses, and treasuries (Av. Zar. 16b). They note that the basilica also served as a hall of justice (Gen. R. 68:12) and as a place for the sale of grain (as in Ashkelon, Tosef. to Oho. 18 end).

An early example of the basilica construction is found in the "Royal Stoa" which Josephus (Ant., 15:411–416) describes as having been erected along the southern wall of the Temple Mount by Herod when he had the Temple rebuilt. This basilica had four rows of pillars each 23 ft. (7 m.) high. According to Josephus, its length was one *stadion* (606 ft. (185 m.)), but it appears to have been longer—about 920 ft. (280 m.). The central hall was 30 cubits wide and 60 cubits high. The width of the side aisles was 20 cubits, and the height, 30 cubits, giving the structure a true basilical form. Two partially carved stone pillars have been found in Jerusalem which by their size indicate that they were destined for this basilica. However, they were cracked and therefore not used. It is possible that Herod modeled his stoa after the Great Synagogue in Alexandria which has been described as "a kind of basilica with a stoa within a stoa" (Tosef. to Suk. 4:6). Conceivably this expression refers to the central area which was constructed between two colonnades. Another interpretation is that this refers to an additional stoa which extended the width of the hall. Such construction was typical of the early synagogues, remains of which have been found at Masada and in Galilee.

The Christians adopted the western form of basilica, and most of the early churches (fourth–sixth centuries) were built on that model, although the term "basilica" was no longer in common usage. In the early Christian basilicas, the apse served as the seat of the priests. The altar was set before it, and this part of the building was separated from the remainder by a grille which crossed the width of the church. Two or more rows of columns extended the length of the building, separating the main hall in the center from the narrower aisles at either side.

The first churches in Palestine and elsewhere, e.g., the Church of the Nativity in Bethlehem and the Church of the Holy Sepulcher in Jerusalem, were built according to this design. In the fifth century a vestibule *(narthex)* was added to the front facade of the basilica churches.

Basilicas were also used for secular purposes in the Jewish community in Palestine. One structure of this nature (135×49 ft. (40×15 m.)) was found in Bet She'arim. It consists of an enclosed paved court, a vestibule, and a basilica with two rows of five columns each. At the far end of the building, opposite the entry, is a low platform. It would appear that this was a hall of justice in the time of R. Judah ha-Nasi.

Bibliography: C. M. Kaufmann, *Handbuch der christlichen Archaeologie* (1913); R. Cagnat and V. Chapot, *Manuel d'archéologie romaine,* 1 (1916), 128–34; H. Kohl und C. Watzinger, *Antike Synagogen in Galilea* (1916); S. Krauss, *Synagogale Altertuemer* (1922), 32–102; E. L. Sukenik, *Ancient Synagogues in Palestine and Greece* (1934); J. B. Ward Perkins, in: *Papers of British School at Rome,* 22 (1954), 69–89; H. L. Gordon, in: *Art Bulletin,* 13 no. 3 (1931); M. Avi-Yonah and S. Yevin, *Kadmoniyyot Arẓenu,* 1 (1955), 200ff.; B. Mazar, in: YMḤEY, 21 (1957), 153–9.

[M.A.-Y.]

BAṢĪR, JOSEPH BEN ABRAHAM HA-KOHEN HA-RO'EH AL-(Yūsuf al-Baṣīr; first half of 11th century), Karaite author and philosopher, who lived in Iraq or Persia. Because he was blind he was euphemistically called al-Baṣīr "ha-Ro'eh" ("the Seeing"). Many Karaite authors confused him with Abū Yūsuf Yaʿqub al-*Kirkisani who lived 100 years prior to him. *Firkovich and later *Harkavy have shown that he lived in the 11th century, since he mentions in one of his works Samuel b. Hophni, who died in 1036, adding "of blessed memory" to his name. Though blind, he traveled extensively, probably as a Karaite propagandist. One of the most important Karaite scholars, he studied Talmud and rabbinic literature. He knew many languages and was well versed in Islamic philosophy. In his philosophic views he followed the Muʿtazilites (see *Kalām). He strongly upholds the belief in the essentially rational character of ethics and gives logical priority to reason over revelation. Only reason can prove God's wisdom and omnipotence, which imply His existence. Other predicates of God are will, oneness and simplicity, incorporeality, and eternity. Of primary importance in al-Baṣīr's philosophy are the questions of God's justice, of the nature of good and evil, and of free will. God does good always because of His wisdom, not by necessity, and even if He inflicts pain it is for the good. Considering God's foreknowledge, al-Baṣīr has no doubt that man is free to determine his actions, though God knows beforehand how he will act. The commandments are God's means of guiding man in the right path and the obedient are eternally rewarded in the next world. If a sinner repents of his evil deeds, it is the duty of God to accept his repentance and remit his punishment. Al-Baṣīr was the author of the following works: (1) *al-Muḥtawī* ("The Comprehensive"). Divided into 40 chapters, the work tries to bring the main principles of the Muʿtazilite Kalām into agreement with the Karaite dogmas. The author polemicizes frequently against Christians, dualists, Magians, Epicureans, and other sects. The book was translated from Arabic into Hebrew under the title *Sefer ha-Ne'imot* or *Zikhron ha-Datot,* probably by Tobiah b. Moses. (2) A compendium of the previous work entitled *al-Tamyīz* ("The Distinction"), also *al-Manṣūrī,* consisting of 13 chapters. This work was translated with some additions by Tobiah b. Moses under the title *Makhkimat Peti.* In a final chapter the author criticizes the esoteric book *Shi'ur Komah* and rejects the doctrine of Benjamin al-*Nahāwendī that the world was created by an angel. It is apparent that al-Baṣīr was familiar with and used Saadiah's *Emunot ve-De'ot* since a number of passages correspond with those found in the *Makhkimat Peti.* (3) *al-Istibṣār* ("Careful Examination"), dealing with the precepts. Several sections of the work, among them those dealing with inheritance and ritual purity, are extant in the British Museum, though without the name of the author. The section concerning the holidays, which contains a polemic in 8 chapters against Saadiah, was translated by Tobiah b. Moses. Al-Baṣīr mentions other writings of his but these are no longer extant. The Karaites considered al-Baṣīr as one of their most important authorities. Judah *Hadassi, Aaron b. Joseph ha-Rofe, Bashyazi, and other Karaite authors often cite his halakhic views and his scriptural interpretations. His philosophic views were also esteemed by later Karaite scholars down to *Aaron b. Elijah in the 14th century, who often cites him in his *Eẓ Ḥayyim.* Of special significance is the reform, encouraged by him, of the Karaite law of consanguinity. This reform was developed further and made effective by his pupil *Jeshua b. Judah, who was likewise an important Karaite authority.

Bibliography: P. F. Frankel, *Ein muʿtazilitischer Kalam aus dem 10. Jahrhundert* (1872); Steinschneider, Arab Lit, 89–91; S. Poznański, *Karaite Literary Opponents of Saadiah Gaon* (1908), 46–48; Guttmann, Philosophies, 78–81 and passim; Husik, Philosophy, 48–55 and passim.

[I.M./L.N.]

"Crow" by Leonard Baskin, 1960, wood, height $46\frac{3}{4}$ in. (119 cm.). Waltham, Mass., Brandeis University Art Collection.

BASKIN, LEONARD (1922–), U.S. printmaker and sculptor. Baskin was the son of a leading orthodox rabbi, Samuel Baskin, in New Brunswick, New Jersey, and was sent to a yeshivah. Later, he received an artistic training in the U.S., Italy, and France. He was influenced in his early years by Ben Shahn. From 1953 he taught printmaking and sculpture at Smith College, Northampton, Massachusetts. Baskin's frequent subject is anxiety-ridden man. His rather precise pen-and-ink drawings, and his much looser brush drawings, vibrant with energy, all used black, sometimes heavily, sometimes delicately, to capture on paper the story of man's torment. However, he preferred wood as a medium. He respected the texture of the material, knowing its character and limitations. The squareness of his figures and an emphasis of gesture bear witness to Baskin's debt to expressionist artists. Many of his drawings and prints concern Jewish subjects. [A.W.]

BASLE (Basel, Bâle), Swiss city. The earliest information on a Jewish community dates from the beginning of the 13th century when Basle was still a German free city. The medieval Jewish cemetery was discovered in recent years and the remains were transferred in 1938 to the present Jewish cemetery. In the Middle Ages the Basle Jews were free to acquire and sell real estate. They engaged in commerce and moneylending, sometimes providing loans to the bishops of Basle. Juridically they were under imperial protection: according to a roster of 1242 the Jews of Basle had to pay the crown an annual tax of 40 marks. During the *Black Death they were accused of poisoning the wells; the members of the city council attempted to defend them, but finally yielded to the guilds who demonstrated before the town hall. Six hundred Jews, with the rabbi at their head, were burned at the stake; 140 children were forcibly baptized. This ended the first Jewish community in Basle (Jan. 16, 1349).

In 1362 a Jew from Colmar in Alsace was permitted to settle in Basle; he was soon followed by others. In 1365 the emperor transferred his prerogatives over the Jews of Basle to the town. The second half of the 14th century was a period of prosperous growth despite restrictions imposed by the Church. However, in 1397, the slander of well poisoning was renewed. The Jews fled in panic and the community again came to an end. In 1434 a *Church Council held in Basle introduced compulsory attendance of Jews at conversionist sermons.

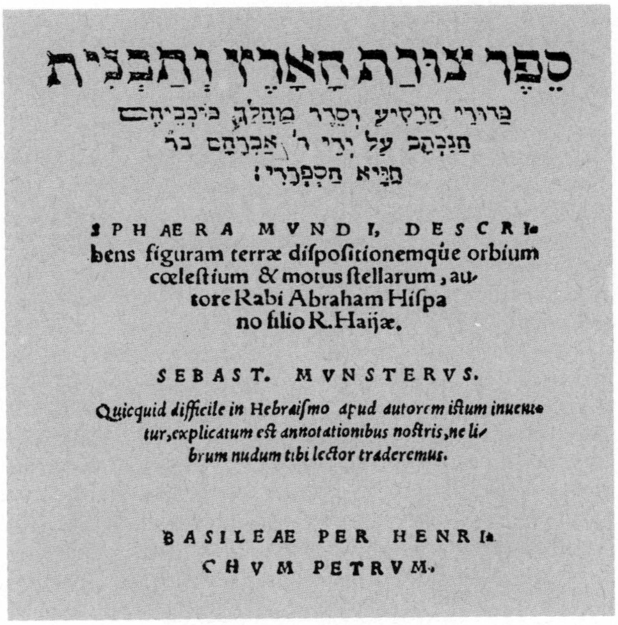

ספר צורת הארץ ותבנית
ברורי הרקיע וסדר מהלך כוכביהם
חברה על ידי ר' אברהם בר
חייא הספרדי:

SPHAERA MVNDI, DESCRIbens figuram terræ dispositionemque orbium cœlestium & motus stellarum, autore Rabi Abraham Hispano filio R. Haijæ.

SEBAST. MVNSTERVS.

Quicquid difficile in Hebraismo apud autorem istum inuenitur, explicatum est annotationibus nostris, ne librum nudum tibi lector traderemus.

BASILEAE PER HENRICHVM PETRVM.

Figure 1. Title page of *Ẓurat Ha-Areẓ ve-Tavnit Kaddurei ha-Raki'a* by Abraham b. Ḥiyya (Ḥayya) ha-Sefardi, printed in Basle in 1546 by Henricus Petrus. This edition of the 12th-century work on astronomy has a Latin translation by Sebastian Munster. Jerusalem, J.N.U.L.

Figure 2. The Basle synagogue consecrated in 1868 and renovated after World War II.

For four centuries there was no Jewish community in Basle. From the mid-16th century Basle authorities alternately issued residence permits to individuals and expulsion edicts. At the end of that century Basle became a center for Hebrew printing. The printing houses were owned by Christians, but they had to have recourse to Jewish proofreaders for whom they obtained residence permits. Johannes *Froben published the Psalms in 1516. His son Jerome in 1536 published a Bible in Hebrew. In 1578–80 Ambrosius Froben was permitted to print a duly censored edition of the Talmud, which had been banned under Pope Julius III in 1553 and placed on the Index in 1559. Also printed there were the works of Johannes *Buxtorf (father and son) who taught Hebrew at Basle University (1591–1664). In 1789, when anti-Jewish propaganda was rife in Alsace, many Alsatian Jews fled to Basle and were permitted to stay there temporarily. On the request of the French government the city authorities in 1797 exempted French Jews entering Basle from payment of the "body-tax" usually imposed on Jews, and in 1798 the tax was abolished completely. Under Napoleon several Jews, mainly French citizens from Alsace, settled in Basle. They numbered 128 in 1805 and were organized in a community. In 1845, however, they were expelled when the French government broke off relations with the canton. Some of the Jews returned after a brief interval, but in 1854 were again forced to leave. After the granting of emancipation to the Jews of Switzerland in 1866 Jews were able to return and settle in Basle. A synagogue was consecrated in 1868.

The first Zionist Congress was held in Basle in 1897 where the "*Basle Program" was adopted; other Zionist Congresses were subsequently held there: the second (1898), the third (1899), the fifth (1901), the sixth (1903), the seventh (1905), the 17th (1931), and the 22nd (1946). Prominent members of the Basle community were Z. Dreyfuss-Brodsky, representative of Swiss Jewry in the Jewish Agency (d. 1942), and the lawyer Marcus Mordecai

Cohn (1890–1953), an active Zionist and rabbinical scholar, who later became adviser on Jewish law to the Ministry of Justice in Israel. Other prominent Basle Jews were the chemist Markus Guggenheim (1885–) and Tadeus *Reichstein (1897–), who was awarded the Nobel Prize for Medicine in 1950. During World War II Basle served as a temporary refuge for many Jewish refugees. Most of them left after the war. The second largest Jewish community in Switzerland, Basle had 2,291 Jews in 1960 and 838 Jewish families in 1969. The community maintains a community-house and an old-age home. The Orthodox community (founded in 1927), with a membership of approximately 70 families, has its own rabbi and network of activities. The Union of Jewish Women in Switzerland is centered in Basle and there are also WIZO and other Zionist organizations. A Jewish day-school and a small, but excellent, Jewish museum are maintained by the community. Since 1940 the weekly *Juedische Rundschau Maccabi* has been published.

Bibliography: A. Wedler-Steinberg, *Geschichte der Juden in der Schweiz* (1966), passim; A. Wolf, *Juden in Basel: 1543–1872* (1909); M. Ginsburger, in: REJ, 87 (1929), 209–11; idem, in: *Basler Zeitschrift fuer Geschichte und Altertumskunde,* 8 (1909); Nordmann, *ibid.*, 13 (1913); idem, in: *Basler Jahrbuch* (1914, 1929); *Jahresberichte der Israelitischen Gemeinde Basel* (1938–1953). PRINTING: K. Y. Luethi, *Hebraeisch in der Schweiz* (1926), 4ff., 21ff.; R. N. N. Rabinowitz, *Ma'amar al Hadpasat ha-Talmud* (1952), 75ff., 121; J. Prijs, *Die Basler hebraeischen Drucke (1516–1828)* (1952); idem, *Der Basler Talmuddruck (1578–80)* (1960); A. M. Habermann, *Ha-Sefer ha-Ivri be-Hitpattehuto* (1968), index; B. Friedberg, *Ha-Defus ha-Ivri be-Eiropah* (1937).

[Z.AV./ED.]

Figure 4. The Basle municipal casino, venue of the First Zionist Congress, 1897, and five subsequent congresses. Jerusalem, Central Zionist Archives.

Figure 3. Theodor Herzl leaving the Basle synagogue, 1903. Jerusalem, Central Zionist Archives.

BASLE PROGRAM, original official program of the Zionist Organization, named after the city where the First Zionist Congress (see *Zionism) was held (August 23–31, 1897), and where the program was formulated and adopted. Its first sentence, stating the objective of the Zionist movement, was followed by a four-point program: "Zionism seeks to establish a home for the Jewish people in Palestine secured under public law. The Congress contemplates the following means to the attainment of this end: 1) The promotion by appropriate means of the settlement in Palestine of Jewish farmers, artisans, and manufacturers. 2) The organization and uniting of the whole of Jewry by means of appropriate institutions, both local and international, in accordance with the laws of each country. 3) The strengthening and fostering of Jewish national sentiment and national consciousness. 4) Preparatory steps toward obtaining the consent of governments, where necessary, in order to reach the goal of Zionism," while the term "Basle Program" includes both the statement of aim and the enumeration of means, the phrase is frequently used to refer solely to the first fundamental sentence.

The text of the Basle Program was prepared by a special commission set up by the Preliminary Conference that met in Basle two days before the opening of the Congress. It consisted of Nathan *Birnbaum, Max *Bodenheimer, Siegmund Mintz, Siegmund Rosenberg, Saul Rafael *Landau, Hermann *Schapira and Max *Nordau—all except the last two being lawyers. The draft constituted a compromise between opposing viewpoints, and a synthesis of various elements. One of these was Herzl's London Program, proposed during his visit to London in July, 1897, according to which the aim of Zionism was "the acquisition of a territory, in accordance with the Law of Nations, for those Jews who are not able or willing to assimilate themselves." Also of importance in the genesis of the Basle Program were Schapira's ideas on the colonization of Palestine and, in particular, the theses of the Cologne Nationaljuedische Vereinigung, headed by Bodenheimer, which postulated a Jewish commonwealth guaranteed by international law, the furtherance of the colonization of Palestine, dissemination of Jewish knowledge, and improvement in the social and cultural position of the Jews.

Not only Herzl in his *Judenstaat* (1896) but others, such as Bodenheimer, had expressly advocated a Jewish state, but the commission regarded it as prudent to refrain from using the word "state" in the official Zionist program. They felt that it was liable to antagonize Turkey, from which Herzl hoped to obtain the charter, and might also frighten certain Jewish circles. They therefore employed the term *"Heimstaette"* (home, or more exactly, homestead), suggested by Nordau, who submitted the draft proposal of the program to the Congress. This draft spoke of a "home secured by law" *(rechtlich gesicherte Heimstaette)*.

Representatives of the younger generation, such as Fabius Schach and Leo *Motzkin—who spoke on this subject in the plenary session of the Congress—took exception to the term and proposed replacing it by "secured by International Law" *("voelkerrechtlich gesicherte Heimstaette")*, wishing to emphasize the political character of the World Zionist Organization and to distinguish it clearly from the *Ḥibbat Zion*, whose cautious approach and exclusively philanthropic methods they strongly resented. It was Herzl himself who provided a compromise formula, which he had already used in his speeches—*"oeffentlich-rechtlich gesicherte Heimstaette"* ("home secured by public law") and this formula met with universal approval. With this amendment the commission's draft proposal was unanimously passed by the Congress and became the official program of the World Zionist Organization for more than half a century. Parts of the first sentence of the Basle Program were incorporated into the *Balfour Declaration (1917) and the League of Nations Mandate over Palestine (1922).

After the declaration of Israel's independence (1948), it was felt that the Zionist program should be adapted to the new situation created by the establishment of the State of Israel, which had fulfilled the main postulate of Zionism. The most important among the proposals for a new Zionist program were those drafted by a committee established by the Zionist Organization of America and headed by the jurist Simon Rifkind, and another put forward by the American Section of the Jewish Agency Executive (both in 1949). These proposals assumed that the establishment of the state was a step toward, rather than a full realization of, the Zionist goal.

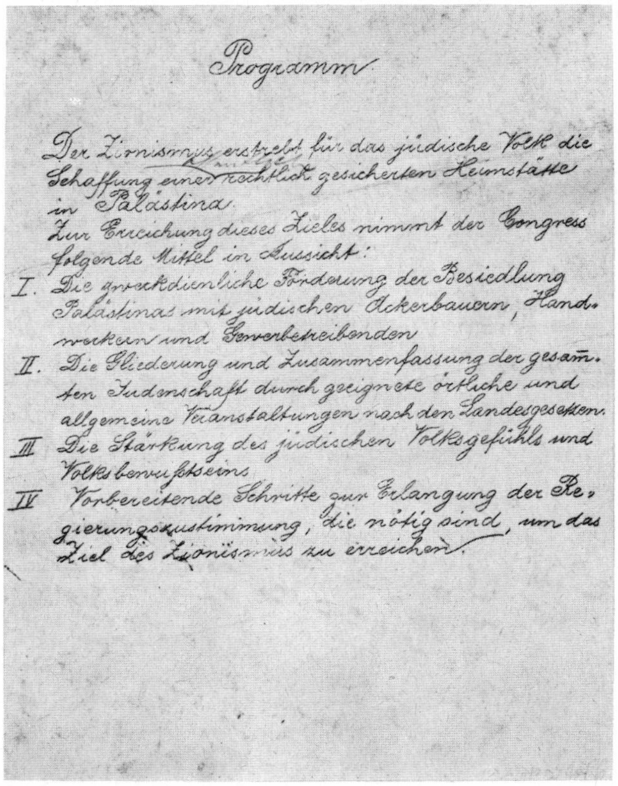
Programm

Der Zionismus erstrebt für das jüdische Volk die Schaffung einer rechtlich gesicherten Heimstätte in Palästina.
Zur Erreichung dieses Zieles nimmt der Congress folgende Mittel in Aussicht:
I. Die zweckdienliche Förderung der Besiedlung Palästinas mit jüdischen Ackerbauern, Handwerkern und Gewerbetreibenden
II. Die Gliederung und Zusammenfassung der gesammten Judenschaft durch geeignete örtliche und allgemeine Veranstaltungen nach den Landesgesetzen.
III Die Stärkung des jüdischen Volksgefühls und Volksbewußtseins
IV Vorbereitende Schritte zur Erlangung der Regierungszustimmung, die nötig sind, um das Ziel des Zionismus zu erreichen.

The Basle Program distributed to delegates to the First Zionist Congress, 1897. Jerusalem, Central Zionist Archives.

The question of the Zionist program figured high on the agenda of the 23rd Zionist Congress (Jerusalem, 1951), the first to meet after the proclamation of the state. The Congress committee charged with reformulating the Zionist program was headed by Ezra Shapiro (U.S.). Rather than abolishing the Basle Program and replacing it by a new one, the committee proposed completing it by a declaration that was officially styled "the task of Zionism." Generally known as the Jerusalem Program, this document reads as follows: "The task of Zionism is the consolidation of the State of Israel, the ingathering of the exiles in Ereẓ Israel and the fostering of the unity of the Jewish people." The Basle Program was retained and its first sentence—as well as the whole Jerusalem Program—was incorporated into the new constitution of the World Zionist Organization of 1960. There were several reasons for the affirmation of the Basle Program. First, a majority could not be found at the Congress for an entirely new reformulation of the goal and aim of Zionism. There were differences of opinion between the delegates from the United States and other English-speaking countries on the one hand and Israel and some Diaspora countries on the other, concerning the "Redemption of Israel through the Ingathering of Exiles" and other propositions. Further, it was felt that, at a time when little more than 10% of the Jewish people were living in the State of Israel, the "home" mentioned in the Basle Program could not be regarded as fully established. The desire to observe a time-honored tradition and to emphasize the continuity of the Zionist movement also played a part in the decision to retain the original platform of the Zionist Organization.

After the Six-Day War in 1967, when the Jewish people all over the world had shown its solidarity with embattled Israel, at least two points of the Jerusalem Program—those regarding the consolidation of the state and the unity of the Jewish people—had become common ground for the overwhelming majority of all Jews. It was felt, therefore, by many Zionists that the Jerusalem Program had lost much of its distinctive Zionist character, precisely because it was so widely accepted. The demand was increasingly voiced to keep the Basle Program unchanged but to revise the Jerusalem Program by making it more outspokenly Zionist. This revision, prepared by the Zionist Executive, was accomplished at the 27th Zionist Congress (Jerusalem, 1968). The Revised Jerusalem Program read as follows: "The aims of Zionism are: the unity of the Jewish people and the centrality of Israel in Jewish life; the ingathering of the Jewish people in its historic homeland Ereẓ Israel through *aliyah* from all countries; the strengthening of the State of Israel which is based on the prophetic vision of justice and peace; the preservation of the identity of the Jewish people through the fostering of Jewish and Hebrew education and of Jewish spiritual and cultural values; the protection of Jewish rights everywhere." This Revised Jerusalem Program was not merely an amplification and elaboration of the 1951 version; it introduced new points, some of which had been included in minority proposals at the 23rd Congress but had not been passed by the Plenary Session. These are the postulates of immigration from all lands; of Jewish and Hebrew education, as well as emphasis on the centrality of Israel in the life of the Jewish people and, consequently, of every Zionist.

Bibliography: H.H. Bodenheimer, *Toledot Tokhnit Basel* (1947); A. Bein, *Theodor Herzl* (1962[2]), index; B. Halpern, *Idea of the Jewish State* (1969[2]), index; L. Jaffe (ed.), *Sefer ha-Kongress* (1950[2]).

[A.Z.]

°**BASNAGE, JACQUES CHRISTIAN** (also called **Basnage de Beauval;** 1653–1725), Protestant divine and historian. Basnage was born in Rouen, France. In 1676 he became pastor there but after the revocation of the Edict of Nantes he accepted a call first to Rotterdam (1686) and later to the Hague (1691). He wrote several books, the most famous being *L'histoire et la réligion des Juifs depuis Jésus Christ jusqu'à present* (5 vols., 1706–11; Eng. *The History and Religion of the Jews from the time of Jesus Christ to the Present,* 1708), which was praised by Voltaire. The book was intended to supplement and continue the history of Josephus, but is marred by the author's inadequate knowledge of Hebrew, which obliged him to rely on Latin translations of Jewish sources and authors. He made use of the works of Buxtorf and Arias Montano and other Christian scholars. Despite Basnage's dry style and occasional inability to control the vast material, his book enjoyed great popularity and was the basis for later, more informed Jewish histories. In 1713 Basnage published another book on Jewish history *Antiquités judaïques ou Remarques critiques sur la république des hébreux.* His books are important as the first comprehensive and truly erudite history of the Jews in the Christian era, filling a gap between early Jewish historical writings and modern Jewish historical research.

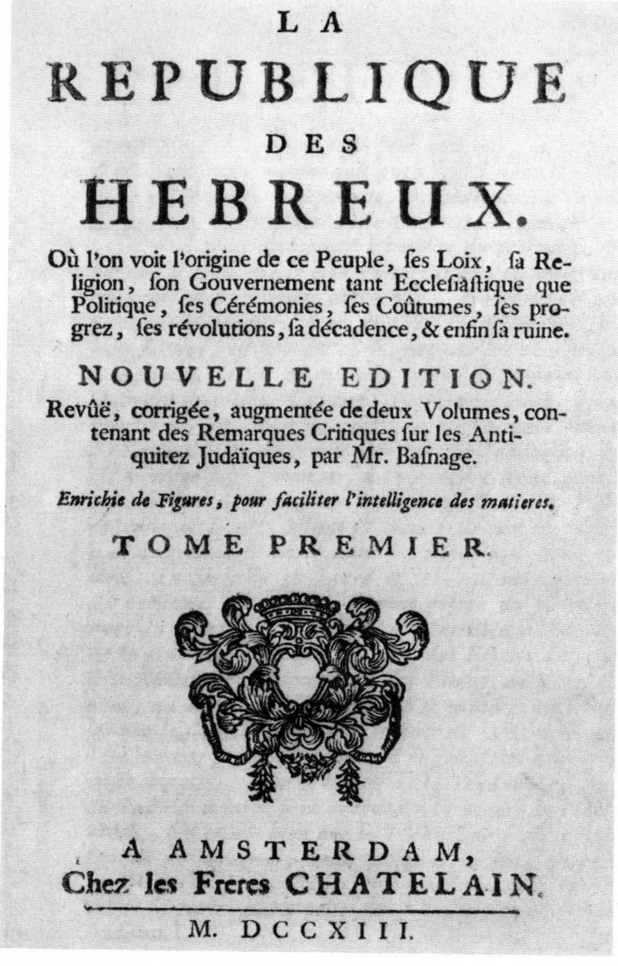
LA
REPUBLIQUE
DES
HEBREUX.
Où l'on voit l'origine de ce Peuple, ses Loix, sa Religion, son Gouvernement tant Ecclesiastique que Politique, ses Cérémonies, ses Coûtumes, ses progrez, ses révolutions, sa décadence, & enfin sa ruine.
NOUVELLE EDITION.
Revûë, corrigée, augmentée de deux Volumes, contenant des Remarques Critiques sur les Antiquitez Judaïques, par Mr. Basnage.
Enrichie de Figures, pour faciliter l'intelligence des matieres.
TOME PREMIER.
A AMSTERDAM,
Chez les Freres CHATELAIN.
M. DCCXIII.

Title page of the first volume of *La république des hébreux* by Jacques Christian Basnage, Amsterdam, 1713. Jerusalem, J.N.U.L.

Bibliography: Bernfeld, in: *Ha-Shilo'aḥ,* 2 (1897), 198–201; E.A. Mailhet, *Jacques Basnage, théologien, controversiste, diplomate et historien: sa vie et ses écrits* (1880); Graetz, Hist, 6 (1949), index; *Dictionnaire de biographie française,* 5 (1951), 734.

[B.D.]

BASOLA, MOSES BEN MORDECAI (I) (1480–1560), Italian rabbi and traveler. Basola was apparently of French extraction, since he signed himself **"Ẓarefati"** ("The Frenchman"); it has been conjectured that his surname is identical with Basilea, i.e., Basle. Born in Pesaro, Basola served as rabbi there. He supported his pupil Immanuel *Benevento in his endeavor to publish the Zohar and his authorization was included at the beginning of the *Tikkunei ha-Zohar* (Mantua, 1558). In 1521 Basola went on a pilgrimage to Palestine, remaining there for more than a year and a half. His account of his journey, *Shivḥei Yerushalayim* ("Praises of Jerusalem") was edited by Jacob b. Ḥayyim and published in 1938 by Izhak Ben-Zvi, the first to identify its author. The work is remarkable for its clarity, critical faculty, and clear delineation of economic and social conditions. At the end are appended an account of the organization of Jewish communal life in Jerusalem, reports on the (mythical) river *Sambatyon, and advice to Jewish sea travelers. On his return Basola took up residence in Ancona as rabbi, and in 1555 led the opposition against the boycott of the port of Ancona, which was organized by Gracia *Nasi to avenge the persecution of the Marranos there. He appealed to the Turkish rabbis either to withdraw the excommunication on those who traded with Ancona or allow every community to decide for itself. Basola was also in touch with the French Christian kabbalist Guillaume *Postel, who termed him the man "who by his outstanding erudition was renowned as pope and chief of all the Jews of this century." Shortly afterward he returned to Palestine and settled in Safed, where he died.

MOSES BASOLA (II) (16th century), kabbalist originally from Safed and possibly the grandson of Moses Basola I, settled in Italy, where he edited, together with Gedaliah b. Moses Cordovero, *Or Ne'erav* (a compendium of *Pardes Rimmonim,* Venice, 1587) and *Tomer Devorah* (Venice, 1589), both by Moses Cordovero.

MOSES BASOLA (III) (16th century), properly Della Rocca, was grandson through his mother of Moses Basola I. He was the teacher of Leone *Modena at Ferrara (1582–84). Subsequently he went to Cyprus where he died. Modena wrote a poem in his memory, which can be read either as Hebrew or Italian.

Bibliography: C. Roth, *The House of Nasi: Doña Graciá* (1947), ch. 7; I. Ben-Zvi, *Masot Ereẓ Yisrael le-Moshe Basola* (1938); F. Secret, *Le Zôhar chez les kabbalistes chrétiens de la Renaissance* (1958), 55; S. Bernstein (ed.), *Divan Yehudah Aryeh mi-Modena* (1932), 51f.

[C.R.]

BASRA, port in southern Iraq, on the Shaṭṭ al-Arab, the outlet into the Persian Gulf of the rivers Tigris and Euphrates. Jews settled there under the *Umayyad regime and one of the nine canals near the town is called Nahr al-Yahūd ("River of the Jews"). Jews also settled in Ubulla, then the port of the town of Basra and now the site of Basra. Toward the end of the Umayyad caliphate, Māsarjawayh, a Jewish physician from Basra, gained fame for his Arabic translations of Greek medical books. In the first generation of Abbasid rule, the court astrologer was the Jew, Misha b. Abra, called Māshāallah. Besides many artisans and merchants, the Basra Jewish community comprised many religious scholars, including Simeon Kayyara of Ṣabkha (suburb of Basra), who wrote *Halakhot Gedolot* about 825. The sages of Basra were in close contact with the academy of *Sura, to which the community sent an annual contribution of 300 dinars. In the tenth century when the academy closed, the last *gaon,* *Joseph b. Jacob, settled in Basra. But until about 1150 the Jews of Basra continued to direct their questions on religious matters to the heads of the yeshivah in Baghdad, and especially to *Sherira Gaon and his son *Hai Gaon. From these questions, it appears that the Jews of Basra had close commercial ties with the Jews of Baghdad. Both a Rabbanite and a Karaite community existed in Basra. A Karaite, Israel b. Simḥah b. Saadiah b. Ephraim, dedicated a *Ben-Asher version of the Bible to the Karaite community of Jerusalem. In the 11th century, Basra was gradually abandoned as a result of civil wars in Mesopotamia; and many of its Jews emigrated. Solomon b. Judah (d. 1051), head of the Jerusalem yeshivah, mentions religious scholars and physicians from Basra in Palestine and Egypt.

However, throughout the Middle Ages there remained an important community in Basra. *Benjamin of Tudela (c. 1170) reports that approximately 10,000 Jews, including many wealthy men and religious scholars, lived in the town. He also mentions the grave north of the town, believed to be that of *Ezra and also venerated by the Muslims. According to an early 13th century letter by Daniel b. Eleazar b. Nethanel Ḥibat Allah, head of the Baghdad yeshivah, there was also a synagogue in the town named for Ezra. When the Mongols conquered Iraq in the mid-13th century, Basra surrendered and was not severely damaged. However, when Tamerlane conquered Mesopotamia in 1393, many Jews were killed and all the synagogues in the town were destroyed. Nevertheless, a small community continued to exist.

The community regained its importance during the 18th century. Its wealth increased; rich landowners in the community liberally distributed alms and even sent contributions to Ereẓ Israel. The liturgical poem *Megillat Paras* ("Persian Scroll,") by the emissary from Hebron, Jacob Elyashar, describes the siege of Basra by the Persians and the town's deliverance in 1775, when the Jewish minister of finance, Jacob b. Aaron, who had been captured, was released. Afterward, Nisan 2nd—the day on which the siege was lifted—was celebrated in Basra as the "Day of the Miracle." Jews played such a vital role in the commercial life of Basra that in 1793 the representative of the East India Company was forced to live in Kuwait for nearly two years, because he had quarreled with the Jewish merchants. In 1824 David d'Beth Hillel reported 300 Jewish households belonging to merchants and artisans in Basra and a Jewish finance minister. During the persecutions of Jews which took place under the rule of Dā'ūd Pasha in the early 19th century, several wealthy members of the Basra community emigrated to India. The traveler, Benjamin II, mentions that in 1848, he found about 300 Jewish families in Basra. But in 1860 Jehiel Fischel, an emissary of the rabbis of Safed, reports 40 Jewish families in the town out of a population of 12,000. After the British occupation in 1914, the number of Jews increased from 1,500 to 9,921 in 1947, when Jews constituted 9.8% of the total population. Most of the Jews were traders and many worked in the administration service of the railroads, the airport, and the seaport. The legal status of the community was regulated by a 1931 law, according to which a president and a chief rabbi were assigned to head it. A boys' school was founded by the Alliance Israélite Universelle in 1903, and later became a high school. In 1950 it had 450 pupils. In 1913 an Alliance Israélite Universelle girls' school was founded, and attended in 1930 by 303 pupils. All schools were under the supervision of the community committee. In the 1930s, a

מגלת פרס

על הנס שנעשה בעיר בצרה יע"א

יום ב' ניסן שנת התק"לה

והוספנו בה את המעשה אשר נעשה

בזמן ההוא וגם מעשה שני יום הנס

העושים פה בגדאד יע"א בקמדה

י"ר שנשמח בביאת הגואל צדק בב"א :

פה בגדאד יע"א

שנת שמחה וישׂשון ליהודים לפ"ק

בדפוס ה' עזרא דנגור ס"ט

Title page of *Megillat Paras,* the story of the Basra "Purim" commemorating the town's deliverance from the Persians in 1775, Baghdad, 1906. Jerusalem, Ben-Zvi Institute.

theosophical group was formed and headed by the Jew Kadduri Elijah 'Aani (who went to Palestine in 1945 and died in Jerusalem). The community excommunicated this group, and its Jewish members were forced to establish their own synagogue, cemetery, and slaughter-house. A Zionist association, formed in Basra in 1921, was not allowed freedom of action. [E.A.]

Modern Period. From 1942, the clandestine He-Ḥalutz and Haganah organizations were active spreading Hebrew, organizing *aliyah,* and in anticipation of pogroms, instructing young people in the use of weapons. These organizations were dissolved in 1951. On September 23, 1948, a Jewish millionaire, Shafīq ʿAdas, was hanged in Basra, having been sentenced to death and fined £5,000,000 for selling British army surplus scrap metal to Israel. The Jews shut themselves in their houses, while thousands of Muslims watched the public hanging; but there were no attacks on Jews. All attempts to save ʿAdas failed, despite his connections in government circles. In 1949–50, Basra served as a center for the flight of Jews to Iran. Thousands were helped by smugglers to cross the Shaṭṭ al-ʿArab to the Iranian shore. The few who were caught were sentenced to imprisonment. By 1968 less than 500 Jews were living in Basra. On Jan. 27, 1969, 4 persons were hanged there, having been accused of espionage for Israel. [H.J.C.]

Bibliography: Sassoon, in: JQR, 17 (1926/27), 407–69; A. Ben-Yaacov, *Yehudei Bavel* (1965), index (bibliography: 388–415); S. Landshut, *Jewish Communities in the Muslim Countries of the Middle East* (1950), 44–45, passim; Y. F. Kestelman, *Masot Sheli'ah Ẓefat be-Arẓot ha-Mizraḥ* (1942), 56–58; H. J. Cohen, *Ha-Pe'ilut ha-Ẓiyyonit be-Irak* (1969), index.

BASS (Bezprozvany), HYMAN B. (1904–), Yiddish educator and essayist. Born in Vilna, Bass emigrated to New York in 1922 and taught in Yiddish schools. From 1953 he served as executive secretary of the *Congress for Jewish Culture and in 1966 as president of the Jewish Book Council of America. He edited textbooks for Yiddish schools and wrote extensively on Jewish education. His book of essays *Unzer Dor Muz Antsheydn* ("Our Generation Must Decide," 1963), embodied his ideas on Jewish education and cultural survival. S. Dubnow, Y. L. Peretz, and Chaim Zhitlowsky were his mentors and he adapted their ideas to the mid-20th century American Jewish scene.

Bibliography: LNYL, 1 (1956), 355–9. [S.L.]

BASS (or **Bassista;** Heb. מְשׁוֹרֵר), **SHABBETAI BEN JOSEPH** (1641–1718), the first Jewish bibliographer. Bass's parents were killed in a pogrom in Kalisz (Poland) by the Cossacks in 1655, but he and his elder brother were saved and fled to Prague. Possessing a pleasant voice, Bass was engaged as an assistant singer (hence his nickname Bass) to the cantor Loeb at the Altneu synagogue (Altneuschul) in Prague. In Prague he acquired a thorough knowledge of the Talmud, and also a general education which included Latin. His love of books and a critical spirit drew him to publication and printing. In 1669 in Prague he printed a revised edition of the Yiddish commentary on the Pentateuch and the Five Scrolls by Moses Saertels, *Be'er Moshe,* with an appendix on "grammatical rules." As there was no complete list in Hebrew of Jewish literature, he undertook to compile one. Between 1674 and 1679 Bass visited libraries in Poland, Germany, and Holland. In Amsterdam he studied the art of printing and proofreading, and published: *Massekhet Derekh Ereẓ,* a guide book for travelers (1680); the Pentateuch with a super-commentary on Rashi, *Siftei Ḥakhamim* (1680), a popular commentary often reprinted; and *Siftei Yeshenim* (1680), a list in Hebrew of some 2,200 Hebraica and Judaica. This was the first Jewish bibliography in Hebrew giving, apart from the names of the books, the name of the author, content, format, place and year of printing, and sometimes also where it could be found. He also listed manuscripts. In some copies a prayerbook was appended to the list. In 1688 Bass obtained a permit to set up a Hebrew printing press at Auras, and this was shortly afterward transferred to *Dyhernfurth. The first book printed by Bass was Samuel b. Uri Shraga's commentary *Beit Shemu'el* (1689), on Shulḥan Arukh *Even ha-Ezer.* He also successfully engaged in bookselling. When the Jesuits accused Bass of spreading hatred against the Christians and the government, he at first succeeded in refuting the accusations; but in 1712 the Jesuits repeated the accusations and he was arrested. In the trial he succeeded in proving the ignorance of his accusers, and was released. His sons and grandsons continued to print books at Dyhernfurth up to the second half of the 18th century.

Bibliography: Bloch, in: *Studies in Jewish Bibliography*... (1929), index; Shunami, Bibl, index. [A.M.H.]

BASSAN, ABRAHAM HEZEKIAH BEN JACOB (18th century), proofreader and poet. Abraham's father, Jacob, was the rabbi of the Spanish and Portuguese community of Hamburg. From 1735 to 1756 Jacob lived in Amsterdam and in 1755 published an order of service for the fast day proclaimed on the occasion of the great earthquake in Lisbon.

Abraham Hezekiah was proofreader for the Hebrew press in Amsterdam. He is mentioned as the proofreader of Benjamin Raphael Dias Brandon's *Orot ha-Mitzvot* (1753) to which his father wrote an approbation, and to which Abraham contributed an introduction and poem consisting of 13 stanzas. Other poems by Abraham were published in works by various authors: in the *Gemul Atalyah* (1770) of David *Franco-Mendes, in the *Se'ah Solet* (1757) of Raphael b. Gabriel Norzi, and in the *Maskiyyot Kesef* (1760) of Mordecai b. Isaac Tamah. In about 1773 he moved to Hamburg where he succeeded his father as rabbi of the local Spanish and Portuguese community. He was the author of a book of eulogies, *Sermões Funebres* (Amsterdam, 1753) written in Spanish. It is doubtful that he is the author of the *Yashresh Ya'akov* (Nuremberg, 1768), a work on grammar and the text of the prayer book, as has been conjectured (see Benjacob, Oẓar, 234 no. 503).

Bibliography: Ghirondi-Neppi, 10 no. 40; Kayserling, Bibl, 26. [Y.Ho.]

BASSANI, GIORGIO (1916–), Italian author. Bassani, who was born in Bologna, lived for many years in Ferrara. His first published work was a small volume of stories and poems entitled *Una città di pianura* (1940), which, because of the Fascist anti-Semitic laws, was printed under the pseudonym "Giacomo Marchi." In 1945 he made his reputation with a book of elegiac, nostalgic poems about Ferrara and the surrounding countryside, *Storie di poveri amanti.* His collection of short stories, *Cinque storie ferraresi* (1956), deal with his persecution as a Jew, his experiences during World War II, and the struggle against Fascism. These stories give a subtle picture of the contrast between the little world of the Ferrara Jewish bourgeoisie and that of the workmen and peasants of the area. They also deal with the theme of spiritual loneliness and lack of communication between individuals and between individuals and society, which Bassani developed further in his psychological novels. The two most famous of these, which are in the tradition of Henry James, are *Una lapide in via Mazzini* (1953) and *Gli occhiali d'oro* (1958; *The Gold-Rimmed Spectacles,* 1960). The former is the story of a survivor of a concentration camp who finds it impossible to resume life in his native town because the people there regard him as an embarrassing reminder of a tragedy they wish to forget. The latter deals with the tragedy of two men rejected by society, one because he is a homosexual, the other because he is a Jew. *Il giardino dei Finzi Contini* (1962; *The Garden of the Finzi Contini,* 1965) was translated into a number of languages, including Hebrew. This dealt with the author's youth in Ferrara, and told the story of an aristocratic Jewish family unable to come to terms with the present, or to face the social upheaval brought about by Fascism and the war. Bassani's Proustian style is even more marked in *Dietro la porta* (1964), a novel recollecting the transition from adolescence to maturity. He also wrote *L'airone* (1968; *The Heron,* 1969). Among his nonfictional writing is another book of verse, *L'alba ai vetri* (1963), and a collection of essays, *Le parole preparate* (1966). From 1948 to 1961 he edited the literary review, *Botteghe Oscure,* and from 1964 to 1965 was a vice-president of the Italian radio and television.

Bibliography: G. Pullini, *Romanzo italiano del dopoguerra* (1961), 177–9, 183–92; G.C. Ferretti, *Letteratura e ideologia* (1964), 17–65 (includes bibliography); Acerbi, in: *Aevum,* 1–2 (1966), 177–88;

Bertacchini, in: *Figure e problemi di narrativa contemporanea* (1960), 303–38; Bertacchini, in: *Letterature Moderne* (March–June 1962); Romano, in: *Scritti... L. Carpi* (1967), 109–202.

[J.B.S.]

BASSANI, MORDECAI (**Marco** in Italian; the name **Hezekiah** was added on the occasion of his last illness, c. 1632–1703, Italian rabbi and polemicist. In 1666 he became preacher to the Ashkenazi community of Verona, and in 1680 he became its rabbi; in 1695 he was appointed rabbi of the entire Verona community. He was the author of *Sefer Bikkurim* (Venice, 1710) containing deathbed prayers and usages (adapted from *Ma'avar Yabbok* of *Aaron Berechiah ben Moses of Modena, and *Shenei Luḥot Ha-Berit* of Isaiah *Horowitz) written for the Bikkur Ḥolim fraternity of Verona, but later widely adopted. His treatise on divorce, entitled *Mikhtav le-Ḥizkiyyah,* and one on *ḥaliẓah,* entitled *Ma'amar Mordekhai,* were included by his great-grandson Menahem Navarra in his *Penei Yiẓḥak* (Verona, 1743). In his will he mentions a collection of "moral sermons" which he had compiled (*Avnei Binyan,* 1 (1938), 65). He was friendly with the Roman Catholic polemicist Fra Luigi Maria Benetelli. His criticisms of Benetelli's polemical work, *Le saette di Gionata...* (Venice, 1703) together with those of Samson *Morpurgo and Abraham Joel *Conegliano prompted Benetelli's rejoinder, *I dardi rabbinici infranti...* (Venice, 1705). In this work Benetelli speaks in the highest terms of the gentle manner, great charity, and admirable character of Bassani. Bassani is also the author of a lengthy responsum on the relationship between the Ashkenazi community of Verona and the smaller Sephardi community there.

Bibliography: S. Baron, in: *Sefer... S. Krauss* (1936), 217–54; Sonne, in: *Zion,* 3 (1938), 123ff.; Simonsohn, in: KS, 35 (1959), 127 n. 1; 253 n. 109; C. Roth, *Gleanings...* (1967), 203, 206–7, 213.

[C.R.]

BASSANO, small town in northern Italy. The first known Jew in Bassano made loans on mortgage from 1252 to 1265. Subsequently, other Jews lent money on pledge, but at the end of the 13th century, Jews were prohibited from practicing moneylending in the town. At the beginning of the 15th century, shortly after Bassano passed under Venetian rule, Jewish moneylenders of German origin settled in Bassano but underwent many vicissitudes. In 1475, following the ritual murder charge concerning Simon of *Trent, the municipality of Bassano unsuccessfully requested permission from Venice to expel the Jews. During the War of the League of Cambrai (1508), the Jews in Bassano paid a heavy tribute, but this did not prevent their expulsion from Bassano at the end of the war in 1509.

Bibliography: G. Chiuppani, *Gli ebrei a Bassano* (1907); Roth, Italy, index; Milano, Italia, index. [A.MIL.]

BASSANO (**Bassan, Bassani**), name of Italian family deriving from the town *Bassano. In the 17th and 18th centuries, it produced several rabbis and scholars, outstanding among whom are: MORDECAI *BASSANI (c. 1632–1703), rabbi of Verona and ISAIAH BEN ISRAEL HEZEKIAH (d. 1739), rabbi in Cento, Padua, Ferrara, and Reggio Emilia. Many of his responsa are included in the second volume of *Todat Shelamim* by his son Israel (see below) and in the *Paḥad Yiẓḥak* of Isaac *Lampronti. His other responsa, glosses on the Talmud, a number of poems, notes on the gospels, sermons, and a book, *Kur le-Zahav,* comprising critical notes on Solomon *Algazi's *Halikhot Eli,* remain in manuscript. His pupils included Moses Ḥayyim *Luzzatto. His son, ISRAEL BENJAMIN (1701–1790), one of the outstanding Italian Jewish poets of his day, published two collections of Hebrew poetry accompanied by Italian versions. He dedicated both to Francesco III of Este, duke of Modena (1750–53), calling the second *Corona Estense.* His *Todat Shelamim* (Venice, 1741, 1791) includes his own halakhic writings and responsa by his father. According to the Christian scholar G. B. *De Rossi, he was highly esteemed in Jewish circles.

Bibliography: I. Sonne, in: *Zion,* 3 (1938), 160–9 (where Israel Benjamin Bassano's will is published); Baron, in: *Sefer ha-Yovel... S. Krauss* (1937), 217–54; C. Roth, in: JQR, 15 (1924/25), 430 (=*Gleanings* (1967), 203, 206–7); Ghirondi-Neppi, s.v.

[C.R.]

BASSEVI OF TREUENBERG (**Treuenburg**), **JACOB** (1570–1634), Court Jew descended from a noted Prague family. He was probably the first European Jew outside Italy to be ennobled. Bassevi and his brother Samuel engaged in large-scale trading and in 1599 obtained a safe-conduct from the emperor exempting them from the restrictions imposed on most Jews. In 1611 Matthias II confirmed Bassevi's privileges and added the right of settling in Vienna. In 1622 because of the emperor's increased need of money during the Thirty Years War, Bassevi formed a consortium with Prince Liechtenstein and the imperial general Wallenstein, which leased the mint for an enormous sum and issued debased coinage. Bassevi, whose profit per silver mark was the lowest within the consortium, provided the financial expertise, and bought most of the necessary silver abroad. When currency dropped to one-seventh of its former value, the depreciated thaler was nicknamed the "Schmilesthaler", the Thaler of Shmil. In 1622 Ferdinand II granted Bassevi a coat of arms. This, however, evidently still did not endow Bassevi with unqualified noble rank, for shortly afterward he requested other privileges connected with his new status, which were nearly all granted.

Coat of arms of Jacob Bassevi, 17th-century head of Prague Jewry. Prague, State Jewish Museum.

Like other Court Jews, Bassevi took an active part in Jewish communal life. After the imperial troops left Prague in 1620, Bassevi organized a guard to defend the Jewish quarter from pillage. He obtained for the Jews in Prague in 1623 some 40 houses bordering on the Jewish quarter which had been confiscated from the rebels. He also paid 12,000 Reichsthaler toward the enormous indemnity demanded from Yom Tov Lipmann *Heller in 1629. As head of Prague Jewry for several years, Bassevi was largely responsible for apportioning the communal taxes, as a result of which the opposing faction complained about him to the authorities. After Prince Liechtenstein's death in 1627 the authorities took steps against the former members of the consortium, the complaints providing a welcome excuse for confiscating Bassevi's property and arresting him (1631). However, because of Bassevi's privileged status, Wallenstein succeeded in securing his release (1632). Bassevi then lived at Wallenstein's residence in Jicin, as fiscal administrator of his duchies. Bassevi survived the murder of Wallenstein in 1634 by only a few weeks and was buried at Mlada Boleslav. After his death all his privileges were declared illegal and abrogated.

Bassevi, who maintained his Jewishness while holding his high position, was considered a "princely Jew" ("Judenfuerst") by his fellow Jews—a fact which seems to have been of some comfort to them in those dark days.

Bibliography: S. Hock, *Die Familien Prags* (1892), 61–63, 367; Bondy-Dvorsky, 2 (1906), nos. 734, 818, 824, 948, 1044, 1045; Spiegel in: *Die Juden in Prag* (1927), 138–45; L. S. Porta, in: *Juedische Familien-Forschung*, 1 (1925–27), 12–15; H. Schnee, *Die Hoffinanz und der moderne Staat*, 3 (1955), 234–6; NDB, 1 (1953), 625; Hofmann, in: *Zeitschrift fuer die Geschichte der Juden in der Tschechoslowakei*, 4 (1934), 1–5; Polák-Rokycana, *ibid.*, 1 (1930–31), 253–6; Baron, Social[2], 14 (1969), 231–33.

[R.K.-G.]

BASSIN, MOSHE (1889–1963), Yiddish poet. Bassin, who was born in Nivki, Belorussia, immigrated to New York from Russia in 1907. From 1909 he contributed lyrics, folk ballads, and children's songs to American Yiddish journals. His reputation rests on two works: a two-volume, 600-page anthology, *500 Yor Yidishe Poezye* ("500 Years of Yiddish Poetry"), with notes on the earlier selections by Ber Borochov, which became a standard work; and an anthology of American Yiddish poetry *Amerikanishe Yidishe Poezye* (1940), encompassing 31 poets. Bassin's own lyrics appeared in various periodicals but were never collected in book form.

Bibliography: *Insich* (1940), 164–76; LNYL, 1 (1956), 228; J. Leftwich, *Golden Peacock* (1939), 411.

[M.R.]

°**BASSUS, LUCILIUS** (d. 72 C.E.), Roman governor of Judea after the fall of Jerusalem in 70 C.E. Bassus was instructed to subdue the fortresses of *Herodium, *Machaerus, and *Masada, which still remained in Jewish hands. He first attacked Herodium, which fell without a battle. Then he marched on Machaerus, which was so strongly fortified as to "inspire its occupants with high hopes of security." The defenders fought bravely until one of their leaders, Eleazar, was captured and the Romans threatened to crucify him opposite the walls. The defenders then agreed to surrender the fortress if Eleazar's life were spared. Bassus kept his promise and allowed the occupants to escape, but followed some *Sicarii who had escaped to a forest called Jardes, where they were all killed. Bassus died as he was preparing to begin operations against Masada. It was during his administration of Judea that Jewish-held lands were confiscated to become imperial domain, and that the poll-tax of the *Fiscus Judaicus was put into operation.

Bibliography: Jos., Wars, 7:163–5, 190–216, 252; Klausner, Bayit Sheni, 5 (1951[2]), 285ff.; Pauly-Wissowa, 26 (1927), 1640–42 (22).

[E.E.]

BAS-TOVIM, SARAH (c. 17th century), author of *tkhines* ("Yiddish prayers for women"). Her prayer pamphlet *Shloyshe Sheorim* ("Three Portals," 1838) deals with the three main *mitzvot* prescribed for women (*ḥallah, mikveh*, and kindling Sabbath and festival candles). It records the following biographical facts: Sarah was born in the Ukraine; her father Mordecai was the grandson of the

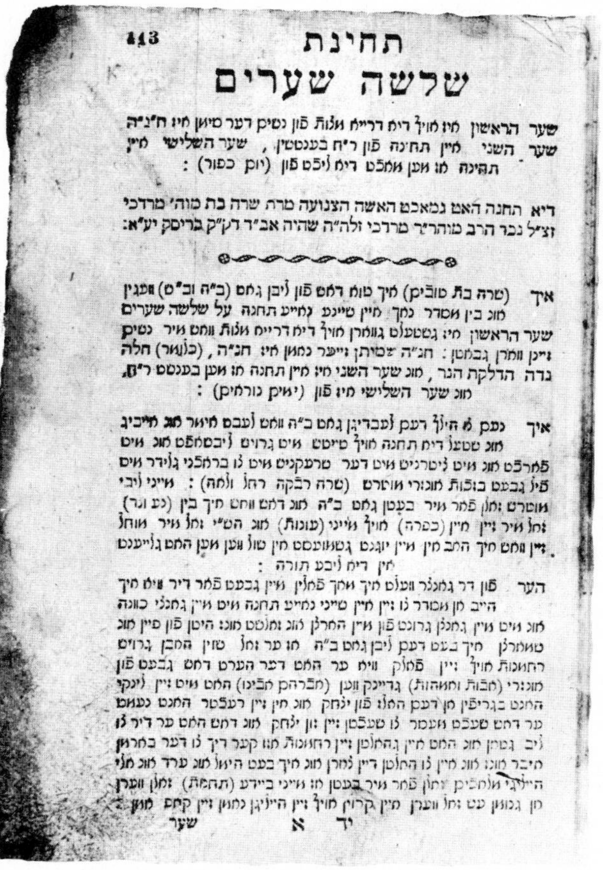
143

תחינת

שלשה שערים

די״א התחנה האט גמאכט האשה הצנועה מרת שרה בת מוה׳ מרדכי
זצ״ל נכר הרב מוהר״ר מרדכי זלה״ה שהיה אב״ד דק״ק בריסק יע״א:

Opening page of Sarah Bas-Tovim's Yiddish prayer pamphlet, *Shloyshe Sheorim*, printed 1838. Jerusalem, J.N.U.L.

rabbi of Brisk (Brest-Litovsk); she grew up in a wealthy home and loved to go to synagogue to display her jewelry; impoverished in her old age, she wandered from place to place. Her *tkhines* taught ethical laws and commandments in rhymed verse. *Shloyshe Sheorim* was already popular in the 18th century and Sarah's fame led to the publication of later *tkhines* under her name by others, including the Haskalah writers I. M. *Dick, Joshua *Meisach, Naftali Maskileison, and M. A. Shatzkes.

Bibliography: S. Niger, *Bleter-Geshikhte fun der Yidisher Literatur* (1959), 83–85.

[M.S.]

BAT (Heb. עֲטַלֵּף, *atallef*). About 20 species of insect-eating bats are found in Israel and one, the *Rousettus aegyptiacus*, which feeds on fruit. The bat is actually a mammal, but because of its wings which enable it to fly, the ancients were in doubt whether it was to be classified with birds or mammals. In the Bible it is last in the list of the unclean birds (Lev. 11:19) but the Talmud declares that "although it lays eggs, it suckles" (Bek. 7b). Apparently the rabbis attributed to the bat the eggs laid by other birds in their caves. The bat is long-lived (up to 30 years) and many legends were woven about its development (BK 16a). The bat causes extensive damage to fruit trees, particularly the date palm, as is indicated in the Jerusalem Talmud (TJ, Pe'ah 8:1, 20d).

Bibliography: Lewysohn, Zool, 102–5; F.S.Bodenheimer, *Ha-Ḥai be-Arẓot ha-Mikra,* 2 (1956), index; J. Feliks, *Animal World of the Bible* (1962), 47; S.Lieberman, in: *Leshonenu,* 29 (1965), 132–5.

[J.F.]

°**BATE, JULIUS** (1711–1771), English Christian Hebraist. As a member of the Hutchinsonians (a Christian sect) he was involved in a controversy with Bishop William Warburton (1698–1779) on the latter's *Divine Legation of Moses* (1737), and with Benjamin Kennicott (1718–1783) on the published emendations of the masoretic text (1751). Bate's mastery of the Hebrew Bible is demonstrated in his most famous work *Critica Hebraica* (1767), a Hebrew-English dictionary in which the biblical words are reduced to their original roots and their specific forms illustrated and exemplified by passages cited at length from the Scriptures. A strong Christian piety pervades this work and his translation of the Bible which goes to the end of II Kings (1773). He wrote various pamphlets in defense of biblical mysticism. [Z.G.]

BATH, spa in Somerset, England. A fashionable resort from the 18th century, Bath early attracted Jewish residents, among them the physician Isaac *Schomberg, as well as visitors. Shortly after 1800, Moses Samuel, formerly warden of the Great Synagogue in London who had retired to Bath, organized a congregation there, and on his death in 1839 left money for building a synagogue. The community subsequently dwindled, and regular services had ceased by 1874. Short-lived congregations have since been set up more than once, but by the 1960s there was no Jewish community in Bath.

Bibliography: C. Roth, *Rise of Provincial Jewry* (1950), 27–29.

[C.R.]

BATH, BATHING. Bathing is referred to in the Bible not only for physical cleanliness but also for ritual purposes. Jacob charged his family to wash themselves before they built the altar at Beth-El (Gen. 35:3). Before the revelation at Sinai, the entire Jewish nation was bidden to sanctify themselves by washing their bodies and their garments (Ex. 19:10). Ritual immersion was associated with levitical purity and was stressed in the Book of Leviticus (see *Mikveh). When Jeremiah described the sinfulness of Israel, he exclaimed, "For though thou wash thee with niter, and take thee much soap" (Jer. 2:22), it still would not remove the sins of the nation.

Talmudic Period. The Talmud declared it forbidden for a scholar to reside in a city which did not contain a public bath (Sanh. 17b). Rome was said to contain 3,000 public baths (Meg. 68) and despite the animosity to the Romans they were praised by the rabbis for constructing baths in Palestine (Shab. 33b). It is related that Rabban Gamaliel utilized the Bath of Aphrodite in Acre although the image of the idol adorned the bath (Av. Zar. 3:4). Originally the baths were communal institutions (Ned. 5:5). Afterward, smaller baths were also built by private individuals (BB 1:6; 10:7), and competition between them to attract customers was permitted (BB 21b). The bath attendants received checks or tokens from intending patrons so they would know in advance how many to expect and what preparations to make (BM 47b and Rashi ad loc.). The larger baths contained separate areas for bathing in lukewarm water, hot water, and steam baths (Shab. 40a). On entering the bathhouse, the rabbis ordained the following prayer: "May it be Thy will, O Lord, my God, to

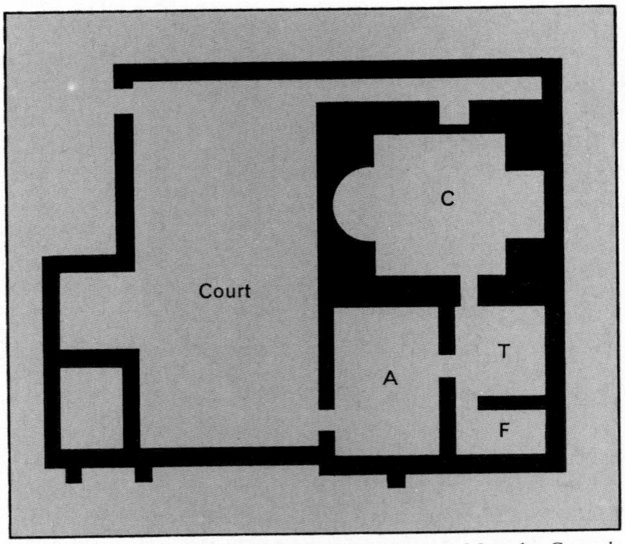

Plan of the large bathhouse from excavations at Masada. C=*caldarium* (hot room). T=*tepidarium* (tepid room). F=*frigidarium* (cold room). A=*apoditerium* (disrobing room). Yigael Yadin, Jerusalem.

deliver me from the flames of the fire and the heat of the water, and to protect me from a cave-in." Upon leaving, the individual recited, "I thank Thee, O Lord, my God, for having delivered me from the fire" (TJ, Ber. 9:6, 14b; cf. Ber. 60a). Hillel the Elder told his disciples that he considered bathing in the communal bathhouse a religious duty for just as the custodians scour and wash the statues of the kings, likewise must man, created in God's image and likeness, do to his body (Lev. R. 34:3).

Middle Ages and Modern Times. The public bath and adjoining *mikveh* were maintained by Jewish communities throughout the Middle Ages as part of the institutions of Jewish social life and welfare. Hygienic habits and the ritual requirements of the Jewish religion made the Jews regard bathing as part of their living routine during a period when bathing was generally considered a form of rare luxury in Europe. By the end of the 11th century, some Jewish communities erected imposing buildings to house their baths and regularly attended to their servicing and upkeep. The refusal of Christians to allow Jews to share the municipal baths and the fear that Jewish women might be molested there increased the need for separate institutions. The fact also, that, with the exception of Poland, Jews were prohibited from bathing in the same river as Christians finally led them to build their own bathhouses, which often became landmarks, such as the *Badehaus* of the Jews of Augsburg, or "Bakewell Hall" in London, which was probably originally "Bathwell Hall." In Moslem Spain, Ramon Berenger IV allowed his court physician, Abraham, to build the only public bathhouse in Barcelona, which his family ran from 1160 to 1199. In the Middle East, and in modern times, particularly in Eastern Europe, Jews became addicted to the "Turkish bath" which has found its way into Jewish folklore. Several ancient baths have been discovered in Ereẓ Israel such as the swimming pool and hot baths that Herod built at *Herodium, which had waiting rooms, dressing rooms, hot rooms, and cool rooms with all the comforts of the baths at Rome. Among the best-preserved and beautifully finished baths that have been uncovered in Ereẓ Israel are those on Masada, where no less than four baths and one swimming pool were built by Herod. In the northern palace there is a small, private bathhouse finished in Roman style, and south of the palace there is a large swimming pool with cubicles for keeping clothes; Herod built a small bathhouse in the west palace as well, which was unusually heated by an oven in an adjoining room and fitted with a niche for an oil lamp. More important, however, are the remains of the large bathhouse near the north palace where more than 200 stands, the remnants of the piping system for the hot air, were discovered, as well as elaborate facilities for steam baths, cold baths, etc., adorned with frescoes and mosaics. At a later period the Zealots built a large bathhouse in the southern corner of Masada, consisting of a small *mikveh* and two connecting larger ones, which conform to *halakhah*. Near Tiberias are the remains of the hot, mineral baths of *Hamath of the Roman period.

See also *Ablution, Tractate *Mikva'ot, *Mikveh, *Purity and Impurity, Ritual.

Bibliography: Y. Brand, *Kelei ha-Ḥeres ba-Sifrut ha-Talmudit* (1953), 27–35; G. Krauss, *Talmudische Archaeologie* (1910); U.E. Paoli, *Das Leben im alten Rom* (1948); J. Carcopino, *Daily Life in Ancient Rome* (1940); Th. Birt, *Zur Kulturgeschichte Roms* (1917); Baron, Social², 4 (1956), 37; I. Abrahams, *Jewish Life in the Middle Ages* (1932), 89, 426.

[Ed.]

BATH-SHEBA (Heb. בַּת־שֶׁבַע, in I Chron. 3:5 בַּת־שׁוּעַ), wife of *David and mother of *Solomon. Bath-Sheba was originally the wife of *Uriah the Hittite, one of David's warriors. During the war against Rabbath-Ammon (II Sam. 11), David saw Bath-Sheba and ordered her brought to his palace. When David knew that she was pregnant by him, he attempted to return Uriah to his house (see II Sam. 11:6–13). Failing to do so, he sought and found a pretext to have Uriah killed in battle (11:14–27); he then married Bath-Sheba. The prophet *Nathan rebuked David for this act (12:1–12), but subsequently took Bath-Sheba's side and supported the enthronement of her son Solomon (I Kings 1:8ff.). She later agreed to present to Solomon *Adonijah's request for David's concubine *Abishag. In addition to Solomon, Bath-Sheba gave birth to at least three other sons, Shimea, Shobab, and Nathan (I Chron. 3:5). It seems that her first son, who died soon after his birth because of the sin of his father, is included in this list (II Sam. 12:13ff.).

According to II Samuel 11:3, Bath-Sheba was the daughter of Eliam, and according to I Chronicles 3:5, she was the daughter of Ammiel, who the rabbis of the Talmud (Sanh. 69b) identify with Eliam son of *Ahithophel the Gilonite (II Sam. 23:34); hence the opinion of early commentators (Kimḥi and Levi b. Gershom) and several recent scholars that the opposition of Ahithophel to David during the revolt of Absalom stemmed from his wish to avenge Uriah's death. Others believe that these opinions are unacceptable, because, if indeed Eliam was the son of the famous Ahithophel, the Bible would not have failed to mention the fact. It is also difficult to believe that Ahithophel, if he was the grandfather of Bath-Sheba, would have taken part in such an action which would undoubtedly have endangered the position of his granddaughter and her son in the royal court. On the other hand, there is reason to suppose that Bath-Sheba was of a family that existed in Jerusalem before its conquest by David. [Y.M.G.]

In the Aggadah. If she was Ahithophel's granddaughter, the prophecies which he believed foretold his own royal destiny, in fact applied to her (Sanh. 101b). Bath-Sheba was predestined for David; his sin was that he took her before the appointed time (Sanh. 107a). She was not guilty of adultery since it was the custom that soldiers going to war gave their wives bills of divorce which were to become valid should they fail to return and Uriah did fall in battle (Ket. 9b). She was a prophet in that she foresaw that her son would be the wisest of men. She is numbered among the 22 women of valor (Mid. Hag. to Gen. 23:1).

For Bath-Sheba in Arts see *David in Arts. [Ed.]

Figure 1. David espies Bath-Sheba at her bath. An historiated initial letter "B" at the beginning of the 13th-century *St. Louis Psalter*. In the lower section, David prays to God. Paris, Bibliothèque Nationale, Ms. Lat. 10525, fol. 85v.

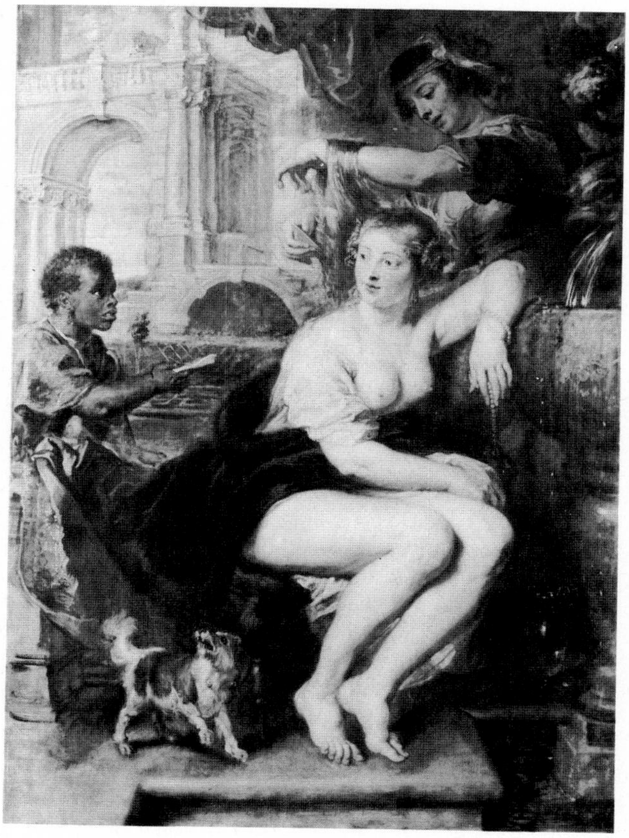

Figure 2. "Bath-Sheba at the Fountain" by Peter Paul Rubens, c. 1635. Oil on wood, 5 ft. 9 in.×4 ft. 1 in. (1.75×1.26 m.). Dresden, State Art Collection.

Bibliography: Bright, Hist, 181, 188n., 189, 230; de Vaux, Anc Isr, index; M. Z. Segal, *Sifrei Shemu'el* (1964²), 299, 326–7; S. Yeivin, *Meḥkarim be-Toledot Yisrael ve-Arẓo* (1960), 198–207, 230–1; Noth, Personennamen, 146–7. IN THE AGGADAH: Ginzberg, Legends, 4 (1947), 94–95, 103–4; 6 (1946), 256–7, 264–5.

BATHYRA, place in the toparchy of Batanea (i.e., *Bashan, east of Golan) founded by Jewish military settlers from Babylonia. Desirous of defending his borders from attacks by the neighboring Trachonites, *Herod decided to settle a large number of Jews in the area of Bathyra with the further intention that it would serve also as a base for his own military offensives. Upon learning that *Zamaris, a Jew from Babylon, had crossed the Euphrates with five hundred horsemen and was staying near Antioch under the patronage of Saturninus, the governor of Syria, Herod offered them the territory for the proposed buffer-zone, promising to rescind all taxes and tributes. The Babylonians took possession of the land, building fortresses and a village named Bathyra. The settlers defended not only the local population from Trachonite brigandage, but also Jewish pilgrims from Babylonia on their way to Jerusalem.

The family of Zamaris became a major ally of Herod, supporting his policies as well as those of the two Agrippas. Although Bathyra remained their base, members of the family also resided throughout the neighboring territories. Relatives of Philip, grandson of Zamaris, were among the prominent residents of Gamala at the beginning of the Roman War (66 C.E.). Philip played a vital if somewhat ambiguous part during that uprising, as well as in the events in Jerusalem on the eve of the outbreak of the war in 66. It was his task to secure Batanea from insurrection against Agrippa II and the Romans. Numerous scholars have made the connection between Bathyra and the rabbis referred to in the Talmud as "the sons of *Bathyra," who held high offices in Jerusalem until they were superseded by Hillel. However, it is improbable that there was any connection between the warriors of Bathyra and the rabbinical "sons of Bathyra."

Bibliography: Jos., Ant., 17:23ff.; Jos., Life, 46ff., 177ff.; H. Graetz, in: MGWJ, 1 (1851), 115ff.; Stern, in: *Tarbiz*, 35 (1965/66), 251–3; Neusner, Babylonia, 1 (1965), 38ff. [I.G.]

BATHYRA, SONS OF (according to TB; in TJ known as "Elders of Bathyra"), members of a famous Jewish family who were prominent from the first century B.C.E. to the second century C.E. Some scholars conjecture that the family was named after the city of *Bathyra in northern Transjordan. It is inferred from talmudic sources that members of this family were the religious authorities of their time, but that when Hillel demonstrated his superior knowledge of Torah (on the question of whether the paschal offering overrides the Sabbath) "they set him at their head and appointed him *nasi* over them" (TJ, Kil. 9:4, 32b; Pes. 66a; BM 85a). As a result of this abdication they were regarded exemplars of humility; Judah ha-Nasi said of them "whatever I am bidden I am prepared to do except what the Elders of Bathyra did for my ancestor (Hillel), namely abdicating from their high office in order to elevate him" (TJ, Ket. 12:3, 35a). The talmudic sources do not specify their names. According to the Jerusalem Talmud they were *nesi'im*. In other talmudic sources, while they were not specifically designated as such, it is implied that they held the patriarchate before Hillel was appointed. According to Halevy, the Sons of Bathyra carried out the functions of the patriarchate when the Sanhedrin was not functioning (possibly at the beginning of Herod's rule). Apparently members of this family exercised influence even after the destruction of the Temple, when the Sanhedrin was in Jabneh. Johanan b. Zakkai was said to have consulted the Sons of Bathyra in regard to certain legal rulings. A number of *tannaim* known by this patronymic, e.g., Judah b. Bathyra, Joshua b. Bathyra, and Simeon b. Bathyra, presumably belonged to this family.

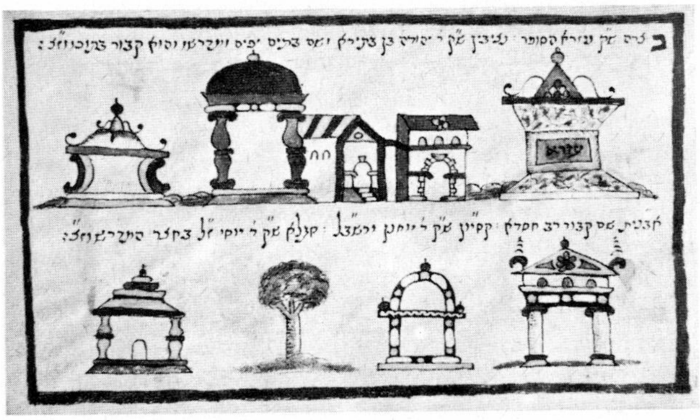

Neẓivin (Nusaybin, Turkey) is described as the burial place of R. Judah b. Bathyra in a page from a travelogue of Palestine and other holy sites, Casale Monferrato, Italy, 1598. Cecil Roth Manuscript Collection, *Casale Pilgrim*, folio 10v.

Bibliography: Halevy, Dorot, 1 pt. 3 (1923), 36–89; 1 pt. 5 (1923), 190–9; Hyman, Toledot, 365ff.; Graetz, in: MGWJ, 1 (1851), 115–20; Klausner, Bayit Sheni, 4 (1950²), 56, 143; Neusner, Babylonia, 1 (1965), index, s.v. *Bathyrans*. [Z.K.]

BAT KOL (Heb. בַּת קוֹל; lit. "daughter of a voice"), a heavenly or divine voice which revealed God's will, choice, or judgment to man. According to rabbinic tradition, the *bat kol* was already heard during the biblical period. It proclaimed Tamar's innocence; declared that the prophet Samuel had not materially benefited from his public position; and validated Solomon's judgment in awarding the child to the true mother (Mak. 23b). Before the death of Moses, a heavenly voice proclaimed that God Himself would attend to his burial (Deut. R. 11:10), and after his death a *bat kol* heard over an area 12 miles square announced his demise (Sot. 13b). A *bat kol* informed David that Rehoboam and Jeroboam would divide his kingdom (Shab. 56b); and when Solomon sought to emulate Moses a heavenly voice rebuked him (RH 21b). According to the Talmud a *bat kol* was often heard at the death of martyrs. After the death of the mother and her seven sons (see *Hannah and Her Seven Sons), a voice proclaimed: "A joyful mother of children" (Ps. 113:9; Git. 57b). When Ḥanina b. Teradyon was cruelly executed, a *bat kol* called out: "R. Ḥanina b. Teradyon and the Roman who hastened his death have been assigned to the world to come" (Av. Zar. 18a). After R. Akiva's execution, a "heavenly voice" resounded: "Happy art thou, R. Akiva, that thou art destined for the life of the world to come" (Ber. 61b). When a Roman officer sacrificed his life so that R. Gamaliel II would be spared, a *bat kol* declared: "This high officer is destined to enter into the world to come" (Ta'an. 29a).

With the cessation of prophecy, the *bat kol* remained the sole means of communication between God and man (Yoma 9b). In most instances, where reference is made to a *bat kol*, it refers to an external voice which is heard by the recipient of the message. However, at times the *bat kol* was only perceived in dreams (cf. Ḥag. 14b). The "heavenly voices" mentioned in stories concerning R. Bana'ah (BB 58a) and Rabbah b. Bar Ḥana (BB73b–74a) also were heard in dreams (see Chajes in bibl.).

The authority granted to a *bat kol* in determining *halakhah* is discussed in two different talmudic passages. In one instance, after three years of controversy between Bet Shammai and Bet Hillel, the sages accepted a *bat kol's* pronouncement that "the words of both are the words of the living God, but the *halakhah* is in agreement with the rulings of Bet Hillel" (Er. 13b). However, R. Joshua refused to abide by a *bat kol* which ruled in favor of R. Eliezer in his dispute with the sages regarding the ritual purity of the oven of *"Akhnai"* (BM 59b). R. Joshua explained that the Torah "is not in heaven" (Deut. 30:12), and therefore no attention is given to a "heavenly voice" and it is rather the majority of the sages who determined the *halakhah.* Later commentaries accepted R. Joshua's viewpoint, and explained that the *bat kol* was only effective in determining the ruling in the Bet Shammai and Bet Hillel controversies since the sages were themselves in doubt whether to rule in accordance with the larger school of Bet Hillel or the more profound thinkers of Bet Shammai (Tos. to Er. 6b s.v. כאן).

Bibliography: A. Guttmann, in: HUCA, 20 (1947), 363–406; E. E. Urbach, in: *Tarbiz,* 18 (1946/47), 23–27; idem, *Ḥazal* (1969), 516; S. Lieberman, *Hellenism in Jewish Palestine* (1950), 194–9; Z. H. Chajes, *Student's Guide to the Talmud* (1960²), 212–3.

[A.Ro.]

BATLANIM (Heb. בַּטְלָנִים; "men of leisure"), originally an honorable title conferred on those who either wholly or partly abstained from work to free themselves for community service. In ancient as well as medieval times there existed the institution of the *asarah batlanim* ("ten men of leisure"). The Mishnah (Meg. 1:3) states that a town was regarded as large if it had "ten *batlanim*" who "frequent the synagogue" (TB Meg. 5a; TJ, Meg., 1:6, 70b) and "abstain from work" (TJ, *ibid.*). Among the population of 120 who make a town "eligible for a Sanhedrin" (Sanh. 1:6) are included "the ten *batlanim* of the synagogue" (Meg. 17b). The ten verses of the Torah read publicly on Mondays and Thursdays "correspond to the ten *batlanim*" (BK 82a). R. Judah, characterized the "ten *batlanim*" as "those who, like ourselves, have no need of our studies" (TJ, Meg. loc. cit.), meaning, probably that they needed no occupation in addition to their studies. The ten *batlanim,* at that time, were scholars. Rashi explains that they refrain from work and are supported by the community in order to attend prayers in the synagogue (Meg. 5a; cf. Rashi to Sanh. 17b). R. Nissim notes that they need not "abstain from work and be supported by the community" for their town to be reckoned a large one in connection with the variant practices concerning the reading of the scroll of Esther. It is sufficient if they attend prayers in the synagogue both mornings and evenings (commenting on Alfasi; beginning of *Megillah*). Elsewhere (BK 82a) Rashi states that an additional function of the ten *batlanim* is to occupy themselves with the needs of the community, and Maimonides sees them as "assigned to the synagogue for communal needs" (Yad, Megillah 1:8). Benjamin of Tudela records that in 12th-century Baghdad, the ten heads of the yeshivah "are called *batlanim,* their sole occupation being to engage in communal affairs . . . . They render decisions on legal and religious questions for all the Jewish inhabitants of the country." In later Yiddish usage the term became pejorative and meant a man who was lazy, loafed, and could not make his way in the world.

Bibliography: R. Hutner, in: *Yavneh,* 1 (1946), 21–24. [Z.K.]

BAT-MIRIAM (Zhelezniak), YOKHEVED (1901–), Hebrew poet. Born in Keplits, Belorussia, Yokheved Bat-Miriam attended the universities of Odessa and Moscow. Although her poems began appearing in 1923, her first volume of poetry *Me-Raḥok* ("From Afar") was published in 1932, four years after she settled in Ereẓ Israel; it was followed by six other volumes of poetry. The bulk of her poetry was written between the two world wars against

Yokheved Bat-Miriam, Hebrew poet. Bronze by Batya Lishansky.

the background of the Jewish tragedy of this period, and her personal experiences as a child in Russia and a settler in Israel. Influenced by Russian symbolist poetry, her verse is written against a dreamlike landscape, charged with nature symbols drawn from the world of childhood. One image fades into another, with past and present merging. This coalescing of imagery is reinforced by a similar shifting of her idiom by means of assonance, alliteration, and other sonal devices. Her works include: *Ereẓ Yisrael* (1937); *Re'ayon* (1949); *Demuyyot me-Ofek* (1942); *Mi-Shirei Rusyah* (1942); *1943—Shirim la-Getto* (1946); and *Shirim* (1963). A list of her works translated into English appears in Goell, Bibl. She was awarded the Israel Prize in 1972.

Bibliography: *Kitvei Shimon Ginzburg,* 1 (1945), 285–95; D. Miron, in: *Haaretz* (Feb. 22, 1963); A. Bernstein, in: *Keshet,* 8 (Winter 1966), 184–7; Band, in: S. Burnshaw et al., *The Modern Hebrew Poem Itself* (1965), 84–88.

[Ed.]

BATO, LUDWIG YOMTOV (1886–), Zionist and writer. Bato was born in Dolní-Kubín in Slovakia (then Hungary) and in 1904 edited the first Zionist publication in Hungarian. While a student in Turin (1906–07), he founded the Piedmontese Zionist Federation. Returning to Hungary in 1908, he joined the editorial board of the Zionist newspaper *Zsidó szemle.* In 1910 he went to Vienna, where he lived until 1933. There he was one of the leaders of the Austrian Zionist Federation and from 1914 to 1918 edited its organ *Juedische Zeitung.* With O. *Abeles he published the literary almanac *Juedischer Nationalkalender* (6 vols., 1916–22). Between 1933 and 1940 Bato was director of the Jewish National Fund in Rumania and in 1940 he settled in Tel Aviv. Bato wrote *Die Juden im alten Wien* (1928) and *Don Yosef Nasi* (Heb., 1942).

Bibliography: MB (Feb. 11, 1966). [G.K.]

BATSHAW, HARRY (1902–), Canadian Zionist and jurist. Batshaw was born in Dubrovno, Russia, and was taken to Canada in 1905. After practicing law for 25 years, Batshaw was appointed judge of the Superior Court of Quebec in 1950. Batshaw, who had been president of Canadian Young Judea (1931–34), was president of the Canadian Friends of Alliance Israélite Universelle, and was active in Canadian Zionism. He attended the World Conference on Human Rights in Teheran (1968) as a member of the Canadian delegation. [B.G.K.]

Justice Harry Batshaw, Canadian jurist.

BAT SHELOMO (Heb. בַּת שְׁלֹמֹה "Daughter of Solomon"), Israel moshav in the Manasseh Hills northeast of Zikhron Ya'akov. It was founded in June 1889 by the administration of Baron Edmond de *Rothschild, to provide farmsteads for children of Zikhron Ya'akov settlers. The small village, with wine grapes as its principal branch of farming, made little progress. After the establishment of the State of Israel, immigrants from Hungary and Yemen settled in Bat Shelomo. The village was named for Baron James (Jacob) Rothschild's wife, whose father was Solomon Mayer Rothschild of Vienna. [E.O.]

BATSHEVA and BAT-DOR DANCE COMPANIES, two dance companies founded and financed by Baroness Batsheva (Bethsabee) de *Rothschild in Tel Aviv, to foster the art of dance in Israel. The first company was started in 1964, using techniques based on the method of the American dancer Martha Graham, who became its artistic adviser. The company made its first overseas tour in 1968. In 1965, Baroness de Rothschild also founded the Batsheva Studios for Dance, with Jeannette Ordman as director and with classical ballet among the basic training methods. In 1968 she decided that a company more closely linked with the studios was needed to provide scope for developing an indigenous style. The studios moved to new premises, were renamed the Batsheva Bat-Dor Studios, and a new company, called the Bat-Dor Dance Company, was formed. Jeannette Ordman became artistic director of both the company and the studios. [D.L.S.]

The Batsheva Dance Company's production of the ballet "Endor," with the choreographer, Moshe Efrati, as Saul and Zelilah Goldstein as the Witch. Photo Mula & Haramaty, Tel Aviv.

BATTAT, REUBEN (1882–1962), Iraqi jurist. Battat studied law in Baghdad and in Constantinople and served as judge in various courts of Iraq. In 1923 as judge in Basra, he handed down a decision in favor of transferring the property of the Jewish philanthropist Gourji Shemtov to the Keren Hayesod. That decision was used against him in 1949, when he was tried by a military tribunal on charges of being a Zionist and sentenced to three years imprisonment. He was, however, released after four months. From 1924 Battat represented the Jews of Iraq for several terms in parliament; he was also one of the supporters of the Zionist organization in Baghdad. Before 1936 he published an important work about the constitution of the kingdom of Iraq (in Arabic). He died in Switzerland.

Bibliography: *Hed ha-Mizraḥ* (Oct. 5, 1945). [H.J.C.]

BATUMI (until 1936 **Batum**), port on the eastern shore of the Black Sea; capital of the Autonomous Adzhar Republic, within the Georgian S.S.R. A Jewish community was established there in 1878 after the town was incorporated into Russia. In 1889 many of the Jews living there without official authorization (see *Pale of Settlement) were expelled. According to official statistics there remained 31 Jewish families, and according to unofficial sources about 100 Jewish families. The number, however, again increased rapidly. By 1897 there were 1,179 Jews living in Batum. One of the oil refineries was owned jointly by the Rothschild family and Jewish investors in Russia. The Jewish population numbered 3,700 in 1923 (6.1% of the total population). Subsequent data are unascertainable. [A.J.Br./Ab.A.]

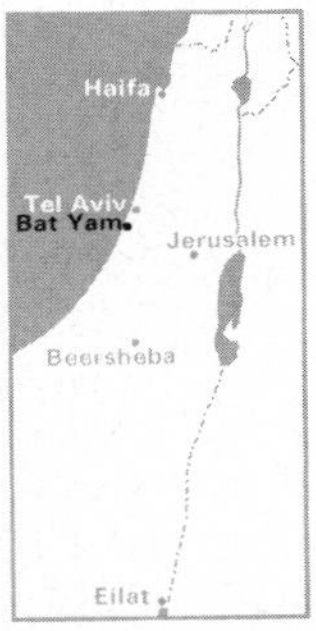

BAT YAM (Heb. בַּת יָם; "Daughter of the Sea"), city in central Israel, on the seashore south of Tel Aviv-Jaffa, founded in 1926 by 24 religious families who called themselves and the quarter they established "Bayit va-Gan" ("House and Garden"). In the 1929 Arab riots, this isolated group found refuge in Tel Aviv, returning to their homes in 1931. From 1933 the population increased as immigrants from Germany built their homes there. In 1937 the quarter received the status of a local council and changed its name to Bat Yam. In the War of Independence (1948), the town, then numbering approximately 1,000 inhabitants, had to defend itself against strong Arab attacks. With the mass immigration following the founding of Israel, the population grew rapidly. The inhabitants numbered 10,000 at the end of 1953 and 62,000 in 1967. Bat Yam, which received city status in 1958, forms part of the Tel Aviv conurbation, bordering on the city of Tel Aviv-Jaffa in the north, Holon in the east, and Rishon le-Zion in the south. Manufacturing and recreation

Bat Yam, aerial view. Tel Aviv, Government Press Office.

facilities are the mainstay of its economy. The food branch (light beverages, beer, ice cream) is outstanding among its 170 factories and workshops. It is a popular resort with a seashore of 2 mi. (3.2 km.), three-quarters of it open for bathing. It has a municipal museum, art galleries, and the Sholem *Asch House. Asch resided in Bat Yam in his last years. [Si.M.]

°**BAUDISSIN, WOLF WILHELM, Graf Von** (1847–1926), German Bible critic and historian of religion. Baudissin was born in Holstein and taught at the universities of Leipzig from 1874 to 1876; Strasbourg 1876–1881; Marburg, 1881–1900; and Berlin, 1900–1921. He belonged to the Wellhausen school of thought as regards the understanding of the Pentateuch as a whole, but he departed from its philosophy in his *Die Geschichte des alttestamentlichen Priesterthums* (1889) where he argued for the priority of P, the pre-Exilic Priestly Source, over the D, Deuteronomic, Source. In *Kyrios als Gottesname im Judentum und seine Stelle in der Religionsgeschichte* (4 vols., 1929), published posthumously, Baudissin championed the theory that the substitution of Adonai for YHWH first originated among Greek-speaking Jews. His main contributions in the area of comparative religion are *Studien zur semitischen Religionsgeschichte* (2 vols., 1876–78); *Jahve et Moloch* (1874); and *Adonis und Esmun* (1911). These studies deal with the influence of the Canaanite cult on the history of Israel.

Bibliography: ZAWB, 33 (1918) (=*Festschrift . . . Baudissin*) includes bibliography; O. Eissfeldt, *Kleine Schriften*, 1 (1962), 115–42, 234–8. [Z.G.]

°**BAUER, BRUNO** (1809–1882), German Protestant theologian, philosopher, and historian. He became influenced by the philosophy of Hegel while a student in Berlin, and because of radical criticism of the New Testament expressed in numerous works, was dismissed from his post as lecturer at Bonn in 1842. Bauer then returned to Berlin where he devoted himself to writing historical works and critical studies of the rise of Christianity. He also wrote on contemporary political issues, defending Prussian conservatism, and strongly opposed granting emancipation to the Jews in Germany. In his essay *Die Judenfrage* ("The Jewish Question," 1843), he stresses, like Hegel, the Oriental character of the "Jewish national spirit" *(Volksgeist)* which failed to comprehend the ideals of freedom and reason and saw its highest duty in fulfilling unreasonable ceremonies. In particular, Bauer attacked the representatives of Reform Judaism, who called for a return to a pure or purified "Mosaism." In his view, "pure Mosaism" was only possible in the land of Canaan, and only in a sovereign Jewish state. It was therefore impossible in contemporary circumstances. Bauer argued that the observance of Jewish laws made faith illusory and that Judaism was exclusive and unrealistic. As long as Jews were not ready to forsake their specific character, their emancipation was out of the question. The work gave rise to sharp controversy in which Abraham *Geiger, Gabriel *Riesser, Samuel *Hirsch, and Karl *Marx, among others, took part.

Bibliography: N. Rotenstreich, in: YLBI, 4 (1959); 3–36; Ẓ. Rosen, in: *Zion*, 33 (1968), 59–76; K. Marx, *A World Without Jews* (1959). [R.M.]

BAUER, HANS (1878–1937), scholar of Semitic languages. Bauer, who was born in Bavaria, studied theology and Semitic languages and in 1922 was appointed professor of Semitic languages at the University of Halle. After working on medieval Arabic philosophy (especially Al-Ghazālī), and other Arabic studies, he turned to Hebrew grammar in the context of the other Semitic languages, employing the methods developed by Indo-Germanic linguists. In his book *Die Tempora im Semitischen* (1910), he dealt with the Semitic tenses. He worked on the assumption (which others had made before him) that the imperfect was in the early stages of the language the only defined verbal form (i.e., the all-tempora: Aorist), while the perfect was orginally a nominal form (i.e., a type of participle: nominal), and thus close in meaning to the present tense. The nominal participle has two temporal qualities, according to the meaning of each verb: an act done now or continuously; or an act, completed in the past, whose results are felt in the present. The second quality *(perfectum praesens)* is likely to develop into the *praeteritum*. In each of the Semitic languages, one of these qualities became the primary: in Akkadian, the former (Bauer equates the form *ikasad* with the perfect of the other languages); in Aramaic, Arabic, Ethiopic, and even Phoenician, the latter. As a result the semantic field of the all-tempora form became limited in its meaning. In Akkadian it is used as the perfect, but in the other languages as the present-future. Biblical Hebrew, which Bauer considered a mixed language, in this respect stands midway: the conversive tenses reflect the Akkadian usage, while the regular tenses are comparable to the use in other Semitic languages. His view of the mixed nature of Hebrew ("early Canaanite base," close to Akkadian, with a "late layer" which is closer to the other Semitic languages) derives from certain cases of phonetic inconsistency, such as the vowels after the *kof* in קָם *(kam)* as opposed to מָקוֹם *(makom)* which both are in Arabic *ā (qām, maqām)*. This problem is discussed in his book *Zur Frage der Sprachmischung im Hebraeischen* (1924). With Pontus Leander, he wrote the *Historische Grammatik der hebraeischen Sprache des Alten Testaments* (1922; repr. 1965). They also collaborated in writing the *Grammatik des Biblisch-Aramaeischen* (1927). In 1930 he succeeded in deciphering most of the Ugaritic alphabet embodying the results of his study in *Die alphabetischen Keilschrifttexte von Ras Shamra* (1936); others followed him in completing this work. Bauer also wrote a book on the origins of the alphabet, *Der Ursprung des Alphabets* (1937).

Bibliography: Wehr-Halle, in: ZDMG, 91 (1937), 175–84, obituary and bibliography; NDB, 1 (1952), 639. [H.J.P.]

BAUER, JACOB (Jehiel ben Gershom; 1852–1926), *ḥazzan* of the Turkish-Israelite Temple in Vienna and adaptor of its liturgical music. Bauer was born in Szenice, Hungary, and went as a youth to Vienna. During his school days in that city, he was a soprano singer with the *ḥazzan* Pesaḥ

Feinsinger. After regular training of his adult voice, Bauer was employed as *ḥazzan* at Ottakring, a suburb of Vienna, Szigetvar (Hungary, 1875), and Graz (1878). In 1880, the governors of the Vienna Sephardi congregation decided to adapt the musical part of their service "to the needs of modern times." They commissioned Bauer and the choir-director Isidor Loewit to arrange their melodies and to organize a temple choir. At first this modernized service was, more or less, in the common Ashkenazi style. In the course of time, Bauer and Loewit worked on arrangements of the original Turco-Sephardi melodies which were published as *Schir-Hakawod* in 1889.

Bauer founded and edited the *Oesterreichisch-Ungarische Kantoren-Zeitung* from 1881 to 1898, and was co-founder and temporarily chairman of the Oesterreichisch-Ungarischer Kantoren-Verband from 1883.

Bibliography: Friedmann, Lebensbilder; E. Zaludkowski, *Kultur-Treger fun der Yidisher Liturgye* . . . (1930), 196.

[H.Av.]

BAUER, OTTO (1881–1938), Austrian socialist leader; first foreign minister of the Austrian Republic (1918–19). Bauer, the son of a Jewish industrialist, joined the socialist movement, as did many young Jewish intellectuals of his time. In 1907, together with Karl Renner and Adolf *Braun, he founded the monthly *Der Kampf,* which became a forum for socialist discussion. In his famous study *Die Nationalitaetenfrage und die Sozialdemokratie* (1907) he contended that no socialist could disregard the problem of nationalities. He provided an original definition of the nation: "the totality of men united through a community of fate into a community of character." Bauer favored the granting of cultural autonomy to every national group in the Austro-Hungarian Empire. He praised the Jewish role in history, but argued that the Jews could not be regarded as a nationality, especially in Western Europe. He advocated assimilation and was sharply criticized by Zionists in consequence. In November 1918, with the collapse of the Austro-Hungarian Empire at the end of World War I, Bauer became foreign minister of the new Austrian Republic. He resigned in 1919 when his main objectives, a merger with Germany and retention by Austria of the German-speaking parts of the Tyrol, failed to materialize. When the Dollfuss regime came to power in 1934, Bauer took a leading part in the uprising of the workers in Vienna. On its suppression, he took refuge in Czechoslovakia. In May 1938 he fled to Paris and died there a few weeks later—on the day the London *News Chronicle* published his appeal to world conscience to save the 300,000 Jews of Austria. Bauer was an outstanding figure within the Socialist International, where although he was an opponent of Communism, he represented the Marxist left wing. He was a prolific writer on socialist problems, his books including *Bolschewismus oder Sozialdemokratie?* (1920), in which he contrasted the economic conditions of Soviet Russia and Western Europe, and *Kapitalismus und Sozialismus nach dem Weltkrieg* (1931), which was intended to be his magnum opus. After his death, his *Die illegale Partei* was published in Paris by Friedrich *Adler (1939).

Otto Bauer, foreign minister of Austria, 1918–1919. Jerusalem, Schwadron Collection. J.N.U.L.

Bibliography: J. Braunthal, *Eine Auswahl aus seinem Lebenswerk, mit einem Lebensbild Otto Bauers* (1961); V. Reimann, *Zu gross fuer Oesterreich* (1958).

[R.W.]

BAUM, HERBERT (1912–1942), German Communist and anti-Nazi fighter. Baum was a member of the German communist youth movement from 1932 and led a clandestine Jewish communist cell in Berlin from 1936. In 1937 he and his wife Marianne organized a political circle with communist leanings frequented by young Jews (both party members and others), including some Zionists. According to communist sources, this group continued its activities even after the outbreak of World War II by mimeographing leaflets and illegal newspapers and establishing contacts with French and Belgian forced laborers in Germany, mainly in the Siemens plant in Berlin where Baum worked. On May 18, 1942, Baum and a number of his comrades set fire to the Nazi propaganda exhibit *Das Sowjetparadies* ("The Soviet Paradise"). Shortly afterward Baum and members of his group were arrested. He died in jail, probably by his own hand, while his comrades were tried and sentenced to death or deported to death camps. At the request of the group's sole survivor, Charlotte Holzer, Baum and his comrades were buried in the Jewish cemetery at Weissensee, East Berlin.

Bibliography: E. Maoz, *Yalkut Moreshet,* 3 (1944), 79–88; M. Pikarski, *Sie bleiben unvergessen* (1968); L. Steinberg, *La revolte des justes—les juifs contre Hitler* (1970), 51–77; B. Mark, in: *Bleter far Geshikhte,* 14 (1961), 27–64 (Eng. summary in Y. Suhl (ed.), *They Fought Back* (1967), 55–68).

[L.St.]

BAUM, OSCAR (1883–1941), Czechoslovak author who wrote in German. Baum was a member of the Prague circle of Max *Brod and Franz *Kafka. Losing his sight as a boy, Baum was trained at the Vienna Institute for the Blind as an organist and pianist, and subsequently became a music critic. Brod took down in shorthand his first short stories and persuaded Baum to publish them. *Uferdasein* (1908), *Das Leben im Dunkeln* (1909), and *Nacht ist umher* (1929), hailed by Stefan *Zweig as the "most moving document in German from the lightless world" were all taken from the life of the blind. They reflect his opposition to the compassion displayed by society and his call for equality of opportunity, which influenced modern education of the handicapped. Baum's *Die boese Unschuld* (1913) has acquired significance as a document of Jewish life in Bohemia against the background of the Czech-German nationality struggle. Baum also wrote a drama, *Das Wunder* (1920). His last novel, *Das Volk des harten Schlafes* (1937), ostensibly a story about the Jewish kingdom of the *Khazars, actually deals with problems of Jewry in the first years of Nazi rule. It was dedicated to Baum's "son and friend" Leo, who was later killed in the King David Hotel explosion in Jerusalem (1946).

Bibliography: M. Brod, *Der Prager Kreis* (1966), 118–32; A. Schmidt, *Dichtung und Dichter Oesterreichs im 19. und 20. Jahrhundert,* 1 (1964), index.

[Ed.]

BAUM, VICKI (1888–1960), novelist. Born in Vienna, Vicki Baum began her career as a professional harpist but her success as a short story writer led her to leave music. In 1921 she became an editor in the Berlin publishing house of Ullstein. Of her 25 novels, the best known is *Menschen im Hotel* (1929; *Grand Hotel,* 1930), which became a worldwide best seller and a popular film. In 1931 she settled in the U.S.A. Vicki Baum often repeated the pattern of *Grand Hotel*—a montage of stories of interrelated characters—in her novels, for which she chose a wide range of historical, sociological, and psychological themes. Her autobiography, *Es war alles ganz anders* (1962), was published posthumously.

Bibliography: J. Bithell, *Modern German Literature* (1959[3]), 333–5; *Britannica Book of the Year 1961* (1962), 511. [S.L.S.]

BAUMGARDT, DAVID (1890–1963), philosopher. In 1924 he was appointed lecturer in philosophy at the University of Berlin where he later was professor (1932–35). In 1935 he was visiting professor at the University of Madrid where he lectured on Maimonides at the congress organized by the Spanish government to commemorate the eighth centenary of Maimonides' birth. From 1935 Baumgardt taught at Birmingham (England) and from 1939 at Pendle Hill, Wallingford, Pennsylvania. From 1941 to 1954 he was consultant on philosophy to the Library of Congress in Washington. Baumgardt, a Zionist from his early youth, conceived the idea of founding a Hebrew philosophical journal. In his earlier works (particularly in his *Das Moeglichkeitsproblem der Kritik der reinen Vernunft, der modernen Phaenomenologie und der Gegenstandstheorie,* 1920) he treated the modalities (possibility, reality, and necessity) in the philosophy of Kant, Husserl, and Meinong (the late 14th-century German philosopher). He then turned his attention to historical studies, particularly to the history of philosophical romanticism in Germany at the beginning of the 19th century. This culminated in the publication of his book on Franz von Baader and philosophical romanticism (1929). Another work of Baumgardt is devoted to an investigation of the relations between Mendelssohn and Spinoza (1932). In *Der Kampf um den Lebenssinn unter den Vorlaeufern der modernen Ethik* (1933) he relates the systematic study of ethics to the study of history. In this book he undertakes a penetrating critique of Kant's system of ethics, showing that Kant's ethical system was derived from the basic idea of a Higher Unity pervading all human striving but that this derivation is merely a formal one, devoid of content. Baumgardt examines Hermann Cohen's attempt to rescue Kant's ethics but even here he arrives at negative conclusions. He likewise examined the attempts, undertaken by thinkers at the end of the 18th century (Herder, Hemsterhuis, Jacobi), to create a system of ethics possessed of content. In opposition to Kant, Herder extolled Hebrew ethics because they preserve man's unity. In connection with this investigation, Baumgardt assembled the literary material relevant to the relations between Herder and Spinoza. His search for ethical fundamentals possessing content led him to become particularly interested in Bentham's ethical system, to which he devoted a large volume on *Bentham and the Ethics of Today* (1952). In 1961 Baumgardt published *Great Western Mystics; Their Lasting Significance.* He sought a reconciliation of the ethics of force and the ethics of love.

David Baumgardt, philosopher, Jerusalem, Schwadron Collection, J.N.U.L.

Bibliography: J. Frank, et al., *Horizons of a Philosopher: Essays in Honor of David Baumgardt* (1963); YLBI, 10 (1965), 239–65. [SH.H.B.]

BAUMGARTEL, ELISE J. (1892–), Egyptologist. Elise Baumgartel, who was born in Berlin, became a leading figure in the field of Egyptian prehistory. She left Germany for England during the Hitler era, and from 1948 to 1950 was keeper of the department of Egyptian antiquities at Manchester University. In 1951 she went to Oxford, where she engaged in research at the Griffith Institute until 1955. She then went to live in the United States, and became a member of the Oriental Institute in Chicago, Ill. Elise Baumgartel's major publications are *Culture of Prehistoric Egypt* (2 vols., 1948–50) and the chapter on "Predynastic Egypt" in the *Cambridge Ancient History* (1963). [P.P.K.]

BAUMGARTEN, EMANUEL MENDEL (1828–1908), economist, communal leader, German and Hebrew journalist, poet, writer, and publisher. Born in Kremsier (Kroměříž, Moravia), Baumgarten studied at yeshivot and, later, economics at the University of Vienna. Apart from contributing to the German and Jewish press, he edited the economic paper *Der Fortschritt* and in 1865–66 the Hebrew periodical *Beit ha-Midrash* (with I. H. Weiss). As a successful businessman, Baumgarten was elected to the council of the Israelitische Allianz (1873) and the Jewish Theological Seminary of Vienna (1893). He did much to assist Russian and Rumanian pogrom victims seeking refuge in Austria. He assisted P. *Smolenskin with his monthly *Ha-Shaḥar* and Jehiel *Brill with his colonization plans in Palestine. Among Baumgarten's published works are: the first translation into German of Baḥya ibn Paquda's *Ḥovot ha-Levavot* with an appendix entitled *Arugat Peraḥim,* containing biographies by S. G. Stern of Baḥya, ibn Tibbon, and J. Kimḥi (1854); a Hebrew poem, *Ruth* (1865); and *Juden in der Steiermark* (1903). Baumgarten edited some apologetic works about the blood libel and in defense of the Talmud; Israel Fraenkel's *Yeshu'at Yisrael,* a chronicle of Moravian Jewry (1898); and Abraham Broda's *Megillat Sedarim,* on the expulsion of the Jews from Aussee (1895; cf. his "Zur Maehrisch-Ausseer Affaere," in *Gedenkbuch zur Erinnerung an D. Kaufmann,* 1900). In 1899, on the occasion of his 70th birthday, his sons published a *Festschrift* in his honor, *Unserem theueren Vater, Emanuel Baumgarten an seinem 70. Geburtstag.*

Bibliography: A. Frankl-Gruen, *Geschichte der Juden in Kremsier,* 2 (1896), 153–6; J. S. Bloch, *Erinnerungen aus meinem Leben,* 1 (1922), 207–11; B. Wachstein, *Hebraeische Publizistik in Wien* (1930), 9–10, 296. [G.K.]

°**BAUMGARTNER, WALTER** (1887–1970), Swiss Bible scholar and orientalist. Baumgartner studied classical and Oriental philology and theology, and taught at the University of Marburg from 1916 (professor, 1928). From 1947, he was professor of Semitic languages at Basle. Baumgartner's position among biblical scholars and orientalists is assured by the results of his work in the field of Bible and Semitic philology. His important studies on the Aramaic sections of the Bible include: *Das Buch Daniel* (1926) and the Aramaic sections of L. Koehler and W. Baumgartner's *Lexicon in Veteris Testamenti Libros* (1953, 1958, 1967 ff.). In his doctoral dissertation, *Die Klagegedichte des Jeremia . . .* (1916), he employed critical methodology to prove that the monologues of Jeremiah were not later additions but may be attributed to the prophet himself. In his monographs *Alttestamentliche Religion* (1928) and *Israelitische und altorientalische*

Weisheit (1933) he helped pioneer the study of ancient Near Eastern religion and wisdom literature. His book *Zum Alten Testament und seiner Umwelt,* a collection of previously published essays on the Bible and Oriental studies, was published in 1959 in honor of Baumgartner's 70th birthday (includes complete bibliography, pp. 1–26) and the jubilee volume *Hebraeische Wortforschung* was presented to him on his 80th birthday.

Bibliography: Y. Kutscher, in: *Haaretz* (March 13, 1970).

[Z.G.]

BAUR, HARRY (1883–1943), French actor. Born of poor Alsatian parents, Baur was compelled at the age of 12 to work on the Marseilles docks, but managed to study at the Marseilles Conservatory of Music. He appeared briefly on the Paris stage but after the outbreak of World War I joined

Harry Baur, French actor.

the army. Wounded, he returned to civilian life, continuing to act on the stage until movies became his chief interest. The French called Baur the "king of the character actors," and indeed, his heavy features and bushy brows lent themselves to a great range of parts including Beethoven in the *Life and Loves of Beethoven.* He also played in *Rasputin* and in *The Golem.* Baur was arrested in Berlin in 1942 on charges of forging a certificate of (Aryan) ancestry. Ironically, the Germans had to destroy a costly film because Baur had the main role. He was subsequently tortured for 4 months and died shortly after his release from prison.

[L.C.]

BAUSKA (Yid. **Boysk**), town in S. Latvian S.S.R., near the Lithuanian border. Originally in the duchy of *Courland, it was incorporated in Russia in 1795 and became a district town in the government (province) of Courland. Jews were permitted to settle there by a special law of 1799. At first their right of residence was restricted to a suburb on a bank of the river Aa (Lielupe), but the restriction was lifted in the 1820s. The community, most of whose members came from Lithuania, retained its "Lithuanian" character, with its stress on Torah learning and Orthodoxy. It numbered 2,669 in 1835 but by 1850 had decreased to 2,226 as a result of the settlement of 82 families (692 persons) from Bauska in the agricultural colonies in the province of Kherson in 1840 and of an outbreak of cholera in the area in 1848. The Jewish population numbered 2,745 in 1897 (42% of the total population). During World War I many Jews were forced by the Russian military authorities to evacuate Bauska, which was in the area of hostilities, for the Russian interior. Many did not return after the war and by 1920 there remained only 834 Jewish inhabitants. Well-known rabbis who officiated in the community in the second half of the 19th century were Mordecai *Eliasberg and Avraham Yitzḥak *Kook. The Jews in Bauska were murdered during the first weeks of the German occupation in summer 1941.

Bibliography: L. Ovchinski, *Toledot Yeshivat ha-Yehudim be-Kurland* (1911[2]), 48–55; Z. A. Rabiner, in: *Yahadut Latvia* (1953), 244–76; M. Bove, *Perakim be-Toledot Yahadut Latvia* (1965).

[S.K.]

BAVA BATRA (Aram. בָּבָא בָּתְרָא, "last gate"), tractate of the Mishnah with *Gemara* in the Jerusalem and Babylonian Talmuds. The tractates **Bava Kamma,* **Bava Meẓia,* and *Bava Batra* were originally one large tractate, *Nezikin.* The division into three apparently took place in Babylonia: in the Babylonian Talmud there are indications that the *Gemara* of each of the three sections was edited by a different hand, while in the Jerusalem Talmud they are uniform.

Chapters 1–3 of *Bava Batra* deal essentially with laws relating to ownership of real estate. Chapter 1 discusses the division of a courtyard held by joint owners whose homes open onto it. They may build a stone partition, each owner contributing an equal amount of land for its construction. Consequently, if the partition falls, "the place and the stones belong to them both." This law is similar to *Bava Meẓia* 10:1, for the last chapter of *Bava Meẓia* opens the discussion on ownership continued here. A courtyard containing several houses is a small community, and the Mishnah discusses the obligations of the individual to this community. Next, the mutual obligations of "neighbors" are presented for the dwellers of one city. The Tosefta adds to these communal obligations: "The citizens of a town can compel each other to build a synagogue, and to purchase a scroll of the Torah and the Prophets. The citizens are permitted to fix price ceilings and control weights and measures . . . " (Tosef., BM 11:23). In chapter 2, the Mishnah imposes limitations upon the actions of the property owner within the bounds of his own property, when such acts are a source of damage or nuisance to neighbors. Personal privacy is protected by a law prohibiting construction of windows which command a close-range view into a neighbor's windows. The section on ownership concludes with chapter 3, which discusses the rules of **ḥazakah,* according to which evidence of three years' undisturbed use of property can serve as proof of ownership. The Babylonian Talmud records many actual cases involving *ḥazakah* and disputed ownership, indicating the wide application of these laws in the area of Jewish real estate in Babylonia.

Concerning the acquisition of real estate, chapter 4 gives precise definitions of terms, so as to prevent a dispute between buyer and seller over what was included in the purchase. The list of legal definitions is continued in chapter

Illustration of the section of the tractate *Bava Batra* dealing with the division of a courtyard between joint owners whose houses open on it. Detail from a title page of a Hebrew and Latin edition of the Mishnah, Amsterdam, 1700–1704. Jerusalem, J.N.U.L.

5 and extended to cover sale of moveables. The variety of objects thus treated presents a wealth of precise Hebrew terminology and a rich description of the *realia* of Palestine during the mishnaic period. The remainder of this chapter expands on the requirement of justice in weights and measures (Lev. 19:35–36; Deut. 25:13–16), a topic related to purchase. Chapter 6 returns to definitions of objects of sale, not with regard to extent of inclusion but with regard to quality, i.e., to what degree the seller is required to replace inferior goods. The remainder of the chapter defines the minimum legal dimensions of various structures and tombs. Definitions of specific quantities of land mentioned in the sale of real estate are presented in chapter 7. This concludes the unit of "definitions," which began with chapter 6. The chapters discussed above deal with acquisition of property through purchase; chapters 8 and 9 consider acquisition of property by inheritance.

Chapter 10 contains rules for the proper preparation of legal documents by scribes, as well as the correct interpretation by the court of certain legal documents, especially bonds of indebtedness. This is a fitting conclusion to the tractate, since legal documents figure in acquisition, ownership, and other matters discussed in earlier chapters. The last Mishnah was intended, perhaps, as an apt conclusion for the entire tractate of *Nezikin* (the three *Bavot, Bava Kamma, Bava Meẓia,* and *Bava Batra*): "He that would become wise, let him occupy himself in cases concerning property, for there is no branch of law greater than they, for they are like a welling fountain" (10:8).

The Tosefta of *Bava Batra* contains 11 chapters. Generally the Tosefta follows the Mishnah, supplementing and paralleling it, but there are chapters where the sources of the Tosefta are richer than the Mishnah and have an original and interesting order of their own.

The first chapter, dealing with the prevention of torts, parallels chapter 2 of the Mishnah (ch. 1 of which is paralleled by the second half of the Tosef., BM 11). Chapter 2:1–14, paralleling the Mishnah 2:1–6, deals with *ḥazakah;* while 2:14–17, paralleling Mishnah 2:2–8, is a supplement to chapter 1 of the Tosefta. It is probable that the connection between this supplement and the preceding section is *Samuel b. Meir's definition of a Tyrean window (14a) and the prohibition against opening a window facing that of a neighbor (14b). Chapters 3–4, paralleling Mishnah 4:1–5:5, deal with the regulations of selling; 5:1–6:21, paralleling Mishnah 5:6–6:3, deal with commercial honesty; the last part of this section differs from the Mishnah, in that the transition to the following two sections is clearly recognizable. Thus the subject of 6:22–23, paralleling the Mishnah at the end of chapter 6, deviates only slightly from the main discussion on commercial honesty, as it deals with the language used by a seller, a subject covered previously, and the subject of Tosefta 6:24–28, parallels the Mishnah of chapter 7. Chapters 7–10, discussing the *halakhot* of inheritance, contain a wealth of sources on details not mentioned at all in the parallel Mishnah (ch. 8 and 9). Chapter 11, dealing with deeds, parallels Mishnah chapter 10.

The rabbinic tradition regarding the order and authorship of the books of Scripture is recorded in *Bava Batra* 14b. The report of the travels of Rabbah bar Bar Ḥana (BB 73–74) contains fantastic descriptions of marvelous creatures and visions of the corpses of the Israelites who left Egypt and died in the wilderness of Sinai.

In the standard printed editions of the Babylonian Talmud more pages are found in this tractate than in any other (BB's last page is numbered 176). However, there are other tractates whose talmudic text is longer (see *Talmud). The size of the *Bava Batra* volume is due to the fact that the commentary of *Rashi is printed through page 29a only (in the Pesaro edition the termination of the commentary is marked: "Here died Rashi"), and the remainder of the tractate contains the more lengthy commentary of Samuel b. Meir. An English translation of the Talmud was made by I. Epstein (Soncino edition, 1935).

Bibliography: Epstein, Amora'im, 187–270; A. Weiss, *Studies in the Law of the Talmud on Damages* (1966), 16–25; Ch. Albeck, *Shishah Sidrei Mishnah*, 4 (1959), 111–6; R. Yaron, *Gifts in Contemplation of Death in Jewish and Roman Law* (1960); D. Daube, in: *Tulane Law Review* 18 (1944), 390–404.

[SH.F.]

BAVA BEN BUTA (first century B.C.E.), sage and judge during the reign of *Herod. Bava, although a disciple of Shammai, agreed with Hillel, that the "Laying of Hands" (cf. Lev. 3:2) on sacrifices during festivals is permissible and was instrumental in establishing this law (Beẓah 20a–b). As a judge, Bava was noted for his thorough investigations and for his just decisions (Git. 57a). He offered daily guilt-offerings prescribed in cases of doubtful trespass, for fear that he had committed a sin (Ker. 6:3). This sacrifice came to be called "the guilt-offering of the pious." Bava overlooked an insult to himself to make peace between husband and wife (Ned. 66b). According to another legend Bava was the only Jewish sage who was not put to death by Herod; instead, Herod blinded him so that he could seek his counsel incognito. When Herod finally disclosed who he was and asked how he could make amends, Bava advised him to rebuild the Temple (BB 3b–4a). Josephus refers to "The Sons of Bava," who were among the noblemen of Jerusalem, and were beloved by the people. They were strong opponents of Herod, and for a long time "The Sons of Bava" remained in hiding for fear of him. Ultimately they were executed by him (Ant., 15:260–6).

Bibliography: Schuerer, Gesch, 1 (1901[4]), 386–7; Klausner, Bayit Sheni, 4 (1950[2]), 27–28; Hyman, Toledot, 261–2.

[Z.K.]

BAVA KAMMA (Aram. בָּבָא קַמָּא), tractate of the Talmud, the first of the order *Nezikin.*

Name. *Bava Kamma* was originally not a separate tractate, but the first part of a larger tractate, whose name was identical with the name of the order. The title *Bava Kamma* is the abbreviated form for *Bava Kamma de-Massekhet Nezikin* ("the first gate (section) of the tractate *Nezikin*"). Tractate *Nezikin* ("torts") comprised 30 chapters, covering the entire range of pecuniary law *(dinei mamonot).* However, according to the Midrash, the size of *Nezikin* discouraged the student: "What does the fool say?

Illustration of the opening section of the tractate *Bava Kamma,* which deals with liability for damage done by an animal. Detail from a title page of a Hebrew and Latin edition of the Mishnah, Amsterdam, 1700–1704. Jerusalem, J.N.U.L.

'Who can study the Torah? *Nezikin* has 30 chapters; *Kelim* has 30 chapters!'" (Lev. R. 19:2). For this reason *Nezikin* was divided into three sections, each consisting of ten chapters. The second and third parts are now called *Bava Meẓia* ("the middle gate") and *Bava Batra* ("the last gate"). The division seems to have taken place in Babylonia (*bava* as "gate" is unique to Babylonian Aramaic; see: Ned. 66b), where the size of *Nezikin* must have interfered with the regular practice of the academies to study one tractate each term. Palestinian sources indicate no division. (*Genizah* fragments of the Jerusalem Talmud treat it as one tractate.)

A similar division took place in the Tosefta, where the original tractate *Nezikin*, which contained 33 chapters, was divided into three sections of 11 chapters each. The mechanical nature of this division is evident from the fact that chapter 11 of Tosefta *Bava Meẓia* contains some material that parallels the last chapter of Mishnah *Bava Meẓia* and some that parallels the first chapter of Mishnah *Bava Batra*.

Contents. The first three *mishnayot* of *Bava Kamma* belong to one of the most ancient strata of mishnaic material, and contain, in succinct phrases, the underlying laws of *Torts (see *Avot Nezikin): "There are four *avot* (lit. "fathers" or "main categories") of torts—the *shor* ("ox"), the *bor* ("pit"), the *maveh* ("man" or "tooth") and the *hever* ("fire"). . . . If I am responsible for the care of a thing, it is I who make possible the injury it may do . . . Assessment of the monetary equivalent [of an injury] must be made before a court of law, based upon the testimony of witnesses. . . . The laws of torts apply equally to women. . . ." The antiquity of this section is indicated by the use of numerical listing (four *avot*), first person constructions, biblical phrases, archaic forms, and terse rules. One of the earliest of the Babylonian *amoraim*, Rav, alluded to the character of this section when he stated: "The *tanna* of this Mishnah was a Jerusalemite, who taught in a terse style" (BK 6b).

The list of four *avot* in the Mishnah is a convenient summary of the various sources of damage mentioned in Exodus 21:28–22:5. In the *beraitot*, other lists of *avot nezikin* are found, one containing 13, and others 24, according to varying schemes of inclusion (see BK 4b; Tosef. to BK 9:1).

CHAPTERS 1:4–3:7. Chapter 1:4 is another ancient Mishnah, again in the form of a numbered list, dealing, now in greater detail, with the *avot* of "horn," "tooth," and "foot," and, finally, "man." In chapter 2 each entry on the list in 1:4 is defined and expanded. For example, if an animal, while walking, kicks some pebbles, which hit another object and cause damage, this is "foot," but only half of the damage is to be paid. Thus, chapter 2 of the Mishnah is a sort of *"Gemara"* on 1:4.

The first laws in chapter 3 come under the category of "pit": "If a man left a pitcher in the 'public domain,' and another stumbled over it . . . the owner is liable for the injury." The middle part of chapter 3 deals with "man": "If two potvendors [carrying their wares] were walking, one behind the other, and the first one stumbled . . . " The end of chapter 3 again deals with "horn" and appears to be a new discussion of the same subject covered in chapter 2. It has therefore been suggested by A. Weiss that 1:4–3:7 was originally an independent Mishnah section, dealing with the *avot* of "ox" ("horn," "tooth," "foot"), "pit," and "man." It would thus appear to be an expansion of the list of *avot* at the beginning of chapter 1, until *maveh*, in consonance with the interpretation that *maveh* is "man."

CHAPTER 3:8–6 END. This is another section, treating in detail the categories "horn," "pit," "tooth and foot," and "fire." It, too, is an expansion of 1:1, taking "ox" as "horn," and *maveh* as "tooth and foot." Thus the dispute between Rav and Samuel as to the meaning of *maveh* (BK 3b) did not originate with them; it had its origin in the underlying organizational scheme of early *mishnayot* which are independent expansions of the ancient Mishnah: "There are four *avot*. . . ."

CHAPTER 7. Chapter 7 is a comprehensive treatment of the laws of theft. It concentrates on the fines of "double," and "four or five" fold found in Exodus 22:3 and 21:37. Virtually each aspect of the theft and subsequent trial of the thief is scrutinized; each term of the pertinent scriptural verses is carefully defined and analyzed. In respect to the fine of "four or five" fold imposed by Scripture for the sale or slaughter of a stolen animal, the Mishnah determines that if the thief sold part of the animal but retained partial ownership, however minute, he is not liable to the fine of "four or five fold," but only to that of "double." Thus "sells it" in the scriptural verse is defined as the sale of the entire animal. Similarly, "if he slaughtered it and it became unfit under his hand [through a ritually improper slaughtering]" (7:5), he is exempt from the fine of "four or five" fold, such an act not being properly deemed "slaughter."

CHAPTER 8. This chapter is a comprehensive unit devoted to the laws of assault and battery.

CHAPTERS 9–10. Chapters 9 and 10 deal with laws of robbery. It would appear that a more natural position for these chapters would be after chapter 7, which deals with the related subject of theft. Their position is perhaps determined by their concentration upon the regulations governing transference of ownership of the stolen object through physical alteration or the original owner's despair of recovery, which makes them more closely related to the laws of acquisition and ownership in the succeeding chapters (see *Bava Meẓia) than to the laws of torts in the preceding ones.

It has been suggested that the function of "monetary law" in rabbinic sources is to prevent offenses of law, and to instruct the common man in moral behavior, rather than merely to provide for redress after a wrong has been committed (i.e., that such law is duty-oriented, rather than right-oriented, as explained by Silberg). Along these lines, types of damages are described in *Bava Kamma* for which one is "not liable according to human law, but guilty according to the laws of heaven" (55b–56a). Since there are acts which, even though not rendering one liable to suit, are morally wrong, it becomes an act of piety to take extreme care in preventing harm to the person or property of others. R. Judah held that the study of the laws of damages in *Bava Kamma* is a prerequisite for achieving true piety (30a).

Jerusalem Talmud. S. Lieberman has shown that the tractate *Nezikin* in the Jerusalem Talmud is of a different nature from the rest of that Talmud. The differences are attributed to its having been edited in Caesarea, no later than 350 C.E., while the rest of the Jerusalem Talmud was edited in Tiberias, some 50 years later. Among its distinguishing features are: the short, pithy nature of the discussions, indicating a minimum of editing; a more primitive talmudic terminology; archaic Hebrew words; a relatively wider use of Greek and Latin (Caesarea was the seat of the Roman government in Palestine); and a distinctive orthography (e.g.,— לָ for לָא). Anonymous statements in *Nezikin* are quoted elsewhere in the Jerusalem Talmud in the name of "the sages of Caesarea," or in the name of specific *amoraim* who lived in Caesarea. When points of law relating to *Nezikin* are discussed elsewhere in the Jerusalem Talmud, the treatment differs from the parallels in *Nezikin*. Conversely, sections of *Nezikin* which discuss matters relating to other tractates do not correspond to the material found in the relevant section of those tractates, although it is reasonable to assume that they were present in the corresponding tractates of the Talmud collection used by the editor of *Nezikin*. All this leads to the conclusion that *Nezikin* differs from the other tractates of the Jerusalem Talmud and constitutes the only existing remnant of the "Talmud of Caesarea."

The tractate in the Babylonian Talmud was translated into English by E. W. Kirzner in the Soncino Talmud (1935).

Bibliography: A. Weiss, *Diyyunim u-Verurim be-Vava Kamma* (1966); S. Lieberman, in: *Tarbiz*, 2 (1931), Suppl. 4; L. Jacobs, *Studies in Talmudic Logic and Methodology* (1961), 132–5; M. Silberg, *Harvard Law Review*, 75 (1961), 307–31; Epstein, Amora'im, 279–87; S. Lieberman, *Sifrei Zutta* (1968); S. Friedman, (ed.), *Jonathan ha-Kohen's Commentary to Bava Kamma* (1969).

[SH.F.]

BAVA MEẒIA (Aram. בָּבָא מְצִיעָא, "middle gate"), tractate of the Mishnah, with *Gemara* in the Jerusalem and Babylonian *Talmuds. Originally *Bava Meẓia* was not a separate tractate but the second part of the tractate *Nezikin* (see **Bava Kamma*). Chapters 1 and 2 deal with the laws of *acquisition *(kinyan)* of lost or abandoned articles and describe the cases in which the article may not be acquired by the finder but must be held until claimed. These regulations are thus related to the laws of the last two chapters of *Bava Kamma,* which determine how and under what circumstances stolen articles may be legitimately acquired and under what circumstances they must be returned. Great religious importance is attached to the commandment of returning lost property: if a man return a lost animal and it escapes again, he must continue to return it, even "100 times" (31a). Nonetheless, exemption is granted from this commandment if its performance would require violation of a ritual prohibition, entail behavior which is an affront to the personal dignity of the finder, or require the finder to neglect his own work and thereby sustain a financial loss greater than the object's value (30a). Chapter 2:9 reads like a new beginning and probably represents the incorporation of a new source, originally a Midrash on Deuteronomy 22:1. It closes with a section which is religious and moral in tone, thus marking the end of a unit.

An unpaid guardian, with whom goods were deposited for safekeeping, is discussed in chapter 3. He resembles one who guards found property (ch. 2), and also must, on some occasions, sell perishables deposited with him and hold the proceeds for the owner. If the guardian misuses the object, he is considered a robber and must assume all responsibility for subsequent damage. Chapter 4 opens with the general rules for acquiring movable property in a business transaction. Transfer of title to the buyer occurs, not at the time of payment, but only when the buyer takes the item (or symbolically "draws" it to himself). This means that the sale can be legally canceled even after payment, as long as the goods have not been "drawn"; but the sages said, "He that exacted punishment from the generation of the Flood . . . will exact punishment from him that does not abide by his spoken word" (4:2). However, R. Johanan held that originally payment of some amount of money effected the transfer of title, but that since this law led to abuse—the seller would not deliver but say, "Your wheat was destroyed by fire in the storeroom"—the rule was changed to its present form (46b). The remainder of the chapter contains a detailed section on *ona'ah,* unfair and illegal business practices (based on Lev. 25:17). Much attention is given to overcharging; the law guarantees redress to the party defrauded of one-sixth or more of the value of the purchase.

Chapter 5 is a self-contained unit dealing with the laws of interest (see Lev. 25:36); it appears here probably by virtue of its association with the regulations on commerce found in chapter 4, and closes with a section emphasizing the ethical seriousness of the prohibition (see Tosef. 6:17). Chapter 6 opens with cases of deception between employer and craftsmen, which can be considered a continuation of the theme of *ona'ah* found in chapter 4. The first Mishnah is followed by a series of *mishnayot* each beginning with the words, "If a man hired. . . ." They deal with breach of contract in cases of hiring craftsmen or work animals. The final section concerns itself with craftsmen who work with others' material but on their own premises; they have the status of "paid guardian" and are responsible for loss or theft. Chapter 7 gives rules of labor relations and the right of the employee, especially the agricultural worker, to eat from the produce of the field. This law reflects the

Illustration of the opening of the tractate *Bava Meẓia* showing a dispute over a found garment. Detail from a title page of a Hebrew and Latin edition of the Mishnah, Amsterdam, 1700–1704. Jerusalem, J.N.U.L.

interpretation that Deuteronomy 23:25–26 refers specifically to the agricultural worker and not to any passerby, for granting to the latter the rights of eating the field's produce would not yield a viable situation for the owner (92a). The duty of the farmer to allow his animal to eat of the produce (Deut. 25:4) is also treated. The discussion of the right of those who guard produce (but do not work with it) to partake of the food is the occasion to introduce an ancient Mishnah delineating the laws of the four kinds of guardian: an unpaid guardian, a borrower, a paid guardian, and a hirer (Ex. 22:6–14). The beginning of chapter 8 continues the subject of guardians, specifically elaborating on Exodus 22:14—that the borrower of an animal may not be liable for payment on unavoidable accidents when he had also borrowed or hired the personal services of the lender. The chapter closes with laws of renting houses (related to "hiring" above).

Chapter 9 opens with a related issue: leasing of a field where the lessee gives the owner a percentage of the produce, or a fixed amount of produce, instead of rental money. The last two parts of the chapter complement laws found earlier in the tractate; they deal with the duty to pay employees promptly and limitations of the creditor's right to exact a pledge from the borrower. The religio-moral tone of this section is typical of the close of a unit. Chapter 10 does indeed open a new topic, the ownership of real estate (continued through **Bava Batra*), and deals basically with the property rights of neighbors whose properties are situated one above the other.

Among several aggadic passages in *Bava Meẓia,* the section beginning at the bottom of 59a is of special interest. R. Eliezer's arguments regarding the purity of a certain oven did not convince his colleagues. He then called for a series of miraculous acts to vindicate him. Although heavenly interventions were forthcoming, the miracles were deemed valueless in settling legal disputes. R. Eliezer then declared," If the law is according to my opinion, may it be proved from heaven." A heavenly voice *(*bat kol)* issued forth saying, "Why do you challenge R. Eliezer, for the law is according to his opinion in all matters?" Whereupon R. Joshua rose and declared, "It is not in the heavens" (Deut. 30:12) " . . . since the giving of the Torah at Mt. Sinai, no attention is paid to a heavenly voice, but the opinion of a majority of the scholars determines authentic law." An English translation of the Talmud was made by S. Daiches and H. Freedman (Soncino edition, 1935). A students' edition, vocalized, with translation, commentary and notes in English, appeared as part of the *Talmud El-Am.*

[Sh.F.]

The Tosefta of *Bava Meẓia* contains 11 chapters. The *beraitot* in the Tosefta, in addition to giving supplementary and sometimes parallel passages to the Mishnah, also contain much more material than the Mishnah, dealing with entire subjects not mentioned in it, since the editor of the Tosefta had before him complete sources that were not available to the editor of the Mishnah.

Chapter I of the Tosefta parallels chapter 1 of the Mishnah, but it ends with a series of laws dealing with deeds and surety. They begin with the words (1:15), "if two have hold of a bill, the one saying it is mine but I lost it" etc., which are directly connected with the main subject of the chapter; since the editor did not want to fragment the source, he gives it in full on account of the first *halakhah.* Chapter 2 parallels Mishnah chapter 2, but from its last *halakhah* (33) it can be inferred to whom lost property need not be returned—"heretics, apostates, and informers" (cf. Av. Zar. 26b; and see Ch. Albeck, *Meḥkarim be-Varaita ve-Tosefta,* 1944, 138 n.4). Chapter 3:1–12, parallels chapter 3 of the Mishnah, and 3:13–29 parallels chapter 4 of the Mishnah. Chapter 5 of the Mishnah dealing with interest is paralleled by chapters 4–6 of the Tosefta. Tosefta 7:1–14 parallels 6:1–5 of the Mishnah, dealing with *ona'ah* in the hiring of laborers and cattle and the requirement not to deviate from traditional custom in the conditions of hire; while Tosefta 7:14–19 parallels Mishnah 6:6–8, dealing with the *halakhot* of craftsmen in respect of guarding articles in their care. It is probable that this chapter preserves richer and more original sources than those contained in the Mishnah.

Chapter 8:1–12, parallelling Mishnah 7:1–7, deals with the duties and rights of laborers, as well as the rights of cattle employed in work (in respect of eating the produce). Tosefta 8:13–26 deals with the four bailees and parallels Mishnah 7:8–8:5, but here too the Tosefta appears to preserve a more original order. It is not clear whether Tosefta 8:25–26 was brought in because of the previous cases of conflicting statements by the two litigants or whether it is merely the supplement of the body of *halakhot* in 7:1–14. Tosefta 8:27–33 parallels Mishnah 8:6–9 and discusses the laws of the hiring and borrowing of houses, inns, and shops. Tosefta chapter 9 deals with hiring and the renting and tenant-hiring of fields. (The Mishnah has nothing on hiring, whereas from the Tosefta the connection (in the Mishnah) between the renting of houses and the leasing of fields becomes clear.) Chapter 10:1 ("He who lends to his fellow") may be a supplement to the previous chapter (9:14, 20–21: "one may not deviate from local custom") or it may have been brought in because of the laws which follow dealing with remuneration for hire. Tosefta 10:2–7, dealing with the laws of hired men and their hire, parallels accordingly Mishnah 9:11–12, and subsequently 8–11 parallels Mishnah 9:13 in dealing with the taking of a pledge. Tosefta chapter 11, dealing with the laws of partners and neighbors, parallels chapter 10 of Mishnah *Bava Meẓia* together with chapter 1 of *Bava Batra.*

[M.D.H.]

Bibliography: Epstein, Amora'im, 279–87; D. Daube, in: *Tulane Law Review,* 18 (1944), 377ff.; Ch. Albeck, *Shishah Sidrei Mishnah,* 4 (1959), 57–63; A. Weiss, *Diyyunim u-Verurim be-Vava Kamma* (1966), 10–16, 26; B. De Vries. *Meḥkarim be-Sifrut ha-Talmud* (1968), 96–101; S. Albeck, in: *Sinai,* 62 (1968), 229ff.

BAVARIA, *Land* in S. Germany, including Franconia. Jews are first mentioned there in the *Passau toll regulations of 906. Their settlement was apparently connected with the trade routes to Hungary, southern Russia and northeastern Germany. A Jewish resident of Regensburg is mentioned at the end of the tenth century. The communities which had been established in *Bamberg and Regensburg were attacked during the First Crusade in 1096, and those in *Aschaffenburg, *Wuerzburg, and *Nuremberg during the

Figure 1. The main synagogue in Fuerth, Bavaria, built in 1616. An engraving made in 1839. Fuerth Municipality. Photo Knut Mayer.

Second Crusade in 1146–47. Other communities existed in the 13th century at Landshut, Passau, *Munich, and *Fuerth. The Jews in Bavaria mainly engaged in trade, dealing in slaves, gold, silver and other metals, and in moneylending. In 1276 they were expelled from Upper Bavaria and 180 Jews were burned at the stake in Munich following a *blood libel in 1285. The communities in Franconia were attacked during the *Rindfleisch persecutions in 1298. The *Armleder massacres, charges of desecrating the *Host at *Deggendorf, Straubing, and Landshut, and the persecutions following the *Black Death (1348–49), brought catastrophe to the whole of Bavarian Jewry. Many communities were entirely destroyed, among them *Ansbach, Aschaffenburg, *Augsburg, Bamberg, *Ulm, Munich, Nuremberg, Passau, Regensburg, *Rothenburg, and Wuerzburg. Those who had fled were permitted to return after a time under King Wenceslaus.

Figure 2. Ark of the Law from the synagogue in Westheim, Bavaria, c. 1725. The ark was latterly in the Wuerzburg Museum, which was destroyed in World War II. Photo Gundermann, Wuerzburg.

In 1442 the Jews were again expelled from Upper Bavaria. Shortly afterward, in 1450, the Jews in Lower Bavaria were flung into prison until they paid the duke a ransom of 32,000 crowns and were then driven from the duchy. As a result of agitation by the Franciscan John of *Capistrano, they were expelled from Franconia. In 1478 they were expelled from Passau, in 1499 from Nuremberg, and in 1519 from Regensburg. The few subsequently remaining in the duchy of Bavaria were expelled in 1551. Subsequently, Jewish settlement in Bavaria ceased until toward the end of the 17th century, when a small community was founded in *Sulzbach by refugees from *Vienna. During the War of the Spanish Succession (1701–14) several Jews from Austria serving as purveyors to the army or as moneylenders settled in Bavaria. In this period a flourishing community grew up in Fuerth, whose economic activities helped to bring prosperity to the city. After the war the Jews of Austrian origin were expelled from Bavaria, but some were able to acquire the right to reside in Munich as monopoly holders, *Court Jews, mintmasters, and physicians. Several Court Jews belonging to the *Frankel and *Model families became prominent in Ansbach and Fuerth for a while in the 18th century, particularly because of their services in managing the state's economy.

In the Napoleonic era Jewish children were permitted to attend the general schools (1804), the men were accepted into the militia (1805), the poll tax was abolished (1808), and Jews were granted the status of citizens (1813). However, at the same time their number and rights of residence were still restricted, and only the eldest son in a family was allowed to marry (see *Familiants Laws). In 1819 anti-Jewish disorders broke out in Franconia (the "*Hep! Hep!" riots). Owing to the continued adverse conditions and the restrictions on families a large number of young Bavarian Jews emigrated to the United States. A second wave of emigrants left for the U.S. in the reaction following the 1848 Revolution. In 1861 the discriminatory restrictions concerning Jews were abolished, and Jews were permitted to engage in all occupations. However, complete equality was not granted until 1872 by the provisions of the constitution of the German Reich of 1871. Certain special "Jewish taxes" were abolished only in 1880. The chief occupation of Bavarian Jews in the 19th century was the livestock trade, largely in Jewish hands (see *Agriculture). By the beginning of the 20th century Jews had considerable holdings in department stores and in a few branches of industry.

A number of Jews were active after World War I in the revolutionary government of Bavaria which was headed by a Jew, Kurt *Eisner, who was prime minister before his assassination in 1919. Another Jew, Gustav *Landauer, who became minister of popular instruction, was also assassinated that year. In the reaction which followed World War I there was a new wave of anti-Semitism, and in 1923 most of the East European Jews resident in Bavaria were expelled. This was the time when the National Socialist Movement made its appearance in the region, and anti-Semitic agitation increased. Jewish ritual slaughter was prohibited in Bavaria in 1931.

The size of the Jewish population in Bavaria varied relatively little from the Napoleonic era to 1933, numbering 53,208 in 1818 and 41,939 in 1933. A Bavarian Jewish organization, the Verband bayerischer israelitischer Gemeinden, was set up in 1921 and included 273 communities and 21 rabbinical institutions. In 1933 the largest and most important communities in Bavaria were in Munich (which had a Jewish population of 9,000), Nuremberg (7,500), Wuerzburg (2,150), Augsburg (1,100), Fuerth (2,000), and Regensburg (450). At this time the majority of Bavarian Jews were engaged in trade and transport (54.5%) and in industry (19%), but some also in agriculture (2.7% in 1925 compared with 9.7% in 1882). Over 1,000 Jews studied at the University of Bavaria after World War I, a proportion ten times higher than that of the Jews to the general population.

Regensburg was a center of Jewish scholarship from the 12th century. Regensburg was the cradle of the medieval Ashkenazi *Ḥasidism and in the 12th and 13th centuries the main center of this school. The traveler *Pethahiah b. Jacob set out from there in about 1170. Prominent scholars of Bavaria include *Meir b. Baruch of Rothenburg (the leading authority of Ashkenazi Jewry, 13th century); Jacob *Weil (taught at Nuremberg and Augsburg, beginning of the 15th century); Israel *Bruna (settled in Regensburg, mid-15th century); Moses *Mintz (rabbi of Bamberg, 1469–1474); and the Renaissance grammarian Elijah *Levita (a native of Neustadt). In the 19th/20th centuries there lived in Munich the folklorist and philologist Max M. *Gruenbaum; Raphael Nathan Nata *Rabinovicz, author of *Dikdukei Soferim;* and Joseph *Perles, rabbi of Augsburg, 1875–1910.

Figure 3. Wall paintings in the synagogue of Bechhofen by Eliezer Sussmann, 1733. The synagogue was restored in 1914 by the Bavarian Commission for National Art Treasures and was destroyed by the Nazis. Jerusalem, Israel Museum Archives.

The Jews in Bavaria were among the first victims of the Nazi movement, which spread from Munich and Nuremberg. Virulent and widespread anti-Semitic agitation caused the depopulation of scores of the village communities so characteristic of Bavaria, especially after the *Kristallnacht in 1938, which was particularly destructive in Bavaria, a hotbed of Nazism and home of many Nazis. The first concentration camp was established at *Dachau in Bavaria and many Jews from Germany and other countries in Europe perished there.

After World War II thousands of Jews were assembled in displaced persons' camps in Bavaria; the last one to be closed down was in Foehrenwald. Almost all of the 1,000 Bavarian Jews who survived the Holocaust were saved because they were married to Germans or were born of mixed marriages. A year after the end of hostilities a Nazi underground movement remained active in Bavaria, and the neo-Nazi anti-Jewish demonstrations of June 1965 started in Bamberg. Anti-Semitic sentiment was also aroused when the minister of Jewish affairs, Philip Auerbach, was prosecuted for misappropriation of funds in 1951.

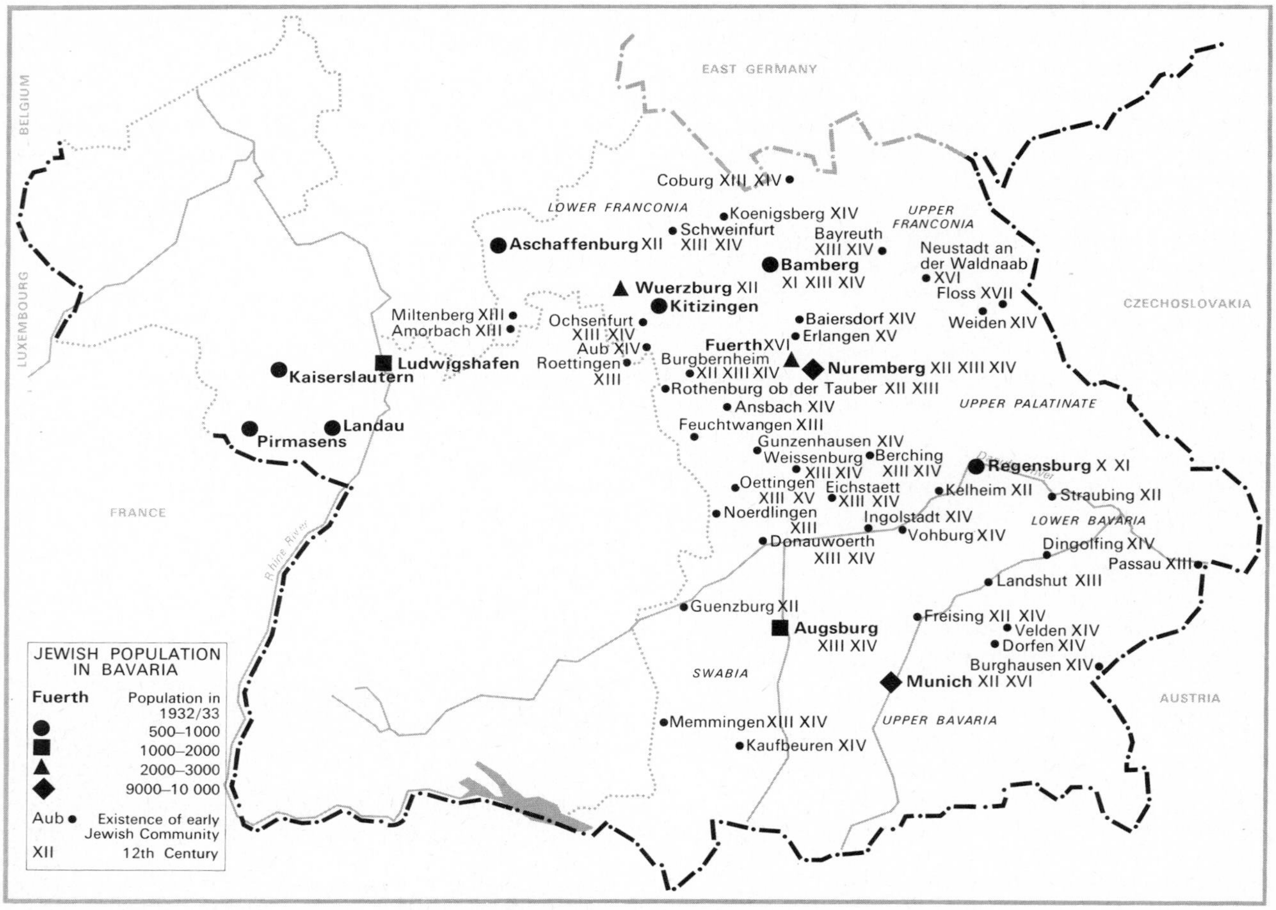

Map of Bavaria showing Jewish population centers from the tenth century to 1932–33.

In 1969 there were in Bavaria about 4,700 Jews, forming 13 communities, the majority from the camps of Eastern Europe. The largest communities were in Munich (3,486), Nuremberg (275), Wuerzburg (141), Fuerth (200), Augsberg (230), and Regensburg (150). There were smaller numbers of Jews in *Amberg, Bamberg, *Bayreuth, Straubing, and Weiden.

See also *Germany.

Bibliography: S. Taussig, *Geschichte der Juden in Bayern* (1874); Germ Jud, 1 (1963), 22–24; 2 (1968), 57–60; S. Schwarz, *Juden in Bayern im Wandel der Zeiten* (1963); R. Strauss, *Regensburg and Augsburg* (1939); H. B. Ehrmann, *Struggle for Civil and Religious Emancipation in Bavaria in the First Half of the 19th Century* (1948), 199; H. C. Vedeler, in: *Journal of Modern History*, 10 (1938), 473–95; P. Wiener-Odenheimer, *Die Berufe der Juden in Bayern* (1918), 131; H. Schnee, *Die Hoffinanz und der moderne Staat*, 4 (1963), 187ff.

[Z.Av./Ed.]

BAVLI (Rashgolski), HILLEL (1893–1961), Hebrew poet and educator. Bavli, who was born in Pilvishki, Lithuania, attended yeshivot in Kovno and Vilna. In 1912 he immigrated to the United States and studied at Canisius College and Columbia University. From 1918 he taught modern Hebrew literature at the Jewish Theological Seminary of America, after 1937 with the rank of professor. Bavli's first poems appeared in a children's periodical, *Ha-Peraḥim*, in 1908. His first book of poetry, *Neginot Ereẓ* ("Melodies of the Land"), was published in 1929. Subsequent collections of his poetry, *Shirim* ("Poems," 1938), *Shirim le-Raḥelah* ("Poems for Raḥelah," 1950), and *Adderet ha-Shanim* ("The Mantle of Years," 1955), also appeared in Israel. Conservative in style and structure, Bavli covers a broad range of themes: personal love; love of his people; love of Ereẓ Israel. He was one of the first Hebrew poets to deal with the American milieu. "Mrs. Woods" is an idyll about an American woman of simple tastes and honest demeanor. Bavli's critical essays *Ruḥot Nifgashot* ("Winds Meet," 1958), deal mainly with Hebrew and American writers. Bavli translated Dickens' *Oliver Twist* (1924) and Shakespeare's *Antony and Cleopatra* into Hebrew (1952). He also translated works by the Negro writers James D. Corrothers, W. Burghardt du Bois, and Claude McKay into Hebrew. He edited a miscellany *Nimim* (1923), a

Hillel Bavli, Hebrew poet.

yearbook *Massad* (2 vols, 1933–1936), the Ẓevi Scharfstein Jubilee Volume (1955), and several modern Hebrew classics for school use. He published a number of articles in English on modern Hebrew literature, including *The Growth of Modern Hebrew Literature* (1939) and *Some Aspects of Modern Hebrew Literature* (1958).

Bibliography: A. Epstein, *Soferim Ivrim be-Amerika*, 1 (1952), 104–24; E. R. Malachi, *Zekher le-Hillel* (1962); J. Kabakoff, in: JBA, 20 (1962/63), 76–83; Waxman, Literature, 5 (1960[2]), 190–2.

[El.S.]

BAVLI, MENAHEM BEN MOSES (fl. 16th century), rabbi and kabbalist of the Safed school. There is little information about his descent. The title *"Bavli"* (Babylonian) probably stands for "Roman," and it is possible that he came from Italy. In 1522 and in 1525 he signed himself as *dayyan* in Trikkala, Greece. Later he immigrated to Ereẓ Israel and in 1531 he was in Safed together with his father and brother Reuben (responsa R. Moses b. Joseph di Trani, 1 (1641), no. 43). They made their living in the wool-dyeing trade. Menahem was considered one of the great scholars of the town. One of his responsa was published in the responsa collection *Maran le-Even ha-Ezer* (no. 14) and in it he quotes a ruling of R. Jacob *Berab whom he calls "our teacher the Great Rabbi," which suggests that Bavli may have been a student at Berab's yeshivah in Safed. After 1553 he was in Egypt. From Safed Bavli went to Hebron probably in connection with the expansion of the Jewish settlement there, in which the scholars of Safed took part. In the introduction to his *Peri Ḥevron (Ta'amei ha-Mitzvot)* (Lublin, 1571), he wrote that he dedicated the income of this book to "Hebron, as a contribution for its reconstruction."

Bibliography: Benayahu, in: KS, 29 (1954), 173f.; A. N. Z. Roth, *ibid.*, 31 (1956), 399; Benayahu, *ibid.*, 399–400; Dmitrovsky, in: *Sefunot*, 7 (1963), 67.

[Ed.]

°**BAYAZID II** (c. 1447–1512), sultan of Turkey 1481–1512, son and successor of Sultan Muhammad II, conqueror of Constantinople. After the expulsion from Spain and Portugal, great numbers of Jews streamed into the Ottoman Empire and settled in various towns of the Balkans and Anatolia. Sultan Bayazid issued an order to the governors of the provinces not to refuse the Jews entry or cause them difficulties, but to receive them cordially. Imanuel *Aboab attributes to Bayazid the famous remark that the Catholic Monarchs (Ferdinand and Isabella) were considered wise, but wrongly so since they impoverished Spain (by the expulsion of the Jews) and enriched Turkey. During the reign of Bayazid the position of rabbi in the capital was held by R. Moses *Capsali, who was succeeded by R. Elijah *Mizraḥi. Joseph *Hamon was the sultan's physician and influential at court. European sources accuse Hamon of complicity in the sudden death of Bayazid after his forced abdication in favor of his son.

Bibliography: M. Franco, *Essai sur l'histoire des Israélites de l'Empire Ottoman...* (1897), 35–40; Rosanes, Togarmah, 1 (1930), 59–90.

[A.H.]

BAYHAN (Bayḥān, also **Beihan)**, territory and name of two towns in South Arabia. In antiquity this area formed the center of the flourishing kingdom of Qataban. In the 12th century Benjamin of Tudela described Jews near Aden who lived in inaccessible mountain recesses and occasionally went down to the plains, taking booty to their hills where no one could pursue them. In *Korot ha-Zeman* (1893), Ḥayyim *Ḥabshush tells of a false messiah who appeared in 1495 during the rule of Imam Amir ibn ʿAbd al-Wahhāb of Yemen (1488–1517). The pretender was defeated only after wars which resulted in the disappearance of the Jews from Bayhan. Ḥabshush's report is confirmed by a South Arabian chronicle which gives a detailed account of a Jewish revolt in Bayhan in the Muslim year 905 (1499–1500). The leader, who rode horses with golden or silver saddles (in the manner of Muslim nobility), attracted many Jews, especially forced converts to Islam. They were overcome by a ruse. Ḥabshush's remark that no Jews were found in Bayhan at his time is partly borne out by a contemporary traveler, who states that Jews were not permitted to live in Bayhan ad-Dawla, the capital of the Yemeni part of the Bayhan. Some Jews lived in nearby Bayda, its commercial center, in the late 19th century. In the second town, Bayhan al-Qasab, c. 1895 Count Carlo Landberg found a Jewish quarter of fifty houses whose inhabitants were mostly silversmiths, weavers, and leather workers. At the time of the exodus from Yemen in 1949, only 88 Jews were in Bayhan. They were flown from the airstrip of the British Air Force in Bayhan to Aden and later to Israel.

Bibliography: Goitein, in: KS, 14 (1938), 266; idem, in: *Haaretz* (Nov. 17, 1950); Serjeant, in: *Bulletin of the School of Oriental and African Studies*, 13 (1950), 294; W. Phillips, *Qataban and Sheba* (1955), 56, passim.

[S.D.G.]

BAYLIS, LILIAN MARY (1874–1937), English theatrical manager and founder of the "Old Vic" in London. Her parents were singers, who took her to South Africa in 1890; there she taught dancing, violin, and banjo. In 1898 she returned to London to assist her aunt Emma Cons, who was running the Victoria Theater as the Coffee Music Hall. Under Miss Baylis' guidance, the "Old Vic" became famous as "the home of Shakespeare" in London. She became sole manager in 1912, and in 1931 took over the derelict Sadler's Wells theater and made that famous for opera and ballet.

Lilian Baylis, founder of London's "Old Vic" theater.

Bibliography: L. M. Baylis and C. M. Hamilton, *The Old Vic* (1926).

[Ed.]

BAYONNE, town in southwestern France. The first Jewish settlement in Bayonne, in the suburb of Saint-Esprit, consisted of *Marranos originally from Spain and Portugal, who settled there early in the 16th century. In 1550 they were granted rights of residence as "New Christians" by the central authorities, but the Bayonne merchants prohibited them from retail trading. In 1636 several Marrano families were expelled from Bayonne, and some of them found refuge at Nantes. From the middle of the 17th century, the Bayonne community organized a congregation, *Nefuẓot*

Bayonne synagogue, dedicated in 1837.

Yehudah ("The Dispersed of Judah"). Their cemetery was established in 1660. The right of the community to observe Judaism openly was not officially recognized until 1723. Rabbis of Bayonne in this period included Ḥayyim de Mercado in the second half of the 17th century, succeeded by Raphael *Meldola (1730–1792) of Leghorn, and Abraham David Leon, author of *Instrucciones sagradas y morales* (1765). At the beginning of the 18th century the community numbered 700, and 3,500 in 1753.

The Bayonne community claimed jurisdiction over the small communities in Bidache, Peyrehorade, and other places in the vicinity. Marranos from Spain and Portugal continued to settle in Bayonne until late in the 18th century. The regulations of the community were drawn up in 1752, and confirmed by the "intendant du roi." Bayonne Jewry helped to introduce the chocolate industry into France; in the mid-18th century the import of salt and glue into Bayonne was in Jewish hands. Bayonne Jews were among the first to establish trade connections with the French West Indies. About one-third of the municipal tax revenue was derived from the Jewish residents. Despite opposition from their Christian neighbors, the Jews participated in the elections to the States-General in 1789. They were recognized as French citizens in 1790, with the rest of the "Portuguese, Spanish, and Avignonese" Jews in France. During the Reign most of the members of the *Comité de surveillance* of Saint Esprit (known then as "Jean Jacques Rousseau") were Jews; it is noteworthy that no guillotinings took place. In the Napoleonic period the community benefited from the city's increasing prosperity. The Jewish population nevertheless fell to 1,293 in 1844, and by 1926 had decreased to 45 families. [Z.Av./Ed.]

Holocaust Period. After the Franco-German armistice (June 1940) Bayonne became a stopover for innumerable Jewish refugees, particularly from *Belgium and *Luxembourg. A great many could not get to Spain, and the official police census of March 15, 1942, registered 308 Jewish families there at that time. In April 1943 the majority of them were expelled, while 193 Jewish possessions were confiscated. However, the Ark, built in the style of Louis XVI, and the Torah scrolls, some of which were of Spanish origin, were hidden in the Basque Museum, and restored to the synagogue after the Liberation. Few of Bayonne's Jews survived the war. The rabbi of Bayonne, Ernest *Ginsburger (1876–1943) directed religious activities on behalf of the Jews interned in French concentration and labor camps. He was subsequently deported and murdered by the Germans. In April 1943, almost all the Jews in Bayonne and the surrounding district were forcibly evacuated.

After the war the community slowly rebuilt itself, with about 120 families recorded living in the city in 1960. With the arrival of immigrants from North Africa, the Jewish community more than doubled, so that in 1969 close to 700 Jews lived in Bayonne. The community maintains an old-age home. A rabbi was engaged to preside over regular community services, led according to the ancient Sephardic ("Portuguese") rites of the 100 year old synagogue which was restored. The old Jewish cemetery, dating back to 1660, was still in use (1969). The Basque Museum maintains two rooms with a large display of Jewish religious objects and historic documents relating to the Bayonne Jewish community. René *Cassin, the Nobel Prize winner and president of *Alliance Israélite Universelle, was born in Bayonne in 1887. [G.Le.]

Bibliography: L. F. de Beaufleury, *Histoire de l'établissement des juifs à Bordeaux et Bayonne* (1799); H. Léon, *Histoire des juifs de Bayonne* (1893); Gross, Gal Jud, 92f.; M. Schwab, in: REJ, 38 (1899), 272–4; Liber, *ibid.*, 64 (1912), 254–61; Genevray, *ibid.*, 74 (1922), 127–47; E. Ginsburger, *Le Comité de surveillance de Jean-Jacques Rousseau* (1934); Szajkowski, in: PAAJR, 24 (1955), 137–64; idem, in: HUCA, 30 (1959), 217–32; *Guide religieux de la France* (1967), 982f.

BAYREUTH, city in Bavaria, W. Germany, and former principality. Jews lived in the principality of Bayreuth at the beginning of the 13th century and are mentioned in *Meir b. Baruch of Rothenburg's responsa. In 1248 several Jews were admitted into the city of Bayreuth. In the course of the riots accompanying the *Black Death (1348–49) many Jews in the principality were killed. After this, the emperor Charles IV entrusted authority over the Jews of Bayreuth to the margrave. In 1372 the latter appointed a chief rabbi for all his territory, including at that time the communities of Kulmbach and Hof. Until the end of the 15th century the Jews were permitted freedom of movement and the right to bring claims against Christians before a mixed tribunal. In 1409 a charter was granted to the Jews of Neustadt an der Aisch (where 71 Jews had perished in the massacre of 1218) and in 1421 Jewish trade in the principality was regulated. In 1422 the Jews were compelled to renounce all claims against Christians and subsequently left the principality. However, six Jewish families resettled in the "Jewish lane" of the city of Bayreuth in 1441, and the position of the Jewish residents improved. A number of refugees from *Bamberg were admitted into the towns of Pegnitz, Steinach, *Baiersdorf, Erlangen, Neustadt an der Aisch, and Kulm (now Chlumec, Czechoslovakia), and several *Court Jews were in the margrave's service at Bayreuth. In 1488 the Jews were again made to cancel all the debts owing to them as a condition for setting aside an expulsion order. Nevertheless, they were expelled several times from various parts of the principality during the 16th and 17th centuries, though most of the expulsion orders were short-lived.

Their position began to improve as a result of the influence of the Court Jew, Samson of Baiersdorf. In 1695 the margrave granted concessions and protection to Jewish tradesmen. The seat of the provincial rabbinate was

Baiersdorf since Jews had been excluded from the city of Bayreuth from 1515. Further improvements followed after 1735, in the main a reflection of the liberal attitude of Margrave Frederick, who had a Jewish chess player and a Jewish painter at his court. The Jewish population of the principality rose from 135 families in 1709 to 346 families (1,727 persons) in 1771. Ten Jewish families were admitted into the city of Bayreuth in 1759, and there were 65 families (401 persons) resident in the city in 1771. In 1805 there were 2,276 Jews living in the principality, which was incorporated into Bavaria two years later. During the 19th and the beginning of the 20th centuries the number of the Jews declined. In spite of their shrill anti-Semitism, Richard *Wagner and his circle in Bayreuth did not affect the position of the Jews there. In 1933 the Jewish population of Bayreuth numbered 261 (0.7% of the total).

On Nov. 10, 1938, the synagogue (built in 1760) was ransacked and homes and shops were pillaged by the S. A. The populace committed further acts of vandalism the next day and the cemetery was desecrated beyond recognition. On Nov. 27, 1941, 50 persons were deported to *Riga; on Jan. 12, 1942, the last 11 were transported to *Theresienstadt. After World War II a new community was established which numbered 550 in 1949 and had decreased, through emigration, to 40 in 1967. Part of the communal archives are in the Jewish Historical General Archives in Jerusalem.

Bibliography: A. Eckstein, *Geschichte der Juden im Markgrafentum Bayreuth* (1907); FJW (1928–29), 125f.; Germ Jud, 1 (1963), 24; 2 (1968), 60–61; Y. L. Bialer, *Min ha-Genazim*, 2 (1969), 54–58; PK.

[Z.F.]

BAY TREE. The *oren*, mentioned only once in the Bible (Isa. 44:14), is identified in the Talmud (RH 23a) with *ara*, the bay tree. It is mentioned in the Mishnah (Par. 3:8) among the trees that were used in preparing the fire for the burning of the red heifer. From it (according to one reading) long poles were made for the beacons that were kindled to announce the New Moon (RH 2:3). In Israel it is an important forest-tree that grows extensively on moist mountain slopes. An evergreen, its aromatic leaves are used for seasoning food, and were, according to the Talmud, an ingredient in a cure for intestinal worms (Git. 69b). In modern Hebrew *oren* denotes the pine tree, an identification that is based on the Septuagint, but the pine is the biblical *eẓ shemen*. The translation of *oren* as "ash" (AV) or as "cedar" (RV) is untenable, the latter being the biblical *erez*. In modern Hebrew the bay tree is called *dafnah* or *eẓ aẓil*.

Bibliography: Loew, Flora, 2 (1924), 119–23; J. Feliks, *Olam ha-Ẓome'aḥ ha-Mikra'i* (1957), 92.

[J.F.]

BAZA (Arabic **Basta**), town N.E. of Granada in S.E. Spain. Baza was annexed to Granada after Almeria's defeat by the army under *Samuel b. Joseph ha-Nagid's command (c. 1039). In the 11th century there was a Jewish community in Baza whose residents were employed mostly in the silk industry. The Jewish quarter was located opposite the present-day cathedral of Santiago. A *mikveh* with three bath chambers has been uncovered and is a good example of 11th-century Arabic bathhouse architecture.

Bibliography: EI, 1 (1960²), s.v. *Basta;* M. Gómez-Moreno, in: *Al Andalus*, 12 (1947), 151–5; Ashtor, Korot, 2 (1966), 92–93.

[Ed.]

BAZELON, DAVID L. (1909–), U.S. judge. Bazelon was born in Superior, Wisconsin, and was educated in Chicago. Admitted to the Illinois bar in 1932, he practiced law until 1949. In 1946 Bazelon was appointed an assistant attorney general of the U.S., and in 1949 President Truman appointed him judge of the U.S. Court of Appeals for the District of Columbia. He became chief judge of the court in 1962. An authority on the relationship between law and psychiatry, Bazelon held several university lectureships, and in 1962 was elected honorary fellow of the American Psychiatric Association. From 1960 he was a member of the board of trustees of the Jewish Publication Society of America.

[Ed.]

BDELLIUM (Heb. בְּדֹלַח) twice mentioned in the Scriptures, once in the description of the land of Havilah, which contained "gold, bdellium, and onyx stone" (Gen. 2:12), and again in the description of the manna, "its appearance was as the appearance of bdellium" (Num. 11:7). In both passages the Septuagint understands it as the name of some precious stone, as do Rashi, who interprets it as "a precious stone, crystal" and Saadiah Gaon, as "pearls." The Midrash gives two opinions. According to one, it is a precious stone, and according to the other the reference is to "the *bedolaḥ* of perfumers." In Genesis the Midrash decides in favor of the first interpretation because there it is associated with gold and onyx (Gen. R., 16:2). Josephus (Ant. 3:28) explains that "the manna resembled the spice bdellium." The reference is presumably to the sweet-smelling sap called in Greek βδέλλιον and in Latin *bdellium*, a semi-transparent resin extracted from trees of the genus *Commiphora*. According to Pliny (*Historia Naturalis*, 12:36) the best variety is Bactrian bdellium from Baluchistan, which is similar to that obtained from Nubia. In effect the sap of both the Bactrian, *Commiphora roxburgii*, and the Nubian, *Commiphora africana*, were used as incense. The former variety is known among Arabs as *mokul*, a name they also give to the resin issuing from the tree *Hyphaene thebaica*, a species of palm with a branching trunk that grows in the Arabah (at the approach to Elath), and in Sinai. The Arabs call it "Jewish bdellium." It is apparently this species that is referred to by Dioscorides as "the bdellium imported from Petra" (*De Materia Medica*, 1:80).

Bibliography: Loew, Flora, 1 (1928), 304f.; J. Feliks, *Olam ha-Ẓome'aḥ ha-Mikra'i* (1968²), 259.

[J.F.]

°**BEA, AUGUSTIN** (1881–1968), Catholic prelate. Born in Baden, Germany, Bea joined the Jesuit Order and had a distinguished ecclesiastical and scholarly career. From 1930 to 1949 he was rector of the Pontifical Bib-

Cardinal Bea (right) with Rabbi Abraham J. Heschel at private conference with Jewish leaders at the American Jewish Committee headquarters in New York, April, 1963.

lical Institute in Rome, and editor of the periodical *Biblica* from 1930 to 1951. During World War II, he served as confessor to Pope Pius XII. He was created cardinal by Pope John XXIII in 1959. Pope John had already begun preparing for an ecumenical council to meet at the Vatican, and he appointed Bea head of the Secretariat for the Promotion of Christian Unity. Among his tasks was the preparation of a statement on the relation of the Catholic Church to non-Christian religions, including Judaism. The declaration, submitted to the Council's second session, met with considerable opposition on political and religiously conservative grounds. Bea accepted some changes, but continued to work for a forceful draft, which he submitted at the Council's third session in 1964. It was again deferred, over the protest of the large liberal element among the churchmen present. At the fourth session in November 1965, the statement, though weaker than Bea and other liberals had hoped for, was adopted by an overwhelming vote. Placed now in the context of friendly declarations on the church's attitude toward Islam and other religions, that on the Jews made two important points: that Jews of today should not be burdened with the guilt of the crucifixion of Jesus, and that the church "decried" anti-Semitism and hostility in any form. It further expressed the hope that friendly dialogue between Christians and Jews would in time eradicate all hostility. After the council's adjournment, Cardinal Bea wrote *The Church and the Jewish People* (1966), explaining the declaration and emphasizing its favorable aspects.

See *Church Councils. [S.G.]

BEANS. Ancient Jewish sources refer to several species of beans under the Hebrew name of *pol* qualified by various epithets. *Pol* itself is the broad bean *(Vicia faba)* which was included in the food brought to David's forces by his loyal supporters from Ammon and Gilead (II Sam. 17:28). Its flour was added to the bread that Ezekiel was commanded to eat to symbolize the approaching destruction of Jerusalem (Ezek. 4:9). In mishnaic and talmudic times the broad bean was widely grown, being a cheap food popular especially among the poor (Tosef., BM 3:9; Sof. 21:4) and eaten with or without the husk. Another important plant was the *pol ha-miẓri* which, identified with the cowpea *(Vigna sinensis),* is a creeper which grows in summer. In mishnaic times it was highly regarded as a food for human consumption (Ned. 7:1; Shev. 2:8–9), but is now grown as fodder. To the botanical genus *Vigna* belongs another plant called *pol he-ḥaruv* which is the legume known as the yard-long bean *(Vigna sesquipedalis),* its Hebrew name being derived, according to the Jerusalem Talmud (Kil. 1:2, 27a), from the shape of its pods, which resembles that of the carob *(ḥaruv).* Another variety of the cowpea is called *she'u'it* (Kil. 1:1); this is the legume *Vigna nilotica,* which grows wild in Israel climbing river banks, or is sown as fodder. The Mishnah *(ibid.)* states that it is not a *mixed species *(kilayim)* with *pol ha-lavan,* the hyacinth bean *(Dolichos lablab),* the seed of which is used as food.

Bibliography: Loew, *Flora* 12 (1924), 492f.; J. Feliks, *Olam ha-Ẓome'aḥ ha-Mikra'i* (1957), 156–8, 318; idem, *Kilei Zera'im* (1967), 41–43. [J.F.]

BEAR (Heb. דֹּב; *dov*). In ancient times the Syrian brown bear, *Ursus arctos syriacus,* had its habitat within the borders of Ereẓ Israel; it was found in the forests of Lebanon until World War I, and is still occasionally reported in Lebanon and northern Syria. The bear is omnivorous, and when driven by hunger, it preys on large animals, including the ox or cow (cf. Isa. 11:7). In the Bible the bear is portrayed as an animal dangerous to man, like the lion. Especially emphasized is the danger of a (female) bear bereaved of its cubs (II Sam. 17:8; Hos. 13:8). This was a frequent occurrence as the cubs were taken from the dam to be trained. The bear was common in the period of the Mishnah, which forbids their sale to Gentiles (Av. Zar. 16a). One of the miracles ascribed to R. *Ḥanina b. Dosa was that after being attacked by bears, each of his goats came home with a bear on its horns (Ta'an. 25a). Because the second world kingdom of Daniel 7 was identified as the Persian one, the fact that it is represented by a bear (Dan. 7:5) is explained by the observation that the Persians "eat and drink like the bear, are fat like the bear, are hairy like the bear, and are restless like the bear" (Kid. 72a).

The Syrian brown bear *(Ursus arctos syriacus)* in the Jerusalem Biblical Zoo. Photo David Harris, Jerusalem.

Bibliography: Lewysohn, Zool, 99; Tristram, Nat Hist, 40–49; F. S. Bodenheimer, *Ha-Ḥai be-Arẓot ha-Mikra,* 2 (1956), index; J. Feliks, *Animal World of the Bible* (1962), 39. [J.F.]

BEARD AND SHAVING. The characteristic manner in which the beard and hair were shaved, cut, curled, or groomed identified specific peoples in the ancient world. Egyptian, Assyrian, and Babylonian monuments depict the unique way various peoples treated facial hair, thereby illustrating their ethnic identity. The Semites appear with thick beards or with thin and groomed beards; the Lybians are shown with pointed beards, while the Hittites, Ethiopians, and Sea Peoples are portrayed as clean-shaven. The Babylonians and Persians are represented with curly and groomed beards, and the majority of the images of Egyptian males reveal clean-shaven faces, with the exception of a number of pharaohs who appear with plaited beards extending from the chin only. Shaving was performed either by the individual himself or by a barber (Heb. *galav*) who also attended to bodily ailments in a quasi-medical fashion. Razors were made entirely from metal or from flint blades fixed in a stone handle. Shaving was also connected with cosmetic treatment of the face (see *Cosmetics). According to Leviticus 19:27 and 21:5 in an apparent reference to the hair between the head and the cheeks (sidelocks) it is forbidden to destroy the "corners" of the beard. It is difficult to determine the reason for the ban, but it is possible that it was promulgated in order to differentiate Israelites from other peoples. Another possible explanation is that shaving specific areas of the face was associated with pagan cults or symbolized those who ministered to their gods and just as the Bible opposes imitation of pagan practices so it opposes this form of ritual shaving. In the Bible shaving of the head and beard is considered a sign of *mourning (e.g., Job 1:20) and degradation. Shaving was identified with the spontaneous plucking of the beard, an expression of great sorrow (Ezek.

5:1ff.). To humiliate a man, it was the practice to forcibly shave half of the beard as in II Samuel 10:4, where the elders, because of this humiliation, were commanded to hide in Jericho until their beards grew again. Shaving is also part of rituals of purification (Lev. 14:8; Num. 6:9; 8:7). Priests were forbidden to shave the "edges" of their beards (Lev. 21:5), and "the priests, the Levites, the sons of Zadok" (Ezek. 44:15) were allowed neither to shave their heads nor let their locks grow long, but only to trim their hair (*ibid.* 44:20). [Z.Y.]

In Talmudic Times. The Talmud regards the beard as "the adornment of a man's face" (BM 84a); a man without a beard was compared to a eunuch (Yev. 80b; Shab. 152a). Young priests whose beards had not yet grown were not permitted to bless the people (TJ, Suk. 3:14, 54a). *Sennacherib was punished by God by having his beard shaved off (Sanh. 95b–96a). Rabbinic authorities permitted only those who had frequent dealings with the Roman authorities to clip their beard with forceps (*kom;* BK 83a). Objection to the removal of the beard was on the ground that God gave it to man to distinguish him from woman; to shave it, was therefore an offense against nature (see Abrabanel to Lev. 19:27).

In the Middle Ages. Jews living in Islamic countries cultivated long beards whereas those in Christian Europe clipped them with scissors. This was permitted by *halakhah* (Sh. Ar., YD 181:10). Rabbinical courts punished adulterers by cutting off their beards (C. M. Horowitz, *Toratan shel Rishonim,* 1 (1881), 29; 2 (1881), 18). The post of *ḥazzan* was only bestowed upon a man with a beard (*Baḥ,* OḤ 53). Kabbalists ascribed mystical powers to the beard (and hair). Isaac *Luria refrained from touching his, lest he

A head with unshaven *pe'ot* (corners) forms part of the illuminated opening of the chapter on shaving in Maimonides' *Mishneh Torah.* The manuscript was written in Spain, early 14th century and illuminated in Perugia (?), Italy, c. 1400. Jerusalem, J.N.U.L., MS Heb. 4° 1193, fol. 27r.

should cause any hairs to fall out (*Ba'er Hetev,* YD 181:5). With the spread of kabbalism to Eastern Europe, trimming the beard was gradually prohibited by leading rabbinic authorities (*Noda bi-Yhudah, Mahadura Tinyana,* YD 80) and with the rise of Ḥasidism, the removal of the beard became tantamount to a formal break with Jewish tradition. Nevertheless, from a strictly traditional point of view, shaving was permitted as long as it was done in a certain fashion. *Halakhah* forbids only the shaving proper of the beard; this is defined as the act of removing the hair with an instrument with one cutting edge. Chemical means (depilatory powder), scissors, or an electric shaver with two cutting edges, are permitted. Although it is customary not to use a single-edge razor to shave any part of the beard, the strict letter of the law forbids its use only for five parts of the face. Considerable difference of opinion among the rabbis as to the exact location of these five places had led to the practice of not using a single edge at all. In Western Europe and especially among Sephardi Jews, rabbinic authorities (S. D. *Luzzatto among others), consented both to the trimming of the beard and even of its entire removal by chemical agents. This became the accepted custom (from the second half of the 17th century). The question of cutting and shaving the beard on *ḥol ha-mo'ed,* prohibited by the Talmud (MK 3:1), was a matter of much controversy at the turn of the 19th century. R. Isaac Samuel *Reggio tried to prove that this talmudic injunction no longer applied because of changed circumstances (*Ma'amar ha-Tiglaḥat,* 1835) but the traditional opinion of the Shulḥan Arukh (OḤ 531) prevails among strictly observant Jews, who also refrain from cutting their beard (and from shaving) during the *Omer period *(Sefirah)* and the *Three Weeks (see also *Mourning Customs). To trim the beard (and have a haircut) in honor of the Sabbath and the festivals is regarded as a pious duty. Several rulers (e.g., Nicholas I of Russia) tried to force the Jewish population to cut off their beard and earlocks; others (e.g., Maria Theresa of Austria) ordered Jews to have beards so as to be easily singled out as a foreign element by their Christian neighbors. [Ed.]

Bibliography: Bible: G. A. Reisner, *Mycerinus* (1931), pl. 45d; A. J. Tobler, *Excavations at Tepe Gawra,* 2 (1950), pl. 176, fig. 18; University of Pennsylvania Museum, *Buhen* (1911), pl. 64, no. 10313; E. Lefébure, *Le tombeau de Seti 1er,* 2 (1886), pls. 4, 5; P. E. Newberry, *Beni Hassan,* 1 (1893), pls. 28, 30, 31; Chicago Oriental Institute, *The Epigraphic Survey; Medinet Habu,* 2 (1932), pl. 125A; E. F. Schmidt, *Persepolis I* (1953), plates 31B, 32B. Post-Biblical: Benzinger, Archeologie, 94, 134, 351; J. Wellhausen, *Reste arabischen Heidentums* (1897²), 195–200; ET, 11 (1965), 118–28; W. Mueller (ed.), *Urkundliche Beitraege . . . der maehrischen Judenschaft* (1903), 68–72; I. Abrahams, *Jewish Life in the Middle Ages* (1932).

BEARSTED, MARCUS SAMUEL, FIRST VISCOUNT (1853–1927), founder of the Shell Oil Company. Marcus Samuel was educated at Jewish schools in London and Brussels before joining the firm established by his father Marcus Samuel, who had prospered in the Far Eastern trade, principally from selling fancy shells and ornamental shell boxes. In 1878, the younger Marcus Samuel formed his own business partnership with his brother Sam (1855–1934), who later sat as a member of parliament for 20 years. Marcus Samuel successfully traded in the Orient, particularly Japan. Subsequently he became London banker to the Japanese government. Samuel entered the oil trade in 1892, built a fleet of tankers, and founded the Shell Transport and Trading Company in 1897. His neglect of his business during his year as lord mayor (1902–03) resulted in Shell's amalgamation with the Royal Dutch Petroleum Company on what seemed disadvantageous terms, but, in the event, he proved indispensable to the new organization. This move served Britain well in World War I. Another momentous war service was the supply of toluol, an essential ingredient in explosives. Marcus Samuel made wide benefactions both to Jewish and non-Jewish charities. The Bearsted Memorial Hospital, a maternity hospital in London, bears his name and was financed by him. Samuel was lord mayor of London in 1902–03, the fifth Jew to hold this office. In 1921 he was made baron, and in 1925, Viscount Bearsted. Although holding no important Jewish communal offices, Samuel used his influence to help persecuted Jews. While lord mayor of London he refused, in the face of opposition, to invite the Rumanian ambassador to the lord mayor's banquet as a protest against Rumania's treatment of its Jewish citizens.

His son WALTER HORACE SAMUEL, SECOND VISCOUNT BEARSTED (1882–1948) succeeded his father as chairman of Shell in 1920. A notable art collector, he was chairman of the trustees of the National Gallery in London. He also held various Jewish communal offices. The third viscount MARCUS RICHARD SAMUEL (1909–), was chairman of the Bearsted Memorial Hospital and president of the Jewish Home and Hospital.

Bibliography: R. Henriques, *Marcus Samuel, First Viscount Bearstead...* (1960); *Times* (Nov. 10, 1948); JC (Jan. 21, 1927 and Nov. 12, 1948). [V.D.L.]

BEATITUDE (Heb. הַצְלָחָה, *hazlahah*), the blissful state of the soul in the World to Come (**Olam ha-Ba*). Medieval Jewish philosophy adopted the terms and formulations of rabbinic eschatology, but invested them with new shades of meaning which were conceptual rather than pictorial. In the theology of Jewish *Kalām, the bliss of the next world is still unconnected with philosophical notions. Thus, *Saadiah Gaon interprets the rabbinic statement, "In the world to come... the righteous will sit with their crowns on their heads and enjoy the splendor of the *Shekhinah*" (Ber. 17a) to mean that life in the hereafter consists in the enjoyment of a specially created luminous substance which sustains the righteous and burns the sinners (*Beliefs and Opinions*, 9:4–5). In Jewish neoplatonism, however, an entirely different concept prevails. Here the bliss of the world to come is understood as the climax of the soul's ascent from its entanglement in matter to union with the supernal world. Isaac *Israeli was the first to link traditional Jewish eschatology with neoplatonic mysticism. Holding that the soul in its ascent passes through three stages, purification, illumination, and union with the supernal light, Israeli identifies the bliss experienced in the afterlife with the last of these stages. However, this union can already be achieved in this world, provided that man withdraws from the influence of the flesh and of the lower souls. The union achieved by the soul at its highest stage is not union with God (though Israeli speaks of the soul's being attached to God), but with "wisdom" which, together with "first matter," occupies a place just below God in Israeli's metaphysical scheme. Israeli identifies the soul's final stage with the religious notion of "Paradise" (*Book of Definitions*, in A. Altmann and S. M. Stern (eds.), *Isaac Israeli* (1958), 25–26). By contrast with his spiritual concept of human blessedness, he provides a more physical account of punishment in the hereafter. The soul of the sinner will be sad, in pain, tortured by fire (*ibid.*, 26–27). Some prominent features of Israeli's eschatology occur also in Joseph Ibn *Ẓaddik's *Olam Katan*.

In the 11th century, both Solomon ibn *Gabirol and *Baḥya ibn Paquda followed essentially the same pattern of neoplatonic thought. Ibn Gabirol saw the goal of the existence of man in the "attachment" of his soul to the supernal world, that is the "return of like to like." This goal is to be reached by "knowledge," i.e., the contemplative life of the intellect, and by "work," i.e., the practice of the ethical virtues. Both activities together free the soul from the captivity of nature, and purify it from its turbidity and darkness (*Mekor Ḥayyim*, 1:2). Ibn Gabirol holds that knowledge leads to works, which, in turn, enable the soul to rise to the contemplation of the spiritual world. The highest level of contemplation consists in the ecstatic vision of the "first universal matter" in which all supernal forms are contained (3:56–58). There is, however, a still higher goal to be attained. Beyond universal matter (and universal form) there exists, in Ibn Gabirol's ontological scheme, the "will" of God and, in the final passage of his *Mekor Ḥayyim*, he speaks of a progress of knowledge leading to a knowledge of the "will." Holding that a still higher stage may be achieved, Ibn Gabirol calls for an ascent to the "will's" beginning and source, i.e., God. The fruit of this effort is freedom from death and man's "attachment" to the "fountain of life" (*mekor ḥayyim*), i.e., communion with God. Beatitude in the hereafter is, in Ibn Gabirol's view, not a mere continuation of the bliss of the contemplative life, but a gift of God (5:43, end). Baḥya, too, sees the upward way as the "road to felicity" (*Ḥovot ha-Levavot*, 1:7), passing through the stages of purification, illumination, and the vision of the "supernal and exalted forms" (8:4). He identifies the love of God with the soul's longing for union with the supernal light, i.e., supernal wisdom (10:1), holding that it arises from the purifying effects of the ascetic life (10:11) and from the scrutiny of the soul (10:8). According to Baḥya, man is an "exile" in this world (8:3), and the "bliss of the next world" should be his most cherished goal (4:4, end). The reward promised for

The righteous in a state of beatitude in Paradise. Full-page miniature from the Hebrew *Ambrosian Bible*, S. Germany, 1236–38. The animal heads, a sign of holiness in the Middle Ages, were adopted by the 13th-century south German school of Jewish illumination as a means of avoiding the depiction of human figures. The top frame depicts the fare on which the righteous will feast: the mythical ox, leviathan, and the bird *ziz*. Milan, Ambrosian Library, Ms. B. 32. inf., fol. 136.

the hereafter is said to consist in the "utmost distinction [conferred on man] by God" and in the "approximation to the supernal light" (4:4). This definition combines the notion of reward as a gift from God with the neoplatonic concept of illumination and union as a result of the soul's ascent. *Judah Halevi teaches that the bliss of the world to come is essentially identical with the supreme stage attainable in this world. This stage is conceived in neoplatonic terms as an "attachment" to the "supernal world" and to the "divine light" (*Kuzari,* 1:103; 3:20), and is more sharply defined as a suprarational prophetic stage. In Halevi's view the life of piety is essentially of the same order as the prophetic stage of illumination and communion with God. Accordingly, the pious man can achieve the bliss of attachment to God already in this world.

In Jewish Aristotelianism the concept of beatitude in the next world became problematical. While Jewish Aristotelians identified immortality with the existence of an incorporeal intelligence, they disagreed on whether immortality is individual or collective, reflecting thereby a difference of opinion which also existed among Islamic philosophers. Among the Muslims, al-*Farabi (in his earlier works) and *Avicenna affirmed that the individual human intellect becomes immortal once it has achieved the stage of the "acquired intellect" (see *Intellect), while *Avempace and *Averroes held that in the afterlife there exists one intellect for all men, denying thereby that anything individual remains after death. Closely related to the question of immortality was that of man's "ultimate felicity," a state which Aristotelians generally identified with the "conjunction" of man's "acquired intellect" with the "agent intellect," or sometimes even with God. Reflecting the differences of opinion concerning immortality, those affirming that immortality was individual allowed for "ultimate felicity" in this world and the next, while the proponents of collective immortality held that "ultimate felicity" was possible only in this world. The position of *Maimonides concerning immortality cannot be easily determined. In his *Guide of the Perplexed* (1:74, the seventh method), the discussion implies that he inclines to Avempace's doctrine of the unity of souls in the hereafter, which amounts to the denial of individual immortality. By contrast, he speaks of the "acquired intellect" as "separate from the organic body" (1:72), and sharply distinguishes the potential intellect with which man is born, and which is a "mere disposition," from the actual intellect, which remains after death, thus implying that immortality is individual (1:70; see also 1:41). Moreover, the whole tenor of his description of the state of man's attachment to God (3:51) points in the direction of an individual afterlife. Concerning man's beatitude, Maimonides holds that "ultimate felicity" is possible in this world, as well as in the next. Man, while still in his bodily state, may achieve the state of continually being with God (whereby Maimonides seems to refer to "conjunction" with the agent intellect), by means of the intellectual worship of Him. Among men, Moses achieved this state in the most excellent manner, but it is also possible for others. This stage of ultimate felicity is continued in the afterlife. Maimonides' endeavor to impress his readers with the spiritual character of the bliss of the afterlife is particularly pronounced in his discussion in his commentary on the Mishnah (introd. to Sanh., *perek Ḥelek*), and reappears in his *Mishneh Torah* (*hilkhot Teshuvah,* ch. 8). Maimonides interprets the meaning of the previously cited rabbinic dictum: "In the world to come there is no eating, no drinking, no bathing, no anointing, no sexual intercourse; but the righteous sit with crowns upon their heads and enjoy the splendor of the *Shekhinah*" in the following manner: "'crowns upon their heads' means the survival of the soul by virtue of the survival of knowledge, the two being one and the same thing; 'enjoying the splendor of the *Shekhinah*' means taking delight in the intellection of the Creator, even as the holy *ḥayyot* and the other angelic orders delight in their comprehension of His existence." Maimonides, it should be noted, distinguished between the world to come, which is an incorporeal state, and Paradise, which is a place here on earth. The treatise known as *Perakim be-Haẓlaḥah* ("Chapters on Beatitude") has been wrongly ascribed to Maimonides, but it expresses views similar to his. Affirming that felicity is possible in this world and the next, the treatise distinguishes between the ecstatic experience of prophecy and the ultimate felicity of the soul's union with God in the next world. Prophecy is described as the stage of man's perfection at which his rational soul, like a polished mirror, reflects the light of the supernal world. At this stage man is happy, though his joy is tempered with the fear of God. Prophecy can be reached only after a search for wisdom and after subjecting the senses to a rigorous discipline. Imagination functions at this level under the complete control of the intellect (cf. Maimonides' letter in *Koveẓ Teshuvot ha-Rambam,* 2:39b, where the same motif is quoted in the name of Abraham ibn Ezra's commentary on Ex. 23:20). The ultimate felicity, on the other hand, is the reward which all righteous may expect in the next world according to the measure of their worthiness. The author adds that this view of the afterlife is in agreement with the views of the philosophers, whereby he seems to refer to al-Farabi (in his earlier works) and Avicenna. The author assures his reader that every man can rise to a rank close to Moses' (for which there is a parallel in Guide, 3:51), and, echoing neoplatonic traditions, he states that ultimate felicity consists in the union with God following the purification of the soul and its illumination by the supernal light.

The concept of a twofold felicity, i.e., one in this world and one of a still higher degree in the hereafter, persists in 13th-century Jewish philosophy. It is found in Shem Tov ibn *Falaquera's *Sefer ha-Ma'alot* (ed. L. Venetianer (1894), 15–19), where the "true happiness of the soul at its ultimate perfection" is said to lead to the eternal life. Invoking the notion of a twofold felicity, *Hillel b. Samuel in his *Tagmulei ha-Nefesh* (Lyck, 1874) states that man, through the perfection of the moral and intellectual virtues, may achieve a rank even higher than that of the angels, but the beatific vision becomes possible only after death. Man is then illumined by the "eternal light," rises from rank to rank, and at the end is granted the vision of God. This state, in Hillel's view, is the meaning of Paradise (*ibid.,* 23a–24a). Jewish Averroists either openly or implicitly denied the validity of the belief in individual immortality. Thus, for example, Samuel ibn Tibbon appears to subscribe to Averroes' doctrine of the unity of souls, when in his *Ma'amar Yikkavu ha-Mayim* (ed. M. Bisliches, Pressburg, 1837) he says of the soul which has become perfect and separate from matter at death that it conjoins with the agent intellect, and that "they become one single thing, for now the soul becomes divine, of a superior and immortal order, like the agent intellect with which it is united" (p. 91). It may be assumed, especially in the light of his commentary on Ecclesiastes, that Ibn Tibbon speaks here of a "total fusion" which leaves no room for individual survival (see G. Vajda, *Recherches sur la philosophie et la Kabbale* (1962), 27 n. 3). *Levi b. Gershom, on the other hand, upheld the notion of individual immortality and of individual degrees of bliss in the hereafter. In his *Milḥamot Adonai* (1:13) he says that the "degrees of the happy ones" vary greatly according to the degree of unity achieved by the acquired intellect in its conception of the intelligibles.

The degree of bliss in the hereafter—identified by him with Paradise—depends on the degree and type of knowledge achieved while on earth.

Traditionalist Reaction. The pronounced intellectualism of the philosophers' concept of beatitude provoked a great deal of indignant protest from the traditionalists who regarded the life of piety rather than intellectual pursuits as the gateway to eternal felicity. The kabbalist Jacob b. Sheshet *Gerondi (in his *Meshiv Devarim Nekhoḥim;* see Vajda, op. cit., 110–1) attacked Samuel ibn Tibbon's interpretation of the ladder in Jacob's dream as an allegory of man's intellectual progress. Ḥasdai *Crescas, in his *Or Adonai* (3:3), rejects the theory that the soul achieves its immortality only through the process of knowledge. The degrees of bliss in the hereafter correspond to the degrees of love of God and attachment to him. The anti-intellectualist attitude gained ground in the last phase of Jewish life in Spain.

See also *Afterlife; *Garden of Eden; *Gehinnom; *Reward and Punishment; *Olam ha-Ba; *Soul, Immortality of.

Bibliography: A. Altmann (ed.), *Biblical and Other Studies* (1963), 222ff.; idem, in: *Harry A. Wolfson Jubilee Volume,* 1 (1965), 47–87; A. Altmann and S. M. Stern, *Isaac Israeli* (1958), index s.v. *union;* J. Guttmann, *Die Philosophie des Salomon ibn Gabirol* (1889), 165ff., 264, and passim; I. Heinemann, *Die Lehre von der Zweckbestimmung des Menschen* (1926), passim; S. Horovitz, in: *Jahresbericht des juedisch-theologischen Seminars* (Breslau, 1906), 146, 198ff.; (1912), 244ff.; D. Kaufmann, *Studien ueber Salomon ibn Gabirol* (1889), 19ff. and passim; S. Pines, in: *Tarbiz,* 27 (1957/58), 218–33; M. Z. Schreiner, in: *Mi-Mizraḥ u-mi-Ma'arav,* 4 (1889), 26ff., 37; G. Vajda, *La théologie ascétique de Baḥya ibn Paquda* (1947), 131ff.; idem, *L'amour de Dieu dans la théologie juive du moyen âge* (1957), index s.v. *adhésion.* [A.Alt.]

BEAUCAIRE (Heb. בלקיירי), town in France. Documents attest the existence of a Jewish community in Beaucaire in the 12th century; its Jews served the counts of Toulouse as fiscal administrators. After the death of Count Raymond in 1194 there were anti-Jewish outbreaks. With the annexation of lower Languedoc to France in 1229 the privileges formerly enjoyed by the Jews in Beaucaire were revoked. In 1294 Philip the Fair relegated the Jews to a special quarter, between the fortress and the present Rue Haute, today the Roquecourbe quarter. A year later he ordered the imprisonment of several Jews in order to extort money from them. The Jews had to leave Beaucaire when they were expelled from France in 1306. They were allowed to return in 1315, when their resettlement was supervised by Christian and Jewish agents sent by the king. In 1317 the Jews in Beaucaire were required to wear the Jewish *Badge. They were again expelled in 1322. The further rehabilitation of the community after 1359 came to an end with the general expulsion of the Jews from France in 1394; most of the exiles settled in Provence, then outside French administration, and in the Papal State of the *Comtat-Venaissin, where many Jews retained Beaucaire as a family name. The former Jewish quarter of Beaucaire was demolished during a siege in 1578.

The poet Judah Al-Ḥarizi, on his visit to Beaucaire in about 1210, found poets and philosophers living there. In about 1321, Samuel b. Judah of Marseilles (Marseilili) finished his Hebrew translation of *Averroes' "middle" commentary on Aristotle's *Ethics* while imprisoned in the fortress of Beaucaire. Moses b. Solomon of Beaucaire translated Averroes' long commentary on the *Metaphysics* (1342); Beaucaire was also the birthplace of the translator Tanḥum b. Moses.

Bibliography: G. Saige, *Les Juifs du Languedoc* (1881); Steinschneider, Uebersetzungen, 171, 217, 666; Gross, Gal Jud, 119–21; Kahn, in: REJ, 65 (1913), 181–95; 66 (1913), 75–97; G. Caro, *Social- und Wirtschaftsgeschichte der Juden,* 1 (1924), 386–90, 510; Z. Szajkowski, *Franco-Judaica* (1962), index.

[Z.Av./Ed.]

BEBAI.

(1) Third-century Palestinian *amora.* Bebai studied under R. Johanan (BK 61a), Resh Lakish (TJ, Nid. 3:3, 50d), R. Eleazar b. Pedat (Zev. 70b), and R. Joshua b. Levi (Ber. 62b). He was a close associate of Ammi and Assi (Shab. 74a; TJ, Ter. 8:5, 45c). He interpreted Deuteronomy 28:66 in terms of his own poverty: " 'The life you face shall be precarious'—this refers to him who purchases provisions from one year for the next; 'You shall be in terror night and day'—refers to him who purchases provisions from one Sabbath eve to the next, 'with no assurance of survival'—refers to him who is dependent upon the bakery." Although Bebai engaged chiefly in *halakhah,* his opinions being frequently cited in both Talmuds, he was also a competent aggadist. Particularly well-known is his application of the commandment, "You shall not swear falsely by the name of the Lord God" (Ex. 20:7), to hypocrites: "Do not don *tefillin,* wrap yourself in a *tallit,* and then commit a sin" (PR, 22:111b).

(2) Fourth-century Babylonian *amora.* Bebai studied under R. *Naḥman and the Talmud quotes halakhic problems that he discussed with his teacher (BM 23b; BB 36b). He taught *beraitot* in the school of Naḥman (Ḥag. 22b; Yev. 12b) and sat before Hamnuna (Nid. 27a). He transmitted teachings in the names of Rav and Samuel and was endorsed by R. Joseph: "Adopt the version of Bebai" (Meg. 18b). He was friendly with R. Joseph (Kid. 81a), who placed him in charge of religious affairs in his city (Kid. 76b). The exilarch Isaac was his sister's son (Yev. 115b).

Bibliography: Hyman, Toledot, 264ff. [Y.D.G./Z.K.]

BEBAI BAR ABBAYE (fourth century), Babylonian *amora.* Bebai was a son of *Abbaye, head of the Pumbedita academy, and studied under him and R. *Joseph. He served as *dayyan* in Pumbedita and appears to have succeeded his father (Yev. 75b). According to the Talmud (Ket. 85a) his colleagues, R. *Papi and R. *Huna b. Joshua who sat with him as judges, at times opposed his rulings with the words, "Because you are a descendant of short-lived people your words are incomplete, lacking a beginning and making no sense" (referring to his descent from Eli the priest whose descendants were condemned to die young, cf. I Sam. 2:32; see *Arukh,* s.v. *mal*). However, R. Papi greatly respected him, referring to him as "master" even in his absence (Ḥul. 43b). Bebai was a prosperous farmer, leasing land in addition to his own (BM 109a; BB 137b). Many legends are related of him. According to one, the angel of death visited him frequently and disclosed to him the secrets of the other world (Ḥag. 4b–5a). Another relates that he perceived demons at work, and was stricken down, whereupon the scholars prayed for him and effected his recovery (Ber. 6a).

Bibliography: Hyman, Toledot, 265f. [Y.D.G.]

BECHER, SIEGFRIED (1806–1873), Austrian economist. Becher was born in Plany (Bohemia) and educated in Prague and Vienna. He became professor of geography and history at the Vienna Polytechnic and was frequently consulted by the Austrian authorities on statistical and tariff questions, and represented his country in several international negotiations. In 1848 he was made a counsellor at the Ministry of Commerce, and later was granted the title of "Hofrat" (court counsellor). In addition to statistical investigations Becher's interests centered on labor and population economics. His publications include *Handelsgeographie* (2 vols., 1836–37); *Oesterreichisches*

Search for leaven, on the evening before Passover Eve. A man using a feather to brush crumbs from a cupboard into a bowl. A decorated page from the *First Cincinnati Haggadah,* copied by Meir ben Israel Jaffe. South Germany, c. 1480–90. Cincinnati, Hebrew Union College, fol. 1v ($13\frac{3}{8} \times 9\frac{7}{8}$ ins/33.8 × 25 cm.).

Muenzwesen 1524–1838 (1838); *Die Bevoelkerungsverhaeltnisse der oesterreichischen Monarchie* (1846); *Organisation des Gewerbewesens* (1849); and *Die Volkswirtschaft* (1853). [J.O.R.]

BECHYNE (Ger. **Bechin**), town in Bohemia (Czechoslovakia). Legends are connected with R. Ḥayyim, living in Bechyne in the 16th century, who apparently forbade the building of a burial hall at the cemetery. Five Jewish taxpayers are mentioned in 1570. In 1685 the representatives of Bohemian Jewry complained that the community of Bechyne had failed to comply with its ordinances. In 1695 the Jews there were prohibited from residing in the same building as Christians. The community numbered 81 persons (14 families living in six houses) in 1715, and 56 persons in 1725. In 1898 the community's German-language school was closed down. The community numbered 145 persons in 1902, 39 in 1927, and 47 in 1930. It was liquidated by the Nazis in 1942. There were also Jewish communities in the vicinity in Bernartice and Stadlec.

Bibliography: Chleborád, in: H. Gold (ed.), *Juden und Judengemeinden Boehmens* (1934), 23–25. [Ed.]

BECK, KARL ISIDOR (1817–1879), Hungarian-born poet, writing in German, who gave voice to the Hungarian people's struggle for liberation against the Austrian Empire. His work was filled with despair and disillusion with the state of Jewry and the world. His first poems, *Naechte, Gepanzerte Lieder* (1838), and *Stille Lieder* (1840), contained such glowing rhetoric, passionate imagery, and consuming love of freedom that he was hailed as a new Byron. When his *Lieder vom armen Mann* appeared in 1846, Friedrich Engels saw in him a future Goethe. The *Lieder vom armen Mann* are lyrics of great depth of feeling and clarity of vision, ranging from savage invective against social injustice to pathetic pictures of starvation in working-class homes. Beck prefaced the volume with the allegation that Rothschild had enslaved the masses with his gold and had failed to liberate his own unredeemed people. Beck was the first German lyric poet to write about slum conditions; in his lyrics there broods a vague hope of better days to come and a fear of impending social strife. Beck's Jewish despair found utterance in a cycle of poems entitled *Das junge Palaestina*, that bewail his unreciprocated love for Germany. His biblical drama *Saul* (1840) has as its climax David's vision of the Jewish people: he sees them as eternal fugitives who have become mere caricatures of a people that was once pure, simple, and glorious. His verse epic, *Jankó, der ungarische Rosshirt* (1841), contains some excellent descriptions of Hungarian life. The refrain of one of his poems, "an der schoenen blauen Donau" inspired Johann Strauss' famous "Blue Danube" waltz. Although he was baptized in 1843, Beck continued to be haunted by the fate of Jewry. He sank into a state of pessimistic resignation, which was intensified by the failure of the Hungarian rising of 1848. Filled with bitterness, he made his peace with the Austrian government, renounced his radical activities, and virtually ceased writing poetry for the rest of his life.

Bibliography: S. Liptzin, *Lyric Pioneers of Modern Germany* (1928), ch. 3; E. Thiel, *Karl Becks literarische Entwicklung* (1938). [S.L.]

°**BECK(IUS), MATTHIAS FRIEDRICH** (1649–1701), German Lutheran orientalist. Beck studied at Jena under Frischmuth, a converted rabbi (1668), and in 1670 received an academic appointment there. His competence in oriental languages was very wide, Jewish interests being reflected in his translation into Latin of the Targum to Chronicles (1680) and a publication of Jewish antiquities discovered in Augsburg (*Monumenta antiqua judaica Augustae Vindelicorum reperta*, 1686). His voluminous unprinted works include a translation of Benjamin of Tudela's travelogue.

Bibliography: J. B. Luhn, *Memoria M. Fr. Beckii* (Wittenberg, 1703); H. Pipping, *Memoria Theologorum* (Leipzig, 1705), 911f.; ADB, 2 (1875), 218. [Ra.L.]

°**BECK, MICHAEL** (1653–1712), German Lutheran theologian and Hebraist. Beck studied in Jena, like his namesake M. F. *Beck, under the apostate Frischmuth. He left a tract on the Masoretic accents as a hermeneutic device (Jena, 1678; repr. in G. Menthen, *Thesaurus theologico-philologicus*, 1, 1701), as well as *Hannahatan ve-Ḥaliẓatan shel Tefillin* or *Usus Phylacteriorum* (Jena, 1675), which is a public dissertation on phylacteries by Beck with the reply of Matthew Kreher.

Bibliography: J. G. W. Dunkel, *Historisch-critische Nachrichten von verstorbenen Gelehrten*, 3 vols. (1753–57); A. Weyermann, *Nachrichten von Gelehrten . . . aus Ulm* (1798); ADB, 2 (1875), 218; J. C. Adelung, *Allgemeines Gelehrten-lexicon*, 1 (1784), 1580 (bibl.). [Ra.L.]

BECK, MORITZ (**Meir**; 1845–1923), rabbi, educator, and leader of Rumanian Jewry. Born at Pápa in Hungary, Beck studied at the University of Breslau and the Breslau rabbinical seminary. He went to Rumania in 1873, and was appointed preacher (in 1900, rabbi) at the "Choir Temple" and principal of the Loebel Jewish School for Boys in Bucharest. Beck was considered rabbi of the progressive elements in the Bucharest community. He promoted the expansion of Jewish education in Rumania, encouraging the formation of new schools with adequate financial support. He also helped establish social welfare institutions, and worked toward the renewal of the Bucharest community organization, which had disintegrated in the second half of the 19th century (see *Rumania). Beck took a prominent part in the fight against anti-Semitism and discrimination in Rumania and for the emancipation of Rumanian Jews. He contributed to the general and Jewish press, and published the journal *Revista Israelită* from 1886 to 1892 and from 1908 to 1910. Aside from his sermons and numerous articles on various subjects, Beck compiled a Hebrew-Rumanian dictionary of the Torah (1881). Toward the end of his life he was attracted by Zionism.

Bibliography: *M. Beck, Cuvânt de omagiu: Viaţa şi opera* (1925); A. Stern, *Insemnări din viaţa mea*, 2 (1921), passim. [El.F.]

BECKELMAN, MOSES W. (1906–1955), U.S. social worker. Beckelman was born in New York City. He was lecturer in social work at the City College of New York

Moses W. Beckelman, director general of the "Joint" in Europe, 1951–55.

(1927–30), and managing editor of the *Jewish Social Service Quarterly* (1936–39). At the outbreak of World War II Beckelman was sent by the *American Jewish Joint Distribution Committee to Lithuania, where he helped large numbers of refugees to emigrate, until he was forced to leave in 1941. In 1942 Beckelman joined the U.S. Office of Strategic Services, and in 1943 directed a refugee camp in Morocco for UNRRA. After serving as an assistant director of the Intergovernmental Committee on Refugees, from February 1945, he rejoined the "Joint" in 1946 and became its director general in Europe in 1951. Until his death Beckelman supervised the liquidation of the displaced persons camps, the establishment of *Malben in Israel for the social care of immigrants, and extensive social work programs for Jews, especially in Morocco and Iran. [Ye.B.]

BECKER, U.S. family of bankers and philanthropists. Abraham G. Becker (1857–1925), U.S. banker and philanthropist, was born in Warsaw, Ohio, and eventually settled in Chicago. He organized his own commercial paper house, A. G. Becker and Company, which pioneered in the syndication of large loans. Active in communal affairs, Becker helped found the Associated Jewish Charities of Chicago and served as its president for eight years. He was a trustee of Hebrew Union College and the Chicago Orchestral Association and bequeathed large sums to the Chicago Art Institute and the Chicago Jewish charities. His son, James Herman (1894–1970), was also a banker and communal leader. In 1914, while an undergraduate at Cornell University, he helped convoke the original Jewish War Relief Conference in Chicago. Becker served with the U.S. Army in Europe from 1918 to 1921, assisting war victims through the American Relief Association and later as director general of the American Jewish Joint Distribution Committee in Europe. Upon his return to America in 1921, Becker joined his father's firm, becoming director (1926), president (1947), and chairman (1961). He also directed several other companies and served with many Jewish organizations. In 1936 he was chosen president of the Chicago Jewish Welfare Fund, a post that he held for nearly 30 years. [E.Gr.]

BECKER, JULIUS (1882–1945), Zionist journalist. Becker, who was born in Breslau, studied at Berne University, where he joined Chaim Weizmann's Zionist group. He acted as editor of the central Zionist organ, *Die Welt*, and of the German Zionist newspaper, *Juedische*

Julius Becker, Zionist journalist.

Rundschau. Immediately after the Young Turk Revolution in 1908, he worked in Constantinople with Richard *Lichtheim and Vladimir *Jabotinsky, in order to win the new regime's support for Zionism. After 1919 Becker was correspondent of the Berlin newspaper *Vossische Zeitung* at the League of Nations and was for a time chairman of the press correspondents assigned to the League. He extended considerable help to the Jewish Agency delegate to the League of Nations, Victor *Jacobson, taking over Jacobson's post at the latter's death in 1934. In 1935 Becker organized the Chinese Information Service in Shanghai for the Kuomintang government. In 1937 he returned to Switzerland. However, as a stateless person, he had to emigrate to the United States in 1941 and died in New York.

Bibliography: M. Waldman, in: *Haolam* (July 5, 1945); *Sefer Sokolow* (1943), 353–60; R. Lichtheim, *Geschichte des deutschen Zionismus* (1954), 157, 195. [G.K.]

BECKER, LAVY MORDECAI (1905–), Canadian communal leader. Becker was born in Montreal. He graduated from McGill University and the Jewish Theological Seminary. Becker served as rabbi and social worker in Detroit, New Haven, New York, and Boston during 1930–47. He worked with the American Jewish Joint Distribution Committee in Germany (1945–46). Later he was president of the Allied Jewish Community Services, Montreal, and chairman of the national executive committee of the Canadian Jewish Congress. He was president and spiritual leader of the Reconstructionist Synagogue, Montreal. In 1967 he was chairman of the National Interfaith Committee, Canadian Centennial Commission. [B.G.K.]

BEDA (Fritz Loehner; 1883–1942), Viennese journalist, satirist, and operetta librettist. Beda wrote satirical verse ridiculing Jews who were attempting to assimilate into Austrian society. His works became extremely popular. Several provoked scandals, and quotations from them became household words. The satires were published in contemporary Zionist periodicals, and subsequently collected in *Getaufte und Baldgetaufte* ("Baptized and Newly Baptized," 1908); and in *Israeliten und andere Antisemiten* ("Israelites and Other Anti-Semites," 1909). A collection of personal lyrics is *Ecce ego* (1920). His best-known libretti (with co-authors) were for Franz Lehar's *Land of Smiles* (1929) and Paul Abraham's *Ball in Savoy* (1932). He was active in the Zionist student organization *Kadimah, and president of the *Hakoah sports club, for whose benefit he organized the "Beda-Abende," one of the highlights of the Vienna season. Beda was deported to *Buchenwald concentration camp in 1938. He organized cultural activities there and in a competition initiated by the camp commandant for a "camp song," Beda's entry (submitted in a "kapo's" name) was chosen. The "Buchenwaldlied" became widely known as a reaffirmation that "whatever our fate we still say 'yes' to life." Beda died in *Auschwitz.

Bibliography: A. Baar (ed.), *50 Jahre Hakoah* (1959), 27, 227–8, 258–60; W. Bartel et al., *Buchenwald* (Ger. 1960), index; S. Czech, *Schoen ist die Welt* (1957), 34, 258–86, 292; MGG. [Ed.]

BEDACHT, MAX (1885–), U.S. Communist leader. Bedacht was born in Munich, Germany. He emigrated to New York City in 1908, moving to Detroit and then to San Francisco (1919), where he worked as an editor for the German press. In the same year he was made a member of the national executive committee of the newly formed Communist Labor Party, renamed the American Communist Party in 1921. In this capacity Bedacht was sent as a delegate to the Comintern Congress in Moscow (1921), from which he returned an apostle of the militant new line. While primarily a labor agitator, Bedacht rose to serve on the central executive committee's secretariat (1927–29), and in 1933 was named general secretary of the International Workers Order. He built its Jewish fraternal section into the party's largest auxiliary, while editing its publication *The New Order*. In 1946, following the post-World War II changes in Communist leadership, Bedacht was expelled from the party for factionalism, and retired to become a poultry farmer in New Jersey. In 1949 he appeared before a hearing of the House Un-American Activities Committee to deny charges made against him by the former Russian espionage agent Whittaker Chambers that for many years he had served as a permanent link between Soviet military intelligence and the central committee of the American Communist Party.

Bibliography: D. Bell in: D. Egbert (ed.), *Socialism and American Life*, 1 (1952), index; T. Draper, *Roots of American Communism* (1957), index; Whittaker Chambers, *Witness* (1952), index.

[E.GR.]

BEDARIDA, GUIDO (1900–1962), Italian author and historian. Born in Ancona of a family of south French origin, Bedarida ultimately settled in Leghorn. The Jewish environment had a deep influence on him, inspiring his poetical and literary work and his eagerness to proclaim his Jewish and Zionist identity. Most of Bedarida's poems deal with Jewish subjects. His first collection of verse, *Io Ebreo* (1927), appeared under the pen name of Eliezer ben David which he thereafter used frequently. Bedarida wrote plays such as *La casa vuota* (1928) and *Io t'ho chiamato* (1930), and three in the Jewish dialect of Leghorn: *Lucilla fa da sé* (1924), *Vigilia di sabato* (1934), and *Il siclo d'argento* (1935). In the verse dialogues *Alla "banca di Memo"* and *Il lascito del sor Barocas* (1950) and in a collection of sonnets, *Ebrei di Livorno* (1956), he gave a lively picture of the life of the Jews of Leghorn and the local Jewish dialect. His *Ebrei d'Italia* (1950) described the Jewish contribution to Italian culture.

Bibliography: E. Toaff, in: *Scritti... in memoria di G. Bedarida* (1966), 5–13 (complete bibliography on p. 15).

[G.R.]

BÉDARRIDE, ISRAËL (1798–1869), French jurist and historian. In 1823 Bédarride won a prize from the Institut de France for his essay on the Jews in the Middle Ages, which he later enlarged and published as *Les juifs en France, en Italie et en Espagne* (1859). The following year Bédarride became a lawyer in Montpellier, and was reputed to be one of the best jurists of southern France. He wrote many articles on legal subjects, but Jewish history remained his main interest. In 1867 he published his *Etude sur le "Guide des égarés" de Maimonide*, and in 1869 his *Etude sur le Talmud*. Bédarride was also interested in contemporary Jewish life and wrote against proselytism and in favor of religious liberty, *Du proselytisme et de la liberté religieuse, ou le judaisme au milieu des cultes chrétiens dans l'état actuel de la civilisation* (published posthumously). He was the author of *Harcanot et Barcanot*, a comedy on life in Carpentras, written in the local Jewish dialect (1896, 2nd edition 1925).

Bibliography: M. E. Lisbonne, *Etude nécrologique sur Israël Bédarride* (Montpellier, 1870); Felix, in: AI, 30 (1869), 717–23; Z. Szajkowski, *The Language of the Jews in the Four Communities of Comtat Venaissin* (New York, 1948), 32–36 (Yid. with Eng. summary).

[S.Z.]

BÉDARRIDES, village in the department of Vaucluse, near Avignon, S. France. The small Jewish community established in Bédarrides in the Middle Ages was expelled by the vice-legate of Avignon in 1694. One of the prominent Jewish families of southern France originated in Bédarrides. Its members include: GAD BEN JUDAH OF BÉDARRIDES, who composed a hymn for a local Purim established at *Cavaillon to commemorate escape from rioters in 1713; JASSUDA BÉDARRIDE (1804–1882), jurist, who became mayor of Aix-en-Provence after the 1848 revolution; ISRAËL (ISAIAH) *BÉDARRIDE; and GUSTAVE EMANUEL BÉDARRIDES (1817–1899), magistrate, the first French Jew to be appointed public prosecutor *(procureur général)* at Bastia, in Corsica (1862), and vice-president of the Central Consistory from 1872. A branch of the family which established itself in Italy assumed the name-form *Bedarida.

Bibliography: Bauer, in: REJ, 29 (1894), 254–65; Gross, Gal Jud, 105; *Dictionnaire de Biographie Française*, 5 (1951), 1256f.

[C.R.]

BEDDINGTON, English family of businessmen, philanthropists, and soldiers, descended from Maurice Moses who changed his name to Beddington in 1868. The family was in the tobacco business and founded the Abdullah cigarette company. ALFRED HENRY BEDDINGTON (1835–1900) was active in the life of the London Jewish community. In World War I, 37 members of the family served in the British Forces. They included Lieutenant-Colonel CLAUDE (1868–1940) who fought in the South African War and was in command of the Mounted Troops of the 20th Division in France in World War I. He became an enthusiastic yachtsman. SIR EDWARD HENRY LIONEL (1884–1966) was a career officer in the British cavalry and, after having taken part in World War I, retired from active service in 1920. At the outbreak of World War II he rejoined the army, beame deputy director of Military Intelligence, and rose to the rank of brigadier. WILLIAM RICHARD (1893–) entered the British army shortly before World War I, served in France and the Mediterranean area, and was wounded in action. In 1939 he became officer commanding the 2nd Royal Dragoon Guards (The Queen's Bays). He held various staff appointments in the Middle East, Italy and North Africa, and finally joined Supreme Headquarters, Allied Expeditionary Forces (SHAEF). In 1946 he rose to the rank of major general and retired in 1947.

Bibliography: P. H. Emden, *Jews of Britain* (1943), 447, 449, 548; J. Ben Hirsh, *Jewish General Officers* (1967), 76–77.

[ED.]

BEDERSI, ABRAHAM BEN ISAAC (c. 1230–c. 1300), Hebrew poet in southern France. The designation "Bedersi" indicates that he originated from Béziers (Heb., בדריש). He may be identical with the Abraham Mosse de Montepessulano (Montpellier; otherwise Abram de Sala) mentioned in secular documents. Abraham settled as a youth in Perpignan where he was a pupil of Joseph Ezobi. He stayed for some time in Arles and once took refuge in Narbonne, but apparently lived most of his life in Perpignan, then under Aragonese sovereignty. The Jewish community there had been granted a charter of privileges by James I to protect them from molestation. Abraham is the conjectured author of a letter from the community to the Jews of Barcelona, appealing to them to persuade the king through the medium of the bishop of Huesca to uphold the rights granted under the charter and reduce the communal tax obligations. Letters of recommendation written by Abraham in the name of the Perpignan community on behalf of petitioners and fund-raising emissaries have also been preserved. In 1275 Todros b. Joseph ha-Levi *Abulafia, who had accompanied the Castilian monarchs to France, spent some time in Perpignan and the two exchanged verses. Abraham also composed for Todros a poem in the style of the Passover *Haggadah*, the first attempt to parody it. He gave some financial assistance to the poet Isaac Gorni, although deriding his literary talents. Abraham wrote numerous poems and satires, apparently collected by his son *Jedaiah ha-Penini (mostly still in manuscript; the most complete manuscript is in the British Museum (Add. Ms. 27, 168); others are in Vienna, Amsterdam, and Leningrad). Despite his bombastic style, Abraham's works contain interesting historical details and provide an insight into the contemporary cultural scene. Between 1290 and 1295 he wrote *Ha-Ḥerev ha-Mithappekhet* ("The Revolving Sword"), a lengthy poem of 210 verses (according to the numerical value of the Hebrew letters in *ḥerev).* In it, Abraham mentions his birthplace and his father, and comments on the Hebrew poets who preceded him in Provence and Spain. He considered himself their inferior. He did, however, contend that he was the best poet of his generation and challenged his contemporaries to a competition for which he proposed judges. Abraham also composed *Ḥotam Tokhnit,* the first dictionary of Hebrew synonyms in the Bible. Both works were published in 1865, the latter with a commentary by Samuel David Luzzatto. There is some doubt whether Abraham or his son Jedaiah composed the prayer *Elef Alfin* (so called because its thousand (Heb. *elef*) words all begin with the letter *alef;* published in *Kerem Ḥemed,* 4 (1839), 57–65) and *Shir ha-Lamedin* (Frankfort on the Oder, 1812), a *bakkashah* for the Day of Atonement, in which each word contains the letter *lamed,* and all subsequent letters of the alphabet are excluded.

Bibliography: Baer, in: *Devir,* 2 (1924), 313–6; Baer, Spain, 1 (1961), 119, 142, 162; Schirmann, Sefarad, 2 (1956), 466–71, 695; idem, in *Sefer . . . Y. Baer* (1961), 154–73; Bergmann, in: MGWJ, 42 (1898), 507–17; I. Davidson, *Parody in Jewish Literature* (1907), 16ff.; Davidson, Oẓar, 4 (1933), 352; Regné, in: REJ, 62 (1911), 59ff.; Gross, Gal Jud, s.v. *Béziers;* Renan, Rabbins, 707–19; Doniach, in: JQR, 23 (1932/33), 63–69, cf. 349–56.

[J.H.SH./Z.AV]

BEDFORD, English county town. In the Middle Ages a small community existed in Bedford, which housed one of the *archae* for registration of Jewish debts. Local Jews suffered from violence during the Barons' Wars in 1263 and again in 1274. Three Jews were hanged for coin clipping in 1278. By the time of the expulsion of the Jews from England in 1290, the community seems to have been almost extinct. Jews resettled in Bedford at the end of the 18th century, and a tiny community existed from 1803 to 1827 and from 1837 to c. 1879. Organized Jewish life was revived briefly in 1903 and again during the evacuation from London in 1939–45. In 1968 there were 55 Jews in Bedford.

Bibliography: C. Roth, *Rise of Provincial Jewry* (1950), 29–31; Roth, England, index; M. Lissack, *Jewish Perseverance* (1851); Rigg-Jenkinson, Exchequer.

[C.R.]

BEDIKAT ḤAMEẒ (Heb. בְּדִיקַת חָמֵץ, "searching for leaven"), ceremony of searching for leaven, instituted in order to ensure that not even the smallest particle of **ḥameẓ* remains in the house during Passover. The biblical injunction, "Even the first day shall ye put away leaven out of your house" (Ex. 12:15), was interpreted by the rabbis as referring to the eve of Passover, i.e., the 14th of Nisan. The ceremony of *bedikat ḥameẓ* takes place on the 13th of Nisan (or the 12th if the 13th should be on a Friday). It follows the *Ma'ariv* prayer immediately after nightfall and before any other kind of activity is undertaken. The ceremony is preceded by the blessing: "Blessed art Thou O Lord our God, King of the Universe, Who hast sanctified us by Thy commandments and commanded us concerning the removal of the leaven."

By the light of a wax candle, with a wooden spoon and a whisk made of several chicken or goose feathers tied together, the master of the house searches every corner in the house for stray crumbs. Every room into which *ḥameẓ* may have been brought during the past year has to be searched. Since a blessing must never be recited without good reason, a few crumbs of bread are deliberately left on window sills and in other obvious places. The ceremony of *bedikat ḥameẓ* takes precedence even over the study of Torah on that evening. If the husband is not available, the

The search for leaven in a Dutch household. Pen and wash drawing by Bernard Picart, 1725. Amsterdam, Stedelijk Museum.

ceremony has to be performed by the wife or another member of the family. The kabbalistic school of R. Isaac Luria used to hide ten pieces of bread for *bedikat ḥameẓ*. Leaven to the mystics symbolized the ferment of base desires and evil impulses which had to be purged. Upon completion of *bedikat ḥameẓ*, the leaven collected is put away in a safe place and the master of the house recites the formula: "May all leaven that is in my possession, which I have not observed, searched out or had cognizance of, be regarded as null and be common property, even as the dust of the earth." On the morning of the 14th of Nisan, not later than 10 a.m., the leaven is burned and a similar Aramaic formula is recited. This observance is called *Bi'ur ḥameẓ*—the removal or the burning of *ḥameẓ*. The laws concerning *bedikat ḥameẓ* are codified in Shulḥan Arukh (OḤ 431 to 445).

See *Ḥameẓ; Sale of *Ḥameẓ; *Passover. [H.RA.]

BEDZIN (Pol. **Będzin,** Yid. **Bendin**), town in Silesia, Poland. A Jewish settlement existed in Bedzin from the beginning of the 17th century. In 1765 the Jewish population numbered 446; in 1856, 2,440 (58.6% of the total); in 1897, 10,839 (45.6%); in 1909, 22,674 (48.7%); in 1921, 17,298 (62.1%); and in 1931, 21,625 (45.4%). A large number of Jewish workers were employed in Bedzin's developing industries at the beginning of the 20th century, and the town became the center of Jewish and Polish socialist activity during the 1905 Russian revolution. After World War I Jews took a considerable part in iron-ore mining, metallurgy, zinc and tin processing, and the production of cables, screws, nails, and iron and copper wire. Jewish-owned undertakings included chemical works and factories for paints, candles, and bakelite products, in particular buttons for the garment industry, which expanded in the area during 1924–31. A Jewish school and gymnasium (secondary school) were supported by the community with the help of donations from local Jewish industrialists. The chain of credit cooperatives and free loan societies established in Bedzin through the American Jewish Joint Distribution Committee had a membership of nearly 1,000. [N.M.G.]

Holocaust Period. The German army entered the town on Sept. 4, 1939, and five days later they burned the Great Synagogue in the Old City. About 50 houses surrounding the synagogue, which were inhabited exclusively by Jews, went up in flames and a number of Jews were burned to death. During 1940–41 the situation in Bedzin was considered somewhat better than in most other places in occupied Poland (Bedzin and its neighbor *Sosnowiec were for a long time the only large cities in Poland where no ghetto was established). For this reason thousands of Jews from central Poland sought refuge there. Several thousand Jews from the district were expelled and forced to reside in Bedzin, among them all the Jews from Oswiecim (German name—Auschwitz), who arrived in April-May 1941, prior to the construction of the Auschwitz camp. In May 1942 the first deportation took place in which several thousand people were sent to their death in Auschwitz. On Aug. 1, 1942, in a second deportation, about 5,000 Jews were sent to Auschwitz, while others were shot on the spot for disobeying German orders. In January 1943 a ghetto was established in the suburb of Kamionka. During the spring and summer of 1943 a few smaller deportations took place, but on Aug. 1, 1943, the liquidation of the ghetto began. The *Aktion* lasted for about two weeks due to the population's resistance. Only a limited number of Jews survived the concentration camps by hiding. The Jewish underground resistance in Bedzin became active at the

The Ark of the Law in the Great Synagogue in Bedzin, Poland. Photo Israel Museum Archives, Jerusalem.

beginning of 1940. They circulated illegal papers and made contact with the Warsaw Ghetto underground. After the establishment of the ghetto, the underground concentrated mainly on preparations for armed resistance. A unified fighting organization came into being with strong ties with the Jewish Fighting Organization of the Warsaw Ghetto. On Aug. 3, 1943, during the last deportation, some armed resistance broke out. Among the fighters who fell in battle was the leading Jewish partisan Frumka Plotnicka. Deportees from Bedzin played a major role in the underground and uprising in the Auschwitz death camp (among them—Jeshajahu Ehrlich, Moshe Wygnanski, Ala Gertner, and Rosa Sapirstein). Although some Jewish survivors settled in Bedzin after the war (in 1946 the Jewish population numbered 150 people), all of them left after some time. In 1969 organizations of former Jewish residents of Bedzin were active in Israel, France, Australia, Canada, and the United States. [S.KR.]

Bibliography: *Yidishe Ekonomik* (1938), 488–90; B. Mintz and I. Klausner (eds.), *Sefer ha-Zeva'ot,* 1 (1945), 122–5; A. S. Stein (ed.), *Pinkas Bendin* (Heb. and Yid., 1959); F. Mazia, *Re'im ba-Sa'ar* (1964).

BEE (Heb. דְּבוֹרָה). Beekeeping was early practiced in the Mediterranean region. However, there is no reference to it in the Bible where the bee is mentioned only four times and only once in connection with honey (Judg. 14:9). References to bees stinging those who approach them (Deut. 1:44; Ps. 118:12) may refer to the gathering of wild honeycombs, and the finding of honey is mentioned (I Sam. 14:25; Prov. 16:4). Bees swarm when the land is desolate and untilled, so that a child will then eat "butter and honey" (Isa. 7:22). On the other hand, the honey of "a land flowing with milk and honey" (Deut. 8:8) is date honey according to the rabbis. There are frequent references to beekeeping in the talmudic era. The rabbis give detailed accounts of the beehives which were made of wicker and attached to the ground with clay (Oho. 8:1; Uk. 3:10) and discuss the number of honeycombs which it was permitted to take from the hives in the case of a man who acquires them for one year only (BB 5:3). Bee honey is permitted as food and the rule "that which derives from the unclean is itself unclean" does not apply to it. The reason adduced is that the bee does not produce the honey but sucks it from the flowers and discharges it through the mouth (Bek. 7b). The bee referred to is the *Apis mellifica* whose sting is specially acute. For this reason in recent times the Italian species *Apis ligustica*, which is easier to handle, has been introduced into Israel.

Bibliography: Lewysohn, Zool, 301; Dalman, Arbeit, 7 (1942), 291ff.; F. S. Bodenheimer, *Ha-Ḥai be-Arẓot ha-Mikra*, 2 (1956), index; J. Feliks, *Animal World of the Bible* (1962), 120. [J.F.]

°**BEEK, MARTINUS ADRIANUS** (1909–), Dutch Bible scholar and orientalist. He was minister of the Dutch Reformed Church and professor of biblical exegesis at the University of Amsterdam.

Beek's scholarship in the area of Bible was mainly traditio-historical research on the growth of certain literary sections of the Prophetic books. He also wrote critical evaluations of the literature of the Bible (1959), and on the nature of the Apocalypse (1941). He wrote several studies in the history of Israel (*Geschiedenis van Israel*, 1957; *A Short History of Israel*, 1963), and published valuable studies in the area of Mesopotamian culture, including *Aan Babylons stromen...* (1956), *Bildatlas der assyrisch-babylonischen Kultur* (1961), and *Atlas van het tweestromenland* (1960; *Atlas of Mesopotamia*, 1962). In 1954 he wrote *Het Boek der Vromen*, a critical but sympathetic commentary on the *Sefer Ḥasidim* by Judah b. Samuel he-Ḥasid of Regensburg. He was also the author of a sensitive and scholarly study on Josephus (*Het leven van Herodes*, 1959) as well as on Martin Buber (1964). [Z.G.]

BEER (Heb. בְּאֵר; "a well"), the name of several biblical localities. (1) One of the stations where the Israelites stopped during the Exodus, north of the Brook of Zered in Transjordan (Num. 21:16–18). It is possibly identical with Beer-Elim (Isa. 15:8) in southern Moab. (2) The place where *Jotham, son of *Gideon, sought refuge when he fled from his brother Abimelech (Judg. 9:21). As this place is associated with the history of *Gideon's family, it is generally located north of the Jezreel Valley. The Septuagint mentions Beeroth, in the inheritance of Issachar, between Shion and Anaharath, i.e., in the vicinity of Mount Tabor (Josh. 19:19), where the Arab village of al-Bīra is located. Nearby is Khirbat al-Bīra, where remains of the early Israelite period have been discovered. The village was abandoned by its inhabitants during the War of Independence.

Bibliography: F.-M. Abel, in: JPOS, 17 (1937), 42ff. (Fr.). [M.A.-Y.]

BEER, AARON (1739–1821), German cantor, composer, and collector. Beer was born near Bamberg and was known as *"der Bamberger ḥazzan."* He had a tenor voice of unusually wide range. While still a youth he became cantor of the Paderborn congregation and at the age of 26 was appointed chief cantor of the Heidereutergasse Synagogue in Berlin, a position he held until his death. Beer was known for his extensive repertory of liturgical melodies, including many of his own composition. Tradition credits him with 1,210 items. He made a habit of varying his tunes for regular prayers in order to discourage the congregation from joining in his singing, a practice of which he

Aaron Beer, "the Bamberg ḥazzan." Mezzotint by Benedict Heinrich Bendix, 1808, after a painting by J. C. Frisch. Kuschtein, *Juedische Graphiker*, 1918.

profoundly disapproved. Beer's collection of 447 festival prayer melodies was passed down to his successor, Asher Leon (1776–1863) and thereafter to Cantor Moritz Deutsch of Breslau (1818–1892), H. Schlesinger, and Cantor E. Birnbaum (1855–1920). It is now in the library of the *Hebrew Union College in Cincinnati.

Bibliography: Idelsohn, Melodien, 6 (1932), 1–194 (for Beer's preface in Hebrew, see after title page); Sendrey, Music, nos. 6042–43; Friedmann, Lebensbilder, 2 (1921), 27–29; J. Meisl et al. (eds.), *Pinkas Kehillat Berlin, 1723–1854* (1962), 229, 230, 232, 280; Idelsohn, Music, index. [J.L.N.]

BEER, BERNHARD (1801–1861), German scholar, community leader, and bibliophile. For nearly 30 years Beer served as head of the Dresden Jewish community and its schools. He founded various charitable organizations, and in 1829 joined in establishing a Mendelssohn Society for the furtherance of scholarship, art, and trades among Jewish youth. Through his writings and personal active efforts, Beer was able to wage an eventually successful struggle for the civic equality of the Jews in Saxony. Although he observed traditional practice and was emotionally attached to Jewish customs, Beer rejected Orthodoxy intellectually and aesthetically in favor of moderate reforms, especially in liturgy. He was the first Jew to give a German sermon in a Dresden synagogue. Beer's religious views were similar to those of his close friend, Zacharias *Frankel. Nevertheless the reformers *Geiger and *Holdheim also accorded him respect and admiration, and Beer was regarded as a mediating influence between the proponents of tradition and those of reform. Beer wrote numerous scholarly articles and reviews which appeared in Frankel's *Zeitschrift* and *Monatsschrift* as well as in *Orient*, *Kerem Ḥemed*, and other journals. His books include *Das Buch der Jubilaeen und sein Verhaeltniss zu den Midraschim* (1856), *Juedische Literaturbriefe* (1857), and *Leben Abrahams nach Auffassung der juedischen Sage* (1859). He also translated into German, with additions, Solomon

Munk's *La Philosophie chez les Juifs* (Leipzig, 1852). The extensive and valuable library which Beer acquired during his lifetime was divided after his death between the Breslau Seminary and the University of Leipzig, where Beer received his doctorate in 1834.

Bibliography: Frankel, in: MGWJ, 11 (1862); G. Wolf, *Ohel Issakhar,* Catalogue of B. Beer's Library in Dresden (Ger. and Heb., 1863) includes bibliography and biography.

[M.A.M.]

BEER, GEORGE LOUIS (1872–1920), historian and publicist. Born in Staten Island, N.Y., during his twenties he was successful in the tobacco business, from which he retired in 1903 to devote himself to research on the theme which commanded all his work as an historian: the economic features of 17th- and 18th-century British colonial policy. His writings include: *Commercial Policy of England toward the American Colonies* (1893); *British Colonial Policy, 1754–65* (1907); *The Origins of the British Colonial System, 1578–1660* (1908); and *The Old Colonial System, 1660–1754* (2 vols., 1912). Beer's basic theses were that English colonization had aimed at setting up a self-sufficient commercial empire of interdependent and complementary areas; that British commercial policy toward the American colonies had promoted their growth; and that the removal of the French from Canada encouraged the American colonies to assert themselves and seek independence. During World War I, Beer supported the British cause. He expressed the hope, particularly in *The English Speaking Peoples* (1917), that Great Britain and the U.S. would ultimately rejoin in a political union, to ensure the progress of the postwar world. He served as chief of the colonial division of the American delegation at the Paris Peace Conference, and helped draft the treaty provisions dealing with the former German colonies. He urged the establishment of "mandates" to promote the welfare of the natives. His *African Questions at the Paris Peace Conference* was published in 1923. A participant in many communal and charitable activities, Beer was a director of the Jewish Protectory and Aid Society.

Bibliography: *George Louis Beer ...* (1924); DAB, s.v.; Scott, in: *Marcus W. Jernegan Essays ...* (1937), 313–22; Cockroft, in: H. Ausubel et al. (eds.), *Some Modern Historians of Britain* (1951), 269–85.

[A.S.E.]

BEER, ISRAEL (1912–1966), military commentator and Soviet agent in Israel. Beer went to Palestine from Vienna in November, 1938. He joined the *Haganah and was appointed to the Central Training Bureau. During the War of Independence he served on the General Staff with the rank of lieutenant colonel. After retiring from the army in 1949, he became noted as a military commentator in Israel and abroad. Later, when he held the chair of military history at Tel Aviv University, *Ben-Gurion commissioned him to prepare the official history of the War of Independence. In 1961 Beer was arrested and accused of having contact with a Soviet intelligence agent. He was found guilty of treason and sentenced to 15 years' imprisonment. He died in prison. The true facts of Beer's biography until his arrival in Palestine are difficult to establish, since he himself gave varying versions. Apparently, he was born in Vienna and studied literature and philosophy at the University of Vienna. He claimed to have simultaneously joined the Schutzbund (the military organization of the Austrian Social-Democratic Party) and the government militia, and to have graduated from a course at Wiener Neustadt Military Academy with the rank of lieutenant in 1935. He also alleged that, at the outbreak of the Spanish Civil War in 1936, he had been ordered by the Social-Democratic Party to join the International Brigade, being finally promoted to the rank of lieutenant colonel. He wrote *Der Nahe Osten, Schicksalsland zwischen Ost und West* (1960), and *Bithon Yisrael—Etmol, ha-Yom, Mahar* (1966; "Israel's Security—Yesterday, Today, Tomorrow").

[J.WA.]

BEER, MAX (1864–1949), German socialist, historian, and journalist. Beer was born in Galicia and in 1889 emigrated to Germany where he became assistant editor of the Social-Democrat publication of Magdeburg, *Die Volksstimme* ("Voice of the People"). One of his articles led to his imprisonment. On his release Beer left Germany and settled in London where he became the correspondent of the Munich *Post,* the New York Jewish *Arbeiter-Zeitung,* and later *Vorwaerts,* the central organ of the German Social-Democratic Party. He also worked on the staff of the *Jewish Encyclopaedia* in New York from 1899 until 1901. After World War I Beer returned to Germany where he began writing on British and international socialism. He continued his research in England after his expulsion from Germany in 1934. Beer had a profound knowledge of the British labor movement and his *Geschichte des Sozialismus in England* (1913; *History of British Socialism,* 1919) is regarded as a standard work. His other writings include *Allgemeine Geschichte des Sozialismus und der sozialen Kaempfe* (1919–1923^2), *Life and Teachings of Karl Marx* (1924), and his autobiographical work, *Fifty Years of International Socialism* (1935).

[ED.]

BEER, MICHAEL (1800–1833), German poet and playwright; brother of the composer Giacomo *Meyerbeer and of the astronomer Wilhelm *Beer. In one of his earliest works, the classical tragedy *Klytemnestra* (1823), he attempted to gain sympathy for a heroine who murders her husband. Beer's play was successfully performed in 1819 at the Berlin Hoftheater and later in Vienna. His second

Michael Beer, German poet and playwright. Anonymous lithograph. New York, Leo Baeck Institute.

tragedy, *Die Braeute von Aragonien* (1823), inspired by Goethe's ballad *Die Braut von Korinth*, was staged in several German theaters with only moderate success. In 1825, he achieved a triumph with the poetic drama *Der Paria*, a protest against Jewish suffering and a plea for Jewish emancipation, which won high praise from Goethe. Beer moved to Paris in 1824, and in 1827 settled in Munich, where he enjoyed the goodwill of King Ludwig of Bavaria and the friendship of Eduard von Schenk, the minister of interior. *Struensee*, generally regarded as his best play, was produced by the Bavarian Royal Theater in 1828, when it was well and wittily reviewed by Heine. The incidental music for *Struensee* was composed by his brother Meyerbeer. Beer's narrative poems include one with a Jewish theme, a legend entitled *Der fromme Rabbi*. His collected plays and poems appeared in 1835, with an introductory biographical sketch by Eduard von Schenk and verse tributes by Schenk and M. G. *Saphir.

Bibliography: Kahn, in: YLBI, 12 (1967), 149–60. [S.L.]

BEER, PETER (**Perez;** pen name: **Theophil Nikodem;** 1758 (or 1764)–1838), Austrian educator and author, representative of radical *Haskalah in the Hapsburg Empire. Beer, who had a traditional Jewish education, also learned Latin and German. He attended the Prague and Pressburg (Bratislava) yeshivot, and from 1780 studied pedagogy at Vienna University, being one of the first Jews to train as a teacher within the educational reform program introduced by Emperor *Joseph II. From 1784 he taught at *Mattersdorf, then at his native *Nový Bydžov, and from 1811 until his death at the new Prague "Normalschule." Beer was also appointed "teacher of morals" to the Jewish pupils at Prague high schools in 1813, being probably the first Jew appointed to hold a government appointment and entitled to wear a government employee's uniform. In 1796 Beer published his *Toledot Yisrael*, a history of the Jews, omitting chapters likely to be unpalatable to enlightened circles, such as the slaying of the prophets of Baal by Elijah, as well as the entire talmudic period. It became the blueprint of biblical history textbooks used by teachers of the Enlightenment school in Europe for many years, both in the original and in translation (the last Russian translation was published in 1905). In 1809 Beer published *Dat Yisrael* and in 1810 *Emet ve-Emunah*, religious manuals in German. His two-volume *Geschichte, Lehren und Meinungen aller religioesen Sekten der Juden und der Geheimlehre oder Kabbala* (1822–23) is even now interesting for the material on the *Frankists and *Ḥasidism. In them, he developed an ideology of "Mosaism," which, parallel to "Christianity" that embraces Catholicism, Protestantism, etc., covers all different Jewish sects. Beer wrote several appeals, some anonymously, to the authorities on matters of public interest, including the question of military service and the establishment of a rabbinical seminary in Prague. He contributed to the periodicals **Sulamith, Ha-Me'assef* (see *Me'assefim), and **Bikkurei ha-Ittim*, and published a prayer book for "educated women" (1815). He was instrumental in opening the Reform synagogue in Prague and in inviting Leopold *Zunz to serve as preacher. He published a commentary on Genesis intended for readers of all creeds, drawing heavily on contemporary Protestant commentators. Only one installment of his translation of Maimonides' *Guide* was published (1834). It was sharply criticized by Joseph *Derenbourg. Beer was highly esteemed by the Austrian authorities and was awarded a decoration. However, his educational activities were viewed with suspicion by the majority of Jews. His autobiography, edited by Moritz Hermann, was published in 1839.

Bibliography: Z. Scharfstein, *Toledot ha-Ḥinnukh*, 1 (1945), 135–6; R. Kestenberg-Gladstein, *Neuere Geschichte der Juden in den boehmischen Laendern*, 1 (1969), index; A. Rubinstein, in: KS, 38 (1962/63), 271; 39 (1963/64), 128; R. Fahn, *Pirkei Haskalah* (1937), 148–54; R. Mahler, *Ha-Ḥasidut ve-ha-Haskalah* (1961), index; G. Wolf, in: ZGJD, 5 (1892), 40–43; G. Scholem, in: YLBI, 7 (1962), 248–9; F. Roubík, in: JGGJČ, 5 (1933), 313–37; 9 (1938), 411–47. [Ed.]

BEER, RACHEL (**Richa;** 1858–1927), owner and editor of the *Sunday Times*, London, 1893–1904. Rachel Beer was born in Bombay, the daughter of Sasson David *Sassoon and Flora (Farḥa) Reuben of Baghdad. She was an infant when the family settled in England. In an age which afforded women little scope, she displayed both character and talent. For two years she worked as an unpaid hospital nurse, and in 1887 married Frederick Arthur Beer, owner of the *Observer*. She became a contributor to the paper, and later its editor. In 1893 she bought its rival the *Sunday Times* which she edited while retaining her position on the *Observer*. Under her control the *Sunday Times* changed its outlook from independent liberal to non-partisan. She was also a composer and published a piano sonata and a piano trio.

Bibliography: C. Roth, *The Sassoon Dynasty* (1941); B. Falk, *Bouquets for Fleet Street* (1951). [Ed.]

BEER, SAMUEL FRIEDRICH (1846–1912), Czech sculptor. Beer studied in Vienna and quickly gained some recognition as a portraitist. His friendship with Theodor Herzl inspired his Jewish subjects, such as the monumental

Samuel Beer's medal commemorating the Second Zionist Congress, 1898. Bronze, diam. 2½ in. (6 cm.). N.Y., Dan Friedenberg Collection.

group, "Shema Israel." He designed the medal issued on the occasion of the Second Zionist Congress at Basle. He later worked in Paris, Rome, and Florence.

Bibliography: Roth, Art, 868; T. Zlocisti, in: *Ost und West*, 5 (1905), 78, 82, 83ff., includes reproductions. [Ed.]

BEER, WILHELM (1797–1850), German astronomer and brother of Giacomo *Meyerbeer, the composer and Michael *Beer, the poet. Wilhelm Beer joined and later succeeded his father in the family banking house. His leisure hours were spent in studying astronomy in an observatory he had constructed in his garden. Together with J. H. Maedler he studied the planet Mars during the

1828, 1832, 1835, and 1837 oppositions and their findings were published. Later they made a map of the moon; over many years they recorded every aspect of the moon surface and published their findings in *Der Mond nach seinen kosmischen und individuellen Verhaeltnissen, oder allgemeine vergleichende Selenographie* (2 vols., 1837). This was the standard work for many years. When Maedler left and joined a university, Beer went into politics and in 1846 was elected to the Prussian Chamber of Deputies. A mountain on the moon is named for him. [Ed.]

BEER-BING, ISAIAH (1759–1805), one of the leaders in the struggle for the "regeneration" of the Jews of France. He wrote a number of pamphlets including a refutation of an anti-Jewish pamphlet by Aubert Dufayet (*Lettre du Sr I.B.B. . . . à l'auteur anonyme d'un écrit intitulé: Le cri du citoyen contre les juifs,* 1787, 1805²). Beer-Bing was appointed to the commission headed by Malesherbes to improve the status of the Jews in 1788. In 1799 he drew up a memorandum on the community of his birthplace Metz. He was a member of the municipal council of Metz from 1790, and became the administrator of the saltworks in eastern France. He was on the editorial committee of the *Décade philosophique.* Beer-Bing translated the *Phaedon* of Moses *Mendelssohn from German into French and Hebrew (*Sefer Hasharat ha-Nefesh,* 1786–87, republished many times), a *Song of Zion* by Judah Halevi from Hebrew into French, and a fragment from the *Beḥinat Olam* by *Jedaiah ha-Penini (in *Essai sur la régénération . . . des juifs* by his friend the abbé *Grégoire, 1789).

Bibliography: E. Carmoly in: *Revue orientale,* 2 (1842), 337f.

[M.C.]

BEER-HOFMANN, RICHARD (1866–1945), Austrian poet and playwright. The son of a Moravian lawyer, Beer-Hofmann was adopted by his uncle, the Viennese industrialist Alois Hofmann. After graduating in law at the University of Vienna, Beer-Hofmann was drawn into the "Young Vienna" literary group, which included many of his close friends, Arthur *Schnitzler, Peter *Altenberg, Hermann Bahr, Theodor *Herzl, Hugo von *Hofmannsthal, and Felix *Salten. He first attracted attention in 1893 with *Novellen,* and in his earliest lyric, *Schlaflied fuer Miriam* (1898), the poet recognizes behind the apparently chaotic structure of the universe a mysterious purpose and a continuity of existence. He sees each individual as a link in the chain of man's ascent to a progressively higher level of culture. This continuity of existence was a theme of the play *Der Graf von Charolais* (1905). In a biblical trilogy, Beer-Hofmann seeks to restate for modern man the Hebraic position on fundamental questions. In the first play, *Jaakobs Traum* (1918), he depicts the patriarch's inner crisis during the night at Bethel, when he accepts for himself and his offspring the blessing and the attendant burden offered him by God. In the second, *Der junge David* (1933), he expounds the belief that the individual is valuable only insofar as he contributes to the well-being of others; and a people is important only to the extent that it confers its creative gifts upon other peoples, coordinating its own welfare with that of humanity at large. Of the third play, only a small part, *Vorspiel auf dem Theater zu Koenig David* (1936), was ever completed. In his sole novel, *Der Tod Georgs* (1900), the hero is an epicurean who decides to abandon his self-centered existence, discovers himself as a Jew, and is thrown into the midst of his people's struggle for justice. Beer-Hofmann was forced to leave Austria in 1939 and emigrated to New York. His *Verse* (1941) contains all the poems that he wanted preserved. His posthumous fragment, *Paula* (1949), a tribute to his wife, recaptures the autumnal mood of Austria as it influenced his own life and shaped his personality.

Bibliography: S. Liptzin, *Richard Beer-Hofmann* (1936); O. Oberholzer, *Richard Beer-Hofmann* (1947); E. Kahler, *Verantwortung des Geistes* (1952), 131–42; M. Buber, Introduction to Beer-Hofmann's *Gesammelte Werke* (1963); A. Werner, *Richard Beer-Hofmann* (1936); Baum, in: *Juden in der deutschen Literatur,* ed. by G. Krojanker (1922), 198–206.

[S.L.]

BE'ERI (Heb. בְּאֵרִי), kibbutz in S. Israel, in the N.W. Negev, affiliated with Ha-Kibbutz ha-Me'uḥad. It was one of 11 settlements in the Negev and the south founded during the night of October 6, 1946. The founding settlers, members of Ha-No'ar ha-Oved (Israel Working Youth Movement), were joined by other settlers, mainly from Iraq. Its economy is based on milch cattle, orchards, field crops, and a printing press. The name commemorates the labor leader Berl (Be'eri) *Katznelson. [E.O.]

BE'ER ORAH (Heb. בְּאֵר אוֹרָה), training camp of *Gadna (the Israel pre-military youth corps) founded in 1950 in the southern Negev, 14 mi. (20 km.) north of Eilat. Youth are brought here in groups for periods of a fortnight or longer to combine nature study and farming with excursions, sports, and small-arms training. Be'er Orah, meaning "Well of Light," is a reversal of the former Arabic Bīr (Be'r) Ḥindīs, "Pitchblack Well," so called by the Bedouin because the strong magnesia content of the local well's water was likely to cause illness. [E.O.]

Be'er Orah, the Gadna training camp in the Negev. Photo Jewish Agency Photographic Service, Jerusalem.

BEEROTH (Heb. בְּאֵרוֹת; "wells"), one of the Gibeonite cities mentioned as part of a confederacy together with Gibeon, Chephirah, and Kiriath-Jearim (Josh. 9:17). Beeroth is listed with the cities of Benjamin (Josh. 18:25); part of its population had previously fled to Gittaim (II Sam. 4:3). One of David's heroes came from Beeroth (II Sam. 23:37; I Chron. 11:39), as did the assassins of Ish-Bosheth (II Sam. 4:2). The town was resettled after the return from Babylon (Ezra 2:25; Neh. 7:29). Birea, where Bacchides encamped in 161 B.C.E. before the battle with Judah Maccabee (I Macc. 9:4), has been identified with the biblical locality. Beeroth is commonly identified with the

Arab town al-Bīra near Ramallah, 9 mi. (14 km.) north of Jerusalem; Bronze Age remains have been found nearby, at Ra's al-Ṭaḥūn. Several attempts to identify Beeroth with Tell al-Naṣb (Mizpeh?) or al-Jib (Gibeon) have been disproved by recent excavations. It has been proposed to locate Beeroth at Nebi Samwil, 1 mi. (1½ km.) south of el-Jib. Although this identification has not yet been confirmed by archaeological findings, it is strengthened by the statement of Eusebius (Onom. 48:9) that a village with this name was situated 7 mi. from Jerusalem on the road to Nikopolis (Emmaus; but according to Jerome, on the road to Neapoli, i.e., Shechem), and its possible appearance on the *Madaba Map.

Bibliography: D. A. Alt, in: ZDPV, 69 (1953), 1–29; K. Elliger, *ibid.*, 73 (1957), 125–32; idem, in: *Mélanges . . . A. Robert* (1957), 82–94; EM, 2 (1965), 8–9; Albright, in: AASOR, 4 (1924), 102–11; Z. Kallai, in: *Eretz Israel*, 3 (1954), 111–5. [M.A.-Y.]

BE'EROT YIZḤAK (Heb. בְּאֵרוֹת יִצְחָק), kibbutz in central Israel on the Coastal Plain, east of Lydda. Affiliated with Ha-Kibbutz ha-Dati, it was originally founded on Aug. 9, 1943, southeast of Gaza by a group of religious pioneers from Germany and was the first settlement in the Negev. During the War of Independence in May, 1948, it was all but razed by shelling from the Egyptian army. The settlers put up strong resistance and drove the attackers back from buildings they had already occupied. Although never abandoned during the fighting, it was so utterly destroyed that it was decided not to rebuild the place and in August 1948 the settlers reestablished their kibbutz on its present site, the former German Templar village of Wilhelma (whose inhabitants were interned there during World War II and later deported from the country). The economy of the kibbutz was, in 1969, based on highly intensive farming and a factory for treating metals against corrosion. The name, meaning "Isaac's Wells," both refers to the wells sunk by the Patriarch (Gen. 26:18ff.) in the part of the Negev where the group first settled, and also commemorates Yizḥak *Nissenbaum. [E.O.]

BEERSHEBA (biblical: Beer-Sheba; Heb. בְּאֵר שֶׁבַע), city in the *Negev on the southern border of Judah; its name has been preserved in the Arabic form Bīr (Beʾr) al-Sabʿ. Beersheba was first settled in the Chalcolithic period. Excavations conducted in its surroundings by J. Perrot uncovered remains of cave dwellings dug in the earth from this age. The inhabitants of the caves engaged in raising cattle and the manufacture of metal tools. Their pottery and stone vessels and figurines carved out of ivory and bone display a highly developed craftsmanship. Evidence of the beginnings of a religious cult was also found.

According to the Bible, Abraham and Isaac dug wells at Beer-Sheba and also formed alliances there with *Abimelech "king of the Philistines." The allies bound themselves under oath to observe the treaties, and in one source Abraham set aside seven ewes as a sign of the oath, which the Pentateuch explains was the origin of the name of the city (*Be'er*, "well"; *Sheva*, "oath" or "seven"; see Gen. 21:31; 26:33). The sanctuary of "the Lord, the Everlasting God," which was apparently located there in very early times, was invested with great importance in the patriarchal

Figure 1. Basalt bowls of the Chalcolithic period found at Tell Abu Maṭar near Beersheba. Jerusalem, Israel Museum. Photo Hillel Burger.

period (Gen. 21:33; 26:23–24, 32–33; 46:1). After the Israelite conquest, Beer-Sheba became a city of the tribe of Simeon and was later incorporated into the tribe of Judah (Josh. 15:28; 19:2). It appears to have been a center of the Israelite settlement in the Negev in the time of Samuel since his sons were sent there as judges (I Sam. 8:1–3). The sanctuary at Beer-Sheba was regarded as the extreme southern point of the country in contradistinction to the sanctuary at Dan which was held to be the northern point (Amos 5:5; 8:14). Thus the phrase "from Dan to Beer-Sheba" (Judg. 20:1, etc.) was the customary designation, at least until the days of David and Solomon, for the entire area of the country. After the division of the monarchy, Beer-Sheba continued to be the southern frontier of the kingdom of Judah; the expression "from Dan to Beer-Sheba" was then replaced by "from Beer-Sheba to the hill-country of Ephraim" (II Chron. 19:4) or "from Geba to Beer-Sheba" (II Kings 23:8). Zibiah, the mother of Jehoash, king of Judah, originated from Beer-Sheba (II Kings 12:2). Elijah set out on his journey to Horeb from Beer-Sheba, the gateway to the desert (I Kings 19:3, 8). The city was settled by Jews after the return from Babylon (Neh. 11:27, 30). The biblical town of Beer-Sheba is to be sought at Tell al-Sabʿ (Tell Beer-Sheba), 2½ mi. (4 km.) northeast of the new town, where remains of a fortress and potsherds from the Iron Age to the Roman period were found in excavations begun in 1969 by Y. Aharoni.

After 70 C.E. Beersheba was included in the Roman frontier-line defenses against the Nabateans and continued to be a Roman garrison town after the Roman annexation of the Nabatean kingdom. A large village existed then at its present site, where many remains have been found including mosaic pavements and Greek inscriptions (including a sixth-century C.E. ordinance regarding tax payments, which was issued to the south of the country, and a synagogue inscription). In the fourth and fifth centuries C.E., Beersheba first belonged to the district of Gerar and was later annexed to "Palaestina Tertia." The town was abandoned in the Arab period. [M.A.-Y.]

Modern Beersheba. The modern settlement dates from 1900, when the Turkish government set up an administrative district in southern Palestine separate from that of Gaza and built an urban center in this purely nomadic region. The Turks were motivated by the need to strengthen governmental authority over the Bedouin at a time when Turkey was struggling with Britain over the delineation of the Egyptian border in Sinai. German and Swiss engineers aided in laying out a city plan. Both a city and a district council were set up, and Bedouin sheikhs held seats on them. Until 1914, however, progress was slow, and Beersheba had about 800 Muslim inhabitants and some Jewish families, one of whom ran a flour mill. In World War I, the town became the principal base for the Turko-German Army fighting on the Suez and Sinai front.

Fortifications were laid out around the town and more settlers, including Jews, came and provided services to the army. A branch of the Jerusalem-Jaffa railway line was constructed and led beyond Beersheba to the southwest. On Oct. 31, 1917, the town was taken by Allied forces under General *Allenby's command, with Australian and New Zealand units prominent in the battle. Allied losses were considerable; the British War Cemetery at Beersheba has about 1,300 graves. When Beersheba's strategic role ended, its economy dwindled and the railway was dismantled. In 1920, a few Jewish laborers planted a tree nursery and eucalyptus grove there and experimented with cultivating vegetables and other crops. In 1922, the population reached 2,356, among whom were 98 Jews. By 1931, the number of Jews decreased to 11. The last Jews left during the 1936–39 riots, but efforts were intensified to purchase land for Jewish settlement in the Negev. During the *War of Independence the invading Egyptian army made Beersheba its headquarters for the Negev. When the town was taken by Israel forces on Oct. 21, 1948, it was totally abandoned by its inhabitants. Early in 1949, Jewish settlers, mostly new immigrants, established themselves there. The population, which totaled 1,800 at the end of 1949, reached 25,500 in 1956, 51,600 in 1962, and over 70,000 in 1968. The vast majority of its inhabitants were new immigrants, mainly from North Africa, Iraq, India, Rumania, Poland, Hungary, and South America. The first arrivals took over the abandoned houses, but from 1951 large new suburbs were built extending mainly to the north and northwest, while to the east a large industrial area sprang up. Arab Beersheba of Turkish times now became a small "old city" in a large modern town. The municipal area of about 6,600

Figure 2. The University of the Negev, Beersheba, 1970.

acres was extended in 1967 to 12,350 acres. Beersheba became the capital of Israel's Southern District, and a hub of communications linking up with the main roads and the railway lines Lydda-Kiryat Gat and Dimonah-Oron. A pumping station of the Eilat-Haifa oil pipeline is located there. Its largest industries (ceramics, sanitary ware, fire-resistant bricks, pesticides and other chemicals, and bromide compounds) exploit Negev minerals. There is also a large textile factory, flour mill, machine garage, and smaller plants for building materials, diamonds, metals, and other industries. The city has several academic, scientific, and cultural institutions, of which the Negev Hospital and the Municipal Museum were the first. In 1957, the Negev Institute for Arid Zone Research was established, which experiments with water desalination by electrodialysis, exploitation of solar energy, cloud seeding, adaptation of plants to aridity, hydroponics, and human behavior under desert conditions. The Institute for Higher Education opened in 1965 was formally recognized as the University of the Negev in 1970 and had 1,600 students. Beersheba also has a Biological Institute mainly for the study of plant life in the desert. Beersheba serves as a market center for the Negev bedouin, and a compound has been built for the purpose. The city also develops tourism and has several large hotels. [G.S./E.O.]

Another Beersheba was situated on the border of Upper and Lower Galilee (Jos., Wars, 3:39). It was fortified by Josephus, together with other places in Galilee in 66–67 C.E., for defense against the Romans during the Jewish War (*ibid.*, 2:573). It is located at Ḥorvat Beer-Sheba (Khirbat Abu al-Shabaʿ) between Parod and Kafr ʿInān near the Acre-Safed highway, where remains from the Second Temple period have been found. [ED.]

Bibliography: G. Dalman, *Sacred Sites and Ways* (1935), index; S. Klein (ed.,) *Sefer ha-Yishuv*, 1 (1939) s.v.; Albright, in: JPOS, 4 (1924), 152; Alt, *ibid.*, 15 (1935), 320; L. Woolley and T. E. Lawrence, *Wilderness of Zin* (1915), 45ff., 107 ff.; Perrot, in: IEJ, 5 (1955), 17, 73, 167; Contenson, *ibid.*, 6 (1956), 163, 226; Dothan, in: *Atiqot*, 2 (Eng., 1959), 1ff.; EM, 2 (1965), 6–8 (incl. bibl.); Press, Ereẓ, 1 (1951), 62–63.

BE'ER TOVIYYAH (Heb. בְּאֵר טוֹבִיָּה), moshav in the southern Coastal Plain of Israel, affiliated to Tenu'at ha-Moshavim. It was founded in 1887 by Jews from Bessarabia with the aid of Baron Edmond de *Rothschild and for years it was the southernmost Jewish settlement in the country. The village did not prosper, due to the scarcity of water, lack of capital and experience, distance from other Jewish centers, enmity of neighboring Arab villagers, and, particularly, the strained relations between the settlers and the Baron's administrators. It was nearly abandoned, but in 1896 the Ḥovevei Zion Association of Odessa (see *Ḥibbat Zion) purchased the land and new settlers came. They too endured hardships and in World War I were forced to leave temporarily by the Turkish authorities. The village was abandoned after it suffered losses in an Arab attack in the 1929 riots. The land was then taken over by the Jewish National Fund and the village was founded anew in 1930 by veteran agricultural laborers. Ground water was discovered and mixed farming introduced. Be'er Toviyyah soon became one of the most populous and prosperous moshavim in the country. In 1939 a second moshav, Kefar Warburg, was established on part of its land. After the Arabs abandoned the entire region during the Israel *War of Independence (1948), Be'er Toviyyah became the center of a densely settled farming area, to which such urban agglomerations as Kiryat Malakhi and Ashdod were later added. Many of the settlers of Be'er Toviyyah came from East Europe and Germany, others were Israel-born. In 1968 the population was 645, and the economy was mainly based on citrus and intensive farming. The village was initially called Qastīna, after a neighboring Arab village. It became Be'er Toviyyah in 1896, the name being adapted from the Arabic name of the site, "Bīr (Biʾr) Taʿabya." [E.O.]

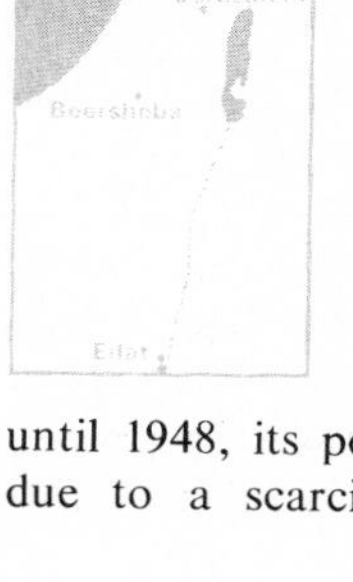

BE'ER YA'AKOV (Heb. בְּאֵר יַעֲקֹב), town in the Coastal Plain of Israel, W. of Ramleh, founded in 1907 by a group of 56 Jews from Russia (most of them "Mountain Jews" from Dagestan). Some of the settlers were peasants in their country of origin and preserved their picturesque dress and customs throughout the decades. Initially, almond orchards constituted Be'er Ya'akov's principal farming branch. In 1925, 20 families from Turkey settled in the village, but until 1948, its population did not exceed 400 inhabitants due to a scarcity of land. After the Israel *War of

Independence (1948), however, new immigrants were absorbed in local housing projects and in two moshavim, Be'er Ya'akov Pittu'aḥ and Talmei Menasheh, which were subsequently integrated into the municipal area. The population rose to 3,950 in 1968. Citrus orchards, poultry, and dairy cattle were prominent branches and constituted an important part of Be'er Ya'akov's economy. It is the site of three large hospitals (Asaf ha-Rofe, Shemu'el ha-Rofe, and a mental hospital) which in 1969 employed over 1,000 persons; and of industrial enterprises, among them a crate factory employing hundreds of laborers. Be'er Ya'akov's educational institutions also attract pupils from other localities, e.g., the Johanna Jabotinsky agricultural high school, a religious girls' teachers seminary, and yeshivot. The name, "Well of Ya'akov," commemorates the spiritual leader of the founders, Rabbi Ya'akov Yiẓḥaki of Dagestan. [E.O.]

BEET. The plant referred to in rabbinic literature as *tered*, or *selek* (Er. 29a) is the spinach beet (*Beta vulgaris*, var. *Cicla*). The present varieties, red beet, sugar beet, and fodder beet, were unknown to the ancients. Although the long white root of the beet was sometimes eaten, it was the leaves which were mainly used as food. The rabbis, in common with the Greek and Roman naturalists, praised it highly for its nutritive and medicinal value. Thus the Talmud states: "A dish of beets is good for the heart and good for the bowels and especially for the small bowels" (Ber. 44b). It was also held to account for the absence of skin diseases and of leprosy in Babylonia (Ket. 77b). It is a winter plant, but due to its nutritive value attempts were made to grow it also in summer, and Solomon's servants were said to have been able to supply summer beets for his table (Deut. R. 1:5).

Bibliography: Loew, Flora, 1 (1926), 346–52; J. Feliks, *Kilei Zera'im* ... (1967), 82–83. [J.F.]

BEGGING AND BEGGARS. Although the Bible is concerned with the poor and the needy, there is hardly a reference to begging or to beggars, and there is, in fact, no biblical Hebrew word for it. The needs of the poor were provided by the laws of **leket, shikhḥah*, and *pe'ah* which were the perquisites of the *ani*, the "poor man," or the *evyon*, the "needy." The only possible references are not to actual begging and beggars, but are contained in the complementary assurances that whereas the children of the righteous will not have to "seek bread" (Ps. 37:25), the children of the wicked will, after his untimely death, be vagabonds "and seek their bread out of desolate places" (Ps. 109:10).

During the talmudic period, however, the itinerant beggar who goes from house to house figures with some prominence. So characteristic does it seem to have been of social life in those times that the first Mishnah of tractate *Shabbat* employs the example of the beggar receiving his pittance from the householder, and the various ways in which it might be handed to him, to illustrate the important laws concerning the carrying of articles from a private to a public domain on the Sabbath. The Mishnah also deals with the rights of the beggar who "goes from place to place" and who had sometimes to be provided with lodging for the night (Pe'ah 8:7). It was regarded as immodest for women to beg, with the result that the Mishnah lays it down that if a man left insufficient means for his children, the daughters should remain at home and the sons go from door to door (Ket. 13:3). The New Testament describes the blind beggar Bartimeus sitting by the roadside and begging (Mark 10: 46) and a lame beggar soliciting alms at the entrance to the Temple (Acts 3:2). The rabbis are censorious of those beggars who used to feign such afflictions as "blindness, swollen belly, and shrunken leg" in order to arouse the compassion of the charitable (Pe'ah 8:9; Tosef., Pe'ah 4:14). Nevertheless one rabbi takes a charitable view of those impostors, pleading that they perform the useful function of exercising the charitable instincts of the people (Ket. 68a). Nor was the cheerful impudent beggar unknown, as the following story in the Talmud indicates: "A beggar once came to Rava who asked him 'What do your meals usually consist of?' 'Plump chicken and matured wine' answered the beggar. 'Do you not consider this a burden on the community?' asked Rava. The beggar retorted: 'I do not take from them—I take what God provides.' At that moment Rava's sister, who had not seen him for 13 years, appeared bringing him a fat chicken and matured wine. 'Just what I told you!' said the beggar" (Ket. 67b).

Nevertheless two factors tended to keep begging within bounds. The one was the delicate custom of sending food to the poor in order to spare their feelings (see the examples, Ket. 67b), and the other was the highly organized system of collection for and distribution to the poor through the official *kuppah* ("charity fund") and *tamḥui* ("soup kitchen"). As a result it was laid down that relief was actually to be withheld from those who went begging and they forfeited their rights to organized charity, although a compromise was arrrived at not to send such a mendicant away completely empty-handed (BB 9a).

In the early Middle Ages this was established as the actual *halakhah* (Yad, Mattenat Aniyyim 7:7; Sh. Ar., YD 250:3); *Rashi (to BB 9a) explains that it is "because he has accustomed himself to make the rounds, he must suffice with that." On the other hand Solomon b. Adret, in answer to an enquiry from a community overburdened with beggars, ruled that although "the poor are everywhere

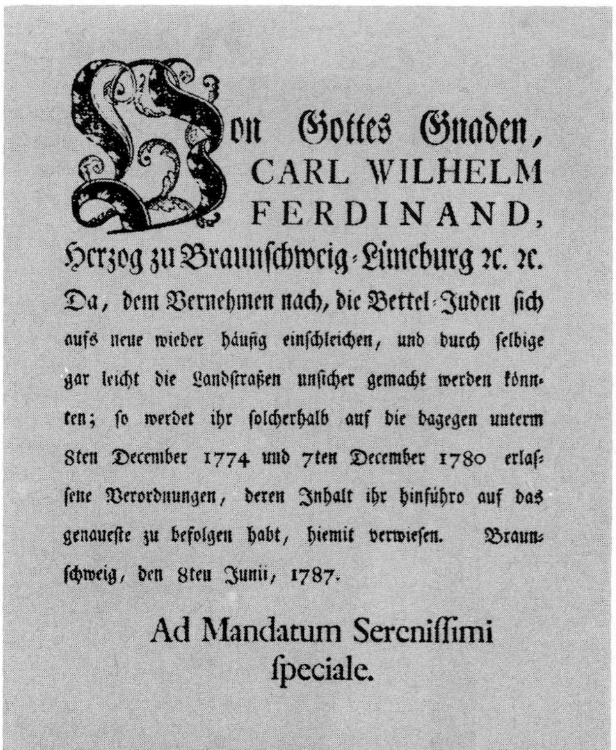
Von Gottes Gnaden,
CARL WILHELM
FERDINAND,
Herzog zu Braunschweig-Lüneburg ꝛc. ꝛc.
Da, dem Vernehmen nach, die Bettel-Juden sich aufs neue wieder häufig einschleichen, und durch selbige gar leicht die Landstraßen unsicher gemacht werden könnten; so werdet ihr solcherhalb auf die dagegen unterm 8ten December 1774 und 7ten December 1780 erlassene Verordnungen, deren Inhalt ihr hinführo auf das genaueste zu befolgen habt, hiemit verwiesen. Braunschweig, den 8ten Junii, 1787.

Ad Mandatum Sereniſſimi
ſpeciale.

v. Münchhausen. Feronce v. Rotenkreutz. v. Hardenberg Reventlow.

Figure 1. Order issued by Carl Wilhelm Ferdinand, duke of Brunswick, on June 8, 1787, confirming earlier regulations against the *"Betteljuden,"* since "these Jewish beggars may become a threat on the highways."

Figure 2. A Jewish beggar and child. Drypoint etching by E. M. Lilien (1874–1925).

supported from the communal chest, if they wish in addition to beg from door to door they may do so, and each should give according to his understanding and desire" (Responsa, pt. 3 no. 380). In Cracow, however, in 1595 and in the Spanish and Portuguese congregation in London in the second half of the 17th century, begging by mendicants was completely outlawed (Balaban, in JJLG, 10 (1913), 342; Barnett, *El Libro de los Acuerdos* (1931), 9).

This admirable system of organized relief for the poor (cf. Yad, loc. cit., 9:3: "We have never heard of a community which has no charity fund for the relief of the poor, though some have no *tamḥui*") seems almost to have eliminated beggars until the 17th century. Launcelot Addison (*The Present State of the Jews,* p. 212) goes out of his way to dispel the belief prevalent in his time that "the Jews have no beggars," which he attributed to the "regular and commendable efforts" by which they supplied the needs of the poor. A notable literary description of the English Jewish beggar is Zangwill's *King of the Schnorrers.*

It would seem that an increase in Jewish mendicancy took place as an aftermath of the *Chmielnicki pogroms when hundreds of Polish communities were destroyed and thousands of penniless and destitute Jews roamed over Europe. From this time dates *"shnorrer,"* the accepted Yiddish term for a beggar which became a characteristic feature of Jewish life. Sometimes the *shnorrers* openly collected for themselves, at other times for dowering a poor bride (see **Hakhnasat Kallah*) or to restore a house which had been burnt down in one of the many conflagrations of wood-built houses. If the 18th century has been styled "a century of beggary" as a whole, it certainly applies to the impoverished Jewish communities of Central and Eastern Europe up to the dawn of the modern period.

Beggary, which was rife in Ereẓ Israel before the establishment of the State of Israel, has been largely eliminated in the streets, as a result of the increased activities of the Ministry of Social Welfare. It is still, however, a feature of the synagogues during the morning services. The beggars consist of two groups, genuine beggars and students of the old-fashioned yeshivot who are to some extent encouraged by the authorities of the yeshivah, not only as a source of subsistence but to afford the worshipers an opportunity of combining prayer with charity. A similar sentiment is held toward beggars in cemeteries. Despite objections that they disturb worshippers, opinion among the Orthodox is opposed to their removal.

See *Charity.

[L.I.R.]

Social Aspects. Begging as a social phenomenon is associated with migrations. It became prevalent in Jewish history during the period of the Mishnah and the Talmud and especially after the destruction of the Second Temple. This came about as a result of persecutions under Roman rule, as well as the physical and economic insecurity which impoverished the rural class and reduced the urban population to ruin. Yet, despite the increase in the numbers of poor and those reduced to begging, nothing is heard about Jewish mendicants forming a society and developing their own subculture, as did occur within the non-Jewish world at that time.

Jewish beggars wandering from place to place are more frequently found throughout the Middle Ages. In the Cairo *Genizah* a large number of letters from beggars complaining of their misfortunes and seeking support have been found. The documents indicate that these itinerant poor wandered from community to community, and from land to land. The *Or Zaru'a* (*hilkhot Ẓedakah* 11) of R. *Isaac of Vienna mentions that these destitute people customarily equipped themselves with "documents," i.e., letters of recommendation which they would present in their travels as proof of their trustworthiness.

In medieval times there is found another class of wanderers who went from place to place, relying upon the hospitality of others, namely, the yeshivah students who moved from one center of Torah study to another. A parallel phenomenon (goliards, vagrant scholars) is found within the student community of the Christian society of that time.

At the end of the 17th century, a relatively large class of Jewish beggars, called in non-Jewish sources *"Betteljuden,"* and *orḥei porḥei* ("flotsam and jetsam") in Jewish literature, developed throughout Europe, especially in Germany. The size of this class is not known exactly, but it has been estimated at as much as 20% of the total Jewish population. Although the reasons for the formation of this class are still not completely clear, it is assumed to have resulted from: (a) the natural growth of the Jewish population; (b) the limited number of Jews permitted to reside in any individual place by the local authorities; and (c) the unstable economic conditions which brought about drastic changes from extreme wealth to great poverty. The *Betteljuden* constituted a section within the large class of non-Jewish itinerant poor. These Jewish vagabonds, like their Christian counterparts, eventually united into societies, religiously intermixed at times, developing their own subculture. This class became a source of manpower and information to the bands of thieves which were rampant at that time. The authorities treated these groups of Jewish mendicants very harshly. They condemned them for thievery and for causing diseases and plagues in various places. As a result of these accusations, local authorities sought to banish the beggars. The Jewish communities were very ambivalent vis-à-vis these mendicants. On the one hand, they strove to obey the local powers-that-be, for they also saw in the beggars a social danger, not only because of their associations with thieves, but also because of their licentiousness. Yet, on the other hand, they not infrequently had feelings of compassion and brotherliness toward these unfortunates. The manner in which the communities handled these *orḥei porḥei,* therefore, corresponded to their ambivalence toward them. In general, the community accomodated them in the homes of its residents for one night (for two nights over the Sabbath), and afterward sent them along with a sum of money for travel expenditures. Special lodgings for mendicants, particularly for the sick among them, were also set up in the *hekdesh* ("poor house"). After the Emancipation, with residence restrictions for Jews lifted, and areas in which Jews were permitted to work widened, this impoverished class was largely integrated with other social classes. However, the phenomenon itself did not disappear from Jewish communal life, and it continued to exist especially in Eastern Europe, if not to the same extent. [M.F.]

Bibliography: I. Abrahams, *Jewish Life in the Middle Ages* (1932²), 331ff., 346f.; Baron, Community, 1 (1942), 131f., 363; 2 (1942), 321–5; Urbach, in: *Zion,* 16, nos. 3–4 (1951), 1–27; R. Glanz, *Geschichte des niederen juedischen Volks in Deutschland* (1968); Scheiber, in: M. Zohary and A. Tartakower (eds.), *Hagut Ivrit be-Eiropah* (1969), 268–75.

BEGHI, family of Karaite scholars in Constantinople (15th–17th centuries). Its members include: ELIJAH AFIDAH (AFDAH) BEGHI (d. before 1641). Elijah wrote *Hilkhot Sheḥitah,* on the rules of slaughtering; *Be'ur Asarah Ikkarim,* on the ten principles of Karaite faith (Bodleian Library, Ms. Opp. Add. 4° 121); *Mikhtav Eliyahu,* poems, verse compositions and tales; and *Me'irat Einayim,* a brief commentary on the Bible. JOSEPH BEN MOSES (15th–16th centuries). Joseph was the pupil of the Karaite scholar Abraham Bali, who in 1505 wrote for Beghi and his fellow student, Joseph b. Caleb, his *Issur Hadlakat Ner be-Shabbat,* on the Karaite prohibition of kindling lights on the Sabbath. The cordial relationship between the Karaites and *Rabbanites at that period is attested by Joseph's correspondence with Rabbanite scholars. Two letters by Moses b. Jacob (evidently *Moses of Kiev *"ha-Goleh"*) to Beghi are preserved. Joseph wrote *Iggeret Sukkah,* on Sukkot; *Keter Kehunnah,* six homilies; *Iggeret Kiryah Ne'emanah* especially directed against the identification of the Karaites with the Sadducees, a work of literary and historical value since it mentions a number of earlier Karaite scholars; *Iggeret Kelulah,* an explanation of a problem in marriage law. Simḥah Isaac b. Moses Lutzki mentions two important works of Joseph which are no longer traceable: *Shulḥan Ḥaverim,* a book of precepts, and *Safah Berurah,* a philosophical work. MOSES BEN BENJAMIN (second half of the 16th century), wrote *Mitzvot Moshe,* a book of precepts including two essays *"Ohel Moshe"* on the calendar, and *"Masat Moshe"* on the Sabbath laws, published in *Pinnat Yikrat* by the Karaite *Isaac b. Solomon (1834). Benjamin also composed liturgical poems, several of which have been included in the Karaite prayer book.

Bibliography: A. Neubauer, *Aus der Petersburger Bibliothek* (1866), 46n, 122; Danon, in: JQR 15 (1924/25), 337–39; HB, 17 (1877), 12; Mann, Texts, 2 (1935), 294n, 300, 302; Simḥah Isaac b. Moses (Lutzki), *Oraḥ Ẓaddikim* (1966), 98, 99, 107, 109; Z. Ankori, *Karaites in Byzantium* (1959), 36n, 58, 279. [I.M./ED.]

BÉGIN, EMILE-AUGUSTE (1802–1888), French physician, historian, and librarian. Bégin, who was born in Metz, studied medicine at the Military College in Strasbourg. He soon gave up his position as a regimental physician in favor of a literary career. His early writing dealt mainly with the history of northeastern France. He became well-known for his four-volume *Biographie de la Moselle* (1829–32) and his literary and political periodical *L'Indicateur de l'Est* (1830). His historical research embraced Jewish communities, and some of his findings appeared under the title *"Recherches pour servir l'histoire des Juifs dans le Nord-Est de la France"* in *Revue Orientale,* 1–2 (1841–42). Bégin settled in Paris in 1846 and became a contributor to publications of the Academy of Medicine. In 1850 he cooperated in the official edition of the papers of Napoleon I and in 1853–54 produced a laudatory five-volume biography, *L'Histoire de Napoléon Ier,* based on hitherto unpublished personal papers. Napoleon III rewarded him with an appointment as librarian at the Louvre, where he remained until 1871. In 1874 Bégin became librarian at the Bibliothèque Nationale, Paris.

Bibliography: *Dictionnaire de biographie francaise,* s.v.; *L'Austraisie,* 7 (July, 1907), 3–26 (suppl.); Wininger, Biog, 1 (1925), 284. [H.A.S.]

BEGIN, MENAHEM (1913–), Israel statesman and former commander of the Irgun Ẓeva'i Le'ummi (I.Z.L.). Begin was born and educated in Brest-Litovsk. He graduated in law at Warsaw University. After a short association with Ha-Shomer ha-Ẓa'ir he joined Betar, becoming a member of its leadership in Poland in 1931, and head of the movement in that country in 1938. During the Palestine riots of 1936–38, Begin organized a mass demonstration near the British Embassy in Warsaw and was imprisoned by the Polish police. When the Germans occupied Warsaw, Begin escaped to Vilna, where he was arrested by the Soviet authorities and sentenced to eight years hard labor in the Arctic region. Because he was a Polish citizen, Begin was released at the end of 1941, and arrived in Palestine in 1942 with the Polish army formed in the U.S.S.R. Toward the end of 1943, after having been released from the Polish ranks, Begin became commander of I.Z.L., declared "armed warfare" against the Mandatory government at the beginning of 1944, and led a determined underground struggle against the British (who offered a reward for his apprehension). Begin tried, at the same time, to avoid violent clashes within the *yishuv.* He was on board the I.Z.L. ship *Altalena* when it approached Tel Aviv with a consignment of arms during the Arab-Israel ceasefire of June 1948 and was shelled by order of the Israel government (see *Irgun Ẓeva'i Le'ummi). In 1948 Begin founded the *Ḥerut Party and became its leader. He led the party's protest campaign against the reparations agreement with West Germany in 1952. He was instrumental in establishing the *Gaḥal faction in the Knesset in 1965. In May 1967, on the eve of the Six-Day War, Begin was named minister without portfolio in the Government of National Unity. However, he and his Gaḥal colleagues left the government in 1970 when the majority accepted the U.S. initiative for peace talks with the Arabs implying the evacuation by Israel of territories occupied in the course of

Menahem Begin, Israel statesman, who commanded the Irgun Ẓeva'i Leummi.

the Six-Day War (see *Israel, Historical Survey). His writings include *Ha-Mered* (1950; *The Revolt,* 1964), which describes the struggle of I.Z.L.; *Be-Leilot Levanim* (1953; *White Nights,* 1957), reminiscences of his imprisonment in Russia; and *Ba-Maḥteret: Ketavim u-Te'udot* (4 vol., 1959–61), a collection of writings from his days in the underground.

[Y.BA.]

BEHAK, JUDAH (1820–1900), Hebrew writer. Behak, who was born in Vilna, was a member of the Vilna group (M. A. *Guenzburg, A. D. *Lebensohn, S. J. *Fuenn, and I. E. *Benjacob) which had a decisive influence on the Haskalah movement in Lithuania. He wrote for *Pirḥei Ẓafon,* the first Lithuanian Haskalah journal, and for *Ha-Karmel.* In 1848 he joined the staff of the newly established Vilna Rabbinical Seminary, and in 1856 moved to Kherson (most of his writings were signed *Ish Vilna be-Kherson,* "A Vilnaite in Kherson"). Behak devoted himself to the study of the Hebrew language. His main work was *Eẓ Yehudah,* linguistic studies of the Bible and the Talmud (5 vols., 1884–1901, Vilna, Odessa, Berdichev). His book *Yod ha-Rabbim,* a study of Aramaic, was published posthumously (1901). Behak also edited J. L. Ben-Ze'ev's *Talmud Lashon Ivri* (with Ẓ. H. Katznellenbogen, 1848) and S. Levisohn's *Meḥkerei Lashon* (with A. D. Lebensohn, 1849), and wrote commentaries for I. E. Benjacob's and A. D. Lebensohn's Bible, *Mikra'ei Kodesh* (1848–53).

Bibliography: E. R. Malachi (ed.), *Kitvei P. Turberg* (1953), 52–62; P. Sandler, *Ha-Be'ur la-Torah shel M. Mendelssohn ve-Si'ato...* (1941), 178–9.

[G.K.]

BEHAR, NISSIM (1848–1931), founder of modern Hebrew education in Ereẓ Israel and public figure in Jewish life in the U.S.A. Behar was born in Jerusalem. He graduated from the *Alliance Israélite Universelle teachers institute in Paris in 1869 and taught in Syria, Bulgaria, and Turkey. He headed the Alliance school in Constantinople from 1873 to 1882. There he introduced the direct method of teaching Hebrew, *"Ivrit be-Ivrit."* In 1882 Behar initiated the founding of the new Alliance school in Jerusalem, Torah u-Melakhah ("Torah and Work"), and became its headmaster. One of the teachers there was Eliezer *Ben-Yehuda, and its first students included David *Yellin and Yosef *Meyuḥas. Its modern methods were eventually applied in Hebrew schools throughout the country. Behar was an outstanding leader of the *yishuv,* especially as a liaison with the Turkish authorities. He attempted, with the help of Baron Edmond de *Rothschild, to regain the Western Wall for the Jewish community, but failed because of rabbinical opposition. The rabbis' hostility to Behar resulted from his educational innovations and he was eventually relieved of his duties as headmaster (1897) and sent to represent the Alliance in the U.S.A. (1901). In his attempts to organize the work of the Alliance in the U.S.A., Behar encountered difficulties from Jewish institutions which looked askance at the activities of a large, foreign Jewish organization. American Jewish leaders did not approve of his intense propaganda, public meetings, and protests. Nevertheless, Behar soon became a public figure in American Jewry. He expounded the idea that political organizations should speak for American Jewry, and in 1906 founded the National Liberal Immigration League, directing it until 1924. In 1908 Behar traveled to Europe and back in order to learn how immigrants to the U.S. were treated on the boats. He was one of the founders of the Federation of Jewish Organizations. Behar was active in the *Histadrut Ivrit in the U.S.A. from its beginning. He died in New York and his remains were reburied in Jerusalem a year later.

Bibliography: Z. Szajkowski, in AJHSP, 39 (1950), 406–43; A. Goldberg, *Pioneers and Builders* (1943), 188–93; H. Debrest, in: *Jewish Forum* (1928), 522–6; M. Ribalow, in: *Hadoar,* 6 (1925), 118; M. D. Gaon, *Yehudei ha-Mizraḥ be-Ereẓ Yisrael,* 2 (1938), 151–9; E. Cohen-Reiss, *Mi-Zikhronot Ish Yerushalayim* (1967[2]), index.

[ED.]

BEHEMOTH (intensive plural of Heb. *behemah,* "beast"), creature described in the Book of Job (40:15–24). It is depicted as an animal that eats grass like an ox, is all muscles and strength, lives in the marsh in the shade of the *ẓe'elim* ("*jujube"), eats huge quantities of food, and can swallow the waters of the Jordan. In the light of the description of other animals in these chapters, it would seem that the reference is to an existing animal, to which legendary details have been added. In later Jewish literature, however, it appears as a purely mythical creature. One of the mammoths fashioned on the fifth day of creation (Targ. Yer., Gen. 1:21; II Bar. 29:4), he is the male counterpart on land of the female *Leviathan in the sea (IV Ezra 6:49–52). He is said to dwell in the wilderness of Dendain (or Dudain), east of Eden (I Enoch 60:7–8), or else, by a fanciful interpretation of Psalm 50:10, to span "a thousand hills" (IV Ezra 6:49–52; Lev. R. 21). At the end of the world's existence he will be slain and served, along with his mate, at a banquet tendered to the righteous (*ibid.;* Targ. Yer., Num. 9:6; PdRE 11; cf. TB, BB 75a). It has been suggested that this reflects the Iranian belief that at the Resurrection the righteous will obtain immortality by drinking a nectar made out of the fat of the mythical ox Hadhayosh mixed with *haoma* (a plant; Bundahishn 19:13, 20:25; Dadistan-i-Denik 37:119); but it is undoubtedly inspired also by the statement in Psalms 74:14 that God once fed the flesh of Leviathan "to the people." The hippopotamus *(Hippopotamus amphibus)* has been identi-

The fight of the mythical Behemoth and Leviathan at the end of the world, depicted in the illuminated opening page of the prayers for Sukkot, from the *Leipzig Maḥzor,* S. Germany, c. 1320, Leipzig, University Library, ms. V 1102, vol. II, fol. 181v.

fied with Behemoth. It is the largest land animal in the Middle East, weighing up to three tons. It has powerful sinews, an enormous head, and a wide mouth with huge molars. Once it inhabited Ereẓ Israel; skeletal remains of it have been found in the vicinity of the Yarkon River. In ancient Egypt it was a favorite quarry of hunters and its capture with spears is often depicted.

Bibliography: Lewysohn, Zool, 355; Tristram, Nat Hist, 50–53; J. Feliks, *Animal World of the Bible* (1962), 24.

[J.F./Th.M.G.]

BE-ḤOZAI, a district extending E. of *Mesene, S.E. of Babylon, and N. of the Persian Gulf. Geographically, Be-Ḥozai did not belong to Babylonia, but to Persia. Despite the great distance between them (Ta'an, 21b; BK 104b), very close ties (including commercial) existed between the Jews of Babylonia and those of Be-Ḥozai. The district had a plentiful supply of water, and rice, extensively grown there, was used for bread by its inhabitants (Pes. 50b). It was an important station for goods in transit between Babylonia and Persia (Shab. 51b; BK 104b; Ket. 85a). Many problems were addressed to the Babylonian scholars by its sages, the names of some of whom are known, e.g., Avimi (Nid. 5b), Aḥa (BM 39b), Beroka (Ta'an. 22a), Avram Ḥoza'ah (Git. 50a), Ḥanina (Shab. 130b). The Babylonians had a generally poor opinion of the common people of Be-Ḥozai (Ned. 22a). The Babylonian Talmud mentions, among other localities in the region, Be Lapet (Syriac for Be Shafat), where many Jews lived (Ta'an, 22a), and Shushan (Meg. 2b), or "Sus," its widely used Syriac abbreviation (Sanh. 94a).

Bibliography: J. Obermeyer, *Landschaft Babylonien* (1929), 204–14.

[M.Be.]

BEHR (Beer), ALEXANDER (first half of 19th century), teacher in Munich. Behr composed a Jewish catechism in German, *Lehrbuch der mosaischen Religion* (1826), intended to introduce systematic religious instruction on modern lines among Jews. It was published under the supervision of the rabbi of Wuerzburg, Abraham *Bing, and authorized by the Bavarian government as the official textbook for Jewish religious instruction. An abridged version was published in the same year, entitled *Hauptlehren der mosaischen Religion.* The works were criticized by Elkan *Henle (1827), who pointed out errors and inaccuracies in the translation of Hebrew texts, and deficiencies such as the omission of the Decalogue, and neglect to stress the duty of patriotism. Behr also published the traditional prayer book with a German translation (1827).

Bibliography: M. Eliav, *Ha-Ḥinnukh ha-Yehudi be-Germanyah* (1960), 251; JE s.v.

[It.G.]

BEHR (Baer), ISSACHAR FALKENSOHN (1746–1817), Polish poet who wrote in German. Born in Zamosc, Behr was raised in a traditional, Yiddish-speaking home. He was a failure as a petty tradesman and, leaving his wife and family in order to seek an education, wandered to Koenigsberg and reached Berlin in 1764. There he learned German, Latin, and French, and studied mathematics, philosophy, and medicine. Daniel *Itzig became his patron and introduced him to the Berlin intellectuals. He soon wrote excellent German verse and in 1772 published his *Gedichte von einem pohlnischen Juden,* a pioneer achievement for an East European Jew. Goethe reviewed this strange collection of lyrics in the *Frankfurter Gelehrten-Anzeiger.* In 1773, Behr completed his medical studies at the University of Halle and devoted himself to medical practice in Courland; thereafter, he wrote no more poetry.

Bibliography: M. Kayserling, *Der Dichter Ephraim Kuh* (1864), 43–47.

[S.L.]

BEHREND, JACOB FRIEDRICH (1833–1907), German jurist. Behrend became a law clerk in 1859, in 1864 he was appointed lecturer at the University of Berlin, and in 1870, associate professor of jurisprudence. From 1873 to 1887 he was professor of law at the University of Greifswald, and in 1887 became a member of the Supreme Court, one of the few Jews to achieve this distinction. He was an ackowledged expert on German and Roman law and specialized in the early sources of law. Behrend published many important works on jurisprudence which were highly regarded by scholars. His first published work was the *Magdeburger Fragen* ("Magdeburg Problems," 1863) which dealt with the jury system. Later Behrend edited numerous works on jurisprudence, including *Zeitschrift fuer die deutsche Gesetzgebung und fuer einheitliches deutsches Recht* ("Journal for German Legislation and for a Unitary German Law," 1880). His major work, *Lehrbuch des Handelsrechts* ("Textbook of Commercial Law"), was regarded as the first comprehensive work on this subject. Although he managed to complete only the first volume, this was for many years an invaluable source of research.

Bibliography: *Deutsche Juristen-Zeitung* 12 (1907), 170.

[B.M.A.]

BEHRENDS (Behrens), LEFFMANN (1634–1714), Hanover Court Jew. Behrends, who began as a small merchant supplying luxuries to the court, gradually established himself as moneylender, diplomatic mediator, and coin minter. His position was strengthened under Duke Ernest Augustus (1679–98), for whom he procured the title of elector, and under George, elector of Hanover (1698–1727), the future George I of England. He established business and marital connections with the *Oppenheimers and *Wertheimers of Vienna and stationed his agents, usually his relatives, in the main German cities. An ardent talmudist, and father-in-law of David b. Abraham *Oppenheim, he supported talmudic studies. For many years he was head *(Vorsteher)* of the community of Hanover-Neustadt, the majority of whose members were connected with his household. In 1673 he acquired the right to open a cemetery, and in 1703 built a synagogue and presented it to the community. In 1687 at his request the duke agreed to permit the Jews of Hanover to appoint a *Landesrabbiner.* In 1700 he obtained the support of the elector in suppressing the writings of Johann *Eisenmenger. Behrends attempted to murder a relative of his who became an apostate, but he was able to use his influence to evade being brought to trial. His sons and grandsons, also Court Jews, carried on the family firm; their bankruptcy in 1721 shook the European financial world and took more than a century to settle legally. The trial revealed that Behrends had left his estate in a sorry condition. His descendants settled in Copenhagen.

Bibliography: S. Stern, *The Court Jew* (1950), index; H. Schnee, *Die Hoffinanz und der moderne Staat,* 2 (1954), 13–67; 5 (1965), 54–81.

[Ed.]

BEHRMAN, MARTIN (1864–1926), U.S. public official. Behrman was born in New York City and taken to New Orleans in 1865 by his parents, who died when he was 12. At 19 he became a traveling salesman for a large grocery concern. Turning to politics, Behrman was elected president of the State Board of Assessors, a member of the New Orleans Board of Education (1892–1906), state auditor (1904–05), and mayor of New Orleans in 1904, serving four terms until his defeat in 1920. Behrman was director of the American Bank and Trust Company. He was a leading state Democrat and was chairman of the Louisiana delegation to the national Democratic convention in 1908. Behrman was active in civic and Jewish affairs. He was a member of the Louisiana Constitutional Conventions of 1898 and 1921, and president of the League of American Municipalities (1917–18).

[E.GR.]

BEHRMAN, SAMUEL NATHANIEL (1893–), U.S. playwright. Behrman was born in Worcester, Mass. He graduated from Harvard, where he joined G. P. Baker's Drama Workshop, and from Columbia University. It took him 11 years to sell his first play, *The Second Man* (1927). It was a great success and marked the beginning of a prolific

S. N. Behrman, U.S. playwright.

and brilliant career. Intellect, technique, wit, and charm apparent in this early work marked his later writings. His plays, including *End of Summer* (1936), *No Time for Comedy* (1939), and *Jacobowsky and the Colonel* (in collaboration with Franz *Werfel; 1943), are distinguished by warmth and respect for human values. Behrman was far ahead of his fellow playwrights in showing awareness of totalitarian evils, as in *Rain from Heaven* (1936) and *Wine of Choice* (1938). Behrman turned to biography with *Duveen* (1952), the career of the famous British art dealer. This was followed by the autobiographical *Worcester Account* (1954), a charming description of an American Jewish boyhood with an immigrant background. In *Portrait of Max* (1961), he recorded his conversations with Sir Max Beerbohm. Behrman returned to the theater in 1958 with a dramatization of his autobiography under the title *The Cold Wind and the Warm.* He also adapted the Duveen biography as a play, *Lord Pengo* (1963). In 1964 he was one of three American authors whose new works were chosen for the opening season of the Lincoln Center Repertory Theatre in New York. Behrman's play was *But For Whom Charlie* (1964), a comedy about a conflict of temperaments. His novel *The Burning Glass* (1969) was set in pre-World War II Salzburg.

Bibliography: S. J. Kunitz (ed.), *Authors Today and Yesterday* (1934²), 56–57; B. Mantle, *Contemporary American Playwrights* (1941), 108–15; J. Mersand, *Traditions in American Literature* (1939), 51–67.

[B.G.]

BEI AVIDAN, meeting place in talmudic times where scholars of various nations and faiths met for religious discussions and disputations. Enjoying the protection of the authorities, the institution was visited by some of the Jewish sages, while others, such as *Joshua b. Hananiah (Shab. 152a) and Eleazar b. Perata (Av. Zar. 17b), refrained from doing so, for which they were compelled to apologize to the authorities. Similarly, the *amora* Rav did not enter a *Bei Avidan,* whereas his colleague Samuel did (Shab. 116a). The *Bei Avidan* is mentioned in this context in association with a *Bei Niẓrefei* (or *Bei Naẓrufei*), to which neither Rav nor Samuel would enter, and which was apparently an idolatrous house of worship (cf. Er. 80a). R. Abbahu was asked whether it was permitted to save the books of a *Bei Avidan* from a fire on the Sabbath (Shab. loc. cit.). It apparently contained books of the Bible (see R. Hananel, ad loc.), but since it was not known whether a Jew or a sectarian had copied them, the doubt arose whether or not they could be saved on the Sabbath. Various theories have been advanced to explain the origin of the word. According to S. J. L. Rapoport (*Erekh Millin* (1852), 3), it derives from the Persian *abdan* ("a forum"), the meeting place there being called *Bei Avidan* (i.e., "house of"). L. Ginzberg (*Festschrift . . . Schwarz,* 1917, 329) suggests that the word derives from the name of a person, possibly the astrologer Abidas-Abidan, who was active in Persia at the beginning of the third century. L. Loew (*He-Ḥalutz,* 2 (1853), 100ff.) contends that the correct reading is *"Bei-Evyoni,"* i.e., the meeting place of the Ebionites in the Land of Israel. However, the fact that the word *"Bei Avidan"* is not found in Palestinian sources and that, furthermore, the statement about Joshua b. Hananiah and Eleazar b. Perata are in Aramaic indicate that the *Bei Avidan* originated in Babylonia and that the term was adopted by the rabbis to apply to the institution in Ereẓ Israel.

Bibliography: Levy J., Neuhebr Tal, 1 (1924²), 9; Jastrow, Dict. 1 (1950), 5; Neusner, Babylonia, 1 (1966), 73ff. (citing further literature).

[Y.D.G.]

BEILIN, ASHER (1881–1948), Hebrew and Yiddish journalist, author, and editor. Beilin was born in Kiev. He worked intermittently as *Shalom Aleichem's secretary (1901–05). In 1906 he moved to London, where he engaged in journalism, and in 1933 settled in Jerusalem. Beilin contributed extensively to the Hebrew and Yiddish press, edited Yiddish papers, and in his latter years wrote for the Tel Aviv Hebrew daily newspaper, *Davar.* His writings include reminiscences of J. Ḥ. *Brenner (1943), with whom he collaborated for many years, and Shalom Aleichem (1945), a novel *Al Belimah* ("On Nothing," 1928), and a play *Banim li-Gevulam* ("Sons to their Border," 1945). His selected works were published in 1956.

Bibliography: *Kol Kitvei G. Shofman,* 4 (1960), 283; 5 (1960), 168; LNYL, 1 (1956), 287–8.

[G.K.]

BEILINSON (Belinson), MOSES ELIEZER (1835–1908), Hebrew and Yiddish writer and publisher. He was born in Dubrovna (Russia). In 1860 he published a brochure *Ẓevi la-Ẓaddik* containing an apologia for Judaism and an attack upon Christianity and Karaism. He translated Ludwig Philippson's novel *Die Vertreibung der Juden aus Spanien und Portugal* into Hebrew as *Galut Sefarad* in 1860. In the 1860s he established a Hebrew printing press in Odessa, and published *Alei Hadas,* a literary and scholarly periodical (1865), in which he printed his correspondence with Philippson on the situation of the Jews in Russia. Only four issues appeared. Perez *Smolenskin published his first pamphlets at Beilinson's press (1862–67); Beilinson wanted to "correct" Smolenskin's style, but most of his corrections were rejected. *Kol Mevasser* (1871), the first Yiddish weekly published in Russia, was also printed at Beilinson's press and Beilinson succeeded Moshe Leib *Lilienblum as its editor, using the pseudonym "M.E.B.N." He composed three genealogical histories (including one on his own family): *Megillat Yuḥasin* (1891), *Yalkut Mishpaḥot* (1892), and *Millu'im le-Koveẓ Yalkut Mishpaḥot* (1893). He published *Toledot ha-Rav Yosef Shelomo Rofe Delmedigo mi-Kandia* (1864), a biography based on Abraham Geiger's *Melo Ḥofnayim* (German section); and *Shelomei Emunei Yisrael,* three brochures dealing with literary and scientific topics (1898–1901). He also edited *Koveẓ Yagdil Torah* (1879–85) and *Koveẓ Mekhilta de-Rabbanan* (1885), dealing with halakhic matters. Beilinson adapted Longfellow's

Judas Maccabaeus into a Yiddish Ḥanukkah play (1882), and also adapted Philippson's above-mentioned novel (1888). He also published a *Nutslikher Fremdvorterbukh* (Part 1, 1887), a dictionary of foreign phrases used in Yiddish.

Bibliography: Zeitlin, Bibliotheca, 18–19; Rejzen, Leksikon 1 (1928), 328–30; Wachstein et al., *Hebraische Publizistik in Wien*, 1 (1930), 11, 293. [G.El.]

BEILINSON, MOSHE (1889–1936), Hebrew writer, journalist, and one of the chief spokesmen of the labor movement in Ereẓ Israel. Beilinson, who was born in Veprika, Russia, qualified as a doctor in 1913. A supporter of the Russian socialist movement, he was won over to Zionist socialism by Z. Shazar and B. Katznelson. After World War I he settled in Italy, where he became active in the Zionist movement. He also published a series of translations into Italian of books of Jewish interest, including: Buber's *Reden ueber das Judentum* (1923); R. Travers Herford's *Pharisees* (1925); and (with Dante *Lattes) Joseph Klausner's *Kiẓẓur Toledot ha-Sifrut ha-Ivrit ha-Ḥadashah* (1926). In 1924 he settled in Petaḥ Tikvah and soon afterward joined the editorial board of the newly founded **Davar*. Here Beilinson published articles and notes, discussing problems of the Palestinian labor movement. He first wrote in Russian but changed to Hebrew in 1926. His style was simple and fluent. Beilinson wrote: *Bi-Ymei Massah*, on the Jewish-Arab question

Moshe Beilinson, Zionist labor writer.

(1930); *Bi-Ymei Teḥiyyat Italyah* (1930); *Be-Mashber ha-Olam* (published in 1940, with essay on Beilinson by B. Katznelson) and *Ba-Derekh le-Aẓma'ut* (1949). One of the main hospitals in the Tel Aviv area was named after him.

Bibliography: *Ẓiyyun le-Moshe Beilinson* (supplement to *Davar*, fasc. no. 3792, Nov. 9, 1937, includes a bibliography of his writings). [G.K.]

BEILIS, MENAHEM MENDEL (1874–1934), victim of a *blood libel charge in Russia in 1911. On March 20, 1911, the mutilated body of Andrei Yushchinsky, a 12-year-old boy, was discovered in a cave on the outskirts of Kiev. The monarchist rightist press immediately launched a vicious anti-Jewish campaign, accusing the Jews of using human blood for ritual purposes. At the funeral of Yushchinsky, leaflets circulating the blood libel were distributed by members of the reactionary "Black Hundred" ("*Union of Russian People") organization. Meanwhile the police investigation traced the murder to a gang of thieves associated with a woman, Vera Cheberiak, notorious for criminal dealings. However, the reactionary anti-Semitic organizations led by the "Black Hundred" pressured the anti-Semitic minister of justice, I. G. Shcheglovitov, to channel the investigation as a ritual murder charge. Accordingly, the chief district attorney of Kiev disregarded the police information and instead looked for a Jew on

The Beilis family in 1914.

whom to shift the crime, through whom the entire Jewish people could be publicly indicted.

In July 1911, a lamplighter testified that on March 12, the day Yushchinsky disappeared, he had seen him playing with two other boys on the premises of the brick kiln owned by a Jew, Zaitsev. He also alleged that a Jew had suddenly appeared and kidnapped Yushchinsky, pulling him toward the brick kiln. On the strength of this testimony, Mendel Beilis, the superintendent of the brick kiln, was arrested on July 21, 1911, and sent to prison, where he remained for over two years. A report was submitted to Czar Nicholas II that Beilis was regarded by the judiciary as the murderer of Yushchinsky.

The case attracted universal attention. Protests and addresses by scientists, public and political leaders, artists, men of letters, clergymen, and other liberal-minded men were published in all the civilized countries of Europe and the United States affirming that the blood libel was baseless. The trial of Beilis took place in Kiev from Sept. 25 through Oct. 28, 1913. The chief prosecutor A. I. Vipper made anti-Jewish statements in his closing address and defended the Cheberiak gang against the charge of Yushchinsky's murder. Beilis was represented by the most able counsels of the Moscow, St. Petersburg, and Kiev bars: Vassily Maklakov, Oscar O. Grusenberg, N. P. Karabchevsky, A. S. Zarundy, and D. N. Grigorovitch-Barsky. The lamplighter and his wife, on whose testimony the indictment of Beilis rested, when questioned by the presiding judge, answered, "We know nothing at all." They confessed that both had been confused by the secret police and made to answer questions they did not comprehend. "Scientific" foundation for the blood libel was supplied at the trial by a Catholic priest with a criminal record, Justin Pranaitis, who stated that the murder of Yushchinsky had all the characteristics of ritual murder enjoined by the Jewish religion. His arguments were refuted by the rabbi of Moscow, Jacob Mazeh, who proved that Pranaitis was ignorant of the talmudic texts cited. Two Russian professors of high standing, Troitsky and Kokovtzoff, also spoke on behalf of the defense in praise of Jewish values and exposed the falsity of the ritual murder hypothesis. The jury, composed of simple Russian peasants, after several hours of deliberation unanimously declared Beilis "not guilty."

Beilis, who still remained in danger of revenge by the "Black Hundred," left Russia with his family for Erez Israel. In 1920 he settled in the United States. Bernard *Malamud's novel *The Fixer* is based on the Beilis case.

Bibliography: M. Samuel, *Blood Accusation: the Strange History of the Beiliss Case* (1966); M. Beilis, *Story of My Sufferings* (1926); AJYB, 16 (1914/15), 19–89; A. D. Margolin, in: *Jews of Eastern Europe* (1926), 155–247; A. B. Tager, *The Decay of Czarism: The Beiliss Trial* (1935); Z. Szajkowski, in: PAAJR, 31 (1963), 197–218. [C.T.]

BEIM, SOLOMON BEN ABRAHAM (1817–1867), Karaite scholar. Like his father, Solomon was *ḥazzan* of the Odessa Karaite community, an office corresponding more or less to that of rabbi. Solomon Beim first officiated as *ḥazzan* in Chufut-Kale where, in addition to Bible and Hebrew, he also taught secular subjects, a new departure for Karaites at that time. Beim endeavored to raise the educational level of the Karaites, but when he attempted to ease the severe Karaite laws he met with strong opposition. He wrote several treatises in Russian on the Karaites which, however, have little value, being based on the doubtful findings of Abraham *Firkovich. Solomon's younger brother, Isaac, succeeded him as *ḥazzan* of the Odessa Karaite community. He published the third edition of *Adderet Eliyahu* by Elijah *Bashyazi (1870).

Bibliography: Gottlober, in: *Ha-Maggid*, 8, nos. 20–21 (1864); S. Poznański, in: YE, 4 (c. 1910), 41. [I.M./Ed.]

BEIN, ALEXANDER (1903–), archivist and historian of Zionism. Bein was born at Steinach and studied at Erlangen and Berlin. From 1927 to 1933 he served on the staff of the German State Archives. In 1933 he settled in Palestine where he became assistant director of the General Zionist

Alexander Bein, Israel state archivist.

Archives in 1936. In 1955 he was appointed director, and in addition from 1956 was state archivist of Israel. Apart from studies in general history, *Die Staatsidee Alexander Hamiltons in ihrer Entstehung und Entwicklung* (1927), Bein devoted his efforts to the history of Zionism and modern anti-Semitism. Among his works are *Toledot ha-Hityashevut ha-Ẓiyyonit* (1945^{2}); *The Return to the Soil* (1952); and his biography of Theodor Herzl (1934) which was translated into several languages. Bein also edited a new Hebrew edition of Herzl's writings in Hebrew which appeared in ten volumes in 1960–61. He contributed articles to scholarly journals on the history of modern anti-Semitism and Zionism.

Bibliography: Kressel, Leksikon 1 (1965), 230. [I.M./Ed.]

BEI-RAV (Aram. בֵּי־רַב), term in talmudic literature designating an academy of higher learning (e.g., Sanh. 17b; Yev. 83b), lesser academies generally being referred to as *bet rabban* (e.g., Shab. 119b). the students at the *bei rav* also lived there (Ber. 25a). The academies of Rabbi *Akiva in Ereẓ Israel and later of Rav, in Sura, were called Bei-Rav (Ket. 62b; BM 102b). *De-Vei-Rav* is also used by some *amoraim* as a term for certain collections of tannaitic literature. *She'ar Sifrei de-Vei-Rav* ("Other Books of Bei-Rav") mentioned by some *amoraim* (Yoma 74a; BB 124b), are explained by Rashi as the tannaitic commentaries on Numbers and Deuteronomy, although Solomon b. Abraham *Adret and *Gershom b. Judah include the Midrash on Exodus as well. For them, the Midrash on Leviticus (*Sifra de-Vei Rav*) was the book of Bei-Rav as everyone was so well versed with it, whereas the other works were somewhat less well-known. Zunz identifies **Sifra* and *Sidra de-Vei-Rav* (also known as *Torat Kohanim*) with the commentary on Leviticus, and *Sifrei* and *Sifrei de-Vei-Rav* with the commentary on Numbers and Deuteronomy. Known under the single name of **Sifrei*, these midrashic commentaries were taught for the first time by Rav in Babylonia (Zunz, Vortraege, 49f.). Maimonides and Menahem Meiri after him considered Rav the author of these works. M. Friedmann, in his introduction to the **Mekhilta* (1870; xviff.), identifies *Sifra* with *Torat Kohanim* (i.e., the commentary on Lev.) and *Sifra de-Vei-Rav* with miscellaneous **baraitot* of Rav, or of the academy of Rav. D. Hoffman (*Zur Einleitung in die halachischen Midraschim* (1887), 13–20, and *Mar Samuel* (1873), 68f.), subscribes to the view that the term "*tanna de-Vei-Rav*" embraces the *Sifra* and *Sifra de-Vei-Rav*, a collection of the teachings of the sages at the academy of Rabbi Huna (cf. Sanh. 17b). The general opinion is that the term *Bei-Rav* applies to all sorts of halakhic Midrashim taught at the Babylonian academies or to all those traditions (*Sifra, Sifrei*) upon which they are based (cf. Ch. Albeck, *Untersuchungen ueber die halakischen Midraschim* (1927), 87ff.).

See also Rabbi *Ishmael.

Bibliography: Weiss, Dor, 2 (1904^{4}), 206f.; Bacher, Bab Amor, 2; idem, *Ergaenzungen und Berichtigungen* . . . (1913), 5; Gruenhut, in: *Sefer le-David Ẓevi (Festschrift . . . D. Hoffmann)* (1914), 1–11 (Heb.); J. Z. Lauterbach (ed.), *Mekhilta*, 1 (1933), xxi ff. (Eng. and Heb.); J. N. Epstein, *Mevo'ot le-Sifrut ha-Tanna'im* (1957), 646ff., 728ff.; Ch. Albeck, *Mavo la-Talmudim* (1969), 102–6.

[Ed.]

BEIRUT, capital city and chief port of Lebanon. From the second century B.C.E. Jews lived in its vicinity, and probably in the city itself. The Chronicle of Joshua the Stylite mentions the existence of a synagogue in Beirut at the beginning of the sixth century. *Abiathar b. Elijah (late 11th century) includes Beirut and Gebal (Byblos) among the cities subject to the gaonate of Palestine. At the time of the Crusader conquest (1100) Beirut contained 35 Jewish families and *Benjamin of Tudela (c. 1170) found 50 households there. According to Isaac of Acre many Jews were killed during the Muslim capture of the city in 1291. Jews frequently visited Beirut on their way to Ereẓ Israel, but a pupil of *Nahmanides who stopped there at the beginning of the 14th century did not note the presence of Jews in the city. An anonymous pupil of Obadiah *Bertinoro wrote in a letter (1495) "At Baroto (Beirut) there are no Jews, and I do not know the reason, because the Ishmaelites at Baroto are better than all the other people of the Kingdom and are very well-disposed toward the Jews." However Jews settled again in Beirut after the expulsion from Spain in 1492. Moses *Basola, who visited the city in 1521, found 12 Jewish families from Sicily. Abraham Castro was in charge of customs. During Basola's stay in the city, the activity of David *Reuveni, whom a Jewish merchant encountered at Gaza, excited the Jews. *David d'Beth Hillel, who visited Syria in 1824, relates "There are [in Beirut] some 15 families [of] Jewish merchants, natives of the country [i.e., the place] who speak Arabic and have a small synagogue, their customs resembling those of the Jews of Palestine."

In 1856 Ludwig August *Frankl stated that he found in Beirut 500 Sephardi Jews, mostly merchants and porters. In course of time other Jews went to Beirut from Damascus, Smyrna, Aleppo, Constantinople, and ultimately also from Russia. In 1878 the *Alliance Israélite opened a girls' school and the following year, one for boys. In 1901, 271 pupils were studying at the latter, and 218 at the former. In 1897 the Alliance opened a crafts school for girls.

Pupils of the Alliance Israélite Universelle's girls' school in Beirut. A photograph taken in the early 1950s.

In 1862 and in 1890, blood libels resulted in Christian attacks on the Jewish quarter. In 1890 order was restored by the Turkish authorities and the rioters were arrested. At that time Beirut contained a synagogue and 12 *batei midrash*.

After World War I the Jewish population grew in Beirut, the newly established capital of *Lebanon. The community was regarded as the most highly organized in Lebanon and Syria. The principal synagogue Magen Avraham was the center of the communal institutions, which included the schools of the Alliance and of the congregation, the B'nai B'rith Lodge and the Maccabi Club.

The Jews of the city belonged mostly to the middle class. They were not concentrated in special quarters, but the poorer Jews resided in streets formerly part of the Jewish quarter. When the State of Israel was established, an anti-Jewish demonstration was held and infuriated mobs advanced on the Jewish quarter, but the Christian community dispersed the demonstrators. The Jewish paper *al-ʿAlam al-Isrāʾīlī* ("The Israelite World") changed its name to *Et al-Salām* ("Peace"). The Jewish community was compelled to contribute a sum of money to the fund of the Arab League but in general the Jews were not molested.

In 1880 there were about 1,000 Jews in Beirut; in 1889 1,500; between 1892 and 1906 there were 3,000; between 1907 and 1910 their number reached 5,000. [S.Mar.]

From 1948. The number of Jews rose from 5,000 in 1948 to 9,000 in 1958, as a result of the emigration of Syrian Jews to Lebanon. However, the numbers were subsequently depleted, especially as from 1967; and in 1969 only about 2,500 were left.

During the Israel War of Independence (1948), the internal unrest in Lebanon (1958), and the Six-Day War (1967), the Lebanese authorities ordered the police to protect the Jewish quarter in Wadi Abu Jamīl. The wealthy Jews living in new suburbs among members of other faiths were unharmed. In contrast to other Arab countries, Jewish life in Lebanon continued almost normally. In 1950 a bomb was planted by extremist Muslim nationalists underneath the *Alliance Israélite Universelle school building, causing the building to collapse. The Alliance administered three other institutions, in which 950 pupils studied in 1965. In addition 250 pupils attended the *talmud torah* and 80 studied at the Oẓar ha-Torah religious school. The Jewish scouts and Maccabi sports organization were closed by the government in 1953. The community council, which had nine members, was elected biennially. The Bikkur Ḥolim committee of the council was responsible for medical treatment of the poor, and their hospitalization if they were not Lebanese citizens. Its income derived from the *Arikha* (assessment) tax, paid by all males, as well as from endowments and from synagogues. Most Beirut Jews were merchants or employees of trading and financial enterprises.

[H.J.C.]

Bibliography: D. Goitein, in: *Eretz Israel,* 4 (1956), 152; G. Scholem, in: KS, 2 (1925/26), 103; I. Ben-Zvi, *Masot Ereẓ Yisrael le-Moshe Basola* (1938), 38–40; A. Yaari, *Masot Ereẓ Yisrael* (1946), 135f., 525f.; index; Ashtor, Toledot, 2 (1951), 121f.; S. Landshut, *Jewish Communities in the Muslim Countries of the Middle East* (1950), 54–56.

BEIT, SIR ALFRED (1853–1906), South African financier and co-founder, with Cecil Rhodes, of Rhodesia. Born in Hamburg, Beit learned the diamond trade in Amsterdam and went to South Africa in 1875. He became prominent in the development of the Kimberley diamond fields and later, of the Witwatersrand gold reefs. In 1889 he formed the partnership of Wernher, Beit, and Company, forerunner of one of the big Rand mining groups. Beit met Rhodes, and their careers became inseparable. His financial talents complemented those of Rhodes, and he became identified with Rhodes' imperial ambitions. Beit stood with Rhodes in the rivalry with *Barnato for the control of the diamond fields. He obtained the assistance of the London Rothschilds, and became a life governor in De Beers Consolidated Mines when it was formed in 1888. With Rhodes he established the British South Africa Company for the administration of the territory that became known as Rhodesia, and had a part in the development of the country second only to that of Rhodes himself. He was implicated in Rhodes' plot against the Kruger regime that ended in the Jameson Raid of 1895. He made generous

Sir Alfred Beit, co-founder of Rhodesia.

donations to South African war relief funds, founded the Beit professorship of colonial history at Oxford, and through the Wernher-Beit bequest stimulated university education in South Africa. Other bequests included

£1,200,000 for education and communications in Rhodesia and thirty fellowships in medical research. His brother, Otto John Beit (1865–1930), was associated with him in his financial activities and benefactions.

Bibliography: G. S. Fort, *Alfred Beit...* (1932); P. H. Emden, *Randlords* (1935), index; G. Saron and L. Hotz (eds.), *Jews in South Africa* (1955).

[D.L.S.]

BEIT JANN, Druze village in Upper Galilee, Israel. Lying at 3,082 ft. (940 m.) above sea level on the western slope of Mt. Meron, it is one of Israel's highest inhabited places. Although the identification of the village with the town Beth-Dagon of the tribe of Asher is no longer regarded as correct, Beit Jann seems to be the Galilean village Bet Dagan, reported in talmudic times as producing a certain late-ripening vegetable (Tosef., Shev. 7:13). In 1839 Scottish missionaries found here a few Jewish families, who apparently had moved from Safed 6.2 mi. (10 km.) to the east after the 1837 earthquake. With 4,110 inhabitants in 1968, Beit Jann is one of the major Druze centers in Israel. Its economy is based on fruit, beef cattle, and tobacco.

Druze village of Beit Jann, from the west. Jerusalem, J.N.F.

[E.O.]

BEIT JIMĀL, monastery and agricultural school in the Judean Foothills, 3 mi. (5 km.) S. of Bet-Shemesh, founded in 1881 by Salesian Fathers from Italy on the supposition that R. *Gamaliel I lived there and that the place was called after him. The site is supposed by some scholars to be identical with *Kefar Gamala, where the tomb of St. Stephen was located in the fifth century. Remnants of a church with a mosaic floor were discovered there in 1916.

[E.O.]

BEJA, town in S. Portugal; one of the seats of the subordinate rabbinates set up under the general control of the **Arraby Moor* in the 15th century. When the kingdom of Portugal was established in the 12th century, Jews are said to have been living already in Beja. In the charter *(foro)* granted to the town in the 13th century, nine clauses deal with the Jews, both resident and transient; most of them speak of established local usage. After the expulsion of the Jews from Portugal in 1496–97, Beja became a center of crypto-Judaism and many natives of the city appeared at autos-da-fé or escaped abroad. In the early years of the 18th century, a physician named Francisco de Sá e Mesquita spitefully denounced persons from Beja—on one occasion 66, on another 92—who, he said, had come together to observe Jewish rites. The name Beja was common among the Sephardim of the Orient: e.g., Ḥayyim Beja (c. 1810–1870) of Salonika, who subsequently became rabbi of Tyria in Asia Minor; and the scholar-preacher Isaac b. Moses *Beja.

Bibliography: J. Mendes dos Remedios, *Os judeus em Portugal,* 1 (1895), 422f.; Rosanes, Togarmah, 3 (1938), 115–7; A. da Silva Carvalho, *Noticia sôbre alguns medicos judeus do Alentejo* (1930), 47–48.

[C.R.]

BEJA, ISAAC BEN MOSES (c. 1570–1628), preacher in Salonika and Nikopolis (Bulgaria). Beja studied in Salonika. He was compelled to wander from one community to another until he was invited to teach at the yeshivah of Nikopolis. He arrived there after the city had been damaged in the war between the Turks and the Walachians (1595–99). Beja's homilies and eulogies, blended with Kabbalah, were published under the title *Bayit Ne'eman* (Venice, 1621); he also wrote poetry, and four of his poems appear in this work. His work displays originality both in thought and in his homiletical approach. His homily on the building of the synagogue of Nikopolis was reprinted under the title *"Keter Torah"* in *Le-Ohavei Leshon Ever* (Paris, 1628). There were two contemporaneous Salonikan scholars both named Isaac Beja; one died in 1635, the other in 1647.

Bibliography: Rosanes, Togarmah, 3 (1938^2), 115ff.; M. Molḥo, *Be-Veit ha-Almin shel Yehudei Saloniki,* 4 (1933), 13; I. S. Emmanuel, *Maẓẓevot Saloniki,* 1 (1963), 250f., 270.

[ED.]

BEJERANO, family of Israel industrialists. The brothers MOSHE (1902–1951) and SHIMON (1910–1971) BEJERANO were born in Plovdiv, Bulgaria, and educated in Switzerland. In 1921 they moved with their family to Milan, where they became active Zionists. Shimon settled in Palestine, in 1936, followed by Moshe three years later. Together they founded a cigarette factory, and acquired the Assis factory in Ramat Gan, which they developed into one of the largest syrup and canning enterprises in Israel. They became leaders of the Manufacturers' Association of Israel. Moshe served as Israel's first commercial attaché in Moscow and devoted himself to the development of commercial relations between Israel and the Far East. Shimon was active in the General Zionist Party, which he represented in the Second and Third Knessets.

[A.A.]

BEJERANO, BEKHOR ḤAYYIM BEN MOSES (1850–1931), Bulgarian rabbi and scholar. Bejerano was born in Eski-Zagra, Bulgaria, and studied under Zechariah ha-Levi of Salonika. He learned, in addition to his regular Torah studies, languages and other secular subjects. In 1880, he moved to Rushchuk, where he served as head of the community and where Solomon *Rosanes was one of his pupils. During the Russo-Turkish War (1878), Bejerano found a haven in Choumla. He afterward moved to Bucharest, where he was both a *dayyan* and principal of the school of the Sephardi community. His years in Bucharest were his most fruitful, both in terms of literary productivity and of personal gratification. He maintained close ties with Queen Elizabeth of Rumania and served as the official interpreter for Semitic languages of both the Rumanian royal house and of the official government institutions. His publication of several books in Rumanian earned him a government decoration. In 1908, Bejerano was chosen chief rabbi of Adrianople and in 1922, chief rabbi of Constantinople, a position he held until his death. Bejerano was famous for his generosity and was greatly honored in his lifetime. He was a corresponding member of the Spanish and French academies. His Hebrew articles appeared in *Ha-Maggid, Ḥavaẓẓelet, Ha-Me'assef,* and *Ha-Miẓpeh,* etc. He left many works in manuscript.

Bibliography: M. D. Gaon, *Yehudei ha-Mizraḥ be-Ereẓ Yisrael,* 2 (1938), 143f.

[Y.Al.]

BEKACHE, SHALOM (1848–1927), printer and publisher. He was born in Bombay of Baghdad origin. After studying in Safed, he became a rabbi in Acre and then migrated to Algeria, where he was rabbi of the Ben-Thoa Synagogue, the oldest in Algiers, for 40 years. He contributed to the Hebrew periodicals *Ha-Maggid, Ha-Meliẓ,* and *Ha-Ẓefirah.* In 1885 he published in Leghorn in Judeo-Arabic *Mevasser Tov,* a historical, geographical, and literary miscellany, which was followed by a monthly bulletin *Or ha-Levanah,* dedicated essentially to the history and geography of Ereẓ Israel; five issues were published. In about 1888 he established a small printing press in Algiers, which produced some 20 books in Judeo-Arabic, edited and translated by himself. These works, which deal with the history of the Jews of Babylonia and the kingdom of the Khazars in fictional form, were adapted to the intellectual standard of the Algerian Jews of that time and were useful in widening their historical knowledge. In 1891–93 Bekache published a weekly newspaper in Judeo-Arabic, *Beit Yisrael. Niẓẓahon ha-Or al ha-Ḥoshekh* ("Triumph of the Light over the Darkness," 1896) is a philosophical thesis in Hebrew presented in the form of a controversy between the Pharisees and the Sadducees.

Bibliography: ZHB, 2 (1897), 37–38; 7 (1903), 153–4.

[R.At.]

BEKEMOHARAR, family of 18th–19th century rabbis of Adrianople. MENAHEM BEN ISAAC ASHKENAZI (1666–1733) was born in Temesvár; he was two years old when his parents moved to Adrianople. He used to sign his name בכמוהר״ר (*BKMOHRR*=**B**en **K**evod **M**orenu **h**a-**R**av **R**abbi), to which abbreviation each of his descendants appended the initial letter of his own father's name. When Abraham Gheron was appointed rabbi of Adrianople in succession to his father-in-law Abraham Ẓarefati, six of the 13 congregations, disapproving the appointment, appointed Menahem b. Isaac as head of the *bet din.* He headed a large yeshivah and wielded great influence, the surrounding communities subjecting themselves to his authority. His works on Maimonides' *Mishneh Torah,* on Jacob b. Asher's *Arba'ah Turim,* and on Isaac b. Abba Mari's *Ha-Ittur,* as well as a homiletic work, were destroyed in a fire that broke out in Adrianople after his death. Another homiletic work, responsa, and novellae on the Talmud were saved. A small portion of the responsa that were saved was published in *Mikhtav Shelomo* by his grandson Solomon Bekemoharar. Menahem was also a kabbalist and a poet; his poem recited at circumcisions is well-known throughout Turkey and the Balkan states.

His son, MORDECAI B. MENAHEM (d. 1748), rabbi and halakhist, succeeded his father. Most of his *Ma'amar Mordekhai,* a commentary to Mordecai b. Hillel's commentary to tractates Yevamot and part of Ketubbot was destroyed by fire. The first three chapters of Yevamot which were rescued, were published (Salonika, 1874) with the text; appended are novellae on Maimonides' *Mishneh Torah* with assorted addenda. Still in manuscript are homilies and a talmudic commentary. Several of his responsa were published in his son's *Mikhtav Shelomo.*

MENAHEM (II) B. MORDECAI (d. 1781) succeeded his father. He was a halakhist and kabbalist and his halakhic decisions are still in manuscript. His son was Mordecai (II). NISSIM (a name added later) SOLOMON BEN MORDECAI

(1732?–1770?) began to write halakhic responsa at an early age. His works include: *Ḥeshek Shelomo* (Constantinople, 1768) on the first 68 chapters of *Ḥoshen Mishpat, Mikhtav Shelomo,* responsa (vol. 1, Salonika, 1855; vol. 2, appended to his father's *Ma'amar Mordekhai*), and *Beit Shelomo,* only a small part published in his grandson Menahem (IV)'s *Devar Emet.* His *Mirkevet ha-Mishneh,* on Maimonides' Yad, was almost identical with Aaron *Alfandari's work of the same name and as soon as Alfandari's work was published in Smyrna in 1755, Bekemoharar stopped working on his. His son, MORDECAI SIMEON BEN NISSIM SOLOMON (d. 1814?), rabbi and halakhist, traveled extensively between the communities in Turkey and the Balkans. He wrote *Matteh Shimon,* one of the most important works on the *Ḥoshen Mishpat* (till §258; in 3 vols.; Salonika, 1797–1819; volume three consists of responsa).

MORDECAI (II) BEN MENAHEM (II) (d. 1821) succeeded his father. Some of his halakhic decisions were published in *Mera Dakhya* (appended to vol. 3 of Mordecai Simeon b. Solomon's *Matteh Shimon*). The Jewish concessionaires in Constantinople appealed against his monopoly of the laudanum concession. In 1802, after a controversy in which the rabbis of Constantinople and Adrianople took part, his rights to the concession were reaffirmed. His son, MENAHEM (III) (d. 1810), was a member of the rabbinate during his father's lifetime, from about 1800. In 1801 a new congregation was formed in Rushchuk, comprising settlers from Adrianople, Vidin (Bulgaria), Belgrade, and Niš (Yugoslavia), which chose Menahem as rabbi. He left several works in manuscript.

JOSEPH RAPHAEL B. MORDECAI (II) (d. 1849) also served in the rabbinate during his father's lifetime. In 1839 the sultan Abdul Mejid appointed him head of all the congregations in Adrianople and its environs. His eldest son, MOSES RAḤAMIM (d. 1878), succeeded him in his lifetime (1846). Moses wrote responsa to questions addressed to his father and published *Nitpal la-Kodesh,* a compendium of his own responsa, together with the *Ma'amar Mordekhai* of Mordecai (I) b. Menahem. During the Russo-Turkish War (1878), he escaped to Constantinople, where he died. He was succeeded by his son, RAPHAEL (d. 1899), who was a member of the Bulgarian parliament. When independent Bulgaria was founded, the communities that came under Bulgarian rule severed their ties with the Adrianople rabbinate.

His son, MENAHEM (IV) B. MORDECAI SIMEON (1810?–1887), preacher and halakhist, was productive as a writer and as a publisher of the works of his family. His works include *Devar Emet* (Salonika, 1843), on the laws of Torah scrolls; *Devar Menaḥem* (2 vols., 1866–69), on Oraḥ Ḥayyim; *Devar ha-Mishpat* (Smyrna, 1874); *Menaḥem Avelim* (1880), on the laws of mourning. He was employed in a bank. During the Russo-Turkish War (1878), he escaped to Constantinople; in 1880, he immigrated to Ereẓ Israel, where he died. His grandson, YOM TOV, a scholar and a *maskil,* contributed in his youth to *Ha-Maggid,* participated in communal endeavors, and was a Bulgarian Zionist leader.

Bibliography: A. Danon, *Yosef Da'at* (1886), 66–67, 71–72, 82–88; Rosanes, Togarmah, 4 (1935), 252–3; 5 (1938), 34–40, 102–3, 149–52; 6 (1945), 109ff.; Marcus, in: *Mizraḥ u-Ma'arav,* 5 (1930–32), 173–84; idem, in: *Sinai,* 21 (1947), 48–63; Azuz, in: *Ḥemdat Yisrael . . . Ḥ. H. Medini* (1946), 164–7.

[Ed.]

BÉKÉSCSABA, city in S. E. Hungary. An organized community was formed there at the beginning of the 1830s. A synagogue was built in 1846, and another in 1893. A school was opened in 1855. After the schism in Hungarian

Jewry of 1868, the congregation of Békéscsaba joined the Orthodox party. In 1872 it became a status quo ante congregation, and in 1883 a separate Orthodox congregation was formed which in 1894 built its own synagogue and a school. The status quo congregation joined the "congress" organization in 1909. The Jewish population numbered 97 families in 1857, 2,322 persons in 1926, and 2,433 (4.6% of the total) in 1941. They were mainly occupied in commerce, especially grain dealing and industry; some owned factories. The Tevan (now Kner) printing press was founded in Békéscsaba in 1903. The scholar Eleazar *Gruenhut served as rabbi of the city. During World War II, 3,200 Jews (both local and others concentrated there) were deported from Békéscsaba, of whom 350 returned. In 1968 there were 151 Jews living there. The Orthodox synagogue still exists; the neologist synagogue was sold in 1961.

Bibliography: F. Révész, *A békéscsabai izraelita hitközség multja és jelenje* (1926).

[AL.SCH.]

BEKHOROT (Heb. בְּכוֹרוֹת; "Firstborn"), fourth tractate in the Mishnah, in the order of *Kodashim,* dealing in nine chapters, with the laws relating to the *firstborn, both of men and animals, and with allied subjects. The Scriptural regulations (Ex. 13:2, 11–13; 22:28–29; 34:19–20; Lev. 27:26; Num. 3:12–13; 18:15–18; Deut. 14:23; 15:19–23; Neh. 10:37) distinguish between three kinds of firstborn: (a) the firstling of unclean animals; (b) the firstling of clean animals; and (c) the firstborn of man. Numbers 18:15 seems to imply that the firstlings of all "unclean beasts" are to be redeemed, and this was the view of Philo, Josephus, and also the Karaites (see Albeck, Mishnah, *Seder Kodashim,* 153). But talmudic *halakhah,* relying on Exodus 13:13 and 34:20, both of which explicitly single out the ass, restricts the application in the case of unclean animals to the firstling of the ass, the subject of the first chapter of *Bekhorot.* Chapters 2–6 deal with the firstlings of clean animals. The question of blemish, which makes the firstling unfit as a sacrifice (Deut. 15:21), gets wide treatment. Chapter 7 digresses to discuss the kinds of blemish which make a kohen unfit for the priestly service (see Lev. 21:17–23). Chapter 8 deals with the firstborn of man. Apart from the question of redemption of the firstborn *(pidyon ha-ben),* it also deals with the privileges of the firstborn with regard to inheritance (Deut. 21:15–17). The concluding chapter presents an apparent deviation from the general subject of this tractate as it deals with the tithing of cattle (Lev. 27:32; II Chron. 31:6). This subject is, however, alluded to in preceding chapters (2:2 and 5:1), and there are, indeed, many points of similarity between the laws relating to the firstborn of clean animals and those relating to the tithing of cattle (see Albeck, *ibid.,* 154 and esp. 156 note 9).

Illustration of the first chapter of the tractate *Bekhorot,* which deals with the laws relating to the firstborn issue of man and of animals. Detail from a title page of a Hebrew and Latin edition of the Mishnah, Amsterdam, 1700–1704. Jerusalem, J.N.U.L.

The Babylonian *Gemara* widens the scope of the mishnaic discussion, but has comparatively few aggadic digressions. The strange legend about a supposed encounter and dispute between R. Joshua b. Hananiah and the Athenian sages (8b) deserves particular mention. Palestinian *Gemara* is missing for the whole order of *Kodashim* and it is a matter of controversy whether any ever existed. S. Friedlander's "discovery" of this *Gemara* (the first part of which, published in 1902, included *Bekhorot*) has proved a forgery (see H. L. Strack, *Introduction to the Talmud,* 1931, 68). The Tosefta covers the whole material of the Mishnah in seven chapters.

Bibliography: H. L. Strack, *Introduction to the Talmud and Midrash* (1945), 56, 263; P. Blackman (ed. and tr.) *Mishnayoth,* 5 (Eng., 1954), 241–2.

[A.Z.E.]

BEKHOR SHOR, JOSEPH BEN ISAAC (12th century), northern French exegete, tosafist, and poet. Referred to as Joseph Bekhor Shor, he has been identified with Joseph b. Isaac of Orleans, an identification which has been proved despite the doubts of various scholars. The designation Bekhor Shor ("Firstling Bullock") derives from the expression applied to Joseph (Deut. 33:17). He was the pupil of R. *Tam, who esteemed him greatly and referred to him in terms of high praise. Abraham b. Joseph of Orleans, mentioned several times in *tosafot,* was apparently his son. Joseph's commentary on the Pentateuch, parts of which previously appeared in various publications, was issued in its entirety by Joseph Gad (1956–60), while excerpts from his commentary on Psalms have been published in *Revue des Études Juives* (vol. 58 (1909), 309–11). In his exegesis, he adopted his French predecessors' method of literal interpretation—that of Rashi, Joseph Kara, and particularly Samuel b. Meir upon whom he largely based himself. Nevertheless, in many respects he pursued a new and original course, although in his efforts to produce novel interpretations his comments are sometimes rather strange and pilpulistic, particularly in the manner in which he relates passages to one another. He dwells at length on the biblical figures and investigates the motives for their actions but at times interprets these somewhat in terms of contemporary social conditions (Gen. 27:40). In many respects his exegesis is similar to that of the Spanish commentators, this being apparent in his efforts to explain away anthropomorphic expressions (Gen. 1:2; Num. 23:19); in defending the actions of the Patriarchs and rejecting any calumnies against them (Gen. 30:33); in interpreting miracles as almost natural phenomena (Gen. 19:26; Ex. 9:8); and in giving, to a greater extent than his French predecessors, a rational basis for the Commandments (Ex. 30:1; Lev. 19:27).

He pays little regard to grammar, nor is he as extreme as Samuel b. Meir in his homiletical comments, adding these occasionally alongside the literal interpretation (Gen. 3:24; Ex. 25:29). He makes use of *gematria* (Ex. 22:16), and at times incorporates in his comment a lengthy halakhic discussion of a passage, in these two respects being close to the exegetical method of the tosafists. He sharply opposes the allegorization of the Commandments, any neglect of which he vehemently assails (Lev. 17:13), adopting a similar attitude as regards the precepts of the *tefillin* and *mezuzah* (Deut. 6:9). This did not however prevent him from giving a literal interpretation of some passages contrary to the accepted *halakhah* (Ex. 23:19), which he naturally neither repudiates nor controverts. Joseph knew Latin, and both in speech and in writing refuted the christological interpretation of biblical passages, attacking in his comments both apostates and Christians, against whom he argued a great deal rejecting all attempts to find in the Bible allusions to Christian dogmas. He similarly repudiated their allegorical explanations that deny the validity of the Commandments. "Although they have translated the Bible from the holy tongue into the vernacular, the Lord has given them neither a heart to understand, nor eyes to see, nor ears to hear" (Num. 12:18). In his commentary on Genesis and Exodus he adds at the end of each weekly portion a brief poem in which he expresses his hopes and those of the Jewish people. He also wrote *piyyutim* in the style of the German and northern French *paytanim*, describing in them the sorrows that afflicted his generation. Several of these were published by Habermann in *Tarbiz* (vol. 9, 1937/38); others have not yet appeared in print.

Joseph of Orleans, i.e., Bekhor Shor, is mentioned in the *tosafot*; four of his halakhic questions addressed to R. Tam are preserved in *Sefer ha-Yashar*, while excerpts of many others are quoted by earlier authorities.

Bibliography: Liber, in REJ, 58 (1909), 307–14; N. Porges, *Joseph Bechor Schor* (Ger., 1908); S. Poznański (ed.), *Perush al Yeḥezkel u-Terei Asar le-R. Eli'ezer mi-Belganẓi* (1913), lv-lxxv; Urbach, Tosafot, 113–22; Abraham ben Azriel, *Arugat ha-Bosem*, ed. by E. E. Urbach, 4 (1963), index; G. Walter, *Joseph Bechor Schor, Der letzte nordfranzoesische Bibelexeget* (1890).

[Av.G.]

BEKKER (Baruch), PAUL (1882–1937), German music critic and writer. Bekker started his career as a violinist and conductor in his native Berlin, and from 1906 wrote music criticism for Berlin papers and was chief music critic of the *Frankfurter Zeitung* from 1911 to 1925. He did much to promote acceptance of the works of Gustav *Mahler, Franz Schreker, and Paul Hindemith. As supervisor of the State Theater in Cassel (1925–29), and at Wiesbaden (1929–32), he continued to foster contemporary music, especially operatic. In his books on music history and aesthetics he pioneered the application of sociological criteria to the understanding of musical creation and performance. His critical biography of Beethoven (1911, first English translation 1926) is considered a major contribution to the analysis of the creative process in music. In 1934 Bekker emigrated to the United States and became music critic of the *New Yorker Staatszeitung und Herold*. His other books include biographies of Oscar Fried (1907) and *Offenbach (1909); studies of the symphonies of Beethoven (1911, Eng. trans. 1925) and Mahler (1921), and the life of Wagner (1924, Eng. trans. 1931); *Neue Musik* (1923); *Musikgeschichte als Geschichte der musikalischen Formwandlungen* (1926); *Materiale Grundlagen der Musik* (1926); *Wandlungen der Oper* (1934; *The Changing Opera*, 1935); and *The Story of the Orchestra* (1936).

Bibliography: MGG s.v.; Baker, Biog Dict. s.v.

[B.B.]

BELAIS(H), ABRAHAM BEN SHALOM (1773–1853), Tunisian rabbi. At one time treasurer to the bey of Tunis, he had to leave the country following business reverses and settled in Jerusalem. For a time he was rabbi in Algiers, then, moving to Europe, he managed to secure the patronage of persons high in public life. He was appointed by the king of Sardinia rabbi of Nice, against the wishes of the community, with whom he promptly quarreled. In 1840, he went to London where before long he again got into financial difficulties and quarreled with the authorities. He was ultimately given a minor communal office and sat occasionally on the *bet din*. He published a large number of books, apart from his sycophantic odes in honor of European crowned heads and other influential persons. The following deserve mention: *Yad Avishalom* (1829), on *Oraḥ Ḥayyim; Peraḥ Shushan Beit Levi* (1844), sermons with English translation; *Petaḥ ha-Bayit* (1846), commentary and alphabetical index to part of the Shulḥan Arukh; responsa *Afrot Tevel* (1850); and an English translation of Ecclesiastes with his commentary. His undoubted scholarship was marred by his serious defects of character. Another Abraham (b. Jacob) Belaish (d. Jerusalem, c. 1828) was rabbi in Jerusalem and wrote a number of religious works.

Bibliography: JC (Sept. 2, 1853); A. M. Hyamson, *Sephardim of England* (1951), 208–9, 291; D. Cazès, *Notes bibliographiques sur la littérature juive-tunisienne* (1893), 20ff.; G. Levi, in: RMI, 12, no. 3–4 (1937/38), 129–62.

[D.Co.]

BEL AND THE DRAGON, two stories appearing in different versions in the Apocrypha, the Septuagint, and Theodotion; they appear as a continuation of the Book of Daniel. In "Bel," Daniel challenged the divinity of the idol Bel, which was reputed to eat and drink. By scattering ashes on the temple floor, he revealed the footprints of the priests who secretly removed the sacrifices placed before the idol. As a result the Persian king, Cyrus, destroyed the idol and killed the priests. In "The Dragon," Daniel caused the death of a dragon worshiped by the Babylonians, by feeding it a mixture of pitch, fat, and hair. Thrown into the lion's den at the crowd's demand, he was miraculously unharmed and survived for a week without food, after which he was fed by the prophet Habakkuk who was miraculously transported to Babylon (see Prophecy of *Habakkuk). The king thereupon praised God and had Daniel's accusers thrown to the lions who devoured them. The object of these stories is to portray the futility of idolatry. The suggestions that they are either a "Jewish version" of the Babylonian Marduk and Tiamat legend, or propaganda against Hellenistic idolatry, seem improbable. They appear to be popular works composed in Babylon when Bel was no longer worshiped, i.e., between the destruction of the temple of Babylon by Artaxerxes (485–465 B.C.E.) and its rebuilding by Alexander the Great (332 B.C.E.). Snakes (= dragons) were used in the Babylonian cult, and the stories were perhaps a midrashic elaboration of Jeremiah 51:34, 44. The two Greek versions seem to be translations from an Aramaic original. A version from the *Midrash Bereshit Rabbati* of R. Moses ha-Darshan (published by A. Neubauer, Book of Tobit (1878), Hebrew portion p. 39–40) as well as by Ch. Albeck (1940, p. 175) is found in the *Pugio Fidei* of Raymond *Martini (p. 957). These two versions are almost identical with the Syriac *Peshitta*. An Aramaic version of Bel and the Dragon in the *Chronicle of Jerahmeel* is based on Theodotion. A Hebrew fragment is preserved in Genesis R. 68:20 and a Hebrew version is found in *Josippon (3).

[Y.M.G.]

BELASCO, DAVID (1859–1931), U.S. theatrical producer and playwright. Born in San Francisco, Belasco came from a Portuguese-Jewish family named Valasco. As a boy in Victoria, British Columbia—where his father, a one-time clown, owned a store—he joined a circus. At the age of 11 he appeared at the Victoria Theater in Charles Kean's production of *Richard III.* Working as a stage manager on the Pacific Coast, he devised melodramas with fires and battles and a passion play with real sheep. In 1879 he went to New York, where his name became associated with sensational scenic effects. He was a pioneer in the use of electricity for stage lighting. Belasco's first melodrama, *La Belle Russe,* was produced at Wallack's Theater in 1882. He established the Lyceum School of Acting and produced successes such as *Du Barry* and *Zaza.* In 1902 he opened the first of two theaters, both called "The Belasco," where he introduced innovations such as footlights sunk below stage level. His 374 productions displayed a passion for flamboyant realism. His greatest successes as a playwright were *Madame Butterfly* (1900, based on a story by J. L. Long) and *The Girl of the Golden West* (1905), both turned into operas by Puccini. Belasco's work was primarily in melodrama and though the literary worth of his plays was slight, he was able to satisfy the contemporary demand for spectacular staging. His production of *The Merchant of Venice* (1922), with David *Warfield as Shylock, was regarded as the finest artistic achievement of his career.

[B.G.]

BELAYA TSERKOV (Heb. שְׂדֵה לָבָן; "White Field"), ancient town in Kiev oblast, Ukrainian S.S.R., center of a fertile agricultural region. A community was formed there toward the end of the 16th century; 100 houses in Jewish ownership out of a total of 800 are recorded in 1646. The community was destroyed during the *Chmielnicki rising in 1648, and again suffered at the beginning of the *Haidamack rising in 1703. Subsequently, Jews again began to settle there, in 1765 numbering 1,876 polltax-payers in the town and its vicinity. After Belaya Tserkov had been attacked by the hordes under Cossack general Gonta (1768) only 223 Jewish inhabitants remained. The community increased to 1,077 in 1787; 6,665 in 1847; and 18,720 in 1897 (54% of the total). The grain trade and sugar industry contributed to the growth of the town during the 19th century. The Jews there suffered from pogroms in 1905. During the civil war of 1919–20 about 850 Jews were massacred in Belaya Tserkov by Ukrainian troops, bands of peasants, and soldiers of the White Army. The religious and cultural life of the community, which numbered 15,624 (36.4%) in 1926, came to an end with the establishment of the Soviet government. In August 1943, after the Nazi occupation of the town, the approximately 3,000 Jews who remained in Belaya Tserkov and the surrounding districts were killed. There were 5,600 Jews listed in Belaya Tserkov in the 1959 census. Its sole synagogue was closed in 1962 and thereafter Jews conducted private prayer services. During the 1965 High Holidays, militia broke into such *minyanim,* arrested participants and confiscated religious articles. In 1970 the Jewish population was estimated at 15,000. In Jewish folklore Belaya Tserkov is also referred to as the "Black Abomination" (Yid. *Shvartse Tume*), a play on its name in Russian ("White Church").

Bibliography: S. Ettinger, in: *Zion,* 21 (1956), 107–42; *Die Judenpogrome in Russland* 2 (1909), 406–8; A. D. Rosenthal, *Megillat ha-Tevaḥ,* 1 (1927), 78–81; *Eynikeyt,* no. 24 (1945).

[Y.S.]

BELCHATOW (Pol. **Bełchatów**), small town 28 mi. S. of Lodz, central Poland, in the district of Piotrkow. Seven Jews are recorded as living in Belchatow in 1764. Jewish settlement increased after the formation of Congress *Poland. By 1897 there were 2,897 Jewish residents out of a total population of 3,859, mainly engaged in the flourishing textile industry which developed in the 19th century. In 1921 the Jewish population numbered 3,688 (59% of the total), and in 1939, 6,000, constituting one-third of the total population.

[Ed.]

Holocaust and Postwar Periods. The German army took the town during the first week of the war, during the High Holidays. Many Jews dressed in *tallit* and *kittel* were humiliated in the streets and photographed by German soldiers. The Torah Scrolls and other liturgical objects were taken from the local synagogues and burned while the congregation was forced to dance around the pyre. Jewish property was looted, goods in Jewish warehouses were confiscated, and the Jews were evicted from their homes and sent on forced labor. There was no formal ghetto, but a few streets were earmarked as the Jewish district. Numerous refugees from the smaller towns and villages were crowded into this small area. Frequent German raids took place in which able-bodied men were kidnapped and deported.

The final liquidation of the Jewish community took place in August 1942 when close to 1,000 able-bodied Jews were sent to the *Lodz ghetto and 5,000 Jews were deported to the death camp in *Chelmno. No Jewish community was established in Belchatow after the war.

[De.D.]

Bibliography: I. Trunk, in: *Bleter far Geshikhte,* 2 no. 1–4 (1949), 64–166; D. Dabrowska, in: BŻIH, no. 13–14 (1955); idem (ed.), *Kronika getta lodzkiego,* 2 vols. (1965–66), passim; *Belkhatov Yisker Bukh* (Yid., 1951).

BELED, village in Sopron county, Hungary. Jews settled there in the mid-18th century. A synagogue and cemetery were established about 1790. Beled subsequently became the main Jewish organizational and cultural center for the district, its cemetery serving the communities at Szil and neighboring villages. The congregation remained strictly Orthodox. The Jewish population formed 3.7% of the total population of Beled in 1785, and numbered 209 in 1828 (10.2%), 278 in 1865 (11.7%), and 336 in 1930 (11.3%).

During World War II there were 350 Jews living in Beled. They were subsequently sent to forced labor camps or deported to *Auschwitz in July 1944. The synagogue was destroyed by the vandalism of the German army and *Arrow Cross organization. Forty-two survivors returned in 1945. Most emigrated or left. In 1968 there was one Jewish resident in Beled.

Bibliography: M. Stein, *Magyar Rabbik,* 3 (1907), 1f.; 5 (1909), 3f.; M. Raab, in: *Soproni Szemle* (1957), 244–52.

[L.H.]

°**BELEV, ALEXANDER** (1900–1944), first commissar for Jewish affairs in *Bulgaria (1942–43). He was one of the founders of the anti-Semitic organization Ratnik, and became an official of the ministry of the interior. Belev was sent in 1941 to Germany to study methods of enforcing anti-Jewish legislation and, in September, 1942, he became head of the Commissariat for Jewish Affairs. He collaborated closely with Dannecker, *Eichmann's representative in Bulgaria, with whom he signed an agreement on Feb. 22, 1943, to deport 20,000 Jews. Belev implemented the anti-Semitic "Law for the Protection of the Nation" (which had been passed on Dec. 24, 1940) with cruelty and sometimes exceeded his authority in order to gain his end—the deportation of all Bulgarian Jewry, but he succeeded only in deporting "to the East" the Jews from the Yugoslav and Greek territories under Bulgarian military occupation. His wide powers earned him the nickname

"King of the Jews." When Bulgaria was conquered by the Soviet Army in September, 1944, Belev attempted to flee with the Germans, but he was caught by the militia and disappeared without a trace. He was sentenced to death *in absentia* by a People's Court in Sofia in 1945.

Bibliography: B. J. Arditi, *Yehudei Bulgaryah bi-Shenot ha-Mishtar ha-Naẓi 1940–44* (1962), index; EG, 10 (1967).

[O.A.]

BELFAST, capital of Northern Ireland. The earliest reference to Jews in Belfast dates from 1652. Mention of a "Jew Butcher" in 1771 suggests the existence of the nucleus of a community. Jews are again recorded in the 1840s. D. J. Jaffe, who settled in Belfast in 1851, established a congregation in 1869 and built its first synagogue in 1871/72. Joseph *Chotzner was the first minister (1869–80; and again 1893–97). After 1881 the community increased with the arrival of Jewish refugees from Russia. These at first formed their own congregation but in 1903 joined the main congregation. A municipal Jewish elementary school was established in 1898. Sir Otto *Jaffe, twice lord mayor and once high sheriff, served for many years as the congregation's president and built its second synagogue in 1904. Isaac *Herzog served as rabbi of Belfast from 1915 to 1919, followed in 1926 by Jacob Shachter, and in 1954 by Alexander Carlebach (until 1965). In 1967 the Jewish population numbered about 1,350. In that year, a new synagogue building was consecrated.

Interior of the Belfast synagogue consecrated in 1967. Architect: Yorke Rosenberg Mardall.

Bibliography: B. Shillman, *Short History of the Jews in Ireland* (1945), 134–6; Carlebach, in: JHSET, 21 (1968), 261ff.; idem, in: JC, Suppl. (July 30, 1965); L. Hyman, *Jews of Ireland* (1972).

[C.R.]

BELFORT, capital of the territory of Belfort, eastern France. A grant of privilege conferred on the city in 1307 authorized Jewish residence. Persecutions of Jews living in Belfort are recorded in 1336. They were subsequently expelled and readmitted in 1689. During the French Revolution anti-Jewish excesses took place in the region but the Jews in Belfort remained unharmed. The Jewish population increased considerably after the Franco-Prussian war (1870–71) with the arrival of Jews from Alsace-Lorraine (then annexed to the German Empire) who wished to remain French.

Holocaust and Postwar Periods. The Belfort Jewish community was destroyed under Nazi occupation. Out of a total of 700 Jews, about 245 were killed. A monument bearing the names of those who perished was erected in the Jewish cemetery after the war. The community was dynamically rebuilt after World War II, and together with the Montbeliard Jewish community numbered about 1,300 persons in 1969. It had a synagogue with an acting minister, a communal center, a network of institutions, and a quarterly bulletin.

The synagogue in Belfort, built in 1862.

Bibliography: Salfeld, Martyrol, 68, 240; A. Corret, *Histoire pittoresque et anecdotique de Belfort* (1855), 263–72; Z. Szajkowski, *Analytical Franco-Jewish Gazetteer* (1966), 165.

[R.Be.]

BELFORTE, SOLOMON (19th century), printer of Leghorn. Belforte was both a scholar and an able businessman; he established a new printing house in Leghorn in 1834. In addition to books for the religious needs of Italian Jewry, such as the Pentateuch, Mishnayot, *maḥzorim*, and other books in Hebrew and Italian, Belforte printed prayer books for the Jewish communities of North Africa and even for the Jews of Yemen. At the end of the 19th century he was also a partner in a bookselling business. In 1926 the printing house employed 100 workers and published several catalogs. After the establishment of the State of Israel, all the equipment of the printing house, including the many matrices, were transferred to Tel Aviv.

[A.M.H.]

BELGIUM, West European kingdom.

The Medieval Community. Jews first appeared in the southern Netherlands during the early 13th century, although the exact date of their settlement there cannot be ascertained. They arrived from the east, most probably from the large Rhenish communities, and did not migrate further south than *Brussels and Mechlin (*Malines). Most of the immigrants settled along, or within proximity of the Cologne-Bruges axis. Jews are mentioned in Jodoigne (in Brabant province) in about 1200; in Louvain, where a small community lived precariously, in about 1220; in Tirlemont in about 1230; and in Brussels shortly before 1260. In his will (1261) Duke Henry III ordered that "all Jews and usurers be expelled from the province of Brabant. They are to be totally extirpated until not even one remains, unless they undertake to engage in commerce after the fashion of other merchants and agree to cease their practice of moneylending and usury." Apparently their expulsion was not implemented. When consulted, Thomas *Aquinas recommended that the Jews should be taxed moderately, so as not to deprive them of the necessary means to lead a decent existence. He added that it was preferable to compel them to earn their livelihood by manual labor rather than become wealthy by the practice of usury. The fact remains that they were not disturbed in any of their occupations. The organization of a crusade in 1309 brought this comparative tranquillity to an end. After the massacre of Jews in Louvain who had refused baptism, Duke John II took the survivors under his protection. Jews later returned to Louvain, and in 1311 had their own rabbi. The number of Jews throughout Brabant during this period was not large.

As a result of the expulsion from France in 1306, a number of exiles found refuge in the province of Hainaut. They were scattered in about ten localities, the community in Mons being the most important. In 1326, a converted Jew was put to death in Cambron, on a charge of stabbing an image of the Virgin. In 1337, the count of Hainaut renewed his protection of the Jews. A census on this occasion showed 18 Jewish families, comprising 35 adults. They subsequently scattered in other cities in Hainaut, but their numbers remained small. The Black Death (1348–49) calamitously disrupted the existence of these communities. Accused of having introduced the plague by poisoning the wells, the Jews were either massacred by the populace or executed by the authorities. Almost all the Jews in Brabant were done to death. In Brussels the community ceased to exist. The massacre may have spread to *Antwerp, and few communities in Hainaut remained unscathed.

Thus the Jews disappeared almost completely from Hainaut. In Brabant, however, tiny communities were reestablished. There were seven families living in Brussels in 1368 and two in Louvain. In 1370 the Jews in Brussels and Louvain were accused of desecrating the Host, and after confessions extracted by torture a number were burned at the stake. The Jews thus disappeared also from Brabant. The role and number of the Jews in medieval Belgium were unimportant. Mainly petty moneylenders, their restricted numbers prevented them from wielding any influence in the economic life of the country. They were generally regarded as foreigners and as such exposed to violent hostility.

The Resettlement Period. It is only in the early 16th century that Jews again appeared in the southern Netherlands. At that time, Portuguese merchants made their way to the north, attracted by the economic development of the Netherlands, first to Bruges and then to Antwerp. Possibly the majority of them were *Marranos whose presence was sanctioned by a safe-conduct accorded to the New Christians in 1526. The newcomers consolidated their presence in Antwerp, notwithstanding a number of inconsistent measures concerning them. For a number of them, such as the future Duke of Naxos, Joseph *Nasi, or the physician *Amatus Lusitanus, Antwerp was only a place of transit en route to the hospitable Turkish haven. The Marrano population of Antwerp gradually increased with the intensification of their persecution in Portugal. However, with the establishment of an open Jewish community in *Amsterdam, the main tide of Marrano settlement was diverted to that place and to Holland generally. On the other hand, the Dutch Jews now not infrequently visited Brussels or Antwerp, sometimes for prolonged periods, without suffering serious inconvenience. When Antwerp passed under Austrian rule in 1713, the community was at last able to profess Judaism more openly. With the occupation of the Netherlands by the French revolutionary armies in 1794, Jews were able to settle freely in Brussels and Antwerp. From the early 18th century, there was also a slight immigration of Ashkenazi Jews to Belgium. The authorities took care to limit their numbers by the imposition of special taxes which aroused vehement protests by the Dutch Jews, who rejected this attempt at discrimination.

Under French domination, Belgian Jewry, which then numbered some 800 persons, was incorporated into the *Consistory of Krefeld; the administrative framework disappeared with the downfall of Napoleon's empire. The principal communities in Belgium at the time were in Antwerp, Brussels, Herentals, Liège, and Mons. From 1831, once Belgian independence was achieved, the Jewish religion received official recognition, religious freedom being an integral part of the constitution guaranteed by the Concert of Europe. However, the synagogue councils were not officially recognized until 1870. The organization of Belgian Jewry remained strongly influenced by the Napoleonic prototype. Centralized in Brussels, it was administered by the Consistoire Central Israélite de Belgique.

Throughout the 19th century, Belgian Judaism developed on the French pattern. At the end of the century, however, as a result of the influx of immigration from Central and Eastern Europe, Belgian Jewry underwent a process of bipolarization which has lasted to the present day. Brussels was the center of French influences while in the Antwerp community Yiddish influences, and accessorily Flemish, were equally strong; occasionally conflicts arose between the two. In 1900, Antwerp numbered some 8,000 Jews, the greater part intending emigrants en route to the United States. The sudden impetus given to the diamond industry by the discovery of mines in South Africa opened numerous possibilities of employment in Antwerp. After an interruption during World War I, when part of the Jewish population migrated to Holland, the increase was resumed. The massive immigration to Antwerp, as well as the local particularism, rapidly resulted in a marked difference in character between Antwerp Jewry and the main body in Belgium, not only from the economic aspect,

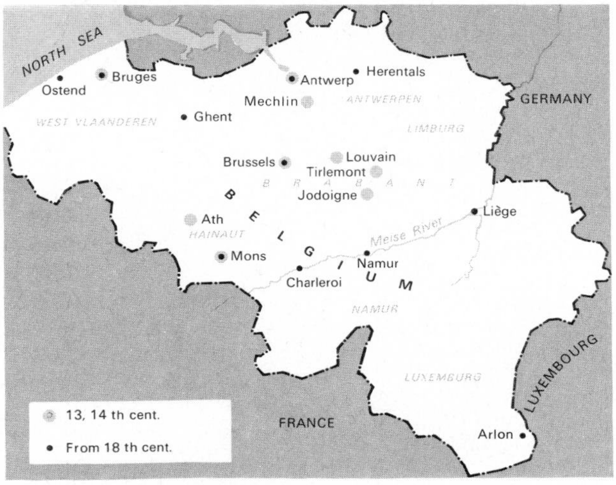

The Jewish communities of Belgium.

but also from the aspect of its anxiety to retain the traditional forms of Jewish life. As a result the Antwerp community resisted assimilation with more success than neighboring Brussels. This was also due to the care taken to ensure that almost every child should attend a Jewish school. The Jewish community of Antwerp remained faithful to its East European origins and was rightly considered as a bulwark of European Judaism. The Brussels community, as well as the smaller communities, had also benefited from a strong numerical contribution from Eastern Europe, but this had little effect on its structure or character. The Belgian government's restrictive naturalization policies encouraged the continued cohesion of the Antwerp community, whose members represented some 75% of the local manpower employed in the diamond industry and commerce.

[S.Sch.]

Holocaust Period. The study of the Holocaust in Belgium has been complicated by lack of unified research and by contradictory accounts. Furthermore, as the Belgian Constitution does not allow any mention of religion on documents of civil status, exact official data are lacking.

When the German army invaded on May 10, 1940, between 90,000 and 110,000 Jews lived in Belgium, among whom there were probably about 20,000 German refugees. Only 5–10% of the Jews in Belgium were of Belgian nationality, while the majority of Jews who immigrated to Belgium from other countries had to remain foreign nationals. Antwerp had at that time at least 55,000 Jews, forming Belgium's largest, and economically, socially, and culturally most closely knit Jewish community, and thus suffered more heavily than the loosely knit community in Brussels (at least 35,000) and the other smaller communities: Charleroi, with at least 2,000 Jews; Liège, 2,000; Ghent, 300; and Namur, 50. At the time of the invasion, the adult males among the German-Jewish refugees were treated as suspect aliens although many had volunteered for the Belgian Army. They were rounded up by the Belgian police and interned in the Gurs camp in France. Their families remained behind, many reliant on the social welfare committees of the Jewish communities.

The majority of Jews from Belgium fled the country, mainly southward toward France. Some managed to escape German occupation and emigrated overseas; others were overtaken by the German armies and ordered to turn back. Many who reached unoccupied France were lured back to Belgium a few months later in accordance with Nazi policy at the time to assuage the fears of the Jews and prevent the rise of antagonism among the non-Jewish population. Belgium capitulated on May 28, 1940, and was held under military rule until the liberation in September 1944. The German military occupation set up a Belgian administration in charge of civilian affairs, which was instructed by the Wehrmacht to carry out anti-Jewish measures. This situation was more favorable than that for the Jews in the *Netherlands, where the *Gestapo was in charge of carrying out anti-Jewish measures. The anti-Jewish policy was executed in two stages. The preparatory phase circumscribed the Jewish population, ordered their geographic fixation, and brought about gradual economic and social paralysis. The exterminatory phase, which began on July 22, 1942, consisted of labor call-ups, followed by roundups and razzias for internment in the Dossin assembly camp near Mechlin (Malines). From there, the inmates were deported to extermination camps in the east.

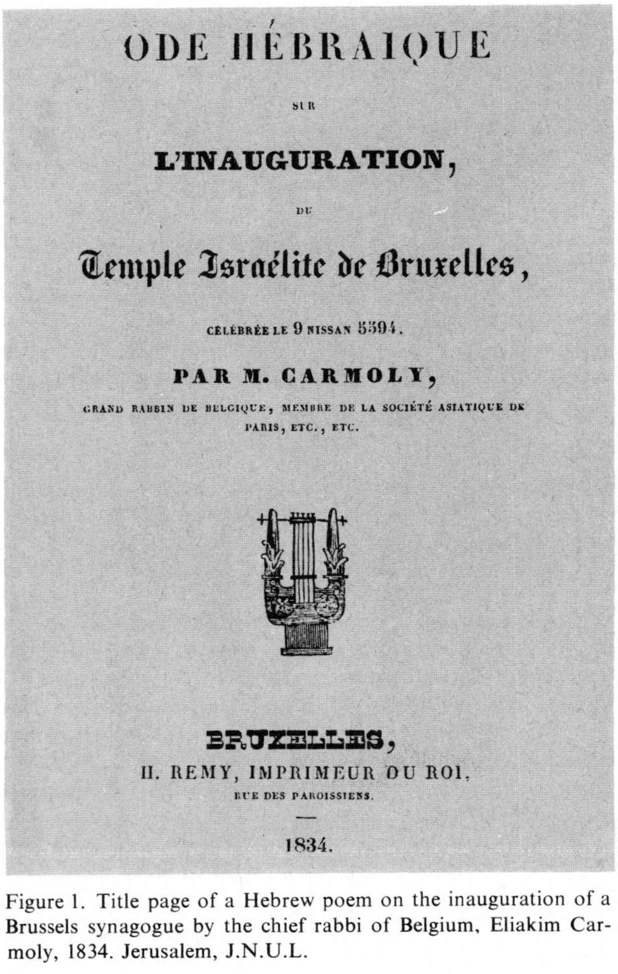
ODE HÉBRAIQUE

SUR

L'INAUGURATION,

DU

Temple Israélite de Bruxelles,

CÉLÉBRÉE LE 9 NISSAN 5594.

PAR M. CARMOLY,

GRAND RABBIN DE BELGIQUE, MEMBRE DE LA SOCIÉTÉ ASIATIQUE DE PARIS, ETC., ETC.

BRUXELLES,

H. REMY, IMPRIMEUR DU ROI,

RUE DES PAROISSIENS.

1834.

Figure 1. Title page of a Hebrew poem on the inauguration of a Brussels synagogue by the chief rabbi of Belgium, Eliakim Carmoly, 1834. Jerusalem, J.N.U.L.

The succession of edicts followed that in other Nazi-occupied countries, though what the Germans termed the "lack of understanding of the local population," and the courageous and well-supported Jewish resistance did slow up the persecution somewhat. The tragic and still not forgotten experience in Belgium of German occupation during World War I brought about more immediate and efficient resistance than in the Netherlands. The first edicts were issued in October 1940. Ritual slaughter was forbidden (Oct. 23, 1940). The first sign of racial discrimination was the ordinance of Oct. 28, 1940, which defined who was a Jew and prohibited the further return of Jews to Belgium. It required all Jews above the age of 15 to register at the communal administration and have the letter J stamped on their identity cards. The registration affected about 42,000 Jews; apparently 10,000–13,000 Jews did not register at all. Jewish property had to be registered, and was not transferable. Notices of Jewish ownership in three languages (Flemish, French, and German) had to be posted. Jews in the fields of law, education, and communication were prohibited from practicing their professions. The first protest was raised by the Belgian associates of Jewish professional men and the Belgian administration in the case of discriminatory legislation bearing on Jews in the professions. They objected to the anti-constitutional character of the anti-Jewish legislation and claimed they were unable to carry it out. The Belgian government in exile, residing in London, laid down a decision on Jan. 10, 1941, that all laws imposed by the German occupation which contradict the Belgian Constitution would be annulled at the time of liberation.

In 1941, further edicts were issued to restrict and paralyze Jewish life: edicts for confiscation of radios (May 31); enforced declaration of bank holdings (June 10); prohibition against residing outside the four large cities of Antwerp, Brussels, Liège, and Charleroi (August 29); and a curfew between 8 p.m. and 7 a.m. (August 29). On Nov. 25, 1941, the German military commander for Belgium and northern France ordered the formation of a Judenrat, called Association des Juifs en Belgique (AJB), under the pretext of organizing Jewish social welfare for the community and furthering Jewish emigration. A national committee of seven representatives was to encompass all Jews and take over existing Jewish bodies and their property. Rabbi T. S. Ullman, the only rabbi of Belgian nationality, accepted the presidency only after consultation with high Belgian authorities. Local committees were formed in Brussels, Antwerp, Charleroi, and Liège. Although no documents attest to the modes of constitution of these committees, there are indications that the Germans held sway over the choice of their members. In the course of time, the members of the AJB committees were utilized by the Germans as a front for carrying out their own aims. On Dec. 1, 1941, the Judenrat was ordered to set up an educational system for Jewish children who were expelled at that time from the public schools by the Germans.

The AJB was ordered to hold another census of the Jews and, by March, forced to take charge of the distribution of call-ups to be accompanied by covering letters pressing for conformance to the orders. In September 1942, the AJB leaders were interned in the concentration camp of Breendonck and charged with insufficient diligence in carrying out German orders. The AJB president was released after a week and resigned. Razzias now replaced call-ups, and the AJB's job was largely limited to mitigating the suffering of the deportees. Officially, however, they were permitted to continue their activities. They set up children's homes and old-age homes, and their employees and administrators were "protected," i.e., not liable for deportation. The underground took advantage of this status by introducing some of its people into positions within the AJB and utilized its resources, despite all the risks involved.

On May 27, 1942, the Nazis issued an order for every Jew to wear the yellow badge. The Belgian administration refused to promulgate the order and the Germans were forced to do it themselves, but a few days later they imposed the task on the AJB. The Belgian population showed its hostility to this discriminatory measure, expressing its sympathy in various ways. By June 1, 1942, Jewish doctors, dentists, and nurses were forbidden to practice, except for Jewish patients. Previously (March 2 and May 8), forced labor for the Nazi organization Todt had been imposed theoretically on all the unemployed, but was in fact aimed at the Jews, who had been evicted from all economic pursuit. The underground issued pleas not to submit to these labor call-ups. By July 1942, summonses were issued to unemployed Jews to report to Malines for "work in the east." At first the summonses were meekly obeyed, but the resistance movements' warnings started taking effect and people went into hiding. As the call-ups provided insufficient numbers of "volunteers," the Germans commenced their razzias. The first convoy of 1,000 Jews left on Sept. 2, 1942. Within five weeks, 10,000 had been deported. Later, the deportations slowed down. By July 31, 1944, 25,631 victims had been deported in 31 convoys. Only 1,244 of the deportees returned after the war. Belgian leaders, among them the queen mother Elisabeth and Cardinal van Roey, intervened on behalf of the small number of Jews of Belgian nationality, and the Germans agreed to omit them from expulsion as long as they would not transgress German laws. This show of tolerance was short-lived. On Sept. 3, 1943, the Jews holding Belgian citizenship were all rounded up and deported.

Resistance. The Jewish population required time to organize resistance. Some Jews individually joined the ranks of the Belgian underground. But after the dissolution of Jewish organizations, the former social and political groups started regrouping, mainly for the purpose of mutual social help. Anti-fascist elements grasped the significance of the persecutions sooner and formed a group of about 70 Jewish armed partisans, many of whom fell in the line of duty. An estimated 140 fell, including those who fought as individuals in the general armed resistance. The Committee for Jewish Defence (CDJ, recognized officially after the war as a civilian resistance group affiliated to the Front de l'Indépendance) comprised a complete range of Jewish groups and individuals. It soon realized the need to hide Jews, and called upon all the Jews to resist and disobey any German edicts as well as instructions from the AJB. The Committee developed a vast, well-organized network of activity for hiding children (an estimated 3,000 children were thus saved) and adults (an estimated 10,000). In fact, in Belgium a high proportion of Jews was saved compared to other occupied countries. Places of hiding, identity papers, food ration tickets, and money were obtained, and escape routes established toward Switzerland and Spain. The cultural aspect of the Jewish resistance groups was

Figure 2. A pro-Israel demonstration in Brussels on June 6, 1967, the second day of the Six-Day War. Photo *Le Soir*, Brussels.

remarkable. They distributed information and propaganda material, established a lending library, and maintained a Jewish illegal press. The Yiddish paper *Unzer Vort* appeared 28 times, and *Flambeau* in French and the *Vrije Gedachte* in Flemish appeared with the help of the Belgian illegal press.

Contacts were made with numerous non-Jewish organizations who helped, including Oeuvre Nationale de l'Enfance, Jeunesse Ouvrière Catholique, the Red Cross, a number of Catholic institutions, and underground resistance movements. As time went on, more and more money was needed to keep alive those in hiding. Millions of francs were contributed by local Jews and non-Jewish organizations and credit was allotted. Later, large sums were secretly obtained through Switzerland, and some came from the Belgian government in exile. A number of people managed to escape from deportation trains in a feat unique to occupied Belgium. The 20th convoy departing on April 19, 1943, was attacked in a well-organized action initiated by the CDJ together with Georges Livchitz and partisans of Group "G" (an armed resistance group). It enabled several hundred to escape, although many of them were caught or killed by the Germans. Another Jewish underground group, the Ninth Brigade, was organized under the aegis of the Mouvement National Belge, a more rightist group. A little-known and rather circumscribed resistance activity was carried out by the federation of the Zionist parties, which succeeded in obtaining through Switzerland a few immigration certificates to Palestine which protected the holders from deportation. At one point (1941–42) a *hakhsharah* (agricultural training program) for members of Zionist youth movements was provided. According to partial studies and reports by former participants, there were innumerable cases (not generally known) of underground activity, including armed attacks on collaborators, sabotage, and withdrawing those children in hiding who were exposed and in danger of arrest by the Gestapo.

The Catholic Church on many occasions intervened on behalf of the Belgian Jews through the work of Cardinal van Roey, who acted mainly through his secretary Canon Leclef. On Aug. 4, 1942, he alerted the Vatican to the inhumanity of the racial laws, pointing out that even Catholics of Jewish origin were affected. The Church was largely efficacious through its request to Catholic institutions to hide Jewish children and to refrain from baptizing them, unless specific permission was given. When the German-Jewish refugees in Antwerp were deported at the end of 1940 to the province of Limburg, the priests instructed the local population to help them. When the Jews were compelled to wear the yellow badge, priests denounced this discriminatory act and elicited the sympathy of large parts of the population. The Belgians made attempts to allay Jewish suffering, though prior to the invasion, the Germans had encouraged Flemish nationalism and separatism and fanned anti-Semitism. For this reason the persecutions met with greater success in the mostly Flemish Antwerp region. [R.BA.]

Contemporary Period. In 1945 the Jewish population was composed of those who had remained in the country, had returned from exile, or were liberated from prisons and camps. Until about 1955, thousands of Jewish refugees from Eastern and Central Europe resided in Belgium for a limited time, awaiting immigration permits to other countries of permanent settlement. In the 1960s both emigration and immigration considerably decreased. The number of Jews in Belgium in 1970 was about 40,000. This population, essentially urban, was distributed approximately as follows: Brussels, 18,000; Antwerp, 12,000; Liège, 1,000; Charleroi, 500; Ghent, Ostend, and Arlon, 1,000; the remainder was dispersed among other cities. As the Jewish population has become stable, social and economic integration within Belgian society has improved in many respects. It is not especially difficult to obtain citizenship, and a great number of immigrants and their descendants are therefore Belgian citizens. Although many arrived in the country without independent resources, within a short period they have displayed great social mobility. The majority now belong to the middle class and are active in the fur and textile industry, wholesale and retail trade, crafts, and the manufacture of clothing and leather goods. Antwerp Jewry has been professionally concentrated for a long time in the diamond industry and trade. Since the end of World War II, more young people have undertaken university studies, resulting in the growth of the professional and white-collar classes. Though the country's economic progress benefited the Jewish population, there is still a small number of underprivileged persons and social cases, most of whom are cared for by the community. The favorable attitude of the government and communal authorities, as well as the population as a whole, has facilitated the integration of Jews in Belgium, though from time to time certain manifestations of anti-Semitism have been provoked by small factions of the extreme right.

The Jewish religion is legally recognized along with the Catholic and the Protestant religions. Belgian laws also guarantee public Jewish worship. There are 12 recognized Jewish communities in the country: four in Brussels, three in Antwerp, and one each in Liège, Charleroi, Ghent, Ostend, and Arlon. Two of these communities are Sephardi, the others are Ashkenazi. The rabbis, cantors, and synagogue boards are elected by the members of the community. Each community has proportional representation at the Consistoire Central Israélite de Belgique, which represents the communities in their relations with the state. Though this institution, of Napoleonic origin, supervises the administration of synagogue properties and examines their budgets and accounts, it generally does not intervene in their internal affairs but is called to ratify the nomination of rabbis and *ḥazzanim.*

The chief rabbi is appointed by the Consistoire to act as the supreme authority on Jewish religious affairs. Cultural differences between communities represented in the Consistoire are evident. Some older communities reflect many formal aspects of the Reform movement, which spread through Belgium during the 19th century, but whose influence was reduced by East European Jews. The result of the contact between the two elements was the widespread practice of Conservative Judaism. Other communities remain faithful to an Orthodoxy imbued with Yiddish Ashkenazi traditions. In spite of the differences, most blatant in the contrasting character of the Brussels and Antwerp communities, the Consistoire preserves a sense of unity. The state provides the salaries of the chief rabbi, the four recognized rabbis and 14 cantors, and the 24 state-recognized teachers, who provide religious instruction in public primary, secondary, and technical schools throughout the country. The state also subsidizes four Jewish day schools—two in Brussels and two in Antwerp—in which courses of Jewish content are taught in addition to the compulsory general curriculum. The state's contribution to various religious and educational institutions illustrates concretely the recognized position of the Jewish religion, which gives observant and nonobservant Jews a feeling of security and confidence.

About 100 Jewish organizations, either revolving around the recognized communities or developing on the fringe, are active in every facet of Jewish life. The main types of organizations are welfare and philanthropic, Zionist and pro-Israel, communal bodies, youth movements, and independent religious, political, cultural, and sport-oriented groups. Welfare and philanthropic organizations are united for fund raising purposes in Brussels and are absorbed into a central body in Antwerp. These two centralizing institutions collaborate at the national level in La Conférence Permanente des Oeuvres Sociales Juives de Belgique. Youth movements are grouped in La Fédération de la Jeunesse Juive de Belgique. Very influential before the war, the Zionist Federation of Belgium continues to concern itself with the renewal of its structure and with the aim of expanding its membership; but since the creation of the State of Israel, the distinction between Zionists and non-Zionists within the community has lost much of its acuteness. Indeed, most Belgian Jews express their support of Israel, and for many of them it has developed into a component of their identity. Manifestations of this support are shown in various ways: financial contributions, collective trips to Israel, the study of modern Hebrew, and hosting Israel experts on communal and educational matters. The favorable attitude toward Israel is widely shared by non-Jews as well. During the Six-Day War (1967), non-Jews walked side by side with Jews in public demonstrations to proclaim solidarity with Israel, and the Belgian press as a whole supported Israel's point of view. [MA.G./W.B.]

Relations with Israel. Important circles in Belgium displayed sympathy for Zionism and supported the struggle of the Zionist movement almost from its beginning. Noteworthy were the active support of Queen Elisabeth and of various Socialist leaders, including Emile Vandervelde, Camille Huysmans, de Brouquère, and Paul Henri Spaak. On Nov. 29, 1947, Belgium voted in the U.N. in favor of the establishment of a Jewish state and it was among the first countries to establish diplomatic relations with Israel (de facto Jan. 31, 1949, and de jure in January 1950). These relations were subsequently elevated to the ambassadorial level. The Israel ambassador in Brussels is also accredited in Luxembourg, which is tied to Belgium through a customs' pact, and is attached to the European Economic Community, whose seat is in that city. Trade relations between Belgium and Israel have developed satisfactorily and in 1968 reached the scope of $8,000,000, with exports from Israel to Belgium slightly greater than imports. Tourism from Belgium has also increased and reached 8,000 people in 1968. Belgium fills a specific role in Israel's foreign relations because of its special position in the process of European integration and the fact that

Brussels has become a sort of "capital of Europe." Many of Israel's diplomatic efforts directed toward the European Community pass through Belgium, which is either a host or an active participant in the creation of the new European identity. The official ties between the two countries included the visit of Queen Elisabeth and a short visit of King Baudouin, which was mainly a pilgrimage to the Holy Land, and the visits of President Izhak Ben-Zvi and prime ministers David Ben-Gurion and Levi Eshkol to Belgium.

[Y.ME.]

Bibliography: E. Ouverleaux, *Notes et documents sur les Juifs de Belgique sous l'ancien régime* (1885); S. Ullmann, *Studien zur Geschichte der Juden in Belgien bis zum XVIII. Jahrhundert* (1909); idem, *Histoire des Juifs en Belgique jusqu'au 19e siècle* (1934); E. Ginsburger, *Les Juifs en Belgique au XVIIIe siècle* (1932); J. Stengers, *Les Juifs dans les Pays-Bas au moyen âge* (1950); E. Schmidt, *Geschiedenis van de Joden in Antwerpen* (1963). HOLOCAUST PERIOD: R. Hilberg, *Destruction of the European Jews* (1961), 382–9; C. Reitlinger, *Final Solution* (1968²), 398–408; Belgium, Commission d'enquête sur la violation des règles du droit des gens . . . , *Les crimes de guerre commis sous l'occupation de la Belgique 1940–1945: la persécution antisémitique* (1947); Gutfreund, in: *Yalkut Moreshet*, 2 no. 4 (1965), 43–55; Liebman, in: *Centrale* (Bruxelles, March 1964); B. Garfinkels, *Les Belges face à la persécution raciale 1940–1944* (1965); Steinberg, in: *Regards*, nos. 29 and 30 (Aug.–Oct. 1968); E. Schmidt, *Geschiedenis van de Joden in Antwerpen* (1963). CONTEMPORARY JEWRY: Centre National des Hautes Études Juives, *La vie juive dans l'Europe contemporaine* (1965), with Eng. summ.; J. Gutwirth, in: JJSO, 10 no. 1 (1968), 121–37; idem, in: *Les Nouveaux Cahiers*, no. 7 (1966), 56–63; C. Lehrer, in: *L'Arche*, no. 62 (1962); S. Brachfeld, *Het Joods Onderwijs in België* (1966); A. Tartakower, *Shivtei Yisrael*, 2 (1966), 225–37.

BELGOROD-DNESTROVSKI (formerly **Akkerman;** Rum. **Cetatea-Albă**), city in Ukrainian S.S.R., in the region of *Bessarabia, on the river Dniester; in Rumania 1918–40 and 1941–44. It is referred to in Jewish sources as Weissenburg and *Ir Lavan* (both meaning "White City"). Karaite scholars, including apparently Caleb *Afendopolo, lived there in the early 16th century, attesting to the existence of a cultured Karaite settlement during this period. A Rabbanite community is first recorded in Belgorod-Dnestrovski in 1591. In 1808, 18 heads of Jewish families were registered in Belgorod-Dnestrovski. According to tradition, a *bet midrash* was built there in 1815 and a synagogue in 1828. The community grew considerably in the 19th century with the arrival of Jews in Bessarabia from other regions of the *Pale of Settlement. The Jewish population numbered 2,422 in 1864 and 5,613 in 1897 (19.9% of the total). The Jews in Belgorod-Dnestrovski were influenced in social and cultural spheres by the important Jewish center in *Odessa. Most of the Jews earned their living in the grain trade, which was mainly concentrated in Jewish hands, but many engaged in crafts. In 1905 there was a pogrom in which eight Jews were killed. After Bessarabia passed to Rumania in 1918, the Jews in Belgorod-Dnestrovski developed a flourishing communal and cultural life, and established cultural and welfare institutions. Jewish institutions before World War II included a hospital (founded in 1882), an old-age home, a kindergarten, and a Hebrew elementary *Tarbut school. In 1930 there were in Belgorod-Dnestrovski 4,239 Jews (12.3% of the total population).

[EL.F.]

Holocaust Period and After. In July 1940, during the Soviet occupation, all Jewish life was disbanded, and a few months later, the great Remasline synagogue became a government archive. Prominent and wealthy Jews were arrested and tried or disappeared altogether. On the night of June 13, 1941, dozens of families were exiled to Siberia, most of whom did not survive. When the fighting drew near, in 1941, about 4,000 Jews fled the city, mostly for nearby Odessa. Those who remained were the sick and the old and pious Jews. The entry of German and Rumanian troops was preceded by the murder of Jews and the plunder of Jewish property on the part of the local peasants. As soon as the town was occupied, all the remaining Jews were gathered in Remasline synagogue where they were kept for three days without food and water. They were taken to the Liman River where they were all shot to death; 600–800 Jews were killed in the slaughter. The Jews who had fled to Odessa met the same fate as the other Jewish inhabitants of that city. About 500 of the prewar population of Belgorod-Dnestrovksi survived the war, and about half of these eventually returned. In 1970, the Jewish population was estimated at 300 families. The last synagogue was confiscated in the 1950s but there was still a Jewish cemetery.

[J.AN.]

Bibliography: I. Feldman, *Toledot ha-Yehudim be-Besarabyah ad Sof ha-Me'ah ha-Tesha-Esreh* (1970), index; idem, in: *Tarbiz*, 38 (1968/69), 61–74; Y. Schildkraut, *Al Ḥurvot Besarabyah* (1954), 17–191.

BELGRADE (Serb. **Beograd**), capital of Serbia and *Yugoslavia. Several Jews from Italy and Hungary settled in Belgrade in the 13th and 14th centuries. They were joined by Sephardi Jews after the Turkish conquest in 1521. They lived mostly in the Jewish *mahala* ("quarter") near the citadel, and were physicians, weaponsmiths, tanners, and merchants. The Jews lived in comfortable circumstances and were allowed to own land. The community enjoyed a degree of judicial autonomy. It numbered 800 in 1663. Between 1642 and 1688, the Belgrade yeshivah became

לאלהי מעוזים רני תודות
בני ישראל ק"ק מנטובה
מספרים תהלותיו ועזוזו ונפלאותיו אשר עשה לארונינו
המלך והקיסר ג׳וסיפי סיקונדו
כי הצליחו צבאות חילו במלחמה גם שחה לפניהם קריה
נשגבה וילכדו עיר מבצר בלגראדו

DIVOTISSIME AZIONI DI GRAZIE
UMILIATE A DIO SIGNORE
DALLA NAZIONE EBREA DI MANTOVA
PER LE SEGNALATE VITTORIE
RIPORTATE DALLE ARMI INVITTE DI S. M. I.
L' AUGUSTISSIMO NOSTRO SOVRANO
IMPERATORE E RE
GIUSEPPE SECONDO
E SEGNATAMENTE PER L' ACCLAMATA PRESA DI
BELGRADO

M. D. CC. LXXXIX.
Con Permissione.

Title page of a Hebrew poem in honor of the capture of Belgrade in 1788 by Emperor Joseph II of Austria, Mantua, 1789. Cecil Roth Collection. Photo David Harris, Jerusalem.

widely known under the rabbis Judah *Lerma, Simḥah b. Gershon Kohen, and Joseph *Almosnino.

With the start of the decline of the Turkish Empire in the late 17th century, a long series of catastrophes befell the Jews of Belgrade. In 1688, at the approach of the Austrians, Turkish janissaries plundered and burned the Jewish quarter. After the capture of the city, Austrian soldiers burned, looted, and killed the Turkish and Jewish population. The community was totally destroyed; some Jews managed to flee to Bulgaria, but the majority were taken prisoner and deported to Austria to be sold as slaves or offered to Jewish communities for ransom.

Shortly after, a number of Jews returned to the city and rebuilt the synagogue. However, since Belgrade became the key fortress against the Turks, under Austrian rule (1717–39) Jewish residence was restricted. The town was captured again by Turks in 1739 and by 1777 the number of Jews had increased to 800. In 1795 irregular troops of Pazvan Oglu, pasha of *Vidin, attacked Belgrade, burning the synagogue and many Jewish houses in the *mahala*. Nevertheless, the Jews remained prosperous: in 1798 all the Belgrade guilds together paid 1,600 grush in taxes, while the Jewish community alone paid 10,000 grush.

A series of rebellions and wars by the Serbs against the local Turkish despots, who had made themselves semi-independent of Constantinople, began in 1803, continuing intermittently for nearly 30 years. Belgrade changed hands many times, the Jews suffering each time. In 1807 the Serbs expelled the Jews from Belgrade. The anti-Jewish measures were revoked at Russian intervention. Some Jews had been allowed to stay, and more returned between 1811 and 1813, but were forced to leave once more when an abortive rebellion broke out in 1813. When in 1815 Milosh Obrenovich was recognized ruler of Serbia the situation of the Jews improved. There were some 1,300 Jews (200 Ashkenazim) in 1831. Prince Milosh's Serbian State Press, founded in 1837, had Hebrew type too. The works, mostly liturgical or ritual, were printed in Ladino, or in Hebrew with a Ladino translation. The Ladino periodical *El Amigo del Pueblo* was established in 1888 and appeared in Belgrade throughout the 1890s. Milosh's successor, Alexander Karageorgevich (1842–58), introduced a series of restrictions on Jewish residence, professions, and acquisition of property.

After obtaining full rights following the Congress of Berlin in 1878, the wealthier Jews gradually became absorbed into Serbian society. They spoke Serbian, their children went to state schools and universities, and became physicians, civil servants, etc. In 1907 they built the new Sephardi synagogue, Bet Yisrael, in the upper town. There was a Hebrew school from the 1850s. Most Jews lived in the *mahala* until World War I when it was partly destroyed. After World War I, when Belgrade became the capital of independent Yugoslavia, the younger generation gradually left the *mahala* to enter the professions, banking, the stock exchange, and the garment industry.

Holocaust Period. When the Germans entered Belgrade in April 1941, 12,000 Jews were living there. The 20,000 Volksdeutsche (ethnic Germans) of Belgrade led the Germans to Jewish shops and homes, looting all that the Germans left. Jews were evicted and their property confiscated. The Ashkenazi synagogue was turned into a brothel; the Bet Yisrael synagogue became a storehouse for looted Jewish property and was blown up before the German retreat. All communal activities were forbidden, but the *Vertretung* ("Representation"), nominated by the Germans, contrived to organize public kitchens, medical services, etc. for the local Jews and for the 2,500 Jews from the Banat region who were expelled to Belgrade. All men between the ages of 14 and 60 and all women between the ages of 14 and 40 were forced to work in the town, not only without payment but also providing their own food.

With the beginning of armed resistance in Serbia, the Germans began executing hostages, mostly Jews. The first mass execution took place on July 29, when 122 "Communists and Jews" were shot. The "final solution" began with the mass arrest of some 5,000 Jewish men between August and October 1941. After being imprisoned in two camps in Belgrade, the men were then taken in groups of 150 to 400 "to work in Austria" and shot in nearby forests by regular German army units. The remaining 6,000 Jewish women and children were arrested in December 1941 and transported to the Saymishte camp, a former commercial fairground on the left bank of the Sava. Food was scarce, and many froze to death in the winter of 1941–42. Between February and May 1942, the remainder were killed in gas vans. Patients of the Jewish hospital in the *mahala* were also liquidated in 1942.

Resistance. Immediately after the German occupation Jewish youth, mainly from Ha-Shomer ha-Ẓa'ir, joined the resistance movement, sabotaging enemy installations, disseminating propaganda, and collecting funds and medical supplies. In August 1941 they joined partisan units in the forests, but not before considerable numbers of them had been arrested and shot. A monument to fallen Jewish fighters and victims of Fascism was set up after the war in the central cemetery of Belgrade.

Contemporary Period. Immediately after the liberation of Belgrade in October 1944 the Jewish community resumed its activities by opening a soup kitchen, a center for returnees, and medical services. The Ashkenazi synagogue was reconsecrated in December 1944, with the Ashkenazi and the Sephardi communities merging. In 1947 the community had 2,271 members, half of whom emigrated to Israel shortly after. In 1969 there were 1,602 Jews in Belgrade. The community center ran an internationally known choir, a youth club, and a kindergarten. It also housed the Federation of Jewish Communities of Yugoslavia. The Yugoslav Jewish Historical Museum contains material on all Jewish communities in Yugoslavia.

Bibliography: A. Hananel and E. Eškenazi, *Fontes Hebraici*... 1 (1958), 219, 468–71, and index; 2 (1960), 177–8, 258–60, and index; D. Djurić-Zamolo, in: *Jevrejski Almanah 1965–67*, 41–76; A. Alkalay, in: *Jevrejski Almanah 1961–62*, 82–97; Moses Kohen, *Et Sofer* (Fuerth, 1691). Holocaust Period: Savez Jevrejskih Opština, *Zločini fašističkih okupatora*... (1952), 1–9 (Eng. summary); G. Reitlinger, *Final Solution* (1961), 385–92; R. Hilberg, *Destruction of European Jewry* (1961), 435–42.

[D.F.]

BELIAL (Heb. בְּלִיַּעַל; lit. "worthlessness"). In the Bible a common noun characterizing persons who behave in a dissolute manner, give false testimony, or hatch infamous plots. It is used in apposition to such words as "son" (Deut. 13:14; I Sam. 2:12), "daughter" (I Sam. 1:16), "man" (I Sam. 30:22; Prov. 16:27), "witness" (Prov. 19:28), and "counsellor" (Nah. 1:11). A "matter of *beliyyaʿal*" is a base thought (Deut. 15:9), and "rivers of *Belial*" (Ps. 18:5) are hellish currents of adversity. In post-biblical literature—especially in the pseudepigrapha—Belial (usually written Beliar) is the name of the Prince of Evil, i.e., *Satan—a view which no doubt underlies the practice of the Vulgate (and of Theodotion, Judg. 9:22) to reproduce the word by transliteration in certain passages of Scripture. Belial is the spirit of darkness (Test. Patr., Levi 19:1; 1QM 13:12). Evil men are dominated by him or his attendant spirits (Test. Patr.: Ash. 1:8; Levi 3:3; Joseph 7:4; Dan. 1:7; Ben. 6:1), and the world is currently under his sway (1QS 1:18, 24; 2:5, 19; 1

QM 14:9; Mart. Isa. 2:4). His will opposes God's (Test. Patr., Naph. 3:1), and he wields a sword which causes bloodshed, havoc, tribulation, exile, death (or plague?), panic, and destruction (*ibid.*, Ben. 7:1–2), or catches men in the snares of lewdness, lucre, and profanity (Zadokite Document 4:13ff.). Belial will ultimately be chained by God's holy spirit (Test. Patr., Levi 18:12) or cast into the all-engulfing fire (*ibid.*, Judah 25:3), and his attendant spirits will be routed (*ibid.*, Iss. 7:7; *ibid.*, Dan 5:1), and discomfited by the Messiah (*ibid.*, Dan 5:10; *ibid.*, Ben. 3:8). There will be a final war in which he and his partisans will be defeated by God and God's partisans, aided by heavenly cohorts (1QM 1:5; 15:3; 18:1, 3). The latter now abide in the second of the seven heavens (Test. Patr., Levi 3:3).The concept of Belial as the opponent of God probably owes much to Iranian dualism, where the eternal antagonists, Asha (Right) and Druj (Perversity) are portrayed as destined to engage in a final "Armageddon," aided respectively by heavenly and earthly partisans, *ashovans* and *dregvants*. (In 1QS (2:20–21; cf. 4:23; 9:21), these terms are reproduced exactly as *benei ẓedek*, "sons of righteousness," and *benei ʿawel*, "sons of perversity.") The Iranian picture was validated, however, by the authority of the biblical text Zechariah 14:5, "The Lord my God will come and all the holy ones [will be] with you" (LXX: "and all His holy ones with Him"). In the third book of the *Sibylline Oracles* (65–74), Belial is identified with a deceiver and miracle-monger whose line hails from Sebaste, i.e., Samaria. This is thought to refer to Simon Magus.

Bibliography: Tur-Sinai, in: EM, 2 (1965), 132–3; Gaster, in: IDB, 1 (1962), 377.

[Th.H.G.]

BELIEF.

The Bible. In the Bible there are no articles of faith or dogmas in the Christian or Islamic sense of the terms. Although trust in God is regarded as a paramount religious virtue (Gen. 15:6; Isa. 7:9; cf. Job 2:9), there is nowhere in Scripture an injunction to believe. Even a verse like II Chronicles 20:20 "believe *(ha'aminu)* in the Lord your God, and you will be established; believe His prophets, and you will succeed" expresses only King Jehoshaphat's advice to the people; it is not a religious commandment. Furthermore, the verb *he'emin* (האמין "to believe"), the noun *'emunah* ("belief"), and other forms derived from the stem *'mn* (אמן) mean to trust, have confidence; and faithfulness; and in this sense are used both of God and of man (Gen. 15:6; Deut. 32:4; Prov. 20:6; Job 4:18). This usage is in striking contrast to the concept of "belief" in the New Testament (e.g., John 3:18). It is only in the Middle Ages, when Jewish theologians began to formulate articles of faith, that derivations of the root *'mn* came to be used in a dogmatic sense.

The reason for the absence of a catechism in both the Bible and the rabbinic tradition is probably twofold: in Judaism the primary emphasis is not on profession of faith but on conduct (Avot 1:17); and speculative and systematic thinking is not characteristic of the biblical or the rabbinic genius. Dogmatics entered Judaism as a result of external pressure; contact with alien religious systems, which had formulated theological doctrines, compelled Jewish thinkers to state the basic creeds of their own faith. In a sense, Jewish dogmatics forms part of the larger category of Jewish apologetics.

No religion, however, is conceivable without fundamental doctrines or axiomatic principles, and Judaism, in its scriptural as well as rabbinic aspects, is no exception. Indeed, the Bible contains certain summary statements that might be considered incipient dogmas. The **Shemaʿ* (Deut. 6:4), underscoring the unity of God; the Ten Command-

Moses receiving the Tablets of the Law at Mount Sinai while the Israelites stand behind a fenced mountain. A marginal illustration to the mishnaic tractate *Avot*. Florence, Italy, 1492. New York, Jewish Theological Seminary, *Rothschild Maḥzor*, fol. 139.

ments (Ex. 20:1 ff.; Deut. 5:6 ff.), providing an epitome of Jewish precepts; the formulation of the divine attributes in Exodus 34:6–7; Micah's sublime summary of human duty (6:18); and the majestic simplicity of the Lord's assurance to Habakkuk "but the righteous shall live by his faith" (2:4) are a few examples culled from many. But valuable as these formulations are, they do not embrace the complete range of fundamental biblical teachings. Only an analysis of scriptural doctrines against the background of the entire complex of biblical thought can yield the essential religious beliefs, moral ideals, and spiritual truths that underlie the faith expounded by the Scriptures.

That "God is" is axiomatic. He is One (Deut. 6:4) and incomparable (Isa. 40:18); there are no other gods (Deut. 4:39). He is omnipotent (Job 42:2), omnipresent (Ps. 139:7–12), omniscient (Job 28:23 ff.), and eternal (Isa. 40:6–8; 44:6). Even more important is the doctrine that He is the God of justice and love (Ex. 34:6–7); it is His moral nature that makes Him holy (Isa. 5:16). In His might He willed the creation of the universe (Gen. 1), and in His love He continues to sustain it (Ps. 104; 145:14 ff.). He made the laws of nature; the miracles are exceptions to these cosmic rules, but both the normal and the abnormal conform to the Divine Will. Mythology, except for idiomatic phrases, is excluded from biblical teaching. Magical practices are forbidden (Deut. 18:10); unlike miracles, they do not issue from the will of God, but seek to overrule divinely established laws of nature.

The apex of creation is man, created in the divine image. This "image" is reflected in the moral and spiritual qualities of human nature. In man creation achieves a new dimension—a moral personality endowed with freedom of will. The relationship between God and man has a voluntaristic ethical character. It is an encounter between the Divine Person and His human counterpart, between Father and child. Ideally it is an "I—Thou" relation. But man may disobey; sin is spiritual treason, which transforms the "nearness" of God into "estrangement." The divine "Thou" then becomes "It."

Human freedom of choice (Deut. 30:15, 19) is the source of man's responsibility, upon which are predicated rewards and penalties, both collective and individual. Divine retribution is a corollary of God's righteousness; but its purpose is primarily not punitive but educative and reformative; it aims to restore the "I—Thou" nexus. Thus God does not desire the destruction of the wicked, but their return to the path of goodness (Ezek. 18:23, 32), and heaven's grace far exceeds the measure of divine punishment (Ex. 20:5–6; Deut. 5:9–10). Hence all the predictions of the prophets are conditional (cf. Jonah). The Heavenly Father hopes for His punitive decrees to be nullified. Conceptually there appears to be a contradiction between God's omniscience and omnipotence on the one hand, and man's freedom of action on the other. But the Bible harmonizes them in a supreme historic event. Human rebellions will ultimately end in a great reconciliation. In the messianic era Zion's teaching will become a universal heritage (Isa. 2:2 ff.; Mic. 4:1 ff.). "In the end of days" the divine design of history will be realized as perfectly as His cosmic plan.

Human waywardness was manifest from the beginning of history. Man has constantly been tempted to do wrong: "every imagination of the thoughts of his heart was only evil continually" (Gen. 6:5). To aid humanity to persevere along the path of righteousness, divine revelation was necessary. Its purpose was to direct and supplement the basic sense of right and wrong innate in every human being (cf. Gen. 39:9). Certain spiritual geniuses—the patriarchs, the prophets—learned to know the will of God in given situations. But the complete revelation was vouchsafed to the Children of Israel at Sinai. It comprised many elements—legal and ritual, moral and spiritual, national and universal—each component being necessary to its educative and purifying intent. The precepts were neither to be augmented nor diminished (Deut. 4:2); the law was immutable. Intrinsically the prophets did not add to the Torah. The glory of Hebrew prophecy consists not in preaching new ideas, but in elucidating the historic covenant and applying its teachings to the circumstances of their time. In particular they stressed the moral and spiritual values of religion, and the universal conception of the consummation of history in the kingdom of God.

By accepting the Torah, Israel became the "treasured people" of the Lord, a holy nation in the service of the Holy God (Ex. 19:5; Lev. 19:2). They entered into a covenant with Him (Ex. 24:7; Deut. 29:11, 12), calling for unswerving obedience on their part and protective providence on the part of God. The election of Israel was not an act of favoritism. On the contrary, it represented a mission involving special responsibility and corresponding retribution. "You only have I known of all the families of the earth; therefore I will visit upon you all your iniquities" (Amos 3:2). Nor was God's providential care limited to Israel; there was a Philistine and Aramean exodus comparable to that of Israel (*ibid.*, 9:7). The covenant with Israel was an integral part of God's universal historic plan of salvation (Isa. 49:6). Hence the Israelites were as indestructible as the cosmos (Jer. 33:25–26). Their sins would be punished, but redemption would succeed every disaster. The national hope of restoration and return to the Land of Israel is thus indivisibly linked with the redemption of all mankind. Jewish nationalism and universalism are not opposed but complementary biblical ideals.

Since ethics occupies a central position in scriptural theology, theodicy greatly exercised the minds of the prophets and sages of Israel. The thought "shall not the Judge of all the earth do justly?" (Gen. 18:25) is echoed in various forms throughout the Scriptures. It is an essential aspect of the dialogue between man and God. To criticize and challenge God in sincerity is not viewed by Scripture as a sin (witness Abraham, Moses, Jeremiah, Habakkuk, and Job); only hypocrisy and smugness are iniquitous (Job 42:7). The biblical answers to the problem of suffering are varied: it is accounted for by sin, by the concept of "the suffering servant," by the limitations of human knowledge. Man's view is too short; however long the process, righteousness triumphs in the end (Ps. 92:8). In the final analysis God's purpose is beyond man's understanding (Isa. 55:8; Job 42:3). Until the ultimate reconciliation at "the end of days," the Incomprehensible God can be apprehended only in faith (Hab. 2:4).

Hellenistic Literature. The encounter with Greek culture in the Hellenistic period brought the challenge of new concepts and philosophic methodology to Judaism. But the impact was transitory, and *Philo, "the first theologian," was the only one among the Greco-Jewish writers to formulate Jewish dogmas. He enumerates five tenets: (1) God exists and rules the universe; (2) He is one; (3) the world was created; (4) creation is one; (5) Divine Providence cares for the world (Op. 61). Josephus asserts that the antagonism between the Sadducees and Pharisees was based on doctrinal differences, such as the question of providence, the immortality of the soul, and the belief in resurrection with the concomitant idea of the final judgment (Wars, 2:162–5). Modern scholarship, however, is inclined to give a political and national interpretation to these disputes.

Rabbinic Literature. Rabbinic theology is marked by an overwhelming diversity of opinion. Since the sages' method of study was essentially based on argumentation and controversy, it is by no means easy to determine at all times its fundamental ideas. Furthermore, while the rabbis sought to give clear definition to the *halakhah*, the *aggadah* remained vague, unsystematized, and contradictory. Nevertheless in Talmud and Midrash, as in Scripture, it is possible to discern ground patterns of thought and basic concepts that constitute the foundations of the tannaitic and amoraic ideology. It is axiomatic that rabbinic teaching rests firmly on biblical doctrine and precept. Here, as in the Bible, God is the transcendent Creator; the Torah is the unalterable embodiment of His will; providence is motivated by moral principles; there is an "I—Thou" relationship between man and God; the election of Israel, linked to the immutable covenant of the Torah, is a paramount idea; and the prophetic promise of Israel's ultimate redemption and the establishment of the kingdom of God upon earth is the national-universal denouement of the drama of history. But rabbinic theology is a superstructure founded on scriptural faith, not a copy of it; there are evolutionary differences in talmudic Judaism that distinguish it from biblical norms and give it its distinctive qualities.

Rabbinic Judaism produced no catechism; but external cultural pressures and internal heresies gave rise to certain formulations of a dogmatic character. Sanhedrin 10:1, for example, in defining those who have no share in the world to come, gives to the belief in resurrection and in the divine origin of the Torah credal status. Similarly Hillel's dictum "That which is hateful to thee do not do unto others" (Shab. 31a) constitutes in its context the principal Jewish dogma. In discussing the precepts of the Torah the rabbis spoke of various figures who reduced the number of precepts (from the traditional 613), ending with Habakkuk who subsumed them all under one fundamental principle, "but the righteous shall live by his faith" (Hab. 2:4; cf. Mak. 24a). But in rabbinic, as in scriptural, literature, the root-ideas can be reached only by a careful examination of the complete compass of the tradition and a comparative study of its beliefs.

A new mysticism, emanating from the doctrines of *ma'aseh bereshit* ("work of creation") and *ma'aseh merkavah* ("work of the chariot"), now attaches to the concept of God. Gnostic influence, despite the general opposition of the sages to Gnostic ideas, is discernible. But these esoteric notions were reserved for the few only (Ḥag. 2:1). On the other hand, the broad-based popular approach, found in numerous *aggadot,* inclines toward an anthropopathic presentation of the Deity. The Holy One of Israel suffers all Israel's tribulations; He too is exiled (Sif. Num. 84; Ber. 9b). Man is conceived as a dualism: his soul, which is immortal, gives him a place among the angels; his body makes him akin to the beasts (Sif. Deut. 309). But the body is not contemned as a source of evil, nor may the material things of this world be left unenjoyed (TJ, Kid. 4:12, 66d). They are the work of God and inherently good. Indeed, God is to be served with both lower and higher impulses (Sif. Deut. 32; Ber. 54a). Man's freedom of choice, however, is fully recognized: "All is in the power of heaven except the reverence of heaven" (Ber. 33b), though the omniscient God foresees all (Avot 3:15). But this freedom is the basis of responsibility and the justification of retribution. To err is human, but penitence is the great shield that protects man (*ibid.* 4:13). Hence it was created even before the world (Pes. 54a).

The Torah, as the will of God, is immutable, and the sages regarded it as their supreme task to expound and determine its provisions, giving precedence, where needed, to moral principles over strict legalism (e.g., TJ, BM 2:5, 8c). To be holy and to walk in the Lord's ways implied in particular the practice of lovingkindness (Sifra 19:1; Sif. Deut. 49), which was equal to all the precepts put together (TJ, Pe'ah 1:1, 15b). The purpose of the commandments is to purify man (Gen. R. 44:1), and the true spirit of observance seeks no reward beyond the service of God (Avot 1:3). But there are two Torahs: the Oral Law, which was also revealed at Sinai, supplements and elucidates the Written Law. On the basis of Deuteronomy 17:11 (Ber. 19b), the sages claimed the right to enact laws of their own *(mi-de-rabbanan),* chiefly with a view to their serving as a "fence" (protection) to the biblical ordinances *(mi-de-oray-ta).* The most daring principle of all originated by the rabbis was their right to interpret the Torah in conformity with their understanding and to decide (by majority vote) accordingly. It was they, not the heavenly court *(familia),* that fixed the calendar (TJ, RH 1:3, 57b). Even if a halakhic ruling ran counter, so to speak, to the view of heaven, the rabbis still maintained that theirs was the right to decide, for the Torah, having been vouchsafed to man, was now subject to human judgment. Nor did this principle displease the Holy One, Blessed Be He, for He smiled indulgently when His children outvoted Him (BM 59b). The sages went so far as to declare "the suppression of the Torah may be the foundation thereof" (Men. 99). Thus the rabbis evolved theological machinery for adapting the *halakhah* to historical changes and needs without discarding an iota of the scriptural tradition. Theologically they justified this procedure by the theory that all that the rabbis taught was already inherent in the Sinaitic revelation (Lev. R. 22:1; TJ, Pe'ah 2:6, 17a), that the sages did not innovate but discovered already existing truths.

The rabbinic exaltation of Torah study was a natural corollary of their attitude to the Scriptures. The Mishnah lists the things whose fruits a man enjoys in this world, while the capital is laid up for him in the world to come, and declares "the study of the Law is equal to them all" (Pe'ah 1:1). The rabbis (BB 12a) elevate the sage (with his restrained, reflective approach) above the prophet (with his incandescent, intuitive consciousness). Nevertheless the truth that Judaism is life and that learning must lead to deeds was not lost sight of: "Great is the study of the Torah, because it leads to [right] action" (Kid. 40b).

Israel's election is a leading theme in rabbinic thought. It brought comfort and renewed courage to a suffering people. God's ultimate salvation was never doubted. The messianic era, despite the preceding tribulation, would bring redemption to Israel and the land. This belief suffuses the entire aggadic literature and inspires every facet of the liturgy. Great emphasis is placed on the importance of Ereẓ Israel in Talmud and Midrash and the prayer book. The rabbis exhaust the language of praise and indulge in unrestrained fantasy in depicting the future glories of the land. One dictum even avers that "he who dwells outside the Land of Israel is as one who serves idols" (Ket. 110b). This hyperbole was intended not only to encourage Jewish settlement in Ereẓ Israel, but also to strengthen the hope of national restoration. Jewish nationalism did not, however, exclude universalist ideals. "The pious of all nations have a share in the world to come" (Tosef., Sanh. 13:10). "Whoever repudiates idolatry is called a Jew" (Meg. 13a); and the greatest Torah principle is enshrined in the verse "This is the book of the generations of Adam"—the brotherhood of man (TJ, Ned. 9:4, 41c).

In the Talmud, as in the Bible, the problem of theodicy is a major theme. The sages range the entire gamut of possible explanations for human suffering. In the ultimate analysis they propound the profoundest conception of all: suffering deriving from divine love (Ber 5a). Human suffering is an essential element in human spiritual advancement. It is an aspect of God's grace. Another cardinal rabbinic belief offered a collective historical solution to the question of divine justice. The concept of resurrection (Sanh. 10:1) was closely linked with the advent of the Messiah and the last judgment (Shab. 152b; Ḥag. 12b; Sanh. 91a–b). Bygone generations would, if worthy, share in the sublime joy of the kingdom of God upon earth. Maimonides, however, interprets the resurrection in a purely spiritual sense *(Ma'amar Teḥiyyat ha-Metim).* Going beyond biblical theology, the rabbis envisaged yet another world, where the imbalance of earthly justice is rectified. The immortal soul is judged after the death of the body in the hereafter ("world to come") and is requited according to the individual's deeds upon earth (Sif. Deut. 307; Ber. 28b; Shab. 153a; Ber. 17a). In this solution time is transcended. God's ultimate justification is a function of eternity.

These norms of rabbinic faith provided the basis of medieval Jewish theology and philosophy. Their lack of definition gave later Jewish thinking flexibility and their emphasis a firm framework.

[I.ABR.]

Medieval Jewish Philosophy. In medieval philosophy belief is a general philosophical category belonging to the theory of knowledge, of which religious belief is one specific kind. The medieval philosophers distinguished between two activities of the mind: the formulation of propositions, and the affirmation that propositions in the mind correspond to a reality outside the mind, and identified belief with the latter activity. In line with this account *Maimonides defines belief as ". . . the notion that is represented in the soul when it has been averred of it that it is in fact just as it has been represented" (*Guide of the Perplexed,* 1:50). In somewhat less technical language *Saadiah defines belief as "... a notion that arises in the soul in regard to the actual character of anything that is apprehended. When the cream of investigation emerges, and is embraced and enfolded by the minds and, through them acquired and digested by the souls, then the person becomes convinced of the truth of the notion he has acquired" (*Book of Beliefs and Opinions*, introd.). Belief defined in this manner may still be true or false, and hence it is necessary to add criteria by means of which true beliefs may be distinguished from false ones. Saadiah, discussing this issue, lists four criteria which enable one to establish that a belief is true: sense perception, self-evident propositions, inference, and reliable tradition (*ibid.*, introd.; cf. Maimonides, "Letter On Astrology," in: R. Lerner and M. Mahdi (eds.), *Medieval Political Philosophy: A Sourcebook* (1963), 228). This conception of belief as the affirmation or conviction that propositions within the mind correspond to reality outside the mind can be traced to Greek philosophy, particularly to the Stoics.

Belief for medieval Christian, Muslim, and Jewish thinkers meant, in the first instance, religious belief, that is, the conviction that the teachings of Scriptures are true and that their truth is guaranteed by the authority of their respective traditions. At the same time they noted that philosophers also investigated some of the same issues that interested them, e.g., the existence of God, the creation of the world, principles of human morality, and they further noted that there was a similarity between the teachings of religion and human reason. Hence the question arose how the teachings of religion, that is, religious beliefs, are related to the teachings of philosophy, that is, philosophical beliefs. There were essentially three views concerning this interrelation. There were those who, denying that the term belief applies to philosophic teachings, affirmed that this term in its strict sense refers only to propositions accepted on the basis of religious authority; there were those who permitted the application of the term only to propositions known by way of demonstration; and there were still others, who were prepared to use the term belief for describing both. In line with these distinctions H. A. *Wolfson classifies the attitudes toward religious belief in a threefold fashion: the double faith theory, according to which the acceptance of propositions based both on religious authority and rational demonstration constitutes belief; the single faith theory of the authoritarian type, according to which the acceptance of propositions based on authority alone constitutes belief; and the single faith theory of the rational type, according to which the acceptance of propositions based on demonstration alone constitutes belief (JQR, 33 (1942), 213–64).

Saadiah, a proponent of the double faith theory, accepts the notion of belief as applying to things known both by way of authority and by way of demonstration. He maintains that the doctrines of Scripture coincide with those of philosophy, and that an affirmation of these doctrines, whether based on revelation or on rational demonstration, constitutes belief. While Saadiah advocates speculation about the truths of religion, he, nevertheless, maintains that it is forbidden to ignore Scripture entirely and to rely solely on one's reason, for the reason is not infallible, and may lead to erroneous conclusions.

*Judah Halevi, a representative of the single faith theory of the authoritarian type, maintains that belief applies only to things known by means of authority. According to him, belief is an acceptance of the doctrines of Scripture based on authority, i.e., on the fact that these doctrines of Scripture were divinely revealed. For example, in connection with sacrifices Halevi states categorically that "... he who accepts [sacrifices], without examination or reasoning is better off than he who resorts to research and analysis" (*Kuzari*, 2:26; see also 1:64–65, and 3:7).

Maimonides, on the other hand, is a representative of the single faith theory of the rationalist type. He maintains that belief applies only to things known by way of demonstration. While he does not state categorically that an acceptance of the doctrines of Scripture based on authority is not belief, he definitely considers an acceptance based on demonstration to be a more perfect form of belief. Belief is more than verbal acceptance; it requires understanding and a rational basis. Providing an example, Maimonides writes that someone who utters with his lips that he believes in the unity and incorporeality of God, while at the same time maintaining that God has positive attributes, cannot be said to believe truly in God's unity. That he can maintain that God has attributes indicates that he does not understand the principle of God's unity, and there is no belief without understanding (*Guide*, 1:50). According to Maimonides the precept "You shall love the Lord, your God," cannot properly be fulfilled without an understanding of metaphysics. Love of God, according to Maimonides, is "proportionate to apprehension" (*Guide*, 3:51; cf. Yad, Yesodei ha-Torah, 4:12).

*Levi b. Gershom shares the view of the Maimonidean school that there is no opposition between reason and belief. He holds that priority should be given to reason where its demands are unambiguous, for the meaning of Scripture is not always clear and is subject to interpretation (*Milḥamot Adonai*, introd.).

See also *Allegory, *Revelation, *Philosophy.

[J.H.]

Modern Jewish Philosophy. While in medieval philosophy the description of faith formed an integral part of the theory of knowledge, the rise of modern science and the concomitant decline of the belief in the divine revelation of Scriptures have made faith a matter of trusting in God rather than of the affirmation of certain propositions. Characteristic of this attitude in recent Jewish thought are the views of Franz *Rosenzweig, according to whom religious belief arises from the experience of personal revelation, for which man must always strive and be prepared. This view was anticipated by Hermann *Cohen in his theory of correlation. Similarly, Martin *Buber and Abraham *Heschel see faith as a relationship of trust between man and God, which arises from, and manifests itself in, personal encounters between man and God, and man and man, which Buber calls I—Thou relationships.

Another tendency among modern thinkers, which reflects the influence of psychology, is to view belief as a psychological state which is valuable insofar as it motivates man to act in an ethical manner. Mordecai *Kaplan, a representative of this naturalistic view, implies that faith is a kind of "self-fulfilling prophecy" insofar as it leads to the redemption of human society. According to the others embracing a naturalistic view, faith is good in that it infuses meaning and purpose into an otherwise meaningless and cruel existence. This point is taken up strongly by Richard *Rubenstein, who has been concerned with the challenge to Jewish faith posed by the Holocaust. [Ed.]

Bibliography: S. Schechter, *Studies in Judaism*, 1 (1911), 147–81; I. Efros, in: JQR, 33 (1942/43), 133–70; A. Heschel, *ibid.*, 265–313; G. F. Moore, *Judaism*, 2 (1946), 237–8; H. A. Wolfson, *Philo*, 1 (1948), 155–6; M. Buber, *Two Types of Faith* (1951); W. Eichrodt, *Theology of the Old Testament*, 2 (1967), 277–90; E. E. Urbach, *Ḥazal* (1969), 15–28; S. H. Bergman, *Jewish Philosophy in Modern Times* (1968), 177–9.

BELINFANTE, Sephardi family. Its founder, Joseph Cohen Belinfante, escaped from Portugal to the Balkans in 1526. The family lived in Belgrade, whence MEIR ḤAYYIM left for Amsterdam in 1721. His son ẒADDIK (1675–1750), author of works on the Talmud, settled in Amsterdam, where he became chief rabbi. Of his seven children the most noted, ELIJAH HEZEKIAH and MOSES, moved via London to Holland where they played an important part in the Jewish community. ISAAC *BELINFANTE (d. 1780), son of Elijah Hezekiah, was a Hebrew poet and a bibliographer. MOSES BEN ẒADDIK (1761–1827), grandson of Moses, was born at The Hague. An accomplished linguist, Moses as a young man served as a diplomatic interpreter. After his father died in 1781 he became principal of the Jewish school for the poor in The Hague, where he introduced modern methods of teaching. In collaboration with friends he published a translation of the prayer book. He was active in the struggle for Jewish *emancipation in Holland, and published a Jewish paper (Amsterdam, 1806–08). In 1806 Moses moved to Amsterdam and became editor of the official gazette of the Kingdom of the Netherlands. He also took part in the controversy concerning the formation of a special Jewish militia. He continued to write, translate, and publish Jewish works. JACOB (1780–1845), brother of Moses, was editor of the official gazette between 1807 and 1837. His publications include Jewish almanacs and the *Jaarboeken voor de Israeliten in Nederland* (The Hague, 1835–40).

Bibliography: FAMILY: Carmoly, in: *Revue Orientale*, 3 (Brussels, 1843–44), 134–44; ESN, 52–57. MOSES AND JACOB: Somerhausen, in: AI, 8 (1847), 339–47, 398–407; Baron, in: HJ, 5 (1943), 1–26.

[J.M.]

BELINFANTE, ISAAC (d. 1780), precursor of the Haskalah movement. Belinfante, who was preacher in an Amsterdam synagogue, wrote poetry, mostly dedicated to famous people and events, and bibliographical studies (in manuscript). Only a fraction of the latter was ever printed, some in the books of his pupil, David *Franco Mendes. A list of works associated with his name, including hitherto unprinted manuscripts, and two poems (*Ha-Lomed be-Veit Limmudo* and *Sha'ar ha-Yesod*) were published by H. G. Enelow.

Bibliography: Malachi, in: *Tagim* (1969), 78–87; H. G. Enelow, in: *Studies . . . A. S. Freidus* (1929), 5–30.

[G.K.]

BELISHA, Moroccan family of merchants and financiers. In 1817 MOSES BELISHA (1788–1851) settled in Marseilles where he acquired a large fortune. He became "Merchant of the sultan of Morocco" and a benefactor of the Jewish community. His activities extended to Gibraltar and to Manchester. Moses was assisted by his son BARROW who traded with India, Egypt, and Mogador, where the philanthropists JESHUA and SOLOMON had remained. Moses' nephew, ISAAC, merchant and industrialist, became president of the Manchester Sephardi community in 1872. Isaac's grandson was Leslie *Hore-Belisha.

Bibliography: J. L. Miège, *Maroc*, 1 (1961), 94, 144, 574; A. Hyamson, *Sephardim of England* (1951), 359, 397.

[D.Co.]

BELKIN, SAMUEL (1911–), U.S. rabbi, educator, and scholar. Born in Swislocz, Poland, Belkin studied at the yeshivot of Slonim and Mir, and was ordained in Radun (1928). He immigrated to the U.S. in 1929 and received his Ph.D. at Brown University in 1935. He joined the Yeshiva College faculty as instructor in Greek and Talmud (1935–37), becoming secretary of its graduate school (1937) and member of the College Executive Committee (1939). Appointed professor and dean of Yeshiva's Rabbi Isaac Elchanan Theological Seminary in 1940, Belkin became president of the RIETS and Yeshiva College in 1943. He launched a far-reaching program of academic and physical expansion which enlarged Yeshiva University from 850 students and a faculty of 94 to 8,000 students and a faculty of some 2,200 with teaching centers throughout New York City. Fourteen constituent schools were founded, and in 1945 the college became *Yeshiva University.

Belkin, an authority on Jewish law and Hellenistic literature, especially Philo and early Midrashic sources, published many scholarly studies. In his major work, *Philo and the Oral Law* (1940), he stressed that "the oral law which originated in Palestine was also known and practiced among the Jews who lived outside of Palestine, and that Philo's *halakhah* is based upon the Palestinian oral law as it was known in Alexandria." He further showed that "there prevailed a great interdependence of thought between the Alexandrian and Palestinian Jewish communities and that we cannot regard them as two entirely separate forms of Judaism." His later works also demonstrate Philo's dependence upon ancient rabbinic traditions. Belkin wrote *Essays in Traditional Jewish Thought* (1956) and *In His Image* (1960), in which he formulated a religious philosophy of Judaism as reflected in the *halakhah*. Numerous articles of his have been published in learned periodicals, both in Hebrew and in English.

Samuel Belkin, president of Yeshiva University, N.Y.

As an educator Belkin stresses that "Torah is the source from which all human obligations spring." He has especially enunciated the religious philosophy of Judaism as reflected in the *halakhah*. To him its basic principles are the sovereignty of God and the sacredness of the individual. Hence, many legal and spiritual institutions in Judaism can be understood only by these fundamental teachings based on belief in divine kingship and the finite worth of the human personality. Though recognized as a modernist Orthodox spokesman, Belkin generally maintained rapport with all groups in Judaism, promoting the unity of peoplehood.

Bibliography: G. Klaperman, *History of Yeshiva University* (1969); *Hadoar* (Kislev 6, 5728); *Hapardes* (Tammuz 5728); Yeshiva University, *The Inauguration of Rabbi Samuel Belkin* (1945).

[S.B.H.]

BELKIND, Ereẓ Israel family of the First *Aliyah.

MEIR BELKIND (1827–1898), one of the first teachers of the modern Hebrew school system in Ereẓ Israel. Belkind, who was born in Logoisk, Belorussia, followed his sons, Israel and Shimshon, to Ereẓ Israel at the beginning of the 1880s. He settled first in Jaffa and later in *Gederah, where he served as rabbi for the new settlers. Although a traditional Jew himself, he defended the *Bilu'im against the attacks of the religious zealots. When his son Israel established the first Hebrew school in Jaffa in 1889, Belkind became its teacher for religious subjects, thus molding the method of religious instruction in the modern schools of Ereẓ Israel.

ISRAEL (1861–1929), one of the founders of Bilu. Israel was born in Logoisk. In 1882, while studying at Kharkov

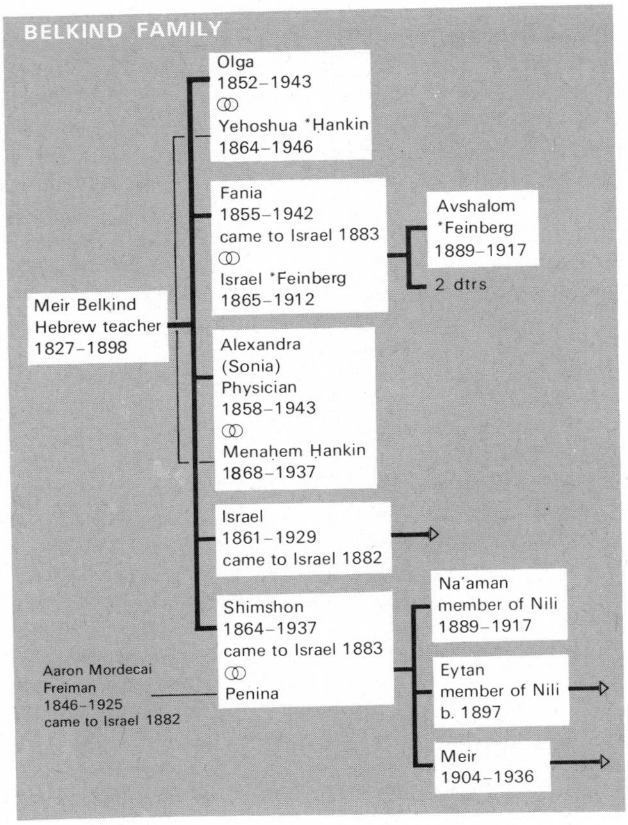

University, he was among the students who founded the Bilu movement and went to Ereẓ Israel at the head of its first group. He led the opposition against Baron Edmond de *Rothschild's officials and, on being expelled by them from Rishon le-Zion, settled in Gederah. In 1889 Belkind opened a private Hebrew school in Jaffa. He was accepted as a teacher at the *Alliance Israélite Universelle in Jerusalem in 1892, and there published several textbooks. In 1903 he founded an agricultural training school at Shefeyah (near Zikhron Ya'akov) for orphans of the Kishinev pogroms whom he brought to Ereẓ Israel. However, the school was forced to close down in 1906 because of lack of funds. During World War I Belkind was in the U.S., where he published his memoirs in Yiddish, *Di Ershte Shrit fun Yishuv Erets Yisroel* ("The First Steps of the Jewish Settlement of Palestine," 1918).

Apart from numerous articles and popular pamphlets, Belkind published a geography of Palestine, *Ereẓ Yisrael ba-Zeman ha-Zeh* ("The Land of Israel Today," 1928). He died in Berlin, where he had gone for medical treatment. His remains were interred in Rishon le-Zion.

Figure 1. A Belkind family group, 1912. Shimshon is seated and Israel is on the right. Jerusalem, Central Zionist Archives.

Shimshon (1864–1937), Bilu pioneer. Shimshon was born in Logoisk. He joined the Bilu movement in Russia and settled in Ereẓ Israel in 1883. He worked at various crafts in Jerusalem, Mikveh Israel, and Rishon le-Zion, and in 1888 moved to Gederah, where he was a farmer. His sons Na'aman and Eytan were members of *Nili.

Figure 2. Na'aman Belkind, a member of Nili. Jerusalem, Central Zionist Archives.

Na'aman (1889–1917), member of Nili, executed by the Turks. He was employed in the Rishon le-Zion wine cellars, where he came into contact with visiting Turkish officers. He joined Nili together with his cousin Avshalom *Feinberg. In September 1917, while attempting to reach Egypt to investigate the circumstances of Feinberg's death, he was caught by Bedouin who handed him over to the Turkish authorities. He was taken to Damascus, tried, convicted for spying, and hanged in the winter of 1917, together with Yosef *Lishansky. He was later buried in Rishon le-Zion.

Bibliography: D. Idelovitch (ed.), *Rishon le-Ẓiyyon* (1941), 76–81; M. Smilansky, *Mishpaḥat ha-Adamah*, 2 (1944), 128–32; A. Yaari, *Goodly Heritage* (1958), index; A. Engle, *Nili Spies* (1959), index. [Y.S.]

BELKOWSKY, ẒEVI HIRSCH (**Grigori**; 1865–1948), Zionist leader and jurist. Belkowsky was born in Odessa, where his father died of wounds received during the 1881 pogroms. He was admitted to a Russian high school and

Ẓevi Hirsch Belkowsky, Russian Zionist leader and jurist. Raphaeli Collection, Tel Aviv.

graduated *cum laude* from the University of Odessa law faculty. He was offered a post at the university on condition that he convert to Christianity. He refused, and became a lecturer and later professor at the University of Sofia in Bulgaria (1893–97). As a university student he had joined the *Ḥibbat Zion movement, and from 1891 was in contact with the pre-Herzl Zionist circle surrounding Nathan *Birnbaum in Vienna. When Herzl's *Judenstaat* was published in 1896, Belkowsky joined Herzl's group and helped organize the First Zionist Congress (1897). At the Third Congress he was elected to the General Council and appointed representative to the St. Petersburg district of the movement. He was among the leaders of the opposition to the *Uganda Scheme. Belkowsky published a series of pamphlets on Zionist subjects. He also initiated the publication of a bibliographical work in Russian entitled *Ukazatel literatury o sionizme* ("A Guide to Zionist Literature," 1903). Belkowsky continued his Zionist activity during the Russian Revolution. He was adviser to the British consul in Moscow on matters regarding Palestine immigration certificates, and chairman of the Zionist Central Committee of Russia (1920–22). In 1924 he was arrested for his Zionist activities and sentenced to deportation to Siberia, but the sentence was commuted to banishment from the Soviet Union. He settled in Palestine in 1924 and was active in the Federation of General Zionists. He wrote his memoirs *Mi-Zikhronotai* (1940).

Bibliography: *Enziklopedyah le-Ẓiyyonut*, 1 (1947), 143–6; A. L. Jaffe (ed.), *Sefer ha-Congress* (1950²), 299.

[Y.S.]

BELLOW, SAUL (1915–), U.S. novelist. The son of Russian immigrants to Canada, Bellow was born in Lachine, Quebec, and raised in Montreal and in Chicago, Ill. His trilingual childhood included Yiddish as well as English and French. After studying anthropology at Chicago and Northwestern universities, he began his career

Saul Bellow, U.S. novelist.

as a writer in 1940. He spent three years (1943–46) on the editorial staff of the Encyclopaedia Britannica, taught creative writing at Princeton University (1952–53), and subsequently held a professorial appointment with the Committee on Social Thought at the University of Chicago. Bellow's first novel, *Dangling Man*, appeared in 1944. Of the works that followed, *The Victim* (1947) was an original treatment of the theme of anti-Semitism; the prize-winning *Adventures of Augie March* (1953), a picaresque novel about the adventures of a Jewish boy from Chicago during the depression of the 1930s; *Seize the Day* (1956), a sensitive study of loneliness and the onset of middle age; and *Henderson the Rain King* (1959), an excursion into the fantastic about a wealthy American's search for ultimate reality among primitive African tribesmen. Bellow's most widely acclaimed work was the novel *Herzog* (1964), an international best seller that gained the "Prix International de Littérature." Its hero, an endlessly ruminating Jewish professor, struggles comically but futilely to relate with humanistic values to a dehumanized modern world; like all Bellow's protagonists, he is doomed to live out the contradiction between an inner world of romantic aspiration and an outer one of less than romantic fact. Universally considered one of mid-century America's leading novelists, Bellow published his first play, *Analysis*, in 1965; a volume of short stories, *Mosby's Memoirs and Other Stories* (1968); and *Mr. Sammler's Planet* (1970). Bellow also edited *Great Jewish Short Stories* (1963).

Bibliography: M. Klein, *After Alienation* (1964), 33–70; H. M. Harper, *Desperate Faith* (1967), 7–64; K. M. Opdahl, *The Novels of Saul Bellow: an Introduction* (1967); J. J. Clayton, *Saul Bellow: in Defense of Man* (1968); I. Malin (ed.), *Saul Bellow and the Critics* (1967); idem, *Saul Bellow's Fiction* (1969); H. Fisch, in *Judaism*, 17 (1968), 42–54.

[Ed.]

BELMONT, AUGUST (1816–1890), U.S. banker, diplomat, and politician. Belmont was born in Alzey (Hesse), but claimed descent from the distinguished *Belmonte family of Portugal. His enemies later circulated the story that his original name was Schoenberg. He began his career as an apprentice in the Frankfort banking house of *Rothschild and was soon transferred to the Naples office, where he conducted the Rothschilds' financial negotiations, including those with the Vatican. After an assignment to Havana, Cuba, in 1837, Belmont served the Rothschild interests in New York. Later he opened his own banking house, August Belmont & Co., which continued to represent the Rothschilds in the United States until the beginning of the 20th century. In 1844 he was appointed honorary Austrian consul general in New York, but resigned in 1850 in protest against the Vienna regime's brutal treatment of the Hungarian rebels, particularly their leader, Louis Kossuth. Belmont represented the United States at The Hague as chargé d'affaires (1853–55), and as minister (1855–58). At the conclusion of his foreign service, Belmont returned to New York and became active in political life. He supported the Union during the Civil War and raised and equipped the first German-born regiment in New York. He enlisted the support of European bankers and merchants for the Union cause during visits to Europe in 1861 and 1863. As Democratic National Committee chairman from 1860 until his retirement from politics in 1872, he exercised great influence in his party and American society. He introduced thoroughbred racing and became the founder of the U.S. Racing Club. One of New York's largest horseracing tracks carries his name. Belmont severed his Jewish ties and married the daughter of Commodore Matthew C. Perry. One son, Perry (1850–1947), became a lawyer, diplomat, congressman, and an author on United States history and politics. The other, August (1853–1924), succeeded his father as head of the bank, and played an important role in financing public transportation in the United States.

Bibliography: R. J. H. Gottheil, *The Belmont-Belmonte Family* (1917), 173–5; I. Katz, *August Belmont . . .* (Eng., 1968).

[J.O.R.]

BELMONTE, town in northern Portugal near the Spanish frontier. Its medieval community is seldom mentioned in the contemporary records, but there is preserved a Hebrew synagogal inscription of 1296–97, probably originally intended to be placed above the synagogue Ark. After the forced conversion of the Jews in Portugal at the end of the 15th century, Belmonte became a major center of New Christian life. A number of well-known families of the Marrano Diaspora bearing this name originally derive from this place. It was here that S. Schwarz first established contact with the surviving Marranos in 1917. The crypto-Jewish traditions are more faithfully preserved here than in any other place in Portugal, and there are some approaches to an organized religious life.

Bibliography: Roth, Marranos, index; A. Novinsky and A. Paulo, in: *Commentary* (May, 1967), 76–81; S. Schwarz, *Os Christãos – Novos em Portugal no século XX* (1925), 9–12; idem, *Inscrições hebráicas em Portugal* (1923), 23–28; N. Slouschz, *Ha-Anusim be-Portugal* (1932), 94–99; ESN, 1 (1949), 59.

[C.R.]

BELMONTE, Dutch Sephardi family of poets and diplomats of Marrano extraction. The first member of the family to figure in Jewish life was Jacob Israel (1570–1629). Born in Madeira as a Marrano under the name of Diego Nuñez Belmonte, he was one of the founding members of the Amsterdam Jewish community. According to Daniel Levi (Miguel) de *Barrios, he wrote a satire in Spanish directed against the Inquisition and a poem on Job, both now lost. His son MOSES (17th century), drew and engraved a portrait of his mother Simḥah (Gimar) Vaz. It is impossible to establish their family relationship with ISAAC NUÑEZ (alias MANUEL) BELMONTE (d. 1705), a wealthy merchant who served from 1664 as Spanish agent general in the Netherlands and from 1674 as resident minister. In 1693 he was created count palatine by Emperor Leopold III, while at the same time the king of Spain conferred on him the title of baron. In 1676 Isaac Nuñez Belmonte founded a poetic society in Amsterdam, the *Academia de los Sitibundos* and in 1685 the *Academia de los Floridos*. In 1684 he was appointed one of the two deputies to represent the Sephardi community in cases before the Dutch authorities. Unmarried, he was succeeded after his death, both in his title and his diplomatic post, by his nephew Baron FRANCISCO (ISAAC) XIMENES (d. 1713) who, in turn, was followed by his son, MANUEL XIMENES (d. 1730) who died childless, and the title became extinct. JACOB ABRAHAM BELMONTE (alias Franz van Schoonenberg; b. 1757), Dutch diplomat, also was connected with this family, but it is impossible to establish the exact relationship. ISAAC NUÑEZ BELMONTE (18th–19th centuries), a scholar of Smyrna, presumably belonged to a branch of this family which had emigrated to Turkey. He was author of *Sha'ar ha-Melekh* (Salonika, 1771; Bruenn, 1801; Lemberg, 1859), a commentary on the first and second parts of Maimonides' *Mishneh Torah*.

Bibliography: Brugmans-Frank, 1 (1940), 455; Roth, Marranos (1959), 304, 332, 337f.; J. Caro Baroja, *Los Judíos en la España moderna y contemporanea*, 2 (1961), 152; ESN, 1 (1949), 59; I. da Costa, *Israel en de Volken* (1848), 287; idem, *Noble Families among the Sephardic Jews* (1936), index; R. J. H. Gottheil, *The Belmont-Belmonte Family* (1917).

[K.R.S.]

BELOFF, MAX (1913–), English historian and political scientist. Beloff, who was born in London, graduated in modern history from Oxford in 1935. From 1939 he taught history at Manchester University and returned to Oxford in 1946 as reader in the comparative study of institutions. During World War II he served in the Royal Signal Corps. In 1957 he became professor of government and public administration at Oxford and a fellow of All Souls' College. The author of numerous works on European history, American government, and Soviet foreign policy, Beloff also wrote extensively about developments in contemporary international relations, particularly concerning Western Europe after World War II. In *The United States and the Unity of Europe* (1963) he considered the prospects of European unity and the interdependence of Western Europe and the U.S. Two works on Soviet foreign policy, *The Foreign Policy of Soviet Russia 1929–41* (1947–49) and *Soviet Policy in the Far East 1944–51* (1953) were among the pioneering attempts to present a documentary and historical assessment of the Soviet Union's role and aims in international politics and are considered standard works in this field. Beloff's studies of American government, including *The American Federal Government* (1959), concentrated on the historical roots of American federalism and how its evolution shaped the structure and functioning of contemporary American politics and institutions. Among his other works are: *The Age of Absolutism, 1680–1815* (1954); *Europe and the Europeans* . . . (1957), a report prepared at the request of the Council of Europe; *The Great Powers: Essays in 20th Century Politics* (1959); and *The Balance of Power* (1967). [B.K.]

BELORUSSIA, territory located between the rivers Neman (west) and Dnieper (east) and the rivers Pripet (south) and Dvina (north). Between the 14th and 18th centuries part of *Poland-Lithuania, from the partitions of Poland (1772–95) until the 1917 revolution it was part of the "northwestern region" of Russia, and much of it was included in the three "guberniyas" (provinces) of Minsk, Mogilev, and Vitebsk. Under Soviet rule Belorussia became a political entity as the Belorussian Soviet Socialist Republic.

Up to Soviet Rule. In Jewish history Belorussia is part of "Lita" (Lithuania), its Jews being considered "Litvaks." Jewish merchants apparently first visited Belorussia in transit between Poland and Russia as early as the 15th century. Jews were acting as toll collectors in Nowogrodek (1445), *Minsk (1489), and *Smolensk (1489). In 1495 the Jews in Belorussia were included in the expulsion of Lithuanian Jewry, returning with it in 1503. An important role in developing Belorussia was played by Jews from *Brest-Litovsk as large-scale farmers of the customs dues and wealthy merchants. Their agents were often the pioneers of the communities of Belorussia. A community was established in *Pinsk in 1506. By 1539 there were Jews settled in *Kletsk and Nowogrodek, and subsequently in Minsk, *Polotsk, *Vitebsk, *Mogilev, and *Orsha. The Christian citizenry consistently opposed the permanent settlement of Jews within the areas of the cities and towns under municipal jurisdiction. In Vitebsk, for instance, they were not granted permission to build a synagogue until 1630. Within the framework of the Council of Lithuania (see *Councils of the Lands), Pinsk was one of the three original principal communities; most of the communities in Belorussia came under the jurisdiction of the Brest-Litovsk community, while several were subject to that of the Pinsk community. In 1692 the *Slutsk community also achieved the status of a principal community. Smaller communities also grew up under the protection of the landowners who rented their towns, villages, taverns, or inns to Jewish contractors (see *Arenda). These made constant attempts to break away from the jurisdiction of the older communities and manage their communal affairs independently.

Down to the period of the partitions of Poland the communities in Belorussia were constantly exposed to the danger of Russian incursions, which were accompanied by wholesale massacres and forced conversions. Such occurred in 1563 in Polotsk, and in many other communities between 1648 and 1655.

The relative strength of the Belorussian communities in the middle of the 18th century is shown by the amounts levied on them as listed in the tax register of the Council of Lithuania for 1761: for the communities in the eastern part of Belorussia, 16,500 zlotys; Polotsk and environs, 3,000 zlotys; the area around Minsk (including 40 small communities), 4,260 zlotys; Slutsk and its environs, 2,420 zlotys; Druya and its environs, 750 zlotys; Nowogrodek, 300 zlotys. According to the government census of 1766, there were 62,800 taxpaying Jews living in Belorussia, forming 40% of Lithuanian Jewry. The largest communities were in Minsk (1,396 Jewish inhabitants) and Pinsk (1,350).

After Belorussia passed to Russia in the late 18th century *Shklov became an important commercial center on the route between Russia and Western Europe. Although a small group of Jews acquired wealth as building contractors, army suppliers, and large-scale merchants, the vast majority of Jews in the region of Belorussia were relatively destitute. Nevertheless their numbers grew. There were 225,725 Jews living in the three "guberniyas" of Belorussia in 1847, and 724,548 in 1897 (13.6% of the total population), forming the majority in the principal cities of the region. There were 47,561 Jews in Minsk (52.3% of the total population); 34,420 in Vitebsk

(52.4%); 32,369 in *Daugavpils (46.6%); 21,539 in Mogilev (50%); 21,065 in Pinsk (74.2%); 20,759 in *Bobruisk (60.5%); and 20,385 in *Gomel (54.8%). The Jews in the cities and townships of Belorussia had associations with the village and rural economy in a variety of ways. Both the wealthy and poorer Jews engaged in the development and trade of forest industries, and established small or medium-sized timber enterprises. They also developed leather and allied industries on a similar scale. Another Belorussian Jewish occupation was peddling combined with the buying up of village produce, such as flax, hemp, and bristles, which the Jewish peddler sold to Jewish merchants who exported these commodities to the West. Because of the prevailing conditions of poverty large numbers of Jews emigrated from Belorussia to the Ukraine or southern Russia, and, from the 1880s, to the United States.

In the cultural sphere, the Jews of Belorussia were influenced by the centers in Vilna, Volhynia, and Podolia. In general the **Mitnaggedim* trend predominated in the north and west of the region. Most of the celebrated Lithuanian yeshivot were in Belorussia, those of *Volozhin and *Mir, among others. Ḥasidism penetrated Belorussia from the south. Two of the fathers of Ḥasidism, *Menahem Mendel of Vitebsk and *Shneur Zalman of Lyady, were active there. Belorussia was the cradle of *Ḥabad Ḥasidism. In southern Belorussia the influence of the ḥasidic rabbis of the *Karlin and *Stolin dynasties was strong. By the mid-19th century Haskalah penetrated the larger towns from Vilna. The pogroms in Russia of 1881 to 1883 did not spread to Belorussia. The Ḥovevei Zion found adherents mainly in the larger and average-size communities. Toward the end of the 19th century Zionism and the Bund movement began to spread among Belorussian Jewry. Zionism found its main adherents among the middle-class professionals and white-collar workers or working men from the ranks of traditional Judaism. It was in Belorussia that Labor Zionism originated, its centers being Minsk, Bobruisk, Gomel, and Vitebsk. The second convention of Russian Zionists was held in Minsk in 1902. The Bund won converts mainly among Jewish artisans and workers, but also among radicals of the intelligentsia. During the revolution of 1905 the Bund headed the revolutionary movement in Belorussia. Self-defense organizations to protect the Jews during the wave of pogroms in this period were established by the Bund and the Labor Zionists at this time in every town in the region. The first move toward organized Jewish self-defense there was made to combat a gang of rioters in Gomel in the fall of 1903. As a result only a few communities in Belorussia were harmed.

The revolution precipitated far-reaching changes in the internal life of the Jews of Belorussia which contributed to the breakup of the traditional Jewish social and spiritual patterns and loyalties. Zionism resulted in the development of modernized *ḥadarim* and Hebrew schools. After the outbreak of World War I a stream of refugees and émigrés from Poland and Lithuania passed through Belorussia, and were warmly received by the Jews there. The 1917 February Revolution aroused great expectations among the Jewish public, and the Jewish political parties emerged from underground. A number of Jewish journals were issued in Minsk, including the Zionist *Der Yid* and the Bundist *Der Veker.* In the Minsk district the Zionists received 65,400 votes in the elections to the All-Russian Constituent Assembly as against 16,270 votes for the Bund and the Mensheviks. After the October Revolution and the Peace of Brest-Litovsk, Belorussia became a battlefield between the Red Army and the Polish army. The Jewish communities suffered severely both from the general wartime conditions and from attacks by the Polish Army when Jews were killed indiscriminately on the charge of spying and helping the Red forces. The victims of these atrocities included 35 Jews in Pinsk in April 1919. Russian volunteers under the command of General Bulak-Balakhovich terrorized the Jews in the small towns and villages. After the Treaty of Riga in March 1921, Belorussia was divided between the Soviet Union and Poland.

Under Soviet Rule (until 1941). During the first years of Soviet rule, the Jews of Belorussia found themselves in an exceptional situation. Among the Belorussian people, mainly poor and uneducated peasants, nationalist feelings were just beginning to crystallize. The anti-Jewish tradition, which poisoned relations between the Jews and non-Jews in Poland and the Ukraine, was little felt among the peasant masses of Belorussia. On the other hand, there were no cultural ties between the Belorussians and the Jews. The Jewish poet, Samuel Plavnik (1886–1941), known by the pseudonym Zmitrok *Byadulya as one of the creators of Belorussian literature even before the October Revolution, was a rare phenomenon. The Jewish population in Belorussia existed in conditions conducive to a flourishing cultural and social life of its own. Relatively, the largest concentration of Jews in the Soviet Union was that of the Belorussian Republic, with a solidly based social structure and culture, Yiddish being its main language. According to the census of 1926, the 407,000 Jews in Belorussia formed 8.2% of the republic's total population. A considerable proportion of the urban population was Jewish. There were 53,686 Jews (40.8%) in Minsk; 37,745 (43.7%) in Gomel; 37,013 (37.5%) in Vitebsk; and 21,558 (42%) in Bobruisk. The Belorussian government, in its policy of reducing the predominance of the Russian language in the towns, which was to no small extent a language used by the Jews, encouraged the promotion of Yiddish among the Jewish population. For some time the slogan "Workers of the World Unite!" was also inscribed in Yiddish, in addition to Belorussian, Russian, and Polish, on the emblem of the Belorussian Republic.

With the consolidation of the Soviet regime in Belorussia, the old economic structure of the Jewish population was overturned. The abolition of private trade and the restrictions on the small artisan created a large class of citizens "deprived of rights" *("Lishentsi")*. Attempts to integrate these elements into the agricultural and industrial sectors failed to solve the problem. A partial solution was however achieved by the continuous Jewish emigration from Belorussia to the interior of Russia, especially to Moscow and Leningrad. According to the census of 1939, there were only 375,000 Jews living in Belorussia, and their proportion in the general population had decreased to 6.7%.

The *Yevsektsiya (Jewish section of the Communist Party) was particularly active in Belorussia in its violent campaign of propaganda and persecution against the Jewish religion and way of life and Jewish national solidarity. *Ḥadarim* and yeshivot were closed down, and synagogues turned to secular use. Yet, even in the late 1920s religious Jews still fought courageously for the right to publish *siddurim,* calendars, etc., and to maintain synagogues. *Ḥadarim* and yeshivot were maintained secretly. A relentless war was also waged on Zionism, which was deeply entrenched in Belorussia. Underground Zionist youth movements (*Kadimah, *Ha-Shomer ha-Ẓa'ir, *He-Ḥaluẓ) continued their activities in Belorussia until the late 1920s. It was only after repressive measures and systematic arrests that the movements were suppressed.

On the other hand, the Jewish Communists attempted to create a framework for promoting a Soviet-inspired secular national-Jewish culture in Belorussia. A network of Jewish schools giving instruction in Yiddish was established, which, in 1932–33, was attended by 36,650 children, 55% of the Jewish children of school age. A number of Yiddish newspapers were also established, the most important of which were the daily *Oktyaber* and the literary journal *Shtern*. In 1924 a Jewish department was set up in the Institute of Belorussian Culture of Minsk, with philology, literature, and history sections. There was also an institute for Jewish teachers at the Belorussian University. In 1931, proceedings were conducted in Yiddish in ten Soviet law tribunals. A center for Yiddish literature was created in Minsk of which the most outstanding members were the writers Izzie *Kharik, Moshe *Kulbak, and Selig *Axelrod. During the 1930s, there was a sharp decline in this cultural activity with the abolition of the Yevsektsiya. The Jewish cultural and educational institutions gradually degenerated, and toward the end of this decade most were liquidated. The systematic "purge" of Jewish intellectuals in Belorussia also began in the late 1930s (Izzie Kharik and Moshe Kulbak in 1937, and Selig Axelrod in 1941).

Western Belorussia under Polish and Soviet Rule. In the western part of Belorussia, which was under Polish rule from 1920 to 1939, Jewish life developed on entirely different lines. The old economic order was maintained, and the Jews continued to engage in commerce and crafts, most living in great poverty. Jewish culture however was able to develop naturally. *Ḥadarim* and yeshivot, including yeshivot whose members had fled from the Soviet sector, such as the yeshivah of Slutsk that transferred to Kletsk, continued to expand. A Hebrew school network (Tarbut, Yavneh) was established. The Zionist movement was well organized and many of the youth joined the Zionist bodies, from Ha-Shomer ha-Ẓa'ir to Betar. Many were also members of the illegal Communist movement which was rigorously repressed in this border region. Yiddish remained the spoken language of the Jewish masses and knowledge of Hebrew was widespread. In the cultural sphere the Jews there looked to the important centers of Vilna, Brest-Litovsk, Bialystok, and Warsaw.

In September 1939, when western Belorussia was annexed by the Soviet Union, hundreds of thousands of Jews in whom religious and nationalist feelings were strong augmented the numbers of Belorussian Jewry already under Soviet rule. They also included groups of refugees from the Nazi-occupied zone. Even though the Soviet authorities immediately began to liquidate the practice of religion and the Zionist movement, signs of awakening were evident among the "older," "Soviet" Jews. In Bialystok a nucleus of Jewish writers and intellectuals was formed. The Hebrew schools were converted to Yiddish. The higher authorities however were prompt to give the signal to liquidate this "reactionary evolution." Arrests of "bourgeois elements" and expulsions to the interior of Russia followed, and every effort was made to press forward with the liquidation and assimilation carried out over 20 years in eastern Belorussia. The German invasion of Belorussia in June 1941 interrupted this activity, then at its height. The Jews in Belorussia, most of whom had not succeeded in escaping eastward, were now caught in the trap of the Nazi occupation.

For their subsequent history, see *Russia, Holocaust Period, Contemporary Period.

Bibliography: Dubnow, Hist Russ; N. P. Vakar, *Belorussia—the Making of a Nation* (1956); idem, *Bibliographical Guide to Belorussia* (1956); W. Ostrowski, *Anti-Semitism in Belorussia and its Origin* (1960); H. Shmeruk, *Ha-Kibbutz ha-Yehudi ve-ha-Hityashvut ha-Yehudit be-Belorussia ha-Sovietit—1918–1932* (1961), Eng. summ.; *Vitebsk Amol* (Yid., 1956); *Slutzk and Vicinity* (Heb., Yid., Eng., 1962); *Sefer Bobruisk* (Heb., Yid., 1967); *Sefer Pinsk* (1969). [Y.S.]

BELSHAZZAR (Heb. בֵּלְשַׁאצַּר בֵּלְאשַׁצַּר; the Akkadian name *Bel-šar-uṣur*, "O Bel, guard the king"; LXX, Βαλτασάρ), son of *Nebuchadnezzar and the last king of Babylon, according to the Book of Daniel. The biblical account (Dan. 5) relates that Belshazzar gave a banquet for his high officials at which the wine was drunk from the sacred vessels captured by Nebuchadnezzar from the Temple in Jerusalem amid songs to the idols of gold, silver, etc. While they were thus engaged, a mysterious hand appeared and wrote on the wall words which none of the Chaldeans was able to read or interpret but which Daniel, on being summoned by the king, read as **Mene Mene, Tekel Upharsin*, and interpreted as a warning to Belshazzar of the impending downfall of his kingdom. That night Belshazzar was killed and was succeeded as world ruler by *Darius the Mede (5:30; 6:1). Two of Daniel's visions are dated as occurring in the first and third years of Belshazzar's reign (7:1; 8:1). While the details given in Daniel appear historically inaccurate, Babylonian texts mention a Bēl-šar-uṣur as the son, crown prince, and regent of *Nabonidus, the last king of Babylon (556–539 B.C.E.). In Nabonidus' absence, Babylon was captured by the armies of *Cyrus, king of Persia. Neither Nabonidus nor Belshazzar was directly descended from Nebuchadnezzar. Presumably because he was a regent, Belshazzar's name is coupled with that of Nabonidus in Babylonian prayer formulae (in the prayer for the king's health in I Bar. 1:11, it is coupled—unhistorically—not with Nabonidus but with Nebuchadnezzar) and in two legal documents (12th and 13th years of Nabonidus), where an oath is sworn by their lives. While the Greek historians Herodotus (1:191) and Xenophon (*Cyropaedia*, 3:5, 15) do not mention Belshazzar, they share with Dan. 6 the—hardly historical—tradition that the Babylonians were engaged in revelry at the time when the Persians entered the city (corresponding to the time when Belshazzar was killed in the biblical account).

In the Aggadah. Belshazzar is often linked in the *aggadah* with two of the other Babylonian rulers mentioned in the Bible, Nebuchadnezzar and *Evil-Merodach. Thus the "three-year-old heifer" that Abraham was commanded to offer up (Gen. 15:9) is said to be a reference to these three kings (Gen. R. 44). The occasion of Belshazzar's feast was his miscalculation that the "seventy years" (Jer. 25:11–13) of exile before the redemption had passed without any sign of God's help to His people, a calculation that he made from the date of Nebuchadnezzar's accession to the throne, instead of from the destruction of the Temple (Dan. 9:2; Meg. 11b). Darius and Cyrus were the doorkeepers of Belshazzar's chamber. On the night after he had seen the handwriting on the wall, the king commanded them to kill anyone who tried to enter, even if he should claim to be king. Belshazzar himself, however, had cause to leave the room during the night by a private entrance, and when he attempted to reenter through the usual entrance, Darius and Cyrus, in accordance with his own instructions, slew him (Song. R. 3:42).

In the Arts. Christian writers and artists of the Middle Ages saw in Belshazzar a prefiguration of the antichrist. Belshazzar's feast is described in the *Ordo Prophetarum*, a medieval mystery cycle, in the section dealing with the prophet Daniel. From Renaissance times onward, however, the theological aspect of the story faded, and its dramatic and spectacular character was invariably emphasized. The great Spanish playwright Pedro Calderón de la Barca (1600–1681) devoted one of his innumerable *autos sacramentales* to the theme, his *La Cena de Baltasar* (written c.1634), combining fine poetry with excellent stagecraft. In England Hannah More included a *Belshazzar* in her *Sacred Dramas* (1782); Lord *Byron wrote the poem "Vision of Belshazzar" (in his *Hebrew Melodies*, 1815); and the poet and historian Henry Hart

"Belshazzar's Feast" by Rembrandt, 1634. London, National Gallery.

Milman, who became dean of St. Paul's Cathedral, produced *Belshazzar; a Dramatic Poem* (1822), a melodramatic verse-play not intended for the stage. Another English work inspired by the biblical story was *The Impious Feast* (1828), a poem by Robert Eyres Landor. Lord Byron's interpretation is said to have inspired the poem *Belsazar*, one of the earliest works of Heinrich *Heine, which appeared in his *Buch der Lieder* (1827). Another writer who dealt with the theme was the Spanish playwright and novelist Gertrudis Gómez de Avellaneda, author of the romantic tragedy *Baltasar* (1858).

In the visual arts treatment of the Belshazzar episode followed the same pattern as in literature. The antichrist interpretation occurs in medieval manuscript illumination, notably the 11th-century *Saint-Sever Apocalypse*, and in sculpture at Vézelay, France (12th century), and Amiens and Magdeburg (13th century). By contrast, the spectacular aspect is dominant in later painting, notably the dramatic portrayal by *Rembrandt (1634). [Ed.]

The biblical story has also inspired orchestral and vocal music. Handel's powerful oratorio *Belshazzar* (1745; text by Charles Jennens) did not deter later composers from attempting versions of their own. The most successful of these was William Walton's oratorio *Belshazzar's Feast* (1931; text arranged by Osbert Sitwell). Other treatments of the theme were Sibelius' *Belsazars gästabud* (1906), written as incidental music to a drama by the Finnish-Swedish poet Hjalmar Procopé and reworked as an orchestral suite in 1907; and a setting of Heine's *Belsazar* by Bernard van Dieren (1884–1936). The incidental music to a play on the theme which Joseph *Achron composed in 1928 was later reworked as two tableaux for large orchestra. **[B.B.]**

Bibliography: In the Bible: J. A. Montgomery, *Daniel* (ICC, 1949²), 66, 261; R. P. Dougherty, *Nabonidus and Belshazzar* (1929), passim; H. L. Ginsberg, *Studies in Daniel* (1948), 25–26. In the Arts: L. Réau, *Iconographie de l'art chrétien*, 2 pt. 1 (1956), 408–9; Sendrey, Music, nos. 7504, 9083.

BELTESHAZZAR (Heb. and Aram. בֵּלְטְשַׁאצַּר ; בֵּלְטְאשַׁצַּר; LXX, Βαλτασάρ; Vulg., Baltassar), name given to *Daniel in Babylonia (Dan. 1:7). Foreigners introduced into court life were often given native names; e.g., in Egypt *Joseph became known as Zaphenath-Paneah (Gen. 41:45). Popular etymology related the name Belteshazzar to Bel (Dan. 4:5) but it probably derived from *Balaṭ-šarri-uṣur* ("Protect the life of the king").

Bibliography: J. A. Montgomery, *The Book of Daniel* (ICC, 1949²), 123; W. Baumgartner, *Hebraeisches und aramaeisches Lexikon zum Alten Testament* (1967), 127.

[B.Po.]

BELTSY (Rum. **Bălti**), city in Bessarabia, Moldavian S.S.R.; in Rumania 1918–40 and 1941–44. Jews were invited there in 1779 when an urban nucleus was formed in the village. Their rights and obligations were established by an agreement of 1782. There were 244 Jewish families living in Beltsy in 1817. The community subsequently increased through immigration; after the *May Laws were issued in 1882, many Jews expelled from the neighboring villages settled in Beltsy. The community numbered 3,124 in 1864, and had grown to 10,348 in 1897 (56% of the total population) even though Jewish domicile was limited by legislation and Jews were often expelled from the city as illegal residents. As an outcome of these expulsions, coupled with economic difficulties, many Jews from Beltsy emigrated toward the end of the 19th century, including a group to Ereẓ Israel.

In 1847 a Jewish state school was opened in Beltsy. A *talmud torah*, founded in 1889, provided instruction in both

Jewish and general subjects. By the 1930s Jewish educational institutions included a kindergarten, three elementary schools, and two secondary schools, for boys and girls. Welfare institutions included a hospital and old-age home. The Jews in Beltsy were mainly occupied in commerce and crafts; some living in the vicinity engaged in agriculture. The 1,539 members of the local Jewish cooperative loan-bank in 1925 included 656 occupied in business, 441 in crafts, and 156 in agriculture. The Jewish population numbered 14,259 (46% of the total) in 1930. When Bessarabia passed to Soviet Russia in June 1940, the communal organization was disbanded. [El.F.]

Holocaust Period and After. In June 1941, about two-thirds of the town's buildings were destroyed in German and Rumanian air raids. The Jews fled to the nearby villages, mainly to Vlad. On July 7, a gang of Vlad peasants fell upon homes sheltering the refugees, murdered the occupants, and set fire to the houses. The next day, a group of Rumanian soldiers came upon 50 Jews on the road to Beltsy, drove them into the swamps and shot them to death. Beltsy was captured by the Germans on July 9 and those Jews who had returned were deported to a concentration camp. The same day ten Jews who had been taken as hostages were executed. The Gestapo also asked the ghetto committee to furnish it with a list of 20 "Jewish communists" who were to be put to death. When they refused to do so, all the committee members, together with another group of 44 Jews, were forced to dig their own graves and shot. Twenty more Jews were shot by the Germans on July 16. On July 11, 1941, all the surviving Jews were concentrated in the courtyard of the Moldova Bank. The Rumanian troops who took over transferred them from there to an internment camp in the Răuţel forest, some 7½ mi. (12 km.) from the town. Many of the inmates died from starvation and disease. By August 30, 1941, only 8,941 Jews were left in the entire district (as against the 31,916 residing there according to the 1930 census). They were concentrated in three camps, and later on all were deported to *Transnistria. Even the Jewish tombstones were removed from the Jewish cemetery in Beltsy to erase all traces of the Jewish inhabitants of the town. Jews returned to Beltsy after the war. The only synagogue was closed by the authorities in 1959 and the Jewish cemetery was badly neglected. In 1962 militia broke into a house where Jews had assembled for prayer; those attending were taken to the public square where communist youth had been gathered to jeer them. Their children were expelled from school. The city has retained a certain Jewish character and Yiddish is often heard on its streets. Its estimated Jewish population in 1970 was 15,000. [J.An./Ed.]

Bibliography: E. Schwarzfeld, *Din istoria evreilor ... in Moldova* (1914), 36–39; M. Carp, *Cartea Neagră*, 3 (1947), index; Feldman, in: *Sefer Yahadut Besarabyah* (in press); M. Mircu, *Pogromurile din Basarabia* (1947), 5, 17, 160.

BELZ, small town in Lvov oblast, Ukrainian S.S.R. (between the World Wars, Poland). The Jewish settlement in Belz dates from the beginning of the 16th century. About 200 Jews inhabiting 32 houses are recorded in 1550. Belz was devastated in 1655. It later revived and became famous as a center of Ḥasidism. The *rebbes* of the Rokeaḥ dynasty (see next entry) officiated as rabbis of the Belz community. Other noted rabbis of Belz include Joel *Sirkes, Zechariah *Mendel, and Jonah *Te'omim. In 1921 the Jews numbered 2,104 (50.7% of the total population). In February 1942 during the Nazi occupation about 1,000 Jews from Belz were deported to death camps. In May 1942 an additional 1,540 were deported. The remaining were hunted down and deported in September of that year. In 1970, Jews lived in the town and there was one synagogue.

Bibliography: *Bleter far Geshikhte*, 1–2 (1950), 78, table 5.

[N.M.G./Ed.]

BELZ, one of the most important ḥasidic dynasties of Galicia, so called after the township where it took up residence (see previous entry). The founder of the dynasty, Shalom Roke'aḥ (1779–1855), came from a distinguished family descended from R. Eleazer *Roke'aḥ of Amsterdam. Orphaned as a child, Shalom studied under his uncle, Issachar Baer of Sokal whose daughter he married. At Sokal he was introduced to ḥasidic teachings by *Solomon of Lutsk, a devoted follower of *Dov Baer, the *maggid* of Mezhirech. Later Shalom became a disciple of *Jacob Isaac Horowitz, ha-Ḥozeh ("the Seer") of Lublin, Uri of *Strelisk, the *maggid* Israel of *Kozienice, and *Abraham Joshua Heschel of Apta. On the recommendation of Horowitz, Shalom was appointed rabbi in Belz. After Horowitz' death in 1815, Shalom was recognized as a *zaddik* as his following increased. He built a splendid *bet midrash* in Belz. Thousands of Ḥasidim flocked to him, including rabbis and well-known *zaddikim*, and Belz became the center of Galician Ḥasidism. Many legends tell of the miracles he performed. Shalom was also considered an authoritative talmudist; he stressed the importance of talmudic study and strengthened the principle of learning in Ḥasidism. Active in public affairs, he served as a spokesman for Galician Jewry, taking part in the struggle to improve the severe economic conditions, and opposing Haskalah. Excerpts from his teachings have been frequently quoted. They are collected, with legends and tales of his activities, in *Dover Shalom* (1910). Many of Shalom's descendants served

The Belz *rebbe*, Issachar Dov, on his way to the Western Wall, 1970. Photo Weiss, Jerusalem.

as *zaddikim*, including his son-in-law Henikh of Olesko and his son Joshua (1825–1894) who succeeded him. The latter provided Belz Ḥasidism with the organizational framework which maintained it as the focus of Ḥasidism in Galicia, and ruled his community strictly. One of the leaders of Orthodox Jewry in Galicia, he was prominent in the opposition to Haskalah. He initiated the establishment of the Maḥazikei ha-Dat organization and the Orthodox newspaper *Kol Maḥazikei ha-Dat*. As a result of the cultural and social tensions in Galician Jewry, the Belz *zaddikim* adopted an extreme stand and resisted every new idea emanating from non-Orthodox circles. Some of Joshua's teachings are published in *Ohel Yehoshu'a* (printed with *Dover Shalom*, 1910). Joshua's successor Issachar Dov (1854–1927) was greatly influenced by Aaron of Chernobyl although Aaron taught a form of Ḥasidism that differed radically from that of the Belz school. Issachar Dov was an exacting leader of Galician Orthodoxy and also headed the Maḥazikei ha-Dat. In particular he opposed the Agudat Israel and denounced any innovations. He strongly opposed Zionism in any form. In 1914, when the war front reached Belz, he fled to Hungary and lived in Újfehértó where he succeeded in winning many Hungarian Jews to Belz Ḥasidism. In 1918 he moved to Munkács (*Mukacevo) and became embroiled in a bitter quarrel with the *zaddik* of Munkács which gave rise to a voluminous exchange of polemics. In 1921 Issachar Dov returned to Galicia and settled first in Holschitz, near Jaroslaw, moving back to Belz in 1925.

His son and successor Aaron (1880–1957) deviated little from the pattern set by his father. He lived an ascetic life, and instituted a lengthy order of prayers. The influence of Belz Ḥasidism had considerable impact on Jewish life in Galicia because its adherents entered all spheres of communal affairs and were not afraid of the effects of strife within the community. Many rabbis accepted the authority of the Belz *zaddikim*. In the parliamentary elections the Belz Ḥasidim did not join the Jewish lists, but voted for the Polish government party. On the outbreak of World War II, Aaron escaped to Sokol and then to Przemysl where 33 members of his family were murdered. After confinement in the ghettos of Vizhnitsa, Cracow, and Bochnia, he was sent to Kaschau (now *Kosice), then in Hungary, at the end of 1942 and subsequently to Budapest. In 1944 he managed to reach Ereẓ Israel. There he revised his political views and directed his followers to support the Agudat Israel. He established yeshivot and *battei midrash* throughout the country. His home in Tel Aviv became the new center for the followers of Belz Ḥasidism throughout the world. His grave is a place of pilgrimage where many gather on the anniversary of his death. He was succeeded by his nephew, Issachar Dov (1948–), who established a *bet midrash* in Jerusalem.

Bibliography: L. I. Newman, *Hasidic Anthology* (1934), index; M. I. Guttman, *Rabbi Shalom mi-Belz* (1935); A. Y. Bromberg, *Mi-Gedolei ha-Ḥasidut*, 10 (1955); M. Prager, *Hazzalat ha-Rabbi mi-Belz mi-Gei ha-Haregah be-Polin* (1960); Y. Taub, *Lev Same'aḥ Ḥadash* (1963); N. Urtner, *Devar Ḥen* (1963); B. Landau and N. Urtner, *Ha-Rav ha-Kadosh mi-Belza* (1967); M. Rabinowicz, *Guide to Ḥassidism* (1960), 93–96.

[Y.AL.]

BELZEC (Pol. **Bełżec**), small Polish town in the Lvov district; site of German labor camps and an extermination camp during World War II. In 1921 Belzec had 1,960 inhabitants, of whom 124 were Jews. In September 1939, after the partition of Poland between Germany and the Soviet Union, Belzec became part of the German-occupied territory, subsequently called the General-Gouvernement, and was incorporated in the Lublin District. In early 1940 Himmler decided to implement his Eastern Wall *(Ostwall)* plan on the border separating the German and Soviet "spheres of influence," and to use Jewish labor conscripts for this purpose. He obtained the approval of the German Army High Command, and a central labor camp was set up in Belzec shortly after. The first transport of 190 Jews from Lublin and the surrounding areas reached Belzec on May 29, 1940, even before accomodation or food had been prepared for them. In the following months additional transports with more than 7,000 persons arrived from Lublin, Warsaw, Radom, and adjacent areas. By the middle of August 1940 the number of forced laborers had reached 11,000. Jews were sent to auxiliary camps as well as to the three camps in Belzec itself. Living conditions in the camps were abominable, rations were extremely meager, and hundreds died of overwork, hunger, and disease, and from Nazi brutality. The Lublin Judenrat set up a Central Relief Committee in Belzec, and similar committees were established in each camp. The councils of localities from which Jews had been deported to Belzec sent assistance in various ways, but this aid could not satisfy their minimal needs. The camps were gradually liquidated by December 1940 and the surviving conscript laborers were sent back to their homes; but not everybody returned. According to an official German document, some 400 persons "disappeared," of whom "it is impossible to assume that all were shot." Records from the Warsaw ghetto describe the health of the returnees as so poor that many died soon after. The tank ditches dug by the Jews proved to be useless in the course of the war between Germany and the Soviet Union. They became mass graves for those who were gassed in the death camp set up at Belzec in the first half of 1942.

Jews in Zamosc waiting for deportation to the Belzec extermination camp, 1942. Jerusalem, Yad Vashem Museum.

The first mention of Belzec as an extermination camp occurs in a German document dated March 17, 1942. The camp was said to be able to handle four to five transports of 1,000 persons each a day, of whom "none will ever return to the General-Gouvernement." Deportations from Lublin and surrounding areas began at this time and approximately 20,000 Jews were brought to Belzec and put to death. Transports from other places, mainly in east Galicia, subsequently arrived in Belzec. Jews transported from Germany, Czechoslovakia, and Rumania were also exterminated at Belzec, after first being sent to the neighboring ghetto in Izbice. The camp functioned until the end of 1942. More than 600,000 people died at Belzec, including some 2,000 non-Jews. Their valuables and all other belongings were sent to Germany. The Jews in the ghettos, such as Warsaw, learned of what was happening at Belzec. After the war it became known that gas issuing from diesel engines in six special cells had been used for extermination.

The Germans liquidated the camp in the spring of 1943. The bodies were removed from their graves and cremated. Telltale signs were eliminated and *Volksdeutsche were settled on a farm established on the site. Only a few inmates succeeded in escaping from the camp, and of these, only one survived the war. The absence of survivors and the paucity of German documents referring to Belzec make a detailed history of the camp impossible. In consequence, the German staff of the camp could not be traced after the war, with the sole exception of the camp commandant's aide. The camp was directed by Odilo *Globocnik. His predecessor, Hermann Dolp, had previously been commandant of the Belzec labor camp. Other commandants were Gottlieb Hering and Christian *Wirth.

Bibliography: R. Hilberg, *Destruction of the European Jews* (1961), index; N. Blumental (ed.), *Te'udot mi-Getto Lublin* (1967), index; K. Gerstein, in: *Vierteljahreshefte fuer Zeitgeschichte*, 1, no. 2 (1953), 177–94; R. Reder *Bełżec* (Pol., 1946); E. Szrojt, *Biuletyn głownej komisji badania zbrodni niemieckich w Polsce*, 3 (1947), 29–45; Blumental, in: *Dokumenty do dziejów okupacji niemeckiej w Polsce*, 1 (1946), 215–24.

[N.B.]

BELZYCE (Pol, **Bełżyce**), small town in Lublin province, Poland. A charter of privileges granted to Belzyce in 1432 designated it a compulsory halting stage for merchants traveling to the Lublin fair. Jews settled there at the beginning of the 16th century, probably connected with this traffic. The physician *Jacob Naḥman lived in Belzyce at the end of the 16th century. The Council of Four Lands convened in Belzyce in 1643. The community suffered heavy losses during the *Chmielnicki massacres of 1648–49. The ḥasidic rabbi Gedaliah Samuel Jacubson lived in Belzyce in the second half of the 19th century. In 1764 the Jewish population numbered 949; in 1897, 1,705 (out of 3,182); in 1921, 1,882 (over half the total population); and in 1939, 2,100.

[N.M.G.]

Holocaust Period. The German army entered the town in mid-September 1939, and the Jewish population became subject to the persecution and terror carried out throughout Lublin Province. In February 1940 about 300 Jews from Stettin (then Germany) were deported to Belzyce. In February and March 1941 about 500 Jews from Cracow and another 500 from Lublin were forced to settle there. On May 12, 1942, several thousand Jews from central Germany (Sachsen and Thuringen) arrived. The town's Jewish population grew to about 4,500 by the time the mass deportations to the death camps began. On Oct. 2, 1942, the Germans conducted an *Aktion* to liquidate the remaining Jews in Belzyce. They rounded up over 3,000 Jews for extermination at Majdanek. Subsequently the Germans established a concentration camp in Belzyce in a few houses around the destroyed synagogue. At the end of March 1943 the Belzyce camp was liquidated. Several hundred Jews, mostly women and children, were shot, while another 250 women and 350 men were deported to the concentration camp in Budzyń, where only a handful survived. After the war the Jewish community in Belzyce was not reconstituted.

[S.Kr.]

Bibliography: T. Bernstein, in: *Bleter far Geshikhte* (Jan.–June 1950), 51–78.

BE-MOẒA'EI MENUḤAH (Heb. בְּמוֹצָאֵי מְנוּחָה; "at the close of the rest (day)," i.e., the Sabbath), name of a *piyyut* in acrostic style of unknown authorship. It forms part of the *Seliḥot service on the first day of the *Seliḥot* cycle preceding Rosh ha-Shanah. It consists of eight verses which close with the refrain "Hear our supplication and our prayer." The initial words of the first stanza as well as other expressions indicate that it was composed for the first day of *Seliḥot*, which always falls on a Saturday night–early Sunday morning. A song of a similar name, *Be-Moẓa'ei Yom Menuḥah*, forms part of the traditional hymns for the closing of the Sabbath. Its author is the liturgist Jacob de *Lunel ("Ya'akov min Yeriḥo").

English translation in *Seliḥot*, published by the Rabbinical Assembly, N.Y. (1964), 33–35; I. G. Glickstein and S. Braslavsky, *Midnight Service* (1931), 15ff.; A. J. Rosenfeld, *Authorized Selichot* (1957), 13. Text and melody in A. Nadel, *Zemirot Shabbat, Die haeuslichen Sabbatgesaenge* (1937), 44 (Hebrew part 16).

[M.Y.]

BEMPORAD, AZEGLIO (1875–1945), Italian astronomer. Bemporad, who was born in Siena, was appointed director of the Capodimonte Observatory near Catania in Sicily in 1912. Some of his first publications were of a purely mathematical nature, and until c. 1924 his main interest was the complex study of the extinction of starlight within the earth's atmosphere. He was also concerned with observational and theoretical studies of solar radiation, of variable stars, solar and lunar eclipses, and occultations. From 1925, he published discussions on the progress of the compilation of the *Catalogo astrofotografico . . . di Catania* as part of the international enterprise of mapping the sky. Bemporad wrote about the history of astronomy. In 1946, a commemorative volume of his life work was published.

[A.Be.]

BEMPORAD, ENRICO (1868–1944), Italian publisher. At an early age he joined the Florentine publishing company of the brothers Alessandro and Felice *Paggi. After the death of his father, Roberto, in 1891, he became the head of the firm which had, in the meantime, changed its name into R. Bemporad and son. Under his direction the publishing house became one of the most important in Italy. Bemporad established branch offices in many towns and extended the company's activities from educational and scholastic publications to wider literary fields. His company published the works of Giovanni Verga and Luigi Pirandello, as well as the initial edition of Dante's works for the Italian Dante Society. Bemporad was at various times president or managing director of other Italian publishing companies, including Lattes of Turin, Sansoni of Florence, and Zanichelli of Bologna. During the Nazi occupation Bemporad was compelled to abandon his publishing work. He went into hiding and died a few days after Florence was liberated.

[G.R.]

BENA'AH (**Benaiah**; third century C.E.), Palestinian scholar in Tiberias at the end of the tannaitic and the beginning of the amoraic era. Most of his dicta are transmitted in the Talmud by his disciple *Johanan Nappaḥa, but some are also cited in collections of tannaitic literature. His extant sayings are chiefly of an aggadic character: e.g., "Whoever occupies himself with the Torah for its own sake makes learning an elixir of life" (Ta'an. 7a); "The Pentateuch was given scroll by scroll" (Git. 60a). Bena'ah acquired a great reputation for wisdom, juridical ability, and the unraveling of complex legal cases, as a result of which the Roman authorities appointed him a judge. He was the author of an enactment according to which any judge found guilty even in a civil case was deemed unworthy of continuing in his judicial office (BB 58a-b). According to the biographer of the emperor Alexander Severus, the introduction of a similar statute in Roman law was the result of the Jewish precedent (*Scriptores Historiae Augustae*, Alexander Severus, 45:7). Bena'ah used to mark burial caves to keep the unsuspecting from defilement. In this connection, the talmudic aggadah relates some wondrous tales such as that of his visit to the grave of Adam (BB 58a). Bena'ah was the head of an academy in Tiberias, which apparently continued to function after his death. His disciple, Johanan, taught there (TJ, Shab. 12:13c). Some scholars maintain that it was because of this college that Tiberias was selected as the site of the central academy in Palestine.

Bibliography: Bacher, Tann; Hyman, Toledot, 280–1. [Z.K.]

BEN-ADIR (pen name of **Abraham Rosin;** 1878–1942), writer and Jewish socialist leader, born in Krucha, Belorussia. He received a traditional Jewish education from his grandfather Jacob Aaronson and his uncle Solomon *Aaronson. At the age of 16 he went to Odessa to sit for the university examinations as an external student, and then moved to Minsk. In 1896–97 he became influenced by A. *Liessin who advocated a Jewish national brand of socialism. After the First Zionist Congress in 1897, Ben-Adir published an article advocating political Zionism in opposition to the ideology of *Aḥad Ha-Am. In 1901 he moved to Paris where he studied at the Free Russian University, and later returned to Russia. After the *Kishinev pogrom of 1903 Ben-Adir published a call for the formation of a Jewish party which would combine the aims of revolutionary socialism with national Jewish aspirations. Ben-Adir was one of the founders and ideologists of the *Vozrozhdeniye group, and of its successor of the Sejmists (*Jewish Socialist Workers' Party) whose program included Jewish national-political autonomy while envisaging *Territorialism as a remoter aim. He edited its organs *Serp* (Russian) and *Folkśshtime* (Yiddish). After the February 1917 Revolution, Ben-Adir became a leader of the *United Jewish Socialist Workers' Party. Also in 1917 he published *Kehile Fragen,* a pamphlet envisaging the *kehillah* as an instrument of national Jewish *autonomy. Ben-Adir withdrew from the united party in 1919 when the communist trend predominated, and in 1921 left Russia for Berlin. His *In Khaos fun Lebn un Denken* ("Whirlwind of Life and Thought"), a collection of essays on socialist problems, in particular an argument against communism, was published in 1925. Ben-Adir stayed in Ereẓ Israel between 1925 and 1927 but returned to Berlin, leaving for Paris in 1933. After the French defeat by the Nazis in 1940 he went to the United States. In Paris and New York he coedited the *Algemeyne Entsiklopedye* ("General Encyclopedia in Yiddish") to which he also contributed.

Bibliography: LNYL, 1 (1956), 336–9; Rubin, in: *Asufot,* 1 (1945), 21–25. [Ed.]

BEN-AHARON (NUSSENBAUM), YIZḤAK (1906–), Israel labor leader. Ben-Aharon was born in Zoinitza, then Austrian Bukovina. A student of political science and economics in Berlin, he was also a leader of the *Ha-Shomer ha-Ẓa'ir movement. Ben-Aharon settled in Palestine in 1928, and was in kibbutz *Givat Ḥayyim from 1933. In 1940 he joined the British Army Pioneer Corps, serving as an officer, and was prisoner of the Germans, 1941–45. Active in the Yishuv's struggle against the British after the war, he was court-martialed, and discharged from the army in 1946, and was among the Jewish leaders arrested on "Black Sabbath" (June 29, 1946). Ben-Aharon became a leader of *Aḥdut ha-Avodah after its secession from *Mapai, representing it in the *Histadrut. He was elected to the Knesset several times, and in 1956–62 served as minister of communications and transport. In 1962 he called for the unification of all Zionist labor parties in Israel in order to revive the declining pioneering spirit. He became a prime initiator of the trend that culminated in the creation of the united Israel Labor Party after the Six-Day War

Yiẓhak Ben-Aharon, Israel labor leader.

(1967). In 1969, he was appointed secretary-general of the Histadrut. His writings include an explanation of Zionism for non-Jews, *Listen Gentile* (1947).

Bibliography: D. Lazar, *Rashim be-Yisrael,* 2 (1955), 149–53. [B.J.]

BENAIAH (Heb. בְּנָיָהוּ, בְּנָיָה; "YHWH has built"), son of Jehoiada, one of David's warriors and Solomon's commander in chief. Benaiah came from Kabzeel in Judah. Famous for his individual acts of valor, the killing of two warriors, the slaying of a lion in a pit in the snow, and the defeating of an Egyptian giant, he was one of David's most honored warriors (II Sam. 23:20–23; I Chron. 11:22–25). It is reasonable to attribute some of these deeds to the period of David's outlawry or to the first part of his reign. David appointed Benaiah as the head of his bodyguard (II Sam. 23:23; I Chron. 11:25), identified by some scholars with the Cherethites and Pelethites (II Sam. 20:23, according to the *keri;* I Chron. 18:17; cf. II Sam. 8:18; I Kings 1:38), whose commander was also Benaiah. After the death of *Ahithophel, he served as counselor to David, together with the priest *Abiathar (I Chron. 27:33–34, where the order of the names should be reversed according to some versions: "Benaiah son of Jehoiada" instead of "Jehoiada son of Benaiah"). Benaiah opposed *Adonijah's attempt to seize the crown at the end of David's reign and, together with the priest *Zadok and the prophet *Nathan, he proclaimed Solomon king (I Kings 1:8–44). He later carried out the liquidation of *Shimei, of Solomon's rival *Adonijah, and of the latter's supporter *Joab (2:25–46), in whose stead Solomon appointed Benaiah commander-in-chief.

Bibliography: Bright, Hist, 189–90; de Vaux, Anc Isr. 127–8, 220–1; Dinaburg (Dinur), in: *Zion,* 11 (1946), 165ff.; Mazar, in: *Sefer D. Ben Gurion* (1964), 248–67. [Y.M.G.]

BENAIM (Heb. בן נאיים), name of North African families of rabbis and merchants. Jacob Ḥayyim Benaim (d. 1803), rabbi in Fez, Morocco, author, and halakhic authority, left

Fez about 1760 for Algeria on his way to Ereẓ Israel, but remained in the city of Mascara, where he was appointed rabbi and *dayyan.* In 1764 he moved to Algiers to become *av bet din,* a position he held for 18 years; eventually, however, his harsh exercise of this office provoked opposition from noted scholars in the community and he left. He settled in Leghorn in 1782 and there had his works printed, including *Zera Ya'akov,* responsa (1784); *Yeshu'ot Ya'akov,* sermons (1795); and an edition of the Zohar (1795). His novellae to the Talmud were published posthumously in *Ḥesed ve-Emet* (Salonika, 1813). He also composed *piyyutim* for a local Purim of Algiers to commemorate the victory over the Spanish.

MOSES (19th century), merchant, emigrated from Algiers to Marseilles, France. In 1819 he established the Dramont commercial house for Franco-Moroccan trade; his good relations in the two countries proved beneficial to the business affairs of his Jewish compatriots. His son Makhluf founded another commercial company with the later Rif rebellion leader Abd el-Kader. RAPHAEL ḤAYYIM MOSES (c. 1850–1920), was born in Tetuan, but emigrated to Palestine in his youth. He was a member of the *bet din* of Tiberias. In the 1870s he traveled to Turkey and North Africa as an emissary to collect charitable funds for Palestine. In Gibraltar he was chosen chief rabbi (1881), and held this position until his death. His publications include *Raḥamim* [initials of Raphael Ḥayyim Moses (son of) Isaya (and) Masudah] *Peshutim,* responsa (Tunis, 1910; but according to the preface not published before 1914), and other rabbinical works.

JOSEPH (1882–1961), rabbi and clerk to the *bet din* of Fez, Morocco, was a lifelong bibliophile, who collected the largest library of books and manuscripts in Morocco. His own works include a bio-bibliographical dictionary of rabbis of Morocco, *Malkhei Rabbanan, Kevod Melakhim* (Jerusalem, 1931); a collection of sermons, *Millei Me'alyata* (in manuscript); and many other writings left in manuscript. After his death his library was sold to the Jewish Theological Seminary of New York. DAVID (1888–1968), son of Raphael Ḥayyim Moses, was the leader of the Jewish community in Gibraltar after his father's death. He became a member of the Government Council of the Colony, and in 1954 was appointed honorary consul of Israel for Gibraltar.

Bibliography: J. M. Toledano, *Ner ha-Ma'arav* (1911), 185, 193; Yaari, Sheluḥei, 656, 859; R. H. M. Benaim, *Raḥamim Peshutim* (1910), preface; A. Cahen, *Juifs dans l'Afrique septentrionale* (1867), 105–6; Hirschberg, Afrika, 2 (1965), index; H. Z. Hirschberg, *Me-Ereẓ Mevo ha-Shemesh* (1957), 212–4; *Oración Fúnebre . . . J. Ibn Naim* (Leghorn, 1803); Miège, Maroc, 2 (1961), 160, 156.

[D.O.]

BEN ʿALĀN, JOSHUA (ninth century?), author of a Hebrew treatise on the Jewish calendar. Excerpts from the treatise are found in a polemical essay by the Karaite scholar Hasan b. Mashi'aḥ (Ms. Leningrad), in which the latter refers to Ben ʿAlān as "the rabbinical scholar who is the best versed in the science of the calendar." This is the only source for Joshua's name; a grammarian by name of Judah b. ʿAlān, who lived in Tiberias at the beginning of the tenth century, may have been Joshua's brother, as Harkavy assumes.

Bibliography: Harkavy, in: *Ha-Goren,* 4 (1903), 75–80; Poznański, in: REJ, 44 (1902), 176–7; Bornstein, in: *Ha-Tekufah,* 9 (1921), 224–5; Z. H. Joffe, *Korot Ḥeshbon ha-Ibbur* (1931), 86ff., 94ff., 129ff.

[M.N.Z./ED.]

BEN-AMI (Shieren), JACOB (1890–), actor and director. Ben-Ami's long stage career began in his native Minsk, Belorussia, before he was a teenager. After traveling with many Yiddish acting companies through Eastern Europe, Ben-Ami went to the United States in 1912 to appear with Rudolph Schildkraut and Sarah Adler in Yiddish plays. In 1918, together with Maurice *Schwartz, he founded the Yiddish Art Theater in New York. Ben-Ami's reputation as an actor and director grew, and in 1920 he made his English-language acting debut in *Samson and Delilah,* a drama written by a Dane, Sven Lange, that Ben-Ami had played and directed in Yiddish in New York and in Russia. The following year he made his Broadway debut in Peretz Hirshbein's *The Idle Inn,* and many leading roles followed. Ben-Ami played more parts on the English-speaking stage than on the Yiddish, but he did not appear in a commercial success until almost 40 years later, when he played a grandfather in Paddy Chayefsky's *The Tenth Man* (1959). In the interim, Ben-Ami toured extensively in South America, in South Africa, and in the United States where he did Yiddish plays and Yiddish translations of Russian, European, and American plays.

[S.KA.]

BEN-AMI (Dankner), OVED (1905–), founder and long-time mayor of Netanyah. Ben-Ami, who was born in Petaḥ Tikvah, served as secretary of Benei Binyamin (1924–28), an organization of the sons of early Jewish settlers, which was instrumental in establishing several new settlements. Ben-Ami founded the town of Netanyah in

Oved Ben-Ami, founder of Netanyah. Bronze by Duda (David Edelstein), 1965.

1928–29, and the settlement of Even Yehudah in 1932. He was mayor of Netanyah continuously from 1930 with minor interruptions. During that time Netanyah became a major resort and the center of Israel's diamond industry. In 1947 Ben-Ami and other Jewish mayors and *yishuv* leaders were arrested by the British Mandatory authorities in reprisal for Jewish underground activities. Ben-Ami was a member of the Liberal Party and a part owner of *Ma'ariv,* the daily evening paper. From 1958 to 1961 he was active in the establishment of the new town of Ashdod, heading the

Ashdod Development Company. He wrote the books, *Netanyah, Birat ha-Sharon* (1940), and *Unbreakable Spirit of Our Jewish Heritage* (1964).

Bibliography: Tidhar, 2 (1947), 1024–25. [B.J.]

BEN-AMITAI, LEVI (1901–), Hebrew writer. He received a general education in his native Belorussia and in 1917 joined the He-Ḥalutz movement. In 1920 he emigrated to Palestine, where he worked as a manual laborer. He became a member of Kibbutz Deganyah Bet in 1925, and worked there first as an agricultural laborer, then as a teacher. His stories and sketches in Hebrew periodicals began to appear in 1925. His books of poetry include: *Ha-Shibbolim Penimah* (1934); *Leilot ba-Maẓor* (1939); *Ba-Kevuẓah* (1938); *Sadot she-ba-Emek* (1950); *Oholivah* (1959); *Mi-Midbar Mattanah* (1962), poems about the Essenes; and *Osfei Kayiẓ* (1966). He edited the anthologies *Deganiyyot* (1955) and *Ha-Sofer ba-Kevuẓah* (1956), and was coeditor of a collection of short stories by writers in cooperative agricultural settlements, entitled *Al Admatam* (1959). Ben-Amitai's poetry is distinguished by its short verses, and restrained, almost prosaic style. The agricultural-folk setting takes on symbolic dimensions by virtue of the connotative language he chooses. Much of his writing is charged with strong religious accents that evoke a prayerful mood. [G.K.]

BEN-AMMI (Rabinowicz), MORDECAI (1854–1932), author and journalist writing in Russian. A traditional Jewish education and the harsh circumstances of his life after early losing his father are reflected in his stories. At Odessa he attended a yeshivah where the curriculum included languages and sciences. Influenced by Perez *Smolenskin he became a *maskil,* and entered a Russian secondary school and thereafter the University of Odessa. When the pogroms broke out in southern Russia in 1882, Ben-Ammi took part in organizing Jewish self-defense in Odessa. He campaigned against the czarist regime for organizing the pogroms and the Russian press for condoning them, also castigating the Jewish intelligentsia for failing to defend its people. In 1882 he went to Paris to obtain assistance from the Alliance Israélite Universelle for the victims of the pogroms. From there he sent his "Letters from Paris" to the Russian-Jewish monthly *Voskhod* (signed "Resh Galuta"), which reflect his deep appreciation of Jewish values. The same year Ben-Ammi moved to Geneva where he began to write stories depicting the joyous spirit of the festivals and legends associated with them. In 1883 he completed the stories *Priezd Tsadika,* and *Ben Yukhid,* the latter reflecting the atmosphere of the days of the Cantonists, and in 1884 a long story *Baal Tefila.* The stories became popular among Jews who read Russian. In 1887 Ben-Ammi returned to Odessa, where he remained until 1905, and published the autobiographical story *Detstvo* ("Childhood"), in which he describes the Jewish background of his youth. In articles published in *Voskhod* he attacked the czarist authorities for their anti-Jewish discrimination. He also criticized the Jewish intelligentsia for having renounced Jewish values and for leaving their persecuted brethren to their fate. He also published a collection of stories for Jewish juvenile readers with illustrations, as well as a series of stories in Yiddish. Ben-Ammi became a member of the committee of Ḥovevei Zion in Odessa on its foundation in 1890, and was a delegate to the First Zionist Congress and other congresses convened by Theodor Herzl. His esteem for Herzl was so great that on his death Ben-Ammi mourned him as for a close relative. While living in Odessa, he taught in the Jewish school directed by Mendele Mokher Seforim, whose faithful friend he remained throughout his life. On the outbreak of the Russian revolution of 1905, Ben-Ammi returned to Geneva. In 1923 he settled in Ereẓ Israel. Ben-Ammi's stories portray the traditional Jewish way of life from the inside. Despite a certain sentimentality and romanticization, the sincerity and spirit of piety permeating them made an appeal, especially to the young. Several were translated into Hebrew by Ḥ. N. Bialik.

Bibliography: Aḥad Ha-Am, *Al Parashat Derakhim,* 3 (1921), 64–65; J. Klausner, *Yoẓerei Tekufah u-Mamshikhei Tekufah* (1956), 107–17; *Haolam,* no. 17 (1911), 2–3; LNYL, 1 (1956), 349; I. Klausner, *Mi-Katoviẓ ad Basel,* 2 (1965). [I.K.]

BEN-AMOTZ, DAHN (1923–), Israel author and humorist. Born in Poland, he was taken to Palestine with a group of children in 1938, escaping the fate of his parents who were murdered in the Holocaust. He joined the British Navy during World War II. After the war he volunteered for the Palyam, the marine branch of the Palmaḥ, where he first established himself as a humorous writer. Though his earliest publication is a volume of "serious" stories *Arba'ah ve-Arba'ah* (1950), he won fame with a collection of Palmaḥ lore—half fact, half tall story—entitled *Yalkut ha-Kezavim* ("Bag of Lies," 1956), which he wrote jointly with the poet Ḥayim *Ḥefer. His other humorous writings, initially published in the Hebrew press, are collected in *Mah Nishma* ("What's New," 1959) and *Eikh La'asot Mah* ("How to do What," 1962). Besides writing, Ben-Amotz made a reputation for himself as a witty radio personality, a sharp-tongued interviewer, and manager of "Ḥamam," a satirical stage. In 1968 he published his first full-scale novel, *Lizkor ve-Lishko'aḥ* ("To Remember and to Forget") which, though laced with humor, is basically a return to serious writing. A semi-autobiographical story, it constitutes the author's attempt to confront a past he had tried to ignore, his non-*sabra* origin, the murder of his parents, and his own responsibility as their son. The questions of the German people's guilt, the existence of the "other Germany," and the moral justification for accepting German Reparations are all widely explored in this book. [Mi.A.]

BENAMOZEGH, ELIJAH BEN ABRAHAM (1822–1900), Italian rabbi and philosopher. Benamozegh was born in Leghorn of Moroccan parents, members of a wealthy Moroccan family of merchants and rabbis. He served as rabbi in Leghorn and as professor of theology in the rabbinical school of that city, and wrote numerous works in Hebrew, French, and Italian, in which he attempted to present a systematic exposition and interpretation of the doctrines of Judaism, and to point out the affinities between Judaism and contemporary secular philosophy. Benamozegh was influenced by the culture of the Jews of Morocco and the East, in which the Kabbalah played an important role, and by the secular philosophy of his day, in particular by the Italian philosophers Rosmini-Serbati and Gioberti. He regarded the Kabbalah as an essential component of Judaism, defending it against the attacks of many of his contemporaries. Regarding Judaism as a synthesis of the universal eternal truths which are scattered throughout the religions, philosophies, and mythologies of other peoples, he believed that the study of Judaism was essential for the solution of the religious questions of mankind at large.

Among Benamozegh's Hebrew works are: (1) *Eimat Mafgi'a,* a refutation of Leone *Modena's attack on the Zohar and the Kabbalah (1855); (2) *Ger Ẓedek,* explanatory notes to Targum Onkelos (1858); (3) *Ner le-David,* a commentary on Psalms (1858); (4) *Em la-Mikra,* a commentary on the Pentateuch, incorporating the findings of comparative philology, archaeology, and ancient history (1862–65); (5) *Ta'am le-Shad*, a refutation of Samuel David *Luzzatto's *Vikku'aḥ al ha-Kabbalah*, in which Luzzatto had disputed the antiquity of the Zohar (1863); (6) *Ya'aneh ba-Esh*, on the prohibition of the cremation of the dead (1886); (7) a general introduction to the Oral Law for use by the rabbinical students at the seminary in Leghorn (in *Ha-Levanon*, 1 (1864), 73ff.). In Italian, Benamozegh published a collection of lectures on Essenes, entitled *Storia degli Esseni* (1865), and *Teologia dogmatica e apologetica*, on theology (1877). In French he wrote *Morale juive et morale chrétienne* (1867; Hebrew translation *Bi-Shevilei Musar*, 1966), and *Israël et l'humanité*. The preface to this work was published in 1885. The complete work, with an introduction by Hyacinthe Loyson, appeared in 1914, a shortened version in 1961, and a Hebrew translation in 1967.

Bibliography: Fuenn, Keneset, 100; W. Zeitlin, *Kiryat Sefer* (1891–95), 19; Benjacob, Oẓar, 35, no. 678, 398, no. 178; D. Lattes, *"Ani Ma'amin" shel Filosof Yehudi* (1943); G. Lattes, *Vita e opere di Elia Benamozegh* (1901); U. Cassuto, *Gli studi giudaici in Italia negli ultimi cinquant' anni* (1913), 4–6; A. Pallière, *Le sanctuaire inconnu* (1926); Maynard, in: *Jewish Institute of Religion Quarterly*, 4 (1928), 15-19.

[M.N.Z./Ed.]

BENARDETE, MAIR JOSÉ (c. 1895–), philologist. Benardete was born in Turkey and emigrated to the United States in 1910. He taught at Hunter College, New York. Benardete wrote a number of volumes in the field of Spanish literature and civilization. Several Loyalist ballads are presented in English translation in *And Spain Sings* (1937), which he prepared in collaboration with the poet Rolfe Humphries. His *Hispanic Culture and Character of the Sephardic Jews* (1952, Spanish, 1963) is an analysis of the Sephardi Jews.

Bibliography: H. V. Besso, in: I. A. Langnas and B. Sholod (eds.), *Studies in Honor of M. J. Benardete* (1965), 459–86 (including bibliography).

[V.A.M.]

BENARES, capital of Benares district, India. This sacred city of the Hindus became the residence of Anglo-Jewish merchants toward the end of the 18th century because of its proximity to the diamond mines. Among these early Jewish merchants was Jacob Barnet, an English diamond merchant who moved from Madras to Benares in 1780. His clients in London included the merchant-house of Israel Levin *Solomons. In 1786 Lyon Prager was sent by this firm to Bengal and established his headquarters in Benares. Prager also became inspector and purchaser of drugs, indigo, and other commodities for the English East India Company. After his death in 1793 his activities were continued by his brother George Prager, who moved from Benares to Calcutta. The Jewish association with Benares was maintained by the affluent Anglo-Portuguese Jewish diamond merchant Benjamin d'Aguilar (d. 1813), and Pellegrine Treves (d. 1825), who obtained permission to settle in Bengal in 1774.

Bibliography: W. J. Fischel, in: REJ, 123 (1964), 433–98.

[W.J.F.]

BEN-AROYA, AVRAHAM (1887–), Greek socialist and one of the founders of the labor movements in Salonika and Macedonia. Born in Vidin, Bulgaria, Ben-Aroya was a teacher and in 1908 went to Salonika, then under Turkish rule, where he taught Bulgarian and worked as a printer. Already an enthusiastic socialist, Ben-Aroya found in Salonika's large Jewish working class a ready audience for his doctrines. While his views were close to those of the small revolutionary Bulgarian group, he was drawn to the exploited and unorganized Jewish workers in the city, especially the tobacco workers with whom he shared common interests. In 1909 he formed the Salonika workers' organization later known as the *Federación Socialista Laboradera* ("Socialist Workers' Federation"). Under Ben-Aroya's direction the Federation founded the first workers' newspaper in Turkey, *El Journal del Laborador*,

Avraham Ben-Aroya, Greek labor leader.

and later a weekly Ladino newspaper, *Solidarità Oberadera*. After the Balkan war, Ben-Aroya joined with Greek socialists in Athens. He formed *La Bursa del Laboro* ("Jewish Syndicate Center") and was elected chairman of its executive. He was also a leader of the Greek Socialist Party, but when the Party split in 1924 Ben-Aroya helped to found the Social Democratic Party and its newspaper *The New Period* (in Greek). Subsequently, Ben-Aroya published numerous political pamphlets including tracts on *Social Democracy and the Jewish Question* (Bulgarian) and *The Workers' Movement in Turkey* (Hebrew tr. 1910). In 1953 Aroya emigrated to Israel. Although bitterly opposed to Zionism for many years, the rise of Nazism and World War II changed his views, while his decision to emigrate to Israel reflected his disillusionment with socialism, which he had previously believed would resolve the Jewish question.

[B.U.]

BENARUS, ADOLFO (1863–1958), Portuguese writer. His grandfather David Bensabat, born in Morocco, was the first Jew to settle (1815) in the Azores Islands. Benarus was born there, at Angra do Heroísmo. He was a painter and philologist and taught English in the faculty of letters of the Uni-

Adolfo Benarus, Portuguese writer.

versity of Lisbon and in other educational institutions. He was active in communal life and was honorary president of the Jewish community of Lisbon. He wrote: *Israel* (1924); *Os Judeus, Historia Estranha deste Povo* ("The Jews, the Strange Story of This People," 1927); *A Tragédia da Historia* ("The Tragedy of History," 1937); *Antisemitismo* (1948); as well as pamphlets on Jewish festivals.

[M.B.A.]

BENAS, BARON LOUIS (1844–1914), English banker and communal worker. Born in London, he settled in Liverpool early in life where he carried on the family banking business. He established in 1867 the Liverpool branch of the *Alliance Israélite Universelle, which later became the local branch of the *Anglo-Jewish Association, serving as its president until his death. He was chairman of a commission set up in 1882 by the London Russo-Jewish Committee to supervise the emigration via Liverpool to the United States of refugees from Russia. He was elected president of the Liverpool Literary and Philosophical Society in 1890 and wrote several papers for that and other learned societies, including *Records of the Jews in Liverpool* (1899). His son, BERTRAM BENJAMIN BARON (1880–1968), practiced as a chancery barrister from 1906. A well-known figure in legal circles, he was appointed bencher of the Middle Temple in 1953, and was also chairman of the Liverpool Bar Association. He served as president of the Merseyside Jewish Representative Council (1944–46) and of the Jewish Historical Society of England (1951–53). He was the author of a number of books and papers, including supplements to his father's pioneering monograph on Liverpool Jewish history.

Bibliography: JC (Feb. 6, 13, 1914, on Baron Louis; Dec. 13, 1968, on Bertram Benjamin); Roth, Mag Bibl, index; Lehmann, Nova Bibl, index.

[S.D.T.]

BEN-ASHER, AARON BEN MOSES (called Abu Sa'id in Arabic; first half of tenth century), last and most important of a family of masoretes active in Tiberias for six (or five) generations, from the second half of the eighth century. That Ben-Asher lived in the first half of the tenth century may be deduced from a list in the *Keter,* a biblical manuscript formerly in Aleppo, now in Israel. This states that Ben-Asher vocalized and *masar* (i.e., wrote the *Masorah of) the *Keter,* which was written by Solomon b. Bouya'a, a well-known scribe, who wrote another Bible dated 930. It is also known that Ben-Asher was no longer alive in 989, since the scribe of the manuscript of the Former Prophets from that date says of him: "may he rest in the Garden of Eden" (Leningrad, Firkovich II, Ms. 39). Ben-Asher was apparently an elder contemporary of *Saadiah Gaon, who wrote the anti-Karaitic critique *"Essa Meshali,"* against Ben-Asher.

The controversial question, as to whether or not Ben-Asher was a Karaite, was seemingly settled when this reply of Saadiah (mentioned in Dunash's objections on Saadiah, p. 21, no. 72) was discovered. In this reply it is clear that the Ben-Asher who was Saadiah's opponent worked on masorah, and it seems, therefore, that he was identical with Aaron Ben-Asher, the well-known masorete. The assumption that he was a Karaite serves to explain his attitude to the Bible and its authoritativeness in matters of *halakhah* (for example, *Dikdukei ha-Te'amim,* ed. A. Dotan (1967), ch. 2: "The prophets ... complete the Torah, are as the Torah, and we decide Law from them as we do from the Torah") and to vocalization, opinions rooted in Karaite thought. It appears from the parallel ideas and style used in the *Maḥberet Ben-Asher* (see below), from the "Wine Song" written by his father, and from the list which his father appended to the codex of the Prophets (kept in the Karaite synagogue, Cairo), which he wrote "827 years after the destruction of the Second Temple" (i.e., in 895), that his father, Moses Ben-Asher, was also a Karaite, and it is probable that Karaism was a family tradition. (Note, however, that Dotan (*Sinai,* 41 (1957), 280ff.) and M. Zucker (*Tarbiz,* 27 (1957/58), 61ff.) hold that Aaron Ben-Asher and his family were not Karaites.) It is noteworthy that the founder of the family, "Asher the Great Sage," apparently lived in the first half of the eighth century and was a contemporary of Anan, the founder of Karaism.

Ben-Asher rapidly gained fame as the most authoritative of the Tiberias masoretes, and in 989, the scribe of the above-mentioned manuscript of the Former Prophets vouched for the care with which his copy was written by the fact that he had vocalized and added the masorah "from the books that were [vocalized] by Aaron ben Moses Ben-Asher." Maimonides, by accepting the views of Ben-Asher (though only in regard to open and closed sections), helped establish and spread his authority. Referring to a Bible manuscript then in Egypt, he writes: "All relied on it, since it was corrected by Ben-Asher and was worked on *(ve-dikdek bo)* by him for many years, and was proofread many times in accordance with the masorah, and I based myself on this manuscript in the *Sefer Torah* that I wrote" (Yad, Maim. Sefer Torah, 8:4). It is generally agreed that the codex used by Maimonides is that formerly in Aleppo.

Proof for this is adduced from Saadiah b. David Al-Adni, who wrote in his commentary on the Yad (*ibid.*): "The Codex that the Gaon [i.e., Maimonides] used is in Zoba, called Aleppo, and is called the *Keter* ... and at the end is written, 'I Aaron Ben-Asher proofread it ... I saw and read it'" (Oxford, Bodleian Library Ms. Hunt. 372, fol. 138b; cf. P. Kahle, *The Cairo Genizah* (1947), 58). However, Cassuto, who studied the *Keter* in Aleppo, was doubtful. An attempt was made to refute these doubts by M. Goshen-Gottstein (*Textus,* 1 (1960), 1ff.), but A. Dotan further supported Cassuto's position (*Tarbiz,* 34 (1964/65), 136ff.) It is not certain that it was Ben-Asher who vocalized and added the masorah to the *Keter* of Aleppo, since the note in the manuscript was written after his death. The masorah has been vocalized and added by "the lord of scribes, the father of wise men and the first of teachers ... the unique Rabbi Aaron ben Rabbi Asher, may his soul be bound up in the bond of eternal life" (the latter being an epithet applied to a person who has died).

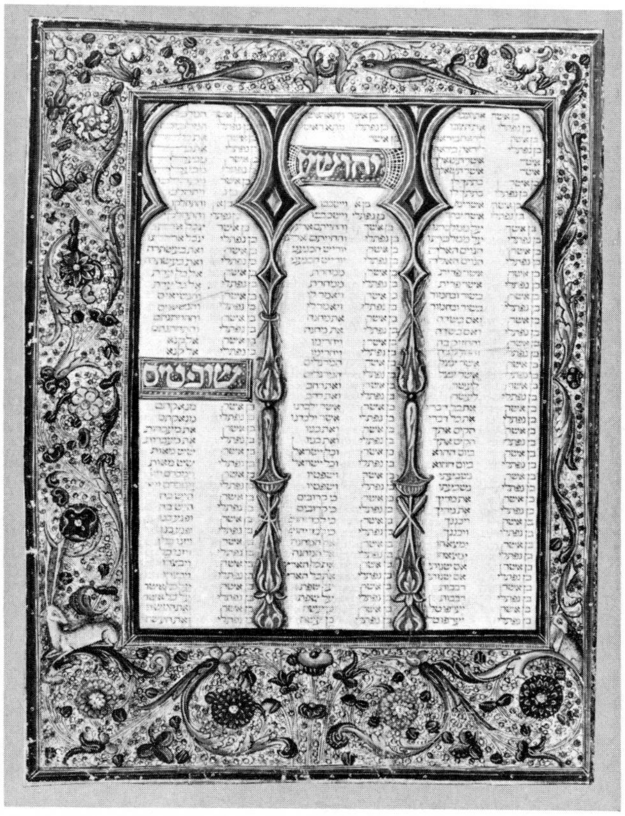

List of masoretic differences between Ben-Asher and Ben-Naphtali, from the *Aberdeen Bible,* Italy, 1493. Scotland, University of Aberdeen Library, ms. 23, fol. 3r.

The tradition of Ben-Asher is the one accepted in the Jewish Bible, but this does not mean that the version of the Bible found in the common editions is exactly the same as that which Ben-Asher produced. The differences between the printed editions and the various manuscripts assumed to be written in the Ben-Asher tradition are mainly in the placing of the accents, especially the use of the *meteg*, different uses of the *sheva* and *ḥataf* in certain grammatical forms, all differences that are unimportant for the average reader. These differences developed over the years, usually as a result of grammatical assumptions that were not always correct. Furthermore, certain divergences in vocalization and masorah are found even in manuscripts that are accepted as Ben-Asher codices. This fact, combined with the evidence of Mishael b. Uzziel in his *Kitab al-Khulaf*, indicates that Ben-Asher used different systems of vocalization at different times in specific words. It may be said, therefore, that different Ben-Asher manuscripts reveal a continual development in his method of vocalization.

Ben-Asher was one of the first to lay the foundations of Hebrew grammar. His *Sefer Dikdukei ha-Te'amim* (or the *Maḥberet Ben-Asher*, as *David Kimḥi called it in his commentary on Judg. 6:19) is a collection of grammatical rules and masoretic information. Grammatical principles were not at that time considered worthy of independent study. The value of this work is that the grammatical rules presented by Ben-Asher reveal the linguistic background of vocalization. The book was first published in the *Mikra'ot Gedolot* (1516–18), and again in 1879 by S. I. Baer and Strack, who edited the material according to topics, in a manner different from that in the first edition. Until recently all studies relating to Ben-Asher's system of grammar and masorah were based on this edition. A. Dotan's edition (1967), which includes a commentary and studies on the content of the book, changed the previous conception of *Dikdukei ha-Te'amim* as it had been understood for 90 years. Many of the phonological and morphological topics which had been commonly attributed to *Dikdukei ha-Te'amim* are not included. The main theme discussed in the book is the relationship of the biblical accents to the rules of vocalization and pronunciation. The *sheva* and its pronunciation play a major part in this work.

Except for certain parts, including masoretic lists, the book is written in a rhymed poetic style, using paytanic language. It can be assumed that the parts not written in this style were not by Ben-Asher. The language of the book shows a certain Arabic influence, particularly with regard to grammatical terms. Even in its more limited form *Dikdukei ha-Te'amim* is important not only for showing how the different vocalizers determined the correct vocalization, but also for a clearer understanding of the grammatical world of the later masoretes, who laid the foundations for Hebrew grammar in later generations.

Bibliography: Fuerst, Karaeertum, 1 (1862), 112; Graetz, in: MGWJ, 20 (1871), 1–12, 49–59; Bacher, in: ZAW, 15 (1895), 293–304; Mann, Egypt, 2 (1922), 43–49; P. Kahle, *Masoreten des Westens*, 1 (1927); idem, in: VT, 1 (1951), 161–8; idem, in: *Donum Natalicium H.S. Nyberg* (1955), 161–70; L. Lipschuetz, *Der Bibeltext der Tiberischen Masoretenschule* (1937); K. Levy, *Zur masoretischen Grammatik* (1936); Teicher, in: JJS, 2 (1950/51), 17–25; S. Pinsker, *Likkutei Kadmoniyyot* (1860), 32; Schorr, in: *He-Ḥalutz*, 6 (1862), 67ff.; J. Saphir, *Even Sappir*, 1 (1866), 11–20; 2 (1874), 185ff.; B. Z. Bacher, *Nizzanei ha-Dikduk* (1927), 27–41; D. Yellin, *Toledot Hitpatteḥut ha-Dikduk ha-Ivri* (1945), 6–29; M. H. Segal, *Mevo ha-Mikra*, 4 (1952³), 896–9 and esp. notes 15, 17; Ben-Ḥayyim, in: *Leshonenu*, 18 (1953), 92–94; B. Klar, *Meḥkarim ve-Iyyunim* (1954), 276–319; Cassuto, in: *Haaretz* (April 15, 1949).

[Z.B.-H.]

BEN-ASHER, MOSES (second half of ninth century), scribe and masorete. Moses was the fourth in the line of well-known masoretes descended from Asher the Elder, and the father of the last, Aaron. A manuscript by him of the former and latter prophets has survived, written, pointed, and furnished with accents and masoretic notes. Found today in the Karaite synagogue in Cairo, it has been photographed a number of times (one photocopy is in Jerusalem). A colophon by Ben-Asher at the end of the manuscript testifies that he wrote it in Tiberias in the year 827 after the destruction of the Second Temple (i.e., 896 C.E.). The manuscript is a beautiful one, embellished with drawings and illuminations, the work of an expert artist, in a style which, according to the latest investigations, constitutes an ancient specimen of Islamic decorative art, perhaps the most ancient of this type.

The vowel-points, the accents, and the masoretic notes are marked with the stamp of antiquity, but deviate greatly from the method of pointing of his son Aaron, whose method is nowadays called "the school of Ben-Asher" (see *Ben-Asher, Aaron). A comparison of the readings in the manuscript with the list of variants in the *Kitāb al-Khulaf* of Mishael b. Uzziel shows that in almost two-thirds of the cases the manuscript follows the reading of *Ben-Naphtali, and only in one-third, that of Aaron Ben-Asher (see *Masorah). At times it also maintains its own independent reading. In about a quarter of the cases in which the two authorities agree, according to Mishael, he differs from both their readings. He points בִּישְׂרָאֵל (Jer. 29:23) and לְיִרְאָה (Jer. 32:39). Accordingly the Ms. displays a great measure of affinity with what was later termed "the school of Ben-Naphtali." On the other hand it contains a great number of *ge'ayot* (i.e., *metegs;* "secondary stress"), more than was usual in other manuscripts of his time, particularly *ge'ayot* in open syllables (known as *ga'ayah gedolah* "major *ga'ayah*"). There are also other anomalies in the pointing, such as some *degeshim* in the letter א (בְּלוֹאֵי, Jer. 38:12; תְּלוּאִים, Hos. 11:7). It follows that the actual tradition of pointing was not uniform throughout the generations of the Ben-Asher family; it was only the occupation with the masorah that they had in common. Another possibility, suggested by A. Dotan, is that the pointing and accents of the manuscript are by a different scribe and that Moses Ben-Asher only wrote the consonantal text. In any event the

Colophon page of Moses Ben-Asher's manuscript of the Prophets, Tiberias, 895 C.E. The original is in the Karaite synagogue in Cairo.

fragment entitled "The order of Scripture," which he copied at the end of the manuscript (p. 583), was certainly not written by him.

No other works by Moses have survived, but his name is mentioned in an Arabic *genizah* fragment (Cambridge, Ms. T.-S. Arabic 9/5): "and Moses Ben-Asher, may God have mercy upon him, has already written a large book . . ." Because that fragment also mentions, though without any connection with M. Ben-Asher, the expressions מצותה ("vowel"), אלז׳ מצותאת ("the seven vowels"), Allony conjectured that the large book attributed here to M. Ben-Asher is the anonymous *Kitāb al-Muṣawwitāt* mentioned in several places in the writings of Jonah *ibn Janaḥ. Mention of it has also been discovered in Nissim Gaon's *Megillat Setarim* (see *Nissim b. Jacob b. Nissim), where it is ascribed to Ben-Asher (with no first name). At present there is not sufficient evidence to accept this conjecture. It would appear that he also wrote *piyyutim* and composed the "Song of the Vine," in which the people of Israel is compared to a vine whose roots are the patriarchs, and from which come forth the prophets and sages. Mention is also made there of the masorah, the accents, and the work of the masoretes. Most of the poem is extant, in three manuscripts (one of which is Ms. Leningrad B 19a) only its end is missing. The initial letters of the remnant verses form the acrostic משה בן אש . . . ("Moses Ben-Ash . . ."). This poem contains one of the decisive proofs that M. Ben-Asher was not a Karaite.

In some places the name has been corrupted as a result of a faulty completion of the abbreviation "Ben-Asher," as in the commentary *Migdal Oz* on Maimonides' Yad, Sefer Torah 8:4, where "Moses Ben-Asher" occurs instead of Aaron, and as in the British Museum manuscript (Or. 4227, p. 274b) where "Moses b. Aaron Ben-Asher, the great scribe," occurs instead of Aaron b. Moses.

Bibliography: J. Saphir, *Even Sappir,* 1 (1866), 14a–17a; 2 (1874), 185–91; R. Gottheil, in: JQR, 17 (1905), 639–41; E. S. Artom (Hartom), in: *Ha-Kinnus ha-Olami le Madda'ei ha-Yahadut,* 1 (1952), 190–4; B. Klar, *Meḥkarim ve-Iyyunim* (1954), 309–14; Pérez Castro, in: *Sefarad,* 15 (1955), 3–30; A. Dotan, in: *Sinai,* 41 (1957), 288–91, 295–9, 357–62; idem (ed.), *The Diqduqé Haṭṭeʿamim of Ahāron ben Mōse ben Ašér,* 1 (1967), 70f.; M. Zucker, in: *Tarbiz,* 27 (1957/58), 61–82; P. E. Kahle, *The Cairo Geniza* (1959²), 82–86, 91–105; idem, *Der hebraeische Bibeltext seit Franz Delitzsch* (1961), 51–76; R. H. Pinder Wilson and R. Ettinghausen, *ibid.,* 95–98; N. Allony, in: HUCA, 35 (1964), 1–35 (Heb. pt.); idem, in: *Sefer Segal* (1964), 271–91; idem, in: *Leshonenu,* 29 (1964/65), 9–23, 136–59; I. Yeivin, *Keter Aram-Ẓovah* (1968), 360f.

[A.Do.]

BENATZKY, RALPH (1884–1957), composer. Benatzky was born in Moravske-Budejovice and studied in Prague and Munich. A composer of light music, he wrote about five thousand songs and 92 operettas. The best known was *Im Weissen Roessl* (1930), which became famous throughout the world as *White Horse Inn.* Benatzky went to live in the United States in 1938, but later returned to Europe and settled in Zurich. He wrote the scores for about 250 films.

Bibliography: Riemann-Gurlitt; Baker, Biog. Dict.

[D.L.S.]

BEN-AVI, ITHAMAR (1882–1943), Hebrew journalist and Zionist. He was the son of Eliezer *Ben-Yehuda, from the initials of whose name Ben-Avi formed his Hebrew name. Ben-Avi was one of the first modern Jews whose mother tongue was Hebrew. In his early youth he began publishing in Hebrew periodicals edited by his father. He studied at the Teachers' Seminary of the Alliance Israélite Universelle in Paris and at the Institute for Oriental Studies at the University of Berlin. On his return to Ereẓ Israel in 1908, he joined the editorial board of Ben-Yehuda's *Ha-Ẓevi* and *Ha-Or,* bringing to them something of the flamboyant spirit of popular European and American journalism. During World War I he lived with his family in the U.S.A. Returning after the war he founded the daily **Do'ar ha-Yom* in Jerusalem in 1919 and continued to edit it until 1929. From 1924 onward he was also editor of the English-language *Palestine Weekly,* and served as the Jerusalem correspondent for the London *Times* and *Daily Mail* and several French newspapers. An accomplished speaker in several languages, Ben-Avi visited various

Ithamar Ben-Avi, Hebrew journalist and Zionist.

countries on behalf of the Jewish National Fund and the settlement projects of the native generation of moshavot farmers, of whose organization, *Benei Binyamin, he was a co-founder. In 1939 he went to the U.S.A., where he later died. His remains were interred in Jerusalem in 1947. Impetuous by nature, Ben-Avi advocated bold innovations, such as the writing of Hebrew in Latin characters, in which he published the weekly *Deror* (1934) and a biography of his father (*Avi,* 1927). In the 1930s he campaigned for the partitioning of Palestine into Jewish and Arab cantons. His political and cultural aim was the transformation of the Jewish people into an independent "western" nation.

Bibliography: H. Ben-Yehuda, *Nosei ha-Degel* (1944), includes bibliography.

[G.El.]

BENAYAH (Benaiah), family of scribes, who lived in Sanʿa, Yemen, in the 15th century. The books copied by members of the family, particularly the Scriptures, are noted for accuracy and beauty, and to this day Yemenite Jews remember Benayah as the greatest scribe in their history. The members of the family known to have been scribes are Benayah, his sons David and Joseph, and his daughter Miriam. Benayah's signature was "Safra (writer) Benayah b. Sa'adiah b. Zechariah."

According to Yemenite Jewish tradition, the Benayah family copied some 400 books for synagogues and private individuals, some of which are still extant. Most of them are unilingual Pentateuchs *(Tijān),* which include the large and small masorah in the margins and *Maḥberet al-Tijān,* which deals with matters affecting the traditional reading of the scriptural text and with grammar. Apart from Pentateuchs, they also copied books of *haftarot* with Aramaic translations and prayer books; one such prayer book, containing a wealth of songs and *piyyutim,* which had been copied by Joseph, is in the Royal Library in Berlin (Heb. Ms. 103).

The periods during which members of the family engaged in their work can be determined from the dates given by the

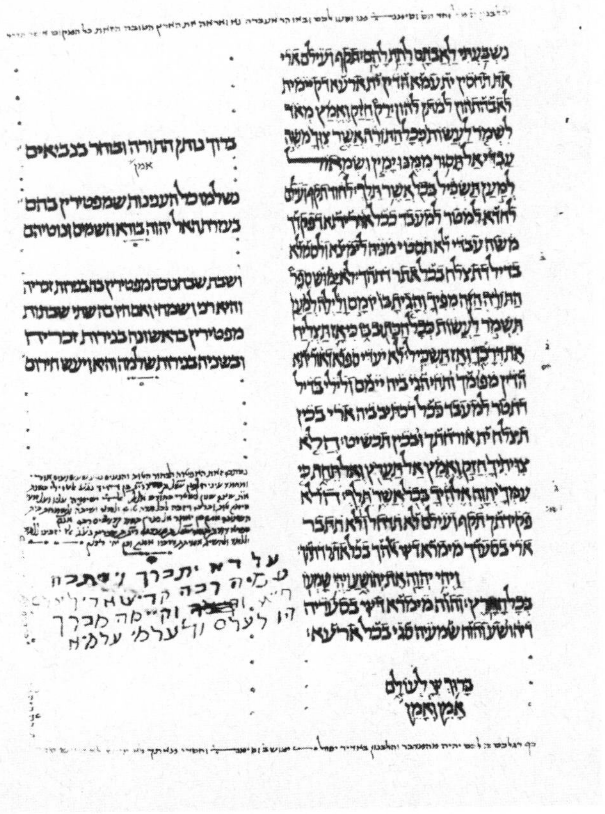

Colophon page of the *haftarot* written by the Yemenite scribe David b. Benayah, 1484. London, British Museum, ms. Or. 1470, fol. 78v.

inscriptions in the books: Benayah, 1470; David, 1484–1510; and Joseph, 1485–1508. Miriam, Benayah's daughter, was a phenomenon in Yemenite society and culture, where, as a rule, women were illiterate. Jacob *Saphir, who visited Yemen in 1859, describes a Pentateuch that Miriam copied, and which contains an apology by her at the end: "Do not condemn me for any errors that you may find, for I am a nursing woman; Miriam, the daughter of Benayah the scribe."

Two other scribes by the name of Benayah are known: Benayah b. Kalev b. Maḥpuẓ al-Bauli, around 1342 (J. L. Nahum, *Mi-Ẓefunot Yehudei Teiman* (1962), 252); and Benayah b. Saida b. Joseph, around 1587 (Moscow, Guenzburg Ms. 1306).

Bibliography: Margoliouth, Cat, 4 (1935), index s.v. *Benaiah*; J. Saphir, *Massa le-Teiman*, ed. by A. Yaari (1951), 173–4; D. S. Sassoon, *Ohel Dawid* (1932), 606–8; *Haaretz* (May 26, June 2, 16, July 14, 1961; Jan. 5, Feb. 2, 1962). [Y.R.]

BENAYAHU, MEIR (1926–), Israel scholar. The son of the Israel chief rabbi Isaac *Nissim, Benayahu was a member of the team of senior workers at the Ben-Zvi Institute for Research on Oriental Jewish Communities, which was founded in 1947, and from 1964 he was its director. A prolific researcher he published numerous studies and documents. His works include: *Marbiẓ Torah* ("Propagator of the Torah"), on the authority, functions, and status of the bearer of the title *Marbiẓ Torah* in Oriental countries (1951); *Rabbi Ḥayyim Yosef David Azulai* (1959), a comprehensive monograph; *Rabbi Ya'akov Elyashar ve-Ḥibburo Megillat Paras* ("R. Jacob Elyashar and His Work The Scroll of Persia," 1960); *Sefer Toledot ha-Ari* ("Biography of R. Isaac *Luria," 1967). He also published a new edition of *Zimrat ha-Areẓ* of Jacob *Berab (the Third) on the beginnings of the Jewish settlement in Tiberias during the mid-18th century. Benayahu was an editor of the yearbook *Yerushalayim* (Jerusalem), comprised of studies on Ereẓ Israel (vols. 3–5; 1951–55). The first seven volumes of the scientific periodical of the Ben-Zvi Institute, *Sefunot* (begun in 1957), were jointly edited by Izhak *Ben-Zvi and Benayahu, while from the eighth volume onward he was the sole editor. [Ed.]

BEN AZZAI, SIMEON (early second century C.E.), *tanna* who lived in Tiberias, generally referred to in talmudic literature simply as "Ben Azzai." He was presumably a disciple of *Joshua b. Hananiah since he transmitted rulings in his name (Yoma 2:3) and was also a "disciple–colleague" of R. Akiva (BB 158b). It was said of him: "With the passing of Ben Azzai, diligent scholars passed from the earth" (Sot. 9:15). Although he declared that whoever abstains from procreation is regarded as though he had shed blood (Yev. 63b), he himself never married, so as not to be distracted from his studies. When accused of not practicing what he preached, he answered: "What shall I do if my soul yearns for Torah? The world can be perpetuated by others" *(ibid.)*. Some state that he married, but separated from his wife (Sot. 4b). According to another tradition he was betrothed to Akiva's daughter who, as her mother had done, made it a condition of marriage that her husband devote himself to the study of the Torah (Ket. 63a). Apparently, however, the marriage never took place (Tos. to Ket. 63a). Ben Azzai was one of the four "who entered the Garden" (*pardes*, i.e., engaged in esoteric speculation); and it is reported of him that "he caught a glimpse and died," i.e., was led astray by mystical teaching (Ḥag. 14b). It seems that Ben Azzai was never ordained, possibly because of his early death. He is thus never referred to as "rabbi" and is spoken of, not as one of the "sages," but as one of the "disciples" who argued in the presence of the sages (Sanh. 17b). He was an outstanding scholar, and later generations of scholars used to underscore their own scholarship by claiming: "I am like Ben Azzai in the marketplace of Tiberias" (Kid. 20a). His aphorisms included: "Be quick in carrying out a minor commandment as in the case of a major one, and flee from transgression; for one good deed leads to another good deed and one transgression leads to another transgression; for the reward for a good deed is another good deed and the reward for a transgression is another transgression" (Avot 4:2). While R. Akiva said that the verse "Thou shalt love thy neighbor as thyself" (Lev. 19:18) is a great principle of the Torah, Ben Azzai declared that the verse "This is the book of the generations of man" (Gen. 5:1) embodied an even greater principle, i.e., of the common origin of mankind (Sifra 7:4 and parallel passages). Ben Azzai was renowned for his saintliness; it was said: "He who sees Ben Azzai in his dreams may look forward to achieving saintliness" (Ber. 57b). He is numbered by some among the *Ten Martyrs (Lam. R. 2:2, no. 4).

Bibliography: Bacher, Tann; Ḥyman, Toledot, 1206–09. [Z.K.]

BEN BAG BAG, *tanna*, apparently of the first century C.E. His most famous dictum: "Turn it and turn it [the Torah], for everything is in it, and contemplate it, and grow grey and old over it, and stir not from it, for you can have no better rule than this" (Avot 5:25) is elsewhere attributed to Hillel (ARN 12, 11). A number of halakhic statements are reported in Ben Bag Bag's name in various *baraitot* (e.g., Er., 27b; Tosef., BK 10:38). On the question whether a person is permitted to take the law into his own hands he states: "do not enter your neighbor's courtyard in stealth to take what belongs to you without his permission, lest you appear to him a thief; rather break his teeth [i.e., enter openly] and say to him, 'It is my own property that I take' " (BK 27b). Some scholars identify Ben Bag Bag with Johanan b. Bag Bag, who sent a question to Judah b. Bathyra in Nisibis, and whom the latter eulogized as "an expert in the chambers of the Torah" (Tosef., Ket. 5:1). Some incline to the view that the name is symbolic like that of *Ben He He (Avot 5:26) with whom he has been identified, and that he was a proselyte (Ḥag., 9b and Tos., s.v. *Bar He He*). Some identify him with the proselyte who came to Hillel and asked to be taught the Torah "while standing on one leg," which occasioned the famous reply of Hillel: "What is hateful to thee do not do to thy fellow."

Bibliography: Bacher, Tann; Frankel, Mishnah, 100f.; Hyman, Toledot, 672 s.v. *Yoḥanan b. Bag Bag.* [Z.K.]

BEN CHANANJA, the first Hungarian Jewish learned periodical, published in German between 1844 and 1867. *Ben Chananja* was founded and edited by Leopold *Loew. It first appeared in Leipzig as a quarterly in 1844; resumed publication in Szeged, Hungary, in 1858; and became a weekly in reduced format in 1861. *Ben Chananja* advanced the scientific development of Jewish studies and stimulated interest in Jewish questions. Its contributors were scholars of prestige in Hungary and abroad. The periodical presented biblical exegesis, commentary on the Talmud, historical studies, educational information, and literary news. It also considered religious and social problems, advocating the establishment of a rabbinical seminary and legislation for Jewish emancipation. Among the contributors were Simon Bacher, Abraham Hochmuth, Solomon Buber, S. D. Luzzatto, and Leopold Dukes. The academic material was supplemented with topical articles, editorials, Jewish communal news, and occasional poems. *Ben Chananja* had correspondents in Jerusalem, Berlin, New York, and in most cities with large Jewish communities in Europe and America. [J.Z.]

BENCHETRIT, AARON (1886–1967), physician and communal leader. Born in Tetuán, Spanish Morocco, Benchetrit spent his childhood in Caracas, Venezuela, and studied in Paris and Caracas. He was the medical director and administrator of the Leproserías de Venezuela (1921–26). In 1927 he moved to Bogotá, Colombia, where he was in charge of all leprosy cases in the country from 1927 to 1935 and directed many scientific researches on leprosy. He published several medical works including *Disertaciones de un estudiante de medicina* (1917), *La epidemia febríl de Caracas* (1919), *Nuevas disertaciones* (1921), and *Disertaciones acerca de la lepra* (1922). He also wrote on Zionism in *Disertaciones acerca del sionismo.* Benchetrit was president of the Centro Israelita of Bogotá and was president of the Zionist Federation of Colombia, 1943–44. [Ed.]

BENCHIMOL, Moroccan family. The descendants of Abraham Benchimol, one of the leaders of the community in Fez (1700), established a business of international repute in Tangiers at the end of the 18th century. For four generations the family played a leading role in Morocco's political and economic life. As diplomats, they were entrusted with many missions by the French or the sultans. Ḥayyim (1834–1915), who lived in Tangiers, was the founder of freemasonry in Morocco. There he organized and supported the *Alliance Israélite Universelle. He also established the first newspapers in Tangiers for the defense of human rights and of the Jews in particular. His influence provoked attacks by the anti-Semite Edward *Drumont. A philanthropist and a founder of charitable institutions, Ḥayyim headed the Jewry of northern Morocco.

Bibliography: J. M. Toledano, *Ner ha-Ma'arav* (1911), 124, 133; F. Rey, *De la protection diplomatique et consulaire dans les échelles du Levant et de Barbarie* (1899), 515–7; A. Laredo, *Memorias de un viejo Tangerino* (1935), 435–449; Miège, Maroc, 2 (1961), 85ff.; 210; 3 (1962), 443, 498; 4 (1963), 49–50; Hirschberg, Afrikah, 2 (1965), 313.

[D.Co.]

BENDA, JULIEN (1867–1956), French writer and philosopher. Benda studied history and philosophy at the Sorbonne. His first book *Dialogues à Byzance* (1900), offered a bold analysis of the manifestations of corruption in French society, which formed the background of the Dreyfus Trial. Benda wrote several novels, especially in the first years of his literary activity, including *L'Ordination* (1911), which reveal his rationalistic outlook and rigorous morals. But Benda was first and foremost a philosopher who preferred to express his ideas in essays defending reason, science, and responsible thinking against the cult of intuition. In *Le Bergsonisme, ou une philosophie de la mobilité* (1912) and in other works, Benda attacked Bergson's irrationalism; in *Belphégor* (1919; Eng. tr. 1929), Benda rejected most contemporary writers, such as Romain Rolland, Paul Claudel, Maurice Barrès, George Sorel, and Charles Péguy, his former friend. Benda's militancy increased in his most famous book *La trahison des clercs* (1927; *The Great Betrayal*, 1928), in which he castigated contemporary thinkers and writers, including the intellectuals and the professionals. He accused them of having sold reason or of having left it to the state, to society, to the parties, to the family, etc. He charged them with having forsaken service to reason and to the perennial truth, all for the sake of temporary success. The rigorous conclusions which oppose any compromise are the basis of his views in theology, history, and aesthetics, in his last books such as *Essai d'un discours cohérent sur les rapports de Dieu et du monde* (1931) and *La France byzantine; ou Le triomphe de la littérature pure . . .* (1945). This last work was sharply criticized. Although Benda did not convert to Christianity, he was completely isolated from Jewish life, and considered his Jewish origin a burden. He had to seek refuge during World War II in southern France. However, he regarded the Jewish problem as only a minor aspect of the war.

Bibliography: H. E. Read, *Julien Benda and the New Humanism* (1930); P. Brodin, *Maîtres et témoins de l'entre deux guerres* (1943); C. Mauriac, *La trahison d'un clerc* (1945); R. J. Niess, *Julien Benda* (Eng., 1956).

[H.P.]

BENDAVID, LAZARUS (Eleazar; 1762–1832), German mathematician, philosopher, and educator. He attended the universities of Goettingen and Halle, and spent from 1792 to 1797 in Vienna where he delivered public lectures on Kantian philosophy. In 1802 he became political editor of the newspaper *Haude- und Spenersche Zeitung.* In 1806 he was appointed honorary director of the Juedische Freischule in Berlin, which he headed until 1826. The school attained a high reputation and a large proportion of its students were Christian until 1819, when the government forbade the enrollment of non-Jews. Bendavid began his scientific work in 1785 with an investigation of the theory of colors. In 1786 he published *Ueber die Parallellinien,* and in 1789 *Versuch einer logischen Auseinandersetzung des mathematischen Unendlichen.*

In 1795 his *Vorlesungen ueber die "Kritik der reinen Vernunft"* appeared. Bendavid held that philosophy had attained the pinnacle of its development in the Kantian system. From 1796–98 he wrote a series of works explaining Kant's philosophy. In 1799 he published *Versuch einer*

Geschmackslehre, containing his theory of aesthetics based on Kant. In 1801 the Royal Academy of Sciences in Berlin awarded him a prize for his study, *Ueber den Ursprung unserer Erkenntnis,* and published it in 1802.

With this work, Bendavid's philosophical labors came to an end. During his remaining thirty years he wrote solely on Jewish problems. These writings reflect the struggles of the first post-Mendelssohnian Jewish generation with the problem of being Jewish. Bendavid regarded Reform Judaism as the only means of stemming the tide of conversion to Christianity. In his work *Etwas zur Charakteristick der Juden* (1793), he advocated the abolition of the ritual laws and the cultural and social assimilation of Jews. Nevertheless, he eschewed conversion to Christianity. Kant wrongly interpreted Bendavid's attitude as counseling Jews to accept Christianity and advised them, on the strength of Bendavid's views, openly to adopt the religion of Jesus and thus at long last attain a religious ethic and through it a religion (cf., Kant, *Der Streit der Fakultaeten;* also, the pertinent remarks of Hermann *Cohen in his *Kants Bergruendung der Ethik* (1901), 49). Bendavid's biblical studies are in the spirit of extreme Haskalah rationalism. In an essay in 1797 he attempted to show that the Ark of the Covenant was an electrical device which helped to kindle the wood on the altar. He published studies on the jubilee year, the prohibition of usury, the mixture of wool and linen, the belief in the Messiah, and the written and oral Law. In his article on the Messiah he sought to demonstrate, by investigating the theory of the transmigration of the Messiah's soul, that the belief in the coming of the Redeemer is not a dogma of Judaism and that the bestowal of equal rights upon the Jews would signify that the "Messiah" had come.

Bibliography: Dubnow, Divrei, 8 (1940^3), 142, 162; 9 (1941^3), 62; S. Maimon, *Versuch ueber die Transcendentalphilosophie* (1790), 275, 291; A. Goerland and E. Cassirer, *Hermann Cohens Schriften zur Philosophie und Zeitgeschichte,* 2 (1928), 117ff.; Jakob Guttmann, in: MGWJ, 61 (1917), 26–50, 176–211. [SH.H.B.]

BENDEMANN, EDUARD JULIUS FRIEDRICH (1811–1889), German painter. Bendemann, who was born in Berlin and studied under Gottfried von Schadow, later became a member of the original Duesseldorf School. He revealed his talent early in a portrait he painted of his grandmother before he was 20. In 1830 he accompanied Schadow to Italy, where for one year he devoted himself exclusively to the study of Raphael and Michelangelo. Bendemann produced his best-known paintings between 1831 and 1835, among them "The Exiles of Babylon in Mourning" (1832), and "Jeremiah at the Destruction of Jerusalem" (1836). In 1835 Bendemann married Schadow's sister and converted to Christianity. He was appointed professor at the Academy of Fine Arts of Dresden in 1838 and executed a number of murals for the royal palace there. In 1859 he succeeded his former teacher as director of the Academy in Duesseldorf, remaining there until 1867. He was commissioned to paint portraits of well-known figures, and a large number of his works are exhibited in Berlin museums. In addition, his illustrations in the neo-classical style appear in such literary works as the *Nibelungenlied* and Lessing's *Nathan der Weise.* His son RUDOLF (1851–1884) was also a well-known painter. His elder son FELIX (1848–1915) was an admiral and chief of Naval Staff.

Eduard Bendemann, German painter. Lithograph by C. Eppelin after a painting by Metz. N.Y., Leo Baeck Institute.

Bibliography: Roth, Art, 544; J. Schrattenholz, *Eduard Bendemann* (Ger., 1891). [P.N.]

BENDER, ALFRED PHILIP (1863–1937), South African minister. The son of a minister of the Dublin Hebrew Congregation in Ireland, he was the recognized leader of Cape Town Jewry for many years, both in religious and secular affairs. He was minister of the Cape Town Hebrew Congregation, the "mother congregation" of South Africa, from 1895 for 42 years and was responsible for initiating many educational, social, and cultural activities, including special services for children, confirmation services for girls, Sunday morning classes for women, and debating and social clubs for young men, taking a special interest in Jewish university students. Although very English in outlook and not sympathetic to the ways of "foreigners," he always gave generous assistance to East European immigrants in their settlement problems. He was long opposed to the principle of a representative lay body for South African Jewry, and in consequence his congregation did not affiliate with the Board of Deputies until 1919. He was also unsympathetic to the Zionist movement, but supported it after the Balfour Declaration. In the general community he was prominent in numerous educational and philanthropic endeavors, giving long service to the Cape Town hospital board, the school board, the council of the Cape Town University, and a variety of undenominational philanthropic organizations.

Bibliography: I. Abrahams, *Birth of a Community* (1955), index; G. Saron and L. Hotz (eds.), *Jews in South Africa* (1955), index. [G.SA.]

BENDER, LAURETTA (1897–), U.S. research psychiatrist. Born in Butte, Montana, Bender contributed to the study of genetic factors and growth patterns involved in the development of childhood schizophrenia, and employed electroconvulsive shock therapy in the treatment of childhood schizophrenia. She made an early contribution to an understanding of the psychological effects of deprivation in institutionalized children. Her research led to the development of the "Bender Gestalt Test," one of the most reliable means of measuring the visual-motor coordination in young people essentially as an aid to diagnosing impaired development or damage to the brain. She is the author of *A Visual Motor Gestalt Test and its Clinical Use* (1938), and is the author and editor of *Bellevue Studies in Child Psychiatry.* She served on the research staffs of Johns Hopkins Hospital, Columbia College of Physicians and

Surgeons, and the New York State Department of Mental Hygiene.

Bibliography: A. M. Freedman and H. I. Kaplan (eds.), *Comprehensive Textbook of Psychiatry* (1967), index; Centre International de l'Enfance, Travaux et documents, 2, *Psychiatrie Sociale de l'Enfant* (1951), 474, 525, incl. bibl.

[Ed.]

BENDER, MORRIS BORIS (1905–), U.S. neurologist. Bender, who was born in Russia, was taken to the United States in 1914. After graduating in medicine he trained in neurology and psychiatry in several New York hospitals. He was research fellow in neurophysiology at Yale University (1936–38) and New York's Mount Sinai Hospital (1938–42). He then served as head of the laboratory of experimental neurology at New York University (1942–50). He joined the faculty of neurology at the New York University College of Medicine in 1938, becoming professor of clinical neurology in 1953. In 1966 he was appointed professor and chairman of the department of neurology of the Mount Sinai School of Medicine. He was also clinical professor of neurology at Columbia University's College of Physicians and Surgeons from 1953 to 1967. Bender's major research interests are the physiology of the visual and oculomotor systems and behavioral neurology, especially consciousness and perception. His major works are *Disorders in Perception* (1952) and *Visual Field Defects after Penetrating Missile Wounds of the Brain* (in collaboration with others, 1960); he also edited *The Oculomotor System* (1964) and *The Approach to Diagnosis in Modern Neurology* (1967). [F.R.]

BENDERLY, SAMSON (1876–1944), U.S. educator. Benderly, who was born in Safed, Palestine, emigrated to Baltimore in 1898. He received a medical degree at Johns Hopkins University. During his internship Benderly became interested in modern Jewish education in Baltimore and abandoned his medical career. In 1910 he was appointed director of the first Bureau of Jewish Education in the United States, in New York. This agency outlasted its parent body, the *kehillah* of New York City, and was molded by Benderly's lifework. Benderly conceived of a comprehensive educational program to raise the level of Jewish life in America. He was the American organizer of *Ivrit be-Ivrit* pedagogy—the use of Hebrew as the language of instruction. He initiated pilot schools which developed curricula and experimented with new ideas. He organized school board representatives, formed principals' and teachers' study groups, and initiated a leadership training program to make Jewish education a profession. Benderly also pioneered in the education of Jewish girls, and in adolescent and secondary Jewish schooling. He experimented with Jewish educational camping, initiated home-study projects for the preschool child, and designed extension programs for the unschooled. His bureau structure was the prototype for similar agencies throughout America, and the personnel he trained became foremost leaders of Jewish education in America.

Bibliography: N. H. Winter, *Jewish Education in the Pluralist Society* (1966), incl. bibl.

[N.H.W.]

BENDERY (Rum. **Tighina**), city in Bessarabia (in Rumania 1918–40; 1941–44), Moldavian S.S.R. The presence of Jews there is first recorded in 1769 and a burial society, whose *pinkas* (register) is still extant, was founded in 1793. There were 101 Jewish families living in Bendery in 1808 (out of 331). In 1814 the *ẓaddik* Aryeh Leib Wertheim, son of Simeon Solomon of *Savran, became rabbi of Bendery; the descendants of the dynasty of *ẓaddikim* which he founded served as rabbis of Bendery until World War II. The Jewish population increased with the influx of immigrants into Bessarabia in the 19th century, numbering 4,297 in 1864 and 10,644 in 1897 (33. 5% of the total). Institutions of the community included a hospital founded in 1885, an old-age home, a secondary school founded in 1912, and an elementary school. In 1925, of the 1,526 members of the local Jewish cooperative loan-bank, 701 were occupied in commerce, 363 in handicrafts, and 49 in agriculture. According to the official census the community numbered 8,294 (26.4% of the total population) in 1930. The communal organization was dissolved and its institutions were abolished or nationalized when Bessarabia passed to Soviet Russia in June 1940.

The synagogue in Bendery, Moldavia.

[E.F.]

Holocaust Period. Under Soviet occupation (1940–41), the wealthy Jews were exiled to Siberia, as were wealthy non-Jews. Owing to its location far from the front and near the shores of the Dniester, many families managed to cross the river and get through to the interior of the U.S.S.R. Those who stayed behind (perhaps 40 families) were all killed by the invading Rumanian troops, who retook Bessarabia in 1941, and buried in a common grave near the town fortress. In Bendery an agreement was signed between Germany and Rumania, on August 31, 1941, concerning the plan to deport Jews to Transnistria. [J.An.]

Bibliography: Taubman, in: *Kovez Besarabyah* (1941), 90–96; Feldman, in: *Sefer Yahadut Besarabyah.*

BENDIX, BENEDICT HEINRICH (1768–1828), German engraver, known for his portraits of leaders of German Jewry in the early 19th century. Bendix was born in Berlin and studied engraving. He portrayed various contemporaries such as the Duke and Duchess of Mecklenburg and the mathematician Abraham Wolff. His only mezzotint (1808) portrays Aron Beer, the first cantor to be appointed to the Berlin Jewish community. Among his most important works are two plates, each consisting of three medallions: one depicting Napoleon I, Frederick William III, and Alexander I of Russia, and the other Empress Josephine, Queen Louise, and Empress Elizabeth of Russia. Bendix also executed an engraving of Nathan and the Templar (1806), a subject taken from *Lessing's play *Nathan the Wise.* When the Berlin Jewish community opened a school in 1825 Bendix was engaged as teacher of drawing. He remained in that position until his death by suicide.

Bibliography: S. Kirschstein, *Juedische Graphiker,* (1918), 28–38.

[Ed.]

BENDIX, REINHARD (1916–), U.S. sociologist. Born in Berlin, Bendix left Germany after Hitler's rise to power and emigrated to the U.S.A. In 1943 he began his academic career as an instructor at the University of Chicago. He taught at the University of Colorado (1946–47) and then at the University of California at Berkeley. In 1956 he became full professor and the chairman of the Department of Sociology. He was president of the American Sociological Association.

Reinhard Bendix, U.S. sociologist.

Bendix approached sociological problems typologically. He used the theories of Max Weber as a basis for his sociological explorations and refined and advanced them considerably. His book *Max Weber: An Intellectual Portrait* (1960) is largely biographical but his primary interests, as is shown in most of his books and numerous articles in sociological journals, were in political and industrial sociology, social stratification, and sociological theory. His book, *Class, Status and Power* (1953; 1967[2]), a collection of readings in stratification edited jointly with Seymour Martin *Lipset, became a standard work in the field. A later publication was *Social Mobility in Industrial Society,* which he also coauthored with Lipset. His best-known book, for which he received the MacIver award, is *Work and Authority in Industry: Ideologies of Management in the Course of Industrialization* (1956). It is based on historical data from England, the United States, Russia and East Germany. Another work, *Nationbuilding and Citizenship* (1964), analyzes the processes leading to the formation of new nations. Bendix is the author of numerous scholarly papers, chiefly on topics of a theoretical nature.

[W.J.C.]

BEN-DOR, IMMANUEL (1901–1969), archaeologist. Ben-Dor, who was born at Okopy, Poland, was a member of the archaeological expeditions of the University of Pennsylvania in Beth-Shean, Egypt, Mesopotamia, and Italy and also took part in the American School of Oriental Research excavation at Beth-El and that of the University of Liverpool at Jericho. He served as assistant keeper (1935) and librarian (1939) of the Palestine Archaeological Museum and conducted excavations at Nahariyyah and al-Zīb. From 1948 to 1954 he was assistant director of the Israel Department of Antiquities and was also archaeologist to the Link Underwater Expedition at Caesarea. From 1958 to 1968 he was professor of biblical archaeology and Semitics at Emory University, Atlanta. He published articles on aspects of Palestinian archaeology.

[M.A.-Y.]

BENE-BERAK (Heb. בְּנֵי בְרַק). (1) A biblical city 5 mi. (8 km.) E. of Jaffa. It is included in the territory of the tribe of *Dan together with Jehud and *Gath-Rimmon (Josh. 19:45), but it was no doubt in the area controlled by the

Philistines until the period of the united monarchy. Assyrian sources describing Sennacherib's invasion in 701 B.C.E. speak of Bene-Berak as subject to *Ashkelon (together with Jaffa, Beth-Dagon, and Azur). After the destruction of the Second Temple, Bene-Berak became a center of Jewish learning when R. *Akiva established his school there, which was attended by such well-known pupils as Judah, Meir, and Simeon b. Yoḥai (Tosef., Ber. 2:14; Tosef., Shab. 3:3; Sanh. 32b; Gen. R. 95:30). The Passover *Haggadah* preserves an account of a famous *seder* held there by R. Akiva. When Eleazar b. Azariah accompanied Akiva to the public baths at Bene-Berak, it gave rise to a halakhic query (Tosef., Shab. 3:4). Echoes of religious persecution by the Romans (under Hadrian) are contained in both the passage in the *Haggadah* and in the Tosefta (Tosef., Ber. 2:14). Even after the *Bar Kokhba War (132–35 C.E.), Bene-Berak remained a Jewish city; Judah ha-Nasi visited it and was impressed by the extraordinary fertility of its orchards and vineyards (Mid. Tanḥ. to 26:9; TJ, Pe'ah 8:4, 20b). The same impression is reported by the *amora* Rami b. Ezekiel (third century C.E.), who applied to it the biblical phrase "a land flowing with milk and honey" (Ket. 111b). The Crusaders called the city Bombrac and built a fortress there to protect the approaches to Jaffa.

[M.A.-Y.]

(2) One of the ten towns in Israel which form the metropolitan area of Tel Aviv, about 3 mi. (5 km.) northeast of downtown Tel Aviv, bordered on the north by the Yarkon River, on the east by the main highway to the south and north, and on the south and west by Ramat Gan. Bene-Berak was established in 1924 by a group of 13 Orthodox families from Warsaw, Poland, under the leadership of Rabbi Y. Gerstenkorn, who later became the town's first mayor. Until 1936 affairs were run by a local committee, and from 1936 to 1949 by a local council, but since 1950 Bene-Berak has been a township, comprising about 1,775 acres (7,100 dunams). The founders engaged mostly in farming and by 1929 the settlement grew to 100 families; in 1941 Bene-Berak had 4,500 inhabitants; in 1948—8,800, in 1955—25,000, and was in 1968 the eighth largest town in Israel with 64,700 inhabitants. Its dynamic growth was due to its proximity to Tel Aviv, and its special position as a place for a thoroughly Orthodox population and way of life. As a suburb, Bene-Berak is interrelated with the Tel Aviv nucleus for its public transportation, wholesale and retail trade, entertainment, education on the university level, and for employment—especially for white collar workers in Tel Aviv who live in Bene-Berak. Bene-Berak is known for its numerous yeshivot, headed by the Ponevezh Yeshivah, founded in 1941 by Rabbi Joseph *Kahaneman. It is also known for the strict public observance of the Sabbath, holidays, and Jewish laws, one consequence of which is that all its roads are closed to traffic on the Sabbath and holidays. There are more than 200 synagogues, many of them for ḥasidic *rebbes,* and closed ḥasidic neighborhoods like Zikhron Meir, Vizhnitz, and Satmar (see *Satu Mare). Bene-Berak was the home of Ḥazon Ish (Rabbi Abraham I. *Karelitz).

Bene-Berak became one of Israel's important industrial areas and had in 1969 about 150 factories and numerous workshops for food preserves, cigarettes, wool textiles, and other branches, among them several of the country's largest such enterprises, employing about 8,000 workers. The yearly budget in 1969 amounted to IL20,000,000 ($5,714,286) out of which 6% was earmarked for religious

A pottery incense stand of the Chalcolithic period (4,000–3,200 B.C.E.) found in Bene-Berak. Jerusalem, Israel Department of Antiquities and Museums.

affairs, 12% for welfare, and 38% for education. The yeshivot had about 4,000 students in 1969, a large percentage of them from abroad. The land for the municipality of Bene-Berak was purchased from the Arab village Ibn-Ibrāq. [AL.C.]

Bibliography: D. D. Luckenbill (ed.), *The Annals of Sennacherib* (1924), 31; S. Klein (ed.), *Sefer ha-Yishuv*, 1 (1939), s.v.; EM, 2 (1965), 174; Press, Ereẓ, 1 (1951), 109; A. Cohn, *The Development of Bene-Berak as a Satellite Town of Special Features* (Thesis, Technion Haifa, 1969), Hebrew with English synopsis.

BENEDEK, THERESE F. (1892–), U.S. psychoanalyst and psychiatrist. Born in Eger, Hungary, Therese obtained clinical experience in Budapest and Leipzig, and emigrated to the United States in the early 1930s. She was appointed a staff member at the Chicago Institute for Psychoanalysis in 1936. In her research she concentrated on studying the psychological implications of female sexual functions and the personal disturbances associated with their impairment. She wrote (with B. B. Rubenstein) *The Sexual Cycle in Women* (1947), *Psychosexual Functions in Women* (1952), and *Insight and Personality Adjustment* (1946). [ED.]

°**BENEDICT,** name of 15 popes, several of whom had significant contacts with Jews. BENEDICT VIII (1012–1024) ordered the execution of a number of Roman Jews in 1020 or 1021, on a charge that they had mocked the cross and thereby caused an earthquake which killed a number of Christians. BENEDICT XII (1334–1342) gave proof of his conversionary zeal when in 1320, while still bishop of Pamiers, he argued with a certain Baruch who had been forced into Christianity during the *Pastoureaux persecutions. He displayed the same zeal in 1338 by urging all Christians to aid in the pursuit of converted Jews who changed their places of residence in order to revert to Judaism. In 1335 he ordered the destruction of a synagogue in Posen because it had been erected too near a Cistercian chapel. He complained to King Pedro of Aragon in 1340 that Jews and Muslims were erecting too many synagogues and mosques and were enjoying too many contacts with Christians. At the same time, he was deeply concerned over the report by Albert II, duke of Austria, in 1338, that the Jews of *Passau had been falsely accused of having desecrated the *Host. A similar charge in *Nuremberg a few years previously had also proved false. The pope now ordered the bishop of Passau not to permit the Jews to suffer if they had been unjustly accused. BENEDICT XIII (Peter de Luna, 1394–1417) does not belong to the apostolic succession, since he is counted as an anti-pope during the Great Schism of the Church. His hostility to Jews and Judaism was evident during his period in Avignon (1394–1411). In 1396 he acted upon the accusation that the Jews of Geneva were enjoying many privileges under the protection of the local authorities; he also charged the leaders of the Avignon Jews with exceeding their powers. In 1403 he granted a three-year moratorium on debts owed by Christians to Jews. He did grant the Jews of Toro (Castile), in 1404, the right to have a synagogue in place of the two they had had before the persecutions in Spain in 1391, but this had already been granted them by the king of Castile. His attempt in 1410 to calm the excessive zeal of the inquisitors in Majorca may also have been due to the exigencies of diplomacy rather than to personal good will. His really spectacular anti-Jewish activity began when, expelled from Avignon, he moved to his native Spain, still claiming to be the only legitimate pope. The depressed condition of the Spanish Jews at the time persuaded him that he could startle Christendom by obtaining the conversion of all Spanish Jewry. The Disputation of *Tortosa was the result. When it was concluded in May 1415, Benedict issued his Bull *Etsi doctoribus gentium* imposing every conceivable restriction on Jewish life. It condemned the Talmud and ordered it expurgated of every statement that might appear uncomplimentary to Christianity, and it made contact between Jews and Christians all but impossible. The Bull's enforcement lapsed after Benedict XIII was deposed by the Council of Constance in 1417; but its spirit remained alive and found echoes in a number of *Bulls by later popes. BENEDICT XIII (1724–1730) used every pressure, especially economic, on the inhabitants of the Roman ghetto to become converted to Christianity. He personally participated in the ceremonious baptism of 26 of them. He tried to limit Jewish trade to nonessentials. BENEDICT XIV (1740–1758) was deeply interested in the rigid interpretation and enforcement of Canon Law. Consequently, while reaffirming the right of the Jews of Avignon to trade in cloth, he increased the onus of the Jewish badge for the Jews of Rome by ordering them to wear it even when on a journey. A mere suspicion of consent was now enough to declare a Jew properly baptized; while a child, even if baptized without parental consent, was compelled to remain a Christian. Converts were limited to marrying only born Christians. Twice during his pontificate, in 1753 and 1755, Jewish books were confiscated and examined for anti-Christian statements. Yet he recognized that Jewish taxation was too heavy. Moreover, it was under his auspices that Lorenzo Ganganelli (later Pope *Clement XVI) drew up his memorandum concerning the *blood libel, and Benedict subsequently wrote to the authorities in Poland deploring the recent wave of accusations.

Bibliography: Benedict VII: Roth, Dark Ages, 76, 119; Vogelstein-Rieger, 1 (1896), 213. Benedict XII: Grayzel, in: HJ, 17 (1955), 89–120; MHJ, 1 (1903), 62, no. 36; Baron, Social², 11 (1967), 170f., 267. Benedict XIII (anti-pope): Baer, Spain, 2 (1966), 155, 167, 229ff., 393f.; M. Simonsohn, *Kirchliche Judengesetzgebung im Zeitalter der Reformkonzilien von Konstanz und Basel* (1912). Benedict XIII: E. Rodocanachi, *Le Saint-Siège et les Juifs* (1891), 220, 284; Roth, Italy, 381. Benedict XIV: C. Roth, *Ritual Murder Libel and the Jew* (1934); Roth, Italy, 379, 411; Rodocanachi, op. cit., 266, 284, 292; Vogelstein-Rieger, 2 (1895), 242, 245ff.; *New Catholic Encyclopedia,* index.

[S.G.]

BENEDICT, SIR JULIUS (Isaac; 1804–1885), composer and conductor, born in Stuttgart. After conducting in Vienna (1823–25) and later in Naples, he settled in London in 1835. He accompanied Jenny Lind on her American tour (1850–52) and conducted at Drury Lane and Covent Garden. Of his operas, the most successful was "The Lily of Killarney" (Covent Garden, 1862). Although a convert to Protestantism (1826), he set to music Psalm 84 (first verse) for the inauguration of the first British Reform Synagogue (West London) in 1840. His works include cantatas, symphonies, and piano concertos. He wrote biographies of Felix Mendelssohn (1853²) and Carl von Weber (1881), whose pupil he was. He was knighted in 1871.

Sir Julius Benedict's house in Manchester Square, London, bears one of the London County Council's commemoration plaques. Photo M. Ninio, Jerusalem.

Bibliography: P. H. Emden, *Jews of Britain* (1943), 514–15; Raphael, in: BLBI, 11 no. 41 (1968), 32–37; Grove, Dict; Riemann-Gurlitt; Baker, Biog Dict; Sendrey, Music, indexes.

[D.L.S.]

BENEDICT BEN MOSES OF LINCOLN (d. 1278), English financier, in secular records called Magister Benedictus filius Magistri Mossei de Lincolnia. Benedict came from a family of scholars: his great-grandfather, Moses of Bristol (later of Oxford), had been a patron of letters; his grandfather, Yom Tov (apparently also known as Simeon), composed the lost *Sefer ha-Tena'im;* and his father, R. *Moses b. Yom Tov of London, was the leading Hebrew and talmudic scholar of his day in England. One of Benedict's brothers was Hagin (Ḥayyim), *archpresbyter of English Jewry from 1257 until his death in 1280; another was R. *Elijah Menahem b. Moses of London. Benedict's business activities in Lincoln date from 1252 and are often referred to in the records of subsequent decades. It is conjectured that the *blood libel at Lincoln in 1255 took place when a number of Jews from all over England were assembled to celebrate the marriage of Benedict's daughter Bellasset. Benedict was among those arrested. After his family had procured the intervention of the Castilian ambassador, Benedict was released in December 1255 and his sequestered property restored to him. In Hebrew Benedict was known as R. Berechiah of Nicole (Lincoln). He was regarded as one of the outstanding Anglo-Jewish halakhic scholars of his day, and was mentioned with veneration long after his death. R. Berechiah was also known as an exegete. His name occurs along with those of other English rabbis of the 13th century in the works of several tosafists.

Bibliography: J. Jacobs, in: JHSET, 1 (1893–94), 101–2; C. Roth, *ibid.,* 15 (1946), 29ff.; idem, in: JJS, 3 (1952), 56–61; Rigg-Jenkinson, Exchequer, index; Urbach, Tosafot, 402; J. Ḥazzan, *Ez Ḥayyim,* ed. by I. Brodie, 1 (1962), 141, 310; 2 (1964), 179; E. E. Urbach, in: *Sefer ha-Yovel Tiferet Yisrael . . . Brodie* (1967), 1ff.

[Ed.]

BENEDICTIONS (Heb. sing. בְּרָכָה, *berakhah;* pl. בְּרָכוֹת, *berakhot*), formulas of blessing or thanksgiving, in public and private services. The Hebrew noun *berakhah* is derived from the verb *brkh* ברך ("to fall on one's knees"). The Talmud ascribes the institution and formulation of the benedictions to "the Men of the Great *Synagogue" (Ber. 33a), to the sages of old (Sif. Deut. 33:2; Mid. Ps. 17:4), or to the "120 elders" at the head of the community in the time of *Ezra (Meg. 17b; TJ, Ber. 2:4, 4d). These references, however, cannot be considered historically authentic, although they are indicative of the fact that benedictions were known to have been instituted in very ancient times. In the Bible, mention is made of a number of individual benedictions (Gen. 24:27; Ex. 18:10; Ruth 4:14; I Sam. 25:32; II Sam. 18:28; I Kings 1:48; 5:21; 8:15, 56; I Chron. 16:36; II Chron. 2:11; 6:4; Ps. 28:6; 31:22). After the victory of the Maccabees over Nicanor, the people exclaimed, "Blessed be He who has kept His holy place undefiled" (II Macc. 15:34). According to the Book of Enoch (36:4), each time Enoch beheld some of the wonders of nature he "blessed the Lord of Glory, Who had made great and glorious wonders to show the greatness of His work to the angels and to spirits and to men, that they might praise His work and all His creation."

The Origin of the Berakhot. Elbogen and other scholars have shown that the various benedictions probably originated in different congregations and localities. The formulas ultimately adopted by all Jews were selections from, and combinations of, local customs and traditions. The attempts of other scholars to establish a definite date for the formulation of each benediction and to reconstruct an "original" wording appear to lack foundation. There are indications which suggest that different formulas were known and used simultaneously. Similarities to the 18 benedictions which comprise the **Amidah* prayer are, for instance, to be found in various sources: the hymn recorded in Ecclesiasticus 51:12, and the prayer found in Ecclesiasticus 36:1ff. The latter contains a series of benedictions petitioning for the ingathering of the exiles and the salvation of Israel. It also expresses the hope that Zion and the Temple may be filled with God's glory. The "eight benedictions," recited by the high priest on the Day of Atonement (Yoma 7:1; TJ, Yoma 7:1, 44b), and the order of the morning service of the priests in the Temple (Tam. 5:1), are also examples of this procedure.

The End of the Second Temple Period. By the end of the Second Temple period, certain "orders of benedictions" had become the generally accepted custom in most communities. Prominent among these were the seven benedictions which comprise the *Amidah* for Sabbaths and festivals, the nine for Rosh Ha-Shanah (Tosef., Ber. 3:14), and most likely also the 18 benedictions for the weekday *Amidah.* The number and contents of the benedictions before and after the *Shema, and the three benedictions of the *Grace after Meals were also standardized about this time. The "redaction" of the regular, prescribed prayers and benedictions under Rabban *Gamaliel II at Jabneh (Ber. 28b ff.), at the end of the first century C.E., gave official sanction to what had been in essence the prevailing custom for a considerable time, and probably established the order and content of the benedictions. It did not, however, become the single, authoritative version.

THE TALMUDIC PERIOD. At the earliest, prayers were written down by the end of the talmudic period, and many alternative formulations of the same benediction are known from talmudic sources (some are in use in different rites to the present day). The order of prayer was still relatively flexible, for while the general outline and the motifs of the prayers and blessings were well defined, their recital involved an element of improvisation and free composition. The latter was seen as a safeguard against mechanical prayer. Some *amoraim* were singled out for praise because they recited "a new prayer" or "a new benediction" every day (TJ, Ber. 4:3, 8a). During talmudic times, however, only the requirements for the wording of each benediction were fixed in greater detail, and various subsidiary motifs which had to be included in some of them were enumerated. Consistent attempts at establishing one single authoritative version of all prayers only came later.

The Benediction Formula. Every blessing opens with the words *Barukh Attah Adonai* ("Blessed art Thou, O Lord"). When the benediction occurs at the beginning of a prayer, the words *Eloheinu Melekh ha-Olam* ("our God, King of the Universe") are added. There are three types of formulas for benedictions: The first is a short blessing (*matbe'a kaẓar,* "short formula") which, after the above opening, is followed by a few words of praise specific to the occasion, e.g., the benediction over bread: *ha-moẓi leḥem min ha-areẓ* ("who brings forth bread from the earth"). The second is a long blessing (*matbe'a arokh,* "long formula"), in which the opening is followed by a more elaborate text, e.g., in the first section of the Grace after Meals, after which a concluding benediction formula must be recited at the end of the prayer, e.g., *Barukh Attah Adonai ha-zan et ha-kol* ("Blessed art Thou O Lord, Who feedest all"). The third type of benediction forms part of a series (*berakhah ha-semukhah le-ḥavertah,* "contiguous blessings"). The opening formula is omitted (except in the first benediction of each series), and only the conclusion is phrased in the benediction style. The second section of the Grace after Meals, for instance, begins with the words *Nodeh Lekha* ("We thank Thee"), and ends with the benediction *Barukh Attah Adonai al ha-areẓ ve-al ha-mazon* ("Blessed art Thou O Lord, for the land and the food"; TJ, Ber. 1:8, 3d). The mention of God as "King of the Universe" (known as *Malkhut*) occurs only in the first two forms, and not in the third. It is totally absent from the *Amidah,* and probably did not become customary before the second century C.E. (Ber. 40a). The introduction of *Malkhut* into the opening phrase of the formula may have been motivated by the desire to stress the exclusive kingship of God, as a protest against the Roman cult of emperor worship. Since most of the obligatory prayers, e.g., the *Amidah,* and the benedictions preceding and following the *Shema,* consist of a series of blessings, the form occurring most frequently in the synagogue service is the third, in which the benediction formula is used only as a conclusion.

The standard benediction formula occurs only twice in the Bible (Ps. 119:12; I Chron. 29:10); other formulas such as *Hodu la-Adonai* ("Praise God"), *Odekha Adonai* ("I will thank Thee, O Lord") are more frequent, as is the phrase *Barukh Attah* (without *Adonai*). The benedictions in Ecclesiasticus 51:12, for instance, are introduced by *Hodu la-Adonai,* and in the Dead Sea Scrolls the benediction formula is used interchangeably with *Odekha Adonai,* and the like (e.g., Thanksgiving Scroll, cf. 2:20, 31; 4:5, with 11:28, 30; 16:8; and especially 5:20, where the latter formula has been struck out by the scribe and replaced by the former). Nor do the Dead Sea Scrolls yet distinguish between the use of the divine names *Adonai* and *El* in benedictions. The Talmud also retains some traces of formulas other than the standard ones (Ber. 40b and 54b; Tosef., Ber. 4:4–5). The ultimate choice of the formula containing both the Tetragrammaton and the direct address of God in the second person was deliberate. It reflects the personal and even intimate relationship of the worshiper with God. It also ensures that supplications and petitions (such as the intermediary benediction of the *Amidah*) invariably conclude with words of praise. After asking for forgiveness, the prayer concludes: "Blessed art Thou . . . who dost abundantly forgive."

Laws of Benedictions. The Talmud (Ber. 40b) quotes Rav as saying that every benediction must have the name

Figure 1. Second title page of *Seder Berakhot* ("Order of Benedictions"), a Sephardi compilation of blessings, prayers, and supplications, Amsterdam, 1687. The page introduces the *me'ah berakhot*—the hundred daily blessings enjoined by the Talmud—and illustrates benedictions connected with the five senses: upper right, on seeing the new moon; upper left, on hearing the *shofar;* lower right, on smelling the *havdalah* spices; lower left, on performing a circumcision; center, the grace after meals. The bottom register depicts Isaac reaping the hundredfold harvest with which he was blessed by the Lord (Gen. 26:12). Cecil Roth Collection.

Figure 2. "The Blessing over the Candles" by Isidor Kaufmann (1853–1921). New York, Oscar Gruss Collection. Photo Frank J. Darmstaedter, New York.

of God, and R. Johanan as saying that each benediction must also contain the attribute of God's kingship. It is also obvious from this talmudic passage that a benediction could be recited in the vernacular and did not have to be an exact translation of the Hebrew formula. A shepherd, Benjamin, is quoted as having said in Aramaic, "Blessed be God, the master of this bread," and Rav agreed that it was sufficient (Ber. 40b). Particular stress is laid upon the closing formula (Ber. 9:5; Ta'an. 2:3; Tosef., Ber. 7:21–22). While the benediction formula is obligatory in every one of the prescribed prayers, its use is precluded in spontaneous free prayers: "He who recites a blessing which is not necessary is considered to transgress the prohibition 'Thou shalt not take the name of the Lord Thy God in vain'" (Ex. 20:7; Ber. 33a). Maimonides (Yad, Berakhot 1:4) divides the benedictions into three types: those which are recited before enjoying a pleasure (e.g., food); those which are recited for the performance of a religious duty (e.g., hearing the *shofar*); and those which are forms of liturgical thanksgiving and praise (e.g., Grace after Meals).

*Abudarham distinguished four classes or types of benedictions: those recited in the daily prayers; those preceding the performance of a religious duty; blessings offered for enjoyments; and those of thanksgiving or praise (*Abudarham ha-Shalem, Berakhot*).

Many benedictions, though obligatory and therefore couched in the characteristic *berakhah* formula, are not recited in congregational worship but by the individual in private prayer. Prominent among them are three groups: benedictions before and after the partaking of food and drink; benedictions to be recited before the performance of most *mitzvot;* and benedictions of praise for various occasions (the morning benedictions which express man's gratitude for awakening in possession of all his faculties were originally of this type). Since all three types of benedictions are essentially of a private character, no *minyan* is required for their recital. (The Grace after Meals is, however, preceded by a special introduction when said in company.)

Benedictions Recited Before the Performance of a Mitzvah. All benedictions recited before the observance of a *mitzvah* begin with the formula "Blessed . . . who has sanctified us through his commandments and commanded us . . . ," and mention the specific *mitzvah* about to be performed. The same formula is also used before the performance of commandments of rabbinic origin (e.g., the lighting of candles on the Sabbath or on Ḥanukkah) since such commandments are implied in the biblical injunction to observe the teaching of the sages (Deut. 17:10; Shab. 23a). The actual benediction over the *mitzvah* is sometimes followed by further benedictions (e.g., on kindling the Ḥanukkah candles, the benediction "who has performed miracles for our fathers in days of old at this season" is recited). When a *mitzvah* is performed for the first time in the year, the *She-Heḥeyanu* benediction ("who has kept us alive and preserved us and enabled us to reach this season") is also added. No blessings are recited after the observance of *mitzvot,* unless they involve public reading from the Scriptures (e.g. Torah, Prophets, *Hallel*). It is, however, recorded that the Palestinian scholars used to recite one on taking off the *tefillin.*

In practice, a benediction is not recited before the performance of every *mitzvah.* Some commentators have suggested that the determining principle is that no benediction should be recited before *mitzvot* which do not involve any action (e.g., leaving the corner of the field for the poor; Lev. 19:9), or the observance of which is possible only in undesirable circumstances (e.g., divorce, or the return of stolen goods). In the case of other *mitzvot* (e.g., the giving of alms), however, the reason for the absence of a benediction is not readily apparent, and there is no general agreement regarding the underlying principles. Custom on the matter seems to have varied as late as geonic times.

Benediction of Praise on Various Occasions. Among the many benedictions prescribed for various special occasions, those to be recited on hearing good and bad tidings, on witnessing awesome natural phenomena, on visiting a place where miracles have been performed in the past (in Ereẓ Israel) are prominent. The blessing *Ha-tov ve-ha-metiv* ("Blessed is He Who is good and does good") is recited by an individual upon hearing good news which will also benefit others, such as when hearing news that one has received an inheritance or when rain begins to fall after a drought. It is also recited when partaking of additional wine which is different in kind from that drunk previously. The *Birkat ha-Gomel,* a blessing recited upon individual salvation from danger, is included in this category. Known generally as "blessings of praise," the main purpose of these benedictions is "to make us remember our Creator at all times" (Maim. Yad, Berakhot 1:4). While the benedictions over food are evidently intended to sanctify the physical act of taking nourishment, and those recited before *mitzvot* serve to prevent the performance of the *mitzvah* in a thoughtless routine manner, the recital of the "benedictions of praise" is practically an end in itself. These benedictions serve to illuminate the educational function of blessings which transform a variety of everyday action and occurrences into religious experiences designed to increase awareness of God at all times. R. Meir went so far as to declare that it is the duty of every Jew to recite 100 benedictions daily (Men. 43b), a custom which, according to one tradition, was instituted by King David (Num. R. 18:21). The rabbinical discussions of benedictions are contained in the Mishnah tractate **Berakhot,* and the *gemara* in both Talmuds.

See also: *Prayer; *Liturgy; *Morning Benedictions; *Birkat ha-Torah; Names of *God.

Bibliography: Abrahams, Companion; Ch. Albeck (ed.), *Shishah Sidrei Mishnah: Berakhot* (1952); Elbogen, Gottesdienst; Finkelstein, in: JQR, 16 (1925/26), 1–43, 127–70; 19 (1928–29), 211–62; L. Ginzberg, *Perushim ve-Ḥiddushim ba-Yerushalmi,* 4 vols. (1941–61); J. Heinemann, *Ha-Tefillah bi-Tekufat ha-Tanna'im ve-ha-Amora'im* (1966[2]); idem, in: JSS, 5 (1960), 264–80; idem, in: JJS, 13 (1962), 23–29; Idelsohn, Liturgy; Kohler, in: HUCA, 1 (1924), 387–425; Liebreich, *ibid.,* 21 (1948), 176–209; 34 (1963), 125–76; idem, in: PAAJR, 18 (1948/49), 255–67;

Liber, in: JQR, 40 (1949/50), 331–57; Mann, in: HUCA, 2 (1925), 269–338; A. I. Schechter, *Studies in Jewish Liturgy* (1930); Zunz, Vortraege; Petuchowski, in: HUCA, 37 (1966), 175–89.

[Ed.]

BENEDIKT, MORITZ (1835–1920), Austrian neurologist, anthropometrist, and criminologist. Born in Eisenstadt, Hungary, Benedikt served as a surgeon in the Austrian army during the wars with Italy and Prussia in 1859 and 1866. Appointed a lecturer at the University of Vienna, he rose to become professor of neurology. He achieved eminence for his varied contributions to neuropathology, the localization of brain function, and electrotherapeutics, a field in which he made important innovations. His interest in electricity was not confined to its medical application but extended to generic physics, and he produced a number of significant studies on magnetism and electric current. He contributed to various branches of medical research, including the physiology and pathology of the circulatory system, and was one of the founders of electrotherapy.

Benedikt also engaged in anthropometric studies of criminals, devoting particular attention to cephalometry and brain pathology and to criminal psychology. His studies in physical anthropology are to be found in his *Anatomische Studien an Verbrecher-Gehirnen* (1879; *Anatomical Studies upon Brains of Criminals,* 1881) and *Kraniometrie und Kephalometrie* (1888). These made him, together with Cesare Lombroso, one of the pioneers of criminal anthropology.

Moritz Benedikt, Austrian neurologist. Jerusalem, J.N.U.L.

Of diverse cultural interests and activist liberal propensities, he wrote on current affairs and contemporary literature and aesthetics, and participated actively in various reformist movements, notably the extension of women's suffrage. His memoirs, *Aus Meinem Leben,* appeared in 1906.

Bibliography: S. R. Kagan, *Jewish Medicine* (1952), 374.

[E.Fi.]

BENEDIKT, MORITZ (1849–1920), Austrian journalist. Benedikt studied law and economics and in 1872 was appointed to the financial staff of the *Neue Freie Presse,* the most influential newspaper in the Austro-Hungarian Empire. In 1881 he became chief financial editor and later part owner. After the death of his partner Eduard Bacher in 1908, Benedikt determined the paper's editorial policy. He was able to exert considerable influence on Austrian affairs,

Moritz Benedikt, Austrian journalist.

advocating compromise between Austria and Hungary and supporting the German Liberal Party. Regarding himself as a German, he violently opposed Zionism and would not permit Theodor *Herzl, then literary editor of the *Neue Freie Presse,* to publish anything in support of Zionism in his newspaper. Benedikt was appointed to the upper house of the Austrian parliament in 1917.

Bibliography: J. Walter, *Moritz Benedikt und die "Neue Freie Presse"* (1950); R. Patai (ed.), *Complete Diaries of Theodor Herzl,* 5 vols. (1960), index.

[E.M.J.]

BENEI AKIVA (Heb. בְּנֵי עֲקִיבָא, "Sons of Akiva"), the youth movement of *Ha-Po'el ha-Mizrachi, named after the *tanna* R. *Akiva. It was founded in Jerusalem in 1929. Chief Rabbi Avraham Yiẓḥak *Kook served as the spiritual leader of the movement.

"Torah va-Avodah" ("Torah and Labor"), religion and pioneering—represented by the yeshivah and the kibbutz—are the two major guidelines of Benei Akiva's educational work and direct its activities. As early as 1931, two years after the establishment of the movement, the first attempt was made to found a Benei Akiva *kevuẓah* at Kefar Avraham (next to Petaḥ Tikvah). The *kevuẓah* became the center of the young movement, but it was a focal point without a circumference, as the movement was still weak organizationally and educationally. After three years of economic and social difficulties, the *kevuẓah* was disbanded. Following the failure of the first experiment, efforts were made to establish a training farm for members of Benei Akiva. The cornerstone of a permanent settlement was laid in 1938, with the establishment of a pioneers' nucleus for training at Kefar Gideon. In 1940 the members of this group moved to *Tirat Ẓevi and *Sedeh Eliyahu, for further training. After another year, this group, together with another from a work camp at Nes Ẓiyyonah, established the *kevuẓah* *Alummot near Netanyah as the first Benei Akiva settlement of its kind. Two years later the group moved to Herzliyyah, and in 1947 it established its permanent home, Kibbutz Sa'ad, in the northern Negev. Since that time, the movement has succeeded in establishing six *kevuẓot,* three moshavim, four *Naḥal settlements, and 64 settlement groups throughout Israel.

In the sphere of religious education, the movement established a yeshivah in 1940 at *Kefar ha-Ro'eh. It served as the basis for a network of Benei Akiva yeshivot throughout Israel, today encompassing 16 yeshivot at the high school level. These institutions introduced a new approach to the study of the Torah by the young generation, which aroused widespread interest in circles hitherto uninterested in religious education. In addition,

Symbol of the Benei Akiva youth movement used as an official postal cancellation during the world conference at Mikveh Israel, 1958.

four religious schools for girls were established. At the end of 1969, the movement had 160 branches, about half of which were in new settlements, with a total of about 25,000 members. The basic characteristics of a youth movement are found in Benei Akiva. Scouting is cultivated, and each summer large camps are operated. The Passover school vacation is dedicated to hikes throughout the country. The movement also publishes literary material and educational literature. Since 1936 the quarterly *Zera'im* has been published. After the *Six-Day War (1967), Benei Akiva established Yeshivat ha-Kotel near the Western Wall, and members of the movement were the first to resettle within the walls of the Old City of Jerusalem.

Benei Akiva sponsors a variety of activities in the Diaspora through the dispatch of emissaries, the training of Diaspora leaders through seminars in Israel, and the establishment of branches in various countries. In 1954 the world framework of Benei Akiva was established. In 1970 it had 20,000 members in 28 countries and in 60 cities on five continents. Hundreds of its graduates settled in Israel annually; hundreds of others go for a year's training on settlements, and many join settlement groups of *Ha-Kibbutz ha-Dati.

[Y.Go.]

BENEI BINYAMIN (Heb. בְּנֵי בִנְיָמִין, "Sons of Benjamin"), association of second-generation farmers in the veteran moshavot of Palestine, active from 1921 to 1939. It engaged mainly in promoting economic and cultural interests, along with matters of security and self-defense. Benei Binyamin was founded by Alexander *Aaronsohn, and was named in tribute to Edmond (Binyamin) de *Rothschild and Theodor (Binyamin Ze'ev) *Herzl. The association had as its motto: "To preserve the existing and to rebuild the destroyed." It was active in such veteran settlements as Petaḥ Tikvah, Rishon le-Zion, Nes Ẓiyyonah, Ekron, Ḥaderah, Zikhron Ya'akov, Rosh Pinnah, Mishmar ha-Yarden, and Yesud ha-Ma'alah. The Benei Binyamin Cooperative Bank, opened in 1924, loaned money to members for agricultural development, which the association constantly encouraged. In the same year Benei Binyamin began publication of its own newspaper, *Yedi'ot ha-Va'ad ha-Merkazi shel Histadrut Benei Binyamin*. Netanyah, Kefar Aharon, Even Yehudah, and part of Herzliyyah were founded by Benei Binyamin. Its active supporters in the U.S. included Nathan *Straus (in whose honor Netanyah was named). Alexander Aaronsohn was its president, and Oved *Ben-Ami served as its secretary for a number of years.

Bibliography: Dinur, Haganah, 2 pt. 3 (1964), index; Benei Binyamin, *Likerat ha-Binyan* (1922).

[Ed.]

BENEI DAROM (Heb. בְּנֵי דָּרוֹם), moshav shittufi east of Ashdod, Israel, affiliated with the Ha-Po'el ha-Mizrachi Moshavim Association. It was founded in 1949 by members of *Kefar Darom who had defended it during the War of Independence, until it fell and remained within the Egyptian-controlled Gaza Strip. In 1961 the settlers decided to change from the kibbutz to the moshav shittufi form of settlement. Some settlers originated from Germany and North America, others were born in Israel. Its economy is based on intensive farming including citrus orchards and irrigated field crops. In 1968 its population was 144.

[E.O.]

BENEI DEROR (Heb. בְּנֵי דְּרוֹר; "Sons of Freedom"), moshav in the southern Sharon, Israel, affiliated with Tenu'at ha-Moshavim, founded in 1946 by World War II veterans who were joined by immigrants from Turkey in 1949. Its economy is based on citrus plantations and milch cattle. In 1968 its population was 231.

[E.O.]

BENEI MOSHE (Heb. בְּנֵי, "Sons of Moses"), secret order of Ḥovevei Zion founded in Russia in 1889 to ensure personal dedication to the spiritual renaissance of the Jewish people and the return to Ereẓ Israel. Benei Moshe, founded on the seventh of Adar, the traditional birth date of Moses, was active in Russia and Ereẓ Israel until 1897. Its originator was Yehoshua Barzillai (Eisenstadt), who returned from Ereẓ Israel dissatisfied with the situation of Jewish agricultural settlement and the general state of depression in the small new *yishuv*. Barzillai's views conformed to those of *Aḥad Ha-Am, as expressed in his historic article *"Lo Zeh ha-Derekh"* ("The Wrong Way"), then still in manuscript but known to a limited circle. Barzillai and Avraham *Lubarsky persuaded Aḥad Ha-Am to accept leadership of the order. In his article *Derekh ha-Ḥayyim* ("Way of Life," 1889) and its supplements, Aḥad Ha-Am outlined the aim of the association: the return of the Jews to their historic homeland, but with prior spiritual preparation. The name Moshe (Moses) was to serve "as a sign to all members ever to keep in mind this chosen son of our people," a symbol of humility and morality. In this spirit, the order attempted "to broaden the scope of nationalism, elevating it to an ethical ideal based on the love of Israel, and embracing moral values."

Benei Moshe chapters consisted of at least five members, headed by leaders and advisers. A member was initiated in a ceremony in which he vowed to adhere faithfully to the statutes. The language used was Hebrew, and knowledge of Hebrew was a prerequisite for membership eligibility. The minimal eligibility age was 20. Members were called "brothers." Despite its very small membership (about 160), the order exerted considerable influence on the Ḥibbat Zion movement, whose leaders were, in fact, members of Benei Moshe. However, it had many opponents, namely those who advocated the primacy of practical settlement work in Ereẓ Israel above everything else (among them Moses Leib *Lilienblum); as well as Orthodox circles that conducted a fierce campaign against what they regarded as the secular ideology of Benei Moshe (among them Jehiel Michael *Pines and Ze'ev Wolf Jawitz).

Benei Moshe's practical achievements were in the field of modern Hebrew education in Ereẓ Israel and elsewhere (e.g., the modernized Hebrew-speaking *ḥeder* called *ḥeder metukkan*); in helping to found the settlement *Reḥovot; and in the establishment of the Hebrew publishing house Aḥi'asaf. The order helped publish the Hebrew anthologies *Kavveret* (1890) and *Pardes* (2 vols., 1892, 1895) in Russia. In Ereẓ Israel they published *Mikhtavim me-Ereẓ Yisrael* ("Letters from Ereẓ Israel," 1893–94), edited by Barzillai under the pen name Beit ha-Levi.

In 1891 Aḥad Ha-Am left the leadership of the order, although he remained its spiritual guide throughout its existence. The Benei Moshe headquarters moved to Jaffa in 1893. The order gradually abandoned its secret form, and in 1895 Aḥad Ha-Am suggested that it become a political party. However, by this time, the order was embroiled in bitter controversy both with its opponents and within its own ranks. Neither changes in the statutes nor the opening of the association could remove the feeling of frustration and reinvigorate it, and in 1896 Aḥad Ha-Am himself suggested that Benei Moshe be dissolved. This came about naturally with the rise of political Zionism, particularly with the convening of the First Zionist Congress in Basle (1897), which gave a new impetus to the Jewish national movement. The aims of Benei Moshe were sustained in Aḥad Ha-Am's continued opposition to Herzl's political Zionism.

Bibliography: Aḥad Ha-Am, *Essays, Letters, Memoirs*, ed. by L. Simon (1946), index; *Kol Kitvei Aḥad Ha-Am* (1947), index; Aḥad Ha-Am, *Iggerot*, 6 (1960), index; idem, *Selected Essays*, ed. by L. Simon (1962); B. Halpern, *The Idea of the Jewish State* (1969[2]), 26, 83f.; S. Tchernowitz, *Benei Moshe u-Tekufatam* (1914); Malachi, in: *Hadoar* (1955/56), nos. 37–42; Kressel, Leksikon, 1 (1965), 60–71; I. Klausner, *Mi-Katoviẓ ad Basel*, 2 (1965), index.

[G.K.]

BENE ISRAEL, Jewish community in India.

In India. The origins and date of the arrival of the Bene Israel in India are shrouded in legend. The Bene Israel claim that their ancestors left Galilee because of the persecution under *Antiochus Epiphanes (175–163 B.C.E.). Their ship was wrecked in the Indian Ocean and the seven men and seven women who survived were cast ashore near the village of Nawgaon on the Konkan coast, about 26 mi. (32 km.) south of Bombay, where they and their descendents remained for centuries isolated from Jewish life elsewhere. Thus, they forgot much of the Hebrew language, prayers, and ceremonies, and adopted the names, customs, and dress of their Hindu neighbors, and their language, Marathi, as their mother tongue. Throughout the centuries, they clung, however, to some fundamentals of the Jewish tradition and observed circumcision, dietary laws, the Sabbath and some fasts and festivals, and recited the *Shema*. In their new surroundings the Bene Israel turned to the pursuit of oil-pressing and agriculture and became known to their neighbors as *Shanwar Telis* ("the Sabbath-observing oilmen"), indicating both their occupation and their religious observance. The presence of a special Jewish group in the Konkan region remained unknown to outsiders and only casual references to them were made from the middle of the 18th century by European visitors such as the Danish missionary Sartorius. Various theories about their origin were propounded in the 19th century conjecturing that the Bene Israel were an offshoot of the Jewish settlements in Yemen, refugees from the persecution of the Jews by Muhammad, or descendants of the Babylonian-Persian Diaspora.

The existence of the Bene Israel became generally known outside India when some of the group moved from their villages in the Konkan to *Bombay, probably as a result of the unstable political situation in the Konkan and the economic opportunities which Bombay seemed to offer under British rule.

The British authorities were anxious to recruit reliable soldiers to their "native" regiments. A number of the Bene Israel enlisted, since some had apparently served as soldiers under Konkan potentates. Some of the Bene Israel rose to officer rank and established a reputation as good fighters in the Anglo-Mysore, Anglo-Afghan, and Anglo-Burmese wars of the 18th and 19th centuries. They were also efficient civil servants.

The Bene Israel apparently remained unaware of the existence of any other Jewish group in India even after settling in Bombay. Their first contact was with the *Cochin Jews in the mid-18th century when David *Rahabi helped to obtain the release of the Bene Israel officer, Samuel Ezekiel *Divekar, who had been taken prisoner during the Anglo-Mysore wars and was subsequently brought to Cochin. Divekar was impressed by the community there and their synagogues and it was on his initiative that a synagogue was established in Bombay in 1796, known as Sha'ar ha-Raḥamim ("Gate of Mercy"). The first confrontation with Cochin Jews became transposed in the Bene Israel legendary tradition. It tells of a learned and pious Jew David Rahabi, said to have arrived from Egypt "about the year 1,000," who taught the community Jewish ways. This figure is apparently the same David Rahabi of the 18th century. A further impetus to their return to traditional Judaism was given to the Bene Israel through the

Figure 1. Ezekiel Samuel, a 19th-century Bene Israel officer in the British Indian Army. Ernakulam, Cochin. E. Elias Photo Collection.

Figure 2. Bene Israel baking *mazzah*, from a *Haggadah* with Marathi translation, Poona, 1874. From A. Yaari, *Bibliography of the Passover Haggadah*, 1960.

cooperation of Cochin Jews who visited Bombay and the Konkan villages, and through the new wave of immigration of Arabic-speaking Jews from Baghdad to Bombay in the early decades of the 19th century. Prominent among these Jews was D. S. *Sassoon, who liberally supported religious philanthropic and educational establishments for their benefit. The Sassoon family established a special school for the Bene Israel in 1875. The education of the Bene Israel was also considerably influenced by the American Mission Society, established in Bombay in 1810 by Rev. J. Wilson of the Free Church of Scotland, and by a Cochin Jew who became converted to Christianity, Michael Surgun, who devoted his energy to their education in the Marathi language. A number of schools were established in Bombay as well as in the Kolaba district together with prayer houses. The books of Genesis and Exodus were translated into Marathi and a Hebrew grammar in Marathi was published by J. Wilson (1832).

The communal organization of the Bene Israel was headed by a secular leader, the Mucaddam, and by the Cazi, the religious leader. Additional synagogues established for the Bene Israel in Bombay include Sha'ar Raẓon (1839), Etz Ḥayim (1888), Tifereth Israel (1923), and Magen Chassidim (1931). The occupations of the members of the community varied. Apart from serving in the British "native" regiments, they were employed as civil servants in government, railway, postal, and customs offices, engaged in trade and commerce as shopkeepers, artisans, carpenters, masons, and in agriculture. Many who attended the University of Bombay and the Elphinstone College, which introduced Hebrew into their curriculum, became known as engineers, lawyers, scientists, physicians, educators, architects, artists, and writers. E. Moses, a Bene Israel Jew, was mayor of the city of Bombay in 1937–38. Prominent among the leaders and educators were Ḥayyim Samuel *Kehimkar, historian of the community, and Joseph Ezekiel *Rajpurkar, writer and translator of Hebrew liturgical works into Marathi. One of the earliest liturgical works to be printed was by a Yemenite Jew from Cochin, Solomon Shara'bi, "*Seliḥot* according to the Sephardi rite" (1841). It was followed by the publication of the Hebrew calendar (*Lu'aḥ*, 1845) and the first Passover *Haggadah* (1846, facsimile reprinted W. J. Fischel, 1968) with a Marathi translation. From the last decade of the 19th century the Bene Israel published a number of short-lived journals and periodicals in Marathi and English. Military and commercial assignments led to a considerable dispersion of the Bene Israel from the *Alibag and other Konkan villages and Bombay to other places in India such as Ahmadabad, Baroda, Poona, Panvel, New Delhi, and Karachi (today Pakistan). They also settled beyond the borders of India in Burma and Aden, where there was a Bene Israel synagogue up to 1964, as well as other places.

In recent years efforts have been made by American Jewish organizations to obtain the affiliation of the existing synagogues of the Bene Israel with the World Council of Synagogues (Conservative), the Union of Orthodox Jewish Congregations, or the World Union for Progressive Judaism (Reform). The Jewish Religious Union (London) established the Rodef Shalom congregation in 1925 with a modern Sunday school which attracted a small educated group of the Bene Israel and was successively led by two American Reform rabbis. The Hebrew education of the Bene Israel was later mainly fostered by Israel teachers sent by the *Jewish Agency, who have established a wide network of Hebrew instruction. They have also stimulated *aliyah* to Israel. The first contacts of the Bene Israel with the modern Zionist movement go back to the time of Theodor Herzl. In 1897 the Bene Israel were invited to participate in the First Zionist Congress. They refused with the explanation that the community was waiting for "the Divine Hand" to bring them back to Zion. The first Bene Israel Zionist Association was founded in Bombay in 1919. Visits of Zionist leaders such as Israel *Cohen in 1921, the first Zionist emissary to India on behalf of the World Zionist Organization, and subsequently of Immanuel Olswanger, and others, stimulated the community's interest in and support of the Jewish National Home.

The number of Bene Israel in India was approximately 7,000 in 1881, increasing to about 24,000 in 1947, falling to 15,000 in 1961. It was estimated in 1969 at approximately 12,000–13,000, when it was declining. The decrease in number is mainly due to emigration to England and especially to Ereẓ Israel. [W.J.F.]

In Israel. Between 1948 and 1952, approximately 2,300 Bene Israel emigrated to Israel. As a result of sit-down strikes and hunger strikes (see below), the Jewish Agency returned a total of 337 individuals, in several groups, between 1952 and 1954. Most of them were brought back to Israel by the Jewish Agency after several years. From the establishment of the state until 1969, over 12,000 Bene Israel emigrated to Israel. They were mainly absorbed into the branches of industry in which they were occupied in India, such as textiles and metals, as well as into public services. They settled mainly in Beersheba, Dimonah, Ashdod, and Eilat. Some settled in kibbutzim and moshavim.

SOCIAL-RELIGIOUS CRISIS. The Bene Israel became the focus of a controversy which arose in 1954 over the basic

Figure 3. A Bene Israel family, c. 1890. Bombay, B. G. Israel.

question of the personal status of the Bene Israel regarding marriage with other Jews. Although the Chief Rabbinate had laid down in essence that "the sect of the Bene Israel in India is of the seed of the House of Israel without any doubt," several rabbis in Israel refused to marry Bene Israel to other Jews. This standpoint was based on halakhic decisions that had been given for Jews from Baghdad who had settled in India, and who denounced intermarriage with those whom they considered to belong to an inferior caste. On first coming to India in the 18th century, the Baghdadi Jews had prayed in the synagogues of the Bene Israel and buried their dead in their cemeteries. However, as they became more settled and acquired a higher status and education, they began to keep apart and to question whether the Bene Israel were legitimately Jewish. They considered that association with the Bene Israel should be debarred for fear of illegitimacy *(mamzerut)* since the latter were unfamiliar with the Jewish laws of divorce *(gittin)*, absolved themselves from levirate marriage, and did not practice *ḥaliẓah*. Not one of the rabbis outside India who returned a negative decision concerning the Bene Israel in previous generations had ever visited there or met representatives of the Bene Israel community in order to obtain knowledge of their customs or information directly from them. In Israel the controversy arose between those who rejected the Bene Israel and those who regarded them as Jews in every respect. In 1962, the Israel Chief Rabbinate appointed a commission of four rabbis who were charged with meeting representatives of the Bene Israel. From the evidence of the leaders of the community who appeared before the rabbis and from earlier sources, it became clear that the Bene Israel had not been accustomed to divorce women at all, in the same way that divorce was not practiced among Indians other than Muslims until about a century ago. It was only on the arrival in India of rabbis from Baghdad and Yemen who were experts on the Jewish laws of divorce that a number of Bene Israel had approached them. Concerning widows the Bene Israel generally followed the custom of their Indian neighbors and did not permit them to remarry, so that the question of levirate marriage or *ḥaliẓah* did not arise. On Oct. 18, 1962, the council of the Chief Rabbinate decided that marriage with Bene Israel is permissible. However, the rabbi registering the marriage was bound to investigate, as far back as three generations at least, the maternal ancestry of every applicant of the Bene Israel, man or woman, wishing to marry outside the community, in order to establish to what extent there were not intermixed in the family persons who were non-Jews or proselytes. The rabbi concerned was also bound to establish as far as possible that neither the parents of the applicant nor his grandparents had remarried after a previous divorce, and that they were not within the prohibited degrees of kinship.

These directives aroused fierce resentment, culminating in a stormy strike in Jerusalem in the summer of 1964, in which several hundred of the Bene Israel from all over Israel participated. Subsequently, the prime minister, Levi Eshkol, issued the statement that "the government of Israel reiterates that it regards the community of the Bene Israel from India as Jews in every respect, without any restriction or distinction, equal in their rights to all other Jews in every matter, including matters of matrimony."

To these troubling afflictions had been added the difficulties of absorption of the Bene Israel into a society totally different from that to which they had been accustomed in India, and the difficulties of finding employment and of language. When the first groups of Bene Israel encountered the difficulties of absorption, they reacted by sit-down strikes of groups and individuals. The

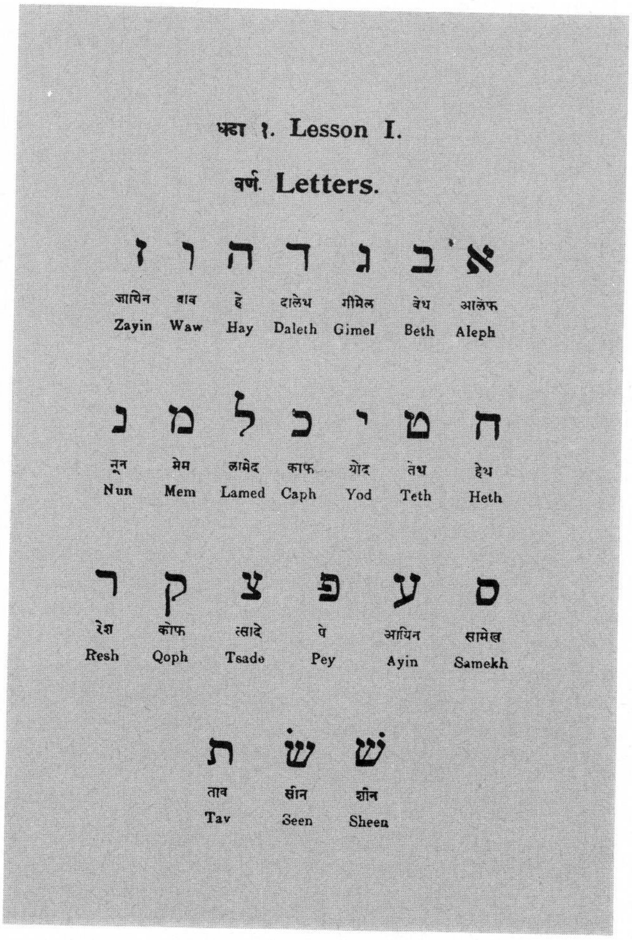

Figure 4. First page of *The Elementary Hebrew Reader*, a textbook by B. S. Ezekiel for the use of the Bene Israel. Jerusalem, Rabbi Ze'ev Gotthold.

presence of Bene Israel strikers at the doors of the offices of the Jewish Agency became a regular feature of the 1950s. In the Indian Parliament, a debate upon discrimination against Indian Jews in Israel took place at the beginning of the crisis. On Sept. 8, 1952, a statement of the Indian deputy minister for external affairs, Shri Anil R. Chanda, was read in answer to a question in the Indian Council of States in New Delhi, as follows: "The government of India has received complaints from some Indian Jews who had returned from Israel that there was discrimination against them on account of their color. The government has not verified any of these complaints, and in any event, such individual complaints do not justify a general statement that there is a color bar in Israel." The young generation of Bene Israel has become integrated into Israel society and found its place in all fields of Israel life. Their communal attachment is still strong and finds particular expression at meetings on festivals. [N.B.-G.]

Bibliography: H. S. Kehimkar, *History of the Bene Israel of India* (1937); M. Ezekiel, *History and Culture of the Bene Israel in India* (1948); R. Reuben, *Bene Israel of Bombay* (1913); L. I. Rabinowitz, *Far East Mission* (1952); N. Bar-Giora, *Massa be-Hodu* (1953); W. J. Fischel, *Ha-Yehudim be-Hodu* (1960); idem, in: *Essays . . . Abba Hillel Silver* (1963), 170–85; S. Strizower, *Exotic Jewish Communities* (1962), 48–87; I. Nissim, *Benei Yisrael, Piskei Halakhah* (1962); B. J. Israel, *Religious Evolution among the Bene Israel of India since 1750* (1963); S. Shellim, *Treatise on the Origin and Early History of the Bene Israel* (1963); R. Dafni, *Indian Jews in Israel* (1969).

BENEI ZION (Heb. בְּנֵי צִיּוֹן), moshav in central Israel, in the southern Sharon, affiliated with Ha-Iḥud ha-Ḥakla'i middle-class settlements association; founded in 1947 by veteran farmers, later joined by immigrants from Poland, Rumania, and North Africa. Its economy was based on citrus plantations and intensive farming. The moshav is named after the B'nai Zion Order of America, which contributed funds toward the acquisition of the land. [E.O.]

BEN ELIEZER, MOSHE (1882–1944), Hebrew editor, author, and translator. Ben Eliezer, who was born in Shchuchin, near Vilna, became attracted to the Haskalah while studying at Mir yeshivah, and joined the staff of the Hebrew daily *Ha-Zeman*. From 1906 to 1910 he lived in the

Moshe Ben Eliezer (standing, left) with some fellow Hebrew writers, c. 1910. Next to him is Yehudah Karni and in front (left to right) are A. M. Berachyahu, Peretz Hirschbein, and A. Druyanow.

United States, where he established *Shibbolim* (1909), a journal devoted to modern Hebrew literature. Returning to Poland he edited several Hebrew journals for young people, and spent some time after World War I in Kovno as press officer for the Lithuanian Ministry for Jewish Affairs. Immigrating to Palestine in 1925, he joined the editorial staff of the newspaper *Haaretz*. His stories, feuilletons, and translations appeared in the Hebrew press of various countries and he also wrote and edited several series of books for children. His works include the historical novels *Yerovam u-Reḥavam* ("Jeroboam and Rehoboam," 1939) and *Don Yosef Nasi* (1945), the novel *Gavri'el* (1945), and translations of works by Scott, Dickens, Conrad, Hawthorne, and others.

Bibliography: N. Goren, *Demuyyot be-Sifrutenu* (1953), 69–74; H. Weiner, *Pirkei Ḥayyim ve-Sifrut* (1960), 94–95; F. Lachower, *Shirah u-Maḥashavah* (1953), 236–8; Rabbi Binyamin, *Mishpeḥot Soferim* (1960), 312–3. [G.K.]

BENESCH, ALFRED ABRAHAM (1879–), U.S. attorney and civic leader. Benesch was born in Cleveland, Ohio, the son of Bohemian immigrants. He established a law practice in Cleveland, and was elected to the Cleveland City Council in 1912. In 1914–15 he served as public safety director in Mayor Newton D. Baker's cabinet. In 1922 Benesch gained prominence as a libertarian for his fight against a proposed quota system for Jews at Harvard. His public career was highlighted by 37 years of continuous service on the Cleveland Board of Education (1925–62); he was its president in 1933–34. Benesch made an immediate impact on school policy when he successfully opposed compulsory reserve military training in the city's public high schools. He was Ohio State Director of Commerce during 1935–39. Benesch held many public and civic offices, and was equally active as a Jewish communal leader, serving as a trustee of many local Jewish agencies. [JU.R.]

BENEŠOV (Ger. **Beneschau**), town in Bohemia (Czechoslovakia). The community, first mentioned in 1419, was among the earliest to be established in a seignorial town in *Bohemia. Five Jewish families were living there in 1570. A community is again mentioned there in 1845, numbering seven families in 1852. It was officially registered in 1893 with 786 persons (including those living in 27 surrounding villages). Benešov was a center of the Svaz *Čechů-židů, Czecho-Jewish movement, and of the struggle against the German-language Jewish school at the end of the 19th century. In 1930 the community numbered 237 (2.8% of the total population), 24 of whom declared their nationality as Jewish. The anti-Jewish laws imposed during the German occupation were sometimes not enforced in Benešov. The community was deported to the Nazi extermination camps in 1942. Only two Jews returned. The synagogue equipment was sent to the Central Jewish Museum in Prague; two cemeteries still remain. No community has been reconstructed. [J.HER.]

BENEVENTO, town in southern Italy. Jews were living in Benevento at least from the 9th century, when the miracle worker *Aaron of Baghdad visited the town. Later, members of the *Ahimaaz family resided in Benevento, Hananeel b. Paltiel establishing his yeshivah there. In 1065, Landolfo VI, prince of Benevento, forced a number of Jews to become converted to Christianity, being reproved for this by Pope *Alexander II. When *Benjamin of Tudela visited Benevento about 1159 he found 200 Jewish families. They were living in a fairly ample quarter; in 1198 three churches in Benevento were known as "de Judeca." Jewish economic activities included weaving and especially dyeing, on which taxes were paid to the archbishop. Later Jews engaged in moneylending. In the early 16th century they also dealt in corn. Benevento being a Papal enclave, the Jewish community which now maintained two synagogues was not disturbed at the time of the general expulsion from southern Italy in 1541. Nevertheless, after the election of Pope *Paul IV in 1555, their position sharply deteriorated. In 1569 they were expelled from Benevento as from the other small towns in the Papal States. The municipal council readmitted Jews in 1617, but in 1630 they were accused of poisoning the wells. Thereafter, the organized Jewish community ceased to exist.

Bibliography: P. M. Lonardo, *Gli ebrei a Benevento* (1899); idem, in: *Vessillo Israelitico*, 67 (1917); Roth, Dark Ages, index; Milano, Bibliotheca, no. 1041 and index. [A.MIL.]

BENEVENTO, IMMANUEL BEN JEKUTHIEL (16th century), Italian grammarian and kabbalist. Benevento, who lived in Mantua, was the pupil of R. Moses *Basola of Pesaro. He wrote *Livyat Ḥen* (Mantua, 1557) on Hebrew grammar and poetry and published *Ma'arekhet ha-Elohut*, the kabbalistic work of Perez b. Isaac Gerondi (of Barcelona), which he annotated with his own commentary (Mantua, 1558). He also published the first printed edition of the major parts of the Zohar (Mantua, 1558–60), based upon a comparative study of several Zohar manuscripts.

Bibliography: Steinschneider, Cat Bod, 541, no. 3492, 1055, no. 5266; J. Perles, *Beitraege zur Geschichte der hebraeischen und aramaeischen Studien* (1884), 220; G. Scholem, *Bibliographia kabbalistica* (1927), 166, 177. [U.C./ED.]

BENEVENUTUS GRAPHEUS HIEROSOLYMITANUS (c. 12th century), the most famous medieval non-Arab oculist. Probably Jewish, he practiced and lectured in Southern Europe. His work on ocular diseases was the best-known textbook until well into the 16th century. Twenty-two manuscripts and 18 printed editions are still in existence, differing in length and completeness. According to a Vatican Latin codex, the work was "translated from the Hebrew into Latin." The Latin *editio princeps* is the Ferrara incunabulum (1474). Benevenutus' knowledge of anatomy and his physiological and pathological conceptions follow closely Galen's teachings. In therapy, however, he reflects ophthalmological knowledge of his own time. His description of seasonal ophthalmia is an indication of his having been a "Hierosolymitanus" (Jerusalemite), since it conforms surprisingly well with the summer and autumn epidemics of conjunctivitis in Ereẓ Israel. His therapy is empirical and free from irrational elements. Among his numerous remedies some carry the adjective "Jerusalem." From his descriptions of couching for cataract, the radical treatment of trichiasis, dacryocystitis, and "scabies" of the eyes (trachoma), Benevenutus must have been an experienced and skillful surgeon. He describes an astonishingly modern method for dealing with ocular injuries; embryos from freshly embryonated eggs, removed and reduced to a pulp, and regularly used as an ointment, "bring about a good consolidation of the wound." Of the many names of Benevenutus, Grapheus seems to be the correct one. It would appear to be a stylized derivation of the Hebrew *rofe* ("physician"). In the Paris codex he is called *"Bien Venu Raffe."* The various Christian invocations in his writings were probably later insertions and are not proof that he was not Jewish, nor does the frequently repeated assertion "nos Salernitani" prove that Benevenutus taught in Salerno.

Bibliography: J. Hirschberg, in: A. Graefe-T. Saemisch, *Handbuch der gesamten Augenheilkunde*, 13 (1908); C. A. Wood (ed.), *Beneventus Graffus, De Oculis* (Eng., 1929); H. Friedenwald, *Jews and Medicine*, 2 (1944), 539–40; Feigenbaum, in: *Acta Medica Orientalia*, 14 (1955), 26–29, 75–82.

[A.F.]

BENFELD, town south of Strasbourg, eastern France. In 1349, a regional assembly of feudal lords was held in Benfeld to finalize measures to be taken against the Jews who were accused of spreading the *Black Death. Shortly afterward the Jews living in Benfeld were murdered or expelled. A new community was established in 1830, numbering 236 in 1836. A synagogue was built in 1845. It was one of the few in Alsace not desecrated during World War II under the German occupation, when 31 Jews were deported from Benfeld. In 1968, the community numbered 75 persons.

Bibliography: E. Scheid, *Histoire des Juifs d'Alsace* (1887), 36–37, 286–7; R. Berg, *La persécution raciale* (1947), 181. [R.Be.]

BENFEY, THEODOR (1809–1881), German comparative philologist and Sanskritist. Benfey was born in Noerten, near Goettingen, and lived in Goettingen from his childhood. His first works in classical philology were produced hastily and contained many inaccuracies (as in his *Griechisches Wurzellexikon*, 1839–42). As a young scholar he interested himself in the relationship of Egyptian to Semitic languages, on which he wrote *Ueber das Verhaeltniss der aegyptischen Sprache zum semitischen Sprachstamm* (1844), his sole work on Semitic linguistics. He also dealt extensively with the recurrence of certain motifs in narrative literature, tracing their derivation from Oriental, especially Indian, sources. His work turned increasingly to Indian linguistics, a field in which he became a recognized authority. His two Sanskrit grammars, the complete (1852) and the short (1855), for many years served as basic texts in this field. Though Benfey was a pioneer in the study of the language of the Veda, he never completed the Vedic grammar on which he worked for many years. In 1834 Benfey was appointed a lecturer at the University of Goettingen; in 1848, after converting to Christianity, he was appointed associate professor; and in 1862 full professor. A noted teacher, his students included Jacob Wackernagel and Theodor Noeldeke. For the Bavarian Academy's history of sciences in Germany, Benfey wrote the volume *Geschichte der Sprachwissenschaft und orientalischen Philologie* . . . (1869), with an outstanding chapter on the beginnings of comparative linguistics and its spiritual background.

Bibliography: T. Benfey, *Kleinere Schriften*, 1 (1890), biography by M. Benfey; 2 (1892), 133–56 (bibliography).

[H.J.P.]

BENGALIL (Abengalel), family which flourished in Spain and North Africa in the 13th century. Joseph Bengalil was a rabbi probably living in Ceuta, Morocco, who corresponded with Solomon b. Abraham *Adret. His sons Abraham and Samuel both served on diplomatic missions for the Aragonese kings to Granada and Morocco. Abraham resided in Valencia, and was authorized to conduct business there in 1276 by James I at the request of the sultan of Tunis, apparently also using his official journeys for business purposes; in 1280, when his goods were impounded by the Castilian authorities, Pedro III retaliated in kind against Castilian merchants visiting Aragon. In 1291 Abraham took his family with him on a mission to Tlemçen (Algeria).

Bibliography: J. M. Toledano, *Ner ha-Ma'arav* (1911), 41; J. Ben-Naim, *Malkhei Rabbanan* (1931), 57; Baer, Spain, 1 (1961), 410; Corcos, in: JQR, 54 (1963/64), 65; Hirschberg, Afrikah, 1 (1965), 281–2.

[D.Co.]

BEN-GAVRIEL, MOSHE YA'AKOV (originally **Eugen Hoeflich;** 1891–1965), Israel author who wrote in German. Born into an assimilated Viennese family, Ben-Gavriel went to Palestine during World War I as an Austrian liaison officer with the Turkish forces in Jerusalem, and after the British occupation he returned to Vienna. From there he

Moshe Ben-Gavriel, Israel author.

contributed to Martin Buber's *Der Jude* and became an active Zionist. In *Der Weg in das Land* (1918), *Feuer im Osten* (1920), and *Die Pforte des Ostens* (1923), Ben-Gavriel presented Zionism as a pan-Asian movement, the *yishuv* being the link between East and West. Later he adopted the outlook of the Berit Shalom without actually joining the group. Returning to Palestine in 1927, Ben-Gavriel was until 1933 the local representative of the Deutsches Nachrichtenbuero and later worked for the Swiss press. His World War II experiences in a Palestinian unit of the British Army inspired the Schweik-like hero of *Frieden und Krieg des Buergers Mahaschavi* (1952; *Mahaschavi in Peace and War*, 1960). After 1948 Ben-Gavriel, living in Jerusalem, was successful in writing and broadcasting about the State of Israel in West Germany, where his many books on the Middle East, many of them styled as oriental tales, such as *Kumsits* (1956), were bestsellers. His novels include *Das Haus in der Karpfengasse* (1958), set in Nazi-occupied Prague, which had appeared in Hebrew in 1944. Two volumes of early recollections were *Zahav ba-Ḥuẓot* (1946) and *Die Flucht nach Tarschisch* (1963).

Bibliography: Tidhar, 4 (1950), 1948. [Ed.]

BENGHAZI, port city in the district of Cyrenaica, Libya. In ancient times it was called Hesperides, but was later renamed Berenice. After 74 B.C.E. it was part of Roman Cyrenaica, but according to an inscription of 13 B.C.E., found at Benghazi, the Jews of Berenice were considered citizens (as in the rest of Cyrenaica) but were ruled by their own Jewish archons and not by an ethnarch as in other parts of the Diaspora. Furthermore they are described as a "municipal community," and appear from the inscription to be observant of the festivals (CIG 3:2, no. 5361). Another inscription found in 1938, gives thanks to certain donors for helping to dedicate a synagogue in Berenice in 56 C.E. In both this and the previous inscription the majority of the names mentioned are non-Jewish, testifying to a fair degree of hellenization, as in Egypt. During the revolt of the Jews of *Cyrene in 115 and during the Byzantine era the Jews of Berenice suffered the same fate as those of Cyrene in general. After the Arab conquest in 660, Berenice was mostly deserted. In the 14th century it was called by its Arabic name Benghazi. In the beginning of the 16th century, many Jews from Tripoli helped to repopulate it, earning their livelihood by trade with North Africa and the Mediterranean area, or as smiths or tailors. [Ed.]

Following the Turkish occupation of 1640, Jewish families from Tripoli were attracted to the city. In 1745 epidemics and poverty drove out the inhabitants, but about 1750 some members of the previous Jewish community returned and reorganized the community, which began to flourish about 1775 with the arrival of Jewish families from Italy. In the 18th and 19th centuries Benghazi had 400 Jewish families divided into two clans: those of the town and the surrounding region *(Kahal Benghazi)* and those who were born in Tripoli and Italy. Although both groups recognized the authority of one rabbi, each had its own synagogue. The Muslim Brotherhood of the Sanusiya, whose influence was considerable in the country, was well disposed toward the Jews of Benghazi. They enjoyed complete freedom and were not forced to live in a special quarter. They lived in affluence, and because of their commercial activity the town became an important trading center for Europe and Africa. Several wealthy families occupied high positions in the service of the Turkish authorities. Among scholars of this community were Elijah Lavi (1783–1883), author of *Sefer Ge'ullot Adonai* (1864) and other works written in Hebrew or Judeo-Arabic; Moses Ḥakmon; and Isaac Khalfon. The *talmud torah* was organized under the leadership of Elia Juili (1890), Ḥai Teshuba, and many others. In 1909 when a large fire broke out in the bazaar, the Turkish soldiery, who were supposed to extinguish it, looted and attacked the population, especially the Jews. Because of this, several families moved back to Tripoli. From 1911 Italian rule attracted more Jews from the interior of the country, as well as from Italy, to Benghazi, and in 1935 the Jewish population numbered 2,236. Until 1936 life under Italian rule proceeded peacefully for the Jews. In 1936, however, the Italians began to enforce fascist legislation. Jews were removed from municipal councils and their papers stamped with the words "Jewish race." When Benghazi fell to the British on Feb. 6, 1941, the Jews were overjoyed, but suffered in attacks by hostile Muslim youth when the city was recaptured by the Italians on April 3, 1941. On Dec. 24, 1941 the British retook the city but Italian-German forces once again conquered it on Jan. 27, 1942. This again resulted in anti-Jewish attacks, the systematic plunder of all Jewish shops, and the promulgation of a deportation order. Almost all the Benghazi Jews were deported to Giado, 149 miles (240 km.) south of Tripoli, a camp in the desert where they were forced to perform hard labor in road construction under severe conditions. 562 of them died of starvation and typhus. The condition of the Jews in Giado improved only when the British entered the camp in January 1943. In 1945 and 1948 the community suffered anti-Jewish pogroms at the hands of Arab nationalists. Thereafter, the majority of the community of 2,500 persons emigrated to Israel. Before the Six-Day War of 1967, there were approximately 200 Jews left in Benghazi. Unlike other areas of Jewish settlement in Libya, the authorities reacted fairly rapidly to protect the Jews in Benghazi. Almost immediately after word of Israel-Arab fighting came, the Jews were rounded up and put into protective custody in army barracks outside the city. Subsequent to the Six-Day War most of the remaining Jews in Benghazi emigrated.

Pupils at the Hebrew School at Benghazi organized by a unit of the Jewish Brigade after the recapture of the town by the British in 1943. Jerusalem, Central Zionist Archives.

For bibliography see *Libya. [D.Co.]

BENGIS, SELIG REUBEN (1864–1953), Lithuanian rabbi. Bengis studied in Volozhin under Naphtali Ẓevi Judah *Berlin and Ḥayyim *Soloveichik. In 1894 he was appointed rabbi of Bodki and, in 1912, of Kalvarija, Lithuania. At the outbreak of World War I he went to Smolensk, but in 1915 he returned to Kalvarija. In 1938 he was appointed head of the *bet din* of the separatist Orthodox community Ha-Edah ha-Ḥaredit of Jerusalem, and in 1949, on the death of Joseph Ẓevi *Duschinsky, became its rabbi. Despite the fact that his community consisted of active religious extremists, he succeeded in directing its affairs into practical channels and in curbing its most extreme wing, the *Neturei Karta. He also served as head of the Ohel Moshe Yeshivah in Jerusalem. Bengis' mastery of rabbinic literature, and his memory, were phenomenal; he could unhesitatingly give the source of any random quotation from the Talmud, Rashi, or *tosafot.* He published *Li-Felagot Re'uven* (in 7 parts, Kaidan, Riga, Jerusalem, 1924–46), consisting of **hadranim,* i.e., discourses delivered on completing the study of a talmudic tractate, interwoven with his novellae. He justified the unusual form of his work by maintaining that while novellae are little read, there was a considerable interest in this form of talmudic learning. Bengis himself stated that he had written, under the same title, a commentary on Alfasi, and sermons, which remained in manuscript. Some of his halakhic articles appeared in *Tevunah* (Jerusalem, 1941).

Bibliography: S. Schurin, *Keshet Gibborim* (1964), 40–43.

[Y.AL.]

BEN-GURION, DAVID (1886–), Israel statesman; first prime minister and defense minister of Israel; an outstanding leader of the pioneering labor movement in Ereẓ Israel, he headed the struggle for Jewish independence in Palestine.

Early Years. Ben-Gurion was born in Plonsk (then in Russian Poland). His father, Avigdor Gruen, was a "legal adviser" (i.e., a nonqualified lawyer), an adherent member of Ḥovevei Zion, and a fervent Zionist, whose house was the center of Zionist activity in the town. Ben-Gurion's mother Sheindel (née Friedman) died when he was 11 years old. He was educated in a modernized Hebrew-language *ḥeder,* and studied secular subjects with private tutors. At the age of 14 he was among the founders of a Zionist youth group, "Ezra." He joined the *Po'alei Zion movement in 1903, traveling and speaking on its behalf in Plonsk, Warsaw, and smaller towns. During the revolution of 1905–06 he was arrested twice but released at the intervention of his father. In September 1906 Ben-Gurion settled in Ereẓ Israel, working in the orange groves of Petaḥ Tikvah and in the wine cellars of Rishon le-Zion. He was elected to the central committee of Po'alei Zion, which at the time numbered only a few score members. In October 1906 he took part in a conference at Ramleh which formulated the party's first platform in a distinct Marxist spirit in accordance with Ber *Borochov's teachings.

In his party Ben-Gurion preserved an independent point of view, stressing the obligation of every member to settle in Ereẓ Israel and the right of the immigrants and settlers to manage their own affairs without interference from the Diaspora. Demanding that Hebrew be the sole language of the party and indeed of Jewish public life, he refused to collaborate with the Yiddish party organ (*Der Anfang,* 1907), energetically supporting the historic decision of the third conference of Po'alei Zion in Ereẓ Israel (September 1907) that all party activity be in Hebrew.

Figure 1. David Ben-Gurion (first row, marked X) in a Po'alei Zion group in Plonsk, c. 1905. His father, Avigdor Gruen, is framed in the right-hand window. Jerusalem, Central Zionist Archives.

The years 1907–10, when Ben-Gurion was an agricultural worker and watchman in Lower Galilee (Sejera, Milḥamiyyah (later: Menaḥemiyyah), Kinneret) and in Zikhron Ya'akov, left an indelible impression on his life. He became convinced that "the settlement of the land is the only true Zionism, all else being self-deception, empty verbiage, and merely a pastime" (B. Habas (ed.), *Sefer ha-Aliyyah ha-Sheniyyah* (1947), 353).

In 1910 Ben-Gurion joined the editorial staff of the new party organ *Aḥdut* ("Unity") in Jerusalem, which included among others Izhak *Ben-Zvi and Raḥel Yanait (later Ben-Zvi). Here he published his first articles under the name "Ben-Gurion." Their central theme was that the *yishuv,* including the workers, must organize as a political force, together with Jews in other parts of the new Turkey (after the 1908 Young Turk revolution), and strive for Jewish autonomy in Palestine. In 1911 he and Ben-Zvi were elected delegates to the 11th Zionist Congress. They also participated in the third world conference of Po'alei Zion in Vienna.

In the same year, Ben-Gurion joined a group of young Zionists and Po'alei Zion who went to study at Turkish universities. Their object was to establish close ties with the educated ruling circles in Turkey and join in their political struggle, thereby advancing the development of Ereẓ Israel as a center of the Jewish people. At first he lived in Salonika, where he came in contact with the large Jewish community there, but when Salonika was taken by the Greeks in 1912, Ben-Gurion moved to Constantinople to continue his law studies.

1914–1921. When World War I broke out, Ben-Gurion and his party favored loyalty to Turkey and adoption of Ottoman citizenship. However, with the advent of the anti-Zionist persecutions by the Turkish administration, both he and Ben-Zvi were arrested and accused of conspiring against Ottoman rule in order to establish a Jewish state. Exiled to Egypt in March 1915, they met Joseph *Trumpeldor, who was engaged in forming the "Zion Mule Corps" within the British Army, an activity which Ben-Gurion and Ben-Zvi opposed because it was likely to endanger the *yishuv* without benefiting the Zionist cause.

Later in 1915 Ben-Gurion and Ben-Zvi proceeded to New York, where their main efforts were directed to the establishment of the *He-Ḥalutz organization, preparing young Jews for settlement in Palestine immediately after the war. In 1917 Ben-Gurion married Paula Munweis (born in Minsk, Russia, 1892), a nurse in New York, and an active member of Po'alei Zion. She was a devoted wife until her death in 1968.

After the *Balfour Declaration Ben-Gurion was among the first in the United States to call for the formation of Jewish battalions to liberate Palestine. Volunteering for the British Army in May 1918, he reached Egypt in August as a soldier in the *Jewish Legion (the 39th Battalion of the Royal Fusiliers). There he met volunteers from the labor movement in Palestine; all generally agreed on the necessity for a united workers' movement to prepare for the great days of Jewish mass immigration and settlement that lay ahead after the liberation of the country from Ottoman rule. At the 13th conference of Po'alei Zion in Palestine (Jaffa, February 1919), Ben-Gurion called upon Jewish workers in Palestine and abroad to unite in forming a political force that would direct the Zionist movement toward the establishment of a new Jewish socialist society in Palestine, based upon the collectivist principles embodied in

Figure 2. David Ben-Gurion as a law student in Constantinople, c. 1915. Jerusalem, Central Zionist Archives.

the *kevuẓot* (see *Kibbutz Movement). In 1919, Ben-Gurion opened the founding conference of *Aḥdut ha-Avodah in Petaḥ Tikvah. He also participated in the world delegation of Po'alei Zion which prepared a blueprint for the future development of Ereẓ Israel. After the Jerusalem riots of Passover 1920, Ben-Gurion went to London, where he and Shelomo *Kaplansky headed the political bureau of Po'alei Zion, which established ties with the British Labor Party.

Building the Histadrut. On his return to Palestine at the end of 1921, Ben-Gurion was elected secretary-general of the *Histadrut (founded in 1920) which he and Berl *Katznelson headed for nearly 14 years. He was active on all levels—the organization of strikes, the struggle for the improvement of workers' conditions, the employment of Jewish workers in the general labor market, including their due share in government works, and provision for the unemployed. Since Ben-Gurion's objective was to turn the Histadrut into an instrument for settlement, as well as an economic and political body, he proposed that it become a cooperative "workers' society" *(ḥevrat ovedim)* which would undertake both agricultural settlement and the promotion of industry and building. All the workers would pool their money, and would thus be provided with their necessities. When this proposal, in a modified and limited version, was adopted by the second Histadrut conference in 1923, Ben-Gurion and his colleagues ran the Histadrut as a centralized organization, opposing all attempts to decentralize its functions.

In the early 1920s Ben-Gurion tried to develop economic relations between the Histadrut and the Soviet trade unions and economic bodies, in the hope that such relations would facilitate the existence of the He-Ḥaluẓ movement in that country, and further emigration of Russian Jews to Palestine. He visited the U.S.S.R. in 1923, when the Histradrut participated in the Moscow Agricultural Exhibition. However, these efforts at gaining Soviet friendship proved abortive.

At the end of the 1920s, the middle class, both in Palestine and in the Zionist movement, gained in strength and the *Revisionist movement declared its opposition to the idea of an all-embracing socialist workers' organization, Vladimir *Jabotinsky even calling for the "breaking" of the Histadrut. Ben-Gurion was in the vanguard of resistance to this right-wing pressure. He reached the conclusion that the labor movement must secure a key position, and even hegemony in the World Zionist Organization. The increased unity in the labor movement which Ben-Gurion called for was further advanced by the merger of Aḥdut ha-Avodah and *Ha-Po'el ha-Ẓa'ir into *Mapai in 1930.

In the years 1930–34 Ben-Gurion led the struggle to prevent the Revisionists from gaining ascendancy in the Zionist movement. At the 18th Zionist Congress in 1933, in which labor comprised 44% of the delegates, Ben-Gurion became a member of the Zionist and *Jewish Agency Executive. In an attempt to prevent a split in the Zionist movement, he reached a tentative agreement with Jabotinsky. The first stage was to be an accord on labor matters between the Histadrut and the Revisionist workers. This agreement, however, was decisively rejected by a plebiscite of the members of the Histadrut. Ben-Gurion regarded the rejection as a "grave error," but abided by its decision. As chairman of the Jewish Agency Executive from 1935 to 1948, Ben-Gurion, together with Chaim *Weizmann, directed all Zionist affairs.

In an effort to reach agreement on Jewish-Arab peace and cooperation, Ben-Gurion established contact with the leaders of the Arab national movement which continued even during the Arab rebellion in Palestine in 1936. However, nothing was decided at these meetings.

Toward the Founding of the Jewish State. The proposal to partition Palestine into an Arab and a Jewish state, recommended by the Royal Commission of Enquiry in June 1937, was accepted by Ben-Gurion in the belief that even a small Jewish state would be a powerful instrument for the realization of Zionism. His position was shared by Weizmann and Moshe *Sharett, but many of his closest colleagues, including Berl Katznelson and Yiẓḥak *Tabenkin, were among its opponents. When the British government abandoned the partition plan, Ben-Gurion participated in the political negotiations held by the British in London with Jews and Arabs separately (the "Round Table" talks), which ended in 1939 with the declaration of a new anti-Zionist policy (the White Paper of 1939). The essentials of the policy were the restriction of *aliyah* and of Jewish rights to acquire land. Ben-Gurion condemned the White Paper as a betrayal and called for active resistance to its implementation. He proposed the intensification of "illegal" immigration, involving incidents with British coastal guards, and settlement of land in areas prohibited to Jews.

At the outbreak of World War II Ben-Gurion defined the position of the *yishuv* and of the Zionist movement in these words: "We must assist the British in the war as if there were no White Paper and we must resist the White Paper as if there were no war." He expected the new anti-Zionist policy to be shelved for the duration of the war. Thus, the implementation of the Land Transfer Regulations in February 1940, accompanied by severe harassment of the *Haganah, was regarded by Ben-Gurion as an act of bad faith on the part of the British, who, he felt, exploited the war to suppress Jewish aspirations in Palestine. He initiated a strong protest movement, involving stormy anti-British demonstrations, but the protest was ended in June 1940 when Italy entered the war, opening a second front against the British in the Mediterranean.

Ben-Gurion then set out on a Zionist political and propaganda campaign, mainly in the United States. In May 1942 he headed the group that drew up the *Biltmore Program. It formulated the new political program of the Zionist movement, calling for the opening of Palestine to Jewish immigration and settlement, and defining as the movement's objective that Palestine be established as "a Jewish Commonwealth integrated in the structure of the new democratic world." When the dissident underground organizations *Irgun Ẓeva'i Le'ummi (I.Ẓ.L.) and *Loḥamei Ḥerut Israel (Leḥi) organized armed attacks against the British government in Palestine toward the end of the war, Ben-Gurion ordered the *yishuv* institutions and the Haganah to take vigorous measures to curb them. He even went so far as to cooperate with the British authorities in apprehending members of the dissident organizations, a step which aroused much controversy in the ranks of the Haganah.

When, soon after World War II, it became clear that the British government had no intention of abandoning the White Paper policy, Ben-Gurion led the political struggle against the British and authorized the sabotage activities of the Hebrew Resistance Movement (Tenu'at ha-Meri ha-Ivri), which comprised the Haganah, I.Ẓ.L., and Leḥi. Encouraging "illegal" immigration, he visited the camps of Jewish survivors in Germany, and at their conference in 1946 (see *Bergen-Belsen), he declared: "We shall not rest until every one of you who so desires joins us in the land of Israel in building a Jewish state." In the months immediately following the war he ordered the Haganah leaders to begin acquiring large quantities of arms in preparation for the contingency of an armed clash with the Arabs.

Ben-Gurion, who was in Europe on "Black Saturday" (June 29, 1946), when the members of the Jewish Agency Executive in Palestine were arrested by the British, opposed the moderate elements in the Zionist movement who favored an attempt to reach a compromise with the British. But he did give the order to halt the armed struggle in Palestine. Ben-Gurion's policy was approved at the 22nd Zionist Congress (December 1946), at which Weizmann failed to be reelected as president of the World Zionist Organization. Ben-Gurion was reelected chairman of the Jewish Agency Executive and was also given the defense portfolio. Returning to Palestine, he devoted himself to studying security problems and strengthening the Haganah for effective resistance not only to the Arabs in Palestine but also to the armies of the Arab states in case of invasion. Ben-Gurion was one of the chief Zionist spokesmen before the Anglo-American Enquiry Commission (1946) and the United Nations Special Commission on Palestine (UNSCOP, 1947).

War of Independence, 1947–1948. When the *War of Independence broke out in December 1947, Ben-Gurion headed the defense effort, organizing the raising of financial support, the acquisition of arms, the recruiting of military experts, and the preparation of operational plans. During the course of the war he molded the character and structure of the Israel Army, which was officially formed in May 1948. In this undertaking he had to decide between two systems in the Haganah, represented mainly by the commanders of the *Palmaḥ on the one hand and the veterans of the British Army on the other. Ben-Gurion also had to deal with the activity of the dissident organizations I.Ẓ.L. and Leḥi, which were finally liquidated in the summer of 1948 after the *Altalena* (see *Irgun Ẓeva'i Le'ummi) episode and the murder of Count *Bernadotte. In his determination to free the newly established army from all separatist influences, Ben-Gurion ordered the disbanding of the Palmaḥ command and the complete integration of all Palmaḥ units in the general framework of the army. His opinion was the decisive factor in all the fateful events of the war that determined the borders of the state: the conquest of the northern Negev (October 1948), the retreat from Sinai (January 1949), and the occupation of Eilat (March 1949).

1948–1956. In the spring of 1948, despite great pressure from the U.S. government and the doubts of many of his colleagues, Ben-Gurion insisted upon the establishment of the Jewish state immediately upon the termination of the British Mandate. On May 14, 1948, he proclaimed the rebirth of the independent Jewish nation. He became prime minister and minister of defense in the provisional government, continuing in these posts after the election to the first Knesset in 1949. Since no single party obtained an overall majority, Ben-Gurion formed a coalition government, which set the pattern for future governments. In December 1949, he declared Jerusalem the capital of Israel. Ben-Gurion devoted most of his efforts to strengthening the army, to establishing civilian control over it, and to winning the support of the powers for Israel's struggle to consolidate a position of security. In 1951 he went to the United States where he launched the first Israel Bond Drive . He gave the full weight of his authority to the *Reparations Agreements with West Germany, which met with serious opposition from large sectors of the population.

Ben-Gurion had a formative influence on the emergent character of the State of Israel, making the ingathering of

Figure 3. David Ben-Gurion in Jewish Legion uniform, 1918. Jerusalem, Central Zionist Archives.

Figure 4. David Ben-Gurion speaking at the laying of the foundation stone of the Bet ha-Po'alim in Jerusalem, 1924. Jerusalem, Central Zionist Archives.

the exiles a supreme principle in the ideology of the state; introducing free education in an effort to weld the diversified elements of Israel into one nation and using the army as an educational medium; and placing the advancement of science and research as a central factor to the development of the country and its people.

In December 1953 Ben-Gurion announced his resignation from the government. After many years of political work he felt he needed a rest from the tensions of high office. By joining the new non-party kibbutz *Sedeh Boker in the heart of the Negev, he wished to set an example for personal pioneering, particularly in the Negev, which he regarded as foremost in importance for the future of Israel. He later founded a regional high school there, as well as an institute of higher studies which he hoped would eventually become "the Yavneh and Oxford of Israel."

In February 1955, following the collapse of an Israel intelligence network in Egypt, Defense Minister Pinḥas *Lavon resigned, and Ben-Gurion was recalled to serve as minister of defense in the government headed by Moshe Sharett. Ben-Gurion's return to the Defense Ministry came at a time when Israel's security and political situation had deteriorated as a result of the Bandung Conference of Afro-Asian states (April 1955) and the Czechoslovak-Egyptian arms deal concluded under Soviet auspices (September 1955). Israel's neighbors were increasing terrorist activity within her borders. Ben-Gurion decided upon systematic reprisal actions beyond the armistice lines. After the elections in November 1955, Ben-Gurion again assumed the twofold functions of prime minister and minister of defense. In his search for allies, he established close relations with France. These ties became closer when Nasser antagonized

Figure 5. David Ben-Gurion giving evidence before the Anglo-American Commission of Enquiry on Palestine, Jerusalem, 1946. Jerusalem, Central Zionist Archives.

the Western powers by nationalizing the Suez Canal in July 1956. In October 1956 Ben-Gurion went to France for a secret meeting with the representatives of the French and British governments, at which concerted military action against Egypt was planned. On Oct. 29, 1956, the Israel Army moved into the Sinai Peninsula, and within a week the military objectives had been achieved (see *Sinai Campaign). After taking a strong political stand, Ben-Gurion was compelled to agree to the withdrawal of Israel forces from Sinai and the Gaza Strip as a result of heavy international pressure, especially from the U.S. and the Soviet Union. This withdrawal was completed in March 1957. The main achievements of the campaign were the cessation of terrorist raids into Israel from Egyptian-controlled territory, the stationing of United Nations forces in the Gaza Strip, and the opening of the sea route to Eilat.

1956–1963. After the Sinai Campaign Ben-Gurion's efforts were directed to consolidating Israel's international position. His policy of obtaining economic and military aid from West Germany aroused considerable public controversy. During Ben-Gurion's election campaign at the end of 1959, the main issue was electoral reform. He favored the system of personal election by constituencies, which he regarded as the cure for Israel's political ills, rather than the existing system of proportional representation. The elections, however, produced no significant change in the composition of the Knesset, and no majority could be found for changing the electoral system.

During 1960–62 Ben-Gurion traveled to the United States, Western Europe, Burma, and the Scandinavian countries. During this period he met with Chancellor Adenauer (1960) and with President Kennedy (1961) in New York and with President de Gaulle in Paris (June 1960).

In September 1960 the government and the country were shaken by the "Lavon Affair." Suspicions arose concerning the authenticity of certain documents that had been brought before the government six years earlier, which had attributed the responsibility for the failure of Israel intelligence in Egypt to Pinḥas Lavon, then minister of defense. Lavon demanded that his name be cleared, and a commission of seven ministers who examined the relevant documents acquitted him of any responsibility in the affair. Ben-Gurion refused to accept this verdict. He submitted his resignation in January 1961 and requested that his party choose between himself and Lavon. After considerable controversy in the party and in the press, the central committee of Mapai decided by a 60% majority to dismiss Lavon from his office as secretary-general of the Histadrut. Mapai received fewer votes in the elections of August 1961, and it was only after lengthy negotiations that Ben-Gurion succeeded in forming a new coalition government.

Ben-Gurion in Retirement. In June 1963 Ben-Gurion again resigned from the government, recommending Levi *Eshkol as his successor. He again retired to Sedeh Boker and devoted himself to writing the history of the rebirth of Israel. It seemed as if Ben-Gurion's public career had come to an end. But in the spring of 1964, he returned to the public arena by again raising the question of the "Lavon Affair" and demanding a judicial inquiry. He renewed his advocacy of a change in the electoral system, expressed his opposition to the alignment between Mapai and Aḥdut ha-Avodah, and attacked Levi Eshkol and other members of the government. At a conference in January 1965, Mapai decided against Ben-Gurion by a majority of 60%. As a result, Ben-Gurion organized his followers in an independent list for the 1965 elections to the Histadrut and the Knesset, the Israel Workers List (Reshimat Po'alei Israel, or *Rafi), thus seceding from Mapai. He was joined by

Figure 6. The proclamation of the State of Israel, May 14, 1948, in Tel Aviv. David Ben-Gurion is flanked by the members of his provisional government, including (left to right) Bechor Shitreet, David Remez, Pinḥas Rosen, Pereẓ Naftali, Rabbi Y. L. Maimon (Fishman), Moshe Shapiro (behind microphone), Moshe Sharett, Eliezer Kaplan, Mordekhai Bentov, and Aharon Zisling. Photo Government Press Office, Tel Aviv.

Moshe *Dayan, Shimon *Peres, and Yosef *Almogi, among others.

The results of the elections (10% in the Histadrut and 8% in the Knesset) were a disappointment to Ben-Gurion and his supporters. Rafi rejoined the government on the eve of the Six-Day War (June 1967) and, shortly after the war, joined with Mapai and Aḥdut ha-Avodah to form the reunited *Israel Labor Party (Mifleget ha-Avodah). Ben-Gurion did not participate in the negotiations and did not join the new party. He continued his demand for a renewed inquiry into the "Lavon Affair," which he regarded as a moral fight for truth and justice. He remained a solitary figure, whose preeminent and single-minded role in the establishment and building of the state assured him a unique position in public life and in the affection of the people.

In the October 1969 elections to the Knesset Ben-Gurion and a group of his followers (under the name of Reshimah Mamlakhtit, the "State list") received four mandates, retaining a strong oppositional attitude toward the Alignment of the Israel Labor Party and Mapam. Ben-Gurion resigned from the Knesset the following year.

Figure 7. David Ben-Gurion with his wife, Paula, after receiving an honorary doctorate at New York University, 1967. Abraham I. Katsh is on the left and James Hester, president of N.Y.U., on the right.

Ben-Gurion's personality embodied great spiritual forces and tremendous willpower. As an orator, publicist, and forceful debater, he strove to strengthen both the labor movement in Ereẓ Israel and the Zionist movement, and to organize institutions designed to advance their objectives. His intellectual interests were wide, embracing not only a thorough study of the Bible, but also Greek philosophy, Buddhism, and the philosophy of Spinoza. By conviction an intransigent democrat, he rejected any suggestion that he use his great influence to introduce undemocratic methods of government. From his youth he insisted that Zionism could be realized only by personal presence in Ereẓ Israel. After the founding of the state, he bitterly attacked the Zionists who remained in the Diaspora. Both admirers and opponents, Jews and non-Jews, have regarded Ben-Gurion as foremost among the founding fathers of modern Israel.

Figure 8. David Ben-Gurion in retirement. Photo Government Press Office, Tel Aviv.

BEN-GURION'S WORKS: *Rebirth and Destiny of Israel* (1952); *Israel: Years of Challenge* (1963); (ed.), *The Jews in Their Land* (1966); *Anaḥnu u-Shekheneinu* (1931); *Mi-Ma'amad le-Am* (1933); *Ba-Ma'arakhah*, 5 vols. (1947–49); *Be-Hillaḥem Yisrael* (1950); *Ḥazon va-Derekh*, 5 vols. (1951–57); *Ẓava u-Vittaḥon* (1955); *Ma'arekhet Sinai* (1959); *Pegishot im Manhigim Arviyyim* (1967); *Mikhtavim el Paula ve-el ha-Yeladim* (1968); *Medinat Yisrael ha-Meḥuddeshet* (1969).

Bibliography: S. Lachower, *Kitvei David Ben-Gurion* (a bibliography, 1960); R. St.-John, *Ben-Gurion* (Eng., 1959); B. Litvinoff, *Ben-Gurion of Israel* (1954); M. Edelman, *Ben-Gurion, A Political Biography* (1964); M. Pearlman, *Ben-Gurion Looks Back* (1965); O. Zmora, *Days of David Ben-Gurion* (1967); M. Bar-Zohar, *The Armed Prophet: A Biography of Ben-Gurion* (1967); J. Comay, *Ben-Gurion and the Birth of Israel* (1967); B. Ḥabas, *David ben-Gurion ve-Doro* (1952).

[Y.S.]

BEN-HADAD (Heb. בֶּן הֲדַד; "Son of Hadad"), the name of three kings of *Aram (see *Damascus), as Hebraized in the Bible. In Aramaic inscriptions the name appears as *Brhdd* (ברהדד), with the native word *br* (then pronounced *bir*, later *bar*) instead of the Hebrew *ben*.

BEN-HADAD I, son of Tabrimmon son of Hezion (I Kings 15:18), was a contemporary of King *Asa of Judah and King *Baasha of Israel. Like his father (cf. I Kings 15:19; II Chron. 16:3), he was bound by alliances to the kings of both Israel and Judah. However, when war broke out between Baasha and Asa, the latter won him to his cause by sending him treasures from the Temple and the royal palace. Ben-Hadad invaded the kingdom of Israel, conquering *Ijon, *Dan, *Abel-Beth-Maacah, the region of Chinneroth, and all the land of Naphtali (I Kings 15:20). It was possibly this Ben-Hadad who set up the votive stele, found in the vicinity of Aleppo, which was dedicated to the Tyrian god Melqart (Pritchard, Texts, 501).

BEN-HADAD II, a contemporary of *Ahab, dominated the smaller kingdoms of Aram: in his war against Israel he is said to have been accompanied by 32 vassals (I Kings 20:1). On three occasions he waged war against Ahab, succeeding in the first conflict in besieging Samaria (20:2ff.). Ahab resolved to resist when the demands of Ben-Hadad became excessively harsh, and managed to defeat him. Later Ben-Hadad again opened hostilities against Ahab, but was defeated a second time at *Aphek and taken prisoner (I Kings 20:26ff.). By the terms of the friendly alliance which he subsequently concluded with Israel, he undertook to return the Israelite towns under his dominion and to put bazaars in Damascus at the disposal of the merchants of Israel. After three years of peace, Ahab, with the assistance of *Jehoshaphat, the king of Judah, embarked on a new war against Aram in Ramoth-Gilead, during which he met his death (I Kings 22, where the king of Aram is referred to only by his title). It seems that between the second and the last war against Ahab, Ben-Hadad (who is referred to in Assyrian inscriptions as Adad-Idri, i.e., probably Hadadezer, perhaps his personal name as distinct from his throne name) led an alliance consisting of the kings of Syria, Phoenicia, and Palestine (including Ahab) in a war against Shalmaneser III, king of Assyria, near *Qarqar in 853 B.C.E. After the war of Qarqar the coalition split up and the last war with Israel took place. Afterward Ben-Hadad resumed the leadership in an alliance against Assyria and thus succeeded in temporarily removing the Assyrian threat (848, 845 B.C.E.). Shortly after *Jehu's accession to the throne of Israel, Ben-Hadad was assassinated on his sickbed by Hazael (II Kings 8:15), who seized the throne of Aram (II Kings 8:7–15; cf. I Kings 19:15).

BEN-HADAD III, son of Hazael, was the contemporary of *Jehoahaz and *Joash, kings of Israel (814–800 and 800–784 B.C.E.). During the early years of his reign the greater part of the kingdom of Israel was occupied by Aram. It is also possible that Ben-Hadad added to the conquests of his father because he headed an alliance of north Syrian and neo-Hittite kingdoms (e.g., *Que, Sam'al) who attacked Zakir, king of Hamath and Luath, and besieged Hadrach, though without success. In 806–805, Adad-Nirari III, king of Assyria (810–782), renewed the war against Aram, besieged Damascus in 802, and imposed a heavy tribute on Ben-Hadad (whom the Assyrian inscriptions refer to by the Aramean title of *Mari*, "Lord"). It was this setback of Aram that enabled Israel to throw off the Aramean yoke. In the reign of this Ben-Hadad, Damascus lost its dominant position in Syria, and for a generation after, the kings of Israel and Judah were the predominant force there. [I.G.]

H. Winckler and E. Meyer (followed in the 1940s by W. F. Albright) believe that there were only two kings of Aram by the name of Ben-Hadad, the Aramean contemporary of Baasha being identical with that of Ahab.

Moreover, while the chronology of the books of Kings has been followed above, H. L. Ginsberg has suggested that, though there are bound to be differences as to just

A votive stele dedicated by Ben-Hadad of Aram (Damascus) to the god Melqart, 9th century B.C.E. It is the first known monument of any significance bearing the name of a king of Damascus. Height 4 ft. 4 in. (1.62 m.). Aleppo, Syria, National Museum.

what adjustments need to be made, the distribution of the incidents during the Aramean wars among the various kings of Israel cannot be correct in all respects. If the Aramean incident of I Kings 20 took place under the dynasty of Jehu, the above Ben-Hadad II is identical not with the above Ben-Hadad I but with the above Ben-Hadad III, and Ahab's Aramean ally had only the one name Adad-Idri Hadadezer, for there is no difficulty in assuming that this legend in II Kings 8:15 is in error regarding the name of Hazael's predecessor. Also, the elaborate story in I Kings 20:1–35 about the anonymous king of Israel who dies in his chariot of an arrow wound sustained in a battle with the Arameans, in which he was assisted by King Jehoshaphat of Judah, at Ramoth-Gilead bears a strong resemblance to the palpably historical account in II Kings 8:25–9:24. This tells of how King Jehoram of Israel, while recuperating (at Jezreel) from wounds sustained in a battle with the Arameans, in which he was assisted by King Ahaziah of Judah, at Ramoth-Gilead, is shot dead in his chariot with an arrow from the bow of Jehu, who follows him (to Jezreel) from the camp at Ramoth-Gilead. Thus one wonders if the suspicion that the former is a legendary parallel to the latter and has nothing to do with Ahab has not been voiced before. (The incident in the former, with the various prophets, probably contains a core of history, but also pertains to Jehoram and Ahaziah, not to "Ahab" and Jehoshaphat.)

See also *Ahab, *Jehoahaz, *Joash, *Jehoram, and *Jehu, and the bibliography below under Jepsen. [H.L.G.]

Bibliography: Bright, Hist, 215, 221, 223–4, 228, 235, 237; A. Dupont-Sommer, *Les araméens* (1949); E. Kraeling, *Aram and Israel* (1918); M. F. Unger, *Israel and the Arameans of Damascus* (1957); A. Jepsen, in: AFO, 14 (1941–4), 153–72; W. F. Albright, in: BASOR, 87 (1942), 23–40; 90 (1943), 32; 100 (1945), 10–22.

BEN-HAIM (originally **Frankenburger**), **PAUL** (1897–), Israel composer. Ben-Haim, who was born in Munich, was a theater conductor and assistant to Bruno Walter and Hans Knappertsbusch before settling in Tel Aviv in 1933. There he worked as a teacher, accompanist, and conductor until he could afford to devote himself mainly to

Paul Ben-Haim, Israel composer.

composition. Many of Israel's younger generation of composers studied with him. As a westerner living in the east, Ben-Haim regarded it as his task to contribute to a synthesis of western and eastern music. One of Israel's outstanding composers, he helped to create the Eastern Mediterranean school of composition. He strove to incorporate in his work the atmosphere of the traditional music of the Near East, with its florid melodies, its intricate rhythms, and its characteristic instrumental playing. Most of his work is lyrical, though in his biblical cantatas—notably *Hymn from the Desert* (1962), based on an ancient hymn discovered in the Dead Sea Scrolls—it often rises to dramatic heights. His work generally exudes the pastoral atmosphere of the Israel countryside and the youthful spirit of its population. At the same time it reflects deep meditation and feeling. Ben-Haim's works include two symphonies (1940 and 1945); *Evocation* for violin and orchestra (1942); concertos for piano (1949), violin (1960), and cello (1962); the symphonic movements *Sweet Psalmist of Israel,* which were awarded the Israel Prize in 1957; *Liturgical Cantata* (1950); the cantatas *Vision of a Prophet* (1959), *Three Psalms* (1952), and *Kabbalat Shabbat* (1967); as well as songs, chamber music, and pieces for the piano.

Bibliography: P. Gradenwitz, *Music and Musicians in Israel* (1959[2]), 60–72; *P. Ben Haim* (Heb., 1967), biography and bibliography.

[P.E.G.]

BEN HA-MELEKH VE-HA-NAZIR (Heb. בֶּן הַמֶּלֶךְ וְהַנָּזִיר "The Prince and the Hermit"), Hebrew version by Abraham b. Samuel ha-Levi *Ibn Ḥasdai of an original Hindu tale about a prince who eventually became an ascetic. Balauhar and Budasaph, the names of the heroes of the tale in the old Pahlavi version, became Barlaam and Joasaph in the Greek version and Barlaam and Josaphat in the oldest Latin version (1048) and in later European translations. The Hebrew work is based on an Arabic version, but whether it is a translation or an adaptation cannot be determined until the Arabic text is established. *Ben ha-Melekh ve-ha-Nazir* is the account of a prince, Joasaph, sent by his father to a luxurious palace on an island in an effort to avert the fulfillment of a prophecy that he would become a Christian monk. When the prince discovers the reason for his confinement, he implores his father to allow him to return to the mainland. The king

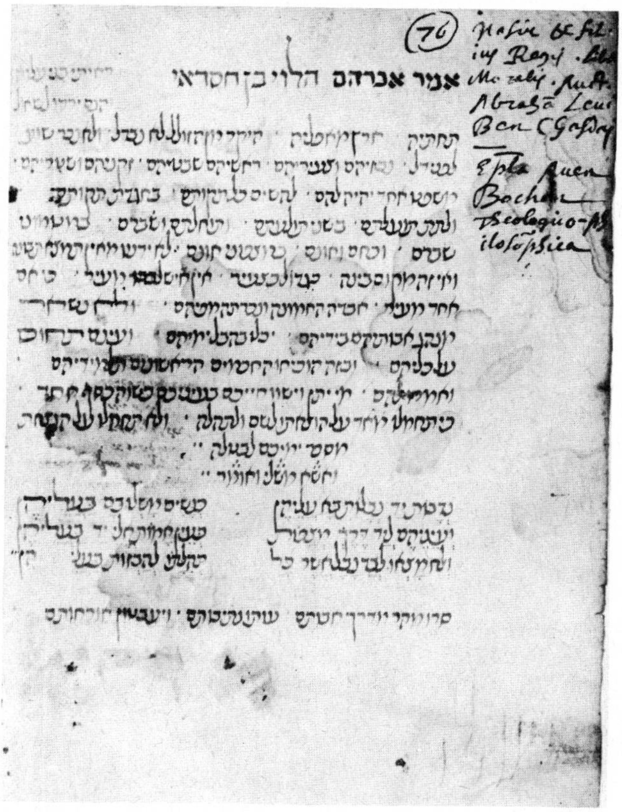
אמר אברהם הלוי בן חסדאי

Introduction page of a copy of *Ben ha-Melekh ve-ha-Nazir* ("The Prince and the Hermit") made in Bologna, Italy, 1423. The opening words give the name of the author of the Hebrew version as Abraham ha-Levi ben Ḥasdai. Jerusalem, J.N.U.L.

yields, and the son soon becomes aware of evil in the world, with consequent unrest in his heart. A monk, Barlaam, who comes disguised as a merchant (monks being prohibited in the land) gains access to the prince and gradually teaches him to realize the vanity of this world and the advantages of the ascetic life. Unlike the Greek and the Arabic tales, the Hebrew does not reintroduce the father, nor does it relate his efforts to undo the effects of the monk's instruction. Instead, it continues the discussion on philosophic and theological questions until the monk is obliged to leave and the prince feels bereft and lonely. The course of transmission of the original tale until it evolved into a world classic is complicated, with many problems still unresolved. In the European texts, the prince adopts the Christian faith of his preceptor. The Hindu original is obviously modeled after the life of Buddha. The Hebrew version is attractively written, and the prose narrative is interspersed with versified aphorisms.

Bibliography: H. Peri (Pflaum), *Der Religionsdisput der Barlaam-Legende* (1959); Abraham b. Ḥasdai, *Ben-ha-Melekh ve-ha-Nazir*, ed. by A. M. Habermann (1951); F. Liebrecht, *Zur Volkskunde* (1879), 441–60; Steinschneider, Uebersetzungen, 863–7; E. A. W. Budge, *Barlaam and Jewâsaf* (1923); D. M. Lang, *The Wisdom of Balahvar* (1957); J. Jacobs, *Barlaam and Josaphat* (1896).

[M.PL.]

BEN ḤAYYIM (Goldmann), ZE'EV (1907–), Hebrew scholar and linguist. Born in Mościska, Galicia, he emigrated to Palestine in 1931 and in 1934 became secretary of the Va'ad ha-Lashon. In 1948 he was appointed lecturer (1955, professor) of Hebrew language at the Hebrew Uni-

Ze'ev Ben Ḥayyim, Hebrew scholar.

versity and in 1961 was elected vice-president of the *Academy of the Hebrew Language in Jerusalem. Ben Ḥayyim specialized in the Samaritan Hebrew dialect, literature, etc., on which he published *Ivrit ve-Aramit Nusaḥ Shomeron* ("The Literary and Oral Tradition of Hebrew and Aramaic among the Samaritans," 4 vols., 1957–67). In this book, he discusses the evolution and historical development of the Samaritan language, starting from its earliest literary sources through the linguistic tradition preserved in the modern idiom. It contributed not only to the recognition of this particular dialect, but also to the clarification of important aspects of the history of the Hebrew and Aramaic languages and their development.

In his pamphlet *Lashon Attikah bi-Meẓi'ut Ḥadashah* ("Ancient Language in a New Reality," 1953) he deals with problems of the growth and development of modern Hebrew as the living language in the State of Israel. He was the editor of the historical dictionary of the Hebrew language—one of the major projects of the Academy. He also edited Hebrew dictionaries containing modern Hebrew terms in the fields of mathematics, anatomy, technology, etc., and contributed articles to leading linguistic journals on problems of Hebrew grammar and on the systems of Hebrew grammarians. He received the Israel Prize in 1964. A full list of Ben Ḥayyim's works and scientific publications appeared in *Leshonenu* (vol. 32, Tishri-Tevet 1967/68), the publication of the Academy, edited by Ben Ḥayyim from 1955 to 1965.

[ED.]

BEN HE HE (c. first century), *tanna*. In *Avot* (5, end) appears a maxim in the name of Ben He He: "According to the labor is the reward." The same maxim is quoted as a popular saying in the name of Hillel the Elder (ARN[1] 12:28; ARN[2] 27:28), while a similar version occurs in Samaritan literature (see S. Liberman, *Greek in Jewish Palestine* (1942), 160, p.113). The Talmud (Ḥag. 9b), implying that he may have been a pupil of Hillel, contains questions addressed to Hillel by Bar He He (see *Seder ha-Dorot*, s.v. *Ben Bag Bag*; cf., however, Liberman, loc. cit.). His name is said to have originated from his having been "a proselyte, i.e., the son [*ben*] of Abraham and Sarah, to each of whose names the letter ה [*he*] was added" (cf. Gen. 17:5, 15; Tos. to Hag. 9b; *Maḥzor Vitry*, ed. Hurwitz (1923), 563–4). Bacher (Tann, 1 (1903²), 8–9) suggests that he was converted under the influence of Hillel. He is also identified with *Ben Bag Bag (Tos. and *Maḥzor Vitry*, loc. cit.).

Bibliography: Hyman, Toledot, 285.

[Z.K.]

BEN-HORIN, MEIR (1918–), U.S. Jewish educator. Born in Koenigsberg, East Prussia, Ben-Horin was assistant professor of education at the Boston *Hebrew Teachers College from 1951 to 1957. From 1957, he headed the department of education of Dropsie College (now *Dropsie University) in Philadelphia, with the rank of professor from 1962. Ben-Horin wrote *Max Nordau: Philosopher of Human Solidarity* (1956) and *Common Faith—Uncommon People* (1970). Together with Judah *Pilch he coedited *Judaism and the Jewish School* (1966). In applying to Jewish education the Reconstructionist view of Judaism as a religious civilization, Ben-Horin follows the educational and philosophical thinking of Dewey, M. M. Kaplan, and Theodore Brameld.

[L.SP.]

BENIDER, Moroccan family. ABRAHAM BENIDER (first half of 18th century), a native of Tetuan, later a resident of Gibraltar and Tangiers, was chandler to the British fleet and official interpreter. His son JACOB, born in Gibraltar, served as interpreter in the British consulates in Tetuan, Tangiers, Salé, Mogador, Safi, and Agadir. In 1768 he was vice-consul in Salé. In 1772 the sultan of Morocco sent him as his ambassador to London on a special mission. However, Benider was not successful in his mission. Apparently he did not return to Gibraltar or Morocco.

Bibliography: C. Roth, in: JHSEM, 2 (1935), 84–90; Hirschberg, Afrikah, 2 (1965), 285, 288–91; idem, in: *Essays . . . I. Brodie*, 2 (1967), 165–81.

[D.CO.]

BENIOFF, HUGO (1899–1968), U.S. seismologist. Born in Los Angeles, Benioff was assistant at the Mount Wilson observatory from 1917 to 1924. In 1923–24, he carried out seismological research at the Carnegie Institute in Washington. He then joined the staff of the California Institute of Technology in the seismological research department, where he was professor from 1950. He designed instruments for measuring movements of the earth's crust on land and in the sea. Benioff applied his knowledge as consultant to building firms to help plan against earthquake destruction, and to the U.S. Navy submarine section. He was adviser to the geophysical department of the U.S. Air Force.

[ED.]

BENISCH, ABRAHAM (1814–1878), author, scholar, and precursor of Zionism. Benisch was born in Drossau, Bohemia. As a student of medicine at the University of Prague he joined Moritz *Steinschneider, who founded a student organization for the purpose of "reestablishing Jewish independence in Ereẓ Israel." Continuing his studies in Vienna in 1838, Benisch, and Albert *Loewy, established a secret society, *Die Einheit,* whose purpose was to initiate organized Jewish immigration to Ereẓ Israel. With this aim in mind he talked to Adolphe *Crémieux and, in 1841, proceeded to London with a letter of recommendation from the House of Rothschild to influential Jewish circles. Receiving no tangible support, Benisch nevertheless continued to promote his views in the periodical *The Voice of Jacob* (1841–48), and in 1853 started the *Hebrew Observer* as a rival to the then 12-year-old *Jewish Chronicle.* In 1854 the paper was merged with the *Jewish Chronicle,* which for the next 13 years, and again from 1875 to 1878, was edited by Benisch, under the title *Jewish Chronicle and Hebrew Observer.* During these years Benisch utilized every opportunity, including the *Damascus Affair and the Crimean War, to raise the question of Jewish revival in Ereẓ Israel. He collaborated with Charles *Netter in founding the *Mikveh Israel agricultural school. He was one of the founders and first directors of the *Anglo-Jewish Association and carried on an unceasing campaign for the rights of the Jews in Russia and the Balkan countries. In his articles before and during the Congress of Berlin (1878), Benisch stressed the importance of Jewish settlement of Ereẓ Israel as integral to the solution of Near Eastern problems. Benisch published a Hebrew commentary on the Book of Ezekiel (1836), and wrote *Two Lectures on the Life and Writings of Maimonides* (1847). He translated the Bible into English (1851), and in the same year also translated into English the *Travels* of *Pethahiah b. Jacob of Regensburg. He wrote a Hebrew grammar and a scripture manual in 1852, entitled *Bikkurei ha-Limmud,* and *An Essay on Bishop Colenso's Criticism of the Pentateuch and Joshua* (1863). A collection of his lectures entitled *Judaism Surveyed* appeared in 1874.

Bibliography: *Jewish Chronicle: 1841–1941* (1949), ch. 5; S. W. Baron, in: *Jewish Studies in Memory of G. A. Kohut* (1935), 72–85; N. M. Gelber, in: *Prague vi-Yrushalayim* (1954), 42–44; idem, *Shivat Ẓiyyon,* 1 (1950), 106–30.

[N.M.G.]

BENJACOB, ISAAC (1801–1863), first modern Hebrew bibliographer. He was born near Vilna and spent most of his life in that city. After publishing original works and republishing several medieval writers, including *Ḥovot ha-Levavot* by *Baḥya ibn Paquda (with a commentary of his own), Benjacob published, with Abraham Dov *Lebensohn (Adam ha-Kohen), a 17-volume edition of the Hebrew Bible (1848–53). It included Rashi's commentary, Mendelssohn's German translation (in Hebrew script), a new commentary by Lebensohn, as well as Benjacob's own *Mikra'ei Kodesh,* an abridged version of *Tikkun Soferim* ("the scribes' emendations to the biblical text"). This edition helped spread Haskalah among Russian Jewry, and was utilized not only for the study of Scriptures, but also for learning German. Benjacob then began his magnum opus of 20 years' duration, *Oẓar ha-Sefarim* (Vilna, 1880; repr. New York, 1965), one of the greatest bibliographic achievements in Hebrew literature. The work lists approximately 8,480 manuscripts and approximately 6,500 books published up to 1863, with a description of their contents. Benjacob also wrote a collection of epigrams, poems and literary essays, *Mikhtamim ve-Shirim Shonim* (1842). His son JACOB (1858–1926) was a merchant, banker, and Zionist. After first publishing his father's work *Oẓar ha-Sefarim* with the assistance of M. *Steinschneider (1877–80), he began recruiting and expanding it, using new bibliographical methods but retaining its original chronological limit (1863). His son-in-law Moses *Schorr reported that the new edition contained 60,000 entries and comprised 12 volumes. Both Benjacob and Schorr tried unsuccessfully to have it published. The manuscript was lost during the Holocaust in Poland.

Bibliography: Benjacob, Oẓar, xxi–xxvii; B. Nathanson, *Sefer ha-Zikhronot* (1876), 112–5; Habermann, in: *Yad la-Kore,* 3 (1952/53), 1–6; Schorr, in: *YIVO Bleter,* 8 (1935), 138–46; idem, in: *Soncino Blaetter* (1927), 38–40; Waxman, Literature, index.

[B.D.]

BENJAMIN (Heb. בִּנְיָמִין), youngest son of *Jacob by *Rachel (Gen. 35:16–18), and the eponym of the tribe of Benjamin. Benjamin was the only one of Jacob's sons to be born in Canaan. Little is known of his life and personality, though he is frequently mentioned in the stories about Jacob, not only because he was the youngest son and born of the beloved wife Rachel but also because he was, as

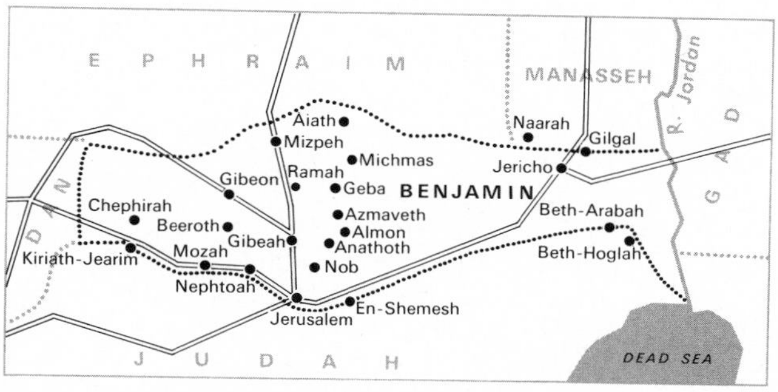

Territory of the tribe of Benjamin.

*Joseph's only full brother, closest to him. Jacob did not send Benjamin to Egypt with the other brothers to procure food during the famine, but when they applied to Joseph for rations he insisted that Benjamin should be sent for. Much against Jacob's will Benjamin eventually accompanied his brothers to Egypt after Judah had undertaken to be responsible for him. When Benjamin was presented, Joseph was overcome with feeling and went into a room and wept there. He invited his brothers to dine and favored Benjamin with extra portions. Joseph, however, put his brothers' integrity to the test and did not make himself known to them. He instructed his steward to conceal a silver goblet in Benjamin's bag and later to overtake the brothers on their journey home and accuse him of stealing it. The brothers interceded for Benjamin, and Judah declared himself ready to sacrifice his liberty in exchange for Benjamin's release to spare their father's grief if he failed to return. Then Joseph finally disclosed his identity to them, and sent an invitation to his father to settle in Goshen with his family (Gen. 42–45).

Rachel had named her son Ben-Oni which could mean either "son of my vigor" or "son of my suffering," though the second meaning better fits the context as her labor was hard and she died in childbirth. The father, however, named the baby Benjamin, which literally means "son of the right hand," and can be understood as having an auspicious sense. It could also mean "son of the south" (cf. Ps. 89:13), either because this son was the only one born in the south, that is in Canaan (all his brothers were born in Aram-Naharaim), or because the legacy of Benjamin was south (i.e., to the right) of that of his brother Joseph. A parallel to the name Benjamin used in the sense of "southerners" is to be found in the *Mari documents referring to West Semitic tribes called *DUMU*^{meš} *(=binu-)*

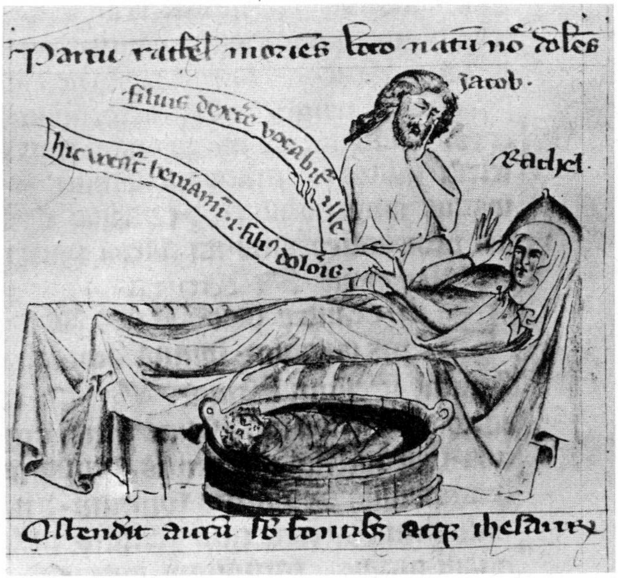

Figure 1. The birth of Benjamin, with Jacob standing by the dying Rachel. From a Latin Bible, *Biblia Pauperum,* first half of 15th century. Lilienfeld, Austria, Abbey Library, Codex 151. Photo Wagner.

Yamina, meaning "sons of the [right, or] south," in contrast to another group of tribes called *DUMU^{meš} Sim'al,* "sons of the [left, or] north" (Sim'al, "left"). Opinion is divided on the possible connection between the Bini-Yamina tribes of the Mari documents (18th century B.C.E.) and the Israelite tribe of Benjamin.

The Genealogies. The Bible contains genealogical lists of the tribe of Benjamin which in part do not correspond with one another either in respect of the number of clans or their names (Gen. 46:21; Num. 26:38–41; I Chron. 7:6–12; 8:1–40; 9:35–44). The variations arise from the fact that some are fragmentary and that the lists may reflect differing traditions about the lineage of the tribe as well as periodic changes in its composition and in territorial boundaries. Beriah, for example, appears in the genealogical lists of Benjamin (I Chron. 8:13–16), Ephraim (*ibid.* 7:21–23), and Asher (Gen. 46:17; Num. 26:44–45). If in each case the reference is to the same clan then this reflects a movement of Beriah from south to north or the reverse. Huppim and Shuppim are included in the genealogical lists of the tribes of both Benjamin (Gen. 46:21, where the latter is Muppim; Num. 26:39; I Chron. 7:12) and Manasseh (I Chron. 7:15). In view of the close ties between Benjamin and the east bank of the Jordan (see below) it seems that the duplication reflects the migration of one or two clans from Benjamin to Manasseh or the reverse. I Chronicles 8:29–40 and 9:35–44 preserve two parallel lists of the family of Saul which place "the father of Gibeon" in the genealogical records of Benjamin. The city of Gibeon was inhabited by the Gibeonite descendants of the Hivites and included in the territory of Benjamin, and the relationship of Saul to Gibeon in these lists indicates the intermingling of the Gibeonite population with the Benjamites. However, some scholars believe that "Gibeon" is a scribal error for "Gibeah," the city of Saul (I Sam. 11:4).

The Tribal Territory. The territory of Benjamin, which extended from the hill country of Ephraim to the hill country of Judah, is described in great detail in Joshua 18:11–28. The description of its southern border fits that of the northern border of Judah (Josh. 15:5–11), while the picture of its northern border accords with that of the southern border of the House of Joseph (Josh. 16:1–3, 5). The northern boundary began at the Jordan and continued in an almost straight line westward to Jericho, which it bypassed to the north; it then ascended the mountains in a west-northwesterly direction, encompassing Beth-El, turning south and continuing to the southwest, and circumventing lower Beth-Horon on the south. The western border of Benjamin is unclear; however, from the description of the territory of Dan, it would seem that it did not reach the sea, but ended in the vicinity of the valley of Aijalon, with the area of lower Beth-Horon and Kiriath-Jearim marking its northern and southern extremities (cf. Josh. 18:28 with 15:60). The southern border ran "from the outskirts of Kiriath-Jearim" (Josh. 18:15), eastward via the "spring of the Waters of Nephtoah" (Lifta) to Jerusalem, which was included in the territory of Benjamin; for the border passed Jerusalem on the south and descended east by way of En-Rogel, En-Shemesh, "the Stone of Bohan son of Reuben," and Beth-Hoglah to the Dead Sea, near where the Jordan enters it. The eastern border was the Jordan.

The list of Benjamite towns (Josh. 18:21–28) does not accord with the northern border of the tribe as described in Joshua 18:12–13 since Beth-El, Zemaraim, Ophrah, and Mizpeh are elsewhere included in the territory of Ephraim (cf. Josh. 16; II Chron. 13:4, 19). Possibly the list of cities and the list of border points are not from the same period and reflect fluctuating territorial and historical situations. It is generally believed that the list of border points antedates the period of the monarchy, whereas the list of cities is of later date. A westward expansion of the Benjamites—possibly as early as the end of the period of Judges, but perhaps taking place during the monarchy—can be inferred from the list of Benjamite towns in Nehemiah 11:31–35. Non-Israelite enclaves existed within the territory of Benjamin; the Jebusites dwelt in Jerusalem (Josh. 18:28), and there were four cities of the Hivites in the western portion. Echoes of the conflicts between the Benjamites and the indigenous population are discernible in II Samuel 21:1–2 and possibly in I Chronicles 8:6–8.

The History of the Tribe. Despite the fact that the territory of Benjamin was smaller than that of most of the other tribes and although Benjamin was regarded as the youngest tribe (see the *Tribes of Israel), it played an important part in the history of the unification of the tribes of Israel during the period of the Judges and the beginning of the monarchy. One of the first judges who arose to save Israel was *Ehud son of Gera, of the tribe of Benjamin (Judg. 3:15), and the first king to rule Israel was *Saul the Benjamite (I Sam. 9:1). Benjamin's importance was due to the strategic position of its territory, through which the divide (watershed) of the central hill country passed. The territory's main north-south road ran along the divide; a

Figure 2. Jacob entrusting Benjamin to Judah. From the Byzantine *Vienna Genesis,* early sixth century. Vienna, Austrian National Library, Ms Theo. Gr. 31, fol. 42.

main highway connecting Transjordan with the west also passed through Benjamin's territory. It was this road that the Israelites used after they crossed the Jordan. When *Eglon king of Moab extended the boundaries of his rule westward, the oppressive effects were felt mainly by the tribe of Benjamin, since the corridor connecting regions on the banks of the Jordan was situated in its territory. Therefore it was not just by chance that the judge who saved Israel from Moab came from the tribe of Benjamin (Judg. 3:12ff). The close ties between the Benjamites and the people of Jabesh-Gilead (Judg. 20–21; I Sam. 11; 31:11–13; Obad. 19) are also explained in part by the Benjamites' easy access to Transjordan. In the days of *Deborah the Benjamites joined in the war against Jabin and Sisera (Judg. 5:14). After forcing the tribe of Dan to move northward, Philistine pressure focused upon the territory of the Benjamites because of the strategic importance of the area. The *Philistines dominated the entire central part of the country and placed a garrison in Gibeath-Benjamin (I Sam. 10:5; 13:3). Opposition to Philistine rule was thus centered in Benjamin, and so it is hardly surprising that the first king, *Saul, whose primary task it was to save Israel from the Philistines (cf. I Sam. 9:16), was a Benjamite. This is also in keeping with Benjamin's reputation for military prowess, as expressed in Jacob's blessing: "Benjamin is a ravenous wolf; in the morning he consumes the foe, and in the evening he divides the spoil" (Gen. 49:27).

A count of Benjamites made before the intertribal war that followed the affair of the concubine in Gibeah (Judg. 19–21) revealed "twenty six thousand men that drew the sword . . . Among all these were seven hundred picked men who were left-handed; every one could sling a stone at a hair and not miss" (Judg. 20:15–16; cf. I Chron. 8:40; 12:1–2). According to the account, Benjamin was defeated and its civilian population massacred. The survival of the tribe was only insured by seizure as wives for the 600 remaining warriors of the unmarried women of Jabesh-Gilead and Shiloh (Judg. 21). The kingdom of Judah established by David did not include Benjamin (see *Ish-Bosheth), and when Israel also chose David as its king, Benjamin continued to belong to "the House of Joseph" (II Sam. 19:17–21). The tribe retained some rancor against David as the supplanter of the House of Saul, as is shown by the episode of *Shimei son of Gera and the revolt of *Sheba son of Bichri (II Sam. 16:5–13; 20:1–2). Under Solomon, too, the territory of Benjamin constituted one of the administrative divisions of Israel (I Kings 4:18). After Solomon's death and the revolt of Israel, the Davidides tried to regain as much of Israel as they could, and according to II Chronicles 13 for a time pushed the northern limit of their dominion well beyond Benjamin. Ultimately, however, they had to be content with the Benjamite watershed as a buffer between Israel and their place of residence, Jerusalem (I Kings 15:22). [B.O.]

In the Aggadah. Benjamin, according to one opinion, was the image of his mother, Rachel (Tanḥ. B. 1:197), and according to another resembled his father (Tanḥ., Mi-Keẓ 10). He alone of all the brothers took no part in the sale of Joseph; as a result he was privileged to have the Temple built on the territory of his tribe (Gen. R. 99:1). Another reason is that he was not yet born when his father and brothers prostrated themselves before Esau (Targ. Sheni to Esther 3:3). Although he knew of Joseph as having been sold into slavery, he never revealed it to his father (Mid. Ps. 15:6). The four additional portions given by Joseph to Benjamin (Gen. 43:34) consisted of one each from Joseph, Asenath, and their sons, Ephraim and Manasseh (Gen. R.

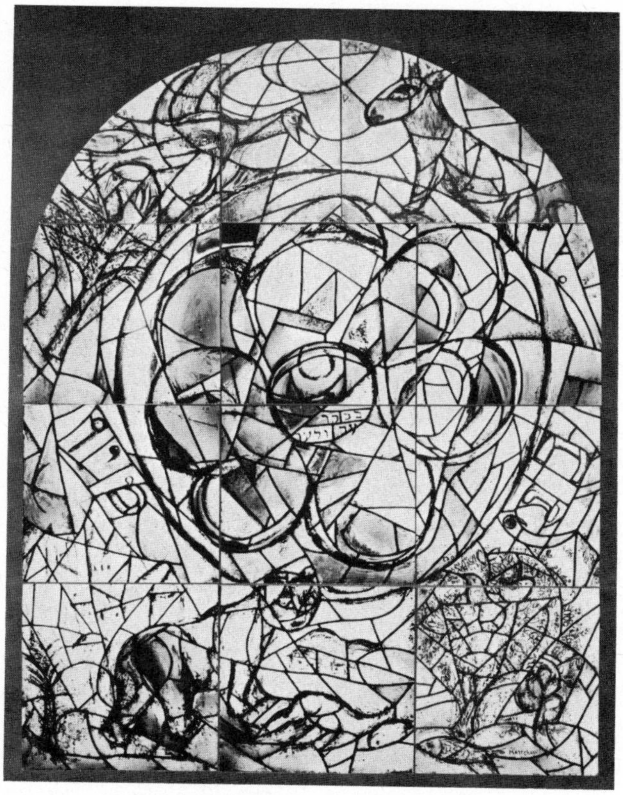

Figure 3. The Tribe of Benjamin. One of the twelve stained glass windows designed by Marc Chagall for the synagogue of the Hadassah Hebrew University Medical Center in Jerusalem, 1961. $11 \times 8\frac{1}{2}$ ft. (338×251 cm.)

92:5). After Joseph's silver cup was found in Benjamin's sack, his brothers struck Benjamin on the shoulder saying, "O thief and son of a thief, thou hast brought the same shame upon us that thy mother brought upon our father when she stole the teraphim that were her father's" (Tanḥ. B. 1:198). Jacob's deathbed blessing to Benjamin contained the prophecy that his tribe would provide Israel with its first and its last ruler, both Saul and Esther being of the tribe of Benjamin (Gen. R. 99:3). He was untainted by sin (Shab. 55b), and when he died his corpse was not exposed to the ravages of worms (BB 17a). [ED.]

In Islam. Though Muhammad does not mention the name Benjamin in the Sura of Yūsuf (Sura 12, verse 69ff.), there is no doubt concerning the identity of the brother whom Joseph wishes to bring to him in Egypt. The Koran continues with the biblical account (cf. Gen. 42–43), according to the version derived from the *aggadah.* Not only Reuben but all the brothers guarantee Jacob that they will bring Benjamin back (sura 12, 66; cf. Tanḥ. *Mi-Keẓ,* 8). There are many accounts in Muslim legends of the threats made by Benjamin's brothers when Joseph wanted to imprison him (cf. Gen. 44:17). [H.Z.H.]

Bibliography: W. F. Albright, in: AASOR, 4 (1922–23), 150–5; J. Muilenburg, in: JBL, 75 (1956), 194–201; Z. Kallai, in: VT, 8 (1958), 134–60; E. A. Speiser, *Genesis* (1964), 273–4; K. D. Schunck, *Benjamin* (Ger., 1963); idem, in: ZDPV, 78 (1962), 143–58; H. L. Ginsberg, in: *Fourth World Congress of Jewish Studies, Papers,* 1 (1967), 91–93. IN THE AGGADAH: Ginzberg, Legends, index. IN ISLAM: Tabari, *Tafsir,* XIII, 6–20; al-Kisā'ī, *Qiṣaṣ* (1922), 169–76; Vajda, in: EIS, s.v. *Binyamin.*

BENJAMIN II (originally **Israel Joseph Benjamin;** 1818–1864), Rumanian explorer and writer; born in Falticeni, Moldavia. He engaged first in the lumber trade but, after some initial success, he lost his fortune at the age of 25. Influenced by his failure and by the romantic trends of the time, he decided to emulate the medieval traveler *Benjamin of Tudela. He styled himself Benjamin II and, in 1845, took to the road in search of the remnants of the *Ten Lost Tribes. He traveled first to Egypt, from there through Ereẓ Israel and Syria and then to Armenia, Iraq, Kurdistan, Persia, India, and China. He came back by way of Afghanistan to Vienna (1851) and from there again to Italy and on to Tripoli, Tunisia, Algeria, and Morocco. Wherever his travels took him, he made a point of assembling information concerning the Jewish settlement in that place—the number of Jews of that community, how they earned their livelihood, their customs, and folklore. Although unscientific, his approach was simple and direct, and earned the praise of scholars like A. von Humboldt and A. Petermann. He described his experiences in a Hebrew travelogue, first published in French under the title *Cinq années de voyage en orient 1846–1851* (1856; Eng. 1859). The Hebrew edition of the book, *Sefer Masei Yisrael,* as revised by David *Gordon, was published in Lyck, in 1859. He published at his own expense in 1863 Nathan Hannover's *Yeven Meẓulah* on the 17th-century Chmielnicki massacres in Poland. Over and above his literary endeavors, Benjamin undertook to ease the plight of the Jews of Morocco. He also appealed to Turkey, France, and England in an attempt to ameliorate the condition of the Jews of Kurdistan and Persia. In 1859 Benjamin II began on a three-year journey through the United States describing his travels in *Drei Jahre in Amerika* (1862; republished in English in 1956 by the JPSA). He died in London in abject poverty while preparing another trip to the Orient.

Bibliography: JC (May 13, 1864), p. 5; I. J. Benjamin, *Three Years in America* (1956), introduction by O. Handlin. [Ed.]

BENJAMIN, BARUCH BEN ISRAEL (17th century), Jerusalem rabbi. After studying under his father, Baruch proceeded to the yeshivah of Isaac Gaon, where Kabbalah was included in the curriculum. He was a signatory to the regulation of 1646, which exempted rabbinic scholars from taxation (A. Ankawa, in *Kerem Ḥemed* 2 (1871), 22b). In 1657 he, together with other Jerusalem kabbalists, endorsed the certificate which declared that Baruch Gad, the Jerusalem messenger to the East, had visited the Ten Lost Tribes. Some of his responsa were published in *Mishpetei Ẓedek* (1945, nos. 66, 95, 98, 100, 131, 133) of his friend, Samuel *Garmison. While serving as *dayyan* in Jerusalem he wrote a work on divorces (Jerusalem Ms. Heb. 8°199). Toward the end of his life he traveled to Egypt, possibly as an emissary, and he died there.

Bibliography: J. Sambari, *Likkutim mi-Sefer Divrei Yosef,* ed. by A. Berliner (1896), 66; Frumkin-Rivlin, 2 (1928), 29; A. Yaari, in: *Sinai,* 6 (1940), 170–5. [Ed.]

BENJAMIN, ERNEST FRANK (1900–1969), British army officer and commander of the *Jewish Brigade in World War II. Born in Toronto, Canada, Benjamin was educated in England at the Royal Military Academy, Woolwich, and at the Staff College, Camberley. He was commissioned in 1919 and served in Turkey, Malaya, and Madagascar. During World War II Benjamin commanded the marine division of the Royal Engineers and later the Combined Training Center for the Middle East and Italy. From 1944 to 1946 he commanded the Jewish Brigade which went into action in north Italy in 1945 as part of the Eighth Army. Brigadier Benjamin later served in Hong Kong and retired in 1950. He was joint honorary treasurer of the Jewish Lads Brigade.

Bibliography: J. Ben Hirsh, *Jewish General Officers* (1967), 78; E. Rubin, *140 Jewish Marshals, Generals and Admirals* (1952), 252–6. [Ed.]

BENJAMIN, ISRAEL (c. 1570–1649), *posek* and kabbalist, who was among the greatest of Egyptian and Jerusalem scholars of his century. According to David *Conforte he was also called "Israel Eliakim." Benjamin was a disciple of R. Eleazar Monzalavi and his friend *Samuel b. Sid, and corresponded with Jacob Castro of Egypt (*Oholei Ya'akov,* 1738, no. 58). According to Conforte a collection of more than a hundred legal decisions and a book of scriptural exegesis by Benjamin was in the possession of his son Baruch Benjamin in Jerusalem. Ḥ. J. D. Azulai also saw a manuscript of his responsa. Abraham Azulai quotes new rulings by Benjamin in his annotations. He was a disciple of the kabbalist *Joseph ibn Tabul in Egypt. In the manuscript *Oẓerot Ḥayyim* by Ḥayyim *Vital (Ms. Jerusalem 8° 370) there are annotations by Benjamin, as well as statements of Ibn Tabul which the latter heard from Isaac *Luria. Benjamin taught Kabbalah in Egypt and Jerusalem. His disciples include Meir *Anaschehon and Meir *Poppers. They had Benjamin's annotations to other writings of Isaac Luria, as well as a *maḥzor* based on the Kabbalah; these are found in *Beit Mo'ed* in the manuscripts of Solomon b. Benjamin ha-Levi. Ḥayyim Vital's *Sefer ha-Gilgulim* contains glosses by Benjamin. An immigrant from Carpi who went to Jerusalem in 1625 found manuscripts of Luria in the possession of Benjamin. He served in Jerusalem as *dayyan* and was one of the prominent scholars in the town. In 1623 he signed an agreement not to cause division in the community and in 1625 he signed an agreement to exempt the scholars from taxes. In that year the Jews of Jerusalem suffered from the oppressive rules of Ibn Farruk, and Benjamin signed a circular entitled *Ḥurvot Yerushalayim* which was handed to emissaries who were sent to the Diaspora with the aim of collecting money for the reconstruction of the community. His signature is also found in a letter to Fez in 1630. In 1646 he was the head of the Jerusalem rabbis. In 1649 he signed first on the endorsement (**haskamah*) of Joseph *Caro's *Maggid Meisharim* (vol. 2, Venice 1649).

Bibliography: Conforte, Kore, 48b–49a; S. Ḥazzan, *Ha-Ma'alot li-Shelomo* (1894), 45a–b; *Yerushalayim* (ed. by A. M. Luncz), 2 (1887), 147–8; 5 (1901), 73–85; Azulai, 1 (1852), 114, no. 406; J. M. Toledano, in: HUCA, 4 (1927), 464–6 (Heb.); Frumkin-Rivlin, 2 (1928), 27–29; 3 (1929), 13. [Ed.]

BENJAMIN, JUDAH PHILIP (1811–1884), U.S. lawyer and statesman. Benjamin was undoubtedly the most prominent nineteenth-century American Jew. He was a noted lawyer, whose services were requested in connection with some of the most significant legal disputes of the time, a powerful politician who was a leader in the cause of Southern rights and on behalf of the short-lived Confederacy.

Born in St. Thomas, Virgin Islands, of British parents, Benjamin was a British subject. His family moved to Charleston, South Carolina, while he was still a boy. He was at Yale University for two years, but studied law privately in New Orleans while earning a meager living as a tutor in English and as a clerk in a business establishment. Deprived of a happy home through an unsuccessful marriage to a non-Jewess, Natalie St. Martin, who left him to live in Paris, he was free to devote himself to law and politics. His legal eminence brought him wealth, and his political activity fame. He was the first professing Jew to be elected to the United States Senate, as a Whig in 1852, and as a Democrat (after the Democratic Party espoused the cause of Southern rights) in 1856. He became a leading member of the school of Southern politicians which favored secession from the Union as the only safeguard for Southern survival, and delivered a number of major addresses in the Senate defending slavery. When Louisiana seceded, he withdrew from the Senate, and was immediately called to the cabinet of the newly created Confederate government (March 1861) as attorney general. President Jefferson Davis relied heavily upon Benjamin's companionship and counsel and appointed him to the more important position of secretary of war in September 1861. Benjamin's apparent responsibility for a number of military disasters, which involved shortages of ammunition and other equipment which could not be made public, however, brought about his resignation in March 1862. Davis promptly put the lie to a large number of anti-Semitic attacks upon Benjamin by appointing him secretary of state, a position which he held until the collapse of the Confederacy. In this role Benjamin came close to obtaining recognition of and help for the Confederacy from England and France. But the Confederacy's cause was doomed from the first, and after Lee's surrender to Grant (April 1865) Benjamin was the only leading Confederate to choose exile rather than live in the defeated South. He escaped to England through Florida and Nassau, and there made for himself a distinguished career as barrister (he was appointed Queen's Counsel), which in many ways outshadowed his prewar American legal career. Ill health forced his retirement from active work in 1882 and he died two years later in Paris where he had finally rejoined his wife and daughter.

Benjamin took no interest in Jewish affairs, although he never denied his origin and was never converted to the Catholic faith of his wife. There is no record of membership on his part in any synagogue, nor did he ever give support to any Jewish cause or organization.

Bibliography: B. W. Korn, *American Jewry and the Civil War* (1951), index; idem, *Eventful Years and Experiences: Studies in Nineteenth Century American Jewish History* (1954); R. Douthat Meade, *Judah P. Benjamin, Confederate Statesman* (1943).

[B.W.K.]

BENJÁMIN, LÁSZLÓ (1915–), Hungarian poet, born in Budapest. His first poems were published in the left-wing press and in such anthologies of working-class poetry as *Tizenkét költő* ("Twelve Poets," 1940). Benjámin's early poetry was based on the hopelessness preceding World War II and, during and immediately after the war itself, on the class struggle. The collections of this period include *A csillag nem jött fel* ("The Star Did Not Come Forth," 1939), *Betüöntók diadala* ("The Victory of the Typecasters," 1946), and *A teremtés után* ("After the Creation," 1948). When the Hungarian Communist government was formed in 1949, Benjámin became one of its chief literary spokesmen. From 1953 his writing changed, and he turned to themes of self-criticism and personal confusion. This later poetry appears in *Éveink múlása* ("The Passing of our Years," 1954), *Egyetlen élet* ("Only During One Lifetime," 1956), and *Ötödik évszak* ("The Fifth Season," 1962).

Bibliography: *Magyar Irodalmi Lexikon*, 1 (1963), 136–7; *Hét évszázad magyar versei*, 3 (1966), 686–740.

[I.Y.-K.]

BENJAMIN, MOSES (first half of the 18th century), rabbi and kabbalist in Baghdad. He was the first of the Baghdad scholars known to have studied much Kabbalah and was an expert in Lurianic Kabbalah. Very little is known about his life; his wife and children died in an epidemic before 1737, and he never fulfilled his desire to immigrate to Jerusalem. He apparently served as rabbi, because he mentions among his writings "some legal rulings." His book *Ma'aseh Rav* (Constantinople, 1736) is a kabbalistic commentary on the sayings of *Rabbah b. Bar Ḥana. In the introduction he mentions the following of his own works: *Matteh Moshe*, a commentary on the masorah, as well as an explanation of rabbinic verses and sayings; *Ho'il Moshe*, a homiletical interpretation of the Pentateuch; and a collection of sermons which he preached on Sabbaths and various occasions. His kabbalistic works are *Tefillah le-Moshe* and *Sha'arei Yerushalayim*, completed in 1731 (author's manuscript; Sassoon Library, 771). The latter contains kabbalistic principles according to the *Zohar and Isaac *Luria. These two books were stolen while en route to the publishers and the author was left with only the first draft.

Bibliography: D. S. Sassoon, *Ohel Dawid*, 1 (1932), 442–3; A. Ben-Jacob, *Yehudei Bavel* (1965), 95–96.

[Ed.]

BENJAMIN, WALTER (1892–1940), German philosopher and literary critic. Born in Berlin, Benjamin attended Haubinda, a country educational establishment, where he met the radical school reformer Gustav Wyneken. From 1910 to 1914 Benjamin took an active part in the youth movement influenced by Wyneken and was for some time the students' president at Berlin University. He published his first articles under the pseudonym Ardor in *Der Anfang* edited by Wyneken. In 1915 Benjamin broke off with Wyneken and his movement because of their acceptance of World War I. Benjamin studied philosophy in Freiburg, Berlin, Munich, and Berne. He returned to Germany in 1920 and lived there till 1933. His thesis written to obtain the qualification to teach aesthetics and history of literature at the university in Frankfort was not accepted. Today, however, this work on the origin of the German drama (Berlin, 1928) is regarded as one of the most important philosophical interpretations of this field. In 1929 Benjamin joined Bertold Brecht (*Versuche ueber Brecht*, 1966), with whose ideas he identified himself to a large extent. Benjamin felt his Jewishness intensely and had for several years toyed with the idea of going to Palestine. When the Nazis came to power he first went to the Balearic Isles and then to Paris. At the outbreak of World War II he was interned as a German citizen, but was released in November 1939. He fled to the south of France and, with a group of refugees, crossed the Spanish border. When the police chief of the border town Port-Bou threatened to send them back to France, Benjamin took his own life.

Between 1914 and 1924, he did not publish much. Then he wrote a long essay, *Goethe's Wahlverwandtschaften* (publ. by H. v. Hofmannsthal in *Neue deutsche Beitraege*, 1924–25; in book form 1964), and continued his intensive activity as essayist and literary critic, especially in the *Frankfurter Zeitung*, *Literarische Welt*, and *Die Gesellschaft*. During his lifetime, Benjamin published only two books: a volume of philosophical aphorisms *Einbahnstrasse* (Berlin, 1928), and, during the Nazi era, under the pseudonym Detlev Holz, *Deutsche Menschen, eine Folge von Briefen* (Lucerne, 1936), an annotated collection of 25 letters from 1783–1883), in which he discussed the flowering and the first decadence of German bourgeois culture. The first collection of his writings appeared posthumously in 1955 (*Schriften*, 2 vols., Frankfort), edited by Theodore Adorno who had always stressed Benjamin's importance as a philosopher. *Illuminationen* (1961; *Illuminations*, 1969), *Angelus Novus* (1966), *Das Kunstwerk im Zeitalter seiner technischen Reproduzierbarkeit* (1963), *Staedtebilder* (1963), and *Zur Kritik der Gewalt* (1965) contain more of his essays, some taken from his literary legacy. G. Scholem and Th. Adorno published a selection of his correspondence (2 vols., 1966).

Benjamin is considered as the most important critic in

the German language between the two wars, and his importance is growing. His thought, formed by Kant and the religious-philosophical current, had been metaphysically oriented in the beginning. Later, especially from 1930 on, Benjamin showed an inclination toward Marxism, whose ideas he, however, interpreted in a highly personal way. Benjamin considered himself as a philosophical commentator of important literary events, stressing especially historical, philosophical, linguistic, and social motives. Intellectually, he was extremely independent, a fact felt in everything he wrote, even in the short book reviews. His concentrated prose makes him difficult to read. He had a strong poetic streak, expressed clearly in his *Berliner Kindheit um Neunzehnhundert* (first published in Frankfort, 1950). Benjamin was also important as a translator, especially of French literature, which attracted him deeply. He translated from Baudelaire (*Tableaux Parisiens,* 1923), several volumes of Proust (1927–30), and several novels by M. Jouhandeau.

Bibliography: G. Scholem, *Walter Benjamin* (= *Leo Baeck Memorial Lecture,* no. 8, 1965); R. Tiedemann, *Studien zur Philosophie Walter Benjamins* (= *Frankfurter Beitraege zur Soziologie,* vol. 16, 1965), includes bibliography; W. Kraft, in: *Merkur,* 21 (Ger., 1967), 226–32; H. Heissenbuettel, *ibid.,* 232–44; R. Alter, in: *Commentary* (Sept. 1969), 86–93; H. Holz, in: *Sinn und Form,* 8 (1956), 514–49; P. Missac, in: *Critique* (Aug.–Sept. 1966), 692–710 (Fr.).

[G.Sch.]

BENJAMIN BEN AARON OF ZALOZCE (late 18th century), East European homilist. In his sermons he commented pointedly on the social and religious life of his time. His didactic works include instructions on personal behavior and on the conduct of Jewish community leaders. He was involved also in the controversy concerning the spiritual value of immigration to Ereẓ Israel, which was a main issue among Jewish thinkers in the 1760s and 1770s. His writings include some important quotations from *Israel b. Eliezer Ba'al Shem, the founder of Ḥasidism, and other early ḥasidic teachers. His three main works are: *Amtaḥat Binyamin,* a homiletic exegesis on Ecclesiastes (Minkowitz, 1796); *Ahavat Dodim,* on Song of Songs (Lvov, 1795); and *Turei Zahav,* a major collection of sermons on the weekly portions of the Pentateuch, and on the holy days (Mogilev, 1816).

Bibliography: B. Dinur, *Be-Mifneh ha-Dorot* (1955), index s.v. *Binyamin me-Zeloziẓ;* I. Werfel, *Ha-Ḥasidut ve-Ereẓ Yisrael* (1940), 39–46.

[Ed.]

BENJAMIN BEN AZRIEL (11th century), liturgical poet, who apparently lived in France. His name and his father's are known only from his *piyyutim,* which are written in the spirit of the earlier *paytanim.* While the influence of Joseph *Bonfils and *Moses b. Kalonymus is apparent in the language of his *piyyutim,* Benjamin at times introduced new terms into the vocabulary of the *paytanim.* His hymns are found in the old French *maḥzor* and have not as yet been published. It is almost certain that a number of hymns signed merely "Binyamin" are his.

Bibliography: Zunz, Lit Poesie, 144–5; Davidson, Oẓar, 4 (1933), 371.

[A.M.H.]

BENJAMIN BEN ELIEZER HA-KOHEN VITALE OF REGGIO (1651–1730), Italian kabbalist. Benjamin, who was among the leading disciples of Moses *Zacuto in Mantua, was rabbi in his native town of Alessandria, Piedmont, until 1682 and afterward in Reggio. He became well-known as a preacher and poet, but in particular as a kabbalist; he was considered one of the major exponents of Isaac *Luria's Kabbalah in Italy. Most of his *piyyutim* (*Et ha-Zamir,* Venice, 1707) were kabbalistic. He also wrote numerous notes and glosses on Luria's works, some of which were published together with the writings of Luria (particularly in the Korets editions). His books are written in the spirit of ascetic kabbalah. Benjamin was a close friend of Abraham *Rovigo in Modena, and desired to immigrate with him to Ereẓ Israel. However, these plans failed. Both he and Rovigo were among the believers in *Shabbetai Ẓevi even after the latter's apostasy and for decades he was among the leading secret Shabbateans in Italy, without, however, relinquishing his ascetic way of life. Benjamin was among the chief proponents of a modern "ḥasidic" Shabbateanism which sought to combine traditional Judaism with the belief in the messianic character of Shabbetai Ẓevi. He did not openly express his Shabbatean views in print, but in *Allon Bakhut* (on Lamentations, Venice, 1712) he dared to explain the lamentations as joyful hymns on the Redemption, on the Shabbatean supposition of the change in their meaning in "the days to come." Many leading Shabbateans met in his home; he also made a point of collecting information about the "faith" and was greatly interested in every new manifestation of a Shabbatean prophet. While his Shabbateanism was still moderate, Benjamin was the teacher of Ḥayyim *Malakh. In his writings Benjamin kept apart the Lurianic Kabbalah from the new Shabbatean Kabbalah of *Nathan of Gaza. He refused to join in the persecution of the Shabbatean Nehemiah *Ḥayon (1714). One of his Shabbatean pamphlets, *Sod Adnut Adonenu* ("The secret of the Lordship of our lord [Shabbetai Ẓevi] according to Nathan"), was published by A. Freimann. Isaiah Bassan, his son-in-law and successor as rabbi of Reggio, was Moses Ḥayyim *Luzzatto's teacher. When the aging Benjamin learned of Luzzatto's revelations in Kabbalah, he wrote asking him about the root (*"shoresh"*) of his soul, and its restitution (*"tikkun"*). A small part of the correspondence between Benjamin and Moses Zacuto, is extant in *Iggerot ha-Remaz* (Leghorn, 1780). Others are still in manuscript. A large collection of his sermons (*Gevul Binyamin*) was published in his old age (Amsterdam, 1727). Some of his halakhic rulings were published in *Lampronti's *Paḥad Yiẓḥak.* Benjamin's responsa, *She'elot u-Teshuvot ha-Re* (1970) were published by Chief Rabbi Yitzḥak *Nissim.

Bibliography: A. Freimann (ed.), *Inyanei Shabbetai Ẓevi* (1912), 93–108; G. Scholem, *Ḥalomotav shel ha-Shabbeta'i R. Mordekhai Ashkenazi* (1938), chs. 7, 11; I. Tishby, *Netivei Emunah u-Minut* (1964), 95–98, 230–32; S. Ginzberg, *Ramḥal u-Venei Doro* (1937), 5–8, 36–40, 45–48, 56; Sonne, in: *Sefer ha-Yovel . . . A. Marx* (1943), 93–95; D. Kaufmann, in: MGWJ, 41 (1897), 700–8.

[G.Sch.]

BENJAMIN BEN ELIJAH (18th century), *Karaite pilgrim to Ereẓ Israel. A resident of *Chufut-Kale (Bakhchisarai), in the Crimea, Benjamin made a vow to "cross seas and deserts and brave great hardships" in order to visit Jerusalem, where a small Karaite community had been revived in 1744. He embarked with six other Karaites from Eupatoria on June 27, 1785, and reached Jerusalem on October 18. After a month's stay there Benjamin returned by way of Jaffa and Constantinople. Benjamin described his nine-month journey in his account, in which he relates, among other matters, that contributions from Crimean Karaites to those in Jerusalem were concealed from the Turkish authorities in order to prevent extortion of money. Some hymns by Benjamin are included in the Karaite liturgy.

Bibliography: H. J. Gurland, *Ginzei Yisrael be-St. Petersburg,* 1 (1865), 44–54; J. D. Eisenstein, *Oẓar ha-Massa'ot* (1926), 212–8; A. Ya'ari, *Masot Ereẓ Yisrael* (1946), 459–78, 775f.

[A.Ya.]

BENJAMIN BEN ḤIYYA (Jehiel; 11th–12th century), liturgical poet. Benjamin lived in Germany during the First Crusade and was among the refugees from Neuss, Bacharach, and Speyer. The horrors of the Crusade constitute the theme of his poetry. According to a 13th-century commentary, his three-line *seliḥah* beginning *"Berit Kerutah"* refers to the claim made by two monks to have brought back from the Holy Sepulcher a document in which the extermination of the Jews is urged. It is probable that other *piyyutim* which bear the name Benjamin are attributable to him.

Bibliography: Zunz, Lit Poesie, 158; Zunz, Poesie, 139, 166, 197; Landshuth, Ammudei, 52; Davidson, Oẓar 2 (1929), 77, no. 1717.

[Ed.]

BENJAMIN BEN JAPHETH (fl. third century), Palestinian *amora.* Benjamin studied under R. Johanan and transmitted legal rulings in his name (Ber. 33a, et al.). R. Zeira praised him for a report he transmitted in the name of Johanan (Shab. 53a). However, he would not rely upon him when he contradicted the tradition of Ḥiyya b. Abba in whom Zeira placed greater trust (Ber. 38b). Benjamin also

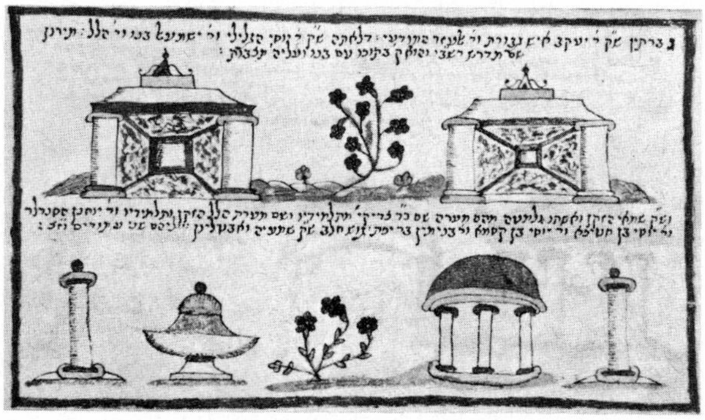

Benjamin b. Japheth, the third-century Palestinian amora, is mentioned among the rabbis buried at Meron in the *Casale Pilgrim* travelogue. Italy, Casale Monferrato, 1598, fol. 7v. Cecil Roth Manuscript Collection.

transmitted many sayings in the name of R. Eleazar b. Pedat, noteworthy among them his comment on the fact that Jacob bowed to his son Joseph (Gen. 47:31), viz., "Bow to the fox in his season" (i.e., if you behold fortune favoring the fox, bow down to him, meaning that one should submit to an inferior person when he is in a position to convey a favor; Meg. 16b).

Bibliography: Hyman, Toledot, 282f.

[Y.D.G.]

BENJAMIN BEN SAMUEL HA-LEVI (of Coutances; early 11th century), rabbi and liturgical poet. Benjamin lived in Coutances, Normandy. His poems are composed in the style of the old *piyyutim* and are, at times, of considerable artistic distinction. Benjamin wrote *piyyutim* for the three pilgrimage festivals, Rosh Ha-Shanah, and the Day of Atonement. Some of his poems are included in the *Maḥzor Romania.* Benjamin was regarded as a talmudic authority and was often quoted by contemporary talmudic scholars.

Bibliography: Landshuth, Ammudei, 53; Zunz, Lit Poesie, 115ff.; Graetz, Gesch, 6 (1894[3]), 53 (calls him Benjamin b. Samuel of Constance); Gross, Gal Jud, 553; Davidson, Oẓar, 4 (1933), 371; Moses b. Jacob of Coucy, *Sefer Mitzvot Gadol* (1905), no. 42; Mordekhai, RH, no. 720; Tos. to Ḥag. 12a; Shelomo b. Yiẓḥak (Rashi), *Pardes,* ed. by Ehrenreich (1923), 229; S. Bernstein, *Piyyutim u-Faytanim Ḥadashim me-ha-Tekufah ha-Bizantinit* (1947), 44–57; H. Merḥaviah, in: *Sefer Ḥayyim Schirmann* (1970), 195–212.

[Ed.]

BENJAMIN BEN ZERAH (c. 1050), liturgical poet. Benjamin probably lived in France or in Germany. He composed liturgical poetry of various sorts in the style of the earliest *paytanim,* but his works already contain the names of angels and other holy appellations. Because of the esteem accorded to him, he was designated *Ha-Gadol* ("the Great"). He was also called *Ba'al ha-Shem* ("Master of the Divine Name"), possibly on account of the numerous names of God and the angels in his poems. About 60 of his *piyyutim* are known, many being included in the Ashkenazi and Italian liturgies.

Bibliography: Landshuth, Ammudei, 52; Davidson, Oẓar, 4 (1933), 371; Zunz, Lit Poesie, 120–3, 239–43, 615.

[A.M.H.]

BENJAMIN NEHEMIAH BEN ELNATHAN (16th century), Italian Jewish chronicler. A resident or perhaps rabbi of Civitanova near Ancona, he was arrested with five other members of the Jewish community in the summer of 1559 on a charge of being implicated in the conversion of a Catholic priest. They were sent to Rome for trial by the Inquisition but were released with the other prisoners of the Holy Office on the death of Pope *Paul IV. On Benjamin's return he wrote a vivid account of his experiences, viewing them in the historical context of Paul IV's persecution of the Jews and Marranos of Ancona, which he apparently witnessed. He wrote his account in fine, idiomatic Hebrew, and it is an important contribution to Hebrew literature as well as to Jewish history. The chronicle was discovered by I. Sonne and published in *Tarbiz* (vol. 2, 1930/31), and again in his *Mi-Paolo ha-Revi'i ad Pius ha-Ḥamishi* (1954).

[C.R.]

BENJAMIN OF BRODY (18th century), preacher. Benjamin was the official preacher of the Jewish community in Berdichev for 17 years, after which he moved to Brody. His sermons were collected in the book *Imrei Binyamin* (Tarnopol, 1814) by his grandson, Meir Eliezer b. Phinehas. Benjamin's sermons, which follow the order of the weekly Torah portions, are undoubtedly edited versions of those he had originally delivered orally. Rabbinic in character, they deal frequently with halakhic problems, interpretations of talmudic sayings, and moralistic preaching.

[Ed.]

BENJAMIN OF CAMBRIDGE (12th–13th century), English scholar, pupil of R. *Tam. A number of Benjamin's opinions on *halakhah,* grammar, and exegesis are preserved in scattered secondary sources. He is referred to as "Benjamin of קנטבריי״א," formerly interpreted as Canterbury, but without doubt designating Cambridge ("Caunbrigge"). His English origin is confirmed by the citation of one of his opinions by *Elijah Menahem b. Moses of London. He is to be identified with "Magister Benjamin" of Cambridge, mentioned in English records, who maintained the local synagogue.

Bibliography: C. Roth, *Intellectual Activities of Medieval English Jewry* (1948), 136, 149; H. P. Stokes, *Studies in Anglo-Jewish History* (1913), 113–4; J. Jacobs, *Jews of Angevin England* (1893), 54, 281; S. Eppenstein, in: MGWJ, 40 (1896), 178; 41 (1897), 222; Urbach, in: *Essays . . . I. Brodie* (Heb. vol., 1966), 13ff.

[C.R.]

BENJAMIN OF TIBERIAS, leader of Palestinian Jewry at the beginning of the seventh century C.E. At the time of the Persian invasion of Ereẓ Israel in 614, Benjamin appears to have been among the Jewish leaders who negotiated with the Persians; as a result of these contacts, the Persian armies received Jewish military support. Benjamin then considered the Christians to be the enemies of his people; however, when the armies of Heraclius, the Byzantine emperor, reconquered the country in 628, he was compelled to receive them on friendly terms. Benjamin, who was exceedingly wealthy, accomodated the emperor in Tiberias and then succeeded in obtaining a general pardon from him for those Jews who had committed offenses against Christians under Persian rule. Benjamin accompanied Heraclius to Jerusalem in 629, and on the way the emperor succeeded in persuading him to be converted. He was baptized in the house of Eustathios, an influential Christian living in Neapolis (now Nablus). In Jerusalem the members of the Christian clergy influenced Heraclius to break the promise which he had given to the Jews through the intervention of Benjamin; the emperor condemned many of them to death, and prohibited the Jews from living in Jerusalem or within a three-mile radius of the city. There is no further mention of Benjamin in historical sources.

Bibliography: M. Avi-Yonah, *Bi-Ymei Roma u-Bizantyon* (1952^2), 190, 200f.

[M.A.-Y.]

BENJAMIN (Ben Jonah) OF TUDELA (second half of 12th century), the greatest medieval Jewish traveler. Nothing whatsoever is known about him except that which emerges from his famous *Sefer ha-Massa'ot (Book of Travels).* He is frequently called "Rabbi" by non-Jewish writers, but there is no authority for this except that the conventional abbreviation "ר" is prefixed to his name in the Hebrew sources. From internal evidence the beginning of his journeys has been dated either about 1159 or about 1167, and he returned to Spain in 4933 (1172/73). His journeys lasted therefore a minimum of 5 and a maximum of 14 years. Since he spent at least a year on the last lap of his journey, from the time he left Egypt to the time of his return to Spain, the latter conjecture is more probable. In any case, he obviously had leisure to spend some time in the places he describes. The object of his journey is unknown, though it has been suggested that he was a gem-merchant—he more than once shows an interest in the coral trade. His *Book of Travels,* largely impersonal, was based on the materials which the author noted down in the course of his travels. From Tudela in northern Spain Benjamin traveled by way of Saragossa and Tarragona to Barcelona, and thence via Gerona into Provence. He gave a fairly full account of the cities and especially the scholars of this region (Narbonne, Beziers, Montpellier, Lunel, Posquières, Arles), paying adequate attention to economic life. From Marseilles he went by sea to Genoa, and thence through Pisa to Rome. Here he must have spent a fairly long time, for he has a detailed description of the antiquities of the city. Many of these he, like other writers of the period, interpreted as being associated with Jewish history. He also writes about the Rome Jewish community and their relations with the much-opposed Pope Alexander III. It is clear therefore that he was there either shortly after the beginning of Alexander III's pontificate in September 1159, or in the brief period between November 1165 and July 1167, when this pope was again securely established in the city. From Rome, Benjamin went southward, traveling throughout southern Italy and describing, sometimes at length, conditions in many places in this region such as Salerno, Amalfi, Melfi, Benevento, Brindisi. He embarked at Otranto, sailing by way of Corfu to Arta, and then through Greece, where he noted the Jewish silkweavers in various places, and the agricultural colony at Crissa on Mt. Parnassus. He seems to have spent a particularly long time in Constantinople, where his lively picture, excelled by no other medieval traveler, is of great importance for knowledge of non-Jewish as well as Jewish conditions. Thence by sea through the Aegean archipelago (Mytilene, Chios, Samos, Rhodes) to Cyprus whence he crossed to the mainland, making his way south via Antioch, Sidon, Tyre, and Acre into Ereẓ Israel, at that time under the rule of the Crusaders. He traveled throughout the country, giving a detailed account of the Holy Places (which he calls in many instances by their French names: thus Hebron is St. Abram de Bron). It is a document of primary importance for the Palestinian history of this period. His record of the

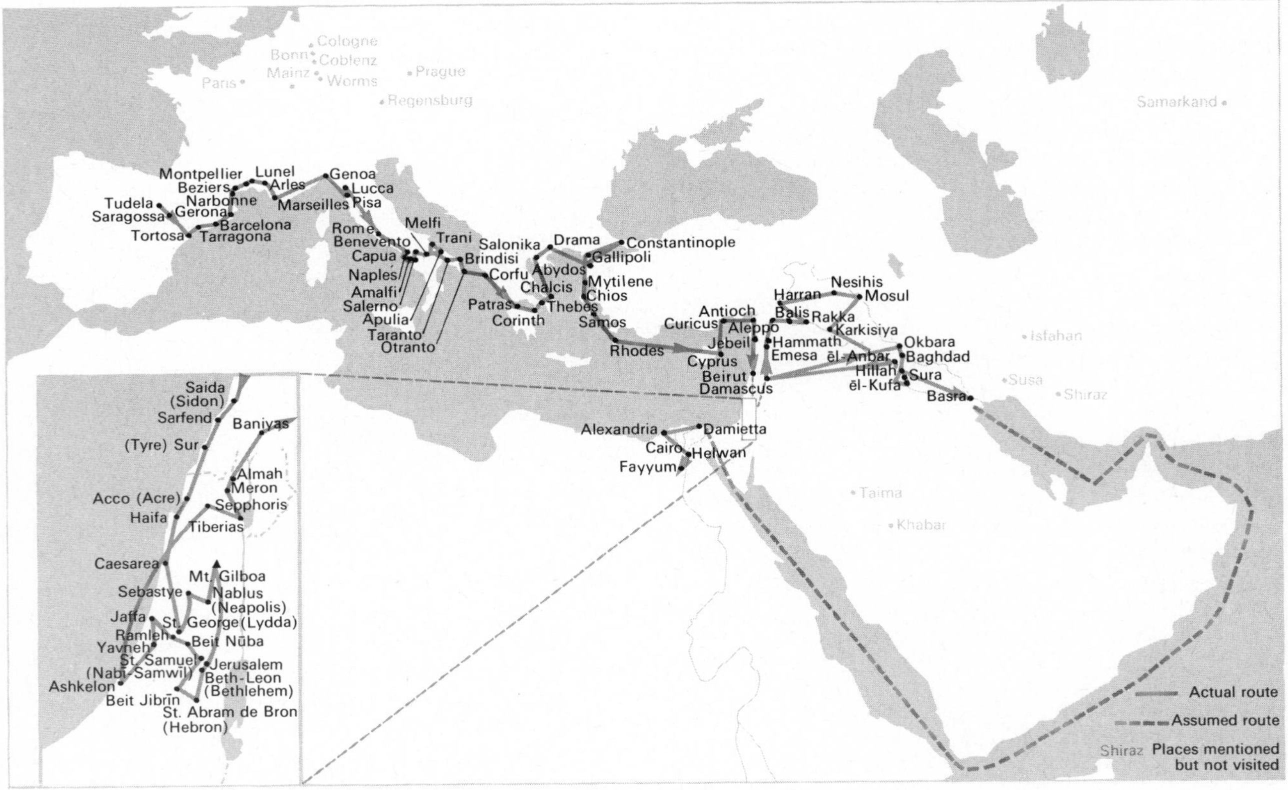

Map showing the travels of Benjamin of Tudela.

Samaritans, although highly disapproving, is characteristic. On the whole, his descriptions are far more objective than those of Christian pilgrims of the age, and he shows himself to peculiar advantage in his account of Jerusalem and its monuments. On leaving Tiberias he traveled north to Damascus, and thence through Aleppo and Mosul—it is not easy to trace his precise route—to Baghdad. His account of the Druze is the first in the non-Arabic literature. Of Baghdad he gives a longer account than of any other city on his itinerary. He draws a graphic picture of the court of the caliph and the charitable foundations of the city. He also tells us of the organization of the still-surviving talmudic academies and the glories and functions of the Exilarchate. He seems to have traveled widely about Mesopotamia and into Persia, though his account of conditions here contains much legendary material. A good deal of space is devoted to the story of the pseudo-Messiah David *Alroy which was, until recently, almost the sole historical source about his career. It is not probable that he ventured beyond this area, but he speaks with some fantastic detail of China, India, and Ceylon. His personal impressions are obviously resumed in his admirable and detailed account of Egypt in general and its Jewish life in particular, especially in Cairo and Alexandria, which he visited on his return voyage. After this he reembarked for Sicily, his account of Palermo being both accurate and picturesque. From here he probably made his way back to Spain by sea, though the itinerary as we have it ends with an idealized picture of Jewish life in northern France and Germany, presumably based on hearsay. He reentered Spain, as is specifically stated, through Castile, having left it by way of Aragon.

There is no general account of the Mediterranean world or of the Middle East in this period which approaches that of Benjamin of Tudela in importance, whether for Jewish or for general history. Most of his record is concise and clear, presumably only a precis of the ampler material he brought back with him. He indicates the distances between the various towns he visited, tells who stood at the head of the Jewish communities, and who were the most notable scholars. He gives the number of Jews he found in each place, though it is not clear in many instances whether he is speaking of individuals or of householders, and in some cases such as Baghdad, the figures seem to be exaggerated. This may be due to the corrupt state of the text as we now have it. He notes economic conditions, describing the activity of merchants from various lands in Barcelona, Montpellier, and Alexandria, and speaking frequently of the occupations of the Jews—the dyers in Brindisi, the silkweavers in Thebes, the tanners in Constantinople, and the glassworkers in Aleppo and Tyre. He was deeply interested in Jewish scholarship, and his account of intellectual life in Provence and Baghdad is of singular importance, as is his characterization of the organization of synagogal life in Egypt. Sects, too, engage his attention, not only the Samaritans in Palestine, but also the Karaites in Constantinople and a heretical sect in Cyprus which he relates observed the Sabbath from dawn to dawn. His characterizations of non-Jewish life are vivid, and sometimes very important. He speaks of the internecine fighting at Genoa and Pisa, the constant wars between these two republics, the embarkation ports of the Crusaders in south Italy, the palaces and pageants of Constantinople and the wealth and the weaknesses of the Byzantine Empire. His somewhat highly colored account of the Assassins of Lebanon and of the Ghuzz Turks are primary historical sources, and he is said to be the first European of modern times to mention China by the present name. The importance of the work can be gauged from the fact that it has been translated into almost every language of Europe, and is used as a primary source-book by all medieval historians.

Bibliography: The *Itinerary of Benjamin of Tudela* was first published at Constantinople in 1543 and, according to a much-differing manuscript, at Ferrara in 1556. The standard editions are those edited by A. Asher, with very valuable notes and excursus and much additional material (London, 1840–41; reprinted New York, 1927, includes list of editions); and by M. N. Adler (London, 1907, with critical Heb. text and Eng. tr.; reprinted from JQR, vols. 16–18, 1904–06; reprinted 1964); there is also an edition by L. Gruenhut and M. N. Adler (Jerusalem-Frankfort, 1903–04) and another edition by H. Haddad (Baghdad, 1945). See also: E. Carmoly, *Notice historique sur Benjamin de Tudèle* (1852), followed by J. Lilewel, *Examen géographique de ses voyages;* R. Luria, in: *Vessillo Israelitico,* 36 (1888), 56–58; Borchardt, in: JJLG, 16 (1924), 139–62; idem, in: *Journal of Roman Studies,* 26 (1936), 68–70; C. R. Beazley, *Dawn of Modern Geography* 2 (1897), 218–64; Andréadès, in: *Byzantinische Zeitschrift,* 30 (1929–30), 457–62; Reissner, in: *Zeitschrift fuer Religions- und Geistesgeschichte,* 6 (1954), 151–5; E. García de Herreros, *Quatre voyageurs espagnols à Alexandrie d'Egypte* (1923). Most works dealing with the history of the Jews in Italy, Palestine, Byzantium, Mesopotamia, and the Middle East in the 12th and 13th centuries use and comment upon Benjamim's material.

[C.R.]

BENJAMIN ZE'EV BEN MATTATHIAS OF ARTA (early 16th century), *dayyan* and halakhist. He first engaged in business but later became a member of the *bet din* at Arta (Epirus). After living at Larissa (1528) and Corfu (1530), Benjamin Ze'ev settled in Venice; but toward the end of his life returned to Arta (1538). As a result of his lenient decisions on an *agunah,* Benjamin Ze'ev was severely criticized by David ha-Kohen, Joseph Taitaẓak, and others. He replied in his *Binyamin Ze'ev,* containing 450 legal decisions and responsa, completed in 1534 at Venice, where it was published five years later. It constitutes an important source for a knowledge of the economic conditions and religious life of the Jews of Greece, Turkey, and Asia Minor. His legal decisions reflect his independence in halakhic matters, which led to the opposition of German and Italian rabbis to his book. He was hostile to Marranos who willingly "follow the laws of the Gentiles and transgress all the commandments of the Torah," and stated that "they are less than the Gentiles"(*Binyamin Ze'ev,* 203, end). Contemporaries, such as Isaac Gershon of Venice and David ha-Kohen, questioned his authority in legal decisions; while Solomon Luria (*Yam shel Shelomo,* BK 78) expressly states that "no one should follow Benjamin Ze'ev, unless he has made a thorough study of the relevant talmudic passages and the halakhic authorities." Several prominent rabbis, among them the rabbis of Salonika, agreed with Benjamin. Following the intensification of the dispute between Benjamin and his opponents at Arta (1530), the views of the Italian rabbis were sought by both sides. Some, including Azriel Diena (Dayyena), favored Benjamin Ze'ev's dismissal from the rabbinate. The dispute continued until 1532, but Benjamin nevertheless continued as rabbi at Arta after that date. His son Mattathias, who died in 1541, wrote a poem to mark the completion of his father's book (*Binyamin Ze'ev,* 573a).

Bibliography: Graetz, Gesch, 8 (c. 1900[4]), 70, 443–7; Bruell, Jahrbuecher, 1 (1874), 88–90; Rosanes, Togarmah, 1 (1930), 114, 155–8; Assaf, in: KS, 15 (1938/39), 113–9.

[Y.Ho.]

BEN KALBA SAVU'A (1st century C.E.), wealthy man of Jerusalem. He was renowned for his generosity, and he fed whoever came to his house (Git. 56a). During the Roman siege of Jerusalem, he and his two wealthy friends, Nakdimon b. Guryon and Ben Ẓiẓit ha-Kassat, provided food and other necessities for the inhabitants over a number of years, until the zealots set fire to their stores, in an attempt to force the people to make a desperate effort to break the siege *(ibid.)*. Josephus mentions the burning of "provisions that would have sufficed . . . for a long siege," although he does not mention Ben Kalba Savu'a and his associates (Wars, 5:25). The Talmud relates that Rachel, Ben Kalba Savu'a's daughter, married R. *Akiva, who in his youth had been Ben Kalba Savu'a's shepherd. This was against the wishes of her father, who disinherited them. When Akiva had become famous as a great scholar, his father-in-law was reconciled to him and bequeathed him half of his wealth (Ket. 62b–63a; Ned. 50a).

Bibliography: Hyman, Toledot, 274; Z. Vilnay, *Maẓẓevot Kodesh be-Erez Yisrael* (1963), 281–5.   [Z.K.]

BEN-KIKI, Moroccan family. REUBEN (late 17th and 18th century) participated in 1719 in negotiations with Great Britain; in 1721 he assisted Ibn Attar, the Moroccan royal treasurer, in concluding a peace treaty with Great Britain. After the death of the king of Morocco Ahmad al-Dhahabi in 1729, he became one of the ministers of the new king Abdullah. His brother ELEAZAR had been appointed ambassador to Holland by Ahmad al-Dhahabi to take charge of the peace talks, and was in Gibraltar on his way to Holland, when the king died. He was not allowed to continue his journey, nor to return to his country until 1730. After Reuben was appointed a minister in Morocco, he succeeded in sending his brother to Holland, but the latter was unable to negotiate a treaty.

Bibliography: Hirschberg, Afrikah, 2 (1965), 273, 276, 284; idem, in: *Essays . . . I. Brodie* (1967), 161–2, 164.   [A.D.]

BEN LA'ANAH (Heb. בֶּן לַעֲנָה), name of the author of an unknown apocryphal work. The Jerusalem Talmud (Sanh. 10:1, 28a), includes the book of Ben La'anah among the works forbidden to be read (cf. Eccles. R. 12:12 where the reading is Ben Tiglah). However, except for a reference by David Messer Leon in the 16th century to an apocryphal work called *Ben Ya'anah* (בֶּן יַעֲנָה), which may be identical with Ben La'anah, nothing is known about the book or the author. Various scholars have tried to identify him either with the pagan philosopher Apollonius of Tyana (M. Joel), or with the author of a collection of fox fables *Mishlei Shu'alim* (J. Fuerst), but none of these theories is regarded as satisfactory.

Bibliography: Perles, in: REJ, 3 (1881), 116–8; Kaufmann, *ibid.*, 4 (1882), 161; Klein, in: *Leshonenu,* 1 (1928/29), 340, 344.   [ED.]

BEN MEIR, AARON (early tenth century), scholar and *rosh yeshivah* in Erez Israel. Aaron lived apparently in *Ramleh, and traced his descent to the former *nesi'im* ("patriarchs") of Palestinian Jewry. His relations with the *Karaites in Palestine were extremely strained. In about 920 he went to Baghdad to complain to the central authorities of the malicious Karaite attacks upon the Rabbanites. After his return, Aaron conceived the idea of strengthening the religious hegemony of Palestine, which had been weakened by the Babylonian yeshivot. To achieve this, Aaron attempted to restore to the Palestinians the sole authority to fix the calendar, as they had had until the middle of the ninth century. On Hoshana Rabba 921 he proclaimed on the Mount of Olives to all communities of Palestine and of the Diaspora that the months of Marḥeshvan and Kislev would be defective, i.e., consisting of only 29 days. As a result, Passover of 922 would fall on Sunday and the New Year of 922 would fall on a Tuesday instead of on the following Thursday as it would have done were these months to contain the full 30 days (see *Calendar).

This proclamation aroused the opposition of several scholars, notably of *Saadiah, who was on his way to Baghdad. The latter tried repeatedly to convince Aaron that there was no justification for opposing the Babylonian calendar calculations. Aaron stood his ground, however, and gave publicity to his proclamation. Fearing that the Jewish festivals might be celebrated at different times in different places, Saadiah addressed himself to the Diaspora communities warning them against acceptance of Aaron's proclamation, but he could not prevent a split. In 922 the Jews of Palestine, and, apparently, also those of Egypt, celebrated Passover two days before the Jews of Babylonia, fixing also the date of the following Rosh Ha-Shanah accordingly. This split caused considerable agitation throughout Jewry. References to it are to be found even in Syriac literature. Thus, the Syrian, Elias of Nisibis, wrote: "The year 309 [of the Hijra] began on the Sabbath, Iyyar 12, 1232 of the Seleucid era; in that year dissension broke out between the Jews of the West [Palestine] and those of the East [Babylon] with regard to the calculation of their holidays. The former fixed the New Year on a Tuesday and the latter on a Thursday" (Baethgen, *Fragmente syrischer und arabischer Historiker* (Leipzig, 1884), 84). The Karaite Sahl b. Maẓli'aḥ sought to prove from this controversy that the Rabbanite calendar calculations were altogether groundless.

The controversy between Aaron and his opponents on this issue continued for some time thereafter, ending in Aaron's defeat, and with it the failure of the attempt to strengthen the sole religious authority of the Palestinian scholars.

Bibliography: H. Malter, *Saadia Gaon* (Eng., 1921), 69–88, 409–19; Mann, Egypt, 1 (1920), 50–55, 61–66; 2 (1922), 49–57; Mann, Texts, 2 (1935), index; American Academy for Jewish Research, *Saadia Anniversary Volume* (1943), index; Abramson, Merkazim, 29–33; H. J. Bornstein, *Maḥaloket Rav Sa'adyah Ga'on u-Ven Me'ir* (1904), printed also in *Sefer ha-Yovel . . . N. Sokolow* (1904), 19–189.   [N.G.]

BEN-NAPHTALI, MOSES (or Jacob) BEN DAVID, masorete. He is assumed to have been a contemporary of Aaron b. Moses *Ben Asher, who dates from the ninth or tenth century C.E., and an inhabitant of Tiberias. Although nothing about him is known, except his name, there survives a list of some 850 minor differences from the reading of Ben Asher in vowels and accents in the Hebrew Bible. These differences, especially as recorded by Mishael b. Uzziel, with considerable deviations in detail in the different traditions (published by L. Lipschuetz), reveal no systematic features, and may be nothing but a gathering of traditional variants. The very name Ben-Naphtali is suspect: Naphtali in the Bible is the son of Jacob born after Asher, and the series "Ben-Asher, Ben-Naphtali" resembles the standard series of random names, "Reuben, Simeon." In the Orient of that period it was a common feature to systematize differences by assigning them to two "schools," only one of which existed. The closest parallel, as shown by Gotthold *Weil, is the invention of a Kufan School of Arabic grammar as a foil for the Basrian School.

There are, indeed, a number of Bible manuscripts with a type of Tiberian vocalization rather different from that of the Ben-Asher school (which itself is not entirely monolithic), but the slight similarity these manuscripts share with some variant readings ascribed to Ben-Naphtali in Mishael's list is not sufficient to substantiate the claim that they are representative of the Ben-Asher School.

See also: *Masorah.

Bibliography: C. D. Ginsburg, *The Massorah* (1880–1905); idem, *Introduction to the Massoretico-Critical Edition of the Hebrew Bible*

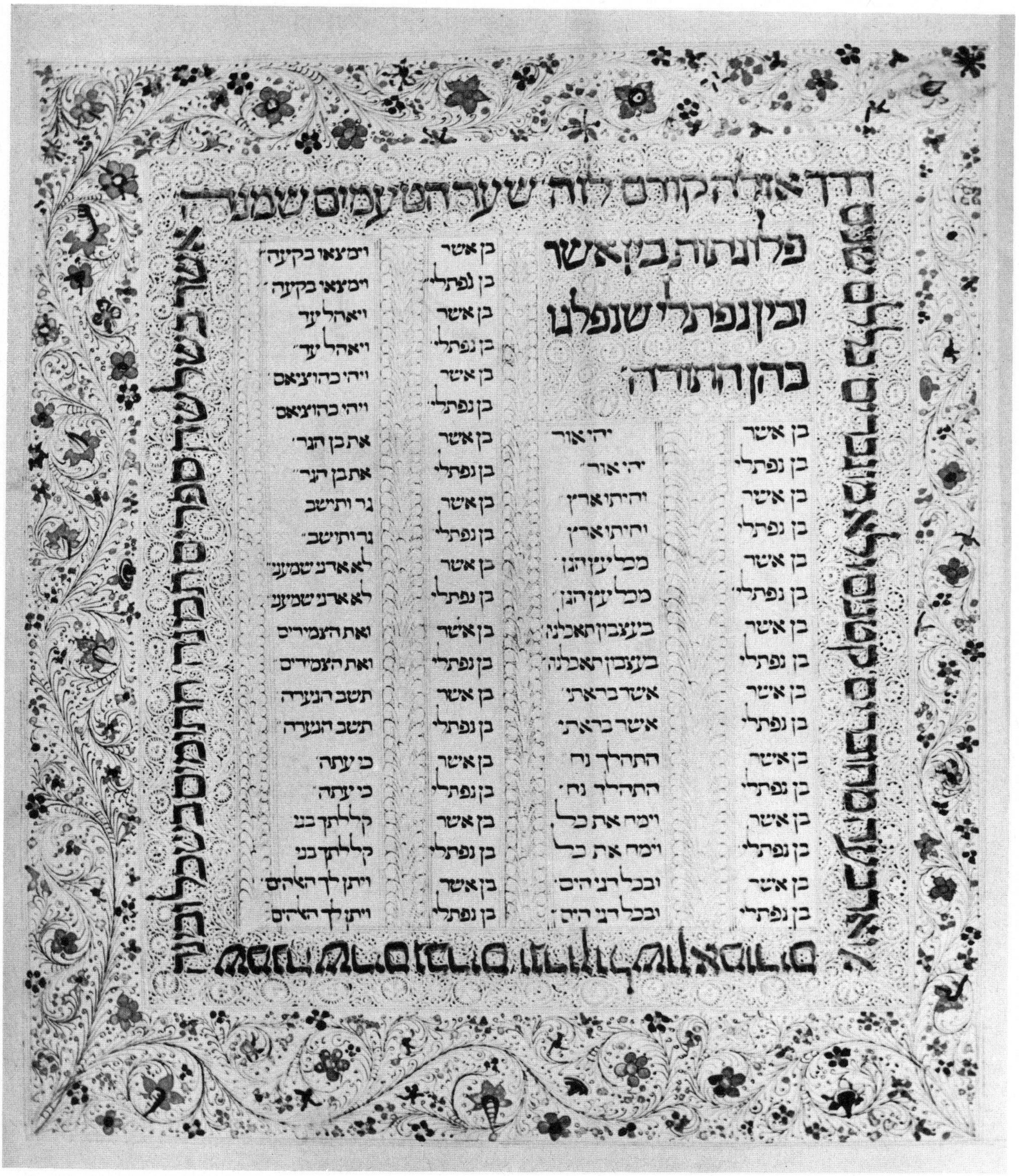

List of masoretic differences between Ben-Asher and Ben-Naphtali in the *Lisbon Bible,* 1482/83, London, British Museum, Or. 2626–28, fol. 185.

(1897), 241–86; Mann, Egypt, 2 (1922), 43–49; Edelmann, in: P. Kahle, *Masoreten des Westens,* 2 (1930), 45–68; idem, *The Cairo Geniza* (1947), 67–76; L. Lipschuetz, in: *Textus,* 2 (1962), Heb. pt. 3–58; 4 (1964), 1–29; Morag, in: JSS, 4 (1959), 216–37; idem, *The Vocalization Systems of Arabic, Hebrew, and Aramaic* (1962), 34, 38–41; idem, in: *Leshonenu,* 29 (1965), 203–9; G. Weil (ed.), *Abu'l-Barakāt ibn al-Anbāri, Die grammatischen Streitfragen der Basrer und Kufer* (1913), 48–93.

[Ch.M.R.]

BENNETT, ARCHIE (Aaron Baehr; 1891–), Canadian community leader. Bennett was born in Malech in the Brest-Litovsk district of Belorussia and was taken to Canada as a child. He was raised in Kingston, Ontario, where he became co-owner of a large real estate and building firm. In the summer of 1912 Bennett served as editor of the *Canadian Jewish Times* in Montreal. He began writing in Yiddish in that same year for the *Keneder Adler.* At this time in Montreal he became part of the circle of young intellectuals around Reuben *Brainin, and wrote for the latter's short-lived *Der Veg* in 1914. In 1914 he settled in Toronto. In 1919 he was a delegate to the first Canadian Jewish Congress in Montreal, where he delivered a paper on nationality minority rights. In 1922 Bennett reorganized the structure of the Zionist movement in Ontario and instituted the province's first Keren Hayesod campaign. Bennett, in that same year, began writing for the *Canadian Jewish*

Review, then published in Toronto. He helped establish the Menorah Society at the University of Toronto and from 1922 to 1924 was a faculty adviser to the Jewish students. In 1933–34 he led in the reorganization of the Canadian Jewish Congress and in the World War II years was president of its central region, Ontario, active in refugee aid, war efforts, and community relations. Writing for the Jewish press was Bennett's lifelong avocation. In 1914 he began writing editorials for the *Canadian Jewish Chronicle* which absorbed the *Canadian Jewish Times.* During the 1930s and until the early 1940s he wrote regular columns for the *Canadian Jewish Review;* and from the mid-1940s in the *Jewish Standard.* [B.G.K.]

BENNETT, SALOMON YOM TOV (1761–1838), English engraver and writer. Bennett was born in Polotsk, Belorussia. In 1792 he went to study in Copenhagen. Three years later he moved to Berlin, where he was admitted to the Royal Academy and engraved portraits of Frederick the Great, the king and queen of Prussia, and others. In 1799 he settled in London. However, as his standard of religious observance was open to criticism he found himself cold-shouldered in official circles. He began to attack the chief rabbi, Solomon *Hirschel, in books and pamphlets. Bennett produced a series of polemical, theological, and

Self-portrait of Salomon Bennett appearing as a frontispiece to one of his pamphlets attacking the leaders of London Jewry, published in 1818. Cecil Roth Collection.

exegetical works, including: *The Constancy of Israel* (1809); *Discourse on Sacrifice* (1815); *The Temple of Ezekiel* (1824); *The Molten Sea* (1824); *Critical Remarks on the Authorized Versions of the Old Testament* (1824); and *A Theological and Critical Treatise on the Primogeniture and Integrity of the Holy Language* (1835). He began to prepare a new English translation of the Bible of which only the first two parts, comprising Genesis chs. 1–41, appeared (1841). As a frontispiece to the *Temple of Ezekiel* Bennett included an engraved portrait of himself painted by another artist. The work is illustrated by a fine and erudite reconstruction of the general view and ground plan of the Temple.

Bibliography: Barnett, in: JHSET, 17 (1951–52), 91–111; S. Kirschstein, *Juedische Graphiker aus der Zeit von 1625–1825* (1918), 15–27; Roth, Mag Bibl, index; A. Barnett, *The Western Synagogue Through Two Centuries* (1961), 51–54; Roth, Art, 532–3.

[ED.]

BENOLIEL, Moroccan family. ELIEZER, a leading citizen of Fez (1730), established his family in Gibraltar; there JUDAH (d. 1839) was consul-general of Morocco (1817), the only agent of the sultan in the service of the European powers, signed the treaty with Austria in 1830, and was later the representative of that country. Judah negotiated with Sweden, Norway, Denmark, and Belgium and reestablished peace between Sardinia and Morocco. As president of the Gibraltar Chamber of Commerce, he enjoyed the confidence of European financiers. His financial interests were widespread and at his death he left a fortune estimated at about three million gold dollars. He was president of the Jewish community in Gibraltar and founded charitable institutions in Morocco. At his request the sultan authorized the reconstruction of the synagogue in Tangiers. JOSEPH *BENOLIEL was a scholar and bibliophile.

Bibliography: J. Davidson, *Notes Taken During Travels in Africa* (1839), 3–6; H. de La Martinière, *Souvenirs du Maroc* (1919), 26, 123; *Report of Anglo-Jewish Association* (1877/78), 113; Miège, Maroc, 2 (1961), 29, 89, 161, 191–3, 249; Kayserling, Bibl, 26–27; A. I. Laredo, *Memorias de un viejo tangerino* (1935), 262–5.

[D.Co.]

BENOLIEL, JOSEPH (**José;** 1888–1937), Portuguese scholar and bibliophile. Benoliel was born and died in Tangiers but spent most of his life in Lisbon. He was a distinguished philologist, fluent in Hebrew, Arabic, Spanish, French, and Portuguese. After studying in a yeshivah in Morocco and in the Oriental School of the Alliance Israélite Universelle in Paris, he taught for a time at Mikveh Israel in Palestine. He then became professor of French and Hebrew at the University of Lisbon as well as official translator for the Portuguese Ministry of Foreign Affairs. He wrote many books, including French grammars and French and Portuguese dictionaries, a volume of poetry, and studies on the *Lusiadas* of Camões, parts of which he translated into Hebrew.

[M.B.A.]

BEN PETURA (also **Ben Peturi, Ben Peturin;** early second century), *tanna.* He is best known for his dispute with R. Akiva: "Two men are traveling in the desert; one has a pitcher containing enough water to enable one of them to reach a place of habitation. If they share the water both will die; if one drinks, his life will be saved." Ben Petura taught: "It is better that both drink and die than one witness the death of his companion." But R. Akiva expounded: "It is written: that thy brother may live with thee (Lev. 25:36) this means that 'thy life takes precedence over that of thy brother'" (BM 62a; Sifra 9:5, with slight variations).

Bibliography: Bacher, Tann; Aḥad Ha-Am, *Al Parashat Derakhim,* pt. 4 (1947[3]); Kaminka, in: *Keneset le-Zekher Bialik,* 4 (1939), 352–3, no. 41; S. Pines, in: *Tarbiz* 16 (1944/45), 238–40.

[Z.K.]

BENREMOKH (**Rimokh, Remoch, Rimoc, Ramukh**), family in Spain and Morocco. SOLOMON BENREMOKH (1285) was a communal leader in Lerida, Spain. The exegete ABRAHAM BEN ḤAYYIM was born in Barcelona. He wrote a commentary on Psalms, to which he appended an autobiography containing information on the situation of the Jews in southern Europe. In 1391 his home was pillaged, his possessions stolen, and he himself imprisoned. He participated in the disputation of *Tortosa in 1413–14. In the 15th century the Benremokh family fled to Morocco, where it attained a position of leadership in the community before 1492. ḤAYYIM BEN SHEM TOV (d. after 1526) was one of the spiritual leaders of the indigenous communities of the kingdom of Fez, and SHEM TOV BEN ABRAHAM was their *nagid.* A dictatorial person, his dispute with the Spanish exiles of 1492 on questions concerning ritual slaughter created a friction of long duration between them and the native Jewish community. Dismissed from office in 1527, he was replaced by his relative SAUL BEN SHEM TOV who remained *nagid* until after 1563. YAMIN, confidential adviser to King Mūlay Zaydān, was sent on a mission to London in 1615 and in 1624 to Holland, where he remained until 1628. SHEM TOV (II) was *nagid* of Fez until his death in 1648. In 1650 his brother bought the position from the king against the will of the community, to which he caused great suffering. Thereafter, the family gave up political activity but remained among the most respected members of the Fez community. Part of the family settled in Gibraltar in 1785 and in London.

Bibliography: Baer, Urkunden, 2 (1927), index, s.v. *Rimoch;* Baer, Spain, 2 (1966), 131, 218ff., 472, 484, 500; SIHM, Angleterre, 2 (1925), 490; Pays-Bas, 3 (1912), 498; 4 (1913), 72, 111, 143–6, 202–3; J. M. Toledano, *Ner ha-Ma'arav* (1911), 65–80, 101; Hirschberg, Afrikah, 2 (1965), 235–6.

[D.Co.]

BENRUBI, ISAAC (1876–1943), philosopher. Born in Salonika, he was a member of a well-known Turkish family which produced rabbis and rabbinic emissaries. After serving as a teacher in a public school in Philippopolis (Plovdiv) in Bulgaria, he left for Jena, Germany, where he studied philosophy with Rudolf Eucken. In 1900, while attending the Sorbonne, he became interested in contemporary French philosophy. His participation in the Second International Congress of Philosophy in Geneva (1904) brought him into personal contact with the leaders of the philosophic schools in France. Benrubi decided to devote himself to the study of modern French philosophy and to disseminate its ideas abroad, especially in Germany, where almost nothing was known of French philosophy after Comte. In addition, he was eager to spread knowledge of the German philosophy of idealism in France. From 1907 to 1914 he attended the lectures of Bergson in Paris, where he was asked to prepare a German translation of Bergson's book *Matière et Mémoire* (1896). Benrubi undertook this task with the assistance of Bergson. He engaged in frequent conversations with Bergson on philosophical, religious, social, and political questions, keeping current notes of these conversations, which took the form of his book *Souvenirs sur Henri Bergson* (1942), an important source for an understanding of Bergson's personality. During World War I, he lectured at the University of Geneva on contemporary French and German philosophy. After the war, he finally completed the first part of his original project: an exposition of modern French philosophy, which was first published in an abridged version both in English, *The Contemporary Thought of France* (1926), and in German, *Philosophische Stroemungen der Gegenwart in Frankreich* (1928). In 1933 the complete work appeared in French, under the title, *Les sources et les courants de la philosophie contemporaine en France.* Benrubi wrote this book, on the basis, among other things, of the comprehensive conversations he had had with the thinkers of whom he wrote. After his death, his friend, Axel Stern, published a book of selections illustrating his views on epistemology and ethics, *Connaissance et Morale* (1947).

[SH.H.B.]

BEN-SASSON, HAIM HILLEL (1914–), Israel historian. Ben-Sasson was born in Volozhin, Lithuania, and emigrated to Palestine in 1934. He taught at the Hebrew University, Jerusalem, from 1949 and became a full professor in 1970. Among Ben-Sasson's published works are: *Millon le-Munaḥei ha-Politikah* (1941), a Hebrew political dictionary; *Perakim be-Toledot ha-Yehudim bi-Ymei ha-Beinayim* (1958), a history of the Jews in the Middle Ages; and *Hagut ve-Hanhagah* (1959), on the social concepts of Polish Jewry at the end of the Middle Ages. He also edited the textbook of Jewish history *Toledot Am Yisrael* (3 vols., 1969–70). From 1966 he was one of the editors of the Hebrew historical quarterly *Zion;* he was also editor of the history division of the *Encyclopaedia Judaica.*

[ED.]

BENSAUDE, Moroccan-Portuguese family. ABRAHAM BENSAUDE (1790–1868) left Morocco after the creation of a mellah in his hometown of Rabat in 1807. In 1819, he settled in São Miguel, in the Azores and founded the first Jewish community on the island. He was joined by his brother ELIAS and his cousin SOLOMON, who established the firm of Bensaude and Company. Under the direction of the latter's son, ABRAHAM, this became one of the most important enterprises in Portugal, with its head office in Lisbon. By the mid-19th century the Bensaude family had established a network of commercial relations between branches in Mogador, Gibraltar, Hamburg, London, Manchester, and Lisbon. The family of the first Abraham Bensaude contributed to the economic development of San

Joaquim Bensaude, Portuguese historian.

Miguel for over a century. His son JOSÉ (1835–1922) established the tobacco industry and promoted the culture of pineapples, tea, and flax. José's son JOAQUIM (1859–1952) was a distinguished Portuguese historian, noted for his research into the history of Portuguese scientific navigation, *L'astronomie nautique au Portugal à l'époque des grandes découvertes* (Berne, 1912). He disproved Alexander von Humboldt's thesis concerning the German origin of scientific navigation in Portugal. In particular, he pointed out the important part played by Jewish astronomers and astrologers in the Iberian peninsula during the Middle Ages, from which scientific navigation in Portugal originated.

Bibliography: A. Bensaude, *Vida de José Bensaude* (1936); Miège, Maroc, 2 (1961), 96, 574.

[J.A.N.]

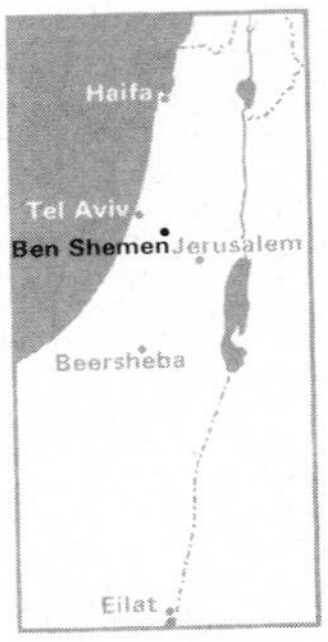

BEN SHEMEN (Heb. בֶּן שֶׁמֶן), youth village and moshav in central Israel, in the northern Judean foothills, 1.8 mi. (3 km.) east of Lydda. Land bought here in 1904 by the Anglo-Palestine Bank was transferred to the *Jewish National Fund in 1907, thus becoming one of its first holdings in the country. "Atid," a Jewish company for oil and soap production, founded a factory here in 1905. A year later, Kiryat Sefer, a children's village, was established for orphans of the *Kishinev pogrom, under the direction of Israel *Belkind. In 1908 the Palestine office of the Zionist Organization set up a training farm for agricultural workers; they planted groves of olives and other fruit trees. These plantations were then named "Herzl Forest." Ten Yemenite families were settled at Ben Shemen in 1911 to combine farming with arts and crafts in the style of the *Bezalel School of

Figure 1. The Bezalel workshop at Ben Shemen, 1912. Jerusalem, Central Zionist Archives.

Jerusalem. During World War I Ben Shemen was a battlefront between the German-Turkish and the Allied armies. It was abandoned and largely destroyed. In 1921 one of the first moshavim was founded at Ben Shemen. In 1927 an agricultural school was opened under the direction of Siegfried *Lehmann and in 1934 it was among the first institutions to be included in the framework of *Youth Aliyah. Early in 1948, during the War of Independence, both the school and the moshav came under siege and the school was evacuated to the Ḥefer Plain until the end of the

Figure 2. Moshav Ben Shemen, 1966. Photo Government Press Office, Tel Aviv.

year, there constituting the basis for the Ne'urim Youth Village. In 1952 a new moshav (affiliated with Tenu'at ha-Moshavim) was established by settlers from Rumania, whose main occupation was dairy farming and citrus plantations. In 1968 Ben Shemen had 920 inhabitants, of whom 720 were in the youth village. The name is taken from Isaiah 5:1. [E.O.]

BENSHEN, Ashkenazi term, probably derived (via Old French) from the Latin *benedicere,* meaning "bless" or "pronounce a benediction." It is mainly used for *Grace after Meals which, when recited by three adult males, is introduced by a formula, of which the Yiddish version is *Raboysay, mir volen benshen* ("Gentlemen, let us say Grace"). It is also used as a designation for the Prayer for the New Moon, *Rosh Ḥodesh benshen,* and for the benediction recited by a person who has had a perilous escape, *gomel benshen.* The kindling of Sabbath and festival lights is called *likht benshen.* The blessing of children by parents is also called *benshen.* The term corresponds to the Sephardi *bencao.* [Ed.]

BEN SIMEON, RAPHAEL AARON (1848–1928), rabbi. Ben Simeon, who was born in Jerusalem, became chief rabbi of Cairo in 1891. Toward the end of his life he returned to Palestine and settled in Tel Aviv. Ben Simeon wrote a number of works, mainly dealing with questions of *halakhah* and ritual. They include *Nehar Miẓrayim* (1908), on the ritual followed by the Jews in Egypt, and *Sha'ar ha-Mifkad* (1908–19), on the various rituals observed by the Jerusalem communities. His collection of responsa, *U-mi-ẓur Devash* (1912), includes rulings by his father David; *Tuv-Miẓrayim* (1908) gives genealogies of Egyptian rabbis.

Bibliography: Frumkin-Rivlin, 3 (1929), 307–8. [E.A.]

BEN SIRA, ALPHABET OF, a narrative, satirical work, written probably in the geonic period in the East. The *Alphabet of Ben Sira* is one of the earliest, most complicated, and most sophisticated Hebrew stories written in the Middle Ages. Four versions of the work have been printed: (a) the usual text found in most editions and manuscripts, edited with notes by Steinschneider and published in Berlin in 1858; (b) a fuller version of part of the work that was discovered by Steinschneider in a manuscript in Leiden (parts of it were added as notes to his edition); (c) a totally different version printed by Loewinger and Friedman from a Kaufmann manuscript in Budapest, published in Vienna in 1926; and (d) part of a fourth version discovered by Habermann in a manuscript in Jerusalem and published in 1958. There are more than 50 extant manuscripts of the work, in full or in part, many of which contain different versions and additional stories.

There is no reason to doubt the unity of the work as a whole, despite the fragmentary character of the different versions. All the versions share a special, satirical, and even heretical, character, and this indicates that they all were written by a single hand. They seem to reflect varying degrees of censorship on the part of editors and copyists. The complete work contains four parts. The first part is the biography of Ben Sira from his conception until the age of one year. This story, omitted in many editions, explains how Jeremiah, the prophet, was simultaneously Ben Sira's father (the numerical value of Ben Sira's name equals that of Jeremiah), and grandfather. Ben Sira's mother was Jeremiah's daughter. The old prophet was forced to an act of onanism by wicked men, and his daughter conceived from his emissions when she came to bathe. The form of this story is based on a biblical verse that tells the glories and wonders of God's deeds; thus the story satirizes not only Jeremiah, but God's deeds as well.

The second part is more sophisticated in form. It tells how Ben Sira, now one year old, meets with his teacher, who tries to teach him the alphabet. Instead of repeating each letter of the alphabet after his teacher, Ben Sira responds with an epigram beginning with that letter. The epigrams lead the teacher to tell the story of his life. It may be assumed that the original structure of this part was 22 + 12 paragraphs, each containing a letter, an epigram, and a part of the story.

The third part is the longest and contains most of the narrative material in this work. It recounts the story of Ben Sira's life and adventures in the court of Nebuchadnezzar, king of Babylonia. It also includes stories told by Ben Sira himself as answers to the king's questions. These stories often include pornographic elements, as well as derogatory descriptions of biblical figures, like King Solomon or Joshua. Some of the stories in this section contain motifs from international folklore and may be based on folktales, but they were adapted to the special framework of the work and satirical elements were added to them. Examination of the various versions indicates that here, too, there were 22 stories, arranged according to the letters of the alphabet, to which 12 other stories were added.

The fourth part, which is found in most versions and gave the work its name, contains 22 alphabetically arranged epigrams attributed to Ben Sira that serve as material for discussion and interpretation by Ben Sira's son, Uzziel, and his grandson, Joseph b. Uzziel. The contents are satirical and even heretical. It may be assumed that this part was constructed in the same manner as the two previous ones—22 + 12 sections. The work, therefore, displays elements of unity both in structure and in its ideological aims. It is all but impossible, however, to discover the background upon which such a work could have been written. Some scholars (L. Ginzberg and others) believe that it aimed at ridiculing the story of Jesus' birth; but the basis for such a conclusion may be found only in the first part, and even this is not very clear, for the irony seems to be directed more against God than against Jesus. It is hardly possible that the author was a Karaite, as some of the abusive stories are directed against biblical figures, and not only against the Talmud and Midrash. It seems likely that the author did not belong to any organized group or definable ideological movement, but was merely a writer with an anarchistic tendency who used satire to ridicule all the institutions of established religion in his day.

Another difficult problem is the relationship between this pseudepigraphal work and the original proverbs of Ben Sira. Some of the proverbs and epigrams included in the work are originally in the work of Ben Sira, but many such proverbs are found in talmudic literature, and the author probably took them from there. The author of the pseudepigraphal work did not even know Ben Sira's first name. There is only one slight connection that might be accidental: the Wisdom of *Ben Sira has a preface written by the author's grandson, who edited the work, and in the pseudepigraphal work the figure of a grandson is also present.

It is impossible to fix even the approximate date of this work. It has been suggested that a quotation from the work is included in the tenth-century *Arukh,* but this now seems very doubtful. The *Alphabet,* however, seems to have been written in the East after the rise of Islam.

Maimonides and other authorities attacked the work vigorously, but it was generally accepted as part of the midrashic tradition, to the extent that a circle of Ashkenazi ḥasidic mystics in the 12th and 13th centuries attributed some of their mystical compilations to works and theories received from Joseph b. Uzziel, who inherited the wisdom of Ben Sira and Jeremiah. The anarchistic and heretical elements in the work went unrecognized, probably because of the censorship exercised by copyists, who prevented the full version from being known to readers.

Bibliography: M. Steinschneider (ed.), *Alpha Betha de-Ben Sira* (1858); D. Z. Friedman and D. S. Loewinger (eds.), *Alpha Betha de-Ben Sira* (1926) (= HHY, 10 (1926), 250–81); A. M. Habermann in: *Tarbiz,* 27 (1957/58), 190–202; I. Reifman, in: *Ha-Karmel,* 2 (1873), 123ff.; A. Epstein, *Mi-Kadmoniyyot ha-Yehudim* (1957), 111–5; J. L. Zlotnick, in: *Sinai,* 18 (1946), 49–58; S. Lieberman, *Sheki'in* (1939), 32–42.; J. Dan, in: *Molad,* 23 (1965), 490–6; Lévy, in: REJ, 29 (1894), 197–205; Zunz, Vortraege, 106–11; S. H. Kook, *Iyyunim u-Meḥkarim,* 1 (1959), 231–3.

[Y.D.]

BEN SIRA, SIMEON BEN JESUS (second century B.C.E.), Hebrew aphorist, sage, and scribe, the author of Wisdom of *Ben Sira (Ecclesiasticus). Ben Sira was a younger contemporary of the high priest Simeon (50:1ff.), apparently Simeon the Just, who according to the Talmud and Josephus (Ant., 12:43, 157) lived at the beginning of the third century B.C.E. In the introduction to the Greek translation of the Wisdom of Ben Sira, the author is referred to as Jesus, by which name he is generally known in the Christian tradition. In the more authoritative Hebrew version, however (50:27; 52:end), his full name is given as Simeon b. Jeshua b. Eleazar b. Sira. The book was translated into Greek by Ben Sira's grandson after his arrival in Egypt in 132 B.C.E. From this date, given by the grandson in the preface to his translation, it may be reckoned that Ben Sira completed the book about 170 B.C.E. Apparently Ben Sira's life was at one time in jeopardy because of a false charge leveled against him, from which, however, he was saved (51).

Bibliography: S. Schechter and C. Taylor, *The Wisdom of Ben Sira* (1899); R. Smend, *Die Weisheit des Jesus Sirach erklaert* (1906–07); M. H. Segal, *Sefer Ben-Sira ha-Shalem* (1958^2); E. S. Hartom, *Ha-Sefarim ha-Ḥiẓonim: Ben-Sira* (1963).

[M.H.S./Ed.]

BEN SIRA, WISDOM OF (also called **Ecclesiasticus**), a work of the Apocrypha, which, though usually known by this name, may have been called by its author, "The Words of Simeon b. Jeshua," the title found on the Hebrew fragments. In Greek the book is called Σοφία (Ἰήσου υἱοῦ) Σειράχ), "Wisdom of (Jesus son of) Sirach," and hence in Latin it was known as Siracides (i.e., Sira's son). Its common name in modern times, Ecclesiasticus (abbr. Ecclus.) dates from the 4th-century custom of naming certain homiletical books *libri ecclesiastici* (i.e., books for (reading in) the church). The book is divided into eight sections, each introduced by a poem in praise of wisdom or of the wise man. The last section (Hebrew version 44–50), called "The Praise of the Fathers," eulogizes the great figures of the Bible, with the exception of the final chapter which is devoted to praise of Simeon b. Johanan the priest, i.e., *Simeon the Just. The greater part of the work consists of maxims, poetic in form, like those in the book of Proverbs. It also contains psalms of supplication and of thanksgiving (36:1–17 (33:1–13; 36:16–22); 42:21–35 (15–25), 43, et al.), these latter being characterized by a lofty poetic style and by elevated thought (cf. 42:21 (15); 43:33 (58). (References are given to two editions: the first to the Hebrew edition by M. H. Segal (1958^2), the second to the standard edition in the Greek text of the Apocrypha). The work also includes didactic poems on subjects of daily life and on historical events, after the manner of certain psalms (13; 15; 16; 18; 34:19–35; 40; 41; et al.), and concludes with an epilogue

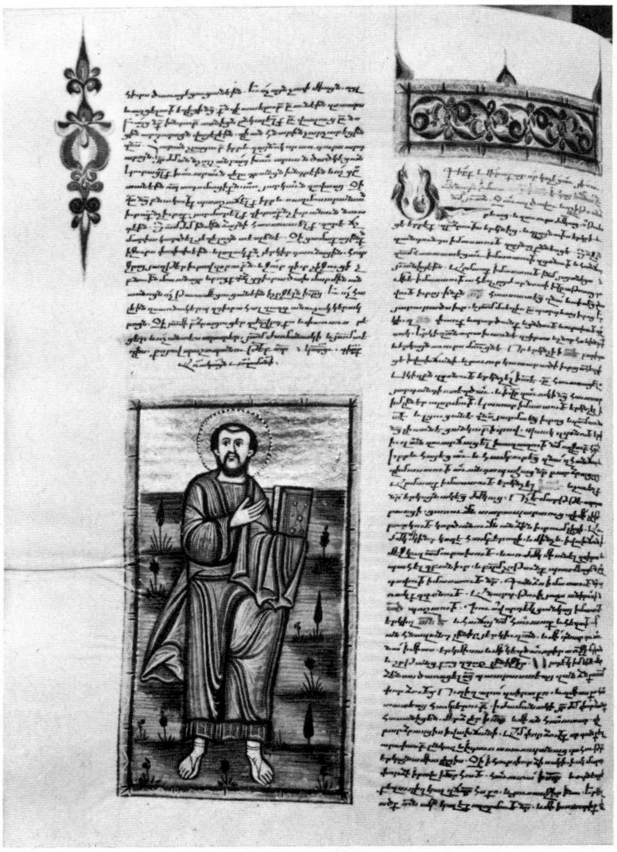

Simeon ben Sira holding his book. Miniature from an Armenian illuminated Bible, Constantinople, 1649 or 1653. Jerusalem, Library of the Armenian Patriarchate, MS. 1927, fol. 293v. Photo David Ḥarris, Jerusalem.

comprising two poems of praise and thanksgiving, and an alphabetic poem on the importance of acquiring wisdom.

The Wisdom of Ben Sira directs man to the love of wisdom and ethical conduct, teaches him virtue and good deeds, and proper behavior in eating and drinking, speech and silence, work and commerce, studying and teaching, poverty and wealth, health and sickness. It also seeks to instruct man to perform all his actions with intelligence and understanding, moderation, care and wisdom, so that his deeds may bring to him and others the appropriate benefit. It teaches man how to behave within his family circle: toward his father and mother, his wife, his sons, and his daughters. It guides him in his conduct toward all men. It stresses, as does the book of Proverbs, that the fear of the Lord is the beginning and the end of all wisdom. The work, though written in the spirit of the Bible and in the language of the later biblical books, bears a contemporary impress of the second century B.C.E., and its faith, in general, is that of subsequent Pharisaic Judaism (everything is foreseen but man has freedom of choice: 15:15–17; cf. Avot 3:15). It also reveals some influence of Greek literature and idiom: men grow and fall like leaves on a tree (14:19; cf. Iliad 6:146–9); he becomes wise who is unfettered by affairs, corresponding to the σχολαστικός, the Greek man of leisure. The work also contains a trace of the Greek gnosis and perhaps also of its philosophical thought (cf. 42:29–33 (20–23)). Unlike other books of proverbs, in which the authors address themselves to youth, the Wisdom of Ben Sira attaches prime importance to the well-ordered family, the effective basis of which is the father. It is primarily to him that the author addresses himself, advising and instructing him. A man should marry a suitable wife, beautiful and kindly-spoken, who, assisting him, will bring him supreme happiness. He should rear his sons in the Torah, marry off his daughters while they are young, and deal faithfully with his fellowman.

From a literary viewpoint, the work is well constructed. Most of the maxims are arranged according to subject matter, and the various sections have headings such as "The fear of the Lord," "Honoring parents," "Humility," "Lovingkindness," and the like. For the rabbis of the early talmudic period the work had an importance almost equal to that of the book of Proverbs. Its aphorisms, quoted either in Ben Sira's name or anonymously, are scattered throughout talmudic literature and are cited by both *tannaim* and *amoraim,* such as R. Levitas of Jabneh (Avot 4:4, cf. Ecclus. 7:13), Akiva, and Rav. Several of Ben Sira's maxims are to be found in other books of the Apocrypha, the New Testament, the Syriac version of the book of *Aḥikar, as well as in the writings of early medieval Jewish scholars. Ben Sira's influence on ancient Hebrew prayers and *piyyutim* is particularly great. Although the Wisdom of Ben Sira is quoted in talmudic literature with the introductory phrase "as it is written," ordinarily reserved for biblical quotations, and is once explicitly mentioned among the books of the Hagiographa (BK 92b; cf. Ecclus. 27:9), it was not included in the canon. Some *amoraim* even forbade it to be read (Sanh. 100b; TJ, Sanh. 10:1, 28a). In the book of Proverbs the ethics are personal and worldly, and its general character is bound up with its secular origin, even though the religious content of the book is of prime importance. In the Wisdom of Ben Sira there is a notable difference. Wisdom, which is spoken of in the book of Proverbs as a primordial fascinating entity, is in Ben Sira identified with the Torah given to Israel, emphasizing that it is the true basis of all divine and human wisdom. In the Wisdom of Ben Sira there occur for the first time a number of ideas subsequently found in the *aggadah,* such as that Israel as well as the Torah was among the first acts of God's creation (cf. Ecclus. 36:15 and Gen. R. 1:4) and that the people of Israel (37:29 (25)), the Temple (17:20 (13)) and the priesthood of Aaron and of Phinehas (45:26, 45 (15, 24)) will endure forever (cf. Sif. Num. 92; Lev. R. 2:2). Ben Sira is also the original source for several customs which are later found in the *halakhah* (e.g., the blessing on seeing a rainbow—43:13 (11)), and contains the earliest reference to the accepted basis of the Eighteen Benedictions and the like. The sages delivered homilies based on Ben Sira's maxims, but changing their form and language. They were even rendered at times in the mishnaic Hebrew or Aramaic spoken by the sages. Excerpts from these maxims, current among the masses, were collected in small compilations, not always in the original order, and they included not only biblical verses but some aphorisms which were not Ben Sira's. As a result these verses and aphorisms were erroneously ascribed to Ben Sira by the rabbis.

The original Hebrew text was no longer extant after the time of Saadiah Gaon (10th century). In the 19th century the work was translated from the Greek into Hebrew by Judah Leib *Ben-Zeev, S. I. Fraenkel, and others. In 1896, however, S. Schechter discovered among the *Genizah* fragments in Cairo a page of the original Hebrew work. During the next four years, Schechter and other scholars found many other fragments from various manuscripts, comprising about two-thirds of the entire book. In 1929 Joseph Marcus found a fragment from a fifth manuscript containing 46 verses; in 1957 J. Schirmann found a new folio, and in 1959 yet another folio of manuscript B, as well as two folios of manuscript C. These fragments consist at times of no more than portions of verses, and contain many mistakes, omissions, and corruptions, as well as numerous additions and repetitions. Nonetheless, they presumably preserve an early or even original version. Some fragments of the Hebrew original (6:20–31) were discovered in Qumran Cave II. In 1964 Yigael Yadin discovered at Masada fragments containing chapters 39:27–44:25, which indicate that manuscript B of the *Genizah* represents substantially the original Hebrew version of the book. The Wisdom of Ben Sira was included in the Septuagint, from where it made its way into the Christian Bible. It was translated into Syriac in about 300 C.E. by a Christian (apparently a Jewish apostate). Although these versions contain very many mistakes, by comparing them with the Hebrew version it is generally possible to establish the original text of the work. On the question of the date of the author and the book, see *Ben Sira, Simeon son of Jesus.

See also *Apocrypha and *Bible, Canon. [M.Z.S./ED.]

In the Arts. In literature and art the Wisdom of Ben Sira has not inspired great creativity. In music, by contrast, Ben Sira's work has proved to be of considerable importance. The use of its texts may be considered under three headings: (a) The Priestly Office. The text beginning *Ecce sacerdos magnus* ("This is the high priest"), a paraphrase based on the praises of Moses and Aaron in chapters 44 and 45, is used in the Catholic liturgy for the commemoration or welcome of high ecclesiastical dignitaries, especially popes and bishops. The traditional plainchant melody was used by Palestrina as a *cantus firmus* (compositional foundation) in the first of his published masses (1554), which was dedicated to Pope Julius III; and also for festive motets on the text itself, such as those written by Constanzo Porta (book of motets for 6 voices, 1585, dedicated to Pope Sixtus V) and Tomas Luis de Victoria (4 voices, in his *Motecta festorum totius anni . . .* 1585). The last, like the Palestrina mass, has since been sung at many papal coronations. An *Ecce sacerdos* motet appears in the *Opus musicum* by Jacob Handl (Gallus; 1550–1591), in which other settings of Ben Sira texts also appear. It may be assumed that the attention of composers was drawn to Ben Sira as a text-source by the feeling of obligation, which the Counter-Reformation inspired, that no part of the liturgical cycle be neglected by composers. (b) "Now praise the Lord." The short hymnic passage in ch. 50:22–24, adopted by the Anglican *Book of Common Prayer,* was set by William Byrd (1545–1623) as an impressive six-voiced anthem, *Behold now praise the Lord.* The rhymed German paraphrase *Nun danket alle Gott,* by Martin Rinkart (first published by him in 1636 as a grace at table), became famous as the "German *Te Deum*" when it was sung on the occasion of the peace treaty ending the Thirty Years' War in 1648 to a chorale-melody composed by Johann Crueger (first published in the same year). Translated by Catherine Winkworth in 1858 as *Now thank we all our God,* it became popular in the English-speaking church; and both the German and the English versions have been sung on many historic occasions. Bach used the chorale-melody for his cantata no. 192, *Nun danket alle Gott,* and at the conclusion of his cantata no. 79. Felix *Mendelssohn adapted it for the *Festgesang* which he wrote for the 500th anniversary of the invention of printing, celebrated at Leipzig on June 25th, 1840. (c) "Let us now praise famous men." The opening passage of the "Praise of the Fathers," ch. 44, in the English version of *The Book of Common Prayer,* has been set for choir by Ralph Vaughan Williams (1923), Cyril Scott (1935), and other English-speaking composers.

Settings of other texts include those by Heinrich Schuetz; the rhymed Dutch paraphrase *Ecclesiasticus* by Jan Fruytier (1965), which used the tunes of Clemens non Papa's famous *Souterliedekens* ("Little Psalter Songs," 1556); and the three-voiced canon on "Non impedias musicam" ("Do not impede the music," ch. 32, 5 [2]), in G. B. Martini's *Storia della Musica* (vol. 1, 1757). [B.B.]

Bibliography: M. H. Segal, *Ḥokhmat Ben Sira* (1933); idem, *Sefer Ben Sira ha-Shalem* (1958[2]), contains detailed bibliography; idem, in: *Tarbiz,* 29 (1959/60); Grinz, in: *Beḥinot,* 6 (1953/54), 85–93; Schirmann, in: *Tarbiz,* 27 (1957/58), 440–3; A. Kahana *Ha-Sefarim ha-Ḥiẓonim,* 2 (1959); Charles, Apocrypha; A. A. Di Lella, *Hebrew Text of Sirach* (1966); C. C. Torrey, in: *Alexander Marx Jubilee Volume* (1950), 585–602; Yadin, in: *Eretz Israel,* 8 (1967), 1–45.

BEN STADA, a person mentioned in talmudic sources "who brought witchcraft from Egypt by means of scratches upon his flesh" (Shab. 104b). Attempts to identify him have been based mainly on expansions of the above text, found in manuscripts and in early uncensored editions of the Talmud: " 'Was he then ben ("the son of") Stada? Surely, he was the son of Pandira.' R. Ḥisda said 'The husband was Stada; the paramour was Pandira,' 'Was not the husband Pappos ben Judah, and his mother, Stada?' 'His mother was Miriam, a woman's hairdresser. As they say in Pumbedita 'This one has been unfaithful *(satat da)* to her husband' " (Dik. Sof., Shab. 104b).

A similar passage appears in manuscripts of Sanhedrin (67b), but with the following introduction: "They hanged Ben Stada in Lydda on the eve of Passover." An opinion, mentioned by Rabbenu Jacob b. Meir *Tam (in early editions of *tosafot* to Sanh.), identifies Ben Stada with Jesus. This suggestion, based on the allusion to Pandira (alleged to be the real father of Jesus), and strengthened by the mention of a Passover execution and of a mother named Miriam (Mary), is nevertheless unacceptable. R. Tam himself points out that Pappos b. Judah lived a century after Jesus. Furthermore, Jesus was executed in Jerusalem and not in Lydda. It appears that the very name "Ben Stada" emerges from the Babylonian Talmud's exegesis (סטת דא). Almost all the parallel passages in Tosefta (Shab. 11:15) and the Jerusalem Talmud (Shab. 12:4, 13d) read בן סטרא (see S. Lieberman, *Tosefta ki-Feshuta,* 1 (1955), 179–80). It has also been suggested that Ben Stada was the Egyptian prophet who, during the administration of the Roman procurator Felix, persuaded "large crowds to follow him to the Mount of Olives," where at his command, "Jerusalem's walls would fall down and he would provide an entrance to the city" (Jos., Ant., 20:169ff.; Acts, 21:38). The only real link between the two, however, is the mention of Egypt. Josephus claimed that the prophet disappeared, whereas Ben Stada was executed in Lydda, possibly in the second century C.E. (see Derenbourg, *Essai sur les formes des pluriels arabes* (1867), 468–71). It would appear, therefore, that too little is known of Ben Stada to permit a definite identification.

Bibliography: R. T. Herford, *Christianity in Talmud and Midrash* (1903), 37, 344ff.; J. Klausner, *Jesus of Nazereth* (1929), 20–23; Schoeps, in: HUCA, 21 (1948), 258ff.; Chajes, in: *Ha-Goren,* 4 (1903), 33–37.

[I.G.]

BENSUSAN (Ibn Sūsān or **Shoshan,** also **Cohen ibn Sūsān** and **Levy Bensusan)**, Moroccan family that can be traced to the 12th century. JUDAH IBN SŪSĀN (d. 1165) was Maimonides' teacher in Fez; he was martyred there by the Almohads. During the 13th and 14th centuries, members of the Ibn Sūsān family held important posts as rabbis, astronomers, physicians, financiers, and diplomats in Christian Spain. Their descendants returned to Morocco after 1391. Some time before 1539, the Moroccan mathematician ISSACHAR B. MORDECAI IBN SŪSĀN settled in Jerusalem and later in Safed, where he wrote *Tikkun Yissakhar* (Salonika, 1564), which was reedited under the title *Ibbur Shanim* ("Intercalation of the Years," Venice, 1578). The book includes two treatises on the rituals to be followed according to yearly variations of the Jewish calendar, and the apportioning of the *haftarot* according to the rites of different communities. NATHAN LEVI BENSUSAN was a leader of the *toshavin* ("native") community in Morocco in the early 16th century. Several of his descendants were scholars who were often named in the statutes of the Fez community.

The family constituted a powerful merchant clan in Rabat-Salé, and often acted against the interests of other members of the community. During the 17th and 18th centuries their activities extended to London, where they were active in the Sephardi community. In the 19th century they reinforced their position in trade in Morocco, especially in Mogador and Marrakesh, where JOSHUA LÉVY-BENSUSAN (19th cent.) represented France in about 1881. SAMUEL LEVY BENSUSAN (1872–1958), who lived in Essex, England, wrote a number of books about the English countryside, such as *Annals of Maychester* (1936), and also published studies of great artists. He traveled widely and wrote about Morocco, Spain, Paris, Germany, and the haunts of Shakespeare. Bensusan edited a weekly newspaper, *The Jewish World* (1897–98), and *The Theosophical Review* (1925–28).

Bibliography: A. Hyamson, *Sephardim of England* (1951), 247, 336, 397; J. M. Toledano, *Ner ha-Ma'arav* (1911), 25ff., 41, 63, 109, 191; REJ, 6 (1941), 12–25; Miège, Maroc, 2 (1961), 550; 3 (1962), 208; 4 (1963), 304. [D.Co.]

BEN TEMALYON, name of a demon. According to talmudic legend it accompanied R. *Simeon b. Yoḥai on his journey to Rome where he pleaded with the authorities to annul the decree compelling the Jews to have intercourse with their menstruating wives, to desecrate the Sabbath, and not to circumcise their children. The demon entered into the Roman emperor's daughter and when Simeon b. Yoḥai exorcised it, his request was granted (Me'il. 17b). A more detailed account of this miracle is contained in **Halakhot Gedolot* (ed. Hildesheimer, 603–4), where, however, the demon is called "Shamdon" or "Ashmedai." The story frequently recurs in medieval folklore, sometimes with an anti-Jewish bias. Some scholars have attempted to identify Ben Temalyon (or Bar Temalyon) with the apostle Bartholomew about whom a similar legend is related in connection with his missionary voyage to India.

Ben Temalyon (or Telamyon) is also the name of a person who technically avoided perjury by concealing a hundred dinars which he owed to a plaintiff, in a hollowed cane which he asked the latter to hold, and taking an oath that he had returned him the money (cf. Ned. 25a).

Bibliography: I. Lévi, in: REJ, 8 (1884), 200–2; 10 (1885), 66–73; Halevy, *ibid.*, 60–65; R. Margoliouth, *Malakhei Elyon* (Jerusalem, 1945), p. 222. [ED.]

BENTOV (Gutgeld), MORDEKHAI (1900–), Israel politician; *Mapam leader. Bentov, born in Grodzisk, near Warsaw, settled in Palestine in 1920, working for several years in road building and draining swamps. He graduated

Mordekhai Bentov, Israel politician.

from the government law classes in Jerusalem and later became a member of Kibbutz *Mishmar ha-Emek. A leader of the *Ha-Shomer ha-Ẓa'ir movement, Bentov served as its representative in central bodies of the *Histadrut and the Zionist Movement. He was a member of the Jewish delegation to the 1939 Round Table Conference with the British government to discuss the future of Palestine. In 1947 he became a member of the Political Committee representing the Jewish Agency in the U.N. He served as editor of the Mapam daily, *Al ha-Mishmar,* from 1943 to 1948. In the 1948 provisional government of Israel he was minister of labor and reconstruction, and sat in the Knesset as a Mapam member from 1949 until 1965. During 1955–61 he was minister of development, and in the years 1966–69 minister of housing. He published articles on various political and economic topics, and the following books: *Constitutional Development of Palestine* (1941); *The Road for Bi-national Independence for Palestine* (1947), which presented the Mapam viewpoint; and *Israel Economy at the Crossroads* (1965).

Bibliography: Tidhar, 2 (1947), 1002. [B.J.]

BENTWICH, English Zionist family who settled in Palestine during the 1920s.

HERBERT BENTWICH (1856–1932), British Zionist leader and lawyer. An authority on copyright law, for many years he edited the *Law Journal.* Bentwich was born in London. He became a leading member of the English Ḥovevei Zion and one of the first followers of Theodor *Herzl in England. In 1897 Bentwich organized the first pilgrimage to Ereẓ Israel of the Order of the Ancient Maccabeans, on whose behalf, in 1923, he acquired land for settlement at Gezer, near Ramleh. Bentwich was a founder of the English

Herbert Bentwich, English Zionist, 1856–1932.

Zionist Federation in 1899 and for some time served as its vice-chairman. He was a legal adviser for the *Jewish Colonial Trust. From 1916 to 1918 he served on the Zionist political advisory committee under Chaim *Weizmann. Bentwich settled in Palestine in 1929, spending most of his time at the family home in Zikhron Ya'akov.

His son, NORMAN DE MATTOS BENTWICH (1883–1971), English Zionist, lawyer, and scholar, was born in London where he practiced law from 1908 to 1912. In 1913 he was appointed commissioner of courts in Egypt and lecturer at the Cairo Law School. During World War I he served in the British Army on the Palestine front and was demobilized with the rank of major. From 1920 until 1931 Bentwich was attorney general of the Mandate government in Palestine, and in this capacity was active in modernizing the country's courts and introducing British law and procedure to replace those of the former Turkish regime. In 1930 an attempt was made on his life by an Arab terrorist. The Mandate government's anti-Zionist policy led him to resign in 1931.

The following year Bentwich was appointed professor of international relations at the Hebrew University of Jerusalem. He advocated Arab-Jewish rapprochement, sharing the views of the *Berit Shalom group. He served as director of the League of Nations' Commission for Jewish Refugees from Germany between 1933 and 1936. In 1951 he retired from the Hebrew University and returned to

England where he was active on behalf of the Hebrew University.

Bentwich was a prolific writer. His books on Zionism and Israel include: *Palestine of the Jews: Past, Present and Future* (1919); *England in Palestine* (1932); *Fulfillment in the Promised Land* (1938); *Palestine* (1946[2]); *Jewish Youth Comes Home, 1933–1943* (1944); *Israel* (1960[2]); *Israel and her Neighbors* (1955); *Legislation of Palestine* (1926); *The Criminal Law of Palestine* (1928). On international relations: *The Religious Foundations of Internationalism* (1959[2]); *From Geneva to San Francisco* (1946); *A Commentary on the Charter of the U.N.* (1950); *The Mandates System* (1930). On Hellenism: *Hellenism* (1919); *Josephus* (1914); *Philo-Judaeus of Alexandria* (1910). Biographies: *Solomon Schechter* (1938); *For Zion's Sake* (on J. L. *Magnes, 1954); and on Brigadier F. Kisch. *Wanderer in the Promised Land* (1932), *Wanderer Between Two Worlds* (1941), and *Wanderer in War* (1946) are all autobiographies as is *My 77 Years* (1961). *Mandate Memoirs 1918–1948* (1965) was written in collaboration with his wife Helen, and a biography of his father, *The Pilgrim Father* (1940), in collaboration with his sister Margery. Bentwich's wife, Helen Caroline (née Franklin; 1892–1972), was chairman of the London County Council in 1956–57, and alderman from 1958 to 1965. She wrote *Our Councils, the Story of Local Government* (1962).

Norman Bentwich, Zionist, lawyer, and scholar.

JOSEPH BENTWICH (1902–), another son of Herbert Bentwich, was an Israel educator. Bentwich was born in London and settled in Palestine in 1924. From 1928 to 1948 he served as inspector of schools for the Mandate government, and from 1943 to 1948 as assistant director of the Department of Education. Bentwich was principal of the Reali High School in Haifa from 1948 to 1955 and from 1955 to 1958 lectured on education at the Hebrew University. In 1962 he was awarded the Israel Prize for his contribution to Israel education. Bentwich was a leader of the Amanah ("Covenant") group, established to study and promote new interpretations of Judaism. He edited *Yalkut ha-Datot* ("Anthology of Religions," 1964) and *Yahadut, Mikra'ah* ("Judaism, a Reader," 1967). He published several textbooks for teaching English and mathematics and *Education in Israel* (1965). [B.J./C.R.]

Herbert Bentwich's ninth child, THELMA (1895–1959) was a cellist. Born in London, she went to Palestine in 1920, and married Eliezer Yellin the son of David Yellin. Thelma Yellin was an active pioneer of the musical life of the capital. In 1921 she helped to organize the Jerusalem Musical Society; in 1922, together with Emil *Hauser, she founded the Jerusalem String Quartet; in 1932 she was cofounder of the Jerusalem School of Music and Visual Arts, which a year later became the Palestine Conservatoire and eventually the Rubin Academy of Music. Thelma Yellin herself was the cellist of the Jerusalem String Quartet until it disbanded in 1950, and the following year joined the Israel String Quartet. She also appeared often with the Philharmonic and radio orchestras. During all this time, she continued to teach, until 1942 at the conservatoire in Jerusalem and afterward mainly at the Tel Aviv academy. Her plans for a "music gymnasium" for talented children, originally projected by Bronislaw *Huberman, began to be realized at the Israel Academy of Music in Tel Aviv in 1958, and the music high school of the academy, finally opened in 1962, was named the Thelma Yellin Gymnasium. [B.B.]

Bibliography: Margery Bentwich, *Thelma Yellin, Pioneer Musician* (1954).

°**BENTZEN, AAGE** (1894–1953), Danish biblical scholar, He was appointed professor of biblical studies at the University of Copenhagen in 1929. He was the first president of the International Organization of Old Testament Scholars, which was established in Leiden in 1950, and was instrumental in helping to establish its journal, *Vetus Testamentum*, in the same year.

Bentzen was a prolific scholar, expert in all phases of biblical exegesis. Since he observed little agreement between the J and E documents, and regarded them as independent of one another, he preferred to write in terms of etiological legends, myths, and cultic songs. He almost completely ignored the older classification of literary criticism, including the Documentary Hypothesis, and was inclined instead to emphasize historical narrative, historiography, and strata of traditions. Typical of Bentzen's methodology and thought is his *Messias—Moses redivivus—Menschensohn* (1948; *King and Messiah*, 1955), where he attempts to assess the contributions of the English and Scandinavian myth and ritual schools in regard to the cultic situations in the life of the king of Israel. Bentzen criticizes both schools and argues for the impact of history on the cultic myth. Furthermore, it is the "Urmensch" idea which underlies the role of the king, the priest, the prophet, and the messiah in Israel. He also wrote *Introduction to the Old Testament* (2 vols., 1948–49, 1961[6]).

Bibliography: VT, *Congress Volume* (1953), vii-xv (incl. complete bibliography). [Z.G.]

BENVENISTE (also **Bienveniste, Benvist, Abenbenist,** etc.), personal name and surname of a widespread Sephardi family. The name originated in Spain and Provence and means "welcome." It is first mentioned in documents from Barcelona in 1079. After the expulsion from Spain in 1492, the family was dispersed, especially throughout the Ottoman Empire.

Prominent members, in addition to those to whom separate articles are devoted, include: BENVENISTE IBN BENVENISTE (early 14th century), translator of medical works from Arabic into Catalan during the reign of James II, king of Aragon (1291–1327); IZMEL (ISHMAEL) of Barcelona (early 14th century), physician, father of the physician Samuel *Benveniste; ADZAY (=ḤASDAI) BENVENIST (mid-15th century), member of the communal council in Saragossa; JUDAH B. ABRAHAM (1460–1515), born in Toledo, a descendant of Abraham *Benveniste of Soria, who, after the expulsion from Spain, was active in Salonika; and NISSIM (15th century), a scholar whose halakhic queries to Isaac *Aboab were published by Abraham Meldola in *Ziv ha-Einayim*.

Bibliography: Baer, Urkunden, 1 pt. 2 (1936), index, s.v. *Bienvenist;* Baer, Spain, index; Cantera-Millás, Inscripciones, 180, 193–4; *Sefarad,* index to vols. 1–15 (1957), 399, 401. [Ed.]

BENVENISTE, ABRAHAM (1406–1454), "court rabbi" in Castile mentioned in crown documents dating from about 1430. The young king, John II, handed over the government of Castile to two noblemen, who appointed Benveniste, a native of Soria, to restore its shaky fiscal administration. Benveniste acted as tax farmer general of the realm and organized the levy of the taxes and customs duties with the assistance of subordinates, mainly Jews. He also supplied the army with money and grain. In 1432, at the request of the Jewish communities of the Castile, the king appointed Benveniste chief justice and tax superintendent of Castilian Jewry, with the title of *Rab de la Corte.* The same year he convened the representatives and scholars of the Castilian communities in Valladolid, and framed a number of ordinances designed to strengthen the status of Spanish Jewry, which had been undermined by the recent tragic events. These enactments were directed toward maintaining religious instruction, the fair administration of justice in Jewish courts, equitable tax apportionment, defense against informers, and curbs on extravagance in dress and entertainment. Benveniste was conservative in his approach to religious problems. He opposed the rationalist philosophical trends widespread among Jewish scholars, and strove for the rehabilitation of Jewish communal life through strict observance of the precepts of Judaism.

Bibliography: Graetz, Hist, 4 (1949), 228–9, 280, 341, 351; Baer, Urkunden, 1 pt. 2 (1936), 305–6, 309; Baer, Spain, index; Neuman, Spain, index; Finkelstein, Middle Ages, 103, 349. [Z.Av./Ed.]

BENVENISTE, ABRAHAM (18th century), rabbi and communal leader in Smyrna. Benveniste was a son-in-law of Ḥayyim Ventura and of Abraham ibn Ezra, both outstanding scholars of Smyrna. His communal activity brought him into contact with the scholars of Italy, and his correspondence with Moses Ḥayyim Morpurgo of Ancona during the years 1746–50 is extant. Morpurgo asked him to supply a list of books recently published in Turkey and to keep him informed of any new publications, while Benveniste on his part sent Morpurgo a list of books which he asked him to acquire for him in Venice. It is possible therefore that Benveniste was in the book trade.

Bibliography: M. Benayahu, in: *Aresheth,* 1 (1958), 224–6, 231–9. [Ed.]

BENVENISTE (or **Benvenist**), **ḤAYYIM BEN ISRAEL** (1603–1673), Sephardi rabbinic scholar and codifier. Benveniste studied in his native Constantinople mainly under Joseph b. Moses of Trani, and also under Joseph *Samegah. In 1624, when he was only 21, he began to write his detailed commentary on the *Sefer Mitzvot Gadol* of *Moses b. Jacob of Coucy, which he called *Dina de-Ḥayyei* ("Law of the Living"). The same year he was appointed to decide cases dealing with ritual law *(Issur ve-Hetter).* Benveniste was rabbi in Tirya, near Smyrna, from 1643 to 1655 when he settled in Smyrna. When Chief Rabbi Joseph Escapa of Smyrna reached an advanced age, Benveniste was appointed in 1661 to act for him in matters of ritual and matrimonial law, and succeeded him after his death the following year. In 1665 the council of the city's scholars (with Benveniste's consent) appointed Aaron *Lapapa in charge of civil cases, but at the end of the same year the latter was deposed by the many admirers of Shabbetai Ẓevi, whom Lapapa had excommunicated and condemned to death. After Shabbetai Ẓevi's conversion to Islam a small

Title page of Ḥayyim Benveniste's Passover treatise, *Sefer Pesaḥ Me'ubin,* Venice, 1692. Cecil Roth Collection.

section of the Smyrna community unsuccessfully attempted to reinstate Lapapa. As a result, Benveniste became involved in a dispute with Lapapa. Benveniste's attitude to the Shabbatean movement as a whole was entirely negative, but he sought to avoid controversy in the interest of communal harmony, and was not resolute enough in certain instances to oppose openly the majority of his community, who followed Shabbetai Ẓevi and his followers.

Benveniste's role in this episode however did not detract from his dignity and authority as one of the greatest of the Jewish codifiers. Among his many disciples were Solomon ibn Ezra, Isaac Algazi, Ḥayyim Algazi, and Abraham b. Aaron de Boton. His principal work *Keneset ha-Gedolah,* was accepted by both Ashkenazi and Sephardi rabbis as an authoritative work of great practical value. In his work, which comprises eight large volumes, Benveniste cites and methodically explains all the conclusions and legal novellae to be found in the responsa and other halakhic works of the outstanding authorities after the time of Joseph *Caro, as well as some of the decisions of earlier scholars whom Caro had failed to cite.

In Benveniste's lifetime only three parts of the work were printed: on *Oraḥ Ḥayyim* (Leghorn, 1658); *Sheyarei,* addenda on *Oraḥ Ḥayyim* (Smyrna, 1671); and on *Ḥoshen Mishpat* (part 1, Smyrna, 1660). After his death there appeared the volume on *Yoreh De'ah* (3 parts, Constantinople, 1711–17); on *Even ha-Ezer* (Smyrna, 1731, new ed. Lemberg, 1861); on *Ḥoshen Mishpat,* part 2, with several appendixes by other authors (Smyrna, 1734). Also his *Dina de-Ḥayyei* was published posthumously from a defective manuscript (Constantinople, 2 pts. 1747). Additional legal novellae on the *Ḥoshen Mishpat* are to be found in Ḥayyim b. Menahem Algazi's *Benei Ḥayyai* published in Orta-koi (near Constantinople) in 1712. Benveniste also wrote important responsa (*Ba'ei Ḥayyei,* "Needs of the Living"), on the four parts of the *Turim,* the following of which have been published: on *Oraḥ Ḥayyim* (part 2, Salonika, 1783), on 211 sections of *Yoreh De'ah* and on 24 of the *Even ha-Ezer* (*ibid.*, 1788), as well as on the *Ḥoshen Mishpat*, in two parts (*ibid.*, 1791). Benveniste also wrote novellae on a number of tractates: that on *Sanhedrin* which he called *Ḥamra ve-Ḥayyei*, only part of which is extant, was published, together with notes and extracts from the manuscripts of the novellae of the earlier halakhic authorities, under the title of *Ḥemer Ḥivver Attik* (Leghorn, 1802). Benveniste's son Israel (1644–1729) succeeded him as chief rabbi of Smyrna.

Bibliography: J. J. Emden, *Torat ha-Kena'ot* (1752), 4b; J. Sasportas *Ẓiẓat Novel Ẓevi*, ed. by I. Tishby (1954), index, s.v. *Benvenisti, Ḥayyim;* Conforte, Kore, 51a; Bernfeld, in: *Kobez al Jad*, 9 (1899), 1–11 (third pagination); A. Freimann (ed.), *Inyanei Shabbetai Ẓevi* (1912), 142, no. 20; Rosanes, Togarmah, 4 (1935), 42–47, 160–4; Benayahu, in: *Zion*, 12 (1946/47), 44–48; idem, in: *Reshumot*, 5 (1953), 197–211; idem, in: *Sinai*, 34 (1954), 167, 200–2; Scholem, Shabbetai Ẓevi, index; Sonne, in: *Sefunot*, 34 (1960), 48, 50, 57 s.v. *Benvenest;* Molho and Amarijlio, *ibid.*, 214–6 (Eng. summ.). [M.N.Z./ED.]

BENVENISTE, ISAAC BEN JOSEPH (d. c. 1224), physician to James I of Aragon and *nasi* of Aragonese Jewry. He was the leading figure in the representative congresses of the Jewish communities convened at Montpellier and Saint-Gilles in 1214 and 1215 to consider protective measures in view of the approaching *Lateran Council. Subsequently he secured for the Aragonese communities a temporary suspension of the obligation to wear the Jewish *badge. In 1220, he received from Pope Honorius III a warm letter of recommendation to the king and the archbishop of Tarragona notwithstanding Isaac's "erroneous" views in matters of religion.

Bibliography: Neuman, Spain, index; Solomon ibn Verga, *Shevet Yehudah*, ed. by A. Shochat (1947), 147, 223; S. Grayzel, *The Church and the Jews* (1966^2), index. [C.R.]

BENVENISTE, JOSEPH BEN MOSES DE SEGOVIA (second half of the 16th century), rabbi and author. Benveniste spent most of his life in Safed but died in Brusa, Turkey. His principal teacher was Elisha *Gallico, but he also studied under Isaac *Luria and Samuel b. Isaac de *Uceda. Joseph *Ganso, rabbi of Brusa, was his pupil. He wrote many works which were lost. Benveniste mentions two of them: *Be-Ẓel ha-Kesef*, an ethical work modeled on the *Kad ha-Kemah* of *Baḥya b. Asher and *Yakhol Yosef* (also erroneously called *Yevul Yosef*) containing various novellae. A number of his biblical comments, including interpretations he heard from Isaac *Luria, are quoted in the *Dovev Siftei Yeshenim* (Smyrna, 1671) of his grandson Nissim Solomon *Algazi.

Bibliography: Scholem, in: *Beḥinot*, 9 (1956), 82; Tamar, in: *Tarbiz*, 27 (1957/58), 105–8; M. Benayahu, *Sefer Toledot ha-Ari* (1967), 362–4. [A.D.]

BENVENISTE, JOSHUA RAPHAEL BEN ISRAEL (1590?–1665?), Turkish rabbi, physician, grammarian, and poet; brother of Ḥayyim *Benveniste. Joshua was born in Constantinople and was a disciple of Joseph b. Moses *Trani and Abraham *Alegre. He studied grammar under Isaac *Uzziel, and medicine under Isaac Caro, the physician. While serving as rabbi in Constantinople, he accepted the rabbinate of Sophia, after the community had agreed to all of his conditions, but the Constantinople community objected and prevailed upon him to remain. For some years Joshua was rabbi of Bursa. Many communities, even Karaites, addressed their problems to him, and responsa written by him, as early as 1610, are extant. Benveniste was a versatile author and many of his works are still regarded as basic in their fields. He devoted himself particularly to the Jerusalem Talmud, which was largely neglected in his day. His commentary on it, *Sedeh Yehoshu'a*, was published with the text. Joshua's method was first to explain all difficult words according to the Babylonian Talmud, the *Arukh*, etc., and then to explain the passage, comparing it with the parallel passage in the Babylonian Talmud or explaining it according to the context where no such parallel exists. Where the *halakhah* differs in the two Talmuds he decided according to the Babylonian, "since it is the essential one." He also collected explanations which he found in works of *rishonim* and halakhists and added his own. He deals only with the halakhic portions, ignoring the *aggadah*. His language is very prolix. This may explain why the commentary did not become widespread among the scholars of Eastern and Western Europe.

His commentary to the following tractates was published: *Berakhot, Pe'ah, Orlah, Ḥallah*, and *Bikkurim* of the order *Zera'im* (Constantinople, 1662); a number of tractates of *Mo'ed, Nashim*, and *Nezikin* (Constantinople, 1749). The commentary has frequently been reprinted together with the text. His *Seder ha-Get* and *Seder Ḥalizah* were published in *Get Pashut* (Constantinople, 1719) of Moses ibn Ḥabib. According to Ḥayyim Joseph David *Azulai, his four volumes of responsa, *Sha'ar Yehoshu'a*, were destroyed by fire after 1677. Some of his 97 responsa on *Ḥoshen Mishpat*, which have remained in manuscript (Jewish Institute, Warsaw, no.13), were published in Husiatin in 1904 and many of his responsa were published in the books of his contemporaries. His other published works are *Oznei Yehoshu'a* (Constantinople, 1677), sermons, and *Avodah Tammah* (Constantinople, 1691–95), an exposition of the **Avodah* in the Day of Atonement liturgy, and a clarification of the variant readings. The following remain in manuscript: *Mishmeret ha-Mitzvot* (JTS, Ms. 0347), a poetic arrangement of the commandments in accordance with the enumeration of Maimonides; *Levush Malkhut*, describing the greatness of the Creator as evinced in the human anatomy, written in the style of the *Keter Malkhut* of Solomon ibn Gabirol; *Perek be-Shir* (Montefiore Ms. 377), on prosody and meter; and a treatise on medicine.

Bibliography: L. Ginzberg, *Perushim ve-Ḥiddushim ba-Yerushalmi*, 1 (1961), introduction (Eng.) liii-liv; N. Allony, *Mi-Torat ha-Lashon ve-ha-Shirah bi-Ymei ha-Beinayim* (1944), 85–92; idem, *Mi-Sifrut Yemei ha-Beinayim* (1945), 39–42; Benayahu, in: *Aresheth*, 3 (1961), 151. [ED.]

BENVENISTE, MANUEL (**Immanuel**; 17th century), Hebrew printer in Amsterdam. Benveniste's name appears in an entry in the *Puiboken* of that city, dated Feb. 10, 1640: "Immanuel Benveniste of Venice, 32 years old, parents still living . . ." Among the 65 works he printed between 1640 and 1670 are *Midrash Rabbah* (1641–42), *Mishnah* (1643), and Alfasi's *Halakhot* (1643). His outstanding production, however, was the Talmud (1644–48), which restored some passages expunged by the censor in previous editions. As correctors Benveniste employed Moses di Cordova b. Isaac of Constantinople (for the *Midrash Rabbah*) and the Amsterdam rabbi Abraham b. Joshua of Worms (for the Alfasi edition). Benveniste's editions can usually be recognized by the title page frame of a gate of prism-shaped stones with his printer's mark, a castle flanked by a lion with a star superimposed.

Bibliography: J. S. da Silva Rosa, *Geschiedenis der portugeesche Joden te Amsterdam 1593–1925* (1925), 29ff.; ESN, 62; Brugmans-Frank, 469, 476; Wolf, Bibliotheca, 2 (1721), 903—4. [E.J./ED.]

BENVENISTE, MOSES (second half of the 16th century), Turkish physician. As medical attendant to the grand vizier, Siavouch Pasha, Benveniste attained considerable influence in Turkish politics. In 1582 he was largely responsible for reinstating Peter the Lame as *gospodar* (ruler) of Moldavia. In 1583, in conjunction with Nissim, the Jewish director of the mint, he recommended the currency reform which led to a revolt of the Janissaries. Later, he was associated with the Jew David *Passi and the Italian Paolo Maria in unsuccessful intrigues with the English ambassador Barton against Solomon *Abenaes, Duke of Mytilene. In 1598 Benveniste, who had always favored the pro-Spanish party in Turkish politics, was one of the three Turkish plenipotentiaries in the peace negotiations with Spain. Having exceeded their instructions, they were banished. Benveniste unsuccessfully tried to escape this sentence by embracing Islam, but died a political prisoner in Rhodes.

Bibliography: Rosanes, Togarmah 3 (1938[2]), 8, 13, 356–8, 363; C. Roth, *House of Nasi, Duke of Naxos* (1948), 200, 204, 211 215; A. Galanté, *Turcs et Juifs* (1932), 101; idem, *Juifs de Rhodes* (1935), 109f.; E. Charrière (ed.), *Négociations de la France dans le Levant*, 4 (1966), 246f.

[C.R.]

BENVENISTE, SAMUEL (d. after 1356), physician and translator, living in Tarragona and Saragossa, Spain. Benveniste was a familiar at the court of King Pedro IV of Aragon, being physician to his brother, Don Manuel. In about 1300 he translated into Hebrew Maimonides' *Sefer ha-Kaẓẓeret* ("Treatise on Asthma"), apparently from a Latin translation; his rendering is colloquial and fluent, although the surviving manuscripts are carelessly copied. Some scholars ascribe to Benveniste a translation of Boethius' *Consolations of Philosophy*.

Bibliography: HB, 8 (1865), 85, 125f.; 9 (1869), 91; 10 (1870), 84; Steinschneider, Uebersetzungen, 496, 767; Baer, Urkunden, 1 (1929), 172, 434; Sanchez Real, in: *Sefarad*, 11 (1951), 347.

[Ed.]

BENVENISTE, SHESHET BEN ISAAC BEN JOSEPH (also called **"Perfect de Pratis"**; c. 1131–1209), Spanish financier, physician, and poet; grandson of Sheshet ha-Nasi of Barcelona. In his youth, Benveniste entered the service of the count of Barcelona. Subsequently, he served the kings of Aragon Alfonso II and from 1196 Pedro II as physician, translator into Arabic, political adviser, and diplomatic envoy. He also took an active part in the fiscal administration, and received certain state revenues in return for loans to the royal treasury. Like the nobility of the kingdom, Benveniste was exempted from taxes and enjoyed legal immunity from the jurisdiction of both the crown authorities and the local Jewish community. He received a royal grant of privileges on the basis of which he regulated the affairs of the Barcelona synagogue. His signature in Hebrew figures on official documents. Benveniste apparently had a wide knowledge in many subjects. He wrote Hebrew poetry, was in touch with Muslim scholars, knew general history, and wrote medical works still preserved in manuscript. Benveniste regarded the *Mishneh Torah* of Maimonides as the basic authority on *halakhah* and vigorously championed the latter's philosophical views. *Benjamin of Tudela and Judah *Al-Ḥarizi, who met Benveniste in Barcelona, praise him highly. He was a patron of poets and scholars, such as *Isaac b. Abba Mari, and Joseph *ibn Zabara, who dedicated to him his *Sefer ha-Sha'ashu'im*.

Bibliography: Baer, Spain, 1 (1961), 91, 100; D. Kaufmann, in: REJ, 39 (1899), 62–63; Marx, in: JQR, 25 (1934/35), 406–7.

[Z.Av./Ed.]

BENVENISTE DE PORTA (d. 1268), financial official in Aragon during the reign of James I, from Villafranca del Panadés. Benveniste dealt in grain and owned flour mills in Barcelona. In the 1250s and 1260s he served the crown as *baile* (bailiff) in Barcelona and elsewhere. In exchange for the sums he lent to the king and his ministers, Benveniste received concessions on royal revenues in Catalonia and the Balearic Islands. At one time, he provided the silver for the Barcelona mint. In 1264 his brother Astrug de Porta was accused of blaspheming Jesus during a religious discussion but, through Benveniste's influence, the sentence of banishment was commuted to a fine.

Bibliography: F. de Bofarull y Sands, *Los judiós en el territorio de Barcelona* (1910); Neuman, Spain, index; Baer, Spain (1961), 146, 156.

[Z.Av.]

BENWAISH, ABRAHAM (16th–17th centuries), banker to the sultan of Morocco Aḥmad al-Manṣur in Marrakesh (south Morocco) and later superintendent of finances (until 1627). Benwaish was extremely influential and it was because of him that members of the *Pallache family were appointed ambassadors of Morocco to Holland. He was responsible for one of his relatives, Abraham Buzaglo-Azulay, being sent to Venice in 1606 to buy expensive goods for the ruler. Benwaish was appointed *nagid* of the Jews of the kingdom of Marrakesh and promoted study there. In his capacity as superintendent of finance he discriminated against the English and Dutch Christians in favor of his coreligionists, a policy which brought protests from the European governments. Accused of embezzlement, he had no difficulty in clearing himself. His descendant Samuel (1738–1817), *dayyan* of Meknès, was renowned for his piety. His responsa are extant in manuscript.

Bibliography: SIHM, Angleterre, 2 (1925), 233, 363, 441, 468; 3 (1936), 64, 66, 68–70; Pays-Bas, 1 (1906), 343, 500; J. M. Toledano, *Ner ha-Ma'arav* (1911), 106, 111, 196; J. Ben-Naim, *Malkhei Rabbanan* (1931), 121; Hirschberg, Afrikah, 2 (1965), 225.

[D.Co.]

BEN-YEḤEZKI'EL, MORDEKHAI (1883–1971), Hebrew essayist and adapter of folktales. Born in Galicia, he moved in 1906 to Lvov where he was both student and tutor. After visiting Western Europe, he taught for a time in Lvov, and immigrated to Palestine in 1920. At first he taught at the Tel Aviv Teachers' Seminary and from 1925 was an instructor of Hebrew, Bible, and Literature at the Mizrachi Teachers' Seminary in Jerusalem. After the publication of his first article on *Ḥasidism in *Ha-Shilo'aḥ* in 1904, he wrote regularly on language, literature, Ḥasidism, etc., in the Hebrew press and was encouraged by Ḥ. N. *Bialik to publish his adaptations of various folktales, which appeared as *Sefer ha-Ma'asiyyot* ("Book of Folk Tales"; four volumes 1926–29; expanded edition in six volumes, 1957).

Bibliography: G. Bader, *Medinah va-Ḥakhameha* (1934), 76; *Kitvei A. Barash* (1957), 131; A. Korekh, *Kehillat Glina* (1950), 77–80; E. M. Lipschuetz, *Ketavim*, 3 (1957), 181–4.

[G.K.]

BEN-YEHUDA, ELIEZER (1858–1922), Hebrew writer and lexicographer, generally considered the father of modern Hebrew, and one of the first active Zionist leaders. Born Eliezer Yiẓḥak Perelman in Luzhky, Lithuania, he officially adopted the pseudonym Ben-Yehuda, which he had previously used in his literary activities, when he went to Palestine. Ben-Yehuda's father, a *Ḥabad Ḥasid, died when Eliezer was five years old. At the age of 13, he was sent to his uncle to attend the yeshivah in Polotsk. The head of the yeshivah, a *maskil* in secret, introduced him to secular literature. To save him from heresy, his uncle sent him to study in Glubokoye, in the Vilna district, where Ben-Yehuda made the acquaintance of Samuel Naphtali Herz Jonas, also a Ḥabad Ḥasid, who was writing for

Figure 1. Eliezer Ben-Yehuda, pioneer of modern Hebrew, with his wife, Ḥemdah, 1912. From Ben Dov Collection by courtesy of Israel State Archives.

Hebrew periodicals. Jonas persuaded him to prepare for secondary school matriculation, and his eldest daughter, Deborah, taught him Russian. After a year of preparation he entered the Dvinsk Gymnasium from which he graduated in 1877.

The Russo-Turkish War (1877–78) and the struggle of the Balkan nations for liberation planted in Ben-Yehuda the idea of the revival of the Jewish people on its ancestral soil. He maintained that the Jewish people, like all other peoples, had a historic land and a historic language. What was needed was to actuate a national movement that would restore Israel to its land and to its language. He wrote in the preface to his dictionary: "In those days it was as if the heavens had suddenly opened, and a clear, incandescent light flashed before my eyes, and a mighty inner voice sounded in my ears: the renascence of Israel on its ancestral soil." He determined to settle in Ereẓ Israel, and in 1878 went to Paris to study medicine so that he might have a profession to sustain himself. He discussed his plan for a Jewish national movement with some Hebrew writers; they, however, were not interested. His article *"She'elah Lohatah"* ("A Burning Question") was published in P. *Smolenskin's *Ha-Shaḥar* in 1879 (after *Ha-Maggid* had refused to accept it) under the name "E. Ben-Yehuda." For the first time the idea of a national spiritual center in Ereẓ Israel was clearly propounded. Ben-Yehuda linked the Jewish national revival with the general European awakening and said that the Jewish people should learn from the oppressed European peoples that were fighting for political freedom and national revival. The Jewish people must establish a community in Ereẓ Israel that would serve as a focal point for the entire people, so that even those Jews who would remain in the Diaspora would know that they belong to a people that dwells in its own land and has its own language and culture. In this essay, the fundamental principles of spiritual Zionism are anticipated: the settlement of the land not for the return of the entire people from the exile, but for the creation of a national center designed to save from assimilation those Jews that are scattered all over the Diaspora.

In Paris, Ben-Yehuda met George (Getzel) *Selikovitch, a Jewish journalist, who told him that in his travels through Asia and Africa he had spoken Hebrew with the Jews of these lands, so that in fact Hebrew was not dead. When Ben-Yehuda contracted tuberculosis in the winter of 1878, he decided to discontinue his medical studies and make his home in the more favorable climate of Ereẓ Israel. He enrolled in the teachers' seminary of the Alliance Israélite Universelle, to qualify for a teaching post in *Mikveh Israel. There he attended the lectures of the Assyrologist Joseph *Halevy who in the periodical *Ha-Maggid* had advocated the coinage of new Hebrew words as early as the 1860s. As his health deteriorated, Ben-Yehuda entered the Rothschild Hospital in Paris, and there he met the Jerusalem scholar A. M. *Luncz who spoke Hebrew to him in the Sephardi pronunciation, and told him that the members of the various Jewish communities in Jerusalem were able to converse with one another only in Sephardi Hebrew. This reinforced Ben-Yehuda's opinion that the Jews could not hope to become a united people in their own land again unless their children revived Hebrew as their spoken tongue. The Hebrew living language must have Sephardi phonetic sounds because that was the pronunciation which served in the transliteration of biblical names in ancient and modern translations of the Bible. In 1880 he published two articles in *Ha-Ḥavaẓẓelet* in which he advocated that Hebrew rather than the various foreign languages become the language of instruction in the Jewish schools in Ereẓ Israel. In 1881, he left for Palestine. He traveled by way of Vienna, where he was joined by his childhood acquaintance, Deborah Jonas, whom he married in Cairo. In October 1881, they arrived in Jaffa where Ben-Yehuda informed his wife that henceforth they would converse only in Hebrew. The Ben-Yehuda household thus was the first Hebrew-speaking home established in Palestine, and his first son, Ben-Zion (later called Ithamar *Ben-Avi), the first modern Hebrew-speaking child.

To ingratiate himself with the Orthodox Jews who knew written Hebrew and could, therefore, readily learn to speak the language, Ben Yehuda at first adopted their customs. He grew a beard and earlocks, and prevailed upon his wife to wear a *sheytl* ("wig"). This did not last very long because the Orthodox Jews of Jerusalem soon sensed that for Ben-Yehuda Hebrew was not a holy tongue, but a secular, national language, and that his purpose for introducing spoken Hebrew was solely nationalist and political. They began to suspect him, and Ben-Yehuda became an extremist in his antireligious attitude. He registered as a national Jew "without religion."

As early as 1881 Ben-Yehuda, together with Y.M. *Pines, D. *Yellin, Y. *Meyuḥas, and A. Mazie, founded the society Teḥiyyat Israel based on five principles: work on the land and expansion of the country's productive population; revival of spoken Hebrew; creation of a modern Hebrew literature and science in the national spirit; education of the youth in a national and, at the same time, universal humanistic spirit; and active opposition to the **ḥalukkah* system. During the period 1882–85, Ben-Yehuda worked on *Ha-Ḥavaẓẓelet* and put out a supplement to the periodical under the name *Mevasseret Ẓiyyon*. At the same time, he taught in the Jerusalem Alliance school, which post he accepted only after he was permitted to use Hebrew exclusively as the language of instruction in all Jewish subjects. The school was thus the first in which at least some subjects were taught in Hebrew. In 1885, Ben-Yehuda published a geography of Palestine, called *Ereẓ Yisrael* (only part 1 appeared). Toward the end of 1884, he founded a weekly, *Ha-Ẓevi,* which later became a biweekly, under the new name, *Ha-Or.* In 1908, it became a daily, known first as *Ha-Ẓevi,* and from 1910 onward as *Ha-Or;* it appeared until 1915. For several years, from 1897, Ben-Yehuda also published a weekly (from 1904, biweekly) called *Hashkafah.* In his periodicals he fought against the *ḥalukkah* system, championed agricultural labor, the new settlement, and, especially, the revival of spoken Hebrew. He spared no effort to enrich the language by coining new terms and introducing transliterations from foreign tongues. Financial difficulties in the economically poor Jerusalem environment were mainly responsible for the shortcomings of his magazine. Despite all its defects, however, Ben-Yehuda's periodical was the first in Hebrew to meet European standards. It removed the barrier between strictly Jewish topics and secular subjects, and discussed, insofar as the strict Turkish censorship permitted, all aspects of general political and cultural life.

In 1891, Ben-Yehuda's wife died, and about six months later he married her younger sister. She adopted the Hebrew name Ḥemdah. A constant companion to her husband in his literary activity, Ḥemdah Ben-Yehuda published translations and original Hebrew stories in his periodicals. It was she who incited Ben-Yehuda's extremism against the Jewish tradition. Ben Yehuda's unorthodox behavior, and the campaign which he waged in the columns of his periodicals against the *ḥalukkah* system and its administrators, aroused the vehement opposition of the extreme Orthodox Jews. Seeking a pretext for revenge, they found it in an article by Jonas in the 1894 Ḥanukkah number of *Ha-Ẓevi,* which contained the phrase "let us gather strength and go forward." Some of Ben-Yehuda's more bigoted enemies distorted its meaning and interpreted it to the Turkish authorities as "let us gather an army and proceed against the East." Ben-Yehuda was charged with sedition and sentenced to a year's imprisonment. The affair

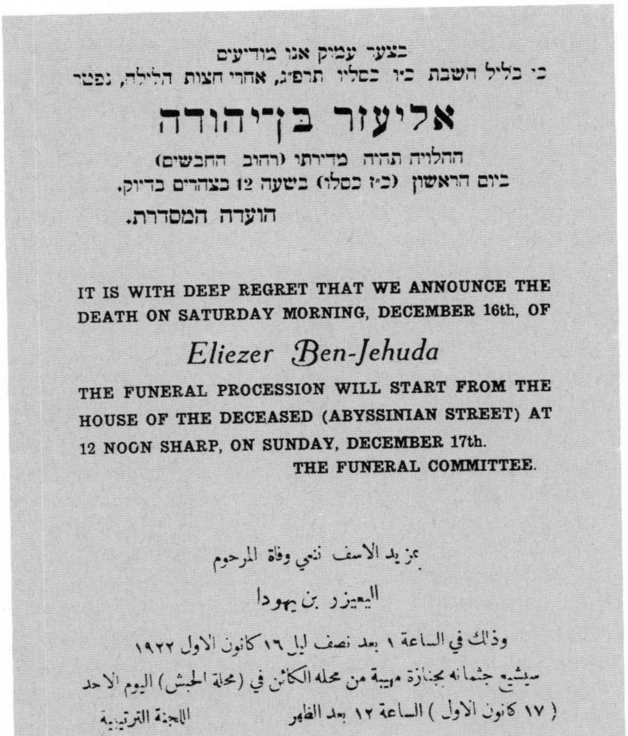
בצער עמיק אנו מודיעים
כי בליל השבת כ״ו כסליו תרפ״ג, אחרי חצות הלילה, נפטר
אליעזר בן־יהודה
ההלויה תהיה מדירתו (רחוב החבשים)
ביום הראשון (כ״ז כסלו) בשעה 12 בצהרים בדיוק.
הועדה המסדרת.

IT IS WITH DEEP REGRET THAT WE ANNOUNCE THE DEATH ON SATURDAY MORNING, DECEMBER 16th, OF

Eliezer Ben-Jehuda

THE FUNERAL PROCESSION WILL START FROM THE HOUSE OF THE DECEASED (ABYSSINIAN STREET) AT 12 NOON SHARP, ON SUNDAY, DECEMBER 17th.
THE FUNERAL COMMITTEE.

بمزيد الاسف ننعي وفاة المرحوم
اليعيزر بن يهودا
وذلك في الساعة ١ بعد نصف ليل ١٦ كانون الاول ١٩٢٢
سيشيع جثمانه بجنازة مهيبة من محله الكائن في (محلة الحبش) اليوم الاحد
(١٧ كانون الاول) الساعة ١٢ بعد الظهر
اللجنة الترتيبية

Figure 2. Notice of the death of Eliezer Ben-Yehuda on December 16, 1922, in Hebrew, English, and Arabic. Cecil Roth Collection.

created a great stir throughout the Jewish world; an appeal was lodged and he was released.

Turkish censorship of *Ha-Ẓevi,* however, became more stringent from then on. As a result, Ben-Yehuda began to concentrate more on linguistic questions to which the censors could make no objection. He became increasingly engrossed in his dictionary for which he had begun to collect material from the day he arrived in Ereẓ Israel. In order to conduct research and raise funds for its publication, Ben-Yehuda traveled several times to Europe, and later also to the United States where he worked in American libraries. In 1910, assisted by various sponsors, he began to publish his *Complete Dictionary of Ancient and Modern Hebrew* volume by volume; after his death, his widow and his son Ehud continued his publication which was completed in 1959 (17 vols.), with an introductory volume *Ha-Mavo ha-Gadol* ("Prolegomenon").

In 1890, together with David Yellin, Mazia, and others, Ben-Yehuda founded the Va'ad ha-Lashon over which he presided until his death. This *va'ad* was the forerunner of the *Academy of the Hebrew Language which Ben-Yehuda had also suggested in 1920.

Ben-Yehuda was among the supporters of the *Uganda proposal; he wrote articles in *Ha-Ẓevi* advocating the idea, and even a special pamphlet called *Ha-Medinah ha-Yehudit* (1905). His views incurred many enemies for him among those who were not prepared to exchange Zion for any other country. On the other hand, he won general respect when he led the fight (1913–14) against the plan of the *Hilfsverein der deutschen Juden to introduce German as the language of instruction in its secondary schools in Palestine and in the technical college which was about to be established in Haifa.

During World War I, when Jamal Pasha, the Turkish commander in Palestine, outlawed Zionism, Ben-Yehuda left for the United States. There he wrote his book *Ad Eimatai Dibberu Ivrit?* ("Until When was Hebrew Spoken?" 1919). He returned to Palestine in 1919. Together with M.*Ussishkin, he prevailed upon Herbert *Samuel, the British high commissioner, to declare Hebrew one of the three official languages of the country. He founded Sefatenu, a society for the propagation of Hebrew, and also served as secretary of the Planning Committee of the Hebrew University. A number of his writings were collected and published posthumously: the anthology *Yisrael le-Arẓo ve-li-Leshono* (1929) and *Avot ha-Lashon ha-Ivrit;* part 1: *Rabbi Akiva* (1945).

Ben-Yehuda's cultural activities and achievements fall into four divisions: (1) The revival of spoken Hebrew. Hebrew was spoken before the days of Ben-Yehuda, but only intermittently. The very sanctity with which the language was invested prevented its daily use. Ben-Yehuda made Hebrew speech a national goal. He was convinced that a living Hebrew, spoken by the people in its own land, was indispensable to the political and cultural rebirth of the nation. In this view Ben-Yehuda differed from *Smolenskin, *Lilienblum, and *Herzl, who were able to envisage a Jewish homeland without Hebrew as its mother tongue. Ben-Yehuda fought untiringly and uncompromisingly for this ideal. He lived to see his vision realized: the revival of the *Hebrew language as a spoken tongue after more than two thousand years. (2) The creation of a simple, popular style in Hebrew literature. Ben-Yehuda fought against the use of inflated rhetoric and the archaic expressions and forms which had lost their appeal. He demanded simplicity and concreteness in Hebrew prose which, until then, had been rhetorical and florid. With this objective in mind, he translated a number of stories from various languages into plain, unadorned Hebrew. (3) Ben-Yehuda was the first to make a regular and systematic practice of coining Hebrew words. Neologism was not new to Hebrew, but it had never been done methodically and specifically to meet the practical demands which were constantly being made on the language in daily speech, in journalism, in science, and in literature. (4) His dictionary complemented his achievement of the revival of spoken Hebrew. The dictionary attempts to include all the Hebrew words used in the different periods and developmental stages of the language. It is also arranged in the manner of modern European language dictionaries, and not according to word roots, as was customary in former Hebrew dictionaries. A characteristic feature of the dictionary is its bold omission of all Aramaic words, as well as other foreign words found in the Bible, Talmud, Midrash, and other works that are not of Semitic origin.

Bibliography: R. St. John, *The Tongue of the Prophets* (1952); R. Brainin (ed.), *Sefer Zikkaron le-Eliezer Ben Yehuda* (1918); D. Yellin, *Ben Yehudah and the Revival of the Hebrew Language* (c. 1924); I. Ben-Avi, *Avi* (1927); J. Kena'ani, *Eliezer Ben Yehuda* (Heb., 1929), contains bibl.; Ḥ. Ben Yehuda, *Ben Yehuda, Ḥayyav u-Mifalo* (1940); idem, *Ha-Loḥem ha-Me'ushar* (1932); J. Klausner, *Eliezer Ben Yehuda, Toledotav u-Mifal Ḥayyav* (1939); A. Herzberg, *The Zionist Idea* (1960), 158–65; J. Fichman, *Be-Terem Aviv* (1959), 195–203, 215ff.; R. Sivan, in: *Leshonenu la-Am*, 12 (1961/62), 35–77; G. Kressel (ed.), *Ḥol va-Ru'aḥ* (1964); idem, *Toledot ha-Ittonut ha-Ivrit be-Ereẓ Yisrael* (1964²), 67–100; Kressel, Leksikon, 1 (1965), 275ff. (includes bibl.).

[J.KL./ED.]

BEN-YEHUDA, ḤEMDAH (1873–1951), Hebrew author; wife of Eliezer *Ben-Yehuda. Her sister Deborah was Ben-Yehuda's first wife. After she died, Ḥemdah went to Jerusalem from Lithuania and married Ben-Yehuda in 1892. She aided her husband in his literary work, wrote

Ḥemdah Ben-Yehuda, Hebrew author.

articles and stories for his papers, and after his death in 1922 concerned herself with the continued publication of his multi-volume dictionary. Her two main works were *Ben Yehuda, Ḥayyav u-Mifalo* (1940), a life of Ben Yehuda, and *Nose ha-Degel* (1944) on her stepson Ithamar *Ben-Avi.

Bibliography: J. Harari, *Ishah va-Em be-Yisrael* (1959) 273–7.

[G.K.]

BEN-YEHUDAH, BARUKH (1894–), Israel educator. Ben-Yehudah, who was born in Marijampole, Lithuania, settled in Ereẓ Israel in 1911. During World War I he joined *kevuẓat* Deganyah, teaching there and at Rosh Pinnah. He then studied at the University of Brussels and, after receiving a degree in mathematics and physics in 1924, returned to teaching. He became principal of the Herẓlia Gymnasium in Tel Aviv. In 1927 he helped found the pioneering high school youth movement Ḥugim (later known as Maḥanot Olim). He also founded the Teachers' Council for the Jewish National Fund. He was director of

Barukh Ben-Yehudah, Israel educator.

the education department of the Va'ad Le'ummi in 1947, and the first director-general of the Ministry of Education and Culture of the State of Israel (until 1951). His books include *Toledot ha-Ẓiyyonut* ("The History of Zionism," 1943); *Ha-Keren ha-Meḥannekhet: Tenu'at Morim Lema'an Ẓiyyon u-Ge'ulatah* ("The Educating Fund: The Teachers' Movement for Zion and its Redemption," 1949, 1952); *Ta'amei ha-Mikra le-Vattei Sefer* ("Biblical Cantillation for Schools," 1968); *Kol ha-Ḥinnukh ha-Ẓiyyoni* ("The Voice of Zionist Education," 1955); and *Yesodot u-Derakhim* ("Fundamentals and Ways," 1952). He also wrote on teaching mathematics: *Hora'at ha-Matematikah be-Veit ha-Sefer ha-Tikhon* ("The Teaching of Mathematics in High School," 2 vols., 1959–60) and mathematics texts.

[A.A.]

BEN YIẒHAK, AVRAHAM (pen name of **Avraham Sonne;** 1883–1950), Hebrew poet. Born in Galicia, Ben Yiẓḥak received a traditional Jewish and secular education, and then studied at the universities of Vienna and Berlin. From 1913 to the summer of 1914, he was visiting lecturer in Hebrew literature and psychology at the Jerusalem Teachers' Seminary. After a brief career in the Zionist organization, he served as teacher and later principal at the Hebrew Pedagogium (Teachers' Academy) in Vienna, founded by H. P. *Chajes. After the Nazi Anschluss of Austria in 1938, he emigrated to Ereẓ Israel and settled in Jerusalem. Although he published only 11 poems during his lifetime Ben Yiẓḥak is considered a distinguished figure in modern Hebrew poetry. Most of his poems appeared before World War I and immediately attracted attention. His first poem, *"Ḥoref Bahir"* ("Bright Winter") was published in *Ha-Shilo'aḥ* in 1908. His last poem, *"Ashrei ha-Zore'im ve-Lo Yikẓoru"* ("Happy Are They That Sow But Shall Not Reap") in 1928, a farewell to his craft, concludes with the words, "And their everlasting lot shall be silence." His refusal to publish further remains a mystery. Later poems were found among his effects, but others, which he had read to his friends, are lost. Some of his work has been translated into English and various European languages. Ben Yiẓḥak wrote according to the Sephardi pronunciation (the one adopted in Ereẓ Israel) long before it was adopted by other Hebrew poets, who wrote in the Ashkenazi accent used by Hebrew-speaking European Jews. Ben Yiẓḥak's lyrics, with their terse style and biblical diction, focus on nature, meditation, and love. Though the form of BenYiẓḥak's poems is occasionally reminiscent of the Psalms, their content expresses a modern outlook on life and poetry, and he is considered by many to be the first truly modern Hebrew poet. His prose works included anonymous articles in German-Jewish periodicals and an essay on *Mendele Mokher Seforim in *Der Jude*, 3 (1918–19). One of the most scholarly and sensitive thinkers of his generation, Ben Yiẓḥak's personal influence on both Jewish and non-Jewish writers and philosophers was profound, yet he always declined to publish his obiter dicta. His collected poems appeared posthumously.

Bibliography: A. Ben Yiẓḥak, *Shirim* (1957), original poems with English translation, biography and essay by Benzion Benshalom Katz; L. Goldberg, *Pegishah im Meshorer* (1952); S. Burnshaw et al. (eds.), *Modern Hebrew Poem Itself* (1965), 50–53. [LE.G.]

BEN-YOSEF (Tabachnik), SHELOMO (1913–1938), first Jew executed by the British in Palestine. Ben-Yosef, who was born in Lutsk, Poland, joined *Betar in 1928. In 1937 he reached Palestine as an "illegal" immigrant, and joined the Betar work brigade at Rosh Pinnah. Ben-Yosef and two of his comrades, Shalom Zurabin and Avraham Shein, decided to retaliate for the murder of Jews by Arab terrorists, and on April 21, 1938 tried to attack an Arab bus on the Rosh Pinnah-Safed road. The attack failed and the three were arrested and brought before a military court.

The monument in memory of Shelomo Ben-Yosef.

Ben-Yosef and Shein were sentenced to death and Zurabin to imprisonment. Shein was reprieved because of his youth. All efforts to save Ben-Yosef from execution were in vain. He went to the gallows at Acre prison on June 29, 1938 singing Betar songs. On the day of his execution, riots broke out in Tel Aviv when demonstrators clashed with the British police. Ben-Yosef was buried at Rosh Pinnah, and after the establishment of the State of Israel a monument was erected in his memory on the Rosh Pinnah-Safed road.

Bibliography: Y. Nedava, *Sefer Olei ha-Gardom* (1952); Dinur, Haganah, 2 pt. 3 (1964^2), index; Tidhar, 4 (1950), 1764–66; D. Niv, *Ma'arkhot ha-Irgun ha-Ẓeva'i ha-Le'ummi*, 2 (1965), 61–74. [D.N.]

BENZAMERO, Spanish-Moroccan family. Its best-known members in Spain lived chiefly in Seville. JUDAH BEN EPHRAIM (1245–1330); MOSES (I) and his son EPHRAIM, were 14th-century financiers; and SOLOMON (I) and MEIR (I), 14th-century physicians. ISAAC (I) settled in Badajoz, Spain, where shortly before the 1492 expulsion Ferdinand and Isabella intervened to ensure that the large sums he had advanced them for the war against Granada would be repaid. He was probably the same Isaac Benzamero who after 1496 settled in Safi (Morocco). He became the treasurer of the Portuguese governors there, exercising important political influence, and was entrusted with many diplomatic missions, both to the king in Lisbon and to the Moroccan leaders. With his relative ISHMAEL he led 200 Jewish soldiers who took part in the defense of Safi when it was besieged by the sharif of Marrakesh in 1510.

Isaac's brother ABRAHAM BEN MEIR (d. c. 1530), paytan, physician and diplomat, lived in Granada and Malaga, and then in Tlemcen and Oran. In 1493 in Oran he wrote philosophic poems, quoted by Abraham *Gavison in his *Omer ha-Shikhḥah*. Later he settled in Safi, and there, in 1510, by decree of King Emmanuel I, was appointed chief rabbi with wide powers. Abraham b. Meir's political role in Portuguese affairs in Morocco was preeminent. He was highly regarded both by his coreligionists and the Muslims. He was also esteemed by King John III of Portugal, who received him at his court, and by the sultans of Fez and the sharifs of Marrakesh. David *Reuveni made his acquaintance in Lisbon.

In the 16th century JUDAH and SLIMAN held eminent positions in commerce. A letter is extant from their nephews SAMUEL and his brothers, which mentions the existence of independent Jewish warrior tribes in the western Sahara, a fact which is confirmed in other sources. AARON (16th century) was deputy governor of Agadir (Morocco), where he built a synagogue that received the former Marranos from the Canary Islands. ABRAHAM, who was official interpreter in Mazagan (1527), was evacuated to Arzila when the Portuguese lost their southern Morocco territories (after 1541).

The Benzameros then settled in Fez. Even before 1560 SOLOMON (II) had undertaken official functions, for which he received secretly large sums of money from Jeanne d'Autriche. MOSES (II) converted at the Escorial (the Spanish royal palace), took the name Pablo de Santa-Maria, and became a royal councillor. This caused a great scandal but the family continued to hold a leading position in Moroccan Jewish affairs. ISAAC (II), rabbi and *dayyan*, signed *takkanot* of Fez, when DAVID was *nagid* (1600–05). JOSEPH published *Divrei David* by *David b. Solomon ibn Abi Zimra at Leghorn in 1828, when his own work *Hon Yosef* appeared also. In Safi the family burial vaults, called the "Seven Zamero sons," were until recent years the site of frequent pilgrimages.

Bibliography: I. Loeb, in: REJ, 22 (1891), 104; Baer, Urkunden, 1 pt. 1 (1929), 182, 404; 1 pt. 2 (1936), 127, 162, 384–9; J. Caro Baroja, *Los judíos en la Espãna moderna*, 1 (1962), 80; Suárez Fernández, Documentos, 401; J. M. Toledano, *Ner ha-Ma'arav* (1911), 88–89; J. Ben-Naim, *Malkhei Rabbanan* (1931), 25, 31–32, 72; SIHM, Portugal, 1–5 (1934–53), passim; SIHM, Espagne, 3 (1961), 11–13; Hirschberg, Afrikah, 1 (1965), 319–21; Corcos, in: *Sefunot*, 10 (1966), 57, 59–69. [D.Co.]

BEN ZAQEN, Moroccan family descended from Spanish exiles. SAMUEL BEN ZAQEN (c. 1670–1745) lived in Fez, and studied under R. Judah Uzziel and R. Judah b. Attar. His works include *Peri Eẓ ha-Gan* (2 volumes, 1904), on the Bible and Midrash, *Gefen Poriyyah* (1904), also on the Midrash, and responsa. A part of the family emigrated from Morocco to Gibraltar in 1741, and from there some went to America, where, before 1750, they were well-established merchants in New York. JACOB BEN SAMUEL BEN ZAQEN was a communal leader in Gibraltar between 1834 and 1851. His cousin ISAAC BEN VIDAL BEN ZAQEN sent financial assistance to the Jewish poor in Rabat, Morocco. JOSEPH BEN ZAQEN served as *nagid* and was appointed the Swedish and Norwegian consul in Tetuan c. 1836. LEON BEN ZAQEN (1905–) studied medicine in Paris and became an ophthalmologist. He was much respected by his fellow Jews and had considerable influence with King Mohammed V of Morocco. When Morocco gained independence he was appointed minister of posts (1956–58).

Bibliography: Rosenbloom, Biogr Dict, 12; J. M. Toledano, *Ner ha-Ma'arav* (1911), 76, 144, 188; Samuel b. Zaqen, *Gefen Poriyyah* (1904), introd.; J. Ben-Naim, *Malkhei Rabbanan* (1931), 123a; Miège, Maroc, 2 (1961), 91, 95, 168.

[D.O.]

BEN ZE'EV, JUDAH LEIB (1764–1811), grammarian and lexicographer; the first Jewish scholar to apply Western research methods to the study of Hebrew. Born near Cracow, Ben Ze'ev received a traditional Jewish education, but covertly, on his own, studied Hebrew philology and secular subjects. He belonged to the group of Polish-Jewish writers that published *Ha-Me'assef,* a literary organ in the spirit of the early Haskalah. Later, in 1787, when he moved to Berlin, he was admitted to the circle of Haskalah scholars there. In Berlin, he devoted himself to secular studies but returned to his native city which he was forced to leave when persecuted by Orthodox Jews because of his liberal opinions. He settled in Breslau and worked as a proofreader in a Hebrew publishing house. Later he moved to Vienna where he was employed in the same capacity, in the Hebrew printing establishment of Anton von Schmid.

Ben Ze'ev's versatile literary activities spread over a number of fields: grammar and phonetics, lexicography, Bible exegesis, translations, poetry, parodic works, and the editing of medieval texts. *Talmud Leshon Ivri* (Breslau, 1796), probably his best-known work, is a grammar which served as the main source for the study of Hebrew in Eastern Europe for a hundred years; it was frequently reissued and exerted considerable influence on subsequent grammarians. In it, Ben Ze'ev discusses phonetics (and vocalization); the theory of forms (parts of speech); the noun, the verb, the particles; selected aspects of syntax (particularly the combination of sentences); aspects of literary theory (parallelism, rhyme, and meter); and the theory of *ta'amei ha-mikra* ("biblical accentuation and cantillation"). In his study of phonemes, he followed the line of thought of S. Z. Henau; in the definition of the parts of speech that of M. Mendelssohn; in his description of the noun and the verb the ideas of Elijah *Levita and in his discussion on syntax the foundations of David Kimḥi in *Sefer ha-Mikhlol.* Ben Ze'ev applied the methods used in the study and research of European language grammars; his rules, based on logic, are organized in a manner suitable for instruction. Many of the concepts in his books are original, not to be found in any previous grammatical work: especially, a new terminology in the field of composition and syntax; innovations in syntax; and the study of poetry. His most important achievement is *Oẓar ha-Shorashim* (Vienna, 1807–08), a Hebrew-German and German-Hebrew dictionary which was inspired by the works of David Kimḥi. It is arranged in alphabetical order, e.g., in the German section, verbs with prefixes are listed alphabetically according to the prefixes; the definitions of the terms often include synonyms and examples of usage taken either from the Bible directly or cited in sentences formulated in biblical style; the German terms are written in Hebrew characters. Ben Ze'ev laid the basis for the modern Hebrew terminology in linguistics, translating grammatical terms from German into Hebrew and indicating their German equivalent.

Among his translations is Ecclesiasticus rendered into Hebrew (Breslau, 1798; at a time when the Hebrew text had not yet been discovered). When later parts of the Hebrew text were recovered it was found that Ben Ze'ev's translation in a biblical gnomic style was imbued with the very spirit of the author. *Meliẓah le-Furim,* a collection of ironic prayers and *seliḥot* for Purim (Breslau, 1800), containing also many clever parodies on well-known Jewish texts and poetic writings, mainly in the genre of the fable, is among his literary creative works. Ben Ze'ev lacked a poetic flair and it is in his grammatical studies that he excelled.

Bibliography: Klausner, Sifrut, 1 (1952[2]), 178–90; R. Fahn, *Tekufat ha-Haskalah be-Vinah* (1919), 38–46; G. Bader, *Medinah va-Ḥakhameha* (1934), 44–46; Waxman, Literature, 3 (1960[2]), 125–7.

[M.Z.Ka.]

BENZER, SEYMOUR (1921–), U.S. molecular biologist. Born and educated in New York, Benzer was appointed to the staff of his alma mater, Purdue University, Indiana, in 1945 and became professor of biological sciences from 1958 to 1961 and Stuart Distinguished Professor from 1961. He specialized in work on the gene.

Working with a bacteriophage, Benzer developed techniques for carrying out genetic analysis on a finer scale than had previously been possible. He was able to make detailed maps of the internal structure of the gene. By this method he showed that a gene could be divided into distinct regions, called cistrons, that can function independently of each other.

[N.Lev.]

°BENZINGER, IMMANUEL (1865–1935), German Protestant theologian and Orientalist. Benzinger was born in Stuttgart and served as lecturer in biblical studies at Berlin University from 1898 to 1902. He taught in Jerusalem at various Christian institutes and at the Ezra Society School from 1902 to 1911. Thereafter he was professor of Bible in Toronto, Canada (1912–15), Meadville, Pa. (1915–18), and Riga, Latvia (from 1921 until his death). His principal work, *Hebraeische Archaeologie* (1894, 1927[3]), is a comprehensive reference book of biblical archaeology. His *Buecher der Koenige* (1899) and *Buecher der Chronik* (1901) are commentaries on the books of Kings and Chronicles. His other major works include *Bilderatlas zur Bibelkunde* (1905), *Geschichte Israels bis auf die griechische Zeit* (1904, 1927[3]), and *Jahvist and Elohist in den Koenigsbuechern* (1921). At the outset of his scholarly career, Benzinger followed the *Wellhausen school of biblical criticism, but later became an adherent of the Pan-Babylonian school.

[M.A.-Y.]

BEN-ZION (Weinman; 1897–), U.S. painter known for his unconventional interpretation of biblical themes. Ben-Zion was born in the Ukraine, the son of a cantor, and at one time planned to enter the rabbinate. He wrote poetry plays and fairy tales in Hebrew before turning to art, which he studied in Vienna. In 1920 he settled in America, where he joined "The Group of Ten," which included such progressive artists as Adolph *Gottlieb and Mark *Rothko. The group exhibited together until 1942. In his first drawings, Ben-Zion became preoccupied with line, which dominated all of his work with its use of black. During the

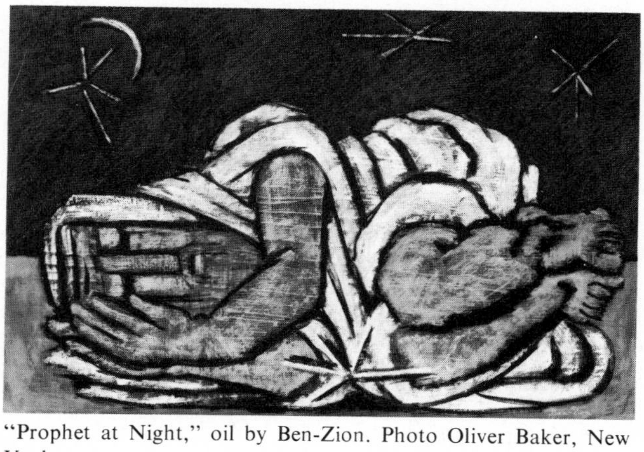

"Prophet at Night," oil by Ben-Zion. Photo Oliver Baker, New York.

depression years of the 1930s he received several commissions from the Works Project Administration and was given his first important exhibition in the Artists' Gallery, New York, in 1936. Over 150 of Ben-Zion's paintings are interpretations of biblical themes, reflecting the education of his early years in a Ukrainian yeshivah. They stress a strong linear structure with a reduced color scheme and limited shadow casting. These qualities lent themselves to the technique of etching in which Ben-Zion executed his main biblical compositions. [S. KAY.]

BEN-ZION, S. (pseudonym of **Simḥah Alter Gutmann;** 1870–1932), Hebrew and Yiddish author. Ben-Zion, who was born in Teleneshty, Bessarabia, settled in Odessa in 1889. He taught there with Bialik, at the modern elementary school, where modern Hebrew was the language of instruction. With Bialik and *Rawnitzki, he founded the publishing house *Moriah and was editor of its juvenile division. The three also collaborated in the writing of Bible stories for children. Ben-Zion published the widely used reader, *Ben Ammi* (3 parts, 1905–11). From 1905 until his death he lived in Palestine, where he edited various journals and miscellanies; *Ha-Omer* (Jaffa, 1907–09); *Moledet* (1911); *Shai* (1918–19), the literary supplement of the weekly *Ḥadashot me-ha-Areẓ; Ha-Ezraḥ* (1919); and, for a short period (1930–31), the weekly *Bustanai.* Ben-Zion was also active in public life and was one of the founders of the Aḥuzzat Bayit suburb, out of which Tel Aviv developed. Ben-Zion's main achievement was as a short story writer. He began as a realist, influenced by *Mendele Mokher Seforim, but his realism had none of Mendele's social satire. The main theme of his early works is the decline of the Bessarabian small Jewish town at the end of the 19th century. The younger generation longed to escape from the poverty and ignorance of their parents, but found themselves unequipped to do so. Their approach to life was blighted by an excessive leaning toward abstraction and they lacked a realistic approach to everyday problems. Ben-Zion's memories of his own childhood and youth occupy a prominent place in these stories. In *Nefesh Reẓuẓah* ("A Crushed Soul," 1952), he denounces the anguish inflicted upon the Jewish child, crushed in the stifling atmosphere of the *ḥeder.* Ben-Zion's emigration to Palestine marked a turning-point in his writing. Sensing that the true essence of Zionism at the time was to be found not in the reality but in the vision, he abandoned his realism for poetic lyricism and visionary symbolism. In this vein, he wrote his prose-poems *Raḥel* and *Leviyyim* which, though artistically imperfect, nevertheless represent a milestone in modern Hebrew literature. Toward the end of his life Ben-Zion wrote two lengthy historical novels, *Megillat Ḥananyah,* set in the period of the Second Temple, and *Ma'aseh ha-Nezirah,* the story of Judith and Holophernes. He also excelled as a translator and rendered several of the classical works of German poetry into Hebrew: Goethe's *Hermann und Dorothea* (1917); Schiller's *Wilhelm Tell* (1924); *Ẓelilim,* a selection of Heine's poems (1923); Heine's *Deutschland, ein Wintermaerchen* (1938), published posthumously. In addition, Ben-Zion wrote monographs on the Biluim and the colonies of Nes Ẓiyyonah and Gederah; edited an anthology entitled *Ha-Kotel ha-Ma'aravi* ("The Western Wall," 1929) and published *Zemirot li-Yladim* ("Songs for Children") with music by Joel *Engel (1923). His collected writings were first published in 1914 (in two volumes), and were later reissued in a single large volume (1949), with a complete bibliography, and illustrations by his son, Naḥum *Gutmann (1949).

Bibliography: I. Klausner, *Yoẓerim u-Vonim,* 2 (1929), 183–99; J. Rawnitzki, *Dor ve-Soferav,* 2 (1937), 106–14. [G.EL.]

BEN ẒIẒIT HA-KASAT (or **ha-Kassaf;** "silversmith"), wealthy and prominent citizen of Jerusalem at the time of the destruction of the Second Temple (Git. 56a; Gen. R. 42:1; Lam. R. 1:5, no. 31). It is related that Ben Ẓiẓit and his associates undertook to provide the needs of the inhabitants of Jerusalem throughout the war with Rome, but the Zealots burned their stores (see also *Ben Kalba Savu'a). Ben Ẓiẓit is possibly the Hebrew equivalent of the Latin *crispus* ("curly-headed").

Bibliography: Graetz, Gesch, 3 pt. 2 (1906[5]), 528; Epstein, in: MGWJ, 63 (1919), 262ff.; Klein, in: *Leshonenu,* 1 (1928/29), 343. [Z.K.]

BEN ZOMA, SIMEON (second century), *tanna.* A contemporary of *Akiva, he appears to have studied under *Joshua b. Hananiah (Ḥag. 15a; Naz. 59b). He was regarded as no more than "a disciple of the sages" (Kid. 49b and Rashi *ibid.*), and as one of those "who discussed before the sages" (Sanh. 17b and Rashi *ibid.*). Nevertheless, he was considered an outstanding scholar, so that it was said that whoever sees Ben Zoma in a dream "may hope for wisdom" (Ber. 57b). The Mishnah says that he was the last of the authoritative biblical expositors (Sot. 9:15). Among the aggadic statements in his name is: "In what labors was Adam involved before he obtained bread to eat? He had to plow, sow, reap, bind the sheaves, thresh and winnow and select the ears of corn; he had to grind them and sift the flour, to knead and bake, and only then could he eat; whereas I get up and find all these things prepared for me. And how much Adam had to labor before he found a garment to wear. He had to shear, wash the wool, comb it, spin and weave it, and only then did he acquire a garment to wear; whereas I get up and find all these things done for me. All kinds of craftsmen come early to the door of my house, and I rise in the morning and find all these things before me" (Ber. 58a). Many of his sayings became proverbs, such as "Who is wise?—he who learns from every man. Who is mighty?—he who subdues his evil inclination. Who is rich?—he who rejoices in his lot. Who is honored?—he who honors his fellow men" (Avot 4:1). He was one of the *tannaim* who occupied themselves with mystical speculation, the *ma'aseh bereshit* ("cosmogony") and the *merkavah* ("divine chariot of Ezekiel"). He was one of the four sages who "entered paradise" (i.e., engaged in mystical studies), and of him it is said that "he cast a look and became demented" (Ḥag. 14b; in TJ, Ḥag. 2:1, 77b: "he cast a look and died"). The Tosefta (Ḥag. 2:5) states that when Ben Zoma told R. Joshua what he had seen in the *ma'aseh bereshit,* the latter exclaimed to his pupils: "Ben Zoma is already without." A few days later Ben Zoma died (cf. TJ, loc. cit.).

Bibliography: Bacher, Tann; Hyman, Toledot, 1172–73; S. Lieberman, *Tosefta ki-Feshutah,* 5 (1962), 1294. [Z.K.]

BEN ZUTA (Ben Zita), ABU AL-SURRĪ (tenth century), Karaite exegete. A number of his explanations of the Scripture are sarcastically dismissed by Abraham *ibn Ezra in his commentary on the Pentateuch (e.g., on Ex. 20:23; 21:35; 22:28) and his *Sefer ha-Ibbur.* In the absence of corroboration from Karaite sources, Ibn Ezra's citations remain a principal source for particulars about Ben Zuta's life. A passage in an anonymous Arabic commentary on Samuel suggests, however, that Ben Zuta lived in Jerusalem and at a somewhat later period than had been conjectured. Judah *ibn Bal'am also mentions Ben Zuta and cites his objection to an interpretation of Anan b. David, the founder of Karaism, to Ezra 18:6.

Bibliography: M. Friedlaender, *Essays on the Writings of Abraham Ibn Ezra,* 4 (1877), 70 (Heb. appendix); J. Israelsohn, in:

REJ, 23 (1891), 132–3; S. Poznański, in: MGWJ, 41 (1897), 203–12; Mann, Texts, index, s.v. *Alī Surri Hakkohen b. Zuta.* [Ed.]

BEN-ZVI, IZHAK (1884–1963), *yishuv* leader, second president of Israel. Ben-Zvi was a founder and leader of Zionist Socialism, of the pioneering Zionist labor movement, and of Jewish self-defense, both in Russia and in Ereẓ Israel. He also made important contributions to the historiography of Ereẓ Israel and of ancient and remote Jewish communities. His personal simplicity, modesty, and empathy for all the communities and sects of the country endeared him to the citizens of Israel.

Ben-Zvi was born in Poltava, Ukraine, the eldest son of Ẓevi Shimshelevich (Shimshi). His father, a member of *Benei Moshe, went to Ereẓ Israel in 1891 to explore possibilities for settlement. Educated in both a traditional and a modernized *ḥeder,* Ben-Zvi later studied at a Russian gymnasium (1901–05). He visited Ereẓ Israel for the first time in 1904 for a period of two months. He entered the University of Kiev in 1905, but studies were interrupted by the general strike that year. During the November pogroms he was active in the Jewish self-defense organization in Poltava. In 1906 he attended the founding conference of *Po'alei Zion-Zionist Social Democrats of Russia, held in Poltava where his childhood friend, Ber *Borochov, proposed the founding program of the party. Ben-Zvi served on the committee of three that formulated the final version of the program and was himself responsible for the points dealing with Palestine.

In June 1906 a search of Ben-Zvi's parents' home by the Russian police revealed a cache of weapons belonging to the self-defense organization that Ben-Zvi headed. His father was sentenced to lifetime exile in Siberia (he eventually settled in Ereẓ Israel after serving 16 years of his sentence). His aunt, his sister, and his brother Aaron *Reuveni were also imprisoned, but Ben-Zvi himself escaped to Vilna where he participated in the clandestine activities of the central committee of Po'alei Zion. He traveled to Germany, Austria, and Switzerland to try to influence Jewish students there. In Vienna he organized the first ties between Po'alei Zion branches in different countries. At the end of 1906 he returned to Vilna, which, after Borochov's imprisonment, had become the center of the movement.

Figure 1. Izhak Ben-Zvi in 1918, as a soldier in the Jewish Legion, with his wife, Raḥel. Jerusalem, Central Zionist Archives.

Figure 2. Izhak Ben-Zvi, bronze by Batya Lishansky, 1954. Lifesize. Photo I. Zafrir, Tel Aviv.

Ben-Zvi settled in Ereẓ Israel at the beginning of 1907. In the same year he was a Po'alei Zion delegate from Ereẓ Israel to the Eighth Zionist Congress held in the Hague. Ben-Zvi participated in the founding of the Bar Giora organization (in Jaffa, 1907), and in 1909 of *Ha-Shomer, along with Raḥel Yanait (*Ben-Zvi), who had settled in Ereẓ Israel in 1908. (They were married in 1918.)

After the second Turkish revolution (1909), Ben-Zvi traveled to Turkey on behalf of Po'alei Zion. He visited Smyrna, Constantinople, and Salonika, as well as Beirut and Damascus, establishing ties with the Jewish communities and with Jewish labor movement leaders. In Salonika he first encountered the remnants of the Shabbatean sect, later to become a subject for his research.

In 1910 Ben-Zvi, together with Raḥel Yanait, Ze'ev Ashur, and others, founded the first Hebrew socialist periodical in Ereẓ Israel, *Aḥdut* ("Unity"), Jerusalem (1910–15). With the outbreak of World War I, Ben-Zvi interrupted his studies at the University of Constantinople and returned to Ereẓ Israel. During the persecution of Jews by Jamal Pasha, the Ottoman governor, *Aḥdut* was closed down, and Ben-Zvi, together with David *Ben-Gurion, was

Figure 3. President and Mrs. Ben-Zvi in Leopoldville during their state visit to the Democratic Republic of the Congo, 1962. Photo Government Press Office, Tel Aviv.

imprisoned. They were both deported, and eventually made their way to New York. There they founded the He-Ḥalutz movement of America (1915), establishing branches in many cities.

Before the British offensive on the Palestine front, Ben-Gurion and Ben-Zvi initiated a volunteer movement for Jewish battalions in the U.S., and were among the first volunteers. They arrived in Egypt in 1918, and from there went to Ereẓ Israel as soldiers of the *Jewish Legion in the British Royal Fusiliers. During the Arab riots in Jerusalem (1920, 1922, 1929), Ben-Zvi was active in the ranks of the *Haganah, while also representing the *yishuv* in negotiations with the authorities.

He was elected to the central committee of the *Aḥdut ha-Avodah Party at its founding convention. During the summer of 1920 he participated in the world conference of Po'alei Zion held in Vienna, in which the movement split under the impact of the Bolshevik revolution in Russia. Ben-Zvi was instrumental in its reorganization on a firm Zionist platform.

In October 1920 Ben-Zvi was appointed by Sir Herbert *Samuel to the Palestine Advisory Council, which had been set up as a substitute for an elected representative body. But with the Jaffa riots of May 1921 and the subsequent suspension of *aliyah,* he resigned from the council in protest against Mandatory government policy.

Ben-Zvi was elected to the secretariat of the *Histadrut at its founding (1920), and, in July 1925, together with Ben-Gurion and Chaim *Arlosoroff, he represented the Histadrut at a conference of British Empire labor. Ben-Zvi devoted a considerable part of his public activity to Jerusalem and its Jewish population. He was first elected to the Jerusalem Municipal Council in 1927, but after the riots of 1929 he resigned from the municipality in protest against the stand of the city's Arab administration. In September 1934 he was reelected to the municipality.

From the beginning of the establishment of the Va'ad Le'ummi (1920), Ben-Zvi was elected to its leadership, first as a member, later as chairman (1931), and finally as president (from 1945). He participated as a delegate in all the Zionist Congresses during the 1920s, and as chairman of the Va'ad Le'ummi he represented the Jewish community of Palestine at the coronation ceremonies of King George VI (1937) as well as at the Round Table Conference on Palestine in London (1939). Ben-Zvi became known as a prolific journalist, and his many articles, published under his own name as well as under various pseudonyms, appeared in a variety of newspapers.

After the establishment of the State of Israel, Ben-Zvi was elected as a *Mapai member to the First (1949) and Second (1951) Knesset. Upon the death of President Chaim *Weizmann, Ben-Zvi was elected president of the state (1952), and in 1957 was returned by the Knesset to that office for five more years. His state visits abroad included Holland and Belgium (1958), Burma (1959), and various African countries (1962). In 1962 he was elected president for a third term. He died in office on April 23, 1963.

Ben-Zvi headed the Institute for the Study of Oriental Jewish Communities in the Middle East, which he founded in 1948 and which was named the Ben-Zvi Institute (1952). His research on the history of the people of Israel, begun in his youth (1904), was to be a lifelong endeavor. The scholarly works that he published were devoted mainly to research on communities and sects (such as the Samaritans, Karaites, Shabbateans, Jewish communities in Asia and Africa, the mountain Jews, and others) and to the geography of Ereẓ Israel, its ancient populations, its antiquities, and its traditions. His brochure *Ha-Yishuv ha-Yehudi bi-Kefar Peki'in* ("The Jewish Yishuv in Peki'in Village," 1922) was the beginning of a series of studies on the Jewish villages in Ereẓ Israel that preceded modern Jewish settlement, most of which were included in his book *She'ar Yishuv* ("The Remnant of the Yishuv," 1927) and in vol. 2 of his writings. His studies of communities were greatly facilitated by his direct contact with the subjects and by their willingness to reveal historical documents previously unpublished. Ben-Zvi's collected surveys on the non-Jewish communities of Israel appear in *Ukhlosei Arẓenu* ("Populations in our Land," 1932), which, together with his book on the Jewish population of Israel, *Ukhloseinu ba-Areẓ* ("Our Population in the Land," 1929), is included in vol. 5 of his writings (1937). His studies on the history of the Samaritans, *Sefer ha-Shomeronim* (1935, and new enlarged edition 1970), is a basic work. Ben-Zvi also published *Masot Ereẓ Israel le-Rav Moshe Basola* ("Journeys of R. Moses Basola in Ereẓ Israel"), based on an original manuscript. This study, he believed, had enabled him to identify the unknown traveller in the *Masot ha-Nose'a ha-Almoni mi-Livorno mi-Shenat Resh Peh Bet* ("Journeys of an Unknown Traveler from Leghorn, from the Year 1521/22"). His book *Niddeḥei Yisrael* was translated into English (*The Exiled and the Redeemed,* 1958 and 1961), Spanish, French, Italian, Swedish, and Yiddish. The most important of his many studies on the history of the *yishuv* is *Ereẓ Yisrael ve-Yishuvah bi-Ymei ha-Shilton ha-Ottomani* ("Ereẓ Israel and Its Yishuv during

Figure 4. President and Mrs. Ben-Zvi welcomed by Premier David Ben-Gurion and Foreign Minister Golda Meir on returning from their tour of Africa, 1962. Photo Government Press Office, Tel Aviv.

the Ottoman Empire," 1955), which is based on Turkish documents and rabbinical responsa of the period. A large part of this work appears in English translation in L. Finkelstein (ed.), *The Jews, their History, Culture and Religion* (1960), pp. 602–88. His book *The Hebrew Battalion Letters* (1969) also appeared in English. A volume of his memoirs, *He-Ḥazon ve-Hagshamato* appeared in 1968. His complete works, including diaries, letters, and articles were republished, starting in 1965, by Yad Izhak Ben-Zvi, a memorial institute founded to perpetuate Ben-Zvi's interests and works.

Bibliography: Yad Izhak Ben-Zvi, *In Memoriam* (1965); R. Ben-Zvi, *Coming Home* (1963); S. Shunami, *Bibliografyah shel I. Ben-Zvi* (1958), with a biography by S. Z. Shazar; Y. Carmel, *I. Ben-Zvi: mi-Tokh Yoman Beit ha-Nasi* (1967).

[Z.SH.]

BEN-ZVI, RAḤEL YANAIT (1886–), labor leader and writer; from 1918, wife of Izhak *Ben-Zvi. Born in Malin, Ukraine, Raḥel Yanait was educated in Russia and in Nancy, France, where she pursued studies in agronomy. After helping to create the *Po'alei Zion labor movement in Russia, she settled in Ereẓ Israel as a teacher in 1908, and was a cofounder of the Hebrew Gymnasium in Jerusalem, the second modern high school in the country. She played a pioneering role in *Ha-Shomer and Tenu'at ha-Po'alot (Women's Labor Movement), and coedited the weekly *Aḥdut*, the first Hebrew organ of the Po'alei Zion movement in Ereẓ-Israel, from its founding in 1910. After World War I, she became a founder of *Aḥdut ha-Avodah labor party and a leader of the *Haganah in Jerusalem, continuing her career as an educationist, and in 1920 established near Jerusalem's Talpiot quarter a girls' agricultural high school of which she was the first principal. In 1948, she was the guiding spirit behind the founding of an agricultural youth village in Ein Kerem. After her husband became president of Israel in 1952, she assisted him in his official duties and worked particularly to make the president's home a popular meeting place for all the communities of Israel. Upon her husband's death in 1963, she became an active member of Yad Ben-Zvi, his memorial institute. Her memoirs have been published: *Anu Olim* (1959; *Coming Home*, 1963) and *Eli* (Heb., 1957), a book written together with her husband about their son, who died in the Israel War of Independence. She also coedited her husband's writings, which began to appear in 1965.

Raḥel Yanait Ben-Zvi (middle row, second from right) with members of the Po'alei Zion, Jerusalem, 1924. Izhak Ben-Zvi is on her right. Jerusalem, Central Zionist Archives.

Bibliography: H. M. Sachar, *Aliyah: The Peoples of Israel* (1961), 115–51.

[G.K.]

BEN-ZVI, ZEEV (1904–1952), Israel sculptor, whose work influenced a generation of sculptors. Ben-Zvi was born in Ryki, Poland and studied at the Warsaw Academy of Art before emigrating to Palestine in 1924. He entered the *Bezalel School in Jerusalem that year and studied under Boris *Schatz. Ben-Zvi specialized in portrait heads in beaten copper and molded plaster, which he treated in a cubist manner. When the New Bezalel School was opened in 1936 Ben-Zvi was appointed teacher of sculpture. On the outbreak of World War II, he executed the first model of "Outcry"—a hand lifted to the heavens. "Outcry" symbolized the horror and rebellion of Jews against the Holocaust in Europe—a subject to which Ben-Zvi frequently returned. In 1947, he executed his moving monument, *In Memory of the Children of the Diaspora*, at Mishmar ha-Emek. From 1947 to 1949 he tried to alleviate the hardships of the illegal immigrants detained by the British government in the Cyprus detention camps by teaching them art. Ben-Zvi's works are to be found in museums and private collections in Israel and Great Britain.

Bibliography: H. Gamzu, *Ben-Zvi, Sculptures* (1955).

[F.S./ED.]

BEOBACHTER AN DER WEICHSEL (Ger., "The Watcher by the Vistula"; Pol. title *Dostrzegacz Nadwislański*), the first Polish Jewish newspaper; published in Congress Poland from 1823 to 1824. Its editor was Anton *Eisenbaum, who approached the authorities for permission to publish a paper to serve the ideals of Enlightenment (see *Haskalah). Permission and financial backing were granted, but only on condition that a translation into Polish would be provided. The first issue of the paper accordingly came out at the end of 1823 with a Polish translation accompanying the Yiddish text (which was in fact German in Hebrew transcription). Some items, calculated to please the authorities, were printed in Polish only. The paper was divided into five sections: official announcements and general news from Poland; foreign news and descriptions of Jewish life in other countries (including descriptions of Jewish agricultural settlement in Kherson province); commercial news; miscellaneous items including biographies of famous Jews such as Josephus, Maimonides, Moses Mendelssohn, and Rothschild; announcements. Official announcements were published without comment or criticism. Discussion of actual problems facing Jewry seems to have been deliberately avoided. Eisenbaum had no assistants and virtually brought out the paper by himself. It was apparently difficult to find suitable candidates since the few Jewish writers who could write in Polish seem to have preferred non-Jewish platforms. The paper appeared for less than a year, from Dec. 3, 1823 to Sept. 29, 1824: altogether only 44 issues, the circulation never exceeding 150. The paper had to close down when the grant it had received from the government was exhausted. It failed to gain increased circulation because the typical advocates of the Enlightenment were not particularly interested in Jewish problems, while the Jewish masses found the quasi-Yiddish incomprehensible. The extreme assimilationist views of the paper and its negative attitude toward Jewish religious traditions made it objectionable to the majority of the Jewish population of Warsaw.

Bibliography: J. Shatzky, *Geshikhte fun Yidn in Varshe*, 1 (1947), 290–1; S. Łastik, *Z dziejów oświęcenia żydowskiego* (1961), 176–8.

[M.LAN.]

BERAB (Beirav), JACOB (c. 1474–1546), halakhic authority and leader of the Jewish communities of Palestine, Egypt, and Syria during the first half of the 16th century. Berab was born in Maqueda near Toledo, Spain, and went to Morocco after the expulsion of Jews from Spain in 1492. According to his own statement, he was only 18 years old when he was appointed rabbi of Fez. A few years later Berab left Fez and traveled to Egypt, Palestine (Jerusalem, Safed), and Syria (Aleppo, Damascus) in connection with business concerns, which proved very successful. During these sojourns Berab also taught Torah, gathering wide circles of pupils, who respected him greatly. He considered himself superior to the majority of scholars in Egypt, Palestine, and Syria, and tried to impose his authority on questions of *halakhah* that were brought before him, or that he undertook on his own initiative. Although Berab had close associations with many of his contemporaries, his domineering tendency brought him into conflict with scholars who would not submit to him.

Berab was swept along with the messianic current of the early 16th century, which resulted in large measure from intensive study of the Kabbalah. Berab himself gave some impetus to messianic anticipation by trying to revive the institution of **semikhah* ("rabbinical ordination"). According to Maimonides (Yad, Sanhedrin 1:3), the establishment of a "great *bet din*" will take place before the coming of the messiah. Since an institution competent to give *semikhah* had not existed for several hundred years, Maimonides provided instructions for its establishment. He authorized the rabbis of Ereẓ Israel to nominate one among them who would be the first *samukh* (ordained rabbi). In turn, that rabbi would have the authority to ordain others, who could then form a Sanhedrin (Yad, Sanhedrin 4:11). The Spanish expulsion and the ingathering of many Jews in Ereẓ Israel was interpreted as a sign that redemption was imminent.

Berab, while still in Egypt, conceived the idea of renewing *semikhah.* As the Palestinian settlement became stronger and the number of scholars increased, Safed became the seat of the messianic impetus. In 1538 Berab, who had been living in Safed periodically from at least 1524, succeeded in winning over the scholars there, including R. Joseph *Caro and R. Moses of *Trani, to his point of view. The scholars of Safed decided to renew the *semikhah* and they designated Berab as the first *samukh.* Immediately after this decision was taken, a messenger was sent to R. *Levi b. Ḥabib in Jerusalem, asking him to give his consent to the renewal of the *semikhah* and to accept the ordination of Berab. Not only did Levi b. Ḥabib, with whom Berab had had various disputes, refuse to accept the *semikhah* of Berab, but he also opposed the decision of the rabbis of Safed on halakhic grounds. He also insisted that Maimonides' statement concerning the reestablishment of *semikhah* did not represent a decision but only an opinion, and that Maimonides had retracted it later (Yad, Sanhedrin 4:2). The protests of Levi b. Ḥabib delayed Berab's project. Discussions on the question of *semikhah* among the rabbis of both towns had been in progress for three months when Berab was forced by the Turks to leave Palestine. Apparently, he had become embroiled in a private affair, as a result of which his enemies denounced him to the Turkish authorities in Safed.

According to *halakhah, semikhah* could not be given outside Palestine. Berab feared that he might not be able to return and that all his plans would come to an end. Before he left, therefore, he gave *semikhah* to four rabbis of Safed, among whom were Joseph Caro and Moses of Trani. Levi b. Ḥabib, considering this to be a disregard of his protests, then publicly opposed the *semikhah.* From Damascus Berab conducted the discussion of the question in a vigorous manner, even by personal attacks on his adversary. Levi b. Ḥabib replied in kind and he was supported by an important ally—R. *David b. Solomon ibn Abi Zimra, who lived in Egypt. Thus, the project of establishing the "great *bet din*" came to an end; even the validity of the *semikhot* already given was in doubt. Nevertheless, those who had been ordained by Berab ordained other scholars after his death.

Berab wrote a commentary to all those parts of Maimonides' work not dealt with in the *Maggid Mishneh* commentary by *Vidal Yom Tov of Tolosa. However, only a small part was published (by Y. L. Maimon (Fishman) in *Sinai,* 36 (1955), 275–357). His responsa and his novellae to tractate *Kiddushin* were published together (1663). These novellae were republished from a manuscript in an enlarged form by Michael Rabinowitz (in Y. L. Fishman (eds.), *Sefer ha-Yovel . . . B. M. Levin* (1939), 196–299). Many of his halakhic decisions are reported in the works of his contemporaries, especially Joseph Caro.

Berab's grandson, Jacob Ben Abraham (d. 1599), rabbi and halakhic authority, studied under Joseph Caro and was ordained by him. From 1563 he is mentioned in documents with the more important rabbis of Safed. By 1593 he was the most prominent of Safed's scholars and it was he who gave *semikhah.* He ordained R. Moses Galante, R. Eliezer Azikri, his own brother R. Moses Berab, R. Abraham Gabriel, R. Yom Tov Ẓahalon, R. Ḥiyya ha-Rofe, and R. Jacob Abulafia, all of Safed. In 1599 these seven rabbis reached an agreement not to ordain any other person without his approval. None of his writings remains, but his approvals of the decisions of his contemporaries, as well as some of his responsa scattered in the works of contemporary scholars, are known.

Bibliography: J. Newman, *Semikhah* (Eng., 1950), includes bibliography; Graetz, Hist, 6 (1949), index, s.v. *Jacob Berav,* Gruenhut, in: *Ha-Ẓofeh me-Ereẓ Hagar,* 2 (1912), 25–33; Katz, in: *Zion,* 16 nos. 3–4 (1951), 28–45; Benayahu, in: *Sefer Yovel . . . Y. Baer* (1960), 248–69; Dimitrovsky, in: *Sefunot,* 6 (1962), 117–23; 7 (1963), 41–102; 10 (1966), 113–92; *Teshuvot RaLBaḤ* (Venice, 1565), including a report of the controversy at the end.

[Ed.]

BERAB (Beirav), JACOB BEN ḤAYYIM (end of 17th–18th century), poet and hymnologist. A descendant of R. Jacob *Berab, Berab was born in Safed. He left Palestine with his father-in-law R. Ḥayyim b. Moses *Abulafia before 1710 and settled in Smyrna (Izmir), Turkey. In 1740 they returned to Palestine and helped found the new Jewish settlement at Tiberias. Berab recorded all the events of the journey to Tiberias and their subsequent settlement in *Zimrat ha-Areẓ* (Mantua, 1745, etc). He also noted interesting details of the wars between the governor of Damascus, Soliman Pasha (1741–43), and the sheikh of Galilee, Dahr al ʿAmr. The purpose of his work was to call to the attention of the Diaspora the importance of the resettlement in Tiberias. Appended to the published editions were 12 of his poems in Hebrew and Ladino praising the resettlement and Tiberias. Some of these poems were, until recently, sung to a special folk tune in the Balkan countries.

Bibliography: J. b. Ḥ. Berab, *Zimrat ha-Areẓ,* ed. by M. Benayahu (1946), introduction; Shalem, in: *Hed ha-Mizraḥ,* 2 no. 9 (1943), 9; Baron, in: *Sefer ha-Yovel . . . A. Marx* (1943), 79; Ben Zvi, Ereẓ Yisrael, 308–11.

[A.D.]

BERAḤ DODI (Heb. בְּרַח דּוֹדִי; "make haste my beloved," Song 8:14), *ge'ullah piyyut* in the morning prayer of the first day of Passover in the Ashkenazi rite. It consists of three stanzas based upon the allegorical interpretation of the central motif of *Song of Songs according to which "the beloved" is the people of Israel and the "lover" is God. Israel implores the "lover" to hasten his return to his "beloved." It made use, at the end of each stanza, of the text of Song of Songs: "Behold he standeth behind our wall" (2:9); "Hark! my beloved! behold, he cometh" (2:8); "This is my beloved, and this is my friend" (5:16). On the basis of the initials interwoven in this *piyyut* (שלמה יגדל בתורה חזק), the authorship has been ascribed to the tenth-century liturgical poet Solomon b. Judah ha-Bavli. Another *ge'ullah piyyut* in the morning prayer of the second day of Passover recited outside Ereẓ Israel (Ashkenazi rite), and composed by *Meshullam b. Kalonymus (c. 1000 C.E.), bears the same name. This *piyyut* of four stanzas is based upon the same motif as the aforementioned one. A third *piyyut* by the same name is recited on the Sabbath during the Intermediate Days of Passover. This was composed by Simeon b. Isaac, who also lived in the tenth century.

Bibliography: *Service of the Synagogue,* tr. by I. Zangwill (London, 1954), 202.

[Ed.]

BERAKHAH, ISAAC (d. 1772), rabbi and preacher in the Aleppo community. The support and encouragement of Elijah Silbirah enabled Berakhah to pursue his studies until he became a noted scholar. His *Berakh Yiẓḥak* (Venice, 1763), a book of homiletics, contains several sermons for each weekly Reading of the Law; they deal mostly with halakhic problems. He often mentions Maimonides' *Yad ha-Ḥazakah,* Samuel Eliezer *Edels, the *tosafot,* and the responsa of *Isaac b. Sheshet. In addition to halakhic problems, he deals with such questions as the *kavvanah* and joy with which one should perform the *mitzvot.* Some of Berakhah's responsa were published in S. R. Laniado's *Beit Dino shel Shelomo* (Constantinople, 1775). Abraham Antibi, one of his many pupils, eulogized him at his death. Berakhah's sons Ḥayyim and Elijah were also rabbis in Aleppo.

Bibliography: Steinschneider, Cat Bod, 1096 no. 5321; D. Laniado, *Li-Kedoshim Asher ba-Areẓ* (= Aram-Zobah, i.e., Aleppo; 1952), 37.

[Ed.]

BERAKHOT (Heb. בְּרָכוֹת; "Benedictions"), talmudic tractate. *Berakhot* is the first tractate of the *Talmud. In its first three chapters, *Berakhot* elaborates on the component parts of the **Shema,* i.e., Deuteronomy 6:4–9, 11:13–21, and Numbers 15:37–41. *Berakhot* also discusses the implications of passages which allude to the recital of prayers and suggests that prayers should be recited three times daily (Ps. 55:18, and more explicitly Dan. 6:11). Prayer in the context of this tractate refers specifically to the **Amidah (Shemoneh Esreh),* and the subject is discussed in chapters 4 and 5. Benedictions over food, especially the *Grace after Meals (Deut. 8:10), are discussed in chapters 6–8. Scriptural "hints" apart, benedictions in general (and especially those treated in chapter 9) are attributed to post-biblical *takkanot* ("regulations"; see *Liturgy). More specifically, the contents of the nine chapters of the Mishnah tractate *Berakhot* are as follows:

Chapter 1: the time for the recital of the *Shema* in the evening and the morning; the controversy between *Bet Hillel and Bet Shammai as to the position of the body (standing, reclining, sitting, etc.) during the recital; the benedictions before and after the *Shema.*

Chapter 2: *kavvanah* ("proper inner intention") in the recital of the *Shema;* whether reading silently can be considered recital; whether incorrect pronunciation or other mistakes invalidate the recital; permission for laborers to say the *Shema* while at work; a newlywed's dispensation from the *Shema,* because of his inability to recite it with *kavvanah.*

Chapter 3: mourners' exemption from the *Shema* and from the *Amidah;* non-obligation of women, slaves, and

Illustration of the tractate *Berakhot* (Benedictions), the first tractate of the Talmud. Detail from a title page of a Hebrew and Latin edition of the Mishnah, Amsterdam, 1700–1704. Jerusalem, J.N.U.L.

minors from the *Shema* (but not from the *Amidah*); the obligation of a person in a state of ritual uncleanness to recite the *Shema, Amidah,* and other benedictions.

Chapter 4: the time to recite the *Amidah,* in the morning, afternoon, and evening; the summary *Amidah* and its wording; praying with devotion; reciting the *Amidah* while riding or driving; stress on the *Amidah* of the Additional Service *(Musaf).*

Chapter 5: *kavvanah* in the *Amidah* and the prohibition to make interruptions; insertion of specific supplications (e.g., for rain) in the *Amidah;* procedure when the reader makes a mistake in reciting the *Amidah.*

Chapter 6: benedictions over various kinds of food.

Chapter 7: Grace after more males have dined together *(zimmun).*

Chapter 8: differences between Bet Hillel and Bet Shammai time regulations, especially as to the order of the various benedictions; *Kiddush* and *Havdalah* are also discussed.

Chapter 9: benedictions for a variety of occasions, e.g., on the occasion of earthquakes and storms, over good and evil things ("But to cry over the past is to utter a vain prayer"). In conclusion, various additional instructions are given: to ensure respect to the Temple mount and to the name of God in personal salutations ("The Lord be with you"); to resist heresy by stressing belief in the world-to-come.

The Babylonian *Gemara* elaborates on and supplements the mishnaic *halakhah,* but the aggadic digressions are much more extensive here than in any other tractate. Interesting details are given about the dietary customs and table manners of the Persians (8b), of the Babylonian Jews (chap. 6), and of the Palestinian Jews (chap. 8), the latter showing similarities with those of the Romans. The controversy between R. Joshua and the Patriarch Rabban *Gamaliel, which led to the latter's temporary removal from office, is also recorded here (27b–28a). Chapter 9 deals largely with interpretation of *dreams. On the disproportionate *aggadah, tosafot* comments are few and short, and *Berakhot* appears in the current printed editions of the Babylonian Talmud as a medium-sized tractate (64 folios) despite the fact that its *Gemara* text is one of the largest.

There is also a Palestinian Gemara and a Tosefta (the latter divided into seven chapters). *Berakhot* appears at the beginning of order **Zera'im* ("seeds"). Since the subject of benedictions is unrelated to agricultural laws, the reasons for linking *Berakhot* with *Zera'im* have been widely discussed by talmudic scholars, medieval and modern (see Ch. Albeck, *Mishnah, "Seder Zera'im,"* 1–3). In the sequence of the mishnaic orders, *Zera'im* was not always seen as the first, neither was tractate *Berakhot* always linked with *Zera'im* (e.g., in the Ms. Munich). What is significant is that it emerged as the opening tractate in all standard editions of the Mishnah, Tosefta, and Talmud. As the subject of *Berakhot* is Divine worship (starting with the *Shema,* which proclaims the belief in one God), it is logical that this tractate should serve as the prelude to the Talmud. An English translation of the Mishnah was made by H. Danby (1933) and of the Talmud by M. Simon in the Soncino edition (1948), and the first part of the Talmud appeared with English commentary in the El Am edition of A. Z. Ehrman.

Bibliography: L. A. Rosenthal, *Mischna, Aufbau und Quellenscheidung* (1906–09), pt. 1, *Die Ordnung Seraim;* H. Strack, *Introduction to Talmud . . .* (1945), 29–34; P. Blackman, *Mishnayot,* 1 (Eng., 1951), 23.

[A.Z.E.]

BERBERS, indigenous North Africa tribes who originally spoke dialects of the Berber language. Medieval Arab writers ascribed the ancestry of the Berbers to *Goliath the Philistine and maintained their Canaanite origin. The Phoenician colonization of Africa, the long Carthaginian domination, and the survival of Punic, a language closely related to Hebrew, supported these legends which spread among the Berbers themselves. Similar tales are found in the writings of Greek and Latin authors and in the Talmud which spread the legend that the Canaanites emigrated of their own free will to North Africa. It is said that the survivors of the Jewish revolt in *Cyrenaica (115–116 C.E.) found refuge among the Berbers of Western Libya. Scholars have frequently claimed that the Jews' desire to proselytize found a favorable atmosphere among the Berbers from the first to the seventh centuries. African Christianity, whose early converts were Jews, clashed with Jewish proselytism. Archaeological discoveries, epigraphs, and writings of the Christian scholars Tertullian and St. Augustine, indignant at the growing Berber conversions to Judaism, attest to these facts. The persecutions by the Byzantines forced Jews to settle among the Berbers in the mountain and desert regions. Ibn Khaldun confirmed the existence of a large number of proselyte Berbers at the time of the Arab conquest of Africa. The Islamization of

Figure 1. Berber Jewish women of Talouet, in the High Atlas, dancing the *haouach.* Jerusalem, Israel Museum Photo Collection, Department of Ethnography. Photo Shulman.

Figure 2. Jewish Berbers from Tikrit, in the Siroua region of Morocco, wearing the black goatskin *akhnif.* Jerusalem, Israel Museum Photo Collection, Department of Ethnography. Photo Besencenet.

these countries, however, did not abolish all previous beliefs. Christianity was abandoned rapidly; Judaism continued to exist and from Tripolitania to *Morocco, modern ethnographers and anthropologists encountered small groups whom they called "Jewish Berbers." These isolated groups of Jews lived in the high mountains of North Africa until the last few decades. Some scholars designated them as the descendants of Berber proselytes. In most cases they eventually intermingled with the rest of the population. However, the survival of such groups to the present is now doubted.

Bibliography: H. Fournel, *Les Berbères* (1875), 32–41; S. Gsell, *Histoire ancienne de l'Afrique du Nord,* 1 (1920), 236–343; E. F. Gauthier, *Le passé de l'Afrique du Nord* (1942), 140ff., 225–44, 270ff., 439; Simon, in: *Revue d'histoire et de philosophie religieuses* 26 (1946), 1–31, 105–45; M. Simon, *Verus Israel* (Eng. 1948), index; Hirschberg, in *Zion,* 22 (1957), 10–20; idem, in: *Journal of African History,* 4 (1963), 313–39; Hirschberg, Afrikah, 2 (1965), 9–36; N. Slouschz, *Hébraeo-Phéniciens et Judéo-Berbères* (1908); idem, *Travels in North Africa* (1927), 453–88, passim; A. N. Chouraqui, *Between East and West* (1968).

[D.Co.]

BERCOVITCH, PETER (1879–1942), Canadian legislator. Born in Montreal, Bercovitch entered practice as an advocate in 1901. In 1911 he was appointed king's counsel and in 1916 he was elected as a Liberal to the first of seven consecutive terms in the Quebec Assembly, thus becoming the first Jew to be seated in that body. There he introduced measures for the improvement of the conditions of the poor and in 1923 was largely responsible for defeating a bill designed to deprive Quebec's Jews of equal public school rights, against which he argued before the Privy Council in London. A strong champion of Jewish rights in the Quebec school system, he opposed separate schools for Jews. He was responsible for the authority given rabbis in Quebec to keep marriage registers. He resigned to be elected to the House of Commons of the Dominion Parliament by popular acclaim. Highly active in Jewish life as well, he was

Peter Bercovitch, Canadian legislator.

the first president of the Jewish Immigrant Aid Society and honorary vice-president of the Canadian Jewish Congress.

[Ed.]

BERDICHEV, town in the historic region of Volhynia, now in Zhitomir oblast, Ukrainian S.S.R. Apart from two single references to individual Jews from Berdichev in 1593 and 1602, there is no evidence that a Jewish community existed in Berdichev before 1721. In 1732, the owner of the town granted a charter to the Jewish guild of tailors freeing them from interference by the communal authorities *(kahal).* The Jewish population gradually increased with Berdichev's development as a fair town from 1765. According to the census of 1765, the Jews in Berdichev numbered 1,220 (out of a total population of 1,541) including Jews living in the vicinity; they numbered 1,951 in 1789 (out of 2,460). In 1794, Prince Radziwill, the owner of the town, deprived the rabbis of their right of civil jurisdiction, which was transferred to a court to be elected by majority Jewish vote. Berdichev had become an important center of Volhynian *Ḥasidism in the last quarter of the 18th century, and the Ḥasidim were thus able to secure the election of *dayyanim* so as to free themselves from the jurisdiction of the *kahal* and its *Mitnaggedim* rabbis. As the town grew, a number of noted scholars served as rabbis of Berdichev, including Lieber "the Great," Joseph "the Ḥarif," and, from the end of the 18th century until his death in 1809, *Levi Isaac of Berdichev.

In 1797, Prince Radziwill granted seven Jewish cloth merchants the monopoly of the cloth trade in Berdichev, and in the first half of the 19th century the town's commerce was concentrated in Jewish hands. Jews founded scores of trading companies and banking establishments there, with agencies in the Russian interior and even abroad. Jews also served as agents of the neighboring estates of the nobility, whose agricultural produce was sold at the Berdichev fairs. The expatriation of Polish nobles and decline of the Polish nobility after the uprising of 1863 dealt a blow to Jewish commerce in Berdichev. The economic position of most of the Berdichev Jews was further impaired by the restrictions imposed on Jewish settlement in the villages by the "Temporary Regulations" (*May Laws) of 1882 and other government restrictive measures.

The main increase in the Jewish population of Berdichev occurred in the first half of the 19th century. There were 23,160 Jews living in Berdichev in 1847, and 46,683 in 1861. It was then the second-largest Jewish community in Russia. Shortly afterward the numbers began to decline, and in 1897 Berdichev had 41,617 Jewish residents (80% of the total population). The 1926 census shows 30,812 Jewish residents (55.6% of the total); about the same number were probably living there in 1939. Until World War I, emigration was balanced by the natural increase in the Jewish population; after the 1917 Revolution the proportion of Jewish residents steadily decreased through emigration.

At the end of the 19th century, about half of the Jewish wage earners were employed in manual trades, mostly in tailoring, shoemaking, carpentry, metalwork, etc. About 2,000 were hired workers, while the remainder gained their livelihood from trade. Berdichev became one of the foremost centers of the *Bund. After the 1917 Revolution, the proportion of hired workers increased, while a considerable number of Jews were absorbed by the state administration.

The ideas of Enlightenment (*Haskalah) began to spread in Berdichev early in the 19th century, especially among the wealthier families. The Galician Haskalah pioneer and Hebrew author Tobias *Feder Gutmann settled in Berdichev toward the end of his life. Influenced by Isaac Baer *Levinsohn a group of *maskilim* was formed there in the 1820s, in which the physician Israel Rothenberg was to be particularly active. Among the opponents of the *maskilim* was the banker Jacob Joseph Halpern, who had great influence in ḥasidic circles and was close to the government. The first public school in Berdichev giving instruction in Russian was opened in 1850. With the economic decline of Berdichev, the wealthier *maskilim* left for the larger cities. Because of the poverty of the majority of the Jewish population a large number of children were even unable to attend *ḥeder.* According to the 1897 census, only 58% of Jewish males and 32% of Jewish females were able to read or write any language.

In Russian and Jewish literature and folklore, Berdichev epitomizes the typical Jewish town. It had some 80 synagogues and *battei midrash* and its cantors were celebrated throughout the Ukraine. It serves as the model for the town depicted in the writings of *Mendele Mokher Seforim and *Shalom Aleichem *(Gants Berdichev),* as well as in *Der Nister *(Mishpokhe Mashber).* During the 1917 Revolution and the civil war of 1917–19 the head of the community and mayor of the town was the Bundist leader D. Lipets. In early 1919, the Jews in Berdichev became victims of a pogrom perpetrated by the Ukrainian army.

Under the Soviet government, most of the synagogues were closed. Yiddish continued to receive official acknowledgment and Yiddish schools were opened in Berdichev. In 1924, a government law court was established there, the first in the Ukraine to conduct its affairs in Yiddish. According to the 1926 census, of the 30,812 Jews in Berdichev 28,584 declared Yiddish as their mother-tongue. However, by the early 1930s, complaints were heard about curtailment of the use of Yiddish in government offices in Berdichev. A

A Jewish house in Berdichev, photographed in 1967.

Yiddish periodical *Der Arbeter* appeared in Berdichev about twice weekly until the middle of the 1930s. All Jewish cultural activities there were suspended before World War II.

The Nazis established an extermination unit in Berdichev early in July 1941. Immediately afterward wholesale massacres began, and a ghetto was set up in the city. It was liquidated on Oct. 5, 1941, after all the inhabitants were murdered. One report states that there were about 6,000 Jews in Berdichev after the war (March 1946).

Although *mazzah* baking was prohibited in the early 1960s, it was resumed after a few years. In 1970, there were an estimated 15,000 Jews in Berdichev with a synagogue, a cantor, and a ritual poultry slaughterer. The cemetery was reported to be neglected but the Jews had erected a fence around the grave of Levi Isaac of Berdichev. [S.Ett.]

Hebrew Printing in Berdichev. In 1807 Samuel C. Isachar Ber, who had printing presses in several towns, set up a press in Berdichev, initially as a branch of his Ostraha house. Samuel and, after 1817, his son Jacob Funkelmann, operated there until 1820, when the business was transferred to Szdelkow. Altogether they printed over 30 works on Ḥasidism, Kabbalah, and *halakhah* in addition to prayer books and popular books in Yiddish. Another printing house was established by Israel *Bak in 1815–21. Before his emigration to Ereẓ Israel in 1831 he produced 26 works on roughly the same subjects, most of them set in a new typeface designed and cut by Bak himself, with his own illustrations. Other Berdichev printers were M. H. Rothenberg (1834–36) and H. J. Sheftel (1885–1910); the latter published a great number of scholarly works, including a popular edition of the Babylonian Talmud (with Rashi) in one volume (1894). [A.Ya.]

Bibliography: Horodezky, in: *Ha-Me'assef* (1902), 106–9; A. Zederbaum, *Di Gehaymnise fun Berdichev* (1870); M. Morgulis, in: *Voskhod,* 15 no. 4 (1895), 21–35; Lestschinsky, in: *Blaetter fuer demographische Statistik und Wirtschaftskunde der Juden,* 2 (1923), 37–48; M. Osherowitch, *Shtet un shtetlekh in Ukraine,* 1 (1948), 92–104; *Yalkut Volin,* 2 (1951), 12–13; Yaari, in: KS, 10 (1934/35), 100ff., 296f.; H. D. Friedberg, *Toledot ha-Defus ha-Ivri be-Polanyah* (1950²), 133ff.

BERDUGO, family name of many distinguished rabbis in Morocco, chiefly in Meknès. According to tradition, the family was of Davidic descent through the exilarch *Bustanai. Yaḥya (or Ḥiyya) Berdugo (d. 1617) endorsed an ordinance in Fez in 1605, later left for Tetuan and was nominated deputy rabbi there in 1614. A Yaḥya Berdugo was known in Meknès about the same time but it is not certain whether they are identical or not. Moses ben Abraham, called "Mashbir" (c. 1679–1730), was head of the rabbinical court in Meknès, where the Berdugos settled after leaving Fez. Famous for his sense of justice (compilation *Or ha-Ḥayyim* to Deut. 1:15), he was the author of *Rosh Mashbir,* novellae on the Pentateuch and on some of the Talmud tractates (1840); *Kenaf Renanim I,* commentaries and novellae to the Bible (1909), and *Kenaf Renanim II,* an anthology of homilies (1932); and *Divrei Moshe,* responsa (1947). Other unpublished writings are at the National Library, Jerusalem (Ms. Heb. 8° 1446), Ben-Zvi Institute, Jerusalem (Ms. 736), and in private possession. Judah ben Joseph I (1690–1744), *dayyan* in Meknès (1730) following Moses b. Abraham Berdugo the Mashbir, was the author of *Mayim Amukkim,* a commentary on the Pentateuch and *haftarot* (1937). Some of his responsa have been published in the responsa of Jacob ibn Ẓur. Mordecai ben Joseph, "Ha-Marbiẓ" (1715–1762), brother of Judah, was the grandnephew, pupil, and son-in-law of Moses b. Abraham, and a noted *dayyan* (after 1748) in Meknès. He wrote many works, of which, however, only *Mordekhai* has been published (1948); others are still extant in manuscript. Raphael (1747–1821), son of this Mordecai, *dayyan* and scholar, was the author of the following works: *Mishpatim Yesharim,* responsa (2 vols., 1891), *Torot Emet,* commentary on the Shulḥan Arukh (1939); bound with the latter are *Kiẓẓur ha-Takkanot* and *Minhagei Terefot;* and *Mei Menuḥot,* a commentary on the Pentateuch (2 vols., 1900–42). Other works are still in manuscript, including translations of the Bible from Genesis to the end of Isaiah into Arabic, under the title *Leshon Limmudim.* Maimon "the Mevin" (1767–1824), son of Raphael, was a *dayyan* and the author of responsa and other works, including *Lev Mevin* and *Penei Mevin* (issued together 1951). His novellae to the Talmud are in manuscript.

Pethahiah Mordecai ben Jekuthiel (1764–1820) was the author of *Nofet Ẓufim,* responsa (1938), and *Pittuḥei Ḥotam,* a commentary on the Talmud (unpublished). Jacob (1783–1843), his brother, *dayyan* and poet, was known for his stand against the rabbis of Tiberias in favor of the Jerusalem rabbis in the controversy of 1836 over participation in the *ḥalukkah.* His works include *Shufrei de-Ya'akov,* responsa (1910); *Gallei Amikta,* a commentary on *Mayim Amukkim* of Judah Berdugo (1911); *Kol Ya'akov,* liturgical poems (1844). *To'afot Re'em* or *Karnei Re'em,* on Rashi and Elijah *Mizraḥi, is still in manuscript (Ms. Jerusalem National Library, Ms. Heb. 8° 3839, and 1448). Joseph (1802–1854), *dayyan* in Meknès, was a scholar whose works include a lexicon of Hebrew grammatical roots and their derivatives, *Ketonet Yosef* (3 vols. 1922–43). Other works are unpublished. Jacob ben Mordecai (d. 1901), brother of Joseph, was an *av bet din* in Meknès. Solomon ben Daniel (1854–1906), halakhic authority and poet, was a rabbi in Meknès and in 1897 was appointed rabbi of the community. He was the author of *Dei Hashev, Em le-Masoret,* responsa, a collection of laws and Torah novellae; appended are *Musar Haskel* and *Shirei Shelomo* (1950). Jekuthiel Ḥayyim ben Elisha (1858–1940), great-grandson of Mordecai b. Joseph, was born in Rabat, and appointed *dayyan* there in 1893. The French government appointed him in 1922 a member of the supreme *bet din* (court of appeal) which had its seat in Rabat, the capital of Morocco. In 1934 he deputized for Raphael *Ankawa, chief rabbi of Morocco, during his illness, and he succeeded him after his death. In 1935 he was made president of the Supreme *bet din.* Joshua ben Jacob (1878–1953) became chief rabbi of Meknès in 1904 and in 1941 chief rabbi of Morocco, where he served until his death. He had a strong personality and on a number of occasions was in conflict with the leaders of the Church and with members of the French government, by whom he was respected. The communal rules and regulations adopted during this time were published in the pamphlets of "The Council of Moroccan Rabbis" (Casablanca). None of his books was published.

Bibliography: J. M. Toledano, *Ner ha-Ma'arav* (1911), index; idem, *Oẓar Genazim* (1960), 167; J. Ben-Naim, *Malkhei Rabbanan* (1931), passim; Yaari, Sheluḥei, index; M. Benayahu, in: *Minḥah le-Avraham Elmaleh* (1959), 35. See also introductions to published works of members of the family. [D.O./Ed.]

BERDYCZEWSKI (later: **Bin-Gorion**), **MICHA JOSEF** (1865–1921), Hebrew writer and thinker. Born in Medzibezh, Podolia, Berdyczewski was the descendant of a line of ḥasidic rabbis. His father served as the rabbi of Medzibezh during Berdyczewski's childhood. Berdyczewski began to read Haskalah writers in his adolescence and the ensuing struggle between modern ideas and the concepts and forces of traditional Judaism was to animate his writings throughout his life. His first marriage (1883–85) ended when his father-in-law would not tolerate his preoccupation with modern Hebrew books. Shortly thereafter he moved to the yeshivah of Volozhin to study for over a year. Here he began his literary career and incurred the wrath of his teachers with his writings.

His first article was *"Toledot Yeshivat Ez Ḥayyim"* (in *Ha-Asif*, 1887) and his first story *"Heziz ve-Nifga"* (in *Ha-Meliz*, 1888). Most of his publications in this period were polemical articles, some popular and some scholarly, which contain many of the ideas he developed later. He often expressed his views in lyrical outbursts rather than in connected logical statements—a style which marked much of his writing throughout his life.

Berdyczewski left Russia for Germany (1890) and stayed two years in Breslau, studying at the rabbinical seminary and the university. He met frequently with David *Frischmann who strove to expand Berdyczewski's intellectual horizons and cultivate his literary taste. In 1892 he moved to Berlin and combined both Jewish and secular studies but continued the lonely existence of the poor, foreign university student. In Germany Berdyczewski's chaotic, revolutionary ideas were given shape under the impact of his studies in philosophy. The influence of Schopenhauer can be noticed in his famous article *"Reshut ha-Yaḥid Be'ad ha-Rabbim"* ("The Individual and the Community," in *Ozar ha-Sifrut*, 1892), in which he defended the claims of individual freedom and creativity against the stultifying demands of such abstractions as tradition, religion, public consensus and will, history, and ideology. Here and in other articles, Berdyczewski attacked the limited scope of much of Hebrew literature, the inadequacies of Haskalah, Aḥad Ha-Amism, and Ḥibbat Zion. After two years of studies in Berne, Berdyczewski returned to spend four years (1896–1900) in Berlin, one of the most productive periods in his life. Stimulated by his opposition to both *Aḥad Ha-Am and *Herzl, and

Micha Josef Berdyczewski, Hebrew writer. Engraving by M. Aryeh.

encouraged by his friends and other Hebrew writers there, Berdyczewski published in many of the leading Hebrew journals, vigorously attacking all accepted ideological positions and calling for a "transvaluation"—in the Nietzschean sense—of Judaism and Jewish history, and the expansion of the canons of Hebrew literary taste. His impulsive tone won him the admiration of the young and the scorn of the older, more conservative readers, mostly the admirers of Aḥad Ha-Am. The famous Aḥad Ha-Am versus Berdyczewski debate appeared in *Ha-Shilo'aḥ* (1897). In 1900 Berdyczewski firmly established himself in the history of Hebrew literature with the publication of nine volumes of articles and stories.

The year 1900 was also significant in Berdyczewski's personal life; he married Rachel Romberg, a dentist. During the next 20 years she assisted him in his literary and scholarly work and together with their son Immanuel Bin-Gorion continued to edit his writings after his death. With his bride he returned home for a brief visit to the Russian Pale of Settlement for the first time in ten years. The renewed confrontation with the harsh realities of Jewish life in the Pale both modified his stridency and rekindled his interest in the narrative possibilities afforded by this rapidly disintegrating organic community.

After a short stay in Warsaw, he returned to Germany and Breslau (1901–11) and, in self-imposed isolation from colleagues and current affairs, devoted himself to intense literary work which he carried out through many periods of poverty and infirmity until his death. In Breslau, where some of his finest works were written between 1906 and 1909, he continued to write in Hebrew, but embarked upon several new ventures—he wrote articles and stories in Yiddish; systematically collected rabbinic legends; studied the origins of Judaism with particular emphasis upon the Samaritan tradition; and began a still unpublished diary in German. His collected Yiddish writings were published in 1912. After moving to Berlin in 1911, he edited anthologies of legends, reworked his previous writings for the Stybel edition (1921–25), and studied Jewish history of the biblical and Christian period. The years after 1914 were particularly difficult: his health failed; his travel was restricted since he was a Russian citizen; and after the war he was deeply shocked at the news of the pogrom in Doubovo and his father's murder. Nevertheless, Berdyczewski wrote some of his major stories after the war, notably his short novel *Miryam* which he completed shortly before his death.

Though Berdyczewski's writings are commonly divided into four groups: essay, fiction, folklore anthologies, and scholarship, the borders between them are often quite arbitrary. Written over a period of 35 years and edited by the author for the Stybel edition, Berdyczewski's literary output is rich but its ambivalent attitudes are the mark of an uprooted, marginal man capable of simultaneously embracing logically contradictory positions and emotions. Many of Berdyczewski's paradoxes can be understood in terms of the dialectical stages of his development, each a reflection of *fin de siècle* European moods.

In his literary criticism, Berdyczewski derided exhibitionistic mannerism and the submission of a writer's artistic individuality to the demands of ideology. He showed little appreciation for the outstanding literary figures of his day, *Mendele Mokher Seforim, *Aḥad Ha-Am, Ḥ. N. *Bialik, and J. *Klausner, but supported younger writers like J. H. *Brenner and M.Z. *Feuerberg and others devoted to their art. He held literature to be one of the vital forces in human experience and reacted to it impressionistically in often fragmentary critical essays, replete with intemperate outbursts and bitter irony; hence his critical point of view is far from consistent.

Berdyczewski wrote more than 150 Hebrew stories, many in Yiddish, and several in German. These stories deal with two central subjects: life in the Jewish towns of Eastern Europe in the last decades of the 19th century and the life of the Eastern European Jewish students in the cities of Central and Western Europe. Heavily autobiographical, many of his pre-1900 stories are often impressionistic, emotional monologues with essayistic digressions.

The *shtetl* ("Jewish town") served as the background for dramatic situations embodying Berdyczewski's philosophical outlook. He was obsessed with exceptional, individualistic types—lonely, rebellious, and ostracized, and the inevitable clash between them and the intolerant community. The archetypal topography of the town with its Jewish and gentile quarters separated by a river is symbolic of the psychological and social tensions in dozens of stories. Often there is an implied protest against pre-arranged marriages and other forms of coercion within the Jewish community which cause misery, particularly for the women. Life is often depicted as a struggle between light and darkness, beauty and ugliness, refinement and crudeness, and in this struggle the good and beautiful are vanquished. The stories after 1900 consciously strive to erect a literary monument to a fading society or to comprehend human existence in literary terms. Increasingly, the *shtetl* is comprehended as a society in the grip of a blind, cruel force.

In his fiction one can discern basic patterns and archetypal figures which appear in various forms: the gracious woman who is callously given to a commonplace or vulgar husband; the uprooted student; the undistinguished, almost impotent male; the virile, ruddy man. Berdyczewski attempted to discover the basic psychological features of his protagonists as they function in plausible, realistic situations and thus added a new dimension to the Hebrew short story. The recurring typology, however, and the use of key epithets and motifs organized his more successfully integrated stories and opened them to symbolic interpretation. In their structure they resemble the rabbinic legends whose concrete situations and symbolic implications had always fascinated Berdyczewski. During his most rebellious period (1896–1900) he collected ḥasidic legends which he published as a separate volume in 1900. The vitality, individuality, and aesthetic sensibility of the Ḥasidim attracted him since they were the antithesis of rabbinic Judaism. Both the Hebrew and the German editions of these anthologies substantially expanded the library of Jewish literature available to the average reader.

One of the most seminal figures in both modern Hebrew literature and Jewish thought, Berdyczewski exerted a subtle yet crucial influence upon many readers since the turn of the century because he embodied, both in his personality and in his writing, the painfully ambivalent attitudes toward both traditional Judaism and European culture shared by many Jewish intellectuals. Characteristically, Berdyczewski rebelled against his religious background, but could never completely reject it.

Berdyczewski's collected works are *Kol Kitvei*, Stybel edition (20 vols. (1921–25)), and various other later editions; collected Yiddish works *Yidishe Ksurim* (1924); rabbinic legends; *Me-Oẓar ha-Aggadah* (2 vols., 1913; *Mi-Mekor Yisrael* (5 vols., 1930–45)). A list of his works translated into English appears in Goell, Bibliography, 63, 94.

His son IMMANUEL BIN-GORION (1903–), writer and translator, was born in Breslau. In 1936 he settled in Tel Aviv where he served as director of Bet Mikhah Yosef (a municipal library based on his father's collection). His writings in Hebrew and German include essays, literary criticism, and studies of folklore. He edited and published his father's writings. His Hebrew books include *Shevilei ha-Aggadah* (1950) and *Ḥidot ha-Sheloshah*, ancient Indian legends.

Bibliography: Waxman, Literature, 4 (1960), 113–24, 382–93; Kressel, Leksikon, 1 (1965), 322–5; S. Spiegel, *Hebrew Reborn* (1930), 331–74; Y. A. Klausner, *Major Trends in Modern Hebrew Fiction* (1957), 124–43; *Kol Kitvei J. Ḥ. Brenner*, 3 (1967), 34–54; Fishmann, in: *Kol Sippurei Bin-Gorion (Berdyczewski)* (1951), 13–28; Y. Kaufmann, *Golah ve-Nekhar*, 2 (1954), 386–404; Y. Keshet, *M. J. Berdyczewski* (Heb., 1958); Lachower, Sifrut, 3 (1963), 71–139, bibliography 217–9; Meron, in: *Moznayim*, 19 (1954), 248–58; I. Rabinovitz, *Major Trends in Modern Hebrew Fiction* (1968), 124–44. [D.ALM./A.J.B.]

BERECHIAH (fourth cent.), Palestinian *amora;* sometimes referred to in the Midrash as R. Berechiah ha-Kohen. His father's name was apparently Ḥiyya (Tanḥ. B. Gen. 60, cf. Lev. R. 31); was a pupil of R. *Ḥelbo, whose aggadic sayings, as well as those of other scholars, he reported. His many aggadic sayings are found mostly in the Midrashim and in the Jerusalem Talmud, but he is also mentioned in the Babylonian Talmud. R. Berechiah preached and taught in his own *bet midrash* (TJ, Ber. 7:6, 11c). In his homilies he stresses the virtues of charity and the uniqueness of the Jewish people (Lev. R. 27:7; Ta'an. 4a). "God said to Israel: 'My children: If you see the merit of the patriarchs declining and the merit of the matriarchs diminishing, go and cleave to acts of charity' " (TJ, Sanh. 10:1, 27d). He gave voice to the expectation that God would exact vengeance upon Israel's enemies (Lam. R. 5:1). Although only a few of his *halakhot* are mentioned, it is clear that his views in the field of *halakhah* were regarded as authoritative (TJ, RH 3:1, 58d). Some scholars think that there was an earlier Palestinian *amora* (third century) called Berechiah or Berechiah Sabba ("old").

Bibliography: Bacher, Pal Amor, s.v.; Hyman, Toledot, 296–8; Z. Rabinowitz, *Sha'arei Torat Bavel* (1961), 368; Frankel, Mevo, 69. [Z.K.]

BERECHIAH BEN NATRONAI HA-NAKDAN (end of 12th–13th century), fabulist, translator, thinker, copyist, and grammarian. Some have identified him with Benedictus le Puncteur of Oxford, who presented a gift to Richard I in 1194, though many deny this. Berechiah lived in Normandy and at a certain period also in England. His title *ha-Nakdan* testifies to the fact that he punctuated Hebrew books. He also knew foreign languages and translated and adapted several books into Hebrew, including *Quaestiones Naturales* by Adelard of Bath, a popular 12th-century book on natural sciences. Berechiah entitled it *Dodi ve-Nekhdi* or *Ha-She'elot* (ed. by H. Gollancz, 1920). His collections of ethical treatises *Sefer ha-Ḥibbur* and *Sefer ha-Maẓref* (ed. by Gollancz, *The Ethical Treatises of Berachyah, son of Rabbi Natronai Ha-Nakdan*, 1902) summarized the opinions expressed in Saadiah Gaon's *Emunot ve-De'ot* (of which Berechiah used the old, unprinted translation in Hebrew), as well as the opinions of other *geonim*. In these essays he invented several Hebrew terms for philosophical concepts. He also wrote *Ko'aḥ Avanim* (unpublished), a translation-adaption of a Latin book about the magical powers in stones.

His most famous work is *Mishlei Shu'alim* (English translation by M. Hadas *Fables of a Jewish Aesop*, 1967), a collection of fables translated mostly from the French fable collection *Ysopet* by Marie de France (c. 1170), and also from the lost Latin translation of Aesop, *Romulus*, as well as from other collections of Oriental origin. Berechiah writes in his preface: "These fables are well-known to all mankind and are in books by people of all languages, but my faith differs from theirs." The preface contains an

משלי
שועלים
להחכם השלם
רבי ברכיה הנקדן
נדפס פעם שנית בתכלית היופי
בק"ק ברלין
להבין משל ומליצה .
דברי חכמים וחידותם

Figure 1. Title page of Berechiah ha-Nakdan's *Mishlei Shu'alim*, Berlin, 1756. A. M. Habermann, *Title Pages of Hebrew Books*, 1969.

appraisal in rhyming puns of the low moral state of English Jewry as seen through Berechiah's eyes: "The wicked are saved, the righteous groan, the bitter are sweetened, the evil rise, while the great are cast down, and prayer is tasteless, glory is folly, and the sacrifice is wicked." He concludes, "I would prefer toil and a dry crust to sharing my lot with them." *Mishlei Shu'alim* has appeared in 18 editions, most of them, including the first (Mantua 1557–59), being incomplete. Berechiah has been identified with Krespia or Crispia (Heb. קרשפיא, קרישפיה, קרישפיהו) the grammarian, one of whose fables (Fable 119) was included in *Mishlei Shu'alim*, but this identification is unfounded. Berechiah's son, Elijah, who lived in "the city of Radom" (Darom, i.e., Dreux) was a copyist and grammarian. In those of his texts which have survived he expresses his feeling of honor at his father's respected position and refers to him as "the *tanna* and pedant."

Bibliography: A. M. Habermann (ed.), *Mishlei Shu'alim* (1946), complete edition, based on manuscripts; Davidson, Oẓar, 4 (1933), 373; W. I. H. Jackson, in: *Fables of a Jewish Aesop* (ed. M. Hadas, 1967); C. Roth, *Jews of Medieval Oxford* (1951), 118–9; idem, *Intellectual Activities of Medieval English Jewry* (1949), 48–50; J. Jacobs, *Jews of Angevin England* (1893); Steinschneider, Uebersetzungen, 958–62; Porges, in: HB, 7 (1903), 36–44; Gross, Gal Jud, 180–5; Fuenn, Keneset, 202–3.

[A.M.H.]

FABLES
OF A JEWISH AESOP
Translated from the Fox Fables
of Berechiah ha-Nakdan
by MOSES HADAS
Illustrated with Woodcuts by Fritz Kredel
1967
Columbia University Press
New York & London

Figure 2. Title page and frontispiece of the English translation of *Mishlei Shu'alim*, 1967.

BERECHIAH BERAKH BEN ELIAKIM GETZEL (c. 1670–1740), rabbi and author. Born in Cracow, Berechiah Berakh served as a rabbi in Klementow and later as a preacher in Yaworow (Yavorov). The leader of Polish Jewry, Abraham Isaac *Fortis (Ḥazak), allowed him to preach in every place without previously obtaining the permission of the local rabbi. His eloquent sermons belong to the end of the period of the Council of Four Lands. He spoke out against the low moral standards prevailing in the upper strata of Polish Jewry in the first half of the 18th century. He criticized rabbis who took gifts from the parents of their pupils, judges who accepted remuneration beyond that permitted by law, and preachers and communal leaders who accepted gifts in return for their efforts. He also criticized the practice of lending money at interest. His outspokenness earned him many opponents. Isaac Eisik of Szydlowiec withdrew an approbation he had given to Berechiah's book of responsa when he learned that the latter, whose words were misinterpreted, prohibited a certain marriage permitted by Solomon *Luria. As a result, the above-mentioned book, together with four others on which Berechiah had labored for more than 22 years, were forcibly taken from him and he had to flee. Only a small part of his works (on the Pentateuch, Psalms, Talmud, and *Turim*) survived, and was published by Berechiah in two volumes, entitled *Zera Berakh* as a supplement in two parts to the work of the same name in two volumes by his grandfather *Berechiah Berakh b. Isaac Eisik. The first consists of explanations and homilies to Genesis (Halle, 1714), and the second of novellae to the tractate, *Berakhot* (Frankfort on the Oder, 1731). A commentary on the Pentateuch, *Zera Berakh*, part 4 (mentioned *ibid.*, part 3) has remained in manuscript.

Bibliography: Michael, Or, 299, no. 647; H. N. Dembitzer, *Kelilat Yofi*, 2 (1893), 50a–52b; Halpern, Pinkas, 477–9; A. Yaari, *Meḥkerei Sefer* (1958), 445–9.

[Sh.A.H./Ed.]

BERECHIAH BERAKH BEN ISAAC EISIK (d. 1663), called "the Elder" in differentiation from his grandson *Berechiah Berakh b. Eliakim Getzel; rabbinical scholar, *dayyan*, and preacher in Cracow; his father-in-law was Yom Tov Lipmann *Heller. Berechiah studied under the kabbalist Nathan Shapiro, and became a *dayyan* of the *bet din* of *Joshua Heshel of Cracow. He officiated as chief preacher to the community in Cracow, belonging to a category of preachers held in high esteem. His sermons were published under the title *Zera Berakh* in two parts: the first (Cracow, 1646) includes Berechiah's exposition of Genesis concluding with the portion *Masei*, and the second (1662) completes the commentary to the end of Deuteronomy and includes sermons on the Five Scrolls, and the Passover *Haggadah*. His commentaries are not only representative of homiletics in 17th-century Poland-Lithuania, but provide wide-ranging disquisitions on central problems of Jewish society, such as, on the causes of the Chmielnicki massacres in 1648/49. He also composed a special elegy, entitled *"El Male Raḥamim,"* on the martyr's death suffered by Mattathias *Calahora in Cracow in 1663, which was introduced in the Cracow liturgy. Berechiah died in Constantinople on his way to Ereẓ Israel.

Bibliography: H. H. Ben-Sasson, *Hagut ve-Hanhagah* (1959), index.

[Ed.]

BEREGI, ÁRMIN BENJAMIN (1879–1953), Hungarian Zionist. Born in Budapest, Beregi was a relative of Theodor *Herzl and knew him from childhood. He graduated as an engineer in 1901 and worked in factory construction in various parts of Europe and later in Palestine. At Herzl's request he organized a Zionist student movement in Hungary. He served as president of the Hungarian Zionist Organization from 1911 to 1918. A Jewish defense force that he organized in 1918 for protection against pogroms was authorized by the Hungarian government. Beregi headed the Palestine Office (see *Jewish Agency) in Budapest from 1925 to 1935, when he settled in Palestine. The last years of his life were spent in Tel Aviv as construction manager of a brick factory. In 1933 he published a two volume novel about life in Palestine, entitled *Isten árnyékában* ("In the Shadow of God").

Bibliography: *Ha-Olam* (Feb. 28, 1950); Tidhar, 13 (1963), 4223–24.
[G.K.]

BEREGOVO (Cz. **Berehovo;** Hg. **Beregszász**), city in Sub-Carpathian Ruthenia (now in Ukrainian S.S.R.). Toward the end of the 18th century Jews were first permitted to settle there on the estates of the counts Schoenborn and to pursue trade. Most of them originated from Poland. By 1795 there was an organized community with a synagogue and *ḥevra kaddisha.* Abraham Judah ha-Kohen *Schwarz officiated as rabbi from 1861 to 1881, and Solomon Sofer (Schreiber) from 1884 to 1930. A Hebrew elementary school was opened after 1918, while Beregovo was within Czechoslovakia. There were 4,800 Jews living in Beregovo in 1914, and 5,680 in 1930, of whom 4,069 declared their nationality as Jewish. A number of Jews owned brick kilns and vineyards, and supplied the international market as vintners. After the Hungarian takeover in 1938 the Jews were deprived of their business licenses. The males were sent to labor battalions. In 1941 about 500 Jews from Beregovo were deported and flung into the river Dniester. The big synagogue was confiscated while service was being held during Passover 1959 in order to house the local theater. After that time, services were held in a rented room. The number of Jewish families was estimated at 300 in 1970.

Bibliography: Y. Erez (ed.), *Karpatorusyah* (1959); *Yedi'ot Yad Vashem*, nos. 10–11 (1956), 20, 31.
[O.K.R.]

BEREGOWSKI, MOSES (Moshe-Aaron) YAKOVLEVICH (1892–1961), Soviet Russian musicologist. Born in the Ukraine, Beregowski was the son of a *melammed* and reader *(ba'al kore).* In 1919 he founded and directed the music section of the Jewish Kultur Lige in Kiev, which was closed three years later. In 1917 he was placed in charge of the music section of *An-Ski's second ethnographical expedition, and from 1930 until its liquidation in 1948 was head of the ethnomusicological section of the Institute for Jewish Proletarian Culture established by the Ukrainian Academy of Sciences. There he assembled the material collected by the Kultur Lige, the recordings and notes of An-Ski's expeditions, the greater part of Joel *Engel's archives, and his own recordings, which totaled more than 7,000 items. Beregowski's studies and publications were oriented to prevailing Soviet politico-cultural tenets, emphasizing the "proletarian" themes in East European Jewish folksong before and after the Russian revolution. He also stressed the Jewish folksong's musical and textual connections with the surrounding culture, and opposed the "clerical-bourgeois" approach of Jewish musicology and Jewish musical composition outside Russia. However, the quantity and variety of the material which he collected and its scholarly publication assured the value of his contribution to the study of Jewish music beyond the ideological framework to which he adhered both by choice and by circumstance.

Beregowski's most important folksong publications were *Yevreyskiy musikalny folklor* and its Yiddish edition (in Latin characters), *Jidisher Muzik Folklor* (both 1934), the second volume of which, scheduled for 1935, was never published; *Yidishe Folkslider,* edited with Itzik *Fefer (1938), which contained 298 items; and the first volume of a projected multi-volume anthology of Jewish folklore (vocal, instrumental, theatrical, dance), which was edited by S.V. Aksiuk (1962).

Bibliography: Sendrey, Music, index; LNYL, 1 (1956), 414–5, includes bibliography; *Sovetish Heymland,* 3 no. 5 (1963), 124–6; 7 no. 7 (1967), 160; *Spravochnik Soyuza Kompozitorov S.S.S.R.* (1960), 174.
[H.B.-D.]

BERENBLUM, ISAAC (1903–), pathologist specializing in cancer research. Berenblum was born in Bialystok, Poland, and was taken to England in 1914. As a student he became interested in cancer research, and from 1936 to 1948 was a member of the School of Pathology at Oxford University and in charge of the Oxford Research Center of the British Empire Cancer Campaign. During this period he developed the theory of the two-stage mechanism for the production of tumors. He found that in addition to the chemical which causes cancer, another chemical is required for the promotion of a tumor. He continued the development of this research theme at the National Cancer Institute at Bethesda in the United States from 1948 to 1950. In 1950 he joined the staff of the Weizmann Institute at Rehovot, where he set up the department of experimental biology. He developed an internationally recognized school of cell biologists and cancer workers. He served for three years (1965–68) as a member of the scientific council of the international agency for cancer research. Berenblum was deeply interested in the public aspects of cancer, and was chairman of the Israel society for the fight against the disease. He wrote *Science Versus Cancer* (1946; U.S. ed. *Man Against Cancer,* 1952) and *Cancer Research Today* (1967).
[J.GR.]

Isaac Berenblum, Israel pathologist.

BERENDT, GOTTLIEB MICHAEL (1836–1920), German geologist. Berendt was born in Berlin, where he studied mining geology. The results of his early field work in the Berlin area were published in his first major book *Die Diluvialablagerungen der Mark Brandenburg* (1863). This research made him an ardent protagonist of the new, and at the time controversial, glacial theory, for which he adduced additional evidence by a study of the Harz Mountains. In 1873 he was appointed professor at the University of Koenigsberg, and in 1875 professor at the University of Berlin. He was one of the first Jews to join the Prussian Geological Survey, where he directed the department for the North German Lowlands. Berendt engaged in extensive geological mapping, particularly of glaciated areas. His geological map of the province of Brandenburg was the first of its kind. Notwithstanding his open mind on modern geological theory, he was an opponent of Darwin whose theory of evolution he tried to refute in *Die Theorie Darwins und die Geologie* (1870).

Bibliography: NDB, 2 (1955), 69–70. [Y.K.B.]

BERENICE (1) (last half of first century B.C.E.), daughter of *Salome, sister of *Herod and of Costobar the Edomite. She was the wife of *Aristobulus (son of Herod and Mariamne). Berenice bore Aristobulus three sons (*Herod, who became king of Chalcis; Agrippa, who became *Agrippa I; and *Aristobulus) and two daughters (Mariamne and *Herodias, the second wife of *Antipas (Herod Antipas)). Berenice did not live harmoniously with her husband, who was proud of his descent from the Hasmonean Mariamne. She was used by Salome to obtain information about her husband so as to arouse Herod's enmity against him. After Aristobulus had been put to death in 6 B.C.E., Berenice was given in marriage to Theudian, brother of *Doris, the first wife of Herod and mother of his son Antipater. She spent her last years in Rome, where she gained the friendship of the emperor *Augustus and *Antonia, the widow of Drusus. On the strength of this friendship Antonia was well disposed toward the young *Agrippa I, even to the extent of assisting him with large sums of money when he was heavily in debt.

(2) (b. 28 C.E.), the oldest daughter of *Agrippa I. At the age of 13 she was married to Marcus, son of the *alabarch Alexander Lysimachus. After the death of Marcus she was married to *Herod, king of Chalcis, her father's brother. Two sons were born of this marriage—Berenicianus and Hyrcanus. On the death of her husband in 48 C.E., Berenice went to stay with her brother *Agrippa II, who had succeeded Herod. The residence of brother and sister under one roof gave rise to calumny. Berenice was married a third time, c. 65 C.E., to Polemon II, then king of Olba in Cilicia. However, she left him after a short time and returned to the house of her brother. She was in Caesarea with Agrippa in 60 C.E. when Paul was put on trial before the governor Festus (Acts 25:13–26;30). The Jerusalem riots of 66 C.E. found Berenice in the city in fulfillment of a Nazirite vow made when she was ill. She risked her life in an attempt to keep Gessius Florus from provoking the multitude, but was unsuccessful. When she attempted to pacify the rioters, they burned down her palace, forcing her to flee. Later, when the Syrian governor *Cestius and his army marched on Jerusalem, she went over to him with her brother. She remained in the Roman camp even when Vespasian commanded the army fighting against the rebels. Titus, son of Vespasian, fell in love with Berenice who was 39 years old at the time. She was with him during the siege of Jerusalem and witnessed the horrors of its destruction. In

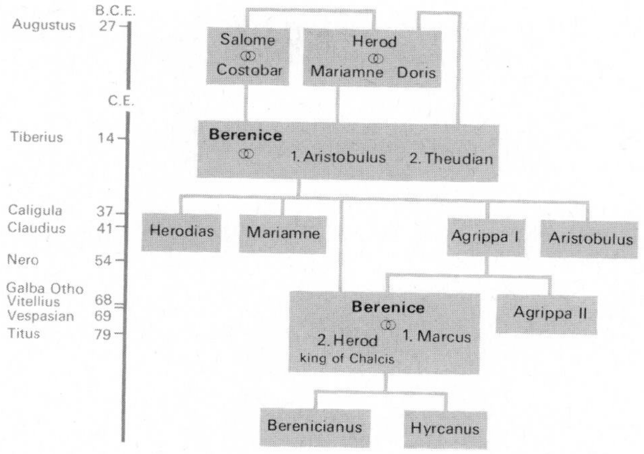

75 C.E. Titus established her in the royal palace at Rome and conducted himself toward her as if she were about to become his legal wife. The ruling circles in Rome, however, did not look favorably upon the affair and when Berenice began to act like an empress, the opposition to her deepened and Vespasian compelled Titus to send her away. After Vespasian's death in 79 C.E., she returned to Rome. However, her previous relationship with Titus was not renewed. The Greek inscription in honor of Berenice by the civic leaders of Athens dates apparently from the period of her travels between Italy and Judea.

Her story has been the subject of fiction as in Leon Kolb's *Berenice, Princess of Judea* (1959) and Lion Feuchtwanger's *Josephus* trilogy.

For Berenice in art, see *Titus.

Bibliography: BERENICE DAUGHTER OF COSTOBAR: Schuerer, Hist, 152, 215f.; Pauly-Wissowa, suppl. 3 (1918), 203, no. 19; A. Schalit, *Hordos ha-Melekh* (1964[3]), 287, 292; Klausner, Bayit Sheni, 4 (1950[2]), 270. BERENICE DAUGHTER OF AGRIPPA I: Pauly-Wissowa, 5 (1897), 287–9, no. 15; Schuerer, Hist, 238–42, 245, 248; Klausner, op. cit., 35; 5 (1951[2]), 20, 140–4, 265, 281; A. H. M. Jones, *Herods of Judea* (1938), index. [A.SCH.]

BERENIKE (Gr. Βερενίκη), the name of several ancient cities founded (or restored) by the Ptolemaic kings and named in honor of Egyptian queens. One of these cities, in the territory of Israel, was Ailane on the Gulf of Eilat (Jos., Ant., 8:163). Another was in Cyrenaica (see *Benghazi).

Bibliography: Pauly-Wissowa, 5 (1897), 280–2; Avi-Yonah, Geog, 175. [ED.]

BERENSON, BERNARD (1865–1959), U. S. art historian and art connoisseur. Berenson was born Valvrojenski in the Lithuanian village of Baltramentz, where his father, an ironmonger and grain and lumber merchant, was one of the leaders of the Jewish community. When Berenson was ten, the family emigrated to the United States, where they changed their name. Berenson was sent to the Boston Latin School and, with the financial assistance of the art collector, Isabella Stewart Gardner, was able to go to Harvard University. After graduating he went to London, Oxford, Berlin, and finally Italy, where he made his home for the rest of his life.

Berenson made a thorough study of Italian Renaissance art, and was soon able to purchase important masterpieces for his patron. Through his books—his earliest, *The Venetian Painters of the Renaissance,* appeared in 1894—he became known as an authority. In 1907 he began his long association with the English art dealer, Joseph (later Lord) *Duveen. This connection enabled Berenson to amass a fortune by providing Duveen's pictures with "Berenson

Bernard Berenson, U.S. art historian.

passports," certifying the expensive paintings as genuine. He and his wife, who came from a wealthy American Quaker family, acquired an old villa near Florence and filled it with art treasures and a vast library. Here Berenson's research into Renaissance art came to fruition in a number of important books, among them *The Study and Criticism of Italian Art* (in three series, 1901, 1902, and 1916), *Essays in the Study of Sienese Painting* (1918), and *Italian Pictures of the Renaissance* (1932). Berenson was a prolific writer. His bibliography, published on his 90th birthday, listed 73 pages of books and articles. Although he destroyed some time-hallowed attributions, he also rediscovered artists forgotten for hundreds of years whose works had been credited to better-known masters. He managed to bring light into the jungle of naïve or careless credits that prevailed in Renaissance connoisseurship when he began his career.

Berenson experienced a certain conflict in his relationship to Judaism. As a young man he contributed essays on Jewish topics to the *Harvard Monthly*, and throughout his long life never denied being a Jew and even boasted of carrying on the Jewish "traditions of great learning." However, he joined the Episcopalian church as a young man, and later became a Catholic, although he never publicized these conversions. As an American citizen he was not affected by the anti-Semitic legislation in Italy before and during the Nazi domination. However, he became apprehensive for the safety of his art treasures, and in 1942 went into hiding until the German retreat from the country. In his autobiographical writings he vacillated between an enormous racial pride and a sharp condemnation of the Jewish people. One of his last autobiographical books was *Sketch for a Self-Portrait* (1949), which contained reminiscences of his childhood in Lithuania. For many years he was an anti-Zionist, but in his old age he accepted Zionism and the necessity for a Jewish state. He bequeathed his villa "I Tatti," with all its treasures, to Harvard, to be available to young scholars so that they could "live" art there as he had lived it.

Bibliography: S. Sprigge, *Berenson* (1960); N. Mariano, *Forty Years with Berenson* (1966); H. Kiel (ed.), *Bernard Berenson Treasury* (1962).

[A.W.]

BERENSON, LEON (1885–1943), Polish lawyer and diplomat. Berenson was born in Warsaw, and started his legal practice there in 1905 as defense counsel in political cases in which he showed himself a brilliant and courageous fighter for social justice. He soon became one of Poland's most famous lawyers. In 1914 he joined the Party for Civic Equality which favored Jewish assimilation through the establishment of Jewish secular educational institutions. He was elected to the Warsaw Municipal Council in 1916 as the representative of this party. When the Polish state was established in 1918, Berenson, as an official in the Ministry of Justice, helped to organize the Polish judiciary. In 1920 he entered the Foreign Ministry and served in Washington until 1923 and later in the U.S.S.R. Berenson resigned from the foreign service in 1930, when the fascist National Democratic Party became a powerful force in the ruling Pilsudski regime. He resumed his legal practice and was defense counsel in several political trials of historical significance. He died in the Warsaw ghetto. His writings include *Z sali śmierci: Wrożenia obróncy politycznego* ("From the Death Cell: Memoirs of a Defense Counsel in Political Cases," 1929).

Bibliography: Hafftka, in: I. Schiper et al. (eds.), *Żydzi w Polsce odrodzonej*, 2 (1933), 250; EG, 1 (1953), 249–50.

[Ed.]

BERÉNY, RÓBERT (1887–1953), Hungarian painter and graphic designer. Born and educated in Budapest, Berény studied in Paris and Italy. On his return he joined the *"Nyolcak,"* a progressive group of artists searching for new forms of pictorial expression. In 1948 he was appointed professor at the Academy of Creative Arts in Budapest. Berény's early work reflects the influence of Cézanne, while

Róbert Berény's portrait of himself in the 1940s, oil on canvas (49.5×45.5 cm.). Budapest, Hungarian National Gallery.

his later work is more expressionistic. He painted a wide variety of subjects, including life studies and landscapes. He was an outstanding graphic artist whose posters maintained a high standard. His "Self-portrait with Straw Hat" (1906), "The Lady Cellist" (1929), "The Scrawl" (1933), "Ice-Carrying" (1937), and "The Student Painter" (1947) are in the Hungarian National Gallery. His portrait of Béla Bartók is in the Bartók Archives, New York.

[J.Z.]

BERESTECHKO (Pol. **Beresteczko**), small town in Volhynia, Ukrainian S.S.R.; until 1795 and from 1921 to 1945 within Poland. An assembly was held in Berestechko by Jewish communities in the district in 1523, but Jewish settlement there is first mentioned in 1569. About 200 families perished in Berestechko during the *Chmielnicki massacres in 1648–49. In the battle fought at Berestechko between the Cossacks and Poles in 1651 some 1,000 Jews fought on the Polish side, according to Nathan Nata *Hannover. There were 872 Jews registered in the community in 1765, of whom 632 lived in the town. It was devastated by a pestilence at the end of the 18th century. Rehabilitated shortly afterward, the community numbered 1,957 in 1847; 2,251 in 1897 (45% of the total population); decreasing to 1,975 by 1921.

[Ed.]

Holocaust Period. When war broke out on Sept. 1, 1939, the Polish authority in the area disintegrated. In the period before the Soviet Army arrived, the Jewish community organized self-defense to forestall Ukrainian attacks. The vast changes introduced by the Soviet regime inevitably affected Jewish life. Private businesses were closed; the Hebrew Tarbut school was shut down; social welfare bodies of the community were disbanded; and cooperatives of carpenters, shoemakers, and tailors were set up. Leaders who were suspected of disloyalty to the regime were deported to Lutsk, and from there sent to Baranovichi. Zionist youth leaders sought refuge in Lutsk to avoid arrest.

On June 22, 1941, the Germans captured the city. At the end of July, German police with the help of the local Ukrainians rounded up 300 Jewish men and executed them in the vicinity. In the fall of 1941 the Jews were concentrated in a specially designated area. The artisans were housed in separate quarters. Only craftsmen and the men in charge of burying the dead were allowed to leave the ghetto. These same persons smuggled food into the ghetto for the destitute population. In Sept. 1942 most of the inhabitants were murdered and the ghetto closed down. Berestechko was recaptured by the Soviet Army on April 24, 1944. The few survivors who returned from the Soviet Union found their homes in ruin. A society of emigrants from Berestechko functions in Israel and published a memorial book, *Hayeta Ayyarah* . . . (1961).

[A.W.]

BERETTYÓUJFALU, town in east Hungary. It had 75 Jewish residents at the beginning of the 19th century. They formed a community, maintained a synagogue, and subsequently opened an elementary school. By 1920 a ḥasidic congregation had also been established. The Jewish population numbered 125 around 1830 (2.3% of the total), 811 in 1891 (11.8%), and 1,038 in 1930 (9.5%). Rabbis of Berettyóujfalu include Amram *Blum (1883–1907), and his son Bela Benzion Blum, who perished in the ghetto of Budapest during the Holocaust. About 1,000 Jews were living in Berettyóujfalu in 1944. The men were sent to forced labor camps, and the women and children to the assembly center at Nagyvárad (Oradea) before being deported to *Auschwitz. About 850 Jews from Berettyóujfalu perished. After the war 150 survivors returned. Most subsequently moved away or emigrated. In 1968 there were some 20 Jews living in Berettyóujfalu. The synagogue was sold in 1964.

Bibliography: M. M. Stein, *Magyar rabbik*, 3 (1907), 12; 5 (1909), 5f.; Z. Nadányi, *Bihar vármegye* (1938), 454; S. Kiss, *Berettyóujfalu és környéke* (1940), 6, 15.

[L.H.]

BEREZA (also **Kartusskaya Bereza**; Pol. **Bereza Kartuska**), town in Brest oblast, Belorussian S.S.R.; until 1795 and between the two world wars in Poland. A Jewish community existed there from the beginning of the 17th century. Erection of a synagogue was authorized in 1629. The community numbered 242 in 1766, 515 in 1847, and 2,623 in 1897 (42.1% of the total population). Although it had decreased to 2,163 by 1921 the Jews still formed 61.3% of the total population. A number of noted rabbis served in Bereza, including Isaac Elhanan *Spektor who officiated there when a young man (1839–46), and Elijah *Klatzkin (1881–94).

[Ed.]

1939–1941. After the outbreak of World War II and the Soviet-German agreement on the division of Poland, Bereza fell to Soviet rule. Jewish communal life was adversely affected under the new regime. All public, independent political activity of a national character was forbidden. The Jews' sources of livelihood were reduced by the creation of a network of government-owned stores and heavy taxation of private enterprise. Attempts were made by the Jews to enter the cooperatives and government service.

Holocaust Period. On June 23, 1941, a day after the outbreak of war between Germany and the U.S.S.R. German forces entered Bereza. The Jews were physically attacked and their property robbed. On June 26 the synagogue and the houses nearby were burned down. The community faced kidnappings for forced labor, starvation, and disease throughout that winter (1941–42). In July 1942 a ghetto was established, comprising two sections: ghetto "A" for "productive" persons employed by the Germans; and ghetto "B" for the "nonproductive," nonworking members of the community. On July 15, 1942, the inmates of ghetto "B" were taken to Brona Góra and murdered. Some of the Jews in ghetto "A" attempted to flee to the forests, or to *Pruzhany Ghetto, which was still free from deportations. On Oct. 15, 1942, the Germans carried out an *Aktion* to liquidate ghetto "A." In defiance the Jews set the ghetto ablaze. That day some of the members of the *Judenrat committed suicide at their last meeting. Many of the inmates were murdered in the ghetto itself, while about 1,800 were taken and killed outside the town. The community was not reconstituted after World War II.

[Ar.W.]

Bibliography: *Słownik geograficzny krolestwa polskiego*, 1 (1880), 140–1; *Regesty i nadpisy*, 1 (1899), no. 781; NLYL, 1 (1956), 18–19; *Pinkes fun Finf Fartilikte Kehiles* (1958), 687–91, 327–464.

BEREZHANY (Pol. **Brzeźany**), town in the Ukrainian S.S.R. (formerly in E. Galicia). Jews had settled there by the 18th century. Jewish representatives from different communities met at the fairs held in Berezhany, e.g., in September 1740. There were 90 Jews living in Berezhany in 1765, in 1900, 4,305 (over 40% of the total population), and 3,580 in 1921. Of the 825 pupils attending the German high school in Berezhany in 1908, 186 were Jews. Before World War I the flour trade was mainly in Jewish hands. The community had a hospital and old-age home. Among the rabbis of Berezhany was Shalom Shvadron. During the Holocaust, in the fall of 1942, some of the Jews in Berezhany were transferred to the extermination camp in Belzec; and on April 12, 1943, those who remained were shot by the Germans. No further information on this community can be procured. Presumably the community was not revived after World War II.

Bibliography: J. Kermisz, *"Akcje" i "Wysiedlenie"* (1946), index; *Bleter far Geshikhte,* 4 no. 3 (1953), 104; Bauer, in: *Midstream,* 4 (1968), 51–56. [ED.]

BEREZINO, small town east of Minsk, Belorussian S.S.R. The Jews there suffered during the *Chmielnicki uprising in 1649. In 1702, during the Swedish campaign, the Jews were fined for failing to pay their post duties which had been imposed by the Polish Sejm (diet) in 1673. The community numbered 266 in 1766; 1,289 in 1847; and 3,377 in 1897 (69.3% of the total population). It suffered in 1920 when Berezino was on the front line between the Polish and Soviet armies. In 1926 there were only 1,565 (53%) Jewish residents registered in Berezino. The community was annihilated during the Nazi occupation (1941).

Bibliography: *Yevrei v SSSR,* 4 (1929[4]). [ED.]

BEREZOVKA, town in Odessa oblast, Ukrainian S.S.R. A Jewish community was established there by the first half of the 19th century. On April 4, 1881, the Jews were attacked in a pogrom and out of the 161 buildings owned by Jews only the synagogue and pharmacy were undamaged. The local population prevented another pogrom from occurring in October 1905. The Jewish population numbered 3,458 (56.2%) in 1897 and 3,223 (42.6%) in 1926. The Jews there all perished during the German occupation in World War II.

Bibliography: *Yevrei v SSSR* (1929[4]), 50; *Eynikeyt* (May 4, 1945). [ED.]

BERG, former duchy in West Germany. A number of Jews took refuge in towns of Berg after their expulsion from *Cologne in 1424; the former rabbi of Cologne settled in *Deutz. The Jews were temporarily expelled from the duchy in 1461. Early in the 15th century, after the amalgamation of Berg with *Juelich, a joint communal organization was established for both communities. Assemblies were held at specified intervals to deliberate questions of tax allocation, rabbinical appointments, the prohibition of resort to the general law courts, and the maintenance of adequate facilities for Torah study. In the 18th century they were held every four years, except in time of war. The Grand Duchy of Berg established by Napoleon comprised a number of localities with ancient communities such as *Duisburg and Siegburg (dating from the early 12th century), *Dortmund, *Essen, *Soest, and Hamm (13th century), and *Recklinghausen and Unna (14th century). After the dissolution of the grand duchy in 1815, its territory was incorporated into *Prussia.

Bibliography: Kaufmann, Schriften, 1 (1908), 199–200; idem, in: *Ozar ha-Sifrut,* 3 (1889), 7–16; C. Brisch, in: *Der Israelit* 20 (1879), 97ff., 145f., 174f. [Z.AV./ED.]

BERG, LEO (1862–1908), German essayist. A founder of the Berlin literary group *Durch* (1887) and editor of its *Akademische Zeitschrift,* he popularized the aesthetic principles of German naturalism. Berg called attention to the importance of Ibsen's innovations in *Henrik Ibsen und das Germanentum in der modernen Literatur* (1887). In the essays of *Zwischen zwei Jahrhunderten* (1896) he maintained his skeptical attitude toward established German writers. He defended *Heine against anti-Semitic detractors, and espoused the cause of Tolstoy. Berg prophesied that national literatures would give way to a common European literature as the expression of the emerging "good European." In his volume, *Der Uebermensch in der modernen Literatur* (1897; *Superman in Modern Literature,* 1916), he revealed his adoption of Nietzschean doctrines. [S.L.]

BERGAMO, city in northern Italy; ruled mainly by Venice between 1430 and 1797. Jewish moneylenders in Bergamo are mentioned in the 15th century. The anti-Jewish sermons preached there by the Franciscan *Bernardino da Feltre in 1479 led to the temporary expulsion of the Jews. By the beginning of the 16th century, Jews in Bergamo still owned houses and real estate. When Louis XII of France captured the city in 1509 the Jewish inhabitants were expelled, but they were permitted to return when it reverted to Venice in 1559. There has been no Jewish community in Bergamo in recent times.

Bibliography: Milano, Italia, 208, 277. [U.C./ED.]

BERGEL (Abergel), Moroccan family. The Bergels came from Safi. They settled in Tangiers, Marseilles, and Gibraltar, where before 1810 MOSES founded a powerful commercial organization. His son YOM TOV (1812–1894), an outstanding figure in western Mediterranean Jewry, served as president of the Gibraltar community from 1860. He helped the Péreire family in establishing the Compagnie Générale Transatlantique in Morocco. Yom Tov and his son MOSES of Marseilles obtained the monopoly for the sale of specialized Moroccan products in Europe.

Bibliography: JC (Oct. 26, 1894); Miège, Maroc, 2 (1961), 121, 250, 511; 3 (1962), 487. [D.CO.]

BERGEL, JOSEPH (1802–1884), physician, poet, and author. Bergel, who was born in Moravia, was a practicing physician, publishing papers in medical journals. He was a Hebrew poet of note and his poems appeared in the journals *Bikkurei ha-Ittim* and *Kokhevei Yiẓḥak* and in a collection *Pirkei Leshon Ever* (1873). In these poems he was the first to scan by Ashkenazi word accent. He also translated German and Latin poems into Hebrew, including those of Goethe and Schiller. Probably his most important contribution to Jewish scholarship was *Medizin der Talmudisten* (1885), with an appendix on *Anthropologie der alten Hebraeer.* He also wrote *Studien ueber die naturwissenschaftlichen Kentnisse der Talmudisten* (1880); *Eheverhaeltnisse der alten Juden im Vergleich mit den griechischen und roemischen* (1881); *Der Himmel und seine Wunder* . . . (also published under the title *Mythologie der alten Hebraeer,* 1882); and a history of Hungarian Jewry, *Geschichte der Juden in Ungarn* (Ger. and Hg., 1879).

Bibliography: Carmilly-Weinberger, in: *Aresheth,* 4 (1966), 400–1. [ED.]

BERGELSON, DAVID (1884–1952), Russian Yiddish writer. Born in Okhrimovo, near Uman, in the Ukraine, Bergelson was the son of a prominent lumber and grain merchant, who died when Bergelson was only nine; his mother died five years later. He then went to live with older brothers in Kiev, Odessa, and Warsaw. His traditional *ḥeder* education was supplemented by private instruction in secular subjects. In 1907–08, he studied as an external student in Kiev, but failed the examinations, and then audited courses in dentistry, without taking a diploma.

Bergelson read Hebrew and Russian literature before he was in his teens, and began writing in those languages. His early literary efforts, a Hebrew story *"Reikut"* and a Yiddish story *"Der Toyber,"* submitted to several periodicals, did not meet with success. *"Der Toyber,"* however, was later published in his collected works (4 vols., 1922–23); it was dramatized under the name *"Di Broyt*

Mil" (1930), and was staged in Russia and in America. His first full-length work, *Arum Vokzal* ("By the Depot"), published in Warsaw in 1909 at his own expense, was warmly received by major critics; Bergelson thereafter wrote only in Yiddish, devoting himself to Yiddish literature and belles lettres. The novel *Nokh Alemen* (1913) was hailed as a masterpiece; it established his reputation as a gifted author of prose whose major theme was the slow decay of the Jewish bourgeoisie in village and town.

Bergelson was very active in Jewish cultural circles and he was one of the founding directors of the dynamic Yidishe Kultur Lige, a Jewish cultural organization established after the Russian Revolution. He coedited two of its most influential publications: the literary miscellanies *Oyfgang* (1919, in which his work "*In Eynem a Zumer*" appeared) and *Eygns* (1920, in which his story "*Opgang*" was published).

In his critical publications, Bergelson stated that art should not be a tool of the new social order and provide "naked abstractions" for propaganda, but should draw on tradition in the creation of its subtle personalized images.

In 1920, Bergelson moved to Berlin where he coedited the journal *Milgroym* with *Der Nister, then *In Shpan*, the title suggesting a new political orientation. Writing for the New York Jewish daily *Forward* until 1925, he later became a correspondent for the Moscow *Emes* and the New York communist paper, *Morning Freiheit*. In marked contrast to his earlier views, his writings of this period show an identification with Soviet ideology, including the need for literature to toe the proletarian line. His novels and stories of those years dealt with revolutionary themes.

Bergelson traveled widely: in 1924, through the Jewish communities of Rumania, under the auspices of ORT; to the Soviet Union in 1926, where he declared himself a "Soviet writer"; to Paris; to the United States for six months during 1929; through Poland on a lecture and reading tour; and to Copenhagen for a brief stay, in 1933. In 1934, he settled in Moscow after a visit to the Jewish autonomous region of Birobidzhan. His major work of the 1930s, *Baym Dnieper*, is a modified, partly autobiographical *Bildungsroman* (2 vols., 1932–36). Like most Jewish and other Soviet writing of the decade, Bergelson's work adapted itself increasingly to the thematic and stylistic demands of socialist realism.

After 1941, and for the duration of World War II, Bergelson was active in the *Anti-Fascist Committee; his wartime stories appeared in its publication, *Eynikeyt*. Two dramas, *Prints Reuveni* and *Mir Viln Lebn*, were written and performed during this time: the first in Moscow, the second by the Habimah Theater in Tel Aviv. Early in 1949, Bergelson was imprisoned (apparently without trial) with other leading Yiddish writers—including P. *Markish, I. *Feffer, D. *Hofstein—and together with them was shot on August 12, 1952, his 68th birthday. A Soviet edition of his collected works, published in 1961, indicated his subsequent "rehabilitation."

Bergelson's early theme—the decline of individual initiative in a period of widespread stagnation—finds its precise tonal correlative in his style: indirect quotation, passive verb forms, adjectival repetition, periodic sentences, and similar devices create a fatalistic atmosphere in his fiction that subordinates character and emphasizes the pessimistic curve of the plot. This style persists even in his "revolutionary" writing of the 1920s, but becomes more straightforwardly dramatic in his stories about Birobidzhan and Soviet progress. His wartime fiction, collected in *Naye Dertseylungen* (1947), shows an interesting variation of his early impressionism. Yiddish criticism considers Bergelson one of its foremost modern prose writers.

Bibliography: Rejzen, Leksikon, 1 (1926), 347ff.; LNYL, 1 (1956), 379–83; E. Dobrushin, *David Bergelson* (Yid., 1947); Finkelstein, in: *Sovetish Heymland*, 4 (1964), 148–50, includes bibliography; Kressel, Leksikon, 1 (1965), 317–8; Kh. Shmeruk et al. (eds.), *A Shpigl oyf a Shtayn* (1964), contains complete bibliography on Bergelson's life and works; I. Howe and E. Greenberg (eds.), *A Treasury of Yiddish Stories* (1953, English notes on Bergelson); C. Madison, *Yiddish Literature* (1968).

[Ru.W.]

BERGEN-BELSEN, Nazi concentration camp near Hanover, Germany, called *Aufenthaltslager* ("transit camp"). Bergen-Belsen was established in July, 1943, in part of a prisoner-of-war camp, and intended for Jews whom the German government wished to exchange for Germans in allied territory. The camp was run by the S.S., whose commandants were Adolf Haas, Siegfried Seidle, and Josef Kramer. Its inmates were Jews possessing passports or citizenship papers of Latin American states, entry visas for Palestine (or the official promise of visas), hostages, prisoners who had paid a ransom, collaborators, and others. Between July, 1943 and the end of 1944 more than 9,000 Jews from Poland, Greece, Holland, North Africa (Benghazi), France, Yugoslavia, and Hungary were transported to Bergen-Belsen. More than 1,300 of these prisoners were sent elsewhere, and most died. However, even during the war, two prisoner exchanges took place: 301 persons were sent to Switzerland (165 were detained on their way, and only 136 arrived in Switzerland) and 222 to Palestine.

There was room in the camp for 10,000 inmates, and conditions, though difficult, were at first better than in other camps. But during 1944 there was a change for the worse. Food rations were reduced to below the minimum nutritional requirement, and the prisoners were forced to do hard labor and were cruelly beaten. In addition, whether from malicious intent or for lack of administrative facilities, the camp authorities failed to provide even essential services. When most of the prisoners had reached the point of physical and spiritual collapse, they were joined by prisoners removed from other camps as a result of the German retreat. The camp population swelled rapidly from 15,000 in December 1944 to 41,000 in March 1945; during the last few weeks there was an additional massive influx of prisoners from the East. The new prisoners, who arrived after forced marches sometimes lasting weeks, were starved and disease-ridden. Epidemics broke out, but there was no medical attention. The death rate was high: in March 1945 nearly 20,000 people died (including Anne *Frank). A total of 37,000 died before the liberation.

Though Bergen-Belsen was taken by the British on April 15, 1945—the first camp to be liberated by the Allies—the

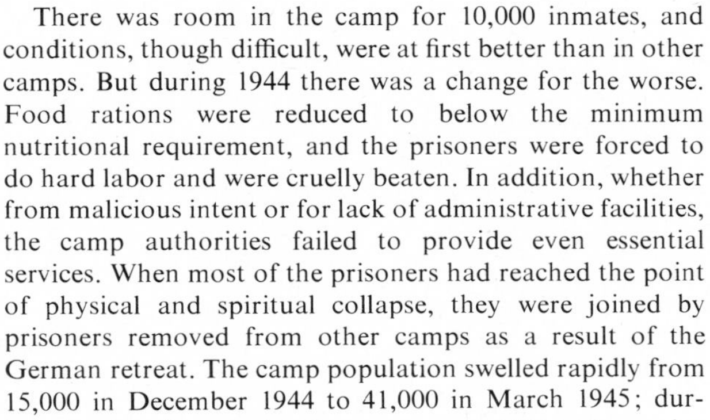

Dr. Klein, Nazi doctor of Bergen-Belsen, photographed in front of the remains of victims after the liberation of the camp. Jerusalem, Yad Vashem Archives.

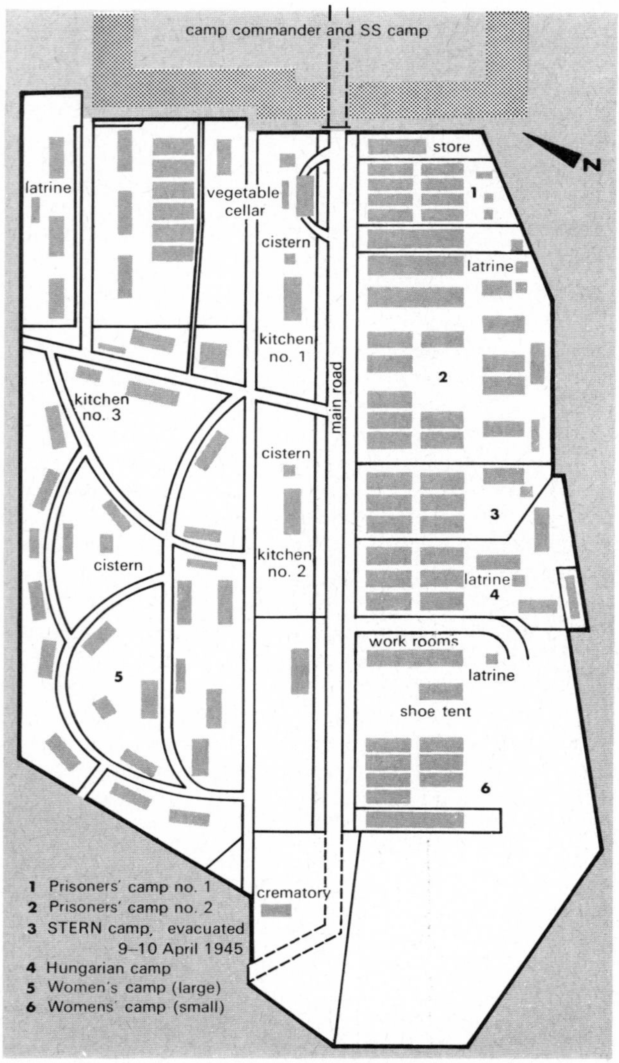

Plan of Bergen-Belsen, February-April, 1945. From *Bergen-Belsen* by Eberhard Kolb.

suffering of the inmates was not at an end. Another 14,000 of the remaining 60,000 died, while the rest were in need of medical care. The horrors, which deeply shocked the British soldiers, received widespread publicity in the West. The British arrested the S.S. administrators, including the commandant, Josef Kramer, and almost all were put to work clearing and burying the thousands of corpses. Twenty of them died doing this work, probably from infectious diseases. The rest were tried at the end of 1945. Eleven were condemned to death, 19 to imprisonment, and 14 were acquitted.

Immediately after the liberation, a Jewish camp committee was established headed by Joseph Rosensaft, from Bedzin, Poland. It actively assisted the early rescue work, while the Red Cross transported 6,000 sick women to Sweden. The Jewish Relief Unit representing the Jewish Agency, Anglo-Jewish, and American-Jewish organizations, was also active in the camp. There was a struggle with the British authorities to gain permission for Bergen-Belsen to be separately organized as an autonomous Jewish camp, whereas other camps were administered by the Allies. This was not achieved until May 1946, when the Polish prisoners left.

Representatives of Jewish communities in the British zone of occupation joined the camp committee, and a central committee for the whole zone was established, also headed by Rosensaft. Schools were opened for the 600 children who had survived thanks to the dedicated efforts of a few women. A newspaper, *Undzer Shtime,* was published from July 12, 1945, and was widely circulated both in Germany and abroad. Later it was replaced by a weekly *Vokhenblat.* Youth movements and Zionist parties opened branches in the camp, and religious life was organized. In 1946 and 1947 the *American Jewish Joint Distribution Committee (AJDC) supplemented the rations distributed by the British army through UNRRA. At two large assemblies, where 40 camps and communities from Germany were represented (September, 1945 and July, 1947), the inmates expressed their identification with the Zionist movement and reelected their committees.

From October 1945 refugees from Poland came to Bergen-Belsen. Many of them passed through to the American zone, the rest joined the thousands of original camp inmates. In the summer of 1947, Bergen-Belsen inmates helped the "illegal" immigrants on the ship *Exodus,* and resisted strong British anti-Zionist pressure. From April 9, 1946 "legal" transports of children also left for Palestine. Most of the camp inmates went to Palestine between 1947 and 1949. The rest migrated elsewhere, mainly to the United States. The camp was closed in September, 1950, and its last inmates left for the United States on August 15, 1951. The Bergen-Belsen inmates are represented in Israel by their organization, Irgun She'erit ha-Peletah me-ha-Ezor ha-Briti (Bergen-Belsen; "Organization of Survivors from the British zone, Bergen-Belsen"). A memorial has been erected on the site of Bergen-Belsen, together with a special memorial to Anne Frank.

Bibliography: S. A. Bloch (ed.), *Holocaust and Rebirth, Bergen-Belsen 1945–1965* (1965); E. Kolb, *Bergen-Belsen* (Ger., 1962); R. Phillips (ed.), *Belsen Trial* (1949); Irgun She'erit ha-Peletah me-ha-Ezor ha-Briti, *Belsen* (Eng., 1957); L. H. Hardman, *The Survivors* (1958).

[J.M./Ye.B.]

BERGEN COUNTY, district located in the northernmost part of the state of New Jersey, U.S., bordering the Hudson River, and including 70 individual municipalities. Bergen County's population in 1969 was about 950,000, of which approximately 100,000 were Jews. The first Jewish settlers in Bergen County arrived in Englewood in the 1880s and the 1890s. They came primarily from Lithuania and Russia and made their living as farmers and small businessmen. The first religious service in Bergen County was held on Rosh Ha-Shanah, 1896, in Englewood and was conducted by Benjamin Sher, a native of Lithuania. This group became the first congregation, Congregation Ahavath Torah, in Bergen County. Early Jewish settlers in other towns eventually built their own synagogues, most of them immediately after World War I, in Park Ridge, Hackensack, Ridgefield Park, and Westwood. A number of descendants of the early settlers still live in the county. The Jewish population of Bergen County grew slowly, with some spurts after World War I, until the completion of the George Washington Bridge in 1931, which opened the door for a huge migration from New York City. The greatest increase in Jewish population took place after World War II with the housing boom. By 1950 there were approximately 20,000 Jews in the general population of 540,000. In the following two decades the Jewish population more than quintupled, whereas the general population had not quite doubled. In 1969 Teaneck, the largest municipality in Bergen County, had nearly 45,000 people and 12,000 Jews; Fair Lawn with a general population of 40,000 had close to 7,500 Jews; and Englewood with 27,500 residents had 7,000 Jews. The Jewish community is affluent and well educated. It has an unusually high proportion of industrialists and professionals, especially among those affiliated with New York City businesses and universities and with the growing number of educational facilities and commercial enterprises in the county.

Jews have been prominent in the political life of the county. Matthew Feldman, a native of neighboring Hudson County, who served as mayor of Teaneck, 1959–66, and as state senator, 1966–67, was chairman of the County Democratic Party in 1969. Nelson Gross of Upper Saddle River was appointed chairman of the County Republican Party in 1966 and chairman of the State Republican group in 1969. Nat Feldman was elected councilman in Englewood in 1969 and was mayor of Englewood (1970). Alvin Moskin, a descendant of one of the earliest settlers, served as mayor of Englewood, 1956–59. Martin Kole of Fair Lawn and Abraham Rosenberg of Bogota were appointed to judgeships on the county bench in 1966. Franklin H. Cooper was elected to the Bergen County Board of Freeholders on the Republican ticket (1969). Jews also participate in the social and cultural life of the area to a great extent. These developments represent a radical change from the 1930s and the early 1940s, when the county was a hotbed of activity for pro-German Bundists. Although several country clubs are reported to discriminate against Jews and other minority groups, there is very little overt anti-Semitism.

Organizational life is very active. There are 25 Conservative synagogues, nine Reform, and five Orthodox. There are Jewish day schools in Englewood and in neighboring Passaic County, which also serve the local area. There are over 100 known Jewish organizations. During the late 1960s there was an increase of coordination among them. The Bergen County Rabbinical Association was organized in 1968. A Community Relations Council of Bergen County came into being in 1969 to help unify the work of the various Jewish organizations in this field. In 1969 the Jewish Welfare Council, which conducts over 15 individual campaigns for local causes, had begun to coordinate its fund raising efforts, and national United Jewish Appeal, which sponsors various local campaigns, was also discussing area coordination. [M.M.K.]

BERGER, VICTOR (1860–1929), U.S. journalist, socialist leader, and congressman. Berger was born in Nieder-Rehbach, Austria. In 1880 he immigrated to the United States and settled in Milwaukee, where he taught German and also taught Sunday School at the Bnei Yeshuron synagogue. In 1892 Berger became editor of the *Milwaukee Daily Vorwaerts,* a German-language socialist paper, and in 1897 he helped to found the American Socialist Party. A conservative socialist influenced by the writings of Eduard Bernstein, Berger joined ranks with Morris *Hillquit in opposing the influence of the communists and such radicals as Daniel *De Leon in the socialist camp. In 1908 he became editor of the weekly *Social Democratic Herald,* which was later replaced by the daily *Milwaukee Leader,* a newspaper that he then headed until his death. In 1911 Berger was elected to Congress from Wisconsin, thereby becoming the first avowed socialist to serve in the U.S. House of Representatives, where he was known for his advocacy of labor legislation and social reform. His opposition to America's entry into World War I led the postmaster general to revoke the mailing privileges of his *Milwaukee Leader* on the grounds of its being a subversive journal, and Berger himself was indicted under the Espionage Act. A court conviction led to a 20-year sentence, as a result of which the House refused to seat him when he won the off-year election in 1918 and again the following year when he won in a rerun. In 1921, however, the Supreme Court reversed his conviction, and a year later, in consequence of this ruling and the general abatement of war hysteria, the House allowed him his seat which he continued to hold until 1928. At the time of his death he was chairman of the National Executive Board of the American Socialist Party. [ED.]

BERGH, HERMAN VAN DEN (1897–), Dutch poet. Van den Bergh was born and educated in Amsterdam, and for many years earned his living as a journalist. He lectured in Italian cultural history at the University of Amsterdam and published many essays on Romance studies. Van den Bergh was one of the founders of the Dutch expressionist school represented by the magazine *Het getij* ("The Tide"), and championed the avant garde. His own poetry expresses a love of nature in vigorous, rhythmical language. His verse collections *De boog* ("The Bow," 1917), and *De spiegel* ("The Mirror," 1925) were among the earliest works of expressionist poetry in Holland. Later Van den Bergh wrote *Het lidteken van Odysseus* ("The Scar of Odysseus," 1956), *Verstandhouding met de vijand* ("Collusion with the Enemy," 1958), and *Stenen tijdperk* ("Stone Age," 1960). In these mature works, a deeply felt emotion is brilliantly expressed. Some of the poet's critical essays were collected in *Nieuwe tucht* ("New Discipline," 1928).

Bibliography: C. van Wessem, *Mijn broeders in Apollo* (1941), 35–51. [G.A.-T.]

BERGH, VAN DEN, Dutch family of industrialists. Originally from Prussia, the family moved to Brabant and settled at Heerenberg on the Dutch-German border, commonly called "den Bergh," from which the family name derives. SIMON VAN DEN BERGH (1818–1906), founder of the family concern, was born at Geffen (Germany). He entered his father Zadok's business, bartering groceries and dry goods for butter supplied by peasants from the surrounding countryside. In 1872, Simon, helped by his sons Arnold, Henry, Isaac and Jacob, started production of "artificial butter," or oleomargarine in a factory in Oss (Holland), later replaced by a bigger one at Rotterdam. Henry and Jacob opened a branch in London. In 1888 a margarine factory was built by the Van den Berghs in Cleves. Subsequently, the firm developed rapidly and became one of the leading margarine manufacturers in Europe. In 1930 the Van den Bergh Margarine Union Ltd. merged with Lever Bros. Ltd., forming Unilever Ltd., which expanded into a giant international concern. Other members of the family include George van den Bergh and Samuel van den Bergh. SIDNEY J. (b. 1898), son of Samuel, was born in Rotterdam and became active in public affairs. After serving as a commissioner for UNICEF, he was appointed minister of defense in 1959.

Bibliography: C. Wilson, *Story of Unilever* (1954). [ED.]

BERGHEIM, village N. of Colmar in Alsace, E. France. Jews are first mentioned there in connection with the persecutions in the 14th century by the *Armleder gangs and following the *Black Death. During the Burgundian wars (1476–78) they again suffered severely. By the beginning of the 16th century, however, Bergheim had the largest Jewish community in Alsace. The Jewish settlement was pillaged by rebel peasants in 1525, and an anti-Jewish outbreak in 1784 followed the abolition of the "body tax" on Jews. The Jewish population declined from 327 in 1784 to 40 in 1926. In 1968 there were no Jews living in Bergheim.

Bibliography: M. Ginsburger, *Les Juifs à Ribeauvillé et à Bergheim* (1939). [Z.Av.]

BERGMAN, SAMUEL HUGO (1883–), philosopher. Bergman studied philosophy in Prague and Berlin. During his student days at Prague, he was a member of the Zionist student circle, Bar Kochba, and in 1903 began to publish articles on Zionist themes. During this period he came into contact with Martin *Buber who had a lasting influence on him. From 1907 to 1919 Bergman was librarian at the University Library at Prague, except during World War I when he served in the Austrian army. In 1920 he emigrated to Palestine where he was the first director of the National and University Library, a position he held until 1935. He helped found the *Histadrut ha-Ovedim and was elected a member of its executive council. In 1928 he became a lecturer in philosophy at the Hebrew University, in 1935 professor, and from 1935 until 1938 he served as its first rector. One of the founders and editors of *Kirjath Sepher,* he was the editor of general philosophy for the *Encyclopaedia Hebraica,* and an editor of the philosophical quarterly *Iyyun.* He was a member of *Ha-Po'el ha-Ẓa'ir and later of *Berit Shalom of which he became the main spokesman. He headed the Jewish delegation from Palestine to the Pan-Asiatic Conference held in New Delhi in 1947.

Bergman's two main intellectual interests were science and religion. Two periods can be distinguished in his attitude to scientific problems. During the first he was influenced by Brentano and he applied himself chiefly to an analysis of the phenomena of perception and evidence, while during the second he was influenced by the neo-Kantian school, especially by Hermann *Cohen and Ernst *Cassirer. In Hebrew he wrote on Kant, Maimon, and thinkers of the 20th century, as well as on epistemology. In 1954 he was awarded the Israel Prize for Humanities for his work on logic, *Mavo le-Torat ha-Higgayon* ("Introduction to Logic," 1953).

In his views on faith and religion, Bergman departed from the prevailing rationalism and anthropocentricism. His attitude to religious problems has been influenced by Rudolf Steiner, Martin Buber, and Franz *Rosenzweig, as well as by Christian thinkers and Indian philosophers, such as Aurobindo. Bergman has striven to live his faith as a direct experience, as a "meeting" with God. He has stressed the "dialogic" nature of this meeting and sees the chief forms of its expression in prayer and listening to the voice of God. His observations on questions of religion are found in his *Hogim u-Ma'aminim* ("Thinkers and Believers," 1959). He also wrote *Faith and Reason: An introduction to Modern Jewish Thought* (1961) and *Philosophy of Solomon Maimon* (1967).

Bibliography: B. Shohetman and S. Shunami (eds.), *Writings of Shmuel Hugo Bergman: A Bibliography 1903–1967* (1968); S. Shunami, in: *Library Journals,* 85 (1960); *Hagut: Teshurah li-Shemuel Hugo Bergman* (1944); N. Rotenstreich, in: *Moznayim,* 17 (1944), 154–7; D. Lazar, *Rashim be-Yisrael,* 2 (1955), 205–10.

[Na.Ro.]

Students honoring Samuel Hugo Bergman on his 85th birthday, 1968. Jerusalem, Hebrew University. Photo Werner Braun, Jerusalem.

BERGMANN, ERNST DAVID (1903–), Israel organic chemist. Bergmann was born in Karlsruhe, Germany, the son of Judah *Bergmann. He obtained his doctorate at the University of Berlin and joined the staff of the Chemical Institute of the university. In 1933 he moved to London, and began his long and close association with Chaim Weizmann. After working in the Featherstone Laboratories in London, he was made responsible for the planning of the Daniel Sieff Research Institute in Reḥovot, Palestine, and in 1934 went there to become its scientific director. In 1939 Bergmann went to France to work in the Ministry of Armaments and in 1940 to London, to work in the Grosvenor Laboratories of the Ministry of Supply. Weizmann and Bergmann developed the "catarole process" for making aromatic hydrocarbons from petroleum, and also worked on fermentation and a process for making isoprene. Bergmann returned in 1946 to the Daniel Sieff Institute and, when this was incorporated in the Weizmann Institute in 1949, was named scientific director. In 1948 he became scientific director of the science department of the Israel Ministry of Defense, a position he held for nearly 20 years. He resigned his position at the Weizmann Institute in 1951 and the following year was appointed professor of organic chemistry at the Hebrew University in Jerusalem. From 1953 to 1966 he was chairman of Israel's Atomic Energy Commission. He was a member of Israel's National Council for Research and Development and the Israel Academy of Sciences and Humanities. In 1968, he was awarded the Israel Prize for Natural Sciences. His output of scientific work covered a wide range of topics, including polycyclic aromatic hydrocarbons, carcinogenic agents, the addition of sodium to double bonds, dipole moments, molecular rearrangements, photochemistry, and insecticides. Bergmann and W. Schenk wrote *Ausfuehrliches Lehrbuch der organischen Chemie* (2 vols., 1932–38; Bergmann's name was deleted from the title page). In 1948 he published *The Chemistry of Acetylene Compounds* and *Isomerisation of Organic Compounds.*

Ernst David Bergmann, Israel organic chemist. Photo R. M. Kneller, Jerusalem.

Bibliography: *Israel Journal of Chemistry,* 1 (1963), 323–50 (includes list of publications until 1962); D. Lazar, *Rashim be-Yisrael,* 2 (1955), 211–5.

[S.A.M.]

BERGMANN, JUDAH (1874–1956), rabbi and author. Born in Brzezany (Galicia), Bergmann served as rabbi at Karlsruhe and Frankfort on the Oder and from 1908 with the Berlin Jewish community. Bergmann took an early interest in Jewish scholarship and published various articles on Jewish history and folklore in Jewish scholarly journals. Among his published works are *Juedische Apologetik im neutestamentlichen Zeitalter* (1908), in which he described the self-defense of Palestinian Judaism against emerging Christianity; *Legenden der Juden* (1919), a study on the nature and sources of *aggadah; Ha-Am ve-Ruḥo* (1938), studies and essays on the problems of scholarship and life; *Ha-Ẓedakah be-Yisrael* (1944), a study on the history and institutions of charity among the Jews; and *Ha-Folklor ha-Yehudi* (1953), about the popular knowledge, beliefs, characteristics, and customs of Jewish people. He was one of the founders of the Freie Juedische Volkshochschule in Berlin. When the Nazis seized power in 1933, he emigrated to Jerusalem. His son was E. D. *Bergmann. [A.M.H.]

BERGMANN, MAX (1886–1944), chemist, best known for his research in leathers. Bergmann was born in Fuerth, Bavaria. He obtained his doctorate in 1911 at Berlin, where he became the assistant to the organic chemist Emil Fischer. In 1920, Bergmann was appointed head of chemistry at the Kaiser-Wilhelm Institut fuer Faserstoff-Forschung in Berlin, and in 1921, director of the Kaiser-Wilhelm Institut fuer Lederforschung in Dresden and professor of the Technische Hochschule there. He held these positions until forced to leave Germany in 1934. His main area of research was in the chemistry and structure of proteins. Bergmann went to the United States where he became a member of the Rockefeller Institute for Medical Research.

Bibliography: *Journal of the Chemical Society* (1945), 716–8; H.T. Clarke, in: *Science,* 102 (1945), 168–70; J.C. Poggendorff, *Biographisch-litterarisches Handwoerterbuch der exakten Naturwissenschaften,* 7B (1967), 335–7. [S.A.M.]

BERGNER, ELIZABETH (1897–), actress. She first became known as an actress in Berlin. However, most of her greatest triumphs were in English-speaking roles in London and New York. She studied in Vienna, and acted there and in Berlin for Max Reinhardt and gained an international reputation in the title role of Shaw's *Saint Joan.* She toured Europe and made her first appearance in London in *Escape Me Never.* This was an immediate success, which she repeated two years later in New York. Bergner played the title roles in *The Boy David* (1936), which Sir James Barrie wrote for her, and *The Duchess of Malfi* in New York in 1946. Under the direction of her husband, Paul Czinner, she appeared in a number of films. Her films included *Der traeumende Mund, As You Like It* (as Rosalind), and *Stolen Life* (1939). She was not a success in Hollywood films. After World War II she toured in Germany and Austria. [P.N.]

Elizabeth Bergner in the BBC's television production of Brecht's *The Jewish Wife,* 1968.

BERGNER, HERZ (1907–1970), Yiddish novelist. The younger brother of Melech *Ravitch, Bergner grew up in Galicia and emigrated to Melbourne in 1938. From 1928 he published short stories in leading Yiddish periodicals in Europe, Israel, Australia and the United States. His novels, *Tsvishn Himel un Vaser* (1946; *Between Sky and Sea,* 1946) dealing with a boatload of Jewish refugees, and *Likht un Shotn* (1960; *Light and Shadow,* 1963) describing the struggle of a Jewish family for acceptance in an Australian community, were translated into English. Bergner's short stories, especially his volume *Vu der Emes Shteyt Ayn* ("Where the Truth Lies," 1966), realistically mirror Jewish life in Melbourne and focus on the Jewish immigrants who arrived in Australia after World War II.

Bibliography: LNYL, 1 (1956), 379; M. Ravitch, *Mayn Leksikon* (1945), 43–45. [S.L.]

BERGNER, YOSSL (Yosef; 1920–), Israel painter, son of the Yiddish poet and essayist Melech *Ravitch. Bergner was born in Vienna and grew up in Warsaw. In 1937 he emigrated to Australia, and in 1951 settled in Israel with his wife Audrey Bergner, also a painter. He lived first in Safed, and many of his expressionist paintings of this period feature high walls perforated by windows in which strange, anonymous figures enact dramatic scenes. Later work suggested the emotional world of the early Russian settlers in Palestine. Sophisticated figures in 19th-century costume were incongruously placed in Middle Eastern settings. This world had its characteristic symbols: halves of apples, butterflies, birds of ill omen, waiting or weeping figures, looming horizons, marshes, and stormswept skies. After 1961, Bergner's paintings tended toward abstraction. Bergner illustrated Kafka and other authors and made designs for various theaters. He contributed to the Venice Biennales of 1956, 1958, and 1962, and the São Paulo Biennale of 1957.

Bibliography: Y. Fischer, in: *Ariel,* no. 11 (1965), 16. [Ed.]

BERGSON (Berkson), assimilated Warsaw family, descended from the court factor Samuel *Zbitkower (d. 1800). Most of the children of his second wife, Judith Levi of Frankfort on the Oder, were given a secular education, and became converted to Christianity, founding the Fraenkel, Oesterreicher, and Flatau families which played an important role in Polish economic life. Ber (Berek), Zbitkower's son by his first wife, alone remained Jewish, and under Prussian rule adopted the family name Sonnenberg. He and his wife, Tamar (Temerl), built a synagogue in the Praga suburb of Warsaw in 1807. Their home became a meeting place for the Ḥasidim in Poland. Their sons, Jacob, Leopold, and Michael, took the name Bergson (or Berkson, "son of Berek"). Members of the family included Joseph Bergson (1812–?), lecturer in medicine at Warsaw University (1841–61) and the musician Michael *Bergson (1820–1898), father of the most celebrated member of the family, the philosopher Henri *Bergson. Active in the Warsaw community was Michael

Bergson, the son of Leopold, who served as president of the community from 1896 to 1918. Others were bankers and manufacturers.

Bibliography: A. N. Frenk, *Meshumodim in Poyln,* 1 (1923); I. Schipper (ed.), *Żydzi w Polsce odrodzonej,* 1 (1932), 481; J. Shatzky, *Di Geshikhte fun Yidn in Varshe,* 3 vols. (1947–53), index; A. Levinson, *Toledot Yehudei Varshah* (1953), 204; EG, 1 (1953), 235–54.

[N.M.G.]

BERGSON, ABRAM (1914–), U.S. economist and expert on the Soviet Union, born in Baltimore, Maryland. From 1937 to 1940 Bergson was an instructor at Harvard, and from 1940 to 1942 assistant professor at the University of Texas. He spent 1942 to 1946 as an economist in various agencies of the U.S. government, and as chief of the division for the Office of Strategic Services, was a U.S. delegate to the Moscow Reparations Conference (1945). For the next ten years he was at Columbia University, but returned to Harvard in 1956 as professor of economics, and

Abram Bergson, U.S. economist.

in 1964 was appointed director of its Russian Research Center. His knowledge of Soviet economic policies and practices qualified him as the outstanding expert before congressional committees dealing with the Soviet economy. He wrote extensively on this special field of interest and his published works include: *The Structure of Soviet Wages* (1944); *Soviet National Income and Product in 1937* (1953); *Soviet Economic Growth, Conditions and Perspectives* (1953); *Soviet National Income and Product 1940–48* (1954); *The Real National Income of Soviet Russia Since 1928* (1961); *The Economics of Soviet Planning* (1964); *Essays in Normative Economics* (1966); and *Planning and Productivity Under Soviet Socialism* (1968). He was also the editor of *Economic Trends in the Soviet Union* (1963). [J.O.R.]

BERGSON, HENRI LOUIS (1859–1941), French philosopher. His father, Michael *Bergson, came from a distinguished Warsaw family; his mother from England. He was born in Paris and from 1881 taught philosophy at the Angers Lycée and subsequently at Clermont-Ferrand, where he gave his famous lectures on laughter, and where, after long meditations in the countryside, he first devised the idea of the vital, continuous, and generative impulse of the universe. From the age of 25, Bergson devoted himself to elaborating this theory in various forms. In 1889 he returned to Paris, published his Ph.D. thesis *Essai sur les données immédiates de la conscience* (*Time and Free Will,* 1910), and lectured at the Lycée Henri IV and the Ecole Normale Supérieure. In 1900 he was appointed professor of philosophy at the Collège de France. His lectures were popular and were attended by the elite of Paris society. These lectures, like his books, especially *L'Evolution créatrice* (1907; *Creative Evolution,* 1911), were distinguished by their lucid and brilliant style and established his fame in France and throughout the world. In 1914 he became a member of the French Academy and in 1928 was awarded the Nobel Prize for Literature. Bergson was also politically active, especially in foreign affairs, and headed a French delegation to the U.S. He was president of the League of Nations' Committee for Intellectual Cooperation. In 1940, after the French surrender to the Nazis, Bergson returned all his decorations and awards, and, rejecting the French authorities' offer to exclude him from the edicts against the Jews, queued for many hours to register as a Jew although he was weak and ill. In his latter years he was attracted to Catholicism but remained a Jew in order to maintain his identification with the persecuted. He died a Jew in 1941.

Most of his works deal with the conception and explication of the notions of "duration" and "movement," not as static concepts defined by the mind but as experiences, conceived by the intuition when it is freed from the limitations which the intellectual consciousness imposes upon the conceiver and the conceived. According to Bergson, the dynamic element of the duration, the flowing time, is the sole penetrator of real existence. "Time" abolishes the static world of the conscious mind and the concept of "duration" may be defined as the continual change which takes place in time. This change is not transcendentally motivated but results from an inner energy—the vital impulse *(élan vital)* which derives from an unlimited source. The actual duration of the vital impulse is the basic element of the universe, while matter and awareness are only momentary manifestations or creations of the central stream. The consciousness can grasp the essence of reality, both in its primary purity as a duration and in its consolidation and objectification as matter in space. In the same manner consciousness can also reach self-knowledge in two different ways: through intellectual static self-consciousness, and through an intimate awareness of its essence as a conscious duration, a vital and fluctuating spirit, regenerating and developing continuously. From this it follows that the factor fashioning consciousness is memory. Memory comprises the duration for it accumulates all past achievements and within it "the past grows into the present." Through the intuition, which is the essence of the memory, man grasps his personal essence as a vital and conscious duration, and, similarly, grasps the creative duration, which is absolute reality.

Bergson's view also appears in his theories on the functions of instinct, intellect, and intuition. Life evolution advances in three directions: vegetative, instinctive, and rational. The instinct is the capability of utilizing organic instruments, but this function is merely a blind practical knowledge. The intellect has the ability of execution and of utilizing inorganic instruments, and it introduces, therefore, the knowledge of the qualities of objects, accompanied by self-knowledge. When the intellect has time enough to develop its knowledge, it judges all objects as if they were inorganic instruments, thus viewing the living reality itself in a mechanical, devitalized mirror. This perverted conception can be corrected by intuition, which is a developed instinct with self-awareness. Bergson conceived the intuition as the only means by which it is possible to inject a primary flexibility into fossilized scientific methods and draw them closer to reality.

Bergson recognized that the potential capability for immediately grasping reality is actualized only in a few select men. Strong fetters of habit tie man down to the social, moral, and conceptual reality of his environment, and only an elite few are capable of extricating themselves. Therefore, Bergson admired the great mystics (see his *Les deux sources de la morale et de la religion,* 1932; *Two Sources of Morality and Religion,* 1935).

Henri Bergson, French philosopher and Nobel laureate. Medal by H. Kautsch, 1913. $2\frac{3}{4}\times2$ in. (7×5 cm.). New York, Dan Friedenberg Collection.

Bibliography: A. D. Lindsay, *The Philosophy of Bergson,* 1911; H. Wildon Carr, *Henri Bergson: The Philosophy of Change,* 1912; Hugh S. Elliot, *Modern Science and the Illusions of Professor Bergson,* 1912; V. Jankelevitch, *Henri Bergson,* 1931; A. Keller, *Eine Philosophie des Lebens* (1914); J. Maritain, *La philosophie Bergsonienne* (1914); A. Thibaudet, *Le Bergsonisme* (1923); J. Chevalier, *Bergson* (Fr., 1948); A. Pallière, *Bergson et le Judaïsme* (1932); I. Benrubi, *Souvenirs sur Henri Bergson* (1942); B. Scharfstein, *Roots of Bergson's Philosophy* (1943); A. Cresson, *Bergson, sa vie, son oeuvre* (1950); R. M. Mossé-Bastide, *Bergson éducateur* (1955); idem, *Bergson et Plotin* (1959); I. W. Alexander, *Bergson, Philosopher of Reflection* (1957). [P.H.]

BERGSON, MICHAEL (1820–1898), Polish pianist and composer, born in Warsaw. He was the father of the French philosopher Henri *Bergson. Michael's opera *Luisa di Montfort* was produced in Florence (1847) and in Hamburg (1849); his operetta *Qui va à la chasse, perd sa place* in Paris (1859). For ten years he was piano professor, then director of the Geneva Conservatory. In 1873 he settled in London, where he collaborated with M. Hast in the compilation and editing of synagogue music. A pupil of Chopin, he composed in Chopinesque style, for which Schumann criticized him. One of his works, *Scena ed Aria,* is still widely played by military bands.

Bibliography: Baker, Biog Dict; Grove, Dict; Sendrey, Music, indexes. [D.L.S.]

BERGSTEIN, FANIA (1908–1950), Hebrew poet. Born in Szczuczyn, near Lomza, Poland, she received a Hebrew and a Russian education. In her youth she became active in the Zionist youth movement He-Ḥalutz ha-Ẓa'ir, immigrated to Palestine in 1930, and joined kibbutz Gevat. Her books include: *Bazir* (1939), poems; *Avim Ḥolefot* (1950), poems; *Asif* (1955), collected poems; and *Reshimot* (1952), collected prose, edited by M. Poznański. Among her ten volumes of poems, stories, and plays for children is *Tekhelet ve-Adom* (1961). A list of her works that have been translated into English appears in Goell, Bibliography, index.

Bibliography: *Fania* (Heb., 1950), memorial brochure, issued by kibbutz Gevat; N. Goren, *Demuyyot be-Sifrutenu* (1953), 144–9; Y. Harari, *Ishah va-Em be-Yisrael* (1959), 455–7. [G.K.]

°**BERGSTRAESSER, GOTTHELF** (1886–1933), German Semitic scholar and linguist. Bergstraesser was born in Oberlosa (Thueringen). During World War I, while professor at the University of Constantinople, he studied the spoken dialects in Palestine and Syria on which he later published several scholarly works: *Sprachatlas von Syrien und Palaestina* (1915); *Zum arabischen Dialekt von Damaskus* (1924); *Neuaramaeische Maerchen und andere Texte aus Maʿlula* (1915); *Glossar des neuaramaeischen Dialekts von Maʿlula* (1921). Bergstraesser began to work on an edition of Gesenius' *Hebraeische Grammatik* of which only two parts appeared (*Einleitung, Schrift- und Lautlehre,* 1918; *Verbum,* 1929). He also edited a Hebrew reader *Hebraeische Lesestuecke aus dem Alten Testament* (1920). In addition to the linguistic studies which earned him international repute (*Einfuehrung in die semitischen Sprachen,* 1928), Bergstraesser engaged in research on textual criticism and reading of the Koran, Arabic translations from Greek, especially of Galen, and on Islamic law. A fierce opponent of Nazism, Bergstraesser spoke out strongly against anti-Semitism.

Bibliography: M. Meyerhof, in: *Isis,* 25 (1936), 60–62 (Eng.); H. Gottschalk, in: *Der Islam,* 24 (1937), 185–91 (with partial bibliography). [M.Pl.]

BERGTHEIL, JONAS (1819–1902), pioneer in Natal, South Africa. Bergtheil emigrated to Cape Colony from Bavaria in 1834 and moved in 1843 to Durban, where he formed a company to bring settlers from Europe and grow cotton for the first time in South Africa. To encourage immigration to South Africa he took a Zulu to Germany in 1847 as an example of the indigenous population and recruited 188 non-Jewish settlers whom he took to Natal. The 47 families concerned were each given 250 acres of land at New Germany in the Pinetown district some 15 mi. (24 km.) from Durban. Although cotton growing was initially a failure, the settlement prospered. Bergtheil was also director of a company which built the first railway line in South Africa, a short stretch starting in Durban. He was elected in 1857 to the first legislative council in Natal, holding the seat until 1866. He was one of the founders of the Cape Town Hebrew Congregation in 1841. In 1866 he left to settle in England.

Bibliography: G. Saron and L. Hotz (eds.), *Jews in South Africa* (1955), index; *Jewish Affairs,* 9 (Johannesburg, 1954), no. 6. [L.Ho.]

BERIḤAH (Heb. בְּרִיחָה; "flight"), name of an organized underground operation moving Jews out of Poland, Hungary, Czechoslovakia, Rumania, Yugoslavia, the Baltic countries, and the U.S.S.R. into Central and Southern Europe between 1944 and 1948 as a step toward their—mostly "illegal"—immigration to Palestine: also name of the spontaneous mass movement of Jewish survivors from Europe toward Ereẓ Israel.

In 1939, Jewish refugees fleeing from the Germans were illegally crossing frontiers into Soviet-occupied Poland and thence to Lithuania or, in the south, to Rumania. While this movement was in the main chaotic, Zionist, Bundist, and Orthodox groups provided some organized nuclei. The same holds true of Jews fleeing from Slovakia to Hungary

BERIḤAH

The Beriḥah operation which, at the end of World War II, moved hundreds of thousands of survivors of the Holocaust across the frontiers of Europe to a new life in Ereẓ Israel. Photos: Tel Aviv, E. Dekel Collection.

Figure 1. The beginning of the journey: waiting for transport.

Figure 2. A Jewish officer of a British army unit organizing a convoy.

3

Figures 3 and 4. Youngsters traveling by rail.
Figures 5 and 6. On foot to the frontier: through the forest and over the mountain.
Figure 7. The end of the journey: "illegal" immigrants arrive in Ereẓ Israel, pulled ashore by members of the Haganah.

4

6

5

7

8

Figure 8. Injured during a struggle with intercepting British troops, one "illegal" immigrant ends his journey in Haifa. The other passengers on this battered vessel were later transported to a detention camp in Cyprus.

Figure 9. Some of the forged identity documents used by Ephraim Dekel, European commander of Beriḥah from 1946.

9

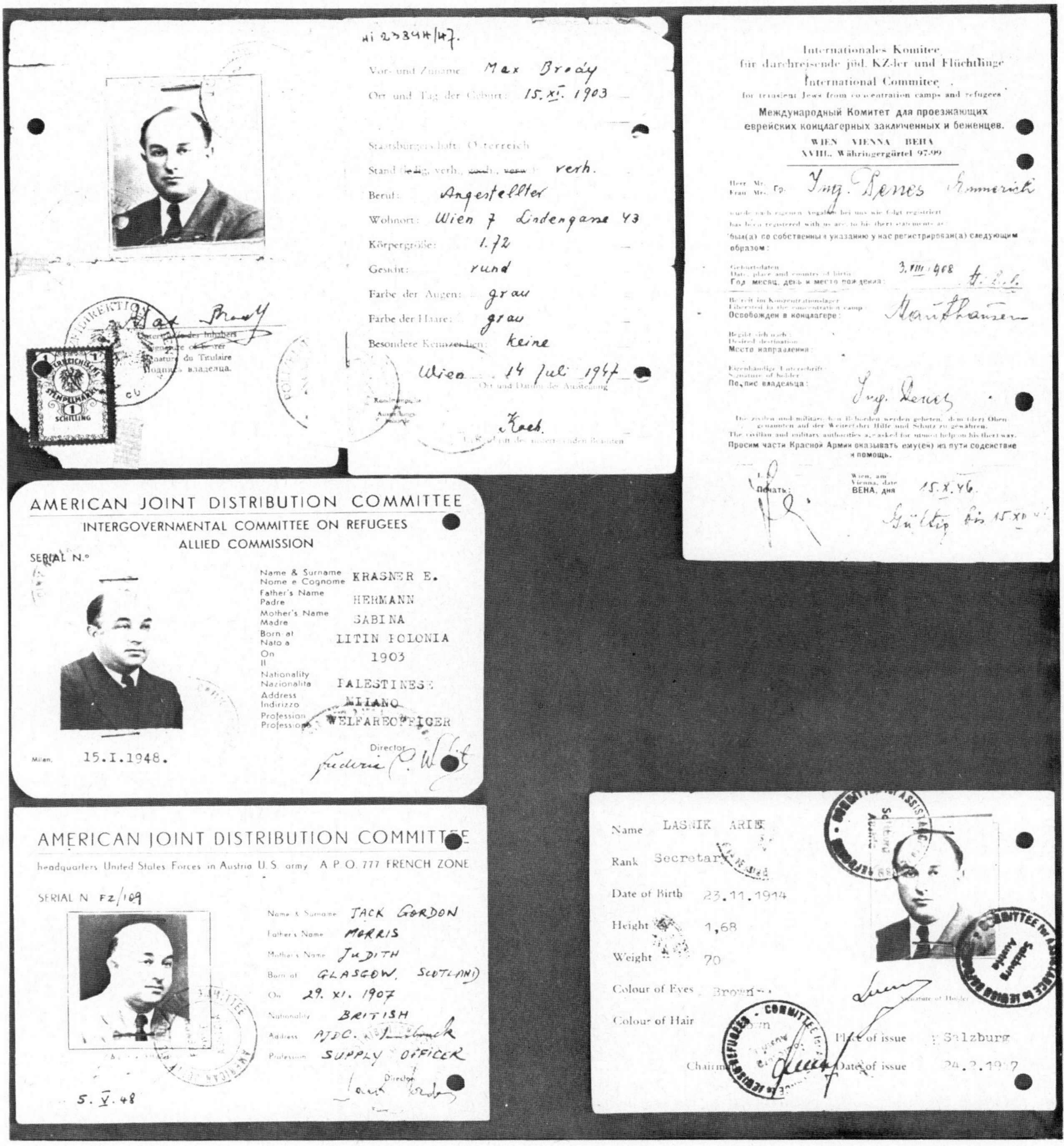

in 1942, and from Hungary back into Slovakia and into Rumania in 1944. At the end of World War II, tens of thousands of Jews found that they could not remain in the countries of Central Europe either because of their memories of the *Holocaust and the destruction of their homes or because of the anti-Semitic atmosphere that prevailed in these countries. A mass migration of the remnants of the Holocaust began. It was partially spontaneous and partially organized as an attempt to find a way to reach Palestine. The first initiators of the organized Beriḥah came from among the leaders of Jewish resistance groups, partisans, and organizers of Zionist underground groups who already had participated in illegal border crossings in Nazi-occupied Eastern Europe during the war years.

In 1944, with the liberation of Rovno in Volhynia and Vilna by the Soviet Army in February and April, respectively, illegal groups of former Jewish partisans were formed independently of each other. Their aim was to take out the remnants of the Jewish population and bring them to Ereẓ Israel. They were joined by Zionist groups returning from Soviet Asia, and met in Lublin in December 1944 under the leadership of Abba *Kovner. In January 1945, they were joined by the remnants of the Warsaw ghetto fighters under Yiẓḥak *Cukierman, and founded the Beriḥah organization under the leadership of Kovner. The first groups were sent to Rumania in the middle of January 1945, in the hope of reaching Ereẓ Israel with the help of emissaries (*sheliḥim*) of the *yishuv* staying at the time in Bucharest. During the first months after the war, before the borders of Central European countries were redrawn and closed and when millions of *Displaced Persons were returning to their homes, the movement of Jews searching for a way to Palestine also began. An event connected with this mass movement was the "Rescue Train," which, under the auspices of the International Red Cross, set out for Poland to return to Rumania Jews who had been deported by the Germans. This project succeeded in returning from Poland to Rumania about 5,000 Jews, including many children. But hopes of reaching Palestine from Rumania had soon to be discarded, and in May, Kovner had instead established transit points in Hungary and Yugoslavia, moving his people toward Italy, which he himself reached in July. Polish Jews were now coming via Slovakia to Budapest, and thence to Graz in Austria, hoping to cross the Italian border from there. In August, however, the British occupation forces stationed there closed the border and 12,000 people were stranded in the Graz area. They managed to cross the border in small groups only in the winter of 1945/46.

A center (*Merkaz la-Golah*) for smuggling Jews into Italy from the liberated concentration camps in Germany and Austria was established by Palestinian Jewish soldiers stationed in Europe, both from the *Jewish Brigade and from other army units. It started its activities in June 1945 and brought in some 15,000 people till August, when British forces sealed the border. Financing in this early period was from *Jewish Agency funds. The first attempt to organize the migration of Jewish survivors throughout Europe was made at a meeting of Beriḥah activists in Bratislava in March 1946. A central committee of the Beriḥah was chosen with Mordechai Surkis from the Jewish Brigade and Pinḥas Rashish, head of the Palestine aid delegation to Poland, as its heads. This committee exercised an ill-defined and shadowy control over Beriḥah activities in Europe until the end of 1946.

From August 1945 onward, a movement started out of Poland into the Displaced Persons (DP) camps of Czechoslovakia; the various routes led to the U.S. zone in Austria and into Bavaria. From October onward an alternative route operated via Szczeczyn (Stettin), Berlin, and the British zone (northern Germany) to the U.S. zone in the south. Transit through Czechoslovakia, Austria, and Hungary was controlled by Levi Kopelevich (Argov), a *shali'aḥ* from Palestine, who from March 1946 headed the Beriḥah secretariat in Bratislava. Movements were coordinated with the Beriḥah in Poland under Isser Ben-Ẓvi, a *shali'aḥ* who had taken over in October 1945. In the winter of 1945/46, funds began to be received from the *American Jewish Joint Distribution Committee for food and clothing for stranded refugees. The control over Beriḥah exercised heretofore through Surkis was now acknowledged to be in the hands of the "Mosad le-Aliyah Bet" (or "Mosad," center for "*illegal" immigration) in Palestine, whose head, Shaul *Avigur, moved his office to Paris in 1946.

The movement was largely organized by Zionist youth movements whose representatives in Poland formed the Beriḥah "center," to which the commander was responsible. The movements and Zionist parties formed groups, many of which were influenced by the kibbutz idea and therefore known as "kibbutzim." The groups were directed to border towns where Beriḥah teams accommodated them in "stores" (temporary lodgings). There they were provided with slips of paper containing a code *("parol")* and sent to the actual border station ("point") where the local Beriḥah team smuggled them across. Until 1946, forged Red Cross documents were employed to identify people as Greek refugees. In Czechoslovakia, an informal agreement was obtained not to hamper the movement of Jews, and UNRRA and the Czech government paid the train fares from the Polish border to either Bratislava or As on the Czech-German frontier. On the Szczeczyn-Berlin route, Soviet or Polish truck drivers were bribed into smuggling people in, and exit from Berlin to the British zone was effected either through UNRRA officials whose sympathy was obtained or with the help of forged documents. From October 1945 onward, the operation in Austria was under Asher Ben-Nathan, and in Germany under Ephraim Frank, both *sheliḥim* from Palestine. In Vienna a series of transit camps were clustered around the Rothschild Hospital, receiving refugees passing from Bratislava to the U.S. zone of Austria. From the U.S. zone of Austria transit was effected either to Italy (until about May 1946), directed by Issachar Haimovich, or to the U.S. zone in Germany.

The U.S. Army did not encourage entry of Jewish refugees into their zones. However, poor conditions in DP camps in these zones had caused an investigation to be made by Earl G. Harrison in August, 1945, and the report that was published on Sept. 30, 1945, reflected badly on the army. To avoid arousing public opinion in the United States the army acquiesced in Jewish refugee movements, provided no very large numbers were involved. Simon H. Rifkind and Philip S. Bernstein, advisers on Jewish affairs to the U.S. command in Germany, played a large part in persuading the army to maintain its tolerant attitude.

The murder of 41 Jews in a pogrom at *Kielce (Poland) on July 4, 1946, created a wave of panic among Polish Jews, who now included the 150,000 repatriates from the U.S.S.R. who came out from February 1946 onward (before that there had been only 80,000 Jews in Poland). Pressure was exerted on Beriḥah by panic-stricken Jews to take them out of Poland. In July this was still done by the usual illegal means. But the Polish government, which arrived at the conclusion that it would not be able to restrain the outbursts against the Jews, saw their exodus from Poland as a solution to the problem. In late July, negotiations conducted by Yiẓḥak Cukierman with Polish government agencies led to an oral understanding whereby

Jews were allowed to leave Poland without hindrance through the Silesian border into Czechoslovakia. Simultaneously (on July 26) the Czech government, largely through the influence of Jan Masaryk, the foreign minister, decided to open its frontier to Jews fleeing from Poland. In the three months of July, August, and September 1946 more than 70,000 Jews fled through Czechoslovakia. Transport was paid for by the Czechs, against an UNRRA promise to return the money later; food was obtained largely from the JDC and UNRRA. The exodus of those months was joined by 15,000 Hungarian Jews and some 1,000 Rumanian and Czech Jews. Despite Polish insistence that only the Silesian route should be used after the July agreement, Beriḥah continued to send also large numbers of Jews via Szczeczyn to Berlin, a route which was controlled by Jewish Brigade soldiers. Others went from Szczeczyn to Luebeck and Hanover in the British zone by train or boat through PUR, the Polish agency expelling Germans from Poland: the Jews posed as Germans and were thus enabled to leave by "being expelled." The total number leaving Poland from July 1945 to October 1946 was estimated at 110,000, excluding PUR and a large number of people who came out not with the organized Beriḥah but with professional smugglers, Jews as well as non-Jews. From the beginnings of the Beriḥah until October 1946 no less than 180,000 people were involved in the migratory movements.

After some hesitation, and due again largely to the intervention of Rabbi Philip Bernstein, the U.S. Army allowed the large scale move into the U.S. zones of Germany and Austria to take place in the summer of 1946. Movements out of Germany into Italy were limited, especially during the second half of 1946, until the route was reestablished in early 1947 through the Valle Aurina. In early 1947 the Polish government terminated the arrangement at the border; movement via Szczeczyn had almost come to a standstill in November 1946. During 1947, less than 10,000 Jews managed to leave Poland via Beriḥah routes. In Germany, Beriḥah cooperated with the committees of Jewish DPs to arrange for social and political absorption of the refugees into the camps. Beriḥah's orientation was clearly Zionist, but there were refugees who declared their preference for migration to countries other than Palestine.

The Beriḥah movement from the Soviet Union was a special case. Many Jews who had lived in prewar Poland left the U.S.S.R. with their families as part of the Polish repatriation program. The position of veteran citizens of the Soviet Union was a more difficult one. Nonetheless, activities of the Beriḥah were organized by a number of bodies, which, inter alia, brought out many Lubavich Ḥasidim from the Soviet Union. When the new Soviet border was definitely sealed in 1946, the Soviet authorities began to seize the Beriḥah organizers, some of whom were arrested and sentenced to long prison terms. At the end of 1946 a meeting of Beriḥah commanders was held at Basle during the 22nd Zionist Congress. Shaul Avigur, head of the "Mosad," was present. There a new European commander of the Beriḥah, Ephraim Dekel, a former head of *Haganah Intelligence in Palestine, was nominated. Under Dekel Beriḥah became more closely linked with the "Mosad," but the numbers coming in from Eastern Europe were falling. In the spring of 1947 economic crisis and fear of anti-Semitism caused a panic flight of some 15,000 Rumanian Jews to Hungary and Austria. On April 21, 1947, the U.S. Army decreed that no more Jews would be accepted into existing DP camps, but Beriḥah poured the refugees into the Viennese transit camps until the American authorities relented and allowed the people entrance into camps in the U.S. zone in contravention of the decree. The tension in Palestine between the *Haganah and the dissident underground organizations, *Irgun Ẓeva'i Le'ummi (I.Ẓ.L.) and *Loḥamei Ḥerut Israel (Leḥi), sometimes influenced the work of the Beriḥah as well, and in September 1947 a Beriḥah man was murdered at a "point" near Innsbruck by I.Ẓ.L. members. In general, however, the *Revisionists were part of the current of the Beriḥah and the "illegal" immigration to Palestine.

In 1948, Meir Sapir took over from Dekel as Beriḥah commander, and Beriḥah was slowly wound up, though Beriḥah points still operated on certain eastern borders in 1949. In the west, Beriḥah points existed on the German-French and, briefly, on the Belgian, frontier, and the 4,500 *Exodus* passengers passed through these in June 1947. However, entry into France was regulated by the "Mosad" rather than Beriḥah. The total number of people who left Eastern Europe between 1944 and 1948 can be estimated at about 250,000, and of these about 80% at least came with the organized Beriḥah. The Beriḥah was a prime factor in the struggle for the establishment of the Jewish State from 1945 to 1948. It dramatically underscored President Truman's demand for a speedy admission of 100,000 Jewish refugees to Palestine (August 1945) and was reflected in the conclusions of the Anglo-American Committee (May 1946). It created a reservoir of people from which came the masses of immigrants that fought together with the *yishuv* to open the gates of Palestine to Jewish immigration and to establish the State of Israel. (See also *Displaced Persons and "*Illegal" Immigration).

Bibliography: Y. Bauer, *Flight and Rescue* (1970); J. and D. Kimche, *The Secret Roads* (1954); *"Brycha" 1945–1948* (Pol., 1950?), an album; E. Dekel, *Bi-Netivei ha-"Beriḥah"* (1958); idem, in: *Seridei Ḥerev* (1963); A. Gefen, *Poreẓei ha-Maḥsomim* (1961); L. W. Schwarz, *The Redeemers* (1953), 232–45; R. Korchak, *Lehavot ba-Efer* (1965), 303–7.

[YE.B.]

BERIT SHALOM (Heb., lit. "Covenant of Peace"; English name "The Peace Association"), society founded in Jerusalem in 1925 to foster amicable Jewish-Arab relations and to seek a joint solution for the future of Palestine. Among its charter members were Arthur *Ruppin, *Rabbi Binyamin, Samuel Hugo *Bergman, Ḥayyim Kalvariski, Joseph *Lurie, Jacob *Thon, and Hans *Kohn. Gershom *Scholem and Abraham Katznelson (later *Nissan) were among those who joined its ranks. Though Berit Shalom's membership was confined to a small circle of intellectuals, political leaders such as Henrietta *Szold, Meir *Dizengoff, David *Yellin, David *Ben-Gurion, Joseph *Sprinzak, and Berl *Katznelson occasionally took part in its deliberations on Jewish-Arab relations. From the start there were differences concerning the purpose of the society. Ruppin wanted it to be a research group that would present the results of its studies to the Zionist leadership, while others urged that it formulate and attempt to implement its own political program. Berit Shalom favored a "bi-national state" in the whole of Palestine, with Jews and Arabs having an equal share in the administration regardless of the size of their respective populations. Rabbi Binyamin, the first editor of its monthly, *She'ifatenu* ("Our Aspiration"), who demanded an agreement with the Arabs on the basis of unlimited Jewish immigration, was replaced when a majority of the members declared themselves ready to accept a temporary limitation of immigration to facilitate an agreement with the Arabs. In 1930 Berit Shalom published (in English) a *Memorandum on an Arab Policy for the Jewish Agency,* and *Practical Proposals for Cooperation Between Jews and Arabs in Palestine.* Berit Shalom was attacked by most of the Zionist parties, especially the *Revisionists, and, by the mid-1930s, virtually ceased to exist. An attempt to revive the organization was made in 1936 and again later on the eve of World War II, when the League for Jewish-Arab Understanding was founded. This was a society of leading politicians, mainly of the left *Po'alei Zion and *Ha-Shomer ha-Ẓa'ir, as well as public figures such as Moshe *Smilansky. It disintegrated when, in 1945, the struggle against the Mandatory government began. A further society of this kind, Iḥud ("Unity"), was founded in 1942 by Judah L. *Magnes, Martin *Buber, Rabbi Binyamin, Menaḥem Raphael Cohen, Ernst *Simon, Moshe Smilansky, Mordecai Reiner, and Heinrich Strauss. Politically more unified than its predecessors, Iḥud's program was intended to win support from Arab and Jewish intellectuals. It published a periodical called *Be'ayot* ("Problems"). With the outbreak of the Arab-Israel War and the death of Magnes in 1948, Iḥud's activities temporarily ceased. It was revived once more in the early 1950s under the leadership of Rabbi Binyamin, who edited its monthly, *Ner* ("Candle"). After his death, the paper was edited by Simon Shereshevsky, until it ceased publication in 1964. Iḥud, whose membership was still predominantly intellectual, devoted its energies to organizing group discussions, and had as its main purpose the search for mutual understanding and compromise between Israel and the Arab states, and the protection of the rights of Israel's Arab minority.

Bibliography: *She'ifatenu*, 1–3 (1927–33). [EH]

BERKMAN, ALEXANDER (1870–1936), U.S. anarchist and writer. Born in Russia, Berkman emigrated to the United States in 1888 where he joined the "Pioneers of Freedom," one of the first Jewish anarchist groups founded by Russian immigrants. Later he joined the German anarchist movement; he and Emma *Goldman were considered leaders of the anarchist movement in America. During a steelworkers' strike in Homestead, Pasadena, in 1892, he shot and wounded the director of the steelworks as a protest against the treatment of the workers. He was condemned to 22 years hard labor but was released after serving 14 years in prison. During World War I, Berkman was convicted for engaging in propaganda against conscription and was returned to prison. He was deported to the U.S.S.R. on his release in 1919 but was disappointed with the Bolshevik regime, which he could not reconcile with his own libertarian principles, and left Russia, settling in Germany (1922) and then in France (1925). Eventually he committed suicide. Berkman's numerous publications include *Prison Memoirs of an Anarchist* (1912); *The Kronstadt Rebellion* (1922); *The Bolshevik Myth* (1925); and *Now and After, the ABC of Communist Anarchism* (1929).

Bibliography: R. Drinnon, *Rebel in Paradise* (1961), passim.

[Ed.]

BERKOVITS, ELIEZER (1900–), rabbi and theologian. Berkovits was born in Oradea (Nagyvarad), Transylvania, and was ordained at the Hildesheimer Rabbinical Seminary (1934). After serving in the rabbinate in Berlin, he left Germany for England in 1939, where he was a rabbi in Leeds during 1940–46. He officiated in Sydney, Australia, from 1946 to 1950, then went to the United States, where he served until 1958 as a rabbi in Boston and subsequently as chairman of the department of Jewish philosophy of the Hebrew Theological College in Chicago. As both a modern Orthodox theologian and a Zionist, Berkovits was deeply concerned with the tensions between a secular Jewish nationalism and Jewish religious tradition, a subject to which his *Towards a Historic Judaism* (1943) is largely devoted. He is also the author of *Was ist der Talmud* (1938), *God, Man and History* (1959), *Jewish Critique of the Philosophy of Martin Buber* (1962), and *Judaism: Fossil or Ferment* (1956), a reply to British historian Arnold Toynbee's negative treatment of Jewish history. A

Eliezer Berkovits, U.S. theologian.

collection of his sermons was published in 1945 under the title *Between Yesterday and Tomorrow*.

[H.H.]

BERKOWICZ, JOSEPH (**Józef**; 1789–1846), Polish army officer, the son of Berek *Joselowicz. In 1809 he joined Napoleon's Polish Legion, and took part in the battle of Kock, where his father was killed. For his distinguished service in Napoleon's Russian campaign of 1812, in which he was severely wounded, Joseph was awarded two crosses for valor. Retiring because of his war injuries he was employed in forestry, becoming chief forester in various localities in Poland. At the time of the 1830–31 uprising he called upon the Jews to take up arms and fight for their Polish fatherland. After the Polish defeat, he left with his son Leon for France, where he lived in Besançon. He later moved to Liverpool, England, where he wrote a novel which he himself translated into English, *Stanislaus or the Polish Lancer in the Suite of Napoleon* ... (published posthumously by his sons, 1846).

Bibliography: A. Kraushar, *Syn Berka Joselowicza* ... (1889); E. Tuniński, *Berek Joselewicz i jego syn* (1909), 51–109; M. Balaban, in: *Nowy Dziennik* (April 12, 1933); *Polski Słownik Biograficzny*, 1 (1935), 454–5; A. Levinson, *Toledot Yehudei Varshah* (1953), 122–3.

[Ed.]

BERKOWITZ, HENRY (1857–1924), U.S. Reform rabbi. Berkowitz was born in Pittsburgh, Pa. He was a member of the first graduating class of *Hebrew Union College in 1883. After occupying pulpits in Mobile, Alabama, and Kansas City, where he succeeded his brother-in-law Joseph *Krauskopf, Berkowitz became rabbi of Congregation

Henry Berkowitz, U.S. rabbi.

Rodeph Shalom, Philadelphia (1892). Despite opposition he eliminated many traditional forms from the practice of his congregation and brought it within the mainstream of advanced Reform. Berkowitz established in Philadelphia the Jewish Chautauqua Society, an educational and interfaith organization, and was its chancellor until his

death. He took an active part in the establishment of the
Federation of Jewish Philanthropies in Philadelphia in 1901
and the Philadelphia Rabbinical Association in the same
year. He was the first secretary of the Central Conference of
American Rabbis. Among his publications are *Kiddush or
Sabbath Sentiments in the Home* (1898) and *Intimate
Glimpses of a Rabbi's Career* (1921).

Bibliography: W. Rosenau, in: AJYB, 26 (1924/25), 448–58;
M. E. Berkowitz, *Beloved Rabbi* (1932); O. Levitas, in: AJA, 14
(1962), 3–19.   [S.D.T.]

BERKOWITZ, YITZHAK DOV (1885–1967), Hebrew and
Yiddish novelist, editor, and translator of *Shalom
Aleichem. Born in Slutsk, Belorussia, Berkowitz studied
in *ḥeder* and educated himself in secular subjects. In 1903 he
made his way to Lodz. He became friendly with Itzhak
*Katzenelson. One of his first stories, *"Moshkele Ḥazir,"*
was printed in *Ha-Zofeh* in 1903 and won a literary prize. In
1905 he became literary editor of *Ha-Zeman,* and his
articles and stories appeared in most of the Hebrew and
Yiddish journals of the day. In 1906 Berkowitz married
Shalom Aleichem's daughter, Ernestina, spent 18 months
in Switzerland, and visited the U.S. in 1908. While there, he
contributed to the local Yiddish and Hebrew press. In 1909
he moved to Warsaw, where he edited the literary page of
the Yiddish journal, *Di Naye Velt.* Several volumes of his
collected stories were published in Hebrew and Yiddish
from 1910 onwards.

In 1913 he went to the United States where he edited the
weekly *Ha-Toren* as well as *Miklat* (1920–21). He settled in
Palestine in 1928, and became one of the first editors of the
weekly, *Moznayim.* Berkowitz published his translation of
the collected works of Shalom Aleichem and his
masterfully written reminiscences of the great Yiddish
writer and his generation, under the title *Ha-Rishonim
ki-Venei Adam* (1933–48).

While his contemporaries, G. *Schoffman, J. Ḥ *Brenner, and U. N. *Gnessin revolted against the style of
*Mendele Mokher Seforim and Ḥ. N. *Bialik, Berkowitz
remained true to the older prose writing tradition,
displaying his individuality in the choice of subject,
methods of characterization, and structure of the story.
Although his less conformist contemporaries were not
always accepted by the literary establishment, he himself
was praised by Bialik. Berkowitz's stories, novels, plays,
and memoirs appeared in Yiddish and Hebrew. The bulk of
his work was written in Hebrew.

Berkowitz is important as a writer of short stories. In his
early years he wrote realistic stories under the influence of
Mendele, Bialik, and Chekhov but soon was captivated by
the technique and style of Shalom Aleichem. The influence
of the greater writer tended to weaken Berkowitz's
originality. Berkowitz's stories were written out of the
context of the social crisis which shook Eastern European
Jewry in his day. Among his central themes are: (1) the
weakening of parental authority: *"Lifnei ha-Shulḥan"*
("Before the Table"); *"Pere Adam"* ("The Ill-Mannered
One"); *"Malkot"* ("Lashings"); *"Ba'al Simḥah"* ("The
Feted"); *"Maftir"; "Moshkele Ḥazir";* (2) the problems
resulting from changes in the protagonists' social status and
from their cultural isolation: *"Viddui"* ("Confession");
"Talush" ("Severed," in *Israel Argosy,* 1936); *"Kelei
Zekhukhit"* ("Glass," in *Reflex,* 1927); (3) problems resulting from emigration: *"Karet"* ("The Outcast," in *The Jewish Standard,* 1936); *"El ha-Dod ba-Amerikah"* ("To Uncle
in America," in *B'nai Brith Magazine,* 1930); *"Yarok"*
("The Greenhorn," in *The American Jewish Chronicle,*
1917); *"Mi-Merḥakim"* ("From Afar"); (4) problems from
the social pressure of a strange world: *"Pelitim"* ("Refu-

Yitzḥak Dov Berkowitz, Hebrew and Yiddish writer.

gees"); *"Ruḥot Ra'ot"* ("Evil Spirits"). The characters,
generally unable to face up to the crisis, are "anti-heroes"
who collapse under pressure, victims of social and
psychological situations beyond their control. It is not the
plot, but the social and psychological situation expressed
through the plot, which is the main point of Berkowitz's
stories. His characterization is not introspective (as is the
case with J. Ḥ. Brenner and U. N. Gnessin), but external.
The inner world of the protagonists is revealed through
mannerism, habits, and dialogue. In many cases wider basic
situations are implied through the specific case by the
symbolic expansion of landscapes or verbal hints, extending
the significance of the dialogue or characters. The
background of most of Berkowitz's stories is Russia at the
turn of the century, and the effect of the social and general
crisis of the time on the country's Jews. Some of the stories
deal with the place of immigrants of the old generation in
the U.S., others with the impact of Erez Israel on new
immigrants: *"Amerikah Olah le-Erez Yisrael"* ("America
Comes to Erez Israel," 1946); *"Ha-Nehag"* ("The Heart of
a Chauffeur," in *Commentary,* 1953).

There is a change in direction as regards technique and
theme in Berkowitz's novels. In the first of these, *Menaḥem
Mendel be-Erez Yisrael* ("Menahem Mendel in Erez Israel,"
1936) he attempted to transfer one of Shalom Aleichem's
characters to the new environment of Erez Israel,
continuing the epistolary technique. The correspondence is
one-sided; Menahem Mendel writes to his wife, Sheine
Sheindel; she does not reply. The theme is the ideological
struggle between fathers, who still belong to the Diaspora in
their way of thinking and try to make easy money out of the
building boom in the Tel Aviv of the 1930s, and the sons,
who are committed to the ideal of pioneer labor. The mode
is satirical rather than humoristic. *Yemot ha-Mashi'aḥ*
("Messianic Days," 1938) is a description of the emigration
of Dr. Menuḥin, a Zionist intellectual, from the United
States to Erez Israel. At times it reads like a *roman à clef,* in
which the writer hints at real characters and at the struggle
between the *Revisionist (right-wing Zionist) and the Labor
movement. His hero, Menuḥin, is searching for a new truth
and a new way of life, and he eventually finds a wife
(Yehudit), after overcoming various prejudices, and
discovers the attractions of "labor Palestine." The ideology

of the labor movement is one of the important aspects of the novel and events are judged by its light.

Berkowitz also wrote several plays of different types, some of which appeared in a separate volume in 1928. The fourth, *Mirah,* was published in 1934. His play, *Ba-Arazot ha-Reḥokot* ("In the Distant Lands," 1928), is a comedy on the life of immigrants to the United States. The appearance of Anton, a Russian farmer, in the midst of a Jewish family, causes various romantic complications and errors. *Oto ve-Et Beno* ("He and His Son," 1928), a realistic "somber drama," is a continuation of the story *"Moshkele Ḥazir."* Moshke, a convert to Christianity who had a son, Jacob, by a non-Jewish wife, is nevertheless still tied to his Jewish origins. During a pogrom in the midst of the Russian Revolution, Moshke hides Jews in his home and this act brings about a clash between him and his son, in which Moshke murders Jacob and commits suicide. The play is written in realistic, Ibsenesque style and is well made; it was produced by the Habimah Theater in 1934. *Mirah* was influenced by Ibsen's *A Doll's House,* and deals with the status of women in the United States immigrant society, contrasting the heroine's moral qualities, despite her sin, with her husband's imperfections. In old age, Berkowitz published reminiscences, both of his childhood in Russia, *Pirkei Yaldut* ("Childhood Episodes," 1966), and of Ereẓ Israel in the 1930s, *Yom Etmol Ki Avar* ("Yesterday," 1966). He also translated Tolstoi's *Childhood* (1912) and Chekhov's *Youth* (1922).

Berkowitz was received with enthusiasm by the critics of his time. Bialik praised him warmly while Brenner regarded him with mixed feelings, praising his clarity and freshness but noting his limitations. A later generation dealt with the relationship between naturalism and realism in his work (Y. Keshet), emphasized the central psychological dilemma in his work, which confronts the little man with a situation beyond his control (D. Sadan), and described the alienation of his intellectual heroes (S. Halkin). The young Israeli critics have not devoted much attention to his work. Some have stressed the sociological aspect in his work (i.e., the breakup of the home—G. Katznelson) and others have studied in detail his technique in story and playwriting (G. Shaked). He has had little influence on the writers of his own and the subsequent generation or on the young Israeli writers. A list of his works translated into English appears in Goell, Bibliography.

Bibliography: Ḥ. N. Bialik, *Iggerot,* 1 (1938), 263; idem, *Devarim she-be-al-Peh* (1935), 188–90; *Kol Kitvei J. Ḥ. Brenner,* 2 (1960), 380; D. A. Friedman, *Iyyunei Perozah* (1966), 143–60; S. Halkin, *Arai va-Keva* (1942), 95–112; D. Sadan, *Bein Din le-Ḥeshbon* (1963), 163–8; J. Fichmann, *Benei Dor* (1952), 226–53; Y. Koplewitz (Keshet), *Be-Dor Oleh* (1950), 13–24; G. Katznelson, in: *Gilyonot,* 30 (1954), 239–43; G. Shaked, *Al Arba'ah Sippurim* (1964), 11–33; idem, *'Oto ve-Et Beno' ve-ha-Maḥazeh ha-Re'alisti: Al Sheloshah Maḥazot* (1968), 9–38; A. Komem-Kominkovsky, in: *Me'assef le-Divrei Sifrut,* 4 (1964), 243–53; R. Wallenrod, *Literature of Modern Israel* (1956), 162–6, 169.

[G.Sh.]

BERKSON, ISAAC BAER (1891–), U.S. educator and philosopher. Berkson, who was born in New York, began his teaching career at the Central Jewish Institute in New York, of which he was appointed director in 1917. From 1918 until 1927 he supervised the schools and extension program of the city's Bureau of Jewish Education. In 1927 he began teaching education at the Jewish Institute of Religion (later merged with the Hebrew Union College), and in the same year accepted the invitation of Henrietta Szold, who headed the Palestine Executive's department of education, to survey Jewish schools in Palestine. After completing his survey, he remained in Palestine from 1928 to 1935 as superintendent of the Jewish school system. In 1938 Berkson began lecturing in the philosophy of education at the City College of New York (professor, 1955). Though a follower of the progressive education ideas of John Dewey and W. H. Kilpatrick, Berkson only partially accepted their pragmatic-instrumentalist philosophy. His merger of these views with his own, which were a reflection of the ideals and values of his Jewish heritage, was given expression in his book *The Ideal and the Community* (1958). In dealing with the specific problems of Jewish education he advanced the "community theory." According to him, the Jewish communities of the world constitute the "Knesset Israel," which has its own "heritage of cultural, social, and spiritual values." The cultivation of the individual's Jewish personality must therefore combine loyalty to his own community—the "Knesset Israel," including the State of Israel—and sharing with his fellowmen in the "realm of universal ideals." Berkson's *Theories of Americanization* (1920) was an important influential statement of the American theory of cultural pluralism which he applied specifically to the problems of Jewish education. Berkson's other works include: *Preface to an Educational Philosophy* (1940), *Education Faces the Future* (1943), and *Ethics, Politics and Education* (1968).

Bibliography: S. Dinin, in: *Jewish Education,* 32 (1962), 134; E. Schwarcz, *ibid.,* 29 (1958), 56; J. Pilch (ed.), *Judaism and the Jewish School* (1966), 42.

[Er.S.]

BERLEWI, HENRYK (1894–1967), Polish painter, inventor of "Mechano Faktura." Born in Warsaw, Berlewi studied in Warsaw, Antwerp, and Paris. On his return to Poland he spent some time studying the old masters and was active in Polish art circles. He organized a corporation of Jewish artists and exhibitions of their work. After World War I, Berlewi moved to Berlin, where he became spokesman for the avant-garde. He exhibited with the Novembergruppe in the "Der Sturm" gallery, directed by Herwarth *Walden. In 1922 he developed an abstract painting known as "Mechano-Faktura" ("mechanical painting"). This form of painting attempted to reflect the mechanical processes of industry and was characterized by geometric simplicity and a total lack of representation. Berlewi published a Mechano-Faktura manifesto in Warsaw in 1924. In 1926, however, he returned to representational art and painted realistic *trompe l'œuil* still-life compositions. He reverted to abstract painting in his later years. From 1928 onward he lived in Paris.

Bibliography: *Berlewi, Témoignages* (1965), catalog of the Centre d'Art Cybernétique, Paris.

[Ed.]

BERLIAND, SHLOMO MEIR (1868–1941), one of the first members of the Ḥovevei Zion in Bessarabia and a founder of the *Odessa Committee, the center of the Ḥovevei Zion in Russia (1890). Berliand was born in the Ukraine. In 1920 he became the secretary of the committee for aiding Jewish refugees from the Ukraine. From 1927 until 1940 he was chairman of the Zionist Federation, the central committees of *Keren Hayesod, and of *Tarbut in Bessarabia, Rumania. Head of the Wissotzky Tea Company's agency throughout this period, he worked for the Zionist movement wherever he traveled, and aided Jacob *Bernstein-Kogan in his Zionist activities. At the outbreak of World War II Berliand refused to join his sons in London. When Bessarabia was conquered by Soviet Russia (June 1940) he was forced to leave Kishinev. In June 1941 he was arrested in Czernowitz, along with a group of Zionists, and sent to forced labor in Komi where he died.

Bibliography: *Haolam* (Feb. 24, 1938); M. Landau et al. (eds.), *Al Admat Bessarabia,* 2 (1962), 13–14.

[D.V.]

BERLIGNE, ELIYAHU MEIR (1866–1959), *yishuv* leader and a founder of Tel Aviv. Berligne was born in Mogilev, Russia. He was a delegate to several Zionist congresses and at the Fifth Congress in 1901 joined the Zionist *Democratic Fraction under the leadership of Chaim *Weizmann. In 1907 Berligne settled in Ereẓ Israel, where he established industrial plants producing olive oil and soap. He was one of the founders of Tel Aviv, served on its first administrative committee, of which he was appointed chairman in 1909, and was made an honorary citizen of the city in 1946. Berligne was a member of the board of Herzliah High School in Tel Aviv. In 1919 he was a member of the *yishuv* delegation to the Paris Peace Conference. He was active in the Provisional Council of Palestinian Jewry (Ha-Va'ad ha-Zemanni), was a member of the Va'ad Le'ummi from 1920 to 1948, also serving as its treasurer, and was a signatory of Israel's Declaration of Independence in 1948. He was a member of the General Zionists ("A" Group) which later (1949) became the Progressive Party.

Bibliography: Tidhar, 4 (1950), 1736–38; M. Attias (ed.), *Sefer ha-Te'udot shel ha-Va'ad ha-Le'ummi* (1963), index; A. Druyanow (ed.), *Sefer Tel Aviv* (1936). [B.J.]

BERLIJN, ANTON (Aron Wolf; 1817–1870), Dutch composer, born in Amsterdam. He was for many years conductor and director of the Royal Theater, and was made a member of the Order of Merit by King William III of the Netherlands. Other monarchs (of Belgium, Denmark, Greece, Sweden, and Austria) also decorated him. He founded many choral groups, wrote liturgical works for the synagogue, and composed a large body of other music. His compositions included nine operas (of which *Die Bergknappen* and *Proserpina* became popular), an oratorio *Moses auf Nebo,* a symphony (performed by Spohr at Cassel, 1857), seven ballets, and a cantata. His archives, including correspondence with Mendelssohn and Meyerbeer, among others, are preserved at the National and University Library, Jerusalem.

Bibliography: Grove, Dict; Baker, Biog Dict; Riemann-Gurlitt; Sendrey, Music, index. [D.L.S.]

BERLIN, largest city in Germany. The capital of Germany until 1945, it is now divided into West Berlin and East Berlin.

The Old Community (1295–1573). Jews are first mentioned in a letter from the Berlin local council of Oct. 28, 1295, forbidding wool merchants to supply Jews with wool yarn. Suzerainty over the Jews belonged to the margrave who from 1317 pledged them to the municipality on varying terms, but received them back in 1363. Their taxes, however, were levied by the municipality in the name of the ruler of the state. The oldest place of Jewish settlement in "Great Jews' Court" (Grosser Judenhof) and "Jews' Street" had some of the characteristics of a Jewish quarter, but a number of wealthier Jews lived outside these areas. Until 1543, when a cemetery was established in Berlin, the Jews buried their dead in the town of Spandau. The Berlin Jews engaged mainly in commerce, handicrafts (insofar as this did not infringe on the privileges of the craft guilds), moneychanging, moneylending, and other pursuits. Few attained affluence. They paid taxes for the right to slaughter animals ritually, to sell meat, to marry, to circumcise their sons, to buy wine, to receive additional Jews as residents of their community, and to bury their dead. During the *Black Death (1349–50), the houses of the Jews were burned down and the Jewish inhabitants were killed or expelled from the town.

From 1354, Jews again settled in Berlin. In 1446 they were arrested with the rest of the Jews in *Brandenburg, and expelled from the electorate after their property had been confiscated. A year later Jews again began to return, and between 1454 and 1475 there were 23 recorded instances of Jews establishing residence in Berlin in the oldest register of inhabitants. A few wealthy Jews were admitted into Brandenburg in 1509. In 1510 the Jews were accused of desecrating the *Host and stealing sacred vessels from a church in a village near Berlin. 111 Jews were arrested and subjected to examination, and 51 were sentenced to death; of these 38 were burned at the stake in the new market square together with the real culprit, a Christian, on July 10, 1510. Subsequently, the Jews were expelled from the entire electorate of Brandenburg. All the accused were proved completely innocent at the Diet of Frankfort in 1539 through the efforts of *Joseph (Joselmann) b. Gershom of Rosheim and Philipp *Melanchthon. The elector Joachim II (1535–71) permitted the Jews to return and settle in the towns in Brandenburg, and Jews were permitted to reside in Berlin in 1543 despite the opposition of the townspeople. In 1571, when the Jews were again expelled from Brandenburg, the Jews of Berlin were expelled "for ever." For the next 100 years, a few individual Jews appeared there at widely scattered intervals. About 1663, the Court Jew Israel Aaron, who was supplier to the army and the electoral court, was permitted to settle in Berlin.

Beginnings of the Modern Community (to 1812). After the expulsion of the Jews from *Vienna in 1670, the elector issued an edict on May 21, 1671, admitting 50 wealthy Jewish families from Austria into the mark of Brandenburg and the duchy of Crossen (Krosno) for 20 years. They paid a variety of taxes for the protection afforded them but were not permitted to erect a synagogue. The first writ of privileges was issued to Abraham Riess (Abraham b. Model Segal) and Benedict Veit (Baruch b. Menahem Rositz), on Sept. 10, 1671, the date considered to mark the foundation of the new Berlin community. Notwithstanding the opposition of the Christians (and also of Israel Aaron who feared competition) to any increase in the number of Jewish residents in Berlin, the community grew rapidly, and in the course of time the authorities granted letters of protection to a considerable number of Jews. In addition, many *unvergleitete* Jews (i.e., without residence permits) infiltrated into Brandenburg. The first population census of 1700 showed that there were living in Berlin at that time 70 Jewish *vergleitete* families with residence permits, 47 families without writs of protection, and a few peddlers and beggars (about 1,000 persons). The refugees from Austria now became a minority, and quarrels and clashes broke out within the community (see below). The Jews of Berlin engaged mainly in commerce. The guilds and merchants were bitterly opposed to them and they were accused of dealing in stolen goods. The Christians demanded the expulsion of the foreign Jews or restriction of their economic activity to dealing in secondhand goods and pawnbroking, not to be conducted in open shops. The government responded only partly to such demands, being interested in the income from the Berlin Jews. It imposed restrictions upon the increase of the Jewish population in the city and issued decrees increasing their taxes, making the community collectively responsible for the payment of protection money (1700), for prohibiting Jews from maintaining open shops, from dealing in stolen goods (1684), and from engaging in retail trade in certain commodities except at fairs (1690). Nevertheless, the number of Jewish stores grew to such an extent that there was at least one in every street. The Jews were subsequently ordered to close down every store opened after 1690, and all other Jews were forbidden to engage in anything but dealing in old clothes and pawnbroking. They could be exempted from these restrictions on payment of 5,000 thalers.

Elector Frederick III, who became King Frederick I of Prussia in 1701, began a systematic exploitation of the Jews by means of various taxes. The protection tax was doubled in 1688; a tax was levied for the mobilization and arming of an infantry regiment; 10,000 ducats were exacted for various misdemeanors; 1,100 ducats for children recognized as *vergleitete;* 100 thalers annually toward the royal reception in Berlin; 200–300 thalers annually in birth and marriage taxes; and other irregular imposts. Frederick William I (1713–40) limited (in a charter granted to the Jews on May 20, 1714) the number of tolerated Jews to 120 householders, but permitted in certain cases the extension of letters of protection to include the second and third child. The Jews of Berlin were permitted to engage in commerce almost without restriction, and in handicrafts provided that the rights of the guilds were not thereby infringed. By a charter granted in 1730, the number of tolerated Jews was reduced to 100 householders. Only the two oldest sons of the family were allowed to reside in Berlin—the first, if he possessed 1,000 thalers in ready money, on payment of 50 thalers, and the second if he owned and paid double these amounts. *Vergleitete* Jews might own stores, but were forbidden to trade in drugs and spices (except for tobacco and dyes), in raw skins, and in imported woolen and fiber goods, and were forbidden to operate breweries or distilleries. They were also forbidden to engage in any craft, apart from seal engraving, gold and silver embroidery, and Jewish ritual slaughter. Land ownership by Jews had been prohibited in 1697 and required a special license which could be obtained only with great difficulty. Jews might bequeath their property to their children, but not to other relatives. On Jan. 22, 1737, Jews were forbidden to buy houses in Berlin or to acquire them in any other fashion. In 1755 an equal interest rate was fixed for Jews and Christians.

The Jews in Berlin in the 18th century primarily engaged as commercial bankers and traders in precious metals and stones. Some served as *court Jews. Members of the *Gomperz family were among the wealthiest in Berlin. In the course of time, all trade in money in Berlin was concentrated in Jewish hands. One of the pioneers of Prussian industry was Levi Ilf, who established a ribbon factory in Charlottenburg in 1718. At the same time the royal policy continued of restricting the Jewish population of Berlin, and even decreasing it as far as possible. When in 1737 it became evident that the number of Jewish families in Berlin had risen to 234, a decree was issued limiting the quota to 120 families (953 persons) with an additional 48 families of "communal officers" (243 persons). The remainder (584) were ordered to leave, and 387 did in fact leave. However in 1743 Berlin had a Jewish population of 333 families (1,945 persons).

*Frederick the Great (1740–86) denied residence rights in Berlin to second and third children of Jewish families and wished to limit the total number of protected Jews to 150. However, the revised *Generalprivilegium* and the royal edict of April 17, 1750, which remained in force until 1812, granted residence rights to 203 "ordinary" families, whose eldest children could inherit that right, and to 63 "extraordinary" families, who might possess it only for the duration of their own lifetime. A specified number of "public servants" was also to be tolerated. However, during his reign, the economic, cultural, and social position of the Jews in Berlin improved. During the Seven Years' War, many Jews became wealthy as purveyors to the army and the mint and the rights enjoyed by the Christian bankers were granted to a number of Jews. In 1763, the Jews in Berlin were granted permission to acquire 70 houses in place of 40. While their role in the retail trade decreased in importance because of the many restrictions imposed, the number of Jewish manufacturers, bankers, and brokers increased. On May 2, 1791, the entire *Itzig family received full civic rights, becoming the first German Jews to whom they were granted. At the same time, the king compelled the Jews to supply a specified quantity of silver annually to the mint at a price below the current one (1763), to pay large sums for new writs of protection (1764), and, in return for various privileges and licenses, to purchase porcelain ware to the value of 300–500 thalers from the royal porcelain factory and sell it abroad.

As a concomitant of economic prosperity, there appeared the first signs of cultural adaptation. Under the influence of Moses *Mendelssohn, several reforms were introduced in the Berlin community, especially in the sphere of education. In 1778 a school, *Juedische Freischule (Ḥinnukh Ne'arim), was founded, which was conducted along modern comprehensive principles and methods. Mendelssohn and David *Friedlaender composed the first German reader for children. The dissemination of general (non-Jewish) knowledge was also one of the aims of the Ḥevrat Doreshei Leshon Ever ("Association of Friends of the Hebrew Language"), founded in 1783, whose organ *Ha-Me'assef* (see **Me'assefim*) began to appear in Berlin in 1788. Mendelssohn's home became a gathering place for scholars, and Berlin became the fount of the Enlightenment movement (*Haskalah) and of the trend toward *assimilation. The salons of Henrietta *Herz, Rachel *Varnhagen, and Dorothea *Schlegel served as rendezvous for both Jews and Christians of the social elite of Berlin. However, progress toward legally recognized civil equality was slow. After the new Exchange building was erected in Berlin in 1805, a joint "corporation" of Christians and Jews was

Figure 1. The burning of the Jews in the new market, 1510. Woodcut from a contemporary pamphlet published in Frankfort on the Oder.

established in which the latter were in the majority and had equal rights. In 1803–04, during the literary controversy over the Jewish question, the government took no action whatever on behalf of the Jews, but after the Prussian defeat by Napoleon the Municipal Act of Nov. 19, 1809, facilitated their attainment of citizen status. Solomon *Veit was elected to the Berlin municipal council and David Friedlaender was appointed a city councillor. The edict of March 11, 1812, finally bestowed Prussian citizenship upon the Jews; all restrictions on their residence rights in the state, as well as the special taxes they had to pay, were now abolished.

Internal Life (17th–18th Centuries). The fierce controversies that had broken out in the Jewish community during the communal elections in 1689 resulted in governmental intervention in the administrative affairs of the community. Thus the decree of January 24 and the statute of Dec. 7, 1700, included government-approved regulations for the Jewish community. The communal leaders *(parnasim),* elected for three years, were empowered to impose fines (two-thirds of which went to the state treasury and one-third to the communal charity fund) and to excommunicate members with the consent of the local rabbi and government. The "chief *parnas*" acted as mediator between the Jews and the state. In 1717, complete anarchy in the conduct of communal affairs became evident; the *parnasim* were deposed and a fine was imposed on the community amounting to 10,000 thalers, later reduced to 6,500. In 1722 and in 1723 new statutes were promulgated regulating the organizational structure of the community. Apart from the chief *parnasim,* who were appointed by the king and functioned under the supervision of a Jewish commission, a communal committee of three, four, or five *parnasim* was set up which would coopt to itself two optimates *(tovim)* and two alternates *(ikkurim)* for handling particularly important matters. To decide on matters of extreme importance larger committees were appointed of 15, 18, or 32 members. In 1792 a supervisory committee was created consisting of three members to supervise the fiscal aspect of communal administration.The first rabbi, elected at the time of the erection of the Berlin synagogue in the Heiderentergasse, was Michael Ḥasid (officiated 1714–28). His successors include Jacob Joshua b. Ẓevi Hirsch *Falk of Cracow (1731–34), author of *Penei Yehoshu'a,* David *Fraenkel (1743–62), author of *Korban ha-Edah* on the Palestinian Talmud and teacher of Moses Mendelssohn, and Ẓevi Hirsch b. Aryeh Loeb (Hirschel *Levin, 1772–1800), known for his opposition to Haskalah.

From the Edict of Equality to the Accession of the Nazis. The political history of the Jews of Berlin after 1812 becomes increasingly merged with that of the Jews of *Prussia and *Germany as a whole. In the 1848 Revolution the Jews played an active role as fighters on the barricades and members of the civic guard, as orators and journalists, and the like. Despite the edict of 1812 Jews continued to be hampered by a number of restrictions, and formal civic equality was not attained until July 1860. Subsequently, Jews began to enter Berlin's political and social life in increasing numbers, and the Berlin municipality was for a long time a stronghold of liberalism and tolerance. About one-fifth of Berlin's newspapers were owned by Jews. The *Berliner Tageblatt* and the *Vossische Zeitung,* whose publishers and editors were Jewish, were read abroad with particular attention, although it was known that they did not express the opinions of circles close to the government. Berlin Jews played a prominent part in literature, the theater, music, and art. Their successes aroused fierce reaction among the more conservative elements and Berlin became a center of anti-Semitism. The "Berlin Movement"

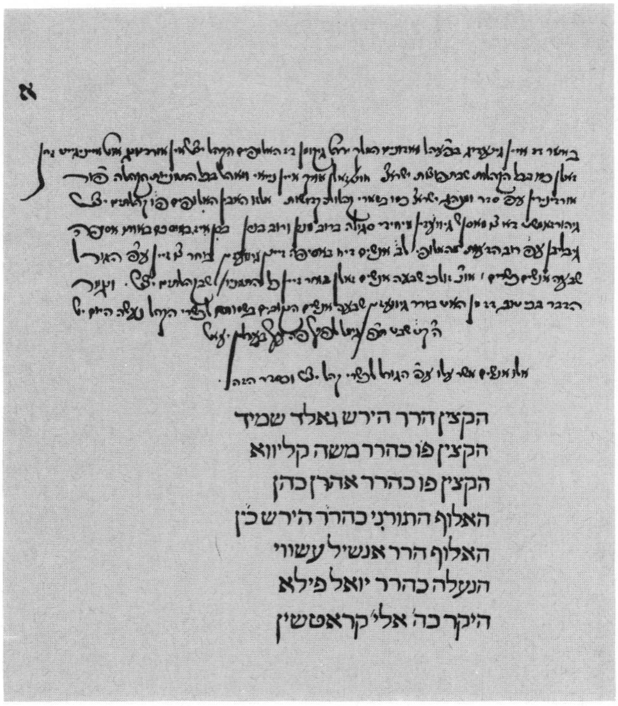
א

הקצין הרר הירש גאלד שמיד
הקצין פו כהרר משה קליווא
הקצין פו כהרר אהרן כהן
האלוף התורני כהרר הירש כ״ן
האלוף הרר אנשיל עשווי
הנעלה כהרר יואל פילא
היקר כה' אלי' קראטשין

Figure 2. First page of the minute book of the Berlin community, 1723. Jerusalem, C.A.H.J.P.

founded by Adolf *Stoecker incited the masses against the Jews by alleging that they were the standard-bearers of capitalism and controlled the press (see *Anti-Semitic Political Parties and Organizations).

The Jewish population of Berlin numbered 3,292 in 1812; 11,840 in 1852; 108,044 in 1890; and 172,672 in 1925. Thus, within a century it had increased more than fiftyfold. The Jews comprised about 2% of the total population in 1840, 5.02% in 1890, and 4.29% in 1925. The Jews in Berlin comprised 1.4% of German Jewry in 1811–28, 7.03% in 1871, and 30.6% in 1925. Despite the increasing instances of intermarriage, renunciation of Judaism, and conversion to Christianity, and the decline in the Jewish birthrate, the Jewish population of Berlin continued to grow through the arrival of Jews from provincial centers, especially from the province of Posen (Poznan) and from Eastern Europe. As Berlin grew in importance as a commercial and industrial center, Jews played an increasingly important role in the city's economic life, especially as bankers (*Mendelssohn, *Bleichroeder, and others), owners of department stores (*Wertheim, *Tietz, Jandorf), and in the grain and metal trades, the textile and clothing industries, building construction, the manufacture of railway engines and cars, the brewing of beer, and other branches of the economy. Ludwig *Loewe headed a large armaments factory in Berlin. The General Electric Company (A.E.G.) was founded by the Jewish engineer Emil *Rathenau, and both his son Walter *Rathenau and Felix Deutsch were active in it. In 1861 53.17% of the Jews in Berlin engaged in commerce, and 17.3% in industry and the manual trades; by 1910 the percentage of those occupied in commerce had decreased to 41.61%, while 35.16% earned their livelihood in industry and the manual trades.

Internal Life of the Berlin Community (1812–1933). Following the partitions of Poland-Lithuania, 1772–95, the Berlin community became increasingly influenced by the steady stream of Eastern European Jews *(Ostjuden)* who first arrived from the Posen district. This influx made up for the losses to the Jewish communities through assimilation and apostasy. Later there was growing immigration from the *Pale of Settlement. From the second half of the 19th century the increasing colony of Russian, mainly Jewish, students exerted a powerful cultural influence in Berlin. The organizational structure of the Jewish community was undermined after the emancipation of the Jews in 1812. The old regulations were abolished by the 1812 edict and no new regulations were instituted. For some time the community was not allowed to collect dues and faced disintegration. A statute issued in July 1837 permitted the renewal of normal communal life, and from then on the Berlin community was administered by a committee of seven members and three alternates and a council of 21 members and ten alternates. The first elections to the council took place in February 1854, and the community's first constitution was ratified in August 1860. During this period, the community was thrown into a ferment as a result of the aspiration of David Friedlaender and others for extreme liturgical reforms. The *Reform program was temporarily restrained by a decree of Dec. 9, 1823, which laid down that all divine worship was to take place in the local synagogue and according to accepted custom without any innovations in the language, ritual, prayers, and liturgy.

In 1819, the *Verein fuer Kultur und Wissenschaft des Judentums ("Society for Jewish Culture and Learning"), was founded in Berlin by Leopold *Zunz, I. M. *Jost, and Eduard *Gans, with Heinrich *Heine among its members (see *Germany). In the meanwhile, far-reaching changes had been introduced in education. The Ḥinnukh Ne'arim school was closed at the end of 1825 for lack of funds, and was replaced in 1826 by a new school for boys, founded by the community; Zunz was principal of this school until 1830. In 1835 the community founded a school for girls. There were also several Jewish private schools in Berlin, such as that of H. M. Bock (founded in 1807), whose principals were Jost (1816–35) and Sigismund *Stern (1835–45). R. Meir b. Simḥah Weyl, who charted a conservative course in education, opened a teachers' seminary in 1825. From 1840 to 1850 a teachers' seminary functioned under the direction of Zunz. A teachers' training institute was established in 1859 under the rectorship of Aaron *Horowitz.

In 1844 Michael Jehiel *Sachs was invited to be the third *dayyan* and preacher of the community. Although a Conservative, he was not opposed to moderate reform. In the wake of the foundation of the second Kulturverein ("cultural association"; 1840), Aaron *Bernstein founded the Reform Society in 1845, and later the Reform Congregation, which introduced far-flung liturgical reforms, especially during the rabbinate of Samuel *Holdheim (1847–60). At first, divine worship was held both on Saturdays and Sundays and later only on Sundays. The Reform Congregation was unsuccessful in its attempt to secede from the official community, but the latter was obliged to give very substantial financial support to the Reform Congregation since many of its members were among the largest taxpayers. The Berlin community was again violently shaken when many of its members pressed for the introduction of an organ and modification of the liturgy in the New Synagogue. The appointment of Abraham *Geiger as rabbi of the Berlin community (officiated 1870–74) met with strong opposition from Orthodox circles, and in 1869 Azriel (Israel) *Hildesheimer and his adherents left the main community and established the Adass Yisroel congregation, which received official recognition in 1885. Abraham Geiger had stipulated as a condition of his appointment that an institute for Jewish research be established in Berlin, and in 1872 the *Hochschule fuer die Wissenschaft des Judentums was opened there. A year later, Hildesheimer opened a rabbinical seminary for Orthodox Judaism (*Rabbinerseminar fuer das orthodoxe Judentum). Between 1880 and 1930, eight large synagogues were erected by the Berlin community, among them that in the Fasanenstrasse which was one of the most magnificent synagogues in the world. In all, the community owned 16 synagogues, seven of them Orthodox and the remainder Liberal and Reformist. Thirty rabbis served in Berlin after Abraham Geiger (12 Orthodox and the remainder liberal). In addition, most religious groups which were supported by the community had their own rabbis.

Berlin was the center of the national German-Jewish organizations, such as the *Deutsch-Israelitischer Gemeindebund (founded in 1869), Verband der deutschen Juden (1904), the *B'nai B'rith (1883), *Central-Verein deutscher Staatsbuerger juedischen Glaubens (1893), *Hilfsverein der deutschen Juden (1901), Zentralwohlfartsstelle der deutschen Juden (1917), and others. Likewise, Jewish newspapers and periodicals were published in Berlin, including the communal organ, whose circulation reached 60,000 copies. The Berlin communal institutions and their activities in every field served as a model for Jewish communities throughout the world. The annual communal budget in the 1930s was about 10,000,000 marks (as against 5,000,000 marks in 1914). About 70,000 Jews in Berlin paid dues to the community.

For about 80 years the Liberals were predominant in the Berlin community. But Liberals and Orthodox worked together in full harmony in the central organizations in which, at least for a certain period, the Zionists also participated. The *Ḥibbat Zion movement met with but a lukewarm reception in Berlin, especially among the Orthodox, and the opposition to political Zionism was particularly keen. The Berlin rabbi S. *Maybaum was among the leaders of the "*Protest Rabbis," and the Central-Verein and the *Vereinigung fuer das liberale Judentum launched a concerted effort against the Zionistische Vereinigung fuer Deutschland and its organ, the **Juedische Rundschau.* When the procedure for communal elections was changed after World War I, four representatives of the *Juedische Volkspartei (a coalition of Zionists, *Mizrachi, and the Verband der ostjuedischen Organizationen) and one of the *Po'alei Zion were elected in 1920 to the representative council (Repraesentantenversammlung), which consisted of 21 members; two Zionists sat on the communal committee (Gemeindevorstand). In the 1926 election, a coalition of the Juedische Volkspartei, the Conservatives, and the Mittelpartei won a majority. For three years, the Zionist Georg Kareski headed the communal committee. However, in the elections of November 1930, 24 Liberals were elected to the representative council, 14 from the Juedische Volkspartei, and three from among the small parties; seven Liberals, three Zionists, and one Conservative sat on the communal committee. Max Naumann and his faction were the spearhead of the extremist anti-Zionist faction which rejected all cooperation with non-German Jews and demanded that the Zionists be deprived of their German citizenship and permitted to reside in Germany only as aliens. In 1922, at the initiative of the Berlin community, the Preussischer Landesverband juedischer Gemeinden was founded, comprising 655 communities, not including the Orthodox communities which formed their own association. A great boon to the Berlin community was the government support which was granted for the first time during the inflation of late 1923, without which it could not have survived. In later years, the government subsidy to the community was insufficient.

After the murder of Karl Liebknecht and Rosa

Figure 3a. The famous Fasanenstrasse Synagogue in Charlottenburg, Berlin, designed by E. Hessel, 1912. Berlin Municipality. Photo State Picture Office, Berlin.

*Luxemburg in January 1919, anti-Semitic propaganda in Berlin increased. The Kapp putsch (March 1920) had blatant anti-Jewish undertones. Walter Rathenau, the German foreign minister, was assassinated by anti-Semitic nationalists on June 24, 1922. On Nov. 5, 1923, anti-Semites attacked the Jews living in Grenadierstrasse and Dragonerstrasse, which were centers of Jewish residence. In 1926, after the appointment of Joseph *Goebbels as *Gauleiter* in Berlin, anti-Jewish rabble-rousing increased. On the eve of the Jewish New Year (Sept. 12, 1931), Jews returning from synagogue in Kurfuerstendam were assaulted by gangs of Nazis, organized by Count Wolff Heinrich von Halldorf (later chief of police in the Third Reich).

[J.Mel./Ed.]

1933–39. At the time the Nazis seized power, Berlin's organized Jewish community numbered about 172,000 persons. In 1933 the Nazi boycott (April 1) affected Jewish shop owners; legislation against non-Aryans led to dismissal of Jewish professionals; while "aryanization" of Jewish firms and the dismissal of their Jewish employees was carried out by the exertion of steady economic pressure. The Jewish officials not affected by these measures were eventually ousted under the provisions of the *Nuremberg Laws (1935). During this early period, such incidents as the murder of a Jewish physician, Dr. Philippsthal (spring 1933), and the suicide of Rudolf S. Mosse after mistreatment in prison (fall 1933), the first such incidents of their kind, caused great consternation among the Jews. In these initial years, when the members of the Jewish community were being methodically deprived of their economic standing and civil rights, Jewish religious and cultural life in Berlin underwent a tremendous upsurge. Jewish children, most of them excluded from the public schools, attended schools set up and maintained by the Jewish community or private schools. Eight elementary Jewish schools were maintained at one period to meet the community needs, as well as the famous college for Jewish studies, the *Hochschule fuer die Wissenschaft des Judentums. Jews were later forbidden to attend theaters and public places of entertainment. The Juedischer Kulturbund ("Jewish Cultural Society") was established. In the summer of 1935 yellow benches for the segregation of Jews were set up in parks and inscribed *nur fuer Juden* ("only for Jews"). Signs inscribed *Juden unerwuenscht* ("Jews not wanted") were displayed in public places. These were removed for the duration of the Olympic Games then being held in Berlin (summer 1936). Throughout this period, raids and arrests became frequent occurrences and were accelerated in 1938. Until November 1938 Jewish newspapers and books were published on an unprecedented scale. Notable among the newspapers was the *Berliner juedisches Gemeindeblatt,* a voluminous weekly published by the community. Zionist work was in full swing, especially that of He-Ḥalutz, and in February 1936, a German Zionist convention was held in Berlin (the last to meet there), still reflecting in its composition the vigorous party life of German Zionists. From March 28, 1938, the Jewish community was deprived of its status as a recognized public corporate body. The Berlin community was made a "private" organization, denied the right to collect dues from the community, and renamed the Juedische Kultusvereinigung Berlin ("Jewish Religious Society").

In June 1938, mass arrests of Jews took place on the charge that they were "asocial," e.g., had a criminal record, including traffic violations, and they were imprisoned in *Sachsenhausen concentration camp. On November 9–10, **Kristallnacht* marked a turning point in the affairs of Berlin Jewry: synagogues were burned down, Jewish shops destroyed, and 10,000 Jews from Berlin and other places were arrested and imprisoned in Sachsenhausen. The *"Bannmeile"* was decreed, which restricted Jews to an area within a certain radius from their place of residence; banished them from most of the main thoroughfares, and the area in which government offices were located; and evicted Jews from their apartments, a step which had begun earlier, but was now accelerated. Jewish newspapers had to cease publication. The only paper was the new *Das juedische Narchrichtenblatt* which was required to publish Gestapo directives to the Jews. Meetings of bodies of the Jewish community were no longer permitted, and the Jewish community's executive council had to conduct its affairs from then on without consulting any representative group. Religious services, when resumed, were now restricted to three synagogues (on Levetzow, Luetzow, and Kaiser Streets) and a few small halls. Most of Berlin's rabbis left Berlin before *Kristallnacht:* the last three rabbis to stay were Leo *Baeck (who was later sent to Theresienstadt camp), Felix Singerman (died in Riga in 1942), and Martin Salomonski (died in Auschwitz in 1944). At the end of January 1939, the Gestapo established a Zentralstelle fuer juedische Auswanderung ("Central Bureau for Jewish Emigration") in Berlin. The Berlin community, presided over by Heinrich *Stahl, was the largest and most dynamic German-Jewish community, and was incorporated along with the Reichsvertretung der deutschen Juden into the Nazi-imposed Reichsvereinigung der Juden in Deutschland, established on July 4, 1939. After its incorporation into the Reichsvereinigung, the Berlin community maintained its autonomous function for some time.

1939–45. After the outbreak of war, the living conditions and situation of the Jews worsened. Emigration was still permitted and even encouraged, and existing organizations and institutions (Kulturbund, Jewish schools) were able to continue functioning. However, Jews were drafted for forced labor at wages far below the prevailing rate and with no social benefits, but this at least provided them with a minimum income and delayed their deportation. On Jan. 31, 1940, a special Arbeitsamt fuer Judenarbeiter ("Labor Exchange for Jew-Workers") was set up. In the spring of 1940 Stahl was removed from his post in the Reichsvereinigung by the Nazi authorities and replaced by Moritz Henschel, a former attorney. In September 1941, a drastic turn for the worse came about. First the *Judenstern* ("Jewish star," i.e., yellow *badge) was introduced. Two weeks later, on the Day of Atonement, in the middle of a sermon by Rabbi Leo Baeck, the president of the community was summoned to the Gestapo and told that the community would have to prepare for a partial evacuation from the city, that large apartments still occupied by Jews would have to be cleared, that many additional parts of the city would now be out of bounds to Jews, and that the Levetzowstrasse synagogue would be turned into a *Sammellager* ("assembly camp") for 1,000 persons. In due course more such assembly camps were added. Legal emigration was prohibited on October 23. The last transport of emigrants left Berlin on October 18 for Lisbon. In the preceding months (May–October), 1,342 emigrants had been permitted to leave. Between October 23 and the end of the year only 62 persons managed to leave, and in 1942 only nine Jews were permitted to go abroad. There were five major phases in the process of deportation: (a) Between fall 1941 and January 1942 the deportees were sent to Riga, Minsk, Kovno, and Lodz. (b) Those deported in spring 1942 were sent to Lublin (Trawniki). (c) Between summer 1942 and February 1943 their destination was Theresienstadt, Auschwitz, Riga, and Tallinn (Rasiku). (d) Auschwitz was the destination of the deportees of March–April 1943. (e) Those deported from spring 1943 until the end of the war were sent to Bergen-Belsen, Ravensbrueck, Sachsenhausen, and Auschwitz. Altogether there were 63 *Osttransporte* carrying some 35,000 victims to death camps in the east, and 117 *Alterstransporte,* transporting some 15,000 (mainly older) persons to Theresienstadt. It is believed that about 95% of the first and 90% of the second group perished. (For lists of transport numbers, dates, numbers of deportees and destinations, see bibliography, Sellenthin, 84–85.) All through 1942 the deportations were kept up, although community employees and persons employed on forced labor were still excluded. In November and December 1942, the infamous commissar Alois Brunner (see Adolf *Eichmann) from Vienna was employed in Berlin and was responsible for organizing the picking up of the candidates for deportation in their homes, "distinguishing" himself by his extraordinary cruelty. Eventually, the deportations came to include groups of community employees, and from the fall of 1942, only those Jewish laborers who were employed in vital war production were still safe from deportation. At the beginning of 1943, the Gestapo persuaded the military administration to relinquish these workers, which resulted on February 27–28 in the so-called *"Fabrikaktion"*—marked by exceptional cruelty—in which all the workers were taken straight from the factories and deported from Berlin. Those Jews arrested in this "action" who had gentile wives were taken to a special camp for onward deportation, but when their wives carried out violent street demonstrations, the Gestapo yielded and set their husbands free. On May 13, 1942, an anti-Jewish exhibition, "Soviet Paradise," was opened in Berlin, and was attacked by a group of Jewish communists, led by Herbert *Baum. The group was caught and hardly any of them survived. Two hundred and fifty Jews—50 for each German who had been killed in the attack—were shot, and another 250 were sent to Sachsenhausen and perished there. The community offices were closed down on June 10, 1943, and six days later the "full" Jews among the members of its executive council were deported to Theresienstadt. The remaining Jews were looked after by the Neue Reichsvereinigung, which took up its seat in the Berlin Jewish Hospital. While the deportations went on, many Jews tried to stay on illegally, a very difficult undertaking, owing to the need for frequent change of hideouts, and the lack of ration cards; many were caught and deported. The "illegals" were given temporary help on an organized basis, by groups of people who were of mixed parentage *(Mischlinge)* and as such were not liable for deportation themselves; there were also some Germans who at the risk of their lives put their apartments at the disposal of the Jews who were hiding out. One group of Jewish youngsters and their instructor managed to hide in Grunewald for an extended period, spending their time in the study of Zionist subjects. No exact figure is available for the number of "illegal" Jews who survived in Berlin, and estimates vary from 2,000 to 4,000. Berlin became officially *"judenrein"* ("clean of Jews") on June 16, 1943. On June 30, 1943, there were in fact 6,700, and on March 31, 1945, 5,990 Jews, comprising 4,790 Jews who had non-Jewish spouses, 992 *"Geltungsjuden"* (persons of mixed parentage, professing Jewish religion), 46 Jews from non-enemy countries, and 162 "full" Jews, most of whom were employed in the Jewish Hospital. The Jewish cemetery had remained in use—several Torah Scrolls were hidden there, to be restituted after the war.

Size of the Jewish Population. The diagram shows the decrease in the Jewish population of Berlin between 1925 and 1945. The statistics before 1933 refer to persons designated as members of the Jewish faith, whereas the later figures for the most part also include Jews "by race" (as defined by the Nuremberg Laws):

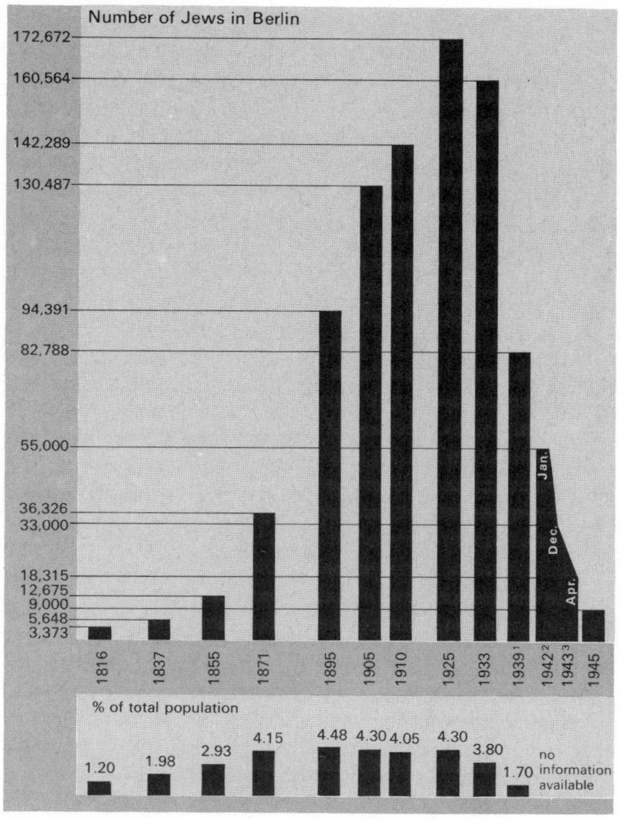

[1] Including Jews by "race"— decrease due mainly to emigration but in small measure also to a mortality rate higher than the birth rate. Emigration figures were actually higher for Berlin Jewry, but were offset by the influx of Jews from the provinces.

[2] Decrease due to deportation.

[3] Decrease due to final mass deportations.

In 1967 there were 6,000 Jews in West Berlin and approximately 1,500 in East Berlin.

The Jewish population of Berlin, 1816–1945.

[K.Y.B.-K./ED.]

Contemporary Period. On July 15, 1945, the Jewish community was officially reconstituted. At first it was headed by Erich Nelhans, a former *Mizrachi leader, and from the fall of 1945 by Hans Erich Fabian, who had returned from Theresienstadt, the only member of the Reichsvereinigung to survive the war. Also active in the

Figure 3b. A synagogue in flames on *Kristallnacht,* November 9–10, 1938. Jerusalem, Ansbacher Collection.

leadership of the community were Alfred Schoyer, a member of the Berlin Jewish Community Council before his deportation; Heinz Galinski, who had returned from Bergen-Belsen; and Julius Meyer, a survivor of Auschwitz. At the beginning of 1946, the community had a registered membership of 7,070 people, of whom 4,121 (over 90% of all married members) had non-Jewish spouses, 1,321 had survived the war by hiding, and 1,628 had returned from concentration camps. The Jews were dispersed throughout Berlin, a third of them living in the Soviet sector. The community was assisted by the military government, as well as by the *American Jewish Joint Distribution Committee (JDC), which initiated its activities in Berlin in the autumn of 1945. Several synagogues were opened, the Jewish Hospital resumed its work (although most of its patients and staff were not Jews), and three homes for the aged and a children's home were established. There was no local rabbi or religious teachers, but American Jewish army chaplains volunteered their services. The general assumption at this time was that the Jews would not be able to reestablish themselves in Berlin (or anywhere else in Germany) and that the community's principal task was to help them to emigrate from the country. The community was thus defined as a "liquidation community" *(Liquidationsgemeinde).*

In addition to the organized Jewish community, Berlin also became a center for Jewish *Displaced Persons (DPs). Toward the end of 1945 and during the first half of 1946, the main *Beriḥah route from Poland led through Stettin and the Soviet Zone to Berlin, from where it continued through the remaining part of the Soviet Zone and the British Zone to the American Zone. It was a very arduous route, especially during the harsh winter months, and temporary shelter had to be provided in Berlin. A small camp was established in the Wittenau district of the French sector of the city in the autumn of 1945 with a capacity of 200; at the beginning of 1946 a large camp was established at Schlachtensee in the American sector, which could hold 4,000 refugees, and a third camp was established in the summer of 1946 in the Tempelhof district of the American sector. In July 1946, however, the Beriḥah from Poland took on a quasi-legal character and was rerouted through Czechoslovakia and Vienna to the American Zone in Germany and Austria. As a result the refugee population of Berlin became fairly stabilized. By the end of 1946, there were 6,785 DPs in the three Berlin camps. When the Soviet blockade of Berlin was lifted, the Occupation authorities decided to evacuate the DPs, and between July 23 and Aug. 1, 1948, 5,456 Jewish refugees were airlifted from Berlin to various camps in the American Zone.

By this time the Jewish community had reached a measure of consolidation, in spite of the difficult economic and political conditions in the city. Although a few hundred members had emigrated overseas and mortality exceeded the birthrate, the total number of Jews had increased as a result of the influx of Jews returning from abroad. Prominent among the returnees was a group of 500 refugees who had spent the war years in *Shanghai. The welfare services extended by the community were greatly improved; the return of confiscated property, a process which was initiated at this time, also helped raise the standing of the community. In 1946, upon the initiative of Fabian, the community established its own weekly, *Der Weg,* later to be merged with the Jewish weekly appearing in Duesseldorf. Jewish organizations in the United States arranged for American rabbis to undertake several years' service in Berlin. In 1949 Galinski was elected as chairman of the community council.

The growing tension between the Western and Soviet Occupation authorities also had its effect upon Berlin Jewry. In 1947 Nelhans was arrested by the Soviets on the charge of aiding Soviet military personnel to desert; he was sentenced to 15 years imprisonment and was not heard of subsequently. Although the city administration was split in two, the Jewish community remained unified until the end of 1952, when its own split became inevitable. In the following years, the situation of the Jews and the community in West Berlin was greatly improved as a result of the rising economic prosperity in West Germany (which also affected West Berlin) and the return of confiscated

Figure 3c. The Jewish community center erected by the West Berlin municipality on the Fasanenstrasse site in 1959. The portal and column are relics of the synagogue. Photo State Picture Office,

property and the indemnification of victims of Nazi persecution. The Berlin City Senate showed great concern for the rehabilitation of the community and its individual members; Joachim Lipschitz, the senator for internal affairs (who was the son of a Jewish father and a Christian mother), in particular did his utmost to help the development of the community. There are four synagogues in Berlin. In 1959, the City of Berlin erected a large Jewish community center on Fasanenstrasse at the site on which one of Berlin's most magnificent synagogues had stood until 1938. In 1954 the Zionist Organization and the Israel Appeal renewed their activities in Berlin. There exists an active Jewish women's organization, a B'nai B'rith lodge, a Jewish students' organization, and a youth organization. There are also several organizations dedicated to the fostering of interfaith relations. The Juedischer Verlag Publishing Company has been reestablished.

In 1954 the community had a membership of about 5,000 and by January 1970 this figure had risen to 5,577. The demographic composition of the community is marked by relatively high average age (4,080 are above the age of 41), a low birthrate, and a great number of mixed marriages.

East Berlin. In 1946 the number of Jews in the Soviet sector was 2,442, while in 1966 it was estimated at 850 (according to figures given by the community's president, Max Schenk). Although there is no restriction on religious practice and the authorities support the community (the great synagogue on Rykestrasse has been reconstructed), the prevailing anti-religious atmosphere of a communist state has a detrimental effect upon the community.

[Ch.Y.]

Hebrew Printing in Berlin. The first Hebrew printer in Berlin was the court preacher and professor D. E. Jablonsky, as Jews could not obtain the necessary license; nevertheless, the manager J. L. Neumark, and most of the setters and proofreaders were Jews. The first book published by them was the Book of Psalms (1697), followed by the complete Bible (1699), and other scholarly and liturgical works. An application by Rabbi Mirels for permission to print the Talmud in Berlin was refused by Frederick I, king of Prussia; the permission to publish Maimonides' Code was not taken up, as this was just being printed in Amsterdam by J. *Athias. But a Talmud edition was issued by Gottschalk and Jablonski, in partnership with a Frankfort on the Oder printer, 1715–22. Among other printers to be mentioned are Baruch Buchbinder (Radoner) of Vilna (1708–17), who printed a number of important works such as the *Tzena Urena* and works by the Shabbatean Nehemiah *Ḥayon (1713), a Mishnah with Rashi and Jacob Ḥagiz's commentary (1716–17), and a *Ḥoshen Mishpat* (1717). Nathan, son of the aforementioned J. L. Neumark, was active 1719–27, while his son-in-law Aaron b. Moses Rofe of Lissa built up an important press, 1733–62, publishing a series of well-known rabbinic works, above all the second Berlin Talmud edition 1734–39. Aaron's press was continued for a while by his grandson Moses b. Mordecai. An annual *Lu'aḥ* began to appear probably from 1725 but not later than 1738. Of some importance was the press of Isaac b. Jacob Speyer (1764–70), a son-in-law of the Berlin rabbi David Fraenkel, who printed notable rabbinic works—Steinschneider calls it "the highlight of Hebrew printing in Berlin"; and that of Mordecai Landsberg, also from 1764. The prolific writer and editor Isaac *Satanow took over Landsberg's press in 1772 and issued a considerable number of books, particularly his own (until 1804). In 1784 David Friedlaender and his friends founded the Verlag der juedischen Freischule, managed by A. *Wolfsohn-Halle who bought the Landsberg press and obtained a license to print and sell books. Pupils of the society were taught the craft of printing and a number of books were published from 1796 with the imprint "Orientalische Druckerei." During these years Berlin became the center for the printing of Enlightenment literature, notably the writings of M. Mendelssohn, N. H. Wessely, D. Friedlaender, etc. Mendelssohn's edition of the Pentateuch appeared here in 1783.

In 1830 the Landsberg press was bought by Isaac Levent. In that

Figure 4. A bench in a Berlin park, "For Aryans Only," 1938. Jerusalem, Yad Vashem Museum.

year the printer Trevitsch and son moved to Berlin from Frankfort on the Oder. In 1834, the year of his death, David Friedlaender founded his own press and published a number of important books; the scholar D. *Cassel worked there as a proofreader. In 1836 the apostate Julius Sittenfeld set up a printing house which published the complete Talmud (1862–68), Maimonides' Code (1862), and other works. In the late 19th and early 20th century H. Itzkowski, Siegfried, Arthur and Erich Scholem were active as general, Jewish, and also Hebrew publishers and printers in Berlin. In 1930 a Pentateuch was printed for the *Soncino-Gesellschaft by the "Officina Serpentis" with a new Hebrew type cut for this occasion.

[A.M.H.]

Bibliography: J. Meisl (ed.), *Pinkas Kehillat Berlin 1723–1854—Protokollbuch der juedischen Gemeinde Berlin* (Heb. and Ger., 1962); idem, in: *Arim ve-Immahot be-Yisrael,* 1 (1946), 80–140; H. G. Sellenthin, *Geschichte der Juden in Berlin* (1959); Germ Jud, 2 (1968), 68–73; E. L. Landshuth, *Toledot Anshei Shem* (1884); P. von Gebhardt (ed.), *Das aelteste Buergerbuch 1453–1700* (1927); L. Geiger, *Geschichte der Juden in Berlin* (1871); D. Kaufmann, *Die letzte Vertreibung der Juden aus Wien* (1889), 206–21; L. Davidsohn, *Beitraege zur Sozial- und Wirtschaftsgeschichte der Berliner Juden vor der Emanzipation* (1920); M. Stern, *Beitraege zur Geschichte der juedischen Gemeinde zu Berlin,* 6 vols. (1926–34); *Gemeindeblatt der juedischen Gemeinde zu Berlin* (1911–38); *Juedisches Jahrbuch fuer Gross-Berlin* (1926–28) and *Juedisches Jahrbuch* (1929–33); D. Friedlaender, *Akten-Stuecke, die Reform der juedischen Kolonien in den Preussischen Staaten betreffend* (1793); I. Freund, *Die Emanzipation der Juden in Preussen,* 2 vols. (1912); S. Stern, *Der preussische Staat und die Juden,* 2 vols. (1925, repr. 1962); W. Heise, *Die Juden in der Mark Brandenburg bis zum Jahre 1571* (1932); H. Rachel, *Das Berliner Wirtschaftsleben im Zeitalter des Fruehkapitalismus* (1931); H. Rachel et al., *Berliner Grosskaufleute und Kapitalisten,* 3 vols. (1934–39); J. Jacobsohn (ed.), *Die Judenbuergerbuecher der Stadt Berlin, 1809–1851* (1962); M. Sinasohn (ed.), *Adas Jisroel, Berlin* (1966); H. Seeliger, in: YLBI, 3 (1958), 159–68; I. Eisenstein-Barzilay, in: PAAJR, 25 (1956), 1–37; 29 (1960–61), 17–54; idem, in: *Essays on Jewish Life and Thought* (1959), 183–97; Barzilay, in: PAAJR, 29 (1960–61), 17–54; idem, in: JSOS, 21 (1959), 165–92; E. Hurwicz, in: YLBI, 12 (1967), 85–102. Holocaust Period: P. Littauer, *My Experiences During the Persecution of the Jews in Berlin and Brussels, 1939–44* (1945); Irgun Olej Merkas Europa, *Die letzten Tage des deutschen, Judentums* (1943); Ball-Kaduri, in: *Yad Vashem Studies,* 3 (1959), 261–81; 5 (1963), 271–316; H. Gaertner, in: YLBI, 1 (1956), 123–42; F. Friedlaender, *ibid.,* 3 (1958), 187–201; S. Shiratzki, *ibid.,* 5 (1960), 299–307; *Nachrichtenblatt der juedischen Gemeinde von Gross-Berlin D. D. R.* (1961). Hebrew Printing: H. D. Friedberg, *Toledot ha-Defus ha-Ivri be-Arim Augsburg . . .* (1935), 87ff.; R. N. Rabinowitz, *Ma'amar al Hadpasat ha-Talmud* (1952), 108f., 152f.; Steinschneider, in: ZGJD, 1 (1887), 377ff.; 2 (1888), 200ff.; 3 (1889), 84ff., 262ff.; A. M. Habermann, *Ha-Sefer ha-Ivri be-Hitpattehuto* (1968), index.

BERLIN, ARYEH LOEB BEN ABRAHAM MEIR (1738–1814), German rabbi. Berlin, the younger brother of Noah Ḥayyim Ẓevi Hirsch *Berlin, was born in Fuerth where his father, a well-to-do merchant, was communal leader of Franconian Jewry. Like his brother, he was appointed *dayyan* in Fuerth but Aryeh Loeb was at the same time rabbi of Baiersdorf in Bavaria. From 1789 he was rabbi of Bamberg, where his duties included that of civil judge. While there he was involved in an unpleasant lawsuit when the heirs of a large estate of which he was appointed executor accused him of abusing his office, exacting illegal fees, and not accounting for certain expenditure. He was acquitted of dishonesty, but made to pay a fine. The publication of the relevant documents by Eckstein (see bibl.) shows that the charges were groundless. In 1794 Berlin was appointed chief rabbi of Hesse-Kassel, but owing to the opposition of his detractors in Bamberg he was unable to leave and did not assume his post until the following year. When the kingdom of Westphalia, with Kassel as its capital, was created by Napoleon in 1807 and given to Jerome Bonaparte, Berlin delivered a sermon in Hebrew welcoming the new king and composed a hymn of praise in Hebrew (published under the title *Davar be-Itto Mah Tov,* with a German translation, Kassel, 1807). In 1808, when the Jewish *consistory was organized on the basis of the French consistories he was appointed chief rabbi of the kingdom. The president of the consistory was Israel *Jacobsohn, and Berlin, despite the protests of the more extreme rabbis, agreed to certain relaxations of the strict laws of Passover, in particular permitting the eating of peas and beans on Passover.

Berlin's annotations to the Talmud appear in the three volumes of the Fuerth edition (1829–32) which were published, and his annotations to the tractate *Shevu'ot* are in the Romm-Vilna edition. Some of his novellae appear as an appendix to his brother's *Aẓei Almuggim* (Sulzbach, 1779).

Bibliography: A. Eckstein, *Geschichte des Juden im ehemaligen Fuerstbistum Bamberg* (1898), 176–9, and Nachtraege (1899), 3–44; E. Kohn, *Kinat Soferim* (1892), 896f. [Ed.]

BERLIN, CONGRESS OF, gathering of the great European powers in 1878 to settle problems concerning the Balkans and Near East arising after the war between Russia and Turkey in 1877. Held between June 13 and July 13, 1878, it was attended by representatives of Austria-Hungary, France, Great Britain, Italy, Russia, and Turkey, with some participation of representatives of the Balkan states (Greece, Montenegro, Rumania, and Serbia). Among its most influential members was the head of the British delegation, Benjamin *Disraeli (Lord Beaconsfield). The position of the Jews in the Balkan countries (Rumania, Serbia, and Bulgaria) was also placed on the agenda on the initiative of the "Zion" society in Bucharest, led by Adolf Weinberg and Adolf *Stern; these joined with the *Alliance Israélite Universelle in Paris and the Council for the Defense of Rumanian Jews in Berlin, led by Moritz *Lazarus. The Jewish community of Berlin petitioned the chairman of the congress and head of the German delegation, Count *Bismarck, on Feb. 28, 1878, to raise the question of equal rights for Rumanian Jews at the congress. As a result, the German representatives were instructed to demand equal civil rights for the members of all religions in the Balkan countries and the inclusion in the peace treaty of special paragraphs to this effect explicitly providing for their implementation. The question of equal rights for the Jews in these countries was also discussed in the parliaments of France, Italy, Austria, and Hungary, and the representatives of these countries at the congress were requested by special resolutions to ensure an appropriate settlement.

To deal with the Jewish questions a special council was established in Berlin consisting of the representatives of the Committee for Jewish Affairs in Berlin (Gerson von *Bleichroeder, M. Lazarus, Jacob *Bernays, and Berthold *Auerbach), representatives of the Alliance (Sacki Kann, Charles *Netter, and Emanuel *Veneziani), the delegation of Rumanian Jews (Adolf Stern, Marco Brociner, Taussig, and Hermann *Hirsch), and representatives of the Alliance in Berlin (Salomon Neumann, the banker Julius Platho, and Hermann Goldschmidt). This committee formulated a memorandum which was submitted to the entire congress, followed by a second memorandum to Bismarck. The memoranda contained a description of the plight of the Jews in the Balkan countries accompanied by a request that the members of all creeds and races should be guaranteed equal civil rights in the peace treaty (stipulated in special clauses). Special steps were also taken to submit the Jewish requests to the representatives of the different governments. To this end Baron Maurice de *Hirsch and Sir Moses *Montefiore began negotiations with the representatives of England and France, and Bleichroeder turned his attentions to Bismarck and the Russian representative, Count Shuvalov.

The members of the united committee also visited the representatives of the Balkan countries (Rumania, Serbia, Bulgaria), who were not officially represented at the congress but were working behind the scenes. The Rumanian representative, Kogălniceanu, endeavored to persuade the Jewish representatives not to appeal to the congress since the question of equal civil rights for Jews was an internal affair of the Rumanian government. Threats against the Jews of Rumania appeared in Rumanian newspapers which also attempted to influence the Western Jews to withdraw their demands. These tactics, however, were vehemently condemned and rejected by the representatives of the Alliance.

On June 24, 1878, the Jewish problem came up for discussion as part of the general consideration of Bulgarian affairs. The French representative, Waddington, proposed that a clause be inserted in the peace treaty recognizing the independence of Bulgaria on condition that it granted equal civil rights to members of all races and religions. The proposal was accepted. On June 28, during the discussions on Serbia, the Turkish representative, Karatheodori (Caratheodory) Pasha, and the English representative, Lord Salisbury, demanded that a similar clause be inserted in the peace treaty as a condition for the recognition of Serbian independence. The Russian representative, Prince Gorchakov, opposed this resolution on the ground that the Jews of Serbia, Rumania, and Russia could not be put in the same category with the Jews of Paris, London, Berlin, and Vienna. Despite his opposition it was decided to insert in the peace treaty a clause (par. 35) guaranteeing equal rights.

Also during the discussions on Rumania it was proposed by Waddington that recognition of that country's independence should be made contingent on her granting equal rights to the members of all religions within her borders. The proposal received the full support of Beaconsfield, Count Andrássy of Austria-Hungary, and Bismarck, and even the agreement of Shuvalov. By a separate resolution, introduced into paragraph 44 of the peace treaty, equal rights were granted to the members of all religions in Rumania. This principle was also to be binding, according to a resolution introduced by Salisbury, on Turkey, Greece, and Montenegro.

The question of the future of Palestine was also touched upon by the congress indirectly. In June 1878 a group of Jews submitted a memorandum to the congress (addressed to Bismarck and Beaconsfield) requesting that the Jews in Palestine should be given their independence (in the same manner as had been restored to the Balkan peoples) and permitted to establish a constitutional Jewish monarchy in that country. This memorandum was listed in the protocol of documents submitted to the congress but was not discussed on the floor. Before the congress assembled, there were discussions in the English press concerning the political resurgence of the Jews in Palestine. After the congress was concluded, Serbia and Bulgaria complied with the clauses of the peace treaty obliging them to grant equal rights to their minorities, and even incorporated these clauses in their constitutions. Rumania refused to meet her obligation, and the struggle to implement paragraph 44 of the peace treaty in this country extended over decades.

Bibliography: Kohler and Wolf, in: AJHSP, 24 (1916), ix; 1ff.; 40; J. Brociner, *Die Judenfrage in Rumaenien und ihre Loesung* (1879); B. Segel, *Rumaenien und seine Juden* (1918); L. Wolf, *Notes on the Diplomatic History of the Jewish Question* (1919), 23–26, 52; Gelber, in: HJ, 2 (1940), 39–48; idem, in: YLBI, 5 (1960), 221–48; idem, in: *Sefer Yovel . . . S. Federbush* (1960), 117–64; idem, in: *Sefer Yugoslavyah* (Tel Aviv, 1962); J. Meisl, *Die Durchfuehrung des Artikels 44 des Berliner Vertrages in Rumaenien und die europaeische Diplomatie* (1925); N. Leven, *Cinquante ans d'histoire . . . ,* 1 (1911).

[N.M.G.]

BERLIN, DAVID BEN (Judah) LOEB (d. 1771), German rabbi and talmudic authority. The brother of Isaiah *Berlin, he was probably born in Eisenstadt (Hungary). After serving as rabbi of Dessau and Marktbreit (Bavaria) and as chief rabbi of Schwarzburg, Berlin was appointed rabbi of the three united congregations of Altona, Hamburg, and Wandsbeck. In 1769 when the Danish government, at the instance of the Hamburg Town Council, sought to separate the Altona Jewish community from that of Hamburg, Berlin was elected a member of the delegation whose successful intercession with the Danish king resulted in the continuation of the status quo. His learned correspondence with his brother-in-law, Joseph Steinhardt, was published in the latter's work, *Zikhron Yosef* (EH 4:11; ḤM 1:2); a number of his responsa have been published in *Or Yisrael* of Israel b. Eliezer *Lipschuetz (Cleves, 1770) and in *Beit Evel u-Veit Mishteh* of Samuel Palaggi (Altona, 1770). Some of his talmudic novellae and homilies are in manuscript at the Bodleian Library.

Bibliography: A. Berliner, *Rabbi Jesaja Berlin* (Ger., 1879), 8; Fuenn, Keneset, 227f., s.v. *David b. Aryeh Leib Berlin;* E. Duckesz, *Ivah le-Moshav,* 59–63; Neubauer, Cat, no. 526; L. Loewenstein, *Index Approbationum* (1923), 47, no. 825.

[Jo.H./Ed.]

BERLIN (Baline), IRVING (Israel; 1888–), U.S. popular song writer. Berlin was born in Kirghizia, Russia, the son of a cantor, and was taken to New York in 1893. His first regular job was as a "singing waiter," and it was then that he wrote the lyrics of his first song "Marie from Sunny Italy" in 1907. His second song "Dorando" (1908) brought him $25 and a job with a music company. He became a partner in the firm and later established his own music publishing house. Berlin had no musical training and never learned to read music. His technique remained primitive, and when he composed at the piano he did it only in one key; modulations were effected by a special set of pedals. His first big success was "Alexander's Ragtime Band" (1911). His melodies, for which he wrote the lyrics, were infectious, sentimental, and have maintained their popularity. He composed more than 1,000 songs. Films for which he wrote the songs included *Top Hat* (1935); *Follow the Fleet* (1936); *On the Avenue* (1937); *Holiday Inn* (1942); and *Easter Parade* (1948). Among the Broadway shows for which he wrote the music, the best known were *Annie Get Your Gun* (1946) and *Call Me Madam* (1950). In 1954 Berlin received a special gold medal from President Eisenhower for his patriotic song "God Bless America."

Bibliography: A. Woollcott, *Story of Irving Berlin* (1925); D. Ewen, *Story of Irving Berlin* (1950); Baker, Biog Dict; Sendrey, Music, nos. 3605–07.

[N.S.]

BERLIN, SIR ISAIAH (1909–), English philosopher and political scientist. Born in Latvia, Berlin was taken to England as a boy. He later studied at Oxford, where he lectured in philosophy from 1932 and became the first Jewish Fellow of All Souls College in 1938. During and after World War II he served with the British Information Services in New York and with the British embassies in Washington and Moscow. From 1957 Berlin was professor of social and political theory at Oxford, and in 1966 he was appointed the first president of the newly founded Wolfson College in Oxford. His work was characterized by a strongly liberal attitude to social and political questions. His *Karl Marx* (1939) examines Marx's thought within the context of the intellectual atmosphere of the 19th century. In his *The Hedgehog and the Fox* (1953), Berlin considers Tolstoy as a writer who vainly sought some unifying thread in history. In *Historical Inevitability* (in: *Auguste Conte Memorial Lectures 1953–62,* 1964) he opposes the notion that events are inevitable and therefore predictable, and that political conditions are not capable of being changed by individuals. In *Two Concepts of Liberty* (1958), Berlin distinguishes between those thinkers who have sought to found liberty within a framework of mutual restraints while at the same time recognizing the diversity of human needs and behavior, and those who, espousing one all-embracing and dogmatic notion of liberty, seek to "force men to be free" and thus end by enslaving them. Among his other writings are *The Age of Enlightenment* (1956), *The Life and Opinions of Moses Hess* (1959), *Four Essays on Liberty* (1969), and numerous essays. Berlin earned a considerable reputation as a scholar, teacher, and conversationalist, and influenced generations of students in Britain and in the United States, where he was visiting professor at several universities. His long-standing ties with Israel and Zionism

Sir Isaiah Berlin, English philosopher and political scientist.

were distinguished by personal friendships with a number of Zionist leaders including Chaim *Weizmann. He was a member of the editorial board publishing the Weizmann letters and was a governor of the Hebrew University of Jerusalem. [B.K.]

BERLIN, ISAIAH BEN JUDAH LOEB (Isaiah Pick; 1725–1799), rabbi and author. Berlin was known also as Isaiah Pick after his father-in-law, Wolf Pick of Breslau, who supported him for many years. He was born in Eisenstadt, Hungary, but his father, an eminent talmudic scholar (who later became rabbi of Pressburg), moved to Berlin where the young Berlin studied under him. Later he studied under Ẓevi Hirsch Bialeh (Ḥarif), the rabbi of Halberstadt, at the latter's yeshivah. In 1755 Berlin moved to Breslau where he engaged in business. In 1793, when already advanced in years, he was elected to a rabbinical post, being appointed to succeed Isaac Joseph Te'omim as rabbi of Breslau. His election was marked by a dispute between the members of the community and the local *maskilim,* who had begun to organize themselves as a body and opposed Berlin, who, despite his love of peace, openly attacked their ideas. Berlin was elected by an overwhelming majority. According to ḥasidic sources, Berlin was sympathetically disposed toward that movement and extended a friendly welcome to one of its emissaries, Jacob Samson of Spitsevka. Berlin was renowned for his conciliatory attitude and for his avoidance of all disputes. Characteristically, he called a work *She'elat Shalom* ("A Greeting of Peace"), for "all my life I have been careful not to treat my fellow men with disrespect, even to the extent of not slighting them by faint praises." As a result of this moderation, leaders of the Breslau *maskilim,* such as Joel Brill and Aaron Wolfsohn, frequently visited him. Berlin corresponded on halakhic subjects with his brother-in-law Joseph *Steinhardt, Ezekiel *Landau of Prague, Eleazar b. Eleazar *Kallir, and Ephraim Zalman *Margolioth of Brody, among others. His chief claim to fame rests not on his rabbinic and halakhic but rather on his extensive literary activities devoted to glosses and textual notes on talmudic literature. He commented on the Bible, Mishnah, Talmud, Alfasi, Maimonides, the *Arukh,* and the whole corpus of the earlier halakhic authorities. Of his collated texts, in which he notes parallel passages and variant readings, the most important is that on the Talmud, entitled *Masoret ha-Shas* ("Talmud Tradition"), which supplements an earlier work by Joseph Samuel, rabbi of Frankfort. First published at Dyhernfurth (1800–04), it has since been printed in every edition of the Talmud. Berlin not only cites parallel passages, but also amends and compares texts, displaying an acute critical faculty and a profound grasp of history.

His other works are: (1) *She'elat Shalom* (Dyhernfurth, 1786), a commentary on Aḥai of Shabḥa's *She'iltot,* with sources and notes entitled *Rishon le-Zion;* (2) *Hafla'ah she-ba-Arakhin,* glosses and annotations to Nathan b. Jehiel of Rome's *Arukh* (first published, part 1, Breslau, 1830, part 2, Vienna, 1859), and thereafter in many editions of the *Arukh;* (3) *Minnei Targima,* expositions on Targum Onkelos (Breslau, 1831); (4) *Tosefot Rishon le-Ẓiyyon,* notes and brief comments on the Mishnah (first published at Sulzbach, 1783–85, and often reprinted); (5) *Kashot Meyushav* (Koenigsberg, 1860), in which all talmudic passages concluding with the word *kashya* ("difficulty") are answered; (6) *Omer ha-Shikhḥah,* containing talmudic *halakhot* not mentioned by the codifiers. This work, first published as an addendum to *Kashot Meyushav,* was later printed separately (Johannisberg, 1866).

There was no early work to which Berlin did not write glosses and explanations, as he was in the habit of annotating every book that he read. Thus he wrote glosses to: (7) the Bible (Dyhernfurth, 1775; Lemberg, 1861); (8) the prayer book in *Tikkun Shelomo* (Dyhernfurth, 1806); (9) Alfasi (Pressburg, 1836); (10) Maimonides' Yad (Dyhernfurth, 1809); (11) Elijah Baḥur's *Tishbi* (his annotations appearing in Moses Koerner's *Birkat Moshe,* Berlin, 1834); (12) Malachi b. Jacob's *Yad Malakhi* (Berlin, 1852); (13) Elijah b. Moses de Vidas' *Reshit Ḥokhmah* (Dyhernfurth, 1811).

His unpublished works include: (14) *Yesh Seder la-Mishnah,* a commentary in several volumes on the Mishnah; (15) *Tena Tosefta,* a commentary on the Tosefta; (16) *Keneset Ḥakhmei Yisrael,* responsa; (17) *Shetarei ha-Me'uḥarin,* novellae on Rashi and *tosafot* to the Talmud, dealing with those passages where proof was deduced from later biblical verses but could equally well have been inferred from earlier ones; (18) glosses and notes on the minor tractates.

Berlin was the first in Germany to interest himself in the history of post-talmudic literature. He was also the first to offer a solution to the problem of the identity and the period of the *paytan* Eleazar *Kallir, and although his conclusions are not accepted by scholars, they all use the extensive material cited by him (see J. Steinhardt's *Zikhron Yosef* to OḤ 13–15).

Bibliography: A. Berliner, in: MWJ, 6 (1879), 65–89; Y. A. Kamelhar, *Dor De'ah* (1935^2), 87–89. [Y.AL.]

BERLIN, ISRAEL (1880–?), Russian-Jewish historian, descended from a distinguished ḥasidic family. Berlin was educated at Lithuania yeshivot and moved to St. Petersburg where he became a member of the editorial board of the Russian Jewish Encyclopedia (*Yevreyskaya Entsiklopediya,* vols. 9–16) for which he edited the sections on the geonic period and rabbinic literature. He also contributed many basic articles on other topics, among them the Hebrew language, the Zohar, Ḥasidism, the Khazars, and Judaizers. He also contributed to the periodical *Yevreyskaya Starina.* In his fundamental study "Historical Settlements of the Jewish People on the Territory of Russia" (1919), Berlin attempted to explain the origins of Jewish settlements in Russia and trace their history up to the end of the 16th century. This work, based on copious literary and documentary material, was not completed. Berlin's fate under Soviet rule is not known.

Bibliography: B. Z. Dinur, *Be-Olam she-Shaka* (1958), 151–3.
[Y.S.]

BERLIN, MOSES (1821–1888), Russian scholar and civil servant, born in Shklov, Belorussia. Berlin wrote his first paper in Hebrew under the Latin title *Ars logica* (1845). In 1849 he was appointed teacher in the government school for Jews in Mogilev and in 1853 he became adviser on Jewish affairs to the governor-general of Belorussia. He subsequently held the post of adviser on Jewish matters at the Department of "Foreign Religions" (1856–66). Berlin translated into Russian Joshua b. David's *Ẓok ha-Ittim* on the *Chmielnicki massacres. For his work on the ethnography of the Russian Jews, *Ocherk etnografii yevreyskogo naseleniya v Rossii* (1861), Berlin was elected a member of the Imperial Russian Geographical Society. Berlin responded to the attacks on Jews and the Talmud, made in Russian literature and the press by anti-Semites. He was also active in the St. Petersburg community.
[ED.]

BERLIN, NAPHTALI ẒEVI JUDAH (known as **ha-Neẓiv** from the initials of his name; 1817–1893), one of the leading rabbis of his generation, and head of the yeshivah at

*Volozhin for some 40 years. He was born at Mir and already in his early youth was famed as a great talmudic scholar. In 1831 he married the daughter of R. Isaac b. Ḥayyim *Volozhiner who headed the large and important yeshivah in that town. When R. Isaac died in 1851 he was succeeded by his elder son-in-law Eliezer Isaac. When the latter died in 1854, Berlin succeeded him, transforming that institution of learning into a spiritual center for the whole of Russian Jewry. In his day, the yeshivah at Volozhin was attended by more than 400 students, among whom were many men of great talent and unusual intellectual caliber. He taught the whole of the Babylonian Talmud in the order of its arrangement, without omission and with a commentary of his own, in which he followed the system and method of R. Elijah b. Solomon the *gaon* of Vilna. He avoided hairsplitting *pilpul,* being concerned only with determining the plain meaning of the text as well as establishing its accuracy by reference to parallel passages in the Jerusalem Talmud and in the halakhic Midrashim. Early in life he wrote a commentary on *Sifrei* (published 1959–61 in Jerusalem, in three volumes, under the title *Emek ha-Neẓiv*). He ascribed great importance to the study of geonic literature and the works of the early authorities who lived close to the time of the Talmud. This accounts for his special interest in the *She'iltot* of R. *Aḥa of Shabḥa which he published with a commentary. It was the most comprehensive of its kind on this work, and was titled: *Ha'amek She'elah* (Vilna, 1861, 1864, 1867; second edition with addenda and corrigenda from Berlin's manuscripts, Jerusalem, 1948–53). Berlin also devoted considerable attention to the interpretation of the Scriptures, following again in the footsteps of the Vilna *gaon.* In the yeshivah he gave a daily lesson in the weekly portion of the Reading of the Law, an unusual innovation in the yeshivot of his day. His commentaries on the Torah, *Ha'amek Davar,* were published (Vilna, 1879–80; second edition with addenda from manuscripts, Jerusalem, 1938) as were those on the Song of Songs, *Rinnah shel Torah* (Warsaw, 1886). In his Bible commentaries, he sought to demonstrate the consonance of the interpretations of the Pentateuch as transmitted in talmudic sources with the plain meaning of the Written Law and the rules of Hebrew grammar and syntax. In the course of his long years as head of the yeshivah at Volozhin, Berlin dedicated his energies to that institution. He adamantly opposed any modernization of the yeshivah and the introduction of secular studies in its curriculum, as demanded by the *maskilim* in Russia, who were supported by the authorities. He feared that such innovation might detract from the purpose and mission of the yeshivah—the education of scholars of the traditional type. He did not negate secular learning per se, but regarded the study of the Torah and the production and maintenance of talmudic scholars as the very foundation of Jewish existence. He exhibited the greatest solicitude over any form of neglect of Torah study and professed a fatherly love for all his students, who in turn admired and revered him greatly, including those who later departed from his way of life and outlook. Bialik's poem *"Ha-Matmid"* reflects in large measure his personal impressions of his student days at Volozhin. Bialik describes the heart-warming personality of the "head of the yeshivah," and stresses his great love for the students of the Torah.

Berlin was keenly interested in the general community and its needs. He wrote many detailed responsa to questions arriving from various communities throughout the world on matters of *halakhah* and on general public affairs. A small part of his responsa was collected in his *Meshiv Davar* (2 vols., Warsaw, 1892) which revealed his general breadth of outlook. He completely rejected the demand of certain religious circles to establish separatist orthodox communities, stressing that "such advice is as painful as a dagger in the body of the nation," for all Jews are commanded to form "one union" (*Meshiv Davar,* vol. 1 responsum 42). He joined the *Ḥibbat Zion movement from its very inception, and at the Druzgeniki Conference (1887) was elected "counseling member" of its executive. In many letters he urged observant Jews to join the movement and to support the settlement of Jews in Ereẓ Israel, even though some were nonobservant. At the same time, he stressed that "our contributions do not go to settle the land of the Philistines, but to restore the desolation of our Holy Land . . . so that the Torah and the precepts be observed among its inhabitants" (*Meshiv Davar,* vol. 2, responsum 3). With that end in view, he urged that a religious person be appointed supervisor of the settlers in the colonies in Ereẓ Israel to ensure they conduct themselves in accordance with the Torah and the precepts. He also suggested that "secular" members of the Jewish settlements (referring to the Bilu'im in Gederah) be enabled to return to their countries abroad and that their place be taken by observant Jews from the old *yishuv* in Jerusalem. Later, however, he withdrew this suggestion, and even defended the Bilu'im because they had "improved their ways." Berlin was opposed to the permission granted by other rabbinic authorities for fields to be worked during the sabbatical year by means of the legal fiction of "selling" the land to non-Jews.

In his last years, he came into conflict with the Russian authorities as a result of their instructions both for a reduction in the number of students at the yeshivah of Volozhin and the introduction of secular subjects, especially the study of Russian, in the curriculum. Very much against his will, he reduced the student roll somewhat and introduced the study of Russian. However, even after these steps, the number of students at the yeshivah remained double that permitted by the Government, with few students among them attending the lessons in Russian. As a result the yeshivah was closed down by government decree in 1892 and Berlin and his family were exiled. They moved first to Minsk and later to Warsaw. The closing down of the yeshivah seriously affected his health and he was unable to carry out his desire to settle in Ereẓ Israel. He died in Warsaw about 18 months after his departure from Volozhin. His sons were R. Ḥayyim Berlin and R. Meir *Bar-Ilan.

Bibliography: Berdichevsky, in: *Ha-Asif,* 3 (1886), 231–42; A. J. Slutzky (ed.), *Shivat Ẓiyyon,* 1 (1891), 17–18; 2 (1891), 5–8, 18–19, 28–30; I. Rivkind, *Ha-Neẓiv ve-Yiḥuso le-Ḥibbat Ẓiyyon* (1919); idem, *Iggerot Ẓiyyon* (1923), 73–103; idem, in: *Reshumot,* 5 (1927), 262–375; M. Berlin, *Mi-Volozhin ad Yerushalayim,* 1 (1939); idem, *Rabban shel Yisrael* (1943); S. Y. Zevin, *Ishim ve-Shitot* (1958), 9–37; J. Litvin, in: L. Jung (ed.), *Men of the Spirit* (1964), 285–99; Waxman, Literature, 3 (1960), 730–3.

[Z.K.]

BERLIN, NOAH ḤAYYIM ẒEVI HIRSCH (1734–1802), German rabbi and halakhist. Berlin was born in Fuerth and was the son of Abraham Meir Berlin, the communal leader of Franconia. He became a *dayyan* at Fuerth in 1764 and later served as rabbi in Bayersdorf and Bayreuth. In 1783 Berlin was appointed rabbi of Mainz and the surrounding district. His appointment was ratified by the prince elector. He established a yeshivah at Mainz, and lived there until 1799 when he succeeded Raphael ha-Kohen as the rabbi of the united communities of Altona, Hamburg, and Wandsbeck. Berlin showed skill and tact in uniting the various elements in these communities. Wolf *Heidenheim was his most outstanding pupil. Berlin wrote *Aẓei Almuggim* (1779), a commentary on the hand-washing ritual, *eruvei ḥaẓerot,* and marriages forbidden by rabbinical enactment; *Aẓei Arazim* (1790), a commentary on the Shulḥan Arukh, *Even ha-Ezer; Ma'yan ha-Ḥokhmah* (1804), on the 613 commandments (in verse and with a commentary). This work, unfinished by Berlin, was completed by his brother Aryeh Loeb *Berlin. Two further works, *Aẓei Besamim* and *Aẓei Levonah,* remained unpublished. He wrote glosses to the tractates of *Berakhot* (1829), *Shabbat* (1832), and *Shevuot.* The last was published in the Vilna edition of the Talmud. There is a rational basis to his explanation of the *halakhah,* and he makes use of the Jerusalem Talmud.

Bibliography: Fuenn, Keneset, 346; E. Duckesz, *Ivah le-Moshav,* 1 (1903), 74–77, 139–40, xxvi; I. Wolfsberg, in: *Arim ve-Immahot be-Yisrael,* 2 (1948), 33; idem, *Die Drei-Gemeinde* (1966), 66; A. Eckstein, *Nachtraege zur Geschichte der Juden im ehemaligen Fuerstbistum Bamberg* (1899), 5; Loewenstein, in: JJLG, 3 (1905), 233; *ibid.,* 8 (1910), 72.

[Y.Ho.]

BERLIN, SAUL BEN ẒEVI HIRSCH LEVIN (also called **Saul Hirschel;** 1740–1794), German rabbi. His father was Hirschel *Levin (Ẓevi Hirsch) and his brother, Solomon *Hirschel. At the age of 20, he was ordained by some of the greatest rabbis of the time. In 1768 he was serving as *av bet din* in Frankfort on the Oder. In 1778 he wrote an approbation for Moses Mendelssohn's commentary on the Torah *Biur* (*Be'ur;* Berlin, 1783). Some time before 1782 Berlin, becoming disenchanted with what he considered antiquated rabbinical authority, retired from the rabbinate and settled in Berlin. There he joined the Haskalah group whose members, known as the *Me'assefim,* were the pupils and admirers of Mendelssohn. He was also an ardent supporter of Naphtali Herz *Wessely at a time when the most eminent rabbis of Germany violently opposed him. After the publication of Wessely's *Divrei Shalom ve-Emet* (Berlin, 1782), Berlin wrote a satire *Ketav Yosher* (published anonymously after his death, 1794), in which he sharply criticized the methods of education and the scholarship of his time as well as the customs and superstitions which had spread among the people. It also sought to dispel the rabbis' opposition to the work of Wessely. In 1784 he traveled to Italy, ostensibly to seek a cure for his rheumatism, but, quite conceivably, to meet those rabbis who had placed themselves in Wessely's camp. In Italy Berlin wrote a provocative anonymous pamphlet of objections to the *Birkei Yosef* of R. Ḥayyim Joseph David *Azulai (Leghorn, 1772), to which the latter replied in his book *Maḥazik Berakhah* (*ibid.,* 1785). Interesting himself in manuscripts, Berlin began to edit the *Or Zaru'a* of *Isaac b. Moses of Vienna, to which he added his own notes and novellae; these were omitted, however, from the posthumously published version in 1862. In 1789 his book *Miẓpeh Yokte'el* appeared in Berlin under the pseudonym of Obadiah b. Baruch Ish Polonyah. It contained the most extreme criticism of the novellae to *Yoreh De'ah,* entitled *Torat Yekuti'el,* by Raphael b. Jekuthiel Susskind *Kohen, rabbi of the united communities of Altona, Hamburg, and Wandsbeck. Berlin's book, in which Raphael is accused of plagiarism and of condoning corruption, stirred up a storm among the rabbis, including Berlin's own father, who placed a ban upon the book and upon its author. When the identity of the author became known, his father regretted his action and tried to protect his son. However, before the storm had subsided, another of his books, *Besamim Rosh,* appeared in Berlin in 1793 and touched off a new tempest. The book contains 392 responsa purporting to be by Asher b. Jehiel and his contemporaries: on the title page it was stated that these responsa had been collected and prepared for publication by R. Isaac di Molina. Although Berlin maintained that he had copied the book from a manuscript in Italy and that he had only added his own notes and novellae *(Kassa de-Harsana),* it soon became evident that the statements attributed to Asher and the other rabbis quoted were full of strange leniencies which actually bordered on antinomianism. The suspicion was soon raised that the whole book was fictitious and that its author was Berlin. The first to attack him was R. Wolf Landsberg in his pamphlet *Ze'ev Yitrof* (Frankfort on the Oder, 1793). After him came R. Mordecai Benet, who wrote to Berlin's father and to other rabbis. A massive rabbinical campaign then followed which branded Berlin as an atheist who sought to uproot the foundations of the Torah. Berlin's father came again to his aid, requesting the rabbis to retract their accusations against his son, and even attempting to establish the genuineness of the manuscript and R. Raphael ha-Kohen and his circle as the source of the libel. It seems that he succeeded in appeasing the rabbis, but not those scholars who held no rabbinical position. Disappointed, Berlin began to wander from one country to another. According to his relative Ẓevi Horowitz (*Kitvei ha-Ge'onim,* 1928), Berlin went to London in 1794 to take up the position of rabbi of the Ashkenazi community there but died before he was able to assume the office. His literary remains present many bibliographical problems, some of which have not yet been solved. He left critical essays which have been published in various places. He is probably the author of *Ha-Orev* (Vienna, 1795), attributed to R. Baruch *Jeiteles.

Bibliography: C. Roth, *The Great Synagogue London 1690–1940* (1950), 108–24, 180–201; Samet, in KS 43 (1967/68), 429–41; M. Wunder, *ibid.,* 44 (1968/69), 307–8.

[A.D.]

BERLINER, ABRAHAM (1833-1915), scholar and author. Berliner's vast knowledge of rabbinic literature and of ancient and modern languages was mostly self-taught (cf. his autobiographical *Aus meiner Knabenzeit,* JJGL, 16 (1913), 165ff.). After succeeding his father as teacher in his native Obersitzko, he became preacher and teacher in Arnswalde (both in the province of Posen, then Germany). From 1858 to 1865 he lectured at the *bet ha-midrash* of the Berlin Talmudic Society out of which developed the Rabbinical Seminary, founded by Azriel *Hildesheimer in 1873. Here Berliner lectured in Jewish history and literature and was also librarian. In subsequent years he paid frequent visits to the important libraries of Germany, England, Holland, France, and, above all, Italy, in search of their Jewish treasures. He prepared the first critical edition of Rashi's commentary on the Pentateuch, giving Rashi's sources and explanatory notes (1866). In the completely revised second edition (1905) he added a vocabulary of foreign words used in the commentary. Berliner pursued his Rashi studies in a number of important monographs and also turned his attention to other medieval commentators (*Peletat Soferim,* 1872, 1966[2]). He also provided a modern edition of *Targum Onkelos* (1884). Berliner's historical studies were chiefly devoted to Italian Jewry, as shown by his three-volume *Geschichte der Juden in Rom* (1893). On the history of German Jewry, he wrote *Aus dem Leben der deutschen Juden im Mittelalter* (1861, second revised and enlarged edition 1900, 1937[3]; Hebrew translation, 1900). Complementary to this work was a monograph *Persoenliche Beziehungen zwischen Juden und Christen im Mittelalter* (1882). Berliner also wrote biographies of Israel *Isserlein and of Isaiah *Berlin and a defense of *Maimonides against the accusation of apostasy (*Moses ben Maimon, sein Leben* . . . 2 (1914), 103ff.). Berliner published many bibliographical studies and works on liturgy and Talmud. He discovered in Rome parts of commentaries on the Bible and the Talmud by *Hananel b.

Ḥushi'el and *Gershom b. Judah and was instrumental in the inclusion of both commentaries in the Vilna (Romm) Talmud edition. In 1874 Berliner began to publish a *Magazin fuer juedische Geschichte und Literatur* which two years later became the *Magazin fuer die Wissenschaft des Judentums* (with a Hebrew supplement, *Oẓar Tov*), which he edited with David *Hoffmann until 1893. In 1885 he revived the *Mekiẓe Nirdamim society. On his 70th birthday he was awarded the title of professor by the Prussian government. On that occasion too appeared a *Festschrift* in his honor, edited by A. Freimann and M. Hildesheimer (*Birkat Avraham*, 1903) with a bibliography of his writings. A three-volume collection of Berliner's writings was planned but only the first appeared in 1913. A two-volume collection was published in Hebrew (1945–49). Berliner was a staunch supporter of Orthodoxy and an opponent of Reform. He supported Hildesheimer in the establishment of the *Adass Jisroel* secessionist congregation and acted as the chairman of its council for many years. Yet in his *Randbemerkungen* he had suggested certain changes in prayer texts and customs, which were not to the liking of some of his Orthodox friends.

Bibliography: M. Reines, *Dor ve-Ḥakhamav* (1890), 50ff.; Eppenstein, in: *Jeschurun* (Wohlgemuth), 2 (1915), 457ff.; J. Wolfsberg (Aviad) in: *Ḥokhmat Yisrael be-Ma'arav Eiropah*, ed. by S. Federbush, 1 (1958), 101ff.

[A.C.]

BERLINER, EMILE (1851–1929), inventor. Born and educated in Wolfenbuettel, Germany, Berliner emigrated to the U.S.A. in 1870. He worked in New York and Washington, D.C., as a clerk, salesman, and assistant in a chemical laboratory. He studied electricity and in 1876 began experimenting with Bell's newly invented telephone, which he succeeded in refining with his invention of the loose-contact telephone transmitter or microphone and the use of an induction coil. The Bell Telephone Company immediately purchased the rights to his invention, which for the first time made the telephone practical for long-distance use. Berliner was appointed chief electrical instruments inspector of the company. In 1887 he improved Edison's phonograph by introducing a flat disc instead of a cylinder and the use of a shallow groove. The patent was acquired by the Victor Talking Machine Company and served as the basis for the modern gramophone. In his later years he engaged in aviation experiments and introduced the use of a revolving cylindered light engine. Between 1919 and 1926 he built three helicopters which he tested in flight himself. Berliner also interested himself in public matters, particularly in the field of health and hygiene. In 1890 he founded the Society for the Prevention of Sickness. In 1907 he organized the first milk conference in Washington, whose efforts contributed to the pasteurization of milk and an improvement in its quality. He played a leading part in the fight against the spread of tuberculosis, and wrote a number of articles on hygiene and preventive medicine. He set out his agnostic ideas on matters of religion and philosophy in his book *Conclusions* (1902). Toward the end of his life Berliner supported the rebuilding of Palestine and was active on behalf of the Hebrew University of Jerusalem.

[Gr.L.]

Emile's son Henry Adler Berliner (1895–), aeronautical engineer, did pioneering work with his father on helicopter construction during and after World War I. He was president of Berliner Aircraft, Inc. in Washington and from 1930 to 1954 chairman of Engineering and Research Corporation. In 1955 he became president of the Maryland firm of Tecfab Inc. In World War II, during which he lost an arm, he was chief of war plans for the Eighth Air Force.

[S.A.M.]

Bibliography: F. W. Wile, *Emile Berliner, Maker of the Microphone* (1926); C. J. Hylander, *American Inventors* (1934).

BERLINER, YIẒHAK (1899–1957), Mexican-Yiddish poet. Born in Lodz, Berliner emigrated to Mexico in 1922, and earned a precarious livelihood as a peddler in the Mexican provinces. In 1927 he and two other Mexican-Yiddish poets, Moses Glikovski and Jacob *Glanz, published a volume of lyrics *Drei Vegn*. His second volume *Shtot fun Palatsn* (1936) was illustrated by the Mexican painter Diego Rivera. His national elegies *Ad Mosai?* (1941) were followed by *Shtil Zol Zayn* (1948) and *Gezang fun Mentsh* (1954). In style, imagery, use of neologisms, and rich rhythms, Berliner was influenced by his Lodz fellow poet Moshe *Broderzon, but Berliner was more socially conscious. In many lyrics he cries out vehemently against the abysmal poverty of the Mexicans around the Tepito Market in the heart of the "City of Palaces."

Bibliography: LNYL, 1 (1956), 392–3; S. Kahan, *Yidish-Meksikanish* (1945), 211–23; idem, *Meksikaner Viderklangen* (1951), 106–201; idem, *Meksikaner Refleksen* (1954), 228–31. [M.Rav.]

BERMAN, ADOLF ABRAHAM (1906–), socialist Zionist. Born in Warsaw, he was the son of Isser Berman, a well-known Zionist and member of the Ḥovevei Sefat Ever society, and a brother of Jacob *Berman. Adolf Berman joined the Left Po'alei Zion as a student and edited both its Polish language organ and its Yiddish weekly, *Arbeter Tsaytung*. After the outbreak of World War II he was for some time chief director of "Centos," the organization for social welfare in Warsaw, and was active in the Polish underground movement. Upon the establishment of the Anti-Fascist Bloc in 1942, he became one of its leaders and coeditor of its paper *Der Ruf*. He left the ghetto after the mass deportation of Jews to Treblinka in the summer of 1942, and established himself in the so-called "Aryan" side of Warsaw where he cooperated with the left-wing political groups. He was a member of the presidium of the Jewish National Committee and its representative with the Polish underground organization. He fought in the Warsaw uprising of 1944 and after the liberation of Poland was a member of the Polish temporary parliament.

In 1947 Berman became president of the central committee of Polish Jews, but three years later he emigrated to Israel. Here he joined Mapam, and in 1951 was elected to the Knesset. In 1954 he left Mapam and became a member of the Communist Party. He was elected to the party's central committee and edited its Yiddish language weekly, *Frei Israel*. In 1956 he became a member of the general council and bureau of the International Resistance Organization.

[A.We.]

BERMAN, JACOB (1901–), Polish Communist leader. Born in Warsaw, a brother of Adolf *Berman, Jacob graduated in law and then undertook research into the economic and social history of Poland. Some of his articles on these subjects dealt with Jewish problems, and in 1926 he published a dissertation on the tasks of the historical section of the Jewish Scientific Institute (YIVO). From 1928 to 1939 he worked for the Jewish Telegraphic Agency. Berman joined the Polish Communist Party in 1928, becoming one of its most active workers. During World War II he took refuge in the Soviet Union, and in 1943 helped to organize the Soviet-sponsored Union of Polish Patriots. He was a member of the political staff of the Polish Army in the U.S.S.R. and of the Polish National Liberation Committee. After the war he returned to Poland and was undersecretary of state in the presidium of the Council of Ministers from 1945 to 1952. From 1952 to 1956 he was a deputy premier. In these years Berman was a leading figure in the Political Bureau and a close colleague of the Polish president, Boleslaw Bierut. In 1956, when Wladislaw Gomulka came to power, Berman was accused of Stalinism and removed from all his government and party posts. From 1958 to 1968 he worked as editor in a publishing house but in 1968, during the anti-Semitic campaign, he was forced to retire. [A.WE.]

BERMAN, LOUIS (1903–), U.S. astronomer and astrophysicist. Born in London, Berman moved to the United States where he worked at the California Lick Observatory on Mount Hamilton. His early publications were mainly concerned with observations of minor planets, comets, and double stars, and with the determination of orbits of visual and spectroscopic binaries. Berman then did important research on the determination of star temperatures, the analysis of spectral lines, and the effect of space reddening on the spectra of planetary nebulae. His later work dealt with the rotation of the Milky Way. [A.BE.]

BERMAN, MORTON MAYER (1899–), U.S. Reform rabbi and organization executive. Berman was born in Baltimore, Maryland. He was ordained by the Jewish Institute of Religion in 1926 and served as rabbi in Davenport, Iowa (1927–29), the Free Synagogue in New York City (1929–37), and Temple Isaiah Israel in Chicago (1937–57). During World War II Rabbi Berman was a chaplain in the Pacific with the U.S. Navy. From 1939 to 1957 he played leading roles in such national organizations as the Jewish National Fund, the Zionist Organization of America, and the American Jewish Congress. In 1957 he settled in Jerusalem, where he became director of the department of English-speaking countries for Keren Hayesod. Rabbi Berman wrote *Jew's View of the Crucifixion* (1929), and *Role of the Rabbi* (1941). [ED.]

BERMAN, SIMEON (1818–1884), precursor of Jewish agricultural settlement in Ereẓ Israel. Berman, who was born in Cracow, founded a Jewish agricultural settlement society there in 1851. He emigrated to the United States in 1852, and settled in New York. There and in other cities he attempted to found societies for agricultural settlement, but received no support. In 1870 he went to Ereẓ Israel and proposed that Mikveh Israel land be set aside for an agricultural settlement, but his proposal was rejected. Berman sent a request, through the U.S. consul, to the Ottoman government asking to be allowed to buy land in Ereẓ Israel. The request was granted, and Berman moved to Tiberias, where he founded the cooperative Holy Land Settlement Society. He received messages of encouragement from rabbis Ẓevi Hirsch *Kalischer and Elijah *Guttmacher, who also promised funds. A parcel of land on the shores of Lake Kinneret was chosen for settlement, and Berman went abroad to propagate the scheme. His Yiddish book *Masot Shimon*, published in 1879, relates his experiences in Ereẓ Israel. In 1882 Berman returned to Tiberias where he died. Toward the end of his life he witnessed the establishment of the first settlements in Judea and Galilee. Their founders, as the early settlers David Schub and Moshe *Smilansky testify in their memoirs, had been influenced by his book.

Bibliography: A. Yaari, *Masot Ereẓ Yisrael* (1946), 593–610, 780; EẒD, 1 (1958), 420–8 (includes bibliography); *Hadoar*, May 16, 1958. [A.YA.]

BERMANN, RICHARD ARNOLD (1883–1939), Austrian author and journalist. Bermann was born into an assimilated Viennese family. From 1912 he was correspondent of the *Berliner Tageblatt* under the pseudonym of Arnold Hoellriegel, and traveled widely as a foreign reporter. He visited Palestine with Arthur Rundt, and their book *Palaestina* (1923) was a glowing account of early Zionist achievements. Both men were careful, however, to disclaim any personal adherence to Jewish nationalism. Bermann's most popular book, *Das Urwaldschiff* (1927; *The Forest Ship*, 1931), described an adventurous trip up the Amazon. The subject of *Derwischtrommel* (1931), which appeared in English as *The Mahdi of Allah* (1931) with an introduction by Winston Churchill, was the Sudanese struggle against the British in the days of General Gordon and Lord Kitchener. When the Nazis occupied Vienna in 1938, Bermann fled to the U.S. He continued his struggle against the Nazis as director of the American Guild for German Cultural Freedom, in New York. [S.L.]

BERMANN, VASILI (Ze'ev Wolf; 1862–1896), one of the first members of Ḥovevei Zion in Russia. He was born in Mitava, Russia (today Jelgava, Latvia) and studied at the Russian-Jewish school run by his father Eliezer Bermann, who published the Russian-Jewish newspaper *Russkii Yevrei* in St. Petersburg. He graduated as a lawyer from St. Petersburg University. After the 1881 pogroms in South Russia, he joined the Ḥibbat Zion movement. He published and edited the Russian-language anthologies *Palestina* (1884, with A. Flekser, Volynsky) and *Sion*, which expounded the intellectual basis for the Ḥibbat Zion ideology. Bermann attended the Ḥovevei Zion Druskiniki

Vasili Bermann, an early member of *Ḥovevei Zion* in Russia. Jerusalem, Central Zionist Archives.

conference (1887) and aided in the efforts to obtain an official permit for the Ḥovevei Zion society to operate in Russia. He was secretary of the founding assembly of the society in Odessa (1890). Convinced that organized emigration was essential for Russian Jewry, Bermann supported Baron de *Hirsch's plans to organize the mass exit of Jews from Russia, and regarded this as supplementing the settlement project in Ereẓ Israel. He became secretary of the ICA (*Jewish Colonization Association) founded by Baron de Hirsch, conducted a comprehensive survey of the problem of Jewish emigration, and established and headed the ICA's emigration department. Bermann was also a founder of the Historical-Ethnographical Committee of the Society for the Spreading of Enlightenment among the Jews in Russia. He contracted tuberculosis and went to live in Cairo, where he died.

Bibliography: *Lu'aḥ Aḥi'asaf*, 4 (1896), 46–50; Katznelson, in: *Ha-Meliẓ*, no. 76 (1896), 3–4; A. Raphaeli (Zenziper), *Pa'amei ha-Ge'ullah* (1951), 28, 88. [Y.S.]

BERMUDA CONFERENCE, Anglo-American Conference on Refugees in 1943. During World War II, Jewish and general public opinion in the U.S. and the British

Commonwealth urgently demanded that the Allied governments rescue the victims of the Nazi regime. Under pressure from parliament, churches, and humanitarian organizations, the British Foreign Office, on Jan. 20, 1943, proposed joint consultation between Britain and the U.S.A. to examine the problem and possible solutions. After an exchange of diplomatic notes, the Anglo-American Conference on Refugees was held in Bermuda from April 19 to 30, 1943. The American delegation was headed by Harold Willis Dodds, president of Princeton University; the British delegation, by Richard Law, parliamentary undersecretary of state for foreign affairs. No private organizations or observers were admitted but interested Jewish organizations in America and England prepared memoranda proposing rescue measures. Chaim *Weizmann submitted a document on behalf of the *Jewish Agency for Palestine, underlining the importance of Palestine in the solution of the problem of Jewish refugees, and demanding abandonment of the British White Paper Policy of May 1939. The delegates, however, anxiously avoided referring to the Jews as the Nazis' major victims. Disagreement between the two governments about continuing the Intergovernmental Committee of Refugees, founded at the *Evian Conference in July 1938, took up most of the time but it was decided eventually to extend its mandate to deal with postwar problems. British plans for opening up camps in North Africa as a haven for refugees during the war proved impracticable. After seven months—on Dec. 10, 1943—the report of the conference was published. Its only positive decision—to revive the Evian Committee—came too late to save a single Jew from the Nazi Holocaust.

Bibliography: M. Wischnitzer, *To Dwell in Safety* (1948), 245–8; Adler-Rudel, in: YLBI, 11 (1966), 213–41; A. D. Morse, *While Six Million Died* (1968), index; World Jewish Congress (Australian Section), *Bermuda Conference on Refugees* (1943); A. Tartakower and K. R. Grossmann, *The Jewish Refugee* (1944), index.

[S.A.-R.]

°BERNADOTTE, FOLKE, EARL OF WISBORG (1895–1948), Swedish statesman. Bernadotte was the youngest son of Prince Oscar August of Sweden, a brother of King Gustav V. During World War II he organized an exchange of disabled prisoners of war between Germany and the Allies on behalf of the Swedish Red Cross. He became vice-chairman in 1943, and president in 1946, of the Swedish Red Cross. Stimulated by Norwegian and Danish intervention on behalf of their civilian prisoners in German concentration camps, he negotiated on behalf of the Swedish Red Cross with *Himmler who was persuaded to release more than 7,000 Scandinavians during March and April 1945, including over 400 Danish Jews, from *Theresienstadt. Following negotiations with a representative of the *World Jewish Congress in Sweden, Norbert Masur, he also effected the release of several thousand Jewish women from various countries interned in the Ravensbrueck concentration camp. Most of those released were transferred to Sweden. Subsequently, at a meeting in Luebeck on April 24, 1945, Himmler tried to use Bernadotte's good offices to forward peace proposals to the Allies. Bernadotte transmitted the Allies' rejection of these proposals to Himmler on April 27, in Flensburg.

On May 20, 1948, the Security Council of the United Nations appointed Bernadotte mediator in the Arab-Israel conflict. He succeeded in bringing about the first four-weeks truce on June 11, but failed to achieve Arab consent for its prolongation. Overextending his assignment as mediator, Bernadotte worked out a peace plan that deviated substantially from the UN partition resolution, suggesting, *inter alia*, the incorporation of Jerusalem and the whole Negev in Transjordan in exchange for the inclusion of Western Galilee in Israel. These proposals, which became public a few days after Bernadotte's death, met with stiff opposition by Israel and failed to achieve endorsement by the UN General Assembly in November 1948. On Sept. 17, 1948, Bernadotte was assassinated in Jerusalem. His assailants have not been identified, but are believed to have been connected with *Loḥamei Ḥerut Israel. A forest named in his honor has been planted by the *Jewish National Fund in the Judean Hills. Among his books are *The Curtain Falls: Last Days of the Third Reich* (1945) and *To Jerusalem* (1951).

Bibliography: R. Hewins, *Count Folke Bernadotte: His Life and Work* (1950); Yachil, in: *Yad Vashem Studies*, 6 (1967), 181–220; B. Nadel, *Reẓaḥ Bernadotte* (1968); M. Sharett, *Be-Sha'ar ha-Ummot 1946–1949* (1958), index.

[L.Y.]

BERNAL, Sephardi family of Marrano extraction. Its members included ABRAHAM (Manuel Nuñes) BERNAL (c. 1612–1655), a native of Almeida in Portugal, who was the leader of the crypto-Jewish group at Écija (Spain). After trial by the Inquisition at Córdoba he was burned at the stake for his faith, proclaiming his adherence to Judaism to the end. When the news reached Amsterdam the local Jewish poets collaborated in a volume in his memory under the title *Elogios que zelosos dedicaron á la felice memoria de Abraham Nuñez Bernal,* which was published by his cousin JACOB BERNAL. This volume also includes a sermon in honor of Abraham by Isaac *Aboab da Fonseca, and a prose account of the imprisonment and death of Abraham's nephew MARCO (Ishac de Almeida) BERNAL who was martyred also in 1655 at the age of 22. It ends with a sermon by Jacob Abendana in honor of both martyrs. In the course of the 18th century, some of the family settled in London. JACOB ISRAEL BERNAL, a West Indian merchant (d. 1766), served as a warden of the Spanish and Portuguese Jewish community there in 1745, but resigned in protest in 1752 when the synagogue authorities objected to his marriage to an Ashkenazi woman. His son JACOB (d. 1811) dissociated himself from the community and denounced its methods as inquisitorial when he failed to be elected to office; he did not formally abandon Judaism. In the course of time, however, the family left the Jewish community. His son RALPH (1783–1854), brought up as a Christian, was a politician and member of parliament from 1820 to 1853. In 1853 he was president of the British Archaeological Society and a renowned art collector. His son RALPH BERNAL-OSBORNE (1808–1882) was a noted wit and Liberal politician, who was secretary to the admiralty (1852–58). The physicist JOHN DESMOND BERNAL (1901–   ) is also descended from this family. The Jewish origin of MESTRE BERNAL, who accompanied Columbus' first expedition to America, is hypothetical.

Bibliography: A. M. Hyamson, *Sephardim of England* (1951), 170–1, 197–8; C. Roth, in; REJ, 100 (1936), 38–51; Roth, Marranos, index; I. S. Revah, in: REJ, 124 (1965), 368, 426; P. H. D. Bagenal, *Life of Ralph Bernal Osborne* (1884); DNB, 2 (1921–22), 373–4; A. B. Gould, in: *Boletín de la Real Academia de la Historia,* 90 (1927), 532–60; J. Picciotto, *Sketches of Anglo-Jewish History* (1956²), 149, 198–201.

[K.R.S.]

°BERNARD, EDWARD (1638–1697), English Orientalist and bibliographer. He had already studied Hebrew at school (in London), and at Oxford, when his mathematical ability secured him the professorship of astronomy at Oxford, first as Wren's deputy, and for one year (1676) he acted as tutor to Charles II's sons. He was devoted, however, to the study of Oriental languages. Bernard was one of the earliest students of Samaritan; he traced all alphabets to this script as putative parent (1689). His planned edition of Josephus foundered after the early books of the *Antiquities* (Oxford, 1700); he had written on the Septuagint and Letter of Aristeas (*ibid.*, 1692) and published W. Guise's translation of part of Mishnah *Zera'im* (*ibid.*, 1690). The wider scholarly world knows Bernard as author of the still important combined catalog of English and Irish manuscript collections (*ibid.*, 1697). His publications and manuscript *reliquiae* are listed by A. Wood (*Athenae Oxonienses*, ed. by P. Bliss, 4 (London, 1813–20), 703), and a printed auction-catalog of his library survives in the British Museum.

Bibliography: DNB, 2 (1921–22), 378–80. [RA.L.]

BERNARD, ḤAYYIM DAVID (1782–1858), Polish physician and ḥasidic leader. Born in Dzialoszyce, near Piotrkow, Bernard is reputed to have been the son of the poet and physician Issachar Falkensohn *Behr. At the age of 14 Bernard arrived in Berlin and later qualified as a physician in Erfurt. The liberal policies of King Frederick William II enabled him to become court physician at Potsdam and a medical officer in the Prussian Army—a considerable achievement for a Jew. After Napoleon's conquest of Poland, Bernard was appointed medical inspector for the western regions of the Grand Duchy of Warsaw (1807–15). A typical product of the German-Jewish Enlightenment, he at first remained aloof from Polish Jewry, but a spiritual crisis led him to approach R. David of *Lelov, who introduced him to R. Jacob Isaac ha-Levi *Horowitz, the Seer of Lublin. Bernard, known thereafter as R. Ḥayyim David, became a strictly Orthodox Jew and a follower of the Seer. He grew a beard, although he retained western dress, and never mastered Yiddish. As the Warsaw Jewish archives have shown, he was a leading communal figure and later worked in collaboration with R. *Simḥah Bunem of Przysucha. Among the Jews and Christians whom he treated, Bernard was venerated as a saint and he spent the rest of his life in Piotrkow, both as head of the local hospital and as a "wonder-working" Ḥasid. Although his wife opposed the Seer's wish to designate her husband as his successor, Bernard was widely regarded as the Seer's spiritual heir and for decades after the physician's death his grave was a center of ḥasidic pilgrimage.

Bibliography: *Maḥanayim*, no. 123 (1969), 174–8. [ED.]

BERNARD, TRISTAN (1866–1947), French playwright and novelist. Born in Bestançon, Bernard began his career as a sports writer, but soon turned to the theater, where he was able to exercise his talent for comedy good-humored satire, and witty observation of the man in the street. His *bons mots* were so famous that for three decades he was credited with many of the jokes current in France. Bernard wrote several novels, notably *Mémoires d'un jeune homme rangé* (1899), *Amants et voleurs* (1905), and *Mathilde et ses mitaines* (1912). He is best remembered, however, as the author of such hilarious comedies as *Les pieds nickelés* (1895), *L'anglais tel qu'on le parle* (1899), *Le petit café* (1911), *Le prince charmant* (1923), *Jules, Juliette, et Julien* (1929), *Le sauvage* (1931), and *Que le monde est petit* (1935). Tristan Bernard combined the wit of the French with the bitter humor of the Jew. *Le Juif de Venise* (1936) attempts to reinterpret the character of Shakespeare's Shylock. He was arrested by the Nazis during World War II but was released, following the intervention of influential friends. His son, JEAN-JACQUES BERNARD (1888–), also wrote a number of popular plays including *Martine* (1922) and *L'invitation au voyage* (1924). Though a convert to Catholicism, he was imprisoned at Compiègne for part of the Nazi occupation. His war experiences were recorded in *Le camp de la mort lente* (1945) and are reflected in the story, *L'Intouchable* (1947).

Bibliography: R. Blum, *Tristan Bernard* (Fr., 1925); P. Blanchart, *Masques*, 11 (1928); idem, *Tristan Bernard, son oeuvre* (1932); J. J. Bernard, *Mon père, Tristan Bernard* (1955). [M.C.]

°**BERNARDINO DA FELTRE** (1439–1494), *Franciscan friar, born at Feltre, N. Italy. From 1471 Bernardino began to attain a great reputation throughout northern Italy as a preacher, especially of the Lenten sermons urging the people to repentance. Pursuing the policy of his order, Bernardino inveighed against the Jews and supported the foundation of public loan-banks (**Monte di Pietà*) in order to displace Jewish moneylenders. His preaching was mainly responsible for the blood libel at *Trent in 1475. In the following year, he made a similar attempt at Reggio, and then in Bassano and Mantua; in 1485 he instigated the expulsion of the Jews from Perugia, and in 1486 from Gubbio. In 1488 he was expelled from Florence to prevent disorders. In 1491 in Ravenna he succeeded in having the Jews expelled and the synagogue destroyed. In 1492 he secured the expulsion of the Jews from Campo San Pietro, and from Brescia in 1494. Shortly after his death he was beatified.

Bibliography: E. Lazzareschi, *Il beato Bernardino da Feltre, gli Ebrei e il Monte di Pietà in Lucca* (1941), Roth, Italy, 170–6, passim; Milano, Italia, index; U. Cassuto, *Gli Ebrei a Firenze nell' età del Rinascimento* (1918), 52–53, 56–60, 62–63. [C.R.]

°**BERNARDINO DA SIENA** (1380–1444), Franciscan friar, celebrated for his powerful oratory. One of the main themes urged by Bernardino in his sermons was the return of the Church to its original purity and the exclusion of any form of association between Christians and Jews. Hence, Bernardino ruthlessly upheld the application of anti-Jewish restrictions, including segregation, exclusion from money-lending, limitation of economic activities, and wearing of the Jewish badge. He preached throughout Tuscany, Umbria, and Abruzzi, culminating in inflammatory sermons delivered at Aquila in 1438, attended by King René of Anjou. Almost everywhere, Bernardino's sermons resulted in a deterioration of the relationships between Christians and Jews and often provoked disorders. The circle of disciples which formed around Bernardino assiduously propagated his anti-Jewish doctrine. Most important of those whom he influenced were Barnabas of Terni, Giacomo della Marca, and *Bernardino da Feltre.

Bibliography: V. Facchinetti, *Bernardino da Siena* (It., 1933); Roth, Italy, 162ff.; Milano, Italia, 162f., 684. [A. MIL.]

°**BERNARD OF CLAIRVAUX** (1090–1153), French Cistercian, homilist, and theologian. In 1146, when preaching the Second Crusade, he intervened orally and in writing to protect the Jews in the Rhineland from persecution incited by a certain monk Radulph, declaring that an attempt on the life of a Jew was a sin tantamount to making an attempt on the life of Jesus. A letter addressed by Bernard to the Germans implicitly repudiates the policy urged by *Peter the Venerable, abbot of Cluny, against the Jews (although without expressly naming the abbot) by emphasizing the difference between Jews and Muslims; Bernard, while considering it right to take up arms against Muslims, maintains that it is forbidden to attack Jews. While Peter wished to expropriate the wealth of the Jews to finance the Crusade, Bernard limited himself to recommending the abolition of interest on credit they had advanced to crusaders. He finally recalled in his epistle the fate of Peter the Hermit and his followers, who had persecuted the Jews during the First Crusade and led his supporters into such peril that practically none had survived. Bernard warned that the present crusaders might well suffer similar Divine retribution: "It is to be feared that if you act in like manner, a similar fate will strike you." Jewish chroniclers stress Bernard's disinterestedness in his defense of the Jews.

Bibliography: A. Neubauer (ed.), *Hebraeische Berichte*... (1892), 58ff., 187ff.; Blumenkranz, in: K. H. Rengstorf and S. von Kortzfleisch (eds.), *Kirche und Synagoge* (1968), 119ff.

[B.BL.]

BERNAYS, family originating in Germany with branches elsewhere in Central Europe and the U.S.

ISAAC BEN JACOB BERNAYS (1792–1849), rabbi of Hamburg, Germany, was born in Mainz, studied at Wuerzburg University and at the yeshivah of Abraham Bing, and was appointed rabbi of Hamburg in 1821. In his struggle against Reform in the community, Bernays formulated a "modern orthodoxy" which influenced the views of his disciple, Samson Raphael *Hirsch. Bernays held that "Judaism should be explained according to science, which is common to all nations, and that its religious precepts should be observed for the sake of mankind." In 1842 Bernays interdicted the Reform prayer book, then republished, stating that "this is a prayer book, but not a Jewish prayer book." In his opinion, the immutability of the Jewish people was dependent on their mission. Thus he considered that the repudiation of the messianic belief by the Reform movement undermined the very existence of the Jewish people. *Der biblische Orient,* the only work attributed to him, is considered by many to have been written by Kalb, a Christian friend of his. I. Heinemann has supported Bernays' authorship on the ground that the main content of the work conforms closely with Bernays' views. He was related to Heine who often mentions him in his letters.

Isaac's eldest son JACOB (1824–1881), born in Hamburg, was a philologist and classicist. He taught Greek at Bonn University (1848–53), at which time he published the Teubner edition of Lucretius' *De Rerum Natura* (1850), *Heraklitische Studien* (1850), and *Ueber Spinozas hebraeische Grammatik* (1850). Unlike his younger brother, Michael, Jacob was attached to Judaism and when, because of it, he could not gain promotion at Bonn he left and helped to found the *Breslau Rabbinical Seminary in 1853. Jacob arranged the curriculum and taught classics, German literature, Hebrew poetry, and Jewish philosophy. He encouraged the publication of treatises with the annual report, himself contributing three (on the poetic fragments of Phocylides, 1856; on the *Chronicle* of Sulpicius Severus, 1861; and Theophrastus' lost work *On Piety,* 1886). His greatest work, *Grundzuege der verlorenen Abhandlung des Aristoteles ueber die Wirkung der Tragoedie* (1857), on Aristotle's treatise which preceded the *Poetics,* aroused considerable criticism. In 1866 Jacob finally overcame the prejudices at Bonn and was appointed assistant professor and chief librarian, but still maintained an interest in the seminary at Breslau. His collected works were issued in 1885 (edited by Usener).

[Y.HO.]

Isaac's younger son, MICHAEL BERNAYS (1834–1897), was a distinguished literary critic and historian. He was professor of German literature at the University of Munich (1874–90) and wrote pioneering textual studies of Goethe. His hatred for Judaism led him to convert and break with his family in 1856. Isaac's other son BERMAN BERNAYS (d. 1879), merchant and secretary to the Viennese economist, Lorenz von Stein, was father of MARTHA BERNAYS (1861–1951) who married Sigmund *Freud.

[G.S.]

PAUL ISAAC BERNAYS (1888–), mathematician, is best known as the coauthor with D. Hilbert of *Grundlagen der Mathematik* (2 vols., 1934–49), which is considered a classic work. Bernays, who was born in London, became Hilbert's assistant in Goettingen in 1917, and was appointed professor in 1933. In 1934 Bernays left Nazi Germany for Zurich, Switzerland, where he became professor at the Polytechnicum. In the postwar era, Bernays was mainly concerned with the philosophy of mathematics. In "Some Empirical Aspects of Mathematics," he argued that his discipline has an objective ("phenomenological") reality distinct from the natural world. Bernays wrote numerous papers on this subject, coauthored with A. H. *Frankel *Axiomatization of Set Theory* (1958), and coedited *Information and Prediction in Science* (1965). A book in his honor entitled *Logica, Studia Paul Bernays Dedicata* was published in Switzerland in 1969.

[GA.W.]

EDWARD L. BERNAYS (1891–) was a public relations expert whose methods revolutionized the field of public relations and who coined the term "public relations counselor." Born in Vienna, a nephew of Sigmund Freud, he went to the U.S. at an early age. After graduating from Cornell (N.Y.) Agricultural College in 1912, Bernays worked as a medical

Edward L. Bernays, U.S. public relations counselor.

journalist before becoming a show business publicity agent. He used public relations techniques to overcome opposition to Brieux's controversial play, *Damaged Goods.* Bernays also did publicity work for Enrico Caruso, Otis Skinner, and Diaghilev's Russian Ballet. He was a key staff member of George Creel's World War I U.S. Committee on Public Information. Bernays' first private client was Thomas G. Masaryk, father of Czechoslovak independence. After 1920 Bernays was recognized as the leading public relations "counselor" for major corporations. He wrote the first book on public relations, *Crystallizing Public Opinion,* in 1929 and taught the first college course on the subject in 1930.

[B.P.]

Bibliography: Fuerst, in: MGWJ, 58 (1914), 516–8; Bach, *ibid.*, 83 (1939), 533–47; Duckesz, in: JJLG, 5 (1907), 297–322; Heinemann, in: *Zion,* 16 (1951), 44–90; M. Fraenkel, *Jacob Bernays* (Ger., 1932); L. Wickert, in: *Historische Zeitschrift,* 205 (1967), 269–94.

BERNBACH, WILLIAM (1911–), U.S. advertising executive. Born in the Bronx, N.Y., he served in the U.S. Army in World War II and then worked at Grey Advertising. In 1949 he joined with Ned Doyle, another Grey vice-president, and with Maxwell Dane, a small agency owner, to form a partnership. They specialized in subtle, intelligent copy and graphics. So successful were these efforts that in less than 20 years the agency had become the sixth-largest in the U.S. Bernbach's influence on the contemporary advertising industry was profound. His creative leadership won him many awards. Some of his most famous slogans were "You don't have to be Jewish to love Levy's" (rye bread); "Think Small" for a small-car manufacturer; and "We Try Harder Because We're Only Number 2" for a car-rental company.

[I.BA.]

William Bernbach, U.S. advertising executive.

BERNE (Ger. **Bern**), capital of Switzerland. Jews in Berne, engaged in moneylending, are first mentioned in a document of 1262 or 1263. In 1293 or 1294 several Jews were put to death there in consequence of a *blood libel, and the remainder expelled from the city. However, an agreement was made with the citizenry through the intervention of Adolph of Nassau permitting the Jews to return, against a payment of 1,500 marks and a moratorium on debts owed to them. During the *Black Death (1348) the Jews in Berne were accused of poisoning the wells, and a number were burnt at the stake. The Jews were expelled from Berne in 1392 after Christians were permitted to engage in moneylending (1384). Although between 1408 and 1427 Jews were again residing in the city, the only Jews to appear in Berne subsequently were transients, chiefly physicians and cattle dealers. After the occupation of Switzerland by the French revolutionary armies and the foundation of the Helvetian Republic in 1798, a number of Jews from Alsace and elsewhere settled in Berne. They required a special license to engage in commerce, and were obliged to keep accounts in German or French instead of their customary Alsatian Judeo-German. These restrictions were removed in 1846. An organized Jewish community was officially established in 1848: a synagogue was consecrated in 1855, and a cemetery in 1871. Berne University was one of the first German-speaking universities (1836) to allow Jewish lecturers without requiring a change of professed faith, and many Jews subsequently held academic positions there. The university was attended by numerous students from Russia and Hungary before World War I, including Chaim Weizmann. The famous trial in which evidence was brought that the "Protocols of the *Elders of Zion" was a forgery was held in Berne in the 1930s. In 1969, 230 families were declared members of the Berne Jewish community (although the total number of Jews living there is presumably greater).

Bibliography: M. Kayserling, in: MGWJ, 13 (1864), 46–51; Tobler, in: *Archiv des historischen Vereins des Kantons Bern*, 12 (1889), 336–67; *Festschrift zur Jahrhundertfeier der juedischen Gemeinde zu Bern* (1948).

[Z.AV./ED.]

BERNFELD, SIEGFRIED (1892–1953), psychoanalyst and educator. Born in Lvov, he studied at the universities of Freiburg and Vienna. A pupil of Sigmund Freud, Bernfeld was also influenced by Gustav Wyneken, the German educator and philosopher. He practiced and taught psychoanalysis in Vienna and Berlin and later in Menton, France. Leaving France in 1936, he settled in San Francisco, California. Bernfeld was active in Austrian and German youth movements, applying in practice the conclusions he drew from his psychoanalytic studies. During World War I, he organized the Zionist youth movement in Austria, and published the Zionist youth periodical *Jerubaal* in Vienna (1918–19). Among his other works of Jewish interest are *Das juedische Volk und seine Jugend* (1920). He was a founder of the Hebrew Paedagogium at Vienna and the Jewish children's home at Baumgarten. Bernfeld wrote extensively on a variety of topics. His examination of infant psychology and of Freud's childhood, and also his attempts at educational reform, are noteworthy.

Bibliography: S. Wininger, *Grosse juedische National-Biographie*, 1 (1925), 344; 6 (1931), 465; *Journal of the American Psychoanalytic Association* 2 (1954), 378–9 (obituary by Norman Reider); *International Journal of Psychoanalysis* 36 (1955), 66–71 (obituary by Hedwig Hoffer); A. Grinstein (ed.), *Index of Psychoanalytic Writings*, 1 (1956), 142–7; Hoffer, in: YLBI, 10 (1965), 150–67.

[S.Z.L.]

BERNFELD, SIMON (1860–1940), rabbi, scholar, and author. Bernfeld was born in Stanislav, Galicia, and was educated in Koenigsberg and Berlin. In 1886 he was appointed chief rabbi of the Sephardi community of Belgrade, Serbia; he remained there until 1894, when he returned to Berlin and devoted himself to scholarly pursuits. He continued his literary work until his death, despite blindness in his later years. Bernfeld wrote several monographs in Hebrew on Jewish history and philosophy, the earliest published when he was only 19 (in *Ha-Maggid*, 1 (1879), 91ff.). His best-known work is *Da'at Elohim* ("Knowledge of God," 2 vols., 1897), a history of religious philosophy. He also wrote *Toledot ha-Reformazyon ha-Datit be-Yisrael* (1900), a history of the Reform movement; *Benei Aliyyah* (2 vols., 1931), a collection of monographs on famous Jews of various periods; *Sefer ha-Dema'ot* ("Book of Tears," 3 vols., 1923–26), an anthology of historical sources in prose and verse on the persecution of Jews from the earliest periods until the Ukrainian pogroms of 1768, still an important reference work; and *Mavo Sifruti-Histori le-Khitvei ha-Kodesh* (3 vols., 1923–25), an introduction to the Bible from the viewpoint of biblical criticism. Bernfeld also wrote in Hebrew on the history of the Haskalah in Germany and Galicia, *Dor Tahapukhot* (1897–98) and monographs on Muhammad (1898) and on the Crusades (1899). Bernfeld's works in German include *Juden und Judentum im neunzehnten Jahrhundert* (1898); *Der Talmud, sein Wesen, seine Bedeutung und seine Geschichte* (1900); and *Kaempfende Geister in Judentum* (1907). His German translation of the Bible, which follows traditional translations, was published in several editions. Bernfeld edited *Die Lehren des Judenthums* (4 vols., 1920–24 and later editions; Eng. tr. of vol. 1 by A. H. Koller, *Teachings of Judaism* (1929), vol. 1: *Foundations of Jewish Ethics*, with new introduction by S. E. Karff, 1968). Although not original in his ideas, Bernfeld popularized and disseminated much important literary and scientific knowledge.

Bibliography: I. Klausner, *Yozerim u-Vonim*, 1 (1944[2]), 290–8; idem, *Yozerei-Tekufah u-Mamshikhei Tekufah* (1956), 153–61; EIV, 9 (1958), 870–2; M. J. bin-Gorion, *Kitvei . . . Bi-Sedeh-Sefer*, 2 (1921), 52–63; Voyeslavsky, in: *Gilyonot*, 2 (1934/35), 478–84; S. B. Weinryb, in: *Bitzaron*, 1 (1939/40), 502–11; Hodess, in: *New Judea*, 16 (1940), 73–74.

[J.KL./ED.]

BERNHARD, GEORG (1875–1944), German journalist. A native of Berlin, he wrote for financial columns and after entering the Reichstag as a Social Democrat in 1913, founded the financial journal *Plutus* (1904), which he published until 1925. In 1908 he also became publishing editor of the *Berliner Morgenpost* and the *Berliner Zeitung*

Georg Bernhard, Berlin newspaper editor. Oil painting by Gertrud Sax-Bernhard. N.Y., Leo Baeck Institute.

am Mittag, and in 1913 editor in chief of the *Vossische Zeitung.* Bernhard was active in German-Jewish communal organizations. In 1933 he left for Paris, and there edited the emigrant journal *Pariser Tageblatt.* He wrote *Die deutsche Meister und Dilletanten im Kapitalismus im Reiche der Hohenzollern* (1936), and, in collaboration, *Warum schweigt die Welt?* (1936). He was interned by the French in 1940 but succeeded in escaping to the U.S.A. in 1941.

Bibliography: *Revue mondiale* (Jan. 1931), 198–202. [Ed.]

BERNHARDT, SARAH (Rosine Bernard; 1844–1923), French actress. Fathered by a Frenchman (Edouard Bernard), she was the eldest of three illegitimate daughters born to Judith Van Hard, a Dutch-Jewish music teacher. When Sarah was ten years old she was sent to the convent of Versailles and baptized. However, she remained proud of her Jewish heritage. She made her debut at the Comédie Française in 1862 as Iphigénie in Racine's *Iphigénie en Aulide.* She acted at the Odéon from 1866 to 1872, and achieved popular acclaim in Coppée's *Le Passant* as the page Zanetto, her first male role. Returning to the Comédie Française, she became one of the greatest interpreters of Racine, playing *Andromaque* in 1873 and *Phèdre* in 1874. Temperament and impatience with authority ended her career at the Comédie in 1879. She embarked on a series of tours abroad and drew crowds wherever she appeared. She acted in a London season almost annually until as late as 1922. She visited the U.S. nine times, and acted in Germany, Russia, Latin America, and Australia. Everywhere she conquered her audience with *La Dame aux Camélias* by Alexandre Dumas, fils. Forming her own company, she appeared in both classical and modern works, and excelled in Sardou's *Fédora* (1882), *Théodora* (1884), and *La Tosca* (1889), all of which he wrote for her. Almost every role she acted became her personal triumph. In Edmond Rostand's *L'Aiglon* she played the part of Napoleon's 21-year-old son when she was herself 55. In 1899 she took over a large Paris theater, renamed it Théâtre Sarah Bernhardt, and directed it until her death. Here she presented *Hamlet* and herself played the title role. A neglected knee injury resulted in complications, and in 1914 Bernhardt was obliged to have her right leg amputated. She continued to appear in roles which permitted her to sit, such as Racine's *Athalie.* The "Divine Sarah," as she was called by Victor Hugo, died while at work on a film. Her autobiography *Ma Double Vie* was published in 1907.

Bibliography: L. Verneuil, *Fabulous Life of Sarah Bernhardt* (1942); J. Agate, *Madame Sarah* (Eng., 1945); J. Richardson, *Sarah Bernhardt* (Eng., 1959); C. O. Skinner, *Madame Sarah* (Eng., 1967). [L.G./Ed.]

BERNHEIM, HIPPOLYTE (1840–1919). French neurologist. Born in Alsace, he was appointed professor of internal medicine at Nancy University in 1878. In 1884 he began to devote himself to nervous and mental disease and was one of the first to concentrate systematically on the problems of psychotherapy. His methods included suggestion and hypnosis. He was regarded as head of the Nancy school of psychiatry, as opposed to the Paris school headed by Charcot, which saw hypnosis as an investigative method and not as a method of treatment. Bernheim based treatment on persuasion—the doctor's psychological influence on the course of the neurosis. His methods became outdated but his activities were instrumental in winning acceptance for psychotherapy by the medical profession. Bernheim's most important work was *De la suggestion et de ses applications à la thérapeutique* (1886). His other works include *Hypnotisme, suggestion et psychothérapie* (1890). His work laid the foundation for an understanding of the human personality in the light of psychopathology rather than of philosophy. Bernheim recognized "automatisms" which were not under conscious

The Sarah Bernhardt stamp issued by the French Post Office in 1945.

control. He absolved the will as being the origin of mental disease and crime—thus attacking the stigma attaching to insanity and opening the road to the principle of "irresistible impulse"—in the penal code.

Bibliography: S. R. Kagan, *Jewish Medicine* (1952), 375–6; Zilbourg, *A History of Medical Psychology* (1941), 367–9.

[J.O.L.]

BERNHEIM, ISAAC WOLFE (1848–1945), U.S. distiller and philanthropist. Bernheim was born in Schmieheim, Baden. He emigrated to the U.S. in 1867 and settled in Paducah, Kentucky, where he worked as a salesman and bookkeeper. In 1872 Bernheim, together with a brother, established a distillery. The business was moved to Louisville, Ky., in 1882, and became one of the most important in the country. Bernheim made several gifts to public causes. In 1889 he organized the first YMHA in Louisville and contributed its first home. He contributed to Hebrew Union College its first library building (1912), and later helped subsidize its second. Other benefactions included an addition to the Louisville Jewish Hospital (1916), sculpture for Louisville and the Statuary Hall in Washington, a 13,000-acre nature reserve near Louisville, and gifts to the village of his birth. Bernheim was rigid and autocratic in temperament. Particularly hostile to Zionism, in 1918 he addressed a letter to the Central Conference of American Rabbis urging the founding of a "Reform Church of American Israelites" to consist of "100 percent Americans." In a 1921 address to the Union of American Hebrew Congregations, of which he was a vice-president and for over 40 years member of the executive board, he called for a Sunday Sabbath and argued that the terms "Jew and Judaism" were a "reservoir from which is fed the perennial spring of hatred, malice, and contempt." Likewise he urged that foreign terms such as "temple" and "synagogue" strengthened the accusation that the Jews were a "foreign and indigestible element." From 1906 to 1921 Bernheim was treasurer of the American Jewish Committee. He wrote two autobiographical works, *Bernheim Family* (1910) and *Closing Chapters of a Busy Life* (1929). He also wrote *History of the Settlement of the Jews in Paducah and the Lower Ohio Valley* (1912). [S.D.T.]

BERNHEIM, LOUIS (1861–1931), Belgian army officer. Born in Saint-Josse-ten-Noode, Bernheim was commissioned in the Grenadiers and was transferred to the general staff in 1888. Later he returned to the Grenadiers and on the outbreak of World War I commanded the 7th Infantry Regiment at Antwerp. At the battle of the Marne, Bernheim commanded a Belgian brigade in the First Division and later defended Antwerp against German attacks. He subsequently took command of the First Division. He was seriously wounded in September 1915 but was promoted to lieutenant general in the following year and in 1918 commanded three Belgian divisions in Flanders in the final advance on the German lines. Bernheim received numerous awards and honors and was given a state funeral. After his death a statue was erected in his honor in a Brussels square.

Bibliography: *New York Times* (Feb. 14, 20, 21, 22, 1931).

[Ed.]

BERNHEIMER, CARLO (1877–), Italian scholar. Born in Leghorn, Bernheimer taught Sanskrit at the University of Bologna from 1906 to 1938, when he was dismissed under the Fascist racial laws. Bernheimer devoted himself especially to the study of Hebrew paleography, and bibliography. In his *Paleografia ebraica* (1924) he set himself the task "of illustrating . . . everything that concerns Hebrew manuscripts." He also published catalogs of the Hebrew and cognate manuscripts in the *talmud torah* of Leghorn (1915), the Ambrosian Library of Milan (1933), and the Biblioteca Estense of Modena (1960). [A.M.R.]

BERNHEIMER, CHARLES LEOPOLD (1864–1944), U.S. businessman and explorer. Bernheimer was born in Germany. He was educated in Switzerland and emigrated to the United States in 1881. He began his career as an office boy for a relative, Adolf Bernheimer, a dry goods wholesaler in New York City. Seventeen years later he became president of the firm. In 1911 he was appointed chairman of the Committee on Arbitration of the New York Chamber of Commerce; his ability to successfully arbitrate disputes involving large sums won him a reputation as "the father of commercial arbitration." He

Charles L. Bernheimer, U.S. businessman and explorer. Oil painting by Louis Betts, 1925. New York Chamber of Commerce Collection.

helped write the New York State and Federal arbitration laws. Bernheimer's hobby was exploration. He made eight expeditions between 1915 and 1923 to northern Arizona and the Utah "Bad Lands" for the American Museum of Natural History. In Utah Bernheimer discovered the most perfect set of dinosaur tracks ever known and cliff-dwelling ruins. Bernheimer undertook expeditions to Guatemala, Yucatan, and southern Mexico. His books include: *A Business Man's Plan for Settling the War in Europe* (1915); *The Advantages of Arbitration* (1926); and *Rainbow Bridge* (1924). [Ed.]

BERNHEIMER, CHARLES SELIGMAN (1868–1960), U.S. social worker. Bernheimer, who was born in Philadelphia, Pa., served with Jewish welfare and educational organizations during six decades, holding such posts as business secretary of the *Jewish Publication Society of America (1890–1906), executive director of the Hebrew Educational Society of Brooklyn (1910–19), and director of community studies for the *National Jewish Welfare Board (1921–40). He also edited the information bulletin of the Jewish Welfare Board, *The Jewish Center,* for many years. As assistant head worker of the University Settlement in

New York City (1906–10), Bernheimer played a prominent role in support of the workers in the Shirtwaist Strike of 1909 that helped establish modern trade unionism in the garment trades. Bernheimer edited the pioneer study *The Russian Jew in the United States* (1905), in which he wrote the chapters on Philadelphia. He was coauthor of the book *Boys' Clubs* (1914) and contributed to many periodicals. His memoirs *Half a Century in Community Service* were published in 1948.

[I.Y.]

BERNHEIM PETITION, petition against Nazi anti-Jewish legislation, signed by Franz Bernheim on the initiative of Emil *Margulies and submitted to the League of Nations on May 17, 1933, by representatives of the *Comité des Délégations Juives (Leo *Motzkin, Emil Margulies, and Nathan Feinberg). At the same time they presented to the League a similar petition signed by the Comité, the American Jewish Congress, and other Jewish institutions. Since there was a special procedure regarding petitions addressed by inhabitants of German Upper Silesia, Bernheim's petition alone was immediately considered by the League. When the Nazis came to power, Bernheim, a warehouse employee in Upper Silesia, was dismissed from work as a result of racial discrimination, and took up temporary residence in Prague. In his petition he complained that the anti-Jewish legislation of the Third Reich was also being applied to Upper Silesia, in violation of the German-Polish Convention of May 15, 1922 (Geneva Convention), which guaranteed all minorities in Upper Silesia equal civil and political rights. The petition requested the League to state that all the anti-Jewish measures, if and when applied in Upper Silesia, infringed upon the Geneva Convention and were therefore null and void, and that Upper Silesian Jews be reinstated in their rights and receive compensation for damages. Bernheim's petition was placed on the agenda of the 73rd session of the League Council on May 22, 1933. The German representative, von Keller, lodged an objection denying Bernheim's right to submit the complaint, a plea that was rejected by an ad hoc committee of jurists. Four days later von Keller declared in the name of his government that internal German legislation did not in any way affect the General Convention and that if its provisions had been violated, this could only have been due to errors and misconstructions on the part of subordinate officials. The purpose of this public apology was to prevent a general debate on the petition, but these tactics failed, and in two public sessions (May 30 and June 6) the persecution of Jews in Germany was fully discussed. Many of the speakers severely censured Germany for the treatment of its Jews and demanded that they be accorded minimum human rights. In a unanimous decision, Germany and Italy abstaining, the Council adopted a resolution noting the German government's declaration and requesting it to furnish the Council with information on further developments. On September 30, 1933, the German government submitted a letter in which it claimed to have fulfilled its obligations, and that the rights of the Jews of Upper Silesia had been restored. The main objective of the Comité des Délégations Juives in bringing the petitions before the League was to focus world attention on the anti-Jewish legislation of Nazi Germany and the persecution of its Jews, and to have it condemned. The discussions in the League Council, and especially the declaration of the German government, helped the Jews of Upper Silesia in their struggle for their rights before such local bodies as the Mixed Commission established under the Geneva Convention. Until the expiration of the Convention on July 15, 1937, the Jews of Upper Silesia continued to enjoy equality of rights, and even *sheḥitah*, forbidden in the Third Reich, was permitted them.

Bibliography: G. Kaeckenbeck, *International Experiment in Upper Silesia* (1942); *Question des Juifs allemands devant la Société des Nations* (1933); G. Weissmann, in: BLBI, 61 (1963), 154–98; N. Feinberg, *Ha-Ma'arakhah ha-Yehudit Neged Hitler al Bimat Ḥever ha-Le'ummim* (1957).

[N.F.]

BERNSTEIN, ARNOLD (1888–), German shipbuilder. Born in Breslau, Germany, Bernstein served in the German Army during World War I and was awarded the Iron Cross. After the war he began a small shipping business. His first successful venture came as a result of his construction of ships, called "floating garages," on which uncrated automobiles could be shipped without risk of damage. The process involved a substantial saving in automobile transportation, and at one time his ships carried more than half the automobiles exported from America to Europe. With the sharp decline in tourism in the difficult economic period of the early 1930s, Bernstein converted his ships into combined freight-passenger vessels and introduced one-class tourist cabins. He bought the Red Star Line with the profits from this venture. Shortly thereafter he established the Palestine Shipping Company, which included the *Tel Aviv*, the first ship fully manned by a Jewish crew. During a visit to Germany in 1937 he was arrested by the Nazis on the charge that he had violated currency regulations. A prison sentence and a fine of $400,000 were imposed on him. The Holland-America Line gained control of all his ships in return for payment of the fine, except those belonging to the Palestine Shipping Company. Some months later the latter went into bankruptcy. Upon Bernstein's release in 1939 he moved to New York where he organized the Arnold Bernstein Shipping Company and in the 1950s, the Atlantic Banner Line. This failed because it could not meet the competition of the airlines.

[ED.]

BERNSTEIN, ARON DAVID (1812–1884), German political and scientific writer and one of the founders of Reform Judaism in Berlin. Born in Danzig, he was the son of a rabbi and had a thorough religious education but no secular schooling of any kind. At the age of 20 he went to Berlin, where he taught himself the German language, and literature and science. He earned his living for some years as an antiquarian bookseller, but began writing in German in 1834, when he published an annotated translation of the Song of Songs. Bernstein combined progressive thought in politics, science and religion with a nostalgic affection for Jewish ghetto life. His main interest was natural science, of which he became a successful popularizer. He promoted the Jewish Reform Movement in Berlin and edited its monthly, *Die Reform-Zeitung*. Bernstein's widely read stories, written in the German-Jewish dialect *(Judendeutsch)*—*Voegele der Maggid* and *Mendel Gibbor* (1860; reissued 1934, 1935)—were forerunners of a literary genre which sentimentalized the Jewish lower middle class in small-town ghettos. They were translated into several languages. During the Prussian liberal era, Bernstein, who wrote under the pseudonym of A. Rebenstein, was influential as a political journalist. A champion of democracy, he fought on the barricades during the Prussian revolution of 1848. In 1849, when the revolutionary tide receded, he founded the *Urwaehlerzeitung*, an organ advocating moderate political reform. This brought him into conflict with the authorities, and in about 1852 the newspaper was suppressed and he was sentenced to four months' imprisonment. As a successor to the *Urwaehlerzeitung*, Bernstein founded the influential daily, the *Berliner Volkszeitung*, where his political editorials and articles on popular science appeared for nearly 30 years. A selection of his political articles was published in 1883–84. His essays on science, *Naturwissenschaftliche Volksbuecher*, were published in 21 volumes (1855–56), and a Hebrew translation (mainly by David Frischmann) entitled *Yedi'ot ha-Teva* appeared in Warsaw from 1881 to 1891. Bernstein himself was a practical scientist and experimented widely in telegraphy and photography.

Bibliography: S. Holdheim, *Geschichte ... der juedischen Reformgemeinde in Berlin* (1857); A. Geiger, in: JZWL, 7 (1869), 223ff.; S. Kaznelson, *Juden im deutschen Kulturbereich* (1959), 28, 574. [R.W.]

BERNSTEIN, ARYEH LEIB (1708–1788), chief rabbi of Galicia, and merchant; born in Brody. While a young man he served for a brief period as rabbi of Zbarazh, subsequently returning to Brody where he entered commerce. The 1740s was a period of prosperity for Brody; the Jews there began to establish commercial links abroad. Bernstein succeeded in concentrating a large part of the trade in his hands. When in 1776 the election of a chief rabbi (*Oberlandesrabbiner*) of Galicia was about to take place, the rabbi-designate Ezekiel *Landau remained in Prague, and Bernstein was appointed. At his new place of residence in Lemberg, Bernstein took over control of the religious functionaries and the administration of taxes in the communities under his jurisdiction. His authoritarian ways and interference in the administration of the communities aroused opposition which was exacerbated by his financial dealings, which he continued while serving as chief rabbi. His opponents complained bitterly against him, and in 1785 an investigation was begun. However, through his influence, the charges were dropped and his accusers were punished. Despite this, his authority was undermined. The increasing dissatisfaction among the mass of Jews, coupled with the inclination of the authorities to abolish the centralistic chief rabbinate, led to its abrogation on Nov. 1,1786. Bernstein, who was permitted to retain the title only, did not succeed in his intention to continue to manage religious affairs. He subsequently devoted himself mainly to commerce and left a large fortune to his heirs. [M.LAN.]

His father, ISSACHAR BER (d. 1764) was also a distinguished scholar, rabbi, and communal leader. Issachar Ber's first position was as a rabbi of the Kehillat Ḥayyatin ("Congregation of the Tailors") in Brody. In 1750, he was elected *rosh ha-medinah* ("head of the province") of Brody, and also was appointed "a trustee of the Council of Four Lands and *parnas* of Rydzyna Province." Despite the intense opposition of some communities, he remained a trustee until 1763. [Y.AL.]

Bibliography: N. M. Gelber, *Aus zwei Jahrunderten* (1924), 14–37; idem, in: JQR, 14 (1923/24), 303–27; S. Buber, *Anshei Shem* (1895), xixff.

BERNSTEIN, BÉLA (1868–1944), Hungarian Jewish historian. Bernstein was born in Várpalota; he graduated in 1892 from the Jewish Theological Seminary of Budapest, and received his doctorate in 1890 in Leipzig. He served as rabbi in Szombathely from 1892 to 1909 and then became rabbi in Nyiregyháza. He tried to introduce a uniform religious education in Hungary in 1901. Bernstein wrote works devoted to the history of the Jews in Hungary: *Az 1848–49-iki magyar szabadságharc és a zsidók* ("The 1848–49 Hungarian Revolution and the Jews" (1898), preface by Mór Jókai); "The History of the Jews in Vasmegye" in: *Magyar Zsidó Szemle*, vols. 30–32 (1913–15); and *"Die Anfaenge der Judengemeinde in Nyiregyháza"* in *Semitic Studies in Memory of Immanuel Loew* (1947). In his last years Bernstein worked on his memoirs. He was deported to Auschwitz by the Nazis in 1944 and died there.

Bibliography: *Magyar Zsidó Szemle*, 49 (1932), 235–8. [AL.SCH.]

BERNSTEIN, EDUARD (1850–1932), German socialist theoretician, spokesman for the so-called revisionist group which challenged orthodox Marxist doctrines. Born in Berlin, Bernstein was the son of a Jewish engine driver. He joined the Social Democratic Party in 1872 and was forced to leave Germany after the enactment of the anti-socialist legislation of 1878. He lived first in Switzerland, where he edited the *Sozialdemokrat*, and then in London. It was while he was in London that he published his principal work *Die Voraussetzungen des Sozialismus und die Aufgaben der Sozialdemokratie* (1899; *Evolutionary Socialism*, 1909), in which he set out his nonconformist Marxist interpretation of history. Bernstein contested the view of the inevitable collapse of capitalism and urged the socialists to become a party of reform. His views were vehemently opposed as heretical by most of the party but gained numerous adherents. In 1901 Bernstein returned to Germany and sat in the Reichstag from 1902 to 1906 and from 1912 to 1918. In World War I his pacifist views led him to disassociate himself from the right-wing faction and join the left-wing independent socialists who opposed the war. He returned to the majority party in 1918 and sat as a Social Democrat from 1920 to 1928. In common with many Jewish socialists of the time, Bernstein left the Jewish community because the party disapproved of all religious affiliations. During World War I, however, he came under the influence of *Po'alei Zion leaders, including Zalman Rubashov (later *Shazar, president of Israel), and began to appreciate the special position of the Jewish people. In his book *Die Aufgaben der Juden im Weltkriege* (1917) he argued that because of their dispersion and universalist ideas, the Jews should be the pioneers of an internationalism which would unite nations and prevent war. Toward the end of his life, he came to support the concept of a Jewish national home in Palestine and became a leader of the "International Socialist Pro-Palestine Committee." Bernstein's writings include: his autobiography *Erinnerungen eines Sozialisten* (1918; *My Years of Exile*, 1921); *Ferdinand Lassalle* (1919); *Die Deutsche Revolution* (1921); and *Sozialismus und Demokratie in der grossen Englischen Revolution* (1922; *Cromwell and Communism*, 1930).

Bibliography: G. Lichtheim, *Marxism* (1961), index; P. Angel, *Eduard Bernstein et l'évolution du socialisme allemand* (1961); P. Gay, *The Dilemma of Democratic Socialism: Eduard Bernstein's Challenge to Marx* (1952); E. Silberner, in: HJ, 15 (1953), 3–48. [R.W.]

BERNSTEIN, HENRI-LEON (1876–1953), French playwright. Bernstein was born in Paris, and during his early period (1900–1914) wrote powerful, realistic plays depicting the cruelty of modern life and society. The best known of these are: *La Rafale* (1905), *Le Voleur* (1907), *Samson* (1908), *Israël* (1908), and *Le Secret* (1913). Some of his plays deal with the Jew's position in modern society. There are echoes of the *Dreyfus case in *Israël*, which deals with one of the tragic results of assimilation. The young leader of an anti-Semitic movement discovers that his own father is a Jew. Overwhelmed by the revelation and unable to accept his new status, the young man is eventually driven to suicide. The plays written from 1918 to 1938 place increasing emphasis on the psychological problems of their heroes. To this period belong *Judith* (1922), *Félix* (1926),

Mélo (1929), and *Espoir* (1936). The theme of anti-Semitism periodically recurs, and Nazism is attacked in *Elvire* (1940). During World War II, Bernstein lived in the United States. Although he continued writing after 1945, tastes had changed, and his plays declined in popularity.

Bibliography: L. Le Sidaner, *Henri Bernstein* (1931); P. Bathile, *Henri Bernstein, son oeuvre* (1931); H. Clovard, *Histoire de la littérature française du symbolisme à nos jours*, 1 (1947). [D.R.G.]

BERNSTEIN, HERMAN (1876–1935), U.S. journalist, born in Neustadt-Schirwirdt (Vladislavov), Lithuania; one of the first to expose *The Protocols of the *Elders of Zion* forgery. Bernstein went to the United States from Russia in 1893 and wrote in Yiddish and English. His first book was *With Master Minds* (1912), a collection of interviews with European personalities. In 1914 he founded the Yiddish daily *Der Tog (The Day)*, which became a recognized organ of liberal Jewish opinion. He was its editor until 1916 and editor in chief of the **American Hebrew* until 1919. During World War I, Bernstein made an on-the-spot study of Jewish conditions in Eastern Europe and stimulated the organization of relief for Jewish war victims. In 1917, when he was correspondent of the *New York Herald*, he discovered 65 telegrams which had been exchanged between the German kaiser and the czar between 1904 and 1907, and published them as *The Willy-Nicky Correspondence* (1918). In 1921 Bernstein published *The History of a Lie* (1928), a book which was among the first exposures of the notorious *Protocols of the Elders of Zion* as a forgery. He also instituted legal proceedings against Henry Ford, who had helped to circulate the *Protocols* and had allowed anti-Semitic articles based on them to appear in his weekly *The Dearborn Independent*. Bernstein's postwar interviews for the daily press were reprinted as *Celebrities of Our Times* (1925) and *The Road to Peace* (1926). He wrote a study of Herbert Hoover in 1928. Bernstein served as United States envoy to Albania from 1931 to 1933. [S.L.]

BERNSTEIN, IGNATZ (1836–1909), Yiddish folklorist and collector of proverbs. Bernstein was the son of a wealthy family of sugar merchants, and as a rich industrialist in Warsaw he was able to indulge in his hobby of collecting the folklore of many peoples. He accumulated one of the world's richest libraries in this field. Bernstein published a two-volume illustrated catalog of his collection of books and manuscripts (1900, 1968[2]). He traveled through Europe, North Africa, and Palestine, and for 35 years collected Yiddish proverbs current among the Jews of Russia, Poland, and Galicia. He published 2,056 Yiddish proverbs in Mordecai Spector's annual *Hausfreund* (1888–89). Two decades later the number of proverbs had grown to 3,993, which he published in a magnificent volume *Juedische Sprichwoerter* (1908, 1912, 1948). In the same year he published his collection of 227 Yiddish proverbs concerned with sex under the Latin title *Erotica et Rustica* (1909, 1918[2]). Bernstein helped to found, and also supported, the central Jewish library in Warsaw.

Bibliography: Rejzen, Leksikon, 1 (1928), 373–5; LNYL, 1 (1956), 407–8; J. Shatzky, *Geshikhte fun Yidn in Varshe*, 3 (1953), 325–8. [S.L./C.C.]

BERNSTEIN, ISSACHAR BERUSH BEN ARYEH LOEB (1747–1802), German rabbi and author. Bernstein studied under his father, the son of Jacob Joshua *Falk, and Ẓevi Hirsch Levin of Berlin. In 1788 he succeeded his father as rabbi of Hanover. Legend attributes Bernstein's untimely death to his having insulted the son of Jonathan *Eybeschuetz, R. Wolf Eybeschuetz, who, as a young man, had held heretical views but had subsequently recanted. Several of Bernstein's novellae were included in his father's *Penei Aryeh* on *Bava Kamma* (printed with Jacob Joshua Falk's *Penei Yehoshu'a;* Fuerth, 1780, together with Bernstein's rejoinders to critical comments made by R. Judah Leib Friedenburg on this work were also included). His *Hadrat Ḥakhamim*, discourses delivered on the conclusion of the study of talmudic tractates, is still in manuscript. Of his sons, the best known is Samuel (d. 1839) who succeeded his father-in-law, Jacob Moses b. Saul, as rabbi in Amsterdam, becoming the fifth member of the family to hold this position. Samuel wrote an approbation to the *Arẓot he-Ḥayyim* of Malbim (1836), and corresponded with Moses *Sofer on halakhic matters. Samuel's son Berush was a *dayyan* in Amsterdam and later rabbi in The Hague.

Bibliography: A. Walden, *Shem ha-Gedolim he-Ḥadash* (1864), 116, no. 33; H. Dembitzer, *Kelilat Yofi*, 1 (1888), 115a; S. Knoebil, *Gerem ha-Ma'alot* (1921[2]), 55; De Vries, in: *Ba-Mishor*, 271 (1945), 8. [Y.Al]

BERNSTEIN, JACOB NAPHTALI HERZ (1813–1873), Polish communal leader born in Lvov, descendant of a distinguished rabbinical family. Bernstein led the Orthodox Jews in Lvov in resisting the establishment of a *Reform temple and a secular Jewish school. He opposed the reforms introduced into the community in 1848 and its first Reform rabbi, Abraham *Kohn. However, his efforts to force Kohn to resign were unsuccessful. Kohn was later poisoned, and Bernstein, who was included among the suspects, remained in custody for a year. After his release he continued to oppose the Reform and Germanizing trends, with the backing of the Polish nobility. A street has been named after him for the services he rendered to the Lvov municipality. Bernstein was the grandfather of the Jewish scholar J. N. *Simchoni. The play *Herzele Meyukhes* by M. Richter is based on Bernstein's life.

Bibliography: M. Balaban, *Dzieje Żydów w Galicyi i w Rzeczypospolitej Krakowskiej, 1772–1868* (1914); F. Friedman, *Die galizischen Juden im Kampfe um ihre Gleichberechtigung* (1929), 51, 60–63; N. M. Gelber, in: EG, 4 pt. 1 (1956), 247–64; J. Tenenbaum, *Galitsye Mayn Alte Heym* (1952), 50. [Ed.]

BERNSTEIN, JULIUS (1839–1917), German physiologist and medical educator, who laid the foundations of neurophysiology. Bernstein, the son of Aron *Bernstein, was born in Berlin and began his research career under DuBois Reymond in his native city, continued his investigations into electrophysiology at Heidelberg, and was appointed professor of physiology in Halle in 1872. Through his novel application of physical instrumentation, such as differential rheotome and photography, to the study of nerve and muscle function, Bernstein developed the concept of the polarized membrane as the major focus of the excitation process. His view that the impulse is a self-propagating wave of depolarization deriving from permeability changes forms the foundation of modern neurophysiology. Though best known for his *Untersuchungen ueber den Erregungsvorgang im Nerven- und Muskelsystem* (1871), Bernstein also published books on medical education, toxicology, electrobiology, and the significance of mechanism in biology. [G.H.F.]

BERNSTEIN, LEONARD (1918–), U.S. composer and conductor. Bernstein, who was born in Lawrence, Mass., studied composition at Harvard, piano in Philadelphia, and later joined the conducting class of Serge *Koussevitzky at Tanglewood, Mass. In 1943 he was appointed assistant conductor of the New York Philharmonic; he attracted national attention by acquitting himself brilliantly when

Leonard Bernstein conducting the Israel Philharmonic Orchestra in the Mann Auditorium, Tel Aviv, May, 1970. Photo Isaac Freidin, Tel Aviv.

called upon to conduct a difficult program at short notice. In 1958 he was appointed music director and conductor of the N.Y. Philharmonic, the first American-born musician to occupy this post. He retired in 1969 to devote himself to composing. Among his symphonic works are the *Jeremiah Symphony,* with a vocal solo to the Hebrew text of Lamentations (1944); *The Age of Anxiety,* after a poem by W. H. Auden, utilizing jazz rhythms; *Kaddish* (in Hebrew), oratorio for narrator, chorus, and orchestra, which he conducted for the first time in Tel Aviv in 1963; and *Chichester Psalms* (also in Hebrew), for chorus and orchestra (1965). Bernstein had his greatest popular triumph with *West Side Story* (1957), which owed much of its success on both stage and screen to his dynamic music. Other shows for which he wrote the music were *On the Town* (1944), *Wonderful Town* (1953), and *Candide* (1956). He was a brilliant lecturer on music, and a collection of his talks from his exceptionally popular series of young people's concerts (which reached wide audiences through television) was published under the title *The Joy of Music* (1959).

Bernstein was closely associated with Israel from 1947, when he conducted his first concerts in the country. After the establishment of the State he was instrumental in creating the Koussevitzky music collection at the National Library in Jerusalem. Over the years he made periodic guest appearances with the Israel Philharmonic Orchestra, both in Israel and on its tours abroad.

Bibliography: D. Ewen, *Leonard Bernstein* (Eng., 1960, 1967), includes bibliography; J. Briggs, *Leonard Bernstein, the Man, his Work and his World* (1961); A. L. Holde, *Leonard Bernstein* (Ger., 1961); J. Gruen (text) and K. Heyman (phot.), *The Private World of Leonard Bernstein* (1968).
[N.S.]

BERNSTEIN, LUDWIG BEHR (1870–1944), U.S. social worker. Bernstein was born in Jelgava (Mitau), Latvia, and emigrated to the United States in 1892. Bernstein taught languages in the New York City public schools for several years, and in 1903 became managing director of the Hebrew Sheltering Guardian Orphan Asylum in Pleasantville, New York. His contributions to Jewish child welfare administration included the development of a cottage home plan and the organization of the Home Bureau of the Hebrew Sheltering Guardian Society—a pioneer experiment in foster home placement. In 1919–20 Bernstein served as executive director of the Bureau of Jewish Social Research, supervising studies in child welfare and delinquency in the Jewish communities of Chicago, Philadelphia, and New York. He moved to Pittsburgh in 1921 as executive director of the Federation of Jewish Philanthropies. During the 1930s Bernstein was a pioneer in the movement to establish Jewish community councils in American cities. [R.Lu.]

BERNSTEIN, PEREZ (Fritz; 1890–1971), Zionist leader, publicist, and Israel politician. Bernstein, who was born in Meiningen, Germany, studied commerce. In his youth he went to Rotterdam, Holland, where he entered business. In 1917 he joined the Dutch Zionist organization, and soon attained a prominent position. He later served as secretary of the Dutch Zionist Federation and as its president for four years. From 1930 to 1935 he was chief editor of the Dutch Zionist weekly, in which he fought for "unconditional Zionism," both in relations with non-Jews and in debate with the socialist and the religious Zionists. In his major work *Der Antisemitismus als Gruppenerscheinung* (1926; *Jew-Hate as a Sociological Problem,* 1951) he tried to prove that anti-Semitism is a sociological phenomenon which cannot be eliminated by better knowledge, by persuasion, or by education. He also rejected the theory that the Jews in the Diaspora have negative traits which encourage anti-Semitism. Another of his books is: *Over Joodsche Problematiek* (1935). In 1936 Bernstein settled in Palestine and became editor of the General Zionist newspaper *Ha-Boker.* From 1941 he was chairman of the Union of *General Zionists which, in 1946, elected him a member of the Jewish Agency, where he was responsible for commerce and industry. Bernstein was a member of the Knesset from its inception until 1965, and minister of commerce and industry in 1948–49 and from 1952 to 1955.

Perez Bernstein, Israel politician.

When the Liberal Party was established he was elected one of its two presidents. Following the party split in 1964, he became honorary president of the larger faction which retained the name of the Liberal Party. Bernstein continued his journalistic activities during his political career. He often opposed the left wing in his articles and advocated a business-oriented policy.

Bibliography: Y. Nedava (ed.), *Sefer Perez Bernstein: Mivḥar Ma'amarim u-Massot* (1962); D. Lazar, *Rashim be-Yisrael,* 1 (1953), 62–66; Tidhar, 3 (1958²), 1395.
[J.M.]

BERNSTEIN, PHILIP SIDNEY (1901–), U.S. rabbi. Bernstein was born in Rochester, N.Y., and was ordained in the first graduating class of the Jewish Institute of Religion (1926). He served as rabbi of Rochester's Congregation B'rith Kodesh from then. During World War

II he was executive director of the committee on Army and Navy religious activities of the Jewish Welfare Board. With the liberation of Nazi concentration camps at the end of World War II, Bernstein was appointed by President Truman as Jewish adviser to U.S. Army commanders in

Philip S. Bernstein, U.S. rabbi.

Europe (1946–47) where he played a significant role at the time of the *berihah. He was president of the Central Conference of American Rabbis (1950–52). He was chairman (1954–68), and subsequently honorary chairman, of the American Israel Public Affairs Committee. He is the author of *What the Jews Believe* (1951). [M.H.St.]

BERNSTEIN, SIDNEY LEWIS, LORD (1899–), British television pioneer and publisher. Born in Ilford, Essex, Bernstein inherited his interest in show business from his father, Alexander Bernstein (d. 1921), who owned a group of cinemas. Sidney Bernstein was a founder of the Film Society in 1924, and started his Granada chain of cinemas at Dover in 1930. During World War II he was film adviser to the British Ministry of Information (1940–45) and chief of the film section, S.H.A.E.F. (Supreme Headquarters, Allied Expeditionary Force; 1943–45). Bernstein introduced additional entertainments into his cinemas, including art exhibitions, and established links with Hollywood. However, his most important interest eventually became the Granada group of television companies operating mainly from Manchester. Bernstein had seen the possibilities of television in 1948, but could not obtain a license until the British Television Act of 1954. The Granada companies made many endowments to universities. He and his brother, Cecil Bernstein (a fellow director), gave £300,000 in 1965 for the establishment of a Northern Arts and Sciences Foundation. After 1961 he acquired a substantial interest in the publishing companies of Rupert Hart-Davis, McGibbon and Kee, and several others. He was awarded a life peerage in 1969. [J.M.S.]

BERNSTEIN, SIMON (1884–1962), journalist and Hebrew scholar. Bernstein was born in Latvia. From 1908 to 1911 he was Hebrew secretary of the Society for Spreading Enlightenment Among the Jews of Russia. In 1912 he joined the staff of the World Zionist Organization, being attached to the head office in Berlin until 1915, to the Copenhagen Bureau 1915–20, and to the London office 1921–22. In 1922 he settled in the United States, becoming editor of *Dos Yiddishe Folk*, organ of the Zionist Organization of America. He held this post until 1953. Bernstein was a prolific writer. Apart from his newspaper articles and Zionist pamphlets, he devoted himself to scholarly research, especially in the field of Hebrew poetry. He brought to light unpublished *piyyutim* of Spanish, Italian, and Byzantine poets; altogether he published over 3,000 such poems. Bernstein's major books are *Be-Ḥazon ha-Dorot* (1928), a volume of Hebrew essays; editions of *Divan Rav Immanuel ben David Frances* (1932); *Divan Yehudah Aryeh mi-Modena* (1932); *Shirei Yehudah ha-Levi* (1944), selected liturgical and secular poems; *Divan Shelomo Da Piera* (1942); *Al Naharot Sefarad* (1956), lamentations in the Sephardi rite on the destruction of Jerusalem and other calamities; and *Shirei ha-Kodesh* (1957), the collected liturgical poetry of Moses ibn Ezra.

Bibliography: J. Modlinger, *Simon Bernstein* (1949); M. Glenn, in: *Or ha-Mizraḥ*, 11 (April 1963), 40–42; A. Ben Ezra, *ibid.*, 43–44; M. Schmelzer, in: *Hadoar*, 42 (1963), 195. [ED.]

BERNSTEIN, ZVI HIRSCH (1846–1907), publisher, editor, and pioneer of the Yiddish and Hebrew press in the United States. Born in Russia, he received a traditional education and contributed articles to Hebrew literary magazines. In 1870 he emigrated to the United States and founded the first Yiddish paper *Di Post*. (J. K. Buchner's *Di Yidishe Tsaytung*, although published earlier in 1870, appeared only three or four times.) In 1871 Bernstein founded the first Hebrew newspaper in the United States *Ha-Ẓofeh ba-Areẓ ha-Ḥadashah*, which survived until 1876. Afterward he became a successful businessman and a patron of the Yiddish theater.

Bibliography: B. Z. Eisenstadt, *Ḥakhmei Yisrael ba-Amerikah* (1903), 20–22; M. Davis, in: *Sefer ha-Yovel li-Khevod Alexander Marx* (1950), 115–41; Kressel, Leksikon, 1 (1965), 374. [EI.S.]

BERNSTEIN-COHEN, MIRIAM (1895–), actress and pioneer of the theater in Israel. Born in Rumania, the daughter of Jacob *Bernstein-Kogan, she was educated

Miriam Bernstein-Cohen as the mother in Yosef Bar-Yosef's play *Tura*.

in Russia and took a degree in medicine. Turning to the stage she worked for a time in the Russian theater. In 1921 she went to Palestine and joined David Davidow's company known as the "Hebrew Theater." When the group dissolved in 1923, she and other members went to Germany to study stage work. In Berlin she met Menahem *Gnessin and helped him to organize the Teatron Ereẓ Israeli. She returned with the company to Palestine in 1924 and worked with it until its merger with the *Habimah Theater a few years later. Subsequently she appeared with various companies, gave solo performances in Palestine and abroad, and eventually joined the Cameri Theater in Tel Aviv. She translated plays and stories by de Maupassant, Tolstoy, Henri Barbusse, and Pearl Buck. [M.K.]

BERNSTEIN-KOGAN (Cohen), JACOB (1859–1929), Russian Zionist leader. Bernstein-Kogan, who was born in Kishinev, studied medicine in St. Petersburg and Dorpat. After the wave of pogroms in southern Russia in 1881, he devoted himself to Ḥibbat Zion and Zionism. As a delegate to the First Zionist Congress, he was elected to the Zionist Actions Committee. He administered an information center called the Zionist "post office," which informed Zionist branches in Russia, numbering about one thousand, of developments in the movement. He was a leading member

Jacob Bernstein-Kogan, Russian Zionist leader.

and ideologist of the *Democratic Fraction (1901) and was one of the leaders of the Russian Zionist opposition to the *Uganda Scheme. Settling in Ereẓ Israel in 1907, he worked as a doctor in Lower Galilee and in Petaḥ Tikvah. He was a founder of the Medical Association of Ereẓ Israel (1908). Conflicts with the conservative settlers of Petaḥ Tikvah induced him to return to Kishinev in 1910. He moved to Ereẓ Israel again in 1925, but accepted a proposal of the *American Jewish Joint Distribution Committee to serve as a physician in the Jewish agricultural settlements in the Ukraine.

Bibliography: M. Bernstein-Cohen (ed.), *Sefer Bernstein-Cohen* (1946); I. Klausner, *Oppoziẓyah le-Herzl* (1960), index; D. Smilansky, *Im Benei Dori* (1942), 51–59; Tidhar, 1 (1947), 192–3; A. L. Jaffe (ed.), *Sefer ha-Kongress* (1950²), 307–10; J. Yaari-Poleskin, *Ḥolemim ve-Loḥamim* (1964³), 89–92. [Y.S.]

BERNSTEIN-SINAIEFF, LEOPOLD (1867–1944), French sculptor. He was born in Vilna to an Orthodox family. He began to study drawing before moving to Paris at the age of fourteen. In Paris he studied under Rodin and Dalou and first exhibited at the Salon des Champs Elysées in 1890. He executed statues, portraits, groups of figures, and funerary monuments, and made busts in bronze and marble of important figures such as Pope Leo XIII. He received the Order of the Legion of Honor and his sculpture "Ezra Mourning" was acquired by the French nation. When the Germans occupied France they destroyed the sculpture "Youth and Age" to which Bernstein-Sinaieff had devoted over ten years. The Nazis arrested him and sent him to the prison camp at Drancy. Two weeks later he was released, only to be reinterned and sent to an extermination camp where he was killed. [Ed.]

BEROR ḤAYIL (Heb. בְּרוֹר חַיִל), place in southern Israel, 8½ mi. (14 km.) S.E. of Ashkelon. In Byzantine times the town was called Bouriron (Vita Sabeae, 10). It was the place where R. *Johanan b. Zakkai moved and taught after his stay in Yavneh. When the performance of Jewish marriages was prohibited under Emperor Hadrian, in the second century C.E., the inhabitants of Beror Ḥayil announced a clandestine marriage ceremony by putting a candle on the window sill (Sanh. 32b). Beror Ḥayil is now a kibbutz affiliated with Iḥud ha-Kibbutzim. It was founded on May 4, 1948, during the War of Independence, with the aim of reestablishing contact with the Jewish settlements spread over the northern Negev at a point where the Arabs had repeatedly cut off Jewish traffic to and from the south. The kibbutz was set up overnight. The initial settling group, pioneers from Egypt, was later joined by immigrants from Brazil, Uruguay, and other countries. In 1968 the kibbutz had a population of 520, and its economy was based on intensive farming and on a vegetable dehydrating factory. In the early 1960s, the *Ḥeleẓ oilfield expanded southward when reserves were discovered at Beror Ḥayil (their exploitation was in no way connected, however, with the economy of the kibbutz). [E.O.]

BERR, JACOB (c. 1760–1855), French physician and publicist, nephew of *Berr Isaac Berr de Turique. Besides gaining a reputation as a surgeon, Berr was a fervent advocate of equal rights for French Jews. In 1789 he published a refutation of an anonymous pamphlet which contested the right of Alsatian Jews to enlist in the National Guard. Later, in a letter addressed to the bishop of Nancy (1790), he criticized his uncle's project to preserve a special status for French Jews. According to E. Carmoly, *Historie des médecins juifs* (1844), Berr was the first French Jew to marry a Christian without forsaking Judaism. [Ed.]

BERR (de Turique), MICHEL (1781–1843), French lawyer. Born in Nancy, he was the son of *Berr Isaac Berr and became the son-in-law of Isaiah *Beer-Bing. Like his father, Berr was an advocate of Mendelssohnian Enlightenment. He sided with its radical exponents, however, and tended to disregard the national and religious aspects of Judaism while concentrating on the struggle for civic equality for the Jews in their different countries. In this spirit he defended persecuted Jews in a pamphlet entitled *Appel à la justice des nations et des rois* (1801). Berr was the first Jewish lawyer to practice in France. In 1806 he and his father were deputies at the *Assembly of Jewish Notables, and in 1807 Berr was appointed secretary of the Napoleonic *Sanhedrin. He then held an official appointment in the Kingdom of Westphalia and subsequently in the Préfecture of La Meurthe, but his later career was disappointing and he dissipated his talents.

Many important non-Jewish personalities regarded Berr as the ideal type of modern Jew. Berr translated a number of works from Hebrew including panegyrics to Napoleon. His most voluminous work was *Abrégé de la Bible et choix de morceaux de piété et de morale à l'usage des Israélites de France* (1819). At first Berr's attitude toward Judaism tended to be radical and rationalist. He held that once Judaism had detached itself from "talmudic quibbling" it would appear as the universal truth, while Christianity, also freed from its superstitions, would simply merge with Judaism. Later Berr insisted on the retention of what, in his opinion, were essential Jewish practices, which he explained in his *Nouveau précis élémentaire d'instruction réligieuse et morale à l'usage de la jeunesse française israélite* (1839), thus adhering in his eclectic way to Jewish religious reform.

Bibliography: Terquem (Tsarphaty), in: AI, 4 (1843), 721–7; 5 (1844), 109–16, 168–80; Barcinski, in: *Euphorion*, 15 (1908); *Dictionnaire de biographie française*, 6 (1954), 141; Szajowski, in: JJS, 14 (1963), 53–66. [M.C.]

BERR ISAAC BERR DE TURIQUE (1744–1828), leader in the struggle for Jewish *emancipation in France, born in Nancy. His father Isaac Berr had been appointed Jewish "syndic" by King Stanislaus of Poland, duke of Lorraine. Berr himself, a naturalized French citizen, was a tobacco manufacturer and banker. In August 1789 he was chosen as one of six members of a Jewish delegation sent to Paris from Alsace and Lorraine to put the case for granting Jewish civic equality, acting as their spokesman at the bar of the National Assembly. He was a member of the Nancy municipal council from 1792, and in 1806 was a leading delegate in the *Assembly of Jewish Notables, sitting on its "Committee of Twelve." He later became a member of the Napoleonic *Sanhedrin. In 1816 he purchased an estate in Turique, adding Berr de Turique to his name by royal permission. Berr translated N. H. *Wessely's proposals for Jewish educational reform into French under the title *Instructions Salutaires Adressées aux Communautés Juives de L'Empire de Joseph II* (Paris, 1790). He also published letters in defense of Jewish rights, demonstrating the moral value of the Talmud. While supporting certain reforms in Jewish life and customs, including the abolition of Jewish communal and judicial autonomy, Berr did not advocate religious Reform (*Réflexions sur la Régénération Complète des Juifs en France*, 1806).

Bibliography: E. Carmoly, in: *Revue Orientale*, 3 (1843/44), 62–63; L. Kahn, *Les Juifs de Paris pendant la révolution* (1898), 27; Graetz, Hist, 6 (1949), index. [M.C.]

BERSHAD, small town in *Vinnitsa oblast, Ukrainian S.S.R. The Jews there were butchered by one of the Cossack bands during the *Chmielnicki massacres. The community numbered 438 in 1765; 650 in 1787; 3,370 in 1847; 6,600 (out of a total of 8,885) according to the 1897 census; and 7,400 (61%) in 1910. They still formed the majority of the population in 1926 (6,110; 59%), although steadily diminishing. At the beginning of the 19th century, when the *ẓaddik* *Raphael of Bershad lived there, Bershad became a center of Ḥasidism. It became celebrated for its *tallit* weaving industry which came to an end after many of the weavers emigrated to the United States. Most of the plants for sugar refining and distilling, flour mills, and tanneries established in Bershad toward the end of the century were owned by Jews. During the civil war of 1919–20, 150 Jews in Bershad were massacred by Ukrainian gangs and soldiers of Denikin's army. After the German invasion of Russia in 1941 Bershad was included in Transnistria. A ghetto was established in the town and Jews deported from Bessarabia and Bukovina were sent there. Many died of hunger and disease. In 1970, the Jewish population was estimated at 8,000. There were one synagogue and a rabbi, and kosher poultry was available.

Bibliography: A. D. Rozenthal, *Megillat ha-Tevaḥ*, 1 (1927), 100–2, 110; Y. Midrashi, *Bershad ve-ha-Haganah Shellah* (1935); N. Huberman, *Bershad* (Heb., 1956). [S.Ett.]

°**BERSHADSKI, SERGEY ALEXANDROVICH** (1850–1896), historian of Lithuanian Jewry. He became interested in the history of the Jews in Lithuania through his teacher, F. *Leontovich. Bershadski, who for many years worked in official archives, in particular those of the archduke of Lithuania, also lectured in law at the University of St. Petersburg. His first historical study of Lithuanian Jewry was published in the series *Yevreyskaya Biblioteka*, where he also published a collection of sources relating to Jewish history in southwest Russia and Lithuania. In 1882 he published two volumes of documents relating to Jewish history in Lithuania from 1388 to 1569, and in 1883 his book *Litovskiye Yevrei* ("The Lithuanian Jews"), a history covering the same period. His other works on this subject include a Russian history of the Jewish community in Vilna from 1593 to 1649 (*Voskhod*, nos. 10, 11, 1886, and nos. 3–8, 1887), and studies on Abraham Jesofovich, the Lithuanian treasurer (1888), and on Saul Wahl (*ibid.*, nos. 1–5, 1889).

In the 1890s Bershadski began to interest himself in the history of the Jews in Poland, for which he collected material from the central archives in Warsaw. He published several articles on the subject, the documents upon which he drew being published posthumously in *Russko-Yevreyskiy Arkhiv* (vol. 3, 1903). In response to the growing anti-Semitism of the time, Bershadski also undertook a study of the blood libel in Poland and Lithuania in the 16th to 18th centuries, published in *Voskhod* (nos. 1, 9, 11, 12, 1894). Before his death he began publication of a work on the "Jewish Statute" of 1804, but did not complete it.

After he began his researches, Bershadski, who had been formerly radically anti-Jewish, developed an appreciation of the Jewish people and became their warm supporter. In his wish to promote their integration into the Russian state and culture, he attempted to show the antiquity of the Jewish settlement there and that the Jews had made a positive contribution to Russian life and the Russian language. He attributed the isolation of the Jews by the rulers of Poland to the annexation of Lithuania in 1569. Bershadski considered that the union had brought Lithuania "the Talmud, Jewish autonomy, and *Kahal* solidarity." He was, however, not an expert in the internal developments in Jewish history.

Bibliography: M. Vinaver, in: *Voskhod*, 17 no. 5 (1897), 49–54 (second pagin.); Vengerov, in: *Kritiko-Biograficheskiy slovar'*, 3 (1892), s.v. [S.Ett.]

BERSHADSKY (Domashevitzky), ISAIAH (1871–1908), Hebrew novelist. Bershadsky, who was born in Zimoshti, Belorussia, received the traditional Jewish education of the period, and also acquired a knowledge of Russian. His novel *Be-Ein Mattarah* ("To No Purpose") appeared in 1899 (under the pseudonym Bershadsky, an abbreviation of

Isaiah Bershadsky, Hebrew novelist. Tel Aviv, Genazim.

the Hebrew for Ben Reb Shimon Domashevitzky) in the *Biblioteka Ivrit* series founded by Ben Avigdor. It proved a landmark in Hebrew literature. For the first time in the 20 years since the foundation of the *Ḥibbat Zion* movement a novel was published in Hebrew giving a comprehensive view of contemporary society. *Be-Ein Mattarah* is a psychological realistic novel of the type prevalent in the European literature of the period. The background is the Jewish middle class in a town in the Pale of Settlement, and the main characters are the Hebrew teachers. The plot deals with their social and ideological problems arising from the question of a Jewish national rebirth. The hero, Admovitz, in common with Bazarov, Turgenev's nihilist archetype of Russian literature, rejects idealism and favors theorizing and philosophizing. He thus reacts negatively to Zionism and to the concept of a resurrection of the Hebrew language, both of which threw the Pale of Settlement into a ferment in the 1890s. However, his rejection does not lead to any constructive alternative. His attempts to immerse himself in materialistic pleasures are accompanied by agonies of conscience, a result of his religious education. These he tries to hide beneath a mask of cynicism and mockery. His life is joyless and purposeless. In the character of Admovitz, who shares many personality traits with his author, Bershadsky created the prototype of the Jewish social misfit, who became the anti-hero of Hebrew fiction in the first quarter of the 20th century. A two-volume anthology of Bershadsky's stories and sketches was published during 1899 and 1902 under the title *Tippusim u-Ẓelalim* ("Types and Shadows"). His second novel, *Neged ha-Zerem* ("Against the Stream") appeared in 1901 in four parts. Written before *Be-Ein Mattarah*, it depicts the collapse of traditional Jewish life. The hero, Israelson, the representative of Zionist orthodoxy, discovers that the bourgeois youth has surrendered to anarchy, cynicism, and hedonism. He eventually reached the conclusion that no Diaspora-based system of education can contain assimilation. Bershadsky is one of the first modern Hebrew authors to describe the relationship between the sexes realistically. In general, his works mark the entry of realism into Hebrew fiction, ending its tradition of over-moralizing. There are, however, defects in his writing. These include weakly traced plots, an excess of propaganda, usually put into the mouths of the heroes during their numerous arguments, and a dry, unimaginative style, lacking lyrical finesse.

Bershadsky was a member of the editorial board of the periodical *Ha-Zeman* in 1904–05 in St. Petersburg and later in Vilna. He died in Warsaw. His later stories and sketches and his early and unpublished writings were collected and published posthumously in two volumes under the title *Ketavim Aḥaronim* ("Last Writings," 1910).

Bibliography: I. Bershadsky, *Be-Ein Mattarah* (1967), introduction (contains a selected bibliography); I. Bershadsky, *Ketavim Aḥaronim*, 1 (1910), 7–22 (biography by P. Kaplan); A. Sha'anan, *Ha-Sifrut ha-Ivrit ha-Ḥadashah li-Zerameha*, 3 (1964), 322–6; Waxman, Literature, 4 (1960), 85–92.

[G.El.]

BERSOHN, MATTHIAS (1823–1908), Polish art collector and historian. Bersohn was active in the Warsaw Jewish community. He assembled an important collection of Jewish and Polish art in his own home and made generous presents to Polish museums. Since all his children converted to Christianity, he presented his collection and library to the Warsaw Jewish community, which established the "Bersohn Museum for Jewish Antiquities" to house it, at the time the only institution of its kind in Poland. In March 1940 the Germans broke into the museum and robbed it of its treasures. Bersohn's general collection was given to Polish museums. One of the earliest researchers of the history of art in Poland, he wrote a study on the wooden-structured synagogues in Poland (Pol., 3 vols., 1895–1903; Ger., in MGJV, 8 (1901), 159ff.). He also wrote a study of Joseph Nasi (MGWJ, 18 (1869), 422ff.) and one of Tobias Cohen and other Polish-Jewish doctors (1872). His lexicon of Jewish scholars in Poland, 16th–18th centuries (Pol., 1906), and his collection of documents on Polish Jewish history from 1388 to 1872 (1910, ed. posthumously by his son-in-law A. Kraushaar) are not too reliable.

[Ed.]

BERSON, ARTHUR JOSEPH STANISLAV (1859–1942), Austrian meteorologist. Born in Neu-Sandec, Galicia, he worked at the Prussian Aeronautic Observatory later transferred to Lindenberg and Friedrichshafen. In 1899 he introduced new methods for the study of the air strata structure at heights of tens of miles above the earth. Berson employed kites and balloons of rubber and paper filled with hydrogen gas and attached them to thin metal threads. Berson, in balloons of his own design, rose to the upper atmosphere a number of times with instruments for the measurement of the air pressure, the air temperature, and the relative humidity. Berson also carried out his observations over Spitzbergen, the Arctic Ocean, East

Arthur Berson, Austrian meteorologist. Washington, D.C., National Air and Space Museum, Smithsonian Institution.

Africa, Brazil, the Indian Ocean, and Indonesia. From these observations of Berson, the notion of the troposphere and the stratosphere were accepted generally. In 1901 Berson and a companion reached a height of about seven miles without oxygen masks. Berson also sent up unmanned balloons to heights of 18 miles. These balloons contained recording instruments which, if the balloon exploded, came down by means of small parachutes. He also used red balloons sent up at a fixed rate which could be tracked and thus determine the direction of the wind. During World War I this knowledge of the direction of wind at high altitudes was of great importance to the fighter planes. The observations and studies of Berson were first published in three volumes, together with those of R. Assmann, under the title *Wissenschaftliche Luftfahrten* (1899–1900).

[D.Ash.]

°**BERTHOLD OF FREIBURG** (13th century), Dominican preacher and theologian. In his *Summa*, completed in about 1295, the oldest known textbook of canon law in the German language, Berthold contests the validity of forced conversion to Christianity, obtained by "use of arrow or lance," or by "pushing people under the baptismal font against their will." He further prescribes that converts should be allowed to retain their property after baptism, in opposition to the fiscal policy followed by certain princes who commonly confiscated the property of the new converts to compensate for the loss of the Jewish tax.

Bibliography: R. Stanka, in: *Theologische Studien der oesterreichischen Leo-Gesellschaft*, 36 (1937), 146; *Monumenta Judaica* (1963), 162, 165.

[E.B.]

°**BERTHOLD OF REGENSBURG** (**Ratisbon;** before 1210–1272), Franciscan friar, the most celebrated preacher in Germany in the Middle Ages. From 1240 Berthold traveled throughout the German-speaking countries. In

1263 he began to preach the crusade. His sermons, delivered in fields or public squares, drew huge crowds. While preaching against Christian heresies, such as those held by the Cathari and Waldenses, he included the Jews in his attacks. Berthold declared that the heretics together with their allies the Jews, were so powerful that, but for the emperor's opposition, they would have gained control over Germany. He even predicted that a time would come when Christians would have to defend themselves against them in the same way as against the "infidels" (the Muslims). Berthold strongly opposed the practice of usury by the Jews whom he also accused of proselytizing among Christians.

Bibliography: DHGE, 8 (1935), s.v. *Berthold de Ratisbonne;* R. Iannucci, *Treatment of the Capital Sins and the Decalogue in the German Sermons of Berthold von Regensburg* (1942), includes bibliography.

[B.BL.]

°**BERTHOLET, ALFRED** (1868–1951), Swiss Bible scholar and theologian, who taught biblical exegesis at the University of Basle.

Bertholet wrote extensively on the canonical and extra-canonical books of the Bible. His works include commentaries on Leviticus (1901), Deuteronomy (1899), Ezekiel (1897), Ruth (with E. F. Kautzsch, 1923), and Ezra and Nehemiah (1902). His Appendix on the Apocrypha and Pseudepigrapha in the *Geschichte der althebraeischen Literatur* (ed., K. Budde, 1906, 1909²) is considered one of the best in the field. In his works *Der Beitrag des Alten Testaments zur allgemeinen Religionsgeschichte* (1923) and *Das Dynamistische im Alten Testament* (1926) Bertholet maintained that the religion of ancient Israel, characterized by a strong personal conception of the Deity, was unique in a world dominated by dynamistic theories which viewed the universe as essentially constituted by natural and supernatural forces. His other works in biblical studies include: *Die Stellung der Israeliten und der Juden zu den Fremden* (1896), *Die juedische Religion von der Zeit Esras bis zum Zeitalter Christi* (1911), *Kulturgeschichte Israels* (1919), and a second commentary on the Book of Ezekiel (1936). His works in the field of comparative religion include *Buddhismus und Christentum* (1902, 1909²), *Dynamismus und Personalismus . . .* (1930), *Goetterspaltung und Goettervereinigung* (1933), *Das Geschlecht der Gottheit* (1934), *Der Sinn des kultischen Opfers* (1942), *Die Macht der Schrift in Glauben und Aberglauben* (1949), and the posthumous *Grundformen der Erscheinungswelt der Gottesverehrung* (1953).

Bibliography: *Festschrift A. Bertholet* (1950), 564–78, includes a complete bibliography; Baumgartner, in: *Schweizerische Theologische Umschau*, 21 (1951), 121ff.

[Z.G.]

BERTINI, K. AHARON (1903–), poet and editor. Bertini, who was born in Bessarabia, began to publish poetry in 1924, and taught in Hebrew high schools in Bessarabia from 1927. He immigrated to Ereẓ Israel in 1947, where he resumed his teaching career. From 1965 he served as an editor of *Moznayim*, the literary magazine of the Hebrew Writers' Association. His volumes of poetry include: *Temol Deheh* (1939); *Mi-Layil ad Boker* (1951); *Marot al ha-Efer* (1954); *Shevil Kaḥol* (1961) and *Bakbuk al Penei ha-Mayim* (1969). With Z. Rosenthal and D. Vinitsky he edited the literary anthology *Min ha-Ẓad* (1939–40). He translated from French, Rumanian and Yiddish into Hebrew. Among the last are David *Bergelson's play *Prince Reuveni* and Moshe Altman's short story collection *Be-Omek Ha-Re'i* (1967). Bertini also edited an anthology of translations from Yiddish literature for high schools (1958).

[G.K.]

Gary Bertini, Israel conducter. Tel Aviv, Government Press Office.

His son GARY (1927–) is a noted Israel composer and conductor. Born in Bessarabia, he received his musical education in Israel, Italy, and with the composer Honegger in Paris. He founded and directed "Rinat," Israel's leading amateur chamber choir, the Israel Chamber Ensemble, and the Chamber Opera. He frequently conducted in Europe, where he included music by Israel composers. His own compositions include symphonic and chamber music, ballet, and incidental music for the theater, films, and radio.

[H.SH.]

Bibliography: M. Avishai, *Bein Olamot* (1962), 153–6.

BERTINORO, OBADIAH BEN ABRAHAM YARE (Di or **Of;** c. 1450–before 1516), Italian rabbi and Mishnah commentator. The name Yare is an acrostic of the Hebrew יְהִי רְצוּי אֶחָיו (*Yehi Reẓui Eḥav;* "Let him be the favored of his brethren." Deut. 33:24). Little is known of his family, which derived from the town Bertinero in northern Italy. At some time he apparently lived in Città di Castello. His best-known teacher was Joseph *Colon. Much more is known about Bertinoro, after he left this place, from three letters he wrote during 1488–90 in which he described his travels and his early impressions of Ereẓ Israel. Leaving his home at the end of 1485, he went on via Rome to Naples and stayed there and at Salerno for four months. In 1487 he reached Palermo where he stayed three months, preaching every Sabbath. Though pressed to become rabbi, he refused, and sailed by way of Messina and Rhodes for Alexandria, where he arrived early in 1488. He describes at length the Jewish communities of these places and their customs. He proceeded to Cairo, and the *nagid* Nathan ha-Kohen *Sholal received him with great honor. Sholal asked

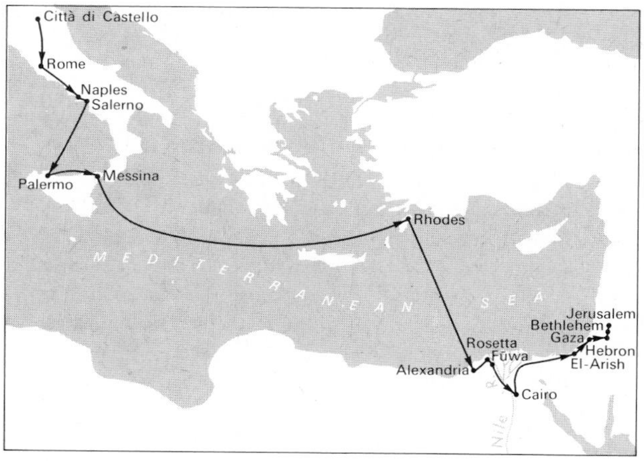

Obadiah di Bertinoro's journey from Italy to Ereẓ Israel, 1485–1488.

Obadiah to remain in Cairo but he refused and continued his journey via Gaza, Hebron, and Bethlehem, reaching Jerusalem just before Passover in 1488. Jacob of Colombano, an Ashkenazi rabbi who had come to Jerusalem from Italy, welcomed him warmly. On his arrival Bertinoro became the spiritual leader of Jerusalem Jewry, and during the period of his rabbinate was successful in uniting the oppressed and divided community. He established regular courses of study and preached twice a month in Hebrew. He even occupied himself with the burial of the dead since no one else was ready to undertake this religious duty. He enacted communal regulations and made himself responsible for the collection of funds from Italy for the support of the poor. Emanuel Ḥai Camerino of Florence, to whom Bertinoro had entrusted his property and who had promised to send 100 ducats a year, added an additional 25 ducats for charity. Bertinoro's wealthy brother also sent contributions. Nathan Sholal put his house in Jerusalem in Bertinoro's charge and authorized him to manage the communal affairs. With the repeal of the communal tax and the arrival after 1492 of refugees from Spain, the community began to grow. An anonymous disciple testifies to Bertinoro's fame in Ereẓ Israel and in the Diaspora. From his third letter in 1490 from Hebron it appears that he left Jerusalem for a time and became rabbi of Hebron. By 1495, however, he was back in Jerusalem. He was buried on the Mount of Olives.

Bertinoro's fame rests on his commentary on the Mishnah which was completed in Jerusalem and published in Venice (1548–49). It has become the standard commentary on the Mishnah as is Rashi's on the Talmud. This commentary was published with the text in almost every edition of the Mishnah. Written in an easy, lucid style, it draws largely on Rashi, often quoting him literally, and on Maimonides, whose rulings he cites. For the sections of Mishnah which have no Talmud he drew on the commentary of *Samson b. Abraham of Sens and of *Asher b. Jehiel. He also wrote *Amar Neke* (published 1810), a commentary on Rashi on the Pentateuch. The three letters mentioned above were written in a flowing, limpid Hebrew to his father, his brother, and possibly his friend, Camerino. They have frequently been published under the title *Darkhei Ẓiyyon* or *Ha-Massa le-Ereẓ Yisrael* and translated into many languages. Other works and exchange of letters as well as poems and prayers remain in manuscript.

Bibliography: *Ha-Me'ammer,* 3 (1919), 93–174; S. Sachs, in: *Jahrbuch fuer die Geschichte der Juden und des Judenthums,* 3 (1863), 193–270; A. Marx, in: *Sefer ha-Shanah shel Ereẓ-Yisrael,* 2–3 (1926), 97–99; Cassuto, in: *Ha-Ẓofeh le-Ḥokhmat Yisrael,* 10 (1926), 296–302; P. Grojewski, *Rabbenu Ovadyah Yare mi-Bartenura* (1938); E. N. Adler, *Jewish Travellers* (1966²), 209–50; Artom, in: *Yavneh,* 3 (1942), 112–24; A. Yaari, *Iggerot Ereẓ Yisrael* (1943), 98–144; M. A. Shulvass, *Roma vi-Yrushalayim* (1944), 31ff.; Ch. Albeck, *Mavo la-Mishnah* (1959), 249ff.; I. Ben Zvi, *Ereẓ Yisrael ve-Yishuvah* (1963), 139ff.

[A.D.]

BERTONOFF, YEHOSHUA (1879–1971), Israel actor. Bertonoff started his career as a teacher in Vilna, but in 1905 turned to the stage and acted with Yiddish and Russian troupes. In 1912 he assisted Nahum *Ẓemach in organizing a group which staged a Hebrew production of Dymov's *The Eternal Wanderer* in Bialystok and Vienna. He then resumed his career as a touring actor, but after the 1917 Revolution was invited to organize the State Jewish Theater in Odessa. Later Bertonoff headed the State Jewish Theater in Minsk and played Shalom Aleichem's *Tevye the Milkman* in Moscow. He went to Palestine in 1927, joined the *Habimah Theater, and became one of its most popular actors, distinguishing himself in folk and patriarchal types. Bertonoff was awarded the Israel Prize in 1959.

Yehoshua Bertonoff in the title role of the 1943 Habimah production *Tevye the Milkman* by Shalom Aleichem. Photo Alexander Studio, Tel Aviv.

His daughter, DEBORAH BERTONOFF (1915–), made a study of national dance techniques and traveled widely giving dance performances with programs which included Jewish subjects. As a result of her travels she wrote *Rikkud elei Adamah* ("Dance toward the Earth").

[M.K.]

BERUREI AVERAH/AVEROT (Heb. בְּרוּרֵי עֲבֵרָה/עֲבֵרוֹת; "the elected [to control] sin"), an institution of Catalonian origin found in the Jewish communities in Spain from the second half of the 13th century and later in the *Sephardi Diaspora in the 16th and 17th centuries. Officers so appointed mainly had the authority to deal with religious and moral transgressions. There were also similar officers *(berurei tevi'ot)* to investigate monetary suits. *Berurei averot* had the authority to impose punishments such as expulsion, excommunication, and flogging on guilty persons. The communities of Catalonia, Valencia, and Majorca had two or three such officers, while in Aragon this function was included in the duties of the **adelantados.* A legend about Isaac b. Solomon *Luria in 16th-century Safed conveys the atmosphere in which this body practiced its activities: "It happened that the sages of Safed appointed ten men concerning transgressions, all of them learned and wise." One of them looked out of his window early in the morning and saw a well-dressed woman. He followed her, and seeing her enter the courtyard of a man of light morals, "immediately after the end of the morning prayers ordered the beadle to call together his fellow appointees over transgressions, and [stated that] he would testify before them concerning a transgression that he had himself seen." While they were in assembly Luria proved miraculously to the accuser that his suspicions were unfounded.

Bibliography: Baer, Urkunden, 1 pt. 1 (1929), index s.v. *berurim do averoç;* Baer, Spain, index; M. Benayahu (ed.), *Sefer Toledot ha-Ari* (1967), 159–60.

[ED.]

BERURYAH (second century), daughter of R. *Hananiah b. Teradyon and wife of R. *Meir. She is famous as the only woman in talmudic literature whose views on halakhic matters are seriously reckoned with by the scholars of her time; cf. "Rightly did Beruryah say" (Tosef., Kelim, BM 1:6). Even in the period of the earliest *amoraim*, stories were current about her great knowledge (Pes. 62b). A number of anecdotes illustrate her moral stature. When certain evil persons antagonized her husband and he prayed for their death, she rebuked him, interpreting Psalms 104:35 as expressive of God's desire for the destruction of sin, and not of sinners, and exhorting him to pray, rather, that they repent of their evil ways (Ber. 10a). Another aggadic passage relates that when two of their sons died on a Sabbath, Beruryah did not inform Meir of their children's death upon his return from the academy, in order not to grieve him on the Sabbath. Only after the **Havdalah* prayer did she broach the matter, saying, "Some time ago a certain man came and left something in my trust; now he has called for it. Shall I return it to him or not?" Naturally, Meir replied in the affirmative, whereupon Beruryah showed him their dead sons. When Meir began to weep, she asked: "Did you not tell me that we must give back what is given on trust? 'The Lord gave, and the Lord hath taken away'" (Mid. Prov. to 31:1). The *aggadah* also tells of her incisive quips. Once, when R. Yose the Galilean, meeting her along the way, asked, "By which road should we travel in order to reach Lydda?" she replied: "Galilean fool! Did not the rabbis say, 'Talk not overmuch with women?' You should have asked: 'How to Lydda?'" (Er. 53b). Another instance of her sharpness is her reply to a sectarian concerning the interpretation of a verse from the Prophets (Ber. 10a). Beruryah also guided students in their study. When she found a student studying in an undertone, she rebuked him, saying: "Is it not stated (II Sam. 23:25) 'Ordered in all things, and sure'?—If the Torah be ordered in the two hundred and forty-eight organs of your body, it will be sure, and if not, it will not be sure" (Er. 53b–54a). Rashi (to Av. Zar. 18b) quotes a legend to the effect that as a result of her pretension of being above feminine weakness she was led astray, with tragic consequences. Beruryah is the heroine of a number of belletristic works in Hebrew and in other languages.

Bibliography: Hyman, Toledot, 294–5; Graetz, Gesch, 4 (1908^4), 172–3.

[Z.K.]

BESALÚ (Latin **Bisuldunum, Bisuldum;** Heb. ביסאלו, בסלו, ביואלדו), town in Catalonia, N.E. Spain. Its Jewish community was one of the oldest in Catalonia, a tombstone dating from 1090 having been found there. In 1258 James I gave permission to the Jews of Gerona and Besalú, then forming a single *collecta* ("tax administrative unit"), to appoint five representatives to act in financial and administrative matters. In 1258 the two communities together paid a tax of 15,000 solidos. The Zabara and Corvida families were among the leading members of the community of Besalú in the 13th through 15th centuries. Several of their number were baptized in 1391. In 1271 the Jews of Besalú were empowered by the Infante Pedro to execute legal contracts in the same way as Christians and Moors. During a heresy hunt in Besalú in 1292 the Dominicans tried to interfere in Jewish affairs, but were prevented by the king. An outbreak against the Jews at Gerona during Easter 1331 had repercussions there. During the anti-Jewish outbreaks that swept Spain in 1391 the Jews were protected by the local authorities. A small Jewish community continued to exist in Besalú in the 15th century, until the expulsion from Spain. A *mikveh* was recently discovered in the old Jewish quarter.

Bibliography: Baer, Studien, 42ff.; Neuman, Spain, index; Cantera, in: *Sefarad*, 9 (1949), 481–2; Millás Vallicrosa, *ibid.*, 25 (1965), 67–69; Cantera-Millás, Inscripciones, 264.

[H.B.]

BESANÇON, capital of the department of Doubs, eastern France; from the 13th century a free city, annexed to France in 1674. The first reference to Jews in Besançon is found in 1245. The Jewish street was in the present Rue de Richebourg, and the cemetery in front of the present Porte de Charmont. Jewish bankers of Besançon are mentioned in the chronicles of the Anglo-French war of 1296–1301. In 1321, and between 1393 and 1404, Jews expelled from *Franche-Comté and *Burgundy reached the city. The Jews left Besançon in the 15th century, and in 1465 the cemetery was sold by the municipality. Jews were denied free access to Besançon from the end of the 17th to the end of the 18th century, a few permits of temporary residence for a limited period being granted to a small number of merchants. A permit of longer duration was issued to an engraver of semiprecious stones.

After the French Revolution the community in Besançon was reestablished. It numbered 20 families in 1807, who sent a delegate to the Assembly of Jewish notables and to the Sanhedrin convened by Napoleon. The community belonged to the *Consistory of Nancy until 1858, and then to that of Lyons. The present synagogue, in Moorish style, was consecrated in 1869. In 1872 an independent consistory was set up at Besançon. The community was increased by Jews who left Alsace after the Franco-Prussian war of 1870. At the beginning of the 20th century there were 170 families living in Besançon.

[Z.Av./Ed.]

Holocaust and Postwar Periods. The community was largely destroyed and dispersed under the Nazi occupation during World War II. One hundred Jews, who did not manage to leave Besançon in May 1940, were deported by the Germans. After the war, the Jewish community slowly revived, and had 120 families in 1960. However, by 1969 their number had practically doubled, due mainly to the influx of Jewish immigrants from North Africa. The community engaged a rabbi and cantor and maintained a number of institutions.

[G.Le.]

The synagogue at Besançon, France, consecrated in 1869.

Bibliography: J. Morey, in: REJ, 7 (1883), 2f., 19f.; 49 (1904), 2–7, 257–61; J. Auscher, in: AI, 31 (1870), 441ff., 472ff., 592ff.; M. A. Gerson, *Essai sur les juifs de la Bourgogne au moyen âge* (1893); A. Castan, *Notes sur l'histoire municipale de Besançon* (1898), 210, 278, 316, 348, 351; Z. Szajkowski, *Analytical Franco-Jewish Gazetteer* (1966), 185; R. Berg, et al., *Guide Juif de France* (1968), 148.

BESEKOW, SAMUEL (1911–), Danish actor, director, and author. After training in Berlin with Max *Reinhardt and Erwin Piscator he became director of a workshop theater in Copenhagen, *Riddersalen*, where he presented works by modern playwrights. During the last years of World War II Besekow was a refugee in Stockholm. After the war he worked as director in theaters in Copenhagen and abroad. Besekow staged Brecht's *Galileo* in Tel Aviv, in 1962, and Molière's *The Miser* for the *Freie Volksbuehne* in West Berlin in 1967. He wrote books about the theater, novels depicting the artist's life; *Guds Göglere* ("God's Jesters," 1954), a novel dealing with Jewish life in Russia, Denmark, and Germany; *Ild brander, eng gror* ("Fire Burns, Meadow Grows," 1958); *Letters to a Theater-Crazy Professor* (1959); *Skrevet i Vand* ("Written in Water," 1962); and *Skrædderens søn* ("The Tailor's Son," 1964). [T.M.]

BESICOVITCH, ABRAM SAMOILOVITCH (1891–), mathematician. Besicovitch was descended from a Karaite family. He began his academic career at St. Petersburg where he worked under Markoff. Owing to difficult conditions caused by the Revolution he moved to Perm in the Urals. Besicovitch left the Soviet Union in 1925 and in 1926 settled in Cambridge. He was elected a Fellow of the Royal Society in 1934 and received its Sylvester medal in 1952. Kekeya's famous problem, the determination of the least area swept out by a straight line which is reversed in direction by a continuous motion in the plane, was solved by Besicovitch who proved the surprising result that there is no least area. He made important contributions to the theories of measure, sets of points, real analysis, surface area, and also to the additive theory of numbers. He was known for producing apparently simple problems which were extremely difficult to solve. His publications include *Almost Periodic Functions* (1955^2).

Bibliography: J. C. Poggendorff, *Handwoerterbuch zur Geschichte der exakten Wissenschaften*, 8 (1966). [B.S.]

BESOR, BROOK OF (Heb. נַחַל הַבְּשׂוֹר), a river valley (wadi) in the Negev that David crossed in pursuit of the Amalekites after their attack on Ziklag (I Sam. 30:9–10, 21). It is commonly identified with Wadi Ghazza-al-Shallāla southwest of Beersheba.

Bibliography: Abel, Geog, 1 (1933), 405; Press, Ereẓ, 4 (1955), 806–7, s.v. *Ziklag*. [Yo.A.]

BESREDKA, ALEXANDER (1870–1940), French immunologist, known for his research on anaphylaxis, local immunization, and immunization in contagious disease. Besredka was the son of a Hebrew writer, Elimelech

Alexander Besredka, French immunologist.

Ish-Naomi. He first studied in Russia, but when it was proposed to him that he convert to Christianity in order to further his scientific career, he refused and moved to France. He completed his medical studies in Paris, became a French citizen, and was appointed a member of the Pasteur Institute of which he was later a director. Besredka maintained his contacts with Judaism all his life, was active in Jewish organizations such as *OSE, and wrote for Jewish scientific journals, including the Hebrew *Ha-Refu'ah*. His anaphylaxis research was based on original concepts, different from the accepted beliefs in immunology. In 1907 he discovered the possibility of eliminating hypersensitivity to foreign serum. His desensitization method was accepted throughout the world as the pretreatment of patients who had acquired a sensitivity toward a serum, in order to prevent anaphylactic shock by repeated serum treatment. Besredka was closely associated with the biologist Metchnikoff and in 1910 was appointed professor at the Pasteur Institute in Paris. His book *Immunisation locale, pansements spécifiques* was published in 1925.

Bibliography: Adler, in *Ha-Refu'ah*, 19 (July–Aug. 1940), 13. [A.L.O.]

BESSARABIA, region between the rivers Prut and Dniester; before 1812 part of Moldavia, with several districts under direct Ottoman rule; within Russia 1812–1918; part of Rumania 1918–40; returned to Russia 1940. The larger (central) part is in Moldavian S.S.R.; the extreme northern and southern sections in Ukrainian S.S.R.

Up to 1812. From the 15th century onward, Jewish Sephardi merchants from Constantinople frequented Bessarabia while using the trade route which crossed the length of the territory, connecting the countries of the East and the Black Sea shores with Poland. Later, Jewish merchants from Poland also began coming to Bessarabia. Some of them settled there, thus laying the foundation of the first Jewish communities in northern and central Bessarabia; in southern Bessarabia Jewish communities were found already in the 16th century. By the early 18th century, permanent Jewish settlements had been established in several commercial centers. Toward the end of the century relatively large numbers of Jews were living in most of the urban settlements and in many villages. Their number was estimated at 20,000 in 1812. The legal status of the Jews in the part of Bessarabia under Moldavian rule was similar to that of the rest of Moldavian Jewry. They were organized in autonomous communities subject to the authority of the *ḥakham bashi* in Jassy. In the parts under Ottoman rule they were subject to the same laws as the other communities under this regime. In the 18th and 19th centuries the Jews in Bessarabia mainly engaged in local commerce and liquor distilling; some traded on a considerable scale with neighboring countries. In the villages main occupations were leasing activities and innkeeping. In the cultural sphere, Bessarabian Jewry in this period was not advanced. The most prominent rabbis of the early 19th century were *Ḥayyim b. Solomon of Czernowitz, rabbi of *Kishinev, and David Solomon *Eibenschutz, rabbi of Soroki. Jacob *Frank exerted an influence from Podolia, and Khotin became a center for Frank and his adherents. Toward the end of the 18th century Ḥasidism penetrated Bessarabia.

1812–1918. After the Russian annexation in 1812, Bessarabia was included in the *Pale of Settlement, and many Jews settled there from other parts of the Pale. The Jewish population, mainly concentrated in Kishinev and district and in the northern part of the region, grew from 43,062 in 1836 to 94,045 in 1867 (excluding New Bessarabia, see below), and to 228,620 (11.8% of the total) in 1897. Of these 109,703 (48%) lived in the towns (of them 50,237, or 22%, in Kishinev), 60,701 (26.5%) in small towns, and 58,216 (25.5%) in the villages. They formed 37.4% of the town population, 55.7% of the population of the small towns, and 3.8% of the village population. Regulations governing the legal status of the Jews of Bessarabia after the annexation were issued in 1818. In conformance with the Russian pattern Jews were required to join one of the three classes: merchants, townsmen, or peasants. All their former rights were confirmed, while the existent Russian legislation concerning the Jews did not apply, since Bessarabia had autonomous status. The regulations even expressly authorized Bessarabian Jews to reside in the villages and engage in leasing activities and innkeeping, in contradiction to the "Jewish Statute" of 1804 (see *Russia). Because of this regional autonomy, the Jews of Bessarabia were spared several of the most severe anti-Jewish decrees issued in the first half of the 19th century. By 1835, when liquidation of Bessarabian autonomy began, the "Jewish legislation" then promulgated in Russia was equally applied to Bessarabian Jewry, although the prohibition on Jewish residence in border regions was not enforced in Bessarabia until 1839, and compulsory military service until 1852. In the second half of the 19th century the restriction on Jewish residence in the border area assumed special importance for the Jews of Bessarabia. By the Treaty of Paris (1856) a territory in the southern part of the region was allocated to Rumania, and many localities, including Kishinev, now fell in the border area. The restrictions were not strictly enforced and thousands of Jews settled in this region, although decreees of expulsion were issued in 1869, 1879, 1886, and 1891. Of these the most severe and extensive was that of 1869. Expulsions of individual Jews also became frequent. The Jews in New Bessarabia—the area incorporated within Rumania by the Treaty of Paris—shared the fate of the other Jews in the country. The anti-Jewish riots which broke out in the towns of this region—*Izmail, Kagul, and Vilkovo—in 1872 aroused both Jewish and non-Jewish public opinion in Europe, and diplomatic intervention was enlisted to alleviate their position. When New Bessarabia reverted to Russia in 1878, the Jews who were then recorded on the Rumanian tax registers were permitted to remain there. The "*May Laws" of 1882 severely affected Jews in Bessarabia as a considerable proportion lived in the villages, and frequent expulsions ensued. In 1903 a frightful pogrom broke out in Kishinev. The wave of pogroms of 1905 swept Bessarabia. Three towns and 68 other localities were struck and 108 Jews were murdered. The damage was estimated at 3,500,000 rubles. The 1917 Revolution in Russia brought civic equality for the Jews of Bessarabia.

During the 19th century the economic structure of Bessarabian Jewry remained basically unchanged. In their old occupations Jews played an important role within the agrarian economy of the region. An increasing number of Jews entered agriculture, and between 1836 and 1853, 17 Jewish agricultural settlements were established in Bessarabia, mostly in the northern districts, on lands purchased or leased from Christian or Jewish landowners. There were 10,859 persons living on these settlements in 1858; 12.5% of Bessarabian Jewry were farmers, and the region became among the largest and most important centers of Jewish agriculture in Russia. There were 106,031 *dessiatines* (276,283 acres) in Jewish ownership in 1880 (2.5% of the arable land of Bessarabia) and an additional 206,538 *dessiatines* (557,652 acres) held by Jews on lease. In time, especially after the application of the "May Laws," most of the settlements were liquidated. According to a survey carried out by the *Jewish Colonization Association (ICA) in 1899, there were 1,492 families (7,782 persons), of whom 53% were landowners, on the six settlements still in

The central committee of the Bessarabian cultural association, *Ḥevrat Tarbut*, 1925. Jerusalem, Central Zionist Archives.

existence. Of these families only 31.5% were engaged in agricultural work. The land in Jewish ownership also diminished. In 1897, 7.12% of the Jews in Bessarabia were engaged in agriculture; 26.81% in crafts and industry; 3.65% in transport; 2.34% in commercial brokerage; 39.53% in commerce (of these 58% engaged in the trade of agricultural produce); 8.9% as clerks or employees in private enterprises, domestics, daily workers, or unskilled laborers; 4.9% in public or government services or the liberal professions; and 6.75% in miscellaneous occupations. The 22,130 Jews engaged in commerce constituted 81.2% of the total number of merchants in the region, and 95.8% of the grain dealers. The proportion of Jewish artisans, mainly tailors, was lower (39%). From the early 1880s the economic situation of Bessarabian Jewry deteriorated as a result of the frequent expulsions from the villages and border areas, and the agrarian crisis in Russia during this period. Many impoverished Jews emigrated overseas. The principal factor in Jewish spiritual life was Ḥasidism. Many of the village Jews of no marked learning adopted much of the way of life and customs of the Moldavian peasantry. A major influence was wielded by the *ẓaddikim* of the Friedman (see *Ruzhin) and *Twersky families. During the 1830s and 1840s Haskalah began to penetrate into Bessarabia. From the end of the 1840s Jewish government schools were opened in Bessarabia. In 1855 there were six such schools, in *Beltsy, Khotin, *Brichany, and Izmail, and two in Kishinev, with 188 pupils. Private secular Jewish schools also began to appear, and from the 1860s Jews in Bessarabia, especially wealthier ones, began to send their children to the general schools. During the 1870s, 30% to 40% of the pupils in some of the secondary schools of the region were Jewish. In 1894, however, 60.9% of Jewish children of school age still attended *ḥeder*. The population census of 1897 revealed that only 27.8% of Bessarabian Jews above the age of ten could read Russian. After the pogroms of the 1880s, Ḥovevei Zion societies were founded in Bessarabia as elsewhere, the most important in Kishinev, led by Abraham *Grunberg and Meir *Dizengoff. Toward the end of the 1880s and early 1890s there was some movement toward pioneer settlement in Ereẓ Israel (*aliyah*). Seven delegates from Bessarabia, of whom six were from Kishinev, took part at the founding meeting of the Ḥovevei Zion Odessa Committee (April 1890). The Zionists of Bessarabia were represented at the First Zionist Congress in 1897 by Jacob *Bernstein-Kogan of Kishinev. Toward the close of the 19th century and the beginning of the 20th, a line of poets and authors emerged on the cultural scene in Bessarabia, many of whom were to play an important role in Yiddish and Hebrew literature, including Eliezer

*Steinbarg, Judah *Steinberg, S. *Ben-Zion, Jacob *Fichman, Samuel Leib *Blank, and Ḥayyim *Greenberg. The chief rabbi of Bessarabia, Judah Loeb *Zirelson, wrote halakhic works.

1918–1941. After the incorporation of Bessarabia into Rumania in 1918, the Jews there automatically received Rumanian citizenship, in accordance with the commitments of Rumania under the Treaty of Paris. However, as a result of the Nationality Law of 1924, many Bessarabian Jews who could not fulfill its requirements were deprived of Rumanian nationality, and defined as aliens. According to a count taken in 1920 there were 267,000 Jews in Bessarabia. As in the other parts of Rumania, they encountered popular hostility, anti-Jewish measures and suspicion on the part of the government, and petty administrative harrassment. In 1938, 21,844 Jewish heads of families in Bessarabia were deprived of Rumanian nationality (according to official statistics). The economic situation of Bessarabian Jewry also deteriorated. The separation of the region from its former Russian markets, the drought which struck Bessarabia three times during this period, the world economic crisis, and the government's policy of exploitation, resulted in a severe crisis in the agricultural economy. Assistance from abroad was provided principally by the *American Joint Distribution Committee and ICA. The savings and credit cooperatives set up before the war supported by ICA also played an important role in this period. In 1930 there were 41 savings and loan banks operating in 39 localities with a membership of 30,202, i.e., two-thirds of Jewish breadwinners in Bessarabia. Of these 12% were farmers, reflecting the development of Jewish agriculture in this period. At the time of the agrarian reform in Bessarabia (1920–23) between 4,000 and 5,000 Jews received seven to ten acres of land each—altogether approximately 120,000 acres were cultivated. In Bessarabia agriculture as a Jewish occupation ranked second after Ereẓ Israel. In 1935, about 3,000 families cultivating a total of approximately 20,000 hectares were supported by ICA. Two new agricultural settlements were established with assistance from ICA.

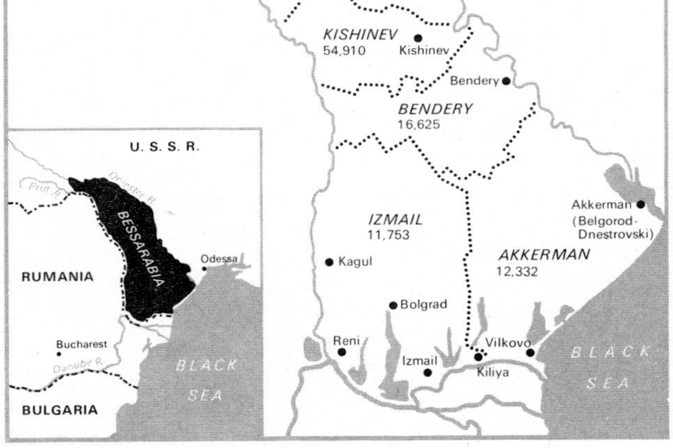

Main centers of Jewish settlement in Bessarabia in 1897, showing total Jewish population according to districts.

Under Rumanian rule, Jewish communal life flourished and leadership revived. A number of political parties, prominent among them the Zionist movements, were active, as well as other organizations. The first conference of Bessarabian Zionists was convened in 1920 in Kishinev, and a central office for the Zionist Organization of Bessarabia was set up in Kishinev. On the basis of the minority treaties signed by Rumania, a ramified network of Jewish elementary and secondary schools with instruction in Yiddish or Hebrew was established in Bessarabia at the beginning of Rumanian rule. In 1922 there were 140 Jewish schools with 19,746 pupils (105 giving instruction in Hebrew with 16,456 pupils). A teachers' seminary was established in Kishinev. However, by the end of 1922 government policy changed. Many of the schools were deprived of their Jewish character and converted into Rumanian schools. By 1929–30, there remained 64 Jewish educational institutions in 30 localities (15 kindergartens, 37 elementary schools, 11 secondary schools, and one vocational school) with 6,381 pupils and 312 teachers. Social welfare institutions in Bessarabia during this period included 13 hospitals, a sanatorium for tubercular patients, societies for assistance to the sick in 25 localities, 13 old-age homes, and four relief institutions for children. From 1923, the *OSE society was also active in Bessarabia where it maintained stations in eight localities. After the entry of the Red Army into Bessarabia on June 28, 1940, life for Jews in Bessarabia was gradually brought in line with the general pattern of Jewish existence under the Soviet regime. On June 13, 1941, a comprehensive "purge" was carried out throughout the region. Thousands of Jews—communal leaders, active members of the Zionist movement, businessmen, and persons suspected of disloyalty to the regime—were arrested and deported to internment camps or exiled to Siberia. [El.F.]

From 1941. The first Soviet occupation of the area lasted from 1940 until the beginning of hostilities between Germany and Russia in June of the following year. Rumania was an ally of Germany. Bessarabia was reconquered by German and Rumanian troops by July 23, 1941, and remained under Rumanian authority until August 1944, when it was reoccupied by the Russians. Central and northern Bessarabia, as well as a narrow strip on the west side of the Dniester, became the Moldavian Soviet Socialist Republic with the capital in Kishinev. When Bessarabia was reoccupied by the Soviets, only a few Jews were still alive. The great majority had been massacred by the Einsatzkommandos and by the German and Rumanian soldiers, while others were deported to *Transnistria, where more than half of them died. Many of the deported Jews preferred to slip back into Rumania, and from there to leave for Israel.

For further information on the Holocaust in Bessarabia see articles on *Russia and the various towns. [Th.L.]

Bibliography: *Die Judenpogrome in Russland,* 1 (1910), passim; 2 (1910), 5–37; N. Sharand, *A Dritl Yorhundert Yidisher Kooperatsye in Besarabye* (1934); J. Starr, in: JSOS, 3 (1941), 57–80; *Besarabyah* (Heb., 1941), essays; A. Ettinger, *Im Ḥakla'im Yehudim ba-Tefuẓot* (1942), 110–70; Sh. Hillels, in: *Shevilei ha-Ḥinnukh* (1943), 3–16, 67–73; idem, in: *Ha-Tekufah,* 30–31 (1946), 786–806; Z. Scharfstein, *Toledot ha-Ḥinnukh be-Yisrael ba-Dorot ha-Aḥaronim,* 3 (1949), 248–59; M. Ussishkin, in: *Pirkei Besarabyah,* 1 (1952), 32–50; *Al Admat Besarabyah,* 3 vols. (1959–63), essays; E. Feldman, *Toledot Ha-Yehudim Be-Bessarabia ba-Me'ah ha-19* (1970); idem, in: *He-Avot,* 12 (1965), 102–20; idem, in: *Zion,* 30 (1965), 206–33.

BESSELS, EMIL (1847–1888), German physician, Arctic explorer and naturalist. After his graduation from the University of Heidelberg in 1865, Bessels was appointed custodian of the Stuttgart Museum of Natural Science. In 1869 he was a member of a German Arctic expedition which studied the influence of the Gulf Stream on areas east of Spitzbergen. Bessels served as a surgeon in the German army in 1870. The following year Bessels sailed on the U.S. vessel *Polaris* as surgeon and naturalist with Captain Charles Francis Hall's expedition to the North Pole. Hall died unexpectedly in 1871 at Thank God Harbor, Greenland, after the *Polaris* had traveled farther north than any other ship. In the following year, the *Polaris* was caught in the polar ice and wrecked near Littleton Island. Nineteen members of the expedition, including Bessels, became separated from the rest of the crew and floated 1,300 miles on an ice-floe to the Bay of Melville off the Labrador coast, before they were rescued by a sealer. On his return to the U.S. in 1873, Bessels was accused by one of the crew of murdering Hall by administering morphine. An inquiry conducted by the surgeon-generals of the U.S. Army and Navy ruled that Hall had died of apoplexy and that Bessels was innocent. Subsequently, Bessels prepared the scientific results of this Arctic expedition (1876), wrote on natural history for scientific journals, and edited reports of the United States Naval Institute. Bessels was a member of an ethnological expedition which sailed on the steamship *Saranac* to the northwest coast of America. The vessel was wrecked in Seymour Narrows, British Columbia. Bessels died in Stuttgart.

Bibliography: C. H. David, *Narrative of the North Polar Expedition, U.S. Ship Polaris, Capt. Charles Francis Hall Commanding* (1876); J. Mirsky, *To The North* (1934).

[Ed.]

BESSIS, ALBERT (1883–), Tunisian politician. Born in Tunis into a distinguished family of writers and *dayyanim*, Bessis qualified as a lawyer and was elected to the Grand Council of Tunisia in 1934 where he became chairman of the committee on legislation. He participated in the negotiations with the French government in the early 1950s which led to the granting of autonomy to Tunisia in 1955. Bessis was minister of housing and town planning from 1954 to 1955 when he became minister of public works. He retained his post following the independence of Tunisia in 1956. He resigned in the following year and retired from public life. Bessis was an active figure in the Jewish community and was president of the Tunisian *ORT and other communal organizations. [D.Co.]

BESSIS, JESHUA (1773–1860), Tunisian scholar. Bessis was appointed chief rabbi of Tunis in 1847 and served in this office until his death. He wrote responsa and a work on the Shulḥan Arukh, only the section on *Yoreh De'ah* being published, part of it under the title *Avnei Ẓedek* (1902), and part as *Avnei Ẓedek u-Me'orot Natan* (1903). Bessis wrote introductions and approbations for the books of Tunisian scholars. He engaged in practical Kabbalah and was regarded as a saint; his grave became a place of pilgrimage.

Bibliography: Arditti, in: *Revue Tunisienne*, 3 (1932), 102–3; Hirschberg, Afrikah, 2 (1965), 148.

[Ed.]

BET (Heb. ב), second letter of the Hebrew alphabet; a voiced bilabial plosive [b] and voiced labiodental fricative [v] (a positional variant); numerical value, 2.

The earliest form of *bet*—in the Proto-Sinaitic inscriptions—is the acrophonic pictograph of a house *(bayit)* ⊏. While in South Arabic its shape is ⊓ and in Ethiopic በ, in the Proto-Canaanite script the main stages of development are → ⊏ → ⊐ → 𐤁. Variants of the latter form survive in the Phoenician (𐤁, 𐤁), Hebrew (𐤁, 𐤁) and Samaritan (ࠁ) as well as in the Greek (8 → B) and Latin scripts.

The Aramaic *bet*—like the *dalet, resh,* and *'ayin*—has an open top already in the seventh century B.C.E. While in the fifth century B.C.E. the downstroke has a diagonal flourish 𐡁, from the fourth century B.C.E. onward the downstroke is vertical curving into a horizontal base; at the same time there is a tendency to straighten the top of the letter: ב. In the early Jewish script the tick on the left side of the top ב is the only remnant of the half-circle-head. Already in the Herodian period, the base of the Jewish *bet* is written occasionally with a separate left-to-right stroke ב. This fashion prevails, becomes common in the Jewish bookhand, and the *bet* does not change its basic shape during the ages: In some cursive trends, as in the period of Bar Kokhba and today, the *bet* is written without lifting the pen: ב. However, the Ashkenazi cursive developed as follows: ב → ב → ב → ב.

Palmyrene *bet* follows the third-century B.C.E. Aramaic ב and develops through ב into Syriac ܒ. The Nabatean *bet* loses its top ﺑ ; this form is adopted for Arabic *ba*, which later is distinguished by a diacritic sign ب from ت (*ta*), ن (*nun*), and ي (*ya*).

See *Alphabet. [Y.N.]

BET AGLAYIM, a place mentioned by Eusebius (Onom. 48:19) 8 mi. (13 km.) S. of Gaza, near the sea coast, which he erroneously identified with the biblical Beth-Hoglah (Josh. 15:6; 18:19–21). Bet Aglayim is most probably the ancient name of the important Tell al-'Ajjūl located about 4½ mi. (7 km.) southwest of Gaza, which was excavated from 1929 to 1931 by Sir Flinders Petrie (who identified it with ancient Gaza). The remains at Tell al-'Ajjūl date mainly from the Middle and Late Bronze Ages and include Hyksos fortifications and graves, and the palace of an Egyptian governor. Rich finds of gold, silver, and jewelry were discovered in the tombs.

Bibliography: W. M. F. Petrie, *Ancient Gaza*, 5 vols. (1931–52); Maisler, in: ZDPV, 56 (1933), 186ff.; Abel, Geog, 2 (1938), 265; Albright, in: AJSLL, 55 (1938), 337–59.

[M.A.-Y.]

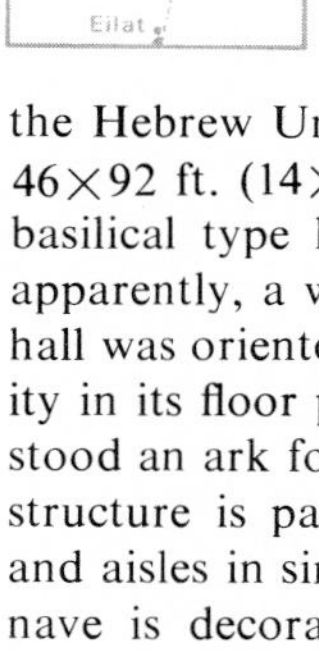

BET ALFA (Heb. בֵּית אַלְפָא), place in Israel in the eastern Jezreel Valley at the foot of Mount Gilboa. The name is historical and has been preserved in the Arab designation of the site Beit Ilfa which may have some connection with the proper name Ilfa or Hilfa which occurs in the Talmud (Ta'an. 21a). The foundations of an ancient synagogue were discovered in 1929 near Bet Alfa by E. L. *Sukenik and N. *Avigad, who were conducting excavations on behalf of the Hebrew University. The synagogue covered an area of 46×92 ft. (14×28 m) and included a courtyard, narthex, basilical type hall with a nave and two side aisles, and, apparently, a women's gallery. The apse at the end of the hall was oriented south toward Jerusalem, and a small cavity in its floor probably served as a *genizah;* above it once stood an ark for Scrolls of the Law. The entire floor of the structure is paved with mosaics: the courtyard, narthex, and aisles in simple geometric designs, and the floor of the nave is decorated with mosaic panels surrounded by a broad ornamental border. Two inscriptions were found at the entrance to the hall: one (in Aramaic) states that the mosaic was made during the reign of Emperor Justin (undoubtedly Justin I, 518–27); the other (in Greek) gives the names of the mosaicists, *Marianos and his son Ḥanina.

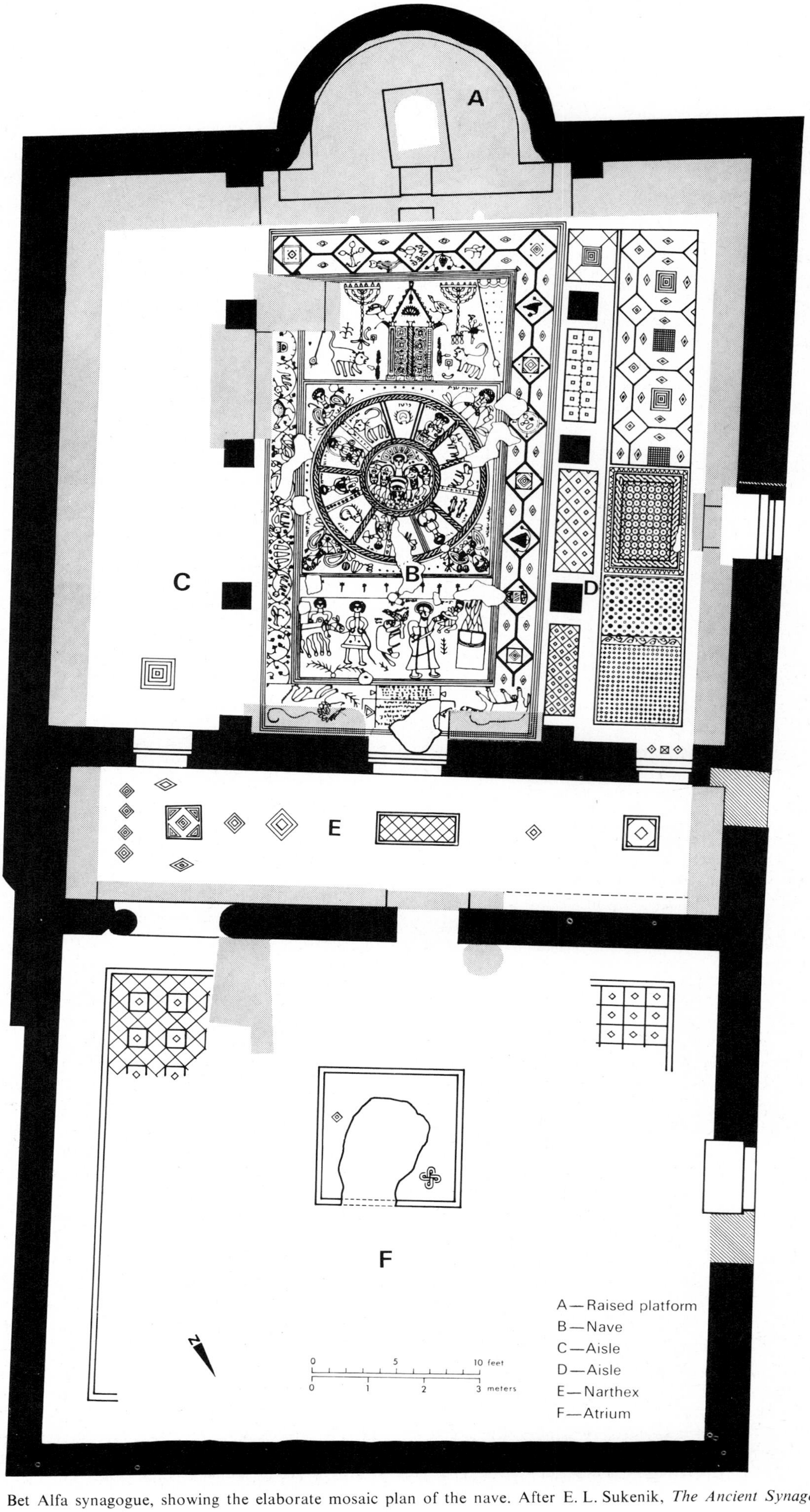

Plan of the Bet Alfa synagogue, showing the elaborate mosaic plan of the nave. After E. L. Sukenik, *The Ancient Synagogue of Beth Alpha.* Jerusalem, 1932.

Symbolic animals are depicted on either side of the inscriptions: a lion on the right and a bull on the left. The three mosaic panels in the center of the hall depict (from north to south): (1) *The Offering of Isaac,* which shows Abraham pointing a drawn knife at Isaac who is bound near an altar; behind Abraham a ram is tied to a tree, and alongside it appears the inscription "And behold a ram." The hand of God is seen between the sun's rays above; Abraham's two servants and donkey stand behind him; a band of palm trees separate this scene from the next one. (2) *The Signs of the Zodiac,* with the sun in the center in the form of a youth riding a chariot drawn by four horses; each sign has its Hebrew designation inscribed above it. In the corners appear the four seasons of the year (Tishri, Tevet, Nisan, Tammuz), each in the form of the bust of a winged woman adorned with jewels. (3) *The Ark of the Synagogue,* in which the ark has a gable roof with an "eternal light" suspended from its top and two birds perched at its corners; on either side is a lion with a seven-branched *menorah* ("candelabrum") and above it and between them are depicted *lulavim* ("palm branches"), *etrogim* ("citrons"), a *shofar* and censers. Curtains adorn the scene on the left and right sides.

The simple but strong style of the mosaic pavement represents a folk art that appears to have developed among the Jewish villagers of Galilee. The figures are depicted frontally and the artist took great pains to make each scene expressive. The mosaics of Bet Alfa are striking in their coloring and stylization and are among the finest examples of Jewish art in the Byzantine period. In 1960 the synagogue structure was renovated and the pavement repaired by the Israel Government. [M.A.-Y.]

The kibbutz of Bet Alfa was founded in 1922 by pioneers from Poland. It was the first settlement of the Kibbutz Arẓi ha-Shomer ha-Ẓa'ir movement. For over 14 years it was the easternmost village of the Jewish region in the central valleys and was exposed to Arab attacks in the 1936–39 riots. In 1968 it numbered 670 inhabitants and its economy was based on intensive and diversified farming. [E.O.]

Bibliography: E. L. Sukenik, *Ancient Synagogue of Beth Alpha* (1932); N. Avigad, *Bikat Beit She'an* (1964), 63–70; E. R. Goodenough, *Jewish Symbols in the Greco-Roman Period,* 1 (1953), 241–53; Roth, Art, 209–13.

BET(H)-ANATH (Heb. בֵּית עֲנָת), Canaanite city named after the goddess *Anath. Beth-Anath may possibly be mentioned in the list of cities conquered by Thutmosis III in c. 1469 B.C.E. (no. 97) but it definitely appears in the records of the campaigns of both Seti I in c. 1300 B.C.E. (between Tyre and Kadesh) and of Rameses II in c. 1280 B.C.E. (before Kanah). Although it is listed with the cities in the territory of the tribe of *Naphtali (Josh. 19:38), this tribe could not overcome it and only imposed tribute on the inhabitants (Judg. 1:33). Some scholars locate it in Lower Galilee at Bu'eina in the valley of Beth-Netophah or at el-Bina in the Bet ha-Kerem valley, but the archaeological survey makes a location in Upper Galilee more probable and its identification with Safd el-Batikh has been suggested. In talmudic times a Beth-Anath is mentioned as a city outside Ereẓ Israel with a mixed Jewish-gentile population (Tosef., Kil. 2:16). The Zeno Papyri from 259 B.C.E. contain a reference to a vineyard at Baitoanaia. It has also been suggested that the Batnaea mentioned by Eusebius (Onom. 30:5; 52:24) refers to the same site. (If so, the Caesarea 15 mi. (24 km.) distant would be Caesarea Philippi.)

Bibliography: Aharoni, Land, index; Avi-Yonah, Land, 143; EM, 2 (1965), 96f.; Press, Ereẓ, 1 (1951²), 95–96; S. Lieberman, *Tosefta ki-Feshutah, Zera'im* (1955), 620. [M.A.-Y.]

BETAR (abbreviated name of **Berit Trumpeldor,** Heb. בְּרִית תְּרוּמְפֶּלְדוֹר, בֵּית״ר), an activist Zionist youth movement founded in 1923 in Riga, Latvia, and attaining significant proportions in the 1930s, mainly in Eastern Europe. Betar played an important role in Zionist education, in teaching the Hebrew language and culture, and methods of self-defense. It also inculcated the ideals of *aliyah* to Ereẓ Israel by any means, legal and "illegal," and of personal dedicaton to the creation of a Jewish state "on both sides of the Jordan." The Betar ideology originated in a fusion of Vladimir *Jabotinsky's "legionism" with the ideas of personal pioneering and defense exemplified in Joseph *Trumpeldor's life and death.

1923–1935. At its inception Betar was a variation of the Zionist trend in East European Jewish youth that led to the Third Aliyah. The group of students and young workers that founded the movement declared themselves a "part of the Jewish Legion to be established in Ereẓ Israel." They organized a farm for the agricultural training of pioneer settlers in Palestine. The first Betar immigrants to Palestine (1925–29) joined the Histadrut and the Haganah as a matter of course. In the 1930s, however, with the growing rift and exacerbated conflict between the Revisionists and the Zionist-Socialist majority, Betar gradually became a bitter rival of Zionist-Socialist youth, both in the Diaspora and in Palestine. Sometimes relations deteriorated into physical clashes on the streets of Tel Aviv. Zionist-Socialist circles pointed to the brown shirts of the members of Betar as tangible proof of its "fascist character," and called for its speedy elimination from public life, whereas Betar spokesmen asserted that the "red-brown" shade of their uniform symbolized the earth of Ereẓ Israel, and in any event its adoption in the early 1920s preceded the rise of the German Nazis.

Betar members constituted a major part of the rank and file of the Union of Zionist Revisionists (from 1935, the New Zionist Organization) and also of the National Labor Federation and the Irgun Ẓeva'i Le'ummi in Palestine. In 1926 the second world congress of the Union of Zionist Revisionists in Paris recognized the Latvian group as the sponsor and provisional center of its youth movement. The first world conference of Betar, which convened in Danzig in 1931 with 87 delegates representing 21 countries, formulated the principles of the movement and elected Jabotinsky as *rosh Betar* ("head of Betar"), empowering him to appoint the overall leadership (*"shilton"*).

Defense training was proclaimed the foremost duty of every member, and those going to Palestine were to enlist for two years in special work brigades. At the second world conference of Betar in Cracow, in 1935, Jabotinsky proposed a codified text of the Betar ideology called *Ha-Neder* ("the Oath"), which stipulated in its first paragraph: "I devote my life to the rebirth of the Jewish State, with a Jewish majority, on both sides of the Jordan." It demanded, in addition to the basic tenets of all Zionist youth movements, a "monistic" conception of Zionism, rejecting any fusion with "alien" creeds (meaning mainly socialism). It also urged the inculcation of a mode of thought and deed called *hadar,* defined by Jabotinsky as "beauty, respect, self-esteem, politeness, and faithfulness."

Betar in Palestine. In Palestine the Betar work brigades (from 1934 called mobilized groups) grew into a network of disciplined units based in villages and settlements. Most of these were in Upper Galilee but, after the outbreak of the Arab riots in 1936, such units were established also in the Jewish quarter of the Old City of Jerusalem and at Naḥalat Yiẓhak, near Jerusalem. These groups engaged in clandestine defense training within the framework of Irgun Ẓeva'i Le'ummi, maintaining themselves collectively as laborers on the farms of old-time Jewish settlers or as wage earners in town. Some members eventually formed the nuclei of the first Betar settlements (Ramat Tiomkin near Netanyah, Tel Ẓur near Binyaminah, and in Mishmar ha-Yarden).

Systematic defense training was introduced in Betar in many Diaspora countries during the early 1930s by Yirmiyahu *Halpern, who established training courses and camps where self-defense, drill, street-fighting, the handling of small arms, boxing, and military tactics were taught. In Poland members of Betar also underwent training in the official paramilitary units of the state. In Shanghai Betar members organized a separate Jewish unit as part of the international force which policed the non-Chinese sections of the city.

The first Betar instructors' school was set up in Tel Aviv in 1928 and its trainees took part in the defense of the city during the riots of 1929. In 1931 Betar units joined dissident Haganah members in Jerusalem in setting up the separate underground organization Irgun Ẓeva'i Leummi. In 1930 a Betar naval unit was founded in Tel Aviv, training with sailboats. A central naval school of Betar was established in Civitavecchia, Italy, functioning there from 1934 to 1937 and graduating 153 cadets. About 50 sailors were also trained by Betar in Latvia between 1935 and 1939. These men later played important roles in the establishment of the Israel Navy and the Merchant Marine. In 1935 Jabotinsky's son Eri, heading a unit of mobilized Betar members in Palestine, constructed the first glider in the country. Flying courses were introduced later by the Irgun Ẓeva'i Le'ummi in Palestine; by 1939, 13 members had graduated as pilots.

Betar underwent rapid expansion during the 1930s as illustrated by the growth of its total world membership from 22,300 in 1931 to nearly 90,000 in 1938. In the late 1930s Betar was actively engaged in the Revisionists' "illegal" *aliyah* operation which, by 1939, took thousands of Jews to Palestine, among them many members of Betar. During World War II many Betar members in Palestine volunteered for the Palestinian units of the British Army and, later, the Jewish Brigade.

After the Holocaust. Most of the European branches of Betar were destroyed in the Holocaust. A few thousand members escaped by joining the anti-Nazi partisans, while Betar and Revisionist units took part in the ghetto uprisings, notably in Warsaw, Vilna, and Bialystok. With the loss of European Jewry, Israel became the center of the movement, which in the late 1960s numbered about 8,000 members, of whom over 4,000 were in Israel, and the rest in 13 other countries, mainly in Latin America, the United States, South Africa, and Australia.

Many members of Betar in Israel, upon joining the army, went into *Naḥal units. The movement in Israel also maintains youth towns in collaboration with *Youth Aliyah. Between 1948 and the late 1960s Betar, in cooperation with the Ḥerut movement, established 12 collective and cooperative settlements, some of them border settlements, such as Amaẓyah in the Lachish area, Mevo Betar near the site of historical *Bethar, *Ramat Raziel in the hills of Jerusalem, and Ẓur Natan in Central Israel.

Betar's membership in Palestine grew rapidly and by 1937 it had its own sports center which enabled its members to play, among other sports, football, basketball, and table tennis, engage in gymnastics, and train as boxers. In 1968 there were 4,500 active Betar members in 74 branches. Betar in Israel is affiliated with the Israel Football Association and the Israel Sports Federation.

Bibliography: H. Ben Yeruḥam, *Sefer Betar, Korot u-Mekorot*, 1 (1969); Brith Trumpeldor, *This is Betar* (1956²); J. B. Schechtman, *V. Jabotinsky Story*, 2 vols. (1956–61); B. Lubotzky, *Ha-Ẓohar u-Vetar* (1946); E. Even, *Songs of Betar* (1966); Brith Trumpeldor, *Generation to Generation* (1958); D. Niv, *Ma'arekhot ha-Irgun ha-Ẓeva'i ha-Le'ummi*, 3 vols. (1965–67), passim. [D.N.]

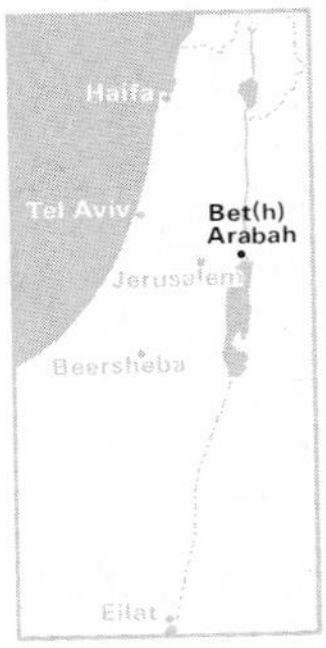

BET(H)-ARABAH (modern **Bet ha-Aravah;** Heb. בֵּית הָעֲרָבָה; "House of the Steppe"), place in southern Ereẓ Israel, in the Jericho Desert of the Lower Jordan Valley. The ancient name is preserved in ʿAyn al-Gharaba, southeast of Jericho near the Jordan River, but no corroborative archaeological remains have been thus far discovered in the vicinity. According to the Bible it belonged to the tribe of Judah on the border of Benjamin (Josh. 15:61; 18:22). More recently it was a kibbutz situated 1,235 ft. (380 m.) below sea level, 1.8 mi. (3 km.) north of the Jordan mouth of the Dead Sea. It was founded on Oct. 8, 1939, by a group of the Maḥanot ha-Olim youth movement and young immigrants from Germany and other Central European countries, on land of the Palestine Potash Company. Bet ha-Aravah was affiliated with Ha-Kibbutz ha-Me'uḥad. The kibbutz succeeded in sweeping its extremely saline soil with fresh Jordan water, making it capable of producing abundant farm crops. The land thus won yielded out-of-season vegetables, fruit, fodder, and other farm products. Carp ponds were also installed. A number of members worked in the potash plant. Members of the kibbutz cultivated friendly relations with the Arab inhabitants of Jericho and even with the nearby villages of Transjordan. Bet ha-Aravah proved that both adults and

Kibbutz Bet ha-Aravah, before its destruction in 1948. Jerusalem, Central Zionist Archives.

children could overcome the health hazards of the torrid climate. In the Israel War of Independence (1948) the completely isolated settlement held out for six months. Eventually the settlers were evacuated by boat to Sodom, at the south end of the Dead Sea. Later its members erected two new settlements in Galilee, *Kabri and *Gesher ha-Ziv. The Arab Legion completely razed the empty settlement. Its soil again became saline, and hardly any vestige of the village could be discerned when Israel forces reached the site in 1967. The following year a *Naḥal group set up a new settlement, Naḥal Kallia, in the general vicinity.

Bibliography: Abel, Geog, 2 (1938), 267; EM, s.v.; Aharoni, Land, 235, 302. [E.O.]

BET(H)-CHEREM (בֵּית הַכֶּרֶם, *"Bet ha-Kerem,"* "The House of the Vineyard"), settlement near Jerusalem in the First and Second Temple periods. It is first mentioned in the Beth-Lehem district at the time of the Judean kingdom in an appendix of the Septuagint to the list of Judean cities in Joshua 15:49 (as Karem). Jeremiah (6:1) speaks of the

Bet din, a panel illustrating a Court of Law in an opening page of *Tur Ḥoshen ha-Mishpat*, the fourth part of the *Arba'ah Turim* ("Four Columns" of law) by Rabbi Jacob ben Asher. Mantua, 1436. Rome, Vatican Library, Cod. Rossiana 555, the verso of an unpaginated folio between fols. 292 and 293 ($13\frac{1}{4} \times 9\frac{1}{4}$ ins/33.5×23.5 cm.).

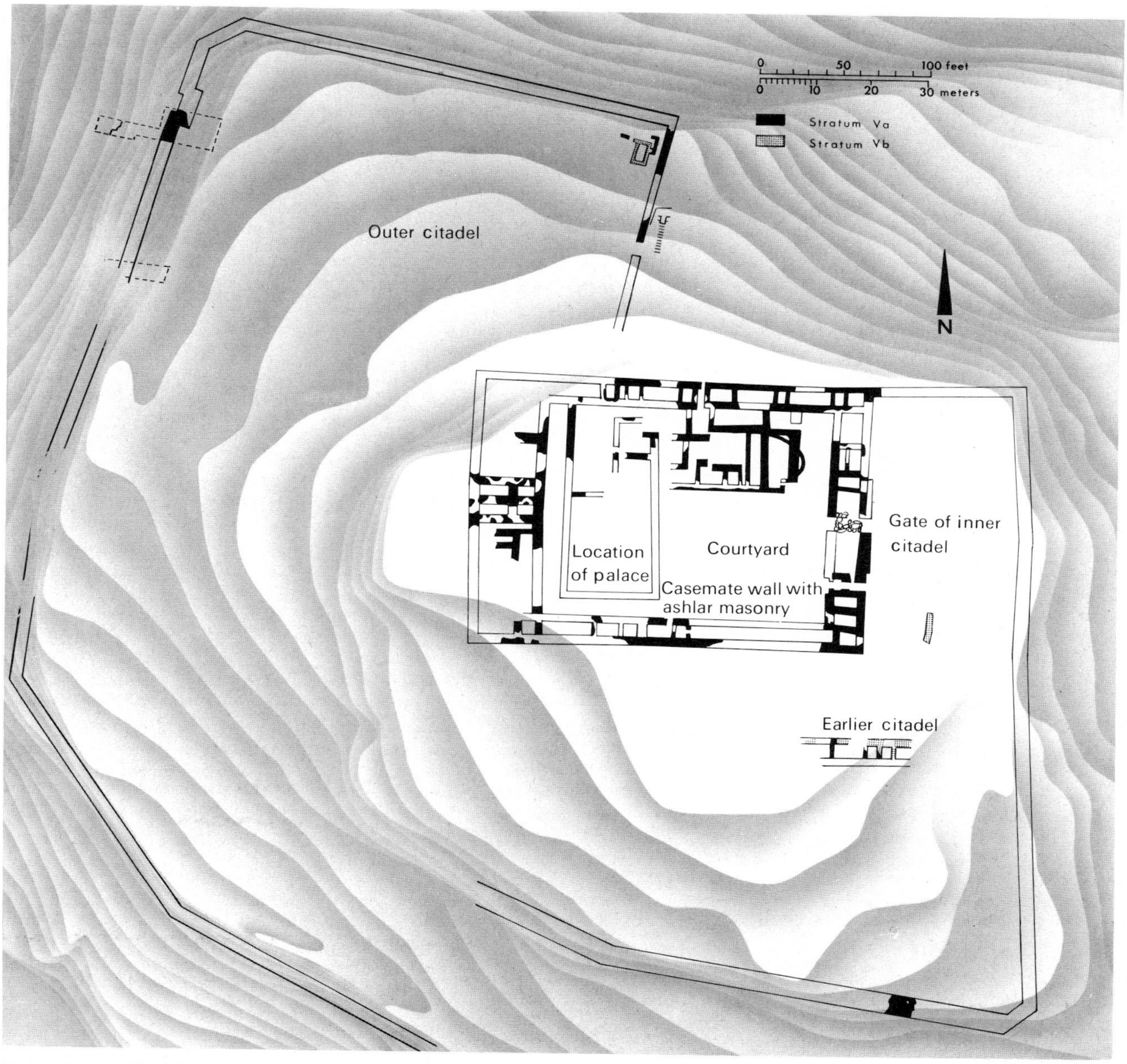

Plan of the citadel of Beth-Cherem. Jerusalem, Y. Aharoni.

town as a fortress near Jerusalem on the way to Tekoa, where beacons were lit in times of danger. It again appears during the time of Nehemiah as the center of one of the Judean districts; Malchijah, son of Rechab, the ruler of the district of Beth-Cherem, took part in building the walls of Jerusalem under Nehemiah (Neh. 3:14). The valley of Beth-Cherem appearing in later sources should apparently be sought near the town. According to the Mishnah (Mid. 3:4), the stones for the temple altar were brought from the valley of Beth-Cherem (Ex. 20:25 (JPS 20:22); Deut. 27:5–6). The town and its valley are also mentioned in two Dead Sea Scrolls from the end of the Second Temple period. In the Genesis Aprocryphon on Genesis 14:17, the "vale of Shaveh—the same is the King's Vale" is identified with "the valley of Beth-Karma." The Copper Scroll, which contains a list of hiding places for treasure, describes Beth-Cherem as located between a place in the "big valley" (Kidron Valley?) and Yad Avshalom (Absalom's monument), which, according to II Samuel 18:18, was located in the King's Valley. The last reference to Beth-Cherem is found in Jerome's commentary on Jeremiah 6:1 (from the fifth century C.E.), where he tells of a place the Jews call Bethacharma situated on a mountain between Jerusalem and Tekoa.

The various sources clearly indicate that Beth-Cherem was located on a height at the southern approaches of Jerusalem. Its usual identification with Ein Karem (in a valley southwest of Jerusalem), based on the similarity of names, neither fits its description in the sources nor has been confirmed by archaeological evidence. Several elevated points in the vicinity of Bethlehem have therefore been suggested, the most probable of which is the tell of *Ramat Raḥel, situated on a dominant hill halfway between Jerusalem and Bethlehem. Its history—as derived from excavations there—corresponds with the facts known about Beth-Cherem. The town was founded in the ninth–eighth century B.C.E., and a royal palace erected there close to the end of the monarchy may be interpreted as "the house of the vineyard" outside the city. This was probably the palace built by Jehoiakim, the son of Josiah, who was vehemently denounced by the prophet Jeremiah (22:13–19), in whose time it was the major stronghold on the southern approach to Jerusalem. The large number of official seal impressions from the Persian period found at Ramat Raḥel indicates that it served as an administrative center at that time, which again agrees with the biblical account of Beth-Cherem's role in the post-Exilic period (Neh. 3:14). (For the excavations, see Ramat

Raḥel.) In modern times the name has been applied to a western suburb of Jerusalem founded by teachers and writers in the early 1920s.

Bibliography: Schick, in: ZDPV, 3 (1880), 91–92; S. Klein, *ibid.*, 33 (1910), 29ff.; Alt, in: PJB, 28 (1932), 11; Abel, Geog, 2 (1938), 295–6; S. J. Saller, *Discoveries at St. John's Ein Karim* (1946), 8; Y. Aharoni, in: BIES, 20 (1956), 44–46; idem, in: IEJ, 6 (1956), 152–5; idem, et al., in: *Excavations at Ramat Raḥel,* 1 (1962), 49–51; 1 (1964), 119–24.

[Yo.A.]

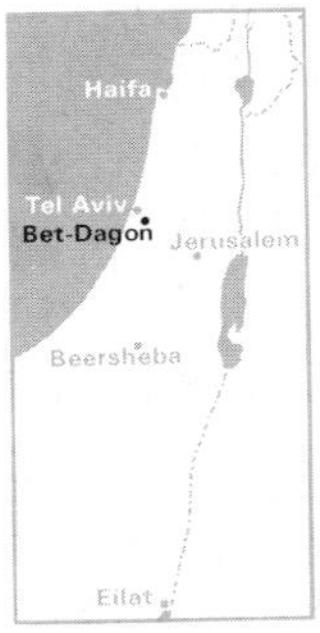

BET(H)-DAGON (Heb. בֵּית דָּגוֹן), several biblical places, named after a house (shrine) of the god Dagon (cf. the Temple of Dagon in Ashdod, I Sam. 5:1ff.). (1) An unidentified city in the southern Shephelah district of Judah (Josh. 15:41). (2) A place in Galilee on the eastern border of the tribe of Asher, northeast of Mount Carmel (Josh. 19:27), which is possibly mentioned in a list of cities of Pharaoh Ramses III. (3) A city mentioned as Bit-Daganna, near Jaffa, in the inscriptions of Sennacherib, king of Assyria, in whose time (701 B.C.E.) it was under the rule of Ashkelon. The Tosefta in reference to it (Oho. 3:9) specifies that it is located "in Judah," and distinguishes it from Beth-Dagon located by Eusebius (Onom. 50:16) "between Diospolis (Lydda) and Jamnia (Jabneh)," but called by him Kefar Dagon. The original name appears on the Madaba Map in the form (Bet)odegana. It was populated by Samaritans, who built a synagogue there in the fourth century; their presence is still attested to in the tenth century. The crusaders erected a castle there, known as Casal Moyen or Castellum de Maen, i.e., "midway" between Jaffa and Ramleh, which was destroyed by Saladin in 1187, but rebuilt by Richard the Lion-Hearted four years later.

[M.A.-Y.]

Modern Period. This site is now the small town of Bet Dagan. In modern times the Arab village Beit Dajan existed there, which increased in population and wealth due to the development of nearby Tel Aviv. Heavy fighting took place there during the War of Independence (1948) to secure Jewish traffic to Jerusalem and the south, and the village was abandoned. It was settled by immigrants from Bulgaria at the end of 1948 and called Bet Dagan ("House of Corn"). This soon developed from a moshav into a semi-urban community. In 1962 the Israel Institute for Meteorology was opened there. The town had 2,680 inhabitants in 1968.

[E.O.]

Bibliography: M. Avi-Yonah, *Madaba Mosaic Map* (1954), 62; Avi-Yonah, Land, 157; 107; Abel, Geog, 2 (1938), 269; G. Beyer, in: ZDPV, 56 (1933), 227; E. Dhorme, in: RHR, 138 (1950), 130–1; Press, Ereẓ, 1 (1951), 79; Aharoni, Land, 337.

BET DIN AND JUDGES (Heb. בֵּית דִּין; lit. "house of judgment"). *Bet din* (pl. *battei din*) is the term, in rabbinic sources, for a Jewish court of law. In modern times it usually refers to an ecclesiastical court dealing with religious matters such as divorce, and supervision of the dietary laws, and acting, with the consent of all concerned, as a court of arbitration. In Israel the term has come to mean the rabbinic court (as opposed to the secular court known as the *bet mishpat*) which has, by act of the Knesset, jurisdiction in matters of personal status in addition to its normal religious function. This article deals with the general meaning as found in rabbinic sources.

[Ed.]

In Jewish Law. Origins. The Bible records that Moses sat as a magistrate among the people (Ex. 18:13) and, either on the advice of Jethro, his father-in-law (Ex. 18:17–23), or on his own initiative (Deut. 1:9–14), he later delegated his judicial powers to appointed "chiefs of thousands, hundreds, fifties, and tens" (Ex. 18:21; Deut. 1:15)—reserving to himself jurisdiction in only the most difficult, major disputes (Ex. 18:22 and 26; Deut. 1:17). It is therefore probable that Israel was one of those civilizations in which the judicature preceded the law, and that some of the later, codified law may have originated in judicial precedents. The earliest reports of such legal decisions already indicate a high standard of judicial practice and qualifications. Judges had to be "able men, such as fear God, men of truth, hating unjust gain" (Ex. 18:21) and "wise men, and understanding and full of knowledge" (Deut. 1:13). They were charged to "hear the causes between your brethren and judge righteously between a man and his brother and the stranger," not be "partial in judgment," but to "hear the small and the great alike; fear no man, for judgment is God's" (Deut. 1:16–17). When the children of Israel settled in their land, the allocation of jurisdiction on a purely numerical basis ("thousands, hundreds, fifties, tens") was to be replaced by allocation on a local basis, i.e., that judges were to be appointed in every town within the various tribes (Deut. 16:18 and Sif. Deut. 144; Sanh. 16b). It is disputed whether this injunction to establish courts in every town applied only in the land of Israel or also in the Diaspora. Some hold that outside the land of Israel courts ought to be established in every district, but need not be established in every town (Mak. 7a); whereas others hold that the injunction applies only in Israel, viz. "in all the settlements that the Lord your God is giving you," but not "in foreign countries in which He has dispersed you" (Maim. Yad, Sanh. 1:2). However, later authorities regard as obligatory the establishment of a court in every community (cf., e.g., *Arukh ha-Shulḥan* ḤM 1:18). In towns with less than 120 inhabitants, there was only a court of three judges—three being the minimum number—so that where opinions were divided, a majority could prevail (Sanh. 3b; Yad. Sanh. 1:4). In towns with 120 inhabitants or more, the court should have 23 judges and be designated as a "Sanhedrin Ketannah" (Sanh. 1:6; Yad, Sanh. 1:10). Courts of 23 judges also sat in the Temple precincts in Jerusalem (Sanh. 11:2; Yad. Sanh. 1:3). The highest court was the "Sanhedrin Gedolah" of 71 judges which sat in the Temple *(Lishkat ha-Gazit)* in Jerusalem (Mid. 5:4; Sanh. 11:2; Yad, Sanh. 1:3 and 14:12), corresponding to the 70 elders and officers who took their place with Moses to "share the burden of the people" (Num. 11:16–17).

The jurisdiction of the various courts was as follows.

(1) Courts of three judges exercised jurisdiction in civil matters generally (Sanh. 1:1), including those which might involve the imposition of *fines (Sanh. 1:1; Sanh. 3a). They also had jurisdiction in matters of divorce (Git. 5b) and *ḥaliẓah* (Yev. 12:1). A court of three judges was required for the conversion of non-Jews (Yev. 46b); for the absolution from vows (Ned. 78a; TJ, Ḥag. 1:8, 76c and Ned. 10:10, 42b); for the circumvention of the law annulling debts in the Sabbatical year ("prosbul"; Shev. 10:4; Git. 32b); for the non-release of slaves after six years (Ex. 21:6; Mekh. Mishpatim 2; Yad, Avadim 3:9); for the enslavement of one who commits a theft and does not have the means to pay for the principal (Ex. 22:2; Yad, Sanhedrin 1:1; Genevah 3:11); and also for the taking of any evidence, even in noncontroversial cases (Yev. 87b; Resp. *Ha-Meyuḥasot la-Ramban* 113; Resp. Rashba vol. 1, no. 749). Compulsory orders in matters of ritual would also

require the concurrence of three judges in order to be valid (Ket. 86a; Ḥul. 132b), as would the imposition of any sanction for disobedience (*Mordekhai* Git. 384).

(2) Courts of 23 judges exercised jurisdiction in criminal matters generally, including capital cases (Sanh. 1:4). They also exercised jurisdiction in quasi-criminal cases, in which the destruction of animals might be involved (e.g., Lev. 20:15–16; Ex. 21:28–29; Sanh. 1:4). Where a case was originally of a civil nature, such as slander, but might in due course give rise to criminal sanctions, such as slander of unchastity (Deut. 22:14), it was brought before a court of 23 (Sanh. 1:1); if the slander was found to be groundless, the matter would be referred to a court of three for civil judgment (Maim. Yad, Sanh. 5:3). According to one view, the imposition of the penalty of *flogging required a court of 23 (Sanh. 1:2), but the prevailing view is that a court of three is sufficient (Sanh. 1:2; Yad, Sanh. 5:4), as it is really a penalty that is not necessarily for criminal offenses (see *Contempt of Court), as well as being the accepted method of judicial admonition *(makkot mardut)*.

(3) The court of 71 judges had practically unlimited judicial, legislative, and administrative powers but certain judicial and administrative functions were reserved to it alone. Thus, the high priest (Sanh. 1:5), the head of a tribe (Sanh. 16a), and presumably also the president of the Sanhedrin *(nasi)*, could, if accused of a crime, only be tried by the court of 71. Certain crimes were also reserved to its jurisdiction, such as the uttering of false prophecy (Sanh. 1:5), rebellious teaching by an elder (*"zaken mamre"*; Sanh. 11:2; see *Majority Rule), and the subversion of a whole town or tribe (Sanh. 1:5); and certain death penalties had to be confirmed by it before being carried out (such as of the rebellious son, the enticer to idolatry, and false witnesses; Tosef., Sanh. 11:7). The *ordeal of a woman suspected of adultery took place in the Great Court at Jerusalem only (Sot. 1:4).

Among the administrative functions reserved to the Great Sanhedrin were the appointment of courts of 23

Figure 1. The entrance to the old *bet din* in Bratislava, Czechoslovakia, photographed in the 1930s. Photo R. Vishniak.

(Sanh. 1:5; Maim. Yad, Sanh. 5:1); the election of kings (Yad, loc. cit. and Melakhim 1:3) and of high priests (Yad, Kelei ha-Mikdash 4:15); the expansion of the limits of the city of Jerusalem and of the Temple precincts (Sanh. 1:5), and the partition of the country among the tribes (according to Ulla; Sanh. 16a); the declaration of war (Sanh. 1:5); the offering of a sacrifice for the sin of the whole community (Lev. 4:13–15; Sanh. 13b); and the appointment and control of priests serving in the Temple (Mid. 5:4; Tosef., Ḥag. 2:9). The legislative functions of the Great Sanhedrin cannot easily be enumerated. It has been authoritatively said that the Great Court of Jerusalem was the essential source of all Oral Law (Yad, Mamrim 1:1). The law as laid down (or as interpreted) by the Great Sanhedrin is binding on everybody, and any person contravening or repudiating it was liable to the death penalty (Deut. 17:12; Sif. Deut. 155; Yad, Mamrim 1:2), even where the law as laid down (or interpreted) by the court might appear misconceived: "even though they show you as right what in your eyes is left or as left what is right—you must obey them" (Sif. Deut. 155; but cf. Hor. 1:1 and TJ, Hor. 1:1, 45d; and see Rabbinical *Authority). As a corollary of their legislative powers, the Great Sanhedrin also exercised advisory functions: wherever in any court any question of law was in doubt, the final and binding opinion of the Great Court at Jerusalem would have to be taken (Sanh. 88b; Yad, Sanh. 1:4). For the question of appeals see *Practice and Procedure.

(4) Apart from the regular courts mentioned above, there sat in the Temple a special court of priests charged with the supervision of the Temple ritual and with civil matters concerning the priests (cf. Ket. 1:5). Mention is also made of a special court of levites, presumably with similar functions (cf. Tosef., Sanh. 4:7). Originally, the priests performed general judicial functions: they were the sole competent interpreters (or diviners) of God's judgment (Ex. 28:15, 30, 43; Num. 27:21; Deut. 33:8–10); later, they adjudicated matters together or alternately with the judges (Deut. 17:9; 19:17; 21:5), and it seems that the litigants had the choice of applying to the priest for the dictum of God or to the judges for judgment according to law; eventually, the judicial functions of the priests were reduced to their simply being allotted some seats in the Great Sanhedrin (Sif. Deut. 153).

(5) While no regular court could consist of less than three judges (Sanh. 3b), recognized experts in the law *("mumḥeh la-rabbim")* were already in talmudical times admitted as single judges (Sanh.5a), albeit in civil cases only and not without express reservations and disapproval—there being no true single judge other than God alone (Avot 4:8; Yad, Sanh. 2:11). No litigant could be compelled to submit to the jurisdiction of a single judge (Sh. Ar., ḤM 3:2).

Appointment of Judges. The appointment of judges presupposed the *"semikhah"* ("laying of hands") by the appointer upon the appointee, as Moses laid his hands upon Joshua (Num. 27:23) thereby making him leader and supreme judge in succession to himself. The tradition is that throughout the ages judges received their authority from their immediate predecessors who "laid their hands" upon them; so it came about that in law the president of the Great Sanhedrin would be the authority conferring judicial powers on graduating judges (Sanh. 5a), in a formal procedure before a court of three in which he participated or which he appointed (Yad, Sanh. 4:5). But judges were also appointed by kings (e.g., II Chron. 19:5–6), a power which appears to have eventually devolved on the *exilarch in Babylonia (Yad, Sanh. 4:13), but was superseded even there by the overriding authority of the heads of the academies (*rashei yeshivot;* cf. A. Harkavy (ed.),

Zikhron . . . Kammah Ge'onim, 80f., no. 180). Courts need not be composed of authorized judges only: any duly authorized judge could form a court by co-opting to himself the necessary number of laymen (Yad, Sanh. 4:11).

The original practice of *semikhah* ceased about the middle of the fourth century and at the present time *battei din* exercise their judicial functions only as agents of, and by virtue of, an implied authority from the Ancients (Git. 88b; BK 84b; Yad, Sanh. 5:8). This "agency" does not extend to capital cases; even for cases involving fines nonauthorized judges would not be qualified (Sh. Ar., ḤM 1:1). It is only because of force of circumstances that the scope of jurisdiction was in practice never restricted, but extended to whatever causes local conditions required (cf. *Netivot ha-Mishpat,* Mishpat ha-Urim, ḤM 1:1; Nov. Ramban Yev. 46b).

One of the consequences of the cessation of the traditional authorization of judges was the adoption in many (mostly Western European) communities of a system of election of judges: in Spain, the judges were elected every year, along with all other officers of the community (cf. Resp. Ribash 207). The leading rabbinical authorities of the period were time and again consulted about election procedures (cf., e.g., Resp. Rashba vol. 3, nos. 417, 422–5; vol. 5, no. 284), so as to ensure that the best and most impartial candidates would be elected. It seems that, when elected, they could not refuse to serve, even though they had not put up their candidature (cf. *Rema* ḤM 25:3; see Judicial *Autonomy; *Mishpat Ivri).

In the State of Israel today, the procedure for appointing rabbinical judges is similar to that for appointing secular judges (*Dayyanim* Act, 5715–1955), but while the qualifications of secular judges are laid down in the law, those of rabbinical judges are in each individual case to be attested to by the chief rabbis on the strength of examinations.

No authorization *(semikhah)* and no appointment of a judge will be valid where the appointee did not possess the necessary qualifications (Maim. Yad, Sanh. 4:15); and the sin of appointing unqualified judges is said to be tantamount to erecting an **asherah* beside the altar of the Lord (Sanh. 7b); and where the man was appointed because he was rich, it was like making gods of silver or gods of gold (*ibid.*), not only causing miscarriages of justice but idolatry (Maim. loc. cit., 3:8); and it is reported that judges appointed because of their money were treated with open contempt (TJ, Bik. 3:3, 65d). "The Sages have said that from the Great Court messengers were sent out all over the country of Israel, and they looked for judges who were wise and feared sin and were humble and clearsighted and of good appearance and good manners, and first they made them judges in their towns, and then they brought them to the gates of the Temple, and finally they would elevate them to the Great Court" (Maim. loc. cit., 2:8).

QUALIFICATIONS. The judicial qualifications have been enumerated by Maimonides as follows: judges must be wise and sensible, learned in the law and full of knowledge, and also acquainted to some extent with other subjects such as medicine, arithmetic, astronomy and astrology, and the ways of sorcerers and magicians and the absurdities of idolatry and suchlike matters (so as to know how to judge them); a judge must not be too old, nor may he be a eunuch or a childless man; and as he must be pure in mind, so must he be pure from bodily defects, but as well a man of stature and imposing appearance; and he should be conversant in many languages so as not to stand in need of interpreters. The seven fundamental qualities of a judge are wisdom, humility, fear of God, disdain of money, love of truth, love of people, and a good reputation. A judge must have a good eye, a humble soul, must be pleasant in company, and speak kindly to people; he must be very strict with himself and conquer lustful impulses; he must have a courageous heart to save the oppressed from the oppressor's hate, cruelty, and persecution, and eschew wrong and injustice (Yad, Sanh. 2:1–7). Playing cards for money or other games of chance and lending money on interest also disqualify a person from judicial functions (Sanh. 3:3). A judge who is a relative of one of the litigants, or has any other personal relationship toward him ("loves him or hates him"), must disqualify himself from sitting in judgment over him (Sanh. 3:4–5). A judge should not engage in manual work, so as not to expose himself to popular contempt (Kid. 70a).

PRINCIPLES OF JUDICIAL CONDUCT. A judge must show patience, indulgence, humility, and respect for persons when sitting in court (Yad, Sanh. 25:1; Sh. Ar., ḤM 7:2–5); he must always hear both parties to the case (Sanh. 7b; Shev. 31a; and Codes); he may not in any way discriminate between the parties (Lev. 19:15; Shev. 30a–31a; Yad, Sanh. 21:1–2; 20:5–7; Sh. Ar., ḤM 17:1 and commentaries ad. loc.); nor may he act under the possible pressures of any undue influence, including *bribery by money or by words (Deut. 16:19; Sanh. 3:5; Shab. 119a; Ket. 105b; and Codes); he must, on the one hand, proceed with deliberation and care, and reconsider again and again before finally pronouncing his verdict (Avot 1:1; Sanh. 35a; Sif. Deut. 16 and Codes), but may not, on the other hand, unduly delay justice (Yad, Sanh. 14:10 and 20:6); and he must so conduct himself that justice is not only done but is also manifestly seen to be done (Yoma 38a; Shek. 3:2) and readily understood by the litigants (ḤM 14:4). Before joining a court, a judge must satisfy himself that the judges sitting with him are properly qualified (Yad, Sanh. 2:14); and no judge should sit together with another judge whom he hates or despises (Sh. Ar., ḤM 7:8). Nor may a judge—especially in criminal cases—instead of considering and deciding the issue before him on his own, rely on the opinion of greater judges in the court and try thus to disburden himself of his judicial responsibility (Tosef., Sanh. 3:8; Yad, Sanh. 10:1).

See also Judicial *Autonomy; *Mishpat Ivri *Takkanot; *Arbitration. [H.H.C.]

Talmudic Period. The rabbis ascribe the development of *battei din* to leading biblical personalities such as Shem, Moses, Gideon, Jephthah, Samuel, David, and Solomon (Mak. 23b; Av. Zar. 36b; RH 2:9; RH 25a). Historical evidence of the existence of a *bet din* in the time of Jehoshaphat is found in *Deuteronomy Rabbah* 19:8. However, the *bet din* belongs essentially to the period of the Second Temple, and its establishment is attributed to *Ezra. He decreed that a *bet din,* which was to sit on Mondays and Thursdays (BK 82a), be established in all populated centers. These were local courts, while the Great Sanhedrin of Jerusalem served as the supreme court (Deut. 17:8–13; Sot. 1:4; Sanh. 1:6). The Sanhedrin existed for the duration of the Second Temple. A decree against immoral behavior is ascribed to the *bet din* of the Hasmoneans (Av. Zar. 36b).

After the destruction of the Temple, *Johanan b. Zakkai established his *bet din* in Jabneh as the cultural and political center of the Jews, and it succeeded the previous Sanhedrin Gedolah. The Jabneh *bet din* was responsible for regulating the calendar and thereby became the religious and national center not only of Ereẓ Israel, but also of the Diaspora. In addition to this central *bet din,* local *battei din* continued to function, particularly in the vicinity of the academies. The Talmud speaks of the courts of R. Eliezer in Lydda, R. Joshua in Peki'in, R. Akiva in Bene-Berak, and R. Yose in

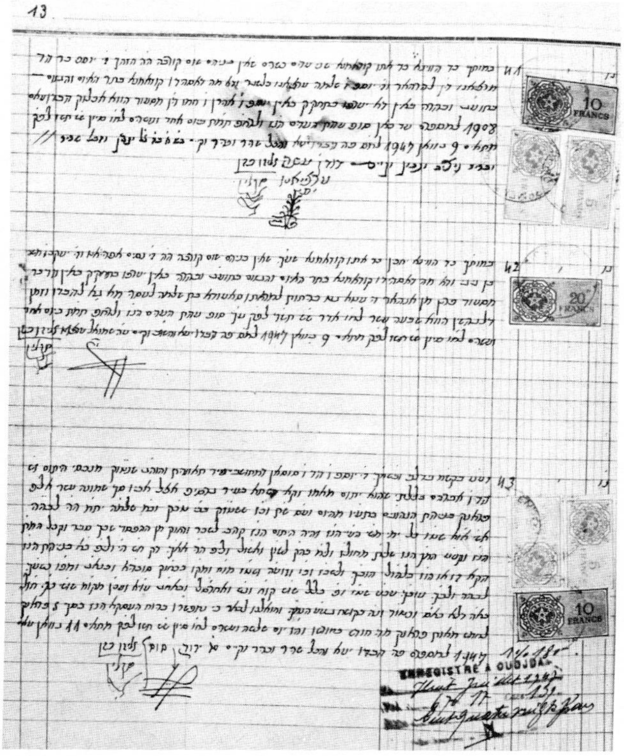

Figure 2. Register of financial transactions executed before the *bet din* of Debdou, Morocco, in 1947. Jerusalem, C.A.H.J.P.

Sepphoris (Sanh. 32b). Under R. Johanan's successor, *Gamaliel II, the power and influence of the central *bet din* increased. The summit of its authority was reached under *Judah ha-Nasi I. His grandson, Judah Nesia, may be regarded as the last *nasi* under whose direction the *bet din* was still the actual center of the Jewish people. The Talmud therefore refers to Gamaliel and his *bet din* (Tosef., Ber. 2:6) and to Judah ha-Nasi and his *bet din* (Av. Zar. 2:6), thereby indicating the central civil and religious authority of the Jews.

Toward the middle of the third century, the *bet din* of the *nasi* gradually lost its importance due to the rise of Jewish scholarship in Babylonia and the increased oppression of Palestinian Jewry under Roman rule. Although the office of the *nasi* continued until the end of the fifth century, his *bet din* was no longer the center of the Jewish people. In Babylonia, no *bet din* ever achieved preeminent authority, even for Babylonia alone. This situation continued throughout the geonic period, as no central *bet din* could be established because of the rivalry between the two academies. [Ed.]

Medieval and Modern Period. The *bet din* became the stronghold of Jewish *autonomy in the Middle Ages, and continued with reduced powers into modern times. It experienced many changes in the various centers of Jewish life in the Diaspora, while retaining the continuity of the principles of talmudic law. A vast literature of rabbinic responsa grew out of the written judgments passed by the scholars of every age on actual cases, thus setting precedents and affording an orderly development of Jewish jurisprudence.

In some exceptional cases Jews resorted to non-Jewish courts. Such occurred in Egypt and Ereẓ Israel in the 11th and 12th centuries, following the decline of the gaonate, and in Spain, Majorca, Tunis, and Algeria in the 14th century. In Germany, Jewish and Christian judges met in the synagogue to adjudicate cases between Jews and Gentiles.

The general rule in the Middle Ages, however, was that Jews were strictly prohibited from taking litigation among themselves to gentile courts. This was achieved partly by the control exercised by the community over the individual and by the conception that "Judgment is God's" and hence that recourse to gentile courts meant "aggrandizing the honor of alien gods," as well as by the fairness, incorruptibility, and swiftness of Jewish justice in the majority of countries and most of the time.

In the first half of the geonic period local judges were appointed centrally in Babylonia by the *exilarchs. Later the country was divided into three domains: one was under the jurisdiction of the exilarch, and the other two under the academies in *Sura and *Pumbedita respectively. The local court usually consisted of three judges, one appointed by the exilarch or by the *gaon* and two more local associates co-opted by him. In Egypt the *nagid* selected local judges.

In the absence of a central authority in the newly developing Jewish settlements in Europe the judiciary became part of the local government of each community. Either the elders themselves constituted a court of justice, or special *dayyanim* ("judges") were selected. In the days of *Gershom b. Judah (tenth century) these local courts were invested with full judicial authority to impose fines and exact penalties. They were mostly constituted of laymen, not necessarily versed in the law. Later, when communities began engaging rabbis, the lay judges were expected to consult them on talmudic law.

In Spain the *bet din* achieved its fullest growth and widest powers. The prerogatives of every *alijama* ("community council") were often defined by a royal charter. The *bet din* thus derived its authority from the king through the *kahal.* The king often appointed a chief rabbi for the realm who was a grandee not necessarily expert in Jewish law, the judiciary being included within his competence. He usually sought the advice and guidance of trained Jewish jurists. The authority of the *bet din* extended to all spheres of Jewish life, social as well as individual, its judgments resting on rabbinic law. It developed a rigorous system of punishments, some of which were far removed from the legacy of ancient Jewish jurisdiction. It assumed, for instance, the right to mete out flagellation, fines (which generally went to the royal treasury), excommunication, chains, imprisonment, exile, and even bodily mutilation, such as cutting off hands or the nose, or cutting out the tongue, as well as the death penalty for *informers *(malshinim).* Hence on the basis of temporary emergency legislation many local Christian legal mores were adopted by the Jewish *bet din.*

During the period when the *Councils of the Lands had jurisdiction over the communities in Poland and Lithuania these bodies included a supreme judiciary selected from among the talmudic scholars of the main communities. In general, appellate Jewish courts existed in many lands, including Spain, Italy, Moravia, Bohemia, Austria-Hungary, and Bulgaria.

Whereas the traditional *bet din* for civil cases consisted of three judges, there were other compositions of this court ranging from one person, usually the local rabbi, to the seven *tovei ha-ir,* the elders of the community. Large cities had more than one *bet din.* A court of arbitration whereby each litigant selected one judge and these two judges appointed the third was very common. Small rural settlements which were administratively allied with a neighboring *kahal* took their litigation to the *bet din* of that *kahal.* Associations within a community, mainly those of artisans, had their own *bet din* for their members by permission of the *kahal.* On the arrival of the Spanish exiles in Turkey after the Expulsion of 1492, each congregation established its own *bet din.*

Figure 3. A sitting of the Jerusalem *bet din*, 1969. Photo Government Press Office, Tel Aviv.

In Russia the *bet din* was especially powerful until the latter part of the 19th century. Before the abolition of the *kahal* there in 1844 the *bet din* not only applied strict penalties to guilty individuals but also had jurisdiction over the *kahal* itself in claims of individuals against it. There is even a record of the imposition of capital punishment upon two informers in Novo-Ushitsa in 1836.

The distinguishing characteristic of the medieval *bet din* was that it served as an arm of the self-governing *kahal* which possessed powers of law enforcement. As emancipation of the Jew in the modern era dissolved the corporative structure, Jews tended increasingly to resort to the general courts. Wherever the *bet din* has survived to this day it enjoys the prerogatives only of a court of arbitration whose decisions are generally upheld by the law of the country. In many countries, in particular in England and its dominions, and to a lesser degree in France, the *bet din* system, headed by the *bet din* of the chief rabbi of the country, still plays a central role in Jewish life. In Ereẓ Israel, under the mandatory government, an elaborate network of *bet din* courts was established under the Supreme Rabbinical Court in Jerusalem. The State of Israel has taken over this system, giving the *bet din* exclusive jurisdiction over the Jewish population in matters of personal status.

See also Judicial *Autonomy. For *bet din* in modern Israel see *Israel, start of section on Legal and Judicial System. [I.L.]

Bibliography: D. Hoffmann, *Der Oberste Gerichtshof in der Stadt des Heiligthums* (1878); J. Jelsky, *Die innere Einrichtung des Grossen Synedrions zu Jerusalem und ihre Fortsetzung im spaeteren palaestinensischen Lehrhause*... (1894); A. Buechler, *Das Synedrion in Jerusalem und das Grosse Beth-Din in der Quaderkammer des Jerusalemischen Tempels* (1902); Schuerer, Gesch, 4 (1911^4), index, s.v. *Gerichtswesen;* Gulak, Yesodei, 4 (1922), index; S. Assaf, *Battei ha-Din ve-Sidreihem Aḥarei Ḥatimat ha-Talmud* (1924); idem, in: *Ha-Mishpat ha-Ivri*, 1 (1925/26), 105–20; A. Feldman, in: *Juridical Review*, 41 (1929); D. M. Shohet, *The Jewish Court in the Middle Ages* (1931); A. A. Neuman, *The Jews in Spain*, 2 (1942), index, s.v. *Courts, Jewish;* Ḥ. Albeck, in: *Zion*, 8 (1942/43), 85–93; I. Levitats, *Jewish Community in Russia 1772–1844* (1943), 198–217; A. Weiss, in: *Sefer ha-Yovel... Ginzburg* (1946), 189–216; Albright, in: *A. Marx Jubilee Volume* (1950), 61–82; Gershoni, in: *Ha-Torah ve-ha-Medinah*, 2 (1950), 72–75; ET, 1 (1951^3), 117–9; 2 (1949), 253; 3 (1951), 150–74, 174–80, 181; 8 (1957), 510–2; S. B. Hoenig, *The Great Sanhedrin* (1953); H. Mantel, *Studies in the History of the Sanhedrin* (1961); Silberg, in: *Molad*, 23 (1965/66), 265–74; Baron, Social², index, s.v. *Courts, Jewish;* Elon, Mafteaḥ, 12–16; J. S. Zuri, *Mishpat ha-Talmud*, 7 (1921), 1–12.

BET(H)-EDEN (Heb. בֵּית עֶדֶן), the biblical name for **Bît Adini,** an Aramean kingdom that extended along the banks of the Euphrates from the mouth of the Sâjūr River in the north to the mouth of the Balikh River in the south (see *Aram). The name Beth-Eden appears in its entirety in Amos 1:5; the short form Eden is found in Ezekiel 27:23; and the phrase children of Eden (*benei* Eden) appears in II Kings 19:12 and Isaiah 37:12. The identification of Beth-Eden with Bît Adini is based on the fact that Beth-Eden is mentioned because of its importance along with the kingdom of Damascus (Amos 1:5). The kingdom was founded in the tenth century B.C.E., and during the first half of the ninth century it was the most important Aramean kingdom in Mesopotamia. It was probably named for the father of the dynasty that founded it, and is first mentioned in the Annals of Adad-nirari II around the year 900. The biblical references to Beth-Eden belong to the period when the kingdom was an Assyrian province (after it was captured in 855 B.C.E.). A. Malamat views the expression "one who holds the scepter [i.e., a ruler] from Beth-Eden" (Amos 1:5) as a reference to Šamši-ilu, the Assyrian governor, who, as is known from a document discovered at Til Barsip, Beth-Eden's major city, was appointed over Beth-Eden in the time of Amos. The words spoken by the messengers of Sennacherib about "children of Eden who were in Telassar" (II Kings 19:12; Isa 37:12) may allude to the conquests of *Tiglath-Pileser III. Telassar was apparently the name of a region in the Assyrian province of Beth-Eden.

Bibliography: A. Malamat, in: BASOR, 129 (1953), 25–26; Pritchard, Texts, 275. [Ed.]

BET(H)-EL (Heb. בֵּית אֵל), Canaanite and Israelite town, 10½ mi. (17 km.) N. of Jerusalem, located at the intersection of the north–south mountain road along the watershed and the east–west road leading to the plains of Jericho and to the Coastal Plain (cf. Judg. 20:31). At present its site is occupied by the small Muslim village of Baytīn, 2,886 ft. (880 m.) above sea level. Excavations were conducted at Beth-El by W. F. *Albright and J. L. Kelso in 1927 and 1934 and resumed by Kelso in 1954, 1957, and 1961.

Settlement at Beth-El apparently began at the turn of the third millennium B.C.E., when it inherited the position of neighboring *Ai (al-Tell), which already lay in ruins. In the 16th century B.C.E. the settlement was enlarged and surrounded by an 11 ft. (3⅓ m.) thick stone wall. The biblical account of Abraham's building an altar to the Lord between Beth-El and Ai (Gen. 12:6–8) is usually assigned to this period. Beth-El's main importance, however, is derived from its traditional association with Jacob's dream. Fleeing from his brother Esau, Jacob spent the night there and dreamed he saw a ladder reaching to heaven with angels of God ascending and descending it. A voice then spoke to him and assured him of God's protection and confirmed the promise that the land on which he rested would be given to him and his descendants (*ibid.*, 28:10–22). Arising the next morning, Jacob erected a *maẓẓevah* ("sacred pillar") over which he poured oil as a thanksgiving sacrifice. The name of the place, which was formerly Luz, was now called Beth-El (i.e., "home of God"; *ibid.*, 5:19; 35:6, 15; 48:3; Josh. 18:13; according to Josh. 16:2, however, Beth-El was east of Luz).

Canaanite Beth-El continued to flourish in the Late Bronze Age (15th–14th centuries, B.C.E.), when it had commercial relations with Cyprus, indicated by the pottery finds. The remains of a house with rooms built around a large courtyard, plastered or stone floors, and masonry sewage channels belong to this period. A burnt layer indicates that the city was captured and burned down around the first half of the 13th century B.C.E. and resettled by an Israelite population (cf. Judg. 1:22ff.; Josh. 12:16). The city was on the southern border of Ephraim (Josh. 16:1–2; 18:13; I Chron. 7:28), but it is also listed as a Benjamite town (Josh. 18:22). There was a decline in the standard of living at Beth-El during the Israelite period, when the building became cruder, but a recovery is noticeable during the reigns of David and Solomon. The stormy epoch of the Judges is reflected in three building phases, while the relatively calm period of the United Monarchy is represented in a single building phase. The Tabernacle and the Ark were set there for a while, and in the conflict with Benjamin the Israelites prayed, fasted, and offered sacrifices there. They invoked the oracle of the Urim and the answer was provided by Phinehas (Judg. 20:18, 28). Deborah lived near the city (Judg. 4:5), and Samuel visited it periodically to judge the people (I Sam. 7:16). During Saul's war with the Philistines, he concentrated his forces in the mount of Beth-El (I Sam. 13:2).

With the division of the Monarchy, Beth-El passed into the possession of Jeroboam I. In order to wean his people away from making pilgrimages to Jerusalem, he erected one of the two principal shrines of his kingdom there (the other one was at Dan), with its own priesthood. The golden calf he set there was apparently designed to serve as a substitute for the cherubim in the Temple of Jerusalem. In the same spirit he ordered the 15th day of the eighth month to be celebrated instead of the Feast of Ingathering (Sukkot), which was observed on the 15th of the seventh month in Jerusalem as the main pilgrim festival (I Kings 12:29–33). This schism aroused vehement opposition among the prophets (I Kings 13) and caused a rift between Jeroboam and Ahijah the Shilonite (I Kings 14:7ff.). The biblical story of Hiel the Bethelite, who ignored the curse of Joshua and rebuilt Jericho on its ruins (I Kings 16:34), and that of the children of Beth-El who mocked Elisha (II Kings 2:23) may serve as proof of the strained relations existing between the inhabitants of Beth-El and the prophetic circles. This antagonism assumed its most acute form in the days of Amos (3:14; 4:4; etc.) and Hosea (10:15), both of whom call Beth-El Beth-Aven ("The House of Iniquity"; Amos 5:5; Hos. 4:15; cf. Jer. 48:13).

Beth-El and its surroundings were conquered by Abijah, king of Judah, in his war against Jeroboam (II Chron. 13:19), but it was returned to Israel not later than the reign of *Baasha and remained there until the fall of the kingdom. In the eighth century B.C.E., Beth-El was enclosed by a thick wall with towers that was repaired in the following century. Even after the destruction of Samaria (721 B.C.E.), priests still served at Beth-El (II Kings 17:28) until Josiah captured it, broke down its altar, destroyed its high place, and defiled the site (II Kings 23:15). Beth-El was destroyed during the Babylonian invasion (587 B.C.E.) and remained in ruins until the Persian period. In the time of Nehemiah, it was included in the territory of Judah (Ezra 2:28; Neh. 7:32). During the Hasmonean revolt, it was fortified by the Syrian general Bacchides (I Macc. 9:50). Beth-El is not mentioned again until its capture by Vespasian in 69 C.E. (Jos., Wars, 4:551). Coins found there date only from the period between 4 B.C.E. and its capture. In the Byzantine period, Beth-El was a village in the territory of "Aelia Capitolina" (Jerusalem), located 12 (Roman) miles from the capital "on the right, as one goes to Neapolis" (Eusebius, Onom. 192 etc.). The Christian traveler the Pilgrim of Bordeaux (333 C.E.) and the Christian writer Theodosius (c. 503 C.E.) also refer to it. According to Jerome (fifth century) a church was erected at Beth-El. On the Madaba Map "Luzah, which is also Beth-El" is also represented as a village north of Jerusalem. Very few remains of the Roman and Byzantine periods have been discovered at the site.

Bibliography: Y. Kaufmann, Religion, index; N. H. Tur-Sinai, *Ha-Lashon ve-ha-Sefer,* 2 (1950), 307; Alt, in: PJB, 21 (1925), 28ff.; Noth, in: PJB, 31 (1935), 7–29; Albright, in: BASOR, 55 (1934), 23–25; 56 (1934), 2–5; 57 (1935), 27–30; 74 (1939), 15–17; U. Cassuto, *La Questione della Genesi* (1934), 284–6, 291–7; Galling, in: ZDPV, 66 (1943), 140–55; 67 (1944), 21–43; H. H. Rowley, *From Joseph to Joshua* (1950), 19, 111, 138; Kelso, in: BASOR, 137 (1955), 5–10; 151 (1958), 3–8; 164 (1961), 5–19; Bright, Hist, index; Aharoni, Land, index.

[M.A.-Y.]

Figure 2. The story of Jacob's journey to Beth-El (Gen. 35) depicted in the Byzantine *Vienna Genesis,* c. sixth century. Upper register: left, Jacob receives God's command to go to Beth-El; right, he orders his household to put away their idols and purify themselves. Lower register: right, the flight to Beth-El; left, Jacob prays before the altar and hides the idols under the terebinth tree. Vienna, Austrian National Library, Theol. Gr. 31, fol. 13.

Figure 1. Ruins of ancient Beth-El, with the Arab village of Baytīn in the background. Photo Richard Cleave, Jerusalem.

BET ESHEL (Heb. בֵּית אֶשֶׁל), former Jewish settlement in southern Israel, southeast of Beersheba. It was founded in 1943 as one of the first three observation outposts in the Negev. The settlers, immigrants from Central Europe, lived as a kibbutz but intended to make Bet Eshel a moshav. They succeeded in growing grain crops with dry farming methods. A water well drilled at the spot enabled them also to grow vegetables and plant fruit orchards, thus proving the feasibility of agricultural settlement in the northern Negev. In the Israel War of Independence, Bet Eshel was besieged for over 10 months (December 1,

1947–October 21, 1948). It suffered heavy losses and was destroyed by continuous shelling. After the lifting of the siege, the settlers consented to leave and they established moshav Ha-Yogev in the Jezreel Valley. "Bet Eshel" means "House of the Tamarisk," this tree being characteristic of the Beersheba desert flora. [E.O.]

BET GARMU, family of bakers who supervised the preparation of the showbread *(leḥem ha-panim)* in the Temple (Shek. 5:1; Tosef., Yoma 2:5). Although the Mishnah states that the memory of the family was in disrepute because they would not teach others how to prepare the showbread (Yoma 38:11), other sources commend them. According to one *baraita,* "the sages sent for specialists from Alexandria of Egypt, who knew how to bake as well as they, but they did not know how to remove the loaves from the oven as well as the Bet Garmu," and as a result the bread became moldy (Yoma 38a). Bet Garmu agreed to return to work only after their remuneration was doubled. When asked why they refused to teach their art to others, they replied: "Our family knows that the Temple will be destroyed and perhaps an unworthy man will learn the process and use it for idolatrous worship" (*ibid.,* Tosef., loc. cit.). The same source praises the family for never using bread made of fine quality flour, lest they be suspected of eating the holy showbread.

Bibliography: A. Buechler, *Die Priester und der Cultus . . .* (1895), 52ff.; Schuerer, Gesch, 3 (1907[4]), 333; S. Klein, in *Leshonenu,* 1 (1928/29), 347. [I.G.]

BET GUVRIN (Heb. בֵּית גּוּבְרִין).

(1) A prominent city in the period of the Second Temple, located in the southern Shephelah. Ancient Bet Guvrin rose to importance after the destruction of Maresha (Marissa) by the Parthians in 40 B.C.E. Betabris, mentioned by Josephus (Wars, 4:447) as one of two villages taken by the Romans in 68 C.E. "right in the heart of Idumea," may possibly refer to Bet Guvrin. In 200 C.E. Septimus Severus conferred on it the privileges of a Roman city and called it Eleutheropolis ("the city of freemen"). The Midrash (Gen. R. 41:10) interprets Mt. Seir of the "Horites" (Gen. 14:6) as Eleutheropolis—an interpretation based on a play of words, since *Ḥori* means both "freeman" and "cave dweller" and the Bet Guvrin region abounds in large caves. Severus also granted the new city a large area encompassing the districts of Bethletepha, western Edom, and Hebron as far as En-Gedi, which made it the largest single region in Roman times, with over a hundred villages. Bet Guvrin also had its own system of dating and coinage. The wealth of its inhabitants is attested to by a mosaic pavement of a Roman house from the fourth century C.E. which depicts a hunting expedition, with representations of animals and the personifications of the four seasons.

The *tanna* Judah b. Jacob (Tosef., Oho. 18:15, 16) and the *amora* Jonathan (TJ, Meg. 1:11, 71b) resided at Bet Guvrin and there were still Jewish farmers in its vicinity in the fourth century. The place was regarded as being outstandingly fertile and the rabbis applied to it the verse from Isaac's blessing of Esau: "And the dew of the heaven above" (Gen. 27:39; Gen. R. 68:6). In matters of *halakhah,* Bet Guvrin was regarded as belonging to Edom and was therefore exempt from the commandments applying only to Ereẓ Israel (TJ, Dem. 2:1, 22c; TJ, Shev. 8:11, 38b). The talmudic region Darom (Gr. *Daromas*) was within the area of Bet Guvrin. An inscription found there records the

Caves in the Bet Guvrin region. Photo David Harris, Jerusalem.

donation of a column to the local synagogue in Byzantine times. Excavations have uncovered the mosaic pavements of two churches from the same period. In 1171, Benjamin of Tudela found three Jewish families living there. [M.A.-Y.]

(2) Kibbutz in the southern Judean Foothills, on the Ashkelon–Hebron road. Bet Guvrin is affiliated with Ha-Kibbutz ha-Me'uḥad. In 1949, after the large Arab village of Beit (Bayt) Jibrīn was abandoned by its inhabitants in the War of Independence, the present settlement was established. In 1968 most of its settlers were Israel-born, and its economy was mostly based on field crops, orchards, milch cattle, and poultry. [E.O.]

Bibliography: Neubauer, Géogr, 122–4; Y. Z. Horowitz, *Ereẓ Yisrael u-Shekhenoteha* (1923), s.v.; S. Klein (ed.), *Sefer ha-Yishuv* (1939), s.v.; Vincent, in: RB, 31 (1922), 259ff.; Abel, *ibid.,* 33 (1924), 593; Beyer, in: ZDPV, 54 (1931), 209ff.; Press, Ereẓ, s.v.; Z. Vilnai, *Israel Guide* (1966), 234ff.

BETH. For entries whose first word is "Beth," see under "Bet." For example, for Beth-Anath, see *Bet-Anath.

BET HA-EMEK (Heb. בֵּית הָעֵמֶק), kibbutz in northern Israel, northeast of Acre, affiliated with Iḥud ha-Kibbutzim. Bet ha-Emek was founded on Jan. 4, 1949, by young survivors of the Holocaust from Hungary and Slovakia. Later, immigrant youth from England and Holland joined the settlement to form the majority of its members. The kibbutz has a number of cultural institutions set up with contributions from England and other countries. In addition to highly intensive, fully irrigated farming, Bet ha-Emek opened an olive-pickling plant. A nearby mound is supposed to be identical with biblical Beth-Emek (Josh. 19:27), which belonged to the tribe of Asher and was also inhabited in the time of the Talmud. The village ʿAmqa, abandoned by its Arab inhabitants during the War of Independence (1948), preserved the ancient name; and antique columns, capitals, ashlars, etc. were used in the construction of its dwellings. In 1970 Bet ha-Emek numbered 286 inhabitants. [E.O.]

BET HA-LEVI (Heb. בֵּית הַלֵּוִי), moshav in central Israel in the Ḥefer Plain, founded in 1945 by settlers from Bulgaria. Its economy was mainly based on citrus plantations, garden crops, and milch cattle. The village bears the name of *Judah Halevi. In 1970 Bet ha-Levi numbered 225 inhabitants.

[E.O.]

BET ḤANAN (Heb. בֵּית חָנָן), moshav in central Israel, west of Nes Ẓiyyonah, founded in 1930 by settlers from Bulgaria. Its economy was based on citrus plantations, poultry, milch cattle, and other farm products. The village's name resembles the former Arabic denomination of the site "Wadi Ḥanīn." In 1970 Bet Ḥanan numbered 374 inhabitants.

[E.O.]

BETHANY (Heb. **Bet Aniyya, Bet Ḥananyah**), a village about 1¾ mi. (3 km.) E. of Jerusalem, frequently mentioned in the Gospels (Mark 11:1; 14:3; Matt. 21:17; Luke 19:29; etc.). According to Christian tradition, it was the home of the sisters Mary and Martha, with whom Jesus lodged, and the scene of the resurrection of their brother Lazarus after he had been interred for four days (John 11). At the end of the fourth century, the Byzantines built a church and adjoining monastery at Bethany which was renovated in the following century. It was named after Lazarus, and from this comes the Arabic name of the village, al-ʿAzariyya. During the Crusader period, the church was regarded as the property of the Church of the Holy Sepulcher, and it underwent extensive alterations. It was destroyed in the 16th century and a Greek monastery stands in its place. The ancient site of the church was apparently near the present Catholic monastery Raʾs al-Shayyāḥ. Remains of ancient buildings and tombs dating from the period of the Second Temple and later have been uncovered there. A cistern from the Second Temple period, which served as a shrine in Byzantine times, has Christian-Greek graffiti on its plastered walls. It was discovered in 1949–53 together with oil presses, cisterns, and numerous tombs of later periods.

Bibliography: G. Dalman, *Sacred Sites and Ways* (1935), index; Benoit and Boismard, in: RB, 58 (1951), 200–50; S. J. Saller, *Excavations at Bethany* (1957).

[M.A.-Y.]

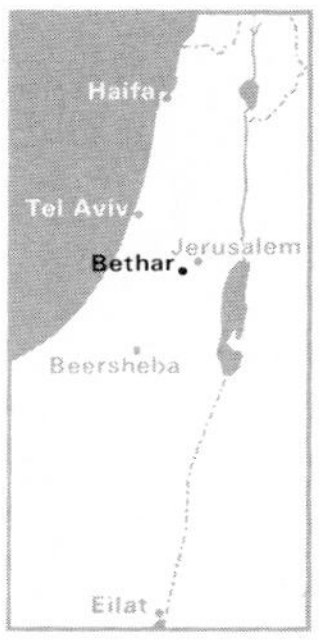

BETHAR (**Betar,** Heb. בֵּיתָר), *Bar Kokhba's last stronghold in his war against Rome. It is identified with Khirbat al-Yahūd ("the Jewish ruin"), an area of ruins on the summit of a steep hill, northwest of the Arab village of Battīr which has preserved the ancient name. Bethar is mentioned in the Septuagint in a verse added after Joshua 15:59 (Βαιθηρ) together with several other cities of Judah, including Beth-Lehem. It also appears in a manuscript of the Septuagint (Version "A") after Beth-Shemesh in the list of levitical cities in I Chronicles 6:44. The various transliterations of the name in the Septuagint and in Eusebius (*Historia Ecclesiastica* 4:6)—Bitter, Better—seem to indicate that it was originally called Bet-Ter (בֵּית־תֵּר). In aggadic literature the name has been preserved in the Aramaic Bei-Ter (בֵּי־תֵר).

Bethar lies on a spur 7 mi. (11 km.) southwest of Jerusalem; it is bounded by the Sorek Valley on the east, north, and west. The upper part of the hill, c. 2,300ft. (700 m.) above the level of the Mediterranean, constitutes the tongue of a plateau, sloping gradually to the north to the steep drop of the Sorek Brook (c. 490 ft. (150 m.)) above the bottom of the valley. The northern half of the spur was a sort of garden suburb of the ancient town and contains few building remains. A spring, the source of water of ancient Bethar and at present of the Arab village of Battīr, flows from a rock southeast of the spur. Part of a defaced Latin inscription on the rock near the mouth of the spring mentions three of the Roman legions which participated in the siege of Bethar. South of the ancient settlement is a fosse about 16½ ft. (5 m.) deep which cuts the narrow saddle between the top of the spur and the main ridge. The rock faces north of the fosse are smoothed to a steep slope and the remains of a wall are traceable above it.

The remains of the upper wall encompass an area of about 8.7 acres and only a small section in the northwest of the city has survived in the form of a regular construction (to a height of about 10 ft. (3 m.)). A gate, about 30 ft. (9 m.) wide, which was probably the city's main gate ("Water Gate") stood near the northeastern corner of the wall. A short distance to the northeast, a narrow postern is still visible, close to a strong square wall tower; the area around it is called Bāb al-Madīna ("City Gate") by the local Arabs. This tower belongs to the late system of fortifications (from Bar Kokhba's time) and was built over the ruins of a much larger square tower from the Herodian period (first century B.C.E.–first century C.E.). The continuation of the wall as it turns to the west and south is defended by a square tower with a huge stone revetment, and semicircular bastions—one single and two pairs. A third gate, 13½ ft. (4 m.) wide, was found between the southern pair of bastions, whose

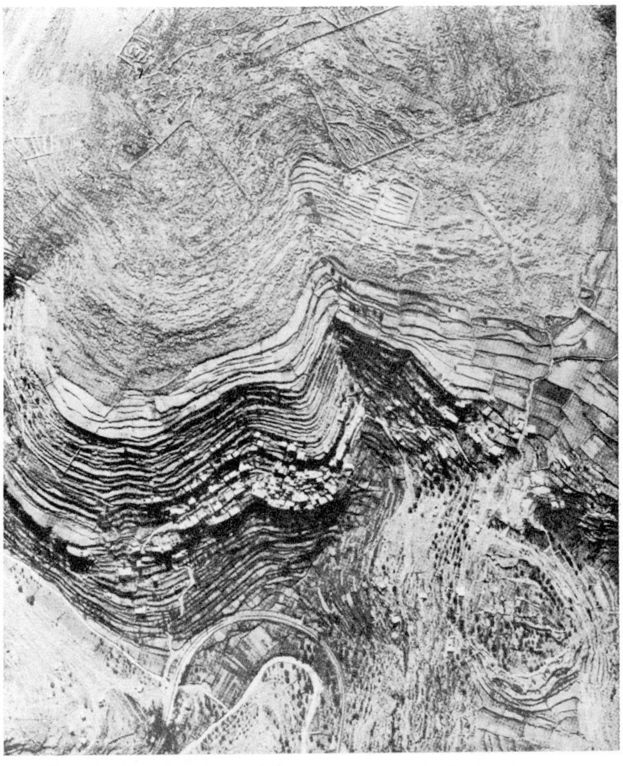

Aerial view of Bethar, showing the rectangular camps of the Roman legions in the upper part of the picture and the fortress in the lower right-hand corner. Jerusalem, Mosad Bialik.

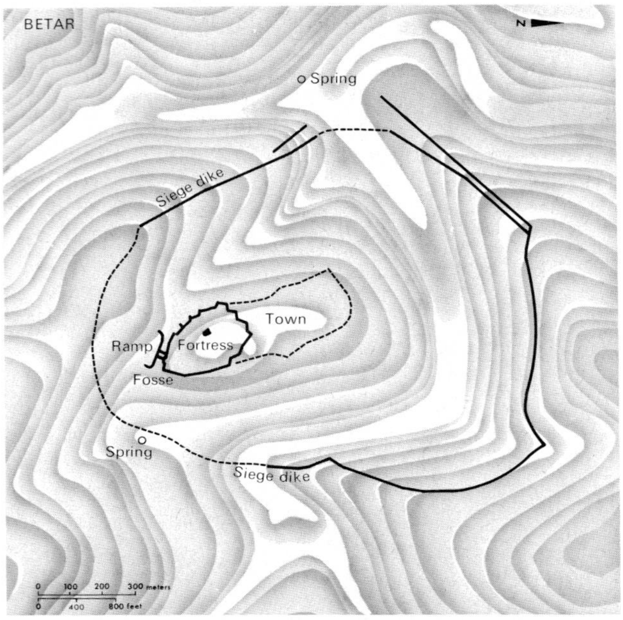

Map of the fortress of Bethar. In: Ministry of Labor and the Bialik Institute, *Atlas of Israel*, 1956.

foundations were defended by revetments with outward batter. Part of the fortifications from the First Temple period, a square tower, was discovered near the northern pair of bastions, with a wall from the same period between them. Bethar's southern defenses survive only in its eastern sector where a semicircular bastion defended by a square revetment still stands. The Romans appear to have attempted to storm Bethar from this side; a siege dam was made in the fosse opposite the bastion. Little has remained of Bethar's wall on the eastern side; in its southern sector, the remains of a wall at a lower level have been dated to the Herodian period. Within the wall of Bethar, no building remains are visible on the surface.

Bethar seems to have been inhabited in the days of the Israelite conquest and settlement and also in the First Temple period, as is indicated by a number of finds from graves. Settlement apparently continued without interruption also in the Second Temple period and up to the end of the Bar Kokhba War.

The inhabitants of ancient Bethar derived their livelihood from the sale of their garden produce in the Jerusalem market as do the fellahin of the Arab village of Battīr today. The relationship between the ruling classes of Jerusalem and the naive villagers of Bethar is indicated in an anecdote cited in several sources according to which the Jerusalemites stripped the people of Bethar of their fields by deceitful means (Lam. R. 2:5).

After abandoning Jerusalem, Bar Kokhba and his army withdrew to Bethar where they were besieged for several months during the summer of 135 C.E. The siege ended, according to tradition, on the Ninth of Av. The Romans surrounded the besieged city with a circumvallation (דָּיֵק, "rampart") whose remains can be traced at several points. The reference to the men "who went down to the rampart of Bethar" (Tosef., Yev. 14:15) may apply to this time. Traces of the fortified camps in which the besieging troops were quartered may also be seen. [E.H.]

Modern Period. In Israel's 1949 armistice agreement with Jordan, most of the village, together with the historical mound, remained on the Jordanian side, but the railway line at the bottom of the gorge and a narrow strip of land with a number of houses and gardens on its southern side were included in Israel territory. A certain area with a few dozen inhabitants belonged to Israel from 1948 but from 1967 the bulk of the village, with 1,445 inhabitants, became part of the territory under Israel administration. [E.O.]

Bibliography: J. K. Sepp, *Jerusalem und das Heilige Land,* 1 (1873), 647ff.; Zickermann, in: ZDPV, 29 (1906), 51ff.; Schuerer, Gesch, 1 (1901[3]), 693ff.; Carroll, in: AASOR, 5 (1925), 77ff.; Schulten, in: ZDPV, 56 (1933), 180 ff.; Reifenberg, in: *Archaeology,* 3 (1950), 40ff.

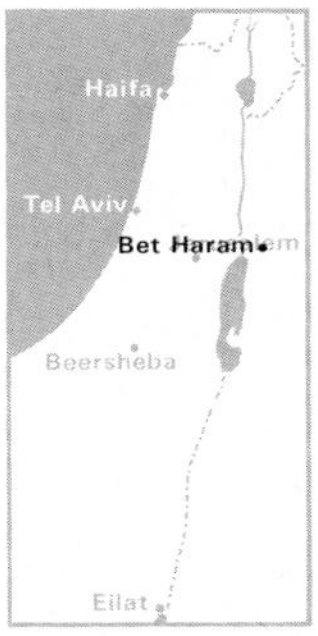

BET(H)-HARAM (or **Haran;** Heb. בֵּית הָרָם, הָרָן), town in the Jordan Valley, N. of the Dead Sea, allotted by Moses to the tribe of Gad and included in the list of its cities (Num. 32:36; Josh. 13:27). It is possibly mentioned in the Egyptian Execration Texts of the 18th century B.C.E. In the Talmud, Beth-Haram is identified with Bet ha-Ramta (TJ, Shev. 9:2, 38d; cf. Shab. 26a) which is also mentioned by Eusebius (Onom. 48:14) as Betharamphtha. *Herod Antipas, who fortified the city, called it Livias, in honor of the empress Livia, and also Julias, as soon as Livia became a member of the Julian imperial family. In 56 C.E. *Agrippa II received Livias and its district from the emperor Nero (Jos., Wars, 2:59, 168, 252; Jos., Ant., 18:27; 20:159). Beth-Haram was the headquarters of a region as late as the Byzantine period. Springs and groves are reported to have existed in its vicinity. The Hellenistic and Roman cities are situated on Tell al-Rāma, in the lower Jordan Valley, which has preserved the ancient name; the Israelite city has been located by Nelson Glueck at Tell Iktanū nearby.

Bibliography: EM, s.v.; Glueck, in: AASOR, 25–28 (1951), 389–95; Press, Ereẓ, 1 (1951), 82; Aharoni, Land, index.

[M.A.-Y.]

BET ḤARODON, locality 3 mi. (5 km.) S. of Jerusalem. It was on the road leading to Bukei'a in the wilderness where the he-goat that was allotted to *Azazel in the Temple ritual on the Day of Atonement was pushed to its death from a cliff (Yoma 4:2ff.; Yoma 66bff.). It has been identified with Khirbat Ḥarazān near the wilderness of Ẓuq. Bet Ḥarodon is also mentioned (in the form Ḥarodona) in a marriage contract from 117 C.E., written in Aramaic, found in the *Murabbaʿat cave.

Bibliography: Avi-Yonah, Geog, 104, 226; P. Benoit et al., *Les Grottes de Murabbaʿat* (1961), 111. [M.A.-Y.]

BETHBASI, locality in Judea identified with Khirbat Beit Bassa south of *Bethlehem where *Simeon b. Mattathias the Hasmonean was besieged by the Syrian general *Bacchides. Simeon managed to raise the siege by burning Bacchides' war engines (I Macc. 9:62ff.). Bethbasi is also mentioned in the Copper Scroll from *Murabbaʿat.

Bibliography: Abel, in: RB, 34 (1925), 211ff.; P. Benoit, et al., *Les Grottes de Murabbaʿat* (1961), no. 24. [M.A.-Y.]

BET ḤERUT (Heb. בֵּית חֵרוּת; "Home of Freedom"), moshav in central Israel, in the Ḥefer Plain, founded in 1933. The settlers, mostly from East and Central Europe, transformed their village in 1966 from a regular moshav into a moshav shittufi. Its economy was based on citrus plantations, garden crops, and milch cattle. In 1970 Bet Ḥerut numbered 290 inhabitants.

[E.O.]

BET HILLEL (Heb. בֵּית הִלֵּל), moshav in northern Israel, in the Ḥuleh Valley, founded in 1940 as one of the settlements then being established on the periphery of the then Ḥuleh swamp. It suffered heavy damage in the War of Independence (1948) and was subsequently rebuilt by a group of demobilized soldiers. The population was composed of immigrants from Eastern Europe and other areas. Its economy was based on milch cattle, field crops, and fruit orchards. The settlement was named after Hillel *Joffe.

[E.O.]

BET HILLEL AND BET SHAMMAI, two schools of exposition of the Oral Law, named after *Hillel and *Shammai who lived at the end of the first century B.C.E. and the beginning of the first century C.E. These two schools existed from the time of these two sages, their founders, until the second generation after the destruction of the Second Temple, i.e., until the beginning of the second century C.E. Tannaitic literature, the *halakhah*, the halakhic Midrashim, and the *aggadah* record the numerous controversies which took place between Bet Shammai and Bet Hillel. These debates comprise the principal content of the Oral Law in the last two to three generations of the Second Temple period. Very little is extant of the teachings of individual scholars as they are frequently cited as part of the overall teachings of Bet Shammai and Bet Hillel. Many of the *halakhot* and tannaitic controversies dating from the generation of Jabneh (c. 70 C.E.) are probably, and a large number are explicitly, based on the views of Bet Hillel which were adopted as the *halakhah* in opposition to those of Bet Shammai (see below), while numerous anonymous *halakhot* are extant which may once have been the subject of dispute between Bet Shammai and Bet Hillel.

Their controversies are concerned with four areas. (1) Halakhic decisions based on judgment and on logical reasoning. For example, in discussing the order of the blessings in the *Kiddush* for Sabbaths and festivals, Bet Shammai declares that the blessing is to be said first over the day (i.e., the Sabbath or festival) and then over the wine; whereas Bet Hillel maintains that the blessing is to be said first over the wine and then over the day (Ber. 8:1). Again, Bet Shammai contends that a woman may not remarry on the evidence of a "mere voice" (i.e., the voice of someone who, testifying to the death of the husband, cannot be identified), while Bet Hillel holds that she may remarry on the basis of such evidence (Yev. 122a). (2) Determining the "fences" around prohibitions, and the extent to which a prohibition is to be applied. For example, with regard to spiced oil, Bet Shammai declares it liable to tithing by one who buys it from an **am ha-areẓ* (a person who in his ignorance is not scrupulous in observing the laws concerning priestly and levitical dues), whereas Bet Hillel exempts it (Dem. 1:3). If one slaughters with a scythe with a forward movement (i.e., not against the serrated edge), Bet Shammai maintains that the slaughtering is invalid, while Bet Hillel declares it valid (Ḥul. 1:2). (3) Halakhic Midrashim. For example, Bet Shammai maintains that in the evening a man should recline (on his side) and recite the *Shema*, and in the morning he should stand, according to the verse (Deut. 6:7), "When thou liest down, and when thou risest up." Bet Hillel, however, declares that a man should recite it as it suits him, since it states *(ibid.)*, "When thou walkest by the way." Why then does the biblical verse state, "When thou liest down, and when thou risest up?" This means at the times when people customarily lie down and at the time they rise up (Ber. 1:3). Again, Bet Shammai say: A man should not divorce his wife unless he finds some unchastity in her, since it says: 'because he hath found some unseemly thing in her" (Deut. 24:1), but Bet Hillel say: even if she has merely spoilt his food, since it says: "because he hath found something unseemly in her" (i.e., anything the husband personally finds unfitting) (Git. 9:10). (4) *Aggadah*, religious philosophy, and ethics. For example, Bet Shammai asserts that it were better if man had not been created at all, whereas Bet Hillel maintains that it is better for man to have been created than not (Er. 13b).

Only three controversies between Hillel and Shammai themselves have been preserved, but more than 350 are reported between Bet Hillel and Bet Shammai, most of which are in the *Zera'im, Mo'ed, Nashim*, and *Tohorot* sections of the Mishnah. They deal with personal life, with blessings and prayers, the separation of priestly dues and tithes, marriage and divorce, levitical cleanness and abstinence, and in a very few instances with sacrifices and the priestly service, and with civil and capital cases. In some of these controversies Shammai himself disputes the opinions of both Bet Shammai and Bet Hillel (Eduy. 1:7, 8, 10, 11). In several instances where the view opposed to that of Bet Shammai is quoted anonymously *(tanna kamma)* or in the name of the sages (Ber. 6:5; Dem. 3:1), the version is late as this is how the opinion of Bet Hillel was recorded after it had been adopted as the definitive ruling. Proof of this is found in a number of cases where the view of the *tanna kamma* or of the sages quoted in a Mishnah occurs in a *baraita* as that of Bet Hillel (cf. Ter. 4:3, with Tosef., Ter. 5:3, et al.). Generally, Bet Shammai is mentioned before Bet Hillel, and tradition sees in this an expression of the latter's humility (Er. 13b).

Many of the controversies between the two schools took place in Second Temple times. There is, for example, the argument whether on a festival hands could be laid on burnt and peace offerings, a subject on which Hillel and Shammai themselves held conflicting views (**Semikhah* on Sacrifices). A dispute concerning this *halakhah* took place in the forecourt of the Temple between Hillel and the pupils of Bet Shammai, and between them and those of Bet Hillel. On this question, the *halakhah* was decided during the existence of the Second Temple (Ḥag. 2:3; Tosef., Ḥag. 2:10–12; and parallel passages). During this period Bet Shammai once achieved ascendancy over Bet Hillel in the Temple Chamber of Hananiah b. Hezekiah b. Garon with the adoption of the "Eighteen Measures"—restrictive decrees that increased the barrier between Jews and non-Jews (TJ, Shab. 1:7, 3c; and parallel passages). This event is believed by several scholars to have taken place shortly before the destruction of the Second Temple. The early date of other controversies is evident from the conflicting views of *tannaim* living in the period of the destruction of the Second Temple in formulating the disputes between Bet Shammai and Bet Hillel (Tosef., Pe'ah 3:2). There are, however, controversies about problems raised by the destruction of the Temple, e.g., procedure at the time of removal of **ma'aser sheni* (Ma'as. Sh. 5:7).

Very little is known about the identity of the pupils of Hillel and Shammai. A *baraita* states that "Hillel the Elder had eighty disciples . . . the greatest of them was *Jonathan b. Uzziel, the least *Johanan b. Zakkai" (Suk. 28a). None of the teachings of Jonathan b. Uzziel has been preserved, and while Johanan b. Zakkai's statements reflect the outlook of Bet Hillel, it is difficult, as a matter of chronology, to assume that he studied under Hillel himself. Several of Shammai's pupils are known, most of them from the period of the Second Temple, their connection with Bet Shammai being stressed in tannaitic literature. They are

Bava b. Buta, a contemporary of Hillel (Tosef., Ḥag. 2:11; and parallel passages); Dostai of Kefar Yatmah who transmitted a tradition he had heard from Shammai (Or. 2:5); Joezer, master of the Temple, who once put a question to Gamaliel the Elder in the Temple court (Or. 2:12); and Johanan b. ha-Ḥoranit of the generation of the destruction of the Temple (Tosef., Suk. 2:3). Sometimes "the elders of" Bet Shammai and Bet Hillel are mentioned (Suk. 2:7; Tosef. RH 4:11; Men. 41b et al.). According to a *genizah* fragment of *Sifrei Zuta* on *Ḥukkat* (*Tarbiz*, 1 (1930), 52), Bet Shammai had Idumean pupils, their halakhic statements corresponding to those of R. Judah who taught the view of Eliezer b. Hyrcanus *"ha-Shammuti"* (Men. 18a). According to Rashi, Nid. 7b, this refers to the fact that R. Eliezer was excommunicated, but this interpretation is inacceptable. As Tos. *in loc* points out, it means "a Shammaite" (cf. also Rashi to Shab. 132b, where he gives this as an alternative). Eleazar b. Hananiah, the general for Idumea in the Jewish War against the Romans (Jos., Wars, 2:566), also followed the line of Shammai (cf. Mekh., Ba-Ḥodesh, 7 with Beẓah 16a).

The circumstance that gave rise to the two schools is given in a tannaitic tradition: "At first there were no controversies in Israel . . . When anyone had need of a *halakhah* he went to the Great Sanhedrin . . . If they had heard (such a *halakhah*), they informed him of it, but if not, they decided the matter by taking a vote . . . From there the *halakhah* would spread in Israel. With the increase in the pupils of Shammai and Hillel who had not sufficiently 'ministered to sages' (i.e. inadequately studied the Torah), controversy increased in Israel" (Tosef., Sanh. 7:1; and parallel passages). Even if the deficient learning of the pupils of Shammai and Hillel is ascribed to various historical factors, such as the dissolution of the Sanhedrin under Herod, or the Sadducean majority in the Sanhedrin which precluded any halakhic decisions being submitted to it by the sages, it is doubtful whether this tannaitic tradition adequately explains the numerous controversies which spanned almost a century. A more likely explanation is in terms of the expansion and crystallization of the *halakhah* involving a clash between different opinions and approaches in interpreting earlier traditions and in creating new *halakhot*. Tannaitic tradition presumably saw in the two views a legitimate expression of conflicting opinions: "Both of them are the words of the living God" (TJ, Ber. 1:7, 3b). It was reasonably permitted to follow the views either of Bet Shammai or of Bet Hillel but "a man who wishes to impose additional restrictions upon himself by adopting the stricter practices of Bet Shammai as well as the stricter practices of Bet Hillel, can be characterized by the verse 'the fool walketh in darkness' " (Eccles. 2:14; Tosef., Eduy. 2:3). It was furthermore stated that "although one school prohibited what the other permitted, or forbade what the other declared eligible, nonetheless Bet Shammai did not refrain from marrying women from [the families of] Bet Hillel, nor Bet Hillel from [the families of] Bet Shammai . . . Nor did either refrain from borrowing the utensils of the other for the preparation of food under conditions of levitical cleanness" (Yev. 1:4). In all this there is no indication that the controversies originated from "insufficiently ministering to sages," but rather have their basis in the process whereby the *halakhah* was created.

Tannaitic tradition emphasizes that Bet Shammai adopted the stricter, Bet Hillel the more lenient view. The Mishnah (Eduy. 4) enumerates 23 (or 24) of their controversies that differ from the others in that they are "instances of Bet Shammai's lenient and of Bet Hillel's restrictive rulings." To these, various sages added a further 17 examples *(ibid.)*. There are others concerning which the Talmud and the commentators try to find an explanation as to why they too were not similarly cited. The total of all of these is about 50. Of Bet Shammai's restrictive rulings the bulk extends the application of a prohibition, Bet Shammai, adopting the stricter view (i.e., the wider application of the prohibition). Bet Hillel usually adopts the more lenient approach.

Many scholars have sought to define the basic principles underlying the divergences between the two schools. The generally accepted explanation is that they reflect the individual traits of their founders, of Hillel who was gentle and kind, and of Shammai who was stern and short-tempered. But this is inadequate, particularly since only a few controversies took place between Hillel and Shammai personally. Another interpretation regards their disputes as a social and economic conflict, holding that Bet Shammai belonged to the upper or middle landed classes, whereas the sages of Bet Hillel were from the lower strata of society with their respective views reflecting the needs and life of these strata. However, this point of view has been attacked by some scholars on the grounds that there is scanty proof that Bet Shammai belonged to the wealthy middle class. It is moreover difficult to accept the interpretation given to the *halakhot* listed by these scholars. It is similarly difficult to accept theories such as that which attributes the difference to the divergent halakhic outlook, conception, and apprehension of the two schools, with Bet Shammai adopting a uniform, systematic approach to the *halakhah*, as against the particularized, heterogeneous viewpoint of Bet Hillel. The weakness of these theories is that they only explain an insignificant number of the controversies. Nor are the explanations suggested the only feasible ones, for these particular instances. Various factors and traditions, as well as different approaches and tendencies, probably combined to produce the divergent views. Difficult though it is to find the social or conceptual bases for the rise of the two schools, a certain line is evident in their homiletical exegesis of biblical passages and in their discussions of many *halakhot*. Bet Shammai tends in the former to the plain and sometimes even to the narrow, literal interpretation of a verse, as opposed to the wider significance assigned by Bet Hillel. Because of the limited number of controversies involving the exegesis of biblical verses it is impossible to ascertain what relation their disputes bear to the seven exegetical principles laid down or formulated by Hillel (Tosef., Sanh. 7:11). Insofar as the *halakhah* is concerned it is evident in many cases that the view of Bet Hillel is characteristic of theoretical *halakhah* which differentiates between principles of jurisprudence and that they decided in *halakhah* in accordance with such principles, in contrast to the view of Bet Shammai which is characteristic of the literal and even the conservative approach, conservative not in the sociological sense but in creativity and in halakhic innovation (cf. Pe'ah 6:1; Eduy. 4:1 and5; Er. 1:2; Beẓah 1:2).

The Mishnah reports several instances in which Bet Hillel retracted its opinion and agreed with that of Bet Shammai (Yev. 15:3; Eduy. 1:12, et al.) But there is not a single instance in which Bet Shammai retracted and agreed with Bet Hillel except once (Ter. 5:4), when it is stated that "after they agreed," i.e., Bet Shammai with Bet Hillel. In matters relating to the Temple the *halakhah* was decided according to the opinion of Bet Hillel on only one occasion (Tosef., Ḥag, 2:11, cf. Pes. 8:8; Tosef., *ibid.*, 7:13, et al.). At Jabneh, in the generation after the destruction of the Temple, Bet Hillel gained the ascendancy (first–second century), whereupon the *halakhah* was laid down according to Bet Hillel. It was then stated that the possibility of making a choice between the two schools applied only "before a *bat kol [heavenly voice] went forth, but once a bat kol went forth, the halakhah was always according to Bet Hillel, and whoever acted contrary to the views of Bet Hillel deserved death. It was taught: A bat kol went forth and declared, 'The halakhah is according to the words of Bet Hillel.' Where did the bat kol go forth? . . . At Jabneh" (TJ, Ber. 1:7, 3b; and parallel passages). The determination of the halakhah according to Bet Hillel was probably not accomplished in a single act but was rather a process that continued during the entire Jabneh period, commencing with Johanan b. Zakkai, soon after the destruction of the Temple (70) and ending with the death of Rabban Gamaliel before the Bar Kokhba war (c. 135). This process was strongly opposed by the last adherents of Bet Shammai (Tosef., Eduy. 1:1; Tosef., Yev. 1:9–10; TJ, Shev. 4:5, 35b). In the amoraic period the halakhah of Bet Hillel was accepted in the schools of the amoraim who declared: "The opinion of Bet Shammai when it conflicts with that of Bet Hillel is no Mishnah" (Ber. 36b, et al.). Several halakhot were, however, decided according to Bet Shammai (see Ber. 51b ff.; Tos. to Suk. 3a, s.v. de-amar), and traces of the decision of Bet Shammai are to be found in various passages in tannaitic and even amoraic literature. The Kabbalah and following it Ḥasidism explained the differences between the two schools in terms of their philosophies: Bet Shammai has its origin in gevurah ("might") and Bet Hillel in ḥesed ("mercy"); in the future (i.e., the world to come) the halakhah will be according to Bet Shammai (Zohar, Ra'aya Meheimna 3:245a; Moses b. Menahem (Graft) Sefer va-Yakhel Moshe 2 (1699)).

Bibliography: A. Schwarz, *Die Erleichterungen der Schammaiten und die Erschwerungen der Hilleliten* (1893); Bacher, Tann 1 (1903²), 11–22; Buechler, in: *Sefer . . . M. Bloch* (1905), 21–30 (Heb. part); Weiss, Dor, 1 (1904⁴), 167–76; M. Guttmann, *Zur Einleitung in die Halacha*, 1 (1909), 36ff.; D. Hoffmann, *Ha-Mishnah ha-Rishonah* (1913), 12–59; Frankel, Mishnah, 47–57, 94; L. Ginzberg, *Perushim ve-Ḥiddushim ba-Yerushalmi*, 1 (1941), 146–7, 152–60; idem, *On Jewish Law and Lore* (1962), 88–124; Sonne, in: *Louis Ginzberg Jubilee Volume* (1945), 275–91; Guttmann, in: HUCA, 28 (1957), 115–26; Gilat, in: *Bar-Ilan Sefer ha-Shanah*, 4–5 (1967), 104–16; Z. Finkelstein, *The Pharisees* (1962³), index s.v. *Hillel and Shammai*. [SH.S.]

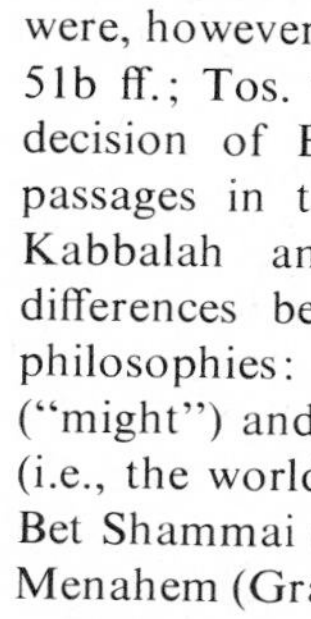

BETHLEHEM (Beth-Lehem; Heb. בֵּית לֶחֶם; Arab. بيت لحم), city in Judah located five mi. (eight km.) S. of Jerusalem. Bethlehem may be mentioned in the *Tell el-Amarna letters (14th century B.C.E.) as a city in the territory of Jerusalem (*Bit ilu Nin. Ib*=the house of the god Ninib=Lahamu?; EA, 290; however, the meaning of the ideogram *Nin. Ib* is not certain). Tradition placed the tomb of *Rachel in the vicinity of Ephrath/Beth-Lehem where Jacob is said to have buried her (Gen. 35:19). Together with its neighboring cities (I Chron. 2:51, 54), Beth-Lehem became the center of the tribe of *Judah and was settled by an important clan claiming descent from Perez, son of Tamar and Judah, among whose descendants were Boaz and Jesse the father of David. In the period of the Judges, the fields of Beth-Lehem were the scene of the idyll of Ruth and Boaz as related in the Book of Ruth. The levite youth in the story of Micah and the graven image (Judg. 17:7), as well as the levite's concubine mentioned in Judges 19, came from this city. *David and some of his warrior-kinsmen, sons of Zeruiah, were also born at Beth-Lehem, and it was there that Samuel anointed David king (I Sam. 16:1–13). The sacrificial act performed by Samuel on that occasion suggests that Beth-Lehem may have been a center for the worship of the

Figure 1. Aerial view of the Church of the Nativity. Photo Government Press Office, Tel Aviv.

Lord. At the end of Saul's reign, Beth-Lehem was occupied for a time by a Philistine garrison. The story of David's men bringing him water from the "well of Beth-Lehem, that was by the gate" (II Sam. 23:15) implies that it was even then a fortified city. Some of the assassins of Gedaliah son of Ahikam, Nebuchadnezzar's governor in Judea after the destruction of the Temple, came from the neighborhood of Beth-Lehem (Jer. 40:8); the remnants of his followers withdrew to the same region before their flight to Egypt (Jer. 41:16–17). With the return from Babylonia, the exiles from Beth-Lehem went back to their city (Ezra 2:21; Neh. 7:26), and Jews inhabited the city until the time of Bar Kokhba. In 135 C.E. a Roman garrison was stationed there to root out the remnants of Bar Kokhba's army (Lam. R. 1:15). Later a gentile population resided in Bethlehem and erected a temple to Adonis (Tammuz) in a grove at the edge of the city (Jerome, Epistle 58 to Paulinus).

On the basis of Micah 5:1, the early Christians identified Jesus' birthplace with Bethlehem (Matt. 2:1, 5; Luke 2:4, 15; John 7:42). The location of this event in a cave east of the city is first mentioned by Justin Martyr (155–160) and by the time of Origen (third century) the site of the cave already corresponded to its present position. At the beginning of the reign of Constantine, his mother *Helena erected a Christian church over the cave. The church was destroyed during the Samaritan uprising against Byzantine rule (529): it was rebuilt by Justinian in the form that it has kept to the present time. On the facade of the building, over the entrance, were depicted the birth of Jesus and his adoration by the kings of the East. Because this picture portrays people in Oriental costume, the Persians are said to have spared the building when they captured Bethlehem in 614. In the fifth century *Jerome settled in Bethlehem and built a monastery there. In preparing his Latin translation of the Bible, the basis of the Vulgate, he was assisted by Jewish scholars who apparently lived in villages in the neighborhood of the city. The grotto in which he is reputed to have lived is still to be seen under the Church of the Nativity. Further evidence of the resumption of Jewish settlement in the hills of Jerusalem is also found in an extant account of the Persian campaign, according to which the invaders were aided by Jewish inhabitants of the hill country.

In the early Arab period Bethlehem suffered no damage. The city fell to Tancred's forces during the First Crusade without fighting. Baldwin I and II, the crusader kings of Jerusalem, were crowned in the church of Bethlehem. The crusaders built a fort in the city that was demolished in 1489

Figure 2. Aerial view of Bethlehem. The Church of the Nativity is marked 1 in the upper right-hand section of the photograph. Photo Government Press Office, Tel Aviv.

during clashes between the Christians of Bethlehem and the Muslims of Hebron. *Benjamin of Tudela visited the city (c. 1160) and found 12 Jewish dyers there. The church of Bethlehem remained in Christian hands during the rule of the Mamluks and the Turks, even though the Muslim rulers oppressed the Christian minority. The Christians continually reduced the size of the entrance to the church for security reasons, so that by now it is just a low and narrow opening. From time to time, the Christian rulers in Europe concerned themselves with the maintenance and repair of the church. The conflicts between the various Christian communities in Bethlehem caused damage to the church and served to motivate international friction; the theft of the Silver Star from the church in 1847 was one of the factors behind the outbreak of the Crimean War. In the middle of the 19th century, the Turkish authorities determined the division of the church among the various Christian communities and the order of their ceremonies, according to previous tradition; this decision has been observed, almost without amendment, to the present.

[M.A.-Y.]

Modern Bethlehem. Until 1948, Bethlehem was a city with a Christian majority. Of its 8,000 inhabitants in 1947, 75% were Christians and the rest Muslims; this ratio, however, subsequently changed as a result of the influx of Arab refugees from Israel who settled there. During the Six-Day War (1967), Bethlehem surrendered to the Israel army without a fight. In the 1967 census taken by Israel authorities, the town of Bethlehem proper numbered 14,439 inhabitants, its 7,790 Muslim inhabitants represented 53.9% of the population, while the Christians of various denominations numbered 6,231 or 46.1%. The 1,874 inhabitants of the refugee camp, lying within the municipal confines, raised the percentage of Muslim citizens to 58.2%. However, the three townships of Bethlehem, Beit (Bayt) Saḥur (the traditional Field of Ruth), and Beit (Bayt) Jala can be considered as a unit, as in 1967 they formed a continuous built-up area and a social and economic entity. Their total population amounted to 27,000, of whom 14,400 were Christians, constituting a 55% majority. The main Christian denominations are the Latins (Roman Catholics) and the Greek Orthodox. Other communities with over 100 adherents include the Syrian-Orthodox, the Syrian-Catholics, and the Melkites. There are also Protestants of various denominations, Maronites, and Armenians. Throughout most of its history, Bet (Bayt) Jālā was an exclusively Christian town. It has numerous churches and Christian institutions, including the Greek Orthodox St. Nicholas Church, the Catholic Patriarchate's Seminary, and a Lutheran secondary school. Nearby is the Cremisan Monastery of the Salesian fathers.

Figure 4. The Grotto of the Nativity. The star marking the traditional spot on which Jesus was born is inscribed *Hic de Virgine Maria Jesus Christus Natus Est.* ("Here Jesus Christ was born of the Virgin Mary.") The 17 lamps above, which burn day and night, belong to the Latin, Greek, and Armenian communities. Photo Government Press Office, Tel Aviv.

The Bethlehem town group has close economic and social ties with Jerusalem. In 1968 farming, trade, and tourism continued to constitute the mainstay of Bethlehem's economy. Inhabitants of the town own olive groves, vineyards, and deciduous fruit orchards. Bethlehem is a market town where bedouin from the nearby Judean Desert trade their produce for local and imported goods. The town has a number of small hotels and restaurants catering to tourists and, more important, many workshops producing Christian souvenirs. Christian institutions contributed to raising the educational level and provided employment to a large number of inhabitants. The main building in Bethlehem is the Church of the Nativity (sections of which are

Figure 3. Part of the mosaic below the present floor of the Church of the Nativity, fourth century. Photo Israel Department of Antiquities and Museums, Jerusalem.

maintained by the Greek Orthodox and the Catholics, the latter holding St. Catherine's Church adjacent to the main basilica). It is a major attraction for Christian pilgrims, especially at the Christmas celebrations of the Latins (Dec. 24 and 25), Orthodox (Jan. 6 and 7), and Armenians (Jan. 19 and 20). Bethlehem has numerous other Christian buildings, including convents of the Franciscans and the Rosary Sisters, edifices above the Milk Grotto, the Syrian-Orthodox Church, the Lutheran Church, parish schools, orphanages, and a French hospital. Near Bethlehem is the traditional "Shepherds' Field." Between Bethlehem and Jerusalem is the Greek Orthodox monastery of Mar Elias, the traditional resting place of Elijah the prophet when he fled from Jezebel.

For Beth Leḥem (Ha-Gelilit) see *Bet Leḥem. [E.O.]

Bibliography: Lewy, in: JBL, 59 (1940), 519–22; EM, 2 (1965), 86–88; Press, Ereẓ, 1 (1951), 88–89; R. W. Hamilton, *Guide to Bethlehem* (1939); L. H. Vincent and F. M. Abel, *Bethléem* (Fr., 1914).

BETHLEPTEPHA, town in Judea which, in the time of Herod, replaced Keilah as the headquarters of one of the toparchies into which the province was divided. It is sometimes written "Betholeptephon," and is mentioned by Josephus (Wars, 4:445) as "Pella." Schuerer regards the name as a distortion of the Hebrew *Bet Netofah (Beit Nattif) a village six miles (10 km.) north of Bet Guvrin. The identification has now been generally accepted, though some identify it with Bet le-Tappu'aḥ (the Tappuah of Josh. 15:34). Vespasian destroyed Bethleptepha and killed all its inhabitants on his way from Emmaus to Edom. A mosaic floor of a fifth-century Byzantine church was discovered there as well as other mosaics, tombs, cisterns, and pillars from the Roman-Byzantine period.

Bibliography: A. Reland, *Palaestina* . . . (1714), 648; Schuerer, Gesch, 2 (1907[4]), 232n.; S. Klein, *Ereẓ Yehudah* (1939), 214; A. Schalit, *Hordos ha-Melekh* (1964[3]), 111ff. [M.A.-Y.]

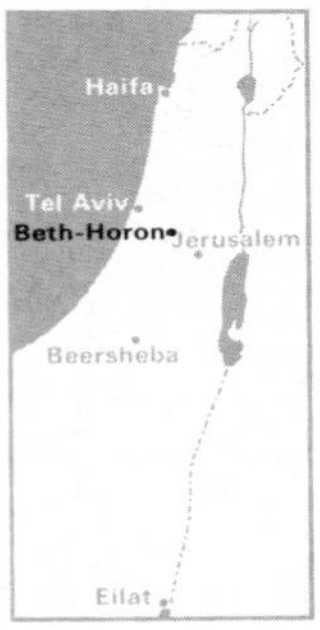

BET(H)-HORON (בֵּית חוֹרוֹן; **Upper,** עֶלְיוֹן *(Elyon),* and **Lower,** תַּחְתּוֹן *(Taḥton)*), two adjacent biblical towns named after the Canaanite deity Horon mentioned in Ugaritic literature and other texts. The towns, known as Upper and Lower Horon, were strategically located on the Gibeon-Aijalon road and guarded the important "ascent of Beth-Horon." Biblical tradition attributes their founding to Sheerah, daughter of Beriah, son of Ephraim (I Chron. 7:24). They were located on the border between the territory of the tribe of Ephraim and that of Benjamin (Josh. 16:3; 18:13–14). One or both of the towns was a levitical city (Josh. 21:22; I Chron. 6:53). Solomon fortified Beth-Horon (the lower town only, according to I Kings 9:17; both towns according to II Chron. 8:5). Beth-Horon is mentioned together with Gibeon in the list of towns conquered by Pharaoh *Shishak (tenth century B.C.E.). It then became part of the kingdom of Judah (cf. II Chron. 25:13). In the Persian and Hellenistic periods, Beth-Horon was in Judea. During the Hasmonean Wars, *Bacchides fortified both towns (I Macc. 9:50). The Mishnah (Shev. 9, 2) states that the Maritime Plain begins at Beth-Horon. It is located by Eusebius (Onom. 46:21) 12 (Roman) mi. from Aelia Capitolina (i.e., Jerusalem) and within its territory; on the *Madaba Map the two villages are marked as one place. Upper Beth-Horon is now identified with the Muslim Arab village 'Ūr al-Fawqā (pop. 298 in 1967) and Lower Beth-Horon with Beit 'Ūr al-Taḥtā (pop. 920 in 1967). The road passing the two and the ascent between them were of military importance in ancient times. *Joshua pursued the Canaanite kings along this ascent after the battle of Gibeon (Josh. 10:10–11); the *Philistines passed this way after their setback at Michmas (I Sam. 13:18); here also *Judah Maccabee defeated Seron, the Seleucid general (I Macc. 3:16), and a Zealot force defeated the Roman governor *Cestius Gallus on his retreat from Jerusalem (Jos., Wars, 2:538ff., 546ff.). Archaeological finds indicate that Lower Beth-Horon, where potsherds from the Late Bronze Age onward have been uncovered, was established before Upper Beth-Horon, where the finds date only from and after the Iron Age (the Monarchy). An ostracon found at Tell el Qasīle (north Tel Aviv) mentions a consignment of gold for "Beth-Horon," but it is uncertain whether the name of the place Beth-Horon is meant or "the temple of [the god] Horon."

[M.A.-Y]

Bibliography: Abel, Geog, 2 (1938), 274; B. Maisler (Mazar), in: JNES, 10 (1951), 266ff.; Mazar, in: VT, Suppl., 4 (1957), 61; Aharoni, Land, index; J. Garstang, *Joshua-Judges* (1931), 224; EM, 2 (1954), 73–75.

BETHPHAGE, village on the Mount of Olives in the immediate vicinity of *Jerusalem; it is named for green figs *(paggim).* In ancient times, it was surrounded by a wall. Bethphage marked the eastern confines of Jerusalem in the Second Temple period (Men. 11:2; Men. 75b). In the New Testament (Matt. 21:1; Mark 11:1) it is mentioned as the place where *Jesus found the she-ass on which he entered Jerusalem. The Crusaders put up many buildings in Bethpage. It has been identified with the village of al-Ṭūr, on the southern of the three hills of the Mount of Olives. According to an ancient tradition the prophetess *Huldah was buried there.

Bibliography: Abel, Geog, 2 (1938), 279; Press, Ereẓ, s.v.

[M.A.-Y.]

BETHSAIDA (Heb. בֵּית צַיָּדָא, **Bet Ẓayyada**), fishing village that was situated on the northeast shore of the Sea of Galilee near the mouth of the Jordan River in the Second Temple period. Philip the son of Herod (*Herod Phillipus) built a Hellenistic city there, naming it Julias in honor of the wife of the emperor Augustus and mother of Tiberius. It was Philip's second capital and he was buried there (Jos., Ant., 18:28, 108; Wars, 2:168; 3:515; Life, 398; cf. Pliny, *Historia Naturalis* 5:15). *Nero later presented it to *Agrippa II. The city is mentioned several times in the New Testament (Matt. 11:21; John 1:44, etc.) in accounts of visits of *Jesus and his disciples to villages on the shores of the Sea of Galilee and as the birthplace of the apostles Peter, Andrew, and Philip. It is also mentioned by Eusebius (Onom. 58:11) and the sixth-century pilgrim Theodosius (ch. 2, ed. Geyer). Bethsaida is the present-day al-Tell (al-Tal) in Golan, not far from where the Jordan flows into Lake Kinneret. Sixteenth-century travelers reported a Jewish fishing village there. Various remains have been found at the site; these include potsherds, building stones, and tesserae.

Bibliography: Alt, in: PJB, 27 (1931), 40; Schuerer, Gesch, 2 (1907), 208; Avi-Yonah, Land, 105; Press Ereẓ, 1 (1951), 99; G. Schille, in: ZDPV, 73 (1957), 142.

[M.A.-Y.]

BETHUEL (Heb. בְּתוּאֵל = בֵּית אֵל; "house of God," cf. *Bati-ilu* in the *Tell el-Amarna letters or—מתואל, "man of God"), the youngest son of *Nahor and Milcah (Gen.

22:21–22) and the father of Laban and *Rebekah (22:23, 24:15, et al.). In the list in Genesis 22 Bethuel appears as head of a tribe of Nahor's descendants and brother of Kemuel the father of Aram, while the appellation "Aramean," used of him in Genesis 28:5, is an anachronism and was applied to him after the domination of Mesopotamia by the Arameans in the 12th century. Bethuel does not play as important a part in the biblical story of Rebekah as does Laban (24:28ff., et al.), and it appears that Bethuel was no longer alive, this being the reason that Laban received Abraham's servant, since in the organization of the patriarchal society that emerges from this story, the firstborn brother was regarded as head of the family. Bethuel is only mentioned in the discussion of the marriage and, even there, only after Laban (24:50). It is quite possible, as has been suggested by scholars, that that is a later addition, for even when Rebekah commences her journey, the members of the family salute her as "Our sister!" (24:60).

In the Aggadah. Bethuel was the king of Haran (Yal., Gen. 109). Bethuel's apparent disappearance in the middle of the negotiations with regard to Rebekah (cf. Gen. 24:50, 55) is explained on the assumption that he died suddenly while they were in progress. There are two Midrashim. According to one, when Bethuel saw the treasures Eliezer had brought with him, he tried to kill him by placing poisoned food before him. While he was telling his story, however, the angel who accompanied Eliezer changed the dishes so that the dish intended for Eliezer was set before Bethuel, who ate of it and died (Yal., Gen. 109). According to the other account, Bethuel had introduced the *jus primae noctis* and his subjects declared themselves ready to submit to this outrage on condition that his own daughters should not be exempt from it. He was about to exercise this right on Rebekah, but to spare her this shame, God caused his death *(ibid.)*. With her approval Eliezer refused to let Rebekah remain in her father's house during the week of mourning (Gen. R. 60:12). From the fact that Rebekah was consulted before she accompanied Eliezer, the rabbis conclude that a fatherless minor girl may not be given in marriage without her consent *(ibid.)*.

Bibliography: E. A. Speiser, *Genesis* (Eng., 1964), 181, 184; de Vaux, Anc Isr, 29; Maisler (Mazar), in: *Zion*, 11 (1946), 7–8 (incl. bibl.); W. W. Baudissin, *Kyrios als Gottesname* . . . , 3 (1929), 300, 304. In the Aggadah: Ginzberg, Legends, 1 (1942), 294–6; 5 (1947), 261–2; L. Rabinowitz, in: JQR, 58 (1967/68), 143–61.

[Ed.]

BETHULIA, the home of Judith, the heroine of the apocryphal Book of Judith, in which it is described as a Jewish city that was besieged by the Assyrian general Holofernes. His death brought the siege to an abrupt end. The name of the city is apparently a form of Beth-El ("House of God"), and the geographic context of the story indicates a location on the northern edge of the hills of Samaria, near Dothan, and Ibleam. Some scholars have identified Bethulia with Jerusalem, Bemeselis (Mithiliyya), or with other localities such as Shechem or Sheikh Shibl above Kafr Qūd. It seems most probable, however, that Bethulia was an imaginary city that was endowed with a theophoric name for the purposes of a historical romance.

Bibliography: Abel, Geog, 2 (1938), 283; J. M. Grintz, *Sefer Yehudit* (1957), 30ff.

[M.A.-Y.]

BET (Bayt) IKSA (Ar. بيت اكسا), Muslim-Arab village in the Judean Hills, west of Jerusalem; population (1967) 633. Located in mountainous terrain, its economy is mainly based on orchards of olives, almonds, and other fruit trees. In the Israel War of Independence (1948), hard

battles were fought over the village which lies close to the Jerusalem–Tel Aviv highway. Israel forces captured Bet Iksā but under the terms of the 1949 Armistice Agreement the village was returned to Jordan, in exchange for small areas elsewhere given to Israel. The stipulation to keep the village demilitarized was not observed by the Jordanians. Bet Iksā was taken by Israel Forces in the Six-Day War. [E.O.]

BET KESHET (Heb. בֵּית קֶשֶׁת), kibbutz north of Mount Tabor, affiliated with Ha-Kibbutz ha-Me'uḥad. Bet Keshet was founded on Aug. 15, 1944 as the first settlement of the then clandestine *Palmaḥ. Most settlers had received agricultural training in the nearby Kadoorie School, while others were demobilized soldiers who had served in World War II. South African immigrants and others joined the kibbutz after 1948. In the War of Independence (1948), hard battles raged around Bet Keshet and a monument was subsequently erected to its members who fell. In 1969 its economy was based on field crops, deciduous fruit, vines, beef cattle, and other farm products. The name, "House of the Bow," refers to the village being founded by pioneer soldiers (cf. II Sam. 1:18). [E.O.]

BET(H) LEḤEM (Ha-Gelilit), place located in western Galilee, near Kiryat Tivon, in the lower Zebulun region (Jos. 19:15; perhaps also Judges 12:8f.). It is referred to as Beth-Leḥem Ẓeriyah (TJ, Meg. 1, 70a), however this name has not yet been given a definitive explanation. Dalman believes that it means the Beth Leḥem which once belonged to Tyre. According to the list of priestly places of residence in Galilee, members of the Malkiya priestly division lived in Beth Leḥem in the 3rd and 4th centuries; it may also have been the home of the amora Kahana bar Malkiya (of the Malkiya priestly division). The biblical name was preserved by an Arab site called Beit Laḥm, southeast of Haifa. At present there is a moshav affiliated with Tenu'at ha-Moshavim near the site. This was founded in 1948 on the land of the former German Templer colony Bethlehem whose inhabitants were interned during World War II and later deported from the country. The population is composed of immigrants from Central and Eastern Europe and native-born Israelis. Its population in 1968 was 270.

Bibliography: IDB, 1 (1962), s.v. Bethlehem, no. 2; *Enziklopediyah le-Geografiyah Mikra'it* 1 (1963), 281–2.

[E.O./Ed.]

BET(H)-MAON (Heb. בֵּית מְעוֹן). (1) See *Baal-Meon. (2) A locality ½ mi. (¾ km.) from Tiberias (Tell Mā'ūn) where Josephus conferred with the men of Tiberias during the Jewish War in 66 C.E. (Life, 64, 67). In talmudic times Beth-Maon is frequently mentioned as a center of opposition to the Patriarchs residing in Tiberias and as a refuge for rabbis antagonistic to them (Gen. R. 80:1, 24; 31:2). The priestly family of Huppah settled there after the destruction of the

Temple (ha-Kallir: *Yashevah Eikhah*). The sources mention a synagogue there (cf. TJ Ta'an, 4:2, 68a).

Bibliography: Avi-Yonah, Geog, 139; Press, Ereẓ, 1 (1951), 90.

[M.A.-Y.]

BET MEIR (Heb. בֵּית מֵאִיר), Israel moshav in the Judean Hills, west of Jerusalem, affiliated with Ha-Po'el ha-Mizrachi moshavim association. In the War of Independence (1948), the Arab garrison entrenched in the then-Arab village had cut off Jewish Jerusalem. The capture of the village by Israel forces opened the "Jerusalem Corridor." Bet Meir was founded in 1950. Its inhabitants came mainly from Hungary, Rumania and Poland. The settlers made use of hydroponics in order to conform with the religious prescription of the *sabbatical year. Bet Meir lies in the center of the Martyrs' Forest. The village is named after Meir *Bar-Ilan. [E.O.]

BET (HA)-MIDRASH (pl. **battei (ha)-midrash;** Heb. בֵּית (הַ)מִּדְרָשׁ, pl. בָּתֵּי (הַ)מִּדְרָשׁ; house of study"), study center where people assembled to listen to words of wisdom and exposition of the Law from very early in the Second Temple period. Esau and Jacob are said to have attended *beit ha-sefer* together until the age of 13, when Jacob continued his studies at *bet ha-midrash;* Esau, instead, frequented idolatrous shrines (Gen. R. 63:10). The Talmud described the 394 courts of law in Jerusalem and the equal number of synagogues, *battei midrash*, and *battei sefer* that existed there (Ket. 105a). Simeon *Ben Sira in the second century B.C.E. invited people to "dwell in my *bet midrash*" (Ecclus. 51:47). In the mishnaic period it was an institution independent of the synagogue and regarded as being more holy. R. *Joshua b. Levi stated that a synagogue may be turned into a *bet midrash*, but not the contrary, for it is "a place where Torah is exalted" in contradistinction to the synagogue which is "a place where prayer is exalted" (Meg. 27a). Sleeping in a *bet ha-midrash* was prohibited, although an exception was made for scholars who spent all their time there (Meg. 28a; Ber. 25a). It was considered ill-omened for a family to eat its Sabbath repast while public study sessions met at the local house of study (Git. 38b). Mothers were praised for sending their children to the synagogue to study, and for waiting up for their husbands who returned late from *bet ha-midrash* (Ber. 17a). One who goes directly from the synagogue (after services) to *bet ha-midrash* (to study) is deemed worthy to welcome the Divine Presence (Ber. 64a); and whosoever enters synagogues and houses of study in this world will be privileged to enter synagogues and houses of study in the world to come (Deut. R. 7:1). The *bet ha-midrash* was the center of instruction for scholars and the common people alike and contributed to disseminating culture widely in Jewish society. In the Middle Ages it tended to be merged with the synagogue, but its specific characteristic was preserved: in the *bet ha-midrash* prayer was a secondary activity, while the study and discussion of Jewish Law and problems concerning Judaism were its main concern, and usually open to all who cared to attend. The *bet ha-midrash* normally had a library with works on various branches of rabbinical literature intended for all sectors of the public. Attendance at the *bet ha-midrash* was not limited as at the **ḥeder* and *yeshivah, and the instructors were often itinerant preachers engaged by the community. The *battei midrash* serving the yeshivot acquired a somewhat cloistered character. The rabbi prayed there with his students when he was not required to join the communal worship. The *bet ha-midrash* also afforded lodging to yeshivah students, and occasionally was used as a hostel for impecunious travelers.

In some *battei midrash* independent study was pursued. In some communities the *bet ha-midrash* became identical with the yeshivah or the synagogue, where scholars taught immediately after morning and evening prayers. Some *battei midrash* were established and maintained by the community, while others were built by philanthropists who bequeathed funds for their maintenance. In Germany, such *battei midrash* were known as *klaus* (from Lat. *clausura*), and in Eastern Europe as *kloyz*. The *Ḥasidim developed a new combination of public instruction and prayer in the **shtibl* ("small room"). In Islamic countries, and some Sephardi communities, the *bet midrash* is called simply *midrash*.

Bibliography: Baron, Community, index; H. H. Ben-Sasson, *Hagut ve-Hanhagah* (1959), index; J. Katz, *Tradition and Crisis* (1961), index; ET, 3 (1951), 210–3. [N.E./A.Ro.]

BET NEḤEMYAH (Heb. בֵּית נְחֶמְיָה), moshav northeast of Lydda. Bet-Nehemyah is affiliated with Ha-oved ha-Ẓiyyoni moshavim association. It was founded in 1950 on the site of the former Beit (Bayt) Nabālā camp of the Arab Legion where a decisive battle was fought in the War of Independence in 1948. Bet Neḥemyah was initially a "work village" whose settlers, immigrants from Iran, were engaged in land reclamation. On its grounds is the site of the Second Temple village Nebellat. The village is named for Nehemiah. In 1970 Bet Neḥemyah numbered 227 inhabitants. [E.O.]

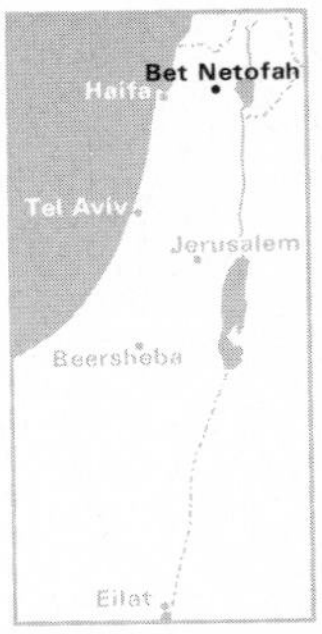

BET NETOFAH (Heb. בֵּית נְטוֹפָה), village in Lower Galilee, north of Sepphoris. It was known in talmudic times as a place where the vetch plant grew later than in other places (Shev. 9:5). Bet Netofah is identified with Khirbat al-Nāṭif, on the northeastern edge of the plain known in Arabic as Sahl al-Baṭṭūf and in Hebrew as the Bet Netofah Valley. Josephus (Life, 207) calls it the Valley of Asochis. High quality clay was found in this valley. In modern times, one of the reservoirs of the National Water Carrier (see *Israel, Water and Irrigation) was built in the valley and is now called the Eshkol Reservoir in honor of Levi *Eshkol.

Bibliography: Abel, Geog, 1 (1933), 410; Press, Ereẓ, 1 (1951), 92, 120–1.

[M.A.-Y.]

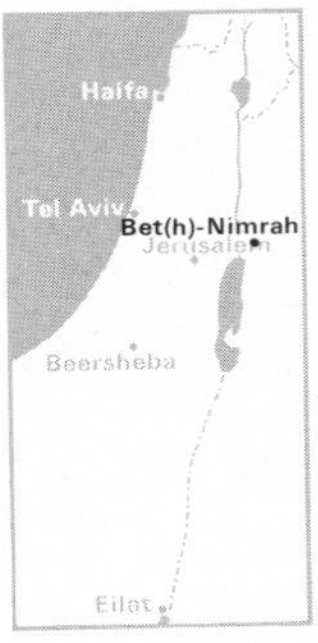

BET(H)-NIMRAH (Heb. בֵּית נִמְרָה), biblical locality in the Jordan Valley opposite Jericho, in the area allotted to the tribe of Gad (Num. 32:36; Josh. 13:27; called Nimrah in Num. 32:3). It is mentioned in the form Bethnambris in the time of the Jewish War with Rome (66–70/73; Jos., Wars, 4:420), after which it continued to exist as a Jewish settlement and is frequently mentioned in talmudic sources (e.g., Pe'ah 4:5, etc.). In Byzantine times it was known as Bethnambris (Eusebius, Onom. 44:17; Johannes Moschus, *Pratum Spirituale, PG*, 87, pt. 3, 2952). The biblical town of Beth-Nimrah has been identified with Tell Balaybil, and the later settlement with Tell Nimrīn, 11 mi. (18 km.) S. W. of *Gadara.

Bibliography: Glueck, in: AASOR, 25–28 (1951), 367–71; Abel, Geog, 2 (1938), 278; Press, Ereẓ, 1 (1951), 92–93; 3 (1952), appendix, 10.

[M.A.-Y.]

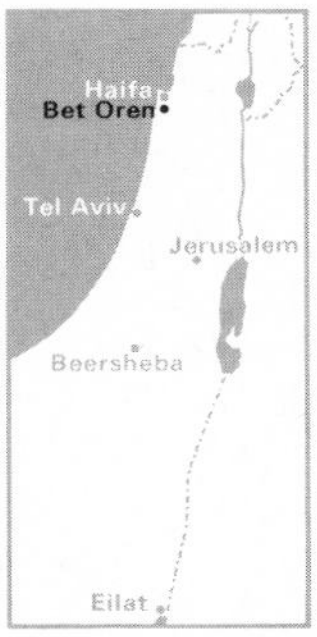

BET OREN (Heb. בֵּית אֹרֶן; "House of Pine Tree"), kibbutz on Mount Carmel, affiliated with Ha-Kibbutz ha-Me'uḥad. Founded in 1939, the settlement was initially isolated and had little land, so that its members had to work as hired laborers in Haifa. During the Mandate regime Bet Oren served as a clandestine training camp of *Haganah. After irrigable land on the Carmel coast was allocated to Bet Oren, it raised milch and beef cattle, fodder, field crops, deciduous fruit, and other products. The kibbutz had a large rest house amid the natural pine and oak forests and nature reserves of the surroundings. In 1970 Bet Oren numbered 220 inhabitants.

[E.O.]

BET OVED (Heb. בֵּית עוֹבֵד), moshav in central Israel, southeast of Nes Ẓiyyonah. Bet Oved, affiliated with Tenu'at Ha-Moshavim, was founded in 1933 by workers from Russia. Its economy is based on citrus plantations, garden crops, and milch cattle. In 1970 Bet Oved numbered 195 inhabitants.

[E.O.]

BET(H)-REHOB (Heb. בֵּית רְחוֹב), biblical city or dynasty that gave its name to one of the *Aramean states existing at the time of the Israelite conquest. In the Bible, Rehob is mentioned at the entrance to Hamath (Num. 13:21) and the city Laish-Dan is placed specifically in the "valley that lieth by Beth-Rehob" (Judg. 18:28). The Arameans of Beth-Rehob were among the mercenaries hired by the Ammonites to fight Israel; they were thoroughly routed first by Joab at Medeba and then by David (II Sam. 10:6ff.; I Chron. 19:6ff.). It has been assumed that *Aram-Zobah already held the other Aramean kingdoms under its sway at that time; the period of Israelite control was broken by *Damascus, who took the lead in revolting against Solomon. The last appearance of Rehob may be in an inscription of Shalmaneser III (853 B.C.E.), which mentions a certain Ba'sa, son of Ruhubi from Amana, in a list of Syrian-Palestinian kings.

Bibliography: EM, s.v.; Bright, Hist, 181.

[M.A.-Y.]

BETROTHAL (Heb. שִׁדּוּכִין, *shiddukhin*).

Definition. In Jewish law *shiddukhin* is defined as the mutual promise between a man and a woman to contract a marriage at some future time and the formulations of the terms (*tena'im,* see below) on which it shall take place. In general parlance, as opposed to legal terminology, it is known as *erusin* (Kid. 63a, Tos.), which is in fact part of the marriage ceremony proper (see *Marriage, Ceremony of). The concept of *shiddukhin* can entail either a promise by the intending parties themselves or one made by their respective parents or other relatives on their behalf (Kid. 9b; Sh. Ar., EH 50:4–6 and 51). The sages regarded *kiddushin* (consecration; see *Marriage) without prior *shiddukhin* as licentiousness and prescribed

A betrothal ceremony. Engraving from Johann Bodenschatz' book on Jewish customs in Germany, *Kirchliche Verfassung der heutigen Juden,* 1748.

that "he who enters into a marriage without *shiddukhin* is liable to be flogged" (TJ, Kid. 3:10, 64b; TB, Kid. 12b; Maim. Yad, Ishut, 3:22 and Issurei Bi'ah, 21:14; Sh. Ar., EH 26:4). *Shiddukhin* as such has no immediate effect on the personal status of the parties—it being only a promise to create a different personal status in the future (Resp. Rosh 34:1; *Beit Yosef* EH 55). Nor does the promise give either party the right to claim specific performance from the other—since a marriage celebrated in pursuance of a judgment requiring the defendant to marry the plaintiff is repugnant to the basic principle that a marriage requires the free will and consent of both the parties thereto.

Gifts (Heb. סִבְלוֹנוֹת, *sivlonot*). The Talmud (Kid. 50b) discusses the question whether the bride's acceptance of gifts from her bridegroom is to be regarded as an indication that *kiddushin* has already been celebrated between them—thus making it necessary for her to receive a divorce, on the grounds of "doubt," in the event she does not marry him and wishes to marry someone else. The *halakhah* was to the effect that the matter be left dependent on local custom—so that any "doubt" as to whether or not *kiddushin* had already taken place would depend on whether or not there was any custom in the particular place where the parties resided to send such gifts before or after *kiddushin.* From the time that it became the general custom for parties to initiate their intended ties with each other by way of *shiddukhin* (when the bridegroom would send gifts to his bride) and for the *kiddushin* and *nissu'in* (the marriage proper; see *Marriage) to take place simultaneously at a later date, there would usually be no opportunity for the bridegroom to send such gifts to the bride after the *kiddushin* but before the *nissu'in,* so the *halakhah* was then to the effect that the giving of gifts per se implied no suspicion of *kiddushin* as mentioned above (Sh. Ar., EH 45:2; *Arukh ha-Shulḥan* EH 45:16–18. See also **Minhag.*

Tena'im (Heb. תְּנָאִים, "conditions"). It is customary, but not generally or necessarily so, for the *tena'im,* or conditions of the *shiddukhin,* to be reduced to writing—

whereby such matters would be prescribed as the date and place of the proposed marriage, the financial obligations of the parties, i.e., the *dowry (Heb. נְדוּנְיָה, *nedunyah*) to be brought by the bride, or the period for which her father undertakes to provide for the couple. All such obligations undertaken at the time of the *shiddukhin* are valid and binding, even without a formal or symbolic *kinyan* (see Modes of *Acquisition), as obligations of this nature are "in these matters effected by mere verbal arrangement" (Ket. 102a; Kid. 9b; See also *Contract). It is also customary to stipulate a sum of money as a penalty to be paid in the event of a breach of promise without good cause. In the Talmud such written instruments are termed *shetarei pesikta*—abbreviated by the *posekim* to *"shetarei"* or *"tena'ei shiddukhin"* or simply *"tena'im"* (Rashi, ad loc.; Sh. Ar., EH 51: *Arukh ha-Shulḥan*, EH 51:13; see also forms: A. A. Rudner *Mishpetei Ishut*, 178f. and Gulak, Oẓar 1–19 (nos. 1–4), 362 (no. 403); see also **Shetar*).

Breach of the Shiddukhin. Consequences of Breach. The party committing a breach of promise, i.e., by not marrying the other party, may be liable to compensate the other party for any actual damage sustained, such as the expenses of the preparations for the marriage, and may also be obliged to return the gifts he received on the occasion of the *shiddukhin*, whether from the other party or from relatives and friends (Sh. Ar., EH 50:3–4; Resp. Rosh, 35:8; *Arukh ha-Shulḥan*, EH 50:20). The offending party may further be liable to pay the penalty stipulated in the *tena'im*—or, if not so stipulated, such amount as a court may determine as proper in the circumstances—having particular regard to the degree of mental suffering, shame, and public degradation suffered by the other party as a result of the breach of promise (Tos. to BM 66a; Sh. Ar., EH, 50:3–4; *Ba'er Heitev* 15). In cases where the sum stipulated in the *tena'im* to be paid by way of compensation exceeds the value of the actual damage caused, so as to make it a real penalty, the *posekim* debate the legal validity of such a condition on the grounds that the promise is tainted with **asmakhta*, i.e., that a promise to pay such a sum by way of compensation might possibly not have been meant seriously, since both parties would have been at the time so certain and confident of fulfilling their respective commitments. Some of the authorities, mainly Ashkenazi, took the view that the law requiring one who shamed another to compensate the latter should be strictly applied in these cases as well, and that the plea of *asmakhta* avails only if the stipulated sum is a highly exaggerated one (Tos. to BM 66a and to Kid. 8b; Resp. Rosh 34:2,4; *Rema* EH 50:6 and *Beit Shemu'el, ibid.*; *Arukh ha-Shulḥan*, EH 50:21f.; *Rema* ḤM 207:16 and *Siftei Kohen, ibid.*). Other sages, primarily Sephardi, held that the plea of *asmakhta* would avail the offending party even in a breach of promise case involving *shiddukhin* (Maim. Yad, Mekhir 11:18; Sh. Ar., ḤM 207:16; *Beit Yosef* EH 50; see also PDR 3:131–154). In order to avoid any doubts, however, in the Middle Ages the Sephardi authorities introduced the practice of two separate agreements between the parties—one whereby each party unconditionally undertook to pay to the other a fixed sum in the event of breach of promise and another whereby each party released the other from the former undertaking upon the fulfillment of all the obligations stipulated in the *tena'im* (Sh. Ar., ḤM, *ibid.*, and EH 50:6; Resp. Maharit, 131). Even if the *tena'im* had not been reduced to writing the court would adjudge the offending party to pay such compensation as may seem proper in the circumstances, having regard to the standing of the parties, provided the terms of the *shiddukhin* had been evidenced by *kinyan* between the parties.

Defenses against Liability. Any justifiable reason for withdrawing from the *shiddukhin* is a valid defense to a claim for compensation. Since the matter in issue is a promise to marry, involving a personal tie between the parties, the court will tend to regard any ground for not entering the marriage as reasonably justified, even if it is not directly attributable to the defendant. For example, if the *tena'im* were agreed by the parents and subsequently the son or the daughter involved refused to accept them, such refusal would be regarded as justified and would not involve him or her in any liability (Resp. Rosh 34:1; Tur and Sh. Ar., EH 50:5, *Arukh ha-Shulḥan* EH 50:29; PDR 5, 322–9). However, if the grounds on which the defendant bases his withdrawal were known to him prior to the *shiddukhin* or if they became known to him thereafter and he did not immediately withdraw, he will be regarded as having waived his objections and such grounds will not later avail him as a defence.

Validity of the Tena'im after Marriage (Nissu'in). Noncompliance with the terms of the *tena'im* after the marriage has taken place does not exempt the parties from the duties imposed on them by law vis-à-vis each other as husband and wife. Thus, the husband is not absolved from his duty to maintain and provide a home for his wife because she or her parents may have failed to honor their undertaking to provide a home for the couple—the husband's duty being imposed on him by law (see *Marriage) and being unconnected with any rights deriving from the *shiddukhin* (*Bayit Ḥadash* EH 52; *Rema* EH 52:1, and *Ba'er Heitev* 5). On the other hand, the existence of the marriage is not necessarily to be regarded as constituting a waiver and cancellation of the obligations created by the *shiddukhin*. In order to avoid such a contention, it is customary for the parties to draw up "secondary" or "new" *tena'im* at the time of the *kiddushin*, whereby they reaffirm the original *tena'im*—or else stipulate specifically in the **ketubbah* that the marriage is based on the terms of the original *tena'im*; the latter form being the customary procedure in the *ketubbah* adopted in the State of Israel (A. A. Rudner, *Mishpetei Ishut*, 179). Such procedures provide either party with a clear cause of action for claiming the specific performance of all obligations undertaken in the *tena'im* after the marriage has taken place. According to some *posekim*, there is no need for the original *tena'im* to be specifically recalled at the time of the *kiddushin*—as it is presumed that the *kiddushin* was entered upon in accordance with the terms of such *tena'im* (PDR 1:289–313; 4:193–9, 289–304).

Customs. The ceremony and the writing of the agreement is called in Yiddish *teno'im shrayben*. The term *knas-mahl* ("penalty meal") was also used because of the penalty (usually 50% of the promised dowry) stipulated in the document to be paid by the party guilty of breach of the promise to marry (Sh. Ar., EH 51).

Though of secondary importance from an halakhic point of view, the "betrothal" remains a significant ceremony in marriage arrangements. According to *Elijah b. Solomon, the Gaon of Vilna, a bridegroom, rather than break the engagement, should marry and then divorce his bride. In certain Jewish circles, a marriage is not contracted with a person who was a party to a broken engagement.

Among the Oriental Jews, the engagement ceremony is a very elaborate affair. Kurdish Jews had the custom of *hatlabba* ("bidding the bride") and those of *Djerba indulged in great festivities. After the engagement, bride and bridegroom would exchange presents, and on Passover, Shavuot, and Sukkot, the groom would send his bride clothing, jewelry, and choice fruits. Similarly among Ashkenazi Jews, as *sivlonot* the groom usually sent the bride clothing or jewelry, and she reciprocated with a new *tallit* or a richly embroidered *tallit* bag she had made herself. At the Ashkenazi *tena'im* ceremony, it is customary to break a plate; the act is parallel to the crushing of the glass at the wedding ceremony.

Bibliography: Buechler, in: *Festschrift... Lewy* (1911), 110–44; Gulak, Yesodei, 2 (1922), 82; 3 (1922), 14–19, 22, 29, 45; Gulak, Oẓar, 1–19 (nos. 1–14), 362 (no. 403); idem, in: *Tarbiz,* 3 (1931–32), 361–76; 5 (1933–34), 126–33, Herzog, Instit, 1 (1936), index; Ch. Albeck, in: *Koveẓ... M. Schorr* (1944), 12–24; ET, 2 (1949), 114; 6 (1954), 610; 7 (1956), 138–49; PD 12:1121–204; 16:2737–40; B. Schereschewsky, *Dinei Mishpaḥah* (1967²), 22–31; idem, *Kenas u-Fiẓẓuyim Ekev Hafarat Ḥozim le-fi Dinei Yisrael* (1960); B. Cohen, in: PAAJR, 18 (1949), 67–135; republished in his *Jewish and Roman Law,* 1 (1966), 279–347, addenda 777–80; H. Schauss, *The Lifetime of a Jew* (1950), 129–31, 150–2, 158–61, 165–9, 182–6; Elon, Mafteaḥ, 326ff.

[B.-Z.SCH.]

BET(H)-SHEAN (Heb. בֵּית שְׁאָן; also **Beisan**), historic city in the fertile valley of Beth-Shean. The city Beth Shean, situated at a main crossroads in a well-watered fertile region, is 390 ft. (120 m.) below sea level.

"Shean" or "Shan" (II Sam. 21:12) seems to be the name of an idol. Some scholars dispute the supposed mention of it in the Egyptian execration texts of the 20th–19th centuries B.C.E. It is mentioned in Egyptian sources from the time of Thutmose III (15th century B.C.E.) to that of Ramses III (12th century B.C.E.). The excavations of Tel Beth-Shean (Ar. *Tell al-Husn*) proved the importance of Beth-Shean as a station for caravans and as a center of Egyptian rule. An Egyptian basalt stele found dating from the reign of Pharaoh Seti I (late 14th century B.C.E.) mentions the Apiru, the Habiru (thought to be Hebrews) of the cuneiform writings, who disturb the peace and undermine government authority in the region of Beth-Shean. Ramses II refortified the city of Beth-Shean and built a temple different from that of Seti I. His basalt stele mentions the suppression of the "Asians and the inhabitants of the sands"; Ramses III also refortified the city and rebuilt its temples. Evidence of Aegean cultural influences, brought by Philistine laborers, was found in the vicinity of the cemetery beyond the tell. It was one of the strong Canaanite cities not captured at the beginning of the Israelite conquest of Ereẓ Israel.

The valley of Beth-Shean was allotted to the tribe of Issachar, but the tribe of Manasseh extended its settlements to this territory (Josh. 17:11). During Saul's reign the city was in the hands of Philistines; they hanged Saul's body on the walls of Beth-Shean (I Sam. 31:10, 12). In the time of Solomon it was included in the district under the authority of Baana the son of Ahilud (I Kings, 4:12). The wall, the gate, and the style of stone cutting found in the hill belong to the Solomonic period. It is thought to have been destroyed by Sheshonk I (the biblical Shishak), king of Egypt.

[JO.BR.]

Excavations conducted there by an American expedition between 1921 and 1933 uncovered 18 levels of occupation extending from the Chalcolithic (fourth millennium B.C.E.) to the early Arab period. The main discovery was a series of temples built by the Egyptians in honor of local deities. These apparently range in date from the el-Amarna period to the reign of Ramses III in the 12th century B.C.E. (strata IX–VI). Two later temples (stratum V) existed until c.1000 B.C.E.; one of them may be identical with the "house of Ashtaroth" in which the Philistines placed Saul's armor (I Sam. 31:10). Various Egyptian inscriptions were found including a stele dedicated to Mekal, the god of Beth-Shean; a lintel bearing the name of an Egyptian builder from the time of Ramses II; and three victory stelae, two from the reign of Seti I and the other from the reign of Ramses II.

A large number of burial caves from different periods were excavated on the slope opposite the tell. Some of these contained anthropomorphic sarcophagi that attest to the presence of the Philistines (or a related group of sea peoples). The blow struck at the Philistines before the war of Deborah (Judg. 3:31; 5:6) may have had the seizure of the Egyptian citadel at Beth-Shean and its mercenary troops as its objective. With the removal of the supreme Egyptian authority, the safety of the roads was disrupted and the opportunity provided for the decisive battle between the Israelites and Canaanites in the north of the country.

[Y.A.]

During the rule of the Diadochi, the successors of Alexander the Great, Beth-Shean received the name of Scythopolis ("city of the Scythians"); this seems to refer to a colony of Scythian mercenaries, who were in the service of the Egyptian king Ptolemy II. It is first mentioned in the campaign of Antiochus Seleucus III, against Egypt in 218 B.C.E. Near the temple for the worship of Dionysus, a temple in honor of Zeus was built. The town accepted Seleucid rule and became a Greek city *(polis)* under *Antiochus IV.

By the time of Judah Maccabee, many Jews lived in Beth-Shean. It was there that *Jonathan, the brother of Judah, met *Tryphon, the Syrian usurper. The city was conquered by the sons of John Hyrcanus I in 107 B.C.E. During the Hasmonean period Beth-Shean became an important administrative center, and Alexander Yannai built ramparts around the city. In 63 B.C.E. Pompey revived the Greek way of life, and Gabinius, proconsul in Syria from 57 to 54 B.C.E., improved the city and enlarged it. It became the capital of the federation of ten Greek cities known as the Decapolis alliance, the other nine centers of which were on the east bank of the Jordan. When the Jewish War broke out in 66 C.E., the Jews also attacked Beth-Shean. The Jewish and gentile inhabitants of the city alike resisted. However, the Gentiles deceived the Jews and massacred some 13,000 of them (Jos., Wars, 2:466–76).

During the mishnaic and talmudic periods (second and third centuries) Beth-Shean was inhabited by Jews (Av. Zar. 1:4; 4:12), whose principal occupations were the manufacture of thin linen garments, field-crops, and olive plantations (TJ, Pe'ah 7:4, 20a). They spoke in the Galilean dialect. At that time Beth-Shean was one of the world centers for the manufacture and export of textiles. Regular performances were held in the theater, amphitheater, and hippodrome. The theater, considerable remains of which are still visible, was built about 200 C.E. and had seating for 4,500–5,000 spectators.

A synagogue excavated north of the Byzantine wall of the city testifies to the presence of a Jewish population from the fourth century onward. The synagogue itself was in use about 200 years and there are signs of renovation. It is built in the form of a basilica and paved with a beautiful mosaic of geometrical and plant patterns, of a beautiful Holy Ark with a candelabrum on each side, ritual horns *(shofarot),* incense bowls, and three Greek inscriptions. In the adjoining rooms of the later Byzantine era a Samaritan inscription was also found. The synagogue seems to have burned down in 624.

At the beginning of the fifth century Beth-Shean became the capital of the province called Palestina Secunda and the seat of the commissioner and the tribunal. It was also the seat of the episcopate and had numerous churches. An

Figure 1. The tell of Beth-Shean. Photo Government Press Agency, Tel Aviv.

Figure 2. Aerial view of the tell of Beth-Shean. Photo Richard Cleave, Jerusalem.

Figure 3. Upper part of an anthropomorphic pottery vessel of the Late Bronze Period (15th–13th centuries B.C.E.) found at Beth-Shean. Jerusalem, Israel Department of Antiquities and Museums.

Figure 4. Statue of the pharaoh Ramses III (1198–1167 B.C.E.) found at Beth-Shean. The cartouche on the right shoulder includes the throne-name, "Powerful for truth is Ra beloved of Amen." The one on the left shoulder gives the ruler's personal name, "Ramses ruler of Heliopolis." Jerusalem, Israel Department of Antiquities and Museums.

interesting mosaic floor from one of these churches, found in the northern part of the city, is preserved in a new building.

During the first centuries of the Arab period (seventh–ninth centuries), Beth-Shean was renowned for its palm trees, vineyards, wine, and rice, which was exported. However, the Crusaders devastated the valley in their wars. The Muslim geographer Yakut found only two palm trees there in 1225. In his time the inhabitants were black-skinned with negroid hair.

The Mamluk period brought new life to Beth-Shean. During the 14th century it became the principal town of a district *(vilayet)* of Damascus, and was a relay station on the postal route from Damascus to Cairo. The "inn" called Khan-al-Aḥmar remains from this period. In the second quarter of the 14th century the town was chosen by *Estori ha-Parḥi as a center for his topographic-historical research. He describes the town as "situated among a plentiful supply of still waters, a blessed and pleasant land, joyously

Figure 5. Part of the lid of an anthropomorphic pottery sarcophagus from the Philistine necropolis at Beth-Shean, 12th century B.C.E. Jerusalem, Israel Museum. Photo Zev Radovan, Jerusalem.

Figure 6. Stele of Seti I from Beth-Shean, 1313 B.C.E. It depicts the pharaoh (left) making votive offerings to the god Horus. The hieroglyphic text describes the repulse of an attack on Beth-Shean. The name of the town has been highlighted in white at the bottom of the stele. Jerusalem, Israel Department of Antiquities and Museums.

satisfied; as the Garden of God she gives forth her bread and her door leads to the Garden of Eden." The last Arab settlement of the town occurred with its conquest by Ibrahim Pasha, the son of the Egyptian ruler, in 1830. Some of the inhabitants of Beth-Shean, as well as Bedouin tribes of the valley, were of Egyptian origin. Most of the lands of the valley were owned by the sultan as *jiftlik* ("state domain") and were leased out. Irrigation was supplied by relays, each lessee having his day of the week.

When the railroad from Haifa to Damascus was laid, Beth-Shean became the lowest railroad station in the world. Beth-Shean reached the lowest ebb in its development at the beginning of the 19th century when it was no more than a miserable village with at most 200 inhabitants. It then grew, albeit very slowly, until World War I. [JO.BR.]

Modern Period. In September 1918, it was captured by British forces. In the 1920–1930s Bedouin from the Beth-Shean Valley settled in the town, which numbered 2,000 inhabitants in 1921 and over 3,000 during the Israel *War of Independence (1948). From the beginning of the 20th century, Jews, mainly from Kurdistan and other Muslim countries, also took up residence in Beth-Shean, but temporarily left during the 1929 Arab riots; the Jewish population of Beth-Shean numbered 94 persons in the spring of 1936. Most of them abandoned the town immediately upon the outbreak of the 1936 riots. The town became a headquarters for Arab bands attacking Jewish villages in the neighboring Harod Valley, but the marauders' position was weakened when Jewish *tower and stockade settlements were established on all sides of Beth-Shean in the years to follow. In the War of Independence, Beth-Shean capitulated on May 12, 1948, to Jewish forces, who found

Figure 7. Pottery stand for burning incense, early Israelite period (1200–1000 B.C.E.), reconstructed from fragments found at Beth-Shean. Jerusalem, Israel Department of Antiquities and Museums.

Figure 8. The Roman theater at Beth-Shean, c. 200 C.E. Photo Richard Cleave. Jerusalem.

Figure 9. Bronze handle in the shape of a *menorah*, believed to have been attached to the rim of an oil lamp, found in the synagogue at Beth-Shean. Jerusalem, Department of Antiquities and Museums.

Figure 10. Detail of the mosaic floor of Byzantine church at Beth-Shean, fourth-fifth centuries C.E. Photo Israel Department of Antiquities and Museums, Jerusalem.

Figure 11. Beth-Shean children running to a shelter during an alert exercise, 1969. Photo Government Press Office, Tel Aviv.

it deserted by its former inhabitants. The settlement of Beth-Shean by Jewish immigrants began in 1949. In 1950, the town numbered 1,200 inhabitants, and in 1968, 12,800—of whom half originated from North Africa (mainly from Morocco), 30% from other Muslim countries (Iran, Iraq, and Turkey), while 20% came from Europe or were Israel-born. As the town had no industry in the initial phase of its resettlement, the inhabitants had to subsist in the 1950s mainly on small trade and on doing hired farm work in the vicinity. Later, a number of industries were established, the largest being a textile mill, followed by a clothing factory, a plastics plant, and by smaller enterprises. A few factories in Beth-Shean are run by local kibbutzim, while the inhabitants of the town are also employed in industry and agriculture in the rural communities of the Beth-Shean Valley. Social and living standards were not satisfactory, however, particularly during the 1965–1967 recession. After the *Six-Day War (1967), Beth-Shean, exposed to the Jordanian artillery positions beyond the Jordan River, suffered from occasional shelling.

[E.O.]

Bibliography: A. Rowe and G. M. Fitzgerald, *Four Canaanite Temples of Beth-Shan,* 2 vols. (1930–40); *Publication of the Palestine Section of the Museum of the University of Pennsylvania,* vols. 1–4 (1930–40); A. Rowe, *Topography and History of Beth-Shan* (1930); G. M. Fitzgerald, *Beth-Shan Excavations 1921–1923* (1931); idem, *A Sixth Century Monastery at Beth-Shan* (1939); J. Braslavi (Braslavsky), *Ha-Yadata et ha-Areẓ,* 1 (1940); 5 (1960); 6 (1964), indexes; Israel Exploration Society, *Bikat Beit She'an* (1962); Aharoni, Land, index; Z. Vilnay, *Guide to Israel* (1966[9]), 398–406; H. Z. Hirschberg (ed.), *Naftali* (1967), 61; Albright, in: AASOR, 6 (1926), 32–38; Wright, in: AJA, 44 (1941), 484–5; B. Maisler, in: BIES, 16 (1951–52), 14–19; N. Zori, in: IEJ, 16 (1966), 123–34; idem, in: *Eretz Israel,* 8 (1967), 149–67.

BET SHE'ARIM (Heb. בֵּית שְׁעָרִים; Gr. **Besara**), ancient city on the southern slopes of Lower Galilee situated on the hill of al-Sheikh Burayk (near Kiryat Tivon on the Nazareth-Haifa road). Although settlement at Bet She'arim apparently started during the period of the divided monarchy, the first mention of the city occurs at the end of the Second Temple period, when it was a center of the estates of Berenice (the daughter of Agrippa I and sister of Agrippa II) in the Plain of Esdraelon. Josephus speaks of it as Besara (Life, 118–9). According to talmudic sources, important *tannaim* and *amoraim* lived there (Tosef., Ter. 7:14; Nid. 27a). Bet She'arim reached a position of great importance and prosperity in the late second century, when *Judah ha-Nasi took up residence there and made it the seat of the Sanhedrin (RH 31a–b). From the beginning of the following century the necropolis of Bet She'arim became a central burial place for Jews of Palestine and the Diaspora (TJ, MK 3:5, 82c). The city was destroyed by Gallus during the suppression of the Jewish revolt in 352 C.E. A small settlement nevertheless continued to exist there during the Byzantine and early Arab periods.

The hill of al-Sheikh Burayk has been partly excavated by B. Mazar (1935–40; 1960) and N. Avigad (1953–58) under the auspices of the Israel Exploration Society. An inscription found there contains the name Besara, confirming the identification of the site with Bet She'arim.

The city of Bet She'arim extended over the entire summit of the hill—an area of some 25 acres (100 dunams), 450 ft. (137 m.) above sea level. It was surrounded by a wall, two sections of which were exposed. Remains of various large buildings were uncovered on the northeastern part of the hill. The most important of these was a spacious basilical-type synagogue, 115×49 ft. (35×15 m.), built of ashlar blocks, of which only two courses have survived. The front of the synagogue was oriented toward Jerusalem and contained three entrances that led into the large columned hall; the bases of the columns have been preserved. The synagogue was decorated in the style characteristic of Galilean synagogues of the third century C.E., and many architectural fragments were found scattered among its ruins: column drums, capitals, jambs, lintels, and decorated friezes. The ruins of other buildings and courtyards were found in the vicinity of the synagogue, including a large two-story building with an outer wall 99 ft. (30 m.) long, built of fine ashlar blocks, as well as the remains of what was apparently a glassmaking workshop. Many small artifacts were found: metal, pottery, and glass vessels, inscribed marble slabs, and some 1,200 bronze coins, all of which were struck in the first half of the fourth century C.E. These coins made it possible to determine the date of the destruction of all the buildings in the area. A gate and an oil press, used chiefly in the Byzantine period, were also found nearby.

The excavations, however, were concentrated mainly in the extensive ancient necropolis that stretched over the slope of the hill northeast, north, and west of the city and

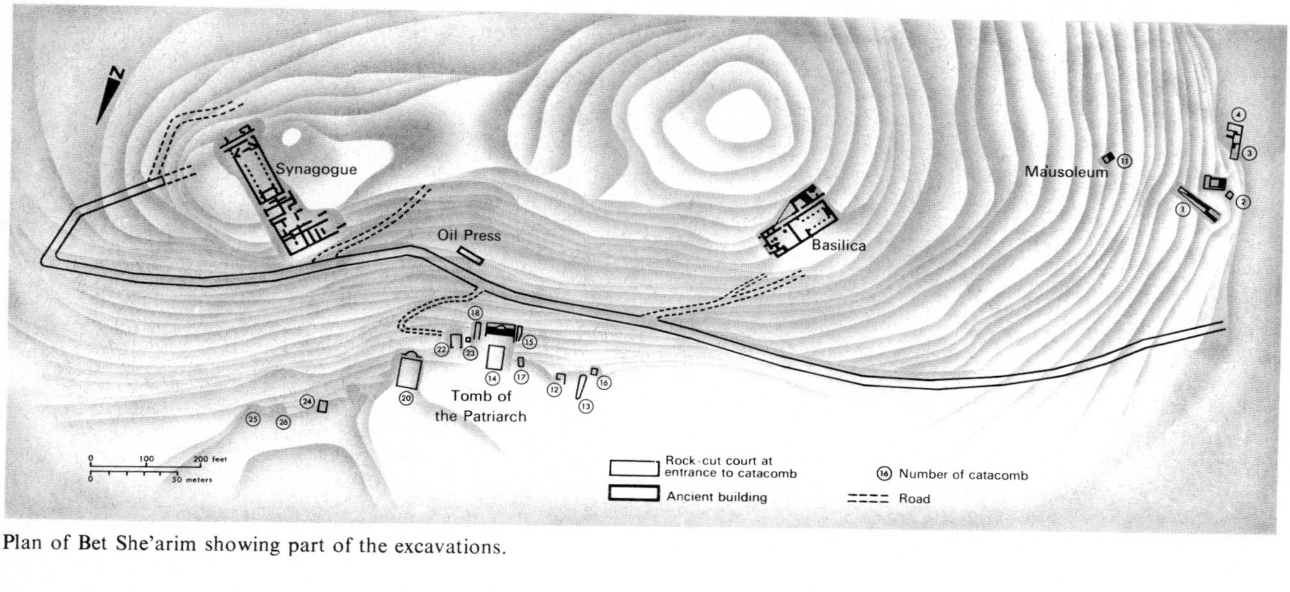

Plan of Bet She'arim showing part of the excavations.

1

2

3

4

Figure 1. Entrance to the main catacomb of the Bet She'arim necropolis, second–fourth centuries C.E. It has been restored with stones found on the site. Photo Government Press Office, Tel Aviv.

Figure 2. The courtyard of catacomb no. 13. Its 12 doors leading to the burial chambers are constructed on three levels. All are made of solid blocks of stone moving on hinges. Photo Israel Department of Antiquities and Museums, Jerusalem.

Figure 3. One of the doors of courtyard no. 13, all but one of which are decorated with carved panels, nailheads, and knockers to resemble wood. Photo Government Press Office, Tel Aviv.

Figure 4. Bas-relief of a *menorah* held by a man dressed in a Roman legionary's tunic. The seven-branched candelabrum is the decoration recurring most frequently among the many wall carvings in the Bet She'arim catacombs. Photo Government Press Office, Tel Aviv.

5

8

6

9

7

Figure 5. Wall carvings in catacomb no. 4. The bas-relief on the left of the burial niche depicts the Ark of the Law, the one on the right probably a shrine in a synagogue. Photo Israel Department of Antiquities and Museums, Jerusalem.

Figure 6. Man leading a horse. One of the many graffiti of the Bet She'arim necropolis.

Figure 7. View of a series of burial chambers and sarcophagi. Photo Government Press Office, Tel Aviv.

Figure 8. The shell sarcophagus, so called because of the distinctive carving on the lid, repeated on the side of the coffin. Photo Government Press Office, Tel Aviv.

Figure 9. Carving of a bearded face on the end of a sarcophagus, possibly representing the Greek god Zeus. Photo Government Press Office, Tel Aviv.

over the slopes of adjacent hills to the north and west. Rock-cut catacombs that were prepared to provide burial places to sell to people from outside Bet She'arim were found in all these areas. Some were family vaults, but the majority were for the general public. Each catacomb contained an open court and a number of tomb halls that were connected by a series of chambers to some of the branch burial compartments containing graves. The openings between the chambers are arched. The usual form of a grave is the *arcosolium*—an arched niche cut into the wall with trough-like graves hewn at the bottom. *Kukhim* (*loculi*—"burial recesses") are also found frequently. Some of the catacombs lack all decoration, but many possess chambers that display a variegated ornamentation. The soft rock easily lent itself to carving and incision. The many reliefs, graffiti, and drawings adorning the walls are generally executed in the primitive style of the Jewish folk art popular in the Roman period. Jewish symbols and ritual objects are very common motifs, particularly the seven-branched candelabrum and the Ark of the Law, complete with columns and steps. The *shofar, lulav, etrog,* and incense shovel are also represented. But secular motifs also occur: human figures, animals, ships, geometric patterns, etc., as well as architectural ornaments that were carved in the rock (columns, capitals, arches, and niches). Ornamental stone doors were decorated to imitate wooden ones, complete with panels, nailheads, and knockers. These were locked by bolts, and lifted by keys. The doors still turn on their hinges. Some of the main entrances are adorned with built arches resting on pillars. The facades of two catacombs (nos. 14 and 20) are built of smooth ashlar stones in the form of an arcade of three arches. Over these facades are structures of monumental steps with prayer niches. A mausoleum was built over catacomb no. 11 and contained rich architectural decorations and reliefs.

Of special importance are the epitaphs, of which some 250 have been discovered. The majority are in Greek and the others are written in Hebrew, Aramaic, and Palmyrean. They are incised in the soft rock of the chamber walls, on the sides of the tombs, on lintels, on stone or marble slabs, or are painted in red or black. Their contents are generally restricted to the name of the deceased and his patronymic (or other family descent), with the addition of a word of affection or praise. The rank or occupation of the deceased, and occasionally his place of origin, are sometimes mentioned. Among the callings and titles are teacher, kohen, banker, goldsmith, government official, perfumer, chief warden of a community, chief of a synagogue, and rabbi (written *ribbi* and *bi-ribbi*). Typical examples of Hebrew inscriptions read: "Shalom to Judah," or "This tomb is (of) Rabbi Isaac bar Makim, shalom." An unusual Aramaic epitaph was found: "He who is buried here [is] Simeon, son of Johanan, and on oath, whoever shall open upon him shall die of an evil end." In catacomb no. 14 the following epitaphs were found: "Rabbi Simeon"; "This is the burial place of Rabbi Gamaliel"; and "Anina [Ḥanina] the Small." As it is known from the Talmud that before his death Judah ha-Nasi appointed his son Simeon *ḥakham,* Gamaliel (his second son) patriarch, and his most outstanding pupil, *Ḥanina b. Ḥama, head of the yeshivah (TB, Ket. 103b), one may assume that this catacomb was the burial place of the patriarch and his family. There are 218 Greek inscriptions and Greek was apparently the common language of the Jews at the time. Pure Greek names occur beside Hebrew ones in Greek transliteration. Some inscriptions express a belief in eternal life. The places of origin appearing in the epitaphs indicate that Bet She'arim was a central burial place for the Jews of Palestine-Elath (Exion-Geber), nearby Arabah and Baka, and of the Diaspora—Tadmor (Palmyra), Antioch, Byblos, Tyre, Sidon, and Beirut in Syria, Meishan in northern Mesopotamia, and Himyar in southern Arabia. Two inscriptions found incised on marble slabs in the mausoleum over catacomb no. 11 and in catacomb no. 18 are arranged in the form of Greek epigrams in the Homeric style. The former reads:

Here lie I, son of Leontius, dead, son of Sappho-Justus,
And after I had plucked the fruit of all wisdom
I left the light, the miserable parents who mourn ceaselessly
And my brothers. Woe to me, in my Besara!
After descending to Hades, I, Justus, lie here
With many of my people, for so willed stern fate.
Be comforted, Justus, no man is immortal.

The mausoleum also contained a reused sarcophagus on which Greek mythological scenes were depicted.

The largest catacomb excavated (no. 20) was comprised of 24 burial chambers with over 200 coffins made of local limestone and many fragments of imported marble sarcophogi decorated with mythological figures. On the coffins birds and animals and even human beings were depicted. The inscriptions found in the catacomb (almost all in Hebrew) reveal that it was occupied by members of the patriarchal family, "holy" rabbis, and other sages.

Additional information on the industrial activities of Bet She'arim was supplied by the discovery of a huge glass slab (11×7 ft. (c. $3\frac{1}{3}\times 2$ m.) and 18 in. (45 cm.) thick, weighing nine tons) in an underground cistern. It possibly served as raw material for village glassmakers in the region. The slab must have been heated for several days at about 1922°F (1050°C) in order to melt it.

Modern Bet She'arim, named after ancient Bet She'arim, which lies 3 mi. (5 km.) further west of it, is a moshav in the northwestern corner of the Jezreel Valley, founded in 1936 by a group of Israel-born and East European settlers. In 1968 the moshav's economy was based on livestock and crops. Its population was 320 in 1968.

Bibliography: B. Mazar, *Bet She'arim ...1936–40,* 1 (Heb., 1957[2]); Avigad, in: IEJ, 4 (1954), 88–107; 5 (1955), 205–39; 7 (1957), 73–92, 239–55; 9 (1959), 205–20; Mazar, *ibid.,* 10 (1960), 264; Brill, *ibid.,* 15 (1965), 261f.; Avi-Yonah, in: *Eretz Yisrael,* 8 (1967), 143–8; Frey, Corpus, 2 (1952), 177–212; M. Schwabe and B. Lifschitz, *Bet She'arim,* 2 (Heb., 1967).

[N.Av.]

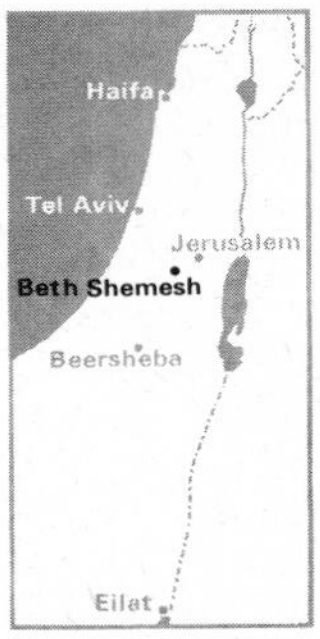

BET(H)-SHEMESH (Heb. בֵּית שֶׁמֶשׁ; "the house [temple] of [the sun-god] Shemesh"), name of a number of places mentioned in the Bible.

(1) A city in the Shephelah on the northern border of the tribe of Judah, between Chesalon and Timnah (Josh. 15:10). Beth-Shemesh appears on the list of cities of the tribe of Dan (Josh. 19:41, as Ir-Shemesh), but it was apparently never actually conquered by it (Judg. 1:35, if the identification of Harheres with Beth-Shemesh is correct). In the list of levitical cities, it is mentioned as belonging to the tribe of Judah (Josh. 21:16; I Chron. 6:44). Beth-Shemesh was located close to the border of Philistia, and the archaeological excavations there have shown that in the period of the Judges, the Philistines exerted a strong influence on the city. The Samson narratives all take place in the vicinity of Beth-Shemesh; his birthplace, Zorah, lay just to the south of it, and the Philistine city Timnah is to the west of it. It has even been suggested that the name Samson itself (Heb. *Shimshon*) indicates a connection with the city. When the Philistines returned the "Ark of God," which they had

captured at the battle of Eben-Ezer, on an ox-driven cart, it was sent along the road that led straight from Ekron to Beth-Shemesh (I Sam. 6). In the period of the monarchy, the city was part of Solomon's second administrative district, which included the former cities of the territory of Dan (I Kings 4:9). The war between Amaziah and Jehoash, kings of Judah and Israel, in about 790 B.C.E. was fought near Beth-Shemesh, and Amaziah was taken prisoner there (II Kings 14:11–13; II Chron. 25:21–23). The last reference to Beth-Shemesh in the Bible occurs during the reign of Ahaz, king of Judah, from whom it was captured by the Philistines in about 734 B.C.E. (II Chron. 28:18).

Beth-Shemesh is identified with Tell al-Rumayla, astride the Wadi al-Ṣarār (biblical Sorek Valley?) on one of the major highways connecting Jerusalem with the seacoast (the modern Jerusalem–Tel Aviv railroad follows this ancient route). The site was excavated by D. Mackenzie (1911–12) and E. Grant (1928–33); G. E. Wright assisted in analyzing the results. The excavations revealed that the first city (stratum VI) of Beth-Shemesh was established toward the close of the third millennium B.C.E. (end of the Early Bronze Age). The next city (stratum V), dating to the Hyksos period (c. 1750–1550 B.C.E.), is characterized by a high level of development. This Middle Bronze Age city was fortified by a massive wall with insets and offsets and towers. In the southern part of the wall, a strong gate was discovered with the entrance between two guardrooms, a style typical of the period. The city continued to flourish in the Late Bronze Age (stratum IV, c. 1550–1200 B.C.E.). In this stratum plastered water cisterns, installations for the manufacture of bronze, numerous imported vessels from the Aegean area and Egypt, an inscription in the Ugaritic cuneiform alphabet, and an ink-inscribed ostracon in early Canaanite-Phoenician script were found. The following stratum (III) dates to the period of the Judges (Early Iron Age). This city shows signs of a decline in the material culture as is also evident in other sites from this period. The decline, however, did not affect the metal industry, which continued to operate at its previous high level. The abundance of Philistine pottery found in this stratum is proof of the strong influence of the Philistines in the area during this period. The destruction of the city by fire in the second half of the 11th century B.C.E. was a result of the wars with the Philistines that preceded the establishment of the monarchy. The city was rebuilt (stratum IIa) sometime in the tenth century and was surrounded by a casemate wall—the typical fortification of Israelite cities in the period of the united monarchy. The large store house and granary erected in the city confirm the biblical description of the important administrative role held by Beth-Shemesh.

Settlement at Beth-Shemesh continued until the end of the First Temple period (strata IIb and IIc). The last city was unfortified. Between IIb and IIc there appears to have been some interruption in the occupation of the site, which may explain the absence of Beth-Shemesh from the detailed city list of Judah, where it would be expected to appear in the Zorah-Azekah district (Josh. 15:33–36). Scholars disagree as to whether the date of this gap in the history of Beth-Shemesh should be ascribed to Pharaoh Shishak's campaign in c. 924 B.C.E. or to the capture of the city by Jehoash, king of Judah, in the eighth century. In Roman times the settlement moved to nearby Ayn Shams, which preserves the ancient name. Talmudic sources describe Beth-Shemesh as a small village (Lam. R. 2:2; etc.) and Eusebius (Onom. 54:11–13) accurately locates it 10 miles from Eleutheropolis (Bet Guvrin) on the road to Nicopolis (Emmaus).

(2) A Canaanite fortress town listed as part of the inheritance of Naphtali (Josh. 19:38) but not settled by the tribe in the early stages of the Israelite occupation of the country (Judg. 1:33). It was most likely located in the northern part of Upper Galilee, where remains of strong Canaanite settlements have been discovered. Some scholars identify it with the Beth-Shemesh of Issachar ((3) below) and accordingly place it in Lower Galilee on the border between Issachar and Naphtali.

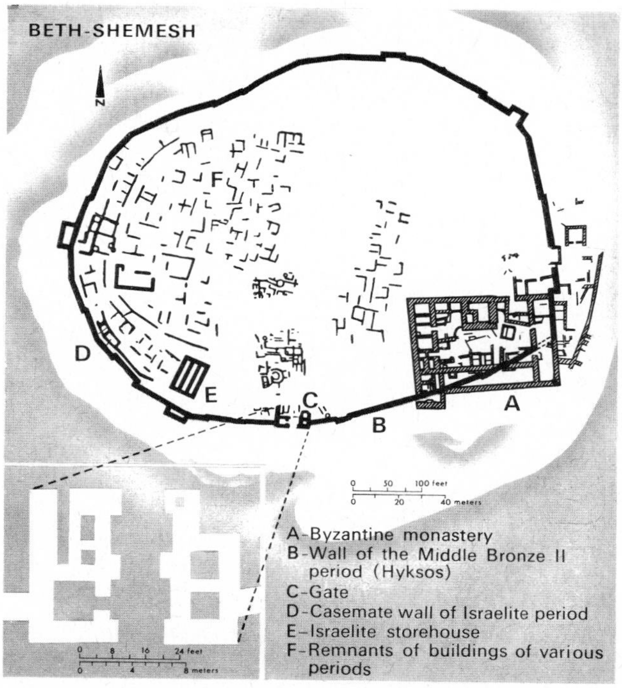

Plan of the excavations at Beth-Shemesh. Courtesy, Mosad Bialik, Jerusalem.

(3) A city in the territory of Issachar, apparently close to the northern border of the tribe (Josh. 19:22). Khirbat Sheikh al-Shamsāwī in the southern part of the valley of Naphtali may preserve the ancient name. Some scholars, however, identify it with al-ʿUbaydiyya, farther east near the Jordan River, on the assumption that it is identical with (2) above.

(4) The city On-Heliopolis in Egypt whose temple to the Egyptian sun-god Re is mentioned in Jeremiah's prophecies against the nations (Jer. 43:13; cf. Isa. 19:18). It is the present-day el-Matariyeh, east of Cairo.

[Yo.A.]

Modern Period. In the vicinity is the modern town of Beth-Shemesh. Its beginnings go back to the village of Hartuv, founded in 1895 by Jews from Bulgaria who bought the land from a training farm set up 12 years earlier by the English Mission of Jerusalem which had tried unsuccessfully to convert Jerusalemite Jews working there. Hartuv made little progress due to its isolation and the lack of water and good soil. In the 1929 Arab riots, the few inhabitants had to leave the village temporarily but soon returned. Shortly before 1948, the Tel Aviv municipality opened a youth training farm there, and construction of the large "Shimshon" cement factory was begun. Beth-Shemesh was abandoned for a few months during the 1948 War of Independence, but finally fell to Israel forces on September 19, 1948. A **ma'abarah* ("immigrant transit settlement") was set up there in 1950, and in 1951 a permanent urban settlement was begun as part of the program of populating and securing the "Jerusalem Corridor." New industrial enterprises developed, including textiles (knitting, shirts), steel (foundry, chains), bicycles, stoves and refrigerators, diamond polishing, and printing. Prominent among later projects were a jet plane engine works and a Murano glass factory. The town numbered 10,000 inhabitants in 1969. [E.O.]

Bibliography: (1) Press, Ereẓ, 1 (1951), 104–5; EM, 2 (1965), 110–8 (includes bibliography). (2) Y. Aharoni, *Hitnaḥalut Shivtei Yisrael ba-Galil ha-Elyon* (1957), 52, 74–5. (3) Abel, Geog, 2 (1938), 282–3; Aharoni, Land, index. (4) EM, 1 (1965), 147; 2 (1965), 119.

BET(H)-SHITTAH (modern **Bet ha-Shittah;** Heb. בֵּית הַשִּׁטָּה), biblical locality mentioned in the description of the Midianites' flight after their defeat by Gideon (Judg. 7:22). Some scholars locate it at the small village of Shatā' (site of a prison), east of the hill of Moreh, but most prefer to place it in the immediate vicinity of the Jordan. There is a kibbutz in the Valley of Jezreel named after the biblical locality of Beth-Shittah. The kibbutz is affiliated with Ha-Kibbutz ha-Me'uḥad. Bet ha-Shittah was founded in 1935 by sabras and pioneers from Germany, later joined by immigrants from other countries. In 1968 Bet ha-Shittah had 885 inhabitants and its economy was based on irrigated field crops, particularly cotton, fodder, fruit orchards, carp ponds, milch cattle, poultry, other farm products, and industrial enterprises such as metal works, wood products, and olive pickling. [E.O.]

BETTAN, ISRAEL (1889–1957), rabbi and scholar. Born in Kovno, he attended Slobodka yeshivah. In 1907 he emigrated to the United States and was ordained as a rabbi by the Hebrew Union College in Cincinnati. Bettan was rabbi of Congregation B'nai Israel, Charleston, West Virginia, from 1912 to 1922 (except for a period as chaplain in World War I). He was appointed professor of Midrash and homiletics at Hebrew Union College in 1922.

Bettan wrote numerous scholarly and popular studies on midrashic literature, liturgy, Jewish preachers, responsa, and on various aspects of Reform Judaism. He also wrote two books: *Studies in Jewish Preaching* (1939) and *The Five Scrolls* (1950). Throughout his career, he was actively involved in the work of the Central Conference of American Rabbis. As a member of its Liturgy Committee, he was one of the major contributors to the newly revised Union Prayer Book. His reports as chairman of the Committee on Responsa (published in the annual volumes of the *CCAR Yearbook*) represent a significant chapter in the development of Reform halakhic literature. Bettan was elected president of the Conference in 1956. The Central Conference dedicated its 1957 yearbook (67) to his memory and also published an *Israel Bettan Memorial Volume* (1961).

Bibliography: Cohon, in: *Israel Bettan Memorial Volume* (1961), 3–27; Wiener, *ibid.*, 52–62. [Eu.M.]

BETTAUER, HUGO (1872–1925), Viennese journalist and novelist. Bettauer went to the United States in his youth, first working in business and later teaching German literature. He later returned to Berlin where he became a journalist for one of the newspapers of the *Ullstein publishing house and was several times imprisoned for offending Emperor William II. Back in New York, he worked on German newspapers published by the Hearst group. After World War I he was sent to Vienna by them and settled there. He wrote several novels, successful in their time, which were also filmed. Most noteworthy of these, *Stadt ohne Juden* (1923; *The City without Jews*, 1926), is directed against anti-Semitism and relates how the State of Austria expels all Jews for racial reasons; as a result it breaks down completely and has to call them back. In 1924 he edited a periodical *Er und Sie* (later *Bettauers Wochenschrift*), advocating sex education and trial marriage. His views made him the focus of attacks from right-wing newspapers. In March 1925 he was murdered by a National-Socialist. [Ed.]

BETTELHEIM, family originating from Pozsony (*Bratislava, Pressburg), formerly in Hungary. According to tradition, one of its forebears frustrated a plot by the count of Bethlen to abduct his wife, and for this feat was called "Bethlen-Jude," which later became Bettelheim. The first noted member of the family, Loeb Bettelheim, served as *dayyan* in Pozsony in 1709. Lipot Leopold (Meyer Leb) Bettelheim (1777–1838) was physician to the count in Galgoc (now Hlohovec) and a noted Hebraist. Moses Bettelheim (beginning of the 19th century) was head of the Jewish community in Pozsony. His son, Fülöp (Raphael), represented the Orthodox Jews in Pozsony at the assembly of Jewish delegates held in Pest in 1868. Samuel *Bettelheim was a journalist and editor. Prominent members of the family outside Hungary include Albert (Aaron) Siegfried *Bettelheim, rabbi, publicist, and physician. Karl Bettelheim (1840–1895), also a physician, became head of a Vienna clinic and the editor of *Medizinisch-Chirurgische Rundschau* (1870–78).

Bibliography: EẒD, 1 (1958), 272–4; S. Federbush, *Ḥokhmat Yisrael be-Ma'arav Eiropah*, 2 (1963), 371–2. [J.Z.]

BETTELHEIM, ALBERT (AARON) SIEGFRIED (1830–1890), U.S. rabbi. Bettelheim was born in Galgoc, Hungary. He served as correspondent on Jewish affairs for several periodicals, director of a network of Jewish schools, editor of a political weekly *Elöre* ("Forward"), and rabbi of a small congregation. Bettelheim's progressive political views brought him into trouble with the government, and he emigrated to America in 1867. He served as rabbi in Philadelphia, and on the faculty of the short-lived Maimonides College. He also acquired a medical degree. In 1875 Bettelheim accepted a pulpit in San Francisco. There he organized a society for Hebrew study for Christian clergymen, and was active in civic affairs, especially prison reform. He coedited a weekly, the *Jewish Times and Observer,* which represented the traditionalists' views. In 1887 he returned East to a pulpit in Baltimore. A foundation to aid needy scholars in Vienna was established in his memory by his daughter Rebekah, wife of Alexander *Kohut. Bettelheim left no complete scholarly work but he wrote many articles on art, medicine, and other subjects and some of his notes and suggestions were incorporated into Kohut's *Arukh*. His son, Félix Albert Bettelheim (1861–1890), a physician, also moved to the United States and initiated the establishment of the first hospital in Panama, serving as head physician between 1883 and 1889.

Bibliography: M. Davis, *Emergence of Conservative Judaism* (1963), 329–31. [J.Ri.]

BETTELHEIM, BRUNO (1903–), U.S. psychologist and educator, best known for his pioneering techniques in the treatment of emotionally disturbed children and his analysis of the psychological aspects of racial prejudice. Born in Vienna, Bettelheim studied at the university there. In 1938 he was sent to the Dachau concentration camp and then to Buchenwald. In 1939 he was released and permitted to leave for the United States. There he worked with the Progressive Education Association and, for a short period, with Rockford College in Illinois. He was subsequently appointed principal of the University of Chicago's Sonia

Shankman Orthogenic School, a residential institution devoted to the education and treatment of children with severe emotional disorders. From 1952 he was professor of educational psychology at that university. In a number of essays and reviews and in a volume entitled *The Informed Heart* (1960), Bettelheim, basing himself on a limited documentation, appears as a stern judge of the Jewish masses who did not revolt against the Nazi terror.

Bruno Bettelheim, U.S. educational psychologist.

Bettelheim has written prolifically on the diagnosis and therapy of emotionally disturbed children. He wrote *Dynamics of Prejudice* (1950) in collaboration with Morris Janowitz, regarded as a vital work in its field. His other major publications included: *Love is Not Enough* (1950); *Truants from Life* (1955), *The Empty Fortress* (1967), and *The Children of the Dream* (1969), an analysis of the rearing of kibbutz children.

Bibliography: J. Robinson, in: *Yad Vashem Studies*, 8 (1970); M. J. Blumenthal, in: *Conservative Judaism* (Spring 1970), 16–19; D. Dempsey, in: *New York Times Magazine* (Jan. 11, 1970), 22–23, 107–11.

[A.J.T.]

BETTELHEIM, SAMUEL (1872–1942), early Zionist and Mizrachi leader in Hungary, later in Czechoslovakia. Bettelheim was born in Pressburg (later Bratislava), where he received a religious and secular education. Under Herzl's influence, he formed the first Zionist association in Hungary. When the Mizrachi movement was founded in 1904, he became one of its leaders. From 1908 he published and edited in Pressburg a Zionist weekly, *Ungarlaendische Juedische Zeitung*. During World War I, the Austro-Hungarian government sent him on a mission to the United States to influence American Jewry in its favor. After the war, he became a leading Zionist in Czechoslovakia. However, Bettelheim, who opposed the political and cultural activities of the Zionist Organization, soon joined Agudat Israel, taking an extreme anti-Zionist stand. He edited their newspaper *Juedische Presse* in Bratislava and Vienna and from 1922 *Juedische Zeitung* in Bratislava, where he propounded Agudat Israel. In 1934–35, he published in Bratislava a German-language monthly called *Judaica*, devoted to Jewish literature and history and containing material on Jewish and Zionist history in Hungary. In his last years he lived in Budapest.

Bibliography: S. H. Weingarten, *Toledot Yehudei Bratislava* (1960) 139–40; EZD, 1 (1958), 272–4.

[SH.W.-H.]

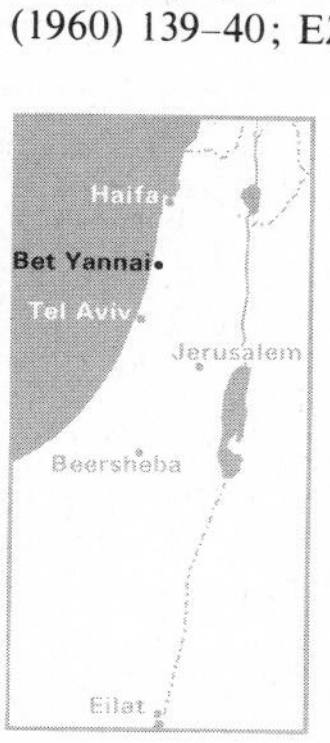

BET YANNAI (Heb. בֵּית יַנַּאי), coastal moshav in the Ḥefer Plain, affiliated with Tenu'at ha-Moshavim; founded in 1933. Its settlers came from Poland, Lithuania, and North America. Its economy is based on farming (mostly citrus plantations) and tourism (the moshav has also become a seaside resort). It is named after the Hasmonean king Alexander Yannai. In 1968 its population was 229.

[E.O.]

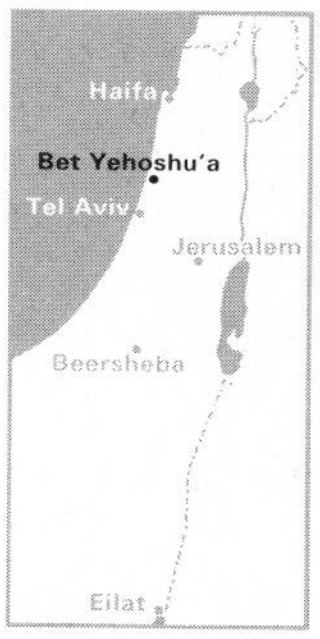

BET YEHOSHU'A (Heb. בֵּית יְהוֹשֻׁעַ), moshav shittufi in central Israel, in the southern Sharon, affiliated with Ha-Oved ha-Ẓiyyoni. It was founded as a kibbutz in 1938 by pioneers from Poland. Its economy is based mainly on citrus plantations and milch cattle. The village's name commemorates the Zionist leader Osias (Yehoshu'a) *Thon. In 1968 its population was 260.

[E.O.]

BET YERAḤ (Heb. בֵּית יֶרַח), large Canaanite city on the shore of the Sea of Galilee extending over a tell of approximately 50 acres, from the site of the present-day moshavah *Kinneret, to the outlet of the *Jordan River from the lake near *Deganyah. This location is based on the Jerusalem Talmud (Meg. 1:1, 70a) which speaks of two autonomous cities surrounded by walls, Bet-Yeraḥ and Ẓinabri (*Sennabris), in the vicinity of the Sea of Galilee. An additional reference is found in *Bekhorot* 51a, which states that the Jordan River "began" at Bet Yerah. Inasmuch as Sennabris is usually identified with Ḥaẓar Kinneret, it is probable that Bet Yeraḥ was situated on the site known to the Arabs as Khirbat al-Karak. Although not mentioned in the Bible, the name points to an ancient Canaanite settlement whose deity was a moon god. Excavations were conducted there in 1944–46 by the Jewish Palestine Exploration Society and, from 1949, by the Department of Antiquities and the Oriental Institute, University of Chicago.

The earliest settlement at Bet Yeraḥ is dated at the end of the Chalcolithic and the beginning of the Early Bronze Age

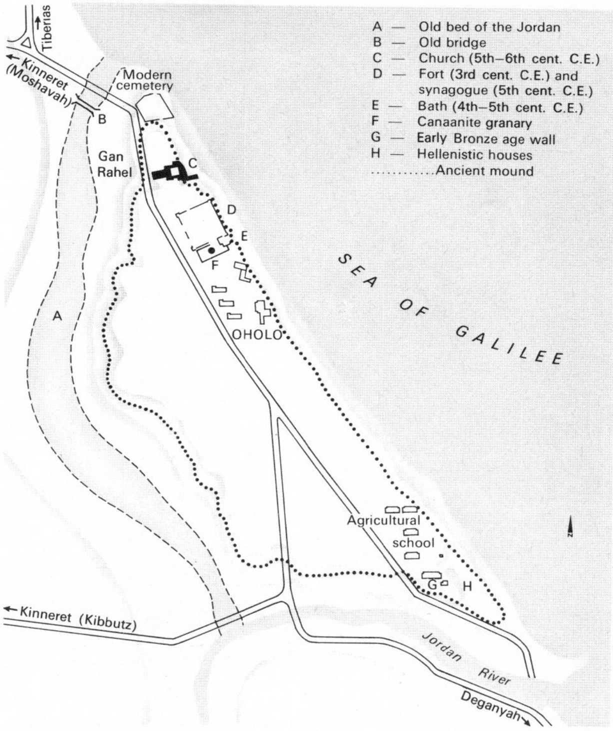

Map showing the site of the Canaanite city of Bet Yeraḥ in relation to the modern Oholo. After P. Delougaz and R. C. Haines, *A Byzantine Church at Kirbat Al-Karak*, 1960.

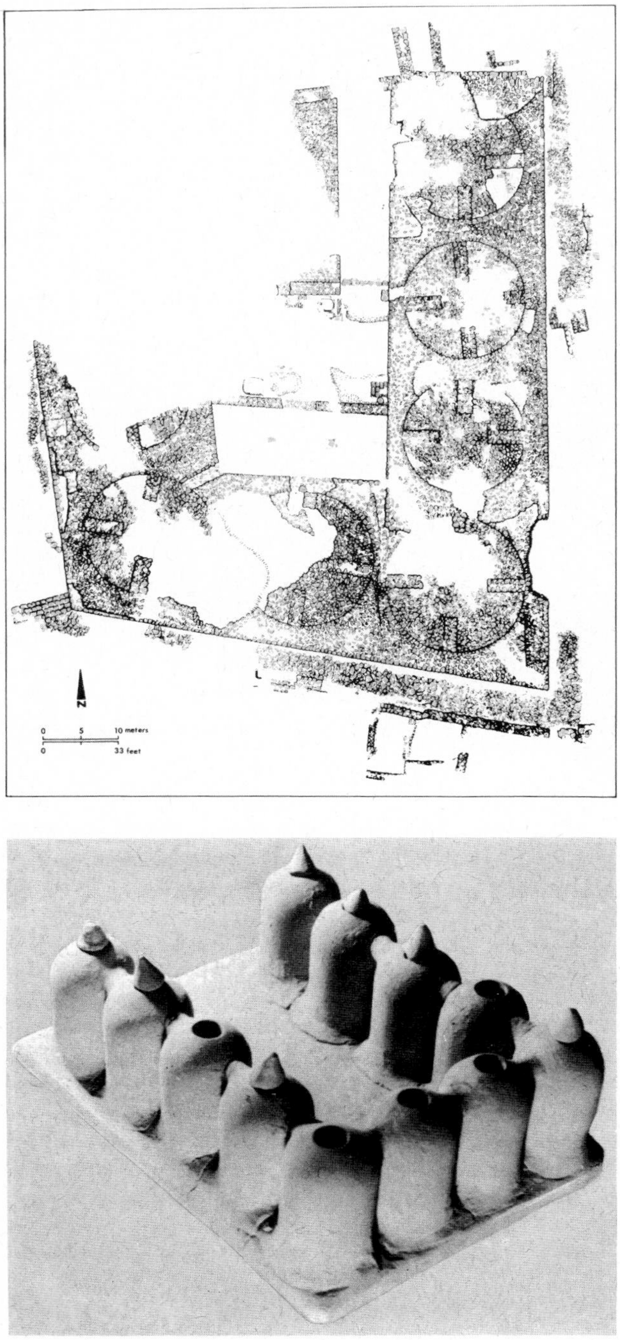

Figure 1. Above: Drawing of the base found at Bet Yeraḥ for a set of grain containers. Diam. 6 in. (15 cm.). Below: Model of a similar set of containers from the tomb of Kamena at a-Kab, Upper Egypt, c. 2613–2494 B.C.E. Diam. 11 in. (28 cm.), height 15¼ in. (39 cm.). Haifa, Dagon Museum.

I (c. 3200 B.C.E.). The inhabitants lived in huts some of which were sunk into pits dug to a depth of about 11½ ft. (3.5 m.). Traces of pavements and ovens were found in the pits. The erection of a brick wall, the first of Bet Yeraḥ's fortifications, was followed by the building of mud-brick houses and in the 29th century B.C.E. (Early Bronze Age II), stone houses made their appearance. A tomb from this period found at moshavah Kinneret contained gold ornaments in the style of Asia Minor. The settlement reached its zenith in the Early Bronze Age III (26th–24th centuries B.C.E.), when a large granary, 3,936 sq. ft. (1,200 sq. m.) in area, was constructed to the north of Bet Yeraḥ, indicating that at that time it was already the center of a large region of irrigated farmlands. The pottery of this epoch is light red or red-black burnished ware (a type common in Syria and Asia Minor) and its presence is apparently to be attributed to influences of northern peoples who penetrated through trade or invasion. In the Middle Bronze Age I the settlement was concentrated in the southern part of Bet Yeraḥ. No settlement existed there after that for about 1,500 years until the Persian period; to this period belong several graves found there. The city's location in ancient times east of the Jordan, on a narrow tongue between the river and the Sea of Galilee, necessitated building the main fortifications on the southern side. Here, where the Jordan now flows, the city lacked natural defenses in ancient times. The settlement at Bet Yeraḥ flourished again in the Hellenistic period. It has been identified with Philoteria, a Ptolemaic center, captured by *Antiochus III in 198 B.C.E. and also mentioned among the cities conquered by Alexander *Yannai (according to George Synkellus, 1:559). Remains uncovered from this period include a stone wall with vaulted openings and several houses, some with floors, plastered and painted walls, and windows overlooking the lake; numerous Rhodian stamped jar handles were also discovered.

In the early Roman period, a large Roman structure, covering an area of 105×59 ft. (32×18 m.), was erected on the ruins of the Hellenistic houses on the south. A large rectangular fort built of dressed masonry with towers at its corners was constructed on the northern part of the tell in the third century C.E. From this period there are several reports of a mixed Jewish-gentile population at Bet Yeraḥ (TJ, Meg. 1:1, 70a). After the Bar Kokhba war, priests of the Haaziah family settled there. The verse "Naphtali is a hind let loose" (Gen. 49:21) was interpreted by rabbis of the time as referring to Bet Yeraḥ, the territory of which was "entirely irrigated" (Gen. R. 98:22). The statement in the Jerusalem Talmud (loc. cit.) "The city was destroyed and became the possession of gentiles" also alludes to some event which occurred in the third century at Bet Yeraḥ or in its vicinity. In the fourth and fifth centuries, the fort seems to have been abandoned and its southern wall was used as the northern wall of a bathhouse. Excavations have shown that the bathhouse, the water for which was conducted through earthenware pipes from the aqueduct of *Tiberias, had a central hall with a circular pool in the center and heated rooms. In the fifth century, a synagogue was built within the fort. It was basilical, with an apse oriented to Jerusalem, and was one of the largest contemporary synagogues in the country, 121×72 ft. (37×22 m.). Its foundations have survived as well as part of its mosaic floor depicting a citron tree, a man and a horse (possibly a representation of the story of Mordecai and Haman), and also the base of a column incised with a seven-branched candelabrum.

North of the synagogue, a Christian church was built, basilical in form, with a central hall and two aisles; an atrium containing a well lay on its west side. The church had been enlarged to the north by a baptistery with a mosaic pavement dating from 529 C.E. Bet Yeraḥ was resettled in the seventh century after having been destroyed during the Persian or Arab invasion, but it was abandoned shortly afterward and reoccupied only in recent years. In 1945 an agricultural secondary school for the settlements of the Jordan Valley was built south of the tell and in 1949 Oholo, a conference and study center in memory of Berl *Katznelson, was erected north of it. Oholo opened in 1957 on the initiative of Ben Zion Yisreeli of Kevuẓah Kinneret, a leading personality of the labor and kibbutz movement. It houses courses for soldiers after their discharge; a teachers' seminary, principally for students hailing from Middle Eastern countries who intend to teach

Figure 2. Pottery bowl of the Early Bronze Age III (26th–24th centuries B.C.E.) from Bet Yeraḥ, a typical specimen of the red and black burnished "Bet Yeraḥ ware." Jerusalem, Israel Department of Antiquities and Museums.

in immigrant villages and development towns; and a field school of the Society for the Preservation of Nature.

Bibliography: Maisler et al., in: IEJ, 2 (1952), 165–73, 218–29; P. Bar-Adon, in: *Eretz Israel,* 4 (1956), 50–55; Albright, in: AASOR, 6 (1926), 27ff.; idem, in: JPOS 15 (1935), 200; Sukenik, in: JPOS, 2 (1922), 101ff.; P. Delougaz and R. C. Haines, *Byzantine Church at Khirbat al-Karak* (1960).

[M.A.-Y./E.O.]

BET YIẒḤAK (Heb. בֵּית יִצְחָק), moshav in central Israel, in the Ḥefer Plain. It was founded in 1940 as an unaffiliated middle-class settlement by immigrants from Germany, many of whom were formerly members of academic professions. Later, Bet Yiẓḥak merged with the neighboring moshav Nirah, most of whose settlers came from Czechoslovakia and Austria. In 1968 Bet Yiẓḥak had a population of 825, and its economy was based on citrus orchards, a fruit preserves factory, and intensive farming. Its name commemorates the German Zionist Yiẓḥak Feuerring, whose bequest was instrumental in financing the settlement. [E.O.]

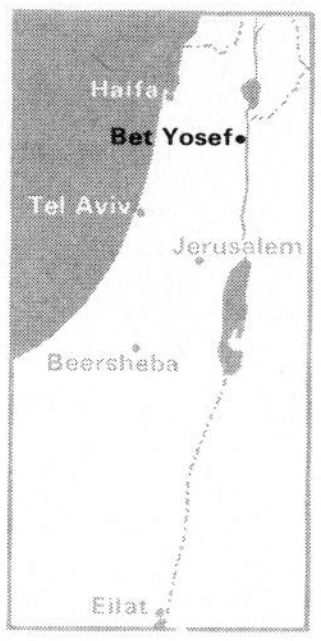

BET YOSEF (Heb. בֵּית יוֹסֵף), moshav in Israel, in the north of the Beth-Shean Valley near the Jordan River, affiliated with Tenu'at ha-Moshavim; founded on April 9, 1937 as a "*tower and stockade" settlement. Its inhabitants came from Kurdistan. Its economy was based mostly on livestock and field crops, including cotton. Following the Six-Day War in June 1967, Bet Yosef frequently suffered from Jordanian artillery fire and acts of sabotage. Its name commemorates the Israel labor leader, Yosef *Aharonovitch.

[E.O.]

BET ZAYIT (Heb. בֵּית זַיִת), moshav west of Jerusalem, affiliated with Ha-Mo'aẓah ha-Ḥakla'it association of "middle-class" settlements. Bet Zayit was founded in 1949 by immigrants from Yugoslavia, Rumania, and Hungary. Later, immigrants from Egypt settled in the village. Its economy was based on fruit orchards, vegetables, poultry, and other farm products. Bet Zayit lies on the fringe of the Jerusalem Forest Park and operates a swimming pool. Near the village is the Ein Kerem dam built to store winter flood waters. The name, "House of the Olive Tree," refers to the extensive olive groves on the slopes around the village. In 1970 Bet Zayit numbered 468 inhabitants. A place of the same name mentioned in the books of the Maccabees stood further north, possibly at the site of the Arab village Bīr al-Zayt, north of Ramallah. [E.O.]

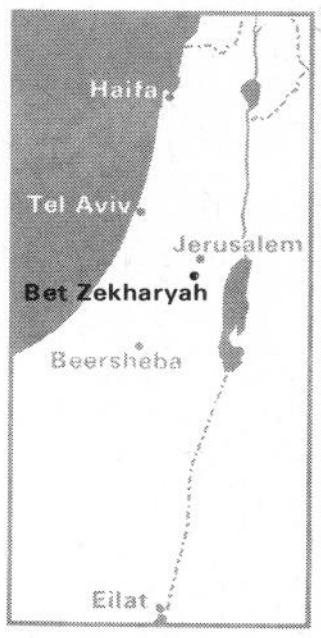

BET ZEKHARYAH (Heb. בֵּית זְכַרְיָה), site 10 mi. (16 km.) S.W. of Jerusalem and 6 mi. (9½ km.) N. of Beth-Zur, where the Hasmonean army clashed with that of Antiochus V Eupator, king of Syria, in 162 B.C.E. In this battle *Eleazar, a brother of *Judah Maccabee, was crushed to death by one of the enemy's elephants whom he attacked, believing it to be carrying the king. The Jewish force was compelled to retreat (I Macc. 6:32–3; Jos., Ant., 12:369ff.). Bet Zekharyah is present-day Khirbat Beit Zakarya, 2.2 mi. (4 km.) S.W. of Solomon's Pools.

Bibliography: Jos., Wars, 1:41ff.; Avi-Yonah, Geog, 103; Abel, in: RB, 33 (1924), 212ff.; Ploger, in: ZDPV, 79 (1958), 173.

[M.A.-Y.]

BET ZERA (Heb. בֵּית זֶרַע, "House of Seed"), kibbutz in Israel, 1¼ mi. (2 km.) S. of Lake Kinneret, affiliated with Kibbutz Arẓi ha-Shomer ha-Ẓair, founded in 1927 by pioneers from Germany who had previously participated in establishing *Mizra in the Jezreel Valley. It received part of the Umm Jūnī lands (among the first acquired in the country by the Jewish National Fund), ceded by nearby Deganiyyah when it intensified its farming methods. The settlers developed a farming economy adapted to the hot climate, including bananas and other tropical fruit. It also owns a factory that manufactures plastic goods. In 1968 Bet Zera had 660 inhabitants. In its initial years, the settlement was named also Kefar Nathan Laski, after the English communal leader. The site is supposed to be that of Kefar Agun of talmudic times, home of R. Tanḥum b. Ḥiyya (Gen. R. 100:7). [E.O.]

BET ẒERIFA, Jewish family of the Second Temple period. According to the Mishnah "there was a family of Bet Ẓerifa in Transjordan and Ben-Zion rejected it by force" (Eduy. 8:7; see also TJ, Yev. 8:3, 9a: TJ, Kid. 4:1, 65c). Scholars are divided as to whether this implies that Ben-Zion (of whom nothing more is known) had it ejected from the priesthood because he questioned its legitimacy. Possibly the learned Judah, son of Sariphaeus (Ẓerifa), who—according to Josephus—incited his disciples to pull down the golden eagle erected by Herod the king over the temple gate, belonged to this family, as well as R. Judah son of Ẓipporai, also known as Ben Ẓerifa.

Bibliography: Jos., Ant., 17:149; Jos., Wars, 1:648; Buechler, in: *Festschrift A. Schwarz* ... (1917), 137ff.; S. Klein, in: MGWJ, 64 (1920), 180ff.; J. N. Epstein, *ibid.*, 65 (1921), 89–90.

[I.G.]

BET(H)-ZUR (Heb. בֵּית צוּר), ancient city in Ereẓ Israel, 4½ mi. (7 km.) N. of Hebron, and, according to Eusebius (Onom. 52:1–2), 20 Roman miles south of Jerusalem, on the Hebron–Jerusalem road. The name has been preserved at Khirbat Burj al-Ṣūr but the ancient city was located nearby at Khirbat al-Ṭubayqa, on a high isolated plateau.

Beth-Zur seems to have first been settled during the Early Bronze Age (third millennium B.C.E.). The earliest city, however, was apparently established by the *Hyksos in the second half of the Middle Bronze Age (c. 18th century B.C.E.). Only meager traces of the Late Bronze Age have been discovered. The site was rebuilt during the period of the Israelite settlement and appears to have been associated with the rule of the sons of *Caleb and the tribe of Judah (Josh. 15:58; I Chron. 2:45). The Israelite city was destroyed by fire c. 1,000 B.C.E., apparently in one of the Philistine attacks. Rehoboam included Beth-Zur in his system of fortifications (II Chron. 11:7). In the days of *Nehemiah, it was the capital of a sub-district. Its ruler, Nehemiah, son of Azbuk, took part in the rebuilding of the walls of Jerusalem (Neh. 3:16). From this time onward, Beth-Zur served as a defense post on the southern frontier of Judea against the Idumeans in the Hebron district. It played an important role in the Hasmonean wars; a Seleucid garrison stationed there from 175 B.C.E. was routed by *Judah Maccabee in 165 B.C.E. This victory and Judah's fortifications of Beth-Zur as a border stronghold of Judea made possible the resumption of the service in the Temple and its rededication (I Macc. 4:29). Two years later, the Syrians regained control of the city and thereby of the road to Jerusalem (I Macc. 6:60). Their general *Bacchides rebuilt its fortifications, c. 160 B.C.E. (I Macc. 9:52), but after a prolonged siege it was finally captured by the Hasmonean *Simeon son of Mattathias in the mid-forties of the second century B.C.E. and its defenses were strengthened. Remains of the Maccabean fortress, containing large rock-hewn cisterns, were uncovered in excavations conducted in 1931 and resumed in 1957. The city was destroyed and abandoned, apparently during *Vespasian's campaigns, but as shown by the Madaba Map, it was reestablished in the Byzantine period, probably on the opposite hill, Khirbat Burj al-Ṣūr, whose ruins date from Crusader times.

Bibliography: O. R. Sellers, *Citadel of Beth Zur* (1933); Lapp, in: BASOR, 151 (1958), 16–27; Aharoni, Land, index; Avi-Yonah, Geog, index. [M.A.-Y.]

°**BEUGNOT, AUGUSTE ARTHUR** (1797–1865), French lawyer, senator (1841), and delegate to the National Assembly (1848). Beugnot was keenly interested in the improvement of the situation of the Jews in France. In 1822, together with J. B. Capefigue and G. B. Depping he won a French Academy competition for a paper *Juifs d'occident, ou recherches sur l'état civil, le commerce, la littérature des Juifs en France, en Espagne et en Italie, pendant la durée du moyen âge* (Paris, 1824). Beugnot showed thorough knowledge of Jewish history and concluded his study with an exposition of the contributions of the Jews to the growth of European economies and culture. He asserted that whatever negative traits the Jews possess can be blamed on the Christians. In 1824 the Institute of Science, Agriculture, and Art in Strasbourg announced a competition under the patronage of an anonymous Jew, which had as its purpose to find "the most helpful ways in enabling the Jewish population of Alsace to enjoy the accomplishments of civilization." Beugnot won first prize but his submitted work never appeared in print. A resumé of his "Quels sont les moyens les plus propres à faire jouir la population israélite de l'Alsace des bienfaits de la civilisation?" appeared in *Journal de la Société des Science, Agriculture et Arts du Departement du Bas Rhin* (1 (1824), 114–6; 2 (1825), 297–320). He proposed that a council of Alsatian Jews be formed, under state sponsorship, to form committees for schools, publication of textbooks, experimental farms, trade, and charity. He argued that it was necessary to found a modern theological school and also proposed changing the Sabbath to Sunday. [N.GR.]

°**BEVAN, EDWYN ROBERT** (1870–1943), historian and philosopher. He was educated at Oxford and became lecturer in Hellenistic history and literature at King's College, London. Bevan's main publications of Jewish interest are *The House of Seleucus*, 2 vols. (1902) and *Jerusalem under the High Priests* (1904), still a standard work. He also was coeditor (with Israel Abrahams and Charles Singer) of the *Legacy of Judaism* (1928^2), to which he contributed the article on Hellenistic Judaism. His brother, ANTHONY ASHLEY BEVAN (1859–1933), taught Oriental languages at Cambridge University. His chief interests were Arabic and Hebrew and he wrote a commentary on the Book of Daniel (1892). [ED.]

°**BEVIN, ERNEST** (1881–1951), British trade union leader and statesman. He was a member of the British War Cabinet in World War II (1941–45), and foreign secretary in the Labor government (1945–50) when Palestine was transferred de facto from the aegis of the Colonial Office to that of the Foreign Office. Bevin's Palestine policy was based on two premises: first, he felt that since the vast majority of the Middle East population was Arab, nothing should be done against their will, lest this set the Arab world against Great Britain and the West in their global struggle with the U.S.S.R. and Communism; second, he believed that Palestine could not essentially solve the Jewish problem as Jews should continue residing in Europe and contributing to its welfare. Rather than impose a Jewish state on the Arabs, he desired some kind of settlement between Jews and Arabs. In an attempt to obtain U.S. government approval for his Palestine policy, Bevin proposed appointing an Anglo-American commission whose task would be to plan a solution to the Palestine question. In the summer of 1946 he rejected the committee's proposals for the immediate admission of 100,000 Jewish refugees from Europe and the annulment of the provisos in the Macdonald White Paper restricting the acquisition of land by Jews. As a result, the situation in Palestine deteriorated, and Bevin began applying severe repressive measures against the *yishuv*. Leading members of the Jewish Agency and the Va'ad Le'ummi were arrested, "illegal" immigrants were deported to detention camps in Cyprus, and the *Exodus*, bearing 4,500 such immigrants, was shipped back to Germany. At the same time, Bevin proposed other ways of solving the problem. One of these was the cantonization of Palestine, better known as the Morrison Scheme, which allocated about 17% of the country to the Jews; another was the Bevin Plan to give the British government a five-year trusteeship over Palestine with the declared object of preparing the country for independence. On Feb. 15, 1947, after both plans had been rejected by Jews and Arabs, Bevin announced that he was referring the entire matter to the United Nations. As a result, the United Nations Special Committee on Palestine (UNSCOP) was appointed and, on Nov. 29, 1947, the UN voted to divide Palestine into a Jewish and an Arab State. Bevin gradually became reconciled to the idea of a Jewish state; in January 1949, eight months after the proclamation of the State of Israel, he granted it de facto recognition.

Bibliography: F. Williams, *Ernest Bevin* (Eng., 1952); J. H. Hurewitz, *The Struggle for Palestine* (1950); R. H. S. Crossman, *A Nation Reborn* (1960), ch. 2; idem, *Palestine Mission*

(1946); B.C.Crum, *Behind the Silken Curtain* (1947); Jewish Agency, *The Jewish Plan for Palestine* (1947). [M.R.]

BEYTH, HANS (1901–1947), *Youth Aliyah leader. Beyth, who was born in Bleicherode, Germany, was active in his youth in the *Blau-Weiss Zionist youth movement. In 1935 he went to Palestine, where he worked as Henrietta *Szold's assistant in Youth Aliyah. His resourcefulness in rescuing and warmth in educating the Youth Aliyah wards made him an outstanding personality in the organization. He was instrumental in the establishment of Youth Aliyah institutions in communal settlements, and in the absorption

Hans Beyth, Youth Aliyah leader.

of many wards into kibbutz life. Beyth was sent to Europe at the end of World War II to prepare the emigration and absorption of surviving Jewish children. In the last year of his life he arranged for the care of 20,000 wards. Beyth was murdered by Arabs in December, 1947 while on his way home to Jerusalem from Haifa and Athlit, where he had been welcoming children on their arrival from a youth village in Cyprus.

Bibliography: *Hans Beyth, Ish Aliyyat ha-No'ar* (1951); *Im Gedenken an Hans Beyth,* (1948), published by the Jewish Agency.
[A.L.]

BEẒAH (Heb. בֵּיצָה; "egg"), a tractate (so called after its opening word) of the order *Mo'ed,* in the Mishnah, Tosefta, Babylonian Talmud, and Jerusalem Talmud. The tractate deals with the laws of festivals, but whereas each of the other tractates of the order *Mo'ed* deals with a specific festival, *Beẓah,* in the main, discusses the laws common to festivals in general; for this reason this tractate is also called *Yom Tov* ("festival"). The tractate consists of five chapters in both the Mishnah and the Talmud, but of only four in the Tosefta. The halakhic content of the Mishnah, of which the first two chapters consist chiefly of differences of opinion between Bet Shammai and *Bet Hillel, derives in part from Temple times (e.g. 2:7; 3:8; 5:5) and in part from the period of Jabneh (2:6). The Mishnah gives for the most part the opinions of various *tannaim* who were disciples of R. *Akiva, but it also contains many anonymous mishnayot of later *tannaim* who were contemporaries of Judah ha-Nasi. *Beẓah* in the Babylonian Talmud contains many teachings of Palestinian scholars who reached Babylon by way of the **neḥutei,* but which do not appear in the Jerusalem Talmud. Conversely, the text of the tractate in the Jerusalem Talmud contains statements of Babylonian scholars which are not found in the Babylonian Talmud. *Beẓah* contains many additions of the *savoraim* (26a, 27a, 35b), as well as older material revised by them. There is an English translation of the Talmud text in the Soncino translation (1938) by M. Ginsberg.

Illustration of the opening of the tractate *Beẓah,* which deals with the laws relating to an egg laid on a festival. Detail from a title page of a Hebrew and Latin edition of the Mishnah, Amsterdam, 1700–1704. Jerusalem, J.N.U.L.

Bibliography: P. Blackman (ed. and tr.), *Mishnayot,* 2 (Eng., 1952), 349–75 (with introd. and notes); H. Strack, *Introduction to the Talmud and Midrash* (1959²), 39–40; Epstein, Tanna'im, 354–62; Epstein, Amora'im, 24–44; H. Albeck, *Shishah Sidrei Mishnah, Seder Mo'ed* (1958), 281–6.
[Z.K.]

BEZALEL (Heb. בְּצַלְאֵל; "in the shadow [under the protection] of God," cf. Ps. 91:1; similar to the Akkadian *ina-ṣilli-Bēl* ("in the shadow of Bel"), *ina-ṣilli-Nabû,* "in the shadow of Nabu," and the like), son of Uri, son of Hur of the tribe of Judah; an expert in metalwork, stonecutting, and woodcarving. Moses appointed Bezalel head of the artisans who were employed both in the construction of the

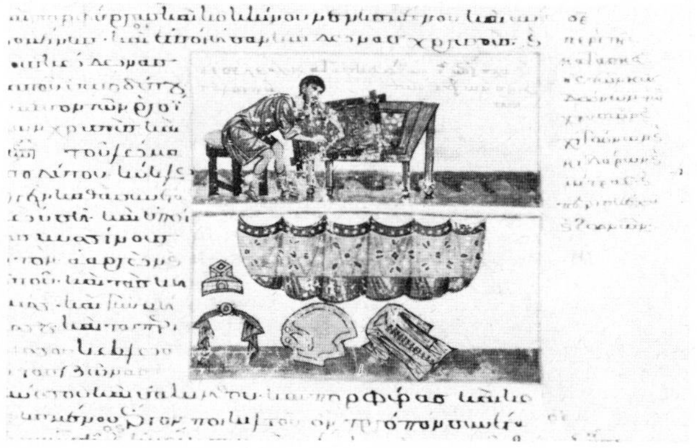

Bezalel stretching hides for the Tabernacle. The lower register shows the priestly vestments. Illumination from a Byzantine Octateuch, 12th century. Rome, Vatican Library, Gk. 746.

*Tabernacle and its equipment and in designing the priests' vestments (Ex. 31:1–11; 36–39). He was assisted by *Oholiab son of Ahisamach the Danite, who was an expert craftsman and embroiderer (31–6; 35:34–35).

The Bible views Bezalel's construction of the Tabernacle and its equipment as the execution of a plan that the Lord detailed to Moses on the Mount (Ex. 25:9, 40; 26:30; 27:8; Num. 8:4). The idea that the Temple's construction should be detailed according to a divine plan is also found in Ezekiel's vision concerning Jerusalem and the Temple (40:2ff.). Similarly, the author of I Chronicles (28:19) asserts that the instructions for building the First Temple were given "in writing, by His hand." Parallel notions are to be found in the literature of other nations as, for

Bezalel and Oholiab building the Tabernacle. Woodcut from the *Koberger Bible*, Nuremberg, 1483. Jerusalem, Israel Museum Archives.

example, in the inscriptions of Gudea, king of Lagash, concerning certain structures he erected in his land, and in Babylonian inscriptions dealing with the temple of Marduk. Drawing upon Exodus 31:3, which describes Bezalel as being endowed with "... a divine spirit of skill, ability, and knowledge ...," Philo viewed Bezalel as a symbol of pure knowledge (II Gig. 23). He inferred from the name "Bezalel" that he knew God by seeing the divine shadow, that is, by seeing only God's works, and not God Himself, as had Moses (ILA 3:102). [Y.M.G.]

In the Aggadah. When Moses was instructed to erect the Sanctuary and fashion its vessels, God showed him the name of Bezalel written in the Book of the Generations of Adam (Gen. 5:1), in which are inscribed all the deeds of future generations, as the divinely appointed architect. Nevertheless he was told to obtain the approval of the Children of Israel for the appointment, in order to teach that no leader should be appointed without the consent of

Bezalel sculpting the cherubim, inspired by the hand of God. On his left, Moses receives the tablets of the Law. Carved wood relief by Milton Horn on the doors of the ark at Temple Israel, Charleston, W. Va., 1960. Height 7 ft. (2.1 m.). Photo Estelle Horn.

the people (Ber. 55a; cf. Jos., Ant., 3:104). At the side of Bezalel, who belonged to the aristocratic tribe of Judah, worked Oholiab, of the lowliest tribe, that of Dan, to show that before God "the great and the lowly are equal" (Ex. R. 40:4). God filled Bezalel with wisdom (Ex. 31:3) "because he already possessed wisdom," since "God does not grant wisdom save to those who already have wisdom" (Tanḥ. Va-Yakhel, 2; Ber. 55a). Bezalel had five other names: Reaiah ("the seer"), Shobal ("the builder of the dovecote," a synonym for the Tabernacle), Jahat ("the dreadful"), Ahumai ("the unifier of Israel"), and Lahad ("one who beautified Israel," or "one who was near to the poor"; Ex. R. 40:4).

Bibliography: Ginzberg, Legends, index.

[E.E.H.]

BEZALEL, academy of Arts and Design in Jerusalem. Generally regarded as the national institution for studies in these fields, it was formerly designated the Bezalel School of Arts and Crafts and was under the supervision of the Ministry of Education. It achieved its present status as an academy in November 1969 and is now under the aegis of the National Council for Higher Education. Its diploma, awarded after four years of study, is officially recognized as equivalent to a B.A.

Bezalel, named after the biblical artisan *Bezalel, son of Uri, who constructed and decorated the Ark of the Covenant (Ex. 36:2), was founded in 1906 by the sculptor Boris *Schatz, court sculptor to King Ferdinand of Bulgaria, who brought six of the first students from that country. It was installed in a romantic crenellated stone structure built as an orphanage at the turn of the century. Schatz's aim was to establish a center that would affect the cultural life of the *yishuv* and create craft industries; each fine arts student was also required to learn a craft and, if possible, to play an instrument. At the same time he founded the Bezalel Museum as part of the school for the benefit of both students and public. Initial financial support came principally from Otto *Warburg and a group of German Zionists who also helped to find outlets for the weaving, needlework, metalwork, and wood and ivory carvings produced at the school. Schatz imposed what he intended to be both a Jewish and an economically viable style on the students. In 1911, when there were 460 students and craftsmen at the school and its workshops, an abortive attempt was made to settle some of them in a workers' colony at *Ben Shemen, where the families of 14 Yemenite silversmiths were to work on the land. The school fell on hard times when support from Germany failed during World War I and the school was destroyed and Schatz, together with other Jewish public figures, was held as a hostage by the Turks. After the war, Schatz left on a fund-raising mission, and succeeded in reconstructing the school. He died abroad, and the school was closed (1932), but reopened the following year when a new wave of immigrants, refugees from Hitler's Europe, provided not only a new need for such an institution, but also a new impetus and a new staff.

Arthur *Ruppin headed a committee which obtained funds from the Jewish National Fund, the Jewish Agency and the Mandatory government, and the "New Bezalel" was reopened in 1935 under Joseph *Budko as an institution separate from the adjoining museum. Among the teachers were Ze'ev *Ben Ẓvi, Mordecai *Ardon, Jakob *Steinhardt, Yeraḥmiel *Schechter, and Isidor *Aschheim, who succeeded each other as directors of the school, followed by Felix Darnell and Dan Hoffner, a Bezalel graduate, who became director in 1963. Hoffner modernized the academy, putting the accent on design. The student

Figure 1. Teachers and students of the Bezalel School of Arts and Crafts with Boris Schatz, seated in the center of the second row, c. 1910. From Ben Dov Collection, by courtesy of Israel State Archives.

body grew from 26 in 1936 to 300 in 1969. Financial support comes from interested ministries (education, industry, labor) and the America-Israel Cultural Foundation.

The major professional subjects are painting, sculpture, industrial design, interior and furniture design, graphic design and packaging, typography, lettering, book illustration, jewelry, metalwork (chiefly silver and goldsmithing), theater design, ceramics, enameling, etching, lithography,

Figure 2. A students' show at the Bezalel Academy. Photo Ephraim Dagani, Jerusalem.

silk-screen printing, and photography; there are also courses in metallurgy, psychology, theory of creation, sociology, and economics.

For Bezalel National Art Museum see *Museums.

[Me.R.]

BEZALEL BEN MOSES HA-KOHEN (1820–1878), Lithuanian rabbi and unofficial rabbi of Vilna. At the age of 11, Bezalel already knew by heart two of the six orders of the Talmud; at 13, he had covered the entire Talmud and amazed his listeners with his original halakhic discourses. A sermon which he delivered before the rabbis of Vilna at the age of 18 was subsequently published in his *Reshit Bikkurim.* His novellae were collected in a work *Torat Yisrael* which is no longer extant. In 1843 although only 23 years of age, Bezalel was chosen as one of the rabbis of Vilna in succession to Joseph Shiskes. He soon became the leading *"moreh ẓedek"* of Vilna, an office equivalent to that of rabbi of the city. Bezalel was well versed in secular subjects, particularly mathematics and engineering. *Reshit Bikkurim,* responsa and comments on the *Sifra* (1868), reveals his extensive scholarship and his firm attitude in halakhic questions. His glosses on the Talmud, *Mareh Kohen,* bearing the same title as his notes on *Yoreh De'ah,* were published in the Vilna edition of the Talmud (1884). His commentary on the *Sefer ha-Mitzvot* of Maimonides appeared in the Vilna edition of 1866. He also published a pamphlet entitled *Hora'at Hetter,* dealing with the permissibility of using *etrogim* from Corfu on Sukkot (1876). Many of Bezalel's responsa appear in the works of his contemporaries and a number of his writings are still in manuscript.

Bibliography: H. N. Maggid-Steinschneider, *Ir Vilna,* 1 (1900), 55–61; J. L. Maimon, *Middei Ḥodesh be-Ḥodsho,* 4 (1958), 12–16.

[Y.Al.]

BEZALEL BEN SOLOMON OF KOBRYN (17th century), preacher and author. Bezalel was active in Slutsk (Minsk region), Boskowitz (Moravia), and Przemysl. The following of his books are worthy of note: (1) *Pelaḥ ha-Rimmon* (Amsterdam, 1659), consisting of 20 different expositions of various Midrashim; (2) *Ammudei ha-Shivah* ("Seven Pillars," Lublin, 1666), sermons on obscure Midrashim. The "Seven Pillars" are Abraham, Isaac, Jacob, Moses, Aaron, David, and Solomon, and each section has in its title a biblical verse containing the respective names of these worthies. In his introduction the author states: "I found favor in the eyes of the rulers and leaders of the country [Lithuania], who were moved to make a large contribution toward the publication of the book, and it also received the approbation of the Council of the Four Lands." Selections from the book were published by Joshua Abraham b. Israel of Zhitomir under the title *Nofet Ẓufim* (Lemberg, 1804). (3) *Korban Shabbat* (Dyhernfurth, 1691), homilies on the Sabbath precepts and customs, compiled from the halakhic authorities and works of Kabbalah. Other of his works are still in manuscript.

Bibliography: Michael, Or, 289, n. 613; Halpern, Pinkas, 78–79, 99; *Pinkas Slutsk* . . . (1962), 19, 33, 272.

[Y.Ho.]

BEZEK (Heb. בֶּזֶק), place-name mentioned in the Bible. Saul mustered his army there before undertaking his campaign to relieve *Jabesh-Gilead, which was being besieged by the Ammonites under Nahash (I Sam. 11:8). Bezek has been identified (following Eusebius, Onom. 54:8) with Khirbat Ibzīq, 15 mi. (24 km.) north of Shechem on the road leading to Beth-Shean. Its position on the road descending from the hill country of Ephraim to the Jordan Valley would explain its choice as a mobilization point.

A Bezek is also mentioned in Judges 1:4–5, as the place where the tribe of Judah defeated the Canaanites and Perizzites. Their dying overlord, Adoni-Bezek, was taken to Jerusalem. Attempts to locate this Bezek in the vicinity of Jerusalem have so far been unsuccessful. Some scholars accept its identification with the other Bezek, assuming that the tribe of Judah crossed the Jordan Valley in the direction opposite to that taken by Saul and then continued south to its inheritance.

Bibliography: Clermont-Ganneau, Arch, 2 (1899), 239ff.; Alt, in: PJB, 22 (1926), 48ff.; EM.

[M.A.-Y.]

BEZIDUL NOU (Hg. **Bőződújfalu**), village in Transylvania, Rumania, inhabited by Szeklers, a distinctive ethnic group. In the 17th century it was an important center of the Sabbatarians. In 1868–69, after equal rights had been granted to Hungarian Jewry, the Sabbatarians, then numbering approximately 100, mostly poor farmers, openly practiced Judaism. The seal of the community they established was inscribed the "Proselyte Community Congregation of Jeshurun." At the beginning of the 20th century a few Jews by birth settled in the village and intermarried with the proselytes. In 1940 Bezidul Nou passed from Rumania to Hungary and there followed a period of disaster. The authorities ordered the demolition of the synagogue; under pressure from the local clerics and the authorities, most of the community became converted to Unitarianism. From 1940 the leaders of the congregation tried to obtain exemption for their members from the anti-Jewish racial laws. On Oct. 3, 1941, the Hungarian minister of justice signed an order enabling the descendants of Sabbatarians to obtain certificates of exemption. There were then 94 proselytes living in Bezidul Nou, while an additional 30–40 persons originating from the village or the vicinity also obtained certificates. These were still being issued by the Hungarian ministry of justice in spring 1944, a few days before the German occupation. When ghettos were established, the proselytes were deported to the ghetto of Tîrgu Mureş. Some of their leaders succeeded in reaching Budapest and obtained certificates for a small number already confined in the ghetto, who were subsequently released. Those who did not wish to accept the certificates were deported to *Auschwitz.

After World War II Bezidul Nou reverted to Rumania; those who survived the Holocaust remained formally Christians, although some continued to follow Jewish observances. In 1960 they began to emigrate to Israel, where by 1968 they numbered approximately 50. Only five families, all aged persons, remained in the village in 1969, formally belonging to the Unitarian Church. They observe the Sabbath and their wives light candles on Sabbath eve; they maintain close contact with their relatives in Israel. A small cemetery with a few hundred tombstones attests to the past existence of the community. The Hebrew inscription (*Ger Ẓedek*, "proselyte") appears next to the name on many of the tombstones, most of which bear the *menorah* and a *Magen David*.

Bibliography: S. Kohn, *A szombatosok* (1889), 336–7; Beck, in: *Dr. Blochs Oesterreichische Wochenschrift* (1912), 704–5, 738–40, 754–6; Gy. Balázs, in: *Libanon*, 6 (Hg., 1941), 18–22. [Y.M.]

BÉZIERS (Heb. בדרש; based on the Latin form), city in the department of Hérault, France. Natives of the city were known as בדרשי normally transliterated as "Bedersi." An estate near Béziers belonging to Jews *(Guardia Judaica)* is mentioned in a document of 990. In the 11th century, the Jews lived in both parts of the city, which was divided between the bishop and the count. They paid the count taxes on honey, cinnamon, and pepper. The synagogue was built in 1144 or 1164 in the present rue de la Promenade. Its mosaic pavement, with Hebrew inscriptions and its foundation stone, were discovered in the first half of the 19th century. The cemetery was situated outside the city walls to the east and two Hebrew tombstones were discovered there. A rue de la Juiverie recalling one of the medieval Jewish quarters still exists. Both the count and the bishop made use of Jewish commercial and financial agents. In 1160 the bishop abolished the ancient local custom of stoning the houses of the Jews on the Sunday before Easter. In return, the Jews undertook to pay an annual tax. Count Roger II was kindly disposed toward the Jews, even entrusting them with administrative functions. The Christian inhabitants of Béziers, who had *Albigensian leanings, were also, as a rule, favorably disposed. About 200 Jews were among the victims of the massacre of the Albigenses in

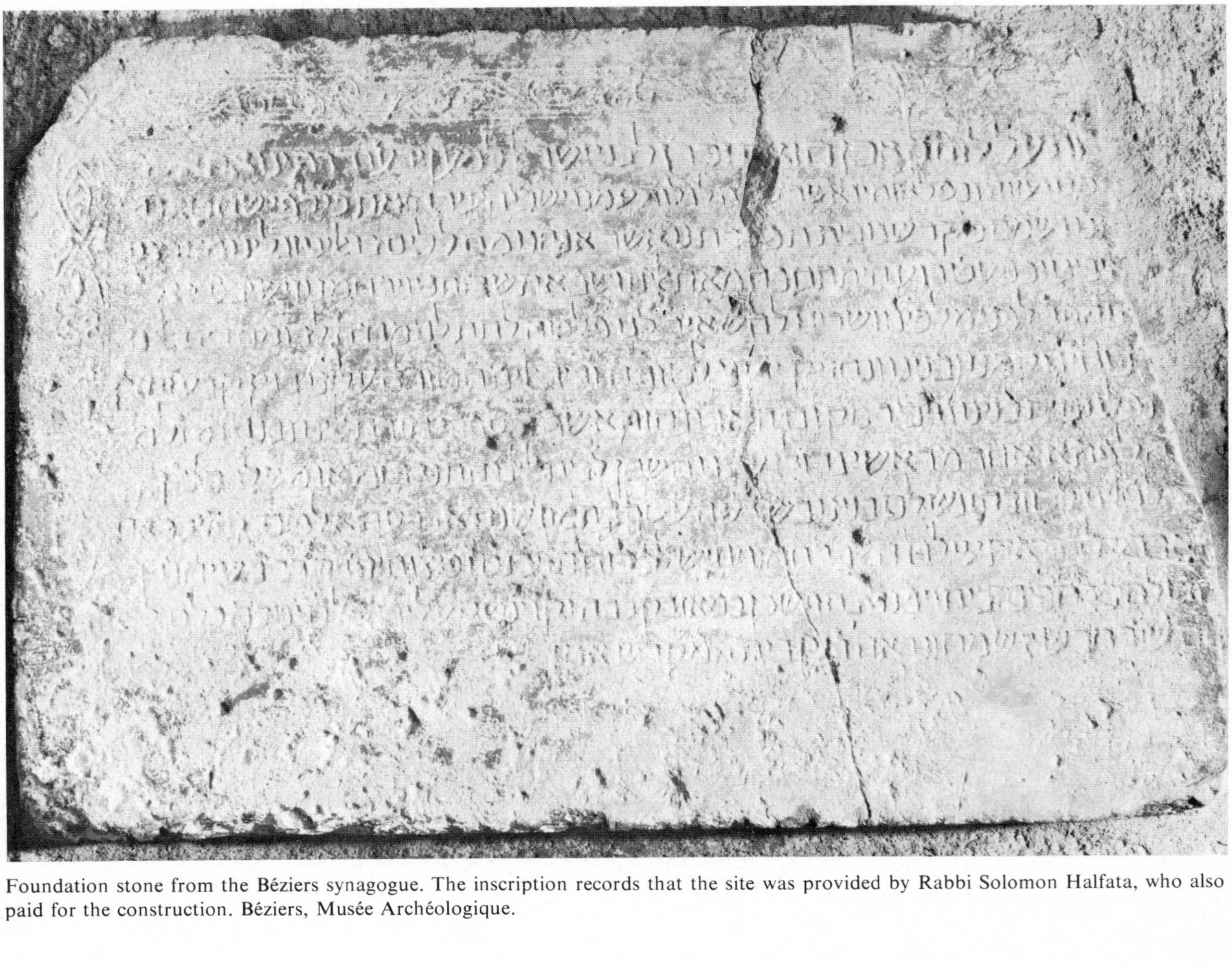

Foundation stone from the Béziers synagogue. The inscription records that the site was provided by Rabbi Solomon Halfata, who also paid for the construction. Béziers, Musée Archéologique.

Béziers in 1209. Most of the Jewish population had previously fled from the city. Some of the refugees settled in Narbonne; some apparently in *Gerona, Spain; an inscription apparently intended for the synagogue they founded there has been discovered in Gerona. The revenues formerly derived by the counts of Béziers from the Jews now went to the king. The bishop however retained his right, and even built a new synagogue in the part of the city under his jurisdiction in an effort to attract Jews from the area. In 1278, however, the king compelled him to destroy the synagogue and ordered the Jews who had moved to the bishop's territory to return.

Béziers was known to the medieval Jews as "the little Jerusalem." Abraham *ibn Ezra stayed there for some time in about 1155; he dedicated his *Sefer ha-Shem* to two scholars of Béziers. Benjamin of Tudela, visiting the town in about 1165, remarked on "a congregation of learned men." The best known of these are the liturgical poet Abraham b. Isaac *Bedersi, his son *Jedaiah ha-Penini, and *Meshullam b. Moses. The poets Eleazar Hanan Ezobi, Astruc of Béziers, and Meshullam Ezobi also lived in Béziers. Samuel ibn *Tibbon lived there for some time. Solomon b. Joseph ibn Ayyub of Granada and Jacob b. Moses, translators of Arabic works into Hebrew, settled at Béziers.

The Jews were expelled from Béziers in 1306. An indication of the scope of the Jewish settlement there is provided by three deeds of sale which have been preserved concerning the subsequent liquidation of their real estate on the king's behalf. The documents mention at least 13 houses which had belonged to some ten Jews. In 1367 the community was renewed by an agreement made by a number of Jews with the bishop. The general expulsion of the Jews from France in 1394 again forced them to leave. During World War II, 300 Jewish refugees stayed in Béziers, where they had two prayer rooms at their disposal, until 1943. A new community was formed after the war which in 1968 comprised some 400 persons, mostly from North Africa.

Bibliography: Graetz, Hist, 6 (1949), index; Roth, Dark Ages, 136, 146; Gross, Gal Jud, 96–105; Z. Szajkowski, *Franco-Judaica* (1962), no. 309; idem, *Analytical Franco-Jewish Gazetteer* (1966), 198; Millás Vallicrosa, in: *Sefarad*, 10 (1950), 341–3; Catane, in: *Tarbiz*, 24 (1954/55), 232f.; H. Vida, *Episcopatus . . . Béziers* (1951).

[Z.Av./Ed.]

BIALA, town in W. Galicia, S. Poland, on the river Biala opposite the Silesian town *Bielsko with which it was amalgamated in 1950 to form Biala-Bielsko. The two were closely connected through their joint textile industry. In 1765 the Jews were expelled from Biala. Many of them subsequently returned and formed a community in conjunction with the Jews in the suburbs which until the middle of the 19th century remained under the jurisdiction of the Oswięcim community. A cemetery was established in 1849 and an independent congregation constituted in 1872. The Jews in Biala numbered about 2,600 in 1929. With the exception of the *ḥevra kaddisha* the charitable and cultural institutions were maintained jointly with those of the Bielsko (Bielitz) community. For Holocaust period see *Bielsko.

[Ed.]

BIAŁA PODLASKA, town in Lublin province, Poland. The first mention of Jewish settlement in Biała Podlaska dates from 1621 when 30 Jewish families were granted rights of residence there. In 1841 there were 2,200 Jews out of a total population of 3,588; in 1897, 6,549 out of 13,090; and in 1921, 6,874 out of 13,000. Four Yiddish newspapers were published there between the two world wars.

Holocaust Period. On Sept. 26, 1939, the Soviet army entered the town, but withdrew a month later when the Soviet-German boundary agreement was reached. About 600 Jews left the town together with the Soviet army. The remaining Jewish population was immediately subjected to Nazi persecution and terror. At the end of 1939 about 3,000 Jews from Suwalki and Serock were forced to settle here. A few months later about 1,000 Jewish prisoners of war who had served in the Polish army were brought to Biała Podlaska from the prison camp in Czarne near Chojna. Several score of them were murdered during the march on foot to Biała Podlaska. They were imprisoned on arrival in a forced labor camp and about a year later were transferred to a Lublin prisoner of war camp. During 1940 and 1941 further deportations to Biała Podlaska took place. Several hundred Jews from Cracow and Mlawa were dispatched there. As a result of all the "resettlements" the Jewish population in the town grew to about 8,400 in March 1942. At the end of June 1941 a certain number of Jews were sent to the concentration camp in *Auschwitz for giving bread to Soviet prisoners of war marching through the town. They were among the first Jewish victims to perish in Auschwitz.

On June 6, 1942, the first deportation from Biała took place. About 3,000 people were sent to *Sobibor death camp and exterminated. On Sept. 26, 1942, a second deportation was carried out in which the entire remaining Jewish population was deported to the ghetto in Miedzyrzecz, and from there to *Treblinka death camp in November 1942. Only 300 Jews were left in Biała Podlaska in a newly established forced labor camp. This was liquidated in May 1944 and all its inmates transferred to *Majdanek concentration camp, where only a few survived. Several hundred Jews fled to the woods during the deportations, but only about 30 of them survived in hiding until the liberation of the region in July 26, 1944. After the war the surviving Jewish remnant, together with a few hundred former residents who came back from the Soviet Union, tried to rebuild the Jewish community, but were forced to leave the town in the summer of 1946 because of anti-Semitic manifestations among the Polish population. In June 1946 Polish anti-Semites killed two young Jews and destroyed the monument which the Jewish survivors had erected in memory of the murdered Jewish community. Societies of former Biała Podlaska residents are active in Israel, the U.S.A., Argentina, France, Canada, and Australia.

Bibliography: M. I. Feigenbaum (ed.), *Sefer Biała-Podlaska* (1961).

[S.Kr.]

BIALEH, ẒEVI HIRSCH BEN NAPHTALI HERZ (1670–1748), German rabbi and *rosh yeshivah*. Bialeh was born in Lemberg. He served as rabbi of Biala (hence his name) and then as head of a yeshivah in Lemberg. In 1718 he was appointed to Halberstadt (hence his other appellation Ẓevi Hirsch Halberstadter) where he remained until his death. Because of his acumen he was also called Hirsch Ḥarif ("sharp"). He established a large yeshivah in the town and among its pupils were such outstanding rabbis of the following generation as Akiva *Eger, Isaiah *Berlin, and Mordecai *Halberstadt. He refused to publish his novellae on the grounds that through the continual publication of works by *aḥaronim*, students would neglect the *rishonim*, but glosses and responsa by him can be found scattered in various works of his contemporaries. His works, which were published only after his death, are: *Ateret Ẓevi* (1804), comprising responsa, sermons, eulogies, and novellae; *Kos Yeshu'ot* (1902), Part 1 novellae on *Bava Kamma* and *Shevu'ot*, Part 2 on *Bava Meẓia* and other material. He preferred to penetrate deeply into the understanding of the sources, stress the plain meaning of the Talmud, and avoid excessive *pilpul.* Five of his children were rabbis: Solomon Dov Berush in Glogau; Naphtali Herz in Dubno; Abraham in Rawicz; Samuel in Halberstadt; and Simḥah in Dessau. His brother, Israel b. Naphtali Herz (d. 1744) lived in Cleves, Offenbach, and Hanau. His talmudic novellae are contained in his brother's *Ateret Ẓevi.*

Bibliography: Michaelson, in: Ẓevi Hirsch Ḥarif, *Kos Yeshu'ot,* 1 (1902), appendix *(Toledot ha-Meḥabber);* Israel Moses b. Ḥayyim Joshua, *ibid.,* 2 (1910), appendix *(Toledot ha-Meḥabber);* B. H. Auerbach, *Geschichte der israelitischen Gemeinde Halberstadt* (1866), 64–70; S. Buber, *Anshei Shem* (1895), 196, 240, 247f., I. T. Eisenstadt and S. Wiener, *Da'at Kedoshim* (1897–98), 141f.; Loewenstein, in: JJLG, 14 (1921), 19; Frankel, in: *Naḥalat Ẓevi,* 7 (1937), 321f.; Meisl, in: *Reshumot,* 3 (1947), 190; *Sefer Biala-Podlaska* (1961), 19, 270.

[Y.Ho.]

BIALIK, ḤAYYIM NAḤMAN (1873–1934), the greatest Hebrew poet of modern times, essayist, storywriter, translator, and editor, who exercised a profound influence on modern Jewish culture. Born in the village of Radi, near Zhitomir (Volhynia), Bialik's development as a poet was influenced by his environment—the simplicity and fervor of a folk spirituality—which characterized Volhynian Jewry, and the ḥasidic ambience, alive with mystic lore, in which it was steeped. His father, Isaac Joseph, came of scholarly stock and had been engaged in the family timber trade and in flour milling before coming down in life through his impracticality. For his father as well as his mother, Dinah Priva, this was a second marriage, both having been widowed previously. Despite his family's dire economic circumstances, Bialik retained many happy memories of the first six years of his childhood in Radi. In some of his best poems, *"Zohar"* ("Radiance," 1901) and *"Ha-Berekhah"* ("The Pool," 1905), attempting to recapture the lost paradise of childhood, he idealizes the enchanted hours which he spent romping in the dazzling light of the fields and in the secret shade of the forest. Others have fewer happy references and are marked by loneliness, parental neglect, and the almost narcissistic withdrawal of a sensitive, artistic child, e.g., the prose poem *"Safi'aḥ"* ("Aftergrowth," 1908).

Childhood Period (1880–1890). When Bialik was six, his parents moved to Zhitomir in search of a livelihood and his father was reduced to keeping a saloon on the outskirts of town. Shortly thereafter, in 1880, his father died and the destitute widow entrusted her son to the care of his well-to-do paternal grandfather, Jacob Moses. For ten years, until he went to yeshivah in 1890, the gifted, mischievous Ḥayyim Naḥman was raised by the stern old pietist. At first he was instructed by teachers in the traditional *ḥeder* and later, from the age of 13, pursued his studies alone. He was a lonely figure in the almost deserted house of study on the edge of town, for the expanding modernization of Jewish life had restricted the traditional study of Torah to a secluded nook. Passionate and solitary dedication to study shaped traits of character that Bialik was to exalt: "A fertile mind, lively logic, a trusting heart when the knee falters." From this experience of his adolescence stems the sense of vocation of the chosen individual who dedicates his life to an ideal, sacrificing youth and the delights of the world in order to remain faithful to the last. This theme of vocation was to become central to Bialik's thinking and his poetry is a spiritual record of the paradoxical struggle to free himself from his calling and at the same time to remain faithful to it. During this period too his reading of medieval theology and Haskalah works stimulated ambitions for secular knowledge, moving him to seek a more comprehensive education. He dreamed of the rabbinical seminary in Berlin, and of acquiring the cultural tools that would give him entrance to modern European civilization.

Figure 1. Bialik stamp, with the poet's autograph, issued by the Israel Post Office in 1958.

Volozhin Period. Convinced by a journalistic report that the yeshivah of *Volozhin in Lithuania would offer him an introduction to the humanities, as well as a continuation of his talmudic studies, Bialik persuaded his grandfather to permit him to study there. In Volozhin, a center of *Mitnaggedim,* his hopes for a secular academic training were not fulfilled since the yeshivah concentrated only on the scholarly virtues of talmudic dialectic and erudition. For a short time Bialik immersed himself in the traditional disciplines. In some of his poems the image of his stern grandfather merges with the image of the uncompromising *rosh yeshivah,* becoming a symbol of the burning imperatives of traditional Judaism. In the end, however, modernist doubts triumphed over traditionalist certainties. Bialik began to withdraw from the life of the school and lived in the world of poetry. At this time, he read Russian poetry and started his acquaintance with European literature. During the following year in Volozhin and later in Odessa, he was deeply moved by Shimon Shemuel Frug's Jewish poems, written in Russian, and many of Bialik's early motifs echo him. His first published poem *"El ha-Ẓippor"* ("To the Bird") was written in Volozhin. In the yeshivah Bialik joined a secret Orthodox Zionist student society, Neẓaḥ Israel, which attempted to synthesize Jewish nationalism and enlightenment with a firm adherence to tradition. Bialik's first published work (in *Ha-Meliẓ,* 1891) is an exposition of the principles of the society and reflects the teachings of Aḥad Ha-Am's spiritual Zionism.

Aḥad Ha-Am's Influence. Aḥad Ha-Am, whose thinking had a profound impact on Bialik and his generation, first began publishing his essays in 1889. They provided a framework of ideas that helped his contemporaries translate their Jewish loyalties from a religious context into a modern, philosophically oriented humanist rationale for Jewish existence. Bialik recognized Aḥad Ha-Am as his great teacher. He wrote of this period, "... the day a new essay of Aḥad Ha-Am's appeared was a holiday for me." Bialik later wrote a poem in tribute to his mentor: "Receive our blessing for each seed of... idea/That you have sown... in our desolate hearts." But Aḥad Ha-Am also had an inhibiting influence on Bialik's poetic imagination. Preferring a classical and lucid style, Aḥad Ha-Am discouraged many of Bialik's ventures into more modernist or more experimental poetry.

First Stay in Odessa. The break with tradition occurred in the summer of 1891 when amid disruptions in the yeshivah, Bialik left for Odessa, the center of modern Jewish culture in southern Russia. He was attracted by the literary circle that formed around Aḥad Ha-Am and harbored the dream that in Odessa he would be able to prepare himself for the entrance to the modern Orthodox rabbinical seminary in Berlin. Penniless, alone, unemployed, and hungry, he earned a livelihood for a while by giving Hebrew lessons. He continued to study Russian literature, reading and admiring the poetry of Pushkin and Frug, as well as the stories and novels of Dostoevski and Gogol. He was tutored in German grammar and read works of Schiller and Lessing. At first the shy youth did not become involved in the literary life of the city but when he showed his poetry to Moses Leib *Lilienblum the latter commended the poem *"El ha-Ẓippor"* to Aḥad Ha-Am who passed it on to Yehoshua Ḥana *Rawnitzki to be published in the first volume of *Ha-Pardes* (1892, p. 219f.). The poem, a song longing for Zion written in the style of the poets of the Ḥibbat Zion era, was favorably received by the critics. During the six months he spent in Odessa, Bialik wrote several poems and made the acquaintance of prominent literary figures with whom he was to establish lasting relationships. He was especially close to Rawnitzki and their friendship was to develop into a unique collaboration in literary and publishing endeavors.

Return to Zhitomir. When Bialik learned, early in 1892, that the yeshivah of Volozhin had been closed, he cut short his stay in Odessa and hurried home in order to spare his dying grandfather the knowledge that he had forsaken his religious studies. On returning home he found that his older brother too was dying. Dejected by the whole atmosphere, which for him embodied the chronic despair and spiritual squalor of Jewish life, he wrote "You have not changed from what you were/Old oldness, nothing new/Let me join your company, my brothers,/Together we will rot till we stink" (*"Bi-Teshuvati,"* "On my Return," 1892). Another poem of this period which is reminiscent of Frug *"Mi-Shut ba-Merḥakim"* ("From Wandering Afar") also develops the theme of unfulfilled return. The alienated son, full of youthful vitality, is repelled by the melancholy of a moribund traditionalist society. The death of Judah Leib *Gordon, the last significant poet of the Haskalah period, in the summer of 1892, closed an era. Rawnitzki asked Bialik to compose an elegy for the second volume of *Ha-Pardes* (1893, p. 248f.) and he complied with *"El ha-Aryeh ha-Met"* ("To the Dead Lion"). Like other early poems, it still showed the influence of the Haskalah poets and was omitted from the collected poems. The elegiac mood characterizes a considerable part of Bialik's early work and tears are a recurring motif in the first volume of poems (1901). Before leaving Odessa he wrote *"Hirhurei Laylah"* ("Night Thoughts," 1892; "My song is a bottle of tears, a bottle of tears"), and in a later poem *"Shirati"* ("My Song," 1901) he describes his mother's tear falling into the dough she is kneading and it is this tear that enters his bones and is transformed into poetry.

1893–1896. In the spring of 1893, after the death of his brother and grandfather, Bialik married Manya Averbuch and for the next three years joined her father in the timber trade in Korostyshev, near Kiev. Since business kept him in the forest for long stretches, he read widely and broadened his education considerably during this lonely period. At that time he wrote *"Al Saf Beit ha-Midrash"* ("On the Threshold of the House of Study," 1894) which predicts the ultimate triumph of Israel's spirit. While the themes of the poem, which poignantly speaks of the abandoned house of study, are vocation and return, the underlying priestly symbolism, relating to the Ninth of Av, the date on which the poem was written, endows the house of study with the universal metaphor of ancient ritual. In the hymn *"Birkat Am"* ("The Blessing of the People," 1894), written several months earlier, which is permeated by intricate allusions to Temple ritual, the poet metamorphoses the builders of Ereẓ Israel into priests and Temple builders. Temple imagery seems to be a predominant symbol both of Bialik's thought and of his poetry and is a basic point of reference of his brilliant cultural interpretation of the two Jerusalems—the earthly and the celestial—in his address at the opening of the Hebrew University (1925).

1897–1900. In the spring of 1897, failing in business, Bialik found a position as a teacher in Sosnowiec, near the Prussian border. The pettiness of provincial life depressed him and he wrote several satires that were published under

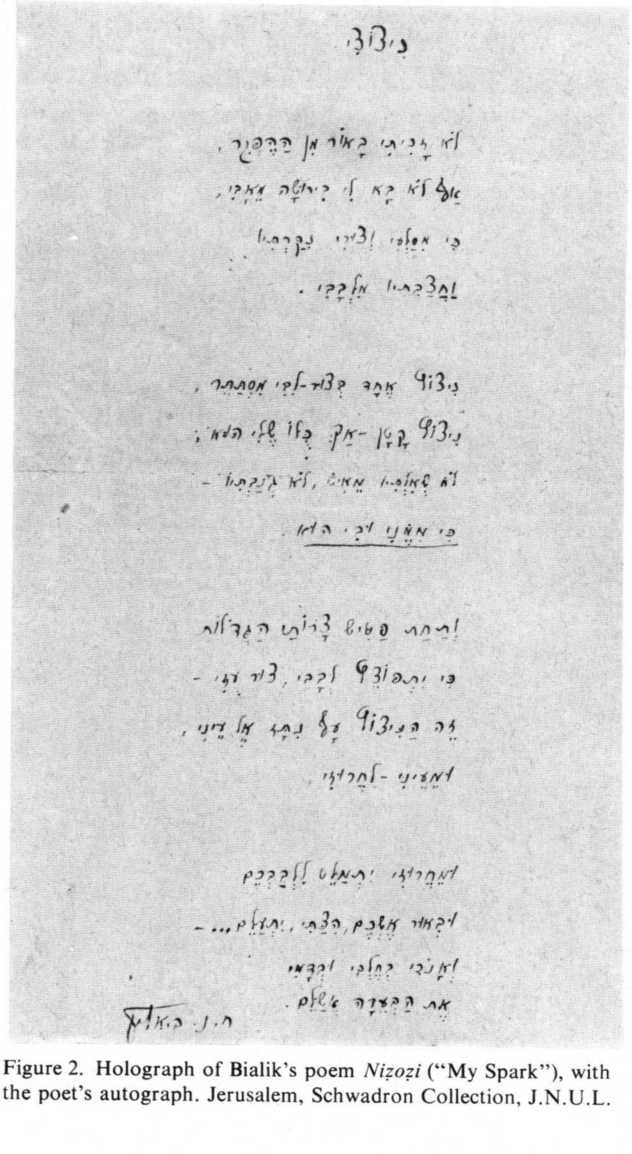

Figure 2. Holograph of Bialik's poem *Niẓoẓi* ("My Spark"), with the poet's autograph. Jerusalem, Schwadron Collection, J.N.U.L.

pseudonyms. During this period he started to write stories (e.g., *"Aryeh Ba'al Guf,"* 1899) and to experiment with Yiddish writing. Some of his poems appear to reflect the life-affirming themes of the "new way" embraced by the writers of the 1890s, although Bialik remained wary of what he felt was the literary pretensions of its members. The poet's ire against Jewish apathy to the rising national movement found expression in *"Akhen Ḥaẓir ha-Am"* ("Surely the People is Grass," 1897) in which he called out to the people "Even when the horn be sounded and the banner raised/Can the dead awaken, can the dead stir?" Widely acclaimed, it was the first of his poems of wrath and reproof in which he speaks to the people in the tones of prophetic visions. While biblical themes were not uncommon in the period, Bialik's unequaled mastery of the prophetic diatribe added a dimension of authenticity to his utterances and he began to be considered the national poet. Other poems indicate his preoccupation with the implications of the First Zionist Congress. Welcoming the high tide of national enthusiasm, as in *"Mikra'ei Ẓiyyon"* ("Convocation of Zion," 1898), he was at the same time faithful to Aḥad Ha-Am's spiritual ideology and wrote a satire against Herzl's political Zionism, *Rabbi Zeraḥ* (1912), which, because of its tone of levity, Aḥad Ha-Am refused to print in *Ha-Shilo'aḥ*. *"Al Levavkhem she-Shamem"* ("On Your Desolate Hearts," 1897), his most profound response to the Zionist Congress, gives vent to Bialik's despair with contemporary Jewish life. In it he develops his own set of symbols which were to recur throughout his poetry; the cat which first appears in *"Levadi"* (1902) as a symbol of boredom and despair; the sanctuary as the symbol of tradition; and the spark of fire, appearing in many poems in various forms (a burning coal or candle, a twinkling star, or flaming torch), represents the true ideal. *Ha-Matmid* ("The Talmud Student," 1894–95), his first long poem, apparently begun in Volozhin, was an immediate triumph. In the poem Bialik traces the inner struggles of the dedicated student who represses his natural inclinations and sacrifices life, movement, change, nature, and family for the ascetic study of Torah. This was an ideal figure who captured the imagination of the reader. He embodied the moral qualities that build societies and preserve cultures. The ability to sublimate for the sake of higher values was a basic idea in Bialik's conception of vocation. The key metaphor of the poem is, characteristically, the twinkling light.

Settling in Odessa. In 1900 Bialik finally succeeded in finding a teaching position in Odessa where he lived until 1921, except for a year's stay in Warsaw (1904), where he served as literary editor of *Ha-Shilo'aḥ*. He was drawn into the circle of writers and Zionist leaders that gathered around Aḥad Ha-Am, *Mendele Mokher Seforim, and Simon *Dubnow. Other members of the group were Mordecai (Ben-Ami) Rabinowicz, Ḥayyim *Tchernowitz, and Alter Druyanov. As Bialik gained a reputation, young poets such as Zalman Shneour, Jacob *Fichmann, and Jacob *Steinberg went to Odessa to meet him. Working with Mendele, he translated the latter's *"Fishke the Lame"* into Hebrew from the original Yiddish. He had tried his hand at Yiddish poetry before leaving Sosnowiec and now his work with Mendele, a master in Hebrew and Yiddish literatures, turned him to Yiddish again. His realistic stories in Hebrew, *"Aryeh Ba'al Guf"* and *"Me-Aḥorei ha-Gader"* ("Behind the Fence," 1909), were influenced by Mendele's realism of style—indeed they came into being because Mendele had forged a new and pliant Hebrew idiom. Bialik's poetry, however, including the prose poem *"Safi'aḥ,"* was relatively free of his mentor's influences. Together with Rawnitzki, Simḥah *Ben-Zion, and Elḥanan Leib Lewinsky he founded the Moriah Publishing House which produced suitable textbooks for the modern Jewish school written in the spirit of Aḥad Ha-Am's educational ideals. In his dark rooms in Odessa Bialik created nature poems that evoke a childhood intoxicated with light (e.g., *"Zohar,"* 1901). During this period also a self-imposed challenge to cast folk expression into Hebrew, only a literary language then, led the poet to write the first of a series of folk songs. In his first decade in Odessa he wrote poems of wrath in Yiddish *"Fun Tsa'ar un Tsorn"* ("Of Sorrow and Anger," 1906) and in Hebrew *Ḥazon u-Massa* ("Vision and Utterance," 1911). Both were products of that critical period in Jewish life when the initial impetus of Zionism was retarded and other movements and ideologies, such as Yiddishism and territorialism, offered different solutions to national problems. When Bialik's first volume of poems appeared in 1901, Joseph Klausner hailed him as "the poet of the national renaissance." In 1902 he wrote *"Metei Midbar"* ("The Dead of the Desert"), a long descriptive poem whose motifs are taken from the legend that the generation of the Exodus did not die but slumbers in the desert. Gigantic in stature, they awaken from time to time to utter defiance against the divine decree which consigned them to their state of living death, and to fight for their own redemption. It may also reflect the universal predicament of modern man whose struggle for the right to determine his own destiny involves the desperate rejection of the divine imperative.

Kishinev. The Kishinev pogroms in 1903 deeply shocked the whole civilized world. Bialik on behalf of the Jewish Historical Commission in Odessa went to Kishinev to interview survivors and to prepare a report on the atrocity. Before leaving he wrote *Al ha-Sheḥitah* ("On the Slaughter," 1903) in which he calls on heaven either to exercise immediate justice and, if not, to destroy the world, spurning mere vengeance with the famous lines "Cursed is he who says 'Revenge'/Vengeance for the blood of a small child/Satan has not yet created." Later he wrote *"Be-Ir ha-Haregah"* ("In the City of Slaughter," 1904), a searing denunciation of the people's meek submission to the massacre, in which he is incensed at the cowardliness of the people, bitter at the absence of justice, and struck by the indifference of nature—"The sun shone, the acacia blossomed, and the slaughterer slaughtered."

Influence of Warsaw. In 1904 Bialik became the literary editor of *Ha-Shilo'aḥ* and moved to Warsaw, where, among the members of the circle of Isaac Leib *Peretz, he found a lighter mood. They were less cautious and less involved with higher principles than the Odessa group. In Warsaw he wrote several memorable love poems. The symbolist emphasis of Peretz may have influenced the poem *"Ha-Berekhah"* ("The Pool," 1905), most of which was written during the Warsaw stay. The pool, guarded by the forest, reflects the changing moods of nature and the observer, meditating on the "riddle of the two worlds," objective reality and reality as it is reflected in the pool, ponders which is primary—the external manifestation, or the inner conception of the soul (of art). This was Bialik's most prolific period and *"Ha-Berekhah"* was followed by his most enigmatic and experimental work, *"Megillat ha-Esh"* ("The Scroll of Fire," 1905). The work is a prose poem which fuses elements drawn from Jewish legend (*aggadah*) and Jewish mysticism. Its overt theme is the destruction of the Temple and of Jerusalem, and the exile which followed. The destruction of the Temple appears to represent the destruction of the poet's soul on one level and that of the religious faith of an entire generation on the other. The youths, marooned on the island, as they are transported into exile may symbolize spiritual isolation; at the same time the two youths represent the struggle between faith and despair which is the poem's central theme. The chosen youth himself is caught between the call to preserve the last spark of redemption and the lure of *eros*, the girl. Torch in hand, he moves toward the girl and plunges into the abyss.

Silence. After *"Megillat ha-Esh"* Bialik fell into a period of silence, writing few poems and becoming occupied with manifold cultural activities: public lectures, essays, criticism, translating, and editing. The growing tension and the stark dichotomies in his poetry point to an inner crisis; the lonely poet can no longer find solace either in his individual talent or in his God. The radical split of personality in the autobiographical prose poem *"Safi'aḥ"* (1908), in which the child's inner self is abandoned by its double who accompanies the crowd, marks the farthest development of Bialik's ambivalent attitude to tradition and religion. Baruch Kurzweil has shown that the change in the motif of return in *"Lifnei Aron ha-Sefarim"* ("Before the Book Case," 1910) marks a turning point in Bialik's poetry. The poet desperately realizes that his attempt to return and to repent fails because there is no one to return to, and no condition of dialogue with God or the world. The flame of the study candle has died, the people's past is a graveyard that offers nothing, and the returning son, despairing, welcomes death and departs. Bialik's poetry now becomes acutely personal. The poet, sensing his strangeness in the world, retreats and longs for death. Having lost the purity of childhood and the grace of the chosen, he is preoccupied with death—a broken, useless twig, dangling from its branch, *"Ẓanaḥ lo Zalzal"* ("A Twig Fell," 1911). Before his death Bialik wrote the cycle *"Yatmut"* ("Orphanhood" poems, c. 1933) in which the existential predicament is fused with the poignancy of his own orphaned childhood.

Berlin and Palestine. Bialik lived in Odessa until 1921 when Maxim Gorki interceded with the Soviet government to permit a group of Hebrew writers to leave the country. Bialik went to Berlin, which had become a center of Jewish émigré writers, engaging in publishing and editing, until he settled in Tel Aviv in Palestine in 1924 where he spent the rest of his life. He died in Vienna where he had gone for medical treatment.

Essays. A series of essays written between the years 1907 and 1917 secures Bialik's place as a distinguished essayist. In it he charts the course of modern Jewish culture: the state of Hebrew literature, the condition of Hebrew journalism, the development of language and style, the existential function of language, and the role of authority in culture. *"Ha-Sefer ha-Ivri"* ("On the Hebrew Book," 1913) propounds his basic idea of selecting and collecting the best of classic Jewish literature.

Cultural Role. After 1905, he became more active in public affairs, devoting his abundant vigor, vision, and charm to the preservation and advancement of Jewish culture. He participated in Zionist Congresses (1907, 1913, 1921, and 1931) and the Congress for Hebrew Language and Culture (1913). His cultural missions took him to the United States (1926) and to London (1931). From 1928 on, ill health forced him to spend his summers in Europe and these trips became occasions for the promotion of Jewish culture. He was active in the work of the Hebrew University, served as president of the Hebrew Writers Union and of the Hebrew Language Council, and initiated the popular *Oneg Shabbat*, a Sabbath study project.

Editor and Translator. Bialik was the literary editor of several periodicals, *Ha-Shilo'aḥ* (1904–09), *Keneset* (1917), *Reshumot* (1918–22), and he founded *Moznayim* in Palestine (1929). Together with Rawnitzki he compiled a selection of rabbinic lore, *Sefer ha-Aggadah* (1908–11) and the collected works of the medieval poets Solomon ibn *Gabirol (1924) and Moses *ibn Ezra (1928). In 1932 he published a commentary to the first order of the Mishnah. His masterful translations of *Don Quixote* (1912) and *Wilhelm Tell* (1923) are an integral part of his work. After his death some of Bialik's lectures and addresses were collected in *Devarim she-be-Al Peh* (2 vols., 1935) and part of his huge correspondence was published in *Iggerot* (5 vols. 1938–39).

For English translations of his work see Goell, Bibliography, index. [S.LE.]

Evaluation. Bialik's literary career is a watershed in modern Hebrew literature; when he arrived on the scene, Hebrew poetry was provincial and by and large imitative. It could not free itself of the overwhelming biblical influence which had dominated it for centuries and, except for the poetry of a few, the stylized florid biblical *meliẓah* (ornate phrase) had a stifling effect on the creativity of the Haskalah poets. At the same time most of these poets slavishly imitated in subject and in genre the European models—mainly German romantic poetry. Bialik, who more than any other Hebrew poet since *Judah Halevi had a thorough command of Hebrew and the ability to use the many resources of the language, forged a new poetic idiom which enabled Hebrew poetry to free itself from the overwhelming biblical influence and yet, at the same time, retain its link with "the language of the race." While his Hebrew remained learned and "literary," he anticipated the conversational verse which was to become the hallmark of the Palestinian poets (e.g., in his folk poems and children's verse). Not an experimenter, Bialik nevertheless opened new vistas when on rare occasions he abandoned the accepted accented syllabic meter for purely biblical cadences, or when he developed the Hebrew prose poem. While he wrote his serious verse in the Ashkenazi accent, he was among the first to try out the Sephardi accent in his children's verse. He freed Hebrew poetry from its didactic and propagandistic tendency. Although his works are often filled with fervent Jewish hopes, memories, and ideals, content is always subordinate to aesthetic criteria. Early Bialik criticism invariably reads all his poems as expressions of national ideas, but many of his poems are purely lyrical and have been misinterpreted by critics whose love of ideals exceeded their literary taste. Lyric poems like *"Ẓanaḥ lo Zalzal"* or *"Im Dimdumei ha-Ḥamah"* are among the finest

Figure 3. Bialik's first visit to Ereẓ Israel, Jaffa, 1909. Standing, right to left: S. Ben-Zion (Simḥa Alter Gutmann), Pesaḥ Auerbach, Bialik, Mrs. Auerbach. Seated, right to left: Yehoshua Ḥana Rawnitsky, Mrs. Gutmann and her son Naḥum, later to become a painter. Photo: Bet Bialik, Tel Aviv.

in Hebrew literature. Bialik's dominant theme is the crisis of faith which confronted his generation as it broke with the sheltered and confined medieval Jewish religious culture of its childhood and desperately sought to hold on to a Jewish way of life and thought in the new secularized world in which it found itself. He adopted the ethico-humanist reading of Judaism which was proferred by Aḥad Ha-Am, but as Kurzweil has pointed out, he often had grave misgivings as to its efficacy in bridging the traditional and the modern. His doubts find conscious and unconscious expression in his writings. Despite his moments of despair, Bialik did not completely abandon the Aḥad Ha-Amian hope of reconciling modernism with tradition within the context of a new national Jewish culture (Kurzweil's view on this is to the contrary).

Bialik's poetry, growing out of the cultural milieu of Eastern European Jewry in a particular area, is in a sense regional, but because of its great artistic merit has become the concrete expression of the general crisis of faith which faced an entire generation of Europeans. His poetry can be read on three levels: the individual, the Jewish, and the universal. As an individual, the poet emerges as a sensitive artist who seeks to preserve the purity of his "calling" in the face of the materialism and the erotic drive of modern man. He loses his purity as he leaves the security of his childhood Eden and vainly attempts to recapture it. At times he is not sure whether his preoccupation with society, with his people and its ideals, may not actually hinder his self-fulfillment as an artist. On the Jewish level, the poet becomes the spokesman of his generation. Born in the pious world of the East European Jewish town, he is cast into a secular materialist world which questions the old values. He strives to reconstruct a way of life in which he can survive as a Jew and thus fulfill Judaism's historical mission. On the universal level, the poet, a product of a preindustrial rural world, is driven into the secular city, driven out of the Eden of good order and faith. He is left to agonize about his loneliness, his barrenness, and his ultimate death.

Searching out new and further vistas yet rooted in the rich Jewish heritage, Bialik is both the product and the dominant motivator of the cultural revolution of his age, embodying its very essence—to carve out of the past the foundation on which the people might build with dignity in the future. In answering the silent cry of a people needing articulation in a new era, he has gained its permanent recognition. As a poet his genius and spirit have left an indelible imprint on modern Hebrew literature. [E.Sp.]

Bibliography: I. Efros, *Hayyim Nahman Bialik* (Eng., 1940), incl. bibl.; F. Lachower, *Bialik, Ḥayyav vi-Yẓirotav* (1950²); J. Fichmann, *Shirat Bialik* (1946); Z. Shapiro, *Bialik bi-Yẓirotav* (1951); idem, *Derakhim be-Shirat Bialik* (1962); J. Klausner, *Bialik ve-Shirat Ḥayyav* (1951); D. Sadan, *Avnei Boḥan* (1951), 60–77; E. Kagan, *Marot Shetiyyah be-Shirat Bialik* (1959); R. Zur, *Devarim ke-Ḥavayatam* (1964); A. Zemach, *Ha-Lavi ha-Mistatter* (1966); B. Kurzweil, *Bialik ve-Tchernichowsky* (1967); E. Schweid, *Ha-Ergah li-Mele'ut ha-Ḥavayah* (1968); J. Haephrati, in: *Ha-Sifrut*, 1 (1968/69), 101–29; M. Perry, *ibid.*, 607–31; I. Avinery, *Millon Ḥiddushei Ḥ.N. Bialik* (1935); A. Avrunin, *Meḥkarim bi-Leshon Bialik ve-Yalag* (1953); B. Benshalom (Katz), *Mishkalav shel Bialik* (1945); A. Avital, *Shirat Bialik ve-ha-Tanakh* (1952); A. Even Shoshan and Y. Segal, *Konkordanẓyah le-Shirat Bialik* (1960); Z. Fisman, in: *En Hakore*, 2–3 (1933), 97–134, incl. bibl.; M. Ungerfeld, *Ḥ.N. Bialik vi-Yẓirotav: Bibliografyah le-Vattei ha-Sefer* (1960); E. H. Jeshurin, in: Ḥ. N. Bialik, *Oysgeklibene Shriftn* (1964), Bialik's bibliography; Shunami, Bibl, nos. 3261–72.

BIALOBLOCKI, SAMUEL SHERAGA (1888–1960), talmudic scholar born in Pilwiszki (western Lithuania). Bialoblocki studied for many years at the Lithuanian yeshivot of Telz, Slobodka, and Ponevezh; at the last he studied under Isaac Jacob Rabinowitz and Isaac *Blaser. After World War I he entered the Bet Midrash Elyon of Ḥayyim *Heller in Berlin. He also attended various universities and graduated from Giessen with a thesis on *Materialien zum islamischen und juedischen Eherecht*... (1928) and became instructor in modern Hebrew. Between 1928 and 1934 he was one of the contributors on talmudic subjects to the German *Encyclopaedia Judaica*. With the advent of the Nazis he emigrated to Palestine where first he taught at the Mizrachi Teachers' Training College in Jerusalem but later ventured into the real estate business, though continuing to devote most of his time to his studies. When Bar Ilan University was opened in 1955, Bialoblocki was appointed head of its Talmud department; he also served as chairman of the University's Senate.

Bialoblocki, though a profound scholar of vast erudition, did not publish much; his importance lay chiefly in his influence as a teacher. His method, both in teaching and writing, expressed a spirit of conservative criticism. He began to prepare an anthology of early commentaries on the Talmud with notes on the variants and sources for the Makhon ha-Talmud ha-Yisre'eli ha-Shalem, of which a first part was published posthumously (*Bar Ilan, Sefer ha-Shanah*, 2 (1964), 65–69). In Germany he published his *Beziehung des Judentums zu Proselyten und Proselytentum* (1930, Heb. tr., 44–60). Various learned articles of his appeared in: *Keneset*, 6–8 (1942–44); *Yovel Shai... S. J. Agnon* (1958); and *Alei Ayin* (*Sefer Yovel... S. Schocken* 1952). He contributed the article on Personal Status *(Ishut)* to the *Encyclopaedia Hebraica*. Bialoblocki also contributed articles on the Torah centers in Lithuania and on his teacher I. J. Rabinowitz in: *Yahadut Lita*, 1 (1960), 185ff., 394ff.

Bibliography: H. Z. Hirschberg and S. J. Agnon, in: *Bar-Ilan, Sefer ha-Shanah*..., 2 (1964), 7–43 (Eng. summaries); Ungerfeld, in: *Ha-Ẓofeh* (Jan. 2, 1970). [Y.Ho.]

BIALOBLOTZKY, CHRISTIAN HEINRICH FRIEDRICH (1799–1868), hebraist and missionary. Bialoblotzky converted to Christianity as a young man and studied theology and philosophy at Goettingen, where he also was active as preacher. He traveled in Asia and Africa on behalf of the Protestant mission, and after serving as head of a private school in England, became lecturer at the University of Goettingen. Among his published works are: *Das Biblische Unterrichtswesen* (1828); *The Chronicles of Joseph b. Joshua Meir the Sephardi* (2 vols., 1835–36), a translation with introduction and notes of *Joseph ha-Kohen's *Sefer Divrei ha-Yamim;* a Hebrew lexicon, *Oẓar ha-Shorashim* (*Lexicon radicum hebraicarum*, 1843), in Hebrew and Latin as well as in Hebrew and English; and *Psalms* (first book 1846), Hebrew, Greek, and English, as part of Origen's *Hexapla*. [Ed.]

BIALOSTOTZKY, BENJAMIN JACOB (1892–1962), Yiddish poet and folklorist, born in Pumpenai, Lithuania. Bialostotzky was the son of the famed "Posvoler Maggid" of Lithuania. He immigrated to the United States in 1911, taught in Yiddish schools, coedited Yiddish journals and, from 1922, wrote for the Yiddish daily *Forward*. In 1953 he edited the memorial volume for the poet David *Edelstadt. His own volume of poetry *Lid tsu Lid* ("Song to Song," which includes his bibliography by E. H. Jeshurin, 1958), is predominantly nationalistic in tone. His folklore studies resulted in several collections of legends: *Fun Golus Bovel bis Roym* ("From the Babylonian Exile to Rome," 1949), *Di Mesholim fun Dubner Maggid* ("Parables of the Maggid of Dubno," 1962); *Yidisher Humor un Yidishe Leytsim* ("Jewish Humor and Jewish Jesters," 1963).

Bibliography: LNYL, 1 (1956), 277ff.; S. D. Singer, *Dikhter un prozaiker* (1959), 105; M. Bassin, *Amerikaner Yidishe Poezye*

[M.RAV.]

BIALYSTOK (Rus. **Belostok**), industrial city in N.E. Poland; latterly one of the principal Russian/Polish Jewish centers; incorporated into Russia between 1807 and 1921 and administered by the U.S.S.R. between 1939 and 1941, reverting to Poland in 1945. Originally the Bialystok community formed part of the *Tykocin (Tiktin) community. Jewish settlement in the village of Bialystok was encouraged by the manorial overlords, the counts of Branicki. In 1745 the Bialystok community became self-governing, although remaining within the Tykocin province. The heads of the Jewish community were permitted to take part in municipal elections in 1749. In 1759 the Jews had to contribute two-thirds of the funds required to provision the armies in transit through Bialystok. The character of the craft guilds explicitly admits Jewish membership. Communal affairs were regulated by the counts in 1749 and 1777. By 1765, there were 765 Jews living in Bialystok.

The position of the Jews deteriorated when Bialystok passed to Prussia (1795), and subsequently to Russia. Its situation on the western border was favorable for developing trade with Russian markets, however, and the Jews were able to earn a livelihood as army purveyors or importers of tea and other commodities. The economic situation deteriorated when there was an influx of Jews expelled from the neighboring villages in 1825–35 and 1845, under the 1804 discriminatory legislation (see *Russia), who crowded into Bialystok. There was a steep increase in the Jewish population which in 1856 numbered 9,547 out of a total population of 13,787, many of them homeless or unemployed. Welfare institutions were established in an attempt to alleviate matters.

The development of the large textile industry in Bialystok after the Napoleonic wars owes much to Jewish enterprise. A number of the soldiers from Saxony were expert weavers and spinners who settled in Bialystok and established workshops largely financed by Jews; textile mills were erected by two Jews in 1850. As they acquired spinning, weaving, knitting, and dyeing skills, Jews replaced the German specialists. In 1860, 19 of the 44 textile mills in Bialystok were Jewish owned, with an output valued at 3,000,000 rubles; in 1898, of the 372 mills in Bialystok, 299 (80.38%) were Jewish owned, while 5,592 (59.5%) of the workers were Jewish. Of the total output of the Bialystok mills for this year, valued at 12,855,000 rubles, the Jewish share amounted to 47.3%.

The Jewish labor movement found strong support in Bialystok, and in 1897 many Jewish workers there became members of the *Bund. The Bialystok Jewish workers issued an underground newspaper, *Der Byalistoker Arbayter,* the same year. The intensive activities of the labor movement in Bialystok during the Russian revolution of 1905–06 provoked savage acts of reprisal by the Russian authorities. The *pogroms in Bialystok that occurred between June 1 and 3, 1906, were the most violent of the mob outbreaks against Russian Jewry that year, resulting in 70 Jews being killed and 90 gravely injured. The commission of inquiry later appointed by the Duma to

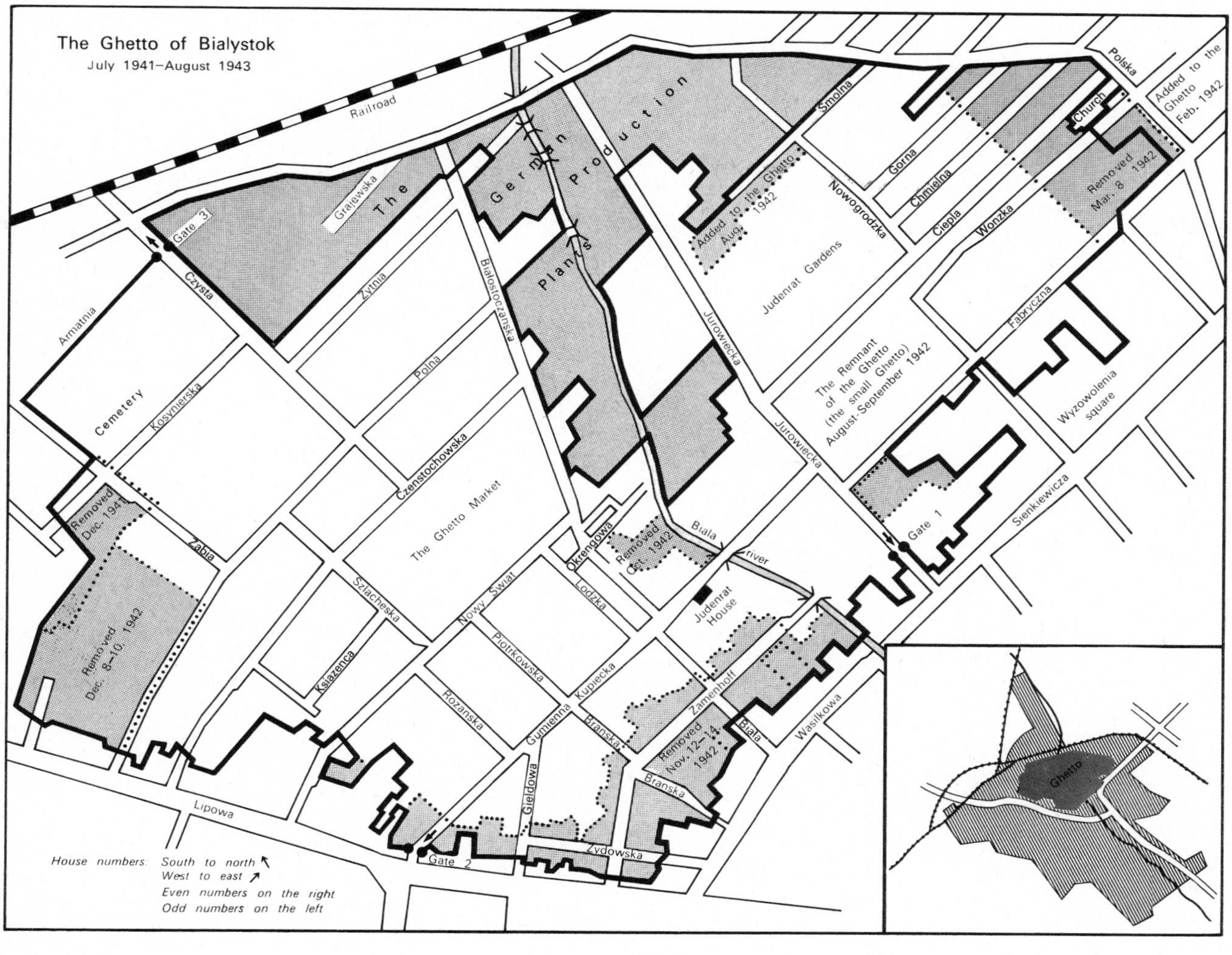

investigate the circumstances surrounding the pogrom held both the local police and the central authorities to blame for the tragedy. A prolonged crisis in Bialystok's trade and industry followed.

The contacts with German Jewry during the period that Bialystok was governed by Prussia had introduced the spirit of Enlightenment (*Haskalah) into Jewish circles in Bialystok. Prominent in the movement were members of the *Zamenhof family; Abraham Schapiro, author of *Toledot Yisrael ve-Sifruto* (1892); Jehiel Michael Zubludowsky, a contributor to *Ha-Karmel* and author of *Ru'aḥ Ḥayyim* (1860); and the poet Menahem Mendel *Dolitzki. A Ḥovevei Zion group was formed in Bialystok in 1880. Zionism in its manifold ideological ramifications subsequently gained numerous supporters. The Bialystok Zionists were led by Samuel *Mohilewer, and later by Joseph *Chasanowich. Rabbis living in Bialystok in the 19th century included Aryeh Leib b. Baruch Bendit (1815–20), author of *Sha'agat Aryeh;* Yom Tov Lipmann Heilpern (1849–79); and Samuel Mohilewer (1883–98).

Modern Jewish elementary schools, such as the modern *ḥeder (ḥeder metukkan),* a girls' school, and institutes for commerce and crafts were founded while Bialystok was part of Russia; the language of instruction was Russian, but Hebrew was also taught. The first Hebrew kindergarten was founded in 1910. Hebrew elementary and high schools were established after World War I.

In 1895 the Jewish population numbered 47,783 (out of 62,993). Of the 3,628 merchants and shopkeepers in the city in 1897, 3,186 (87.8%) were Jews. In 1913 the Jewish population numbered 61,500 (out of 89,700). In 1921, 93% of the businessmen were Jewish, and 89% of the industrial plants were Jewish owned; later the proportion of Jews in business decreased (to 78.3% in 1928). In 1932 there were over 39,165 Jews (out of 91,207) in Bialystok. [N.M.G.]

Holocaust Period. Shortly after the outbreak of the war, the Germans entered Bialystok, first occupying it from Sept. 15 until Sept. 22, 1939, when it was transferred to the Soviets. The second German occupation was from June 27, 1941, to July 27, 1944. At that time some 50,000 Jews lived in Bialystok, and some 350,000 in the whole province. On the day following the second German occupation, known as "Red Friday," the Germans burned down the Jewish quarter, including the synagogue and at least 1,000 Jews who had been driven inside. Other similar events followed in rapid succession: On Thursday, July 3, 300 of the Jewish intelligentsia were rounded up and taken to Pietrasze, a field outside the town, and murdered there; on Saturday, July 12, over 3,000 Jewish men were put to death there. Their widows were later known in the ghetto as *"die Donnershtige"* ("the ones from Thursday") and *"di Shabbesdige"* ("the ones from Saturday"). A *Judenrat was established on German orders (July 26, 1941), and chaired by Rabbi Rosenmann, but his deputy, Ephraim *Barash, was the actual head and served as its liaison with the German authorities. On August 1, some 50,000 Jews were segregated into a closed ghetto. The three gates in the barrier were guarded by armed gendarmes.

For administrative purposes, Bialystok was incorporated into the Reich (end of July 1941), as an autonomous district *(Bezirk)* of East Prussia under *Gauleiter* and *Oberpraesident* Erich Koch, one of Hitler's trusted men. Under this setup various Nazi authorities in Berlin, Koenigsberg, and Bialystok issued frequently contradictory orders concerning the fate of the Jews of the ghetto. The first year, there was relative quiet and order in the ghetto (except for the deportation of 4,500 of the poorest Jews

Figure 1. A synagogue in Bialystok, 1901. Jerusalem, Israel Museum.

to Pruzhany) as the Germans wished to exploit the ghetto to a maximum in industrial production for the army. Every Jew in the 15–65 age group was forced to work, and the Germans meted out physical punishment, including death sentences, to anyone attempting to avoid or resist forced labor. The only remuneration was a daily bread ration of 500 grams, which was later reduced to 350 grams. In addition, the Germans confiscated property, imposed forced "contributions," and collected a head and apartment tax; the Judenrat collected its own taxes to cover its expenses. There were private factories in the ghetto, owned by a German industrialist, Oskar Stefen; Jews were also employed in various German enterprises outside the ghetto. Two thousand persons were employed by the Judenrat, not including those in charge of the ghetto's economic enterprises. Over 200 men served in the "Jewish Police." The Judenrat maintained important departments: industry and artisans, labor, finances, and supply; its other departments dealt with health, welfare, housing, culture, and vegetable gardening for staples for a small segment of the ghetto; in the main, however, the Judenrat concentrated on factories engaged in war production in the hope of thus prolonging the survival of the ghetto inhabitants. The deputy chairman of the Judenrat, Barash, knew the truth about the deportations and death camps and had also read German documents containing plans to liquidate the ghetto. Nevertheless, up to his last day, he trusted in the idea that the inmates' hard work and economic "usefulness" would delay their destruction or even save them. Most of the inhabitants of the ghetto trusted Barash and shared his illusions. He stayed at his post until he was deported to Majdanek and murdered.

The Germans embarked upon the liquidation of the Jews on Feb. 5–12, 1943, when the first *Aktion* in the ghetto took place. The Jews were dragged from their homes and hiding places. One thousand of them were killed on the spot, while 10,000 were deported to Treblinka death camp. The period following the first *Aktion* was marked by Jewish underground preparations for armed resistance in the event that the deportations would be resumed. At this time the local German authorities, who were interested in prolonging the existence of the ghetto for economic reasons, were negotiating with the Berlin and Koenigsberg authorities on the date for the liquidation of the ghetto. The differences of opinion were resolved in the latter's favor, leading to the final destruction of the ghetto on Aug. 16, 1943.

Resistance. An underground came into existence in the early days of the ghetto and expressed itself mainly through sabotage acts at the members' places of work. It lacked, however, a uniform plan of action and a clear idea of its aims. Finally, in November 1942, Mordecai *Tenenbaum (Tamaroff), sent by the *Warsaw Jewish Fighting Organization to organize resistance in Bialystok Ghetto, arrived in the city and gave the movement direction. The underground's main problems were the lack of arms and disunity in the ranks. The ghetto stood alone in its struggle, for no help could be expected from the Polish underground. Arms had either to be stolen from the German armories or purchased at high prices outside the ghetto; only the hand grenades were of home manufacture.

In the early stage, Barash supported the ghetto underground and supplied it with finances and information through Tenenbaum. Barash also passed on copies of the Judenrat's minutes and proclamations as well as copies of German documents for the underground's secret archives. These archives were established by Tenenbaum on the model of the *Ringelblum *Oneg Shabbat* archives in the Warsaw Ghetto. Tenenbaum wrote a great deal himself and also collected diaries, depositions, historical articles, folklore, and Judenrat and German documents. These archives were hidden outside the ghetto and uncovered after the war; most of its contents are now in the custody of *Yad Vashem in Jerusalem. Until January 1943, the Bialystok underground maintained regular contact with the Jewish Fighting Organization in Warsaw, *Vilna, and other ghettos.

Barash supported the underground, however, only as long as the Germans were unaware of its existence. When the first *Aktion* took place, in February 1943, the underground was not yet ready. However it stepped up its activities. The men were trained in the use of arms, more weapons were acquired, and attempts were made to establish contact with the partisans in the forests. Several sentences of death were also carried out on Jews who acted as informers or otherwise cooperated with the Gestapo. The ghetto youth were greatly attracted to the forests, where there was a chance of fighting and personal salvation. Three small groups left the ghetto for the forests (January, March, and June 1943). But the Jewish partisan groups there were in a difficult situation, for they had few arms, and there was no Soviet partisan activity in the vicinity in this period. The ghetto therefore remained the base for the provision of food, medical aid, clothing, and arms to the small number of Jewish partisans.

One of the weaknesses of the underground, disunity, stemmed from differences in the members' political background and views on the underground's character and goals. Some were convinced that the minimum conditions necessary for military operations could not exist inside the ghetto, and that in fighting in the forests, side by side with the other partisans, the Jews could contribute to the common struggle against the Nazis. Tenenbaum on the other hand, adhered to the view that the underground had to concentrate on the struggle inside the ghetto, and that only after they had carried out this national duty could the members of the underground continue the struggle in the forests. It was not until July 1943, after the break with the Judenrat chairman, that the various underground movements in the ghetto united, on the basis of Tenenbaum's views, in a united fighting organization. Tenenbaum was elected its chairman, and Daniel Moszkowicz deputy chairman. Other prominent members of the underground were Zerach Zylberberg, Hershel Rosenthal, Haika Grosman, and Israel Margulies.

The united Jewish underground called upon the Jews to disregard the orders for deportation, and join the active resistance. Most of the Jewish population, however, stupefied by the Germans' surprise attack, which launched the final liquidation of the ghetto on Aug. 16, 1943, obeyed the orders given. The Germans were aware of the existence of the underground and therefore made careful secret preparations for the *Aktion,* for which a special commando unit from *Lublin was brought under the command of Odilo *Globocnik. The Jewish Fighting Organization tactics were to open battle, prevent the Jews from leaving the ghetto for the deportation trains, break through the German ranks, and seek refuge in the forests. German fire, however, supported by tank action, crushed the rebellion. After a day of fighting, 72 fighters retreated to a bunker in order to organize their escape to the forests. The Germans discovered the bunker and killed all the fighters, with a single exception. The ghetto fighters held out for another month, and night after night the gunfire reverberated through Bialystok. The commanders, Tenenbaum and Moszkowicz, presumably committed suicide when the revolt was quashed. A month later the Germans announced the completion of the *Aktion,* in which some 40,000 Jews were dispatched to Treblinka and Majdanek. The members of the Judenrat were among the last group to be deported. A few dozen Jews succeeded in escaping from the ghetto and joined the partisans in the forests. The revolt made a deep impression upon the Poles and the Germans. After the ghetto's liquidation, six Jewish girls remained who had posed as "Aryans." They acted as underground couriers, and now helped those who escaped to reach the partisans. After suffering many losses, the Jewish partisans in the forests united to form a single group, "Kadimah." They in turn were absorbed into a general partisan movement led by Soviet parachutists at the end of 1943.

After the war there remained 1,085 Jews in Bialystok, of whom 900 were local inhabitants, and the rest from the neighboring villages. Of the ghetto inhabitants 260 survived, some in the deportation camps, others as members of partisan units. The community presumably dwindled and dissolved.

[B.KL.]

אבל-עם!!!

יעדער איד פילט און באקלאגט מיט בלוטיגע טרערן דעם
שרעקליכן מורדערישן אומגליק פון די לעצטע פאגראמען. יעדער
איד וואס אין זיינע אדערן פליסט נאר יודישעס בלוט נעמט גע-
וויס דעם גרעסטן אנטהייל אין דעם גרויזאמען אומגליק פון גאנצן
כלל ישראל. נאר יעדער טרויערט אין זיין ווינקיל, יעדער קרעכצט
באזונדער. עס איז אבער נייטיג דאס דער קרעכץ פון גאנצן כלל
זאל זיך צונויפגיסען אין איין מעכטיגען געשריי. אלע טרערן
וואלען זיך צונויפקלייבן צו איין יאמערליכן הימעלשרייענדען
ים של דמעות. עס איז וויכטיג צו ווייזן דאס דער אידישער הער-
צער לעבט און פילט דען שמערץ פון יעדער גליד. דארום אום
צו ווייזן השתתפות בצער האומה, איז געבליבן בהסכם בד"צ דפה
ובדעת אסיפה גדולה אז מארגען מאנטאג ו' כסליו זאל זיין א
תענית ציבור, אין אלע בתי מדרשים וועט מען זאגן סליחות של
כ' סיון. און מאכען איין אזכרה די אלע הרוגים פון די לעצטע
פאגראמען, און צו מנחה זאל מען לייענען ויחל. אויסער דעם
וועט זיין א אזכרה בבהמ"ד הגבוה ברחוב וואשליקאווער ברוב עם
בשעה 11½ בבוקר, די קראמען דארפען זיין געשלאסען ביז זייגער 1
נאך מיטטאג.

דער וואס קען ניט פאסטען דארף געבען פדיון לטובת אחינו השדודים און
אריינטראגען אין קאמיטעט, ובזכות השתתפותנו בצער אומתנו ישמרנו ד'
מכל שד ושבר ולא ישמע עוד כל פרץ וצוחה ברחובותנו.

Figure 2. Yiddish notice calling on the Bialystok community to observe a day of fasting and prayer after the pogroms of June 1906. Jerusalem, C.A.H.J.P.

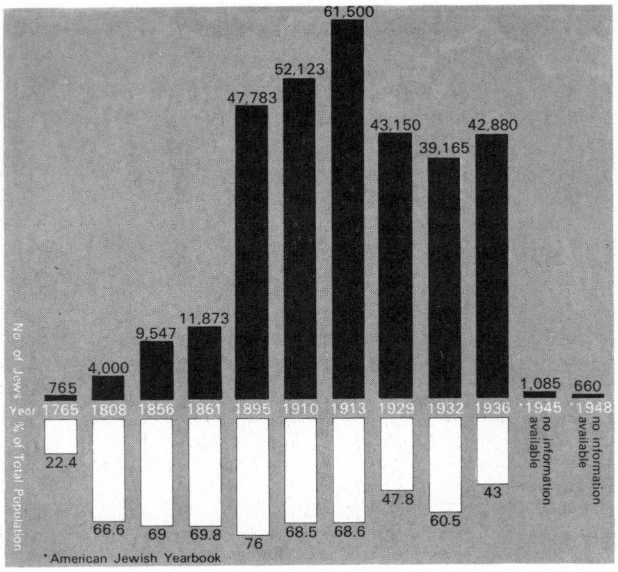

Jewish population of Bialystok, 1765–1948.

Bibliography: A. S. Hershberg, *Pinkas Bialystok* (1949); J. Lestschinsky, in: EJ, 4 (1928), 471–9; I. Schipper (ed.), *Żydzi w Polsce odrodzonej,* 2 (1933), 495–6, 523; B. Wasiutyński, *Ludność żydowska w Polsce w w. xix i xx* (1930). Holocaust Period: Klibanski, in: *Yad Vashem Studies,* 2 (1958), 295–329; M. Tenenbaum-Tamaroff, *Dappim min ha-Delekah* (1948); H. Grossman, *Anshei ha-Maḥteret* (1965²); N. Blumental, *Darko shel Yudenrat: Te'udot mi-Getto Bialystok* (1962); R. Raizner, *Umkum fun Byalistoker Yidentum 1939–1945* (1948); B. Mark, *Oyfshtand in Byalistoker Geto* (1950); D. Sohn (comp.), *Byalistok Bilder Album ...* (1951), with English captions; S. Datner, *Walka i zaglada bialostockiego getta* (1946).

BIARRITZ, coastal town in southwestern France. The Jewish community dates to the beginning of the 17th century. In 1619, after disorders in St. Jean-de-Luz, many *Marranos left that town to settle in Biarritz; according to the contemporary Pierre l'Ancre they numbered 2,000. In the census of Jews taken in 1942, 168 families were registered in Biarritz. The present synagogue, built in 1904, contains the Torah scrolls, the Ark, and the silver candelabrum from the former synagogue of Peyrehorade. In 1968, the Biarritz community had 150 members, many of whom originated from North Africa.

Bibliography: Roth, Marranos, 223ff.; Laborde, in: *Le Républicain du Sud Ouest* (1963); Loeb, in: REJ, 22 (1891), 111; Z. Szajkowski, *Analytical Franco-Jewish Gazetteer* (1966), 241.

[R.Be.]

BIBAGO, ABRAHAM BEN SHEM TOV (15th century), Spanish scholar, religious philosopher, commentator on Aristotelian works, and preacher. Bibago was born in the province of Aragon. He first resided in Huesca, where, in his youth, he completed a commentary on Aristotle's *Posterior Analytics* (1446). He later settled in Saragossa, where he was head of the yeshivah, and preached publicly on Sabbaths and festivals. He engaged in numerous disputations with Christian scholars at the court of Juan II, king of Aragon, on the Trinity and other Christian tenets, and for this reason kept abreast of Christian theology and scholastic philosophy. He probably died shortly before the expulsion of the Jews from Spain.

His "Derekh Emunah" and Philosophy. Bibago may be regarded as "a rational believer" (Steinschneider). On the one hand, he sharply denounced the bigoted zealots "who retain the shell but reject the kernel, posing as pious before the multitude, while vilifying and mocking the master (i.e., Maimonides) and his disciples" (*Derekh Emunah* 45:4). On the other hand, however, he sharply criticized the destructive tendency of some of the rationalists in their pursuit of philosophy and free enquiry. Bibago's chief work is *Derekh Emunah* ("Path of Faith"), on the principal tenets of Judaism (Constantinople, 1521). It is divided into three treatises. The first discusses the acts of God, His knowledge, and His providence; the second the intellect and its objects, faith and reason, sin, and related topics; and the third, the principles of the Jewish religion, miracles, creation, and special articles of faith.

Bibago's views influenced Isaac *Arama, who refers to them, without, however, mentioning the author's name. It appears that Arama gained this knowledge through personal contact rather than through reading the *Derekh Emunah* (Wilensky, *Yiẓḥak Arama,* 44–5; cf. J. S. Delmedigo, *Maẓref la-Ḥokhmah,* 8b). Arama describes Bibago as "one of the most important scholars and philosophers of our people" (*Akedat Yiẓḥak, Gate 80*). Isaac *Abrabanel quotes the *Derekh Emunah* in his *Rosh Amanah,* without, however, mentioning its author's name. Jacob ibn *Habib speaks highly of Bibago's scholarship, although he objects to his allegorical interpretation of talmudic passages (*Ein Ya'akov,* end of tractate *Berakhot*).

Other Works. Bibago's only other published work is his homily on creation and the Sabbath, *Zeh Yenaḥamenu* (Salonika, c. 1522/23?), but many other works exist in manuscript. The most important of these is his extensive commentary on the *Metaphysics* of Aristotle based upon the Middle Commentary of *Averroes. Bibago knew Arabic and Latin and had an extensive knowledge of Hebrew, Arabic, and scholastic philosophic works, quoting extensively from them. It is evident that Bibago knew most of Aristotle's works, as well as the commentaries of Averroes. He quotes Euclid, Galen, Ptolemy, two commentators on Aristotle (Alexander of Aphrodisias and Themistius), Apollonius of Perga, and others. Of Arabic philosophers he mentions, besides Averroes, al-Fārābī, Avicenna, al-Ghazālī, Ibn Tufayl, and Avempace. Among Christian writers he refers to Eusebius and several of the scholastics, including Duns Scotus and William of Ockham. Bibago also delved into the Kabbalah.

His commentary to Aristotle's *Posterior Analytics* preserved in Vatican Ms. 350 is believed by some scholars to be in his own hand. Bibago mentions this work in his commentary on the *Metaphysics* in which he refers also to his commentary on Aristotle's *Physics,* which has not survived. Of his other works, mention should be made of his *Eẓ Ḥayyim,* on the creation of the world, which he mentions several times in his *Derekh Emunah,* and in which he attempts to rebut Aristotle's and Averroes' proofs for the eternity of the world. Some are of the opinion that Bibago's *Zeh Yenaḥamenu,* as well as other treatises in manuscript are portions of the *Eẓ Ḥayyim* which was a collection of his homilies. He also wrote a treatise in which he refuted the arguments of *Naḥmanides against the exegetical method used by Maimonides in his *Guide of the Perplexed* (*Derekh Emunah,* 38:1).

Bibliography: Baer, Spain, index, s.v. *Abraham Bivach;* Munk, Mélanges, 507; Graetz, Gesch, 8 (1890³), 219ff.; Steinschneider, in: MGWJ, 32 (1883), 79ff., 229; Steinschneider, Uebersetzungen, 89ff., and passim; S. Wilensky (Heller), *Yiẓḥak Arama u-Mishnato ha-Filosofit* (1956), index.

[M.N.Z./Ed.]

BIBAGO (Bivach), ISAAC (d. 1489), physician in Huesca, Spain; brother of Abraham *Bibago. In the 1460s he and others of his circle helped to bring back to the faith Jews who had been forcibly converted to Christianity (see **Anusim*). These included the wealthy converso *Juan de

Opening and closing pages to the Pentateuch portion of *Shelaḥ Lekha* ("Send thou", Num. 13–15). Top—opening pages (fol. 3v–4) are decorated with gold bars on the top and at the bottom of the single text column and have gold motifs in the margins. The masorah, magna and parva, the traditional textual apparatus of the Bible, are written in the borders. Bottom—closing pages have a carpet page (fol. 33v) and a framed colophon (fol. 34). The small manuscript was written by Isaac ben Abraham ha-Levi in 1106, probably in Egypt. Jerusalem, Jewish National and University Library, ms. Heb. 8°2238, fol. 3v–4 and 33v–34 (5 × 4 ins/12.5 × 10 cm.).

3·

3·

Ciudad, who spent some time as a guest of the Bibago brothers in order to be instructed by them in the principles of Judaism. In 1489 the Inquisition uncovered the Huesca community's proselytizing activities, and Isaac was among the few suspects still living at the time. He was arrested and was condemned to be burned at the stake. However, as he accepted baptism he was strangled before his body was consigned to the pyre; his fellow prisoners were burned alive.

Bibliography: Baer, Spain, 2 (1966), 297–9, 385–9; Baer, Urkunden, 1 pt. 2 (1956), 488ff.

[Ed.]

BIBAS, family of rabbis and physicians originating in Spain. After 1492 the Bibas family fled to Morocco where its members became spiritual leaders of important communities. Abraham Bibas was one of the leaders of the Castilian community in Fez in 1526. Ḥayyim became *dayyan* of Tetuan in 1575; there he built the Great Synagogue, which was destroyed by the Muslims in 1667. His direct descendants succeeded him as leaders of the community until after 1700. Other members of the family were *dayyanim* in Salé. Known for their piety and learning, they exercised great influence and had many disciples. Their decisions and responsa were collected and many of them were published with others of their works. Members of the Bibas family settled in Safed, Jerusalem, Cairo, Leghorn, Amsterdam, and Gibraltar. Shem Tov was a member of Joseph Caro's *bet din* in Safed. Joseph was one of the leading rabbis in Safed at the end of the 17th century. He was the father-in-law of the Shabbatean Nehemiah Ḥayyon who found in his library an old manuscript of the Zohar, attributed to Benjamin ha-Levi. Samuel (d. 1793), a friend of Ḥ. J. D. *Azulai, was *dayyan* in Salé. His son Judah (1780–1852), a prominent rabbi and precursor of Zionism, was born in Gibraltar, and studied there and in Leghorn, Italy. He received a secular education in Italy and was apparently granted a doctoral degree by an Italian university. Between 1805 and 1832 he lived in Gibraltar, London, and Leghorn, gaining a reputation as a Jewish scholar. In 1832 he was appointed rabbi of Corfu, where he reorganized the Jewish community and its education system, and introduced reforms which aroused opposition from some of the heads of the community. He traveled through Europe in 1839, visiting Turkey, the Balkans, Vienna, and Prague. In Zemun he met Judah *Alkalai, from whom he learned of the new concept of *teshuvah* as a return to the Land of Israel, and not merely as "repentance." Alkalai incorporated his impressions of Bibas in his book *Darkhei No'am.* Two Scottish missionaries, A. Bonar and R. M. M'Cheyne, relate of a visit to the Holy Land in their book *Narrative and Mission of Inquiry to the Jews in 1839* (1878), that Jews in Rumania quoted Bibas as saying: "The Jews must be instructed in sciences and in arms so that they may wrest the land of Palestine from the Turks under the conduct of the Messiah, as the Greeks wrested their country." It appears that Bibas conceived the idea of the return to Zion in active, contemporary terms, on a religious basis. In 1852, after a stay in London and another ten-year period in the rabbinical post in Corfu, Bibas went to Ereẓ Israel and settled in Hebron.

Bibliography: I. R. Molho, *Ha-Rav Y. Bibas* (1957); I. Ben-Walid, *Va-Yomer* (1875), 11, nos. 103–5. J. M. Toledano, *Ner ha-Maarav* (1911), 60, 89–90, 152–3, 158; J. Ben-Naim, *Malkhei Rabbanan* (1931), passim; I. R. Molho, in: *Oẓar Yehudei Sefarad,* 3 (1960), 112–5; M. Benayahu, *ibid.,* 95–111; Hirschberg, Afrikah, 1 (1965), 314; EẒD, 1 (1958), 276–80; T. Preschel, in: *Sinai,* 53 (1963), 174–5.

[D.Co./G.K.]

BIBLE. The entry is arranged according to the outline below. Bibliography for a section is indicated by (†).

THE CANON, TEXT, AND EDITIONS

CANON

General Titles. There is no single designation common to all Jews and employed in all periods by which the Jewish Scriptures have been known. The earliest and most diffused Hebrew term was *Ha-Sefarim* ("The Books"). Its antiquity is supported by its use in Daniel in reference to the prophets (Dan. 9:2). This is how the sacred writings are frequently referred to in tannaitic literature (Meg. 1:8; MK 3:4; Git. 4:6; Kelim 15:6; et al.). The Greek-speaking Jews adopted this usage and translated it into their vernacular as *τὰ βιβλία*. The earliest record of such is the Letter of *Aristeas (mid-second century B.C.E.) which uses the singular form (v. 316, *ἐν τῇ βίβλῳ*) for the Pentateuch. The translator of The Wisdom of *Ben Sira into Greek (c. 132 B.C.E.) similarly employs "The Books" to designate the entire Scriptures (Ecclus., prologue, v. 25 "*καὶ τὰ λοιπὰ τῶν βιβλίων*"). It is from this Hellenistic Jewish usage of *τὰ βιβλία*, which entered European languages through its Latin form, that the English "Bible" is derived.

The term *Sifrei ha-Kodesh* (*Sifre ha-Qodesh;* "Holy Books"), although not found in Hebrew literature before the Middle Ages, seems to have been used occasionally by Jews even in pre-Christian times. The author of I Maccabees (12:9), who certainly wrote in Hebrew (c. 136–135 B.C.E.), speaks of "the Holy Books" (*τὰ βιβλία τὰ ἅγια*). In the early first century C.E., the Greek writer of II Maccabees 8:23 mentions "the Holy Book" (*... τὴν ἱερὰν βίβλον*) and toward the end of that century, both Josephus (Ant., 20:261) and Pope Clement I (*First Epistle,* 43:1) refer to "the Holy Books" (*αἱ ἱεραὶ βίβλοι*). The appelation is rare, however, since the increasing restriction of *sefer* in rabbinic Hebrew to sacred literature rendered superfluous any further description. On the other hand, *Kitvei ha-Kodesh* (*Kitve ha-Qodesh;* "Holy Writings"), is fairly common in tannaitic sources as a designation for the Scriptures (Shab. 16:1; Er. 10:3; Yad. 3:2, 5; 4:6; BB 1:6; Par. 10:3). Here the definition is required since the Hebrew כתב *(ktb)* did not develop a specialized meaning and was equally employed for secular writing (cf. Tosef., Yom Tov 4:4). The title "Holy Writings" was also current in Jewish Hellenistic and in Christian circles, appearing in Greek as *αἱ ἱεραὶ γραφαί* (Philo, Fug. 1:4; Clement's *First Epistle* 45:2; 53:1), as *τὰ ἱερὰ γράμματα* (Philo, Mos. 2:290, 292; Jos., Ant., 1:13; 10:210; et al.; and as *γραφαί ἄγαι* (Rom. 1:2). Closely allied to the preceding is the title *Ha-Katuv* ("The Scripture"; Pe'ah 8:9; Ta'an. 3:8; Sanh. 4:5; Avot 3:7, 8, et al.) and the plural *Ha-Ketuvim* ("The Scriptures"; Yad. 3:5 et al.). These, too, were taken over by the Jews of Alexandria in the Greek equivalent, probably the earliest such example being the Letter of Aristeas (vv. 155, 168, *διὰ τῆς γραφῆς*). This term was borrowed by the early Christians (*ἡ γραφή* John 2:22; Acts 8:32; II Tim 3:16 et al.; *αἱ γραφαί* Mark 12:24; I Cor. 15:34 et al.; *τὰ γράμματα* John 5:47).

These uses of the Hebrew root *ktb* ("to write") to specify the Scriptures have special significance, for they lay emphasis on the written nature of the text in contradistinction to the oral form in which the rabbinic teachings were transmitted. In the same way, *Mikra* (*Miqra';* lit. "reading"), another term for the Bible current among the rabbis, serves to underline both the vocal manner of study and the central role that the public reading of the Scriptures played in the liturgy of the Jews. The designation is found in tannaitic sources (Ned. 4:3; Avot 5:21; TJ, Ta'an, 4:2, 68a), but it may be much older, as Nehemiah 8:8 suggests. It is of interest that *Miqra'* as the Hebrew for "Bible" achieved wide popularity among Jews in the Middle Ages

The acronym תנ״ך *(TaNaKh)*, derived from the initial letters of the names of the three divisions of the Bible *(Torah, Nevi'im, Ketuvim)*, became similarly popular.

Still another expression for the Scriptures is *Torah, used in the widest sense of the term as the revelation of religion. While it is only occasionally so employed for the Bible in rabbinic literature (cf. MK 5a with respect to Ezek. 39:15; Sanh. 91b citing Ps. 84:5; PR 3:9, in reference to Eccles. 12:12), the fact that νόμος, the Greek rendering of Torah, is found in the New Testament in the same way (John 10:34, quoting Ps. 82:6) indicates that it may once have been in more common use among Jews.

Thoroughly Christian is the characterization "Old Testament" (i.e., Covenant; II Cor, 3:14; cf. Heb. 9:15–18). This term is used to distinguish the Jewish Bible from the "New Testament" (i.e., Covenant; I Cor. 11:25; II Cor. 3:6; Christian interpretation of Jeremiah 31:30–32). At the same time, it is possible that the designation "Testament" (i.e., "Covenant," Gr.: διαθήκη) may have been a reflection of an extended use among Jews of the Hebrew *berit* ("covenant") or *Sefer ha-Berit* ("Book of the Covenant"; Ex. 24:7; II Kings 23:2, 21). Jeremiah (31:30–32) himself uses "covenant" and "Torah" synonymously, and the "Book of the Torah" found in the Temple (II Kings 22:8, 10) is alternatively styled the "Book of the Covenant" (*ibid.* 23:2, 21). The Wisdom of Ben Sira (24:23) actually uses the latter term βιβλως διαθήκης) parallel with Torah (νόμος), and a similar usage is found in I Maccabees 1:56–57.

The Canon. The term as applied to the Bible designates specifically the closed nature of the corpus of sacred literature accepted as authoritative because it is believed to be divinely revealed. The history of the word helps to explain its usage. Of Sumerian origin, it entered into Semitic languages with the meaning of "reed" or "cane" (Heb. קנה), later used for "a measuring rod" (cf. Ezek. 40:5), both of which senses passed into Greek (κάννα, κανών). Metaphorically, it came to be used as a rule or standard of excellence and was so applied by the Alexandrian grammarians to the Old Greek classics. In the second century, κανών had come to be used in Christian circles in the sense of "rule of faith." It was the Church Fathers of the fourth century C.E. who first applied "canon" to the sacred Scriptures.

No exact equivalent of this term is to be found in Jewish sources although the phrase *Sefarim Ḥizonim* ("external books"; Sanh. 10:1), i.e., uncanonical, is certainly its negative formulation. However, tannaitic literature does employ the phrase *mettame et ha-Yadayim* ("rendering the hands unclean") to convey what is commonly understood by "canonical." According to rabbinic enactment, hands that came into direct contact with any biblical book contracted uncleanness in the second degree, so that if they then touched *terumah* without prior ritual washing they rendered it unfit for priestly consumption (Kelim 15:6; Yad. 3:2; 4:6). Whatever the true origin and purpose of this legislation (Yad. 3:3–5; Tosef., Yad. 2:19; Shab. 13b–14a; TJ, Shab. 1:6, 3c), the effect was to make the phrase "rendering the hands unclean" synonymous with canonical. Hence, rabbinic discussions about the full canonicity or otherwise of Ecclesiastes, Song of Songs (Eduy. 5:3; Yad. 3:5; Tosef., Yad. 2:14), Esther (Meg. 7a), Ben Sira, and other books (Tosef., Yad. 2:13) are expressed in terms of this formula.

The Significance of the Canon. The concept enshrined in the "canon" is distinctively and characteristically Jewish. Through it Israel became the "People of the Book" and the Bible became the animating force of Jewish existence, its precepts and teachings impressed upon the

First page of the Book of Judges with Targum Jonathan and commentaries by David Kimḥi and Levi b. Gershom in an incunabulum printed by Samuel d'Ortas in Leiria, Portugal, 1495. Incunabula list, no. 34.

mind and soul of the nation. The canonized Scriptures were looked upon as the faithful witness to the national past, the embodiment of the hopes and dreams of a glorious future, and the guarantee of their fulfillment. They constituted, in time, the main source for the knowledge of Hebrew and typified the supreme standard of stylistic excellence. Through the instrumentality of the Oral Law they represented the force of truth, wisdom, law, and morality. In short, the development of the canon proved to be a revolutionary step in the history of religion, and the concept was consciously adopted by Christianity and Islam.

The Process of Canonization. It should be noted, however, that the above refers to the canon solely in respect of its religious connotation. There is evidence that as early as the second half of the second millennium B.C.E., the classical literary texts of Mesopotamia were beginning to assume standardized form. There emerged a widely diffused, recognizable body of literature with fixed authoritative texts, the sequence and arrangement of which were firmly established. This discovery is significant because it provides an important precedent for the external features of canonical literature and it means that the process of canonical development could have begun quite early in Israel's history. Unfortunately, there is no direct information about the origins of the canon, nor can the criteria of selectivity adopted by those who fixed it be ascertained.

It is clear that the books that make up the Bible cannot possibly have comprised the whole literary production of ancient Israel. The Scriptures themselves bear testimony to the existence of an extensive literature which is now lost. The "*Book of the Wars of the Lord" (Num. 21:14) and the "*Book of Jashar" (Josh. 10:13; II Sam. 1:18) are certainly very ancient. Prophetic compositions are ascribed to Samuel, Nathan, and Gad (I Chron. 29:29) of the early monarchy period and to Ahijah, Jedo/Iddo, and Shemaiah from the time of the division of the kingdom (II Chron. 9:29; 12:5; 13:22). The references to the chronicles of King David (Chron. 27:24), of Solomon (I Kings 11:41), and of the Kings of Israel and Judah (*ibid.* 14:19, 29; I Chron. 9:1; II Chron. 16:11; 20:34; 27:7; 32:32; 33:18) all bear witness to royal annalistic sources no longer extant. A category of literature called "Midrash" (II Chron. 13:22; 24:27) is also ascribed to the times of the monarchy, and a book of dirges to the end of that period (II Chron. 35:25). While it is true that in many of these instances it is possible that the same work has been referred to under different titles and that the caption *sefer* might indicate a section of a book rather than the whole, it cannot be doubted that numerous other works must have existed which were not mentioned in the Bible. In fact, the very concept of a scriptural canon presupposes a process of selection extending over a long period.

The quantitative disproportion between the literary productions and the literary remains of ancient Israel is extreme. The main factor at work was the natural struggle for survival. The absence of mass literacy, the labor of hand copying, and the perishability of writing materials in an inhospitable climate all combined to limit circulation, restrict availability, and reduce the chances of a work becoming standard. In addition, the land of Israel was more frequently plundered and more thoroughly devastated than any other in the ancient Near East. At the same time, in the historical realities of the pre-Exilic period Israel's cultural productions had scant prospects of being disseminated beyond its natural frontiers. Developments within Israel itself also contributed. The change of script that occurred in the course of Persian hegemony doubtless drove out of circulation many books, while the mere existence of canonized corpora almost inevitably consigned excluded compositions to oblivion.

Certainly there were other books, including some of those cited above, which were reputed holy or written under the inspiration of the divine spirit, but why they did not enter the canon cannot be determined. The possibility of chance as a factor in preservation cannot be entirely dismissed, though it is extremely unlikely. Some works probably survived because of their literary beauty alone. A very powerful instrument must have been scribal and priestly schools which, by virtue of their inherent conservatism, would tend to transmit the basic study texts from generation to generation. Similarly, the repertoire of professional guilds of Temple singers would be self-perpetuating, as would the liturgies recited on specific occasions in the Jerusalem Temple and the provincial shrines. Material that appealed to national sentiment and pride, such as the narration of the great events of the past and the basic documents of the national religion, would, particularly if employed in the cult, inevitably achieve wide popularity and be endowed with sanctity. Not everything that was regarded as sacred or revealed was canonized; but sanctity was the indispensable ingredient for canonicity. It was not, in general, the stamp of canonization that conferred holiness upon a book—rather the reverse. Sanctity antedated and preconditioned the formal act of canonization, which in most cases, simply made final a long-existing situation. Of course, the act of canonization, in turn, served to reinforce, intensify, and perpetuate the attitude of reverence, veneration, and piety with which men approached the Scriptures, and itself became the source of authority that generated their unquestioned acceptance as the divine word.

Contents and Titles of the Books. The Jewish Bible is composed of three parts, designated in Hebrew: *Torah* (תורה), *Nevi'im* (נביאים), and *Ketuvim* (כתובים). The earliest name for the first part of the Bible seems to have been "The Torah of Moses." This title, however, is found neither in the Torah itself, nor in the works of the pre-Exilic literary prophets. It appears in Joshua (8:31–32; 23:6) and Kings (I Kings 2:3; II Kings 14:6; 23:25), but it cannot be said to refer there to the entire corpus. On the other hand, there is every likelihood that its use in the post-Exilic works (Mal. 3:22; Dan. 9:11, 13; Ezra 3:2; 7:6; Neh. 8:1; II Chron. 23:18; 30:16) was intended to be comprehensive. Other early titles were "The Book of Moses" (Ezra 6:18; Neh. 13:1; II Chron. 35:12; 25:4; cf. II Kings 14:6) and "The Book of the Torah" (Neh. 8:3) which seems to be a contraction of a fuller name, "The Book of the Torah of God" (Neh. 8:8, 18; 10:29–30; cf. 9:3).

With the widespread dissemination of the Torah in the generations following the activities of *Ezra and *Nehemiah, it became customary, for strictly nonliturgical purposes and for convenience of handling, to transcribe the work on five separate scrolls; hence the Greek name ἡ πεντάτευχος (βίβλος), "the five-volumed [book]," which has passed into English as Pentateuch. In rabbinic literature the Hebrew equivalent is "The Five Books of the Torah" (*Ḥameshet Sifrei Torah;* TJ, Meg. 1:7, 70d; *Ḥamishah Sifrei Torah;* TJ, Sot. 5:8, 20d), or "The Five Fifth-parts of the Torah" (*Ḥamishah Ḥomshei* (popularly, but inaccurately called *Ḥumshei*) *Torah;* Ḥag. 14a; TJ, Sanh. 10:1, 28a; Sanh. 44a).

The English names for the books of the Torah—Genesis, Exodus, Leviticus, Numbers, and Deuteronomy—derive from those of the Latin Bible which, in turn, have their origins in titles current among the Greek-speaking Jews, who translated Hebrew designations in use among their coreligionists in Palestine. These titles are descriptive of the contents or major theme of the respective books and they have partly survived in rabbinic literature and medieval Hebrew works in these forms: *Sefer Beri'at ha-ʿOlam* ("The Book of the Creation of the World"); *Sefer Yeẓi'at Mizrayim* ("The Book of the Exodus from Egypt"); *Torat Kohanim* ("The Book of the Priestly Code"); *Ḥomesh ha-Pekuddim* (*Ḥomesh ha-Pequddim;* "The Book of the Numbered"), *Mishneh Torah* ("The Repetition of the Torah"; cf. TJ, Meg. 3:7, 74b et al.). Another method of naming was to entitle a book by its opening word or words, or by its first significant word; cf. the Babylonian "When on High" and "I will Praise the Lord of Wisdom." This was common in rabbinic sources (*Elleh ha-Devarim;* "These Are the Words" = Deuteronomy, Sot. 7:8; Gen. R. 3:5; TJ, Meg. 3:1, 74a) and has remained the most popular mode of designation in Hebrew to the present time. Finally, there is also evidence that ordinal numbers were used (cf. Gen. R. 3:5; TJ, Meg. 3:1, 74a).

The second division of the Bible is known as *Nevi'im* ("Prophets"), later subdivided into "Former Prophets" and "Latter Prophets." This distinction, one of convenience only, serves to differentiate between the narrative, historical works—Joshua, Judges, Samuel, and Kings—and the (largely poetic) literary creations of the prophetic orators Isaiah, Jeremiah and Ezekiel, and the Twelve "minor" prophets—Hosea, Joel, Amos, Obadiah, Jonah, Micah, Nahum, Habbakuk, Zephaniah, Haggai, Zechariah, and Malachi. The popular epithet "minor" in connection with these twelve has a solely quantitative connotation and is no indication of relative importance. The names of the books are based upon the central figure or reputed author. The subdivision of the Prophets into "Former" and "Latter" was not known in the modern sense in talmudic times. The rabbis employed "former" in reference to the prophets up to the destruction of the First Temple (Sot. 9:12; Ta'an. 4:2; Sot. 48b; cf. Zech. 1:4; 7:7, 12), and reserved "latter" exclusively for the postexilic prophets; Haggai, Zechariah, and Malachi (Tosef., Sot. 13:2; Sot. 48b).

The *Ketuvim* ("Writings," Hagiographa), the third division of the Bible, is a varied collection comprising liturgical poetry—Psalms and Lamentations; secular love poetry—Song of Songs; wisdom literature—Proverbs, Job, and Ecclesiastes; and historical works—Ruth, Chronicles, Ezra, Nehemiah, Esther, and a blend of history and prophecy in the Book of Daniel.

This tripartite division of the Scriptures is simply a matter of historical development and does not, in essence, represent a classification of the books according to topical or stylistic categories. The Hellenistic Jews, apparently sensitive to the more or less random nature of the organization of biblical literature, attempted to effect a more systematic arrangement (see Hellenistic Canon, below).

The Tripartite Canon. The earliest sources consistently refer to the three corpora of scriptural books. *Ben Sira, approximately 180 B.C.E., speaks of "the Law of the Most High," "the wisdom of the ancients," and "prophecies" (Ecclus. 39:1). His grandson who wrote the Prologue to the Book of Ben Sira (c. 132 B.C.E.) refers explicitly to "the Law and the Prophets and the others that followed them," "the law and the prophets and the other books of our fathers," "the law . . ., the prophecies and the rest of the books." The author of II Maccabees (2:2–3, 13) mentions "the Law," "the kings and prophets, the writings of David . . ." *Philo is familiar with the Law, the "Prophets and the Psalms and other Writings" (Cont. 25). Josephus knows of the "five books of Moses," "the Prophets" and "the remaining . . . books" (Apion, 1:39–41). The same threefold arrangement is specified in the New Testament. To the author of Luke (24:32, 44) the Scriptures consist of "the Law of Moses and the Prophets and the Psalms."

From these sources it becomes clear that the third collection of Scriptures was not known by any fixed name. In fact, it was often not referred to by any name at all. IV Maccabees (18:10) mentions simply the "Law and the Prophets" even though Daniel, Psalms, and Proverbs are included in the designation (18:13–16). It must have been a widespread practice to refer to the entire Bible in this manner for it is encountered in the most diverse sources, rabbinic (Tosef., BM 11:23), New Testament (Matt. 5:17· 7:12; 11:13; 22:40; Luke 16:16; John 1:45; Rom. 3:21), and the Scrolls from the Judean Desert (1QS 1:2–3). All this can mean only one thing: the *Ketuvim* were canonized much later than the Prophets and the tripartite canon represents three distinct and progressive stages in the process of canonization. This is not to say, however, that there is any necessary correlation between the antiquity of the individual books within a given corpus and the date of the canonization of the corpus as a whole. Further, a clear distinction has to be made between the age of the material and the time of its redaction, the period of its attaining individual canonicity and the date that it became part of a canonized corpus.

The Canonization of the Torah (Pentateuch). Nowhere is this differentiation more applicable than in respect of the Torah. A clear distinction must be made between the literature of the Torah and the Torah book. Whatever the details of the incredibly complex history of the pentateuchal material, it is beyond doubt that much of it, at least, is of great antiquity and was venerated at a very early period. The traditional doctrine of Mosaic authorship of the entire Torah has its source in Deuteronomy 31:9–12, 24, more than in any other passage. But the reference here seems more likely to be to the succeeding song (Deut. 32),

Division	Section	Book	Chapters
The Law *Torah* **Pentateuch**		Genesis	50 Chapters
		Exodus	40
		Leviticus	27
		Numbers	36
		Deuteronomy	34
The Prophets *Nevi'im*	Former Prophets	Joshua	24
		Judges	21
		I Samuel	31
		II Samuel	24
		I Kings	22
		II Kings	25
	Latter Prophets	Isaiah	66
		Jeremiah	52
		Ezekiel	48
		The Twelve Prophets:	
		Hosea	14
		Joel	4
		Amos	9
		Obadiah	1
		Jonah	4
		Micah	7
		Nahum	3
		Habakkuk	3
		Zephaniah	3
		Haggai	2
		Zechariah	14
		Malachi	3
The Writings *Ketuvim* **Hagiographa**		Psalms	150
		Proverbs	31
		Job	42
	Five Scrolls *Megillot*	Song of Songs	8
		Ruth	4
		Lamentations	5
		Ecclesiastes	12
		Esther	10
		Daniel	12
		Ezra	10
		Nehemiah	13
		I Chronicles	29
		II Chronicles	36

as is indicated by verses 19 and 22. The Torah itself contains no explicit statement ascribing its authorship to Moses, while Mosaic attribution is restricted to legal and ritual prescription and is hardly to be found in connection with the narrative material. Moreover, the term "Torah" (which, by the way, means teaching and is by no means limited to laws) has to be examined in each case in its own context and in no instance can it be unequivocally understood in its later, comprehensive sense. In fact, the phrase "Torah of Moses" is not pentateuchal.

An important stage in the history of the pentateuchal canon is the chance finding of the "book of the Torah" in 622 B.C.E. as described in II Kings 22–23; II Chronicles 34. It is highly significant that there is no suggestion that the book is new. On the contrary, it is called the "Torah" and its authenticity and authority is at once recognized and acknowledged by the high priest and King Josiah alike. The enquiry of the prophetess Huldah and her reply relate not to the authenticity of the book but to the subject of divine punishment for the infringement of its prescriptions. The "Torah" was publicly read and accepted as binding in a national covenant ceremony. The identity of the book is not given, nor is it termed Mosaic in direct speech (II Kings 23:25 and II Chron. 34:14 are editorial remarks). Yet insofar as the ensuing reform of the cult expresses precisely the leading motifs of *Deuteronomy, it may be assumed that the ceremony described represents the formal canonization of that book and the beginning of the formation of the Pentateuch, not as literature, but as a sacred book.

This conclusion is strengthened by the remarkable fact that neither Kings nor Chronicles includes the reading of the Torah in the detailed descriptions of the great assemblies in the Jerusalem Temple held in connection with its dedication by Solomon (I Kings 8; II Chron. 5–7) and the national religious reform of Hezekiah (II Chron. 29–30). The absence of any retrojection of later practice into these narratives, despite the Chronicler's great emphasis on the "Torah of Moses," constitutes important evidence for the history of the canon. The first report of the reading of the Torah in public assembly subsequent to Josiah comes from the post-Exilic period, namely, the ceremony conducted in Jerusalem by Ezra, approximately 444 B.C.E. (Neh. 8–10). This ceremony cannot be the occasion of the canonization of the Pentateuch, as has often been claimed, since the initiative for the public reading comes from the people and there is no hint that the promulgation of a new law is involved. The book is called "the book of the Torah of Moses which the Lord commanded Israel" (Neh. 8:1) and the emphasis is on its dissemination and exposition.

Further evidence that the Torah had already been canonized by this time is provided by the Chronicler and by Samaritan tradition. The former, writing approximately 400 B.C.E., frequently appeals to the "Torah of Moses" and shows familiarity with every book of the Pentateuch. The Samaritans adopted the entire Torah together with the belief in its Mosaic authorship. Since hostility to the Judeans was already acute in Ezra's time and since the Samaritan-Jewish schism could not have taken place much after this, it follows that the canonization of the Pentateuch could not then have been a very recent event.

It may safely be assumed that the work of final collection, fixing, and preservation of the Torah took place in the Babylonian exile (cf. Ezra 7:14, 25). If some formal ceremony or act of canonization occurred, tradition has preserved no recollection of this momentous event.

THE CANONIZATION OF THE PROPHETS. The existence of the Torah Book served as a stimulus to the collection and organization of the literature of the prophets. A consistent tradition, repeatedly formulated in rabbinic sources, regards Haggai, Zechariah, and Malachi as the last of the prophets, the "divine spirit" having ceased to be active in Israel with their death (Tosef., Sot. 13:2; Sot. 48b; Yoma 9b; Sanh. 11a). Indeed, the absence of prophecy was regarded as one of the features that characterized the Second Temple period as opposed to the First (TJ, Ta'an. 2:1, 65a; Yoma 21b). Josephus, too, reflects this same tradition (Apion, 1:39–41). By the middle of the second century B.C.E., the institution was accepted as having lapsed (I Macc. 9:27; cf. 4:46; 14:41).

That contemporary prophecy was falling into discredit soon after the return from the exile is clear from Zechariah 13:2–5, and it is quite likely that the closing verses of the last prophetic book (Mal. 3:22–24) are actually an epilogue to the entire collection indirectly expressing recognition of the cessation of prophecy and the hope of its eschatological renewal (cf. I Macc. 4:45; 14:41; 1QS 9:11). The ideological background to this state of affairs was the consciousness of prophecy as the expression of the special and unique relationship between God and His people. This inevitably led to the notion that the disruption of this relationship would bring with it the cessation of prophecy as part of the spiritual punishment that Israel must endure for its sins (Jer. 18:18; Ezek. 7:26; Amos 8:11–12; Micah 3:6–7). The restoration from exile saw a brief revival of prophetic activity, but the Second Temple did not fulfill the messianic hopes and the movement waned.

The tradition declaring the prophetic canon to have been closed during the era of Persian hegemony, i.e. by 323 B.C.E., can be substantiated by several unrelated facts. That Chronicles belongs to the *Ketuvim* and neither displaced nor supplemented Samuel-Kings in the Prophets can be explained only on the assumption that the latter were already sealed at the time Chronicles was canonized. Similarly, the omission of Daniel from the Prophets (cf. Sanh. 94a) would be inexplicable if their canonization occurred in Hellenistic times. The absence of Greek words or of any reference to the historical fact of the downfall of the Persian empire and the transition to Greek rule provides further evidence. Moreover, no rabbinic disputes are recorded concerning the canonicity of any of the prophetic books. The tannaitic discussions about Ezekiel (Ḥag. 13a) have nothing to do with the history of canonization. The suggestion to relegate the book to the bibliocrypt *(lignoz)* was intended solely to remove it from common use. In fact, only sacred things could be so treated. On the other hand, some time must have elapsed between the canonization of the Torah and that of the Prophets, since only the former and not the latter were publicly read at the great assemblies described in Nehemiah 8–10, while the Samaritans, who became schismatic in the days of Ezra or soon after, received the Torah but not the Prophets.

THE CANONIZATION OF THE KETUVIM (HAGIOGRAPHA). The third collection of biblical books does not constitute a unified entity either contextually or ideologically. Many of the books were certainly written while the prophets were still active and the books were individually canonized quite early. They were excluded from the prophetic collection because their inspiration appeared to be human rather than Divine, or because they did not otherwise conform to the special ideological content or historical-philosophic framework of that corpus. This would be true of such works as Psalms and Proverbs. Other books, like Ezra, Chronicles, and Daniel, must have been written too late for inclusion in the Prophets. They were certainly canonical, as was Job too, by the generation before the destruction of the Second Temple (Yoma 1:6). On the other hand, there is plenty of evidence to show that the collection of the *Ketuvim* as a whole, as well as some individual books within it, was not accepted as being finally closed until well into the second century C.E. As noted above, the practice of calling the entire Scriptures the "Torah and Prophets" presupposes a considerable lapse of time between the canonization of the second and third parts of the Bible. The fact that the last division had no fixed name points in the same direction. Even the finally adopted designation *"Ketuvim"* is indeterminate, since it is also used in rabbinic Hebrew in the two senses of the Scriptures in general and of individual texts in particular.

Other indications of lateness are the fact that the Song of Songs contains two Greek words (3:9, אַפִּרְיוֹן = *φορεῖον* = palanquin; 4:4, תַּלְפִּיּוֹת = *τηλῶπις* = far-off), as does Daniel (3:5, 15, סוּמְפֹּנְיָה = *συμφωνία* = bagpipe; 3:5, 7, 10, 15, פְּסַנְתֵּרִין = *ψαλτήριον*) קיתרס = *κίθαρις* which even refers to the breakup of the Greek empire (by name 18:21; 11:2) and which most likely did not achieve its final form before approximately 167 B.C.E. (For the influence of Persian and Greek on the Book of Ecclesiastes see *Ecclesiastes.) Ben Sira (c. 180 B.C.E.), who shows familiarity with all other biblical books, does not mention Daniel or Esther. The latter book, in fact, seems not to have been accepted among the sectarians of Qumran; at least no fragments of it have yet turned up among the scrolls from the Judean Desert. Indeed, that there was once a certain reserve in respect of the sanctity of the Book of Esther is apparent from rabbinic discussion (Meg. 7a; cf. Sanh. 100a).

The ambivalent attitude on the part of the rabbis to the *Wisdom of Ben Sira* is highly significant. The fact that in the middle of the second century C.E. it was necessary to emphasize the uncanonical status of this book (Tosef., Yad. 2:13) and to forbid its reading (TJ, Sanh. 10:1, 28a) proves that the corpus of *Ketuvim* was still fluid at this time, and that Ben Sira had acquired a measure of sanctity in the popular consciousness. Despite the ban, the book continued to achieve wide circulation. The *amoraim* even quote from it, employing the introductory terminology otherwise exclusively reserved for Scripture (cf. Nid. 16b *di-khetiv;* Ber. 55b *she-ne'emar*). In one instance, a third-generation Babylonian *amora* actually cites Ben Sira as *Ketuvim* as opposed to Torah and Prophets (BK 92b).

It is true that in the generation after the destruction of the Temple the author of IV Esdras 14:41–46 (cf. Joseph., Apion, 1:39–41) seems to imply a closed biblical canon of 24 books; nevertheless, tannaitic and amoraic disputes about the canonicity of Proverbs, Song of Songs, and Ecclesiastes (Eduy. 5:3; Yad. 3:5; ARN 1:2), as well as of Esther (Meg. 7a), show that the widely held, though unsupported, view that the formal and final canonization of the *Ketuvim* occurred at the Synod of Jabneh (c. 100 C.E.) has to be considerably modified. More probably, decisions taken on that occasion came to be widely accepted and thus regarded as final in succeeding generations.

The Hellenistic Canon. The needs of the Hellenistic Jews, whether of Alexandria in particular or of the Greek-speaking Diaspora in general, led to the translation of the Bible into Greek. Beginning with the Torah about the middle of the third century B.C.E. the process took many centuries to complete. The formation of much of the Greek canon was thus coeval with the emergence of the Hebrew Bible as a sealed collection of sacred literature. The final product, however, diverged from the Hebrew—apart from the problem of the text—in two important respects. It adopted a different principle in the grouping and sequence of the biblical books, and it included works not accepted into the normative Hebrew canon. It must be understood, however, that, with the exception of a few fragments, all extant manuscripts of the Greek Bible are of Christian origin, and while it is reasonable to assume a Jewish prototype, the content and form of the Hellenistic Jewish canon cannot be known with certainty.

The Greek Ben Sira (prologue) clearly shows that the Palestinian tripartite division of the Bible was known in Alexandria in the second century B.C.E.; yet the Greek Bible does away with the *Ketuvim* as a corpus and redistributes the books of the second and third divisions according to categories of literature, thus creating a quadripartite canon of Torah, history, poetic and didactic writings, and prophecy. The sequence of books in the Greek Bible varies greatly in the uncial manuscripts and among the different patristic and synodical lists of the Eastern and Western churches. The Torah, however, always takes priority, followed by the Former Prophets. Ruth is attached to Judges, sometimes before, sometimes after it. The Minor Prophets invariably appear as a unit, though in slightly different order (Hosea, Amos, Micah, Joel, Obadiah, Jonah, etc.) and frequently preceding the three major prophets. Lamentations is affixed to Jeremiah, its reputed author. Of those books excluded from the Hebrew canon but included in the Greek Bibles, the number varies, but the following are found in the fullest collections: I Esdras (Ezra), Wisdom of Solomon, Wisdom of Ben Sira, Judith, Tobit, Baruch, the Letter of Jeremiah, I–IV Maccabees, and the Psalms of Solomon.

The order of the books in the Greek Bibles is illustrated by the following (the order in the Hebrew Codex Aleppo is given for comparison):

CODEX VATICANUS (B) 4th century	CODEX ALEXANDRINUS (A) 5th century	CODEX ALEPPO (C) 10th century
Genesis-Judges	Genesis-Judges	Genesis-Judges
Ruth	Ruth	I-II Samuel
I-IV Kings	I-IV Kings	I-II Kings
(Samuel, Kings)	I-II Chronicles	
I-II Chronicles		Isaiah
I Ezra (apochryphal)	Hosea	Jeremiah
II Ezra	Amos	Ezekiel
(Ezra-Nehemiah)	Micah	Hosea
	Joel	Joel
Psalms	Obadiah	Amos
Proverbs	Jonah	Obadiah
Ecclesiates	Nahum	Jonah
Song of Songs	Habakkuk	Micah
Job	Zephaniah	Nahum
Wisdom of Solomon	Haggai	Habakkuk
Wisdom of Sirach	Zechariah	Zephaniah
Esther	Malachi	Haggai
Judith	Isaiah	Zechariah
Tobit	Jeremiah	Malachi
	Baruch	
Hosea	Lamentations	I-II Chronicles
Amos	Letter of Jeremiah	Psalms
Micah	Daniel	Job
Joel	Ezekiel	Proverbs
Obadiah		Ruth
Jonah	Esther	Ecclesiastes
Nahum	Tobit	Lamentations
Habakkuk	Judith	Esther
Zephaniah	I Ezra	Daniel
Haggai	II Ezra	Ezra
Zechariah	I-IV Maccabees	
Malachi	Psalms	
Isaiah	Job	
Jeremiah	Proverbs	
Baruch	Ecclesiastes	
Lamentations	Song of Songs	
Letter of Jeremiah	Wisdom of Solomon	
Ezekiel	Wisdom of Sirach	
Daniel	Psalms of Solomon	

The Number of Books. By dividing Samuel, Kings, and Chronicles into two books each, and by individually enumerating Ezra, Nehemiah, and the twelve minor prophets, English Bibles usually list 39 books. This reckoning, however, is not traditional, for the twelve were written on a single scroll and counted as one; Ezra and Nehemiah were likewise treated as a unit, and the convenient bisection of Samuel, Kings, and Chronicles was unknown in Hebrew Bibles before the Bomberg edition of 1521 (see Editions, below). In this way a total of 24 books is traditionally obtained.

This number is consistently specified in the literature of the *amoraim* (cf. Ta'an. 5a) and is implicit in the tannaitic listing of the biblical books (BB 14b). It must be quite ancient for it is expressly mentioned as something well understood in IV Ezra 14:45, a passage deriving from about 100 C.E. On the other hand, from about this same period derives a variant tradition of Josephus limiting the canon to 22 books (Apion, 1:39–41). It is possible that the Song of Songs and Ecclesiastes were not yet included in Josephus' Bible. More likely, however, the difference is to be explained by the practice of attaching Ruth to Judges or Psalms, and Lamentations to Jeremiah. Since many of the Church Fathers also mention a 22-book canon (cf. Origen in Eusebius, *Historia Ecclesiastica,* 6:25, 1), it must be assumed that the observation of Josephus reflects a fairly widespread, if minority, Jewish scribal tradition that persisted for several centuries. Either way, the specified number really refers to the sum of separate scrolls used in transcribing the corpus of canonized literature. The artificiality of the number 24 and the absence of any authentic tradition to explain its origin are clear from the homiletics of the *amoraim,* who variously connected it with the like number of ornaments in Isaiah 3:18–24 (Ex. R. 41:5; Song. R. 4:11; Tanḥ. B., Ex. 111–117), of priestly and levitical courses in I Chron. 23:28; 24:4 (Num. R. 14:18; Eccles. R. 12:11; PR 3:9), and of the bulls brought as dedicatory offerings by the chieftains of the tribes (Num. 7:88; Num. R. 14:18).

It has been suggested, but with little probability, that Jewish practice may have been influenced by the pattern set by the Alexandrian division of the Odyssey and Iliad of Homer into 24 books each, an innovation itself dictated as much by the practical consideration of avoiding the inconvenience of handling a scroll containing more than 1,000 verses as by the desire to create a correspondence with the number of letters in the Greek alphabet. The 24-book division may have been regarded as a model for the national classics, especially because it is a multiple of 12, a number which was charged with special significance in the ancient world, even in the literary sphere. This is evidenced by the 12-tablet division of the Gilgamesh Epic, the 12 sections of the Theogony of Hesiod and the Laws of the Twelve Tablets. The 22-book division might well have been an adaptation of Greek practice to the Hebrew alphabetic enumeration.

The Order of the Books. In considering the arrangement of the biblical books in a specific sequence, two distinct problems have to be differentiated. The first relates to the very meaning of "order," the second to the underlying rationale of the diverse arrangements found in literary sources and manuscripts. The earliest list of biblical books is that preserved in an anonymous tannaitic statement (BB 14b):

> Our Rabbis taught: the order of the Prophets is Joshua, Judges, Samuel, Kings, Jeremiah, Ezekiel, Isaiah, and the Twelve . . . ; The order of the *Ketuvim* is Ruth, the Book of Psalms, Job, Proverbs, Ecclesiastes, the Song of Songs, Lamentations, Daniel, the Scroll of Esther, Ezra, and Chronicles.

As long as the normative practice restricted scrolls to individual works and did not combine several books into single volumes, it is difficult to understand what is meant by "order." Such a term would be applicable only after the rise of the codex form. However, the above-cited *baraita* cannot be later than the end of the second century C.E., whereas the codex was not accepted by Jews until many centuries later. The solution is probably to be sought in the library practices of the Mesopotamian and Hellenistic worlds.

The steady growth of collections, whether of cuneiform tablets or papyrus rolls, necessitated the introduction of rationalized and convenient methods of storing materials in ways that facilitated identification and expedited usage. At the same time, the requirements of the scribal schools engendered an established sequence in which the classic works were to be read or studied. This combination of library needs and pedagogic considerations is probably what lies behind the fixing of the order of the Prophets and *Ketuvim* as recorded in the list above. The reference would be to the order in which the individual scrolls in these two corpora were shelved and cataloged in the Palestinian archives and schools. The silence about the Pentateuch in the *baraita* is due to the fact that its priority in its long fixed order was so universally known as to make it superfluous. As to the underlying principles that determined the sequence, it is clear that the historical books of the prophetical division are set forth as a continuous, consecutive narrative with Jeremiah and Ezekiel following in chronological sequence. The anomalous position of Isaiah after Ezekiel reflected also in some manuscripts (see Table 1) has been variously explained. According to the *Gemara* (BB 14b) contextual considerations were paramount:

> The Book of Kings ends with a record of destruction; Jeremiah deals throughout with destruction; Ezekiel commences with destruction and closes with consolation, while Isaiah is entirely consolation. Therefore, we juxtapose destruction to destruction and consolation to consolation.

Table 1.
The Order of the Latter Prophets

1. Talmud and three mss.	2. Two mss.	3. Eleven mss.	4. Five Early Editions
Jeremiah	Jeremiah	Isaiah	Isaiah
Ezekiel	Isaiah	Jeremiah	Jeremiah
Isaiah	Ezekiel	Ezekiel	Ezekiel
The Twelve	The Twelve	The Twelve	The Twelve

1. (1) The Babylonian Talmud; (2) 1280 C.E. Madrid, National Library, ms. no. 1; (3–5) London, British Museum, mss. Orient. 1474, Orient. 4227, Add. 1545.
2. (1) 1286 C.E. Paris, National Library; (2) London, British Museum, Orient. 2091.
3. (1) 916 C.E. Leningrad codex; (2) 1009 C.E. Leningrad ms.; (3–11) London, British Museum, mss. Orient. 1246 C.E., Arund. Orient. 16, Harley 1528, Harley 5710–11, Add. 1525, Add. 15251, Add. 15252, Orient. 2348, Orient. 2626–8.
4. (1) The first printed edition of the entire Bible, 1488 Soncino; (2) The second edition 1491–93 Naples; (3) The third edition, 1492–1494 Brescia; (4) The first edition of the Rabbinic Bible, edited by Felix Pratensis, 1517 Venice; (5) The first edition of the Bible with the Masorah, edited by Jacob b. Ḥayyim, 1524–25 Venice.

This explanation is hardly adequate since Jeremiah contains prophecies of comfort and the observation on Isaiah applies only to chapters 40–66. Nor is it likely that the late exilic origin of the last 27 chapters of Isaiah determined its place after Ezekiel, since there is no evidence that the rabbis recognized the heterogeneous nature of the book. More persuasive, perhaps, is the thesis that the sequence Jeremiah, Ezekiel, Isaiah, and the Twelve was conditioned by their respective lengths in decreasing order. There may have been a tendency to place in close proximity prophets who were considered to have been contemporaries so that the great similarity between Isaiah 1:1 and Hosea 1:1 might well have been responsible for the juxtaposition of the books of Isaiah and the Twelve.

The *baraita* gives no list of the Minor Prophets. It simply designates them "the Twelve," implying that the order was well-known and universally accepted. The same conclusion is to be drawn from Ben Sira's reference to "the twelve prophets" (Ecclus. 49:10). Doubtless, the arrangement of the 12 small books, always written on a single roll, was based on chronological principles as understood by the religious authorities responsible for the canonization of the prophetic corpus. The present sequence is uniform in all Hebrew manuscripts and printed editions.

No reason for the tannaitic order of the *Ketuvim* is given in the *Gemara,* but it may be noted that the 11 books are arranged chronologically in groups according to rabbinic notions of their authorship. Ruth, which closes with the genealogy of David, precedes Psalms, which was ascribed to that king. Job follows, probably because of a tradition assigning the book to the time of the Queen of Sheba (BB 15b; cf. Job 1:15). Proverbs, Ecclesiastes, and Song of Songs were all attributed to Solomon; Lamentations was thought to have been written by Jeremiah; Daniel was credited to the exilic period and the last two to the Persian era. Notwithstanding the tannaitic notice, it would seem that the sequence of the *Ketuvim* was never really fixed, for the manuscripts and printed editions exhibit a variety of systems (see Table 2). Nevertheless, the differences are restricted to specific books or clusters of books. In the manuscripts and early editions, Chronicles never appears other than at the beginning or end of the corpus. Ezra-Nehemiah is invariably either the penultimate or final book depending on the position of Chronicles. The three larger works: Psalms, Job, and Proverbs, always constitute a group, with Psalms invariably first and the other two interchanging. The Talmud itself lists the "three larger books of the *Ketuvim*" as Psalms, Proverbs, and Job (Ber. 57b), a variant possibly conditioned by the view that Job was among those who returned from the Babylonian exile (BB 15a).

The most unstable books in respect of their order in the *Ketuvim* are the five Scrolls *(Megillot).* Their position varies in the manuscripts and printed editions both as part of the corpus of *Ketuvim* and as separately attached to the Pentateuch (see Table 3). Nowhere in rabbinic sources are all five listed in immediate succession, nor is the term "Five *Megillot*" used. The chronological sequence, according to reputed author, that underlies the tannaitic listing is essentially reflected in another talmudic source which identifies "the three smaller books of the *Ketuvim*" as the Song of Songs, Ecclesiastes, and Lamentations, in that order (Ber. 57b). In fact, six of eight main variations basically preserve this chronological principle (Table 2, cols. 1–5, 7). The practice of grouping all five *Megillot* together has its origin in the custom of reading these books on festival days: the Song of Songs on Passover, Ruth on Pentecost, Lamentations on the Ninth of Av, Ecclesiastes on Sukkot, and Esther on Purim (cf. Soferim 14:1, ed. Higger, p. 251–2). This is the order as it crystallized in the early printed Hebrew Bibles and in some manuscripts and early printed editions of the Pentateuch, to which all five *Megillot* have been attached.

The final position of Chronicles is most remarkable since Ezra-Nehemiah follows naturally in continuation of the narrative. The anomaly is emphasized by the widespread support it received in the manuscripts and early printed editions. It would appear that the New Testament, too,

Table 3.
The Order of the *Megillot* after the Pentateuch

1. mss. Nos. 1, 2, 3	2. mss. Nos. 4, 5, 6	3. mss. Nos. 7, 8	4. mss. No. 9	5. Early Editions
Song of Songs	Esther	Ruth	Ruth	Song of Songs
Ruth	Song of Songs	Song of Songs	Song of Songs	Ruth
Lamentations	Ruth	Ecclesiastes	Lamentations	Lamentations
Ecclesiastes	Lamentations	Lamentations	Ecclesiastes	Ecclesiastes
Esther	Ecclesiastes	Esther	Esther	Esther

The nine mss. collated for this Table are the following in the British Museum: (1) Add. 9400; (2) Add. 9403; (3) Add. 19776; (4) Harley 5706; (5) Add. 9404; (6) Orient. 2786; (7) Harley 5773; (8) Harley 15283; (9) Add. 15282.
The fifth column represents the order adopted in the first, second and third editions of the Hebrew Bible (see Table 1), as well as that of the second and third editions of Bomberg's Quarto Bible (Venice 1521, 1525), in all of which the five Megillot follow immediately after the Pentateuch.

Table 2.
The Order of the Hagiographa

	1. Talmud and Six mss.	2. Two mss.	3. Add. 15252	4. Adat Devorim and three mss.	5. Ar. Or. 16	6. Or. 2626–28	7. Or. 2201	8. Five Early Editions
1	Ruth	Ruth	Ruth	Chronicles	Chronicles	Chronicles	Psalms	Psalms
2	Psalms	Psalms	Psalms	Psalms	Ruth	Psalms	Job	Proverbs
3	Job	Job	Job	Job	Psalms	Proverbs	Proverbs	Job
4	Proverbs	Proverbs	Proverbs	Proverbs	Job	Job	Ruth	Song of Songs
5	Ecclesiastes	Song of Songs	Song of Songs	Ruth	Proverbs	Daniel	Song of Songs	Ruth
6	Song of Songs	Ecclesiastes	Ecclesiastes	Song of Songs	Song of Songs	Ruth	Ecclesiastes	Lamentations
7	Lamentations	Lamentations	Lamentations	Ecclesiastes	Ecclesiastes	Song of Songs	Lamentations	Ecclesiastes
8	Daniel	Esther	Daniel	Lamentation	Lamentations	Lamentations	Esther	Esther
9	Esther	Daniel	Esther	Esther	Esther	Ecclesiastes	Daniel	Daniel
10	Ezra-Nehemiah	Ezra-Nehemiah	Ezra-Nehemiah	Daniel	Daniel	Esther	Ezra-Nehemiah	Ezra-Nehemiah
11	Chronicles	Chronicles	Chronicles	Ezra-Nehemiah	Ezra-Nehemiah	Ezra-Nehemiah	Chronicles	Chronicles

1. (1) The Talmud; (2) 1280 C.E. Madrid, University Library, codex no. 1; (3–7) London, British Museum, mss. Harley 1528, Add. 1525, Orient. 2212, Orient. 2375, Orient. 4227.
2. (1) 1286 C.E. Paris, National Library, mss. no. 1–3; (2) London, British Museum, Orient. 2091.
3. London, British Museum, Add. 15252.
4. (1) 1009 C.E. Leningrad ms.; (2) 1207 C.E. *Adat Devorim;* (3–4) London, British Museum, mss. Harley 5710–11, Add. 15251.
5. London, British Museum, Arund. Orient. 16.
6. London, British Museum, Orient. 2626–28.
7. 1246 C.E. London, British Museum, Orient. 2201.
8. The five early editions, see Table 1, note 4.

reflects this arrangement (Matt. 23:35; Luke 11:51). As an explanation, it might be suggested that the position of Chronicles represents the chronology of canonization, though there is no evidence to support this. More likely, it resulted from a conscious attempt to place the biblical books within a narrative framework. Genesis and Chronicles both begin with the origin and development of the human race and both end with the promise of redemption and return to the land of Israel. The two books actually employ the same key verbs in this connection (Gen. 50:24–25; II Chron. 36:23; פקד, עלה; *pkd (pqd)*, *ʿlh*). Indeed, the messianic theme of the return to Zion as an appropriate conclusion to the Scriptures was probably the paramount consideration in the positioning of Chronicles. Further evidence that the arrangement of the Scriptures was intended to express certain leading ideas in Judaism may perhaps be sought in the extraordinary fact that the initial chapter of the Former Prophets (Josh. 1:8) and of the Latter Prophets (Isa. 1:10) and the closing chapter of the prophetical corpus (Mal. 3:22), as well as the opening chapter of the *Ketuvim* (Ps. 1:2), all contain a reference to Torah.

The Languages of Scripture. The books of the Bible have come down in the Hebrew language with the exception of two words in Genesis (31:47), a single verse in Jeremiah (10:11), and sections of Daniel (2:4b–7:28) and Ezra (4:8–6:18; 7:12–26), all of which are in Aramaic. The problem of the language of Scripture is, however, more complicated than would appear on the surface and it constitutes part of the larger issue of the history of the growth and formation of the canon. Some scholars, for instance, regard Job, Ecclesiastes, and Chronicles, as well as the Hebrew sections of Daniel and Ezra-Nehemiah as translations, in whole or part, from Aramaic. This implies that the original is lost, and at once raises the possibility of error in the course of rendition from language to language. It should be noted, though, that in dealing with the problem of translation care must be taken to distinguish between Aramaisms and Aramaic influence on Hebrew style on the one hand, and a translation that may betray its Aramaic substratum on the other.

Even works unquestionably composed in Hebrew are not without their linguistic history. It is the almost unanimous scholarly view that the spoken language of the patriarchs and most of the tribes was not Hebrew, but some form of Aramaic (cf. Deut. 26:5) and that the language of Canaan, or Hebrew, was adopted only later. Whether the process of linguistic metamorphosis was completed by the time of the conquest is uncertain, but it is clear that if the earliest traditions of Israel go back to northern Mesopotamia and to the formative period of Israel's history, then again these traditions must have undergone translation at some stage of their oral preservation.

In dealing with biblical Hebrew it must be remembered that the language of Scripture represents a period of creativity covering several hundred years during which internal development inevitably took place. In general, it may be said that the poetic texts in the historical books have preserved the earliest strata of the language (Gen. 49; Ex. 15; Num. 23–24; Deut. 32; 33; Judg. 5), while the Hebrew of those works deriving from the postexilic period—like Haggai, Zechariah, Malachi, Ecclesiastes, Chronicles, Ezra-Nehemiah, and Daniel—exhibits features that distinguish the known characteristics of postbiblical Hebrew. In between there are several linguistic layers, the isolation of which is complicated by the relatively small amount of material available for comparison, the difficulties in dating the different documents, and the problem of distinguishing between the age of the material and the period of the final stage of its redaction. Also, it is not known to what extent the editors "modernized" the language of the material they worked with. Comparative Semitic phonology and morphology make it certain that the present system of vocalization of the Hebrew consonants reflects the stage of Hebrew pronunciation more or less as it had crystallized in the Second Temple period. It can be said from internal biblical evidence (cf. Judg. 12:6) and from several inscriptions that there were important differences in dialect between northern Israel and southern Judah. Consequently, since much of the biblical literature originated in the north but was mediated through the Judean scribes, it must have been stylistically transformed to conform to the standard Jerusalemite dialect. Finally, in evaluating the language of the Bible, the problem of the reliability and integrity of the Hebrew consonantal text tradition cannot be overlooked.

TEXT

The History of the Biblical Text. In the medieval codices of the Hebrew Bible, as in the printed editions to the present times, the text generally comprises three distinct components. These are the consonants, the vowel symbols, and the liturgical, diacritical notations. The latter two elements were invented by the masoretes (see *Masorah) while the history of the consonantal text, with which this section is exclusively concerned, represents the crystallization of a textual critical process of very great antiquity and of remarkable complexity. The second edition of the Rabbinic Bible, edited by Jacob b. Ḥayyim and published by Daniel *Bomberg (Venice 1524/25), served as the model for all future printed editions (see Printed Editions, below). Between this date and that of the most ancient fragments of the Hebrew Scriptures found in the Judean Desert intervenes a period of approximately 2,000 years, and many more centuries of textual transmission separate the earliest documents from the *editio princeps* of a biblical book.

THE EARLIEST PERIOD (up to c. 300 B.C.E.). It is no longer possible to reconstruct the textual evolution of the Hebrew Scriptures between the time of the composition of an individual work and the age of the first known witnesses, approximately 300 B.C.E. The existence of divergent texts of the same books may be postulated since this is the only way to explain the variants in the many passages duplicated in the Bible. (II Sam. 22 = Ps. 18; II Kings 18:13–20:19 = Isa. 36–39; II Kings 24:18–25:30 = Jer. 52; Isa. 2:2–4 = Micah 4:1–3; Ps. 14 = 53; 40:14–18 = 70; 57:8–12 = 108:2–6; 60:7–14 = 108:7–14; 96 = I Chron. 16:23–33; Ps. 105:1–15 = I Chron. 16:8–22; 106:1, 47–48 = I Chron. 16:34–36; the parallels between Sam.-Kings and Chron.).

As late as the 13th century traditions were still preserved about a period of disorder in biblical texts and the textual-critical activities of the "Men of the Great Assembly" (David Kimḥi, preface to his commentary on Joshua). This conclusion is reinforced by the findings from caves in Qumran. Here a plurality of text-types has been discovered—a situation which must represent a state of affairs much older than its earliest documentation. On the other hand, it may be argued that the very idea of canonicity carries with it an attitude of reverence for the text and fosters care and accuracy in its transmission. This would be particularly true of a written text since scribal activities would naturally be restricted to a relatively small circle of specialists. Furthermore, the use of sacred literature in public worship and in the curriculum of influential schools would tend to endow a certain version of a scriptural text with greater prestige. All these factors would tend to work in the direction of inhibiting the multiplication of textual versions and would serve to give some text-types greater prominence than others.

The situation presupposed here finds support in the history of Mesopotamian literature, where all the evidence points to the emergence of authoritative standard versions of the classical texts by the end of the second millennium B.C.E. As a consequence of this development, the great cuneiform literary texts appear in very limited editions despite wide geographic distribution and considerable chronological variability. A similar state of affairs is discernible in connection with the Greek classics. As early as the sixth century B.C.E. the production of a definitive text of the Odyssey and the Iliad was commissioned by Pisistratus, tyrant of Athens, though this is not necessarily the text that finally became predominant. From the third century B.C.E. on, considerable textual-critical work on the manuscripts of Homer in order to determine the correct readings was undertaken by scholars at the museum library of Alexandria. There is no reason why the textual history of the sacred Scriptures of Israel should have been more anarchic than that of the Mesopotamian and Greek classics. In fact, the existence of a fixed text of at least part of the Torah before the close of the pentateuchal canon is presupposed by the injunction in Deuteronomy (17:18–19) that the king have a copy of the law transcribed for himself for purposes of regular study, as well as by the prescription to hold a periodic public reading of the Law from an official copy deposited in the central sanctuary (Deut. 31:9–12, 26). There is no way of knowing, however, whether any one recension achieved greater national importance or prominence within this period. It can only be concluded that since the prototype of the text-family that ultimately achieved hegemony is present at Qumran, the history of that text must be much older.

THE SECOND PERIOD (c. 300 B.C.E.–first century C.E.). The starting point, it should be noted, is somewhat arbitrary and is conditioned by the fortuitous existence of manuscript documentation; and the limiting point is fixed by the observation of a radical change after the destruction of the Temple. The evidence for development within this period involves Hebrew sources and Greek translations and is both direct and indirect. It is characterized by the diversity of text-types, though the number seems to have been very limited and each family of manuscripts appears to have maintained its homogeneity over a long period of time.

Until the discovery of the *Dead Sea Scrolls, the evidence of textual diversity in this period consisted mainly of the Samaritan *Pentateuch and the Septuagint; the latter must have been translated from a Hebrew source at variance with the received text. Further evidence for a still fluid state of the text is provided by the citations of Scripture found in the books of the *Apocrypha and by rabbinic traditions about the activities of the **soferim*. These latter are credited with responsibility for textual emendations (*tikkunei soferim*, Mekh., Shira, 6; Sif. Num. 84), for marking dislocated verses (*ibid.;* Shab. 115b–116a) and suspect readings (ARN[1] 34, 100–1; ARN[2] 37, 97; Sif. Num. 69), as well as for deletions (*itturei soferim*, Ned. 37b). Other rabbinic traditions tell of the need for "book correctors" *(maggihei sefarim)* in Jerusalem attached to the Temple (Ket. 106a; TJ, Shek. 4:3, 48a) and even of divergent readings in pentateuchal scrolls kept in the Temple archives (TJ, Ta'an 4:2, 68a; Sif. Deut. 356; ARN[2] 46, 65; Sof. 6:4).

This fluidity of text is precisely the situation that was revealed at Qumran, particularly Cave IV which has yielded about 100 manuscripts, complete or fragmentary. The outstanding phenomenon is the ability of the sect to tolerate, with no apparent disquiet, the simultaneous existence of divergent texts of the same book, as well as verbal and orthographic variety within the scope of a single recension. Clearly, an inviolable, sacrosanct, authoritative text did not exist at Qumran. Whether the identical conclusion is also valid for the normative Jewish community of Palestine in this period is less certain. It is true that there is nothing specifically sectarian about the Qumran Bible scrolls, either in the scribal techniques and conventions employed or in the nature of the divergent readings, which are decidedly neither tendentious nor ideological. Nevertheless, caution must be exercised in the use of the Qumran evidence for reconstruction of a generalized history of textual development in this period. The lack of more examples of the masoretic text-type may be solely accidental. It is also possible that this is less a library than a *genizah* which would tend to preserve discarded texts and so present a distorted picture. In many instances, the fragments are very small and are only *disjecta membra*, making the derivation of overall characteristics very hazardous. Finally, the isolated, cloistered, and segregated existence led by the sect of "covenanters," with its implacable hostility to the Jerusalem religious establishment, could well have insulated Qumran from normative developments elsewhere in Judea, where a less tolerant approach to textual diversity may have prevailed.

In fact, the rabbinic testimony cited above demonstrates the existence of a movement away from a plurality of recensions and toward textual stabilization. The textual-critical activities of the *soferim* are all directed to this end and they are expressly reported to have worked on a text fixed even in respect of the number of its letters (Kid. 30a). Whatever its intrinsic worth this talmudic tradition could not have arisen among the rabbis had the fixing of the text been recent. The presence of Temple-sponsored "book correctors" implies the acceptance at some point in the Second Temple period of an authoritative text by which the accuracy of other scrolls was measured (Ket. 106a; TJ, Shek. 4:3, 48a; Sanh. 2:6, 20c). The record of the variant Temple scrolls is a tradition concerned with an attempt to ensure just such a standardized recension. Indeed, that there existed an official Temple Scroll *(Sefer ha-Azarah)* which enjoyed high prestige is amply attested in rabbinic sources (TJ, Sanh. 2:6, 20c; Shek 4:3, 48a; MK 3:4; Kelim 15:6; cf. Jos., Wars, 7:150, 162), though it is not possible to tell exactly to what period they refer. Certainly, the seven rules of biblical hermeneutics, compiled but not invented by Hillel the Elder (Tosef., Sanh. 7:11; ARN[1] 37, 110; cf. Pes. 66a; TJ, Pes. 6:1, 33a), take the history of textual stabilization at least back to the time of Herod.

Soon after the destruction of the Temple, Josephus (Apion, 1:8) wrote about the inviolate nature of the text of the Jewish Scriptures and it is clear that he regarded this as a virtue of long standing. Further proof for the existence of the notion of an authoritative text is provided by the Letter of Aristeas which is well aware of the circulation of carelessly written books of the Law (Arist. 30) and has Ptolemy send to the high priest in Jerusalem for a Hebrew text from which to make the Greek translation (*ibid.*, 33–40, 46; cf. 176). Once produced, this translation itself came to be regarded as sacrosanct by the Jews of Alexandria (*ibid.*, 311). Nevertheless, there is evidence from Qumran that the Greek translation was the object of much recensional activity, the purpose of which was to bring it into line with developments in the Hebrew texts current in Palestine. This phenomenon reveals, once again, both that the Hebrew text was still fluid and that there was a movement toward textual stabilization.

Within this period the notion of an authoritative text was well rooted outside the Qumran community. A very limited number of textual families is discernible, probably each having achieved local authority. Each family, however, exhibits internal textual variety. The religious leadership in Jerusalem appears to have recognized a fixed text and to have been engaged in textual-critical activity aligning divergent exemplars with it. The beginnings of this movement may probably be traced to the Maccabean victories. At any rate, the recensional family that ultimately crystallized into what came to be known as "masoretic" is well represented among the Qumran collection, the most outstanding example being the Isaiah scroll (1QIsb).

THE THIRD PERIOD (first century C.E.–ninth century C.E.). The existence of an official text with binding authority from the generation of the destruction of the Temple is clearly reflected in halakhic discussions. Zechariah b. ha-Kazzav, who was apparently a priest in the Temple (cf. Ket. 2:9), based legal decisions on the presence of a conjunctive *vav* (Sot. 5:1). *Nahum of Gimzo, of the first generation of *tannaim*, employed the principle of "extension and limitation" in the interpretation of certain Hebrew particles (Ḥag. 12a; Pes. 22b), a hermeneutical system later developed to the full by R. *Akiva to whom not a word of the Torah, nor even a syllable or letter, was superfluous. Hence, he could derive a multiplicity of rules from each tittle on the letters of the Torah (Men. 29b). He, too, warned against teaching from "uncorrected" books (Pes. 112a) and emphasized the importance of the protective devices (masoret) for the Torah text (Avot 3:13). Further, it was in Akiva's day that the question arose as to whether the established consonantal text or the traditional manner of reading was to determine the halakhic interpretation (Mak. 7b; Sanh. 4a; Pes. 86b; Kid. 18b). R. *Ishmael, his contemporary, formulated the 13 *hermeneutical norms (Sifra 1:1) which presuppose a fixed recension. He also advised R. Meir to be extraordinarily meticulous in his work of transcribing sacred texts lest he omit or add a single letter (Er. 13a). This period is distinguished from its predecessors in that a single stabilized text attained unimpeachable authority and achieved hegemony over all others. This development seems to have occurred in the course of the first century C.E., probably as a consequence of the need for religiocultural cohesion and national unity following the destruction of the Temple. Before long, all other Hebrew recensions were discarded and passed into oblivion, leaving only a few traces behind.

It is true that in the generation after R. Akiva copies of the Torah made by R. Meir might still contain a few textual oddities (Gen. R. 9:5; 20:12), and medieval tradition could retain a record of variant readings found in a Torah scroll stored in the synagogue of Severus in Rome (*Bereshit Rabbati*, ed. Albeck, p. 209). It is also true that rabbinic literature has preserved several hundred deviations from the received text in scriptural quotations and in reconstructed readings underlying a specific piece of midrashic exegesis, while the same phenomenon may be discernible in citations in Jewish Palestinian apocryphal and pseudepigraphical literature, in the New Testament, and in the Church Fathers. Even in the third century C.E., R. Ammi, a Palestinian *amora*, might still find it necessary to warn against the retention of "uncorrected books" for more than 30 days (Ket 19b). Nevertheless, at this period all this constitutes a survival and not a living tradition.

The hegemony of the masoretic-type text is amply attested, apart from halakhic sources, by two independent classes of witnesses. On the one hand, the Hebrew biblical scrolls and fragments discovered at Masada (66–73 C.E.), at Wadi Murabbaʿat, and at Naḥal Ḥever (both from c. 132–35 C.E.) are all practically identical with the received text. On the other hand, the Jewish Greek translation of the Minor Prophets found in Naḥal Ḥever, and the second-century Greek translations of the Bible attributed to *Aquila, *Symmachus, and *Theodotion all testify to revisions of the Septuagint attempting to bring it closer to a masoretic-type Hebrew text which had become exclusively authoritative. Whether this development resulted from an official promulgation by accepted religious authorities, or whether it was the culmination of a long period of growth during which the masoretic type had always represented the mainstream of tradition can no longer be determined. Whatever the case, no further developments of any significance in the biblical Hebrew consonantal text took place during the 600 years that elapsed between the latest manuscripts from the tannaitic period (c. 200 C.E.) and the earliest medieval ones (c. ninth century C.E.). None of the medieval manuscripts and codices, and not even the thousands of Bible fragments from the Cairo **Genizah* represent a recension different from the received text.

See also **Masorah*, **Poetry* in the Bible.

Bibliography: F. Buhl, *Canon and Text of the Old Testament* (1892); C. D. Ginsburg, *Introduction to the Massoretico-Critical Edition of the Hebrew Bible* (1897), repr. 1966 with a prolegomenon by H. M. Orlinsky; V. Aptowitzer, *Das Schriftwort in der rabbinischen Literatur* (1906–15); H. E. Ryle, *The Canon of the Old Testament* (1909); H. B. Swete, *An Introduction to the Old Testament in Greek* (1968²); L. Ginsberg, in: JBL, 41 (1922), 115–36; M. L. Margolis, *Hebrew Scriptures in the Making* (1922); G. F. Moore, *Judaism*... (1927–30); A. Geiger, *Urschrift und Uebersetzungen der Bibel*... (1928); S. Zeitlin, in: PAAJR, 4 (1932), 169–223; R. Gordis, *Biblical Text in the Making* (1937); J. Ph. Hyatt, in: BA, 6 (1943), 71–80; E. Urbach, in: *Tarbiz*, 17 (1945/46), 1–11; B. J. Roberts, *Old Testament Text and Versions* (1951); Y. Kaufmann, Toledot; E. A. Parsons, *The Alexandrian Library* (1952); M. H. Segal, in: JBL, 72 (1953), 35–47; idem, *Mevo ha-Mikra* (1956); L. J. Liebreich, in: HUCA, 25 (1954), 37–40; C. H. Robert, in: *British Academy Proceedings* (1954), 169–204; M. Weitemyer, in: *Libri*, 6 (1955–56), 217–38 (Eng.); M. Greenberg, in: JAOS, 76 (1956), 157–67; P. Katz, in: ZNW, 47 (1956), 191–217; M. Haran, in: *Tarbiz*, 25 (1955/56), 245–71; I. L. Seligmann, *ibid.*, 118–39; P. W. Skehan, in: VT Supplement, 4 (1957), 155–60; W. Hallo, in: IEJ, 12 (1962), 13–26; idem, in: JAOS, 83 (1963), 167–76; 88 (1968), 71–89; S. Lieberman, *Hellenism in Jewish Palestine* (1950); D. Barthélemy, *Les Devanciers d'Aquila* (1963); F. M. Cross, in: HTR, 57 (1964), 281–99; idem, in: IEJ, 16 (1966), 81–95; idem, in: BA, 28 (1965), 87–100; E. Wuerthwein, *Text of the Old Testament* (1957); M. H. Goshen-Gottstein, *Text and Language in Bible and Qumran* (1960); idem, in: *Textus*, 2 (1962), 28–59; 5 (1966), 22–23 (Eng.); idem, in: A. Altmann (ed.), *Biblical and Other Studies* (1963), 79–122; idem, in: *Biblica*, 48 (1967), 243–90 (Eng.); P. Kahle, *The Cairo Geniza* (1959²); S. Talmon, in: *Textus*, 1 (1960), 144–84; 2 (1962), 14–27; 4 (1964), 95–132 (Eng.); F. G. Kenyon, *Our Bible and the Ancient Manuscripts* (1965⁴); N. M. Sarna, in: *Essays in Honor of I. E. Kiev.*

[N.M.S.]

PRINTED EDITIONS (HEBREW)

The story of the printing of the Hebrew Bible begins with the 1477 edition of the Psalms, most probably produced at Bologna. Each verse is followed by the appropriate passage from David *Kimḥi's commentary, an arrangement which does not appear again in Hebrew Bibles. Since the first printers had considerable difficulty with the vowel-points, they abandoned them after Psalm 4:4, excepting only three consecutive verses, 5:12–6:1. Many words are printed *plene* (with vowel letters (*matres lectionis*, Heb. *immot ha-keri'ah*), including even *yod* for *segol*. There are frequent errors, whole verses (108), half verses (3), and odd words (43) are omitted, and there are dittographs both of letters and of words.

The next venture was due to the *zedakot* ("charities") of the rich and pious Joseph b. Abraham Caravita. Knowing that the vigor of Judaism depends on serious and continued reading and study of the Bible, many wealthy Jews employed scribes to copy manuscripts in order to foster this study. In Spain they continued using scribes, but Jews in Italy quickly realized that the invention of printing with movable type would enable them to ensure the more

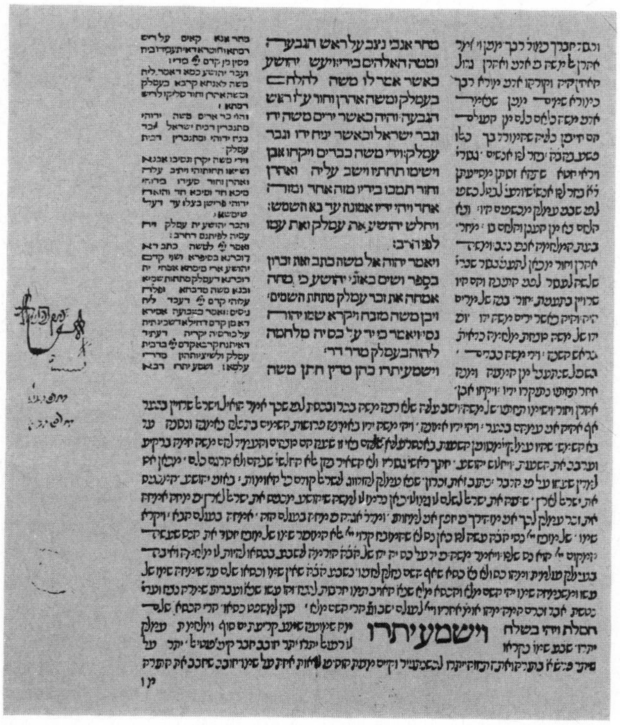

Page from the Pentateuch with Targum Onkelos and Rashi's commentary, printed on parchment by Solomon Salmatic b. Maimon, Hijar, Spain, 1490. The layout is that used for pages of the Babylonian Talmud. Jerusalem, J.N.U.L.

effective dissemination of the Bible. In 1479–80 Joseph b. Abraham invited from Ferrara to Bologna Abraham b. Ḥayyim di Tintori, a master craftsman who had largely solved the problems of both vowel-points and accents. The result of this move was the Bologna Pentateuch of 1482, which set the pattern for many future editions, culminating in the Bomberg rabbinic Bibles of the next century. The folios consist of Rashi's commentary across the page, top and bottom, with the Hebrew text in the inner and wider column and Targum Onkelos in the outer column. The type is larger than that of the 1477 psalter, but, as in some Ashkenazi manuscripts, the final letters *kaf, nun,* and *pe* do not extend below the base-line of other consonants, so that it is virtually impossible to distinguish between *dalet* and final *kaf.*

A little later, a certain Israel Nathan b. Samuel moved to Soncino, a small town in the duchy of Milan. There he set up a printing press for his son, and this was the beginning of the great firm of Joshua Solomon *Soncino and his nephews, Moses and Gershom. Attracting Abraham b. Ḥayyim from Bologna, they produced the first complete Bible, the Soncino Bible of 1488, with vowels and accents, but without a commentary, as was the custom of the Soncinos. The Soncino brothers also were responsible for the 1491–93 Naples Bible, in which the vowel-points and accents are better placed than before. Gershom Soncino moved to Brescia, where he produced the 1495 Brescia Bible, an improved edition of the 1488 Soncino Bible, but, more important, in small octavo format, making it a pocket edition specifically produced for the persecuted Jews who, perpetually moving from place to place, found it difficult to carry the huge and costly folio Bibles. It was this edition which Martin Luther used when he translated the Bible into German.

In Spain a Hebrew Pentateuch with Targum and Rashi was printed by Solomon Salmatic b. Maimon in 1490 at Ixar. There were also printing presses in Portugal, where in 1487 the Faro Pentateuch was produced. In this edition the printer was unable to solve the problem of placing a dot in the middle of a consonant, so there is no *dagesh.* This was followed in 1491 by the Lisbon Pentateuch in two volumes with the Targum and Rashi's commentary, and in the next year by Isaiah and Jeremiah at Lisbon and Proverbs at Leira. The expulsion of the Jews from Spain (1492) put an end to the printing of new editions of the Bible, both in Portugal and Italy, for wealthy Jews needed all their means to help the refugees, over a quarter of a million of them. The Portuguese tradition was revived in Salonika 23 years later in an edition of Psalms, Proverbs, Job, and Daniel with Don Judah Gedaliah as patron and Joseph b. Mako Golphon as printer. The first Bible to be printed in Spain was the 1514–17 Complutensian Polyglot printed at Alcalá de Henares (Lat. *Complutum*) under the patronage of Cardinal Ximenes de Cisneros, founder of the university there, regent of Castile, and archbishop of Toledo. The project was completed in 1517, but it was nearly three years before Pope Leo X authorized the work and a further two years before publication, by which time Cardinal Ximenes had been dead for five years. Accents were deliberately rejected; other signs were introduced to mark the colons and the penultimate accented syllables. The vowel-points are far from reliable.

By the year 1511 the Soncinos, now at Pesaro, were able to make a new start and in stages they completed a fourth edition of the complete Bible. Gershom had used the interval to perfect his technique and this edition is the best produced by Ashkenazi Jews in Italy. Around this time Daniel *Bomberg, a Christian merchant of Amsterdam, arrived in Venice and established his printing office there. In 1516–17 he published the first Great Rabbinic Bible, edited by Felix Pratensis, who was born a Jew but was baptized in 1506. The work is in four volumes, with Targums and commentaries. For the first time the *kerei* is given, but in the variants in the margin (see *Masorah). The last volume contains additional material, notably Maimonides' "Thirteen Articles" and the treatise on accents entitled *Dikdukei ha-Te'amim* said to be by *Ben Asher and here printed for the first time. Here also for the first time in Hebrew Samuel and Kings were each divided into two books in imitation of the Vulgate. The strangest thing about this edition is the statement made to the pope when his *imprimatur* was sought; it claimed that the many previously printed Bibles "contain as many errors as words" and that "no one had attempted it before." Daniel Bomberg and Felix Pratensis duly received the pope's blessing, though it proved more of a hindrance than an asset. Even before this four-volume Bible was published, Bomberg realized that he had made two bad mistakes: employing an apostate Jew as his editor, and requesting the pope's *imprimatur.* He therefore remade the columns as soon as the folios of the large Bible had been run off and issued a quarto edition at the same time, this time without any mention of either editor or pope. A second edition was called for within four years, when the whole was reset; on this occasion the two sons of Baruch Adelkind were mentioned as printers, and great emphasis was laid on the fact that they were Jews, thoroughly Orthodox and already engaged in printing the whole of the Talmud. However, something had to be done about the Great Rabbinic Bible, and, as though divinely guided and certainly opportunely, Jacob b. Ḥayyim ibn Adonijah arrived in Venice after his family had been driven out of Spain and again out of Tunis. After seven penurious years of wandering Jacob b. Ḥayyim found work with Bomberg in Venice. The chief fruit of the partnership was the second Great Rabbinic Bible of 1524–25, the text of which became the standard masoretic text and continued as such for 400 years. Jacob b. Ḥayyim was very conscious of the importance of the masorah as the guarantee of the correct text, and he went to great pains and undertook several journeys to secure as many codices with a masorah as possible. Thus, for the first time, there was a printed Hebrew Bible with a marginal masorah. As the editor discovered that "the masorah did not harmonize with the majority of the codices," he had to exercise his discretion. The edition was in four volumes, with Targums, and with commentaries by Rashi, Ibn Ezra, David and Moses Kimḥi, and Levi b. Gershom. A third Bomberg quarto edition appeared in 1525–28, the text being a combination of that of Felix Pratensis and that of Jacob b. Ḥayyim.

Daniel Bomberg's tribulations were not over, for soon after 1525 Jacob b. Ḥayyim became a Christian. In 1527 Elijah *Levita, a refugee originally from Neustadt near Nuremberg, came to Venice and found employment with Bomberg. No more is heard of Jacob b. Ḥayyim, Elijah Levita being henceforth chief adviser to the Bomberg firm. In subsequent reprints of the 1524–25 Bible, there is no mention of the editor. Bibles printed after 1525 all follow substantially the text of Jacob b. Ḥayyim ibn Adonijah until *Buxtorf's small-format Bible of 1611 and his four-volume rabbinic Bible of 1618–19, printed at Basle, in which the text was influenced by Sephardi traditions, and not dominated by the Ashkenazi ones as were all previous editions printed under Jewish auspices. The text was edited by Jablonski in 1699, but the most important edition based on the Buxtorf text is that of J. H. Michaelis in 1720. It is a critical edition, quoting 19 printed editions and five Erfurt manuscripts, especially the very important Erfurt 3 with its masorah, and containing also *Okhlah ve-Okhlah,* an 11th century masoretic work of great importance then printed for the first time. The critical notes and the variants provided by Michaelis indicate a masoretic tradition different from that of the 1524–25 Bible of Jacob b. Ḥayyim. They form a pattern, already discernible in Jablonski's 1699 edition, but more clearly in *Lonzano's *Or Torah* and *Norzi's *Minḥat Shai.* Norzi depended mostly on the de Rossi codex 782, which had a strange, disturbed history, though *de Rossi (vol. 1, p. 128) recognized it as "the most perfect examplar of the masoretic text." This tradition must have come to Spain at a comparatively early date, and it is firmly established in Sephardi tradition. It is responsible for at least some of the differences between the Complutensian Polyglot and the standard text based on Ashkenazi codices. Michaelis' critical edition is an early and neglected precursor of the modern editions of the Hebrew Bible, those by P. Kahle and N. H. Snaith.

The story of modern times begins with Seligmann *Baer, who published the Hebrew Bible in single volumes with notes, except for Exodus to Deuteronomy (for which see the Roedelheim Pentateuch, a popular edition without notes). The dates of these volumes are 1869–1895. Baer believed that the masorah is supreme, that firm rules can be established, and that these must be rigidly followed, whatever the manuscripts may say. In this he is the literary descendant of Elijah Levita and his *Masoret ha-Masoret.* Baer, who regularly followed a masorah or a rule against the codices and frequently "corrects an error," worked according to the rules laid down by Jekuthiel in *Ein ha-Kore,* and later by Heidenheim. Baer was supported by Franz *Delitzsch, whose authority was immense. In his books on the accents, W. Wickes (*Verse Accents,* 1881; *Prose Accents,* 1888), similarly makes and adopts fixed and rigid rules. In contrast, C. D. *Ginsburg (British and Foreign Bible Society edition, 1911–26) followed Jacob b. Ḥayyim; where the various masorah traditions disagreed either with the text or with each other, he exercised his judgment, with the result that he paid more attention to the manuscripts than to either masorah or to Jacob b. Ḥayyim. With the third edition of R. Kittel's *Biblia Hebraica* (1936), a new signpost was erected. P. Kahle was responsible for the text, based on the Leningrad codex (Firkovich collection B 19a) which Kahle claimed was a true, accurate, and genuine Ben Asher codex. Ever since Maimonides supported the Ben Asher tradition against *Saadiah b. Joseph Gaon, who favored the *Ben Naphtali tradition, it had been agreed that a true masoretic Bible must follow Ben Asher.

The 1928 Foreign Society (N. H. Snaith) edition was based mainly on British Museum's mss. Orient. 2626–28, a beautifully illustrated codex, close to the notes of Lonzano, Norzi, and the tradition found in the 1720 Michaelis Bible. The text, though compiled from completely different sources, is very close to the Kahle text. This indicates that the Ben Asher text is to be found not only in Leningrad manuscript but also in the best Sephardi manuscripts (in the first hand, and not as corrected by a second hand to the Ben Ḥayyim tradition, as often happened after 1492 when the exiled Jews came into close contact with the other traditions). The same type of text will be found in the Hebrew University Bible Project based on the Aleppo codex, which has been hidden and so preserved from "correction." Indeed the severe strictures that W. Wickes made against it are the reasons why it is to be accepted as what H. M. Orlinsky calls "a masoretic text." Bibles containing the original Hebrew text (or Greek in the case of New Testament) together with the important ancient versions arranged in parallel columns are termed polyglots. They were at one time important in ascertaining correct readings or meanings of the text. The oldest one in print is the *Complutensian Polyglot,* mentioned above

The first page of Genesis from the *Soncino Bible,* printed in Naples by Joshua Solomon b. Israel Nathan Soncino, 1491–93. Jerusalem, J.N.U.L.

containing the Hebrew masoretic text, the Vulgate, the Aramaic Targum (with a Latin translation), and the Septuagint (with a Latin translation). The most comprehensive are Brian Walton's *London Polyglot* (1654–57) which contained texts in Hebrew, Samaritan, Aramaic, Greek, Latin, Ethiopic, Syriac, Arabic, and Persian (all with Latin translations), and Samuel Bagster's *Polyglot* (1831) in Hebrew, Greek, Samaritan, Latin, Syriac, German, Italian, French, English, and Spanish. More modern polyglots have contented themselves with giving the texts in Hebrew, Greek, Latin, and a modern language.

Bibliography: C. D. Ginsburg, *Introduction to the Massoretico-Critical Edition of the Hebrew Bible* (1897), repr. 1966 with introd. by H. M. Orlinsky; E. Levita, *Massoreth ha-Massoreth and the Introduction of Jacob ben Chayyim ibn Adoniyah to the Rabbinic Bible of 1525*, ed. by C. D. Ginsburg, introd. by N. H. Snaith (1967). [N.H.S.]

TRANSLATIONS

ANCIENT VERSIONS

Aramaic: the Targumim. The word *targum* (תַּרְגּוּם) means "translation," corresponding to the verb *tirgem* (תרגם; "translate"), of which passive participle, *meturgam*, occurs in Ezra 4:7, where it seems to have the special meaning of "composed" ("written in Aramaic characters and composed in the Aramaic language"). *Tirgem* is a denominative verb, being derived from the noun *turgeman* ("interpreter") whence, ultimately, the English *dragoman*—a word of Akkadian origin (Akk. *targumānu* or *turgumānu*, from the verb *ragāmu*, "to call"). In Aramaic and Hebrew the word *turgeman* exists alongside a more native-looking Hebrew adaptation, *meturgeman*. In tannaitic and amoraic Hebrew *tirgem* is said of translating from Hebrew into any other language (TJ, Kid. 1:1, 59a; TJ, Meg. 1:11, 71c), but the noun *targum* does not seem to occur with reference to any but Aramaic versions of the Bible (Shab. 115a; TJ, Kid. 1:1, 59a; TJ, Meg. 1:11, 71c). In fact, the Mishnah (Yad. 4:5) refers to the Aramaic originals of certain sections of Daniel and Ezra as *targum*.

Origin of the Targums. The Jewish diaspora in Babylonia must have exchanged Hebrew for Aramaic as its vernacular in only a few generations. In Palestine the process was much more gradual, but Aramaic was probably the language of the majority of Jews there before the end of the Persian period. During the period of Persian domination (539–333 B.C.E.), Aramaic was the language of the Persian administration and the lingua franca of southwestern Asia. The bilingual character of the books of Ezra and Daniel presupposes the Jews' equal familiarity with both languages. The practice of translating the Bible reading into Aramaic in the synagogue is attributed to Ezra by *Rav (third century C.E.), who interprets the word *meforash* in Nehemiah 8:8 to mean an interpretation of the Hebrew text of the Bible in Aramaic translation (Meg. 3a; Ned. 37b; cf. TJ, Meg. 4:1, 74d), but both the meaning of the word and the reliability of the account in Nehemiah 8 are subjects of controversy. At any rate the custom of interpreting the synagogue reading of the Bible text with the Targum after each verse (or after each three verses) in the presence of the congregation, so as to permit a translator to repeat it in Aramaic, is attested in the Mishnah.

Manner of Usage. The professional translator of the Hebrew Bible text in the synagogue was called *meturgeman* (Meg. 4:4). His oral explanations were given along with the reading of the Sabbath lesson. The rules for reading the Targum are formulated in the *halakhah* (Meg. 4:4–10; Meg. 23b–25b; Tosef., Meg. 4:20–41). The Targum was to be read after every verse of the *parashah* of the Pentateuch and after every third verse of the reading from the Prophets. There is no mention in this source of reading from a written Targum, and elsewhere (TJ, Meg. 4:1, 74d) the use of such writings was forbidden, at least for the Pentateuch, for the Sabbath worship service, but the preparation and use of them by individuals for private study and school instruction was permitted. Although certain portions of the Bible were read but were not translated (as Gen. 35:22), others were neither read nor translated (as Num. 6:24–26; II Sam. 11–13). *Judah b Ilai, the pupil of Akiva, declared that whoever rendered a verse of Bible in its original form was a liar, while he who made additions was a blasphemer (Tosef., Meg. 4:41; Kid. 49a). In *Sifrei* (Deut. 161), the Targum is mentioned as a branch of study that falls between the Bible and the Mishnah. The Targums as a whole are not always primarily literal translations of the corresponding Hebrew text; they are often intermingled with various paraphrases and aggadic supplements such as one meets in exegetical or homiletic works like the Talmud and the Midrash. They also contain explanations and alterations adapted to secure the sense of the masoretic text current among the rabbinical authorities, offering it to the people in an intelligible form. In this period the main feature of Jewish criticism and exegesis was the anxiety to remove or tone down all references to God that could lead to misunderstanding in the popular mind. The Targum thus contains various devices to obviate the appearance of a very distinct anthropomorphic character of God.

Date of Targum. There are early indications that the Targum was committed to writing, although for private use only. A tannaitic tradition refers to an Aramaic translation of the book of Job which existed in written form at the time of *Gamaliel I (first century C.E.) and which, after being withdrawn from use, reappeared in the lifetime of his grandson Gamaliel II. Targum Onkelos, which was made the official Targum of the Babylonian schools, was committed to writing and redacted as early as the third century C.E., since there is a masorah to it which dates from the first half of that century (see below). When the Aramaic language was displaced as the vernacular of the Jews of Palestine late in the second century C.E., the oral recitation of the Targum ceased. In the meantime, however, its written text had been definitely fixed, so that the traditional renderings would not be forgotten and excesses in its oral recitation would be prevented. The official recognition of a written Targum and the final redaction of its text, however, belong to the post-talmudic period, thus not earlier than the fifth century C.E.

Liturgical Use of the Targum. Two Palestinian *amoraim* of the third century C.E. (Ber. 8a–b) urged that in private worship the Hebrew text of the weekly *parashah* be read twice and the Targum once, exactly as was done in public worship. There are still pious Jews who do this before the Sabbath, although Aramaic is no longer the vernacular of the Jews. The Yemenite Jews have even retained the public reading of Targum Onkelos (see below). Targums to all the books of the Bible except Daniel and Ezra-Nehemiah (this constituting in Jewish tradition a single book of Ezra) have survived to this day.

Targums to the Pentateuch. Targum Onkelos. The official Targum to the Pentateuch, the only such Aramaic version that was subjected to a unified and scholastic redaction, is known by the name of Targum Onkelos. The origin of this name is derived from the Babylonian Talmud (Meg. 3a), where the Targum to the Torah is attributed to the proselyte *Onkelos, who is said to have composed it under the guidance of R. Eliezer and R. Joshua. The Jerusalem Talmud, however (Meg. 1:11, 71c), contains the statement: "Aquila the proselyte translated the Pentateuch in the presence of R. Eliezer and R. Joshua," in a context which shows that a translation into Greek is meant. These accounts are obviously related: in the Babylonian Talmud only the name Onkelos occurs, while Aquilas (= Akylas, the Greek adaptation of the Latin Aquila) alone is found in the Jerusalem Talmud. The latter is historically reliable—Aquila did compose a scrupulously exact and literal Greek translation of the Bible, and Targum Onkelos, however, is almost a literal Aramaic translation of the Pentateuch. In addition to this, a great deal of what is revealed about Onkelos in Babylonian sources is attributed to Aquila in the Jerusalem ones. Two important works that discuss the identity of Onkelos and Akylas (= Aquila) are those of M. Friedmann and A. E. Silverstone. The former believes that they were two different personalities, while the latter, with many other scholars, arrives at the conclusion that they are one and the same person, but that the Babylonian teachers applied to the Aramaic translation, which attained official status among them, the tradition current in Palestine regarding the Greek version of Aquila.

The Aramaic of this Targum exhibits a mixture of the Western and Eastern features. This combination gave rise to a variety of opinions about the Targum's place of origin. A. Berliner, T. Noeldeke, G. Dalman, and E. Y. Kutscher believe that it originated in Palestine, while its final redaction took place in Babylonia. The opposing view is held by P. Kahle and his followers, who consider this Aramaic version to have originated entirely in Babylonia. Essentially, the content of the Targum shows that it was composed in Palestine (particularly in Judea) sometime in the second century C.E., since both the halakhic and aggadic portions betray the influence of the school of Akiva. After the destruction of the Second Temple and the suppression of the Bar Kokhba revolt, which destroyed the cultural centers of Judea, Targum Onkelos disappeared from Palestine. The old standard literary Aramaic was superseded by the local Western Aramaic dialects, and since the center of Jewish life shifted to Galilee, a new Targum in the Galilean dialect evolved in the course of time. Kutscher has cited the vocabulary of the Qumran Genesis Apocryphon and the Aramaic Bar Kosiba Letters as evidence for the Western origin of Targum Onkelos. At the beginning of the Amoraic period (end of second century C.E.), before it had disappeared from Palestine, Targum Onkelos was imported, along with the Mishnah and the Tosefta to Babylonia. There it underwent final revision during the third century C.E. and was recognized as the authoritative Aramaic version of the Pentateuch for the local Jewish population. In the Babylonian Talmud (Kid. 49a) it is mentioned as "our Targum" or by the expression "as we translate." A special masorah prepared for it contains statements concerning the divergencies between the Babylonian academies of *Sura and *Nehardea.

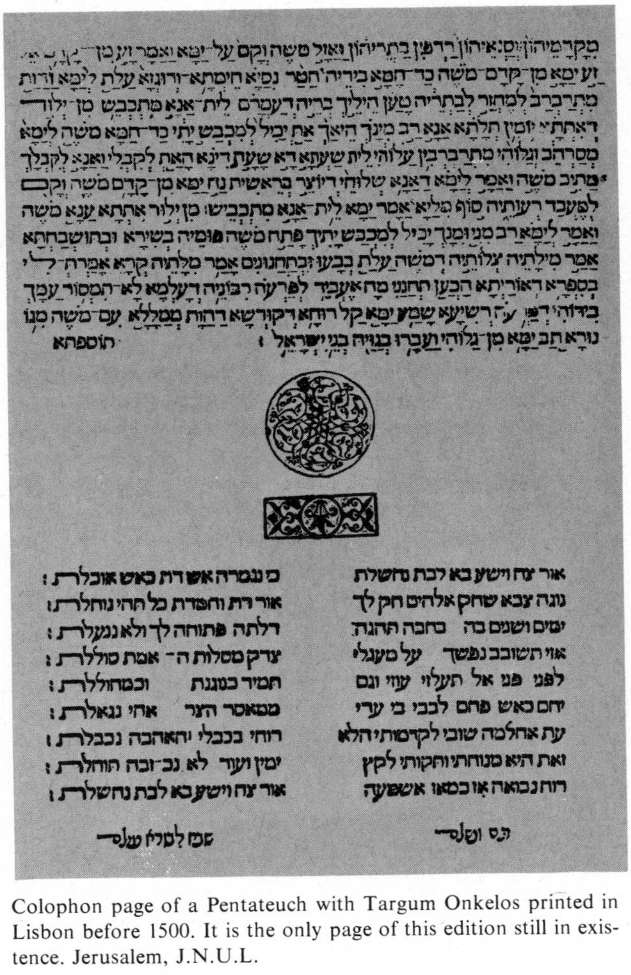

Colophon page of a Pentateuch with Targum Onkelos printed in Lisbon before 1500. It is the only page of this edition still in existence. Jerusalem, J.N.U.L.

This Targum is the most literal translation of the Pentateuch. The text from which it was prepared was in all essentials the masoretic one. The principal objective was to conform the Targum as closely as possible to the original text, and the grammatical structure of the Hebrew was thus followed closely. One prominent example of this is the use of the particle *yat* as a sign of the accusative for the corresponding Hebrew particle *ʾet*. Yet there are numerous exceptions where the Targum does not adhere to the original. Paraphrase occasionally takes the place of translation: in the poetic portions (e.g., Gen. 49) there are aggadic supplements of moderate size, while halakhic regulations are often read into the legal portions (e.g., Ex. 21:16). Offensive or disagreeable material is paraphrased or rendered by some sort of circumlocution (e.g., Gen. 20:13; Ex. 24:11). The paraphrastic style of translation affected by the Targums in general, in order to obviate anthropomorphisms and anthropopathisms in reference to God, is observed with special care in the Targum Onkelos. Figurative language, as a rule, is not translated literally but is explained (e.g., Gen. 49:25; Ex. 15:3, 8, 10; 29:35). Geographical names are sometimes replaced by those current at a later time (e.g., Gen. 10:10; Deut. 3:17). Apart from *Megillah* 3a (previously mentioned), all the references to Onkelos as the author of the Aramaic translation of the Pentateuch originated in the post-talmudic period, although they are all based on this passage in the Babylonian Talmud. The earliest of those is in the late midrashic work known as *Pirkei de-R. Eliezer* (38), where the targumic passage on Genesis 45:27 is cited in the statement "Onkelos has translated." The ninth-century *gaon* *Sar Shalom (*Sha'arei Teshuvah,* 29) names Targum Onkelos as the Targum that was in circulation in the Jewish community at that time and as having more claim to sanctity than any other existing Targums. The *gaon* *Natronai (*Seder Rav Amram,* Warsaw (1865), p. 29) attributes this Targum to the rabbis of the Talmud and attaches a canonical value to it. Accordingly, the designation "Targum Onkelos" was firmly established in the early part of the geonic period.

Noteworthy is the fact that the Jews of Yemen received this Targum, like that of the Prophets, with the Babylonian supralinear punctuation. A critical edition of Targum Onkelos to the Pentateuch (as well as Targum Jonathan to the Prophets) with supralinear punctuation according to Yemenite manuscripts has been edited by A. Sperber (see bibliography). Yemen and Yemenite synagogues in Israel are the only places where the reading of Targum Onkelos has continued to accompany that of the Pentateuch on Sabbaths into the 20th century. Elsewhere, some pious Jews still observe the custom of going over the weekly portion of the Torah privately on the eve of the Sabbath, verse by

A carpet page from the *Damascus Keter*. The foliage scrolls are painted in gold while the leaves and background are in magenta wash. The scrolls and leaves are outlined by micrographic masorah (the traditional textual apparatus of the Bible) and this in turn is surrounded by a frame of masorah in large letters. This bible was written by Menahem bar Abraham Ibn Malik (?) in 1260, probably in Toledo. It was for many centuries the pride of the Damascus Synagogue. Jerusalem, Jewish National and University Library, ms. Heb. 4° 790, fol. 310 ($11\frac{7}{8} \times 10\frac{5}{8}$ ins/30.2 × 27 cm.).

verse in Hebrew, Targum, and Hebrew again (Ber. 8a–b; Sh. Ar., OḤ, 285).

Palestinian Pentateuch Targums. *Codex Neofiti I.* Since 1930, there has been great progress in the recovery of the old "Jerusalem," properly speaking, Galilean, Targums. In that year Kahle edited for the first time some *genizah* fragments of such Targums (see bibliography) dating from between the seventh and ninth centuries C.E. Because they overlap, they exhibit divergences which show that their text, unlike that of Targum Onkelos, was never fixed. Further texts have since been published by A. Diez-Macho, Y. Komlos, and W. Baars. In 1956 Diez-Macho announced the discovery of a complete Palestinian Targum to the Pentateuch called Neofiti I, which he had found in the Vatican Library (VT Supplement, 7 (1960), 222–245).

Prior to the discovery of Neofiti I, the Galilean Targum was represented by two main recensions: Targum Yerushalmi I (TY I), also known as Targum Jonathan or Targum Jonathan b. Uzziel in Hebrew and hence as Pseudo-Jonathan in Western languages; and Targum Yerushalmi II (TY II), the so-called Fragmentary Targum. More correct than Targum Yerushalmi, "Jerusalem Targum," is Targum Ereẓ Israel, "the Palestinian Targum," by which it is designated in a responsum by R. Hai Gaon, but it is already called "the Targum of the People of the Holy City" by *Menahem b. Solomon, the 12th-century author of the *Midrash Sekhel Tov.* With the appearance of Neofiti I, three principal Galilean Aramaic versions of the Pentateuch are now in existence. Whereas Neofiti I is complete, 15 verses are missing from Targum Yerushalmi I, and Targum Yerushalmi II contains only 850 verses of the Pentateuch. Codex Neofiti I differs from other Galilean Targum manuscripts in orthography, grammar, and range of paraphrase. It also contains a large number of marginal and interlinear variants.

Targum Yerushalmi I (Pseudo-Jonathan). The ascription of this Targum to *Jonathan b. Uzziel is believed to date back to the 14th-century commentator Menahem b. Benjamin Recanati, who erroneously analyzed the abbreviation," ת״י(Targum Yerushalmi) as Targum Jonathan. W. Bacher believed that Recanati probably misinterpreted a passage in the Zohar (1:89a) according to which Jonathan translated *ha-mikra* (הַמִּקְרָא), which in this case refers to the Prophets rather than to the whole Bible (hence the Pentateuch). The name Targum Ereẓ Israel is found in writers of the 11th century. The Tosafot cite the Galilean Pentateuch Targum variously as Targum Jonathan (to Ḥag. 27a), Jonathan b. Uzziel (to Av. Zar. 59a), and Targum Yerushalmi (to Ber. 8b). The language of this version of the Pentateuch is Galilean Jewish Aramaic (outside the manuscript it was not transmitted in its pure form). Its most distinctive characteristic is the free aggadic handling of the text. Like the other Targums, it sets aside figurative speech and eliminates all anthropomorphic expressions referring to God. Early geographical names are replaced by those current in a later age. This Targum contains abundant information on most of the religious and dogmatic teachings of Judaism of the talmudic period. One finds the later Jewish doctrines of the being of God, His dwelling place, His revelation in the Torah, angels, creation, sin, death, the messianic kingdom, resurrection of the just and the future life, gehenna, and the world to come.

This Targum is not later than the seventh–eighth century C.E., although it contains material which is much earlier than the date of its final compilation and redaction. A very ancient date has been claimed for the following passages: Genesis 15:19, Numbers 24:21, the interpretation of "Kenites" as Salmeans, contemporaries and allies of the Nabateans, and Deuteronomy 33:11, the reference to Johanan (b. Hyrcanus) the high priest. Indications of a late date of composition, however, occur in Exodus 26:9, in which reference is made to the Six Orders of the Mishnah; in Genesis 21:21, where the Hebrew names of the two wives of *Ishmael (regarded as the ancestor of the Arabs) are rendered respectively by עישא or חדישא, i.e., the name of Muhammad's wife Ayesha or of his wife Khadijah, and פטימא, the name of his daughter Fatima; and in Genesis 49:26 and Deuteronomy 33:2, where Edom (i.e., Byzantium or Christian Europe) and Ishmael are spoken of as world powers in a way that was possible only in the seventh century at the earliest.

Targum Yerushalmi II (the Fragmentary Targum). This Targum contains renderings of only certain verses, phrases, or words of the Pentateuch, estimated at about 850 verses altogether. Three-fourths of these are on the historical sections of the Pentateuch, while the remaining fourth is on the legislative sections in Exodus, Leviticus, and Numbers. There are about 14 chapters which have no translation at all, while for some 90 verses there are translations of only a single word of the Hebrew text. The earliest known fragments were first published in Bomberg's Great Rabbinic Bible in 1516–17, based on Vatican Codex 440 (a good portion of the fragments had already appeared under the title "Tosefta Yerushalmi" in the Lisbon Bible of 1491). In 1899 M. Ginsburger edited a number of other fragments from manuscript sources, expecially from Paris Codex 110, as well as from quotations from the Targum Yerushalmi found in early works, under the title *Das Fragmententhargum.* This work also contained numerous fragments that occur under the title *Nusḥa Aḥarena* in the Venice Bible of 1591. These plus other variants are sometimes referred to as Targum Yerushalmi III. The language of this Targum is Galilean Jewish Aramaic, and it includes many foreign loan words. Its fragmentary condition has been accounted for in various ways.

The fragments are not all contemporaneous. The text of the majority of them is older than Pseudo-Jonathan. Many of these fragments, especially the aggadic paraphrases, agree with Pseudo-Jonathan, which may, on the other hand, be older than some of them. Similarly, aggadic additions were made to the text of the Targum in later centuries, so that a North African manuscript of 1487 alludes to the capture of Constantinople by the Turks in 1453. Early in the 12th century, *Judah b. Barzillai wrote of these additions: "The Jerusalem Targum contains aggadic sayings added by those who led in prayer and who also read the Targum, insisting that these sayings be recited in the synagogue as interpretations of the text of the Bible." These numerous additions to the Jerusalem Targum and the majority of the fragments are all of a later date than Onkelos, yet both Pseudo-Jonathan and the Fragmentary Targum contain much that has survived from a very early period. According to W. Bacher, the nucleus of the Jerusalem Targum is older than the Babylonian one, which was, in his opinion, redacted from it.

The Targums to the Prophets. Targum Jonathan. This Targum also originated in Palestine and in the early centuries of the common era was brought to Babylonia, where it underwent a series of revisions by the Babylonian academies and became recognized as the official Aramaic version of the Prophets. According to P. Churgin, its final redaction was accomplished by the seventh century C.E. in the form in which it is now known. Like the Targum to the Pentateuch, it originated in the synagogue, where it was recited after every three verses from the Hebrew text of the Prophets during that part of the service. During the persecution of the Jews by *Antiochus IV Epiphanes, when it was forbidden to read the Pentateuch in the synagogue, portions of the Prophets were read instead. This may have been the beginning of a Targum to the Prophets. According to the Babylonian Talmud (Meg. 3a), it was written by Jonathan b. Uzziel "at the dictation of Haggai, Zechariah, and Malachi." The account continues to relate that because of this translation the entire land of Israel was shaken and a voice from heaven cried out: "Who has revealed my secrets to man?" The story adds that Jonathan wished to translate the Hagiographa as well, but that a heavenly voice bade him to desist. According to W. Bacher the Targum to Job, which was withdrawn from circulation by Gamaliel I, may have resulted from Jonathan's attempts to translate the Hagiographa. Jonathan b. Uzziel is named as *Hillel's most prominent pupil in the first century B.C.E. and was a contemporary of Gamaliel I. In the Babylonian Talmud, this Targum is quoted quite frequently by R. Joseph b. Ḥiyya (270–333 C.E.), head of the Pumbedita Academy (MK 28b; Sanh. 94b; Meg. 3a). Thus, as early as the beginning of the fourth century, the Targum to the Prophets was recognized as being of ancient authority. Hai Gaon (commentary to *Tohorot,* quoted in *Arukh ha-Shalem,* 2 (1926), 293a) regarded R. Joseph as its author, since he cited passages from it with the words "Rav Joseph has translated."

As it originated in Palestine and was then revised and redacted in Babylonia, this Targum contains Eastern as well as Western Aramaic linguistic traits. It has a few Persian loan words, such as *dusteqa* or *dastega* (Persian, *dastah;* Judg. 3:22) and *idron* (Persian, *enderun;* Joel 2:16). Its style is very similar to that of Targum Onkelos, especially in the Former Prophets—the historical narratives. In the prose sections one meets an occasional reading which is not in the masoretic text (Josh. 8:12) or an apparent conflation of two variants (*ibid.* 8:16). Proper names are sometimes transformed into their (often, surely, merely guessed) up-to-date appellations (*ibid.* 7:21, where Shinar is interpreted as Babel and Jer. 46:25, where No (נא) is interpreted as Alexandria), but for the most part they are taken over unchanged from the Hebrew text. The usual rules of targumic interpretation are observed in the rendering of anthropomorphic expressions and figurative language (Hos. 1:3). Poetic passages are drastically paraphrased (e.g., Judg. 5; I Sam. 2:1–10). The same holds true for difficult passages, where paraphrasis is specially employed in an attempt to explain the Hebrew text (cf. I Sam. 15:23; 17:8; II Sam. 14:11; 20:18). The rendering in the Latter Prophets is more paraphrastic on the whole than the Former Prophets, which is to be expected in view of their more exalted and rhapsodic style (cf. Targum Jonathan's amplification of the Heb. text of Isa. 29:1 and Jer. 10:11; for instances of *aggadah* in this Targum see Isa. 12:3; 33:22; 62:10; Micah 6:4). The careful revision this Targum underwent in Babylonia is apparent from its unity of style and character throughout the historical as well as the prophetic books. This can be seen, as Gesenius pointed out, from a comparison of the passages II Kings 18–19 (=Jer. 36–39) and Isaiah 2:2–4 (= Micah 4:1–3), which are translated alike with only slight variations, and from other features, such as the rendering of Tarshish by Yama, which is common to Jonah, Jeremiah, and Ezekiel.

A conspicuous affinity exists between Targum Jonathan and Targum Onkelos, as seen from certain passages which are word for word identical. Most of the early writers on this subject recognized this identity but differed in their conclusions. Thus, while de Rossi and Herzfeld were certain that Onkelos knew the Targum to the Prophets, L. Zunz took the view that Jonathan and Onkelos before him had quoted it in Judges 5:8 (= Deut. 32:17), I Samuel 12:3 (= Num. 16:15), II Kings 14:6 (= Deut. 24:16), and Jeremiah 48:46 (= Num. 21:28–29). Especially noteworthy is Targum Jonathan's translation of Judges 5:26, which brings to mind Targum Onkelos of Deuteronomy 22:5.

Targum Yerushalmi to the Prophets. The existence of such a Targum is inferred mainly from the frequent citations from it by early authors, especially Rashi and David Kimḥi. Fragments from the books of Joshua, Judges, Samuel, Kings, Isaiah, Jeremiah, Amos, Jonah, and Zechariah are contained in Codex Reuchlinianus, written in 1105 (ed. Lagarde, *Prophetica Chaldaica,* 1872), in the form of 80 extracts. W. Bacher investigated their character in his detailed article "Kritische Untersuchungen zum Prophetentargum" (in ZDMG, 28 (1874), 1–58). The language is Palestinian in character, yet its aggadic additions are frequently traceable to the Babylonian Talmud. This Targum thus belongs to a later period, when the Babylonian Talmud began to exercise a considerable amount of influence on Palestinian literature. There are also "Toseftas" (additions) to the Prophet Targum that are similar to the Targum Yerushalmi and are also cited by Kimḥi (see esp. A. Sperber, *The Bible in Aramaic,* 2 (1959), ix–x, 3 (1962), xi, 23–25, 462–5, 479–80; for Tosefta to Targum Onkelos, see 1 (1959), xvii–xviii, 354–357).

Targums to the Hagiographa. Although there are extant Targums to the Hagiographa, they did not enjoy official recognition. They did not originate until a later period, and were written at different times by various authors, yet they contain old material. W. Bacher considers them to have originated in Palestine, since they contain expressions known in the Jerusalem Talmud and the Midrash, although in the Targums to the Five Scrolls many linguistic features of the Aramaic of the Babylonian Talmud occur. Their unofficial status was probably due to the fact that they were not used in the public synagogue service (with the exception of Esther, though in later times all Five Scrolls were used in the liturgy of the synagogue) or school. The Targum to the Book of Job, which existed in the first century C.E. according to the Babylonian Talmud (Shab. 115a), cannot be identified with the Targum to this biblical book in existence now, which is a product of a much later period. Its relation to the Aramaic translation of Job from Qumran (see below) is a matter for speculation. The various Targums of this part of the Bible may be conveniently classified into three categories: Targums of Job, Psalms, and Proverbs; of the Five Scrolls; and of Chronicles.

Job. This Targum and that of Psalms may have had a common origin, in view of the many similarities between them. Both aim at giving a fairly faithful rendering of the Hebrew text, and although aggadic additions are present from time to time, they are brief and can easily be separated from the translation itself. Each Targum contains a number of double renderings (Job has between 40 and 50, Psalms has fewer); the second rendering is introduced by ת"א *(targum aḥer)* and is considered by some the original one. In such cases, one of the translations is generally aggadic, while the other is more literal. About six verses in Job even have a third rendering. An indication of an early date is contained in Job 4:10, where the word שני which the masoretic pointing interprets, in accordance with the context, as *shinnei* ("the teeth of") is interpreted by the translator as *shenei* ("the two"), apparently alluding to Rome and Constantinople as the two capitals of the Roman Empire—a fact which would indicate that the work was composed before the fall of Rome in 476 C.E. (cf. the Targum on Ps. 108:10). Another common feature of these two Targums is the fact that between them they contain about a hundred variants in vowels and even consonants from the masoretic text, a feature not found with such frequency in the other Targums. Since a number of these same variants also occur in the *Peshitta and the *Septuagint, they offer adequate proof of an early date of composition for these two Targums. In both the two constant themes are the law of God and its study, as well as the future life and its retribution. A Targum to Job was among the many finds discovered among the *Dead Sea Scrolls in 1947. A preliminary study on some of the fragments was published by J. P. M. van der Ploeg (see bibliography; see also A. S. van der Woude, in VT Supplement, 9 (1962), 322–31).

Psalms. This Targum is partly allegorical and partly literal; thus it was probably the work of more than one hand. The paraphrase in it is explanatory rather than simply expansive (e.g., 29:1; 46:4). An indication of an early date is Psalms 108:10, which still mentions the Western Roman Empire. In Psalms 18 the targumist has availed himself of the Targum to II Samuel 22, although without adopting the linguistic peculiarities of the Babylonian recension of Targum Jonathan.

Proverbs. A unique feature of this Targum is its striking similarity to the Peshitta. Various explanations have been offered for this phenomenon. Some think that the Targum was influenced by the Peshitta and was actually a Jewish recension of it; others consider the possibility of both versions being separate reworkings of an older Aramaic version. About one third of the verses in this Targum agree with the Peshitta against the reading of the Hebrew original (e.g., 1:7; 4:26; 5:9; 7:22, 23; 9:11; 12:19; 16:4, 25).

Five Scrolls. The Targums of these books are essentially a collection of Midrashim, and consequently they are exclusively paraphrastic and verbose in form. Only in a few instances, where no Midrash can be utilized, are they literal in their approach. The exception is the text of the Targum Esther in the Antwerp Polyglot, which is almost a literal translation; the text of the London Polyglot, which is essentially the same as that of the Antwerp Polyglot but has many aggadic additions, is now the standard Targum text to Esther. The Targums of Ruth and Lamentations are somewhat less paraphrastic than those of Esther, Ecclesiastes, and Song of Songs. An additional Targum exists to the Book of Esther (Targum Sheni). It is much more voluminous than the first Targum of this scroll and is regarded as an amalgam from other Targums and Midrashim. The commentators refer to it as *"aggadah"* and as "Midrash." The earliest mention of Targum Sheni occurs in tractate **Soferim* (13:6), and it was probably not completed before 1200 C.E. The Targum of Song of Songs interprets the biblical book as an allegory on the relation between God and Israel and on the history of Israel. The types of paraphrase employed by the various Targums to the Five Scrolls may be summarized as follows: historical parallels; motives and reasons to explain the occurrences of events; etymology and explanation of proper names; figurative language rendered into prose and allegory in the place of narrative; the Sanhedrin, as well as the study of the law, frequently mentioned; appendance of elaborate genealogies to names; and general statements related to names of particular individuals, such as the Patriarchs, Nimrod, Pharaoh, Nebuchadnezzar, Titus, Alexander, and the Messiah.

Chronicles. No Targum to this book was known to exist until the appearance of the Polyglot Bibles. It was first published, in a somewhat incomplete form, in 1680–83 from an Erfurt manuscript of 1343 and edited with notes and translation by M. F. Beck. In 1715 a more complete form of the text was edited by D. Wilkins on the basis of a Cambridge manuscript of 1347, which contained a later revision of the targumic text. This Targum is essentially a literal rendering of the Hebrew original, although midrashic amplifications are also employed at times (e.g., I Chron. 1:20, 21; 4:18; 7:21; 11:11, 12; 12:32; II Chron. 2:6; 3:1; 23:11). Instances where the author made use of "Jerusalem" Targums to the Pentateuch are: Genesis 10:20 and I Chronicles 1:21, and Genesis 36:39 and I Chronicles 1:43. Similarly, acquaintance with Targum Jonathan to the Prophets is suggested when one compares the readings from the books of Samuel and Kings to the readings from the Targum in the synoptic passages in Chronicles, only slight variations occurring between them. The date of the Targum may be surmised from the translation of geographical names, as well as their rendering into modern forms. The final redaction of the Erfurt manuscript has been assigned to the eighth century, and that of the Cambridge manuscript to the ninth century C.E. (M. Rosenberg and K. Kohler in bibliography).

R. Joseph and the Authorship of the Hagiographa Targums. The 1680–83 Augsburg edition of Targum to Chronicles carries the title "Targum Rav Yosef." This fact is related to the view that prevailed in early times that R. Joseph b. Ḥama, the Babylonian *amora* who had the reputation of being thoroughly versed in the Targums of the Prophets, was the author of the Targum of the Hagiographa. Thus, a quotation from Targum Sheni to Esther 3:1 is introduced as *kedimtargem Rav Yosef* in tractate *Soferim* 13:6. Furthermore, the Breslau Library manuscript of 1238 appends the following statement to apocryphal additions to Esther known as *"Ḥalom Mordekhai"*: "This is the end of the book of the Targum on the Hagiographa, translated by R. Joseph." The 12th-century commentator *Samuel b. Meir quoted passages on Job and Proverbs in the name of R. Joseph (see Ex. 15:2; Lev. 20:17). In the Talmud, the phrase *kedimtargem Rav Yosef,* "as R. Joseph has translated," occurs frequently, but it occurs only with reference to passages in the Prophets and once in the Pentateuch (cf. Sot. 48b). It was inferred that R. Joseph was also the author of the known Hagiographa Targums, but on the basis of the basically Palestinian linguistic character of the Hagiographa Targums, as well as the variety of the translation techniques, which mitigate against the view of one author for all of them, this opinion has been rejected as historically without basis. Furthermore, the *Tosafot* (Shab. 115a) assign the origin of the Hagiographa Targums to tannaitic times (cf. Meg. 21b).

Bibliography: Editio Princeps: Targum Onkelos: Bologna, 1482, Sabbioneta, 1557; Targum Pseudo-Jonathan: Venice, 1591; Fragmentary Targum: *Rabbinic Bible,* Venice, 1518; Targum Jonathan: Leira, 1494, Venice, 1518; Targum to Hagiographa: Venice, 1517; Ms. *Neofiti I-Genesis* (A. Diez-Macho), Madrid-Barcelona, 1968. Critical Editions: A. Sperber, *The Bible in Aramaic,* 1–3 (1959–62); M. Ginsburger, *Pseudo-Jonathan* (1903); idem, *Das Fragmententhargum* (1899); A. Diez-Macho, *Biblia Polyglotta, Matritensia IV/5 Deuteronomium Caput I* (1965), 1–23; P. Kahle, *Masoreten des Westens,* 2 (1930), 1–65; J. F. Stenning, *The Targum of Isaiah* (1953²); P. de Lagarde, *Hagiographa chaldaica* (1873); R. H. Melamed, *The Targum to Canticles According to Six Yemen Mss. (1921).* Lexicons, Translations, Grammars, and Concordances: Jastrow, Dict; S. Krauss, *Griechische und Lateinische Lehnwoerter im Talmud, Midrasch und Targum,* 2 vols. (1898–99); J. W. Etheridge, *The Targums of Onkelos and Jonathan ben Uzziel on the Pentateuch with the Fragments of the Jerusalem Targum* (1862–65, 1968); G. H. Dalman, *Grammatik des Juedisch-Palastinischen Aramaeisch* (1905, 1960); H. J. Kassovsky, *Oẓar ha-Targum* (1940). General Works: Geiger, Urschrift, 159–70; M. Ginsburger, *Die Anthropomorphismen in den Thargumim* (1891); H. Z. Hirschberg, in: *Sefer ha-Shanah shel Bar-Ilan,* 1 (1963), 16–23; M. R. Lehman, in: *Revue de Qumran,* 1 (1958), 249–63; M. McNamara, in: CBQ, 28 (1966),

1–19; M. Martin, in: *Orientalia et Biblica Lovaniensia*, 4 (1962), 425–51; S. Maybaum, *Die Anthropomorphien und Anthropopathien bei Onkelos und die spaeteren Targumim* (1870); A. Sperber, *The Bible in Aramaic*, 4 (1969); G. Vermes, in: *Annual of the Leeds University Oriental Society*, 3 (1960–61), 81–114; Zunz, Vortraege; P. Nickels, *Targum and New Testament, a Bibliography* (1967). TARGUM ONKELOS: A. Berliner, *Targum Onkelos*, 1–2 (1884); M. Friedmann, *Onkelos und Akylas* (1896); S. D. Luzzatto, *Ohev Ger* (1830); A. E. Silverstone, *Aquila and Onkelos* (1931); A. Sperber, in: *Jewish Studies in Memory of G. A. Kohut* (1935), 554–64; PALESTINIAN TARGUM: Geiger, Urschrift, 451–80; A. Diez-Macho, in: VT Supplement, 7 (1960), 222ff.; idem, in: CNFI, 13 pt. 2 (1962), 19–25; M. McNamara, *The New Testament and the Palestinian Targum to the Pentateuch* (1966). TARGUM JONATHAN: Z. Frankel, in: MGWJ, 21 (1872), 192ff.; P. Churgin, *Targum Jonathan to the Prophets* (1907). HAGIOGRAPHA TARGUMIM: W. Bacher, in: MGWJ, 21 (1872), 408–16, 463–73; 20 (1871), 208–23, 283–4; P. Churgin, *Targum Ketuvim* (1945); Y. Komlos, in: *Sefer M. H. Segal* (1964), 265–70; J. P. M. van der Ploeg, *Le targum de Job de la grotte 11 de Qumran* (1962); M. Rosenberg and K. Kohler, in: JZWL, 8 (1870), 72–80, 135–63, 263–78; J. Shunary, in: *Textus*, 5 (1966), 133–44; A. S. van der Woude, in: VT Supplement, 9 (1963). [BE.G.]

Greek: The Septuagint. NAME AND DESCRIPTION. The Greek version of the Bible known as the Septuagint (*Interpretatio septuaginta seniorum*, i.e., "translation of the seventy elders") probably owes its name to a story related in the *Letter of *Aristeas*, according to which 72 scholars, summoned from Jerusalem by Ptolemy II Philadelphus, achieved a perfect Greek translation of the Pentateuch, which was deposited in the Alexandrian library. This story was embellished with time until the 72 interpreters were credited with the translation of the entire Hebrew Bible. It was maintained that although each of them had worked independently, their finished versions were identical and, moreover, superior to the original as a result of divine inspiration.

Together with the New Testament, the Septuagint constituted the Bible of the Christian church, and it still is the Bible of the Greek Orthodox Church. The number of extant manuscripts is therefore considerable. Over 30 uncials, dating from the fourth to the ninth century, and about 350 cursives, ranging from the ninth to the fifteenth century, are in existence. They have been supplemented by recently discovered papyri fragments, which generally date from the second to the ninth century; a few of them date back to the second century B.C.E., and a number of fragments from the Qumran caves also bear witness to the pre-Christian Septuagint (see *Dead Sea Scrolls).

The Old Testament contains a translation of all the books of the Hebrew canon. Some of them have different titles, some have discrepancies in the order of the chapters (especially Jeremiah), and others have additional sections (Esther, Jeremiah, Daniel). It also embodies the deuterocanonical books of the Catholic Church (Judith, Tobit, I and

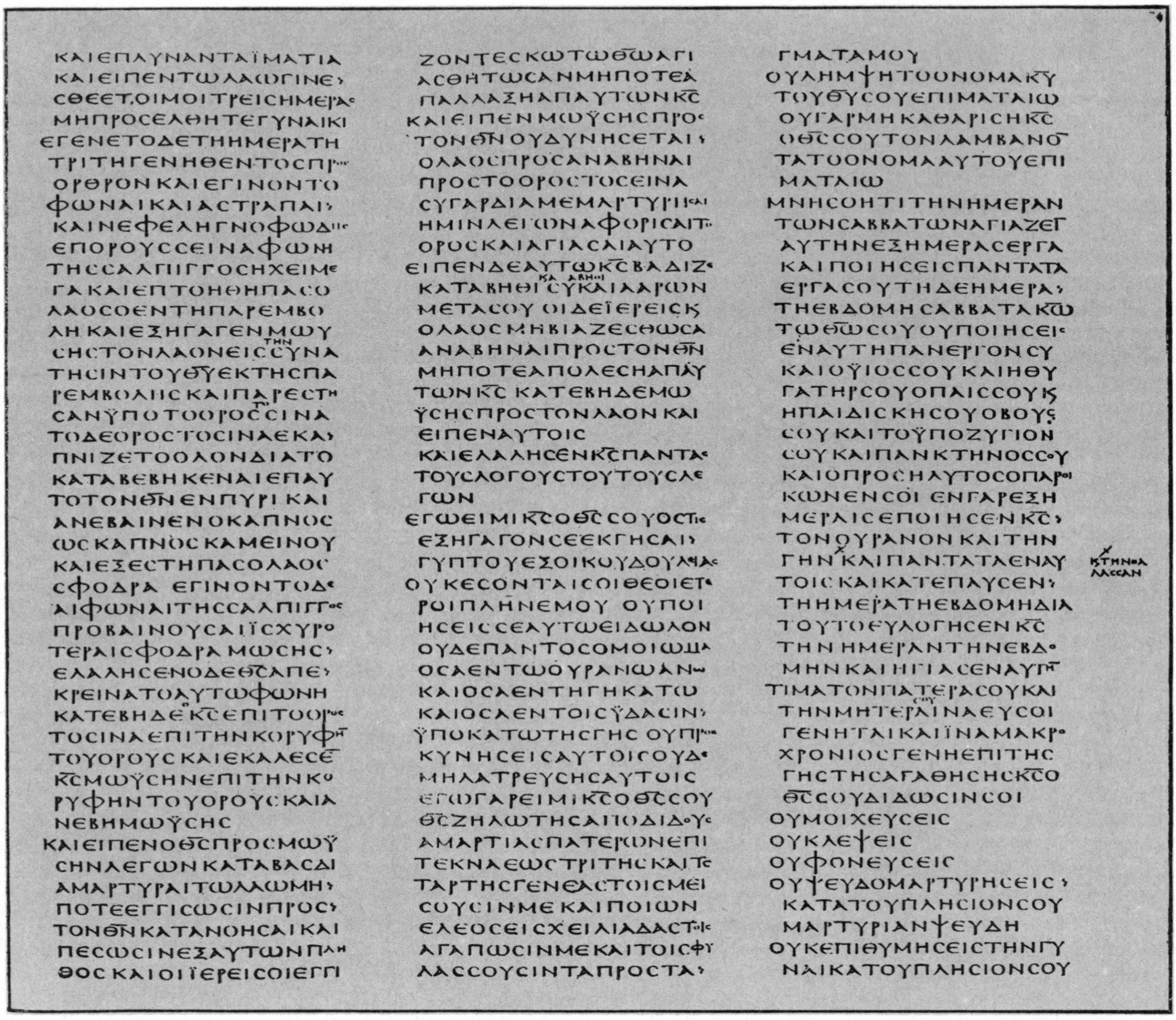

Manuscript of the Septuagint, fifth century. The page is from Exodus 19:14–20:17. Codex Vaticanus, Rome, Vatican Library.

II Maccabees, Wisdom of Solomon, Ben-Sira, I Baruch) and a few other Apocryphal books (I Esdras, III and IV Maccabees, the Odes, and the Psalms of Solomon). The sequence is based on a literary classification: law, history, poetry, prophecy.

Origin and History. It is widely accepted that what the *Letter of Aristeas* relates about an official translation of the Pentateuch, made in Alexandria at the beginning of the third century B.C.E., may be taken as valid. However, it is assumed that the project was initiated by the Greek-speaking Jewish community itself, which needed a version of the Pentateuch for worship and instruction. This version, which was undoubtedly a collective undertaking, perhaps based on previous written or oral attempts, was hailed with enthusiasm by the community. It was followed by translations of the other books of the Hebrew Bible. According to Thackeray, the liturgical needs of the Alexandrian Jews led to a gradual translation of the Latter Prophets, followed by that of the Former Prophets, during the second century, while the books of the Hagiographa were translated separately in the first century B.C.E. or later. However, it is more generally held that the versions of the Former and Latter Prophets must be placed before the end of the third century B.C.E., and that at least some of the Hagiographa were already translated at the beginning of the second century B.C.E., since the prologue to the Greek Ben-Sira (132 B.C.E.) refers to an already existing version of the "the Law, the Prophets, and the other writings." It is therefore accepted that a complete version of the Hebrew Bible existed at least at the beginning of the first century C.E. All or nearly all of it was of Egyptian origin, but as each component emerged, it was disseminated throughout the Hellenistic Diaspora and Palestine. There must have been considerable confusion in its transmission, due to the normal scribal corruptions and a growing incomprehension of the intentions of the translators, who had used a rather flexible technique and had not worked on a standard original. The resulting deviations were all the more disconcerting when the Hebrew canon was definitely fixed. This may explain the dissatisfaction of the Jews for the Septuagint, an attitude which was doubtless aggravated by the enthusiastic use of it by the Christians. As a result, new versions were made in the course of the second century by *Aquila, Theodotion, and Symmachus (see below).

A short time later *Origen became alarmed at the state of the Greek text of the Bible: the latter not only differed considerably from the Hebrew text of the Jews, which he believed to be the original one, but it appeared in a wide range of forms in the manuscripts current among the Christians. His purpose in producing his enormous work known as the Hexapla ("the sixfold," completed in 245 C.E.) was to reconstitute and standardize the "genuine" text of the Septuagint, essential both to sound exegesis and effective apologetics. The Hexapla consisted of six parallel columns: the first—the standard Hebrew text, the second—the same transcribed in Greek characters, the third, fourth, and sixth—the versions of Aquila, Symmachus, and Theodotion respectively; the critical text of the Septuagint compiled by Origen made up the fifth column. It was often recopied separately and enjoyed wide circulation in Palestine. However, it did not become preeminent throughout the Christian world, since, at the end of the fourth century, Jerome referred to the existence of two other recensions, one Egyptian by Hesychius, and the other made in Asia Minor by Lucian. The existence of these three versions might in itself afford a sufficient explanation of the many discrepancies displayed by the Septuagint manuscripts.

The Proto-Septuagint. The authentic text of the Alexandrian version must be sought at a period before the vicissitudes of this long history. Despite the alternative theory of "the Greek Targum" held by P. Kahle, who aimed to prove that such a version never existed, the consensus of opinion continues to favor the Proto-Septuagint, whose text should be reconstitutable from a critical study of the sources. This is, moreover, the assumption on which the two great modern editions of the Septuagint are based, although their fundamental principles differ. The Cambridge Septuagint, containing the Pentateuch and the historical books (9 vols., 1906–1940), presents the text of the Codex B or *Vaticanus* (the gaps in which are filled from the *Alexandrinus* (A), and the *Sinaiticus* (S)); it includes an immense critical apparatus based on the collation of the uncials and a large number of the cursives, and using data from the versions derived from the Septuagint (in particular the *Vetus Latina,* and the Coptic, Ethiopic, Armenian, and Syro-Hexaplaric versions), together with the quotations of Philo, Josephus, and the Church Fathers. The Goettingen Septuagint claims to provide a restored original text, although it generally comes back to B as the best source. It includes with this text a vast critical apparatus in which the sources are grouped as far as possible in families.

The Importance of the Septuagint. Long venerated by the Catholic Church as much if not more than the Hebrew text, the Septuagint has also enjoyed the favor of critical exegetes, who saw it as precious evidence of a Hebrew text far older than the oldest extant manuscripts. However, the more favorable opinion of the masoretic text which prevails today, and a fuller understanding of the problems inherent in the traditional Greek text have led scholars to believe that the possible use of the Septuagint in retrieving the original Hebrew text can only lie in the future. It is realized that only when a reliable text of the Proto-Septuagint has been constituted, and the language, technique, and actual intentions of its authors are better understood, will it be possible to reconstitute the original Hebrew text used with sufficient credibility so that it can be compared with the extant text.

It is therefore clear that, though still associated with biblical studies, contemporary research on the Septuagint has acquired an undoubted autonomy. Moreover, apart from the prestige of its antiquity and the influence it exercised throughout the centuries, the Alexandrian version is of great value in itself. It is one of the most extensive collections of texts in Hellenistic *Koiné.* Although its style is distinctly influenced as a whole by the Hebrew, the language is genuinely Greek, as has been shown by a comparison with contemporary sources. As it has the twofold advantage of dealing with matters which are much more varied than the papyrological documents, and of not being subject to the imitation of traditional styles, as the literary works of the period, it may claim to represent a precious relic of the living language of Ptolemaic Egypt.

As the first attempt to translate the Bible into another tongue, the Greek Pentateuch is also worthy of close attention. The translation is strikingly faithful, even adapting to the dimensions of the original and attempting to reproduce the order, as well as the number of words and the nature and construction of clauses in a sentence. Yet it is not servile to the original. Not only is the syntax of the Greek respected and its resources judiciously exploited, but the vocabulary also is used with remarkable independence. Far from seeking to show the etymology of Hebrew terms, the translators do not hesitate to give a word a different Greek equivalent according to the context, and to make the same Greek term serve for two or more Hebrew words. This plasticity of vocabulary enabled the translators to avoid paraphrase, and greatly contributed to the continuous but infinitely unobtrusive commentary, which they offered in their desire to eliminate the obscurities and reduce the apparent contradictions in the text, while emphasizing the whole range of intentions. This technique, which might be called targumic inasmuch as its objectives are essentially didactic, is constantly found, although in differing degrees, in most of the books which succeeded the Alexandrian Bible. However, in some, and particularly in the Hagiographa, two new tendencies emerge. The extreme freedom of the version of Proverbs, for example, contrasts with the literalism of that of Ecclesiastes or Song of Songs. Despite this evolution to two opposite trends in the philosophy of translation, it must be noted that the stylistic tradition established by the Greek Pentateuch remained remarkably strong, and that the influence of its vocabulary, in particular, is still felt even in the rival versions of the second century C.E.

With its general desire to explain the Hebrew text, the Alexandrian version offers enlightening interpretations in many places. In this first monument of Jewish exegesis, at a particularly important period in the religious history of Israel, it is not unusual to find interpretations similar to those offered by rabbinical sources. Z. Frankel drew attention to these convergencies in the last century, and if their study were pursued it would undoubtedly throw fuller light on the extent of the spiritual links between the Egyptian Diaspora and the religious center of Palestine.

Minor Greek Versions. The Greek translations of the second century are known essentially from annotations to certain Septuagint manuscripts and from patristic quotations, in particular those of *Jerome, who still had access to the *Hexapla* and had willingly used it for guidance when he produced his own translation, the Vulgate. To these fragments (last edited by F. Field in 1875) must be added a few more recent discoveries: 150 verses of the Psalms in the five last columns of the Hexapla and a few fragments of Kings and Psalms according to Aquila. The Theodotion version of Daniel is given by practically all of the Septuagint manuscripts with the exception of the Alexandrian.

The patristic and rabbinical sources agree in regarding Aquila as a proselyte, and this fact, together with the similarity of their names, has suggested that Aquila and the targumist Onkelos were the same person. Aquila's version, which was probably made in Palestine at the beginning of the second century, was highly rated by the Jewish communities, and a novella of the emperor Justinian authorizing its use for synagogal reading bears witness to its vitality as late as the sixth century. Aquila strove to keep as close as possible to the letter of the Hebrew text, reproducing even the etymology of words and the wording of idioms. Some of his devices, such as his frequent use of *syn* to render the particle *ʾet,* could also reflect the influence of the exegesis of R. Akiva, whose disciple he is said to have been. As this demand for strict literalism is already noticeable in the Alexandrian version of certain Hagiographa, Aquila's version might be considered to be a result of a long process, rather than an entirely new enterprise.

Theodotion, whose name likewise recalls that of a targumist, Jonathan, probably flourished toward the end of the second century. He was a Diaspora Jew who may have been a Christian for some time before returning to his original faith. He apparently concerned himself mainly with revising the Septuagint, in order to bring it nearer to the standard Hebrew text, harmonize its renderings, and eliminate the midrashic elements. A noteworthy feature of his work is the use of transliterations. Recent research suggests that Theodotion may have used an earlier version *(Ur-Theodotion).*

Detail from a Greek Octateuch manuscript, Byzantine, 12th century. The illumination shows Adam and Eve and the serpent in the Garden of Eden. Rome, Vatican Library, Ms. Gr. 746.

Symmachus, whom the Church Fathers make either a Samaritan converted to Judaism or a Christian, must have come still later. He must be assumed to have been at least of Jewish origin or training, in order to explain the influence which contemporary rabbinical exegesis clearly had over him. He seems to have been guided eclectically by the previous versions, although he adopted a personal technique. He carefully avoided literalism and made skillful use of the resources of the Greek language, resorting frequently to idiomatic renderings.

Mention must finally be made of the existence of three other anonymous versions, called, respectively, the *Quinta, Sexta,* and *Septima,* in reference to the place they occupied in the Tetrapla ("the fourfold," an abridged edition of the Hexapla without the first two columns). Only tiny fragments testify to their existence, but recent theories regarding predecessors of Aquila and Theodotion have drawn greater attention to them.

Bibliography: H. B. Swete, *An Introduction to the Old Testament in Greek* (1914²); R. Ottley, *A Handbook to the Septuagint* (1920); H. St. John Thackeray, *Some Aspects of the Greek Old Testament* (1927); H. H. Rowley, in: JQR, 33 (1942/43), 497–9; H. M. Orlinsky, in: H. R. Willoughby (ed.), *The Study of the Bible Today and Tomorrow* (1947), 144–61; idem, *The Septuagint, the Oldest Translation of the Bible* (1949); idem, in: JBL, 78 (1959), 26–33; G. Gerleman, *Synoptic Studies in the Old Testament* (1948); E. J. Bickerman, in: *A. Marx Jubilee Volume* (1950), 149–78; B. J. Roberts, *The Old Testament Text and Versions* (1951), 101–87; F. F. Bruce, in: *The Bible Translator,* 4 (1953), 129–35; L. H. Brockington, in: ZAW, 66 (1954), 80–86; F. G. Kenyon, *Our Bible and the Ancient Manuscripts* (1958⁴), 52–79, 89–97; P. Kahle, *The Cairo Geniza* (1959²), 209–64; idem, in: JBL, 79 (1960), 111–8; J. Ziegler, *Die Septuaginta. Erbe und Auftrag* (1962); S. Jellicoe, *The Septuagint and Modern Study* (1968).

[Su.D.]

Latin. Evidences of early Latin Bible translations are numerous but fragmentary. No single manuscript exists of a complete ancient Latin Bible, but various Latin text-forms of biblical verses, passages, and books can be derived from Latin Bible manuscripts exhibiting a pre-Vulgate text (see below); from the lower texts of palimpsests; from quotations by Latin Church Fathers; and from marginal annotations on Vulgate and the like. It is still a matter of dispute whether these extant texts ultimately go back to one original or rather reflect different versions made in several places. At any rate, the customary subsumption of these diverse elements under the name of *Vetus Latina,* or the Old Latin Version (OL), though convenient, is not accurate. While it is hard to prove conclusively, it is possible that the starting-point of the OL was a Jewish translation. Tombstones of Jewish catacombs in Rome bear Bible verses in Latin (first centuries C.E.; see Cassuto in bibliography); some manuscripts of the OL are based in a number of instances on the Hebrew Bible (see Weber in bibliography). In the main, however, the OL is a translation from the Greek Septuagint and thus constitutes only a secondary witness to the wording and meaning of the Hebrew Bible, and it includes features of clearly Christian inspiration. The first mention of an OL occurs in North Africa between the second and third centuries; later, an actual version of this sort appears in southern Gaul and in Rome. By the end of the fourth century C.E. accumulated textual corruptions and alterations gave rise to a need for a uniform and reliable Latin Bible text on which the Western Church could base its teaching (see Roberts in bibliography).

This task was entrusted to *Jerome (c. 345–420), the leading biblical scholar of the day and secretary to Pope Damasus I. Jerome was a master of Latin and Greek and had a remarkable knowledge of Hebrew. First he set out to revise the existing Latin texts in light of the Hebrew and Greek originals; among the portions of this revision that have survived are the books of the New Testament, the Psalms, Job, and the Song of Songs. Through his work Jerome became increasingly aware of the innumerable instances where the Septuagint diverged from the Hebrew Bible, and he thus decided to prepare an entirely fresh Latin translation from the "original truth of the Hebrew text," the *Hebraica veritas*. This great work he carried out in Bethlehem where he had settled in 386. His translation reveals the influence of various sources, especially that of his Jewish teachers (see Rahmer in bibliography) and that of his predecessors, the Greek translators; it thus sheds light on these sources as well as on the Hebrew text of the day. However Jerome's work also testifies to his linguistic skill: the translation varies, but on the whole Jerome succeeded in combining an elegant and intelligible Latin with fidelity to the original (see Kedar in bibliography). Jerome's translation of the Hebrew Bible in conjunction with his revision of the New Testament and the OL text of the Apocrypha became the standard Latin translation commonly called the Vulgate, from which at first all translations of the Bible into West European languages were made and from which some Roman Catholic translations, e.g., that of Ronald Knox into English, have continued to be made until most recent times (Knox's New Testament in 1944, his Old Testament in 1949 and 1950, with a revision of the Psalms in 1955).

Page from the Book of Numbers in an illuminated Latin Bible, France, 12th century. The initial letter "H" depicts Moses speaking to the Israelites. Paris, Bibliothèque Nationale. Ms. Lat. 167, fol. 47.

Bibliography: B. Fischer (ed.), *Vetus Latina*, 1–2 (1949–54); M. D. Cassuto, in: *Sefer Johanan Lewy* (1949), 161–72; R. Weber (ed.), *Les anciennes versions latines du deuxième livre des Paralipomènes* (1945); B. J. Roberts, *The Old Testament Text and Versions* (1951), 237–46; M. Rahmer, *Die hebraeischen Traditionen in den Werken des Hieronymus*, 1–2 (1861–1902); B. Kedar-Kopfstein, *The Vulgate as a Translation* (1968); F. Stummer, *Einfuehrung in die lateinische Bibel* (1928).

[B.KE.]

Syriac (Eastern Aramaic): Peshitta and Other Versions. The term "Peshitta" means "simple, straightforward, direct," and it is descriptive of the general characteristic of this major Bible version—its close conformity to the Hebrew text. The name was first used by Moses b. Kefa (d. 913) and then by Gregory *Bar Hebraeus. Almost every assertion regarding the authorship of the Peshitta and the time and place of its origin is the subject of controversy among scholars. Christian tradition ascribes the origin of the Peshitta to Abgar, king of Edessa, who is said to have sent scholars to Palestine to translate the Bible into Syriac (cf. Bar Hebraeus, Commentary to Ps. 10). That this Abgar was identical with King Izates II of Adiabene who, together with his entire family and household, converted to Judaism in the first century C.E. was first postulated by Wichelshaus and finds support in Josephus (Ant., 20:69–71), who states that Izates sent his five sons to Jerusalem to study the language and learning of the Jews. Other traditions assign the work to the time of Solomon, and ascribe the translation to an order of Hiram, king of Tyre, or to the priest Assa sent by an Assyrian king to Samaria (II Kings 17:27–28). Burkitt (*Early Eastern Christianity*, 71ff.) states that the Syriac translation of the Hebrew Bible was the work of Jews who lived in Edessa toward the beginning of the Common Era. Most scholars now agree that Edessa was the place of origin of the Peshitta because of the style of the language, which points to Syria. The translation of the Pentateuch is said to have started in the first century C.E., continued in the second (as Melito of Sardis speaks of a Syriac version of the Hebrew Bible) and third centuries, the entire Hebrew Bible being completed by the fourth century (since it is mentioned more and more frequently by the fourth century Church Fathers Augustine and Ephraem Syrus).

The controversy regarding the authorship of the Peshitta may be summarized as follows: Noeldeke maintains that it was Christian with Jewish help, basing his opinion on three arguments: (1) Peshitta is never mentioned in the Talmud; (2) the superscriptions of Psalms and the translation of certain verses of Isaiah are Christian in spirit; (3) the language of the Peshitta translation of the Hebrew Bible closely resembles that of the New Testament Peshitta. Dathe considers it to be the work of a Judeo-Christian sect. Other scholars (R. Simon, J. Perles, M. Seligson, C. Heller) assign it to Jewish hands, basing their contention on the following points: (1) Its abundant Judeo-Aramaisms which were certainly not understood by Christians; (2) it was originally written in Hebrew characters until Ephraem Syrus forbade it; (3) the halakhic and aggadic interpretations contained in it were certainly for synagogue consumption (e.g., Ex. 22:30 and Ḥul. 102b; Lev. 16:7

and Ḥul. 11a; Lev. 18:21 and Meg. 25a; Lev. 24:8 and Men. 97a); (4) Peshitta on Psalms is divided into five books like the Hebrew original. J. Perles goes as far as to say that the text was used in the synagogue since it was divided into weekly lessons for the Palestinian triennial cycle; the portions read in the synagogue on the festival are indicated (Lev. 23:1; cf. Meg. 30b); and the superscriptions to Exodus 20:1 עסרא פתגמין ("Ten Commandments") and Leviticus 17 נמוסא דקורבנא ודדבחא ("The Law of Offerings and Sacrifices") are in the rabbinical spirit (cf. Meg. 30b). Noeldeke's evidence for a Christian authorship is questioned by M. Seligson, who contends that the Peshitta may very well have been alluded to in the Talmud (Shab. 10b; RH 33b; Meg. 10b); and that the Christian superscriptions and translations were probably added later by Christian revisers. The Hebrew Bible known to the early Syrian Church was substantially that of the Palestinian Jews. It contained the same number of books but in a different order: Pentateuch, Job, Joshua, Judges, I and II Samuel, I and II Kings, Psalms, Proverbs, Ecclesiastes, Ruth, Song of Songs, Esther, Ezra, Nehemiah, Isaiah, 12 Minor Prophets, Jeremiah, Lamentations, Ezekiel, Daniel.

The current text is believed to have been translated not from the Hebrew but rather from the Septuagint, especially from the Septuagint of the Hexapla, except for the Wisdom of Ben Sira, which is said to have been translated from the Hebrew. In style, the translation of the Pentateuch (especially Genesis), Isaiah, the 12 Minor Prophets, and partly Psalms, show the influence of the Septuagint; Ezekiel and Proverbs are in close agreement with the corresponding Jewish Targums; Job is literal, Ruth is midrashic, and Chronicles is partly midrashic and of a late period.

Recent research into the history of the Peshitta text indicates that it was the accepted Bible of the Syrian Church from the end of the third century C.E. Ephraem Syrus, who died in 373, speaks of it as an old translation. In the fifth century theological differences divided the Syrian Christians into two distinct groups, the Nestorians and the Jacobites. Each group then proceeded to formulate its own Peshitta text based upon previous versions, with the result that there are two different text forms of the Peshitta: Western Syriac and Eastern Syriac. In the fifth and sixth centuries the Melchites (Palestinian Syrians) attempted to make the Eastern Syriac version conform with the Septuagint, the official text of the region, thus creating a text which was a mixture of the Peshitta and the Septuagint.

Knowledge of these versions, recently augmented by finds of textual fragment, is important for an understanding of the evolution of the Peshitta and subsequently in the assessment of the masoretic text. The oldest manuscript dates back to 464. It was first published in the Paris Polyglot Bible of 1645. This edition did not contain the Apocrypha which were later added in the London Walton Polyglot of 1657. In 1823, the Peshitta was printed separately by the British Foreign Bible Society in London and known as the Lee Edition. This edition, in Jacobite characters, practically reproduces the London Polyglot which itself was based on the Paris Polyglot. Two editions were prepared by American missionaries: The Urmia edition of 1852, and the Mosul edition of 1887–91 (1951[2]), both in Nestorian characters: the first work was proved to be influenced by the Lee edition, while the second is dependent on the Lee and Urmia editions and corrected according to the Vulgate. Attempts to publish the Peshitta in Hebrew characters include Hirsch's edition of the Five Scrolls (1866), Eisenstein's edition of the first two chapters of Genesis (1895), and Heller's Genesis (1928).

[BE.G.]

THE CHRISTIAN-PALESTINIAN VERSION. Around the end of the fourth century the Melchites in Palestine published a translation in the local Aramaic dialect in old Syriac characters (Estrangelo). It is generally admitted that this translation was rendered from the Greek and was influenced by the Peshitta and the Palestinian Targum.

THE PHILOXENIAN VERSION. In an attempt to displace the Peshitta, Philoxenus, the Jacobite bishop of Mabbugh, ordered a translation of the Septuagint (Lucian's version) and the Greek New Testament. Polycarp, his coadjutor, finished the work in 508. Of this translation only fragments from the Old Testament (Isaiah) were preserved, while five books from the New Testament entered into the printed edition of the Peshitta. A century later a version with marginal notes, taking into account various Greek manuscripts, was published by Thomas of Heraclea. It is not known whether in this work Thomas revised the Philoxenian Version completely or confined himself to adding the marginal notes.

THE SYRO-HEXAPLA. Commissioned by the patriarch Athanasius I, Paul, the bishop of Tella (near Alexandria), prepared a translation based on the fifth column of Origen's Hexapla. The translations of Aquila, Theodotion, and Symmachus were taken into account in marginal notes. This translation was completed in about 617. A manuscript of this work from the eighth or ninth century is extant in Milan. Paul of Tella's Syro-Hexapla, as it is called, is of great importance since Origen's Hexapla, upon which it was based, was almost completely destroyed. [ED.]

Bibliography: TEXTS OF THE PESHITTA: A. M. Ceriani *Biblia Sacra juxta versionem simplicem, quae dicitur Pschitta* (1951[3]); The Peshitta Institute of the University of Leiden, *Vetus Testamentum Syrice et Neosyrice* (1954); idem, *Peshitta... Specimen edition* (1969); for biblical Peshitta manuscripts see VT vol 12 and following; T. Noeldeke, in: *Archiv fuer wissenschaftliche Erforschung des Alten Testaments*, 2 (1871), 246–9; STUDIES: R. Duval, *Anciennes Littératures Chrétiennes*, vol. 22: *La Littérature Syriaque* (1899); F.C. Burkitt, *Early Eastern Christianity* (1904), 39–78; H. Mager, *Die Peschittho zum Buche Joshua* (1916); A. Baumstark, *Geschichte der syrischen Literatur* (1922), idem, in: BZ, 19 (1931), 257–70; P. Kahle, *Masoreten des Westens*, 2 (1930); idem, *The Cairo Geniza* (1959[2]), 265–313; C. Moss, in: *Le Muséon*, 46 (1933), 55–110; C. Peters, *ibid.*, 48 (1935), 1–54; 52 (1939), 275–96; idem, in: *Biblica*, 22 (1941), 25–34; P. Churgin, in: *Horeb*, 2 (1935), 259–79; I. Nobel, in: *ibid.*, 10 (1948), 77–104; M. Black, in: BJRL, 33 (1950/51), 203–10; A. Vogel, in: *Biblica*, 32 (1951), 32–56, 198–231, 336–63, 481–502; M. Goshen-Gottstein, in: BJRL, 37 (1954/55), 429–45; idem, *Text and Language in Bible and Qumran* (1960); A. Vööbus, *Peschitta und Targumim des Pentateuchs* (1958); idem, in: *Le Muséon*, 68 (1955), 215–8; E. R. Rowlands, in: VT, 9 (1959), 178–91; J. A. Emerton, *The Peshitta of the Wisdom of Solomon* (1959); W. Baars, in: VT, 10 (1960), 224–7; 13 (1963), 260–8; 18 (1968), 548–54; P. Wernberg-Møller, in: *Studia Theologica*, 15 (1961), 128–80; idem, in: JSS, 7 (1962), 253–66; J. A. Emerton, *ibid.*, *204–11*. THE CHRISTIAN PALESTINIAN VERSION: J. P. N. Land, in: *Anecdota Syriaca*, 4 (1862–75), 103–224; A. S. Lewis, *A Palestinian Syriac Lectionary...* (1897); J. T. Milik, in: RB, 60 (1953), 526–39; L. Delekat, in: ZAW, 71 (1959), 165–201. THE PHILOXENIAN VERSION: A. M. Ceriani (ed.), *Monumenta Sacra et Profana* vols. 1, 2, 3, 5, 7 (1866–74); L. Delekat, in: ZAW, 69 (1957), 21–54. THE SYRO-HEXAPLA: Ceriani, op. cit. vols. 2, 5, 7; A. P. de Lagarde, *Veteris Testamenti ab Origene recensiti fragmenta* (1880); J. M. Vosté, in: *Biblica*, 26 (1945), 12–36.

Ethiopic. Aramaic-speaking Christian missionaries enriched Ethiopic with Aramaic loanwords to express new Christian concepts, and Ethiopic Bible translations consequently show signs of Syriac influence. The earliest of these translations produced in the fifth or sixth century C.E. but known only from 13th-century manuscripts, are mainly almost word for word translations of the Greek Septuagint.

These were often awkward and their inadequacies account for the literal reproduction of various designations and technical terms. The Greek originals were themselves carelessly copied, resulting in even further textual confusion. These errors were not entirely corrected when a revision was undertaken with the sanction of the Church, in the course of which Coptic and Arabic (including *Saadiah's) translations were consulted. The Ethiopic Bible is unique among translations of the Bible in that it consists of the Octateuch, i.e., the five books of Moses, together with Joshua, Judges, and Ruth. From the very beginning, many Apocryphal writings were also included, but only the Book of *Enoch and Jubilees survive in their entirety. In the course of time, translations were made of all the books of the Bible and the New Testament Gospels, including in addition the Apocrypha and ten other noncanonical books, which enjoyed wide popularity in Ethiopia. Apart from these Ethiopic versions, there are translations of the Bible and the New Testament into Amharic (the modern language of the country), which have mainly been produced by European missionaries.

Bibliography: H. Ludolf, *Psalterium Davidis aethiopice et latine*... (1701); A. Dillmann, *Biblia Veteris Testamenti Aethiopica* (1853–94), R. M. J. Basset, *Les apocryphes éthiopiens* (1893–1900); J. O. Boyd, *The Octateuch in Ethiopic* (1901–); O. Loefgren, *Die aethiopische Uebersetzung des Propheten Daniel* (1927); idem, *Jona, Nahum, Habakuk, Zephanja, Haggai, Secharja und Maleachi aethiopisch*... (1930); B. J. Roberts, *The Old Testament Text and Versions* (1951), 234–5; B. Cotte, in: DBI, Supplement, 6 (1960–66), 825–9.

[Ed.]

Egyptian (Coptic). Coptic translations of the Bible from the earliest Greek versions were probably in existence by the end of the third century C.E. They have been preserved in various dialects. The portions of the Bible translated into the Bohairic (Alexandrian) and Sahidic (upper Egyptian) dialects have survived and have been published almost in their entirety. On the other hand, only fragments of the Faiyoumic (or Memphitic; Middle Egyptian) and Akhmimic Bible translations are known and have been edited. The surviving versions have their source in the Greek translations; the Sahidic version of Job, which shows no trace of a Hexaplar reading, is of particular importance for the Septuagint text of the Book of Job.

Bibliography: G. W. Horner, *The Coptic Versions in Southern Dialect (Sahidic)* (1911–24); E. A. T. W. Budge (ed.), *Coptic Biblical Texts in the Dialects of Upper Egypt* (1912); H. S. Gehman, in: JBL, 46 (1927), 279–330; O. H. E. Burmester and E. Dévaud, *Les Proverbes de Salomon... Texte Bohairique*... (1930); W. H. Worrell, *The Proverbs of Solomon in Sahidic Coptic according to the Chicago Manuscript* (1931); F. H. Hallock, in: AJSLL, 49 (1932–33), 325–35; J. Simon, in: *Zeitschrift fuer die neutestamentliche Wissenschaft und die Kunde der aelteren Kirche*, 37 (1938), 205–11; B. J. Roberts, *The Old Testament Text and Versions* (1951), 229–33.

[Ed.]

Armenian. According to Armenian tradition the Bible was the first book translated into that language. The translation was undertaken directly after the invention of the Armenian alphabet in 406 C.E.; the story of the translation is preserved in the Armenian tradition for which the prime source is the "Life of Mesrop," written by Koriun (or Goriun). The initial translation, which according to these sources was made from Syriac, was subsequently revised twice in the light of Greek manuscripts brought from Constantinople and Alexandria. The work was completed by c. 450.

The translation of the Bible as preserved by the Armenian Church is predominantly Hexaplaric in character, equipped with Hexaplaric signs and showing a full text.

Page from an Armenian illuminated Bible, c. 1650, with miniature of Joseph and his wife, Asenath. Jerusalem, Library of the Armenian Patriarchate, Ms. 1927, fol. 40v.

Further relationships of the versions have been studied only for few books, where it has been demonstrated that it reveals relationships with certain non-Hexaplaric Greek text types and with the Peshitta. There is also evidence for the existence of two recensions in certain books, such as Chronicles and Ben Sira, and Revelation in the New Testament. Khalatianz (Moscow, 1899) published a version of Chronicles apparently reflecting the translation made from Syriac prior to the revision according to Greek manuscripts. The translation has been characterized as "queen of the versions" and its closeness to the Greek original is reflected in sentence structure and word order. It is one of the central works of the golden age of Armenian literature.

The first edition is that of Oskan, published in 1666 in Amsterdam. The best is that published in Venice in 1805 by J. Zabrabian who based his work on eight complete Bible manuscripts and certain additional manuscripts for Isaiah and Psalms. His edition is no longer adequate for scholarly purposes today. There are numerous manuscripts still unstudied. The earliest complete Bible codices date from the 13th century but there are psalters of an earlier date.

The canon is substantially that of the Septuagint. IV Ezra, Testaments of the Twelve Patriarchs, and the Book of Joseph and Asenath are often included in Bible manuscripts. The canon of Zabrabian's version however is that of the Vulgate.

Bibliography: F. C. Conybeare, in: DB, 1 (1911), 151–3; H. Hyvernat, in: DBI, 1 (1912), 1010–15; H. B. Swete, *An Introduction to the Old Testament in Greek* (1914^2), 118–20; H. S. Gehman, in: ZAW, 48 (1930), 82–99; idem, in: JAOS, 54 (1934), 53–59; B. Johnson, *Die armenische Bibeluebersetzung als hexaplarischer Zeuge im 1. Samuelbuch* (1968).

[M.E.S.]

Arabic. Since it is an established fact that Jews and Christians lived in the Arabian Peninsula in pre-Islamic times, and it is reasonable to surmise that their vernacular was Arabic, it has been conjectured that Arabic translations of the Bible or of some of its books were available in the time of Muhammad; however, nothing actually exists to substantiate this. More likely, an oral tradition of explanation in Arabic may have begun to develop among Arabic-speaking Jews at an early date, and subsequently may have been recorded in writing. The Muslim traditionalist Abu Hurayra (not too reliable a witness) reports that the Jews read the *Tawrāt* (i.e., Bible) in Hebrew and rendered it into Arabic for followers of Islam. Biblical stories in the Koran and anecdotes termed *Isrāʾīliyyāt* in the *Hadīth bear testimony to the likelihood of an oral tradition.

After predominantly Christian western Asia with its Jewish minorities came under Muslim domination in the seventh century, the gradual Islamization and Arabization of the area created an ever greater need for an Arabic Bible, both for followers who could not read it in the original and for Muslims who were prompted by curiosity or by polemical motives. It is reported that Ḥunayn ibn Iṣḥāq (c. 800–873), the celebrated Christian translator of Greek and Syriac works into Arabic, prepared an edition of the entire Bible in that language (cf. al-Masʿūdī, *Kitāb al-Tanbīh* (ed. M. J. de Goeje), 112). He most probably made it from the Septuagint, just as later Christian translators based themselves on the Greek Bible and the Peshitta or other Syriac renderings. Nothing has survived of Ḥunayn's labors.

The first and best-known translation of probably the entire Bible from the Hebrew was prepared by *Saadiah b. Joseph Gaon (882–942). Perhaps written in Arabic characters for the purpose of placing it at the disposal of non-Jews (see Ibn Ezra, comm. to Gen. 2:11) or of Jews who could not read Hebrew script (cf. examples of biblical texts transcribed in Arabic characters in the Cairo *Genizah*), it sought to offer a rendition of the Hebrew Bible that would be rationally acceptable and would also read smoothly. To the former end, Saadiah eliminated all anthropomorphisms or suggestions of them; for the latter, he followed Arabic, rather than Hebrew syntax and usage in translating the Hebrew, adding words when he felt they were needed for the sense desired and omitting others for the sake of Arabic idiom; he even introduced Arabic names of places or persons when he believed they would shed light on the text. Many of his versions of biblical books are no longer extant. Searchers of the *Genizah* collections in the last few decades have brought to light considerable portions of his commentaries on biblical texts. These include renditions of verses or passages not otherwise preserved.

Some anonymous versions (e.g., Bodleian 206) show the influence of Saadiah's work. In the 13th century, a Jew from Africa prepared an Arabic Pentateuch, also based on Saadiah. Judah b. Isaac ibn Ghayyat translated Ecclesiastes into Arabic.

Among the Karaites, Japheth b. Eli ha-Levi (tenth century), a prolific writer, translated the entire Bible into Arabic and provided it with lengthy commentaries, and Abu al-Faraj Furqān ibn Asad (Joshua b. Judah; 11th century) is credited with an Arabic version of at least the Torah (Brit. Mus., Ms. Or. 2491).

The Samaritan Arabic translation of the Pentateuch, made by Abu Saʿīd (13th century), has been shown to be indebted to Saadiah's version, although it undoubtedly utilized an oral tradition of interpretation current in the Samaritan community. Ezekiel ben Shemtov David published an Arabic rendition of the Bible in 1895. There are numerous Christian renditions by members of the several Oriental churches, as well as by modern missionaries who seek to reach Arabic-speaking groups. Best known in the West are those which are included in the Paris Polyglot Bible and which were copied from the latter in the London Polyglot Bible. The most complete source for this class of writings by Christians was published by Georg Graf (see bibliography).

See also *Pentateuch, Samaritan.

Bibliography: J. Derenbourg, *Version arabe du Pentateuque de R. Saadia ben Josef al Fayyoūmi*... (1893); Steinschneider, Arab Lit, 46–69; A. P. de Lagarde, *Materialen zur Kritik und Geschichte des Pentateuchs*, 1 (1867); M. L. Margolis. *The Story of Bible Translations* (1917), 53–55; H. S. Gehman, in: JBL, 44 (1925), 327–52; O. Loefgren, *Studien zu der arabischen Danielueberset-zung*... (1936); M. Kattan, in: REJ, 101–102 (1937), 115–9; E. Robertson, in: *Saadya Studies* (1943), 166–76; G. Graf, *Geschichte der christlichen arabischen Literatur*, 1 (1944), 85–195; B. J. Roberts, *The Old Testament Text and Versions* (1951), 266–9, 314; P. Kahle, *Die arabischen Bibeluebersetzungen*... (1904).

[A.S.H.]

MODERN VERSIONS

Introduction. The Bible has been translated more than any other major literary work, and, in part, or as a whole has appeared in almost all the languages and dialects of the world. Christianity spread knowledge of the Bible throughout the ancient world and, in time, to almost every known country and people. The Reformation gave a further impetus to translation of the Bible, the reformers often basing their work on the original texts. Since the Roman Catholic Church was at first disinclined to promote Bible study in any text but the Latin Vulgate, Protestantism soon took a commanding lead in the dissemination of the Bible, which was systematically translated into many vernaculars. By the 1960s, the British and Foreign Bible Society alone had published complete Bibles in well over 200 languages, and translations of individual biblical books in about five times that number. Protestant translations are often based on the English Authorized Version; Catholic editions, generally, on the Vulgate. Complete Bibles and separate biblical books have appeared under Jewish auspices from earliest times, in many languages, although the missionary purpose of some of the first Jewish translators were zealously suppressed by Christian authorities in many countries. Jewish translators have therefore tended to direct their work to the Jewish reader. From time to time, however, Jewish Bible translations have influenced Christian scholars.

Judeo-Persian. As *Maimonides *(Iggeret Teiman)* attests, a Persian translation of the Pentateuch was in existence centuries before Muhammad. In fact, theological works of the Sassanid period (*Dinkard* and *Shikand Gumanik Vigar*) contain biblical quotations which point to the existence of a Pahlavi version. Nevertheless, this fact and even the reference to the reading of the Book of Esther in the dialects of Media and Elam (Meg. 18a) provide no firm evidence for the existence of a complete or partial translation of the Bible into these languages. The earliest such text is a Pentateuch of 1319 written in *Judeo-Persian, and there are also manuscripts of the Pentateuch, Psalms, and even fragments of the Apocrypha, all predating the 16th century. Their stylistic uniformity suggests that there may possibly have been a school of Judeo-Persian Bible translation in the 14th–15th centuries. The earliest printed text is the Pentateuch of Jacob b. Joseph *Tavus, apparently based on a 13th-century version, which appeared in the Polyglot Pentateuch of Constantinople (1546); here the Judeo-Persian is printed in Hebrew characters. There are also some modern Bible translations in this dialect, notably versions of Psalms, Proverbs, and Job published by a Bokharian Jew, Benjamin Kohen, in

1883, and Simeon *Ḥakham's translation of the Pentateuch (5 vols., 1901–02).

See also *Judeo-Persian Literature. [ED.]

Judeo-Tatar. The Bible translations into Judeo-Tatar (not to be confused with *Judeo-Tat, spoken by the "Mountain Jews" of Daghestan and the Caucasus) originated among the Karaites of the Crimea, Russia. Authorship of the Tatar translation claimed by the Karaites has been disputed by the Krimchaks (Rabbanite Jews of the Crimea), who also used such texts. There are manuscript copies of this version in the Firkovich collection (Leningrad Library) and elsewhere. Fragments of the Judeo-Tatar Bible are contained in Benjamin *Mussafia's *Zekher Rav* (1831), which includes translations of certain words into Turkish by Joseph Solomon of Eupatoria, a Karaite *ḥakham.* A Hebrew Pentateuch intended for the Karaites of Turkey and the Crimea, containing a translation into Judeo-Tatar (i.e., in Hebrew characters), was published in Constantinople (1836). A complete Judeo-Tatar Bible (ed. Mordecai Tirishkan) followed soon after (4 vols., 1841–42). [I.M./ED.]

Judeo-Romance Languages. During the Middle Ages, there were Jewish translations of the entire Bible in the Romance languages. They appear to have a common source—a traditional version of the Bible in Low Latin, which the Jews of imperial Rome used in the synagogue and for the purposes of study. This translation was probably transmitted orally, and in time the text underwent morphological and phonetic modifications as Low Latin developed into the various Romance languages in various countries. The Judeo-Romance Bible translations are therefore as old as the Romance languages themselves, and much older than the manuscripts containing them or the glosses relating to them. This development may be traced most fully in Italy, where the Jews lived uninterruptedly from Roman times. Traces of the old Latin translation have been discovered in Jewish funerary inscriptions at Rome and in southern Italy dating from early Christian times; a novella of Justinian (553 C.E.) mentions a Jewish Bible translation in the vernacular. Hebrew works from the 11th century onward contain glosses, and in the 13th century the rabbis of Rome decided that for liturgical purposes, Italian versions of the Bible might be considered equivalent to the Targum. From the 15th century onward, Romance dialect versions of the Bible and of the prayer book were preserved in manuscript, as well as handwritten glossaries and a Bible dictionary in Hebrew, Italian, and Arabic *(Makre Dardeke),* which was first printed (at Naples?) in 1488. Their impact has been felt in modern translations.

Several Judeo-Romance versions of biblical books are extant, including a 14th-century *Judeo-Provençal fragment of the Book of Esther by Crescas du Caylar, and manuscript translations of Song of Songs (the oldest dating from the 13th century) and of the entire Bible written in *Judeo-Italian. Although the Old French versions have been lost, their existence is attested by six 13th-century glossaries and two complete biblical dictionaries in *Judeo-French. There may also have been Jewish translations of portions of the Bible in Catalan, since (as in the case of Old French and Judeo-Provençal) biblical glosses *(*La'azim)* and glossaries in this dialect have inspired scholarly research (see below).

Ladino (Judeo-Spanish). Judeo-Spanish translations of the Bible dating from the 13th to 15th centuries were among the earliest Castilian versions of the Bible, and three manuscripts have been preserved in the Escorial Library, Madrid. These early works were invariably written in Latin characters, as was the famous Ferrara Bible (1553), published by Abraham *Usque, of which there were separate editions for Jews and Christians. After the Spanish expulsion, however, Ladino versions of the Bible were mainly printed in Hebrew characters for the use of Jewish refugees in the Sephardi Diaspora. These translations, which were clearly distinguishable from Spanish Christian editions, include Psalms (Constantinople, 1540), the Pentateuch (in the Polyglot Pentateuch, Constantinople, 1546), and Prophets (Salonika, 1572). Judeo-Spanish Bible translations were later produced by Manasseh Ben Israel (1627) and Abraham b. Isaac Assa, whose complete Bible (Constantinople, 1739–45) was long the most popular work of its kind among Sephardi communities of the Orient (see also *Ladino Literature). [U.C./ED.]

Yiddish. The oldest Yiddish versions of the Bible stem from the scholarly work of German rabbis who produced Yiddish (or Judeo-German = *Juedisch-Deutsch*) glosses of biblical texts from the 13th century. These were subsequently inserted in rabbinical commentaries and specialized glossaries were prepared, five dating to the 13th–14th centuries and four to the 14th–15th centuries. Copies of these have been preserved in various German libraries. Prose translations of various biblical books were written from the 14th century onward, and these were specifically designed for the unlearned and for women, in view of the widespread ignorance of Hebrew. Such *"Teitsch"* versions include a 14th–15th century translation of Proverbs, Job, and Psalms (the oldest extant); one of Psalms (before 1490); and others of Psalms, Proverbs, and the Pentateuch. These are literal and awkward, and appear to derive from a 13th-century source.

Rhymed Yiddish translations of the Bible, which also appeared in medieval times, owe their origin to the influence of the Bibles and chronicles in rhyme produced by German writers from the ninth century onward. There are also rhymed Yiddish paraphrases of the Bible, which flourished in the 14th century, predating the rhymed translations. These paraphrases, unlike the translations, go beyond the original text and show the influence of German epic minstrelsy. The best-known work of this type is the so-called **Shemuel Bukh,* a rhymed paraphrase of I and II Samuel, the prototype of which appeared no later than about 1400, although the first printed edition is of a much later date (Augsburg, 1543). The *Shemuel Bukh* served as the model for a host of other biblical paraphrases in rhyme, including: three 14th-century paraphrases of Esther; one of Judges (14th–15th centuries); paraphrases of the five *Megillot,* which were apparently the work of Abraham b. Elijah of Vilna (15th–16th centuries); paraphrases of Judges and Isaiah by Moses b. Mordecai of Mantua (before 1511); and poetic reworkings of the account of the death of Moses and the *Akedah.* The last two display great originality, adorning the biblical stories with legendary motifs drawn from the midrashic *aggadah,* and endowing the biblical personalities and events described with medieval characteristics. By the 15th century there were also prose paraphrases of certain biblical books, most of which have, however, been lost. The existence of such literary works is indicated by the late 15th-century *Ma'asiyyot* ("tales"), stories in prose about the *Akedah,* Jonah, and King Solomon.

From the 16th century onward no new type of Bible translation made its appearance. The only noticeable development was the steady displacement of other genres by the prose paraphrases. Three notable Yiddish glossaries of the Bible, all rooted in medieval scholasticism, were the so-called *Sefer R. Anschel* (Cracow, 1584), Moses Saertels'

Be'er Moshe (Prague, 1605–05?), and *Lekaḥ Tov* (Prague, 1604). The same scholastic tradition characterizes the oldest printed Yiddish editions of the Pentateuch with *haftarot* and the five *Megillot:* that of the convert Michael Adam (Constance, 1544); another by the convert Paulus Aemilius (Augsburg, 1544); a revision of the Constance edition by Leo Bresch (Cremona, 1560); and a further translation based on the preceding Cremona edition, together with a summary of Rashi's commentary in Yiddish (Basle, 1583). The publishers rarely did more than bring the Yiddish translations up to date, and this was also true of the Yiddish version of Psalms by Elijah *Levita (Venice, 1545), which closely followed earlier editions by Moses b. Mordecai of Brescia (before 1511) and Joseph Yakar (*siddur,* Ichenhausen, 1544). Two further Yiddish translations of the 16th century were Shalom b. Abraham's Judith and Susanna (Cracow, 1571) and an edition of Isaiah with extracts from Kimḥi's commentary (Cracow, 1586). Toward the end of the 17th century, two complete Yiddish Bibles appeared almost simultaneously: one by Jekuthiel b. Isaac Blitz (Amsterdam, 1676–78) and another by Josef Witzenhausen (Amsterdam, 1679), which was more significant than the first.

Rhymed Yiddish translations were rare after the 16th century. They include one of Judges (Mantua, 1564); one of Genesis (Venice, 1551); Moses Stendal's edition of Psalms (Cracow, before 1586); a 17th-century version of Psalms (the *Teitsch-Hallel*), whose author copied the verse form of contemporary German church hymnology; and *Mizmor le-Todah* (Amsterdam, 1644) rhymed translations of stories from the Pentateuch and the *Megillot* by David b. Menahem ha-Kohen. Rhymed paraphrases of various biblical books were still popular in the 16th and 17th centuries, the outstanding example being the *Shemuel Bukh* (see above), of which there were at least seven editions during the years 1543–1612. Another work of this type was a version of the Pentateuch, Joshua, and Judges, written by *Jacob b. Isaac ha-Levi of Roethelsee (*Kehillat Ya'akov,* 1692).

Later, Yiddish prose paraphrases of the Bible were much in favor. Some notable examples were the so-called *Lang Megile* on Esther (Cracow, 1589); the *Teutsch-Khumesh* by *Isaac b. Samson ha-Kohen of Prague (Basle, 1590), a paraphrase of the Pentateuch with Midrashim; the *Ẓe'enah u-Re'enah* (*Tsenerene;* cf. Song 3:11) by Jacob b. Isaac *Ashkenazi (Lublin, 1616), a reworking of the Pentateuch filled with edifying and instructive material drawn from the Talmud, the Midrash, and folklore; and the *Sefer ha-Maggid* by the same author (Lublin, 1623), an adaptation of the Prophets and Hagiographa with Rashi's commentary.

The most famous of these was *Ẓe'enah u-Re'enah,* which ran to many editions and continued to serve as a second Bible among East European Jewry during the 19th century. An extract was translated into Latin by Johann Saubert in 1661, and the whole work into French by A. Kraehhaus in 1846. A German version (with an introduction by A. Marmorstein) was serialized in 1911.

With the decline of Yiddish among German Jewry, from the early 19th century onward, these Bible translations and paraphrases were read only by the Jews of Eastern Europe and the U.S. Mendel *Lefin (of Satanow), an early 19th-century Polish apostle of the Enlightenment, produced an excellent Yiddish version of Proverbs (Tarnopol, 1817). Bible translations of outstanding linguistic and artistic merit were later written by two leading Yiddish poets of the 20th century—I. L. *Peretz (the Five Scrolls, 1925) and *Yehoash (Yiddish Bible, 1910ff.). The latter, in particular, was considered a great masterpiece of the Yiddish language. It became a standard work for Yiddish-speaking homes throughout the world. In 1929 Yehuda Leib (Zlotnick) *Avida translated Ecclesiastes into Yiddish. See also *Yiddish Literature. [Ed.]

English. Earliest Versions. The Latin Bible, in an essentially Italian form, first reached England in the sixth or seventh century; however, it should be understood that until the late Middle Ages, the "Bible" of the West comprised, for practical purposes, only the Gospels, Catholic (i.e., canonical) Epistles, and Psalms. Codices of the complete Latin Bible were almost unknown before approximately 800 C.E. From the Latin, Bede (d. 735) translated the Gospel according to John into Anglo-Saxon, and Aelfric of Eynsham made abridgments of the Old Testament from Genesis to Judges and of some other books. Caedmon wrote an Anglo-Saxon verse paraphrase of Genesis and other portions of the Bible (c. 670) and Alfred the Great attached an Anglo-Saxon version of the Ten Commandments and parts of the Pentateuch to his legal code. The earliest attempts, however, took the form of continuous interlinear glosses to the Latin, e.g., as in the Lindisfarne Gospels (ca. 700; British Museum, coll. Cotton, Ms. Nero D. IV). Psalters with interlinear glosses seem to have been used, particularly in women's convents (coll. Cotton, Ms. Vespasian A. I. from the ninth century, perhaps being the earliest surviving work). Eadwine's Canterbury Psalter (Trinity College, Cambridge, Ms. R. 17. 1) dates from the middle of the 12th century. The Psalter of Richard Rolle of Hampole (c. 1300–49) enjoyed wide popularity and ecclesiastical approbation up to the Reformation.

The Lollard Bible. The first comprehensive English translation was produced late in the 14th century; it is connected with the Wyclifite movement, whose adherents were nicknamed Lollards and were treated by the Church as heretics. John Wyclif was himself responsible, though not necessarily as a translator, for the earlier version (before 1384) made from the Latin. The Old Testament was translated, at least in part, by Nicholas of Hereford, whose translation is characterized by a slavish adherence to the Latin. John Purvey is assumed to have been mainly responsible for the later version (c. 1388), the preface to which acknowledges the use made of Nicholas de *Lyra's commentary on the Old Testament. This version is consequently the first point at which the English Bible was subjected, albeit at one remove, to the influence of Jewish exegesis. Numerous manuscripts of the Lollard Bible are extant, and it was disseminated in part by word of mouth because of ecclesiastical hostility. There was no printed English Bible before the Reformation.

The 16th–17th Centuries. Several interacting factors afford the background to the "classical" period of English translations, which may be dated from W. Tyndale (1537) to the Authorized Version (1611). The revival of learning meant the provision of chairs for teaching Greek and Hebrew at Oxford and Cambridge, as well as the dawning of a critical approach to the texts of both the Greek New Testament and the Latin Vulgate, printed editions of which were prepared by Erasmus. Estienne (Stephanus) in Paris also published scholarly texts. The polyglot Bible editions made it easier to compare the ancient versions. The new (or rediscovered) methodology of textual criticism demonstrated the importance of basing vernacular versions on original and not on secondary texts; Reuchlin and Luther in Germany were pioneers of the new scholarship. A new theology was to lead, in the reformed churches, to the recognition that ultimate Christian authority lay in Scripture, rather than in the tradition of the Church, and conversely, in the Catholic Church it led to insistence by the Council of Trent in 1546 on the "authentic" quality of the Latin Vulgate, notwithstanding the possibly greater accuracy of contemporary Latin versions of the Bible. Finally, the period—which embraces the age of Shakespeare—witnessed the spectacular advance of the English language as a literary medium.

TYNDALE AND HIS SUCCESSORS. William Tyndale (martyred in 1536), considered the father of the Bible of the English-speaking world, was educated at Oxford, and subsequently at Cambridge, where he learned Greek and was influenced by the writings of Erasmus and, perhaps, by Luther. By the time his New Testament appeared in 1535, Tyndale had already learned enough Hebrew to publish the Pentateuch (1531), followed by Jonah (1531) and further lectionary Old Testament material (1534); Joshua-II Chronicles, left by Tyndale in manuscript, was printed in the *Matthews Bible* of 1537.

Tyndale's Bible, a factor in promoting the English Reformation, raised hostility less by its content than by its Luther-inspired prefaces and provocative notes. Not long after Tyndale's martyrdom, his prayer at the stake—"Lord, open the King of England's eyes"—was answered when Henry VIII broke definitely with the Church of Rome. In 1535 Miles Coverdale, Tyndale's assistant, produced an English Bible under royal auspices, which was actually a private enterprise, and was based not on the original texts but on the Vulgate, together with Pagninus' literal Latin rendering of the Old Testament, and other versions including those of Luther and Erasmus. Another translation—Tyndale's, except for Ezra, Malachi, and the Apocrypha, which were by Coverdale—was published pseudonymously (Matthews) by J. Rogers, Tyndale's friend, with controversial notes (1537). This in turn was the basis of the "Great" Bible of 1539, known also as Cranmer's from the preface to the 1540 edition, which Henry VIII had ordered to be placed in every parish church. M. Coverdale was editor, but some of his earlier provocative inclusions were dropped, and although surplus words found in the Vulgate Latin were rendered into English, they were typographically distinguished. Some Latinisms of diction crept in. The translation of the Old Testament was improved by reference to *Muenster's Hebrew-Latin Bible of 1535. This edition's Psalter is that which has been retained ever since in Anglican church usage.

ANGLICAN, CALVINIST, AND CATHOLIC BIBLES, 1560–1610. In spite of the radicalism of his ecclesiastical politics, Henry VIII was doctrinally a moderate conservative; the successors of his "Great" Bible, produced under Elizabeth I and James I, reflected the "Anglican Compromise." The *Bishops' Bible* (1568) was fathered by Archbishop Parker, himself responsible for translating Genesis, Exodus, and some of the New Testament. It was intended to offset the pressures of the returned exiles of Mary's reign for an English church settlement on Calvinistic lines and the popularity of their Geneva version from which, however, the Bishops retained some notes and renderings. The contributors were enjoined to avoid polemical exegesis, and were directed to correct the Great Bible, following Pagninus and Muenster for the Hebrew. The main significance of this Bible lies in its forming the basis of the Authorized Version of 1611.

The Scotsman John Knox was the most prominent Briton to take refuge from the Catholic restoration of Mary, in Geneva, where he began to study Hebrew. At the time, not only was *Calvin himself teaching there, but French and Italian Bible-making was also in progress. English versions of Psalms were issued from 1557 on, corrected, and finally superseded by the complete *Geneva* or *"Breeches" Bible* (so-called from its rendering of Gen. 3: 7) of 1560. Additional words which were idiomatically essential were printed in italic type; the remainder, in roman instead of the black letter of earlier prints. For the Hebrew, as well as the new Latin versions, of this Great Bible, the translation of Leo Jud (Zurich, 1543) was drawn upon, as was Castellio's French translation (1555). The influence of David Kimḥi's commentaries may be observed in this version, which was reprinted until 1644.

English Catholics who fled to Flanders under Elizabeth I produced their own New Testament at Rheims (1582), followed by the Old Testament printed at Douai (1609–10). This version—characterized by the outspokenly apologetic tone of its editorial matter—was naturally based on the Latin Vulgate.

THE KING JAMES, OR AUTHORIZED, VERSION, 1611. The incomplete success of the *Bishops' Bible* had made James I sympathetic to pleas from scholars—especially, perhaps, the Hebraist Hugh *Broughton—for a fresh translation; after its publication in 1611, printing of the *Bishops' Bible* was discontinued, and thus the King James version became—without any explicit declaration—the "Authorized" Version, i.e., that "appointed to be read in churches." The work of translation was done by a team of 54, in Westminster, Oxford, and Cambridge; the 47 identified translators including most of the best English Orientalists (although Broughton was himself too cantankerous to be included) and Greek scholars. By now there were much-improved tools of biblical scholarship in the shape of dictionaries and The Antwerp Polyglot Bible *(Biblia Regia)* of 1572, and the team included experts in the cognate Oriental languages, particularly Syriac and Arabic. In addition, the translators paid substantial attention to the Latin version of the Hebrew by the apostate Jew Immanuel *Tremellius (1579), who had settled in England and taught at Cambridge. The *Bishops' Bible* was the basis; that of Geneva contributed something in precision, and that of Rheims, some Latinizing vocabulary, although standard Anglican ecclesiastical terms were retained. Caution sometimes relegated the correct translation to the status of a marginal variant. Further editorial treatment—other than chapter summaries and headlines—was excluded *a priori.* By 1611, the diction and grammar were slightly archaic, and although the Geneva version was far from being superseded—Lancelot *Andrewes, himself one of King James' translators, continued to use it in his sermons—the Authorized Version ultimately achieved, and has retained, a preeminent and quasi-sacrosanct position within the English-speaking world. Of other unofficial English ventures in translation prior to the late 19th century none achieved widespread popularity save H. Ainsworth's Psalms (1612), introduced by the Pilgrim Fathers to America, and sundry metrical Psalters such as that of Tate and Brady (1696).

1611–1970. Subsequent nonofficial translations have been inspired partly by doctrinal and sectarian considerations (for Jewish enterprises), partly by a scholarly desire for improved accuracy, and partly by the motive of either "improving" the literary quality of the English (e.g., E. Harwood, New Testament, 1768) or colloquializing it (e.g., D. Mace, New Testament, 1729). A Revised Version of the Bible was published in Britain in 1881 (New Testament) and 1885 (Old Testament) in order to modernize the 17th-century language of the King James and to revise it in accordance with 19th-century scholarship. The American Standard Version, in cooperation with the Revised, appeared in 1901. Both translations soon proved of great importance to scholarship, but were not widely employed in worship. Recent endeavors are those of J. Moffatt (1913–24; revised 1935), E.J. Goodspeed (New Testament, 1923) and J. W. Powis Smith with others (Old Testament, 1927), and J. B. Phillips (New Testament, 1958). Modern official undertakings (i.e., those sponsored by the Anglican

Church, sometimes in association with Nonconformist bodies) have essayed to reconcile all three factors according to various priorities. Of Catholic versions, mention may be made of that (from the Vulgate) by Ronald A. Knox (1944–49). *The Bible in Basic English* (1941–49) with a vocabulary of only 1,000 words was produced by S. H. Hooke. The "Revised Standard Version" (1946–52) marks a new departure. For the first time a panel of translators from all the non-Catholic American Christian communities included also a professing Jew. Secondly, the Hebrew consonantal text, not always as masoretically vocalized, was taken as basic, and was corrected, not only in the light of the *Dead Sea Isaiah scroll and of the ancient versions, but also (in default of satisfactory versional restoration) by cautious emendation. In the U.S. New Catholic Bible, the so-called Confraternity Version (1949ff.), proper names are given in their Hebrew form, rather than the old Latinized spelling. Some 20th-century projects are the Anchor Bible (1964ff.) edited by D. N. Freedman and W. F. Albright; the English version of the French *Bible de Jérusalem* (A. James (ed.), *Jerusalem Bible*, 1966); and *The New English Bible*, sponsored jointly by the major non-Catholic churches of Great Britain. The New Testament appeared in 1961; the Old Testament (ed. G. R. Driver) in 1970. A novel feature is the association of a literary panel which scrutinized the scholars' proposed version, the aim being to produce a Bible in contemporary English that avoids both archaisms and transient neologisms. But the participating scholars (all Christians) were accorded ultimate freedom in matters of literary taste and theological dogma. The distinct, but parallel Revised Psalter, tentatively sponsored by the Church of England (1963), retains the style of Coverdale's translation (1535) and cautiously emends the Hebrew text "where manifestly corrupt," particularly in the light of the Septuagintal Greek.

ANGLO-JEWISH VERSIONS. From the early 18th century, progressive anglicization of Jewish settlers in England and America rendered first the Spanish, and ultimately the Yiddish, translations inadequate for educational needs. The King James Version became current in spite of the christianizing tendency of some of its "headlines" to the Prophets. The Pentateuch with *haftarot* published in London by David Levi (1787) appears to be the King James Version but without offending captions and with Jewish annotations. An earlier Pentateuch was produced by A. Alexander in 1785. In the U. S. Isaac *Leeser published a Pentateuch (5 vols., 1845) and subsequently a complete Old Testament in English (1853), which incorporated matter from the Mendelssohn school's German translation. C. G. *Montefiore's *Bible for Home Reading* was published in 1896. A. *Benisch issued a *Jewish School and Family Bible* (1851–61) and M. *Friedlaender's *Jewish Family Bible* (1881) used the Authorized Version. After the Revised Version of 1885 had appeared, the London Jewish Religious Education Board published (1896) a pamphlet listing essential emendations to make that version acceptable for Jewish use. These modifications were among the material utilized for the version published by the *Jewish Publication Society of America in 1917, which also took into account 19th-century Jewish Bible scholarship and rabbinical commentary (e.g., *Malbim); the edition—issued by a committee representative of both traditional and Reform Judaism—was basically the work of Max L. Margolis. The New Jewish Version, in the course of translation by an American Jewish team presided over by H. M. Orlinsky, while probably being more open than any earlier Jewish version to the findings of non-Jewish biblical scholarship, still remains tied to the masoretic text, even

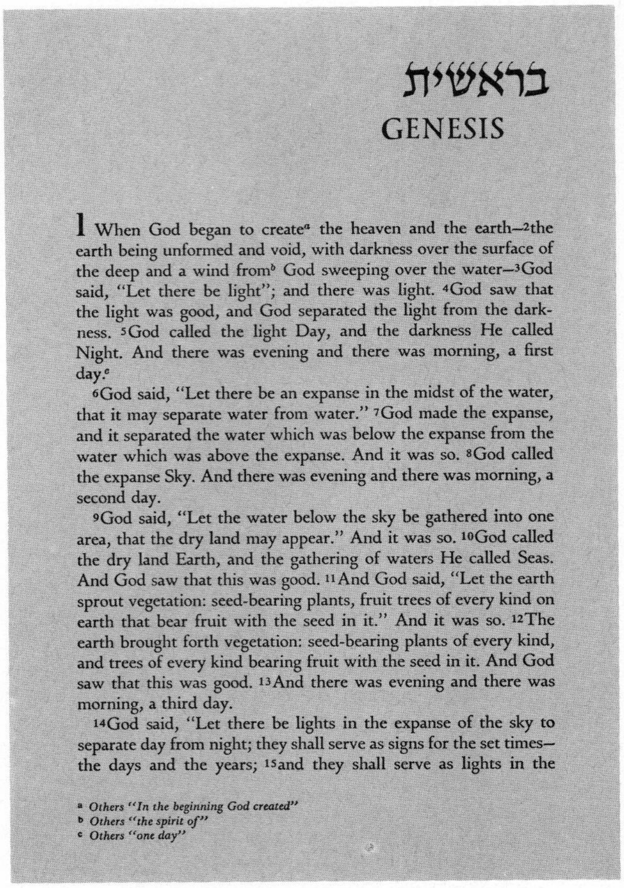
בראשית
GENESIS

1 When God began to create[a] the heaven and the earth—2the
earth being unformed and void, with darkness over the surface of
the deep and a wind from[b] God sweeping over the water—3God
said, "Let there be light"; and there was light. 4God saw that
the light was good, and God separated the light from the darkness. 5God called the light Day, and the darkness He called
Night. And there was evening and there was morning, a first
day.[c]
6God said, "Let there be an expanse in the midst of the water,
that it may separate water from water." 7God made the expanse,
and it separated the water which was below the expanse from the
water which was above the expanse. And it was so. 8God called
the expanse Sky. And there was evening and there was morning, a
second day.
9God said, "Let the water below the sky be gathered into one
area, that the dry land may appear." And it was so. 10God called
the dry land Earth, and the gathering of waters He called Seas.
And God saw that this was good. 11And God said, "Let the earth
sprout vegetation: seed-bearing plants, fruit trees of every kind on
earth that bear fruit with the seed in it." And it was so. 12The
earth brought forth vegetation: seed-bearing plants of every kind,
and trees of every kind bearing fruit with the seed in it. And God
saw that this was good. 13And there was evening and there was
morning, a third day.
14God said, "Let there be lights in the expanse of the sky to
separate day from night; they shall serve as signs for the set times—
the days and the years; 15and they shall serve as lights in the

[a] *Others "In the beginning God created"*
[b] *Others "the spirit of"*
[c] *Others "one day"*

First page of Genesis from *The Torah: The Five Books of Moses*, a new translation of the Bible published by the Jewish Publication Society of America in 1962.

though it incorporated on its margin emendations based on evidence gathered from ancient versions of Hebrew manuscripts. The Pentateuch, published in 1962, has consequently met with substantial criticism from Orthodox Jewish circles. Two modern Pentateuchs are the *Pentateuch and Haftorahs* edited by Chief Rabbi J. H. Hertz (1929–36), which first used the Revised Version and later the American Jewish translation, and I. Levi's Hirsch Pentateuch (1958–62), translated from the German. [RA.L.]

German. BEFORE LUTHER. Only a few verses (from Ezra and Nehemiah) are extant of the Old Testament portion of the Bible translation by the Gothic bishop Ulfilas (Gothic *Wulfila*; 311–383). According to old tradition, Ulfilas (who, according to the Byzantine church historian Socrates (d. c. 450), invented the Gothic alphabet for the purpose of his translation) wrote a complete version of the Bible, excluding only I and II Kings because of the warlike disposition of the Goths.

In fragments of an Old Saxon Genesis in alliterative verse, a parallel to the Teutonic paraphrase of the New Testament Gospels (the so-called *Heliand*, c. 830) has been found, although it was probably not written by the same author. The surviving fragments cover the biblical narrative from Adam to the destruction of Sodom.

Early in the 11th century, Notker Labeo, a monk of St. Gallen, translated the Psalms and the Song of Songs, as well as the Book of Job, which has been lost. Later in the same century, William of Ebersberg also wrote a commentary on Song of Songs (c. 1065) in Middle High German (critical edition, 1967). Subsequently many other partial translations of the Bible appeared, mainly versions of the Psalter.

Toward the end of the 14th century, a second German

Bible (restricted to the Old Testament), renowned for its improved style, made its appearance; the earliest manuscript copy of this translation, written by Martin Rother, was the so-called *Wenzel Bible* (Vienna, after 1389).

The first German Bible to appear in print was Johann Mentel's edition (Strasbourg, 1466), probably written about a century before. This translation, based on the Vulgate, was frequently revised and reprinted, inspiring 13 further pre-Lutheran editions. In 1477 the first Bible in Low German appeared in print. Johann Rellach of Resoem, who may have prepared the original of the 1466 edition, translated Joshua, Judges, and Ruth.

LUTHER AND THE PROTESTANT BIBLES. The classic German Bible is that of Martin *Luther, who transformed it into a German literary work. His translation, which created literary German and consolidated the Reformation, was the basis of all subsequent German versions and also of most other European translations. Luther's Bible, based on the Brescia Hebrew edition of 1495, continued the work of his pioneering New Testament (1522), with the Pentateuch, historical books, Hagiographa (1523–24), Prophets (1532), and Apocrypha (1534). His first complete Bible, *Biblia, das ist: die gantze Heilige Schrifft Deudsch* (6 vols., Wittenberg 1534), underwent 11 successive revisions during his lifetime. The last of these (1544–45) was reproduced at Halle in seven volumes (1845–55) and later reprinted in 1926–28. Over the years, Luther's Bible, which became the canonical version of the German Protestant church, also underwent linguistic revision. The so-called Lutheran Bibles that followed include the Uniform Bible *(Einheitsbibel)* of 1581, the Stader Bible of 1695, the so-called *Probebibel* (1883), and the revised editions of 1892 and 1912. Textual modifications affected not only the German style but also certain concepts that were clarified and explained in the light of later scientific research.

While Luther was engaged in his work, an Anabaptist translation of Prophets, by Ludwig Haetzer and Johann Denck, appeared at Worms in 1527. Until Luther's version reached completion there also appeared several, so-called, "Combined Bibles," in which those portions of the Bible which Luther had not yet completed were supplemented by other translations. The Zurich (Swiss-German) Bible (1527–29) of the Swiss Reformed Church largely preserved a suitable text reworked by Luther; the Prophets were translated by the "Zurich preachers"; and the Apocrypha were translated by Leo Jud, who also headed the project. This edition, repeatedly revised (1755–56, 1772, etc.), increasingly deviated from Luther's version. The so-called (Johannes) Piscator Bible (Herborn, 1602–03) was based on Latin translations and became the Berne Church Bible. Other Protestant editions were J. F. Haug's pietistic Berleburg Bible (8 vols., 1726–42), an adaptation of Luther's with reference to the Zurich text, and three others by J. Saubert (Helmstedt, 1665), Triller (Amsterdam, 1703), and Junckkerot (Offenbach, 1732).

From the 18th century onward, many other German Protestant Bibles made their appearance. Johann Lorenz Schmidt's so-called Wertheim Bible (1735), the first rationalist translation, again referred to the original Hebrew, as did J. D. *Michaelis' scholarly ecclesiastical edition (Goettingen, 7 vols., 1769–85). The translation produced by J. C. W. Augusti and W. M. L. de Wette (1809–14) was the first Bible to proceed from modern biblical investigation, but another translation by Bunsen (9 vols., 1858–70) was a more popular work. Later German Bibles include the edition of P. W. Schmidt and F. von Holtzendorff (1872); the sectarian Elberfeld Bible (1855); scholarly editions by Eduard Reuss (7 vols., 1892–94) and E. F. Kautzsch (1894; 1900; 1922–23[4]); and two popular works, F. E. Schlacter's *Die Heilige Schrift; Miniatur Bibel* (1905, 1952[20]) and Hermann Menge's Bible (1929; 1963). There are also scholarly translations in the exegetical works of W. Nowack, E. Sellin, and H. L. Strack and O. Zoeckler; and poetical versions by other scholars, such as H. Ewald's *Die Dichter des Alten Bundes* (2 vols., 1866–67), J. Wellhausen's *Die kleinen Propheten* (1893[2]), Duhm's *Die poetischen und prophetischen Buecher des Alten Testaments . . .* (4 vols., 1897–1910), and H. Gunkel's *Ausgewaehlte Psalmen* (1917[4]). Some leading German poets also turned their attention to the Old Testament, Goethe and Herder translating the Song of Songs (1778), and F. Rueckert attempting a metrical version of Isaiah 40–66 and the Minor Prophets (*Hebraeische Propheten,* 1831).

CATHOLIC BIBLES. The earliest complete German Catholic Bible was that of Johann Dietenberger (Mainz, 1534), which was partly modeled on the works of Luther and Leo Jud. The second was by Luther's opponent, Johann Eck (Ingolstadt, 1537), who followed the Vulgate. Caspar Ulenberg's edition (Cologne, 1630), based on Dietenberger and the Vulgate, long remained the standard Catholic text and was often revised, the subsequent translations of T. A. Erhard (1722), G. Cartier (1751), Rosalino (1781), Seibt (1781), I. Weitenauer (1777–81), and Fleischuetz (1778) also referring occasionally to the original Hebrew. Another Catholic Bible appeared anonymously at Vienna in 1794. Heinrich Braun's version (1788–1805) provided the basis for the widely distributed edition of J. F. von Allioli (1830–37), which was revised by Arndt and furnished with notes indicating textual divergences between the Vulgate and the original (1898–99). C. M. Brentano

Opening page of Genesis from the *Koberger Bible,* Nuremberg 1483. It depicts the creation of Eve. Free Library of Philadelphia.

made a translation from the original text (1797), and Jaeck, one from the Vulgate (1847), while Leander van Ess's Bible (1822; 1950–55) and that of V. Loch and W. Reischl (1851) enjoyed the success of Allioli's earlier translation. Modern Catholic editions include those of Nivard Schloegl (1920), which was the first critical edition under Catholic auspices. F. Feldmann and H. Herkenne (1923), J. Nikel (1911–33), P. Riessler (1924), and Pius Parsch (1952).

A work of special interest was the so-called *Biblia Pentapla* of 1710–12 (3 vols.), which compared the texts of Martin Luther, Caspar Ulenberg, and Johannes Piscator, the two remaining columns containing Joseph Witzenhausen's Judeo-German version and the Dutch *Statenbijbel* version. A parallel Bible of 1887–88 contained Luther's text together with a literal translation in modern German.

Jewish Bibles in German. The first Jew to translate the Bible into High German was Moses Mendelssohn, whose work was fiercely attacked by the rigidly Orthodox (notably Ezekiel Landau and Phinehas Horowitz of Frankfort) and repeatedly placed under a ban. Mendelssohn's closest collaborators were Solomon Dubno, Hartwig Wessely, Naphtali Herz Homberg, and Aaron Jaroslaw. The translation, printed in Hebrew characters, appeared under the title *Netivot ha-Shalom,* together with the original Hebrew and a commentary, designated *Be'ur (Biur).* Mendelssohn himself translated the Pentateuch (1783), Psalms (1785–91), Ecclesiastes (1770), and Song of Songs (1788; ed. J. Loewe and A. Wolfsohn), and he also prepared a version of the Song of Deborah. The project was completed by his collaborators and successors, the "Biurists." Translations of separate portions of the Bible were supplied by various scholars. A complete edition of the Minor Prophets, prepared by Moses Philippson (Arnswalde), Josef Wolf, Gotthold Salomon (S. Lipman), Israel Neumann, and Joel Loewe, appeared as *Minḥah Ḥadashah* (1805) and reappeared in Moses Israel Landau's edition of the complete Bible (1833–37). Aside from what Mendelssohn had himself prepared, the translation of the remaining biblical books was the work of M. J. Landau, Josef Weisse, Salomon Sachs, Wolf Mayer, Abraham Benisch, and Marcus Goldmann. Mendelssohn's Bible translation also appeared in German orthography (Genesis, 1780; Pentateuch, 1815). In contrast to Luther, who based his rendering of God's name, "der Herr," on the Greek *kyrios* of the Septuagint and the Latin *dominus* of the Vulgate, Mendelssohn wrote "der Ewige" ("The Eternal"), a term which was accepted by German-speaking Jews.

The next translator of the Bible was Josef Johlson, who furnished his text with scholarly notes (1831–36; only the first half was actually published). Separate biblical books were translated by A. A. Wolf, Phoebus Philippsohn. A. Bernstein (A. Rebenstein), S. H. Auerbach, L. Herzberg, L. H. Loewenstein, and Heymann Arnheim and Michael *Sachs (the combined work of the latter two was later retained in the Bible of Leopold Zunz). With the support of I. N. Mannheimer, Gotthold Salomon published *Deutsche Volks- und Schul-Bibel* (1837), the first complete German Bible under Jewish auspices. In his *Die vierundzwanzig Buecher der Heiligen Schrift* (2 vols., 1837; 1935[17]) L. Zunz only translated Chronicles, the remainder being the work of Arnheim, Julius Fuerst, and Sachs. Solomon *Herzheimer's edition (4 vols., 1841–48) was intended for Christians as well as Jews. Jacob Auerbach's *Kleine Schul- und Haus-Bibel* (1858) had a very wide distribution. *Die israelitische Bibel* (3 vols., 1839–54) of Ludwig Philippson was revised by W. Landau and S. I. Kaempf and illustrated with pictures by Doré; this had been preceded in 1865 by an Orthodox edition produced under the auspices of Isaac Dov (Seligman Baer) Bamberger, A. Adler, and M. Lehmann. Orthodox approval was also given to I. Cosman's Pentateuch (1847–52) and, above all, to Samson Raphael *Hirsch's translations of the Pentateuch (5 vols., 1867–78; 3 vols., 1956–58) and Psalms (1882; 1960), to which the latter's son, J. Hirsch, added a version of Isaiah (1911). Other editions were an *Illustrierte Pracht-Bibel* (1874) by J. Fuerst; a Pentateuch (1899, 1939[7]) by J. Wohlgemuth and I. Bleichrode; and a complete Bible (1902; 1929[5]) by Simon Bernfeld and H. Torczyner (4 vols., 1935–37).

Apart from the foregoing, there were also many German Jewish translations of individual books of the Bible, such as L. I. Mandelstamm and M. Kirschstein's edition of Genesis (3 vols., 1862–64). H. Graetz's version of Psalms (1881), and D. Z. Hoffmann's translation and commentary on Leviticus (2 vols., 1905–06) and Deuteronomy (2 vols., 1913–22). An isolated modern attempt to reproduce the Old Testament in German verse was that of M. A. Klausner's *Die Gedichte der Bibel* (1902). Two outstanding modern editions are Lazarus Goldschmidt's *Die heiligen Buecher des Alten Bundes* (the Pentateuch, historical books, and Prophets having appeared by 1923), which referred to rabbinic exegesis, and *Die Schrift und ihre Verdeutschung* (15 vols., 1926–37?) by Martin *Buber and Franz *Rosenzweig, which endeavored to do justice to the language and rhythm of the Hebrew text.

See also *German Literature. [Ed.]

Dutch. There were several medieval Dutch versions of biblical books, but the first Dutch Bible—the complete Bible except for the Psalms—dates from a Flemish work (c. 1300) and was a translation from the Vulgate (published Delft, 1477). A Dutch version of Psalms, produced by another translator, was frequently reprinted from 1480 onward. Later, there was a Dutch translation of Luther's Bible (Antwerp, 1526), and an Old Testament based on Luther and the Delft Bible appeared in 1525. Claes (Nicholas) van Winghe's Dutch Catholic Louvain Bible (1548) underwent many revisions and remained in use well into the 19th century. The Dutch Protestants—Reformed, Lutheran, and Mennonite—all pursued their own adaptations of the Bible, but the first editions based on the original Hebrew appeared only in 1614 and 1623. Early in the 17th century the Dutch States-General commissioned the famous *Statenbijbel* (Leyden, 1636–37), the text of which was later published in the German *Biblia Pentapla;* frequently revised, it remained in use until the mid-20th century. Three modern Dutch Bibles are the versions of A. van den Schuur and H. van Rhijn (2 vols., 1732); I. van Hamelsveld (1802–03), based on the original languages; and J. H. van den Palm (2 vols., 1818–19). A. *Kuenen's (with I. Hooykaas, W. H. Kosters, and H. Oort) "Leidsche Vertaling," translation and interpretation of the Bible, appeared in Leiden in 1899–1901. A Catholic Bible was published in 1936–37 by the Petrus Canisius Society and a Bible published by the new Katholieke Bijbelstichting St. Willibrord is in preparation (Psalms, 1963). An entirely new Protestant Old Testament was published in 1951 and Dutch Jews have translated selected Psalms (tr. by M. Levie, 1966) and most of the Old Testament (1826–38, etc.). A new translation of the Pentateuch by I. Dasberg was published in 1970.

See also *Dutch Literature. [Ed.]

Danish. Although Hans Tausen's Pentateuch (Magdeburg, 1535) is thought to have been only part of a complete Danish translation of the Bible, the earliest surviving complete edition—the so-called Christian III Bible (1550; 1950)—was a reworking by Christiern Pedersen of Luther's German Bible. Like its prototype, the latter was written in an extraordinary pithy style and had a significant impact on

A double page from the *Hispanic Society Bible,* showing the end of II Kings and the opening chapter of Isaiah. The shield at the bottom of the right hand page is the combined coat of arms of Leon, Castile and Aragon. Portugal, late 15th century. New York, Hispanic Society of America, ms. B.241, pages 288–289 ($11 \times 8\frac{3}{8}$ ins/28×22 cm.).

the Danish language. It was later revised as the Frederick II Bible (1588–89) and the Christian IV Bible (1632–33). Meanwhile, the need for a translation from the original languages had been recognized, and in 1607 professor (later bishop) H. P. Resen published an edition of the Bible that was linguistically distinct from its predecessors. Revised by the professor (later bishop) Hans Savning in 1647, this remained until modern times the "authorized" Danish version of the Bible. There were also innumerable translations of separate portions of the Bible; and various private biblical projects, two of which were a translation by C. A. H. Kalkar (1847), who was a Jew by birth, and a more significant version by the orientalist and theologian J. C. Lindberg (1837–54). The first Danish Bible to take cognizance of modern biblical criticism was that produced by Frants Buhl and his associates in 1910; this was in part the basis for a new translation, directed by Bishop Goetzsche, of which the Old Testament appeared in 1931. Another new version of the Old Testament in Danish appeared in 1931, and Catholic Bibles based on the Vulgate were published in 1893 and 1931. There have also been some Danish translations under Jewish auspices, notably the Pentateuch of Chief Rabbi A. A. *Wolf (1891), published with the Hebrew text. A new edition, revised by the Jewish education authorities and to which the *haftarot* were added, appeared in 1894. Chief Rabbi Friediger also published Esther with a Danish translation in 1924.

Norwegian. The pre-Reformation *Stjórn* of Iceland (see below) was the first biblical work current in Norway. Norway subsequently turned to Denmark for translations of the Bible, even after the political separation of the two countries in 1814. With minor modifications, Hans Savning's revised Danish Bible of 1647 was Norway's standard text during most of the 19th century (rev. 1819, 1830, and 1873). After many tests the Norwegian Bible Society's new *Riksmål* (Danish-Norwegian) translation made its appearance in 1891. The scholars collaborating in this project included the theologian and orientalist C. P. Caspari, who was of Jewish birth. Linguistically, this Norwegian Bible still remained close to literary Danish. A complete Protestant Bible in *Landsmål* (pure Norwegian) appeared in 1921 (revised in 1938). A Norwegian Catholic *Riksmål* Bible, based on the Vulgate, appeared in 1902 (revised in 1938).

Icelandic. Although there was no Icelandic translation of the Bible during the Middle Ages, the *Stjórn* ("Guidance") was, as a partial paraphrase of the historical books of the Old Testament, woven together with some later biblical books (republished 1956). Following the Reformation, Gudbrandur Thorláksson, bishop of Hólar, made a complete translation of the Bible (Holum, 1584). Like the Danish Bible of 1550 (Christian II Bible), this had marked literary power and mainly drew from Luther's translation. It was revised by a later bishop of Hólar, Torlak Skulasson, who referred to the Danish Christian IV edition of 1644. Bishop Steinn Jonsson's Icelandic version of H. P. Resen's Danish translation was so unsuccessful that the old edition of Skulasson had to be printed. Headed by the philologist S. Egilsson, an Icelandic commission later undertook a thorough revision of the Icelandic Bible (1841); the work was continued by Haraldur Nielsson in collaboration with other scholars (1912).

Swedish. There was no complete Swedish translation of the Bible during the Middle Ages, although individual biblical books were translated during the 14th and 15th centuries. However, after the Reformation, the Gustav Vasa Bible, directed by the archbishop Laurentius Petri, appeared in 1541 and was widely used for some time. A revised version, the Charles XII Bible (1702–03; 1961ff.), which was more closely modeled on Luther's translation, was Sweden's authorized "Church Bible" for a considerable time. A thorough revision of this work, the product of more than a century's research (1773–1878), never received official recognition. A new translation, produced by many scholars, including the philologist Tegnér, enjoyed greater success and, on its completion in 1917, received royal approbation. The outstanding private translation of the Bible was that of H. M. Melin. A Swedish Catholic translation of the Bible, based on the Vulgate, appeared in 1895.

Finnish. Because of the linguistic separation of Finland from the rest of Scandinavia, Finnish biblical translation has had an independent history. In 1551 Bishop Michael Agricola published a revised Lutheran version of Psalms, but it was not until 1642 (Stockholm) that a complete Finnish Bible, translated from the original texts, made its appearance. This has since undergone various revisions.

[D.J.Sl./Ed.]

Italian. The earliest Italian versions of the Bible, preserved in manuscript, mostly contain only a traditional text, which perhaps originated in northern Italy during the 13th century, but which was also conceivably derived from Waldensian heretical circles. The version gave rise to the two Italian editions of the Bible (based on the Vulgate), which were published in Venice in 1471. Antonio Brucioli's translation (Venice, 1532) labored under the suspicion of heresy (in fact it inspired the Geneva Protestant Bible of 1562). It was followed by the 1607 Geneva version of the Italian Protestant, Giovanni Diodati, based on the original texts; widely distributed, this version has periodically been republished. Archbishop Antonio Martini's authoritative Catholic translation (based on the Vulgate) first appeared in 1776–81. Translations of separate biblical books include editions by G. B. de Rossi and G. Ugdulena in the 19th century, and modern ones by S. Minocchi, di Soragna, G. Ricciotti, and F. Valente, as well as new versions of the complete Bible by the Waldensian Protestant, G. Luzzi (4 vols., 1921–30), and by the Pontifical Biblical Institute (1923–58).

During the 16th and 17th centuries, Jewish Bible translations in Italian were undertaken by David de Pomis, whose Ecclesiastes appeared in 1571 (Job and Psalms were never printed), and C. Rieti (Proverbs, Venice, 1617). Leone Modena also compiled a glossary of the Old Testament entitled *Galut Yehudah* (1612). Jewish translations of the 19th century include those of I. Reggio (Pentateuch, 1821), Lelio della Torre (Psalms, 1854), Samuel David Luzzatto (Job, 1853; Isaiah, 1855–67; Pentateuch, 5 vols., 1858–60), and David Castelli (Ecclesiastes, 1866; Song of Songs, 1892; Job, 1897). A complete Bible was produced by Luzzatto and his disciples in 1866–75 and revised in 1960.

See also *Italian Literature.

Spanish. Translations of the Bible into Spanish were undertaken in the 13th century, Jews and Christians collaborating in versions antedating 1250. Since the Old Testament translations were based on the original Hebrew rather than the Vulgate (and perhaps also because of the interreligious scholarly activities), Juan I of Aragon prohibited further Bible translations in 1233, suspecting them of heretical tendencies. However, the more tolerant Alfonso the Wise (Alfonso X of Castile and Leon) encouraged the translation of the Bible into Spanish, but only parts of this version have been preserved. Numerous Bible manuscripts dating from the 14th century onward are extant, and these Spanish versions—some based on the Vulgate, others on the original Hebrew—were the work of

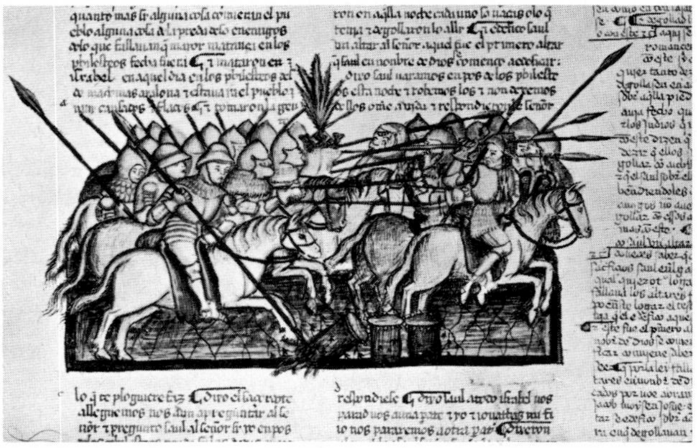

Jonathan, the son of Saul, fighting the Philistines. Detail from a page of the *Alba Bible,* a Spanish translation by the 15th-century Jewish scholar, Moses Arragel. Madrid, Duke of Alba Collection. Photo Oronoz.

Jews or Jewish apostates. The most important of these was the Alba Bible (1422–33), which Moses *Arragel produced at the command of Don Luis de Guzmán, grand master of the Order of Calatrava; an edition of this Bible appeared in Madrid in 1920–22. During the 16th–18th centuries, Spanish Catholic scholars only translated the Psalms, the biblical "Songs," and the Wisdom Books, although Fray Luis de León wrote a version of Song of Songs (c. 1561; printed, Madrid, 1798) based on the original Hebrew. Two Protestant translations of the complete Bible (based on the Hebrew text) were Cassiodoro de Reina's (Basle, 1567–69) and an edition by Cipriano de Valera (Amsterdam, 1602). Later Catholic Bibles by Felipe Scio de San Miguel (Valencia, 1790–93) and Felix Torres Amat (1823–25) appeared, as well as translations of separate biblical books by Garcia, Carvajal, and other scholars. The last great Jewish Bible project in Spanish, Abraham Usque's Ferrara edition of 1553, was based on Arragel's 15th-century version and is thought to have inspired translators in Christian Spain. Two modern Spanish Bibles have been produced by E. Nácar Fuster and A. D. Colunga (1944; 1959^{9}) and J. M. Bover and F. Cantera Burgos (2 vols., 1947).

Portuguese. The only notable early Portuguese translations of the Old Testament were the Protestant edition of João Ferreira d'Almeida (Batavia, 2 vols., 1748–53) and a Catholic Bible based on the Vulgate by Antonio Pereira de Figueiredo (Lisbon, 23 vols., 1778–90). A modern edition was published by M. Soares (1927–30), and new Brazilian Portuguese Bibles appeared by the Liga de Estudos Biblicos in 1955 and *Bíblia Ilustrada* is being published.

See also *Spanish and Portuguese Literature and *Ladino Literature.

Catalan. A Catalan Bible, probably based on a French prototype, was prepared in 1281–91 at the request of Alfonso III of Aragon, but this has not been preserved and perhaps remained unfinished. Various Catalan translations—Psalms (14th–15th centuries), part of Genesis (14th century), a complete Bible by Sabruguera (14th century), and other 15th-century Bibles—were made from the Vulgate using the French and Provençal versions. Sabruguera's Bible was revised by Jaime Borrell and by Bonifacio Ferrer (c. 1400), the printed edition of 1477–78 reproducing the work of the latter, which was destroyed by the Inquisition. During the 16th century, some biblical books were translated from the original Hebrew. In 1832 a complete Catalan Bible was made by the Protestant scholar J. M. Prat (published by the British and Foreign Bible Society). Various Catholic translations appeared in the 20th century, including those by Clascar (1915), the monks of Montserrat (1926), and the Catalan Biblical Foundation (1928–48). [U.C./Ed.]

French and Provençal. French. Although there were two early French (Anglo-Norman) versions of Psalms (c. 1100) and a 12th-century version of Samuel and Kings, the first to possess a complete and accurate translation of the Old Testament in spoken French—and to make regular use of this in teaching and worship—were the Jews. Religious scruples may have prevented the Jews from setting down their whole text in writing, but it did not preclude their compiling explanatory glossaries in the vernacular *(la'azim).* A few of those which have survived, in whole or part, contain fairly long Hebrew commentaries. The glossaries were an aid to teachers instructing children in the Bible according to the traditional word for word method; they also served as an aid to scholarly commentators *(poterim)* working at a higher level, who debated the meaning of a text and, relying upon the glossaries, proposed more subtly phrased translations. Lastly, these glossaries were used by translators officiating in the synagogue.

By contrast, the Church always looked askance at unsupervised reading of the Bible. Herman de Valenciennes' metrical version of the Bible (c. 1190) was followed in 1199 by Pope Innocent III's edict prohibiting any reference to the suspect French Bible. Although the Church declared its opposition to the translation of the Bible into any vernacular at the Council of Toulouse (1229), Louis IX commissioned a French version of the complete Bible (c. 1230), and in the 14th century it was revised by order of John II and Charles V. Nevertheless, the biblical text was submerged, during the later Middle Ages, under a mass of scholastic glosses and amplifications. The most famous medieval French version was the late 13th-century *Bible*

Page from the *Queen Mary Psalter,* England, 14th century, showing God renaming Abram, Abraham, and telling Sarah of the divine command. London, British Museum, Royal Mss. 2B VII, fol. 10v.

historiale of Guiard des Moulins, a paraphrase based on the scholastic compilation of Pierre Comestor. This Bible, much revised and often versified, was one of the earliest French printed books (1478). Only the Psalms inspired fairly accurate translations.

The first Bible translation of the 16th century, which returned to the original Latin—suppressing accumulated glosses and interpolations—was that of Jacques Lefèvre d'Etaples (1528). It was rightly suspected by Rome, Lefèvre's earlier Psalter (1509) having influenced Martin Luther. In its revised form (Louvain, 1550), Lefèvre's Bible ran to more than 200 editions. However, the Louvain Bible, too, contained borrowings from the first Protestant version by Pierre Rovert Olivétan (Neuchâtel, 1535; rev. 1724), which was based on the original Hebrew and Greek texts. Olivétan's version (known from its place of publication as the Serrières Bible) was the outcome of the religious fervor which the Bible had roused among the Waldenses. The Bible of Sebastian Castellio (Châteillon, d. 1555), the tolerant French humanist and theologian who opposed the severity of Calvin, appeared at Basle in 1555. This was written in a style uniquely designed to convey the original meaning of the Hebrew.

In the 17th century the Protestant translation of G. Diodati (Geneva, 1644) is known to have inspired more than one passage in the Jansenist Port-Royal version (Paris, 1672–95), which was mainly the work of Louis Isaac Le Maistre, known as de Sacy. Unfortunately, however, the *Bible de Sacy*, no less than the many versions subsequently based on it, was no more than a paraphrase, overburdened with notes and commentaries. Among the versions of individual biblical books produced at this time was J. B. Bossuet's French edition of Song of Songs (1695).

It was only during the second half of the 19th century that French lay scholars began to devote their attention to the Bible: Ernest Renan published editions of Job (1859), Song of Songs (1862), and Ecclesiastes (1882), and F. Lenormant produced a translation of Genesis (1883). The 19th-century Catholic Bibles of Genoude, J. J. B. Bourassé (illustrated by Doré), Jean Baptiste Glaire, and others possessed little elegance or accuracy and were eventually displaced by better versions: the *Bible de Maredsous* (1949), the J. T. Crampon Bible (1894–1904; 1960), and especially *La Sainte Bible de Jérusalem* (43 vols., 1948–52; in 1 vol., 1956). These modern Catholic translations nevertheless still remained hampered by notes and directions as to "what must be understood from the text."

Despite their wish to preserve textual accuracy, French Protestants were not content with Olivétan's ponderous style and accordingly produced various revisions, the most widely distributed of which were those of D. Martin (Amsterdam, 1707), and J. F. Ostervald (Amsterdam, 1747), and the French *Geneva Bible* (1802–05); perhaps the most successful was the version of Louis Segond and H. Oltramar (2 vols., 1874). French Protestants generally use the officially approved *Version synodale* (1910), although the *Bible du Centenaire* (by Société Biblique de Paris, 1916–47; 1950) is considered to be the finest text produced by the Reformed Church.

The 19th century also saw the appearance of critical Bible editions, notably that of E. Reuss (11 vols., 1874–81), whose substantial annotations display with unerring, though by now, dated erudition the whole historical and philological background of the biblical text. Two other critical editions are those of P. Giguet (1872), based on the Septuagint, and the more recent, penetrating, and lucid version of E. Dhorme (2 vols., 1956–59).

Modern French Jewish translations only appeared toward the end of the 18th century, and these were followed by the biblical passages and books (Psalms, Job, Five Scrolls) which Mardochée Venture included in his *siddur* (4 vols., Nice, 1772–83). In the 19th century, Samuel Cahen published *La Bible, traduction nouvelle* (7 vols., 1831–51), a remarkable achievement of its kind, in which he secured the collaboration of other modern Jewish commentators. Half a century later this was superseded by the French rabbinate's own clear translations of the Bible, produced under the supervision of Zadoc Kahn (*La Bible du rabbinat français*, 2 vols., 1899–1906; 1966). Though without "claims to great learning," this was faithful to the masoretic tradition and to rabbinic interpretation; combining the letter and the spirit of the Bible in a lucid and stirring style, it succeeded in "satisfying the reader who wishes for religious and moral inspiration from the Bible." Partial translations of the Bible under Jewish auspices include L. Wogue's rather constricted version of the Pentateuch (5 vols., 1860–69), and editions of Psalms by A. Ben-Baruch Créhange (1858), B. Mossé (1878), and André Chouraqui (1956).

See also *French Literature.

PROVENÇAL. In southern France the reformist movements of the Albigenses (Cathars) and Waldenses (Vaudois) promoted the translation of the Bible from the 12th century onward. This partly accounts for the hostile attitude toward vernacular Bibles displayed by the Church of Rome. Provençal versions of Psalms and of a portion of Genesis are known from the 14th century, and a translation of the historical books of the Bible was made from the French during the 15th century. As part of the Félibrige movement for the revival of Provençal culture from the mid-19th century onward, Frédéric Mistral produced an original translation of Genesis (1906). The Waldenses, who survived various persecutions to join French Protestantism, were active from the early 14th century as translators of the Bible. Their dialect versions cover Proverbs, Song of Songs, Ecclesiastes, and parts of Genesis and Job. It has been surmised that there were connections between the translators of the Provencal and Vaudois biblical books, and between them and the scholars who prepared the earliest texts in Italian.

Romansh (Raeto-Romance). The neo-Latin dialects known as Romansh, Friulian, Ladin(o), etc., once spoken widely in Austria, northern Italy, and Switzerland, gave rise to Bible translations from the 16th century onward. A complete Romansh Bible was prepared by Vulpi and Dorte (1617) and another by later scholars in 1719.

Rumanian. Among the earliest documents preserved in Rumanian are two manuscript versions of the Psalms: the *Psaltirea Scheiană* (1482) and the *Psaltirea Voronețeană* (1580). After the invention of printing, various editions of Psalms appeared. The first (1578, 1580) was produced by Coresi, a friar of Brasov; there subsequently appeared a translation in verse by the Moldavian metropolitan Dosoftei Uniev (1673) and a prose version by the metropolitan Antim Ivireanu (1694). Translations of the Psalter multiplied during the 18th century. The Prophets (1673) were soon followed by the first complete Rumanian Bible, *Biblia lui Şerban* (Bucharest, 1688; revised, 1795), which was based on the Septuagint. This version of the Bible had a decisive impact on the Rumanian language and greatly influenced later translations of the Bible. Other Rumanian Bibles include those by Samuil Micu (1795), Ion Eliade Rădulescu (1858), and the outstanding modern Orthodox edition by Gala *Galaction and Vasile Radu (1938). The *Palia (Paloea)*, a Rumanian version of Genesis and Exodus containing much legendary material, appeared in 1882. A 20th-century Rumanian Protestant Bible, printed in both Cyrillic and Latin characters, was published by the British and Foreign Bible Society. Two modern Rumanian editions of the Pentateuch intended for Jewish readers were those of A. Gold (1902) and Moscovic.

See also *Rumanian Literature. [Ed.]

Hungarian. In the 15th century the Hussite movement assailed the Latinity of the Church. Behind the heresy lay, among other social aims, the wish to make the Bible available to the masses, so that people might know the world of the Bible even in the oppressive reality of feudalism, and so become acquainted with the admonitions of the biblical prophets. The oldest Hungarian Hussite Bible translations are preserved in the late 15th-century Vienna codex (Ruth, Esther, Minor Prophets) and the Apor Codex (Psalms). The Codex of Dobrente contains the translations of the Song of Songs and Job (1508). The first Catholic Pentateuch survives in the Jordanszky Codex (1516–19). The Hungarian reformers translated the Bible in the spirit of Erasmus and also emphasized its social message. Unlike the Catholics, who adhered to the Vulgate, Protestant scholars referred to the Hebrew text of the Old Testament. Gáspár Heltai and four Protestant colleagues translated the entire Bible, but several books of the Hagiographa did not appear in this edition (Kolozsvar, 1552–65). The first complete, and most readable, Bible translation was that of Gáspár Károlyi, a Calvinist preacher (Vizsoly, 1590); revised by Albert Szenczi Molnár (1608), it became the official text of the Hungarian Protestant Church and was the basis of a modern (London) Bible Society version.

The Reformation enhanced the ecclesiastical importance of the Psalms, most translations of which were, however, merely paraphrases. Christian terminology and political references were inserted into the text, to the detriment of the original. The first renderings were those of Sztáray (1575), a more poetical version being that of Balint Balassa (1554–94). Accumulated accretions were eliminated by Miklós Bogáti Fazekas, a Unitarian preacher, in his unpublished versified translation of Psalms (1587). Protestant translations of Samuel, Kings, and Job were produced by Peter Melius Juhász in 1565–67.

The Bible translations of the 15th and 16th centuries were stimulated by social motives, while in the 17th century religious concern proved to be the creative force. The greatest accomplishment of Hungarian Protestantism at the time was the *Psalterium Ungaricum* of A. Molnár (Hanau, 1608). This was the first complete Hungarian translation of the Psalms in verse, running to more than 100 editions and it is still extant. It endured because of the beauty of its style and because of its faithfulness to the original text. Simon Péchi, the most renowned member of the Hungarian *Szombatos* (Sabbatarian) sect, who had a good command of the Hebrew language, interpreted the biblical text and his translation adhered strictly to the original (1624–29). The first complete Hungarian Catholic Bible was published by the Jesuit György Káldi (Vienna, 1626). Toward the end of the 17th century a new Protestant Bible translation was prepared by György Csipkés of Komorn (often called György Komáromi, 1675; published Leiden, 1719), who was widely known for his Hebrew sermons.

In time Károlyi's Bible was reworked and his text improved, while Samuel Kámory produced a new version of the Bible for Hungarian Protestants (1870). Poets began to be interested in the Psalms from an aesthetic point of view, the translations of Benedek Virág and Ferenc Versegi having a classical mood in antique verse form. More significant translations of Psalms were those by Károly Kálmán (1883), Sándor Sik (1923), and Béla Teleki (1929). Two versions of the Song of Songs were those of Károly Kerényi, which was based on the Latin text (1941), and István Bernáth (1962).

Although Mór Bloch (Ballagi) produced a Pentateuch in 1840, there was for a long time no demand for a Hungarian Jewish Bible, since the Jews of Hungary used Yiddish and German. The first complete Bible translation under Jewish auspices was that of the Jewish Hungarian Literary Society (IMIT), published in 1898–1907 (in 4 vols.), with Vilmos Becher, József Bánóczi, and Samuel Krauss as editors. Earlier partial translations were József Mannheim's Psalms (1865); H. Deutsch's Pentateuch and *haftarot* (1888); Mór Stern's Psalms (1888); Ignác Füredi's Joshua and Judges (1893); and the Füredi-Stern Pentateuch (1894–95). Bernát Frenkel edited and published the "Holy Scriptures for Family and School" (1924–26) and the IMIT began publishing a Bible for the young, which remained incomplete, only the first and second volumes being printed (1925). During the years 1939–42 the IMIT published a Hungarian version of the Pentateuch edited by Britain's chief rabbi, J. H. Hertz; this was the work of Michael Guttmann, Simon Hevesi, Samuel Loewinger, and others.

Hungarian Jewish prose versions of the Psalms began with Mór Rosenthal's translation (1841); later there were versified translations by József Kiss, Immanuel Loew, Emil Makai, and Arnold Kiss. The translations of Attila Gerö (1894) and Endre Neményi (1917) both displayed an original approach. Other versions of individual biblical books include Immanuel Loew's Song of Songs (1885) and Simon Hevesi's versified Lamentations (1916).

See also *Hungarian Literature.

Slavonic. Church Slavonic. The oldest Slavonic version of the Bible is that of the missionary monks Cyril and Methodius (ninth century C.E.). Cyril, who first acquired a knowledge of Hebrew on a journey to the *Khazar kingdom, borrowed some Hebrew characters for the Slavic alphabet which he invented (see *Bulgarian Literature), and it is thus reasonable to suppose that he was familiar with the original Hebrew text of the Old Testament. It was probably toward the middle of the ninth century that the entire Book of Psalms and liturgical extracts from other biblical books (mainly the Pentateuch, Job, and the Prophets) were translated into Old Moravian, almost certainly with the assistance of Cyril. Presumably these Scriptural portions were first rendered into the Old Moravian tongue and only then into Old Bulgarian (Church Slavonic). According to some accounts, the work of Cyril (d. 869) was completed by his brother, Methodius (d. 885). Although neither the text nor the language of these translations has survived, it may be assumed that they were written in Moravian-Bulgarian. The historical influence and dissemination of the so-called Cyril-Methodius translation among the Slavic peoples passed from the Moravians to the Bulgarians, Serbs, and Poles, and then to the Russians. The Old Bulgarian biblical and liturgical texts reached the Russian Slavs in the second half of the ninth century C.E.—the era of Christianity's spread to the Kiev region. A manuscript Bible in Church Slavonic, dated 1499 and named after Archbishop Gennadi of Novgorod, is extant; revised editions of this translation appeared in 1581, 1663, and 1751.

Czech and Slovak. The earliest known translations of isolated biblical books into Czech probably date from the 13th century, but it was only in the 15th century, under the impact of the Hussite movement, that the entire Bible was first translated into Czech. John Huss revised and modernized earlier Czech versions at the beginning of the 15th century. The first Czech printed edition (1475) was based on the Vulgate. An impressive Czech version of the Scriptures, based on the original Hebrew and Greek texts, was Jan Blahoslav's *Kralice Bible* (1579–93). Another classic Czech translation was the Catholic Bible edited by Durich and Prochaska at the request of Empress Maria Theresa (1778). Other Czech versions include the Jesuit *Wenceslas Bible* (1677–1715) and that of Sýkora, which was revised by Hejčl and, in 1947, by Col and Josef Heger (1925–48), the latter noted for its stylistic distinction. The first complete Slovak Bible by J. Palkovič (1829–32) was followed by other Catholic versions based on the Vulgate. J. Rohaček's complete Protestant Bible (1926) was also a Slovak translation.

POLISH. Until the 13th century, Polish translations of the Bible were, it is believed, written in Polish Cyrillic rather than Latin orthography. By the end of the 13th century the earliest Polish versions in Latin script made their appearance: the so-called Queen Margaret Psalter and the Bible of Queen Sophia (also known as the Szaros Patak Bible). These texts were written in rather clumsy Polish and based on Czech prototypes. Two early Polish biblical translations were the 14th-century Florian Psalter (published 1834; critical edition by W. Nehring, 1883) and the 15th-century Puławy Psalter (published 1880). With the onset of the Reformation in Poland during the 16th century, various printed editions made their appearance: some Psalters, the first complete Bible in Polish, known as the Cracow Bible (or the Leopolita Bible) of Jan Leopolita (1561), the so-called Radziwill or Brésć Bible of the Polish Calvinists (1563), and S. Budny's Unitarian Nieśwież Bible (1572). Budny's was perhaps the most famous of these. They were followed by the classic Catholic edition of J. Wujek (Cracow, 1599), which was also used by Protestants and has been compared with the King James (Authorized Version) Bible in English. Wujek's edition greatly influenced the development of Polish as a literary language. Another Protestant translation was the Gdansk Bible (Danzig, 1639, reprinted in 1944). The Old Testament had a notable impact on many Polish writers from the 16th century onward. Jan Kochanowski's verse rendering of the Psalms (Cracow, before 1578) inspired a later version by Maciej Rybiński (1605) and paraphrases by Mikołaj Sęp-Szarzyński (*Rytmy*, 1601) and other authors. Two 20th-century versions were the Poznan Bible (1926–32) and the new Cracow Bible (1935; ed. by S. Styś and J. Rostworowski); in 1965 a new edition of the Scriptures was in preparation (to be called the Tyniec Bible). Jewish translations of the Old Testament include those of J. Cylkow (1883–1914); F. Aszkenazy (1927–30); J. Mieses (1931); and S. Spitzer (1937). A modern version of Psalms was written by the émigré poet Janusz Artur Ihnatowicz.

See also *Polish Literature.

SERBIAN AND CROATIAN; WENDISH. Until 1847 the literary language of the Serbs was Old Slavonic, and Church Slavonic remained dominant in the Serbian Orthodox Church. The earliest complete translation of the Old Testament was produced by the reformer Primož Trubar in Slovenia during the late 16th century; a Croatian Lutheran edition appeared in Tuebingen (1563), and two 19th-century versions were prepared by Matia Petar Katančić in Croatia (1831) and by G. Daničić in Serbia (1865; revised, 1932, 1933). A modern Serbian Bible was that of Petar Vlasić (1923–25).

The oldest Protestant translation of part of the Old Testament into the South Lusatian dialect of the Wends (a declining Slav people isolated in eastern Germany) was an edition of Psalms by Pastor Wille (Guben, 1753); a complete Bible was published by Johann Gottlieb Fritz (Cottbus, 1796). There were earlier translations into the North Lusatian Wendish dialect: Psalms by Paul Pretorius, and later Proverbs, Ecclesiastes, Song of Songs, and Daniel by Christian Leonhardi Georg Dumisch (Loebau, 1719). A complete Bible by Johann Lange, Matthaeus Jockisch, and Johann Boehmer (Bautzen, 1727–28) was prefaced by an introduction in German. The Catholic Wends have no printed versions of the Bible apart from an edition of Psalms translated from the Hebrew by Johann Lara (1872).

See also *Yugoslav Literature.

BULGARIAN. Translations of the Bible that have been preserved among the Bulgarians are almost exclusively written in Old Church Slavonic. The revival of the old Bulgarian literary and ecclesiastical tradition had its origin in 16th-century Russia. Two modern Bulgarian Bibles are those of P. R. Slaveykov (Constantinople, 1860–64) and of the Orthodox synod (1925).

RUSSIAN AND UKRAINIAN. During the early pre-Mongol period of the Church Slavonic Bible in Russia (before 1240), there was, according to the hypothesis of Golubinski, a whole complex of Old and New Testament writings that were adopted by the Bulgarians. However, only fragments of these have been preserved, mainly the Psalms. On the other hand, a host of biblical texts from the post-Mongol period (15th century onward) has survived. The so-called Judaizing sects of the 15th century gave the strongest impetus to the codifications of the Bible. Adherents of the sects in Novgorod were in possession of a complete Russian Bible, and this moved the archbishop Gennadi to compare the texts of the Greek Orthodox Bible (Septuagint) with those of the Judaizers (see also above on Church Slavonic). With the exception of Esther, all the missing biblical books were translated from the Vulgate. Esther and Psalms were once thought to have been translated from the original Hebrew by the convert Fyodor (Theodore) the Jew, but this has been disputed by Harkavy. Gennadi's great achievement was to produce, for the first time in the annals of Church Slavonic literature, a complete and unified text of the Bible unconnected with the liturgy of the Orthodox church. The 16th-century Bible of the Moscow metropolitan Makari reverted to the former liturgical orientation and order of the biblical books. The first printed Psalter in Russian appeared in 1564–68. The first complete Ukrainian Bible, commissioned by Prince Constantine of Ostrog (1581), followed the text of Gennadi. The first Moscow edition of the Russian Bible (1663) was a more elegant version of the Ostrog text. Soon after this, an attempt was made by Avraami Firsov in his Psalter (1683) to translate the Scriptures into lively Russian. In 1714 Peter the Great commissioned a Church Slavonic Bible, whose text was compared with the Septuagint; this revision (the Czarina Elizabeth Bible) appeared in 1751 and was edited by Valaam Lyaschevski. Here the Old Testament was based on the Septuagint and those biblical books which had earlier appeared only in a translation based on the Vulgate were also translated from the Greek text.

Bible translations of the first half of the 19th century are linked with the activity of the Russian Bible Society. This development was impeded by the political reaction which marked the last years of the reign of Alexander I and the entire reign of Nicholas I. Translations of several biblical books from the original Hebrew, undertaken by the first Russian Hebraist Pavski in the mid-19th century, were placed under a ban. However, the Moscow metropolitan Philaret managed to obtain the Russian Orthodox synod's authorization for a Russian version of the Scriptures in 1860. From 1868 onward a complete translation of the Bible was undertaken by Daniel A. Chwolson; later collaborators in the project included Gulyayev and Bashanov. By virtue of its accuracy and style, this so-called Synodal Bible (1875) is the best available in the Russian language. Canonical books were translated from Hebrew; non-canonical portions, from the Greek and Latin.

Ukrainian Bible translations were first attempted in the late Middle Ages, the earliest printed edition being that published at Ostrog in 1581. An Ukrainian version of Psalms appeared at Vilna in 1526, and complete Bibles were printed at Pochayev (1798) and Przemysl (1859), both of these being based on the Russian Czarina Elizabeth Bible of 1751. A 20th-century version was that of P. Kulish, I. S. Levytski, and J. Puluj (1903); another Orthodox Bible was by Metropolitan (John Ohienko) Ilarion (1962); and a third was the Catholic Bible of Ivan Khomenko (1963). All were translated from the original Hebrew and Greek texts. A Russian Protestant Bible, printed in London in 1875, was first banned in Russia, but a reprint prepared there was later permitted. A new illustrated Russian Old Testament, the first of its kind since the 1917 Revolution, was issued in 100,000 copies by the Soviet State Publishing House in 1967.

Among Jewish scholars various attempts were made from the 1860s onward to produce Russian translations of the Bible. Leon Mandelstamm published a Pentateuch in Berlin (1862), the second edition (1872) being accompanied by his version of Psalms. Pumpyasnski also issued a translation of Psalms (1872), which was followed by Proverbs in 1891. Meanwhile, the Society for the Enlightenment of the Jews in Russia had published a new version of the Pentateuch (1875), which was prepared by J. Herstein with the assistance of the Hebrew poet J. L. Gordon. Another version of the Pentateuch, that of Joshua Steinberg, appeared under the Society's auspices in 1899, and in 1906 Steinberg published translations of Joshua, Judges, and Isaiah.

See also *Russian Literature.

Arabic. Catholic and Protestant Arabic Bibles were, until the second part of the 19th century, based on the 1671 edition of the (Vatican) Congregation of Propagation of the Faith when three new versions appeared. The American Protestant missionaries in Beirut published in 1864 a translation in modern Arabic, which was started by Eli Smith and finished by C.V.A. van Dyck, with the help of Arab scholars, especially Sheik Nasif el-Yāzijī. This version was reprinted in 1869 and became known as the Oxford Arabic Bible. The Dominicans of Mosul published a four volume Bible based on C.J. David's version (1874–78). About the same time (1876–80) the Jesuits in Beirut published a translation in classical Arabic, in three volumes. The Arabic Bibles in circulation among Christians are based on those versions.

Other Languages. Complete Bibles and portions of the Old Testament have also been translated into hundreds of other languages in recent centuries; versions in many of the more remote languages and dialects were the work of Protestant missionary groups, particularly the British and Foreign Bible Society, during the 19th and 20th centuries. Maltese Bible translations include M. A. Camillari's edition of Psalms based on the Hebrew text (1845), R. Taylor's Psalms and Song of Songs (1846), C. Cortis' Ruth (1924), and P. P. Saydon's complete Maltese Bible, *Il-Kotba Mkaddsa bil-Malti* (1929–59). The earliest modern Greek translations of the Old Testament, consisting of the Pentateuch and other biblical books, were probably the work of an unknown Jewish scholar of the 14th century. There were also two early versions of Jonah in *Judeo-Greek. Two early Judeo-Greek works printed at Constantinople were a translation that appeared in the Polyglot Pentateuch (1547) and Job (1576) by Rabbi Moses b. Elias Pobian. A Greek Christian version of Psalms, based on the Septuagint, was published in 1543. The first complete Bible in modern Greek was the Protestant edition of 1840, and an entirely new version was in preparation in Athens during the 1960s, but this was denied general distribution owing to the hostile policy of the Greek government. A Protestant Basque Bible (1859–65), based on the Vulgate was published in London, and Catholic Lithuanian Bibles appeared in 1922 and 1936.

Celtic versions of the Scriptures were first attempted in the Middle Ages, the earliest being a partial translation in Welsh (1346). The English Reformation gave a considerable impetus to Celtic Bible translation. The first complete Welsh Bible was produced by William Morgan and others in 1588 (revised 1620 by R. Parry and J. Davis), and this remained in use with only slight modifications well into the 20th century. An interdenominational Welsh Bible project was begun in 1926 and again after World War II. The first complete Irish (Erse) Bible, based on the English Authorized Version, was produced by Bishop William Bedell and others (1685), and inspired the Scots Gaelic edition of 1783–1801. A new Irish Protestant Bible appeared in 1817. An Irish Catholic Pentateuch, based on the Vulgate, was published in 1861 together with an annotated English text. Two Breton Bibles of the 19th century were Le Gonidec's Catholic edition of 1866 and G. Le Coat's Protestant version of 1889.

The more exotic translations include versions of the Scriptures in Chinese, Japanese, and American Indian dialects. There have been pioneering Bible translations in Sanskrit (1822), Chinese (1823), and Burmese (1834), as well as many translations into the dialects of India. The first Japanese Protestant Bible appeared in the late 19th century (1887), a Catholic version being published only in 1959. A widely distributed Japanese Protestant edition, the work of Japanese scholars, was published in 1955, and the first complete Catholic Bible, in 1964. In North America, John Eliot produced the earliest Amerindian Bible for the Massachusetts Indians in 1663, and by 1830 parts of the Bible had been translated and printed in the Creek and Cherokee languages of the "Five Civilized Tribes," using the alphabet devised by the Cherokee chief Sequoyah. [Ed.]

Bibliography: JUDEO-PERSIAN: A. Kohut, *Kritische Beleuchtung der persischen Pentateuch uebersetzung des Jacob ben Joseph Tawus* (1871); E. Nestle, in: *Realencyklopaedie fuer protestantische theologie und Kirche*, 3 (1897), 124–5. JUDEO-ROMANCE LANGUAGES: S. Berger, *La Bible Française au Moyen-Age* (1884); D. S. Blondheim, *Les parlers judéo-romans et la Vetus Latina* (1925); M. L. Margolis, *The Story of Bible Translations* (1917). YIDDISH: W. Staerk and A. Leitzmann, *Die juedisch-deutschen Bibeluebersetzungen von den Anfaengen bis zum Ausgang des 18 Jahrhunderts* (1923). ENGLISH: B. F. Westcott, *A General View of the History of the English Bible*, ed. by W. A. Wright (1905[3]); F. F. Bruce, *The English Bible: A History of Translations* (1961); S. L. Greenslade (ed.), *The Cambridge History of the Bible: The West from the Reformation to the Present Day* (1963); C. C. Butterworth, *The Literary Lineage of the King James Bible, 1340–1611* (1941); International Council of Religious Education, *An Introduction to the Revised Standard Version of the Old Testament* (1952); E. H. Robertson, *The New Translations of the Bible* (1959); R. Loewe, in: HUCA, 28 (1957), 205–52; M. T. Hills (ed.), *The English Bible in America . . . 1777–1957* (1961); A. S. Herbert (ed.), *Historical Catalogue of Printed Editions of the English Bible, 1525–1961* (1968); H. Pope, *English Versions of the Bible* (1952); D. Daiches, *The King James Version of the English Bible* (1941); H. M. Orlinsky (ed.), *Notes on the New Translation of the Torah* (1969). GERMAN: E. Nestle, in: *Realencyklopaedie fuer protestantische Theologie und Kirche*, 3 (1897), 59–84; W. Streitholz, *Die gotische Bibel* (1919); W. Walther, *Die deutschen Bibeluebersetzungen des Mittelalters*, 3 vols. (1889–92); F. Rosenzweig, *Die Schrift und Luther* (1935); S. L. Greenslade (ed.), *The Cambridge History of the Bible* (1963), 94–109, 339–47; E. P. Arbez, in: CBQ, 16 (1954), 343–7; A. Risch, *Die deutsche Bibel in ihrer geschichtlichen Entwickelung* (1907); W. Weintraub, *Targumei ha-Torah la-Lashon ha-Germanit* (1967). DUTCH: J. van Kasteren, in: DBI, 4 (1912), 1549–57; S. L. Greenslade (ed.), *The Cambridge History of the Bible: The West from the Reforma-*

tion to the Present Day (1963); E. P. Arbez, in: CBQ, 16 (1954), 201–9; E. Nestle, in: *Realencyklopaedie fuer protestantische Theologie und Kirche,* 3 (1897), 119–24. SCANDINAVIAN: C. J. Brandt, *Udsigt over vore danske bibeloversaettelsers historie* (1889); H. Nielsson, in: *Festskrift . . . Buhl* (1925); S. L. Greenslade (ed.), *The Cambridge History of the Bible: The West from the Reformation to the Present Day* (1963), 135–40, 355–8, 541. ITALIAN: S. Minocchi, in: DBI, 3 (1912), 1012–38; A. Vaccari, in: *Enciclopedia Italiana,* 6 (1930–38), 899–903. SPANISH: S. Berger, *Les Bibles castillanes* (1899); F. Pérez, *La Biblia en España,* ed. by B. Orchard (1956), 83–97; J. Llamas (ed.), *Biblia medieval romanceada judío-cristiana* (1950–55); S. L. Greenslade (ed.), *The Cambridge History of the Bible: The West from the Reformation to the Present Day* (1963), 125–9; 540–1. PORTUGUESE: A. Ribeiro dos Santos, in: *Memória da Litteratura Portugueza,* 7 (1806), 23–57; J. Pereira, in: DBI, 5 (1912), 562–5; G. L. Santos Ferreira, *A Bíblia em Portugal: Apontamentos para uma monographia, 1495–1850* (1906); H. Wendt, *Die portugiesische Bibeluebersetzung: Ihre Geschichte und ihre Aufgaben mit besonderer Beruecksichtigung des A. T.* (1962). CATALAN: P. Bohigas, in: *Saggi e ricerche in memoria di Ettore Li Gotti* (1962); L. Arnaldich, *Los estudios bíblicos en España desde el año 1900 al añ 1955* (1957). HUNGARIAN: T. Kardos, *A huszita biblia keletkezése* (1952); M. Ballagi, *Tanulmányok a magyar bibliafordítások körül* (1865); A. Boros, *Zsoltárfordítás a kódexek korában* (1908); E. Császár, *A magyar protestáns zsoltárköltészet a XVII és XVIII században* (1902); L. Blau, in: *Magyar Zsidó Szemle* (1910); F. Balogh, in: *Realencyklopaedie fuer protestantische Theologie und Kirche,* 3 (1897), 115–8. POLISH: E. Dabrowski (ed.), *Prodreczna encyklopedia biblijna,* 2 (1959); L. Stefaniak, in: *New Testament Studies,* 5 (1958–59), 328–38. RUSSIAN: M. Spinka, in: JR, 13 (1933), 415–32; A. Osroff, in: *Bible Translator,* 7 (1956), 56–65, 98–101; J. Schweigl, in: *Biblica,* 18 (1937), 51–73; J. Schmid (ed.), *Moderne Bibeluebersetzungen* (1960). MODERN ARABIC: T. H. Darlow and H. F. Moule, *Historical Catalogue of the Printed Editions of Holy Scripture,* 2 (1911), 62–84; G. Graf, *Geschichte der christlichen arabischen Literatur,* 1 (1944), 85–297.

EXEGESIS AND STUDY

TALMUDIC LITERATURE

The voluminous body of talmudic literature—the *Oral Law—is essentially a compilation of hermeneutic, interpretative, and analytic exegesis of the Bible—the Written Law. According to rabbinic tradition, Moses not only received the Oral Law on Mount Sinai, but also the definitive explanation of the meaning buried in the Torah's compact and cryptic literary style. "Moses received the Torah from Sinai and transmitted it to Joshua" (Avot 1:1), providing the material on which generations of exegetes worked, creating the vast store of talmudic literature. According to the talmudic tradition, *Ezra, upon his arrival in Palestine, founded the institution of the *scribe *(sofer),* whose contribution to the teaching and understanding of the Bible has been fundamental. "These early scholars were called *soferim* [which can mean "scribes" or "reckoners"]" the Talmud relates, "because they used to count all the letters in the Torah" (Kid. 30a). In order to certify a biblical text as traditionally correct, the *soferim* first counted the letters to ascertain omissions or additions. The scribal appellation has been associated with certain facets of talmudic interpretative work (see above, The History of the Biblical Text).

The scribes continued their work until the end of the period of the Great Assembly. The **tannaim,* who emerged toward the end of the scribal era (second century B.C.E.), together with the *amoraim* (third–sixth centuries C.E.), devoted their efforts to teaching their disciples the true meaning of Scripture. They practiced their exegetical methods on such subjects as theology, ethics, lexicography, homiletics, and religious and civil law. The body of their work is incorporated in the Talmud corpus, comprising the Mishnah, *Gemara,* Tosefta, and *baraita.* An important repository of exegetical work is the midrashic literature, which is made up of a number of collections reflecting different approaches to the task of transmitting the essence of the biblical text; one approach is the halakhic, which produced a collection of Midrashim in order to explain the legalistic (ritual and tort) portions of the Bible and the manner in which the commandments were to be fulfilled. Notable among the collection of halakhic Midrashim are the **Mekhilta,* **Sifrei,* and **Sifra.* Collections exemplifying the aggadic approach, or use of parable and anecdote to explain the text, include, among others, **Genesis Rabbah* and **Ecclesiastes Rabbah.* **Pesikta* and **Tanḥuma* are collections of Midrashim representing the homiletical approach. Based on the Sabbath Torah reading, homilies are arranged according to the text of the weekly portion. Methodologically, a complex system of exegesis was employed. It consisted of a diversified analysis of the text by one or all of the elements of **pardes,* an acronym representing the following: *peshat,* literal translation; *remez,* implied meaning; **derash,* homiletic comprehension; and *sod,* mystical, allegorical meaning. *Peshat* and *derash* are the more popular methods of exegesis, since they are comprehensible to most, while *remez* and *sod* represent the esoteric, mystical, and kabbalistic approaches. These latter exegetical methods were at times considered dangerous for use by the unscholarly man, who might arrive at misinterpretations and risk heresy. *Peshat* is an objective method of obtaining the literal meaning of a passage by analysis of the language, whereas *derash* is a subjective method which attempts to make the text applicable to the time of the exegete. The sages believed that the Oral Law accompanied the receipt of the Written Law, and that it renews itself in each era, i.e., the interpretation of the Oral Law, which is a continuous process, reformulates the Bible's eternal verities, giving them continuing applicability.

*Shemaiah and Avtalyon were among the earliest expositors of the law. Their disciple, *Hillel, formulated the seven *hermeneutical precepts by which exegesis could be accomplished. These precepts were subsequently expanded by R. *Ishmael into 13 principles, and finally by R. *Eliezer into 32 rules. Two great schools of midrashic interpretation emerged, those of R. Ishmael and R. *Akiva. R. Ishmael's approach was didactic and literal, because he believed that the Torah is written in the language of ordinary usage, and, therefore, holds no hidden meanings. R. Akiva, however, analyzed each word (see above, The History of the Biblical Text). These two schools produced the material collected in *Mekhilta, Sifrei,* and *Sifra.* At times, the lines between the respective schools were not clear because disciples were not above enlisting other methods, perhaps more suitable for a particular topic.

Bibliography: Zunz, Vortraege; M. Soloweitschik and Z. Rubashov, *Toledot Bikkoret ha-Mikra* (1925); H. L. Strack, *Introduction to the Talmud and Midrash* (1945); H. Zernowitsch, *Toledot ha-Halakhah,* 4 (1950); M. Z. Segal, *Parshanut ha-Mikra* (1952[2]); Waxman, Literature, 1 (1960[2]), 45–138; B. M. Casper, *An Introduction to Jewish Bible Commentary* (1960).

[AB.Z.]

MEDIEVAL RABBINIC COMMENTARIES

From the period of the *geonim* until the age of the Haskalah (about 1,000 years), Bible exegesis constituted one of the main themes of Jewish literature, not only in books especially devoted to biblical exegesis, but also in those dealing with philosophy or linguistic research, which often included interpretations of biblical verses. Generally speaking, two broad approaches to biblical exegesis are discernible—the literal and the homiletical. In the former the commentator bases himself on the plain meaning of the text and on the context, and the interpretation is objective.

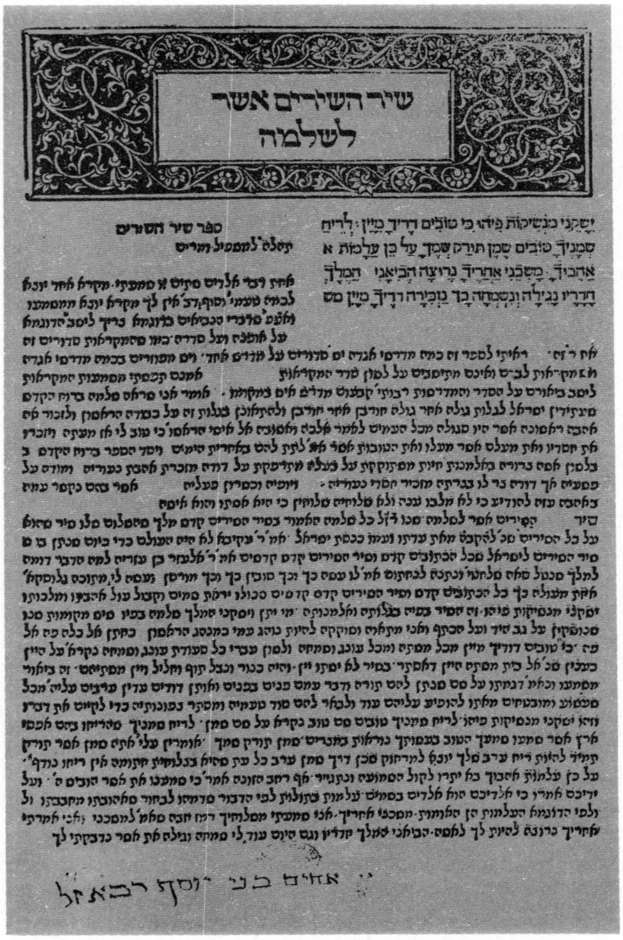

First page of the Song of Songs with Rashi's commentary, printed in Naples, 1487. Jerusalem, J.N.U.L.

In the homiletic approach the commentator strives to interweave his ideas with the text even if the simple meaning of the language and the context are at variance with his interpretation, and his interpretation is subjective. Homiletic commentary developed because of various cultural requirements and because of the necessity of finding a correspondence between scriptural views and the prevailing opinion in different ages.

A considerable portion of the exegesis of the geonic period consisted of assembling and editing material, much of which had accumulated through traditions handed down over the generations. Included in this material were midrashic collections and the masorah. The task of the masorah scholars, particularly in establishing vocalization and cantillation, was of the utmost importance, providing as they did the most valuable interpretation of the Bible. Vocalization and cantillation insured correct reading of the biblical text and were established, as a rule, in accordance with the *peshat,* the literal meaning. The greatest commentators such as *Rashi, Abraham *ibn Ezra, and others, based their interpretations on the masorah.

In additon to this work of collation new and original works were created in the geonic period, opening up fresh paths in the field of exegesis and powerfully influencing succeeding generations. Two historic events led to this development: the expansion of Islam and the rise of *Karaism. The efflorescence of learning and science among the Muslims influenced the Jews living among them to participate in philosophic enquiry and linguistic research. Along with the decline of Aramaic as the vernacular came a decline in the use of Aramaic translations of the Bible. The intensification of the Karaite-Rabbanite controversy over readings and interpretations of biblical texts also contributed to this development. The Karaites produced a number of commentators, among them *Anan, the founder of Karaism, who in his interpretations frequently applied the hermeneutic methods of the tannaitic Midrashim, and Benjamin *Nahawāndī, who made use of allegorical explanations. The Rabbanites were thus compelled to intensify their biblical research and to seek new methods of exegesis.

The Work of Saadiah Gaon and Its Influence. The new era was ushered in by *Saadiah Gaon, a considerable portion of whose extensive literary work is connected with Bible commentary. Saadiah endeavored to prove the impossibility of explaining the Scriptures without the masorah and to show that the Midrashim and *halakhot* of the rabbinic sages were based on the literal meaning of scriptural texts. In this context, Saadiah's Arabic translation of the Bible and his commentaries are noteworthy. The translation is actually a paraphrase of the text. His commentaries, particularly those on the Pentateuch, include a wealth of material: explanation of the text, linguistic and philosophic research, and polemics, directed primarily against the Karaites. He even composed a special work against the extreme and heretical views of *Ḥiwī al-Balkhī on biblical subjects.

As a result of Saadiah's biblical studies, Bible commentary emerged from the sphere of homiletics to embark upon the pursuit of direct and close exposition of the biblical text. In his linguistic and philosophic approach Saadiah provided directives for scholars who came after him. That influence is particularly noticeable in *Samuel b. Hophni and his son-in-law *Hai. Samuel b. Hophni, an unusually prolific writer, engaged extensively in Bible commentary. In addition to translating the Scriptures into Arabic, he applied himself to philosophic inquiry. His attempts to explain miracles as natural phenomena were attacked by Hai.

In Spain. A significant flowering of Bible commentary took place in Spain, which had its basis in the researches of *Menahem b. Jacob ibn Saruq, his critic *Dunash b. Labrat, and Menahem's pupil, *Judah b. Ḥayyuj (tenth century). Although their works are mainly concerned with grammatical and linguistic considerations, they are interspersed with numerous elucidations of verses and individual words in Scripture. The novelty of their approach lies in its philological orientation.

Particularly important are the investigations of *Jonah ibn Janāḥ (Abu al-Walīd) in *Sefer ha-Rikmah* and *Sefer ha-Shorashim.* In illustrating and elucidating his philological and grammatical rules, he cites many biblical passages, explaining them in a profound and original manner. He is unfettered in his inquiry, at times ignoring the masoretic text, and, in some instances, even transposing and emending biblical texts. Though his deviation from the masorah provoked much opposition, his influence on later commentators was very great.

Ongoing progress in Hebrew linguistics produced the philological commentary, two of whose famous exponents were Moses ha-Kohen *Jikatilla and Judah ibn Balʿam (11th century). The former is characterized by his freedom and originality, interpreting, for example, the predictions of the prophets as applying strictly to their own times and not to the Messianic era. Judah ibn Balʿam opposed his approach, writing in a far more conservative spirit. In a class by itself stands the Bible research of Moses *ibn Ezra. Though his book *Shirat Yisrael* was expressly written as a guide to the composition of poetry, his analysis of the various literary forms—"The Twenty Portals of Poetic Embellishment"—is rich in biblical references. Ibn Ezra's investigations bear the strong impress of Arabic poetry and of the scholarship in that area. Belonging to a completely different class of commentary, which was also greatly influenced by Arab culture, is philosophical commentary (see below).

Literal Commentary. Of a quite different nature is the literal commentary, fostered by Rashi and his disciples, which flourished in northern France, and which is relatively free of outside influence. The Jews of France, though occasionally engaging in discussion with Christians on the interpretation of biblical passages, had only limited cultural relations with their neighbors, whose standards in this area in any event were quite low. Thus, their commentaries do not contain such philosophical or philological elements as abound in the commentaries of the Spanish school. The commentary of this school is characterized by the search after the plain meaning, although a certain conflict is discernible between the inclination toward homiletical exegesis and the conscious effort to explain biblical passages according to their plain meaning.

The interpretations of *Menahem b. Ḥelbo contain much homiletics. Rashi, too, introduced many ancient rabbinic Midrashim, but only in addition to the plain meaning, frequently remarking that they were not to be taken as representing the literal meaning of the passage. Rashi often reiterates as his aim the explanation of the text according to its plain meaning or according to the closest aggadic interpretation. This tendency becomes even more marked with Rashi's successors Joseph *Kara, *Samuel b. Meir, *Eliezer of Beaugency and Joseph *Bekhor Shor. It is somewhat surprising that this phenomenon should exist particularly in northern France. Samuel b. Meir and Joseph Bekhor Shor, for example, who are outstanding exponents of literal commentary, are also among the foremost tosafists, and their method with regard to their biblical exegesis is in contrast to that adapted by them in their talmudic exposition. In some instances they even assigned to a biblical text a meaning at variance with the *halakhah*, despite the fact that the *halakhah* was unquestioningly accepted by them, their serene spirit and unswerving faith ruling out any feeling of strain or conflict. A contributing factor to the growth of literal exposition may have been the need felt to counter christological interpretations of certain biblical passages, although these commentators—and particularly Rashi—had a definite influence on some of the Christian biblical exegetes.

Synthetic Commentary. Certain commentators embody all the above methods of interpretation. The main representatives of this synthetic approach are: Abraham ibn Ezra, David *Kimḥi and Naḥmanides. Their commentaries include philological, philosophical, literal, homiletical and, in the case of Naḥmanides, even kabbalistic elements.

While Ibn Ezra bases his commentary principally on the philologic method, contributing much to linguistic research, he also introduces many philosophical explanations. In dealing with halakhic material, he accepts the rabbinic **Midrash Halakhah*, but opposes *Midrash Aggadah* when it is in conflict with the plain meaning of Scripture. He argues that homiletical explanations should not always be taken literally, there being even in *halakhah* instances of derivations which are only formally associated with a biblical verse.

Joseph *Kimḥi was active in Narbonne at the same time, and was followed by his sons, Moses and David. The latter's work constitutes a kind of melting pot for the various methods of commentary. From Spain he borrowed the topical, philological, and philosophical commentary, and from Franco-Germany the literal and homiletic methods. He very frequently quotes Midrashim, but gives the literal interpretations with it. He has little recourse to philosophic commentary, resorting to it only when he sees a special need to do so.

An important turning point is reached with the introduction by Naḥmanides of Kabbalah into his Bible commentary. Naḥmanides' approach, too, is eclectic, a blend of the Franco-German school with that of Spain, but the emphasis is less on philological commentary than on a penetrating investigation of the context. Though he discusses the problems raised by philosophers, he does not regard the rational aspect as paramount, and in many places attacks the Aristotelian approach. On occasion, along with other interpretations which he considers acceptable, Naḥmanides quotes from the "Secret Discipline," the Kabbalah, but he employs it sparingly. It is included as an adjunct only, mostly by way of mere allusion and intended solely for those with a knowledge of Kabbalah.

Later Commentary. Philosophic commentary enjoyed a resurgence despite Naḥmanides' opposition, especially in the 14th century. This trend was continued, with certain limitations, by Isaac *Abrabanel in 15th-century Spain. Though he resorts to philosophic explanations, he is at the same time often opposed to the rational approach to Bible commentary. He does not touch on philological questions in his interpretations, confining himself to the conceptual problems arising from Scripture.

In the 16th and 17th centuries occupation with biblical exposition diminished. Two commentators, however, who stand out in this period are David and Hillel *Altschuler, who wrote literal commentaries on the Prophets and the Hagiographa. Their commentaries, *Meẓudat David* and *Meẓudat Ẓiyyon*, attained wide circulation, though they were for the most part gleanings from the works of others (see also *Malbim). Gradually, under the influence of the *pilpul* which characterized Torah study in Poland, there was

פירוש התורה שחבר
רבי אברהם בן עזרא
בשם האל הגדול והנורא אחל לפרש פי' התורה

First page of the commentary on the Pentateuch by Abraham b. Meir ibn Ezra, printed by Joseph b. Jacob Ashkenazi of Gunzenhausen, Naples, 1488. Jerusalem, J.N.U.L.

introduced into biblical commentaries the method of "novellae and ingenious interpretations." A fundamental change in biblical exegesis took place in the Haskalah period. It is characterized by the great influence of Christian Bible commentary on Jewish exposition and, in the wake of this, the expansion of Bible criticism. These are discussed below.

Bibliography: W. Bacher, *Die Bibelexegese der juedischen Religionsphilosophen des Mittelalters vor Maimuni* (1892); idem, *Die juedische Bibelexegese vom Anfang des zehnten bis zum Ende des fuenfzehnten Jahrhunderts* (1892); S. Poznański, *Mavo al Ḥakhmei Ẓarefat Mefareshei ha-Mikra,* in: *Perush al Yeḥezkel U-Terei-Asar le-Rabbi Eliezer mi-Belganẓi* (1913); D. Yellin, *Toledot Hitpatteḥut ha-Dikduk ha-Ivri* (1945); M. Z. Segal, *Parshanut ha-Mikra* (1952); M. Zucker, *Al Tirgum R. Sa'adyah ha-Ga'on la-Torah* (1959); B. Smalley, *The Study of the Bible in the Middle Ages* (1964), H. Malter, *Saadia Gaon* (Eng., 1921), L. Nemoy (ed.), *Karaite Anthology* (1952), H. Hailperin, *Rashi and the Christian Scholars* (1963). [Av.G.]

ALLEGORICAL INTERPRETATIONS

Allegorical interpretation of Scripture is concerned with the "inner" or "spiritual" meaning of the biblical text. Used consistently in the writings of Philo, the Church Fathers, the medieval Jewish philosophers, and the kabbalists down to the ḥasidic teachers, this method does not necessarily discard the literal meaning *(peshat),* but tends to prize the allegorical one more highly. While the Bible itself makes occasional use of allegory, the allegorists claim the right to treat the Bible as a whole or certain of its parts, as a series of allegorical expressions.

(1) Rabbinic *aggadah* and Midrash employed the allegorical method in an uninhibited homiletic rather than in a systematic manner. Their guiding motive was not, as that of the allegorists, a concern for the true, inner meaning of the text, but a pious endeavor to find "everything" (Avot 5:22), in Scripture, to make every biblical passage or word (Sanh. 34a) yield as many "meanings" *(te'amim)* as necessary. Thus while the *aggadah* and Midrash contain many instances of allegorism (*mashal* or *dugma*), these fail to exhibit, as I. Heinemann has shown, any pattern of consistency. The only exceptions are the allegorical interpretations of Proverbs 31:10–31 (the "woman of valor" being understood as the Torah) and of the Song of Songs. But even in the interpretation of the Song of Songs at least three different allegorical themes are apparent: the love between God and Israel; the exodus; interpretations of Jewish laws. Ezekiel's vision of the resurrected dry bones (ch. 37) and the figure of Job are described as allegories (BB 15a; Sanh. 92b), but no detailed allegorical interpretation of these texts is provided. Nor was Proverbs, in spite of its suggestive title *(mishlei),* expounded allegorically, except for a few passages (including 31:10ff.) and terms (e.g., "father," God; "mother," Israel). Systematic, philosophical allegory was absent in rabbinic literature because no philosophical system presented a real challenge to the literal meaning of Scripture.

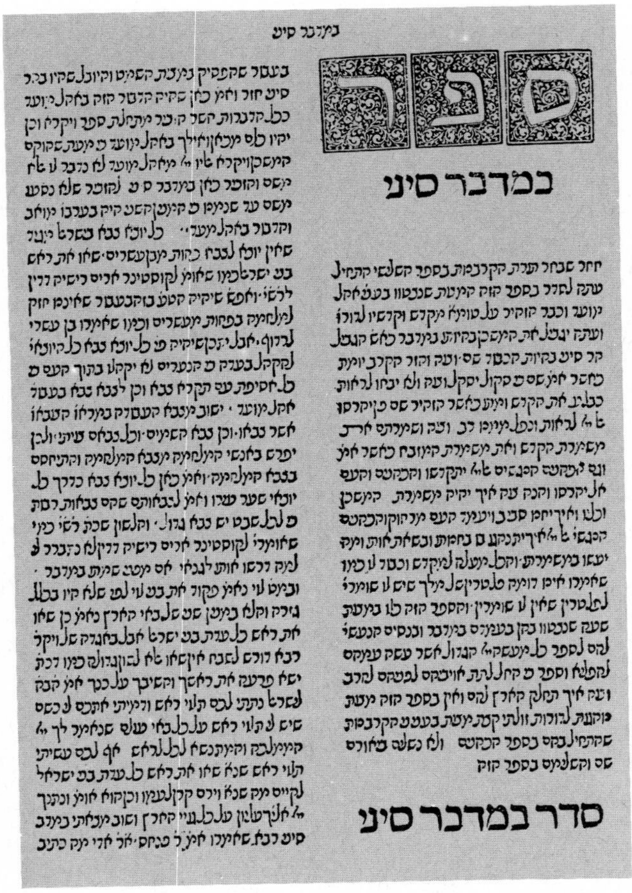
ספר

במדבר סיני

סדר במדבר סיני

Page from a Bible with Targum Jonathan and the commentaries of David Kimḥi (Radak) and Levi b. Gershom (Ralbag), printed in Leiria, Portugal, 1494. Jerusalem, J.N.U.L.

(2) The situation, however, differed radically among Hellenistic Jews, many of whom felt the need to prove that the teachings of the Bible are consonant with Greek wisdom. Here the allegorical method, which had been used by the Stoic philosophers to interpret the old Greek myths, provided a means of harmonization. It appears, however, that at first Hellenistic Jewish writers were reluctant to use allegory. The Greek version of the Bible, the Septuagint (see above), shows hardly any traces of it. *Aristobulus of Paneas, who is considered an allegorist (see Eusebius, *Praeparatio Evangelica,* 8:10, 2), does distinguish between "mythical" expressions in the Bible and their allegorical sense, i.e., their "physical" or cosmological meaning. However, he only offers metaphorical interpretations of anthropomorphic descriptions of God. The Letter of *Aristeas, on the other hand, emphasizes the symbolic meaning of Jewish law and ritual, and does so for apologetic reasons. Similarly, the *Wisdom of Solomon uses allegorical interpretations: the garments of the high priest, for instance, are said to represent an image of the entire cosmos (18:19). The sect of the *Therapeutae is likewise described by Philo (Cont. 78) as employing the allegorical exposition of Scripture. Nevertheless, it is only in Philo himself that the method comes into its own. According to *Philo, the true significance of Scripture lies in the "underlying meaning" (*hyponoia,* also termed *allegoria*), which is "obscure to the many" and comprehensible only to "the few who study soul characteristics rather than bodily forms." According to H. A. Wolfson, "everything in Scripture, from names, dates, and numbers to the narration of historical events or the prescription of rules for conduct, is to Philo subject to allegorical interpretation" (*Philo,* 1 (1947), 116). Yet this does not mean that the historicity of the Bible or, for that matter, its legal validity is dissolved; its literal meaning is upheld. Thus, the three men who appeared to Abraham (Gen. 18), while representing metaphysical symbols, are still to be regarded as real beings; and, the laws of the Pentateuch, no matter how spiritual in significance, are still to be observed. In fact, Philo denounced those allegorists who regarded practical observances as superfluous (Migr. 93). His main concern, however, was to impress the authority of the Bible upon Jews and Gentiles by showing that its symbolic language concealed profound metaphysical and psychological truths; and that its laws were meant to guide the soul toward the contemplation of God by

freeing it from material attachments. His allegorism bears all the marks of a deeply personal spiritual religion.

(3) In the medieval period allegorism in its proper sense, as distinct from the mere employment of metaphorical interpretation, was applied by Jewish neoplatonic and Aristotelian philosophers and kabbalists. By contrast, the Jewish theologians following the methods of Islamic *Kalām, did not engage in allegorism, but were content to treat biblical anthropomorphism as metaphors *(taʾwīl)*. *Saadiah Gaon laid down the philosophic position on the propriety as well as the limitations of metaphorical interpretation *(taʾwīl)* and it was later acknowledged by Abraham *ibn Daūd and *Maimonides. According to Saadiah, the literal meaning of a biblical text is to be discarded in favor of *taʾwīl* in four instances only: if it is contradicted by sense perception, by reason, by some other explicit text, or by rabbinic tradition qualifying its apparent meaning. He argued that if license were given for metaphorical interpretation in other than these four instances, all the commandments of the Torah and all the miraculous events narrated in Scripture might be explained as mere metaphors (*Book of Beliefs and Opinions,* 7). Saadiah upholds the literal meaning of passages presumably referring to the resurrection of the dead, but insists on the metaphorical sense of the anthropomorphic descriptions of God. His use of the *taʾwīl* method is sufficiently restricted to prevent allegorism on any significant scale.

(4) Under the impact of neoplatonic and Aristotelian philosophy the situation changed fundamentally. Having expanded the meaning of *taʾwīl* to include the philosophic interpretation of doctrinal matters, the Islamic neoplatonic and Aristotelian philosophers distinguished between the "inner" *(bāṭin)* and "apparent" *(ẓāhir)* meaning of certain words and teachings of the Koran, treating the "apparent" meaning as an allegory replete with philosophic truth. Concurrent with this distinction it was often held that the philosophical truths contained in the allegory should be kept secret from the multitude. Following this tradition Moses *Maimonides insists that the true meaning of certain biblical passages, such as Ezekiel's vision of the Chariot, and chapters in Proverbs, etc., lies in the philosophical truths which they express in allegorical fashion and which should not be revealed to the philosophically untrained. Applying the simile of Proverbs 25:11 ("A word fitly spoken is like apples of gold in settings of silver"), he said that "the inner meaning bears the same relation to the apparent one as gold to silver" (*Guide,* introd.). Here allegory proper comes into its own. The "inner" meaning is considered superior to the "apparent" one since it alone establishes "the truth in all its reality" *(ibid.)*. Philosophic truth, as far as it is demonstrable, is thus made the arbiter of biblical exegesis. Maimonides was less radical when he interpreted anthropomorphic or spatial terms applied to God as either homonyms or metaphors. Maimonides cites the rabbinic phrase, "The Torah speaks in the language of men" (BM 31b), in the sense that Scripture speaks of God in terms appropriate to the mental capacity of the multitude (*Guide* 1:26). This phrase had already been applied in this sense by earlier exegetes and theologians such as *Judah ibn Quraysh, *Jacob b. Nissim, *Baḥya ibn Paquda, *Judah Halevi and others. The question of the legitimacy of the allegorical method had been raised by Abraham *ibn Ezra, who rejected the search for hidden meanings *(sodot; ḥidot)* in passages whose plain meaning did not conflict with reason or sense perception. He also asserted that the apparent and the inner meaning should be allowed to coexist, like body and soul (Commentary on the Torah, introd., method no. 3).

The issue of the merits or demerits of allegorism became

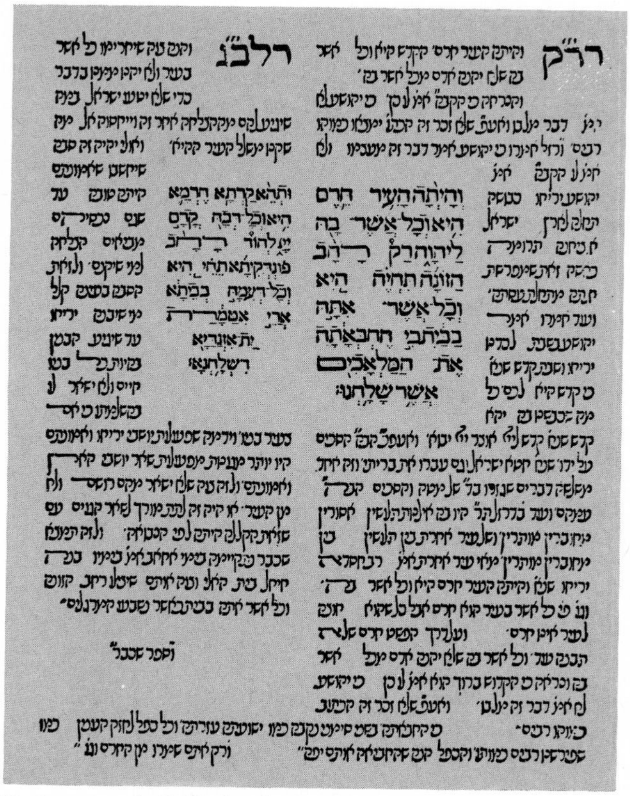

First page of *Ḥiddushei ha-Torah,* the commentary on the Pentateuch by Naḥmanides (Ramban), Lisbon, 1489. This was the first book to be printed in the Portuguese capital. Jerusalem, J.N.U.L.

pronounced at the close of the 13th century and was keenly contested in the polemical literature of the second *Maimonidean controversy. While Maimonides declared as allegorical all biblical passages (1) announcing a change in the laws of nature (in the messianic age), (2) dealing with the resurrection of the dead, and (3) foretelling the ultimate destruction of the world, he warned (as reported by Joseph ibn *Aknin) against allegorizing biblical laws. Maimonides interprets Ezekiel's vision of the Chariot as an allegory of metaphysical doctrines conforming to his neoplatonic brand of Aristotelianism, but he saw no compelling reason to allegorize the biblical account of the createdness of the world, maintaining that Aristotle's view of the eternity of the world had not been demonstrated. Other instances of allegorism in Maimonides are: the ladder in Jacob's dream means the ascent of prophetic knowledge; the adulterous wife in Proverbs 7 is an allegory of matter; the Song of Songs is an allegory of man's love for God. Some of Maimonides' successors went beyond the limitations he had imposed upon himself. Following the more radical allegorism of *Averroes, Isaac *Albalag interpreted the biblical account of the creation in the sense of eternal creation. *Levi b. Gershom, taking his cue from Maimonides' cryptic remarks in the *Guide* 2:30, saw in the story of Paradise an allegory of the human soul, its faculties and its rise to felicity. Jacob *Anatoli and *Levi b. Abraham of Villefranche (author of *Livyat Ḥen*) were frequently denounced as radical allegorists. There is, however, little evidence in their works to justify this accusation. The animosity toward allegorism shown by the traditionalists (e.g., Solomon b. Abraham *Adret) stemmed chiefly from their observation that the philosophical interpretation of Scripture tended to weaken practical religious observance. *Jacob b. Reuben, author of *Milḥamot ha-Shem* (12th century), had already polemicized against those who "twist the verses of Scripture by the allegorical method" *(be-derekh* *dimyon u-mashal)* and thereby "bring themselves into disrepute" (*le-mashal ve-li-sheninah;* ed. J. Rosenthal (1963), 37). The more orthodox type of Jewish philosophy, aroused by the dangers of Averroism, on the one hand, and the rising power of Kabbalah, on the other, did not discard allegorical interpretation but made it subservient to dogmatic beliefs, strongly emphasizing the validity of the literal meaning side by side with the allegorical. Joseph *Albo (*Sefer ha-Ikkarim,* 3:21) pointed out that the Torah was called "testimony" *(edut),* and as such should be taken as literally as would be a witness in court. Hence, its narratives and laws must not be negated through allegorism, notwithstanding the right to see in them symbols of something higher and more precious than the literal sense. Philosophizing preachers like Joshua *ibn Shuʿayb, Joseph b. Shem Tov *ibn Shem Tov and his son Shem Tov, Isaac *Arama and others were eager to plumb the deeper meaning of Scripture and rabbinic *aggadah,* laying particular stress on the themes of creation and providence. Their sermons are an interesting blend of homiletics *(derash)* and allegory *(mashal; sod).* Some of them exhibit strong traces of Kabbalistic influence. *Baḥya b. Asher's commentary on the Torah exemplifies the trend to make use of philosophic and kabbalistic interpretations alike. It offers interpretations (1) by the literal method; (2) by the homiletical method; (3) by the method of reason *(sekhel),* i.e., the philosophical method; and (4) by the method of Kabbalah. Allegorism, then, in its strict sense is here two-faced, rational and mystical.

Bibliography: W. Bacher, *Die Bibelexegese der juedischen Religionsphilosophen des Mittelalters vor Maimuni* (1892), 8–14; idem, *Die Bibelexege Moses Maimunis* (1897), 8–22; I. Goldziher, *Die Richtungen der islamischen Koranauslegung* (1920); J. Guttmann, in: MGWJ, 80 (1936), 180–4; I. Heinemann, in: *Bericht des juedisch-theologischen Seminars, Breslau* (1935); idem, in: *Mnemosyne,* 5 (1952), 130–8; idem, in: HUCA, 23 pt. 1 (1950–51), 611–43; W. Jaeger, *Early Christianity and Greek Paideia* (1961), 46–68, 127–36; D. Kaufmann, in: *Jahresbericht der Landes-Rabbinerschule in Budapest* (1899), 63–79; H. Lewy (ed.), *Philosophical Writings of Philo* (1946), 12–16; A. Schmiedl, *Studien ueber juedische, insonders juedisch-arabische Religionsphilosophie* (1869), 215–36; L. Strauss, *Philosophie und Gesetz* (1935), 68–86; G. Vajda, *L'amour de Dieu dans la théologie juive du moyen âge* (1957), index, s.v. *Cantique des Cantiques,* and review by A. Altmann in: KS, 34 (1958/59), 53–54; idem, in: *Sefarad,* 10 (1950), 25–71; H. A. Wolfson, *Philo,* 1 (1947), 115–38; A. S. Halkin, in: PAAJR, 34 (1966), 65–76; idem, in: A. Altmann (ed.), *Jewish Medieval and Renaissance Studies* (1967), 165–84; I. Husik, in: JAOS, 1 (1935), Supplement, 22–40; L. Ginzburg, *On Jewish Law and Lore* (1955), 127–50; B. Smalley, *The Study of the Bible in the Middle Ages* (1952).

[A.ALT.]

EXEGESIS AMONG JEWS IN THE MODERN PERIOD

Jewish biblical exegesis in the period of the Enlightenment must be understood mainly against the background of the period itself. The main concern of the Enlightenment among Western European Jewry was the enlightenment and education of the Jews—and the Bible served as a means for achieving this goal. Moses *Mendelssohn, the "father of the Enlightenment" among the Jews and its earliest spokesman, was also the father and founder of the biblical exegesis of the time, through his bilingual project, the German translation of the Bible and its Hebrew *Biur* (*Be'ur;* "commentary"; see above: Translations, German). Mendelssohn's purpose in undertaking this project was twofold. On the one hand, he wished to open to the Jews a gateway to general culture, since he believed that the Bible could serve as a cultural bridge between European Jews and non-Jews. On the other hand, Mendelssohn wanted to educate the Jews toward good taste and to help them develop an aesthetic outlook, especially toward the Bible.

Mendelssohn's German translation of the Bible introduced nothing new in terms of content, but was novel in terms of form. It is written in a literary, ornate German which is aimed at removing the Jews from Yiddish and at bringing them closer to the Enlightenment through a knowledge of the German language and its literature. The writing of the Hebrew "commentary" to the Torah was actually carried out by various people who were commissioned by Mendelssohn, but Mendelssohn's stamp and his viewpoint are manifest in the commentary (particular mention should be made of Solomon *Dubno, who interpreted Genesis, and Naphtali Hirz Wessely, who interpreted Leviticus). The method and approach of Mendelssohn and his group were influenced by contemporary Christian biblical research and commentary. It should be pointed out that in 1753, approximately 15 years before the beginning of the project, three basic works were published which ushered in a revolution in biblical research, each of which reflected a particular approach: R. *Lowth's book on form criticism (*Praelectiones academicae de sacra poësi Hebraeorum; Lectures on the Sacred Poetry of the Hebrews,* 1829); J. *Astruc's work on source criticism *(Conjectures sur les mémoires originaux dont il paroit que Moyse s'est servi pour composer le livre de la Genèse);* and C. F. Houbigont's work on text criticism (*Biblia hebraica cum notis criticis et versione latina ad notas criticas facta,* 4 vols.); (see below, Bible research and criticism). A short while later J. G. Herder's book on Hebrew poetry (*Vom Geist der hebraeischen Poesie,* 1782) and J. G. Eichhorn's introduction to the Old Testament (*Einleitung in das Alte Testament,* 3 vols., 1780–83) were published.

Mendelssohn's "commentary" was first intended to be an explanation of the reasons for translating the Bible, but it broadened into a comprehensive commentary on the entire Pentateuch. The "commentary" places emphasis on grammatical points, cantillations, and elements of style, and is based both on traditional Jewish exegesis and biblical research. In matters of style, the commentary relies mainly on Lowth and Herder (see the summary of Mendelssohn's aesthetic views in the preface to Ex. 15). The "commentary" on the Pentateuch was written in simple language and in a scholarly Hebrew style, and despite the fact that five authors collaborated in its composition, the unity of language and style was preserved because of Mendelssohn's editing. In the "commentary" Mendelssohn was attempting to establish a single and homogeneous method for the study of the Bible among the Jews, and for this reason early Jewish commentaries do not appear alongside his commentary (for it is, essentially, an eclectic exegesis). The commentary was very popular and was reprinted about 20 times.

Mendelssohn's followers continued with the method established in the "commentary" in interpreting the Prophets and the Hagiographa, but they made no innovations. These interpretations are only a collection of commentaries, particularly from the medieval commentators, but the introductions to these commentaries were influenced by biblical research, especially by Eichhorn's introduction to the Old Testament.

In the generation after Mendelssohn, young Jews studied in the German universities and adopted the critical method which was prevalent there. Thus they moved to critical interpretation, which was also written in German. In the 19th century, German Jews wrote a number of works on biblical research, but the only one who also dealt with exegesis was H. Graetz in his commentaries to the Song of Songs, Ecclesiastes (1871), and Psalms (1881). The

Mendelssohnian Enlightenment's view of the Bible as an independent aesthetic, religious, and moral tract found expression only in Western Europe and Italy (see below), while in Central and Eastern Europe, the Bible was viewed mainly from a talmudic perspective, and the approach to the Bible took on the form of "lower criticism," rather than "higher criticism."

Most noteworthy among the commentaries of Eastern Europe is that of Meir b. Jehiel Michael *Malbim. While it was written in the period of the Enlightenment, and reflects, in a number of places, influences of the Enlightenment, this commentary is nonetheless an authentic and typical work of "the culture of the ghetto as it developed among the outstanding and brilliant scholars of Eastern Europe" (Segal). This commentary, which follows the method of *pilpul,* contains *halakhah* and *aggadah,* philosophy and Kabbalah, philological investigation and moralistic homilies. Despite his declaration that he was interpreting the text in accordance with its literal meaning, Malbim did not recognize the boundaries between literal and homiletical exegesis. He collected investigations of style and language, classifying them into 613 rules, corresponding to the number of the commandments of the Torah. He gathered these rules from the Midrash, and added to them some of his own.

In Western Europe, in contrast to Eastern and Central Europe, the Enlightenment penetrated Italy and influenced Jewish Italian commentators, such as Samuel David *Luzzatto (ShaDaL) and others. Luzzatto combined a comprehensive knowledge of traditional Jewish exegesis in all its forms with a knowledge of non-Hebrew biblical research. He did not, however, tread the beaten path, but was both independent and original, disagreeing with both early and late commentators. He drew on early and late commentaries, ancient translations, and Semitic philology. He had a poetic bent, and understood biblical poetry. Like Mendelssohn's, his work was bilingual and included translation and interpretation. He translated and interpreted the Book of Isaiah (1855). His commentary on the Torah was collected for publication from his lectures in the rabbinical seminary in Padua (1871). His commentaries on Jeremiah, Ezekiel, Proverbs, and Job were published by his son (1876).

Luzzatto introduced many new elements in his interpretations and investigations, but at the same time he relied on his predecessors. He introduced the method of textual emendation in Hebrew biblical analysis, his emendations following his own rules of interpretation. The textual emendations which he allowed himself to make were based on the incorrect separation of words in the traditional text, similar letters in the ancient Hebrew script and square (Aramaic) characters, dittography, haplography, incorrect vocalization and cantillations, metathesis, and abbreviations. In these emendations Luzzatto used translations and manuscripts of the Bible. His emendations serve as fundamental touchstones in biblical research.

While non-Hebrew biblical research reached its peak and culmination at the end of the 19th century, its influence on Hebrew interpretation was gradual. At the end of the 19th century and at the beginning of the 20th century there were three Hebrew commentators whose exegesis was novel and original: Meir *Friedman (Ish-Shalom), Benjamin *Szold, and Arnold *Ehrlich. Friedman and Szold did not rely in their commentaries on non-Hebrew criticism, though they were acquainted with it, but rather on the rabbinic scholars and traditional exegesis, while Ehrlich displayed originality, both in relation to traditional Jewish exegesis and non-Hebrew biblical research.

Arnold Ehrlich's writing was bilingual. His biblical commentary on difficult passages, *Mikra ki-Feshuto* (3 vols, 1899–1901), was written, according to him, "in Hebrew for the sake of my brethren and my people who only know Hebrew." He later published an expanded version of this work in German: *Randglossen zur hebraeischen Bibel* (7 vols., 1908–14). He had a free attitude toward the Bible and his approach was almost secular. He directs sharp criticism against the method of the non-Jewish critics, but emphasizes that in his system "interpretation is primary while criticism is secondary." Though he does engage in biblical criticism in a few places, exegesis remains the major and decisive basis of his work. With his erudition, his knowledge of Semitic languages, and especially his intuition, his interpretations are often very much to the point. Ehrlich's contribution is described by Orlinsky in the following manner: "The Randglossen by A. B. Ehrlich ranks as one of the more important and better-known contributions to biblical studies textual and contextual." While his Hebrew commentary contains some minor emendations, Ehrlich's German commentary is replete with emendations. Haran says of Ehrlich's place in the history of Jewish biblical exegesis: "In his partially secular approach to the Bible he did not lag behind the period of the Enlightenment but rather anticipated the national revival. This moment assures his place at the crossroad of the two periods."

In the period of the Enlightenment, Judaism did not liberate itself from dogmatical approach to the Bible. The extent of the criticism of Jewish scholars depended on the degree of holiness of the particular section of the Bible with which they were dealing. Thus, they dealt mainly with the Hagiographa, less with the Prophets, and very little with the Pentateuch. As has been stated, this investigation dealt with "lower criticism" and not with "higher criticism," which is concerned with the character of the author, the composition of the work, its editing, and its time. The national revival brought about a change and new evaluation of the Bible. Non-Hebrew biblical criticism made deep and incisive incursions into Hebrew literature. The depth of this penetration is reflected in the thought of *Aḥad Ha-Am, "the father of spiritual Zionism," and it was he who wished for the publication of a Hebrew modern, critical interpretation of the Bible. This desire was actually fulfilled by the exegetical activity of Abraham *Kahana.

Abraham Kahana surrounded himself with the best Jewish scholars of Eastern and Western Europe and divided the labor among them (Samuel by M. Z. Segal; Isaiah by S. Krauss; the Minor Prophets by J. B. Weinkopf, D. S. Loewinger, G. Hirschler, M. L. Margolis, and P. Chajes; Psalms by P. Chajes; Song of Songs by A. Kaminka; Lamentations by F. Perles; Esther by G. Hirschler; Daniel by M. Lambert). He himself interpreted much of the remainder (Genesis, Exodus, Numbers, Jonah, Haggai and Zechariah, Proverbs, Job, Ruth, Ecclesiastes, and Ezra and Nehemiah). Although the commentary was not completed (it was published in 1904–1930), it remains the only critical commentary on the Bible in Hebrew. This series is not uniform and includes interpretations of varying value (the best are those of Chajes on Psalms and Krauss on Isaiah). It gives very clear expression to the conclusions of non-Hebrew analytical investigation in Hebrew and Semitic philology, in comparative literature, based on the great discoveries in the ancient East, and in the Documentary Hypothesis in the study of the Pentateuch.

N. H. *Tur-Sinai (Torczyner), who engaged extensively in the study of the Bible and the Hebrew language, collected his commentaries and summarized his studies in this area in his book *Peshuto shel Mikra* (4 vols. in 6, 1962–68). There is a similarity in name, content, and method, between this work and that of Ehrlich. Tur-Sinai's work also reflects a broad knowledge of Semitic languages together with a familiarity with rabbinic scholarship and the early translations, but numerous textual emendations are suggested in his commentary. Of these suggested emendations, there are some which have been accepted by many scholars. Tur-Sinai wrote a special commentary to the Book of Job, which has been published in various corrected editions (2 vols., 1941, 1954; Eng., 1957). This work, which is the crowning achievement of his exegetical career, is also marked by the same characteristics; and the argument that Job was translated from Aramaic sometimes dictates the interpretation. M. Z. *Segal, who interpreted the Book of Samuel within the framework of Kahana's project (1919, 1922), returned to it later and published a new interpretation (1956), which is very different from the original one. Segal also published many investigations on various books of the Bible. Umberto *Cassuto intended to compose a broad and comprehensive interpretation of the Pentateuch, but did not succeed in completing the work. He did interpret the entire Book of Exodus (1952, Eng., 1967) but only managed to reach chapter 13 of his interpretation of Genesis (2 vols., 1944–49; Eng., 2 vols., 1961–64). Cassuto opposed the Documentary Hypothesis in his comprehensive Italian investigation (*La questione della Genesi,* 1934), and briefly in his Hebrew work (*Torat ha-Te'udot,* 1941; *The Documentary Hypothesis,* 1961). A conception of the unity of the Torah and its form served as a basis for Cassuto's philologic-aesthetic approach. In addition to his monumental work *Toledot ha-Emunah ha-Yisre'elit,* Y. *Kaufmann also engaged, toward the end of his life, in interpreting the books of Joshua (1959, 1963^2), and Judges (1962), which actually only served to complete and consolidate the foundations of his theories, both on the history of Israelite religion and on the antiquity of the writing and editing of the books. In these outstanding analytical interpretations Kaufmann inveighs strongly against the German school of biblical analysis of Wellhausen and his circle. In his comprehensive introductions, both to the two commentaries as a whole and to the various chapters, he presents a knowledgeable discussion of the Bible and its research. He attempted to prove that his own method was correct and was the one to be preferred. In his commentaries he demonstrated that the method of omitting and the division of verses into various sources and different editions is not essential. It is possible in most instances through fine analysis to recognize the perfection and harmony of the text. The need for a new Hebrew analytical interpretation of the Bible has been emphasized on many occasions, and there have been attempts to implement this aim. A "new interpretation of the Bible," to be written by a staff of scholars under the editorship of B. Mazar, was planned in the 1950s, but this plan was not realized, except for the interpretation of Ecclesiastes by H. L. *Ginsberg (1961).

Bibliography: M. Soloveitchik and S. Rubashov, *Toledot Bikkoret ha-Mikra* (1925), 126–61; P. Sendler, *Ha-Be'ur la-Torah shel Moshe Mendelssohn ve-Si'ato* (1941); H. Sheli, *Meḥkar ha-Mikra be-Sifrut ha-Haskalah* (1942); M. Z. Segal, *Parshanut ha-Mikra* (1944), 109–26; M. Diman (Haran), in: *Bitzaron,* 21 (1950), 110–4, 174–8, 256–62; 22 (1951), 189–96; 23 (1952), 38–41, 115–26, 187–93; M. Haran, *Biblical Research in Hebrew* (1970); idem, in: *Molad,* 26 (1970), 97–106; H. M. Orlinsky, in: JQR, 45 (1954/55), 374–412.
[Is.A.]

BIBLE RESEARCH AND CRITICISM

"Research and criticism" of the Bible is, in one sense, as old as, if not older than, the traditional Bible. Some modern scholars have devoted great efforts to the attempt to trace the details of the process whereby the older semi-canonical materials which went into the final shaping of the canon itself were reapplied and made relevant to their day. After the closing of the canon, quite similar methods continued to be used for centuries (see above, Canon). That is to say, from a purely literary or external (as distinguished from a religious or theological) viewpoint, the distinction between canonical and non-canonical literature is in this respect quite artificial—a statement, which, in itself, exemplifies the difference between traditional and modern critical approaches.

Increasing attention has been devoted to the study of the history of the interpretation of the Bible as methods and schools have proliferated, and especially as the "hermeneutical" question has come to the fore. It may be observed that, *mutatis mutandis,* the problem has always been essentially what it still is today: how to be both historically faithful to the text's original significance as well as adequately to convey its meaning and relevance to the contemporary situation. Furthermore, it may be asserted that, in general, the precise methods used in this task at any given time tend, up to a point, to be quite similar in both Judaism and Christianity. Thus a certain common influence exerted by the prevailing philosophy of the time is often noticeable: the strong Platonic influences of the early Common Era: the mystical and Aristotelian influences of the Middle Ages: the philosophical impetus provided by the Renaissance: and the rationalism, historicism, and existentialism of more modern periods. Correspondingly, the precise methods in the two communities also often have much in common: the multiple (and often fourfold) senses ascribed to a text in the Middle Ages as well as the specific types of literary and historical investigation employed in modern times.

Nor is it surprising to note a fair amount of interaction and cross-fertilization: developments within Christianity tended to set the general cultural tone and atmosphere, while there was always much in Judaism's retention of the grammatical text (even when interpreted allegorically) which Christianity, especially with its early preference for the Septuagint, was always in danger of forgetting. Jewish influence on Christian interpretation is especially clear in the case of the dependence of the Antiochene school and of Jerome on the rabbis, and the influence especially of Rashi via Nicholas of Lyra and Reuchlin upon Luther, not to speak of the many contributions by modern Jewish scholars. These generalizations begin to hold true as soon as the two streams diverge. It has long been realized that New Testament principles of interpretation had much in common with that of the mainstream of rabbinism (classically in H. L. Strack and P. Billerbeck, *Kommentar zum Neuen Testament aus Talmud und Midrasch,* 1922–56, and J. Bonsirven, *Exégèse rabbinique et exégèse paulinienne,* 1939). More recently, it has become clear from Qumran that the specific apocalyptic motifs of the Essenic stream of Jewish thought were also very influential in early Christianity (see F. F. Bruce, *Biblical Exegesis in the Qumran Texts,* 1959).

Early Moves Toward Critical Study. Much of the intellectual endeavor of both Judaism and Christianity, until well after the Reformation, was directed to Bible study. In retrospect, various individuals and schools seem to stand out as precursors of modern biblical study. Among these must be noted: the Christian school of Antioch and especially Theodore of Mopsuestia (d. c. 428); the philological accents of Saadiah Gaon under the influence of especially the Aristotelian revival in the Muslim world; its sequel in a sense when Aristotelianism conquered the West in the rationalism of Maimonides and somewhat related manifestations in Rashi, David Kimḥi, and Abraham ibn

Ezra within Judaism, and the 12th-century Victorine School and Nicholas of Lyra among the Christian expositors.

With the Reformation came a tremendous upsurge of emphasis upon literal, "grammatical" exegesis. "Allegory" and multiple interpretations were indignantly rejected—although, by most modern definitions, sometimes retained under a different title. Simultaneously, the Renaissance and its resurgent humanism were placing great stress upon early sources and plain meanings; in comparison with the ecclesiastical revolution it was sometimes hard to say what was cause and what effect. Most significant, however, in terms of future developments, were the extra-ecclesiastic philosophies which began to appear and slowly gained momentum to usher in the "modern" era. The fundamentally new situation which was gradually developing was that the major context of Bible study would no longer be the synagogue or the church, but the secular university. Among the major names which must be mentioned are: René Descartes (d. 1650), who with his *Cogito ergo sum* virtually provided the creed of the rationalism which dominated the century after his death; Benedict *Spinoza, who applied the new thought more specifically to biblical study, including a portentous questioning of the Mosaic authorship of the Pentateuch; Hugo *Grotius, a Dutch jurist, whose probings have sometimes earned him the title of the "father" of the historical-critical method; Gotthold Ephraim *Lessing, with his famous pronouncement that "accidental truths of history can never become proof of necessary truths of reason"; and Immanuel *Kant, whose emphasis upon "practical reason," i.e., man's conscience and its ethical judgments, was to be of incalculable influence in succeeding years. With Kant's divorce of the "phenomenal" and "noumenal" worlds, the stage was set for that loss of the authority of an inspired Scripture and of a sense of the transcendent in general, which dominated most of the succeeding centuries. Much of the new mood was introduced into Judaism especially through Moses Mendelssohn. In both Judaism and Christianity, there was (and sometimes still is) uncompromising resistance to "higher criticism" (i.e., those aspects of biblical criticism which deal with literary analysis and historical and ideological considerations; as opposed to "lower criticism" which deals with the text, canon, etc.) because of its original connection with rationalistic and other anti-supernaturalistic philosophies. However, although the problem and the risk remain, many of even the very conservative members of both faiths generally recognize today that much of great benefit can be salvaged from this approach, or aspects of it.

In this climate, precursors of the more technical aspects of the critical study of the Bible also began to appear, especially Isaac *la Peyrere and Richard *Simon, who postulated various authors of the Pentateuch, and perhaps particularly the 18th-century Jean *Astruc, who first used criterion of different Hebrew names for the deity in Genesis. These and other preliminary critical investigations were, in a sense, summarized and ordered by Johann *Eichhorn in a three-volume work on the Old Testament. Two 18th-century scholars were especially important in developing further the theoretical foundations of the movement, specifically in breaking away from the restraints of ecclesiastical dogma and tradition. Johann Semler (d. 1791), especially in his *Abhandlung zur freien Untersuchung des Kanons*, campaigned for an approach to the Bible exactly "like another book," free from all dogmatic pre-assumptions. Similarly Johann Gabler (d. 1787), often known as the father of "biblical theology" because of the distinction he advocated between that discipline and the traditional dogmatic theology, urged that the latter should concentrate on biblical teachings of universal relevance, while "biblical theology" should concern itself with historically and temporally conditioned matters.

Nineteenth-Century Pentateuch Criticism and Wellhausen. Critical investigations into the Pentateuch in particular continued throughout the 19th century by scholars like Martin de Wette (d. 1843), the first to isolate Deuteronomy as a separate source and associate it with Josiah's reformation (II Kings 22), and Heinrich Ewald (d. 1875), a prolific writer who changed his own position repeatedly, thus typifying the exploratory nature of that period's investigations. By 1850, late datings for Daniel, Second Isaiah (i.e., Isaiah 40–66), the second part of Zechariah, and Psalms had become generally accepted (all except the latter still widely held today), but no unanimity had been reached on the Pentateuch. W. Vatke's recognition of the lateness of the *Grundschrift* (the later "Priestly Document") eventually provided the needed breakthrough, but his thoroughgoing Hegelianism and Ewald's rejection of his views led to a stalemate which was broken only by Wellhausen and his congeners. When this intermediate period (after Eichhorn) came to an end, a certain "critical orthodoxy" was introduced (which, with various modifications, is still very influential today) in the epoch-making *Prolegomena to the History of Israel* of Julius Wellhausen in 1878 (Eng. tr. 1965). Others beside Wellhausen were influential in the formulation of the final hypothesis and others worked alongside him in its subsequent elaboration, but Wellhausen's work so succesfully presented and popularized the approach that few dispute the appropriateness of epithets like "Wellhausenian," "classical criticism," etc.

The great significance of Wellhausen's achievement lay in the fact that it represented not only the latest in a series of isolated critical investigations, but that these were integrated into an entirely new synthesis and reconstruction of the total course of Israel's religious history, to the stages of which the various literary documents were related. Although L. Perlitt (*Vatke und Wellhausen*, 1965) has attempted to disprove it, it still seems that, however indirect, the ultimate philosophical inspiration of Wellhausen's reconstruction was the idealistic monism of Hegel. (For better or for worse, much of the historicism and immanentalism of this period survived even in the later corrections, and it is doubtful if even the most determinedly conservative today have remained uninfluenced by this "Copernican revolution" which stresses that things can be understood only when their history is known.)

Wellhausen postulated a slow evolutionistic rise from the animism of the earliest, "patriarchal" periods to the "ethical monotheism" of especially the eighth-century prophets. The purest of the pentateuchal sources, from this perspective, was judged to be J or the Yahwist (which used the divine name YHWH), dated to the ninth century, followed by a slow but sure degeneration toward formalism and institutionalism in the subsequent sources, E or the Elohist (using the divine name *Elohim*) perhaps a century later, D or the Deuteronomist (the author of the Book of Deuteronomy) with his incipient "biblicism," writing in connection with Josiah's abortive ventures shortly before the fall of Judah, and P (author of the Priestly document) during or after the Exile, providing the constitution for the small semi-independent hierocracy within the vast Persian empire. All of the sources were understood as providing reliable information primarily only of the period of composition, not of the earlier periods which they described. The Pentateuch was allegedly given its final shape by circles akin to P about the time of Ezra. It was asserted that during the same period, and indeed down to that of the Maccabees, the earlier prophecies of doom were supplemented by more optimistic oracles, and most of the psalms, understood mostly as gems of individualistic piety, were also composed. Vast modifications of Wellhausen's synthesis continue to be made, and the underlying unilinear notion of progress in history has been almost totally repudiated; nevertheless, very little scholarship has turned its back on him completely and his influence is still to be widely detected in biblical research.

In general, it is probably true that much Jewish scholarship, even that which was not totally traditionalistic, was initially and, to a degree, still remains rather cool toward the standard results of German biblical scholarship, well aware of the subtle anti-Judaism, if not anti-Semitism, which by no means necessarily but very often *de facto* accompanies any depreciation of the Old Testament—and it is undeniable that such implications were often present in much of the "classical" critical literature. U. *Cassuto attacked the hypothesis frontally, and a coolness is apparent in the works of Y. *Kaufmann, M. H. *Segal and others.

The Influence of Archaeology. Probably the major development which led to a modification of the Wellhausenian synthesis was archaeology (and it is perhaps in this area and the subsidiary philological ones that modern Jewish scholars, both in Israel and elsewhere, have made their major contributions). Apart from the various particulars, archaeology's contribution can be summed up by saying that it provided an actual, historical context for interpreting ancient Israel's life and literature instead of the *a priori*, philosophic one on which Wellhausen had largely depended. Especially at the hands of some of its leading practitioners such as W. F. *Albright and Nelson *Glueck, the general net effect of archaeological discoveries has been to enhance the general trustworthiness and substantial historicity of the biblical tradition, although not in the naïve, uncritical sense sometimes expressed by the "prove the Bible true" slogan. Where archaeological influence was (and is) felt, the basic viewpoint tended to shift from an ideological (i.e., not only heuristic) skepticism to an inclination to give tradition the benefit of the doubt unless there was clear evidence to the contrary. New hypotheses soon sprang up to come to terms with the new archaeological data, but often these in turn mushroomed far beyond what the evidence would support, so that archaeology was frequently both the major source of raw materials for new hypotheses as well as their major critic.

Gunkel and "Form" Criticism. The first "school" to exploit the new resources was that of *Religionsgeschichte* and, closely allied with it, that of form criticism. In both cases, Hermann *Gunkel was probably the leading spirit, and his name can be used to symbolize a considerable diversity almost to the extent that Wellhausen's name can be of the preceding era. Not only the newer discoveries, but also the tradition of romanticism, as exemplified in the studies of Johann *Herder of ancient Hebrew poetry and to a certain extent the theology of Friedrich Schleiermacher (d. 1834), were highly influential in determining the direction of his work. Various anthropological investigations contributed to the new climate as well. During his lifetime, Gunkel's approach often won only very slow and grudging acceptance from his German colleagues schooled in the more classical approaches, but today it can safely be said that even in Germany, Gunkel generally determined the direction of current biblical research far more directly than Wellhausen.

In essence, Gunkel's thesis was that in ancient society each *Sitz im Leben* ("life-setting") had its own *Gattung* or "form" (pattern, outline, style, etc.), and the latter could really be understood only in the light of the former. In his *Die Sagen der Genesis* (1901) and *Einleitung in die Psalmen* (1933) and a host of other works, he proposed categories which, in the main, are largely still accepted today. A certain sympathy for the ancient literature on its own terms tended to result, as well as a disposition to date the literature, or at least its roots, much earlier than had previously been the case. Even the cult began to receive more sympathetic treatment as indisputably an important component of pre-secular cultures. Similarly, the recognition of the role of memory in ancient cultures, preceding and continuing alongside written materials, led to consideration of the nature of oral tradition as well as of scribal habits and strictly textual criticism. All these aspects of the new movement were developed, especially by Gunkel's successors, in different ways by various groups and individuals too numerous to detail here.

Perhaps the greatest weakness of the central form-critical effort was its very concentration on individual units, thus, ironically, often leading to an atomism quite similar to the older "scissors-and-paste" literary criticism which it had sought to correct. The subsequent corrective movement of "tradition criticism" (so-called if it dealt with oral materials; often called "redaction-criticism" if the subject was written texts) has attempted to compensate for this weakness by trying to ascertain the "laws" and the process by which the individual units were united. Another weakness was the tendency—in practice at least—to assume the non-historicity of the material unless there was overwhelming evidence to the contrary, or at least to argue that the question itself was irrelevant. The more archaeologically oriented scholars in particular took exception to this tendency, arguing that "external evidence" was required in order to test factuality, something which mere literary techniques could never do, and that Israel's own subjectivity made the question of factual reality something which could not simply be ignored. This division of opinion probably remains the most serious of all within the ranks of contemporary biblical scholarship. Many aspects of the division as concerns the early (pre-monarchical) history of Israel are exposed in the two major current histories of Israel by John Bright (1959) and Martin *Noth (1950). The disposition of some "biblical theology" writers (especially Gerhard von Rad), to argue that Israel's original theological interpretations stand even if there are no factual traditions behind them, only raises more questions than it answers.

Certain of the *religionsgeschichtliche* developments stemming from Gunkel's work were at least as problematic. Whereas Wellhausenianism and classical liberalism had solved the problem of distance and relevance by a drastic reductionism to what allegedly had timeless truth and value (mostly ethics!), *Religionsgeschichte* tended to accentuate—and often exaggerate—the distance of the material from modern man and its strangeness to him and evidenced little or no concern for the questions of the relevance and factuality of the material, or for the contemporary philosophical and theological debates in general. Furthermore, the exploitation of the many parallels between Israel and her neighbors easily developed into a "parallelomania" (Sandmel) which judged Israel almost totally in the light of her neighbors. The "pan-Babylonianism" of A. *Jeremias, Friedrich *Delitzsch, and H. *Winckler was one of the major manifestations of this mood, but it continued to some extent in the later "myth and ritual" school of S. H. Hooke, the Uppsala school of I. Engnell, and in the works of Sigmund *Mowinckel. (Not quite so all-encompassing and pretentious were the collections of comparative materials in the many works of J. *Morgenstern and T. H. *Gaster.) Impressive theories were developed about "divine kingship" in Israel and about an alleged autumnal "New

Feast of the Righteous in Paradise. Top—leviathan, wild ox and the mythical bird *ziz,* the legendary food of the Righteous in Paradise. Bottom—crowned, animal-headed Righteous people eating, drinking, discussing, and listening to music played by two animal-headed musicians standing on either side of the table, which is laid with vessels of food and wine. The last page of the giant three-volume *Ambrosian Bible* written in Ulm, South Germany, in 1236–38. Milan, Ambrosian Library, ms. B.32, inf. fol. 136 (18 × 13$\frac{5}{8}$ ins/45.3 × 34.3 cm.).

Year" festival, strongly patterned along foreign lines. Rival theories, drawing more upon the biblical sources as they now stand, were developed especially by Artur Weiser and Hans-Joachim Kraus. While few would deny some measure of truth to many of these theories, especially in the heavily syncretistic days reported by the Books of Kings, it remains to be seen how many of the specifics will stand the test of time, especially as concerns normative or mainstream Israel (assuming, against Wellhausen, that there was such a thing before the Exile). One of the most devastating critiques ever leveled against the cultic "patternism" common to many of these efforts was H. *Frankfort's *Kingship and the Gods* (1948).

Furthermore, in connection with many of the theories of this type, the common assumption was that the cult created its own supporting stories which were later "historified," rather than celebrating historical events to begin with. Similarly, many traditio-historical theories saw the cult as the major factor in not only the production of the stories but in their canonical ordering and interrelationship as well. One of the more curious developments in the attempt to understand biblical antiquity on its own terms was the attempt to isolate "Hebrew thought," especially in contrast to "Greek" (classically perhaps in T. Boman, *Hebrew Thought Compared With Greek,* 1960). While this line of investigation was helpful in excluding certain alien concerns of Western philosophy and rationalism, it easily left the impression that the difference was intrinsically linguistic or ethnic, rather than a matter of pre-secular and pre-philosophic (not "prelogical"!) forms of expression. Sometimes this approach was confused with "biblical theology," and at other times it confused the "mytho-logic" of paganism with Israel's "empirical logic" (the terms are Albright's) in an indiscriminate "primitivism" (the weakness of J. Pedersen's *Israel* (1926), which, however, is still useful). James Barr leveled especially devastating critiques at this approach. H. Frankfort's *The Intellectual Adventure of Ancient Man* (1946; later reprinted under the title *Before Philosophy*) remains an outstanding study.

"Biblical Theology." In a way, the last of the supplements to classical Wellhausenianism, although it often overlapped with the movements already noted above, was that of "biblical theology." Its roots lay in the post-World War I disillusionment with both the reductionism of the earlier liberalism and the deliberate "irrelevance" of *Religionsgeschichte* (as expressed also in the "neo-orthodoxy" of Karl Barth in particular). While unwilling to return to the pre-Kantian "orthodoxy" of an objective norm in an inspired Scripture, this movement did strongly affirm the truth of the Bible's "record of revelation" because it allegedly "rang true" to man's existential condition. It revolted especially against the earlier critical tendency to limit criticism to questions of date, authorship, sources, etc., without pressing on seriously to consider the message. No doubt, since Gabler's manifesto, most "biblical theology" had in actuality been little but "history of Israel's religion."

Most work in this field tended to have somewhat of a *Heilsgeschichte* character. However, no unanimity at all was reached concerning the order or system which was most appropriate, and on this reef the movement itself eventually foundered. Among the major names may be mentioned: Edmond Jacob (1955) who produced a theology using quite traditional categories; Walther Eichrodt (1933) who tried to arrange his material around the internal biblical category of *covenant; and Gerhardt von Rad (1957), author of the last and perhaps the greatest of the works of this school, who attempted to return to a more strictly chronological arrangement, thus abandoning all attempts to find any real internal unity in the material. Hence it became plain that this movement too had come full circle, and in subsequent years works on the "religion" of Israel again began to supplant "theologies."

Many speak of the demise of biblical theology in the early 1960s; but it is too early to say whether any major new phase has been entered. A vast amount of activity continues on almost all fronts but with no easily discernible unity. Fohrer's introduction (1965) laments the centrifugality of the current situation and seems to lean toward a return to a modified Wellhausenianism, while R. K. Harrison's massive study (1969), from a very conservative standpoint, calls for a fresh start on new, more empirical foundations. Perhaps the major new symptom is the current interest in Israel's wisdom literature, reflecting the radically humanistic and immanentistic mood of the times, often bolstered by appeals to some sort of "process" philosophy.

Finally, there is the ecumenical spirit of the age, which has seen not only Roman Catholicism join most of the rest of Western Christendom in the historical-critical enterprise, but often Judaism as well. To the extent that this cooperation has progressed beyond theologically neutral philological matters, probably two traditional blindspots of the previously dominant Protestantism appear to be increasingly corrected: its disregard of cult and ritual, and its tendency to view "Torah" as essentially legalistic and thus a different religion from Christianity.

Major Results of Biblical Research.

WISDOM LITERATURE. Turning to a survey of some of biblical criticism's major results or the current status of the investigation, wisdom literature is a logical place to begin, because of the great interest it has attracted recently. The canonical wisdom books like Job and Ecclesiastes seem to indicate the relatively marginal role this movement played in the totality of Israel's life and thought. The motivation which excluded Ben Sira and the Wisdom of Solomon from the canon, even though those books made the identification of Wisdom and Torah much more explicit than previously, was undoubtedly justified because of the extent to which those same works were amenable to Gnostic and other Hellenistic syncretisms. Similarly, "biblical theology" was at a loss how to understand these materials because of their minimal attention to the specific themes of Israelite history, religion, and ethics. Recent studies have not so much answered these questions as considered them relatively unimportant. The major study of H. H. Schmidt (*Wesen und Geschichte der Weisheit,* 1966) argues in rather existentialist fashion that, in general, wisdom was primarily concerned with "historicality," which gives man his full self-understanding, etc. Schmidt and others have labored to demonstrate the antiquity of wisdom within Israel and its importance in all periods. Others (Richter, Gerstenberger) have argued that the origins of Israelite law lay in the same secular settings as early wisdom, not in the cultic milieu postulated by Alt and many since him. Strenuous efforts have also been devoted to attempting to trace wisdom influence on Israel's historical and prophetical literature.

ISRAEL'S EARLY HISTORY. Parallel to the pride of place occupied by the Pentateuch in the labors of the literary critic is the concentration of the historian on Israel's early (pre-monarchical) history and religion. In Germany especially, much of the earlier skepticism about the reliability of any of the biblical traditions on these early periods still lingers, but in America and Israel, and in particular among the archaeologically oriented, much greater credence is generally granted them. In general, Jewish scholars have tended to hold even more conservative opinions here. The strictly historical question is inseparable from that of what was taking place in general in Canaan throughout much of the second millennium B.C.E., and a great deal is still very unclear in this area. Although there is much circumstantial evidence, it is not yet possible to make any incontrovertible points of contact between the patriarchal narratives in the Bible and extra-biblical evidence. Nelson Glueck and W. F. Albright especially have argued strongly for dating Abraham in the Middle Bronze I period (c. 21st to 19th centuries B.C.E.), on the grounds of the archaeological evidence that the Negev, where Abraham is generally situated, was unoccupied for nearly 1,000 years in either direction except for this period. Albright (BASOR, no. 163, pp. 36ff.) has even attempted to see Abraham as a "donkey caravaneer," a leader in the thriving trade of that period, first between Ur and Haran, later between Damascus and Egypt. Others (Gordon, Kenyon, van Seters) have challenged this entire association of the patriarchs with the Amorite settlement in Middle Bronze I. Many aspects of patriarchal life can be illustrated from the great Amorite city of *Mari, but others are elucidated by the later and non-Semitic (Hurrian) culture of *Nuzi, thus possibly pointing toward the Late Bronze Age (1500 on) and closer to the main Israelite advent.

PATRIARCHISM AND MONOTHEISM. Patriarchal religion is even harder to elucidate in the present paucity of concrete information, but there is no want of theories. Most current exploration of the subject builds on Albrecht *Alt's essay (1929), "The God of the Fathers" (pp. 1–66 in *Essays in Old Testament History and Religion*) which explained the patriarchal deities as of a "family god" type, by comparison with allegedly comparable types found among Nabatean and Palmyrene travelers of later periods. Frank Cross (HTR, 55 (1962), 225ff.) has gone further and postulated a synthesis of the family god (personal, historical) traditions of the patriarch's Amorite past with the "high," creator-type, god of Canaan, as perhaps evidenced in the various El-compounds by which the Bible refers to the patriarchal deity. U. Oldenburg (*El and Baal,* 1969) argues for an older, purer El monotheism which the patriarchs and their heirs had preserved in spite of its degeneration elsewhere in Canaan because of the influence of the (originally Amorite) Baal cult. Ephraim *Speiser in his *Anchor Bible* commentary on Genesis (1964) argues for a monotheistic impulse behind Abraham's initial decision to leave Ur itself. As against this, M. Haran stresses the non-monotheistic character of the patriarchal religion ("The Religion of the Patriarchs: An Attempt at a Synthesis," ASTI (1965), 30–55).

The question of *monotheism, of course, has a far wider history of debate than merely the patriarchal period. The Wellhausenian dogma had been that it was not possible to speak of "ethical monotheism" until the prophetic period, and even then essentially of only an impersonal philosophical monism. Of course, such a reconstruction is dependent on many other decisions with respect to Israel's early history, which cannot all be considered here. Suffice to say that for years W. F. Albright, especially in his *From the Stone Age to Christianity* (1940) has been one of the staunchest champions of Mosaic monotheism. That judgment is not unrelated to his widely accepted—but by no means unchallenged—interpretation of the Tetragrammaton, "YHWH," as originally a causative form *(Hifil),* meaning "He who causes to be," i.e., "Creator," etc.

FROM THE CANAANITE CONQUEST TO THE FALL OF JERUSALEM. Questions of the Israelite conquest of Canaan are no less vexed. As noted above, probably the dominant critical position from Wellhausen to Martin Noth has remained essentially unchanged: it is really not possible to speak of "Israel" in any meaningful sense until the immediate pre-monarchical period and whatever may have happened earlier is beyond recovery. This position, of course, clashes with the biblical memory of that period as one of massive apostasy rather than of creativity and innovation. Noth's hypothesis that there was an Israelite organization in that period of an "amphictyonic" type, after both Greek and many other ancient Near Eastern parallels, has found virtually unanimous acceptance, but other aspects of the traditional critical reconstruction are open to serious question. Neither the biblical reports nor the archaeological evidence are monolithic in the picture they leave of the nature of the Israelite conquest. The net result of both is probably that at least three major factors must be reckoned with: (1) a slow infiltration over a lengthy period of time—with apparent success perhaps especially in the central area in and around Shechem; (2) sporadic revolts of native Canaanite peasants against the petty city-states; and (3) a few lightning campaigns by Joshua, probably often administering the *coup-de-grâce* to any lingering resistance. The related Philistine problem has received some clarification from excavations at Ashdod, and the current status of that problem has been masterfully summarized in a work by Trude Dothan (*Ha-Pelishtim ve-Tarbutam ha-Ḥomrit,* 1967).

As concerns the biblical literature which reports most of Israel's history between the conquest and the fall of Jerusalem (the "former prophets"), the earlier critical tendency to trace the four major Pentateuchal strands into Joshua and often through Kings seems to have been largely set aside. Instead, Noth's hypothesis of a "deuteronomic history," beginning with the Book of Deuteronomy itself, is widely followed; the "deuteronomist" appears to allow his sources to speak for themselves, but the overall framework and theological interpretations seem to be his own (at least in final form). The weakest link in this theory is undoubtedly the Book of Samuel, where the alleged "deuteronomic" evidences are often difficult to find. It is interesting to note, however, that the major division in Noth's theory after Numbers instead of after Deuteronomy (a "Tetrateuch" instead of a "Pentateuch") corresponds generally to the Uppsala school's proposal of a "D-work" and a "P-work," both allegedly oral and fluid in nature until quite late. If there is any truth in these proposals, there may be merit, however, in proposed adjustments (similar to older views which often thought of a "Hexateuch" i.e., the Pentateuch and Joshua) which view some of the present Book of Joshua as the original "fifth book," or, at least, the record of the "fulfillment" (in the conquest) of the promises which figure so prominently in the preceding material. The present telescoping of the beginning of the later work and the end of the earlier one may then have taken place in conjunction with the later exaltation of Moses and/or the concern of the post-Exilic Judahite community to convince the Persian authorities that they were not seditiously urging any campaign of total independence.

Archaeological Evidence. The contributions of archaeology, beyond those already mentioned, are especially significant in the area of lexicography and textual criticism. In general, the literary finds discovered since 1929 at Ras Shamra (the ancient *Ugarit destroyed in the 12th century B.C.E.) on the northern Phoenician coast are easily the most important for biblical studies. Here in three major epics and much other literature, there are not only classical versions of the paganism which was Yahwism's major competitor, but also the "language of Canaan" as it was spoken at a time and place not too far removed from "biblical Hebrew" (i.e., mostly, the pre-Exilic dialect of Jerusalem). As a result, all sorts of obscurities in the older biblical text (e.g., Ex. 15, Judg. 5, etc.) can be clarified, as well as many features in even younger texts where tradition apparently transmitted the consonantal text faithfully, but using idioms which the masoretes or other later commentators no longer understood (e.g., an "enclitic *mem*," various meanings of *lamed*, etc.)

H. L. Ginsberg was among the earliest to recognize and explore the potential here. Probably the first major studies utilizing these resources have appeared in some commentaries of the *Anchor Bible* series, perhaps especially those of Mitchell Dahood on Psalms (1966) and Marvin Pope on Job (1965). Undoubtedly, not all their suggestions will stand—but here progress is being made on the basis of concrete empirical evidence and not mere speculation. It should also be noted that these discoveries have made it credible that many of the psalms (not to speak of Job and Proverbs) are pre-Exilic in date and not inconceivably literally "Davidic," at least in their roots.

The *Dead Sea Scrolls have been of great importance for an understanding of the complexities of the Judaism of the times as well as of the origins of Christianity. For the Old Testament, however, their significance is largely limited to the field of textual criticism—where their influence has been nearly revolutionary. Above all, since the oldest manuscripts previously known had been nearly a millennium younger, the Qumran scrolls eliminated with one stroke much of the great skepticism which had previously reigned in some quarters concerning the age and reliability of the texts. At the same time, the variation in detail in some of the Hebrew manuscripts showed that no absolutely standardized and uniform text had been fixed at the beginning of the Christian era.

Even more significant, in a way, was the discovery of Hebrew manuscripts in recensions agreeing with the Septuagint and the Samaritan Pentateuch. In the past, the pendulum had swung from one extreme to another in the comparative evaluation of the Hebrew text and the versions; in general, "Wellhausenianism," true to its anti-traditional stance in general, had preferred the versions, while some later correctives discounted them almost entirely. Now it increasingly became plain that all three streams had equally ancient roots, that no *a priori* preferences could be maintained in favor of any of the three, and that, in all likelihood, the original tradition was richer than any one of its three major later derivatives. That is, in contrast to much of the textual criticism of the 19th century which attempted, often on the basis of highly subjective assumptions, to eliminate all the later additions and restore the original "pure" text, it now seems likely that the text has suffered more from losses than from glosses. Apparently, as an official rabbinic or masoretic text gradually came into existence around the beginning of the Christian era, at least three major attempts to revise the Septuagint in conformity with it can be traced. (See F. M. Cross, "The Contribution of the Qumran Discoveries to the Study of the Biblical Text," in IEJ, 16 (1966), 81ff.)

The Dating of Psalms. The study of Psalms has been affected at various points by the developments sketched above. In addition to the textual studies, there has developed a general disposition to date the psalms earlier than previously, not only because of the many Ugaritic parallels, but because of the demonstration that, as in virtually all other ancient societies, poetry in Israel was generally much older than prose (precisely the opposite of Wellhausen's assumption). It should also be noted that the cultic emphasis of many scholars (quite apart from any specific reconstructions of the Israelite liturgy) has tended also to de-emphasize the individualistic light in which both precritical tradition and the early critics usually viewed them. Instead of a search for the precise personal or political situation in which a psalm was supposedly uttered or composed, the attention has shifted to the "cultic situation" and to some impersonal professional liturgical figure who composed and/or uttered the psalm. Simultaneously, a more "realistic" view of what "cult" generally meant in pre-secular cultures was also posited for ancient Israel; rather than seeing a collection of individuals identifying with the past or merely in vertical communion with the divine, emphasis was put more on a sacramental "representation," "actualization," or the like of earlier redemptive events. The exact point of departure varied widely from the heavily nature- and mythology-oriented types (classically in Mowinckel's *The Psalms in Israel's Worship*, 1951), usually strongly influenced by *religionsgeschichtliche* parallels (cf. above), to those emphasizing firmly the presumed native Israelite theme of "covenant renewal," usually related to similar investigations into the nature of the early "amphictyonic" ceremonies, and developed in connection with the psalms, especially in the commentary of Artur Weiser (1962). The theme of "theophany" also tends to be prominent in the latter approach. Naturally, all of these various reconstructions of the cult influenced the detailed exegesis of the individual psalms at many points. One curious factor in all of these reconstructions is striking: namely the almost total neglect of the sacrificial context. While there have been some thorough studies of sacrifice (excellently summarized in R. de *Vaux's *Ancient Israel*, 1958), and while there has been a waning of the older evolutionistic notion that sacrifice, especially of the piacular type, was a late intrusion into Israel, these studies of sacrifice were virtually never integrated into the mainline investigations of the cult.

Research on the Prophets. The same cultic emphases sometimes also heavily influenced the interpretation of the prophets. In contrast to the virtual dogma of almost total antithesis of prophet and priest in Wellhausenianism, *Religionsgeschichte* again drastically narrowed the distance, sometimes all but eliminating it (see especially A. Johnson, *The Cultic Prophet in Ancient Israel*, 1962. The prophets became simply cultic functionaries, and elaborate theories, especially in the Uppsala tradition, were developed to explain many of the prophetic books as liturgies. This did have the happy result of making the older mechanical distinction of "genuine" and "ungenuine" somewhat beside the point, but it tends to be conceded on all sides today that much of the "cultic" stress on the prophets was overdone. The residue that seems to survive is the realization that the prophets certainly did utilize and quote cultic materials to a large extent and may, indeed, at times have had certain official connections with it, but that their major stance was to protest in favor of a basically good institution (including its "false prophets") that had become unfaithful. Another major fruitful line of research on the prophets has been the realization of the extent to which the prophet understood himself as the divine messenger who had been privileged to join Yahweh's heavenly council temporarily and who had then to proclaim the "covenant lawsuit" which he had heard there (see especially various essays in the J. Muilenburg *Festschrift*, 1962). As an independent study of the prophets, Abraham J. *Heschel's book *The Prophets* (1962) must also be mentioned.

Apocalyptic Literature. Finally, a few words on the apocalyptic literature. Classical criticism dealt very harshly with this material, arguing basically that its otherworldly accent on God's immediate intervention beyond history was a perversion of classical prophecy's stress on an intervention mediated by and within ordinary history (a thesis often bolstered by a radical literary criticism of the prophetic books which excised as late and protoapocalyptic anything which seemed to veer in that direction).

Extra-Israelite (especially Iranian) influences and an alleged "dualism" were heavily accented (see the many works of R. H. Charles for fairly classical statements of this stance). Recent studies have moderated this position somewhat, but much of it lingers, for example in Von Rad's *Theology of the Old Testament* (vol. 2). Perhaps the best recent study is that of Russell, *The Method and Message of Apocalyptic* (1964). Plaguing the entire discussion also is lack of basic agreement on a working definition of "eschatology"; if it is not simply equated with the apocalyptic form, it is hard to see how eschatology of some sort can be denied to pre-Exilic Israel, and various recent studies have even labored to demonstrate that it was inherent in Israel's basic covenant- and election-thought from the very outset Mitchell Dahood in his commentary on Psalms in the *Anchor* series even argues that Israel had a far more developed idea of afterlife than has been supposed in most modern criticism.

Bibliography. Major works relating to the subject at hand have been included in the text above. Much further recent bibliography and summary of the last century's developments are found in Herbert Hahn, *The Old Testament in Modern Research,* with a survey of recent literature by H. D. Hummel (1970²). Major essays by specialists on recent developments up to publication date are found in H. H. Rowley (ed.), *The Old Testament in Modern Study* (1951). Many of the pioneering essays themselves are reprinted and interpreted in Samuel Sandmel's handy *Old Testament Issues* (1968). Other major studies include: L. Diestel, *Geschichte des Alten Testaments in der christlichen Kirche* (1869); F. W. Farrar, *History of Interpretation* (1886); H.-J. Krauss, *Geschichte der historisch-kritischen Erforschung des Alten Testaments von der Reformation bis zur Gegenwart* (1969²); C. Kraeling, *The Old Testament since the Reformation* (1955); B. Smalley, *The Study of the Bible in the Middle Ages* (Oxford, 1952²); R. Grant, *A Short History of the Interpretation of the Bible* (New York, 1963²), and various articles in the *Interpreter's Dictionary of the Bible* (1962) and vol. 1 of *The Interpreter's Bible* (1952).

[H.D.H.]

RELIGIOUS IMPACT

IN JUDAISM

In Hellenistic Judaism. Hellenistic Jewish literature, dating from about 250 B.C.E. to 40 C.E., may be regarded as the fusion of the biblical tradition with the Greek language and culture. The literary activity included paraphrases and analyses of biblical narratives, philosophical commentaries, epic and dramatic poetry. Some of these writings are strictly monotheistic; in others the pagan influence is pronounced; and there are a few remnants whose contents supposedly run counter to the current concepts of monotheism. But, except in one or two instances, the "Jewishness" of these fragments seems assured. The common characteristic that distinguishes these writings from the apocryphal and pseudepigraphal literature is that the names of the authors, though sometimes pseudonymous, are almost invariably known.

The tradition of the translation of the Torah by the Seventy during the reign of Ptolemy Philadelphus presupposes the existence of a professional cadre of translators in Alexandria, who were the first Hellenistic Jewish literati. They coined the term "Holy Bible" (ἡ ἱερὰ Βίβλος), recorded for the first time during the last two decades of the third century B.C.E. The Bible, or rather what is now known as the Pentateuch, was also called the Law (a translation of Torah), to which epithets were attached such as "the Holy," "God's," "Moses'," or "Israel's."

*Demetrius, who flourished during the reign of Ptolemy IV Philopater (221–204), may be regarded as a representative of the Alexandrian school whose immediate antecedents go back to the Septuagint translators. "Someone asked," he says, "'After having come here unarmed, how did the Israelites have weapons?' (Ex. 13:18)." This suggests that his question had been raised by other biblical commentators. It also shows that the question and answer method, current among Alexandrian pagan exegetes, was adopted by the Jews. Their rendition of the Hebrew word *va-ḥamushim* (Ex. 13:18) differed from that of the known versions of the Septuagint, which translate the term as the fifth generation (of the Israelites in Egypt). In general, in the extant fragments at least, Demetrius devotes most of his comments to chronological and genealogical problems. Chronology was also of great concern for a certain Philo, who may not be identical with *Philo the Elder, mentioned in *Josephus (Apion, 1:218), or Philo the Epicist; *Eupolemus, and Josephus' rival—*Justus of Tiberias.

In contrast to Demetrius and *Aristeas, the author of a history *On the Jews,* who show no direct awareness of the pagan world, writers such as *Pseudo-Eupolemus and *Artapanus reflect syncretistic traditions of biblical Hellenistic historiography. Pseudo-Eupolemus identified Enoch with the Hellenic Atlas, the reputed discoverer of astrology; Noah with Belus, the traditional founder of Babylon; and Melchizedek with the king and priest of the temple on Mount Gerizim. The last identification indicates that syncretistic and Euhemeristic tendencies were prevalent also among the Samaritans. Artapanus, who flourished during the second century B.C.E., represents the most extreme syncretistic school. According to him, Abraham, Joseph, and primarily Moses developed Egypt's science, statecraft, and religion. The story of Moses' war against Ethiopia, found in Artapanus and Josephus (Ant., 2:238–53), may be due to a common source. There is no evidence for the suggestion, maintained by Freudenthal, that Artapanus was a Jew who paraded as an Egyptian priest.

Alexandrian scholars in the middle of the second century B.C.E. also published commentaries that began to interpret Scripture allegorically, somewhat as many Greek exegetes explained Homer. *Aristobulus, "the teacher of Ptolemy" (II Macc. 1:10), argued that anthropomorphic expressions of the Bible such as "God's hand" must be understood as God's power. This may not seem to be quite allegory as the term is now understood, but Aristobulus' censure of the literalists' understanding of Scripture suggests the beginnings of a symbolic exegesis of Scripture (see above Allegorical Interpretations). Interestingly, Aristobulus says that there had existed a Greek translation of the Torah prior to the Septuagint which Homer, Hesiod, Pythagoras, Socrates, Plato, Hecataeus of Abdera and others had allegedly utilized. This indicates that the Jewish forgeries of Greek poets that extolled Jewish religion antedate the middle of the second century B.C.E.

From a literary point of view, the great achievement of the Greco-Jewish writers was in the field of poetry and drama. Philo the Elder composed an epic in Homeric hexameters on Jerusalem; short fragments on Abraham, Joseph, and the fountains and canals of Jerusalem survive. An epic by a Samaritan, *Theodotus, recounts the rape of Dinah (Gen. 34). Without introducing radical changes in the biblical story, there is considerable invention in the remaining 48 lines, attesting to a high degree of poetic inspiration and technical proficiency. Hellenistic Jewish literature attained its zenith in the drama *Exagoge (Exodus)* by *Ezekiel the Poet. In a sense this work seems but a paraphrase of the relevant chapters of the Septuagint Book of Exodus. But the dramatist was able to weave into the play interpretations that had been proposed by biblical commentators. Thus Zipporah, Moses' wife, is said to have been identical with the "Ethiopian woman" (Num. 12:1), a view earlier put forward by Demetrius. The heathen environment supplied Ezekiel the Poet with the forms of the play; the Torah, with its content and meaning. The same may be said of most of the Greco-Jewish literature—it was primarily Jewish and secondarily Greek.

See also *Apocrypha, *Josephus, *Pseudo-Philo.

[B.-Z.W.]

Talmud and Medieval Times. With the famous convocation of the people called by Ezra in the fifth century B.C.E., at which the Bible was solemnly and publicly read to the assembled people—"they read in the book, in the law of God, distinctly, and they gave the sense and caused them to understand the reading" (Neh. 8:8)—the Bible became for centuries the main, and for a long time the sole, intellectual preoccupation of the Jewish people. The talmudic interpretations (Meg. 3a) that "they read in the book" refers to the Hebrew text, and "distinctly" (or "with an interpretation") to its translation into the Aramaic vernacular are probably correct, and serve to indicate that for the first time the Bible had become the common cultural and religious possession of the entire Jewish people. This determination to spread knowledge of the Bible among the entire people is probably reflected in the adage of the Men of the *Great Synagogue, who carried on the activity thus initiated: "Set up many disciples" (Avot 1:2).

In discussing the Bible among the Jews it is essential to make a sharp distinction between their preoccupation with the Pentateuch and with the other sections of the Bible. The purpose of the study of the Pentateuch was mainly for the systematic development of the *halakhah*, the "way of life" which the Jew was to follow, and secondarily for homiletical exegesis. The former gave rise to the **Midrash Halakhah* and the latter to the **Midrash Aggadah*. The Pentateuch was regarded as the main authoritative source for the *halakhah*, and verses from the prophets and the Hagiographa were regarded merely as giving secondary support to it. They were called "Kabbalah" (tradition) and it was laid down that "no inference may be drawn concerning statements of the Pentateuch from statements found in the Kabbalah" (Ḥag. 10b). As a result, for the purpose of *halakhah* the entire weight was laid on the Pentateuch, and from the time of Ezra until the compilation of the Mishnah, the Pentateuch was practically the sole textbook for study. Since the purpose of that study was to arrive at the *halakhah*, this became the main subject of study with the compilation of the Mishnah.

A somewhat different situation existed with regard to the study of the Bible by the aggadists. Although their main preoccupation was also with the Pentateuch, they added to it the other portions of the Bible which were publicly read in the **haftarot* and the Five Scrolls. In addition to that, however, they deliberately sought to acquaint their listeners with the Bible as a whole, and almost invariably selected as the text of their proem a verse from the Hagiographa, linking it with the scriptural portion. As a result the entire Bible was gradually subjected to intensive study. This process is reflected in the statement of the Midrash: "Ben Azzai was engaged in stringing together verses of the Pentateuch to those of the prophets, and of the prophets to the Hagiographa, and the words of the Torah rejoiced as on the day they were given on Mt. Sinai" (Lev. R. 16:4; cf. Song R. 1:10 where the same is said of "Abba b. Mimi and his colleagues"). As a result of this extensive exegesis, it was possible for later authors to compile Midrashim on individual books of the Prophets and Hagiographa, as well as on the entire Bible, of which the **Yalkut Shimoni* is the outstanding example. Their principal sources were the Midrashim to the books which formed part of the synagogue lectionary and exegesis found in the Talmud. Consequently a large proportion of the non-pentateuchal portion of the Bible is commented on in Talmud and Midrash. It should be pointed out, however, that this exegesis was overwhelmingly homiletical and midrashic. Literal exegesis was almost entirely neglected during this period. It is true that R. Kahana stated that "a verse does not lose its interpretation according to the *peshat*" (Shab. 63a), but it is highly doubtful whether *peshat* in this context has the meaning "literal interpretation" given to it in later ages, probably first by Rashi. It seems to mean "the accepted interpretation as given in the schools." Certain interpretations referred to as "*peshat*" in one passage appear as "*derash*" in parallel passages; moreover, in *Ketubbot* 111b, R. Dimi, after giving a homiletical interpretation of Genesis 49:11 in answer to a question as to the "*peshat* of that verse," gives one which is much more midrashic than his previous one. As stated, the importance attached to the study of the Bible was conditioned by its liturgical use. Pride of place was given to the Pentateuch, which was not only read completely from beginning to end (in one year in Babylon and in a triennial cycle in Ereẓ Israel), but also was the basis of the *halakhah*. Next came the Five Scrolls which alone of the Hagiographa are read in their entirety in the synagogue. Of the prophets only the portions selected as the *haftarot* were read. Such portions were chosen from all the books of the Prophets with the exception of Joel, Nahum, Haggai, and Zephaniah. Until recent times it was the traditional and almost invariable practice for the Jewish preacher to select the text of his sermon from the scriptural reading of the week, either expounding its theme or applying his interpretation of the verse to the theme on which he was preaching (see *Preaching).

Insofar as concerns the Bible in the liturgy, one of its interesting aspects is the gradual increase of the number of Psalms included in the liturgy. In talmudic times, apart from the six Psalms of **Hallel* and the seven daily Psalms, one of which was recited daily as "the Psalm which the Levites used to say in the Temple," the Psalms did not form part of the daily liturgy, and in fact, the only biblical passages included in the actual prayers were the three paragraphs of the **Shema*. As against this, the *Standard Authorized Daily Prayer Book*, current among Ashkenazim in England, gives an index to the 72 Psalms included therein. Of these, 53 belong to statutory services. In addition to the above, the bulk is made up of seven Psalms in the *Pesukei de-Zimra* of weekdays (100 and 145–150) and nine (in the Sephardi rite 11) additional ones for Sabbaths and festivals, six (95–99 and 29) for the Inauguration of the Sabbath, and 16 (104 and 15 Songs of Degrees 120–134) for Sabbath afternoon in winter. The balance comprises Psalm 30 as an introduction to the *Pesukei de-Zimra;* Psalms recited when the Scroll of the Law is returned to the ark (already included in the above); Psalms 6 (in **Taḥanun*) and 20 in the concluding part of the daily service; Psalms 144 and 67 for the conclusion of the Sabbath; Psalm 27 during the month of Elul and until Hoshana Rabba; and a number of voluntary additional Psalms. Psalms are also included in every type of non-statutory service, e.g., in the night prayer, the service for the consecration of a house, for sickness, in the house of mourning, at the setting of a tombstone. A number of the above are recited on more than one occasion.

Various other sections of the Bible have also found their way into the prayer book. I Chronicles 16:18–36 is included in the *Pesukei de Zimra* (in the Sephardi rite it precedes them) as are I Chronicles 24:10–13, Nehemiah 9:6–11, and the Song of Moses (Ex. 14:30–15, 18). The last chapter of Proverbs has been instituted for home reading on Friday night. Among other biblical verses, mention should be made of the ten verses each of **Malkhuyyot, Zikhronot* and *Shofarot*—of which four are from the Pentateuch, three from the Prophets, and three from the Hagiographa—and Psalm 47 recited before the sounding of the *shofar* on Rosh ha-Shanah. The individual biblical verses introduced into the liturgy are too numerous to be detailed.

The intensive preoccupation with the aggadic and homiletical interpretation of the Pentateuch, brought in its wake a profound familiarity with the Bible, in which, however, the Midrash was paramount. The worthies of the Bible were regarded not as figures from the past but almost as living contemporaries. Abraham's smashing of the idols of his father and his deliverance from the fiery furnace, Esau as the embodiment of wickedness and the prototype of the archenemy of Israel, Aaron as the personification of the love and pursuit of peace, Judah as the mighty warrior, David as the wholly righteous monarch without sin or flaw, all of them the creation of the Midrash, appeared as real, if not more so, than the literal portrayal of them in the biblical narrative. In the Talmud it is laid down (Ber. 8a–b) that one should revise the weekly scriptural reading during the preceding week "twice in the original and once in the Aramaic translation [Targum]." It was later laid down (Tur., OḤ 2:285) that the commentary of Rashi could be substituted for the Targum. This injunction was widely followed throughout the ages, with the natural result that the ordinary Jew acquired an unparalleled and intimate acquaintance with the Pentateuch. Nevertheless, it was emphasized that the study of the Oral Law took precedence over and was regarded as more meritorious than that of the Bible. "Those who occupy themselves with the Written Torah (alone) are of but indifferent merit (lit. "a quality and not a quality"); but they do receive their reward; with Mishnah, are wholly meritorious, with **Gemara*—there can be nothing more meritorious" (BM 33a). Tractate *Soferim* expands this with the statement, "the Bible is compared to water, the Mishnah to pepper, the *Gemara* to spices." The world needs all three, and the wealthy man can indulge in all, but "happy is the man whose occupation is with *Gemara,*" the only rider being that the study of Bible should be thorough and not a mere springboard ("jumping") to the study of the Oral Law (15:8–9).

The Talmud declares that a person should divide his time into three equal portions, one of which should be devoted to the study of the Bible. Rashi maintains that one should therefore devote two days weekly to the study of Bible, but his grandson R. Tam, while applying the division to each day rather than the week, makes the significant comment that "a person who studies Talmud can ignore that of Bible since Bible is 'intermingled' in it" (Av. Zar. 19b and Rashi and Tos. in loc.). Maimonides, however (Yad. Talmud Torah 1:11), posits the talmudic injunction in its literal sense, which is probably the reason that knowledge of the Bible—indeed its memorization—has been much more widespread among oriental Jews than among Ashkenazi Jews. The close study of the biblical text, pursued with meticulous care and devotion by the masoretes, who not only set themselves the task of establishing the correct text but provided both punctuation and accents, was of immense service in establishing the accepted and standard text. It became the basis of the independent study of the Bible which was to characterize the Middle Ages.

The other non-Pentateuchal books of the Bible were also studied in the talmudic period. Every child was given a specific verse of the Bible which was, so to speak, regarded as "his own" (Ḥag. 15a–b; Esth. R. 7:13). (It may, however, refer to the verse he had studied that day.) The verses quoted in these two passages alone are from Isaiah (four verses), Jeremiah (two verses), Psalms and Proverbs. The child was introduced to the study of the Bible at an early age. The standard age of five is given in *Avot* (5:21), but a certain amount of flexibility was permitted (BB 21a—see *Education). The Mishnah, however, continues "the age of 10 for the study of Mishnah and of 15 for gemara," evidence that the study of the Bible was regarded as belonging to elementary education, although it was insisted that it be studied thoroughly (Sof. 15:9).

In the Middle Ages and After. The stimulus behind the emergence of the study of the Bible as an independent discipline was largely the result of the challenge provided by biblical exegesis of the *Karaites. Rejecting the entire corpus of talmudic tradition as incorporated in the Oral Law, and calling themselves "Benei Mikra" ("students of the Scripture"), they paid especial attention to the investigation of the biblical text and the derivation of new rules of conduct from it. There is no doubt that it was this challenge which stimulated Saadiah Gaon to branch out into what was to become the new intellectual activity of independent biblical exegesis, which largely took the form of literal exegesis. He was followed, among the Babylonian *geonim,* by Samuel b. Hophni and his son-in-law Hai Gaon, and they may be said to have laid down the foundations for literal exegesis of the Bible. (For the history of subsequent exegesis see above section on Exegesis.) An aspect of this study of the Bible in medieval times as an independent discipline is the fact that from Rashi onward biblical commentary covered the entire Bible. The commentary to the Pentateuch and Early Prophets of Isaac Abrabanel can be regarded as marking the close of this period.

The influence of the close study of the Bible, especially in Spain, is also evident in the neo-Hebrew poetry which developed during this period. Unlike the *paytanim* of Ereẓ Israel and the Franco-German school, the poets of Spain, particularly Solomon ibn *Gabirol, Moses *ibn Ezra and *Judah Halevi confined themselves to classical biblical Hebrew in their works, paying close attention to the rules of grammar and displaying a perfection and finish which reveals a thorough knowledge of the Bible. Mention must be made of a different approach to the study of the Bible which left a permanent mark. This is the kabbalistic exegesis of the Bible, which reached its full development in the *Zohar, "the Bible of the Mystics." This famous work can be regarded as a midrashic commentary to the Pentateuch, but the interpretation is mystic (*sod*; see *Kabbalah). It is difficult, however, to determine whether the burgeoning of the study of the Bible as a whole, and particularly in France (and Spain) was confined to scholars, or whether it encompassed the entire people. The remarkable explanation given by Rashi, who wrote commentaries on practically the entire Bible, of the deathbed statement of R. Eleazar: "Keep your children from *higgayon*" (meditation)—"Do not accustom them to excessive study of the Bible, because of its attractiveness" (Ber. 28b)—certainly seems to point to a discouragement of the "excessive" study of the Bible as a whole.

The 16th to the 18th centuries are characterized by an almost complete neglect of the study of the Bible as such. Talmud and Kabbalah became almost the sole subjects of study. Only in Italy was the study of the Bible as such pursued, and it produced such epoch-making works as Elijah *Levita's *Masoret ha-Masoret,* Azariah dei *Rossi's *Me'or Einayim,* Abraham *Portaleone's archaeological researches, and the commentaries of Obadiah *Sforno and Moses Ḥefez (*Gentili). Otherwise, biblical commentary consisted largely of novellae, supercommentaries and homiletical disquisition. Various attempts were made, e.g., by *Judah Loew b. Bezalel of Prague, to revive the study of the Bible, but with little effect.

Modern Times. The revival of the study of the Bible among Jews was inaugurated by the pentateuchal commentary of Moses *Mendelssohn, the *Biur*. That commentary heralded the return to the study of the Bible *per se*, with emphasis upon the literal interpretation of the Bible according to its natural meaning. Basing itself largely upon the classic rabbinical commentators of the Bible, Rashi, Samuel b. Meir (Rashbam), Ibn Ezra, and Naḥmanides, it eschewed homiletical interpretation entirely and confined itself solely to establishing the literal meaning of the text. However, this renewed interest in the study of the Bible was confined to scholars. The number engaged in it was small, and it had little effect on renewing interest in the Bible, and hardly penetrated into the consciousness of the Jewish masses. There were theological inhibitions which prevented the introduction of the fruits of modern biblical study, and those scholars who did engage in it had largely to make their contributions in European languages, in which almost all biblical study was developed. The prohibition against women studying Torah enunciated by R. Eliezer (Sotah 3:4) and accepted as *halakhah* (YD 246:6) was regarded as applying only to the Oral Law, and not to the Written. Women were, nevertheless, not encouraged to study the Bible; "she should not be taught in the first instance, but if she was so taught it is not regarded as obscenity" (YD loc. cit. Yad. Talmud Torah 1:13). Thus there was no special study of the Bible by women, yet the **Ẓe'enah U-Re'enah*, a midrashic exposition of the Bible in Yiddish especially written for women, achieved an immense popularity.

An almost dramatic transformation took place with the rise of the national movement after the end of the 19th century. On the one hand, the revival of Hebrew as a spoken language made possible the study and teaching of the Bible in the language in which it was written, and on the other hand, for the first time among the Jewish masses, that study was liberated from the theological confines to which it had been limited. A secular approach to the Bible, which regarded it solely as the greatest cultural and literary monument of Jewish culture, the outstanding achievement of the Jewish people when it lived a full national life in its own homeland, was adopted. It gave impetus to the most striking aspect of study in modern Israel, the restoration of the study of the Bible *per se*. The Bible and its study has come into its own in modern Israel. It is studied with equal interest both in religious and non-religious schools, with the obvious difference, however, that whereas in the former the religious aspect is paramount and there is a complete absence of any reference to biblical criticism, in the latter it is studied from the point of view of literature and history. Its study can be regarded almost as a national pastime. It has become a significant feature of Israel life; it is divided into daily readings so that the entire Bible is read in the course of the year, and those readings (for Prophets and Hagiographa), with a topical commentary, are the subject of a daily broadcast. Biblical "quizzes," whether among youth, in the army, among the general populace, or international have become a popular feature. Criticism has been leveled against this phenomenon in that it tends to emphasize a wide and comprehensive knowledge of the text alone, with no consideration given to its more profound aspects. But for the first time a public exists which employs the language of the Bible as its vernacular and which has a considerable knowledge of the text. As a result, practically for the first time since biblical study became an independent discipline, the possibility has been created for that study to be undertaken and disseminated in Hebrew. It has been suggested that the great enthusiasm for the Bible in Israel is a search for roots. It is witnessed in the popular interest in Bible conferences, in archaeological digs, in the revival of biblical place- and personal-names. Contact with the land of the Bible and its distinctive natural features and tangible conditions has had a distinct influence, for example, in the fields of topography, the history of settlement in Israel, and biblical realia, which have been intensified in recent years. [L.I.R.]

The annual International Bible Contest held in Jerusalem, 1969. Photo Eliahu Kaminer, Holon.

Bibliography: Hellenistic Judaism: J. Freudenthal, *Hellenistische Studien*, 2 vols. (1874–75); J. Wieneke, *Ezechielis Judaei poetae Alexandrini fabulae...* (1931); Eusebius, *Praeparatio Evangelica*, ed. by K. Mras, 1 (1954), 419–554; 2 (1956), 165–256; English translation: E. H. Gifford's edition, 3 (1903); F. Jacoby (ed.), *Die Fragmente der griechischen Historiker*, 3C, pt. 2 (1958), 666–713, nos. 722–37; N. Walter, *Der Thoraausleger Aristobulos* (1964); Wacholder, in: HUCA, 34 (1963), 83–113; idem, in: HTR, 61 (1968), 451–81. Modern Times: M. Haran, in: *Ha-Universitah*, 14, no. 3 (1969), 10–12; idem, *Biblical Research in Hebrew* (1970).

IN CHRISTIANITY

Christianity began as a conventicle in Judaism, with a complete and unquestioned acceptance of what had come to be the foundation stone of Judaism's serious view of itself as the one true revealed religion, destined to be the religion of all mankind. Through the years the confidence had matured that in the Bible was the complete and all-embracing record of all that men would ever need to know. Here stood revealed the full and complete will of God: all that men were to do and to be had been revealed to them. Their conduct toward one another and toward Him, the way they were to worship Him and regard Him, even their attitudes of mind and will, all had been revealed and was man's for the knowing. No circumstance could ever arise that had not been anticipated, no question for which the certain answer had not been given. Even before the moment of creation it had stood in the mind of God. Subsequently the blueprint for all time had been revealed by God to men through the agency of Moses and the other specially designated and inspired agents. The Bible was not 24 books, as it might superficially seem to be to Jewish eyes, or 29, to those of the Christians. It was fundamentally one book, with God its one author.

As the movement eventually to be styled Christianity became separate from the parent, it never lost this confidence in the nature of its inherited Scriptures, which, as the true Israel it regularly conceived itself to be, it easily came to believe were actually primarily its own, not the parent's, "for," as *Justin Martyr phrased it in his *Dialogue with Trypho* (ch. 29): "we believe them, but you, though you read them, do not catch the spirit that is in them."

Gradually, in the course of almost exactly 100 years, a large number of additional chapters, so to speak, were produced. As the years passed, many of these later writings became dear to an ever-increasing body of believers, with the result that by the middle of the fourth century 27 more writings had come to be widely regarded and formally accepted as a part of God's Revelation, of which He was the actual author, having seen fit to reveal His mind through the records which evangelists and apostles had written at His dictation.

Through the centuries this view was maintained. It is this which is meant by the statement in the twentieth of the still-authoritative Thirty-Nine Articles that the Bible is "God's word written." In the 18th century Locke was asserting nothing new when he insisted: "It has God for its author, salvation for its end, and truth without any mixture of error for its matter." A century later, an Oxford theologian, Dean Burgon, spelled it out: "The Bible is none other than the voice of Him that sitteth upon the throne. Every book of it, every chapter of it, every word of it, every syllable of it (where are we to stop?), every letter of it, is the direct utterance of the Most High. The Bible is none other than the Word of God, not some part of it more, some part of it less, but all alike the utterance of Him who sitteth upon the throne, faultless, unerring, supreme" (*Inspiration and Interpretation* (1861), 89).

This view of Scripture, despite two centuries of inquiry during which in the eyes of an increasingly large group it has been discredited or drastically qualified, is still with nuances the verdict of Christianity, Orthodox, Roman Catholic, and Protestant alike. The Protestant Reformation did not affect the matter in the slightest. There was and is no real difference between Catholics and Protestants as to the proper attitude toward the Bible or the basis on which they rest their creeds. The sole difference lay—and still lies—in the fact that to the Catholic (and Orthodox) Scripture is not the sole authoritative and infallible source of belief. Scripture (i.e., Old and New Testament including the deuterocanonical books) and tradition are the source of God's revelation. For the Protestants the Scriptures alone can have such a claim. Both, however, accept the Bible as the authoritative and infallible statement of revealed truth. Actually, Protestant scholars at times went to greater extremes in their stress upon biblical interpretation than did Catholics. During the years, ecclesiastical infallibility and scriptural infallibility had grown up together. As a result of the Reformation, ecclesiastical infallibility was thrown overboard by Protestants. The infallibility of the Bible was set up as a bulwark against the rejected infallibility of the Church. It is accordingly not surprising that in consequence a literal view of inspiration, like that enunciated by Dean Burgon, resulted.

Thus the real and distinctive note in the Christian attitude toward the Old Testament has never been whether the Old Testament is or is not Scripture, to be accepted and prized, for this acceptance has been universal. Rather, the problem has always been how the Old Testament is to be interpreted and used.

Beginning, and continuing for many years, as a part of Judaism, sounding the proclamation of Jesus, whom they believed to have been raised from the dead by God and to be with him in heaven soon to return to establish the speedily expected new age, which, like him, they styled the kingdom of God, the Christians' main differences from the rest of orthodox Jewry were their developing views of Jesus himself. So far as fundamentals were concerned, they remained orthodox Jews, in their views of the unity of God, of His relation to Israel, of His complete revelation in Scripture.

With their basic view of the all-inclusive content of the Divine Revelation in Scripture it was not unnatural that Christians saw prophesied therein their movement and their Christ. As the movement came more and more to be separate from Judaism, the conviction deepened that Judaism, which failed to see in the predictions in the Old Testament the Christian Jesus and the success of the movement resulting from his preaching, was blind to the real content of the Scriptures, which Scriptures they were confident were theirs. The Old Testament, according, for example, to the *Epistle of Barnabas*, has meaning only when it is understood in terms of the gospel. It was held that God's covenant has always been made with Christians, and the Old Testament has always been misunderstood by the Jews. This in no wise minimized the Old Testament. "All scripture is inspired by God and helpful for teaching," as the author of II Timothy 3:16 was to insist; but it must be rightly understood.

Much has been written about Paul's rejection of the Mosaic law, but although this is true, it is far from meaning that he rejected the Old Testament. It remains Scripture for Paul and of the profoundest value, as his constant citation to establish or buttress this contention or that indicates, but it is no longer letter but spirit, no longer law but a ministry of grace. By the aid of the Spirit he holds, the Old Testament can be interpreted as a spiritual book—the reason others cannot do so is because they have not received the gift of the spirit. They have been blinded by Satan; true understanding of the Old Testament comes only from God. Paul is adept in finding "spiritual meaning" in the most unlikely texts. He does not view the Old Testament as the Christian's moral guide, for his break with the law, ceremonial and moral alike, was complete. Rather this standard or guide is to be found based on what he calls Jesus' law of love, more exactly, what is worthy of one in Christ. The point often overlooked is that the kind of life which Paul felt worthy of in Christ is precisely the type of life which as a Jew he had been from birth trained to revere, as he had found it revealed in Scripture.

The whole insistence in the *Epistle of Barnabas* is that Christians must avoid a Judaistic conception of the Old Testament. Despite Barnabas' blistering criticism of the literal understanding of passages regarding sacrifices and the food laws, he never thinks of giving up the Old Testament or its divine Creator, as Marcion and most of the Gnostics were subsequently to do. Instead his pages are filled with such words as "Moses received these doctrines concerning food and thus spoke of them in the Spirit; but they [the Jews] received them as merely referring to food, owing to the lust of their flesh" (*Epistle of Barnabas,* 10). His reference to gnosis and his anti-Judaism do not mean that he was either a Gnostic or that he rejected the Old Testament. Gnosis, as he uses the term, is simply deeper insight into the truths of Christianity with the aid of allegorical interpretation of the Old Testament which allowed him to find what he sought to discover. His allegorization constantly does violence to the meaning of the text and resolves historical events into exaggerated fantasy. Nor is Barnabas alone. Justin Martyr indicates the same naive and uncritical attitude toward the Old Testament. That he revered it as inspired Scripture is evident in every page; his devotion to allegorical interpretation, which can find Jesus clearly predicted in the most impossible passages and the cross prefigured not alone throughout the Scriptures—the paschal lamb roasted on a spit (*Dialogue with Trypho,* 40), the extended hands of Moses (*ibid.,* 90), the serpent in the wilderness (*First Apology,* 60), the horn of the unicorn (*Dialogue with Trypho,* 91)—but also in the nautical rig of masts and yardarms, in the plow and tools of the farmer and mechanic, in the more obscure and misty discourses of Plato, or in the nose which juts from the face which enables the prophet to say, "The breath before our face is the Lord Christ" (*First Apology,* 55), reveals vividly, if to a modern age grotesquely, the early Christian confidence that the Old

Testament was primarily a Christian book, at least of a sort which must be rightly read to be properly understood. Like Paul, Justin does not deny the historical reality of God's relationship with Israel. What he insists upon is that the earlier covenant looks forward to being superseded. The prophets herald a new covenant with God, and in Christianity with its two predicted advents of Christ—the one already experienced, the other yet to come—their predictions are fully realized.

The Alexandrian school, notably *Origen, deeply indebted to Philo, sets forth most thoroughly the principles or purport of Christian allegorization, and with far less of the bizarre overemphasis of a Barnabas or Justin Martyr. For Origen the fulfillment of prophecy is the proof of its unquestioned inspiration. Thus, in the advent of Jesus the inspiration of the prophetic words and the truly spiritual nature of Moses' law come into full light. The purpose of Scripture is to reveal intellectual truths, not to show God's working in history. Actually history often conceals truth. This, Origen sees clearly evidenced in the pages of both Old and New Testaments. In addition—for, like Philo, Origen was in many ways a very practical and down-to-earth man—much of the legislation in both Testaments cannot be literally observed. Such passages must, accordingly, reveal other important, if less obvious, values. But Origen is far more restrained than were some of his predecessors: the passages which are historically true, he is sure, far outnumber those which are composed with purely spiritual significance—that is, which are not historically true. In sum, all Scripture has a spiritual meaning. It should be observed that Origen is a scholar and thinks and writes as such. His protests against what he terms the literal meaning are directed essentially against the superficial and often absurd misinterpretations put upon Scripture by ignorant people who cannot understand metaphors and parables and who thus regularly read poetry as pedestrian prose.

The allegorical method of interpreting Scripture, which was the outgrowth of the Christian confidence that their movement and their Christ were of course revealed in the all-inclusive Scriptures, and that it was their task to set forth these facts clearly so that when their Lord returned from heaven he would find faith on the earth, encountered much criticism. Marcion, a devoted if misguided Christian—and in no small degree driven to his rejection of the Old Testament as a Christian book by these absurd excesses of allegorization—insisted on a literal understanding of the Hebrew Scriptures, the better to emphasize their crudity. In his eyes the Old Testament was not a Christian book, and no amount of allegorization could make it such. Jesus was not foreseen in any of the prophecies of the Old Testament, nor did his coming in any sense fulfill them; rather, he had come to destroy both the law and the prophets. Marcion stands alone in this rejection, and many interpreters have denied that he was a Christian in any sense of that word.

Others, notably the group of scholars styled the Antiochian school and *Jerome, had a profound respect for the literal meaning of Scripture. Jerome had earlier been an allegorist, as his first biblical commentary clearly shows, but his contacts with Jewish teachers had been influential in his change of front. It is not too much to say that wherever the influence of the Synagogue is to be seen—as in Dorotheus, head of the catechetical school in Antioch, who painstakingly learned Hebrew—there was a tendency toward a literal understanding of the Old Testament. This was not to deny the deeper meaning of Scripture, which was to them unquestioned. Rather, the deeper meaning was built onto the literal, not flatly opposed to it as Barnabas had fulminated.

The most influential of the school of Antioch was Theodore of Mopsuestia. He insisted on the historical reality of biblical revelation. In the prophecies of Christ's coming, allegory is not to be seen, as the Alexandrians had maintained. Rather, the prophets actually foresaw what was to come to pass in Israel and announced it, but in addition they saw—or some of them did—the ultimate coming of Christ. Nor could Alexandria rightly claim Paul's words in Galatians 4 and I Corinthians 10 as its support. Despite Paul's phrase, he was not indulging in allegory. His words were typological. The incident was real, but in addition it typified a deeper truth. The events had taken place; nonetheless they were comparisons and so he could use them as warning examples. Actually Theodore insisted that only four of the Psalms (2, 8, 44, 109) are in any sense to be seen as predictive of Jesus, and that they are not truly messianic but rather give glimpses of the incarnation. Only books containing a prophetic element are to be regarded as canonical; thus Job, Chronicles, Ezra-Nehemiah, and Esther, as well as all the books of the Apocrypha, are to be seen as containing human wisdom alone and are to be rejected from the canon. This exclusion of any of the books of the Hebrew canon was most unusual, and a century later Theodore's writings were burned as heretical—in part because of the views of his pupil Nestorius, for which he was held responsible, and in part because of his exclusion of books universally revered as canonical, quite regardless of the way they were interpreted.

As the Christian movement spread into the gentile world, it was but natural that the current Greek version of their inherited Scripture became their Bible. Because of the confidence that Jesus and the Christian movement were to be found in its pages and because of the Christian conviction that the Jewish understanding of the Scriptures was in error regarding what to them was palpably a Christian book, it is not surprising that the Septuagint speedily lost all authority in Jewish eyes and that the second century saw several new Greek translations (Aquila, Symmachus, Theodotion) stemming from Jewish feelings of outrage that their Scripture was being so crassly misused and turned into a weapon against them. One of the most significant achievements by any early Christian scholar, well indicating the universal Christian acceptance of the Old Testament as a part of their inspired Scripture, was the gigantic Hexapla, with the Old Testament standing in six parallel columns (cf. above, Ancient Versions, Greek). Well aware of the fact, as he was, that frequently the Septuagint and the Hebrew diverge, Origen sought to indicate this. Material in the Septuagint but not in the Hebrew was indicated by warning obeli; material in the Hebrew but not in the Greek was indicated by asterisks. In addition to this monumental work by Origen, other recensions of the Septuagint (Hesychian and Lucianic) were subsequently made. Occasionally Christian scholars in the early days had some knowledge of Hebrew and made use of Hebrew texts, although regularly chided by Jewish scholars for employing inferior and corrupted texts; by and large until the 16th century, when knowledge of Greek and Hebrew became a scholarly must, study of the Old Testament was based upon the Greek texts. Although translations of both Testaments into Latin and Syriac were made early, Greek continued to be the usual medium until the fourth century. Gradually Latin became the common Christian tongue, and a standard authoritative Latin version of both Testaments became necessary to bring order out of the chaos which had arisen and of which Augustine remarked: "Whenever in earlier days a Greek manuscript came into any man's hand, provided he fancied that he had any skill at all in both languages, he did not hesitate to translate it." After completing his revision of the Latin text of the New

Testament at Rome at the behest of Pope Damasus, Jerome went to Bethlehem and produced a version of the Old Testament. He claimed that it was a new translation into Latin of the Septuagint on the basis of Origen's hexaplaric text, that is, the fifth column of the Hexapla. Whether this was actually a fresh translation, as Jerome claimed, or simply a revision of the Old Latin text, is uncertain, for Jerome's claims are often unreliable. At any rate, he speedily became convinced of the need of a fresh translation of the Old Testament from the Hebrew text. This he made and, except for the Psalms, it is the present Vulgate (cf. above, Ancient Versions, Latin). His translation of the Hebrew Psalter was never likely to oust in popular regard his earlier translation from the Greek (Gallican Psalter). In consequence of his work, Jerome became convinced that only the books in the Hebrew Bible had warrant to be considered part of the Bible. Despite his arguments and insistence, the Roman Church continued to use the Apocrypha, which had been regularly regarded as canonical by Christians to whom the Septuagint was their Bible; the Apocrypha continued to be, as it is today, an unquestioned part of the Bible of the Roman Catholic Church, not collected at the end, but interspersed, as it was in the Septuagint, among the other Old Testament books. Jerome's objections eventually found acceptance in Protestantism. Luther relegated the Apocrypha to the end of the Old Testament. Subsequently British and American churches came to exclude these books, even as a separate collection, from printed editions of the Bible, although in the 20th century they have regained a measured popularity as valuable reading. They are not, and they have not been since the Reformation, a veritable part of the Bible in Protestant eyes (see also *Luther; *Reformation; *Protestantism). For many centuries the basic contention of both Judaism and Christianity maintained that the Bible is totally different from all other books, and in consequence the rules and procedures for studying and appraising other writings do not apply here. The past three centuries have seen the rise and development of a direct challenge to this contention, in what is commonly styled Higher Criticism. The source analysis of the first six books of the Old Testament, from Astruc and De Wette to Colenso and Wellhausen, has resulted in far more than just a transfer of authorship from Moses to a host of nameless men at a distinctly later date or dates. It has brought these books into clear view as the record of centuries of achievement and of the long pilgrimage of men and women, constantly confronted with the tasks and problems of life, making their mistakes, achieving new and sounder insights. In short, to many Christians the Old Testament now stands as the longest and best record of man's evolution and the growth of his ideas about himself and his God, and the record of the development of morality, politics, and religion, which have, for better or worse, very definitely molded our own culture and patterns of thought.

Bibliography: A. von Harnack, *Bible Reading in the Early Church* (1912); H. R. Willoughby (ed.), *The Study of the Bible Today and Tomorrow* (1947); R. M. Grant, *The Bible in the Church* . . . (1948); B. Smalley, *The Study of the Bible in the Middle Ages* (1952[2]); E. G. Kraeling, *The Old Testament since the Reformation* (1955); I. M. Price, *The Ancestry of our English Bible* (1956[3]); G. Burkhardt (ed.), *Five Essays on the Bible* (1960); S. L. Greenslade (ed.), *The Cambridge History of the Bible* (1963); E. C. Colwell, *The Study of the Bible* (1964[2]).

[M.S.E.]

IN ISLAM

The presence of Jewish and Christian communities in the northern and southern Arabian Peninsula during the centuries which preceded the advent of *Muhammad is sufficient explanation that the Arabs already knew of the existence of the Bible in these communities during the period of the *Jāhilīyya* ("ignorance"), i.e., before the "Prophet of Islam" began to herald his religion. The pre-Islamic poets saw the books of the Bible in the possession of the Jewish *ḥakhamim* and the Christian clergymen and monks, and since the overwhelming majority of them could not read or write—Muhammad also prided himself on his ignorance in this field (Sura 7:156; cf. also 4:162; 40:78)—the letters appeared to them as the "faded traces of abandoned campsites" which could only be distinguished with difficulty (but see Brockelmann, Arab Lit, supplement 1 (1937), 32 n. 2). The poets mention the *zabūr*—the definition of which appears to be (the book of) Psalms (of David); Muhammad later pluralized it as *zubūr* in the Koran to denote the whole of the Bible (see Sura 17:57; 26:196). Muhammad knew of the Torah (*tawrāt;* e.g., Sura 3:58, 87), which was given to *ahl al-kitāb* ("the people of the book," i.e., Jews and Christians) and like the Koran it is a revelation of the word of God. The *tawrāt* is held as a way of uprightness and light. According to the book of Allah, the Prophets—who were loyal to Allah—as well as the rabbis and the *aḥbār* (Jewish *ḥakhamim*), judged the Jews (Sura 5:48). Even though it is obvious that Muhammad had heard much of the contents of the Bible, there is no doubt that all of his knowledge was acquired from teachings and tales told to him by Jews and Christians. It appears that he was not the only one in his time who repeated these to his followers. His opponents therefore often mocked him because he told them *asāṭīr al-awwalīn,* stories of the ancients which had been heard more than once (see e.g., Sura 6:25; 8:31; 16:26; et al.). It was natural that such religious sermons—whether their contents were intended for the purpose of teaching or amusement—be delivered in a free style (i.e., not verbatim). Accurate translations of the Bible or enlargements with aggadic paraphrases (similar to Targum Jonathan) were however certainly to be found among the *ahl al-kitāb*—if not in writing, then at least in a fixed oral tradition. Nonetheless, it is doubtful whether Muhammad heard these verbatim—at least not during the first years of his appearance. Even though the Koran relies on the words of the *kitāb* ("the Book")—and in many Suras there is a clear allusion to the Pentateuch and the Prophets—the instances which may be regarded as (rather free) translations of the Bible are very few: in Sura 3:87 "all food was lawful to the children of Israel save what Israel (i.e., Jacob) made unlawful to himself before the law was revealed" (see Gen. 32:33; Sura 5:49; cf. Ex. 21:25–26; both Suras belong to the Medina period). Only in Sura 21:105 (of the Mecca period) can one find a quotation from Psalms (37:29) with the mention of the source: "And already have we written in *zabūr* [Psalms] . . . 'The earth shall my righteous servants inherit.' " ("The righteous shall possess the land, and dwell upon it forever.")

Muhammad points out that Allah gave The (Holy) Book to Mūsā (=Moses; Sura 25:37; 2:81, 140–1, et al.). However, even before Mūsā, *ṣuḥuf* ("holy scrolls") were given to Ibrāhīm (= Abraham; Sura 53:37–38; 87:19; 19:42) and to Ismāʿīl (=Ishmael; 19:55), and their contents were also revealed to earlier generations (20:13; 87:18). According to Sura 20:133, these scrolls contain clear proofs of the prophecy and the mission of Muhammad; they are identical with the *kitāb,* the original book being in Heaven; it was revealed to the prophets and is the source of all revelations. This book is the *umm al-kitāb* (the "mother of the [Holy] Book," 43:3; 85:21). All the deeds of men from the Creation of the World until the final Day of Judgment are also inscribed in this book. According to Speyer (p. 334) the origin of this expression lies in a Midrash ("Torah . . . which is called a mother to its students"). The notion of the "Book" preserved in Heaven, in which everything is written and which also serves as a register for the deeds of all creatures, is found in the Bible (Ex. 32:32; Isa. 4:3; et al.); Muhammad received it from Judaism (cf. Hirschberg, *Diwan des as-Samau'al,* 24, 52–58).

When Muhammad met face to face with the *aḥbār,* the Jewish *ḥakhamim,* at *Yathrib-Medina, they began to doubt his prophetic mission, and particularly ridiculed his lack of knowledge of the tales of the Bible. Muhammad then accused the Jews (and also the Christians) of having altered *(ḥarrafa)* the words of the Torah and having substituted *(baddala)* what was written in it (Sura 2:56, 70, 73; 4:48; 5:16; 61:6). At Yathrib-Medina, the sharp turning point in Muhammad's attitude toward the Jews occurred. Indeed, Muhammad's lack of familiarity with the Old and New Testaments was particularly revealed in his Bible tales, because with regard to true monotheistic beliefs there are hardly any conflicts with Jewish views; this is not the case with respect to the divinity of Jesus and the Trinity. In the Bible tales, however, the inexactitudes, changes, lack of consistency, and even errors on almost every subject are conspicuous. However, during the years of Muhammad's activity, many changes also occurred in his approach to the Bible tales, which he sometimes deliberately adapted to the new conditions that had emerged; some of these were political, others were connected with information acquired from others or conclusions which he had reached himself. The commentators of the Koran later attempted to explain some of these faults, but with regard to others they did not conceal the truth. The cause of these errors is sometimes the defective source from which Muhammad drew his information, but one may also assume that Muhammad did not attribute much importance to these details. He employed the narrative material as a creator who sought to form a new structure from it, and therefore often adapted it to his requirements. The function of the tales of the Prophets on the events in antiquity and the attitude toward the emissaries who had preceded him was to explain his mission, his war against the inhabitants of Mecca, his policy, and also his failures. Hence the phenomenon that there is no uniform system in the Koran concerning the tradition of the Bible tales.

(A) Certain figures are mentioned by their names, but with occasional changes in the pronunciation which have been influenced by the Greek or Syrian languages, e.g., Ilyās—Elijah; Ismāʿīl—Ishmael; Sulaymān—Solomon; Firʿawn—Pharaoh. Other changes are due to Muhammad's affection for the creation of paronomasian couples, such as Hābīl and Qābīl (Abel and Cain), Hārūn and Qārūn (Aaron and Korah), Jālūt and Ṭālūt (Goliath and Saul), Yājūj and Mājūj (Gog and Magog), etc. Other changes must be attributed to Arabic writing, which as of yet did not have the diacritic marks, e.g., *Qiṭfīr instead of Poti-Phar; Asiya (wife of Pharaoh; see *Firʿawn) instead of Asenath (the daughter of Poti-phera). (In both cases the difference in the reading lies in the placing of the diacritic mark.)

(B) Some figures are alluded to in the Koran in such a way that there is no doubt as to whom Muhammad referred, even though they are not mentioned by their biblical name, e.g., the three (or four!) sons of *Noah (Sura 11:44–49), and Joshua son of Nun (5:23–29). This anonymity at times stems from Muhammad's obvious tendency to use insinuations. In some cases, however, the name was not sufficiently clear to him and he then preferred not to name the person (see: e.g., the Sura on *Balaam son of Beor, in the identification of which the commentators of the Koran also encounter difficulties, 7:174–5).

(C) In contrast to this anonymity, some figures are mentioned in the Koran with different names from those in the Bible; figures from the world of fantasy are cited as well: e.g., *Terah, the father of Abraham, is named Āzar; a figure from the world of folklore is the prophet to whom *Moses went during his journey with his servant. The third Sura of the Koran known as the Sura of ʿAmrān Family, i.e., Amram. It refers to a man whose wife (known as Hannah in post-Koranic legend) gave birth to *Mary (Miriam), the mother of Jesus, the messiah, as is apparent from the continuation of the tale (3:31ff.). Miriam, the sister of Aaron and Moses, is not referred to by her name in the Koran. Parenthetically, it should be noted that the space allocated in the Koran to the tales and legends of the New Testament is disproportionately small, a fact which has drawn the attention of all researchers (Hirschberg, *Juedische und christliche Lehren,* 64–66). On the other hand, Christian influence is discernible in the descriptions of some of the biblical characters, such as Lot, Solomon, and Jonah. Many attempts, some of them successful, have been made in the post-Koranic Muslim literature to correct the curiosities in the tales of the Koran, to clarify the intentionally or unintentionally obscure places, to call by their correct names those figures who are mentioned by incorrect names or only by allusion, and to complete that which has been omitted in the continuity of the Bible tales. It is remarkable that in spite of the excessively large number of biblical characters referred to by the title of prophet because God spoke to them, and the figures of the prophets who were sent to the Arab tribes (e.g., *Hud, Ṣāliḥ), the three great prophets, Isaiah, Jeremiah, and Ezekiel, are unknown. Speyer has already noted that Muhammad does not allocate a place of importance to women in the Koran, especially not to unmarried girls. In his opinion this is the reason why the rescue of Moses is attributed to Asiya, the wife of Pharaoh (Sura 28:8), and not his daughter. Similarly, there is no mention in the Koran of the names of Sarah, Hagar, Rebekah, Leah, and Rachel (to whom there is a distinct allusion in Sura 4:27), or to Zipporah, the wife of Moses. He presents the wives of Noah and Lot in dreadful disgrace and describes the wife of Pharaoh as a righteous woman (Sura 66:10–12). In the post-Koranic literature all the above women are mentioned by their names and even Keturah, the wife of Abraham, is not forgotten. This process of exegesis and completion began within the circle of Muhammad's friends and supporters immediately after his death. Similar to the *Hadith collections (traditions dealing with *sunnat al-nabī*—the ways of the Prophet, his practical conduct *(halakhah)*—and based on *isnād,* i.e., an unbroken line of transmission which has been handed down from mouth to mouth beginning from the companions of the Prophet or the Prophet himself) they also began to insert, according to the same system, the explanations, commentaries, and legendary additions of the Koran. The legends which originated in Judaism were called **Isrāʾiliyyāt* and are to be found in three literary categories: (1) *The commentaries on the Koran,* the most renowned, detailed, and ancient of which is that of the historian Abu Jaʿfar Muhammad al-Ṭabarī (838/9–992). Al-Ṭabarī published a 30-volume anthology of commentaries in accordance with the Hadith system; he presents the various opinions then prevalent on many subjects (see: e.g., in the entry "Isaac" concerning the question of who was bound by Abraham). Al-Ṭabarī, however, was also familiar with the Bible and knew the details of the story of the conquest of Canaan by Joshua. (2) *Arabic history books.* Again the first volume of the detailed historical work by al-Ṭabarī is a rich source of Bible tales, as they were current among the Arabs and the Muslims in general. (3) A third source is the **Qiṣaṣ al-Anbiyāʾ* ("Legends of the Prophets"), in which the tales were also collected in chronological order. The first to gather these tales in writing appears to have been *Wahb ibn Munabbih, the author of the *Isrāʾīliyyāt* which have been lost and are only known from quotations. The detailed work which has been printed many times is that of al-Thaʿlabī (d. 1035), who presents his subjects according to the Hadith system. In addition to the legends, his work contains literal translations and paraphrases from the Bible. A second collection which was published is that of al-Kisāʾī (lived during the 11th century). A third collection is extant in manuscript in the Vatican (Cod. Borgia 165); it is the earliest of the collections and belongs to ʿUmāra ibn Wathīma (eighth century). His work does not attain the completeness of those mentioned above. Much romantic material, which cannot be traced to the Bible or to Jewish literature, has also entered into these tales: e.g., the story of Jarāda, the daughter of the king of Sidon, whom Solomon took for his wife after he had defeated her father and whom he loved more than all his other wives because of her beauty (Ṭabarī, *Taʾrīkh*, 1 (1357 A. H.), 351–352). She continued to worship the idols and Āṣaf ibn Barakhyā, the righteous adviser of Solomon who frequented his palace, rebuked him for this. According to the commentators, there is an allusion to this Āṣaf in Sura 27:40, in the story of *Bilqīs, the queen of Sheba.

Abundant and rich biblical material has entered Arabic and Muslim literature by the way of the Koran and tales of *aggadah*. Some of the Bible tales, as well as Muhammad's accusations against the changes *(tabdīl)* and the forgeries *(taḥrīf)* in the Bible in order to refute the prophecy of his coming—found in the Holy Scriptures of the Jews and the Christians—served as the Islamic *polemic against Judaism (and Christianity) in Muslim literature. *Ibn Ḥazm used this particular method when he argued with Samuel ha-Nagid (11th century), and also the Jewish apostate al-Samawʾal al-Maghribī (Samuel b. Yaḥya; 12th century). One may see the last echo of this polemic in the words of R. David ibn Abi Zimra, who laments: "The Arabs . . . regard our prayer as heresy and they say that we have added to, subtracted from, and changed our Torah . . ." (responsa, vol. 4 (Sudilkov, 1836), 21c).

See also *Koran; *Aggadah (in Islam).

For biblical tales in Islam see also the following articles: *Aaron (Hārūn); *Abraham (Ibrāhīm); *Adam (Ādam); *Balaam (Balʿam ibn Bāʿūrā); *Benjamin (Binyāmīn); *Cain and Abel (Qābīl wa-Hābīl); *Canaan (Kanʿān); *Daniel (Dāniyāl); *David (Dāʾūd); *Elijah (Ilyās); *Elisha (Alyasaʿ); *Enoch (Idrīs); *Eve (Ḥawwāʾ); *Ezekiel (Ḥizqīl); *Ezra (Uzayr); *Gog and Magog (Yājūj and Mājūj); *Goliath (Jālūt); *Haman (Hāmān); *Isaac (Isḥāq); *Isaiah (Shaʿyā); *Isrāʾīliyyāt; *Ishmael (Ismāʿīl); *Jacob (Yaʿqūb); *Jeremiah (Irmiyā); *Job (Ayyūb); *Jonah (Yūnus); *Joseph (Yūsuf); *Joshua (Yūshaʿ); *Korah (Qārūn); *Lot (Lūṭ); *Miriam (Maryam); *Moses (Mūsā); *Nebuchadnezzar (Bukhtanaṣr); *Nimrod (Namrūd); *Noah (Nūḥ); *Pharaoh (Firʿawn); *Potiphar (Qiṭfīr) *Queen of Sheba (Bilqīs); *Samaritans (Sāmirī); *Samuel (Shamwīl); *Saul (Ṭālūt); *Seth (Shīth); *Solomon (Saleiman); *Terah (Āzar).

Bibliography: A. Geiger, *Was hat Mohammed aus dem Judenthume aufgenommen* (1833); G. Weil, *Biblische Legenden der Muselmaenner* (1845); H. Hirschfeld, *Beitraege zur Erklaerung des Koran* (1886); M. Steinschneider, *Polemische und apologetische Literatur in arabischer Sprache zwischen Muslimen, Christen und Juden* (1877); M. Gruenbaum, *Neue Beitraege zur semitischen Sagenkunde* (1893); W. Rudolph, *Die Abhaengigkeit des Qorans von Judentum und Christentum* (1922); J. Horovitz, in: HUCA, 2 (1925), 145–227; idem, *Koranische Untersuchungen* (1926); T. Andrae, *Der Ursprung des Islams und das Christentum* (1926); R. Bell, *The Origin of Islam in its Christian Environment* (1926); J. W. Hirschberg, *Der Dīwān des as Samauʾal ibn ʿAdijāʾ* (1931); idem, *Juedische und christliche Lehren im vor- und fruehislamischen Arabien* (1939); D. Sidersky, *Les origines des légendes musulmanes dans le Coran et dans les vies des prophètes* (1933); Ch. Cutler Torrey, *The Jewish Foundation of Islam* (1933); A. Jeffery, *The Foreign Vocabulary of the Qurʾān* (1938); H. Speyer, *Die biblischen Erzaehlungen im Qoran* (1961²); E. I. J. Rosenthal, *Judaism and Islam* (1961); A. I. Katsh, *Judaism and the Koran* (1954).

[H.Z.H.]

IN THE ARTS

LITERATURE

Although the Greek Septuagint translation of the Old Testament inspired a few writers in classical times, the Hebrew Bible's first significant impact on the secular literature of other nations really dates from the Middle Ages with the beginning of drama. Old Testament episodes figured in various cycles of Sacred Mysteries or Miracle Plays sponsored by the Church (mainly in England, France, and Germany), the vernacular eventually replacing Latin dialogue. During the Reformation, writers in many countries produced biblical epics which expressed the national aspirations and religious yearnings of their people. New scope was given to original treatment of Old Testament themes through the appearance of numerous *Bible translations (largely the works of Protestant scholars in Switzerland, Germany, England, Hungary, and other lands); and these not only popularized the Bible stories, but also very often had linguistic repercussions. From the Renaissance era onward, biblical works increasingly contained political and social overtones. Although *Yiddish literature is several centuries old, Yiddish fiction based on biblical themes other than *Purim plays is of recent date. Some notable treatments of Old Testament themes are dramas by Abraham *Goldfaden (*Akeydas Yitskhok*, 1897) and Sholem *Asch's novels *Moses* (1951) and *The Prophet* (1955). *Judeo-Provençal contains a late 17th-century *Tragediou de la Reine Esther* by Mardochée Astruc, revised and published by Jacob *Lunel (The Hague, 1774);

Figure 1. Page from a manuscript of the Judeo-Persian paraphrase of stories from the Pentateuch by the 14th-century poet, Maulana Shahin of Shiraz, written by Nehemiah b. Amshal in Tabriz, 1686. The illustration shows the finding of Moses in the bullrushes. Jerusalem, Israel Museum.

*Ladino literature the early 15th-century *Poema de Yoçef* and Abraham de Toledo's *Coplas de Yoçef* (Constantinople, 1732); and *Judeo-Persian literature four poetic paraphrases of Bible stories by the 14th-century writer Maulana *Shahin of Shiraz, who was emulated by the poet *Imrani in the 16th century and by Yusuf *Yahudi in the 18th century. In other literatures, Jewish writers either followed conventional approaches to Old Testament subjects, or, more frequently, reinterpreted the biblical stories in the light of issues such as Jewish emancipation, religious toleration, and political Zionism.

In *English literature a vast array of biblical figures appear in poetry and prose from the seventh century C.E. onward. Among the Puritans, John *Milton was outstanding (*Paradise Lost,* 1667; *Samson Agonistes,* 1671), biblical motifs also dominating some works by John Dryden (*Absalom and Achitophel,* 1681). After a lull in the 18th century, the impact of the Bible was again evident in Lord *Byron (*Hebrew Melodies,* 1815) and the scholarly Robert *Lowth and Matthew Arnold; while a more mystical vein appeared in the writings of William *Blake. The 19th century saw the emergence of a reckless biblicism in various works by the *British Israelites. With the exception of Isaac *Rosenberg, Jewish writers in England have largely avoided biblical themes. Some later non-Jewish authors who drew inspiration from the Bible were G. B. Shaw (*Back to Methuselah,* 1921); J. M. Barrie (*The Boy David,* 1936); James Bridie (plays including *Tobias and the Angel,* 1930); and Christopher Fry (*A Sleep of Prisoners,* 1941). The Old Testament's first significant impact on *French literature can be traced to the late 16th century, when French Protestants wrote epics of biblical grandeur, notably Salluste *Du Bartas (*La semaine ou création du monde,* 1578; *La seconde semaine,* 1584) and Agrippa d'Aubigné (*Les Tragiques,* 1577–94; published 1616). Biblical dramas of the same era were written by Jean de la Taille (*Saül le furieux,* 1562) and Robert Garnier (*Sédécie ou les Juives,* 1589). An epic poet of the Renaissance whose works were full of biblical and kabbalistic allusions was Guy *Le Fèvre de la Boderie. In the 17th century, Bossuet and *Pascal were profoundly influenced by the Bible, as was the dramatist Jean *Racine (*Esther,* 1689); *Athalie,* 1691). The 18th-century French philosophers were mainly hostile to the Old Testament, but later writers favorably reassessed the Bible, notably Chateaubriand, and the poets Lamartine, de Vigny, and Victor Hugo. Biblical themes also attracted the Catholic writers Léon *Bloy, Paul *Claudel, and Charles *Péguy. In the 20th century, there were plays by André Obey (*Noé,* 1931), and André Gide (*Saül,* 1903), and poems by Pierre Emmanuel and Jean Grosjean. Among Jewish writers, Edmond *Fleg, André *Spire, Gustave *Kahn (*Images bibliques,* 1929), and Benjamin *Fondane were outstanding interpreters of the Bible. The impact of the Old Testament in *Italian literature was rather more limited, although the ex-Marrano poet Solomon *Usque wrote a Purim play about Queen Esther (performed in Venice, 1558), which was both successful and influential. Originally written in Portuguese or Spanish it was reworked in Italian and published by Leone *Modena (1619). Giambattista Andreini's drama *Adamo* (1613) is thought to have inspired the character of Satan in Milton's *Paradise Lost;* and biblical themes dominated some works by Feo Belcari, Pietro Metastasio, and Vittorio Alfieri (*Saul,* 1782; *Abele,* 1797). Two Jewish writers who turned to the Bible for inspiration were David *Levi, the author of an allegorical drama about Jeremiah (*Il profeta,* 1866), and Guido *Bedarida, whose *La bella ridestata* (1927) was a Zionist allegory invoking the figure of Abishag the Shunamite. In *Spanish and Portuguese literature, more

Figure 2. An engraving by William Blake, 1825, illustrating Job, 2:7–12, shows the afflicted Job with his wife and his three friends, Eliphaz, Bildad, and Zophar. London, Tate Gallery.

than a quarter of the biblical *autos* of the Madrid Codex (1550–75) deal with Old Testament themes. During the Renaissance Luis de *Léon, a humanist of partly New Christian descent, wrote biblical poems and translations, while Usque's Purim play was staged at Venice. Two leading 17th-century dramatists who used biblical motifs were Tirso de Molina (*La venganza de Tamar,* 1634) and Calderón. Marrano and Jewish writers were, however, more prominent as interpreters of Old Testament themes in Spanish during the 17th and 18th centuries. They include the eminent preacher Felipe *Godínez; Francisco (Joseph) de *Caceres; Antonio Enríquez *Gómez (*El Sansón nazareno,* 1651; *La Torre de Babilonia,* 1649); and João (Mose) *Pinto Delgado. Like Pinto Delgado, Isaac Cohen de *Lara was attracted to the story of Esther, publishing a *Comedia famosa de Aman y Mordochay* (Leiden, 1699). Although many Jewish writers made their appearance in Latin America from the late 19th century, few, if any, paid more than cursory attention to biblical motifs.

The Old Testament was a prime cultural influence in *Dutch literature, the Calvinists of Holland seeing themselves as Israelites engaged in a war of liberation against Catholic Spain. The outstanding Dutch biblical writer of the 17th century was, however, a Protestant convert to Catholicism, Joost van den Vondel, whose many biblical dramas include *Joseph in Egypten* (1640), *Salomon* (1648), *Jephta* (1659), *Koning David hersteld* (1660), *Adam in Ballingschap* (1664), and *Noah* (1667). After some decline of interest in the 18th and 19th centuries, biblical writing revived with works such as H. de Bruin's epic drama about Job (1944). Three Jewish writers of the 20th century who dealt with biblical themes were Israël *Querido (*Saul en David,* 1915; *Simson,* 1927), Abel *Herzberg (*Sauls dood,* 1958), and Manuel van *Loggem (*Mozes in Egypte,* 1960). Old Testament themes in *German and Austrian literature have been traced back to the 11th century but, apart from the Miracle plays found also in England and France, the Bible's influence was more important during and after the Reformation. Biblical themes attracted first Sixtus Birck and Hans Sachs, then Christian Weise (*Nebukadnezar,* 1684; *Athalia,* 1687; *Kain und Abel,* 1704) and Johann Bodmer (*Die Synd-Flut,* 1751). Their successors included Solomon Gessner, Friedrich Klopstock, and J. K. Lavater (*Abraham und Isaak,* 1776). Biblical culture exerted varying degrees of influence on *Herder, *Schiller, and *Goethe (whose *Faust* owes much to the book of Job). Old Testament motifs also preoccupied some of the leading 19th-century dramatists, notably Franz Grillparzer (*Esther,* 1877). In the 20th century, Georg Kaiser, Frank Wedekind (*Simson oder Scham und Eifersucht,* 1914), and Thomas *Mann (*Joseph und seine Brueder,* 1933–43) were only three of the many leading writers who turned to the Bible. The Bible also inspired a remarkably large number of Jewish authors from the 19th century onward. Biblical poems were written by *Heine; plays by Karl *Beck (*Saul,* 1841), Arno *Nadel (*Adam,* 1917), Richard *Beer-Hofmann (*Jaakobs Traum,* 1918; *Der junge David,* 1933), Sammy *Gronemann, Max *Brod, Stefan *Zweig (*Jeremias,* 1917), and many others; and biblical novels were published by Joseph *Roth (*Hiob,* 1930), and Lion *Feuchtwanger (*Jefta und seine Tochter,* 1957). The European Holocaust, however, put an end to this vast and creative literary output. In *Hungarian literature, too, biblical influences were at work during the Middle Ages and the Reformation. Biblical themes inspired Protestant epics of the 16th century, and 18th-century dramas, notably *Izsák házassága* ("The Marriage of Isaac," 1704) by Ferenc Pápai Páriz. The Hungarian national revival in the 19th century prompted works by Mihály Tompa (*Samson,* 1863) and Imre Madách (*Mózes,* 1860); and biblical poems were composed by 20th-century writers such as Endre Ady and Attila József. Jewish writers who reinterpreted biblical themes included Emil *Makai, Lajos *Palágyi, Lajos *Szabolcsi and Károly *Pap (*Batséba,* performed 1940; *Mózes,* performed 1944). Several Jewish writers in Hungary also dealt with biblical motifs after World War II. Themes from the Bible have received differing emphases in the Balkan lands. A classic drama of modern *Greek literature was Vikentios Kornaros' *I Thysia tou Abraam* ("The Sacrifice of Abraham, c. 1675), a humanistic interpretation of the **Akedah* story. One 20th-century Greek work of biblical inspiration was the drama *Sodhoma kye Ghomorra* (1956) by Nikos Kazantzakis and books by Jewish writers, such as Joseph *Eliyia and Nestoras *Matsas. In *Rumanian literature, one of the earliest biblical works was J. A. Vaillant's *Legenda lui Aman şi Mardoheu* (1868). Alexandru Macedonski and Cincinat Pavelescu wrote the tragedy *Saul* (1893); the book of Job inspired poetic works by G. Gârbea (1898) and N. Davidescu (1915); while Eugen Lovinescu wrote the play *Eliezer* (1908). Rumania's most prominent biblical writer was the Christian Zionist Gala *Galaction. Among Jewish authors, those who dealt with Old Testament motifs included Enric *Furtuna (*Abişag,* 1963), Camil *Baltazar, and Marcel Breslaşu, who wrote an oratorio based on the Song of Songs. Some of the outstanding figures in *Yugoslav (Serbo-Croatian) literature sought biblical inspiration from the 16th century onward, notably the Ragusan poet Mavro Vetranović. Later Milovan Vidaković composed Serbian epics about Joseph (1805) and Tobias (1825), while Aron Alkalaj, a Jewish banker of Belgrade, wrote a biographical work about Moses (1938). One of the early classics of *Bulgarian literature was Ioan (John) the Exarch's ninth-century *Shestodnev* ("The Six Days"), based on the Creation story. During the later Middle Ages, many biblical works were written by the heretical Bogomils. In the 20th century, Emanuil Pop Dimitrov published *Rut* and *Deshcherite na Yeftaya* ("Jephthah's Daughter"). In *Czechoslovak literature two outstanding biblical works by non-Jews were *Vůdce* (1916; *The Leader,* 1917), a drama about Moses by Stanislav Lom, and *Adam stvořitel* (1927; *Adam the Creator,* 1929), a play by the brothers Josef and Karel Čapek. However, Old Testament themes proved more attractive to Jewish authors. Julius *Zeyer (*Sulamit,* 1883), Jaroslav *Vrchlický, and Eduard *Leda were among the most prominent of these. Biblical works were also written by two later Jewish authors, Ivan *Olbracht and Jiří *Orten. The treatment of Old Testament subjects in early *Polish literature was largely colored by the religious controversies of the Reformation. The Calvinist Mikołaj Rej, who versified the Psalms, wrote a work on Joseph (*Żywot Józefa z pokolenia żydowskiego,* c. 1545) and his contemporary, Jan Kochanowski, who also translated the Psalter, produced epics on the Flood (1558) and Susannah (1562), as well as the biblical *Threny* ("Lamentations," Cracow, 1580). Later Polish writers whose biblical themes symbolized the fate of their homeland were Adam *Mickiewicz, Kornel Ujejski (*Pieśni Salomona,* 1846; *Skargi Jeremiego,* London 1847), *Melodye biblijne,* 1852; and the dramatist Stanisław Wyspiański (*Daniel,* 1908). Since Yiddish was Polish Jewry's cultural language before the Holocaust, Jewish treatments of the Bible in Polish fiction are rare. In *Russian literature, on the other hand, biblical motifs were generally less prominent, although many leading writers were clearly steeped in the language of the Old Testament. The 11th-century *Primary Chronicle* begins with an account of the Tower of Babel, while in the 15th century Bible translations and even some rabbinic motifs appeared in the writings of various Judaizing sects. Modern Russian drama is largely the creation of Semyon Polotski and the German Lutheran pastor Johann Gottfried Grigori, who wrote biblical plays for the Moscow court, where a drama about Esther was staged in 1672. Old Testament themes have been reinterpreted in the 20th century by the writers Alexander Kuprin (*Sulamif,* 1908) and Leonid Andreyev; and by two Jewish authors of the post-Stalin "thaw," Semyon *Kirsanov and Joseph *Brodski.

The Bible and the associated traditions of the Midrash were a major source of Moslem legend. Though in general unspectacular, the Islamic sphere of *Oriental literature also produced a few works on biblical subjects, beginning with poems by the 9th-century Hejaz poet *Samuel b. Adiya (Al-Samwʾal Ibn ʿĀdiyā). There are also biblical allusions in the poems of a 13th-century Spanish Arabic author, *Ibrāhīm b. Sahl al-Andalūsī (Abu Isḥāq). A 20th-century writer who versified the Old Testament was the Egyptian Karaite Murād *Faraj. The literary use of biblical motifs in *United States literature is very much more recent. Old Testament influence may be seen in the writings of major 19th-century authors such as Emerson, Hawthorne, Whitman, and Whittier. Two best-selling religious romances by Joseph Holt Ingraham were *The Pillar of Fire* (1859) and *The Throne of David* (1860). Some writers of the 20th century who dealt with Old Testament themes were William Vaughn Moody (*The Death of Eve,* 1912), and Archibald MacLeish (*Nobodaddy,* 1926; *J.B.,* 1958). Marc Connelly's play *The Green Pastures* (1930) was a Negro reinterpretation of the Bible stories. American Jewish writers were prominent among those who sought new ideas in the Old Testament. They include the novelists Robert *Nathan (*Jonah,* 1925), Irving *Fineman (*Jacob,* 1941; *Ruth,* 1949), Howard *Fast (*Moses, Prince of Egypt,* 1958), and Maurice *Samuel; the playwrights Clifford

*Odets (whose *The Flowering Peach,* 1954, reinterpreted the story of Noah) and Paddy *Chayefsky (*Gideon,* 1961); and poets such as James *Oppenheim, Charles *Reznikoff, Delmore *Schwartz (*Genesis,* 1943), and Louis *Untermeyer. In *Canadian literature the poets Irving *Layton and Eli Mandel made much of biblical imagery; and Adele Wiseman (in *The Sacrifice,* 1956) retold the story of the *Akedah* in a prairie setting.

The Hebrew Bible has been one of the most powerful literary stimuli of the past millennium, inspiring poems, plays, novels, and stories in many languages. The Old Testament's portrayal of the human condition and of man's relation to the Divine remains an inexhaustible source of inspiration for Jews and non-Jews alike, wherever the Bible is freely taught and imbibed. [ED.]

MUSIC

The musical setting of biblical texts or subjects is a basic element in both the Jewish and the Christian cultures. A biblical text may be attached to a simple melodic pattern and incorporated in the liturgy, or it may be set, with the technical resources of art music, for an ensemble of voices and instruments for performance on the concert stage. The extent of quotation may range from the repetition of a single verse—chosen for its overt or symbolic content—to an exposition of entire chapters or even books, which may vary from the simplest to the most complex. Finally, the "musicalization" of a biblical text or story-subject may serve as a means of carrying both performer and listener away from everyday reality, to the reenactment of a religious or historical experience; or it may be intended to achieve the exact opposite, drawing the traditional words, stories and characters into the contemporary world (as in the **Purimspiel,* the Negro Spiritual, or the contemporary Israel "verse-song"). The mere enumeration of the repertoire of "The Bible in Music," even within the limits of printed sources of European art music, is a virtually impossible task, although partial lists have been published. The situation is further complicated by the use of mixed texts, especially in motets and cantatas, where biblical quotations, texts from the New Testament and ecclesiastical literature, and new poetic creations, alternate and complement each other symbolically.

There is no field of Western art music in which the Bible has not been reflected at one time or another; the major forms are the Mass, oratorio, cantata, motet, and opera and operetta. Biblical subjects have also furnished the inspiration for various forms of instrumental music (such as Johann Kuhnau's "Biblical Sonatas" in the 18th century), as well as ballet.

The problem of censorship has left its imprint on the history of the "Bible in Music," as it has on the spoken and visual arts, and especially in those forms intended for actual stage representation. Even when biblical characters were permitted to appear, move and sing, the appearance of God was often forbidden, even as a disembodied voice. The late development of oratorio in France, for instance, is directly connected with such a ban, which was relaxed officially only about the middle of the 18th century. In Russia the prohibition against representing biblical characters in a sung work was in force until the end of the Czarist regime.

See also separate articles on individual characters, subjects and books of the Bible and Apocrypha, and on: *Cantillation; *Haggadah; *Hallel; *Hallelujah; *Music; *Priestly Blessing; *Psalms (Music); *Shema. [B.B.]

ART

The Hebrew Bible has been a continual source of inspiration to artists from classical antiquity until the present day, and was a major source until the 17th century. In early Christian wallpaintings in the Roman catacombs and in the carvings on sarcophagi certain images including "Sacrifice of Isaac," "Moses striking the Rock," the "Three Men in the Fiery Furnace" (Shadrach, Meshach and Abed-Nego), and "Jonah and the Whale" continually recur. These images, which were associated with Christian doctrines concerning the life to come, have their artistic origins in pagan art and also, perhaps, in Jewish visual representations of the Bible, such as those that survive in the wallpaintings of the synagogue at *Dura-Europos. In the East Roman (Byzantine) empire, the visual interpretation of the Bible was dominated by the icon, or "holy image," whose form, credited with a divine origin, was preserved unchanged for hundreds of years. This precluded the development of any narrative interest. The characteristic art-form of Byzantium was the mosaic, but the troubled condition of the West after the fall of Rome discouraged ambitious schemes of architectural embellishment and favored instead the more modest illuminated manuscript. This was at first somewhat stylized, but the Carolingian period of the ninth century witnessed a renaissance of creativity. Traditional images were transformed, iconography was developed, and a number of important schools of illumination came into being. Until the close of the Middle Ages, Christian representations of the Bible were governed by certain dogmatic considerations. Scenes from the Old Testament were held to prefigure episodes from the New, and were generally depicted in that light. Thus, the sacrifice of Isaac was taken to be symbolic of the Crucifixion of Jesus; the story of Jonah and the whale as a prefiguration of the Resurrection. In the age of the great Romanesque and Gothic cathedrals, from the 12th century onward, most of the arts tended to be subordinated to a total architectural ensemble. Gradually, however, each art began to regain a life of its own. The static carved figures round the cathedrals began to converse in groups; in Italy they were placed in niches which isolated them in an independent area of space. The same tendency was to be seen in other arts.

Figure 1. Mosaic in the church of Santa Maria Maggiore, Rome, early fifth century, depicting Abraham's visitation by the three angels. Above, the appearance of the angels; below, Abraham orders Sarah to prepare food, which he then serves to the angels. Photo Alinari, Florence.

Figure 2. Gothic sculptures of Adam and Eve, c. 1235, from the exterior of Bamberg Cathedral, Germany. Photo Emil Baur, Bamberg.

The Gothic architecture of the North eliminated wallspace in order to let in the light, so that frescoes were replaced by stained-glass windows. In Italy wallpainting continued to develop but, instead of remaining subordinate to the architectural scheme, it became increasingly of equal importance to its setting. This tendency reached its culmination in Michelangelo's great biblical frescoes in the Sistine Chapel in Rome. In the same way, illuminations which had formerly been integral to the text of a manuscript now developed into miniature paintings, in which an artist's individuality could be expressed. Other changes occurred. Images no longer depended to the same degree on their purely symbolic significance. Artists sought to treat figures naturalistically, placing them in their natural settings. More and more, the biblical subject provided an opportunity for the study of contemporary life. Paintings developed a third dimension, with colors that were naturalistic rather than symbolic. The interest in the natural setting finally developed into landscape-painting. By the 17th century, the landscape in the paintings of Nicholas Poussin was given the same importance as the biblical figures, and in the paintings of his contemporary Claude Lorrain it is given even more. Some of Poussin's biblical scenes are primarily studies of nature; thus his "Ruth and Boaz" (c. 1660–64, Paris, Louvre) is in reality a portrait of summer.

National schools of painting developed, each with its own characteristics. The Italians rendered space according to the laws of perspective and took inspiration for their figures from the art of antiquity. French painters such as Claude utilized standardized compositions resembling stage-sets. The Germans sometimes divided up the picture-plane into a number of sections according to the theme. Italian painters favored boldly constructed landscapes and interiors, showing man as the master of space. Italian interiors were clearly visible and well defined, whereas northern interiors could be dark and mysterious, with filtered light such as is found in the works of *Rembrandt. The Italian Renaissance glorified man. In his "Creation of Adam" (1511, Vatican, Sistine Chapel), Michelangelo depicted Adam as the perfect man, the image of God. Michelangelo created several of the most famous interpretations of Old Testament figures. His sculpture of Moses on the tomb of Pope Julius II (c. 1513–16, Rome, S. Pietro in Vincoli) and David (at the Florence Academy) and his painting of Jeremiah (c. 1511) in the Sistine Chapel frescoes are particularly noteworthy. In the 17th century, Rubens treated biblical themes with great dramatic freedom, and Rembrandt restored an element of supernatural mystery to painting, from which it had been banished by the development of naturalistic representation. Rembrandt lived in the heyday of Protestantism, which had brought the Old Testament into favor but at the same time disapproved of paintings of the Bible. Nevertheless, it was a major theme in Rembrandt's work. In his biblical paintings, he abandoned the longstanding tradition of typology and treated each episode on its merits and not as a prefiguration of something else. His tender, emotional treatment often suggested a subject rather than described it. His famous painting of David and Saul, for example, depicts their psychological relationship but not an exact textual passage. He also made many biblical etchings and drawings.

After the late 18th century there was no longer a universally accepted style of painting, and hence no longer a language through which a painter of biblical subjects could easily communicate with the public. Morever, the authority of the Scriptures was no longer unquestioningly accepted. Paintings of the Bible became sporadic, and largely anecdotal or antiquarian. In the 19th century, however, major Jewish artists treated the subject for the first time, and, in the 20th century they accorded it a far more comprehensive treatment. Thus the Old Testament has been the subject of over 40 paintings and numerous etchings by Marc *Chagall and of many works by *Ben Zion, which

Figure 3. The prophet Jeremiah. Fresco by Michelangelo in the Sistine Chapel in the Vatican, Rome. Photo Alinari, Florence.

Two full-page frontispiece panels from the three-volume "giant" *Bishop Bedell Bible.* On the first page is the ornamented letter *shin* alluding to the original patron, Shabbetai ben Mattathias. The inscription on the second page reads: "a crown of beauty, Pentateuch, Prophets and Hagiographa." Written by Abraham ben R. Yom Tov ha-Kohen in Rome, 1284. Belonged to William Bedell, Bishop of Kilmore and Ardagh (1571–1642). Cambridge, Emmanuel College, ms. 1.1.5 (also 6, 7), folios Iv–II ($13\frac{1}{4} \times 9\frac{3}{4}$ ins/33.6 × 24.5 cm.).

Figure 4. "Adam and Eve in Paradise" by the two 17th-century Flemish masters, Peter Paul Rubens and Jan Breughel the Elder. The Hague, Collection Royal Picture Gallery, Mauritshuis. Photo A. Dingjan, The Hague.

bear witness to the fascination the Bible continues to exert on artists up to the present time.

Islamic Art. In Islamic art Bible figures often occur in manuscript illustration, but in less than profoundly religious context, being encountered in histories, scientific works, or the type of book called *Stories of the Prophets.* The important period for this art was from the 14th to the 17th centuries, and the area was that under Persian influence. Various Genesis topics recur—Adam and Eve, Abel, Noah's Ark, and especially Joseph and Potiphar's wife. Moses and Solomon, both part of the Muslim canon, appear, and also Jonah and the whale. Style changes reflect those in the Persian secular miniature, and the manner is equally sensuous and realistic. [Ed.]

Figure 5. Adam and Eve depicted in an Islamic illuminated manuscript, *Manafi al-Hayawan* ("The Usefulness of Animals"), Iran, 1294–99(?). New York, Pierpont Morgan Library, M 500, fol. 4v.

ILLUSTRATED BIBLES IN MEDIEVAL ILLUMINATED MANUSCRIPTS

Pictorial biblical cycles in the early Middle Ages probably grew out of early Jewish art. Similarly, iconographical elements of the surviving biblical representations in Jewish monumental art of the third and fourth centuries, and some Christian Greek and Latin illumination, suggest an earlier Jewish prototype. Representations of the midrashic *aggadah* in medieval Christian illumination also point to the same ancient source. It is not known whether the original source for biblical representation was architectural art, such as the third-century fresco cycle in the synagogue of *Dura-Europos, or an illustrated biblical text. No ancient or early medieval Hebrew illuminated Bible has survived, although this does not exclude the possibility that there may have been one in scroll or codex form before the 3rd century. The Cotton Genesis, fragments of a Greek fifth-century Bible probably from Egypt (B. M. Cotton Ms. Otho. B. VI) is the earliest surviving illustrated biblical manuscript. Its framed miniatures, placed within the text pages, may allude to an illustrated scroll as an archetype. The direct iconographic relation of the Cotton Genesis to the mosaics in the church of Sta. Maria Maggiore in Rome further suggests a common prototype. The Cotton Genesis Recension maintained its influence during the Middle Ages in Eastern and Western biblical representations, such as 13th-century mosaics of S. Marco in Venice, and the 12th-century *Hortus Deliciarum,* formerly in Strasbourg. Byzantine biblical representations apparently belonged to

Figure 1. The men of Sodom call upon Lot to deliver up the two angels. Illustration from the fifth-century Greek *Cotton Genesis,* the earliest illustrated Bible extant. London, British Museum, Cotton Ms., Otho B VI.

Figure 2. Miniature from the Greek *Vienna Genesis,* Byzantine, c. sixth century. It depicts Joseph's brothers finding the money hidden in their sacks and revealing their discovery to Jacob. Vienna, Austrian National Library, Ms. Vindobon Theol. Gr. 31.

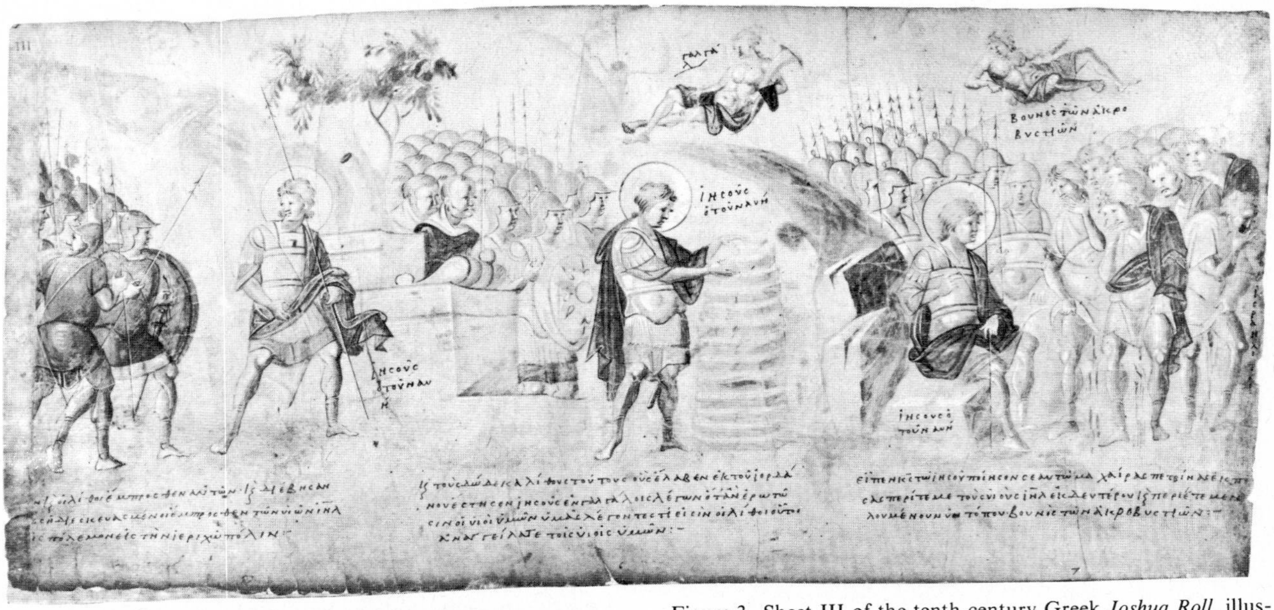

Figure 3. Sheet III of the tenth-century Greek *Joshua Roll,* illustrating Josh. 4–5. Rome, Vatican Library, Ms. Palat. Grec. 431.

Figure 4. Full page miniature of scenes from Genesis, Chapter 25, in the Latin *Ashburnham Pentateuch,* seventh century. Upper register: Isaac being told of Rebekah's going to inquire of the Lord during her pregnancy. Lower register: left, Rebekah giving birth to Esau and Jacob; right, Esau sells his birthright to Jacob. Paris, Bibliothèque Nationale, Nouv. Acq. Lat. 2334, fol. 22v.

Figure 5. The vision of Ezekiel depicted in continuous narrative in the ninth-century Greek manuscript, *Sermons of St. Gregory of Nazianzus.* Paris, Bibliothèque Nationale, Ms. Grec. 510, fol. 438v.

Figure 6. David, inspired by a personified Melodia, playing the lyre. Full page miniature from the tenth-century *Paris Psalter*, Paris. Bibliothèque Nationale, Ms. Grec. 139, fol. 1v.

another recension related to an important Greek manuscript, the Vienna Genesis (Vienna National Library Ms. Theo. Gr. 31). The incomplete text paraphrases the Book of Genesis, and illustrations appear at the bottom of each page. The position of the illustrations suggests a scroll archetype for the manuscript, since classical scientific scrolls were illustrated in this way. It has been suggested that the manuscript was made for a child's biblical education. This theory accounts for the textual paraphrase, the legendary material, and many everyday scenes. Since the manuscript was painted on purple-tinted vellum, it was probably meant for a child of royal family. The style and motifs date it to the time of Justinian (sixth century). The Cotton and Vienna Genesis manuscripts are but two surviving examples of an important Eastern school of illumination in Alexandria, Antioch and Constantinople. The "Joshua Roll" in the Vatican Library (Palat. Grec. 431), probably of the tenth century, has a very shortened Greek text as captions to the consecutive pictorial episodes from the Book of Joshua, painted on a scroll. The style, iconography and some Classical motifs suggest a prototype which may go back to the second century C.E.

Biblical illustrations of the Western tradition are best exemplified by the full-page illustrations of the Latin Ashburnham Pentateuch (Bib. Nat. Nouv. Acq. Lat. 2334). Dating from the seventh century, but of unknown origin, this manuscript contains iconography different from the Eastern tradition of the Cotton and Vienna Genesis recension, although a complete comparison is not possible because most of the full-page miniatures have been cut out.

In the early Middle Ages illustrations existed in the East and West for books of the Bible other than the Pentateuch. There were, for example, the fifth-century "Itala Fragments" illustrating episodes from I Samuel, and the Syrian Book of Kings of 705 C.E. (Paris, Nat. Ms. Syr. 27). The "Itala Fragments" (Berlin Ms. Theo. Lat. fol. 485), which use a Latin translation earlier than that of St. Jerome, were found in a 17th-century binding. Some of the color had disappeared, exposing written instructions by the scribe to the artist regarding what he should illustrate in the miniatures. These instructions suggest the possibility that the illustration of Bible manuscripts may have been a matter of individual choice. By the pre-Iconoclastic period, Byzantine illuminators had developed a system of consecutive biblical illustrations. Such pictures were used, for example, to illustrate the book of Christian Topography by Cosmas Indicopleustes. As soon as the Iconoclastic bans were lifted after 843 C.E., biblical representations returned to Byzantine illumination, fashioned after the surviving Early Christian and Antique representations. One example is the manuscript of the Sermons of St. Gregory of Nazianzus (c. 880 C.E.), which has extensive biblical illustrations. Consecutive cycles also continued in post-Iconoclastic times, mainly in illuminated psalters. Psalters illustrated the life of David, episodes from the Exodus from Egypt, and other passages mentioned in the text. The two main types were the "aristocratic," with full-page miniatures and the "monastic," with marginal illustrations. Among the best known Byzantine biblical manuscripts are the Greek Octateuchs, which contain the Pentateuch and the books of Joshua, Judges, and Ruth. The 11th- to 13th-century Octateuchs have small miniatures within the text.

Figure 7. Full page miniature illustrating the story of Jacob, from the *Psalter of King Wenceslas of Hungary and Bohemia,* Paris, c. 1260. Left: top, Jacob wrestling with the angel; middle, Jacob drawing water; bottom, Jacob meeting Laban. Center: top, Jacob offering his services to Laban; bottom, Jacob receiving his symbol of servitude from Laban. Right: top, Laban marrying Jacob to Leah; middle, Jacob tending sheep; bottom, Laban marrying Jacob to Rachel. Formerly Dyson-Perrins Collection, ms. 32, fol. 12r. Photo, Courtauld Institute of Art, London.

In the West, the most famous Carolingian center for biblical illustration was the French city of Tours. The Bibles of this school illustrate the life of the first men and Moses with the Israelites in the desert. It is possible that the large Bibles from Tours were inspired by a biblical illuminated manuscript of the Cotton Genesis recension and also by the Ashburnham Pentateuch, which was probably in Tours by the ninth century. Psalters were also illustrated in Carolingian art centers, the most notable being the Utrecht Psalter and the Stuttgart Psalter, which contain illustrations above each psalm. For an unknown reason, no consecutive cycle of biblical episodes existed in Ottonian illumination, and the few biblical representations were usually symbolic. Other regional schools, such as the Anglo-Saxon, Franco-Saxon and Italian, followed the same symbolic method. In Spain, however, a system of biblical text illustrations survived from later antiquity, and formed the Catalan school of illumination of the 10th to 13th centuries. Artists used this system to illustrate the commentaries of Beatus of Liébana on the Apocalypse, as well as complete Bibles. It was only through the influence of Byzantine art that biblical cycles were reestablished in the other parts of Western Europe during the 12th century. Most French, German and English Bibles of the 12th century had a few illustrations, probably all derived from Byzantine prototypes. The custom of adding a sequence of full-page biblical illustrations to the psalter was possibly also derived from Byzantine aristocratic psalters. The spread of biblical cycles attached to psalters from England to France during the 13th century is parallel to the development of the Gothic style in illuminated manuscripts. A complete series of biblical illustrations from the Creation to the building of the Second Temple was produced in France, mainly in Paris, during the reign of *Louis IX. The best examples are the Pierpont Morgan Picture Bible and the *Psalter of St. Louis.* This biblical series quickly spread from France to most European countries, and was incorporated into other types of books, such as the German *Weltchroniks* and *Armenbibel,* the French *Histoire Universelle, Bible Moralisée, Biblia Pauperum* and *Speculum Humanae Salvationis,* and the Hebrew Spanish *Haggadot.* During the early part of the Italian Renaissance, it became fashionable to illustrate biblical texts with elaborate miniatures on the first page of each book. Their iconography is mainly based on central and south Italian tradition, which preserved the most classical iconography, both in miniatures and in the monumental art of the period. Examples are the Pantheon Bible of the 12th century, the Padua Bible of the 14th century, and the Bible of Borso d'Este of the 15th century. The early printed bibles mainly used the 15th-century system of Italian illuminated bibles and some of the early printed Gutenberg Bibles were hand decorated as if they were manuscripts. The printed editions of the Poor Men's Bibles mainly followed the hand-produced examples of this type. [B.N.]

Illuminated Hebrew Manuscripts. The *halakhah* explicitly forbids the decoration of the Scroll of the Law read in the synagogue. (Tradition condemns the Jerusalemites of Alexandria for adorning their scroll with the name of God in gold; Sof. 1:8.) However, Hebrew Bibles in codex form, not used for reading in the synagogue, may have been decorated and illustrated in antiquity, though no such manuscripts have survived. Those illuminated Hebrew Bibles which still exist belong to a later period. They consist of four regional types: Oriental, Spanish, Ashkenazi, and Italian. Their styles

Figure 1. Fragment of a carpet page depicting the Tabernacle and its implements from the *First Leningrad Bible,* an illuminated Hebrew manuscript, Egypt (?), 929 C.E. Leningrad Public Library, Firkovich collection, ms. II, 17.

differ but they share iconographic and formal elements.

Oriental Bibles may have originated in the first or second century and may have served as a model to the surviving illuminated Bibles. A comparison of ninth- and 13th-century illuminated manuscripts with first- and second-century monuments, such as wall paintings and floor mosaics, suggests that illuminated Bibles consisted of textual illustrations, *implements of the Temple, and fully decorated pages which, from their likeness to designs on Oriental carpets, are known as carpet pages. The wall paintings in *Dura Europos may be an example of a cycle inspired by Bible manuscripts. Later medieval Greek, Latin, and Hebrew illuminated manuscripts contain similar iconography. The Jewish legendary material *(*aggadah)* depicted in early synagogues and in later manuscripts may allude to an illustrated paraphrase of the Bible, rather than to the canonic text. The early identification of the Temple portal and implements of the Temple with messianic and national aspirations made them an important subject of decoration in minor cult objects as well as in synagogal art. Another element which appears in early synagogal decoration, such as the Aegina and the *Bet Alfa floor mosaic, is the framed carpet-like area decorated with geometrical, repetitive patterns. The reappearance of such decorations in later illuminated Bibles makes it plausible that early Hebrew Bibles might well have been similarly illustrated.

ORIENTAL. Most of the existing Oriental illuminated Hebrew Bibles come from Egypt. The earliest illuminated Bibles, of the ninth and tenth centuries, are of *Karaite rather than *Rabbanite origin. Of these, the earliest existing illuminated manuscript is a ninth- or tenth-century codex of the Latter Prophets, found in the Karaite synagogue in Cairo. This manuscript, together with two Pentateuch fragments of 929 C.E. (Leningrad, Firkovich collection, II, 17) and 951 C.E. (Ms. Firkovich, II, 8), and a tenth-century Karaite Pentateuch written in Arabic characters (British Museum, Ms. Or. 2540) help to establish the system of decorating Oriental Hebrew Bibles from the ninth to the 13th centuries. The style is Oriental and may be either Palestinian or Mesopotamian. Preceding the biblical text, there are fully decorated pages, colored in gold, green, red, and blue, either carpet pages or decorated pages containing patterned masoretic micrography. The carpet pages are

Figure 2. Double carpet from a Karaite Bible, Palestine, tenth century. London, British Museum, Or. ms. 2540, Fols. 2v and 3r.

Figure 3. The *Second Gaster Bible,* Egypt (?), 12th century, with rounded motifs marking the end of *parashot*. London, British Museum, Or. ms. 98880, fol. 34.

Figure 4. The end of the Book of Numbers, with decorative panel giving the number of verses it contains, Persia, 11th century. The panel resembles the Sūra headings in the Koran. London, British Museum, Or. ms. 1467, fol. 78r.

Figure 5. The second song of Moses (Deut. 32), set out in verse form and framed by a decorative border, Persia, 11th century. London, British Museum, Or. ms. 1467, fol. 118r.

Figure 6. The opening words of each of the Ten Commandments are given next to the text of the commandments inside a double frame symbolizing the tablets of the Law in a Pentateuch with Targum, Persia, 11th–12th century. London, British Museum, Or. ms. 2363, fol. 73v.

composed of repeated geometric designs or a central motif with ornamented frame. In several manuscripts, such as the Cairo Karaite Latter Prophets, there are two geometrical, patterned carpet pages which have an additional palmette motif on the outer border. The origin of such carpet pages is unknown, but similar types can be found in the eighth-century Christian sacred books of Hiberno-Saxon and Northumbrian origin, such as the *Lindisfarne Gospels.* In Hebrew Bibles they are directly related to the traditional opening and closing pages of Koran manuscripts of the same period.

The other type of fully decorated pages in Oriental Bibles incorporates floral and geometric motifs outlined in micrography. The text of the minute script is usually the *masorah magna. Some masoretic pages have a portal-like motif, although most have round, square, or rhomboid shapes. Floral and geometric elements sometimes frame dedicatory and colophon pages. In addition to the carpet pages, the Pentateuch manuscript dated 929 C.E. has two pages with a display or plan of the sacred implements of the tabernacle and Temple. These consist of the seven-branched candelabrum, shovels, the table of shewbread, jars, basins, Aaron's flowering staff, and a highly stylized triple arcade, perhaps symbolizing the facade of the Temple, as well as a stylized Ark of the Covenant. The exposition of the *menorah,* the Ark, the jar of manna, and the triple-gate facade of the Temple probably originated in late Hellenistic tradition. All these elements appear on minor Jewish art objects of the first to the third centuries, such as clay oil lamps, painted gold-leaf glasses, and coins, as well as in monumental wall-painting in synagogues and catacombs and in later synagogal floor motifs.

Within the text of the Oriental Bibles, traditionally written in three columns, divisional motifs demarcate the end of books, portions *(parashot),* and verses. At the end of books, there is usually an ornamental frame containing the number of verses in the book. Sometimes, these frames were extended to decorative panels, like the Sūra headings in the Koran. Decorated roundels or other motifs, occasionally with mnemonic devices, mark the different *parashot* as well as the chapters of the Psalms. The roundels resemble the *'ashira* (division into verses), and the *sajdah* (pause for prostration) signs in contemporary Korans. Other sections contain similar decorations. Most frequent is a paisley motif, derived from the Arabic letter *ha,* which resembles the *khamise* (five-verse section) notation in Korans. The Songs of Moses (Ex. 15; Deut. 32) are traditionally written in a distinct verse form, sometimes framed by decorative geometric and floral bands. An example is an 11th-century Persian Bible in the British Museum (Or. Ms. 1467, fols. 117v–118v). Of the few existing examples of Oriental Bibles that contain text illustrations, two are 11th-century Persian Pentateuchs. One has pictures of sacred vessels between the text columns of the page, illustrating the text's description of the princes' gifts to the tabernacle in the desert (Num. 7:1; Brit. Mus., Or. Ms. 1467, fols. 43–43v). The other has an illustration of the two tablets of the law inscribed with the opening words of each Commandment, next to the text of the Ten Commandments (Ex. 20:2–17; Brit. Mus., Or. Ms. 2363, fol. 73v). Portions of the Bible, especially the Pentateuch, intended for educational use were also decorated in the same manner. One example is the Jerusalem *Shelaḥ Lekha* portion of 1106 C.E. Oriental Bibles of the 12th and 13th centuries carry on the tradition of carpet pages, decorated micrography, and divisional signs.

SPANISH. The illumination of Spanish Bibles is derived from the Oriental ones. Like them, they contain carpet pages, illustrations of the Temple implements, divisional signs for books, portions, and verses, and patterned masorah. Spanish Bibles also contain innovations, mainly in the comparative masoretic tables. No illuminated Bible from the Islamic "Golden Age" in Spain has survived. The extant Bibles of Christian Spain suggest a link between them and the early Oriental Bibles because of their similar plan and iconography. The carpet pages of 13th- and 14th-century Spanish Bibles are placed mainly at the beginning and in the major divisions of the Bibles. These carpet pages combine painted motifs with figurated masorah and are framed by verses in monumental scripts.

The earliest recognizable Spanish school of Bible illustration developed in Castile during the second half of the 13th century. Examples of illuminated Bibles from this school indicate an Oriental origin in both the type of decoration and the main floral, geometric, and micrographic motifs. The carpet page from the *Damascus Keter,* in the National and University Library in Jerusalem, a Bible copied in Burgos in 1260 by Menahem b. Abraham ibn Malik, is a good example of the Spanish style. The Oriental flavor of the foliage scroll, outlined by micrography, is somewhat subdued by the Western touch of a burnished gold filling and magenta-brown background. Other Bibles from Castile, such as the 14th-century codex from Cervera, near Toledo (Lisbon, National Library, Ms. 72) reveal more Westernized taste, and were probably influenced by the southern French schools of illumination; Provence should be regarded both culturally and socially as part of the northern Spanish schools.

The most common illustrations of the Spanish Bibles are the implements of the Temple. They are usually shown in a double-page spread in front of the manuscript, next to the carpet pages, rather than in the form of a plan of the Temple or tabernacle. A Bible copied in Perpignan in 1299 (Paris, Bibliothèque Nationale, cod. héb. 7) contains one of the earliest full-page expositions of the implements of the tabernacle. The implements are arranged arbitrarily within frames. The first page (fol. 12v) shows the seven-branched *menorah* and its tongs and fire pans, with two step-like stones on either side of the base, the jar of manna, the staff of Moses and Aaron's flowering rod, the Ark with the tablets of the law deposited in it, the two winged cherubim over the Ark-cover, and the table with the shewbread—two

Figure 7. Carpet page from the *First Joshua Ibn Gaon Bible,* Spain. 1301. Paris, Bibliothèque Nationale, Cod. Heb. 20, fol. 9v.

rows of six loaves—above which are two incense ladles. On the second page (fol. 13) are the gold incense altar, silver trumpets, the horn, the sacrificial altar with a leaning ramp, the laver on its stand, vessels, basins, pans, shovels, and forks. An earlier Bible of the same type from Toledo (1277) is in the Biblioteca Palatina, Parma (Ms. 2668).

The *Farḥi Bible* (Sassoon Collection, Ms. 368), one of the richest Bibles of the 14th century, was both copied and decorated by Elisha b. Abraham b. Benveniste b. Elisha, called Crescas (b. 1325). It took him 17 years, from 1366 to 1382, to complete the work which, as his colophon reveals,

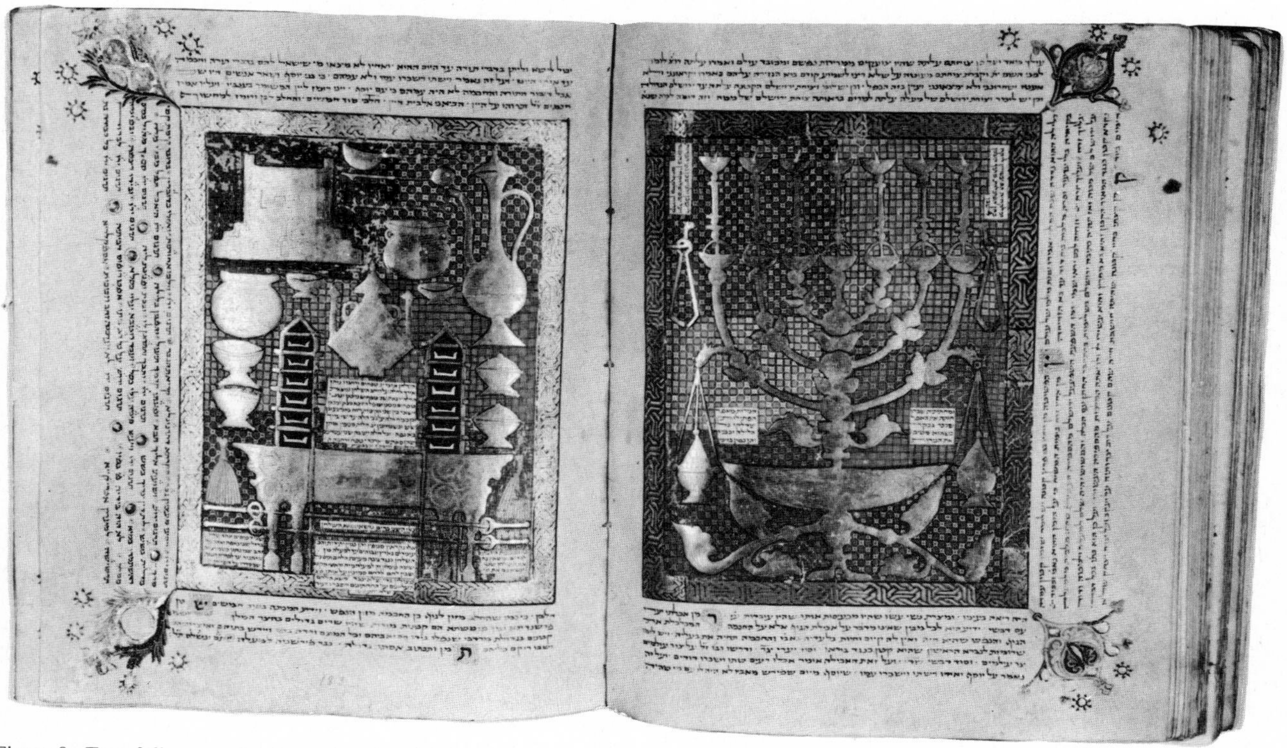

Figure 8. Two full-page miniatures showing the implements of the Tabernacle. From the *Farḥi Bible,* a 14th-century Hispano-Provençal manuscript. Letchworth, England, Sassoon Collection, Ms. 368, pp. 182–3.

Figure 9. The masoretic differences of Ben Asher and Ben Naphtali set in a triple arcade in a 14th-century Bible from Spain. London, British Museum, Add. 15250, fol. lv.

he undertook for his own use. The manuscript was previously in the possession of the Farḥi family of Damascus and Aleppo. The actual biblical text is preceded by 192 fully decorated pages, 29 of which are carpet pages and nine, full-page miniatures. Among the illustrations are several pages of drawings of the implements. The Bible became a substitute for the Temple and was called *Mikdashiyyah* ("God's Temple"). Thus, in Spanish Bibles the implements symbolize the messianic hope for the rebuilding of the Temple. A tree on a hill representing the *Mount of Olives, where tradition states that the precursor of the Messiah will appear, is included among the implements—a further indication of the messianic intent of the illustration. Plans of the Temple also exist in Spanish illumination. One early example is attached to the *First Ibn Merwas Bible* of Toledo, 1306 (British Museum, Ms. Or. 2201). A large fragment, executed by Joshua b. Abraham *ibn Gaon in Soria (1306), is bound together with the *Second Kennicott Bible* (Oxford, Bodleian Library, Ms. Ken. 2). It contains all the implements and vessels of the Second Temple arranged in ground-plan form, unlike the more common random arrangement.

A few Bibles have other illustrations next to the carpet pages. The *Farḥi Bible* has several, among which are the labyrinth of the seven walls of Jericho and the tents of Jacob and his wives. Two novel features appear in the carpet pages of Spanish Bibles. One is the calendar page, according to the Jewish year. Most of the calendars are circular, similar to the zodiac form; some, such as that in the *First Joshua Ibn Gaon Bible* of 1301 (Paris, Bibliothèque Nationale, cod. héb. 21), consist of movable disks. Contemporary calendars were also added, usually beginning with the year in which the manuscript was written. The second major novelty is the comparative tables of the masorah. The different versions of the masorah of *Ben Asher and *Ben Naphtali are written in columns framed by arcades which resemble the early medieval canon tables. In some manuscripts, the tradition of the fully arcaded pages persists even though the text is different. The *First Kennicott Bible,* a masterpiece of Spanish-Jewish art (Oxford, Bodleian Library, Ms. Ken. 1), was copied, punctuated, and edited according to the masorah by Moses Jacob ibn Zabara, and completed, as his colophon shows, on July 24, 1476, in the Spanish town of Corunna, for Isaac son of Don Solomon de Braga. The manuscript was planned and fashioned in scope and decoration on the model of the *Cervera Bible* (1300, Lisbon, Univ. Lib. Ms. 72). The illumination was done by Joseph *ibn Ḥayyim, who fashioned his colophon in zoo- and anthropomorphic letters, similar to those of *Joseph ha-Ẓarefati, the artist of the *Cervera Bible.* Joseph ibn Ḥayyim however, added many new elements to his work. These additions include 14 fully decorated carpet pages, some illustrating the traditional array of implements of the tabernacle. As in the *Cervera Bible,* a number of pages are decorated with arcades which serve as frames for David *Kimḥi's grammatical compendium. Some of these arcades have pictorial borders, such as an army of hares besieging a wolf in a castle (fol. 443).

The Spanish artists, following the Oriental tradition, used divisional signs for books and *parashot* although in a more elaborate way and with some text illustrations. These can be seen as early as 1260, in some *parashot* signs in the *Damascus Keter*. The *First Kennicott Bible* has several such illustrations (e.g., Phinehas brandishing his spear). Unlike Oriental Bibles, the beginnings of books in some Spanish manuscripts have a text illustration. The *Kennicott Bible* presents Jonah and the whale (fol. 305). The *Cervera Bible* has several text illustrations. The indicator for *Parashat Ki-Tavo* (Deut. 26) displays a basket of fruit, illustrating the offerings of the first fruit in the Temple; above it are an

Figure 10. A portion of David Kimḥi's grammatical compendium, *Sefer Mikhlol,* which opens the codex of the *First Kennicott Bible,* Corunna, Spain, 1476. Oxford, Bodleian Library, ms. Kennicott 1, fol. 6r.

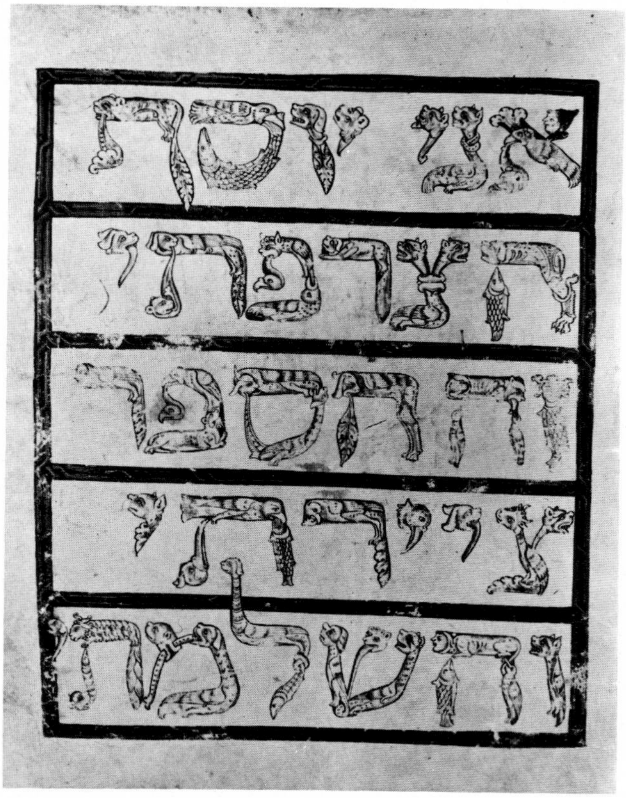

Figure 11. Colophon of the artist Joseph ha-Ẓarefati, illuminator of the *Cervera Bible*, Spain, 1300. Lisbon, National Library, ms. 72, fol. 449.

elephant and castle, the royal arms of Castile. At the end of Exodus there is a panel showing the *menorah* (fol. 60). A stag is painted alongside Psalm 42 (fol. 326), and a lamenting grotesque decorates Lamentations (fol. 371v). Zechariah (fol. 316v) is illustrated by his vision of the two olive trees providing oil for the *menorah*. Jonah (fol. 304) opens with a picture of a ship with sailors, under which the prophet is being swallowed head first by a whale—a not uncommon scene in illuminated Spanish Bibles.

A similar picture of a sailing vessel is found at the beginning of Jonah in a Bible written in Soria (1312) by Shem Tov b. Abraham ibn Gaon, probably a brother of Joshua ibn Gaon (Sassoon Collection, Ms. 82). Further resemblances between the *Shem Tov Bible* and the *Cervera Bible*, such as the grammatical and masoretic treatises written within columns and the crouching lions at the bases of arcades, suggest that they are based on a common model. These two manuscripts are also related in artistic style. The numerous text illustrations in the margins and between the columns of the *First Joshua Ibn Gaon Bible* (Paris, Bibliothèque Nationale cod. héb. 20) include Noah's ark (fol. 13), the dove holding an olive branch (fol. 14), Hagar's water jug (fol. 20), Abraham's sacrificial knife (fol. 20v), the goblet of Pharaoh's butler (fol. 133), David's sling with Goliath's sword, and the bear and lion killed by David (fol. 170). Of all the 15th-century Bibles, the *First Kennicott Bible* has the largest number of text illustrations. At the opening of the Book of Jonah (fol. 305), the traditional picture of the prophet being swallowed head first by a whale, beneath a decorated ship, is depicted in a way similar to that in the *Cervera Bible*. There is also an illustration of King David at the beginning of II Samuel (fol 185) in the *Kennicott Bible*. Floral and geometric shapes composed of micrographic masorah decorate the margins of some text pages. As in the Oriental Bibles, the two songs of Moses are often written in a special form and sometimes have a frame decorated with colors or micrography, which is also used in the ornamentation of carpet pages from the 13th to the 15th centuries.

Hebrew illustrated Bibles must have been so common in Spain that Castilian translations of the Bible may have used their illustrations as early as the 13th century. Jewish iconography is also predominant in the Castilian **Alba Bible*.

The 15th-century Yemenite school of illumination, like the Spanish, follows the Oriental school. Many Yemenite Bibles contain carpet pages ornamented with floral and animal motifs in micrography of colors (e.g., Brit. Mus., Or. Ms. 2348 of Sana'a, 1469, and Or. Ms. 2211 of 1475). The micrography in these manuscripts is of biblical verses and Psalms, not the masorah.

ASHKENAZI. Hebrew Bibles of the Ashkenazi school fall into two categories: one consists of complete Bibles, mostly in large, even giant, format, such as the *Ambrosian Bible* (Ulm, 1236–38), written in large script with Aramaic translation incorporated into the text after each verse; the other contains the Pentateuch with its Aramaic translation, the five scrolls, **haftarot*, parts of Job, and sometimes the "passages of doom" in Jeremiah (2:29–3:12; 9:24–10:16). Ashkenazi Bibles are illuminated in a different fashion from the Oriental and Spanish ones. Most are decorated by the punctuator-masorete in micrography and pen drawing, either in large initial-word panels or in the margins of the text area. Illuminated Bibles of the Ashkenazi tradition do not contain carpet pages and only occasionally have expositions of the Temple implements. What sometimes

Figure 12. Carpet page with floral and fish motif in micrography from a Yemenite Bible, San'a, 1469. London, British Museum, Or. ms. 2348, fol. 39r.

Figure 13. Carpet page with painted foliage scroll work and border. According to the Arabic inscription in the top and bottom borders, the manuscript, written by the scribe Benaiah, was ordered for the synagogue of San'a, Yemen, 1475. London, British Museum, ms. Or. 2211, fol. 1v.

appears like a carpet page is in fact an excess of masoretic material copied in decorative shapes, either at the beginning or the end of books of the Bible. Implements of the Temple are very rare. One example occurs in the *Regensburg Pentateuch* of about 1300, now in the Israel Museum, Jerusalem, which has an exposition of the tabernacle implements, including Aaron in his robes extending his arm to light a very large *menorah,* which is depicted on the facing page.

The most common illuminations of French and German Bibles are initial-word panels, which sometimes include text illustrations. The Rashi commentary on the Pentateuch from Wuerzburg, 1233 (Munich, Cod. Heb. 5) has initial-word panels to each *parashah* which includes a text illustration. The *Ambrosian Bible* (Mss. B. 30–32 inf.) has illustrated panels to most of the books. At the end of the third volume, this manuscript has full-page eschatological illustrations, which depict the Feast of the Righteous in Paradise, and a cosmological picture. The *British Museum Miscellany* (Ms. Add. 11.639) of c. 1280 contains three cycles of full-page miniatures of biblical episodes, which were probably intended to illustrate a northern French Bible. Painted initial-word panels also exist and sometimes extend to a full page, as in the *Duke of Sussex Pentateuch* in the British Museum. Sometimes these painted panels illustrate the text, but a few are merely decorative. The 46 medallions of the frontispiece to Genesis in the *Schocken Bible* in Jerusalem depict episodes from the entire Pentateuch, beginning with Adam and Eve by the Tree of Knowledge and ending with Balaam being stopped by an angel while riding his ass.

The other most prominent type of decoration in the Ashkenazi Bible is the elaborate marginal micrography. The masoretic micrography sometimes contains text

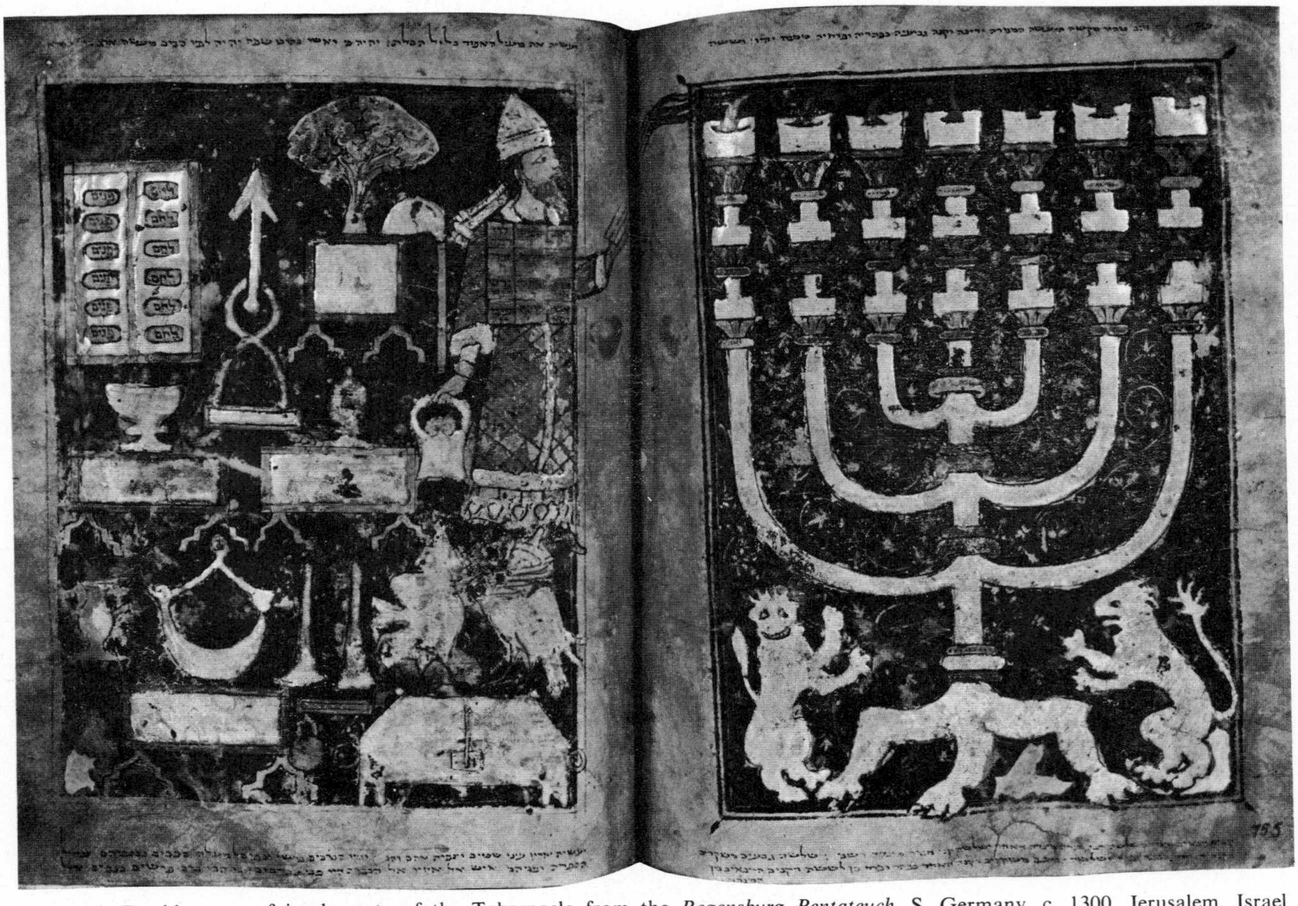

Figure 14. Double page of implements of the Tabernacle from the *Regensburg Pentateuch,* S. Germany, c. 1300. Jerusalem, Israel Museum, ms. 180/52, fols. 155v-156r.

illustrations. Some opening panels and colophons are also decorated by micrography, and the micrography within the text sometimes forms an illustration of the text. The *Duke of Sussex Pentateuch* (fol. 28) shows the ram caught in a thicket alongside the text of the sacrifice of Isaac. A Bible in the British Museum (Ms. Add. 21160, c. 1300), has some interesting examples of such illustrated micrography; e.g., Joseph riding a horse (fol. 192), Pharaoh's baker carrying a triple basket on his head (fol. 43), the four beasts of Ezekiel's vision (fol. 285), and Jonah being spewed from the mouth of the whale and seated under a tree (fol. 292–292v). However, most of the masoretic variations surrounding the text form grotesques. Ashkenazi Pentateuchs of the second half of the 14th century are smaller and illustrated in a manner differing from that of the earlier period—the *Coburg Pentateuch* of 1369, is an example of this later type.

ITALIAN. Very few illuminated Italian Bibles of the 13th century survive, and most of them are of Roman origin. The *Bishop Bedell Bible* of 1284 (Cambridge, Emmanuel College) is a typical example. It contains two full-page decorated panels, which include some inscriptions. Decorated arches surround the opening pages or text columns of the different books, and the initial word is written in a larger script. *Parashot* signs in the margin follow the Oriental type. A two-volume Bible in the British Museum (Ms. Harl. 5710–11), from about 1300 preserves the two typical techniques of decoration—watercolor pen drawings and painted illuminations. The openings of each book of the Bible are headed by painted initial-word panels and surrounded by foliage scrolls—either around the whole page or one text column. The foliage scrolls are wiry and incorporate animals, birds, fish, and grotesques in a style which was common in the province of Emilia and influenced mainly by the Bolognese school. This Bible contains a few text illustrations. Under the initial-word panel of Genesis (fol. 1), there is a painted panel containing seven medallions, five of which represent the creation of heaven and earth, the sun, moon, and stars, water, trees, and beasts. Each medallion shows the hand of God emerging from segments of the sky. At the end of the Pentateuch (fol. 136), there is a full-page drawing of a delicately formed *menorah* painted in red, green, ocher, and brown. The entire page is framed and filled with painted foliage scrolls combined with grotesques and dragons. Another delicately painted manuscript of Emilian style, from the end of the 13th century, is a psalter in the Biblioteca Palatina in Parma (Ms. 1870). Many of the chapter openings have small initial-word panels with grotesques and animals in the margins. Some illustrate the text: weeping people, with their violins hung upon a willow, illustrate Psalm 137, "By the waters of Babylon there we sat down . . . We hung our harps upon the willows in the midst thereof"; a man conducting a choir illustrates Psalm 149, "Hallelujah, sing to the Lord a new song." Italian Bibles of the 14th and 15th century are decorated by initial-word and -letter panels, with marginal ornamentation and some illustrations.

The Aberdeen Bible (University of Aberdeen, Ms. 23) was completed probably in Naples in 1493 by Isaac b. David Balansi (i.e., Valensi), presumably a Spaniard who had been expelled from Spain in 1492. While the Spanish influence is evident in the manuscript's masoretic micrography and *parashot* indicators, it does not appear in the fully decorated pages containing the comparative tables of masorah, initial-word panels, and border illumination; these are purely south Italian. The heavy borders, decorated with foliage scrolls, animals, birds, and large pearls framing the table of *haftarot*, are typical of the other illuminated pages in this Bible.

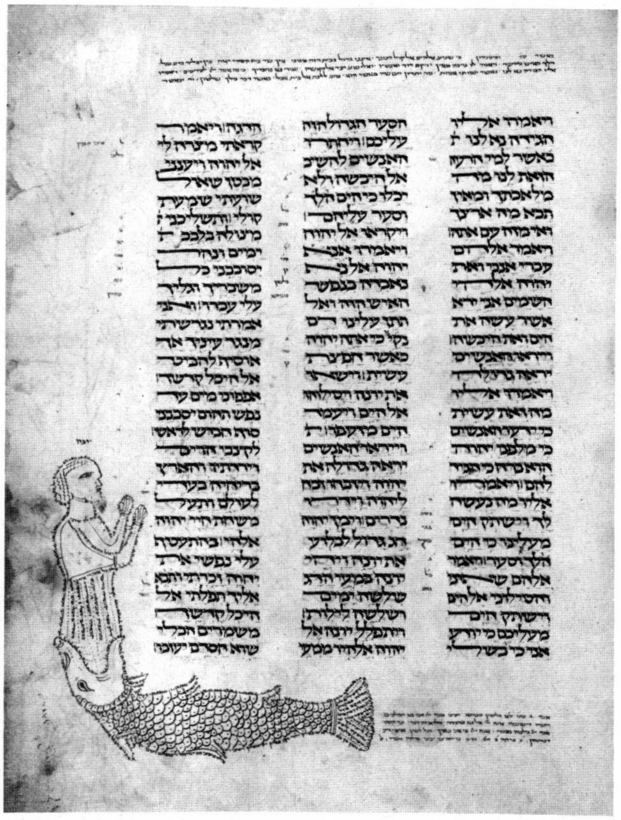

Figure 15. Jonah and the whale depicted in an elaborate micrographic marginal masorah in an Ashkenazi Bible, Germany, c. 1300. London, British Museum, Add. 21160, fol. 292.

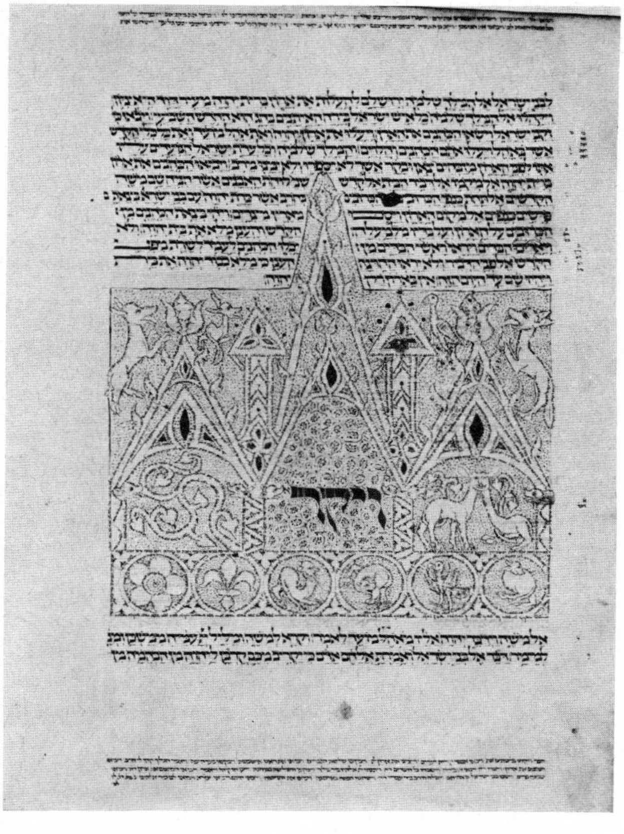

Figure 16. Masoretic micrography used as outlines for the illustrations in an initial word panel for the beginning of Leviticus. Germany, 1290. Copenhagen, Royal Library, Cod. Heb. XI.

Figure 17. Miniature of a teacher admonishing his pupil from the *Coburg Pentateuch*, Germany, 1396. London, British Museum, Add. 19776, fol. 72v.

With the Renaissance in Italy, Hebrew illumination reached its artistic peak. It developed through the ready patronage of affluent Jewish loan-bankers who supported such fine illuminators as those who produced the *Rothschild Miscellany* (Ms. 24, Jerusalem, Israel Museum) and the Bibliothèque Nationale's *Portuguese Bible* (Ms. héb. 15). Unique in the richness of their decoration, these manuscripts were in great demand, but only a few families could afford the single productions.

With the invention of the printing press, by the end of the 15th century handwritten Bible illumination practically ceased. The decoration of printed Bibles developed a different form and content, except for the illuminated scrolls of Esther, which evolved a specific tradition.

See also *Illuminated Manuscripts, Illuminated **Haggadot*, and illuminated **maḥzorim*. [B.N.]

For more information on individual biblical figures in the arts see also the articles on the following: *Abraham, *Absalom, *Adam, **Akedah*, *Athaliah, *Babel, Tower of, *Balaam, *Belshazzar, *Cain (and Abel), *Creation, *Daniel, *David, *Deborah, *Decalogue, *Elijah, *Esther, *Ezekiel, *Gideon, *Habakkuk, *Hezekiah, *Hosea, *Isaac, *Isaiah, *Jacob, *Jephthah, *Jeremiah, *Jerusalem, *Job, *Joel, *Jonah, *Joseph, *Joshua, *Lamentations, *Melchizedek, *Moses, *Nebuchadnezzar, *Noah, *Psalms, *Rachel, *Ruth, *Samson, *Samuel, *Saul, *Sodom (and Gomorrah), *Solomon, *Song of Songs, *Temple.

Bibliography: In Literature: N. J. E. Rothschild, Baron de, *Le mistère du Viel Testament*... 6 vols. (1878–91), includes extensive bibliography of biblical plays in French; A. Sakheim, *Das juedische Element in der Weltliteratur* (1924); L. Finkelstein (ed.), *The Jews*, 2 (1960³), 1452–86; M. Roston, *Biblical Drama in England* (1968); Shunami, Bibliography, 248–58

Figure 18. Tables of the masorah of Ben Asher and Ben Naphtali with panels giving the names of the books and decorative border illumination. From the *Aberdeen Bible*, Italy, 1493. Scotland, University of Aberdeen Library, ms. 23, fol. 7v.

Figure 19. The Judgment of Solomon as an illustration to the opening of the Book of Proverbs. From a Hebrew manuscript of Psalms, Job, and Proverbs, Florence, 15th century. Jerusalem, Israel Museum, ms. 180/55, fol. 186v.

passim. IN MUSIC: JL, 1 (1927), col. 997–9. IN ART: J. Leveen, *The Hebrew Bible in Art* (1944); R. Wischnitzer, in: L. Finkelstein, *The Jews*, 2 (1960³), 1322–48; T. Arnold, *The Old and New Testaments in Muslim Religious Art* (1932); JL, 1 (1927), 985–9; *Encyclopedia of World Art*, 2 (1960), 483–516; D. S. Berkowitz, *In Remembrance of Creation: Evolution of Art Scholarship in the Medieval and Renaissance Bible* (1968). ILLUSTRATED BIBLES: Mayer, Art, index; G. Hareloff, in: ZAW, 69 (1957), 103–29; S.C. Cockerell, and M.R. James, *A Book of Old Testament Illustrations of the Middle of the Thirteenth Century* (1927); A. de Laborde, *Etude sur la Bible moralisée illustrée*, 5 vols. (1911–27). ILLUMINATED MANUSCRIPTS: Gutmann, in: *Gesta*, 5 (1966), 39–44; D.S. Sassoon, *Ohel Dawid*, 1 (1932), 6–14, pl. 1; *B. Narkiss, in: Catalogue of the Israel Museum*, 40 (1967), nos. 1, 2, 3, 4, 16, 18, 19; idem, *Hebrew Illuminated Manuscripts* (1969), index; C. O. Nordström, in: *Byzantion*, 25–27 (1955–57), 487–93; idem, *The Duke of Alba's Castilian Bible* (1967); M. Gengaro, F. Leoni and G. Villa, *Codici decorati e Miniati dell'Ambrosiana* (1957), 13–62; Mayer, Art, nos. 53, 523, 670A, 800, 876, 1071, 1190, 1721, 2003, 2074, 2207, 2221, 2223, 2525, 2547, 2775, 2776.

BIBLE SOCIETIES, associations intended to propagate the Christian Bible, i.e., the Old and New Testaments. The first association of this kind was founded in 1719 in Halle an der Saale, and from 1775 was called the Cansteinsche Bibelanstalt. Numerous Bible societies were founded from the beginning of the 19th century in the wake of the missionary societies established between 1792 and 1800 in England, Holland, and Germany. The British and Foreign Bible Society was founded in 1804, the Bible Society of Basle in 1804, that of Berlin in 1805, Holland in 1814, Norway in 1815, the American Bible Society in 1816, and the Société Biblique de Paris in 1818. Other important societies are the American Board of Commissioners for Foreign Missions, the American and Foreign Bible Society, the Baptist Missionary Society, the Bible Translation Society, the Church Missionary Society, the National Bible Society of Scotland, the Society for Promoting Christian Knowledge, and the Trinitarian Bible Society. In general, these societies publish the biblical texts without commentaries, but they have also issued emended texts of existing translations and editions. They have also published the Greek and Latin editions of Nestlé (1879), Kittel's *Biblia Hebraica* (1905; the Bible Society of Wuerttemberg), and the *Bible du Centenaire* (1916–48; Société Biblique de Paris). Photographic reproductions of the British and Foreign Bible Society Hebrew Bible have been issued in various formats by some Jewish publishers. The masoretic Bible of C. D. *Ginsburg was published by the same society in 1926 in London.

Bibles published by these societies are disseminated by the mission societies or by large-scale retailing. Since the beginning of the 19th century, over a thousand million copies of biblical texts in over a thousand languages have been thus published and distributed. The British and Foreign Bible Society alone has published texts in 700 languages and dialects and distributed a total of 550,000,000 copies, 130,000,000 of which were of the Old Testament. In a single year before World War II, this society distributed 11,000,000 copies of the Bible, the National Bible Society of Scotland 4,000,000, and the American Bible Society 7,000,000. In China, before the accession to power of the Communists, 9,000,000 copies of biblical texts were distributed annually. Owing to the low prices they charge, these societies frequently succeed in selling their Hebrew editions of the Bible, with or without translation, to Jews. The issue of equally low-priced Hebrew Bibles by Jewish authorities or institutions, with or without translations, to counteract this disguised missionary activity of the Bible societies is a relatively recent undertaking. The edition of the New Testament in Hebrew translation is more openly designed for missionary work among Jews. The first New Testament in Hebrew was published in 1817 by the London Society for Promoting Christianity among Jews (better known as the London Jews' Society). The translation of the New Testament by F. *Delitzsch appeared between 1877 and 1892 in at least 13 editions. Other translations openly intended for Jews have been published in Yiddish, Judeo-Arabic, Judeo-Persian, and Ladino.

Bibliography: T. H. Darlow and H. F. Moule (comps.), *Historical Catalogue of the Printed Editions of Holy Scripture in the Library of the British and Foreign Bible Society*, 2 vols. in 4 (1903–11, repr. 1963); S. de Dietrich, *Le Renouveau Biblique* (1949²), 89ff.; Bouyer, in: *Bible et Vie Chrétienne*, 13 (1956), 7–21.

[B.BL.]

°**BIBLIANDER (Buchmann), THEODOR** (1504–1564), Swiss Hebraist and theologian. In 1531, Bibliander succeeded Zwingli as lecturer in Septuagintal studies, but his denial of absolute predestination cost him his post. His publications include a Hebrew grammar (1535), a commentary on the Hebrew text of Nahum (1534), and a treatise interpreting Ezra with reference to Roman history (1553?). Bibliander left Basle with a projected translation of the Koran (of which he published an interpretation, 1543) when the enterprise encountered local difficulties; he was also a collaborator of Leo Juda in his Latin version of the Bible (1543).

Bibliography: J. J. Christinger, *Theodor Bibliander* (Ger., 1867); *Dictionnaire historique et biographique de la Suisse* (1921–34); J. Prijs, *Die Basler hebraeischen Drucke, 1492–1866* (1964), 102, 128.

[RA.L.]

BIBLIOGRAPHY. As in general bibliography, the development of Hebrew bibliography is characterized by the transition from brief listings to more detailed catalogues. The listing of the books of the Bible which appears in the Talmud (BB 14b, 15a) had as its purpose the fixing of an authoritative order for the biblical books as a guide for the copyists. Lists of books for broader purposes, among them those of the Cairo *Genizah*, have come down from the 11th century. Sometimes these listings contain only the name of the book; in other cases, the author's name is also included. In some of the later booklists, short annotations also appear. Bibliographical lists within the biographical listings are found in genealogical works of the 16th century, as in *Sefer Yuḥasin* by Abraham *Zacuto and in *Shalshelet ha-Kabbalah* by Gedaliah *ibn Yaḥya. In the early part of the 17th century several important ventures in the field of bibliography were undertaken. Johannes *Buxtorf the elder published *De abbreviaturis hebraicis, liber novus et copiosus* (Basle, 1613) in which he included a section on rabbinic literature entitled *Bibliotheca rabbinica ordine alphabetico disposita*. This listing of 324 works, arranged in alphabetical order by titles, is the first bibliographic catalogue of rabbinic literature. *Manasseh Ben Israel, in his listing of sources used by him in the first part of his *Conciliador* (Frankfort, 1632), distinguished six categories of Hebrew literature: Talmud and Midrash; commentaries on these; commentaries on the Bible; Kabbalah; *posekim* and responsa; sermons, grammar, chronology, and legal literature. The first, however, to compile a true bibliography of Hebrew literature was Giulio *Bartolocci in his *Bibliotheca Magna Rabbinica* (4 vols., Rome, 1675–93; repr. 1969). The Christian scholar Carlo Giuseppe Imbonati added a fifth volume, *Bibliotheca Latina Hebraica* (Rome, 1694). Bartolocci's work is arranged in alphabetical order of authors, supplemented by a list of subjects in Latin and an abridged listing in Hebrew.

Leone *Modena assisted the bishop of Lodève, J. Plantavit de la Pause: in his *Bibliotheca Rabbinica* (appended to his *Florilegium Biblicum*, 1645) by supplying him with a list of 500 names of rabbis, which he used for his alphabetic dictionary of 780 Hebrew books. The first Jewish bibliographer was Shabbetai *Bass whose *Siftei Yeshenim* (Amsterdam, 1680) contains a bibliography arranged by title, followed by the name of the author, the date and place of publication, the format, and some indication of content. The approximate number of listings in this bibliography is 2,200, including manuscripts. The third important pioneer bibliographer was another Christian, Johann Christoph *Wolf. He utilized the two previous bibliographies in compiling his own four-volume work, *Bibliotheca Hebraea* (Hamburg, 1715–33; repr. 1969). He corrected some of the material found in the earlier works, using the library of David b. Abraham *Oppenheim. The genealogical reference work of David *Conforte *Kore ha-Dorot* (1746, 1846[2]) contains much valuable bibliographic material. It should be noted, also, that Jehiel *Heilperin included in his *Seder ha-Dorot* (Karlsruhe, 1769) the names of the books which are referred to in Bass' bibliography, though generally he omitted the place and year of publication, even when these were included in the *Siftei Yeshenim*. Especially valuable from a bibliographical standpoint is the Ḥ. J. D. *Azulai's *Shem ha-Gedolim* (1774–86, 1853, 1876), which contains an alphabetical listing of Hebrew books and manuscripts. Azulai noted every unusual Hebrew book or manuscript, even those in non-Jewish collections, which came to his notice in the course of his extensive travels without, however, always giving the date and place of publication. The major work of the Christian scholar G. B. de *Rossi, *Annales Hebraeo-Typographici Seculi XV* (Parma, 1795), dealing with Hebrew incunabula, together with his *Annales Hebraeo-Typographici ab anno 1501 ad 1540* (Parma, 1799), and the *Dizionario storico degli autori Ebrei e delle loro opere* (2 vols., Parma, 1802), as well as assorted lists of Hebrew publications from various Italian cities, serve as a transition to modern bibliography.

With the development of Jewish studies, Hebrew bibliography became a scientific discipline in its own right. L. *Zunz's *Zur Geschichte und Literatur* (1845) contains a complete section on bibliography (pp. 214–303), including material on the dates found in books; on printers and typography in Mantua from 1476 to 1662; and on Hebrew printing in Prague from 1513 to 1657. This work laid the foundation for modern Hebrew bibliography. In 1849 Julius *Fuerst published the first part of his *Bibliotheca Judaica* (3 vols., 1849–63). The book is neither all-inclusive nor completely accurate, but it is important in view of its comprehensiveness. It is arranged according to author, commentator, editor, and publisher, with an alphabetical index to the Hebrew works appended to the end of the third volume. The format of each book is noted, and sometimes the number of pages as well. The preceding bibliographies are overshadowed by the works of Moritz *Steinschneider, in particular by his *Catalogus Librorum Hebraeorum in Bibliotheca Bodleiana* (1852–60) and *Die hebraeischen Uebersetzungen des Mittelalters* (1893). These works set the definitive standard for modern Jewish bibliography. Another important bibliography is Isaac *Benjacob's *Oẓar ha-Sefarim*, (1877–80), listing Jewish books and manuscripts until 1863, and published by the author's son Jacob, together with notes by Steinschneider. By the late 19th century Jewish bibliography, comprising Jewish literature in all languages, had undergone considerable development and today compares favorably with general bibliography. Aaron *Walden, who followed Azulai with the *Shem ha-Gedolim he-Ḥadash* (1864) included a section entitled, "A Catalogue of Books," which includes ḥasidic works absent from earlier listings. However, this listing was not done scientifically. William *Zeitlin, in his *Kiryat Sefer, Bibliotheca Hebraica post-Mendelssohniana* (1891–95), listed the works of the Haskalah movement to that date (more than 3,500 volumes). Ḥayyim David Lippe published a catalogue called *Asaf ha-Mazkir* (1881–89), "a complete listing of all the books, treatises, and Hebrew periodicals which appeared during the period 1880–1887." He also issued a follow-up catalogue, *Asaf ha-Mazkir he-Ḥadash* . . . (1899), "listing all the books, treatises, and periodicals which appeared during the period 1882–1898." From 1928 to 1931 H. D. *Friedberg published his *Beit Eked Sefarim*, a bibliographical lexicon covering the general field of Hebrew literature, with particular attention to books written in Hebrew and Yiddish; but also including works written in Italian, Latin, Greek, Spanish, Arabic, Persian, and Samaritan, and printed in Hebrew characters from 1475–1900, with their general content, author, date, place of publication, and number of pages. An expanded edition of this work appeared in 1951–54. Though not truly scientific in its approach, it is still very useful. The many, important studies of Abraham Yaari include *Meḥkerei Sefer* (1958), containing among its studies in Hebrew booklore a section on the catalogue of Israel (see above). M. *Kasher and Dov Mandelbaum compiled a bibliography of works covering the years 500–1500 called *Sarei ha-Elef* (1959). Important monographs and articles in the field of Hebrew bibliography have been written by S. *Wiener, I. *Sonne, S. *Seeligmann, D. *Chwolson, A. *Jellinek, A. M. *Habermann, C. *Lieberman, A. *Marx, M. *Roest, G. *Kressel, J. *Zedner, I. *Rivkind, S. Shunami, N. Ben-Menahem, and others. The indispensable handbook today is S. Shunami's *Bibliography of Jewish Bibliographies* (1936, 1965[2]; repr. 1969, with supplement) which also includes sections on Jewish and Modern Hebrew literature (nos. 1146–1240; 4875–85) as well as on Judeo-German and Yiddish (nos. 1241–1357; 4586–95). In 1960 the Hebrew University, in cooperation with Mosad Bialik and the Ministry of Education and Culture, initiated the Institute for Hebrew Bibliography under the direction of N. Ben-Menahem. Its aim is to compile a definitive bibliographical listing of every Hebrew book which has been published up to 1960 (specimen brochure, 1964).

The first scholar to publish a special periodical devoted to Hebrew and Jewish bibliography was Steinschneider: *Ha-Mazkir, Hebraeische Bibliographie, Blaetter fuer neuere und aeltere Literatur des Judenthums* (HB, 1858–65, 1869–82). Nehemiah *Bruell continued Steinschneider's project in the bi-monthly *Centralanzeiger fuer juedische Literatur* (1890) but succeeded in publishing it only during one year (6 issues). At the same time M. *Kayserling published his bibliographical dictionary of Spanish and Portuguese works on Judaism and Jews (the *Biblioteca española-portugueza judaica*, 1890). A few years later the *Zeitschrift fuer Hebraeische Bibliographie* (ZHB; 1896–1921) appeared. The editor of volumes 1–3 was H. Brody; volumes 4–9 were edited jointly by Brody and A. Freimann; and the remaining volumes appeared under the editorship of Freimann alone. The two great authorities on the bibliography of Anglo-Jewish history are C. Roth's *Magna Bibliotheca Anglo-Judaica* (1957), and R. P. *Lehmann's *Nova Bibliotheca Anglo-Judaica* (1961), the latter dealing with the years 1937–60. The most important contemporary bibliographical journal is *Kirjat Sepher* (KS), a quarterly published since 1924 under the auspices of the Jewish National and University Library. Editors during the

Opening page to the book of Isaiah, from a Bible written and partly decorated in Portugal in the 15th century. This and other opening pages were later executed in Florence, probably by Attavante delli Attavanti, illuminator to Matthias Corvinus, King of Hungary. Paris, Bibliothèque Nationale, ms. Heb. 15, fol. 251 ($12\frac{5}{8} \times 9\frac{3}{4}$ ins/32×24.7 cm.).

first two years were S. H. Bergmann and H. Pick, and after that I. B. Joel. Since 1953 a new bibliographical magazine, *Studies in Bibliography and Booklore* (SBB), has been published by the Hebrew Union College Library, Cincinnati. The *Jewish Book Annual* (JBA; founded in 1942) published in New York also contains useful bibliographical material. Of Jewish bibliographic periodicals whose life-span was limited, the following deserve mention: *En Hakore*, edited by D. A. Friedman and Z. *Woyslawski, three issues (Berlin, 1923); *Soncino-Blaetter, Beitraege zur Kunde des juedischen Buches*, edited by H. *Meyer (3 vols., Berlin, 1925–30); and *Journal of Jewish Bibliography*, a quarterly edited by Joshua *Bloch (New York, 1938–43).

The first bookdealers' catalogue of secondhand Hebrew books was published in Amsterdam around 1640 by Manasseh Ben Israel, but no copy is now extant (cf. Roth in *Aresheth*, 2, 413–4). In 1652 his son Samuel published *Catalogo de los Libros que Semuel ben Israel Soeiro vende, estampados todos na sua Typographia, adjuntos os preços, para que cada qual saibo o que valem.* In this catalogue 65 books are noted together with their prices in Dutch currency. The earliest known auction sale catalogues are those of the libraries of two Amsterdam rabbis, Moses Raphael d'*Aguilar (1680) and Isaac *Aboab da Fonseca (1693). The only earlier commercial listings of Hebrew books are in manuscript form, such as some found in the *Genizah*, or the catalogue of Hebrew books printed in Venice prior to 1542, which came into the possession of Konrad Gesner and appeared in his *Pandectarum sive partitionum universalium libri xxi* (20 vols., Zurich 1548–49; cf. ZHB, 10 (1906), 38–42). A catalogue of books compiled for business purposes was printed as an appendix to the collection of responsa by Joseph ibn Lev (vol. 4, Fuerth, 1692). Another commercial book listing, called *Appiryon Shelomo*, was published in 1730 by Solomon Proops, printer and bookdealer of Amsterdam. The advance in the field of Hebrew bibliography resulted in the publication of improved commercial catalogues (see *Booktrade). A number of these newer catalogues are of definite scientific value such as those of M. *Roest, R. N. N. Rabinowitz, L. Schwager and D. Fraenkel, J. Kauffmann, N. W. Bamberger and Wahrmann, Rosenthal (Munich, Oxford), and others. In addition, the detailed catalogues of such libraries as those of Oxford, Amsterdam, Leiden, Leningrad, Frankfort, the British Museum, and the Bibliothèque Nationale, Paris, have proved extremely useful.

Bibliography: C. Roth, in: *Jewish Studies in Memory of Israel Abrahams* (1927), 384–93; Shunami, Bibl, xiv–xv (Eng.), 7ff.; Urbach, in: KS, 15 (1938/39), 237–9; Assaf, *ibid.*, 18 (1941/42), 272–81; Yaari, *ibid.*, 21 (1944/45), 192–203; Zulay, *ibid.*, 25 (1948/49), 203–5; Sonne, in: SBB, 1 (1953–54), 55–76; Aloni, in: *Sefer Assaf* (1953), 33–39; idem, in: *Aresheth*, 1 (1958), 44–60.

[A.M.H.]

BIBLIOPHILES. Little is known about private book collectors in antiquity and in the early Middle Ages. It might be assumed, however, that patrons of learning, such as *Ḥisdai ibn Shaprut, collected important Hebrew and other books. Historical sources refer to the library of *Samuel ha-Nagid. Judah ibn *Tibbon's advice on how to care for a library is well known. Unfortunately, little is known about the titles of the books making up his collection. Several book lists, some compiled for auctions after the owner's death, were found in the Cairo **Genizah*, the best known being that of R. *Abraham b. Samuel he-Ḥasid. His collection consisted of 27 Hebrew books and a number of volumes on medicine, probably in Arabic. The most remarkable of known medieval Jewish book collectors was the world traveler and physician Judah Leon *Mosconi of Majorca. His library included Hebrew and Arabic books in many branches of learning. Two catalogues have been preserved, one of them drawn up for the auction after his death in 1377. The king of Aragon ultimately canceled the sale and seized the library for himself. In Renaissance Italy there were many enthusiastic book collectors, such as *Menahem b. Aaron of Volterra (15th century), whose library is now in the Vatican. The library of Solomon *Finzi, son of the Mantuan scientist Mordecai (Angelo) *Finzi, contained 200 volumes, at that time a number considered worthy of a great humanist. Elijah *Capsali, a Cretan scholar of the 16th century, possessed a famous collection of Hebrew manuscripts, now at the Vatican. The largest Jewish library in the Renaissance period was that built up in successive generations by the family of Da *Pisa. They were outdone in the 17th century by Abraham Joseph Solomon *Graziano, rabbi of Modena, who wrote the initials of his name *ish ger* (איש גר) in vast numbers of books now scattered in Jewish libraries throughout the world. His contemporary Joseph Solomon *Delmedigo, a physician who traveled widely, boasted that he collected no fewer than 4,000 volumes, on which he had expended the vast sum of 10,000 (florins?). Doubtless, many of these were in languages other than Hebrew.

The first printed sale catalogues of private Hebrew libraries emerged in Holland in the 17th century, for example, the one printed for the disposal of the collections of Moses Raphael d'*Aguilar, the earliest such publication known to Jewish booklore, and that of Isaac *Aboab da Fonseca's collection, comprising about 500 volumes, many in Spanish, French, and even Greek and Latin, including some classics and the writings of the Church Fathers. Other book collectors of that period in Amsterdam were *Manasseh Ben Israel and Samuel Abbas. One of the greatest Jewish book collectors of any period was David *Oppenheim, rabbi of Prague, who in 1688 compiled the first catalogue of his collection, comprising the 480 books he owned at the time. Ultimately, he acquired 4,500 printed works in addition to 780 manuscripts, possibly the most important Jewish library in private ownership that has ever been assembled. It was purchased in 1829 by the Bodleian Library in Oxford. The Italian Catholic abbé Giovanni Bernardo de' *Rossi, a Hebrew scholar of repute and a book collector of genius, had opportunities in Italy that were unequaled elsewhere. His great collection of Hebrew manuscripts, catalogued by him and including several superb illuminated codices, is now housed at the Palatine Library in Parma, having been acquired after his death by the ruler of that petty principality. What the printed book collection includes is still barely known, but one example of its treasures is the only known copy of the earliest of dated Hebrew printed books—Rashi's Commentary printed at Reggio di Calabria in 1475. The next century produced a large number of more self-conscious collectors, such as Heimann Joseph *Michael, a Hamburg businessman, not very affluent but a considerable scholar. The learned catalogue he composed, still a standard work of reference, describes 860 manuscripts and 5,400 printed books, which in due course joined the Oppenheim collection in Oxford. At about the same time Solomon *Dubno of Russia and Holland assembled some 2,000 printed books and about 100 manuscripts, which were sold by auction in Amsterdam in 1814. Another scholarly collector was Solomon *Halberstam of Poland. Business reverses compelled him to dispose of his manuscript collection, part going to the Montefiore Library (now in the library of Jews' College, London), and part to the library of the Jewish Theological Seminary, New York. The most valuable part of his collection of printed books was sold to the library of the Vienna Jewish community; the bulk was acquired by Mayer Sulzberger and presented to the Jewish Theological Seminary in New York. Eliakim *Carmoly, rabbi in Brussels, who destroyed the value of everything he owned by embellishing it with ingenious, but sometimes transparent, forgeries possessed some 1,200 printed volumes and 290 manuscripts. His manuscripts can be found in Oxford, the British Museum, and the Guenzburg Library in Moscow.

In Russia David *Guenzburg of St. Petersburg built up a magnificent manuscript collection, which is now in the Lenin State Library, Moscow. In the United States Mayer *Sulzberger, assisted by the dealer Ephraim *Deinard, built up an important collection. In 1903 Sulzberger gave his collection of 3,000 rare books to the Jewish Theological Seminary. Moritz *Steinschneider's library in Berlin, some 4,500 books and manuscripts, was important both for the caliber of its contents and for the copious, scholarly annotations that Steinschneider added to his books. His collection passed into the ownership of the Jewish Theological Seminary, most of it being destroyed by fire in 1966. Judaica was only part of the great library which Salman *Schocken assembled in Germany, but in that field he concentrated on Hebrew poetry and rare printed books. This collection is now housed in the Schocken Library, Jerusalem, in recent years enriched by some remarkable illuminated manuscripts. A specialized library of another sort was that of David *Montezinos of Amsterdam, who created a unique collection of works, largely in Spanish and Portuguese, illustrating the history of that community. He gave it to the Sephardi synagogue, where he then became librarian. This library worked in friendly competition with the Bibliotheca Rosenthaliana in that city for many years. The latter, the library of Leiser *Rosenthal, a rabbi, was given by his son George to the city of Amsterdam; it is now a constituent of the University Library. Another outstanding rabbinical bibliophile was the Hungarian scholar David *Kaufmann whose remarkable collection, largely of Italian provenance, including some splendid illuminated manuscripts, was presented by his widow to the Hungarian Academy of Sciences. Elkan Nathan *Adler, an English lawyer, who traveled around the world in the course of his business affairs, built up a library of incunabula, rare printed works, and manuscripts, which for bulk, if not for quality, was perhaps the greatest collection assembled by a private person. Just after World War I in order to make good the defalcations of a business associate, he was compelled to sell his library to the Jewish Theological Seminary, thus elevating it to a foremost place among the Jewish libraries of the world. Adler's collection also contained some 30,000 fragments from the Cairo *Genizah,* which he had visited even before it achieved fame. Moses *Gaster, *haham* of the English Sephardi community, also built up a great collection of manuscripts reflecting every side of his versatile interests. Toward the end of his life he sold the bulk to the British Museum. Some of the remainder was ruined during the German air raids on London in World War II; what remained, including the Samaritan manuscripts, was acquired by the John Rylands Library in Manchester to add to its already remarkable Hebrew collection. David Solomon *Sassoon of London had the advantage of great wealth, close connections with the Orient, and a family tradition of book collecting. He assembled his collection of manuscripts with scholarly discrimination and described it in an elaborate catalogue, perhaps the most exhaustive work of its type that has appeared in print. This collection went into the possession of his son Solomon David Sassoon in Letchworth, England. The important collection of Berthold Strauss of London (1901–1962), catalogued in part in his *Ohel Barukh* (1959), was acquired after his death for Yeshiva University, New York. The 20th-century scholars whose private collections have become part of established libraries include Israel *Davidson (Jewish Theological Seminary, where it was destroyed by fire), Hyman *Enelow (Jewish Theological Seminary), Lazarus *Goldschmidt (second collection, Royal Library, Copenhagen), Mordecai *Margolioth (Bar Ilan University), and Alexander *Marx (Jewish Theological Seminary, partly destroyed). Other large private collections were assembled by Saul *Lieberman, Cecil *Roth, and Gershom *Scholem. Significant private collections were also built up by ḥasidic dynasties, e.g., Gerer, Sadagorer, and Lubavitcher. Christian scholars and collectors who owned many important Hebrew books included Johannes *Buxtorf, Bishop Huntington, Bishop Kennicott, Sir Thomas Phillips, Edward Pococke, the Duke of Sussex, and Aldis Wright. Other important private collections belonged to Abraham *Merzbacher (now in Frankfort City and University Library), Nathan *Porges, Israel *Solomons (Jewish Theological Seminary and Hebrew Union College libraries), Mathias Straschun (part in Heikhal Shelomo, Jerusalem), and Michael Zagayski. Among other collectors, mention should be made of Fritz *Bamberger (New York), Ludwig Jesselson (New York), Jacob Lowy (Montreal), and Israel Mehlman (Jerusalem). A very important collection of early Yiddish literature was that of Judah A. Joffee (Jewish Theological Seminary).

Bibliography: Zunz, Gesch, 230–48; M. Steinschneider, *Vorlesungen ueber die Kunde hebraeischer Handschriften* (1897), ch. 3; A. Marx, *Studies In Jewish History and Booklore* (1944), 198–237; Shunami, Bibl, 38–76, 788–9; C. Roth, in: JBA, 25 (1967/68), 75–80; S. Simonsohn, *Toledot ha-Yehudim be-Dukkasut Mantovah;* 2 (1964), 495–8; KS, 41 (1967), suppl., index to vols. 1–40; Allony, *ibid.,* 43 (1967/68), 121–39; Szulvas, in: *Talpioth,* 4 (1949), 600–2; Padover, in: J. W. Thompson (ed.), *The Medieval Library* (1939), 338–46; Sonne, in: SBB, 1 (1953–54), 55–76; 2 (1955), 3–19, 156–9.

[M.SCH.]

BIBLIOTHÈQUE NATIONALE, French national library founded in the 14th century. There was no trace of Hebrew books there before 1544; however, by 1739 there were 516 manuscripts mainly from the collections of Catherine de' Medici, Cardinal Richelieu, and Gilbert Gaulmin. The catalogue of works printed in Hebrew and prepared by Nicolas Rigault remains unedited. The reforms brought about by the French Revolution resulted in several important collections being transferred to the National Library. These consisted of books and manuscripts from convents and from the Sorbonne library. Through the efforts of Solomon *Munk still further acquisitions were added. A description published in 1866 by Herman Zotenberg (*Catalogue des Manuscrits Hébreux et Samaritains de la Bibliothèque Impériale,* based on the preliminary work by Solomon Munk, Joseph *Dernbourg, and Adolphe *Franck), numbers 1,313 works in Hebrew and 11 in Samaritan. In 1968 there was a total of 1,459 manuscripts, including some discovered at Qumran, and 61 Samaritan manuscripts. A new catalogue, prepared by a team from the Institute of Research and History of Texts, was in preparation. There was no complete catalogue of Hebrew books printed. Recent acquisitions are registered in the *Catalogue général des livres imprimés* and in *Ouvrages imprimés en caractères hébraïques* (1967).

Bibliography: Schwab, in: REJ, 36 (1898), 112–4; 37 (1898), 127–36; 61 (1911), 82–87; 121 (1962), 194–209; M. Schwab (ed.), 64 (1912), 153–6, 280–1; 66 (1913), 290–6; I. Adler, *ibid., Manuscrits hébreux de l'Oratoire* (1911); I. Adler, *Incunables hébraïques de la Bibliothèque Nationale* (1962).

[G.V.]

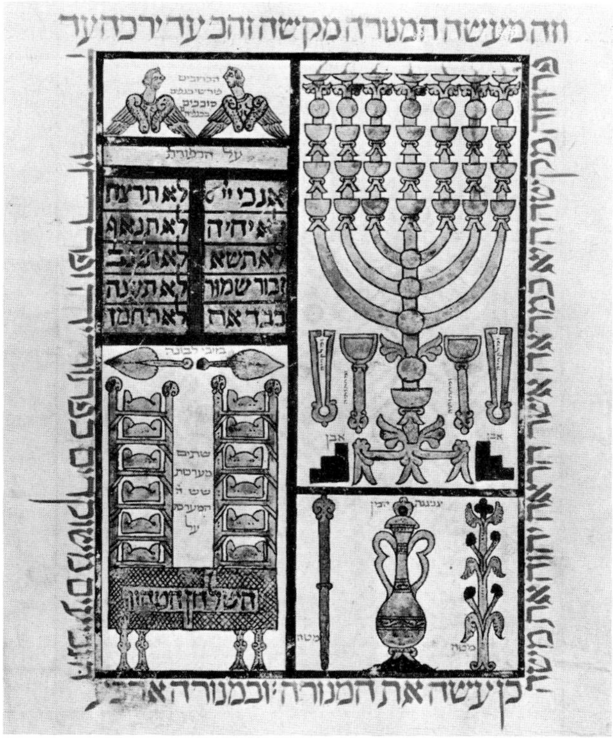

A page from the *Perpignan Bible*, 1299, one of the many illuminated Hebrew manuscripts in the Bibliothèque Nationale, Paris. The illumination shows the *menorah* and implements of the Tabernacle. Paris, Bibliothèque Nationale, Ms. héb. 7, fol. 12v.

BICK, JACOB SAMUEL (1772–1831), Hebrew writer and one of the pioneers of *Haskalah in Galicia. Bick, a friend of Solomon Judah *Rapoport, translated French and English poems into Hebrew and published delightful, satirical letters in *Bikkurei ha-Ittim, Kerem Ḥemed,* and in the anthology *Ha-Ẓefirah,* edited by *Letteris. Bick, like other Galician *maskilim* of his day, began by scoffing at the boorish Ḥasidim, but his strong attachment to the common people and his love of tradition led to a change in his views. When Tobias *Feder published his pamphlet *Kol Meḥaẓeẓim* (1816), criticizing Menahem *Lefin (Levin Mendel of Satanov) for having translated the Book of Proverbs into Yiddish, Bick defended Lefin and argued that one should be pleased that the book had been made accessible to the people in a language that they understood. Most of Bick's literary works were destroyed by fire. However, shortly before World War II, Dov Sadan discovered the manuscripts of three anti-ḥasidic Hebrew plays written by Bick in the Joseph Perl library in Tarnopol. These plays probably belong to Bick's early period.

Bibliography: S. Werses, in: *YIVO Bleter,* 13 (1938), 505–36; G. Bader, *Medinah va-Ḥakhameha* (1934), 36–7; D. Sadan, *Mazkeret Levi* (1953), 96–108.

[G.El.]

BICKEL, SHLOMO (1896–1969), Yiddish essayist and literary critic. Born in eastern Galicia, Bickel was an officer in the Austrian army during World War I. As an active Labor Zionist, he was editor of *Di Freyheyt* (1920–22), the Yiddish organ of the Po'alei Zion of Bukovina, and later editor and coeditor of Yiddish literary periodicals in Rumania. Emigrating to the United States in 1939, he served, from 1940, as literary critic of the New York Yiddish daily, *Der Tog (The Day)* and in the 1960s as head of *YIVO's Commission on Research.

Among his ten books, which appeared between 1936 and 1967, the following are the most significant: *A Shtot Mit Yidn* (1943, 1960), a survey of the vanished culture of Kolomyya—written with mild irony, deep sympathy, and tolerant understanding—which highlights acts of moral greatness and poetic, joyous moments in the lives of ordinary Jews; *Dray Brider Zaynen Mir Geven* (1956), further recollections of Kolomyya's Jews; *Remenye* (1961), which chronicled developments of Jewish cultural life in Rumania between the two world wars, intimately experienced by the author; *Shrayber fun Mayn Dor* (2 vols., 1958–65), essays on Yiddish writers.

Bickel was one of the foremost literary critics and essayists. He set each writer in his specific environment, defining his uniqueness at the same time. A jubilee volume, *Shlomo Bickel Yovel-Bukh* (1967) summarized and evaluated his role in Yiddish literature, including numerous poetic and prose tributes to him.

Bibliography: LNYL, 1 (1956), 300–2; J. Glatstein, *In Tokh Genumen* (1956), 473–9; A. Glanz-Leyeles, *Velt un Vort* (1958), 233–40; S. D. Singer, *Dikhter un Prozaiker* (1959), 303–12; D. Sadan, *Avnei Miftan* (1962), 279–84; S. Liptzin, *Maturing of Yiddish Literature* (1970), 230–2.

[S.L.]

BICKELS-SPITZER, ZVI (1887–1917), Yiddish dramatist and literary critic. Bickels-Spitzer was born in Lemberg. He was a pioneer of the nascent Galician branch of modern Yiddish literature, which became prominent in the early 20th century. The *Czernowitz Language Conference of 1908 awakened the interest of Galician youth in Yiddish. In 1910, Bickels-Spitzer was an editor of the first modern Yiddish literary collection of the Galician region, *Yung-Galitsyaner Almanakh.* He also wrote dramas; the most noteworthy was *Der Goyel* ("The Savior"). His selected writings were posthumously published in Hebrew translation, edited by Dov Sadan (1948).

Bibliography: LNYL, 1 (1956), 302; *Sefer Ẓevi Bickels-Spitzer* (1948); Neugroeschel, in: *Fun Noentn Over,* 1 (1955), 355–62; D. Sadan, *Avnei Miftan* (1961), 87f.

[M.Rav.]

BICKERMAN, ELIAS JOSEPH (1897–), historian. Bickerman was born in Kishinev, Russia, and studied at the University of Petrograd (Leningrad). In 1918 he escaped to Germany, studied at the University of Berlin until 1926, and taught there from 1929 until 1932, when he emigrated to France. He was *chargé de cours* in the Ecole Pratique des Hautes Etudes from 1933 to 1940 and in the Centre National de Recherche Scientifique from 1937 on. After the German conquest of France he again escaped, this time to the United States. There he taught at the New School for Social Research and the Ecole Libre in New York (1942–46), was research fellow at the Jewish Theological Seminary (1946–50), taught at the University of Judaism in Los Angeles (1950–52) and was professor of ancient history at Columbia University (1952–67). After his retirement from Columbia he taught at the Jewish Theological Seminary.

Bickerman wrote innumerable articles in scholarly journals in many fields of ancient history, notably law, religion (especially Judaism), epigraphy, chronology, and the political history of the Hellenistic world. Outstanding among his many books are: *Der Gott der Makkabaeer* (1937; *The Maccabees,* 1947; also as part 2 of his *From Ezra to the Last of the Maccabees,* 1962) which revolutionized the historical understanding of the Maccabean revolt; *Institutions des Séleucides* (1938); and *Chronology of the Ancient World* (1968)—the last two being the fundamental works on their respective subjects.

[M.Sm.]

BIDACHE, village in the department of the Basses-Pyrénées, S. France. A Jewish community composed of

Marrano refugees from Spain and Portugal was established there from the beginning of the 17th century. The duke of Gramont granted his protection to the Jews of Bidache in statutes of 1665 and 1668. When at the beginning of the 18th century the Auch district authority wished to conduct a general tax assessment on the Portuguese Jews in the area, the duke of Gramont intervened on behalf of the Jews in Bidache, including those not of Portuguese origin, who "enjoyed the privilege of nonassessment." The Jewish community dispersed after the French Revolution and was never reestablished. The former cemetery lies on the Port Road outside Bidache and contains tombstones often with epitaphs in both Hebrew and Portuguese.

Bibliography: Gross, Gal Jud, 114; J. Labrit, *Les Gramont, souverains de Bidache* (1939), 97–99. [B.BL.]

BIDNEY, DAVID (1908–), U.S. anthropologist and philosopher. Born in the Ukraine, Bidney was educated in Canada. He taught philosophy at Toronto, Yeshiva, and Yale universities and then gradually shifted the focus of his academic interest to anthropology. Between 1942 and 1950 he was research associate anthropologist with the Wenner-Gren Foundation for Anthropological Research and was then appointed professor of anthropology and philosophy at the University of Indiana. His major interest in philosophy was in interpreting Descartes and Spinoza, as shown in his *Psychology and Ethics of Spinoza* (1962^2). In anthropology Bidney was concerned primarily with the philosophical foundations and implications of the discipline, which appeared in his *Theoretical Anthropology* (1967^2). He interested himself in the history of anthropological thought, theory of myth, primitive religion, and comparative ethics and law. The symposium he organized, and the papers of which he edited, on *The Concept of Freedom in Anthropology* (1963), surveyed freedom in the framework of diverse cultures. [E.FI.]

BIEBER, HUGO (1883–1950), German literary historian. Bieber was born in Berlin, where he studied German literature and philosophy. He was for many years editor of the *Volksverband der Buecherfreunde,* Germany's most important book club. Bieber wrote a history of the intellectual and literary movements of the 19th century, *Der Kampf um die Tradition* (1928). *Confessio Judaica* (1925), an anthology of Heinrich *Heine's opinions on Jews and Judaism, demonstrates Heine's unbroken adherence to his Jewish heritage. Bieber wrote another work entitled *Heinrich Heine* which was translated into English and edited by M. Hadas (1956). After the rise of Hitler, Bieber emigrated to New York. [R.K.]

BIEBER, MARGARETE (1879–), archaeological scholar and teacher. Born in Schoenau, West Prussia, she studied at Bonn, and then was some years an assistant at the German Archaeological Institute in Athens. On her return to Germany she worked at the archaeological museum in Cassel until 1919, when she joined the University of Giessen, where she was appointed professor in 1931. She left Germany in 1933, and after a period at Oxford settled in New York, where she first lectured at Barnard College and then became associate professor in the Fine Arts department of Columbia University. After her retirement she was a visiting lecturer at Princeton (1949–51). Bieber concentrated on Classical and Hellenistic art, and was distinguished for her profound knowledge of Greco-Roman sculpture and her penetrating insight into archaeological problems. During the first phase of her career her publications included the catalog of the Cassel Museum (1915) and two handbooks, *Die Denkmaeler zum Theaterwesen im Altertum* (1920; *The History of Greek and Roman Theater,* 1939), and *Griechische Kleidung* (1928), on ancient Greek dress. In America, her books include *German Readings in the History and Theory of the Fine Arts* (1946), and the monumental *Sculpture of the Hellenistic Age* (1955). [P.P.K.]

BIEDERMANN (Freistaedtl), MICHAEL LAZAR (1769–1843), Austrian financier, entrepreneur, and communal leader. Born in Pressburg, Biedermann first took up engraving. He settled in Vienna when a youth, and in 1798 was commissioned to engrave the imperial seal. In 1800 he opened a store for jewelry and antiques. He subsequently turned to the wool industry into which he introduced modern production methods. In business with L. A. *Auspitz, Biedermann succeeded in transferring the center of the wool trade in the Hapsburg Empire from Budapest to Vienna. He founded one of the first banks in Austria, and in 1816 gave the emperor an interest-free loan of 300,000 florins to combat famine in Vienna. In 1830 he became court jeweler. Biedermann played a leading role in organizing a congregation in Vienna, of which he became a representative in 1806. He was instrumental in the foundation of a Jewish school in 1812 and of the first synagogue in Vienna (the Seitenstettengassetempel) in 1826. He encouraged welfare activities and built a hospital. I. N. *Mannheimer was invited to Vienna to officiate as rabbi on his recommendation. An advocate of moderate *Reform, Biedermann was one of the leaders in the struggle for Jewish *emancipation.

Bibliography: S. Husserl, *Gruendungsgeschichte des Stadttempels der Israelitischen Kultusgemeinde Wien* (1906); A. F. Pribram, *Urkunden und Akten zur Geschichte der Juden in Wien,* 2 vols. (1918), index; M. Rosenmann, *Isak Noah Mannheimer* (Ger., 1915^2); B. Wachstein, *Die ersten Statuten des Bethauses in der inneren Stadt* (1926), 12; idem, *Inschriften des alten Judenfriedhofes in Wien,* 2 (1917), 514; L. Bato, *Juden im alten Wien* (1928); M. Grunwald, *Vienna* (Eng., 1936); J. Fraenkel (ed.), *Jews in Austria* (1967), 11. [ED.]

BIEGELEISEN, HENRYK (1855–1934), Polish literary historian and ethnographer. On his mother's side a grandson of Naḥman *Krochmal, Biegeleisen was assimilated and even made his sons convert. He was for many years principal of a girls' school run by the Jewish community at Lvov. Biegeleisen published a number of studies and monographs on Polish romantic literature. These include *Pan Tadeusz Mickiewicza* ("Mickiewicz's Pan Tadeusz," 1884); *Lirnik mazowiecki* ("The Bard of Mazovia," 1913) on the poet Teofil Lenartowicz; and *Ilustrowane dzieje literatury polskiej* ("An Illustrated History of Polish Literature," 5 vols., 1898–1901). He also edited the works of Słowacki, *Mickiewicz, and Fredro, and a Polish translation of Shakespeare. In the field of ethnography Biegeleisen wrote a number of original studies, among them *Matka i dziecko w obrzędach, wierzeniach i zwyczajach ludu polskiego* ("Mother and Child in the Rites, Beliefs, and Customs of the Polish Folk," 1927); *Wesele* . . . ("Wedding . . . ," 1928); *U Kolebki—przed ołtarzem—nad mogiłą* ("At the Cradle—Before the Altar—By the Tomb," 1929); *Lecznictwo ludu polskiego* ("Popular Cures of the Polish Folk," 1930); and *Śmierć w obrzędach, zwyczajach i wierzeniach ludu polskiego* ("Death in the Rites, Customs, and Beliefs of the Polish Folk," 1931). One of his sons, BRONISLAW BIEGELEISEN-ŻELAZOWSKI (1881–), was professor of psychology in various Polish universities, and published works in his field.

Bibliography: *Polski Słownik Biograficzny,* 2 (1936), 30–32; F. Pajączkowski, in: *Pamiętnik Literacki,* 31 (1934), 244–7 (bibl.); *Wielka Encyklopedia Powszeczna,* 1 (1962), 779–80 (on Bronislaw; incl. bibl.). [MO.A.]

BIEL, township near Uncastillo, Aragon, Spain. The earliest information on the community of Biel dates from 1294, when a Christian girl disappeared; rumors were spread that the Jews were responsible, and the Jews of Biel were arrested. It was only after the intervention of James II that the charge was withdrawn. In 1305, however, Açac de Çalema, the wealthiest Jew of Biel, was accused of having derided the Christian religion. He was arrested and brought to trial before the Dominicans, and his property was confiscated. In 1294 and in 1305, the Jews of Biel paid an annual sum of 250 *solidi,* amounting to a quarter of the income derived by the king from the locality. In 1361, the king requested Solomon de la *Cavallería to annul an irregular Jewish marriage at Biel. A Jewish community continued to exist until the expulsion of the Jews from Spain in 1492.

Bibliography: Baer, Studien, 131; Baer, Urkunden, 2 (1936), 184f., 375, 917; Baer, Spain, 2 (1966), 7–8.

[H.B.]

BIEL (Bienne), town in the Swiss canton of Berne. Citizenship (Buergerrecht) was granted to several Jewish families in 1305, although Jews probably settled in Biel earlier. They were allowed to trade freely and engage in moneylending, until their expulsion from the city, the date of which is unknown. Communal life revived after 1848, when several Jewish families from *Alsace-Lorraine settled in Biel. A synagogue was built in 1882. In 1969 the community consisted of 227 people and had its own rabbi.

Bibliography: A. Welder-Steinberg, *Geschichte der Juden in der Schweiz,* 1 (1966), 68; Schweizerischer Israelitischer Gemeindebund, *Festschrift 1904–1954* (1954), 313.

[Ed.]

BIELEFELD, city in North Rhine-Westphalia, West Germany. Jews there were massacred during the *Black Death, 1348–49. In 1370 a few Jews again settled in Bielefeld. The prohibition of 1554 on Jewish residence in the duchy of *Juelich also applied to Bielefeld, but Jews resettled there in 1586. Their main occupations were commerce and moneylending. Jews from Bielefeld attended the fairs at *Leipzig at the beginning of the 18th century. The cemetery continued in use from 1665, until a new one was opened in 1891. In 1905 a synagogue to seat 800 was consecrated. The Jewish population numbered 65 in 1783 and 800 in 1933. On Nov. 10, 1938, the synagogue was burned down. About 400 members of the community perished during the *Holocaust. Only 12 survivors returned to Bielefeld after the war. A few Jews settled there from other places, and there were 66 Jews living in Bielefeld in 1955. A new synagogue was inaugurated in 1951.

Bibliography: Germ Jud, 2 (1968), 82; MGDJ, 3 (1912), 14–21; U. Niemann (ed.), *Ueberblick ueber die Geschichte der juedischen Gemeinde in Bielefeld* (mimeo 1962); H. A. Maass, in: *Historischer Verein fuer die Grafschaft Ravensburg,* 65 (1966–67), 79–94.

[Z.Av./Ed.]

BIELSK, town in N.E. Poland. Jews are mentioned there in 1487. An organized community existed in Bielsk in the early 16th century and a synagogue was built in 1542. In 1564 a Jewish tax-collector in the town was condemned to death following a blood libel. The Jewish population numbered 94 in 1816; 298 in 1847; and 4,079 in 1897 (54.6% of the total).

[Ed.]

Holocaust Period. In 1921 Bielsk had 2,392 Jews, but under Soviet rule (1939–41) its Jewish population increased to 6,000 when large numbers of refugees arrived from the western parts of Poland occupied by the Germans. In the summer of 1940 a number of refugees were exiled to the Soviet interior. In the spring of 1941 young Jews were drafted into the Soviet Army. When the war broke out between Germany and the U.S.S.R. (June 22, 1941), groups of Jews attempted to flee eastward with the retreating Soviet forces, but few of them succeeded. The Germans entered Bielsk on June 24, 1941. Within ten days they assembled 30 of the Jewish leaders and intellectuals and put them to death. The Germans exacted a fine of four kilograms of gold and 200,000 rubles from the Jewish community. They also imposed a Judenrat, headed by Shlomo Epstein. At the end of 1941 an "open" ghetto was established. In February 1942 the ghetto was surrounded by barbed wire and closed off from contact with the outside. On Nov. 2–11, 1942, the Germans rounded up over 5,000 ghetto inhabitants for Treblinka death camp and murdered 200 old and sick Jews in the local Jewish cemetery. About 40 experts and skilled craftsmen were picked out and sent to *Bialystok Ghetto, where they were eventually liquidated along with the rest of the Jewish inmates. The community was not reconstituted after the war.

[Ar.W.]

Bibliography: I. Schipper (ed.), *Dzieje handlu żydowskiego na ziemiach polskich* (1937), index.

BIELSKO (Ger. **Bielitz**), town in S. Poland on the river Biala opposite *Biala, amalgamated with Biala in 1950 to form the city of Biala-Bielsko. A community existed in Bielsko in the first half of the 19th century, which was authorized to open a prayer hall in 1831 and a cemetery in 1849. It became an independent community in 1865. The Jewish population numbered 1,977 in 1890 increasing to 3,955 by 1921, and approximately 5,000 in 1939; most were German speaking. According to the 1921 census, 2,737 declared their nationality as Jewish, of whom 513 declared Yiddish as their mother tongue. The Jews in Bielsko took an important part in the city's commerce and woolen textile industry. Most of the communal institutions were maintained jointly with the Biala community. Michael Berkowicz, Theodor Herzl's Hebrew secretary, taught religious subjects in the secondary school at Bielsko, and attracted many Jews to Zionism. The Hebrew scholar and bibliophile S. Z. H. *Halberstam lived in Bielsko and the scholar Saul *Horovitz officiated as rabbi there from 1888 to 1895.

[A.J.Br.]

Holocaust and Post-War Periods. The German army entered the town on Sept. 3, 1939, and immediately initiated an anti-Jewish terror. On Sept. 13, 1939, on the eve of Rosh Ha-Shanah, the Nazis burned down both synagogues in Bielsko and the Ḥ. N. Bialik Jewish cultural home. A few days later the Germans burned down the two synagogues in nearby Biała, and its Orthodox Jews were forced to throw the holy books into the fire. In the summer of 1941 a ghetto was established in Bielsko. The ghetto was liquidated in June 1942 when the town's entire Jewish population was deported to the death camp in Auschwitz. Bielsko was amalgamated with *Biała in 1950 to form the city of Bielsko-Biała. After the war a few hundred Jews settled in Bielsko-Biała. A children's home for orphans, survivors of the Holocaust, functioned there for a few years. The Jewish Cultural Society ran a club until June 1967 when the Polish government initiated its anti-Semitic campaign. After that date almost all the remaining Jews left Poland.

[S.Kr.]

Bibliography: M. Aronsohn, *Die israelitische Kultusgemeinde in Bielitz 1865–1905* (1905). Holocaust Period: J. Kermisz, *"Akcje" i "wysiedlenia"* (1946), index; *Megillat Polin* (1961), 164; T. Berenstein and A. Rutkowski, in: BŻIH, no. 38 (1961), 3–38, passim; *Yad Vashem Archives,* 0–3/1251.

BIEN, JULIUS (1826–1909), U.S. lithographer. Julius was born in Naumburg, Germany, where he studied lithography. After participating in the unsuccessful revolution of 1848, he fled to New York where he established a small lithographic business in 1850. His abilities soon earned him most government contracts for engraving and printing major geographic and geological publications, including a map of the territory west of the

Julius Bien, U.S. lithographer. B'nai B'rith photo.

Mississippi River, which was standard for 25 years. He produced the maps and atlases accompanying the federal census reports from 1870 to 1900, as well as atlases of New York State (1895) and Pennsylvania (1900). Bien was president of the National Lithographers' Association (1886–96). A director of the Hebrew Technical Institute and Hebrew Orphan Asylum in New York, he was president of the B'nai B'rith order (1854–57, 1868–1900) and instrumental in forming its international structure. Julius' brother HERMAN M. BIEN (1831–1895), U.S. rabbi and author, founded a Hebrew school in San Francisco and served as rabbi of Temple Emanu-El until 1860. He then moved to Virginia City, Nevada, where he organized a school and was elected to the state legislature (1863–65). Moving to New York, he became a merchant in Fort Henry. In 1881 he was appointed rabbi of Congregation Beth Shalom in Chicago, but moved to Vicksburg, Mississippi, in 1885. Among his numerous works are the drama *Samson and Delilah* (1857), and *Ben Beor* (1891), a portrayal of anti-Semites. [E.GR.]

BIENENFELD, FRANZ RUDOLF (1886–1961), lawyer, writer, and Zionist. Born and educated in Vienna, Bienenfeld became an active figure in Zionist and in Jewish communal affairs. He succeeded Robert *Stricker as chairman of the Austrian section of the *World Jewish Congress. Under the nom de plume Anton von Mueller, Bienenfeld published *Deutsche und Juden* (1934; *The Germans and the Jews,* 1939), an analysis of the relationship between Jews and Germans in the period of Hitler, and followed it with *Religion der religionslosen Juden* (1938; *Religion of the Non-Religious Jews,* 1944). In 1939 he fled to England where he worked on the staff of the World Jewish Congress, later becoming a member of the executive, and drafted the claims for German *reparations after World War II. His book, *Rediscovery of Justice* (1947) argued the claim of the Jews to compensation. His writings on Austrian civil law include *Die Haftung ohne Verschulden* (1933). [J.J.L.]

BIENENSTOCK, MAX (1881–1923), writer, educator, and Zionist leader of the labor movement. Bienenstock was born in Tarnow, Galicia, and educated at an Austrian high school. He graduated as doctor of philosophy from Cracow University. He taught in government high schools from 1904 until the collapse of the Hapsburg monarchy. From his early youth he was an active Zionist. During the short-lived Jewish autonomy in western Ukraine (1918–19), he was director of the Department of Education and Culture. When the Ukrainian Republic was overthrown by the Polish army, he was arrested for a few months as a political criminal. Afterwards the Polish authorities refused to confirm his appointment as teacher and director of the Hebrew high school in Cracow. From then on, he devoted his efforts to writing and to Zionist education. Attracted by the socialist ideology, Bienenstock formed and led the Hitaḥadut party in eastern Galicia. In the Polish parliamentary elections of 1922, his party, in the framework of the Jewish national bloc, elected him to the senate for the Lvov district. Bienenstock was a progressive educator and a gifted writer in Polish, German, and, later, Yiddish. He published two books, *Das juedische Element in Heines Werke* (1910), and *Henrik Ibsens Kunstanschaungen* (1913). He translated Polish classics into German, including *The Ungodly Comedy* by Krasinski. He wrote essays on Zionist socialist topics and, in his last years, on Yiddish literature. He died in Lvov.

Bibliography: M. Bienenstock, *A Zamelshrift Wegn Zeyn Leben un Shafen* (1924); N. M. Gelber, *Toledot Ha-Tenu'ah ha-Ẓiyyonit be-Galiẓyah,* 2 (1958), 757–8; D. Sadan, *Avnei Zikkaron* (1954), 98–110. [A.TAR.]

BIENSTOK, JUDAH LEIB (Leon; 1836–1894), Russian writer and community leader. He was born in Volhynia and educated in Zhitomir at the government-sponsored rabbinical seminary. He served as government-appointed rabbi at Zhitomir from 1859 to 1862. Afterward he worked as a specialist for Jewish affairs in the office of the governor of Volhynia. He wrote for the Jewish press in Russian and Yiddish. In 1879 he went to St. Petersburg where for a time he became the secretary of both the Jewish community and the "Society for the Spreading of Enlightenment." As a friend of *Mendele Mokher Seforim, he translated his *He-Avot Ve-ha-Banim* ("Fathers and Children") into Russian and collaborated with him on a few popular pamphlets in Yiddish, also writing one of the first biographical articles about him (*Voskhod,* 12, 1884). In 1891 he published a study of the Jewish agricultural settlements in the district of Yekaterinoslav (now Dnepropetrovsk). In 1892 when Vladimir *Tiomkin resigned from his post as Ḥovevei Zion representative in Ereẓ Israel, the *Odessa Committee appointed Bienstok in his place. He assisted in the establishment of modern schools in the country and the founding of the Sha'arei Zion library in Jaffa.

Bibliography: Tidhar, 3 (1958), 1280–81; LNYL, 1 (1956), 297–8. [Y.S.]

BIERER, RUBIN (1835–1931), one of the first active Zionists and members of Ḥovevei Zion in Galicia, Austria, and Bulgaria. Bierer, who was born in Lemberg, completed his studies in medicine in 1863. He was a founder of the Jewish association Shomer Israel in Galicia. From the early 1880s he lived in Vienna, where he was a founder of the Jewish student organization *Kadimah (1882). In the same year, he was one of the founders of the Ahavat Zion society for the settlement of Ereẓ Israel, of which both Pereẓ *Smolenskin and Zalman Spitzer, the leader of the Orthodox Viennese community, were members. He published articles on the idea of Jewish nationhood and settlement of Ereẓ Israel in most of the German Jewish periodicals. Invited to Belgrade to serve as court physician, he transferred his Zionist activities there, and thereafter to Sofia, where he later lived. In Bulgaria he was a devoted assistant to *Herzl, who sent him the first copy of *Der Judenstaat,* inscribed "to the first pioneer of the Zionist idea." He returned to Lemberg in 1905, and continued his Zionist activities almost until his death.

Bibliography: T. Herzl, *Complete Diaries,* 5 (1960), index; N. M. Gelber, *Toledot ha-Tenuah ha-Ẓiyyonit be-Galiẓyah,* 2 (1958), index; *Haolam* (Dec. 22, 1931), 1003; EG, 10 *(Bulgariya)* (1967), index.

[G.K.]

BIESENTHAL, JOHANN HEINRICH (born **Raphael Hirsch;** 1800–1886), Hebraist and theologian. Biesenthal, who converted to Christianity, became a Protestant missionary first in Berlin and later (1844) in London. Biesenthal wrote *A Hebrew and Chaldaic Vocabulary of the Old Testament* (1836–37) and a Bible dictionary including a history of the church and archaeology (*Biblisches, kirchenhistorisches, und archaeologisches Handwoerterbuch,* 1841). He published (together with F. S. Lebrecht) a new edition of David Kimḥi's *Sefer ha-Shorashim* ("Book of Roots," 1838), and a collection of quotations from the Zohar (based on T. A. Tholuck's compilation) with German translation (1876[4]). He also published the first part of a Judaistic encyclopedia entitled *Chrestomathia rabbinica . . .* (Berlin, 1844). On the occasion of the *Damascus blood libel he wrote a pamphlet (under the pseudonym Karl Ignaz Corvé) denouncing the legend of ritual killing of which the Jews were accused (1840). Among his works dealing with the history of the Christian church are critical editions with commentary on Romans (1855) and Hebrews (1857 and 1878) in which he tried to prove that Paul wrote these letters originally in Hebrew to his Jewish brethren.

Bibliography: J. de le Roi, *Geschichte der evangelischen Judenmission,* 1 (1898[2]), 90ff., 156; Fuerst, Bibliotheca, 1 pt. 1 (1863), 115; Zeitlin, Bibliotheca, 31.

[Jo.H./Ed.]

BIGAMY AND POLYGAMY. In Jewish law the concept of bigamy (or polygamy) can involve either (1) a married women *(eshet ish)* purporting to contract a second marriage to another man (or to other men) during the subsistence of her first marriage; or (2) a married man contracting marriages to other women during the subsistence of his first marriage. These two aspects must be considered separately.

(1) Relating to Women. The general principle is that "a woman cannot be the wife of two [men]" (Kid. 7a and Rashi). In relation to a wife the term *kiddushin* implies her exclusive dedication to her husband. There can therefore be no *kiddushin* between her and another man while the first *kiddushin* subsists, and a purported marriage to another man is thus totally invalid. Nevertheless, such a bigamous "marriage" does incur severe legal consequences—primarily because of the law that sexual intercourse between a married woman and a man other than her husband (i.e., adultery) results in her subsequently being prohibited to both men forever and she then requires a *get* ("divorce") from both of them (see *Divorce, *Adultery). She requires a divorce from her husband, *mi-de-Oraita* ("according to biblical law"), because, although her adultery renders her prohibited to him, her legal marriage to him continues to subsist. To resolve this paradox she needs a *get.* She also requires a divorce from her adulterous "husband," *mi-de-Rabbanan* ("according to rabbinical enactment")—even though her marriage to him is invalid—so that people, ignorant of the true facts and perhaps under the impression that her second "marriage" was a valid one, should not be misled into thinking that she is free of him without a proper divorce (Yev. 88b and Rashi; Maim. Yad, Gerushin 10:5; Sh. Ar., EH 17:56).

Notwithstanding her divorce by both men, on the death of either of them she continues prohibited to the survivor forever (Sot. 27b; Yev. 87b and 88b; Yad, Gerushin, 10:4–5; Sh. Ar., EH 17:56). The aforementioned consequences result whether the bigamous "marriage" was intentional or inadvertent; e.g., if the woman was incorrectly informed by two witnesses of her legal husband's death (Yev. 87b; Yad, Gerushin 10:4 and Sh. Ar., EH 17:56). If, in spite of the said prohibitions, she does subsequently contract a later marriage with either of the two men, such a later marriage is a prohibited one (see Prohibited *Marriages) and must be dissolved (Maim. Yad, Gerushin 10:4). Further legal consequences of a woman's bigamous "marriage" are that her children of the second, adulterous, union are classed as **mamzerim* according to biblical law and also that her financial rights are affected (Yev. 87b).

(2) Relating to Men. The law is different in the case of a married man who purports to take a second wife while still married. According to Jewish law this second marriage (and any others) is valid and can therefore only be dissolved by death or divorce (Yev. 65a; *Piskei ha-Rosh, ibid.,* 17; Yad, Ishut, 14:3; Sh. Ar., EH 1:9; 76:7). Permitted according to biblical law, polygamy was practiced throughout the talmudic period and thereafter until the tenth century (*Piskei ha-Rosh* to Yev. 65a; Sh. Ar., EH 1:9). Already in amoraic times, however, the practice was frowned upon by the sages, who prescribed that polygamy was permissible only if the husband was capable of properly fulfilling his marital duties toward each of his wives (see *Marriage). The opinion was also expressed that if a man takes a second wife, he must divorce his first wife, if the latter so demands, and pay her *ketubbah* (Yev. 65a; Alfasi, *Piskei ha-Rosh,* and Sh. Ar., EH 1:9). Similarly, according to talmudic law, a man may not take a second wife if he has specifically undertaken to his first wife, e.g., in the *ketubbah,* not to do so (Sh. Ar., EH 76:8). Taking a second wife is also forbidden wherever *monogamy is the local custom since such custom is deemed an implied condition of the marriage, it being presumed that the wife only wishes to marry in accordance with local custom (Sh. Ar., EH 1:9; *Beit Shemu'el, ibid.,* 20; *Ḥelkat Meḥokek, ibid.,* 15, 76:8). Generally, the husband can only be released from this restriction with his wife's consent (loc. cit.; *Darkhei Moshe,* EH 1:1, n. 8; Sh. Ar., EH 76).

Ḥerem de-Rabbenu Gershom. Substance of the Ban. In the course of time and for varying reasons (*Oẓar ha-Posekim,* EH 1:61, 2), it became apparent that there was a need for the enactment of a general prohibition against polygamy, independent of the husband's undertaking to this effect. Accordingly, relying on the principle of endeavoring to prevent matrimonial strife (which principle had already been well developed in talmudic law) Rabbenu *Gershom b. Judah and his court enacted the **takkanah* prohibiting a man from marrying an additional wife unless specifically permitted to do so on special grounds by at least 100 rabbis from three "countries" (i.e., districts; see below). This *takkanah,* known as the *Ḥerem de-Rabbenu Gershom,* also prohibited a husband from divorcing his wife against her will. Various versions of the *takkanah* exist (*Oẓar ha-Posekim,* EH 1:61, 1) and, indeed, scholars have even questioned the historical accuracy of ascribing its authorship to Rabbenu Gershom. This, however, does not in any way affect its validity.

Since the prohibition against polygamy is derived from this *takkanah* and not from any undertaking given by the husband to his wife, she is not competent to agree to a waiver of its application, lest she be subjected to undue influence by her husband (Sh. Ar., EH 1:10; *Oẓar ha-Posekim,* EH 1:61, 5). Nevertheless, if the husband does enter into a further marriage it will be considered legally valid (Tur, EH 44; *Darkhei Moshe, ibid.,* n. 1; Sh. Ar., EH 44; *Beit Shemu'el* 11), but as a prohibited marriage, and the first wife can require the court to compel the husband to divorce the other woman. Since the first wife cannot be obliged to live with a *zarah* ("rival"), she may also ask that the court order (but not compel) the husband to give her (i.e., the first wife) a divorce (Sh. Ar., EH 154; *Pitḥei Teshuvah,* 5; PDR vol. 7, pp. 65–74, 201–6). The husband continues to be liable to maintain his wife until he complies with the court's order—even though they are living apart—because as long as he refuses to divorce her he is preventing her from remarrying and thus being supported by another husband (*Keneset ha-Gedolah,* EH 1, Tur 16–17; PDR vol. 7 p.74). However, if the first wife and the husband agree on a divorce and this is carried out, he is then released from his obligation to divorce his second wife, although his marriage to her in the first place was in defiance of the prohibition (Sh. Ar., *Pitḥei Teshuvah,* 5; *Ozar ha-Posekim,* EH 1:80, 1 and 2).

Applicability of the Ḥerem as to Time and Place. Many authorities were of the opinion that the validity of the *ḥerem* was, from its inception, restricted as to both time and place. Thus, it is stated: "He [Rabbenu Gershom] only imposed the ban until the end of the fifth millennium," i.e., until the year 1240 (Sh. Ar., EH 1:10); others, however, were of the opinion that no time limit was placed on its application. At any rate, even according to the first opinion the *ḥerem* remained in force after 1240, since later generations accepted it as a binding *takkanah.* Accordingly, the *ḥerem,* wherever it was accepted (see below), now has the force of law for all time (Resp. Rosh 43:8; Sh. Ar., EH 1:10; *Arukh ha-Shulḥan,* EH 1:23; *Ozar ha-Posekim,* EH 1:76). In modern times it is customary, in some communities, to insert in the *ketubbah* a clause against the husband's taking an additional wife "in accordance with the *takkanah* of Rabbenu Gershom...." However, the prohibition is binding on the husband, even though omitted from the *ketubbah,* as such omission is regarded as a "clerical error" (*Keneset ha-Gedolah,* EH 1, Tur 17; *Arukh ha-Shulḥan,* EH 1:23).

The *ḥerem* did not extend to those countries where it was apparent that the *takkanah* had never been accepted (Sh. Ar., EH 1:10). In a country where the acceptance of the *takkanah* is in doubt, however, its provisions must be observed (*Arukh ha-Shulḥan,* EH 1:23). In general it can be said that the *ḥerem* has been accepted as binding among Ashkenazi communities, but not among the Sephardi and most of the Oriental communities. This is apparently because in those countries where Ashkenazim formed the main part of the Jewish community, as in Europe, America, or Australia where European Jews migrated, polygamy was also forbidden by the dominant religion, Christianity, and therefore by the secular law. This was not the case in Oriental countries, as in Yemen, Iraq, and North Africa, polygamy being permitted in Islam (*Arukh ha-Shulḥan* and *Ozar ha-Posekim,* loc. cit.). Thus, Maimonides, who was a Sephardi, makes no reference at all to the *ḥerem.* In practice, therefore, to prohibit polygamy Oriental communities would customarily insert an express provision in the *ketubbah,* whereby the husband was precluded from taking an additional wife except with the consent of his first wife or with the permission of the *bet din.* As this provision was a condition of the marriage, any breach thereof entitled the wife to demand either that her husband complied with the provision, i.e., by divorcing the second wife, or that she be granted a divorce with payment of her *ketubbah* (*Sedei Ḥemed,* Asefat Dinim, Ishut 2; *Keneset ha-Gedolah,* EH 1, *Beit Yosef* 13, 16; *Ozar ha-Posekim, ibid.,* 1:80, 8; PDR 7:65).

People who move from a country where the *ḥerem* is binding to a country where it is not, or vice versa, are subject to the following rules: (1) the ban adheres to the individual, i.e., it accompanies him from place to place and he always remains subject to it (*Arukh ha-Shulḥan,* loc. cit.; *Ozar ha-Posekim,* EH 1:75, 1; Sh. Ar., EH 1); (2) local custom is followed, so that if the *ḥerem* applies to a particular country it is binding on everyone, irrespective of their country of origin (*Arukh ha-Shulḥan, ibid.; Ozar ha-Posekim, ibid.* and 1:75, 3; *Keneset ha-Gedolah,* EH, *Beit Yosef,* 22). Both these rules are strictly applied with the intent of extending the operation of the *ḥerem* as widely as possible. On the other hand, if a man legally married two wives in a country where this was permitted, he is not obliged to divorce either of them on arriving in another country where the *ḥerem* is in force, as the law is only infringed by his taking an additional wife and not when a man already has two (*Arukh ha-Shulḥan, ibid.*).

Release from the Prohibition. The object of prohibiting bigamy is to prevent a man from marrying a second wife as long as he is not legally entitled to dissolve his first marriage. Thus, in order to avoid any circumvention of the prohibition, the *ḥerem* also generally prohibits divorce against the will of the wife. This double prohibition may, however, result in the husband being unjustifiably fettered in circumstances where he would not otherwise be required by law to maintain his ties with his wife—and yet may not divorce her against her will. This can, therefore, be obviated by the availability of a *hetter* ("release") from the *ḥerem* against bigamy, which is granted by the *bet din* in the appropriate circumstances. This *hetter* does not mean that the first wife is divorced, but that the husband is granted exceptional permission to contract an additional marriage. Naturally, such a step is only taken if the court, after a full investigation of the relevant facts, is satisfied that a release is legally justified. Thus, for example, a release would be granted in a case where a wife becomes insane. Her husband cannot, therefore, maintain normal married life with her, a fact which would ordinarily entitle him to divorce her; this he cannot do because of her legal incapacity to consent. However, as the first marriage must continue to subsist, the husband remains liable to support his wife—including medical costs—but he is permitted by the court to take an additional wife (Baḥ, EH 119; Sh. Ar., EH 1; *Beit Shemu'el* 1, n. 23; 119, n.6; *Ḥelkat Meḥokek, ibid.,* 10–12; *Ozar ha-Posekim,* EH 1:72, 19). Should the first wife subsequently recover her sanity she cannot demand that her husband divorce his second wife, as he married her in accordance with the law. On the contrary, the husband would be entitled—and even obliged—to divorce his first wife, so as not to remain with two wives, and if she refuses to accept his *get* he would be free from any further marital obligations towards her, save for the payment of her *ketubbah* (Sh. Ar., EH 1; *Beit Shemu'el, ibid.; Ozar ha-Posekim,* EH 1:72, 17–18; PDR 3:271). However, the *hetter* would be revoked if the first wife recovered her mental capacity before the second marriage took place (Sh. Ar., EH 1, *Pitḥei Teshuvah,* 16, concl.; *Ozar ha-Posekim,* EH 1:72, 14).

On the strength of the aforementioned rule, a release from the *ḥerem* may also be obtained by a man whose wife refuses to accept a *get* from him, despite the court's order that she does so, e.g., in the case of her adultery or where the marriage is a prohibited one (Sh. Ar., EH 1:10; *Ḥelkat Meḥokek, ibid.,* 16; *Ozar ha-Posekim,* EH 1:63, 7). Some authorities are of the opinion that in the event of the wife's adultery the husband only requires a *hetter* from a regular court and not from 100 rabbis, since the *ḥerem* was not meant for such a case (*Ozar ha-Posekim,* EH 1:73, 2). A *hetter* would be justified where a wife who has had no children during a marriage which has subsisted for at least ten years—a fact which entitles the husband to divorce her—refuses to accept the *get* and thus prevents her husband from remarrying and fulfilling the *mitzvah* to "be fruitful and multiply." In such a case the husband is obliged to take another wife to fulfill the *mitzvah* and so he would be entitled to the *hetter* (Sh. Ar., EH 1:10; *Oẓar ha-Posekim*, EH 1:68; *Arukh ha-Shulḥan*, EH 1:25).

As has already been stated, in Oriental communities for a husband to take a second wife requires either his first wife's consent or the court's permission. The wife is required to give her consent before a regular court (not 100 rabbis) and the court will permit the second marriage only if satisfied, after a thorough investigation of the facts, that the wife has consented wholeheartedly, without anger or under undue influence (*Oẓar ha-Posekim*, EH 1:61, 5, subsec. 3; *Sedei Ḥemed*, Asefat Dinim, Ishut 2). Without her consent, the court will generally only grant a release to the husband in such cases where it would do so were the *ḥerem* to apply (*Sedei Ḥemed; Oẓar ha-Posekim, ibid.*), since it is presumed that the husband's undertaking the *ketubbah* is given on the understanding that no circumstances shall exist which, if the *ḥerem* were to apply, would warrant his release from the prohibition (*Sedei Ḥemed, ibid.; Oẓar ha-Posekim*, EH 1:72, 9).

Procedure for Granting the Hetter. After the court has decided that a release from the *ḥerem* should be granted, the matter is referred to 100 rabbis of three "countries" (*Oẓar ha-Posekim*, EH 1:61, 9) for approval and, if so approved, the *hetter* takes effect. As a preliminary, the husband is required to deposit with the court a *get* for his first wife, together with an irrevocable authority for the court to have the *get* delivered to his first wife as soon as she is able and willing to receive it from an agent appointed by the husband at the request of the court. However, in the case where the *hetter* is given because of the first wife's insanity, it is customary to give her a new *get* when she recovers, rather than the one previously deposited with the court, as some doubt could be cast on the latter's validity, since it was the wife's insanity that made it impossible to deliver the *get* to her originally and there may therefore possibly be other legal objections to its validity. The deposited *get* is usually only delivered to her if she is in danger of becoming a deserted wife (see *Agunah; *Arukh ha-Shulḥan*, EH 1:26; *Oẓar ha-Posekim*, EH 1:72, 30–31). Furthermore, the husband is also generally required to deposit with the court the amount of the wife's *ketubbah* in cash or provide adequate security (Baḥ, EH 119; Sh. Ar., EH; *Beit Shemu'el* 1, n. 23; *Arukh ha-Shulḥan*, EH 1:25; *Oẓar ha-Posekim*, 1:72, 23–24). Some authorities are of the opinion that the husband must also deposit with the court, or adequately secure in like manner, such sum as the court may determine to cover the wife's maintenance and medical expenses (*Oẓar ha-Posekim*, EH 1:72, 29).

State of Israel. At a national rabbinic conference called in 1950 by the chief rabbis of Israel, an enactment was passed making monogamy (apart from the above-mentioned permissions) binding upon all Jews irrespective of their communal affiliations. This *takkanah*, however, does not render a second marriage invalid according to biblical law, and therefore, if such a marriage does take place, it can be dissolved only by divorce. The criminal law of the state, however, renders it an offense on pain of imprisonment for a married person to contract another marriage (Penal Law Amendment (Bigamy) Law, 5719-1959). Nevertheless, for Jewish citizens no offense is committed if permission to marry a second wife was given by a final judgment of a rabbinical court and approved by the two chief rabbis of Israel. The latter's approval is accepted as conclusive proof that the permission was given according to the law. Special provisions relating to the grant of this permission are laid down in the *Takkanot ha-Diyyun be-Vattei ha-Din ha-Rabbaniyyim be-Yisrael*, 5720–1960.

See also *Monogamy.

Bibliography: L. Loew, in: *Ben Chananja*, 3 (1860), 317-29, 529–39, 657–67; 4 (1861), 111–5, 257–9, 271–3 (reprinted in his *Gesammelte Schriften*, 3 (1893), 33–86); F. Rosenthal, in: *Jubelschrift... Hildesheimer* (1890), 37–53; Finkelstein, Middle Ages, 111–26, 205–15; A. Ḥ. Freimann, *Seder Kiddushin ve-Nissu'in* (1945), passim; M. Elon, in: *Hed ha-Mishpat* (1957), 233–5; S. Lowy, in: JJS, 9 (1958), 115–38; I. Glasner, in: *Ha-Peraklit*, 16 (1960), 274–80; Z. W. Falk, *Nissu'in ve-Gerushin...* (1961), passim; P. Tishbi, in: *Tarbiz*, 34 (1964/65), 49–55; S. Eidelberg, *ibid.*, 287f.; I. Schepansky, in: *Hadorom*, 22 (1965), 103–20; I. Ta-Shema, in: *Tarbiz*, 35 (1965/66), 193; E. Berkovitz, *Tenai be-Nissu'in u-ve-Get* (1966), passim; B. Schereschewsky, *Dinei Mishpaḥah* (1967^2), 61–80; M. Elon, *Ḥakikah Datit* (1968), 34–36, 104–16, 122–7.

[B.Z.Sch.]

BIHALJI MERIN, OTO (1904–), Yugoslav writer and art historian. He studied painting in Belgrade and Berlin. In 1929, he founded the Belgrade progressive publishing house "Nolit," with his brother Pavle Bihalji, who was shot by the Nazis in 1941. Bihalji Merin was taken prisoner by the Germans (1941–45) and became one of the leaders of the Yugoslav resistance in prisoner-of-war camps. In 1945 he returned to Belgrade and with his wife successfully resumed his publishing career. He edited the house magazine and monographs of the publishing firm "Jugoslavija," one of whose notable editions was the **Haggadah* of Sarajevo. An authority on naive art, he helped to keep Yugoslav thinking in touch with new trends. Many of his works have been translated into major languages, the more important being: *Modern German Art* (1938); *Das naive Bild der Welt* (1959; *Modern Primitives: Masters of Naive Painting*, 1961); *Umetnost naivnih u Jugoslaviji* (1963); and *Adventure of Modern Art* (1968).

[Zd.L.]

BIHARI, ALEXANDER (1856–1906), Hungarian *genre* painter. The son of a poor housepainter, Bihari studied in Budapest and Vienna. In 1883, a wealthy patron made it possible for him to travel to Paris, where he fully assimilated the style of the French naturalist or realist masters, such as Jules *Adler. Upon his return to Hungary, Bihari settled in Szolnok, an agricultural center in the great Hungarian plains, rather than in a fashionable Budapest studio. He continued to paint *genre* pictures and was soon recognized as Hungary's leading painter in this field. A quality of Parisian wit seemed to guard him against the temptation of overt sentimentality. Using broad brush strokes, Bihari grouped and painted his figures as he saw them in their everyday surroundings. Bihari's masterpiece is

"Sunday Afternoon" by Alexander Bihari, 1893, oil, 47×60 ins. (119×153 cm.). Budapest, Hungarian National Gallery.

perhaps his "Sunday Afternoon" which showed the influence both of Courbet and the impressionists. His work is represented almost exclusively in Hungarian collections. [E.R.]

BIJUR, NATHAN (1862–1930), U.S. jurist and communal leader. Bijur achieved prominence in corporation law and participated in the reorganization of many large companies. In 1909 he was elected, with Republican Party endorsement, for a 14-year term as New York State Supreme Court justice and was reelected in 1923 without opposition. His judicial decisions included important questions of constitutional law involving the extension of legal doctrines to meet modern conditions. Bijur's civic activities included service on the New York State Prison Commission and a special commission which established a municipal ambulance service in New York City. He was among the founders of the National Conference of Jewish Charities and the *American Jewish Committee, and he was a trustee of the Baron de Hirsch Fund and the Hebrew Free Trade School. In 1905 he was elected president of the New York Conference of Charities. Bijur was a supporter of the Hebrew Sheltering and Immigrant Aid Society and was often consulted on legal questions involving Jewish immigration. [Mo.Ro.]

Nathan Bijur, New York State Supreme Court justice. New York, State Library.

BIKAYAM, MEIR BEN ḤALIFA (d. 1769), kabbalist and crypto-Shabbatean. The family name is rare, and the origin of the family is unknown. Bikayam lived in Smyrna. He studied Kabbalah under Jacob *Wilna, belonged to his circle, and was initiated by him into the "mystery of the Godhead" revealed by *Shabbetai Ẓevi (Ms. 2262, Ben-Zvi Institute). Bikayam received from his teacher the kabbalistic works of *Solomon ha-Levi which the latter had received from his father, Benjamin ha-Levi. Some of the most learned and pious of the Smyrna community belonged to his circle. Bikayam was a close friend of Ḥayyim *Abulafia and Isaac ha-Kohen Rappaport, the rabbis of the community. One of the wealthy Jews of the town, Solomon *Ardit, supported him and his circle, and even in his old age (c. 1745) the latter studied Kabbalah under him. The wealthy leader of the Constantinople community, Samuel ha-Levi, and Moses b. Joshua *Soncino of Smyrna supported and financed the publication of his books. When he went to Salonika in 1747, Abraham Enriques Miranda and Joseph Enriques Miranda, wealthy men of the community, welcomed him with great honor. There he also taught Shabbatean Kabbalah to a group of devotees and published two of his books. He returned to Smyrna about 1747. His books are all concerned with Kabbalah; his Shabbatean leanings are hinted at, but never explicitly revealed. He wrote the following books: (1) *Golel Or*, on the doctrine of **gilgul* ("transmigration"; Smyrna, 1737); (2) *Me'ir la-Areẓ*, on the portions of the Pentateuch, according to the principles of Lurianic Kabbalah (Salonika, 1747); (3) *Magen Avot*, on *Pirkei Avot* (Salonika, 1748); (4) *Me'orei Or*, on the Pentateuch, based on Lurianic Kabbalah (Salonika, 1752); (5) *Kera Mikreh* (Salonika, 1752); (6) *Me'ir Bat Ayin*, on *Ein Ya'akov* (Smyrna, 1755). He composed esoteric as well as nonesoteric prayers. His books contain *piyyutim* on the Redemption which he apparently expected in the year 1740 or before.

Bibliography: A. Freiman (ed.), *Inyanei Shabbetai Ẓevi* (1912), 145; M. Benayahu, in: *Yerushalayim*, 4 (1952/53), 203–4. [Ed.]

BIKERMAN, JACOB JOSEPH (1898–), U.S. physical chemist. Bikerman was born in Odessa, Russia, and attended the University of St. Petersburg (Leningrad). He held a variety of academic and industrial positions in the U.S.S.R., Germany, and Britain before going to the U.S. in 1946. From 1956 to 1964 he was head of the Adhesives Laboratory of the Massachusetts Institute of Technology. Bikerman contributed many papers to scientific journals, dealing with adhesion, electrokinetics, colloids, rheology, surface tension, contact angles, lubrication, and friction. His works include *Kapillarchemie* (with H. Freundlich, 1932); *Foams: Theory and Industrial Applications* (with J. M. Perri a.o., 1953); *Surface Chemistry* (1958^2); *The Science of Adhesive Joints* (1961); and *Contributions to the Thermodynamics of Surfaces* (1961). [S.A.M.]

BIKERMAN (Bickermann), JOSEPH (1867–1941), journalist active in Jewish political life. Born in Okny, Podolia, Bikerman graduated in philology at Odessa University in 1903. In an article written in 1902 in the monthly *Russkoye Bogatstvo* he strongly opposed Zionism, and called upon Jews to join with the progressive elements in Russia to help in the country's rebirth. His article aroused a controversy in which V. *Jabotinsky and B. *Borochov took part. He contributed to the democratic journal *Yevreyskiy Mir*, and wrote studies in Russian on the Pale of Settlement (*Cherta yevreyskoy oszedlosti*, 1911), and on Jews in the grain trade (*Rol yevreyev v russkoy khlebnoy torgovle*, 1912). After the Bolshevik revolution, Bikerman settled in Berlin. He was one of the founders of the short-lived "Patriotic Union of Russian Jews Abroad," which supported the ideal of the restoration of the Russian monarchy. His views on Jewish political problems are summarized in his Russian pamphlet on the self-knowledge of the Jew (*K samopoznaniyu yevreya*, 1939). He was the father of the historian Elias J. *Bickerman and the scientist Jacob J. *Bikerman.

Bibliography: B. Dinur, *Bi-Ymei Milḥamah u-Mahpekhah* (1960), 66–68; J. Frumkin (ed.), *Russian Jewry* (1966), index. [Ed.]

BIKKUREI HA-ITTIM (Heb. בִּכּוּרֵי הָעִתִּים; "First Fruits of the Times"), Hebrew literary-scientific annuals, published in Vienna for 12 successive years (1821–32), and a central forum for *Haskalah literature. The editor of the first three volumes, Shalom b. Jacob *Cohen, sought to continue in this publication the tradition of *Ha-Me'assef*, the journal which initiated Hebrew periodical publications in the Haskalah period. (He had previously published and edited the last three volumes of *Ha-Me'assef he-Ḥadash*.) The first volumes also contained a German section (transcribed into Hebrew letters), which was later discontinued. The editors following Cohen were: Moses *Landau (vols. 4–5), Solomon Pergamenter (vol. 6), Issachar Baer Schlesinger (vols. 7–8), Isaac Samuel *Reggio (vols. 9–10), and Judah Loeb *Jeiteles (vols. 11–12). All the various literary genres were represented in these volumes—e.g., fiction, research, as well as translations of world literature (but mainly from German)—and were contributed by writers from Italy, Bohemia, Austria, Galicia, and Hungary. Reprints of a selection of works from *Ha-Me'assef* were also included. The standard improved in the last volumes, especially with S. J. *Rapoport's publication of his biographical monographs on geonic medieval Jewish scholars and authors. Other contributors included S. D. *Luzzatto and Isaac *Erter. With the discontinuation of these annuals, M. E. *Stern attempted in 1844 to publish *Bikkurei ha-Ittim,* and Reggio together with Isidore *Bush, *Bikkurei ha-Ittim ha-Ḥadashim* in 1845. While these attempts were unsuccessful, another annual, *Kokhevei Yiẓḥak,* did succeed. Its publication began in 1845 in Vienna, under the editorship of M. E. Stern, and lasted until 1873.

Bibliography: B. Wachstein, *Die hebraeische Publizistik in Wien* (1930), xiii–xl (introduction); R. Fahn, *Kitvei Re'uven Fahn,* 2 (1937), 100–41 *(Pirkei Haskalah).*

[G.K.]

BIKKURIM (Heb. בִּכּוּרִים; "First Fruits"), last tractate of the Mishnah order of **Zera'im,* dealing with laws relating to first-fruit offerings (Deut. 26:1–11; cf. also Ex. 23:19; 34:26; Num. 18:13). The first chapter discusses the duty of offering first fruits and the formula to be recited upon offering them. Normally a Jew brings the fruits of his own land and makes the prescribed declaration. If the fruit is not of his own land (e.g., it is from that of a tenant), he neither brings nor recites the declaration in view of the phrase "the choicest first fruits of thy land" stressing the "thy." A proselyte brings the offering but does not recite, because the formula contains the phrase "the land which the Lord swore unto our fathers." Although it would appear from the Bible that all fruit is subject to the Law of *Bikkurim,* rabbinical tradition applies it only to the seven fruits enumerated in Deuteronomy 8:8.

The second chapter opens with a comparison between the laws of first-fruit offerings, heave offerings, and the second tithe, but then digresses into other matters, e.g., the method of classifying fruits and animals.

The third chapter contains a beautiful description of the first-fruits procession from the country to Jerusalem and of the ceremony at the Temple. The archaic language of the chapter, as well as the reference to King *Agrippa II, would seem to place it as early as the period of the Temple.

In current Talmud editions, and also in some earlier Mishnah editions, there follows here a fourth chapter dealing with the halakhic problems of the hermaphrodite (the **androgynos*) mentioned in the first chapter as one who may bring the first fruit, but is not to recite. The Tosefta (Bik. 2:3–7) also gives a detailed treatment of this subject along the lines of the fourth chapter. There is no Babylonian *Gemara* on *Bikkurim* but there is a Palestinian *Gemara* which shows a strong dependence on the Tosefta.

Bibliography: H. L. Strack, *Introduction to the Talmud and Midrash* (1945), 33–34; P. Blackman (ed. and tr.), *Mishnayot,* 1 (Eng., 1951), 463–5; H. Danby, *Mishnah* (Eng., 1933), 93–98.

[A.Z.E.]

BILBEIS, capital of the "Eastern Province" of Egypt (Sharqīya) during the Middle Ages. It had a well-organized Jewish community, mentioned in a letter written about 1100 by the *dayyan* Abraham b. Shabbetai to all Jews of the area, and also in a letter written by his son and successor Shabbetai later in the 12th century. When Ashkelon was conquered by the Crusaders in 1153, many Jews fled to Bilbeis; 15 years later Bilbeis was itself captured by the Crusaders and the Jewish community undoubtedly suffered. At the end of the 12th century Bilbeis was still considered one of the chief Jewish communities of Egypt. In a community law dated 1187 R. Judah ha-Kohen is mentioned as *dayyan* of Bilbeis (Maimonides, Responsa, ed. by J. Blau, 2 (1960), no. 346). Documents of the early 13th century found in the Cairo *Genizah* contain his signature as head of the rabbinical court. In a letter from R. *Abraham b. Moses b. Maimon the Bilbeis community was asked for financial assistance for the Jews in Jerusalem. Other documents mention Jews from Jerusalem who were visiting Bilbeis. Throughout the Fatimid and Ayyubid caliphates the Jewish community in Bilbeis had its own customs, such as concerning the indication of the value of a bride's dowry in the *ketubbah.* According to a late Jewish source, the persecution of Jews in Egypt in 1301 resulted in the conversion of all the Jews in the city to Islam, and of the synagogue into a mosque. However, in the late 15th century, Meshullam da Volterra mentions 50 families in the city in 1481, while Obadiah di Bertinoro estimated them at 30 a few years later.

Bibliography: Mann, Egypt, 2 (1922), 25, 327, 329; R. Gottheil and W. H. Worrell, *Fragments from the Cairo Genizah . . .* (1927), 13ff., 139; S. D. Goitein, in: *Eretz Israel,* 4 (1956), 153ff.; Sambari, in: Neubauer, Chronicles, 1 (1887), 136; A. Yaari, *Iggerot Ereẓ Yisrael* (1943), 60, 124; Ashtor, Toledot, 2 (1951), 423; 3 (1970); idem, in: JJS, 18 (1967), 23–27.

[E.A.]

BILDERSEE, ADELE (1883–), U.S. educator and author. Adele Bildersee was born in New York City. After teaching in New York City's elementary and secondary school

Illustration of the third chapter of the tractate *Bikkurim,* which describes the procession carrying the first fruits up to Jerusalem on the festival of Shavuot. Detail from a title page of a Hebrew and Latin edition of the Mishnah, Amsterdam, 1700–1704. Jerusalem, J.N.U.L.

system (1903–11), she was appointed instructor of English at Hunter College and remained there for the next 20 years, becoming acting dean in 1926. In 1931 she became dean of women at Brooklyn College, where she was also director of admissions from 1944 until her retirement in 1954. She also served as principal of the Temple Beth-El and Emanuel religious school, and wrote several textbooks for Jewish children. Among her published works are *Jewish Post-Biblical History Through Great Personalities* (1918), *Bible Story in Bible Words* (6 vols., 1924–30), *Hidden Books: Selections from the Apocrypha for the General Reader* (1956), and *Imaginative Writing: A Course in College Composition* (1927).

[Ed.]

BILETZKI, ISRAEL ḤAYYIM (1914–), Yiddish poet and Hebrew essayist. Born in Kobrin, Biletzki went to Ereẓ Israel in 1934. From his first book of Yiddish verse *Umru* (1937) to his seventh lyric volume *Lider Tsum Mensh* (1967), he displayed impeccable artistry in simple rhymed quatrains as well as in sophisticated free rhythms. His poems were translated into Hebrew by Mordecai Amitai and Avigdor Greenspan, but Biletzki himself used Hebrew primarily as a prose medium. He published several volumes of critical essays in Hebrew calling attention to Yiddish masterpieces and their authors (Eng. translation, *Essays on Yiddish Poetry and Prose Writers,* pt. 1 (1969)).

Bibliography: M. Ravitch, *Mayn Leksikon* (1958), 85–86; LNYL, 1 (1956), 292; Kressel, Leksikon, 1 (1965), 229.

[S.L.]

BILGORAJ, small town in Lublin province, Poland. A Jewish community had been established there by the second half of the 17th century. Many of the Jews perished during the massacres of 1648–49. In 1765 Jewish poll-tax payers in Bilgoraj and the vicinity numbered 661. The Russian prohibition on Jewish settlement of the western border area (see *Russia) halted the growth of the community until the restriction was rescinded in 1862. The Jewish population numbered 1,637 in 1841; 3,486 in 1897; and 3,715 in 1921. The brothers I. J. *Singer and I. *Bashevis Singer, Yiddish writers, were born in Bilgoraj. A Hebrew printing press was established there in 1909 and continued to publish numerous Hebrew and Yiddish books until the Holocaust.

[Ed.]

Holocaust Period. It is estimated that over 5,000 Jews lived in Bilgoraj before the outbreak of World War II, constituting more than half the town's population. On Sept. 11, 1939, almost the whole Jewish quarter was set on fire in a heavy bombardment by the German air force. A few days later German troops entered the town and immediately organized anti-Jewish pogroms. On September 29 the German army withdrew, but the occupying Soviet army had to cede the town to the Germans a week later. About 20% of the town's Jewish population left for the Soviet Union together with the retreating Soviet troops. On June 25, 1940, a ghetto was established. In the course of 1941 and 1942 a number of deportations took place; on Nov. 2, 1942 almost all the remaining Jewish population was deported to *Belzec death camp. On Jan. 15, 1943, the last 27 survivors who had remained in hiding were shot. A group of young men organized a small partisan unit which operated in the surrounding forests. The Jewish community was not reestablished after the war.

[S.Kr.]

Bibliography: T. Brustin-Bernstein, in: *Bleter far Geshikhte,* 3 no. 1–2 (1950), 65–76, table 3; *Khurbn Bilgoraj* (1957).

BILHAH (Heb. בִּלְהָה), servant girl presented to *Rachel by her father (Gen. 29:29). Bilhah was given by Rachel to her husband Jacob as a concubine (see *Nuzi). Bilhah bore two children by him, *Dan and *Naphtali (30:1–8). Reuben cohabited with her while his father was still alive, apparently by way of asserting his right of primogeniture (35:22). This offense is given as the reason for the loss of the birthright by Reuben (Gen. 49:3–4; I Chron. 5:1). The meaning of the name is uncertain. It may be derived from the Arabic root *balaha* which means "to be confused" or "lacking in understanding" (cf. Heb. *bhl*), perhaps having some symbolic connotation relative to the status of the tribes descended from this concubine (see also: The Twelve *Tribes, *Patriarchs).

[E.H.]

In the Aggadah. The *aggadah* indicates Bilhah's righteousness by the statement that, after the death of Rachel and Leah, the *Shekhinah* (which had been continuously present in their households) passed to abide with Bilhah (Zohar 1:175b). After the death of Rachel, Jacob moved Bilhah's bed into his chamber. Bilhah is identified as the "messenger" (Gen. 50:16) sent by the brothers to Joseph, to inform him of his father's will (Tanḥ.B. 3:18).

[Ed.]

Bibliography: C. H. Gordon, in: RB, 44 (1935), 35–36; Noth, Personennamen, 10; S. Yeivin, *Meḥkarim be-Toledot Yisrael ve-Arẓo* (1960), 149–50.

BILL-BELOTSERKOVSKI, VLADIMIR NAUMOVICH (1885–1966), Soviet Russian playwright. Born to a poor, Yiddish-speaking family in the Ukraine, Bill-Belotserkovski received little traditional Jewish education. At the age of 16 he ran away to sea and spent the years from 1911 to 1916 in the United States (hence the nickname "Bill," which he eventually adopted as part of his name). After his return to Russia in 1917, Bill-Belotserkovski fought in the Civil War and was one of the founders of the Communist propaganda theater as well as the author of some of the best-known plays in its repertory. These plays, called *agitki,* were primitive one-act dramas, designed to rally audiences to the Communist cause; their artistic value was slight. Bill-Belotserkovski's best play, *Shtorm* ("The Storm," 1925), dealt with the Civil War. Its effectiveness was enhanced by its documentary, matter-of-fact style and coarse humor. In later years he tried to tackle social and moral topics, but his tendency to see everything in terms of clearcut contrasts, his aversion to intellectual subtlety, and his fondness for heroics limited his range. After World War II, Bill-Belotserkovski, who had earned a reputation as an "American expert," was commissioned to produce a number of anti-American works, the best known of which was *Tsvet kozhi* ("The Color of Skin," 1948). In 1937 Bill-Belotserkovski wrote *Pogranichniki* ("The Frontier Guards"). The play's hero, a Soviet army officer, is a Jew named Kogan. Interrogated by anti-Soviet intelligence agents, Kogan proudly emphasizes his Soviet, Communist Jewishness ("My father is the best pig-breeder in Birobidzhan") and, in the end, not unlike the biblical Samson, succeeds in killing himself and his jailers. During the anti-Semitic, anti-cosmopolitan purges of 1947–53 the play was revived, but the Soviet censorship carefully obliterated all references to Kogan's Jewishness other than his Jewish-sounding name.

Bibliography: *Teatral'naya entsiklopediya,* 1 (1961), 581–82; M. Friedberg, in: *American Slavic and East European Review,* 13 (Feb. 1954).

[M.F.]

BILLIG, LEVI (1897–1936), Arabist. Born in London, he compiled *An Arabic Reader* with Avinoam *Yellin (1931, 1963) which is still one of the best introductions to classical Arabic. In 1926 he was appointed the first lecturer in Arabic language and literature at the Hebrew University. Billig also studied Shi'a and spent time in Persia for this purpose. During the Palestine riots of 1936 he was shot to death by an Arab terrorist while working in his home. His untimely death prevented him from finalizing a study of the theory of the Imams (the successors of Muhammad).

Bibliography: *The Times* (London, Aug. 22 and 25, 1936).

[S.D.G.]

BILLIKOPF, JACOB (1883–1950), U.S. social worker. Billikopf, born in Vilna, emigrated to the United States in the late 1890s. He was a son-in-law of Louis *Marshall. An imaginative administrator and fund raiser, receptive to fresh ideas, Billikopf became professionally active in labor relations as well as Jewish social work. He served as superintendent of the Jewish Settlement, Cincinnati (1904–05), of the United Jewish Charities of Milwaukee (1905–07), and of the United Jewish Charities, Kansas City, Missouri (1907). While in Kansas City Billikopf played an important role in the establishment of the pioneering municipal Board of Public Welfare. During World War I Billikopf directed the campaign to raise $25 million for Jewish war relief and in 1918 he directed the National Coordinating Committee for Aid to Refugees and Emigrants. He was appointed executive director of the Federation of Jewish Charities, Philadelphia (1919), which became his base for many services in the labor field. He was the impartial chairman of the Men's Clothing Industry, New York City, and the Ladies' Garment Industry, Philadelphia. In the 1930s he was appointed impartial chairman of the federal Regional Labor Board. Billikopf also served as vice-president of the American Association for Old Age Security, chairman of the Committee of One Hundred on Unemployment Relief, Philadelphia (1930–31), and board chairman of the New York Clothing Unemployment Fund. [R.Lu.]

°**BILLROTH, THEODOR** (1829–1894), Viennese surgeon. His remarks in a work on the study of medicine in German universities, *Ueber das Lernen der medizinischen Wissenschaften an den Universitaeten der deutscher Nation* (1876; the Eng. translation (1924) tones down the vehemence of the original) gave considerable impetus to anti-Semitism in student organizations. Billroth attacked Jewish students from Galicia and Hungary, alleging that they were driven to study medicine by vanity and ambition. Stating also that Jews could never be Germans, he added that he did not want to be considered a *Judenschimpfer* ("Jew-baiter"). The book caused rioting at Vienna University and a fierce controversy ensued, in which Berthold *Auerbach participated. Billroth's allegations were answered by the German naturalist Matthias Jakob Schleiden in his essay *Die Bedeutung der Juden fuer Erhaltung und Wiederbelebung der Wissenschaften im Mittelalter* (1877; *The Importance of the Jews for the Preservation of Learning in the Middle Ages,* 1911). Billroth later acknowledged that he had been wrong and even became a member of the Verein zur Abwehr des Antisemitismus. [Ed.]

BILTMORE PROGRAM, declaration of policy by the World Zionist movement during World War II (May 1942), to the effect that the cause of Zionism could no longer be advanced by the existing British Mandatory regime. It urged, as the next step, that Palestine be established as a Jewish commonwealth and that the Jewish Agency replace the British Mandatory administration's authority for developing the country. The name of the program was derived from the New York Biltmore Hotel where the Extraordinary Zionist Conference was held from May 6 to May 11, 1942. Since no Zionist Congress could be convened because of the war, this conference was practically vested with the authority of a Congress. Its delegates came from every American and Canadian Zionist organization and included all available leaders from Palestine and Europe, among them the president of the World Zionist Organization Chaim *Weizmann. The main speaker was David Ben-Gurion, chairman of the Jewish Agency Executive, who went to New York specifically for the Conference. He explained that the Jews could no longer depend on the British administration to facilitate the establishment of a Jewish National Home in Palestine as promised by the *Balfour Declaration of 1917, and that unless Jewish authority were established over Palestine progress would cease. He stressed the need for immigration and settlement, maintaining that no other regime could accomplish as much in these spheres as the Jews if they were given the required authority. The Biltmore Program was the object of controversy in Zionist and non-Zionist ranks before and after its adoption as official policy by the Zionist General Council (October 1942). The opposing minority included those who objected to the idea of a Jewish state, and others who considered the demand premature and would have preferred to work for the abolition of British restrictions (contained in the White Paper of 1939) and let a Jewish majority gradually develop in the country, or who would have turned over the Mandate to the United Nations. Still others insisted that the whole of Palestine should become an independent "bi-national" Jewish and Arab state, because a Jewish state would include only part of the country. In fact, neither in the resolution itself nor in Ben-Gurion's address was there any mention of the boundaries of the proposed Jewish Commonwealth. However, the Biltmore Program was in time adopted not only by the organized Zionist movement but by nearly all Jewish organizations in America and formed the basis for the political struggle of the Zionist movement from 1943 until the establishment of the State of Israel in 1948.

Bibliography: J.C. Hurewitz, *Diplomacy in the Near and Middle East,* 2 (1956), 234–5; idem, *Struggle for Palestine* (1950), chs. 10, 12; Weizmann, in: *Foreign Affairs,* 20 (Jan. 1942), 324–38; D. Ben-Gurion, in: *Tav-Shin-Gimmel* (1944), 154–65; B. Halpern, *The Idea of the Jewish State* (1969), ch. 2.

[M.Z.F.]

BILU (Heb. בִּיל״וּ, Hebrew initials of *Beit Ya'akov Lekhu ve-Nelkhah;* "House of Jacob, come ye and let us go," Isa. 2:5), an organized group of young Russian Jews who pioneered the modern return to Ereẓ Israel. Bilu was a reaction to the 1881 pogroms in southern Russia, when the ideology of Jewish nationalism began to replace that of assimilation, which was prevalent among the youth. At first not linked with any particular country, the Bilu ideology soon came to mean a return to Ereẓ Israel. One of the first Bilu'im, Ḥayyim *Hisin, testified: "The recent pogroms have violently awakened the complacent Jews from their sweet slumbers. Until now, I was uninterested in my origin. I saw myself as a faithful son of Russia, which was to me my raison d'être and the very air I breathed. Each new discovery by a Russian scientist, every classical literary work, every victory of the Russian kingdom would fill my heart with pride. I wanted to devote my whole strength to the good of my homeland, and happily to do my duty, and suddenly they come and show us the door, and openly declare that we are free to leave for the West."

Statuts
pour
la Société
"בית יעקב לכו ונלכה"
Viens maison Israel
concernant l'organisation des
Colonies en Syrie et Palestine,
et soignante pour l'avenir
de l'Emigration Israélite

§ 1. But de la Société. Le but de la Société est de rétablir la situation politique-économique non moins spirituelle nationale du peuple Hébreu par colonisation en Syrie et Palestine.

§ 2. Pour réaliser ce but, c'est que la Société tache à l'union de toutes les personnes qui rendent hommage à cette grande idée sans regard à leur état ou religion, et effectuera l'application d'un œuvre basé sur la raisonabilité dans les pays ci-devant mentionnés.

§ 3. C'est pour cela que la Société

Figure 1. The first version of the regulations of the Bilu organization, written in French. Jerusalem, Central Zionist Archives.

The reawakening of the Jewish spirit coincided with the increasing waves of emigrants and fugitives leaving Russia as a result of the pogroms. Jewish leaders devised various solutions, one of which was settlement of Ereẓ Israel, but most of the emigrants were attracted to the United States. Although a thin stream of settlers flowed to Ereẓ Israel, anticipating the Bilu group by a few months, Bilu was the first organized group of pioneers to go there. Lacking financial resources, they desired only to work, and especially, to work the land.

Founding of Bilu. Bilu was initiated when a fast was held by the Jewish communities in Russia on Jan. 21, 1882, as a result of the pogroms. Israel Belkind, then a student, invited a group of young Kharkov Jews to his home to discuss the state of Russian Jewry. Unlike the *Am Olam Group, which was organized for the purpose of emigration to the U.S., Belkind's group decided to settle in Ereẓ Israel. It first called itself Davio, Hebrew initials for *Dabber el Benei Yisrael ve-Yissa'u* ("Speak unto the Children of Israel that they go forward," Ex. 14:15), but later changed the name to Bilu for, according to Belkind, "instead of advising the people to go to Ereẓ Israel, we decided to go there ourselves."

Founded with only a handful of members, Bilu rapidly increased its membership to over 500 as a result of effective recruitment campaigns, though only a few were ready to leave for Ereẓ Israel. Kharkov became the Bilu headquarters, and Belkind its leader. Bilu ideology was expressed in different and even contradictory ways. Of the many statutes formulated by the group, one defined the aim as the creation of "a political center for the Jewish people," while another stated that the society pursues "an economic and national-spiritual aim" for the Jewish people "in Syria and Palestine." Ze'ev *Dubnow, a member of Bilu, wrote: "The aim of our journey is rich in plans. We want to conquer Palestine and return to the Jews the political independence stolen from them two thousand years ago. And if it is willed, it is no dream. We must establish agricultural settlements, factories, and industry. We must develop industry and put it into Jewish hands. And above all, we must give young people military training and provide them with weapons. Then will the glorious day come, as prophesied by Isaiah in his promise of the restoration of Israel. With their weapons in their hands, the Jews will declare that they are the masters of their ancient homeland."

Eventually, headquarters were moved to Odessa, from where the pioneers intended to sail. The leaders of the Jewish national movement in Russia were generally opposed to the *aliyah* of the Bilu'im and urged them not to go. Among the Bilu'im themselves two trends emerged. One advocated immediate *aliyah* to Ereẓ Israel in order to work there. The other contended that no practical settlement should be begun so long as Jews had no political guarantees from the Turks. The internal debate between the two trends in Bilu lasted for about two years, diminishing the strength of the group and hindering the first efforts of the group that went to Ereẓ Israel. At first the Bilu'im hoped to receive support from wealthy Russian Jews. Disappointed by their lack of interest, they turned to Laurence *Oliphant, then living in Constantinople and rumored to have close relations with the sultan's court. However, they discovered that Oliphant could give them no practical help, and again split into divergent groups. Some advocated continuing political activity in Constantinople to gain recognition from the Ottoman authorities, while the rest, led by Belkind, decided to go to Ereẓ Israel immediately.

In Ereẓ Israel. The first to arrive in the country was Ya'akov Shertok (father of Moshe *Sharett), who preceded the first group of 14 Bilu'im by a few weeks. The group, led by Belkind, reached Jaffa on July 6, 1882. The day after their arrival they began work at the *Mikveh Israel agricultural school where they lived in a commune,

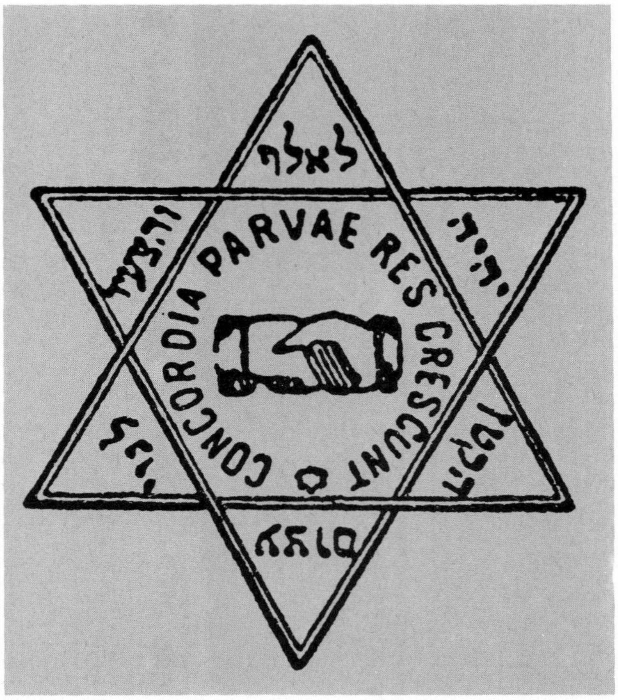

Figure 2. The stamp of the Bilu organization. The Hebrew text is "The smallest shall become a thousand, and the least a mighty nation" (Isa. 60:22). Tel Aviv, Raphaeli Collection.

Figure 3. Bilu veterans at the 40th anniversary of the founding of Rishon le-Zion, 1922. Jerusalem, Central Zionist Archives.

the household being run by the only woman in the group. There they underwent great hardships, as they were unused to physical labor, received meager wages, and were subject to oppression by the director of the school. However, they found a great friend in Charles *Netter, the founder of Mikveh Israel, who adopted a paternal attitude to the Bilu'im, encouraged them, and openly identified himself with their aims. With Netter's death that same year (1882), the Bilu'im were again without a patron, until Yeḥiel *Pines, a writer and public figure, came to their assistance. Elected by the Bilu'im as their leader and guide, he transferred some of them from Mikveh Israel to Jerusalem to become artisans. The Bilu group in Jerusalem called itself "Shehu" (שהו), the initial letters of *Shivat he-Ḥarash ve-ha-Masger* ("Return of the Craftsman and the Smith," cf. II Kings 24:16), and they established a carpentry and woodcraft workshop. However, the scheme eventually failed because of lack of experience, and the Jerusalem members of Bilu dispersed elsewhere in Ereẓ Israel.

In November 1882 some of the members of Bilu, under Belkind's leadership, moved to *Rishon le-Zion, working as hired laborers, sharecroppers, and manual laborers for the village council. Poor yields and difficult relationships between the settlers and hired laborers in the village were greatly disappointing, especially as the Bilu'im hoped to found their own settlement eventually. They continued their search for satisfactory work between Rishon le-Zion and Mikveh Israel. Even the Russian Ḥovevei Zion disappointed them, for they failed to provide them with the means for settlement. After a steady decline in their number abroad, the Bilu association in Russia died out. In June of 1883, about a year after *aliyah,* Bilu numbered 28 members in Ereẓ Israel, of whom 13 were at Rishon le-Zion, seven at Mikveh Israel as hired laborers, and three in Jerusalem. They met on festivals and holidays, organizing a trip on Passover of 1884, together with Eliezer *Ben-Yehuda, speaking Hebrew among themselves and singing Hebrew songs.

When the Bilu members who were in Constantinople realized that their political activities had failed, they also went to Ereẓ Israel (1884). However, their economic situation deteriorated steadily. They worked for a while as laborers at Mikveh Israel, but were soon dismissed, and the director of the school even supplied them with means to emigrate to America. At the very last moment, Pines succeeded in saving them by acquiring the land of the Arab village Qaṭra in the Judean foothills, an area of 3,300 dunams (c. 800 acres). Borrowing the money, Pines sent an envoy abroad to sell the land parcels to Zionist associations, on condition that each of them hand over their parcel to the Bilu'im. The Bilu settlement of *Gederah was thus founded, and the Bilu members who had worked at Mikveh Israel and Rishon le-Zion settled there in December of 1884. Although a few Bilu'im settled in Rishon le-Zion and elsewhere, Gederah became known historically as the Bilu settlement.

An estimated total of 53 Bilu members left Russia for Ereẓ Israel during the early 1880s. Some returned to Russia or went on to the U.S., while others remained faithful to the ideal of settling Ereẓ Israel, and some of them later became leaders in the public life of the country.

Bibliography: N. Sokolow, *Hibbath Zion* (Eng., 1935), ch. 42; idem, *History of Zionism,* 2 vols. (1919), index; B. Halpern, *The Idea of the Jewish State* (1961), 27, 131, 255; M. Meerovitch, *Bi-Ymei Bilu* (1942); idem, *Mi-Zikhronotav shel Aharon ha-Bilu'im* (1946); A. Druyanow (ed.), *Ketavim le-Toledot Ḥibbat Ẓiyyon,* 3 vols. (1919–32), index; I. Klausner, *Be-Hitorer Am* (1962), index; S. Jawnieli (Yavnieli), *Sefer ha-Ẓiyyonut,* 2 vols. (1961[2]); Z. D. Levontin, *Le-Ereẓ Avoteinu* (1950[3]), passim.

[G.K.]

BIMAH (Heb. בִּימָה; "elevated place"), platform in the synagogue on which stands the desk from which the Torah is read. Occasionally the rabbi delivers his sermon from the *bimah,* and on Rosh Ha-Shanah the *shofar* is blown there. In Sephardi synagogues the *ḥazzan* conducts most of the service from the *bimah.* In some Ashkenazi synagogues, the *ḥazzan* has a separate reading stand immediately in front of and facing the ark from which he conducts the service. Alternative names are *almemar* (from the Arabic *al-minbar,* "platform") or, among Sephardi Jews, *tevah* ("box"). The use of the *bimah* as a pulpit for reading the Torah in public was known as early as the times of Nehemiah (Neh. 8:4). Raised platforms were also known in Second Temple times (Sot. 7:8). The Talmud mentions a wooden pulpit in the center of the synagogue of Alexandria in Egypt (Suk. 51b). In Orthodox synagogues of the Ashkenazi rite the *bimah* is often in the center, with some intervening seats between the *bimah* and the ark (based upon the opinion of Maimonides,

Figure 1. The *bimah* as a wooden platform on columns. Full page miniature from the *"Sister" to the Golden Haggadah,* Spain, 14th century. London, British Museum, Or. ms. 2884, fol. 17v.

Figure 2. Baroque *bimah* set in a semicircular niche in the Canton Synagogue, Venice, 1532. Photo Fotostampa-Zago, Venice.

Figure 4. *Bimah* in the synagogue in Harburg, Bavaria, 18th century. Photo Bayerisches Landesamt fuer Denkmalpflege

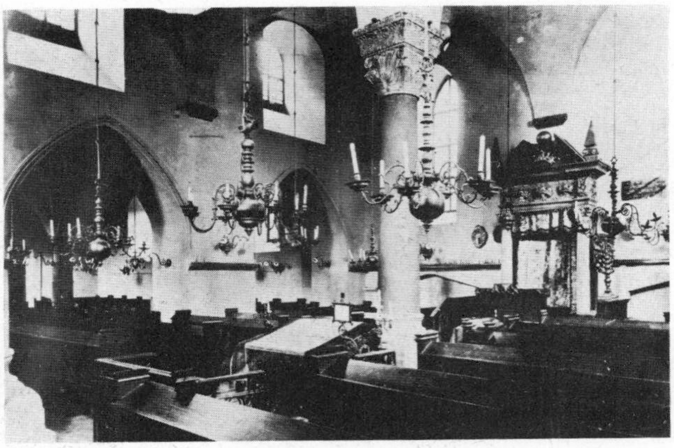

Figure 3. The *bimah* of the synagogue built in Worms, Germany, in 1175 was placed in the center of the room. The synagogue was destroyed in 1938. Jerusalem, Yad Vashem Archives.

Figure 5. The 17th-century *bimah* in the Altneuschul, Prague (c. 1270), is enclosed in a wrought iron cage.

in Yad, Tefillah, 11:3; Tur., OḤ 150, and *Rema,* OḤ 150:5). In Sephardi and Oriental synagogues the *bimah* is placed in the middle of the room opposite the ark and without intervening seats. The location of the *bimah* close to the western wall in Sephardi synagogues was permitted by Joseph *Caro. In his commentary *Kesef Mishneh* (to Maimonides, *loc. cit.*), he wrote: "It is not essential to place the *bimah* in the center; all depends upon the place and time." However, a heated dispute resulted from moving the *bimah* from the center toward the ark in Liberal synagogues after the inception of the Reform movement. The most vehement antagonists of this innovation were Moses *Sofer (*Ḥatam Sofer,* OḤ 28), and Ezekiel *Landau (*Noda bi-Yhudah Mahadura Tinyana,* OḤ 18). Their protest led to a proclamation by 100 rabbis prohibiting worship in a synagogue that does not have the *bimah* in the center (see *Sedei Ḥemed,* Assefat Dinim, Bet ha-Keneset no. 13). Almost all modern Reform and Conservative synagogues combine the *bimah* with the ark.

Forms of the Bimah. Examples of the *bimah* surviving from early times are simple in form and built close to the ground. For instance the *bimah* at the synagogue at Bet Alfa (sixth century) is one step high. In medieval Spain the *bimah* was a wooden platform raised high above the ground on columns. It was sometimes surmounted by a canopy and reached by an attached stairway. Until the Renaissance the *bimah,* which was placed in the center of the synagogue, had a more dominant position than the ark. In Italy from the 16th century, they were given equal emphasis by being placed at opposite sides in the center of the hall. The ark in the synagogue at Worms, Germany (1175), was placed on

Figure 6. Centrally placed *bimah* in the Orthodox synagogue of the Congregation Sons of Israel, Lakewood, New Jersey, designed and executed by Ludwig Y. Wolpert.

the central axis, between the two main columns. This became the usual arrangement among Ashkenazi Jews in Central and Eastern Europe. In this area, a new form of *bimah* came into being in the late 17th century. The four central pillars which supported the vaulted ceiling of a synagogue were used as the framework of the *bimah* which thus became a roofed structure. The *bimah* assumed curved,

Figure 7. In the contemporary Temple Beth El, South Orange, New Jersey, the *bimah* and pulpit are on a dais on either side of the ark. Architects: Davis, Brody, and Wisnewski. Photo Congregation Beth El of the Oranges and Maplewood, N.J.

circular, octagonal, and other forms, and was made of many materials such as stone, wood, bronze, marble, and wrought iron. In Eastern Europe from the 16th century it could be found enclosed by a wrought iron cage.

Bibliography: Elbogen, Gottesdienst, 473ff.; EJ, 2 (1928), 371–84; S. Freehof, *Reform Jewish Practice,* 2 (1952), 16–20; ET, 3 (1951), 112–3.

[Ed.]

BIMKO, FISHEL (1890–1965), Yiddish dramatist and novelist. Born in Kielce, Poland, Bimko's first realistic narrative, *Di Aveyre* ("The Transgression"), was published in 1912 and his first play, *Oyfn Breg Vaysel* ("On the Shores of the Vistula"), was staged in Lodz in 1914. Thereafter his plays were produced in the Yiddish theaters of Europe and America. Especially popular were *Ganovim* ("Thieves," 1921), a realistic play depicting the Polish-Jewish underworld, and *East Side* (1938), a naturalistic drama of Jewish life in New York, where Bimko settled in 1921. His selected dramas were published in seven volumes in 1936, and his selected narratives in three volumes in 1941 and 1947.

Bibliography: Rejzen, Leksikon, 1 (1926), 270–2; LNYL, 1 (1956), 293–5; A. Beckerman, *F. Bimko Dramaturg un Realist* (1944); B. Rivkin, *Undzere Prozaiker* (1951), 297–320.

[S.L.]

BINDER, ABRAHAM WOLF (1895–1966), U.S. composer. Born in New York, son and grandson of cantors, Binder became a choir director at the age of 14. In 1916 he formed the Hadassah Choral Union, and in 1917 he organized a music department, the first of its kind, at the 92nd Street YMHA in New York. In 1921 he became instructor in Jewish music at the Jewish Institute of Religion, and in 1922 music director at the Stephen Wise Free Synagogue. Here he was able to reintroduce the traditional chanting of the Bible, while keeping to the spirit

Abraham W. Binder, U.S. composer of liturgical music.

of the Reform movement. In his revision of the *Union Hymnal* (1932) he also encouraged contributions by contemporary American Jewish composers. When the Jewish Institute of Religion was combined with the Hebrew Union College in New York, Binder was appointed professor of Jewish liturgical music there and helped to found its School of Sacred Music (1948). A prolific composer, he wrote synagogal services and songs, Hebrew and Yiddish songs, nine cantatas and oratorios (including *Amos on Times Square* and *The Legend of the Ari*), and piano, violin, chamber, and orchestral music. His music library and manuscripts were bequeathed to kibbutz Ein ha-Shofet.

Bibliography: I. Heskes, *A. W. Binder, his Life and Work* (1965); Sendrey, Music, indexes; L. Appleton (ed.), *The Music of A. W. Binder; a bibliography* (mimeographed, 1964).

[B.B.]

BING, name of a number of Jewish families from the *Bingen community, which branched out in Germany, Lorraine, England, and the Netherlands. Bingen Jews are mentioned in *Frankfort in the early and middle 15th century. Expulsions in the 16th and 17th centuries helped to disseminate the name in northeastern France and southwestern Germany; four families from Bingen settled in Frankfort around 1530 and ten additional families named Bing settled there by the end of the 17th century. *Court Jews named Binge were active in *Hanau and elsewhere. In the late 18th century persons bearing the name were prominent in the community of *Metz. Abbé *Grégoire wrote (February 1789) to Isaiah *Beer-Bing of Nancy encouraging him to avail himself of the opportunity offered by the meeting of the General Estates "to take counsel with other members of your nation, in order to claim the rights and advantages due to citizens. . . ." Prominent also were the physician SOLOMON, born in Bingen (1615), a pupil of Joseph Solomon *Delmedigo; JOSEPH, of Mons, who fought in 1786 for the abolition of the Jewish tax; ABRAHAM, renowned talmudist (b. 1752), Rabbi of Wuerzburg from 1798 to 1839; and ALBERT (1844–1922), Austrian ear specialist. The Danish and English Bing families are not necessarily connected with them.

Bibliography: A. Dietz, *Stammbuch der Frankfurter Juden* (1907), 31–39; R. Z. Gruenfeld, *Geschichte der Juden in Bingen* (1905); R. Anchel, *Napoléon et les Juifs* (1928), index; AI, 5 (1844), 416–7; REJ, 5 (1882), 148; 8 (1886), 211; C. Roth, *The Great Synagogue London 1690–1940* (1950), 69, 193, 224, 267; P. Levy, *Les noms des Israélites en France* (1960), index; H. Schnee, *Die Hoffinanz und der moderne Staat*, 2 (1954), 279, 355–7; 4 (1960), 170.

[ED.]

BING, ISAAC BEN SAMUEL (17th century), scholar. Born in Jerusalem, he went to Europe after his sons had died in a plague, and during 1645–46 wandered from town to town in Poland. In 1646 he arranged for the printing in Lublin of the first part of the *Maggid Meisharim* of Joseph *Caro on the basis of an incomplete manuscript which he had brought with him. In 1654 he was still in Europe and, together with Elisha Ḥayyim b. Jacob Ashkenazi (father of Nathan of Gaza), who had brought the remainder of the manuscript from Jerusalem, published it in Venice (Friedberg, Eked II 546 no. 471; but see Werblowsky, p. 25 and n.5). Bing should not be confused with the Isaac b. Baruch Bing who lived in Safed during the first quarter of the 17th century.

Bibliography: I. Bing, in: J. Caro, *Maggid Meisharim* (Lublin, 1646), introd.; Yaari, Sheluḥei, 271; R. J. Z. Werblowsky, *Joseph Karo, Lawyer and Mystic* (1962), 24ff.

[A.YA.]

BINGEN, town in Rhenish Hesse, West Germany. *Benjamin of Tudela (mid-12th century), heard of a community there. The Christian burghers attacked the small Jewish quarter on the Jewish New Year's day of 1198 or 1199, and its inhabitants were then driven from the city. Jews are again found in Bingen as moneylenders in the middle of the 13th century under the jurisdiction of the archbishop of Mainz. In 1343 French Jews settled in Bingen. During the *Black Death (1348–49) the Jews in Bingen, too, suffered severely. They were later placed under the jurisdiction of the church in order to save them from further excesses (1365). In 1405, however, the archbishop declared a moratorium on one-fifth of the debts owed to Jews by Christians, and subsequently the archbishops repeatedly extorted large sums. Noted rabbis who taught in the small community include Seligmann Oppenheim, who convened the Council of Bingen (1455–56) in an unsuccessful attempt to establish his authority over the whole of Rhineland Jewry. After the proposal was opposed by Moses *Minz, the matter was referred to Isaac *Isserlein, who rejected the project. The Jews were again

The synagogue of Bingen, W. Germany, built in 1905. All but the outer walls were destroyed by bombs in World War II. Municipality of Bingen. Photo Guenter Kleinz.

expelled from Bingen in 1507, and did not return until the second half of the 16th century. There were 21 Jewish families living in Bingen in 1689, and 343 in 1754. The Jewish population numbered 596 in 1933, and 222 in 1939. By 1942, only 169 Jews remained in Bingen. The majority were deported and only four ultimately returned. The synagogue was demolished in 1945, and the community was not reestablished after the war. Part of the communal archives (1674–1938) are now in the Central Archives for the History of the Jewish People in Jerusalem. Jewish families with the name Bing probably originated in Bingen.

Bibliography: R. Gruenfeld, *Zur Geschichte der Juden in Bingen am Rhein* (1905); Germ Jud, 1 (1963), 26f.; 2 (1968), 82–85; PK.

[Z.AV./ED.]

BINSWANGER, ISIDORE (1820–1890), U.S. businessman and communal leader. Binswanger was born in Wallerstein, Bavaria. He immigrated to the United States in 1841, living first in Baltimore, then in Philadelphia, and finally in Richmond, Virginia. In 1869 he became president of the Richmond Granite Company, a position he held until shortly before his death. Binswanger was chairman of the board and later president of the Hebrew Education Society in Philadelphia, and president of the board of trustees of Maimonides College. He was also active in various aid societies and helped organize relief measures in the early 1880s for Jewish immigrants from Russia. His three brothers, Lewis, Samuel, and Harry S., settled in Richmond too, where they also went into business and were active in local Jewish life.

Bibliography: H. S. Morais, *Jews of Philadelphia* (1894), 250–2; I. Markens, *Hebrews in America* (1888), 200.

[ED.]

BINYAMINAH (Heb. בִּנְיָמִינָה), village in central Israel, at the southern spur of Mt. Carmel, founded in October 1922 by the Palestine Jewish Colonization Association (PICA). The first settlers were immigrants from East Europe. Later, immigrants from Bulgaria, Georgia (USSR), and other countries were housed in a new quarter. Naḥalat Jabotinsky, a moshav founded nearby by the *Revisionist movement in 1947, was later incorporated into the village. In 1969, the economy of the village was based on intensive farming, principally fruit plantations. Prominent among its industrial enterprises is a wine and liquor factory. In 1968 Binyaminah had 2,570 inhabitants. It is named after Baron Binyamin (Edmond) de *Rothschild.

[E.O.]

View of Binyaminah in 1928. Jerusalem, Jewish National Fund.

BIOGRAPHIES AND AUTOBIOGRAPHIES. Apart from the Book of *Nehemiah, which may well be considered an autobiography, *Josephus' apologetic *Vita,* and *hagiographic works, autobiographies and biographies are completely unknown among Jews in ancient times. The first biography known is that of *Saadiah Gaon which was written by his two sons She'erit and *Dosa at the request of *Ḥisdai ibn Shaprut (published by J. Mann, JQR, 11 (1920/21), 423–8, and by A. Scheiber in KS, 40 (1964/65), 571).

[Ed.]

In Medieval Hebrew Literature. The biographic genre was also unknown to medieval Hebrew literature and there is almost no writing in the field. The lack of development of this literary vehicle is rooted in two main aspects of medieval Hebrew culture. Historians and chroniclers were mainly concerned with events and not personalities as such; a person was important only insofar as he influenced or participated in a major historical event. The lives of major Jewish personalities are, therefore, outlined only briefly in Jewish historiography, and there is no full biography in the modern sense. Historiographers, who were mainly interested in the process of the transmission of the Torah, tended to list scholars and rabbis in chronological order, briefly describing the achievements of each in the field of learning, and only mentioning by the way such details as birthplace, travels, family, and death. Jewish historiography, focusing primarily on historical events, developed the art of historical description at the expense of biography.

The Influence of Hagiography on Biography. Hagiography, however, influenced the fate of biographic literature probably more than historiography. Hebrew medieval writers who concentrated on an historical figure and gave some biographic facts, usually added legendary or panegyric details and thus turned their accounts into hagiographies. Medieval Judaism viewed the actions of an outstanding personality as model behavior to serve as an exemplum. No full description of his life and personality (his faults and his virtues) was, therefore, needed. The only interest the medieval writer and reader could find in the story of a great personage was in the moral to be drawn from his actions and his character. This ethical and didactic approach, driven to the extreme, rendered almost all Hebrew writings about major personalities into heroic legends and not authentic biographies. The cycle of stories about such figures as Abraham *ibn Ezra, *Naḥmanides, *Rashi, *Judah b. Samuel he-Ḥasid, Isaac *Luria, *Israel b. Eliezer Ba'al Shem Tov, and many others are legendary hagiographies, having little direct historical data and giving a partial portraiture of the protagonist. Historians like Abraham *ibn Daud, author of *Sefer ha-Kabbalah,* only briefly mention the sages and scholars who transmitted the Torah. When he dwells on actual personalities, like the scholars in "The Four Captives," his description is purely hagiographic. The same is true of Gedaliah *ibn Yaḥya and many others, including the first Hebrew medieval chronologist, *Sherira Gaon. Personal accounts sometimes formed polemic material in a religious conflict, e.g., the biography of Anan, the founder of the Karaite sect. Sherira describes him as a frustrated, ambitious, evil man; the Karaites wrote hagiographies to extol his deeds. Biographic elements are scattered throughout Hebrew epistolary, hagiography, and historiography, but as a literary form, biography came into its own only in modern Hebrew literature. An exception to this, however, is the biographical introduction to the *Ma'yenei ha-Yeshu'ah* of Isaac *Abrabanel by Baruch Uzziel b. Baruch Forti (Ḥazketto) in 1551. The author probably gleaned Abrabanel's autobiographical fragments from his introductions to commentaries to Joshua, Kings, and Deuteronomy, and from his responsa to Saul Kohen. *Ahimaaz b. Paltiel wrote his *Megillat Yuḥasin* in the middle of the 11th century on the history of his family.

Historiography Written as Personal Experience. The autobiographic genre was a more apt vehicle of literary expression than the biography in the Middle Ages. This was mainly due to the intrinsic nature of the art itself. The need for self-scrutiny (the characteristic of autobiography) has greater impetus than the biographic sketches of authors. Medieval and Renaissance writings, letters, introductions to books, apologies, and personal diaries contain autobiographic elements and sketches much more than biographic elements. In these works, however, the writer also focused on the historical event and the part he had played in it rather than on his own personal life. Maimonides, describing his life in his letters, gives an account of his daily working schedule and of certain aspects of his life. Azariah dei *Rossi, in the introduction to his *Me'or Einayim* (Mantua, 1574), describes the Ferrara earthquake of 1570 which he witnessed and which in part was the stimulus of the book.

Legendary Autobiography. Since the early Middle Ages, another aspect of autobiography was known in Jewish writings: the legendary autobiography. *Eldad ha-Dani, the first writer of this autobiographic form (appeared in Babylonia in the late ninth century), claimed to be a member of the tribe of Dan. In his work, he describes the life of the Ten Lost Tribes in detail. This, however, forms only part of his whole account, much of which is devoted to his various adventures in faraway lands among strange peoples. This narration is typical of imaginary or legendary autobiography.

The thread of this literary expression was picked up centuries later by a much more accomplished autobiographer, David ha-*Reuveni. In a detailed autobiography he describes his birthplace in the lands of the Ten Lost Tribes, his numerous adventures on his way to Italy and especially in Palestine, and his political and diplomatic efforts to organize an army to conquer Palestine. He even includes in his work a detailed expense account, listing his expenditures at every step of his travels. His autobiography is, in fact, an apology: he blames various treacherous friends for the failure of his venture.

Another autobiography, also an apology, is *Gei Ḥizzayon* by Abraham *Jagel (16th century). It is an imaginative vision of the afterworld containing autobiographical elements. Jagel, in prison, relates his life story and how he came to be imprisoned, to his dead father who appears to him in a dream and takes him on a trip to the various heavenly spheres. This autobiography is probably the first to be written in Hebrew by a minor writer about a comparatively trivial life. The focus is not on any major historical event, nor on the author's participation in a noteworthy adventure. Jagel used the autobiographic form to express his misery and to complain about the injustice done to him. Due to its concentration on the personal, *Gei Ḥizzayon* may be described as the first autobiography to be written in Hebrew. Earlier works belong more to the field of historiography which were written as personal experience.

Modena's Ḥayyei Yehudah. Probably the most representative work of the genre and literally the best-developed autobiography written in Hebrew during the Middle Ages is *Ḥayyei Yehudah* ("The Life of Judah"), by Leone (Judah Aryeh) *Modena. In short passages and sometimes long stories, Modena describes in detail a 20-year span in his life. The sincere revelation of the inner self in Modena's account has not been equaled by any Hebrew writer until modern times. He candidly describes his addiction to card-playing, which repeatedly threw him into debt and obliged him to use any means and choose any work to earn enough to cover them. He depicts in detail the tragic fate of his three sons: one was killed in an unsuccessful alchemic experiment, the second, in a street fight, and the third left Italy after being condemned to row in the galleys without his father ever learning of his whereabouts. His various illnesses, those of his wife and of his relatives, are discussed in detail, as well as his dreams, his visions, and his astrological beliefs. A profound cynical skepticism can be discerned in his writings. Modena's work may also be seen as an apology: the apology of a man who saw himself as a failure in every way (history today contradicts this judgment). He blamed the stars for the tragedies he had suffered and the misfortunes which befell him. Probably his belief in astrological determinism psychologically allowed him to lay bare unashamedly the different facets of his character (of which he was far from proud).

Other Autobiographic Elements and Sketches. In line with Modena's work, almost full autobiographies can be reconstructed from the letters of R. Moses Ḥayyim *Luzzatto, and from the letters of other writers. Some autobiographic elements and sketches are to be found in ḥasidic literature where various rabbis sincerely describe their own spiritual development, e.g., R. *Naḥman of Bratslav. In kabbalistic literature, another type of autobiography is to be found: kabbalists describing their visions and the development of their mystical insight. The most noteworthy among these are the visions of Solomon *Molcho which, together with some actual autobiographical passages, form a full spiritual autobiography in the modern sense (Abraham b. Joseph Rothenburg, *Ḥayyat Kaneh, Ḥazon Shelomo Molkho,* ed. by A. S. Aescoly, 1938). Such elements are found also in *Maggid Meisharim,* R. Joseph *Caro's diary on his heavenly revelations, and in other writings of kabbalists. [Y.D.]

Memoirs and Introductions. Memoirs, from those of *Glueckel of Hameln of the 17th century to the diary of Anne *Frank, may be termed "unconscious autobiographies" which were not intended for publication. The valuable autobiographical material, which was sometimes included in the introduction to halakhic works, is the nearest approach to autobiographies of the rabbis. Notable among them are Isaac *Abrabanel's introductions to his biblical commentaries, and those which were produced under the stress of two great catastrophes which overtook European Jewry, the expulsion from Spain in 1492 and the *Chmielnicki massacres of 1648. Prominent among those who described their sufferings in the expulsion from Spain was the author Isaac *Caro (see H. H. Ben-Sasson, in *Zion,* 26 no. 2 (1961), 23–64). Shabbetai b. Meir ha-Kohen and Moses b. Abraham *Mat of Przemysl (in *Matteh Moshe*) are among those who described the period of the Chmielnicki massacres.

Modern Times. With the dawn of emancipation and enlightenment, real biographies began to make their appearance. Among the first of these was Isaac *Euchel's

Toledot Rambaman on Moses Mendelssohn. *Ezekiel Feivel's *Toledot Adam* on Solomon Zalman b. Isaac of Volozhin (1801), and Moses Kunitz's *Beit Rabbi* on Judah ha-Nasi (1805). Dov Ber *Birkenthal of Bolechow wrote his *Zikhroynes*, an important source for material on Jews of Galicia in the 18th century (Heb., Eng., Yid., 1922). Solomon Maimon's autobiography (1792) was revolutionary in more than one sense and evoked the approval of such literary giants as Goethe and Schiller. The autobiography of L. *Bendavid (1804) also belongs here. The scholarly impulse given by the movement for Wissenschaft des Judentums and the related Haskalah in Eastern Europe prompted men like L. *Zunz and S. J. *Rapoport to write biographical sketches of the great Jewish scholars of the past, whose lives—as distinct from their scholarly work—had remained obscure. Zunz wrote a "Life of Rashi," a task that was later taken up by Maurice Liber and Eliezer Meir Lipschuetz. Rapoport published a series of biographical sketches *(Toledot Gedolim)* covering Eleazar Kallir, Saadiah Gaon, *Hananel b. Ḥushi'el, Nissim b. Jacob, and others. Since then, biographies or lengthy monographs have been written about many of the significant figures in Jewish history and literature. Some, like Louis Finkelstein's *Akiba*, have been major studies, as is the two-volume work in history on *The House of Nasi* by Cecil Roth *(Dona Gracia, The Duke of Naxos)*, while Louis *Ginzberg wrote a series of penetrating biographical studies of famous scholars. In recent years some biographies of ḥasidic rabbis, who were previously described in a distinctly hagiographic character, have been written on a rational and scientific basis, an example of which is *The Zaddik* on *Jacob Joseph of Polonnoye, by S. H. Dresner. The list is too numerous to be given, but mention may be made of what may be called biographical anthologies. Israel Kammelhar has written biographies of all the great figures of medieval German Ḥasidim. The *Sarei ha-Me'ah* on the rabbis of the 19th century by Rabbi J. L. Fishman (*Maimon), though sometimes uncritical, is a treasurehouse of biographical material. Much biographical material from prominent Jewish characters of the 18th–20th centuries is contained in the last three volumes of "The Jewish Library" series, edited by Leo Jung (vol. 6, *Jewish Leaders 1750–1940*, 1953; vol. 7, *Guardians of Our Heritage*, 1958; vol. 8, *Men of Spirit*, 1964). Naturally the general vogue of compiling biographies of contemporary Jewish figures after their decease is as marked among Jews as in general literature, but it contains no specific Jewish aspect. From the end of the last century autobiographies have become more common. Mention may be made of those of Isaac Hirsch Weiss, J. L. Gordon, Ḥ. N. Bialik, Chaim Weizmann, Cyrus Adler, and Nahum Goldmann. H. Ribalow has published an anthology of autobiographies of American Jews (1965). Other collections have included Leo W. *Schwarz's *Memoirs of my People* (1943) and H. Bach's *Juedische Memoiren aus drei Jahrhunderten* (1936).

[ED.]

Biographical Lexicons. Although much biographical material about Jews can be found in the medieval Jewish chronicles, the first lexicon of Jewish biographies did not appear till the end of the 18th century. S. Shunami's *Bibliography of Jewish Bibliographies* (1965) contains sections on biographical dictionaries of Jews in general (nos. 2594–2661), of Jews in Zionism (nos. 1872–76), Jews in America (nos. 2172–83), Jews in the Holocaust (nos. 2539–44), Jews in Palestine and Israel (nos. 2017–27, 2057–66a), as well as on biographical literature (nos. 2662–67). The following is a list of dictionaries of the history of the lives of individual Jews:

GENERAL JEWISH BIOGRAPHICAL LEXICONS

S. Wininger, *Grosse juedische National-Biographie* (7 vols., 1925–36), the most comprehensive work of this kind;

Juedischer Plutarch; oder biographisches Lexikon der markantesten Maenner und Frauen juedischer Abkunft (2 vols., 1848);

Juedisches Athenaeum. Galerie beruehmter Maenner juedischer Abstammung und juedischen Glaubens (1851), limited to the preceding century;

H. S. Morais, *Eminent Israelites of the Nineteenth Century* (1880), 100 biographies, mainly of rabbis and community leaders, but also of some Jews prominent in public life;

A. Kohut, *Beruehmte israelitische Maenner und Frauen in der Kulturgeschichte der Menschheit* (2 vols., 1901), classified by professions, such as writers, composers, etc.

RABBIS AND TALMUDISTS

J. Heilprin, *Shemot Ba'alei Meḥabberim* (1769);

Ḥ. J. D. Azulai, *Shem ha-Gedolim* (2 vols., 1774–86, reprinted and revised several times, latest edition 1967);

H. J. Michael, *Or ha-Ḥayyim* (1891, reprint 1965). The author, who died in 1846, left incomplete a bio-bibliographical work including over 1,200 entries, covering the same ground as Azulai, but with more modern scientific tools. The work also had the benefit of being edited by the great scholar Leopold Zunz;

A. Hyman, *Toledot Tanna'im ve-Amora'im* (2 vols., 1964^2), sages of the Talmud;

M. *Margaliot, *Enẓiklopedyah le-Ḥakhmei ha-Talmud ve-ha Ge'onim* (2 vols., 1945–46), sages of the Talmud and the *geonim;* idem, *Enẓiklopedyah le-Toledot Gedolei Yisrael* (4 vols., 1945–50), Jewish scholars from the 9th to the 18th centuries;

S. J. Fuenn, *Keneset Yisrael* (1886), scholars from the geonic period up to the present; incomplete, ending with the Hebrew letter *Yod;*

Abraham Stern, *Meliẓei Esh* (3 vols., 1930–38; 1962^2), medieval and modern rabbis and scholars;

A. Walden, *Sefer Shem ha-Gedolim he-Ḥadash* (1865), continuation of Azulai (see above);

B. Eisenstadt, *Dorot ha-Aḥaronim* (vol. 1, 1913–15; vol. 2, 1937–41), rabbis of the recent past;

I. Lewin, *Elleh Ezkerah* (6 vols., 1956–65), rabbis and scholars who perished during World War II;

S. Federbusch, *Ḥokhmat Yisrael be-Ma'arav Eiropah* (3 vols., 1958–65). Vol. 3 also deals with East European scholars.

ḤASIDIM

Y. Raphael, *Sefer ha-Ḥasidut* (1955^2).

MODERN HEBREW WRITERS

G. *Kressel, *Leksikon ha-Sifrut ha-Ivrit be-Dorot ha-Aḥaronim* (2 vols., 1965–67);

W. Zeitlin, *Kirjath Sepher, Bibliotheca hebraica post-Mendelssohniana* (1891–99).

YIDDISH WRITERS

Z. Rejzen, *Leksikon fun der Yidisher Literatur, Prese un Filologye* (4 vols., 1926–30);

Leksikon fun der Nayer Yidisher Literatur (7 vols., 1956–68), in progress; ed. by Saul Raskin.

YIDDISH THEATER

Z. Zylbercweig, *Leksikon fun Yidishn Teater* (6 vols., 1931–69), in progress.

ZIONISTS

S. L. Zitron, *Leksikon Ẓiyyoni* (1924).

AUSTRO-HUNGARY

M. Fruehling, *Biographisches Handbuch der in der k.k. oesterreichisch-ungarischen Armee aktiv gedienten Offiziere juedischen Stammes* (1911), on Jewish officers in Austria-Hungary.

GERMANY

S. Osborne, *Germany and Her Jews* (1939);

E. G. Lowenthal, *Bewaehrung im Untergang* (1966^2), German Jews who perished during World War II;

E. Duckesz, *Ḥakhmei AHW* (1908), religious leaders of Altona, Hamburg, and Wandsbek; with German summary.

ITALY

M. *Mortara, *Indice alfabetico dei rabbini e scrittori israeliti in Italia* (1886).

PALESTINE AND ISRAEL

D. Tidhar, *Enẓiklopedyah le-Ḥaluẓei ha-Yishuv u-Vonav* (18 vols., 1947–67, in progress), for 19th and 20th century; a combination of national biography and current Who's Who.

POLAND AND RUSSIA

S. Buber, *Anshei Shem* (1895), lay and rabbinic leaders in Lemberg (Lvov) from 1500–1900;

P. Kaplan, *Byalistoker Leksikon; Biografyes fun Byalistoker Yidishe Perzenlekhkeyten* (1935), for Bialystok.

United States

J. R. Rosenbloom, *A Biographical Dictionary of Early American Jews, Colonial Times Through 1800* (1960).

Contemporaries

Who's Who in World Jewry (1955, 1965);

World Jewish Register (1955–56), same material as in *Who's Who in World Jewry* (1955), arranged by professions.

Rabbis and Scholars

B. Eisenstadt, *Dor, Rabbanav ve-Soferav* (6 vols., 1895–1903). Volume 5 is devoted exclusively to the United States;

S. N. Gottlieb, *Oholei Shem* (1912), mainly for Eastern Europe.

Israel

Sefer ha-Ishim (1937) and *Palestine Personalia* (1947);

Who's Who in Israel (1945/46–1967/68), title of first edition: *The Near and Middle East Who's Who*, published almost every year;

Ishim be-Yisrael (1960, 1966), personalities in Israel.

United States

J. Pfeffer, *Distinguished Jews of America* (1917–18). Volume two was also published separately under the titles: *Eminent Jews of America* and *Prominent Jews of America; Who's Who in American Jewry* (1925, 1926, 1928, 1938/39);

Biographical Encyclopedia of American Jews (1935);

American Jews, their Lives and Achievements (1947, 1958);

Israel Honorarium (5 vols., 1968). Volumes 2–5 contain biographical sketches of American Jews.

[Th. W.]

Bibliography: S. W. Baron, *Bibliography of Jewish Social Studies* (1941), 324–48, 214–8; C. Roth, Mag Bibl, 114–56; Waxman, Literature, 2 (1960²), 506–16; 3 (1960²), 575; 4 (1960²), 838–66, 1044–47, and index s.v. *biography, memoirs;* H. U. Ribalow, *Autobiographies of American Jews* (1965), 3–14 (introd.); J. Mazeh, *Zikhronot*, 4 (1936); L. W. Schwarz, *Memoirs of My People* (1943), introduction, 13–26, a popular survey of autobiographies.

BIOLOGY. This entry is arranged according to the following outline:

In the Bible and Talmud
- Reproduction
- Embryology—the Development of the Fetus
- Heredity
- Ecology

Middle Ages and Modern Times
- The 19th Century
- The Modern Period

In the Bible and Talmud. Problems relating to biology are raised in various passages in the Bible—in the creation chapter, in laws concerning levitical cleanness and uncleanness, in parables taken from the life of nature and agriculture, and in accounts of God's providence over His creatures. In the literature of the sages, where these areas are enlarged in *halakhah* and *aggadah*, there is a wide range of views and descriptions of fauna and flora, some derived from observation and experience, others from the folklore of ancient peoples as also from Greco-Roman science, which made a profound impression on the mishnaic and talmudic period. Many subjects in the sphere of biology are dealt with in various articles on fauna and flora in the Encyclopaedia, while the article on *evolution refers to the different views of the sages on the problems of the creation. Here several basic questions in biology will be considered: reproduction, embryology, heredity, and ecology.

Reproduction. In the creation chapter it is stated on the third day: "And God said: 'Let the earth put forth grass, herb yielding seed, and fruit tree bearing fruit after its kind, wherein is the seed thereof, upon the earth'" (Gen. 1:11). On the fifth day, after the creatures in the water and the birds were created, it is said: "And God blessed them, saying: 'Be fruitful, and multiply, and fill the waters in the seas, and let fowl multiply in the earth'" (1:22). After the creatures on land and finally Adam and Eve were created, it says: "God blessed them; and God said unto them: 'Be fruitful, and multiply, and replenish the earth, and subdue it'" (1:28). To all organisms, flora, fauna, and man, the injunction to reproduce applies "after their own kinds" as repeatedly emphasized in the Pentateuch; that is, each organism has to multiply within the framework of its own species, on which some based the prohibitions against hybridization in fauna and flora (see below).

The assumption therefore is that every organism, plant and creature, develops from its conspecies created during the six days of creation. In the literature of the sages statements are, however, sometimes to be found about the production of living organisms from inorganic substance through spontaneous generation, a notion that was current in Greco-Roman science. This view was accepted particularly as regards the reproduction of certain insects, which were thought to be created from the soil or from the matter on which they subsist (see *Evolution). Miraculous deeds are related in the *aggadah*, such as the claim of the *amora* *Joshua b. Hananiah that he was able to create a deer and gazelle from gourds and watermelons, or the story of an *amora* that he saw a man throw into the air a stone which turned into a calf, but this was declared to be merely sleight of hand (TJ, Sanh. 7:19, 25d). There it is asserted that "if all the human beings were to join together, they would be unable to create one gnat and imbue it with a soul," while in respect of human beings it is stated that "it is impossible for a person [to be born] without a woman, and

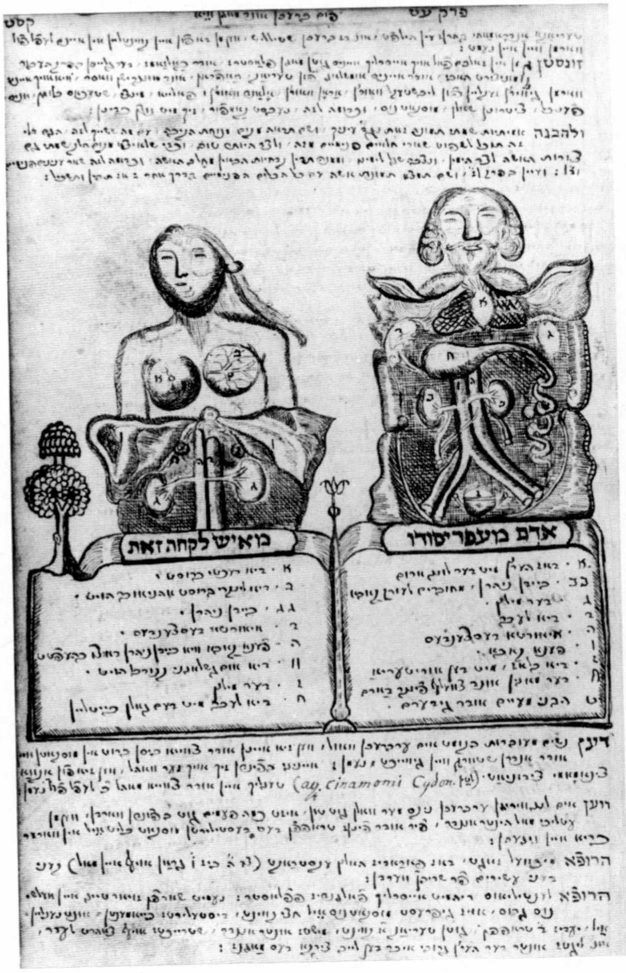

Anatomical drawing of male and female organs from a Yiddish medical manuscript, *Sefer Etz ha-Sadeh*, by Mordekhai b. Jehiel Mikhel ha-Cohen, Germany, 1751–53. Jerusalem, J.N.U.L., Ms. Heb. 56, p. 169.

it is impossible for a woman [to become pregnant] without a man, and both are impossible without the Divine Presence" (TJ, Ber. 9:1, 12d; this statement was made in controversy with the sectarians, i.e., the Christians).

The phenomenon of sexual reproduction was known to the sages also in respect of small creatures, of "the flea which reproduces" and of "creeping things which reproduce" (Shab. 107b). The sages knew of external insemination among fish (TJ, Kil. 1:6, 27a), and declared that "three copulate face to face, a fish, a man, and a serpent" (Bek. 8a). With regard to the fish, they may have reached this conclusion from observing the sexual orifices on its abdomen; or they may have referred to those species in which there is internal procreation, as in some cases of fish without fins and scales, which do not lay eggs, but, procreating internally, breed living progeny, and hence the principle that "a prohibited fish breeds, a permitted fish lays eggs" (Bek. 7b). The sages further declared that "in any species which has its testicles on the outside, [the female] gives birth [to its young], but where the testicles are inside, [the female] lays eggs" (Bek. 8a), a rule that holds good for all mammals (except piscatory), which have testicles externally, in contrast to birds, fish and reptiles which have them internally. The sages thus distinguished between terrestrial and aquatic mammals, both of which produce living young. That snakes of the genus Viper breed living progeny *(vivo-paria)* was also known. Since the biblical *ẓifoni* is the viper, scholars were faced with the problem of explaining the verse: "They hatch vipers'[JPS "basilisks"] eggs . . . he that eateth of their eggs dieth" (Isa. 59:5). It has however been established that the species *Vipera palaestina* does indeed lay eggs, from which the young are hatched only after some time.

Yet another rule was enunciated by the sages: "Whatever has its male genital externally, [the female] gives birth, but whatever has its male genital internally, [the female] lays eggs." The latter statement applies to fowls, the male of which has no protruding sexual organ (though here, too, there are exceptions among aquatic birds, such as the duck). The quotation continues: "Whatever copulates in daytime, gives birth in daytime. Whatever copulates in the night, gives birth in the night" (Bek. 8a). The former instance is illustrated by the cock (the hen laying its eggs during the daytime), the latter by the bat, concerning which the sages asserted: "Whatever gives birth, gives suck, and whatever lays eggs, feeds it brood by picking up [food for its young], except the bat which, although it lays eggs, suckles [its young]" (Bek. 7b, end). It is now known that the bat, like all mammals, gives birth to living progeny, but since it procreates in dark caves, the manner of its procreation was unknown to the ancients, who ascribed to it the fowls' eggs found in caves. On the other hand, the sages were aware that "dolphins reproduce like human beings" (Bek. 8a), for although having the appearance of fish, they give birth and suckle like human beings. This is apparently referred to in the verse: "Even the whales [which is sometimes the meaning in the Bible of *tannin;* JPS, "jackals"] draw out the breast, they give suck to their young ones" (Lam. 4:3).

The sages distinguished between reptiles' eggs which have "the white and the yolk mixed up" and those of fowls in which "the white is outside and the yolk in the center" (Ḥul. 64a). They held that a hen, even though fructified not by a cock but by friction with the ground, could lay eggs (Beẓah 7a). However, it is also stated that without fructification it does not lay eggs (Yoma 69b; Rashi, *ibid.* queries this). Actually a hen can lay eggs without having been mated (the eggs are then unfertilized) and without friction with the ground.

Alongside accurate perceptions there are also erroneous ones, such as the assumption that "the human being's *membrum virile* has two channels, one of which discharges urine and the other semen, and the distance between them is no more than the [thickness of a] peel of garlic" (Bek. 44b). In fact, however, both have a common outlet channel. The raven, according to the *aggadah,* impregnates the female by expectorating his seed into her mouth (e.g., Sanh. 108b; Gen. R. 36:7), a fiction mentioned already by Aristotle (*Historia animalium,* 5:47).

Although coition is essential for procreation, the sages believed that it was possible for a virgin "to conceive in a bath," through semen, which had issued from a male, entering her womb (Ḥag. 15a). They held that during coition the woman, too, "emits semen," apparently on the assumption that the glandular secretions which the woman discharges are homologous with the man's semen. Thus the verse: "If a woman emit semen [JPS, "be delivered"], and bear a man-child" (Lev. 12:2), was interpreted by the sages that "if the woman emits her semen first, she bears a male child; if the man emits his semen first, she bears a female child" (Nid. 31a), this being apparently the basis of the statement that "one who desires all his children to be males should cohabit twice in succession" (Nid. 31b). The aim here may have been educational in that the man who desires male children should allow his wife time to obtain sexual satisfaction that she may "emit her semen first." Several statements mention the importance of conciliating the woman prior to the sexual act. This the man should learn from the cock "who first coaxes and then mates," strutting round the hen with outstretched wings, the tips of which touch the ground, as though saying to her, "I shall buy you a dress reaching down to your feet" (Er. 100b).

Impregnation is done by *shikhvat zera* ("a flow of semen"), *tippah shel zera* ("a drop of semen"), or *tippah seruḥah* ("a fetid drop"), while *tippat keri* ("drop of pollution") is the semen emitted by the male not during coition, these being the customary terms used in the literature of the sages. In the Bible semen is referred to as *shikhvat zera* (Lev. 15:16), *shekhovet* (Lev. 18:20), *zirmah* (Ezek. 23:20). *Tippah rishonah* is the first semen from which the firstborn is begotten (Gen. R. 99). The origin of "twin brothers" is explained as due "to one drop that divided itself into two" (Yev. 98a). Semen is also called *tippah shel loven* ("a drop of white substance"), and the Midrash (Tanḥ., Tazri'a, 3) mentions the fact that "the peacock, which has 360 kinds of colors, is formed from a drop of white substance. And this applies not only to a fowl but even to a human being, who is likewise created from a drop of white substance" (Gen. R. 7 refers to the *ẓavo'a* (= hyena), which is born from a drop of white substance and has 365 colors).

The literature of the sages contains a great deal of material on sexual defects: the person of indeterminate sex *(tumtum),* the hermaphrodite *(androgenos),* the masculine woman *(eilonit),* and others. There is a strict prohibition against impairing the ability to procreate, the Pentateuch forbidding emasculation (Lev. 22:24, according to the rabbinic interpretation). Josephus declares emphatically: "You shall castrate neither man nor beast" (Ant. 4:291), it being prohibited to castrate even a dog (Ḥag. 14b). Some held that the Noachides, too, are forbidden to practice castration (BM 90b), as was extensively done by non-Jews to animals that they should be more amenable to work *(ibid.).* Female animals were also gelded, and it is told that "no cow or sow leaves Alexandria of Egypt before its womb is cut out that it may not breed" (Bek. 4:4), such sterilization having been done to prevent the breeding of a high quality species in a foreign country.

The ancients were ignorant of the ways in which

flora reproduces. Greco-Roman agricultural literature occasionally speaks of a male or female tree, referring however not to its sex but to its shape. The sages were aware that in trees the fruit develops from the blossom and even laid down "the gestation periods" of various trees, that is, from the time of blossoming to the ripening of the fruit (60 days for the apple, for example), but in the case of wheat (six months), they reckoned from the time it is sown (Bek. 8a) and not from when it flowers (which is not very obvious on its spike). Only one plant—the date tree—was known in ancient Babylonia to have male and female trees, and that to obtain fruit from the female tree, near which was no male, it had to be artificially pollinated, this being referred to in the Mishnah as the "grafting" of date trees, which for fear of financial loss was permitted on the eve of Passover even when work was prohibited (Pes. 4:8), and was done "by putting the pollen in florescence over the female trees" (Pes. 56a). The Midrash tells of a female date tree (called *temarah*) which bore no fruit and "looked toward Jericho" to a male date tree to impregnate her, for "a female date tree has sexual desire" (Gen. R. 41). The vegetative propagation of flora by shoots, by bending a branch and covering it with earth to strike new roots, and by grafting was well-known to the ancients, who, however, assumed that different species of trees could be grafted so as to produce hybrids. Prevalent in the literature of the sages, this view has no basis in fact (see Heredity, below).

*Embryology—The Development of the Fetus. It is now known that the sex of the embryo is determined when the ovum is impregnated by the spermatozoon. The fact that the sex of the embryo is established at the time of coition is mentioned by some sages (Nid. 31a; "If the woman emits her semen first she bears a male child"; see above). Another view, however, has it that "within the first three days a man should pray that the seed should not putrefy; from the third to the fortieth day he should pray that the child should be a male" (Ber. 60a). According to this, the sex of the embryo is not finally fixed until the 40th day, for "until the 40th day the embryo is merely fluid" (Yev. 69b). The Mishnah (Ber. 9:3) declares that "if a man's wife is pregnant and he says, 'God grant that my wife bear a male child,' he utters a vain prayer." This *halakhah* was explained by some as referring to the time "when she is seated on the travailing chair," that is, to the actual time of birth, but prior to that a prayer is apt to change the sex of

Herman J. Muller, U.S. biologist, awarded the Nobel Prize in 1946. Photo Scientific Products, Bloomfield, Indiana. (See col. 1031.)

the embryo (TJ, Ber. 9:4, 14a; cf. Ber. 60a). In fact the sages were aware that "all women who give birth bear a half of males and a half of females" (Yev. 119a).

The embryo is a living entity from the moment of impregnation: "From the instant that [God] decreees [its destiny], a soul is given to it," on which point R. Judah ha-Nasi was enlightened by the emperor Antoninus (Sanh. 91b). A concept which has no basis in reality and with which the *halakhah* dealt is the time when the embryo is fully developed. This is, according to one view, the same for a male and a female, namely 41 days, while according to another opinion "a male is fully fashioned on the 41st and a female on the 81st day" (Nid. 3:6). The Tosefta (Nid. 4:17) tells that "it once happened that Cleopatra the queen of Alexandria took her handmaids, who had been sentenced to death by the king, and operated on them, whereupon it was found that the male [embryo] was fully fashioned on the 41st and the female [embryo] on the 81st day." Another *baraita,* however, states that in both instances she found that the embryo was fully fashioned on the 41st day (Nid. 30b).

Though the sages were aware that the embryo is enclosed in the fluid of the amnion (TJ, Nid. 3:3, 50d), their descriptions of the embryo in its early stages—referred to as *shafir merukkam,* that is, an amnion whose limbs are fashioned—are a mixture of fantasy and fact. "What is meant by an amnion whose limbs are fashioned? Abba Saul said, 'Its two eyes are like two drippings of a fly, its two nostrils are like two drippings of a fly, its mouth is as narrow as a stretched hair, its membrum is the size of a lentil, and in the case of a female her organ has the appearance of the longitudinal [slit] of a barley grain, its hands and feet have not yet developed'" (Tosef., Nid., 4:10; for a somewhat similar statement, see Nid., 25b; and cf. TJ, loc. cit.). More accurate are the descriptions of the embryo in its more advanced stages of development: "What does an embryo resemble when it is in its mother's bowels? It resembles a nut floating in a bowl of water . . . During the first three months the embryo occupies the lowest chamber, during the middle ones the middle chamber, and during the last months the uppermost chamber. And when its time to emerge arrives, it turns over and then emerges" (Nid. 31a). "What does an embryo resemble when it is in the bowels of its mother? It resembles a folded writing tablet. Its hands rest on its two temples, its two elbows on its two legs, and its two heels against its buttocks. Its head lies between its knees, its mouth is closed, and its navel open, it eats what its mother eats and drinks what its mother drinks, but produces no excrements, since otherwise it might kill its mother. As soon however as it sees the light of the world, the closed organ opens and the open one closes, for if this were not to happen, the embryo could not live even a single hour" (Nid. 30b).

A woman's period of gestation was declared by Samuel to be 271–3 days (Nid. 38a; TJ, Nid. 1:4,49b; 271–4 days), figures which are quite accurate (usually 280 days elapse from the time of the menses). The fact is mentioned that a child prematurely born at six and a half months is viable (Yev. 42a). On the other hand the sages adopted the fallacious view of the Greeks that a child born at eight months is not viable, and hence the *halakhah:* "For a seven month embryo the Sabbath laws are suspended, for an eight month one the Sabbath laws are not suspended" (Tosef., Shab. 15:5).

The *halakhah* dealt with the possibility, which is unrealistic, of an animal of one species bearing progeny that resembled another species, such as, for example, "if a cow gave birth to a species of ass, or an ass gave birth to a species of horse" (Bek. 1:2) or "a camel that was born of a cow" (Tosef., Bek. 1:9). In the case of "one who, having slaughtered a [permitted] animal, found in it a pig," the sages held divergent views whether the latter may be eaten (TJ, Ter. 8; 5, 45c). In such instances they assumed that the male was of the same species as the female, since it is a general rule that "a forbidden animal does not bear from a permitted one, nor a permitted animal from a forbidden one, nor large from small cattle or small from large cattle, nor a human being from all of these or all of these from a human being" (Tosef., Bek. 1:9). This principle is undoubtedly correct, although in certain instances the sages assumed the possible crossbreeding of animals of different and remote species (see Heredity, below).

The sages gave reasonable figures for the gestation period of domestic animals, but for that of wild animals the figures are unrealistic. Thus it is stated in the Tosefta (Bek. 1:10; and somewhat similarly in TB, Bek. 8a): "Small permitted animals bear at five months; large permitted cattle at nine months; large forbidden cattle at twelve months." While these figures are correct, this is not so with regard to other animals: "A dog bears at 50 days" (actually 60–63 days); "a cat at 52 days" (actually 56); "a pig at 60 days" (actually 116); "a fox or jackal and creeping things [insects, small rodents, etc.] at six months" (actually for a fox or jackal it is 60 days; as for "creeping things," for a mouse it is 18–20 and for a rat 21–25 days). Entirely fanciful is the statement that the gestation period of "the wolf, lion, bear, leopard, cheetah, elephant, monkey, and hedgehog [according to the TB, the small ape] is three years" (actually in the case of the wolf it is 63 days; of the lion, 108–13 days; the bear, 6–7 months; the leopard, 92–95 days; the cheetah, 95 days; the elephant, 18–22 months; the monkey and small ape, 5–9 months). The statement continues: the gestation period of "the snake is seven years," and in this connection a dispute is recorded (Bek. 8b) between R. Joshua and "the emperor" who, controverting this view, declared that the sages of Athens had coupled a male and a female snake which gave birth after only three years. To this R. Joshua replied that the snake may already have been pregnant for four years. In point of fact the gestation period of snakes (including the laying and hatching of the eggs) is several months only. It is similarly preposterous that the gestation period of "the carpet viper is 70 years" (Bek. 8a). Indeed, the ancients ascribed no importance to the figures they gave for the gestation period. Thus Aristotle states in one passage (*Historia animalium,* 5:12) that the female camel is pregnant for five months and in another (*ibid.,* 6:25) for ten months. The actual period is 12 months.

The sages also stated the period that elapses between blossoming and the ripening of the fruit, as for example: "Small permitted animals bear at five months, and corresponding to them among trees is the vine. Large permitted cattle bear at nine months, and corresponding to them among the trees is the olive tree" (Bek. 8a). The passage further enumerates the periods that elapse between blossoming and the ripening of fruits corresponding to the gestation of the animals mentioned above. The figures given are largely correct, although no uniform criterion was used in respect of flora, for whereas the period that elapses until the ripening of the fruit of the vine, olive tree, fig tree, apple tree, and mulberry tree was reckoned from the appearance of the blossoms, with regard to wheat (six months) it was reckoned from the time of sowing, and with regard to the date tree (12 months) apparently from the appearance of the inflorescence inside the trunk. The period of three years for *benot shu'aḥ,* which is the fruit of the *pine, is accurate. For an explanation of the statement that the carob begins to bear fruit only after 70 years, see *Carob.

Heredity. The fact that parents transmit some of their characteristics to their offspring was known early in historical times and perhaps even many centuries before that. But the laws of heredity were formulated only in 1865 by Gregor Mendel. Possibly these laws were already known to Jacob in his handling of Laban's sheep (see below). Yet even if this assumption is accepted, it is clear that for thousands of years mankind erred in its quest for the apparently simple laws of heredity, due to two reasons: to the views on the disparate share of the male and female in transmitting their characteristics to the child, and to the different approaches to the question of the inheritance of acquired characteristics.

The roots of the view concerning the unequal share of the male and the female in transmitting their characteristics to their offspring go back to very ancient times; this view was developed mainly by the philosophers and naturalists of Greece and Rome, according to whom the woman is merely the receptacle for the growth and nourishment of the embryo, whereas the characteristics of the child, especially if it is a male, derive from the father. This theory was also applied to the heredity of animals. The literature of the sages echoes this view, though in a somewhat sublimated form. There is, for example, the statement that a fixed division exists between the father and the mother in transmitting their characteristics to the child's various tissues and limbs: "The white substance [the spermatozoa] is supplied by the man, from whom come [the child's] brain, bones, and sinews; the red substance [the blood from which the embryo develops] is supplied by the woman, from whom come [its] skin, flesh, and blood; the spirit, the soul, and the animation come from the Holy One Blessed Be He; and the three of them are partners in the child" (TJ, Kil. 8:3, 31c; and similarly in Nid. 31a).

Despite the "topographical" distribution of the tissues transmitted by each of the parents, it was clear to the sages that the influence of the father's semen is not localized and limited to certain limbs, since "the seed is mixed up"—that is, it is involved in the formation of all the tissues, "for if this were not so, the blind should produce blind offspring, and the crippled a crippled offspring" (Ḥul. 69a). Despite the importance which the sages attached to the characteristics transmitted to the child by its father, in the case of animals they differed whether "we must take the seed of the male into account," while ascribing the main influence in the formation of the offspring to the mother (*ibid.*). It is nowadays clear that the character of the offspring is determined by the totality of both parents' characteristics.

The second problem that impeded a comprehension of the laws of heredity is the transmission of acquired characteristics. On this point there is a clash between common sense and the conclusions of science that the characteristics acquired by an organism during its lifetime are not transmitted by heredity to its offspring. It is a basic assumption in the Bible that during the six days of creation all the organisms, flora and fauna, were created. With regard to the flora, it is said that the third day saw the creation of "grass, herb yielding seed after its kind, and tree bearing fruit, wherein is the seed thereof, after its kind" (Gen. 1:12), that is, every seed produces flora like its progenitors. The sages enunciated the principle: "If a man puts different seeds in a bed, each grows in conformity with its own particular species" (Nid. 31a). This had been proved by experience: "Is it possible that you sowed wheat and barley came up?" (Sif. Deut. 306). These sources thus speak of the stability of the species in transmitting hereditary characteristics unchanged from generation to generation. On the other hand, the literature of the sages contains views, most of which were current in the contemporary

Greco-Roman agricultural literature, that the characteristics of flora are liable to change under the influence of the environment, and that these changes are transmitted to the progeny. So, for example, the Mishnah (Kil. 1:1) declares that "wheat and tares do not constitute diverse kinds one with the other," the reason being (TJ, Kil. 1:1, 26d) that "fruits degenerate," that is, a man sows wheat which turns into tares, a prevalent view among the ancients. Galen even asserted that his father had proved it experimentally (*De alimentorum facultatibus,* 1:37), but against this Basilius (*Hexameron,* 5) rightly argued that tares and wheat are two different, discordant species. If tares are found growing among wheat, this is simply because seeds of the former, mixed with the grains of the latter, were sown together.

To this sphere of the relation between heredity and environment belong the *halakhot* according to which it is possible to obtain hybrids by grafting trees of different species. It is now known that in flora, as in fauna, hybrids can be produced by sexual impregnation, which in the case of the former means the transference of pollen to the stigma. But the ancients believed that by grafting a shoot of one species on the stock of another, hybrids could be obtained that would produce fruit and seed bearing the intermediate characteristics of both species. Thus, for example, it is asserted (TJ, Kil. 1:4, 27a) that by grafting an almond tree on a terebinth, it is possible to obtain the pistachio, a fruit which resembles the almond but belongs to a different, remote family. Greco-Roman agricultural literature gives advice on how to produce new species by grafting different species of trees. This advice, which belongs to the province of agricultural folklore, penetrated into the *aggadah,* the Tosefta, and the Jerusalem Talmud, but Judah ha-Nasi, having apparently sifted these *halakhot,* omitted them from the Mishnah.

The characteristics and attributes of the seed determine the quality of the crop, a notion that is often applied metaphorically in the Bible to man (e.g., Hos. 10:12; Prov. 11:18, 22:8; Job 4:8). To this realm belongs the principle that "a Jew, even though he sins, is still a Jew" (Sanh. 44a), that is, his actions do not preclude him from being considered one. Even the offspring of an apostate are regarded as Jews, for the negative characteristics acquired by a person because of environmental influences cannot change the characteristics of his offspring. Thus Jeremiah (31:29) and Ezekiel (18:2) already protested against those who declared: "The fathers have eaten sour grapes, and the children's teeth are set on edge." Even the positive characteristics and knowledge which a man acquires in his lifetime are not transmitted by heredity to his offspring: "Why is it not usual for scholars to have sons who are scholars? That it might not be said, 'Among them the Torah is inherited'" (Ned. 81a). Hence everyone must start anew to learn the Torah and an occupation. Nor is it possible even by prayer to change the sex of the embryo in its mother's womb (Ber. 9:3).

On the other hand, the literature of the sages contains statements, according to which other factors and not only heredity are liable to determine the characteristics of the child. Thus the time of coition has an influence: those who have sexual intercourse in the daytime have red-spotted children (Ber. 59b); a woman who solicits her husband to the marital obligation will have sons who are scholars (Er. 100b); a child's characteristics and fate depend upon the day on, and the constellation under which, it is born (Shab. 156a). The *aggadah* tells that R. Johanan, who was famous for his beauty, would sit near the ritual bath for women, so that when they came from it they might look at him and have children as beautiful as himself (Ber. 20a). The Midrash relates that when a white son was born to an Ethiopian couple, Judah ha-Nasi explained to the father that this was because his wife had gazed at white mirrors in their home (Gen. R. 73). By placing objects before a cow's eyes when it was being mated, a red heifer could be obtained (Av. Zar. 24a). The principle that characteristics acquired by an organism during its lifetime are likely to be transmitted by heredity to its progeny was current in the folklore and literature of the ancient peoples of Greece and Rome, and persisted in the theories of Darwin and Lamarck, according to whom evolution is the product of the transmission of acquired characteristics. Refuted by modern experimental science, these theories are contrary to the Mendelian laws, whose principle is that heredity characteristics are stable and not liable to changes due to environmental factors.

This problem of the relation between heredity and environment is to be found in the biblical account of what Jacob did with Laban's sheep (Gen. 30:31–43; 31:7–12). According to the accepted interpretation it was the rods, in which Jacob peeled white streaks and which he set "over against the flocks," that led to the birth of sheep with different colored skins (30:37). But this interpretation is entirely fallacious. From the biblical passage it emerges that the laws of heredity were revealed to Jacob when the angel of God, appearing to him, opened his eyes to a comprehension of the subject (31:12; for a comprehensive article by J. Feliks in *Teva va-Areẓ,* see bibliography). On the basis of this assumption, the passage can be satisfactorily explained. Jacob suggested to Laban: "I will pass through all thy flock today, removing from thence every speckled and spotted one, and every dark one among the sheep, and the spotted and speckled among the goats; and of such shall be my hire" (30:32). The sheep in this region are usually white in the places where the wool grows, only about a quarter of them having brown spotted wool; while the goats usually have black hair and only about a quarter of them have white or brown spots. The entirely white sheep and the completely black goats are designated as "monochrome" and the spotted sheep and goats as "spotted." Jacob suggested that Laban separate from the monochrome sheep all the spotted ones and take them for himself, and he, Jacob, would tend only the monochrome ones. As his remuneration ("and of such shall be my hire") he would receive all the spotted young that would be born from the monochrome sheep and goats.

Laban readily fell in with this suggestion, assuming that the monochrome sheep would bear only a trifling percentage of spotted young, and such indeed would have been the case were it not that Jacob adopted a special method of selection, as will be explained later. Laban removed all the spotted sheep which constituted 25% of the entire flock and put his sons in charge of them (30:35). For fear that there might be contact between these sheep and those tended by Jacob, he set the two flocks far apart from each other (30:36). In the flock tended by Jacob there were ostensibly only monochrome sheep. This was so in respect of phenotype, but as regards genotype a third of them were pure monochromes (homozygotes) and two-thirds heterozygotes, that is, they contained the gene of "spottedness." And since the gene of "monochromeness" is dominant, all the sheep appeared monochrome. In order to obtain spotted young, Jacob had to see that only the heterozygotes were crossed among themselves, and these according to the laws of heredity bore 25% spotted sheep, which became Jacob's property. But all this was on condition that the monochrome heterozygotes were not crossed with the monochrome homozygotes, from which only monochrome sheep would be born.

Bifurcation in crossbreeding the offspring of pure white sheep (A) with brown spotted sheep (b). The pure white gene is dominant over the spotted.

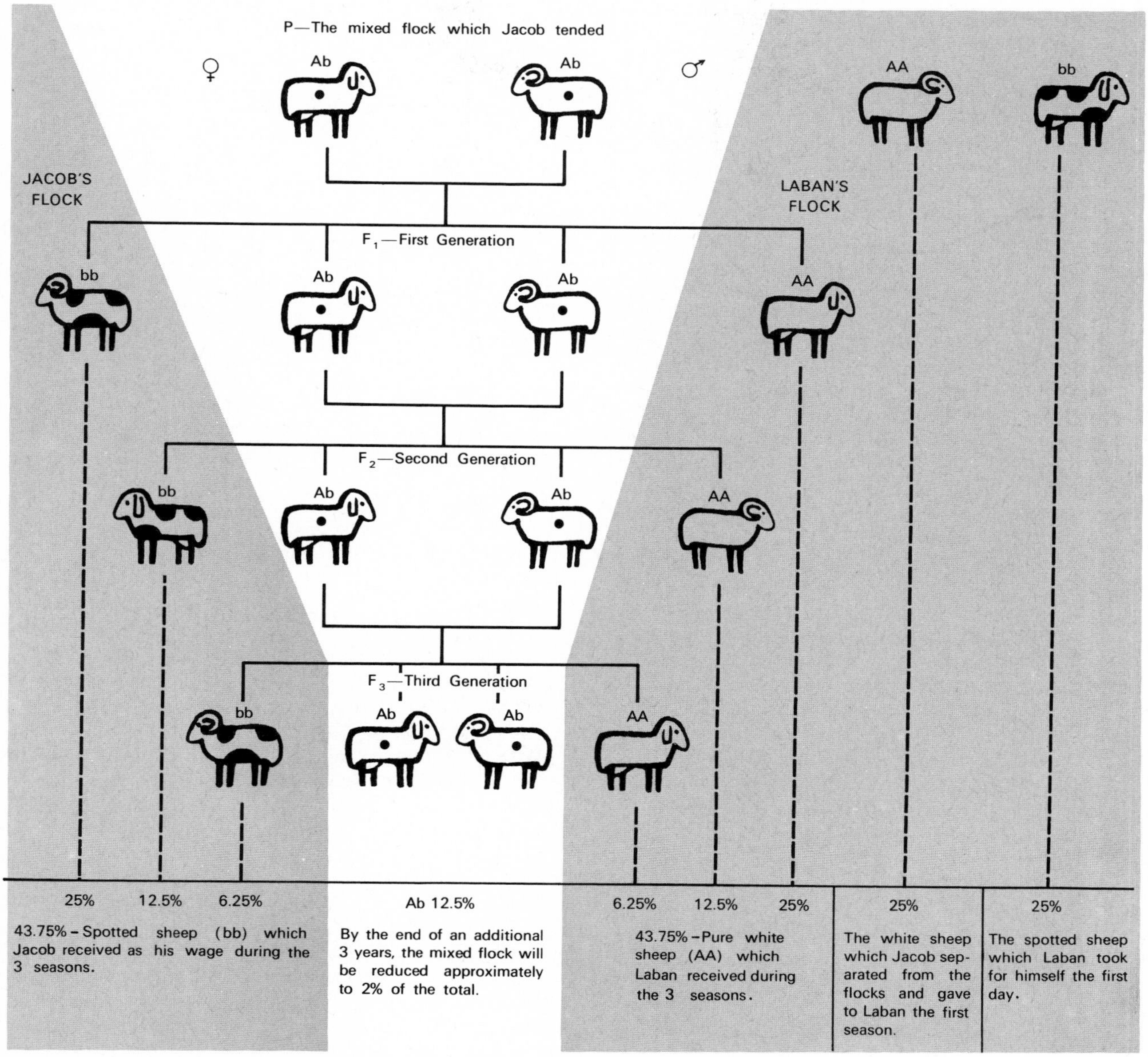

Jacob's crossbreeding of Laban's flock (Gen. 30). Chart by Jehuda Feliks, Jerusalem.

How he could distinguish between the heterozygotes and the homozygotes was revealed to Jacob in his dream by the angel. "Lift up thine eyes, and see, all the he-goats which leap upon the flock are streaked, speckled, and grizzled" (31:12). Ostensibly, that is, all the he-goats were monochrome but in some the characteristic of "spottedness" was recessive. This characteristic could be detected by the phenomenon of the hybrid's excessive potency (hybrid vigor-heterosis), that is, the monochrome sheep carrying the genes of "spottedness" conceived earlier than the homozygotes. Those that showed this hybrid vigor-heterosis are called in the Pentateuch *mekusharot* ("the stronger") and the others *atufim* ("the feebler"). According to the biblical narrative, Jacob laid the peeled rods before "the stronger" sheep that they might conceive, but not "when the flock were feeble," that is, not before those that conceived later (30:41–42); and the passage concludes: "So the feebler were Laban's and the stronger Jacob's," that is, Jacob handed over to Laban all the homozygote monochromes which had not revealed heterosis—these in addition to the spotted ones which Laban had received when the flocks were divided. The peeled rods which Jacob laid before the conceiving sheep were intended only to pretend to Laban that he was following the usual procedure of shepherds (which is also done nowadays), whereas in point of fact he had adopted a method of selection unknown to Laban.

Accordingly, in the first season Jacob was left with 50% of Laban's sheep. During the following seasons (extending over six years, according to 31:41) he obtained from the sheep that he tended nearly 50% spotted ones and Laban received about the same percentage. Hence Laban was left with a total of 75% of all the sheep, while Jacob got 25% of them, a percentage which Laban had not expected and which no shepherd could have obtained without a precise knowledge of the laws of heredity.

Genesis 30–31 thus represents the earliest document on a practical familiarity with the laws of heredity and heterosis. The Bible gives a detailed account of all the stages in this episode, perhaps to controvert the prevalent view that man can influence heredity by rods and similar objects. Another episode in the same chapter, that is, the incident of the *mandrakes (30:14–17), is also apparently intended to emphasize that conception and birth are a divine gift and cannot be influenced by charms, such as the fruit of the mandrakes. And indeed the biblical passage stresses that Leah, who gave the mandrakes to Rachel, became pregnant and bore a son, and not Rachel who received them.

Ecology. The mutual relations of organisms between themselves and their environment are dealt with in various passages in the Bible and in the literature of the sages, there being a wide spectrum of views and *aggadot* on the subject. On the conclusion of the creation it is said: "And God saw everything that He had made, and, behold, it was very good" (Gen. 1:31). It was then, too, that Adam was told that his food would be fruit and edible herbs (Gen. 1:29), which the sages (Sanh. 59b) interpreted as meaning that Adam and his sons were prohibited from eating flesh, this being allowed only after the flood to Noah and his sons (cf. Gen. 9:2–3). The passage mentions that "every green herb" would be the food of creatures (Gen. 1:30), from which some Church Fathers inferred that before the Fall there were no beasts of prey in the world (cf. Novatianus, *De cibis Judaicis,* 2). Isaiah's vision of the end of days when "the wolf shall dwell with the lamb . . . and the lion shall eat straw like the ox" (Isa. 11:6–7) may allude to that wholly good world of the creation in which there was neither carnivorous animal nor prey.

The Bible has numerous descriptions of animals and their ecological background, and these generally contain praise of the harmony in God's providence of His world even when the mode of life of animals of prey is described. Thus, for example, it is said: "Thou makest darkness, and it is night, wherein all the beasts of the forest do creep forth. The young lions roar after their prey, and seek their food from God" (Ps. 104:20–21). This psalm describes the habitat of the stork, the wild ass, the ibex, the hyrax, and the leviathan, who all live in harmony under God's providence: "All of them wait for Thee, that Thou mayest give them their food in due season." Mention is also made of the cycle of life and death among living things (Ps. 104:27–30), which is also a part of this harmony. An expression of the Creator's concern for all His creatures is to be found in the sages' statement that "the Holy One Blessed Be He sits and sustains [all creatures], from the horns of wild oryx to the eggs of lice" (Shab. 107b).

As regards each organism's specific conditions of survival, R. Akiva on the verse: "How manifold are Thy works, O Lord!" (Ps. 104:24) commented: "You have creatures that live in the sea and You have creatures that live on the land. If those of the sea were to come up on the land they would straightway die, and if those of the land were to go down into the sea they would straightaway die" (Ḥul. 127a). This passage also mentions creatures "that live in fire," the reference being to the legendary salamander.

There are indeed strange creatures in the world. What purpose they serve, particularly since they also include pests, is apparently doubtful. In reply to just such a question the Midrash asserted: "Even things which one regards as superfluous in the world, such as flies, fleas, and mosquitos, are included in the creation of the world, and the Holy One Blessed Be He conveys His message with everything, even by means of a snake, even by means of a mosquito, even by means of a frog" (Gen. R. 10). Some saw in these "insects and creeping things," a reminder to God who, "when human beings sin, looks at them and says, 'If I preserve these of which there is no need, how much more should I preserve those of which there is need.' " According, however, to another view "There is still a need of them, the fly for the hornet, the flea for the leech . . . ," that is the bite of the one is an antidote against the poison of the other (TJ, Ber. 9:3, 13c). This statement is quoted in the Babylonian Talmud in the name of the *amora* Rav (Shab. 77b), who concluded that "of all which the Holy One Blessed Be He created in this world, He created nothing without a purpose"—the very words used by Aristotle (*De Caelo,* 1:4).

There exists an accord between an animal's limbs and its mode of life and environment, as stressed by R. Judah when asked questions on this subject: "Why is a camel's tail short?—Because it eats thorns [in which its tail is liable to get caught]. Why is an ox's tail long?—Because it grazes in meadows [marshy pastures] and has to beat off mosquitos [with its tail]. Why are the antennae of a locust soft [flexible]?—Because it lives among the reeds and if they were hard [inflexible] they would be dislocated and it would go blind. Why does a fowl's [lower] eyelid curve [and close] upward?—Because it lives among the rafters and if smoke entered [its eyes] it would go blind" (Shab. 77b). Similar answers that connect the structure of the limbs with the environmental conditions were given by Hillel to one who asked him questions to provoke him: "Why are the eyes of the Palmyreans without lashes?" Hillel answered him: "You have asked a great question. It is because they live in sandy regions." Another question was: "Why are the feet of the Africans wide?" To this Hillel replied: "Because they live in marshes" (Shab. 31a).

Every creature has its appropriate habitation. "As for the stork, the junipers [JPS, "fir trees"] are her house. The high mountains are for the wild goats; the rocks are a refuge for the hyrax" (JPS, "conies"; Ps. 104:17–18). The wild ass has for "His house . . . the wilderness, and the salt land [for] his dwelling place" (Job 39:6). The mountains of Lebanon are "the lion's dens . . . the mountains of the leopards" (Song 4:8). The lion dwells in the thickets of the Jordan (Jer. 49:19), the desert is the habitation of "the lioness and the lion, the viper and flying serpent" (Isa. 30:6). Nocturnal birds dwell in waste places (Isa. 34:11–17). Migratory birds arrive in Ereẓ Israel at fixed times—"Yea, the stork in the heaven knoweth her appointed times; and the turtle and the swift [JPS "swallow"] and the crane observe the time of their coming" (Jer. 8:7). The hawk, too, is migratory: she stretches "her wings toward the south" (Job 39:26).

The sages stated the principle that "whatever is in the inhabited land is in the desert; there are many in the desert that are not in the inhabited land. Whatever is on land is in the sea; there are many in the sea that are not in the land. The species of rat is not in the sea" (Tosef., Kil. 5:10). Every creature has its suitable habitat: "The animal of the mountain does not thrive in the valley nor does the animal of the valley thrive in the mountain." Every creature is accustomed to its food: "The animal in Judea does not thrive on the fruit of Galilee nor does the animal in Galilee thrive on the fruit of Judea." In this connection mention is made of a creature's deep attachment to its habitat, even as a person has for his birthplace: "Diocletian oppressed the inhabitants of Panias with taxes. They said to him: 'We shall go from here.' Whereupon a sophist told him: 'They will not leave, and if they do, they will ultimately return—if you wish to test this, take gazelles, send them to a distant land, and in the end they will return to their old locality.' He did so. He took gazelles, covered their horns with silver, and sent them to Africa. At the end of 30 [another version: three] years they returned to their former places" (TJ, Shev. 9:2, 38d).

Some sages displayed a special interest and ability in observing nature. Several times it is mentioned that the *tanna* Simeon b. Ḥalafta was "an experimenter in things," that is, he used to conduct experiments with animals. He investigated the effect of heat on a fowl's change of feathers (Ḥul. 57b), observed the nesting habits of the hoopoe (Lev. R. 22), experimented with ants to find out how their work was organized (Ḥul. 57b) and established their developed sense of smell (Deut. R. 5). The *nasi* Simeon b. Gamaliel, too, showed an aptitude for observing the ways of animals and plants, and even suggested an original method of waging "biological warfare" against ants: "How may ants' holes be destroyed? Earth is fetched from one hole and put in another and they [the ants of the two nests] strangle one another" (MK 6b). This R. Simeon also set down the phytogeographic areas of Ereẓ Israel: "An indication of mountainous country is the presence of tall oaks; an indication of valleys is palm trees; an indication of streams is reeds; an indication of lowlands is sycamore trees" (Tosef., Shev. 7:6; Pes. 53a). The sages laid down the principle that "where the sycamore does not grow is Upper Galilee . . . where the sycamore grows is Lower Galilee" (Shev. 9:2; the sycamore thrives in the heat and not in mountainous regions).

Under some conditions weeds can be indicators of a plant's suitability for a certain soil. From the verse: "Let thistles grow instead of wheat, and Ridolfia [JPS, "noisome"] weeds instead of barley" (Job 31:40), R. Hoshaya inferred: "The Torah teaches one a worldly occupation. A field that produces thistles is suitable for sowing under wheat, a field that produces Ridolfia weeds is suitable for sowing under barley" (Tanḥ. Re'eh, 13). The local species, which is adapted to the ecological conditions of the region, is to be preferred to an apparently superior species from some distant place, as asserted by the sages: "If the wheat in your locality [is mixed] with tares, sow them" (Gen. R. 59). Of Joseph it is said: "The food of the field, which was round about every city, laid he up in the same" (Gen. 41:48), which is explained by the Midrash that it is advisable to store produce in its own vicinity, "since every country preserves its own fruits" (Gen. R. 90). This refers to the storing of seeds which are less affected by local pests since, as is well-known, there is an ecological equilibrium between the pests and the creatures that feed on them.

As regards the ecology of man it must be pointed out that the ancients did not appreciate trees planted in a town. Thus the Mishnah teaches: "Trees must be kept at a distance of 25 cubits from a town, carobs and sycamore trees 50 cubits. Abba Saul says, 'All non-fruitbearing trees must be kept at a distance of 50 cubits'" (BB 2:11). The reason for this is (BB 24b) that "the beauty of the town may be preserved," and Rashi explains: "Because a town is beautified if it has an open space in front of it." Other passages indicate that the term for "beauty" נוי *(noi)* derives from נוה *(naveh)* which also has the meaning of "climate." And such is the reason given for this *halakhah* in the Jerusalem Talmud (BB 2:7, 13c): "Because [the tree] stands and darkens [the town] or adversely affects its climate." Under the crowded housing conditions of those days, it was important to allow the sun to penetrate everywhere and act as a disinfectant (which is apparently the reason why there are almost no trees in Arab villages).

Other sources refer to gardens and orchards at the outskirts of a town and in the courtyards of the wealthy (cf. Meg. 5b), while in Jerusalem there was a "king's garden" (II Kings 25:4). According to an early *baraita* a regulation was in force in Jerusalem "that neither gardens nor orchards may be cultivated there, except for the garden of roses which existed from the days of the former prophets" (BK 82b), the reason for this prohibition being "on account of the bad odor" of manure and rotting leaves. Particular insistence was laid in Jerusalem on levitical cleanness and sanitation, and it was therefore prohibited to accumulate heaps of garbage, to build kilns, or to breed fowls there *(ibid.)*. As for other towns, an *amora* declared: "It is forbidden to live in a town in which there is no garden or greenery" (TJ, Kid., 4:12, 66d). Even as it was prohibited to plant trees within the town limits, so threshing floors had to be placed at a distance from a town, that the chaff carried from them by the wind should not dirty it. It was furthermore laid down that "carrion, graves, and tanneries must be kept 50 cubits from a town. A tannery must be placed only on the east side of a town" (since an east wind is not a prevailing one; BB 2:8–9).

Many passages in the Bible and in the literature of the sages deal with matters relating to *hygiene. On the communication of diseases mention may be made of two statements: "R. Johanan issued the warning, 'Beware of the flies of one afflicted with *ra'atan*'" (Ket. 77b), the reference being apparently to a certain skin disease, communicated, so it was thought, by flies. In Babylonia R. Judah, when informed that a plague had broken out among pigs, decreed a fast, "because their intestines are like those of human beings," and hence there was a danger that people might catch their disease (Ta'an. 21b). [J.F.]

Middle Ages and Modern Times. In the Middle Ages, a number of Jewish writers, in common with their more famous Arab counterparts, played a part in the transmission of Greek science to Europe. While not primarily biological, these writings are nevertheless of interest to the student of the history of science. The *Sefer ha-Aẓamim,* ascribed to Abraham *ibn Ezra, includes a chapter on animals. The aim of this short treatise is not to instruct the reader about animals, but rather to advance the Aristotelian thesis that a directive force guides the harmonious course of embryonic development and the self-protective activities of animals. Abraham *ibn Daud included a discussion of animal senses in his *Emunah Ramah.* He largely follows Galen in his treatment of the sensory functions, the nerves, and the relation of the brain to the sense organs. *Gershon b. Solomon of Arles was the author of an encyclopedia called *Sha'ar ha-Shamayim,* compiled c. 1280. The first part of this work deals with natural history and includes treatises on plants, quadrupeds, birds, insects, spiders, and fishes, as well as human anatomy.

Jews apparently played no part in the renaissance of modern biology. One reason for this was the existence of anti-Jewish legislation and the exclusion of Jews from the universities. The first Jew to figure prominently in the history of biology was Marcus Eliezer *Bloch, a physician who devoted himself to zoological research. He published a number of studies on the structure, habits, and economic importance of the fish of Germany.

The 19th Century. Biology as a conceptually unified science dates from the early 19th century, with the formulation of the cell theory and growing recognition of the common protoplasmic basis of plant and animal organization. A number of Jews figured prominently in these advances. Robert *Remak, a physician and embryologist, originated the terms ectoderm, endoderm, and mesoderm for the three primary layers of embryo. Jacob *Henle laid the foundations for modern histology with his *Allgemeine Anatomie.* Ferdinand Julius *Cohn of Breslau has rightly been called the father of bacteriology. To Cohn also belongs the credit for recognizing (1850) that the protoplasm of plant cells and that of animals (then called "sarcode") were identical. Nathan Pringsheim was a botanist who made significant contributions to the study of lower plants. He clarified the life history of a number of species of algae, applying to them the concept of alternation of generations and demonstrating the phenomenon of sexual reproduction by isogametes, i.e., male and female sex cells of almost identical appearance. Julius *Sachs, one of the greatest botanists of the 19th century, was a professor at Wuerzburg. During his 30 years' tenure there, his laboratory became a world center for the study of plant physiology.

During the last quarter of the 19th century the basis for modern cell biology was established by the discovery of far-reaching generalizations: the universality of the phenomena of cell division, the role of the nucleus in heredity, and the nature of fertilization. In these revolutionary advances two biologists of Jewish descent played a crucial part. Eduard *Strasburger, a professor at the University of Bonn, was eminent in plant cytology. In his pioneer work, *Zellbildung und Zellteilung* (1875), and during the years following its publication, he elucidated the process of mitosis in plants, correctly describing the behavior of the chromosomes, and he called attention to the role that the nucleus must play as a carrier of hereditary factors. Leopold *Auerbach at Breslau observed the fusion of sperm and egg nuclei in a nematode worm and perceived that fertilization must involve contributions of nuclear material from both male and female parents which are distributed to the cells of the zygote. In the United States, Jacques *Loeb sought to explain fertilization and other cellular phenomena in physico-chemical terms. Much of the teaching of American biology today echoes his influence.

The Modern Period. In recent times, the number of Jews who have made important contributions to biology has grown enormously. More than 100 Jews are members of the U.S. National Academy of Sciences and of 46 Nobel Prizes in the biological sciences between 1950 and 1967, 11 recipients were Jews.

Herman J. Muller (1890–1967), a student of T. H. Morgan, was a member of the group that pioneered in developing animal genetics through experimental studies with the fruit fly, *Drosophila melanogaster.* Muller devised a technique for measuring the mutation rate in *Drosophila* and discovered the effect of X-rays in increasing the rate of mutation. His 1927 paper marks the first clear example of the artificial induction of mutations. It was shortly followed by confirmation by L. J. Stadler (1896–1954), who demonstrated the same effect in barley. For his discovery, Muller was awarded the Nobel Prize in medicine in 1946. From his first account, Muller insisted that high-energy radiation is dangerous not only to the exposed individual, but to his descendants as well. This far-sighted conclusion became a matter of public concern with the onset of the nuclear age and the wide dissemination of radioactive isotopes. Curt Stern (1902–) demonstrated that the recombination of genetic traits seen in crosses is accompanied by the physical exchange of pieces of chromosome. He showed that the process of crossing-over occurs not only in sex cells but in somatic (body) cells as well. (For photograph of H. J. Muller see col. 1019)

The problem concerning the way in which the genetic endowment of the fertilized egg is translated into the physical features of the individual constitutes the science of developmental genetics. An outstanding leader in this field was Richard B. *Goldschmidt. Through crosses between European and Japanese races of the gypsy moth, *Lymantria dispar,* he showed that the development of sexuality depended on genetic factors which differed in strength in various populations and could shift the development toward maleness or femaleness to various degrees. I. Michael *Lerner made important contributions to the field of population genetics. Lerner wrote *Genetic Homeostasis* (1954), *The Genetic Basis of Selection* (1958), and other works.

The field of biochemical genetics attempts to answer the question of how genes act in terms of their effects on the biochemical activities of the organism. One of the first experimental approaches to this problem was the work of George Beadle and Boris *Ephrussi. Joshua *Lederberg shared the Nobel Prize with Beadle and Tatum for his discovery of sexuality in bacteria. The first step in solving the genetic code (by which sequences of the units of DNA "spell out" instructions for the synthesis of proteins) was accomplished by Marshal W. *Nirenberg and his colleagues at the National Heart Institute at Bethesda, Md. Nirenberg was awarded a Nobel Prize in medicine in 1968. Other major strides were made by Arthur *Kornberg, who synthesized DNA in a cell-free preparation and with his colleagues later succeeded in obtaining the replication of DNA in a test tube. Kornberg received the Nobel Prize in 1959. Other important workers in molecular biology are Sol *Spiegelman, professor of microbiology at the University of Illinois, Matthew Meselson (1930–) of Harvard University, and, in France, F. *Jacob and Elie *Wollman.

Activity of the nervous system is accompanied by changes measurable in two ways: alterations in the electric potential across the membrane of the nerve cell, and liberation of chemical mediators, or transmitter substances, at the nerve endings. The properties of the nerve cell membrane were studied by Julius Bernstein (1839–1917). Later Joseph *Erlanger and Herbert *Gasser developed the use of the cathode ray oscillograph to monitor the nerve impulse and demonstrated the highly differentiated properties of single nerve fibers. This work earned them the Nobel Prize in 1944. The first demonstration that a nerve may act by liberating a chemical substance was accomplished by Otto *Loewi in 1921. In an experiment he proved that the vagus nerve, when stimulated, released a substance (later identified as acetylcholine) that transmits the inhibitory impulse slowing the heart beat. In recognition of his discovery Loewi was given the Nobel Prize in 1936. Studies of neural transmitter substances were carried out by Bernhard *Katz of University College, London (Nobel Prize, 1970), and David Nachmansohn (1899–) at Columbia University. The chemical and biophysical aspects of vision were studied by Selig *Hecht and his student George *Wald; the latter's investigation of the light-sensitive pigments rhodopsin and porphyropsin and their relation to vitamin A won him a Nobel Prize in 1967.

One of the triumphs of 20th-century biology was the elucidation of the complex chain of events by which the green plant makes sugars and starch from carbon dioxide and water, using light energy. Many Jewish scientists helped to solve different aspects of this problem. James *Franck, a Nobel laureate in physics, interested himself in the energy requirements of photosynthesis in terms of quantum mechanics. Otto *Warburg, who was a prolific investigator responsible for much of the present knowledge of the enzymatic mechanisms of cellular respiration (Nobel Prize in 1931), found that the efficiency of photosynthesis was increased in intermittent light. Samuel Ruben (1913–1943), William Zev *Hassid, and Martin Kamen (1913–) were the first to apply the method of isotopic tracers to a study of photosynthesis. Daniel Israel *Arnon found that the light energy in photosynthesis is used by the plant to create high-energy phosphate bonds. The sequence of biochemical steps by which organic compounds are built up was convincingly demonstrated by Melvin *Calvin, whose achievement was recognized by a Nobel award in 1961.

Among the pioneers in the development of biological sciences in Ereẓ Israel were Otto *Warburg, Israel *Aharoni, Alexander *Eig, and Israel Reichert; also Karl Reich (1902–), a hydrobiologist and F. S.

*Bodenheimer, entomologist, ecologist, and historian of biology. With the establishment of the Hebrew University, the Weizmann Institute of Science, and Tel Aviv University, their biology departments became active centers for research and advanced training in botany (M. *Evenari, M. *Zohary, at the Hebrew University), zoology (George *Haas at the Hebrew University), and cell biology (I. *Berenblum at the Weizmann Institute). Research is also carried out at government laboratories such as the Institute for Biological Research at Nes Ẓiyyonah and the Negev Institute for Arid Zone Research in Beersheba. A comprehensive review of accomplishments in Israel in the biological sciences has been edited by M. Prywes, *Biological and Medical Research in Israel* (1959). [M.L.G.]

Bibliography: In The Bible and Talmud: Lewysohn, Zool; J. Preuss, *Biblisch-talmudische Medizin* (1911); Ginzberg, Legends, 1 (1909); J. Feliks, *Animal World of the Bible* (1962); idem, in: *Teva va-Areẓ*, 7 (1965), 330–7; idem, *Olam ha-Ẓome'aḥ ha-Mikra'i* (1968); idem, *Kilei Zera'im ve-Harkavah* (1967). Middle Ages and Modern Times: F. S. Bodenheimer, *Biologist in Israel* (1959); B. Dawes, *Hundred Years of Biology* (1952); M. L. Gabriel and S. Fogel, *Great Experiments in Biology* (1955); E. Nordenskjöld, *History of Biology* (1935); H. Schueck et al., *Nobel: the Man and His Prizes* (1962).

BIRAM, ARTHUR (Yiẓḥak; 1878–1967), Hebrew educator. Biram, who was born in Bischofswerda, Germany, attended Berlin University and the *Hochschule fuer die Wissenschaft des Judentums in Berlin. From 1909 to 1913 he taught classics in German high schools. An early member of the Zionist movement, he went to Ereẓ Israel in 1914 and was appointed by the Zionist Executive principal of the Reali High School in Haifa. After serving with the German Army in Palestine during World War I, Biram became in 1918 deputy principal of the Hebrew Teachers' College in Jerusalem. He returned to Haifa in 1920 and again became principal of the Reali High School, where he also taught Bible, until 1948. During his tenure, the school was enlarged and its activities diversified. In 1937 he initiated the paramilitary training program of high school pupils, called *Ḥagam* (abbreviation for *Ḥinnukh Gufani Murḥav,* i.e., "extended physical education"), later renamed *Gadna.* In 1943 he established and headed a teachers' seminary at the Reali High School and, in 1953, initiated the establishment of a military academy there. He wrote the three-volume *Divrei Yemei Yisrael bi-Zeman ha-Mikra be-Misgeret Toledot ha-Mizraḥ* ("History of Israel in Biblical Times in the Context of Near Eastern History," 1962–64), based mainly on his own method of teaching the Bible. For Biram the training of pupils toward fulfilling their duties as citizens, and the inculcation of discipline, order, and precision, were educational principles which could determine the fate of the nation. He devoted special attention to physical education, military training, and scouting. Under his direction, the course of studies at the Reali High School consisted of six years of primary and six years of secondary education, the latter being divided into two stages, permitting specialization in the senior grades. Some of Biram's reforms were later incorporated into the educational system of the country. Biram received the Israel Prize for Education in 1954.

Bibliography: *Sefer Biram* (1956); Tidhar, 4 (1950), 1696f.

[J.B.]

BIRANIT (Heb. בִּירָנִית; "small fortress"), kibbutz in Israel, on the Lebanese border. Biranit was planned as the large rural center of a group of settlements including Zarit, Netu'ah, Shetulah, and Yakinton, in the framework of the Central Galilee Development Project inaugurated in 1963. Its nucleus was established on Dec. 1, 1964, by a Naḥal group affiliated with Ha-Kibbutz ha-Me'uḥad. The center's initial tasks consisted of land reclamation, afforestation and restoration of ancient woodlands, planting of fruit orchards, road building, and other development work.

[E.O.]

BIRIYYAH (Berai; Heb. בִּירִיָּה; בֵּרַי), in the talmudic period an important Jewish town in Upper Galilee, 1 mi. (1½ km.) N. of Safed. After Safed's importance decreased in the first century C.E. as an outcome of the Jewish war against Rome, Biriyyah took over its role as a regional center and became an important place of learning. Both in the Jerusalem and Babylonian Talmuds (Er. 45a, Git. 34a, TJ Meg. 2:3, 73b et al.) six sages who were residents of Biriyyah are mentioned. The Talmud also relates several episodes from the life of "Benei Berai," i.e., Biriyyah's inhabitants. In Biriyyah, R. Abba Sha'ul, one of the important sages of the Mishnah, is assumedly buried together with his wife, a fact mentioned by a number of travelers as late as 1876. According to kabbalist tradition, the tomb of Benaiah son of Jehoiada, one of the commanders of King David, is also to be found near Biriyyah. The *genizah* literature testifies that Jews lived at Biriyyah also between the 11th and 13th centuries C.E., and it is possible that their descendants continued to be inhabitants of the village until the 16th century, when Biriyyah entered a new phase of ascendancy as many Jews expelled from Spain settled in Safed and its vicinity. It was then that Joseph *Caro completed at Biriyyah the first part of the *Shulḥan Arukh on the 2nd of Elul 5315 (1555 C.E.). The local Jews of that time were farmers and tradesmen, as were the Jewish inhabitants of neighboring villages. At the beginning of the 17th century, there were no longer any Jews living at Biriyyah, but the local synagogue existed until the 18th century, serving the Jewish community of Safed in case of need; its keys were kept by local Arabs who showed great reverence for the synagogue.

After the 1837 earthquake that destroyed Safed, a Hebrew printing press was temporarily brought to Biriyyah before being transferred to Jerusalem. It was the site of an Arab village Bīryā. In January 1945 a group from *Benei Akiva founded a kibbutz on top of Mt. Biriyyah at an elevation of 3,135 ft. (1950 m.) above sea level, working principally on land reclamation. On March 5, 1946, British Mandatory authorities carried out an arms search and, after discovering weapons, arrested the settlers and occupied the village. Ten days later 3,000 youths went up the mountain, set up a tent camp near the village, and started clearing stones. The British moved up strong military forces and drove the settlers away, but they returned the following night, setting up a new camp. The whole *yishuv* supported

A protest against the occupation of Biriyyah by British forces in 1946.

Some of the youths who helped to defy the occupation of Biriyyah.

the settlers, and the British gave in, first permitting the camp to remain, then releasing the imprisoned settlers, and finally (June 7, 1946) evacuating the village buildings. In September 1948, a new religious kibbutz took over the site and was replaced in 1949 by a moshav founded by immigrants from Tripolitania (Libya). The moshav supports some hill farming, but most of its inhabitants work in Safed and elsewhere. A large forest (with nearly 6 million trees in 1968) has been planted on Mt. Biriyyah.

[E.O.]

BIRKAT HA-MINIM (Heb. בִּרְכַּת הַמִּינִים, "benediction concerning heretics"), the 12th benediction of the weekday **Amidah.* This benediction, which varies in wording among the different rites, invokes divine wrath upon "slanderers," "wickedness," "Thine enemies," and the "kingdom of arrogance," and adores God, "who breakest the enemies and humblest the arrogant [sectarians]." Prevailing scholarly opinion, based upon Ecclesiasticus 36:7, holds that this prayer originated during the Syrian-Hellenistic oppression in the time of the Second Temple, and that it was directed against those Jews who collaborated with the enemy. At that time, the prayer was known as the "Benediction to Him Who humbles the arrogant." A century later the imprecation was directed against the Sadducees, and it was designated as the "Benediction concerning the Sadducees." Under Rabban Gamaliel II (first century C.E.) this prayer was invoked against the Judeo-Christian and Gnostic sects and other heretics who were called by the general term **min* (plural *minim*). To avoid any suspicion of heresy, the *ḥazzan* had to be certain to recite this prayer in public worship. If he omitted it by error, he had to return and recite it, although such a regulation does not apply to any other benediction (Tanḥ. B., Lev. 2a). Although some scholars hold that there were only 17 benedictions prior to the inclusion of this prayer into the *Amidah,* others contend that *Birkat ha-Minim* was the 19th.

The formulation of this prayer is ascribed to *Samuel ha-Katan, who revised its text after it had fallen into oblivion (Ber. 28b). The many different historical situations in which this prayer was used are reflected in the variant readings still extant. The text has been further confused as a result of censorship during the Middle Ages. In geonic times, this prayer was invoked against *poshe'im* ("sinners") or, as Maimonides read it, against *apikoresim* ("heretics"), whereas in the *Maḥzor Salonika* and in the *Roman Maḥzor* it refers to *meshummadim* ("the apostates"). This term was further changed into *ve-la-poshe'im,* which later became *ve-la-malshinim* ("slanderers"). In some versions other expressions were substituted for the word *minim:* e.g., "all doers of iniquity," regardless of origin and nationality. The Sephardi ritual retained *minim.* Instead of the passage "and all the enemies of Thy people," as in older versions, the modified Ashkenazi and Roman rites read: "and they all." The phrase *malkhut zadon* ("kingdom of arrogance") by which the Roman Empire was meant, was changed by *Amram b. Sheshna (Amram Gaon) into "the arrogant," as in most rites. The concluding phrase "who breakest the enemies and humblest the arrogant" *(Siddur Amram Ga'on)* was replaced in some versions, by: "who breakest the evildoers" (*Siddur Sa'adyah Ga'on* and Maimonides). From the historical evidence, it is clear that this prayer was never meant to be directed against non-Jews in general, but rather against Jewish heretics and gentile persecutors of the Jews. Nevertheless Jews were often accused of including a special imprecation against Christians in their statutory prayers. In modern times, the text has further been adjusted and many prayer books substitute the impersonal "slander" and "evil" for "slanderers" and "evil doers." In several Reform rites, the prayer has been modified or omitted.

Bibliography: Elbogen, Gottesdienst, 35, 51ff.; J. Heinemann, *Ha-Tefillah bi-Tekufat ha-Tanna'im ve-ha-Amora'im* (1966²), 141–3; E. Munk, *World of Prayer,* 1 (1954), 140–4; JE, 11 (1905), 281; Abrahams, Companion, lxiv–lxv; J. J. Petuchowski, *Prayerbook Reform in Europe* (1968), 223–5.

[M.Y.]

BIRKAT HA-TORAH (Heb. בִּרְכַּת הַתּוֹרָה), the blessing over the Law. The study of the Law was always regarded as a foremost religious duty and hence had to be preceded by a formula of benediction. This requirement applies both to the liturgical reading of the Torah and to ordinary study. Various formulas are given in the Talmud (Ber. 11a–b) in the name of several rabbis and all have been integrated into the traditional liturgy. These benedictions were instituted in talmudic times based upon Deuteronomy 32:3 (see TJ, Meg. 4:1, 74d) and by *a fortiori* inference from the duty to recite Grace after Meals (TJ, Ber. 7:11a; TJ, Meg. loc. cit.). Three blessings over the Law are pronounced at the beginning of the daily morning prayer. The first praises God for granting Israel the privilege and the duty of studying Torah; the second is a prayer that the study of Torah may be pleasant and that it should be cultivated by one's offspring and the whole house of Israel; the third is identical with the benediction recited before the Reading of the Law in the synagogue service: "Who has chosen us from all nations and hast given us Thy Law." They are followed by selections from Scripture (Num. 6:24–27), the Mishnah (Pe'ah 1:1) and the Talmud (Shab. 127a), recited in symbolic fulfillment of the duty to study Torah. Jacob b. Asher interpreted the words, "Torah of truth" to refer to the written Torah, and the words, "everlasting life" to refer to the oral tradition. These benedictions contain 40 words, said to symbolize the 40 days Moses spent on Mount Sinai (Tur OḤ 139). The benedictions over the Law have uniform wording in all modern rituals, including that of Reform Judaism. Only the Reconstructionist trend, which repudiates the notion of the election of Israel, has changed the wording of the middle part of the benediction to read "who hast brought us close to Thy service" instead of "who hast chosen us."

Bibliography: ET, 4 (1952), 615–31; J. Heinemann, *Ha-Tefillah . . .* (1964), 105–8; E. Levy, *Yesodot ha-Tefillah* (1952²), 130, 315–6; Hertz, Prayer, 12–17, 190–3; E. Munk, *World of Prayer* (1961), 41–49, 174–5.

[ED.]

BIRKENTHAL (Brezhover), DOV BER (Ber of Bolechow; 1723–1805), Hebrew writer and memoirist. Born in Bolechow, Birkenthal adopted a German name in accordance with the decree of Joseph II in 1772, when the city passed from Polish to Austrian rule. He received a traditional Jewish education, but his father, who was a winedealer and had contact with Polish and Hungarian nobles and priests, agreed to engage a non-Jewish tutor—an unusual step for the time—who taught him Polish, Latin, German, and French. Birkenthal took over his father's business, and became the leader of the Bolechow community. In the debate with the followers of Jacob *Frank, which was held in the main church of Lemberg in 1759, Birkenthal served as interpreter and adviser to R. Ḥayyim b. Simḥah ha-Kohen Rapoport, the chief rabbi of Lemberg. His main literary work, *Imrei Binah,* is a study of false-Messiah movements in Jewish history, and the debate with the Frankists occupies a central position in it. The work was discovered in 1910, long after his death, and published by A. J. Brawer in *Ha-Shilo'aḥ* (vols. 33 and 38). A manuscript of his memoirs was discovered in Jews' College, London, in 1912 and was published—with introduction—in 1922 in Berlin by M. Wischnitzer. It was published in Yiddish *(Ber Bolekhovers Zikhroynes)* and in English translation *(The Memoirs of Ber of Bolechow)* in the same year. These two works contain valuable information for the study of Jewish history in Galicia in the 18th century, not only for the Frankist movement but also for the history of the Council of the Lands, the Jewish census in Poland (1764), and for Jewish economic history of that period.

Bibliography: Zinberg, Sifrut, 5 (1959), 109–11; Wischnitzer, in: JQR, 12 (1921/22), 1–24; Balaban, in: *Festschrift . . . S. Poznański* (1927), 25ff.

[A.J.Br./Ed.]

BIRMINGHAM, city in Alabama, U.S. Although Jews were among the first settlers, Jewish communal life did not begin to develop until 1882 when Birmingham had a population of 3,086.

The East European Jews, who moved to Birmingham in large numbers, experienced a period of difficult struggle from 1900 to 1920. Most of the immigrants had a poor command of English and were impoverished. Yet they adjusted quickly, became acculturated, and showed great flexibility and ingenuity in meeting their daily problems. After 1920 several important changes took place in the Jewish community. Anti-Semitism became more pronounced, there was a sharper division between the generations, and there was an increased pace at which Jews moved from their old neighborhoods. There was also the beginning of a united, local Jewish community, despite the continuance of a sharp cleavage between the German Jews and the East European Jews. Temple Emanu-El, Reform, was founded in 1882. Morris Newfield served as rabbi of Temple Emanu-El for 45 years and was an acknowledged civic and cultural leader. K'nesseth Israel Synagogue,

The Jewish Community Center building in Birmingham, Alabama. Photo John A. Farmer.

Orthodox, was founded in 1899. Temple Beth-El, Conservative, was founded in 1906 by 44 K'nesseth Israel members, who wanted a more liberal liturgical policy.

Numerous Jewish community activities and events take place in the new Jewish Community Center, which serves over 4,000 members. Formerly known as the YMHA, organized in 1906, it moved to its present site in 1958. The Federation of Jewish Charities, the United Jewish Fund, founded in 1936, and the Jewish Community Council, which serves as a community relations and social planning agency, are all housed in the Jewish Community Center building. In 1969, the two Jewish country clubs, the Hillcrest Club, which was organized in 1883, and the Fairmont Club, which was founded in 1920, merged to form the Pinetree Country Club. There are also many other Jewish organizations. Birmingham has been fertile ground for a number of extremist groups, but the 1960s saw a trend toward improvement in interracial and interfaith group relations. Jews participate fully in the city's commercial and civic life. They include bankers, manufacturers, and retail store owners and are active in real estate, insurance, and the professions. In 1967, there were 4,100 Jews in Birmingham.

[H.E.K.]

BIRMINGHAM, city in England. The Jewish community there is believed to have come into existence around 1730. The early Jewish settlers included peddlers who used Birmingham as a base. The first known Birmingham glass furnace was set up by Meyer Oppenheim (or Opnaim) in or

The Central Synagogue, Birmingham, England, built in the 1960s. Photo Simon Livingstone Studios, Birmingham.

about 1760. In 1783 a synagogue existed in "The Froggery." A new synagogue, constructed in Severn Street in 1809, was wrecked in the riots of 1813 along with the Nonconformist chapels but was rebuilt and enlarged in 1827. Internecine strife at this period resulted in the formation of a second congregation, but the two groups united to build the Singers Hill Synagogue, consecrated in 1856, and still in use. There were then about 700 Jews in Birmingham. The Jewish community included jewelers, merchants, and manufacturers. In the 20th century Jews were leading figures in property development and in the entertainment world. On the other hand, immigration from Eastern Europe affected Birmingham less than other large cities. Rabbis of the community included M. J. *Raphall (1841–49) and George J. Emanuel (1863–1911), succeeded by Abraham *Cohen (1913–49). To serve the East European Jews who settled in Birmingham a *bet midrash* was opened in 1901, which later became the Central Synagogue. The Hebrew Philanthropic Society, established in 1838, and the Board of Guardians, in 1870, were consolidated in 1926 in the Birmingham United Jewish Benevolent Board. The Birmingham Jewish Representative Council was established in 1937. Jews have played a prominent part in the civic and business life of Birmingham. Sir David Davis served as lord mayor in 1922 and 1923, as did Louis Glass in 1963–64. Birmingham, whose Jewish population numbered approximately 6,300 in 1967, has the lowest percentage of Jews of any great city in England.

Bibliography: C. Roth, *Rise of Provincial Jewry* (1950), 32–33; C. Gill and A. Briggs, *History of Birmingham* (1952). [S.D.T.]

BIRNBAUM, ABRAHAM BAER (1864–1922), cantor and composer. Birnbaum, who was born in Pultusk, Poland, was regarded as an *illui* ("prodigy") in Talmud. He studied the violin in Lodz with Ḥayyim H. Janowski, founder of the Ha-Zamir choral society. At the age of 19, he accepted a position as cantor in Hethar, Hungary, but in due course returned to Poland as chief cantor in Czestochowa. His *Hallel ve-Zimrah,* consisting of Sabbath eve melodies arranged for choir and organ, was published in 1897. His main work, which much enriched synagogue music, *Ommanut ha-Ḥazzanut,* was a treatment of liturgical music for cantor and choir, written in two parts (1908, 1912). He composed a "Romance for Violin and Piano" and set to music poems of Bialik, Frischmann, Yaakov Cohen, and Frug. Birnbaum's activities included publishing, and he brought out four numbers of *Yarḥon ha-Ḥazzanim* ("Cantors' Monthly") in 1897, textbooks on music, in Yiddish and Hebrew, written for the cantorial school he opened at Czestochowa (1907) and for the Lodz teachers' seminary. He organized the conference of cantors held in Warsaw for the purpose of founding the Aguddat ha-Ḥazzanim ("Cantorial Association"). His musical collection is in the Hebrew Union College Library, Cincinnati.

Bibliography: Sendrey, Music, indexes; Friedmann, Lebensbilder, 3 (1927), 58–61; Sherman, in: A. H. Rosen, *Di Geshikhte fun Khazones* (1924), 210–1. [J.L.N.]

BIRNBAUM, EDUARD (Asher Anshel; 1855–1920), German cantor and one of the early research workers in Jewish music. Born in Cracow, he spent three years in Vienna studying *ḥazzanut* with Solomon *Sulzer. In 1872 he was appointed assistant cantor of the Magdeburg community. Two years later he became chief cantor of Beuthen, where his duties allowed him to travel to other cities and meet cantors and scholars. He started to collect printed and manuscript music, literature and documents, which became source material for his research and led directly to his critical essay on the *Baal T'fillah* of Abraham *Baer (*Das juedische Literaturblatt,* nos. 24 and 27, 1878). In 1879, Birnbaum succeeded Ẓvi Hirsch Weintraub as chief cantor of Koenigsberg and held this position till his death. Many young cantors came to study with him and some were stimulated to undertake research. He conducted educational work among cantors and teachers by means of lectures and the publication of printed material (*Liturgische Uebungen,* 2 vols., 1900, 1912). He also composed liturgical works, some of which were published after his death (*Aseh le-Ma'an, Ha-Melekh, Kedushah, Lekhah Dodi* in the supplements of *Der juedische Kantor,* 1927–31). Birnbaum's most important achievements were his writings and the "Birnbaum collection," subsequently acquired by the Hebrew Union College, Cincinnati. These contain his thematic catalogue of synagogal melodies, comprising about 7,000 cards, and his collection of references to music in rabbinic texts.

Bibliography: Sendrey, Music, indexes; A. Friedmann, *Dem Andenken Eduard Birnbaums* (1922); E. Werner, in: HUCA, 18 (1943–44), 397–428. [H.B.-D.]

BIRNBAUM, NATHAN (1864–1937), writer (early pen name: **Mathias Acher**), philosopher, one of the originators of Zionist ideology, later a leader of religious Judaism. Born in Vienna of parents of Galician and Hungarian origin, his rabbinical ancestry can be traced back to the Middle Ages. At school he became estranged from observant Judaism. He did not, however, follow the assimilationist path of that period, but conceived the idea that the Jews were an ethnic entity, a people, and propagated his ideas among his schoolmates. In his first year at the Vienna university he founded, together with Reuben *Bierer and Moritz *Schnirer, Kadimah, the first Jewish nationalist students' organization (1882). In 1884 his first publication appeared, a pamphlet called *Die Assimilationssucht, Ein Wort an die sogenannten Deutschen, Slaven, Magyaren etc. mosaischer Confession von einem Studenten juedischer Nationalitaet.* In 1885 he founded and edited the first Jewish nationalist journal in German, *Selbstemanzipation,* where he coined the term "Zionism." The policy and name of the journal came from Leo *Pinsker's pamphlet "Autoemanzipation." Birnbaum was, during the decade 1885–1895, "the most distinguished intellectual personality in Jewish national circles in Austria and Germany" (Bein). In 1893 he published *Die nationale Wiedergeburt des juedischen Volkes als Mittel zur Loesung der Judenfrage, Ein Appell an die Guten und Edlen aller Nationen,* a summing up of his first Zionist phase. He now gradually passed to a cultural conception of Zionism, as evidenced by his publication *Die juedische Moderne* (1896) and his official address, *Zionism as a Cultural Movement,* at the First Zionist Congress (1897). After a short period of service as chief secretary of the central Zionist office run by *Herzl, ideological disagreements broke out between the two, and after the Second Zionist Congress (1898)

Nathan Birnbaum, writer and philosopher. Etching by Joseph Budko, 1912. London, J. Fraenkel.

Birnbaum became a spokesman for "diaspora nationalism," publishing articles in which he severely criticized Herzl's "diplomatism," the "inorganic" nature of the Zionist movement, and the Zionist "negation of the Diaspora." He gradually withdrew from Zionism, affirming that "Israel comes before Zion," i.e., that the striving for Ereẓ Israel must not entail neglect of the Jewish People itself. His concept was now that of an interterritorial nation, comprising and integrating all existing Jewish groups which had a cultural life of their own. The most important group in his eyes was the Yiddish-speaking one in Eastern Europe. The political aspect of these ideas found expression in a demand for the cultural autonomy of the Jews, in conformity with the autonomy principle for the various peoples of the Austro-Hungarian Empire which was then gaining ground. One of its cornerstones was language. In the case of the Jews this was Yiddish. Birnbaum set about working for its recognition as a language in its own right and an important cultural value, mainly through articles in his weekly *Neue Zeitung* (1906–1907). He learned Yiddish himself and used it as a literary medium. In 1907 he was the Lemberg Zionist candidate to the Austrian Reichsrat, but was defeated by the Polish candidate. In 1908, while on a visit to America, he proposed that a world conference on behalf of Yiddish should be called. This took place in Czernowitz in 1908 with the participation of the leading Yiddish writers. A resolution was passed there declaring Yiddish to be a (not the) national language of the Jewish people. From 1908 to 1911 Birnbaum lived in Czernowitz, publishing the newspapers *Dos Folk* and *Vokhen-Blat*.

Birnbaum's acquaintance with East European Jewry was now deepening and he "arrived at the religious core of the nation." His basic attitude underwent a change. The atheism of his materialist philosophy as well as his secular nationalism were gradually replaced by the conviction that the vocation and destiny of the Jewish People was a religious one. Finally, "God entered into his consciousness." The turning point seems to have been an intimate religious experience in 1908. He later wrote that he had not "sought" God but that God had "sought" him. During the next few years before World War I his writings and lectures dealt with problems of religion. He gradually accepted the Jewish tradition and way of life, and finally joined the ranks of religious Jewry as a practicing Jew. However, he did not feel satisfied with the state of affairs he met with there. He maintained that religious Jewry was not making a serious attempt at fulfilling its world mission as an exemplary people living on the basis of God's Word. He outlined a program toward effecting a change. Those things in the environments, occupations and habits of the Jews which were barring the way to spiritual advancement must be altered. The highest authority of the Jewish nation was to be vested in a body of Guardians of the Faith. The first step would be the founding of a small community of "Those Who (want to) Ascend" (Ḥever Olim), who would act as a nucleus, and for whom he laid down a scheme for disciplined living. These ideas were embodied in *Et La'asot* ("The Time Has Come for Action") and *Divrei ha-Olim* ("The Words of Those Who (want to) Ascend," both in 1917, Heb. and Yid.). He repudiated his own former "pagan-Jewish" life in *Gottes Volk* (1917), further editions in 1918 and 1921). In *Vom Freigeist zum Glaeubigen* (1919) he described his spiritual development. Upon the refounding of the *Agudat Israel World Organization (1919) he became its first general secretary. At that time, after the war, revolution, and pogroms in Eastern Europe, he devoted much effort to the problem of emigration and endeavored to enlist general Jewish cooperation toward regulating on a big scale what amounted to an organized, panic mass flight.

His book *Im Dienste der Verheissung* (1927) contains a critical analysis of the "activism" of the Orthodox as a grafting of fashionable ideologies onto an organism that was inherently of a different nature and suggested to the "activists" a more fruitful field—the gigantic task of creating the necessary material preconditions toward effecting a metamorphosis. Nearness to God can only result from a complete inner transformation of the masses through their sociological restratification in favor of a life based mainly on agriculture, and this is to be achieved by the large-scale colonization of sparsely populated or practically uninhabited territories. The anarchy in the life of the Jewish community can be remedied by the establishment not of an interterritorial, state-like organization but of an interterritorial "All Israel Congregation," under authoritative spiritual leadership. The next publication devoted to these ideas was the journal *Der Aufstieg* (1930–1933), many of whose pages were written by himself. At the advent of Hitler (1933) he left Berlin where he had lived most of the time since 1911, and settled in the Hague-Scheveningen, where he published a journal *Der Ruf* (1934–1937). A series of articles were republished in a booklet, *Rufe* (1936), his "testament to the Jewish People." "The great ideal is to create the new Jew, based in the Torah, near to nature and to God, creative, harmonious, happy." There are three books of selections from his writings: from his secular period, *Ausgewaehlte Schriften zur juedischen Frage* (1910), from his early religious phase, *Um die Ewigkeit* (1920) and from the later one, *Et La'asot* (1938, in Yid.). His son, Solomon *Birnbaum, edited a selection of his works, *The Bridge* (1956).

Bibliography: S. Birnbaum, in: L. Jung (ed.), *Men of the Spirit* (1964), 519–49; J. Fraenkel, in: JSOS, 16 (1954), 115–34; A. E. Kaplan and M. Landau (eds.), *Vom Sinn des Judentums* (1925); *Der Freistaat* (May and June 1914); A. Boehm, *Die zionistische Bewegung*, 1 (1935), 135–8; L. Hermann, *Nathan Birnbaum* (Ger., 1914); *Davar, Literary Supplement* (May 7, 1937); J. Fraenkel, in: *Shivat Ẓiyyon*, 2–3 (1953), 275–99; Kressel, *ibid.*, 4 (1956), 55–99; L. S. Dawidowicz (ed.), *The Golden Tradition* (1967), index.

[ED.]

BIRNBAUM, PHILIP (1904–), U.S. author and translator. Birnbaum was born in Kielce, Poland, and went to the United States in 1923. He supported himself by teaching Hebrew and directing Hebrew schools. Birnbaum's annotated editions of the *Daily Prayer Book* (1950) and the *High Holyday Prayer Book* (1951), which he also translated, won wide acceptance. Among his many other publications are *The Arabic Commentary of Yefet Ben Ali on Hosea* (1942), *Hebrew-English Abridged Edition of the Rambam's "Mishneh Torah"* (1942), *A Book of Jewish Concepts* (1964), and *Ha-Siddur ha-Shalem—Nosaḥ Sefarad* (1969). Birnbaum contributed numerous articles to English and Hebrew periodicals and newspapers. [ED.]

BIRNBAUM, SOLOMON ASHER (1891–), paleographer and Yiddish philologist. The son of Nathan *Birnbaum, he studied architecture in his native Vienna. After World War I, during which he was seriously wounded, he specialized in Oriental languages in various European universities. Birnbaum was lecturer in Yiddish at Hamburg University from 1922 until he immigrated to England in 1933. There he taught Yiddish and Hebrew paleography at the London School of Oriental Studies (1936–57) and at the School of Slavonic and East European Studies (1939–58). He wrote for Yiddish newspapers and journals and published a German work on Yiddish grammar (1919, 1966[2]) and *Specimens of Yiddish from the Eighth Century Onward* (1965). Birnbaum translated stories of Mendele Mokher

Seforim from Yiddish into German (1924–25) and Max Brod's novel *Tycho Brahes Weg zu Gott* into Yiddish (1921). From *Shivḥei ha-Besht* he adapted *Leben und Worte des Balschem* (1920; *Life and Sayings of the Baal Shem,* 1933), and edited a selection of essays by his father, *The Bridge* (1956). Birnbaum's major work is in paleography.

Solomon Asher Birnbaum, paleographer and philologist.

His *Hebrew Scripts* (parts 2–4, 1954–57), contain examples of Hebrew manuscripts in the form of charts illustrating the evolution of Hebrew script. He also wrote *The Qumran (Dead Sea) Scrolls and Paleology* (1952).

Bibliography: Rejzen, Leksikon, s.v.; LNYL, s.v. [A.M.H.]

BIRNBAUM, URIEL (1894–1956), poet and artist; son of Nathan *Birnbaum. Born in Vienna, he embarked on his career as an artist and poet at a very early age. His graphic and literary output continued throughout World War I, even after he was severely wounded when fighting in the Austrian Army. His war experiences found expression in a volume of sonnets, *In Gottes Krieg* (1921). Between the wars he published several portfolios and volumes of lithographs and paintings: *Weltuntergang* (1921), *Das Buch Jona* (1921), *Der Kaiser und der Architekt* (1924), *Moses* (1924). When Austria was occupied by Nazi Germany he was granted entry to the Netherlands, upon the intervention of leading Dutch artists. Here he continued to write but had to give up

"Jonah preaching to the Ninevites," from Uriel Birnbaum's volume of lithographs, *Das Buch Jona,* 1921. Jerusalem, J.N.U.L.

his graphic work for lack of artists' materials. A selection he made from his poetical output *(Gedichte, eine Auswahl),* appeared in 1957. Birnbaum had very early in life turned away from the materialistic philosophy of the period and became a believer. He developed into an uncompromising fighter against fashionable modern ideologies. He was also opposed to nationalism and approved of the multinational state of old Austria.

Bibliography: A. Polzer-Hoditz, *Uriel Birnbaum Dichter-Maler-Denker* (1936); A. Horodisch, *Die Exlibris des Uriel Birnbaum* (1957). [Ed.]

BIRNBOIM, MOSES JOSEPH (1789–1831), secret agent of the czarist police and blackmailer. He started to work for the Warsaw police in 1820, in charge of about 30 servants set to spy on their employers, mostly persons prominent in Polish political and economic life. Later sent to Germany, he mixed in Polish student circles purporting to be an opponent of czarist absolutism in order to gain the students' confidence. He subsequently returned to Warsaw, using his position to blackmail Jews, exploiting the czarist anti-ḥasidic legislation, and earning the hatred of both Jews and Poles, until he himself was denounced to the police. In an effort to save himself he apostatized and adopted the name Mateusz Józef, but was arrested in 1824 and in 1830 sentenced to ten years' imprisonment. During the Polish uprising of 1831, Birnboim, along with many traitors and others hated by the Poles, was taken from prison by Jews, brought to Franciszkańska Street in Warsaw, where most of his Jewish victims lived, and hanged on a lantern.

Bibliography: Warszawski, in: *YIVO Historishe Shriftn,* 2 (1937), 335–54; J. Shatzky, *Geshikhte fun Yidn in Varshe,* 1 (1947), 327–8. [Ed.]

BIRÓ (Blau), LAJOS (1880–1948), Hungarian author and playwright. Biró was born in Vienna. He studied in Hungary, and became a journalist working for the liberal *Budapesti Napló* and the radical *Világ.* In 1906, for political reasons, he went with his family to Berlin, but returned to Budapest in 1909. During the October Revolution of 1918, Biró was appointed secretary of state at the Foreign Ministry. However, he left Hungary and finally settled in Great Britain, where together with Sir Alexander *Korda he founded the London Film Production Company, of which he remained a director until his death. Biró's Hungarian writing covered short stories and drama. The former included *Huszonegy novella* ("Twenty-one short stories," 1908) and *Kunszállási emberek* ("People of Kunszállás," 1912), and among his plays were *Sárga liliom* ("Yellow Lily," 1912) and *Hotel Imperial* (1917). In his later years he turned to writing film scripts, of which the most famous were *The Way of All Flesh* and *The Private Life of Henry VIII.* In 1921, when living in Vienna, he published *A bazini zsidók* ("The Jews of Bazin"), a story about a blood libel in 1529, when the entire Jewish community of a village near Pressburg was tortured and burned to death. In this vivid description. Biró depicts the fate of the Jew in the Diaspora. In his essay, *A zsidók útja* (1921, "The Way of the Jews") he rejected both assimilation and Jewish nationalism, defining the Jewish question as unanswerable, but enthusiastically accepting the existence and continuity of the Jewish people.

Bibliography: *Magyar Zsidó Lexikon* (1929), 126; *Magyar Irodalmi Lexikon* (1963), 165–6. [B.Y.]

BIROBIDZHAN, colloquial name of the region (oblast) in the Russian S.F.S.R., for which the official designation is the "Jewish Autonomous Region" *Avtonomnaya Oblast).* Part of the Khabarovsk territory

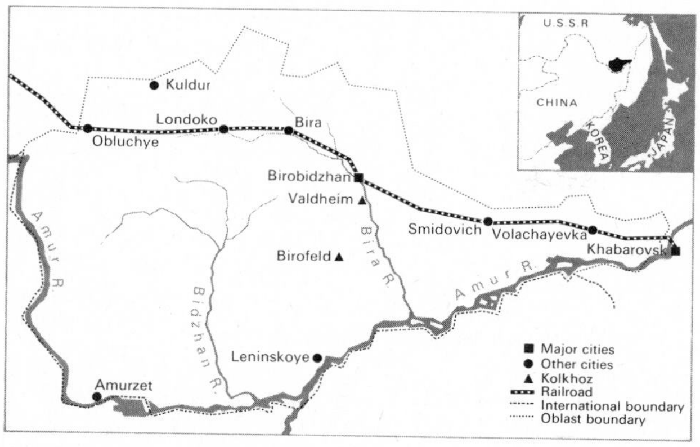

Map of the Birobidzhan region.

(kray) in the Soviet Far East, the region is located between 47° 40′–49° 20′ N. and 130° 30′–135° E. To the west, south, and southeast, it is bordered by the Amur River, the boundary between the U.S.S.R. and Manchuria (China). Its area is 13,900 sq. mi. (36,000 sq. km.). On Jan. 1, 1961, the estimated population of the region numbered 179,000 and that of the capital, the city of Birobidzhan, 49,000. The Jewish population of the region numbered 14,269 (8.8% of the total) in 1959, of these 83.9% lived in cities and urban settlements while 16.1% lived in villages. (By 1970, the Jewish population was thought to have dropped further.) The capital is located on the Bolshaya Bira River and on the Trans-Siberian Railroad which cuts through the northern sector of the territory from west to east. Its industries include farm machinery, transformers, textiles, clothing, and furniture. The climate is influenced by the prevailing monsoons and the surrounding mountains to the west and north. It improves progressively southward, the most favorable conditions prevailing in the Amur River strip in the southern part of the region. The winter is cold and dry with little snow, spring is mild, summer is hot and humid, and fall is dry and pleasant. Birobidzhan has numerous rivers and lakes abounding with fish. Most of its area is composed of heavy soils with an excess of moisture. A considerable part consists of swamps and about one-third is covered with forest. Birobidzhan has abundant mineral wealth, for the most part not commercially exploited, except for tin ores which are the basis of a large national metallurgical works, the "Khinganolovo." Grains, pulses, potatoes, vegetables, and other crops are grown. However, at the time when Jewish settlement began there, the region suffered from an almost complete absence of roads and land suitable for agriculture, insufficient and poor living accommodations, harsh climatic conditions, *"gnus"* (local name for bloodsucking insects), and unsanitary conditions. The Soviet decision to select Birobidzhan for Jewish settlement was influenced by several factors, the decisive one being the desire to strengthen the security of the Soviet Far East, in view of its proximity to Japan and the danger of penetration by the Chinese. The settlement of Birobidzhan became of particular importance to the U.S.S.R. after the Japanese occupation of Manchuria in 1931–32. Since the Soviet government attempted in the late 1920s and early 1930s to improve its relations with the West, the Birobidzhan project could have also played a role in influencing Jewish and pro-Jewish public opinion there. The association of Jews with the settlement of Birobidzhan was also meant to obtain financial support from their conationals abroad, and thus alleviate the allocation of Soviet resources for this purpose. Moreover, such settlement seemed to provide a partial solution to the economic difficulties facing Soviet nationalities. To some of those active in the *Yevsektsiya (the Jewish Section of the Communist Party), Birobidzhan seemed to constitute an ideological alternative to the Zionist idea. The first official step toward implementation of the project was the dispatch of a scientific delegation to Birobidzhan in the summer of 1927, to investigate the feasibility of an agricultural settlement there. Its recommendations led to a resolution by the presidium of the central executive committee of the Soviet Union on March 28, 1928, to entrust Komzet (committee for settling Jews on the land) with the supervision of Jewish settlement in the region. On May 7, 1934, the "Birobidzhan district" *(rayon)*, which had been established in 1930, was granted the status of the "Jewish Autonomous Region" (J.A.R.), by a decree of the central executive committee.

Jewish immigration to Birobidzhan began in April 1928, and continued at a varying rate. Colonization proceeded under most difficult conditions, especially at the beginning. The first year proved particularly difficult, with heavy rains, floods, and an outbreak of anthrax (horse disease). In the following years a comparatively large number of Jewish settlers arrived in Birobidzhan. However, the unsuitable absorption facilities and difficult climatic conditions seriously affected the rate of those who stayed there permanently. Out of prospective settlers who arrived between 1928 and 1933 more than half left. The Birobidzhan project aroused a controversy among those active in Jewish settlement in the U.S.S.R. and among the Yevsektsiya leaders. Among the critics were Mikhail (Yuri) *Larin and Abraham Bragin, both active in the Jewish settlement movement. Larin argued that other areas of the Soviet Union, especially the Crimea, were far more suitable for Jewish colonization. The Birobidzhan project found an ardent supporter in Mikhail Kalinin, the titular head of state. In a speech delivered at a congress of the society for Jewish agricultural settlement, Ozet, in 1926, before the Birobidzhan project was born, he had declared: "The Jewish people now faces the great task of preserving its nationality. For this purpose a large segment of the Jewish population must transform itself into a compact farming population, numbering at least several hundred thousand souls." In a reception given to representatives of Moscow workers and the Yiddish press in May 1934, he suggested that the creation of a Jewish territorial center in Birobidzhan would be the only way to normalize the national status of Soviet Jews. He also expressed his hope that "Within a decade Birobidzhan will be the most important and probably the only bulwark of national Jewish socialist culture," and that "the transformation of the region into a republic is only a question of time." The visit of Lazar *Kaganovich, a Jew and member of the Politburo, to Birobidzhan in February 1936, greatly encouraged the Jewish leadership of the region. Birobidzhan aroused wide interest in world Jewry,

Figure 1. The Birobidzhan railroad station, c. 1935. Jerusalem, C.A.H.J.P.

especially among those who believed in Jewish *territorialism. The fact that Jewish settlement in Birobidzhan coincided with the intensification of anti-Jewish repressions in Nazi Germany also contributed to support of the idea by Jews outside the Soviet Union. Almost all sectors of the Zionist movement opposed it. Jewish organizations outside the U.S.S.R. which participated in Jewish colonization projects in the Soviet Union, such as Agro-Joint (American Jewish Joint Agricultural Corporation), and the *Jewish Colonization Association (ICA) generally took a neutral stand. The *Ort-Farband lent limited assistance to the development of industry and workshops. Those Jewish organizations abroad whose membership consisted mostly of Communists and their sympathizers supported the plan without reservation. Among the most active organizations was Icor (the American Association for Jewish Colonization in the Soviet Union), which cooperated closely with Ozet. In 1929 Icor organized a scientific delegation consisting of American specialists in agriculture and settlement to investigate the possibilities for further colonization of Birobidzhan. Ambidjan (American Committee for the Settlement of foreign Jews in Birobidzhan) supported Jewish settlement in Birobidzhan for a short period in the mid-1930s and after World War II. Jewish organizations supporting Birobidzhan existed in Canada, Western Europe, and South America. Representatives of the Argentinian Jewish organization Procor (Society to assist the Productivization of the economically ruined Jewish Masses in the Soviet Union) visited Birobidzhan in 1929. These organizations, besides holding meetings, issuing publications, and collecting money, also propagandized the colonization of Birobidzhan by Jews from abroad. Thus, about 1,400 Jewish immigrants from countries outside the Soviet Union arrived in Birobidzhan in the early '30s from the United States, South America, Europe, Palestine and other countries.

From the beginning of Jewish colonization in Birobidzhan, and particularly in the mid-1930s, much was accomplished to promote the Jewish character of Birobidzhan. Jewish collective farms were established and Jewish village councils organized. Jews served in key positions of the region. Y. Levin, formerly active in the party apparatus in Belorussia and in the secretariat of Ozet, was appointed as first party secretary of the Birobidzhan district in 1930. After the establishment of the J.A.R. in 1934, another Jew, M. Khavkin, was appointed first secretary of the regional party committee. Joseph Liberberg, head of the Jewish section of the Ukrainian Academy of Sciences, was appointed at the same time chairman of the regional executive committee. He was one of those intellectuals, who, by settling in Birobidzhan, inspired others in their pioneering efforts. A number of resolutions were passed regarding the use of Yiddish as the official language of the region, along with Russian. Schools were established with Yiddish as the language of instruction, and experiments were made to teach Yiddish even in non-Jewish schools. Street signs, rail station signs, and postmarks appeared in both Russian and Yiddish. A Yiddish newspaper and periodicals were published. In 1934 a Jewish state theater was established. A regional library, named after Shalom Aleichem, containing a sizable collection of Judaica and Yiddish works, was founded in the city of Birobidzhan. The mid-1930s was a period of great expectations for Birobidzhan's development as a center of Jewish settlement and culture in the Soviet Union. However, the purges of 1936–38 delivered a severe blow to the developing and rather weak framework of the nascent Jewish statehood in the J.A.R. Leading Jewish personalities of the region, such as Liberberg, were denounced as nationalists and Trotskyites, demoted from their posts, and liquidated. The purges particularly affected the immigrants from abroad. As a result, the late 1930s witnessed a shattering setback in the development of the region. Despite the optimistic plans for continuous settlement of Jews in Birobidzhan, their number did not exceed 20,000 on the eve of World War II. The Soviet annexation of the Baltic states and parts of eastern Poland and Bukovina in 1939–40 resulted in a sudden increase in the Jewish population of the U.S.S.R. During that period plans were initiated to transfer Jewish settlers from the annexed territories to Birobidzhan. However, the outbreak of the Soviet-German war in 1941 put a fast end to these plans. Although the war years did not witness any sizable increase in the Jewish population of the region, the very idea of Birobidzhan as a center for Jewish statehood in the Soviet Union received new meaning.

The Holocaust and growth of anti-Semitism in the U.S.S.R. during the war resulted in revived interest in the J.A.R. among Soviet Jews. The growth of national feelings and the difficulties faced by Soviet Jews who had fled to the East, upon their return to their prewar homes in the western parts of the U.S.S.R. caused some to turn to Birobidzhan. Moreover, since the hopes for a planned settlement of Jews in the Crimea did not materialize, Birobidzhan remained the only alternative for a compact Jewish settlement. Numerous requests for immigration to Birobidzhan were received by the J.A.R. authorities in the postwar years, and a flow of new Jewish settlers reached the region between 1946 and 1948. Articles in the *Eynikayt,* organ of the Jewish anti-Fascist Committee, emphasized the idea of Jewish statehood in Birobidzhan. The Soviet Jewish writer *Der Nister, who accompanied a trainload of new settlers, wrote: "There are some travelers whose intentions are only materialistic, and there are others whose intentions are different, of a national character . . . and there are also burning enthusiasts, ready to give up everything in order to live there . . . and among them a former Palestinian patriot. . . . Although in his fifties, he hustles about during the day and is sleepless at night, hoping to see his new enterprise come true. . . ." The short postwar migration to Birobidzhan increased the local Jewish population by one-third, and by the end of 1948 it was estimated at about 30,000, the largest ever in the region. The postwar period witnessed an increase in the number of Jews in the local administration and an intensification of Jewish cultural activities. Among local Jewish writers active in the "Soviet Writers' Association of the J.A.R." were Buzi Miler, Israel *Emiot, Ḥayyim Maltinski, Aaron *Vergelis, and others. Assistance from Jews abroad was permitted once again. The revival of Birobidzhan as a Jewish center came to a halt toward the end of 1948, as a result of Soviet policy to suppress Jewish activities throughout the U.S.S.R., and purge those involved. While the purges of the late 1930s mainly affected individual Jews holding official positions, those of 1948 and thereafter aimed to destroy any sort of Jewish activity in the region. Thus, most of the local Jewish writers were imprisoned, the Birobidzhan Jewish theater

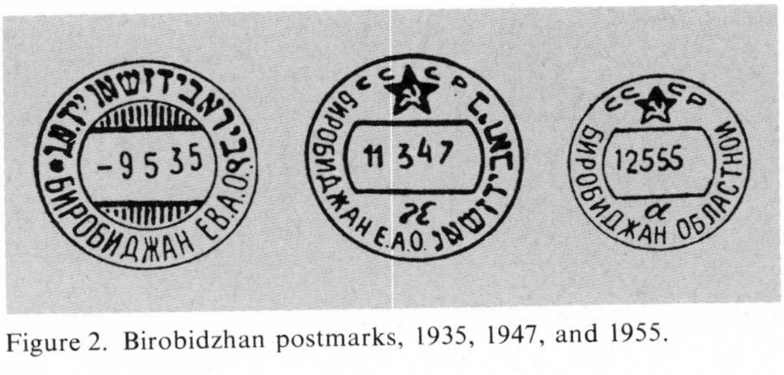

Figure 2. Birobidzhan postmarks, 1935, 1947, and 1955.

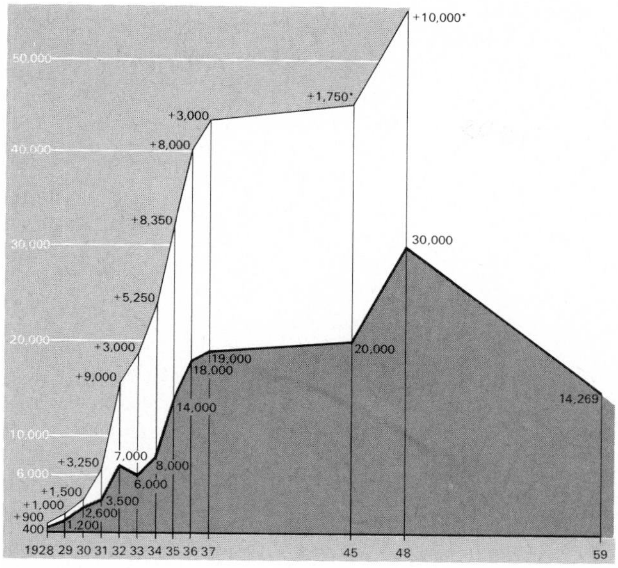

Jewish population of Birobidzhan, 1928–59. The lower graph shows the total Jewish population, the upper one the immigration into the region.

was closed, teaching of Yiddish in local schools was discontinued, and a great number of Yiddish books were removed from the Shalom Aleichem Library. Jewish immigration to Birobidzhan ceased, and its Jewish population shrank considerably. The post-Stalin period did not bring any substantial changes to Jewish life in Birobidzhan. Jewish inhabitants comprised less than one-tenth of the general population of the region in 1959, party and administrative positions were not generally held by Jews, and Jewish agriculture was almost nonexistent. The sole kolkhoz with a comparatively large Jewish membership is that of Valdheim in the vicinity of the capital; but it is now only a branch of the large kolkhoz "Ilich's Wills" and its Jewish population is diminishing. Such key positions as secretary or chairman of the local party regional and district committees (the region is divided into five administrative districts) are generally not held by Jews although in 1970 Lev Shapiro was appointed first secretary of the regional Communist Party organization. Of the five deputies to the Council of Nationalities of the U.S.S.R. only a minority is Jewish. The sole expression of Jewish cultural activity in 1970 was a two-page Yiddish newspaper, *Der Birobidzhaner Shtern,* nearly devoid of all Jewish content, which appeared three times weekly and had a circulation of 1,000. There were also a few street signs in Yiddish, and Shalom Aleichem Street remained one of the thoroughfares of the capital. There was one synagogue. All official and public business was conducted exclusively in Russian. N. S. Khrushchev, Soviet premier and first party secretary, stated in an interview for *Le Figaro,* which appeared on April 9, 1958, that "It must be admitted that if we strike a balance we would have to state that the Jewish settlement in Birobidzhan was a failure." He further put the blame for it upon the Soviet Jews, who, according to Khrushchev, never liked collective work and group discipline. It is difficult to ascribe the failure of the Birobidzhan experiment to one single cause. In the history of the Jewish people it belongs to the series of other futile attempts at planned Jewish mass settlement, based on agriculture, whose failure is often attributed to its implicit or explicit negation of the ultimate return to Zion. However, viewed in the context of Soviet Jewish reality, the immediate cause of its failure was undoubtedly the fact that twice, in 1936–37 and in 1948–49, the Stalinist purges put a brutal end to the short periods of developing a Jewish autonomous life and culture in Birobidzhan.

Bibliography: S. Schwarz, *The Jews in the Soviet Union* (1951), index; idem, in: J. Frumkin (ed.) *Russian Jewry 1917–1967* (1969), 342–95; A. L. Eliav (Benami), *Between Hammer and Sickle* (1969), 176–88; S. W. Baron, *The Russian Jew under Tsars and Soviets* (1964), index; J. Lvavi, *Ha-Hityashevut ha-Yehudit be-Birobidzhan* (1965); A. G. Duker, *Jewish Survival in the World Today* (1939), 47–59; idem, in: *Contemporary Jewish Record* (March–April 1939), 24–26; J. Emiot, *Der Birobidzhaner Inyen* (1960); *Jews in Eastern Europe* (1966ff.), index; Z. Katz, in: *Bulletin on Soviet Jewish Affairs,* 2 (July, 1968); C. Abramsky, in: L. Kochan (ed.), *Jews in Soviet Russia since 1917* (1970), 62–75 (incl. bibl.).

[J.Lv./Shi.R.]

BIRTH. The injunction to "be fruitful and multiply" (Gen. 1:28) is regarded as the first commandment of the Bible. As a consequence of the disobedience of Eve in the Garden of Eden, the pangs of childbirth were foretold (Gen. 3:16). References to pangs of travail as the most intense of pains are very frequent in the books of the prophets (e.g., Jer. 6:24; 22:23; 49:24; 50:43; and Micah 4:9–10). Midwives assisted in the delivery (Gen. 35:17), and it seems that a birthstool, called *ʾovnayim,* was often used (Ex. 1:16). The Bible records the deaths of Rachel (Gen. 35:18) and the daughter-in-law of Eli (I Sam. 4:20) in childbirth. The Talmud states that Michal (II Sam. 6:23) also died during childbirth (Sanh. 21a).

Biblical law regarding birth is confined to laying down the period of ritual impurity of the mother (Lev. 12). The mother of a male child is unclean for seven days, followed by a 33-day period of impurity; these periods are doubled in the case of a female child. At the conclusion of these periods a sin-offering and burnt-offering were brought by the mother. According to the Talmud, the sin-offering is incumbent upon her because during the anguish of childbirth, she foreswears any future relations with her husband, which she later regrets (Nid. 31b).

In the Talmud. The sages attributed death during childbirth to neglect of the laws of family purity, failure to separate the dough-offering, and carelessness in kindling the Sabbath lights (Shab. 2:6). Viability began from the time the fetus was six months and one day old, although it was considered as a fact that an eight-month-old fetus was not viable (Tosef., Shab. 15:7; see *Abortion). Before

Figure 1. A protective prayer for women in childbirth engraved by Abraham b. Jacob, Amsterdam, late 17th century. The central panel depicts Adam and Eve in Eden. The Hebrew text says, "Adam and Eve—out Lilith! Sanoi and Sansanoi, and Samnaglof the Angels—destroy Satan!" According to legend Lilith was the queen of demons and Adam's first wife, and was thought to wish to kill newborn children.

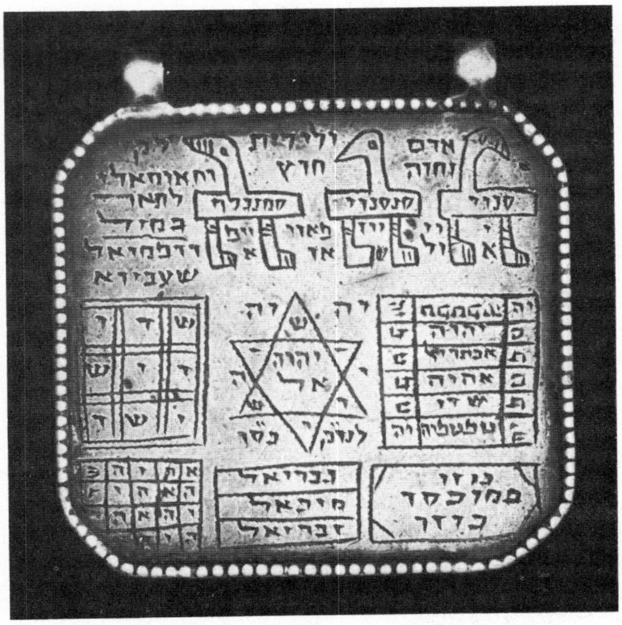

Figure 2. Silver amulet for the protection of a newborn child, Persia, 18th century. The *Magen David* with the Tetragrammaton, intended to invoke the holy Name, is flanked by magic acrostics, and below are the names of the angels Gabriel, Michael, and Zavdiel. Tel Aviv, Einhorn Collection.

birth, it is permissible to perform an embryotomy when the mother's life is in danger, since "her life comes before that of the child." Once the greater part of the child has been born, or his head alone has emerged from the birth canal, he is considered a living being and the mother's life no longer takes precedence (Oho. 7:6). The child is not considered viable until it is 30 days old. No death penalty is therefore incurred for killing a newborn child unless it is certain that he could otherwise have lived for 30 days (Nid. 5:3, Nid. 44b). All work necessary for the delivery of a child may be performed on the Sabbath (Shab. 18:3); if the mother dies during labor, the Sabbath must still be desecrated and all attempts made to save the unborn child (Ar. 7a).

For the purposes of birthdate and setting the time of circumcision, birth is determined by the projection of the fetus' head out of the birth canal (Nid. 42b). The delivery of a child by Caesarean section was not regarded as "an opening of the womb" (Ex. 13:2), and the child had neither the privileges nor the obligations of the firstborn (Bek. 8:2).

Birth—Customs and Folklore. Most of the customs surrounding birth belong to the category of popular folklore, much of which is not specifically Jewish but was adapted from local cultural surroundings (Tosef., Shab. 6:4; Sh. Ar. YD 178). The following biblical selections were recited for a woman in labor: Psalms 20; I Samuel 1; or Genesis 21:1–8 (Sephardi custom). A magic circle was drawn with chalk or charcoal on the floor of the room to guard against evil spirits. As a good omen for easy and speedy delivery, all the ties and knots in a woman's garments were undone and all doors in the house were opened wide. If her travail was difficult, the keys of the synagogue were placed in her hand, she was girded with the band of a Torah Scroll, and prayers were recited at the graveside of pious relatives. At times the circumference of the cemetery walls was measured and according to the length a number of candles were donated to the synagogue. Mother and child were surrounded by various charms and talismans from the moment of birth until the circumcision. Most of these charms were to guard them against the female demon *Lilith, and they were known by different names, such as *kimpetsetl* (from *kindbet*, "child bed" and *tsetl*, "a note"), *Shir Hamalos-Tsetl* (from *Shir ha-Ma'alot*—the Song of Degrees), and *Shmir-Tsetl* (from *shemirah*, "guarding"). They were placed above the bed of the woman and above the doorposts of the room.

A popular custom until modern times, in the case of the birth of a male child, was the vigil ceremony which was performed every night. In Oriental communities it was called *taḥdid*. Friends and relatives nightly gathered at the home of the newborn to recite the **Shema* in order to protect the child from demons. Schoolchildren led by their teachers also participated in this ceremony and were rewarded with apples, nuts, and sweets.

Whereas a boy is named at the circumcision, a girl is usually named in the synagogue when the father can be called to the reading of the Torah. Another custom was to name the child when her mother visited the synagogue for the first time after rising from childbed. An Order of Service was prescribed for this visit (see Hertz, Prayer, 1038–41). In Germany and Western Europe the naming took place in a home ceremony on Sabbath mornings, called *Hohekreisch*, the custom originated in German folklore and superstition.

Oriental Customs. Among the methods utilized to protect the mother and infant from evil spirits—particularly *Broshah*, the female demon who steals newborn children—was the hanging of a *hamsikah*, an *amulet in the shape of the palm of the hand with fingers, or a seven-branched candelabrum. Amulets containing biblical verses were also used, and it was customary to place sweetmeats under the bed so that the evil spirits would be occupied with eating them. In Salonika it was customary to leave the doors of the house and all its cupboards open during pregnancy to ensure that the mother would not miscarry. It was also customary to measure a string seven times around the grave of a renowned rabbi and then bind it around the stomach of the pregnant woman to ensure an easy pregnancy. The mother and her relatives also prayed at the graves of pious men in the fifth month of her pregnancy. To ensure that the child would be a male, the mother pronounced the intended name of a boy every Friday. She

Figure 3. Four engravings of childbirth scenes, with invocations of angels, from *Kirchliche Verfassung der heutigen Juden* by Johann Bodenschatz, Germany, 1748–49. Cecil Roth Collection.

was guarded for 15 days after birth, and blue beads or pieces of ivory and coral were hung above the cradle of the child. Garlic and other plants were hung in the room, and an open hand was painted on the door. An attempt was made to keep the mother awake for the first three days after birth to prevent Lilith from harming her. In Yemen, a festive meal, at which the name was given, was held on the third day. In Kurdistan the mother was not allowed to leave the house after nightfall for 40 days. Since delivery usually takes place now in modern hospitals, most of these traditional customs at childbirth have tended to disappear, particularly since they were primarily based on medieval superstitious folklore. Naming a daughter at the synagogue, however, has been retained in traditional, Conservative, and Reform Jewish practice.

See also *Circumcision.

Bibliography: I. Jakobovits, *Jewish Medical Ethics* (1959), 170–91; M. Perlman, *Midrash ha-Refu'ah,* 1 (1926), 18–25; E. Ilinson, in: *Sinai,* 66 (1969/70), 20–49. Customs and Folklore: Y. Yehoshua, *Yaldut bi-Y'rushalayim ha-Yeshanah,* 2 (1966), 79–91; Molcho, in: *Saloniki, Ir va-Em be-Yisrael* (1967), 188–93; M. Zadok, *Yehudei Teiman* (1967), 213–4; N. B. Gamlieli, *Teiman u-Maḥaneh "Ge'ullah"* (1966); H. Schauss, *The Lifetime of a Jew* (1950), 31–76; S. Schechter, *Studies in Judaism,* 1 (1896), 282–95, 358. [Ed.]

BIRTH CONTROL. Jewish tradition ascribed the practice of birth control to the depraved humanity before Noah (Gen. R. 23:2, 4; Rashi to Gen. 4:19, 23). The sole explicit reference in the Bible to what may be considered as some form of birth control occurs in Genesis 38:9–10: the Lord punished Onan by death because he had "spilled his seed on the ground" to prevent the birth of a child from the *levirate marriage to his deceased brother's wife Tamar. On the strength of this passage, and as constituting a deliberate violation of the first commandment to "be fruitful and multiply" (Gen. 1:28), the Talmud sternly inveighs against "bringing forth the seed in vain," considering it a cardinal sin (Nid. 13a). Legislation on contraception proper is to be found in a talmudic passage which permits (or requires, according to another view) the use of a contraceptive tampon by minor, pregnant, or lactating women, to prevent any danger to their own or their offspring's life resulting from a conception under those circumstances (Yev. 12b). A permissive ruling extended to women, but not to men, also allows for the use of a "cup of roots" or "potion of sterility" (Tosef., Yev. 8:4), probably some oral contraceptive known to the ancients, which was to produce temporary or in certain dosages even permanent sterility. While the medieval codes strangely omit any reference to physical birth control devices, they codify the permissive ruling on the oral sterilizing agent (Sh. Ar., EH, 5:12). It is in the rabbinic responsa, especially those of the past 200 years, that the attitude of Jewish law to birth control is defined and discussed in great detail. The many hundreds of rulings recorded in these responsa consider urgent medical reasons as the only valid justification for certain contraceptive precautions. Jewish law regards such decisions as capital judgments and it would, therefore, insist on dealing with each case on its individual merits and on the evidence of competent medical opinion. Where some grave hazard to the mother, however remote, is feared, as a result of pregnancy, the rabbinic attitude is usually quite liberal, all the more readily if the commandment of procreation (which technically requires having a son and a daughter) has already been fulfilled. Under no circumstances, however, does Jewish law sanction any contraceptive acts or safeguards on the part of the male, nor does it ever tolerate the use or distribution of birth control devices outside marriage. While the law proscribes sexual intercourse among spouses in times of famine (Ta'an. 11a; Sh. Ar. OḤ 240:12; 574:4), this is not to be taken as a recognition of the economic argument in favor of birth control. On the contrary, the restriction from which childless couples are in any case excluded is meant simply to curb the pleasures of marital indulgences at a time of great national suffering, just as conjugal relations are among the experiences of pleasure and comfort forbidden on days of national or private mourning. More characteristic of the spirit, if not the letter, of Jewish law is the story related in a famous 13th-century moralistic work: A poor person complained that he could not afford to support any more children and asked a sage for permission to prevent his wife from becoming pregnant again. The sage said: "When a child is born, the Holy One, blessed be He, provides the milk beforehand in the mother's breast; therefore, do not worry!" But the man continued to fret. Then a son was born to him. After a while the child became ill and the father turned to the sage: "Pray for my son that he shall live!" "To you applies the verse," exclaimed the sage, " 'Suffer not thy mouth to bring thy flesh into guilt' " (Eccles. 5:5; *Sefer Ḥasidim,* ed. R. Margoliot (1957), no. 520). The sources of Jewish law and morals do not present the problem of "the population explosion" as relevant to birth control. According to some rabbinic authorities, the restrictions on birth control do not necessarily apply to non-Jews as the latter are not held to be bound by the commandment to "be fruitful and multiply" (see *Mishneh le-Melekh,* to Maim., Yad, Melakhim 10:7). The threat of a "population explosion" is less likely to agitate a people that for most of its history has been threatened with virtual annihilation and is now haunted by the specter of "the vanishing Jew," due to the gross imbalance between a low natural increase and a high artificial decrease through drift, assimilation, and intermarriage. In recent times, the practice of birth control has invariably been more prevalent among Jews than other groups living in the same general society, as shown by the disproportionately low Jewish birthrates according to the latest comparative surveys in America, in Europe, and notably in Israel. In 1967, in Israel, the Jewish birthrate of 2.5% in the kibbutzim and only 1.3% in a city like Tel Aviv contrasts sharply with the non-Jewish birthrate inside Israel of nearly 5% (see *Statistical Abstract of Israel,* published by the Central Bureau of Statistics, Jerusalem, 1968). The Jewish birthrate is appreciably higher only among the strictly Orthodox who, for religious reasons, refuse to resort to birth control. In common with the attitude of most Protestant denominations, Reform Judaism would generally leave the decision on birth control to the individual conscience, recognizing social and economic factors no less than the medical motivation.

Bibliography: D. M. Feldman, *Birth Control in Jewish Law* (1969); E. Waldenberg, *Ẓiẓ Eli'ezer,* 9 (1967), 208–25 (extensive halakhic treatise); J. Z. Lauterbach, in: CCARY, 37 (1927), 369–84 (early Reform view); I. Jakobovits, *Jewish Medical Ethics* (1959), 167ff., and passim; idem, *Journal of a Rabbi* (1967²), 146–7, 163, 213–20; J. Levy, in: *No'am,* 11 (1968), 167–77. [I.J.]

BIRTHDAY. The celebration of birthdays is unknown in traditional Jewish ritual. A comparatively late exception, however, is the *bar mitzvah and the bat mitzvah. The only reference to a birthday in the Bible is that celebrated by Pharaoh (Gen. 40:20). In Reform and Conservative synagogues, special prayers of thanksgiving are recited on the occasion of significant birthdays (e.g., 50th, 70th, 80th, etc.) and at silver and golden wedding anniversaries.

Bibliography: *Rabbi's Manual* (1928–1962²), 45–49, C.C.A.R. (Reform); J. Harlow (ed.), *Likkutei Tefillah, A Rabbi's Manual* (1965), Conservative, 51–55. [Ed.]

BIRZAI (Lith. **Biržì**; Yid. בירזי), district capital in northern Lithuania, near the Latvian border. It had one of the oldest Jewish communities in northern Lithuania (in the area known as Zhmud = Samogitia) and constituted one of the three leading communities of the "*medinah* [province] of Zamut" (Zhmud) in the mid-17th to mid-18th century. A small Karaite community also existed there. The Jewish population numbered 1,040 in 1760; 1,685 in 1847; and 2,510 in 1897 (57% of the total). In 1915 the Jews were expelled from Birzai by the Russian military authorities. After the war some of the exiles returned. The Jewish community developed during the period of Lithuanian independence (1918–39). There were approximately 3,000 Jews living in Birzai in 1934 (about one-third of the total population), most earning their livelihood from trade in wood products and flax; several factories for weaving and spinning were owned by Jews.

The Jews there were murdered in the summer of 1941 shortly after the occupation of the town by the Germans.

Bibliography: *Yahadut Lita,* 2 (1967), 292–4. [Y.S.]

BIRZULA (from 1935, **Kotovsk**), town in Ukrainian S.S.R. Until May 1903 it was a village, and under the "Temporary Regulations" of 1882 (see *May Laws) Jews were prohibited from settling there. The Jewish inhabitants were attacked in a pogrom in October 1905. In 1919, 50 Jews were massacred in Birzula by the followers of Simon *Petlyura. The Jewish population numbered 2,507 in 1926 (25% of the total). Almost the entire community perished during the Nazi occupation.

Bibliography: *Judenpogrome in Russland,* 1 (1909); E. D. Rosenthal, *Megillat ha-Tevaḥ,* 1 (1927); Jewish Colonization Association, *Rapport pour l'année 1925,* (1927), 160–243. [Ed.]

BISCHHEIM, French town in the department of the Bas-Rhin. Jews settled there after their expulsion from *Colmar in 1512. H. *Cerfberr, one of the general syndics of Alsace Jewry in the second half of the 18th century, lived in Bischheim, as did his brother-in-law, David *Sinzheim. Cerfberr set up a foundation on behalf of the community with a capital of 175,000 livres for charitable activities and education. There were 473 Jews living in Bischheim in 1784. The wooden synagogue, built in 1781, was replaced by a new one in 1838. It was sacked during the German occupation in World War II, destroyed in 1944, and rebuilt in 1959. The Jewish community in 1968 had 360 members. It has a *mikveh* which belonged to David Sinzheim.

Bibliography: M. Ginsburger, *Histoire de la communauté israélite de Bischheim au Saum* (1937); E. Scheid, *Histoire des Juifs d'Alsace* (1887), 102, 175, 249; R. Berg, *La persécution raciale* (1947), 181; Z. Szajkowski, *Analytical Franco-Jewish Gazetteer* (1966), 45, 249. [R.Be.]

°**BISCHOFF, ERICH** (c. 1867–1936), German biblical and talmudic scholar. Bischoff repeatedly served as expert on Judaism in court cases, furnishing memoranda on the *blood libel, the ethics of the Talmud and the Shulḥan Arukh, etc. He refused to be termed either anti- or philo-Semitic, but was criticized by Jewish writers and organizations for his views (cf. C. Bloch, *Blut und Eros im Judentum,* 1935). In his *Klarheit in der Ostjudenfrage* (1916) he suggested the introduction of a special *Ostjuden* tax to be raised by Jewish organizations either to improve the conditions of unwanted Eastern European Jews in Germany or to settle them in Palestine. Among Bischoff's published works are also *Kritische Geschichte der Thalmud-Uebersetzungen aller Zeiten und Zungen* ... (1889); *Rabbinische Fabeln ueber Talmud, Schulchan Aruch, Kol Nidre* ... (1922); *Das Blut im juedischen Schrifttum und Brauch* (1929); and *Das Buch vom Schulchan Aruch* (1942^{4}!). Bischoff also edited and translated—from an Oxford manuscript—the famous anti-Christian tract *Toledot Yeshu* (*Ein juedisch-deutsches Leben Jesu,* 1895). Though Bischoff pretended to be objective in his judgment on Judaism, his work misinterpreted Jewish sources and was fully exploited by the Nazis. [A.Pa.]

BISCHOFFSHEIM, family of bankers in Belgium, Britain, and France. The family's founder Raphael (Nathan; 1773–1814) was born in Bischoffsheim on the Tauber and settled as a young man in Mainz, where he became a prominent merchant and president of the Jewish community. His elder son, Louis (Ludwig) Raphael (1800–1873) found work at a banking house in Frankfort. When he was twenty he moved to Amsterdam where he established a bank. Through his marriage to Amalie Goldschmidt, he became related to Europe's banking aristocracy. His business expanded rapidly and in 1827 he established a branch in Antwerp, in 1836 together with the Goldschmidt family a London branch known as Bischoffsheim and Goldschmidt, and in 1846 another branch in Paris. In 1848 he moved to Paris, where his bank cooperated with great French houses in national and international transactions. At some stages in the development of his banking business, he had the help of his nephew, Ludwig *Bamberger. His many philanthropies were devoted to charitable and educational purposes, including support of the Association Philotechnique of which he was president and the Athenée Theater, which he founded.

His brother, Raphael Jonathan (1808–1883), moved to Brussels in 1830 after Belgium achieved its independence and became one of that country's most influential financial figures. In 1850 he helped found the National Bank of Belgium and served on its board of directors for twenty years. He was adviser to the royal house and in 1862 became a senator, who was regarded by his colleagues as the principal authority in his field. He was an active member of the Jewish consistory and was well known for his benefactions, such as the endowment of a chair for

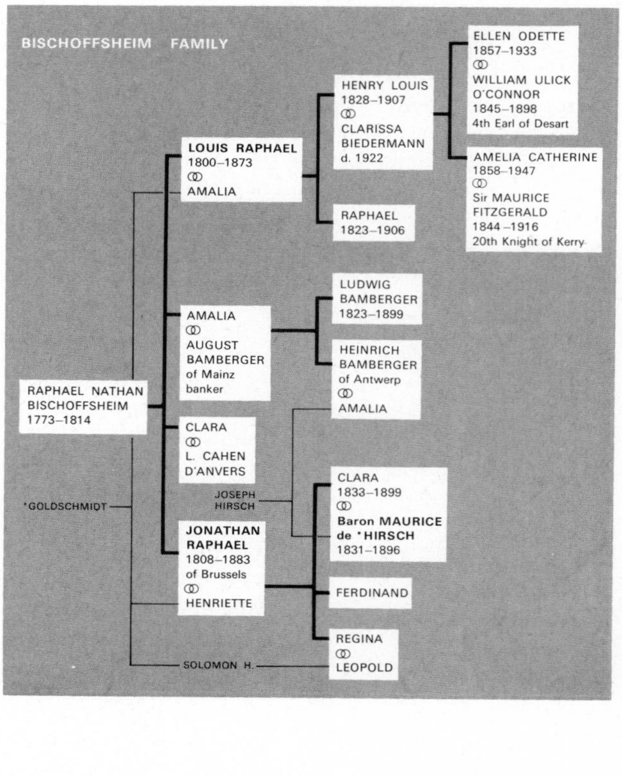

Arabic at the University of Brussels. A street in that city bears his name. His daughter, Clara, married Baron Maurice de *Hirsch in 1855.

Louis Raphael's son RAPHAEL LOUIS (1823–1906), who was born in Amsterdam, succeeded his father as head of the Paris bank. His principal outside interest lay in astronomy, and his generous gifts made possible the building of a number of observatories, the best-known of them at Mont Gras, near Nice. In 1881 he was elected to the Chamber of Deputies.

Louis Raphael's second son, HENRY LOUIS (1828–1907), married Clarissa Biedermann, the sister-in-law of James *Stern of Stern Brothers of London. He headed the London house of Bischoffsheim and Goldschmidt. In conjunction with other financial institutions his bank participated in many international projects, including railway construction in France, Italy, and the Balkans, and the government financing of Turkey, Egypt, and various Latin American countries. In 1881 his eldest daughter, ELLEN ODETTE (1857–1933), married William Ulick O'Connor, the fourth Earl of Desart, and lived at the Desart seat at Kilkenny until her husband's death in 1898. Despite her anti-suffrage agitation, she became the first woman senator of the Irish Free State. This signal honor was the product of her efforts on behalf of Ireland's cultural and economic welfare. Lady Desart remained an active Jewess throughout her life, holding office in a number of Jewish philanthropic organizations and supporting them generously. Her sister AMALIA married Sir Maurice Fitzgerald, 20th Knight of Kerry. She also retained her Jewish interests, was active in support of the work of the Jewish National Fund, and organized a project for the rescue of Jewish children from German-controlled territories in the 1930s.

Bibliography: P. H. Emden, *Jews of Britain* (1943), 536–8; idem, *Money Powers of Europe* (1937).

[J.O.R.]

BISLICHES (Bisseliches), MORDECAI (Marcus) LEIB (1786–1851), bibliophile and rabbinic scholar. Bisliches left his native Brody, Galicia, to lead an unsettled life. In 1816 he went to Paris where he successfully engaged in business. There, in association with his brother Ephraim, he prepared for publication Isaac *Abrabanel's *Yeshu'ot Meshiḥo* from a manuscript in the Bibliothèque Nationale (1828). Bisliches returned home, but soon left again, this time for Holland and England, always searching for rare books and manuscripts. On a third journey he went to Italy where he made many discoveries, and on his return prepared the following works for publication: Shem Tov b. Joseph *Falaquera's *Sefer ha-Nefesh* (1835) and *Moreh ha-Moreh* (1837, 1961²); Samuel ibn *Tibbon's *Yikkavu ha-Mayim* (1837), with a largely autobiographical introduction; *Naḥmanides' novellae to tractate *Shabbat* under the title *Oẓar Neḥmad* (1837); Abba Mari b. Moses (of Lunel)'s *Minḥat Kena'ot* and *Sefer ha-Yare'aḥ* (1838), with a letter concerning Maimonides' Guide; and Abraham *ibn Ezra's *Sefat Yeter* (1838), with an introduction by M. Letteris. In 1846 Bisliches, in partnership with S. G. Stern, sold 111 manuscripts in 102 volumes to the archduchess Marie Louise of Parma for 8,500 lire; they were added to the de *Rossi Collection in the Palatine Library. These manuscripts were basically the collection of the 18th-century bibliophile and bookdealer Moses Benjamin *Foà (b. 1729), who was book purveyor to the dukes of Modena. Bisliches also published *Ha-Palit* (1850), a catalog of 80 of his rare Hebrew manuscripts prepared by L. Zunz with annotations by Senior Sachs.

Bibliography: Loevinson, in: RMI, 7 (1933), 477ff.; Y. Colombo, *ibid.*, 34 (1968), 492.

[ED.]

°**BISMARCK, PRINCE OTTO VON** (1815–1898), Prussian statesman and from 1870 first chancellor of the German Empire. His attitude to Jews and Judaism was ambivalent. Though in 1847 he strongly opposed opening senior governmental positions to Jews, he was later attacked by anti-Semites for "being duped by Jewish financiers" (their main target being G. von *Bleichroeder), and for passing the laws of 1869 and 1871 which abolished restrictions based on religious differences. This legislation, however, was mainly directed by political expediency, while Bismarck's relations with Bleichroeder were financially beneficial to both men. The Jewish Liberal parliamentarians E. *Lasker and L. *Bamberger supported Bismarck in the early years, but when he turned to the Conservatives after 1878 they became his bitter adversaries.

Although Bismarck regarded the rabidly anti-Semitic court preacher Adolph *Stoecker with disdain, he appreciated Stoecker's services in opposing socialism. In 1878, during the Congress of *Berlin, Bismarck generally supported a policy favorable to the Jews, which resulted in the incorporation of written guarantees in the peace treaties assuring their equality in the Balkan states, in particular in *Rumania. A petition (bearing 250,000 signatures) demanding the dismissal of Jews from all government positions (1881) was ignored by Bismarck, who was suspicious of all popular manifestations. However, only apostates were allowed to reach the upper echelons, while the careers of the few Jews employed by the state were severely restricted. In 1885–86, Bismarck supported the expulsion from Germany of around 30,000 Russian and Austrian citizens, one-third of whom were Jews, mainly refugees from the 1883 pogroms. Bismarck, who was contemptuous of all things Polish, despised the East European Jews and adopted the prejudices against *Ostjuden* current even among the Jewish community in Germany. He was also suspicious of the connection between Jewish *Reform in religion and political radicalism, and had a higher opinion of Jewish *Orthodoxy. In the early years of his political career, Bismarck had the support of the vast majority of German Jewry, but he gradually lost it later, as Jews in Germany increasingly turned toward radical liberalism.

Bibliography: O. Joehlinger, *Bismarck und die Juden...* (1921); J. Toury, *Die politischen Orientierungen der Juden in Deutschland...* (1966), index; H. Neubach, *Die Ausweisungen von Polen und Juden aus Preussen, 1885–86...* (1967), index; E. Hamburger, *Juden im oeffentlichen Leben Deutschlands* (1968), index; P. W. Massing, *Rehearsal for Destruction* (1949), index; E. Hamburger, in: YLBI, 9 (1964), 216, 220–2; N. M. Gelber, *ibid.*, 5 (1960), 221–48; D. S. Landes, *ibid.*, 5 (1960), 201–20; P. G. J. Pulzer, *The Rise of Political Anti-Semitism in Germany and Austria* (1964), index; F. Stern, in: *American Historical Review*, 75 (1969), 37–46; U. Tal, *Yahadut ve-Naẓerut ba-Reich ha-Sheni 1870–1914* (1970), index.

[H.W.]

BISTRITA (Rum. **Bistriţa**; Hg. **Beszterce**; Ger. **Bistritz**), town in Transylvania, Rumania; within Hungary until 1918 and between 1940 and 1945. After the prohibition on Jewish settlement there was lifted in 1848, Jews began to settle in Bistrita, mainly from Bukovina and Galicia. The community in Bistrita was Orthodox with a strong ḥasidic element although there were also Jews who adopted the German and Hungarian culture. The first Zionist youth organization in Bistrita in Hungary, Ivriyah, was founded in Bistrita in 1901 by Nissan Kahan, who corresponded with Theodor *Herzl. After World War I the central office of Orthodox Jewry in Transylvania was established in Bistrita. It represented 80 communities (135,000 persons) and was headed by the rabbi of Bistrita, Solomon Zalman

Ullmann, until his death in 1930. There was a large and important yeshivah in Bistrita under the direction of the rabbi.

The Jewish population numbered 718 in 1891 (out of a total of 9,100); 1,316 in 1900 (out of 12,155); 2,198 in 1930 (out of 14,128); and 2,358 in 1941 (out of 16,282). Most of them were deported in 1944 during the Holocaust. The 1,300 Jews who resettled in Bistrita in 1947 included survivors from the camps, former residents of neighboring villages, and others liberated from camps in *Transnistria. Subsequently, the Jewish population declined steadily as a result of emigration to Israel, the United States, and Canada. Two Jewish families remained in Bistrita in 1969.

Bibliography: E. Pistiner, *Bistritz* (Ger., 1953). [Y.M.]

BITAN AHARON (Heb. בִּיתַן אַהֲרֹן), moshav in central Israel, in the Ḥefer Plain, affiliated with Tenu'at ha-Moshavim, founded in 1936 by pioneers from East and Central Europe. Its economy is based principally on citrus plantations. It is also a summer vacationers' center and site of a rest home for civil servants. The village is named after the Canadian Zionist Aharon (Archibald J.) Freiman. [E.O.]

BITHIAH, name given by the rabbis to the daughter of Pharaoh who found the infant Moses. Many legends are told of her in the *aggadah*. The name Bithiah ("daughter of God") was given her as a reward for her devotion in treating Moses as her own child (Lev. R. 1:3). Her purpose in bathing in the Nile was to cleanse herself of the impurity of the idolatry rampant in Egypt (Sot. 12b). When her handmaidens refused to disobey the royal decree and save the Israelite child, her arm was lengthened miraculously so that she could reach the casket in which Moses lay; as soon as she reached it she was cured of her leprosy. She called the child Moses, not only because she had "drawn" him out of the water, but because she knew he would "draw" the children of Israel out of Egypt (Mid. Hag. to Ex. 2:10). Although Moses had many names, God called him only by the name Bithiah gave him (Lev. R. 1:3). At Moses' intercession, Bithiah was not afflicted by any of the ten plagues and therefore was the only female firstborn to be spared in Egypt (Ex. R. 18:3). She became a proselyte and married Caleb because, as she had opposed her father, he would oppose the spies (Lev. R. 1:3). Bithiah was one of those who entered Paradise in her lifetime (Mid. Prov. 31:15). She is numbered among the 22 women of valor (Mid. Hag. to Gen. 23:1, s.v. *Takom*).

Bithiah brings the infant Moses before Pharaoh. Detail from a full-page miniature in the 14th-century Spanish *Golden Haggadah*. London, British Museum, Add. 27210, fol. 10v.

Bibliography: Ginzberg, Legends, 2 (1946), 266ff., 369; 5 (1947), 398ff., 435. [ED.]

BITHYNIA, district of Asia Minor identified in the Talmud with the biblical Tubal (Yoma 10a). There is information, dated from 139 B.C.E., of a Jewish settlement in Amysos which was included in the territory of Bithynia during the period of its expansion (Sampsames in I Macc. 15:23 being identified by Schuerer and others with Amysos in Pontos). Philo, too, testifies to the existence of a Jewish settlement there (*De Legatione ad Gaium,* 281). A Jewish tombstone with a Greek inscription found near the Bosporus marks the burial place of a Jew called Shabbetai who served as elder, scribe, and leader to a Jewish community which is called παλαιοι ("The Ancients," REJ, 23 (1893), 167–71). Talmudic sources (Av. Zar. 2:4; Tosef., Av. Zar. 4:13; Tosef., Shev. 5:9) frequently mention cheeses from Bet-Unyaki which were forbidden "because the majority of calves of that place are offered as sacrifices to idols" (Av. Zar. 34b). This Bet-Unyaki is identified with Bithynia, whose excellent cheeses are also attested to by Pliny (*Natural History* 11:241). The spread of Christianity in Bithynia at the beginning of the second century so alarmed its governor, Pliny the younger (c. 112), that he applied to Trajan for instructions on how to deal with it. The detailed answer given by Trajan exerted a decisive influence for some generations on Rome's policy toward Christianity.

Bibliography: Epstein, Mishnah, 1104–05; Schuerer, Gesch, 3 (1909^4), 23; Frey, Corpus, 2 (1952), 50–52; Neubauer, Géogr, 262–3. [A.SCH.]

BITTELMAN, ALEXANDER (1890–), U.S. Communist leader and journalist. Bittelman was born and grew up in Odessa, Russia. He joined the socialist *Bund* at an early age, then emigrated to America in 1912 and settled in New York City. Bittelman studied engineering, worked for the People's Relief Committee, and in 1919 became editor of *Der Kampf,* the organ of the Jewish Communist Federation. In the same year he joined the American Communist Party, soon becoming its "Jewish specialist." He was sent to Moscow in 1922 to obtain funds for establishing the party's Yiddish paper, the *Morning Freiheit.* From 1923 to 1928 Bittelman worked in the party's national office in Chicago. He traveled to India on a political mission; then edited the *Communist* upon his return. He devoted himself to writing articles of a historical and ideological nature, several of which were published in 1937 in his *Milestones of the History of the Communist Party.* A member of the Communist Party National Committee after World War II, Bittelman also served as general secretary of the Morning Freiheit Association, which he sought to reorganize as a center for Jewish Communist propaganda and culture. Bittelman was indicted under the Smith Act in 1951 for conspiring to overthrow the government, and was jailed in 1955 for a three-year term. Released from prison in 1957, he wrote for the *Daily Worker* until his expulsion from the party for revisionism in 1958. In 1960 he published his personal testament, *A Communist Views America's Future.*

Bibliography: M. Epstein, *Jews and Communism* (1959), 398–403; T. Draper, *Roots of American Communism* (1957), index.

[E.Gr.]

BITTERN (Heron; Heb. אֲנָפָה, *anafah*), mentioned among the unclean birds (Lev. 11:19; Deut. 14:18) and referring to birds of the family *Ardeidae* which are aquatic and marsh birds. Various species occur in Israel such as the white heron *(Egretta alba)* whose span can be as much as a yard. On the other hand the buff-backed heron *(Bulbucus ibis)* is

A white heron, one species of bittern.

much smaller. The latter, as well as many other species of bittern, have greatly increased in recent years in Israel with the spread of fish ponds and irrigation.

Bibliography: Lewysohn, Zool, 169–70; F. S. Bodenheimer, *Ha-Ḥai be-Arẓot ha-Mikra,* 2 (1956), index; J. Feliks, *Animal World of the Bible* (1962), 84.

[J.F.]

BITTUL HA-TAMID (Heb. בִּטּוּל הַתָּמִיד, literally abolition of the daily offering), interruption of prayers and of Torah reading in the synagogue (Heb. עִכּוּב הַקְּרִיאָה, *ikkuv ha-keri'ah* and, therefore, also called *ikkuv ha-keri'ah ikkuv ha-tefillah,* "delay the reading of the Torah," "delay the morning prayers") to seek redress of a wrong, mainly a judicial or moral one. This practice was prevalent mainly in the Middle Ages among Ashkenazi Jewry. The custom of interrupting public religious services was a form of protest and way of arousing public indignation afforded to an individual who felt that an injustice was perpetrated upon him by the constituted authorities or by rich and violent individuals. Ashkenazi *takkanot* of the 12th century set various limits to the exercise of this right to arouse "public scandal for the rights of the individual," while *takkanot* attributed to *Gershom b. Judah sought to regulate it: "If a man summons his neighbor to court and the latter refuses to appear, the plaintiff may not stop the morning prayers and reading of the Torah, unless he has first three times stopped the evening services." A Book of Customs compassionately adds: "However an orphan or a widow may interrupt even the first time until justice is done them." Until 1876 a Jew wishing to protest communal abuses was permitted to rise and say, *"Ich klame."* This privilege was extended to the aggrieved in Eastern Europe also, including cases of complaints against the *kahal* itself. In Russia, after the conscription law of 1827, many a poor mother availed herself of the opportunity to prohibit further prayer until she had stated her protest over the cruel drafting of her male child as a *Cantonist.

Bibliography: Finkelstein, Middle Ages, index s.v. *Interrupting the prayers;* Baron, Community, index s.v. *Interruptions of Prayers;* I. A. Agus, *Urban Civilization in Pre-Crusade Europe,* 2 (1965), index; S. Assaf, *Battei ha-Din ve-Sidreihem* (1924), 25–29; H. H. Ben-Sasson, *Perakim be-Toledot ha-Yehudim bi-Ymei ha-Beinayim* (1962), 115–6.

[I.L.]

BITUMEN (Heb. חֵמָר, *ḥemar* and כֹּפֶר, *kofer;* LXX, ἄσφαλτος), a black, flammable substance which becomes viscous and absorbent on heating. It occurs in almost every part of the world, including Mesopotamia, Iran, and Israel, and is found in various natural forms: in pure form, as in the Dead Sea, where it floats and collects along the coast; as an ore in sandstone; and in semi-solid and fluid forms. The "pits" in the Valley of Siddim referred to in Genesis 14:10 were probably bitumen quarries. In Mesopotamia bitumen was used in building as a mortar which at the same time soaked into the porous bricks, making them stronger. Bitumen was employed too for waterproofing boats, for constructing model boats for cultic purposes, and for sealing water ducts and irrigation canals. It was used in this way to caulk Noah's ark (Gen. 6:14) and the basket which carried Moses (Ex. 2:3). Whether used for strengthening bricks or for sealing against water, bitumen was mixed with sand, chalk, plaster, or with its own ore, since in its pure form it has a low melting point and will not harden unless amalgamated with another mineral.

Bibliography: EM, 3 (1965), 187–90 (incl. bibl.); Staples, in: IDB, 1 (1962), 444.

[Z.Y.]

BIZTHA (Heb. בִּזְּתָא; Gr. Βαζάν, Μαζάν, Βαζεά), one of the seven eunuchs of *Ahasuerus (Esth. 1:10). On the seventh and last day of his feast for the peoples of Susa, when King Ahasuerus was in high spirits from drinking, he sent his seven attendant eunuchs to summon Queen Vashti so that he might display her beauty before the assembled company. The name Biztha is apparently Persian but no agreement has been reached on its meaning (suggestions include: *besteh,* "bound"; *biz-da,* "double gift"; *Mazdā [dā]na,* "gift of Mazda").

Bibliography: L. B. Paton, *The Book of Esther* (ICC, 1908), 67; Gehman, in: JBL, 43 (1924), 323; Duchesne-Guillemin, in: *Le Muséon,* 66 (1953), 107.

[B.Po.]

BIẒẒARON (Heb. בִּצָּרוֹן; "stronghold," cf. Zech. 9:12), moshav in the southern Coastal Plain of Israel, affiliated with Tenu'ot ha-Moshavim, founded in 1931 by pioneers from the Soviet Union whose training farm "Tel Ḥai" in the Crimea had been closed by the Soviet authorities. They themselves had been imprisoned as Zionists, but later permitted to leave. Farming is highly intensive, with citrus plantations as the principal branch. In 1968 its population was 420.

[E.O.]

BLACK, MAX (1909–), U.S. philosopher. Black was born in Baku, Russia, and educated in Germany and England. He taught at the University of Illinois from 1940 to 1946, and afterward at Cornell University. His work deals mainly with problems in contemporary analytical philosophy, ranging from the nature and function of mathematics to the role of ordinary language in the solution of philosophical problems. Though influenced by formalists, his own contributions stress the effectiveness of informalist approaches in the elimination of philosophical perplexity. He edited the influential journal *The Philosophical Review*. Black's major publications include: *The Nature of Mathematics* (1933); *Language and Philosophy* (1949); *Problems of Analysis* (1954); *The Importance of Language* (1962); and *Models and Metaphors* (1962). [A.S.]

BLACK, SIR MISHA (1910–), British architect and industrial designer. Born in Baku, Russia, Black was taken to England as an infant. Before World War II he helped to found the Artists International Association, a radical organization with an anti-Nazi program for assisting refugee artists then attempting to enter Great Britain. In 1933 together with the designer Milner Gray he set up a firm called Industrial Design Partnership in an effort to bring total design methods to Britain. In 1944 they founded the Design Research Unit. Black became a nationally recognized design leader, as coordinating architect for a major part of the 1951 Festival of Britain; he later took part in the design of exhibitions in many other countries. Among the most important activities of the Design Research Unit is the redesigning of British Railways, including Black's designs for a diesel locomotive and an electric train, and supervision of the Victoria Line opened by the London Underground in 1969.

Sir Misha Black, British architect and industrial designer.

Black was appointed professor of industrial engineering design at the Royal College of Art in 1959. He served as president of the British Society of Industrial Arts and Design and as a trustee of the British Museum. His publications on exhibition and interior design include *The Practice of Design* (1946) and *Public Interiors* (1959).

Bibliography: *Art and Industry*, 63 (Sept. 1957), 106.

[Ch.S.S.]

BLACK DEATH, epidemic of various contagious diseases, bubonic, septicemic, and pneumonic, all caused by the same bacillus, *pasteurella pestis*, a combination of which raged throughout Europe between 1348 and 1350. It was the worst plague experienced since the sixth century. Between one-quarter and one-half of the total population perished. In centers with denser populations, such as the monasteries, the proportion of victims was much higher. As the bacteria of this disease live in certain temperatures only, the peak periods of sickness and mortality usually occurred at certain months in the year, according to the local climate.

The impact of this unprecedented catastrophe had a profound effect on the behavior of the population. People reacted by extremes, either seeking recourse to religion through repentance and supplication to God, or reverting to licentiousness, lawbreaking, and savagery. These two types of reaction often combined, in particular where they concerned the attitude of the non-Jewish population to the Jews. Toward the end of 1348 and in early 1349 countless numbers of Jews lost their lives in a wave of massacres which spread throughout Europe as a result of the accusation that the Jews had caused the death of Christians by poisoning the wells and other water sources. According to L. F. Hirst, a leading authority in this field, the Black Death "in all probability . . . originated somewhere in the central Asiatic hinterland, where a permanent reservoir of infection is maintained among the wild rodents of the steppes. Rumors of a great mortality among Asiatics, especially Chinese, reached Europe in 1346, and by the spring of that year bubonic plague had reached the shores of the Black Sea. . . . From ports on the shores of the Crimea besieged by Tatars, who perished in vast numbers from the epidemic . . . the infection was carried on shipboard to Constantinople, Genoa, Venice, and other European ports. The disease spread as rapidly as the transport of those days permitted . . . to the Mainland." At the time of the Black Death no one was aware of this connection and the existence of contagion was only vaguely perceived. By some persons the catastrophe was ascribed to astrological conjunctions; others regarded it as a divine visitation. Pope *Clement VI, in his bull defending the Jews from these accusations, saw it as "the pestilence with which God is afflicting the Christian people." The vast majority of the population, however, was inclined to view it as a *pestis manufacta* (an artificially induced malady), the simplest explanation to the unsophisticated mind, and therefore sought the human agents thought to be spreading the disease. Initially, the Jews were not the only persons accused; strangers of every type were suspected. An Avignonese physician relates: "Many hesitated, in some countries people believed that the Jews intended to poison the whole world and therefore killed them. In other countries they expelled paupers suffering from deformity; and in yet others, the nobles." Sometimes itinerant monks were suspected of placing the poison and spreading the disease, and they were attacked instead.

Well Poisoning Libel. Soon, however, the feelings of helplessness to stem the plague, and the fierce urge to react against the death and destruction it caused, concentrated the force of the populace on the age-old target of popular Christian hostility, the Jews. Anti-Jewish violence was particularly rabid in *Germany, where it had been preceded by a dark half century of anti-Jewish persecution in conjunction with a succession of *blood libels and accusations of *host desecration. This had added to the sinister traits already attributed to the hateful image of the Jew. In France, also, the way had been paved for this accusation by a similar charge leveled during the *Pastoureaux persecutions of 1321. Amid the general atmosphere of hostility, and the cruelty of the persecutions to which the Jews had been subjected, it was almost logical that Christians could imagine that the Jews might seek revenge. Thus, a Jew who was tortured in *Freiburg im Breisgau in 1349, "was then asked . . . 'why did they do it . . . ?' Then he answered: 'because you Christians have destroyed so many Jews; because of what king *Armleder did; and also because we too want to be lords; for you have lorded long enough.' " (". . . *wan umb das, das ir cristen so menigen juden verdarpten, do kuenig Armleder was, und ouch um das, das wir ouch herren wolten gewesen sin, wan ir genug lang herren gewesen sint;" Urkundenbuch der Stadt Freiburg im Breisgau* (1828), nos. 193, 382).

The first occasion on which Jews were tortured to confess

complicity in spreading the Black Death was in September 1348, in the Castle of Chillon on Lake Geneva. The "confessions" thus extracted indicate that their accusers wished to prove that the Jews had set out to poison the wells and food "so as to kill and destroy the whole of Christianity" *("ad interficiendam et destruendam totam legem Christianam")*. The disease was allegedly spread by a Jew of Savoy on the instructions of a rabbi who told him: "See, I give you a little package, half a span in size, which contains a preparation of poison and venom in a narrow, stitched leathern bag. This you are to distribute among the wells, the cisterns, and the springs about Venice and the other places where you go, in order to poison the people who use the water. . . ." This indictment, therefore, shows that his accusers recognized that the plague had spread from the south northward. As the case dragged on, details were extracted telling of further consultations held among the Jews, about messengers from Toledo, and other wild allegations. On Oct. 3, 1348, during the summing up, an allegation providing a motive for the total destruction of Jewry was made; it was asserted that "before their end they said on their Law that it is true that all Jews, from the age of seven, cannot excuse themselves of this [crime], since all of them in their totality were cognizant and are guilty of the above actions" *("asseruerunt praefati Judaei ante eorum ultimum supplicium per legem suam esse vera dicentes quod omnes Judaei a septem annis circum non possint super hoc se excusare, quoniam universaliter sciant omnes, et sint culpabiles in dicto facto")*.

Outbreak of Persecutions. These "confessions" were sent to various cities in Germany. The accusation that the Jews had poisoned the wells spread there like wildfire, fanned by the general atmosphere of terror. The patricians of *Strasbourg attempted to defend the Jews at a meeting of representatives of the Alsatian towns at Benfeld, but the majority rejected their plea, arguing: "If you are not afraid of poisoning, why have you yourselves covered and guarded your wells?" Correspondence on the subject between the authorities in the various cities has been preserved. In general, it reveals a decision to expel the Jews from the locality concerned for good, and to launch an immediate attack to kill them while they still remained. At *Basle the patricians also unsuccessfully attempted to protect the Jews. In various cities Jews were tortured to confess their part in the conspiracy. The defamation, killings, and expulsions spread through the kingdoms of Christian Spain, France, and Germany, to Poland-Lithuania, affecting about 300 Jewish communities (see map). On Sept. 26, 1348, Pope Clement VI issued a bull in Avignon denouncing this allegation, stating that "certain Christians, seduced by that liar, the devil, are imputing the pestilence to poisoning by Jews." This imputation and the massacre of Jews in consequence were defined by the pope as "a horrible thing." He tried to convince Christians that "since this pestilence is all but universal everywhere, and by a mysterious decree of God has afflicted, and continues to afflict, both Jews and many other nations throughout the diverse regions of the earth to whom a common existence with Jews is unknown [the charge] that the Jews have provided the cause or the occasion for such a crime is without plausibility." Both the emperors Charles IV and Peter IV of Aragon also tried to protect the Jews from the

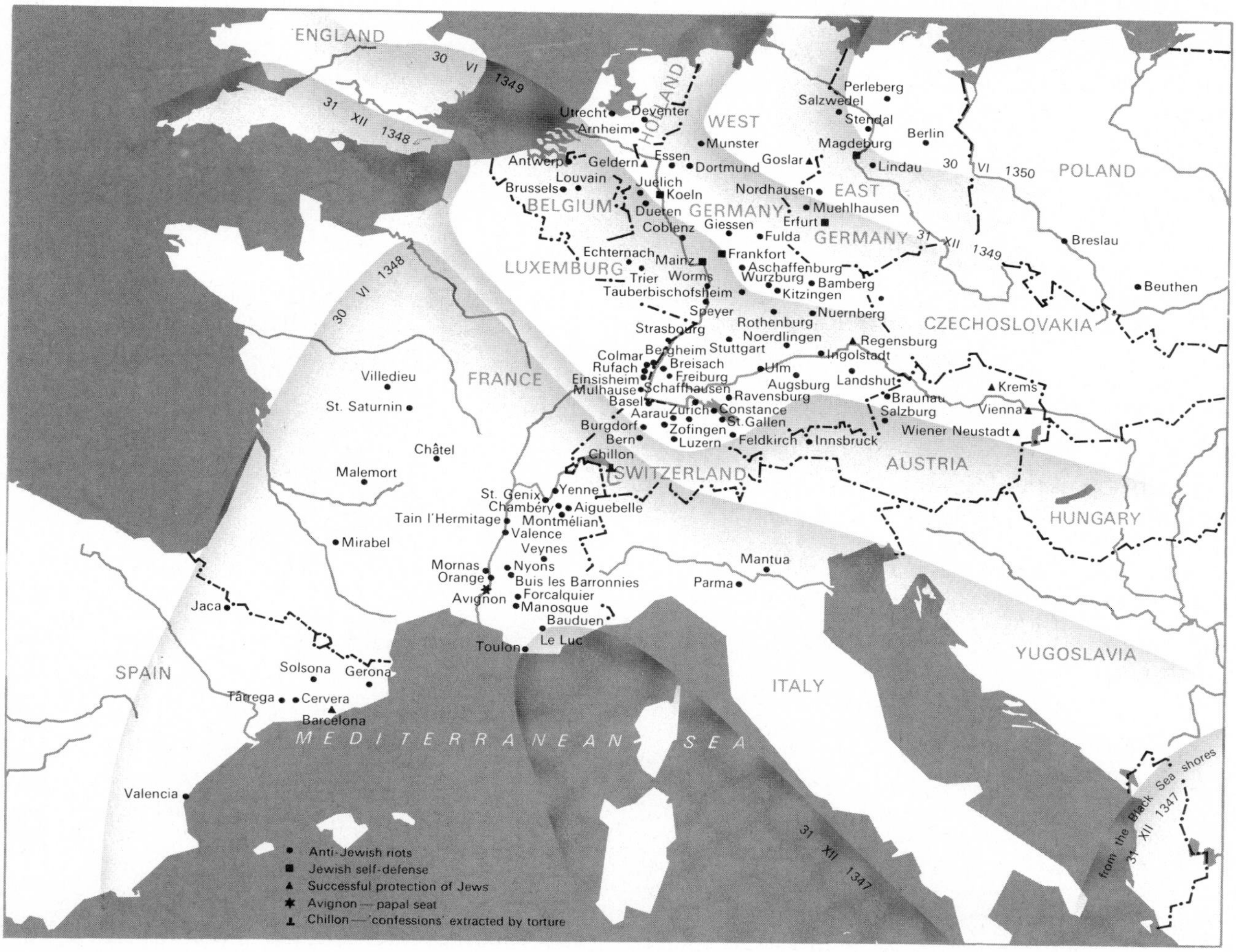

The Black Death. The map shows, in progressive shades of gray, the spread of the plague across Europe in six-month periods from Dec. 31, 1347, to June 30, 1350.

results of the accusation. The arguments generally put forward by the rulers were expressed by the physician Konrad of Megenberg in his *Buch der Natur* arrived at in the light of his own experience: "But I know that there were more Jews in Vienna than in any other German city familiar to me, and so many of them died of the plague that they were obliged to enlarge their cemetery. To have brought this on themselves would have been folly on their part." However, all these appeals to reason were ineffective. The massacres of the Jews continued, and Jewish property was confiscated. Despite his policy of protecting the Jews, in 1350 the emperor Charles IV formally absolved the burghers of *Cheb (Eger) in Bohemia for the killings and robbery they had committed among the Jewish population. In doing so, he stated: "Forgiveness is [granted] for every transgression involving the slaying and destruction of Jews which has been committed without the positive knowledge of the leading citizens, or in their ignorance, or in any other fashion whatsoever." By this time it was well-known that the accusation that Jews had spread the plague was false. In many places Jews were killed even before the plague had visited the locality. Further outbreaks of plague continued later in the 14th century but Jews were no longer accused of being the cause.

The Martyrs. It was recognized by the Jews that the Christians "have opened wide their mouths about me: they have put and spread poison on the water, so they say, in order to libel and attack us," to quote a contemporary dirge. Faced with this overwhelming antagonism, the Jews tried to defend themselves wherever possible and in whatever way they could. In many localities fierce conflicts took place between the Jewish population and their attackers. At *Mainz the Jews set fire to their homes and to the Jewish street: according to some sources, 6,000 Jews perished in the flames. This also occurred at *Frankfort on the Main. In Strasbourg, 2,000 Jews were burnt on a wooden scaffold in the Jewish cemetery. The manner in which the martyrs met their deaths is described in a contemporary Hebrew source concerning "the holy community of Nordhausen. . . . They asked the burghers to permit them to prepare themselves for martyrdom: permission having been given . . . they joyfully arrayed themselves in their prayer shawls and shrouds, both men and women. They [the Christians] dug a grave at the cemetery and covered it with wooden scaffolding . . . The pious ones [among the Jews] asked that a musician be hired to play dancing tunes so that they should enter the presence of God with singing. They took each other by the hand, both men and women, and danced and leapt with their whole strength before God. Their teacher, R. Jacob, went before them; his son, R. Meir, brought up the rear to see that none should lag behind. Singing and dancing they entered the grave, and when all had entered, R. Meir jumped out and walked around to make certain that none had stayed outside. When the burghers saw him they asked him to save his life [by apostasy]. He answered: 'This now is the end of our troubles, you see me only for a while, and then I shall be no more.' He returned to the grave; they set fire to the scaffolding; they died all of them together and not a cry was heard" (*Sefer Minhagim* of Worms). This was the spirit that enabled European Jewry to emerge spiritually unscathed from the avalanche of hatred and cruelty released on the Jews by the Christians in Europe.

The Black Death not only resulted in the immediate destruction of thousands of Jewish lives and the loss of Jewish homes and property in hundreds of communities, but had more far-reaching consequences. Popular imagination invested the already odious image of the Jew with even more horrible characteristics. It was this image that helped to shape the stereotype of the Jew represented by *anti-Semitism and racism in modern times. After the Black Death the legal status of the Jews deteriorated almost everywhere in Europe. Although Jews were frequently received back into the cities where many had been killed or driven out, sometimes within a year of the decision to expel them for good, they usually only gained permission to resettle on worse terms and in greater isolation than before. The position of the Jews in Aragon and Castile (*Spain) deteriorated sharply after 1348–49. The only countries in Europe where the events of the Black Death did not leave a permanent scar on the Jewish communities were Poland-Lithuania. The reconstruction of the Jewish communities and of Jewish life and cultural activity in the second half of the 14th and the beginning of the 15th century clearly evidence the social and spiritual vitality of the Jewish people in Europe in the period.

Bibliography: P. Ziegler, *Black Death* (1969); R. Hoeniger, *Der schwarze Tod in Deutschland* (1882); J. Nohl, *Der schwarze Tod* (1924), 239–73; L. F. Hirst, *Conquest of Plague* (1953); E. Carpentier, in: *Annales,* 17 (1962), 1062–92; E. Littmann, in: MGWJ, 72 (1928), 576–600; J. Trachtenberg, *The Devil and the Jews* (1943, repr. paperback 1961), 97–108; S. Guerchberg, in: S. L. Thrupp (ed.), *Change in Medieval Society* (1964), 208–24; Baron, Social², 9–12 (1965–67).

[H.H.B.-S.]

BLACK JEWS IN AMERICA. The small groups of Black Jews in America who have adopted Judaism are more reflective of the religious cults and charismatic entrepreneurs among American Negroes than of any historical links to the Jewish religion.

Individuals professing Judaism appeared from time to time within the Black community in the antebellum South (AJA, 15 (1963), 3–5). Small numbers of American Negroes converted to Judaism during the post-World War II period, joining established congregations. However, most Black Jews are members of small urban sects that originated in American cities after World War I. One type of sect was led

Ḥizkiyyahu Blackwell, one of the Black Jews who settled in Dimona and Arad. Photo Micha Bar-Am, Tel Aviv, 1970.

Marginal text-illustrations to the *Dragon Haggadah*. Right: A woman giving birth to six children, illustrating a midrashic interpretation of Ex. 1:7. Left: The Egyptian taskmaster striking an Israelite. France, 13th century. Hamburg Staats- und Universitaetsbibliothek, Cod. Heb. 155, folios 23v–24 ($7\frac{1}{4} \times 5\frac{1}{4}$ ins/18.7 × 13.8 cm.).

primarily by West Indian figures interested in the total spectrum of Negro life in America who saw the sect as a politico-religious device for alleviating the general condition of the oppressed Blacks. The second, led primarily by Southern American Negroes, emphasized the more emotional, affective, and purely religious elements common to the Christian sectarian pattern historically predominant among American Negroes. Groups of both types have regularly appeared in urban areas, and for the most part have only faint connections to historically recognizable Judaism. They usually consist of a few dozen individuals (mostly women) who attach themselves to a charismatic figure generally proclaiming a rediscovery of the true lost roots of the Black nation in Judaism by means of visions, kabbalistic sources, and verbal traditions. Their religious practices tend to be highly syncretistic, utilizing elements from both the Christian and Jewish traditions. Knowledge of Hebrew, ritual, and religious sources other than the Bible itself are rudimentary. The groups bear such names as Bnei Israel, the Commandment Keepers, Temple of the Gospel of the Kingdom, Kohel Beth B'nai Yisrael.

No reliable statistics exist for the number of Black Jewish congregations or for total membership, but estimates suggest a few dozen distinct groupings in cities such as New York, Chicago, Philadelphia, Boston, and Cincinnati, with membership between two and six thousand. Relationships with the white Jewish community are generally scant or nonexistent. The largest Black Jewish congregation is believed to be the Commandment Keepers Congregation of the Living God in Harlem, led by West Indian-born W. A. Matthew. In the 1960s a few young Black Jews began studying at Jewish institutions (generally Orthodox), but the prospect for closer integration of Black Jews with other Jews on an institutional level seemed remote (1970). Toward the goal of greater integration, a group comprised predominantly of young adult Black Jews was organized in 1965, with some significant support from white Jews, calling itself Hatza'ad Harishon ("the first step"). In addition to promoting contact between white and Black Jews, this group has sought to enlarge Jewish educational opportunities among the Black Jews (*Jewish Digest,* Dec. 1965, 66–68). At the end of 1969 and the beginning of 1970 several black Jewish families from Chicago arrived in Israel and settled in Dimonah, after having spent some time in Liberia.

It has been suggested that for many Black Jews—as for many Black Muslims—a primary motivation in their religious orientation was to seek a haven from the overwhelming rejection experienced at the hands of white society.

Bibliography: H. Brotz, *Black Jews of Harlem* (1964); idem, in: *Phylon,* 13 (1952), 324–37; idem, in: JSOS, 27 (1965), 10–17; Waitzkin, in: *Harvard Journal of Negro Affairs,* 1 no. 3 (1967), 12–44; Goldreich, in: *Hadassah Magazine* (Jan. 1967), 12–13, 31; Landes, in: JJSO, 9 (1967), 175–89.

[B.Z.S.]

°**BLACKSTONE, WILLIAM E.** (1841–1935), Chicago businessman who became an evangelist, missionary, and ardent supporter of the return of the Jews to Palestine. His "Zionistic" views sprang from his millennarian theology as expressed in his first book *Jesus is Coming* (1878), which was translated into many languages, including Hebrew. He considered the Jewish restoration to Zion as the fulfillment of biblical prophecies signifying the approach of the second Advent of Jesus. After a visit to Palestine in 1888/89, Blackstone organized meetings of Jews and Christians in order to promote his Zionist ideas. In 1891 he initiated a memorandum to President Harrison urging the restoration of Palestine to the Jews as a primary solution to the problem of Jewish persecution in Czarist Russia. The petition was signed by 413 outstanding Jewish and Christian personalities in the United States. In 1916 a similar memorandum was sent to President Wilson which may have influenced his positive attitude to the *Balfour Declaration.

[Yo.M.]

°**BLAKE, WILLIAM** (1757–1827), English poet and engraver. One of the great figures of the English romantic movement, Blake described his poems as prophecies, declaring that his model was the Bible, which he termed "the great code of art." The works of Homer and Ovid were for him, by contrast, perversions of art and imagination. Blake was in touch with various occult circles and shared with them the belief that Britain was the cradle of the Israelite people. This explains his tendency to identify English names and places with those in the Bible. His work is saturated in biblical imagery and allusion. His main biblical poems are *The Four Zoas, Milton,* and *Jerusalem.* The last quatrain of his preface to *Milton* well illustrates Blake's revolutionary mystique: "I will not cease from mental fight/ Nor shall my sword sleep in my hand,/ Till we have built Jerusalem/ In England's green and pleasant land." In freeing his verse from the shackles of classical prosody and adopting for his prophetic books something resembling the syntax of the Bible, Blake may have been influenced by the 18th century Oxford scholar, Robert *Lowth. Although he knew little or no Hebrew, and was not Jewish, Blake was also influenced by ideas which can be traced to the *Kabbalah. His notion of the Giant Albion, whose limbs contain heaven and earth, is derived from the kabbalistic image of **Adam Kadmon* (Primal Man). Equally kabbalistic are his notions of a divine world divided into male and female principles, and his conception of a

William Blake's frontispiece to his book *Jerusalem,* 1804. His symbolic figure, Los, looking like a ḥasidic rabbi and entering the "door of death," bears an interesting resemblance to Lord George Gordon, the convert to Judaism who had led the London "No Popery" riots of 1780, which Blake witnessed.

primordial "Fall" from which all evil flows in both the divine and the human realms. In spite of many Judaistic ideas and currents of feeling, Blake's moral ideas are, paradoxically enough, anti-Judaic, even anti-Semitic. Like the Gnostics, he viewed the Law and the Commandments as an evil system, and he identified the God of Sinai with some evil demiurge.

Bibliography: D. Saurat, *Blake and Modern Thought* (1929); J. Bronowski, *Man Without a Mask* (1944); H. Fisch, *Jerusalem and Albion* (1964), 273–80; D. Hirst, *Hidden Riches* (1964); S. Damon, *Blake Dictionary* (1965); M. Roston, *Poet and Prophet* (1965).

[H.F.]

°**BLANCKENHORN, MAX** (1861–1947), German geologist who became famous principally for his research and publications on the geology of the Near East, Syria, and particularly Ereẓ Israel. Blanckenhorn visited the countries of the Near East many times and worked together with A. *Aaronson and the zoologist Israel *Aharoni. He was also a friend of Otto *Warburg, with whom he worked to deepen and spread knowledge of the natural resources of Ereẓ Israel. As the then almost single expert on the geology of Ereẓ Israel, Blanckenhorn often advised Zionist leaders on matters concerning economic resources of the country. From 1889 to 1940 he published more than 50 pieces of research on the general and structural geology of the Near East, on the stratigraphy, paleontology, prehistory, seismology, climatology, and on mineral resources such as phosphates, bitumen, and the salts of the Dead Sea. He prepared the first geological maps of the Jerusalem area (1905), of the Near East (in International Map of Europe containing the Mediterranean area, 1902–11), and of Ereẓ Israel on a scale of 1:700,000 (1912). Of great importance are his paleontological monographs on the fossils from Ereẓ Israel and Syria. A detailed list of his publications on the Middle East appeared in *Israel Journal of Earth-Sciences.*

Bibliography: A. Avnimelech, in: *Israel Journal of Earth-Sciences*, 12 (1963/64), 1–7. [M.A.A.]

BLANES, JACOB (1877–1943), one of the last cantors of the Portuguese Synagogue of Amsterdam before the Holocaust. He was appointed in 1902. Blanes insisted on full accuracy in recitation, a characteristic feature of Sephardi cantoral singing in Amsterdam. He had a deep knowledge of *Hazande*, including many ancient melodies for the **Kaddish*, etc. He had great influence on younger men anxious to preserve the tradition of *ḥazzanut*, and the few pupils of his who survived World War II were afterward to be found in communities in various parts of the world. Blanes himself died after being deported from Holland in 1943.

Bibliography: ESN, 1 (1949), 70–71. [S.V.]

BLANK, MAURICE (1848–1921), Rumanian banker. Born in Pitesti, Rumania, Blank was one of the first Rumanian Jews to receive diplomas in economics and finance at the Vienna and Leipzig universities. He went to work in Bucharest in the banking house of Jacob Marmorosh who later invited him to become a partner. Marmorosh, Blank and Company became Rumania's largest bank after the Rumanian National Bank. Blank made important connections with East European financial institutions and was instrumental in developing his country's economic relations with the rest of Europe, particularly after Rumania became independent in 1878. His bank shared in developing many of the country's industries, helped to introduce steel trains, and made possible the financing of the great tunnel project at Barbosi. Blank was involved in Jewish and general communal affairs, giving generous support to cultural institutions and founding theaters and publishing houses. His son Aristide Blank (1884–) became general director of the bank on his father's death and was also a supporter of many Jewish and general causes. He published a number of studies on finance.

[J.O.R.]

BLANK, SAMUEL LEIB (1893–1962), Hebrew novelist and short-story writer. Blank, who was born in the Ukraine, spent his formative years in Bessarabia and in 1922 settled in the United States. His early stories described the Jewish farmers of Bessarabia, and his tetralogy *Ẓon, Adamah, Naḥalah* (1930–33) and *Moshavah* (1936) focused upon a simple protagonist, significantly and symbolically called "Bo'az." Blank was not a subtle psychologist, but he vividly depicted the Jewish man of the soil in his primitive surroundings. When he attempted to portray the harsher realities of life after World War I, such as the pogroms in the Ukraine in his *Bi-She'at Ḥerum* (1932) or the maladjusted immigrant in America, as in *Mr. Kunis* (1934) or *Iy ha-Dema'ot* (1941), he verged on melodrama. *Al Admat Amerikah* (1958) and *Eẓ ha-Sadeh* (1961) were among his last works.

Bibliography: Waxman, Literature, 4 (1960^2), 1055–58; 5 (1960^2), 202–4; M. Ribalow, *Im ha-Kad el ha Mabbu'a* (1950), 237–43.

[El.S.]

BLANK, SHELDON HAAS (1896–), U.S. rabbi and Bible scholar. Blank was ordained at Hebrew Union College, Cincinnati, Ohio, in 1923. From 1926 he taught Bible at the Hebrew Union College. Blank published numerous studies on many aspects of biblical scholarship, dealing with questions of the text and of social and political history. He made a special contribution by his insights into the religious experience of biblical personalities, especially the prophets, and by his exposition of their religious ideas. These qualities characterize his books *Prophetic Faith in Isaiah* (1958) and *Jeremiah: Man and Prophet* (1961), as well as such essays as *Men against God, The Promethean Element in Biblical Prayer* (in JBL, 72 (1953), 1–13), *Doest Thou Well to Be Angry? A Study in Self-Pity* (in HUCA, 26 (1955), 29–41), and *Of a Truth the Lord Hath Sent Me, An Inquiry into the Source of the Prophet's Authority* (1955). In these studies he strictly followed the canons of critical scholarship. Elsewhere, however, he sought to reinterpret biblical thoughts in terms of the present day, in: *The Relevance of Prophetic Thought for the Modern Rabbi* (CCARY, 65 (1955), 163–72) and *The Dawn of our Responsibility* (1961).

Bibliography: *Dictionary Catalog of the Klau Library*, 4 (1964), 465–70. [B.J.B.]

BLASER, ISAAC (1837–1907), Russian rabbi and educator. Blaser was one of the foremost disciples of R. Israel *Lipkin (Salanter), whose *Musar (ethicist) movement he helped develop and lead. In the early 1850s, Blaser moved from his native Vilna to Kovno, Lithuania, where he came under the influence of Lipkin. In 1864 he reluctantly accepted the rabbinate of St. Petersburg, hence the name by which he is familiarly known, "Reb Itzelle Peterburger." During this time he wrote halakhic works and responsa, arousing the opposition of the *maskilim*. He left the rabbinate in 1878, returning to Kovno where he headed the *kolel* ("advanced talmudical academy"), and sent emissaries throughout the world to gain support for it. He helped to found the yeshivah of *Slobodka. About 1891, as the result of bitter controversy concerning the Musar movement, he left the *kolel* of Kovno and helped to found other such Musar-oriented schools elsewhere. Increasing opposition to the Musar movement (1896–98) and to Blaser, its chief exponent, forced the yeshivah to leave its premises in Slobodka, and it finally became established in Kelm (1898). In 1904 Blaser, favoring the idea of Jewish colonization of Palestine, emigrated to and settled in Jerusalem, where he died. His main contribution to the Musar movement was his emphasis on acquiring "fear of the Lord" (i.e., piety) by means of emotional meditation in works of *musar*. Unlike other disciples of Salanter, who expounded *musar* intellectually, Blaser held that knowledge and conceptualization were inadequate to the task of curbing man's baser instincts. "Fear of the Lord" could be aroused only by an unsophisticated contemplation of man's physical vulnerability, his moral lowliness, and his punishment for continued disobedience. Since he held that the form of such meditation makes a more lasting impression than the contents, he prescribed the reading aloud of *musar* texts in a melancholy melody, with frequent periods of weeping. Similarly, his preaching was simple, sad, and usually accompanied by tears. Blaser's major literary contribution to the Musar movement, *Or Yisrael* ("Light of Israel"; 1900), was often reprinted, and for several decades was the only available exposition of *musar*. Blaser here expounded the fundamentals of the Musar approach and presented excerpts from the letters of Israel Lipkin, along with evaluations of the teachings of the founders of the Musar movement and of some of its leading personalities. His major halakhic work is *Peri Yiẓḥak* ("Fruit of Isaac"); the first volume was published in Vilna in 1881, some 14 years after he had completed writing it. The second volume was published posthumously in 1912. He contributed numerous articles, both on *halakhah* and *musar*, to the various rabbinic journals of the day. Much of his writing remained unpublished.

Bibliography: D. Katz, *Tenu'at ha-Musar*, 2 (1954), 220–73; S. Bialoblotzki, in: *Yahadut Lita*, 1 (1959), 194–7; Ch. Zaichyk, *Ha-Me'orot ha-Gedolim* (1962), 109–29. [No.L.]

BLASPHEMY, in the broadest (and least precise) sense any act contrary to the will of God or derogatory to His power. Blasphemy is the term employed to translate the Hebrew verbs *ḥeref*, *giddef*, and *ni'eẓ* (e.g., Isa. 37:6, *gdf*, where the servants of the king of Assyria denied the Lord's power to save Israel; and Ezek. 20:27, where it refers to Israel's sacrifices on the High Places). In the narrower and more precise sense, the word is used to mean speaking contemptuously of the Deity. The classic instance in the Bible is Leviticus 24:10–23, where the pronouncement (*nakav, naqav*) of the name of God appears in conjunction with the verb *killel* (*qillel*). God (*Elohim*) also appears as the object of the verb *qillel* in Exodus 22:27 (see also I Kings 21:10, 13, where *qillel* is euphemistically displaced by its antonym *berekh*, "to bless" or "to renounce"; see *Euphemism and Dysphemism). The rabbinic interpretation of Leviticus 24:10–23 and Exodus 22:27 as wishing (i.e., wishing harm, Sanh. 7:5), sets up a definition of blasphemy such as to render the actual perpetration (and the application of the penalty, capital punishment) out of the realm of probability. The verb *qallel* rarely means "to curse." Rather it subsumes a wide range of abuse, often nonverbal in nature. "To curse" the Deity meant to repudiate Him, to violate His norms; blasphemy on the part of an Israelite, in the narrow sense, is a concept alien to biblical thought.

See also *Blessing and Cursing. [H.Br.]

In the Talmud. The Mishnah (Sanh. 7:5), rules that the death sentence by stoning should be applied only in the case where the blasphemer had uttered the *Tetragrammaton and two witnesses had warned him prior to the transgression. In the Talmud, however, R. Meir extends this punishment to cases where the blasphemer had used one of the *attributes, i.e., substitute names of God (Sanh. 56a). The accepted *halakhah* is that only the one who has uttered the Tetragrammaton be sentenced to death by stoning; the offender who pronounced the substitute names is only flogged (Maim., Yad, Avodat Kokhavim, 2:7). In the court procedure (Sanh. 5:7 and Sanh. 60a) the witnesses for the prosecution testified to the words of the blasphemer by substituting the expressions "Yose shall strike Yose" (*yakkeh Yose et Yose*). Toward the end of the hearing, however, after the audience had been dismissed, the senior witness was asked to repeat the exact words uttered by the blasphemer. Upon their pronouncement (i.e., of the Tetragrammaton), the judges stood up and rent their garments. The act expressed their profound mourning at hearing the name of God profaned. The custom of tearing one's clothes on hearing blasphemy is attested to in II Kings 18:37 where it is told that *Eliakim and his associates tore their garments upon hearing the blasphemous words of the Assyrian warlord *Rab-Shakeh (Sanh. 60a). It is codified in Shulḥan Arukh (YD 340:37) that whoever hears a blasphemy whether with the Tetragrammaton or with attributes, in any language and from a Jew, even from the mouth of a witness, must rend his garment. The second and any successive witnesses only testified: "I have heard the same words" (Sanh. 7:5); according to the opinion of *Abba Saul, whoever utters the Tetragrammaton in public, is excluded from the world to come (Av. Zar. 18a). Besides sacrilege of God, vituperation against the king, God's anointed servant, was also considered blasphemy (cf. Ex. 22:27 and I Kings 21:10). Gentiles, too, are obliged to refrain from blasphemy since this is one of the Seven *Noachide Laws (Sanh. 56a, 60a). Maimonides also classified as blasphemy the erasure of God's name written on paper or engraved on stone, etc., which was to be punished by flogging (Yad, Yesodei ha-Torah 6:1–6). After Jewish courts were deprived of jurisdiction in those cases where capital punishment was applied, excommunication (see **ḥerem*) was the usual sanction against a blasphemer (J. Mueller (ed.), *Teshuvot Ge'onei Mizraḥ u-Ma'arav* (1898), 27a, responsum no. 103 by Amram Gaon).

Bibliography: Eisenstein, Dinim, 68. [Ed.]

BLAU, AMRAM (1894–), rabbi, leader of the ultra-Orthodox sect *Neturei Karta. Blau was born in Jerusalem into a noted religious family. He was a leading member of the Agudat Israel youth movement in the early 1930s. Blau and some of his colleagues left the movement in 1935 and founded the extreme anti-Zionist Ḥevrat Ḥayyim, later to become Neturei Karta. His fierce opposition to Zionism and Agudat Israel, sometimes expressed violently, led on several occasions to his prosecution and imprisonment. His anti-Zionist attitude did not change with the establishment of the State of Israel (1948), which he refused to recognize. In 1965, after the death of his first wife, he married a proselyte, Ruth Ben-David, despite the opposition of the ultra-Orthodox *bet din* and some of his followers. [M.Fr.]

BLAU, BRUNO (1881–1954), German lawyer and sociologist. Born in West Prussia, Blau practiced law in Berlin. In 1908 he joined A. *Ruppin as editor, and from 1909 was the sole editor, of the *Zeitschrift fuer Demographie und Statistik der Juden* (1904–19; new series 1924–27), published by the Buero fuer Statistik der Juden, of which Blau was the director. Because of his severe illness, the Nazis did not deport him during World War II but kept him confined in the police section of the Berlin Jewish

Hospital. Blau emigrated to the United States after the war, but he died in Germany. Among Blau's published works are: *Kriminalitaet der deutschen Juden* (1906); *Statistik der Juden* (1918); and *Last Days of German Jewry . . .* (1953). Of particular importance is his work on anti-Jewish Nazi legislation and administrative orders, *Ausnahmerecht fuer die Juden in den europaeischen Laendern* (vol. 1, 1952), which is a collection of documents from Germany and was reprinted as *Ausnahmerecht fuer die Juden in Deutschland, 1933–1945* (1965[3]). [Ed.]

BLAU, FRITZ (1865–1929), Austrian chemist. From 1890 he taught at Vienna University. In 1902 he joined the Auregesellschaft in Berlin, and from 1919 was head of research of the Osram Company in Berlin, at that time one of the foremost industries in Germany. He took out 185 patents, some in organic chemistry, but most dealing with tungsten, incandescent electric lamps, gases, and radiation. This field led to other patented work on wireless telegraphy, electric furnaces, and X-ray machines and techniques. In addition, Blau published many papers in scientific journals on these subjects.

Bibliography: *Zeitschrift fuer technische Physik*, 6 (1925), 278–359. [S.A.M.]

BLAU, JOSEPH LEON (1909–), U.S. educator and historian of ideas. Blau was educated at Columbia University, where he later became a professor of religion. In 1966 he became vice-president of the Conference on Jewish Social Studies. Blau followed the philosophic tradition of naturalistic humanism in the line of John Dewey and his school at Columbia. He carried on their interest in the history of philosophy in America in his book *Men and Movements in American Philosophy* (1952) and in monographic studies.

As a student (and, later, collaborator) of Salo W. *Baron, Blau's approach to Jewish history emphasizes interdisciplinary and cross-cultural influences. He opposes the conventional interpretation that the development of the Jewish religious and philosophical tradition is mainly linear, maintaining that the Jews were not cut off from cross-cultural contact for any significant period of their history. His book *The Story of Jewish Philosophy* (1962) explores the ways in which Jewish thinkers absorbed and modified the ideas current in their cultural environment. In *Modern Varieties of Judaism* (1966), Blau demonstrates the same principle of interplay of tradition and environment in the shaping of Jewish religion since the 18th century. *The Christian Interpretation of the Cabala in the Renaissance* (1944) investigates the flow of ideas in the reverse direction, that is, from Jewish to Christian thinkers. [Ed.]

BLAU, JOSHUA (1919–), Israel Arabist. Blau was born in Cluj, Rumania, and was educated at the Hebrew University of Jerusalem, where in 1962 he was appointed professor of Arabic language and literature. He was an authority on such Arabic dialects as Judeo-Arabic and Christian-Arabic, on which he published important studies. Among them are *Grammar of Judeo-Arabic* (1950; in Hebrew, 1961); *Emergence and Linguistic Background of Judeo-Arabic* (1965); *Grammar of Christian-Arabic* (1966–67); and *Syntax des palaestinensischen Bauerndialekts . . .* (1960). Blau wrote a textbook on Hebrew grammar, *Dikduk Ivri Shitati* (1966[4]), and syntax, *Yesodot ha-Taḥbir* (1966); with A. Burak he wrote *Ha-Lashon ha-Ivrit ha-Ma'asit* ("Everyday Hebrew," 1951). He was among the editors of *Oẓar Leshon ha-Mikra* ("Vocabulary of the Bible"; 2 vols., 1957–59). He also edited *Teshuvot ha-Rambam* (3 vols., 1958–61). [Ed.]

BLAU, LUDWIG LAJOS (1861–1936), scholar. Blau studied at yeshivot, the Jewish Theological Seminary of Budapest, and the University of Budapest. As a student he was invited to teach at the Seminary where in 1889 he became a full professor. In 1914 Blau became director of the Seminary. For 40 years he was the editor of the Hungarian Jewish scholarly journal, *Magyar Zsidó Szemle.* In 1911 he founded the Hebrew review *Ha-Ẓofeh le-Ḥokhmat Yisrael be-Ereẓ Hagar,* which he edited until 1931. Blau was a prolific Jewish scholar who contributed to almost every aspect of Jewish learning. He was a regular contributor to most of the Jewish and non-Jewish scholarly periodicals dedicated to theology and philology. His bibliography includes 887 items and in the *Zsidó Szemle* he reviewed 1,383 books. He was among the first to evaluate the talmudic information on the Bible and the masorah (*Masoretische Untersuchungen,* 1891; *Zur Einleitung in die Heilige Schrift,* 1894). He also investigated the information contained in traditional literature on ancient Hebrew booklore (*Studien zum althebraeischen Buchwesen,* 1902). His works subsequently gained added importance in light of interest in old Hebrew scrolls. Blau enriched general folklore by his book *Das altjuedische Zauberwesen* (1898). Equally his *Juedische Ehescheidung und der juedische Scheidebrief* (2 vols., 1911–12) broke new ground; with the discovery of divorce documents among the Bar Kokhba finds, this work takes on new relevance. Blau was among the first to make use of Greek papyri for the evaluation of talmudic law (*Papyri und Talmud in gegenseitiger Beleuchtung,* 1913; *Prosbul im Lichte der griechischen Papyri und der Rechtsgeschichte,* in *Festschrift der Landes-rabbinerschule,* 1927). He also published the letters of Leone *Modena (*Leo Modenas Briefe und Schriftstuecke,* 2 vols., 1905–06).

Bibliography: S. Hevesi, in: *Ve-Zot li-Yhudah* (1926), 1–9; D. Friedman, in: *Jubileumi emlékkönyv Blau Lajos . . . 65. születésnapja . . . alkalmából* (1926), 14–90 (bibliography); D. S. Loewinger, *Zikhron Yehudah* (1938), 5–45; J. Bakonyi and D. Friedman, *ibid.*, 18–34. [Al. Sch.]

BLAU, MOSHE (1885–1946), *Agudat Israel leader; brother of Amram *Blau. Blau, who was born in Jerusalem, directed the Agudat Israel office there from 1924 until his death. He served as a member of the movement's world executive and edited its weekly *Kol Yisrael* ("Voice of Israel"). From 1933 to 1945 he headed the independent, ultra-Orthodox Edah Ḥaredit (Orthodox community). Despite the community's segregation policy, he cooperated with *yishuv* leaders in representing Jewish interests in dealings with the Mandate government. Blau represented Agudat Israel before various British and international commissions which dealt with the Palestine problem. In 1946, while on a rescue mission to Jewish survivors of the war, Blau fell ill and died in Messina. He was taken to Jerusalem for burial. He wrote *Ammuda di-Nehora* ("Column of Light," 1932), a biography of Rabbi Y. Ḥ. *Sonnenfeld, and *Al Ḥomotayikh Yerushalayim* ("Upon thy Walls, O Jerusalem," 1946), autobiographical notes and memoirs.

Bibliography: A. Blau, *Shomer ha-Ḥomot* (1957); Tidhar, 1 (1947), 175–6. [Z.K.]

BLAUSTEIN, U.S. industrialist family. Louis (1869–1937) was born in Russia, and emigrated to the U.S. in 1888. Starting in business as a kerosene peddler, Blaustein went to work in 1892 for the Standard Oil Company at its Baltimore plant and by 1910 had risen to an executive position. In that year he left Standard Oil and, with a small amount of capital, founded the American Oil Company in

Baltimore. The enterprise flourished due in large part to Blaustein's innovations in oil distribution in a period when the automobile was emerging as the major user of petroleum products. He experimented with new forms of gasoline and claimed the first high-test gasoline developed

Louis Blaustein, founder of the American Oil Company.

in the country. Blaustein's filling stations spread from Baltimore through Maryland and eventually covered the entire East Coast. In 1924 the giant Pan-American Petroleum and Transport Company (later controlled by Standard Oil Company of Indiana) paid $5,000,000 for a half interest in the American Oil Company and merged with it in 1933. Blaustein remained active in the firm as it continued to expand, building steamship terminals and petroleum refineries. During his later years he gave large sums to charity, usually anonymously. JACOB (1892–1970), son of Louis, was associated with his father in the founding of the American Oil Company in 1910, serving in executive positions and as its president during 1933–37. Later he served as president of the American Trading and Production Corporation as well as director and executive committee member of major national companies in the fields of petroleum, insurance, and banking. He was reportedly one of the richest individuals in America. During World War II Blaustein was vice-chairman of the U.S. Petroleum Administration's marketing committee and served on other wartime committees. His civic activities include support of the American Heritage Foundation, United Negro College Fund, and American Association for the United Nations. Blaustein played an active role in Jewish affairs, with a major commitment to the American Jewish Committee, which he served as executive committee chairman (1944–49) and president (1949–54). He served on the boards of the American Friends of the Hebrew University and the Weizmann Institute of Science. His philanthropic activities range from local philanthropy in

Jacob Blaustein, U.S. industrialist and philanthropist.

Baltimore, to the American Jewish Joint Distribution Committee, United Service for New Americans, and the Conference on Jewish Claims Against Germany. He was a member of the American delegation to the tenth U.N. General Assembly and was a leader in the movement to adopt the Convention on Genocide and the Declaration of Human Rights.

Bibliography: LOUIS BLAUSTEIN: in: *New York Times* (July 28, 1937), 19. JACOB BLAUSTEIN: in: H. Frank, *Jewish Digest* (March 1962); *Current Biography Yearbook 1949* (1950), 60–61; *Forbes* (Sept. 15, 1968), 26–28.

[Mo.Ro.]

BLAUSTEIN, DAVID (1866–1912), educator and communal worker. Born in Lida (province of Vilna), Blaustein fled to Germany in 1883 in order to evade conscription. There he worked and studied, moving to Schwerin to continue his religious studies, but in 1886 he left for the United States. In Boston he established a modern German-Hebrew school—the first of its kind in the United States—and continued his studies. From 1892 to 1896 he served as rabbi of a Providence Reform congregation and taught at Brown University.

In 1898 Blaustein was appointed superintendent of the Educational Alliance of New York City, then the most important social-educational institution for the Americanization of foreigners. With the untrained social workers of that institution he worked diligently to raise the standards of social work and to turn it into a profession. Respected by Jews and non-Jews alike, he accompanied Robert Watchorn, immigration commissioner at Ellis Island, to Rumania in 1900 to study the conditions of the Jews there and the causes of the large-scale emigration from that country.

In 1905 Blaustein became the first president of the Society of Jewish Social Workers of New York. Active in Zionist affairs in New York, he was the first *nasi* (presiding officer) of Order of the Sons of Zion. In 1908 he became director of the Chicago Hebrew Institute, and in 1910 took up a lectureship on Jewish, Italian, and Slavic immigration at the New York School of Philanthropy, where a chair had been established for him.

Bibliography: DAB, 2 (1929), 360–1; M. Blaustein (ed.), *Memoirs of David Blaustein* (1913).

[Ju.P.]

BLAU-WEISS ("Blue-White"), first Jewish youth movement in Germany, founded in 1912. It initiated a Zionist program, basing its organizational format on the German youth movement Wandervogel (whose increasing anti-Semitism greatly contributed to the expansion of Blau-Weiss). Before and immediately after World War I Blau-Weiss groups engaged almost exclusively in outings and intimate gatherings, emphasizing nature appreciation and "manliness" in the manner of the German *Jugendbewegung* (youth movement). Instead of the cult of German peasantry and folk traditions, Blau-Weiss introduced new forms of celebrating Jewish holidays outdoors and an interest in the Hebrew language, Hebrew songs, and Yiddish folklore. Blau-Weiss reached its peak in the early 1920s, with about 3,000 members. At this time a pioneering, Palestine-oriented tendency developed in its ranks and became its official program at the Blau-Weiss conference in Prunn (August 1922). The conference decided upon the establishment of a Blau-Weiss settlement in Palestine based not only on agriculture but also on precision workmanship in such fields as tool mechanics. It also decided to streamline the organizational structure of the movement along "hierarchical" lines, and to participate actively in Zionist politics. Subsequent friction with the German Zionist leadership, as well as the economic crisis in Palestine, thwarted this ambitious program. While many members of Blau-Weiss settled in Palestine, some of them prior to the Prunn conference, no specific Blau-Weiss settlement or enterprise materialized. The movement dissolved in Germany in 1929, retaining only the *Praktikantenschaft,* i.e., small *hakhsharah* groups.

Blau-Weiss also existed in Austria, where it flourished for a time. The Czechoslovak branch of the movement, which from 1919 called itself by the Hebrew equivalent, *Tekhelet-Lavan,* continued as a pioneering organization into the 1930s. The main impact of "the Blau-Weiss experience" was felt in Germany in the early 1920s among Jewish boys and girls of assimilated and semi-assimilated families. Alienated from their affluent parents and excluded from the "Aryanized" youth movements, these young people found their way back to the Jewish people and to Zionism.

Bibliography: H. Maier-Cronemeyer, in: *Germania Judaica* (Cologne), 8 (1969), 18–40, 59–64, 67–71; H. Tramer, in: BLBI, 5 (1962), 23–43; W. Laqueur, in: YLBI, 6 (1961), 193–205; W. Preuss, *Ha-Ma'agal Nisgar* (1968); M. Calvary, *Das neue Judentum* (1936), 75–87; F. Pollack (ed.), *50 Jahre Blau Weiss* (1962); Bergmann, in: G. Hanokh (ed.), *Darkhei ha-No'ar* (1937), 155–62.

[Ed.]

BLECH, LEO (1871–1958), German opera conductor and composer. Born in Aachen, Blech studied with the composer Humperdinck. He was conductor at the Aachen Stadttheater from 1893 to 1898. In 1906 he was appointed choirmaster of the Berlin Royal Opera (State Opera from 1918) and from 1913 to 1923 was its general musical director. In 1924 he became first conductor of the Berlin Folk Opera. Blech returned to the Berlin State Opera in 1926 and remained its conductor until 1937, when the Nazis forced him to resign. He left Germany for Latvia and in 1941 fled to Sweden, where he became conductor of the Stockholm Royal Opera. He returned to Germany in 1949 and once again conducted the Berlin State Opera. Blech composed a number of one-act and three-act operas, the latter including *Aschenbroedel* ("Cinderella," 1905) and *Rappelkopf* (1917).

Bibliography: MGG; Grove, Dict; Baker, Biog Dict; Riemann-Gurlitt.

[Ed.]

Leo Blech, German opera conductor. Photo German Press Agency, Frankfort.

BLECHER, MARCEL (1909–1938), Rumanian author. Blecher was born in Botoşani, but spent most of his life in the town of Roman. He was something of a phenomenon in Rumanian literature. Afflicted with tuberculosis of the bone he was bedridden for the last ten years of his short life. His illness led to a heightened sensitivity and an obsession with death which contributed to the artistry of his writing. Blecher's work appeared in various periodicals before he published his first collection of poems, *Corp transparent,* in 1934. His first novel, *Intîmplări in irealitatea imediată* ("Incidents in the Immediate Unreality," 1935), was one of the first attempts at surrealism in Rumanian literature. Despite his remoteness from reality Blecher drew some remarkable portraits of a middle-class Jewish family in a

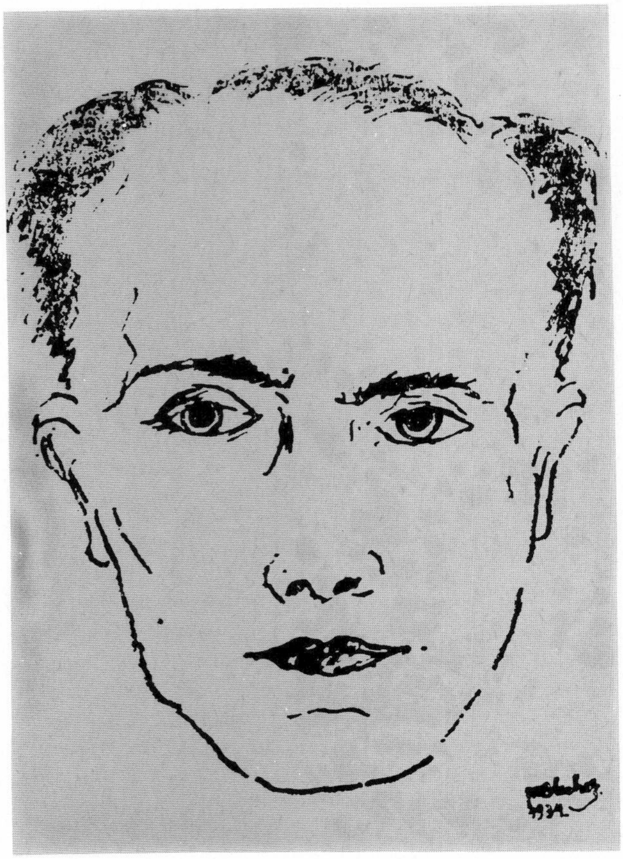

Marcel Blecher, Rumanian author. Self-portrait, 1934.

provincial town and some lively scenes of Jewish customs. In his autobiographical novel *Inimi cicatrizate* ("Scarred Souls," 1937) Blecher described life in the sanatorium at Berck-sur-Mer in France where he spent a long time encased in a plaster cast. In his book he examined with deep psychological insight not only his own spiritual experiences but those of his fellow patients. A Yiddish version of "Scarred Souls" appeared in Rumania and two editions of the original were published in Israel. At the suggestion of André Gide, Blecher began translating the novel into French, but died before he could complete the task. Among his unpublished works, he left the manuscript of a novel on a Jewish theme entitled *Vizuina luminoasă* ("The Bright Vision").

Bibliography: G. Călinescu, *Istoria Literaturii Romîne dela origini pînă inprezent* (1941), 880, 928; C. Baltazar, *Scriitor şi Om* (1946), 29–34; Crohmălniceanu, in: *Preuves,* no. 202 (Dec. 1967), 36–38; Litani, in: *Al ha-Mishmar* (Sept. 20, 1964); Pană, in: *Revista Cultului Mozaic* (March 1, 1968).

[D.L.]

°**BLEEK, FRIEDRICH** (1793–1859), German Bible critic; professor of theology at Bonn from 1829 to 1859. Bleek maintained that the basic document of the Pentateuch is the Elohist (the E document) which has been supplemented by sections from an unconnected Yahwist strand. He argued for the unity of Daniel, and he wrote on the composition of Isaiah, Ezra, Nehemiah, and the Sibylline Oracles. His most important work was in the area of New Testament exegesis, where he was primarily interested in the defense of Christian tradition against the criticism of the Tuebingen school.

Two of his important works are *Einleitung in das Alte Testament* (1860, 1878[4]), and *Einleitung in das Neue Testament* (1866[2]).

Bibliography: Kamphausen, in: ADB, 2 (1875), 701–2.

[Z.G.]

BLEICHROEDER, German banking family. SAMUEL BLEICHROEDER (1779–1855), German banker, the son of a sexton, opened in his native Berlin a money-changing and lottery store in 1803 which developed into the banking firm of S. Bleichroeder. In 1837 the Rothschild banking house of Frankfort appointed him their representative in Berlin. The firm became a member of the Rothschild and the Preussen consortiums.

His son GERSON VON BLEICHROEDER (1822–1893), was born in Berlin. He entered the firm at 17, and became its head upon his father's death. Under his direction the bank developed into one of the leading financial houses in Germany, mainly engaged in issuing, underwriting, and financing railroad loans. During the 1860s Bleichroeder became financial adviser and private banker to Bismarck who relied on his advice and assistance to overcome his difficulties with the Prussian parliament concerning the financial preparations for the 1866 war. Bleichroeder also advised Bismarck regarding the indemnities payable by France after the 1870–71 war. In 1872 Bleichroeder was raised to the nobility. During the Congress of Berlin (1878), he cooperated closely with Sir Moses Montefiore and Adolph Crémieux and successfully invoked Bismarck's assistance for the protection and emancipation of the Rumanian Jews. After Bleichroeder's death, his three sons, HANS, ADOLF (d. 1902), and JAMES (d. 1937), who all abandoned the Jewish faith, continued to run the firm with other members of the family. In 1931 the bank entered into a "community of interest" with the Jewish banking firm of Arnhold Brothers and in 1937 a successor firm was formed in New York under the name of Arnold and S. Bleichroeder, in anticipation of the "Aryanization" of the Berlin house, which took place in 1938. The New York house does not include any bearers of the Bleichroeder name.

Bibliography: O. Joehlinger, *Bismarck und die Juden* (1921); D. S. Landes, in: YLBI, 5 (1960), 201–21; H. Rachel and P. Wallich, *Berliner Grosskaufleute und Kapitalisten*, 2 vols. (1934–38); H. Schnee, *Die Hoffinanz und der moderne Staat*, 3 (1955), index.

[J.O.R.]

BLEJER, DAVID (1913–), Argentine lawyer and politician. Blejer, the son of Jewish colonists in the province of Entre Ríos, was born in Buenos Aires. He was legal adviser to the Argentine Agrarian Institute and lectured on agrarian economics. As a young man he joined the Unión

David Blejer, Argentine politician.

Cívica Radical Intransigente, the party of Arturo Frondizi, who was president of the Argentine from 1958 to 1962. During Frondizi's presidency, Blejer was undersecretary successively of the Ministry of Interior and the Ministry of Labor and Social Security, and then served as ambassador to Mexico.

[I.DR.]

BLEMISH (Heb. מום), a defect in the body of a man or an animal. Defects of conduct too are metaphorically called blemishes (Deut. 32:5; Prov. 9:7; Job. 11:15). A blemished priest was unfit to serve in the priesthood (Lev. 21:16–23) and was precluded from approaching the altar to offer the fire-offerings. He was permitted to carry out only Temple functions not involving actual service at the altar, since he was not standing before the Lord. The Bible forbade a priest who had been blemished to approach the veil (Lev. 21:23), and as a result he was forbidden during the Second Temple period not only to enter the Temple but even to step between the altar and the sanctuary (Kelim 1:9). He was permitted, however, to go into the other parts of the Temple area and even to "eat of the food of his God, of the most holy as well as of the holy" (Lev. 21:22).

Just as the officiating priest had to be unblemished, so no blemished animal was permitted to be offered on the altar (Lev. 22:17–25; Deut. 15:21–23; 17:1; cf. Mal. 1:6ff.). An animal whose blemishes were slight—"with a limb extended or contracted" (Lev. 22:23; see below)—could only be offered as a freewill offering, which was less stringent. A blemished priest was forbidden to approach the veil and approach the altar because "he shall not profane these places sacred to Me" (Lev. 21:23). A blemished sacrifice that was offered would not be acceptable on behalf of the one offering it (Lev. 22:20). Such a sacrifice is called an "abomination" in Deuteronomy 17:1 (cf. the strong words in Mal. 1:8ff. against a prevailing laxness in this regard). The flesh of a blemished animal, however, is permitted as food (Deut. 15:21–22).

The requirement that priests and sacrifices should be without blemish was common to all the ancient civilizations, and there is evidence for this from Egypt, Mesopotamia, Ḥatti (the land of the Hittites), Greece, and Rome. Egyptian documents state that candidates for the priesthood were examined for blemishes, and that the sacrifices were examined in the same way, marking animals fit for sacrifice. Documents from Mesopotamia state that the priests and the sacrifices had to be perfect, without any blemish. The Hittites also regarded the presence at the ceremonial ritual of those blemished as an affront to the gods. The requirement that both priests and sacrifices be without blemish is also known from Greece and Rome.

The following blemishes are enumerated as making priests unfit for service in the Temple (Lev. 21:18–20): *ivver* (*ʿiwwer*), a blind man; *pisse'aḥ*, one injured in the thigh, from birth or as the result of an accident (cf. II Sam. 4:4), in contrast to a man who has a broken leg; *ḥarum*, a man whose nose is sunk in between his eyes; *saruaʿ*, apparently one with hands or feet of unequal length; a man who has a broken leg or broken arm; *gibben* and *dak* (*daq*), whose meanings depend on whether the words are connected with the following (Rashi, Maimonides) or with the previous bone deformities (Ibn Ezra; according to the first explanation *gibben* is one whose eyebrows are long and descend over his eyes and *daq* is one who has a kind of skin (pterygium) over the cornea of his eye; according to the second explanation, *gibben* is a hunchback and *daq* is one whose foot or hand muscles degenerated as a result of corrosion, and are thinner than usual); *tevallul*, a sufferer from cataract; *garav* and *yallefet*, skin diseases, not identified with certainty (*garav* is probably dermatitis and *yallefet* is probably Egyptian herpes, ringworm); *mero'aḥ ashekh*, one with a crushed testicle.

Blemishes that render an animal unifit for sacrifice are (Lev. 22:22, 24): *avveret*, (*awweret*) blindness; *shavur* or *ḥaruẓ*, broken or cracked limbs that cause the animal to be lame; skin diseases (*yabbelet*, a wen, referring to a swelling discernible because of its size; *garav* and *yallefet* (see above)); defects of the testicles due to bruising by hand (*maʿukh*), or cutting with an implement (*katut*), tearing with pincers or a cord *(natuq)*, or even complete severence by castration *(karut)*; *saruʿa* and *qaluṭ*, very slight blemishes, referring to an animal having one leg longer or shorter than the other (these animals may be sacrificed as a freewill offering (Lev. 22:23)). According to some, only *saruʿa* means 'living limbs of unequal length,' whereas *qaluṭ* means "club-footed," i.e., in the case of cattle, sheep, and goats, with the hoof uncloven. [Ed.]

In the Talmud. Blemishes in the Talmud can be divided into four categories: those mentioned in the Bible as physical blemishes disqualifying priests for service; physical blemishes disqualifying animals for sacrifice; nonphysical blemishes in both; and moral blemishes.

Blemishes in Animals. Whereas the Bible enumerates only 12 disqualifying blemishes in animals and 12 in the case of a priest, the Mishnah subdivides them to the minutest detail. The whole of chapter 6 of tractate *Bekhorot* is devoted to an enumeration of those blemishes in an animal. They are divided into permanent and transient blemishes, the former referring to those which continue for 80 days. As an example of the detail, where the Bible merely says "blind," the Mishnah 6:2 enumerates a pierced, defective, or slit eyelid, a speck in the eye, a commingling of the iris and the outer part, various growths in the eye, and rheum, or if its lip is pierced. According to the legend of *Kamẓa and Bar Kamẓa in the Talmud, it was the infliction of one of those two blemishes by Bar Kamẓa in the sacrifice offered up by the Roman emperor "which we count as a blemish and Romans do not," and the obstinate refusal of R. Zechariah b. Avkulas to make any exception, which was the immediate cause of the Roman War (Git. 55b, 56a). The list even includes such blemishes as "if the tail of the animal does not reach the knee joint" or if its lower jaw protrudes beyond the upper. Maimonides lists 50 disqualifying blemishes in man and beast (Yad, Bi'at ha-Mikdash, ch. 7).

Blemishes in Priests. All the blemishes enumerated for animals similarly disqualify priests from serving in the Temple, but chapter 7 of *Bekhorot* gives another extensive list of blemishes which disqualify a priest but which are not considered blemishes in an animal, such as baldness, flat nose, bowleggedness, black skin, red skin or albino, and many others. Maimonides numbers 90 blemishes which particularly apply to man (*ibid.*, ch. 8).

Nonphysical Blemishes. In addition to bodily defects, the Mishnah enumerates some moral blemishes which disqualify a priest: if he has been guilty of homicide or murder, if he has married a woman forbidden to a kohen (though permitted to a non-kohen), or if he becomes ritually unclean by contact with the dead. In the last two cases he can resume his service if he undertakes to separate himself from the woman or undertakes to adhere in the future to the rules of ritual cleanness applying to a kohen. These blemishes originally applied to the actual service in the Temple, and it is explicitly stated that a priest so disqualified could and did participate in reciting the *Priestly Blessing (see Second *Temple, Order of Service). It was, however, laid down that if a kohen had a disfiguration which caused people to stare at him, he was not to recite the priestly blessing, not because the blemish disqualified him but because it would distract the recipients of the blessing. Thus as far as physical blemishes were concerned, this applied only to the hands, and even included a dyer whose hands were dye stained (Mishnah Meg. 4:7). The *Gemara* (Meg. 24b) extends this prohibition to the feet, and even to speech impediments. The test was purely pragmatic; thus if the kohen was so well-known that his blemish raised no curiosity, the ban was removed. A complete list of those "non-statutory" blemishes is given in Shulḥan Arukh, Oraḥ Ḥayyim 128:30. Although the prohibition against a blemished priest officiating in the Temple is given in the Bible, the Talmud justifies it by interpreting the word *shalom*, in Numbers 25:12, as *shalem* ("whole") since according to the masorah the *vav* is written with a break (Kid. 66b).

Moral Blemishes. The word *mum* for a blemish in the Bible also refers to moral blemishes (cf. Deut. 32:5) and is used extensively in this sense in the Talmud: "Do not ascribe to your fellow your own blemish" (BM 59b). If a man falsely accused someone of being a slave, it was evident that he himself was a slave, since "a person stigmatizes another with his own blemish" (Kid. 70b). [L.I.R.]

Bibliography: Pauly Wissowa, 8 (1913), 1417; 18, pt. 1 (1939), 592–4; ERE, 10 (1925), 285; B. Meissner, *Babylonien und Assyrien*, 2 (1925), 54, 83; Jeremias, Alte Test, 423; idem, *Handbuch der altorientalischen Geisteskultur* (1929), 259; E. Dhorme, *Les Religions de Babylonie et d'Assyrie* (1949), 227; H. Bonnet, *Reallexikon der aegyptischen Religionsgeschichte* (1952), 748.

BLESSING AND CURSING. In the Bible these two antonyms have three meanings: (1) the invocation of good or evil; (2) good fortune or misfortune; and (3) the person or thing upon whom or which the fortune or misfortune falls. Thus the first meaning is best represented in English by the terms benediction and malediction or imprecation. The most common formulas of invocation use the terms *barukh* and *ʾarur*. Despite the frequent assertion that words themselves were regarded as intrinsically power-laden, there is little evidence that biblical Israel was any more prone to such a view than is contemporary man. When, in the Bible, man does the invoking, the source of power is (explicitly or implicitly) the Deity; hence both blessings and curses are basic prayers. When the Deity pronounces either good or evil against anyone, the pronouncement is to be understood as a decree rather than a prayer; when man is the subject of the verb *berekh* and the Deity is the object, the verb denotes praise, for nowhere in the Bible is there any indication that the power of God is itself increased by man's pronouncements. As substantive good, blessing is most frequently represented by the terms *berakhah*, *shalom*, and *ṭov*; its most common antonyms are *kelalah (qelalah)* and *raʿah*. Blessings include health, long life, many and enduring progeny, wealth, honor, and victory. The dependence of Palestinian agronomy on rainfall is reflected in the use of *berakhah* for the rains in their due season. Curses, it follows, are sickness and death, barrenness in people and cattle, crop failure, poverty, defeat, and disgrace. That the beneficiary of good fortune or the victim of ill fortune is himself sometimes regarded as a blessing or a curse is reflected in such passages as Genesis 12:2, "be a blessing" and Numbers 5:21, "may the Lord make you a curse." This use of the terms reflects the usage of beneficiaries of good or victims of evil as examples of felicity and disaster in benedictions and imprecations (Gen. 48:20; Jer. 24:9).

Terminology. The basic term for imprecation in the Bible is *ʾalah*. In most instances it represents an adjuration, i.e., a conditional curse upon someone in the second or third person. As "imprecation" the *ʾalah* is implicitly present in every oath *(shevuʿah)*, for an oath is by definition a conditional self-curse. The close relationship between these two terms accounts for the confusion of the two in many translations; indeed, by the operation of metonymy the term *hishbiʿa*, which normally means "to administer an oath," may have the meaning "to adjure." The root *ʾrr* (ארר; and the noun derived from it, *meʾerah*) shows traces of the concept of "spell," a malignant state in which the victim is barred from such benefits as a share of the earth's fertility, participation in a fellowship or society, and the like. Thus where *ʾalah* reflects the curse as formulation, *ʾrr* reflects the curse as operational. The third term most frequently associated with the idea of curse is the verb *kallel* (*qallel*;קלל) and the cognate noun *qelalah*. This term has a far broader connotative range. It reflects attitudes, behavior, and actions all the way from contempt, through verbal abuse, to physical violence; just as *berekh* (ברך) and *kibbed* (כבד; and the nouns derived from them) express respect, compliments and good wishes, and material benefit. The failure to recognize the broad range of meanings expressed by *qillel* resulted in the notion (as early as the Septuagint translation) that *qillel ʾElohim* means to "curse God" (cf. Ex. 22:27; Lev. 24:10–23). To avoid this horrendous formulation the biblical text was altered: in I Samuel 3:13 from *ʾElohim* ("God") to *la-hem* ("to them"); in I Kings 21:13, and Job 1:5, 1:11, 2:9 the original *qillel* is replaced by the *euphemistic antonym *berekh*. The rabbinic tradition in Sanhedrin 7:5 also had recourse to a euphemism in an attempt to understand how imprecation against the Deity is possible in a monotheistic system. In fact, it has been demonstrated that the phrase translated "curse God," *qillel ʾElohim*, usually really means "show disrespect for God"—for the most part by disobeying His moral standards. The antonymous phrase is *yareʾ/yirʾat Elohim*, "to fear God," i.e., show respect for His maxims. Since both blessings and curses are types of prayers, it is not surprising that they are encountered everywhere in the Bible, in everyday contexts, legal and diplomatic proceedings. Salutations of greeting and departure are normally expressions of goodwill, hence the term *b-r-kh* (ברך) for such salutations. Recourse to prayer, i.e., an address to the Deity, is to be expected when human resources are exhausted or, by nature of the situation, unavailing. Hence the employment of oath and adjuration in legal disputes and in treaty formulations.

Ancient Near Eastern treaties exhibit the feature of curses, in that the subjected power invokes its own god or gods to administer punishment in the event of failure to observe the agreed upon (i.e., imposed) terms of the treaty (cf. Ezek. 17:11–19). The formulation of the covenant between Israel and its God follows the pattern of such "vassal treaties." An examination of the curses in Deuteronomy 27:15–26 reveals the essential function of the curse, for all the enumerated breaches of provisions of the covenant are of such a nature that society would be unable to punish them. It follows also that the invocation of God in a curse (be it oath or adjuration) is not only blameless but praiseworthy; for every such invocation is implicitly an acknowledgment of the Deity's sovereignty. This is made explicit in such passages as Deuteronomy 6:13, 10:20, and Isaiah 45:23. Heinous, by contrast, is swearing or cursing "by the name of" other deities. A frequent formulation of biblical curses is *Ko yaʿaseh YHWH ve-kho yosif* ("May the Lord do such-and-such and worse if . . ."). Another formulation invokes the power of both king and Deity or of one of them only: "by the life (Heb. *ḥai*) of the king/the Lord." This formula is a frozen form, that is, a relic of a concept no longer in consonance with the thinking of the people who continue to employ it. The earlier belief was that the life of the king or a god could be put in jeopardy by a solemn pronouncement in support of a promise or of the truth of an assertion; through being thereby involved in the outcome the king or god (and his punitive power) was brought into an issue which might otherwise have been of no concern to him. (This type of thinking remains in evidence today when a person swears "by" or "on" something more precious than his own life, e.g., the head of his child, or his mother's grave.) Alternatives to *ḥai* in cursing/swearing by the life of God or king are *nefesh* "life," "soul") and *shem* ("name"). Thus the Deity Himself is pictured as employing this oath form, swearing "by Myself" (Gen. 22:16, Jer. 22:5; 49:13) or "by My great Name" (Jer. 44:26). [H.Br.]

In the Talmud. The rabbis continued to stress the efficacy of blessings and curses. With regard to the former, they ordained that God's name be utilized in the blessing uttered when meeting or greeting people in accordance with the practice of Boaz (Ber. 9:5; Ruth 2:4). Continuing biblical traditions, the rabbis introduced blessings at circumcisions (Targum Uzziel to Gen. 48:20), at marriages (Gen. 24:60), and upon separating from an acquaintance one was advised to say, "Go unto peace" (Ex. 4:18; MK 29a). The sages declared that even "the blessing or the cursing of an ordinary man should not be lightly esteemed" (Meg. 15a). The Jew was also encouraged to respond "Amen" after the blessing of a Gentile (TJ, Ber. 8:9, 12c). Great stress was placed upon the blessing of an elder, and people were urged to receive their blessings (Ruth R. 6:2). Likewise, people were encouraged to bless the righteous whenever they mentioned them (Gen. R. 49:1). Abraham blessed everybody, and he was constantly blessed by God (Gen. R. 59:5). The ability to bless others was passed on by Abraham to Isaac (Gen. R. 61:6). All blessings were considered as incomplete unless they were also accompanied by peace (Num. R. 11:7).

See also *Benediction; *Blessing of Children; and *Priestly Blessing. [Ed.]

Cursing. According to the Talmud even an undeserved curse by a scholar is effective (Mak. 11a), and an undeserved curse will fall back upon him who utters it (Sanh. 49a and Rashi, ad loc.).

The biblical prohibitions of cursing were elaborated in rabbinic *halakhah* to comprise: (1) The cursing of God (see *Blasphemy). (2) The cursing of parents (Ex. 21:17; Lev. 20:9; cf. Prov. 20:20; 30:11; Sanh. 7:8). This prohibition applies to proselytes toward their unconverted parents (Maim. Yad, Mamrim, 5:11). (3) The cursing of judges and of the chiefs of the people: kings, heads of Sanhedrin, etc. (Ex. 22:27; Eccles. 10:20; Maim. Yad, Sanhedrin, 26:1). (4) The biblical prohibition of cursing the deaf (Lev. 19:14) was interpreted to comprise any poor, physically handicapped, or even any person in his absence (Sanh. 66a; Yad, loc. cit.). (5) The prohibition of cursing is extended to self-cursing (Shevu. 4:13; Yad, loc. cit.) (6) The cursing by a woman of her husband's parents in his presence is a valid reason for divorcing her without the repayment of her *dowry as stipulated in the **ketubbah* ("marriage contract"; Ket. 72a–b; Sh. Ar., EH 115:4). Cursing is permissible only when prompted by religious motives such as the cursing of those who are guilty of reprehensible actions (Men. 64b), or who mislead the people by calculating the date of the coming of the Messiah (*meḥasehvei kiẓẓin*; Sanh. 97b). While rabbinic ethics does not go to the length of the New Testament demand to "bless them that curse you . . ." (Luke 6:27) it disapproves of cursing in general and the Talmud quotes a popular proverb "Be rather of the cursed than of the cursing" (Sanh. 49a). These ideas found their expression in the prayer cited in the Talmud (Ber. 17a) and said thrice daily at the conclusion of the **Amidah*: "O my God, guard my tongue from evil and my lips from speaking guile; and to such as curse let my soul be dumb, yea, let my soul be unto all as the dust. . . ."

The popular belief in the magic power of a curse, even if pronounced unintentionally, has led to the custom of reading the verses of the Bible, Leviticus 26:14–43 and Deuteronomy 28:15–68, called *Tokheḥah* ("chastisement"), in a low voice. Out of fear, people were reluctant to be called up to the Torah reading of these particular sections, so it became customary in some congregations to call for a volunteer *(mi she-yirẓeh)*, or, when a beadle (*shammash*) was hired, it was agreed that it will be his duty to be called up for the reading of the *Tokheḥah* sections (see Isserles to Sh. Ar., OḤ 428:6). Some pious rabbis used to volunteer to be called up to the reading of the *Tokheḥah* to prevent embarrassment to other people. [Ed.]

Bibliography: H. Blank, in: HUCA, 23 (1950–51), 73–95; Speiser, in: JAOS, 80 (1960), 198–200; H. C. Brichto, *The Problem of "Curse" in the Hebrew Bible* (1963); T. Canaan, in: JPOS, 15 (1935), 235–79; J. Scharbert, in: *Biblica*, 39 (1958), 1–26.

BLESSING OF CHILDREN. Belief in the value and efficacy of parental blessing of children is attested in biblical stories, such as those of Noah's blessing of Shem and Japheth (Gen. 9:26–27); Isaac's blessing of Jacob and Esau (Gen. 27, and 28:1–4); and Jacob's blessing of his sons (Gen. 49) and his grandsons, Ephraim and Manasseh (Gen. 48:13–22). The importance of parental blessing is also stressed by Ben Sira (Ecclus. 3:9). The blessing of the children is performed on Sabbath eve either in the synagogue or in the home; on the eves of holy days, of the Day of Atonement, and before leaving for a journey. The blessing is usually given by the father, on special occasions also by the mother, to both small and adult children, by laying the hands upon the head of the child and pronouncing (for a boy) the verse "May God make thee like Ephraim and Manasseh" (Gen. 48:20) or (for a girl) the verse "May God make thee like Sarah, Rebekah, Rachel, and Leah" (cf. Ruth 4:11), followed by the priestly benediction (Num. 6:24–26). From the Middle Ages, the ceremony of blessing children became deeply rooted (see J. Buxtorf, *Synagoga Judaica* (1604), ch. 15, and Jacob *Emden's *Siddur*, 1748). The parental blessing is also recited prior to the child's wedding ceremony and by parents on their deathbed. Where grandparents are still alive, it was customary to receive their blessing, too, especially on the eve of the Day of Atonement and before the wedding ceremony (Abraham Danzig, *Ḥayyei Adam* (1810), 143:19). In some communities the parental blessing was also bestowed after the **Havdalah* ceremony at the end of the Sabbath (Baer, Seder, 309).

Bibliography: Eisenstein, Dinim, 56–57; Abrahams, Companion, cxxxiv–cxxxv. [Ed.]

Figure 1. "The Rabbi's Blessing" by Moritz Oppenheim, the 19th-century German painter. N.Y., Oscar Gruss Collection.

Figure 2. Children being blessed as they leave the synagogue. Miniature from the 14th-century Spanish *Sarajevo Haggadah*. Yugoslavia, Sarajevo National Library, fol. 34.

BLINDMAN, YERUḤAM (c. 1798–1891), cantor and composer. Blindman, who was called "Yeruḥam ha-Koton" ("little") because of his small stature, served as cantor in Kishinev, Tarnopol, and Berdichev. Though not universally admired, his voice was a remarkable lyric tenor with unlimited falsetto range. The public was attracted by his pious appearance in long, white beard and his great artistry in improvisation. His formal knowledge of music was rudimentary, but his own melodies, composed in the spirit of Jewish folksong against a liturgical background, earned him a reputation as a composer of synagogal music. His singing with choir consistently attracted large crowds, including gentiles. He performed with his choir throughout Russia and Austria.

Bibliography: H. H. Harris, *Toledot ha-Neginah ve-ha-Ḥazzanut be-Yisrael* (1950), 404–5; Idelsohn, Music, 302–3; A. Rosen (ed.), *Di Geshikhte fun Khazones* (1924), 97. [J.L.N.]

BLINDNESS. The standard Hebrew term for a blind person is עִוֵּר (*'ivver;* Ex. 4:11; et al.), a noun in the form used for bodily defects. The abstract form is עִוָּרוֹן (*'ivvaron,* "blindness"; Deut. 28:28; Zech. 12:4). The word סַנְוֵרִים (*sanverim;* Gen. 19:11; II Kings 6:18), sometimes incorrectly translated "blindness," means a blinding light causing (possibly temporary) loss of vision (E. A. Speiser).

Eyes which cannot see are described by the verbs כהה ("be dim"; Gen. 27:1; et al.), קום ("be fixed," "still"; I Sam. 4:15; I Kings 14:4), חשך ("be darkened"; Lam. 5:17; et al.), כבד ("be heavy"; Gen. 48:10), and שעע and טחח ("be smeared over;" Isa. 6:10, 32:3; 44:18; et al.). Genesis 29:17 describes Leah's eyes as *rakkot,* but whether this means "tender" or "weak" is moot.

Incidence and Causes. Blindness was widespread in the ancient Near East. Preventive techniques included the application of hygienic ointments, especially kohl, and surgical operations (cf. *The Code of Hammurapi,* 215–20 in Pritchard, Texts, 175). (There is no evidence that the biblical injunction against eating pork was intended or understood to prevent trichinosis or other diseases which cause blindness.) Biblical cases include Isaac (Gen. 27:1), Jacob (Gen. 48:10), Eli (I Sam. 3:2; 4:15), and Ahijah the Shilonite (I Kings 14:4), all of whose eyesight failed in old age. (Deut. 34:7 makes a point of reporting that Moses' eyesight had not failed in old age.) Both Isaac and Jacob in their blindness reversed the status of a younger and an older descendant in blessing them (Gen. 27 (cf. 29:23–6); 48:8–19).

Aside from old age, natural causes of blindness are not mentioned in the Bible. In a few passages blindness is mentioned as a punishment inflicted by God: it is threatened for Israel's violation of the covenant (Deut. 28:28–29; M. Weinfeld takes this passage metaphorically; see below) and for the "negligent shepherd" of Zechariah 11:15–17; Proverbs (30:17) warns that the eye which is disrespectful to parents will be plucked out by birds of prey (cf. *The Code of Hammurapi,* 193, in Pritchard, Texts, 175). Theologically speaking, all cases of blindness are attributed to God (Ex. 4:11), just as the restoration of sight is credited to Him (Ps. 146:8). However, outside of the specific cases mentioned, blindness in general is nowhere stated to be a punishment for sin. In a few passages God strikes His servants' assailants with blinding flashes (Gen. 19:11; II Kings 6:18–20) or permanent blindness (Zech. 12:4; Ps. 69:24) in order to protect His servants.

As a punishment inflicted by human agency one finds the penalty of "an eye for an eye" in the talion formula (Ex. 21:24; Lev. 24:20; Deut. 19:21), although it is debated whether this was ever carried out literally in Israel (cf. *The Code of Hammurapi,* 196–9, where the relation of the law to actual practice is similarly uncertain). Samson and King Zedekiah were blinded, respectively, by the Philistines and Nebuchadnezzar (Judg. 16:21; II Kings 25:7; Jer. 39:7; 52:11). Nahash the Ammonite demanded the putting out of the right eye of all the people of Jabesh-Gilead as a condition for sparing the city (I Sam. 11:2). Several passages speak of the eyes being "spent" or "pining away" from tears and grief. The verb used is usually כלה ("Be spent"); the context makes it clear that soreness rather than blindness is meant (e.g., Lev. 26:16; Deut. 28:65; Jer. 14:6; Lam. 2:11; 4:17; cf. also עשש, Ps. 6:8, "be spent," "waste away").

Effects. Blind persons are naturally helpless in many ways (cf. II Sam. 5:6; Isa. 35:5–6; Jer. 31:7, which invoke the blind, the lame, and the mute as representative examples of helplessness) and subject to exploitation (Deut. 28:29). Biblical ethics warned against exploiting them (Lev. 19:14; Deut. 27:18; Job 29:15).

As a physical defect blindness disqualified priests from sacrificing or approaching the altar (Lev. 21:17–23) and rendered sacrificial animals unacceptable (Lev. 22:21–22; Deut. 15:21; Mal. 1:8). Some have taken the enigmatic saying "the blind and the lame shall not come into the house" (II Sam. 5:8) to indicate that at one time these were forbidden entrance to temples.

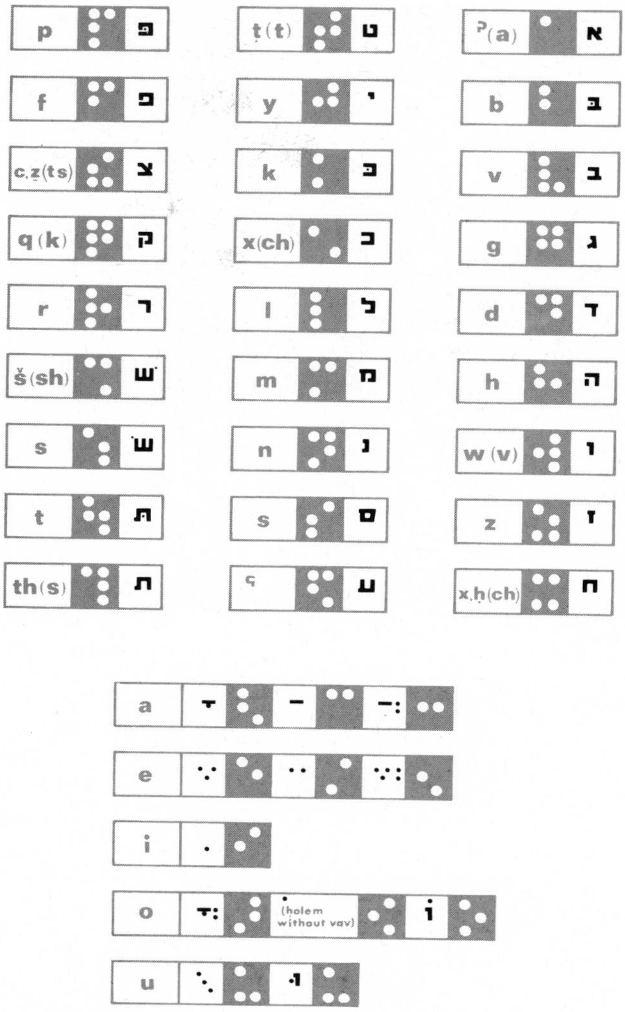

The Hebrew Braille system adopted universally in the 1950s.

Metaphoric Uses. Blindness is used with several metaphoric meanings in the Bible. Frequently it refers to the lack of intellectual or moral understanding (Isa. 29:9–10, 18). Judges are warned that bribes, or gifts, blind the eyes of the discerning (Ex. 23:8; Deut. 16:19). Isaiah is told that his mission is to besmear the eyes of Israel so that it will not "see" and repent and be healed (6:10). In Isaiah 56:10 blindness refers to negligence, while in Numbers 16:14 putting out the eyes is usually taken to mean deceiving. The helplessness and exploitability of the blind made blindness a natural metaphor for oppression and injustice in Deuteronomy 28:28–29 and Isaiah 59:9–10 (cf. Lam. 4:14; M. Weinfeld has noted that the association of blindness and darkness with oppression in these passages also reflects the Mesopotamian association of the sun-god with justice (cf. a related association in II Sam. 23:3–4; Hos. 6:5b; Zeph. 3:5)). A related metaphor is the use of blindness to describe those who dwell in the darkness of prison or captivity (Isa. 42:7, 16–19; 43:8; 49:9; 61:1; cf. Ps. 146:7–8; this use has roots in Mesopotamian royal inscriptions).

[J.H.T.]

In Talmud and Jewish Law. The unusually large number of talmudic sages who were blind probably reflects the wide prevalence of this disability in ancient times. In addition to Bava b. Buta, who was blinded by Herod (BB 4a), mention may be made of Nahum of Gimzo (Ta'an. 21a), Dosa b. Harkinas (Yev. 16a), and R. Joseph and R. Sheshet in Babylon (BK 87a), as well as a number of anonymous blind scholars (cf. Ḥag. 5b; TJ Pe'ah, end). Matya b. Heresh is

Blind youths learning to use Linotype machines at the Amal school of printing, Tel Aviv.

said to have deliberately blinded himself to avoid temptation, but his sight was subsequently restored by the angel Raphael (Tanḥ. B., ed. Buber, addition to *Ḥukkat*). The talmudic name for a blind man is *suma* (Ḥag. 1:1; Meg. 4:6), but the euphemism *sagi nahor* ("with excess of light") is often used (Ber. 58a.; TJ Pe'ah end; and especially Lev. R. 34:13 "the *suma* whom we call *sagi nahor*").

Unlike the deaf-mute, who is regarded in Jewish law as subnormal, the blind person is regarded as fully normal, and most of the legal and religious restrictions placed upon him are due to the limitations caused by his physical disability. The statement (Ned. 64b) based on Lamentations 3:6—"He hath made me to dwell in darkness as those that have been long dead"—that "the blind man is regarded as dead," is of purely homiletic interest and has no practical application. In the second century R. Judah expressed the opinion that a blind man was exempt from all religious obligations, and as late as the time of the blind Babylonian *amora* Joseph (fourth century) the *halakhah* had not yet been determined (see his moving statement in BK 87a), but it was subsequently decided against his view. Even the statement of R. Judah that a person blind from birth cannot recite the *Shema,* since the first of the two introductory blessings is for the daily renewal of light (Meg. 4:6; TB Meg. 24a), was later amended since he enjoys the benefit of light (Rosh, resp. 4:21); the law that a blind man could not be called up to the reading of the Torah, since the passage must be read from the scroll (OḤ 53:14), was abolished with the institution of the *ba'al kore,* who reads the passage for those called up (Taz. to OḤ 141:1). The ruling of Jair Ḥayyim Bacharach (*Ḥavvot Ya'ir* 176) that if there were a person more suitable, a blind person should not conduct the service is an individual opinion and Yehudai Gaon, who himself was blind, gives a contrary opinion (J. Mueller, *Mafte'aḥ li-Teshuvot ha-Ge'onim* (1891), 67).

Similarly, although it was laid down that a totally blind person may not act as a judge, it is stated that when R. Johanan heard of a blind man acting as judge he did not forbid it (Sanh. 34b, cf. ḤM 7:2; for instances in the Middle Ages see *Paḥad Yiẓḥak* s.v. *Suma*). Even as late as the time of Joseph Caro in the 16th century, it was laid down that a blind person is forbidden to act as a *shoḥet* only "in the first instance"; the total prohibition was enacted later (YD 1:9 and commentaries). A special case was the exemption of a blind person from the duty of going up to Jerusalem on the Pilgrim Festivals. The special nature of this law, which is derived from the homiletical interpretation of a word, is seen in the fact that it applied even to a person blind in only one eye (Ḥag. 1:1, and TB Ḥag. 2a).

During the Middle Ages, blinding was imposed by some *battei din* as a form of extrajudicial punishment and was condoned by contemporary rabbis (Assaf in bibl. nos. 97, 98, 135). Blindness was said to be caused by bloodletting at unfavorable times and by the machinations of demons (see Zimmels in bibl., pp. 88 and 153).

The question has been raised in recent times as to the permissibility of removing the cornea of a deceased person and grafting it on a blind person to restore his sight. Halakhic opinion is almost unanimously in favor, and in a responsum I. J. Unterman added the consideration that the danger to the life of a blind person through accidents is such that it can be regarded as a special case of *pikku'aḥ nefesh* (see *Autopsy). [L.I.R.]

Care of the Blind. The Jewish blind have been traditionally assisted by regular communal and voluntary agencies and associations, as well as special institutions. In the United States the New York Guild for the Jewish Blind, founded around 1908, has a home for aged blind, offers integrated services to the visually handicapped, and has initiated a nonsegregated living plan for the blind. In the United Kingdom the central agency is the Jewish Blind Society in London, founded in 1819, and in 1970 caring for the needs of over 1,500 Jewish blind. It maintains four residential and holiday homes, day centers in provincial cities, and a home for infirm Jewish blind.

The special conditions in Israel as a country of immigration created the problem that the proportion of blind persons of working age in the state was three times higher than in Anglo-Saxon countries (1956). Much has been done to alleviate this position, while the blind person is as far as possible not treated as a social case. He is, however, exempted from paying income tax. Special placement officers facilitate his employment. In 1956 the proportion of blind to ordinary residents was estimated at approximately 2.5 per 1,000; 87% of them had immigrated after 1948. Over 85% were born in countries of Asia and Africa where in many cases the blind were not cared for or enabled to work. There was a comparatively high proportion of married women or widows due to marriage of blind girls to elderly men. The Jewish Institute for the Blind in Jerusalem, founded in 1902, cares for the majority of blind children in the country. It includes a kindergarten, elementary school where subjects are taught in braille, and boarding facilities for pupils attending regular secondary school. It also has a vocational school, industrial training shop, a braille printing press, and two houses for mentally or physically handicapped blind adults.

Other agencies and associations for help of the blind in Israel include Migdal Or, the American Israeli Lighthouse Rehabilitation Center for the Blind in Haifa (Kiryat Ḥayyim), which gives casework reorientation, special training and courses, and develops home industries for blind who are physically incapacitated. The Women's League for Israel of New York assists joint projects with the Ministry of Social Welfare for rehabilitation of blind girls and women, and maintains a sheltered workshop, Orah, and a bookbindery, Malben, which in 1951 took over Kefar Uriel, a village for the blind established in 1950 by the Jewish Agency for blind immigrants; in 1962 it had 63 families (about 350 persons). Heads of families are employed in four workshops. The Israel Foundation for Guide Dogs for the Blind in Haifa was established around 1950. A Central Library for the Blind, established in 1952 in Netanya, has over 5,000 volumes in braille and a talking book library.

The Association for the Blind and Prevention of Blindness, founded in 1953, had branches in nine centers.

The National Council for the Blind, established in 1958 for coordinating, research, and planning, is represented on the World Council for the Blind. Voluntary agencies giving assistance from abroad are Hilfe fuer Blinde in Switzerland and Aide aux Aveugles Israéliens in France. Training for non-Jewish blind is also given by the Saint Vincent Roman Catholic hostel in Jerusalem, and at handicraft centers established in Nazareth and Shefaram. Isolated Arab villages are visited by home teachers. [Ed.]

Modern Incidence and Causes. There is no statutory registration of blindness anywhere in the world. All comparative statistics on the incidence and causes of blindness are therefore largely speculative, and this applies in particular to statistics on blindness in Jews, for whom data are usually lacking in whatever national statistics are available. Comparative studies are thus impossible, and little more than some generalizations can be advanced.

The incidence and causes of blindness in most parts of the world are determined essentially by environmental factors. Jews, as a widely dispersed community, therefore suffer from the locally prevailing environmental causes of blindness. In this respect, if the incidence of blindness in a particular Jewish community is different from that in the general population, it will merely reflect the differences found in the various social groupings of the population at large. Thus in all countries where trachoma is endemic, the disease is more prevalent in rural areas, ill provided with sanitation and health services, than in the more developed urban centers with their populations relatively well housed and well served medically. The high incidence of trachoma in Oriental Jews who immigrated into Israel reflects country of origin and social level, rather than their Jewishness.

In the more highly developed countries, infections and other environmental causes of blindness are steadily declining, and most cases of blindness are now due to affections seen in the elderly (such as "senile" cataract and "senile" macular degeneration) or in the middle-aged (such as glaucoma and, to a lesser extent, myopic atrophy, uveitis, and diabetic retinopathy). These are all "constitutional" diseases, and clinical experience in Western Europe and the United States has brought out a greater incidence of three of these affections in Jews: myopia, diabetic retinopathy, and Tay-Sachs disease, a rare lethal disorder. Although adequate statistics are lacking, this clinical experience is probably well-founded and would be readily explained by the fact that these three affections are all genetically determined, generally by recessive or by polygenic inheritance. Although there is no such thing as a Jewish gene pool, it is true that inbred groups—Quakers no less than Jews and royal families no less than village communities—have many features and genes in common. These are readily perpetuated under the prevailing conditions: a recessive mutant gene is much more likely to spread in a closed community than elsewhere. (The gene for Tay-Sachs disease probably originated as such a mutant in a Jewish family in White Russia during the last century, and by emigration, carriers have spread it into the Jewish communities of Great Britain and the United States.) Contrary to early beliefs, the affection is not exclusively Jewish, for it is seen in other ethnic groups as well. These occasional cases do not add substantially to the load of hereditary blindness in Jews, and it is a moot point whether the greater incidence of blindness from high myopia and diabetic retinopathy in Western Jews adds to that load. The numbers involved would be relatively slight, and compensating deficiencies in other hereditary causes are theoretically possible; actual data are lacking, however.

See *Alphabet, Braille. [A.So.]

Bibliography: Gordon, in: *Archives of Ophthalmology*, 9 (1933), 751ff.; E. A. Speiser, *Genesis* (1964), 139 (on Gen. 19:11); idem, in: JCS, 6 (1952), 81ff. (esp., 89 n. 52); Harrison, in: IDB, 1 (1962), 448–9; M. Z. Segal, *Sifrei Shemu'el* (1964), 260, 262 (on II Sam. 5:6, 8); Weinfeld, in: *Biblica*, 46 (1965), 420–1; Paul, in: JAOS, 88 (1968), 182; H. J. Zimmels, *Magicians, Theologians and Doctors* (1952), 461 notes; S. Assaf, *Ha-Onshin Aḥarei Ḥatimat ha-Talmud* (1922), 97–98, 135.

BLIOKH (Bloch), IVAN STANISLAVOVICH (1836–1901), Russian financier, writer, and pacifist. Born in Radom, Poland, Bliokh studied in Warsaw and Berlin. In Warsaw, he engaged in banking, a field he developed extensively in St. Petersburg. He also played a leading role in the construction of the Russian railroads and put their operation on a sound management basis. Bliokh won international fame through his dedication to pacifism, which is the theme of his six-volume publication *Budushchaya voyna v tekhnicheskom, ekonomicheskom i politicheskom otnosheniyakh* (1898; last vol. translated as *The Future of War . . . Is War Now Impossible?*, 1899). He attempted to prove that wars were of no value to a nation because of the massive expenditures involved and the consequent damage to national economies, apart from the human cost. This book, as well as Bliokh's personal endeavors, were among the factors which influenced Czar Nicholas II to convene the 1899 Hague Peace Conference in order to consider the limitation of armaments and the arbitration of international disputes.

Although Bliokh converted to Calvinism, he maintained his interest in the Jewish question and in improving the lot of Russian Jewry. After the pogroms of the 1890s, he fought strenuously in defense of the Jews and pressed the government to end discrimination. In a five-volume work, *Sravneniye materialnago i nravstvennago blagosostayaniya guberniy zapadnykh, velikorossiyskikh i polskikh* ("A Comparison of the Material and Moral Welfare of the Western, Great Russian, and Polish Provinces," 1901), the preparation of which, with the help of many outstanding experts, cost him hundreds of thousands of rubles, he analyzed the economic condition of the Jews in Russia and emphasized their great contribution to the economy. This work constituted a brilliant defense against the government's anti-Jewish arguments, but was confiscated and burned after publication. Fortunately, a number of copies were by chance saved from the censors, and eventually its contents became widely known through a summary by A. P. Subbotin entitled *Yevreyskiy vopros v yego pravilnom osveshchenii* ("The Jewish Question in its Right Light," 1903).

In 1897 Bliokh became involved in the work of the *Jewish Colonization Association (ICA) in Russia and supported it generously. He showed an interest in Zionism and became a friend of Theodor *Herzl, whom he had met in 1899 at the Hague Peace Conference. (Herzl had come to ask the Russian delegates to help him to obtain an audience with the czar. With Bliokh's assistance Herzl met the head of the Russian delegation, de Staal, and other statesmen.) At Herzl's request, in July 1899 Bliokh tried to persuade the Russian authorities to revoke the decree prohibiting the sale of *Jewish Colonial Trust shares. Shortly before his death, Bliokh established the International Museum of War and Peace in Lucerne, Switzerland.

Bibliography: N. Sokolow, in: JC (Jan. 24, 1902), 11. [N.F.]

BLIS, DAVID (1872–1941), Cuban communal leader. Born in Grodno, Poland, he lived in Germany, the U.S., Argentina, and Mexico, before arriving in Cuba in 1913. There he was co-founder (1924) and president of the Centro Hebreo, and the president of the Centro Israelita, which developed from the Centro Hebreo. Blis, who had close ties with the Sephardi Jews in Cuba, was able to understand both the Ashkenazi and Sephardi communities. He was honorary member of the Sephardi Shevet Aḥim, and of Centro Israelita, the organization of East European Jews. From 1933 to 1934 he was president of the Comisión Jurídica, which functioned at the time as the overall Jewish organization in Havana. On Blis's initiative the Cuban Senate unanimously passed a declaration in 1919 supporting a Jewish homeland in Palestine.

Bibliography: B. Sapir, *Jewish Community of Cuba* (1948), 18–21. [Ed.]

°**BLISS, FREDERICK JONES** (1859–1937), British archaeologist. The son of a missionary, Bliss taught for a time at the Syrian Protestant College, Beirut. On behalf of the *Palestine Exploration Fund, he excavated at Tell al-Ḥasī (1891), Jerusalem (1894–97), and (in collaboration with R. A. S. *Macalister) at various mounds in the *Shephelah (1899–1900). At Tell al-Ḥasī Bliss continued the work of Sir Flinders *Petrie and in Jerusalem he discovered the walls of "Mt. Zion" and the wall enclosing the Tyropoeon Valley, in addition to many other minor discoveries. His work in the Shephelah was marked by some important finds but was too hurried to be of lasting value. His publications include: *Mound of Many Cities* (1898); *Excavations at Jerusalem 1894–1897* (1898); *Excavations in Palestine 1898–1900* (1902), with R. A. S. Macalister; *Development of Palestine Exploration* (1906); and *Religions of Modern Syria and Palestine* (1912). [M.A.-Y.]

BLITZSTEIN, MARC (1905–1964), U.S. composer. Born in Philadelphia, Blitzstein studied with Nadia Boulanger in Paris and Arnold Schoenberg in Berlin. Intensely interested in political problems, he developed a genre of operas of "social significance." His short works, *The Cradle Will Rock* (1937) and *No for an Answer* (1941), were important though transitory landmarks in the American "proletarian opera" movement. Among his other works are *The Airborne* (1946), a cantata resulting from his service with the U.S. army in England during World War II, and a musical drama, *Regina,* based on Lillian *Hellman's play *The Little Foxes* (1949). Blitzstein also made an idiomatic American translation of the libretto of Kurt Weill's *Dreigroschenoper.* His opera on the theme of Sacco and Vanzetti, commissioned by the Ford Foundation for production by the Metropolitan Opera, was left unfinished. He died on the island of Martinique of head injuries suffered in an attack by a group of sailors.

Bibliography: Baker, Biog Dict, and 1965 Supplement; Grove, Dict, s.v; MGG, s.v. [N.S.]

BLOC, ANDRÉ (1896–1966), French sculptor and engineer, who was concerned with the relationship of architecture to sculpture. He was the creator of "habitacles" (pieces of sculpture which could be entered) and "constructions," sculptural forms which lie on the borderline between the two arts. Born in Algiers, Bloc studied science in Paris. He then took a degree in engineering, which he practiced from 1930 onward. In 1941 he began to sculpt, and his first important work was executed in 1949. This was a 38-foot "signal" placed outside the Public Works Museum, Paris, on the occasion of the centenary of the invention of reinforced concrete. In 1951 he helped to found the "Espace" group. He was also associated with the foundation of several architectural journals. Bloc died of a fall while visiting a temple in India.

Bibliography: H. Schaefer-Simmern, *Sculpture in Europe Today* (1955); Gisiger, in: *Werk,* 51 (1964), 271–2. [Ed.]

BLOCH, family of U.S. book publishers. The Bloch Publishing Company was founded by Edward Bloch (1816–1881), who emigrated to the United States from Bohemia. He learned the printing trade in Albany, New York, and in 1854 set up a company in Cincinnati which published newspapers and books of specific Jewish interest in English and German. His publications included *The American Israelite* and *Die Deborah.* Later the company diversified its activities and one of its regular clients was a monastery to which he supplied religious books.

In 1885 Edward's son, Charles (1861–1940), established a branch of the company in Chicago. He took over the management of *The Chicago Israelite,* an edition of *The American Israelite,* and in 1891 he co-founded the Chicago-based *Reform Advocate.* He succeeded his father as president in 1901 and moved the Bloch Publishing Company to New York City, where, in addition to publishing, it was also one of the leading bookstores in the U.S. representing several publishing houses. It concentrated on books of Jewish interest. Charles was also highly active during his years in New York in the Reform movement, taking part in 1907 in the founding of the Free Synagogue of New York, of which he later served as president, and in 1922 of the Jewish Institute of Religion. On his death Charles was succeeded by his son Edward (1885–), under whom the company's activities continued to expand.

Bibliography: S. Grayzel, in: JBA, 12 (1953–55), 72–76. [A.M.H.]

BLOCH, CAMILLE (1865–1949), French historian, archivist, and librarian. A professor at the Sorbonne, Bloch was an authority on the French Revolution and its economic and social antecedents; he was secretary-general of the Society for the Study of the French Revolution. He was archivist of the Aude departement (1891–96) and the Loiret departement (1896–1904) and in 1904 became inspector general of libraries and archives. In World War I he became director of the War Library and War Museum in Paris, and historian of the war period. His *Les causes de la guerre mondiale* (1933; *The Causes of the World War,* 1935) is an important work. During the Nazi period, Bloch was hidden in southern France. After 1945 he supervised for the French government the recovery of books looted by the Germans. He left an unfinished study on the Munich Pact of 1938.

Bibliography: P. Renouvin, in: *Revue Historique,* 202 (1949), 147–9; *Dictionnaire de biographie française,* 6 (1954), 677; *New York Times* (Feb. 16, 1949) 25. [H.A.S.]

BLOCH, CLAUDE (1878–1967), U.S. admiral; commander in chief of the United States Fleet. Born in Woodbury, Kentucky, Bloch entered the U.S. Naval Academy in 1895. He served in the Spanish-American war and was decorated for saving Spaniards from burning ships. In 1900, he fought in the Chinese expedition to suppress the Boxer rebellion. During World War I Bloch was naval transport commander of Plattsburg and in 1918 was appointed assistant chief of the Bureau of Ordnance. He was promoted to rear admiral in 1923 and in 1927 he commanded the battleship *California.* After serving as commandant of the Washington Navy Yard, he was promoted to commander of the battle force with the rank of admiral. In 1938, Bloch was made commander in chief of the United States Fleet. Bloch commanded the shore installations of the 14th Naval District, Hawaii, when Pearl

Harbor was attacked, but played no significant role in the events of that day. Retired because of age in 1942, he was retained on active duty as a member of the General Board until 1946.

Admiral Claude C. Bloch, commander in chief of the U.S. Fleet, 1938–40.

Bibliography: E. Rubin; *140 Jewish Marshalls, Generals and Admirals* (1952). [Mo.K.]

BLOCH, ELIJAH MEYER (c. 1894–1955), Lithuanian rabbi and dean of the Telz (Telshe) Yeshivah in the U.S. Bloch, who was born and educated in Telz, Lithuania, was appointed to the faculty of the yeshivah there in 1917. With the Russian occupation of Lithuania, the yeshivah was moved to Cleveland, Ohio, in 1941, under Bloch's leadership. Bloch retained the singular "Telz style" in Talmud study, which stresses precise inductive reasoning. He resisted every attempt at compromise with the Reform elements of the community, yet succeeded in obtaining the support of the Cleveland Jewish Federation for the local Orthodox high school. Active with the Agudat Israel since the Marienbad Conference of 1937, Bloch played a leading role in the American Agudah. He was also a member of Mo'eẓet Gedolei ha-Torah, the international body which guides the World Agudah on questions of Torah principle, where he was known for the universality of his approach. Bloch actively supported Israel.

Bibliography: *Dos Yidishe Vort* (Feb. 1955). [Ed.]

BLOCH, ERNEST (1880–1959), composer. Bloch, who was born in Geneva, revealed his musical gifts as a child and was only ten when he wrote down a vow that he would become a composer and then, in ritual fashion, burned the inscribed paper over a mound of stones. In the face of parental opposition, he left home at the age of 16 and studied music for eight years in Brussels, Frankfort, Munich, and Paris. At that time he composed his first big work, the *Symphony in C Sharp Minor*. Returning to Geneva in 1904, Bloch entered the family clockmaking business. During the next three years he composed his opera *Macbeth*. It was first produced in 1910 at the Opéra-Comique in Paris, and was warmly received. Major works produced during the years immediately following include *Trois Poèmes Juifs* for orchestra (1913), *Schelomo*, a "Hebrew rhapsody" for cello and orchestra (1916), and the *Israel Symphony* for orchestra and five solo voices (1912–16). Bloch first went to America in 1916, as conductor for the dancer Maud Allan, and soon won recognition. Early in 1917, Karl Muck invited him to conduct the *Trois Poèmes Juifs* in Boston, and a few months later a concert of his orchestral works was given in New York. In 1920, he founded and organized the Cleveland Institute of Music. He left it in 1925 to become director of the San Francisco Conservatory of Music. During his five years in this post, Bloch composed a number of large-scale works. Best known of these is *America*, an "epic rhapsody" for chorus and orchestra (1926). A counterpart to this work is *Helvetia*, a "symphonic fresco" written in tribute to Bloch's native land.

One of Bloch's most important works is the *Avodath Hakodesh* ("Sacred Service") for Sabbath morning for baritone, mixed chorus, and orchestra which he wrote in seclusion in Switzerland during 1930–33 (commissioned by Gerald Warburg). He spent the years 1934–38 in a remote French village. From this period came the piano sonata, *Voice in the Wilderness* (symphonic poem with cello obbligato), and the violin concerto. Bloch also composed three string quartets (1916, 1945, and 1951–52). In 1938 Bloch returned to America. After a number of tours as conductor, he finally settled in 1941 in Agate Beach, Oregon. There he spent the rest of his life except for annual lecture visits to the University of California. The manuscripts he left when he died are in the university's music library at Berkeley, where an Ernest Bloch Archive is being set up.

Many honors came to Bloch in his last years. He continued, however, to go his own way without much regard for musical fashion, and ended his career true to the ideals with which he had begun it. As he once stated: "I do not propose or desire to attempt a reconstruction of the music of the Jews. . . . It is rather the Hebrew spirit that interests me—the complex, ardent, agitated soul that vibrates for me in the Bible; the vigor and ingenuousness of the Patriarchs, the violence that finds expression in the books of the Prophets, the burning love of justice, the desperation of the preachers of Jerusalem, the sorrow and grandeur of the Book of Job, the sensuality of the Song of Songs. All this is in us, all this is in me, and is the better part of me. This it is which I seek to feel within me and to translate in my music—the sacred race-emotion that lies dormant in our souls."

Bibliography: M. Tibaldi Chiesa, *Ernest Bloch* (1933), incl. bibl.; D. Z. Kushner, *Ernest Bloch and His Symphonic Works* (unpubl. dissert. 1967); G. Saleski, *Famous Musicians of Jewish Origin* (1949), 18–27; D. Ewen (ed.), *New Book of Modern Composers* (1961), 86–97; G. M. Gatti, in: *Musical Quarterly*, 7 (1921), 20–38; D. Newlin, *ibid.*, 33 (1947), 443–59; California University, *Autograph Manuscripts of Ernest Bloch at the University of California* (1962); Sendrey, Music, index; Grove, Dict; Baker, Biog Dict. [Di.N.]

BLOCH, ERNST (1885–), German philosopher, born in Ludwigshafen. He studied philosophy, philology, and physics. After 1933 he lived as a refugee in various European cities, and from 1938 in the U.S. In 1949 he was invited to East Germany for a professorship of philosophy at Leipzig. Exposed to the attacks of the East German Communists who had previously honored him, he resolved during a visit to West Germany in 1960–61 not to return, and he began lecturing at Tuebingen, where he was appointed professor. Bloch disliked all system-building, and had a dynamic and imaginative literary style. He constantly criticized accepted opinions and ways of life. In his thought he was intent on the future of mankind; it was a pacifist, socialist utopianism, which, though drawn on a wide heritage of religious metaphysics, including mysticism, was progressive, secular, even atheist. Bloch's thought was an enlightened, non-dogmatic, active Marxist humanism—conceived as "humanity in action"—and a philosophy of society and history culminating in an awareness of the not-yet-being, of the really possible which does not yet exist and appears as the actually real. Being in its full truth is before us; still becoming. Bloch's thought culminates in the progressive-creative principle of Hope. He insists on teaching, in free adherence to Marx, that the true task of thinking is the praxis of changing our human life and world, of making it better, of bringing it on the way of progress to perfection and to the realm of freedom. The book *Erbschaft dieser Zeit* (1935, enlarged 1962) describes and criticizes the mentality which made possible the subduing of Germany by the Nazis. *Freiheit und Ordnung; Abriss der Sozial-Utopien* (1946, incorporated later into the main work *Das Prinzip Hoffnung*, 1954–59) contains a chapter *"Altneuland, Programm des Zionismus."* Bloch's main concern is here to criticize Herzl's bourgeois Zionism, and to say that Judaism should not become a territorial nationalism, but acknowledge and preserve the best that was in Moses *Hess's Utopia, and transform it into a messianic international socialism. While having reprinted this chapter Bloch scarcely mentioned the then new state of Israel. But in June 1967 he was the first and in some respects sharpest speaker in a non-Zionist assembly organized at Frankfort University to proclaim Israel's right to live (*Frieden im Nahen Osten*, 1967). Bloch's earlier main work was *Der Geist der Utopie* (1918, revised ed. 1923). In the same period he wrote *Thomas Muenzer als Theologe der Revolution* (1921, revised ed. 1962). Such themes as, e.g., Moses and the Exodus, the prophets, and Jesus are discussed in nearly all of his writings. His other books include: *Subjekt-Objekt, Erlaeuterungen zu Hegel* (1951, enlarged ed. 1962); *Naturrecht und menschliche Wuerde* (1961); *Philosophische Grundfragen; zur Ontologie des Noch-Nicht-Seins* (1961); and *Atheismus im Christentum; Zur Religion des Exodus und des Reichs* (1968).

Bibliography: *Ernst Bloch zum 70. Geburtsag* (1955), incl. bibl.; *Ernst Blochs Revision des Marxismus* (1957); S. Unseld (ed.), *Ernst Bloch zu Ehren* (1965), incl. bibl.; Schilling, in: *Christian Century*, 84 (1967), 1455–58. [O.I.S.]

BLOCH, FELIX (1905–), U.S. physicist and Nobel laureate. Born in Zurich, he studied theoretical physics at its Federal Institute of Technology where, in 1928, Werner Carl Heisenberg was engaged in his fundamental studies of quantum mechanics. Bloch followed him to Copenhagen and worked there with Heisenberg and Niels *Bohr. From there he went to Holland and then to Rome where he worked with Enrico Fermi. It was during his years of work with these leading scientists that Bloch published his own papers on quantum theory, and on the electrical and magnetic properties of crystals. He also made his basic contributions to the study of ferromagnetism and of the energy losses from charged particles in rapid motion. In 1934, after the Nazis came to power in Germany, Bloch emigrated to the U.S.A. and became associate professor of mathematical physics at Stanford University. Here, besides continuing his theoretical studies, he became interested in experimental physics. In 1940, with Luis D. Alvarez, he was the first to determine the magnetic moment of the neutron. During the next few years he did war research in Stanford and in the Los Alamos laboratory. Returning to Stanford, he published his theory in 1946, and, in collaboration with others, an experimental method somewhat similar to that of Isidor Isaac *Rabi at Columbia University. It related to the very precise measurement of nuclear magnetic moments. In 1952 he was awarded the Nobel Prize for physics. Bloch frequently visited Israel and lectured at its institutes of higher learning.

Felix Bloch, U.S. physicist and Nobel Prize winner.

Bibliography: J. C. Poggendorf, *Biographisch-literarisches Handwoerterbuch der exakten Naturwissenschaften*, 7A (1956), 200; *Nature*, 170 (London, 1952), 911–2. [J.E.H.]

BLOCH, GUSTAVE (1858–1923), French scholar in Roman history. He was deeply influenced by his grandfather, Rabbi Alexandre Aron. Bloch taught at the *lycée* in Besançon until 1873, when he joined the new *Académie Française* in Rome. He was so successful there that he was invited to lecture on Greco-Roman antiquities at Lyons University. While at Lyons he received his doctorate for two brilliant theses: *Les origines du Sénat romain* and *De decretis functorum magistratuum ornamentis* (1883). In 1888 Bloch was named *maître des conférences* at the École Normale in Paris, and established his reputation firmly by a series of articles in learned journals and in the classical encyclopedia of Daremberg and Saglio, as well as *la Gaule indépendante et la Gaule romaine* (1900) in the *Histoire de France* edited by Lavisse. In 1904 the post of professor of Roman history was created for him at the Sorbonne. Bloch placed all these honors in jeopardy as an active supporter of *Dreyfus.

Bibliography: R. Lisbonne, in: *Revue Historique*, 145 (1924), 156; *Gustave Bloch* (a pamphlet published on his death). [H.L.A.]

BLOCH, ḤAYYIM ISAAC BEN ḤANOKH ZUNDEL HA-KOHEN (1864–1948), rabbi and scholar. Bloch, born in Plunge, Lithuania, studied at Grubin and Volozhin. In 1894 he founded a yeshivah in his native town where he was appointed rabbi in 1898. He became rabbi of Bausk in 1902,

Ḥayyim Isaac Bloch, rabbi in Lithuania and the U.S.

succeeding Abraham Isaac ha-Kohen *Kook. Bloch was also appointed the official rabbi by the government. During World War I he wandered in Russia, returning to Bausk in 1920. In 1922 he went to the United States and was appointed rabbi in Jersey City, New Jersey, where he remained until his death. In 1932 Bloch was elected honorary president of the Union of Orthodox Rabbis of the U.S. and Canada. During World War II, he was one of the leaders of the Va'ad ha-Hazalah, which worked to save the Jews of Europe. He published *Ḥiddushei ha-Ritba* (*Yom Tov b. Abraham Ishbili) on *Mo'ed Katan, Megillah,* and *Makkot,* giving the sources, together with an introduction and his own notes and corrections, entitled *Divrei Ḥibah* (Ḥayyim Isaac Bloch Ha-Kohen; 1935–39). Under the same title he published in 1941 a work containing some of the halakhic novellae from discourses that he had delivered at the Plungian yeshivah. Bloch was the author of two works on ethics, published anonymously, *Likkutei ha-Rayiv* (1904) and *Ha-Mavḥin* (1928).

Bibliography: D. Kamzon (ed.), *Yahadut Lita* (1959), 45, 200ff.; O. Z. Rand and A. M. Gruenblatt, *Toledot Anshei Shem* (1950), 9ff.

[Mo.Ha.]

BLOCH, HERMANN (Ḥayyim Ben Ẓevi; 1826–1896), rabbi and author. Born in Breslau, Bloch was a grandson of Abraham *Tiktin, chief rabbi of Breslau, whom he mentions in the introduction to his *Mevo ha-Talmud.* He studied in Breslau under his uncle Solomon Tiktin, and then in Hamburg. At various periods of his life he engaged in business and in his later years was a teacher at a *bet midrash* in Breslau. Bloch did research on the development of the Oral Law, and published *Mevo ha-Talmud* (vol. 1, Berlin, 1853). In his view, "the individual character of a *tanna* or an *amora* was the factor which determined his particular teachings or mode of exegesis in all matters, regardless of whether they were financial, ritual, scientific, or ethical" (p. 11). "Nevertheless, the underlying unity of *tannaim* and *amoraim* forms the foundation of 'the chain of tradition' and of 'the unity of the oral law,' whose source is in the written law" (p. 56). He devotes a detailed study, under the title *Hirhurei Torah* (4 pts., 1887–93), to the rule of the majority (based on Ex. 23:2), discussing its application in the Bible and the Talmud. In *Ẓurat ha-Bayit* (1883) he reconstructs the design of Herod's temple according to talmudic sources. He also published *Omrei Inshei* (1855), a collection of 107 parables found in the Babylonian Talmud, accompanied by a German translation.

Bibliography: M. Brann, in: MGWJ, 42 (1898), 529 n.3; Kressel, Leksikon, 1 (1965), 246–7.

[Y.Ho.]

BLOCH, ISSACHAR BAER BEN SAMSON (1730–1798), Austrian rabbi. Bloch was born in Hamburg and studied under Jonathan *Eybeschuetz and Ezekiel *Landau. After serving as rabbi in several communities he was rabbi in Boskovice (1793–96), and later in Mattersdorf where he died. He wrote *Binat Yissakhar* (Prague, 1785), a collection of his sermons with a rhymed appendix on the precepts of the priestly benediction and the redemption of the firstborn. He also wrote glosses on the Mishnah (published in the Lemberg edition, 1869) under the title *Benei Yissakhar.* He carried on a halakhic correspondence with some of the renowned contemporary scholars, to which reference is made in Ezekiel Landau's *Noda bi-Yhudah* (1928, pp. 87–89; cf. also Eleazar b. Aryeh Loeb, *Shemen Roke'aḥ,* (1902), 181–2; and Moses *Sofer, *Ḥatam Sofer,* 7 (1912), nos. 17, 18, 21). Bloch, who was childless, adopted Jacob Patraselka, ancestor of the rabbinical family of Duschinsky and the first rabbi in Nádasd (Hungary), who also carried on a correspondence with Moses Sofer (*Ḥatam Sofer,* OḤ, nos. 104, 106, 139; YD, nos. 243, 305; ḤM, no. 206).

Bibliography: E. Duckesz, *Chachme Ahw* (1908), 24 no. 33 (Heb. section); Eisler, in: *Das juedische Centralblatt,* 11 (1892), 117–8; J. J. Greenwald, *Ha-Yehudim be-Ungarya* (1913), 43 no. 24; idem, *Pe'erei Ḥakhmei Medinatenu* (1910), 94 no. 190; Mandl, in: *Magyar Zsidó Szemle,* 17 (1900), 142; Richtmann, *ibid.,* 22 (1905), 335–6; M. Stein, *Magyar rabbik,* 2 (1905), 103; 3 (1906), 145.

[Sh.A.H./Ed.]

BLOCH, IWAN (1872–1922), German dermatologist and medical historian. After graduating from Wuerzburg University in 1896, Bloch settled in Berlin as a practicing dermatologist. He was one of the first to engage in the scientific study of sex and a leader in the movement for sexual reform. His scientific publications include *Die Praxis der Hautkrankheiten* ("The Practice of Skin Diseases," 1908) and *Ursprung der Syphilis* ("Origin of Syphilis," 1911). In the latter he suggests that the disease was introduced to Europe through the Spaniards after the discovery of South America. Bloch made important contributions to the history of medicine which were published in the monumental *History of Medicine* of Max Neuburger. He also wrote on the history of dermatology and of Indian and Byzantine medicine. Many of his works were written under the pseudonyms of "von Welsenburg" and "Eugen Dühren."

Bibliography: S. R. Kagan, *Jewish Medicine* (1952), 427.

[S.M.]

BLOCH, JEAN-RICHARD (1884–1947), French author and political journalist. Bloch was born into an assimilated family in Paris. His Jewish consciousness was stirred in his boyhood by the anti-Semitism engendered by the Dreyfus Affair, and Jewish themes came to play a significant part in his writing. He was educated at the Sorbonne and became a teacher of history and literature. One of his earliest books was *Lévy* (1912), in which one of the stories deals with the effects of the Dreyfus case on a Jewish family in a provincial town. His most powerful novel, *...et compagnie,* (1918; *...& Co.,* 1929), is the story of Jewish cloth merchants from Alsace who move their business to a small town in western France. This work portrays the conflicts facing the Jew who wishes to maintain his identity while integrating into French culture. In 1910 Bloch founded a literary review, *L'effort libre,* but his work was interrupted by World War I, in which he was wounded three times. During the 1920s and early 1930s he wrote many novels, short stories, plays, poems, and essays. Two of the novels, *La nuit kurde* (1925; *A Night in Kurdistan,* 1930) and *Sybilla* (1932), reflect his fascination with the East. In 1925 he visited Palestine for the inauguration of the Hebrew University, and thereafter wrote a number of articles on the future role of the Jewish people, notably "Quel service les Juifs peuvent-ils rendre au monde?" (in *Palestine,* 1 (1927), 97–102). An essay entitled *Destin du siècle* (1931) showed that his approach to the Jewish problem had become somewhat ambiguous. From his student days, Bloch had been a socialist, and from the mid-1930s his interests centered mainly in politics. He had joined the Communist Party in 1921 and in 1923 helped to found the communist-oriented literary magazine *Europe* and in 1937, together with the poet Louis Aragon, the Communist daily *Ce Soir.* When the Germans occupied France in 1940 Bloch became an active member of the underground and in 1941 escaped the Gestapo by fleeing to Moscow, where he engaged in resistance broadcasts to the French people. He returned to France in 1945. Jean-Richard Bloch was a brother-in-law of André *Maurois.

Bibliography: J. R. Bloch and R. Rolland, *Deux hommes se recontrent* (1964); *Europe* (Fr., June 1966).

[D.R.G.]

BLOCH, JOSEPH (1871–1936), German socialist and journalist. Born in Lithuania, he emigrated to Germany where he edited the *Sozialistische Monatshefte,* a monthly publication whch attracted a team of outstanding writers. Bloch advocated a union of Continental Europe and when the Bolsheviks came to power in Russia, he proposed a Franco-German Union. After the German revolution of 1918, he advocated a system of German democracy based on workers' councils. The *Monatshefte* gave considerable attention to Jewish questions and supported the Zionist movement. Bloch favored mass immigration to Palestine and was highly critical of British policy there. One of the first victims of Nazi persecution in Germany, he never wavered in his belief in the triumph of socialism and the future of the Zionist enterprise. He died a lonely refugee in Prague.

Bibliography: K. Blumenfeld, *Erlebte Judenfrage* (1962), 57, 123.

[ED.]

BLOCH, JOSEPH LEIB (1860–1930), Lithuanian yeshivah head. He showed exceptional ability from childhood and at the age of 14 he traveled to Chelm where he studied under R. Eliezer *Gordon. He continued his studies with Naphtali Ẓevi Judah *Berlin at Volozhin. After his marriage to the daughter of Eliezer Gordon, he moved to Telz, where he assisted his father-in-law, who had been appointed rabbi and *rosh yeshivah.* In 1902, after resigning from the yeshivah in protest against the resistance of a number of the students to the study of *musar,* he was appointed rabbi of Varna, a small village near Telz. He served later as rabbi of Shadova, where he established his own yeshivah. In 1910 Bloch was appointed rabbi of Telz and *rosh yeshivah,* succeeding his father-in-law. Under his leadership, the yeshivah attracted large numbers of students. In addition to his lectures on *halakhah,* Bloch also gave talks on *musar.* He took the unusual step of founding a teachers' seminary, which produced hundreds of educators, and a preparatory school, in which secular studies were taught. Thanks to these auxiliary institutions, the yeshivah of Telz occupied a central position, with an enrollment, at times, of as many as 500 students. Active in communal affairs, Bloch served as a member of the executive of the Association of Lithuanian Rabbis and as one of the leaders of *Agudat Israel. Prominent among his sons were Abraham Isaac, who succeeded his father in Telz, and Elijah Meir, who was one of the yeshivah principals. His other sons and sons-in-law also taught in Telz. Bloch's ethical essays were published in *Shi'urei Da'at* (pt. 1, 1949; pt. 2, 1953; pt. 3, 1956). His halakhic lectures appeared in *Shi'ur Halakhah* (pt. 1, 1932; pt. 2, 1943; pt. 3, 1958).

Bibliography: D. Katz, *Tenu'at ha-Musar,* 5 (1962/63), 17–109.

[Y.AL.]

BLOCH, JOSEPH SAMUEL (1850–1923), rabbi, publicist, and politician in Austria. He acquired distinction for his defense of Judaism against the *blood libel and was praised by Adolf *Jellinek as the "Hercules of the anti-Semitic Augean stables." Son of a poor baker in Dukla (east Galicia), Bloch attended yeshivot at Lemberg and Eisenstadt and then the universities of Munich and Zurich. After officiating in provincial communities, he became rabbi of the Vienna suburb of Floridsdorf and a teacher at Jellinek's *bet ha-midrash.* During the *Tisza-Eszlár blood libel trial in 1883, when August *Rohling undertook to attest on oath that Jews practiced ritual murder, Bloch attacked him in the press. He challenged Rohling's competence as a scholar, accused him of lying, and offered him 3,000 florins for translating a random page of the Talmud. Rohling was forced to sue Bloch for libel, but after two years' investigations withdrew his action 13 days before the trial was due to open.

Bloch was elected in 1884, 1885, and 1891 to the Austrian Parliament from a preponderantly Jewish constituency of Galicia, and was the first parliamentarian to make Jewish affairs his main political concern, regarding himself as an interpreter and defender of Jewish thought to the non-Jewish public. In 1884 he founded a weekly *Dr. Blochs Oesterreichische Wochenschrift* for combating anti-Semitism, which existed until after World War I, and also established the Oesterreichisch-Israelitische *Union (from 1921: Union deutsch-oesterreichischer Juden). He also lectured in social-democratic associations on social conditions in the time of Jesus. Bloch was guided in his political activities by Adolf *Fischhof. He developed a previously unknown militancy and Jewish awareness which brought him into conflict with other Jewish leaders in Austria. In *Der nationale Zwist und die Juden in Oesterreich* (1886) he asked Jews to remain neutral in the struggle of the various nationalities within the Hapsburg Empire and to consider themselves "Austrian Jews" and "Jewish Austrians." He thus supplied the ideology for the Hapsburg patriotism with which the majority of Jews in the realm associated themselves around the beginning of the 20th century. Bloch saw the struggle for Jewish rights as part of the fight for the principle of equality for all nationalities in the empire, which the monarchy would have to recognize in order to exist. He also initiated proceedings against further ritual murder accusations by Franz Deckert and Paulus *Meyer and was active during the *Hilsner case.

Joseph Samuel Bloch, rabbi and member of the Austrian parliament. Jerusalem J.N.U.L.

At first a supporter of Zionism and Theodor *Herzl, Bloch published one of Herzl's articles in 1896 and introduced him to the finance minister Bilinski. However, Bloch preferred the concept of "colonization-Zionism," regarded Jewish nationality as closely linked with the Jewish religion, and refused to close his paper to non-Zionists. Herzl, on the other hand, failed to appreciate Bloch's fight against anti-Semitism. By around 1900 Bloch had become alienated from the Zionists. He visited Ereẓ Israel before his death.

For his work in the Jewish cause Bloch was warmly received on visits to the United States in 1912, and again in 1920. During World War I he raised funds on behalf of the Austrian government in neutral countries. He published a compendium of apologetics *Israel und die Voelker* (1922; *Israel and the Nations,* 1927) based on the evidence of the experts in connection with the Rohling trial and his memoirs *Erinnerungen aus meinem Leben* (1922; *My Reminiscences,* 1927). He also wrote prolifically on Jewish lore.

Bibliography: M. Grunwald, in: *Festschrift des juedisch-theologischen Seminars Breslau,* 2 (1929), 1–12; L. Kolb, in: *Dr. Blochs Wochenschrift* (Nov. 20, 1920), in honor of his 70th birthday; Ch. Bloch, in: *Herzl Yearbook,* 1 (1958), 154–64; J. Fraenkel (ed.), *Jews of Austria* (1967), index; M. Grunwald, *Vienna* (1936), 433–57; W. J. Cahnman, in: YLBI, 4 (1959), 111–39 and passim.

[M.LA.]

BLOCH, JOSHUA (1890–1957), U.S. librarian, bibliographer, and reform rabbi. Born in Dorbian, Lithuania, Bloch went to the U.S. in 1907. He taught at New York University from 1919 to 1928; from 1922 until his death he served as chaplain in several hospitals of the New York State Department of Mental Hygiene. His main work, however, was as head of the Jewish Division of the New York Public Library, a post which he held from 1923 to 1956; under his direction the Library developed as one of the major collections of Judaica in the United States. Bloch arranged many major exhibitions of Judaica there. Many of his bibliographical researches into the history of Hebrew printing were published by the Library, such as *Hebrew Printing in Riva di Trento* (1933; *Bulletin of the New York Public Library,* vol. 37), *Early Hebrew Printing in Spain and Portugal* (1938; *ibid.,* vol. 46). He also founded the quarterly *Journal of Jewish Bibliography* in 1938 and was its editor until 1943. In 1940 he was appointed to the publication committee of the Jewish Publication Society and a year later to the editorial board of the Jewish Apocryphal Literature Series; as a result of these connections he wrote *On the Apocalyptic in Judaism* (1952) and *Of Making Many Books* (1953; an annotated list of the books issued by the Jewish Publication Society, 1890–1952). The following year he published *The People and the Book,* on 300 years of Jewish life in America. His bibliography was collected by Dora Steinglass in *A Bibliography of the Writings of Joshua Bloch (1910–1958)* (1960).

Bibliography: A. Berger et al. (eds.), *Joshua Bloch Memorial Volume* (1960); idem, in: JBA, 16 (1958/59), 102–4; Shunami, Bibl, index.

[AB.B.]

Konrad Bloch, U.S. biochemist and Nobel Prize winner.

BLOCH, JULES (1880–1953), French philologist, specialist in Indic languages. Bloch taught in Paris at the École Pratique des Hautes Études and the École des Langues Orientales Vivantes. His work covered the entire range of Indic languages, ancient, medieval, and —especially—modern. Bloch's main research was into the Indo-European languages of India, on which he wrote *La formation de la langue marathe* (1915) and *L'Indo-Aryen du Véda aux temps modernes* (1934; *Indo-Aryan from the Vedas to Modern Times,* 1965). He also published an important book on Dravidian languages, *Structure grammaticale des langues dravidiennes* (1946; *The Grammatical Structure of Dravidian Languages,* 1954).

[H.H.P.]

BLOCH, KONRAD (1912–), U.S. biochemist and Nobel laureate. Bloch was awarded the Nobel Prize in Physiology and Medicine in 1964 "for discoveries of the mechanism of cholesterol and fatty acid metabolism." He was born in Neisse, Germany, graduated from the Technische Hochschule of Munich in 1934, and went to America two years later. After obtaining his doctorate at Columbia University, New York, in 1938, he became a member of the staff there. His collaboration with R. *Schoenheimer stimulated his interest in the biological origin of cholesterol and he began to concentrate in this field in 1941. Bloch elucidated many of the enzymatic steps which bring about the formation of cholesterol in the animal body. He used the carbon-14 isotope in his long series of researches on terpenes and steroids, and he showed that squalene was a precursor in the biosynthesis of cholesterol.

In 1946 Bloch joined the University of Chicago, becoming professor of biochemistry in 1952, and in 1954 was appointed professor of biochemistry at Harvard University. He was associated with the Committee on Growth of the American Cancer Society, the Biochemical Section of the U.S. Public Health Service, and the National Institute of Neurological Diseases and Blindness. He served as an associate editor of the *Journal of Biological Chemistry,* and published hundreds of papers in this and other scientific periodicals. Apart from topics already mentioned, these dealt with creatinine, glutathione, amino acids generally, proteins, and several metabolic processes.

Bibliography: *Chemical and Engineering News,* 42 (Oct. 26, 1964), 34.

[S.A.M.]

BLOCH, MARC (1886–1944), French historian. Bloch was professor of medieval history at the University of Strasbourg from 1919 to 1936 and then at the Sorbonne. He fought in both world wars and after the fall of France in 1940 was a leader of the Resistance. He was arrested, tortured, and executed by the Gestapo. One of Bloch's most significant works was in the field of French medieval agrarian history, *Les caractères originaux de l'histoire rurale française* (1931; *French Rural History,* 1966). A further contribution to economic historiography was his founding (together with Lucien Febvre) of the important review, *Annales d'histoire économique et sociale.* Bloch's *La société féodale* (1939–40; *Feudal Society,* 1961) became a standard work on feudalism. He did not accept the identification of feudalism with military service, the view held in England and Germany, still less the Marxist oversimplification of feudalism as exploitation of peasants by landlords. Instead, he analyzed the structure of feudal society and the relationship between history and economics during that period. In a posthumous work, *L'étrange défaite* (1946; *Strange Defeat,* 1949) Bloch affirmed his detachment from the Jewish faith and from all other religious dogmas. Nevertheless, he acknowledged his Jewish descent and his admiration for the tradition of the Hebrew prophets. His other works were: *L'Ile-de-France* (1913); *Rois et serfs* (1920); *Apologie pour l'histoire, ou métier d'historien* (1949; *The Historian's Craft,* 1954).

Bibliography: L. Febvre, in: *Les Cahiers politiques* (March, 1945), 5–11. [A.SA.]

BLOCH, MARCUS (Mordecai) ELIEZER (1723–1799), physician and zoologist. He was born in Bavaria, the son of a poor trader. Bloch received a traditional Jewish education and, at the age of 19, he began to learn German, French, and Latin. He was helped by wealthy relatives to study

Marcus Eliezer Bloch. Portrait engraved by Ambroise Tardieu from an original by Antoine Graff.

medicine at Frankfort on the Oder, and received his doctor's degree in 1747. He became a physician in Berlin, and soon gained a reputation at all levels of society. His friends included Moses *Mendelssohn, who was also his patient. Bloch's main achievement was in his morphological and systematic work on fish. He built himself an aquarium and acquired a marine collection which after his death was incorporated in the Berlin Zoological Museum. He wrote his great ichthyological work, *Allegemeine Naturgeschichte der Fische,* in 12 volumes (1781–1795). The work describes and classifies over 1,500 species of fish. Although Bloch's classification system was primitive and superficial, his book retains its scientific value, with its excellent drawings and diagrams. Bloch also wrote several short works on medical and zoological subjects.

Bibliography: Hirschberg, in: *Deutsche Medizinische Wochenschrift,* 39 (1913), 900; *Biographisches Lexikon der hervorragenden Aerzte,* 1 (1929²), 571–2. [ED.]

BLOCH, MARTIN (1883–1954), German expressionist painter, who became a master of British landscape. Bloch lived in Spain during World War I and subsequently spent many summers painting in Italy. In these years he was influenced by Cézanne, the "fauves," and the German expressionists. When Hitler came to power he fled to England, where he was interned during World War II. During his internment he restricted himself to black and white studies in conté crayons heightened with red chalk. His mature style emerged with a period of painting in Dorset in 1947. He developed a deep love of the British landscape, retaining a German expressionist sense of the dramatic but abandoning the tendency to exaggerate. His developed sense of color became subtle and harmonious. A posthumous exhibition held in 1955 established his reputation.

Bibliography: S. Andrews, in: *Studio,* 155 (1958), 40–43. [ED.]

BLOCH, MATTATHIAS BEN BENJAMIN ZE'EV (Wolf) ASHKENAZI (1610/1620–after 1668), preacher and one of the leaders of the Shabbatean movement. Bloch was born in Cracow. His grandfather, Feivel Bloch, was one of the leaders of the community during the first half of the 17th century and its representative at the meetings of the Council of Four Lands in Poland. He studied under the Cracow rabbis Menahem Mendel *Krochmal and Abraham Joshua *Heschel. He suffered during the persecution of the Jews under *Chmielnicki and during the Swedish occupation (1648–57) and was expelled from his town. In 1660 he was in Jassy and in 1665, on his way to Ereẓ Israel, was in Constantinople where he published *Kelal Katan,* a homily on Deuteronomy 32. He relates that he had two important homiletical books in his possession: *Sefer Kelal Gadol,* written in the *peshat* ("literal"), *remez* ("symbolic"), and *derash* ("homiletic-allegoric") styles; and the second, *Sefer Mattityahu,* a kabbalistic commentary on all sections of the Torah. Apparently Bloch became a Shabbatean in 1665 either while he was still in Constantinople or when he arrived in Jerusalem and met Shabbetai Ẓevi before the latter had left Ereẓ Israel. When, at the end of 1665 in Smyrna, Shabbetai Ẓevi appointed kings in a similar order to that of the ancient kings of Israel and Judah, he appointed Bloch "King Asa." In 1666 Bloch was among the leaders of the Shabbatean movement in Egypt. With the failure of the messianic hopes after Shabbetai Ẓevi's apostasy he persisted in his belief, but he left Egypt to settle in Mosul (Iraq) where he was accepted as a rabbi or *dayyan.* His influence spread to the communities in Kurdistan, which he encouraged in their Shabbatean belief. His activities as rabbi of the community as well as a Shabbatean leader are recorded in various letters preserved from 1668. After that year nothing is known about him. According to Jacob *Sasportas, Bloch was already elderly at the start of the Shabbatean movement.

Bibliography: G. Scholem, in: *Zion,* 7 (1942), 175–8, 193–5; Scholem, Shabbetai Ẓevi, index; A. Yaari, in: KS, 36 (1960/61), 525–34. [G.SCH.]

BLOCH, SIR MAURICE (1883–1964), Scottish distiller and philanthropist. Born in Dundee, Bloch settled in Glasgow in 1910. He founded a family distilling business and at the same time played an active role in Jewish communal work. In 1937 he was knighted "for political and social services." In 1954 he gave up his large business to devote himself to civic and Jewish communal affairs. He was president of the Board of Guardians, he represented Scotland on the Chief Rabbinate Council and became chairman of the Queen's Park Synagogue. He was keenly interested in Jewish education and was president of the Glasgow yeshivah, made a generous donation in 1956 to Jews' College, London, and set up a trust fund for the Hebrew University. He also gave sizable gifts to Glasgow University and Royal Faculty of Physicians and Surgeons in Glasgow. In 1948 Bloch was involved in the investigations of the Lynskey Tribunal into the conduct of some ministers of the crown. Throughout Bloch denied corruption though admitting to indiscretions. Nevertheless at the end of the trial his name was removed from the list of magistrates in Glasgow where he had been a justice of the peace for 25 years. [ED.]

BLOCH, MOSES (1815–1909), rabbi and author. Bloch, who was born in Ronsperg, Bohemia, served as rabbi in several cities of Bohemia and Moravia. In 1877 he was appointed together with David *Kaufmann and Wilhelm *Bacher to the academic staff of the newly founded rabbinical seminary in Budapest. Bloch was professor of Talmud and Codes and also the rector of the seminary, in which capacities he served for 30 years. His main work was *Sha'arei Torat ha-Takkanot* (in 7 volumes, 1879–1906) which traces, on the basis of talmudic sources, the development of **takkanot* from Moses to the end of the talmudic period. In a sequel to this work, *Sha'arei ha-Ma'alot* (1908), Bloch gives a detailed exposition of the various states and degrees of holiness, ritual and family purity as defined in the Mishnah and Talmud. Bloch published important monographs, in German and Hungarian on biblical and talmudic law in the yearbooks of the Budapest Seminary. He published the Prague 1608 edition of the responsa of *Meir b. Baruch of Rothenburg, together with notes and indexes (in 1885; 1896[3]), and also some hitherto unpublished responsa of R. Meir for the Mekize Nirdamim (1891).

Bibliography: *Sefer ha-Yovel . . . Moshe Aryeh Bloch* (1905), ix–xxiv; *Jahresbericht der Landes-Rabbinerschule in Budapest*, 31 (1908), 3–4; 32 (1909), iii–x. [M.N.Z./Ed.]

BLOCH, PHILIPP (1841–1923), German historian and Reform rabbi. He was born at Tworog (Silesia) and studied in Breslau. After a period as teacher with the Munich Jewish communal school (1869–71), he became rabbi of the Liberal congregation Bruedergemeinde of Posen where he remained active for some fifty years. When that city reverted to Poland after World War I, Bloch retired from the rabbinate and moved to Berlin. He took a leading part in the association of Liberal rabbis and in the work of German Jewish scholarly societies; in 1905 he was a co-founder of the General Archives of German Jews. Bloch's contributions to Jewish scholarship were concerned mainly with the philosophy of religion, *aggadah*, and Kabbalah; he also wrote about the history of Jews in Poland and the city and province of Posen. Among his works are: a translation of and introduction to the first book of Saadiah's *Emunot ve-De'ot* (1879); a translation of and commentary on the fifth chapter of Book II of Crescas' *Or Adonai* concerning free will (1879); essays on the development of Kabbalah and Jewish religious philosophy for Winter-Wuensche's *Die juedische Literatur* (1894–96); *Die Kabbalah auf ihrem Hoehepunkt . . .* (1905); *Spuren alter Volksbuecher in der Aggadah* (in *Festschrift . . . Hermann Cohen, Judaica*, 1912); and *Piskoth fuer die drei Trauersabbathe*, translation and commentary (in *Festschrift . . . Steinschneider*, 1896).

Bibliography: M. Brann, *Geschichte des juedisch-theologischen Seminars . . . in Breslau* (1904), 146–7, bibliography; A. Warschauer, in: MGWJ, 68 (1924), 1–16; idem, in: MGADJ, 6 (1926), 107–9; J. Guttman, in: KAWJ, 5 (1924), 1–7; N. M. Gelber, in: S. Federbusch (ed.), *Ḥokhmat Yisrael be-Ma'arav Eiropah*, 2 (1963), 59–63.

[Ed.]

BLOCH, PIERRE (1905–), French Socialist politician, writer, and Resistance leader. Bloch, who was born in Paris, contributed to the left-wing journal *Populaire*, and in 1936 was elected Socialist deputy for the Aisne department. In 1937 he was vice-president of a commission of enquiry into the problem of Algeria, which unsuccessfully advocated the consideration of the special demands of the Algerians, then under French tutelage. Bloch volunteered for military service on the outbreak of World War II and was taken prisoner by the Germans in 1940. He escaped and joined the Resistance, becoming one of the leaders of the clandestine French Socialist Party. In 1941 he was condemned to death by the Vichy regime for helping to parachute arms into occupied France. Again he succeeded in escaping and in 1942 reached London, where he became chief of French counterespionage. Later in the war he went to Algiers, where he was appointed assistant commissioner for the interior. After the liberation he was a leading figure in the French Socialist Party (S.F.I.O.) and became director of the Société Nationale des Entreprises de Presse. Later, he was president of the International League Against Anti-Semitism (L.I.C.A.).

A prolific writer, Bloch was the author of *L'Affaire Frankfurter* (1937); *Charles de Gaulle, premier ouvrier de France* (1945); *Liberté et servitude de la presse en France* (1952); *Carnet d'un voyageur en Israël* (1958); and *De Gaulle, ou le temps des méprises* (1969). [S.C.]

BLOCH, SAMSON BEN MOSES (d. 1737), *dayyan* and rabbi of Hamburg. Bloch, known also as "Samson the Ḥasid," was one of the first scholars and teachers and later the principal in the *bet midrash* built by Issachar Baer Kohen in 1707. He was known for his erudition and for his close ties with the great halakhic authorities of his generation. Bloch greatly exerted himself for the benefit of his community and it was through his efforts that the Jews were permitted to escape to Altona during a time of danger. The glosses and novellae which he wrote in the margins of the Shulḥan Arukh, *Oraḥ Ḥayyim* were published under the title *Nezirut Shimshon* (Berlin, 1764), and, again, together with the text of the *Oraḥ Ḥayyim* (Prague, 1785). *Tosafot Ḥadashim* (Amsterdam, 1775), his commentary on the Mishnah, was published with the text and later republished in many editions of the Mishnah. Samson also wrote halakhic novellae which have not been published. His sons were Issachar Baer, and Moses *dayyan* of Mezhirech.

Bibliography: H. Wagenaar, *Toledot Ya'veẓ* (1868), 34, 63; E. Duckesz, *Chachme AHW* (1908), 24–26 (Hebrew section), 9–10 (German section); S. M. Chones, *Toledot ha-Posekim* (1910), 447. [A.D.]

BLOCH, SAMSON (Simson) HA-LEVI (1784–1845), one of the early Hebrew authors of the *Haskalah in Galicia. He was, for a number of years, a student of Naḥman *Krochmal and a close friend of Solomon Judah *Rapoport. In the early 1800s he settled in Zamosc, in Russian Poland. In 1809 he published a new edition of *Iggeret ha-Rashba* (Epistle of R. Solomon b. Abraham *Adret) against the study of philosophy, together with *Iggeret ha-Hitnaẓẓelut* (Letter of Defense) by *Jedaiah ha-Penini on behalf of philosophy. In his introduction, Bloch explained that Adret had objected only to philosophical studies at too early an age. In 1813–14, Bloch worked as proofreader of Hebrew books for the Viennese printer Anton Schmid. He published a Hebrew translation (from the German) of *Manasseh Ben Israel's *Vindiciae Iudaeorum* with the title *Teshu'at Yisrael* ("Israel's Salvation," 1814) with an introduction and the author's biography by David Franco-Mendes. Bloch won his place in Hebrew literature with his *Shevilei Olam* ("Paths of the World"), the first general geography in the Hebrew language. The first two parts of this work, on Asia and Africa, appeared during his lifetime (1822–1827); the unfinished third part, on Europe, was edited by N. M. Schorr and published posthumously in 1855, under the title *Zehav Shebah. Shevilei Olam*, which ran into four editions, is, in the main, an adaptation of German geography books. However, Bloch was able to give his work a popular Jewish flavor by the inclusion of stories about unusual phenomena in far-off lands, mysterious tales and legendary anecdotes, and by special stress on the importance of each country for Jewish history. Bloch's style is extremely florid and stilted even for his own period, and the book as a whole suffers from numerous irrelevant notes. In 1840 Bloch published a Hebrew translation of Leopold Zunz's biography of Rashi, with important emendations and notes. Bloch spent his last years in solitude and illness in his native town of Kulikow (near Lemberg).

Bibliography: Klausner, Sifrut, 2 (1952), 350–68. [G.El.]

BLOCH-MICHEL, JEAN (1912–), French novelist and essayist. Bloch-Michel was influenced by his experiences during the Nazi occupation of France and by the moral confusion and crises of conscience affecting his country after World War II. Both his fiction and his essays show him to be a moralist in the French classical tradition with notable psychological insight. Among his best-known works are *Le témoin* (1949; *The Witness,* 1950); a book of war memoirs, *Les grandes circonstances* (1949); *La fuite en Egypte* (1952; *The Flight into Egypt,* 1957), and *Frosinia* (1966). He also wrote a study of French politics, *Journal du désordre* (1955), and an essay on the contemporary novel, *Présent de l'indicatif* (1963). Bloch-Michel was a contributor to a collective work on capital punishment, *Reflexions sur la peine capitale* (1957). Although culturally assimilated, Bloch-Michel expressed his solidarity with Russian Jewry and the State of Israel.

Bibliography: E. P. Hazard, in: *Saturday Review of Literature* (Feb. 11, 1950); *Évidences,* no. 30 (1953), 8–9. [A. MAN.]

BLOCK, HERBERT LAWRENCE ("Herblock"; 1909–), U.S. newspaper cartoonist. Born in Chicago, Block became an editorial cartoonist for the *Chicago Daily News* when he was 20. For ten years, until 1943, he worked for the N.E.A. Service and was awarded a Pulitzer Prize in 1942. His cartoons, signed "Herblock," became known for their robust style and powerful satire. After World War II

A Herblock cartoon during the Six-Day War, June 1967. "Israel is winning—NOW We Must DO Something!" From *The Herblock Gallery,* Simon and Schuster, 1968.

he joined *The Washington Post,* won the Pulitzer Prize again in 1954, received many other awards, and was made a fellow of the American Academy of Arts and Sciences. Collections of his drawings appeared in book form, among them *The Herblock Book* (1952); *Herblock's Here and Now* (1955); *Herblock's Special for Today* (1958); and *Straight Herblock* (1964). In 1966 he designed the U.S. postage stamp commemorating the 175th anniversary of the Bill of Rights. [ED.]

BLOEMFONTEIN, capital of the Orange Free State, Republic of South Africa. Jewish families played an important pioneering role in the development of Bloemfontein. Isaac Baumann of Hesse-Cassel (1813–1881), one of the first settlers to buy land in the new

Figure 1. Baumann Brothers, the first trading store to be opened in Bloemfontein after the settlement of the township that was to become the capital of the Orange Free State. Johannesburg, South African Jewish Board of Deputies.

township in 1848, established the first trading store. The earliest Day of Atonement services in Bloemfontein were held in his house in 1871. In 1873 marriages by Jewish rites were legalized in the Orange Free State. A Hebrew congregation was formed in 1876, and a synagogue built in 1903. The first president (1902–24) was Wolf Ehrlich. As the East European element increased the communal leadership gradually passed to them, a prominent part being played by Jacob Philips and Henry Bradlow. Jews also took an active part in municipal affairs. Baumann was the second chairman of the Bloemfontein municipal board, the forerunner of the town council. His son Gustav was the first surveyor-general of the Orange Free State. The Baumanns fought on the side of the Boers in the South African War (1899–1902). Moritz Leviseur, who took part in the Basuto War of 1865–66, helped to establish the town's first hospital and founded the National Museum. His wife Sophie wrote *Ouma Looks Back,* an account of the early days, and became known as the "Grand Old Lady of Bloemfontein." Wolf Ehrlich, a friend of the Boer leader General Hertzog (later South African prime minister), sat as a senator in the South African parliament. Jewish mayors of Bloemfontein included Ehrlich (1906–07 and 1911–12), Ivan Haarburger (1912–14), and Sol Harris (1929). The community has a

Figure 2. Moritz Leviseur, founder of the National Museum in Bloemfontein. Johannesburg, South African Jewish Board of Deputies.

well-developed network of institutions, including a fine communal center for cultural and educational activities. A large new synagogue was built in 1965. In 1956 the Hebrew congregation, *ḥevra kaddisha, talmud torah,* and the charitable institutions, combined to form the United Hebrew Institutions of Bloemfontein. Other Jewish institutions include the O.F.S. provincial committee of the South African Board of Deputies and the O.F.S. and Northern Cape Zionist Council. There is also a small Reform group. The Jewish population in 1967 numbered 1,347 out of a total population of 119,000.

Bibliography: G. Saron and L. Hotz (eds.), *Jews in South Africa* (1955), index. [L.S.]

BLOGG, SOLOMON BEN EPHRAIM (c. 1780–1858), Hebrew grammarian and liturgist. He was a teacher at the Jewish community's school at Hanover (Germany) and there founded the Hebrew printing press, Telgener, which was noted for its neatly and accurately printed books. Blogg published Psalms as well as a Passover *Haggadah* (1829) with German translation and his own commentaries. He wrote a history of the Hebrew language and literature with a short study on the Targums, *Korot Leshonenu ha-Kedoshah—Geschichte der hebraeischen Sprache und Literatur* (Berlin, 1826[2]), included also in his *Binyan Shelomo—Aedificium Salomonis* (Ger., 1832), dealing with the history of Hebrew and of the Talmud. Blogg also reedited Solomon London's *Kohelet Shelomo,* a Hebrew work on the liturgy and ceremonial customs according to the Ashkenazi rite. This work was first published in Amsterdam, in Hebrew (1744), then in Yiddish, in Frankfort on the Oder (1790 and 1799). Reedited and translated into German by Blogg (1830), it enjoyed great popularity and was several times reprinted (reedited by A. Sulzbach, 1908). Blogg also wrote: a book of devotion for the sick and for the mourners, *Sefer ha-Ḥayyim* (1856, several times reedited, last in 1930); *Seder ha-Piyyutim,* a German translation of the *piyyutim* (1824); *Massekhet Purim,* a parody of a Talmud tractate with a travesty of evening prayers (*ma'aravit*) and *seliḥot* for Purim (1844); and further minor treatises on Moses the elect prophet (1824), on the Jewish Oath (1826), etc.

Bibliography: Fuerst, Bibliotheca, 1 pt. 1 (1863), 122–3; Steinschneider, Cat Bod, 801, no. 4602; Steinschneider, Handbuch, 23; idem, in: HB, 1 (1858), 16. [M.N.Z./Ed.]

BLOIS, capital of the department of Loir-et-Cher, north-central France. The earliest information concerning Jews in Blois dates from 992. The community is known in medieval Jewish annals for the tragic consequences of a *blood libel in 1171, the first ritual murder accusation to be made in France. 33 members of the community including men, women and children, were burned at the stake on May 26, on the orders of Count Theobald. Jacob b. Meir *Tam established the 20th of Sivan, the date of the martyrdom, as a fast day for the Jews in France, England, and the Rhineland. *Ephraim b. Jacob of Bonn, his brother Hillel, and others composed elegies on the martyrs. The tragedy was the subject of a Hebrew drama by S. D. *Goitein, *Pulẓelinah* (1927). Jews possibly settled in Blois again, for in 1345 a quarter known as *la Juiverie* is reported. The present-day rue des Juifs near the cathedral is probably located on the same site. During World War II a few Jews from Alsace settled in Blois. In 1968 there were 60 Jews living in Blois, mainly from North Africa.

Bibliography: S. Spiegel, in: *Sefer ha-Yovel le-M. M. Kaplan* (1953), 267–87; A. M. Habermann, *Sefer Gezerot Ashkenaz ve-Ẓarefat* (1945); M. Steinschneider, *Die Geschichtsliteratur der Juden* (1905), 34; Zunz, Lit Poesie, 279, 283, 286, 290, 293, 308; Salfeld, Martyrol; Gross, Gal Jud, s.v.; R. Chazan, in: PAAJR, 36 (1968), 13–31. [Z.Av./Ed.]

BLONDES, DAVID, victim of a *blood libel in Vilna in 1900. Blondes, a young Jewish barber, was accused by his Polish housemaid of assaulting her and was subsequently imprisoned. Since the charge was made shortly before Passover, rumors began to circulate that the girl had been wounded to obtain blood for ritual purposes.. The implications of the accusation deeply stirred Russian Jewry, and the eminent non-Jewish lawyers P. G. Mironov and D. V. Spassovich, led by the noted Jewish lawyer Oscar O. *Grusenberg, were engaged to defend Blondes. The trial jury in Vilna convicted Blondes of injurious intent, but acquitted him of intent to murder; he was sentenced to 16 months imprisonment. The ritual implications of the accusation still remained. Grusenberg appealed to the Russian Senate, and the case was reopened before the same court in 1902. Medical experts from St. Petersburg testified for the defense, showing that the woman's injuries were self-inflicted. The jury subsequently returned a verdict of "not guilty."

Bibliography: Dubnow, Hist Russ, 3 (1920), 37f.; *Budushchnost',* 3 (1902), 87–90, 105f.; *Voskhod,* 21 no. 6 (1902), 8f. [C.T.]

BLONDHEIM, DAVID SIMON (1884–1934), U.S. Romance scholar. Born in Baltimore, Maryland, Blondheim studied at Johns Hopkins University where he became professor of Romance philology in 1924. During his studies at the École des Hautes Études in Paris he began to work on the notes left by A. *Darmesteter on the Old French glosses, over 1,000 in number, in Rashi's talmudic commentaries. Blondheim, after collating these with early manuscripts, restored their original form, established their exact meaning and published them as the first volume of his *Les glosses françaises dans les commentaires talmudiques de Raschi* (1929). He then proceeded to study each term in all its ramifications, but on his untimely death left only 125 completed studies. They were published posthumously as the second volume of his *Glosses,* with his biography and a very extensive bibliography (1937). The vast amount of historical and philological documentation gathered by Blondheim offers an invaluable source of information.

Examining, at the same time, the biblical translations in Romance languages in medieval Jewish manuscripts, Blondheim was struck by the particular form of the glosses in the different sources and by the close connection between them. He first published 30 such Old French glosses found in Jewish texts (his doctorate dissertation, in *Romania,* 39 (1910), 129ff.), and went on to prove that the specific traits of these Judeo-Romance texts is encountered also in the earliest Latin Bible translation known as the *Vetus Latina.* This was the theme of his major work *Les parlers judéo-romans et la Vetus Latina* (1925). He concluded that the Jews in the Western Roman Empire must have spoken their own *koiné,* which developed into the various Judeo-Romance dialects; and that Jews were responsible for the translation of the Septuagint in the *Vetus Latina.* Blondheim's views, however, did not obtain general approval, being criticized in particular by Cassuto, Banitt (Berenblut), and Fiorentino.

Blondheim's minor writings included many other contributions to the medieval Judeo-Romance dialects, e.g., medieval Judeo-French hymns. His indefatigable scientific endeavors did not hinder him from taking an active part in Jewish affairs, both philanthropic and Zionist. Blondheim prepared the first English translation of L. *Pinsker's *Auto-Emancipation* (1904, 1916[2]). His life ended on a tragic note. His manuscripts and papers are now in the National and University Library, Jerusalem. [M.BA.]

His son, SOLOMON HILLEL BLONDHEIM (1918–), physician, worked in various New York hospitals and did research into metabolic diseases and bilirubin metabolism before emigrating to Israel in 1951. There he joined the Hadassah-University Hospital in Jerusalem, becoming head of the metabolic unit and laboratory (1957) and associate professor of medicine (1966). [ED.]

Bibliography: H. H. Shapiro, in: *Modern Language Notes,* 49 (1934), 1199ff.; Cassuto, in: *Studi e materiali di storia delle religioni,* 1 (1926), 145ff.; Fiorentino, in: *Archivio Glottologico,* 29 (1937), 138ff.; idem, in: JQR, 42 (1951/52), 57ff.; M. Berenblut (Banitt), *Judaeo-Italian Translations of the Bible* (1949), 197ff.; idem, in: *Revue de linguistique romane,* 27 (1963), 245ff.

BLOOD. In the Bible there is an absolute prohibition on the consumption of blood. The blood of an animal must be drained before the flesh may be eaten (Lev. 3:17; 7:26; 17:10–14; Deut. 12:15–16, 20–24). This prohibition is not found anywhere else in the ancient Near East. Moreover, within Israelite legislation it is the only prohibition (coupled with murder) enjoined not on Israel alone but on all men (Gen. 9:4). It is thus a more universal law than the Decalogue.

That none of Israel's neighbors possesses this absolute and universally binding prohibition means that it cannot be a vestige of a primitive taboo, but the result of a deliberate, reasoned enactment. This is clear from the rationale appended to the law: blood is life (Lev. 17:11, 14; Deut. 12:23). Men (the sons of Noah) are conceded the right to eat meat, if they drain off the lifeblood, which belongs to the Creator (Gen. 9:3–4, see *Noachide Laws). Israel has an additional obligation to drain the blood of sacrificial animals on the authorized altar, "for it is I who have assigned it to you upon the altar to expiate for your lives; for it is the blood, as life, that can expiate" for your lives when you take the animal's life for its flesh (Lev. 17:11; cf. verse 4; see *Atonement).

An unresolved problem is presented by a second blood prohibition, differently worded: *loʾ toʾkhelu ʿal ha-dam* ("do not eat over the blood"; Lev. 19:26; I Sam. 14:32–33; Ezek. 33:25). Various interpretations of this have been offered: in one, *ʿal* is interpreted as "with" (so LXX, ad loc.; for usage, cf. Ex. 12:8; 23:18; Lev. 23:18, 20; et al.). Thus, the two prohibitions are synonymous: both forbid blood as food. A second interpretation holds that *ʿal* means "over," figuratively. The situation envisaged is that the blood has not been consumed, but has been spilled to the ground instead of being brought to the altar. Such a profane disposition of the blood is forbidden by this law. This accords with the requirement of the priestly code (and of King Saul, I Sam. 14:32–33) that all permitted flesh must be sacrificed (Lev. 17:11, above). However, it is not in agreement with the Deuteronomic Code, which allows profane slaughter and expressly orders that blood be spilled upon the ground (Deut. 12:15, 21–22). *ʿAl* has also been interpreted as "over," literally, in which case the prohibition refers to a pagan rite (see Ibn Ezra and Samuel b. Meir (Rashbam) on Lev. 19:26, and Maimonides, *Guide,* 3:46). According to a recent formulation of this view by Grintz, it harks back to the worship of underground deities, who drank the blood out of a pit in which the animal was slaughtered (e.g., Odyssey, 10:530–40).

Blood plays a pervasive role in the cult. When daubed on the horns of the *altar or sprinkled inside the sanctuary (see *Sacrifices), it purges ritual impurity (see *Atonement, Atonement, *Day of). It may also serve this purgative function in the initial rites of purifying the leper (Lev. 14:4–6, 18–29; cf. verses 49–53; see *Leprosy), and in consecrating the priest (Ex. 29:20–21, 33). When dashed upon the side of the altar, as in the case of animals sacrificed for food (see above), its purpose is to expiate sin (see **Kippur*). It also operates as an apotropaic to ward off future harm, e.g., by smearing the paschal blood on doorposts and lintels (Ex. 12:7, 13, 22–23). This usage may also underline the rites of covenanting (*dam berit;* Ex. 24:6–8) and circumcising the Israelites (Ex. 4:24–26; Ezek 16:6).

See also *Bloodguilt. [J.MI.]

In Halakhah. The prohibition of blood enjoined in the Bible is defined by the Talmud as referring to the blood of cattle, beasts, and fowl, and prescribes the punishment of **karet* for the consumption of the minimum amount of the volume of an olive (Ker. 5:1). The blood for which one is so liable is "the blood with which the soul emerges," i.e., the lifeblood, but not the blood which oozes out subsequently, or blood in the meat. Blood of all other creatures, fish, locusts, and human blood, is permitted according to the rabbinical interpretations of biblical law, although according to one source (*Tanna de-Vei Eliyahu Rabbah,* 15) human blood is equally forbidden by the Bible. All authorities agree, however, that it is forbidden by rabbinic law (Maim. Yad, Ma'akhalot Asurot, 6:2). The Talmud uses the peculiar phrase "bipeds" (Ker. 20b), and although all the halakhic authorities regard this phrase as a synonym for humans (Sh. Ar., YD 66:10), J.S. *Bloch, in answer to the *blood accusation whose fomenters quoted this passage in support of their allegation, put forward the intriguing suggestion that it actually refers to simians. Although the content, which enumerates "blood of bipeds, the blood found in eggs, the blood of locusts and of fish" would appear to lend some support to this view, it must be regarded as belonging to the realm of apologetics. Nevertheless, the repugnance felt by Jews for blood caused an extension of the prohibition even of permitted blood "because of appearances" if it were collected in a vessel. Thus it is permitted to swallow the blood from one's bleeding teeth and suck one's bleeding finger, but should a piece of bread, for instance, be stained by blood it must be discarded. Similarly the blood of fish collected in a vessel is forbidden (Ker. 21b).

The prohibition of blood is confined to its consumption; it is, however, permitted for other uses, and the Mishnah (Yoma 5:6) states that the sacrificial blood which flowed into the brook of *Kidron was collected and sold to gardeners as fertilizer. For the most extensive prohibition of blood, the need for its removal from meat before it is fit for Jewish consumption, see *Dietary Laws.

See also **Niddah,* *Circumcision. [L.I.R.]

Bibliography: J. Milgrom, in: *Interpretation* (July 1963), 288–301; E. Isaac, in: *Anthropos,* 59 (1964), 444–56; J. Grintz, in: *Zion,* 31 (1966), 1–17; D. J. McCarthy, in: JBL, 88 (1969), 166–76; M. Greenberg, *Understanding Exodus,* 2 part 1 (1969), 110–22. IN HALAKHAH: ET, 7 (1956), 422–40ff.

BLOOD-AVENGER. A person who is authorized by law, or who is duty-bound to kill a murderer is called *go'el ha-dam*—usually translated as an avenger of blood, but more accurately to be rendered as a redeemer of blood (cf. Lev. 25:25; Ruth 3:12; I Kings 16:11). By putting the murderer to death (Num. 35:19, 21), the avenger expiates the blood shed on the polluted land (Num. 35:33). Originally private revenge was legitimate in Israel, as in other ancient civilizations, not only for homicide but also for mayhem (cf. Gen. 4:23–24) and rape (Gen. 34:25–26);

and the restrictions of the avenger's rights and their legal regulation mark the beginnings of a system of criminal law (see B. Cohen in bibl.). It was laid down that only murder with malice aforethought (Num. 35:20–21; Deut. 19:11–13) or committed with a murderous instrument (Num. 35:16–18; for further examples, see Maim., Yad, Roẓe'aḥ u-Shemirat Nefesh 6:6–9), gave rise to the avenger's right (see Mak. 12a, Sanh. 45b); the unintentional manslayer was entitled to refuge from the avenger (Num. 35:12, 15; Deut. 19:4–6) and was liable to be killed by him only when he prematurely left the city of refuge (Num. 35:26–28). It may be considered a concession to human nature that avenging was not wholly prohibited, but only restricted and regulated: the natural "hot anger" (Deut. 19:6) of the victim's next of kin is left at least some legal outlet.

The avenger's rights were further restricted by being made subject to and dependent on the prior judicial conviction of the murderer—whether the murder was premeditated or not was a question not for the avenger but for the court to decide (Maim. loc. cit. 1:5, following Num. 35:12; "the manslayer may not die unless he has stood trial before the assembly"; but cf. Yad, loc. cit. 5:7–10). Opinions of later jurists were divided as to what the avenger's real function was; some held that he initiated the proceedings, searching for the murderer and bringing him to court for trial (Ramban; Nov.; Sanh. 45b; *Beit ha-Beḥirah* ad loc.); some thought he appeared before the court and participated in the proceedings as a prosecutor (Nissim Gerondi, basing himself on the Targum pseudo-Jonathan who renders *go'el ha-dam* as "claimant of blood"); others relegated the avenger to the role of an executioner, it being his right and privilege to execute the death penalty pronounced by the court (Yad, loc. cit. 1:2; Ritba, Nov., Mak. 10b). That the avenger had a *locus standi* in court appears probable from the scriptural injunction that the court "shall decide between the slayer and the blood-avenger" (Num. 35:24). While the slayer would protest his innocence or, alternatively, his lack of malice, the avenger would plead premeditation (cf. *Malbim* ad loc.); by finding a lack of malice, the court is said to "protect the manslayer from the blood-avenger" (Num. 35:25). Where an alleged murderer stood trial but was not convicted (either because of lack of sufficient evidence or because the verdict had not yet been given) and the avenger killed him, most jurists held that while the killing was unlawful the avenger was not guilty of murder (*Beit ha-Beḥirah,* Sanh. 45b)—the proferred reason being that the avenger had a better right to kill than even the unintentional manslayer (Yad, loc. cit. 6:5), or that Scripture itself recognized the avenger's "hot anger" (Deut. 19:6) as negating premeditation (*Redak* to II Sam. 14:7). However, if the avenger killed the murderer within the walls of the city of refuge, it was murder pure and simple (Tosef., Mak. 3:6).

Any next of kin entitled to inherit the deceased's estate qualified as an avenger (Yad, loc. cit. 1:2). Some later authorities even include maternal relatives although they are not in line for inheritance (*Or Same'aḥ* to Yad, loc. cit., against Maimonides). Women also qualify as avengers (Yad, loc. cit. 1:3). There are biblical instances of a father (II Sam. 13:31–38), a son (II Kings 14:5–6), brothers (Judg. 8:4–21; II Sam. 2:22–23), and also the king (I Kings 2:29–34) as avengers. It was later laid down that where no next of kin was available or came forward, an avenger was to be appointed by the court (Sanh. 45b).

There is little doubt that legally the rights (and duties) of the blood-avenger became obsolete (*Ḥavvat Ya'ir* 146), though the killing by the avenger of a murderer is even today legally regarded by some scholars as no more than unintentional manslaughter (e.g. *Keẓot ha-Ḥoshen* ḤM 2). Apart from the law, the right and duty of avenging the blood of one's nearest is still deeply imprinted on the mind and religious conviction of most Oriental (including many Jewish) communities; notwithstanding repeated efforts from various quarters, blood-vengeance is not, however, recognized in Israel law even as a mitigating circumstance.

Bibliography: M. Duschak, *Mosaisch-Talmudisches Strafrecht* (1869), 19f.; S. Mayer, *Rechte der Israeliten, Athener, und Roemer,* 3 (1876), 36–47; E. Goitein, *Vergeltungsprincip im biblischen und talmudischen Strafrecht* (1891); G. Foerster, *Das mosaische Strafrecht...* (1900), 9ff.; J. Weismann, *Talion und oeffentliche Strafe im mosaischen Rechte* (1913); E. Merz, *Blutrache bei den Israeliten* (1916); ET, 5 (1953), 220–33; J. M. Ginzburg, *Mishpatim le-Yisra'el* (1956), 356–74; EM, 2 (1965), 392–4; B. Cohen, *Jewish and Roman Law,* 2 (1966), 624–7; addenda 793f. [H.H.C.]

BLOODGUILT, liability for punishment for shedding blood. The biblical concept of bloodguilt derives from the belief that deeds generate consequences and that sin, in particular, is a danger to the sinner. The most vivid examples of this belief appear in connection with unlawful homicide, where innocent blood (*dam naki (naqi);* Jonah 1:14) cries out for vengeance (Gen. 4:10), is rejected by the earth (Isa. 26:21; Ezek. 24:7), and pollutes it (Num. 35:33–34). Bloodguilt attaches to the slayer and his family (II Sam. 3:28ff.) for generations (II Kings 9:26), and even to his city (Jer. 26:5), nation (Deut. 21:8), and land (Deut. 24:4). The technical term for bearing bloodguilt *damo bo,* or *damo be-ro'sho* meant originally "his blood [remains] in him/in his head" (Josh. 2:19; Ezek. 33:5), and the legal formula *mot yumat damav bo* (Lev. 20:9–16) means that in the case of lawful execution, the blood of the guilty victim remains on his own person and does not attach itself to his executioners.

The concept of bloodguilt in the Bible pervades all sources, legal, narrative, and cultic, and entails the following system of graded punishments for homicide.

Deliberate Homicide. The penalty is death by man (Gen. 9:6), or failing that, by God (Gen. 9:5; cf. Lev. 20:4–5). A man can be either the direct cause (Num. 35:16–21) or the indirect cause, e.g., the watchman (II Kings 10:24; Ezek. 33:6), the priests (Num. 18:1, 3), the homeowner (Deut. 22:8), or through his subordinate (I Kings 2:31–35). The punishment of the murderer is primarily the responsibility of the *blood-avenger (after court conviction, Num. 35:19; Deut. 19:12), but God is the final guarantor that homicide is ultimately punished. His personal intervention is expressed by the verbs פקד (*pakad (paqad);* "attend to"; Hos. 1:4), נקם (*nakam (naqam);* "avenge"; II Kings 9:7), דרש (*darash,* "exact punishment"; Ezek. 33:6), and שוב (השיב, *heshiv,* "return") in the idiom *heshiv damim ʿal ro'sh* (II Sam. 16:18; I Kings 2:33), which indicates that God will turn back to the head of the slayer the blood of the slain, the punishment for which he thought he had averted. In the Bible, it should be noted, these idioms have become technical terms: the original phrase remains, but without the crudity of its more primitive implications in other ancient sources. God may postpone punishment to a later generation (II Sam. 12:13–14; I Kings 21:21). Man, however, does not have this option (Deut. 24:16; II Kings 14:6) unless divinely authorized (II Kings 9:7, 26).

There is no commutation of the death penalty. The notion that deliberate homicide cannot be commuted is the foundation stone of criminal law in the Bible: human life is invaluable, hence incommutable. This concept is not found in any other law corpus in the ancient Near East.

Accidental Homicide. Since accidental homicide also

results in bloodguilt, the killer may be slain by the *go'el* with impunity (Num. 35:26–27; Deut. 19:4–10). However, as his act was unintentional, the natural death of the high priest is allowed to substitute for his own death (Num. 35: 25, 28). In the interim, he is confined to a *city of refuge to protect him from the blood-avenger (Num. 35:9ff; Deut. 4: 41–43; 19:1–13; Josh. 20:1ff.) In cases where the slayer is unknown, the community nearest the corpus delicti must disavow complicity and, by means of a ritual, symbolically wash away the blood of the slain (Deut. 21:1–9; see **Eglah Arufah*).

Homicidal Beast. The penalty is death by stoning and the shunning of the carcass. The supreme value of human life in the Bible is best expressed in the law that a homicidal beast is also guilty and that not only must it be killed but its carcass, laden with bloodguilt, must be reviled (Ex. 21:28–29; cf. Gen. 9:5).

Unauthorized Slaughter of an Animal. The reverence for life that informs all biblical legislation reaches its summit in the priestly law which sanctions the use of an animal for food on the condition that its blood, containing its life, be drained upon the authorized altar (and thereby be symbolically restored to God; Lev. 17:11). All other slaughter is unlawful bloodshed, punishable by death at the hand of God (Lev. 17:4; see *Atonement, *Blood, **Kipper*, **Karet*).

Exceptions. No bloodguilt is incurred by homicide in self-defense (Ex. 22:1), judicial execution (Lev. 20:9–16), and war (I Kings 2:5–6). The priestly legislation may indicate some qualification of the view that war is justifiable homicide. For example, David was disqualified from building the Temple (I Chron. 22:8).

See also *Homicide.

Bibliography: M. Greenberg, in: *Sefer Yovel Y. Kaufmann* (1960), 5–28; idem, in: IDB, 1 (1962), s.v.; K. Koch, in: VT, 12 (1962), 396–416; J. Milgrom, *Studies in Levitical Terminology*, 1 (1970), 22–33, 56–69.
[J.Mi.]

BLOODLETTING, removal of blood in treating diseases. Bloodletting is frequently mentioned in the Talmud. It was performed not by a physician but by a skilled functionary called *umman* or *gara*, whose status was less than that of a physician. The bloodletter is mentioned in various passages in the Talmud, both favorably and unfavorably (e.g., Ta'an. 21b; Kid. 82a). Some of the directives about bloodletting in the Talmud relate to specific ailments (e.g., Git. 67b; Av. Zar. 29a), but most are in the realm of preventive medicine based on the belief that the regular removal of blood from the body was of hygienic value. Among the ten indispensable requirements of a town, in the absence of which "no scholar should reside there" (Sanh. 17b), is a bloodletter. According to the Talmud, bloodletting is one of the things which should be applied in moderation (Git. 70a), and, in practice, the amount of blood to be let varies with the subject's age. Maimonides (Yad, De'ot 4:18), though in general agreement, suggests, in addition, consideration of the subject's "blood richness" and physical vigor (*Pirkei Moshe*, 12). Many instructions are given in the Talmud with respect to diet and precautions to be taken both before and after bloodletting (e.g., Shab. 129a–b; Git. 70a; Ned. 54b; Av. Zar. 29a; et al.). Maimonides advises moderation in bloodletting: "A man should not accustom himself to let blood regularly, nor should he do so unless he is in great need of it" (Yad, loc. cit.). The views of the Talmud and of Maimonides provide a sharp contrast to those of the ancient and medieval world, where the practice of bloodletting was unrestricted. In late Hebrew literature (e.g., the *Oẓar ha-Ḥayyim* of Jacob *Ẓahalon and the *Ma'aseh Tuviyyah* of Tobias b. Moses *Cohn) directions for bloodletting and cupping are also found.

Bibliography: J. Preuss, *Biblisch-talmudische Medizin* (1923³), 36–39, 289–300; M. Perlman, *Midrash ha-Refu'ah*, 2 (1929), 85–89.
[J.O.L.]

BLOOD LIBEL, the allegation that Jews murder non-Jews, especially Christians, in order to obtain blood for the Passover or other rituals; a complex of deliberate lies, trumped-up accusations, and popular beliefs about the murder-lust of the Jews and their bloodthirstiness, based on the conception that Jews hate Christianity and mankind in general. It is combined with the delusion that Jews are in some way not human and must have recourse to special remedies and subterfuges in order to appear, at least outwardly, like other men. The blood libel led to trials and massacres of Jews in the Middle Ages and early modern times; it was revived by the Nazis. Its origin is rooted in ancient, almost primordial, concepts concerning the potency and energies of *blood.

Origins. Blood sacrifices were practiced by many pagan religions. They are expressly forbidden by the Torah. The law of meat-salting (*meliḥah*) is designed to prevent the least drop of avoidable blood remaining in food. Yet pagan incomprehension of the Jewish monotheist cult, lacking the customary images and statues, led to charges of ritual killing. At a time of tension between Hellenism and Judaism, it was alleged that the Jews would kidnap a Greek

Figure 1. Alleged tomb of Hugh of Lincoln, subject of a 13th-century English blood libel. From D. Tovey's *Anglia Judaica*, Oxford, 1738. Cecil Roth Collection.

foreigner, fatten him up for a year, and then convey him to a wood, where they slew him, sacrificed his body with the customary ritual, partook of his flesh, and while immolating the Greek swore an oath of hostility to the Greeks. This was told, according to *Apion, to King *Antiochus Epiphanes by an intended Greek victim who had been found in the Jewish Temple being fattened by the Jews for this sacrifice and was saved by the king (Jos., Apion, 2:89–102). Some suspect that stories like this were spread intentionally as propaganda for Antiochus Epiphanes to justify his profanation of the Temple. Whatever the immediate cause, the tale is the outcome of hatred of the Jews and incomprehension of their religion.

To be victims of this accusation was also the fate of other misunderstood religious minorities. In the second century C.E. the *Church Father Tertullian complained: "We are said to be the most criminal of men, on the score of our sacramental baby-killing, and the baby-eating that goes with it." He complains that judicial torture was applied to Christians because of this accusation, for "it ought . . . to be wrung out of us [whenever that false charge is made] how many murdered babies each of us has tasted . . . Oh! the glory of that magistrate who had brought to light some Christian who had eaten up to date a hundred babies!" (*Apologeticus*, 7:1 and 1:12, Loeb edition (1931), 10, 36).

Middle Ages. During the Middle Ages some heretical Christian sects were afflicted by similar accusations. The general attitude of Christians toward the holy bread of the Communion created an emotional atmosphere in which it was felt that the divine child was mysteriously hidden in the partaken bread. The popular preacher, Friar Berthold of Regensburg (13th century), felt obliged to explain why communicants do not actually see the holy child by asking the rhetorical question, "Who would like to bite off a baby's head or hand or foot?" Popular beliefs and imaginings of the time, either of classical origin or rooted in Germanic superstitions, held that blood, even the blood of executed malefactors or from corpses, possesses the property of healing or causing injury. Thus, combined with the general hatred of Jews then prevailing, a charge of clandestine cruel practices and blood-hunting, which had evolved among the pagans and was used against the Christians, was deflected by Christian society to the most visible and persistent minority in opposition to its tenets.

As Christianity spread in Western Europe and penetrated the popular consciousness, influencing the emotions and imagination even more than thought and dogma, various story elements began to evolve around the alleged inhumanity and sadism of the Jews. In the first distinct case of blood libel against Jews in the Middle Ages, that of *Norwich in 1144, it was alleged that the Jews had "bought a Christian child [the 'boy-martyr' William] before Easter and tortured him with all the tortures wherewith our Lord was tortured, and on Long Friday hanged him on a rood in hatred of our Lord." The motif of torture and murder of Christian children in imitation of Jesus' Passion persisted with slight variations throughout the 12th century (Gloucester, England, 1168; Blois, France, 1171; Saragossa, Spain, 1182), and was repeated in many libels of the 13th century. In the case of Little Saint Hugh of *Lincoln, 1255, it would seem that an element taken directly from Apion's libel (see above) was interwoven into the Passion motif, for the chronicler Matthew Paris relates, "that the Child was first fattened for ten days with white bread and milk and then . . . almost all the Jews of England were invited to the crucifixion." The crucifixion motif was generalized in the *Siete Partidas* law code of Spain, 1263: "We have heard it said that in certain places on Good Friday the Jews do steal children and set them on the cross

Figure 2. A 15th-century German woodcut showing Jews extracting blood from Simon of Trent, subject of the Italian blood libel of 1475.

in a mocking manner." Even when other motifs eventually predominated in the libel, the crucifixion motif did not disappear altogether. On the eve of the expulsion of the Jews from Spain, there occurred the blood-libel case of "the Holy Child of *La Guardia" (1490–91). There, *Conversos were made to confess under torture that with the knowledge of the chief rabbi of the Jews they had assembled in a cave, crucified the child, and abused him and cursed him to his face, as was done to Jesus in ancient times. The crucifixion motif explains why the blood libels occurred at the time of Passover.

The Jews were well aware of the implications of sheer sadism involved in the libel. In a dirge lamenting the Jews massacred at Munich because of a blood libel in 1286, the anonymous poet supposedly quotes the words of the Christian killers: "These unhappy Jews are sinning, they kill Christian children, they torture them in all their limbs, they take the blood cruelly to drink" (A. M. Habermann (ed.), *Sefer Gezerot Ashkenaz ve-Ẓarefat* (1946), 199). This ironical "quotation" contains an added motif in the libels, the thirst of the Jew for blood, out of his hatred for the good and true. This is combined in 13th-century Germany with the conception that the Jew cannot endure purity: he hates the innocence of the Christian child, its joyous song and appearance. This motif, found in the legendary tales of the monk Caesarius of Heisterbach in Germany, underwent various transmutations. In the source from which Caesarius took his story the child killed by the Jews sings *erubescat judaeus* ("let the Jew be shamed"). In Caesarius' version, the child sings the *Salve Regina.* The Jews cannot endure this pure laudatory song and try to frighten him and stop him from singing it. When he refuses they cut off his tongue and hack him to pieces. About a century after the expulsion of the Jews from England the cultural motif only became the basis of Geoffrey *Chaucer's "Prioress' Tale." Here the widow's little child sings the *Alma Redemptoris Mater* while "the serpent Sathanas, That hath in Jews herte his waspes nest" awakens indignation in the cruel Jewish heart: "O Hebraik peple, allas! /Is this to yow a thing that is honest,/That swich a boy shal waeken as him lest/In your despyt, and singe of swich sentence / Which is agayn your lawes reverence?" The Jews obey the promptings of their

Satanic master and kill the child; a miracle brings about their deserved punishment. Though the scene of this tale is laid in Asia, at the end of the story Chaucer takes care to connect Asia explicitly with bygone libels in England, and the motif of hatred of the innocent with the motif of mockery of the crucifixion: "O yonge Hugh of Lincoln, slayn also / With cursed Jewes, as it is notable, / For it nis but a litel whyle ago; / Preye eek for us."

In the blood libel of *Fulda (1235) another motif comes to the fore: the Jews taking blood for medicinal remedies (here of five young Christian boys). The strange medley of ideas about the use of blood by the Jews is summed up by the end of the Middle Ages, in 1494, by the citizens of Tyrnau (*Trnava). The Jews need blood because "firstly, they were convinced by the judgment of their ancestors, that the blood of a Christian was a good remedy for the alleviation of the wound of circumcision. Secondly, they were of opinion that this blood, put into food, is very efficacious for the awakening of mutual love. Thirdly, they had discovered, as men and women among them suffered equally from menstruation, that the blood of a Christian is a specific medicine for it, when drunk. Fourthly, they had an ancient but secret ordinance by which they are under obligation to shed Christian blood in honor of God, in daily sacrifices, in some spot or other . . . the lot for the present year had fallen on the Tyrnau Jews." To the motifs of crucifixion, sadism, hatred of the innocent and of Christianity, and the unnaturalness of the Jews and its cure by the use of good Christian blood, there were added, from time to time, the ingredients of sorcery, perversity, and a kind of "blind obedience to a cruel tradition." Generation after generation of Jews in Europe was tortured, and Jewish communities were massacred or dispersed and broken up because of this libel (see map). It was spread by various agents. Popular preachers ingrained it in the minds of the common people. It became embedded, through miracle tales, in their imagination and beliefs. This caused in Moravia, in about 1343, "a woman of ill fame to come with the help of another woman and propose to an old Jew of Brno, named Osel, her child for sale for six marks, because the child was red in hair and in face. The Jew simulated gladness, immediately gave three marks to the woman, and invited them to come with the child to a cellar the next day, early in the morning, under the pretext that he had to consult about the buying of the child with the bishop of the Jews and the elders." The Jew invited Christian officials, who imprisoned the women and punished them horribly (B. Bretholz, *Quellen zur Geschichte der Juden in Maehren* (1935), 27–28).

The majority of the heads of state and the church opposed the circulation of the libel. Emperor *Frederick II of Hohenstaufen decided, after the Fulda libel, to clear up the matter definitively, and have all the Jews in the empire killed if the accusation proved to be true, or exonerate them publicly if false, using this as an occasion to arbitrate in a matter affecting the whole of Christendom. The enquiry into the blood libel was thus turned into an all-Christian problem. The emperor, who first consulted the recognized church authorities, later had to turn to a device of his own. In the words of his summing-up of the enquiry (see ZGJD, 1 (1887), 142–4), the usual church authorities "expressed various opinions about the case, and as they have been proved incapable of coming to a conclusive decision . . . we found it necessary . . . to turn to such people that were once Jews and have converted to the worship of the Christian faith; for they, as opponents, will not be silent about anything that they may know in this matter against the Jews." The emperor adds that he himself was already convinced, through his knowledge and wisdom, that the Jews were innocent. He sent to the kings of the West, asking them to send him decent and learned converts to Christianity to consult in the matter. The synod of converts took place and came to the conclusion, which the emperor published: "There is not to be found, either in the Old or the New Testament, that the Jews are desirous of human blood. On the contrary, they avoid contamination with any kind of blood." The document quotes from various Jewish texts in support, adding, "There is also a strong likelihood that those to whom even the blood of permitted animals is forbidden, cannot have a hankering after human blood. Against this accusation stand its cruelty, its unnaturalness, and the sound human emotions which the Jews have also in relation to the Christians. It is also unlikely that they would risk [through such a dangerous action] their life and property." A few years later, in 1247, Pope Innocent IV wrote that "Christians charge falsely . . . that [the Jews] hold a communion rite . . . with the heart of a murdered child; and should the cadaver of a dead man happen to be found anywhere they maliciously lay it to their charge." Neither emperor nor pope were heeded.

Jewish scholars in the Middle Ages bitterly rejected this inhuman accusation. They quoted the Law and instanced the Jewish way of life in order to refute it. The general opinion of the Jews is summed up thus: "You are libeling us for you want to find a reason to permit the shedding of our blood" (the 12th–13th centuries *Sefer Niẓẓaḥon Yashan—Liber Nizzachon Vetus,* p. 159 in *Tela Ignaea Satanae,* ed. J. Ch. Wagenseil, 1681). However, the Jewish denials, like the opinion of enlightened Christian leaders, did not succeed in preventing the blood libels from shaping to a large extent the image of the Jew transmitted from the Middle Ages to modern times. (It was only in 1965 that the church officially repudiated the blood libel of *Trent by canceling the beatification of Simon and the celebrations in his honor.)

Modern Times. From the 17th century, blood-libel cases increasingly spread to Eastern Europe (Poland-Lithuania). The atmosphere at such trials is conveyed by the protocols of the investigation of two Jews and a Jewess who were put to torture in a blood-libel case at *Lublin in 1636: "The Jew Baruch answers: 'I haven't seen the child.' Second torture: 'I am innocent and other Jews are innocent.' Third torture: 'I am innocent and other Jews are innocent, and everything that Joseph [the accuser] said is a lie. Jews need no Christian blood.'" Fegele the Jewess struggled courageously to defend the truth, as evident in the cross-examination: "Judge: 'Are you acquainted with sorcery?' Fegele: 'I never dabble in this. I am a poor widow who sells vodka and *kwas*'; Judge: 'For what purpose do Jews need Christian blood?' Fegele: 'Jews need no Christian blood, either of adults or of children'; Judge: 'Where have you hidden the child's blood?' Fegele: 'The use of blood is forbidden to Jews, even of animal blood'; Judge: 'For what purpose do Jews need Christian blood?' Fegele: 'Jews use no Christian blood.' Judge: 'And are you a sorceress?' Fegele: 'No. I have nothing to do with this.'" She remained unbroken under torture, and even the threat of torture with a red-hot iron. Hugo *Grotius, the Protestant legal philosopher, when told about the case expressed the opinion that the blood accusation was simply a libel generated by hatred of the Jews, and recalled that the early Christians and later Christian sectarians were accused in a similar way (Balaban, in *Festschrift S. Dubnow* (1930), 87–112).

In Eastern Europe, as late as the 17th century, the blood libel is identified with Jewish sorcery in the minds of the accusers, while the motif of the use of Christian blood for Passover *maẓẓot* increasingly comes to the fore. As

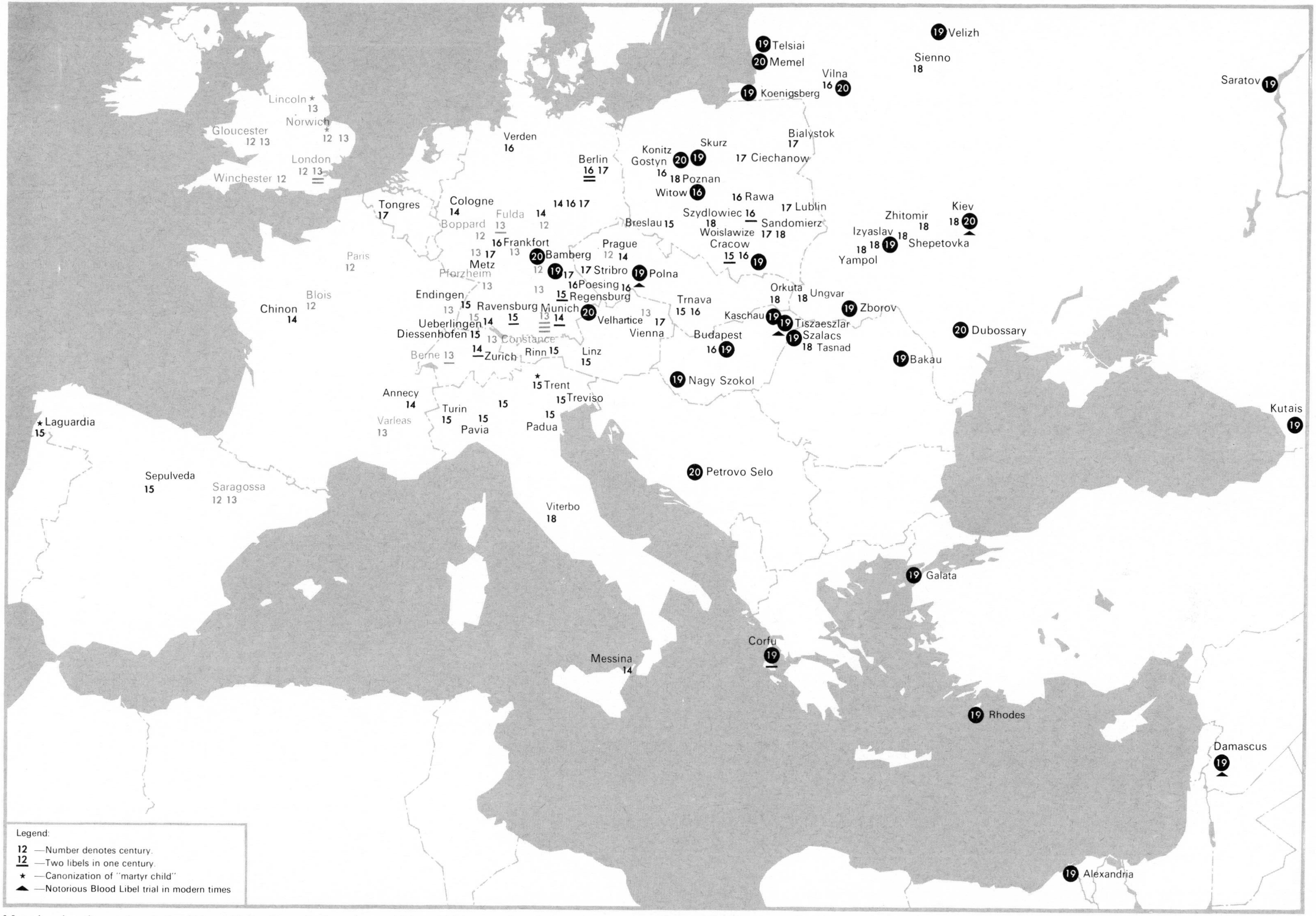

Map showing sites and periods of blood libels. Gray numbers denote 12th and 13th centuries, circled numbers 19th and 20th centuries.

Ritualmord-Nummer

Der Stürmer

...tsches Wochenblatt zum Kampfe um die Wahrheit

HERAUSGEBER: JULIUS STREICHER

Nürnberg, im Mai 1934

1934

Jüdischer Mordplan

gegen die nichtjüdische Menschheit aufgedeckt

Das Mördervolk

Judenopfer

Die Juden sind unser Unglück!

Figure 3. The blood libel revived in the "ritual murder" number of Julius Streicher's Nazi newspaper, *Der Stuermer,* May 1, 1934.

conditions in Poland deteriorated, blood-libel cases multiplied. Through the *Councils of the Lands the Jews sent an emissary to the Holy See who succeeded in having an investigation ordered and carried out by Cardinal Lorenzo Ganganelli, later Pope *Clement XIV. In a detailed report submitted in 1759 Ganganelli examined the veracity of the blood libel in general and of the recent cases in Poland-Lithuania in particular, quoting *in extenso* from former church authorities against the libel. His main conclusion was: "It may be realized with what lively faith we ought to ask God with the Psalmist, 'deliver me from the calumnies of men.' For it cannot be denied that 'Calumny maketh the wise man mad and destroyeth the strength of his heart.' . . . I therefore hope that the Holy See will take some measure to protect the Jews of Poland as Saint Bernard, Gregory IX, and Innocent IV did for the Jews of Germany and France, 'that the name of Christ be not blasphemed' by the Jews" (see bibl., Roth, p. 94).

In the 19th century the ringleaders of Jew-hatred in its modern form of anti-Semitism made conspicuous use of the blood libel for incitement against Jews in various countries. It was also used as a weapon to arouse the uneducated masses for specific political reasons, as occurred, for instance, in the *Damascus Affair (1840) in the struggle among the western powers for influence in the Near East. Anti-Semitic "experts" wrote treatises which set out to prove the truth of the libel from the records of past accusations and Jewish sources. Two such were Konstantin Cholewa de Pawlikowski (*Talmud in der Theorie und Praxis,* Regensburg, 1866) and H. Desportes (*Le mystère du sang chez les Juifs de tous les temps,* Paris, 1859, with a preface by the notorious anti-Semite E. *Drumont). In the blood-libel trials held in the second half of the 19th and early 20th century, such as the *Tiszaeszlar and *Beilis cases, "experts" such as August *Rohling appeared to testify in court; all were irrefutably answered by Jewish and pro-Jewish scholars (J.S. *Bloch, H. L. *Strack, J. *Mazeh). Another weapon developed in the arsenal of anti-Semitism was an insidious way of implying the truth of the blood-libel charge by stating it as a fact without denying it. A notorious example is found in the article *Blut* (in *Handwoerterbuch des deutschen Aberglaubens,* 1 (1927), cols. 1434–42) where it is remarked (col. 1436): *"Moses verbot umsonst das Bluttrinken"* ("Moses in vain prohibited the drinking of blood"), and *"Dass die Frage der juedischen Ritualmorde immer noch nicht verschwunden ist, lehren Prozesse neuerer Zeit"* ("Trials in modern times show the problem of ritual murder has still not disappeared"; col. 1439).

The Nazis unashamedly used the blood libel in full force for anti-Jewish propaganda. They revived old allegations and instituted reinvestigations and trials in territories under their rule or influence: at Memel in 1936; at Bamberg in 1937 (a revival); and at Velhartice, Bohemia, in 1940. On May 1, 1934, the Nazi daily, *Der Stuermer,* devoted a special horrifyingly illustrated number to the blood libel, in which German scientists openly served the Nazi aims. The above-mentioned *Handwoerterbuch* (vol. 7 (1935–36), cols. 727–39) printed an article entitled *Ritualmord* written by Peuckert, a man who remained active and respected in German science, which is throughout simply an affirmation and propagation of the blood libel, although using some cautious phrasing. The epitome appears in the remarkable enquiry: *"Es mag im Anschluss an dieses erschuetternde Register nur noch die Frage behandelt werden: zu welchem Zweck verwendeten die Juden das Blut?"* ("In conclusion to this shocking list, there remains only one question: for what purpose did the Jews use the blood?"; col. 734).

The blood libel, in the various forms it assumed and the tales with which it was associated, is one of the most terrible expressions of the combination of human cruelty and credulity. No psychological or sociological research can convey the depths to which the numerous intentional instigators of such libels, and the more numerous propagators of this phantasmagoria, sank. It resulted in the torture, murder, and expulsion, of countless Jews, and the misery of insults. However, the dark specters it raised were even more harmful in their effects on the minds of Christians. The Jew had only to refer to himself, his upbringing, laws, way of life, and attitude to other people and to cruelty, to perceive the falsity and baselessness of these allegations. In modern times *Aḥad Ha-Am found "some consolation" in the existence of the blood libel, for it could serve as a spiritual defense against the influence on Jewish self-evaluation of the consensus of hostile opinion. "This accusation is the solitary case in which the general acceptance of an idea about ourselves does not make us doubt whether all the world can be wrong, and we right, because it is based on an absolute lie, and is not even supported by any false inference from particular to universal. Every Jew who has been brought up among Jews knows as an indisputable fact that throughout the length and breadth of Jewry there is not a single individual who drinks human blood for religious purposes. . . . Let the world say what it will about our moral inferiority: we know that its ideas rest on popular logic, and have no real scientific basis. . . . 'But'—you ask—'is it possible that everybody can be wrong, and the Jews right?' Yes, it is possible: the blood accusation proves it possible. Here, you see, the Jews are right and perfectly innocent" (*Selected Essays* (1962), 203–4). [H.H.B.-S.]

IN RUSSIA. In modern times Russia has been the principal perpetuator of the blood libel, both medieval and modern factors (see above) combining to enable its deliberate dissemination among the ignorant masses. The first blood-libel case in Russia occurred in the vicinity of Senno, south of Vitebsk, on the eve of Passover 1799, when the body of a woman was found near a Jewish tavern: four Jews were arrested on the ground of the "popular belief that the Jews require Christian blood." *Apostates supplied the court with extracts from a distorted translation of the Shulḥan Arukh and *Shevet Yehudah*. The accused were released through lack of evidence. Nevertheless the poet and administrator G.R. *Derzhavin, in his "Opinion submitted to the czar on the organization of the status of the Jews in Russia," could state that "in these communities persons are to be found who perpetrate the crime, or at least afford protection to those committing the crime, of shedding Christian blood, of which Jews have been suspected at various times and in different countries. If I for my part consider that such crimes, even if sometimes committed in antiquity, were carried out by ignorant fanatics, I thought it right not to overlook them." Thus a semiofficial and "highbrow" seal was given to the libel in Russia at the opening of the 19th century. Official Russian circles were divided in their views on the libel. A number of inquiries into the charges were instituted, while the views of the czars themselves fluctuated; the emperors and popes of the Middle Ages (see above) can be pointed to as models of enlightenment in comparison with the rulers of czarist Russia.

Between 1805 and 1816 various cases of blood libel occurred in places within the *Pale of Settlement, and the investigations always ended by exposing the lie on which they were based. In an attempt to stop their dissemination the minister of ecclesiastic affairs, A. Golitsyn, sent a circular to the heads of the guberniyas (provinces) throughout Russia on March 6, 1817, to this effect. Basing his instruction on the fact that both the Polish monarchs and the popes have invariably invalidated the libels, and that they had been frequently refuted by judicial inquiries, he stated in his circular that the czar directed "that henceforward the Jews shall not be charged with murdering Christian children, without evidence, and through prejudice alone that they allegedly require Christian blood." Nevertheless Alexander I (1801–25) gave instructions to revive the inquiry in the case of the murder of a Christian child in *Velizh (near Vitebsk) where the assassins had not been found and local Jewish notables had been blamed for the crime. The trial lasted for about ten years. Although the Jews were finally exonerated, Nicholas I later refused to endorse the 1817 circular, giving as a reason that he considered that "there are among the Jews savage fanatics or sects requiring Christian blood for their ritual, and especially since to our sorrow such fearful and astonishing groups also exist among us Christians." Other blood libels occurred in Telsiai (Telz) in the guberniya (province) of Kovno, in 1827, and Zaslav (*Izyaslav), in the government of Volhynia, in 1830. The Hebrew writer and scholar I. B. *Levinsohn was stirred by this case to write his book *Efes Damim* (Vilna, 1837), in which he exposed the senselessness of the accusations. A special secret commission was convened by the Russian Ministry of Foreign Affairs to clarify the problem concerning "use by Jews of the blood of Christian children," in which the Russian lexicographer and folklorist V. Dahl took part. The result of the inquiry, which reviewed numerous cases of blood libel in the Middle Ages and modern period, were published in 1844 in a limited edition and presented by Skripitsin, the director of the Department for Alien Religions, to the heads of state. In 1853, a blood libel occurred in *Saratov, when two Jews and an apostate were found guilty of the murder of two Christian children—the only instance in Russia of its kind. The council of state which dealt with the case in its final stages announced that it had confined itself to the purely legal aspect of the case and refrained from "anything bearing on the secret precepts or sects existing within Judaism and their influence on the crime." It thereby *prima facie* deprived the case of its test character as a blood libel. While the case was being considered, between 1853 and 1860, various Jews were accused of "kidnapping" on a number of occasions. The special committee appointed in 1855 had included a number of theologians and orientalists, among them two converts from Judaism, V. Levisohn and D. *Chwolson. The committee reviewed numerous Hebrew publications and manuscripts, and came to the conclusion that there was no hint or evidence to indicate that the Jews made use of Christian blood.

With the growth of an anti-Semitic movement in Russia in the 1870s, the blood libel became a regular motif in the anti-Jewish propaganda campaign conducted in the press and literature. Leading writers in this sphere were H. *Lutostansky, who wrote a pamphlet "concerning the use of Christian blood by Jewish sects for religious purposes" (1876), which ran into many editions, and J. Pranaitis. Numerous further allegations were made, including a case in Kutais (Georgia) in 1879, in which Jewish villagers were accused of murdering a little Christian girl. The case was tried in the district court and gave the advocates for the defense an opportunity of ventilating the social implications of the affair and the malicious intentions of its instigators. The chief agitators of the blood libels were monks. At the monastery of Suprasl crowds assembled to gaze on the bones of the "child martyr Gabriello," who had been allegedly murdered by Jews in 1690. The wave of blood libels which occurred at the end of the 19th century in central Europe, including the cases in Tiszaeszlar in 1881, *Xanten in 1891, Polna in 1899, etc., also heaped fuel on the flames of the agitation in Russia.

A number of works were published by Jewish writers in Russia to contradict the allegations, such as D. Chwolson's "Concerning Medieval Libels against Jews" (1861); I. B. Levinsohn's *Efes Damim* was translated into Russian (1883). Some of the calumniators were also prosecuted (see *Zederbaum v. Lutostansky, 1880). Despite the growing anti-Semitism and its officially supported anti-Jewish policy, the czarist authorities during the reign of Alexander III (1881–94) did not lend credence to the blood libels. It was only at the beginning of the 20th century that further attempts were renewed. These included the *Blondes Case in Vilna, in 1900, and an attempt in *Dubossary, in the guberniya of Kherson, where a Russian criminal tried to pin the murder of a child on the Jews. However, with the victory of the reactionaries in Russia after the dissolution of the Second *Duma in 1907, and the strengthening of the extreme right wing (*Union of Russian People) in the Third Duma, another attempt at official level was made by the regime to use the blood libel as a weapon in its struggle against the revolutionary movement and to justify its policy toward the Jews. An opportunity for doing so occurred in the *Beilis Case engineered by the minister of justice Shcheglovitov. The trial, which continued from spring 1911 to fall 1913, became a major political issue and the focal point for anti-Jewish agitation in the anti-Semitic press, in the streets, at meetings, and in the Duma. The whole of liberal and socialist opinion was ranged behind Beilis' defense, and even a section of the conservative camp. Leading Russian lawyers conducted the defense, and in Russia and throughout Europe hundreds of intellectuals and scholars, headed by V. Korolenko and M. *Gorki, joined in protest against the trial. The exoneration of Beilis was a political defeat for the regime. Despite this, the government continued to assent to the instigation of blood libels and support their dissemination among the masses until the 1917 Revolution. The Soviet government's attitude toward the blood libel was that it had been a weapon of the reaction and a tactic to exploit popular superstition by the czarist regime. The instigators of the Beilis trial were interrogated and tried at an early stage after the revolution. In later years the specter of the blood libel has been raised in the Soviet press in remote regions of the U.S.S.R., such as Georgia, Dagestan, and Uzbekistan, in the context of the violent propaganda campaign conducted by the Soviet government against Judaism and the State of Israel. After these attempts had aroused world public opinion, they were dropped. [Y.S.]

See also: *Host, Desecration of, *Albert II, *Albert V, *Bassano, *Bavaria, *Bedford, *Bernardino da Feltre *Boppard, *Brescia, *Bury St. Edmunds, *Civiltà Cattolica, *Corfu, *Damascus, *Deggendorf, *Dubrovnik, *Endingen, *Fano, *Ferrara, *Frank, Jacob, *Frankfort on the Main, *Gloucester, *Holesov, *Kolin, *Komarno, *Konitz, *Kromeriz (Kremsier), *London, *Masaryk, Thomáš, *Meyer, Paulus, *Nachod, *Noerdlingen, *Northampton, *Nuremberg, *Padua, *Passau, *Pavia, *Pfefferkorn, Johannes, *Premysl Otakar II, *Rome, *Rothenburg, *Ruehs, Christian Friedrich, *Schneider, Ernst, *Sonnenfels, Aloys von, *Treviso, *Veit, Joseph Emanuel, *Verona, *Viterbo, *Winchester, *Wuerzburg.

Bibliography: M. Samuel, *Blood Accusation* (1966); M. Hacohen (ed.) *Mishpatim ve-Alilot Dam* (1967); H. L. Strack, *The Jew and Human Sacrifice* (1909); C. Roth, *Ritual Murder Libel and the Jew* (1935); K. Hruby, in: W. P. Eckert and E. L. Ehrlich (eds.), *Judenhass-Schuld der Christen?* (1964), 281–358; idem, in: *Der Judenchrist* (1960/62); J. Trachtenberg, *Devil and the Jews* (1943), 124–55; Baer, Spain, 2 (1966), 398–423; *Il Piccolo martire S. Domenichino de Val, Patrono di Chierichetti* (1960); M. I. Seiden, *Paradox of Hate* (1967). In Russia: Dubnow, Hist, s.v., *Ritual Murder Libel;* A. D. Margolin, *Jews of Eastern Europe* (1926), 155–247; A. M. Tager, *Decay of Czarism, The Beiliss Trial* (1935).

BLOOM, BENJAMIN SAMUEL (1913–), U.S. educator. Bloom studied at Pennsylvania State University and at the University of Chicago, where he taught from 1940 (professor of education, 1953). He participated in several major educational assessment research efforts, both in America and abroad. His evaluation of school performance among youth of different nationalities was published in *International Study of Achievement in Mathematics; A Comparison of Twelve Countries* (with T. Husen and others, 1966). His other work has been in basic studies of measurement and evaluation procedures in education, analyses of stability and change patterns in human behavior, and the classification of educational objectives. At the invitation of the United States Office of Education Bloom helped set guidelines for federally supported research efforts throughout the United States. He was a member of the Advisory Committee on National Educational Laboratories. In 1965 he was appointed president of the American Educational Research Association, and in 1966 was elected a member of the National Academy of Education. His major publications include *Taxonomy of Educational Objectives, Handbook I and II* (1957–64) and *Stability and Change in Human Characteristics* (1964).

[A.J.T.]

BLOOM, HYMAN (1913–), U.S. painter. Born near Riga, Latvia, Bloom was taken in 1920 to Boston. Some of Bloom's drawings in the Fogg Museum Collection were done when he was only 15 years old. They show human forms in violent action, revealing the birth of an impassioned, deeply religious artist who dedicated himself to chronicles of life and death. During the 1940s he painted impressions of Judaic rituals and synagogue interiors with thick, writhing pigment fragmented into jewel-like tones. This style first won him recognition in 1942 when the Museum of Modern Art, New York, purchased "The Bride" and "The Synagogue." By 1948 the morbid overtones of tragedy hovering beneath Bloom's splendor erupted into a preoccupation with cadavers, whose putrefying flesh and trailing viscera were still the color of crushed jewels. Their extraordinary paint quality rather than their monstrous symbolism was greatly admired.

"The Synagogue" by Hyman Bloom, c. 1940, oil on canvas, $65\frac{1}{4} \times 46\frac{3}{4}$ in. (166×119 cm.). New York, Museum of Modern Art.

Bibliography: O'Doherty, in: *Art in America,* 49 (1961), 45–47.

[R.Bro.]

BLOOM, SOL (1870–1949), U.S. businessman and politician. Bloom, born in Pekin, Ill., was brought to San Francisco by his parents as a child. He was largely self-educated. At the age of 17 he became a theatrical producer, and began successful financial investments. Moving to Chicago, Bloom managed part of the World's Columbian Exposition of 1893 and prospered as a music publisher. In 1903 he moved to New York where he entered the real estate and construction field. Extremely successful in business, Bloom retired in 1920 and went into politics. He was elected to Congress as a Democrat in 1923, and served continuously until his death. As chairman of the Foreign Affairs Committee he strongly supported and advanced President Roosevelt's internationalist policies. He was a member of the American delegation to the 1943 Bermuda conference on refugees during World War II, and was criticized by those who, unlike Bloom himself, found its results unsatisfactory. He was a delegate to the 1945 San Francisco Conference that wrote the UN Charter; to the UN Relief and Rehabilitation Administration Conference of 1946; and to the 1947 Inter-American Conference at Rio de Janeiro. Bloom, who was favorable to Zionism, opposed President Truman's early Palestine policy and took part in gaining American and UN support for the establishment of the State of Israel. His *Autobiography* was published in 1948.

Bibliography: *Current Biography Yearbook 1943* (1944), 55–59.

[S.L.F.]

BLOOMFIELD, LEONARD (1887–1949), American linguist. Bloomfield, chiefly through his book *Language,* became the most influential individual in guiding the development of American descriptive linguistics. He taught at various American universities and from 1940 to 1949 was professor of linguistics at Yale. His interests widened from Indo-European to other language groups and into problems of general linguistics. He published his first inclusive survey of the field *An Introduction to the Study of Language* (1914); later he published *Tagalog Texts with Grammatical Analysis* (1917); and in the early 1920s began his long series of important contributions to the study of the Algonquian languages spoken by many North American Indian tribes. His interest in the practical application of linguistics to the teaching of languages remained strong throughout his life, and he wrote a number of textbooks and a general work, *Outline Guide for the Practical Study of Foreign Languages* (1942). He was one of the founders of the Linguistic Society of America, and served a term as its president. His most important work, *Language* (1933), though outdated in several respects, is still used as a standard textbook in many places. It has provided generations of linguists with a survey of the whole field, an analytical framework, and a basic approach to language as a subject for scientific inquiry.

Bibliography: B. Bloch, in: *Language,* 25 (1949), 87–98.

[H.BL.]

BLOOMFIELD, MAURICE (1855–1928), U.S. expert in Sanskrit. Born in Austria, Bloomfield was taken to the U.S. as a child and received his higher education at the University of Chicago and at Yale, where he studied under the Sanskritist W. D. Whitney. Bloomfield concentrated on research in Vedic language and literature, and after further study at Berlin and Leipzig (1879–81) was appointed professor of Sanskrit and comparative linguistics at Johns Hopkins University. His major works are *A Vedic Concordance* (1906), and *Vedic Variants* (completed after his death by his student and colleague, Franklin Edgerton, and published 1930–34). Bloomfield was president of the American Oriental Society (1910–11).

Bibliography: *Studies in Honor of Maurice Bloomfield* (1920).

[ED.]

BLOOMINGDALE, prominent U.S. family. The founder of the family was LYMAN GUSTAVUS (1841–1905), merchant and philanthropist. He was born in New York, son of German Jewish immigrants. After service in the Civil War in the Kansas Volunteers, he returned to New York where he and his brother Joseph opened a hoopskirt and ladies' notion store. In 1886 Bloomingdale Brothers Department Store was established on its present site in midtown New York City. Lyman was a patron of the arts and a noted philanthropist, with his chief interests the Metropolitan Museum of Art and Montefiore Hospital. JOSEPH BERNHARDT (1842–1904), brother of Lyman, was associated with the family's business endeavors in the West and later in New York. Retiring from Bloomingdale Brothers in 1896, he was president of the Hebrew Technical Institute and one of the founders of Barnard College. EMANUEL WATSON (1852–1928), lawyer and merchant, a third brother, received a law degree from Columbia University and was active both as an attorney and in the family business. His major interests included Republican politics, the New York State Bridge and Tunnel Commission, and the Society for Reformation of Juvenile Delinquents. SAMUEL JOSEPH (1873–1968), son of Lyman, was educated at the Columbia University School of Architecture, but devoted himself to the management of the family's store, serving as its president during 1905–30. An innovator in retailing techniques, he became a director of Federated Department Stores when it absorbed Bloomingdale Brothers in 1930. Samuel was trustee of the Federation of Jewish Philanthropies and active in the American Jewish Committee, also continuing the family association with the Metropolitan Museum of Art and Montefiore Hospital. HIRAM C. (1876–1953), another son of Lyman, served as vice-president of Bloomingdale Brothers and was a leader in the movement to establish standards for accuracy in advertising. Hiram's son ALFRED S. (1916–) was founder and chairman of the Diners Club credit organization.

Samuel Joseph Bloomingdale, U.S. businessman.

[MO.RO.]

BLOWITZ, HENRI GEORGES STEPHANE ADOLPHE OPPER DE (1825–1903), French journalist. As chief Paris correspondent of *The Times,* London, in 1875, he originated the technique of interviewing celebrities (among

Henri de Blowitz, Paris correspondent of *The Times,* London. Sketch by A. Werner, 1878. London, *The Times.*

them Bismarck, the sultan of Turkey, and Pope Leo XIII). In 1875 Blowitz, by now influential in European political circles, exposed plans of the military party in Germany for a second invasion of France. Three years later, he obtained the full text of the Berlin Treaty while it was still being negotiated, enabling *The Times* to print it the day it was signed. Blowitz was born Adolf Opper in Bohemia, but in 1860 added the name of his birthplace to his surname. He left home at 15, traveled, learned several languages, and taught for some years at the *lycée* in Tours and then in Marseilles. He wrote for the Paris newspapers and though sometimes in conflict with the French authorities, became naturalized after the Battle of Sedan. At the close of the Franco-Prussian War (1870–71), he helped to suppress the Commune at Marseilles by maintaining a private telegraph line to Versailles. Blowitz showed an excessive desire to remain detached from the Dreyfus Affair. He wrote short stories, comedies and *My Memoirs* (1903).

Bibliography: F. Giles, *Prince of Journalists* (1962), incl. bibl. [Ed.]

°**BLOY, LÉON** (1846–1917), French Catholic writer whose work contained many Jewish themes. His prose poem, *Le salut par les Juifs* (1892), described by the author as the "only one of my books I would dare to present to God," opens with a condemnation of anti-Semitism and its arch-priest, Edouard *Drumont. However, holding a theory of the identity of opposites, Bloy regards the Jews as both glorious and despicable, at one and the same time the elect of God and "une poignée de boue merveilleuse" ("a handful of wonderful mud"). Among Bloy's later writings, *Le Sang du Pauvre* (1909) contains a moving chapter devoted to the Yiddish poet, Morris *Rosenfeld. Those whom he converted to Catholicism included Jacques and Raïssa *Maritain.

Bibliography: A. Béguin, *Léon Bloy, a Study in Impatience* (1947); J. Petit, *Léon Bloy* (Fr., 1966), incl. bibl.; R. Maritain, *Les grandes amitiés* (1941–44); C. Journet, *Destinées d'Israël à propos du Salut par les Juifs* (1945). [D.R.G.]

BLUESTONE, JOSEPH ISAAC (1860–1934), U.S. physician, Zionist, and Hebraist. Bluestone, who was born in Kalvarija, Lithuania, emigrated to the United States in 1880. Ten years later he graduated from New York University Medical Center and began to practice as a physician on New York's Lower East Side. Bluestone advocated the Ḥibbat Zion movement in America (1882), and in 1889 he edited and published *Shulammit*, a Yiddish weekly devoted to Zionism. He became vice-president of the New York chapter of the Federation of American Zionists upon its formation in 1897, but soon left to form a rival organization, the United Zionists. In 1903 he was a delegate to the Zionist Congress in Basle. Bluestone was active in the order Sons of Zion (later B'nai Zion) and served as its grand master. He also served as secretary of the American Mizrachi upon its formation. Bluestone was involved in Jewish education in New York, notably in the Talmud Torah movement. A Hebraist, Bluestone published a small volume of Hebrew poetry entitled *Shirim u-Meshalim* (1931).

Bibliography: AJHSP, 35 (1939), 53–64; *New York Times* (Nov. 3 and 8, 1934). [H.B.G.]

BLUM, AMRAM BEN ISAAC JACOB (1834–1907), Hungarian rabbi. He served as rabbi of the important communities of Samson, Almas, Mád, Huszt, and Berettyoujfalu, where he died. He studied under his father, who was head of the *bet din* in Nagykaroly, and later in the seminaries of Nagykaroly, and of Abraham Samuel Benjamin Sofer, rabbi of Pressburg. His sons relate that throughout his life he longed to stand at the threshold of the gates of Zion and Jerusalem. He decided to do so once he had married off his sons and daughters. However, he was never able to fulfill this desire. His work *Beit She'arim* (*Oraḥ Ḥayyim*, 1909; *Yoreh De'ah*, 1941) is well-known in rabbinic circles and still of importance as a basic work of *halakhah*. The author formulated his own particular method of research, a method which went to the heart of each problem and explained it with clear reasoning. Blum founded a yeshivah which attracted many students. Blum had five sons and four sons-in-law, almost all of whom were noted scholars and served as rabbis of various communities in Hungary and Transylvania. Prominent among his sons were Isaac Jacob (1858–1938) who succeeded his father; Ben-Zion (1885–1945), rabbi of Szarvas, who published his father's book on the Passover *Haggadah—Arvei Pesaḥim* (1927); Judah Ẓevi (1867–1917), who served as rabbi of Tapoly-Hanusfalva; and Moses Nahum, who held the position of *dayyan* of Nagyvarad. He met his death in Auschwitz in 1944. Moses Nahum arranged the publication of the second volume of his father's *Beit She'arim*.

Bibliography: N. Ben-Menahem, *Mi-Sifrut Yisra'el be-Ungaryah* (1958), 306–9, 314–7; A. J. Schwartz, in: M. Stein, *Even ha-Me'ir* (1909), 83; P. Z. Schwartz, *Shem ha-Gedolim me-Ereẓ Hagar*, 2 (1914), 25a–b; S. Schwartz, *Toledot Ge'onei Hagar* (1911), 15b–20a; *Magyar Zsidó Lexikon* (1929), 130. [N.B.-M.]

BLUM, ELIEZER (pseudonym **B. Alkvit**; 1896–1963), Yiddish poet and short story writer. After living in various European cities Blum went to New York in 1914. In 1920 he joined the introspective movement launched by the poets J. Glatstein, A. *Glanz-Leyeles and N. B. Minkoff, and coedited its organ *In-Zikh*. He worked in a factory and was later associated with the Yiddish daily *Jewish Morning Journal*, in which he published lyrics, mostly in blank verse. His collection of short stories *Oyfn Veg tsum Peretz Skver* ("En Route to Peretz Square," 1958), in common with his lyrics, combines realism and mysticism, an astonishing integration of the people and landscapes of his native Chelm and those of New York. The title story is itself the mystical contemplation of how a small square, bearing the name of Peretz, has somehow strayed into tumultuous New York. His collected poetry was published posthumously.

Bibliography: LNYL, s.v.; J. Glatstein, *In Tokh Genumen* (1956), 443–7; A. Glanz-Leyeles, *Velt un Vort* (1958), 162–5. [M.Rav.]

BLUM, JULIUS (**Blum Pasha**; 1843–1919), Austro-Hungarian banker and Egyptian statesman. Blum, who was born in Budapest, worked for the Austrian *Creditanstalt fuer Handel und Gewerbe*, first in its Trieste branch, and, later, in its affiliate in Egypt. After the bank's liquidation in Egypt, Blum served as undersecretary of finance (1877–90), and was instrumental in the rehabilitation of the country's economy, following the 1875 financial collapse and the British occupation in 1882. In 1890 he resigned his Egyptian post, with high honors, and rejoined the management of the *Creditanstalt* in Vienna where his knowledge of international finance contributed to making the bank a leading institution in Europe. From 1913 Blum was president of the *Creditanstalt*.

Bibliography: J. O. Ronall, in: *Tradition: Zeitschrift fuer Firmengeschichte und Unternehmer-Biographie*, no. 2 (1968), 57–80. [J.O.R.]

BLUM, LÉON (1872–1950), statesman; the first Jew and the first socialist to become premier of France. Son of a wealthy Alsatian merchant, Blum graduated with the highest honors in law at the Sorbonne. At the age of 22, he was recognized as a poet and writer. His publications included *En lisant: reflexions critiques* (1906), *Au Théâtre*, 4 vols. (1905–11), and a book about Stendhal (1914). His *Du Mariage* (1907; *Marriage*, 1937) created a sensation because of its advocacy of trial marriage and was quoted against him years later when he was premier. Blum was also a brilliant literary and drama critic. Blum was appointed to the Conseil d'État, a body whose functions included the settlement of conflicts between administrative and judicial authorities. He rose to the high rank of "Master of Requests," one of the principal offices in the Conseil d'État.

Always conscious of his Jewish origin, Blum was brought into active politics as a result of the *Dreyfus Affair. His close association with Jean Jaurès, whom he greatly admired, led to his joining the Socialist Party in 1899. Blum was first elected to the Chamber of Deputies in 1919. When the party split in December 1920, and the Communist section won a majority, securing the party machine, funds, and press, Blum helped to reconstruct the Socialist Party so successfully that he is considered one of the founders of the modern French Socialist Party.

Blum led the opposition to the government of Millerand and Poincaré and supported Herriot's *Cartel de gauche* in 1924. In the 1928 elections, the Socialist Party won 104 seats but Blum himself was defeated. A year later, however, he was elected for Narbonne, and was reelected for this department in 1932 and 1936. The 1934 Paris riots resulting from the disclosures of the Stavisky financial scandal were an early portent of the danger of fascism, and Blum began to work for the left-wing alliance that became the Front Populaire. In 1936 the Front won a large majority and Blum, its chief architect, became premier (on June 4). His government introduced the 40-hour week, nationalized the Bank of France and the war industries, and carried out a far-reaching program of social reforms. The most difficult problem was that of national defense in the face of the growing power of the Rome-Berlin axis. However, in the face of the challenge of the Spanish Civil War, Blum, confronted with the negative attitude of the British Conservative government to the Republican Forces, decided on a policy of "nonintervention" which was described by his critics as appeasement of the Axis powers. At the same time his social reforms aroused the bitterness of industrialists who openly refused to cooperate with the government. The right wing, which showed pro-German tendencies, conducted a violent campaign of personal vilification against Blum tinged with anti-Semitic undertones. In 1937, on June 21, Blum resigned, after parliament had refused to grant him emergency powers to deal with the country's financial problems. He served as vice-premier in modified Popular Front governments and as premier again, for less than a month, in 1938, during the Nazi invasion of Austria. After the French collapse in 1940, he was indicted by the Vichy government on charges of war guilt and was brought to trial. His brilliant defense confounded the Germans as well as the "men of Vichy" and the former ordered the suspension of the trial. Blum was returned to prison and was freed from a German concentration camp by U.S. forces in May 1945. He was given an enthusiastic welcome both in France and in international labor circles.

Léon Blum, three times premier of France.

After the liberation of France, he emerged as an elder statesman and negotiated the vast U.S. credit to France. In 1946 he formed an all-Socialist "caretaker" government, whose vigorous policy left a deep impression even though it only survived for a month. Blum then retired from public life, except for a brief period as vice-premier in a 1948 government. He is considered one of the great figures in the French Labor movement and an architect of the Socialist International between the two world wars.

Sympathetic to Zionist aspirations, Léon Blum, together with Emile Vandervelde, Arthur Henderson, and Eduard Bernstein, was one of the founders of the "Socialist Pro-Palestine Committee" in 1928. He readily accepted Weizmann's invitation to join the enlarged Jewish Agency and addressed its first meeting in Zurich in 1929. Blum took a leading part in influencing the French government's pro-Jewish vote on the U.N. decision on Palestine in 1947. He was also instrumental in preventing British diplomatic pressure from stopping the flow of Jewish *illegal immigration from Central Europe through France to Palestine.

His son ROBERT LÉON (1902–) was an engineer and industrialist. Born in Paris, he studied engineering at the École Supérieure Polytechnique. In 1926 he joined Hispano-Suiza, manufacturers of automobiles and aircraft engines. In 1968 he retired as president of the company. Robert Léon also served as president of Bugatti, another automobile manufacturing firm. He was president of the Union Syndicale des Industries Aeronautiques et Spatiales.

Bibliography: J. Colton, *Leon Blum: Humanist in Politics* (1966); L. E. Dalby, *Leon Blum: Evolution of a Socialist* (1963); J. Joll, *Three Intellectuals in Politics* (1960); Paris, Bibliothèque Nationale, *Léon Blum* (1962); *Leon Blum before his judges* (1943); J. Moch, *Rencontres avec . . . Léon Blum* (1970). [M.R.]

BLUM, RENÉ (1878–1944), French ballet impresario. A brother of the statesman Léon *Blum, René Blum began his career as a writer and was general secretary of the periodical *Gil Blas*, but gave up writing for art and ballet. When Diaghilev died (1929), Blum was chosen to succeed him as director of the Ballet de l'Opéra de Monte Carlo, and he held the post until the Nazi invasion of France in 1940. He was also associated for four years, from 1932, with Colonel de Basil's Ballet. In 1936 he founded the René Blum Ballets Russes and two years later, joined by Léonide Massine and other members of the de Basil company, he formed the Ballets Russes de Monte Carlo. After the German occupation of Paris, Blum refused to leave for the free zone of France, and at the end of 1941 was interned with nearly a thousand French-Jewish intellectuals in the camp of Compiègne. From there he was sent to Auschwitz, where he died in September 1944. The manuscript of his memoirs, which was in the hands of a Paris publisher in 1940, was not recovered after the liberation.

Bibliography: I. Guest, *The Dancer's Heritage* (1960), 93ff.; S. Lifar, *Histoire du Ballet Russe* (1950), 245, 249. [ED.]

BLUME, PETER (1906–), U.S. painter. He was born in Russia and in 1911 taken to New York. During the 1930s he produced many murals of the American scene under the auspices of the Federal Art Projects of the WPA and earned a high reputation. His work was highly stylized, decorative, and somewhat bizarre. Most paintings were frank fantasy—crisp interpretations of man in the machine age. In "South of Scranton" (1931), now in the Metropolitan

"Excavation" by Peter Blume, 1945, oil on canvas, 21×27 in. (53×68.5cm.). New York, private collection.

Museum of Art, 15th-century technique was applied to create 20th-century images of factories dwarfing man and the slums he lives in. This picture won him a leading place among a growing sect of ultrarealistic propaganda painters called "magic realists." Before the end of the decade his invectives against man's exploitation of man became more vitriolic. In "The Eternal City" (1934–37), also owned by the Metropolitan Museum, he reveals an elaborate panorama of decadence. [R.BRO.]

BLUMENBERG, LEOPOLD (1827–1876), U.S. businessman and soldier. Born in Brandenburg, Prussia, Blumenberg served as a lieutenant in the fighting in Denmark in 1848. He emigrated to the United States in 1854 and developed a successful business in Baltimore. At the beginning of the American Civil War, he helped organize a Unionist Maryland Volunteer regiment, fought with it in the Peninsula Campaign, and was severely wounded while commanding the unit in the Battle of Antietam (1862). Incapacitated by his wounds, he was appointed provost marshall of the third Maryland district and later attained the rank of brevet brigadier general of U.S. Volunteers.

Bibliography: J. Ben Hirsh, *Jewish General Officers*, 1 (1967), 95.
[S.L.F.]

BLUMENFELD, EMANUEL (1801–1878), leader of the Haskalah in Galicia and the first Jew to practice law in Lemberg. Blumenfeld was instrumental in establishing the Reform Temple in Lemberg. He was a member of an unsuccessful delegation sent to the Austrian emperor in 1840 to ask for abolition of the *candle tax and for alleviation of the restriction on Jewish occupations. In 1842 the authorities, wishing to encourage the spread of Haskalah, appointed a community council without holding elections, which Blumenfeld headed. He subsequently reorganized the communal administration and inaugurated wide-ranging educational projects. A secular coeducational Jewish school on the model of the *Perl school in Tarnopol was opened in Lemberg in 1844, and supported by the community. In 1847 Blumenfeld convened an assembly of representatives of the communities of Galicia to discuss alleviation of taxation and the general situation. He was one of the eight Jews elected to the city council for the first time in 1848, and helped to formulate the municipal statute of Lemberg in 1850.

Bibliography: F. Friedman, *Die galizischen Juden im Kampfe um ihre Gleichberechtigung* (1929), 58 n. 146; N. M. Gelber, in: EG, Poland series, 4 (1956), 232–3.
[M.LAN.]

BLUMENFELD, HERMANN FADEEVICH (1861–1920), Russian civil lawyer. He was the son of Rabbi Feitel Blumenfeld of Kherson (1826–1896), who helped to develop the Jewish agricultural colonies in Kherson and Bessarabia. Blumenfeld won a gold medal at the University of Odessa for a thesis on the law of real property. Being a Jew, however, he was not allowed to be called to the Bar and remained formally an articled clerk until 1905 (the formal title in Russian was "assistant lawyer"). In the trials of 1906 following the Kishinev pogroms, the memorandum of the Bar Association submitted to the minister of justice was based on a report drafted by Blumenfeld. In the regime of Alexander Kerensky following the February revolution of 1917, Blumenfeld was made a member of the supreme court. His writings include two books on forms of land ownership in ancient Russia (1884), and on inheritance and authors' rights (1892), and articles on Jewish subjects, including "Economic Activity of the Jews in Southern Russia" in: *Voskhod* (no. 9, (1881), 175–219), and "Jewish Colonies in the Kherson Government" in: *Razsvet* (1880 and 1881). [D.B-R-H.]

BLUMENFELD, KURT YEHUDAH (1884–1963), German Zionist leader. Blumenfeld, who was born in Treuberg, East Prussia, studied law at the universities of Berlin, Freiburg, and Koenigsberg. He joined the Zionist movement in 1904 while still a student and became a student leader of the movement. From 1910 to 1914 he directed the department of information of the World Zionist executive, whose seat was then in Berlin, visiting many countries in the course of his work. In 1913–14 he was the editor of *Die Welt*, and in 1920 was among the founders of Keren Hayesod. He was president of the German Zionist Federation from 1923 to 1933. Blumenfeld settled in

Kurt Blumenfeld, German Zionist leader.

Palestine in 1933 and became a member of the Keren Hayesod directorate. He was a delegate to every Zionist Congress from the ninth (1909) on, and was a member of the Zionist General Council from 1920. His influence on West European personalities, including Albert Einstein, derived primarily from his intellectualism and his specific "post-assimilation" Zionism, i.e., the Zionist ideology he evolved to appeal to Jews who were already assimilated. His memoirs, *Erlebte Judenfrage; ein Vierteljahrhundert deutscher Zionismus* (1962), have been translated into Hebrew.

Bibliography: S. Esh, in: JJSO, 6 (1964), 232–42; *Y. K. Blumenfeld in Memoriam* (1964); *Davar* (April 25, 1962); MB (May 29, 1964).
[A.B.]

BLUMENFELD, RALPH DAVID (1864–1948), British journalist. Blumenfeld was born in Wisconsin, the son of a newspaperman. He became a reporter on the *Chicago Herald* and later on the *New York Herald.* In New York, he entered the typesetting business, sold linotype machines in England, and made a considerable fortune. At the age of 36 he reentered journalism as news editor of the London *Daily Mail,* and transferred to *The Daily Express* as foreign editor in 1902. He was editor, 1904–1932, editor in chief from 1924, and chairman of the London Express Newspaper Company, 1915–1948. Blumenfeld edited *The Daily Express* for mass appeal, used large type in forceful style, stressed the "human angle" wherever possible, and raised the paper's circulation to two million daily. After his retirement in 1932, he visited Palestine, became a supporter of Zionism, and was active against anti-Semitism. Among the books he published were: *R. D. B.'s Diary 1887–1914* (1930); *All in a Lifetime* (1931); *The Press in My Time* (1933), and *R. D. B.'s Procession* (1935). [Ed.]

BLUMENFIELD, SAMUEL (1901–1972), U.S. Jewish educator. Born in Letichev, Russia, Blumenfield was superintendent of the Chicago Board of Jewish Education until 1954, and also headed Chicago's College of Jewish Studies as dean, and later as president. From 1954 until his retirement in 1968, he served as director of the Department of Education and Culture of the Jewish Agency (American Section). Blumenfield is author of *Master of Troyes—A Study of Rashi the Educator* (1946), "Towards a Study of Maimonides the Educator" (HUCA, 23 (1950–51), 555–91), and *Ḥevrah ve-Ḥinnukh be-Yahadut Amerikah* (1965). He was president of Avukah (an American student Zionist Organization) and the National Council of Jewish Education. [L.Sp.]

BLUMENKRANZ, BERNHARD (1913–), historian. Blumenkranz headed a research unit at the National Center for Scientific Research (Paris), and lectured on the social history of the Jews at the École Pratique des Hautes Études in Paris. He was president of the French Commission of Jewish Archives, and director of the bimonthly publication of the Jewish Archives. His works deal principally with the Jewish and Christian relations in the Middle Ages and the history of the Jews in medieval France. His most important books are: *Juifs et Chrétiens dans le monde occidental* (1960); *Les auteurs chrétiens latins du Moyen-Age sur les Juifs et le judaïsme* (1963); and *Le Juif médiéval au miroir de l'art chrétien* (1966). Blumenkranz was a departmental editor of the *Encyclopaedia Judaica.* [C.S.]

BLUMENTHAL, GEORGE (1858–1941), U.S. banker, philanthropist, and patron of the arts. He was born in Frankfort and worked there in the banking house of Speyer. After moving to the United States in 1882, he became senior partner of Lazard Frères and director of various banks and insurance companies. In 1898 he joined other bankers in raising a fund of $50 million to stop the flow of gold from the United States, and after World War I, played an important part in stabilizing the franc.

Blumenthal was director and president of the Mount Sinai Hospital, the largest Jewish hospital in New York. He donated one million dollars to the hospital and a new wing was erected as a memorial to his son. He was active in support of the arts, giving a million dollars to the Metropolitan Museum of Art in New York, of which he became president in 1934. In 1937 he presented a collection of first editions of important French writers to the New York Public Library. [Ed.]

George Blumenthal, U.S. banker and philanthropist. Portrait by Adolphe Deckenaud. New York, Metropolitan Museum of Art.

BLUMENTHAL, JOSEPH (1834–1901), U.S. businessman and a founder of the Jewish Theological Seminary. Blumenthal, who was born in Munich, was taken to the U.S. at the age of five. He was a member of the Committee of Seventy which was responsible for the downfall of the notorious Tweed Ring. He served as New York State assemblyman and as commissioner of taxes and

Joseph Blumenthal, a founder of the Jewish Theological Seminary of New York.

assessments in New York City. Blumenthal served in Jewish communal affairs as president of Shearith Israel Synagogue, president of the Young Men's Hebrew Association, and a leader of B'nai B'rith. He was the first president of the Board of Trustees of the Jewish Theological Seminary, a position he held from its inception in 1886 until his death.

Bibliography: M. Davis, *Emergence of Conservative Judaism* (1963), 331–2. [J.Ri.]

BLUMENTHAL, JOSEPH (1897–), U. S. printer and type designer. In 1926 he founded the Spiral Press in New York City. Blumenthal designed his own typeface, Emerson, which is available for hand and machine setting. At the modern, well-equipped but small Spiral Press,

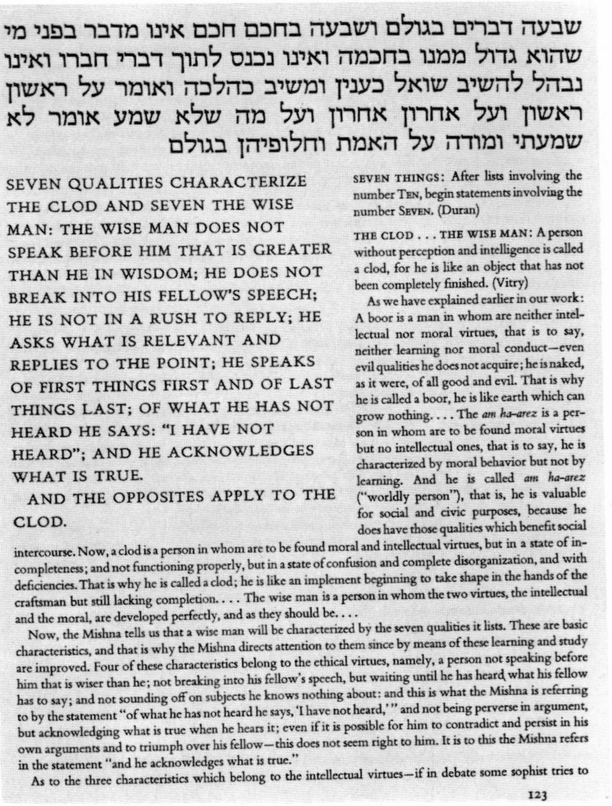

שבעה דברים בגולם ושבעה בחכם חכם אינו מדבר בפני מי
שהוא גדול ממנו בחכמה ואינו נכנס לתוך דברי חברו ואינו
נבהל להשיב שואל כענין ומשיב כהלכה ואומר על ראשון
ראשון ועל אחרון אחרון ועל מה שלא שמע אומר לא
שמעתי ומודה על האמת וחלופיהן בגולם

SEVEN QUALITIES CHARACTERIZE THE CLOD AND SEVEN THE WISE MAN: THE WISE MAN DOES NOT SPEAK BEFORE HIM THAT IS GREATER THAN HE IN WISDOM; HE DOES NOT BREAK INTO HIS FELLOW'S SPEECH; HE IS NOT IN A RUSH TO REPLY; HE ASKS WHAT IS RELEVANT AND REPLIES TO THE POINT; HE SPEAKS OF FIRST THINGS FIRST AND OF LAST THINGS LAST; OF WHAT HE HAS NOT HEARD HE SAYS: "I HAVE NOT HEARD"; AND HE ACKNOWLEDGES WHAT IS TRUE.

AND THE OPPOSITES APPLY TO THE CLOD.

SEVEN THINGS: After lists involving the number TEN, begin statements involving the number SEVEN. (Duran)

THE CLOD . . . THE WISE MAN: A person without perception and intelligence is called a clod, for he is like an object that has not been completely finished. (Vitry)

As we have explained earlier in our work: A boor is a man in whom are neither intellectual nor moral virtues, that is to say, neither learning nor moral conduct—even evil qualities he does not acquire; he is naked, as it were, of all good and evil. That is why he is called a boor, he is like earth which can grow nothing. . . . The *am ha-arez* is a person in whom are to be found moral virtues but no intellectual ones, that is to say, he is characterized by moral behavior but not by learning. And he is called *am ha-arez* ("worldly person"), that is, he is valuable for social and civic purposes, because he does have those qualities which benefit social intercourse. Now, a clod is a person in whom are to be found moral and intellectual virtues, but in a state of incompleteness; and not functioning properly, but in a state of confusion and complete disorganization, and with deficiencies. That is why he is called a clod; he is like an implement beginning to take shape in the hands of the craftsman but still lacking completion. . . . The wise man is a person in whom the two virtues, the intellectual and the moral, are developed perfectly, and as they should be. . . .

Now, the Mishna tells us that a wise man will be characterized by the seven qualities it lists. These are basic characteristics, and that is why the Mishna directs attention to them since by means of these learning and study are improved. Four of these characteristics belong to the ethical virtues, namely, a person not speaking before him that is wiser than he; not breaking into his fellow's speech, but waiting until he has heard what his fellow has to say; and not sounding off on subjects he knows nothing about: and this is what the Mishna is referring to by the statement "of what he has not heard he says, 'I have not heard,'" and not being perverse in argument, but acknowledging what is true when he hears it; even if it is possible for him to contradict and persist in his own arguments and to triumph over his fellow—this does not seem right to him. It is to this the Mishna refers in the statement "and he acknowledges what is true."

As to the three characteristics which belong to the intellectual virtues—if in debate some sophist tries to

123

Page from a Spiral Press publication, *The Living Talmud*, using Joseph Blumenthal's Emerson type.

Blumenthal designed and produced books and exhibition catalogs for the Metropolitan Museum of Art, the Museum of Modern Art, the Pierpont Morgan Library, and similar institutions as well as limited editions such as Ben *Shahn's *Alphabet of Creation* for general book publishers.

[I.So.]

BLUMENTHAL, NISSAN (1805–1903), Russian cantor. Blumenthal was born in Berdichev, Ukraine, where he became cantor at the age of 21. He later served in Yekaterinoslav (Dnepropetrovsk), and from 1841 until his death held the position of chief cantor at the Brody Synagogue in Odessa. His main contribution to the music of the synagogue was the founding of a choir school in Odessa, where he developed choral singing in four voices, an innovation at that time. Contrary to the wishes of the traditionalists, he introduced into the liturgy melodies from German classical music. He was nevertheless a lover of tradition and succeeded in effecting a synthesis of old and new. Few of his melodies appeared in print, but they were preserved by other cantors and some are still sung.

Bibliography: Sendrey, Music, indexes; A. L. Holde, *Jews in Music* (1959), index; H. H. Harris, *Toledot ha-Neginah ve-ha-Ḥazzanut be-Yisrael* (1950), 400–2.

[J.L.N.]

BLUMENTHAL, OSKAR (1852–1917), German playwright. He achieved early notoriety as "Bloody Oskar" for his satirical articles as theater critic of the *Berliner Tageblatt*. In 1888 he helped to found the Lessing Theater in Berlin, and directed many of its productions until 1897. Blumenthal's own plays attacking social foibles were popular for about three decades and in the 1910 season several of his plays were widely performed. The witty comedy *Der Probepfeil* (1884) was often performed in America from 1892 onward as *The Test Case*. His greatest success was *Im Weissen Roessl* (1898), which he wrote in collaboration with Gustav Kadelburg. Transformed into a musical comedy, *White Horse Inn* (1907), it became an international triumph of the mid-1930s.

[S.L.]

BLUMENTHAL, WERNER MICHAEL (1926–), U.S. economist, industrialist, and ambassador. Born in Oranienburg, Germany, Blumenthal left Germany in the 1930s, spent some years in Shanghai where he was interned by the Japanese, and finally went to the United States in 1947. He taught at Princeton from 1954 to 1957, leaving to assume the post of vice-president of Crown Cork International. In 1961 Blumenthal became United States representative to the U.N. Commission on International Commodity Trade, serving simultaneously as deputy assistant secretary of state for economic affairs. In 1963, as President Johnson's deputy special representative for trade negotiations, he was posted to Geneva as ambassador and chairman of the United States delegation to the Kennedy Round of tariff negotiations. After these were completed in 1967, Blumenthal resigned from government service to become president of international operations at Bendix Corporation.

[E.F.]

B'NAI B'RITH, the world's oldest and largest Jewish service organization, with lodges and chapters in 45 countries. B'nai B'rith's total membership numbers (1970) approximately 500,000 Jewish men, women, and youth. There are 1,700 men's lodges, 25% of them outside North America, with a male membership of 210,000, and a U.S. budget of over $13,000,000. Its program encompasses the totality of Jewish concerns and includes many programs in

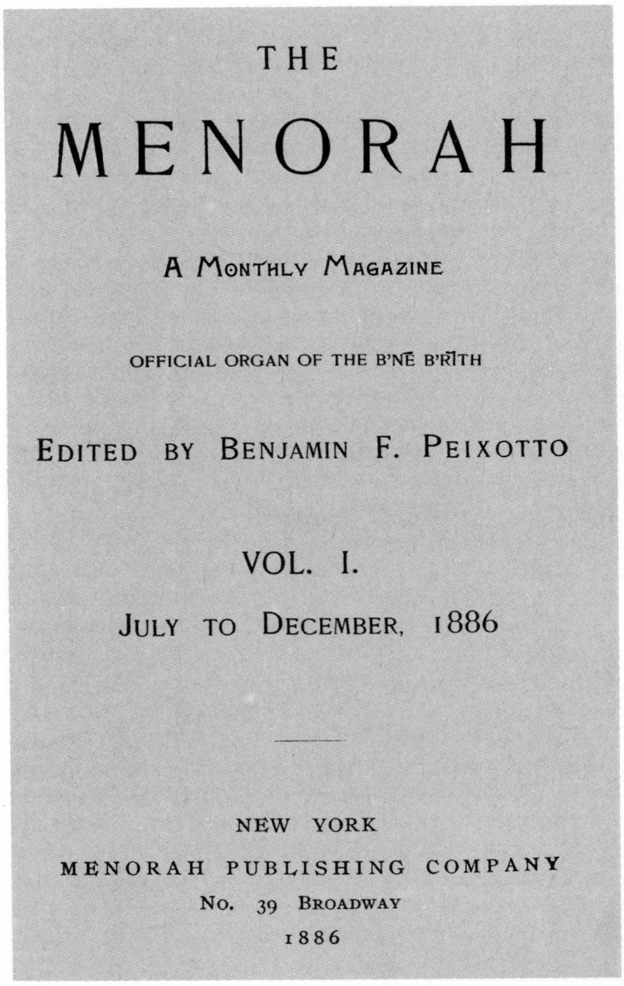

THE

MENORAH

A MONTHLY MAGAZINE

OFFICIAL ORGAN OF THE B'NĒ B'RĪTH

EDITED BY BENJAMIN F. PEIXOTTO

VOL. I.

JULY TO DECEMBER, 1886

NEW YORK

MENORAH PUBLISHING COMPANY

No. 39 BROADWAY

1886

Figure 1. The first collected volume of the B'nai B'rith monthly magazine, *Menorah*. Cincinnati, American Jewish Archives.

Figure 2. The B'nai B'rith national executive with President Taft (center, with medal) at the White House, 1910. They were received to discuss Russian passport restrictions aimed at American Jews. New York, B'nai B'rith. Photo Larry Franklin.

the interest of the wider community. B'nai B'rith was founded on Oct. 13, 1843, by 12 men who met in a cafe on the Lower East Side of New York to establish a new fraternal order for U.S. Jews who then numbered 15,000 souls. The first president was Isaac Dittenhoefer, but Henry Jones, his successor, is credited as the chief founder. The founders chose B'nai B'rith ("Sons of the Covenant") as the name of their new organization and the Menorah as its insignia. They formulated its aims in the following preamble to the B'nai B'rith constitution: "B'nai B'rith has taken upon itself the mission of uniting persons of the Jewish faith [originally: 'Israelites'] in the work of promoting their highest interests and those of humanity; of developing and elevating the mental and moral character of the people of our faith; of inculcating the purest principles of philanthropy, honor, and patriotism; of supporting science and art; alleviating the wants of the poor and needy; visiting and attending the sick; coming to the rescue of victims of persecution; providing for, protecting, and assisting the widow and orphan on the broadest principles of humanity."

These purposes were implemented during the 19th and the early 20th century via a program dominated by mutual aid, social service, and philanthropy. In 1865 the order made a substantial grant to aid cholera epidemic sufferers in Ereẓ Israel, and six years later to provide food, clothing, and medical supplies for victims of the Chicago fire. The organization established orphanages, homes for the aged, and hospitals. After 1881, when the mass immigration from Eastern Europe poured into the country, B'nai B'rith sponsored Americanization classes, trade schools, and relief programs. Hitherto B'nai B'rith had consisted primarily of German Jews, but the changing character of the U.S. Jewish population, and of the 20th century, gave a new complexion to the constituency of the order, its program, and its structure. In 1897, when B'nai B'rith's membership numbered slightly more than 18,000, B'nai B'rith Women came into being with the founding of a ladies' auxiliary chapter in San Francisco. By 1968 B'nai B'rith Women had over 1,000 chapters in 22 countries, with a membership of 135,000, with 90% of the chapters in North America.

B'nai B'rith and the Baron de Hirsch Fund. In 1901, when immigration of Jews from Eastern Europe was at its height, the *Baron de Hirsch Fund established the *Industrial Removal Office in order to relieve the congestion of the eastern cities, especially New York. The purpose was to settle Jews in other parts of the country. B'nai B'rith joined with the Baron de Hirsch Fund in this effort and organized committees outside of New York, especially in the west and the south, to resettle Jews away from the eastern seaboard. In its first year 2,000 persons were moved to 250 different locations. Before the office closed 15 years later, 100,000 Jews were dispersed into every state of the Union, and they in turn attracted new Jewish immigrants to these communities. When anti-Semitism in the United States increased prior to World War I, B'nai B'rith founded its Anti-Defamation League (ADL) in 1913. ADL seeks to strengthen interreligious understanding and cooperation, to improve relations between the races, and above all to protect the status and rights of Jews.

The concern of B'nai B'rith for the preservation of Jewish tradition and values was given new impetus with the establishment in 1923 of the first B'nai B'rith Hillel Foundation to serve the religious, cultural, and social needs of the 400 Jewish students at the University of Illinois. The Hillel movement spread to almost 270 university campuses on six continents. Hillel also sponsors chairs of Judaic studies and faculty programs. About 300,000 Jewish students are enrolled on the campuses served by full-time Hillel Foundations and part-time Hillel Counselorships.

A year later, in 1924, the B'nai B'rith Youth Organization (BBYO) came into being. It has three sections: Aleph Zadik Aleph (A.Z.A.) for Jewish teenage boys, B'nai B'rith Girls for teenage girls, and B'nai B'rith Young Adults. In 1970 BBYO had a membership of 50,000 in 1,500 chapters throughout the world, conducting a program of cultural, religious, community service, social, and athletic activities. To aid young Jewish people in their career planning, in 1938 the order founded the B'nai B'rith Vocational Service. This agency conducts individual and group vocational guidance programs, does occupational research, sponsors career conferences, and publishes career guides.

B'nai B'rith's commitment to Jewish learning found another outlet in its Department of Adult Jewish Education, begun in 1948 and elevated in 1959 to the status

Figure 3. B'nai B'rith leaders with President Truman at the White House after the proclamation of the State of Israel in May 1948. Seated with the President is Frank Goldman, president of the order, and behind are Eddie Jacobson (left) and Maurice Bisgyer. New York, B'nai B'rith. Photo Larry Franklin.

of a commission. Its program includes institutes for the study of Judaism, informal learning groups, and lecture tours by distinguished scholars. The commission also publishes a quarterly magazine, *Jewish Heritage,* and the Great Book Series, and has experimented in new ways of teaching Hebrew to adults. B'nai B'rith has been rendering social services on behalf of war veterans for decades, and has also undertaken citizenship programs. These activities were combined in 1962 into a Commission on Citizens, Veterans, and Community Affairs. Among their activities are service to the disabled, encouragement of employment of handicapped, blood banks, and cooperation with government agencies.

B'nai B'rith has always taken interest in Israel; it fulfilled an important role in support of Israel's independence. The Israel Commission, originally established in 1953, promotes the sale of Israel Bonds and the purchase of trees, especially for the B'nai B'rith Martyrs' Forest near Jerusalem, stimulates tourism to Israel, and in other ways serves as a bridge between the State of Israel and Jews in the Diaspora.

Although founded in the United States, B'nai B'rith has spread throughout the world. Its involvement in world affairs is coordinated through the B'nai B'rith International Council, established in 1959, which has offices in several countries and at the United Nations in New York. Other avenues for B'nai B'rith expression of its international interests are through its membership in the Coordinating Board of Jewish Organizations, the Presidents' Conference, the Conference on Soviet Jewry, the World Conference on Jewish Education, and the Conference of Jewish Organizations. It publishes the *National Jewish Monthly* magazine. B'nai B'rith's presidents have occupied distinguished positions of leadership in the American Jewish community and in international efforts on behalf of world Jewry. Since 1925 B'nai B'rith's international presidents have been Alfred M. Cohen (1925–38); Henry Monsky (1938–47); Frank Goldman (1947–53); Philip M. Klutznick (1953–59); Label A. Katz (1959–65), and Dr. William A. Wexler (1965–). [Be.K.]

In Europe. The first lodge in Europe—and the first outside the United States—was founded in 1882 under the name "Lodge of the German Empire." The order was active in Germany and by 1932 there were 103 lodges numbering 13,000 brethren and a chain of institutions. These lodges formed the B'nai B'rith District Nine. The

Figure 4. Medal commemorating the foundation of the Frankfort lodge of B'nai B'rith, 1902. New York, Dan Friedenberg Collection.

Figure 5. The first home of the Jerusalem lodge of B'nai B'rith, founded in 1888. Jerusalem, Hebrew University. Photo Alfred Bernheim, Jerusalem.

lodge in Rumania was founded in 1911, and here also an independent district was formed—No. Ten. District No. 11 was formed in Czechoslovakia, District No. 12 in Austria, and District No. 13 in Poland. Only after lodges existed in these countries was the English district founded. The first lodge of England, which was also called by this name, was founded in 1910. With the increase of lodges England was recognized in 1926 as an independent district under the name "The District of Great Britain and Ireland." The B'nai B'rith Youth (A.Z.A.) was founded in Britain in 1940. B'nai B'rith work in Europe found expression in Jewish education, the Anti-Defamation League, activity on behalf of Israel, etc. The B'nai B'rith in Bulgaria played a central role in Jewish life there and became an independent district (No. 18), as the B'nai B'rith in Yugoslavia also became an independent district of its own. Individual lodges existed also in other countries in Europe, South Africa, Australia, etc.

The Order of B'nai B'rith in Europe was refounded after the Holocaust (1948). The inaugural meeting was attended by the lodges which survived in Basle and in Zurich, and by lodges that managed to reorganize in Holland, and in France. A representative body was founded, initially headed by Leo *Baeck, later by Edwin Guggenheim of Zurich. An office was established in Paris which by 1952 had inaugurated six lodges in France, two in Belgium, three in Scandinavia, and elsewhere.

In 1955, with an increase of lodges, the lodges in Europe were recognized as an independent district—No. 19. The European district initiated the planting of the Martyrs' Forest in Israel.

By 1970 the European district consisted of 57 lodges in 12 countries, France being the center of an increasing number of lodges.

In Ereẓ Israel. B'nai B'rith was founded in Jerusalem in 1888 by the philosopher Ze'ev *Herzberg. The first lodge was named "Jerusalem." The lodge established a library called Midrash Abarbanel ve-Ginzei Yosef, which ultimately became the National and University Library. It was the first lodge where Hebrew was spoken, and its members included both Ashkenazim and Sephardim. The lodge actively opposed conversion of Jewish children by Christian missions. It inaugurated the first Hebrew kindergarten in Jerusalem, acquired the site for the village *Moẓa near Jerusalem, and established a home for new immigrants. It also initiated other lodges, first in Jaffa, in 1890, the next year in Safed, and, in 1911, in Haifa. A lodge was also founded at Zikhron Ya'akov in 1911, with Aharon *Aaronsohn as master. The lodges established hospitals and libraries, and were instrumental in uniting the various Jewish ethnic groups.

Under the Mandate new lodges were established in Rishon le-Zion, Reḥovot, and Ramat Gan. In 1922 the first women's lodge, Bat Zion, was founded. After 1924 the lodges were grouped as a district, with the authority to establish further lodges without prior approval from the center in Washington. With the immigration from Germany after 1933, B'nai B'rith expanded rapidly, as many of the immigrants had been members in Central Europe. In 1967 B'nai B'rith in Israel numbered 156 lodges, some inactive. It supports No'ar le-No'ar (Youth to Youth), a high school movement for volunteer social work among new immigrants. It also sponsors a council that organizes public demand for *aliyah* from the Soviet Union. It publishes a monthly, *Yedi'on* ("Information"), from January 1966, a quarterly, *Ha-Ra'yon* ("The Idea"), and from 1970, *Moreshet,* a quarterly devoted to Jewish scholarship. [Y.AL.]

Bibliography: E.E. Grusd, *B'nai B'rith: The Story of a Covenant* (1966); M. Bisgyer, *Challenge and Encounter* (1967); I. Alfassi (ed.), *Misdar B'nai B'rith be-Yisrael* (1966); E. Cohen-Reiss, *Mi-Zikhronot Ish Yerushalayim* (1967²), index.

BOARD OF DELEGATES OF AMERICAN ISRAELITES, first national organization of Jewish congregations in the United States, founded in 1859. The immediate occasion of its creation was American Jewish reaction to the *Mortara Case. Under the leadership of Samuel Meyer *Isaacs and Isaac *Leeser, 25 congregations, mostly of a traditional orientation, met in New York City in 1859 to establish an organization modeled on the *Board of Deputies of British Jews, the aim of which was "to gain statistical information, to promote education and literature, to further the cause of charity, to watch over occurrences at home and abroad relating to the Israelites, and to establish a 'Court of Arbitration' for the settlement of disputes between congregations." Apart from joining with the Hebrew Education Society of Philadelphia to found *Maimonides College in 1867, however, the Board largely limited its activities to the defense of Jewish civil and religious rights in America and overseas. Among its efforts in this direction were the raising of funds for the relief of persecuted Jews in Morocco, Tunisia, Persia, Italy, Russia, and Palestine and the presentation of petitions to the U.S. State Department that helped lead to the repeal of discriminatory clauses in American treaties with Switzerland, China, and Japan. Domestically the Board petitioned President *Lincoln in protest against General Ulysses S. *Grant's order expelling Jews from occupied areas of the Confederacy during the Civil War, and strove to have Jewish chaplains appointed to the Union Army. It also took part in the struggle to eliminate religious tests for public office in North Carolina, Maryland, and New Hampshire. In 1878 the Board of Delegates merged with the Union of American Hebrew Congregations, a step which was considered a victory for the left wing of the American Reform movement, which had opposed the Board from its inception. Within the UAHC, however, it continued to lead a separate existence as the Board of Delegates of Civil and Religious Rights until 1925.

Bibliography: M.J. Kohler, in: AJHSP, 29 (1925), 75–135; A. Tarshish, *ibid.,* 49 (1959), 16–32; M. Davis, *Emergence of Conservative Judaism* (1963), 101–8, 197–9, 378–85, and passim.

[H.H.]

BOARD OF DEPUTIES OF BRITISH JEWS, representative organization of British Jewry. The institution dates from 1760, when the Sephardi committee of *deputados*

The Board of Deputies of British Jews in session, 1968.

presented a "loyal address" to George III and were reproached by the Ashkenazi community for acting independently. Both communities then agreed to consult together on matters of mutual interest. Thereafter meetings were intermittent until in 1835 a constitution was adopted. At this time the Board's representative status was recognized by the government. In 1838, Sir Moses *Montefiore became president and, apart from a brief interval, held office until 1874. He opposed representation for the Reform community, which was only achieved in 1886, a year after his death. Membership was based on synagogues, London and provincial, and it was not until the present century that representatives of other communal organizations were added.

In the 19th century, the Board was active in the struggle for political emancipation; in protecting persecuted Jewish communities overseas, to which end the good offices of the British government were enlisted; in ensuring that Jews were absolved from the effects of economic legislation designed to prevent Sunday work; in safeguarding Jewish interests with regard to marriage, divorce, and religious practice generally. It also appointed synagogal marriage secretaries which legalized weddings and, after 1881, was active in projects to integrate the Russo-Polish immigrants.

In 1878, the Board and the Anglo-Jewish Association formed a Conjoint Foreign Committee, which operated successfully until discredited by its anti-Zionist line in 1917, when it disbanded. Reconstituted in 1918 as the Joint Foreign Committee, it continued until the Board was "captured" by a well-organized Zionist caucus and Selig *Brodetsky became president in 1943. With this coup the domination by the Anglo-Jewish "aristocracy" came to an end.

The Board now comprises about 400 members (numbers vary slightly with each election), elected triennially, compared with 65 around 1900. Plenary meetings are held monthly, and the Board works through committees representative of its specific interests: Law, Parliamentary and General Purposes (the oldest); Foreign Affairs; Defense; Education and Youth; Ereẓ Israel; *Sheḥitah;* Aliens; and the Central Lecture Committee. Constitutionally, the Board's "ecclesiastical" authorities are the Chief Rabbi and the Haham, who must be consulted on all religious matters.

Bibliography: C. H. L. Emanuel, *A Century and a Half of Jewish History* (1910); V. D. Lipman (ed.), *Three Centuries of Anglo-Jewish History* (1961), index s.v. *Deputies;* L. Stein, *Balfour Declaration* (1961), index; Brotman, in: J. Gould and S. Esh (eds.), *Jewish Life in Modern Britain* (1964); AJYB, 58 (1957), index; Lehmann, Nova Bibl, index; Roth, England, 222f., 251–5.

[V.D.L.]

BOAS, Dutch banking family, prominent in The Hague in the 18th century. The founder of the family, HYMAN (or Abraham; 1662–1747) was settled in The Hague by 1701. In 1743 he sold his business in jewelry, gold, and textiles for the sum of 80,200 florins to his son TOBIAS (1696–1782), who became one of the most important bankers in the Netherlands. He loaned huge sums to the Dutch government. His children married into the families of the *Court Jews *Gompertz, *Wertheimer, *Oppenheimer, and Kann, with whom he had business relations. Tobias was strictly Orthodox, supported Jewish scholars, and sponsored the publishing of their works. On several occasions he acted as *shtadlan,* representing Jewish interests, in which he was facilitated by his connections with European royalty. As such he took an active part in organizing Dutch and British diplomatic intervention to prevent the expulsion of the Jews from *Prague (1744–45). His sons ABRAHAM and SIMON continued his banking activities. Under the economic stress of the American War of Independence and the French Revolution, however, the firm went bankrupt in 1792. Its failure seriously affected the prosperity of the Jewish community. The family is frequently mentioned in Jewish and non-Jewish memoirs of the period, from the travel diary of Ḥ.J.D. *Azulai to the autobiography of Casanova.

Bibliography: D. S. van Zuiden, *De Hoogduitsche Joden in 's Gravenhage* (1913), passim; Ḥ. J. D. Azulai, *Ma'gal Tov ha-Shalem* (1934), 153–5, 159.

[J.M.]

BOAS, ABRAHAM TOBIAS (1842–1923), Australian rabbi. Boas, the son of a rabbi, was born in Amsterdam and graduated there at the theological seminary. He went to Adelaide, South Australia, as minister of the Hebrew Congregation in 1870 and retired in 1918. While his main interest was education, Boas was also active in civic affairs. He obtained recognition of the Jewish community as a denomination entitled to representation at official functions. He introduced the triennial reading of the Law but later reverted to traditional usage.

His son ISAAC HERBERT (1878–1955) was an Australian timber technologist of international repute. He perfected a method for utilizing the vast eucalyptus reserves for industry. From 1928 to 1944 he was chief of the division of forest products, Council for Scientific and Industrial Research Organization (Melbourne), and during this period his laboratory earned worldwide recognition. Boas served as president of the Royal Australian Chemical Institute. After his death the timber technology research station at Ilanot, Israel, was named after him. Boas was active in the Jewish community, serving as president of the Jewish Welfare Society and the St. Kilda Hebrew Congregation in Melbourne.

[I.P.]

BOAS, FRANZ (1858–1942), U.S. anthropologist who established anthropology as an academic discipline in the U.S.A. Born in Minden, Germany, he taught geography at the University of Berlin, which led to his Arctic expedition to Baffin Land in 1883–84. Gradually his interest in anthropology overtook his interest in cultural geography and in 1885 he became assistant in Bastian's Museum fuer Voelkerkunde in Berlin. Boas developed a major interest in North Pacific culture, which in 1886 took him to British Columbia where he began the study of the Kwakiutl Indians, a subject in which he retained a lifelong interest. In 1887 he settled in New York City, and worked as an assistant editor of *Science* primarily in geography. After some teaching he became affiliated with the American Museum of Natural History, where he served as curator of ethnology 1901–05. In 1899 he was appointed professor of anthropology at Columbia University.

After his monograph on the Central Eskimo (1888) he planned and participated in the Jesup North Pacific expedition. He developed into an authority on the Northwest Pacific coast, the Eskimo and Kwakiutl cultures, American Indian languages, and Mexican archaeology where he was among the first to apply stratographic excavations.

In effect he restructured anthropology into a modern science committed to rigorous empirical method and the fundamental idea of the relative autonomy of the phenomena of culture.

In Boas' view, neither race nor geographical setting have the primary role in forming human beings. Culture is the behavioral environment which forms the patterns of thought, feeling, and behavior, producing habits which are an internalization of traditional group patterns.

In the field of linguistics his studies of American Indian languages and his contributions to modern linguistic techniques in both phonetics and morphology virtually defined American linguistic anthropology.

Franz Boas, U.S. anthropologist.

Boas' studies of race and environmental factors, employing innovative biometric techniques, moved physical anthropology from static taxonomy to a dynamic biosocial perspective. Proceeding to refine the concept of race based on the notion of a permanent stability of bodily forms, he stressed the influence of environmental factors of human cultural life in modifying anatomy and physiology. In this labor his early training in physics and mathematics was of great use to him in his important investigations of changes in cranial and other measurements in children of immigrants. Thus his *Changes in Bodily Form of Descendants of Immigrants* (1912), which measured some 18,000 individuals, comparing European immigrant parents and their children in New York City, demonstrated significant changes in cephalic measurements. He also carried forward pioneer longitudinal studies in human growth and biometrical genetics.

After a lifetime in scientific endeavor and public teaching regarding the dangers of racism, he participated in various efforts on behalf of intellectuals persecuted by the Nazi regime and personally made it possible for many refugees to escape to freedom, while emigration was still possible.

His major works include: *Anthropology and Modern Life* (1932^2); *Race, Language and Culture* (1940); *Race and Democratic Society* (1945); *Primitive Art* (1951); *The Mind of Primitive Man* (1965^3); *The Central Eskimo* (U.S. Bureau of American Ethnology, *Sixth Annual Report 1884–85* (1888), 399–669; issued in paperback, 1964); and *Ethnology of the Kwakiutl* (*35th Annual Report 1913–14* (1921), 41–1481).

Bibliography: M. J. Herskovitz, *Franz Boas, the Science of Man in the Making* (1953), incl. bibl.; R. H. Lowie, in: National Academy of Sciences, Washington, *Biographical Memoirs*, 24 (1947), 303–22, incl. bibl.; A. Kardiner and E. Preble (eds.), *They Studied Man* (1961), 134–59; A. Lesser, in: IESS, 2 (1968), 99–110, incl. bibl.; M. B. Emeneau, in: T. A. Sebeok (ed.), *Portraits of Linguists* (1966), 122–7; R. Jakobson, in: *ibid.*, 127–39.

[E.FI.]

BOAS, GEORGE (1891–), U.S. philosopher, a major figure in the history of ideas movement in America. From 1924 to 1957 he was professor of philosophy at Johns Hopkins University, Baltimore. His major studies were in the areas of aesthetics, the history of thought, and French philosophy. He also translated several works from French. Boas was on the board of editors of the *Journal of the History of Ideas*, from its inception. His major writings include: *The Happy Beast in French Thought of the 17th Century* (1933); *Essays on Primitivism* (1948); *Wingless Pegasus* (1950); *Dominant Themes of Modern Philosophy* (1957); *The Inquiring Mind* (1959); *Rationalism in Greek Philsophy* (1961); and *The Heaven of Invention* (1962). In 1953, at the height of the McCarthy period, Boas helped edit *Lattimore the Scholar*, in defense of Owen Lattimore, who was under attack.

[R.H.P.]

BOAZ (Heb. בֹּעַז), the son of Salmah, great-grandfather of King David. Boaz was descended from Nahshon, the son of Amminadab (Ruth 4:20–22; I Chron. 2:10–15), prince of the tribe of Judah in the generation of the wilderness (Num. 1:7). He lived in Beth-Lehem in the time of the Judges and is described as a "man of substance," that is, a wealthy landowner employing many young men and women on his estate (Ruth 2:1). *Ruth, the Moabite daughter-in-law of Naomi, came to glean in his fields, and Boaz expressed his appreciation for her kindness and devotion to the widowed Naomi. Being a kinsman of Elimelech, Ruth's late father-in-law, Boaz undertook to redeem the latter's inheritance. He then married Ruth (*ibid.*, 2:11–12; 3:12; 4:1–15).

[N.M.S.]

In the Aggadah. Boaz was a prince of Israel (Ruth R. 5:15) and the head of the *bet din* of Beth-Lehem. He is, therefore, sometimes identified with the judge Ibzan of Beth-Lehem (Judg. 12:8) who lost his sixty children during his lifetime (BB 91a). Ruth and Naomi arrived in Beth-Lehem on the day on which Boaz' wife was buried (*ibid.*). He had a vision that Ruth would be the ancestress of David (Shab. 113b). When Ruth told him that as a Moabite she was excluded from marrying him (Deut. 23:4). Boaz answered her that this prohibition applied only to the males of Moab and not to the females (Ruth R. 4:1). Although a prince, Boaz himself supervised the threshing of the grain and slept in the barn in order to prevent profligacy (Ruth R. 5:15). When awakened by Ruth he thought that she was a devil

Opening of the Book of Ruth in the *Tripartite Maḥzor*, Germany, c. 1320. Left: Naomi approaching Boaz. Right: Ruth gleaning. London, British Museum, Add. Ms. 22413, fol. 71a.

and only after touching the hair of her head was he convinced to the contrary since devils are bald (Ruth R. 6:1). The six measures of barley which he gave her were a symbol of her being destined to become the ancestress of six pious men, among them David and the Messiah (Sanh. 93a–b). Boaz was 80 years old and Ruth 40 when they married (Ruth R. 6:2) and although he died on the day after the wedding (Mid. Ruth, Zuta 4:13) their union was blessed with a child, Obed, David's grandfather. In recognition of his merits, certain customs that Boaz originated were retained and received the heavenly approval—the use of the Divine name in greeting one's fellow man (Ruth 2:4; Ber. 9:5) and the ceremony of pronouncing benedictions on the bridal couple in the presence of ten men (Ket. 7a). [Ed.]

Bibliography: S. Yeivin, in: *Eretz Israel,* 5 (1958), 97–104; W. Rudolph, *Ruth* (1962²), 36; J. A. Montgomery, in: JQR, 25 (1934/35), 265; R. B. Y. Scott, in: JBL, 58 (1939), 143ff.; M. Burrows, *ibid.,* 59 (1940), 445–6; F. Dijkema, in: *Nieuw Theologisch Tijdschrift,* 24 (1953), 111–8; EM, 2 (1965), 282–3 (incl. bibl.). In the Aggadah: Ginzberg, Legends, 4 (1947), 30–34; 6 (1946), 187–94.

BOBE-MAYSE, Yiddish expression for a fantastic or incredible tale. The term is based on the title of the Yiddish chivalric romance that Elijah *Levita adapted from *Buovo d'Antona* (the Italian version of *Sir Bevis of Hampton*). This work, popular among Ashkenazi Jews, originally appeared as *Bovo D'Antona* and was subsequently printed as **Bove-Bukh;* in later editions it was titled *Bove-Mayse* (*mayse,* "tale"). The similarity of *Bove* to *Bobe,* the Yiddish word for grandmother, led to the substitution of *Bobe-Mayse* for *Bove-Mayse,* and to the use of the former expression for any grandmother's tale or incredible story, with no necessary connection to the original romance or *chapbook.

Bibliography: Zedner, in: HB, 6 (1863), 22–23; Zedner, Cat, 94; N. B. Minkoff, *Elye Bokher un Zayn Bove Bukh* (1950).

[S.L.]

BOBROVY KUT, Jewish agricultural settlement in Kherson oblast, Ukrainian S.S.R. It was established in 1807 with private funds and settled by families from the province (guberniya) of Mogilev. The settlement numbered 86 families in 1810, and 165 in 1815 (416 men and 327 women). Additional families were transferred there in 1825, 1837, and 1841, and the settlement numbered 1,184 in 1849; 1,248 in 1897; and over 2,000 in 1926. Under the Soviet government, Bobrovy Kut was incorporated in the autonomous Jewish district of Kalinindorf and like the other Jewish agricultural settlements traversed many vicissitudes. It suffered years of hunger, was changed into a kolkhoz, and underwent "internationalization" (i.e., admission of non-Jews). The Jewish settlers were often accused of being "petit-bourgeois," nationalists, or Zionists. Many of the younger settlers were arrested and deported, while most of the older ones left. It was completely destroyed during the Nazi occupation and almost all its settlers perished. Bobrovy Kut was the birthplace of the poet S. *Frug.

Bibliography: V. N. Nikitin, *Yevrei Zemledeltsy 1807–1887* (1887); J. Lestschinsky, *Ha-Yehudim be-Rusyah ha-Sovyetit* (1943), 163–72; Gurshtein, in: *Ḥakla'im Yehudim be-Arvot Rusyah* (1965), 383–6.

[Ed.]

BOBRUISK, capital of Bobruisk oblast. Belorussian S.S.R.; passed to Russia after the second partition of Poland in 1793. Jewish settlement there is first mentioned at the end of the 17th century. The *kehillah* of Bobruisk was included in the jurisdiction of the township of Smilovichi (see *Councils of the Lands). Three hundred and ninety-five Jewish poll tax payers are recorded in Bobruisk in 1766. The community increased appreciably after Bobruisk's accession to Russia. Provisioning of the garrison of the large fortress built there at the beginning of the 19th century became a major Jewish occupation. Toward the middle of the 19th century Jews also took part in lumbering activities, since Bobruisk became an important lumbering center, where timber from the adjacent forests was rafted or entrained to southern Russia or the Baltic ports. The Jewish population numbered 4,702 in 1847; 8,861 in 1861; 20,760 in 1897 (60% of the total); and 25,876 (61%) in 1914, but only 21,558 Jews (42%) in 1926.

There were numerous yeshivot in Bobruisk. Distinguished rabbis who officiated there included leaders of *Ḥabad Ḥasidim (Mordecai Baruch Ettinger, Hillel of Paritch, Shemariah Noah Schneerson) as well as *mitnaggedim* (Jacob David Willowski (Ridbaz), and Raphael Shapiro, afterward head of the Volozhin yeshivah). The Hebrew author M. Rabinson served as "government-appointed" rabbi from 1911. Toward the end of the 19th century, Bobruisk became a center of cultural and political activity for Belorussian Jewry in which both the Zionist and radical wings were prominent. The publishing house of Jacob Cohen Ginsburg became celebrated throughout Russia. The "model" *ḥeder,* established in 1900, provided comprehensive Hebrew instruction and did much to raise the standard of Hebrew education. A popular Jewish library was also opened. After its foundation Bobruisk became one of the main bases of the *Bund; in 1898 its clandestine printing press was seized in Bobruisk by the police.

After World War I, the Jewish population suffered from the frequent changes of government during the civil war and the Soviet-Polish war (1918–21). Subsequently, Jewish activities ceased. J. Ginsburg and other publishers continued to print prayer books and other religious publications in Bobruisk until 1928, the last work of Jewish religious literature to be published in the Soviet Union, *Yagdil Torah,* being printed in Bobruisk. A network of Communist schools giving instruction in Yiddish was established in Bobruisk after the 1917 Revolution and functioned until 1939. Bobruisk was occupied by the Germans in World War II, and on Nov. 7, 1941, 20,000 Jews were sent from there to their deaths. The Jewish population increased after the war, and was estimated at 30,000 in 1970. There was no synagogue, the last one having been closed in 1959. There was a separate Jewish cemetery. Kasher poultry was available. Bobruisk was the birthplace of Pauline *Wengeroff, I. *Nissenbaum, Berl *Katznelson, David *Shimoni, and Y. *Tunkel.

Bibliography: Y. Slutsky (ed.), *Sefer Bobruisk* (Heb. and Yid., 1967).

[Y.S.]

°**BOCCACCIO, GIOVANNI** (1313–1375), Italian author, whose greatest work, *Il Decamerone,* contains a number of Jewish elements. The son of a Florentine merchant, Boccaccio was apprenticed in his youth to a merchant in Naples, and may have come into contact with some of the Jews who were flourishing in Neapolitan commerce at that time. He later introduced Jews into two of the early tales of the *Decameron* (the second and third story of the "First Day" of the cycle). Boccaccio summarized the second story as follows: "Abraham, a Jew, at the instance of Jehannot de Chevigny, goes to the court of Rome, and having marked the evil life of the clergy, returns to Paris and becomes a Christian" (because God would tolerate such conduct only in followers of the true faith). His summary of the third story is: "Melchisedech, a Jew, by a story of three rings, averts a great danger with which he was menaced by Saladin." He uses the character of Abraham to criticize the contemporary ecclesiastical establishment and the corruption of the clergy, and that of Melchisedech to praise human wisdom. Both tales are based on medieval literature, Christian as well as Jewish. A story of three rings or three precious stones, representing the debate as to the relative excellence of the three monotheistic religions, is used by early English, French, and Italian writers. The theme also appears in Jewish literature in the *Shevet Yehudah* (ch. 32) of Solomon *ibn Verga (ed. Y. F. Baer (1947), 78–80). Although this was not published until 1550, the author was undoubtedly quoting a story which was well-known long before he wrote his book. Debates between representatives of Judaism, Christianity, and Islam are often to be found in medieval Hebrew literature.

Boccaccio's choice of Jews as heroes would appear to result from the great emphasis he placed on wisdom and tolerance, both of which he regarded as Jewish characteristics. In his very earliest stories he stressed the keen intelligence of the Jew, his freedom from blind ideology, and his adaptability. Regarding the Jewish character as essentially realistic and individualistic, he also used his two heroes to mock any regimented approach to life. Boccaccio had an important and formative influence on European literature. The strongest echo of his Melchisedech story occurs in *Nathan the Wise* (1779), a play on the theme of religious tolerance by the German dramatist Gotthold Ephraim *Lessing. Some reflection of the "three rings" story has also been detected in the casket scene in *Shakespeare's *Merchant of Venice.*

Bibliography: M. Landau, *Die Quellen des Decameron* (1884); A. Bartoli, *I precursori del Boccaccia* ... (1876); G. Paris, *La leggenda di Saladino* (1896); idem, *La Poésie du Moyen-Age,* 2 (1895); M. Penna, *La Parabola dei tre anelli e la tolleranza nel Medio Evo* (1953); H. G. Wright, *Boccaccio in England* ... (1957); H. Hauvette, *Boccace* ... (1914); R. Ramat et al., *Scritti Su Giovanni Boccaccio* (1964).

[IS.GAR.]

BOCHNIA (from 1939 to 1945 called **Salzberg**), town in Cracow province, Poland, noted for its rock-salt deposits. In 1555 the Jews of Bochnia, who engaged in marketing and contracting for the salt impost, were granted a general privilege by King Sigismund Augustus. Jews there were accused of stealing the Host in 1605 and a Jewish miner, allegedly the instigator, died under torture. Subsequently the Jews were expelled from Bochnia, and the city received the privilege *de non tolerandis Judaeis.* This exclusion of the Jews remained in force until 1860, but Jews were allowed to resettle in the town only in 1862. They numbered 1,911 in 1900 and 2,459 in 1921. [ED.]

Holocaust Period. An estimated 3,500 Jews (20% of the total population) lived in Bochnia in 1939. The German Army entered the town on Sept. 3, 1939, and immediately subjected the Jewish population to persecution and terror. In May 1940 a huge *"Kontribution"* of 3,000,000 zloty ($600,000) was imposed by the Nazis upon the Jewish population. In May 1942 a ghetto was established to which the entire Jewish population from all the surrounding towns and villages was brought. In August 1942 a massive *Aktion* was conducted by police units from Cracow. About 600 Jews were killed on the spot and another 2,000 deported to Belzec death camp. On Nov. 10, 1942, a second deportation took place during which about 70 people were killed and more than 500 deported to Belzec. Afterwards the ghetto was divided into two parts: Ghetto A, which became a forced labor camp; and Ghetto B, which served as a concentration camp. In September 1943 the entire ghetto was liquidated. Those imprisoned in Ghetto B were sent to Auschwitz for extermination while the inmates of Ghetto A were transferred to the concentration camp in Szebnia, where only a few survived. No Jewish community was reestablished in Bochnia after the war.

[S.KR.]

Bibliography: Podhorizev-Sandel, in: BŻIH, no. 30 (1959), 87–109; Steinberg, in: *Dokumenty zbrodni i męczeństwa* (1945), 152.

BOCHUM, city in northern Rhine-Westphalia, West Germany. Jews are mentioned there in 1349. A synagogue, erected in 1594, is mentioned again in 1652. In 1800 there were 27 Jewish residents (1.6% of the total population), mainly cattle merchants and butchers. The number increased to 1,002 by 1900 (0.27%) and to 1,152 in 1933. It maintained two synagogues (one established by the Orthodox Polish community), a *ḥeder,* a Hebrew school, a Jewish elementary school, eight benevolent societies, and cultural organizations. M. David served as rabbi from 1901 to 1936.

Synagogue in Bochum, destroyed by the Nazis on *Kristallnacht,* 1938.

On Oct. 28, 1938, some 250 Polish or stateless Jews were expelled from Bochum, and on Nov. 10—*Kristallnacht*—the main synagogue was blown up, and Jewish shops and homes were looted. Jewish males were arrested and temporarily interned in Sachsenhausen. By June 17, 1939, only 355 Jews remained in the city. During World War II they were deported to *Auschwitz and *Theresienstadt, and to forced labor camps in Eastern Europe. In June and November 1944 two forced labor camps, branches of *Buchenwald, were established in Bochum. About one-third of the 2,000 workers were Jews from Eastern Europe, of whom 60 died there. After the war about 40 Jews returned to Bochum. In September 1955 a new synagogue was consecrated. There were 36 Jews living in Bochum in 1961, mainly pensioners.

Bibliography: PK; *50. Jahre Juedische Gemeinde Bochum* (1892); FJW (1932/33), 158; Germ Jud, 2 (1968), 89–90. [ED.]

BODEK, JACOB (1819–1855), Galician Hebraist. Bodek was born in Lemberg. He and his brother-in-law, A. M. *Mohr, were two of the *maskilim* in Lemberg who published a journal entitled *Ha-Ro'eh u-Mevakker Sifrei*

Meḥabberei Zemannenu ("Criticism of the works of Contemporary Authors," 1838–39), criticizing the works of S. J. Rapoport, S. D. Luzzatto, and I. S. Reggio. He and Mohr later edited a periodical called *Yerushalayim* (1844–45) to which many Galician *maskilim* contributed. Bodek published biblical commentaries and translations of poetry in the periodical *Kokhevei Yiẓḥak*. His letters, which contain valuable material on the historical and cultural background of the early 19th century, were printed after his death in *Ha-Boker Or, Ha-Shaḥar,* and other journals.

Bibliography: Klausner, Sifrut, 2 (1952[2]), index; G. Bader, *Medinah va-Ḥakhameha* (1934), 33. [G.K.]

BODENHEIM, MAXWELL (1893–1954), U.S. poet and novelist. Born in Mississippi, Bodenheim was raised in poverty. He moved to New York, where he first attracted attention with his book of verses *Minna and Myself* (1918). He continued his experiments in free verse with five other volumes. The suppression of his first novel, *Replenishing Jessica* (1925) on the grounds that it was immoral brought him temporary notoriety. His novels of New York's seamy side, such as *Naked on Roller Skates* (1931) and *New York Madness* (1933), endeared him to radical circles. Bodenheim never shunned unpopular causes and continued to pioneer the treatment of unconventional themes. His anguished "Poem to the Gentiles" (1944) cast doubt on the sincerity of many non-Jewish protests against Nazi barbarism. Bodenheim's last days were again spent in poverty. He was murdered by a psychopathic ex-convict.

Bibliography: J. Mersand, *Traditions in American Literature* (1939), 133–6; S. Liptzin, *Jew in American Literature* (1966), 140–1. [S.L.]

BODENHEIMER, FREDERICK SIMON (1897–1959), Israel zoologist. The son of Max Isidor *Bodenheimer, he was born in Cologne, and completed his studies in biology at Bonn in 1921. In 1922 he was appointed entomologist in the new agricultural experimental station of the Jewish Agency in Tel Aviv, where he worked until 1928. In 1927 Bodenheimer carried out an expedition to the Sinai Peninsula. Important among the results of this expedition was his identification of the biblical manna as the honeydew excretion of scale-insects on tamarisk. In 1928 he

Frederick Simon Bodenheimer, Israel zoologist.

was appointed research fellow and in 1931 professor of zoology at the Hebrew University of Jerusalem. From 1938 to 1941 he was visiting professor at Ankara and consultant to the Turkish Ministry of Agriculture. In 1943 he was invited to Iraq to serve as entomological adviser on locust control. In addition to his specialty of agricultural entomology, Bodenheimer's broader biological interests were animal ecology, population dynamics, and the history of science. He was the author of many articles and numerous books, including *Die Schaedlingsfauna Palaestinas* (1930), *Materialien zur Geschichte der Entomologie bis Linné* (2 vols., 1928–29), *Animal Life in Palestine* (1935), *Problems of Animal Ecology* (1938), *Animal and Man in Bible Lands* (1960), *Citrus Entomology in the Middle East...*(1951), *The History of Biology: an Introduction* (1958), and *Animal Ecology Today* (1958). His last book, *A Biologist in Israel* (1959), is an autobiography. [M.L.G.]

BODENHEIMER, MAX ISIDOR (1865–1940), one of *Herzl's first assistants, a founder of the World Zionist Organization, and one of the first directors of the *Jewish National Fund. Bodenheimer was born in Stuttgart and began to practice law in Cologne in 1890. Despite an

Max Bodenheimer, Zionist leader. Jerusalem, Central Zionist Archives.

assimilationist education, he joined the *Ḥibbat Zion movement in his youth. In 1891 he published a pamphlet, *Wohin mit den russischen Juden?* in which he suggested settling Russian Jews in Ereẓ Israel. In 1893 he and David *Wolffsohn founded in Cologne a Ḥibbat Zion society which was the nucleus of the future Zionist Federation in Germany. When Herzl announced his Zionist plans, Bodenheimer joined him immediately. At the First Zionist Congress in 1897 he presented the organizational program of the Zionist movement, and was a member of the committee which prepared the text of the *Basle Program. From 1897 to 1921 and from 1931 to 1933 Bodenheimer was a member of the Zionist General Council. In 1898 he was a member of the Zionist delegation which accompanied Herzl to Ereẓ Israel for an audience with Kaiser William II on his visit there. Bodenheimer put the statutes of the Jewish National Fund into final form and served as its director from 1907 to 1914. The land on which Kinneret, Deganyah, and Merḥavyah were built was among that acquired during his administration; and assistance was also given for urban and rural settlement, including a loan to help found Tel Aviv. During World War I Bodenheimer together with Franz *Oppenheimer and Adolph *Friedemann founded the Va'ad le-Ma'an ha-Mizraḥ ("Committee for the East"), which aimed at serving as a liaison between East European Jewry and the German occupation authorities. He joined the *Revisionist Movement (1931–34) but left when it seceded from the World Zionist Organization. In 1935 Bodenheimer settled in Jerusalem. He published many pamphlets and articles on Zionist matters, and wrote a drama on the life of Jesus (1933). His memoirs appeared posthumously in Hebrew (1952), German (1958), and in English under the title *Prelude to Israel* (1963). His daughter, Hannah, published his correspondence with Hermann Shapira, *Toledot Tokhnit Basel* ("The History of the Basle Program," 1947), and that between him and Herzl in Hebrew and German, under the title *Be-Reshit ha-Tenu'ah* ("At the Beginning of the Movement," 1965). A selection of his writings, *Bi-Mesillat Rishonim,* was published in 1951.

Bibliography: T. Herzl, *Complete Diaries*, ed. by R. Patai, 5 vols. (1960), index; S. Ben-Horin, *Ḥamishim Shenot Ẓiyyonut, Max Bodenheimer* (1946); H. Bodenheimer, *Herzl Yearbook*, 6 (1964–65), 153–81; R. Lichtheim, *Die Geschichte des deutschen Zionismus* (1954), index.

[A.B.]

°**BODENSCHATZ, JOHANN CHRISTOPH GEORG** (1717–1797), German Protestant theologian. Born in Hof, Bavaria, Bodenschatz received his early education at Gera, where through his teacher Schleusner he became interested in biblical and oriental subjects, later studying oriental languages at the University of Jena. He entered the church, became vicar at Uttenreuth, and in 1780 superintendent at Baiersdorf. In his writings Bodenschatz described contemporary Jewish customs in Germany faithfully and without prejudice. His *Kirchliche Verfassung der heutigen Juden, sonderlich derer in Deutschland* (4 vols., Erlangen and Coburg, 1748–49), is an important historical source for Jewish life in Germany in the mid-18th century. A second edition of the book was published in Frankfort in 1756 under the title *Aufrichtig teutsch redender Hebraeer*. Both editions are rich in engravings depicting subjects drawn from contemporary Jewish life in Germany. Some of these engravings were taken from B. Picart's *Cérémonies et coûtumes religieuses de tous les peuples* (1723–37). Bodenschatz is said to have made elaborate models of Noah's Ark and the Tabernacle.

Bibliography: ADB, 3 (1876), 7; I. Abrahams, *By-Paths in Hebraic Bookland* (1920), 160–5.

[Ed.]

Frontispiece of Johann Bodenschatz' *Kirchliche Verfassung der heutigen Juden*, 1748–49. In the library stand Moses, pointing at the Torah, and a Jew in *tallit* and *tefillin*. Cecil Roth Collection.

°**BODIN, JEAN** (1529 or 1530–1596), French historian, economist, and jurist. Bodin took an interest in Judaism in his main works *De Republica* (1576) and *Methodus ad facilem historiarum cognitionem* (1566), but chiefly in a work which he had completed in 1593 but did not publish, *Colloquium Heptaplomeres de rerum sublimium arcanis abditis*

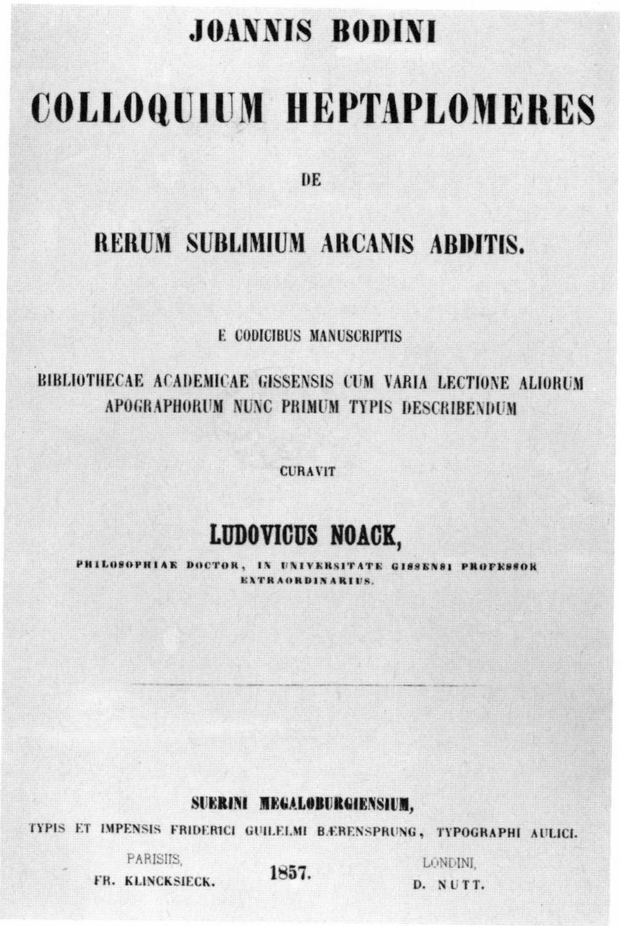

JOANNIS BODINI

COLLOQUIUM HEPTAPLOMERES

DE

RERUM SUBLIMIUM ARCANIS ABDITIS.

E CODICIBUS MANUSCRIPTIS

BIBLIOTHECAE ACADEMICAE GISSENSIS CUM VARIA LECTIONE ALIORUM APOGRAPHORUM NUNC PRIMUM TYPIS DESCRIBENDUM

CURAVIT

LUDOVICUS NOACK,

PHILOSOPHIAE DOCTOR, IN UNIVERSITATE GISSENSI PROFESSOR EXTRAORDINARIUS.

SUERINI MEGALOBURGIENSIUM,

TYPIS ET IMPENSIS FRIDERICI GUILELMI BÆRENSPRUNG, TYPOGRAPHI AULICI.

PARISIIS, FR. KLINCKSIECK. 1857. LONDINI, D. NUTT.

Title page of Jean Bodin's *Colloquium Heptaplomeres*, Schwerin, Paris and London, 1857.

(excerpts first printed in 1841; complete edition 1857). Thanks to the help of three "royal readers" of Hebrew at the College of France in Paris, Cinqarbres, Jean *Mercier, and Paradis, Bodin not only acquired some knowledge of Hebrew and Aramaic but also had translations made of many passages from Hebrew literature, which he used in his works. He referred to the Targum, talmudic authorities, kabbalistic literature, and many medieval writers. The *Heptaplomeres* contains six conversations between seven friends who represented as many religions or attitudes of belief. Toralba, the representative of natural religion, and Solomon Barcassius, the representative of Judaism, are both to some degree the spokesmen of Bodin himself. To Bodin, the Jews were not only the most ancient people but also the most faithful chroniclers of the earliest history of humanity. Bodin inserted into his dialogues a series of Jewish objections to Christianity which he reinforced with his own dialectical skill. Through the interpellations of Solomon he attacked the dogma of the virgin birth. Everything profitable in the writings of the apostles was borrowed from Judaism. The Christians violated the precepts of the Decalogue, which was nevertheless the natural law *par excellence*. Critics accused Bodin of having lost the faith of a real Christian through his dealings with the Jews (although he does not appear to have had any), and called him a half-Jew or secret Jew. This was presumably the source of the baseless supposition that his mother was of Jewish origin.

Bibliography: Guttmann, in: MGWJ, 49 (1905), 315ff., 459ff.; Berg, in: *Revue juive de Lorraine*, 13 (1937), 29ff.; G. Roellenbleck, *Offenbarung . . . und juedische Ueberlieferung bei Jean Bodin* (1964).

[B.Bl.]

BODLEIAN LIBRARY, the official library of the University of Oxford, named after Sir Thomas *Bodley who refounded it. It is one of the world's greatest libraries, and second in importance in England only to the British Museum.

There were Hebrew books and manuscripts in Bodley's original collection, supplemented gradually by gift and purchase in the course of the next two centuries: especially memorable were those from the collections of Archbishop William Laud (1641), John Selden (1654, 1659), Edward Pococke (1691), Robert Huntingdon (1693). In 1829, the University of Oxford purchased for the Bodleian the whole of the fine collection that had formerly belonged to David

Illuminated page from the *Laud Maḥzor* (Germany, c. 1290), part of the Archbishop William Laud Collection in the Bodleian Library of Oxford University. The panel, from the *Shavuot* liturgy, depicts the giving of the Law, Moses sprinkling the Israelites with the blood of the Covenant (Ex. 24:8), and the baking of *maẓẓah.* Oxford, Bodleian Library, Ms. Laud Or. 321, fol. 127.

*Oppenheim, and the library immediately rose to first rank among the Hebrew collections of the world. Later, there were added also the collection of the Hamburg bibliophile Heimann Joseph Michael in 1848, many manuscripts from the collection of Isaac Samuel Reggio in 1853, and in due course large numbers of fragments from the Cairo *Genizah.* The Library now comprises about 3,100 Hebrew and Samaritan manuscripts—still perhaps qualitatively the most important in the world—as well as a remarkably full collection of early printed works. The manuscripts have been described fully in the catalog (vol. I, ed. by A. Neubauer, 1886; vol. II, ed. by A. Cowley, 1906). The printed books formed the material for M. Steinschneider's fundamental work of Hebrew bibliography (*Catalogus Librorum Hebraeorum in Bibliotheca Bodleiana,* 1852–60)—not, however, restricted to books—and of the more succinct recent catalog edited by A. Cowley (1929).

Bibliography: E. N. Adler, in: JHSET, 8 (198), 2ff. [C.R.]

°**BODLEY, SIR THOMAS** (1544/45–1613), English diplomat and bibliophile. Born in Exeter, England, his education began in the Geneva of Calvin and Beza (Bèze) as a Protestant refugee from the Marian persecution. There he learned Hebrew from Chevalier, later continuing his study under Drusius at Oxford. He acquired sufficient competence both to teach Hebrew and to decipher a medieval Anglo-Jewish *shetar.* Bodley traveled widely on the continent, largely on diplomatic missions, and was Elizabeth's permanent resident at the Hague from 1589 to 1596. His quite considerable Hebrew expertise is reflected in the elegy which he contributed to the memorial volume for Bishop John Jewell of Salisbury (*Ioannis Iuelli . . . Episcopi Sarisbuniensis vita et mors* (London, 1573)), in which there occur post-biblical Hebrew terms as applied in Italy and elsewhere to the Catholic hierarchy (*afifyor,* "pope"; *ḥashmannim,* "cardinals"; *hegmon* "bishop"; etc.). Bodley's fame rests upon his munificent restoration of Oxford's public (i.e., university) library, thereafter called the *Bodleian.

Bibliography: G. W. Wheeler (ed.), *Letters of Sir Thomas Bodley to Thomas James* (1926); C. Roth, in: *Bodleian Library Record,* 7 (1966), 242ff.; idem, in: *Oxoniensia,* 15 (1950), 64f.; *Trecentale Bodleianum* (1913), includes *The Life of Sir Thomas Bodley Written by Himself* (London, 1703). [Ra.L.]

BODO (ninth century), French churchman who became a proselyte to Judaism. The scion of a noble family, Bodo entered the church and became deacon of the palace to Louis the Pious. In 838 he left the court with a numerous suite ostensibly to go on pilgrimage to Rome. He instead went to Spain with his nephew and on his way adopted Judaism under the name Eleazar. After spending some time in Saragossa he went on to Córdoba, where he is said to have attempted to persuade the caliph to compel his Christian subjects to abandon their faith in favor of either Judaism or Islam. The details of his career are known mainly through the interchange of correspondence between him and a learned Christian layman of Córdoba, Paolo Alvaro. Alvaro wrote him four polemical letters, printed in various ecclesiastical collections, attempting to convince him of the error of his ways. Bodo-Eleazar's rejoinders and arguments were deliberately destroyed, being taken out of the codex in which they were copied, but B. Blumenkranz has reconstructed them from the quotations in Alvaro's letters.

Bibliography: C. M. Sage, *Paul Albar of Cordoba* (1943); Cabaniss, in: JQR, 43 (1952/53), 313–28; B. Blumenkranz, *Juifs et chrétiens dans le monde occidental* (1960), 166ff. and index; idem, in: RHPR, 34 (1954), 401–13; idem, in: REJ, 112 (1953), 35–42; Roth, Dark Ages, index. [C.R.]

BODROGKERESZTUR, town in N.E. Hungary. A census of 1723–24 records seven Jewish families there. The synagogue is first mentioned in 1833. The Jewish population numbered 13 families in 1753; 36 in 1770; and 73 in 1812; 239 persons in 1833 (13% of the total); 366 in 1850 (20%); and 450 in 1944 (20%). They were mainly occupied as merchants, tradesmen, innkeepers, vintners, and carters; some Jews owned quarries. Rabbis who officiated in Bodrogkeresztur include Ẓevi Hirsch Glanc (1826), grandson of Moses *Teitelbaum, whose influence in the community made it a stronghold of *Ḥasidism. Shaye Steiner (d. 1925), known as Reb Shayele, who lived in Bodrogkeresztur, was revered as a miracle-working rabbi. His grave is still a place of pilgrimage. During World War II many Jews in Bodrogkeresztur were drafted to labor camps. The majority were sent to Sátoraljaujhely assembly center, and in spring 1944 were deported to *Auschwitz.

Nearly all were martyred. The thirty-seven survivors who returned after the war moved later to larger cities or emigrated.

Bibliography: M. Stein, *Magyar Rabbik,* 1 (1905), 3–5; Vadász, in: *Magyar Zsidó Szemle,* 24 (1907), 328; *Új Élet,* 20 (1964), 9; J. Mosolygó, *Tokaj* (1930); MHJ, 7 (1963), 102, 642, 837. [L.H.]

BODY AND SOUL. Jewish theology has no clearly elaborated views on the relationship between body and soul, nor on the nature of the soul itself. Apart from Jewish philosophical and kabbalistic literature on the subject (see *Soul), the major traditional sources for any normative doctrines are the various texts in talmudic and midrashic literature. These latter are not systematic, nor is their interpretation generally agreed on. The talmudic rabbis, as opposed to certain Jewish philosophers of the medieval period, never considered views on such a purely theoretical subject as important. Their interest was focused on the connected, but more practically orientated beliefs, such as in the resurrection of the body and God's future judgment. For the talmudic rabbis the soul is, in some sense, clearly separable from the body: God breathed the soul into the body of Adam (Gen. 2:7; Ta'an. 22b). During sleep the soul departs and draws spiritual refreshment from on high (Gen. R. 14:9). At death it leaves the body only to be united with it again at the resurrection (Sanh. 90b–91a). As a prayer of the morning liturgy, uttered on awakening, expresses it: "O my God, the soul which thou gavest me is pure; thou didst create it, thou didst form it, thou didst breathe it into me. Thou preservest it within me, and thou wilt take it from me, but wilt restore it unto me hereafter" (Hertz, Prayer, 19).

Whether the soul is capable of living an independent, fully conscious existence away from the body after death is unclear from rabbinic sources. The Midrash puts it somewhat vaguely—that the body cannot survive without the soul—nor the soul without the body (cf. Tanḥ. Va-Yikra 11). Although a view is found maintaining that the soul after death is in a quiescent state (Shab. 152b), the predominant view seems to be that the soul is capable of having a fully conscious life of its own when disembodied (see, for instance, Ket. 77b; Ber. 18b–19a). It is even maintained that the soul pre-exists the body (Ḥag. 12b); but how this predominant view is to be interpreted is problematic. Since the various anecdotes and descriptions about the soul in its disembodied state are given in terms of physical imagery, it might be assumed that an ethereal body was ascribed to the soul, enabling it to parallel the most important functions of its embodied state when disembodied. This assumption is unwarranted, however, since the rabbis do not seek conceptual coherence in their theological speculation. Imagery has a homiletic, rather than a speculative, function.

The elliptical and practically oriented aspect of rabbinic teaching is brought out further in the view that the soul is a guest in the body here on earth (Lev. R. 34:3), for this means that the body must be respected and well treated for the sake of its honored guest. The Gnostic idea of the body as a prison of the soul is absent from rabbinic literature; body and soul form a harmonious unity. Just as God fills the world, sees but is not seen, so the soul fills the body, sees but is not seen (Ber. 10a). On the eve of the Sabbath God gives each man an extra soul, which He takes back at its termination (Beẓ. 16a). This is the rabbinic way of emphasizing the spirituality of the soul, its closeness in nature to God, and the extra spirituality with which it is imbued on the Sabbath. The soul is pure as God is pure; its introduction into the human embryo is God's part in the ever-renewed creation of human life (Nid. 31a). Because God originally gave man his soul, it is for God to take it away and not man himself. Thus *suicide, *euthanasia, and anything which would hasten death is forbidden (Job 1:21; Av. Zar. 18a and Tos.; Sh. Ar. YD 345). If man safeguards the purity of his soul by walking in the ways of the Torah, all will be well, but if not God will take his soul from him (Nid. 31a). For his sins, which contaminate the soul, man will be judged; indeed his soul will be his accuser. Nor can the body plead that it was the soul which sinned, nor the soul blame the body, for at the resurrection God will return soul to body and judge them as one. To illustrate this, the Talmud has the following parable: an orchard owner appointed a lame man and a blind man to guard his orchard, thinking that because of his defect each one would be incapable of any mischief. However the two guardians contrived, by means of the lame man sitting on the shoulders of the blind one, to steal and eat the fruit. When accused each pleaded his innocence, the one pointing to his inability to see and the other to his inability to walk. The orchard owner put the lame man on the blind man's shoulders and passed judgment on them thus (Sanh. 91a; Tanḥ. Va-Yikra 12).

See also *Soul, Immortality of the.

Bibliography: K. Kohler, *Jewish Theology* (1918), 212–7; G. F. Moore, *Judaism* (1946), 485–8; 2 (1946), index; A. Marmorstein, *Studies in Jewish Theology* (1950), 145–61; L. Finkelstein, in: *Freedom and Reason* (1951), 354–71. [Ed.]

BOEHM, ADOLF (1873–1941), Zionist and historian of the Zionist movement. When he was still a child Boehm's family moved from his birthplace in Teplitz-Schonau (Teplice), Bohemia, to Vienna where he received his early education. Boehm entered his father's textile factory, which he directed until 1938. His association with the Zionist movement began only after Herzl's death in 1904. Following his visit to Ereẓ Israel in 1907, he became a leader of the "practical" Zionists, whose interest lay primarily in the economic problems connected with Jewish settlement in Palestine. As a result he was particularly active on behalf of the Jewish National Fund. He served for ten years on its board of directors and wrote a book on its activities. During 1910–12, and again during 1927–38 Boehm edited the monthly *Palaestina.* His major effort, however, was *Die Zionistische Bewegung* (1922, enlarged two-volume edition 1935–37) which remains the most exhaustive history of the Zionist movement. In the second edition he brought the history up to 1925. Boehm collected extensive material for a third volume which, however, was never published. Boehm strongly objected to the excessive factionalism within the Zionist movement. At the same time he stressed the importance of the connection between Jewish national and universal human values in a series of articles in *Juedische Rundschau* (1934, nos. 43, 65, 67). Shortly after Hitler's occupation of Austria Boehm fell victim to a mental disorder. He is believed to have died in a Nazi extermination center in Poland.

Bibliography: *Be'anakh ha-Binyan le-Zecher A. Boehm* (1952). [Ed.]

BOERNE, LUDWIG (1786–1837), German political essayist and champion of Jewish emancipation. Born Loeb Baruch, into a prominent Frankfort banking family, he was raised in the Frankfort ghetto. Since medicine was one of the few professions then open to Jews, he was sent to Berlin in 1802 to study under Markus *Herz. After his master's death in 1803 he abandoned medicine and went to study political science at Halle and Heidelberg. He received his doctorate from Giessen University in 1808. In 1811 Boerne became an official in the Frankfort police department; but

Ludwig Boerne, German political essayist. Portrait by Moritz Oppenheim, oil on canvas, $46\frac{1}{2} \times 35\frac{1}{2}$ (119×90 cm.). Jerusalem, Israel Museum.

when the anti-Jewish restrictions of the pre-Napoleonic era were reimposed after Bonaparte's defeat in 1815, he was dismissed. Despite his personal bitterness, Boerne refused to have any part in protests to the Austrian chancellor, Metternich; he pinned his hopes for Jewish emancipation on a political and social revolution that would sweep away the entire system of the Holy Alliance.

In 1818 Boerne converted to Lutheranism, not out of religious conviction but to open the door to wider public activity, and adopted the name by which he was known thereafter. In the same year he founded the periodical *Die Waage.* This journal was ostensibly devoted to art, literature, and social gossip and Boerne earned a reputation with his witty theatrical criticism. But, as a master of innuendo, he managed to inject subversive political allusions into the most harmless subjects. In his *feuilletons,* of which he was a pioneer, he scourged the bureaucracy of Frankfort and ridiculed the whole pompous political structure of Central Europe. He soon ran into difficulties with the political authorities, and in 1821 gave up the editorship of *Die Waage.*

In 1830 constant police interference compelled Boerne to transfer his activities to Paris, where he was generally regarded as the leader of the political émigrés. His *Briefe aus Paris* (1830–1833), described by Heine as "paperbound sunbeams," were literary bullets fired across the German border with the aim of drawing public attention to glaring injustices. Boerne's influence reached its zenith in 1832, when he participated in the Hambach Festival, a gathering of 30,000 liberals from German-speaking states. He allied himself for a time with the influential but conservative Stuttgart editor Wolfgang Menzel, in the struggle against the idealization of Goethe by the Romanticists. But when Menzel espoused anti-Semitism and induced the German Federal Diet in 1835 to ban the works of Young Germany (a group of writers holding liberal views on politics and society), Boerne published his vitriolic diatribe, *Menzel der Franzosenfresser* (1838), a masterpiece of wit and irony.

Sensitive to the Jewish problem, Boerne wanted to be thought of as an individual apart from his Jewishness, and was chagrined when his utterances were attributed to his heredity. The idea that the freedom of mankind as a whole is inextricably bound up with freedom for the Jews recurs constantly in his writings, and he refused to acknowledge the existence of a Jewish problem distinct from the general issue of emancipation. Boerne held that the Jewish mission had been to teach the world cosmopolitanism and that the Jewish nation had disappeared in the most enviable manner; it had merged with mankind as a whole and had given birth to Christian idealism. On Boerne's death, Heine published an uncomplimentary study entitled *Ueber Ludwig Boerne* (1840), in which he expressed resentment against his erstwhile fellow liberal. This provoked Karl Gutzkow's defense of Boerne as a maligned German patriot and led to an extended controversy. Many years later, the old Frankfort *Judengasse* where he had lived was renamed "Boernestrasse" in his honor and, throughout the 19th century, Boerne and Heine were regarded as the major Jewish influences in German literature.

Bibliography: G. Ras, *Boerne und Heine als politische Schriftsteller* (1927); L. Marcuse, *Revolutionaer und Patriot; das Leben Ludwig Boernes* (1929); S. Liptzin, *Germany's Stepchildren* (1944), 27–44; NDB, 2 (1955), 404–6.

[S.L.]

°**BOESCHENSTEIN, JOHANN** (1472–1540), German Hebraist. He was born in Esslingen, and many scholars (such as Wolf, Joecher, Steinschneider, Perles) believed him to be of Jewish parentage, although Boeschenstein himself denied this. With *Reuchlin, Boeschenstein was a pioneer of Hebraic studies among Christians in Germany. He himself was a Hebrew teacher in several German cities

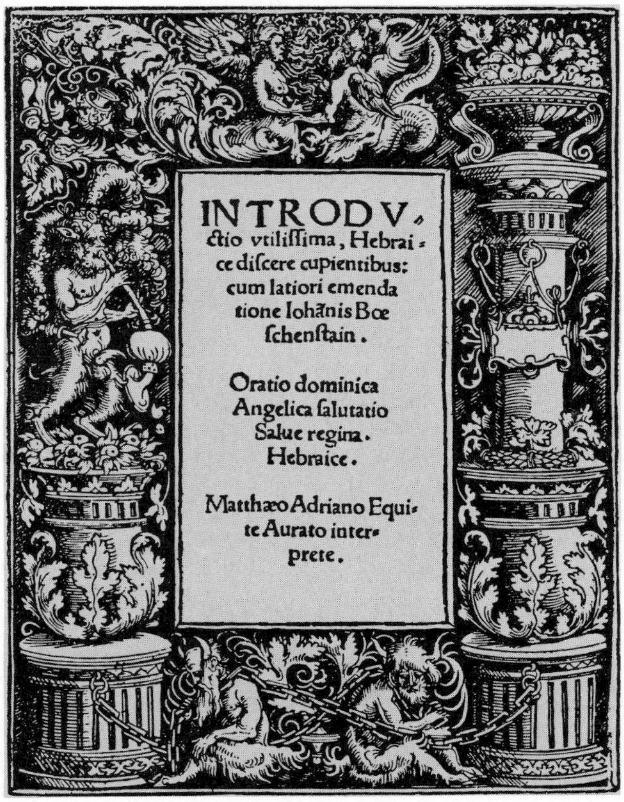

INTRODV-
ctio vtilissima, Hebrai-
ce discere cupientibus:
cum latiori emenda
tione Iohãnis Boe
schenstain.

Oratio dominica
Angelica salutatio
Salue regina.
Hebraice.

Matthæo Adriano Equi-
te Aurato inter-
prete.

Interior title page of *Rudimenta Hebraica,* Johann Boeschenstein's Latin edition of Moses Kimḥi's *Ha-Mehallekh,* Augsburg, 1520. Cecil Roth Photo Collection.

(Ingolstadt, Augsburg, Regensburg) until invited (c. 1519) by *Melanchthon to become professor of Hebrew at the University of Wittenberg. Later he moved to Heidelberg and then to Antwerp, Zurich, Augsburg, and Nuremberg (1525). He died in great proverty at Noerdlingen. Among his students were the noted theologians Caspar Amman, Johann Eck, and Ulrich Zwingli. Boeschenstein published a work on Hebrew grammar, *Hebraicae grammaticae institutiones* (1514, rev. ed. 1519, 1520); a Latin edition of Moses Kimḥi's *Ha-Mehallekh* entitled *Rudimenta Hebraica* (1520); and German translations of general Jewish prayers (*Tefillot ha-Ivrim,* 1525) and of Grace after Meals (1530).

Bibliography: Wolf, Bibliotheca, 4 (1733), 840; J. Perles, *Beitraege zur Geschichte der hebraeischen und aramaeischen Studien* (1884), 27f., 30f.; M. Steinschneider, *Die hebraeischen Handschriften Muenchen* (1895[2]), nos. 72, 259, 329, 401. [H.R.]

BOETHUSIANS, a religious and political sect which existed during the century preceding the destruction of the Second Temple. According to rabbinic tradition the Boethusians and the Sadducees were named after two disciples of *Antigonus of Sokho, Zadok and Boethus. They misinterpreted the maxim of their teacher, "Be not like servants who serve their master in order to receive a reward" as meaning that there was no reward for good works, and thus they denied the doctrine of resurrection and the world to come. They thereupon established the two sects named after them (ARN[1] 13b).

Modern scholars however consider this account to be legendary and they ascribe the origin of the Boethusians to the high priest Simeon b. Boethus who was appointed high priest by Herod the Great in 24 B.C.E. (Jos., Ant., 15:320), in succession to Joshua b. Phabi, in order to afford him a suitable status, as he desired to marry Herod's daughter, Mariamne II. Although in their theological views they closely resembled the Sadducees, some scholars regard them merely as a branch of them (see *Sadducees), and are always mentioned together with them, they did not share their aristocratic background, and whereas the Sadducees supported the Hasmonean dynasty, the Boethusians were loyal to the Herodians. It is they who are apparently referred to in the New Testament as Herodians (Mark 3:16; 12:13). The Boethusians were regarded by the Talmud as cynical and materialistic priests. They hired false witnesses to delude the Pharisees about the new moon (RH 22b; TJ, RH 57d; Tosef., RH 1:15). They maintained that the Omer (Men. 10:3) was to be offered on the first Sunday after Passover, and not on the morrow of the first day and, as a result, differed as to the date of Shavuot which according to them must always fall on a Sunday (Ḥog. 24). They held special views on the preparation of incense on the Day of Atonement (TJ, Yoma 1:39a; Tosef., Yoma 1:8). In terms of the Sabbath ritual, they were not even considered as Jews (Eruv. 68b). The high priestly "House of Boethus" is criticized in the Talmud for its oppression, "Woe is me because of the House of Boethus, woe is me because of their staves" (with which they beat the people—Pes. 57a; cf. Tosef., Men. 13:21).

Other Boethusian high priests included Joezer and Eleazar b. Boethus (Jos., Ant., 17:164, 339), Simeon Cantheras (*ibid.,* 19:297), Elionaeus b. Cantheras (*ibid.,* 19:342), and *Joshua b. Gamala.

Bibliography: L. Finkelstein, *Pharisees,* 2 (1950[3]), 762–79; Klausner, Bayit Sheni, 4 (1950[2]), 43; Schuerer, Gesch, 2 (1907[4]), 478 n. 16. [Ed.]

BOGEN, BORIS DAVID (1869–1929), U.S. social worker. Bogen, born in Moscow, emigrated to the United States in the early 1890s. He studied at the New York University School of Pedagogy in 1897. While working toward his degree, Bogen taught English in the Baron de Hirsch Trade School, and in 1896 accepted a teaching appointment at the Hebrew Technical Institute, the Educational Alliance. Objecting to the school's "pure Americanism" emphasis, Bogen left and became principal of the Baron de Hirsch Agricultural School in Woodbine, New Jersey (1900). He believed he had discovered his mission: "the feet of Jewish youth were to be turned toward a new destiny, leaving behind the peddler's packs and the sweatshops and the slums of their fathers," he wrote in his autobiography. However, the students at the school did not aspire to the status of a rural peasantry; they turned instead to the administrative and scientific aspects of agriculture, and Bogen vehemently dissented from the directors' efforts to reduce the length of study from three years to one and eliminate the scientific component, in order to produce a "contented Jewry working in the fields." Resigning in 1904, he became superintendent of the United Jewish Charities, Cincinnati, and also directed the work of the Jewish Settlement in Cincinnati. In 1913 he became field secretary of the Conference of Jewish Charities. Bogen maintained that the distinctive function of Jewish welfare was to intensify Jewish group consciousness and identity. Following the outbreak of World War I, he turned to problems of international relief, working in Holland, Poland, and Russia for the *American Jewish Joint Distribution Committee from 1917 to 1924. His autobiography, *Born a Jew* (1930), deals mostly with his relief efforts in Eastern Europe. Bogen's philosophy of sectarian social work is summarized in his *Jewish Philanthropy* (1917).

Bibliography: M. Z. Hexter, in: *Jewish Social Service Quarterly,* 6 (1929), 39–40; A. Segal, in: *B'nai B'rith Magazine,* 43 (1929), 315–6. [R.Lu.]

BOGER (Bograshov), ḤAYYIM (1876–1963), educator and *yishuv* leader in Ereẓ Israel. Boger was born in Chernigovka, Crimea. He first received a religious education, and later acquired enough secular education to enable him to receive a degree and teaching diploma from the University of Berne, Switzerland. Boger, an active opponent of the *Uganda Scheme, was a leader of the Ẓiyyonei Zion movement in Russia, and helped organize its conference in Freiburg (1905). In 1906 he settled in Ereẓ

Ḥayyim Boger, Israel educator.

Israel, where he was a founder of the Hebrew Gymnasium Society in Tel Aviv. Deported in 1915 by the Turkish authorities, Boger founded a Hebrew school in Alexandria, Egypt. He returned to Palestine in 1919 and became joint headmaster of the Herzlia Gymnasium, with Benzion *Mossinson. A leading figure in the affairs of Tel Aviv and the *yishuv,* he represented the General Zionists and served as a member of the Tel Aviv municipality, as delegate to the Asefat ha-Nivḥarim ("Elected Assembly"), and later as member of the Second Knesset, whose opening session in 1952 he chaired as its oldest member. He wrote *Ba-Arazot*

Reḥokot ("In Distant Lands," 1930), and *Tiyyul bi-Yhudah* ("Journey in Judea," 1930). In 1921 he helped found the Nordiah district in Tel Aviv for Jews from Jaffa made homeless by the Arab riots of that year. The district's main street is named Bograshov Street in his honor.

Bibliography: D. Smilansky, *Im Benei Dori* (1942), 151–7.

[A.A.]

BOGORAZ, VLADIMIR GERMANOVICH (originally **Mendelvich, Nathan;** 1865–1936). Russian ethnographer, revolutionary, and man of letters. Born in Ovruch, Volhynia, he was expelled from St. Petersburg University for revolutionary activities. He continued his political work under his assumed name of Vladimir Bogoraz, and at the age of 20 converted to Christianity. In 1886 he was arrested in Moscow, imprisoned for two years, and then exiled to Siberia. Here he met Vladimir *Jochelson, who became his lifelong friend and collaborator. It was during his years of imprisonment and exile that Bogoraz began the studies that were to make him an ethnographic authority on the Chukchee and Yakutsk natives of Siberia and on the Paleo-Asiatic peoples generally.

Released in 1889, Bogoraz joined the Jesup North Pacific exploration organized by the American Museum of Natural History in New York City and directed by Franz *Boas, who was to exert a significant influence on his life and achievements. On this expedition, Bogoraz was responsible for investigations of the Chukchee and the Siberian Eskimo. Jochelson was also a member of the expedition, as well as a third Jewish revolutionary, Lev Sternberg. All three men produced reports of precise and reliable scholarship. Bogoraz' included *The Chukchee* (vol. seven of the Jesup North Pacific Expedition Publications) and *Chukchee Mythology* (vol. 8 pt. 1, of the same series).

Bogoraz went back to Siberia to continue his ethnological studies, and made several visits to the United States. He returned to Russia and again involved himself with subversive organizations. For his part in the 1905 revolution he served another term of imprisonment. After the revolution of 1917 he was appointed professor at Leningrad University and curator of the Museum of Anthropology and Ethnography. He also founded and directed various official institutions such as the Museum of the History of Religion and Atheism—actually a museum of comparative religions—in the former Kazan Cathedral in Leningrad. As director of the Northern Peoples Institute in Leningrad he was able to do much to assist the cultural and political development of the peoples of Siberia. Despite their service to the revolutionary regime, Bogoraz and Sternberg were attacked for their views, which were regarded as going beyond the narrow Marxism of their period.

In addition to his academic publications, Bogoraz also produced some creative writing under the nom de plume N. A. Tan, some of it on Jewish themes. He published a pioneering Chukchee-Russian dictionary which appeared in 1937. His literary works include revolutionary poems (1900); *Chukotskiya razskazy* ("Chukchee Tales," 1899); and the novel *Vosem plemyen* ("Eight Tribes," 1902).

Bibliography: Krader, in: IESS, 2 (1968), 116–9, incl. bibl.

[E.Fi.]

BOGOTÁ, capital of *Colombia. Founded in 1538, the city was originally known as Santa Fe de Bogotá. Jews were probably among its first settlers, but corroborative documentation for the period is scarce. The city's isolated geographical location precluded large-scale Jewish immigration until relatively recent years, when improved communications and a sudden influx of European refugees altered the situation. Thus in 1916 there was an estimated total of 80 Jews in all of Colombia; by 1935 Bogotá had 2,000 Jews and by 1942, 3,460. In the 1964 census the Jewish population of Bogotá was 6,506 out of a total population of 1,681,000. The Jewish community is comprised of three congregations: Ashkenazi (the largest), Sephardi, and German—and each has its own communal institution, the Centro Israelita de Bogotá (Ashkenazi), the Comunidad Hebrea Sefaradí, and the Asociación Israelita Montefiori (German). There are also various other cultural and Zionist organizations serving the community, including B'nai B'rith, Wizo, and the Maccabi Sports Club. Bogotá has one Jewish day school with about 1,000 pupils from the kindergarten to pre-university level, and four synagogues. Two Spanish newspapers are published by the community: *Menorah* of Zionist-Revisionist orientation, and *Ideal,* which is Zionist and nonpartisan.

Bibliography: EJC and its volume on contemporary Jewry s.v. *Bogotá* and *Colombia;* J. Shatzky, *Yidishe Yishuvim in Latayn-Amerike* (1952), 195–203 passim; A. Monk and J. Isaacson, *Comunidades Judías de Latinoamérica* (1968), 53–63, and passim; J. Beller, *Jews in Latin America* (1969), 58–69.

[M.N.E.]

BOGROV (Beharav), DMITRI (1888–1911), Russian terrorist and revolutionary, who was executed for shooting the czarist prime minister Stolypin. Bogrov was the grandson of a well-known rabbi and the son of a lawyer. While a law student he joined an anarchist group but later entered the service of the Russian secret police *(Ochrana),* claiming that he did so in the interest of the revolutionary movement. Before he killed Stolypin, Bogrov asked the Social Revolutionary Party to give their approval, but they refused to do so. His true motive was never discovered, but some people believed it to have been to dispel the suspicions aroused by his connection with the secret police.

Bibliography: E. Lazarev, in *Volya Rossii,* nos. 6–7, 8–9 (1926).

[S.K.]

BOGUSLAV, city in Kiev province (oblast), Ukrainian S.S.R., passed to Russia from Poland in 1793. Jews were living in Boguslav from the beginning of the 17th century and an imposing synagogue was built there soon after the community was founded. In 1620 they were restricted in leasing property because the burghers complained that Jews had taken over most of the houses and stores in the marketplace and were competing with the local traders. The Jews in Boguslav suffered during the *Haidamak revolts in the area. During the uprising of 1768 they fled from the city; their homes were destroyed and their property looted. Although 574 Jewish poll-tax payers in Boguslav are recorded in 1765, only 251 remained after 1768. The community developed after Boguslav became part of Russia in 1793. A Hebrew printing press was established there in 1820–21, and Jewish-owned enterprises included textile and tanning factories. Jews also engaged in handicrafts and dealt in grain and fruit. The Jewish population numbered 5,294 in 1847 and 7,445 in 1897 (65% of the total).

After World War I, the Jews in Boguslav suffered severely in the civil war. On May 13, 1919, they were attacked by gangs of marauding peasants and on August 27 *Denikin's "white" army, which occupied the city, pillaged all the houses there, and massacred about 40 Jews. Subsequently a Jewish self-defense force was formed in Boguslav (under the auspices of the Soviet government) which comprised the entire male population of about 1,000 citizens. It fought off the gangs and also took part in punitive actions in the neighboring villages. Boguslav then became an asylum for thousands of Jewish refugees from the towns and villages of the surrounding areas. The self-defense force was disbanded in 1923. The Jewish population numbered 6,432 in 1926 (53% of the total). The community in Boguslav was annihilated after the Nazi occupation of the Ukraine in 1941.

Bibliography: A. Yaari, in: KS, 20 (1943/44), 45–48; M. Korot, in: *Reshumot*, 3 (1923), 140–57; A. Rosenthal, *Ha-Haganah ha-Ivrit ba-Ir Boguslav* (1929).

[Y.S.]

BOHEMIA (Czech, **Čechy**; Ger. **Boehmen**; Heb. בהם, פעהם, פיהם, כנען), independent kingdom in Central Europe, until the beginning of the 14th century, affiliated later in the Middle Ages to the Holy Roman Empire. In 1526 it became part of the hereditary *Hapsburg dominions and in 1620 lost its independence completely. From 1918 it was part of modern *Czechoslovakia (from 1939 to 1945 part of the Nazi protectorate of Bohemia-Moravia).

Early and Medieval Periods. The beginnings of Jewish settlement in Bohemia are much disputed and evidence has to rely on traditions that Jews had settled there before recorded Bohemian history. Trade contacts between the Roman Empire and southern Bohemia certainly brought Jews to the region, and some could have settled there. Presumably the Jewish traders mentioned in the Raffelstaetten Tax Ordinance (906) were also active in Bohemia. In the second half of the tenth century, Jews engaged in the slave trade in Bohemia are mentioned by *Ibrahim ibn Yakub. The Bohemian dukes of the 11th century probably employed Jewish moneyers. The first Bohemian chronicler, Cosmas of Prague, mentions Jews there in 1090. In 1096 many Jews in Bohemia were massacred by the crusaders and others were forcibly converted. Those who reverted to Judaism and attempted to leave were plundered on their departure (1098). According to Cosmas Vicedominus *Jacobus Apella, a high court official reverted to Judaism in 1124. Apparently the communities of *Cheb (Eger) and *Litoměřice (Leitmeritz) were well organized by the end of the 12th century. The places of Jewish settlement and activity in Bohemia are documented from the 13th century onward. The customs dues payable by Jews were regulated in 1222. The plethora of scholars living in Bohemia in this century, including *Isaac b. Jacob ha-Lavan of Prague, *Isaac b. Mordecai (Ribam), Eliezer b. Jacob, *Abraham b. Azriel of Bohemia, and *Isaac b. Moses of Vienna (Or Zaru'a), attests that Jewish culture was already deeply rooted and widespread among the communities there. From here *Pethahiah of Regensburg set out on his travels. The use of Slavic-Bohemian terms in the writings of some of these scholars to explain Hebrew terms indicates the linguistic and cultural ties existing between the Jews and local society. In 1241 the Jewish communities of Bohemia suffered with the rest of the population from the devastations of the Tatar invasion. In 1254 *Přemysl Otakar II granted a charter to the Jews based on the charter of the Austrian duke *Frederick II (1244), appending to it the bull issued by Pope *Innocent IV combating the *blood libel. He reconfirmed it in 1268. The wave of new settlers who went to Bohemia after the havoc wreaked by the Tatars included a number of Jews. These settled in the cities mainly as moneylenders, encouraged by the grant of charters and the status conferred on them as *servi camerae regis*, according them standing and protection at least not inferior to that in their countries of origin. The Altneu synagogue in *Prague was completed around 1270. At the time of the *Rindfleisch massacres in 1298 King Wenceslaus II extorted large sums from Bohemian Jewry for protection. In 1336 King John of Luxemburg ordered the arrest of all the Jews in Bohemia to

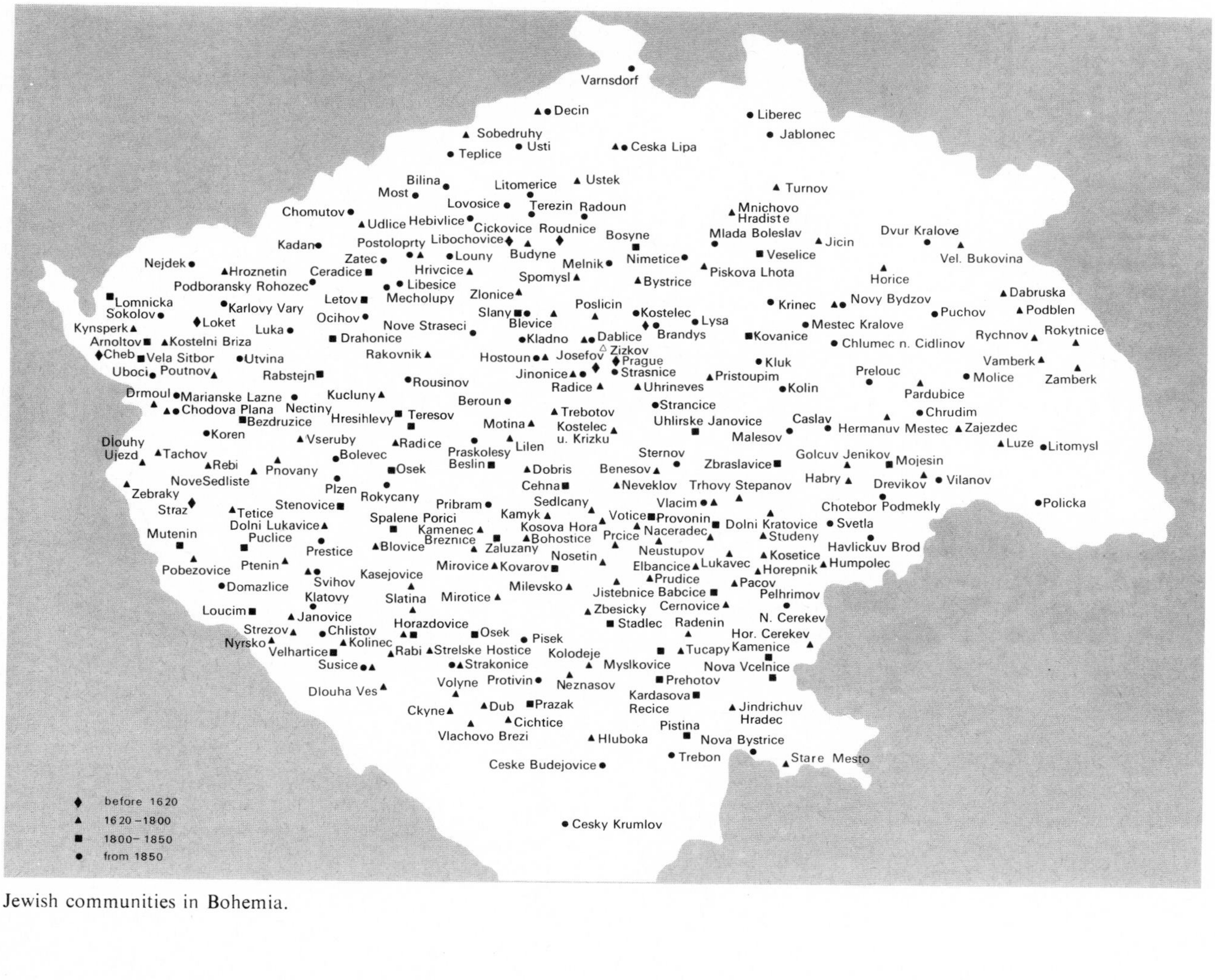

Jewish communities in Bohemia.

extort a ransom. There was a wave of massacres in this period in Čáslav and *Jindřichův Hradec (Neuhaus) in 1337, and also after a Host desecration libel in Kouřim in 1338. The entire Cheb community was butchered in 1350. The atrocities of the 14th century reached a peak with the massacre of the Jews in Prague in 1389. During this period Charles IV confirmed a number of privileges formerly issued to the Jews and in some cases afforded them protection, strictly enforcing their status as serfs of the chamber. Wenceslaus IV protected the Jews from oppression by the local nobility, but on several occasions canceled the debts owed to the Jews, as in 1411. The Jews suffered during the *Hussite uprising in 1419–37. The *Chomutov (Komotau) community was annihilated by the Hussites, while the Jews were expelled from Cheb and Jihlava (Iglau) on the charge of supporting them. In Jewish sources of the late 15th century evidence is found of strong sympathy for the religious reformer John Huss and the Hussites, and in particular for the Taborites, who are regarded as Judaizers and fighting a just national war.

Sixteenth and Seventeenth Centuries. With changes in the religious and social outlook of the burghers, the growing interest in finance and the increasing availability of money, moneylending ceased to be a Jewish monopoly. The competition of Christian moneylenders, abetted by the hypocrisy that forbade Jews to do what they themselves were engaged in, gradually eroded the central position held by Jews in this field. In addition, the weakening of the central royal power threatened the existence of the Jews living in the crown cities. Despite a decision of the Diet to tolerate the Jews (1501) and its confirmation by Ladislas II in 1510, they were eventually expelled from *Pilsen in 1504, and also from Prague, where some individuals were expressly permitted to remain. Their expulsion from the crown cities was formally proclaimed in 1541. Efforts made by *Joseph (Joselmann) b. Gershom of Rosheim to intercede were unsuccessful. The publication of the decree was followed by massacres of the Jews in Litoměřice, Nymburk, *Roudnice nad Labem (Raudnitz), and *Žatec (Saaz). Later a number of Jews returned. The decree of expulsion was renewed in 1557, and the Jews left all the crown cities excepting Prague where a few families remained. Many Jews left for Poland and Turkey.

By the end of the 16th century half of Bohemian Jewry were living in Prague. The rest were scattered throughout the countryside in the villages and small towns under the protection of the local nobility. Jews continued to reside in four towns, *Kolín, Roudnice, Bumsla (*Mladá Boleslav), and *Náchod (known in Jewish sources by their initials קרב"ן). Until the siege of Vienna by the Turks in 1683 the attitude of the authorities toward the Jews was influenced by the fear that they might support the Turks. In 1551 *Ferdinand I enforced the ordinance compelling the Jews to wear the yellow *badge. Four hundred and thirteen Jewish taxpayers are recorded in Bohemia (excepting Prague) in 1570, and over 4,000 Jews at the beginning of the 17th century. Until the development of a mercantilistic policy under *Charles VI, the Jews were almost the only traders in the rural areas. Their function was regarded by the local lords as *versilbern,* i.e., the conversion of the surplus produce of their domains (mainly wool, hides, feathers, and cheese) into money, and the supply of luxuries for their sumptuous households. Despite their frequently small numbers in many localities where they lived, the Jews of Bohemia developed an independent rural way of life and maintained Jewish traditions. Antagonism developed between the Prague community and the rest of Bohemian Jewry, the "Draussige" or "Ḥuẓim" ("outsiders"). The latter became organized in the *Landesjudenschaft.

Conditions improved under *Rudolf II (1576–1612). Subsequently the Prague community increased to attain an importance in the Jewish world far beyond the boundaries

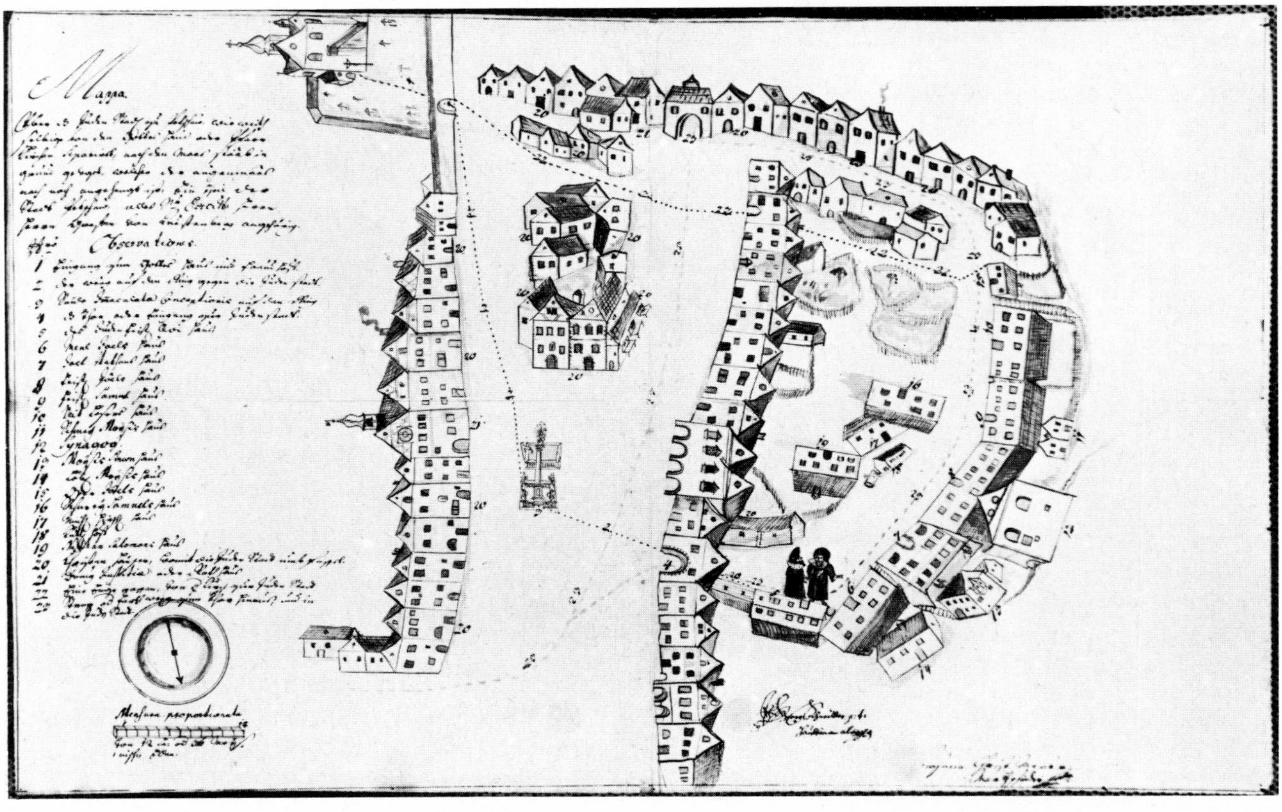

Figure 1. Plan from 1726 of the Jewish quarter of the Bohemian town of Becov (Petschav), near Carlsbad, showing its relationship to Christian areas. Places marked include: 1, Route to Jewish quarter. 4, Entrance to Jewish quarter. 5–11, 13–18, Jewish houses, with names of householders. 12, Synagogue. 20, Christian houses bordering the quarter. 21, Municipality. Prague, C.S.R. State Archives.

of the country. Bohemian Jews gained a reputation as goldsmiths. Hebrew printing flourished in Prague. Mordecai Meisel achieved influence as court banker. Among the prominent scholars of the period were R. *Judah Loew b. Bezalel (Maharal) and the chronicler and astronomer David *Gans. Jacob *Bassevi of Trevenberg was the first Jew to be granted a coat of arms. There was marked reciprocal influence between Bohemian society, in particular the sectarians, and Jews in the social and cultural spheres. Jewish sources express a local Bohemian patriotism. Gans states in his chronicle *Ẓemaḥ David* (Prague, 1595) that parts of his "General History" are written "to the glory [לכבוד] of this land in which I live." He gives a detailed description of Bohemia, its natural resources and its emblem, the lion, declaring "this land is full of God's blessings." He indignantly repudiates an anti-Czech song popular with the German-speaking population: "Ye should know that this song is entirely lies." He refers to the antiquity and beauty of Prague (*Ẓemaḥ David,* 2, fols. 7a, 46b, 49a, 97a).

Jewish life in Bohemia was disrupted by the Thirty Years' War (1618–48). In 1629, *Ferdinand II renewed and extended the privileges accorded to the Jews. However in 1630, he ordered them to attend the conversionist sermons of the *Jesuits. There were 14,000 Jewish taxpayers in Bohemia in 1635. The community absorbed many refugees from the *Chmielnicki massacres in Poland in 1648. In 1650, the Diet decided to curtail the number of Jews permitted to reside in Bohemia and limit their residence to the places where Jews had been living in 1618. This was the beginning of the "Jew-hatred of the authorities," in contrast to the attitude of the nobility who were interested in the income they derived from the Jews. Irksome restrictions were introduced and there were increasing demands for higher taxes. For Prague, a special committee, the *Judenreduktionskomission* ("Commission to Reduce the Number of the Jewish Population") was appointed. The number of the Jews outside Prague was estimated to be 30,000 in 1724. They lived in 168 towns and small market towns and 672 villages.

Familiants Laws. The curtailment culminated in the *Familiants Laws under Charles VI (1726) which only allowed 8,541 families to reside in Bohemia. Jews were segregated in special quarters. Bohemia was divided into 12 district rabbinates *(Kreisrabbinat).* The Jews were expelled from Prague by *Maria Theresa in 1744, but the decree of expulsion was remitted in 1748 and most of the Jews returned. A decree for the whole of Bohemia (1745) was not carried out. There were 29,091 Jews living in Bohemia in 1754, of whom one-third were living in Prague. In the second half of the 18th century some Jews in Bohemia were attracted to the *Frankists. Bohemian Jews took an active part in the industrialization of the country and the development of its trade, among them the *Hoenigsberg family, Simon and Leopold von *Laemel, and the *Popper family.

Toleranzpatent. The Toleranzpatent of *Joseph II for Bohemian Jewry was issued on Feb. 13, 1782. As an outcome, Jewish judicial autonomy was suspended, Jewish schools with teaching in German were opened, and the use of German was made compulsory for business records. Jews were permitted to attend general high schools and universities, and were subject to compulsory military service. These measures were supported by adherents of the *Haskalah movement in Prague, including members of the *Jeiteles family, the *Gesellschaft der jungen Hebraeer, Peter *Beer, Naphtali Herz *Homberg, and Raphael *Joel, among others. They were resisted by the majority of the Jews, led by the rabbis Ezekiel *Landau, Eleazar *Fleckeles,

Figure 2. Synagogue in Hostoun, Bohemia, built in the late 18th century.

Samuel *Kauder, and Bezalel Ronsburg. The legal position of the Jews of Bohemia was summarized in the *Judensystemalpatent* issued in 1797. Bohemian Jews were entitled to reside in places where they had been domiciled in 1725. They were permitted to pursue their regular occupations, with some exceptions, being prohibited from obtaining new licenses for the open sale of alcoholic beverages or from leasing flour mills. New synagogues could only be built by special permission. Rabbis were obliged to have studied philosophy at a university within the empire. Only Jews who had completed a German elementary school could obtain a marriage licence or be admitted to talmudic education. The *censorship of Hebrew books was upheld.

Nineteenth and Twentieth Centuries. The increasing adaptation of individual Jews to the general culture, and their rising economic importance, furthered Jewish assimilation into the ruling German sector. During this period Jews such as Moses and Leopold Porges-Portheim, Aaron and Solomon Pribram, and Moses, Solomon, and Leopold Jerusalem developed the Bohemian textile industry, introducing modern machinery. The discrepancy between the rise in economic and cultural standards and the restrictions imposed on the Jews by their humiliating legal status led to frequent circumvention of the existing legislation.

The budding Czech national renaissance at first attracted the Jewish intelligentsia, enraptured with the new learning, among them Siegfried *Kapper, Ludwig August *Frankl, and David *Kuh, supported by Václav Bolemir Nebeský. However the inimical attitude of Czech leaders such as Karel Havlíček-Borovský, and the outlook of the majority of the Jews moulded by an essentially German education, soon brought them into the German liberal camp, in which Moritz *Hartmann and Ignaz *Kuranda distinguished themselves in the revolutionary tumult of 1848.

In general, however, especially in the small communities, Jewish society continued the traditional way of life and mores despite the persistent trend to assimilation and the changes introduced by such communities as *Teplice. Legislation introduced in the 1840s brought some relief of the humiliating restrictions. In 1841 the prohibition on Jews owning land was waived. The *oath *more iudaico* and the Jewish tax (collected by a much hated consortium of Jewish notables, the "Juedische Steuerdirection") were annulled in 1846. The Jewish orphanage in Prague was built from its surplus funds. The 1848 revolution proved disappointing to the Jews as it was accompanied by anti-Jewish riots in many localities, principally in Prague. The Jews of Bohemia, however, benefited by the abolition in *Austria of marriage restrictions, and by the granting of freedom of residence.

There began a "Landflucht," movement from the small rural communities to the commercial centers in the big towns, in which many of the former communities disintegrated in the process. This was speeded up later by the growing anti-Semitism among Czechs and Germans alike (see below). There were 347 communities in Bohemia in 1850, nine with more than 100 families and 22 with over 50. By 1880, almost half of Bohemian Jewry was living in towns with over 5,000 inhabitants, mostly in the German-speaking area. There were 197 communities in 1890. In 1921 only 14.55% of Bohemian Jewry lived in localities of less than 2,000 inhabitants, and were 0.27% of the population in these localities. Sixty-nine per cent lived in towns of over 10,000. In 1930 46.4% of all Bohemian Jews lived in Prague and the number of Jews in the countryside had decreased by 40% since 1921. During this period, many Jews moved to Vienna or emigrated to the United States. Until 1848, the vast majority of Bohemian Jewry had belonged to the poorest sectors of the population. Subsequently most of them, as a result of their economic activities, moved up to the prosperous and wealthy strata even though their occupations remained essentially in the same sphere as before 1848.

In the second half of the 19th century Bohemian Jewry became increasingly involved in the bitter conflict between the Czech and German national groups. While the elder generation generally preferred assimilation to German culture, and supported the German-orientated liberal political parties, the Czecho-Jewish movement (Svaz *Čechůžidů), initiated and supported by Filip *Bondý, Siegfried Kapper, Bohumil *Bondý, and others, achieved some success in promoting Czech assimilation. By 1900, 55% of Bohemian Jewry declared their mother tongue as Czech and 45% as German. Some Jewish leaders, notably Joseph Samuel *Bloch, advised Bohemian Jews not to become involved in the conflict of the nationalities, but they continued to take sides on this issue until Zionism enabled at least its adherants to remain neutral.

As a result of emigration and a steady decline in the birth and marriage rates among Jews in Bohemia the percentage of the aged rose, and the total population of the community decreased. The vast majority of Jews became indifferent to religion and inclined to total assimilation: the **Yahrzeit*, the Day of Atonement, and a subscription to the *Prager Tagblatt*, the German-liberal daily, was considered by many Jews their only link with Judaism. There was an increase in mixed marriages from 0.15% in 1881 to 1.75% in 1910, and 27.56% in 1930, and many dropped their Jewish affiliation.

Percentage of Jewish Mixed Marriages

1881	0.15
1910	1.75
1930	27.56

Of all persons in Bohemia considered Jewish according to the Nazi standards introduced in 1939, 11.1% were not of Jewish faith. Anti-Semitism became strong in Bohemia at the end of the 19th century. The German population of the Sudetenland, the "Rand-Orls," was the stronghold of the *Schoenerer brand of racial anti-Semitism in the Hapsburg Empire (see also *anti-Semitic political parties and organizations). Czechs saw the Jews as the instruments and partisans of Germanization and the allies of Hapsburg patriotism. The economic anti-Jewish *boycott movement in Bohemia, "Svůj k svému" ("Each to his own kind") was

Jews in Bohemia

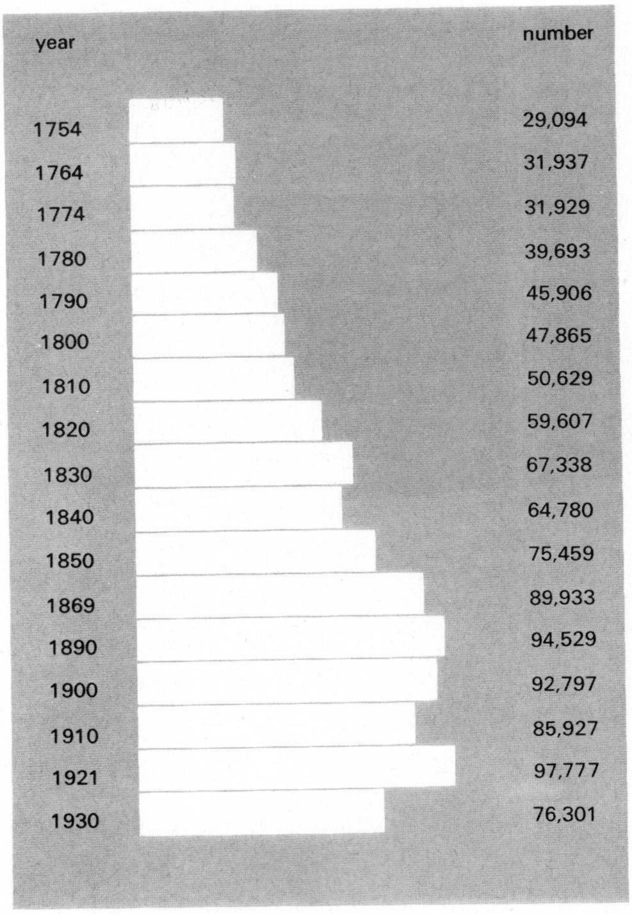

among the first of its sort to emerge in Europe and in particular hit Jewish shopkeepers in the villages. Finally a wave of blood libels, instigated by the Austrian *Christian Social Party, swept Bohemia. These occurred in Kolín and Náchod, among other places, and culminated in the *Hilsner Case. At this time the internal division in Jewry between the parties supporting Czech or German assimilation became increasingly pronounced. Jews joined the liberal and radical parties of both sides. At the end of the 19th century the Czecho-Jewish movement achieved the closure of Jewish schools where teaching was in German. During World War I, Bohemia absorbed thousands of refugees from Eastern Europe. Many settled there permanently and contributed to the revival of Jewish religious and cultural life in the communities. The establishment of independent *Czechoslovakia in 1918 linked Bohemian Jewry with the Jews living in the other parts of the new state. Bohemia attracted many Jews from Carpathian Russia (see *Subcarpathian Ruthenia) and Eastern Slovakia, and the Jews of Bohemia were active in organizing relief for Jews in these impoverished areas. After 1918, there were three federations of communities, one for those of Great Prague and *Ceske Budejovice and *Pilsen, one of Czech-speaking communities, and one of German-speaking communities. From 1926 they were represented, together with the federations of communities in Moravia and Silesia by the "Nejvyšší rada svazu náboženských obcí židovských v Čechách, na Moravě a ve Slezsku" (Supreme Council of the Federations of Jewish Religious Communities in Bohemia, Moravia, and Silesia). In 1930, 46.4% of Bohemian Jewry declared their nationality as Czech, 31% German, and 20.5% Jewish. In 1937 there were 150 communities. In 1938 with the Sudeten-crisis the 29% of Bohemian Jewry living in the Sudeten area became refugees.

Figure 3. Bohemian glass *Kiddush* cup, 19th century. Tel Aviv, Einhorn Collection. Photo David Harris, Jerusalem.

The Jewish State Museum in Prague now has synagogue equipment and archivalia from more than 100 Bohemian communities, most of them brought there in 1942 by Nazi orders when the communities were deported.

For Holocaust and contemporary period see *Czechoslovakia.

Bibliography: *Jews of Czechoslovakia,* 1 (1968), 1–71, 269–438; G. Kisch, *In Search of Freedom* (1949), 333–65 (extensive bibliography); Bondy-Dworský; H. Gold, *Die Juden und Judengemeinden Boehmens . . .* (1934); H. R. von Kopetz, *Versuch einer systematischen Darstellung...*(Prague, 1846); A. Stein, *Geschichte der Juden in Boehmen* (1904); J. Bergl, in: *Sbornik archivu ministerstva unitra,* 6 (1933), 7–64; JGGJČ, 1–9 (1929–38); *Zeitschrift fuer die Geschichte der Juden in der Tschechoslowakei,* 1–5 (1930–38); R. Dán, in: *Zeitschrift fuer die Geschichte der Juden,* 5 (1968), 177–201 (index for the above periodicals); R. Jakobson and M. Halle in: *For Max Weinreich* (1964), 147–72; O. Scheiber, *ibid.,* (1964), 55–58, 153–7; S. H. Lieben, in: *Afike Jehuda Festschrift* (1930), 30, 39–68; B. Bretholz, *Geschichte der Juden in Maehren,* ` (1934), index; Baron, Community, 3 (1942), index; F. Weltsch (ed.), *Prag vi-Yerushalayim* (1954); H. Tykocinski, in: Germ Jud, 1 (1963), 27–46; 2 (1968), 91–93; M. Lamed, in: BLBI, 8 (1965), 302–14; R. Kestenberg-Gladstein, *Neuere Geschichte der Juden in den boehmischen Laendern,* 1 (1969), incl. bibl.; idem, in: Roth, Dark Ages, 309–12, 440–1; idem, in: *Judaica Bohemiae,* 4 (1968), 64–72; idem, in: *Zion,* 9 (1945), 1–26; 12 (1948), 49–65, 160–89; idem, in: JJS, 5 (1954), 156–66; 6 (1955), 35–45; idem, in: *Gesher,* 15 no. 2–3 (1969), 11–82; F. Weltsch, *ibid.,* 207–12; M. Ben-Sasson, *Ha-Yehudim Mul ha-Reformazyah* (1969), 66–68, 102–8; idem, in: *Tarbiz,* 29 (1959/60), 306–7.

[J.Her./M.L.]

°**BOHLE (Bohlius), SAMUEL** (1611–1639), Lutheran Hebraist. Born in Greifenberg (Gryfice), Pomerania, Bohle taught at the University of Rostock, where he wrote an exposition of rabbinic commentaries on Malachi (1637) and a Hebrew grammar (1646). Other publications include an exposition of the seventh chapter of Isaiah, a commentary on Proverbs, and a treatise on the masoretic accents as the key to the verse-allocation of the Decalogue. Some of Bohle's works were published by G. Menthen in *Thesaurus theologico-politicus* (vol. 1, Amsterdam, 1701).

Bibliography: J. Cothmann, *Programma . . . ad exequias . . . Samueli Bohlio,* in: H. Witte, ed., *Memoriae theologorum...,* ser. 4 (1674); *Nouvelle biographie générale,* 6 (1853), 392, Steinschneider, in: ZHB, 2 (1897), 54, no. 113; Steinschneider, Cat Bod, 79, no. 469; 803, no. 4617.

[Ra.L.]

BOHM, DAVID (1917–), U.S. physicist. Bohm, who was born in Philadelphia, studied at the University of California, where he was a research physicist from 1943 to 1947. He was assistant professor at Princeton University (1947–51) and professor at São Paulo University, Brazil (1951–55). He lectured at the Haifa Technion, Israel, from 1955 to 1957 and was a research fellow at Bristol University until 1961, when he was appointed professor of theoretical physics at Birkbeck College, University of London. Bohm's main books are: *Quantum Theory* (1952[2]); *Causality and Chance in Modern Physics* (1957); and *The Special Theory of Relativity* (1965). In his works, Bohm attempted to revive the deterministic interpretation of quantum mechanics, an idea which aroused much discussion among scientists and philosophers though it failed to gain acceptance. Bohm criticized the causal theory of time, i.e., the acceptance of cause and effect as automatically denoting a forward direction of time, and he analyzed the irreversible character of natural processes. He summed up his philosophical position in *Causality* in the words, "the essential character of science is . . . that it moves toward the absolute by studying the relative. . . ." [Ed.]

BOHR, NIELS HENRIK DAVID (1885–1962), Danish physicist and Nobel laureate. He was born in Copenhagen. His father was non-Jewish, a professor of physiology at the University of Copenhagen, and his mother, née Ella Adler, belonged to a prominent Jewish banking family. He obtained his doctorate at Copenhagen in 1911 with a thesis on "Investigations of Metals." In 1912, he worked with J. J. Thomson (the discoverer of the electron) at Cambridge, and then in Manchester with Ernest Rutherford, the discoverer of the atomic nucleus. In 1913, Bohr produced the first of his series of papers which revolutionized conceptions of the structure of the atom. In 1916, Bohr became professor of chemical physics at the University of Copenhagen, and in 1920 head of the university's new Institute of Theoretical Physics. He participated in other important advances, such as the "Correspondence Principle" and the "Principle of Complementarity." In 1922, he was awarded the Nobel Prize, the youngest laureate up to that time. He helped to lead science through the most fundamental change of attitude it has made since Galileo and Newton. In September 1943 he and his family escaped the Nazis by going to Sweden in a fishing boat. In

Niels Bohr, physicist and Nobel Prize winner.

October he was taken to England in the bomb rack of an unarmed Mosquito plane. Bohr was "consultant" to Tube Alloys, the code name for the atomic bomb project. He had determined that the uranium atom which had been split by Hahn and Strassman in 1938 was the rare isotope U-235, a fact of major importance to the project. However, Bohr saw the atom bomb as a threat to mankind. He was given the first Atoms-for-Peace prize of the Ford Foundation in 1956, and was chairman of the Danish Atomic Energy Commission. In the last fifteen years of his life, he was tireless in his work for peace.

He took an active interest in the physics program of the Weizmann Institute of Science at Reḥovot which he visited on several occasions.

Bibliography: W. Pauli (ed.), *Niels Bohr and the Development of Physics* (1955); S. Rozental (ed.), *Niels Bohr; his Life and Work* ... (1967); R. E. Moore, *Niels Bohr: the Man, his Science and the World they Changed* (1966). [S.A.M.]

BOJAN, village in Ukrainian S.S.R., in the region of Bukovina; it belonged to Austria from 1774 to 1918 and to Rumania from 1918 to 1940. In 1807 there were in Bojan only 3 Jewish families, occupied in agriculture. Its situation near the Russian and Rumanian borders contributed to the growth of the community, which numbered 781 in 1880 (14.9% of the total population). It was first affiliated to the community of *Sadagora. An independent community was established in 1860. Bojan became a ḥasidic center when the *ẓaddik* R. Isaac Fridman, a grandson of R. Israel of *Ruzhin settled there in 1886. In consequence of the influx of the Ḥasidim who settled near the *ẓaddik's* home, Bojan developed into an urban settlement. In 1913 the community numbered 2,573. It had a synagogue and four prayer houses. When the Russians occupied Bojan during World War I, the Jewish quarter, including the residence of the *ẓaddik*, was destroyed and most of the Jews there fled. R. Isaac Fridman fled to Vienna where he died.

Bibliography: S. J. Schulson, in: H. Gold (ed.), *Geschichte der Juden in der Bukowina*, 1 (1958), 85–88. [El.F.]

BOJANOWO, small town in Poznan province, western Poland, founded in 1638. Jews were among its early settlers, and traded in textiles and hides. Jewish artisans were employed there by Christians, despite protests from the guilds. For a long time the community was affiliated to that of *Leszno (Lissa). The first synagogue was erected in 1793; a new one was built in 1859. The Jewish population numbered 151 in 1793, 311 in 1840, and 66 in 1905 (out of a total of 2,106). The talmudic scholar Julius *Theodor served as rabbi of Bojanowo. The community ceased to exist after World War I.

Bibliography: A. Heppner and J. Herzberg, *Aus der Vergangenheit und Gegenwart der Juden in den Posener Landen* (1904–29), 308–14. [Ed.]

BOKANOWSKI, MAURICE (1879–1928), French politician. Born in Le Havre into a family of Russian immigrants, Bokanowski studied law in Paris. In 1914 he was elected to the Chamber of Deputies and on the outbreak of World War I joined the French infantry. After the war he was reelected to the Chamber and became a member of the trade and finance commissions. He was appointed minister for the navy in 1924 and from 1926 to 1927 was minister of commerce and industry, signing France's first commercial treaty with Germany after World War I. He was killed in an airplane accident in 1928 and was given a state funeral.

Bibliography: *Dictionnaire de biographie française*, 6 (1954), 879–80. [S.C.]

BOKROS-BIRMAN, DEZSŐ (Desiderius; 1889–1965), Hungarian sculptor and graphic artist. Bokros-Birman was noted for his realistic portraiture and his ability to portray character. He was born in Ujpest and studied in Budapest and Paris. He exhibited first with the KÉVE (Association of Hungarian Creative and Industrial Artists) in 1918. Later he moved to Berlin, where he produced a series of lithographs entitled "Job" (1922). Bokros-Birman then returned to Budapest. During World War II he was a member of the anti-Fascist independence movement and later executed a relief entitled "Independent Hungary."

"Job," lithograph by Dezső Bokros-Birman, 1922. Budapest, Hungarian National Gallery.

Some of Bokros-Birman's better known works are "The 20-Year-Old Ady," "Ujvári Péter," and "The Iron-worker."

Bibliography: *The Statues of D. Bokros-Birman* (1928), introd. by F. Karinthy; *Bokros-Birman* (Hung., 1949), introd. by E. Mihályi. [J.Z.]

BOKSER, BEN ZION (1907–), U.S. Conservative rabbi and scholar. Bokser, born in Lubomb, Poland, was raised in the United States. From 1933 Rabbi Bokser served as rabbi of the Forest Hills Jewish Center, one of the largest Conservative congregations in New York City. He was also associate professor of homiletics at the Jewish Theological Seminary, and for many years editor of its "Eternal Light" radio program. His books, both popular and scholarly, include *Pharisaic Judaism in Transition* (1935), a biography of R. Eliezer b. Hyrcanus; *The Legacy of Maimonides* (1950); *From the World of the Cabbalah* (1954, a study of the life and thought of R. Loew b. Bezalel (the Maharal) of Prague); *Judaism: Profile of a Faith* (1963); and *Judaism and the Christian Predicament* (1967), a study of the relationship between Judaism and Christianity. Rabbi Bokser translated and edited two prayer books, the first for weekday, Sabbath, and festivals, and the second for the High Holidays.

[J.Ri.]

BOLAFFI, MICHELE (or **Michaele**; 1768–1842), Italian musician and composer. In 1793 he composed the music for the religious drama *Simḥat Mitzvah* by Daniel *Terni, written for performance at the inauguration of the synagogue in Florence: the music has not been found. Later, Bolaffi was active at the Leghorn synagogue, where his works continued to be performed until the early years of the 20th century. His works are included in the 19th-century music manuscripts of other Italian communities, notably that of Casale Monferrato. His setting to Psalm 121 is still sung in the Florence synagogue at festivals. Bolaffi also had a career as a secular musician. He went to England, where in 1809 he was employed as "Musical Director to the Duke of Cambridge." He toured Germany in 1816 with the singer Angelica Catalani, and occupied for a short period the post of *Koeniglicher Kapellmeister* at Hanover. Between 1815 and 1818 he was in the service of Louis XVIII as singer with the title "Musicien de S.M. le Roi de France." His compositions include an opera *Saul*, a *Miserere* for three voices and orchestra (1802), a "sonetto" on the death of Haydn (1809), settings for psalms, and other vocal compositions. He also wrote poems, an Italian adaptation of Solomon ibn *Gabirol's *Keter Malkhut* under the title *Teodia* (1809), and Italian translations of Jacques de Lille (1813) and Voltaire (1816).

Bibliography: C. Roth, in: JHSET, 16 (1945–51), 223–4; H. Schirmann, in: *Taẓlil*, 4 (1964), 32f.; Adler, Prat Mus, 125–8.
[I.A.]

BOLAFFIO, LEONE (1848–1940), Italian jurist. Born in Padua, Bolaffio was educated at the Padua talmudical college, and at the University of Padua. He practiced law in Venice for 15 years before becoming a lecturer at the universities of Parma and Bologna. Bolaffio helped revive the study of commercial law in Italy and was a member of the Royal Commission for the Reform of the Commercial Code. His works on commercial law include *Esegesi dell'articolo 58 del Codice di Commercio italiano* (1897) and *Diritto Commerciale* (1918) which became standard textbooks. He also edited the *Commentario al Codice di Commercio* with Cesare *Vivante and founded the law review, *La Temi Veneta*.

Bolaffio established the Italian Society for the Study of Stenography and advocated the introduction of the famous Gabelsberger shorthand system into the public schools of Italy. He himself wrote a manual for this system.

Bibliography: Rotondi, in: *Rivista di diritto privato*, 10 (1941), 150f.
[G.R.]

BOLEKHOV (Pol. **Bolechów**), city in W. Ukrainian S.S.R. since 1945 (formerly in *Galicia; from 1772 to 1919 within Austria, subsequently in Poland). Municipal status was granted to Bolekhov in 1612 by the lord of the town, and the Jews living there were accorded the right to participate in municipal elections for the mayor and council. In 1780 the Austrian government founded a Jewish agricultural settlement near Bolekhov named New Babylon; although the Jews were shortly afterward superseded by Germans, the name was retained. Jewish occupations in Bolekhov in the 18th century included trade in Hungarian wines, cattle, horses, and salt from the local mines. Later they extended to other trades and crafts. Industrial undertakings established by Jews included timber and other mills, tanneries, and furniture, soap, and candle factories. The oil industry founded in Bolekhov after World War I, and its position as a summer resort, also provided sources of Jewish incomes. Bolekhov was a cradle of the Jewish Enlightenment movement (*Haskalah) in eastern Galicia, the Jews there taking an interest in Polish and other foreign languages even in the 18th century. Prominent among its leaders were Dov Ber *Birkenthal, author of a famous autobiography, and Solomon *Rubin, principal of the modern Jewish school, where both Hebrew and German were taught.

The Jews formed a considerable majority of the population until World War II. In 1900 there were 3,323 Jewish inhabitants (78% of the total); in 1925, 2,435. In elections for the Austrian parliament (1867 through 1906), Bolekhov formed part of a constituency with largely Jewish voters. In 1931 there were 2,986 Jews. [N.M.G./Ed.]

Holocaust Period. When World War II broke out, Bolekhov came under Soviet occupation until July 2, 1941, when the town was occupied by Slovak and Ukrainian units under German command. The German commander established a Judenrat, headed by Dr. Reifeisen, who shortly afterward committed suicide. The Jews were segregated in a ghetto established in the autumn of 1941 and the intolerable living conditions there were aggravated by the arrival of refugees from the villages in the district. Relief was organized with great difficulty, and by the spring of 1942 most of them had died of starvation. Some Jews were employed in the local tanneries. Later, Jews were employed in lumber work at a special labor camp. In October 1941, the German police seized over 1,000 Jews. After being tortured for 24 hours, some succumbed and the rest were brought to a mass grave and shot. The second mass liquidation took place in September 1942 when a manhunt was conducted jointly by the Ukrainian and Jewish police for three days. The victims were herded into the courtyard of the city hall, where some 500 persons were murdered by the Ukrainians and some 2,000 dispatched by freight trains to *Belzec death camp where they perished. Most of the remaining Jews, including those from the work camp and some of the Jewish police and Judenrat were killed in December 1942. By 1943 only 1,000 Jews remained in the ghetto, in the work camp, and a few in the Jewish police. These were gradually murdered and only a few managed to escape to the neighboring forests. Some joined the partisans, while others perished there during the first few weeks. By the time of the Soviet conquest (spring of 1944) only a handful of Jews remained alive. In the district of Bolekhov, there was a group of Jewish partisan fighters who operated under the command of a Ukrainian communist. [De.D.]

Bibliography: B. Wasiutyński, *Ludność żydowska w Polsce w w. XIX i XX* (1930), 122; Y. Eshel and M. H. Eshel, *Sefer ha-Zikkaron li-Kedoshei Boleḥov* (1957).

°**BOLESLAV V ("The Pious"**; 1221–1279), Polish prince, son of Ladislas Odonic of the Piast dynasty. Boleslav was prince of Great Poland from 1239, for the first ten years in conjunction with his brother. In 1257, after many vicissitudes, he succeeded in establishing his rule over the whole of Great Poland. During his wars against the Teutonic Order and the rulers of Brandenburg he captured Gdansk (Danzig). The appellation "Pious" denotes Boleslav's good relations with the Church. During his reign Poland was invaded by the Mongols who left the country in ruin after their retreat. Boleslav, like other Polish rulers of the period, invited settlers from Germany, including Jews, to rehabilitate the country, granting various concessions and guarantees to the new settlers. This situation, and the policy to which it gave rise, motivated Boleslav to grant a charter to the Jews of Great Poland, issued on Sept. 8, 1264. It is patterned after, and mainly transcribed from, the charters granted to Jews in Austria in 1244 and Bohemia in

1254. Also known as the Statute of Kalisz, it was the prototype for subsequent Polish legislation concerning the Jews in the Middle Ages, such as that of *Casimir the Great.

The original text of the Statute of Kalisz has been lost, but its content is conveyed in the document of 1506 of the chancellor Jan Laski. About half of the 36 articles of the Statute concern the legal status of the Jews, who were regarded as belonging to the prince's treasury (cf. art. 29: "Whoever robs a Jew . . . shall be considered as robbing Our treasure"). The Jews were protected against the *blood libel. They, their families, their possessions, and their institutions (synagogues, cemeteries) were under the protection of the prince (arts. 8–10, 14, 29) and subject to his jurisdiction (art. 8 denies the municipality any juridical authority over the Jews). The other articles relate to Jewish economic activities, and attest the ruler's special interest in Jewish credit transactions (see *Moneylending) and their organization. Two articles deal with the commercial activity of the Jews. Four articles original to the Statute of Kalisz, i.e., not adopted from earlier documents of this kind, are article 33, permitting the purchase of a horse from a Jew in daytime only; article 34 prohibiting mintmasters from accusing Jews of forging coins; article 35 compelling their Christian neighbors to assist Jews if attacked at night; and article 36 permitting Jews to trade in provisions.

Bibliography: R. Hube, *Przywilej żydowski Bolesława* (1880); Ph. Bloch, *Die Generalprivilegien der polnischen Judenschaft* (1892); I. Schipper, *Studya nad stosunkami gospodarczymi Żydów w Polsce podczas Średniowiecza* (1911); J. Sieradzki, in: *Osiemnaście wieków Kalisza*, 1 (1960), nos. 135–42.

[A.Cy.]

BOLESLAVSKI, ISAAC (1919–), Russian chess grandmaster. Boleslavski was born in the Ukraine. He established himself early as one of the leading players in the U.S.S.R. He achieved his greatest success in the Candidates' Tournament at Budapest in 1950, where he shared first prize with David *Bronstein. The latter won the play-off and so qualified to challenge Mikhail *Botvinnik. From that time Boleslavski distinguished himself in important tournaments. He also achieved celebrity as an analyst of the openings, and many important variations resulted from his experiments in practical play. [G.A.]

BOLIVIA, South American republic. The origins of Jewish settlement in Bolivia can be traced back to the Colonial period, when Marranos from Spain arrived in the country (which then formed part of the Viceroyalty of Peru). Some worked in the silver mines of Potosí, others are known to have been among the pioneers who founded the city of Santa Cruz de la Sierra in 1557 under the leadership of Ñuflo de Chávez. Indeed, certain customs still maintained by old families in that region, e.g., lighting candles on Friday nights and sitting on the ground in mourning when a close relative dies, suggest their possible Jewish ancestry. The only extant documents for the period are those of the Inquisition, which was established in Peru in 1570 and whose appearance signaled the incipient demise of the Marrano community.

There is a similar paucity of information regarding 18th- and 19th-century Jewish immigration to Bolivia. It was not until the present century that substantial Jewish settlement took place there. In 1905 a group of Russian Jews that settled in Bolivia was followed by another group from Argentina and later by several Sephardi families from Turkey and the Near East. The Jewish community nonetheless remained minuscule. It was estimated that in 1917 there were only 20 to 25 Jews in the country, and by 1933, at the beginning of the Nazi era in Germany, only 30 Jewish families lived there. The first tide of Jewish immigration came in the early 1930s, and it was estimated that by the end of 1942 there were 7,000 new immigrants, of whom approximately 2,200 emigrated from Bolivia by the end of the 1940s. The majority settled in La Paz, but by 1939–40 communities had arisen in outlying cities such as Cochabamba, Oruro, Sucre, Tarija, and Potosí and with them the nascent communal organizations that thereafter served the needs of the Jewish population.

Bolivia was traditionally governed by conservative constitutions, and not until 1880 did a more democratic trend appear. The 1938 Constitution recognized Roman Catholicism as the official state religion, but guaranteed general freedom of religion. The Jewish community's relations with the Catholic Church are casual, yet cordial, but there is no intergroup organization servicing the two bodies.

Bolivia's policy on Jewish immigration during World War II vacillated between the granting of mass visas and the total embargo on entry permits. In 1939 the liberal immigration policy was modified, as it had been in other Latin American countries. This move was in keeping with the policy of barring entry to nationals of the Axis powers. In addition, a certain amount of discontent was engendered with the discovery that most of the Jewish immigrants who had entered the country on an agricultural visa were actually involved in commerce and industry. In May 1940 all Jewish visas were suspended indefinitely; nevertheless, immigration did not cease.

After World War II a small wave of Polish Jews who had fled to the Far East after 1939 and abandoned Shanghai in the wake of the communist takeover arrived in Bolivia. The major part of the group remained in La Paz, and was incorporated into the existing *kehillah*. In the early 1950s the demographic trend was reversed and there was not only a decline in immigration but also a consistent exodus, which resulted from a variety of factors, including the political instability in the country. The 1952 revolution that brought to power the National Revolutionary Party (which had been close to the Nazis during the war), aroused anxieties in the Jewish community. These fears were allayed, however, when Jewish rights were not affected. Economic insecurity, health hazards caused by climatic difficulties, and the lack of adequate facilities for higher education also motivated the emigration trend.

Although most of the Jewish immigrants to Bolivia received entry visas as agricultural workers, the majority of them established themselves in commerce and industry. Several colonization projects were attempted, however, under the auspices of the Sociedad Colonizadora de Bolivia (Socobo), founded in 1940, and with the help of the tin magnate Mauricio *Hochschild. The latter spent almost $1,000,000 between 1940 and 1945 on an agricultural development project at Coroico; but, like the one in the Chaparé jungles, it failed. Climatic conditions were exceedingly difficult, and there was a dearth of roads to suitable markets. The early years of the Jewish community in Bolivia were marked by difficult economic conditions, especially for those who did not own business enterprises. Between January 1939 and December 1942 $160,000 were disbursed for relief by the *American Jewish Joint Distribution Committee, by the Sociedad de Protección de los Inmigrantes Israelitas, and by Mauricio Hochschild. The majority of the immigrants entered manufacturing and trade and ultimately played a prominent role in the development of industry, imports and exports, and in the free professions. By the fall of 1939, when immigration had reached its peak, organized Jewish communities had been established in Bolivia. The first organization to be founded was the Círculo Israelita (1935) by East European Jews, followed by the German Comunidad Israelita de Bolivia. During the next few years other organizations were formed, such as B'nai B'rith, the Federación Sionista Unida de Bolivia, etc. The representative roof organization is the Comité Central Judío de Bolivia. Under the auspices of these groups, various communal services have been established: the Ḥevra Kaddisha, the Cementerio Israelita, Bikkur Ḥolim, the house for the aged, Wizo, and Macabi. The La Paz community maintains the Colegio Israelita, a comprehensive school with kindergarten, primary, and secondary grades. Its student body is mixed because the high level of the school attracts also non-Jewish students. Jewish education was one of the prime victims of the emigration trend, and student enrollment, especially in the lower grades, declined drastically.

The community of Cochabamba, which has a Jewish population of about 600, is the second largest in the country. Its history is inextricably linked with its founder, an Alexandrian Jew named Isaac Antaki, who arrived in the 1920s. He established a large textile factory and also built the synagogue which serves the Ashkenazi and Sephardi communities. The Jewish population of the city reached its peak after World War II, but afterward large numbers began to emigrate. The community never managed to establish a Jewish school, and only a kindergarten exists.

The Jewish press in Bolivia consists of sporadic papers and bulletins published by the Colegio Boliviano Israelita, B'nai B'rith, and the Federación Sionista Unida.

Relations with Israel. Bolivia was among the supporters of the 1947 UN resolution on the partition of Palestine. Subsequently, a Bolivian representative was named to the Palestine Commission. In ensuing debates at the United Nations, notably those on the refugee problem, despite changing governments and resultant differences of policy, Bolivia was remarkably consistent in maintaining a friendly attitude to Israel. Israel's first minister presented his credentials in 1957, and an embassy was established in 1964; Bolivia, in turn, established its embassy in Jerusalem in the same year. The two countries engaged in a variety of assistance programs. A technical cooperation agreement between the two countries, signed in 1962, provides for an agricultural mission of Naḥal officers that has been active in Bolivia in cooperation with the Bolivian army in the fields of agricultural settlement and training. Bolivian students on scholarships in Israel included irrigation engineers and youth leaders. An effort in the private sphere is a joint study in medicinal tropical plants undertaken by the School of Pharmacology of the Hebrew University of Jerusalem and its Bolivian counterpart. In 1968 there were 1,700 Jews in Bolivia.

Bibliography: Mangan, in: *Commentary,* 14 (1952), 99–106; N. Lorch, *Ha-Nahar ha-Loḥesh* (1969), passim; Asociación Filantrópica Israelita, Buenos Aires, *Zehn Jahre Aufbauarbeit in Suedamerika* (Ger. and Sp., 1943), 172–98; *Enciclopedia Judaica Castellana* and its volume on contemporary Jewry; J. Shatzky, *Comunidades Judías en Latinoamérica* (1952), 64–69; A. Monk and J. Isaacson, *Comunidades Judías de Latinoamérica* (1968), 36–40.

[N.L.]

BOLM, ADOLPH RUDOLPHOVICH (1884–1951), U.S. ballet dancer and director. Born in St. Petersburg, Russia, Bolm was awarded a first prize at the Imperial Ballet and soon drew public attention with his brilliant dancing and mime. He toured European capitals with Anna Pavlova in 1908 and 1909, and in 1914 went to the U.S. as leading dancer and choreographer in Diaghilev's company. He then settled in New York, where he formed the Bolm Ballet Intime. He produced *Le Coq d'Or* at the Metropolitan Opera in 1918, danced the title role in *Petrouchka,* and established himself as a choreographer. He became maître de ballet at the Chicago Opera in 1922. In 1931, in Hollywood, his ballet *Iron Foundry* (to music by Mossolov) attracted audiences of fifteen to twenty thousand at a time. In 1932 Bolm was appointed ballet master at the San Francisco Opera, and held the post for five years. He later directed a ballet school.

Bibliography: C. W. Beaumont, *Complete Book of Ballets* (1937), 784–90 and index; *Dance Magazine,* 37 (Jan. 1963), 44–50; *New York Times* (April 17, 1951), 29.

[Ed.]

BOLOGNA, city of north central Italy. There is evidence of a Jewish cemetery in Bologna in 302 and 393. Jews are next mentioned in 1171, when they were temporarily expelled. In 1308 they gave the Dominican friar Aymerich, presumably to appease him, an ancient Torah scroll said to date from the time of Ezra. If, in 1366, the Jews of Bologna were confined to a special quarter, as suggested by the documents, the period of segregation must have been brief; for shortly afterward they owned buildings throughout the city and land in the countryside. The city, however, taxed them heavily. In 1394 two brothers of the Roman "Min ha-Ne'arim" or "Delli Putti" family presented the community with a house for a synagogue and ground for a cemetery. In 1416 at the time of the papal election a vigilance committee of Jewish notables from various parts of Italy met in Bologna. In 1417 the bishop of Bologna compelled the Jews there to wear the Jewish *badge and to limit their activities as loan-bankers. The restrictions were confirmed in 1458. Nevertheless, the community flourished. In 1473 *Bernardino da Feltre secured the establishment of a public loan-bank (*Monte di Pietà) in order to undermine the activities of the Jews. It functioned for a short time only, but further attempts were made to establish one in 1505 and 1532.

The Bologna community attained a high cultural level. In the 15th–16th centuries it numbered many rabbis and noted scholars including Obadiah *Sforno, Jacob *Mantino, Azariah de' *Rossi, and Samuel *Archivolti. There were 11 synagogues in Bologna in the middle of the 16th century, even more than in Rome.

Two Hebrew printing presses were set up, the first functioning 1477–82 and the second 1537–40. The first book of the Hebrew Bible to appear in print was the Book of Psalms, with commentary by D. Kimḥi. It was printed in Bologna in 1477 by Meister Joseph and his son, Ḥayyim Mordecai, and Hezekiah of Ventura in an edition of 300 copies. About the same time they printed two small-size editions of the Book of Psalms. In 1482 the Pentateuch with Onkelos and Rashi and the Five Scrolls with commentaries was printed by *Abraham b. Ḥayyim dei Tintori of Pesaro (see *Incunabula). Only the Pentateuch bears the city's name. In 1537 anonymous silk makers in partnership printed a *siddur* of the Roman rite, mostly on parchment, and some other works; and in 1540/41 a *maḥzor* of

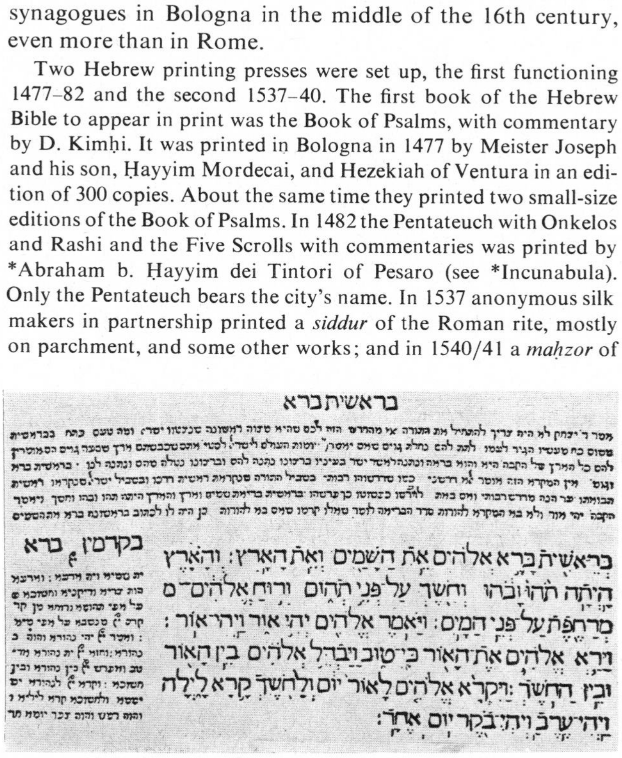

Figure 1. Opening page of the first edition of the Pentateuch to be printed with Onkelos' Aramaic version and Rashi's commentary, Bologna, 1482. New York Public Library.

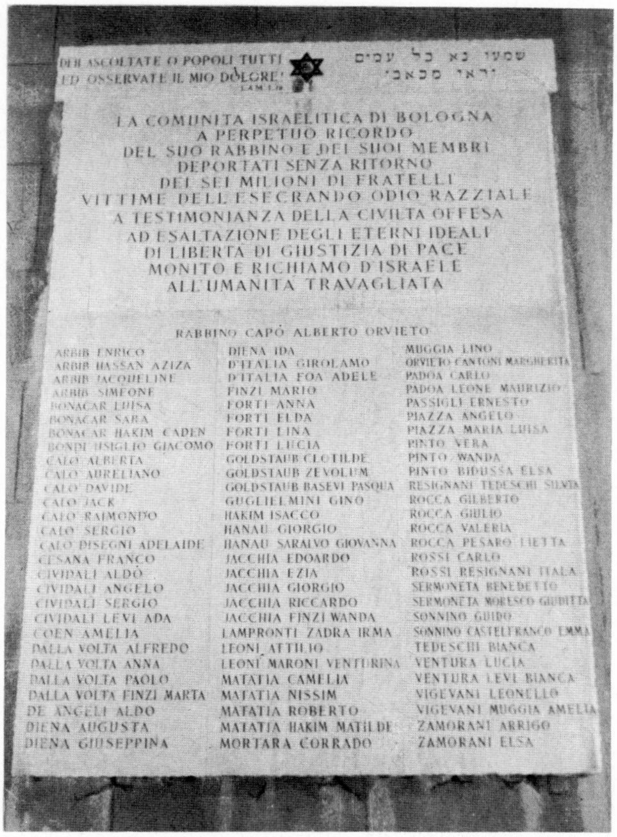

Figure 2. Memorial plaque to the Jews of Bologna sent to extermination camps during World War II. It is headed by the name of the chief rabbi, Alberto Orvieto. Photo J. Shaw, London.

the same rite appeared with commentary by Joseph *Treves. The university library owns an important collection of Hebrew manuscripts and early editions.

Bologna reverted to direct papal rule in 1513, and not long after the community began to suffer from the consequences of the Counter-Reformation. In 1553 the Talmud and other Hebrew works were burned on the instructions of Pope Julius III. In 1556 *Paul IV issued an order confining Jewish residence to a ghetto. Pius V established a House of *Catechumens in Bologna in 1568 and in the following year Bologna was among the towns of the papal states from which the Jews were banished. Eight hundred Jews were forced to leave, paying in addition the enormous fine of 40,000 scudi. The cemetery was given to the nuns of S. Pietro who completely destroyed it in order to use the ground. As a result of the more liberal attitude of Sixtus V, Jews returned to Bologna in 1586, but in 1593 they were again expelled by Clement VIII. On this occasion they removed the bones of their dead, which they reburied in the cemetery of Pieve di Cento.

Subsequently Jews were not able to settle in Bologna for two centuries. In 1796, in the period after the French conquests, several Jews went to live there. They later suffered from the renewed papal rule, and their position progressively deteriorated until in 1836 they were again expelled. It was in Bologna that the kidnapping of the child Edgardo *Mortara took place in 1858, an affair that stirred the civilized world. When the city was annexed to Piedmont in 1859, equal rights were granted to the Jews. [A.MIL.]

The Bologna Jewish community had 860 members in 1931. During the autumn and winter of 1943, 83 Jews (40 men and 43 women) were sent to extermination camps, from which only three returned. The local synagogue was bombed and destroyed, and the rabbi, Alberto Orvieto, was deported and killed. After the war 390 Jews were left in Bologna. By 1970 the number of Jews was reduced to 270 including a number of Israelis studying at the university. The synagogue has been rebuilt. [S.D.P.]

Bibliography: Ravà, in: *L'Educatore Israelita*, 20 (1872), 237–42, 295–301; 21 (1873), 73–79, 140–4, 174–6; 22 (1874), 19–21, 111–3, 296–8; Sonne, in: HUCA, 16 (1941), 35–98; Roth, Italy, index; Milano, Italia, index; H. D. Friedberg, *Toledot ha-Defus ha-Ivri be-Italyah* (1956²), 28ff.; D. W. Amram, *Makers of Hebrew Books in Italy* (1909), 47f.; A. M. Habermann, *Ha-Sefer ha-Ivri be-Hitpattehuto* (1968), 84, 121; L. Ruggini, in: *Studia et Documenta Historia et Juris*, 25 (1959), 186–308 (It.), index.

BOLZANO (Ger. **Bozen**), capital of Bolzano province, northern Italy. Jewish moneylenders began to settle in Bolzano after it passed to the Hapsburgs in 1363. While some originated from Italy, they were predominantly of German origin. The persecutions and expulsions which followed the blood libel in *Trent in 1475 also affected the Jews of Bolzano. A few began to settle in the city again in the first half of the 16th century. In 1754 Ḥayyim David Joseph *Azulai found only two Jewish families in Bolzano. Jewish settlement again increased during the 19th and early 20th centuries. Before World War II there were 100 Jews living in Bolzano. During the German occupation (1943–45), one of the largest concentration camps in Italy was set up in Bolzano, and the Jewish community was annihilated.

Bibliography: Ḥ.Y.D. Azulai, *Ma'gal Tov ha-Shalem*, 1 (1921), 12; J. E. Scherer, *Die Rechtsverhaeltnisse der Juden in den deutsch-oesterreichischen Laendern* (1901); G. Ottani, *Un popolo piange* (1945); G. Canali, *Il magistrato mercantile di Bolzano*... (1942).

[D.C.]

BOMBAY, capital of Maharashtra and the proverbial "gateway to India." Bombay enters Jewish history after the cession of the city to the Portuguese in the middle of the 16th century. Then a small fishing island of no great economic significance, Bombay was leased out around 1554–55 to the celebrated *Marrano scientist and physician Garcia da *Orta, in recognition of his services to the viceroy. Garcia repeatedly refers in his *Coloquios* (Goa, 1563) to "the land and island which the king our lord made me a grant of, paying a quit-rent." After the transference of Bombay to English rule the Jew Abraham *Navarro expected to receive a high office in the Bombay council of the East India Company in recognition of his services. This was, however, denied to him because he was a Jew. In 1697 Benjamin Franks jumped Captain Kidd's "Adventure Galley" in Bombay as a protest against Kidd's acts of piracy; his deposition led to Kidd's trial in London.

The foundation of a permanent Jewish settlement in Bombay was laid in the second half of the 18th century by the *Bene Israel who gradually moved from their villages in the Konkan region to Bombay. Their first synagogue in Bombay was built (1796) on the initiative of S. E. *Divekar. *Cochin Jews strengthened the Bene Israel in their religious revival. The next largest wave of immigrants to Bombay consisted of Jewish merchants from Syria and Mesopotamia. Prominent was Suleiman ibn Yaʿqūb or Solomon Jacob whose commercial activities from 1795 to 1833 are documented in the Bombay records. The Arabic-speaking Jewish colony in Bombay was increased by the influx of other "Arabian Jews" from *Sūrat, who, in consequence of economic changes there, turned their eyes to India.

A turning point in the history of the Jewish settlement in Bombay was reached with the arrival in 1833 of

Figure 1. The Kneseth Elijah Synagogue in Fort, Bombay (interior and exterior), founded in 1888. Bombay, Sir Jacob Sassoon's Charity Trusts.

the Baghdad Jewish merchant, industrialist, and philanthropist, David *Sassoon (1792–1864) who soon became a leading figure of the Jewish community. He and his house had a profound impact on Bombay as a whole as well as on all sectors of the Jewish community. Many of the educational, cultural, and civic institutions, as well as hospitals and synagogues in Bombay owe their existence to the munificence of the Sassoon family.

Unlike the Bene Israel, the Arabic-speaking Jews in Bombay did not assimilate the language of their neighbors, Marathi, but carried their Judeo-Arabic language and literature with them and continued to regard Baghdad as their spiritual center. They therefore established their own synagogues, the Magen David in 1861 in Byculla, and the Kneseth Elijah in 1888 in the Fort quarter of Bombay. A weekly Judeo-Arabic periodical, *Doresh Tov le-Ammo,* which mirrored communal life, appeared from 1855 to 1866 Hebrew printing began in Bombay with the arrival o Yemenite Jews in the middle of the 19th century. They took an interest in the religious welfare of the Bene Israel, for whom—as well as for themselves—they printed various liturgies from 1841 onward, some with translations into Marathi, the vernacular of the Bene Israel. Apart from a shortlived attempt to print with movable type, all this printing was by lithography. In 1882, the Press of the Bombay Educational Society was established (followed in 1884 by the Anglo-Jewish and Vernacular Press, in 1887 by the Hebrew and English Press, and in 1900 by the Lebanon Printing Press), which sponsored the publication of over 100 Judeo-Arabic books to meet their liturgical and literary needs, and also printed books for the Bene Israel.

The prosperity of Bombay attracted a new wave of Jewish immigrants from Cochin, Yemen, Afghanistan, Bukhara, and Persia. Among Persian Jews who settled in Bombay, the most prominent and remarkable figure was Mullā Ibrahim *Nathan (d. 1868) who, with his brother Mūsā, both of *Meshed, were rewarded by the government for their services during the first Afghan War. The political events in Europe and the advent of Nazism brought a number of German, Polish, Rumanian, and other European Jews to Bombay, many of whom were active as scientists, physicians, industrialists, and merchants. Communal life in Bombay was stimulated by visits of Zionist emissaries. [W.J.F.]

Figure 2. The Magen David Synagogue in Byculla, Bombay (interior and exterior), founded in 1861. Bombay, Sir Jacob Sassoon's Charity Trusts.

Contemporary Period. The Jewish population of Bombay was estimated to be 11,000 in 1968, but a strong emigration movement to Israel was gaining momentum. Bombay remained as the last major center of organized Jewish life in India. The Baghdad community, which was the leading element in organized communal life, had decreased to some 500 people, the Bene Israel becoming numerically predominant. Over 80% of the Jews were concentrated in two of the poorer districts of Bombay, 1,500 lived in middle-class suburbs of the town, and another 500 in the best residential areas, Malabar Hill and Kolaba. The small number of European Jews in Bombay lived exclusively in these districts.

The community, with government aid, supported two Jewish schools, and was served by six Bene Israel and two Baghdadi synagogues. These synagogues could be separated into three trends: Orthodox, Conservative (United Synagogue), and Liberal. Membership in a particular synagogue seemed to be a function of social, economic, and educational status as well as of religious difference. The inclusive organization, the Central Jewish Board of Bombay, with which all synagogues, organizations, and institutions were affiliated, served as a spokesman for Indian Jewry as a whole. Similarly, the Bombay Zionist Association was the representative Zionist body in the country. Zionist activities constituted an important part of communal life, and the Jewish Agency provided direct aid in the form of Hebrew teachers and emissaries. All three of the Jewish periodicals in India were published in Bombay. Communal activities were further supplemented by a number of youth, welfare, and charitable organizations. The Israel Consulate is situated in Bombay. [P.Go.]

Bibliography: Fischel, in PAAJR, 25 (1956), 39–62; 26 (1957), 25–39; idem, in: HUCA, 29 (1958), 331–75; S. Jackson, *The Sassoons* (1968), index; C. Roth, *The Sassoon Dynasty* (1941), index; D. S. Sassoon, *History of the Jews in Baghdad* (1949), index; idem, *Massa Bavel*, ed. by M. Benayahu (1955), index; Soares, in: *Journal of the Royal Asiatic Society, Bombay Branch*, 26 (1921), 195–229; A. Yaari, *Ha-Defus ha-Ivri be-Arezot ha-Mizraḥ*, 2 (1940), 52–82. CONTEMPORARY: S. Strizower, *Exotic Jewish Communities* (1962), 48–87; World Jewish Congress, *Jewish Communities of the World* (1963), 40–41; S. Federbush (ed.), *World Jewry Today* (1959), 339–40.

°**BOMBERG, DANIEL** (d. between 1549 and 1553), one of the first and the most prominent Christian printers of Hebrew books. Bomberg left his native Antwerp as a young man and settled in Venice. Rich and well educated, and even having studied Hebrew, he developed a deep interest in books. He probably learned the art of printing from his father Cornelius. In all, nearly 200 Hebrew books were published (many for the first time) at Bomberg's printing house in Venice, which he set up on the advice of the apostate Felix Pratensis. He published editions of the Pentateuch and the Hebrew Bible, both with and without commentaries, and was the first to publish the rabbinic Bible *Mikra'ot Gedolot*, 4 vols., 1517–18, with Pratensis as editor, i.e., the text of the Hebrew Bible with Targum and the standard commentaries. In order to produce this work, he had to cast great quantities of type, and engage experts as editors and proofreaders. As a result of the success of his early work, Bomberg expanded his operations. He published the first complete editions of the two Talmuds (1520–23) with the approval of Pope Leo X (only individual tractates of the Babylonian Talmud having hitherto been published), as well as the Tosefta (appended to the 2nd ed. of Alfasi, 1522). The pagination of Bomberg's editions of the Talmud (with commentaries) has become standard ever since. Similarly, his second edition of the rabbinic Bible (1524–25) edited by *Jacob b. Ḥayyim ibn Adonijah, has served as a model for all subsequent editions of the Bible. He is said to have invested more than 4,000,000 ducats in his printing plant. Bomberg spent several years trying to obtain a permit from the Council of Venice to establish a Hebrew publishing house. He also had to secure special dispensation for his Jewish typesetters and proofreaders from wearing the distinctive Jewish (yellow) hat. In 1515 the Venetian printer P. Liechtenstein printed, at Bomberg's expense, a Latin translation by Felix Pratensis of the Psalms. Apparently, the first Hebrew book to come off his press was the Pentateuch (Venice, Dec. 1516), though there is some evidence that his first work was printed in 1511 (*Aresheth* 3, 93ff.). In 1516 he obtained a privilege to print Hebrew books for the Jews, and went on printing rabbinic books, midrashic-liturgical texts, etc. Among Bomberg's printers, editors, and proofreaders whose names are known were: Israel (Cornelius) *Adelkind and his brother and Jacob b. Ḥayyim ibn Adonijah (all of whom were later baptized); David Pizzighettone, Abraham de *Balmes, *Kalonymus b. David, and Elijah *Levita (Baḥur). It seems that Bomberg's fortunes declined as a result of competition from other publishers. In 1539 he returned to Antwerp, though his publishing house continued to operate until 1548. His distinctive type became popular, and his successors not only lauded his typography but went so far as to print on the title pages of their publications "with Bomberg type," or some similar reference. The name Bomberg which appears in the Plantin Bible published in Antwerp in 1566 almost certainly refers to his son, and from him Plantin obtained a manuscript of the Syriac New Testament on which he based the Polyglot Bible known as *Regia* (8 vols., 1569–73). See *Printing, Hebrew.

Bibliography: A. Berliner, in: JJLG, 3 (1905), 293–305 (= *Ketavim Nivḥarim*, 2 (1949), 163–75, 287–8; A. Freimann, in: ZHB, 10 (1906), 32–36, 79–88; D. W. Amram, *Makers of Hebrew Books in Italy* (1909), 146–224; I. Mehlman, in: *Aresheth*, 3 (1961), 93–98; J. Bloch, *Venetian Printers of Hebrew Books* (1932), 5–16; C. Roth, *Venice* (1930), 246–54; G. E. Weil, *Élie Lévita* (1963), index; C. Roth, in: REJ, 89 (1930), 204; British Museum, Department of Printed Books, *Short-title Catalogue of Books Printed in Italy . . . from 1465 to 1600* (1958), 788–9; H. M. Adams, *Catalogue of Books Printed on the Continent of Europe, 1501–1600, in Cambridge Libraries*, 2 (1967), 397–8. [A.M.H.]

BOMBERG, DAVID (1890–1957), British painter. He was born in Birmingham and brought up in Whitechapel, the Jewish quarter of London. Apprenticed to a lithographer,

"Irrigation, Zionist Development, Palestine" by David Bomberg, 1923. Oil on board, 12½×16 in. (31.7×40.6 cm.). London, Marlborough Fine Arts Gallery.

he attended evening classes and later the Slade School. In 1914 he became a founder-member of the London Group, and participated in an exhibition "Twentieth Century Art" held at the Whitechapel Art Gallery for which he organized an international Jewish section. This was the first collection of modern Jewish art to be seen in England.

In 1923 the English painter, Sir Muirhead Bone, wrote to the British Zionist Federation urging them to employ Bomberg to record pioneering work in Palestine. Bomberg visited Palestine, but fell out with the Zionists, refusing to paint what he regarded as propaganda pictures. He spent six months at Petra, where he developed his taste for sunbaked, desolate landscapes. Later he continued his travels and painted in several countries, particularly in Spain. Bomberg then fell into poverty and neglect as his paintings fell out of favor. In 1954 he returned to Spain, with the intention of founding an artists' colony, but died with the plan still unfulfilled. Bomberg's early paintings show the influence of Cubism, but remain representational; these include some Jewish subjects, such as the "Jewish Theater" (1913), "Family Bereavement" (c. 1913, commemorating his mother's death), and "In the Hold" and "Mud Bath" (1913–14), studies of a Jewish communal bath.

His later work is more emotional, painted in rich, fiery colors. "Hear, O Israel," painted in Spain in 1955, represents a return to Jewish themes of his youth. In 1967 the Tate Gallery honored his memory with a comprehensive memorial exhibition.

Bibliography: W. Lipke, *David Bomberg; a Critical Study of his Life and Work* (1967).

[Ch.S.S.]

BOMZE, NAHUM (1906–1954), Yiddish poet. Bomze was born in eastern Galicia. He made his literary debut in the *Warsaw *Yugent Veker* in 1929, and was a member of the Lemberg literary group *Tsushtayer.* He served with the Russian army during World War II, and settled in the United States in 1948. He published four collections of poetry: *In di Teg fun Vokh* (1929); *Borvese Trit* (1936); *A Gast in Farnakht* (1939); *A Khasene in Herbst* (1949). A selection of his poems with an introduction by H. *Leivick, *Ayvik Bliyen Vet der Traum* was published posthumously.

Bibliography: S. Melzer (ed.), *Al Naharot* (1957), 106, 428; J. Leftwich, *Golden Peacock* (1939); LNYL, 1 (1956), 221–2.

[Sh.B.]

BONAFED (Bonfed), SOLOMON BEN REUBEN (end of the 14th–mid-15th century), Spanish poet and philosopher. According to some scholars, Bonafed served as a rabbi for a time, perhaps in Saragossa, about 1391. Bonafed's forte was satirical verse. Perhaps because of his satirical bent, Bonafed had many enemies with whom he settled his account in his poems and biting epigrams. He believed that he was being persecuted by the community of Saragossa, as his literary mentor Solomon ibn *Gabirol had been before him. His compositions include lyrical poetry, in which the leading motif is his own suffering and that of the Jewish people; didactic poems (such as one containing rules of poetry, reminiscent of Horace); satirical verse, including love poems, following Arabic and Latin modes; Castilian troubadour poetry, frequently coarse; and also liturgical poetry. Among his *piyyutim* are recorded *Shekhunah bi-Neshamah,* a *reshut* for Passover, included in the Montpellier prayer book, and five elegies. Bonafed was also well acquainted with philosophical literature, reading Aristotle in the Latin translation of Boethius.

Although Bonafed mocked the excessively severe rabbinical rulings and many superstitious customs prevalent in contemporary circles, he remained strictly religious and zealous for the Jewish faith. As such, he took part in the disputation of *Tortosa in 1413–14, where many of his poems, generally dedicated to friends who had gathered with him in that city, were written. Bonafed's poems are an invaluable historical source for this event, and illuminate the psychological stresses of the period which resulted in masses of Jews adopting Catholicism. An outstanding defection was that of Vidal de la *Cavalleria, who took a leading part in the disputation. Immediately after his conversion he was appointed to an important official post. Bonafed expressed his distress at Vidal's apostasy: "A precious sun has set in our West—why has it not risen on our horizon?" Many of those who had left Judaism were his former friends, "Scholars who were precious beyond words, who girded themselves with valor . . . How, now that they are gone, shall I erase those pleasant names from my doorposts?" Bonafed addressed a satirical polemic in rhyming prose to the apostate Astruc *Rimoch (Francisco de Sant Jordi), who was attempting to persuade a young acquaintance to follow his example. In it Bonafed raised the anomalies in Christian doctrine, and deduced evidence of their irrationality and untenability. Rimoch's original letter and Bonafed's reply were published by Isaac Akrish as an appendix to the well-known epistle of Profiat *Duran, *Al Tehi ka-Avoteikha* (Constantinople, 1577). Bonafed also condemned the intellectuals who regarded the study of philosophy and sciences as more important than Torah study.

Bonafed's poems are presented in a unique manuscript of over 250 quarto pages, in the Bodleian Library, Oxford (Neubauer, Cat, no. 1984). Part of the *divan* was published by Kaminka in Brainin's *Mi-Mizraḥ u-mi-Ma'arav* (1, 2 (1895), 107–27), with preface and notes.

Bibliography: Zunz, Poesie, 518; Steinschneider, in: HB, 14 (1874), 95–97; Steinschneider, Cat Bod, no. 6904; Neubauer, Cat, 916, 11, 1984A; A.Z. Schwarz, *Die hebraeischen Handschriften in der Nationalbibliothek in Wien* (1925), no. 120, 2; Baer, Spain, index; Schirmann, Sefarad, 2 (1961), 620–43, 699–700.

[B.Su./Ed.]

BONAFOS, MENAHEM B. ABRAHAM (also called **Bonafoux Abraham of Perpignan;** late 14th–early 15th century), philosophical author. Bonafos, who lived in France, is the author of a dictionary entitled *Sefer ha-Gedarim* ("Book of Definitions"), also called *Mikhlal Yofi* ("Perfection of Beauty"), containing precise definitions of technical terms appearing in the Hebrew philosophical and scientific literature, particularly in Maimonides' *Guide of the Perplexed.* The entries under each letter are divided into six sections according to the following classification: ethics and politics, logic, metaphysics, physics, mathematics and astronomy, and medicine. In 1567 the book was first published, with some notes, by Isaac b. Moses ibn Arollo in Salonika, and again in Berlin, 1798, with a commentary and additions by Isaac Satanow.

Bibliography: Renan, Rabbins, 740; Gross, Gal Jud, 476; REJ, 5 (1882), 254; G. B. de' Rossi, *Dizionario storico degli autori arabi* (Parma, 1807), 75; Wolf, Bibliotheca, 1 (1715), 763; Steinschneider, Cat Bod, 1719, no. 6341, 1983, no. 6546; A. Z. Schwarz, *Die hebraeischen Handschriften in der Nationalbibliothek in Wien* (1925), no 150.

[Ed.]

BONAFOUX, DANIEL BEN ISRAEL (c. 1645–after 1710), Shabbatean prophet. Bonafoux was born in Salonika, and settled in Smyrna and served there as a *ḥazzan* in the Pinto synagogue. He was a follower of Shabbetai Ẓevi and even after his apostasy he continued to be a leading believer in him. The Shabbateans accepted Bonafoux as a visionary and a prophet. When Abraham

Miguel *Cardoso came to Smyrna in 1674, Bonafoux, known as Ḥakham Daniel in documents, was at the head of the group of Cardoso's followers. In the 1680s Bonafoux returned to Salonika for a few years, and his opponents claimed that he had joined the *Doenmeh there, but this is doubtful. About 1695 when he returned to Smyrna he caused great confusion by his visionary tricks. He would read questions addressed to him in sealed letters and demonstrate various phenomena of light, etc. Many came to him for answers to their questions, among them critics from abroad who wanted to examine him and to get an idea of his Shabbatean belief. The latter included Abraham *Rovigo, whose letter about his visit to Bonafoux in 1704 is extant (Ms., Jerusalem, 8°, 1466, fol. 196). Bonafoux was a close friend of Elijah ha-Kohen ha-Itamari, the principal preacher of the town, who referred to Bonafoux in *"Yeled,"* his story of a soothsayer (*Midrash Talpiyyot* (1860), 207). In 1702 Bonafoux was expelled on the request of the leaders of the community and he lived for a while in a village near Smyrna. In a letter from the Dutch consul in Smyrna dated 1703, Bonafoux' "oracles" are described in detail. After 1707 he went to Egypt and returned to Smyrna in 1710 with an imaginary letter in praise of Shabbetai Ẓevi from the Lost Ten Tribes, who would reveal himself anew. The letter is found in manuscript (Ben-Zvi Institute, Jerusalem, no. 2263). Until his death, Bonafoux maintained contact with Cardoso who claimed in his letters that the "*Maggid" who talked through the mouth of Bonafoux was the soul of the kabbalist David Habillo.

Bibliography: J. Emden, *Torat ha-Kena'ot* (1870), 55; J. C. Basnage de Beauval, *History of the Jews* (London, 1708), 758f.; A. Freimann (ed.), *Inyanei Shabbetai Ẓevi* (1912), 10; *Sefunot*, 3–4 (1960), index s.v. *Bonafoux* and *Daniel Israel;* G. Scholem, in: *Zion Me'assef*, 3 (1929), 176–8. [G.Sch.]

°BONALD, LOUIS GABRIEL AMBROISE, VICOMTE DE (1754–1840), French political theorist. De Bonald fled France in 1791 during the Revolution. He later became a leading exponent of the Catholic and royalist political school and opposed all liberal tendencies. A logical outcome of his traditionalist views was to regard the Jews as a "deicide nation" and to combat their emancipation. In the *Mercure de France* (23 (1806), 249–67), which he directed with *Chateaubriand from 1806, de Bonald accused the Jews of aspiring to world domination. De Bonald's works, in particular the *Théorie du pouvoir*, formed the ideological arsenal from which the French clerical movement was later to forge its weapons of intolerance and anti-Semitism. See also *Anti-Semitic Political Parties and Organizations.

Bibliography: L. Poliakov, *Histoire de l'antisémitisme*, 3 (1968), index. [Ed.]

BONAN, family of Tunisian rabbis, some of whose members settled in Tiberias and Safed. Mas'ud Bonan (born c. 1705), the first known member of the family, was one of the first scholars of the renewed settlement in Tiberias. In 1748 he was sent as an emissary to Western Europe, and he spent four years in Italy, Holland, England, and Germany. While in Hamburg, he supported Jonathan *Eybeschuetz in his controversy with Jacob *Emden. In 1751 he was in London, where he wrote an approbation to *Mikdash Melekh* by Shalom Buzaglo. From 1752 he made Safed his permanent home. Following the earthquake of 1759, he signed, as chief rabbi of Safed, the letters of the emissaries who traveled to different countries to solicit aid for the rehabilitation of the community. During the wars of Ali Bey, Mamluk ruler of Egypt in 1773, who plundered the Jews, he proceeded to Europe as an emissary, though old and in ill health. The main center of Mas'ud's activity was Leghorn, but he also visited France, Austria, and England. He apparently returned to Safed after 1778. Ḥayyim Mordecai, son of Mas'ud, was sent, together with Israel Benveniste, to Western Europe in 1767 on behalf of the Safed community, and again in 1774 to Syria, Iraq, and Kurdistan. Isaac Bonan (died c. 1810) was an outstanding scholar of Tunis. Of his books the following have been published: *Oholei Yiẓḥak* (Leghorn, 1821), talmudic novellae, together with notes on various halakhic codes. Also included are the halakhic rulings of Isaiah di Trani the Elder on the tractates *Rosh Ha-Shanah, Ta'anit,* and *Ḥagigah; Ohel Yesharim* (Leghorn, 1821), a talmudic methodology, arranged alphabetically (1846); *Berit Yiẓḥak* on the Mekhilta, with its commentaries, *Zayit Ra'anan* and *Shevut Yehudah,* of Judah Najar of Tunis, together with a commentary on the Mishnah of *Berakhot* and the commentary of the tosafists on the Pentateuch. His son David (d. 1850) studied under Isaac Tayib and was a rabbi of the Leghorn community in Tunis. David's books, published by his son Isaac, were: *Dei Hashev* (1857), responsa compiled together with Judah ha-Levi of Gibraltar, to refute Bekhor Isaac Navarro's strictures on the above-mentioned *Oholei Yiẓḥak,* and his own responsa under the different title *Nishal David; Mo'ed David* on the *Avodat ha-Kodesh* of Solomon b. Abraham Adret (Part I, on Festivals, 1887); *Maḥaneh David* (1889), researches on Talmud and *halakhah.* Included are novellae by Isaiah di Trani the Elder and of the son of Naḥmanides on tractate *Beẓah.* David also prepared his father's books for publication and wrote notes on *Berit Yiẓḥak.*

Bibliography: Yaari, Sheluḥei, 460–1, 507–8; M. Benayahu, *Rabbi Ḥ. Y. D. Azulai* (Heb., 1959), 28, 553; Simonsohn, in: *Sefunot*, 6 (1962), 335–6, 346–54; Emmanuel, *ibid.*, 407, 409, 420; D. Cazès, *Notes bibliographiques sur la littérature juive-tunisienne* (1893), 36–59. [Ed.]

BONASTRUC, ISAAC (c. 1400), scholar. Bonastruc was among a group of scholars who settled in Algiers after their expulsion from Majorca in 1391. It seems that he was associated with R. Simeon b. Ẓemaḥ *Duran and R. *Isaac b. Sheshet Perfet in the preparation of the twelve *takkanot* pertaining to marital status (1394) which remained in force for several hundred years (cf. Simeon b. Ẓemaḥ Duran, *Tashbeẓ*, vol. 2 (Amsterdam, 1742), no. 292). Bonastruc had a belligerent, argumentative personality. He was compelled to leave Algiers after 1404, as a result of his slanderous remarks about Saul ha-Kohen *Astruc, the leader of the Algiers community. After the latter's death, Bonastruc settled in Constantine, where again he was the cause of stormy controversies within the Jewish community because of his opposition to its leaders. He was appeased when he received a grant from the community on the recommendation of Isaac b. Sheshet: at the same time Simeon b. Ẓemaḥ asked the local *dayyan*, Joseph b. David, not to oppose him.

Bibliography: I. Epstein, *The Responsa of Rabbi Simon b. Ẓemaḥ Duran* (1968^2), 17–19, 26, 66, 84; A. M. Hershman, *Rabbi Isaac ben Sheshet Perfet and His Times* (1943), index. [A.D.]

BONAVENTURA, ENZO JOSEPH (1891–1948), psychologist. Born in Pisa, Bonaventura was brought to Florence at an early age. Enzo was brought up without any notion of Judaism, but falling under the influence of S. H. Margulies, rabbi of Florence, had himself circumcised when he returned from World War I. In 1922 he was appointed professor of psychology at the University of Florence, where he founded and directed the psychological laboratory. Leader of the Zionist Society of Florence, he settled in Palestine in 1938 and was appointed professor of psychology at the Hebrew University. He was killed in April 1948 during an Arab attack on a convoy on the way to the Hebrew University on Mount Scopus. Bonaventura's views in psychology united the classical and the modern schools of thought and this was apparent in his scientific work, which combined the pursuit of detail within a broad philosophical framework. Bonaventura employed the experimental method in his researches into the problems of time, perception, movement, attention, volition, and conation; he also investigated the problems of mental development, especially in retarded children. His most important works in Italian are: *L'educazione della volontà* (1927); *Il problema psicologico del tempo* (1929); *Psicologia dell'età evolutiva* (1930); *La psicoanalisi* (1938). His important Hebrew works are: *La-Psychologyah shel Gil ha-Ne'urim ve-ha-Hitbaggerut* ("Psychology of Youth and Adolescence," 1943); *Hora'ot le-Morim u-le-Meḥannekhim le-Hadrakhat ha-No'ar bi-Veḥirat ha-Mikẓo'a* ("Instructions to Teachers and Educators in Helping Young People Choose a Profession," 1947). [H.O.]

His father, ARNALDO (1862–1957), was a noted musicologist. He studied law and literature at Pisa, but soon devoted himself to musicology. He became librarian at the music section of the Biblioteca Nazionale Centrale at Florence, and afterward director and librarian at the Instituto Luigi Cherubini in the same town where he also taught music history and aesthetics. Bonaventura's many works include *Manuale di storia della musica* (1898) and *Storia e letteratura del pianoforte* (1918), both of which ran into 13 editions, as well as critical biographies of Paganini, Verdi, Pasquini, Puccini, Boccherini, and Rossini. He also edited the compositions of Peri, Frescobaldi, Strozzi, and Caccini. [C.AB.]

Bibliography: Grove, Dict; Riemann-Gurlitt; MGG; Baker, Biog Dict; Kressel, Leksikon, 1 (1965), 187–8.

BONAVOGLIA, MOSES DE' MEDICI (d. 1446), rabbi and physician in Sicily. A protégé of the House of Aragon, he studied medicine in Padua and on his return in 1420 was appointed chief judge *(*dienchelele)* of the Sicilian Jews. The office, usually held by persons too close to the court, was unpopular among Sicilian Jewry. Hence Bonavoglia was twice removed from this post but was recalled each time. In 1431 he obtained from the king the abrogation of some anti-Jewish legislation. Bonavoglia was the personal physician of Alfonso V and in 1442 followed him when he conquered Naples.

Bibliography: B. and G. Lagumina (eds.), *Codice diplomatico dei Giudei di Sicilia,* 1 (1884), 308f., 361–8; Milano, Italia, 512; Roth, Italy, 238ff., 249. [A.MIL.]

BONDAVIN, BONJUDAS (Bonjusas, or **Judah ben David;** c. 1350–c. 1420), rabbi and physician. Bondavin practiced medicine in Marseilles between 1381 and 1389 as physician to Queen Marie of Provence, and in 1390 settled in Alghero, in Sardinia. Also a talmudic scholar, Bondavin later became rabbi of Cagliari. As such, he enjoyed the favor of the Aragonese authorities. When King Martin II of Aragon visited Sardinia in 1409, Bondavin attended his court, and the king extended his jurisdiction as rabbi to the whole of Sardinia. Bondavin's learning is demonstrated in his correspondence with *Isaac b. Sheshet of Saragossa, centering on a picturesque episode at the royal court.

Bibliography: Bloch, in: REJ, 8 (1884), 280–3; Roth, Italy, 265; Milano, Italia, 182. [A.MIL.]

BONDI (Bondy, Bonte, Ponidi, באנדי, בונדי), family name, a translation of the Hebrew "Yom Tov" (in Romance languages *bon*—"good," *di*—"day"). A Bondia family was known in Aragon in the 13th century. In 1573 an Abraham Bondi lived in Ferrara. Adam Raphael b. Abraham Jacob Bondi and Ḥananiah Mazzal Tov b. Isaac Ḥayyim Bondi were rabbis and physicians in Leghorn in the second half of the 18th century, when the family was also represented in Rome. In about 1600 the family appears in Prague; the first known member was Yom Tov b. Abraham Bondi; subsequently Eliezer, Mordecai, Meshullam (d. 1676), and his son Solomon Zalman Bondi (d. 1732) are mentioned as communal functionaries and scholars. Abraham b. Yom-Tov Bondi (d. 1786) was the author of *Zera Avraham* on the *Even ha-Ezer,* which his son Nehemiah Feivel (1762–1831) published in Prague in 1808 with his own additions. Nehemiah published his own *Torat Neḥemyah* on the Talmud tractate *Bava Meẓia.* Elijah b. Selig Bondi (1777–1860) was a rabbi and preacher in Prague. Although he was strictly conservative, the influence of the *Haskalah is discernible in his sermons (*Sefer ha-She'arim* (1832) and *Tiferet ha-Adam* (1856), both published in Prague). He also published Solomon *Luria's *Yam shel Shelomo* on tractate *Gittin* (1812). Simeon b. Isaac Bondi (c. 1710–1775) moved to Dresden in 1745 and became *Court Jew of the elector of Saxony and head of the Dresden community. Samuel Bondy (1794–1877) was among the founders of the Orthodox congregation in Mainz; his son Jonah (1816–1896) was rabbi there. Members of the family went to the U.S. Among them were August *Bondi and Jonas *Bondi.

Bibliography: R. J. Aumann, *The Family Bondi* (1966; includes genealogies and bibliography); Jakobowits, in: MGWJ, 76 (1932), 511–9. [M.L.]

BONDI (Bondy), AUGUST (1833–1907), pioneer abolitionist, early Jewish settler in Kansas, and supporter of John Brown's military activities. Born in Vienna, Bondi was an adventurer for much of his life. He served in the Vienna Academic Legion at the age of fifteen, and, after the failure of the 1848 revolution, was taken to the U.S. by his parents. He tried to enlist in the Lopez-Crittenden expedition to Cuba and in the Perry mission to Japan in order to escape the monotony that he experienced as a store clerk, the usual experience of a young European Jewish immigrant at that

August Bondi, U.S. abolitionist.

time. With Jacob Benjamin, he established a trading post in Kansas and joined the John Brown abolitionist forces in 1855. His reminiscences and manuscript letters report in colorful detail on the Kansas border warfare and on his later service as a soldier in the Union Army during the Civil War. In both cases, he fought out of the conviction that slavery was a moral evil. In 1866 he settled in Salina, Kansas, where he established himself as an attorney and businessman, and took an active role in civic life. Bondi's reminiscences, published in Galesburg, Illinois, as *Autobiography of August Bondi* (1910), is a fascinating record of an unusual immigrant's life.

Bibliography: G. Kisch, *In Search of Freedom* (1949), index.

[B.W.K.]

BONDI, HERMANN (1919–), British mathematician. Bondi, who was born in Vienna, moved to England in 1937. His studies at Cambridge were disrupted by World War II, when he was interned and sent to Canada as an alien subject. He was allowed to return to England in 1941, and

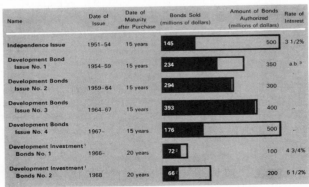

Hermann Bondi, British mathematician.

in the following year joined the Admiralty Signal Establishment to undertake secret research on radar. There he met the astronomer Fred Hoyle, and thus began his interest in cosmology. Bondi was appointed to the chair of applied mathematics at King's College, University of London, in 1954. He was granted leave of absence in 1967 to become director-general of the European Space Research Organization and in 1970 was appointed chief scientist to the Ministry of Defense. In 1959 he was elected a Fellow of the Royal Society. Bondi's writings include numerous papers on stellar constitution, interstellar medium, geophysics, cosmology, and general relativity. In collaboration with Thomas Gold he produced in 1948 the first paper describing the steady-state theory of the expanding universe, with its concomitant process of the continual creation of matter. His books include *Cosmology* (1960[2]) and *The Universe at Large* (1961). Bondi took a great interest in the role of mathematics in secondary school education and in the academic administration of science in the University of London. [B.S.]

BONDI, JONAS (1804–1874), editor, from 1860 until his death, of *The Hebrew Leader,* a Jewish periodical in New York City. Bondi was born in Dresden and educated in Prague. After a business career which ended in failure, he decided to emigrate to America, bringing with him his wife and four daughters. Nathan *Adler, who had been one of his teachers in Germany and who was at the time the chief rabbi of Great Britain, gave him a recommendation on the basis of his Jewish knowledge. This testimonial brought him to the notice of the officers of Anshe Chesed Congregation of New York City in June 1858, shortly after his arrival in the city. Bondi's help in solving some halakhic problems, related to the care of the congregational cemetery, resulted in his appointment as preacher of the congregation, but he served in that capacity for only a year. He then established his journal, which was published both in German and in English. His wife conducted a private school for girls. Bondi was a member of the conservative-historical school and a moderate in theology and practice, who believed that decorum, dignity, and intelligibility were essential if Jewish survival were to be assured, and who balked at the radical changes advocated by the Liberal and Reform leaders and editors. One of Bondi's daughters, Selma, became the second wife of R. Isaac Mayer *Wise two years after her father's death. The fine halakhic reference library which Bondi had assembled was given to the *Hebrew Union College in Cincinnati by I. M. Wise.

Bibliography: M. Davis, *Emergence of Conservative Judaism* (1963), 3321–3; H. Grinstein, *Rise of the Jewish Community of New York* (1945), index, s.v. *Bondy, Jonah;* G. Kisch, *In Search of Freedom* (1949), 89–90, 302–3.

[B.W.K.]

BONDS, STATE OF ISRAEL, Israel government stock floated in various countries for the purpose of raising capital for the economic development of Israel. The Israel Bond Organization was inaugurated in 1951 to enable the government of Israel to provide for the absorption of hundreds of thousands of immigrants who arrived after the proclamation of the state in 1948. From the year of its inception to June 1970, the organization sold a total of more than $1,500,000,000 in bonds, of which $700,000,000 have been redeemed. The proceeds have been used for the development of agriculture and industry; exploitation of natural resources; development of existing harbors at Haifa and Eilat and construction of the deepwater port of Ashdod; housing; electric power plants; and the establishment of new tourist facilities.

Plans for the Israel Bond Organization were formulated at a Jerusalem conference that was convened by Prime Minister David Ben-Gurion in September 1950. The conference, in which some 50 American Jewish leaders participated, agreed to undertake the launching of the first State of Israel Bond issue to be floated abroad. The object was to raise a public loan to relieve the pressure on the Israel government budget caused primarily by mass immigration and rapid development. Prime movers in Israel in the establishment of the new Bond Organization were also Finance Minister Eliezer Kaplan and Golda Meir, then minister of labor. In the U.S., support for the bonds idea was led by former secretary of the U.S. Treasury Henry *Morgenthau, Jr., Rudolf G. *Sonneborn (who became the first president of the new agency), Samuel *Rothberg, Julian Venezky, and Henry *Montor.

Name	Date of Issue	Date of Maturity after Purchase	Bonds Sold (millions of dollars)	Amount of Bonds Authorized (millions of dollars)	Rate of Interest
Independence Issue	1951–54	15 years	145	500	3 1/2%
Development Bond Issue No. 1	1954–59	15 years	234	350	a.b.[3]
Development Bonds Issue No. 2	1959–64	15 years	294	300	
Development Bonds Issue No. 3	1964–67	15 years	393	400	,,
Development Bonds Issue No. 4	1967–	15 years	176	500	,,
Development Investment[1] Bonds No. 1	1966–	20 years	72[2]	100	4 3/4%
Development Investment[1] Bonds No. 2	1968	20 years	66[2]	200	5 1/2%

1. Dollar coupons, Bonds issued to banks, Insurance companies, Labor unions and employee benefit funds.
2. Up to 1969.
3. a. $100–$10,000 (capital appreciation bonds) at 160%
   b. $500–$100,000 (coupon bonds) at 4% in semi-annual sums.

Specimen certificate of the first Israel Bond issue.

In May 1951 Ben-Gurion made a special trip to the United States, his first as prime minister, to inaugurate the Israel bond campaign. The Bond Organization expanded its activities into Canada in 1953, and to certain countries in Western Europe and elsewhere. In 1955 Abraham *Feinberg became president and Abba Hillel *Silver chairman of the Board of Governors, replacing Morgenthau. Joseph J. *Schwartz succeeded Henry *Montor as vice-president and chief executive officer in 1955. Upon Abba Hillel Silver's death in 1963, Louis H. *Boyar became chairman.

The first redemption of matured bonds took place on May 1, 1963. On January 1, 1969, the Israel Treasury paid the lump sum of $48,258,000 to retire all outstanding First Development Coupon Bonds falling due on that date. The total redemption payments until then aggregated $620,000,000. The first (Independence) issue paid 3½% interest per annum. All subsequent issues paid 4%, with the exception of a special issue offered only to banks and other institutions with an interest rate of 5½% per year. By 1970 there were more than two million people who had bought bonds in 35 different countries (though 85% had been sold in the U.S.A.). [M.F.St.]

BONDY, BOHUMIL (**Gottlieb**; 1832–1907), Czech politician, industrialist and author. In 1866 Bondy became head of his father's iron works in Prague, which he expanded considerably. He was elected president of the Prague Chamber of Commerce (1884); the first Jew to be elected to any function on a Czech nationalist ticket. In 1885 he became president of the Industrial Museum. He also was a member of the Bohemian Diet.

In 1906 he published *Zur Geschichte der Juden in Boehmen, Maehren und Schlesien,* a two-volume collection of documents dealing with the period 906–1620, edited by the director of the Bohemian Archives, František Dvorský, in a Czech and a German edition. A projected third volume did not appear. This collection of records is of particular importance, since about three-quarters of its contents were published for the first time. It is still a standard work for the student of Bohemian Jewish history.

Bibliography: Bondy-Dvorský, 1 (1906), 3–4 (preface); Teytz, in: *Česko-židovský kalendář* (1907), 80–81; S. H. Lieben, in: MGWJ, 50 (1906), 627–33; ZHB (1905), 17; *The Jews of Czechoslovakia,* 1 (1968), 4–5.

[O.K.R.]

BONDY, CURT (1894–), German psychologist, educator, and author. Bondy was born and studied in Hamburg. He started his professional career as a research assistant at the Institute of Education of the University of Goettingen and returned to the University of Hamburg in 1925 as an associate professor (full professor, 1930). He did research in social work with special emphasis on the problems of youth and adolescence, and juvenile delinquency. Bondy was compelled to leave Germany in 1933, when the Nazis came to power; he was involved in extensive refugee work in Europe and the U.S.A. until 1940, when he joined the psychology department at the College of William and Mary in Williamsburg, Virginia, becoming head of the department. In 1950 he returned to the University of Hamburg. Bondy wrote extensively for periodicals and professional journals and his major works include: *Die proletarische Jugendbewegung in Deutschland* (1922); *Paedagogische Probleme im Jungend-Strafvollzug* (1925); *Bedingungslose Jugend* (with K. Eyferth; 1952); *Social Psychology in Western Germany 1945–1955* (with K. Riegel; 1956); *Youth in Western Germany* (with O. Hilbig; 1957); and *Probleme der Jugendhilfe* (1957). [Er.S.]

BONDY, FILIP (1830–1907), rabbi in Czechoslovakia; the first to preach in the Czech language. A pupil of S. J. *Rapoport and Aaron *Kornfeld, he graduated from

Bohumil Bondy, Czech industrialist and politician. Portrait bust by Myslbek. Prague, State Jewish Museum.

Prague University and taught in České-Budějovice from 1857 to 1859. He officiated as rabbi in *Kasejovice from 1859 to 1868 and in *Brandýs nad Labem from 1868 to 1876. In 1886 he was appointed preacher at the Or Tamid Synagogue of the Czech-Jewish movement in Prague. His sermons *Hlas Jakubův* ("The Voice of Jacob"; 1886) and part of a Czech translation of Genesis, *Učení Mojžíšovo* ("Teachings of Moses"; 1902), were published.

Bibliography: Vyskočil, in: *Judaica Bohemiae*, 3 no. 1 (1967), 42 (Ger.); Fischer, in: *Kalendář česko-židovský*, 11 (1891/92), 59f.; *Věstnik židovske obcé náboženské*, 9 no. 24 (1947), 145.

[Ed.]

BONDY, MAX (1893–1951), U.S. educator. Bondy, who was born in Hamburg, Germany, was head of several schools in Germany and Switzerland before he emigrated to the United States in 1939. The following year he founded the Windsor School in Windsor, Vermont. This progressive, coeducational school was designed to implement Bondy's educational philosophy. The teaching was on a high level, with special emphasis on languages. The pupils were self-governing and had equal voting rights with the teachers on all important matters. They were also trained to take an active part in the activities of the community. In 1943 the school moved to Lennox, Massachusetts. After Bondy's death, it was directed by his widow. [Er.S.]

BÔNE (**Bona**, ancient **Hippo Regius** or **Hippone**), port of eastern Algeria. Apparently, a Jewish community existed there in the Roman period. In 1153 it was captured by Roger II of Sicily and its Jews were taken into captivity. In the 13th century the trading post established by the Pisan traders attracted the Jews from the surrounding area. Although no Spanish refugees arrived in Bône after 1492, rabbinical responsa from the 15th century onward testify to a strong community life. Use of the port was sometimes granted to citizens of Marseilles, but this practice encountered opposition from the British who were represented in Bône by a Jew, Bensamon (1796). After 1805 his enemy David Bacri obtained the port concession. In the mountains surrounding the city were many Jewish nomads, called **ba-huẓim* ("the outsiders"), and occasionally some nomad families settled in the town. In Bône the revered synagogue-sanctuary called "Ghriba" was visited by many pilgrims, both Jewish and Muslim. With the arrival of the French in 1831 the *ba-huẓim* returned to the mountains. The community was reestablished by Tunisian Jews, numbering 421 in 1839; the community grew to 3,150 in 1941, but they left in the exodus from Algeria in 1962 and by the mid-1960s there were no Jews remaining in Bône.

Bibliography: R. Brunschwig, *Berberie orientale sous les Hafṣides*, 1 (1940), 28, 398, 411; Hirschberg, Afrikah, 2 (1965), index.

[D.Co.]

BONFILS, IMMANUEL BEN JACOB (14th cent.), of Tarascon (in Provence, France), mathematician and astronomer. He is chiefly known for his astronomical tables called *Shesh-Kenafayim* ("Six Wings"—cf. Isa. 6:2) which were written in Hebrew about 1365 and which were subsequently translated into both Latin (in 1406) and Byzantine Greek (c. 1435). These tables are preserved in many manuscript copies and the Hebrew version was published (Zhitomir, 1872). The author is often referred to in Hebrew as *Ba'al ha-Kenafayim* ("Master of Wings"). Each "wing" contains a number of astronomical tables concerning the movements of the sun and the moon for determining the times and magnitudes of solar and lunar eclipses as well as the day of the new moon. The tables themselves are largely based on the tables of the ninth-century Arab astronomer al-Battānī (known in Latin as Albategnius), as the author acknowledges in the preface. But they are presented according to the Jewish calendar and adapted to the longitude and latitude of Tarascon. These tables were consulted by European scholars as late as the seventeenth century. Bonfils is also known to have made astronomical observations, and his discussion of decimal fractions is among the earliest presentations of the subject.

Bibliography: Renan, Ecrivains, 692–99; JE, 3 (1902), 306; M. Steinschneider, *Mathematik bei den Juden* (1964), 155ff.; *The Hexapterygon* [Six Wings] *of Michael Chrysokokhes*, ed. and tr. by P.C. Solon (unpublished thesis, Brown University, 1968); Gandz, in: *Isis*, 25 (1936), 16–45; Saidan, *ibid.*, 57 (1966), 475–89; *Petri Gassendi Opera Omnia*, 5 (1964), 313.

[B.R.G.]

BONFILS (Tov Elem), JOSEPH BEN ELIEZER (second half of the 14th century), author of a supercommentary on the biblical commentary of Abraham *ibn Ezra. Joseph was born in Spain and journeyed to the East. In Damascus, in 1370, at the request of the *nagid* David b. Joshua he wrote a supercommentary, *Ẓafenat Pa'ne'aḥ*, on Ibn Ezra's commentary on the Pentateuch—the most exhaustive and precise of the many supercommentaries on Ibn Ezra. In a clear and comprehensive exposition he solves Ibn Ezra's "enigmas" and defends him against the suspicion of heresy which certain of his critical views (with which Joseph manifestly sympathizes) had aroused against him. The supercommentary was published, but with the omission of the passages dealing with the critical views, under the title *Ohel Yosef*, in *Margalit Tovah* (1722), an anthology of supercommentaries on Ibn Ezra, and later in a critical edition by D. Herzog (1912–1930). From Damascus, Joseph went to settle in Jerusalem.

Bibliography: M.Z. Segal, in: KS, 9 (1932/33), 302–4, no. 1025; Krauss, in: *Sinai*, 5 (Bucharest, 1933); N. Ben-Menahem, in: *Sinai*, 9 (1941), 353–5.

[Ed.]

BONFILS (Tov Elem), JOSEPH BEN SAMUEL (11th century), the first French scholar about whom more than his name is known; called by Rashi's disciples "R. Joseph the Great." A contemporary and colleague of R. Elijah the Elder of Le Mans, he was born in Narbonne, but lived at Limoges and at Anjou. Bonfils was among the early few who shaped the Jewish way of life and halakhic tradition in France and Germany; his principal decisions are frequently quoted by later rabbinic authorities. His positive attitude toward the recitation of *piyyutim* in the prayers (*Shibbolei ha-Leket*, Prayers, 28) and his decisions with regard to taxation exerted particularly great influence, the latter serving as a basis for the later *takkanot* ("regulations") of the Jewish communities in France and Germany. Bonfils copied in his own hand and for his own personal use, some of the more important books of his predecessors, and the later *rishonim* relied heavily on these copies in order to establish correct versions of these texts. Among these books are: *Halakhot Gedolot* (cf. *Semag*, Lavin, 60 end; Tos. to Naz. 59a); *Seder Tanna'im ve-Amora'im* (Tos. to Naz. 57b); *Seder Tikkun Shetarot* (Tos. to Git. 85b); *Hilkhot Terefot* by *Gershom b. Judah and *Teshuvot ha-Ge'onim* (Tos. to Ḥul. 46–47; Tos. to Pes. 30a); as well as works on Hebrew grammar, liturgy and masorah. There is no basis for S.J. *Rapoport's assumption that the collection of geonic responsa published by D. Cassel (*Teshuvot Ge'onim Kadmonim*, Berlin, 1848) is the one copied by Bonfils. Bonfils belongs to the classical French school of *paytanim* and his *piyyutim* are composed in the difficult language adopted by the writers of this genre, all being based on midrashic material, interspersed with numerous *halakhot* concerning the day on which the *piyyutim* are to be recited. Early authorities quoted from his *piyyutim* in order to arrive at halakhic decisions (Tos. to Pes. 115b; *Or Zaru'a* 2:256; Raban, 532). Some of Bonfils' *piyyutim* are to be found in the *maḥzor* according to the French rite, but for the most part they have been superseded by later compositions easier to follow. Of his commentary on the Pentateuch, mentioned by Isaac de Lattes, not even one quotation has been preserved.

Bibliography: D. Kassel (ed.), *Teshuvot Ge'onim Kadmonim* (1848), introd. by S. J. L. Rapoport; Gross, Gal Jud, 308; Davidson, Oẓar, 4 (1933), 404, s.v. *Yosef Tov Elem (ben Shemu'el).*

[I.T.-S.]

°**BONFRÈRE, JAQUES** (1573–1642), Belgian Jesuit, professor of Hebrew and Bible exegesis. Bonfrère wrote a commentary on the Pentateuch (*Pentateuchus Moysis commentario illustratus . . .*, Antwerp, 1625), which has been reedited several times. The book has a strong mystical kabbalistic tendency. He also wrote a commentary on Joshua, Judges, and Ruth (Paris, 1631).

Bibliography: C. Sommervogel et al., *Bibliothèque de la Compagnie de Jésus*, 1 (1890), 1713–15; F. Secret, *Les Kabbalistes chrétiens de la Renaissance* (1964), 232.

[Fr.S.]

°**BONIFACE,** name of nine popes. Only the last two showed significant evidence of concern with the Jews of Europe.

Boniface VIII, 1294–1303, in his Jewish policy displayed an attitude substantially like that of his 13th-century predecessors. In 1295 he commended a citizen of Paris for having established a chapel on the spot where a miracle was said to have occurred when some Jews were supposed to have tortured a consecrated wafer (see Desecration of the *Host). The same year the pope objected to the erection of a new synagogue in Trier, Germany. In 1297 he praised the queen of Sicily for having expropriated the property of Jewish usurers and urged her to use the money for the benefit of the poor. In 1300 he himself ordered the expulsion of Jewish and Christian usurers from *Avignon. But outweighing the above was his favorable response in 1299 to the complaints of the Jews of Rome and Avignon against inquisitors who accused them of illegal acts and then compelled them to answer the charges in some distant court. Claiming that Jews were in the category of those powerful enough to overawe witnesses, inquisitors refused to divulge the names of those who accused Jews of encouraging heresy. Jews, the pope maintained, were not necessarily powerful. One of his decisions became part of Canon Law, namely that Jews, even minors, once baptized must remain Christians.

Boniface IX, 1389–1404, showed exceptional favor to the Jews of Rome. The city had become impoverished because of the absence of the Papal Court for the greater part of the 14th century; subsequently it was further afflicted by a succession of plagues, during which Jewish physicians had shown great skill in serving the sick of all classes. The pope continued and even amplified the favors shown these physicians by his predecessor, Urban VI, especially to Manuel and his son Angelo. He included them among his *familiares* (members of his household), reduced their taxes, and freed them from the obligation of wearing the Jewish *badge. Several other physicians were likewise favored, and the Jews of Rome in general profited from this attitude. The papal chamberlain, acting on behalf of the pope, eased the regulations on the badge, alleviated the tax burden, and even spoke of the Jews as "citizens." The pope could not show an equally friendly attitude to Jews outside the papal territory, since this was the period of the Great Schism in the church and various states wavered in their obedience to the pope in Rome.

Bibliography: M. Stern, *Urkundliche Beitraege ueber die Stellung der Paepste zu den Juden*, 2 vols. (1893–95), passim; Vogelstein-Rieger, 1 (1896), 255–8, 317–9; E. Rodocanachi, *Le Saint-Siège et les Juifs* (1891), passim.

[S.G.]

BONJORN, BONET DAVI(D), called **De Barrio** (14th century), Spanish physician and astronomer. He lived in Perpignan, where he also engaged occasionally in moneylending activities. Here he manufactured astronomical instruments for Pedro IV of Aragon. His wife exerted pressure on him to divorce her by withholding his astronomical instruments. His son, the famous astronomer Jacob Bonet or Jacob Poel drew up astronomical tables for the year 1361 for the latitude of this city. Jacob's son Davi(d) Bonet Bonjorn was authorized to practice medicine at Perpignan in 1390 after examination by two Christian physicians. His baptism in 1391 is said to have occasioned the famous satiric pamphlet *Al Tehi ka-Avotekha* ("Be Not as Your Fathers") by his friend Profiat *Duran.

Bibliography: E. C. Girbal, *Los Judíos en Gerona* (1870); Renan, Ecrivains, 701, 742, 746; Baer, Urkunden, 1 (1929), 259; Baer, Spain, 2 (1965), index; S. Sorbrequés Vidal, *Anales de Estudios Gerundenses* (1947), 1–31; Millás Vallicrosa, in: *Sefarad*, 19 (1959), 365–71; F. Cantera Burgos, *Alvar García de Santa María* (1952), 318f.; Thorndike, in: *Isis*, 34 (1943), 6–7, 410.

[C.R.]

BONN (in medieval Hebrew literature בונא), capital of the German Federal Republic. During the First Crusade in 1096 the Jews in Bonn were martyred. A Jewish community again existed there in the 12th century which, following a murder accusation, had to pay the emperor and the bishop a fine of 400 marks. A *Platea Judaeorum* is recorded in Bonn before 1244. The Jews engaged in moneylending and many became wealthy. In an outbreak of violence on June 8, 1288, 104 Jews were killed. During the *Black Death (1348–49) the community was attacked and annihilated; the archbishop took over its property and pardoned the burghers for the crimes they had committed. Subsequently there is no record of Jewish residence in Bonn until 1381. During 1421/22, there were 11 Jewish families who paid the archbishop of *Cologne an annual tax of 82 gulden. The Jews were expelled in the 15th century, but later returned. In 1578 the Jewish quarter was looted and many Jews were taken captive by a Protestant army besieging Bonn; they were later ransomed. During the 17th century the Jews in Bonn, who lived under the protection of the elector, mainly engaged in cattle-dealing and moneylending. They were attacked in 1665 by students from nearby *Deutz. The Jewish street was destroyed during a siege in 1689, but a

Figure 1. The Bonn synagogue, built in 1878 and destroyed by the Nazis in 1938. Lithograph by Blumberg. Bonn, Municipal Tourist Office. Photo Sachsse.

Figure 2. Plaque marking the site of the Bonn synagogue destroyed by the Nazis. Photo Theo Schafgans.

new Jewish quarter with 17 houses and a synagogue was built in 1715. It was closed at night by guarded gates. Several *Court Jews resided in Bonn; some of them lived outside the Jewish quarter, including the celebrated physician Moses Wolff, the musician Solomon, and the court agent Simon Baruch (the grandfather of Ludwig *Boerne). The Jews in Bonn suffered from a number of anti-Jewish regulations. The Jewish quarter was severely damaged by a flood in 1784.

During the occupation of Bonn by the French revolutionary army (1794), the Jews were declared citizens with equal rights, and the gate of the ghetto was publicly torn down. Two delegates from the Bonn community attended the *Assembly of Jewish Notables convened by *Napoleon in Paris in 1806. A Jewish elementary school with an attendance of 22 boys and 15 girls was opened in 1829; a society for the promotion of Jewish craftsmen was founded in 1840; and there existed several social institutions and associations. The 18th-century synagogue was replaced by a new one in 1878, which followed the *Reform rite. The community numbered 296 in 1796; 536 in 1871; and 1,228 in 1919. From its earliest days the community in Bonn was celebrated as a center of Jewish learning. Among the tosafists who lived there during the 12th century were *Joel b. Isaac ha-Levi (Ravyah), *Samuel b. Natronai, and *Ephraim b. Jacob. Toward the end of the 16th century the rabbi of Bonn was Ḥayyim b. Johanan Treves, a commentator of the *maḥzor*. Ludwig *Philippson and Moses *Hess lived in Bonn, and in 1879 there were five Jewish professors and lecturers at Bonn University.

Figure 3. The new Bonn synagogue, built in 1959. Bonn, Municipal Tourist Office.

During the Nazi era 700 Jews emigrated from Bonn. In 1938 the synagogues were destroyed in the course of the **Kristallnacht*. On Sept. 17, 1939, 512 Jews and 282 persons of mixed parentage remained in Bonn. These were forced out of their homes and into a monastery by August 1941, where they were joined by families evicted from Duisburg, Beuel, and other communities. During June and July 1942 about 400 inhabitants of the monastery were deported; only seven survived. After the war a new community was formed and numbered 155 in 1967, mainly elderly persons. A new synagogue was opened in 1959. Bonn is the seat of the Israel embassy and other official missions to the German Federal Republic.

Bibliography: E. Simons, *Geschichte der juedischen Gemeinden im Bonner Raum* (1959); J. Buecher, *Zur Geschichte der juedischen Gemeinde in Beuel* (1965); Germ Jud, 1 (1963), 46–60; 2 (1968), 93–95; Wiener Library, London, *German Jewry* (1958), 42f.; A. Levy, *Aus Bonner Archiven* (1929), 32; H. Schnee, *Die Hoffinanz und der moderne Staat*, 4 (1963), 267ff.; 6 (1967), 172–90; Neugebauer, in: *Bonner Geschichtsblaetter*, 18 (1964), 158–227; 19 (1965), 196–206; M. Braubach, in: *Rheinische Vierteljahrsblaetter*, 32 (1968), 402–18.

[Z.F.]

BONN, MORITZ JULIUS (1873–1965), German economist. Bonn was descended from a family of bankers whose names appear in the records of Frankfort as early as 1556. After studying economics at Heidelberg, Munich, and Vienna, he went to the London School of Economics, where he specialized in economic-historical studies on England. He did research in this field in Ireland where Horace Plunkett became his mentor. On the basis of these studies, he wrote *Die englische Kolonisation in Irland* (1906). In 1910 he became rector of the College of Commerce in Munich. From 1914 he taught in the United States, and was politically active on behalf of Germany. In 1917, just before America entered World War I, he returned home. In 1921 he was appointed professor at the Berlin College of Commerce, and became its rector in 1931. He was a member of the German delegation to the Versailles peace negotiations, and subsequently adviser to the German chancellor on reparation problems. Bonn criticized the German political situation, which eventually led to the rise of Hitler. He left Germany for Austria soon after Hitler came to power and then went to England where he taught at Oxford, but spent much of his time in the United States teaching, lecturing, and writing. He died in England and, at his request, his remains were taken for burial to Kronberg, near Frankfort. His writings include: *German War Finance* (1916), *Stabilization of the Mark* (1922), *Der neue Plan als Grundlage der deutschen Wirtschaftspolitik* (1930), *Das Schicksal des deutschen Kapitalismus* (1926) and his autobiography, *Wandering Scholar* (1948).

[J.O.R.]

BONNÉ, ALFRED ABRAHAM (1899–1959), Israel economist. Bonné, who was born in Nuremberg, Germany, and studied in Munich, settled in Palestine in 1925. From 1931 to 1936 he directed the Economic Archives for the Near East in Jerusalem. In 1943 he was appointed director of the Economic Research Institute of the Jewish Agency and a year later became professor of economics at the Hebrew University. Bonné was the first controller of foreign exchange of the State of Israel, and from 1955 until his death was dean of the Hebrew University's School of Economics and Social Sciences. Best known among his numerous publications are his studies on the economy of Palestine and Israel; social and economic development in the Middle East; and theoretical and empirical issues of growth in developing areas. Against the background of Jewish experience in Palestine, Bonné developed a theory of implanted development in underdeveloped countries, with particular tasks assigned to government undertakings carried out with the aid of foreign investment. His major publications include: *Palaestina; Land und Wirtschaft* (1932); *Der neue Orient* (1937); *State and Economics in the Middle East; a Society in Transition* (1948); and *Studies in Economic Development* (1957).

Alfred Bonné, Israel economist.

Bibliography: *A Selected Bibliography of Books and Papers of the Late Prof. A. Bonné* (1960). [Z.Y.H.]

BONSENYOR, JUDAH (or **Jafuda;** d. 1331), physician and Arabic interpreter for the Aragonese court. Judah's father, Astruc b. Judah Bonsenyor (d. 1280), had previously served in the same capacity, originally as assistant to Bahye Alconstantini. Judah accompanied Alfonso III as Arabic interpreter during the expedition against Minorca in 1287. In 1294 James II appointed him general secretary for Arabic documents and deeds drawn up in Barcelona. He was commissioned by James II to compile an anthology of maxims from Latin, Arabic, and Hebrew sources and translate them into Catalan—the *Llibre de paraules e dits de savis e filosofs.* Judah also translated a medical treatise from the Arabic.

Bibliography: J. Bonsenyor, *Llibre de paraules e dits de savis e filosofs,* ed. by G. Llabrés y Quintana (1889), pref., 123–32 (documents); M. Kayserling, in: JQR, 8 (1895/96), 632–42; Cardoner Planas, in: *Sefarad,* 4 (1944), 287–93; Baer, Spain, 2 (1966), 6, 460 n.9 (bibliography). [Ed.]

BONYHAD (Hung. **Bonyhád**), town in S. Hungary. The national census of 1746 listed 13 Jewish heads of families with 30 dependents resident there. In 1794 the area where the Jews were living, with the synagogue and communal buildings, was destroyed in a fire. To commemorate the disaster the rabbi of Bonyhad, Abraham Leib (Freistadt), composed an elegy which was recited annually on the first Sabbath after Passover. The impressive synagogue erected subsequently was reputedly built entirely by voluntary Jewish labor. A *bet ha-midrash* was established in Bonyhad in 1802, and a yeshivah shortly afterward. By this time the Jewish population numbered 400 families, mainly occupied in trade, crafts, and peddling. The introduction of Reform into the synagogue in 1868 caused a rift in the community, and a separate Orthodox congregation was formed. The mother community joined the *status quo ante* party (see *Hungary). In 1929 this congregation had 115 members, and the Orthodox congregation 90. The Jewish population in Bonyhad numbered 1,022 in 1930 (14.9% of the total) and 1,159 in 1941.

Rabbis of Bonyhad include Isaac Seckel Spitz of Nikolsburg (d. 1768), author of *Be'ur Yiẓhak* (Pressburg, 1790), a commentary on the *Haggadah;* Israel b. Judah Aryeh Bisenc (d. 1781); Benjamin Ze'ev b. Samuel *Boskowitz; Ẓevi Hirsch *Heller; Isaac Moses *Perles, who, after a long struggle with the pro-Reformists, had to leave Bonyhad; Moses *Pollak (1846–1889), whose yeshivah became famous; Judah Gruenwald (d. 1920), author of *Zikhron Yehudah* (1923); and Eliezer Ḥayyim *Deutsch. The last rabbi in Bonyhad before the destruction of the community in the Holocaust was Aron Pressburger, a saintly scholar who perished in Auschwitz.

With the German occupation, 1,180 people were transferred to the ghetto on May 12, 1944; a week later the occupants of the ghettos in Szekszard and Bataszek were also transferred to Bonyhad. On July 1 the Jews in Bonyhad were deported to Pęcs, and thence on July 6 to Auschwitz. Of these, 1,130 perished. After the war 170 returned, mainly survivors from the forced labor camps. Four Jewish families were living in Bonyhad in 1963; two synagogues have been preserved, but only one small prayer room is in use.

Bibliography: MHJ, 8 (1963), 35 (introd. by A. Scheiber), 802; J. J. Greenwald, *Ha-Yehudim be-Ungarya* (1917); J. Eisner, *A bonyhádi zsidók története* (1965). [A.Schi.]

BOOK OF THE COVENANT (Heb. סֵפֶר הַבְּרִית, *Sefer ha-Berit*), name derived from Exodus 24:7 ("And he took the book of the covenant, and read it aloud to the people . . .") and usually taken to refer to the legal, moral, and cultic corpus of literature found in Exodus 20:22–23:33. This literary complex can be divided into four major units: Exodus 20:22–26, cultic ordinances; 21:1–22:16, legal prescriptions; 22:17–23:19, religious, moral, and cultic instructions; and 23:20–33, epilogue or concluding section. The Book of the Covenant begins (20:22–26) and concludes (23:10–19)—immediately preceding the epilogue—with instructions pertaining to correct ritual procedure. A cultic frame to a juridical corpus is also characteristic of two other biblical corpora, the so-called *Holiness Code of Leviticus (17:1ff. and 26:1–2), and the laws of *Deuteronomy (12:1ff. and 26). The legal corpus proper, Exodus 21:2–22:16, immediately follows the initial cultic prescriptions and contains civil and criminal legislation on the following topics:

I	21: 2– 6	Hebrew Slave
	7–11	Bondwoman
	12–17	Capital Offenses
	18–27	Bodily Injuries (including the laws of talion)
II	21:28–32	Goring Ox
III	21:33–36	Pit and Ox
IV	21:37–22: 3	Theft and Burglary
IV	22: 4– 5	Grazing and Burning
	6–14	Deposits and Bailees
	15–16	Seduction of an Unbetrothed Girl

In sections I and II human beings are the objects; in III and IV property is the object. Most of the individual laws are interrelated, moreover, by means of association and concatenation of similar ideas, motifs, and key words.

Similarity to Cuneiform Laws. In both form and content many of these laws are indebted directly or indirectly to laws found in earlier cuneiform collections, i.e., Laws of Ur-Nammu (LU) and Lipit-Ishtar (LI), written in Sumerian; Laws of Eshnunna (LE) and Laws of Hammurapi (LH), written in Akkadian; Middle Assyrian Laws (MAL); and Hittite Laws (HL). (See *Mesopotamia, Cuneiform Law.) The laws are formulated in the traditional casuistic style. The casuistic formulation of law, which predominates throughout all of the above-mentioned extra-biblical corpora, consists of a protasis, containing the statement of the case, and an apodosis, setting forth the solution, i.e., penalty. The protasis of the main clause is introduced by Hebrew *ki,* and of subordinate or secondary clauses by Hebrew *'im* or *'o* (here meaning "if"). The only exceptions to the casuistic formulation in this section are the prescriptions found in Exodus 21:12, 15, 16, 17, all of which begin (in Hebrew) with a participle.

In content too, this earliest collection of biblical law remains to a great extent within the legal orbit of its cuneiform predecessors. Several possible extra-biblical substrata are still contextually and linguistically identifiable. The formulaic terminology and legal provisions of the law pertaining to the Hebrew slave (Ex. 21:2–6) may be compared to documents from *Nuzi pertaining to the *Habiru. The threefold basic maintenance requirement for a woman (Ex. 21:10) has analogues in LI 27–28 and in legal documents from Ur III down to neo-Babylonian times. The equal division of all assets and liabilities between two owners when one ox gores another to death (Ex. 21:35–36) is identical to LE 53. The laws of talion (punishment in kind; Ex. 21:23–25) are first legislated in LH 196, 197, 200. The Bible, however, does not incorporate vicarious talion (but see Cassuto, *Exodus*, p. 277) as is the practice in LH 116, 210, 230, but does insist, on the other hand, on talion in cases of homicide (Ex. 21:23; according to LH 207, composition is acceptable). The laws of assault and battery (Ex. 21:18–19) are analogous to HL 10 in many respects. The laws pertaining to the seduction of an unbetrothed girl (Ex. 22:15–16) contain several features similar to MAL A 56. The case of an injury to a pregnant woman which results in a miscarriage, or in her own death (Ex. 21:22–23), is dealt with in LH 209–214, MAL A 21, 50–52, HL 17–18, and in earlier Sumerian collections. Another example of a common legal tradition that the biblical corpus shares with its Mesopotamian cogeners is the law of the goring ox (Ex. 21:28–32), in which there are several common features: an official warning, a lack of precaution in spite of the warning, the fatal accident, and the punishment.

Distinguishing Features. Though the legal corpus of the Book of the Covenant emerges as an integral component of ancient Near Eastern law, there are still striking differences to be observed which are due not only to the different composition of the societies, but also to the relative set of values within each society. Though slavery is still a recognized institution within the Bible, the laws in the Book of the Covenant are concerned with the protection of the slave and the preservation of his human dignity: his status is temporary (21:2), his physical being must be guarded against abuse, and he is considered a human being in his own right and not merely his owner's chattel (21:20, 26, 27). In several of the laws the females are put on an equal rank with their male counterparts (a mother, 21:15, 17; a daughter, 21:31; a woman, 21:28, 29; and a female slave, 21:20, 26, 27, 32).

The laws of the goring ox best demonstrate the difference between cuneiform law and the Book of the Covenant, for the biblical version (Ex. 21:28–32) is the only one that preserves an inherent religious evaluation. The sole concern of the corresponding cuneiform laws, LE 54–55 and LH 250–252, is economic; hence, the victim's family is compensated for its loss. The laws are not concerned with the liability of the ox. Only according to biblical law is the ox stoned, its flesh not to be eaten, and the execution of is owner demanded. The stoning of the ox and its taboo status are related in turn to the religious presupposition of bloodguilt (Gen. 9:5–6). A beast that kills a human being destroys the image of God, is held accountable for being objectively guilty of a criminal action, and hence is executed. Furthermore, biblical legislation repudiates the concept of paying an indemnification to the family of the slain man. However, since this is a case of criminal negligence in which the ox alone is guilty of the killing, the owner may redeem his own life, if the slain person's family permits it, by paying a ransom (Ex. 21:30); in this case alone is a ransom acceptable; in other instances of homicide it is strictly forbidden (Num. 35:31). Here, as well as in the other biblical corpora, the sacredness of human life is paramount. Hence, there is an absolute ban on composition (Ex. 21:22), for according to biblical law, life and property are incommensurable. Exodus 21:31 adds another new element to the law by prohibiting the practice of vicarious talionic punishment (contrast LH 116, 210, 230). The religious underpinning of this law reflects the unique feature of biblical law in general. Whereas in Mesopotamia the king is the sole legislator and the law completely secular, in Israel law has a divine authorship. It is the expression of the will of God, who is the sole source and sanction of law, and all of life is ultimately bound up with this will. This explains why in the Book of the Covenant and in other biblical corpora, but not in cuneiform corpora, there is a blending of strictly legal with moral, ethical, and cultic ordinances (Ex. 22:17–23:19).

The next section, Exodus 22:17–23:19, may be subdivided as follows:

22:17–19	Laws Against Idolatrous Customs
20–26	Love and Fellowship Toward the Poor and Needy
27	Reverence Toward God and the Leader of the Community
28–30	Ritual Prescriptions
23: 1– 9	Justice Toward All Men
10–19	Cultic Calendar

This complex is distinguished by the use of the apodictic legal formulation. This formulation is stated as a direct address consisting of a command, whose validity is unlimited, and which obliges one to do, or refrain from doing, a certain action. Though it is present in and outside the Bible in other literary genres, it is unique to biblical juridical corpora, where moral-ethical admonitions and religious-cultic obligations are part and parcel of a comprehensive legal system. Another feature of this section is the presence of motive clauses of an explanatory, ethical, religious, or historical nature. For law in Israel also constitutes a body of teaching, which is set forth publicly and prospectively to the entire community (Ex. 21:1).

The final section, the epilogue, Exodus 23:20–33, consists of two different paragraphs, verses 20–25 and verses 26–33. It contains the promise of God's presence and protection of Israel in the forthcoming conquest of Canaan as long as they remain faithful to His laws. Since several extra-biblical legal corpora (LU, LI, LH) that conclude with epilogues also commence with prologues, the question has been raised whether a prologue can be found in the Book of the Covenant. It has been suggested that in light of the final redaction of the Book of Exodus, chapter 19:3–6 actually serves the function of a prologue by setting forth the prime purpose of biblical legislation, that of sanctification. Thus, Exodus 19:3–6 and Exodus 23:20–33 would form a literary frame that encases the new constitution of Israel and binds the history and destiny of Israel to the discipline of law.

Date. Various dates have been suggested for the compilation of the Book of the Covenant ranging from the period of Moses to prophetic times. Several salient features of this corpus support those who date it very early: archaic vocabulary; predominantly casuistic formulation of the legal section; a societal framework of a non-monarchic tribal polity whose nuclear unit is the family; a pastoral-agricultural (non-urban) society in the process of becoming sedentary; the absence of commercial laws, class distinctions, and professions; the absence of any outside central organization or courts; the fact that laws punishing secular offenses are addressed to the injured party or to the next of kin; the recognition of self-help; and the absence of any reference to Israel or to a king but only to a *nasi*, "tribal chieftain." These characteristics indicate that the collection of laws in the Book of the Covenant is very early, dating from the pre-monarchial period.

Bibliography: M. Greenberg, in: *Sefer Yovel Y. Kaufmann* (1960), 5–28; H. Cazelles, *Etudes sur le Code de l'Alliance* (1946); U. Cassuto, *A Commentary on the Book of Exodus* (1967); M. Haran, in: EM, 5 (1968), 1087–91 (incl. bibl.); S. M. Paul, *Studies in the Book of the Covenant in the Light of Cuneiform and Biblical Law* (1970); O. Eissfeldt, *The Old Testament, an Introduction* (1965), 212–9 (incl. bibl.).

[Sh.M.P.]

BOOK OF JASHAR (Heb. סֵפֶר הַיָּשָׁר, *Sefer ha-Yashar;* "the upright [one]'s book"), one of the lost source books of early Israelite poetry from which the writers in the books of Joshua and Samuel excerpted Joshua's command to the sun and the moon in Joshua 10:12b–13a and David's lament for Saul and Jonathan in II Samuel 1:19–27, as indicated by the accompanying citations. The command to the sun and moon is an archaic poetic unit embedded in the later prose narrative of the victory against a five-king coalition and in defense of Gibeon, a covenant ally. The narrative provides a prosaic interpretation of the couplet, in keeping with the book's presentation of the conquest as a divine miracle and not Israel's victory. In itself the couplet reflects the early Israelite understanding of the Federation's wars as sacral events, with God as commander in chief directing tactics through the agency of heavenly powers who are conceived as members of the divine Sovereign's court (cf. how the stars "fought against Sisera" in Judg. 5:20). The lament for Saul and Jonathan is unquestionably a genuine literary attestation of David's poetic talent and it helps to explain the later attribution of many biblical psalms to David. Probably a third excerpt from the Book of Jashar is found in I Kings 8:12–13, a couplet embedded in Solomon's prayer at the dedication of the Temple, which survives in fullest form in the septuagint version. In the latter, the couplet appears at the end of the prayer and is followed by a notation in verbatim agreement with the one of Joshua 10:13, directing the reader to the book of *Shir* ("Song"). It has been suggested that the latter may stem from an accidental metathesis of letters (*šyr* for *yšr*), which is not uncommon among copyists' errors. See *Book of the Wars of the Lord for another and possibly related anthology, tenth century and earlier, to which historians of Israel and Judah turned for such poetic excerpts. The Talmud (Av. Zar. 25a) homiletically identifies the Book of Jashar with the "book of Abraham, Isaac, and Jacob" (i.e., Genesis), who were "upright." A quasi-historical work of the 13th century bears the same title (see **Sefer ha-Yashar*).

Bibliography: Thackeray, in: JTS (1910), 518–32. [R.G.B.]

BOOK OF LIFE, or perhaps more correctly **BOOK OF THE LIVING** (Heb. סֵפֶר חַיִּים, *Sefer Ḥayyim*), a heavenly book in which the names of the righteous are inscribed. The expression "Book of Life" appears only once in the Bible, in Psalms 69:29 (28), "Let them be blotted out of the book of the living; let them not be enrolled among the righteous," but a close parallel is found in Isaiah 4:3, which speaks of a list of those destined (literally "written") for life in Jerusalem. The erasure of a sinner's name from such a register is equivalent to death (cf. Ps. 69:29, and the plea of Moses, Ex. 32:32–33).

The belief in the existence of heavenly ledgers is alluded to several times in the Bible (Isa. 65:6; Jer. 17:13; 22:30; Mal. 3:16; Ps. 40:8; 87:6; 139:16; Job 13:26; Dan. 7:10; 12:1; Neh. 13:14(?)—the exact meaning of some of these texts, along with I Samuel 25:29, however, is still in doubt), the Apocrypha and Pseudepigrapha (e.g., Jub. 30:19–23; I En. 47:3; 81:1ff.; 97:6; 98:7ff.; 103:2; 104:7; 108:3, 7; I Bar. 24:1), and the New Testament (e.g., Luke 10:20; Phil. 4:3; Heb. 12:23). This belief can be traced to Mesopotamia, where the gods were believed to possess tablets recording the deeds and destiny of men. Examples are the prayer of Ashurbanipal to Nabû, the divine scribe, "My life is inscribed before thee," and of Shamash-Shumukîn, "May [Nabû] inscribe the days of his life for long duration on a tablet." The exact equivalent of the Hebrew *Sefer Ḥayyim* is found in a tablet from the neo-Assyrian period and may also be present in a Sumerian hymn. [Sh.M.P.]

In the Mishnah (Avot 3:17), R. Akiva speaks in detailed terms of the heavenly ledger in which all man's actions are written down until the inevitable day of reckoning comes. On the basis of the above-mentioned reference to the Book of Life in Psalms, however, or, according to another *amora*, of the plea of Moses, the Talmud states "three books are opened in heaven on Rosh Ha-Shanah, one for the thoroughly wicked, one for the thoroughly righteous, and one for the intermediate. The thoroughly righteous are forthwith inscribed in the Book of Life, the thoroughly wicked in the Book of Death, while the fate of the intermediate is suspended until the Day of Atonement" (RH 16b).

This passage has greatly influenced the whole conception of the High Holidays and finds its expression in the liturgy and *piyyutim* of those days. Of the four special insertions in the **Amidah* for the *Ten Days of Penitence, three of them are prayers for "Inscription in the Book of Life" and it is the basis of the moving prayer *U-Netanneh Tokef.* [L.I.R.]

Bibliography: Schrader, Keilinschr, 2 (1903[3]), 400–6, E. Behrens (ed.), *Assyrisch-Babylonische Briefe kultischen Inhalts aus der Sargonidenzeit* (1906), 43; A. Jeremias, *Babylonisches im Neuen Testament* (1905), 69–73; T. H. Gaster, *Thespis* (1961[2]), 288–9; R. F. Harper, *Assyrian and Babylonian Letters,* 6 (1902), let. 545, lines 9–10 (Eng. trans. in L. Waterman, *Royal Correspondence of the Assyrian Empire,* 1 (1930), 386–7); O. Eissfeldt, *Der Beutel der Lebendigen* (1960); N. H. Tur-Sinai, *Peshuto shel Mikra,* 2 (1965), 180.

BOOK OF THE WARS OF THE LORD (Heb. סֵפֶר מִלְחֲמֹת יהוה, *Sefer Milḥamot YHWH*), book, mentioned only once in the Bible (Num. 21:14), which apparently contained an anthology of poems describing the victories of the Lord over the enemies of Israel. The only extant piece contains a fragmented geographical note which is very obscure. According to a tradition preserved in the Septuagint and in the Aramaic Targums the words "The Wars of the Lord" are the beginning of the poetic quotation and are not part of the name of "the Book." The book referred to then would be the Torah. However, according to the Vulgate and medieval and modern exegetes, this is the complete title of a book which, like several other literary works, has not been preserved.

The extent of the actual quotation from this book is debated. Some think it comprises only verse 14 itself, others include verse 15 (JPS), while still others go so far as to include verses 17–20 ("The Song of the Well") and the poem in verses 27–30. The existence of such a book indicates that early written as well as oral traditions have been incorporated within the Pentateuchal documents. The date of the work is variously assigned to the periods of the desert (Kaufmann), Joshua, or David (Mowinckel).

Bibliography: Mowinckel, in: ZAW, 53 (1935), 130–52; Kaufmann Y., Toledot, 4 (1957), 33, 72; N. H. Tur-Sinai, *Peshuto shel Mikra,* 1 (1962), 167–9. [SH.M.P.]

BOOKPLATES, labels, usually inside book covers, indicating the owner of the books. The earliest *ex libris* with Hebrew wording were made for non-Jews. One of the first bookplates was made by Albrecht Duerer for Willibald Pirkheimer (c. 1504) with an inscription in Hebrew, Greek, and Latin of Psalms 111:10. Hector Pomer of Nuremberg had a woodcut *ex libris* (1525) that is attributed to Duerer or his disciple, Hans Sebald Beham, with the Hebrew translation of "Unto the pure all things are pure" (NT, Titus 1:15). "A time for everything" (Eccles. 3:1) in Hebrew is found on the bookplate (1530) by Barthel Beham, of Hieronymus Baumgartner of Nuremberg.

Among the Jewish artists in England who engraved bookplates in the 18th century were Benjamin Levi of Portsmouth, Isaac Levi of Portsea, Moses Mordecai of London, Samuel Yates of Liverpool, and Mordecai Moses and Ezekiel Abraham Ezekiel of Exeter. However, they only made a few bookplates for Jews. The first known *ex libris* of a Jew was made by Benjamin Levi for Isaac Mendes of London in 1746. A number of British Jews in the 18th and 19th centuries had armorial bookplates bearing the family coat of arms, although some of them were spurious. Sir Moses Montefiore had several *ex libris* which bore his distinctively Jewish coat of arms. Among the few Jewish *ex libris* made in the latter half of the 18th century in Germany were those for David Friedlaender, engraved by Daniel N. Chodowiecki in 1774; and Bernhardt Friedlaender, by Johann M. S. Lowe in 1790. In the 18th century Dutch members of the Polack (Polak) family were among the early bookplate artists. A. S. Polak engraved an heraldic *ex libris* for the Jewish baron Aerssen van Sommelsdyk. Isaac de Pinto, a Dutch Sephardi Jew, had a bookplate featuring a huge flower vase with his monogram. The modern Russian-Jewish artist S. Yudovin engraved a number of exquisite woodcut bookplates which are among the relatively few with Yiddish inscriptions. Among other European Jewish artists who have used various graphic media to execute *ex libris* are Uriel Birnbaum, Lodewijk Lopes Cardozo, Fré Cohen, Michel Fingesten, Alice Garman-Horodisch, Georg Jilovsky, Emil Orlik, and Hugo Steiner-Prag. Marco Birnholz (1885–1965) of Vienna, a foremost collector, had over 300 different ones for his own use that were made by many of the European Jewish graphic artists. Bookplates of three Jews are considered to be among the earliest American *ex libris,* dating from the first half of the 19th century. The pictorial bookplate of Barrak (Baruch) Hays of New York incorporated a family coat of arms. Benjamin S. Judah had two armorial bookplates, although there is no evidence that he was entitled to bear a coat of arms. Dr. Benjamin I. Raphael also had two *ex libris*—one showing a hand grasping a surgeon's knife and the other a skull and bones, symbols frequently found on medical *ex libris.* Among the early American college bookplates that have Hebrew words are those of Yale University, inscribed with *Urim ve-Thumim,* Columbia with *Ori El* ("God is my light," alluding to Ps. 27:1), and Dartmouth with *El Shaddai* ("God Almighty"). Many of the major universities in the United States have a variety of bookplates for their Judaica collections. American Jewish artists of bookplates include Joseph B. Abrahams, Joanne Bauer-Mayer, Todros Geller, A. Raymond Katz, Reuben Leaf, Solomon S. Levadi, Isaac Lichtenstein, Saul Raskin, and Ilya Schor. Ephraim Moses Lilien, the "father of Jewish bookplates," designed many for early Zionist leaders which revealed national suffering and hopes. He gave the Hebrew rendering of the Latin term *ex libris—mi-sifrei* ("from the books of") for the numerous *ex libris,* which he created with definitive Jewish significance, and inaugurated a new era in this field that was pursued by other Jewish artists. Hermann Struck drew inspiration from the monuments and landscape of Ereẓ Israel for the *ex libris* he made. Joseph Budko created more than 50 bookplates in aquatints, woodcuts, etchings, and drawings, mostly in a purely ornamental style, leaning heavily on the decorative value of Hebrew script. His artistic *ex libris* are considered among the finest Jewish examples. Jakob Steinhardt also executed a number of bookplates. Among the other modern Israel artists who produced *ex libris* are Aryeh Allweil, David Davidowicz, Ze'ev Raban, J. Ross, Jacob Stark, and Shelomo Yedidiah. Synagogues, Jewish community centers, and institutions of Jewish learning have their own bookplates on which are imprinted names of the donors of books or names of deceased persons who are thus memorialized. Important collections of *ex libris* are at Hebrew Union College, Cincinnati, consisting mainly of the private collections of Israel Solomons and Philip Goodman, and at the Museum of the Printing Arts, Safed, based mainly on the private collection of Abraham Weiss of Tel Aviv.

Bibliography: P. Goodman, *American Jewish Bookplates* (1956), repr. from AJHSP, 45 (1955/56), 129–216; idem, in: JBA, 12 (1953–55), 77–90; *Boekcier,* 9 (Dutch, 1954), 21–26; American Society of Bookplate Collectors and Designers, *Yearbook,* 25 (1955), 14–25; National Union of Printing Workers in Israel, *Katalog le-Ta'arukhat Tavei-Sefer Yehudiyim* (1956); A. Rubens et al., *Anglo-Jewish Notabilities*... (1949); idem, in: JHSET, 14 (1940), 91–129. [PH.G.]

BOOKS.

Production and Treatment. The history of Hebrew bookmaking is as old as the history of the Jewish people and goes back for more than 3,000 years. It may be divided into three periods: from earliest times to the final editing of the Talmud (sixth or seventh centuries); from geonic times to the end of the 15th century and the first printed Hebrew books; and from then to the present day. To the first period belong the books of the *Bible, the *Apocrypha, and the non-biblical texts found among the *Dead Sea Scrolls. Other books are mentioned in the Bible (cf. Eccles. 12:12, "of making many books there is no end") and also in the Talmud, but it may be assumed that in the materials used, the writing techniques, and their format they were no different from books of the Bible. Toward the middle of the geonic period (ninth and tenth centuries) technical changes resulted from Arab influence and the growth of a European Diaspora and—more important still—from the common use of paper as writing material. The revolutionary impact of printing ushered in further developments. (This article will deal with the first period of Hebrew bookmaking; the second can be found under *Manuscripts, and the last under *Printing.)

WRITING MATERIALS. For Bible period see *Writing and Writing Materials.

Papyrus is not mentioned in the Bible, though the Mishnah, Talmud, and Midrash speak of *neyar,* which probably was not made out of the expensive papyrus but from tree bark and similar material. Papyri have also been found in the Dead Sea caves, among them a palimpsest of an eighth century B.C.E. letter. For sacred purposes only animal skin could be used, either in the form of *gevil* ("uncut skin"), which was reserved for Torah scrolls, or *kelaf* ("split skin," "parchment"), which could be used for other biblical books and had to be used for phylacteries, while δύς χιστος ("hard to split"), an inferior kind of parchment, was to be used for *mezuzot* (Shab. 79b; Meg.

Figure 1. Bookplate designed by Albrecht Duerer for a non-Jewish collector, Willibald Pirkheimer, with a quotation in Hebrew, Greek, and Latin from Psalm 111:10 (c. 1504). Cincinnati, American Jewish Archives.

Figure 2. Prayer book bound in silver, bearing the coat of arms for Isaac Mendes by Benjamin Levi of Portsmouth in 1746. Cincinnati, American Jewish Archives.

Figure 3. The *ex libris* of the Viennese bookplate collector Marco Birnholz, with the Bible at the crest of a mountain of books. Cincinnati, American Jewish Archives.

Figure 4. Design for a pediatrician by the U.S. bookplate artist Solomon S. Levadi, 1933. Cincinnati, American Jewish Archives.

Figure 5. Bookplate by Ilya Schor illustrating the saying from the Ethics of the Fathers, "Torah, work, and charity." U.S., 1904. Cincinnati, American Jewish Archives.

Figure 6. The bookplate designed for himself by the artist Ephraim Moses Lilien. Cincinnati, American Jewish Archives.

Figure 7. Bookplate by the Israel artist Ze'ev Raban, for Batya and Shlomo Greenberg. Cincinnati, American Jewish Archives.

Figure 8. The bookplate of the painter and graphic artist Joseph Budko. Cincinnati, American Jewish Archives.

2:2, cf. Arist. 176). Later *halakhah* permitted any parchment for sacred purposes if written on the inside of the skin, while leather was used on the cleaned hair side. Skins used for writing were also distinguished according to the treatment they received: *mazzah, hippah, diftera* (Shab. 79a). The use of Greek terms indicates the origin of the type of parchment or its method of manufacture. For sacred purposes only skins from ritually pure animals could be used (TJ, Meg. 1:11, 71d; Shab. 108a, based on Ex. 13:9); deerskins were preferred (Ket., 103b; TJ, Meg. *ibid.*). Wooden tablets covered with wax (*pinkas*, פִּנְקָס, πίναξ), potsherds (ostraca), tree or plant leaves, and fishskins were for profane use only.

SCROLLS. In antiquity all books, Jewish or non-Jewish, were scrolls. The Torah presented in the third century to Ptolemy II (Philadelphus) of Egypt by the high priest from Jerusalem so that it might be translated into Greek (*Septuagint) was unrolled before him (Arist. 176–7; cf. I. Macc. 3:48; Rev. 5:1). One of the Torah scrolls kept in the Temple (TJ, Ta'an. 4:2, 68a) was carried through Rome among the spoils in the triumphal procession of Titus (Jos., Wars 7:5, 150, 162), but the theory that it is pictured on the Arch of Titus (T. Reinach, in REJ 20, 1894) is not tenable. Talmud and Midrash speak mainly of scroll-books. The high priest on the Day of Atonement read from a scroll during the Temple service and then rolled it up (Yoma 7:1; Sot. 7:7), as was done after each reading of the Law. This was an honor reserved for the leader of the congregation (Meg. 32a). If a man received a Torah scroll in deposit, he had to roll it open for airing once a year (BM 29b). A Torah scroll was rolled from both ends toward the middle, each end being attached to a cylindrical handle called *ammud* ("pillar," BB 14a) or, in later times, *ez hayyim* ("tree of life"), enough parchment being left clear of writing for wrapping round the handle. Other scrolls had only one handle on the right end, while on the left enough parchment was left vacant for wrapping the whole scroll (BB 13b). In the Septuagint the word *megillah* is translated by Κεφαλίς ("head-piece"), referring to the handle, which thus is used to stand for the whole scroll (Ezek. 2:9; 3:1–3; Ps. 40:8). This shows that the handles were already in use in the last centuries B.C.E.

In any event, there is no reference in either biblical or talmudic literature to books in the form of codices with folded pages, unless the *pinkas*, which could have as many as 24 tablets (Lam. R. 1:14), should be regarded as its precursor. The term *tomos* ("volume," from Greek and Latin) is used in the Tosefta (Shab. 13:4; BK 9:31) for which there is a Hebrew synonym *takhrikh* (BM 1:8); but it is not clear whether some sort of codex is meant or the traditional scroll, made of sheets sewn together. *Jerome (fourth century), who speaks of Hebrew Bibles in the possession of Christians, does not mention any Hebrew codex. However, by the fifth century most books, like the earliest Christian ones, are codices. Passages in such late talmudic works as *Soferim* (3:6; cf. ed. Mueller, 46–47) and in the minor tractate *Sefer Torah* (1:2) have been interpreted as referring to codices (Blau, in *Magyar Zsidó Szemle* 21, 1904, 284–8; idem, *Sul libro,* 38–45).

SINGLE AND COMBINED SCROLLS. Biblical books certainly remained in scroll form, and those used in the synagogue have preserved this format. For liturgical use the five books of the Pentateuch had to be written on one single scroll (Git. 60a). According to one tradition, the Torah consisted of seven scrolls, with a division of Numbers at chapter 10:35–36, these two verses making a separate book (Shab. 115b–116a; Lev. R. 11:3; Yad. 3:5). The division of books of the Bible was largely determined by the size of the scroll. Samuel and Kings were probably originally one book but were divided and subdivided for size. The Book of Psalms too was divided into five books at an early date. Ezra, Nehemiah, and Chronicles were originally one book, as suggested by the identity of the last two verses of Chronicles with the first two of Ezra-Nehemiah. Smaller books, such as the two parts of Isaiah and of Zechariah, were combined into one scroll. The fact that the *Minor Prophets were called the Twelve Prophets as early as Ben Sira 49:10 (third–second centuries B.C.E.) proves both their separate and combined entity (see also *Hebrew Book Titles).

Talmudic sources reflect the existence of scrolls containing both single and combined books of the Bible. Single books (Psalms, Job, Proverbs), though much worn, may be given to a widow in payment or part payment of her marriage settlement (Git. 35a). The combination of single books into Pentateuch, Prophets, and Hagiographa respectively is discussed as a halakhic problem. Whether those three could be combined or written in one scroll—at least for liturgical use—was controversial, but the *halakhah* was decided in the affirmative (BB 13b; TJ, Meg. 3:1, 73d–74a; cf. TJ, Yoma 6:1, 44a). According to one opinion Baitos (Boethos) b. Zonin had the eight prophetic books fastened together with the approval of Eleazar b. Azariah; while Judah ha-Nasi reports that his court's approval was given for a complete Bible in this form (BB 13b). Heirs who had inherited biblical books were not allowed to divide between them a single scroll, but could do so if they were separate ones *(ibid.)*. The five books: Song of Songs, Ruth, Lamentations, Ecclesiastes, and Esther (see the Five *Scrolls) are called *megillot* (scrolls), the last one known as "the *megillah*" in Mishnah and Talmud, because it had to be read publicly from a parchment scroll (Meg. 2:2). Like the *Sefer Torah*, the Scroll of Esther retains the scroll form today. At a later stage the custom arose—and is still current—of reading the other four *megillot* on special occasions, in some communities also from scrolls.

NON-BIBLICAL BOOKS. For special purposes excerpts from the biblical books were written in separate scrolls or on one or more sheets *(pinkas)*. The most important example is the *Sefer Aftarta,* the collection of weekly prophetic readings (Git. 60a, see **Haftarah*) which in some communities is still used today. In the same talmudic passage the use of *Sifrei Aggadeta* ("homiletical books") is mentioned as well as the question whether *megillot,* meaning excerpts from the Pentateuch, could be written for teaching purposes. Though the conclusion is negative, it was the practice to copy the **Shema* and the **Hallel* psalms for this purpose (Tosef., Yad. 2:11). According to Numbers 5:23, the curses against the woman suspected of adultery had to be written on a scroll *(sefer)*, and the writing dissolved in water for her to drink. This scroll was called *Megillat Sotah* (Sot. 2:3–4; TB, 17a–18a), for which Queen *Helena of Adiabene presented to the Temple a master copy inscribed on a golden tablet (Yoma 3:10). Genealogical tables current in Temple and talmudic times were called *megillot* or *Sefer Yuhasin* (Yev. 4:13; 49a–b; Mid. 5:4; Pes. 62b; Gen. R. 98:7), and these are also mentioned by Josephus (Life 6; Apion 1:7; see also *Archives). The Mishnah mentions heretical books under the collective name of *Sefarim Hizonim* (i.e., "external books"; Sanh. 10:1), and this has been variously interpreted in Talmud and Midrash (Sanh. 100b and Alfasi *ibid.;* TJ, Sanh. 10:1, 28a; Eccl. R. 12:12 no. 7). Similar books were found among the Dead Sea Scrolls. These discoveries, the oldest Hebrew (or Aramaic) manuscripts in existence—some belonging to the second century B.C.E.—have considerably increased knowledge of this field. Besides manuscripts written on parchment, leather, or papyrus, a *copper scroll was found, on which a Hebrew text is engraved. Y. Yadin (*Megillat Milḥemet* . . . (1958), 107–8) has found that the Dead Sea Scrolls generally conform to the talmudic rules for the writing of sacred scrolls. Though the writing down of the Oral Law was strictly forbidden, this was circumvented by the notes taken down on so-called *megillot setarim,* i.e., private notebooks or such as the *Sifrei Aggadeta* (Shab. 6b; BM 92a; Maas. 2:4, 49d; Shab. 156a; Kil. 1:1, 27a).

Size of Books. From the description in the Mishnah of the reading from the Torah by the high priest on the Day of Atonement (Yoma 7:1) and by the king on the occasion of **Hakhel* (Sot. 7:8), this Temple scroll cannot have been unduly large. The measurements mentioned in the Talmud are 6 by 6 hand-breadths (44×44 cm.) and the scroll was to be of equal height and width—but this was admittedly difficult to achieve (BB 14a). The script had to be correspondingly small—the Torah alone consists of over 300,000 letters. Jerome (*Prologium ad Ezeckielem,* 20) complained that the Hebrew Bible text could hardly be read by daylight, let alone by the light of a lamp, but diminutive script was widely used in antiquity, and Jews were familiar with the Bible from childhood.

Details in Use of Parchment. Usually only one side of the writing material was used. In the Talmud the column is called *daf* ("board"), which is still used today for the double folio of the Talmud, the term for the single page being *ammud* ("pillar"), the common word for page in modern Hebrew, as distinct from *ammudah* for the half-page column. For the writing of Torah and other liturgical scrolls detailed instructions regulate height and width, space to be left between, over, and below the columns, as well as between lines, words, and letters. There are rules for the spacing between the various books of the Pentateuch and of the Prophets, and specific instructions on how many columns a single parchment sheet *(yeri'ah)* should be divided into, how many letters should be accommodated in one line (27), and how many lines in one column (Men. 30a–b; TJ, Meg. 1:11, 71c–d, Sh. Ar., YD 271–8). Poetical passages in the Bible such as the Songs of Moses (Ex. 15; Deut. 32:1–43) and of Deborah (Judg. 5), II Samuel 22, and some lists, such as Joshua 12 and Esther 9:7–10, had to be written in special form of "bricks and half-bricks" (Meg. 16b). The ruling of the parchment—which had to be done with an instrument but not with ink or color—was required for sacred texts (Meg. 18b; Men. 32b) but was general practice as well (see Git. 7a).

Writing Instruments. In talmudic times the *makhtev* (Avot 5:6; Pes. 54a; TJ Ta'an. 4:8, 69a) was used, which corresponds to the Greek γραφίον and the Latin *graphium.* It had one sharp pointed end for writing and one broad end for erasing (Kel. 13:2). For writing on parchment or paper the *kolmos* (κάλαμος) made of reed was more suitable. The Hebrew word for ink *(deyo)* occurs as early as Jeremiah 36:18; this was black Indian ink usually made of lampblack and gum to which occasionally an iron compound was added. Other writing liquids are mentioned in the Talmud, such as *komos* (κόμμι, commis), acacia resin, or gum arabic; *mei afaẓim,* the juice of gallnuts (Shab. 104b; Git 19a), whose use in writing Torah scrolls became a matter of controversy in the Middle Ages; and *kalkantum* (χάλκαντος), copper vitriol, also used as an admixture for Indian ink. For the rabbis the important consideration for sanctioning the use of one ink in preference to another was durability (Shab. 12:5; Git. 2:3). According to the Letter of *Aristeas the Torah scroll presented to Ptolemy Philadelphus and the Torah scrolls used by Alexandrian Jews (in Jerusalem?) had letters written in gold; the rabbis frowned on such ostentation and prohibited it for liturgical use (Shab. 103b; Sof. 1:9; cf. Song R. 1:11). Chrysography was of great antiquity: papyri with gold script of the Twenty-Second Egyptian Dynasty are in the Gizeh museum. Jerome and Chrysostom—like many rabbis before them—criticize the custom of writing Bibles on purple parchment with gold script and the use of precious stones. In his writing kit the scribe had, beside other auxiliary tools, an inkwell (biblical *keset ha-sofer,* Ezra 9:3), talmudic *beit deyo* (Tosef., BM 4:11), or *kalamarin* (Kel. 2:7). Examples of such (Roman type) inkwells were discovered in the ruins of *Qumran, some of them with remnants of a carbon ink still in them. They belonged to the equipment of a special *Scriptorium,* a writing room for the scribes of the Qumran sect. Such an inkwell was also found in excavations in the Old City of Jerusalem.

Keeping of Books. Scrolls, being valuable, were kept with care. Sacred books had to be wrapped in *mitpaḥot* (sing. *mitpaḥat;* Shab 9:6), and it was forbidden to touch them with bare hands (Shab. 14a; 133b; Meg. 32a; cf. II Cor. 3:14–16). The wraps were made of linen, silk, purple materials, or leather. Today's Torah mantle (see *Torah ornaments) has a long history. Some Dead Sea Scrolls were found preserved in linen wrappings. Books were kept in chests, alone or with other things; the synagogue *Ark is a survivor of these chests. Earthenware jars were also used as receptacles for books from Bible times (Jer. 32:14). These have preserved for posterity the treasures of the Dead Sea caves, the *Elephantine Letters, etc. Baskets too were used for keeping books (Meg. 26b).

Genizah. Worn sacred books had to be reverently "hidden away"—in a **genizah*—and were eventually buried (Shab. 16:1; Meg. 26b). This accounts for the fact that so few Torah or Bible fragments have been preserved from antiquity, as parchment, let alone papyrus, decays in the ground. Where the *genizah* was limited to storing away, it made possible such treasure troves as those from the Dead Sea caves and the Cairo **Genizah.* Heretical books too were

Figure 1. Binding for a Bible in leather and embossed silver made by Meir Jaffe of Ulm, 1468. Munich, Bavarian State Library.

condemned to *genizah*, and these included almost anything not admitted to the *Bible canon (Shab. 30b; 115a; Pes. 56a).

Ownership of Books. While books were costly and rare in antiquity, by the second century B.C.E. some Jews possessed their own copies of biblical books. During the persecution preceding the Hasmonean revolt, those caught possessing sacred books were burned with them (I Macc. 1:56–57; 3:48; II Macc. 2:14–15; cf. *Haninah b. Teradyon's martyrdom, Av. Zar. 18a). On the Day of Atonement the burghers of Jerusalem could each produce their *Sefer Torah* for the admiration of all (Yoma 70a). True wealth was books, and it was charity to loan them out (Ket. 50a on Ps. 112:3). Special laws applied to the finding, borrowing, and depositing of books (BM 2:8; BM 29b), whether and under what circumstances it was permitted to sell them (Meg. 27a; see *Book Trade), and the provocative query whether a room filled with books requires a *mezuzah* at its door. This latter question is put into the mouth of Korah (TJ, Sanh. 10:1, 27d). Sacred books were above all owned by municipalities and synagogues (Ned. 5:5; Meg. 3:1). Schoolchildren, too, usually had their own books (Deut. R. 8; TJ, Ta'an. 4:8, 69a). Mention is also made of books being written and owned by gentiles, heretics, and Samaritans (Git. 4:6; 45a–b; Men. 42b). [Ed.]

Bindings. Bookbindings as such first made their appearance toward the end of the fourth century. Sheaves of pages (pen manuscript) were fastened together by means of two covers and a back, and then tied with strings. The early bookbindings from the Cairo *Genizah* were made of parchment with laces sewn on for fastening. Yemenite Jews used similar bindings down to a relatively recent date. These early bindings are without ornamentation. Sometimes parchment or leather ends were left for carrying the book from place to place, and on these ends the name of the copyist or owner occasionally appears.

Middle Ages. In the later Middle Ages examples of Islamic bookbinding arrived in Europe by way of Venice, bookbinders apparently also migrating from Byzantium; these specimens were remarkable primarily for their gold decoration. At about the same time goat-skin binding appeared; formerly it was considered a secret of the Islamic artisans. This led to smaller and lighter bindings. Colored bindings also originated in Islamic countries, and some beautiful examples have survived. Documents from the Cairo *Genizah* reveal that ready-made leather book covers were imported from Europe into Egypt for decoration. A 12th-century list of books speaks of their red, black, and white covers (S. D. Goitein, *Mediterranean Society*, 1 (1967), 112).

The bindings of ancient and heavy parchment volumes were generally not decorated but received "blind-stamping" or gilding only. In the decoration of bindings by Jews the influence of the environment is usually recognizable: that of Islamic countries and Byzantium and that of Christian monastic bookbinders at a later date, in the early and late Middle Ages respectively. The bindings reveal the period of their manufacture, and some book collections were arranged according to the style or origin of the bindings. The 13th-century *Sefer Ḥasidim* (no. 345) advocates binding good books with handsome bindings. It also mentions a case of a Jew learning the craft from a monk, and considers whether to have sacred books bound by a Jew or by a monk, who was the better binder (no. 280). Medieval responsa literature reveals occasional references to bookbinding.

Particular care was bestowed upon the bindings of communal prayer books (e.g., the *Worms Maḥzor* of

Figure 2. Prayer book bound in silver, bearing the coat of arms of a family named Levi, Italy, late 17th century. Cleveland, Ohio, Joseph B. Horwitz Collection. Photo Rebman, Cleveland.

1272) and *Memorbuch, of which some magnificent examples have been preserved, though the date of the bindings is often uncertain. Many communities disposed of special funds to pay for the binding or repairing of books in communal ownership.

Until the 17th century, binders prepared book covers by pasting together paper pages, often using old *manuscripts, cutting them and pasting them together until they achieved the desired thickness (cf. Rashba, Resp. no. 166). Christian binders sometimes used Jewish manuscripts for this purpose, particularly when anti-Jewish riots and the looting of libraries had provided them with the necessary materials. Remnants of valuable manuscripts and *Incunabula have been discovered in such bindings. Books belonging to synagogues or academies had to be carefully guarded and would be attached by iron chains to the table or the shelves in the library.

Medieval Bookbinders. In the 14th century the official bookbinders at the papal court at Avignon were frequently Jews. Cases are recorded of Jews being commissioned to execute the bindings of a missal or a codex of Canon Law to be presented to a friend or relative of the pope. A certain Meir (Makhir) Solomo made artistic bindings for the royal treasury in Aragon (1367–89). From the *bull of the antipope Benedict XIII of 1415, prohibiting Jews from, among other things, binding books in which the names of Jesus or Mary occur, it is evident how important a role Jews played in the craft. On the back of a leather-bound copy of the Perpignan Bible (written in 1299), a calendar was engraved in niello-work about 1470 in honor of the owners, the Kalonymos family (see M. Narkiss, in *Memorial Volume . . . Sally Meyer* (1956), 180).

The most prominent name in this field in the 15th century was that of Meir *Jaffe of Ulm, who belonged to a family of Franconian artisans. Apart from bookbinding, he was also well-known as a manuscript copyist; 15 of his bindings have so far been found (in the libraries of London, Munich, Nuremberg, and Ansbach). He was the master of a special art called *cuir ciselé*. The artist decorated the book covers by cutting ornaments and figures into the moist leather and then, by various methods, raising them into relief. This old-established craft reached its peak in the gothic style of 14th–15th-century Germany. Though it may not have been a Jewish invention, Jews became the supreme practitioners of this method, which became known therefore as "Jewish leather cutting." One of the special features of these bindings of Hebrew books is grotesques, though the genre is found elsewhere in gothic art. Jewish artists preferred "leather-cutting" to the more frequent, simpler, and cheaper method of "blind-stamping." The wandering

Jewish artisan, traveling light by necessity, also may have found the chiseling knife easier to carry than the heavy dies.

Jaffe was responsible for the binding—executed in 1468—of a manuscript Pentateuch (Munich State Library, Cod. Hebr. 212) belonging to the city of Nuremberg. In return the city council gave him permission to stay in the city for several months and follow his calling. This in itself is eloquent testimony to his eminence as a binder (he is called "a supreme artist"), as he must have evoked envy and opposition from the local craftsmen. Though the names of binders rarely appear on medieval books, Jaffe embossed this Bible with the Hebrew inscription: החומש הזה לעידה מנירנברקא שיח׳ מאיר המצייר. "This Pentateuch belongs to the Council of Nuremberg, may they live [long]—Meir [Jaffe], the artist." On another of his works (c. 1470) Jaffe, using calfskin on wooden boards, portrays a scholar on a high chair scanning a book placed before him on a pedestal. The rim of the binding is decorated with flowers. Two metal claps are engraved with the letter *M* in Gothic type, probably being Meir's initial. In 1490 the city of Noerdlingen (Wuerttemberg) made payment to a Jew for binding the *Stadtbuch.* It may well have been Meir Jaffe.

With the invention of printing in the 15th century and the proliferation of books more Jewish bookbinders are found all over Europe. In Poland, during the reign of Sigismund III (1587–1632), Jewish craftsmen were employed by church and state (see M. Kramer, in: *Zion,* 2 (1937), 317). In Italy, in the 17th and 18th centuries, Bibles or prayer books were bound in silver, lavishly decorated, to serve as bridal presents *(sivlonot),* sometimes bearing a representation of a biblical scene relating to the bride's or bridegroom's name, or the coats-of-arms of the two families. The art of filigree binding arose in Italy and France in the 17th century and spread to other European countries. At the same time embroidered or tortoiseshell bindings, though not characteristically Jewish, made their appearance in Holland and Germany, from where they spread eastward. Jews bound their *ritualia,* particularly bridal prayer books, in these beautiful materials. On these bindings metal, usually silver, is used for clasps and corners, and both are often finely engraved and decorated with emblems, monograms, or animal figures representing certain Jewish virtues. These ornately bound books are sometimes inlaid with precious stones and even miniature drawings of the woman to whom they were presented. Similarly bound and decorated books figured as presentations by communities, societies, or wealthy individuals to Jewish or non-Jewish notables on special occasions: a rabbi or communal leader's jubilee, a sovereign's visit, or as a sign of appreciation for favors bestowed or assistance given.

Modern Times. From the 19th century onward, with growing prosperity particularly among Western Jewry, the art of binding Hebrew or Jewish books developed. In Ereẓ Israel, the establishment of the *Bezalel School of Arts and Crafts in Jerusalem in 1906 included a deliberate effort to develop a specifically Jewish style in bookbinding. This produced olive-wood covers for a variety of books. Yemenite artisans too brought with them a tradition of

Figure 3. Silver binding of a *maḥzor* showing Moses and Aaron on the front cover and the sacrifice of Isaac on the back, Germany, 1726. Cleveland, Ohio, Joseph B. Horwitz Collection. Photo Tibor Ardai, New York.

bindings made from leather, silver, and gold filigree, and their productions have retained their popularity. There is, however, a more artistic and less traditional trend which has produced some magnificent bindings, such as that of the *Golden Book* and the *Barmitzvah Book* at the head office of the Jewish National Fund in Jerusalem. [B.M.A.]

Book Illustrations. In the early days of printing the illustrations were far inferior to those in contemporary *illuminated manuscripts. European printing as a whole was preceded by block books, in which the text was subordinate to the illustrations. Hence, the illustrated book existed from the very beginning of printing. In early Hebrew printing nothing of the sort is known; but the very nature of the illustrated book subjected it to more wear than ordinary volumes, and it may well be that some early illustrated works have been thumbed out of existence. There are indeed some surviving wood-blocks showing Passover scenes which were probably printed in Venice c. 1480. These may have been prepared for the illustration of a Hebrew work. The earliest Hebrew printed books, however, while—like other books—leaving a space for illuminated words or letters to be inserted by hand, relied for their decorative effect entirely on the disposition of the type, which was sometimes ornamented. Such is the case with the *Turim* of Pieve di Sacco (1475), the second (dated) Hebrew book to be completed in type.

Decorative Borders. It was only at a slightly later period that, in imitation of the more sophisticated (but not fully illuminated) manuscripts of the period, decorative borders began to be used for the opening—there were no title pages yet—and occasionally also for some of the more significant later pages.

The first Hebrew book to make use of a border was the Pentateuch printed at Hijar in Spain about 1486. The border, however, designed by Alonso Fernandez de *Cordoba, was not on the opening page but appeared as a decoration to the Song of Moses (Ex. 15), as in some Spanish Hebrew Bible manuscripts. This border is outstanding with its beautiful traceries and charming animal figures. It appeared later in the Manuale Saragossanum, one of the great monuments of early Spanish printing, in which Cordoba and the Jewish printer Solomon Zalmati had collaborated. The border around the first page of the *Turim,* printed by Samuel d'Ortas at Leiria in Portugal in 1495, is of particular interest. This, presumably cut by a Jewish artist and incorporating Hebrew letters, elaborates on the similes in the opening passage of the work. About the same time, the Soncino family in Italy were making use of elegant black-and-white borders borrowed from non-Jewish sources. In some cases, in order to comply with the requirements of a Hebrew book, where the opening page needed to have the wider margin on the right rather than on the left, they sometimes broke up the border and in rare cases even had it recut to adjust to the requirements of Hebrew printing. The border used in Baḥya's commentary on the Bible (Ezriel Gunzenhausen, Naples, 1492) appears to have been designed and cut by the Hebrew printer's brother-in-law, Moses b. Isaac. This border also appears in the Italian work *L'Aquila Volante,* produced there at about the same time by Aiolfo de' Cantoni. Many of these borders were transferred from press to press, or taken by the refugees from country to country. Thus the Hijar border referred to above appears in Lisbon in 1489, and later, increasingly worn and indistinct, in various works produced in Turkey between 1505 and 1509. The Naples border was used in Constantinople in 1531/32. There are some superbly designed borders around some pages of the Prague

Figure 4. First page of *Tur Oraḥ Ḥayyim* from the *Arba'ah Turim* of Jacob b. Asher, printed by Samuel d'Ortas in Leiria, Portugal, 1495. Jerusalem, J.N.U.L.

Haggadah of 1526. For the Mantua editions of 1550 and 1560 these were entirely recut, as framework around the identical text. With the development of the engraved title page in the 16th century, the use of borders became an exceptional luxury, as in some of the royal publications of the Mantuan press in the 18th century.

Engraved Title Pages. It is only in 1505 that the first title page appears in a Hebrew book. Thereafter, these also received special care, later being enclosed within an engraved border in the form of a gate (hence the common Hebrew term for title page, *sha'ar,* "gate"), often flanked by twisted columns and later and not infrequently by figures of Moses and Aaron. In due course specially executed vignettes of biblical scenes or Jewish ritual observances were incorporated in these title pages. Printers' marks, first introduced in 1485 in Spain, became common from the 16th century.

Illustrated Works. Illustrations in the conventional sense first figure in a Hebrew book, so far as is known, in 1491, when the Brescia edition of the fable-book *Mashal ha-Kadmoni* by Isaac ibn *Sahula contained a number of cuts illustrating the various fables (repeated in the Barco edition of 1497/98). After this, it was customary to add illustrations to most books of fables, for example the Yiddish *Kuhbuch* (Frankfort, 1687). The prayers for rain and dew recited on the feasts of Tabernacles and Passover were often accompanied in Ashkenazi prayer books with the signs of the Zodiac, which, however, first appear in a far from religious work, the frivolous *Maḥberot Immanuel* by *Immanuel of Rome (Brescia, 1491).

Minhagim Books. Another favorite medium for book illustration was the books of customs or occasional prayers known as *minhagim* books, also following a tradition that goes back to the days of manuscript illustration. The *Birkat ha-Mazon* (Prague, 1514) contains a few woodcuts illustrating the text which are similar to those produced in later *Haggadot.* At the turn of the century, in 1593 and 1601, two *minhagim* books were produced in Italy, lavishly illustrated with woodcuts depicting almost every stage of and event in the Jewish religious year. The later work is the more delicate and its illustrations seem to reflect faithfully the realia of Italian Jewish life of the period. The earlier one, published possibly for export, is more northern European in character, and perhaps for that reason became more popular. These illustrations were constantly reproduced in similar German and Dutch publications down to the middle of the 18th century.

Passover Haggadot. The most popular subject for illumination among Hebrew manuscripts was the Passover *Haggadah, and this tradition naturally continued in the age of printing. The earliest known example of this is in some fragments conjecturally ascribed to Turkey (but obviously printed by Spanish exiles) c. 1515. But the oldest dated illustrated *Haggadah* now extant is that of Prague of 1526, published by Gershon Kohen and his brother Gronem and apparently illustrated in part by their brother-in-law Ḥayyim Schwarz or Shaḥor. This lovely production is one of the most memorable specimens of the 16th-century Hebrew press, the three fully decorated pages being especially noteworthy. It was exactly copied so far as the text was concerned but with fresh borders in the Mantua *Haggadah* of 1560, much improved in the subsequent edition of 1568. After some further experiments, an entirely fresh and more amply illustrated edition of the work was published by Israel Zifroni in Venice in 1609. This continued to be republished with few changes until late in the 18th century and served as the model for the *Haggadot* produced in the Mediterranean basin (e.g., at Leghorn) down to recent times. In 1695, the Venetian *Haggadah* served as the model for the edition published in Amsterdam with copper-plate illustrations by the convert to Judaism who called himself *Abraham b. Jacob. Though the general arrangement of the work and the choice of subjects was strongly influenced by the Venetian edition, the artist based his art to a great extent on illustrations to the Bible and other imaginative details gathered from the publications of Matthew Merian of Basle. The work reappeared with minor changes a few years later (Amsterdam, 1699) and served as the model for a large number of editions produced in central Europe throughout the 18th century and after. The actual illustrations, much deteriorated, continue to be reprinted or copied in popular editions down to the present day. Of the some 3,000 editions of the Passover *Haggadah* which are recorded, over 300 are illustrated. In recent years, artists of great reputation (Arthur *Szyk, Ben *Shahn, etc.) have collaborated in or produced illustrated editions of this favorite work.

Figure 5. Page from the collection of poems, *Sefer ha-Maḥbarot*, by Immanuel of Rome, printed by Gershom Soncino in 1491. This is the first Hebrew book in which the signs of the Zodiac appear. Jerusalem, J.N.U.L.

Other Works. Other Hebrew works which were traditionally enriched with illustrations—in most cases very crude—included the Yiddish pseudo-Josephus (*Josippon), from the Zurich edition of 1547 onward; and the women's compendium of biblical history, *Ẓe'enah u-Re'enah, in numerous Dutch and German editions of the 17th and 18th centuries. On the other hand, for obvious reasons, the Hebrew Bible was never illustrated until a few experiments appeared in the second half of the 19th century.

Portraits. Portraits of an author occasionally appear in Hebrew books printed in Holland and Italy in the 17th and 18th centuries; for example, Joseph Solomon del Medigo in his *Sefer Elim* (Amsterdam, 1629) and Moses Ḥefeẓ (Gentili) in his *Melekhet Maḥashevet* (Venice, 1701). The *Kehunnat Avraham* by Abraham ha-Kohen of Zante (Venice, 1719) has, after the elaborately engraved title page, a portrait which seems to be by the author himself. A portrait of the rabbi Solomon *Hirschell surprisingly accompanied the London prayer book edition of 1809. Judah Leon *Templo's works on the Tabernacle of Moses and the Temple of Solomon (1650 etc.) included fine illustrative engravings. [C.R.]

Bibliography: Production: L. Loew, *Graphische Requisiten und Erzeugnisse bei den Juden*, 2 vols. (1870–71); M. Steinschneider, *Vorlesungen ueber die Kunde der hebraeischen Manuskripte* (1937[2]); L. Blau, *Das althebraeische Buchwesen* (1902); idem, in: *Festschrift A. Berliner* (1903), 41–49; idem, *Papyri und Talmud in gegenseitiger Beleuchtung* (1913); idem, in: *Soncino-Blaetter*, 1 (1025/26), 16–28; Krauss, Tal Arch, 3 (1912) 131–98; H. Strack, *Introduction to the Talmud and Midrash* (1959[6]), 12–20 and notes; S. Lieberman, *Hellenism in Jewish Palestine* (1950), 84–88, 203–8; Beit Arié, in: KS, 43 (1967/68), 411ff.; M. Martin, *Scribal Character of the Dead Sea Scrolls*, 2 vols. (1958); G. R. Driver, *Judaean Scrolls* (1965), 403–10. Bindings; M. Steinschneider, op. cit., 33–35; Husung, in: *Soncino-Blaetter*, 1 (1925/26), 29–43 and 3 pls.; Kurz, in: *Record of the Art Museum, Princeton University*, 24 (1965), 3–11, two facsimiles; C. Roth, in: *Jewish Art* (1961), 350, 503–4; idem, *Jews in Renaissance* (1959), 201–2. Illustrations: C. Roth, in: *Bodleian Library Record*, 4 (1952–53), 295–303; A. Marx, *Studies in Jewish History and Booklore* (1944), 289–300.

BOOKS OF THE CHRONICLES OF THE KINGS OF JUDAH AND ISRAEL, two sets of royal annals, mentioned in I and II Kings but subsequently lost. The historian of Kings refers to these works as his source, where additional information may be found. These references show how the historian of Kings used extensive sources selectively. The books are referred to by this formula, with slight variations: "Now the rest of the acts of [the king], and all that he did, behold, they are written in the book of the chronicles of the kings of Judah/Israel." Frequently references are made to "his might," or "how we warred," and occasionally more specific deeds are mentioned (e.g., I Kings 15:23; II Kings 20:20).

The Israelite annals are mentioned 18 times (I Kings

14:19 (17); 15:31; 16:5; et al.) and the Judean annals 15 times (I Kings 14:29; 15:7, 23; et al.). Of all the kings of Israel, only Jehoram and Hosea are not mentioned as referred to in the Israelite annals. Of the kings of Judah (after Solomon) only Ahaziah, Athaliah, Jehoahaz, Jehoiachin, and Zedekiah are not mentioned in this regard. It is uncertain whether these books were royal records themselves or edited annals based on the records. It seems likely in view of the negative references to certain kings (Zimri, Shallum, and Manasseh), which would not very likely be the product of the king's own recorders, that the books were edited annals. Furthermore, the Judean author of Kings could hardly have had access to all the royal records of the northern kingdom. The content of these books appears identical in character to the Assyrian annals. Probably the mass of facts on royal activities in Kings came from these books. Chronicles mentions the book of the kings of Israel (I Chron. 9:1; II Chron. 20:34) and the book of the kings of Israel and Judah (or Judah and Israel; II Chron. 16:11; 27:7; et al.). The chronicler seems to be referring to the same works, but probably did not actually have them at his disposal.

Bibliography: J. A. Montgomery, *Critical and Exegetical Commentary on the Book of Kings* (ICC, 1951), 24–38; B. Maisler (Mazar), in: IEJ, 2 (1952), 82–88.

[M.Fö.]

BOOK TRADE.

Antiquity. Information on the book trade in antiquity among Jews is very scanty. In biblical and talmudic times the scribe himself was the seller of his products (Tosef., Bik. 2:15; Pes. 50b; Git. 54b). The Tosefta (Av. Zar. 3:7–8) and the Jerusalem Talmud (Av. Zar. 2:2, 41a) speak of a gentile bookseller in Sidon who sold Bibles. While it was forbidden to sell sacred books to non-Jews (Tosef., Av. Zar. 2:4), it was permitted to exceed the current price by half a dinar to buy (really redeem) them from them (Git. 45b). Otherwise a man might buy sacred books from every Jew, but no one should sell his own except for particularly important reasons (Meg. 27a; cf. Sh. Ar., YD 270:1). A Torah scroll is literally priceless and no claim can be made for overcharging (BM 4:9). A story is told from Babylonia in the fourth century of a *Sefer Torah* which was stolen, sold at 80 *zuz* (approx. $1,200), and resold at 120 before the thief was found (BK 115a). A cushion and worn copies of Psalms, Proverbs, and Job were valued at five *minah* (approx.$75; Git. 35a).

Middle Ages. In the Mediterranean area books circulated freely in the early Middle Ages, as can be gathered from documents recovered from the Cairo **Genizah*. Among the wares of Nahrai b. Nissim, a wholesale merchant of high standing in 11th-century Egypt, were a variety of Hebrew and Arabic books: Bible, Talmud, rabbinics and homiletics, grammars, etc. They were transported or shipped in wickerwork crates or other baskets as well as in tin or lead cases. One document reveals the sale by two ladies of a Bible codex for 20 dinars; books were also used as collateral and passed from generation to generation as family heirlooms. In the *Genizah* lists of books have been found with prices attached which are apparently booksellers' catalogs (*Tarbiz,* 30 (1961), 171–85). The (auction?) catalog of the library of Abraham he-Ḥasid of Cairo, sold after his death in 1223 by the Jewish court, has also been preserved.

Individual authors, apart from the professional scribes, sold their own books, while others paid scribes to copy books for them. By the Middle Ages the itinerant bookseller emerged, "rolling" his stock from city to city or country to country in special barrels, and carrying with him booklists, a forerunner of the catalog. They approached bibliophiles whose names were well-known to offer them their wares. Aaron, whose collection, brought back from Spain, was ransacked by *Immanuel of Rome at Perugia around 1300, may have been a bibliophile, not a dealer as is generally stated, though he carried with him a list of his 180 books (*Maḥberot Immanuel ha-Romi,* ed. by D. Yarden (1957), 161–6).

Trade in Printed Books. When books began to be printed from the end of the 15th century onward and were available in greater quantities and at considerably cheaper prices, it became possible to speak of a proper trade in Hebrew or Jewish books. Once more the printers themselves or their agents—as well as the authors—were the principal booksellers. The famous Gershom *Soncino sold his books while moving from place to place, while his great competitor Daniel *Bomberg handed the Swiss scholar Conrad Gesner a list with prices of 75 Hebrew books, printed by himself and others, and Gesner printed the list in Latin in his *Pandectae* (1548). Two Jewish bookdealers on a large scale, David Bono and Graziadio (-Judah?) are mentioned in Naples in 1491, being exempted from tolls and duties like other bookdealers who followed the same calling. The former is recorded as exporting 16 cases of printed books in one consignment. Whether they were in Hebrew is not specifically stated, but is probable. R. Benjamin Zeev of Arta (c. 1500) refers in his responsa to the useful function of the itinerant booksellers of his day. The will of R. *Aaron b. David Cohen of Ragusa (1656) gives some interesting details on how books were diffused: he left money for the publication of his *Zekan Aharon,* of which 800 copies were to be printed: 200 were to be sent to Constantinople, 100 to Salonika, 50 to Venice, 20 to Sofia, 10 to Ancona, 20 to Rome, 50 to Central and Eastern Europe, 50 to Holland, to various places in Italy and to Erez Israel; the last were to be distributed without charge. Issuing works in "installments" was not uncommon in early Jewish publishing, particularly by the Constantinople presses. Thus the responsa of Isaac b. Sheshet (Constantinople, 1547) were printed in sections and sold in this form by the printer to subscribers week by week.

From the 17th century onward the book fairs of Frankfort on the Main became centers for the diffusion of Hebrew books also. Two Jewish booksellers of Frankfort, Gabriel Luria and Jacob Hamel, were in correspondence with the *Buxtorfs with reference to the sale of books. The Buxtorfs were also in contact with Judah Romano of Constantinople, who, whether a professional bookdealer or not, was active in the Hebrew book trade. *Manasseh Ben Israel is known to have attended the Frankfort fair in 1634—the only Jew among 159 Christians—but his application for membership of the Amsterdam booksellers' guild in 1648 was refused. The catalog (in Spanish) published by his son Samuel (1652) includes some books which were apparently printed by other firms. Some years before, Samuel had also distributed a list of secondhand books which he had for sale, copies of which even reached England. Isaac Fundam (Fundao) of Amsterdam produced a printed catalog of books and manuscripts in Spanish and Portuguese (1726), and works purchased from him are occasionally recorded. At the end of the 17th century, the Proops firm of Amsterdam styled themselves in their publications "Printers and Booksellers": their first catalog (*Appiryon Shelomo*) appeared in 1730; they had already been admitted to the booksellers' guild in 1677.

At the end of the 18th century Johanan Levi Rofe ("the physician") was also active in the book trade in Amsterdam. In the 18th century, especially in England, Jewish and Hebrew works were frequently published by subscription, a wealthy person sometimes purchasing several copies. The lists of subscribers printed with the works in question are often important historical sources. The business of distributing books in bulk by the publishers could be complicated. They were not infrequently disposed of by barter, in some instances in exchange for wine. In Eastern Europe the great fairs were the centers for bookdealing, and cheap *chapbooks were sold all over the country by itinerant dealers. The Council of Lithuanian Jewry in 1679 ordered that each community should appoint a person to purchase tractates of the Talmud at the fairs of Stolowicze and Kopyl so as to stimulate study. James Levi, who conducted book auctions in London from about 1711 to 1733, presumably dealt solely in non-Jewish books. On the other hand, Moses Benjamin *Foà (1729–1822), book purveyor to the court of Modena and a dealer on a grand scale, was deeply interested in Jewish literature also, though more as a collector than a merchant. D. Friedlaender and his friends obtained in 1784 a royal license for their *Orientalische Buchdruckerei und Buchhandlung* (for a catalog see Steinschneider, in ZGJD, 5 (1892), 168f.). Heirs to collections of Hebrew books who wished to dispose of them produced sale-catalogs, such as those published by the heirs of David *Oppenheim; two separate catalogs of this famous and outstanding collection were printed: *Reshimah Tammah* (Hamburg, 1782); and *Kehillat David* (*ibid.*, 1826, with Latin translation).

Modern Times. In the 19th century, in Hebrew as in general books, there was a division between printers on the one hand and *publishers and booksellers on the other. In Eastern Europe, however, the three functions remained united in the activities of such firms as Romm in Vilna, who published catalogs as well. In the 20th century, the center of the Jewish secondhand book trade was first Berlin, with the firm of Asher, and then Frankfort with Joseph Baer, Bamberger and Wahrmann (later of Jerusalem), A. J. Hoffmann, J. Kauffmann, and Leipzig with M. W. Kaufmann. The firms of Schwager and Fraenkel (of Husiatyn, later Vienna, Tel Aviv, and New York), F. Muller (Amsterdam), and B. M. Rabinowitz (Munich) made contributions to scholarship through their diffusion of rare books, and sometimes through their learned catalogs, as did Ephraim *Deinard in the United States. The journeys undertaken by some of these booksellers in search of rarities place them almost in the category of explorers. In London Vallentine (later Shapiro, Vallentine) was active from at least the beginning of the 19th century, followed by the firms of R. Mazin, M. Cailingold and Rosenthal, while in Paris the firm of Lipschutz was eminent for many years; in the United States the Bloch Publishing Company has been in existence for over a century and the Hebrew Publishing Company since the 1890s. Important Jewish booksellers in Switzerland were T. Gewuerz and V. Goldschmidt of Basle; in Holland J. L. Joachimsthal and M. Packter of Amsterdam; in Berlin M. Poppelauer and L. Lamm; in Vienna and Budapest J. Schlesinger. Some non-Jewish booksellers, such as O. Harrassowitz (Leipzig, then Wiestbaden) and Spirgates (Leipzig); Mags Brothers and Sothebys (London), have also played a role in the sale of Hebraica and Judaica.

See *Archives; *Libraries; *Manuscripts; *Printing, Hebrew. [C.R./A.M.H.]

Bibliography: A. Yaari, *Meḥkerei Sefer* (1958), 163–9, 430–44; idem, in: KS, 43 (1967/68), 121–2; idem, *Ha-Defus ha-Ivri be-Kushta* (1967), 13–15; S. Assaf, in: KS, 16 (1939/40), 493–5; M. Kayserling, in: REJ, 8 (1884), 74–95; F. Homeyer, *Deutsche Juden als Bibliophilen und Antiquare* (1966[2]); J. Bloch, *Hebrew Printing in Naples* (1942), 6–7; S. Kaznelson, in: idem (ed.), *Juden im Deutschen Kulturbereich* (1962[3]), 131–46; H. Widmann, *Geschichte des Buchhandels vom Altertum bis zur Gegenwart* (1952); S. D. Goitein, *A Mediterranean Society*, 1 (1967), index.

BOORSTIN, DANIEL J. (1914–), U.S. historian. Born in Atlanta, Georgia, he joined the University of Chicago in 1944, and became professor of American history in 1956. His books include: *Lost World of Thomas Jefferson* (1948); *The Genius of American Politics* (1953); *America and the Image of Europe* (1960); *The Image* (1962); *The Americans* (2 vols. 1958/65); *The Decline of Radicalism* (1969); *The Sociology of the Absurd* (1970); and two volumes of the *Landmark History of the American People* (1968/70). Their principal thesis is that American experience was shaped by the environment of the New World. He was editor of the *Chicago History of American Civilization* series. From 1969, he was director of the National Museum of History and Technology at the Smithsonian Institution, Washington.

Daniel Boorstin, U.S. historian.

Bibliography: D. W. Noble, *Historians against History* (1965), 157–75. [A.S.E.]

BOPPARD, town in Coblenz district in West Germany. The earliest reference to Jews there dates from the last quarter of the 11th century. In 1179, 13 Jews in Boppard were murdered following a blood libel. In 1196 eight Jews of Boppard were massacred by crusaders. Subsequently the leader of the community, the learned and wealthy R. Hezekiah b. Reuben, managed to secure the protection of the authorities. A Jewish quarter (*Judengasse, vicus Judaeorum*) is first mentioned in Boppard in 1248–50. In 1287, 40 Jews were massacred in Boppard and Oberwesel: others during the *Armleder persecutions of 1337 and during the Black Death in 1349. In 1312 Boppard ceased to be a free imperial city and the Jews came under the jurisdiction of the archbishops of *Trier. In 1418 all Jews were expelled from the archbishopric. Jews resettled in Boppard in 1532, and by the 1560s numbered approximately 32 families. There were 53 Jews living in Boppard at the beginning of the 19th century, 101 in 1880, 80 in 1895, 108 in 1910, 125 in 1926–27 (out of a total population of 7,000), and 92 in 1932. At this time the community possessed a synagogue, a cemetery, and two charitable institutions. Under the Nazi regime, the Jews who were unable to emigrate from Boppard were deported to the east. On Nov. 9, 1938, the interior of the synagogue was despoiled, although the building was spared because of its proximity to neighboring buildings. The Torah scrolls, ritual objects, and communal archives were thrown into the street and destroyed. On July 27, 1942, the ten remaining Jews were deported to Theresienstadt and Auschwitz, and only one survived. Three Jews settled in Boppard after World War II but subsequently left.

Bibliography: Aronius, Regesten, 162, 311, 338, 572, 576; Germ. Jud, 1 (1963), 61f; 2 (1968), 96f.; Salfeld, Martyrol, 238, 276, 285; Baron, Social[2], 4 (1957), 133; FJW (1932–33), 218; *Israelitisches Familienblatt*, 36 no. 18 (1934), 13; ZGJD, 2 (1930), 109, 286; Kahlenberg, in: *Zwischen Rhein und Mosel, der Kreis St. Goar* (1967), 643ff. [C.T.]

BORAISHA, MENAHEM (pseudonym of **Menahem Goldberg;** 1888–1949), Yiddish poet and essayist. Born in Brest-Litovsk, the son of a Hebrew teacher, he combined a thorough Jewish education with attendance at the Russian school in his birthplace. At the age of 16 he joined the Socialist Zionists and began to write poetry in Russian and Yiddish. When he went to Warsaw in 1905, he published his first poems in Yiddish journals, and wrote drama reviews for the daily *Haynt.* While serving in the Russian Army (1909–11), he published his impressions of barrack-life in both *Haynt* and *Fraynd.* His poem *"Poyln"* (1914) gave expression to the tense relationship between Jews and Poles. In 1914 Boraisha settled in the U.S. and in 1918 he joined the editorial board of the Yiddish daily *Der Tag.* His book of poems *A Ring in der Keyt* (1916) was followed by *Zamd* (1920), a collection of lyrics which included a memorable poem on Theodor Herzl. After a trip to the U.S.S.R. in 1926, he contributed to the Communist daily *Freiheit* but parted company with it in 1929, when it justified Arab attacks on Jews. He then became press officer of the *American Jewish Joint Distribution Committee.

His poem *"Zavl Rimer"* (1923), a rhymed chronicle in 16 chapters, exposed the horror of the postwar Russian pogroms. The narrative structure of the poem restrains his emotional lyricism, though several parts are in the tradition of Yiddish folksong. *Der Geyer* ("The Wayfarer," 2 vols., 1943) is a spiritual autobiography on which he worked for ten years. It describes the progress of its major figure, Noah Marcon, from skepticism to faith and from the profane to the holy. The work is a poetical attempt to summarize the intellectual legacy of Judaism and Jewish history in recent generations. His last poems, *Durkh Doyres* ("Through Generations"), appeared posthumously in 1950.

Bibliography: Rejzen, Leksikon, 2 (1927), 438–41; *Algemeyne Entsiklopedye,* 5 (1944), 230–2; B. Rivkin, *Yidishe Dikhter in Amerike* (1947), 249–64; J. Botoschansky, *Peshat* (Yid., 1952), 151–86; LNYL, 1 (1956), 246–9; S. Bickel, *Shrayber fun Mayn Dor,* 1 (1958), 208–15; E. Biletzky, *Essays on Yiddish Poetry and Prose Writers* (1969), 103–16.

[Sh.N./Ed.]

BORCHARDT, LUCY (1878–1969), German shipping owner and operator. On the death of her husband Richard she became head of the Hamburg Fairplay Tug Company whose craft were known throughout the continent. From 1933 she devoted her energies and resources to enable Jews to escape from Germany. She herself left in 1938 and with her son Karl founded the Fairplay Towage and Shipping Company and the Borchardt Lines in London. With her son Jens she formed the Atid Navigation in Haifa which was liquidated in 1968. After having fallen out with her son Jens she established a competing line to Israel, the Lucy Borchardt Shipping Ltd. "Mother Borchardt," as she was known in shipping circles, took a special interest in the personal needs and welfare of her staff.

[J.O.R.]

BORCHARDT, LUDWIG (1863–1938), German Egyptologist and archaeologist. Borchardt's outstanding career as an Egyptologist rested on his knowledge of architecture as well as Egyptian language. Born and educated in Berlin, he became assistant to the department of Egyptian art in the Berlin Museum. In 1895 he left for Egypt where he examined details in important excavations, and was thus able to revise the interpretation of typical Egyptian building complexes. He was the first to recognize that the pyramid formed an integral part of the temple area. He excavated several pyramids and published monographs on their origin and development. His study of the ancient Egyptian column types and their development helped him to work out the complicated archaeological history of the great temples at Thebes. The structure of the early Egyptian house became the subject of Borchardt's research at the time of his excavations of Tell el-Amarna, the town in which Pharaoh Amenophis IV-Akhenaton (1379–1362 B.C.E.) had lived. In the course of these excavations, he uncovered the workshops of the royal sculptor Thutmose, with many naturalistic portrait models, among them the world-famous painted limestone model head of Queen Nefertiti. Numerous excavations and publications testify to the continuous industry of Borchardt. In 1906 he founded the German Institute for Ancient Egyptian History and Archaeology (Deutsches Institut fuer aegyptische Altertumskunde) in Cairo and was its director until World War I and from 1923 until 1929. Borchardt played an important role in the planning and organization of the great *Catalogue Général des Antiquités Egyptiennes du Musée du Caire* (1897ff., still unfinished). Later he became interested in the question of the identification of Atlantis, the lost continent, which he suggested (at a conference of the Paris Atlantidean Society, 1926) should be identified with *Bahr Atala,* i.e., "Sea of Atlantis," submerged c. 1250 B.C.E., in the northern Sahara, south of Tunis. Among his many publications are: *Die aegyptische Pflanzensaeule* (1897); *Zur Baugeschichte des Amonstempels von Karnak* (1905); *Portraets der Koenigin Nofret-ete aus den Grabungen 1912–13 in Tell el-Amarna* (1923); *Die Enstehung der Pyramide, an der Baugeschichte der Pyramide bei Mejdum nachgewiesen* (1928); and *Die Entstehung des Generalkatalogs und seine Entwicklung in den Jahren 1897–99* (1937).

[P.P.K.]

°**BORCHSENIUS, POUL** (1897–), Danish pastor and author. During the Nazi occupation of Denmark in World War II, Borchsenius was an active member of the underground. He escaped to Sweden, where he engaged in welfare work among his Christian fellow-refugees. He kept

Poul Borchsenius, Danish pastor and author.

in close touch with Jewish fugitives from Denmark and became an enthusiastic Zionist. Borchsenius wrote a series of five volumes on Jewish history after the destruction of the Second Temple: *Stjernesønnen* (1952; *Son of a Star,* 1960), based on the life of *Bar Kokhba; *De tre ringe* (1954; *The Three Rings,* 1963), a history of Spanish Jewry; *Bag muren* (1957; *Behind the Wall,* 1964), an account of the medieval ghetto; *Løste lænker* (1958; *The Chains are Broken,* 1964), the story of Jewish emancipation; and *Og det blev morgen, historien om vor tids jøder* (1960; *And it was Morning, History of the Jews in our Time,* 1962). In two other works, *Sol stat stille* ("Sun, Stand Thou Still," 1950) and *Syv år for Rachel; Israel 1948–1955* ("Seven Years for Rachel," 1955), Borchsenius wrote about the State of Israel. He also published a biography of Israel's first premier, *Ben Gurion: den moderne Israels skaber* ("Ben Gurion, Creator of Modern Israel," 1956) and *Two Ways to God* (1968), a study of Judaism and Christianity.

[T.M.]

BORDEAUX (Heb. בורדיאוש), city in the department of Gironde, S.E. France; in the Middle Ages, capital of the duchy of Guienne. The first written evidence of the presence of Jews in Bordeaux dates to the second half of the sixth century, when it is related that a Jew derided a priest who expected a saint to cure him of his illness. A golden signet ring, dating from the beginning of the fourth century, was found in Bordeaux in 1854 bearing three *menorot* and the inscription "Aster" (=Asterius). Prudence of Troyes relates that the Jews behaved treacherously during the capture of Bordeaux by the Normans in 848. Although based on malice, this anecdote confirms the presence of Jews in the city. From 1072 reference is made to a Mont-Judaique, outside the walls between the present Rues Dauphine and Mériadec, where the Jewish cemetery was located. The Jewish street, called Arrua Judega in 1247 (now Rue Cheverus) lay at the foot of this hill (now leveled off). The present Porte Dijeaux (=Dijeus, de Giu) is referred to as Porta Judaea from 1075. While Bordeaux was under English sovereignty (1154–1453), the Jews were spared the edicts of expulsion issued by the kings of France though they were nominally expelled in 1284, 1305, and 1310–11. The anti-Jewish measures introduced by the English kings were undoubtedly aimed at extorting money, since the Jews continued to reside in Bordeaux and pursue their activities. In 1275 and 1281 Edward I intervened on behalf of the Jews of Bordeaux who were being overtaxed by nobles. However, Edward II issued a further ineffective edict of expulsion in 1313, and in 1320 the Jews were savagely attacked by the *Pastoureaux. Their residence was authorized by Edward III in 1342, when they had to pay an annual due of eight pounds of pepper to the archbishop. The Jews in Bordeaux were organized into the *Communitas Judeorum Vasconie* ("Community of the Jews of Gascony"). It is not certain whether or when they were formally expelled after Bordeaux was incorporated into France in 1453.

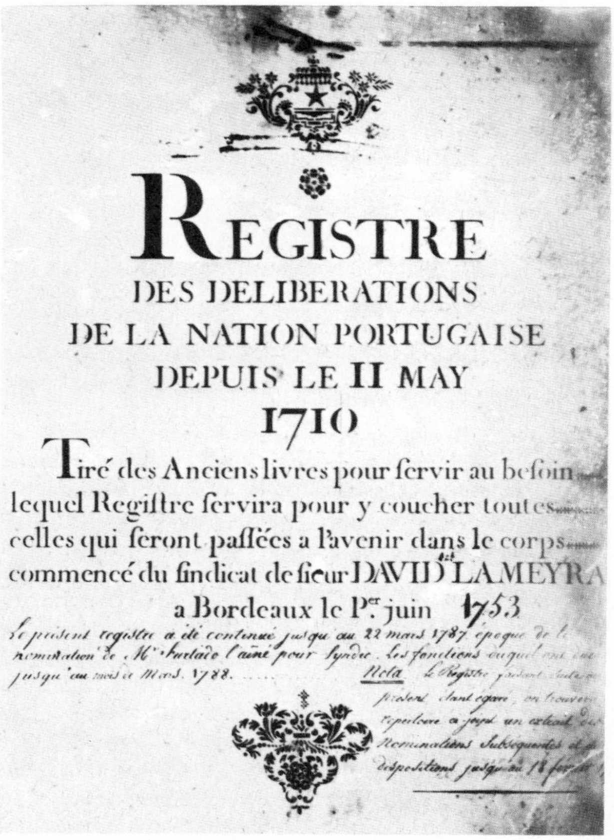
REGISTRE
DES DELIBERATIONS
DE LA NATION PORTUGAISE
DEPUIS LE II MAY
1710
Tiré des Anciens livres pour servir au besoin lequel Registre servira pour y coucher toutes celles qui seront passées a l'avenir dans le corps commencé du sindicat de sieur DAVID LAMEYRA
a Bordeaux le 1er. juin 1753
Le présent registre a été continué jusqu'au 22 mars 1787 époque de la nomination de Mr Furtado l'ainé pour syndic.

Figure 1. Title page of the register of resolutions of the Bordeaux Portuguese "Nation," recording proceedings from 1710 to 1787. Bordeaux, Archives Departmentales de la Gironde.

At the end of the 15th century, Marranos began to arrive in Bordeaux, first coming from Spain and later from Portugal. The Marranos were appreciated for their commercial activities, and in 1550 obtained letters-patent from Henry II authorizing "the merchants and other Portuguese called 'New Christians'" to reside in the towns and localities of their choice. They outwardly practiced Catholicism, and although the general populace suspected them the authorities closed their eyes to possible Judaizing. A more liberal attitude was evinced when in 1604 and in 1612 *Maréchal* d'Ornano, lieutenant-général of Guienne, issued an ordinance forbidding persons to "speak ill of or do evil to the Portuguese merchants." Since they lived mainly in the two parishes of St. Eulalie and St. Eloy, Marranos claimed burial in the cemeteries of the two parish churches, as well as those belonging to the parishes of St. Projet and St. Michel, and in the cemeteries of the Augustine, Carmelite, Franciscan, and St. Francis of Paola monasteries. In 1710 a portion of the Catholic cemetery was reserved especially for them. Their marriages were performed by Catholic priests, and all the formalities, including application for papal dispensation in cases of consanguinity, were duly observed. A change of attitude can be noted in 1710 when the Marranos began to profess Judaism more openly. If the priests continued to register their marriages, they added a note to the effect that the marriage had been or would be performed "in accordance with the customary rites of the Portuguese nation."

At the beginning of the 18th century, a communal institution was established, ostensibly to serve as a charitable organization, named Sedaca. Out of its funds, which were derived from regular contributions paid by its members according to their ability, the organization paid for the maintenance of the Sephardi communities of the "four holy cities" of Ereẓ Israel, for the local poor, and for needy travelers. Subsequently, the Sedaca undertook to provide for the cost of a physician for the poor, as well as to pay for certain officeholders in the community, the teachers of the *talmud torah* (established before 1710), and a rabbi. The first to hold this office was Joseph Falcon (from 1719), followed by Jacob Ḥayyim Athias and the latter's son David. It was only in new letters-patent obtained in 1723 (the previous ones had been granted by Louis XIV in 1656) that the "Portuguese merchants" were for the first time officially referred to as Jews. At the turn of the century, Jews who declared themselves as such more openly had arrived from Avignon and Comtat-Venaissin to settle in Bordeaux. In 1722 they numbered 22 families. For reasons of respectability and other considerations, the "Portuguese" deliberately kept apart from the newcomers. In 1731 the municipal administrator objected to the regulation whereby the "Portuguese" Jews of Bordeaux had to pay protection tax like the Jews of *Metz. Nevertheless, in 1734 this official reminded the Jews of Bordeaux that the practice of the Jewish religion in public was forbidden. A report of 1753 mentions as a "scandal" that the Jewish religion was being practiced in seven synagogues; in fact these were prayer rooms in private dwellings.

Meanwhile, the communal organization of the Portuguese, the Sedaca, had taken the name "Nation." Apart from providing funds for religious and charitable requirements, it also supplied the funds necessary for registering letters-patent, for the salary of a representative in Paris, and other purposes. The "Nation" assumed the capacities of an internal police, in particular expelling paupers or vagrants from Bordeaux. Strictly charitable functions were henceforth discharged by specialized associations, the Yesibot, which included the Hebra or Hermandad for circumcisions and wedding ceremonies, and also attended to visits to the sick and funerals; the Guemilout Hazadim, the association of gravediggers; and the Yesiba Bikour Holim and Misenet Holim, for the care of and visits to the sick (see also *Ḥevrah). From 1728, the "Nation" had its own cemetery (today Cours St. Jean no. 105), acquired by David Gradis in 1724. Burials took place there from 1725 until the French Revolution (this cemetery was closed in 1911), and from 1764 in a second cemetery (now Cours de l'Yser no. 176), which subsequently served the entire Jewish community of Bordeaux. The "Avignonese" owned a cemetery from 1728 on land purchased by David Petit (now Rue Sauteyron no. 49); this cemetery was used until 1805. The status of the "Nation" of the "Portuguese" community was approved by Louis XV on Dec. 14, 1769. The "Avignonese" constituted themselves a "Nation" in 1759, but had, in fact, been an organic body for a long while. The "Portuguese" engaged in financial activities and the supply of marine equipment, the "Avignonese" engaged almost exclusively in the textile and clothing trades, new or secondhand. In 1734 a decree was issued expelling the "Avignonese, Tudesque, or German" Jews from Bordeaux. This, however, they managed to evade by obtaining permission to prolong their stay under various pretexts. New decrees of expulsion were issued in 1740 and 1748. In 1759 six Avignonese Jewish families at last obtained letters-patent similar to those of the "Portuguese."

At the beginning of the 18th century, the Portuguese Jews in Bordeaux numbered 327 families (1,422 persons), while the "Avignonese" Jews numbered 81 families (348 persons).

On the eve of the French Revolution, while the *Malesherbes Commission was engaged in its task of studying the reforms to be applied to the condition of the French Jews, the "Portuguese Nation" of Bordeaux appointed two representatives to attend it in April 1788, S. Lopès-Dubec and Abraham *Furtado. These proposed that clauses be included in the constitution planned for the Jews of France to ensure the maintenance of ancient privileges relating to freedom of residence, economic activities, property, etc. They also envisaged the possibility of differentiating between the legal status of the Spanish and Portuguese Jews on the one hand and of the "German" Jews on the other. Contrary to what was happening elsewhere, the Jews of Bordeaux directly participated in the preparation of the States-General. When on Dec. 24, 1789, this assembly determined to defer a decision on the concession of equal rights to the Jews, a deputation of seven Sephardi Jews from Bordeaux, including David Gradis and Abraham Rodrigues, went to Paris. Their activities resulted in a decree issued on Jan. 28, 1790, declaring that "all Jews known in France under the name of Portuguese, Spanish, and Avignonese Jews . . . shall enjoy the rights of citizens." One of the first manifestations of this equality of rights was on Dec. 6, 1790, when A. Furtado and S. Lopès-Dubec took office on the municipal council of Bordeaux. These two also figured on the Bordeaux Committee for Public Safety formed on June 10, 1793. During the Reign of Terror no Bordeaux Jews were condemned to death but many were imprisoned or ordered to pay heavy fines.

A census of 1806 records 2,131 Jews living in Bordeaux, of whom 1,651 were of Spanish or Portuguese origin, 144 Avignonese, and 336 of German, Polish, or Dutch origin. When the *Assembly of Jewish Notables was convened by Napoleon that year, the department of the Gironde sent two delegates, both from Bordeaux, Abraham Furtado and Isaac Rodrigues: the first became president of the Assembly

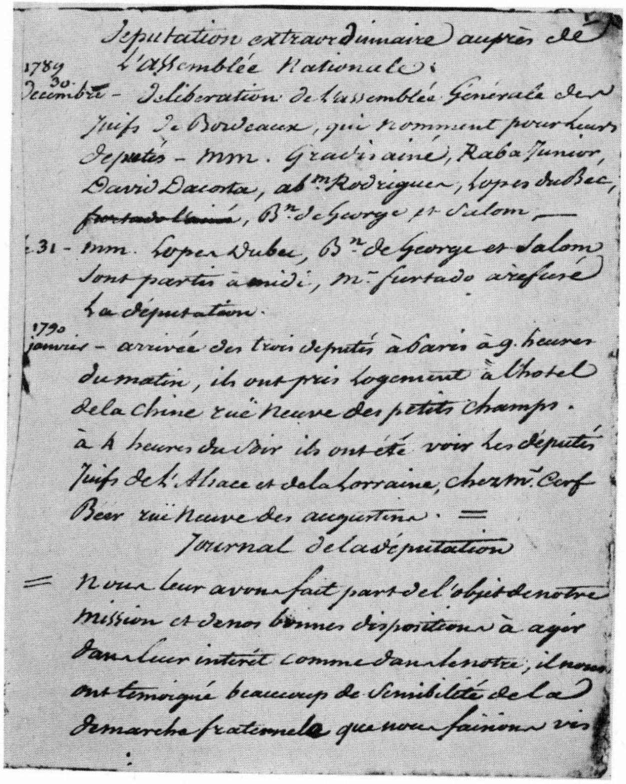
Députation extraordinaire auprès de l'Assemblée Nationale:
1789 30. Décembre – Délibération de l'assemblée Générale des Juifs de Bordeaux, qui nomment pour leurs députés – mm. Gradis ainé, Raba Junior, David Dacosta, abm Rodrigues, Lopes Dubec, ~~furtado l'ainé~~, Bn de George et Salom —
31 – mm. Lopes Dubec, Bn de George et Salom sont partis à midi, m. furtado a refusé la députation.
1790 janvier – arrivée des trois députés à Paris à 9 heures du matin, ils ont pris logement à l'hotel de la Chine rue Neuve des petits champs.
à 4 heures du soir ils ont été voir les députés Juifs de l'Alsace et de la Lorraine, chez mr. Cerf Beer rue Neuve des augustins. =
Journal de la députation
= Nous leur avons fait part de l'objet de notre mission et de nos bonnes dispositions à agir dans leur interêt comme dans le notre; ils nous ont temoigné beaucoup de sensibilité de la demarche fraternelle que nous faisions vis

Figure 2. Beginning of the diary of the Bordeaux Jewish deputation to the French National Assembly, December 30, 1789–January 1, 1790. Jerusalem, C.A.H.J.P.

and the second its secretary. In the consistorial organization (see *Consistory) which was formed following the sessions of the "Great Sanhedrin" (see French *Sanhedrin), Bordeaux became the seat of a Consistory whose jurisdiction extended over ten departments, with 3,713 members. Abraham Andrade was appointed chief rabbi. The private prayer rooms were replaced by a large synagogue (Rue Causserouge), inaugurated on May 14, 1812, and partly destroyed by fire in 1873. Of the 12 members of the municipal council in 1830 two were Jews: Camille Lopès-Dubec and Joseph Rodrigues. Lopès-Dubec was also one of the 15 deputies elected for the department of the Gironde to the National Assembly in 1848. Toward the middle of the 19th century Jewish institutions in Bordeaux included a school for boys and girls, a trade school, and a *talmud torah.* In the second half of the 19th century, many Jews sat on the general council of the department, on the municipal council, and in the chamber of commerce. Adrien Léon was elected to the National Assembly in 1875.

During the 19th century, the Jewish population of Bordeaux dwindled through emigration, numbering only 1,940 in 1900. [B.Bl.]

Holocaust and Postwar Periods. Bordeaux served as a final station for countless Jewish refugees who fled from northern France in May–June 1940. The town, administered within the Occupied Zone after the Franco-German armistice (June 21, 1940), was one of the most important centers of Nazi police and military activities. Two-thirds of the Jewish population, local Jews and refugees alike, were arrested and deported, including the residents of the old-age home. A census of the Jewish population of June 1941 showed only 1,198 persons originating from Bordeaux or from southeastern France out of a total of 5,177; most were refugees from other parts of France and even from abroad. The head office of the international rescue organization HIAS-ICA was transferred to Bordeaux. Between July 1942 and February 1944, 1,279 Jews were deported from Bordeaux by the Germans. A monument has been erected in their memory. In January 1944, French Fascists ransacked the great synagogue, which the Nazis had turned into a detention camp where the victims of their roundups waited to be deported. After the war the survivors of the Bordeaux Jewish community reconstructed the synagogue with the aid of photographs and eyewitness accounts. When the task was completed 12 years later, the Bordeaux synagogue (built in 1882) was restored to its former renown as the largest (1,500 seats) and most beautiful Sephardi synagogue in France. Meanwhile the Jewish population increased with the arrival of new members, including a new Ashkenazi congregation. In 1960 there were 3,000 Jews in the community, and with the arrival of Jewish immigrants from N. Africa, the population doubled, with 5,500 persons in 1969. Bordeaux, the seat of a Chief Rabbinate, maintains a community center and a network of Jewish institutions.

[G.LE.]

Bibliography: L. F. de Beaufleury, *Histoire de l'établissement des Juifs à Bordeaux et Bayonne* (1800); T. Malvezin, *Histoire des Juifs à Bordeaux* (1875); G. Cirot, *Les Juifs de Bordeaux* (1920); idem, in: *Revue historique de Bordeaux . . . ,* 29 (1936); 31 (1938); 32 (1939); Gross, Gal Jud, 111; A. Detcheverry, *Histoire des Israélites de Bordeaux* (1850); Drouyn, in: *Archives historiques de la Gironde,* 21 (1881), 159, 272, 533, 535; 22 (1882), 48, 563, 569, 599, 635, 639; Gaullier, in: REJ, 11 (1885), 78ff.; Bouchon, in: *Bulletin de la Société Archéologique de Bordeaux,* 35 (1913), 69ff.; A. de Maille, *Recherches sur les origines chrétiennes de Bordeaux* (1960), 211ff.; H. G. Richardson, *English Jewry under Angevin Kings* (1960), 232–3; Z. Szajkowski, *Analytical Franco-Jewish Gazetteer* (1966), index; idem, in: PAAJR, 27 (1958), 83ff.

BORDJEL (Burgel), Tunisian family of community leaders and scholars. In the 17th century ABRAHAM amassed a large fortune in Leghorn and returned to Tunis. His son NATHAN (I) (d. 1791), a student of Isaac *Lumbroso, wrote *Ḥok Natan* (Leghorn, 1776–78), reprinted in the Vilna edition of the Talmud. A rabbinical authority, Nathan was consulted by rabbis from Ereẓ Israel and elsewhere. He died in Jerusalem. His son ELIJAH ḤAI (I) wrote *Migdanot Natan* (Leghorn, 1778) in two parts: commentaries on the Talmud and Maimonides' *Yad Ḥazakah;* and treatises and funeral orations. Elijah's son JOSEPH (1791–1857) supported a yeshivah at his own expense and had many disciples. He left two important works: *Zara de-Yosef* (1849) and *Va-Yikken Yosef* (1852). His brother NATHAN (II), scholar and philanthropist, published the first of these works and added a preface. His nephew ELIJAH ḤAI (II) (d. 1898), *caid (maggid)* and chief rabbi of Tunis, published the second. SOLOMON, *caid* in 1853, had great influence on the bey. MOSES (d. 1945) was highly respected for his knowledge, piety, and authority. During the Nazi occupation, Moses served in the difficult position of a leader of the Tunis community.

Bibliography: D. Cazès, *Notes bibliographique sur la littérature juive-tunisienne* (1893), 60–76; Hirschberg, Afrikah, 2 (1965), index.

[D.CO.]

BORGHI, LAMBERTO (1907–), Italian educator and author. Born in Leghorn, Borghi studied at the University of Pisa. He went to the U.S. as a refugee in 1938. In 1952 he returned to Italy to fill the chair of pedagogy at the University of Florence and to direct its Institute of Pedagogy. Borghi showed a keen interest in comparative education and wrote extensively on Italian education. In two of his books, *Educazione e autorità nell'Italia moderna* (1950) and *Educazione e scuola nell' Italia d'oggi* (1958), he discussed the nature and problems of the Italian educational system, including education in the arts and sciences and the limitations imposed by inherited social and economic status on educational opportunities. His books

Lamberto Borghi, Italian educator.

include *Umanismo e concezione religiosa in Erasmus di Rotterdam* (1936); *Education in the U.S.A.* (1949); *John Dewey e il pensiero pedagogico contemporaneo negli Stati Uniti* (1951; Eng. tr., 1952); *Saggi di psicologia dell'educazione* (1951); *Il fondamento dell' educazione attiva* (1952); *Il metodo dei progetti* (1952); *L'educazione e i suoi problemi* (1953); *L'ideale educativo di John Dewey* (1955); and *Educazione e sviluppo sociale* (1962).

Bibliography: G. Z. F. Bereday, *Comparative Method in Education* (1964), 210.

[ER.S.]

BORGIL, ABRAHAM BEN AZIZ (d. 1595?), Turkish rabbinical scholar. Borgil studied in Salonika for many years under Samuel b. Moses *Medina, later becoming head of the yeshivah of Nikopol (Bulgaria), where he employed a unique approach to the teaching of Talmud. His yeshivah became famous and the city became a center of talmudic studies. Borgil's novellae on tractates *Bava Kamma, Bava Meẓia, Ketubbot,* and *Kiddushin* were published under the title *Leḥem Abbirim* (Venice, 1605); the novellae on *Yevamot* which are attributed to him are probably not his. His novellae on *Ḥullin* are extant in manuscript (Moscow, Guenzburg Ms. no. 125). In his novellae, Borgil does not cite his contemporaries or *rishonim* but bases himself, for the most part, upon the tosafists, and, to a certain extent, upon Rashi. It was Borgil's practice to refer to manuscripts of the Talmud for text verification.

Bibliography: M. Benayahu, in: *Sefer ha-Yovel le-Ḥanokh Albeck* (1963), 71–80.

[ED.]

BORINSTEIN, LOUIS J. (1881–), U.S. merchant and civic leader. Borinstein was born in Indianapolis, Indiana. He entered business there and became a partner in the A. Borinstein wholesale iron company in 1920. In 1924 he became vice-president of the Indianapolis Machinery and Supply Company. Active in civic affairs, Borinstein was president of the Indianapolis Chamber of Commerce (1931–36), National Recovery Administration chairman for Indianapolis, and a member of several state and municipal commissions. A president of his B'nai B'rith lodge (1917–18), Borinstein directed the Jewish Welfare Fund and managed Indiana campaigns of the United Jewish Appeal and the American Jewish Joint Distribution Committee. He served as a trustee of the Cleveland Orphan Home (from 1919) and director of the National Hospital in Denver.

[E.GR.]

BORISLAV (Pol. **Boryslaw**), city in Ukrainian S.S.R. (until 1939, Galicia, Poland). Borislav, which at the end of the 19th century was nicknamed the "California of Galicia," in 1920 supplied 75% of the oil in Poland. The industry was pioneered by Jews. About 1880 the numerous wells located by them employed about 3,000 Jewish workers from Borislav and the vicinity. At this time, large Austrian and foreign banks, subsidizing modern techniques, began to squeeze out the smaller enterprises and Jewish labor, although a number of wells were still Jewish owned. In 1898 some of the unemployed workers petitioned the Second Zionist Congress to grant them facilities to emigrate to Ereẓ Israel. At the request of Theodor Herzl, the Alliance Israélite Universelle assisted approximately 500 workers to leave for the United States. The Jewish community of Borislav had been affiliated with the *Drogobych *kehillah*, and became independent in 1928. From 1867 to 1903 Borislav formed part of an Austrian parliamentary electoral district in which the majority of the constituents were Jewish. In 1887 the first society of Ḥovevei Zion was established in Borislav. In 1860 the Jewish population of Borislav numbered about 1,000; in 1890, 9,047 (out of a total of 10,424); in 1910, 5,753 (out of 12,767); in 1921, 7,170 (out of 16,000); and in 1939 over 13,000.

[N.M.G./Ed.]

Holocaust and Postwar Periods. When the town came under Soviet administration in 1939, the Jewish institutions were disbanded and the political parties ceased to function. Jewish merchants were forced out of business, while the artisans were organized into cooperatives. Refugees from western Poland were deported from Borislav to the Soviet interior in the summer of 1940. When the war with Germany broke out (June 1941) many young Jews joined the Soviet army, and others fled with the retreating Soviet authorities. The town fell to the Germans on July 1, 1941, and the following day the Ukrainians staged a pogrom against the Jewish community, killing more than 200 Jews. A *Judenrat was set up, headed by Michael Herz. The first *Aktion* took place on Nov. 29–30, 1941, when 1,500 Jews were murdered in the forests of two neighboring villages. The following winter (1941–42), hunger and disease made inroads on the Jewish community. In 1942 able-bodied Jews were sent to the labor camps of Popiele, *Skole, and *Stryj, and about 5,000 Jews were sent to *Belzec death camp. Two separate ghettos were established, followed by a series of roundups in which hundreds were sent to Belzec. Toward the end of 1942 a special labor camp was established in Borislav for the oil industries. The extermination process of the Jewish community continued with the execution, at the city slaughterhouse, on Feb. 16–17, 1943, of some 600 women, children, and elderly people. During May–August 1943, the remaining Jews were killed and only some 1,500 slave laborers were temporarily spared. Jews who tried to hide in the forests and in the city itself were mostly caught and killed by the Germans, with the cooperation of local Ukrainians belonging mostly to the bands of Stefan Bandera. In April–July 1944 the local labor camp was liquidated and the last surviving members of the Jewish community were brought to *Plaszow labor camp from where they were sent on to death or concentration camps in Germany. There were resistance groups among the young Jews of Borislav, but the only detail known about them is the fact that one of their leaders, Lonek Hofman, was killed while attempting to assault a German foreman. When Soviet forces took Borislav on Aug. 8, 1944, some 200 Jewish survivors were found in the forests and in local hideouts. Another 200 Jews came back later from the Soviet Union and from German concentration camps. A monument was erected to the Jews who fell in World War II but was allowed to fall into disrepair. The Jewish cemetery was closed down in 1959. In 1970, the number of Jews in Borislav was estimated at 3,000. There was no synagogue. A society composed of emigrants from Borislav and Drogobych and the vicinity was set up in Israel. [Ar.W.]

Bibliography: Gelber, in: *Sefer Drohobycz ve-ha-Sevivah* (1959), 171–6; K. Holzman, *Be-Ein Elohim* (1956); T. Brustin-Berenstein in: *Bleter far Geshikhte*, 6, no. 3 (1953), 45–100; *Sefer Zikkaron le-Drohobiz, Borislav, ve-ha-Sevivah* (1959), Heb. with Yid.

BORISOV, town in Minsk oblast, Belorussian S.S.R. Jews were living there in the 17th century; 249 Jewish taxpayers are recorded in Borisov in 1776. The main Jewish occupations were dealing in grain and timber, sent northward by river to Riga via the Dvina and to southern Russia via the Dnieper. Around 1900 Borisov became a center of Bund activity. The Jewish population numbered 2,851 in 1861; 7,722 in 1897 (54.2% of the total); and 10,617 on the outbreak of World War I, subsequently decreasing to 8,358 (32.3%) by 1926. During the German occupation in World War II the Jews in Borisov, first confined to a ghetto, were murdered on Oct. 20, 1941.

Bibliography: Lipkind, in: *Keneset ha-Gedolah*, 1 (1890), 26–32; Eisenstadt, in: *Bleter far Geshikhte*, 9 (1956), 45–70; Office of U.S. Chief of Counsel for Prosecution of Axis Criminality, *Nazi Conspiracy and Aggression*, 5 (1946), 772–6. [S.K./Y.S.]

BORISOV, ANDREY YAKOVLEVICH (1903–1942), Russian orientalist. Borisov made important contributions to the history of medieval Jewish philosophy. Among the *genizah* manuscripts preserved in Leningrad, he discovered manuscripts of Isaac Israeli and the Karaite Yūsuf al-Bāsir. His works include an article on the tractate *Ma'ānī al-Nafs*, the so-called "Pseudo-Baḥya" (in USSR Academy of Sciences, *Izvestiya* (*Otdeleniye obshchestvennykh nauk;* 1929), 775–97), and on Moses ibn Ezra's poetry (*ibid.*, no. 4 (1933), 99–117). He also wrote shorter articles on problems in medieval Jewish literary history. [S.M.S.]

°**BORMANN, MARTIN** (1900–), Nazi leader. He joined the Nazi Party in 1925, after having been active in right-wing organizations. By 1933 he had become chief of staff to Rudolf Hess, Hitler's deputy. In May 1941 he replaced Hess as administrative head of the Party chancellery. By a decree of Jan. 24, 1942, Bormann was given control over all laws and directives issued by Hitler, including the directives of the *Final Solution in all of Hitler's Europe. His representatives participated both at the *Wannsee Conference on Jan. 20, 1942, and at the March 6, 1942, conference that dealt with the fate of Jewish partners in mixed marriages and their offspring. According to the judgment of the International Military Tribunal, Bormann took part in the discussions which led to the removal of 60,000 Jews from Vienna to Poland, signing the order of Oct. 9, 1942, in which he declared that the elimination of Jews from Greater Germany could be solved only by applying "ruthless force" in the special camps in the East. On July 1, 1943, he cosigned an ordinance withdrawing Jews who violated the law from the jurisdiction of the courts and placing them under the jurisdiction of the Gestapo. Goering included him in the group of five "real conspirators" along with Hitler, Himmler, Goebbels, and Heydrich. In 1946 Bormann, who was the "Grey Eminence" of the Third Reich, was sentenced to death in absentia by the International Military Tribunal at Nuremberg. His exact whereabouts after the war remained unknown. The attorney-general of Frankfort opened a case against Bormann and a reward of 100,000 DM was posted for information leading to his arrest.

Bibliography: Office of U.S. Chief of Counsel for Prosecution of Axis Criminality, *Nazi Conspiracy and Aggression*, 2 (1946), 896–915; H. R. Trevor-Roper, *Bormann Letters* (1954); J. Wulf, *Martin Bormann: Hitlers Schatten* (1962); J. McGovern, *Martin Bormann* (Eng., 1968).

[Y.Re.]

BORN, MAX (1882–1970), German physicist and Nobel Prize winner. A son of the anatomist Gustav Born, he was born in Breslau and lectured on physics in Berlin (1915), Frankfort (1919), and Goettingen (1921). Although he had dissociated himself from the Jewish community, Born was dismissed from Goettingen in 1933 because of his Jewish origins. He settled in England working first at the Cavendish Laboratory, Cambridge, and then from 1936 lecturing in applied mathematics at Edinburgh University. On his retirement from teaching in 1953, he returned to Germany.

Born played an important role in the development of modern theoretical physics. He developed the modern mathematical explanation of the basic properties of matter but his outstanding achievement was his work on quantum theory and the use of matrix computations. He was the first to recognize that the function of Schroedinger's waves could be explained as a statistical function which describes the probability of a certain behavior of a solitary molecule in space and time. He examined the problems of probability and wrote a number of books on physics, including *Aufbau der Materie* (1922^2), *Atomtheorie des festen Zustandes* (1923), *Atommechanik* (1925), *Moderne Physik* (1933), *Atomic Physics* (1947^4), and *A General Kinetic Theory of Liquids* (1949). Born was also concerned with the general philosophical problems of natural science, an interest reflected in his works *The Restless Universe* (1936) and *Natural Philosophy of Cause and Chance* (1949). His discussion with *Einstein (a close friend of his) on the meaning of cause and chance in modern science was summarized in his article *Physics and Metaphysics*

Max Born, winner of the Nobel Prize for physics. Lithograph by Harald Isenstein, 1963, 8¾×12½ in. (22.5×32 cm.). Jerusalem, Israel Museum.

(published in *Penguin Science News*, 17 (1950), 9–27). In 1954, Born and W. Bothe were awarded the Nobel Prize for physics for their work on the mathematical basis of quantum mechanics. Eight of Born's essays, revealing his enduring interest in the ethical problems underlying man's vast increase in power through science, were published in 1968 as *My Life and My Views*.

Bibliography: H. Vogel, *Physik und Philosophie bei Max Born* (1968). [M.GOL.]

BORNFRIEND, JACOB (Jakub Bauernfreund; 1904–), painter. Bornfriend was born in a Slovak village. Exposed to the art movements of the period between the two world wars, Bornfriend tried and then abandoned impressionism, cubism, and surrealism. He attained a fair standard in each without finding an individual style. In 1939

"Arctic Birds" by Jacob Bornfriend, 1959. Oil, 25×30 in. (63×76 cm.). London, H. Roland Collection.

Bornfriend escaped to England and worked in factories for six years. He returned to his easel with a personality of his own, combining the formal influence of Picasso with the spiritual influence of Jankel *Adler. Bornfriend retained the warmth and bright colors of his early life, combining a sense of strict laws of form with a deep feeling for human pathos.

Bibliography: Garrett, in: *Studio*, 145 (1953), 160–3; Roth, Art, 831–3. [AV.D.]

BORNSTEIN, ELI (1922–), Canadian artist. Born in Milwaukee, Wisconsin, Bornstein studied in the United States and with Fernand Léger in Paris. He went to Canada in 1950, and later became head of the department of art at the University of Saskatchewan, Saskatoon. Bornstein headed the structurist school, which was centered in Saskatoon, and edited its magazine *The Structurist*. The structurists created a pure, geometric abstract form of art which they felt to be a development of the tradition of Cézanne and the cubists. Their favorite art form was the structurist relief, "a new synthesis of the color of painting and the actual form and space of sculpture." Bornstein received many commissions to execute such reliefs for public buildings and created one in five parts for an exhibition commemorating the centenary of the Canadian Confederation in 1967. [Y.DU.]

BORNSTEIN, ḤAYYIM JEHIEL (1845–1928), authority on the Jewish calendar. Bornstein was born into a ḥasidic family in Kozienice, receiving a traditional Jewish education and studying European languages and secular subjects, especially mathematics, on his own. He worked as an accountant in a sugar factory in the village of Manishev and then settled in Warsaw in 1881. From 1886 on he was secretary of the Tlomackie synagogue in Warsaw. Bornstein's knowledge of chronology, history, and mathematics enabled him to open new avenues in the study of the development of the Jewish calendar. He based his theories on several documents in the Cairo *Genizah*, the importance of which he was the first to recognize. Bornstein advanced the novel claim that the details of the Jewish calendar, with its small cycle of 19 lunar years and its method of reckoning the conjunction of the planets, had not been calculated and accepted until sometime between the mid-eighth and mid-ninth century C.E., and not in the period of the *amoraim* under *Hillel II, as had been generally believed—much less in the first century C.E., as claimed by the German chronologist F.K. Ginzel.

Bornstein published *"Parashat ha-Ibbur"* (*Ha-Kerem*, 1887), *"Maḥaloket Rav Sa'adyah Ga'on u-Ven Meir bi-Kevi'at Shenot 4672–4674"* (*Sefer ha-Yovel Li-khevod Naḥum Sokolov*, 1904), *Ta'arikhei Yisrael* (*Ha-Tekufah*, 1921, nos. 8, 9), and *Ḥeshbon Shematim ve-Yovelot* (*ibid.*, no. 11). M. Teitelbaum's study of *Shneur Zalman of Lyady incorporated an appendix by Bornstein on Shneur Zalman's knowledge of geometry, astronomy, and natural science. Bornstein also translated several classics of general literature into Hebrew, among them the Polish poet Adam Mickiewicz's *Farys* (in N. Sokolow (ed.), *Sefer ha-Shanah* (1900), 326–34), and Shakespeare's *Hamlet* (1926).

Bibliography: A. M. Habermann, in: S. K. Mirsky (ed.), *Ishim u-Demuyyot be-Ḥokhmat Yisrael be-Eiropah ha-Mizraḥit Lifnei Sheki'atah* (1959), 137–244; N. Sokolow, *Sefer Zikkaron* (1889); idem, in: *Ha-Tekufah*, 25 (1929), 528; idem, *Ishim* (1958), 101–43; *Ha-Sifrut ha-Yafah be-Ivrit* (1927); A. A. Akaviah, in: Ẓ. H. Yafeh (ed.), *Korot Ḥeshbon ha-Ibbur* (1931), introduction. [A.H.F.]

BOROCHOV, BER (Dov; 1881–1917), Socialist Zionist leader and foremost theoretician; scholar of the history, economic structure, language, and culture of the Jewish people. A brilliant analyst, in debate as well as in writing, Borochov influenced wide circles of the emerging Jewish labor movement, first in Russia, later in Central and Western Europe and the U.S. He postulated the concept of an organic unity between scientific socialism and devotion to the national needs of the Jewish people. He thus freed many young Jewish intellectuals from their preoccupation with the seemingly irreconcilable contradiction between social revolution and Zionism. Borochov's main theoretical contribution was his synthesis of class struggle and nationalism, at a time when prevalent Marxist theory rejected all nationalism, and particularly Jewish nationalism, as distinctly reactionary. Borochov regarded the mass migration of Jews in his time as an inevitable elemental social phenomenon, expressing the inner drive of the Jewish proletariat to seek a solution to the problem of its precarious existence in the Diaspora, where it is uprooted and separated from the basic processes of production. The task of Socialist Zionism, Borochov maintained, was to prepare "a new territory," i.e., Ereẓ Israel, through a pioneering effort, for the concentration of the masses of Jewish migrants. This would prevent the perpetuation of the Diaspora through continued dispersion in alien lands and economies, creating instead a Jewish national economic body as a framework for the natural class struggle of the Jewish proletariat.

Biography. Borochov was born in Zolotonosha, Ukraine, and grew up in Poltava, where he was educated in a Russian high school. A studious youth, he early displayed a tendency toward philosophic thought and was influenced by the revolutionary socialist trends of his period. Like most Jewish high school graduates, he was denied entrance to a Russian university, which in any case he rejected as alien to his spirit, and embarked on a strenuous process of self-education. He gained erudition in various fields and fluency in several languages. Borochov joined the ranks of the Russian Social Democratic Party, but his interests in specifically Jewish problems led him, in 1901, to establish the Zionist Socialist Workers Union at Yekaterinoslav. The association, which was active in organizing Jewish self-defense and in promoting the interests of Jewish workers, was opposed by both the Russian Social Democrats (who refused to recognize the need for an independent Jewish workers' movement) and some Zionist leaders (who disliked the association of Zionism with socialism).

During the controversy in the Zionist movement about the Uganda Scheme, Borochov took a clear-cut "Palestinist" stand and cooperated closely with Menahem *Ussishkin and other leaders of the "Zion Zionists" who opposed any *territorialism other than in Ereẓ Israel. Borochov traveled throughout Russia to convince the newly founded groups of *Po'alei Zion against territorialist tendencies, which seemed to be gaining increasing influence in Socialist Zionism. He was a delegate to the Seventh Zionist Congress (1905), leading the faction of those Po'alei Zion delegates who were "faithful to Zion." During the ensuing debates among Socialist-Zionists over the territorial issue, the political struggle in the Diaspora, and Sejmism, it was largely Borochov who laid the ideological and organizational foundations of the Po'alei Zion movement. At a conference in Poltava (1906), the movement was renamed the "Jewish Workers' Social Democratic Party Po'alei Zion." Borochov crystallized its doctrine in his treatise "Our Platform" (published as a series in the Po'alei Zion Party organ *Yevreyskaya Rabochaya Khronika* from July 1906) and in supplementary articles and debates with other trends in the Jewish labor movement over the role of the Jewish proletariat and the national problem. In 1907, during the Eighth Zionist Congress at The Hague, Borochov participated in the founding of the World Union of Po'alei Zion, as a separate union *(Sonderverband)* in the World Zionist Organization. After the Eighth Zionist Congress, Borochov insisted on the withdrawal of Russian Po'alei Zion from the Zionist Organization in order to preserve the proletarian independence of Socialist Zionism. From 1907, when he left Russia, until the outbreak of World War I, Borochov worked as a publicist to further the aims of the World Union of Po'alei Zion in Western and Central Europe. He continued his philosophical studies and research into Yiddish language and literature. He left Vienna in 1914 and arrived in the U.S., where he continued his activities as a spokesman for the American Po'alei Zion, as well as for the World and American Jewish Congress movements. He was

Dov Ber Borochov, founder of the Po'alei Zion party in Russia. Jerusalem, Schwadron Collection, J.N.U.L.

also editor of and contributor to the New York Yiddish daily *Di Warheit.* With the outbreak of the Russian Revolution, Borochov returned to Russia, stopping en route in Stockholm to join the Po'alei Zion delegation at a session of an international Socialist Commission of neutral countries. There he helped formulate the demands of the Jewish people and working class in the manifesto for the postwar world order. When he arrived in Russia, Borochov became intensely involved in public activity during the stormy period before the October Revolution. In August 1917, in an address to the Russian Po'alei Zion Conference, Borochov called for socialist settlement in Ereẓ Israel. In September 1917, he read a paper to the "Congress of Nations" in Kiev on "Russia as a Commonwealth of Nations." In the course of a speaking tour he contracted pneumonia and died in Kiev. His remains were taken to Israel in 1963 for reinterment at the Kinneret cemetery, alongside the graves of other founders of Socialist Zionism. A workers' quarter near Tel Aviv, Shekhunat Borochov, now part of the township of Givatayim, was named after him.

Theory. Borochov's Socialist Zionist credo was never dogmatic, parochial, or static; it was universal and dynamic, the evolving product of continuous inquiry and study. In an attempt to analyze the Jewish situation and its problem along Marxist ideological and methodological lines, Borochov sought to probe "beyond the cultural and spiritual manifestations and to examine the deeper concealed foundations of the Jewish problem." The root of the problem, Borochov said, was the divorce of the Jewish people from its homeland. He considered a people "without a country, without an independent economic basis, and trapped in alien economic relations" to be a powerless national minority. The Diaspora was responsible for the fact that the "social physiology of the Jewish people is organically sick." It created the historic conditions in which Jewry was torn between the process of assimilation into, and the isolation from, the host society. The Diaspora had thus divided Jewry's strength, and, because of the ultimate prevalence of "alienating forces," exacerbated the tension between Jews and their non-Jewish neighbors. The growing Jewish migration, while providing relief, was also testimony to Jewry's prolonged and aching conflict between ends and available means. The Jewish worker in the Diaspora occupied a particularly anomalous position. Since he lived in an economy in which petty, backward production predominated and was denied work in the modern, heavy industry, he had a narrow labor front and an abnormal, insufficient "strategic base" for his class struggle. As long as the Jewish economy was detached from those vital branches of production, which are "the axis of the historical wheel," the proletarization of the Jews would continue to be a slow, stunted, and uneven process.

In defining the Jewish problem, Borochov, while keenly aware of the constant threat of anti-Semitic outbursts in the Diaspora, never designated anti-Semitism as the fundamental basis or motivation of Zionism. He chose to view the whole of the Diaspora as a social aberration, reducing the Jews to a permanent state of economic inferiority and political helplessness. Thus, when proposing a solution to the problem, Borochov refused to believe that civil emancipation in the Diaspora, whether in a capitalist or socialist society, could, in itself, solve the Jewish problem. "Even when the State of Freedom will be established—and counterrevolution will be only a memory—the Jewish problem will still have to wait a long time for a specific answer." Assimilation, which Borochov attacked both theoretically and practically, was no less an anathema, whether in its bourgeois inception or in later socialist forms. The origins of assimilation—the mute antagonism between the successful individual and his miserable people—made it morally suspect, and an objective impossibility—the insurmountable objection of non-Jewish society—made it a dangerous daydream. Instead, the solution Borochov envisaged was a unique one, addressed to the particular needs of the Jews: only auto-emancipation, i.e., national self-liberation, could restore "to Jewish existence a healthy socio-economic basis, which is the keystone of national existence and national culture and the basis for a fruitful class struggle and socialist transformation of national life." This, he believed, was the Jewish people's particular road to socialist internationalism, a development which would herald the inevitable exodus from the Diaspora.

For Borochov, the Jewish renaissance and socialism were necessarily mutually interrelated, since Zionism and socialism together served the same purpose—making Jewish life productive again. Zionism was necessary because Jewish migratory movements disperse the Jewish masses into existing societies and economies, thus continuing the traditional Diaspora, instead of concentrating them in their own new territory. The first task, therefore, was to create the conditions necessary for an independent, sovereign national life, through a new trend in Jewish migration toward a new territory. The territory in question was destined to be Ereẓ Israel, Borochov said, for "the general pattern of Jewish dynamism" leads toward an ever-increasing "elemental" (*stychic*) migration to Ereẓ Israel. But this "elemental" mass migration (both his followers and opponents differed over the exact implications of the term) was the culmination of an enterprise which was to evolve from an initial pioneering stage in Ereẓ Israel. Thus, a positive, socialist, yearning for a pioneering way of life had to precede the mere recognition of the negative motives for an exodus from the Diaspora. This was the first task—the historic national mission—that Borochov assigned to the Jewish working class in the realization of Zionism. The Jewish worker was to be a "pioneer of the Jewish future," builder of the road to a territorial homeland for the whole Jewish people.

During his contact with the Jewish population in Western Europe and in the U.S., Borochov broadened many of his earlier concepts. Thus, Ereẓ Israel was to be not merely a strategic base for the class struggle of the Jewish proletariat, but a home for the entire Jewish people. Borochov, increasingly aware of the common fate of world Jewry and the universality of their problem in the Diaspora, also came to oppose any attempts to fragment Jewish history, as well as Jewish demography. He insisted that Jewish history was the chronicle of the Jewish masses' uninterrupted sense of self-pride and will to struggle. He acknowledged the vulnerability of the Jews and analyzed their dangerous position in the face of national renaissance movements on the one hand, and national-social anti-Semitism in Europe, which he perceived even before World War I, on the other. Yet he remained insistent that future international developments also held out hopeful and exciting promises for the Jewish people.

Literary Works. Borochov's literary efforts began in 1902 with a treatise "On the Nature of the Jewish Mind," published in Russian in a Zionist almanac. His 1905 article on "The Question of Zionist Theory," published in the Russian Zionist monthly *Yevreyskaya Zhizn,* decried the attempts of assimilationist Jews to reject Zionism and to rely on universal progress as the solution to the Jewish problem. Characteristically, Borochov raised the level of his polemics against the Uganda Scheme to one of fundamental principle, in his Russian treatise "On the Question of

Zion and Territory" (1905). In it he introduced a materialist-historical analysis of the Jewish problem, establishing Zionism as an elemental force produced by Jewry's plight and sustained by its pioneering elements, becoming the true national-liberation movement of the Jewish people. The pamphlet "Class Factors in the National Question," which he published in the same year, was one of the first ventures at applying Marxist theory to the national question. Drawing a distinction between the nationalism of oppressed peoples and that of oppressing nations, Borochov investigated its expression at various class levels. He concluded that only the oppressing nationalism was "reactionary," whereas nationalism of the oppressed did not obscure class consciousness. On the contrary, this latter nationalism, flourishing among the progressive elements, "impels them toward real liberation of the nation, normalization of the conditions and relationships of production, and the creation of necessary conditions for the true freedom of national self-determination.

Borochov's writings during the 1907–14 period retain special value as contributions to contemporary historiography. His thesis on "The Jewish Labor Movement in Figures" (published posthumously) is a penetrating and original statistical-sociological analysis of the "economic physiology" of the Jewish people. One of the central topics of his ideology, Jewish migration and its social implications, was treated in a brochure published in 1911 in Galicia. He contributed articles to the Russian Jewish Encyclopedia on various aspects of Jewish life and history. He wrote in 1908 "Virtualism and the Religious-Ethical Problem in Marxism" (published posthumously in 1920), a polemical tract against A. Lunacharsky's "Socialism and Religion." His essays *The Tasks of Jewish Philology* (1912–13) and *The Library of the Jewish Philologist* (a bibliography of 400 years of Yiddish research) marked his place among the scholars of Jewish language and culture. Borochov's literary works revealed the wide range of his sustained creativity. There is a vast literature on Borochov the man, his life, and his teachings in Yiddish, Hebrew, and other languages. L. Levite et al. (eds.), *B. Borochov Ketavim,* 3 vols. (1955–66) is the best edition of his works; of special importance are the notes attached to each volume. Also in Hebrew: Z. Shazar (comp.), B. Borochov, *Ketavim Nivḥarim* (1944). There is a short selection in English edited by M. Cohen entitled *Nationalism and the Class Struggle* (1937). In Yiddish: Po'alei Zion New York, *Geklibene Shriften D. B. Borochovs* (1935); B. Locker (ed.), *Geklibene Schriften* (1928); in German: the anthology *Klasse und Nation; zur Theorie und Praxis des juedischen Nationalismus* (1932) and *Sozialismus und Zionismus—eine Synthese; Ausgewaehlte Schriften* (1932).

Bibliography: Duker, in: M. Cohen (ed.), *Nationalism and the Class Struggle* (1937), 17–55; Shazar, in: *B. Borochov Ketavim Nivḥarim* (1944), 19–40 (first pagination); Ben-Zvi, *ibid.*, 7–18 (first pagination); M. A. Borochov, in: B. Locker (ed.), *Geklibene Shriften Borochovs* (1928), 11–29 (first pagination); Ben-Zvi, *ibid.*, 33–48 (first pagination); J. Zerubavel, *Ber Borochov,* 1 (Yid., 1926); A. Herzberg, *The Zionist Idea* (1960), 352–66; M. Minc, *Ber Borochov 1900–Purim 1906* (1968), Heb. with Eng. summ.

[Le.L.]

BORODAVKA (Brodavka), ISAAC (16th century), tax farmer and merchant living in Brest-Litovsk. A grant issued by King *Sigismund August in 1560 entitled Borodavka and his associates to collect the duties on goods and merchandise passing through Minsk, Vilna, Novgorod, Brest, and Grodno for seven years. He was granted the salt monopoly for a similar term in 1561, and was permitted to build distilleries with a monopoly of production in Bielsk, Narva, and Kleszczele; in 1569 the Vilna mint was farmed to him. These concessions excited the envy of Christian competitors, who instigated *blood libels against certain tax collectors employed by Borodavka. Although the charges proved groundless, one of the accused, Bernat Abramovich, paid with his life. The king consequently directed that henceforth all such accusations be laid before the crown, and that those who made false accusations should be punished.

Bibliography: *Russko-yevreyskiy arkhiv,* 2 (1882); 3 (1903), index; *Regesty i nadpisi* (1899).

[Ed.]

BORODIN (Gruzenberg), MICHAEL MARKOVITSCH (1884–1951), Russian communist politician. Born in Yanowitski, Belorussia, Borodin joined the Bund in 1901, but left it for the Bolshevik party two years later. In 1906 he went to England and in the following year to the U.S., where he became a member of the American Socialist Party. Borodin returned to Russia after the October Revolution of 1917 and worked for the Comintern. In 1922 he left for Britain again and was arrested in Glasgow. He was sentenced to six months' imprisonment for incitement and was then deported. From 1923 to 1927 Borodin was an adviser to Sun Yat-Sen, leader of the central committee of the Kuomintang, in China, where he was held in high esteem. When in 1927 the Kuomintang came under the domination of its right wing, led by Chiang Kai-Shek, Borodin was arrested and forced to leave the country. He went back to Russia to become deputy commissar for labor, but after 1932 spent most of his time in journalism. He was successively deputy director of the Tass news agency, editor in chief of the Soviet Information Bureau and editor of *Moscow News.* In 1951 he fell victim to the Stalinist terror and was condemned to death. He was posthumously rehabilitated in 1956.

Bibliography: *Sovetskaya istoricheskaya entsiklopediya,* 5 (1964), 43.

[Ed.]

°BORROMEO, CARLO (1538–1584), Cardinal, archbishop of Milan. In the course of his campaign for reform, which had firmly impressed itself on the spirit of the Council of Trent (1545–63), Borromeo convened a number of provincial councils in Milan of which the first (1565) and the fifth (1579) in particular passed legislation concerning the Jews. Among other provisions, it was stipulated that bishops were to arrange that missionary sermons should be delivered to the Jews by preachers with a knowledge of Hebrew and of Jewish customs. Jewish attendance at the sermons was obligatory, the children being separated from their parents. Those who then declared themselves willing to be baptized would be placed in homes for *catechumens where they would receive the appropriate instruction. The fifth council provided that those who had already been baptized should be given accommodation in homes for neophytes, and imposed a series of special, strictly supervised obligations on the new converts to ensure that they would remain steadfast in the Catholic faith.

Bibliography: *Dictionnaire de théologie catholique,* 2 (1910), s.v. *Charles Borromée;* A. Sala, *Biografia di S. Carlo Borromeo,* 3 vols. (1857–61).

[B.Bl.]

BORSA (Rum. **Borşa**), mountain village in Transylvania, Maramures region, Rumania; within Hungary before 1918 and from 1940 to 1945. Jewish communal life had developed there by 1751. According to local ḥasidic legend, *Israel b. Eliezer Ba'al Shem Tov visited Borsa. At the beginning of the 19th century there were nearly 250 Jewish residents. Ḥasidism was strong in Borsa. Many Jews in

Borsa were occupied in agriculture, forestry, and lumbering as manual laborers; Jews also owned lumber mills and woodworking plants. The community numbered 1,432 in 1891 (out of a total population of 6,219); 1,972 in 1910 (out of 9,332); and 2,486 in 1930 (out of 11,230). On July 4, 1930, the Jewish quarter was destroyed by fire—a clear act of arson prompted by the *Iron Guard.

After the annexation of northern Transylvania to Hungary in 1940, Jewish males of military age were conscripted for forced labor, many Jewish stores were closed down, and Jews were refused business permits. Jews from Borsa were interned in the ghetto of *Vişeul-de-Sus in 1944 and from there were deported to death camps. Of those who returned, 395 were living in Borsa in 1947. Their number subsequently decreased, and only two or three families remained by 1969.

Bibliography: D. Schön, in: *Uj Kelet*, nos. 5382, 5385, 5396, 5401, 5406 (1966). [Y.M.]

BORSIPPA, the modern Birs Nimrud, city in Babylonia, south of the city of Babylon and the river Euphrates, and connected with Babylon by the Barsip canal. In medieval times it was known as Burs (a similar form occurs in Av. Zar. 11b; Kid, 72a). Because of its proximity to Babylon, and possibly also on account of its importance, it was sometimes referred to by the Babylonians as "the second Babylon." Famous in the Hellenistic period for its school of astrologers (Strabo, 16:1,7 (739); cf. also Jos., Apion, 1:151f.), it had, as late as talmudic times, a temple dedicated to Nebo, the deity of the city, which was enumerated among the "five temples appointed for idol worship" (Av. Zar. 11b). The sages held the ruins of the tower at Borsippa to be those of the Tower of Babel (Sanh. 109a; Gen. R. 38:11) and the contemporary Babylon to be located on the site of the ancient Borsippa (Shab. 36a; Suk. 34a). Benjamin of Tudela, who visited the place, relates: "From there (i.e., Hillah which is near Babylon) it is four miles to the Tower of Babel, which was built of bricks by the generation whose language was confounded .... The length of its foundation is about two miles, the breadth of the tower is about forty cubits, and the length thereof two hundred cubits. At every ten cubits' distance there are slopes which go around the tower, by which one can ascend to the top. One can see from there a view twenty miles in extent, as the land is level. There fell fire from heaven into the midst of the tower, which split to its very depths." In talmudic times Borsippa had an important Jewish population with the most distinguished genealogy of all the Babylonian Jews (Kid. 72a).

Bibliography: R. Koldewey, *Die Tempel von Babylon und Borsippa* (1911); idem, *Das wiedererstehende Babylon* (1913); F. Hommel, *Grundriss der Geographie und Geschichte des alten Orients* (1926); J. Obermeyer, *Landschaft Babylonien* (1929), 314–5.

[J.M.G.]

BORSOOK, HENRY (1897–), U.S. biochemist. He was born in London. After working at the University of Toronto until 1929, Borsook went to the California Institute of Technology, becoming professor of biochemistry there in 1935. During World War II he served on the War Production Board, the Committee on Nutrition in Industry of the National Research Council, the War Food Administration, and the Food and Nutrition Board. His contributions to scientific journals were concerned with nutrition, vitamins, amino acids, the biosynthesis of proteins, the thermodynamics, energetics, and kinetics of metabolic reactions, and erythropoiesis. He wrote: *Vitamins—What They Are and How They Can Benefit You* (1940); jointly with W. Huse, *Vitamins For Health* (1942); and *Action Now on the World Food Problem* (1968). Borsook was vice-president of the American Association of Scientific Workers.

Bibliography: *Food Technology*, 12 (Sept. 1958), 18ff.

[S.A.M.]

BOSAK, MEIR (1912–), Hebrew writer. Bosak was born in Cracow, Poland, and studied in Warsaw. During World War II, he was interned in Cracow ghetto and in concentration camps. He emigrated to Israel in 1949 and taught in Tel Aviv. From 1929 he published articles in Polish and Hebrew on the history of Polish Jewry, and wrote essays on Hebrew literature and stories and poems. His works include *Be-Nogah ha-Seneh* (1933), *Ve-Attah Eini Ra'atekha* (1957), *Ba-Rikkud ke-Neged ha-Levanah* (1960; poems), *Aḥar Esrim Shanah* (1963; poems), and *Mul Ḥalal u-Demamah* (1966). [G.K.]

BOSCOVITCH, ALEXANDER URIYAH (1907–1964), Israel composer. Born in Klausenburg, Rumania, Boscovitch studied music in Vienna and Paris, where one of his teachers was the composer Paul Dukas. He became conductor of the Klausenburg opera orchestra, and of a Jewish symphony orchestra which he founded. In 1938 he was invited to Palestine for the first performance of his *Sharsheret ha-Zahav* ("The Golden Chain"), an orchestral suite based on East European Jewish melodies. He decided to remain in the country, and became one of the pioneers of Israel music—songs, chamber music, music for the theater, concertos, and symphonies. In 1942 he composed a violin concerto and the following year an oboe concerto (revised version 1950) which is typical of his attempt to achieve a synthesis of oriental and western forms. His *Semitic Suite* (1946), in two slightly different versions—one for orchestra and one for piano solo—was an experiment in transferring the tone color of oriental instruments to western ones. The composition drew from the folk music of both the Arabs and the Jews in Ereẓ Israel at that time. In 1962 his cantata *Bat Yisrael* ("Daughter of Israel"), based on a text by the poet Bialik, marked the beginning of his preoccupation with the relationship between music and the Hebrew language, which is evident in *Concerto di Camera* (1962) for violin and ten other instruments. His last completed composition, *Adayim*, drew its inspiration from Exodus 15. This work for flute and orchestra utilizes the rhythmic and poetic characteristics of the Hebrew text and the liturgy of Yemenite Jews. Boscovitch was for many years music critic of the daily, *Haaretz*.

Alexander Uriyah Boscovitch, Israel composer. Photo J. Gordon, Tel Aviv.

Bibliography: P. Gradenwitz, *Music and Musicians in Israel* (1959^2), 79–82; Sendrey Music, indexes. [H.SH.]

BOSHAL (Bostal), MOSES BEN SOLOMON (17th century), rabbi. Brought to Safed from Sidon by his father when he was 12 years old, Moses studied there with important rabbis. At age 25, when forced to leave because of a series of calamitous events, Moses moved to Rhodes, becoming a rabbi in that community. His only extant work, *Yismaḥ Moshe* (Smyrna, 1675), written after years of preaching every Sabbath and holiday, contains several sermons for each Sabbath or festival Torah reading. The sermons are primarily commentaries on the Torah text, although explanations of midrashic literature, which he frequently employed, are also found. From his quotations from the Zohar in the introduction to the book—where he also includes an autobiography—Moses appears to have been familiar with kabbalistic literature. Another unpublished work, *Simḥat Moshe*, is mentioned in the proofreader's introduction to *Yismaḥ Moshe*.

Bibliography: Zunz, Vortraege, 445; S. Ḥazzan, *Ha-Ma'alot li-Shelomo* (1968[2]), 55b no. 38. [Ed.]

°**BOSHAM, HERBERT DE** (before 1139–after 1190), companion and biographer of Archbishop Thomas Becket. Born in Bosham, England, he studied in Paris under Peter Lombard, and studied Hebrew probably under Andrew of St. Victor. In addition to editing the Lombard's (thereafter standard) *Great Gloss* to the Pauline Epistles and to the Psalter, he composed (after 1190) a commentary on Jerome's literal Latin translation of the *Psalms (iuxta Hebraeos)*. Herbert's work is replete with midrashic and other Jewish material taken mainly from Rashi, through whom he quotes by name *Menahem b. Jacob ibn Saruq and *Dunash ibn Labrat; but the commentary, which is known from a unique manuscript in London (St. Paul's Cathedral), apparently was ignored until it was recently discovered.

Bibliography: DNB, 9 (1921–22), 617–9, s.v. *Herbert of Bosham;* R. Loewe, in: JHSET, 17 (1951–52), 225–49, includes bibliography; idem, in: *Biblica*, 34 (1953), 44–77, 159–92, 275–98 (Eng.); S. Smalley, *The Study of the Bible in the Middle Ages* (1952), index, s.v. *Herbert of Bosham*. [Ra.L.]

BOSKOFF, ALVIN (1927–), American sociologist. Born in New York, he taught sociology at several universities and from 1964 was professor at Emory University in Atlanta, Georgia. Boskoff's main interest was the application of general sociological theories to specialized researches with particular emphasis on power, decision-making, and processes of social change. His theoretical work is embodied in *Modern Sociological Theory in Continuity and Change* (with Howard Becker, 1957), *Sociology and History* (with Werner J. Cahnman, 1964), and his paper, "Functional Analysis as a Source of a Theoretical Repertory and Research Tasks in the Study of Social Change" in G. K. Zollschan and W. Hirsh (eds.), *Explorations in Social Change* (1964). Boskoff's own specialized research was concerned chiefly with problems of the urban community and with political sociology. He also wrote *The Sociology of Urban Regions, Juvenile Delinquency in Norfolk, Virginia* (1962). Boskoff was an associate editor of the *American Sociological Review*. [W.J.C.]

BOSKOVICE (Ger. **Boskowitz**), town in Moravia, Czechoslovakia. Its Jewish community was one of the oldest and, from the 17th to 19th centuries, one of the most important. A Jewish tombstone there was thought to date from 1069. Jews from Boskovice are mentioned in decisions of the Brno municipal high court in 1243. The community began to flourish after Jews expelled from Brno in 1454 settled in Boskovice. In 1565 Jews there owned real

The synagogue of Boskovice, Moravia, built in 1698.

estate, but were prohibited from doing business in the surrounding villages. The statutes of the *ḥevra kaddisha* were compiled in 1657. There were 26 Jewish houses in Boskovice in 1676. The synagogue was built in 1698, 892 Jewish inhabitants died of the plague in 1715 and the Jewish quarter was put in quarantine for a year. A peculiar custom of the Boskovice community was to bury women who died in childbirth in a special section in the cemetery. A *gabbai* was appointed specially for the members of the *ḥevra kaddisha* who were *kohanim*. The Jews were segregated in a special quarter of the town in 1727. During the revolution of 1848 Jews in Boskovice joined the National Guard. A political community (see *Politische Gemeinden) was established in Boskovice after 1848 which became known for its municipal activities, in particular its fire brigade (founded in 1863). Toward the end of the 19th century many Jews moved away from Boskovice. Between the two world wars Boskovice became a summer resort and was frequented by many Jews.

The community numbered 300 families in 1793; 326 families (1,595 persons) in 1829; 2,018 persons in 1857; 598 in 1900 (when 116 houses were owned by Jews); and 395 in 1930 (6% of the total population), of whom 318 declared their nationality as Jewish. Boskovice was a noted center of Jewish learning. Among rabbis who lived there were Judah Loeb Issachar Baer *Oppenheim (appointed rabbi in 1704), Nathan *Adler (1782), who was followed by his disciple Moses *Sofer, Samuel ha-Levi *Kolin and his son Benjamin Ze'ev *Boskowitz, whose yeshivah made Boskovice celebrated, Abraham *Placzek, who was Moravian *Landesrabbiner* from 1851 to 1884, and Solomon *Funk. The Zionist president of the Vienna community, Desider *Friedmann, and his non-Zionist deputy Josef Ticho, were school friends from Boskovice. Also from Boskovice were the German writer Hermann *Ungar, the Jerusalem eye specialist Abraham *Ticho, the historian Oskar K. *Rabinowicz, and the Brno textile-industrialist *Loew-Beer. The Jews who remained in Boskovice after the German occupation (1939) were deported to the East in 1942 and 1943 via Brno. Ritual objects belonging to the congregation were sent to the Central Jewish Museum in Prague in 1942. Only a few Jews resettled there after the Holocaust, the congregation being administered by the Brno community. The Jewish quarter has been preserved, substantially in its original plan.

Bibliography: Stein, in: *Jahrbuch des Traditionstreuen Rabbinerverbandes in der Slovakei* (1923), 102–34; H. Gold (ed.), *Die Juden und Judengemeinden Maehrens . . .* (1929), 123–36; Flesch, in: JJLG, 21 (1930), 218–48 (ordinances of the *ḥevra kadisha*); I. Reich, *Die Geschichte der Chewra Kadischa zu Boskowitz* (1931); S. Schreiber, *Der dreifache Faden*, 1 (1952), 157–9; J. L. Bialer, in: *Min ha-Genazim*, 2 (1969), 63–154 (ordinances of the community).

[I.Z.K.]

BOSKOWITZ, BENJAMIN ZE'EV (Wolf) HA-LEVI (1740–1818), rabbi and author. Named after his birthplace, he was the son of Samuel *Kolin, the author of *Maḥaẓit ha-Shekel.* In 1785 he was rabbi in Aszod (Pest district), and Prossnitz (Moravia) from 1786 to 1790. From there he returned to Alt-Ofen (Buda, part of Budapest) where he had previously resided. In 1793 he was appointed rabbi of Pest. From 1797 to 1802 he served in Balassagyarmat; he then was invited to the rabbinate of *Kolin (Bohemia), but the government refused him permission to settle there because he was by then a Hungarian subject. From about 1810 he was rabbi in Bonyhad.

Boskowitz' glosses on the Babylonian Talmud were first printed in the Vienna edition of 1830 and frequently ever since. His annotations to Maimonides' *Mishneh Torah* were partly published (to *Sefer ha-Madda* (Prague, 1820), to *Hilkhot Shabbat* (Jerusalem, 1902), to *Hilkhot Shevitat Asor* (1940), and to *Hilkhot Ḥameẓ u-Maẓẓah* (1941)). He also wrote: *Ma'amar Esther*—sermons on the Bible and *aggadah* (Ofen, 1822); *Shoshan Edut,* to the tractate *Eduyyot* (1903–05); and *Le-Binyamin Amar,* a commentary on the sayings of *Rabba b. Ḥana in *Bava Batra* 73 (*ibid.,* 1905). Boskowitz corresponded with R. Ezekiel Landau of Prague on halakhic problems (cf. *Noda bi-Yhudah, Mahadurah Tinyanah,* OḤ 25:60, 61, and YD 14:45, 80, passim).

Bibliography: W. Boskowitz, *Shoshan Edut* (1903–05), introduction; J. J. Greenwald, *Ha-Yehudim be-Ungarya,* 1 (1912); Freimann, in: JJLG, 15 (1923), 39. [M.N.Z./Ed.]

BOSKOWITZ, ḤAYYIM BEN JACOB (18th century), rabbi and author. Little is known of his life, other than that he was born in Jerusalem and apparently lived there for many years. The evidence for this is that when he traveled abroad, apparently with the object of publishing his work, he referred to himself as "from the holy city of Jerusalem." His work, *Toẓe'ot Ḥayyim,* homiletical comments on the Pentateuch, with an exposition of the moral values to be learned from each verse, was published in Amsterdam in 1764. The bibliographer *Benjacob alone gives the date as 1760. The work was printed, along with the Pentateuch, together with the commentaries of Rashi, R. Samuel b. Meir (Rashbam), and Abraham ibn Ezra. A new edition appeared in Vienna in 1794. *Toẓe'ot Ḥayyim* was also published without the Pentateuch, but with various additions, at Zolkiev in 1772. At the time, Boskowitz was living at Brody, Galicia. He seems to have been in Poland as early as 1769, when he wrote an approbation *Leḥem Terumah* of Aaron b. Isaiah on the *Sefer ha-Terumah.*

Bibliography: Fuenn, Keneset, 344; Frumkin-Rivlin, 3 (1929), 83, addenda 45. [Y.Al.]

BOSPHORUS, KINGDOM OF, ancient state, independent until 110 B.C.E. when it became part of the Roman Empire. It is not certain when Jews reached the northern littoral of the Black Sea (the Crimea and the shores of the Sea of Azov within the boundaries of the Cimmerian Bosphorus), but Jews were already living there in the first century, in, among other places, the towns of Panticapaeum (now Kerch), Panagoria, and Tanais. It appears that they lived under congenial conditions. They developed well-organized communities, erected synagogues, which served as communal centers, and were even organized in the "Thiasoi," characteristic of Hellenistic society, by which they were greatly influenced. They, in turn, according to all indications, exercised appreciable influence on non-Jewish circles, and there is reason to believe that they engaged in proselytizing activity. The main source of knowledge of the Jews of the Bosphorus kingdom is from inscriptions. One of the most important, dated 81 C.E., from Panticapaeum, reads, "... I, Chreste ... have manumitted my home-born slave, Herakles ... who may turn whithersoever he desires ... he is not however [to forsake] the fear of heaven and attachment to the synagogue [προσευχή] under the supervision of the community [συναγωγή] of the Jews." In many of the inscriptions there appears a formula of oaths beginning, "I swear by Zeus, Ge, and Helios." There is a difference of opinion as to whether these inscriptions are Jewish.

Bibliography: Schuerer, Gesch, 3 (1909[4]), 23–24; Goodenough, in: JQR, 47 (1956/57), 221–44; Lifshitz, in: *Rivista di filologia,* 92 (1964), 157–62; Bellen, in: *Jahrbuch fuer Antike und Christentum,* 8–9 (1965–66), 171–5. [U.R.]

°BOSSUET, JACQUES BENIGNE (1627–1704), celebrated French preacher. Bossuet was canon in Metz (1652–56), bishop of Condom (1669), tutor to the dauphin (1670–81), and bishop of Meaux (1681). It was chiefly while living in Metz that he had the opportunity to take an interest in the Jews. Many of his sermons from this period of residence in Metz were intended to further missionary work among the Jews. In his sermon on "The Goodness and Severity of God toward Sinners," he emphasized the unhappy state of the Jews, from which, he considered, they could free themselves only by becoming converted to Christianity. He described them as a "monstrous people, without hearth or home, without a country and of every country; once the happiest in the world, now the laughing stock and object of hatred of the whole world; wretched, without being pitied for being so, in its misery become, by a certain curse, scorned even by the most moderate ... we see before our eyes the remains of their shipwreck which God has thrown, as it were, at our doors." The only success of this missionary activity was the conversion of two young brothers: Charles-Marie de Veil, baptized in 1654, and Lewis Compiègne de *Veil, baptized in 1655.

Bibliography: Kahn, in: *Revue Juive de Lorraine,* 7 (1931), 241ff.; E. B. Weill, *Weill—De Veil, a Genealogy, 1360–1956* (1957), 24; J. Truchet, *Prédication de Bossuet,* 2 (1960), 31ff. [B.Bl.]

BOSTON, capital and principal city of Massachusetts. The Jewish population of Greater Boston was estimated at 208,000 (1967), of whom 40,000 lived within the city proper.

Early History. Though Boston is one of the oldest cities in North America, having been first settled in 1628, it was not until the mid-19th century that an organized Jewish community took shape. The records of the Great and General Court of Massachusetts Bay show that in 1649 Solomon Franco, a Jew, proposed to settle in Boston but was paid to leave the province. A 1674 tax list discloses the presence of two Jews. In 1720 Isaac Lopez was elected town constable. Judah *Monis, who later became a Christian and taught Hebrew at Harvard College, arrived in Boston in 1720. Moses Michael Hays (1739–1805) arrived there around 1776 and was a well-known citizen. There is a tradition that some Algerian Jews arrived about 1830 but did not remain.

The first congregation was Ohabei Shalom, established in 1842. It adopted the ritual of Fuerth, which suggests that the members came from southern Germany. In 1844 the Boston City Council, reversing an earlier refusal, permitted the congregation to purchase land for a cemetery. In the following year it held services in a house and in 1852 its first synagogue was erected. A second congregation, established in 1849, was short-lived. In 1854 a secession, apparently of the East German element in Ohabei Shalom, led to the formation of a second congregation, Adath Israel (generally

Figure 1. Temple Ohabei Shalom in Brookline, synagogue of the first Boston congregation, established in 1842. Photo Fay Foto Service, Boston.

known as Temple Israel). A third congregation, Mishkan Israel (later Mishkan Tefilla), was formed of immigrants from East Germany in 1858. German Jews did not settle in such numbers as to build up a community the size of those in the Midwest. In 1875 Boston Jewry was estimated to number 3,000. In 1895, however, the figure was given as 20,000, of whom 14,000 were immigrants. In 1939 the Jewish population numbered 160,000.

Population Trends. The earliest settlers resided in the South End, but from the 1870s onward there was a group of East European Jews in the North End. As the immigration from Eastern Europe increased, the Jewish community spread over to the West End. Both these areas stood at the tip of the peninsula forming the oldest part of the city. Subsequently, the Jewish community spread southward to Roxbury, Dorchester, and Mattapan, westward to Brookline and later to Newton, and northward, across Boston Harbor to Chelsea and Malden. These movements were followed by further dispersion to the outer suburbs and along the shores of Massachusetts Bay, and synagogues were established in those areas.

The substantial immigration and the subsequent dispersal of the community produced a wide variety of organizations. Late 19th- and 20th-century Boston was divided between the Yankees who controlled its social, cultural, and financial institutions, and the Irish who dominated its politics, and this did not make it easy for the largely immigrant Jewish group to find a recognized place. In the early 1940s the anti-Semitic movement inspired by Father Coughlin was active, and this led to the formation of the Jewish Community Council of Metropolitan Boston. In 1969 only 15% of the Jews were immigrants. Whereas at the beginning of the 20th century there was a substantial proletarian element, particularly in the garment industry, by 1969 71% of heads of families were in white-collar occupations.

Religious Developments. Religious reform made itself felt in 1875 when Ohabei Shalom introduced an organ and mixed seating, but remained of a moderate character. Reform of a more radical kind found expression in Temple Israel during the ministry of Solomon *Schindler (1874–93), and was carried further by his successor Charles Fleischer (1894–1911), who eventually left Judaism entirely. Under Harry Levi (1911–39) the congregation, while continuing Sunday services, returned to the Reform pattern usual in its day. After World War II Reform Judaism, which had previously been an isolated phenomenon, developed considerably in the suburbs. Under the leadership of Rabbi Herman *Rubenovitz, who served during 1910–45, Congregation Mishkan Tefilla became the standard-bearer of Conservative Judaism. Rabbi Louis M. *Epstein, who served Kehillath Israel in Brookline during 1925–48, was among the most distinguished scholars in the Conservative movement. The immigration from Eastern Europe produced many Orthodox congregations, great and small. Among the more important were Beth Israel in the North End, Beth Jacob and Shaare Jerusalem, both in the West End, and Adath Israel (the Blue Hill Avenue Shul) in Roxbury. Among the leading Orthodox rabbis were Morris S. Margolies, who served during 1889–1906, and Gabriel Margolis, 1907–10. From 1932 Rabbi Dr. Joseph B. *Soloveitchik, one of the leading figures in American Orthodoxy, was identified with the Boston community.

Of some 75 congregations in the Greater Boston area, 20 are Orthodox, 35 Conservative, and 20 Reform (1969). Several of the Orthodox synagogues are found in districts being vacated by the Jewish population. A survey of religious preferences indicated that 14 per cent of the Jewish population considered itself Orthodox, 44 per cent Conservative, and 27 per cent Reform. A measure of coordination in religious matters, including the supervision of *kashrut,* was attempted by the establishment in 1935 of the Rabbinical Association of Greater Boston (now known as the Massachusetts Board of Rabbis), and in 1941 of the Associated Synagogues of Massachusetts.

Charitable Institutions. The first specifically charitable institution was the United Hebrew Benevolent Association, founded in 1864. To this were added the Hebrew Ladies Sewing Society (1878), the Hebrew Industrial School (1889), the Free Burial Association (1891), and the Hebrew Sheltering Home (1892). The charities established by the German Jews were often paralleled within the Russian community. By 1895 the number of such organizations was great enough to warrant the establishment of the Federation of Jewish Charities, one of the first of its kind in the U.S., later known as the Association of Jewish Philanthropies, later changed to Combined Jewish

Figure 2. The Ark of the Law in the synagogue of the Boston congregation, Mishkan Tefilla, in Newton. Photo Samuel Cooper.

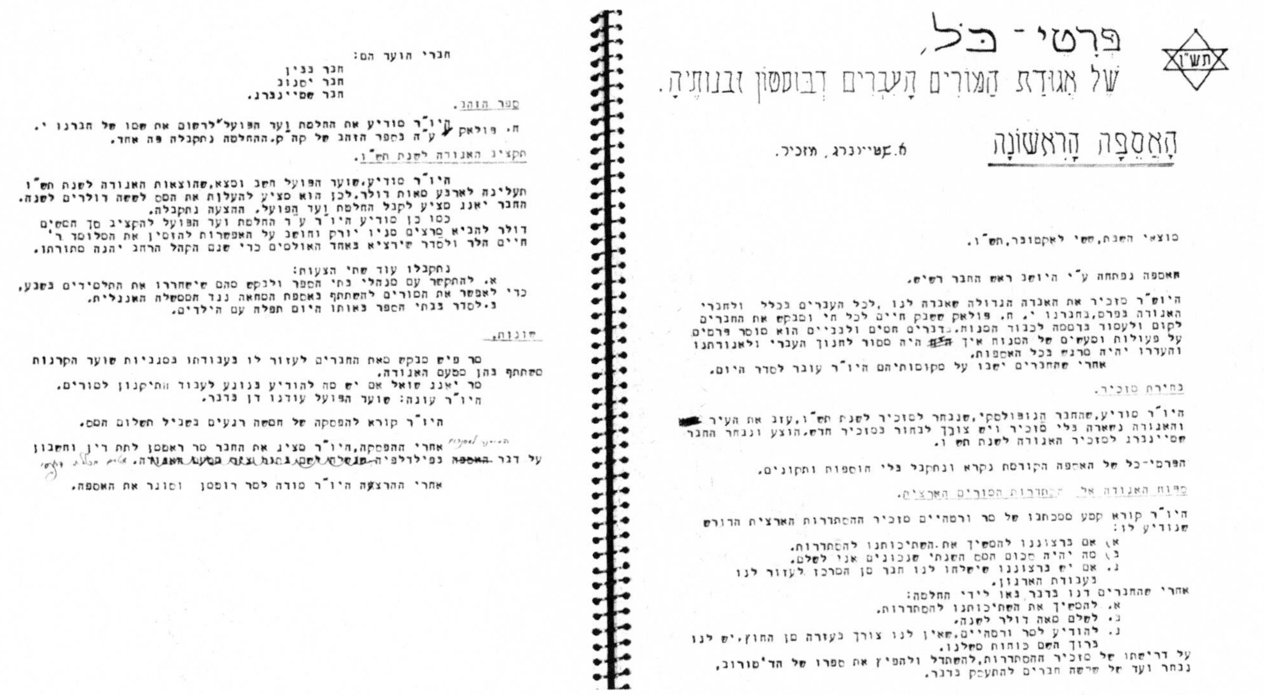

תש"ו

פרטי־כל,
של אגודת המורים העברים דבוסטון ובנותיה.

האספה הראשונה

ח. שטיינברג, מזכיר.

מוצאי השבת, ששי לאקטובר, תש"ו.

האספה נפתחה ע"י היושב ראש החבר רשים.

היוש"ר מזכיר את האבדה הגדולה שאבדה לנו, לכל העברים בכלל ולחברי האגודה בפרט, בחברנו י. ח. פולאק שנפטר חי"ו לכל חי ומבקש את החברים לקום ולעמוד בדממה לכבוד המנוח. בדברים חמים ולבביים הוא מוסר פרטים על פעולות ומעשים של המנוח איך היה מסור לחנוך העברי ולאגודתנו והעדרו יהיה מרגש בכל האספות.
אחרי שהחברים ישבו על מקומותיהם היו"ר עובר לסדר היום.

בחירת מזכיר.

היו"ר מודיע, שהחבר הנופולסקי, שנבחר למזכיר לשנת תש"ו, עזב את העיר והאגודה נשארה בלי מזכיר ויש צורך לבחור במזכיר חדש. הוצע ונבחר החבר שטיינברג למזכיר האגודה לשנת תש"ו.

הפרטי־כל של האספה הקודמת נקרא ונתקבל בלי הוספות ותקונים.

יחוס האגודה אל התחדרות המורים הארצית.

היו"ר קורא קטע ממכתבו של מר ורטהיים מזכיר ההסתדרות הארצית הדורש שנודיע לו:
א) אם ברצוננו להמשיך את השתיכותנו להסתדרות.
ב) מה יהיה סכום המס השנתי שנכונים אנו לשלם.
ג. אם יש ברצוננו שישלחו לנו חבר מן המרכז לעזור לנו בעבודת הארגון.
אחרי שהחברים דנו בדבר באו לידי החלטה:
א. להמשיך את השתיכותנו להסתדרות.
ב. לשלם מאה דולר לשנה.
ג. להודיע למר ורטהיים, שאין לנו צורך בעזרה מן החוץ, יש לנו ברוך השם כוחות משלנו.
על דרישתו של מזכיר ההסתדרות, להשתדל ולהפיץ את ספרו של הד"סורוב, נבחר ועד של שלשה חברים להתעסק בדבר.

חברי הועד הם:
חבר גבין
חבר יסנוב
חבר שטיינברג.

ספר הזהב.

היו"ר מודיע את החלטת ועד הפועל לרשום את שמו של חברנו י. ח. פולאק ע"ה בספר הזהב של קה"ק. ההחלטה נתקבלה פה אחד.

תקציב האגודה לשנת תש"ו.

היו"ר מודיע, שועד הפועל חשב ומצא, שהוצאות האגודה לשנת תש"ו תעלינה לארבע מאות דולר. לכן הוא מציע להעלות את המס לששה דולרים לשנה. החבר יאנג מציע לקבל החלטת ועד הפועל. ההצעה נתקבלה.
כמו כן מודיע היו"ר ע"ר החלטת ועד הפועל להקציב סך חמשים דולר להביא מרצים מניו יורק וחושב על האפשרות להזמין את הפלוסוף ר' חיים הלר ולסדר שירצה באחד האולמים כדי שגם הקהל הרחב יהנה מתורתו.

נתקבלו עוד שתי הצעות:
א. להתקשר עם מנהלי בתי הספר ולבקש מהם שישחררו את התלמידים בשבע, כדי לאפשר את המורים להשתתף באספת המחאה נגד הממשלה האנגלית.
ב. לסדר בבתי הספר באותו היום תפלה עם הילדים.

שונות.

מר פיש מבקש מאת החברים לעזור לו בעבודתו במגביות שועד הקרנות משתתף בהן מטעם האגודה.
מר יאנג שואל אם יש מה להודיע בנוגע לעבוד והתיקנון למורים.
היו"ר עונה: שועד הפועל עודנו דן בדבר.

היו"ר קורא להפסקה של חמשה רגעים בשביל תשלום המס.

אחרי ההפסקה, היו"ר מציג את החבר מר ראסמן לתת דין וחשבון על דבר האספה בפילדלפיה.

אחרי ההרצאה היו"ר מודה למר רוסמן וסוגר את האספה.

Figure 3. Minutes of the meeting of the Boston Hebrew Teachers' Association, October 6, 1946. Among the resolutions is one to request principals to close schools at 7 o'clock on the day of an anti-British protest meeting, to enable teachers to participate. Another calls for prayers with the pupils on that day. Jerusalem, C.A.H.J.P.

Philanthropies. At first the Federation and organized philanthropy made slow headway. Under the leadership of Louis E. *Kirstein (1867–1942) the Federation developed considerably and became more comprehensive in its appeal. In 1902, against considerable opposition from some sections of the Jewish community, the Mt. Sinai Hospital, an outpatient clinic, was established in the West End. This was replaced in 1915 by the Beth Israel Hospital in Roxbury, which in 1928 moved to Brookline Avenue.

Schools and Colleges. In 1858 Congregation Ohabei Shalom established a day school for secular and religious subjects, which closed, however, in 1863. As the community grew, many congregational and other schools were founded. A Jewish Education Society was established in 1915. This organization promoted the association of Boston Hebrew Schools (1917) and the Bureau of Jewish Religious Schools (1918), which merged in 1920 to form the Bureau of Jewish Education. Jewish day schools function under Orthodox and Conservative sponsorship. In 1921 the Bureau established Hebrew Teachers College, and in 1927 the Commonwealth of Massachusetts granted the college a charter enabling it to confer degrees. At first established in Roxbury, it moved to Brookline in 1951. Eisig *Silberschlag, the distinguished Hebrew poet, was dean of the college from 1947 on.

The support given to the Bureau of Jewish Education and Hebrew Teachers College reflects an interest in Jewish culture somewhat more extensive than in most communities. Eighty percent of the adult Jewish population has been found to have had some exposure to Jewish education (1969). Presumably, the well-established culture of Boston itself, including the chairs of Jewish literature and philosophy by Harvard University, helped to exert an influence, along with the establishment in 1948 of *Brandeis University. The contributions to American Jewish history made by Lee M. *Friedman exemplify the application to Jewish affairs of the attitudes cultivated in the Back Bay.

Boston was an early stronghold of the Zionist movement. Under the influence of Jacob *de Haas, who edited the *Jewish Advocate* from 1908 to 1918, Louis D. *Brandeis assumed a leading role in the movement, and his prestige had considerable influence in gaining support for it.

Bibliography: M. Axelrod, et al., *Community Survey for Long Range Planning, A Study of the Jewish Population of Greater Boston* (1967); S. Broches, *Jews in New England,* 1 (1942); A. Ehrenfried, *Chronicle of Boston Jewry from the Colonial Settlement to 1900* (1963); A. Mann (ed.), *Growth and Achievement: Temple Israel, 1854–1954* (1954); Neusner, in: AJHSQ, 46 (1956), 71–85; Reznikoff, in: *Commentary,* 15 (1963), 490–9; B. M. Solomon, *Pioneers in Service* (1956); A. A. Wieder, *Early Jewish Community of Boston's North End* (1962); A. Libman Lebeson, *Jewish Pioneers in America* (1931), incl. bibliography. Various essays by L. M. Friedman are collected in *Early American Jews* (1934), *Jewish Pioneers and Patriots* (1942), and *Pilgrims in a New Land* (1948). Descriptions of the life of the immigrant community are given in novels by M. Antin: *From Polotzk to Boston* (1899), *The Promised Land* (1912), and *They Who Knock at Our Gates* (1914); and in the novels of C. Angoff: *Journey to the Dawn* (1951), *In the Morning Light* (1952), and *Between Day and Dark* (1959).

[S.D.T.]

BOTAREL, MOSES BEN ISAAC (end of 14th–beginning of 15th century), Spanish scholar. After the edicts against Spanish Jewry in 1391, a pseudo-messiah named Moses appeared in Burgos. A letter extravagantly praising this Moses is attributed to Ḥasdai *Crescas; it probably refers to Moses Botarel (A. Jellinek, *Beit ha-Midrash,* 6 (1877), 141–3). There are extant works containing the adverse reactions of opponents to his messianic pretensions. On the strength of his claims, he circulated letters which he introduced with the phrase "Thus says Moses Botarel, occupying the seat of instruction in signs and wonders." Botarel wrote books and pamphlets in every branch of the Torah, *halakhah,* Kabbalah, and philosophy. These works included many "quotations" of scholarly works from the geonic period until his day, but most of his quotations were either spurious or copied from sources entirely different from those which he named. His reasons for this form of pseudepigraphy are unclear. Certainly it did not stem from a desire to enhance the status of kabbalism for he treated purely halakhic material in the same way. Botarel lived for a long time in Avignon, and afterward wandered in France and in Spain. He used to boast of his contact with the Christian scholar Maestro Juan of Paris, insinuating that at the request of the latter he had written a number of his books. His vanity about his achievements was limitless and reached pathological proportions. In 1409 he composed a lengthy commentary on the *Sefer Yezirah,* which was printed in its 1562 edition. His commentary was not kabbalistic, but combined an eclectic miscellany of the sayings of others, mainly fabrications, superficial in content, with selections from earlier kabbalistic works here attributed to nonexistent sources. Apart from a pronounced bent toward practical Kabbalah, there is a marked tendency to reconcile Kabbalah with philosophy.

Two other pamphlets on *halakhah* were published by S. Assaf and J. Sussmann. A treatise of similar type on philosophical matters is found in manuscript (Vatican Ms. 441, fols. 175–9). An essay on the mystical interpretation of vocalization *(nekuddot)* and related lore is in manuscript in Oxford (Neubauer, Cat, no. 1947). Part of another kabbalistic work of 1407 is in manuscript Musaioff, and a collection of writings on practical Kabbalah (subsequently entitled *Ma'yan ha-Ḥokhmah* or *Ma'gelei Yosher)* is in manuscript in the Jewish Theological Seminary, New York.

Many of his kabbalistic remedies are included in collections of writings of practical Kabbalah. The contemporary poet Solomon *Bonafed sharply attacked Botarel's pretensions and falsehoods, and hinted at his literary forgeries (Neubauer, Cat, no. 1984, 4, fol. 66). His fabrications have also misled some scholars who assumed that they were genuine, and utilized them to reconstruct the origins of Kabbalah.

Bibliography: A. Jellinek, *Beitraege zur Geschichte der Kabbala,* 2 (1852), 1–10, 79; Steinschneider, Cat Bod, nos. 6440–41; Assaf, *Tekufat ha-Ge'onim ve-Sifrutah* (1955), 323–40; G. Scholem, in: *Tarbiz,* 32 (1962/63), 260–2; Sussmann, in *Kovez al Yad,* 6 (1966), 269–342; L. Schwager and D. Fraenkel, *Catalog* (1942), list 35, p. 95; A. Aescoly, *Ha-Tenu'ot ha-Meshiḥiyyot be-Yisrael,* 1 (1956), 222ff.

[G.SCH.]

BOTON, ABRAHAM BEN JUDAH DI (1710?–after 1780), Turkish talmudist and halakhist. Born in Salonika, in his youth he was already considered one of its great scholars. Some time before 1753, he was appointed chief rabbi of Monastir (Bitolj), where he served until his death. His responsa and halakhic novellae, together with some by his son, were published under the title *Maḥazeh Avraham* (Salonika, 1795) by his grandson David di Boton who was also chief rabbi of Monastir.

Bibliography: Rosanes, Togarmah, 5 (1938), 122; Azulai, 2 (1852), 78, no. 79.

[ED.]

BOTON, ABRAHAM BEN MOSES DI (1545?–1588), Salonika-born rabbi and halakhist. Boton was related to Moses di Trani and studied under Samuel de *Medina together with Mordecai Kalai. He taught in Salonika and in Apulia. In his youth he began to write a commentary, *Leḥem Mishneh,* to Maimonides' *Mishneh Torah.* In 1575 he obtained a copy of Joseph *Caro's *Kesef Mishneh* on *Mishneh Torah* and from then on he included in his own work only those novellae and comments that had not already appeared in Caro's work. Boton's work, one of the most important commentaries on *Mishneh Torah,* was first published in two volumes (Venice, 1609); it has since been republished with nearly every edition. *Leḥem Rav* (Smyrna, 1660) is a compendium of his responsa. A few of Boton's novellae on tractate *Bava Kamma* were published in Abraham ibn Akra's *Me-Hararei Nemerim* (Venice, 1599). Boton's clarity of expression and his lucid style are particularly evident in his responsa. Some of his responsa are signed "Ḥiyya Abraham b. Moses," the first name having been added after his recovery from a severe illness. Among his pupils were Samuel Ḥayon and Shabbetai Jonah. Boton died during a plague in Salonika.

Bibliography: Conforte, Kore, 43a; S. M. Chones, *Toledot ha-Posekim* (1910), 319; Sokolow, in: *Moznayim,* 3 (1935), 175; Rosanes, Togarmah, 3 (1938²), 53ff.

[A.D.]

BOTON, ḤIYYA ABRAHAM BEN AARON DI (17th century), rabbi and Ereẓ Israel emissary. Ḥiyya di Boton was a grandson of Abraham b. Moses di *Boton, and apparently studied in Gallipoli under his uncle, Meir di *Boton. In 1648 he was in Smyrna, where he was a member of the *bet din* of Joseph *Escapa. His only son and his daughters died in an epidemic there (before 1660). Ḥiyya was a friend of Hayyim b. Israel *Benveniste and corresponded with him as well as with his kinsman Moses *Benveniste. He published *Leḥem Rav* (Smyrna, 1660), the responsa of his grandfather. Boton was among those who opposed Shabbetai Ẓevi in Smyrna. After 1674 he immigrated to Jerusalem, where he became a member of the *bet din* of Moses *Galante, dealing particularly with cases of divorce. He went as an emissary of Ereẓ Israel to Turkey and the Balkans and in 1680 was in Belgrade and in Sarejevo. In 1686 he was in Jerusalem, where in 1700 he was appointed chief rabbi, but he died shortly afterward.

Bibliography: Azulai, 1 (1852), 7 no. 25; Frumkin-Rivlin, 2 (1928), 74 no. 15; Yaari, Sheluḥei, 300–12; Scholem, Shabbetai Ẓevi, 1 (1957), 338.

[ED.]

BOTON, JACOB BEN ABRAHAM DI (1635?–1687), halakhist. Jacob was born in Salonika and was a disciple of Ḥasdai ha-Kohen Peraḥyah. His father, Abraham b. Jacob (b. c. 1610), grandson of Abraham b. Moses di *Boton, was also a disciple of Ḥasdai ha-Kohen Peraḥyah and was appointed chief rabbi of Salonika in 1678. He was among the opponents of Shabbetai Ẓevi. During the lifetime of his father, Jacob acted as *dayyan,* with the specific task of enforcing payments imposed by the *bet din.* He was acquainted with and believed in Shabbetai Ẓevi. When his father died, he failed in his attempt to succeed him as chief rabbi, despite the recommendation of Solomon *Amarillo. Jacob wrote many responsa, the earliest of which is dated 1658. They contain important material on the economic conditions of the time, dealing, among other things, with the guild of dyers to which he himself belonged. He made use of many manuscripts of *rishonim* and quoted early regulations of the Salonika community. A substantial part of his responsa was burnt together with his other writings when he was in Constantinople at the home of Ḥayyim Alfandari. His son-in-law, Solomon Abrabanel, published the remainder of his responsa under the title *Edut be-Ya'akov* (Salonika, 1720). He is known to have written four other books: (1) a commentary on the Mishnah, written during the plague of 1679 when he was in the village of Libada; (2) a commentary on the *Ittur* of *Isaac b. Abba Mari, a part of which was published with the responsa; (3) a work on the novellae of Solomon b. Abraham *Adret and on other topics; (4) commentaries to the Talmud and the *posekim.* A fragment from this work was included in his one printed book.

Bibliography: I. S. Emmanuel, *Maẓẓevot Saloniki,* 2 (1968), 150–2; Azulai, 1 (1852), 86, no. 210; 2 (1852), 106, no. 12; Steinschneider, Cat Bod, 1195, no. 5513.

[ED.]

BOTON, MEIR BEN ABRAHAM DI (c. 1575–1649), rabbi and halakhist. Born in Salonika, he studied under his father, Abraham. b. Moses di *Boton. In his introduction to his father's *Leḥem Mishneh,* he describes the trials and the expulsions he had experienced from his youth. He was appointed rabbi of Gallipoli and served there until his death. Students from all parts of Turkey, among them (Nissim) Solomon *Algazi, streamed to his yeshivah, which became a center of study. Even in his youth, Meir was in correspondence with the greatest halakhic authorities of the day, and problems were addressed to him even from Constantinople. He occupied himself to a considerable extent with communal affairs and also took an interest in poetry. After his death, his library was pillaged. The few responsa which remained in scattered pamphlets were collected and published with other material by his son-in-law, Jesse Almuli (Smyrna, 1660), who added his own valuable notes. Meir di Boton was a close friend of Ḥayyim *Benveniste, who mentions their correspondence in his *Ba'ei Ḥayyei.*

Bibliography: Conforte, Kore, 43a, 51b; Azulai, 1 (1852), 118, no. 6; Rosanes, Togarmah, 3 (1938), 197; Wallenstein, in: *Melilah,* 1 (1944), 62–65. [ED.]

BOTOSANI (Rum. **Botoşani**), town in N.E. Rumania. Up to the end of the 19th century it had the second largest and most important Jewish community in *Moldavia, apparently originating in the 17th century. There was a considerable community in Botosani by the early 18th century. In 1745 merchants in Botosani, including Jews, were granted the right to own their houses by the prince *(gospodar).* In 1799 Prince Alexander Ypsilanti gave a privilege (now in the Central Archives for the History of the Jewish People, Jerusalem) to the Botosani community granting it the status of an autonomous corporation. In 1803 there were 350 Jewish families paying tax in the town. In the 19th century the community increased as a result of Jewish immigration into Moldavia and in 1899 it numbered 16,817 (51.8% of the total population). By the early 19th century the Jews of Botosani had trade connections with Leipzig and Brody, and contributed to the economic development of the town. A growing number engaged in crafts. The Christian population demanded that the authorities should prohibit Jews from these trades. Despite this opposition, by 1899 more than 75% of the merchants and approximately 68% of the artisans in Botosani were Jewish. There were anti-Jewish riots in 1870. Anti-Jewish feelings again flared up during the Rumanian peasant revolt in 1907. When the Jewish communities in Rumania were deprived of their official status at the beginning of the 1860s (see *Rumania), sharp internal conflicts in the Botosani community led to its disintegration and disruption of its activities; many of its institutions closed down. In 1866 Hillel Kahana, the Hebrew writer and educator, founded a secular Jewish school in Botosani, among the first in Rumania. Despite opposition from Orthodox circles and several temporary closures, it existed up to the outbreak of World War II, in part supported by the Alliance Israélite Universelle. The Hebrew writers David Isaiah *Silberbusch, Ẓevi Lazar *Teller, and Israel *Teller taught there. At the beginning of 1882 Silberbush and Teller published the first two numbers of the Hebrew monthly *Ha-Or* in Botosani. After World War I the community was reorganized. It numbered 11,840 in 1930 (36.6% of the total population). Institutions maintained by the community included two primary schools (for boys and girls) and a vocational school for girls. [EL.F.]

Holocaust Period. Under Iron Guard reign (September 1940–January 1941), the 10,900 Jews of Botosani suffered from economic repression and various other restrictions. Many were kidnapped by the Iron Guard, beaten up, and tortured. Even before the forced labor law was enacted in December 1940 (see *Rumania, Holocaust) Botosani's Jewish men between the ages of 15 and 70 were forced into hard labor. Eight thousand Jews were eventually put on forced labor, half of them outside the city. Rumanian authorities deported 42 Jews to Transnistria "on suspicion of communism," most of whom were murdered shortly afterward by the SS and the Rumanian gendarmes. The total number of Botosani Jews deported to Transnistria rose to 148, some being accused of "anti-government agitation or propagating emigration."

The Jewish community dispensed a great deal of aid to the needy. After the occupation of Poland by the Germans, the community took care of the many refugees who came into the town. On the outbreak of war with the Soviet Union (June 1941), 11,000 Jews from villages and towns in the area were evacuated to Botosani, and they too were extended help. As a result of the influx of refugees and the dismissal of Jewish children from public schools, the number of children attending elementary schools maintained by the community grew from 452 in 1940 to 1,050 in 1943. Two high schools were also established, attended by 350 pupils. When the Soviet Army approached the city in April 1944, there was complete anarchy, with German and Rumanian Army deserters terrorizing the inhabitants. The Jewish community then took over municipal functions, established a civilian guard, and ensured the continued functioning of the government hospital and home for the aged. When Soviet forces entered on April 7, the city was handed over by a delegation of the Jewish community. Jews were appointed to all public posts, but the Soviet commander warned them not to turn the city into a "Jewish Republic." After the war, when the evacuees from the villages in the area and those who returned from Transnistria settled in the city, Botosani's total Jewish population numbered 19,550 (1947). A few years later most of the population settled in Israel, leaving 500 families and four synagogues in 1969. The local *shoḥet* also serves as the community's rabbi. [TH.L.]

Bibliography: J. B. Brociner, *Chestiunea Israeliţilor Români* (1910), 169–75; A. Gorovei, *Monografia Oraşului Botoşani* (1926), passim; E. Tauber, in: *Anuarul Evreilor din România* (1937), 151–7. HOLOCAUST PERIOD: PK Romanyah, 29–39; M. Carp, *Cartea Neagră,* 1 (1946), 154, 158.

BOTOSHANSKY, JACOB (1892–1964), Yiddish novelist, journalist, and critic. Botoshansky was born in Bessarabia. He was active in Rumania from 1914 to 1926 as a literary pioneer of Yiddish, and, thereafter, in Buenos Aires as editor of the Yiddish daily *Di Prese.* In 1914–15 he was one of the founders and editors of *Likht,* Rumania's first modern Yiddish periodical, and collaborated with Jacob *Sternberg in writing for the renascent Yiddish theater. In Argentina, Botoshansky played a dominant role in Jewish cultural life and became the community's leading literary figure. He wrote travel sketches of North and South America and of Israel. Two of his dramas, *Hershele Ostropoler* and *Reb Ber Liover* (1928), were staged in Argentina and Soviet Russia. His works include *Mir Viln Lebn* (1948) and *Di Kenigin fun Dorem Amerike* (1962), both fictional travel sketches; *Di Lebnsgeshikhte fun a Yidishn Zhurnalist,* memoirs (3 vols., 1948); and *Pshat,* literary essays (1952).

Bibliography: *Jacob Botoshansky tsu Zayne Zekhtsik Yor* (1955); LNYL, 1 (1956), 211ff.; A. Glanz-Leyeles, *Velt un Vort* (1958) 292–6; S. Bickel, *Rumenie* (Yid., 1961), 356–60. [SH.B.]

BOTVINNIK, MIKHAIL (1911–), Soviet chess master. Born in Saint Petersburg, Botvinnik won the world championship three times. He also achieved great distinction as an electrical engineer. At the end of World War II Botvinnik was decorated by the government for his work in that field. Many times chess champion of the USSR, Botvinnik emerged into international chess when he drew a match with Solomon Mikhailovitch *Flohr in 1933. His first significant success, however, was the sharing of first place with Capablanca at Nottingham in 1936. In the Avro Tournament of 1938, he was a close third behind Reuben *Fine and Keres. His activities were interrupted by the war. After victories at Groningen in 1946, and Moscow (Tchigorin Memorial) in 1947, Botvinnik won the world title, defeating seven other leaders of world chess in a tournament played at the Hague and in Moscow. He defended his title many times. In 1951 he drew with David *Bronstein, and retained the title. In 1954 he similarly drew with Smyslov. In 1957 he lost the title to Smyslov, but in 1958 regained it. In 1960 he lost the title to Mikhail Nekhemovitch *Tal, but in 1961 again regained the title. Finally, in 1963 he lost the title to Petrosian and retired from further attempts at winning it again. Nevertheless, he continued to win tournaments. [G.A.]

BOUCHARA, Algerian family, prominent in the Jewish community life of Algiers from the 17th century. Abraham (early 18th century) was *muqaddim* (leader) of the community and adviser to the deys; his brother Isaac, well-known about 1726, was a shipowner and financier in Leghorn, Genoa, and Algiers. Abraham's son Jacob Raphael (d. 1768) succeeded his father as *muqaddim*. Raphael, who was very wealthy and an associate of the dey, represented Ragusa (*Dubrovnik) as consul (1735). He was one of the principal shipowners of his time, and his commercial activities extended from Alexandria to Venice and from Leghorn to Hamburg. He supported yeshivot and printed Hebrew works at his own expense. His son Joseph was employed by Christian governments to ransom Christian prisoners. Jacob Raphael's other son, Abraham (d. 1801), succeeded him as consul and *muqaddim*, but in 1800 Naphtali *Busnach replaced him in the latter position. Abrahami had disputes with the community, which were eventually settled in his favor by the scholars Jacob *Benaim and Ḥ. J. D. *Azulai. At the beginning of his career, Abraham represented the U.S.A. in her negotiations with the dey. Although involved in commercial affairs, he pursued talmudic and kabbalistic studies. He wrote three works: *Beit Avraham* and *Likkutei Tanakh*, both unpublished, and *Berit Avraham* (Leghorn, 1791), a collection of homilies.

Bibliography: J. Ayash, *Beit Yehudah* (1746), preface; A. Devoulx (J. M. Haddey), *Le Livre d'or des Israélites Algériens* (1871), 52–56, 62–64; E. Plantet, *Correspondence des Deys d'Alger*, 2 (1893), 237–8; I. Bloch, *Inscriptions tumulaires . . . d'Alger* (1888), 62–64, 91–93; Hirschberg, Afrikah, 2 (1965), 62–63, 66.

[D.Co.]

°**BOUDIN, JEAN-FRANÇOIS,** known as **Father Justin** (1736–1811), French Capuchin friar and preacher. Boudin was appointed by Joseph Beni, bishop of Carpentras, at the end of 1783 to deliver the conversionist sermons which the Jews of Carpentras were obliged to attend. Seventeen of the sermons he delivered between 1787 and 1790, as well as his short treatise *Notion du Talmud*, are preserved in a manuscript in the Avignon public library (Ms. 1525).

Bibliography: Barjavel, in: J.-F. Boudin, *Histoire de Guerres . . .* (1859²), xiiff.

[B.Bl.]

BOUGIE (Ar. **Bajaya;** ancient **Saldae**), town in Algeria. Rebuilt in 1067, Bougie attracted Muslim, Jewish, and Christian families, who were exempted from taxes by the Muslim authorities as an inducement to settle there. A port, and often the capital city, its commerce flourished, and it became a great intellectual center. Although the city's inhabitants were spared by the conquering Almohades in 1152, the city later declined. Jews from the Balearic Islands, Italy, and Marseilles settled there in the 13th century, but many members of the indigenous Jewish community emigrated. Later, however, because of the 1391 persecutions, many Jews from Spain and the Balearic Isles took refuge in Bougie and eventually became the town's leading businessmen. As a result Bougie had two separate communities: the older inhabitants and the new refugees. Among those who lived in Bougie were the scholarly rabbis Isaac ʿAbd al-Ḥaqq and Astruc Cohen, the ʿAmmar, Najar, and Stora families, Isaac Nafusi, the astronomer and instrument-maker (originally from Majorca), and the Bacri-Kohen family, which flourished there in the 15th and 16th centuries. When the Spanish conquered Bougie in 1510 Jewish property was pillaged and many Jews were sold as slaves, but the community continued to exist. In 1553 the Turks occupied Bougie, which from then on lost its importance (3,000 inhabitants, of whom 600 were Jews). The Turks granted exclusive trading rights and a concession of the port to David Bacri of Algiers in 1807. With the arrival of the French in 1833 the Jewish community left the town, a few Jews returning in 1838. Thereafter there were never more than 800 Jews in Bougie; none remained by the late 1960s.

Bibliography: R. Brunschwig, *Berbérie orientale sous les Hafṣides*, 1 (1940), 377–84, 398–428; A. Hershman, *Rabbi Isaac bar Sheshet Perfet and his Times* (1943), index; Hirschberg, Afrikah, 2 (1965), index s.v. *Bajaya*.

[D.Co.]

BOULAY, small town in northeastern France; formerly belonging to the Duchy of Lorraine. Jews settled in Boulay in the first half of the 17th century. It was the home of Raphael *Levy, the victim of a *blood libel, executed in 1670. In 1721 Duke Leopold confirmed the right of 19 Jewish families to reside in Boulay and designated the synagogue as the main one for the duchy. A cemetery is mentioned from the end of the 17th century. The Jewish population numbered 137 in 1808, 265 in 1831, and 120 in 1931. During World War II, 11 Jews from Boulay were deported by the Germans and one was shot. The synagogue was destroyed, but was rebuilt in 1956. In 1968, the Jewish population was about 35.

Bibliography: F. Guir, *Histoire de Boulay* (1933), 73f.; C. Pfister, *Histoire de Nancy*, 3 (1909), 318; *Almanach des communautés israélites de la Moselle* (1955), 121f.; Z. Szajkowski, *Analytical Franco-Jewish Gazetteer* (1966), 229.

[G.C.]

BOULE (Gr. Βουλή), in ancient Greece, a state council; in Ereẓ Israel a city council which played an important role during and after the Second Temple period. One of the Hellenistic institutions established in cities founded by Herod and his sons, the Boule later spread to other urban areas inhabited mainly by Jews. There was a Boule also in Jerusalem; inTiberias it consisted of 600 members; and the Boule in Ashkelon is mentioned in a source dating from the end of the third century C.E. (TJ, Pe'ah 1:1, 15c). In some cities the Boule was housed in a special building (Aram. כנישתא דבולי, *Kenishta de-Boulei*), in which the sages delivered public homilies (TJ, Shek. 7:3, 50c; TJ, Ta'an. 1:2, 64a). Various talmudic sources refer to the Boule in southern Judean cities dissolved apparently because of internal friction (TJ, Ned. 3:2, 38a; TJ, Shevu. 3:10, 34d; Git. 37a). The principal function of the Boule was to levy taxes for the Roman administration, for the collection of which the property of members of the Boule was the surety. Since the taxes had frequently to be extorted from the people, wealthy men, appointed against their will, tried various ways to evade serving on the Boule, sometimes by flight, and hence the remark of R. Johanan (middle of the third century C.E.): "If you have been nominated for the Boule, let the Jordan be your neighbor" (TJ, MK 2:3, 81b).

Bibliography: Alon, in: *Tarbiz,* 14 (1943), 145ff. (repr. in his *Mearim,* 2 (1958), 24ff.).

[A. SCH.]

BOURG-EN-BRESSE, capital of the department of the Ain, eastern France. The first mention of Jews in Bourg-en-Bresse dates from 1277 when the Jews and the Cahorsins paid 50 livres to the lady of the manor. An agreement of 1438 between the city guilds and the Jews of Bourg-en-Bresse regarding their share in the expenses for fortifications was signed by 11 heads of families. The Jews then constituted some 3% of the population. The census of 1512 notes that there were no longer Jews living in Bourg-en-Bresse. At the beginning of World War II, 10 to 15 Jewish families were living in the town. Seven of the Jews arrested during the raids of July 10, 1944, were executed. There has been no subsequent Jewish community.

Bibliography: C. Jarrin, *Essai sur l'histoire de Bourg-en-Bresse* (1876), 19, 29; idem, *La Bresse . . . ,* 2 (1885), 21; Gerson, in: *Revue savoisienne,* 26 (1885), 84ff.; J. Brossard, *Cartulaire de Bourg-en-Bresse* (1882), no. 90 (cf. no. 148); Z. Szajkowski, *Analytical Franco-Jewish Gazetteer* (1966), 149.

[B.BL.]

°**BOURGEOIS, JEAN,** son of a Parisian merchant, murdered on August 26, 1652, by members of the secondhand dealers guild which he had insulted by calling it "the synagogue." The affair was taken up in numerous broadsheets, or *"Mazarinades,"* often in verse, which presented the event as if the dealers were Jews guilty of ritual murder. They demanded the expulsion of the Jews from France, although there were then no professing Jews in the country. Prosecution of the accomplices in the crime was stopped in June 1653, by royal writ which expressly noted that all the accused "professed the Catholic religion."

Bibliography: Z. Szajkowski, *Franco-Judaica* (1962), 117f.; R. Anchel, *Juifs de France* (1946), 130ff.

[B.BL.]

BOURGES, capital of the department of Cher, central France. In 570 a Jew, Sigericus, was baptized in Bourges, while at about the same time a Jew practicing medicine there treated a cleric. *Sulpicius, bishop of Bourges, 624–647, attempted to convert the Jews in Bourges to Christianity, and expelled any who resisted his missionary activities. In 1020 a Jewish quarter is mentioned to the south of the city. About 1200 a baptized Jew of Bourges named Guillaume, who had become a deacon, composed an anti-Jewish treatise, *Bellum Domini adversus Iudaeos.* Around 1250 the pope requested the archbishop of Bourges to secure a livelihood for the baptized Jew, Jean. Between the end of the 13th century and 1305 many Jewish names appear on the municipal tax rolls and bailiff court records. A building at 79 Rue des Juifs is believed to have been used as a synagogue in the Middle Ages. The community ceased to exist after the Jews were expelled from France in the 14th century. During World War II, especially after June 1940, hundreds of Jewish refugees were temporarily settled in Bourges.

Bibliography: B. Blumenkranz, *Juifs et Chrétiens . . .* (1960), index; idem, in: *Miscellanea Mediaevalia,* 4 (1966), 278–9; P. Gauchery and A. de Grossouvre, *Notre Vieux Bourges* (1966²), 149; G. Nahon, in: REJ, 121 (1962), 64; Z. Szajkowski, *Analytical Franco-Jewish Gazetteer* (1966), 174; S. Grayzel, *Church and Jews* (1966), index.

[B.BL.]

BOVE-BUKH, a frequently reprinted chivalric romance of the early 16th century composed in ottava rima by Elye Bokher (Elijah Baḥur *Levita). The book is a Yiddish adaptation of the Italian version *(Buovo d'Antona)* of the Anglo-French romance *Sir Bevis of Hampton* of the early 14th century. The 1949 reprint was a facsimile reproduction of the first edition of 1541 (Isny, Germany) with an introduction by Judah A. *Joffe. A crude prose version of Levita's book was published under the title *Bove Mayse* at

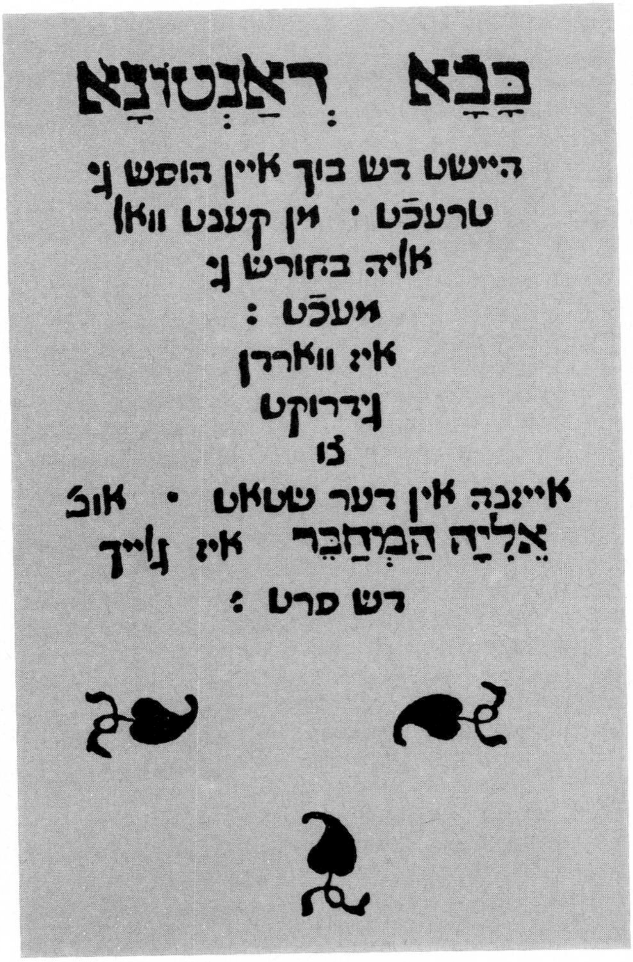

בבא דאנטונא
הייסט דש בוך איין הופש ג׳
טרעכט · מן קענט וואל
אליה בחורש ג׳
מעכט :
איז ווארדן
גדרוקט
צו
אייזנה אין דער שטאט · אוב
אליה המחבר איז גוייך
דש פרט :

Title page of the Yiddish version of *Buovo d'Antona,* from which the expression *Bobe-Mayse* originates. Facsimile of first edition, Isny, Germany, 1541.

the end of the 18th century, and this version remained a popular favorite among the Jewish masses of East Europe. (See also **Bobe-Mayse.*)

Bibliography: M. Weinreich, *Bilder fun der Yidisher Literatur Geshikhte* (1929), 149–71; N. B. Minkoff, *Eliye Bokher un Zayn Bove-Bukh* (1950); G. E. Weil, *Elie Lévita, humaniste et massorète* (Leiden 1963); H. Schwarzbaum, *Studies in Jewish and World Folklore* (Berlin, 1968), 89, n. 61.

[S.L.]

BOVSHOVER, JOSEPH (1873–1915), U.S. Yiddish poet. Bovshover, who was born in Liubavich, Belorussia, immigrated to the United States from Riga in 1891. He worked first in a sweatshop and wrote revolutionary, anarchist poetry which he recited in public. He was influenced by the radical Yiddish poets, Morris *Vinchevsky, David *Edelstadt, and Morris *Rosenfeld, as well as by Heinrich Heine and Walt Whitman. The influence of the Bible can also be discerned in his poetry. Under the name of Basil Dahl he wrote and published 11 poems in English. Despite exaggerated critical praise, he became increasingly melancholic and spent the last 15 years of his life in a home for the mentally ill. Bovshover published essays on Heine, Emerson, Whitman, and Edwin Markham, and translated Shakespeare's *Merchant of Venice* into Yiddish. Bovshover's collected works were published in one volume (1911, 1916[2]).

Bibliography: LNYL, 1 (1956), 207–10; K. Marmor, *Yoseph Bovshover* (Yid., 1952); N. B. Minkoff, *Pionern fun Yidisher Poezie in Amerike*, 1 (1956), 131–91.

[E.SCH.]

BOX, a shrub or tree *(Buxus sempervirens)* that grows wild in Asia Minor. At present it is cultivated in Israel as an ornamental tree. In the Mishnah it is called *eshkero'a*, its excellent wood being used for delicate articles and apparatus, such as the urn which was used in the Temple for the casting of lots to decide the duties of the priests (Yoma 3:9). It has a creamy yellow color and R. Ishmael said that the children of Israel "are like boxwood, neither black nor white, but an intermediate color" (Neg. 2:1). Since he lived in the south of Ereẓ Israel, R. Ishmael was probably referring to most of the inhabitants of that region but no conclusions can be drawn from this statement as regards the color of the skin of the Jews living elsewhere in the country. The box is not mentioned in the Bible although the Targums identify it—without basis—with certain other biblical trees, such as the *te'ashur*.

Bibliography: Loew, Flora, 1 (1926), 316f.; J. Feliks, *Olam ha-Ẓome'aḥ ha-Mikra'i* (1968[2]), 84, 317.

[J.F.]

BOYAR, LOUIS H. (1898–), U.S. real estate developer and philanthropist. Boyar, born in San Francisco, resided in Los Angeles from 1934. He was a pioneer of large-scale home building and community planning in Los Angeles after World War II. Boyar built the city of Lakewood, one of the first and largest planned communities in the U.S. He directed large-scale personal benefactions and fund-raising efforts to the economic and cultural needs of Israel. He served the State of Israel *Bonds organization in many capacities, including that of chairman of the Board of Governors. He also served as chairman of the Board of Israel Investors, Inc. Many educational and social service institutions in Israel were erected by him in memory of his wife, Mae. Boyar was deputy chairman of the Board of Governors of the Hebrew University. Boyar also supported a number of U.S. institutions, particularly in Los Angeles.

[M.V.]

BOYCOTT, ANTI-JEWISH, organized activity directed against the Jews to exclude them from social, economic, and political life. Anti-Jewish boycott pressure has accompanied *anti-Semitism as one of its more dangerous and frequent manifestations. Contacts with Jews were avoided, Jews were not accepted in merchants' guilds, trade associations, and similar organizations. This form of boycott often coincided with legal and administrative restrictions already in force in the country.

Toward the end of the 19th century, the anti-Jewish boycott became one of the basic weapons used for victimizing the Jewish population. The first International Anti-Jewish Congress in Dresden, 1882 (see *Anti-Semitic Political Parties and Organizations), adopted a slogan against Jewish merchants and professionals. In Western Europe, the boycott took the form of excluding Jews from membership of certain societies. In Eastern Europe the rapidly developing "national" bourgeoisie, which formed the mainstay of the rightist parties, soon adopted anti-Semitic tactics in the effort to squeeze out Jewish competitors. The anti-Jewish boycott campaign met with success in many parts of the Austro-Hungarian Empire. The Austrian anti-Semites publicized in the press and at public meetings the slogan, "Don't buy from Jews." When the government declared this slogan illegal, it was changed into "Buy from Christians only." In Bohemia and Moravia the anti-Jewish boycott spread under the slogan "Each to his own" *(svůj k svému)*, at a time when the rising bourgeoisie sought to obtain an exclusive position in the economy, especially in trade.

Shortly before World War I the Ukrainian population of Galicia was swept into a boycott movement instigated because of alleged Jewish collaboration with the Poles. At the same time, some Polish public figures in Galicia (for instance, the priest Stojalkowski) proposed the boycott as a form of defense for the Polish population against alleged Jewish exploitation. In Russia, the boycott did not attain significant proportions, despite the strongly nationalist and anti-Jewish stand of the Russian merchants. The system of legal and administrative restrictions against the Jews already operating in Czarist Russia was more efficient than any form of boycott. A similar situation existed in Rumania, where the Jews had been deprived of all rights of citizenship and were considered "foreigners" in the legal sense. They were not allowed to practice the liberal professions, or keep tobacconist shops (which were a state monopoly), pharmacies, etc. Following the Russian example, Rumania introduced the *numerus clausus* in educational institutions. Jewish factory owners were obliged by law to employ two-thirds non-Jewish workers. In 1907 "foreigners" were prohibited from holding agricultural farms on lease. The anti-Jewish boycott drive was especially intensive in Polish areas, which at that time did not form a national state. The newspaper *Rola*, which began publication in the 1880s, proposed the slogan of "Polonization" of trade and industry. Developments took a decisive turn in the following decade when the National Democratic Party (*Narodowa Demokracja*, "ND," "En-deks"), led by Roman Dmowski, appeared on the political horizon. Initially the Endeks did not come out with anti-Semitic slogans and confined their campaign to the "Litvaks," Jews from Russia, whom they accused of promoting the Russification of Poland.

The crushing of the 1905–07 revolution in Russia was also a major setback to the aspirations of the Polish community for political liberation, and it now began to interest itself exclusively in economic problems. The Endek party campaigns became increasingly aggressive, adopting the slogans "Each to his own," "Don't buy Jewish," and "Buy Christian only." The boycott also spread to cultural life, giving birth to numerous exclusively "Catholic" or "Christian" organizations. The anti-Jewish boycott received wide public support after 1912 in connection with

Figure 1. Nazi pickets outside a German Jewish shop. The placard says, "Germans! Defend yourselves! Don't buy from Jews!"

the elections for the Fourth Russian *Duma. The Jewish voters did not support the candidate put up by the rightist Polish party, and their votes secured the election of the Socialist candidate. In retaliation the rightist press started an intensive anti-Jewish campaign, proclaiming the beginning of the "Polish-Jewish War." The boycott in Polish areas appears to have been coordinated with the anti-Semitic campaign simultaneously unleashed in Russia in connection with the *Beilis case.

Between the two world wars anti-Jewish boycott agitation continued particularly in Poland where the situation deteriorated in the wake of economic difficulties, especially following the depression. In an endeavor to soft-pedal the rising social tension, rightist anti-Semitic circles, with the silent approval of the authorities, pointed at the Jews as the cause of the distress of millions of unemployed. Taking over trade from the Jews was made to serve as a panacea for rampant poverty and unemployment. After the Nazi rise to power in Germany the government publicly announced a general anti-Jewish boycott. Nazi agitators urged boycotting the Jews at mass meetings. On Sunday, April 1, 1933, uniformed Nazi pickets appeared in front of Jewish shops, attacked their clients, and wrote anti-Jewish slogans on their windows. The offices of Jewish doctors, lawyers, and engineers were also picketed. The official German policy roused anti-Semitic circles in neighboring countries to more extreme action. The anti-Jewish boycott in Poland gathered strength in imitation of the Nazi example, and Polish anti-Semitic groups began to adopt active boycott pressure. Pickets appeared in front of Jewish shops and stalls and terrorized the Jewish merchants as well as their non-Jewish clients. The rising number of incidents sometimes resulted in the destruction of shops and goods and also an occasional bloody pogrom, as at Przytyk and Wysokie Mazowieckei.

Anti-Jewish boycott activities received the stamp of official approval in 1937, when Prime Minister Slawoj-Skaladkowski let drop in his notorious statement the slogan "economic boycott?—please!" The Polish government also attempted to step up Jewish emigration from Poland by means of economic strangulation. The boycott did not greatly affect Jewish industrialists and big businessmen, with whom the most rabid propagandists of the anti-Jewish boycott movement not infrequently had secret commercial ties. However, it weighed heavily on hundreds of thousands of small businessmen, artisans, and others. The anti-Jewish boycott—frequently referred to as the "cold pogrom" in the inter-war press—undermined the foundations of the livelihood of hundreds of thousands of Jews.

Figure 3. "Jews not wanted" posters from German cities, 1935. The streamer in the bottom picture reads, "Anyone who buys from a Jew is a traitor." Jerusalem, Yad Vashem Archives.

Figure 2. A 1933 poster warns Berliners to "avoid Jewish doctors and lawyers." Jerusalem, Yad Vashem Archives.

Bibliography: JE, s.v. *Antisemitism;* EJ, s.v. *Antisemitismus;* Dubnow, Weltgesch, 10 (1929), 121 and passim; I. Schipper (ed.), *Dzieje handlu żydowskiego na ziemiach polskich* (1937); Elbogen, Century, 639–44; H. G. Reissner, in: *Jubilee Volume . . . Curt C. Silberman* (1969).

[P.K.]

BOYCOTT, ANTI-NAZI. In protest against anti-Jewish excesses in Germany after the Nazi Party's victory at the polls on March 5, 1933, Jews throughout the world held mass rallies, marches, and a spontaneous anti-German boycott. This boycott developed into an organized movement after the demonstrative all-day boycott of the Nazis against German Jewry on April 1. The boycott proclamation of March 20 by the Jews of Vilna marked the launching of the boycott movement in Europe; Warsaw followed six days later. Soon the movement embraced virtually all Poland and was subsequently consolidated by the United Boycott Committee of Poland. This boycott movement was short-lived, however, for in January 1934,

Poland signed a ten-year nonaggression pact with Hitler, in which cessation of boycott activities was stipulated as a precondition. Under Poland's premier, Józef Pilsudski, the provision was ignored. But in June 1935, about a month after his death, the United Boycott Committee was liquidated.

A mass boycott movement in England first began in the Jewish quarter of London's East End on March 24, 1935. The English-German fur business practically ceased as a result. The boycott groups included the Capt. Weber Boycott Organization, the World Alliance for Combatting Anti-Semitism, the British Anti-War Council, and the Anglo-Jewish Council of Trades and Industries. However, the *Board of Deputies of British Jews opposed the boycott throughout the 1930s.

In France, boycott sentiment was not as intense as in Poland or England; nevertheless, on the eve of the April 1 boycott, French Jewry warned that it would counterboycott the Reich if the Nazis carried out their plans, and they executed their threat by action similar to that of London's East End Jews. Two of France's most active boycott groups were the International League against Anti-Semitism, and the Comité de Défense des Juifs Persécutés en Allemagne. However, the *Alliance Israélite Universelle remained opposed to the boycott. At the end of March 1933, the anti-Nazi boycott movement spread to Rumania and Yugoslavia, eventually encompassing the Jewish communities of Egypt, Greece, Latvia, Morocco, Palestine, several Latin American countries, and the United States.

In the United States the anti-Nazi boycott reached its peak. America's first established boycott group was the *Jewish War Veterans (March 19, 1933), followed by the American League for the Defense of Jewish Rights (ALDJR), a new organization founded by the Yiddish journalist, Abraham Coralnik, in May 1933. Three months later the *American Jewish Congress (AJC) made a boycott declaration and subsequently created a Boycott Committee. In October, the American Federation of Labor, a non-Jewish worker's organization, also announced that it was in favor of the boycott. The ALDJR was first led by Coralnik, and after six months by attorney-at-law Samuel Untermyer. In a move intended to alter the League's Jewish character, Untermyer changed its name to the "Non-Sectarian Anti-Nazi League to Champion Human Rights." In 1934 the *Jewish Labor Committee (JLC) was created claiming to represent about 500,000 Jewish workers, and it immediately initiated a boycott program. Two years later, the organization's central body for boycott activities combined with the Congress' Boycott Committee to form the Joint Boycott Council (JBC). The Council and the League proved to be America's principal boycott organizations; the Jewish Veterans and other boycott groups that arose in the late 1930s cooperated with or joined these two organizations. However, attempts to unite the Council and the League were unsuccessful, the two organizations acting separately in consolidating the boycott on an international level.

The Joint Boycott Council's chairman, Joseph Tenenbaum, obtained passage of a boycott resolution at the *World Jewish Congress (WJC) in 1936. This was a reaffirmation of a worldwide boycott resolution adopted by the Second Preliminary Conference (1933), preceding the establishment of the WJC. Also in 1936, Coralnik and Untermyer convened a World Jewish Economic Conference in Amsterdam to coordinate the growing international boycott movement and help find for the boycotting businessmen substitutes for former German sources of supply. To this end, the Conference created a World Jewish Economic Federation, presided over by Untermyer. In keeping with his view that the boycott was a nonsectarian movement, Untermyer changed the Federation's name to the "World Non-Sectarian Anti-Nazi Council to Champion Human Rights." American Jewry's failure to form a united boycott front did not prevent the movement from achieving success. Thus eventually the department store colossi of Macy's, Gimbel's, Sears and Roebuck, Woolworth, and others gave in to continued boycott pressure.

There is evidence that the Nazis, at least during the first two years of their regime, feared that a tight boycott would cripple their economy. Regarding the United States, for example, a memorandum prepared for Hitler by the Economic Policy Department of the Reich as late as November 18, 1938, cited the following comparative figures, which it attributed partly to the boycott:

Year	1929	1932	1937
Import from the U.S.	1.790*	592	282
Export to the U.S.	991	281	209

* In millions of Reichsmarks

In January 1939 dissolution of the *B'nai B'rith in Germany moved its American counterpart to join the boycott movement. However, the American Jewish Committee remained unalterably opposed to the movement throughout the Nazi era. In the United States, a non-belligerent until Pearl Harbor, the boycott was continued until 1941.

Bibliography: M. Gottlieb, *Anti-Nazi Boycott Movement in the American Jewish Community, 1933–1941* (Ph.D. dissert., Brandeis Univ., 1967); B. Katz, *Crisis and Response* (M. A. thesis, Columbia Univ., 1951); J. Tenenbaum, in: *Yad Vashem Studies,* 3 (1959), 129–46; S. Wise, *Challenging Years* (1949), ch. 15; AJHSQ, 57 (June, 1968).

[M.G.]

BOYCOTT, ARAB. The Arab boycott is a campaign of economic warfare conducted against Israel by the members of the Arab League for the purpose of ruining Israel's economy and thereby weakening its military potential and undermining its political foundation. It consists, first of all, of a complete boycott of Israel and Israel goods by all Arab states and has been extended to apply to countries not involved in the Arab-Israel conflict. The boycott tries to dissuade commercial and industrial firms from establishing economic relations with Israel, or, if such relations have come into existence, to force their abrogation by threatening foreign firms which maintain, or plan to establish, business ties with Israel with blacklisting and exclusion from Arab markets. The boycott is conducted by the Central Office for the Boycott of Israel in Damascus, which is responsible to the Economic Council of the Arab League, and by regional boycott committees in each of the Arab states. The regional committees, although connected with the central office, are under the authority of the respective national governments—the Egyptian War Ministry, the Iraqi Foreign Office, the Lebanese Economic Ministry, etc. Arab diplomatic and consular representatives abroad are also at the disposal of the boycott authorities.

Various documents and certificates are involved in the enforcement of the boycott. Any firm seeking to embark on business activities in an Arab state is required to sign an affidavit declaring that it is not engaged in any "boycottable offense." ("Boycottable offenses," i.e., economic ties with Israel, cover a wide range, from "owning shares in an Israel corporation" to "producing or selling motion pictures which depict Israel or Jewish history in a favorable light"—the anti-Semitic character of the latter provision is noteworthy.) Another document used in the boycott is the "Certificate of Origin," verifying that none of the components or materials of goods shipped to Arab states is made in Israel. A third document is a questionnaire sent by the central boycott office or a regional office (or by the central office and one or more regional offices, for cumulative effect) to a firm suspected of assisting the Israel economy. Such questionnaires usually contain the overt or implied threat of blacklisting in case an unsatisfactory reply, or no reply, is received. The boycott is not only anti-Israel but anti-Jewish in character; Jewish firms are "suspect" and find it difficult to enter into business relations with Arab countries.

The growth of Israel's economy indicates that the Arab boycott has failed to reach its goal; it may even be said to have served as a stimulant to Israel's economic development and its links with foreign markets. When firms have succumbed to the boycott it has not necessarily done lasting harm to Israel; other firms have usually been ready to fill the gap, or Israel has made a special effort to do so on her own. The documentation demanded by the boycott offices—in contravention of established international practice—has been successfully resisted by many governments, chambers of commerce, and individual firms. The attitude of the buying public, especially in countries with large Jewish communities, has also had its effect, especially on large companies, which have had to set off the loss in prestige, local sales, and exports against the threatened loss of Arab markets. The Arabs themselves often compromised where they met with a firm refusal or where their own interests were vitally involved. Much of the success of which the Arab boycott machine boasts has little basis in fact. This is not to say that the effect of the Arab boycott can be discounted. The damage done, however, cannot be estimated, as no statistics can tell what trade was not sought, what investments were not made, and what know-how was withheld.

Israel has defended itself by exposing the hollowness of Arab threats, by pointing up the constant growth of the Israel market, by refusing to cooperate in half-measures proposed in some instances, and by discontinuing trade with firms which have given in to the boycott in any way.

[M.Sh.]

BOZECCO (Bozecchi), BENJAMIN BEN JUDAH (1290–1335), Italian grammarian and biblical exegete, who lived in Rome. His name probably derived from the town Buzecchio in the district of Forli, Italy, from which his family came. In one of his poems *Immanuel of Rome praises him as "the father of all the scholars in mathematics and geometry, preeminent in Bible and *masorah, whose talents and wisdom are unlimited" (cf. D. Yarden (ed.), *Maḥberot Immanuel ha-Romi,* 1 (1957), 229–31). Of his biblical commentaries only those to Proverbs and Chronicles have survived. Written apparently before 1312, they consist mainly of explanations of difficult verses and grammatical comments. He also completed the commentary to Kings left unfinished by *Isaiah Trani the Elder. His exegesis is based upon the literal meaning, and he is considered a pioneer of this method among the Italian Bible commentators. In the introduction to his commentary on Proverbs he emphasizes his opposition to the homiletic method in exegesis, pointing out that most exegetes "follow the method of homiletical exposition *(derash)* instead of the literal, and fail to pay attention to the significance of what the rabbis call *peshat* (literal exposition) i.e., that which is *pashut,* simple and obvious." Among his grammatical works are *Mavo Kaẓar le-Torat ha-Higgui,* on phonetics, published as an introduction to the *Sefer ha-Dikdukim* of Moses Kimḥi (Venice, 1546) and *Mevo ha-Dikduk,* a revised version and extensive summation of the former book (published by S. Loewinger, 1931). A commentary to Ezra and Nehemiah (published by Berger in *Kobez al Jad,* 7 (1896–97); see Alberstamm's note, p. 42) as well as various *piyyutim* are also attributed to him.

Bibliography: Guedemann, Gesch Erz, 2 (1884), 156; W. Bacher, in: REJ, 10 (1885), 123–44; Vogelstein-Rieger, 1 (1896), 388–92; H. Berger, in: MWJ, 16 (1889), 207–54; idem, in: MGWJ, 45 (1901), 138–65, 373–404; Davidson, Oẓar, 4 (1933), 371; S. Loewinger, *Két középkori héber grammatikáról* (1931), 1–34.

[Y.Ho.]

BOZRAH (Heb. בָּצְרָה). (1) A city in *Bashan, south of the *Hauran mountains. It is probably mentioned in the city list of Thutmose III (no. 23) and the *Tell el-Amarna letters (EA 197) as Buzruna. It does not appear in the Bible but may be identical with Bosoa, where Jews lived in the time of the Hasmoneans (I Macc. 5:26). Bozrah's great period began in 106 C.E. when the Nabatean kingdom was annexed to the Roman Empire and Trajan built a highway from Bozrah to Aïla. He also established the camp of the Third Legion, "Cyrenaica," at Bozrah (Ptolemy 5:16,4), and the city was then renamed Nova Trajana Bostra. Hadrian visited it in 129 C.E. Some time later it became the capital of the province of Arabia, a position it retained until the end of Byzantine times (Eusebius, Onom. 10:46). From the third century onward, it was the seat of a Christian archbishopric and in the same century, was elevated to the rank of a Roman colony. In the fourth century, Bozrah was a flourishing city which had trade relations with Persia and Arabia. In the Roman and Byzantine periods, Jews lived at Bozrah and the community included many rabbis, such as Jonah, Eleazar, Berechiah, and Tanḥum; others, among them Resh Lakish and Abbahu, visited the city since the local Jews seem to have been lax in their religious observances. The Babylonian Talmud (Shab. 29b) mentions a synagogue at Bozrah. Bozrah was the capital of the Ghassanid principality under Byzantine suzerainty. It was captured by the Arabs in 635 and retained its status as capital of the Hauran. It is today a village in Jordan called Buṣrā-Askī Shām with about 2,000 inhabitants. The remains of the ancient city include a wall, intersecting streets, a triumphal arch, a well-preserved theater, burial towers, baths (there are springs in the northwest of the city), and a large cistern, 485 × 62 ft. (148 × 19m.), from Roman times. A Christian cathedral, built in 512, contains one of the earliest known examples of a Byzantine dome. A second church has a bell tower and a monastery called Deir (Dayr) Baḥīrā after the monk with whom Muhammad is said to have lodged on his visit there. Around the Roman theater is a citadel erected in 1202 by the Mamluk sultan al-Ādil. (2) A city of *Edom. It is mentioned in the Bible in connection with the list of Edomite kings (Gen. 36:33) and in other passages (Isa. 34:6; Jer. 49:13, 22; Amos 1:12). Archaeological remains ranging in date from the time of the Edomite kingdom to the Arab period have been discovered at a place which the Arabs call Buṣayra. In ancient times Bozrah was a stronghold (hence its name, meaning "fort") guarding the roads from the plateau of Edom to the *Arabah. (3) A village on the southern border of Trachonitis. It is mentioned as Bosor (I Macc. 5:26) and called Buṣr al-Ḥarīrī in Arabic. Jews who settled there in the time of *Judah Maccabee appealed to him for help against their neighbors, and this help was promptly given. The name also occurs in the phrase "Trachonitis in the territory of Bozrah" (instead of "Bozrah in the territory of Trachonitis"?) in the list of the country's borders (Tosef.,

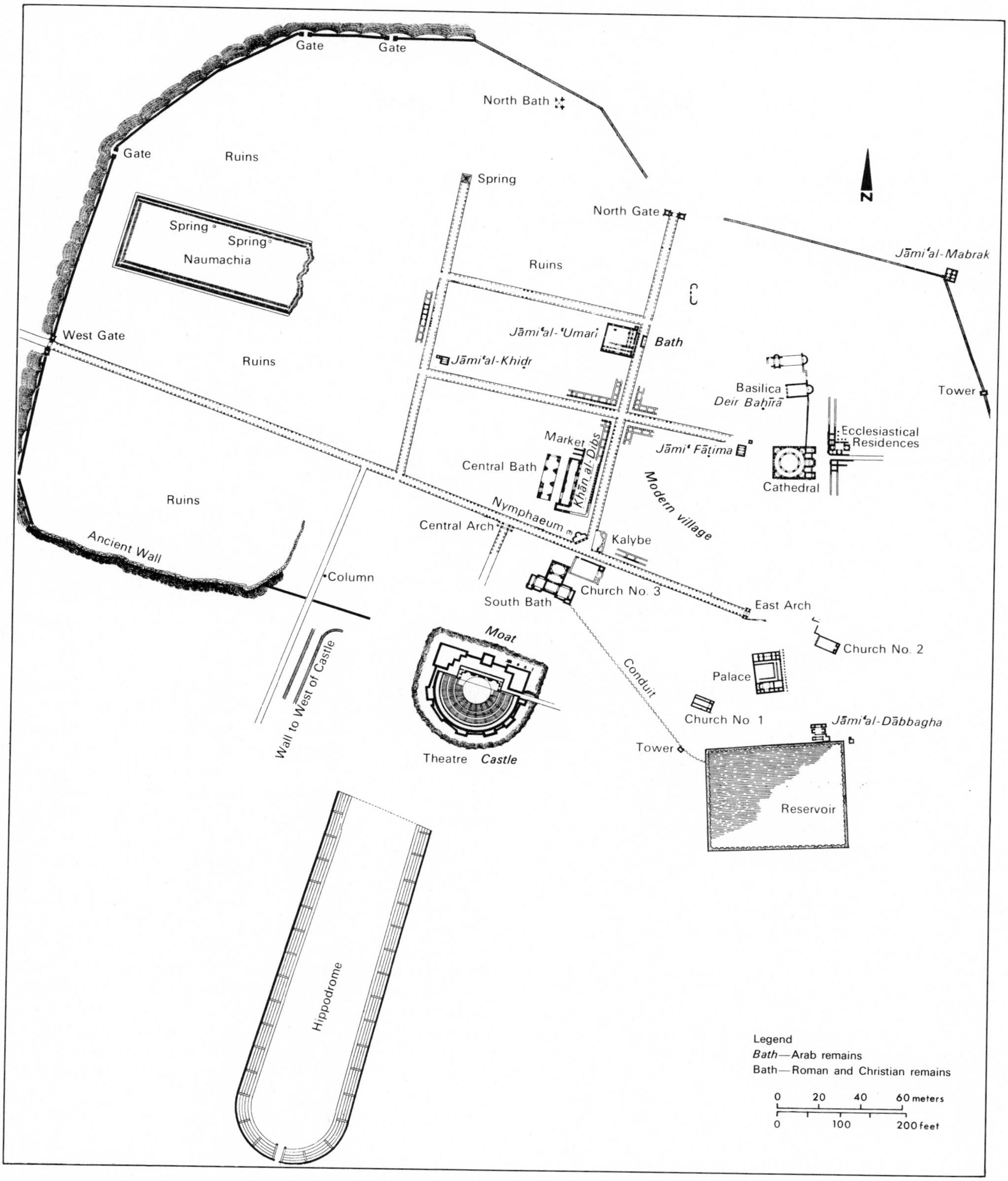

Remains of the ancient city of Bozrah (1). After H. C. Butler, *Architecture and Other Arts*, Princeton University Press.

Shev. 4:11; Sif. Deut. 11:21). There is a modern settlement called *Bozrah about 7 mi. (12 km.) north of Tel Aviv.

Bibliography: (1) R. E. Bruennow and A. V. Domaszewski, *Provincia Arabia*, 3 (1909), 1–84; H. C. Butler, *Syria*, vol. "Architecture" (1919), 215ff.; Abel, Geog, 2 (1938), 286; J. W. Crowfoot, *Early Churches in Palestine* (1941), 37–38; 94–95. (2) Glueck, in: AASOR, 14 (1934), 78–79; 15 (1935), 83, 97–98. (3) Abel, in: RB, 32 (1923), 519; Press, Ereẓ, 1 (1951), 64.

[M.A.-Y.]

BOZRAH (Heb. בָּצְרָה), moshav in Israel in the southern Sharon near Ra'ananah, affiliated with Ha-Iḥud ha-Ḥakla'i, the middle-class settlements association, founded in 1946 by World War II veterans. After the War of Independence

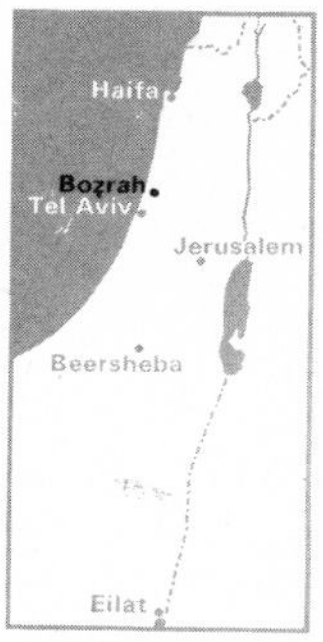

(1948) immigrants from Poland, Rumania, and North Africa joined the settlement. The moshav's economy in 1968 was based on intensive farming. The biblical name of the moshav (literally "fortified place") coincides with that of the Iraqi town Basra, where the first settlers served with the British Royal Engineers Corps and organized themselves for future settlement. In 1969 the moshav numbered 425 inhabitants.

[E.O.]

BOZZOLO, town in Lombardy, northern Italy. Jewish settlement in Bozzolo began in the first half of the 16th century with the arrival of Jewish loan bankers, who had close connections with the Jews in the nearby duchy of *Mantua. During the 17th and the first half of the 18th century, a small but prosperous community existed in Bozzolo, mainly occupied in banking, commerce, and farming of the customs dues. However, after Bozzolo passed to Austrian rule in 1746, its economic importance diminished and the Jews began to leave. There were no Jews left in Bozzolo by the beginning of the 20th century.

Bibliography: S. Simonsohn, *Toledot ha-Yehudim be-Dukkasut Mantovah,* 2 (1965), index; Milano, Italia, index. [D.C.]

BRACH, SAUL (1865–1940), rabbi in Slovakia. He served as rabbi in the Hungarian communities of Nagykaroly and Dunaszerdahely, and, finally, in Košice, Czechoslovakia. His *Avot al Banim* (1926) is prefaced by a violent attack on the Zionist movement (the Mizrachi and Agudat Israel included). Here he states that believers in the law of Moses "should keep their distance from Zionists and Mizrachist homes and avoid eating and drinking with them as they would with gentiles. Further, they ought to be excluded from the community" (p. 27). Although he fully appreciated the Hebrew language, he opposed its secular use (p. 23). In his opinion the Balfour Declaration was "in the interest of the gentile world, its purpose being to rid the nations of the world of the Jews." He was the author of many works, among them: (1) *Mishmeret Elazar* 1897 and subsequent parts, on the festivals and "the excellence of the Holy Land"; (2) *Libba Ba'ei* (1911), novellae on talmudic themes; (3) *Sha'ol Sha'al* (1911), on *Yoreh De'ah;* (4) *Le-Olam ha-Ba* (1938), on *Avot;* and a series of works on the festivals and the month of Elul.

Bibliography: S. B. Sofer-Schreiber, *Ketov Zot Zikkaron,* (New York, 1957), 280. [N.B.-M.]

BRADFORD, city in Yorkshire, England. A Jewish community existed in Bradford by the middle of the 19th century, composed largely of German Jews attracted by the industrial and commercial growth of the city. Services are said to have been held in Bradford in the 1830s, but the first synagogue was built in 1873. A Reform community (after that of London, the second in England) was founded in 1880. The Jewish population was later reinforced by refugees from the Russian persecutions. The German Jewish group was of great significance in the cultural life of the city. The artists Sir William *Rothenstein and Albert Rutherston were born in Bradford. The poet Humbert *Wolfe went to school there and described his childhood in his autobiography (*Now a Stranger,* 1933). Jacob *Moser was lord mayor of Bradford in 1910–11. The Jewish population numbered about 700 in 1968.

Bibliography: V. D. Lipman (ed.), *Three Centuries of Anglo-Jewish History* (1961), 84, 100 n. 48; Lehmann, Nova Bibl. 78, 185, 214. [C.R.]

BRAFMAN, JACOB (c. 1825–1879), Russian apostate and anti-Semitic author. Orphaned at an early age, Brafman fled from his native city of Kletsk to evade being forced into military service by the agents of the community (see *Cantonists). He became embittered by his experiences, and conceived a hatred for the Jewish community and its institutions. At the age of 34 he joined the Greek Orthodox Church and was appointed Hebrew teacher at the government theological seminary in Minsk. He later served as censor of Hebrew and Yiddish books in Vilna and St. Petersburg. Brafman attacked the Jewish communal organization *(kahal)* in Russian periodicals, describing the *Society for the Promotion of Culture among the Jews in Russia, and the *Alliance Israélite Universelle, as "a state within a state." He alleged that they formed part of an international Jewish conspiracy. In 1869, Brafman published with official support and at government expense *Kniga Kagala* ("The Book of the Kahal"), a translation into Russian of the minutes *(Pinkas)* of the *kehillah* of Minsk. A second, enlarged two-volume edition was published in 1875; the first volume, containing essays on Jews and Jewish customs, was published posthumously with an introduction by Brafman's son (1882). The book, translated into French, Polish, and German, created a stir among Jews and Russians. It was presumed by Russian readers to give information about the "secret" customs of the Jews by which they allegedly acquired power over gentiles; anti-Semitic authors used it to justify anti-Jewish outrages. Although Brafman was accused of forgery, in fact his book was a fairly accurate translation of the documents. It has served a number of scholars as a historical source for knowledge of the inner life of Russian Jewry in the 19th century. The impression made by his book is evidence of the extent to which autonomous Jewish community life was alien to modern centralistic political ideas, ideals, and modes of relationship between individuals and the state. The Russian poet V. F. Khodasevich (1886–1940) was Brafman's grandson.

Bibliography: S. L. Zitron, *Meshumodim* (1923), 7–31; Levitats, in: *Zion,* 3 (1938), 170–8; S. Ginsburg, *Meshumodim in Tsarishn Rusland* (1946), 65–79; S. W. Baron, *Russian Jew under Tsars and Soviets* (1964), 49. [Ed.]

°**BRAGADINI,** noble Venetian family; printers of Hebrew books from 1550 to 1710 (see Hebrew printing in *Venice). In 1550 Alvise Bragadini published Maimonides' *Code* with annotations by Meir *Katzenellenbogen of Padua. When the rival house of *Giustiniani issued Maimonides' *Code* in 1550, the resulting dispute, together with Moses *Isserles' decision in favor of Bragadini, led to a prolonged feud and denunciations to Pope Julius III, who eventually decreed the confiscation and burning of all copies of the Talmud in 1553. For ten years the printing of all Hebrew books was prohibited in Venice, and only in 1564 did Alvise Bragadini's press resume its activities. Alvise died in 1575. Hebrew printing continued under his son Giovanni from 1579 to 1614–15, and under Giovanni's son or sons and grandsons until the 18th century. Ḥ. J. D. *Azulai reports a visit to the Bragadini printing works. A great selection of Hebrew literature came from this press.

Bibliography: D. W. Amram, *Makers of Hebrew Books in Italy* (1909), 252–76, 363–75; C. Roth, *Jews in Venice* (1930), 256ff.; J. Bloch, *Venetian Printers of Hebrew Books* (1932), 17ff. and passim; H. B. Friedberg, *Toledot ha-Defus ha-Ivri be-Italyah* (1934), 53–55. [Ed.]

BRAGANZA, town in northern Portugal. The royal privileges of 1187 spoke of the penalty to be inflicted if a Jew who came to the city was assaulted, from which it appears that no community had yet been set up. In 1279 a number of Jews from the city, apparently recently arrived, paid King Denis handsomely for a charter of protection. Thereafter, there are frequent mentions of the community. Under Alfonso IV (1325–1357) there were complaints by the populace against the rate of interest charged by the Jews, which was henceforth limited. In 1429 the *comuna* of the Jews of Braganza were given certain privileges by the Crown, confirmed in 1434 and 1487. In 1461 the community, led by their rabbi, Jacob Cema (Ẓemaḥ), assembled in a public square and appointed representatives to negotiate with the city authorities on matters in dispute.

The rabbi in 1485 was Abraham, the physician who purchased the wines produced by the royal estate adjacent to the "vineyards of the Jews." On the expulsion of the Jews from Spain in 1492, 3,000 exiles arriving through Benavente are said to have established themselves in the region. After the forced conversion in Portugal in 1497, Braganza became one of the most important centers of crypto-Judaism in the country. It was the place of origin of many important Marrano families, and some 800 local Judaizers appeared at various autos-da-fé in Portugal up to 1755. For example, more than 60 appeared in a single *auto* held at Coimbra on May 17, 1716. Traces of crypto-Judaism are still strong there, though attempts to establish some sort of organized Jewish life have failed.

Bibliography: F. M. Alves, *Os Judeus no distrito de Bragança* (1925); J. Mendes dos Remedios, *Os Judeus em Portugal,* 1 (1895), 138–9, 152; M. Kayserling, *Geschichte der Juden in Portugal* (1857), index; Portuguese Marranos Committee, London, *Marranos in Portugal* (1938), 5–8.

[C.R.]

BRAHAM, JOHN (1774 or 1777–1856), English singer. The son of Abraham of Prosnitz (d. 1779), chorister of the Great Synagogue, London. Braham sold pencils in the street before being adopted by his father's associate Meir

John Braham, English singer. Drawing by Robert Dighton. London, National Portrait Gallery.

*Leoni, who introduced him to the Great Synagogue as his assistant. Braham made his first appearance on the stage in 1787 as "Master Braham," and in due course was taken under the patronage of Abraham *Goldsmid, who provided for his musical education. In 1797 he went to Italy and toured Europe with great success together with the celebrated Madame Storace (who bore him a son, later a Church of England clergyman). On his return to England in 1801 he was hailed as the most remarkable singer of the time. It is said that no other English tenor has ever had so wide a vocal range. He himself composed many of the songs he sang, among them "The Death of Nelson," one of the most popular patriotic songs of the period. Although in later life Braham had little contact with Judaism, he collaborated in 1815 with Isaac *Nathan in "Hebrew Melodies" for which Lord *Byron wrote the text. In 1835 Braham built the St. James' Theater in London, but the venture proved disastrous financially and in 1840 he tried, with little success, to recoup his fortunes by a concert tour in America. He continued his platform appearances until shortly before his death. Braham's daughter, Francis Elizabeth, Countess Waldegrave (1821–79), was a notable society and political hostess in the mid-Victorian period.

Bibliography: J. J. M. Levien, *Six Sovereigns of Song* (1948), 7–34; idem, *Singing of John Braham* (1945); C. W. Hewett, *Strawberry Fair* (1955); C. Roth, *Essays and Portraits in Anglo-Jewish History* (1962), 235–7; Sendrey, Music, index; Sands, in: JHSET, 20 (1959–61), 203–14; Grove, Dict.

[C.R.]

BRAHM, OTTO (originally **Abrahamsohn;** 1856–1912), German stage director and drama critic. Brahm was theater critic for the *Frankfurter Zeitung, Vossische Zeitung,* and *Die Nation,* and was one of the most influential champions of Ibsen and the new naturalist school. He was cofounder and first president of Berlin's *Freie Buehne* (1889), a private organization which performed Ibsen and other "modernists" such as Gerhart Hauptmann and Hugo von Hofmannsthal. With the publisher S. Fischer, he founded the monthly *Freie Buehne fuer modernes Leben,* later renamed *Neue Deutsche Rundschau,* as the mouthpiece of the naturalist revolution in literature. In 1894 Brahm took over Berlin's Deutsches Theater, moving to the Lessing Theater in 1904. With his productions of Ibsen, Hauptmann, and Schnitzler, he made Berlin one of Europe's theatrical centers. The "Brahm style," a rigorous stage realism expressing subtle psychological nuances, was adopted by the actors he trained. These included Max *Reinhardt and Albert Bassermann. His greatest triumph

Otto Brahm, Berlin theatrical director.

came in 1909–10 when, at the Lessing Theater, he staged a cycle of Ibsen's 13 sociocritical plays. Paul Schlenther collected Brahm's outstanding reviews and literary essays in *Kritische Schriften* (2 vols., 1913–15), enlarged and revised by Fritz Martini, *Otto Brahm, Kritiken und Essays* (1964).

Bibliography: G. Hirschfeld, *Otto Brahm, Briefe und Erinnerungen* (1925); M. Newmark, *Otto Brahm, the Man and the Critic* (1938); O. Koplowitz, *Otto Brahm als Theaterkritiker* (1936); W. Buth, *Das Lessingtheater in Berlin unter der Direktion von Otto Brahm 1904–1912* (1965).

[O.S.]

BRAILA (Rum. **Brăila,** Turk. **Ibraila**), port on the River Danube, S.E. Rumania; within the *Ottoman Empire from 1544 to 1828, in which year 21 Jewish families were living there. Despite difficulties with the authorities the Jewish population grew after the annexation of Braila to Walachia and its development as an important commercial port. The number of Jews increased from 1,095 in 1860 to 9,830 (17.3% of the total population) in 1899. The majority were occupied in commerce and crafts; in 1889, 24.4% of the shops in the town belonged to Jews, and in 1899, 24.2% of the artisans were Jews. The first Reform synagogue to be established in old Rumania was opened in Braila in 1862. This led to a division of the community until a unified central administration was reestablished in 1905. According to the 1930 census there were 7,134 Jews living in Braila (10.4% of the total population). Communal institutions then included a kindergarten, two elementary schools (for boys and girls), a secondary school for boys, a clinic, and a night shelter. [El.F.]

Holocaust Period. In 1941 there were 5,119 Jews in Braila. During the Iron Guard regime (September 1940–January 1941), the police confiscated Jewish property, 521 buildings and 107 shops, and arrested Jewish youth in the street. Jewish merchants were compelled to admit Iron Guard commissars into their shops and eventually to turn their shops over to the legionaries. The community was very active in extending aid to Jewish refugees who fled from Poland, to a group of Jews from *Jassy who were working as forced laborers in a nearby village, and to Jews who reached Braila from other towns in the district. The Jewish community clinic dispensed medical help to thousands. After the war (1947), 5,950 Jews lived in Braila, among whom were former deportees to Transnistria. This dropped to 3,500 by 1950. In 1969 there was still a Jewish community in Braila, although the majority of the surviving Jews had settled in Israel. [Th.L.]

Bibliography: N. E. Derera, *Monografia Comunității Israelite din Brăila* (1906); S. Semilian, *Evrei în cadrul așerării Brăilei acumi o sută de ani* (1936); *Almanahul Ziarului Tribuna Evreiască pe anul 5698* (1937), 266–9. Holocaust: PK Romanyah, 78–88; M. Carp, *Cartea Neagră*, 1 (1946), index; *Pe marginea prăpăstiei*, 1 (1942), 134, 224; W. Filderman, in: *Sliha*, 1 (1946), no. 4.

BRAILOV, small town in Ukrainian S.S.R. The community numbered 638 in 1765 (living in 190 houses); 2,071 in 1847; and 3,721 in 1897 (43% of the total population). It had a *talmud torah*, a school for boys, and one for girls. In 1918–19, during the civil war, about 100 Jews were massacred in pogroms in Brailov, including a pogrom perpetrated by the gangs of *Petlyura. The Jews in the town succeeded in warding off one attack. The Jewish population numbered 2,393 in 1926. Brailov was occupied by the Germans on July 17, 1941. About 3,000 Jews were murdered there on Feb. 12, 1942.

Bibliography: A. D. Rosenthal, *Megillat ha-Tevaḥ*, 1 (1927), 91–94; *Yevrei v SSSR* (1929^4), 49; B. West (ed.), *Be-Ḥevlei Kelayah* (1963), 58–60. [Ed.]

BRAININ, REUBEN (1862–1939), Hebrew and Yiddish author. Brainin was born in Lyady, Belorussia, and received a traditional Jewish education. His first article was on the last days of Perez *Smolenskin (*Ha-Meliẓ* (1888), no. 59). In 1892 he settled in Vienna where he published an influential but short-lived periodical *Mi-Mizraḥ u-mi-Ma'arav* (1894–99) which was intended to be a bridge between European and Hebrew literature. Only four issues were published at long intervals, with articles on Tolstoy, Nietzsche, Ibsen, and Hebrew scholars such as *Elijah b. Solomon Zalman of Vilna. Brainin also published essays in the annual *Aḥi'asaf*. He attracted wide attention with his caustic critique of Judah Leib *Gordon in the first issue of **Ha-Shilo'aḥ* (1896), edited by *Aḥad Ha-Am. The central theme of Brainin's work was Hebrew literature in the context of world literature. His flair for biography came to the fore in monographs on two great writers of the

Reuben Brainin, Hebrew and Yiddish writer. Etching by Hermann Struck, 1907, $6 \times 8\frac{1}{4}$ in. (15×21 cm.). New York, Leo Baeck Institute.

Haskalah period, Perez Smolenskin (1896) and Abraham *Mapu (1900), which possessed an unusual freshness of tone and approach. He championed the young and unknown Saul *Tchernichowsky, who became one of the great Hebrew poets of the century. In *Ha-Dor* (founded in 1900), Brainin published articles and sketches on contemporary Hebrew writers and artists. There was hardly a Hebrew periodical of the time to which Brainin did not contribute. He also wrote extensively in Yiddish and contributed articles to the Russian-Jewish press. In 1909 Brainin settled in America where he founded the periodical *Ha-Deror*. He spent a few years in Canada, where he edited two Yiddish papers: first the *Kanader Adler* (1912–15), then *Der Weg* (1915–16). He returned to New York and assumed the editorship of *Ha-Toren* (1919–25), first as a weekly, then as a monthly. In New York he also published the first volume of an uncompleted biography of Herzl, *Ḥayyei Herzl* (1919), covering the period up to the First Zionist Congress. Toward the end of his life, Brainin wrote almost exclusively in Yiddish. His championship of the autonomous Jewish province of Birobidzhan in Soviet Russia alienated him from Hebrew writers and Hebrew literature. The three volumes of his selected writings (*Ketavim Nivḥarim*, 1922–40) afford an insight into his activities as a critic, publicist, and writer of sketches and short impressionistic stories. He also translated into Hebrew M. Lazarus' *Der Prophet Jeremias* (1897) and Max Nordau's *Paradoxes* (1901). (For English translations of his works see Goell, Bibliography, 2010, 2763–73.)

His son Joseph (1895–1970) was a U.S. journalist and publicist. Joseph, born in Vienna, served with the Jewish Battalion of the British forces in Palestine during World War I. In 1918 he obtained permission from the Canadian prime minister to form a Jewish legion, which he recruited in Canada and the United States to reinforce the Jewish

Battalion. In 1921 he emigrated to the United States and founded the Seven Arts Feature Syndicate. He served as its editor in chief until 1938. Joseph was associated with the American Committee for the Weizmann Institute of Science from 1953 and became executive vice-president in 1957.

Bibliography: B. Shelvin, *R. Brainin* (Heb., 1922); Waxman, Literature, 4 (1960²), 372–6; Z. Fishman, in: *En Hakore,* 1 (1923), 105–18 (includes bibliography); Lachower, Sifrut, 3 pt. 2 (1963), 3–14; A. Sha'anan, *Ha-Sifrut ha-Ivrit ha-Ḥadashah li-Zerameha,* 2 (1962), 158–66; M. J. Berdyczewski (Bin Gorion), *Bi-Sedeh Sefer,* 2 (1921), 64–70; J. Fichmann, in: *Ha-Tekufah,* 12 (1921), 483–6; Kressel, Leksikon, 1 (1965), 350–3.

[El.S.]

BRAMPTON (Brandon, Brandão), EDWARD (c. 1440–1508), Anglo-Portuguese adventurer. Although his father was a Jewish blacksmith Brampton claimed to be the illegitimate son of a Christian nobleman. He was baptized in England c. 1468, taking the name of his godfather, King Edward IV. Subsequently he received various military and naval commands and was rewarded with mercantile privileges and grants of land; in 1482 he became governor of the island of Guernsey and was knighted in 1484. Having been of service to Alfonso V of Portugal during the latter's exile in France, Brampton later returned to Portugal and was made a member of the Royal Council. His knowledge of the English court enabled him to assist Perkin Warbeck in his bid for the English throne as the alleged son of Edward IV. Brampton's family gained prominence in Portugal but suffered discrimination because of its Jewish origin, which it tried ineffectively to conceal.

Coat of arms of Sir Edward Brampton, 15th-century Anglo-Portuguese adventurer. Cecil Roth Photo Collection.

Bibliography: Roth, in: JHSET, 9 (1922), 143–62; 16 (1952), 121–7; idem, *Anglo-Jewish History* (1962), 68–85; Marques de Sampayo, in: *Anais da Academia Portuguêsa de História,* 6 (1955), 143–65; E. F. Jacob, *Fifteenth Century* (1961²), 592–4.

[C.R.]

BRAMSON, LEON (Leonty; 1869–1941), communal worker and writer. Born in Kovno, Bramson graduated in law from Moscow University, then settled in St. Petersburg, where he practiced, and was active in the *Society for the Promotion of Culture Among the Jews. He was also director of the central committee of the *Jewish Colonization Association from 1899 to 1906. Under his direction a statistical study was carried out on the economic situation of the Jews in Russia (published in Russian in 1904 and in French in 1906–08). He was one of the compilers of the *Sistematicheskiy ukazatel literatury o yevreyakh na russkom yazyke* ("Systematic Guide to Russian Literature About Jews," 1892), and contributed many articles to *Voskhod* and other periodicals on problems of Jewish education, emigration, and colonization. Active in Jewish political life, Bramson was one of the founders of the "Jewish Democratic Group." In 1906 he was elected to the First Duma as a deputy for Kovno province, joining the Labor faction *("Trudoviki").* During World War I, the Revolution, and the Civil War, Bramson was an organizer of the Central Committee for the Relief of Jewish War Sufferers (*YEKOPO). When he left Russia in 1920, he continued to work in Western Europe on behalf of *ORT (with which he had been associated in Russia from 1909), serving as its president from 1923 until his death. Bramson had been a convinced anti-Zionist, but changed his views after a visit to Ereẓ Israel in 1934.

Bibliography: *Yevreyskiy mir,* 2 (1944), 7–54; S. Oron, in: *He-Avar,* 12 (1965), 191–8.

[Ed.]

BRAND, JOEL JENŐ (1906–1964), member of Va'adat Ezrah va-Haẓẓalah, the Budapest Jewish relief committee set up during World War II. Brand, who was born in Naszód, moved to Erfurt, Germany, with his family in 1910. Active in left-wing politics, he was arrested in 1933, but released in September 1934. He escaped to Transylvania and from there went to Budapest, where he joined *Po'alei Zion, and at a Zionist training farm met Hansi Hartmann, whom he married in 1935. From 1938 Brand was active in a semi-clandestine organization for helping Jewish refugees, establishing contact with German Nazi agents who were then secretly working in Hungary. In January 1943 the Va'adat Ezrah va-Haẓẓalah was formally established in Budapest under the leadership of Ottó *Komoly, aided by Rezső (Rudolf) *Kasztner. As a member of this committee, Brand met Adolf *Eichmann, upon whose orders he left for neutral Turkey on May 17, 1944, to present the Jewish Agency with a German proposition (the sincerity of which has never been established) to prevent the extermination of Hungarian Jewry in exchange for a supply of trucks and other equipment. He hoped to meet Moshe Shertok (*Sharett) in Turkey, but Shertok was prevented by the British authorities from traveling to Turkey, and Brand, at the entreaty of Jewish Agency officials in Istanbul, continued to Palestine to conclude negotiations there. He was arrested in Aleppo, Syria, by the British, who claimed

Joel Brand, testifying at the Eichmann trial in Jerusalem, 1961. Tel Aviv, Government Press Office.

that they suspected him of being a Nazi agent, and was taken to Cairo. On October 7, 1944, he was released in Jerusalem, but Hungarian Jews from the provinces had meanwhile been deported to Auschwitz and exterminated. Brand remained in Ereẓ Israel, and after the war devoted himself singlemindedly to tracking down Nazi war criminals. Both Brand and his wife, who was also active in the Va'adat Ezrah va-Haẓẓalah, testified at the Eichmann trial. He died in Frankfort where he was testifying against Hermann Krumey and Otto Hunsche, two of Eichmann's chief aides. The story of Brand's mission was dramatized by Heinar Kipphardt in his play *Die Geschichte eines Geschaefts* (1965).

Bibliography: A. Weissberg, *Advocate for the Dead* (1958); E. Landau (ed.), *Der Kastner-Bericht* (1961); A. Biss, *Der Stopp der Endloesung* (1966).
[Y.M.]

BRANDÃO, AMBRÓSIO FERNANDES (c. 1560–c. 1630), Portuguese author and soldier. Brandão distinguished himself as an officer in the Portuguese campaigns against the French and Indians in northern Brazil. In 1583 he lived in Pernambuco (Recife) where, like many other New Christians of the region, he practiced Judaism in secret. For attending services at a clandestine synagogue Brandão was denounced to the Inquisition in Bahia in October 1591. His name was again mentioned during the trial of another Judaizer, Bento *Teixeira Pinto, in January 1594 and he was once more denounced to the Holy Office in Lisbon in 1606. Brandão nevertheless managed to retain his freedom and eventually settled in Paraíba, where he owned sugar mills during the years 1613 to 1627. There he died prior to the Dutch invasion. Brandão is the reputed author of the *Diálogos das Grandezas do Brasil* (1618), one of the two outstanding works on the history of Brazil composed in the 17th century. In the *Diálogos,* which reflect local conditions in about 1618, conversations are conducted between Brandosio (i.e., Brandão himself) and Alviano (Nuño Alvares, a colleague who was also a New Christian and was similarly denounced to the Holy Office). Brandão claimed that the Brazilian Indians are descended from children of Israel who reached the Americas during the reign of Solomon, but Alviano disagreed with this view. The work contains a number of other references to the Jews.

Bibliography: A. Wiznitzer, *Jews in Colonial Brazil* (1960), 19, 26–8, 32.
[Ed.]

BRANDEIS, LOUIS DEMBITZ (1856–1941), U.S. jurist, the first Jew to be appointed to the U.S. Supreme Court.

Early Years. Brandeis was born in Louisville, Kentucky, the youngest of four children of Adolph and Frederika Dembitz Brandeis. His parents, both of whom were born in Prague, came of old and cultivated Jewish families with a deep interest in European liberalism. Apprehensive of political repression and economic distress after the failure of the 1848 revolutions, both families emigrated to America. Although they had formed the romantic idea of turning to a life of farming, they were dissuaded by Adolph, who had come in advance to explore the possibilities of life in the new country. After a short stay in Marion, Indiana, where a business venture did not prosper, the families moved to Louisville. There Adolph established a grain and produce business which proved highly successful until the depression of the early 1870s.

Louis early showed himself to be a remarkable student. He was brought up in a family environment that cultivated intellectual achievement and spiritual sensibility but in which formal religious training was eschewed. Louis' mother explained this aspect of her children's education: "I wanted to give them something that neither could be argued away or would have to be given up as untenable, namely, a pure spirit and the highest ideals as to morals and love. God has blessed my endeavors." Louis especially admired an uncle, Lewis *Dembitz, a scholarly lawyer and author in Louisville, sometimes known as "the Jewish scholar of the South," who was to become a follower of Theodor Herzl and an active Zionist. In honor of his uncle, Louis changed his middle name from David to Dembitz.

Louis D. Brandeis. Bust by Eleanor Pratt, N.Y. Photo courtesy of Library of Congress, Washington, D.C.

Following his graduation from high school at 15, and after the family business was dissolved because of financial reverses, Louis accompanied his parents in 1872 on an extended trip to Europe. During 1873–75 he attended the Annen Realschule in Dresden. Although he found the demands of the classroom rewarding, the repressive discipline of the place was distasteful. He was eager to return home. "In Kentucky," he said, "you could whistle." On his return, influenced by his uncle's career, Louis entered Harvard Law School. Supported by loans from his older brother and earnings from tutoring fellow students, he completed the course before his 21st birthday with an academic record unsurpassed in the history of the school.

Law Career. Brandeis formed a law partnership in Boston with a former classmate, and by the age of 30 he had achieved financial independence, thanks both to the success of his legal practice and to a deliberately frugal style of living. This simplicity came to be shared and abetted by his wife, Alice, daughter of Joseph Goldmark, a noted Viennese scientist. The wedding ceremony was performed in 1891 by her brother-in-law Felix *Adler, founder of the Ethical Culture Society.

In appearance Brandeis was a figure at once compassionate and commanding—tall, spare, ascetic, with deep-set, dark, penetrating eyes. Many who saw him thought of Lincoln. President Franklin Roosevelt spoke of him as "Isaiah."

As a lawyer Brandeis devoted himself increasingly to public causes and to the representation of interests that had not theretofore enjoyed such powerful advocacy: the interests of consumers, investors, shareholders, and taxpayers. He became known in Boston as the "People's Attorney." When Woodrow Wilson was elected president in 1912 on a platform of the New Freedom, he turned to Brandeis for counsel in translating ideas of political and social reform into the framework of legal institutions. In 1916 Wilson nominated Brandeis as a justice of the Supreme Court, precipitating a contest over confirmation in the Senate that lasted more than four months. The conservatives in that body were unprepared for a nomination to the Court so deeply innovative: the nominee was a Jew, and he was a lawyer of reformist bent. Standing firm against great pressure to withdraw the nomination, Wilson insisted that he knew no one better qualified by judicial temperament as well as legal and social understanding, and confirmation was finally voted on June 1, 1916.

Jewish and Zionist Activities. Brandeis' involvement in Jewish affairs began only a few years before his appointment to the Court. He had never disavowed the faith of his fathers, and had contributed to Jewish philanthropies, but his concerns had been overwhelmingly secular. In 1911, he recounted, his interest in Judaism was stirred by two experiences. One was his service as mediator in the New York garment workers' strike, in an industry dominated on both sides by Jews of humble origin in Eastern Europe. He found a strong sense of kinship with these people, who were remarkable not only for their exceptional intelligence but above all for a rare capacity to see the issues from the other side's point of view. The other experience was a meeting with Jacob *De Haas, then editor of the *Jewish Advocate* in Boston, who had served as Herzl's secretary in London. De Haas was thoroughly familiar with the accomplishments of Lewis Dembitz in Kentucky, and excited in the nephew a new interest in Jewish history and particularly in the Zionist movement. Brandeis, as was his habit, read everything on the subject that De Haas could furnish, footnotes as well as text, De Haas said, and became convinced that, so far from bringing a threat of divided loyalties, American and Zionist ideals reinforced each other. "My approach to Zionism," he said, "was through Americanism. In time, practical experience and observation convinced me that Jews were by reason of their traditions and their character peculiarly fitted for the attainment of American ideals. Gradually it became clear to me that to be good Americans we must be better Jews, and to be better Jews we must become Zionists. Jewish life cannot be preserved and developed," he asserted, "assimilation cannot be averted, unless there be established in the fatherland a center from which the Jewish spirit may radiate and give to the Jews scattered throughout the world that inspiration which springs from the memories of a great past and the hope of a great future."

Brandeis' rise to leadership in the movement was rapid. When war broke out in 1914 and certain leaders of the World Zionist Organization moved to America, Brandeis consented to serve as chairman of the Provisional Committee for General Zionist Affairs. He supported the convening of an American Jewish Congress representing all important Jewish groups in the country to give the widest support to Jewish interests at the peace conference. He thereby brought himself into conflict with eminent non-Zionists in the United States. His close relations with President Wilson and high administrative officials played an important part in securing support for the *Balfour Declaration, and later for the British Mandate, with adequate boundaries.

Conflict Within the Zionist Movement. A turning point in Brandeis' leadership developed out of his relationship with Chaim *Weizmann. The two met for the first time in London in the summer of 1919, when Brandeis was making a trip to Paris, site of the peace conference, and then to Palestine. In Palestine he was exhilarated by the spirit of the settlers but distressed by the debilitating prevalence of malaria and by the lack of business methods and budgetary controls in the handling of Zionist funds. He insisted that priority be given to remedying these physical and financial troubles. In the summer of 1920, at a meeting of the World Zionist Conference in London, Brandeis sought agreement on a plan to concentrate Zionist activity on the economic upbuilding of Jewish settlement in Palestine and to conduct that activity with efficiency and in accordance with sound financial principles. He proposed a small executive body that would include Weizmann and several men of great business experience, including Sir Alfred Mond and James de Rothschild, together with Bernard Flexner, an American lawyer, and others to be co-opted with the aid of Lord Reading. Weizmann was at first attracted to the plan because of the new strength it would give to the movement; but when he found his old colleagues from Eastern Europe offended because of their exclusion from the executive, he felt the tug of divided loyalties and expressed misgivings to Mond and de Rothschild, who withdrew because of the prospect of internal strife.

Brandeis was deeply disturbed by these developments and decided that he could not accept responsibility for the work of the World Organization; he consented to continue as honorary president only when persuaded that his withdrawal would have serious implications for the safety of the Jews in Eastern Europe. In June 1921, at a convention of American Zionists, the controversy brought serious repercussions. Many delegates had strong ties of loyalty to Weizmann and other Eastern European leaders, and shared Weizmann's view that the financial autonomy Brandeis desired for the American organization would weaken the strength of the World Organization. When a majority of the delegates refused a vote of confidence to Brandeis' position, he resigned from any position of responsibility, although not from membership in the organization. In this action he was joined by his principal supporters, including Julian W. Mack, Rabbi Stephen S. Wise, Felix Frankfurter, and Robert Szold.

The ardor of Brandeis' commitment, however, did not slacken. He inspired the organization of the Palestine Cooperative Company, which became the *Palestine Economic Corporation, to work in the investment field on projects that could become self-supporting, and the establishment of the Palestine Endowment Fund to administer bequests and trust funds primarily for projects not expected to yield a financial return. Brandeis contributed generously of his spirit and fortune. In his will the largest bequest was to the Zionist cause. He continued to receive frequent calls for counsel, which he would give, consistent with his judicial office, generally in the form of searching questions that would clarify the problem for the inquirer's own good judgment.

Supreme Court. In his judicial career, as in his Zionist activity, Brandeis was preeminently a teacher and moralist. His important judicial opinions are magisterial in character, notable not merely for their solid craftsmanship and analytical power but for their buttressing with data drawn from history, economics, and the social sciences. At a time when a majority on the Court was striking down new social legislation, Brandeis (together with his colleague Justice Holmes) powerfully insisted that the U.S. Constitution did not embody any single economic creed, and that to curtail experiment in the social sciences, no less than in the natural sciences, was a fearful responsibility. Not only did Brandeis vote to sustain such measures as minimum wage laws, price control laws, and legislation protecting trade unions against injunctions in labor disputes; his dissenting opinions in these cases served to illuminate their basis in experience and in social philosophy. These controversies arose under the vague constitutional standard of "due process of law."

Another notable category of cases concerned the distribution of governmental powers between the national government and the states. Brandeis believed that the American federal system was designed to encourage diffusion and sharing of power and responsibility, and so he was receptive to the claims of the several states to engage in experimental legislation unless Congress itself had plainly exercised authority over the subject matter. Deeply convinced that responsibility is the greatest developer of men, and that even in the ablest of men the limits of capacity are soon reached, he regarded the dispersal of power within a continental domain to be both a moral imperative and a practical necessity.

In one important field Brandeis saw a duty on the Court to be less hospitable to legislative intervention: the area of freedom of thought and expression. Only when speech constituted a genuinely clear and imminent danger to public order would he uphold its suppression. He believed that "the greatest menace to freedom is an inert people; . . . that order cannot be secured merely through fear of punishment for its infraction; that it is hazardous to discourage thought, hope and imagination; that fear breeds repression; that repression breeds hate; that hate menaces stable government; that the path of safety lies in the opportunity to discuss freely supposed grievances and proposed remedies; and that the fitting remedy for evil counsels is good ones" (*Whitney* v. *California,* 274, U.S. Reports 357, 375 (1927)). By the time of his retirement in 1939, he saw the Court well on its way to the adoption of the positions he had for so long taken in dissent.

Bibliography: J. Goldmark, *Pilgrims of 48* (1930); A. T. Mason, *Brandeis: A Free Man's Life* (1946); J. De Haas, *Louis D. Brandeis* (1929); O. K. Fraenkel (ed.), *Curse of Bigness: Miscellaneous Papers of Louis D. Brandeis* (1934); Y. Shapiro, in: AJHSQ, 55 (1965/66), 199–211; E. Rabinowitz, *Justice Louis D. Brandeis, the Zionist Chapter of His Life* (1968); A. Friesel, *Ha-Tenuah ha-Ẓiyyonit be-Arẓot ha-Berit ba-Shanim 1897–1914* (1970), index.

[P.A.F.]

BRANDEIS UNIVERSITY, the first nonsectarian Jewish-sponsored liberal arts institution of higher learning in America. Brandeis University was founded by a group of Jewish communal leaders from New York City on the premises of Middlesex University, a defunct medical school located in Waltham, Massachusetts. Negotiations were consummated a few months after the surprise opportunity came to light, and control changed hands on Feb. 7, 1946. The new university was named in memory of Justice Louis Dembitz *Brandeis. In April 1948 the Board of Trustees appointed Abram Leon *Sachar to the presidency. The actual launching of the university took place in the fall of 1948 with a beginning class of 107 freshmen. The small governing body of trustees, mainly Bostonians, gradually expanded into one of national character.

The basic rationale for the university was contained in Dr. Sachar's inaugural address: a commitment to high standards; rigid objectivity in teaching and research; and an unyielding policy of nondiscrimination on racial, religious, or national grounds in the selection of students, faculty, and staff. The three chapels—Jewish, Protestant, and Catholic—are symbolic of the nonsectarian commitment of the school, but the fact that the Jewish community could at last be hosts satisfied a deeply felt pride and sensitivity. The national headquarters of the American Jewish Historical Society was transferred to the campus.

Brandeis won accreditation for its undergraduate school

Figure 1. Aerial view of Brandeis University, Waltham, Mass., 1967.

Figure 2. The three chapels on the Brandeis campus, designed by Max Abramovitz, symbolize the nonsectarian character of the university. Photo Ezra Stoller.

in arts and sciences within two years after the first class graduated. That same year Brandeis inaugurated its Graduate School of Arts and Sciences, which in 1968 offered advanced degrees in 20 areas. The first professional school, the Florence Heller Graduate School for Advanced Studies in Social Welfare, was established in 1959. A unique complement of institutes and specialized centers for the fine arts, advanced Jewish studies, East European Jewish affairs, the study of violence, and research in communication may be found on campus. There is a special third-year-abroad program in Israel and a heavily subsidized scholarship program for gifted foreign students. Phi Beta Kappa recognition was awarded to the university in 1961. The campus covers approximately 300 acres with nearly 80 buildings. The library contains almost half a million volumes, and in the mid-1960s a special science library, designed to house 250,000 volumes, was dedicated.

At the beginning of the 1969–70 academic year there were 2,841 students, of whom 763 were graduate students and 362 were faculty members. Nearly 200 research grants, totaling eight million dollars, were assigned by major national agencies, with the main concentration in the life sciences. The university has received two six-million-dollar Ford Foundation Challenge Grants for academic excellence, one in 1962, the other in 1964. In 1969 it received a grant from Lewis Rosenstiel to launch a medical research center. Since 1949 it has published the *Brandeis University Bulletin.* [A.L.S.]

BRANDENBURG, German province, now in East Germany. The earliest Jewish community in the mark of Brandenburg was established in Stendal before 1267. In 1297, it received a liberal grant of privileges which served as the model for the other communities there. Most of the communities (*Berlin, Pritzwalk, Salzwedel, Spandau, *Frankfort on the Oder) maintained synagogues but few had rabbis. A liberal charter, granted to the Jews in Neumark in 1344, was later extended to the Jews of the mark of Brandenburg (1420, 1440). The Jews were not restricted to a specific quarter in the cities of the mark and were often granted rights of citizenship. Many of the communities were annihilated during the *Black Death (1349–50). The Jews were expelled from the area in 1446, but permitted to return a year later. Exorbitant taxes were levied in 1473 which only 40 Jews were able to pay. In 1510 a charge of desecrating the *Host developed into a mass trial in which 38 Jews were burned at the stake and the remaining 400 to 500 Jews expelled. Elector Joachim II (1535–71) permitted Jews to trade in Brandenburg (1539) and to settle there (1543) after discovering that the accusations were groundless. The favor he showed toward his *Court Jews *Michel Jud and *Lippold was greatly resented. On Joachim's death anti-Jewish riots broke out and the Jews were again driven out. Jews expelled from *Vienna in 1670 were permitted to settle in Brandenburg, then part of Prussia. The Jewish population in the province of Brandenburg, excluding Berlin, numbered 2,967 in 1816; 12,835 in 1861 (an increase mainly due to immigration from Poland); and 8,442 in 1925.

See also *Prussia; *Germany.

The City of Brandenburg. Jews are mentioned in the city at the end of the 13th century. In 1322 they owned a synagogue and several private houses. Despite the sufferings caused by the Black Death, their numbers increased during the second half of the 14th century; the privilege accorded to them by Elector Frederick II in 1444 mentions their "weakness and poverty." In 1490 mention is made of a Jewish street and in 1490–97 of a Jewish cemetery (*"kiffer,"* a corruption of the Hebrew *kever*). The Host desecration libel in 1510 led to the execution of Solomon b. Jacob and other Jews of Brandenburg (see above). In 1710 five Jewish families with residential rights were living in the city. A community was organized in 1729. It acquired a prayer hall and two cemeteries (1720, 1747). The Jewish population numbered 21 families in 1801 (104 persons; out of the total population of 10,280); 18 families in 1813; 130 persons in 1840; 209 in 1880; and 469 in 1925. It had declined to 253 by 1939 and came to an end during World War II. No Jews returned to Brandenburg after World War II.

Bibliography: Germ Jud, 2 (1968), 105–6; A. Ackermann, *Geschichte der Juden in Brandenburg an der Havel* (1906); *Handbuch der juedischen Gemeindeverwaltung* (1926–27), 10; H. Heise, *Die Juden in der Mark Brandenburg bis zum Jahre 1571* (1932).

[Ed.]

BRANDES (Cohen), CARL EDVARD (1847–1931), Danish author, playwright, and politician; younger brother of Georg *Brandes, Brandes specialized in oriental languages at the University of Copenhagen and received his doctorate in 1879. He published translations from Sanskrit and also Danish versions of Isaiah (1902), Psalms (1905), Job, and Ecclesiastes (1907). However, he openly professed atheism and had no connection with Jewish affairs. Brandes entered politics as a member of the Radical Party. After the split in the party in 1884, he founded a new opposition paper *Politiken* which attained great political and cultural influence. From 1889 until 1894 and from 1906 until 1927 he sat in the Chamber of Deputies. Brandes served as finance minister during 1909–10 and from 1913 to 1920. His diplomatic skill as a negotiator gained him considerable renown, and he acquired further distinction as the administrator of neutral Denmark's finances during World War I. Brandes was also deeply interested in the theater and even tried to become an actor. He wrote on modern Danish and foreign drama, and in his plays fought against conventional morality and hypocrisy in human society.

Bibliography: *Dansk Biografisk Leksikon,* 3 (1934), 614–28; *Dansk Skønlitterært Forfatterleksikon 1900–1950,* 1 (1959), 153–5.

[F.J. B.-J.]

BRANDES, GEORG (Morris Cohen; 1842–1927), Danish literary critic and writer. Brandes was born into an assimilated family which had retained some nominal ties with the Copenhagen Jewish community. As a student of philosophy, he was at one stage strongly attracted to Søren Kierkegaard's Christianity. Turning more and more to literature, Brandes abandoned the idealist philosophy of his time, mainly during a stay in Paris (1866–67), where he was especially influenced by Taine. In 1870 he received his doctorate for a thesis on Taine's aesthetics and at about this time he also became Denmark's leading advocate of the new positivism. A series of public lectures which Brandes delivered in 1871 appeared as *Hovedstrømninger i det 19de Aarhundredes Litteratur* (6 vols., 1872–90; *Main Currents in 19th Century Literature,* 1901–05) and was notable for its new and unorthodox approach. In this work he formulated his opposition to romanticism, and demanded that literature should stimulate the discussion of modern problems. Nevertheless, Brandes' essays on the Scandinavian romantics are among his best works.

Georg Brandes, Danish writer.

Meanwhile, the new naturalist school had gained support and the critic found gifted disciples in Ibsen and Strindberg, among others. However, he encountered strong opposition from conservative and church circles and as a result was denied the chair of aesthetics at the University of Copenhagen. (Years later, in 1902, the title of professor was eventually conferred on him, but without the obligation to lecture.) Bitterly disappointed, Brandes left Denmark and from 1877 until 1882 lived in Berlin. There he became active in the field of German literature, embarking on a new, and ultimately decisive, trend: concentration on personalities rather than on literary currents. Brandes' essays on John Stuart Mill, Renan, Flaubert, and the two great Norwegian writers, Bjørnson and Ibsen, testify to this change, as do his monographs on Lassalle (1877) and Disraeli (1878). In 1883 Brandes returned to Denmark, where friends helped him to secure a livelihood. His new lectures and essays appeared in a selected English edition as *Eminent Authors of the 19th Century* (1886). In 1886 and 1887 travels in Eastern Europe provided him with material for two books, *Indtryk fra Rusland* (1888; *Impressions of Russia,* 1889) and *Indtryk fra Polen* (1888; *Poland, A Study of the Land, People and Literature,* 1903).

In the 1880s Brandes read the still unknown Friedrich Nietzsche and found a message for himself. His Danish article on the German philosopher (1888) was published in Germany (*Aristokratischer Idealismus,* 1890) and marked the starting point of Nietzsche's world fame. Thereafter Brandes indulged in a kind of hero worship. His books on great figures include: *Shakespeare* (1895–96; seven English editions appeared from 1898 to 1924); *Goethe* (1915; Eng. tr. 1924–36); *Voltaire* (1916–17; Eng. tr. 1930); *Julius Caesar* (1918); and *Michelangelo* (1921). When *Eminent Authors* appeared in a new English edition in 1923 as *Creative Spirits of the 19th Century,* it was characteristically enlarged with essays on Swinburne, Garibaldi, and Napoleon. In one of his last works, *Sagnet om Jesus* (1925; *Jesus, a Myth,* 1927), Brandes sought to refute the historical basis of Christianity and launched another attack on early Christianity in *Urkristendom* (1927). His collected works appeared in Danish (1899–1910) and in German (*Gesammelte Schriften,* 1902–1907).

Georg Brandes was one of Denmark's greatest writers and his enormous influence on Danish culture and on European literature is still apparent. He was also one of the outstanding representatives of the greatness and tragedy of the assimilated European Jew. It is significant that the Jewish figures whom he tried to understand and describe were *Heine, *Boerne, *Disraeli, and *Lassalle. Although Brandes created a new type of literary critic and was familiar with all the different national literary and political manifestations in Europe, he himself was never really at home anywhere and his relationship with Denmark was ambivalent. He was never really accepted by the Danes and his ideas still provoke either enthusiasm or disgust. Brandes denounced the progroms in Eastern Europe, but repudiated his own Jewishness and disliked "Jewish" characteristics in others. He defended Dreyfus, but did not take Herzl's *Jewish State* or the Zionist movement very seriously, much to Herzl's dismay. After the Balfour Declaration, Brandes recognized the reality of Zionism. He expressed this change of view in an article entitled "Das neue Judentum" (1918), which later appeared in a biographical study by Henri Nathansen. Here, an intimate friend described the critic's struggle with his Jewish identity.

Bibliography: H. Nathansen, *Jude oder Europaeer: Portraet von Georg Brandes* (1931); J. Moritzen, *Georg Brandes in Life and Letters* (1922); P. von Rubow, *Literære Studier* (1928); idem. *Georg Brandes' Briller* (1932); *Correspondance de Georg Brandes,* 5 vols. (1952–66); H. Fenger, *George Brandes et la France* (1963), contains bibliography and list of works, including posthumous editions of his correspondence; A. Bein and G. Herlitz (eds.), *Iggerot Herzl* 1 (1948), contains Herzl's letters to Brandes.

[F.J.B.-J./L.Y.]

BRANDES, LUDWIG ISRAEL (1821–1894), philanthropist and chief physician of the General Hospital in Copenhagen. Brandes was one of the first Danish doctors to understand and practice physiotherapy, and he wrote a treatise on this subject. He established the first Danish day nursery and a society for children's care. In 1859 he founded a private old-age home called Københavns Sygehjem, which still exists, and initiated several new social projects for the benefit of Danish communal life. His autobiography *Mine Arbejders Historie* ("The Story of My Works," 1891) gives evidence of a great scholar and humanist.

Bibliography: *Dansk Biografisk Leksikon,* 3 (1934), 643–4.

[Ju.M.]

BRANDSTAEDTER, MORDECAI DAVID (1844–1928), Galician Hebrew writer. A successful manufacturer, he became a leading figure in the Tarnow Jewish community, and was appointed lay judge in the district court. His first short stories, *"Eliyahu ha-Navi"* ("The Prophet Elijah") and

Mordecai David Brandstaedter, Hebrew writer. Tel Aviv, Genazim.

"Mordekhai Kizoviz," appeared in *Ha-Shaḥar* (1869), which published most of his subsequent work. Brandstaedter ridiculed the Ḥasidim and their *Ẓaddikim.* He also exposed the foolishness of the so-called "enlightened" Galician Jews, and their shallow materialism. He did not employ the biting satire or the rationalistic didactic moralizing of most

of his contemporaries in the Haskalah movement. He gently mocked his characters' petty and ridiculous activities, without hate or anger. His work bore traces of romanticism; he invented intricate and wonderful plots and idealized characters and situations. Although he did not delve into economic or social problems, he had a grasp of prevailing conditions in the Pale and opposed defects in marriage customs, family life, education, and communal affairs. He derided Jewish petty mercantilism and advocated that Jews engage in craftsmanship and agriculture. In later life, Brandstaedter joined the Ḥibbat Zion movement, and his stories *"Kefar Mezaggegim"* ("The Glaziers' Village"), and *"Zalman Goi"* ("Zalman the Gentile") extolled Zionism and life in Ereẓ Israel. In his work, the dialogue tended to take dramatic form, but occurred naturally within the plot, and avoided lengthy philosophizing and blatant propaganda. Brandstaedter shunned elaborate phrases, and preferred a more concise style. His descriptions were realistic. During World War I Brandstaedter was forced to flee to Vienna. He returned to Tarnow in 1918, and wrote a series of aphorisms, entitled *"Keisamim"* for the New York Hebrew magazine *Hadoar* (1924–29). His autobiography *"Mi-Toledot Ḥayyai"* also appeared in *Hadoar* (1926, nos. 12–20). A three-volume edition of his collected works was published in *Warsaw* (1910–13).

Bibliography: Lachower, Sifrut, 2 (1929), 237–8, 315; Klausner, Sifrut, 5 (1955²), 232–42. [M.Rab./Ed.]

BRANDSTAETTER, ROMAN (1906–), Polish poet and playwright. A grandson of the Hebrew writer Mordecai David *Brandstaedter, he was born in Tarnow. His early verse, collected in *Jarzma* (1928), *Droga pod górę* (1931), and *Węzty i miecze* (1933), was on general themes. During the 1930s he edited Zionist periodicals and began writing poems extolling the return to Zion and the rebuilding of the Jewish national home. Two of his collections at this period were entitled *Królestwo trzeciej świątyni* ("The Kingdom of the Third Temple," 1934 and *Jerozolima światla i mroku* ("Jerusalem of Light and Twilight," 1935). For the first 40 years of his life Brandstaetter was a devoted Jew. In 1936 he published a brilliant attack on anti-Semitism in *Zmowa eunuchów* ("The Conspiracy of the Eunuchs," 1936), and his studies of Jewish interest included one on *Mickiewicz, *Legion żydowski Adama Mickiewicza* ("The Jewish Legion of Adam Mickiewicz," 1932) and another on the writer Julian *Klaczko, *Tragedia Juliana Klaczki* (1933). When he escaped to Palestine in 1940 he was warmly received by the Hebrew writers and his play about anti-Semitism in pre-war Poland was staged. After World War II Brandstaetter moved to Rome and swiftly abandoned all ties with the Jewish people, marrying the relative of a Polish cardinal, and converting to Catholicism. In 1948 he returned to Poland, where he joined the Catholic group of writers. His later works include dramas inspired by Polish history, such as *Powrót syna marnotrawnego* ("The Return of the Prodigal Son," 1948; 1956²); a play about *Rembrandt; and the first part of a novel about Jesus, *Jezus z Nazaretu: Czas milczenia* ("Jesus of Nazareth: The Time of Silence," 1967; 1968²).

Bibliography: E. Korzeniewska (ed.), *Słownik współczesnych pisarzy polskich*, 1 (1963), 260–3 (incl. bibl.). [Mo.A.]

BRANDT, BORIS (Baruch; 1860–1907), Russian Zionist, writer, and economist. Brandt, who was born in Makhnovka (now Komsomolskoye) near Berdichev, Ukraine, was educated in a *ḥeder*. Though he learned Russian only as an adult, he graduated with honors from the law faculty of Kiev University. He wrote many books and articles on economics and taxation and in 1897 was appointed a senior official and later member of the research committee of the Russian ministry of finance. He was an adviser to the minister Count Sergei Witte. Brandt was one of the few Jewish senior officials in the czarist government administration. A convinced and active Zionist, he was forced, as a civil servant, to conceal this activity. He regarded himself as a disciple of Perez *Smolenskin, about whom he wrote a long article. He was a member of the *Benei Moshe, and participated incognito at the First Zionist Congress in 1897 as the delegate of the St. Petersburg Ḥovevei Zion. Brandt regarded emigration as a way of solving the Jewish problem in Russia and persuaded the Jewish Colonization Association to renew its aid to Jewish emigrants. Toward the end of his life, he collected material for a comprehensive study of the economic development and settlement in Ereẓ Israel. He wrote (in Russian, Yiddish, German, and Hebrew) books on foreign capital in Russia, the fight against alcoholism, contemporary woman in Western Europe and Russia, and articles on Zionism and Jewish history for *Russkiy yevrey, Razsvet*, etc.

Bibliography: A. L. Jaffe (ed.), *Sefer ha-Congress* (1950²), 366; N. Sokolow, in: *Die Welt*, 20 (1907), 17. [Y.S.]

BRANDWEIN, YEHUDA ẒEVI (1903–1969), kabbalistic author. A descendant of the ḥasidic dynasty of the rabbi of Stretyn, he was born in Safed and studied in yeshivot in Jerusalem where he was ordained by such great authorities as A. I. *Kook and Ḥ. *Sonnenfeld. Despite the fact that he was a ḥasidic rabbi, he did not want to earn his bread by serving as a rabbi, but preferred manual labor and worked as a builder. At night he would study and meditate on mystical writings. Brandwein was brother-in-law, disciple, and friend of R. Yehudah *Ashlag, who taught him Kabbalah. After Ashlag's death, Brandwein completed Ashlag's commentary on the *Zohar, calling it *Ma'alot ha-Sullam* (1958). He also wrote a commentary on *Tikkunei ha-Zohar* (1960); he published the complete works of Isaac *Luria (1961–64) in 14 volumes, with punctuation, glosses, and references; and republished Moses *Cordovero's *Or Ne'erav* (1965). From 1957, he served as chairman of the Department for the Provision of Religious Requirements in the Histadrut, and was called by many, "the rabbi of the Histadrut." After the Six-Day War, Brandwein settled in the Old City of Jerusalem (1968). [Ed.]

BRANDYS, KAZIMIERZ (1916–), Polish author. Born in Lodz, Brandys studied at Warsaw University and managed to survive the Nazi occupation. After the war he became a leading figure in Polish intellectual life. He helped to found the Lodz weekly *Kuźnica*, and was a member of the editorial board of the Warsaw weekly *Nowa Kultura*. Brandys' works, mainly novels, include *Miasto niepokonane* ("Invincible City," 1946), a book about Warsaw; *Sprawiedliwi ludzie* ("Just People," 1953), a play about the Polish revolt of 1905; *Obywatele* ("Citizens," 1954); *Obrona Grenady* ("The Defense of Granada," 1955); and various short stories. His novel cycle, *Między wojnami* ("Between the Wars"), comprises *Samson* (1948), *Antygona* (1948), *Troja, miasto otwarte* ("Troy, Open City," 1949), and *Człowiek nie umiera* ("Man Does Not Die," 1951). The first part, *Samson*, tells the story of a hunted Jew whose tragic existence is alleviated only when he joins the partisans. After 1955 Brandys tried to assess the effects of the Stalinist era on Poland and to apportion the moral responsibility for his country's social and political situation. An accent of irony marks the volumes of *Listy do pani Z.: Wspomnienia z teraźniejszości* ("Letters to Mrs. Z.:

Memoirs of the Present," 1st ser. 1957–58, 2nd ser. 1959–60; 1968[2]), which contain Brandy's reflections on contemporary issues and attack outdated social, political, and artistic concepts.

His brother, Marian Brandys (1912–), wrote travel books and stories on historical themes. [S.W.]

BRANDYS NAD LABEM (Ger. **Brandeis an der Elbe**), town in Bohemia (Czechoslovakia). The first Jewish settlement in the beginning of the 16th century was located in the suburb of Hrádek. After the general expulsion from Bohemia in 1559, the Jews from Brandys went to *Poznan. However, the Brandys municipality undertook to safeguard Jewish property there for an annual payment of 20 *groschen*. In 1568 the Jews were permitted to return and to reclaim their property. Nine houses in Jewish ownership are

Tombstone from Brandys nad Labem, Czechoslovakia. It marked the grave of Moses, son of Jacob Koppl, who died in 1727.

recorded in 1630. Subsequently a considerable number of the Jews expelled from Prague in 1745 found refuge in Brandys. Filip *Bondy officiated as rabbi from 1856 to 1876. Brandys was one of the first communities in Bohemia to introduce liturgical reforms in its synagogue. The Jewish population numbered 380 in 1893; 272 in 1921 (6% of the total), 13 of declared Jewish nationality; and 139 in 1930. The community ceased to exist during the *Holocaust and was not revived.

Bibliography: Mandl, in: H. Gold (ed.), *Juden und Judengemeinden Boehmens*, 1 (1934), 56–58. [O.K.R.]

BRANN, MARCUS (1849–1920), historian. Brann was born in Rawicz, Poland, where his father was rabbi. He studied under Z. *Frankel and H. *Graetz at the Jewish Theological Seminary and at the University of Breslau. From 1875 to 1883 he served as assistant rabbi in Breslau and from 1883 to 1885 as director of the Berlin Jewish orphanage. He was rabbi in Pless from 1885 to 1891, when he received a call to the Breslau Seminary as Graetz's successor, becoming full professor in 1914.

Brann's early studies dealt with the house of Herod: *Die Soehne des Herod* (1873), and *Megillat Ta'anit* (MGWJ, 25, (1876)). Later he turned to German-Jewish history. He was the first among German-Jewish historians systematically to use Jewish and general archives. Brann made a thorough study of the history of the Jews of Silesia and published in particular *Geschichte der Juden in Schlesien* (6 vols., 1896–1917). He became widely known through some more popular works such as *Geschichte der Juden und ihrer Literatur* (2 vols., 1893–94; 1910–13[3]) and a textbook on the history and literature of the Jewish people, *Lehrbuch der juedischen Geschichte* (4 vols., 1900–03). The historian Dubnow made great use of Brann's work in the first editions of his *History of the Jews*. In addition to the above, Brann (with others) published and annotated the fourth edition of Graetz's *Geschichte der Juden* (1890–1909). In his popular works Brann followed the general pattern established by Graetz; in his independent scientific publications he was a faithful disciple of his mentor in his analysis of the sources and systematic presentation. In 1893 Brann revived the publication of *Monatsschrift fuer Geschichte und Wissenschaft des Judentums* (MGWJ), which had been discontinued in 1887. Until 1899 he was coeditor with David *Kaufmann, continuing alone after the latter's death. Brann also edited: D. Kaufmann's *Gesammelte Schriften* (3 vols., 1908–15); *Gedenkbuch zur Erinnerung an David Kaufmann* (with F. Rosenthal, 1900); *Festschrift zu Israel Lewy's siebzigstem Geburtstag* (with I. Elbogen, 1911); and part 1 (A through L) of volume 1 of the *Germania Judaica* (with A. Freimann, 1917). He also wrote *Geschichte des juedisch-theologischen Seminars in Breslau* (1904); Brann's bibliography was partly reproduced in G. Kisch (ed.), *Das Breslauer Seminar 1854–1938* (1963), 394–5. In addition to his literary activity, Brann was active in various Jewish organizations.

Bibliography: Freimann, in: MGWJ, 63 (1919), 81–97 (incl. bibl.); Elbogen, *ibid.*, 64 (1920), 241–9; W. Cohn, in: *Schlesische Lebensbilder*, 4 (1931), 410–6. [ED.]

BRASLAV (Pol. **Brasław**), small town in Belorussian S.S.R.; in Poland until 1795 and between 1921 and 1945. There was a *Karaite settlement in Braslav and its vicinity. The Jewish population numbered 225 in 1766, 1,234 in 1897 (82% of the total), and 1,900 in 1925. [ED.]

Holocaust Period. In 1941, on the eve of the Holocaust, there were 2,500 Jews in Braslav. The city was captured by the Germans on June 28, 1941, and on the following day the German army and police removed all the city's Jews to the nearby swamp area, where they were held for two days. Meanwhile, all Jewish property had been stolen by the local population. On Aug. 2, 1941, a "contribution" of 100,000 rubles was demanded of the Jews. At the beginning of April 1942, the ghetto was established, and, in addition to the local Jewish population, Jews from Dubinovo, Druya, Druysk, Miory, and Turmont were interned there. The population of the ghetto was divided into two parts: the workers and the "nonproductive." In the first *Aktion*—on June 3–5, 1942—about 3,000 people were killed; local farmers actively helped the Germans in this *Aktion*. After some of the Jews went into hiding, the German commander announced that those Jews who came out of hiding of their own free will would not be harmed, but the handful who responded to this call were executed on June 7. In the autumn of 1942 the ghetto was turned into a work camp in which the remainder of the Jews from the entire area were concentrated. On March 19, 1943, the Nazis began to liquidate the camp, but this time they met with opposition. A group of Jews, fortified in one of the buildings, offered armed resistance. Only after their ammunition ran out did the Nazis succeed in suppressing opposition. The fighters fell at their posts. There were 40 survivors of the Braslav community, some of whom fought in partisan units in the area. After the war a monument was erected to the Jews killed there by the Nazis. In 1970 there were 18 Jewish families with no synagogue. [Ar.W.]

Bibliography: J. J. Kermisz, *"Akcje" i Wysiedlenia,* 2 (1946), index; Yad Vashem Archives.

BRASLAVI (Braslavski), JOSEPH (1896–1972), Israel geographer and author. Braslavi went to Ereẓ Israel from the Ukraine as a boy of ten. During World War I he was an interpreter in the Turkish army. In the early 1920s he taught Hebrew in various kibbutzim. In 1924 he was sent on an exploratory journey to Transjordan and the Negev in connection with the projected settlement of *Ha-Shomer, the Jewish watchmen's organization, in these areas. He went to Berlin to study Semitics in 1927. On his return he resumed his explorations and his lectures on the geography of the country. From 1938 he taught at the Teachers' Seminary inTel Aviv. Braslavi's most important work is his six-volume *Ha-Yadata et ha-Areẓ?* ("Do You Know the Land?" 1940–65), a detailed description of all the regions of Israel. Other books include: *Milḥamah ve-Hitgonenut shel Yehudei Ereẓ Yisrael me-aḥar Mered Bar-Kokhva ve-ad Massa ha-Ẓelav ha-Rishon* (1943); *Le-Ḥeker Arẓenu* (1954); and *Me-Reẓu'at Azzah ad Yam Suf* (1956).

Bibliography: Tidhar, 3 (1958²), 1233–35. [Ed.]

BRAŞOV (Hung. **Brassó;** Ger. **Kronstadt;** between 1950 and 1960 **Oraşul Stalin**), city in Transylvania, central Rumania; until 1918 in Hungary. From 1492 onward Jews are mentioned living there temporarily or passing through Braşov in transit. They took part in the trade between Hungary, Muntenia, and Turkey. In 1826 several Jewish families received permission to settle there permanently. The community numbered 103 in 1865 and 1,198 in 1900. A secular Jewish school was established in 1860. In 1868, the Braşov community became Liberal (see *Neolog). A separate Orthodox community was established in 1877. The school continued to serve both communities. The Jewish population numbered 2,594 in 1930. During World War II, under the Fascist regime, the communal buildings and much Jewish property were confiscated. The rehabilitated community was reorganized in 1949 in accordance with the law on the organization of Jewish communities in Rumania. Instead of two communities, a unified one was established with an Orthodox section. The Jewish population numbered 1,759 in the city of Braşov and 4,035 in the district in 1956, and 2,000 in the city in 1968.

Bibliography: *Magyar Zsidó Lexikon* (1929), 137–8; L. Pap, in: *Sinai,* 3 (Bucharest, 1931), 133–7; 5 (1933), 72–75; PK Romanyah, 291–4. [Y.M.]

BRATISLAVA (Ger. **Pressburg,** Hg. **Pozsony**), capital of *Slovakia, Czechoslovakia; till 1918 in Hungary; former chartered capital of the kings of Hungary. It was one of the most ancient and important Jewish centers in the Danube region. The first Jews possibly arrived with the Roman legions. The **Memorbuch* of the community of Mainz commemorates the "martyrs of Pressburg" who perished in the First Crusade. The first documentary mention of Jews in Bratislava dates from 1251. In 1291

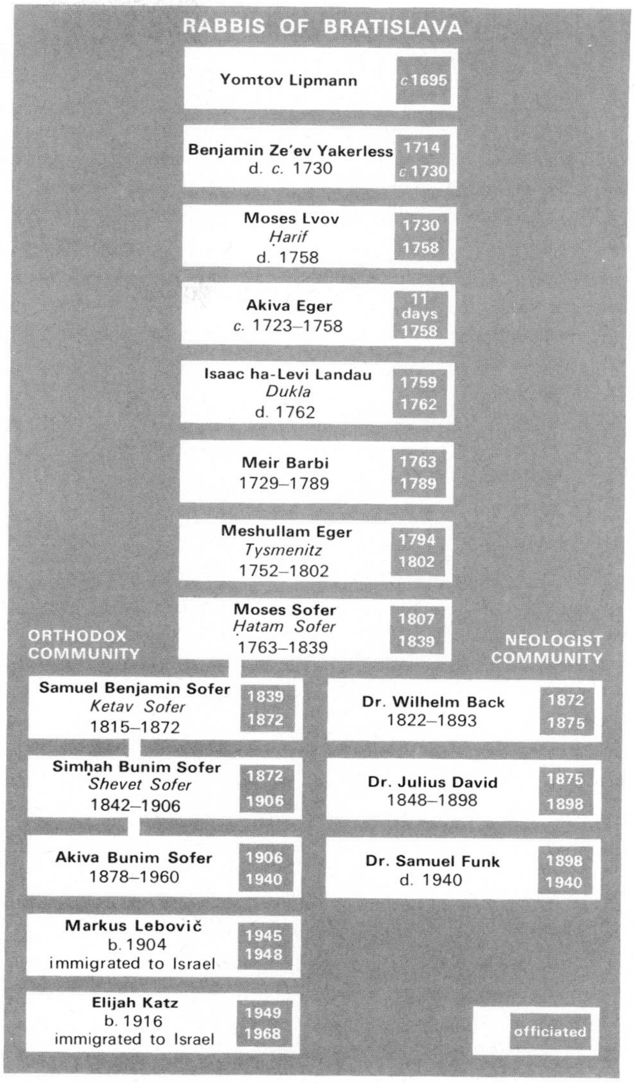

King Andrew III granted a charter to the community, which paid taxes to the royal treasury, and from 1345 also to the municipality. Bratislava Jews mainly engaged in moneylending, but included merchants and artisans, vineyard owners, and vintners. A synagogue is first mentioned in 1335 and was rebuilt in 1339.

In 1360 the Jews were expelled from Hungary, and some of the Jews of Bratislava took refuge in Hainburg (Austria). They returned in 1367 and resumed possession of their homes. In 1371 the municipality introduced the *Judenbuch* regulating financial dealings between Jews and Christians. Isaac *Tyrnau officiated as rabbi in Bratislava about 1410. In 1392 King Sigismund exempted Christians for a year from paying the interest on loans borrowed from Jews; in 1441 and 1450 all outstanding debts owed to Jews were canceled; and in 1475 Jews were forbidden to accept real estate as security. An attempt by many Jews to leave Bratislava in 1506 was prevented by Ladislas II who confiscated the property of those who had already left.

The Jews were expelled from Bratislava in the general expulsion from Hungary in 1526, although they apparently continued to live in several places, including the Schlossberg ("Castle Hill"), outside the municipal bounds. The first Jew subsequently to reside within them was Samuel *Oppenheimer, who received permission to settle in a suburb in 1692. He was followed by other Jews and a synagogue was built in 1695, where the first known rabbi to officiate was Yom Tov Lipmann. In 1699 the *Court Jew Simon Michael, who had settled there in 1693, was appointed head of the community; he built a *bet midrash* and acquired land for a cemetery. By 1709 there were 189 Jews living in Bratislava and 772 by 1736. The Jewish quarter in the Schlossberg remained outside the municipal jurisdiction. It later passed to the jurisdiction of the counts Palffy, who gave protection to the Jews living there. In 1714 they granted a charter of privileges to the 50 families living in its precincts and in Zuckermandel. The Jews in the Schlossberg resided in a single row of houses, but in 1776 the municipality permitted Jews to settle on land owned by the city opposite these houses and thus to constitute a "Jewish street." The Jews living on the Palffy side, however, enjoyed different rights from those under municipal jurisdiction, the former, for instance, being permitted to engage in crafts and all branches of commerce. They enjoyed freedom of religious worship. After the status of the community improved, the customary provision of geese to the Viennese court on St. Martin's Day, formerly an onerous tax, developed into a ceremony (performed until 1917). The Jews in Bratislava pioneered the textile trade in Hungary in the 18th century. Under the direction of Meir Halberstadt the yeshivah became an important center of Jewish learning, while the authority of Moses *Sofer (d. 1839) made Bratislava a center of Orthodoxy for all parts of the Jewish world. During the reign of Maria Theresa (1740–80) the representatives of Hungarian Jewry used to meet in Bratislava to arrange the tax administration.

During the revolution of 1848, anti-Jewish riots broke out. The Jewish quarter was put under military protection and Jews living elsewhere had to retire within it. Jews volunteered to serve in the National Guard but were opposed by the general public. Further outbreaks of anti-Jewish violence followed the *blood libel case in *Tisza-Eszlar in 1882 and 1883. From 1898 tension mounted between the Orthodox and the pro-Reform members of the community (see *Reform; *Hungary). After 1869 the Orthodox, Neolog, and *status-quo-ante* factions in Bratislava organized separate congregations. The Orthodox provincial office *(Landeskanzlei)* later became notorious for its opposition to Zionism. The Neolog and *status-quo-ante* congregations united in 1928 as the Jeshurun Federation. A large part of the Jewish quarter was ravaged by fire in 1913 but was later rebuilt.

Jewish institutions in Bratislava included religious schools, charitable organizations, and a Jewish hospital (founded in 1710; a new building was constructed in 1931). The Hungarian Zionist Organization was founded in Bratislava in 1902 and the World *Mizrachi Organization in 1904, both on the initiative of Samuel *Bettelheim. During the Hungarian Revolution of 1919 anti-Jewish excesses were prevented by a guard formed by Jewish veterans. With the establishment of Czechoslovakia, Bratislava became the center of a number of Jewish national communal institutions and of Jewish national as well as Zionist activities. Bratislava also became the center of *Agudat Israel in Czechoslovakia. During this period, several Jewish newspapers and a Hebrew weekly, *Ha-Yehudi,* were published there. In 1930 the Jewish population in Bratislava numbered 14,882 (12% of the total population), 5,597 of declared Jewish nationality.

In the titularly independent state of Slovakia set up under Nazi auspices in 1939, Bratislava was the seat of the Jewish central office *(Ústredňa židov).* Even before the declaration of the independent state, attacks on the synagogues and yeshivah on Nov. 11, 1938, inaugurated the regime of anti-Semitic terror. Nearly a thousand Jewish students were expelled from the university. Subsequently, anti-Jewish terrorization, restrictive measures, and pogroms increased. On the outbreak of World War II in September 1939 all Jewish shops were confiscated, and in August 1940 the Jews were forced to surrender their homes. Many transports of the "illegal" immigration to Palestine were organized in Bratislava. Numbers of Jews who had fled from Nazi persecution in Vienna in 1938 were put into camps in the Patronka and Petržalka suburbs. In spring 1945, 497 Jews were massacred by the Nazis in Petržalka. Mass deportations of Jews from Bratislava continued until a few weeks before the downfall of Hitler. Only a fraction of the Jewish population survived the Holocaust. The old cemetery was destroyed in a town planning project during the war. A small plot including the tomb of R. Moses Sofer was spared by the fact that a road was built above it.

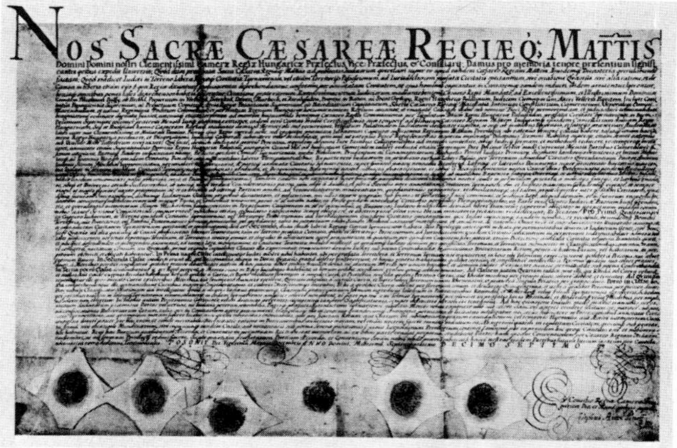

Peace treaty between the city of Tyrnau and Simon Michael, head of the Pressburg (Bratislava) Jewish community, described as "representative of the Jewish people," December 20, 1717. It rescinds the 280-year-old order prohibiting Jews from passing through Tyrnau. Cecil Roth Collection.

Hebrew Printing. Some 340 Hebrew and Yiddish books were printed in Bratislava between 1831 and 1930, the first being *Torat ha-Emunah,* an ethical treatise in Yiddish. But already in 1789 and 1790 two smaller items had been issued here. In 1833 the well-known Vienna printer Anton Edler von Schmidt bought the press of K. Schniskes, and Schmidt's son printed Hebrew books to 1849. He was succeeded by Heinrich Sieber, and he and his heirs were active to 1872, and their successors F. and S. Nirschi to 1878. O. Ketterisch, later K. Ketterisch and Zimmermann, set up a Hebrew press in 1876. The first Jewish printers were Lewy and Alkalay, later A. Alkalay only, whose firm printed from 1877 to 1920. [Sh. W.-H.]

Contemporary Period. On April 15, 1945, a few days after the liberation of the city, the Jewish community of Bratislava was reestablished, and Max Weiss became its chairman. In September, Chief Rabbi Markus Lebovič was installed in his post in a ceremony in the only synagogue that had not suffered damage during the war; the first public prayer services were held there also on the occasion of the High Holidays. In 1946 Bratislava became the headquarters of the 42 reconstituted Jewish communities of Slovakia. Religious functions—ritual slaughter, *mikva'ot,* a kosher butcher and canteen, and religious instruction in the schools—were reintroduced; the Chief Rabbinate also insured the supply of *maẓẓot* and kosher wine. In 1947, when the membership of the Jewish community had grown to 7,000, a second synagogue was opened. One synagogue building serves now as a television studio. International charitable organizations (notably *ORT and the *American Jewish Joint Distribution Committee) played a prominent role in the revival and development of the religious, economic, and social life of the Jewish community. Homes for the aged, youth centers, and a hospital were also established. The *Ha-Shomer ha-Ẓair built training farms *(hakhsharot)* to prepare Jewish youth for settlement in Palestine under the auspices of *Youth Aliyah. Jewish periodicals, notably *Tribuna, Ha-Matḥil,* and *Ha-Derekh,* came into being, and Bratislava became the center of the rapidly developing Jewish life in Slovakia. An archive on the Holocaust period was founded after the war by the Union of Slovakian Jewish Communities and a large section of it was later transferred to *Yad Vashem. Difficulties were encountered, however, in the restitution of Jewish property; the local Slovaks, who had become the "Aryan owners" of such property during the war, did all they could to prevent its return to its rightful owners. Anti-Semitic hate propaganda, which accused the Jews of having been "the tools of Magyarization and exploiters of the Slovak people," resulted in anti-Jewish riots and the plunder of Jewish property (during the summer of 1946 and in March 1948).

The year 1949 was a turning point in the renewed history of the Jewish community. Under the Communist regime Jewish religious and cultural life was gradually restricted, the property of Jewish organizations was nationalized, and the existing social and economic institutions were deprived of their Jewish character. An agreement between Czechoslovakia and Israel facilitated the emigration of about 4,000 Bratislava Jews. In 1949 a new chief rabbi, Elias Elijah Katz, later of Beersheba, and a new community chairman, Benjamin Eichler, were appointed. Any attempts to reactivate Jewish life, however, were nipped in the bud. In January 1952 the Bratislava *Pravda* warned against "Jewish citizens who are in the service of the American imperialists and are trying to undermine Slovak life." Until the end of the decade, the Jewish community, which had been reduced to about 2,000 persons, lived under the threat of dismissal from employment, compulsory manual work, evacuation to different places of residence, and long prison terms. The political changes which took place in 1963 resulted in the immediate resumption of Jewish activities and contact with world Jewry. Several Jews who had been wrongfully imprisoned were rehabilitated, and Jews found it easier to gain employment. Religious instruction was intensified and Jewish ceremonies, such as bar mitzvahs and religious weddings, became a more frequent occurrence. After the Soviet invasion of Czechoslovakia (August 1968), about 500 Jews left Bratislava. The Jewish population of Bratislava in 1969 was estimated at about 1,500. [E.Ku.]

Bibliography: S. H. Weingarten, *Sefer Bratislava* (1960; vol. 7 of *Arim ve-Immahot be-Yisrael*); H. Gold (ed.), *Die Juden und Judengemeinde Bratislava . . .* (1932); O. Neumann, *Im Schatten des Todes* (1956); M. D. Weissmandl, *Min ha-Meẓar* (1960); A. Charim, *Die toten Gemeinden* (1966), 37–42; L. Rotkirchen, *Ḥurban Yahadut Slovakyah* (1961), index; Y. Toury, *Mehumah u-Mevukhah be-Mahpekhat 1848* (1968), index s.v. *Pressburg;* A. Nir, *Shevilim be-Ma'galot ha-Esh* (1967); MHJ, 4 (1938), index. Hebrew Printing: P. J. Kohn, in: KS, 31 (1955/56), 233ff.; N. Ben-Menahem, *ibid.*, 33 (1957/58), 529ff.; *Arim ve-Immahot be-Yisrael,* 7 (1960), 171. Contemporary Period: P. Meyer et al., *Jews in the Soviet Satellites* (1953), 69–204, and passim; *Jewish Studies* (Prague, 1955), passim; R. Iltis (ed.), *Die aussaeen unter Traenen mit Jubel werden sie ernten* (1959), 127–38.

BRATSLAV, small town in Podolia, Ukrainian S.S.R., on the River Bug. A Jew leased the collection of customs duties in Bratslav in 1506, and it appears that a Jewish settlement developed in the town from that time. In 1545 the Jews were exempted from the construction of roads "so that they could travel on their commercial affairs." The Jews underwent much suffering during the attacks of the Tatars on the town during the 16th century (especially in 1551). At the beginning of the 17th century, commercial relations were maintained between the Jews of Bratslav and those of Lvov. In the *Councils of the Lands, Bratslav was attached to the "Land of Russia," of which Lvov was the principal community.

In 1635, King Ladislas IV confirmed the rights of the Jews of Bratslav. At the time of the *Chmielnicki massacres, a number of Jews from Bratslav were murdered in Nemirov and Tulchin, where they had taken refuge. However the community was reconstituted soon afterward. In 1664, when the Cossacks of the Dnieper invaded the land on the western side of the river, they massacred the Jews in Bratslav. At the beginning of the 19th century, Rabbi *Naḥman of Bratslav lived in the town for several years and it became an important ḥasidic center during this period. His disciple, Natan Steinherz set up a Hebrew press in the town in 1819 and published the works of his teacher. At the end of that year the authorities closed down the press after they had been approached by informers. The community numbered 101 according to the census of 1765 (195 including Jews in the surrounding areas) and 221 in 1790 (398 with those in the surrounding areas). After Bratslav's incorporation into Russia (1793), 96 Jewish merchants and 910 townsmen lived in the district in 1797. The Jewish population numbered 3,290 according to the census of 1897 (43% of the total population) and 1,840 in 1926 (23.5%). During the summer of 1919, about 220 Jews in Bratslav lost their lives in pogroms. As a result of the pogroms and the departure of many Jews for the larger towns, the number of Jews in Bratslav gradually decreased between the two world wars. The community was annihilated by the Nazis between July and September 1941. During 1942–43, a concentration camp for Jews from Ukraine, Bessarabia, and Bukovina was set up near Bratslav. The overwhelming majority were murdered by the Nazis. The community has not been rebuilt after the war.

Bibliography: A. D. Rosenthal, *Megillat ha-Tevaḥ* (1927), 98–100; M. Osherowitch, *Shtet un Shtetlekh in Ukraine,* 1 (1948), 118–31; B. West (ed.), *Be-Ḥevlei Kelayah* (1963), 176–7; H. D. Friedberg, *Toledot ha-Defus ha-Ivri be-Polanyah* (1950^2), 155ff.

[S.Ett.]

BRAUDE, ERNEST ALEXANDER (1922–1958), English chemist. Braude was born in Germany and went to England in 1937. He spent his student and working life at Imperial College, London, where he became professor of organic chemistry in 1955. The first field in which Braude specialized was in the spectral properties of organic compounds. He was one of the pioneers of the use of radioactive tracers in organic chemistry, and also of the thermochemical study of organic reactions; he also did research in the field of the chemistry of natural products, discovered lithium alkenyls, worked on the synthesis of vitamin D, and devised a new synthesis for thioacetic acid.

Bibliography: *Proceedings of the Chemical Society* (1957), 297–8.

[S.A.M.]

BRAUDE, MARKUS (Mordekhai Ze'ev; 1869–1949), rabbi, educator and Zionist leader. Braude was born in Brest-Litovsk (then Russia). He was the son of R. Aryeh Leib Braude and his maternal grandfather was the rabbi of Lvov, Ẓevi Hirsch *Ornstein. Braude completed his studies at the University of Freiburg in 1898. An active Zionist from an early age, he attended the First Zionist Congress in Basel (1897), and became a leader of the Zionist Organization in Galicia. On his initiative Galician Zionists decided to take part in the political life of the country, and Braude directed their campaign for election to the Austrian Parliament (1907). Between 1909 and 1939 he was a preacher in Lodz. He founded a network of Jewish secondary schools in Poland and, between 1920 and 1926, was a member of the Polish senate. He was one of the founders of the Institute for Jewish Studies in Warsaw, and of other public and cultural institutions in Poland. Braude settled in Palestine in 1940, was active in the Polish Immigrants' Association, and undertook research in the history of Galician Jewry.

Bibliography: *Sefer ha-Yovel le-M. Z. Braude* (1931); *Zikhron M. Z. Braude* (1960); A. Tartakower, in: S. K. Mirsky (ed.), *Ishim u-Demuyyot be-Ḥokhmat Yisrael* (1959), 287–98. [G.K.]

BRAUDE, MAX A. (1913–), U.S. rabbi and organization executive. Braude was born in Harmony, Pennsylvania. He was ordained at the Hebrew Theological College in Chicago (1941). Braude joined the U.S. Army during World War II, and became the highest-ranking Jewish chaplain with the armed services in Europe, in charge of the welfare of displaced persons. In 1947 Braude joined the International Refugee Organization, with which he remained associated until 1959. In 1951 he became director of the World ORT Union, and in 1957 director general of its international office in Geneva. Frequently called upon as a consultant by the U.S. government, Braude participated in numerous conferences and studies on vocational and refugee problems. [E.Gr.]

BRAUDE, WILLIAM GORDON (1907–), U.S. Reform rabbi and scholar. Braude was born in Telz, Lithuania, and was taken to the United States in 1920. He was ordained at Hebrew Union College in 1931. After a year in Springfield, Ohio, he served as rabbi of Temple Beth El, Providence, Rhode Island, from 1932. Rabbi Braude was one of the leaders of the right wing within the Reform movement and advocated a return to traditional practices and became known as one of the leading students of rabbinics in the Reform movement. He was a leading supporter of the Hebrew day school concept, reintroduced the head covering

William G. Braude, U.S. rabbi. Providence, R.I., Temple Beth El.

at his services, and argued for respect of the dietary laws and other observances. In 1965 he participated in the civil rights demonstration led by Martin Luther King in Montgomery, Alabama. A member of various scholarly bodies, he also served on many civic agencies, and has lectured widely. Rabbi Braude wrote *Jewish Proselyting in the First Five Centuries of the Common Era* (1940); a translation with critical notes of *Midrash on Psalms* (1959); and a translation with critical notes of the *Pesikta Rabbati* (1968). The latter two books represent important contributions to the study of midrashic literature and are based on manuscripts and early printed editions. [J.Ri.]

BRAUDES, REUBEN ASHER (1851–1902), Hebrew novelist and advocate of social and religious reform. Braudes, who was born in Vilna, early established a reputation as a brilliant talmudic student, and published his first articles in the rabbinic periodical *Ha-Levanon* (1869). Leaving Vilna at 17, he spent three years at the rabbinical seminary at Zhitomir before wandering through southern Russia to Odessa, which was then the center of the Haskalah (Enlightenment). Influenced by the critical attitude toward traditional Judaism then dominating Hebrew literature, Braudes began to write articles advocating the religious and social reform of Jewish life such as *Si'aḥ Sha'ah Aḥat Aḥar ha-Mavet* ("A Conversation One Hour After Death"), published in *Ha-Meliẓ* (1870), and in his first short story, *Misterei Beit Ẓefanyah* ("The Mysteries of the Zephaniah Family") which appeared in *Ha-Shaḥar* (1873). In 1875 Braudes left Odessa to spend a year in Warsaw before proceeding to Lemberg where he edited the monthly *Ha-Boker Or* (1876–79). There he published much of his novel *Ha-Dat ve ha-Ḥayyim* ("Religion and Life," 1885), an important work describing the struggle for religious reform that raged within Lithuanian Jewry from 1869 until 1871, as well as many stories, articles, and book reviews.

The years 1879–81 were again spent in Vilna, where he edited most of the first volume of a literary miscellany, *Gan Peraḥim* ("A Garden of Flowers," 1881), which contains an important article on the revival of Hebrew. Shocked by the 1881 pogroms in Russia, he joined the Ḥibbat Zion, although he had previously attacked Smolenskin's advocacy of nationalism in an article *"Beit Yisrael"* which appeared in 1880 in David Gordon's *Maggid Mishneh* (nos. 49–50). After a brief sojourn in St. Petersburg, Braudes fled to Bucharest where from 1882 to 1884 he edited a Yiddish periodical *Yehudit* which advocated Jewish colonization in Palestine. After his expulsion from Rumania as an alien Jew in 1884, Braudes resided in Lemberg until 1891. In 1885 he founded a Hebrew biweekly, *Ha-Yahadut,* of which only four issues appeared. At the same time he participated in a story-publishing venture under the imprint *Eked Sippurim.* Part of his second novel *Shetei ha-Keẓavot* ("The Two Extremes"), which skillfully depicts the clash of contemporary and traditional attitudes and habits within Jewish life in and about Odessa, appeared in the same series, while a finished version was published in Warsaw in 1888. In an introduction to his collection of eight stories (some of which had previously appeared in *Ha-Boker Or*), published under the title *Zekenim im Ne'arim* ("Old and Young," 1886), Braudes laments the dearth of essential vocabulary in Hebrew which limits the scope of the Hebrew story. In 1888 he edited the second volume of the annual *Oẓar ha-Sifrut* published by Shealtiel Isaac Graber in Cracow. His short monograph on Adam Mickiewicz and the Jews (Cracow, 1890) represents the first study in Hebrew of the great Polish poet's attitude toward a Jewish renaissance in Palestine.

From 1891 to 1893 Braudes resided in Cracow, editing a weekly which appeared under the names *Ha-Zeman* and *Ru'aḥ ha-Zeman* in alternate weeks, to avoid paying the duty levied on a weekly. In the former he included the first part of an unfinished novel, *Me-Ayin u-Le'an* ("Whence and Whither") which appeared separately in Cracow in 1891; and in the latter he published a long biographical novel *Shirim Attikim* ("Old Songs"), the finished version of which appeared posthumously in Cracow in 1903. Both novels depict the ideological struggles of contemporary Jewish life.

From 1893 to 1896 Braudes again resided in Lemberg, where from 1894 he edited a Yiddish weekly which also appeared in alternate weeks under the titles *Der Karmel* and *Der Vekker.* With the removal of the duty on weeklies, the journal appeared each week under the name *Juedisches Wochenblatt,* serving as the official Zionist organ in eastern Galicia. Toward the end of 1896 Braudes moved to Vienna where he resided until his death. Here he served as a correspondent for *Ha-Maggid he-Ḥadash*, in which capacity he attended the First World Zionist Congress in 1897. He was appointed editor of the Yiddish edition of the Zionist weekly, *Die Welt*, by Theodor *Herzl. During his last years he composed many articles, sketches and stories, although his plans to complete his unfinished novels were realized only in the case of *Shirim Attikim*.

Braudes' fame as an author rests primarily on the novels, *Ha-Dat ve-ha-Ḥayyim* and *Shetei ha-Keẓavot*, both of which display a highly developed sense of literature. The narrative is clear, concise, and interesting, and the presentation straightforward and direct. The plots, particularly in the case of *Shetei ha-Keẓavot*, are skillfully constructed, with events portrayed in a natural and unforced sequence. In spite of the powerful dramatic tensions and conflicts experienced by the principal characters, the novels are almost entirely free from the crude melodrama and wildly improbable devices to which most of his contemporaries were prone. Both characterization and dialogue are competent within the linguistic limitations of the period. Even the didactic elements which permeate the Hebrew literature of that time are mostly introduced without too much grating on the reader's susceptibilities. Only in the third part of *Ha-Dat ve-ha-Ḥayyim* is the literary aspect deliberately neglected in favor of Braudes' didactic purpose. In *Shetei ha-Keẓavot* the author's advocacy of social reform is introduced with such consummate skill that the novel achieves an artistic unity unrivalled in the Hebrew literature of the period. By utilizing his penetrating knowledge of Jewish life in Eastern Europe, Braudes succeeded in depicting the spiritual conflicts which raged within the community in his time with an uncanny accuracy.

Bibliography: Klausner, Sifrut, 5 (1955²), 345–402; D. Patterson, *Hebrew Novel in Czarist Russia* (1964), 188–209; Waxman, Literature, 3 (1960), 301–8. [D.P.]

BRAUDO, ALEXANDER ISAYEVICH (1864–1924), Russian-Jewish historian and civic leader. After graduating from the University of Dorpat he became head of the bibliographical section of the Historical Society at the St. Petersburg (Leningrad) University and was appointed librarian of the Imperial Public Library. Braudo was active in many associations fighting for social equality and freedom for Russian Jews. He edited *Trudovaya pomoshch* ("Workers' Relief"), cooperated with the *Society for the Promotion of Culture Among the Jews, and was on the editorial staff of the periodicals *Voskhod* and *Perezhitoye*. He was also one of the founders and directors of the publishing house *Rasum*, dedicated to the fight against anti-Semitism. His review *Russian Correspondence*, published in London, Paris, and Berlin, provided information about Russian politics, and especially about anti-Jewish activities of the Russian authorities. Braudo was among the initiators of the massive history of the Jewish people, *Istoriya yevreyskogo naroda*, contributing largely to volumes 11 (1914) and 12 (1921).

Bibliography: *Yevreyskaya letopis*, 4 (1926), 195–6. [Ed.]

BRAUN, ABRAHAM (Sergei; 1881–1940), Bundist leader in Latvia. Born in *Riga, Braun joined the *Bund in 1900 while a student of the Riga Polytechnikum. A brilliant speaker and propagandist, he worked clandestinely on behalf of the party in various towns and was imprisoned several times for revolutionary activities. Braun took part in 1906 in the seventh conference of the Bund in Berne and in its seventh convention in Lvov. He was also sent to South Africa as an emissary of the party. After 1917 Braun renewed his activities in the Bund, and at the eighth party convention that year he was elected to the central committee. From 1921 he lived in Riga where he was active as a speaker and a journalist. After the Fascist take-over in Latvia in 1934, he was sent to a detention camp, and later deported. From 1938 he lived in New York, traveled as speaker for the Arbeiter-Ring (*Workmen's Circle), and contributed to its organ *Friend*.

Bibliography: J. S. Herz (ed.), *Doyres Bundistn* (1956), 298–307.

[M.B.]

BRAUN, ADOLF (1862–1929), German socialist leader, who was active in the Social Democratic Party for more than 40 years. He was the brother-in-law of Victor *Adler. Adolf Braun, son of a wealthy Jewish entrepreneur, joined the socialist movement in Austria as a student. In 1889 he went to Germany and became editor of several socialist newspapers. On his expulsion from Prussia under the anti-socialist laws, he edited the Nuremberg socialist daily, *Fraenkische Tagespost*. Although he belonged to the left wing of the Social Democrats, Braun did not vote against war credits during World War I. He was, however, among the first to demand the abdication of the kaiser in 1918. His articles of that period were reprinted in the book *Sturmvoegel der Revolution* (1919). In 1919 Braun was elected to the National Assembly in Weimar and then to the Reichstag. From 1920 to 1927 he was a member of the Social Democratic Party executive. He wrote on economic, social, and trade union questions. Many socialist journalists received their training in newspaper work under his guidance.

His brother Heinrich Braun (1854–1927) founded, together with Karl Kautsky and Wilhelm Lichtknecht, the periodical of the German Social Democrats, *Neue Zeit*, in 1883. Periodicals devoted to the study of social policy and founded by him included the *Archiv fuer soziale Gesetzgebung und Statistik* of which he was editor until 1903. Braun also edited socialist publications including the *Neue Gesellschaft*. In 1903–04 Braun sat in the Reichstag but his election was declared invalid and his opponent defeated him in the following by-election. His wife was the author Lily Braun, daughter of General von Kretschman.

Bibliography: F. Stampfer, *Erfahrungen und Erkenntnisse* (1957); J. Braun-Vogelstein, *Heinrich Braun, Ein Leben fuer den Sozialismus* (1967).

[Ed.]

BRAUN, FELIX (1885–), Austrian poet, playwright, and novelist. Braun was born in Vienna, and from 1928 taught at the universities of Padua and Palermo, but in 1939, because of his Jewish origin, he had to flee to London. He returned to Austria after the end of World War II. Braun was an impressionist poet, deeply influenced by his friend Hugo von *Hofmannsthal. His first collection of verse was *Das neue Leben* (1913); *Viola d'amore* (1953) contained a selection of his poems spanning the years 1903–53. As a playwright Braun at one time showed a fondness for themes drawn from classical mythology, such as *Tantalos* (1917) and *Aktaion* (1921), and he also dramatized the biblical story of *Esther* (1925). Later, however, he turned to historical subjects, as in the tragedy *Kaiser Karl der Fuenfte* (1936) and *Rudolf der Stifter* (1956). His *Agnes Altkirchner* (1927) is a seven-volume novel depicting Austria's decay and eventual collapse after World War I. Braun's autobiography, *Das Licht der Welt* (1949), and his book of reminiscences, *Zeitgefaehrten* (1963), both provide an insight into Viennese culture in the early years of the 20th century.

Bibliography: F. Lennartz, *Deutsche Dichter und Schriftsteller unserer Zeit* (1959), 98–100. [S.L.]

Felix Braun, Austrian author. Lithograph by Stumpp, 1927. New York, Leo Baeck Institute.

BRAUNER, VICTOR (1903–1966), surrealist painter. Brauner, born in Pietra Neamţ, Rumania, grew up in Bucharest, where he joined the avant-garde of Rumanian artists. In 1930 he settled in Paris where he associated with André Breton and the surrealists and participated in all the major surrealist exhibitions until 1949. During World War II he hid from the Germans in an Alpine village and returned to Paris in 1945. Some of Brauner's early works contain an element of social satire (e.g., "L'étrange cas de monsieur K"). He later elaborated a complex private world of symbolism and mythology, and drew on numerous sources of inspiration in order to make this private world universal. To this end he studied myth, psychology, ethnology, child art, the art of the insane, and that of primitive peoples. In 1948 he made a series of paintings with himself as subject (e.g., "Victor, Empereur de l'espace Infini"). After 1951, in a state of deep depression, he painted his series of "Rectractés": These are people who find no peace in the world. Unable to escape, they turn, instead, a terrifying gaze on the spectator (e.g., "Regard de la lumière"). Many of Brauner's later works were almost abstract, executed with a wry sense of humor.

"Acolo" by Victor Brauner, 1949. From *Quadran*, Vol. 15, Brussels, 1963.

Bibliography: A. Jouffroy, *Brauner* (Fr. 1959); S. Alexandrian, *Victor Brauner, l'illuminateur* (1954); idem (ed.), *Les dessins magiques de Victor Brauner* (1965). [Ed.]

BRAUNSTEIN, MENAHEM MENDEL (pen name **Mibashan;** 1858–1944), Hebrew writer and leading figure in the Zionist movement in Rumania. He received his early education in Jassy and had a broad knowledge of the Bible and of traditional Hebrew literature. After his marriage, however, he took up secular studies and learned several European languages. In 1887 he was one of the founders in Jassy of Doresh le-Zion, an organization which sought to revive the movement of Rumanian Jews to Palestine following the decline which had set in after the relatively large-scale emigration during 1882–83. From 1887, he edited the newspaper *Juedischer Volksfreund* (German in Hebrew script). He helped found Oholei Shem, an association aimed at disseminating knowledge of Jewish history and literature among Rumanian Jewry. For 23 years he taught Hebrew subjects in Jewish schools in various towns in Rumania. He advocated teaching Hebrew through the medium of Hebrew, founded Hebrew libraries, and struggled to overcome the objections of an apathetic public and of assimilationist opponents to the teaching of Hebrew in Jewish schools. He wrote *Divrei ha-Yamim li-Venei Yisrael* ("History of the Jews," Warsaw, 1897, 1904) and *Sefer ha-Moreh* ("The Teacher's Book," Piatra, 1910). From 1885 he also contributed to the Jewish press in German and Rumanian but wrote mainly for the Hebrew press. He settled in Ereẓ Israel in 1914, and continued writing stories and poems, especially for young people. Four volumes of his works were published between 1928 and 1937. Braunstein was one of the last modern Hebrew authors to use a purely biblical style. His translations from European literature include: Lehmann's *The House of Aguilar* (St. Petersburg, 1896); Edmondo de Amici's *Il Cuore* (Warsaw, 1923); and Swift's *Gulliver's Travels* (Tel Aviv, 1944).

Bibliography: Y. Klausner, *Ḥibbat Ẓiyyon be-Romanyah* (1958), 259–68. [Y.S.]

BRAUNTHAL, JULIUS (1891–1972), Austrian journalist, historian, and socialist leader. The son of a bookkeeper who emigrated from Russia, Braunthal joined the Socialist youth movement in Vienna at the age of 15 when he was a bookbinder's apprentice. He participated in the mutiny of the Austro-Hungarian Navy at Cattaro (Boka Kotorska) at the end of World War I, and was appointed adjutant to the undersecretary of state for the armed forces when the Austrian socialists joined the government. His journalistic activities covered a wide range. He was deputy-editor of the *Arbeiterzeitung,* the Austrian socialist daily, founder and editor of the popular daily *Das kleine Blatt*, and for many years editor of the socialist monthly *Der Kampf*. Braunthal was imprisoned for a year by the Austrian government in 1934, and after his release emigrated to England where he joined the staff of *The Tribune*, and later became editor of the *International Socialist Forum*. In 1939 he worked under Friedrich *Adler in the secretariat of the Labor and Socialist International in Brussels and after World War II he became secretary of the reconstructed Socialist International.

Braunthal's enormous literary output includes a massive two-volume *Geschichte der Internationale* (1961–63) and biographies of Victor and Friedrich Adler and Otto *Bauer. He also compiled anthologies of the writings of Victor *Gollancz, Otto Bauer, Friedrich Austerlitz, and Zsigmund *Kunfi and was editor of the *Yearbook of the International Socialist Labour Movement* and of the *Yearbook of the International Free Trade Union Movement*. Braunthal supported Labor Zionism in the Vienna Socialist press. In his autobiography, *In Search of the Millennium* (1945), he stressed the roots of the socialist idea in Jewish messianism and discussed the impact of this Jewish background on certain socialist leaders. [R.W.]

BRAWER, ABRAHAM JACOB (1884–), Israel geographer and historian. Brawer, who was born in Stry, Ukraine, studied in Vienna at the university and at the rabbinical seminary. From 1910 to 1911 he taught at a secondary school in Tarnopol. While there he published Dov Ber *Birkenthal's *Divrei Binah* which dealt with false Messiahs in Jewish history (*Ha-Shilo'aḥ*, 33 (1917); 38 (1921)). In 1911 he settled in Ereẓ Israel and taught at the Ezra Teachers Seminary in Jerusalem. In the summer of 1914 he taught in Salonika and from 1915 to 1918 in Constantinople, where he also served as rabbi of the Ashkenazi congregation.

Abraham Jacob Brawer, Israel geographer.

After pursuing research work in geography at the University of Vienna, he returned in 1920 to the Teachers Seminary in Jerusalem, where he taught until 1949. He wrote *Avak-Derakhim* (2 vols., 1944–46) about his travels in Lebanon, Syria, Iraq, and Persia and his descriptive *Ha-Areẓ* (later *Ereẓ Yisrael*), the first modern regional geography of Ereẓ Israel, was published in 1928 (3rd ed. 1954). Brawer also published several textbooks on geography, an atlas, and maps and was geography editor of the Hebrew Encyclopedia. He was one of the three founding members of the *Israel Exploration Society and its first honorary secretary. [Ed.]

BRAY-SUR-SEINE, village in the department of Seine-et-Marne, central France. In 1190, after the execution of a Christian who had murdered a Jew, a rumor spread that the Jews had crucified the murderer in order to mock the death of Jesus. The king of France, *Philip Augustus, dispatched an armed force to the town, and ordered the entire Jewish community to be burnt at the stake. The identification of the place in question has been disputed, some scholars placing it in Bresmes, other in Brie-Comte-Robert. Toward the middle of the 13th century, Jews were again found living in Bray-sur-Seine. They seem to have returned there in 1315 after the general expulsion of the Jews from France in 1306. The Rue des Juifs was named Rue Emile Zola at the beginning of the 20th century.

Bibliography: Gross, Gal Jud, 123ff.; Neubauer, in: REJ, 9 (1884), 64; L. A. Roubault, *Bray-sur-Seine* (1908), 26ff.; Bouquet, in: *Recueil des Historiens de France*, 17 (1878), n. 769. [B.Bl]

BRAZIL, South American republic.

Colonial Period. When the Portuguese admiral Pedro Álvares Cabral landed in what is now Brazil in 1500, he was accompanied by at least one person of Jewish birth, Gaspar da *Gama, who had been kidnapped and forcibly baptized by the Portuguese in India three years before. In 1502 a consortium of *New Christians headed by Fernando de *Noronha obtained from King Manuel I of Portugal a concession to colonize and exploit the newly discovered land. The main business of the group was to export brazil wood (from which the name of the new land was derived) to Portugal for the purpose of dyeing textiles. There is good reason to believe that New Christians transplanted sugar cane from Madeira to Brazil in the early 16th century. New Christian foremen and workers are said to have been brought over from Madeira and São Tomé when the first sugar plantations and mills were established in Brazil around 1542. One of the first five *engenhos* (sugar plantation and mill) was owned in 1550 by a New Christian, Diego Dias Fernandes. A large number of the 120 *engenhos* that existed in Brazil in the year 1600 belonged to New Christians, many of whom were also administrators. Some of the New Christians were staunch Catholics, but the majority secretly observed Jewish rites and customs and were in fact *Crypto-Jews called *Marranos by the Catholics. The Inquisition was never formally introduced in Brazil. From 1580 on (after Portugal was united with Spain), the bishop of Bahia received investigation powers from Lisbon, and after 1591 the Holy Office in Portugal sent Inquisitional Commissaries to Brazil at intervals. The first commission worked from 1591 to 1593 in *Bahia and afterward until 1595 in Pernambuco; in 1618 a commission again visited Bahia. The investigators of the Inquisition held hearings based on denunciations, and the suspected were arrested and sent to Lisbon to trial. Brazil had about 50,000 European inhabitants in 1624, a high percentage of whom were New Christians. They were owners of *engenhos*, businessmen, importers and exporters, teachers, writers, poets, even priests. Bento Teixeira (also known as Bento Teixeira Pinto), the author of the *Prosopopéia* (Lisbon, 1601)—the first poem written in Brazil—and Ambrósio Fernandes *Brandão, author of *Diálogos das Grandezas do Brasil*—one of the greatest books ever written about that country—were both New Christians.

From the end of the 16th century Amsterdam became an important Jewish religious, cultural, and economic center. When the West India Company, aided by the Dutch government, equipped an expedition to Brazil, Dutch Jews—mainly fugitives from the Inquisition—were its allies. In May 1624 two important forts of Bahia were captured by the Dutch; but a large Portuguese and Spanish expeditionary force arrived shortly after and after two months the Dutch had to surrender (May 1625). All Dutch

Map showing the main areas of Jewish settlement in Brazil.

troops, including some Jews from the Netherlands, could leave Bahia, but five New Christians who had returned to the practice of Judaism during the Dutch occupation were hanged for treason. The West India Company soon prepared another expedition, this time to Pernambuco. The States General at The Hague proclaimed that the liberty of Spaniards, Portuguese, and natives, whether Roman Catholics or Jews, would be respected. Jewish soldiers, traders, and adventurers joined the expedition that successfully landed at the ports of Olinda and Recife in the middle of May 1630. After the arrival of the Dutch, many Marranos who had lived in the northeastern part of Brazil, happy to be able to give up their double life, were circumcised and became professing Jews.

Johan Maurits van Nassau, who was appointed governor-general of Brazil in 1637, gave the inhabitants of Dutch Brazil a sense of security. Jews were enrolled in the militia; one of the four companies was composed entirely of Jews and was exempt from guard duty on Saturday. On the other hand, Johan Maurits and Calvinist preachers tried unsuccessfully to convert Jews and Catholics to Calvinism. In 1636, a synagogue already existed in Recife and a rudimentary congregation in Paraiba. Jews from Recife addressed an inquiry regarding the proper season to recite the prayers for rain to Rabbi Ḥayyim Shabbetai in Salonika, the earliest American contribution to the *responsa literature.

By 1639 Dutch Brazil had a flourishing sugar industry with 166 *engenhos,* six of which were owned by Jews. Jews also became leaders in tax farming (about 63% of it was in their hands) and were largely engaged in the slave trade. The import of Negro slaves from Africa was a monopoly of the West India Company, which sold them at public auctions for cash. Jews purchased the slaves and resold them with great profit (on credit, payable at the next sugar harvest) to the owners of the plantations. Negro slaves generally preferred to work for Jews because under Jewish masters they did not have to work on either Saturdays or Sundays, while the Portuguese allowed them to rest only on Sundays and the Dutch, especially in the hinterlands, required that slaves work seven days a week. Jews were also very active in the export and import business, and all these opportunities attracted many Jews to Dutch Brazil. In 1638 a group of 200 Jews, led by Manoel Mendes de Castro, arrived on two ships. Soon after, the Jews of Recife needed rabbis, Hebrew teachers and *ḥazzanim* and thus invited the famous Rabbi Isaac *Aboab da Fonseca, one of the four rabbis of the congregation Talmud Torah in Amsterdam, and the scholar Moses Raphael d'*Aguilar to come to Brazil as their spiritual leaders. They arrived in Recife at the beginning of the year 1642, by which time two congregations, Zur Israel in Recife and Magen Abraham in Maurícia, already existed. A young Jew by the name of Isaac de *Castro, who had come to Bahia—then under Portuguese rule—from Amsterdam via Dutch Brazil, was arrested for teaching Jewish rites and customs to Marranos. He was extradited to Lisbon and was one of the victims of the auto-da-fé on Dec. 15, 1647.

As early as in 1642 the Portuguese, in collaboration with Brazilian patriots, began preparations for the liberation of northeastern Brazil. In 1645 they began a guerrilla war that lasted nine years. Jews joined the Dutch ranks, and some were killed in action. Scores of persons died of malnutrition. Famine had set in and conditions were desperate when, on June 26, 1649, two ships arrived from Holland with food. On that occasion, R. Isaac Aboab wrote the first Hebrew poem in the Americas, *"Zekher Asiti le-Nifle'ot El"* ("I Have Set a Memorial to God's Miracles"). Soon afterward other ships arrived with 2,000 soldiers and more supplies. The guerrilla war continued, and some Jews taken prisoner by the enemy were sentenced and hanged as traitors; others were sent to Lisbon for trial. The war ended with the defeat and capitulation of the Dutch in January 1654. The Jewish population of Dutch Brazil had reached its peak in 1645, when about 50% (1,500) of the European civilian population was Jewish. Even though during the war many Jews died and many returned to Holland, in 1650 there were still about 650 Jews in Recife and Maurícia.

The minute book of the congregations Zur Israel and Magen Abraham, which was brought back to Holland and has been published, shows that the Jewish community was very well organized along the same lines as the parent body in Amsterdam. All Jewish residents were members of the community and were subject to its regulations, taxes, and assessments. The executive committee *(mahamad)* consisted of five members who were nominated by their predecessors. There was a *talmud torah* and an Etz Haim yeshivah. The relief of the poor was left in the hands of the *mahamad.* The "sedaca" (Heb צדקה = charity) was the general fund of the community. The *mahamad* exercised strict control over the legal aspects of community life, disputes, and civil or commercial suits between members of the community; it also had almost dictatorial powers over law enforcement. The Jewish cemetery was located in the hinterland, separated from Recife and Maurícia by the Capibaribe River. The dead, therefore, had to be transported to the cemetery on boats until 1644, when bridges from Recife to Mauricia and then to the hinterland were completed.

Other parts of Brazil, which were not occupied by the Dutch, such as Bahia, *Rio de Janeiro, *São Paulo, São Vicente, also had New Christians among the population. It was stipulated in the capitulation protocol of Jan. 26, 1654, that all Jews, like the Dutch, were to leave Brazil within three months and had the right to liquidate their assets and to take all their movable property with them. The majority left for Amsterdam, but some sailed to Caribbean Islands (Curacao, Barbados, etc.), where they are believed to have introduced the sugar plant and the sugar industry. A group of 23 Brazilian Jews arrived in New Amsterdam (old name of New York), then under Dutch rule, on the *Saint Catherine* at the beginning of September 1654. They were the founding fathers of the first Jewish community in *New York.

After 1654 there were either few Marranos left in Brazil or they were not discovered. About 25 of them were sent to Lisbon for trial in the second half of the 17th century. Persecutions and extraditions began again in the 18th century. Several hundred Marranos from Brazil appeared at autos-da-fé in Lisbon in 1709, 1711, and 1713. The persecutions, arrests, and confiscation of property brought the manufacture and export of sugar to a temporary standstill and seriously disrupted trade between Brazil and Portugal. The most famous Brazilian Marrano and Inquisitional martyr in the 18th century was *Antonio José da Silva, who achieved prominence as poet and playwright. Altogether dossiers of 18 Brazilian Marranos who suffered the death penalty are found in the Archivo da Tôrre do Tombo in Lisbon. The Portuguese royal decree of May 25, 1773, which declared all legislation discriminating against New Christians null and void, applied also to Brazil. From then on the Inquisition left the New Christians in peace. Mainly because of the high incidence of mixed marriages, the Brazilian Marranos became more and more assimilated and abandoned any residual Jewish beliefs and practices, becoming henceforth good Catholics. Jewish immigration began again only after 1822, when Brazil became independent from Portugal. [A.A.W.]

Agricultural Colonies. Many Jews farmed in northern Brazil during the Colonial Period and probably even introduced the cultivation of sugar cane. More recently, the earliest discussion of a plan for the agricultural settlement of Jews took place in 1891, when the Deutsches Central Comitee fuer die Russischen Juden, established after the expulsion of Jews from Moscow, sent Oswald Boxer—a

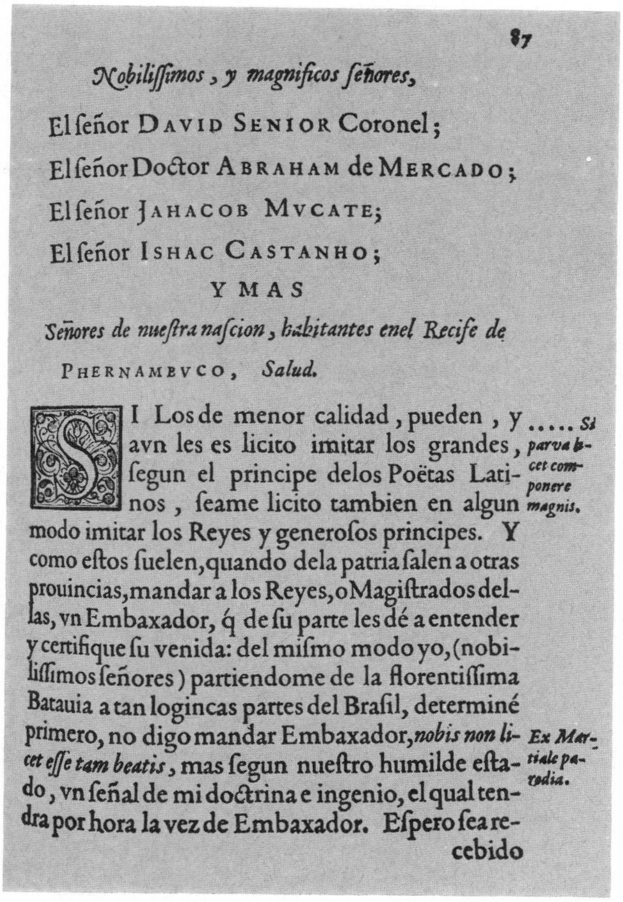
87

Nobiliſſimos, y magnificos ſeñores,

El ſeñor DAVID SENIOR Coronel;

El ſeñor Doctor ABRAHAM de MERCADO;

El ſeñor JAHACOB MUCATE;

El ſeñor ISHAC CASTANHO;

Y MAS

Señores de nueſtra naſcion, habitantes enel Recife de

PHERNAMBUCO, *Salud.*

SI Los de menor calidad, pueden, y aun les es licito imitar los grandes, ſegun el principe delos Poëtas Latinos, ſeame licito tambien en algun modo imitar los Reyes y generoſos principes. Y como eſtos ſuelen, quando dela patria ſalen a otras prouincias, mandar a los Reyes, o Magiſtrados dellas, vn Embaxador, q̃ de ſu parte les dé a entender y certifique ſu venida: del miſmo modo yo, (nobiliſſimos ſeñores) partiendome de la florentiſſima Batauia a tan logincas partes del Braſil, determiné primero, no digo mandar Embaxador, *nobis non licet eſſe tam beatis*, mas ſegun nueſtro humilde eſtado, vn ſeñal de mi doctrina e ingenio, el qual tendra por hora la vez de Embaxador. Eſpero ſea recebido

..... Si parva licet componere magnis.

Ex Martiale parodia.

Figure 1. Page of Manasseh ben Israel's *Conciliador,* Amsterdam, 1651. It dedicated part of the work to leading members of the community of Recife, Brazil, at a time when he was contemplating becoming their rabbi. Cecil Roth Collection.

Viennese journalist and close friend of Herzl—to Brazil to investigate the possibilities of founding agricultural settlements for Russian refugees. Boxer was warmly received by government representatives and after an inspection tour, he reported to the committee that Jewish settlement could indeed prosper in Brazil and that the first settlers could be dispatched as early as March 1892. The revolution of Nov. 3, 1891, and the counterrevolution of Nov. 23, which ended the rule of General Deodoro da Fonseca, invalidated Boxer's forecast, and the project was finally abandoned in 1892, when Boxer died of yellow fever. In 1901, on the initiative of the vice-president of the *Jewish Colonization Association (ICA), who had contacts with the Belgian railway company in Rio Grande do Sul, Brazil again became the objective of Jewish agricultural settlement. The lasting stagnation in the agricultural colonies of Argentina prompted ICA to seek new lands where the expenses of agricultural settlement would be less than in Argentina. In 1902 ICA decided to set up a small experimental colony; 5,400 hectares (13,338 acres) were acquired in the Santa Maria region on the railroad line that later became the international railroad between Montevideo and Rio de Janeiro. In 1904, 37 families (267 persons) from Bessarabia settled at the colony named after its initiator, Philippson. This settlement encountered difficulties from its inception. Despite the *Kishinev pogrom in Bessarabia (April 1903), few Jews wanted to settle in Brazil, and the selection of candidates, who had to be experienced in agricultural work and possess certain financial means, was slow. The 1904 farming season was thus wasted. Frequent changes in the administration, coupled with the lack of agricultural instruction, faulty planning, and insufficient funds prevented the development of the settlement, whose limited size also precluded the improvement of services. Only in 1907 was a qualified teacher appointed and a cooperative formed, but its practical activity was limited. The meager chances of economic success in the settlement, contrasted with the prospect of a comfortable livelihood as a peddler or artisan in Santa Maria, soon caused the settlement's disintegration. In Aug. 1926, the director of ICA in Buenos Aires reported that of the 122 families who settled in Philippson at various periods, only 17 remained, of whom only three worked the land themselves, the others leasing it or employing hired labor. Only 132 hectares (326 acres) were under cultivation, on which corn and beans were grown, and the overall value of the harvest was only £1,060. The report suggested the liquidation of the remaining ICA property in the colony, and this suggestion was adopted. In 1968, two of the offspring of the original settlers, who live in Pôrto Alegre, still owned large tracts of the former colony's land.

Despite the preliminary difficulties at Philippson, on June 5, 1909, the ICA council decided to acquire an additional large tract in northern Rio Grande do Sul. It chose a largely afforested section of 93,850 hectares (231,810 acres) in the Quatro Irmãos area, where a large-scale government settlement was developing. The Quatro Irmãos settlers were to be chosen from among the agricultural laborers in ICA's colonies in Argentina and applicants for settlement specially selected in Russia. While the screening operations met with difficulties because of a lack of confidence in the potential success of the Brazil project, other immigrants reached the colony. By January 1915, 1,678 persons had settled in Quatro Irmãos. Because of the lack of agricultural facilities, the newcomers were either engaged in building or received funds directly from ICA. World War I put an end to any chance of developing the colony. With the help of ICA, the immigrants therefore left the colony for towns in Rio Grande do Sul, Uruguay, and Argentina. By November 1915 only 72 of the original 232 families remained in the colony. Apart from keeping cows and chickens for their own consumption, the settlers had to make a living from their harvests of corn, wheat, beans, manioc, alfalfa, peanuts, and especially yerba maté maté. They also cleared fertile areas of forest and groves *(mato),* which were enriched by the wood ash created by burning the vegetation. The salvaged wood was sold to ICA's sawmills in the area, and, in order to facilitate transportation and marketing, ICA began building an 18-kilometer railroad that joined Quatro Irmãos and the town of Erebango early in 1918. Flour mills and a consumer cooperative organization were also established, and in 1912 a school was built and cultural life began to develop.

Nevertheless, the settlement was undermined by administrative weakness, difficult living conditions, and, most particularly, by the civil war of 1923 (one of whose fiercest battles was fought on the colony's land). By 1926, 40 settlers remained, of whom only 16 lived on their own land and 24 lived in the village of Quatro Irmãos; another ten landowners lived outside the colony. The cooperative and the other public institutions were neglected, and instability reigned in the settlement. In order to make a profit from its investments, in 1920 ICA began selling the land to non-Jewish settlers, mainly Germans and Italians. By 1926, however, it renewed Jewish settlement by establishing five new centers with a total of 97 families. ICA also renewed its efforts to encourage cooperatives, mixed farming, and the establishment of mills, oil presses, and so on. The economic crisis of 1929–30, however, drastically reduced crop prices and prevented the new centers from establishing themselves. From 1930, despite all efforts, the colony began to decline. The ICA report of Dec. 31, 1935, indicated the existence of 104 Jewish families (464 persons) as compared with 419 non-Jewish families (2,080 persons) living in the colony. The severe restrictions on immigration, particularly from 1934 onward, also prevented any further expansion, and Quatro Irmãos remained a huge holding settled mainly by non-Jews and administered, together with its railroad and sawmills, by ICA. The liquidation of this property began in 1958: the railway was closed, more and more land was sold, and the remaining settlers began to disperse. ICA's report for 1965 notes that "the winding up of the Associations affairs in the state of Rio Grande do Sul was virtually completed."

Conditions in Germany in 1935 prompted ICA to make a third attempt at agricultural settlement in Brazil. In 1936, 2,000 hectares (4,940 acres) at Resende, in the state of Rio de Janeiro, were designated for settlers who would engage in mixed farming to provide produce for the local market in Rio. ICA representatives in Germany concurrently selected 20 farming families as candidates for settlement; however, despite continuous contacts with the Brazilian government about the implementation of the plan—which was adapted to the Brazilian immigration laws—the authorities refused to grant the settlers entry permits. The land that had been acquired was meanwhile put at the disposal of 15 other settlers. In 1948 ICA closed its offices in the colony, and in 1952, when part of the area was requisitioned to set up a military school, the Association liquidated the rest of its property there.

Outside the organized settlement, individual Jews farmed in Brazil at Mogi; there are also vine growers from Bessarabia at São Miguel, in the São Paulo state; and in the Bahia state and in the Natal region of the Rio Grande do Norte state Jewish farmers own citrus groves and plantations. In contrast to Argentina, Jewish agricultural settlement in Brazil has not left its mark on Brazilian Jewish literature. [H.A.]

Modern Period. Two years after Brazil declared its independence from Portugal in 1822 it adopted its first constitution. Roman Catholicism remained the state religion, but the constitution proclaimed tolerance of other religions, provided their adherents respected the state religion and public morals and conducted their religious life in private. Non-Catholic religious services were restricted to private dwellings or to buildings whose outward appearance would not disclose their purpose. The new constitution adopted by Brazil in 1891, after the country became a republic, abolished all vestiges of religious discrimination, ensured the civil rights of all citizens, and provided for the introduction of civil marriage and the establishment of nonsectarian municipal cemeteries. The principles of freedom of conscience and religion and of equality before the law have been retained in all the constitutions subsequently adopted by Brazil—in 1934, 1937, 1946, and 1967.

By the time Brazil gained its independence, Brazilian Marranos, i.e., Jews who had originally come to the colony from Portugal, had been absorbed by the general population and were no longer identifiable. There were a handful of Jews of non-Portuguese origin distributed in various parts of the country, but they had little contact with one another, and consequently there was no organized Jewish life in the country. The earliest manifestations of renewed Jewish life in Brazil are to be found in the northern states. The first synagogue, Porta do Céu ("Gate of Heaven"), was established in Belém, the capital of Pará, in 1824 by Sephardi Jews who had immigrated from Morocco at the beginning of the 19th century. Immigrants from Morocco formed small communities in other places in northern Brazil and in 1889 founded a second synagogue in Belém. By World War I, Belém's Sephardi community of about 800 people had its own charitable organizations and social club. There were also small Sephardi communities in Amazonas, another northern state, founded by immigrants who had come toward the end of the 19th century. In the southern part of the country, there were a few Jewish immigrants who had arrived from Eastern Europe in the second half of the 19th century. In Rio de Janeiro a group of Jews from Western Europe founded their own cemetery in 1873. This first step, however, did not lead to the development of organized Jewish life in the city at this stage, when the Jewish population was rather small (in 1890 Rio de Janeiro had about 200 Jews) and indifferent toward communal life. In São Paulo, the first community, also rather restricted in size, was organized in 1897.

The modern Jewish community of Brazil, consisting primarily of East European Jews, had its formal beginnings in 1903, when the first attempts were made to organize agricultural settlement of Jews in the southern part of the country (see above Agricultural Settlements). By World War I, Brazil had a Jewish population of 5,000–7,000. After the war there was a marked increase in Jewish immigration, and in the decade from 1920 to 1930, 28,820 Jews entered the country, mostly from Eastern Europe (according to figures provided by Jewish immigrant aid societies at the time). The year 1930 was a turning point in Brazil's immigration policy, which became increasingly restrictive and had an adverse effect upon the immigration of Jews. In 1937 the tendency to select immigrants on the basis of their ethnic origin was carried to the extreme when a secret order was circulated to Brazilian consulates abroad to reject all visa applications submitted by Jews. Both the 1934 and 1937 constitutions and a decree issued in 1938 provided for a quota system of immigration that was not to exceed 2% (annually) of the total number of immigrants from any particular country in the period 1884–1934 and was to consist of up to 80% agricultural laborers. It was impossible for Jews to exploit even these restricted quotas, in view of the official discrimination practiced against them.

Nevertheless, Jewish immigration, mainly from Nazi-dominated Europe, continued by a variety of means. From time to time special provisions were made for the immigration of people skilled in certain fields or relatives of Brazilian citizens. The law also made it possible for the authorities to accord to tourists the status of permanent residents. In this manner, some 17,500 Jews entered Brazil between 1933 and 1939. In 1940 the Brazilian government, at the request of the Vatican, permitted the entry of 3,000 German refugees who had converted to Catholicism. In the period 1956–57, 2,500 Jews from Egypt, and about 1,000 from North Africa (mainly from Morocco) were admitted, and from time to time smaller groups were able to enter the country. According to the official census, the Jewish population of Brazil in 1940 was 55,668, and in 1950, 69,957; the actual figure was much higher. In 1969, the size of the Jewish population was estimated at 130,000 to 140,000 spread over the large cities: Rio de Janeiro (50,000), São Paulo (50–55,000), Pôrto Alegre (12,000), Belo Horizonte (3,000), Recife (1,600), Curitiba (1,300), Belém (1,200) and Bahia (800). There were 80 families in the new capital Brasilia, and Jews were living in smaller numbers in various other towns.

Communal Life. Apart from the religious and social organizations maintained by the Sephardi communities in the north, in the 20th century improvised prayer houses and *minyanim,* as well as small charitable organizations, existed in the two major cities, Rio de Janeiro and São Paulo. It was at Pôrto Alegre, however, the capital of the southern state of Rio Grande do Sul, that the first officially organized communal activities were introduced. The erstwhile agricultural settlers who had concentrated in that city after abandoning their work on the farm established a variety of religious, charitable, and cultural societies. Pôrto Alegre was also the place where the first Brazilian Yiddish newspaper was published in 1915. Gradually, a properly organized community emerged in the capital (at that time), Rio de Janeiro, especially from the impetus to provide help to the war victims. In 1916 a central aid committee was formed, and all the existing Jewish societies in the city took part in it. Most of these societies had come into being in the six preceding years.

The second city in importance, São Paulo, had at this time a Jewish community (founded in 1915) and several philanthropical and cultural associations. On December 31, 1916, the cornerstone was laid for the first synagogue proper. On a smaller scale, Jewish organizations also came into being in towns near São Paulo, such as Santos, Campinas, Franca, Santa André and São Caetano do Sul.

The large immigration of the 1920s consisted of Jews of a variety of social categories and the whole gamut of ideological orientation. All the Zionist parties were now represented among Brazilian Jewry, and they left their mark upon the community. There was also an organization of Jewish Communists. As a result, Jewish social and communal life was greatly enriched, but each group adhered to its own formula. This was one of the factors which frustrated the efforts by Rabbi Isaiah Raffalovitch (an official of the Jewish Colonization Association, active in social and educational affairs, and in immigrant aid) to create a unified Jewish community in Rio de Janeiro. Further development of Jewish communal activities was brought to a halt by the gradual slow down in immigration and the increasingly nationalistic policy followed by the Brazilian government. The latter resulted in heavy pressure upon the ethnic minorities to assimilate to Brazilian culture.

In April 1938, the government issued a decree prohibiting political activities by foreigners and contacts with foreign organizations; in 1941 foreign-language newspapers were outlawed. The two existing Yiddish dailies had to close down; the same applied to the Zionist Organization. The secular activities of the community, represented mostly by Ashkenazi Jews, were severely curtailed. Although Brazil had never known any organized anti-Semitism, anti-Semitic racist propaganda began to appear in newspapers, and several editions of the Protocols of the *Elders of Zion appeared. This threatening development, however, was brought to a halt before it could result in any serious consequences, thanks to discreet counter-propaganda on the part of the Jews, Brazil's entry into the war on the side of the Allies, and to the basic fact that Brazil's heterogeneous society was not a fertile breeding ground for anti-Semitism.

It was not until 1945, however, on the eve of the proclamation of the new constitution, that a more democratic climate came to prevail in Brazil. The Zionist Organization and other Jewish movements resumed their activities, and the social life of the community functioned once again, albeit at a more subdued pace. The establishment of the State of Israel in 1948 was a source of great encouragement for the Jewry of Brazil. In the period 1946–47, federations of Jewish organizations and institutions were formed in the larger communities, and 1951 witnessed the establishment of the Confederação das Entidades Representativas da Coletividade Israelita do Brasil (Confederation of Jewish Institutions in Brazil)—now known as Confederação Israelita do Brasil (CIB)—to act as the authoritative and representative body of the country's entire Jewish community. Communities in eight states, Rio de Janeiro, São Paulo, Minas Gerais, Paraná, Rio Grande do Sul, Bahia, Recife and Pará, joined the new Confederation. It consists of about 200 institutions and organizations active in the fields of Zionism, education, philanthropy, religion, culture and recreation, sports and interest-free loans.

Education and Culture. The first formally organized Jewish school in Brazil was founded in 1907 in the Philippson agricultural colony; another school was founded in Pôrto Alegre in 1910. São Paulo established a *talmud torah* in 1916. In 1929, there was a total of 27 schools in the country, with about 800 pupils. Figures published in 1967 listed 33 Jewish schools in Brazil attended by 10,409 pupils: 2,907 in kindergartens, 4,611 in elementary schools, 2,383 in junior high schools and 508 in senior high schools and teachers training courses. General studies are held in Portuguese and follow the official curriculum; Jewish studies take up three hours a day, with an emphasis on the study of Hebrew and, in a few cases, of Yiddish. The two major cities each have 13 Jewish educational institutions. There are also courses in Hebrew at the state universities in Rio de Janeiro and São Paulo, which, however, are not held regularly and are not of a high standard. Only an estimated one-sixth of the Jewish children in the two major centers attend Jewish schools, while in the smaller cities the proportion is much higher, sometimes reaching 80 or 90%. The majority of the Jewish schools have a national-secular orientation, while the rest are religious institutions. Most of them are housed in their own buildings.

No central cultural organization exists in the country. There are large Jewish clubs, which from time to time celebrate important cultural occasions; their activities are mainly in the field of sports and recreation. In Rio de Janeiro, the leading Jewish clubs are Hebraica, Monte Sinai, CIB, and ARI; in São Paulo, they are Hebraica, Macabi, Círculo Israelita, and CIP. Neither does the Jewish community of Brazil have a central rabbinate. Each of the two major cities has three chief rabbis who set the tone in religious affairs; in addition, there are various small groups of *Landsmannschaften* with their own rabbi and synagogue. The larger cities have both Sephardi and Ashkenazi synagogues; the Conservative branch (CIP in São Paulo and ARI in Rio de Janeiro) of Judaism has the most members, outnumbering the Orthodox and Reform.

Jewish newspapers, in both Yiddish and Portuguese, came into existence during World War I. In 1915, the first Yiddish-language weekly made its appearance in Pôrto Alegre under the name of *Di Menshhayt* ("Humanity"), and the following year a Portuguese-language monthly, *A Coluna,* was founded in Rio de Janeiro. In 1923 a Yiddish weekly was published in Rio de Janeiro under the name of *Dos Yidishe Vokhenblat,* later changing its name to *Brazilianer Yidishe Presse* (1927). *Di Yidishe Folkstsaytung* also came into existence in Rio de Janeiro in 1927; at first it appeared twice a week, and in 1935, became a daily, appearing as such until 1941, when it ceased publication. The *Yidishe Presse* in Rio de Janeiro, which was founded in 1930, appears mostly as a weekly, and the weekly *Brazilianer Yidishe Tsaytung* was founded in 1952. Two Portuguese-language weeklies are *Aonde Vamos?* and *Jornal Israelita.* São Paulo's Yiddish weekly, *Der Yidisher Gezelshaftlekher un Handels Buletin,* was founded in 1928; a second Yiddish newspaper, *Di San Pauler Yidishe Tsaytung,* was founded in 1931 and later became a daily, appearing as such until 1941, when it was closed down. From 1933 to 1939 São Paulo also had a Portuguese-language periodical, *A Civilisação. Der Nayer Moment,* first published in 1950, appears three times a week. There is also a Portuguese-language biweekly newspaper which appears in São Paulo. In addition, various periodicals in both Yiddish and Portuguese make their appearance from time to time in São Paulo, Rio de Janeiro, and other cities with Jewish communities. The first book in Hebrew, *Ẓiyyun,* was published in 1925. Up to 1969, 20 Jewish titles had been published, mostly in Yiddish. In addition, various books on Jewish themes have been written in Portuguese. There is also a small number of Jewish writers and journalists who have published books on general themes. The publication of books on Jewish subjects in Portuguese has been supported by such institutions as *Biblos* and, since 1966, *Perspectiva* and *Tradição.*

Jewish Participation in Brazilian National Life. Considering its small percentage in the total population the Jewish community plays a relatively important role in the life of the country, especially in the economic sphere. Most of the early Jews became itinerant peddlers, except for a small group of immigrants who worked at their trades as artisans. In the course of time, however, this situation underwent a change. The Jewish tradesmen who settled in the country after World War I soon became manufacturers and industrial pioneers in their fields—especially textile, ready-made clothes, furniture, and, at a later period, construction. An outstanding example of industrial pioneers is the *Klabin family, which leads in paper manufacture and associated industries. The peddlers eventually became wholesalers and retailers, and some also entered industry. No precise data are available on the occupational composition of Brazil Jewry; the majority are engaged in commerce and the rest in industry and services.

Some Brazilian Jews hold administrative posts and others take part in the political life of the country. In the 1966 parliamentary elections, six Jews, representing various parties, were elected to the federal legislature. There are also Jewish members of the state legislatures and the municipal councils. Horacio *Lafer was a leading Jewish political figure and served as finance minister and foreign minister of Brazil. A former federal deputy, Aarão *Steinbruch, was elected senator, the first Jew to be elected to that prestigious post. Jews hold positions in the armed forces and in the judiciary and are active in the arts and sciences. [EL.LI.]

Ties with Israel. A Brazilian statesman, Oswaldo Aranha, presided over the 1947 UN General Assembly, which voted on the partition of Palestine and for the creation of a Jewish state. Apart from casting his delegation's vote in favor of the Partition Resolution, Aranha played a key role in the adoption of the resolution, preventing delaying tactics, and guiding the Assembly to the conclusive vote. In appreciation of his historical role, a street in Tel Aviv and a cultural center in kibbutz Beror Ḥayil (settled by Brazilian Jews) were named after him. Brazil recognized Israel in February 1949 and from 1952 maintained an embassy in Tel Aviv; Israel has an embassy in Rio de Janeiro and a consulate general in São Paulo. Brazil followed the line of the Western Powers on the question of Jerusalem, voting in favor of the internationalization of the city (December 1949) and against its reunification by Israel after the *Six-Day War (July 1967). In the wake of the *Sinai Campaign (1957), Brazil supported the creation of a UN Emergency Force and contributed a contingent to it. In 1967, as a member of the Security Council, Brazil took an active part in the negotiations and debates that followed the Six-Day War and sponsored the Latin American resolution, which in effect blocked the acceptance of anti-Israel proposals.

A cultural agreement between the two countries, signed in 1959, provides the framework for cultural cooperation between Israel and Brazil, and there are institutes for cultural relations in Rio de Janeiro, São Paulo, and Pôrto

Figure 2. Stamp issued by the Brazilian Post Office in honor of the visit by President Shazar of Israel, 1966.

Alegre. Commercial relations between the two countries are still limited: Israel exports to Brazil in 1967 were $1,367,000 and imports were $739,000. On the other hand, extensive technical cooperation exists, now based on an agreement signed in 1962. An Israel mission has worked for years in the Development Authority of the Northeast (SUDENE), establishing a seed farm that specializes in the selection of quality seeds (especially hybrid maize); another team of Israel experts is assisting in the implementation of a pilot project for agricultural and rural development in the state of Piauí (northeastern part of Brazil); Israel has helped the government of Rio Grande do Sul in the development of its water resources; an Israel company has contracted for the laying of railroad lines in the state of Paraná. In 1967 the two countries signed an agreement for scientific cooperation, dealing mainly with the development of atomic energy for peaceful uses. [SH.ER.]

Bibliography: HISTORY: A. Wiznitzer, *Jews in Colonial Brazil* (1960), incl. bibl.; idem, *Records of the Earliest Jewish Community in the New World* (1954); idem, in: AJHSQ, 51 (1962), 168–214, 222–68; C. R. Boxer, *The Dutch in Brazil 1621–54* (1957), incl.bibl.; Emanuel, in: AJA, 7 (1955), 1–64; 14 (1962), 32–68. AGRICULTURAL COLONIES: Jewish Colonization Association, *Rapport de l'administration centrale au Conseil d'Administration* for 1905–1935 and 1957–1967; idem, *Le Baron Maurice de Hirsch et la Jewish Colonization Association* (1931); A. Ettinger, *Im Ḥakla'im Yehudim ba-Tefuẓot* (1942), 136–62; A. Tartakower, *Ha-Hityashevut ha-Yehudit ba-Golah* (1959), 259–65. CONTEMPORARY JEWRY: J. Beller, *Jews in Latin America* (1969), 231–54; E. Lipiner, in: *Algemayne Entsiklopedye, Yidn*, 5 (1957), 385–95, incl. bibl.; M. Kuchinsky, in: *Argentiner YIVO Shriftn* (1945), 189–97; S. Karakuschansky, *Aspektn funem Yidishn Lebn in Brazil*, 2 vols. (1956–57); I. Z. Raizman, *A Fertl Yorhundert Yidishe Prese in Brazil* (1968); J. Shatzky, *Yidishe Yishuvim in Latayn Amerike* (1952), 94–117; I. Raffalovitch, *Ẓiyyunim ve-Tamrurim* (1952), 163–250; D. Landau, in: *Revista do Serviço Público* (1958); E. Lipiner and S. Serebrenick, *Breve História dos Judeus no Brasil* (1962), 113–51; A. H. Neiva, *Estudos sôbre a imigração semita no Brasil* (1945); A. Tartakower, *Shivtei Yisrael*, 3 (1969), 62–79; *Enciclopédia Judaica*, 1 (Port., 1967), 219–50.

BREAD (Heb. לֶחֶם, *leḥem*), a baked commodity from a cereal flour. The primary sense of *leḥem* is "food" in general (Gen. 37:25; Num. 28:2; I Kings 5:2; etc.). The Ugaritic *lḥm* has the same general sense and the same particular sense, while the Arabic *laḥum* has only the specialized sense of "meat" (see relevant lexicons). In biblical times bread was prepared from wheat or barley, but most of the verses mentioning bread do not indicate the exact species used. Bread of *solet* (semolina, the hard particles in the interior of the wheat grain) is mentioned explicitly with reference to sacrifices (Ex. 29:2), and no doubt both the flour and the semolina *(solet)* that were baked in Solomon's ovens were from wheat (I Kings 5:2–3). The well-known fact that barley ripens earlier than wheat no doubt explains why "bread of firstfruits" was baked from it (II Kings 4:42), and for the same reason barley bread was no doubt eaten mainly in the early summer.

It is possible that bread was also made from spelt, as was customary in the ancient Orient and as evidenced by, *inter alia*, the remnants of such bread found in Egyptian tombs. The symbolic bread of Ezekiel—a suggestion of the bread of siege (4:9)—prepared from a mixture of different kinds of crops such as wheat, barley, beans, lentils, millet, and emmer, was no doubt never resorted to except in the extremities of a siege.

Bread was made of flour or semolina which was choicer than ordinary flour (Ex. 29:2; Num. 5:15; I Kings 5:2; II Kings 7:1, 16–18). The flour was made into dough that was baked on coals, like "a cake baked on the hot stones" (I Kings 19:6; Isa. 44:19), or on special devices akin to various types of ovens. Dough to which leaven was added was called *ḥameẓ* (leavened) to differentiate it from *maẓẓah* (unleavened). The baked bread had several names according to its shape and possibly even according to its weight.

Kikkar (Ex. 29:23) was the round flat loaf of the Arab peasant *(fatteh)*. *Ḥallah* (II Sam. 6:19) was probably more like the European loaf and is the term commonly used in scripture. *ʿUgah* (or *maʿog*) seems to have been baked directly on the fuel or on a heated stone but covered with ashes. This explains Ezekiel's squeamishness about the nature of the fuel with which his *ʿugah* was baked (Ezek. 4:12–15). As far as can be seen, the *ʿugah* was not used in ritual ceremonies (e.g., Gen. 18:6; 19:3, etc.). It is possible that *rakik* ("wafer") was similar to the *ʿugah* but thinner (Lev. 8:26; I Chron. 23:29). The word *pat* meant a piece of bread at first (Lev. 2:6; I Kings 17:11), but was sometimes used simply for bread in general (Gen. 18:5; I Sam. 2:36; 28:22). Apparently the *levivah* was also made simply from flour and prepared in a special shape (II Sam. 13:6). Some ate the kernels of fresh corn (called *karmel*) or roasted called *kali*.

Apart from the word "bread," the combination "bread and water" was used to indicate food or was descriptive of man's minimal nutritional needs (e.g., Gen. 21:14; and in a different form in I Kings 19:6). The symbol of poverty is referred to in the Bible as eating "scant bread and scant water" (I Kings 22:27; II Chron. 18:26), or "sparing bread and scant water" (Isa. 30:20). The phrase "bread and *wine" means "food and drink" but implies that at least the drink was not limited to water (Gen. 14:18). Bread is regarded as the mainstay of man's nourishment, as implied by the expression "every stay of bread and every stay of water" (Isa. 3:1) or "the staff of bread" (Ezek. 4:16; etc.; cf. Prov. 30:8, "my allotted bread"). (On the part played by bread in various forms in the meal offerings of the cult, see *Cult and also *Cooking and Baking.) Bread is also used as a metaphor in the Bible, e.g., the ungodly are said to "eat the bread of wickedness" (Prov. 4:17), while the good wife *(ʾeshet ḥayil)* "does not eat the bread of idleness" (Prov. 31:27). [SH.AB.]

In Rabbinic Literature. The rabbis regarded bread as the staple diet and no meal was considered complete without it. They instituted a special benediction to be recited before eating bread made from one of the *five species of cereals grown in Ereẓ Israel. This blessing (popularly called *Ha-Moẓi*) is: "Blessed art Thou, Lord our God, King of the universe, Who bringeth forth *(ha-moẓi)* bread out of the earth" (Ber. 6:1; cf. Ps. 104:14). The benediction is pronounced by the person who presides at the table (Ber. 46a; see also Matt. 14:19, 15:36, 26:26; Acts 27:35). A person who eats alone is also required to say the benediction. After pronouncing this blessing, other food or beverages may be eaten without saying another blessing except for wine and fruits, for which their particular blessings must be recited in all cases (see Sh. Ar., OḤ 167). Before the benediction over bread is said, one is obliged to wash the hands by pouring a quarter "log" (approximately 0.137 lit.) of clean water over them, and drying them properly (OḤ 158–64; see *Ablution). After eating bread at least of the size of an olive the full *Grace after Meals has to be said.

A religious duty of Jewish women when baking is to separate a small portion of the dough about the size of an olive, as *ḥallah* (Shab. 2:6), and to burn it (OḤ 457). From talmudic times, it was the special duty of the housewife to bake the bread for the Sabbath (Ta'an. 24b–25a). This bread, usually prepared from white flour, is called *"ḥallah"* (Heb. for "loaf," or because *ḥallah* was taken from its dough). Two such loaves are placed on the festive Sabbath table as a symbol for the double portion of *manna, which the Israelites in the wilderness received every Friday (Ex. 16:5), or because of the Showbread (see *Temple) in the Temple, which was displayed each Sabbath (Lev. 24:8–9; I Sam. 21:7). The bread for Sabbath is usually of oblong shape, but for Rosh Ha-Shanah it is round. Where wine is lacking, *Kiddush* (but not *Havdalah*) may be made over bread. As a protective measure against assimilation which might lead to intermarriage the rabbis prohibited Jews from eating food cooked by a gentile, or bread baked by a non-Jew *(pat akkum)*. However, this interdiction does not apply to bread sold by a professional non-Jewish baker *(pat palter)*, if the ingredients are not otherwise forbidden by the dietary laws (Sh. Ar., YD 112). Bread must be treated with special regard. Raw meat should not be placed on it nor spilt wine be allowed to spoil it; it should not be thrown across the table nor be used to support another object (Ber. 50b; DER 9). Providing bread for the poor was regarded as a great religious duty (Isa. 58:7; Prov. 22:9); the withholding of it from the hungry, a sin (Job 22:7). Even Micah, the idolater (Judg. 17), was not deprived of his share in the world to come, because he provided bread for the poor (Sanh. 103b). Whenever R. Huna broke bread for a meal, he first opened his door and said, "Let everyone in need come and eat" (Ta'an. 20b), as is done at the beginning of the Passover *seder*. Bread with salt was regarded in midrashic literature as the poor man's food (Ber. 2b) but sufficient for the humble student of the Torah (Avot 6:4) and it has remained a custom to sprinkle a little salt on bread partaken at the beginning of meals. A folk belief ascribed protective power to bread and salt and they were given to newly married couples. [Ed.]

Bibliography: H. Kees, *Aegypten* (1933), 18–70; K. Hintze, *Geographie und Geschichte der Ernaehrung* (1934); Dalman, Arbeit, 3 (1934), passim; F. Blome, *Die Opfermaterie in Babylonien und Israel*, 1 (1934), 248ff.; H. A. Jacob, *Toledot ha-Leḥem* (1950); C. Singer et al. (eds.), *History of Technology*, 1 (1954), 273, 362–70; T. J. Horder et al., *Bread...* (1954); A. Malamat, in: BIES, 19 (1956), 175; M. Noth, *Die Welt des Alten Testaments* (1957), 125–7; G. R. Driver, in: VT Supplement, 4 (1957), 4; M. Haran, in: *Scripta Hierosolymitana*, 8 (1961), 278–9; EM, 4 (1962), 487–95 (incl. bibl.); S. Paul, in: VT, 18 (1968), 114–20; Eisenstein, Yisrael, 6 (1911), 31f.; M. D. Gross, *Oẓar ha-Aggadah*, 2 (1961), 592ff.; Guedemann, Gesch Erz, 1 (1880), 204 n.4; J. Trachtenberg, *Jewish Magic and Superstition* (1939), 160–6.

BRÉAL, MICHEL (Jules-Alfred; 1832–1915), French linguist and educator. A student of F. Bopp, one of the founders of comparative linguistics, Bréal taught comparative grammar at the Collège de France from 1864. From 1879 to 1888 he was inspector general of secondary schools. Bréal was a pioneer in the field of semantics on which he wrote his *Essai de sémantique* (1897; *Semantics: Studies in the Science of Meaning*, 1900). He also published papers on a variety of general linguistic and Indo-European topics.

Bibliography: *Dictionnaire de Biographie Française*, 7 (1956), s.v.; JE, s.v. [Ed.]

BREASTPLATE, metal shield placed in front of the mantle of the Torah scroll in Ashkenazi communities. This custom did not develop in Sephardi communities because their Torah scrolls were kept in a case *(tik)* which did not lend itself to such additional decoration. Symbolic of, and sometimes similar to, the breastplate prescribed for the high priest (Ex. 28:15ff.), the object is often called *ḥoshen mishpat*, the Hebrew for the breastplate. Because of this symbolic identification, the Torah ornament often contained a reproduction of the 12 precious stones which adorned the high priest's breastplate. Since more than one Torah scroll was usually kept in the synagogue Ark, it also became customary during the late Middle Ages to indicate on each scroll the occasion or festival for which it was to be used. From this practical function there gradually developed the practice of including in the breastplate a section specifying the festival on which the scroll was to be utilized. Some of the breastplates are beautiful examples of Jewish *ceremonial art.

See also *Priestly Vestments.

Bibliography: J. Gutmann, *Jewish Ceremonial Art* (1964), 17–18. [Ed.]

BRECHER, GIDEON (1797–1873), physician and scholar. He was born in Prossnitz, Moravia, where he was the first Jew to study for the medical profession. Brecher edited *Judah Halevi's *Kuzari*, in four parts with a Hebrew introduction and commentary (1838–40, including notes by S. D. Luzzatto and J. Weisse). He published *Transcendentale Magie und magische Heilarten im Talmud* (1850); *Beschneidung der Israeliten...* (1845), with an introduction by H. B. Fassel and an appendix by M. *Steinschneider, a nephew of Brecher, on circumcision among the Muslims; and *Unsterblichkeitslehre des israelitischen Volkes* (1857; French tr. by I. Cahen, 1857). Brecher's unfinished concordance of biblical names *(Elleh ha-Ketuvim be-Shemot)* was published posthumously in 1876. [Ed.]

BRECLAV (Ger., **Lundenburg**), town in Moravia, Czechoslovakia. Jews are first mentioned there in 1411. By the middle of the 16th century there was a large Jewish settlement and a synagogue. The community suffered from outbreaks of violence in 1574, 1605, and 1622, and was annihilated when the city was captured by the Swedes in 1643. Jews expelled from the Austrian town of Feldberg settled in Breclav in 1651. In 1697, the council of Moravia (see **Landesjudenschaft*) met there. The 11th of Tevet was kept as a holiday by the Breclav community to commemorate their escape in 1697, when the synagogue roof collapsed while the congregation was waiting to enter. Mordecai *Banet officiated as rabbi there from 1787 to 1789. The historian Heinrich *Graetz taught at the Jewish school from 1850 to 1852. After 1848 Breclav was constituted as a political community (see **Politische Gemeinden*). The Jewish population numbered 30 families, living in 12 houses, in 1702, 66 families in 1726, and 589 persons in 1930 (4.3% of the total population), of whom 432 were of declared Jewish nationality. The entire community was deported in 1942 during the Nazi occupation. None survived the Holocaust. The synagogue appurtenances were sent to the Jewish Central Museum in Prague.

Bibliography: H. Schwenger, in: H. Gold (ed.), *Juden und Judengemeinden Maehrens* (1929), 37–40, 321–9; idem, in: *Zeitschrift fuer die Geschichte der Juden in der Tschechoslowakei*, 1 (1930–31), 171–3; J. Halpern, *Takkanot Medinat Mehrin* (1952), 158–66. [O.K.R.]

BREIDENBACH, WOLF (1751–1829), court agent of several German princes and champion of Jewish emancipation in Germany. He left his birthplace, Breidenbach in Hesse, to attend the yeshivah in Frankfort and then settled in Offenbach. Breidenbach used his connections with the nobility to press for the abolition of the humiliating *Leibzoll* ("body tax") which Jews had to pay on entering places where they had no rights of

BREASTPLATES

Some examples of ornamental silver shields for hanging on Torah scrolls.

Figure 1. Nuremberg, Germany, c. 1700. A double-headed eagle, lions, and unicorns are superimposed on an elaborate background of foliate decoration. New York, Jewish Museum.

Figure 2. Nagyszeben, Hungary, c. 1775. Master, Michael Gross (?). The top section depicts the sacrifice of Isaac. Below, left to right, are Moses, David, Solomon, and Aaron. At the bottom, the Ark of the Covenant is guarded by two cherubim. New York, Jewish Museum.

Figure 3. Augsburg, Germany, c. 1760. Wrought and gilded silver, the *menorah* and Ten Commandments given an architectural setting. The dedicatory inscription is of a later date. Formerly in the Charles Feinberg Collection, Detroit. Photo Manning Bros.

Figure 4. Italy, 1817, The Crown of the Torah is inscribed with the name of the donor, Isaac Luzzatto. Below the Ten Commandments, a phrase from Num. 16:5 indicates the date 1817. London, Jewish Museum. Photo Warburg Institute, London.

Figure 5. Israel, 1940. Silver and enamel, executed by Ludwig Wolpert. The encircling inscription is: "Thy Thummim and Thy Urim be with Thy holy one" (Deut. 33:8). Photo Frank Darmstaedter, New York.

Figure 6. Galicia (probably Brody or Lvov), c. 1780. Silver gilt set with semiprecious stones. The decoration includes mythical griffins and the signs of the zodiac. New York, Jewish Museum.

residence. Thanks to his efforts the toll was abolished in centers such as Isenburg, Hamburg (1803), the electorate of Mainz, Regensburg, Frankfort (1804), and Darmstadt (1805). Breidenbach was a friend of the publisher and scholar B.W.*Heidenheim of Roedelheim, for whose edition of the *maḥzor* he translated several prayers into German. Two of his sons, Moritz and Julius, held high governmental positions and became converted to Christianity after their father's death.

Bibliography: H. Schnee, *Die Hoffinanz und der moderne Staat*, 3 (1955), 127–60; M. Silberstein, in: ZGJD, 5 (1892), 126–45; Graetz, Hist, 5 (1949), 467–8, 472; Brilling, in: BLBI, 7 (1964), 165–68.

[It.G.]

BREISACH (or **Alt-Breisach**), town on the Rhine, West Germany. Jews are first mentioned there in 1301. The community was annihilated during the *Black Death in 1349. Subsequently Jews again settled in Breisach but were expelled in 1424. The community was reestablished in 1550, and a cemetery opened. In 1750 a Jew owned a textile factory in Breisach employing 330 weavers. The synagogue, built in 1756, was destroyed in November 1938. The Jewish population numbered 438 in 1825 (14% of the total), 564 in 1880 (17%), but only 231 in 1933. After the outbreak of World War II, the remaining Jews were expelled from Breisach because of its proximity to the frontier, but they were later allowed to return. On Oct. 22, 1940, 34 Jews were deported to *Gurs concentration camp. In 1967 the sole survivor was a woman who took care of the two cemeteries.

Memorial stone for the Breisach synagogue destroyed in 1938. Stadt Breisach am Rhein. Photo Muehlbauer.

Bibliography: Salfeld, Martyrol, 249; Germ Jud, 2 (1968), 124–5; F. Hundsnurscher and G. Taddey, *Die juedischen Gemeinden in Baden* (1968), index.

[Ed.]

°**BREITHAUPT, JOHANN FRIEDRICH** (1639–1713), German Lutheran Hebraist. Breithaupt, who taught privately at Gotha, published Latin translations of **Josippon* (Gotha, 1707) and of Rashi on the entire Hebrew Bible (3 vols., Gotha 1710–14). No earlier published version of Rashi's commentary had covered more than isolated books or sections, and Breithaupt's gained in importance as, in the 18th and 19th centuries, gentile Hebraists came to restrict themselves more deliberately to biblical Hebrew.

Bibliography: ADB, 3 (1876), 292–4; Steinschneider, Cat Bod, nos. 4625, 6035, 6927.

[Ra.L.]

BREITNER, HUGO (1873–1946), Austrian socialist economist. Born in Vienna, he worked as a clerk in the Landesbank, one of Vienna's leading banks, and was prominent in the bank clerks' union. Breitner became a director of the bank, but relinquished this post in 1918 to take charge of the city's finances at the invitation of the socialist municipal council. He remained in this post until 1932 when he retired through ill health. Breitner was a government adviser during the economic crisis of 1919–22, and persuaded the Austrian government to institute a taxation policy which alleviated the tax burden of the lower classes at the expense of the rich and could provide housing for the poor. The government actually built over 60,000 cheap and comfortable homes for workers which became the model for other European cities. In 1934 Breitner was imprisoned for a time by the fascist government of Dollfuss and fled Austria for the United States shortly before the Nazis entered Austria in 1938. From 1939 to 1942 he worked and lectured on research projects at Claremont College in California.

[Ed.]

BREMEN, city and *Land* in West Germany. There are a few references to Jews in Bremen from 1199. In 1345 Jews were prohibited from trading in Bremen, but Jewish moneylenders are still mentioned in the 14th century. Subsequently Jews were not admitted to Bremen until 1803, when the inclusion of the Hanoverian townships of Barkhof and Hastedt within the boundaries of Bremen brought a viable Jewish community within its jurisdiction. Although Jewish settlement was still officially prohibited in Bremen, at the time of the Napoleonic Wars several Jewish families were living in the city, besides those settled in the two suburbs. The community sent representatives (see Carl August *Buchholz) to the Congress of *Vienna in 1815 to press for Jewish rights in the German cities. The community in Bremen continued to grow, still without official authorization, and numbered 87 in 1821. The situation was regularized by the act of 1848 permitting Jews to settle in the city, and the community moved its institutions from Hastedt into Bremen. A synagogue was built in the Gartenstrasse in 1876. Subsequently, Bremen became an important port of transit for many thousands of Jews emigrating from Eastern Europe to America. The Jewish population in the *Land* Bremen numbered approximately 2,000 in 1933, including 1,314 living in the city. On Nov. 9, 1938, five Jews in Bremen were murdered and all the Jewish men were sent to *Sachsenhausen-Oranienburg concentration camp. Between 1941 and 1942 most of the Bremen Jews were deported to Lodz, Minsk, and Theresienstadt; in all, 915 perished in the Holocaust. A new community was founded after the war, and a new

Figure 1. The Gartenstrasse synagogue in Bremen, Germany. Built in 1876, destroyed by the Nazis in 1938. Israelitische Gemeinde im Lande Bremen.

Figure 2. The new Bremen synagogue, inaugurated in 1961.

synagogue was inaugurated in 1961. There were about 150 Jews living in the *Land* Bremen in 1967.

Bibliography: *Festschrift zum 60 Geburtstag von Carl Katz* (1959); R. Ruethnick, *Buergermeister Smidt und die Juden* (1934); M. Markreich, *Die Beziehungen der Juden zur Freien Hansestadt Bremen von 1065 bis 1848* (1928); idem, in: MGWJ, 71 (1927), 444–61; idem, *Historische Daten zur Geschichte der israelitischen Gemeinde Bremen 1803–1926* (1926); AWJD, 16 (1961/62) no. 22, 25; Germ Jud, 2 (1968), 126.

[Z.F.]

BRENNER, JOSEPH ḤAYYIM (1881–1921), Hebrew writer. A disciple of the "psychology" approach to literature and a writer of the "uprooted" generation, Brenner became a key figure of the school in modern Hebrew literature; he focused and ruthlessly exposed the anxieties, self-probing, and despair of intellectual anti-heroes overwhelmed by life in a society that had lost meaning and direction. His fiction, bleak and fiercely honest, nourishes, however, a belief in artistic truth where faith in all else has failed. A contemporary and friend of G. *Schoffmann and U. N. *Gnessin, Brenner, like them, was also influenced by M. J. *Berdyczewski. In style, he considered himself a follower of Berdyczewski, and in social outlook, a disciple of Mendele Mokher Seforim. Like many Hebrew writers of the early decades of the 20th century, he was mainly influenced by Russian literature, specifically by writers such as Tolstoy and Dostoevski (he frequently mentions the latter in his letters), and by such European writers as Nietzsche and Hauptmann. Brenner, a novelist, critic, philosopher, translator, editor, and publisher, wrote in Hebrew and in Yiddish. He exercised a powerful personal influence, often exceeding his impact as a writer and a critic, on his generation, and on the following one. His colleagues and friends saw in him "a secular saint caught in a world that was not worthy of him" (H. Zeitlin) and he became their moral, social, and artistic yardstick. Brenner's approach to literature demanded a close link between the creative process, the artistic work, and real life.

Born in Novi Mlini (Ukraine), he studied in yeshivot, including that at Pochep where he befriended U. N. Gnessin, the son of the principal of the yeshivah. From there he went to Gomel where he joined the *Bund and published his first story *Pat Leḥem* ("A Loaf of Bread") in *Ha-Meliẓ* (1900). His collection of short stories *Me-Emek Akhor* ("From the Valley of Trouble"), which was similar both in spirit and style to the "social" stories of the *Ḥibbat Zion period, was published in 1901. In *Ba-Ḥoref* ("In Winter," written in 1902 and published in *Ha-Shilo'aḥ*, Jan–Dec. 1903), a short novel, his independent literary personality emerges for the first time.

Brenner lived in Bialystok and Warsaw after 1900 and served in the Russian army from the end of 1901 to the beginning of 1904. At the outbreak of the Russo-Japanese war, with the help of some friends, he escaped to London, where he was active in the *Po'alei Zion movement. He worked in a printing shop and founded the periodical *Ha-Me'orer* (1906). In 1908, he moved to Lemberg where he was editor of the periodical *Revivim* (1908–09), and wrote a Yiddish monograph on the life of Abraham *Mapu. In 1909, he migrated to Ereẓ Israel where he worked in Ḥaderah and later moved to Jerusalem. During World War I, Brenner became an Ottoman citizen so that he would not have to leave the country. He moved to Jaffa in 1915 and taught Hebrew grammar and literature in the *Herzliah high school. When the Jews of Jaffa and Tel Aviv were driven out by the Turkish authorities he moved to Gan Shemu'el and Ḥaderah, returning to Jaffa after the British conquest of Ereẓ Israel. Brenner contributed to two important periodicals of the Second Aliyah: *Ha-Po'el ha-Ẓa'ir* and *Ha-Aḥdut*, and also to the weekly *Kunteres*. He continued publishing *Revivim* (1913–14), was the editor of the monthly *Ha-Adamah* (1920), and one of the founders of the *Histadrut (1920). In 1921, he returned to Jaffa from Galilee and was murdered in the Abu Kabbir district during the Arab riots on May 2, 1921.

Brenner's life and experiences are reflected in his work. In *Ba-Ḥoref*, a young village boy goes to a yeshivah in a larger town, then to a big city where he becomes "enlightened" and participates in the life of the Jewish intelligentsia. These phases are reminiscent of Brenner's life at Pochep and Gomel. The story *Shanah Aḥat* ("One Year," *Ha-Shilo'aḥ*, 1908) reflects Brenner's own army service and the story *Min ha-Meẓar* ("Out of the Straits," *Ha-Olam*, 1908–09) and the play *Me-Ever la-Gevulin* ("Over the Borders," *Ha-Me'orer*, 1907) deal with the life of Jewish workers in London. *Aggav Orḥa* (*Safrut*, 1909) and *Aẓabbim* (*Shallekhet*, 1911) describe the Second Aliyah to Ereẓ Israel; *Bein Mayim le-Mayim* ("Between Water and Water," 1910) and *Mi-Kan u-mi-Kan* ("From Here and There," 1911) depict life in the Ereẓ Israel settlements. In this last work, the main hero is the editor of a Hebrew newspaper, as Brenner had been. Brenner was attacked because of the obvious similarity of his characters to actual people and situations; his critics found parallels between the periodical described in *Mi-Kan u-mi-Kan* and *Ha-Po'el ha-Ẓa'ir* and its editor Joseph *Aharonovitz. *Shekhol ve-Khishalon* ("Bereavement and Failure," complete edition 1920) describes the transition of a pioneer, who did not succeed on the land, from an agricultural settlement to

Joseph Ḥayyim Brenner, the Hebrew and Yiddish writer, with his wife, 1912. From the Ben Dov Collection, by courtesy of Israel State Archives.

Jerusalem. His stories *Ha-Moẓa* ("The Solution") and *Avlah* ("Injustice," 1920) are set in Ereẓ Israel during World War I. *Me-Hatḥalah* ("From the Beginning," *Ha-Tekufah*, 1922) describes life in the Herzliah Hebrew high school. Brenner's writings are directly related to real events; a similar approach is also evident in his attitude to social problems. The societies which he describes are treated in a negative light, whether they be Russian Jewry at the beginning of the 20th century, Jewish workers in England, or Jewish Jerusalem that lived on **ḥalukkah*. His fiction is always concerned with contemporary society and its immediate social problems. The atmosphere of strict authenticity, which is a principal characteristic of Brenner's fiction, is reinforced by the narrative "I" often found in his work. As a consequence, he developed four main literary techniques: (a) The autobiography, in which the narrator recounts his experiences after a lapse of time *(Ba-Ḥoref)*; (b) The "fragmentary" documentary technique, in which the narrator fragmentarily relates a recent event, without observing chronological sequence *(Min ha-Meẓar, Mi-Kan u-mi-Kan)*; here the effect of verisimilitude and authenticity is stressed by the use of a narrator editor; (c) "Edited memoirs." The editor transfers memoirs written in the first person into the third person, and acts as a sort of mediator between the authentic document (in the first person) and the fictitious work (in the third person; *Shekhol ve-Khishalon*); (d) The narrator is a reliable witness to the events, but it is not the main character, e.g., the testimony of the narrator who hears the account of Ḥanina Mintz in *Shanah Aḥat* or the narrator who recounts the story of the hero in *Aẓabbim* as told to him by the latter.

The two novels *Mi-Saviv la-Nekuddah* and *Bein Mayim le-Mayim*, though written in the style of the "omniscient narrator," have an intimate, personal, and confessional tone. The narratives give the impression of being rooted in personal experiences. The authentic technique answers Brenner's demand for "engagé writing." His characters indulge in confessions and in the exposure of their psyche, revealing their unmediated relation to their fate. Brenner's writings are mostly tales of wandering, in which his characters constantly change their abode, deluding themselves that their destiny will also change. The wanderings are in random directions: from town to city *(Ba-Ḥoref,* and *Mi-Saviv la-Nekuddah)*; from Eastern to Western Europe *(Min ha-Meẓar)*; from the *Diaspora to Ereẓ Israel (*Aggav Orḥa, Aẓabbim, Mi-Kan u-mi-Kan)*; and finally in Ereẓ Israel itself, from the village to Jerusalem *(Shekhol ve-Khishalon)*. The hero learns that the change of domicile does not necessarily mean a change of life. He comes to understand that external circumstances are less important than internal factors.

Brenner's protagonists are "anti-heroes" who openly profess their "anti-heroism" *(Ba-Ḥoref)*; some constantly search for a meaning in life, for their identity, and hope to attain these through change (these are roving characters like Feierman, Abrahamson, Mintz, and Oved-Eẓot); others are in despair from the very outset and helplessly submit to their fate (Davidovsky, Menuḥin, and Ḥanokh Hefeẓ). The satirical antagonist is the self-satisfied hero who succeeds in his social and in his sex life (Bursif, Hamilin, and others), in contrast to the protagonists who are failures and forever outsiders.

Brenner in his endeavor to capture reality used in his fiction the "spoken language" (Hebrew) which at the time hardly existed. He improvised by adapting Yiddish, Russian, and German words and phrases; used Yiddish idioms in Hebrew translation, and created local idioms by introducing words from the language where the story is set ("Anglicisms" in *Me-Ever la-Gevulin*, and "Arabisms" in *Aẓẓabim*). He thus broadened the scope of Hebrew. His syntax is also dramatic, close to the spoken word, using parentheses, repetitions, incomplete sentences, and emotive punctuation, e.g., dots, exclamation marks, and hyphens to give the effect of live speech. His language sometimes becomes pathetic through the use of all types of rhetoric repetition. Poetic images come only at climactic points in the narrative where they tend to epitomize the entire work.

In his many articles and essays, he took issue with the views of *Aḥad Ha-Am. The basic point of contention between them was the interpretation of the *galut* (diaspora) concept which to Brenner was a life based on idleness as opposed to a life based on work. He felt that the Jew in the Diaspora was idle and that his salvation was in labor. Productive work for the Jewish people was a question of life. Judaism was not an ideology but an experience of individuals which could only become a collective experience through a change in the social and economic pattern. As a critic, Brenner wrote about major writers of modern Hebrew literature, including Peretz *Smolenskin (1910), J. L. *Gordon (1913), M. J. *Berdyczewski (1913), *Mendele Mokher Seforim (1907 and 1914), Ḥ. N. *Bialik (1916), S. *Tchernichowsky (1912–13), I. L. *Peretz (1915), U. N. Gnessin (1913), *Shalom Aleichem (1916), and others. He also published criticism on Hebrew literature in general: *Ha-Genre ha-Ereẓ Yisre'eli va-Avizeraihu* ("The Genre of Ereẓ Israel and its Paraphernalia," 1911), *Bavu'atam shel Olei Ẓiyyon ba-Sifrut* ("The Image of the Immigrant in our Literature," 1913–19), and wrote about contemporary Hebrew writers, European writers whose works were translated into Hebrew, and on Yiddish literature. In his literary critiques, Brenner insists on "engagé writing" as opposed to art for art's sake. He nevertheless rejected ideological tendentiousness whether it was socialist or Zionist, and advocated the kind of literature that educates by revealing truth. He therefore examined the creative writer on his sincerity and on his ability to harmonize experience and expression. He opposed florid phraseology and verbiage, and also the attempts of the writers in Ereẓ Israel to glorify their actual situation.

Brenner translated into Hebrew: G. Hauptmann's *Die Weber* (1910), *Michael Kramer* (1911), *Einsame Menschen* (1912), *Fuhrmann Henschel* (1913); Dostoevski's *Crime and Punishment* (1924); Tolstoy's *The Landlord and his Work* (1919); A. Ruppin's *The Jews in Modern Times* (1914); and Trumpeldor's diary. He also wrote and translated into Yiddish. In his translations as in his original writings, Brenner used a simple style, avoiding the "elevated" manner of Mendele and Bialik. Contemporary critics received Brenner the writer with mixed feelings. Some condemned his style and his failure to establish aesthetic distance between the author and the aesthetic object (J. Klausner, Lubetzki). Others praised his courageous sincerity and his impact upon society, despite his artistic shortcomings (S. Zemach). Bialik found him to be an important author who wrote rather carelessly, while Berdyczewski stressed the great sincerity of his writings which compensated for his shortcomings as a novelist. Critics of a later generation (D. Sadan) emphasized his complex inner world and his heroes' attitudes to life; others tried to interpret Brenner from a purely sociological point of view. Modern Israel critics tend to refer back to Brenner, some stressing the existentialist aspects of his works (M. Meged, N. Zach), while others praise the structural and stylistic aspects (D. Miron, N. Zach, G. Shaked), pointing out the simplicity, directness, and authenticity of the style. Brenner became the prototype for many young writers who tried to break away from the patriotic literature written in the wake of Israel's War of Independence. Through his writings they found a link with European existentialist literature. List of his works in English translation appears in Goell, Bibliography, 64–87.

Bibliography: *Kitvei Y. Ḥ. Brenner,* 3 vols. (1955, 1960, 1967); J. Yaari-Poleskin, *Me-Ḥayyei Yosef-Ḥayyim Brenner* (1922), bibliography 177–200; A. D. Friedman, *Y. Ḥ. Brenner: Ishiyyuto vi-Yẓirato* (1923); I. Lubetzki, in: *Haolam,* 8 (1908), 118; J. Klausner, in: *Ha-Shilo'aḥ,* 7 (1901), 171–5; H. Zeitlin, in: *Ha-Tekufah* (1922), 14–15, 617–45; J. Rabinowitz, in: *Hedim,* 2 (1923) no. 10, 51–56; Y. Kaufmann, *Golah ve-Nekhar* (1930), 405–17; F. Lachower, *Rishonim ve-Aḥaronim,* 2 (1935), 106–32; J. Fichmann, *Benei Dor* (1951), 9–121; D. Sadan, *Bein Din le-Ḥeshbon* (1963), 137–54; B. Kurzweil, *Bein Ḥazon le-Vein ha-Absurdi* (1966), 261–91; D. Meron, in: *Gazit,* 19 (1961–62) no. 9–12, p. 50–54; N. Zach, in: *Ammot,* 1 (1962), 40–46; G. Shaked, in: *Moznayim,* 13, nos. 3–4 (1961), 242–6; Shunami, Bibl., 3311–3313; Waxman, Literature 4 (1960^2), 92–105. [G.Sh.]

BRENNER, VICTOR (1871–1924), U.S. medalist. Born in Lithuania, Brenner received training in various crafts before going to America in 1890. He settled in New York, worked as a die cutter and engraver of badges, and studied at the Art Students' League and the National Gallery of Design. In 1898 he went to Paris where he studied under Roty and Charpentier, the famous medalists. On his return to the United States he was recognized as one of the country's foremost medalists. He was chosen to model Theodore Roosevelt's head for the Panama Canal medal and Lincoln's for the familiar one-cent piece, which remained unchanged for 50 years. The Lincoln design was well liked, except for the undue prominence given to Brenner's initials. Brenner made many medallions, including Amerigo Vespucci, John Paul Jones, and Whistler. Brenner also displayed a mastery of the nude or draped human figure. His three-dimensional work is less known; an outstanding example is the Schenley Memorial Fountain in Pittsburgh (1916). Of Jewish interest are his engravings of the pianist and composer Rafael Joseffy, the scholar Solomon Schechter, the painter Abraham Walkowitz, and the financiers Jacob Schiff and Solomon Loeb. Brenner is one of the few holders of the J. Sanford Saltus Award of the American Numismatist Society.

Bibliography: *Catalogue of Medals and Plaques by V. Brenner Exhibited at the Grolier Club* (1907); DAB, 3 (1928); Kellogg, in: *Survey* (Oct. 2, 1915); *Numismatist* (May 1924); *New York Times* (April 6, 1924). [Ed.]

BRENTANO, U.S. family of booksellers. August (1831–1886) was the founder of the firm of Brentano's, the largest book-selling firm in the world with bookstores in many cities of the United States, London, and Paris. Born in Austria, Brentano emigrated to the United States in 1853 where he sold newspapers on the streets of New York for two years before setting up a stand for the sale of local and foreign newspapers and magazines. In 1858 he opened a book and stationery store, and in 1870 established the much larger Brentano's Literary Emporium which became New York's leading bookstore, and served at the same time as a meeting place for the literati in New York City. In the 1870s he was joined in his business by his nephews August (1853–1899) who was born in Evansville, Indiana, Arthur (1858–1944), and Simon (1859–1915), the latter two natives of Cincinnati. In 1877 August Brentano sold the business to his nephews, who expanded the firm and incorporated it in 1887. Simon, who had become head of the firm upon his uncle's retirement, devoted much of his time to the study of fire control and wrote a number of books on the subject. His principal work, which was translated into many languages, is entitled *The Control of Fire* (1904). In 1894 August Brentano was forced to retire because of illness, leaving his brothers Simon and Arthur to continue to direct and expand Brentano's, which they converted from a corporation into a partnership, with Simon as president of the company. Simon was later succeeded by his brother Arthur, who was also director of Brentano's Ltd., London, and Brentano's S.A., Paris. Arthur Brentano, a fervent canoeist, founded the American Canoe Association and published its magazine. Lowell (1895–1950), Simon's son, entered the firm after graduation from Harvard in 1918 and took over the responsibility for Brentano's editorial department. He wrote a number of novels and plays, some in collaboration with other writers: *The Spider* (1932); *Family Affairs* (1929); *The Penguin Pool Murder* (1931); *Lady Cop* (1934); and *Torches in the Night* (1937). Some of his books were made into motion pictures.

Bibliography: T. Mahoney and L. Sloane, *Great Merchants* (1966), 133–48. [Ed.]

BRESCH (or **Bres**), **JUDAH LOEB BEN MOSES NAPHTALI** (15th–16th century), author of an adaptation of a Yiddish Bible translation. Born in Poland, Bresch spent part of his life in Germany and Italy. In 1560 he published in Cremona a Yiddish translation of the Pentateuch, the Five Scrolls, and the *haftarot,* to which he added a translation of an excerpt of Rashi's commentary. The work is distinguished for its faithfulness to the text. Steinschneider is of the opinion that Bresch's Pentateuch was an improved version of the Yiddish translation by the convert Michael Adam (Constance, 1544). The Yiddish translation of the Pentateuch published in Basle in 1583 is a facsimile of the Cremona edition.

Bibliography: W. Staerk and A. Leitzmann, *Juedisch-deutsche Bibeluebersetzungen* (1923), 114–5, 129–30; E. Schulmann, *Sefat Yehudit-Ashkenazit ve-Sifrutah* (1913), 9f. [I.Sch./Ed.]

BRESCIA, city in northern Italy. Inscriptions found in Brescia mentioning a *Mater Synagogae,* and an **Archisynagogos,* show that there was a Jewish community

ספר המחברות למר עמנואל ז"ל

Preface to the collection of poems by Immanuel b. Solomon of Rome, *Sefer ha-Maḥbarot,* printed in Brescia by Gershom Soncino, 1491. Jerusalem, J.N.U.L.

there in the late classical period. In 1426, Brescia came under the sovereignty of Venice; in 1444 and 1458 the town unsuccessfully applied to the pope for permission to admit Jewish moneylenders. Later, however, moneylending was evidently permitted. The Jews in Brescia were attacked in 1475 after the blood libel case of Simon of *Trent, but further rioting was prevented by order of the Venetian Senate. In 1481 an attempt to prohibit moneylending in Brescia was unsuccessful. *Bernardino da Feltre preached anti-Jewish sermons in 1494 and a number of Jews were again expelled from the city. After the French captured Brescia in 1509, the houses of the Jews were plundered, moneylending was prohibited, and most of the Jews were expelled. On its reversion to Venice, however, in 1519, they were allowed to return. Most of the Jews were expelled again in 1572 and no Jewish community has since existed in Brescia. Between 1491 and 1494 the printer Gershom b. Moses *Soncino was active in Brescia. His productions included the *Meshal ha-Kadmoni* of Isaac ibn *Sahula, the first illustrated Hebrew book; the *Sefer Maḥbarot le-Mar Immanuel ha-Romi* (1491) of *Immanuel b. Solomon of Rome, and the third complete edition of the Hebrew Bible (1494).

Bibliography: F. Glissenti, *Gli ebrei nel Bresciano . . .* (1890); idem, *Gli ebrei nel Bresciano . . . Nuove ricerche e studi* (1891); Frey, Corpus, 1 (1936), 576; A. Freimann (ed.), *Thesaurus typographiae Hebraicae* (1924), A76–A81; M. Steinschneider and D. Cassel, *Juedische Typographie und juedischer Buchhandel* (1938), 16; D. W. Amram, *Makers of Hebrew Books in Italy* (1909), 70ff.; L. Ruggini, *Ebrei e orientali nell'Italia settentrionale . . .* (= *Studia et Documenta Historiae et Juris*, 25 (1959), 186–308, index).

[U.C./ED.]

The Sklowar synagogue in Breslau, built c. 1790, partially destroyed by the Nazis in November 1938 and later used by them as a winecellar and warehouse. Jerusalem, Israel Museum Archives.

BRESLAU (Polish **Wroclaw**), city in Silesia, Poland (in Germany until 1945). The ownership by Jews of villages in the vicinity of Breslau (Klein-Tinz and Falkendorf) is recorded (1180–1208). The earliest evidence of Jews in Breslau is a tombstone of 1203. In 1267 a church synod decided to restrict the rights of the Jews in Breslau but Duke Henry IV granted them privileges between 1270 and 1290. In 1347 the community was placed under the jurisdiction of the municipality. The medieval community owned synagogues, a bathhouse, and cemeteries, from which a number of tombstones have survived. In the course of the 14th century, Jews were expelled from Breslau several times (1319, 1349, 1360). In 1453, 41 Jews were burned at the stake and the rest expelled after they had been accused of desecrating the *Host by the Franciscan John of *Capistrano. An imperial privilege *de non tolerandis Judaeos* was given to Breslau in 1455 excluding all Jews from the city, excepting those visiting the fair. The prohibition remained in force *de jure* until 1744.

From the beginning of the 16th century Jews began to visit the city, and sometimes stayed longer periods, in order to attend the fairs, which were important for trading throughout the neighboring countries. The municipal council gradually began extending visiting permits to Jews at other times. The Jews also instituted a special type of communal organization for those attending the fair. The "fair treasurers" *(Parnasei ha-Yarid)* represented the Jews to the authorities, levied imposts from them, which they assessed in accordance with Jewish law, and took precautions against thieves and swindlers. Associated with them were the "fair arbitrators" *(Dayyanei ha-Yarid)*, two from Poland and one from Moravia, who were empowered to levy fines and impose the ban. The "fair committee" *(Va'ad ha-Yarid)* supervised dietary requirements for Jews attending the fairs. Functioning "between the fairs" were special officials (the *Schammesse*—שַׁמָּשִׁים) appointed by the Council of the Four Lands. It levied certain sums from Jews attending the fairs, and also farmed out the right to convey *etrogim* for the Jews in Poland via the Breslau fair. These officials eventually became permanent residents of Breslau, as did a number of other Jews who attended the fairs.

In the late 17th century individual Jews succeeded in obtaining limited rights of settlement in Breslau because of their usefulness to the imperial *mint and their importance for trade with Poland and Bohemia-Moravia. The two categories of *Schutzjuden* ("protected Jews") enjoyed either imperial or municipal protection. They were grouped according to their place of origin in various synagogue congregations *(Schulen)*, forming a loose union without a rabbi or cemetery, since there was officially no community in existence. They combined with the congregations formed from about 1670 in the suburbs of Breslau. One of the oldest institutions of the Breslau community was the burial society, established in 1726.

After the capture of the city by the Prussians in 1741, the new authorities permitted the organization of a community limited to 12 families in 1744, and confirmed the appointment of Bendix Reuben Gomperz (Baruch Wesel) as its first rabbi. The community acquired a cemetery in 1761, replacing the cemeteries of *Lissa, *Dyhernfurth, and *Krotoszyn. The importance of the Jews for trade with Poland led the authorities gradually to increase the number of Jews admitted as residents. These held various degrees of restricted rights, and consisted of the "generally privileged" *(Generalprivilegierte)*, the "privileged," the "tolerated," and the *Fix-Entristen*, i.e., those paying a regular fee for temporary sojourn, as well as the *Schutzgenossen*, i.e., persons employed in communal or private service. In 1776, there were nearly 2,000 Jews in Breslau. In 1791 a new regulation divided the Jews into *Generalprivilegierte*, who formed the "community"; their relatives, *Stammnumeranten;* and *Extra-Ordinaere* (i.e., those outside the privileged categories). Although the latter formed the majority, they were not recognized as members of the community. The community was led and controlled by the wealthy "generally privileged" Jews. The leading Breslau families were generally in favor of *Haskalah and *Reform tendencies. Those of this group who stopped short of conversion, either for themselves or their children, attempted to prepare for emancipation by providing what they considered a suitable education for Jews. In order to carry out their ideas, they utilized their connections with tolerant Prussian officials, to establish schools providing a modernized education for the poorer families. Such were the Koenigliche Wilhelmsschule, established in 1791, and the Maedchenschule fuer arme Toechter ("School for Poor Girls," 1801), which were recognized and encouraged by the government. These Haskalah-promoted schools met with resistance from Orthodox Jews.

Modern Community. The division between the majority of the community and its leadership became accentuated after the Prussian Emancipation Edict of 1812. The new communal representatives increasingly tended to work for Reform and assimilation. Their attitude gave rise to serious dissensions within the community. Solomon *Tiktin (d. 1843) and his son Gedaliah (officiated 1843–86) led the Orthodox wing against the Reform wing led by Abraham *Geiger (officiated in Breslau 1840–63). The community, however, remained an "Einheitsgemeinde" (according to the terms of the Statute of March 6, 1856) with two separate religious commissions (*Kultuskommission*), whose Orthodox and Liberal sections each maintained their own rabbis, synagogues, and schools. The "Storch" synagogue (1829), the first large synagogue building to be constructed in Breslau, and the private synagogues were governed by the Orthodox commission. Both sections of the community led an active Jewish religious and cultural life.

Several rabbis of Breslau were distinguished scholars. Noted among the Orthodox section were Joseph Jonas Fraenkel (1705–1793), Isaiah b. Judah Leib *Berlin (Pick), Ferdinand Rosenthal (1887–1921), Moses Hoffmann (1921–38), and B. Hamburger (1938 until his deportation to Poland in 1943). Liberals included besides Abraham Geiger, Manuel *Joel (1863–90), Jacob *Guttmann (1891–1919), Hermann *Vogelstein, and Reinhold Lewin (1938 until his deportation to Poland in 1943). Alongside the talmudic scholars, there gathered a literary circle (Breslauer Dichterschule) of Hebrew essayists and authors (Mendel Broese, Marcus Friedenthal, Raphael *Fuerstenthal, Moses Koerner, Joel *Loewe-Brill, Heinrich Miro, Solomon *Pappenheim, Suesskind Raschkow, and David *Samoszc). A "Bruedergesellschaft" was founded before 1800.

The study and reading circle Israelitischer Lehr- und Leserverein was established in 1842, its library later belonging to the community. The first modern Jewish theological seminary, the Juedisch-Theologisches Seminar, was established in Breslau by Zachariah *Frankel in 1854. With its celebrated library it became a center of Jewish scholarship and spiritual activity until 1938. It also published the first comprehensive Jewish learned journal, **Monatsschrift fuer Geschichte und Wissenschaft des Judentums* (MGWJ). The first Jewish students' fraternity, Viadrina, was founded in Breslau in 1886, as a reaction to the anti-Semitic tone of the general student bodies. The *Juedisches Volksblatt*, later renamed *Juedische Zeitung fuer Ostdeutschland*, was published in Breslau from 1895 to 1937, and the *Breslauer Juedisches Gemeindeblatt* from 1924 to 1938. The *Blau-Weiss youth movement was founded in Breslau by Joseph Marcus in 1912. Jewish cultural activities expanded after World War I. A Jewish elementary school was established in 1921, followed two years later by a Reformrealgymnasium, both of conservative orientation. The "Neuer Juedischer Schulverein" established a school of Liberal orientation. A youth institute and a home for the aged was opened in 1930. Two outstanding personalities of the Breslau community were the historian Heinrich *Graetz, of the theological seminary, and Ferdinand *Lassalle, one of the founders of the German workers movement.

The Jewish population of Breslau numbered 3,255 in 1810; 7,384 in 1849; 13,916 in 1871; 19,743 in 1900; 20,212 in 1910; 23,240 in 1925; 20,202 in 1933; and 10,309 in 1939.

Under Nazi Germany and After. In November 1938, Jewish educational, cultural, and social activities were disrupted. All prayer houses, including the "New Synagogue" (completed in 1872), as well as schools, were destroyed. The "Storch" synagogue was the sole house of worship still standing after November 1938. Beginning in September 1941, Breslau Jews were driven from their homes and crowded into *"Judenhaeuser,"* to be deported a few months later to Gruessau, Tormersdorf, and other places in Silesia, and from there to *Auschwitz. From April 1942 the remaining Jews in Breslau were deported directly to Auschwitz, *Sobibor, *Riga, or *Theresienstadt. By 1943 only partners of mixed marriages and some children remained of the Breslau community. Of the 3,800 deported to Theresienstadt, only 200 survived. Most of the others who were deported also perished. The oldest cemetery, consecrated in 1761, was destroyed. The communal archives, founded in 1924, were preserved in a cemetery building. They were transferred to the Jewish Historical Institute in Warsaw in 1945.

After the war a community in Breslau was established by Jews from Poland, with the "Storch" as its synagogue. In 1960 there were about 1,200 Jewish families living in Breslau, and there were three Jewish producers' cooperatives. In 1967 a Yiddish state elementary school, that also provided secondary education, functioned in the city. After the Six-Day War most of the Jews who lived in the city emigrated to Israel.

Hebrew Printing. Some 190 Hebrew books were printed in Breslau between 1719 and the end of the 19th century. Toward the end of the 18th century the Grassche Stadt-Buchdruckerei was active in face of fierce opposition from the privileged *Dyhernfurth printers. When the Dyhernfurth monopolies lapsed, Loebel Katzenellenbogen-Sulzbach, who had served his apprenticeship in Dyhernfurth, set up a press in 1814, with his son Hirsch as partner from 1825 and sole owner from 1836 to 1877, when it was sold to T. Schatzky.

Bibliography: M. Brann, *Geschichte der Juden in Schlesien*, 6 vols. (1896–1917), passim; idem, in: *Jahrbuch zur Belehrung und Unterhaltung*, 39 (1891), 75–81 (list of Hebrew books printed in Breslau); Germ Jud, 2 (1968), 127–33; Freudenthal, in: MGWJ, 37 (1893), 43ff.; L. Lewin, *Geschichte der israelitischen Krankenverpflegungsanstalt Breslau 1726–1926* (1926); A. Heppner, *Juedische Persoenlichkeiten in und aus Breslau* (1931); Bronsztein, in: JJSO, 7 (1965), 246–75; B. Brilling, *Geschichte der Juden in Breslau von 1454–1702* (1960); M. Freudenthal, in: MGWJ, 37 (1893), 41ff.; J. Landsberger, *ibid.*, 32 (1883), 543–63; R. F. Schaeffer, in: BLBI, 10 (1967), 298–308.

[B.Br.]

BRESLAU, ARYEH LOEB BEN ḤAYYIM (1741–1809), rabbi and author. Aryeh Loeb was born in Breslau but lived from his childhood in Lissa. He served first as rabbi in the *bet ha-midrash* of Daniel Jaffe in Berlin (see responsa *Penei Aryeh*, no. 1), then as rabbi in Emden, and in 1781 succeeded Abraham Lipschutz as rabbi of Rotterdam, where he remained for the rest of his life (*ibid.*, no. 40). He gained a reputation as a profound talmudist, and several of the outstanding scholars of the time, among them Phinehas ha-Levi *Horowitz and Meir *Weyl, addressed halakhic problems to him. He was the author of *Penei Aryeh* (Amsterdam, 1790), responsa, halakhic rulings, and expositions, in which he included *Ma'amar Yesod ha-Shetarot* in 12 chapters. His responsa, distinguished by their simple and clear style and written in a pure Hebrew, reflect his tendency toward a certain degree of independence in halakhic decision. They also contain explanations of various biblical and midrashic passages (no. 60). In connection with a responsum on levirate marriage, he discusses the problem of immortality, stressing that the essence of levirate marriage is connected with the doctrine of metempsychosis and the improvement of the soul (*tikkun ha-nefesh*), and its ultimate perfection (no. 79). Breslau also had a general education, and was in touch with Christian scholars in Holland. The prayers that he composed in Hebrew in connection with the Franco-Dutch war of 1793 were published both in Hebrew (*Tefillot u-Vakkashot*, Amsterdam, 1793), and in a Dutch translation with an introduction by the Christian Jan Scharp (Rotterdam, 1793). One of his poems, *"Mizmor le-Shabbat,"* shows considerable talent. His sons adopted the family name Lowenstamm ("descendant of the lion") in reference to their father's name Aryeh ("lion") Loeb. Two of them, Abraham and Ḥayyim Lowenstamm, followed him in the rabbinate, as did Menahem Mendel, the son of the latter who was rabbi of Rotterdam.

Bibliography: A. Walden, *Shem ha-Gedolim he-Ḥadash*, 2 (1864), 33a, no. 27; D. A. Ritter, in: *Oẓar ha-Sifrut*, 5 (1896), 265–8; L. Lewin, *Geschichte der Juden in Lissa* (1904), 199–200, 251, 258, 339; Z. Hurvitz, *Kitvei ha-Ge'onim* (1928), 22; S. M. Chones, *Toledot ha-Posekim* (1910), 493.

[Y.Ho.]

BRESLAU, JOSEPH MOSES BEN DAVID (1691–1752), German rabbinical scholar apparently born in the city of that name. Breslau studied under Abraham *Broda, whose daughter he married. He served as rabbi in Krefeld and, from 1743 until his death, in Bamberg. He was author of: (1) *Shoresh Yosef* (1730), on the laws and principles of *Migo* (in talmudic law the credence given to a party in a lawsuit on the premise that if he were lying he could have told a more convincing lie); (2) *Ḥok Yosef* (1730), on the laws of Passover, comprising novellae on the *Oraḥ Ḥayyim* sections of the *Shulḥan Arukh (429–94). In it Breslau criticizes the *Ḥok Ya'akov* of Jacob Reischer. The two books were published together under the title *Ḥukkim Tovim* (1767). Reischer wrote a reply entitled *Lo Hibbit Aven be-Ya'akov*, which was published in the 1814 edition of *Ḥukkim Tovim;* (3) *Ketonet Yosef*, sermons, published by his son, Abraham of Muehlhausen, as an appendix to the *Toledot Avraham* (1769) of Broda. His glosses on *Oraḥ Ḥayyim* and on *Yoreh De'ah*, as well as responsa, remain in manuscript.

Bibliography: Fuenn, Keneset, 459; A. Eckstein, *Geschichte der Juden im ehemaligen Fuerstbistum Bamberg* (1898), 171–3; S. M. Chones, *Toledot ha-Posekim* (1910), 262.

[Y.Ho.]

BRESLAW, JOSEPH (1887–1957), U.S. labor leader. Breslaw, who was born in Odessa, went to the United States in 1907. He worked as a cloak presser in the garment industry and joined a local union in 1909. Breslaw was rapidly promoted, and in 1916 became its manager. By 1922 he had become the dominant voice in one of the metropolitan area's most important locals of the International Ladies' Garment Workers' Union, and was elected vice-president of the ILGWU, leading the Union's right wing in the struggle against the communists. Unlike other prominent immigrant Jewish unionists, especially those who went to America after the 1905 revolution, Breslaw did not share a revolutionary tradition or evince socialist sympathies. He acted as a right-wing mainstay for the anti-Communist administration of President Morris Sigman between 1922 and 1925, but was forced off the General Executive Board during the compromise effort with the radical wing. However, upon the collapse of the compromise arrangements with the Communists, Breslaw was called back to office (1929), and a year later was placed in charge of the successful strike in New York City's dress industry. He was a loyal lieutenant to David *Dubinsky. Though more conservative than most garment workers, Breslaw, thoughout his career, was still more radical than the non-Jewish members of the American labor movement. In 1936 he joined the newly founded American Labor Party, and became a member of its state executive committee. Breslaw was prominent in establishing the ILGWU's health center. He also served on various committees to aid Palestine labor colonies, and, for over a decade, was chairman of the American Trade Union Council for the *Histadrut.

[M.D.]

BRESSE, region in France. There is proof of Jewish settlement in Bresse from at least 1275. The main localities inhabited by Jews during the Middle Ages were *Bourg-en-Bresse, Bâgé, Pont-de-Vaux, Louhans, and Pont-de-Veyle. Jews often levied the tolls. They remained longest in Bagé, leaving the town in 1524.

Bibliography: Gerson, in: *Revue Savoisienne*, 26 (1885), 82ff.; idem, in: REJ, 8 (1884), 235ff.; Z. Szajkowski, *Analytical Franco-Jewish Gazetteer* (1966), 288.

[B.Bl.]

BRESSELAU, MEYER ISRAEL (d. 1839), Hebrew writer and one of the leaders of the Reform movement. He was the state notary for the Jews of Hamburg. In 1818, together with I. S. *Fraenkel he edited and adapted a prayer book for the Hamburg Reform Temple under the title *Seder ha-Avodah*. In answer to *Elleh Divrei ha-Berit* (Altona, 1819), a pamphlet which collated the views of the greatest Orthodox rabbis of Western Europe against Reform Judaism and its innovations, he published anonymously his polemic work *Ḥerev Nokemet Nekam-Berit* (Dessau, 1819; reprinted as appendix 4 in S. Bernfeld's *Toledot ha-Reformaẓyon ha-Datit be-Yisrael*, 1900). *Ḥerev Nokemet Nekam-Berit*, a rhymed work written in a satirical biblical style, is remarkable in its witty take-off on the Orthodox rabbis who opposed the reforms in the Hamburg Reform synagogue (temple). It ranks among the best Hebrew polemic literature written at the time of the Haskalah. To counteract Bresselau's polemic work M. L. Reinitz published *Lahat ha-Ḥerev ha-Mithappekhet* (1820).

Bibliography: Zinberg, Sifrut, 5 (1959), 298; Waxman, Literature, 3 (1960^2), 352, 408.

[G.El]

BRESSLAU, ERNST (1877–1935), German zoologist. After taking a medical degree, he studied zoology at the University of Strasbourg, where he subsequently became professor. His major research interests were the origin of the mammary glands and the biology of the turbellarians, a class of flatworms. When in 1918 Strasbourg became part of France, Bresslau went to Frankfort as head of the zoology department of the Institute for Experimental Therapy founded by Paul Ehrlich. In 1926 he became professor of zoology at the University of Cologne, where he established and built up an outstanding research institute. Bresslau left Germany shortly after Hitler's accession to power and in 1934 became professor of zoology at the newly-founded University of Saõ Paulo, Brazil. He started to organize a zoological institute there, but died before his task was completed.

[M.L.G.]

BRESSLAU, HARRY (1848–1926), German historian. Born in Dannenberg, Hanover, he taught at the Philanthropin school at Frankfort and at a Jewish orphanage in Berlin. Bresslau joined the faculty of the University of Berlin in 1872 and was appointed associate professor in 1877. From 1890 to 1918 he was professor at the University of Strasbourg, but when Strasbourg reverted to France in 1918, he was expelled as a German national and spent his remaining years in Heidelberg. Bresslau was a member of the editorial board of the *Monumenta Germaniae Historica* and published a history of the *Monumenta* (1921). He edited the journal of the society for the study of earlier German history *Neues Archiv der Gesellschaft fuer aeltere deutsche Geschichtskunde* from 1889 to 1904 and in 1907 founded the historical records periodical *Archiv fuer Urkundenforschung.* He compiled the volumes dealing with the emperors Henry II and Conrad II in the *Jahrbuecher des deutschen Reiches* (1879, 1884). His manual on the study of records, *Handbuch der Urkundenlehre fuer Deutschland und Italien* (2 vols., 1889–1915), is a basic source-book in its field. Bresslau was a founder and president of the commission for the history of the Jews in Germany and contributed extensively to Jewish historical journals. In 1880 he wrote *Zur Judenfrage,* a reply to *Treitschke's attack. His autobiography was published in *Die Geschichtswissenschaft der Gegenwart in Selbstdarstellung* (1926). Bresslau's daughter, Helena, was the wife of Albert Schweitzer.

Bibliography: P. Kehr, in: *Neues Archiv,* 47 (1927), 255–66.

[Z.Av./Ed.]

BRESSLER, DAVID MAURICE (1879–1942), U.S. social worker and leader in American Jewish efforts to assist Jewish immigrants to the United States, and to aid European Jews during and after World War I. Bressler was born in Charlottenburg, Germany, and was taken to the United States in 1884. He served as manager of the Industrial Removal Office (1900–16), a branch of the Jewish Agricultural and Industrial Aid Society, directing the resettlement of 75,000 immigrant Jews from congested Eastern port cities of the United States to less crowded areas of the country. During World War I Bressler joined the *American Jewish Joint Distribution Committee, in which he played an important role until his death. During the 1920s he headed a number of campaigns to aid European Jews. Bressler served as national chairman of the Allied Jewish Relief campaign of 1930. During the 1930s Governor Herbert Lehman appointed him to important posts in New York State agencies.

[I.Y.]

BREST-LITOVSK (Brisk, Heb. בריסק דליטא; until 1921 Brest-Litovsk; from 1921 until 1945 Brześć nad Bugiem; after 1945 Brest), capital of Brest oblast, Belorussian S.S.R. In the medieval grand duchy of *Lithuania, from the 14th to the 17th centuries, in particular after the union of Poland and Lithuania in 1569, it was the main center of Lithuanian Jewry. Its situation on the River Bug, at the junction of commercial routes and near the borders of the two countries, made Brest-Litovsk an important communications and commercial center. The first Jews settled there under the grand duke Kiejstut (Kestutis; 1341–82). His son Vitold (Vytautas) granted them a generous charter in 1388, which was later extended to all the Jews in the duchy. Jewish merchants from Brest-Litovsk are mentioned in 1423–33 in the muncipal records of Danzig (Gdansk) where they bought textiles, furs, and other goods. The community increased toward the end of the 15th and in the first half of the 16th century, and became one of the largest in Lithuania. It also became the most important organizationally as contacts with Poland steadily expanded. The Jews of Brest-Litovsk engaged in commerce, crafts, and agriculture. Some conducted extensive financial operations, farming the customs dues, taxes, and other government imposts. They also farmed and owned estates. Their business connections extended throughout and beyond the duchy. By 1483 Jews in Brest-Litovsk had established commercial ties with Venice.

In 1495 all Jews who refused to accept Christianity were expelled from Lithuania. Only one convert, of the *Jozefowicz family, remained behind in Brest-Litovsk. The Jews were permitted to return in 1503, and the community regained its former eminence. Michael Jozefowicz played a leading role in its communal affairs in the first half of the 16th century. Records of 1566 show that there were 156 Jewish-owned houses in the town out of a total of 746. Two years later, after the great fire there, the Jews were exempted by King Sigismund Augustus from paying tax for nine years, provided that they thenceforth built their homes of stone only. The Jews in Brest-Litovsk took an increasing share in the Polish export trade to Germany and the import trade from Germany and Austria in the 16th century. Their financial success and the scale and range of the activities of the great merchants, such as the three Jozefowicz brothers, the customs contractor and merchant Michael Rybczykowicz, and many others, was partly due to the combination of customs farming with export and import business. In Brest-Litovsk the Jews could continue to engage in agriculture, and 16% of the real estate was Jewish-owned. The influential Saul *Wahl of Padua, who lived in Brest-Litovsk, established a synagogue and yeshivah in the town.

The satisfactory relationship between the Jews and the townspeople in the 16th century subsequently deteriorated. In 1636 Christian students made a savage raid *(Schuelergelaeuf)* on the Jews. The Lithuanian Council (see *Councils of the Lands) defined it as a "calamity" and treated it as a matter of concern to Lithuanian Jewry as a whole, to be dealt with at its expense. Jewish stores were looted and burned in 1637 by the townspeople, but the Polish authorities compelled the municipality to restore the stolen merchandise to its Jewish owners and punish the rioters. A mixed Jewish-Christian watch was instituted to guard the stores. Despite the increasing anti-Jewish feelings fostered by the clergy, kings Sigismund III and Ladislas IV ratified the Jewish charters. During the *Chmielnicki uprising of 1648–49 many Jews who had the means escaped from Brest-Litovsk to Great Poland and Danzig; hundreds of those who remained were massacred (according to one source, 2,000). Shortly afterward, Jews resettled in Brest-Litovsk and were granted a charter of protection in 1655 from King John Casimir. The wars with Russia, Sweden, and Turkey caused much hardship among the Jews, and many were massacred by the Russian army in 1660. In 1661, in order to relieve their economic distress, the king exempted the Jews from the obligation to billet troops and all other taxes for four years; Jewish debtors were granted a three-year moratorium. In 1669 King Michael Wisniowiecki confirmed the privileges granted in former charters, and permitted the Jews to retain the land and buildings they had owned before the wars, including synagogues, courthouses, public baths, cemeteries, and stores. Jews were permitted to engage in every sphere of commerce and crafts, and required to pay only the same taxes as Christians. The municipality and non-Jewish citizens were ordered to cooperate in suppressing anti-Jewish agitation. The privileges were ratified in 1676 and in 1720. Twenty-two Jewish merchants were recorded in the city in 1662, ten of whom were innkeepers who paid a special tax. By 1676, there were 525 Jews (excluding children under 11) living in Brest-Litovsk. The number grew during the 18th century. The 1766 census recorded 3,353 Jews in the town and its environs. Toward the end of the 18th century there were fresh disturbances between the Jews and the non-Jewish citizens, in particular in 1792. A memorandum was presented by 20 Jewish representatives to the Polish *Sejm* (Diet) urging that the complaints of the Jews in Brest-Litovsk should receive justice.

For many generations the Brest-Litovsk community assumed the lead in communal affairs and cultural activities of Lithuania (see *Councils of Lands). It was one of the three founding communities of the Council of Lithuania (later expanded to four and then to five constituents) in which Brest obtained the widest area of jurisdiction. At first (1623–31) the Council of Lithuania convened in Brest-Litovsk, and 19 of its 42 meetings took place there. The delegates and rabbi of Brest-Litovsk were for long given precedence in the Council. The community represented Lithuanian Jewry before the central authorities according to the following resolution: "It has been thus decided. If His Majesty the King has occasion to visit one of the three principal communities, in the event of his arrival in *Grodno or . . . *Pinsk, they will inform the Brest community. Should the Brest community send their representative to approach His Majesty the King with a gift, then all the expenses incurred thereby shall be defrayed by the Council. Should the Brest community omit to send a representative, then half [only] of the expenses [incurred by the community where the king came] shall be defrayed by the Council, and half by the community concerned" (S. Dubnow, *Pinkas Medinat Lita* (1925). Council Session 1639, par. 398, p. 80). A resolution of 1644 further expresses the precedence accorded to the Brest-Litovsk community: "As to the order of signatures of the honorable members of the Council, it has been thus decided: they shall sign in the following order: first the Council members from Brest . . ." (*ibid.,* Council Session 1644, par. 415, p. 86). The demands of the Brest-Litovsk community that the importance of its institutions and their sacred character should be recognized throughout Lithuania are manifested in the following resolution: ". . . all the members of the sacred conventicle, the conventicle of the Great Synagogue, the Klaus in Brest-Litovsk . . . All know full well that this Great Synagogue is a holy place . . . for many generations its sacredness has been established. . . . He who seeks the Lord, whose spirit is moved to wisdom and understanding, knowledge and fear of the Lord, will come to this Great Synagogue, will take on his shoulders this burden, will bear the yoke of Torah study in groups [of students]." The resolution was moved to persuade the Council to undertake the custody of funds for the institution, and to pay annual sums to it out of the funds (*ibid.,* Council Session 1667, par. 619, pp. 147–8). The leadership assumed by the Brest-Litovsk community in social and economic affairs is instanced by its attempts to control the contracting for vodka-distilling and milling (see **Arenda*) for the good of all the members of the community: "that many should have a living" (Joel Sirkes, Responsa, 1 (1697, 1834), par. 60).

Brest-Litovsk was a stronghold of the **Mitnaggedim* in opposition to *Ḥasidism. Some of the early disputations between the leaders of the two trends took place there. Distinguished rabbis officiating in Brest include Jehiel b. Aaron Luria, the grandfather of Solomon *Luria (mid-15th century); Moses Raskowitz; Menahem Mendel *Frank; Kalonymos, the father-in-law of Solomon Luria (16th century); Solomon Luria; Judah Leib b. Obadiah Eilenburg, author of *Minḥat Yehudah* (1609); Moses Lipschitz; Ephraim Zalman *Schor, author of *Tevu'at Shor* (1613); Joel b. Samuel *Sirkes; Abraham Meir *Epstein; Jacob Schor, author of *Beit Ya'akov* (1693); David *Oppenheim (17th century); *Aryeh Judah Leib, author of *Sha'agat Aryeh;* Abraham b. David Katzenellbogen; Naḥman Halperin; and *Aaron b. Meir, author of *Minḥat Aharon* (18th century); Ẓevi Hirsch b. Mordecai *Orenstein; Moses Joshua Judah Leib *Diskin; Joseph Baer *Soloveichik; his son Ḥayyim; and his grandson Ze'ev (Welvelei; see *Soloveichik family).

After its incorporation into Russia in 1793 the economic importance of Brest-Litovsk diminished. Many historic edifices of the Jewish quarter, including the old synagogue and cemetery, were demolished to give way to the building of a fortress in 1832. The economic position again improved after the completion of the Dnieper-Bug Canal in 1841, and the Jewish community, which handled most of the commerce and industry in the city, began to grow appreciably. A tobacco factory and two large mills were established by Jews in 1845. A hospital was erected in 1838, a new synagogue during 1851–61, and a home for widows in 1866.

The Jewish population numbered 8,135 in 1847 and 27,005 in 1889 (out of a total of 41,625). In 1886, 4,364 Jews were occupied as artisans and 1,235 as merchants (out of 25,000). There were 30,608 Jewish residents in 1897 (out of 46,568), 3,506 of them artisans, who were nearly all Jews at the time, many of them shoemakers and tailors. The city was almost completely destroyed by fire in 1895 and again in 1901. In the pogroms in the wake of the 1905 revolution several Jews in Brest-Litovsk were wounded or killed. A number of Jews there were active in the underground revolutionary groups. However, as elsewhere in Russia, their activities subsided with the failure of the revolution. Although the Jews comprised 70% of the population before World War I, they had only three representatives on the municipal council, while there were 20 non-Jewish members.

The Jews were driven out of Brest-Litovsk on Aug. 1, 1915, by order of the Russian high command. On August 26 the Austro-German army occupied the city, and many of the exiles returned. Shortly afterward, however, they were again expelled by the Germans. After the Poles occupied the region in 1919, Jewish communal life revived. Although more attention was paid to secular aspects, the traditional cultural activities continued to flourish. A communal committee was organized and other institutions were established. Half of the pupils in the general schools (which included a commercial school, a *real-gymnasium,* and a secondary school) were Jewish. In 1921 the Jewish population numbered 15,630 (out of a total of 29,460) and in 1931, 21,440. For several years the deputy-mayor of Brest was a Jew. Prominent in Brest in the late 19th and early 20th centuries were the philologist and talmudist Jacob Nahum *Epstein; Michael *Pukhachewsky, a pioneer farmer in Ereẓ Israel; the journalists Abraham *Goldberg and Noah Finkelstein; and the author and physician Benjamin Szereszewski. [N.M.G.]

Holocaust Period and After. Almost 30,000 Jews lived in Brest in 1941. The Germans first took the city on Sept. 15, 1939, looted, and kidnapped Jews for forced labor. Following the Soviet-German agreement on the division of Poland, however, the city came under Soviet rule (Sept. 22, 1939). The Soviet authorities disbanded the communal bodies, repressed independent political activity, and arrested Jewish leaders. Among those exiled to the Soviet Union was Israel Tenenbaum, the local "Bund" leader. Although the community institutions could no longer function, mutual aid was set up and extended to the Jews who fled from German-occupied Poland and sought refuge in Brest. Immediately following the outbreak of the Soviet-German war the Germans reentered Brest. On June 28–29, 1941, the Germans kidnapped 5,000 Jewish men supposedly for forced labor, but the men were taken outside the city limits and murdered. In the autumn of 1941 the Jews were segregated into a ghetto, and only a few physicians and their families were allowed to remain on the "Aryan" side. Ways were devised to smuggle food in to the starving ghetto. A *Judenrat was imposed, headed by Zvi Hirsh Rozenberg and his deputy, Naḥman Landau. Within the ghetto aid was organized for the needy and various workshops were created to provide the Jews with "productive" work for the Germans in an attempt to prevent their deportation to death camps. At the end of June 1942, a group of 900 skilled artisans were taken away for forced labor in the East. Only 12 of them came back to the ghetto several weeks later. In mid-1942 an underground resistance movement, led by Arieh Scheinman, came into being in the ghetto. Its members raised funds to buy arms to provision fighting groups who would set themselves up in the forests. On Oct. 15, 1942, the Germans began to liquidate the ghetto. Following the *Aktion* the Germans continued a manhunt of those hiding in bunkers. The Jews who had managed to flee the Germans joined the partisan units operating in the forests. A number of Brest's Jews belonged to the "Kotowski" Soviet partisan unit, and Hana Ginzberg of Brest was regarded as an outstanding partisan. When Brest was liberated in July 1944, there were less than ten Jews to be found in the city. After the war a committee set up in the U.S.A. by former residents of Brest provided aid to the approximately 200 survivors of the Holocaust from Brest, dispersed throughout Poland and in displaced persons camps in Germany. Societies of former residents of Brest function in Israel, the U.S.A., Australia, France, and Argentina. The Jewish population of the town was estimated at 2,000 in 1970. It had no synagogue, the last one having been converted into a moviehouse in 1959.

Bibliography: A. L. Feinstein, *Ir Tehillah* (1886); S. Dubnow, *Pinkas Va'ad ha-Kehillot ha-Rashiyyot bi-Medinat Lita* (1925); Halpern, Pinkas; EG, 2 (1954).

BRETHOLZ, BERTHOLD (1862–1936), Moravian historian. He was baptized when young. Bretholz collaborated in the publication of *Monumenta Germaniae Historica* (1886–92). In 1892 he was appointed official historian of Moravia, then director of the Bruenn (Brno) municipal archives and the provincial archives (1900). Bretholz published numerous works on Bohemian and Moravian history. The "Bretholz-theory," expounded mainly in his four-volume work *Geschichte Boehmens und Maehrens* (1921–24), ascribes the descent of the Bohemian and Moravian Germans to Teutonic tribes who had settled the area before the advent of the Czechs and not to medieval colonists. The theory became an important argument of extremist German nationalists in Czechoslovakia. In the last years of his life Bretholz turned to Jewish history; he wrote *Geschichte der Juden in Maehren im Mittelalter* (1934), edited *Quellen zur Geschichte der Juden in Maehren* (1935), and contributed to the yearbooks of the Jewish historical society in Czechoslovakia. His *Geschichte der Stadt Bruenn* (1911) contains a chapter on the Jewish community in Bruenn (pp. 363–81).

Bibliography: NDB, 2 (1955), 601–2; B. Bretholz, *Bruenn* (Ger., 1938), 317–21 (full bibliography, 322–6); Steinherz, in: JGGJČ, 9 (1938), 463.

[Ed.]

BRETHREN OF SINCERITY, EPISTLES OF (Arab. *Ikhwān al-Safā'*), series of Arabic treatises ostensibly covering the spectrum of philosophic studies: mathematics and logic, the natural sciences, metaphysics, and the political and religious organization of society including a discussion of the nature and organization of the "Sincere Brethren." The authors of the work were a group of people belonging to the class of government secretaries and men of letters in tenth-century Baghdad. They were connected with the Ismāʿīliyya movement which opposed the pretensions of the reigning Abbasid caliphs. Their treatises or epistles no doubt also served to propagate their political and religious ideas under the cloak of a philosophic encyclopedia. The level of learning set forth in the encyclopedia is popular and its philosophy is essentially neoplatonic, in contradistinction to the purer Aristotelianism preferred by, e.g., al-Fārābī. Their writings seem to have influenced a number of Jewish philosophers, notably Joseph ibn Ẓaddik and Solomon ibn Gabirol, as well as Moses ibn Ezra. Shem Tov Ibn Falaquera translated excerpts from their writings in his *Sefer ha-Mevakkesh* (1778). In Arles (1316) Kalonymus b. Kalonymus translated a treatise of the *Epistles* into Hebrew under the title *Iggeret Ba'alei Ḥayyim* ("The Epistle of the Animals"). It has been printed a number of times and the Hebrew version has been translated into Yiddish and Ladino.

Bibliography: Steinschneider, Uebersetzungen, 860–2; D. Kaufmann, *Geschichte der Attributenlehre* (1877, repr. 1967); Vajda, in: *Archives d'histoire doctrinale et littéraire du moyen-âge,* 24 (1949), 114 and passim; Stern, in: *Islamic Studies,* 3 (1964), 405–28.

[L.V.B.]

BREUER, ISAAC (1883–1946), theoretician and leader of German Orthodoxy; son of Solomon *Breuer. Born in Papa, Hungary, Breuer was brought as a child to Frankfort, where he studied at his father's yeshivah. He subsequently studied law, philosophy, and history at various universities and practiced as a lawyer in Frankfort. He soon took a leading part in various communal organizations. He defended the communal secession of the Orthodox in his *Preussische Austrittsgesetzgebung und das Judentum* (1913). When Agudat Israel was founded in 1912, Breuer became one of its ideologists and spokesmen. After the Nazis came to power, he settled in Jerusalem (1936), practicing as a lawyer, and devoting himself to organizing Po'alei Agudat

Isaac Breuer, rabbi and one of the founders of Agudat Israel.

Israel, of which he became the president. His appearance on behalf of the Agudah before the Peel Commission (1937) and the Anglo-American Commission (March 1946) made a great impression.

Breuer regarded himself as heir to the work of S. R. *Hirsch, his grandfather. He developed Hirschian thought in his *Messiasspuren* (1918); *Judenproblem* (1922⁴;

also in a condensed English edition, 1947); *Wegzeichen* (a collection of articles, 1923; in expanded form in Hebrew, *Ẓiyyunei Derekh,* 1955); *Das juedische Nationalheim* (1925; English translation, 1926); *Elijahu* (1924); *Die Welt als Schoepfung und Natur* (1926); *Elischa* (1928); *Der neue Kusari* (1934), etc. While opposing Zionism as an attempt to secularize the Jewish nation, with time he saw in this movement, and in the Balfour Declaration and the Jewish National Home, the hand of Providence. To Zionism Breuer opposed his Agudism as the preparation of the Torah nation for renaissance in its ancestral home. After settling in Ereẓ Israel, Breuer began to write in Hebrew (*Moriyyah,* 1944; *Naḥali'el,* 1951), while selected articles appeared posthumously in English (*People of the Torah,* 1956). In the earlier period he had written some—not very successful—novels (*Ein Kampf um Gott,* 1920; *Falk Nefts Heimkehr,* 1923), also as vehicles for his religious concepts. He defended his conception, in the philosophical terms of the 19th century that God's eternal truths were revealed in and to His "Torah people." When historical reality forced itself on his thought, he met its demands with struggle and reluctance.

Bibliography: B. Kurzweil, in: *Haaretz* (Dec. 17, 1943); H. Schwab, *History of Orthodox Jewry in Germany* (1950), 120–2; I. Grunfeld, *Three Generations* (1958), index; S. Ehrmann, in: L. Jung (ed.), *Guardians of Our Heritage* (1958), 617–46. [Ed.]

BREUER, JOSEPH (1842–1925), Austrian physician, neurophysiologist, and precursor of psychoanalysis. Born in Vienna, he taught at the university there from 1875. From 1890, he specialized in diseases of the nervous system. His neurophysiological research on the effect of the vagus on respiration (1868) and the role of the semicircular canals of the ear in the bodily equilibrium (1874) is of great significance. In his treatment of the case of Anna O., an hysteric, which he communicated to Freud, he laid the foundation for the development of Freud's psychoanalytic methods. He and Freud collaborated in writing *Studien ueber Hysterie* (1895) but each later returned to his separate field of research. Breuer remained a widely acknowledged internist and was elected to the Viennese Academy of Science. He was active in Jewish community affairs all his life. [Ed.]

BREUER, JOSEPH (1882–), Orthodox rabbi; son of Solomon *Breuer. Breuer was born in Papa, Hungary. In 1906 Breuer became a lecturer at the yeshivah in Frankfort, heading it after his father's death (1926). He emigrated to the U.S. in 1939 and became head of K'hal Adath Jeshurun in Washington Heights, N.Y., and of its Yeshivah Rabbi Samson Raphael Hirsch (1944), modeled after the Orthodox Jewish community of Frankfort. The *kehillah* which he headed had its own yeshivah, and *kashrut* supervision. Regarded as one of the spiritual heirs of Hirsch, his maternal grandfather Rabbi Breuer wrote extensively in German and English defending staunch Orthodoxy.

Breuer published biblical translations and commentaries on Jeremiah (1914) and Ezekiel (1921); and introductions to S. R. Hirsch's Commentary on the Torah (Ger. 2 vols, 1926; Eng. 2 vols, 1948); translations of and commentaries (with text) on the *piyyutim* for Rosh Ha-Shanah and the Day of Atonement; and wrote *Jewish Marriage* (Ger. 1923; Eng. 1956). A Jubilee Volume was published in his honor on the occasion of his 80th birthday (*Ateret Ẓevi,* Eng. and Heb., 1962, with a bibliography of his writings). [I.B.G.]

BREUER, RAPHAEL (1881–1932), district rabbi at Aschaffenburg, Bavaria; son of Solomon *Breuer. His candidacy for the succession to his father's office led to a bitter struggle in the Frankfort congregation in which the majority, the Israelische Religionsgesellschaft (under Jacob *Rosenheim's leadership), opposed the narrow Orthodoxy with which the name of Breuer had become associated. Raphael Breuer's published works include translations and commentaries (in German) on the Five Scrolls (1908–12; 1924[2]); on the Former Prophets (2 vols., 1915–22); and on Ezra and Nehemiah (2 vols., 1933–38). The literalist interpretation of his commentary on the Song of Songs (1912) caused some scandal among the Orthodox; in the second edition (1923), he gave a more traditional rendering. An appreciation of the ideas of his grandfather S. R. *Hirsch was contained in Breuer's *Unter seinem Banner* (1908). His strong anti-Zionist views were aired in *Nationaljudenthum ein Wahnjudenthum* (1903) and other polemics.

Bibliography: H. Schwab, *Chachme Ashkenaz* (Eng., 1964), 36. [Ed.]

BREUER, SOLOMON (1850–1926), rabbi and author, leader of German Orthodoxy (*Trennungsorthodoxie*). After studying at the Pressburg yeshivah under A. S. B. Schreiber

Solomon Breuer, leader of German Orthodox Jewry.

and at German universities, Breuer officiated as rabbi in Papa, Hungary. He married the youngest daughter of Samson Raphael *Hirsch, and in 1888 he succeeded his father-in-law, in Frankfort. A firm advocate of strict Orthodoxy, Breuer founded the Association of Orthodox Rabbis in Germany, excluding from it Orthodox rabbis who cooperated in communal work with Reform Jews. He was president of the Freie Vereinigung ("Free Union") for the advancement of Orthodoxy and cofounder of the Agudat Israel movement, barring members of mixed Reform-Orthodox communities from the leadership of this movement. In 1890 he founded a yeshivah and directed it for 36 years. In conjunction with Phinehas *Kohn he published the periodical *Juedische Monatshefte* (Hebrew subtitle, *Doresh Tov le-Ammo*) from 1913 to 1920. His writings include *Ḥokhmah im Naḥalah* (4 vols., 1930–35), sermons, and *Divrei Shelomo* (1948), interpretations of *halakhah* and *aggadah*.

Bibliography: S. Breuer, *Divrei Shelomo* (1948), introd.; H. Schwab, *History of Orthodox Jewry in Germany* (1950), index; idem, *Chachme Ashkenaz* (Eng., 1964), 35; I. Grunfeld, *Three Generations* (1958), index. [M.N.Z./Ed.]

BREZNICE (Cz. **Březnice;** Ger. **Bresnitz-Lokschan**), town in Bohemia, Czechoslovakia. Jews settled there in 1592. The Jewish quarter, with a synagogue and cemetery established about 1720, was in the suburb of Lokšany. The synagogue was destroyed by fire in 1821 but subsequently rebuilt. The two "primators" of Bohemian Jewry, Wolf and Joachim *Popper, originated from Breznice. Its rabbis included Isaac Spitz, son-in-law of Eleazar *Fleckeles and author of a volume of poems, *Matamei Yiẓḥak* (Prague, 1843). In 1897 the community adopted Czech as the official language, closing down its German-language school in 1901. The

The synagogue of Breznice, Czechoslovakia, restored as a Jewish memorial museum after World War II. Prague, State Press Office. Photo V. Obereigner.

community numbered 17 families in 1649. In 1731, 22 Jewish houses are recorded. There were 30 Jewish families in 1840, 118 persons in 1900, and 30 persons in 1930. Those remaining on the outbreak of World War II were deported to death camps in 1942. The old Jewish quarter still exists.

Bibliography: S. Krauss, *Joachim Edler von Popper* (1926), 1–14; J. Polák-Rokycana, in: H. Gold (ed.), *Juden und Judengemeinden Boehmens* (1934), 63–69; idem, in: *Českožidovský kalendář*, 42 (1922/23), 114–27; 45 (1925/26), 97–106.

[O.K.R.]

BRIBERY, making a gift to a person in authority, especially a judge. The injunction not to take bribes is several times repeated in the Bible, twice with the reason given that "bribes blind the clear-sighted and upset the pleas of the just" (Ex. 23:8; Deut. 16:19). This was later interpreted to mean not only that a corrupt judge tends to identify the interests of the donor with his own and is thus blind to the rights of the other party (Ket. 105b, Shab. 119a), but also that such a judge would not grow old without becoming physically blind (Pe'ah 8:9). The warning is also sounded that the taking of bribes might lead to the shedding of innocent blood (Deut. 27:25). God is praised as being unreceptive to bribes (Deut. 10:17, et al.), and as human judges are generally exhorted to imitate divine qualities (Shab. 133b; Mekh, Shirah 3) so they are urged to be impartial, and not susceptible to bribes (II Chron. 19:7) and reminded that judicial services should be given free (Bek. 29a). There is no penalty and no non-penal sanction prescribed in the Bible for taking bribes. The donor of bribes is blamed as a tempter or accomplice of the taker (Maim. Yad, Sanhedrin 23:2; Sh. Ar., ḤM 9:1), transgressing the injunction "you shall not place a stumbling block before the blind" (Lev. 19:14). Bribery seems to have been rather widespread (cf. I. Sam. 8:3), or else the prophets would hardly have denounced it so vehemently (Isa. 1:23; 5:23; 33:15; Ezek. 22:12; Amos 5:12; Micah 7:3), but it was in the nature of unethical misconduct rather than of a criminal offense.

Under talmudic law, where no penalty was prescribed in the Bible for the violation of a negative injunction, the transgressor was liable to be flogged (Mak. 16a; Tosef., Mak. 5:16; see *Minḥat Bikkurim* for reading). In the case of bribery this provision was largely academic, as the requisite witnesses would not normally be available—the act being always committed in secret (cf. Ibn Ezra to Deut. 27:14). The rule was therefore evolved that taking a bribe invalidates the judge's decision, and this was extended even to the taking of fees (Bek. 4:6). The invalidation of the proceeding was regarded as a quasi-penalty *(kenas)* imposed on the judge for taking bribes or fees (Tos. to Kid. 58b top; Sma, ḤM 9:5), and it may have counted toward the judge's liability to pay damages where a party had already acted on his judgment. The prohibition against a judge taking fees was mitigated by a renowned jurist, Karna, who allowed both parties to reimburse him in equal shares for the loss he had actually suffered by sitting in court instead of earning his wages as a winetaster (Ket. 105a). This precedent was not applied to a judge who took a fee for the loss of his time without proving actual loss of money: while his decisions remained unaffected he was called "ugly" *(ibid.)*. Other talmudic jurists carried the rule against bribery to extremes by refusing to sit in judgment over any person who had shown them the slightest courtesy, such as helping them to alight from a boat *(ibid.)*.

Originally, judges were remunerated from Temple revenues *(ibid.)*, which furnished the legal basis for their remuneration, in later periods, from communal funds. As all members were required to contribute to the communal funds, so were litigants later—as today in the rabbinical courts in Israel—required to pay court fees, not to any particular judge but into a general fund out of which all court expenses were defrayed. There are, nevertheless, occasional instances of judges demanding exorbitant fees for their services (e.g., the incident reported by Obadiah of Bertinoro to Bek. 4:6).

Bribing non-Jewish rulers, officials, and judges was regarded as legitimate at all times. In view of their bias against Jews it is not difficult to understand such an attitude. Not only was it quite usual to bribe kings (I Kings 15:19; II Kings 16:8; Ber. 28b; et al.), but expenses involved in bribing judges and sheriffs were often expressly included in the expenses recoverable from debtors (cf. Gulak, Oẓar, 237, no. 249).

In the State of Israel the taker and the donor of bribes are equally punishable. Demanding a bribe is tantamount to taking it, and offering or promising one to giving it. Even the intermediary between the donor and the taker (or the intended taker) bears the same criminal responsibility. No extraneous evidence being normally available, the taker is a competent witness against the donor, and vice versa, and though they are accomplices their evidence need not be corroborated (Penal Law Revision (Bribery Offenses) Act, 5712–1952).

Bibliography: ET, 1 (1951^3), 266; 3 (1951), 173f.; M. Elon, in: ILR, 4 (1969), 99f.

[H.H.C.]

BRICEVA, Jewish agricultural settlement in Bessarabia, Ukrainian S.S.R.; in Rumania 1918–40 and 1941–44. Briceva was founded in 1838 on an area of 308 hectares (approx. 760 acres) acquired by colonists originating from Podolia. In 1899 there were 301 families (1,510 persons), of whom 83 owned their holdings (averaging approx. $9\frac{1}{2}$ acres per family), possessing 1,244 sheep and goats. Because of the scarcity of farm equipment plowing was hired out. As a result of the Rumanian agrarian reform of 1922, 72 Briceva farmers received 216 hectares (approx. 533 acres) from the state. In 1924, 176 Jewish families were occupied in agriculture on an area of 1,134 hectares (approx. 2,800 acres of which 1,605 acres were leasehold); in 1930 the Jewish population numbered 2,431 (88.9% of the total).

[El.F.]

Holocaust Period. The settlement's proximity to the Dniester River enabled many Jews of Briceva to escape to U.S.S.R. before the arrival of the Rumanian and German troops in July 1941. Those who stayed, as well as those caught in flight, were deported to *Transnistria, where most of them met their death. After the war, a few dozen families, the surviving remnant of the community, returned to Briceva. None remained there, however, and the land became government property. [J.AN.]

Bibliography: Yakir, in: *Eynikeyt* (Sept. 10, 1946).

BRICHANY (Rum. **Briceni**), town in Bessarabia, Moldavian S.S.R. There were 137 Jewish families living in the town in 1817; another 47 had previously left the village when it was partly destroyed by fire. The community increased in the first half of the 19th century, and by the middle of the 19th century was among the largest in the region. In 1897 there were 7,184 Jews in Brichany (96.5% of the total population). A Jewish state school was opened in 1847. In 1924, 125 Jews were occupied in agriculture on 641 hectares (approx. 1,600 acres) of land, most of it (500 hectares) held on lease. According to the official census figures the Jewish population numbered 5,354 in 1930 (95.2% of the total). Communal institutions on the eve of World War II included a hospital, founded in 1885, and a Hebrew *Tarbut school. [EL.F.]

Holocaust Period. Before the war many Jews from surrounding areas concentrated in Brichany and by 1940 it had a Jewish population of about 10,000. In June 1940, when the city was annexed to the U.S.S.R., Jewish property and community buildings were confiscated and only the synagogue was saved because it was used as a granary. Some 80 Jews, mainly the community leaders, were exiled to Siberia. On July 8, 1941, Rumanian and German troops passed through Brichany and murdered many Jews. Jews from the neighboring towns of *Lipkany and *Sekiryany were brought to Brichany. On July 28, all Jews were dispatched across the Dniester and several were shot en route. When they arrived in Mogilev, the Germans "selected" the old people and forced the younger ones to dig graves for them. From Mogilev the rest were turned back to *Ataki in Bessarabia and then on to Sekiryany. Hundreds died en route. For a month they stayed in the ghetto, only to be deported again to *Transnistria. All the young Jews were murdered in a forest near Soroca. Only 1,000 Jews returned to Brichany at the end of the war. [J.AN.]

Bibliography: M. Carp, *Cartea Neagră*, 3 (1947), 34; M. Mircu, *Pogromurile din Basarabia* (1947), 1; T. Fuchs, *A Vanderung iber Okupirte Gebitn* (1947), 119.

BRICK, DANIEL (1903–), journalist, born in Stockholm, Sweden. He founded a number of short-lived Jewish newspapers and periodicals (some of them together with M. *Ehrenpreis). At the head of a group of young Jewish intellectuals, Brick launched in 1932 the *Judisk Kronika* which at once became the organ of the young Zionist movement in Sweden. Brick was the general secretary of the Zionist Organization in Sweden from 1935 to 1949. In 1957 he established the Judiska Kulturinstitutet in Stockholm, where both Jews and non-Jews attend lectures and participate in discussions on Jewish problems. In 1952 a forest was planted in his honor in Israel.

Bibliography: *Haaretz* (April 18, 1967). [H.V.]

BRICKNER, BARNETT ROBERT (1892–1958), U.S. Reform rabbi. Born in New York, Brickner was a youthful orator in Zionist circles in New York's Lower East Side. He was ordained at Hebrew Union College, Cincinnati, in 1919 and became rabbi of the Holy Blossom Congregation in Toronto in 1920. He also served as president of the Toronto Federation of Jewish Philanthropies and editor of the *Canadian Jewish Review*. In 1925 Brickner moved to Cleveland as rabbi of Congregation Anshe Chesed (Euclid Avenue Temple). There he instituted Sunday services (later discontinued) which attracted large audiences, improved the congregation's educational program, and became active in the life of the city. He was appointed president of the Cleveland Bureau of Jewish Education (1932) and was active in Zionist affairs. In 1942 Brickner became chairman of the Committee on Chaplains of the Central Conference of American Rabbis, which was responsible for recruiting chaplains for the U.S. Armed Forces. Later he was appointed administrative chairman of the Committee on Army and Navy Activities of the Jewish Welfare Board, and undertook a world tour of American military bases. From 1953 to 1955 he served as president of the Central Conference of American Rabbis. His son BALFOUR (1926–), also a Reform rabbi, officiated at Temple Sinai, Washington, D.C. (1952–61). In 1961 he became director of interfaith activities of the Union of American Hebrew Congregations in which position he was prominent as a Jewish spokesman on Jewish-Christian relations in the U.S.

Bibliography: S. M. Silver, *Portrait of a Rabbi* (1959). [S.D.T.]

BRIDEGROOMS OF THE LAW (Heb., sing., חֲתַן תּוֹרָה, *ḥatan Torah*), honorary titles bestowed on those who are called up to the reading of certain sections of the law during the morning service of *Simḥat Torah (which coincides, in Israel, with Shemini Aẓeret), when the annual cycle of the reading of the Torah is concluded and a new one begun. "Bridegroom of the Law" is, strictly, the title reserved for the person called up to the reading of the last portion of the Pentateuch (Deut. 33:27–34:12). The person called up to the reading of the first chapter of Genesis, immediately afterward, is called the "bridegroom of the beginning" (*ḥatan Bereshit* (Genesis) or *ḥatan matḥil*). The Yemenite and Egyptian rites have only one bridegroom, who completes the reading of Deuteronomy, and commences that of Genesis. Other Oriental communities have three: *ḥatan Torah*, *ḥatan Bereshit*, and *ḥatan me'onah* (the first

Pair of carved and gilded chairs designed for the two Bridegrooms of the Law, from the Cazis synagogue, Mantua, Italy, 1775. Jerusalem, Israel Museum. Photo David Harris, Jerusalem.

word of the passage). Where the passage is further subdivided, the second part begins with Deuteronomy 34:1, and the bridegroom is known as *ḥatan va-ya'al*. Some Ashkenazi congregations have four "bridegrooms," giving the title of *ḥatan maftir* to the person called up to the reading of the *haftarah*, and of *ḥatan kol ha-ne'arim* ("bridegroom of all the lads") to the person for whom Deuteronomy 33:22–26 is read. The latter term derives from the fact that the person called up is joined in his *aliyah* to the Torah by children under *bar mitzvah age.

In both the Ashkenazi and the Sephardi rites the bridegrooms of the law are summoned to the Torah reading by special *piyyutim*. These vary in the different rites, but all emphasize, with much poetic hyperbole, the privilege of concluding and beginning the reading of the Torah, and they laud and bless the honored *ḥatanim*.

According to the *Maḥzor Vitry* (ed. by S. Hurwitz (1923²), 458), the term *ḥatan Bereshit* was already known to the disciples of Rashi in the 12th century. The kabbalistic elaboration of the ancient rabbinic image of the Torah as the "betrothed of Israel" (an aggadic interpretation of Deuteronomy 33:4 associates *morashah*, "heritage," with *me'urasah*, "betrothed") may have helped to popularize the custom.

The honor of *ḥatan Torah* was usually given to the rabbi of the congregation or a scholar; and *ḥatan Bereshit*, the president, or a distinguished lay member of the congregation. In some Sephardi and Oriental communities, it was customary to so honor actual bridegrooms of the past year.

In some Oriental rites, candy is showered on the *ḥatanim* as they ascend or descend to and from the reading (cf. Ber. 50b). In medieval Europe, *ḥatanim* made generous donations to charity and threw sweets to the children in the synagogue. In some communities it was customary to erect a baldachin (as for real bridegrooms) on the *bimah* for Simḥat Torah, to decorate the synagogue walls with carpets, and to provide special seats of honor for the bridegrooms. In many congregations it is customary for the *ḥatanim* to entertain the members of the congregation after the service or on the afternoon of Simḥat Torah.

See *Simḥat Torah.

Bibliography: Eisenstein, Dinim, 146; I. Abrahams, *Jewish Life in the Middle Ages* (1932²), 43; H. Schauss, *The Jewish Festivals* (1938), 197–9; J.-T. Lewinski (ed.), *Sefer ha-Mo'adim*, 4 (1952²), 246–52; A. Yaari, *Toledot Ḥag Simḥat Torah* (1964), 63–87, 104–59, 231–6.

[Ed.]

BRIDGEPORT, the second-largest city in the state of Connecticut. A handful of Central and West European Jews settled in the city in the mid-19th century. Most of the Jews went to Bridgeport from Eastern Europe, beginning around 1880. In addition to the predominance of Russian and Polish Jews, a large number came from Hungary and gave Bridgeport proportionately one of the most sizeable Hungarian Jewish populations in America. The city's general population also reflects this ethnic distribution. Most Bridgeport Jews are self-employed, in retail and wholesale business and in the professions. Their economic standing is higher than the average in the city.

In 1968 there were 11 congregations in greater Bridgeport—six Orthodox, four Conservative, and one Reform, nine of which were served by full-time rabbis. Jewish adult organizations totaled 150 in number. In addition, Bridgeport Jewry maintained a Jewish community center, a family and children's agency, a federation, and a home for the aged. It also had one day school, and all but two of the synagogues maintained Hebrew or religious schools; their total enrollment was approximately 1,800.

Park Avenue Temple of the Congregation B'nai Israel, Bridgeport, Conn., dedicated in 1958. Architect: Percival Goodman. Photo Charles Rachum Studio.

After the end of World War II most of the younger families established themselves in the adjacent suburbs of Bridgeport while maintaining their business and professional addresses in the city. The Jewish population of greater Bridgeport was 14,500 (1968). [N.Sk.]

BRIE, LUIS HARTWIG (1834–1919), Argentinian communal leader. Born in Hamburg, Germany, Brie arrived in Brazil in 1847 and enlisted in the Brazilian Legion formed to help General Urquiza in his uprising against Rosas, who held absolute power in Argentina. He participated in the battle of Caseros in 1852, in which Rosas was ousted. He stayed in Argentina and became a citizen in 1871. In spite of the fact that he intermarried and his children were raised in the Catholic faith, Brie was very active in the foundation and organization of the main Jewish institutions in Argentina. He was president of the Congregación Israelita de la República Argentina during the periods 1895–97 and 1904–15, one of the promoters of the *ḥevrah kaddisha* in 1894 (see *A.M.I.), and was its first president during 1894–97. Brie participated in the Argentine war against Paraguay during the 1860s and served in the government's forces against the uprising in 1890. He also held responsible posts in the municipality of Buenos Aires for several decades. [V.A.M.]

BRIEL, JUDAH BEN ELIEZER (1643–1722), exegete, halakhic authority, and polemicist. Appointed a member of the *bet din* of Mantua, Briel succeeded Moses Zacuto (d. 1697) as the rabbi of that community, a position he occupied until his death. Among his pupils was Isaac *Lampronti. In the controversy connected with the banning of the writings of the Shabbatean Nehemiah *Ḥayon, Briel expressed his vehement opposition to Ḥayon in polemical letters. Briel's antipathy to Kabbalah stemmed from his hostility to the Shabbatean movement. Stimulated by the contemporary polemics between Judaism and Christianity and the appearance of numerous anti-Semitic writings, Briel wrote works against Christianity in Italian and Hebrew. Most are still in manuscript. They include: (1) *Discorso Apologetico* (in defense of Manasseh Ben Israel against the attacks of the priest Vincenzo of Ragusa); (2) *Riposta alla Synagoga disingannata dal padre Pinamonti;* (3) *Animadversiones in evangelia* (a criticism of the New Testament). Of his many other works only *Kelalei ha-Dikduk* ("The Rules of [Hebrew] Grammar," Mantua,

1729) has been published. Those still in manuscript include his responsa and his commentary on the Prophets and the Hagiographa. He also wrote occasional poems, such as a sonnet in honor of Isaac Cardoso, and translated the letters of Seneca from Latin into Hebrew.

Bibliography: *Kerem Ḥemed,* 2 (1836), 115, 119; Ghirondi-Neppi, 127–9; *Oẓar Neḥmad* (1860), 168; *Oẓar Tov,* 1 (1878), 84; Steinschneider, in: MGWJ, 44 (1900), 88–89; Rosenthal, in: *Aresheth,* 2 (1960), 158, 166; S. Simonsohn, *Toledot ha-Yehudim be-Dukkasut Mantovah,* 1 (1963), 332, n. 427; Graetz, Gesch, 10 (1897[3]), 297, 329, 502ff.

[Y.Ho.]

The rabbinical diploma granted to Judah b. Eliezer Briel in Venice in 1677. Formerly in the Elkan Adler Collection.

BRIGHTON, town on the south coast of England. Jews began to settle in Brighton in the middle of the 18th century. When the town became a fashionable resort, wealthy Jews flocked there including the *Goldsmid family at the beginning of the 19th century and the *Sassoons at the end. A congregation was first organized in 1800 but soon fell apart. It was reorganized in 1821. There are now in Brighton and its sister-town Hove five synagogues, including one Reform and one Liberal. Jewish affairs are coordinated by the Brighton and Hove Jewish Council. The Jewish population of Brighton and Hove (1968) numbered 7,500.

The oldest synagogue in Brighton, England, consecrated in 1875. Photo Averys, Brighton.

Bibliography: C. Roth, *Rise of Provincial Jewry* (1950), 34ff.

[C.R.]

BRILL, ABRAHAM ARDEN (1874–1948), Austrian-born psychoanalyst. Brill studied with *Freud in Vienna, and to him belongs the main credit for introducing Freud's writings to the English-speaking world. Beginning in 1909 with a translation of *Studien ueber Hysterie* (1895; *Studies in Hysteria,* 1936), written by Freud jointly with J. Breuer, Brill continued over the years to present a systematic translation of most of Freud's work. In 1911 he founded the New York Psychoanalytical Society, and was appointed head of the Psychiatry Clinic at Columbia University.

While Brill's most significant contribution to psychoanalysis was his translation of Freud, he was a talented psychoanalytic practitioner and did some noteworthy research especially on necrophilia. He made an historic contribution to the integration of psychoanalytic concepts into psychiatry. Brill's own writings include *Freud's Contribution to Psychiatry* (1944) and *Psychoanalysis: Its Theories and Practical Application* (1922[3]).

Bibliography: G. Zilboorg, *History of Medical Psychology* (1941), 504–6; *New York Times* (March 3, 1948), 23.

[D.Zo.]

BRILL, AZRIEL (1778–1853), rabbi and scholar born in Zay-Ugróc, Hungary. He studied under Ezekiel *Landau, Moses *Muenz, and Mordecai *Baneth. In 1814 he was appointed teacher of Hebrew, mathematics, and geography at the Jewish school in Pest, and in 1827 became a member of the rabbinate of that city. Brill was the author of *Ein ha-Areẓ* (Buda, 1821), an outline of the geography and history of Hungary in Hebrew; and *Hadrat Kodesh* (1828), a vocalized text of the Mishnah orders *Rosh Ha-Shanah* and *Yoma,* with a German translation and commentary, and the liturgy for the High Holy Days. Azriel's brothers adopted the name Schossberger; one of them, Eliezer, was the ancestor of the barons Schossberger of Tornya. His son, SAMUEL LOEW BRILL (1814–1897), was appointed in 1850 a member of the *bet din* in Pest, which he headed from 1872. His glosses on the Talmud were published by L. Blau (in *Maguar zsidó Szemle,* 1896, and in MGWJ, 1897).

Bibliography: V. Bacher, in: *Magyar Zsidó Szemle,* 9 (1892), 708; A. Loewinger, *ibid.,* 16 (1899), 272–8; L. Blau, *ibid.,* 19 (1902), 40–81, 128–36 (on Samuel Loew).

[AL.SCH.]

BRILL, JEHIEL (1836–1886), pioneer of the Hebrew press in Palestine. Brill left his native Russia in the late 1850s, and after much wandering went to Ereẓ Israel. He married the daughter of Jacob *Saphir, and settled in Jerusalem from where he sent reports to Hebrew newspapers in the Diaspora. Together with Joel Moses Salomon and Michael Cohen he established Jerusalem's second Hebrew printing press, and began publishing the monthly *Ha-Levanon* (1863), the first Hebrew periodical to appear in Palestine. A year later the publication was suspended and Brill went to Paris. There he revived his paper in 1865, first as a biweekly and later as a weekly. After the Franco-Prussian War (1870–71) he moved to Mainz, where he established a Hebrew printing press and published *Ha-Levanon* (1872–82) as a Hebrew supplement to *Der Israelit,* the Orthodox German weekly. *Ha-Levanon* supported the *ḥalukkah* and the Jerusalem rabbis. A staunch defender of religious tradition, Brill also pleaded the cause of settlement in Ereẓ Israel along the lines attempted by members of the old *yishuv*, outside the Jerusalem walls, and in Petaḥ Tikvah. After the Russian pogroms of 1881 and the rise of Ḥibbat Zion, Brill returned to Ereẓ Israel at the head of a small group of Jewish farmers from Belorussia who settled in Mazkeret Batyah (Ekron). However, he became embroiled in an argument concerning the policy of the agricultural school, *Mikveh Israel, and with other settlers and left the country disillusioned. Brill related these experiences in *Yesud ha-Ma'alah* (1883). In 1884 he settled in London and began publishing the short-lived Yiddish weekly, *Ha-Shulamit*. Shortly before his death he revived *Ha-Levanon* in London, but only 11 issues appeared. During his stay in Paris and Mainz, he published several medieval Hebrew manuscripts: *Yein Levanon* (1866, three manuscripts, including one of Maimonides, on tractate *Rosh ha-Shanah*); R. Hananel's commentary on tractate *Pesaḥim* (1868); *Sefer Iggerot* by R. Meir ha-Levi Abulafia (1871), and *Be'er ha-Golah* (1877).

Bibliography: G. Kressel, *Ha-Levanon ve-ha-Ḥavaẓẓelet* (1943); idem, *Toledot ha-Ittonut ha-Ivrit* (1964), 25–47; LNYL, s.v.

[G.K./G.EL.]

BRILL, JOSEPH (better known by his pen name **Iyov of Minsk,** איו״ב ממינסק; derived from the initials of *Ani Yoseph Brill;* 1839–1919), Hebrew writer and humorist. Brill, who was born in Gorki near Mogilev, studied at Lithuanian yeshivot where he began to read modern Hebrew literature clandestinely. He became a *maskil* and took to writing. His first essay appeared in *Ha-Maggid,* 2 (1858), 35–36. From 1858, he published critical essays and satirical *feuilletons* in *Ha-Karmel, Ha-Meliẓ,* and *Ha-Boker Or.* He supported the Socialists against *Smolenskin and published a stinging poem against the latter in *Asefat Ḥakhamim,* 3 (1878). He translated Richard Cumberland's comedy *The Jew* into Hebrew (1878). Particularly popular in their time were Brill's parodies: *Mishnat-Mevakkerim* (*Ha-Shaḥar* (1877), 317–24), a satire on Hebrew writers and the low state of culture among Russian Jews; *Megillat Ta'anit* in *Keneset Yisrael* of Saul Phinehas *Rabinowitz, 1 (1886), 593–605, a satire on assimilationists; a parodied *Kiẓẓur Shulḥan Arukh* for educators and teachers, in *Oẓar ha-Sifrut,* 3 (1889–90), section on "Satire and Humor," 17–34. Some of his letters were published in *Oẓar Mikhtavim ve-Sippurim* ed. by J. Rosenberg (1882).

Bibliography: *Toledot Iyov* (autobiography), in *Oẓar ha-Sifrut,* 4 (1892), 643–50; Klausner, Sifrut, 5 (1955), 117–8.

[G.EL.]

BRILLING, BERNHARD (1906–), German rabbi and scholar. From 1927 to 1939 Brilling was archival assistant and then archivist of the Breslau Jewish community. After settling in Palestine in 1941, he served for a time as archivist of the city of Tel Aviv. From 1957 Brilling pursued various scholarly projects at the Institutim Judaicum Delitzchianum of the University of Muenster. Of his nearly 50 publications in Jewish history, the most important are *Geschichte der Juden in Breslau von 1454–1702* (1960) and, together with Richtering, *Westfalia Judaica 1005–1350* (1967). [M.A.M.]

BRINDISI, seaport in southern Italy. Jews lived in Brindisi from an early period, as testified by several tombstone inscriptions, one of which dates back to 834. About 1165 *Benjamin of Tudela reported that ten Jewish families of dyers lived there. In the first half of the 14th century, the Jews were expelled for unspecified reasons, but were later readmitted. They were then occupied as dyers, moneylenders, and brokers. In 1494–95, when the Jews in the kingdom of Naples were attacked, the Jews of Brindisi attempted to avert disaster by signing over their property to the municipality. However, in 1496 the 50 families living there found it preferable to move from Brindisi to nearby Gallipoli. In 1510 the Jews of Brindisi were included in the general expulsion of the Jews from the kingdom of Naples. A few families were able to return in 1520, but in 1540–41 the decree of expulsion was definitely renewed.

Via Giudea in the Italian seaport of Brindisi. Photo A. Milano.

Bibliography: P. Camassa, *Gli ebrei a Brindisi* (1934); G. Guerrieri, *Gli ebrei a Brindisi e a Lecce* (1900); Milano Italia, index; Roth, Italy, index.

[A.MIL.]

BRINIG, MYRON (1900–), U.S. novelist. His first important work was the novel *Singermann* (1929), which painted a grim picture of the life of second-generation American Jews. Largely autobiographical, *Singermann* tells the story of a Jewish family in Silver Bow (Brinig's fictitious name for Butte, Montana, where he was raised): parental authority collapses and the children drift away, marry non-Jews, and are scattered. This family chronicle was continued in three later novels, *This Man is My Brother* (1932), *Sons of Singermann* (1934), and *The First Book of Michael Singermann* (1935), but these were less successful. Brinig's other works largely reflect memories of life in the American West or in New York. They include *The Sisters* (1937), *Anne Minton's Life* (1939), *The Family Way* (1942), *Footsteps on the Stair* (1950), *The Sadness in Lexington Avenue* (1951), and *Looking Glass Heart* (1958).

Bibliography: S. Liptzin, *Jew in American Literature* (1966), 180–2.

[S.L.]

BRISBANE, capital of Queensland, Australia. The first community was organized there in 1865, and its synagogue, Sha'arei Emunah (now the main synagogue) was consecrated in 1886. There were then 446 Jews in Brisbane out of 724 for the whole of Queensland. The small South Brisbane Congregation, consisting principally of Russian immigrants, was founded in 1928. Another synagogue was opened at Surfers' Paradise, a holiday resort, in 1961. Although religious observance is not strong, all three synagogues are Orthodox. The small congregation in Toowoomba (100 mi. (160 km.) from Brisbane) is now extinct. The main synagogue, to which are attached a hall, classrooms, and a *mikveh,* is the center for social and cultural activities. There is a strong Zionist movement; the overall Zionist body, the State Council, is affiliated to the Zionist Federation of Australia. Relatively few immigrants settled in Brisbane after World War II, and the growth of the community has been slow. In 1966 Brisbane Jewry numbered approximately 1,400; another 400 lived in Sufers' Paradise and other country towns. In 1911, Australian-born Jews represented 64% of the Jewish population in Queensland; Jews from the United Kingdom 16.9%; and from Europe 16.7%. The figures for 1961 were: 53.1%; 11%; and 27.4%.

Bibliography: Bolot, in: *Journal of the Australian Jewish Historical Society,* 1 (1949), 114–6; C. A. Price, *Jewish Settlers in Australia* (1964), 34–35. [I.P.]

Robert Briscoe receiving the mayoral chain from the outgoing Lord Mayor Dockrell in June 1961, after having been elected Lord Mayor of Dublin for the second time. Photo Pat Sweeney, Dublin.

BRISCOE, ROBERT (1894–1969), Irish politician and communal leader who was the first Jewish member of the Irish Dail (parliament) and the first Jewish Lord Mayor of Dublin. He was active in the struggle for Irish independence. From 1917 to 1924 he served in the Irish Republican Army and was sent to the United States to secure financial and moral aid from Irish Americans. He sat in the Dail as a member of De Valera's Fianna Fail Party from 1927 to 1965. From 1928 he was a member of the Dublin Corporation (city council), serving as mayor 1956–57 and 1961–62. Briscoe was an active supporter of the Revisionist movement and a member of the executive of the New Zionist Organization. He gave support to the activities of the *Irgun Ẓeva'i Le'ummi, which utilized his experience of clandestine paramilitary strategy in Palestine. Briscoe was also active in Jewish affairs and was president of the Dublin Board of Sheḥitah. His son Benjamin was elected to the Dail in his father's constituency after the latter's retirement from politics in 1965. Briscoe wrote his autobiography *For the life of Me* (1959). [Ed.]

BRISTOL, seaport in S.W. England. Its medieval Jewish community was one of the more important in England. In about 1183 it was accused of ritual murder (*blood libel) but few details are extant. At the end of the 12th century, an **archa* for registration of Jewish financial transactions was set up. In 1210 all the Jewish householders of England were sent as prisoners to Bristol and a levy of 60,000 (or 66,000) marks was imposed upon them. During

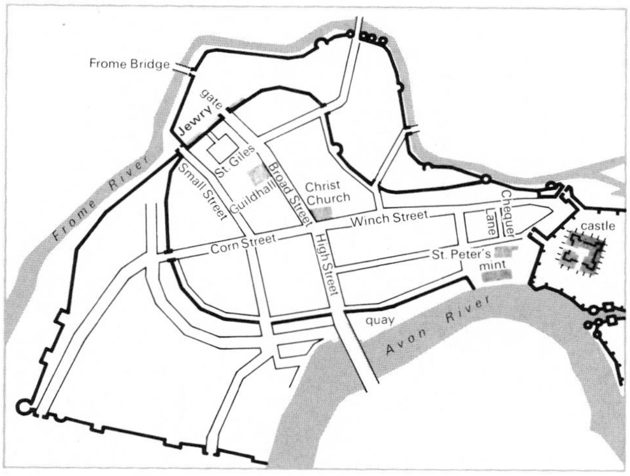

Bristol in 1250, showing the Jewish quarter in the northwestern part of the city.

the Barons' Wars, in 1266, Bristol Jewry was attacked and the *archa* burned. Another attack occurred in 1275, though no lives were lost. At this time the Bristol community received an influx of Jews from Gloucester who were sent there after the expulsion of the Jews from the queen mother's dower-towns. Subsequently several Bristol Jews were hanged for coin clipping. The community came to an end with the expulsion in 1290. Medieval scholars of Bristol include Samuel ha-Nakdan (probably identical with Samuel le Pointur), and Moses, a descendant of R. Simeon the Great of Mainz and ancestor of R. Moses of London and Elijah b. Menahem of London.

In the middle of the 16th century Bristol was the only English town other than London where *Marranos are known to have lived. No organized Jewish community was established, however, until the middle of the 18th century. In 1786 the former Weavers' Hall was taken over as a synagogue. The community leader was Lazarus *Jacobs, a glassmaker, whose work is still sought after by collectors. His son Isaac Jacobs was glass manufacturer to George III. A secessionist community was in existence between c. 1828 and 1835 when it rejoined the parent body. The present synagogue was constructed in 1870. Eastern European Jews arrived after the beginning of the Russian persecutions in 1881, but of late the community has dwindled. The Jewish population numbered 410 in 1968.

Bibliography: M. Adler, in: JHSET, 12 (1928–31), 117–86; idem, *Jews of Medieval England* (1939), 175–251; Rigg-Jenkinson, Exchequer, index; C. Roth, *Rise of Provincial Jewry* (1950), 40–41; idem, in: JHSEM, 2 (1935), 32–56; idem, *Intellectual Activities of Medieval English Jewry* (1948), 47ff.; Wolf, in: JHSET, 11 (1924–27), 5, 34, 92, 104, 109, 111; H. G. Richardson, *English Jewry under Angevin Kings* (1960), 127–8. [C.R.]

BRISZK, family of Transylvanian rabbis.

MORDECAI BEN JOSHUA BRISZK (1884–1944), founder and head of the yeshivah at Tasnad. He was educated in the home of his father who was born at Brest-Litovsk (Brisk), Lithuania, whence he took his family name, but later moved to Hungary, where he became rabbi of Tiszadada. Briszk subsequently studied at the *bet midrash* of Mordecai Loeb Winkler, the rabbi of Mad. In 1908 he was appointed *dayyan* at Marghita, Transylvania, where he had already laid the groundwork for a yeshivah. After he became rabbi of Tasnad in 1919, he expanded his yeshivah, which in 1935 had 450 pupils, making it the largest in Hungary and Transylvania. In his teaching he pursued two basic aims: to equip his pupils with an extensive knowledge of the Talmud and its commentaries, and to prepare them to arrive at halakhic decisions based on a clear understanding of the principles contained in the authorities. Accordingly, he did not limit himself to teaching talmudic themes *(sugyot)* alone, but provided a thorough grounding in the literature of the earlier and the most outstanding later authorities. In 1937 he erected a large building for his yeshivah. Seven years later he and his family were taken to the ghetto at Simleul-Silvaniei. From there he was transported to Auschwitz where he died. Briszk published the work of his father-in-law, Joshua Aaron Ẓevi Weinberger, the rabbi of Marghita, with important addenda of his own, in 1913. He himself was the author of responsa in three parts (Tasnad, 1939), but the printing of the third part was interrupted in the middle and completed in New York in 1963. NATHAN ẒEVI BEN JOSHUA (1883–1944), rabbi and author. The brother of Mordecai and the son-in-law of Naphtali ha-Kohen *Schwarz, he too perished in Auschwitz. From 1909 he was rabbi of Magyarcseke (Ceica), and later of the Orthodox community of Nagyszalonta (Salonta), both in Transylvania. He was the author of several works: *Naḥalat Ẓevi,* on *Avot* (1916); *Naḥalat Avot,* a commentary on the Passover *Haggadah* (1919); *Naḥal Dimah* (1923); *Naḥalat Shivah* (1932), on the festivals and on talmudic themes; and *Ma'amar Esther* (1937), homilies on the Book of Genesis.

Bibliography: Z. Schwarz, *Shem ha-Gedolim me-Ereẓ Hagar,* 2 (1914), 17a; *Elleh Ezkerah,* 2 (1957), 73–80; S. N. Gottlieb, *Sefer Oholei Shem* (1912), 247; N. Ben-Menahem, *Mi-Sifrut Yisrael be-Ungaryah* (1958), 336.

[N.B.-M.]

BRITH ABRAHAM, fraternal order founded on June 12, 1859, in New York City by German and Hungarian Jews. It later attracted also Russian, Polish, and Rumanian Jews. The five original objectives set by Brith Abraham were: (1) aiding members in need, (2) giving medical aid, (3) burying deceased members "in accordance with Jewish Law and ritual," (4) providing for families of deceased members, and (5) assisting members to become citizens. In 1887, 27 delegates to the convention in New York left the order, and at a synagogue on Norfolk Street, under the chairmanship of Jacob Schoen, founded the Independent Order of Brith Abraham. These delegates were dissatisfied with the incompetence of the administration of the original order, and being unable to bring about a change from within, they decided to organize a new order with the same objectives and programs as the old one. In time Brith Abraham became the largest Jewish fraternal order in the world. Yet, though it outnumbered B'nai B'rith, it never equalled the latter in importance. Early in the 20th century, the Independent Order of Brith Abraham reported 302 lodges with a membership of 56,949; by 1909 the number grew to 210,000, but by 1940 the membership declined to 58,000 and since then it has continued to decline. The old Order Brith Abraham had 73,109 members in 1913, but was dissolved in 1927. In 1968 the Independent Order Brith Abraham (which now calls itself Brith Abraham) listed as its activities and objectives: "Fosters brotherhood, Jewish ideals and traditions, and concern for welfare of Jews; provides fraternal benefits to members; supports camps for under-privileged children and senior citizens." It also espoused interest in Zionist and general philanthropic activities. It issued a publication called *The Beacon.*

Bibliography: *History of the Independent Order Brith Abraham* (1937).

[M.A.G.]

BRITISH COLUMBIA, province of Canada bordering the Pacific coast. The discovery of gold on the Fraser River in 1858 brought a population influx into the area, and Jews from all parts of the world were part of the wave which came mainly via California. Josephus Joseph, an Englishman, arrived in Victoria in 1858. His descendants still own property he purchased in Victoria and on the mainland. By the fall of 1858 High Holy Day services were carried on in a private house in Victoria. On May 18, 1859, the tiny community met for the purpose of organizing a burial society, and on June 5 the First Victoria Hebrew Benevolent Society (Chevra Bikur Cholim Ukedusha) was formally established. Early settlers were the Oppenheimer brothers from Germany (see below) via California and Abraham Belasco, father of David *Belasco. In 1863 there were 100 Jews in Victoria who were engaged in various businesses ranging from real estate to seal hunting, and a cornerstone was laid for a synagogue. A rabbi, M. R. Cohen from Sacramento, was engaged to preach for the consecration.

The Jewish community of that area was among the first to provide candidates elected to seats in the legislature. Selim Franklin was elected to the legislature of Vancouver Island in 1860 and became one of the first Jews permitted to hold public office in British North America. In 1866 his brother Lumley Franklin was elected mayor of Victoria, serving one year. In 1870 Henry *Nathan was elected to the last Legislative Council of the Colony of British Columbia. After British Columbia entered the confederation in 1871, Nathan was elected from Victoria to the House of Commons in Ottawa, becoming the first Jewish member of Canada's federal parliament. No permanent Jewish community was established on the mainland until that of *Vancouver at the turn of the century (although individual Jews had lived there from its foundation in 1886). In 1887 David and Isaac Oppenheimer were elected to the Vancouver city council and in 1888 David Oppenheimer was elected as Vancouver's second mayor. David Barrett was elected to the provincial legislature in 1960 and Norman Levi, in 1968. Canada's first Jewish judge, Samuel Scholtz, was appointed to the Vancouver county court in 1914.

The Jewish population of British Columbia in 1941 was somewhat under 3,000. By 1970 it was over 8,000, mostly concentrated in *Vancouver, with only a very small Jewish population in the rest of the province. In Victoria, the cradle of British Columbia's Jewry, the population has been static and even declining, seldom exceeding 200. Prince George, Trail, and Prince Rupert each has less than a dozen Jewish families. No suggestions of anti-Semitism or discriminatory policies have existed in the British Columbia Social Credit government (1952 onward). When incidents have arisen on the part of individuals in the party they have been quickly repudiated. The government passed Fair Employment and Fair Accommodation Practices legislation. British Columbia has the highest proportion of mixed marriages in Canada. It also has the smallest proportion of persons whose mother tongue is Yiddish.

Bibliography: D. Rome, *First Two Years* (1942).

[B.G.K.]

BRITISH ISRAELITES, advocates of the Anglo-Israel theory, which maintains that the English and their ethnic kinfolk throughout the world are descended from the Lost *Ten Tribes of Israel. The theory is based on bizarre theological and linguistic assumptions. Christianity's claim to be the "New Israel" is reinforced by the legend that Joseph of Arimathea established an English church predating that of Rome; the belief that British monarchs, seated at their coronation on the Stone of Scone, are thus in fact consecrated by the patriarch Jacob's stone of Bethel; and the old Puritan idea that the English have refought Israel's battles against God's enemies. By a selective and—according to currently accepted criteria—utterly unscientific interpretation of the Scriptures, British Israelites are able to "prove" that the Japhetic Cymri or Cimmerians are the ancient Britons (*Berit-Ish,* or "Men of the Covenant") and the Saxons, "Isaac's Sons," while the wanderings of the "lost" tribe of Dan are traced from the Dnieper to Denmark and those of the Gadites, from Gotland to Cambria.

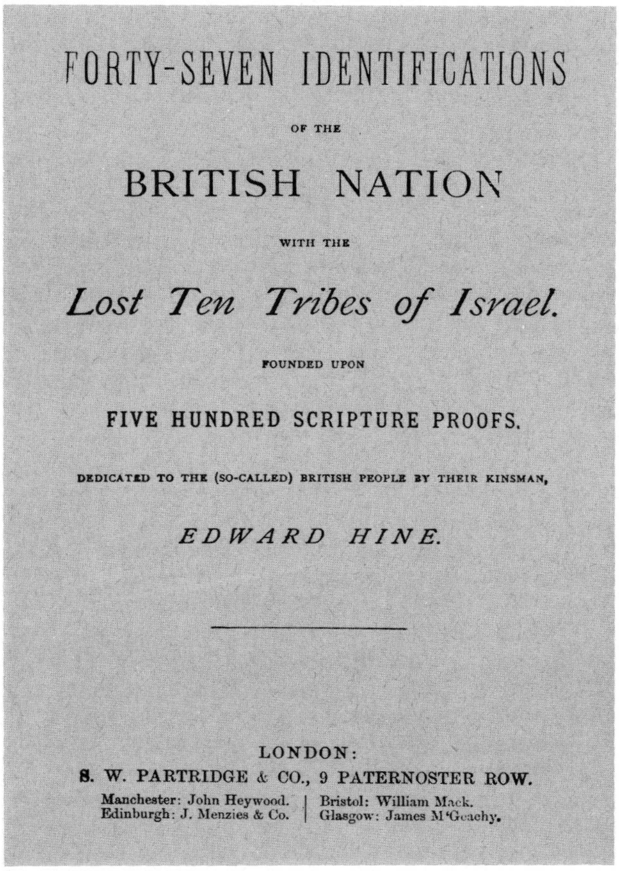
FORTY-SEVEN IDENTIFICATIONS

OF THE

BRITISH NATION

WITH THE

Lost Ten Tribes of Israel.

FOUNDED UPON

FIVE HUNDRED SCRIPTURE PROOFS.

DEDICATED TO THE (SO-CALLED) BRITISH PEOPLE BY THEIR KINSMAN,

EDWARD HINE.

LONDON:
S. W. PARTRIDGE & CO., 9 PATERNOSTER ROW.
Manchester: John Heywood. | Bristol: William Mack.
Edinburgh: J. Menzies & Co. | Glasgow: James M'Geachy.

Edward Hine's book identifying the British people with the Lost Ten Tribes of Israel. London, 1871. Jerusalem, J.N.U.L.

Anglo-Israelism's first manifesto was issued by the Puritan Member of Parliament John Sadler, author of *Rights of the Kingdom* (1649), but the movement began to gather force only at the end of the 18th century, when Richard *Brothers, a messianic prophet and self-styled "Nephew of the Almighty," began publishing a series of pamphlets. A later writer, Edward Hine, published the bestselling *Forty-seven Identifications of the British Nation with the Lost Ten Tribes of Israel* (1871), by which time Anglo-Israelism had crystallized into an organized movement. The British Israel World Federation, with headquarters in London, claims hundreds of thousands of supporters in English-speaking countries; but a kindred organization in the U.S.A., the Anglo-Saxon Federation of America, exploited anti-Semitism in order to further its claims. Anglo-Israelism has become part of the doctrine of various Christian sects, for example the Mormon church.

Bibliography: Hyamson, in: JQR, 15 (1902/03), 640–76; A. Heath, *A Reply* [to] H. L. Goudge, *The British Israel Theory* (1933); C. Roth, *The Nephew of the Almighty* (1933); J. C. James, *Hebrew and English: Some Likenesses, Psychic and Linguistic* (1957).

[G.E.S.]

BRIT IVRIT OLAMIT (Heb. "World Hebrew Union"; Eng. "World Association for Hebrew Language and Culture"), organization for the promotion of Hebrew language and culture. Attempts to organize a world Hebrew-language union had been made during the Sixth Zionist Congress (1903), and by the formation of the Ivriyah Federation at the Hague Conference in 1907, which was attended by Joseph *Klausner. Ḥ. N. *Bialik, and M. *Ussishkin. In 1909 the Hebrew Writers' Circle in Berlin called for a world Hebrew-language congress. The program stipulated that Jewish national bodies should use Hebrew and that Hebrew education should be fostered. The Union consisted mainly of Hebrew-language organizations from Eastern Europe, though affiliated bodies from many Western European countries were also included. There were branches in some 23 countries the world over, including (in 1970), apart from Israel: the United States, Australia, South Africa, and countries in Europe and South America. It was, however, only after the establishment of the State of Israel that the first World Hebrew Congress convened (1950). Izhak *Ben-Zvi and Menahem *Ribalow were elected co-chairmen. Two executives, one in the United States and the other in Israel, were to run the association which was to cooperate closely with the World Zionist Organization and the State of Israel. A second World Congress, held in Jerusalem in 1955, was attended by 270 delegates. The Union and its aims later gained official recognition from the Israel government (1959) and the World Zionist Organization (1960). It actively cooperated with other Jewish bodies (the World Jewish Congress, B'nai B'rith, the British Board of Deputies, and others) whose delegates later attended the Third Congress held in Jerusalem in 1962. Zalman *Shazar was elected president and was subsequently succeeded by Israel *Goldstein, with Arieh *Tartakower as chairman of the executive.

The principal activities of the Brit Ivrit Olamit, which functions in cooperation with the Jewish Agency Department of Education in the Diaspora, consist of promoting spoken Hebrew and modern Hebrew culture, developing Hebrew education, providing material for broadcasting, and issuing a periodical, *Am va-Sefer,* as well

Opening of the third World Congress of the Brit Ivrit Olamit in Jerusalem, 1962. Photo Brit Ivrit Olamit, Jerusalem.

as monographs and written texts for study of the language In the United States it works in cooperation with the Histadrut Ivrit which publishes the Hebrew language weekly *Hadoar.* The organization is financed by the Israel Ministry of Education, the Jewish Agency, and other public and private bodies.

Bibliography: Brit Ivrit Olamit, *Ha-Congress ha-Ivri ha-Olami* (1935, 1955, 1962); *Brit Ivrit Olamit – Ye'udah ve-Darkah* (1965); L. Kuperstein, *Bi-Shelihut ha-Tenu'ah ha-Ivrit* (1964); A. Levinson, *Ha-Tenu'ah ha-Ivrit ba-Golah* (1935); M. Zohary and A. Tartakower (eds.), *Hagut Ivrit be-Eiropah* (1968).

[Is.G.]

BRITTANY (Fr. **Bretagne**), region and former province of western France and ancient independent duchy. Canon 12 of the ecclesiastical Council of Vannes in Brittany (465) forbade clerics to partake in meals with Jews. At about the same time, Nunechius, bishop of *Nantes, welcomed a newly converted Jew. Jews are again found in Brittany from the end of the 12th century living in Ancenis, Clisson, Dol, Guérande, Lamballe, Nantes, and Rennes, and probably also in some other places. By an agreement of Feb. 23, 1222, Pierre Mauclerc, duke of Brittany, confirmed the jurisdiction of the bishop of Nantes over the Jews living in his see. In 1236 many Jews in Brittany were massacred by Crusaders. The remainder were expelled in April 1240 by the duke Jean le Roux who declared a moratorium on all debts owed to Jews and ordered them to return all pledges of chattels or real estate. The duke bound himself and his successors to uphold the decree in perpetuity. For several centuries, therefore, only converted Jews are found living in Brittany. A problem is presented, however, by the Hebrew tombstone (dated 1574) of Solomon b. Jacob Semahes found in Quimperlé. From the beginning of the 17th century, numerous *Marranos settled in Brittany, mainly in Nantes; their Christian competitors failed to have them expelled. During the 18th century, Jewish traders from Bordeaux, Alsace, and Lorraine began to visit the fairs and markets. In 1780, as a result of an isolated incident, they were all expelled. Immediately after the French Revolution, they are found again, notably in Nantes, Brest, Rennes, and Saint-Servan. In 1808, when the *consistories were established, the total number of Jews living in Brittany was only about 30. In 1968 there were communities in Nantes, Brest, and Rennes.

Bibliography: Gross, Gal Jud, 126ff.; Blumenkranz, in: *Etudes d'histoire du droit canonique . . . G. le Bras,* 2 (1965), 1055ff.; L. Brunschvicg, in: REJ, 14 (1887), 84ff.; 49 (1904), 110–20; I. Loeb, *ibid.,* 17 (1888), 92ff.; 33 (1896), 88–121; 43 (1901), 117–22; H. Sée, *ibid.,* 80 (1925), 170–81; J. Montigny, *Essai sur les institutions . . . de Bretagne* (1961); E. Durtelle de Saint-Sauveur, *Histoire de Bretagne* (1957[4]), 230ff.

[B.Bl.]

BRIVIESCA, city in Castile, northern Spain. Briviesca Jewry was closely connected with the communities of *Burgos and *Miranda de Ebro. In 1240 Ferdinand III of Castile ordered the community to continue to pay the amount of 30 denarii annually to the cathedral in lieu of the 30 shekels paid to Judas Iscariot. A number of Jews who had settled in the quarter of Santa Cecilia in Briviesca were conveyed in gift to the monastery of Huelgas by Alfonso X in 1270. Briviesca Jewry was annihilated during the civil war between Pedro the Cruel and Henry of Trastamara in 1366–69, but subsequently reestablished. Records of 1380–81 show Jews of Briviesca engaged in various tax-farming operations. In 1387 the Cortes convened in Briviesca and promulgated a series of anti-Jewish restrictions, including separation of the Jewish, Moorish, and Christian quarters. In 1414 a number of Jewish residents of Briviesca sold land in their possession to a monastery in neighboring Oña. The levy for the war with Granada imposed in 1485 on the Briviesca community and Jews in the vicinity totaled 127 Castilians. No information is available on the fate of the Briviesca Jews after the expulsion from Spain in 1492.

Bibliography: Baer, Urkunden, 1 pt. 2 (1936), index; Cantera, in: *Sefarad,* 2 (1942), 332, 337–8, 360–2; 12 (1952), 68, 71; Huidobro, *ibid.,* 3 (1943), 157–9, 164–6; G. Russell, *English Intervention in Spain and Portugal in the Time of Edward III and Richard II* (1955), 497; Suárez Fernández, Documentos, 66, 75; Baer, Spain, 1 (1961), 365, 420.

[H.B.]

BRNO (Ger. **Bruenn**), capital of Moravia, Czechoslovakia. A community was established there in the first half of the 13th century by Jews invited by the margrave of Moravia. A charter granted in 1254 guaranteed protection to Jewish lives and property, freed Jews from restrictions on trade and occupations, and exempted them from wearing distinguishing dress; the community had to contribute a quarter of the amount required for the upkeep of the city fortifications. The charter was renewed in 1268 and incorporated in the city statutes in 1276. There were about 1,000 Jews living in Brno in 1348. A charter granted in 1345 encouraged Jewish settlement. There was then a Jewish quarter with its own "Jews' Gate." Jewish tombstones have been discovered dating from 1373. In the first half of the 15th century Israel *Bruna officiated as rabbi. The Jews were expelled from Brno in 1454, after John of *Capistrano preached there, and were formally excluded from Brno until 1848 by the privilege *de non tolerandis Judaeis.* Individual Jews, however, paid for permission to attend the markets in the city with an admission fee. This license was extended in 1627 and 1648, but curtailed in 1661. A special inn (leased in 1724 by Jacob Dobruschka) was assigned for Jewish travelers who were officially permitted to spend one night in the city, but often stayed longer illegally. In 1706 the authorities prohibited Jews from holding religious services in public, although these services were tolerated in private. There were then 52 Jews living in Brno. In 1722 the chief representative of Moravian Jewry, the *Landesjudensollicitator,* was permitted to settle near the city gate. The exclusion of the Jews from Brno was renewed in 1745. In 1764 the brothers Hoenig took over the city bank but in the following year, when two of the brothers were permitted to lease houses in Brno, there was an outbreak of rioting. In 1769 Solomon Dobruschka received permission to hold services in his house and to keep a "small" Torah scroll there. However, the authorities still made attempts to prevent the holding of services in public, and in 1812 levied a special tax for "keeping a Torah."

A Hebrew printing press was set up in Brno in 1753 by Franz Joseph Neumann. Jacob *Frank lived in Brno between 1773 and 1786. Following the revolution of 1848 the Jewish community was organized, and received official recognition in 1859. The first rabbi was David Ashkenazi. A cemetery was consecrated in 1852, and a synagogue built in 1855. Baruch *Placzek, when rabbi of Brno, also held the title of **Landesrabbiner* from 1884 until his death in 1922, when it was discontinued. Jewish industrialists, such as Lazar *Auspitz, Julius Ritter von *Gompertz, Loew-Beer, and others, played an important part in developing the textile industry in Brno. During World War I about 16,000 refugees from Eastern Europe were received by the community and many remained there after the war. The Jewish school network established there included the only Jewish high school in western Czechoslovakia. The Jewish population numbered 134 in 1834; 2,230 in 1859; 4,505 in 1869; 7,809 in 1890; and 10,202 (6.9% of the total population) in 1930, of whom 3,295 declared their nationality to be Jewish. Jewish students from Eastern Europe studied at the University of Brno between the two world wars. Largely members of Zionist student groups, they influenced the local Jewish youth in the national spirit. Brno was the seat of the Juedischer Buch- und Kunstverlag and the weekly *Juedische Volksstimme*, founded by Max *Hickl.

During World War II nearly 11,000 Jews were deported from Brno and its surrounding areas to the death camps between Dec. 2, 1941 and July 1, 1943. A memorial plaque to the Jewish victims of Nazism deported from Brno has been affixed to the building where the transports of deportees were concentrated. The survivors who returned to Brno after the Holocaust numbered 1,033 in 1948. The Orthodox synagogue (built in 1932) was restored in the 1950s and was in use in 1968. The rabbi of Brno, Richard *Feder, in 1969 was also chief rabbi of Bohemia and Moravia. The community numbered c. 500 in 1959 and c. 700 in 1969.

Bibliography: Engel, in: JGGJČ, 2 (1930), 50; Kahan, *ibid.*, 9 (1938), 62, 90, 141; M. Brunner, in: H. Gold (ed.) *Die Juden und Judengemeinden Maehrens in Vergangenheit und Gegenwart* (1929), 137–72; L. Levy, *ibid.*, 23–29; B. Bretholz, *Quellen zur Geschichte der Juden in Maehren* (1935), index; idem, *Geschichte der Juden in Maehren im Mittelalter*, 1 (1934), index; idem, *Geschichte der Stadt Bruenn*, 1 (1911), 363–81; Rabinowicz, in: *JQR 75 Years Anniversary Volume* (1967), 429–45; Pick, in: *The Jews of Czechoslovakia*, 1 (1968), 359–438; A. Charim, *Die toten Gemeinden* (1966), 29–36; Cada, in: *Festschrift Guido Kisch* (1955), 261ff.; W. Mueller, *Urkundliche Beitraege zur Geschichte der Maehrischen Judenschaft* (1903); Germ Jud, 2 (1968), 137–40; Freimann, in: ZHB, 20 (1917), 34–44; A. Hellmann, in: A. Engel (ed.), *Gedenkbuch des Juedischen Museums* (1936), 131ff. [I.Z.K.]

BROCH, HERMANN (1886–1951), Austrian novelist. His family were industrialists, and after studying science and engineering he became director of a Viennese textile firm. It was not until he was in his forties that he turned to writing; he established his reputation with his first work *Die Schlafwandler* (3 vols. 1931–32; *The Sleepwalkers*, 1932), a trilogy dealing with the decay of values in the period between 1888 and 1918. Rescued from the Nazis through the intervention of James Joyce and other European writers, Broch settled in Princeton, U.S.A. There he completed his best work, *Der Tod des Vergil* (1945), which he had begun while anticipating death in an Austrian Nazi prison in 1938. This philosophical novel, which appeared simultaneously in an English translation as *The Death of Vergil* (1945) by the poetess Jean Starr *Untermeyer, describes the end of Vergil's life after his return from Greece. Broch's literary style is highly individual and his prose has a lyrical, almost hymn-like quality. His writing is pervaded by the sense of man's mortality; his characters struggle to overcome their constant awareness of their inevitable end. However, he perceives a redeeming spark of divinity which breaks through the contemporary decline of values and allows new hope to spring from apparent despair. Broch's *Gesammelte Werke* appeared in ten volumes (1952–61).

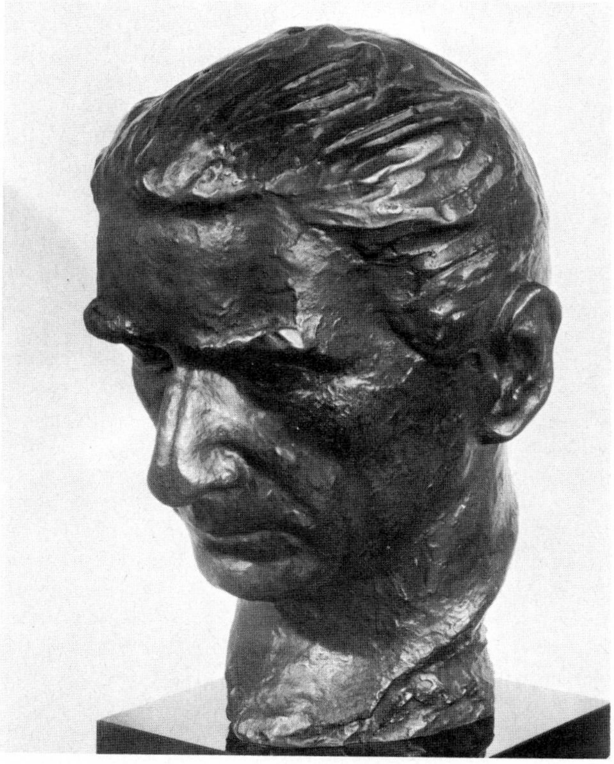

Hermann Broch, Austrian novelist. Sculpture by Irma Rothstein. New York, Leo Baeck Institute.

Bibliography: E. Kahler (et al.), *Dichter wider Willen . . .* (1958); T. Koebner, *Hermann Broch—Leben und Werk* (1965); W. Somm, *Hermann Broch: Geist, Prophete und Mystik* (1965); M. Durzak, *Hermann Broch in Selbstzeugnissen und Bilddokumenten* (1966). [S.L.]

BROCINER, JOSEPH (1846–1918), publicist and communal leader in Rumania and in Jassy. He spent most of his life in Galati and was active in the struggle of Rumanian Jewry for emancipation during and after the Congress of *Berlin (1878). His major contribution was in the sphere of literary polemics. He sought to refute by historical evidence the claim that the Jews were "aliens," adduced against granting them citizenship rights in Rumania. The most important of these works is *Chestiunea Israeliților Români* ("The Rumanian Jewish Question," 1910), because of the many documents published in it, some for the first time. Brociner was also active in reconstructing the officially recognized Jewish communal organization, which had been disorganized since 1862. In March 1896, he convened in Galati a general conference of the representatives of the communities in Rumania, the first in the country, where a plan for communal organization was reviewed. In 1901 he convened a second conference at Jassy, when the "Union of Israelite Communities in Rumania" was founded. He also wrote several publications on the subject, among them a detailed memorandum to the government; these publications also included important historical documents. Brociner was among the first members of Ḥovevei Zion in Rumania. He also became associated with political Zionism and sent a proposal to Theodor *Herzl for the organization of the Zionist movement in Rumania. Brociner's brother MAURICIU (Moritz; 1855–194?) was the first Jewish officer in the Rumanian Army. He distinguished himself in the Rumanian War of Independence of 1877 and later attained the rank of colonel. For many years he filled senior administrative posts at court and served as private secretary to the queen. Another brother was the Austrian author and playwright, MARCO BROCINER (1852–1942).

Bibliography: *J. B. Brociner, Notițe Biografice-Notice Biographique* (1913); S. Wininger, *Artistii, Scriitorii, Savantii, Financiarii, și Intemeietorii Evrei din Romania* (Ms. Jerusalem National Library), 875–83. [EL.F.]

BROCKTON, city in Massachusetts, 20 miles (32 km.) south of Boston. The first Jews to settle in Brockton were immigrants from Eastern Europe who came about 1886. Many found employment in the shoe and leather industry, which then dominated the city's economy. High Holiday services were first held in 1896 and the first synagogue, Agudas Zion, was incorporated in 1899. A Young Men's and Young Women's Hebrew Association was established in 1911 and its Jewish Community Center in 1931.

By the 1960s Brockton had become in effect a suburb of Boston. In 1969 there were three synagogues: Agudas Achim (Orthodox), founded in 1900; Temple Israel (Reform), founded in 1922; and Temple Beth Emunah (Conservative), founded in 1951. In addition the Jewish community maintains a Combined Jewish Philanthropies, a Jewish family service, and The South Shore Hebrew Academy. Many Jews have been prominent in the city's business and political life. Among them were Alvin Jack Sims, mayor 1964–67; Max Coffman who achieved distinction in the discount merchandising field; and Dewey D. *Stone. In 1969 of a total estimated population of 92,000 there were 5,000 Jews living in Brockton. [H.B.E.]

BROD, MAX (1884–1968), Czech-born German author and composer. Born in Prague, Brod studied law at the German university there and then entered the Czech civil service. In 1924 he joined the *Prager Tagblatt* as theatrical and musical editor. He helped found the National Council of Jews of Czechoslovakia in 1918, and became active in the Zionist movement. In 1939, he settled in Tel Aviv and worked as a music critic and drama adviser to *Habimah.

Brod's prolific writings include poetry, fiction, plays, literary criticism, and essays on philosophy, politics, and Zionism. The fundamental thought in all his writing is the problem of dualism, i.e., the difficulty of reconciling a belief in God with the evil that exists in the world. Man's task, he believes, is to strive toward perfection. Judaism, which represents the "miracle of this world," is a critical stage on this road as opposed to the "continuation of this world" in paganism and the "negation of this world" in Christianity. This is propounded in his most influential philosophical work, *Heidentum, Christentum, Judentum,* 2 vols. (1921). Brod's best-known writings are his 20 novels, some of them romantic, others historical. The former include *Schloss Nornepygge* (1908), *Juedinnen* (1911), *Arnold Beer: Das Schicksal eines Juden* (1912), *Die Frau, nach der man sich sehnt* (1927), and *Die verbotene Frau* (1960); among the latter are *Tycho Brahes Weg zu Gott* (1916; *The Redemption of Tycho Brahe,* 1928); *Rëubeni, Fuerst der Juden* (1925); *Galilei in Gefangenschaft* (1948); *Unambo* (1949), about the Israel War of Independence; *Der Meister* (1949)—another version of this book about Jesus appeared in Hebrew in 1956 with the title *Aḥot Ketannah*—and *Armer Cicero* (1955). Brod's plays include *Eine Koenigin Esther* (1918), *Die Retterin* (1919), *Die Faelscher* (1920), and *Klarissas halbes Herz* (1923). He also wrote a biography of Heine (1934).

Brod was the first person to recognize the unique quality of his friend Franz *Kafka, about whom he wrote his novel *Das Zauberreich der Liebe* (1928; *The Kingdom of Love,* 1930). It was Brod who arranged the publication of Kafka's works in the 1930s, a decade after the novelist's death. His biography of Kafka appeared in 1937. He also revealed the genius of Jaroslav Hašek, author of *The Good Soldier Schweik,* and of the composers Leoš Janáček (whose biography he published in 1924–25) and Jaromir *Weinberger, publishing German translations of Janáček's *Jenufa* (1918) and Weinberger's *Schwanda the Bagpiper.*

Many of Brod's books and plays were translated into Hebrew and together with Shin *Shalom he wrote two dramatic works in Hebrew: *Sha'ul, Melekh Yisrael* ("Saul, King of Israel," 1944) and the libretto to Marc *Lavry's opera *Dan ha-Shomer* (1945). Max Brod's musical compositions include a piano quintet, *Requiem Hebraïcum*

Max Brod reading a script to two Habimah directors, Baruch Chemerinsky (center) and Zvi Friedland, c. 1939. Jerusalem, Keren Hayesod-United Israel Appeal Photo Archives.

(words by Shin Shalom), songs, piano pieces, and Israel dances. Brod's last works were his autobiography, *Streitbares Leben* (1960) and reminiscences, *Der Prager Kreis* (1967).

Bibliography: F. Weltsch ed., *Dichter, Denker, Helfer* (Festschrift . . . Brod, 1934), includes bibliography of first editions; E. F. Taussig (ed.), *Ein Kampf um Wahrheit* (Festschrift . . . Brod, 1949); Riemann-Gurlitt, s.v.; Baker, Biog Dict, s.v.; Bergman, in: *Ariel,* no. 11 (1965), 5–11; Weltsch, in: *Judaism,* 14 (1965), 48–59; H. Gold (ed.), *Max Brod–Ein Gedenkbuch* (1969).

[F.W./Ed.]

BRODA, family of rabbis in Lithuania and Slovakia (then in Hungary) from the 17th century on. Ḥayyim Broda, a grandson of Abraham *Broda was rabbi of Janow; his son Aaron was rabbi of Kalvanÿa, Lithuania; and his son Benjamin (d. 1818) was appointed rabbi of Grodno in 1792 and was the last *av bet din* of the city. A dispute between the supporters of Broda and the adherents of Tanḥum b. Eliezer led to the abolition of the office.

Benjamin's son Ḥayyim wrote *Torah Or ve-Derekh Ḥayyim* (Grodno, 1823), on the laws of ritual slaughter, and *Zera Ḥayyim* (published by his grandson Ḥayyim *Heller in 1907), the aim of which was to defend the rulings of the Shulḥan Arukh against the criticisms of *Shabbetai b. Meir ha-Kohen in his *Gevurot Anashim.* Ḥayyim engaged in halakhic correspondence with Abraham *Danzig and *Abraham Abele b. Abraham Solomon Poswoler of Vilna. One of his sons, Dov Ber (d. 1897), was the author of *Divrei Binah* (2 pts., 1888–90) on the tractate *Makkot.* Ḥayyim's son-in-law was Israel Issar b. Mordecai Isserlin (1827–1899), who served as rabbi in Vilna. The following among his works are known: *Shem Yisrael* (1859, published anonymously), a commentary to the Mishnah *Seder Zera'im; Ishei Yisrael* (1864), novellae to the tractate *Shabbat; Tosefot Yerushalayim* (1871), on the Tosefta; *Pitḥei Teshuvah* (1875), on the Shulḥan Arukh, *Oraḥ Ḥayyim.* Another son-in-law of Ḥayyim Broda was Eliezer b. Samuel Landau (1805–1883), who was born in Vilna and served as the head of the Brodno community. He was the author of *Dammesek Eliezer* (1868–70), a commentary in two parts on the expositions of *Elijah b. Solomon Zalman to the Shulḥan Arukh, *Oraḥ Ḥayyim.*

Other important members of the family were (1) Aaron b. Israel (second half of the 17th century), who compiled *Otot le-Mo'adim* (Grodno, 1798), a calendar for the years 5549–5624, appended to which is *Nahara u-Fashta,* a book on customs by Ḥayyim b. Israel Broda. He also wrote *Tekumah,* a digest in rhymed prose of the laws of the Shulḥan Arukh, of which only the section on *Even ha-Ezer, Even Ẓiyyon be-Mishpat,* was published (Shklov, 1784; complete

ספר

פרי החג

כולל רוב הלכות חג הפסח בדברי הגמרא וראשונים · ושרשי דברי היוצאים
מדברי האחרונים · וראשי החומריות הנופלים · ונטפל אליו מחי׳ רעיוני
אשר ברוב יגיעתי חנני השם לתרץ באיזה מקומו דברי רבותינו הראשונים ·
חברתי בעזרת החונן דעת :

הק׳ אברהם בן לאדוני הרבני המופלג בתורה החו״ש כש״ת מוה׳ שלמה זלמן
ברודא ז״ל בן הרב המאור הגדול לד״ק כסגנ כקש״ת מוה׳ מרדכי ברודא
זלה״ל ...
מוהר״ר אברהם ברודא זצ״ל ...
בעל המחבר ... · ומילדי ק״ק אונגהוואר

... ק״ק קליינווארדיין יע״א

אונגהוואר

בשנת אלה מועדי ה׳ אשר תקראו אותם מקראי קודש לפ״ק

Pri Hachag

Ge'rukt in Ungvár bei Karl Jägers Wittwe 1871.

Title page of part one of *Peri he-Ḥag*, a work on the laws of Passover by Abraham b. Solomon Zalman Broda, Ungvár, 1871. Jerusalem, J.N.U.L.

edition by his son Nissim, Vilna, 1818). Other works have remained in manuscript; (2) Ẓevi Hirsch b. David (d. 1820?), rabbi of Szenice, and after 1787 rabbi of Kittsee (Köpcsény), Hungary; was the author of *Ereẓ Ẓevi* and *Te'omei Ẓeviyyah* (pt. 1, Vienna, 1823; pt. 2, Pressburg, 1846), a commentary on chapters 1–65 and 119–178 of the Shulḥan Arukh, *Even ha-Ezer;* and *Shenei Ofarim* (Prague, 1825), sermons, published by his son Aaron; (3) Abraham b. Solomon Zalman (1825–1882) was born in Ungvár (Uzhgorod) and studied in the yeshivah of Moses *Sofer in Pressburg. He lived in Kleinwardein and was rabbi of Nagyberezna from 1876 until his death. He was the author of *Peri he-Ḥag* (2 pts., 1871–76), on the laws of Passover, and *Halikhot Olam* (1874–75, pt. 1 (1927[5]), ed. by I. Gruenwald), in Judeo-German on laws of daily application; (4) Abraham Aaron b. Shalom (d. after 1860) was born in Vilna. He was the author of *Beit Va'ad* (1832), a selection of laws from the four parts of the Shulḥan Arukh, to which was appended *Beit Middot* on weights and measures in the Talmud; and *Bayit ha-Gadol* (1838), a commentary on *Pirkei de-Rabbi Eliezer;* (5) Mordecai b. Nathan Nata (1815–1882) was born in Nádas, Hungary, and from 1864 served as rabbi of Myjava. His *Ḥiddushei She'elot u-Teshuvot Maharam Broda* (1908) was published by his son-in-law Akiva Strasser. His son Joseph, who succeeded him as chief rabbi of Myjava, perished at Auschwitz in the Holocaust.

Bibliography: S. J. Fuenn, *Kiryah Ne'emanah* (1860), 230; S. A. Freidenstein, *Ir Gibborim* (1880), 55–56; H. N. Maggid-Steinschneider, *Ir Vilna* (1900), 277, n. 12, 303; A. Frankl-Gruen, *Geschichte der Juden in Ungarisch-Brod* (1905), 47–48, 50ff.; J. J. Greenwald, *Pe'erei Ḥakhmei Medinatenu* (1910), 44 no. 59, 66 no. 9; idem, *Ha-Yehudim be-Ungarya* (1912), 76; P. Z. Schwartz, *Shem ha-Gedolim me-Ereẓ Hagar* (1913–15), see rabbis and their books; A. M. Broda, *Mishpaḥat Broda* (1938); N. Ben-Menahem, *Mi-Sifrut Yisrael be-Ungaryah* (1958), 109; *Yahadut Lita*, 3 (1967), 26, 65.

[J.Ho.]

BRODA, ABRAHAM BEN SAUL (d. 1717), rabbi and halakhic authority. Broda was born in Bunzlau (Bohemia) and served as rabbi in Lichtenstadt and in Raudnitz. In 1693 he was appointed head of a yeshivah in Prague but left after a dispute with other rabbis of the city. In 1709 he was appointed rabbi of Metz, and in 1713 of Frankfort, where he remained until his death. In these last two cities he established yeshivot which attracted many students. In his approbation to *Eshel Avraham*, Jonathan *Eybeschuetz paid tribute to Broda's contribution to education and teaching: "He was remarkably successful in learning, teaching, and disseminating Torah, and most contemporary scholars of renown were his disciples. Among his outstanding students were Nethanel *Weil, Jonah *Landsofer, and Samuel Helman of Metz. His novellae were noted by his students, who quoted them in their works, or published them together with their own works. Broda's most important work is *Eshel Avraham* (1747), novellae on the tractates *Pesaḥim*, *Ḥullin*, and *Bava Batra*. This reveals his erudition, keen intellect, and methodical treatment of the subject matter. The first part, *Ḥiddushei Halakhot*, summarizes each topic on the basis of the Talmud and its commentaries, and the second, *Ḥiddushei Posekim*, deals with halakhic rulings which derive from these sources. Other works by Broda are *Ḥiddushei Ge'onim* (Offenbach, 1723), on *Bava Kamma*, *Bava Meẓia*, and *Sanhedrin; Ḥiddushei Hilkhot Gittin* (Wandsbeck, 1731), published by his disciple, Jonathan b. Isaac ha-Levi; *Shema'ta Ḥadta* (Frankfort, 1737), novellae and explanations on *Ketubbot* and the second chapter of *Gittin*, and *Toledot Avraham* (Fuerth, 1769), novellae to *Kiddushin* and *Ketubbot* (incomplete). Israel Isserl b. Isaac ha-Levi (beginning of 18th century), a disciple of Broda, published *Asefat Ḥakhamim* (1722), which included novellae by Broda. In a *takkanah* of 1715, Broda deals with the question of modesty, warns against extravagant festivities, and pleads for abstention from extravagance and forbidden foods. His son, Moses (1674–1741), served from 1704 as rabbi of Hanau, and from 1718 as rabbi of Bamberg, transferring to Worms in 1733. He prepared his father's *Eshel Avraham* for publication, adding to it his own glosses, entitled *Ohel Moshe*. The publication was completed by Moses' son Saul.

Bibliography: M. Horovitz, *Frankfurter Rabbinen*, 2 (1883), 79–82, 100 (no. 4427), 103–4; Cahen, in: REJ, 8 (1884), 260–7; Kaufmann, *ibid.*, 19 (1889), 120–9; A. Eckstein, *Geschichte der Juden im ehemaligen Fuerstbistum Bamberg* (1898), 169–70, no. 12; Loewenstein, in: JJLG, 14 (1921), 18–19; Jakobovits, in: JGGJČ, 5 (1933), 79–112, 127–8; N. Netter, *Vingt siècles d'histoire d'une communauté juive (Metz)* (1938), 90–93; A. Broda, *Mishpaḥat Broda* (1938), 27–28; Assaf, Mekorot, 4 (1942), 118–9; Shisha, in: *Ha-Ohel*, 1 (1955), 130–5.

[Y.Ho.]

BRODER (Margolis), BERL (c. 1815–1868), Yiddish balladist and **badhan*, who derived his name from his city of Brody (Galicia). A brushmaker by profession, Broder composed songs and rhymed verses in the style of the *badḥanim*. He later became a buyer for his firm and sang his compositions at various inns where he stopped for the night. In 1855, on an extended business trip to Russia,

Broder entertained his fellow travelers and chance acquaintances with his lyrics. Itinerant minstrels imitated and disseminated his texts and tunes, which influenced Benjamin *Ehrenkranz (Velvel Zbarazher), *Zunser, and Abraham *Goldfaden. In the 1860s Broder organized the first troupe of professional Yiddish folksingers, which traversed Galicia, Hungary, and Rumania, singing in wine cellars and inns. The stage of the *Broder Singers consisted merely of a table with two lit candles. Though their lyrics were at first hardly suitable for such dramatic presentation, the success of their acting and singing was immense, and they paved the way for the Yiddish theater. Their original repertoire, *Draysik Herlikhe Broder Lider in Reyn Yidish Loshn* ("30 Marvelous Brody Songs in Pure Yiddish," Pressburg, c. 1860), was frequently reprinted.

Bibliography: N. M. Gelber, *Aus zwei Jahrhunderten* (1924), 70–100; idem, *Toledot Yehudei Brody* (1957), 227–9; Rejzen, Leksikon, 1 (1926), 395–401; I. Schipper, *Geshikte fun Yidishe Teaterkunst un Drame bay Yiden* (1929), iv, ix; B. Margolis, *Dray Doyres* (1957), contains Berl Broder's songs (and his son's and grandson's also).

[S.L.]

BRODER SINGERS, generic name for small groups of itinerant male Yiddish singers who from the 1850s entertained on weekdays (as distinct from Sabbaths and festivals) on improvised stages in wine cellars and restaurant gardens in Galicia, Rumania, and southern Russia. The name designates a kind of cabaret tradition, its style and repertoire, rather than a specific group or individual. The impact of this tradition on the Yiddish poetic imagination may be gauged in *Peretz' drama *Baynakht oyfn Altn Mark,* and in the works of Itzik *Manger.

The Broder Singers are important in the prehistory of the modern Yiddish theater. They were essentially vocalists (many were former *badḥanim* (see **Badḥan*) and choirboys) who gradually added costume, mimicry, and dance to songs which to begin with were generally dramatic monologues. Solo performance gave way to dramatized duet and subsequently to the musical sketch, with prose recitative linking the songs. The Broder Singers were a source for the first Yiddish stage professionals—Yisroel Gradner, regarded as the first "regular" Yiddish actor, was a Broder Singer before joining *Goldfaden. The reputed "father" of the Broder Singers was Berl *Broder. Though Broder's date and place of birth are disputed, it is almost certain that his association in the years before the Crimean War with the Galician commercial center, Brody (from which he took his name), accounts for the name Broder Singers. Broder composed songs, some of which are extant, but the repertoire was mainly appropriated from the folk poets Eliakum *Zunser and Velvel Zbarazher (Benjamin *Ehrenkranz), from I. J. *Linetzky and the dramatist *Goldfaden, all four of whom were closely linked to the Broder Singers. The repertoire was serious as well as satiric and comic. The prevalence of anti-ḥasidic songs does not justify the often expressed view that the Broders Singers were the poor man's Haskalah, for the principal emphasis was always on entertainment.

Bibliography: Teplitski, in: *YIVO Bleter,* 23 (March–April 1944), 284–7 (contemporary accounts); N. M. Gelber, *Aus zwei Jahrhunderten* (1924), 70–101; Z. Zylbercweig, *Leksikon fun Yidishn Teater,* 1 (1931), 216–36, 508–15; S. Prizament, *Broder Zinger* (1960); D. Sadan, *Avnei Miftan* (1962), 9–17; M. Weinreich and Z. Rejzen, in: *Arkhiv far di Geshikhte fun Yidishn Teater un Drame,* 1 (1930), 455.

[L.P.]

BRODERZON, MOSHE (1890–1956), Yiddish poet and theater director. A descendant of a family of wealthy merchants who were permitted to reside in Moscow,

Title page of Moshe Broderzon's story, *Siḥat Ḥullin,* illustrated by Eliezer Lissitzky, Moscow, 1917. New York, YIVO.

Broderzon received his early education in that city and at a Lodz commercial academy. He lived in Lodz from 1918 to 1938. Active as a journalist, poet, and writer of short plays, he founded little theaters in Lodz: *Ḥad Gadya,* the first Yiddish marionette theater, *Ararat,* and *Shor ha-Bor.* He was head of the literary group Yung-Yidish and discovered many new Jewish talents for the stage. He wrote songs for children, which were frequently reprinted and set to music, and also libretti for operas, including *David and Bath-Sheba* (1924). His final lyrics, which appeared in 1939 with the single letter *Yod* as title, comprise 50 poems of 16 lines each, laden with tragic premonitions of the end of Polish Jewry in a coming world catastrophe. Broderzon returned to his native Moscow in 1939. At the time of Stalin's persecutions of Yiddish writers he was confined and remained in a Siberian work camp from 1948 to 1955. Repatriated to Poland on his liberation, he was enthusiastically acclaimed by the surviving Jews there, but collapsed and died a few weeks later while visiting Warsaw. Broderzon was a consummate master of the Yiddish tongue and of most original Yiddish rhymes. His poems combine Jewish folklore with European expressionism. His wife, the actress Sheyne Miriam Broderzon, described their years of suffering (1939–56) in *Mayn Laydnsveg mit Moyshe Broderzon* ("My Tragic Road with Moshe Broderzon," 1960).

Bibliography: M. Ravitch, *Mayn Leksikon,* 1 (1945), 49–51; LNYL, 1 (1956), 429–32; M. Broderzon, *Oysgeklibene Shriftn* (1959), introd. by S. Rozanski and bibliography by E. M. Jeschurin.

[M.Rav.]

BRODETSKY, SELIG (1888–1954), mathematician and Zionist leader. Brodetsky, who was born in Olviopol, Ukraine, was brought to London by his family in 1893. He received his early education at the Jewish Free School in London, at the same time attending a *talmud torah.* The exceptional ability which he early displayed in mathematics earned him a scholarship to Cambridge. At the age of 20 he was given the honors title of Senior Wrangler. He continued his studies in mathematical astronomy at the University of Leipzig and received his doctorate in 1913. In 1914 he returned to England, where he was appointed lecturer in practical mathematics at Bristol and was professor at the University of Leeds from 1920 to 1949. A highly successful educator, he specialized in theoretical aerodynamics, a field vital for the development of the airplane, dealt with in his *Mechanical Principles of the Aeroplane* (1920). He also wrote on the general theory of relativity, on Newton, as well as popular works on mathematics and the sciences. *The Meaning of Mathematics* (1929) was translated into Dutch,

Spanish, and Hebrew. From his earliest youth Brodetsky was a dedicated Zionist. When the Zionist Association was established in Cambridge in 1907, Brodetsky was appointed its secretary. In Leipzig, he served as president of the Zionist Student Organization. In 1928 he became a member of the executive committee of the Zionist Organization in England, and through it, also of the governing body of the Jewish Agency, serving as head of its Political Department in London. In this position he led the struggle against Lord Passfield's White Paper of 1930. He was a loyal supporter of Chaim *Weizmann. From 1939 to 1949 he was president of the *Board of Deputies of British Jews, the first East European Jew to serve in this capacity. He was responsible for bringing this body closer to Zionism. When Weizmann became president of the new State of Israel, Brodetsky succeeded him as president of the British Zionist Federation. Brodetsky was also a member of the board of trustees and of the academic council of the Hebrew University. In 1949, he succeeded Judah *Magnes as president of the Hebrew University, making his home in Israel. For reasons of ill health and because of differences of opinion over the management of the university, he resigned from this position and returned in 1952 to England. Brodetsky was a Fellow of the Royal Societies of Astronomy (FRAS) and of Aeronautics (FRAeS) and for

Selig Brodetsky, British mathematician and Zionist leader. Jerusalem, Hebrew University. Photo Alfred Bernheim, Jerusalem.

some time was also the president of the Association of University Teachers in England. He was the president of the World Organization of Maccabi. His biographical work, *Memoirs—From Ghetto to Israel,* was published posthumously in 1960. [L.K./Ed.]

BRODIE, SIR ISRAEL (1895–), chief rabbi of the British Commonwealth, 1948–65. Brodie was born in Newcastle-on-Tyne and educated at Jews' College, London, and at Oxford. From 1923 to 1937 he was senior minister at *Melbourne, Australia. He served as a chaplain overseas in both

Sir Israel Brodie, Chief Rabbi of the United Hebrew Congregations of the British Commonwealth, 1948–1965. Photo Blackstone Studios, N.Y.

world wars, becoming senior Jewish chaplain in the British Army in 1944. He was involved in two important controversies: one over his ruling (later modified) that the Israel pronunciation of Hebrew should not be used in synagogues and in classrooms; the other when he decided that the liberal theological views of Louis *Jacobs disqualified him from being appointed as principal of Jews' College or a minister of the United Synagogue. Brodie edited the *Ez Ḥayyim* of *Jacob b. Judah Ḥazzan of London (3 vols., 1962–67). He was the divisional editor for rabbinical literature in the *Encyclopaedia Judaica.*

Bibliography: Shaftesley, in: H. J. Zimmels et al. (eds.), *Essays . . . I. Brodie . . .* (1967), xi–xxxix. [V.D.L.]

BRODSKI, family of industrialists and philanthropists in Russia, whose members played an important role in the Russian economy and Jewish communal life from the middle of the 19th century. It was founded by Meir Schor, a member of the Schor family of distinguished rabbis and communal leaders, who moved from Brody in Galicia to Zlatopol in the province of Kiev in the early 19th century and took the name of Brodski (i.e., "from Brody"). Of his five sons, all wealthy businessmen, the most prominent, Israel (1823–1888), took a leading part in the development of the sugar industry in the Ukraine. During the 1840s, he financed the establishment of several sugar refineries by Russian estate owners in conjunction with other investors. Subsequently, he began to manage them himself and leased or founded additional plants. Brodski introduced many improvements in production methods and an elaborate administration for marketing the sugar within Russia and for export. In 1876 he moved to Kiev, where he became one of the leaders of the community. He built the Jewish hospital and other welfare institutions there. He also helped the *Volozhin yeshivah to establish a *kolel* for young scholars.

His sons Eliezer (Lazar; 1848–1904) and Arieh Leibush (Lev; 1852–1923) enlarged their father's enterprises. In the early 1890s the plants owned by Brodski produced approximately one-quarter of the total amount of sugar refined in Russia. The brothers continued to contribute generously to Jewish and Russian cultural and welfare institutions, and among other benefactions founded the polytechnical and bacteriological institutes in Kiev, donated 300,000 rubles for the establishment of a Jewish school with a department for vocational training, built the great synagogue in Kiev, and gave substantial assistance to victims of the pogroms. The efforts of the Zionist Organization of Russia to persuade Lev Brodski to redeem the area around the Western Wall in Jerusalem were unsuccessful. The Brodski firms employed thousands of Jewish office workers and agents. The Hebrew writers, J. L. *Levin (Yehalal) and Eleazar *Schulmann, were among their employees. After the 1917 Revolution their property was confiscated and Lev Brodski left with his family for Western Europe. Abraham (1816–1884), Israel's brother who settled in Odessa in 1858, contracted to collect the communal meat tax and donated the revenues to Jewish institutions. He also established two Jewish agricultural colonies. Both he and his son Samuel (1837–1897) served as municipal councillors in Odessa.

Bibliography: E. E. Friedman, *Sefer ha-Zikhronot* (1926), 213–4, 221–3, 335–8; H. Landau, in: *YIVO Shriften far Ekonomik un Statistik,* 1 (1928), 98–104; B. Weinryb, *Neueste Wirtschaftsgeschichte der Juden in Russland und Polen,* 1 (1934), 87, 212. [Y.S.]

BRODSKI, ALEKSANDER ILICH (1895–), Russian physical chemist. He was born in Moscow and obtained his doctorate from Moscow University. He joined the Ukrainian Physico-chemical Institute at Dnepropetrovsk about 1930, and from 1938 was director of the L. V. Pisarzhevski Institute of Physical Chemistry of the

Ukrainian S.S.R. Academy of Sciences at Kiev. He became a member of the Academy in 1939 and a corresponding member of the U.S.S.R. Academy of Sciences in 1943. In 1946 he was awarded a Stalin Prize. The major fields with which he concerned himself were: electrochemistry; the refractivity, spectra, and other properties of solutions; radiation chemistry; and the uses of isotopes. His textbook on physical chemistry (*Fizicheskaya Khimiya,* 2 vols., 1932–33) was translated into other Eastern European languages. He also wrote books on electrolytes (1934), on thermodynamic functions (1948), and on isotopes (1952).

Bibliography: J. Turkevich, *Soviet Men of Science* (1963), 66–67. [S.A.M.]

BRODSKI, YOSIF (1940–), Soviet Russian poet and translator. Although he was widely regarded as one of the most promising Soviet poets, none of Brodski's original verse had been allowed to appear in the U.S.S.R. as late as 1970. He was known there only as a translator from several languages, including English, Spanish, and Polish, and as the author of poems printed in the illegal, mimeographed literary journal *Sintaksis* (1958–60). In February 1964, Brodski was tried as a "social parasite" *(tuneyadets)* who changed jobs too frequently, and was sentenced to forced labor in the far north. His trial had pronounced anti-Semitic overtones. Jewish witnesses for the defense, such as the scholars Y. G. Etkind and V. G. *Admoni, were ridiculed for their "strange-sounding" names; and the intercession of such distinguished older writers as Kornei Chukovksi, Samuel *Marshak and Anna Akhmatova also failed to help Brodski. He was later arrested and released several times. Brodski's verse is traditional, though with occasional traces of symbolist and surrealist influence. *Isaak i Avraam,* one of his long narrative poems, is based on biblical motifs, while *Yevreyskoye kladbishche okolo Leningrada* ("The Jewish Cemetery near Leningrad") is one of the most remarkable poems on a Jewish theme ever written by a Soviet author.

Bibliography: G. Stukov, in: Y. Brodski, *Stikhotvoreniya i poemy* (1965), 5–15; Y. Brodski, *Elegy to John Donne and Other Poems* (tr. by N. Bethell, 1967), contains in the introduction part of the transcript of Brodski's trial; the entire transcript appeared in *The New Leader,* Aug. 31, 1964. [M.F.]

BRODSKY, ADOLF (1851–1929), Russian violinist. Brodsky was born in Taganrog and studied in Vienna and Moscow, where he was professor at the conservatory from 1875 to 1879. He was a friend of Brahms, Grieg, and Tchaikovsky, who dedicated his *Violin Concerto* to him. Brodsky gave the first performance of the concerto with the Vienna Philharmonic Orchestra in 1882. From 1883 to 1891 he was a professor in Leipzig, where he formed the noted Brodsky Quartet. He toured widely as a soloist and was leader of the *Damrosch Symphony Orchestra in New York (1891–94) and of the Hallé Orchestra in Manchester, England. On Hallé's death in 1895, Brodsky succeeded him as director of the Royal College of Music in Manchester.

Bibliography: Riemann-Gurlitt; Grove, Dict; Baker, Biog Dict; Sendrey, Music, no. 4788. [D.L.S.]

BRODSKY, ISAAC ISRAELEVICH (1884–1930), Russian painter. Brodsky was born and lived most of his life in St. Petersburg (Leningrad). He studied in Odessa at the School of Fine Arts and later at the Academy. Although he was influenced at first by the modernist trends represented in Odessa mainly by Alexander Exter, Brodsky soon distinguished himself as a virtuoso realist. Under the Soviet regime, he became Russia's most successful portrait painter, and his portraits of Lenin at the Smolny Institute and of other popular Soviet leaders were widely reproduced. Never really a representative of the official Soviet "socialist realist" school of art, Brodsky would have been called, in the Western world, a "magical realist." In his portrait of Lenin, for instance, Brodsky's sobriety in his choice and treatment of significant detail suggests an interest in early Flemish and Dutch art rather than in the application of socialist realist principles. His works thus stand the test of time much better than those of other Soviet artists who, later in the Stalinist era, conformed more strictly to orthodox standards. Nearly all Brodsky's major works are in Soviet museums, especially in Moscow's Tretyakovskaya Gallery.

Bibliography: S. Issakov, *Brodsky* (1945); I. I. Brodsky, *Moy tvorcheskiy put* (1940). [E.R.]

BRODY, city in Lvov district, Ukrainian S.S.R. (in Russia until 1772; in Austria, 1772–1919; and in Poland, 1919–39). An organized Jewish community existed in Brody by the end of the 16th century. In 1648 approximately 400 Jewish families are recorded. The Jewish quarter was destroyed by fire in 1696. Subsequently the overlords of Brody, the Sobieskis, granted the Jews a charter (1699) permitting them to reside in all parts of the town, to engage in all branches of commerce and crafts, and to distill beer, brandy, and mead in return for an annual payment; the communal buildings, including the hospital and the homes of the rabbi and cantor, were exempted from the house tax. The Jews gradually replaced the Armenian commercial element in Brody until by the middle of the 18th century trade was concentrated in Jewish hands. The Jewish artisans in Brody—cordmakers, weavers, and metalsmiths—achieved a wide reputation and exported their products. The Potockis, who subsequently controlled Brody, continued to support the Jews; in 1742 they compelled merchants living on their other estates to attend the Brody fairs.

Adolf Brodsky, violinist. Photo Royal College of Music, Manchester.

Figure 1. The 17th-century fortress synagogue of the Ukrainian town of Brody, destroyed by the Nazis in 1943. Drawing by Georges Leukomski, a Russian authority on East European Jewish religious art. Jerusalem, Israel Museum Archives.

In 1664 the Jewish community of Brody joined with the communities in Zholkva and *Buchach to attain independence from the communal jurisdiction of Lvov, which had extended its authority over the outlying communities. At the session of the provincial council of Russia (see *Councils of the Lands) held at the time, Brody obtained two seats out of seven, and in 1740 the Brody delegate, Dov Babad, was elected *parnas* of the provincial council. For generations a few powerful families controlled the Brody community, among them the Babad, Shatzkes, Perles, Rapaport, Brociner, Bick, Chajes, Rabinowicz, and Bernstein families.

In 1742 the bishop of Lutsk challenged the Brody Jews to a public religious disputation in the synagogue. As he refused to recognize the rights of the representatives of the congregation—the physician Abraham Uziel and the *dayyan* Joshua Laszczower—to participate in the debate, the community leaders invited the surrounding settlements to choose alternative disputants. When the group assembled in Brody, however, it was disbanded by Count Potocki, who arrested several of the Brody communal leaders.

The community in Brody vigorously opposed the Frankist movement (see Jacob *Frank), which found supporters in the area in the middle of the 18th century. Brody was the meeting place of the assembly which excommunicated the Frankists in 1756. A rabbinical assembly convening in Brody in 1772 excommunicated the followers of *Ḥasidism, and ḥasidic works were burned there. In these struggles the circle formed by the Brody *klaus* joined talmudic scholars and mystics as protagonists of Orthodoxy.

During the 1768–72 wars in Poland, the Jews of Brody were ordered to provision the armies passing through the town. The Jewish economic position deteriorated considerably as a result, and to save the community from ruin the overlords of the town granted it a loan. After the annexation of Galicia—including Brody—by Austria in 1772, the lot of the Jewish merchants improved. They were exempted from payment of customs dues on all merchandise in transit through the empire. The guilds of Jewish innkeepers, bakers, and flour dealers were supported by the central authorities in Vienna, in compelling the lord of the town to reduce the taxes. Brody had the status of a free city between 1779 and 1880. After 1880 many Jewish wholesale merchants living in Brody moved to other towns with which they had business connections. A group of Brody Jews had already settled in *Odessa and founded a synagogue there.

In 1756 there were 7,191 Jews living in Brody; in 1779, 8,867 (over half the total population); in 1826, 16,315 (89%); in 1910, 12,188; and in 1921, 7,202.

Rabbis officiating in Brody include: Saul *Katzenellenbogen, appointed before 1664; Isaac Krakover ("from Cracow"), who was the progenitor of the Babad family (end of the 17th century); Eleazar *Roke'aḥ; and Aryeh Loeb *Teomim. In the 19th century Solomon *Kluger exerted a wide influence. The last rabbi of the community was Moses Steinberg (1929–42).

The Jews of Brody, who often traveled to Germany, helped to diffuse the philosophy of the Berlin Enlightenment (*Haskalah) movement in Galicia. Some of its earliest adherents living in Brody were Israel b. Moses ha-Levi of Zamosc Menahem *Lefin, Jacob Samuel *Bick, and Naḥman *Krochmal. The community opened a *Realschule* in 1815 where teaching was in German. Among *maskilim* residing in Brody in the middle of the 19th century were Dov Ber Blumenfeld, Isaac *Erter, and Joshua Heschel *Schorr, who published the Hebrew periodical *He-Ḥalutz* ("The Pioneer") in Brody between 1852 and 1889. Other noted personalities from Brody were the literary historian Marcus Landau, the orientalist Jacob *Goldenthal, the writer Leo Herzberg-Fraenkel, and his son Sigmund Herzberg-Fraenkel, the historian. A folk choir, the "*Broder Singers," was founded by Berl (Margolis) *Broder. Baruch Werber and his son Jacob edited the Hebrew weekly *Ivri Anokhi* (also, *Ivri*) in Brody between 1865 and 1890. As a border town, Brody often served as a point of assembly for the masses of Jewish refugees from the Russian pogroms, intending to emigrate to America or to Western Europe.

Throughout the period of Austrian sovereignty, Brody returned Jewish deputies to the parliament in Vienna. In 1907 the president of the Galician Zionists, Adolf *Stand, was elected as deputy; however, he was maneuvered out of office in 1911 as a result of government pressure and political manipulation by the assimilationist Heinrich *Kolischer. After Brody reverted to Poland in 1919, Jewish communal life was revived under the leadership of Leon Kalir. [N.M.G.]

Holocaust Period. There were approximately 10,000 Jews in Brody when World War II broke out. This area came under Soviet occupation following the partition of Poland in 1939. The town fell to the Germans in July 1941, at which time the Germans set up a Judenrat headed by Dr. Abraham Glasberg. Persecution of the Jews began immediately, and several hundred were murdered by the Nazis and their Ukrainian collaborators. Among the victims were 250 Jewish intellectuals. A ghetto was established in January 1942 for the 6,500 remaining Jews of Brody, who were joined later on (in September 1942) by some 3,000 refugees from the neighboring towns and villages. The unbearable conditions in the ghetto (lack of fuel and foodstuffs), led to the decline of the ghetto population at a rate of 40–50 daily. In the hopes of better chances for survival, a few Jews managed to get into work camps in the vicinity by bribing the guards. Typhoid fever, claiming several hundred victims, broke out in the ghetto which was completely sealed off from contact with the outside.

Mass extermination of the Brody community began with the deportations to *Belzec death camp of several thousand Jews on Sept. 19–21, 1942, followed by several thousand more on November 2. The ghetto and labor camp for Jews were finally liquidated on May 1, 1943, when the surviving 2,500 Jews were deported to *Majdanek.

Resistance. During the Russian occupation and particularly after the Nazis invaded Russia, large numbers of

Figure 2. Jews of Brody, with the synagogue in the background. Drawing by Joseph Pennell, *The Jews at Home*, 1892.

young Jews from Brody joined the Soviet Army. By the end of 1942 a fighting unit (ZOB), consisting of young Jews of all political trends was formed in the ghetto, and led by Jakub Linder, Samuel Weiler, and Solomon Halbersztadt. The ZOB was divided into an urban unit which prepared for armed resistance within the ghetto, and a unit which trained small groups for partisan operations in the neighboring forests. The Jewish fighting organization maintained contacts with the non-Jewish resistance. So far as is known no Jewish community was reconstituted in Brody after World War II. [De.D.]

Bibliography: *Arim ve-Immahot be-Yisrael*, 6 (1955), *Sefer Brody* by N. M. Gelber; J. Pennell, *The Jew at Home* (1892), with many illustrations; T. Brustin-Bernstein, in: *Bleter far Geshikhte*, 6, no. 3 (Warsaw), 1953, 45–153; B. Ajzensztajn, *Ruch podziemny w gettach i obozach, materialy i dokumenty* (1946).

BRODY, HEINRICH (Ḥayyim; 1868–1942), researcher of Sephardi *piyyutim* and medieval Hebrew poetry. Brody was born in Ungvar (Uzhgorod), Hungary, the son of Solomon Zalman *Brody, the grandson of Solomon *Ganzfried, author of *Kiẓẓur Shulḥan Arukh*. Brody studied at the Bratislava (Pressburg) Yeshivah and at the Rabbinical Seminary in Berlin where he also attended university and came under the influence of Abraham *Berliner and Moritz *Steinschneider. In 1894 he published the first part of his proposed edition of the poems of Judah Halevi. Brody continued until 1930 to edit Halevi's poems, with extensive commentaries, but he never completed this edition. Brody intended to publish the works of all the important medieval Hebrew poets. In 1897 he began to publish the poems of Solomon ibn Gabirol, in 1910, those of Samuel ha-Nagid, and in 1926, *Maḥberot Immanuel* of Immanuel of Rome; but for various reasons these editions, too, were not completed. Brody became a Zionist while serving as rabbi in Nachod, Bohemia. After the establishment of the Mizrachi in 1902 he became president of the Hungarian organization. Brody expressed his views on Zionism and the role of religion in a pamphlet (published under the nom de plume H. Salomonsohn) *Widerspricht der Zionismus unserer Religion?* (1898). In 1905 he coauthored with K. Albrecht an anthology of Hebrew poetry of the Spanish-Arabic school entitled *Sha'ar ha-Shir* (English ed., 1906). In 1922, with M. Wiener, he edited an anthology of Hebrew poetry, *Mivḥar ha-Shirah ha-Ivrit*. Brody founded the bibliographical periodical *Zeitschrift fuer hebraeische Bibliographie* in 1896 and published it until 1906 (from 1900 to 1906 together with A. Freimann). He went to Prague in 1905 to head the local *talmud torah* and after the death of Nathan *Ehrenfeld became in 1912 chief rabbi of Prague. When the institute for research of Hebrew poetry (Ha-Makhon le-Ḥeker ha-Shirah ha-Ivrit) was founded in Berlin by S. Schocken in 1930, Brody was invited to head it, and in 1933 he moved with the Institute to Jerusalem. During his years at the Institute he edited the secular poems of Moses ibn Ezra (1935) and *Be'ur la-Divan* (a commentary on the *diwan* of Judah Halevi), a book containing a wealth of information on Hebrew poetry in Spain. He also published the *diwan* of Eleazar bar Jacob (1935) and edited (from 1933 to 1938) the Institute's studies (YMḤSI) in which he printed important original works. Brody published other research papers in Hebrew, German, and Hungarian.

Bibliography: A. M. Habermann, in: *Gilyonot*, 7 (1938), 211–5; J. Klausner, *Yoẓerei Tekufah u-Mamshikhei Tekufah* (1956), 162–66; *Festschrift fuer Heinrich Brody*, *Soncino Blaetter*, 3, nos. 2–4 (1929–30), includes bibliography; Wollstein, in: YMḤSI, 5 (1939); Habermann, in S. Federbush (ed.), *Ḥokhmat Yisrael be-Ma'arav Eiropah* (1958), 92–97; *The Jews in Czechoslovakia*, 1 (1968), index.
[A.M.H.]

BRÓDY, SÁNDOR (1863–1924), Hungarian novelist and playwright. Born in Eger (Hungary), Bródy began his career as a journalist. In 1902 he started his own monthly *Fehér könyv* ("The White Book") and three years later helped to found the weekly *Jovendő* ("The Future"). He portrayed the typical citizen of Pest and his writing helped to mold the characteristic brand of humor associated with Budapest. Bródy's real literary merit lies, however, in the fact that he prepared the ground for the flowering of Hungarian prose in the 20th century. His style was archaic and folkish, interspersed with the emerging idiom of Pest. A number of his stories and plays introduce Jewish characters, and with *Nyomor* ("Misery," 1884) he became the first writer in Hungarian literature to describe the Jewish worker. His letter to Géza Gárdonyi (reprinted in *Haladás*, 1947, no. 17) praises Judaism, and in his last novel *Rembrandt* (1925; Eng. tr. 1928) his own Jewish associations and memories form an integral part of the whole book. His play *Timár Liza* (1914) dramatized the decadence of assimilated Jewish parvenus. Some of Bródy's plays were performed outside Hungary and several were adapted for the screen.

Bibliography: *Magyar Zsidó Lexikon* (1929), s.v.; A. Komlós, *Bródy Sándor: Irók és elvek* (1937); L. Hatvany, *Irodalmi tanulmányok*, 1 (1960); *Magyar Irodalmi Lexikon*, 1 (1963), s.v.
[J.Z.]

BRODY, SOLOMON ZALMAN BEN ISRAEL (1835–1917), rabbi and author. Brody, a member of the well-known rabbinical family of that name, was born in Ungvar (Uzhgorod), Hungary. He was a pupil of Abraham Samuel *Sofer at the Bratislava yeshivah. From 1885 he served as *dayyan* in his native town. Brody became known for his insistence on the strict observance of the law, and in particular took a stand against circumvention of the law of usury. He set out his uncompromising attitude in an essay called *"Neshekh ve-Tarbit"* (*Ha-Maggid*, 23 (1879), nos. 34–38), in which he opposed the practice, then customary, of a *shetar iska* (an agreement between a lender and borrower in connection with an interest-bearing loan applied for trading purposes). Despite his conservative outlook, he took a positive attitude in support of Zionism, to which he devoted an essay, *"Derishat Ẓiyyon"* (first published in D. Z. Katzburg's *Tel Talpiyyot*, 12, 1904), and containing some of his homiletical and halakhic novellae. He also wrote a work called *Divrei Shelomo ha-Yisre'eli*, the manuscript of which was in the possession of his son Ḥayyim, chief rabbi of Prague. Brody was the son-in-law of

Solomon *Ganzfried, the author of the *Kiẓẓur Shulḥan Arukh*.

Bibliography: Ben-Menahem, in: *Sefer ha-Mizrachi, Koveẓ le Zikhro shel J. J. Reines* (1946), 174–5; Weingarten, in: *Mizpeh* (1953), 457; EẒD, 1 (1958), 359–60. [El.Ka.]

BRÓDY, ZSIGMOND (1840–1906), Hungarian journalist and poet. He used his pen in the struggle to attain equal rights for Jews. This was also the theme of his poetry, written under the pen-name, "A Hungarian Jew." His hymns (in Hungarian) for the Neolog Great Synagogue in Pest were in use for some years. Bródy was cofounder of the literary periodical *Pannonia,* which published Hungarian writings in German translations, and became known for his contributions to the papers *Magyar Sajto* and *Pesti Napló.* He was active in Hungary's struggle for equality with Austria under the Hapsburg monarchy and was secretary at the Ministry of Interior in 1871. Resigning the following year, he bought the German-language newspaper *Neues Pester Journal.* In 1896 he was appointed to the Hungarian Upper House as a life member. Bródy made large donations to charitable causes and left most of his estate to a Jewish hospital for children, which was named after his wife Adel.

Bibliography: *Magyar Zsidó Lexikon* (1929), 142; *Magyar Irodalmi Lexikon* (1963), 189. [B.Y.]

°**BROGLIE, VICTOR-CLAUDE, PRINCE DE** (1757–1794), French statesman. Broglie supported the French Revolution, but opposed granting the Jews emancipation, both in writing (*Opinion sur l'Admission des Juifs à l'Etat Civil,* in Bibliothèque Nationale, Paris) and at the Constituent Assembly. Broglie argued that the grant of civil rights to the German-speaking Jews would cause further unrest in *Alsace and Lorraine, that the majority of Alsace Jews were indifferent to citizenship, and that the Jewish claim for citizenship was based on a Jewish plot (January 1791). On Sept. 27, 1791, after a draft resolution demanding equal rights for Jews was approved almost unanimously by the Assembly, Broglie proposed that the Jews be required to swear the Oath of Citizenship ("to Nation, King, and Law"), which amounted to a renunciation of their communal jurisdiction. A modified version of Broglie's amendment was finally approved. Broglie's arguments were among those that inspired *Napoleon Bonaparte's policy toward the Jews and their communal organizations.

Bibliography: L. Kahn, *Les Juifs de Paris pendant la Révolution* (1899); E. Tcherikower (ed.), *Yidn in Frankraykh,* 1 (1942), 109–52. [Ed.]

BROIDA, SIMḤAH ZISSEL BEN ISRAEL (1824–1898), rabbi and moralist. He came from a distinguished family which traced its descent to Abraham *Broda, rabbi of Frankfort. Broida was the outstanding disciple and follower of Israel Lipkin (Salanter), the founder of the *Musar movement. Broida was usually referred to as the "*sabba* (an affectionate term, roughly equivalent to "grand old man") of Kelme." Broida taught the principles of *musar* in Zagare (Lithuania) and St. Petersburg, subsequently founding the *talmud torah* in *Kelme which became the chief center for the spread of the movement. Compelled to leave Kelme as the result of a false accusation, he went to Grobin and founded a *talmud torah* which eventually numbered hundreds of disciples, including noted rabbis of the succeeding generation: Nathan Ẓevi *Finkel, Isser Zalman *Melzer, Aaron Bakst, Moses Mordecai *Epstein, Naphtali Trop, Joseph Leib *Bloch, and Joseph of Nowogródek. His ethical teachings emphasized the need for self-improvement, humility, and making allowance for others. He himself was regarded as a living example of his teaching.

Bibliography: D. Katz, *Tenu'at ha-Musar,* 2 (1958[3]), 26–219, 475; N. Waxmann, in: *Hadorom,* 10 (1959), 55–65; D. Zaritsky, *Torat ha-Musar* (1959), 19–29. [Y.Al.]

BROIDES, ABRAHAM (1907–), Hebrew poet. Broides, who was born in Vilna, settled in Palestine in 1923. He worked for several years as a laborer, an experience which rooted itself in his poetry, and was one of the founders of Ha-No'ar ha-Oved ("Working Youth Organization"). From 1928 until 1964 he was secretary of the Hebrew Writers Association and also edited their publication, *Daf.* Broides first began to publish poetry in the early 1920s in *Ha-Kokhav* and other journals. He began as a proletarian poet describing the anguish and the toil of the poor. Later he wrote landscape poetry with a simple and lyrical line. He is also author of several volumes of children's verse.

Bibliography: *Ha-Tenu'ah ve-ha-Meshorer* (1951); *Ma'gelei Adam va-Shir* (1962, appreciations and autobiography), Kressel, Leksikon, 1 (1965), 136 (detailed bibliography). [G.K.]

BROIDO, EPHRAIM (1912–), Hebrew essayist, translator, and editor. Born in Bialystok, he went to Tel Aviv at the age of 13. From 1931 to 1933 he studied at the University of Berlin, during which time he also contributed articles to *Davar,* was a member of the Central Committee of He-Ḥalutz, and compiled the *Kedem Taschen-Woerterbuch* (1934–35), a Hebrew-German dictionary. In 1934 he returned to Tel Aviv and joined the editorial staff of *Davar,* writing numerous articles on political, social, and literary issues and translating poetry and prose. During World War II he was *Davar's* correspondent in London. In 1948 he founded the influential literary-political monthly *Molad* (from 1968 a bimonthly).

Among the works he edited are *Derekh Ge'ullim* (1935), a selection of M. L. *Lilienblum's writings; and two chrestomathies, *If I Forget Thee* and *The Call of Freedom* (London, 1941). Broido translated Shakespeare's sonnets and several of his plays: *Macbeth* (1954), *The Tempest, A Midsummer Night's Dream, Much Ado About Nothing* (all published in 1964), and *The Comedy of Errors* (1965). He also translated selections from the poetry of W. B. Yeats and of Michelangelo.

Bibliography: D. Feinman, in: *Davar* (Jan. 28, 1966). [E.Sp.]

BROIDO, LOUIS (1895–), U.S. business executive and communal leader. Broido was born in Pittsburgh. He served with the U.S. Army in France, in World War I, then as a member of the U.S. Commission for War Claims in

Louis Broido, chairman of the American Jewish Joint Distribution Committee. Photo, A.J.D.C., N.Y.

France and Italy until 1920. Broido returned to practice law in Pittsburgh and then in New York from 1926 to 1936, when he left the bar to become executive vice-president and later chairman of the advisory commission of Gimbels

Brothers. He retired from this post in 1961 and became managing partner of a private investment company from 1962. Named New York City commissioner of commerce in 1961, Broido was also a New York retail trade leader and a member of several municipal committees. He was vice-chairman of the Union of American Hebrew Congregations for many years, president of the United Jewish Appeal in 1951 and 1952, and from 1965 chairman of the *American Jewish Joint Distribution Committee. His wife, LUCY KAUFMANN BROIDO (1900–1969), helped found the Women's Division of the New York United Jewish Appeal. She was vice-president of the Jewish Education Committee (1946–53), and president of the New York section of the National Council of Jewish Women (1949–53). [E.GR.]

BROKERS. The large variety of commercial intermediaries and agents to which this term refers, in both medieval and modern times, generally included a substantial proportion of Jews. They were particularly numerous at the fairs and in ports which were centers of interregional trade, and later also in the various types of exchanges. In this kind of occupation skill and information, a wide command of languages, and international connections were the chief requirements, and even men with little initial capital of their own could make a living and often a fortune.

Jewish brokers, itinerant and resident, were frequently found in the Mediterranean commercial centers throughout the Middle Ages. In Muslim countries brokerage was often specialized to a high degree. The activity of Jewish brokers was not distinct from that of non-Jews, but benefited periodically from Christian-Muslim political tension. In Christian countries the economic value of brokers was not widely recognized in the early Middle Ages, and their activity was often curtailed. In addition, Jewish traders and brokers suffered from religious animus. Nevertheless Jewish brokers were found in major ports such as Marseilles, Pisa, Barcelona, and Venice. In Spain the position of *corredor* ("broker") was a lucrative one, licensed by the king's bailiffs. Their activity was not limited to the ports, for they were also active in the countryside, particularly on royal and noble estates where they were in charge of selling agricultural produce and buying luxury commodities. The economic and social position of the broker within the Jewish community was generally inferior to that of the merchant. Brokers were excluded from community leadership in Majorca in 1356.

A new era in the history of Jewish brokerage began in the 16th century with the waves of exiles from Spain and Portugal to the ports of Italy, northern Europe, North Africa, the Balkans, and the Ottoman Empire, which coincided with European maritime expansion. Many of the exiles turned to brokerage, utilizing connections between their far-flung places of refuge. In Amsterdam brokerage in goods from the colonies, especially tobacco and sugar, was very profitable; Jewish brokers were allowed to operate unhindered; the entire brokerage of Brazilian sugar was in Jewish hands. In 1612 ten of the 300 authorized brokers were Jewish, and 30 of 430 in 1645. Among the 1,000 unauthorized brokers were many Ashkenazim. Of the 442 Jews who had an annual income exceeding 800 guilders in 1743, 25 were licensed and 100 unlicensed brokers. Marrano brokers had been active in England even before the readmittance (1656). In 1668 there were ten Jewish brokers on the London exchange; in addition there were also many unlicensed ones. An attempt to suppress the activities of unauthorized brokers (and to evict the Jews) led to a parliamentary commission which in 1697 regulated the

"The Lithuanian Stock Exchange." Wood engraving by Bisson from L. Hollaenderski, *Les Israélites de Pologne,* Paris, 1846. Cecil Roth Collection.

number of brokers at 100 Englishmen, 12 aliens, and 12 Jews. Attempts to raise the permitted number of Jews failed in 1723, 1730, and 1739. In Hamburg there were four professional Portuguese-Jewish brokers in the early 17th century in addition to numerous unauthorized ones, mainly Ashkenazi; by 1692 there were 20 Sephardi and 100 Christian brokers. The city council succeeded in lowering the ratio and total number of Jewish brokers in the 18th century.

A different type of Jewish brokerage developed in Poland-Lithuania. During the 16th and 17th centuries domestic commerce as well as export (timber, grain, furs; see *Arenda) and import (cloth, wine, luxuries) were largely in Jewish hands, and brokers played an important role, particularly at the regular fairs (*Lublin and *Jaroslaw). The anti-Jewish polemicist Sebastian *Miczyński wrote in 1618, "A short while ago . . . the Jews made, among themselves, a general agreement and regulation whereby no Jew is to deal with a Christian for their profit, neither to act as intermediary for any merchandise if they request it of him, nor to lead a merchant to Christian merchants or craftsmen, but to Jews alone. And on whoever transgresses this agreement they have applied great bans, curses, and punishments." This is a hostile presentation of a real conflict within the Jewish community. Merchants, who were predominant in community leadership, struggled to preserve their vested interests against brokers.

Tension between brokers and merchants is illustrated by the *Poznan community, where resident brokers dealing with foreign merchants were vigorously harassed. Between 1626 and 1696 the community records dealt with their activity almost annually, but warnings, fines, and excommunications were to no avail for their numbers increased. Their commission was fixed between $\frac{1}{2}$ and 1%, a rate that could be profitable only given a high turnover. Merchants were considered as justified in paying the regular fee only, even when a higher one had been agreed upon; brokers were accused of causing the economic ills of the community, in particular of revealing trade secrets to gentiles; they were sometimes equated with informers. Toward the end of the 17th century pronouncements against brokers became milder and rarer. The community, in economic straits, had acquiesced to a situation in which ever-growing numbers of its members were brokers or prepared to deal in brokerage.

On their arrival in Western Europe and the United States immigrants from Eastern Europe found a niche in several new types of brokerage, among them many new intermediary businesses like real estate brokerage, employment agencies, commodity and security exchanges, and commission agencies. In Central Europe the position of Jewish brokers combined Eastern and Western characteristics. Jews handled a large proportion of the trade between town and country, particularly grain and livestock, but were often excluded from the exchanges in the main cities. The first Jewish merchant to enter the Danzig exchange did so in 1808, accompanied by French gendarmes, after the occupation of the city. In Leipzig, center of the *fur trade, six Jews were appointed brokers for the duration of the fur fair in 1813. By 1818, 28 of 35 fair brokers were Jews, 14 of them from *Brody. Jews were prominent in regional as well as central exchanges in southern and central Germany, Hungary, and Rumania. Their position deteriorated in the 20th century as a result of the rise of producers' cooperatives, which attempted to bypass the middleman, and other developments hostile to small traders.

In Yiddish literature Shalom Aleichem created the figure of the broker Menahem Mendel of Kasrilevke who with his dreams is a kind of Jewish Walter Mitty.

Bibliography: M. Breger, *Zur Handelsgeschichte der Juden in Polen waehrend des 17. Jahrhunderts* (1932), 13ff., 23f.; S. B. Weinryb, *Neueste Wirtschaftsgeschichte der Juden in Russland und Polen* (1934); H. I. Bloom, *Economic Activities of the Jews of Amsterdam* (1937); H. Gousiorowski, *Die Berufe der Juden Hamburgs* (1927), 20–23, 31–32, 45–46, 78–79; D. Abrahams, in: JHSEM, 3 (1937), 80–94; Halpern, Pinkas, index, s.v. *sarsarut*; R. Mahler, *Toledot ha-Yehudim be-Folin* (1946), index, s.v. *sarsurim;* A. Marcus, in: YIVOA, 7 (1952), 175–203; H. Kellenbenz, *Sephardim an der unteren Elbe* (1958); Baer, Spain; W. Harmelin, in: YLBI, 9 (1964), 243ff.; D. Avron (ed.), *Pinkas ha-Kesherim shel Kehillat Pozna* (1966), index, s.v. *sarsurim;* S. D. Goitein, *Mediterranean Society,* 1 (1967), index; A. S. Diamond, in: JHSET, 21 (1968), 53f.; J. Jacobson, in: MGWJ, 64 (1920), 293ff.; S. Mayer, *Die Wiener Juden* (1917), 220ff., 264f., 453f.; W. M. Glicksman, *In the Mirror of Literature* (1966), 203–8.

[H.W.]

BRONFENBRENNER, MARTIN (1914–), U.S. economist. Bronfenbrenner was born in Pittsburgh, Pennsylvania. He taught for some time before going into government service, first with the Treasury and then with the Federal Reserve System. In 1947 he returned to teaching, at Wisconsin, Michigan State, and Minnesota universities successively. In 1962 he joined the Carnegie Institute of Technology in Pittsburgh, and in 1966 became chairman of the economics department at Carnegie-Mellon University. His main interests were the economics of the Far East, particularly of Japan and Korea. His books include *Lessons of Japanese Economic Development* (1961); *Survey of Inflation Theory* (1963); and *Academic Encounter: The American University in Japan and Korea* (1963). [J.O.R.]

BRONFMAN, Canadian family prominent in business and philanthropy. Yehiel and Minnie emigrated from Siroco, Bessarabia, to Manitoba in 1890, where Yehiel opened a hotel. Abe (1882-1968), oldest of the Bronfman sons, worked on behalf of the Mount Sinai Sanatorium (St. Agathe, Que.), United Talmud Torahs, United Jewish Relief Agencies, and the Joint Distribution Committee, all in Montreal. Harry (1886–1963), son of Yehiel, was a founder and supporter of the Canadian Jewish Congress from 1919, and supporter of the Mount Sinai Sanatorium and the YM-YWHA of Montreal. Gerald (1911–), son of Harry, was president and director of various major Canadian businesses. He was squadron leader in the Royal Canadian Air Force during World War II. He supported the Combined Jewish Appeal, Israel Bonds, Federation of Jewish Community Services, YMHA, and Joint Distribution Committee. His other community interests include the Canadian Red Cross Society, Montreal Symphony Orchestra, and Montreal Museum of Fine Arts.

Samuel (1891–1971), son of Yehiel, was a leading Canadian industrialist and philanthropist. Samuel was born in Brandon, Manitoba. He joined his father's hotel business in his teens, then entered the mail-order liquor business. After acquiring control of Canada's distillery Joseph Seagram and Sons Ltd., Samuel made contact with the British Distillers Corporation Ltd. and soon became a major figure in the world distillery industry. His career alternated between his interests as president of the giant Distillers-Seagrams Ltd. and his philanthropic activities in universities, hospitals, charities, and museums. Samuel's pioneer efforts in unified and extensive fund raising for Jewish causes became a byword in the Canadian Jewish community. President of the Canadian Jewish Congress during World War II and for 23 years in all, Samuel made it a model of organization and the accepted representative of Canada's Jewry. He led numerous delegations to various Canadian prime ministers and cabinet ministers, resulting in large immigrations of refugees and war orphans. During this period his services to the government were sought on many matters. At the establishment of the UN in San Francisco in 1945 Bronfman was prominent in the efforts of Jewish organizations seeking the security of Palestine and the incorporation of the Human Rights provisions in the UN Charter. Bronfman was a vice-president of the World Jewish Congress, and its North American Section chairman. He was honored by the Canadian government for his public service. He was a governor of McGill University and founder of its Center for Developing Area Studies. The Biblical and Archaeological Museum in Jerusalem, contributed by Samuel's four children (1965), bears his name. The Samuel Bronfman House in Montreal, headquarters for the Canadian Jewish Congress, was built in 1968. Bronfman's philanthropy extended to many aspects of Jewish social, cultural, and Zionist activities. His wife, Saidye Rosner (1896–), was honored for her wartime services. She was active in the YM-YWHA of Montreal and in the Montreal Museum of Fine Arts. Minda (1925–), daughter of Samuel, married Baron Alain

Samuel Bronfman, Canadian industrialist and philanthropist. Photo De Lutis, Paris.

de Gunzburg of Paris, where she was active in Hadassah-Wizo. Phyllis Lambert (1927–), daughter of Samuel, was an architect in Chicago. She designed and built the Saidye Bronfman Cultural Centre in Montreal. Edgar (1929–), son of Samuel, was president of the U.S. House of Seagram and was active in New York's Mount Sinai Hospital and the Federation of Jewish Philanthropies. Charles (1931–), son of Samuel, was president of Joseph E. Seagram & Sons, Canada, and was on the executive committee of the Allied Jewish Community Services of Montreal. Allan (1895–), youngest of Yehiel's sons, was a vice-president of Distillers Corporation-Seagrams Ltd., and was associated with many Canadian and Israel communal enterprises. He was a cofounder of the Montreal Jewish General Hospital and its president for 25 years. He was an active member of the board of governors of the Hebrew University of Jerusalem and president of its Canadian Friends. [S.Ha.]

BRONOWSKI, JACOB (1908–), British mathematician, philosopher, and writer. Bronowski was born in Poland, and went to England at the age of 12. He was educated at Cambridge and from 1934 to 1942 lectured in mathematics at the University College of Hull. During World War II, he was sent to Washington to work on the Joint Target Group and served as a member of the chiefs of staff mission to Japan in 1945–46. In 1948–49, he was UNESCO's Head of Projects and from 1950 headed the Coal Research establishment of the National Coal Board. In 1964 he became a senior fellow and deputy director of the Salk Institute for Biological Studies and settled in the United States.

He became an authority on the poet William Blake, his books on this subject including *William Blake, a Man without a Mask* (1944). Bronowski wrote a number of experimental radio plays, of which *Face of Violence* won the international Italia Prize for 1951. His philosophical appraisal of the history of ideas appeared as *The Western Intellectual Tradition* (1960). The urgency of the need for the scientist and the humanist to understand each other's language became his preoccupation from the 1950s onward. His works in this field include *The Common Sense of Science* (1951) and *Science and Human Values* (1958). [G.H.F.]

BRONSTEIN, DAVID (1924–), Russian chess grand master, born in Kiev. Bronstein established his place by victories gained in Moscow in 1946, 1948, and 1949, and in Stockholm in 1948. At Budapest in 1950 he shared first place in the Candidates' Tournament with Isaac *Boleslavski, whom he defeated in the play-off. This victory qualified him to play a match of 24 games with Mikhail *Botvinnik, only to draw the match, which left Botvinnik the world champion. He did not win a Candidates' Tournament after 1950 though he was highly placed more than once. Bronstein owed his successes to his exceptional originality. His tremendous efforts of thought in the middlegame often left him too exhausted to do justice to the endgame. [G.A.]

BROOM, the biblical *rotem* (Ar. *ratam*), the wild shrub *Retam roetam,* widespread in the deserts of Israel and in sandy regions. It produces a few leaves in the winter, which it sheds in the summer, its green stalks filling the function of the leaves in photosynthesis. According to R. Meir the shrub under which Hagar left her son Ishmael (Gen. 21:15) was the broom, "since it grows in the desert" (Gen. R. 53:13). Elijah lay down in the shade of a broom in the wilderness "a day's journey from Beersheba" (I Kings 19:3–5), "and he requested for himself that he might die";

A branch of the wild broom shrub, *Retam roetam,* in blossom. Photo Palphot, Herzliyyah.

and indeed it is difficult to find refuge from the powerful rays of the desert sun in the shade of this leafless bush. In the tents of Kedar they used "coals of *rotem*" for fuel and for fashioning arrows (Ps. 120:4–5). The roots are bitter but it is apparently possible to render them edible by roasting. Thus the hungry dwellers in the desert eat the saltwort (Heb. *malu'aḥ,* *Orach) "and the roots of the broom are their food" (Job 30:4; however, some translate *laḥmam* לַחְמָם, "their food" as "to warm themselves thereby" from חמם). According to the *aggadah,* the glowing embers of the broom have a remarkable characteristic: "For all embers are extinguished within [after they die down on the outside] but broom embers still burn within when extinguished on the outside" (Gen. R. 98:19). According to another *aggadah* coals of broom retain their heat for 12 months (BB 74b). Onkelos and the Vulgate translate the *rotem* by *juniper to whose embers Jerome attributes this quality of retaining their heat for 12 months. This identification is however wrong.

Bibliography: Loew, Flora, 2 (1924), 469–73; H.N. and A.L. Moldenke, *Plants of the Bible* (1952), 305; J. Feliks, *Olam ha-Ẓome'aḥ ha-Mikra'i* (1968[2]), 130f. [J.F.]

BROSS, JACOB (1883–1942), lawyer, a founder and leader of the *Jewish Social Democratic Party (Zh. P.S.D.) in Galicia. Bross became known as an orator for the party and the editor of its organ *Social-Demokrat.* The son of a tailor in Cracow, he was attracted to socialism when still at secondary school. His brother, Ignatius, was already active among the Jewish workers during the 1890s. While still in the Polish Social Democratic Party of Galicia, Bross fought against assimilationist tendencies and campaigned for organizational autonomy of the Jewish workers in the party. After demobilization from the Austrian Army in 1918, he did not assume a political function in the Polish *Bund. He lived in Cracow and appeared as an advocate in political trials. He was also active in child and youth welfare. He died in the Holocaust in Kremenets. His essays on the history of the Jewish socialist movement in Galicia were published in *Royter Pinkes*, 2 (1921); a second essay in *Historishe Shriftn*, 3 (1939) was reproduced in *YIVO Annual* (5 (1950), 55–85).

Bibliography: I. S. Hertz (ed.), *Doyres Bundistn*, 2 (1956), 184–7; LNYL, 1 (1956), 445–6. [M.M.]

°**BROTHERS, RICHARD** (1757–1824), founder of the British-Israelite movement. After serving in the Royal Navy (1771–83) Brothers retired on half pay but refused to take the statutory oath on religious grounds. He now began to address letters to the king, the prime minister, and other public personages foretelling the future. He finally regarded himself as the messiah who was to restore the "Hebrews" (i.e., Englishmen who had seen the light of truth) to their land. His name, according to him, signified that he was descended from James, the brother of Jesus, so that he called himself "The Nephew of the Almighty." In 1794 Brothers published the first part of his *A Revealed Knowledge of the Prophecies and Times* foretelling the restoration of the "Hebrews" to Jerusalem in 1798. He had many followers, and large numbers of pamphlets were published supporting or opposing his views. Jews showed no interest, but David *Levi published a derisive pamphlet. Brothers' activities were suspected of being exploited for revolutionary ends and the government had him confined in

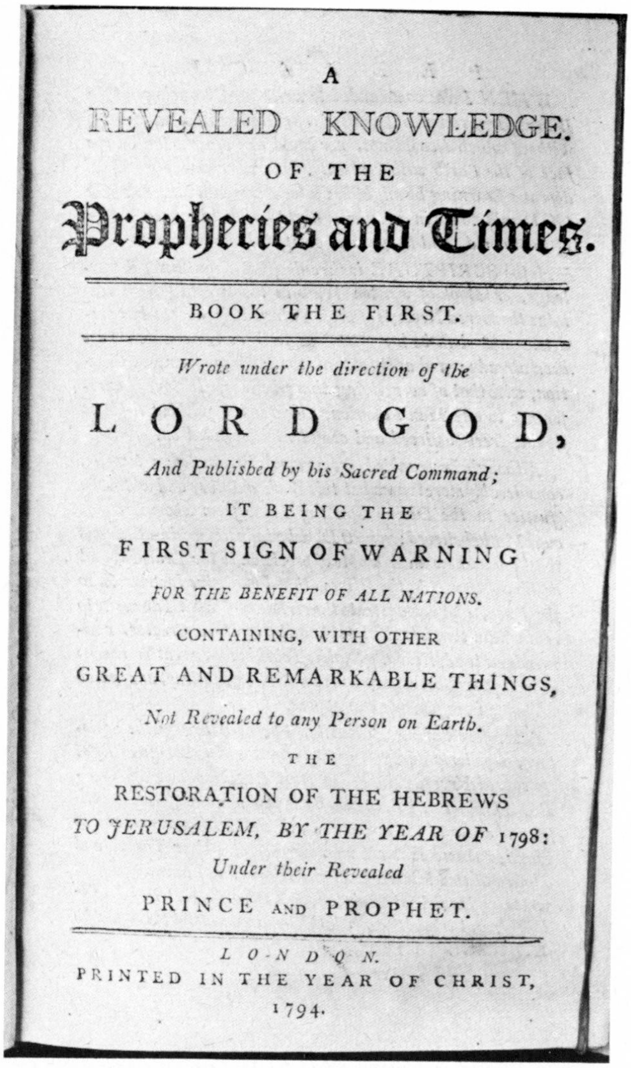

A

REVEALED KNOWLEDGE.

OF THE

Prophecies and Times.

BOOK THE FIRST.

Wrote under the direction of the

LORD GOD,

And Published by his Sacred Command;

IT BEING THE

FIRST SIGN OF WARNING

FOR THE BENEFIT OF ALL NATIONS.

CONTAINING, WITH OTHER

GREAT AND REMARKABLE THINGS,

Not Revealed to any Person on Earth.

THE

RESTORATION OF THE HEBREWS

TO JERUSALEM, BY THE YEAR OF 1798:

Under their Revealed

PRINCE AND PROPHET.

LONDON.

PRINTED IN THE YEAR OF CHRIST,

1794.

Figure 1. Title page of *A Revealed Knowledge of the Prophecies and Times* by Richard Brothers, London, 1794. Cecil Roth Collection.

Figure 2. Anti-Semitic caricature of Richard Brothers leading the Jews to the Promised Land, published in London, 1795. Cecil Roth Collection.

an asylum as criminally insane (1795–1806). Although his prophecies were unfulfilled, this did not affect the faith of his disciples. To the last Brothers continued to compose pamphlets about the government and architecture of the new Jerusalem. Upon his death, leadership of the group passed to John Finleyson (1770–1854).

Bibliography: C. Roth, *Nephew of the Almighty* (1933); Roth, Mag Bibl, 381–9; R. Matthews, *English Messiahs* (1936), 85–126; DNB, 2 (1921–22), 1350–53. [C.R.]

BROUDY, HARRY SAMUEL (1905–), U.S. educator. Born in Filipowa, Poland, Broudy studied at Boston University and at Harvard, where he began teaching philosophy. Between 1937 and 1957 he was professor of philosophy and education at two Massachusetts colleges, North Adams and Framingham. He then became professor of education in the College of Education, University of Illinois. His best-known work, *Building a Philosophy of Education* (1954), reveals his concern with established tradition and his stress on the function of education for intellectual discipline, moral character, cultural conservatism, and national survival. His other books include: *Paradox and Promise* (1961), *Democracy and Excellence in American Secondary Education* (1964), *Exemplars of Teaching Method* (1965), with J. R. Palmer. [Er.S.]

°**BROUGHTON, HUGH** (1549–1612), English Puritan, Hebraist, and controversialist. Broughton studied at Cambridge from 1569, learning Hebrew from A. R. Chevalier; he lived and lectured in London from 1579 to 1589, and thereafter lived mainly in Germany and Holland (Middelburg). Much of his energy was devoted to defense of the scriptural chronology of his first book (*Concent of Scripture*, London, 1588), to the proposing of a new English Bible translation, and to the castigation of the resultant King James' Version (1611). Broughton also projected a Hebrew New Testament, but published *Apocalypse* (Book of Revelations) only (Middelburg?, 1610). He could attract weekly audiences of 100 to lectures on his chronology at St. Paul's Cathedral, and had enough Jewish scholarship to engage in controversy at Frankfort in 1590 with R. Elijah *Loans. This brought him Hebrew correspondence from David *Reuveni of Constantinople, which, together with his reply, was published in English, Latin, and Greek (Amsterdam, 1606, etc.). He was apparently interested in Jewish conversion, and published his controversy with R. David "Farar" on Jesus' genealogy, in Latin (1605) and English (Amsterdam, 1608).

Broughton's works were republished incompletely by J. Lightfoot (London, 1662), with a prefixed "Life"; manuscript material, largely relating to Bible translation, is in the British Museum (Mss. Sloan 3088, Harley 1525; *Lansdowne Catalog*, pp. 220, 331, 332).

Bibliography: DNB, 2 (1921–22), 1367–70; Roth, Mag Bibl, 256, 343–4; S. Greenslade (ed.), *Cambridge History of the Bible* (1963), 164–5; 167–8.

[Ra.L.]

BROWN, BENJAMIN (1885–1939), organizer of U.S. Jewish farm cooperatives. Brown was born in Tulchin, Russia. He immigrated to the United States in 1901 and studied at Philadelphia. Moving to Utah, Brown was president from 1909 to 1915 of the Jewish Agricultural and Colonial Association, which sponsored a farm settlement in the central part of the state, after which he continued to be active in the cooperative movement in Utah, Idaho, and the Pacific Northwest. In 1929 he traveled to Russia as part of an American commission to act in an advisory capacity to Jewish agricultural settlers in Birobidzhan. Upon his return he served as chairman of the Provisional Commission for the Establishment of Jewish Farm Settlements in the United States. In 1936 Brown was instrumental in founding the New Jersey Homestead, a cooperative Jewish settlement near Heightstown, New Jersey. The project was discontinued in 1939, the year of his death. [Ed.]

BROWN, DAVID ABRAHAM (1875–1958), U.S. industrialist and civic leader. Brown, born in Edinburgh, Scotland, was brought to Detroit, Mich., as a child. He became a prominent businessman and community leader, and moved to New York in 1929. There he assumed control of the Broadway National Bank and Trust Co. He published the weekly *American Hebrew* (1930–35). Brown was national chairman of the American Jewish Relief Campaign (1921–22) and the United Jewish Campaign (1925–28), as well as the U.S. division of China Famine Relief (1928–33). He played an active role in the American Jewish Joint Distribution Committee and the Union of American Hebrew Congregations. [R.Ro.]

BROWN, SAUL PARDO (d. 1702), the first known religious leader or *ḥazzan* of New York. Brown (an English alias for Pardo) came to New York in about 1685 from Rhode Island where he had been a merchant. In that year he petitioned Governor Thomas Dongan for permission to engage in retail trade. The privilege was denied to all Jews, but he did receive the right to be a wholesale trader. In 1695 Brown was already *ḥazzan* when he is recorded as ministering to the Congregation Shearith Israel. It is possible that Brown died in Curaçao. The family disappeared from New York records after the death of his wife in 1708.

Bibliography: Rosenbloom, Biogr Dict., 14; M. U. Schappes, *A Documentary History of the Jews in the United States, 1654–1875* (1950), 569; D. and T. de Sola Pool, *An Old Faith in the New World* (1955), 159–60.

[L.He.]

°**BROWNING, ROBERT** (1812–1889), English poet who wrote many works of Jewish interest. Browning's appearance and associations combined to give rise to a report that he was of Jewish extraction, but this was wholly unfounded. Nevertheless, he knew Hebrew, was an assiduous student of the Old Testament (in Hebrew), had some knowledge of rabbinical literature, and always displayed strong sympathy for the Jews. During his long residence in Italy, he witnessed the degradations inflicted by the ghetto system in its last phases. The most famous of Browning's Jewish poems is "Rabbi Ben Ezra" (1864). It sets forth, in the form of a soliloquy, the optimistic philosophy of a Jewish sage, who may perhaps be identified with Abraham *ibn Ezra. "Jochanan Hakkadosh" (1883) is apocryphal legend, Jewish in feeling as well as in title; "Ben Karshook's Wisdom" (1865) is a short, perceptive poem based on R. Eliezer's celebrated injunction that a man should "repent the day before his death" (Avot 2:15); and "Paracelsus" (1835) shows some understanding of the Kabbalah. "Holy Cross Day" (1855), another soliloquy, presents a Roman Jew of the 17th century forced to attend a conversionist sermon at Eastertide. Other poems by Browning of Jewish interest are "Saul" (1845) and "Solomon and Balkis" (1883), while Hebrew phrases or reminiscences are to be found in "Doctor," "The Melon Seller," and "Two Camels." Browning showed his practical sympathy by supporting in 1881 a public protest in London against the persecution of the Jews in Russia.

Bibliography: E. Berdoe, *Browning Cyclopaedia* (1892); J. Jacobs, *Jewish Ideals* (1896), 84–96; J. Kelman, in: *Prophets of Yesterday* (1924), 137–62; J. B. Lieberman, *Robert Browning and Hebraism* (1934).

[C.R.]

BRUCHSAL, town in *Baden, West Germany. The first mention of Jews there dates from 1288. In 1337 the bishop of *Speyer granted them the right of domicile for an annual payment of 700 marks. The community was annihilated during the *Black Death, 1348–49. After a long interval Jews again settled in Bruchsal, but were persecuted during the *Reformation. A prayer room is first mentioned in 1672. The synagogue, built in 1881, was restored in 1923. Between 1886 and 1928, 641 children were educated in the

Synagogue in Bruchsal, Germany, destroyed in 1938. Bruchsal Municipality.

orphanage founded by J.*Eschelbacher. A Jewish district school was opened in 1935–36. The Jewish population numbered 128 in 1814, and 752 in 1885 (6.2% of the total); it had diminished to 501 in 1933, but there were still six benevolent societies. On Nov. 11, 1938, the synagogue was burned down. By 1939 the community had declined to 166. Of those who remained 79 were deported to the *Gurs concentration camp in 1940. The community no longer exists.

Bibliography: Germ Jud, 2 (1968), 135–6; G. Taddey and F. Hundsnurscher, *Die Juedischen Gemeinden in Baden* (1968); FJW (1932/33).

[ED.]

BRUCK, GRIGORI (**Ẓevi Hirsch;** 1869–1922), Russian Zionist. He was born in Chernigov, Ukraine, graduated in 1893 as a physician from Kiev University, and worked as a doctor in Gomel. From his youth, he was a member of the

Grigori Bruck, Russian Zionist. Tel Aviv, Raphaeli Collection.

Ḥovevei Zion and the Zionist movement, and at the Third Zionist Congress he was elected regional representative for Belorussia. In 1901 he became government-appointed rabbi in Vitebsk. In 1905 he was elected to the first Duma on the Constitutional Democratic (Kadet) Party ticket. When the Duma was dissolved, he was a signatory to the protest of the radical delegates (the Viborg Manifesto) and was arrested and removed from his official rabbinical post. Opposing the *Helsingfors Program (1906) which required the Zionists to act as a political party in the Diaspora, he retired from the Zionist leadership. During World War I he served as a doctor in the Russian Army. At the 1917 Russian Zionist Conference in Petrograd he again opposed the participation of Zionists as a party in the Russian Revolution. In 1920 he settled in Ereẓ Israel.

Bibliography: K. I. Silman (ed.), *Z. Bruck, Alim le-Zikhrono* (1929); *Sefer Vitebsk* (1957), 109–28.

[Y.S.]

BRUCKNER, FERDINAND (pseudonym of **Theodor Tagger;** 1891–1958), German poet and playwright. Bruckner was born in Vienna, and studied music and law in Vienna and Paris. In 1923 he founded and became director of the Renaissance-Theater in Berlin. When Hitler came to power, Bruckner emigrated to the U.S., but eventually returned to Berlin, where he died. Bruckner began his literary career as a lyric poet and essayist, but soon became a playwright. Most of his plays were about contemporary life. His technique was much influenced by the cinema. One of his favorite themes was the struggle between the generations, which he dealt with in *Krankheit der Jugend* (1929), *Die Verbrecher* (1929), *Die Rassen* (1934), and *Die Befreiten* (1946). Bruckner also wrote several historical dramas, including *Elisabeth von England* (1931), *Napoleon der Erste* (1937), and *Simon Bolivar* (1945). His last play was *Pyrrhus und Andromache* (1952).

Bibliography: H. Friedman and O. Mann, *Deutsche Literatur im 20. Jahrhundert*, 1 (1961), 162ff.; E. Rieder Laska, *Ferdinand Bruckner* (thesis, Heidelberg, 1961).

[R.K.]

BRUDO, ABRAHAM BEN ELIJAH (known also as **Abraham Chelebi;** 1625?–1717), Turkish rabbi and preacher. Born in Constantinople, he was appointed rabbi there at an early age. When the Shabbatean movement began to spread, he became one of its adherents. In 1666 he was a signatory to a letter of the rabbis of Constantinople and Smyrna supporting Shabbetai Ẓevi's messianic claims. However, a year later they sent another letter now expressing opposition, but apparently some time later the spark of Shabbateanism was rekindled in him. In 1688 or somewhat later, he served as rabbi and preacher in Adrianople, afterward returning to Constantinople. Following the war between Venice and Turkey (1685–87), in which the Venetians conquered the Peloponnese (Morea), he traveled to raise ransom money for the Jews who had fallen captive. In 1694 he was in Leghorn and from there proceeded to other Italian cities. In 1695 he was in Amsterdam, Germany, and Austria, and in 1696, again in Venice. After this journey he settled in Jerusalem, where he spent his remaining years as chief rabbi. Among his disciples were many Ashkenazim, including Nethanel *Weil. In 1697 Abraham published *Birkat Avraham*, a book of sermons on Genesis, in the introduction to which he mentions a book he wrote on the Bible. A few of his numerous responsa were published in works of his contemporaries.

Bibliography: Frumkin-Rivlin, 2 (1928), 103–4; Rosanes, Togarmah, 4 (1935), 191–3; J. Sasportas, *Ẓiẓat Novel Ẓevi*, ed. by I. Tishby (1954), 134, 209; Sonne, in: *Sefunot*, 5 (1961), 292ff.

[A.D.]

BRUDO, MANUEL (c. 1500–c. 1585), Marrano physician and author. His father, Dionysius Rodrigues (d. 1541), was at first physician to the Royal Court in Portugal and later practiced medicine in London and Ferrara. Like his father, Manuel also practiced medicine for some time in London

DE RATIONE VICTVS
IN SINGVLIS FEBRIBVS
secundum Hippocratem,
IN GENERE ET SIGILLATIM
LIBRI III.
AVTHORE BRVDO LVSITANO
Medico, Dionysij filio.

VENETIIS. MDLIX.

Title page of *De Ratione Victus*, Manuel Brudo's book on diet, second edition, Venice, 1559. Cecil Roth Collection.

and later in Italy. His study on diets (*De Ratione Victus*, Venice, 1544, 1559) includes much curious information on the living conditions of the Marranos who escaped to England. He finally settled in Turkey (probably in Constantinople) and openly returned to Judaism. Here he entered the employment of the sultan for whom he composed a work, translated into Turkish under the title, *ʿAsā'-i Pīrān* ("The Walking Stick of the Old"), on the maladies of old age and their cure. There is some doubt as to his authorship of the book *Ta'amei ha-Mitzvot* mentioned by *Ibn Verga in his *Shevet Yehudah* (par. 64) which dealt with the reasons of the sacrifices. Brudo's arguments against Christianity are mentioned admiringly by Abraham ha-Levi ibn Migash in his *Kevod Elohim* (Constantinople, 1585, 127b).

Bibliography: U. Heyd, in: *Eretz-Israel*, 7 (1963), 48, 53: C. Roth, England, 137, 238; idem, in: JHSET, 19 (1960), 4–6; H. Friedenwald, *Jews and Medicine*, 2 (1944); 346, 389, 461, 463–7, 714; Baer, in: *Tarbiz*, 6 (1934/35), 162. [C.R.]

BRUELL, family of Jewish scholars. The first member of the family was JACOB *BRUELL, talmudic scholar. NEHEMIAH (Nahum; 1843–1891) was the son of Jacob. After rabbinical ordination, he continued his studies in Vienna at Jellinek's *bet ha-midrash* under I. H. Weiss and M. Friedmann and at the university. He became associated with the Reform movement, and after serving as rabbi in Bisenz (Moravia), he succeeded A. *Geiger in 1870 as rabbi of the Reform synagogue in Frankfort where he took an extreme standpoint regarding religious matters. Here he found a doughty opponent in S. R. Hirsch. After his failure in the struggle with Orthodoxy, and as a result of heavy personal attacks against him, Bruell eventually left the rabbinate and devoted himself to scholarship. He founded and edited the *Jahrbuecher fuer juedische Geschichte und Literatur* (ten volumes, 1874–90) contributing most of the articles himself. His plan for publishing the *Central-Anzeiger fuer juedische Literatur* as a continuation of *Steinschneider's *Hebraeische Bibliographie*, was cut short after the appearance of the first volume (1891) by his death.

Bruell's monographs in Hebrew and German covered nearly the entire field of Jewish studies, including Bible and Apocrypha, *halakhah* and *aggadah*, talmudic and rabbinic literature, Jewish history, medieval Hebrew, *piyyut* and poetry, and Hebrew grammar and linguistics. His best studies (mostly published in the *Jahrbuch*, as well as in other periodicals and jubilee volumes) include monographs on the literary development of the Babylonian Talmud (in which the contribution of the *savoraim* is well described), the origins and composition of *Avot*, the character of the Tosefta, the *Sifrei Zuta*, foreign words in the Talmud and Midrash, the tractates on mourning, the apocryphal addition to Daniel, and the Jewish (including Yiddish) medieval folk-legends. He had prepared a new edition of Zunz's *Gottesdienstliche Vortraege* (1892), in which his notes were included. Collections of Bruell's sermons and speeches were published in 1869, 1878, 1891, and 1895. Bruell was an astute and profound scholar, whose works on the tannaitic literature and the Babylonian Talmud were an important contribution to research in these fields.

ADOLF (Elhanan; 1846–1908) was another son of Jacob Bruell. Bruell studied at the universities of Vienna, Prague, and Breslau, and at the Breslau Jewish Theological Seminary. From 1871 to 1903 he taught at the Philanthropin Jewish High School in Frankfort. His special field of study was the Samaritan translation of the Pentateuch. Among his published works are: *Fremdsprachliche Redensarten . . . in den Talmuden und Midraschim* (1869); *Trachten der Juden im nachbiblischen Alterthum* (1873); *Kritische Studien ueber Samaritanische Manuscript-Fragmente* (1875); *Zur Geschichte und Literatur der Samaritaner* (1876); and *Beitraege zur Kenntnis der juedisch-deutschen Literatur* (1877). Bruell also edited articles in the *Populaerwissenschaftliche Monatsblaetter zur Belehrung ueber das Judentum fuer Gebildete aller Konfessionen* (1881–1908), to which he contributed numerous articles. He wrote a biography of David *Einhorn and was a contributor to the *Jewish Encyclopedia*.

Bibliography: B. Cohen, in: *Studies . . . in memory of A. S. Freidus* (1929), 219ff. [M.D.H.]

BRUELL, IGNAZ (1846–1907), Austrian pianist and composer. Born in Prossnitz, Moravia, he was taken to Vienna at the age of three, showed early talent, and became famous as a concert pianist. He toured the Continent and gave twenty concerts in London in 1878. As a composer he had most success with "Das Goldene Kreuz" (1875, libretto by S. H. *Mosenthal). Also popular was "Der Husar" (1898). He composed ten operas, two piano concertos, and a body of chamber music. Bruell was a close friend of Brahms and, being a remarkable sight reader, often tried out new works with the composer in four-hand arrangements. He also gave the first public performance of some of them.

Bibliography: H. Schwarz, *Ignaz Bruell und sein Freundeskreis* (1922); Baker, Biog Dict. [D.L.S.]

BRUELL, JACOB (1812–1889), talmudic scholar. Born in Neu-Raussnitz, Moravia, he was ordained by his father-in-law Nehemiah *Trebitsch. From 1843 until his death, he served as rabbi in *Kojetin. Among his disciples were his sons Adolf and Nehemiah *Bruell, and David *Kaufmann, all of whom became renowned Jewish scholars. Bruell developed his own distinctive, scientific, critical approach. His first scholarly work was an annotated and revised edition of Ẓevi Hirsch *Chajes' *Iggeret Bikkoret* on the Targums and Midrashim (1853). His own "addition, corrections, and criticism," were named *Misgeret*. The influence of Zunz's *Gottesdienstliche Vortraege* is noticeable in Bruell's critical notes. His *Doresh le-Ẓiyyun* ("Interpreter of Signs," Ger. *Die Mnemotechnik des Talmuds*, 1864) deals with the mnemotechnical signs in the Babylonian Talmud. Bruell's largest and most important work is his *Mevo ha-Mishnah* ("Introduction to the Mishnah," 2 vols., 1876–85). The first volume deals with the biographies and methods of sages from the time of Ezra to the end of the mishnaic period, and the second, with the method used by Judah ha-Nasi in the arrangement and editing of the Mishnah. Bruell's last work was *Ben Zekunim* (studies in talmudic literature, 1889). He also contributed extensively to the periodicals *Ben Chananja* (ed. by L. Loew) and *Beit Talmud* (ed. by I. H. Weiss).

Bibliography: Zeitlin, Bibliotheca, 43, 54. [M.D.H.]

BRUGGEN, CARRY VAN (1881–1932), Dutch novelist and philosophical writer. Born in Smilde as Carolina Lea de Haan, she was the sister of Jacob Israel de *Haan. Her first husband was the non-Jewish writer Kees van Bruggen, her second, the art historian A. Pit. Carry van Bruggen, who was a school teacher, published her first novel, *De Verlatene* ("The Forsaken Woman") in 1910. This was pitilessly self-analytical and autobiographical, as were *Heleen* (1913), *Het Huisje aan de Sloot* ("The House on the Canal," 1921) and her last novel, *Eva* (1927). Carry van Bruggen displayed an ambivalent and sometimes an antagonistic attitude to Jewish tradition and nationalism, although she described the joys and sorrows of the religious family in which she grew up with great affection. She was an original thinker with a profound knowledge of the history of philosophy, and her main work *Promethus* (1919), an attempt to guide a freethinker in his struggle with the powers of darkness, had a significant influence on leading Dutch writers. She analyzed modern superstition in *Hedendaagsch Fetichisme* ("Fetishism in our Time," 1925). Her novels include *Het Joodje* ("The Little Jew," 1914), *Een Indisch Huwelijk* ("An Indian Marriage," 1921), and *Vier Jaargetijden* ("Four Seasons," 1924). She also published some minor novels under the penname Justine Abbing. Carry van Bruggen spent the last years of her life in a mental hospital.

Bibliography: M. Jacobs, *Carry van Bruggen* (Dutch, 1962).

[M.Roz.]

BRUNA, ISRAEL BEN ḤAYYIM (c. 1400–1480), German rabbi and communal leader. He studied under David of Schweidnitz, and later Jacob Weil, Israel Isserlein, and Zalman Cohen of Nuremberg. His first rabbinical post was in Bruenn, his native city. When R. Goddel of Orenburg arrived there sometime later, and began to exercise rabbinical functions, Bruna lodged a complaint before Isserlein who advised him to resign himself to Goddel's presence. By 1446 he was in Regensburg, where he opened a yeshivah and served as rabbi to his followers, thereby arousing the hostility of a well-known local rabbi, Anshel Segal, who also headed a yeshivah. Despite the decisions of Jacob Weil and Israel Isserlein (Isserlein, *pesak* 128), upholding Bruna's right to work and teach in Regensburg, his rival's supporters made him endure great indignity, which ceased only with R. Anshel's death, at which time Bruna became the acknowledged leader of the community and *av bet-din*. After the death of Weil and Isserlein, he was recognized as the halakhic authority of Germany, and his opinion in communal and rabbinical matters was widely sought. In 1456 Bruna was imprisoned for 13 days, apparently to spur the collection of a "coronation tax" imposed on the Jews of his city by the emperor Frederick III. In 1474 he was imprisoned again, this time the victim of a blood libel; an apostate, Hans Vayol, accused him of buying a Christian youth and killing him to make use of his blood. The church demanded his death, but the community secured the intervention of Frederick III and Ladislav II, king of Bohemia, which led to Vayol's confession and subsequent execution. Bruna was freed only after formally renouncing all claim to compensation for the injustice done to him. His son was *dayyan* in Prague. Bruna's responsa, which provide valuable information on the German Jewish scene of his time, were collected and published posthumously (Salonika, 1788) with many printing errors, again in 1860, with even more errors, and a third edition was published in 1960.

Bibliography: Berliner, in: MGWJ, 18 (1869), 317–8, no. 29; J. Freimann (ed.), *Leket Yosher* (1904), xxxix–xl (preface), no. 82; S. A. Horodezky, *Le-Korot ha-Rabbanut* (1911), 37–44; Zimmels, in: MGWJ, 74 (1930), 57, no. 7; B. Suler, in: JGGJČ, 9 (1938), 101–70; M. Frank, *Kehillot Ashkenaz u-Vattei Dineihen* (1938), index; R. Straus, *Regensburg and Augsburg* (1939), 67–69; S. Eidelberg, *Jewish Life in Austria in the 15th Century* (1962), index.

[I.Z.K./Ed.]

°**BRUNETTI, ANGELO** (known as **"Ciceruacchio"**; mid-19th-century), leader of liberal reform in Rome. Without formal education, Brunetti exerted great influence over the populace. On July 3, 1847, he achieved a reconciliation between the Jews of Rome and the inhabitants of the Regola quarter, near the ghetto, who had always been anti-Jewish. Eight days later, thousands of citizens streamed into the ghetto and publicly fraternized with the Jews. On April 17, 1848, hearing that Pope Pius IX had ordered the abolition of the ghetto, he rallied help to demolish the walls, while the Jews, unaware of his action, were celebrating Passover.

Bibliography: Roth, Italy, 459; Milano, Italia, 360; Vogelstein-Rieger, 2 (1896), 370–4.

[U.C./Ed.]

BRUNNER, ARNOLD (1857–1925), U.S. architect. Brunner was born in New York and graduated from the Massachusetts Institute of Technology. Most of his buildings were of a public character, and included bridges, hospitals, university buildings, and synagogues. They included the Lewisohn Stadium for the College of the City of New York, which is used as an open-air concert hall. Brunner was a pioneer of civic planning, and did valuable work in this field in Baltimore, Rochester, Albany, and Denver. Of his synagogues, Beth El (1891) and Shaaray Tefila (1894) in New York, and Mishkan Israel (1897) in New Haven, were designed in a Romanesque style with

Interior of the Shearith Israel Synagogue, New York, designed by Arnold Brunner in 1897. Photo Charles Kanarian, N.Y.

Islamic and Byzantine elements. This concept of synagogues had originated in Germany and spread to America through the German Jewish congregations. Brunner's later synagogues were built exclusively in a classical style. This change was due, he maintained, to the investigation of ancient synagogues in Galilee, built in a Greco-Roman tradition. An example of this style was the new place of worship Shearith Israel (1897) built for the Sephardi community of New York. He also employed this classical style for the small Henry S. Frank Memorial Synagogue (1901) in the grounds of the Jewish Hospital in Philadelphia. In this case the design was inspired by *Kefar Baram, a second- century synagogue in Galilee.

Bibliography: R. Wischnitzer, *Synagogue Architecture in the U.S.* (1955), 49–60; Roth, Art, 739–40.

[Ed.]

BRUNNER, CONSTANTIN (pen name of **Leopold Wertheimer**; 1862–1937), German philosopher. He lived in Potsdam until 1933, and emigrated to Holland when the Nazis came to power. He constructed his own philosophical system. He followed Plato, and to an even greater extent, Spinoza. His major work is *Die Lehre von den Geistigen und vom Volk* (1908).

Central to Brunner's theory is the characterization of three different aspects of contemplation (including emotion and will): (1) Practical reason, which every human possesses, and which serves one's normal needs. (2) The spiritual faculty, which rises above the relative truth residing in experience and in science, and strives toward a perception of the one eternal and absolute essence. This spiritual faculty finds expression in the artist's inspiration, in the endeavor to penetrate the mysteries of the universe as part of the pursuit of the absolute, and in philosophy as the knowledge of the eternal. Very few are endowed with this faculty. (3) "Superstition"—pseudo-contemplation, which is the mode of contemplation of most ordinary men. Unfounded belief is a distortion of the spiritual faculty. While practical reason recognizes that the "relative" is only "relative," superstition elevates what is relative to the status of the absolute. As part of his theory of society and the state, Brunner argued for total assimilation of the Jews, and staunchly opposed Zionism. Among his admirers were Gustav *Landauer and Walter *Rathenau. In 1924 the Constantin Brunner Society was founded in Berlin. An International Constantin Brunner Institute exists in The Hague. Brunner's other works include *Der Judenhass und die Juden* (1918); *Materialismus und Idealismus* (1928); *Von den Pflichten der Juden und von den Pflichten des Staates* (1930); and *Derentlarvte Mensch* (1951).

Bibliography: Constantin Brunner Gemeinschaft, *Von Constantin Brunner und seinem Werk* (1927); W. Bernard, *Philosophy of Spinoza and Brunner* (1934); L. Bickel, *Wirklichkeit und Wahrheit des Denkens* (1953). [O.I.S.]

°**BRUNNER, SEBASTIAN** (1814–1893), Viennese Catholic priest and anti-Semitic journalist and writer. Ordained in 1838, Brunner was employed in *Metternich's police bureau from 1843 to 1848. He subsequently founded the conservative daily *Wiener katholische Kirchenzeitung* which he edited until 1860. In its pages Brunner claimed, among other allegations, that the Old Testament spirit was vindictive and that Jewish influence endangered Christian morals. In 1860 the Jewish communal leader Ignaz *Kuranda forced Brunner to sue him for libel, claiming that Brunner had merely resurrected the old charges made by Johan Andreas *Eisenmenger and Johannes *Pfefferkorn, and that he was motivated by business interest. Kuranda was acquitted. The proceedings aroused great interest among Eastern European Jewry and were published in Hebrew by David Gordon (*Milḥemet ha-Ḥoshekh ve-ha-Or,* (1861).

Bibliography: P. G. J. Pulzer, *The Rise of Political Anti-Semitism in Germany and Austria* (1964), index; F. Heer, *Gottes erste Liebe* (1967), 232, 303, 354; O. Rommel (ed.), *Der oesterreichische Vormaerz (1816–47)* (1931), 251–79; *Oesterreichisches Biographisches Lexikon.* [Ed.]

BRUNSCHVICG, LEON (1869–1944), French philosopher. In 1909 he was appointed professor of philosophy at the Sorbonne, and in 1920, member of the Académie des Sciences Morales. Brunschvicg, who was a spokesman of the idealistic school of thought in France, published many books, best known of which are: *La modalité du jugement* (1897); *Introduction à la vie de l'esprit* (1900); the valuable historical work *Les étapes de la philosophie mathématique* (1912); another historical work *Le progrès de la conscience dans la philosophie occidentale* (1927); *La Raison et la Religion* (1939); *Spinoza et ses contemporains* (1923); and *Descartes et Pascal, lecteurs de Montaigne* (1944). Brunschvicg published the standard edition of Pascal's writings (1897–1904) and for many years he was also editor of the *Revue de métaphysique et de morale.* In 1945 a memorial collection of essays was published by this journal. Brunschvicg advocated an idealism of consciousness and did not admit any existence outside the realm of consciousness. The irrational, which consciousness confronts and which appears to consciousness to exist independently, is nothing but the limits of consciousness itself, confronted by consciousness with astonishment and pain. As the spirit develops, the limits of consciousness expand—but only in consciousness itself are both truth and existence present together. God is but the "word"—the force which sets consciousness in motion and gives life to it. The development of consciousness in Brunschvicg's conception is very close to Hegel's "spirit of the absolute," though contrary to Hegel, it does not follow an inevitable course; rather it splits into various directions, which are sometimes determined by chance, as an expression of absolute freedom. What Brunschvicg thus attempted was the integration of Hegel's view with Bergson's. Brunschvicg's doctrine is an immanent, monistic philosophy, sometimes reminiscent of Spinoza's. He believed that with the development of consciousness and the elevation of man to higher stages, humanity would reach a "third covenant," which would be able to replace the "second covenant" ("the New Testament"). Brunschvicg saw 20th-century religion as at a crossroad. Religion's past weighs down on it and may smother it. Only a brave decision between its past and future can save it. Religion's past is the religion of personification, which enslaved itself to the selfish aspirations and hopes of man, whereas the future of religion is the pure religion which would free itself from anthropomorphism—a religion of the heart, a pure spiritual religion, a philosophical religion. At a meeting of the French Philosophical Society on March 24, 1928, Blondel, Gilson, and Le Roy debated with Brunschvicg and defended traditional religion. Brunschvicg defended himself against the accusation of atheism. The protocol of this convention was published in Brunschvicg's book *De la vraie et de la fausse conversion, suivi de la querelle de l'athéisme* (1951). His *Ecrits philosophiques,* edited by A. R. Weill-Brunschvicg and C. Lehec, were published in two volumes (1951–54).

Bibliography: Bergman in: *Haaretz* (April 22, 1940); M. Deschoux, *La philosophie de Léon Brunschvicg* (1949); A. Etcheverry, *L'idéalisme français contemporain* (1934); Grenier, in: *Logos,* 15 (1925), 178–96; Vernaux, in: *Revue de philosophie,* 4 (1934), 73–104. [P.H./Ed.]

BRUNSCHVIG, ROBERT (1901–), French orientalist. Brunschvig, who was born in Bordeaux, began his teaching career at Tunis University. In 1932 he became professor of Muslim civilization at Algiers and in 1945 was appointed professor of Arabic language and literature at Bordeaux. Ten years later he went to Paris, where he became director of the Institute of Islamic Studies at the Sorbonne and editor of the journal *Studia Islamica.*

Brunschvig wrote many authoritative works on Islam and Islamic culture, including a monumental political, literary, social, and religious history of the Hafside Kingdom, *La Berbérie orientale sous le Hafṣides, des origines à la fin du XVe siècle* (2 vols, 1940–47). This contains an impressive study of the Jews of Algeria and Tunisia, based on the responsa of North African rabbis. There is also some important historical information about Jews in his *Deux récits de voyage inedits en Afrique du Nord au XVe siècle* (1936).

Always an active Zionist, Brunschvig worked tirelessly on behalf of the persecuted Jews of Algeria during the Vichy regime of World War II. In 1940, when they lost their education rights, he organized primary and secondary schooling for them throughout the country. He was on the executive of the Committee for Study, Aid, and Assistance which saved the lives of many Jews, and in 1942–43 was president of the Committee of Social Studies which played a political role in the face of Algerian anti-Semitism.

Bibliography: M. Eisenbeth, *Pages vécues 1940–43* (1945), passim; M. Ansky, *Les Juifs d'Algerie* (1950), passim. [D.Co.]

BRUNSWICK (Ger. **Braunschweig**), city and former duchy in West Germany. Jews were living in the duchy at the beginning of the 12th century, and in 1137 the emperor gave jurisdiction over them to the duke. The only specific information concerning the Jews living in the duchy before the *Black Death relates to Blankenburg (1223) and Helmstedt (1247), apart from the capital city where a community was established at the end of the 13th century. Both the dukes and the municipality gave the Jews protection and levied taxes. Their economic conditions and legal status were favorable, and Jews from other places in northern Germany moved there. At the beginning of the 14th century the Jews in the capital lived in a street near the market and ducal castle. By the middle of the century they numbered approximately 150. Over half were massacred during the Black Death (1348–49). In 1364 jurisdiction over the Jews passed entirely to the municipality. Jews from Goslar were permitted to settle in Brunswick in 1417. The Jews in the city of Brunswick were accused of desecrating the *Host in 1510, and 16 were expelled. Anti-Jewish riots occurred in 1543, provoked by the polemical writings of Martin Luther, and in 1571 the Jews were expelled from the duchy. The emperor procured their return seven years later, but the decree of expulsion was renewed in 1590. This time the imperial representations were of no avail and the Jews were compelled to leave.

Several Jews were permitted to settle in the duchy at the beginning of the 17th century. Duke Charles William Ferdinand (1780–1806), whom Israel *Jacobson served as *Court Jew, corresponded with Moses *Mendelssohn on philosophical and religious subjects; he invited Mendelssohn for a visit, and encouraged him to write his *Morgenstunden.* In 1805 the duke abrogated the *Leibzoll* ("body tax") hitherto levied on Jews. The school Jacobson founded in Seesen in 1801, the first to educate children in

Synagogue in Brunswick, Germany, consecrated in 1875. Brunswick, Municipal Archives and Library.

the spirit of *Haskalah, was opened under ducal patronage. A second "progressive" school, the Samson school, was opened in *Wolfenbuettel in 1807; I. M. *Jost and Leopold *Zunz were among its pupils. Between 1807 and 1813 Brunswick formed part of the Napoleonic kingdom of Westphalia, and the Jews were granted civic equality. After the downfall of Napoleon in 1814, when the kingdom was abolished, the Jews were again disqualified from holding public office and deprived of the franchise. They acquired the franchise and elective rights in 1832. The "Jewish oath" was abolished in 1845. In 1848 mixed marriages were legalized and Jews were allowed to acquire real property. The civil service remained closed to Jews until 1919. A synagogue was built in the city of Brunswick about 1780 and another in 1784. The Brunswick community adopted *Reform Judaism at the beginning of the 19th century. The rabbi of Brunswick, Levi *Herzfeld (1842–84), convened the first *synod of German rabbis there in 1844. The community in Brunswick numbered 378 in 1812, 258 in 1852 (0.3% of the total), and 1,750 in 1928. However, by 1933 the number had decreased to 682 since the city had become a stronghold of Nazism. Those who remained were deported to the East between 1942 and 1945. A concentration camp was established in Brunswick in which there were a number of Jews at the end of World War II. There were 43 Jews living in the city of Brunswick in 1967.

Bibliography: Germ Jud, 1 (1963), 503; 2 (1968), 87, 108–24, 351; *Brunsvicensia Judaica* (1966; *Braunschweiger Werkstuecke,* no. 35); H. Schnee, *Die Hoffinanz und der moderne Staat,* 2 (1954), 86–109; A. Lewinsky, in: MGWJ, 51 (1907), 214–23; Fischer, in: ZGJD, 8 (1937), 53–64.

[Z.Av./Z.F.]

BRUNSWIG, ALFRED (1877–1927), German philosopher of the school of Theodor Lipps, later influenced by *Husserl. He was born at Plan, taught at Munich (1911–16) and then became professor of philosophy at Muenster. He tried to synthesize psychology and pure logic, and to analyze phenomena to bring together philosophy and experimental research. He was an advocate of critical realism as well as an interpreter of Kant and German idealism. His main works were *Die Frage nach dem Grunde des sittlichen Sollens* (1907); *Das Vergleichen und die Relationserkenntnis* (1910); *Das Grundproblem Kants . . .* (1914), as well as works on Hegel (1922) and Leibniz (1925).

[R.H.P.]

BRUSSELS, capital of *Belgium. A Jewish community existed in Brussels by the mid-13th century. Its cultural standard is attested to by the fine illuminated Pentateuch completed there by the scribe Isaac for Ḥayyim, son of the martyr Ḥayyim, in 1310 (see Figure 1). The Jews of Brussels were massacred during the Black Death (1348–49). A few subsequently resettled, but a further massacre followed an accusation of desecrating the Host (May 1370), and the Jews were officially excluded from Brussels until the end of Spanish rule in Belgium. The memory of the reputed sacrilege was preserved, as the wafers became an object of worship, still commemorated on the third Sunday of July. The episode is depicted in the stained-glass windows of the St. Gudule Cathedral of Brussels. Marranos, however, found their way to Brussels from time to time, such as the Mendes family in the 16th century. In the 17th century several Marranos, including Daniel Levi (Miguel) de *Barrios, served in the Spanish army in Brussels. Some of them later settled in Amsterdam where they openly professed Judaism.

After the Treaty of Utrecht in 1713, Belgium came under Austrian rule and Jews began to settle in Brussels. Decrees of expulsion were issued in 1716 and in 1756, but were

Figure 1. Colophon page of an illuminated Bible with Rashi's commentary, written by the scribe Isaac b. Elisha Ḥazzan, Brussels, 1310. Hamburg, City and University Library, ms. Levy 19, fol. 625.

averted by gifts to the crown. In 1757 the community of Brussels consisted of 21 men, 19 women, and 26 children, many of whom had moved there from Holland. In 1783 Philip Nathan, who received the right of citizenship of Brussels, asked the authorities to assign a site for a new Jewish cemetery. With the annexation of Belgium in 1794 by France, Jews were able to settle freely in Brussels. At the beginning of the 18th century, the Brussels community recognized the authority of the rabbinate of Metz. The Napoleonic edict of March 17, 1808, included Brussels in the *Consistory of Crefeld. When Belgium was united with Holland, Brussels became the head of the 14th religious district of Holland. Belgium became independent in 1830 and the constitution of 1831 accorded religious freedom. Brussels became the center of the Belgian consistories, and Eliakim *Carmoly (1802–1875) was appointed chief rabbi of Belgium in 1832. The community, originally made up primarily of Jews from Holland and Germany, increased through immigration from Poland and Russia and, after 1933, again from Germany. Before World War II, the Brussels community totaled some 30,000, although it remained second in size to Antwerp.

[K.R.S.]

Holocaust Period. The Nazis occupied Belgium in May 1940. A committee of the Association de Juifs en Belgique (A.J.B.) was created in Brussels. All Jews were subjected to direction from this organization under the pretext of providing social relief for their brethren. The local Jews were sent to the labor camp of Mechlin (Malines) and from there they were sent to the extermination camps in the east.

For details see *Belgium: Holocaust Period.

[Ed.]

Contemporary Period. From 1945 until approximately 1950, the Jewish population of Brussels was as large as it had been before World War II (about 27,000), due to the temporary sojourn of thousands of refugees from Eastern and Central Europe there. After that period, however, immigration to Belgium decreased and an important wave of emigration began to the U.S.A., Canada, Australia, and Israel. The total population was not known precisely, but certain statistical data, such as the average family size (which is 2.6 persons), indicated that it did not substantially exceed 18,000. The age distribution, due to a low birthrate and an increasing trend of assimilation, points to the fact that the population has become stationary and is on the road to natural diminution. The community's reconstruction after World War II was severely hampered by Belgium's economic instability and the process of rehabilitating war victims. Furthermore, as the majority of Jews were foreigners, it was difficult for them to obtain work permits. In 1946 a monthly average of 4,500 persons required relief or some form of aid from Jewish agencies, while only a few hundred were still in need in 1970. Priority was given to the creation of general institutions for social assistance and public services, such as L'Aide aux Israélites Victimes de la Guerre (now the Service Social Juif), L'Heureux Séjour, an old-age home; and the Caisse de Prêt de Crédit in order to cope with the needs of the postwar Jewish community. The important contributions of the *American Jewish Joint Distribution Committee and the *Conference on Jewish Material Claims against Germany to the institutions largely supported by them during the last 20 years eventually tapered off. A central fund-raising

Figure 2. The Great Synagogue in Brussels, built 1878. Photo Jewish Community, Brussels.

agency, La Centrale d'Oeuvres Sociales Juives, unifying 15 institutions, was created in 1952.

Brussels has two primary Jewish day schools run on different ideological bases: one is religious-traditionalist, l'École Israélite, and the other, Ganenou, is more specifically Zionist oriented. The Athénée Maimonide high school is run by the same board as the École Israélite. These three schools are recognized and subsidized by the state. Participation in a Jewish curriculum has also been expanded through other endeavors, such as the creation of Sunday schools, a school of Yiddish language and literature, and a number of Hebrew classes. Three ideologically different communal centers also provide educational and leisure activities. Apart from its four legally recognized religious communities (three Ashkenazi and one Sephardi), Brussels has several groups that organize their own religious services. In 1966 Belgian Jews and American Jews residing in Belgium created L'Union Israélite Libérale de Belgique, which has a Progressive ideology. The Centre National des Hautes Études Juives, created by the Free University of Brussels and subsidized by the state, promotes research and studies on contemporary Jewry and plays an active role in the cultural renewal of the community. [MA.G./W.B.]

Bibliography: H. Ouverleau, in: REJ, 7 (1883), 117–38; 8 (1884), 206–34; 9 (1884), 264–89; M. Kayserling, in: REJ, 18 (1889), 276–89; R. Orfinger-Karlin, in: AJYB, 49 (1947), 325–30; JYB (1964), 171; W. Bok, in: *Deuxième colloque sur la vie juive dans l'Europe contemporaine* (1967); W. Bok and H. Helman, in: *Jewish Communal Service* (1967), 69–75; M. Flinker, *Young Moshe's Diary* (1965).

BRUSSILOVSKY, YEVGENI GRIGORYEVICH (1905–), Soviet composer. Born in Rostov-on-Don, he revealed his musical talent during performances while on military service. He studied in Moscow and then moved to Leningrad, where he played the piano in cinemas. From 1926 he studied composition at the conservatory with M. O. Steinberg. His first two symphonies, performed in 1931 and 1932, won instant acclaim. In 1933 he settled in Kazakhstan and began collecting Kazakh folk music as member of the local Music Research Institute. Brussilovsky's first opera, *Kyz-Zhibek* (1934), initiated the development of a Kazakh national opera; it was followed by *Zhalbyr* (1935), *Zolotoye zerno* (1940), and *Dudaray* (1953). He was artistic director of the Kazakh Music Theater (1934–38), and taught at the Alma-Ata conservatory.

Bibliography: B. Yerzakovich, *Brussilovsky* (Rus., 1950); A. Kelberg, *Brussilovsky* (Rus., 1959). [M.GO.]

BRUSTEIN, ROBERT SANFORD (1927–), U.S. drama critic. Brustein wrote for the weekly magazine *The New Republic* and other periodicals, putting forward his belief in the need for a theater that expressed social concerns and political realities. In 1965 he was given an opportunity to test his theories when he was appointed dean of the Yale School of Drama. At Yale he sought to develop a professional repertory theater in which students could learn and work with established actors, playwrights, directors, and stage designers. His unconventional ideas and imaginative productions led to vigorous controversy. He elaborated his theories in *The Theater of Revolt; An Approach to the Modern Drama* (1964). [R.R.]

BRUTZKUS, BORIS DOV (1874–1938), Russian agrarian economist and communal leader. Boris Brutzkus, a brother of Julius *Brutzkus, was born in Palanga, Lithuania. He studied agriculture in Poland and in 1898 became head of the agriculture department of the *Jewish Colonization Association (ICA) in Russia. The following year he took part in the association's investigation of Jewish farming in Poland, Lithuania, Belorussia, and the Ukraine. In 1907 he resigned from ICA because he disagreed with its philanthropic approach, and became a lecturer at the Agricultural Institute in St. Petersburg, where he remained for some 15 years. At the same time he worked for the Russian-Jewish organization *ORT, and came to play an important role in its activities both in Russia and in Germany.

Brutzkus was a leading figure, together with Simon *Dubnow, in the Jewish People's Party *(Folkspartei)*, but nevertheless showed considerable interest in settlement in Ereẓ Israel. In 1922 he left the U.S.S.R. and settled in Berlin, where until 1932 he served as professor at the Russian Scientific Institute. During these years he was active in *YIVO and, together with Jacob *Lestschinsky and Jacob Segall, edited the *Bleter far Yidishe Demografye, Statistik un Ekonomik* (1923–25). When Hitler came to power Brutzkus moved to Paris and from there to Ereẓ Israel. He settled in Jerusalem in 1936, and became professor of agrarian economy at the Hebrew University.

His principal books were: *Professionalny sostav yevreyskogo naseleniya v Rosii* ("Jewish Population in Russia by Professions," 1908); *Yevreyskiye zemledelcheskiye poseleniya Yekaterinoslavskoy gubernii* ("Jewish Agricultural Settlements in Ekaterinoslav," 1913); *Agrarny vopros i agrarnaya politika* ("Agricultural Question and Agrarian Politics," 1922); *Sotsialisticheskoye khozyaystvo* ("Socialist Economy," 1923); *Agrarentwicklung und Agrarrevolution in Russland* (1925); *Di Yidishe Landvirtshaft in Mizrekh-Eyrope* (1926); *Die Lehren des Marxismus im Lichte der Russischen Revolution* (1928); *Der Fuenfjahrplan und seine Erfuellung* (1932); *Economic Planning in Soviet Russia* (1935, a translation and abridgment of the two foregoing works); *URSS, terrain d'expériences économiques* (1937); and *Kalkalah Ḥakla'it* ("Agrarian Economics," 1942), which contains a selected list of his works. [J.O.R]

His son DAVID ANATOL BRUTZKUS (1910–) was an Israel architect. He was born in St. Petersburg and went to Ereẓ Israel in 1935. His public buildings stress their individual function and the character of the site. Brutzkus was also active in town planning. He collaborated with H. *Rau on the first town planning project for Jerusalem after the War of Independence, and after the Six-Day War worked with A. *Sharon on a plan for the Old City and surroundings. [ED.]

Bibliography: Ginzburg, in: *Zukunft* (Feb., 1939), 99–100; B. Dinur, *Benei Dori* (1963), 80–85; I. Gruenbaum, *Penei ha-Dor*, 1 (1957), 326–8.

BRUTZKUS, JULIUS (1870–1951), communal worker, brother of Boris *Brutzkus. He was born in Palanga, Lithuania, and studied medicine at the University of Moscow during the 1880s. Brutzkus was a member of the Benei Zion (see *Ḥibbat Zion) group and worked for an improvement in the condition of the Jews who had been expelled from Moscow in 1891. He settled in St. Petersburg where he participated in the activities of the "Society for the Propagation of Culture Among Russian Jews" and became a member of the editorial board of the Russian-Jewish monthly **Voskhod*. He also took a part in the activities of the ICA (*Jewish Colonization Association) among the Jews of Russia. In 1902 he resigned from *Voskhod* because of its anti-Zionist attitude. In 1905 he became a member of the editorial boards of the Zionist periodicals *Yevreyskaya* *zhizn* ("Jewish Life") and the reestablished **Razsvet* ("Dawn"). During the revolution of 1905 he played a role in the Committee for the Protection of Emancipation of Russian Jews. In 1909 he was elected to the enlarged Zionist organization executive and to the council of the *Jewish Colonial Trust. Brutzkus favored "practical work" in

Julius Brutzkus. Raphaeli Collection, Tel Aviv.

Palestine. In 1917 he was elected to the all-Russian Constituent Assembly as the representative of the "Jewish List" of the Minsk district. In 1921 Brutzkus became the minister for Jewish affairs in the Lithuanian government. In 1922 he was elected to the Lithuanian parliament. After the restriction of Jewish autonomy in Lithuania, he settled in Berlin where he worked with *YIVO, became a vice-president of *OSE, and one of the founders of the Zionist Revisionist Party. When the Nazis came to power in Germany, he emigrated to France. Arrested by the Vichy government, he succeeded in escaping and emigrating to America, and finally to Palestine. As a historian, Brutzkus' activity was principally concerned with the history of the Jews in Russia and Lithuania and the Khazars. His works were published in Russian, Yiddish, and German. His writings include *Ukazatel o russkoy literatury o yevreyakh* ("Bibliographical Guide to Russian Literature on the Jews") in collaboration with L. Bramson (1892); "Documents and Records on the History of the Jews in Russia" (Rus., 1899–1900); *K istorii yevreyev v Kurlyandiyi* ("History of the Jews in Courland"; in *Voskhod*, 1895); "History of the Mountain Jews of Caucasus" (in YIVOA, 1938); and *Pismo khazarskogo yevreya ot X veka* ("Letter from a Khazar Jew of the Tenth Century"; in a special pamphlet in Russian, 1924, and in English, 1935).

[Ab.A./Ed.]

BRYANSK, capital of Bryansk province, Russian S.F.S.R. Under the czars it was outside the *Pale of Settlement, and the community established there in the second half of the 19th century was made up of Jews who were permitted to live outside the Pale (discharged soldiers, registered merchants of the guilds, etc.). In 1896 they were authorized to maintain a synagogue and by 1897 the Jewish residents numbered 1,321. Pogroms occurred in Bryansk in October 1905. After the 1917 Revolution, the Jewish population increased, numbering 2,500 in 1926 (9.1% of the total). When the Germans occupied the city in October 1941 the Jews who had not managed to escape were murdered. The Jewish population of Bryansk province numbered 13,700 in 1959. In 1970, it was estimated that 4–6,000 Jews lived in the town. They had one synagogue but no rabbi.

Bibliography: *Die Judenpogrome in Russland*, 2 (1909), 498–504.

[Y.S.]

BRYER, MONTE (1912–), South African architect. Born in Bloemfontein, he practiced in Johannesburg. His work as an architect was marked by boldness of conception and a flair for experimentation. His outstanding achievement was in 1963, when he headed a team that produced the winning design in an international competition for the new civic center of Johannesburg. Also typical of his technique was a design for a metal industries center, in which he exploited to the full the use of structural steelwork instead of reinforced concrete and of light metals instead of heavy conventional materials. Bryer's other works included the Jewish communal center and synagogue in Bloemfontein. He was president of the Institute of South African Architects (1961–62), and a joint president of the Royal Institute of British Architects, representing the South African Institute on that organization. [L.Ho.]

BRZEG (Ger. **Brieg**), town in Opole province, southwest Poland (until 1945 in Germany). Jews living in Brieg are mentioned in the 14th century. In 1358 certain Jews lent sums of money to noblemen and the duke of Brieg, Ludwig I, who granted the Jews freedom of movement in the duchy in that year. An outbreak of anti-Jewish violence occurred in 1362. In 1423 Ludwig II granted the Jews rights of residence on payment of an annual tax of 20 gulden, but they were expelled from the duchies of Brieg and Liegnitz in 1453 as a result of the inflammatory preachings of the Franciscan John *Capistrano. Among the few Jewish residents in the 16th century was the ducal physician, Abraham. In 1660 a community was again formed. A synagogue was built in 1799, and a rabbi was first appointed in 1816. For many years the popular German yearbooks *Jahrbuch des Nuetzlichen und Unterhaltenden* (from 1841) and *Deutscher Volkskalender und Jahrbuch* (from 1851) were published in Brieg by K. Klein and H. Liebermann, both Jews. The Jewish population numbered 156 in 1785; 376 in 1843; 282 in 1913; 255 in 1933; and 123 in 1939. In the **Kristallnacht* pogroms of 1938 the interior of the synagogue was completely demolished and the Torah scrolls publicly burned; numerous shops were ransacked. The community was not reestablished after World War II.

Bibliography: C. F. Schoenwaelder, *Die Piasten zum Briege* (1855); H. Schoenborn, *Geschichte der Stadt und des Fuerstentums Brieg* (1907); M. Stecker, *Juden zu Brieg* (1938); M. Brann, *Geschichte der Juden in Schlesien*, 1 (1896), passim. [Ed.]

BRZESC KUJAWSKI (Rus. **Brest Kuyavsk**), town in central Poland. A Jewish community is mentioned in 1538; the Jews then owned 15 houses there. On April 15, 1656, 100 Jewish families were massacred by Polish soldiers in Brzesc Kujawski after they refused to be baptized. Between 1822 and 1862 Jewish residence was restricted to certain parts of the town. The Jewish population numbered 164 in 1765; 678 in 1897; 794 in 1921 (out of a total of 3,813); and 633 in 1939.

[Ed.]

Holocaust Period. Under the Nazi occupation Brzesc Kujawski belonged to the Warthegau. At the outbreak of World War II about 630 Jews were living there. A *Judenrat was created, but no ghetto set up. Jews underwent physical suffering, were plundered of all their property, were compelled to perform humiliating work, and endured acts of religious persecution, e.g., the burning of the synagogue. During January-September 1941, able-bodied men and women were deported to slave labor camps in the Posen region. Most of the remaining 400 Jews were then removed to *Lodz ghetto and the rest were sent to the death camp at *Chelmno. [De.D]

Bibliography: I. Schipper (ed.), *Dzieje handlu żydowskiego na ziemiach polskich* (1937), index; L. Lewin, *Die Judenverfolgungen im zweiten schwedisch-polnischen Kriege (1655–1659)* (1901);

D. Dabrowska, in: BŻIH, 13–14 (1955), 122–84; D. Dabrowska and L. Dabroszycki (eds.), *Kronika getta łódzkiego,* 1 (1965), 262.

BRZEZINY, town 2 mi. (3 km.) E. of Lodz in central Poland. Jews are mentioned there in 1564. In 1656, 40 Jewish families were massacred in Brzeziny by Polish soldiers (Czarnecki units). Brzeziny later became a Jewish tailoring center; between 1909 and 1912 its annual production amounted to 50,000,000 rubles. The Jewish population numbered 243 in 1765, 3,917 in 1897 (over half of the total population), 8,214 in 1912, and 4,980 in 1925.

[Ed.]

Holocaust Period. In 1939 there was still a Jewish majority in Brzeziny—6,850 out of a total population of 13,000. During the Nazi occupation Jewish property was confiscated and pillaged; people in the streets or in their homes were kidnapped for forced labor; and community leaders and members of the liberal professions were deported to unknown destinations. In February 1940, a ghetto was established and included over 6,000 inhabitants. In 1942 (Purim?) there was a public execution of ten Jews. The final liquidation of the ghetto took place on May 19–20, 1942. Elderly Jews were sent to *Chelmno extermination camps and others to *Lodz ghetto.

[De.D.]

Bibliography: I. Schipper (ed.), *Dzieje handlu żydowskiego na ziemiach polskich* (1937), index; L. Lewin, *Die Judenverfolgungen im zweiten schwedisch-polnischen Kriege (1655–1659)* (1901), 14; *Bzheshin Yisker-Bukh* (1961); J. J. Kermisz, *"Akcje" i "Wysiedlenia,"* 2 (1946), index; D. Dąbrowska and L. Dąbroszycki (eds.), *Kronika getta łódzkiego,* 2 vols. (1965–66), passim; D. Dąbrowska, in: BŻIH, no. 13–14 (1955), 122–84.

BUBER, MARTIN (1878–1965), philosopher and theologian, Zionist thinker and leader. Born in Vienna, Buber as a child lived in Lemberg with his grandfather Solomon *Buber, the noted Midrash scholar. From 1896 he studied at the universities of Vienna, Leipzig, and Zurich, and finally at the University of Berlin, where he was a pupil of the philosophers Wilhelm Dilthey and Georg Simmel. Having joined the Zionist movement in 1898, he was a delegate to the Third Zionist Congress in 1899 where he spoke on behalf of the Propaganda Committee. In this speech, which bore the influence of modern Hebrew and Yiddish writers, notably of Aḥad Ha-Am, Buber emphasized the importance of education as opposed to a program of propaganda. In 1901 he was appointed editor of the central weekly organ of the Zionist movement, *Die Welt,* in which he emphasized the need for a new Jewish cultural creativity. This emphasis on cultural rather than political activity led, at the Fifth Zionist Congress in 1901, to the formation of the Zionist *Democratic Fraction which stood in opposition to Herzl. Buber, a member of this faction, resigned before the Congress as editor of *Die Welt.* Together with his friends, he founded the *Juedischer Verlag in Berlin, which went on to publish (in German) books of literary quality. At the age of 26 Buber took up the study of Ḥasidism. At first his interest was essentially aesthetic. After attempting to translate the tales of Rabbi *Naḥman of Bratslav into German, he decided to retell them in German in the form of a free adaptation. Thus originated *Die Geschichten des Rabbi Nachman* (1906; *The Tales of Rabbi Nachman,* 1956) and *Die Legende des Baalschem* (1908; *The Legend of the Baal-Shem,* 1955). Later Buber's interest turned from the aesthetic aspect of Ḥasidism to its content. Deeply stirred by the religious message of Ḥasidism, he considered it his duty to convey that message to the world. Among the books he later wrote on Ḥasidism are *Gog u-Magog* (1941, in *Davar;* translated into English under the title *For the Sake of Heaven,* 1945), *Or ha-Ganuz* (1943), and *Pardes ha-Ḥasidut* (1945; translated into English in two volumes *Hasidism and Modern Man,* 1958, and *The Origin and Meaning of Hasidism,* 1960).

In 1909 Buber resumed an active role in public affairs. He delivered three addresses to the Prague student organization, *Bar Kochba, in 1909, 1910, and 1911 (*At the Turning, Three Addresses on Judaism,* 1952; see also Bergman, in *Ha-Shilo'aḥ,* 26 (1912), 549–56), which had a great influence on Jewish youth in Central Europe, and also marked a turning point in Buber's own intellectual activity. With the outbreak of World War I Buber founded in Berlin the Jewish National Committee which worked throughout the war on behalf of the Jews in Eastern European countries under German occupation, and on behalf of the *yishuv* in Palestine. In 1916 he founded the monthly *Der Jude,* which for eight years was the most important organ of the Jewish renaissance movement in Central Europe. In the spring of 1920, at the convention of *Ha-Po'el ha-Ẓa'ir-Ẓe'irei Ẓiyyon in Prague, Buber defined his Zionist socialist position and his adherence to utopian socialism in an address which reflected his affinity to Aharon David *Gordon and Gustav *Landauer. He was opposed to the current concept of socialism which looked upon the state, and not upon a reaffirmation of life and of the relationship between man and man, as the means of realizing the socialist society. Buber envisaged the creation of *Gemeinschaften* in Palestine, communities in which people would live together in direct personal relationship. During the years following World War I Buber became the spokesman for what he called "Hebrew Humanism," according to which Zionism, described as the "holy way," a notion explained in *Der heilige Weg* (1919), was different from other nationalistic movements. Buber also emphasized that Zionism should address itself also to the needs of the Arabs and in a proposal to the Zionist Congress of 1921 stated that ". . . the Jewish people proclaims its desire to live in peace and brotherhood with the Arab people and to develop the common homeland into a republic in which both peoples will have the possibility of free development." In 1923 Buber published his *Ich und Du* (*I and Thou,* 1937) which contains the basic formulation of his philosophy of dialogue. In 1925 the first volumes of the German translation of the Bible appeared as the combined effort of Buber and Franz *Rosenzweig. In *Die Schrift und ihre Verdeutschung* (1936) the translators set forth the guiding principles of their translation: today's reader of the Bible has ceased to be a listener; but the Bible does not seek to be read, but to be listened to, as if its voice were being

Figure 1. Martin Buber, philosopher and theologian. Jerusalem, Hebrew University. Photo Werner Braun, Jerusalem.

spoken today. The Bible has been divested of its direct impact. In the choice of words, in sentence-structure, and in rhythm, Buber and Rosenzweig attempted to preserve the original character of the Hebrew Bible. After Rosenzweig's death in 1929 Buber continued the work of translation alone and completed it in 1961.

In 1925 Buber began to lecture on Jewish religion and ethics at the University of Frankfort, and in 1930 he was appointed professor of religion there, a position he retained until 1933, when with the rise of the Nazis to power he was forced to leave the university. In 1932 Buber published his *Koenigtum Gottes,* which was to be the first volume of a series dealing with the origins of the messianic belief in Judaism. This work was never completed. The third German edition (1956) was translated into English (*Kingship of God,* 1967). In 1933 Buber was appointed director of the newly created Central Office for Jewish Adult Education (Mittelstelle fuer juedische Erwachsenenbildung) established to take charge of the education of Jews after they were prohibited from attending German educational institutions. In the same year he was invited to head the Juedisches Lehrhaus in Frankfort. During the beginning of the Nazi period Buber traveled throughout Germany lecturing, teaching, and encouraging his fellow Jews, and thus organized something of a spiritual resistance. In 1935 he was forbidden to speak at Jewish gatherings. He was then invited to speak at Quaker meetings until the Gestapo prohibited his appearing there as well.

In 1938 Buber settled in Palestine and was appointed professor of social philosophy at the Hebrew University, where he taught until his retirement in 1951. In 1942 his first book written in Hebrew, *Torat ha-Nevi'im* (*The Prophetic Faith,* 1949) was published. This book, a history of biblical faith, is based on the supposition that the mutuality of the covenant between God and Israel testifies that the existence of the Divine Will is as real as the existence of Israel. Another book born out of Buber's efforts to penetrate the essential meaning of the Bible is his *Moses* (1946). Buber in his later years remained very active in public affairs and in Jewish cultural endeavors. He was one of the leaders of Iḥud, formerly *Berit Shalom, which advocated the establishment of a joint Arab-Israel state. Even after the outbreak of the Arab-Israel war, Buber called for a harnessing of nationalistic impulses and a solution based on compromise. Recognizing the importance of the cultural assimilation of immigrants to Israel, especially those from the Islamic countries, Buber was one of the founders of the College for Adult Education Teachers (Beit Ha-Midrash Le-Morei Am) established to train teachers from among the new immigrants themselves. Buber was the first president of the Israel Academy of Sciences and Humanities (1960–62), one of the founders of *Mosad Bialik, and active in many other cultural institutions. In the years following World War II Buber lectured extensively outside Israel, visiting the United States in 1952, and again in 1957–58, and became known throughout the world as one of the spiritual leaders of his generation, making a deep impact on Christian as well as Jewish thinkers. [SH.H.B.]

Figure 2. Hebrew University students celebrate Martin Buber's 85th birthday, 1963. Jerusalem, Hebrew University. Photo David Harris, Jerusalem.

Philosophy of Dialogue. The starting point of Buber's philosophy is not man in himself nor the world in itself but rather the relation between man and the world. In *Ich und Du* Buber distinguished two basic forms of relation—the I–Thou and I–It, into which all man's relations, both with other men and with things in the world, can be divided. The I–Thou relation is characterized by mutuality, openness, directness, and presentness; the I–It, by the absence of these qualities. The I–Thou relation is a true dialogue in which both partners speak to one another as equals. The I–It relation is not a true dialogue in that the partners are not equals but one uses the other to achieve some end. It is impossible to sustain an I–Thou relationship indefinitely, and it is inevitable that every Thou will at times turn into an It. The I–It relation is not evil in itself, for it is only through the I–It relation that objective knowledge will be acquired, and technical advances achieved. In the healthy man and culture there is a dialectical interaction between the I–Thou and I–It relationships. As a result of this dialectical interaction I–Thou relationships become I–It relationships which find their expression in knowledge and art, and these relationships in turn contain within themselves the possibility of becoming once again I-Thou relationships.

In *The Knowledge of Man* (1965) Buber systematically develops his "dialogical theory of knowledge," an epistemology based on the I–Thou relation. While Buber, like Kant, maintains that we cannot have objective knowledge of the universe as it is in itself, and that we know the world only through the categories which are imposed upon it, he does hold that in I–Thou relationships we can have direct contact with objects in the world although we can never know them in themselves. Our sense perception is built on this direct contact, and the I–Thou relation is, therefore, the basis of all our knowledge of the world and of all art.

Eternal Thou and Revelation. Buber's analysis of the I–Thou relation among men leads him to his notion of God as the Eternal Thou, and to his description of the relation between man and God as an I–Thou relation. God, the Eternal Thou, is known not through cognitive propositions, or through metaphysical speculation, but through one's particular I–Thou relationships with persons, animals, nature, and works of art. The Eternal Thou, met in every finite Thou, is itself the very uniqueness and concreteness of each particular I–Thou meeting. It is these meetings with the Eternal Thou which, according to Buber, constitute revelation. Thus revelation is not only something that happened at particular moments in the past, at Mount Sinai or the burning bush, but something that happens in the present, throughout one's life, if one is open to receive it. The revelations described in the Bible differ only in degree, not in kind, from the personal revelations of everyday life. The Bible is for Buber "... a record of the dialogical encounters between man and God ..." (M. Diamond, *Martin Buber, Jewish Existentialist* (1960), 92). Buber maintains that revelation is never a formulation of law. The laws of the Bible are only the human response to revelation, and, therefore, are not binding on later generations (see F. Rosenzweig, *On Jewish Learning* (1955), 109–18, Buber's and Rosenzweig's letters). The Hebrew Bible is not a dead book but living speech, in which the Eternal Thou of the past becomes present again to the one who truly listens. The dialogue between God and the people of Israel is epitomized in the covenant, which lies at the basis of Jewish messianism. God demands of the people of Israel that they become a holy nation and a kingdom of priests, and thereby make real the kingship of God in every aspect of communal life—social, economic, and international. The hasidic influence on Buber is discernible in his hallowing of the everyday, in his seeing God in the particular relationships between men, and in the concomitant refusal to accept a redemption that is anything less than a redemption of this world in all its contradiction and evil. For Buber the essence of the religious life is not the affirmation of religious beliefs but the way in which one meets the challenges of everyday life (*On the Bible: Eighteen Studies,* 1968).

Buber and Christianity. While Buber is far from saying that this dialogical situation is peculiar to Judaism, he does argue that there is no other group that has invested this concept of God and man with so much spiritual force as the Jews. He stresses the gulf between Judaism and certain currents of Protestantism that emphasize the passivity that is demanded of man in his relationship to God, and argues against those Catholic theologians who maintain that Judaism is an activism unmindful of the grace of God. This concept of the life of faith as the life of dialogue between man and God has had a deep influence on contemporary Christian theology. This influence on Catholic theologians is discernible in the writings of Gabriel Marcel, Theodor Steinbuechel and Ernst Michel (the very title of Michel's book, *The Partner of God,* testifies to his proximity to Buber), and on Protestant thinkers, in the works of Paul Tillich, Wilhelm Michel, Walther Nigg, and J. H. Oldham. [Ma.F.]

Bibliography: P. A. Schilpp and M. Friedman (eds.), *The Philosophy of Martin Buber* (1967), includes comprehensive bibliography; M. Friedman, *Martin Buber: The Life of Dialogue* (1955), includes comprehensive bibliography; idem, *Martin Buber: Encounter on the Narrow Ridge,* 2 vols. (1969–70); M. A. Beele and J. S. Weiland, *Martin Buber, Personalist and Prophet* (1968); G. Schaeder, *Martin Buber: Hebraeischer Humanismus* (1966); A. S. Cohen, *Martin Buber* (Eng., 1957); *Der Jude,* 10 no. 1 (1928), special issue for his 50th birthday; H. Kohn, *Martin Buber, sein Werk und seine Zeit* (1961); G. Scholem, in: *Commentary,* 32 (1961), 305–16.

BUBER, SOLOMON (1827–1906), scholar and authority on midrashic and medieval rabbinic literature. Buber was born in Lemberg, Galicia, into a well-known rabbinic family and devoted himself to the publication of scholarly editions of existing Midrashim, printed or in manuscript, and to the reconstruction of those that had been lost. His Midrash editions and those of some medieval works constituted a veritable revolution in the production of reliable texts. Their learned introductions are major research works in themselves, and the annotations give a complete picture of the textual problems and parallel passages. While scholarship in this field has not stood still since Buber's days and his work and method are in part, at

Solomon Buber, rabbinic scholar. Jerusalem, Schwadron Collection, J.N.U.L.

least, outdated, subsequent researchers in this field owe him much.

Buber was a man of independent means and financed his scholarly projects personally. Not only did he pay for the expense of publication, but he also paid for people to visit various libraries to copy manuscripts. Buber's achievement is all the more remarkable in view of his active business life. He was a governor of the Austro-Hungarian Bank and the Galician Savings Bank, president of the Lemberg Chamber of Commerce, and a member of the Lemberg Jewish community's executive council from 1870.

Buber's Midrash editions were: (1) **Tanḥuma* (on the Pentateuch), an older and different version of the previously known and printed Midrash of that name (Vilna, 1885, 1913; repr. 1946, 1964); (2) **Midrash Lekaḥ Tov* or *Pesikta Zutrata* by Tobias b. Eliezer (11th century) on the Pentateuch (part of the work, from Leviticus on, had been printed previously) in Buber's edition with a commentary by Aaron Moses Padua of Karlin (1880, 1884, 1921–24; repr. 1960); (3) *Midrash Aggadah* on the Pentateuch (1894; repr. 1961); (4) *Sekhel Tov* on Genesis and Exodus by Menahem b. Solomon (12th century; 1900–02; repr. 1959, 1964); (5) **Aggadat Bereshit* on Genesis (first published by Abraham b. Elijah of Vilna, 1802), 28 homilies following the triennial cycle of the Palestinian rite (1903, 1925; repr. 1959); (6) *Likkutim mi-Midrash Avkir* on Genesis and Exodus (1883; repr. 1967); (7) a reconstruction of *Midrash Devarim Zuta* in *Likkutim mi-Midrash Devarim Zuta,* on Deuteronomy (1885); (8) **Midrash Shemu'el* (1893, 1925; repr. 1965); (9) **Midrash Tehillim,* or *Shoḥar Tov,* on Psalms (1891; repr. 1966); (10) *Yalkut ha-Makhiri* on Psalms by Machir b. Abba Mari (14th century; 1900; repr. 1964); (11) **Midrash Mishlei* on Proverbs (1893; repr. 1965); (12) *Midrash Zuta* on the Five Scrolls except Esther (1894, 1925; repr. 1964); (13) *Eikhah Rabbah [Rabbati],* on Lamentations (1899; repr. 1964); (14) *Aggadat Ester,* part of *Midrash ha-Gadol* (1887, 1925^2; repr. 1964); (15) *Sifrei de-Aggadata,* three Midrashim on Esther (1887; repr. 1964); and (16) *Pesikta de-Rav Kahana,* a hitherto unpublished selection of homilies for special Sabbaths and festivals by Rav Kahana, first discovered by L. Zunz, from a manuscript written in Egypt in 1565, which Buber found in Safed (now in the Alliance Israélite Universelle in Paris, no. 47; 1868, 1925; repr. 1963). Of these 16 items, numbers 1, 9, and 15 are the most important. Buber also annotated L. Gruenhut's edition of the *Yalkut ha-Makhiri* on Proverbs and of *Yelammedenu* fragments on Genesis (*Sefer ha-Likkutim,* 6, 1903). He also edited many other works by medieval authors as well as some historical works, including a biography and bibliography of Elijah *Levita. Buber also contributed some hundred articles to various periodicals. Martin *Buber was his grandson.

Bibliography: M. Reines, *Dor ve-Ḥakhamav* (1890), 28ff.; S. Bernfeld, in: *Ha-Shilo'aḥ,* 17 (1907), 168ff.; Zeitlin, Bibliotheca, 44ff.; J. K. Miklischansky, in: S. Federbush (ed.), *Ḥokhmat Yisrael be-Ma'arav Eiropah* (1965), 41–58.

[Ed.]

BUBLICK, GEDALIAH (1875–1948), U.S. Yiddish journalist and Orthodox Zionist leader. Bublick was born in Grodno, Russia. He began his literary career in 1899 with an article on Jewish nationalism that appeared in the Hebrew periodical *Ha-Shilo'aḥ.* In 1900 he helped lead a group of 50 Jewish families from Bialystok to Moissville, Argentina, where he worked for four years teaching Hebrew. Settling in New York City in 1904, Bublick joined the editorial staff of the Yiddish-language *Jewish Daily News.* He became editor in chief in 1915, and continued as contributing editor when the paper merged with the *Jewish Morning Journal* in 1928. An active Zionist, Bublick was among the founders of the *American Jewish Congress, of which he became vice-president in 1918, and of the Mizrachi Organization of America. He served on the executive of the World Zionist Organization (1919–26), and of the Jewish Agency for Palestine (from 1929). Among Bublick's publications were *Mayne Rayze in Erets-Yisroel* (1921), and *Min ha-Meẓar* (Yid., 1923), a study of modern Judaism. He was a frequent contributor to Hebrew and Yiddish periodicals.

[E.Gr.]

°**BUCER (Butzer), MARTIN** (1491–1551), German religious reformer. Bucer displayed a characteristically ambivalent approach toward the Jews. Ostensibly preaching understanding for and love toward them, in practice his teachings stirred up hatred—his thesis being that the Jews, having scorned the message of Jesus, had, according to him, forfeited the promised privileges; however they still remained free to embrace Christian teachings, this being the ultimate destiny of Israel and the purpose of its survival. Like Martin Luther, Bucer regarded the Jews as the descendants of the Patriarchs, a people who had received the Commandments from God, but who had been rejected by Him in anger for not fulfilling His will. When Landgrave Philip of Hesse wished to give the Jews in his territories a definitive status (1538), Bucer and six Hesse clergymen offered their written opinion to the effect that the Jews should not be allowed to raise themselves above the Christians but should be confined to the lowest estate. Against the recriminations of Bucer, Joseph (Joselmann) of Rosheim appeared as spokesman on behalf of the Jews.

Bibliography: N. Paulus, in: *Der Katholik,* 3 (1891); *Publikationen aus den Koeniglich-Preussischen Staatsarchiven,* 5 pt. 1 (1880), 56ff. (Butzer's correspondence with Philip of Hesse); M. Maurer, in: K. H. Rengstorf and S. V. Kortzfleisch (eds.), *Kirche und Synagoge,* 1 (1968), 439–41; S. Stern, *Josel von Rosheim* (Eng., 1965), index; *New Catholic Encyclopedia,* 2 (1966), 844; A. K. E. Holmio, *The Lutheran Reformation and the Jews* (1949); C. Cohen, in: YLBI, 3 (1968), 93–101; Baron, Social^2, 13 (1969), 239ff.

[B.M.A.]

BUCHACH (Pol. **Buczacz**), city in Ternopol (Tarnopol) oblast, Ukrainian S.S.R. (until 1939 in Poland). A Jewish settlement there is mentioned in 1572; the earliest Jewish tombstone dates from 1633. In 1672 the town was burned down by the Turks, who killed most of the inhabitants. In 1699 the overlord of the town, Stephan Potocki, renewed privileges previously granted to Buchach Jewry, according to which Jews were not subject to the jurisdiction of the Christian courts; disputes between Jews and Christians were heard by an official appointed by the lord of the town, and inter-Jewish suits by the *bet din.* Jews were free to own and build houses and to trade or engage in crafts, including distilling of brandy and barley beer. In 1765 there were 1,055 Jews living in Buchach and a further 300 in neighboring settlements within the bounds of the Jewish community of Buchach. Jewish economic activities expanded under Austrian rule (see *Galicia), particularly after the grant of equal civic rights in 1867. In the period preceding 1914, most of the large estates in the neighborhood of Buchach were Jewish owned or leased from the Polish nobility. Distilling and commerce remained major Jewish occupations. Between 1867 and 1906 Buchach, Kolomyya, and Sniatyn were combined to form a single constituency and a Jewish deputy was elected to the Austrian imperial parliament. At the beginning of the 20th century, there were approximately 7,000 Jews living in Buchach. During World War I most of the Jewish inhabitants left but many returned later.

Among notable rabbis of Buchach were Ẓevi Kara (18th–19th centuries), author of *Neta Sha'ashu'im;* his son-in-law Abraham David b. Asher *Wahrmann, the "holy" Ḥasid (d. 1841), author of *Da'at Kedoshim* (on the laws of ritual slaughter and dietary laws); Abraham Te'omim, author of the responsa *Ḥesed le-Avraham;* and Samuel Shtark, author of *Minḥat Oni.* The orientalist David Heinrich *Mueller was also from Buchach. Among the writers of the *Haskalah movement before 1914, the best known is Isaac *Fernhof. A Yiddish weekly *Der Yidisher Veker* was published at the beginning of the 20th century, edited by Eliezer *Rokeah of Safed. A large printing press was established in 1907. Descriptions of Jewish life in Buchach are given in the tales of S. Y. *Agnon, the Nobel prizewinning author, who was born in Buchach.

[A.J.Br.]

Holocaust Period. On the eve of the Nazi invasion about 10,000 Jews lived in Buchach (1941). Under Soviet rule (1939–41), Jewish community life suffered and its institutions ceased functioning. All independent political activity was forbidden. Private enterprise was suppressed and the few privately owned stores that remained were subjected to heavy taxes in order to bring about their liquidation. Officially, religious life was not repressed, but synagogues were obliged to pay heavy taxes. The Hebrew education system was disbanded and in its place a Yiddish language school was set up. When war broke out between Germany and the U.S.S.R. (June 22, 1941), Jews were drafted into the Soviet Army. Groups of young Jews also fled to the Russian interior. The Germans invaded Buchach on July 5, 1941. The Ukrainians immediately began murdering and looting the local Jews. On August 25, 350 Jews were killed on Fedor Hill, about a mile (2 km.) from the town. A *Judenrat was set up, headed by Mendel Reich, the head of the former Jewish community organization until its dissolution in September 1939. Jewish refugees began arriving from Hungary and were extended aid by the Judenrat and local community. Young, able-bodied Jews were taken off for forced labor in camps at Velikiye Borki. On Oct. 17, 1942, the Germans carried out a massive *Aktion* in which over 1,500 Jews were rounded up and sent to *Belzec death camp. Over 300 Jews were murdered during the *Aktion.* On Nov. 27, 1942, a second transport with 2,500 Jews was dispatched to Belzec, while about 250 persons were shot in the roundup. On Feb. 1–2, 1943, close to 2,000 Jews were murdered at Fedor Hill on the contention that they were infected with typhus. A labor camp was then set up in a suburb, Podkajecka, for skilled craftsmen. In March–April, over 3,000 Jews were also murdered at Fedor Hill, while other groups were shipped to *Chortkov, Kopiczynce, and Tlusta.

Resistance. A Jewish resistance movement was organized in Buchach at the end of 1942. Arms were obtained and training was given in preparation for a break for the forests. In mid-June 1943 the Germans liquidated the ghetto and labor camp, but met with resistance. Some Jews managed to escape to the forests while others were murdered near the Jewish cemetery. Armed Jewish bands were active in the vicinity, notably attacking Nazi collaborators. On March 23, 1944, when the city was captured by Soviet forces, about 800 Jews came out of hiding and returned from the forests. However, the German Army again took over, and additional Jews fell victim. On July 21, 1944, when Soviet forces definitively entered the city, there were less than 100 Jewish survivors. About 400 Jews returned from the U.S.S.R. After the war most of them emigrated from Buchach to settle in the West or in Israel. The community was not reestablished after the war. [AR.W.]

Bibliography: I. Cohen (ed.), *Sefer Buchach* (1957).

BUCHALTER, LOUIS ("Lepke"; 1897–1944), U.S. racketeer. At the age of 18 he embarked on a criminal career. After serving three years in Sing Sing prison on two burglary convictions, he turned to racketeering, commanding 200 gangsters, who extorted millions of dollars from his victims. He "protected" manufacturers from strikes and unionization of their shops by intimidating workers and using strong-arm measures. He forced unions to do his bidding by installing his own business agents or by creating his own rival unions. In 1933 Buchalter was arrested for violating an anti-trust law. Found guilty, he was fined and sentenced, but a higher court reversed the decision and he was freed on bail. He went into hiding, but in 1939 he surrendered to FBI Director J. Edgar Hoover at a rendezvous arranged by the radio commentator Walter Winchell. He was tried on a narcotics charge and sentenced to 14 years imprisonment, during which he was returned to New York City to be tried on a charge of murder committed in 1936. He was found guilty and executed.

Bibliography: G. Tyler, *Organized Crime in America* (1962); F. Kennedy, *The Enemy Within* (1960); D. Whitehead, *The FBI Story* (1956), 109ff.

[M.M.B.]

°**BUCHANAN, CLAUDIUS** (d. 1815), Christian missionary and collector of Hebrew manuscripts. Buchanan went to Calcutta as chaplain in 1797, and was appointed professor and vice-provost of the College of Fort William. During repeated visits to southern India between 1806 and 1808 Buchanan stayed in Cochin searching for ancient Hebrew manuscripts. His methods alarmed the Jewish population. They claimed that they were being robbed of their records, and sought the intervention of the chief magistrate of Cochin. Buchanan also made a facsimile of Jewish copperplate inscriptions, and was accused of having taken away the original. He deposited the manuscripts, obtained from both Jews and Syrian Christians, in the Cambridge University library.

Bibliography: C. Buchanan, *Christian Researches in Asia* (1812²), 210–49; H. N. Pearson, *Memoirs of the Life and Writings of C. Buchanan,* 2 vols. (1817); T. Whitehouse, *Some Historical Notices of Cochin* (1839), 31–34; T. C. Tychsen, *De inscriptionibus, indicis, et privilegiis judaeorum . . . a Buchanan adlatae* (1819), 12–17; T. Yeates, *Collation of an Indian Copy of the Hebrew Pentateuch* (1812); Schechter, in: JQR, 6 (1893/94), 136–45; Fischel, in: JAOS, 87 (1967), 245–6.

[W.J.F.]

BUCHAREST (Rum. **București**), capital of *Rumania. Before the union of the Danubian principalities (Moldavia and Walachia) in 1859, it was capital of the principality of Walachia. Up to the 19th century almost the entire Jewish population of Walachia was concentrated in Bucharest, where the great majority continued to live subsequently. Thus the history of the Jewish community in Bucharest is essentially the history of Walachian Jewry. The community, consisting of merchants and moneylenders from Turkey and the Balkan countries, is first mentioned in the middle of the 16th century in the responsa of several Balkan rabbis (e.g., Samuel de Medina, nos. 5, 54). When Prince Michael the Brave revolted against the Turks in November 1593, he ordered the massacre of the Jews in Bucharest along with the other Turkish subjects. Toward the middle of the 17th century, a new community, now predominantly Ashkenazi, was established. Many of the Phanariot princes who ruled Walachia in the 18th century maintained close relations with leading Constantinople Jews and brought a number of them to Bucharest, where they attained influential positions (e.g., the Bally family). In the 18th century the Jews were concentrated in the suburb of Mahalaua Popescului, but as the community increased a number began to move to other parts of the city, where they even established synagogues; however, these were closed by the princes. The populace, afraid of Jewish economic competition, was intensely hostile toward the Jews, and in 1793 the residents of the Râzvan suburb petitioned Prince Alexander Moruzi to remove Jews who had recently settled there and demolish the synagogue they had erected. The

Jewish Population in Bucharest

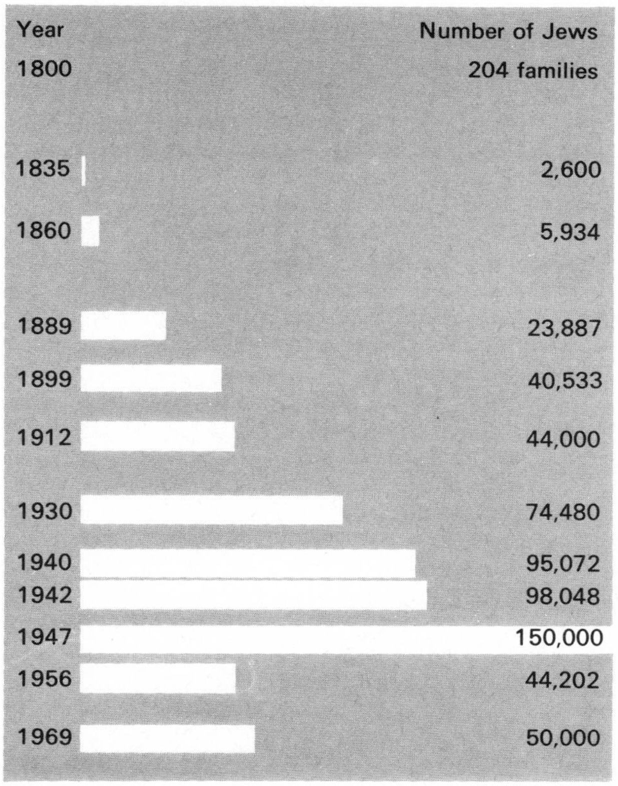

prince ordered the synagogue to be closed (January 1794), but refused to have the Jews removed from the suburb, and a few days later even issued a decree affording them protection. In 1801 there were anti-Jewish riots following *blood libel charges, and 128 Jews were killed or wounded. The community again suffered persecution during the Russian occupation of Bucharest from 1806 to 1812, and in particular during the Greek revolt *(Hetairia)* under Alexander Ypsilanti and its suppression by the Turks in 1821.

During this period, the Bucharest Jews, like those elsewhere in Walachia and Moldavia, were organized as an autonomous Breasla Ovreilor ("Jewish corporation") headed by a *Staroste* ("provost"). The head of the Bucharest community also acted as the deputy of the *ḥakham bashi* (chief rabbi) of Moldavia, whose authority extended over Walachian Jewry as well. In 1818–21, the *Staroste* of Bucharest seceded from the authority of the Moldavian *ḥakham bashi* and assumed the title independently. The few Sephardi Jews, whose numbers began to increase only at the end of the 18th and the beginning of the 19th century, did not then constitute a separate community, although they had their own synagogue in a rented house in Mahalaua Popescului and in 1811 established their own burial society. In 1818 they were granted permission to build a synagogue.

The Bucharest community grew rapidly in the 19th century through immigration. From 127 families registered in Bucharest in 1820 and 594 in 1831, the community grew to 5,934 persons in 1860 and 40,533 (14.7% of the total population) in 1899. Under the *Capitulations system foreign subjects were free from the regular taxation and jurisdiction in Rumania. Hence the immigrants questioned the authority of the community leadership and refused to pay the tax on *kasher* meat, which constituted its sole income. The authorities, drawn into the conflict, at first upheld the traditional rights of the Breasla Ovreilor. However, following repeated complaints from both sides, as well as constitutional changes in the principality resulting from the promulgation of the Organic Statute (see *Rumania) in 1832, the community was given a new constitution in that year which severely curtailed its autonomy and placed it under the direct authority and close supervision of the municipality. The Ashkenazi community was again reconstituted in 1843, and the new statute, which further curtailed the community's autonomy, was confirmed with slight changes by the reigning prince in 1851; although never formally abolished, it fell into disuse in the second half of the century. In the meantime the Sephardi Jews (numbering about 150 families in 1854), had founded their own community. Within the Ashkenazi community, the conflicts between the native and foreign-born members continued. Finally, in 1851, the Prussian and Austrian subjects (about 300 families) were permitted to found a separate community. In 1861, a bitter conflict broke out between the native community and the Russian subjects because some articles had allegedly been removed from the Russian synagogue.

At that time, the Bucharest Ashkenazi community was also torn by violent strife between the *Orthodox and *Progressive wings (the latter led by Julius *Barasch and I. L. *Weinberg). The controversy centered around the modern school opened in 1852 (a year earlier a similar school had been established by Austrian and Prussian subjects) and a proposal in 1857 to build a Choir Temple and introduce certain reforms into the service. The dissension reached its peak when, in 1858, Meir Leib *Malbim was called to the rabbinate. He placed himself at the head of the Orthodox wing and a fierce struggle ensued. The conflict also had a social character since the Progressives were drawn mainly from the well-to-do, while the masses were Orthodox. In 1862 the Progressives achieved success; the government deposed Malbim from the Bucharest rabbinate, and in 1864 he was arrested and expelled from the country. The Temple project was resumed in 1864; it was completed in 1867 and became the center of Progressive Jewry and the focus of a variety of cultural and educational activities. Continued quarrels within the community and repeated complaints to the authorities by each of the competing factions brought about in 1862 the government's decision (which applied to the whole country) not to interfere any more with the internal affairs of the Jewish communities and to withdraw from them their official status. This decision reiterated in 1866, led to the gradual disorganization and dissolution of the Ashkenazi community in Bucharest, which in 1874 had ceased to exist as an organized entity. Several attempts were later made to reconstitute the community, the most serious in 1908. However, it was only in 1919 that an organized Jewish community was again established in Bucharest. Until then various benevolent societies and organizations undertook educational and social welfare activities. Chief among them were the Choir Temple Congregation, formally constituted in 1876 as a separate and independent organization levying its own tax on *kasher* meat, and the Brotherhood Zion of the B'nai B'rith, founded in Bucharest in 1872 by the American consul B. F. *Peixotto. These succeeded in setting up and maintaining a network of educational and charitable institutions, including, in 1907–08, 15 schools, filling the void created by the lack of an organized community. Cultural bodies were also established, and a number of Jewish journals and other publications made their appearance. Bucharest also became the center of Rumanian Jewry's political activity and the struggle for *emancipation. National Jewish bodies, among them the Union of Native Jews, established their headquarters there. Among the most prominent spiritual and religious leaders of the community before World War I were Antoine Lévy and Moritz (Meir) *Beck, rabbis of the Choir Temple Congregation from 1867 to 1869 and 1873 to 1923 respectively, and Yitzhak Eisik *Taubes, rabbi of the Orthodox congregation from 1894 to 1921. The most prominent lay leader was Adolf *Stern.

In the 19th century, a high proportion of the Jews in Bucharest were occupied in crafts. There were 2,712 Jewish artisans in the city in 1899. Others engaged in commerce and several, notably Sephardi Jews, were prominent in banking. During the second half of the 19th century a number of anti-Jewish outbreaks occurred in Bucharest. In 1866, when the legislative assembly was discussing the legal position of the Jews, an excited mob started a riot in which the new Choir Temple, then under construction, was demolished. Another serious riot took place in December 1897, when hundreds of Jewish houses and shops were attacked and looted.

After World War I. In the period between the two world wars the Bucharest community grew in both numbers and importance. The Jewish population of the city, now the capital of greater Rumania and attracting settlers from all parts of the country, increased from 44,000 in 1912 to 74,480 (12% of the total population) in 1930, and to 95,072 in 1940. About two-thirds of those gainfully employed were occupied as artisans, workers, clerks, and shop-assistants; others were active in the liberal professions, especially medicine and law. In 1920, the statute of the reconstituted Ashkenazi community was officially approved, and in 1931, following the publication of the new law for the Organization of the Cults, the community was officially recognized as the legal representative of the city's Ashkenazi Jewish population; at the same time the community's statute was amended to conform to the requirements of the law. The organization of the community was again modified by a new statute in 1937. With the reconstitution of the organized community, all Jewish institutions were brought under its jurisdiction. The community's religious, educational, and welfare institutions included over 40 synagogues, two cemeteries, 19 schools, a library and a historical museum, two hospitals, a clinic, two old-age homes, and two orphanages. The spiritual head of the Ashkenazi community during this period was J. J. *Niemirower, while the outstanding lay leader was W. *Filderman. Like many other Jewish communities in Rumania, the Bucharest community was harrassed during this period by recurrent anti-Jewish outbreaks and excesses varying in intensity in which the university was the focus of anti-Jewish agitation. The Bucharest community and its leaders continued to play an important role in the social and political life of Rumanian Jewry, representing in particular the attitude of the Jews from the Old Kingdom.

Holocaust Period. In September, 1940, with the accession to power of the *Antonescu-*Iron Guard coalition, Bucharest became one of the main centers of the anti-Jewish activities of the new regime and of the Legionnaire terror (see *Rumania). The terror culminated in a bloody pogrom during the Legionnaire rebellion (Jan. 21–24, 1941), when 120 Jews were murdered, thousands arrested and maltreated, Jewish houses, shops, and public institutions destroyed and pillaged, and a large number of synagogues desecrated and devastated.

Until the end of the Antonescu regime (August 1944), Bucharest Jews were subjected to all the restrictions and persecutions which were the lot of the rest of Rumanian Jewry. Thousands of Jews were deprived of employment. In 1942 only 27.2 percent of the city's Jewish population of about 100,000 was registered as gainfully employed, compared with 54.3 percent of the non-Jewish population. In September 1942, several hundred Jews were deported to *Transnistria and killed. At the same time, 5,236 buildings and 14,492 apartments belonging to Jews, including all buildings occupied by Jewish institutions, were expropriated. In January 1942 the community was forced to pay, in money and in kind, a sum amounting to over 760 million lei ($2,550,000). The closing of the government schools to Jews and the growing pauperization of the Jewish population imposed upon the community the need to greatly expand its educational and social-welfare activities. In 1943 the Jewish community maintained 27 schools of various grades and 21 canteens. Bucharest became the center of relief activities for Rumanian Jews, and especially for those deported to Transnistria.

Contemporary Period. After the establishment of the Communist regime in 1947, all Jewish national, cultural, and welfare institutions in Bucharest were gradually closed down. The welfare institutions were nationalized and the schools absorbed in the general educational network. A state Yiddish school was opened in 1949 but closed a few years later. Communal activity is organized by the Federation of Jewish Communities in Rumania. Jewish cultural activities center on the Yiddish theater taken over by the state in 1948. A Yiddish school of dramatic art was established in 1957. Two Jewish newspapers, the Rumanian *Unirea,* followed later by *Viaţa Novua,* and the Yiddish *Ikuf Bleter* were published, but both were discontinued in 1952/53. From October 1956 a periodical in Rumanian, Yiddish, and Hebrew, *Revista Cultului Mozaic* was published on behalf of the Federation of Jewish Religious Communities. The Federation also cares for the religious needs of its members, supplying them with *mazzot,* prayer shawls, prayer books, etc. In the late 1960s there were 14 regular synagogues in Bucharest, including the Choir Temple. There is also a *talmud torah,* a "Hebra-Shas" (weekly courses in Talmud), a Yiddish theater, and a *kasher* restaurant. About 400 Jewish students participate in courses in Hebrew and Jewish history organized by the religious community, but the main problem in this sphere is the lack of competent teachers. Of the 44,202 Jews (3.6% of the total population) registered in the city in the 1956 census, 4,425 declared Yiddish to be their mother tongue. In 1969 it was estimated that 50,000 Jews lived in Bucharest.

Bibliography: M. A. Halevy, *Comunitãţile Evreilor din Jaşi şi Bucureşti,* 1 (1931); idem, in: *Sinai* (Bucharest), 2 (1929), xxix–xxxi; 3 (1931), xvii–xxxiv; 5 (1933), lviii–lxiv; idem, *Monografie istorică a Templului Coral din Bucureşti* (1935); idem, *Templul Unirea-Sfântă din Bucureşti* (1937); E. Schwarzfeld, in: *Anuar pentru Israeliţi,* 9 (1886), 70–83; 19 (1898), 55–62; M. Schwarzfeld, *ibid.,* 9 (1886), 1–30; 10 (1887), 195–9; Barasch, in: *Kalendar und Jahrbuch fuer Israeliten* (1854), 245–80; idem, in: AZDJ, 8 (1844), 750–1; 9 (1845), 94–95, 108–11, 177–9, 444–7, 480–2; Feldman, in: *Zion,* 22 (1957), 214–38; *Anuarul Evreilor din România* (1937), 161–83; *Comunitatea Evreilor din Bucureşti. Raport asupra activităţii cultului mozaic* (1943), typewritten, in Jewish Historical Archives, Jerusalem; M. Carp, *Cartea neagră,* 3 vols. (1946–48), index; Herbert, in: *Journal of Jewish Bibliography* 2 (1940), 110ff.; Ariel, in: *Analele Societăţii Istorice I. Barasch,* 2 (1888), 187–208.

[El.F.]

BUCHBINDER, NAHUM (1895–?), Soviet historian. Buchbinder was born in Odessa. Son of the Yiddish writer Abraham Isaac Buchbinder, he studied from 1916 at the Seminary for Oriental Studies at Petrograd (Leningrad) and began his literary career in the Russian press in Odessa and Simferopol. Buchbinder was one of the first to join the Commissariat for Jewish Affairs after the Revolution, and edited Yiddish Communist newspapers and other publications in Moscow and Minsk. He first wrote on Russian-Jewish literature (studies of Lev *Levanda) and afterward specialized in the history of the Jewish labor movement in Russia, on which he published articles in the learned journals *Krasnaya letopis, Proletarskaya revolutsiya,* and *Yevreyskaya starina.* His main work, *Istoriya yevreyskogo rabochego dvizheniya v Rossii* ("History of the Jewish Labor Movement in Russia," Leningrad, 1925; Yiddish translation, Vilna, 1931), chiefly dealing with the Bund, is based on material from the czarist police archives. Nothing is known of Buchbinder's fate after the 1930s.

Bibliography: LNYL, 1 (1956), 262–3.

[Y.S.]

BUCHENWALD, German concentration camp on the Ettersberg, near Weimar. Opened on July 19, 1937, it was considered the worst of the camps prior to World War II. Its first commander was the notorious Karl Koch, who remained in charge until his transfer to *Majdanek, Poland, on Jan. 22, 1942. Originally erected to house prisoners from several smaller camps that were being disbanded, its first inmates were professional criminals. They were, however, soon followed by political prisoners. The political prisoners, among whom were several Jews, succeeded in appropriating for themselves such administrative posts as were available to prisoners. The first whole group of Jews were political prisoners who arrived in June 1938 as a result of an action against "asocial" Jews. In the summer of 1938, 2,200 Austrian Jews were transferred from *Dachau. Later that year, the mass arrests after the **Kristallnacht* more than doubled the number of Jewish prisoners. The 10,000 new Jewish prisoners, quartered in recently built huts,

Figure 2. Aerial view of the Buchenwald camp.

Figure 3. The main gate to the camp.

Stamp issued by the East German government to provide funds for national memorials at the Buchenwald, Ravensbrueck, and Sachsenhausen concentration camps. The Buchenwald memorial was unveiled on September 14, 1958.

suffered far more than the non-Jews, 244 dying during the first month of their imprisonment. Most of the prisoners were released by the spring of 1939, deprived of their property, and compelled to leave Germany. The outbreak of World War II brought a new influx of prisoners, most of them stateless people from Poland. As Hitler's armies conquered further territory, the camp's population was swollen by prisoners from the occupied countries. Most Soviet prisoners of war were killed upon arrival. Hermann Pister, Koch's successor, remained commander until the camp's liberation in 1945. From the beginning of 1942, Buchenwald, in common with other camps in Germany, became a forced labor camp for war production. The demands of German industry brought transport after transport from all over Europe. On Oct. 17, 1942, all Jewish prisoners, with the exception of 200 building masons, were transferred to *Auschwitz. After December 1942, the camp received German criminals who had been handed over to the *SS by the prison authorities. Most of them became the victims of the pseudo-medical experiments performed in the camp hospital. After May 1944 Hungarian Jews arrived from Auschwitz and were distributed among the various satellite camps, especially the infamous Dora. On Oct. 6, 1944, the number of prisoners reached a peak of 89,143. This increase in numbers diminished the food supplies, led to a further deterioration in the already dangerously unhygienic conditions, and increased the death rate. From the winter of 1944, and especially after January 1945, the camps in the east were evacuated due to the approach of the Soviet Army, and thousands of prisoners, among them many Jews, were transferred to Buchenwald, where they died in great numbers. At the beginning of April 1944 the SS evacuated several thousand Jews. However, the mass evacuation planned for April 5, 1945, to the south, was foiled. During the last weeks of the camp's existence an armed underground movement came into being among the prisoners, and when American troops arrived on April 11, 1945, the members of this movement were in control and handed over the camp to them. Of the 238,380 prisoners the camp held since it was opened, 56,549 had died there or been murdered.

Bibliography: C. Burney, *Dungeon Democracy* (1946); E. Kogan, *Theory and Practice of Hell* (1960); *Buchenwald: Mahnung und Verpflichtung, Dokumente und Berichte* (1960); *Bibliographie zur Geschichte des faschistischen Konzentrationslagers Buchenwald* (Leipzig, 1957[2]).

[Y.Re.]

°**BUCHHOLZ, CARL AUGUST** (1785–1843), German lawyer and author. A champion of Jewish civil rights, Buchholz was an admirer of Moses *Mendelssohn's philosophy. He was appointed by the Jewish communities of *Luebeck, *Hamburg, and *Bremen as their representative at the Congress of *Vienna (1815), the conference of Aachen (1818), and at the Diet of Frankfort. In 1815 he published a collection of laws regarding the improvement of the status of the Jews issued by various German principalities and states *(Aktenstuecke, die Verbesserung des buergerlichen Zustandes der Israeliten betreffend)*, with a foreword which is considered one of the best pleas for Jewish emancipation written in that period by a gentile. He advocated uniform all-inclusive legislation for the Jews in all German states.

Bibliography: J. M. Kohler, *Jewish Rights at the Congress of Vienna*... (1918), index; S. Baron, *Die Judenfrage auf dem Wiener Kongress* (1920), index; S. Carlebach, *Geschichte der Juden in Luebeck*... (1898), 63ff.; H. Spiel, *Fanny von Arnstein* (1962), 437–49; Graetz, Hist, 5 (1949), 468, 472.

[Ed.]

BUCHMIL, JOSHUA HESHEL (1869–1938), Zionist leader. He was born in Ostrog, Volhynia and from 1896 to 1903 studied agriculture and law at the University of Montpellier (France), where he was a member of the Zionist student organization, Atidot Israel. In 1896 Herzl assigned him the task of persuading the Ḥovevei Zion of Russia to participate in the First Zionist Congress, and he succeeded in this, visiting cities and villages in the south of Russia and in Lithuania. A militant opponent of the *Uganda Scheme, Buchmil was a member of the *Democratic Fraction of the Zionist Organization and one of its leading spokesmen. In 1906 he was sent by the *Odessa Committee of the Ḥovevei Zion to Ereẓ Israel to study the economic and legal aspects of Jewish colonization

Joshua Buchmil, Zionist leader. Jerusalem, Central Zionist Archives.

there. After the Revolution of 1917, he joined the Central Zionist Committee of Russia. In 1921 he left for Poland and in 1923 went to Ereẓ Israel where he worked for *Keren Hayesod. He published articles on current topics in the Zionist press in Russian, French, and Yiddish and also wrote *Problèmes de la renaissance juive* (1936), with a biographical essay by Avraham Elmaleh.

Bibliography: Tidhar, 9 (1958), 3287–89; I. Klausner, *Mi-Katoviẓ ad Basel 1890–97*, 3 (1965), index.

[Y.S.]

BUCHNER, ABRAHAM (1789–1869), assimilationist and linguist, born in Cracow. Buchner left Cracow in 1820 for Warsaw at the invitation of the banker Joseph Janasz to teach his children. On his recommendation, Buchner was appointed teacher of Bible and Hebrew in the rabbinical seminary of Warsaw. In his Hebrew works, *Doresh Tov* (Warsaw, 1823), *Yesodei ha-Dat* (*ibid.*, 1836; with Pol. tr.), and *Ha-Moreh li-Ẓedakah* (*ibid.*, 1838), a commentary on the reasons for the *mitzvot* according to Maimonides, Buchner advocates loyalty to the state, religious tolerance, and "productivization" of the Jews. He also compiled *Oẓar Lashon Ivrit* (1830), a Hebrew-German dictionary with an appendix on grammar. His *Kwiaty wschodnie* ("Flowers of the East," 1842) attempts to show the talmudic legends in a positive light. He also praises the Talmud in his Polish "The True Judaism" (Warsaw, 1846). From 1848, however, an inimical tone appears; he was in contact with the anti-Semitic priest *Chiarini, for whom he translated portions of talmudic and rabbinic literature. Buchner's German work *Der Talmud in seiner Nichtigkeit* ("The Worthlessness of the Talmud," 1848) expresses this attitude. His two sons converted to Christianity.

Bibliography: J. Shatzky, *Geshikhte fun Yidn in Varshe,* 2 (1948), 98, 118, 125; R. Mahler, *Ha-Hasidut ve-ha-Haskalah* (1961), 258–61; S. Lastik, *Z dziejów oświecenia żydowskiego* (1961), 184–6; I. Schipper (ed.), *Żydzi w Polsce odrodzonej,* 1 (1932), 444.

[M.LAN.]

BUCHNER, ZE'EV WOLF BEN DAVID HA-KOHEN (1750–1820), Hebrew grammarian and liturgical poet. Buchner, who was born and lived most of his life in Brody, was the secretary of the Jewish community and one of the forerunners of the Haskalah movement. He wrote several epistolary guides in poetic language, e.g., *Zeved ha-Meliẓah* (1774); *Zeved Tov* (1794); and *Ẓaḥut ha-Meliẓah* (1810), all of them dealing with Hebrew style. The last work also contained 120 samples of letters. These works went through several editions. He also wrote religious poems such as *Keter Malkhut* ("Royal Crown," 1794), in the style of Ibn Gabirol's hymn by the same name; *Shir Nifla* ("Wonderful Song," 1802); *Shir Yedidut* ("Song of Friendship," 1810); and *Shirei Tehillah* ("Songs of Praise," 1808^3). The last work consists of two parts. In the first, the roots of all the words have only letters from *alef* to *lamed,* while the second part contains words composed of letters from *lamed* to *tav* only.

Bibliography: Kressel, Leksikon, 1 (1965), 187. [ED.]

BUCHWALD, NATHANIEL (1890–1956), Yiddish theater critic. His work covered much of the "golden age" of the Yiddish theater in the United States. Buchwald contributed to the *Jewish Daily Forward,* but soon became a mainstay of the left-wing daily *Freiheit.* He founded the Freiheit Dramatic Studio, which later achieved eminence under the name *Artef,* producing a number of social problem plays. He also compiled a *Compendium of the Yiddish Theater* (1946). Buchwald tried to avoid the Marxist dogmatism of the thirties. His acceptance of certain plays, such as Maxwell Anderson's *Winterset* (inspired by the Sacco and Vanzetti case), was motivated by humanistic principles. His criticism tended to be both learned and emotional, and he was under fire at times from left-wing partisans for approving plays which they would have preferred him to denounce. [R.SH.]

BUCKY, GUSTAV (1880–1963), radiologist. Born in Leipzig, from 1918 to 1923 he was head of the department of roentgenotherapy of the Berlin University clinic. He emigrated to the U.S. in 1923 but returned to Berlin in 1930 to serve as director of the radiological department and cancer institute of the Rudolph Virchow Hospital. In 1933 he left Germany and served as head of the department of physiotherapy at Sea View Hospital in New York City, consulting physiotherapist at Bet David Hospital, and as clinical professor of radiology at Bellevue Hospital, N.Y. Bucky is known as the inventor of the Bucky diaphragm for roentgenography, which prevents secondary rays from reaching the film, thereby securing better definition. He also invented a camera for medical color photography in radiography and was the originator of grenz ray therapy (infra roentgen rays) called Bucky rays. He wrote numerous scientific articles on his subject and was the author of *Die Roentgenstrahlen und ihre Anwendung* (1918); *Anleitung zur Diathermiebehandlung* (1921) and *Grenzstrahltherapie* (1928).

Bibliography: S. R. Kagan, *Jewish Medicine* (1952), 539.

[S.M.]

BUCOVICE (Cz. **Bučovice;** Ger. **Butschowitz**), small town in southern Moravia, Czechoslovakia. Its Jewish community, one of the oldest in Moravia, increased in importance when Jews expelled from *Brno in 1454 settled in Bucovice. Moravian community synods were held there in 1709, 1724, and 1748. Bucovice was one of 52 communities officially recognized in 1798. A synagogue was built in 1690, and rebuilt in 1853. The community numbered nine families in 1673, 508 persons in 1798, 566 in 1848, 180 in 1900, and 64 in 1930 (2.07% of the total population), 13 of whom declared their nationality as Jewish. Rabbis included Avigdor, son of the "saintly" R. Paltiel (d. 1749), Abraham Hirsch Halberstadt, and Bernard *Loewenstein (1857–1863), author of *Juedische Klaenge* (1862), popular poems which he dedicated to the community. In 1942 the Jews were deported to death camps.

Bibliography: H. Gold (ed.), *Juden und Judengemeinden Maehrens* (1929), 173–6; I. Halperin, *Takkanot Medinat Mehrin* (1952), 176–81, 197–211, 232–7. [O.K.R.]

BUDAPEST, capital of Hungary, formed officially in 1873 from the towns of Buda, Obuda, and Pest, which each had Jewish communities.

Buda (Ger. **Ofen;** Heb. אובן). A community was formed there by the end of the 11th century. Its cemetery was located near the Buda end of the present Pest-Buda tunnel under the River Danube. In 1348 and 1360 the Jews were expelled from Buda but returned after a short interval. As Buda became the royal residence under King Sigismund (1387–1437), its community rose to prominence in the Jewish life of the country. Its leaders were entrusted by the king with the representation of Hungarian Jewry, and the position of Jewish prefect was held by members of the Buda *Mendel family who sometimes took part in royal ceremonies. After 1490 the Jews of Buda were subjected to continual persecution, their property was frequently confiscated and the debts owing them were often unpaid. Following the Ottoman victory over the Hungarians at Mohacs in 1526 many Jews from Buda fled abroad or to the western part of Hungary, while the remainder were deported to Ottoman territory. Shortly afterward, in 1528, Jews were again living in the Jewish quarter of Buda. A census of 1547 showed 75 Jewish residents in Buda and 25 newcomers. During the 150 years of Ottoman rule the Jews were severely taxed, but their numbers continued to increase. A conscription roster of 1580 numbered 88 Jewish families, comprising about 800 persons, including three rabbis, inhabiting 64 houses. They engaged in commerce and finance, and sometime rose to hold official posts in the treasury as inspectors or tax collectors. Jews specialized in the manufacture of decorative braids for uniforms; the family physician of the pasha of Buda was a Jew (c. 1550). In 1660 the community numbered approximately 1,000 and was the largest and wealthiest in Hungary. The ruinous fighting between the Ottoman and Austrian imperial forces put an end to this prosperity. The Jews sided with the Turks; when in 1686 Buda was taken by Austria only 500 Jews survived the siege, the Jewish quarter was pillaged, and the Torah scrolls were burnt.

Jewish residence in Buda was prohibited until 1689, when a few Jews began to resettle there and had a prayer room by 1690. In 1703, when Buda was constituted a free royal city, a struggle began between the Jews of Buda, who preferred to remain under royal protection, and the citizenry which

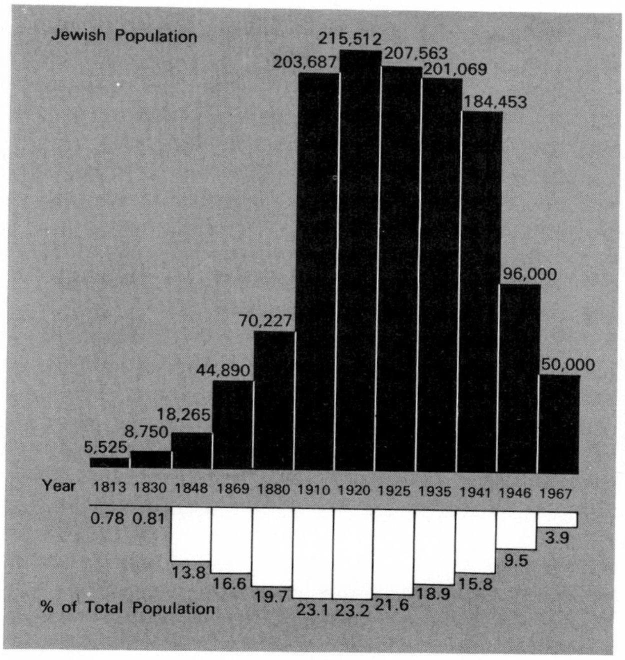

The Jewish population of Budapest, 1813–1967.

made efforts to extend its jurisdiction to the Jewry. This culminated in a decree ordering the expulsion of the Jews in 1712. In 1715 Charles III ordered the burghers to end the continual disturbances and a more tranquil period ensued. A few Jewish families were exempted by the emperor from certain restrictions. The exemptions led to an attack and plunder of Jewish homes in the fall of 1720. Charles, however, again gave them protection. According to a 1735 census, the community numbered 35 families (156 persons), the majority merchants; five families owned open stalls. The repeated accusations of the citizenry bore fruit, however, under *Maria Theresa who in June 1746 issued a decree ordering the expulsion of the Jews from Buda. The obstinate resistance of the burghers was broken by *Joseph II, and in 1783 Jewish residence was again permitted. The antagonism of the guilds recrudesced during the Hungarian revolution of 1848 when renewed demands were made for the Jews' expulsion.

Communal Life. Organized communal life in Buda dates to the 13th century. Under King Matthias Corvinus (1458–90) the head of this community had jurisdiction over the Jews of the entire country. During the Ottoman era, Buda Jewry had Sephardi and Ashkenazi congregations. Two synagogues are known to have existed in 1647.

Rabbis. The first rabbi whose name is recorded was *Akiva b. Menahem ha-Kohen (15th century) known by the honorific of *nasi*. In the second half of the 17th century difficulties in finding appropriate candidates for the rabbinate of Buda compelled the community to employ as rabbis scholars passing through Hungary on pilgrimage to Ereẓ Israel. *Ephraim b. Jacob ha-Kohen, a refugee from Vilna, became rabbi of Buda in 1660. About this time the movement of *Shabbetai Ẓevi gained a large following in Buda; a number of rabbis, among them Ephraim's son-in-law Jacob Sak, supported the messianic movement. The Austrian capture of Buda is recorded in the *Megillat Ofen* of Isaac b. Zalman *Schulhof. Jacob's son was the celebrated Ẓevi Hirsch *Ashkenazi (Ḥakham Ẓevi). Among rabbis of the Haskalah period was Moses Kunitzer. Prominent Jews of Buda in the 19th and 20th centuries include the orator and poet Arnold Kiss (d. 1940), and the scholar and educator Rabbi Bertalan Edelstein (d. 1934).

Synagogues. The synagogue of the Jewish community of Buda fort is mentioned in the Buda chronicle of 1307 as having stood beside the Jews' Gate. It remained in existence until the expulsion of the Jews from Buda in 1360. The second synagogue, built in 1461 in the new Jews' Street, survived until the recapture of Buda. It is mentioned and reproduced in 17th-century engravings. A Sephardi house of worship has been revealed, dating back to the Ottoman era. Subsequently the Jews of Buda could only hold prayer meetings in rented rooms. In 1866 a temple was built in Moorish style in Öntöház Street. In the heyday of assimilationism (from the mid-19th century), especially after the administrative union of Buda and Pest, the Pest community repeatedly tried to impose its hegemony on that of Buda, which, however, succeeded in safeguarding its unique historical character. The Buda community opened an elementary school in 1830.

Obuda (Hung. **Óbuda,** Ger. **Alt-Ofen,** Heb. אובן ישן), "Old Buda," village and later part of Buda. Obuda had a Jewish community in the 15th century which disappeared after the Ottoman conquest in 1526. It was rehabilitated from 1712 on, when the Jews lived under the protection of the counts Zichy, who granted them a charter in 1746, and to whom they paid an annual protection tax. The 1727 census records 24 Jewish families living in Obuda, and the 1737 annual conscription roster, 43. By 1752 there were 59 families, and the community employed two rabbis and three teachers; by 1784 there were 109 families with four teachers. The 1803 conscription list records 527 families. An elementary school was opened in 1784, the first secular Jewish school in the country. Moses *Muenz was rabbi in Obuda from 1781 to 1831. The Jewish linen weavers of Obuda won a reputation for the town; the Goldberger factory had an international reputation. After the revolution of 1848–49 a large contribution was levied on the Obuda community. The old synagogue of Obuda was demolished in 1817 and an imposing new one, still in existence, was consecrated in 1820. Julius *Wellesz was rabbi of Obuda from 1910 to 1915.

Pest. Jews are first mentioned in Pest in 1406; in 1504 they owned houses and land. Records again mention Jews living in Pest from the middle of the 16th century, and a cemetery is known to have existed by the end of the 17th. After the Austrian conquest in 1686, Jewish residence within the city was prohibited. In the middle of the 18th century Jews were allowed to attend the country-wide weekly markets held in Pest, but the only Jews permitted to stay in the city for a specified time were *Magranten* ("transients"; see *Familiants laws). In 1783 Joseph II abrogated the municipal charter with its exclusion

Figure 1. The Heroes' Synagogue in Budapest, built in 1929. Photo C.A.H.J.P., Jerusalem.

privileges and permitted Jews to resettle in Pest. The first "tolerated" Jew received permission to settle within the city walls in 1786 in return for paying a "toleration tax" to the local governorate. Article 38 of the *De Judaeis* law passed in 1790 ratified the legal position of the Jews established under Joseph II. In Pest, however, the law was understood to apply only to Jews living there before 1790, hence new arrivals were not permitted to settle permanently. An attempt was even made to expel the married children of the "tolerated" Jews. In 1833 there were 1,346 Jewish families in Pest. The restrictions on Jewish residence were abrogated by article 29 of the annual national assembly of 1840. Jews had the right to establish factories, and engage in trade and commerce as well as to acquire property. Pest Jewry took the lead in pressing for the abolition of the tolerance tax, and in 1846 the "chamber dues" were abolished. On the outbreak of the Hungarian revolution of 1848, Jews volunteered for civil defense, but the German citizens of Pest objected to their enrollment. On April 19 a mob which attacked the Jewish quarter was repelled by the military. Nevertheless many Jewish youths enlisted in the revolutionary army, and the Jews of Pest gave large financial contributions to the revolutionary cause. After the suppression of the revolt, a huge contribution was levied on the Pest community, and to help the Obuda and Pest communities a collection was made by Hungarian Jewry of 1,200,000 forints. The Pest community played a leading role in the struggle for *emancipation in Hungary. The half century preceding World War I was a period of prosperity and cultural achievement for Pest Jewry. Their numbers increased, and they played a prominent role in the capital's economic development. Max *Nordau and Theodor *Herzl were born there during this period. With the growth of Nazism before World War II Jewish communal and economic life was again restricted.

Communal Life. Active community life is not recorded in Pest until the first half of the 18th century. The first synagogue was opened in 1787, and in 1788 the community received a burial site from the municipality; Moses Muenz of Obuda officiated as rabbi. The first rabbi of Pest (1793), was Benjamin Ze'ev (Wolf) *Boskowitz. Other noted rabbis of the community were Loew *Schwab, S. L. Brill, W. A. Meisel, S. *Kohn, M. *Kayserling, S. *Hevesi, and J. *Fischer. The new constitution for the religious community, approved by the local authorities, came into effect in 1833. The noted Orientalist I. *Goldziher served as secretary of the Neolog community of Pest from 1874 to 1904. A separate Orthodox community was established in Pest in 1871. Koppel *Reich became its rabbi in 1886, and a member of the Hungarian upper house in 1926.

See *Orthodoxy, *Reform, *Hungary.

Synagogues. The Jews of Pest rented a place for worship in the Orczy building in 1796, whose congregation observed the conservative ritual; a more progressive temple existed in the same building, known as the "Kultustempel." In 1859 a double-turreted Moorish-style temple was built in Dohány Street. Construction of the octagonal temple in Rombach Street was completed in 1872. In 1913 the synagogue of the Orthodox congregation was erected in Kazinczy Street.

Educational Institutions. The first Jewish school in Pest was established in 1814 by Israel *Wahrmann. A Jewish girls' school was opened in the fall of 1852 and in 1859 a Jewish teachers' training college was founded. After the attainment of emancipation, a number of Jewish schools closed down, including those in Buda and Obuda. The Orthodox congregation of Pest opened its school for boys in 1873. The Rabbinical Seminary and its secondary school (gymnasium), opened in 1877, helped to make Pest the center of Jewish learning. The Pest community established a comprehensive secondary school in 1891. Following the widespread anti-Semitism aroused by the *Tiszaeszlar blood libel case in 1882, the idea of establishing a Jewish secondary school (gymnasium) found increasing support, and in 1892 Antal Freystaedtler donated one million forints for this project. The school was opened in the fall of 1919 as the Pest Jewish Boys' and Girls' Gymnasium. Because of the existing discriminatory restrictions, the Pest community also opened an engineering and technical college and a girls' technical college. The rabbinical seminary and a secondary school continue to function.

Welfare Institutions. Welfare and communal institutions of the Pest community included a hospital, opened in 1841; the hospital of the Orthodox congre-

Figure 2. The Dohany Street synagogue in Budapest, consecrated in 1859. It is the largest synagogue in Europe, 180 ft. (55 m.) long, 85 ft. (26 m.) wide, and 85 ft. (26 m.) high, and seats a congregation of 3,000. Photos C.A.H.J.P., Jerusalem (exterior), Israel Museum, Jerusalem (interior).

gation, opened in 1920; the Hungarian Jewish Crafts and Agricultural Union (MIKEFE), established in 1842; the Pest Jewish Women's Club, founded in 1868, which established an orphanage for girls in 1867; an orphanage for boys, established in 1869; the deaf and dumb institute, founded in 1876; and the blind institute, founded by Ignác Wechselmann and his wife in 1908. In 1950 the Orthodox community and the communities of Pest, Buda, and Obuda were unified by government order, forming the Budapest Jewish community existing under conditions similar to those prevailing in other communities in Soviet satellite states.

POPULATION. The annual registers of 1735–38, the first to show the number of Jewish families residing in the area which forms Budapest today, recorded 2,531 heads of families of whom 1,139 engaged in commerce. The Jewish population increased with the development of a capitalist economy and the growth of Budapest into a metropolis and reached its highest level in the period preceding and immediately following World War I. Subsequently it declined sharply due to the lowered birthrate, an increasing number of conversions to Christianity, and emigration during the counterrevolution and the *Horthy regime. There were 44,890 Jews living in Budapest in 1869, 102,377 in 1890, 203,687 in 1910, 215,512 in 1920, and 204,371 in 1930. [J.Z.]

Holocaust Period. In 1941 there were about 184,000 Jews in Budapest out of a total population of 1,712,000. Since the number of Christians considered as Jews, in accordance with the anti-Jewish laws then in force (see *Legislation, anti-Jewish, Hungary) was 62,000, the total number of persons subjected to persecutions as Jews was 246,000. From Hungary's entry into the war in the summer of 1941 until the German occupation on March 19, 1944, 15,350 members of Budapest's Jewish population perished in labor detachments and through deportation (see *Hungary). After the Germans entered Hungary, *Eichmann's Sondereinsatzkommando (see *Holocaust, General Survey) and the *Sztójay Government set up the Budapest Jewish Council, deprived the city's Jews of freedom of movement, and, on April 3, 1944, decreed the wearing of the yellow *badge. By the end of July some 200,000 Jews had been herded together in about 2,000 houses distinctly marked with yellow badges. These Jews were to be deported in July–August, after the Jews of the provinces were deported. Rescue actions by neutral states (mainly Switzerland and Sweden) were started by Charles *Lutz and Raoul *Wallenberg in June–July. Thousands of Jews found shelter in so-called "protected houses," or in the legations of the neutral powers.

A certain improvement in the conditions of the Jews was felt in August–September, when Horthy sought contacts with the Allies. Eichmann had to leave Budapest at the end of August, and the deportation was called off. On October 15, 1944, the *Arrow-Cross movement seized power, and, on the same day, began a series of pogroms which decimated the Jewish population. On October 17, Eichmann returned to Budapest, the yellow-badge houses were closed down, and the concentration of Jews into two big ghettos began. By the end of December the population of the Central Ghetto amounted to 70,000. Tens of thousands of Jews possessing safe-conduct passes issued by the neutral powers were crowded into the International Ghetto. Officially, some 7,800 Swiss, 4,500 Swedish, 2,500 Vatican, 698 Portuguese, and 100 Spanish *Schutzpaesse* (safe-conduct passports) were issued. In fact, the number of legal and forged safe-conducts approached 100,000.

On November 5, 1944, the Hungarians began handing over Jews to the Germans. Some 76,000 Budapest Jews were involved in the death march and deportations that followed.

Throughout December the terror grew in intensity. At the beginning of January 1945, the government withdrew its recognition of international safe-conduct passes. Jews were hunted all over Budapest by Arrow-Cross bands and shot by the thousands. The liquidation of the ghettos was planned for mid-January, but the Red Army took the city after long street fighting in January 1945. The International Ghetto was liberated on January 16, and the Central Ghetto two days later.

At the time of Budapest's liberation, some 94,000 Jews remained in the two main ghettos and in the legations of the neutral powers. The number of Jews in hiding was about 25,000. Later, some 20,000 returned from concentration camps and from labor service detachments. Of those Budapest inhabitants considered to be Jews, about 105,000 perished between March 19, 1944, and the end of the war. Since 15,350 Jews died during the period preceding the occupation, almost 50% of Budapest's inhabitants of Jewish origin died during the Holocaust period.

See also *Hungary. [B.V.]

Contemporary Jewry. Approximately 80,000–90,000 Jews remained in Budapest after World War II. During the period of liberalization in 1956 between 20,000 and 25,000 Jews left the city. In 1968, 60,000–70,000 Jews lived in Budapest. Jewish affairs were conducted by the Department of Religious Affairs, controlled by the Ministry of Internal Affairs. Jewish life in Budapest, as in the entire country, was centered around religious life. There were twenty rabbis in the city and in each of the 18 administrative districts in Budapest, there was at least one synagogue, a rabbi, a *talmud torah,* and a meeting hall for lectures. Budapest had the largest European synagogue, and perhaps the largest in the world, that of Dohány Street. Besides the *talmudei torah,* there was an all-day secondary school, with close to 140 students. The language of instruction was Hungarian. The religious community was divided into Orthodox and Neolog branches. The Orthodox one maintained a yeshivah with about 40 students, and the Neolog one supported a rabbinical seminary with approximately ten students. It was estimated that 80% of the community was of Neolog tendency. This phenomenon was probably due to the mass extermination of Orthodox Jews during the Nazi occupation and large immigration of Orthodox Jews to Israel. Religious facilities, such as kosher slaughtering and baking maẓẓah, were freely available. The community maintained a Jewish hospital with beds for 224 patients, staffed by ten Jewish doctors and equipped with a kosher kitchen. In addition, the community supported a home for the aged and a canteen where needy people received free meals. The communal publication was the widely read biweekly *Új Élet,* which was informative about Jewish communal affairs. Although Jewish life was intense, the participation of the youth in communal affairs and in religious life was negligible. [ED.]

Bibliography: A. Buechler, *A zsidók története Budapesten* (1901); A. Fuerst, in: *Arim ve-Immahot be-Yisrael,* 2 (1948), 109–86; S. Scheiber, *Magyarországi zsidó feliratok* (1960), 141–300; F. Grunwald, *A zsidók története Budán* (1938); *Magyar Zsidó Lexikon* (1929), passim; *Új Élet* (fortnightly since 1945), passim; L. Venetianer, *A magyar zsidóság története* (1922), 147–280, 286–303; Z. Groszmann, *A pesti zsidó gyüelekezet alkotmányának története* (1934); S. Eppler, in: *Mult és Jövö* (1935), 329–38; M. H. Szabó and D. Zentai, *Mit mondanak a számok a zsidókérdésben* (1938); E. Duschinsky, in: *The Jews in the Soviet Satellites* (1953); R. L. Braham, *The Hungarian Jewish Catastrophe: a Selected and*

Annotated Bibliography (1962); idem (ed.), *Hungarian-Jewish Studies* (1966–); F. Grunwald and Naményi, in: *A 90 eves Dohány utcai templom* (1949), 19–31; A. Moskovitz, *Jewish Education in Hungary (1848–1948)* (1964), includes bibliography, with additions by B. Yaron, in: KS, 41 (1965/66), 85–88; A. Scheiber, in: *Seventy Years: A Tribute to the Seventieth Anniversary of the Jewish Theological Seminary of Hungary* (1948), 8–30; S. Eppler, in: *A pesti izraelita hitközség* (1925), 55–81; A. Scheiber, in: KS, 32 (1956/57), 481–94; F. Hevesi, in: JBA, 6 (1947/48), 71–75; J. Lévai, *Black Book on the Martyrdom of Hungarian Jewry* (1948), passim; idem, *Eichmann in Hungary* (1961); E. Landau (ed.), *Der Kastner-Bericht* (1961), passim; *Jewish Communities of Eastern Europe* (1968), 30–37; R. I. Braham, *Hungarian Jewish Catastrophe* (1962), bibliography; A. Scheiber, *Héber kódexmaradványok magyarországi kötéstáblákban* (1969).

°**BUDDE, KARL FERDINAND REINHARD** (1850–1933), German Protestant Bible scholar and Hebraist. Budde was born at Bensburg near Cologne. He taught Bible at the universities of Bonn (1873–88), Strasbourg (1889–99), and Marburg (from 1900). With B. Duhm, B. Stade, R. Smend, and Emil Kautzsch, Budde was an ardent supporter of historical criticism as formulated by Eduard Reuss, Abraham Kuenen, Karl Heinrich Graf, and, above all others, Julius Wellhausen, his intimate friend. His detailed study *Die biblische Urgeschichte* (1883) is an attempt to recover the original sources of Genesis 1–11, to clarify their relation to each other, and to determine their origin. During the years 1888–89 Budde delivered a series of lectures at Harvard University on *Religion of Israel to the Exile* (1899), in which he championed the *Kenite hypothesis of the origins of YHWH worship. Throughout his life he was deeply interested in the history of Israel's literature and its literary characteristics. The former received expression in his work *Geschichte der althebraeischen Litteratur* (1906, 1909[2]); the latter, in a series of articles on Hebrew metrics (in ZAW 1882, 1883, 1892) and in his discussion of Hebrew poetry in J. Hastings (ed.), *A Dictionary of the Bible* (vol. 4, 1902). Among his greatest achievements was his treatment of the *kinah,* or lamentation meter.

With the advance of critical studies the need arose for a new series of exegetical commentaries on the Bible, and Budde joined with many other scholars in the publication of the *Goettinger Handkommentar zum Alten Testament.* In addition to those mentioned above, the following are his most important works: *Die Buecher Richter und Samuel, ihre Quellen und ihr Aufbau* (1890); *The Books of Samuel, Critical Edition of the Hebrew Text* (1894); *Das Buch Hiob* (1896, 1913[2]); *Die sogenannten Ebed-Jahwe-Lieder und die Bedeutung des Knechtes Jahwes in Jesaja 40–55, Ein Minoritaetsvotum* (1900); *Der Kanon des Alten Testaments* (1900); and *Die Buecher Samuel* (1902). Budde also translated into German a number of works of Abraham Kuenen, edited several editions of W. A. Hollenberg's *Hebraeisches Schulbuch* and coedited *Eduard Reuss: Briefwechsel mit seinem Schueler und Freunde Karl Heinrich Graf* (1904).

Bibliography: T. H. Robinson, in: *The Expository Times,* 46 (1934–35), 298ff.; H. S. Cadbury, in: JBL, 55 (1936), iiff.; ZAW, 12 (1935), 286–9.

[Ja.Mu.]

BUDKO, JOSEPH (1888–1940), painter and graphic artist. Budko, who was born in Plonsk, received a traditional Jewish education. In 1902 he went to study at the art school in Vilna. In 1910 Budko moved to Berlin where he learned metal-chasing and also studied at the Museum of Arts and Crafts. In Berlin Budko met Hermann *Struck who taught him the technique of etching. Eventually he also took up woodcutting, lithography, and painting. In 1933 Budko settled in Palestine. In 1935 he became the director of the reopened New *Bezalel school of arts and crafts. Budko stressed the teaching of graphic design and utilized the ornamental value of the Hebrew letters. Budko's subject matter was determined by the Jewish environment in which he grew up and to which he returned in Jerusalem. He illustrated books, among them the *Haggadah,* and designed many bookplates.

[E.C.]

"Sitting Old Man" by Joseph Budko, lithograph, 1915. 12¼×9¾ in. (31×24 cm.). Jerusalem, Israel Museum. Photo David Harris.

°**BUDNY (Budnaeus), SZYMON (Simon;** c. 1530–1593), Polish sectarian theologian. During the struggles of the Reformation in Poland-Lithuania he led the Lithuanian anti-Trinitarian ("Arian") wing of the Polish reformist camp which took a radical stand in questions of theology though a conservative one in its acceptance of the social order. Budny translated the Bible into Polish, using the Hebrew text. An original thinker, he was well known to and in contact with Jewish scholars. In the anti-Trinitarian camp Budny represented a trend of opinion, mainly prevalent in Lithuania where he conducted his theological activity, which while stressing the human nature of Jesus opposed many of the other anti-Trinitarians in their advocacy of pacifism and rejection of all secular or ecclesiastical authority. Budny was much concerned with upholding the purity of the biblical canon and preserving it in translation. His social views stemmed from his appreciation of Mosaic law and biblical Jewish society, which he regarded as the paradigms for the ideal Christian society. In support of his appreciation of authority he argued in his *Ourzedzie miecza używającem* (edited in 1932 under this title; first published as *Obrona . . .* in 1583) that "the Lord Jesus Christ is not a law-giver, but he is the interpreter of Divine Law . . . You have to accept that the Divine Law recorded by Moses is excellent in itself. The most that you may say perhaps is that it is not perfect from this aspect, that we cannot fulfill it in its entirety . . . You well know what Jesus says in Matthew chapter 5—that it is not against Moses, or his Law but against the Jewish clergy and the Pharisees (who set up themselves as exponents and were therefore so-called) that the sayings and teachings of Christ are directed . . . He opposes and rejects their commentaries, but not the words of Divine Law . . . Therefore, as the Divine Law is not destroyed and even now exists how can they [i.e., the pacifist Arians] say now there is no need of an office carrying the sword in the Divine Church . . . With every word they usually call out: 'What have we to do with Moses? What is the Old Testament to us? For Christ gave us another law. According to the one it was permitted to kill. According to the second it is even forbidden to be angry.' Now it has been proved that these are monkish legends, inventions and errors—to invent two laws" (ed. by St. Kot (1932), 102–3). In another connection he quotes the argument of his opponents: "You do not quote anything from the New Testament, only everything from the Old Testament" (*ibid.*, p. 53). Budny's contemporary, Isaac b. Abraham *Troki, who was well acquainted with Budny's writings and Bible translations, remarked the Jewish significance of this passage. In his *Ḥizzuk Emunah* (Breslau, 1873, 129), Isaac refers to Budny's "book called *Obrona*" summing up Budny's opinion that Jesus was a commentator on the Law only, and stating, "and he [Budny] adduced there lengthy evidence from the prophets and rational arguments as you will see on page 39 and page 41 and also in other places in this book." While Isaac praises Budny as "the scholar, the latest of Christian translators" (p. 50), elsewhere he refers to him as "our opponent" (p. 65). Altogether there are 24 quotations from Budny in *Ḥizzuk Emunah*.

In his translation of the New Testament, Budny stressed the importance of the knowledge of Hebrew for a proper understanding of the Gospels, "For as the holy Matthew wrote in Hebrew . . . then he could not quote these testimonies . . . except as he read them in the Hebrew books" (H. Merczyng, *Szymon Budny jaro krytyk tekstów biblijnych* (1913), 141). In his other notes to the New Testament Budny bases arguments on proof from the Hebrew spirit and semantics, and accepts many Jewish interpretations. The extent of Budny's Judaizing was limited by his devotion to Jesus. He expressed great indignation at the Jewish custom of pronouncing Christian Hebrew names in a way that tarnished them (*ibid.*).

Budny had a forceful and stirring impact on his contemporaries, but his influence was not permanent. His relative rationalism and broad general culture, as well as his knowledge of Hebrew and deep appreciation of the Hebrew Bible, combine to make him an outstanding figure in the history of reciprocal contacts and influences between Jews and Poles and Judaism and Christian opinion in Poland-Lithuania of the 16th century.

Bibliography: K. Budzyk et al. (eds.), *Nowy Korybut*, 2 (1964), 61–65 (bibl.); St. Kot, in: *Studien zur aelteren Geschichte Osteuropas*, 1 (1956), 63–118; H. H. Ben-Sasson, *Ha-Yehudim Mul ha-Reformazyah* (1969), 100–2.

[H.H.B.-S.]

BUDYNĚ NAD OHŘÍ (Ger. **Budin**), town in Bohemia (Czechoslovakia). Jews are first mentioned there in the 13th century. A Hebrew inscription in a flour mill records that in 1535 the Czech traveler Jan of Hazmburk leased it to a Jew to obtain money for his journey to Palestine. A synagogue was built in Budyně in 1631 (burnt down in 1759 and rebuilt in 1821). The community numbered 49 persons (11 families) in 1638. The old cemetery was closed under *Joseph II and a new one consecrated in 1798. In 1800 the community

The synagogue in Budyně nad Ohří, Czechoslovakia, rebuilt in 1821.

adopted a yellow flag for its insignia, similar to the guild flags. In 1892 it adopted Czech as the official language and closed down its German-language school. There were 176 persons living in 11 localities under the Budyně communal jurisdiction in 1902, and 50 Jews living in Budyně in 1930. The community was liquidated by the Nazis in 1942.

Bibliography: A. Jahda, in: H. Gold (ed.), *Die Juden und Judengemeinden Boehmens* (1934), 78–90 (Cz.).

[O.K.R.]

BUECHLER, ADOLF (1867–1939), theologian and historian. Buechler received his early training in the Jewish seminaries of Budapest and Breslau and was awarded his doctorate in Leipzig in 1890. His earliest studies were in the fields of Hebrew philosophy and masorah. He was ordained rabbi in Budapest in 1892 and held a rabbinic post in that same city for a short time. He spent some time in doing research under the guidance of his renowned uncle, Adolf *Neubauer, after which he was invited to act as instructor in the Israelitisch-theologische Lehranstalt in Vienna. In 1905 he was invited to become chief assistant to Michael Friedlaender, the principal of Jews' College, London, and in 1907 succeeded the latter as principal.

Buechler's main contribution to Jewish learning concerned the history of the Second Temple period, especially the latter part of that era. He wrote the important work on the Great Sanhedrin, *Das grosse Synhedrion in Jerusalem und das grosse Beth-din in der Quaderkammer des jerusalemischen Tempels* (1902). This work contained his theory of the two Sanhedrins. His articles appeared in learned periodicals in several languages. A very important contribution to the history of the synagogue was made during his stay in Oxford and was published in the *Jewish Quarterly Review* (vols. 5, 1893, and 6, 1894), under the title "The Reading of the Law and Prophets in a Triennial

Cycle." Here he displayed an enormous amount of erudition and initiative. His main theological work is *Studies in Sin and Atonement in the Rabbinic Literature of the First Century* (1928). Part of his work included a searching criticism of E. *Schuerer from rabbinic sources, bringing out the religious element in Pharisaism.

The greater part of Buechler's active life was spent at Jews' College. As principal he was a very exacting man. It was admitted even by his admirers that he did not understand the Anglo-Jewish community any more than the community understood him. He was never completely reconciled to the fact that at Jews' College men were being prepared for the ministry of an Anglo-Jewish Community and he overburdened the students with a type of learning in **Juedische Wissenschaft* which so far as that community was concerned was superfluous for its clergy. After a great deal of dissatisfaction on the part of many leaders in the affairs of the college a committee was established to revise the curriculum (1938). Buechler died suddenly during the critical stage of the deliberations. Buechler twice criticized the chief rabbinate at public occasions at Jews' College. He acidly criticized Chief Rabbi Herman Adler in 1911, disagreeing with the evidence given by the latter at the Divorce Law Commission set up by the Parliament. In 1913 he attacked the chief rabbi's court for having granted the rabbinical diploma to a student who, he claimed, should have been examined by the college.

Buechler always had a great interest in raising the standard of Jewish education. He failed nevertheless in his attempt to establish a department of pedagogics at Jews' College.

Apart from the works mentioned above, some of his more important monographs are: *Types of Jewish Palestinian Piety from 70 B.C.E. to 70 C.E.* (1968^2); *The Political and Social Leaders of the Jewish Community of Sepphoris in the Second and Third Centuries* (1909); *Der galilaeische Am Ha'areṣ des zweiten Jahrhunderts* (1906).

Bibliography: Epstein, in: *A. Buechler Memorial Volume* (1956), xiii–xxii; A. M. Hyamson, *Jews College London* (1955); JC (Feb. 24, 1939); M. Ben-Horin, in: AJHSQ, 56 (1966), 208–31.

[A.T.]

BUECHLER, ALEXANDER (1870–1944), Hungarian historian. From 1897 he served as rabbi at Keszthely and also lectured on Hungarian Jewish history at the Budapest university. In 1944 he was deported to the Auschwitz concentration camp, where he died.

Buechler wrote *A zsidók története Budapesten* ("History of Budapest Jewry," 1901). On the basis of archival material he prepared material for a continuation of S. Kohn's *A zsidók története Magyarországon* ("History of the Jews in Hungary," 1884), which covered events to 1526; however, only a few monographs appeared (*Magyar Zsidó Szemle,* 10 (1893), 7–15; A. Wertheimer, et al., *Emlékkönyv . . . Dr. Mahler Ede* (1937), 406–14; A. Scheiber (ed.), *Jubilee Volume . . . B. Heller* (1941), 139–46). Buechler also published letters of such scholars as S. J. *Rapoport in *Shai la-Moreh* (1895), which he edited.

[AL.SCH.]

BUEDINGER, MAX (1828–1902), historian. Buedinger was born in Cassel, Germany, the son of a Hebraist and teacher. After completing his studies—his teachers included the great German historians Leopold von Ranke and Heinrich von Sybel—Buedinger was unable to obtain an academic appointment because of his Jewishness. He tutored private pupils in Vienna (1857–61), traveled widely, and joined the circle of young Austrian historians. In 1861 he obtained a professorship of history at Zurich University, and during his ten years' tenure of the chair raised Swiss historiography to its highest level. After his conversion to Protestantism, he was appointed professor of general history at Vienna (1872–99). A universal historian, Buedinger combined excellent teaching with imaginative writing on ancient, medieval, and modern European history. Among his many books and articles was the first critical history of early Austria from unpublished primary sources (*Oesterreichische Geschichte bis zum Ausgange des 13. Jahrhunderts,* vol. 1, 1858). His major works include: *Die Universalhistorie im Alterthume* (1895); *Untersuchungen zur mittlern Geschichte* (2 vols., 1871); *Untersuchungen zur roemischen Kaisergeschichte* (3 vols., 1868–70); and *Vorlesungen ueber englische Verfassungsgeschichte* (1880). Buedinger shared Ranke's views about the role of ideas in history and the interlinking of civilizations, and combined romantic ideas with historical criticism. An essay on Egyptian influences in Jewish ritual which he published in 1871–73 reflected contemporary scholarly fashion, but was marred by fallacies.

Bibliography: *Festgabe zu Ehren Max Buedingers* (1898); B. L. Mueller, *Max Buedinger, ein Universalhistoriker aus Rankes Schule* (dissert., Munich, 1964).

[H.A.S.]

°**BUEHLER, JOSEF** (1904–1948), Nazi official. After studying law, Buehler was articled to Hans *Frank in Munich in 1930, joined the Nazi Party in 1933, and thereafter was Frank's deputy in the various posts he held. Frank, appointed governor-general of Poland, made Buehler a head of government with the title Staatssekretaer (from 1939 to January 18, 1945). On January 20, 1942, Buehler represented the General Gouvernement of Poland at the *Wannsee Conference and urged the initiation of the "final solution" in the occupied territory, explaining that the transport problem in Poland was negligible, and that Jews constituted a danger there as "carriers of disease." He argued that their black market activities were threatening the economy and that most were in any case "unfit to work." However, the liquidation should be carried out "without upsetting the local population." Buehler managed to leave Cracow before the entry of the Soviet Army, but was arrested in April 1946. He appeared as a defense witness for Frank at the International Military Tribunal at Nuremberg. He was later extradited to Poland and tried there by the People's High Court, charged with planning, organizing, and executing mass robbery and murder of the population in the General Gouvernement. The indictment mentioned the persecution and liquidation of Jews in the territory he administered. The verdict declared that Buehler caused the deaths of an incalculable number of Jews. He was sentenced to death and hanged in Cracow on August 21, 1948.

Bibliography: IMT, *Trial of the Major War Criminals,* 24 (1949), index; *Law Reports of Trials of War Criminals,* 14 (1949), case no. 85, 23–48.

[N.B.]

BUENO (Bueno de Mesquita), family of Marrano origin. JOSEPH BUENO (d. 1641), physician and poet, graduated in medicine at Bordeaux, where he used the alias Ruy Gómez Frontera. In Amsterdam, where he openly professed Judaism, he became noted for his medical skill; in 1625, he attended Prince Maurice of Orange on his deathbed. Bueno was on intimate terms with *Manasseh Ben Israel, contributed a laudatory preface to his *Conciliador* and a prefatory sonnet to the *De la Resurrección de los Muertos.* His son EPHRAIM HEZEKIAH (alias Martin Alvarez; d. 1665) was also a physician, graduating in medicine in Bordeaux in 1642. He edited and subsidized many works; he translated into Spanish and published a good part of the liturgy as well as the Book of Psalms, helped to edit the Shulḥan Arukh of Joseph

Caro, and wrote Spanish poetry. In 1656, with Abraham *Pereira, he founded the Or Torah academy. Bueno's portrait was painted by Rembrandt as "The Jewish Doctor." [K.R.S.]

The Bueno de Mesquita family later became distinguished and its members are found in Amsterdam, London, and America. David Bueno de Mesquita (17th century) was resident in Holland for the margrave of Brandenburg, and was moreover entrusted with various diplomatic missions by the sultan of Morocco. In 1684 he served as agent general of customs of the duchy of Brunswick-Luneburg (Miguel de Barrios, *Aumento de Israel,* p. 172). Jacob (17th century) escaped from the Inquisition and settled in Salé, Morocco, where, in collaboration with his relatives in Amsterdam and London, he established an important business firm before 1670. He was one of those who expected the Messiah to appear in 1672 in Holland, according to an anecdote reported by G. Mouette (*Relations de la captivité,* Paris, 1683). Isaac and Joseph were appointed by the Dutch government in 1682 to negotiate the peace treaty with Morocco that was signed in 1683, as a result of the collaboration of Joseph Maimoran and Joseph Toledano, both Moroccan subjects, and the rich Amsterdam merchants Jacob de Oliveira, Daniel de Mesquita, and Manoel de Belmonte. The famous Jacob *Sasportas also had a hand in the affair, which was of interest primarily to the Jewish Dutch-Moroccan big-business interests. Isaac was sent as the Moroccan ambassador to The Hague in 1729. The monument erected to Benjamin Bueno de *Mesquita, who died in New York in 1683, is one of the oldest in the city. David Bueno de Mesquita (1878–1954) was assistant *ḥazzan* and later *ḥazzan* (1904) of the Spanish and Portuguese congregation of London (1901–45). [D.Co.]

Bibliography: M. Kayserling, *Sephardim* (Ger., 1859), 206, 208, 262, 347; Kayserling, Bibl, 31; J. S. da Silva Rosa, *Geschiedenis der portugeesche Jooden te Amsterdam* (1925), 29, 39, 68; C. Roth, *Life of Menasseh Ben Israel* (1934), 115–6; ESN, s.v.; SIHM, France, 2 (1909), 288; Hirschberg, Afrikah, 2 (1965), 257, 268, 285; I. S. Emmanuel, *Precious Stones of the Jews of Curaçao* (1957), index, s.v. *Mesquita, Joseph.*

BUENO, ISAAC ABRAHAM (17th century), Jerusalem rabbi. Bueno studied under Isaac Zabaḥ, an eminent Jerusalem scholar. His signature appears before that of Moses ibn *Ḥabib on an attestation of 1627. In 1680, he was in Leghorn, where he gave his approval to a halakhic decision of Jacob *Sasportas (*Oholei Ya'akov* (1737), no. 50), and Sasportas corresponded with him in connection with his bitter dispute with the communal leaders of Leghorn. Bueno wrote *Shulḥan Melakhim* (in manuscript) on *Oraḥ Ḥayyim* and *Yoreh De'ah,* in which he incorporated the customs of Jerusalem as well as a selection from the novellae of Jacob *Castro. The work was used to a considerable extent by Jerusalem scholars in succeeding generations, among them Naḥman Nathan *Coronel, in his *Zekher Natan.*

Bibliography: Frumkin-Rivlin, 2 (1928), 68–69; Benayahu, in: KS, 22 (1945/46), 262–5; Tishby, in: *Kovez Al Yad,* 14 (1946), 153–4; J. M. Toledano, *Ozar Genazim* (1960), 213–4. [Ed.]

BUENOS AIRES, (1) the most important province in the Argentinian republic from the point of view of its economic wealth (cattle raising and wheat farming) and the concentration of its population (6,734,548 out of a total population of 20,008,945 in 1960); (2) federal capital of the Republic of Argentina, general population 2,366,816

Figure 1. The Libertad Street Conservative Synagogue, Buenos Aires, built in the late 1920s. Photo Jewish Community Archives, Buenos Aires.

(1960). The Jewish population of the capital and its suburbs ("Greater Buenos Aires"), 350,000–380,000 (1970), constitutes the overwhelming majority of the Jews of Argentina.

The Province. The first colony of the *Jewish Colonization Association (ICA)—Maurício (1891)—was established in Buenos Aires and was followed sometime later by the Baron Hirsch colony (1904–05), one of the largest in Argentina. In 1964 organized Jewish communities in 39 cities of the province were affiliated with the Va'ad ha-Kehillot.

The City. A few Marranos arrived in Buenos Aires during the 16th and 17th centuries, when the city was a small settlement on the border of Spanish America (whose center was at Lima, Peru). There is evidence that the number of "Portuguese" of Jewish descent rose during the 18th century, when Buenos Aires' importance as an administrative center and an Atlantic port grew. However, Jews were not found living openly in Buenos Aires at the time of the revolt against Spanish rule (1810), or at the time of Argentina's declaration of independence (1816). Isolated Jews from Western Europe began to arrive there in the middle of the 19th century, and the first signs of their organized existence date only to 1860 and especially to 1862, when the first *minyan* was held in Buenos Aires. This led to the establishment of the first community organization, the Congregación Israelita de la República Argentina (CIRA). In the decades that followed, Jewish immigrants arrived from North Africa—founding the

Figure 2. Collection of Ḥanukkah lamps in the museum of the Buenos Aires community. Photo Jewish Community Archives, Buenos Aires.

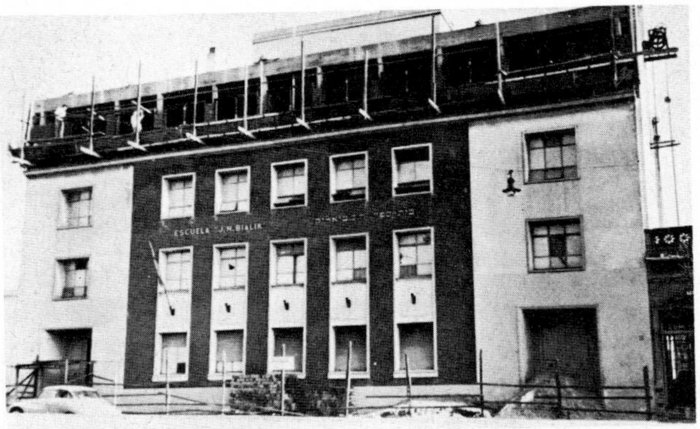

Figure 3. The Bialik School in Buenos Aires. Photo S. Zimberoff.

Congregación Israelita Latina (1891)—and especially from Eastern Europe. The number of East European immigrants increased mainly after the beginning of agricultural settlement in Argentina (1888–89) and the establishment of ICA (1891), which turned Argentina into one of the important immigration countries for Russian Jews.

In 1909 the Jewish population of Buenos Aires was estimated at 40,000, and the framework of the general population, which was heterogeneous and pluralistic from an ethnic and cultural point of view, facilitated the absorption of the immigrants and the establishment of their institutions. In addition to religious and welfare institutions, the Jews of Buenos Aires established a set of political, cultural, and economic organizations. This development was not disturbed by either the manifestations of anti-Semitism in 1910 or the "anti-Bolshevik" pogrom in January 1919, whose main victims were the Jews.

Between the two world wars, Jewish immigration from Eastern Europe and the Near East grew, and after 1933 a large immigration came from Central Europe as well. In the same period, the institutions of each of these communities crystallized. During and following World War II, the government of Argentina no longer permitted Jewish immigration, and, except for a small number of Jews who entered the country in 1956–57, the growth of the Jewish population of Buenos Aires was dependent on natural increase and especially on the important internal migration from towns and provincial cities to the capital.

At present, the community that originated in Eastern Europe, Germany, and other countries of Central Europe is organized in *A.M.I.A., which is the central community organization of Argentinian Jewry and perhaps the largest organization of its kind in the Diaspora. The Sephardim, on the other hand, are split into four separate communities according to their origin: North Africa, Turkey and Greece, Aleppo, and Damascus. In the sphere of religious affairs, the overwhelming majority of East Europeans and Sephardim maintain the Orthodox rite, while most of the

Figure 4. The Ramat Shalom School in Buenos Aires. Photo S. Zimberoff.

German Jews and the long-established organization CIRA and the Bet El community belong to the Conservative movement. In 1964 the Reform movement from the United States established a branch in Buenos Aires—the congregation Emanu-El. Nonetheless, religion does not hold a central position in the life of Jews in Buenos Aires. Jewish identification is based much more on a national consciousness, and the influence of the Zionist parties, loosely federated in their roof organization, O.S.A. (Organización Sionista Argentina), is outstanding in public life.

Jewish education in the city is divided among political orientations and communal organizations. Apart from the communal oriented schools, all the Ashkenazi schools and many of the Sephardi schools are supported by and under the supervision of the Va'ad ha-Ḥinnukh. Since 1967,

Figure 5. The Buenos Aires Hebrew Book Month exhibition, 1969. Photo S. Zimberoff.

Figure 6. Memorial to fallen heroes in Israel's wars erected in Buenos Aires in 1969. The inscriptions are in Hebrew, Spanish, and Yiddish. Photo Jewish Community Archives, Buenos Aires.

education has passed from supplementary schools to day schools, but even so, and in spite of the impressive efforts and budgets invested, it covers only a small portion of the Jewish school-age population. Among the cultural and entertainment institutions, Ha-Koaḥ and Hebraica are worthy of note. Two daily papers in Yiddish and a large number of weeklies, bi-weeklies, and monthlies in Spanish and Yiddish are published in Buenos Aires. A large number of Yiddish books are published there.

See also *Argentina.

For bibliography, see *Argentina. [H.A.]

BUERGER, LEO (1879–1943), U.S. physician born in Vienna, who contributed substantially to knowledge of urology, pathology, bacteriology, and the study of vascular diseases. In 1901 he became pathologist and later surgeon at Mt. Sinai Hospital in New York. In 1930 he was appointed professor of urological surgery in Los Angeles. Buerger gave his name to "Buerger's disease" (thromboangiitis obliterans), a non-inflammatory vascular condition of the extremities which is apt to cause severe occlusion and ultimately even loss of the limb. The disease had been known from 1878 but had not been accurately described in pathological terms until Buerger did so in 1908. It is an infrequent disease and only affects males, generally in middle age. It occurs among all races, but is more common among Jews and for some time was erroneously thought to be a disease peculiar to Jews. [J.O.L.]

BUFFALO, the second largest city in New York State and the seat of Erie Country. Erie County had a Jewish population in 1970 of about 23,500. In heavy industry, the principal support of Buffalo's economy, Jews have occupied relatively minor roles. They are chiefly involved in trade distribution, and professional services. There were 11 congregations in Greater Buffalo in 1970: two Conservative, six Orthodox, one Reconstructionist, and two Reform. The first Jew in the area came during the War of 1812, when Captain Mordecai Myers was assigned to the Williamsville cantonment. In 1825 Mordecai Manuel *Noah launched his short-lived utopian plan for a Jewish homeland, the city of Ararat, near Buffalo. Jewish settlers came to Buffalo in the decades following 1825, a period of great growth for the city. The first Jew to arrive was L. H. Flersheim, who emigrated from Germany in 1835 and taught his native language in the public schools. Jewish merchants and manufacturers soon followed Flersheim. Buffalo's first retail clothing store was opened by Mordecai M. Noah's nephew in the 1840s. Congregation Beth El, composed of Polish and German Jews, was established in 1847. Needy German-Jewish arrivals were aided by the Jacobsohn Society, organized in 1847 on the community self-help idea. The society lasted into the 1860s and also established Buffalo's first Jewish cemetery. Differences in background created dissension in Beth El, and in 1850 the German element seceded to form Beth Zion, one of a succession of splinter groups to emerge from the original congregation. By 1864 the various Reform elements had united to form Temple Beth Zion. Eventually, Beth El became a Conservative congregation.

Most Buffalo Jews are descendants of the Eastern Europeans who came after 1880. These newcomers worked as peddlers, tailors, junkmen, and storekeepers, and with the immigration, the main location of the Jewish residential population shifted from lower Main Street to the East Side. A community house, a Jewish library, and about twelve Orthodox synagogues were set up in the area.

While the synagogues were unable to bring unity into the ghetto, the lodges and charitable organizations were a unifying force. A *ḥevra kaddisha* appeared early in the life of

Figure 1. Foundation stone of Ararat, the Jewish city founded by Mordecai Noah in 1825 near Buffalo, N.Y. Buffalo Historical Society.

Figure 2. Stained glass windows and Tablets of the Law, designed by Ben Shahn, in Temple Beth Zion, Buffalo, N.Y. Photo Sherwin Greenburg, McGranahan and May Inc., Buffalo.

Buffalo Jewry. Montefiore Lodge of B'nai B'rith dates from 1866 and was the first of many groups which provided social companionship and mutual aid. In the 1850s the Buffalo Young Men's Hebrew Association, one of the first in the U.S., aided Jews traveling through the city and also offered cultural programs. Other institutions that were set up included an orphans' home, operated in conjunction with Rochester Jewry, a sheltering house, and Zion House, established by Beth Zion's Sisterhood to care for the newly arrived Russian Jews. Zion House was popularly known as the Jewish Community Building, and formed the nucleus for the Federated Jewish Charities of Buffalo, which was established in 1903. The Federated Jewish Charities incorporated several rival societies and became the direct ancestor of the present United Jewish Federation. While Buffalo Jews early established afternoon and Sunday Hebrew schools, it was not until the late 1920s that a bureau of Jewish education was established. The weekly *Buffalo Jewish Review* has been published since 1917.

Following World War I the Jewish East Side began to deteriorate. Greater Jewish affluence and the increased speed of urban transportation resulted in a general exodus, first to the West Side of the city, then to the Humboldt-Utica-Ferry section of mid-Buffalo, and still later to the North Park-Hertel Avenue part of North Buffalo. The Humboldt area was served by Temple Beth David, established in 1923, and Congregation Ohel Jacob, established in 1926. In North Buffalo, Anshe Zedek, later named Ner Israel, eventually merged with Beth David which had also resettled in the northern part of the city. Temple Emanu-El, Conservative, was founded in the mid-1920s. In 1967, Emanu-El and Beth David joined as Shaarey Zedek. Many of the former East Side congregations are also now situated in the North Park area. As industries expanded in western New York, bringing general prosperity, Jews moved to Kenmore, the town of Tonawanda, Snyder, and other suburban settlements. Beth Am (Reform), Sinai (Reconstructionist), and Beth El (Conservative), are among the congregations in the suburbs.

While Beth Zion decided to rebuild its main sanctuary in the central city after it was destroyed by fire in 1961, the congregation also has a suburban branch. The population shift has continued from North Buffalo to the suburbs. In 1970 the Jewish population was higher in the suburbs than in the city: 55% or 12,510 in the suburbs, compared to 45% or 10,330 in the city.

Bibliography: S. Adler and T. E. Connolly, *From Ararat to Suburbia: History of the Jewish Community of Buffalo* (1960); Falk, in: *Publications of the Buffalo Historical Society,* 1 (1879), 289–304; Plesur, in: *Niagara Frontier* (Summer, 1956), 29–36. [Mi.P.]

BUFFALO (Heb. מְרִיא, *meri;* AV "fat cattle" or "fatling"), animal which in biblical times was sacrificed and the flesh eaten (II Sam. 6:13; I Kings 1:9, 19). The Dead Sea Scroll text of Isaiah 11:6 has *yimru* instead of *meri* ("they shall pasture") for the masoretic reading *"meri"* and this corresponds to the Septuagint reading. The reference is to the water buffalo, the *Bubalus bubalis,* which until the end of the 1940s roamed in the Ḥuleh marsh, where the Bedouin reared it for food. It is also reared in the Beteha valley at the foot of the Golan Heights, the biblical Bashan, which was famed for its buffaloes (Ezek. 39:18). The buffalo originates from a wild species found in India. It is a powerful animal suitable for work, and was employed in Ereẓ Israel for plowing. In addition to the identification of the *meri* with the buffalo (see also the Bible translation of Saadiah Gaon who uses the Arabic word *jamūs*), some have identified the buffalo with the *te'o* (תְּאוֹ) listed as a clean animal (Deut. 14:5) and which Isaiah mentions as being caught in a net (51:20). This identification is improbable, however, since in Ereẓ Israel it was a domesticated and not a wild animal. The *te'o* has also been identified with the bison *(Bison bonasus).* Others have identified the buffalo with the *koi* (כּוֹי) mentioned in the Talmud in connection with the doubt whether it belongs to the category of *behemah* (domesticated cattle) or *ḥayyah* (wild beast), which would involve differing regulations concerning ritual slaughter (cf. Ḥul. 80a, where four opinions are expressed as to its identity).

Bibliography: Lewysohn, Zool, 129; H. B. Tristram, Nat Hist, 56, 72; F. S. Bodenheimer, *Ha-Ḥai be-Arẓot ha-Mikra,* 2 (1956), index; J. Feliks, *Animal World of the Bible* (1962), 20–21. [J.F.]

°**BUGENHAGEN, JOHANN** (also known as **Pomeranus,** i.e., from Pomerania; 1485–1558), German reformer; friend of Martin Luther. In 1517 he became lector in Scripture and patrology in a monastery of the Premonstratensian order in Belbuck. From 1523 onward he served as professor in the University of Wittenberg. He was influenced by the writings of Erasmus and Martin Luther. Bugenhagen was among those who aided Luther in translating the Bible. His most important work is his commentary on the Psalms (*Interpretatio in librum Psalmorum,* Basle, 1524).

Bibliography: G. Geisenhof, *Bibliotheca Bugenhagiana* (1908); E. Goerigk, *Johannes Bugenhagen und die Protestantisierung Pommerns* (1895); W. Leege, *Bugenhagen als Liturgiker* (1925); W. Rautenberg, *Johann Bugenhagen* (Ger., 1958); E. Wolf, *Peregrinatio* (1954), includes bibliography; RGG³, s.v. [Ed.]

°**BUHL, FRANZ PEDER WILLIAM MEYER** (1850–1932), Danish biblical and Semitic scholar. Buhl was born in Copenhagen and educated at the University of Copenhagen, where he taught Old Testament from 1880 to 1890. From Copenhagen he was called to the University of Leipzig, remaining there until 1898, when he was recalled to Copenhagen as professor of Semitic languages (1898–1932). Buhl collaborated in the editing of the 13th (1915) and following editions of *Hebraeisches und aramaeisches Handwoerterbuch ueber das Alte Testament* of Gesenius, and of R. Kittel's *Biblia Hebraica* (where he edited the books of Psalms, 1930, and Esther, 1935). In his article on biblical poetry, "Dichtkunst bei den Israeliten" (in *Realencyklopaedie fuer protestantische Theologie und Kirche,* 4 (1898), 626–38), he anticipated the study of form criticism in his recognition of the literary types *(Gattungen)* and life situations of the poetic compositions. His study of the canon and text of the Old Testament appeared originally in German, *Kanon und Text des Alten Testaments* (1891; English translation by J. Macpherson, 1892) and is among the most influential of his works. Besides the foregoing, he wrote *Den gammeltestamentlige Skriftoverlevering* (1885; German translation, 1891; English translation, 1892); *Jesaja oversat og fortolket* (8 parts, 1889–94); *Gennesaret Sö og dens Omgivelser* (1889); *Palästina i kortfattet geografisk og topografisk Fremstilling* (1890); *Det israelitiske Folks Historie* (1892, 1936⁸); *Geschichte der Edomiter* (1893); *De messianske Forjættelser i det Gamle Testament* (1894); *Til Vejledning i de gammeltestamentlige Undersögelser* (1895); *Geographie des alten Palaestina* (1896); *Die socialen Verhaeltnisse der Israeliten* (1899); *Psalmerne oversatte og fortolkede* (12 parts, 1898–1900); and *Muhammeds Liv* (1903; German translation, 1961³). A *Festschrift* was presented to Buhl on the occasion of his seventy-fifth birthday in 1925. [Ja.Mu.]

BÜHLER, CHARLOTTE (1893–), developmental and clinical psychologist. Born in Berlin, Charlotte Bühler taught at the University of Vienna from 1923, becoming assistant professor in 1929. Leaving Austria in 1938, she was professor at Oslo, Norway, for two years before settling in Los Angeles and, in 1950, retired to private practice. She was associated with the University of Southern California, specializing in the study of the development of children and their social behavior in infancy. Among her numerous published works are: *Soziologische und psychologische Studien ueber das erste Lebensjahr* (1927; *The First Year of Human Life,* 1930); *Kindheit und Jugend* (1928); *Kind und Familie* (1937; *The Child and his Family,* 1939); and *The Course of Human Life; a Study of Goals in the Humanistic Perspective* (1968). [H.E.A.]

BUHUSI (Rum. **Buhuşi**), town in Moldavia, E. Rumania. Jews were invited to settle there around 1823, when the lord of the land of Buhusi, which was then a village, decided to set up a town on its grounds; they numbered 82 in 1831. Buhusi became an important center of Ḥasidism in Moldavia when the *ẓaddik* Isaac Friedman (1835–1896), the grandson of Israel of *Ruzhin, many of whose followers being Bessarabian and Moldavian Jews, made his home there. The community increased from 537 in 1859 to 1,728 in 1899. Welfare associations and educational institutions included a *talmud torah* and a Jewish-Rumanian elementary school, founded in 1897. A yeshivah, founded in 1908 adjacent to the "court" of the *ẓaddik,* existed until 1916. In 1930 there were in Buhusi 1,972 Jews (22.6% of the total population), occupied in commerce and crafts. [El.F.]

Holocaust Period. When the *Iron Guard assumed power (September 1940), Buhusi's 7,207 Jews were forced to contribute to its "Aid Fund," and a large sum was also extorted from the Jewish community funds. At the time of the Legion's (Iron Guard's storm troops) rebellion against *Antonescu (January 1941), the Iron Guard planned a pogrom in Buhusi similar to the one they perpetrated in Bucharest, but their local commander opposed it and restricted himself to extorting more money from the Jews and putting them on forced labor far from the town. An order by the district head for the expulsion of the Jews was also frustrated after the outbreak of war with the Soviet Union (June 1941). On the other hand, Jews were evacuated from neighboring towns and villages to Buhusi, where the community provided for them. In the spring of 1944 a group of 70 Jewish orphans were brought to Buhusi from Transnistria. A part of the "Rebbe's Court" was requisitioned by the Rumanian army and the interior of the synagogue was destroyed. The rabbi himself, Menahem Mendel Friedman, the last of the dynasty, was in need of surgery, but was not permitted to leave for Bucharest and succumbed to his ailment. After the war the Jewish population rose to about 8,000 as some of the people driven out of the nearby villages chose to resettle in Buhusi. Most of these emigrated and by 1969 the town had 50 Jewish families and one synagogue.

[Th.L.]

Bibliography: Kaufman, in: *Cronica communităţilor israelite din Judeţul Neamţu,* 2 (1929), 383–84. Holocaust: PK Romanyah, 21–24; M. Carp, *Cartea Neagră,* 1 (1946), 136, 138.

BUITRAGO, town in Castile, central Spain. The first information about the Jewish community there dates from 1290, when it paid an annual tax of 6,048 maravedis, a relatively inconsiderable sum indicating it was a small community. At the time of the expulsion of the Jews from Spain in 1492, more than 50 Jews owned buildings within the town and valuable properties outside. Don David de Hija was then the majordomo to the duke of Infantado, the local feudal lord—an office occupied in 1482 by Isaac Adarique. The property of the Jews expelled from Buitrago was bestowed by the Catholic Monarchs upon the duke in compensation for his loss of the Jewish revenues. Six files recording prosecutions by the *Inquisition of New Christians in Buitrago between 1514 and 1532 are extant; among them was the municipal councillor *(regidor),* Inigo López de León.

Bibliography: Beinart, in: *Tarbiz,* 26 (1956/57), 77; Baer, Spain, 2 (1966), 247, 485; Baer, Urkunden, 1 pt. 2 (1936), 81, 278, 420ff., 518; J. Amador de los Ríos, *Historia social, politica y religiosa de los judíos de España y Portugal* (1960), 244, 299, 767.

[H.B.]

BUKARAT (Abukarat, Abucarat, Bukrat), ABRAHAM BEN SOLOMON HA-LEVI (late 15th–early 16th century), exegete and poet. Bukarat lived in Malaga, Spain. He was well versed in the natural sciences as well as in Spanish and Arabic. After the expulsion of the Jews from Spain he went to Tunis, where he remained for many years. His *Sefer ha-Zikkaron* (Leghorn, 1845), one of the best supercommentaries on Rashi to the Pentateuch, was completed there in 1507. In it he reveals himself a painstaking scholar, with a sensitive feeling for language. Bukarat utilized his linguistic knowledge to elucidate the meaning of words and concepts and also to collate manuscripts to determine the correct version. Some of his poems are preserved in the Guenzburg collection, Moscow. His elegy on the expulsion from Spain, which was printed by Ben-Sasson, is of considerable importance. In it he describes the situation of those Spanish and Portuguese exiles who came to Morocco and Algeria, giving precise information as to their numbers. According to A. Berliner, Bukarat translated the responsa of Isaac Alfasi from Arabic to Hebrew. Abraham ben Isaac ha-Levi Abukarat, who lived in the following generation in Egypt, may have been his grandson. He was a wealthy scholar, whose library contained important manuscripts.

Bibliography: S. D. Luzzatto (ed.), *Sefer ha-Zikkaron . . . A. Bukrat* (1845), introduction; L. Dukes, in: *Oẓar Neḥmad,* 3 (1860), 151; Scholem, in: KS, 2 (1925/26), 103–4; Ben-Sasson, in: *Tarbiz,* 31 (1961/62), 59–71; Hirschberg, Afrikah, 1 (1965), 300, 325.

[Ed.]

BUKHARA, capital of the former khanate of the same name in Russian Central Asia, now within the Uzbek S.S.R. The name "Bukharan Jews" was applied to one of the communities in the khanate by Ashkenazi Jews and the Russian government. The members of the community customarily referred to themselves as Hebrews, Jews, or Sons of Israel, while the local population called them Dzhugur, an expression of contempt. They speak a Tajiki-Jewish dialect and are at present concentrated in Israel and Soviet Central Asia.

History. The precise date of the first Jewish settlement in Russian Central Asia cannot be ascertained. A tradition current among Bukharan Jews identifies Bukhara with Habor (II Kings 17:6), where the Ten Tribes were exiled. The names of the Bukharan Jews, as well as expressions in their language, suggest that some of them came from Persia and Khiva. Although Benjamin of Tudela, the Jewish traveler (c. 1170), does not mention the town of Bukhara, he speaks of a Jewish community in Samarkand which numbered 50,000. Indeed, according to a Bukharan Jewish tradition, when Samarkand was destroyed during the 16th century, its Jews moved to Bukhara, where they found a small Jewish settlement. The first positive evidence concerning the Jewish community of Bukhara available is that of the 13th-century Arab chronicler, Ibn al-Fūṭī, who relates that in 1240 a fanatic Muslim mystic and magician threatened the Jews and Christians with extermination. Apparently this threat was not carried out, but the Jewish communities endured much suffering under the Tatar-Mongolian rulers and became impoverished. The Jewish settlement in the town of Bukhara appears to have been renewed during the 14th century.

At the end of the 16th century, the Bukharan khanate, which became the propagator of Islam in the area, was established. Jewish residence was restricted to a special quarter, and even there Jews were prohibited from acquiring houses from Muslims. The Jews were compelled to wear a special sign (badge) to distinguish them from the Muslims, and a special tax, which was accompanied by a humiliating slap in the face, was levied from them. In the middle of the 18th century, Muslim fanaticism grew in intensity. Many Jews were compelled to accept Islam and a class of forced converts (see *anusim), which was regarded with suspicion by the Muslim population, came into existence. The missionary J. *Wolff, who visited the town of Bukhara in 1844, found 300 families of forced converts. These conditions made many Jews wish for a Christian government which would alleviate their situation. During the second half of the 19th century, the Russian conquests

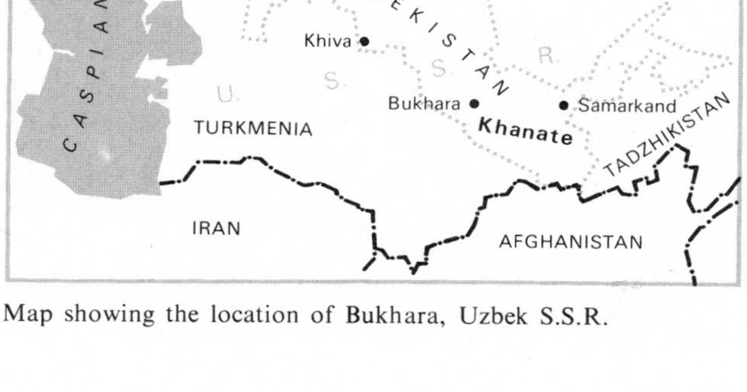

Map showing the location of Bukhara, Uzbek S.S.R.

Figure 1. Leaders of the Bukharan community in Jerusalem, 1928. The men are wearing the kaftan-type *djoma*, the boys, the richly-embroidered barmitzvah cloak modeled on the ceremonial garments of their elders. From the Ben Dov Collection, by courtesy of Israel State Archives.

of the area began, and some regions of the Bukharan khanate (the towns of Samarkand and Tashkent) were incorporated into Russia and included in Turkestanskiy Kray (Turkmenia). In practice, the emir of Bukhara became the representative of the Russian government. In the Bukharan khanate, the general condition of the Jews remained unchanged. On the other hand, within the regions under Russian domination, no special restrictions were imposed on the Jews. As a result of this situation, there was a constant movement of Jews from the Bukharan khanate to the Russian-dominated region of Turkestan. This migration included many forced converts who returned to Judaism once they were under Russian rule. However, from the end of the 19th century, the Russian authorities of the region reacted against the Jews streaming into it from the principalities of Bukhara, Khiva, and Afghanistan. In 1889, the Russian government issued a decree differentiating between the Jews who had lived in the Turkestan region prior to the Russian conquest and those who had arrived afterward. In 1901, the latter were ordered to live exclusively in the three frontier towns of Osh, Katta-Kurgan, and Petro-Aleksandrovsk. At the same time, however, the Russian administration was not excessively severe and was prepared to regard even those who had settled in the region after the beginning of the Russian rule as local Jews. At the same time the Jews made efforts to have the decree abolished and the area of permitted settlement for non-local Jews extended. In fact, the enforcement of the decree was first postponed until 1909, and then until 1910. The area of permitted settlement for non-local Jews was extended to include the towns of Samarkand, Margelan, and Kokand.

From 1905, the anti-Semitic attitude of the government intensified, and Jews were accused of exploiting the local population. With the Revolution of February 1917, all legal restrictions were lifted from the Bukharan Jews. At the same time, the emir of Bukhara proclaimed a constitution in his principality guaranteeing civil rights for all its inhabitants. This proclamation was received with enthusiasm and joyful demonstrations in which the Jews, carrying banners with Hebrew inscriptions, also participated. In March 1918, popular anti-Semitism was manifested in the town of Bukhara in the form of pogroms. The Jews barricaded themselves in the houses of their quarter and the emir sent guards to protect them, so that a large-scale massacre was averted. During the same period heavy taxes were imposed on the Jews for the purchase of arms and provisions for the emir's army in his struggle with the Soviets, but in 1920, the Red Army conquered the principality and established Bukhara as a People's Soviet Republic.

The center of the Bukharan Jews in Palestine also entered upon a period of development from the second half of the 19th century. The emigration of Bukharan Jews to Palestine had begun in 1868. These included wealthy emigrants who endeavored to make Jerusalem a spiritual center for their community. In 1892, the pioneers founded the Bukharan quarter in Jerusalem, which they named Reḥovot: their children remained in Jerusalem to study when they returned home to continue their affairs, visiting Palestine from time to time. World War I brought havoc to the Bukharan Jews in Palestine, most of whom were Russian subjects. The Turks requisitioned their houses for the army. Most of the men left the country and only the women, children, elderly, and disease-ridden remained. In Russia, as a result of the war and the revolutions, many Bukharan Jews became impoverished and returned to Palestine destitute.

Population. At the beginning of the 20th century, there were about 20,000 Jews living in the Bukharan khanate, of whom 4,000–5,000 lived in the city of Bukhara. About 15,000 Bukharan Jews also lived in Turkestanskiy Kray. Toward the end of the 19th century, there were about 180 families of Bukharan Jews in Jerusalem. According to the general population census in the Soviet Union in 1926, there were about 19,000 Bukharan Jews, of whom 18,172 lived in the Soviet Republic of Uzbekistan, including 7,740 in Samarkand, 3,314 in Bukhara, 1,347 in Tashkent, and 746 in Kokand. This census was inaccurate and some estimate the number of Bukharan Jews in the Soviet Union during the mid-1920s at 30–35,000. According to a survey carried out by the *Ozet in 1934, there were over 24,000 Bukharan Jews in the Soviet Republic of Uzbekistan alone, of whom 4,500 lived in villages. In 1936, the Bukharan Jews of Palestine numbered about 2,500, half of whom lived in Jerusalem. According to the 1959 census held in the Soviet Union, the Bukharan Jews numbered approximately 28,000. About 23,000 lived in Uzbekistan, especially in the towns of Samarkand, Bukhara, and the urban centers of the Fergana Valley, and another 5,000 in the Tadzhik S.S.R. However, a 1970 estimate put the figure much lower—10,000 Bukharan and 2,000 Ashkenazi Jews in Bukhara.

Economy. Despite the restrictions imposed on the Jews of Bukhara, there were wealthy merchants among them.

Figure 2. Ark of the Law in a Bukharan synagogue in Jerusalem, built 1898. Photo Government Press Office, Tel Aviv.

J. Wolff relates that most of the Jews were engaged in the dyeing of textiles and the silk trade in 1844. With the Russian conquests, new markets were opened to the Bukharan Jews and many traded with Moscow and other towns of "Great Russia." After 1917 many Jews were ruined as a result of the Revolution and the war between the principality and the Soviets. With the establishment of Soviet rule, thousands of Bukharan Jewish families were deprived of their livelihood. In 1926, the Soviet authorities began to cope with the dire economic plight of the Bukharan Jews by agricultural settlement. About 3,500 Bukharan Jews settled on the land by 1932. The land given to the Jewish settlers was generally of inferior quality and at times they also met with anti-Semitism on the part of the surrounding population. It appears that most of the Jews gradually abandoned the villages. During the late 1920s and early 1930s, cooperatives of Jewish artisans were formed with the assistance of the government. Some of them even had Hebrew names such as *Ḥerut* ("Freedom"), and *Aḥdut* ("Unity"), but these were disbanded in the late 1930s.

Culture and Administration. During the 17th and 18th centuries, Bukharan Jewry produced poets and translators whose works were written in the Tajiki-Jewish dialect. One of the most outstanding was Yusuf *Yahudi. During his lifetime, a school of poets arose who adopted his style in composing poetry in *Judeo-Persian. This literary activity did not influence the mass of Bukharan Jews, and at the end of the 18th century, they were on the verge of spiritual extinction. A fundamental change in the spiritual lives of the Bukharan Jews was brought about by Joseph ha-Ma'aravi, who in 1793 was sent as an emissary of the Safed community to the Bukharan Jews. He gradually introduced reforms in religious usage, brought in a qualified scribe, and sent to Constantinople, Vilna, and Leghorn for books. A further impetus to the awakening of the national and religious consciousness of Bukharan Jewry came from the refugees from *Meshed. During the 1840s, the ancient synagogue in the town of Bukhara, which also served for educational purposes, was renovated. In time, a network of educational institutions for the children of Bukharan Jews was created. *Ḥadarim* for infants, known as *khomla,* where the principal instruction was knowledge of the prayers, were established, while there were also *ḥadarim* for the study of the Torah and Talmud whose graduates generally became *shoḥatim* and teachers. Over the years, the Jews of Bukhara abandoned the Persian liturgy in favor of Sephardi usage. As soon as Bukharan Jews began to settle in Jerusalem, it became their most important spiritual center. Books in the Tajiki-Jewish dialect and in Hebrew were published there for the Bukharan Jews. Until 1939, about 170 such books were published in Jerusalem. The majority were religious works, including prayer books and books of usages, works on Kabbalah and *tikkunim,* Midrashim, and commentaries; the literary works of Persian poets and Hebrew authors were also printed. In 1970 there were several synagogues all in the same compound in a 15th-century building.

With the intensification of religious and communal life among Bukharan Jews, the Jewish internal leadership was also consolidated. The communal administration consisted of 12 assessors who dealt with tax affairs and a *nasi* elected by the *parnasim* of the community whose function was confirmed by the emir. The *nasi* also acted as judge for the members of his community and as its representative to the authorities. In addition to this, a rabbi, known as *ḥakham,* was appointed for the community. He often also held the position of *nasi.* There were also synagogue officials who collected contributions from the wealthy houseowners twice a year for the needy of the community. The first collection was held on the eve of Passover to provide funds for the festival requisites and the second after Tabernacles to pay for the heating of the houses of the poor during the winter. This administration was also maintained in its general lines in the territories conquered by the Russians during the second half of the 19th century. With the widening of contacts between Bukharan and Ashkenazi Jews and the growth of the Zionist movement in the community, schools where the language of instruction was Hebrew were established for Bukharan children. After the Bolshevik Revolution, these schools were placed under the supervision of the Soviet regime but the instruction was continued in Hebrew, and in 1920 a textbook of general geography was even published in Hebrew under the auspices of the Commissar for Education of the Turkestan Republic. It was only at the end of 1921 that the decision of the Commissar for Education to enforce the Tajiki-Jewish dialect as the language of instruction in the Jewish schools was applied. At least until 1923, however, these schools continued to teach Hebrew side by side with the Tajiki-Jewish dialect. In 1920, a seminary for the training of teachers for Bukharan Jewish schools was established in Tashkent. The seminary had boarding facilities, and a kosher kitchen was maintained until the late 1920s. Hebrew was studied as one of the subjects until 1924. In November 1925 *Rushnoy,* a Soviet newspaper in the Tajiki-Jewish dialect, was published in Samarkand. The dialect was written in Hebrew characters, but during the late 1920s and early 1930s, all the Oriental languages of the Soviet Union were transliterated in the Latin alphabet. From the beginning of 1929, a Soviet newspaper in the Tajiki-Jewish dialect, *Bayroki Mikhnat* ("The Flag of Labor"), was published in Samarkand and later in Tashkent. During the middle 1930s Cyrillic letters were adopted for the writing of most of the Oriental languages, including that of the Jews of Bukhara. Throughout this period, a number of works in the Tajiki-Jewish dialect were published. Because of the special conditions in the Soviet Republic of Uzbekistan, the struggle against the traditional forms of Jewish life among Bukharan Jews was not as violent as that waged against Ashkenazi Jews in the Soviet Union. Even though the traditional Jewish administration officially lost its status, its influence continued to be felt and the Jews of Bukhara remained loyal to it. Instruction in prayer continued in semi-secrecy for many years, and the authoritative family framework preserved the national-religious identity of the community. It is due to this that the Bukharan Jews are still one of the most Jewish-conscious groups among Soviet Jewry. In 1970, kosher meat was available and the Jewish cemetery was well kept.

[M.A.R.]

Figure 3. A Bukharan Jewish wedding party, late 19th century. Photo courtesy Lea Levavi, Givatayim, Israel.

Figure 4. Bukharan woman's ceremonial coat, a *kaltshak*. Of gold brocade on a red-pink ground, it is fitted to the body and does not close in front. The long sleeves are very wide at the top, as in a kimono. Jerusalem, Israel Museum.

Costume. Before the Russian Revolution, Bukhara and the other towns of Uzbekistan were distinguished by the splendor of their costumes, jewelry, woven silks, and embroidered fabrics. Restrictions were imposed periodically on Christians and Jews with regard to costume. In earlier periods, they were obliged to wear special colors, in the case of the Jews black and yellow, the black generally an outer garment, worn in the street. Until the 1920s, Jewish men were obliged to wear in the street a cord girdle and a hat trimmed with fur—the *telpak*. The latter was apparently of a special type but its exact shape cannot be ascertained. These two items seem to be the last vestiges of a Jewish costume known only through vague literary descriptions. Apart from these features imposed on their costume, the only garments peculiar to Jewish wear in Bukhara were the white robes worn on the Day of Atonement, and a bridal gown with a special type of veil, both made of bespangled white cotton tulle. Otherwise Jewish costume was similar to Muslim; ceremonial robes were copied from those worn at the court of the emir, who used to present such robes to his distinguished subjects, Muslims and Jews alike.

Men's coats were long garments of the "kaftan" type found in various versions all the way from Eastern Europe to China. Their cut was in simple, straight lines, in a wide, enfolding shape. They wore several coats, one over the other. Women's coats were of three kinds: (1) the *kaltshak*, a long ceremonial coat, narrow at the waist, open in front, with very wide sleeves; (2) the *kamzol*, for more general use, shorter and of a European-style, flared-out cut; and (3) the *frandjin*, a mantle worn in the street, enveloping the whole figure from head to toe. Their dresses were wide, long, shirt-like. They were cut from lengths of cloth without a shoulder seam. The fabrics used were mostly local silks or imported materials.

Ornamentation on the costumes was of various kinds: most common were many-colored edgebands, generally tablet woven, on the borders of nearly all garments. Headgear and the paired bands on the front of women's dresses were embroidered with colored silk threads but also with gold thread, which was used lavishly for ceremonial attire. In private, Jewish men wore various kinds of caps; those current among Bukharan Jews even today are caps heavily embroidered with colored silk or gold. Women had various types of caps, and many kinds of kerchiefs and scarves. Unmarried women at ceremonial or family gatherings wore a *topi-tos*, a soft cap entirely covered with gold embroidery in traditional geometric patterns. For festive dress, mothers and older women bound the forehead with a special kerchief of brocade. On ceremonial occasions Jewish notables wore jeweled belts. In private, Jewish men wore various kinds of the plain cord girdle obligatory on the street. Soft boots of colored, floral patterns were worn indoors and boots resembling black leather galoshes outdoors.

Jewelry. Jewelry formed part of a girl's dowry, and was handed down from mother to daughter. Women normally wore simple earrings, a ring, and a bracelet, but on ceremonial occasions put on a magnificent display of jewels, including various kinds of forehead ornaments, earrings, necklaces, bracelets, and rings. They were made of gold, adorned with pearls, green and rosy stones, and coral beads. The design of jewels for the head and neck comprised two main ornamental elements: (1) solid pieces, originally made of solid gold and later of gold sheet stuffed with a kind of bitumen, studded with semiprecious and precious stones; (2) pendants, known as *poya* ("feet"), made of coiled gold wire threaded with a varying number of pearls, stones, and granulated gold beads.

Bukharan folkways and costumes were long perpetuated by the community in Jerusalem, making it the most colorful and picturesque element in Jerusalem Jewry. In recent years, however, this distinctive dress has been increasingly abandoned, being worn only at weddings and on other festive occasions. [Av.L.]

Bibliography: I. Ben-Zvi, *The Exiled and the Redeemed* (1961), 54–82; Loewenthal, in: REJ, 120 (1961), 345–51; idem, *The Jews of Bukhara* (1961); M. D. Gaon, *Yehudei ha-Mizraḥ be-Ereẓ-Yisrael*, 2 (1938), index; M. Eshel, *Galeryat Demuyyot shel Rashei Yahadut Bukhara* (1966); W. J. Fischel, in: L. Finkelstein (ed.), *Jews*, 2 (1960^3), 1174–76; idem, in: L. Jung (ed.), *Jewish Leaders* (1953), 535–47; A. Yaari, *Sifrei Yehudei Bukhara* (1942), incl. bibl. COSTUME: L. N. Kalontarov, in: S. P. Tolstov et al. (eds.), *Narody Sredney Azii i Kazakhstana*, 2 (1963), 610–30; M. Tilke, *Orientalische Kostueme* (1923), 30–31, plates 111–7; E. Neumark, *Massa be-Ereẓ ha-Kedem* (1947), 3; Israel Museum, *Catalogue, no. 39* (1967), *Bokhara* (incl. bibl.).

BUKOVINA, region between the E. Carpathians and the upper Dniester, part of Ottoman Moldavia until 1775, when it passed to the Austrian Empire (the entire region named Bukovina from 1774); after World War I incorporated into *Rumania; in 1940 the northern part was incorporated into the Soviet Union (west Ukrainian S.S.R.), the southern part remaining in Rumania. The main town of Bukovina is *Chernovtsy, formerly Czernowitz (see entry for some major aspects of Jewish life in the region). Jewish merchants passing through Bukovina are mentioned from the 13th century, and Jews settled there from the 14th century. In 1408 they were granted the right of freedom of movement and commerce along the Moldavian trade routes. The Jewish population increased steadily, and maintained close commercial links with the Jews of *Poland-Lithuania, being mainly occupied in the transit trade and purvey of alcoholic beverages. The Cossack invasion from the Ukraine in 1656 (see *Chmielnicki) caused much suffering in the region.

Jewish communal life in Bukovina developed along the same lines as in the other communities of the Ottoman Empire. From 1710 to 1834 Bukovina Jewry had an independent **ḥakkam bashi*, who held hereditary office, and was also responsible for collecting the taxes imposed on Bukovina Jewry. Another office of the Jewish leadership from 1716 was that of *rosh medinah* (head of the region). From the end of the 17th century the growing Polish-Jewish element imparted a distinct Ashkenazi character to the Bukovina communities. The census of 1776 recorded a Jewish population of 2,906 in the region, now under Austria. Their economic position was satisfactory. That year the government prohibited additional Jews from settling in the communities of Bukovina and limited trade in alcoholic beverages to Jews resident there before 1768. In 1780, when 1,069 Jewish families were recorded in Bukovina, a proposal was made to limit residence of the Jews to three main towns, with permission to settle elsewhere only if they engaged in agriculture. Orders along these lines became effective in 1782, and by 1785 the number of Jewish families had dwindled to 175. They had increased by immigration from *Galicia to 360 in 1791. From 1816 Jews were granted individual residence permits to settle in the region. The number of Jews increased throughout Bukovina after 1848 and the attainment of emancipation (see *Austria), and by 1890 numbered approximately 90,000. Ḥasidism struck roots in Bukovina, one of the early leaders there being *Abraham Joshua Heschel of Apta (Opatow). A branch of the *Ruzhin dynasty of *ẓaddikim* made Sadagora a center of Ḥasidism in the region. Another dynasty originating in Kossow settled in *Vizhnitsa. From the second half of the 19th century Jews in Bukovina tended increasingly to prefer a secular education, in which the Chernovtsy community led the way. They also took part in the political and social life of Bukovina, in general tending toward assimilation into Austro-German culture and identification with its aspirations. Zionism penetrated Bukovina at the end of the century. Jews took an active part in Bukovina's industrial and commercial development, initiated timber and cement industries, and were prominent in railroad construction and banking. A number of these Jewish industrial and financial magnates were awarded Austrian titles. Most owned large estates. The status of Jewish artisans also improved, and certain trades, such as the tinsmiths', were exclusively Jewish. After the incorporation of Bukovina into Rumania the situation of the Jews declined. However there was an upsurge of communal, in particular Zionist, activity. The *Bund gained ground among the growing Jewish proletariat. Among Jews active in politics was the Zionist leader and member of the Rumanian senate, Meir *Ebner. The incorporation of northern Bukovina into the west Ukrainian S.S.R. brought hardship to the Jewish population, and Jewish cultural and social life came to a standstill. On June 18, 1941, 3,800 Jews of the region were deported to Siberia. When in July 1941 northern Bukovina was occupied by the Germans and the Rumanian Fascists, the German and Rumanian soldiers proceeded to massacre the Jewish population. The yellow *badge was introduced, their personal belongings were looted, and all occupation in professions and crafts was prohibited to Jews. Forced labor was imposed. On Oct. 11, 1941, a ghetto was set up in Chernovtsy; 40,000 Jews were deported from there, to be followed by another 35,000 Jews from the surroundings, to the death camps in *Transnistria. On the partition of Bukovina after World War II, the Jews in the northern sector eventually had to conform to the general pattern of Jewish existence under Soviet rule. The more liberal attitude of communist Rumania permitted emigration to Israel from the south where few Jews remain.

Bibliography: H. Gold (ed.), *Geschichte der Juden in der Bukowina*, 2 vols. (1958–62); PK Romanyah, 349–549.

[M.RE./ED.]

BULA, RAPHAEL MOSES (d. 1773), scholar and emissary of the Jerusalem community. During his stay in Constantinople (1752) while on a mission to Turkey, Bula published his homiletical collection, *Ḥayyei Olam*. In 1758 he was one of the scholars at the Neveh Shalom yeshivah in Jerusalem. He wrote *Get Mekushar* (Constantinople, 1767) on divorce, and *Zekhut Moshe* (Salonika, 1818) on ownership rights. Bula is one of the signatories of the letter (1770) authorizing Yom Tov *Algazi and Jacob Ḥazzan to collect funds on behalf of the Jerusalem community. Bula's son SOLOMON (1734–86), a Jerusalem-born rabbi and halakhic authority, left Jerusalem after his father's death and went to Salonika, where he became one of the most renowned scholars. Solomon's work *Leḥem Shelomo* (Salonika, 1795) deals with possession, property rights, and divorce law. His responsa were never published.

Bibliography: Frumkin-Rivlin, 3 (1929), 93–95; Ya'ari, Sheluḥei, 910.

[ED./A.YA.]

BŪLĀN, Khazar king. According to tradition he instituted Judaism in *Khazaria. The "Reply of Joseph" to the letter of *Ḥisdai ibn Shaprut in the "Khazar Correspondence" refers to Būlān as a reforming king who drove the diviners and idolaters (i.e., shamanists) from the land, and accepted monotheism (Judaism) in consequence of a dream or vision. In consequence of another dream or vision he made a successful military expedition south of the Caucasus to Ardabil, from the spoils of which he consecrated cult objects (tabernacle, ark, candelabrum, etc.), still preserved in the time of the writer. After a religious debate held in Khazaria on the merits of Christianity, Islam, and Judaism respectively, Būlān gave his verdict in favor of Judaism which henceforth became the religion of the king and his servants, i.e., apparently the leading Khazars, rather than the people as a whole. Būlān here appears as the Khazar khaqan to whom the beg (Heb. *sar,* "general") is subordinate. M. I. Artamonov makes Būlān the beg. The most probable date for these events, the historicity of which is confirmed at least in part by other sources, is 730–40 C.E. Parallels for the acceptance of a new faith after a religious debate are the conversion of the Uigurs to Manichaeism shortly after 762 and the account of the missions of the Muslims, Latins, Jews, and Greeks to Vladimir I in 986 in the "Russian Chronicle," before Vladimir's final acceptance of Orthodoxy. The name Būlān appears to be Turkish, but there is no agreement as to the meaning. The suggestion of J. *Brutzkus that it is a participial form from the root *bil,* "know," in the sense of "wise," has met with no general acceptance. S. Szyszman, followed by Artamonov, proposes *bulan,* "elk" or "stag" in some Turkish dialects, as the origin of the name, and finds numerous place and personal names in Russia of which *Būlān* is the principal component.

Bibliography: S. Szyszman, in: *Ephemerides Theologicae Lovanienses,* 33 (1957), 68–76; Dunlop, Khazars, index; idem, in: Roth, Dark Ages, 336–40; M. I. Artamonov, *Istoriya Khazar* (Rus., 1962), 276–8; A. Zajączkowski, *Ze studiów nad zagadnieniem chazarskim* (1947), 38–39.

[D.M.D.]

BULAT, JUDAH BEN JOSEPH (c. 1475–c. 1540), talmudist who settled in Turkey after the expulsion from Spain. The first mention of him is in 1510, when he published the second and corrected edition of the *Halikhot Olam* (Constantinople, 1510) of Yeshu'ah b. Joseph ha-Levi. To it he appended *Mevo ha-Talmud,* attributed to Samuel ha-Nagid. He served in Constantinople as a *dayyan.* Bulat was opposed to the practice of basing halakhic rulings on the codes without studying thoroughly the actual circumstances of the case. He tended to disregard stringencies not found in the Talmud. When the Constantinople rabbis decided that a certain bill of divorce was invalid, Bulat declared it valid even against the opinion of Elijah *Mizraḥi. Some of his published responsa testify to serious differences of opinion between him and contemporary scholars. His responsa appear among those of Elijah Mizraḥi (Constantinople, 1560), and in the responsa *Oholei Tam* of Tam ibn Yaḥya, which are included in *Tummat Yesharim* (Venice, 1622). Another halakhic work of Bulat is mentioned in the *Yemin Moshe* of Moses Ventura (Mantua, 1624). He also published *Kelal Kaẓar* (Constantinople, 1532; new ed. 1936), a methodology for the study of the Torah, *halakhah,* and exegesis. He also deals with the classification of the sciences, extending the accepted system to include Jewish studies.

Bibliography: Fuenn, Keneset, 391; Rosanes, Togarmah, 1 (1930[2]), 123–4; Judah ben Joseph Bulat, *Kelal Kaẓar* (1936), introduction by M. Rabinowitz; M. Margaliot, *Sefer Hilkhot ha-Nagid* (1962), 68–73; A. Yaari, *Ha-Defus ha-Ivri be-Kushta* (1967), 86–88.

[ED.]

BULAWAYO, one of the two main commercial and industrial centers in *Rhodesia. Jews were among the earliest pioneers in Bulawayo. The first white child born there (April 1894) was Jewish, and the first newspaper (March 1894), the *Matabele Times and Mining Journal,* was owned and edited by a Jew, William Francis Wallenstein. The Hebrew Congregation was formed in that year and the

Figure 1. Moses Isaac Cohen, first minister of the Bulawayo congregation. Photo Bulawayo Hebrew congregation.

foundation stone of the synagogue building was laid in 1897. A Ḥovevei Zion society was established in 1898. In 1900, when there were 300 Jewish residents (76% of the total Jewish population of Rhodesia), Moses Isaac Cohen (1876–1939) from London became minister of the Bulawayo Hebrew Congregation. He was an active Zionist and the acknowledged leader of the Jewish community. An authority on general education, he helped plan the system

Figure 2. I. Hirschler, the first mayor of Bulawayo. Photo Central African Jewish Board of Deputies, Bulawayo.

of public education in Rhodesia and was also a mediator in industrial disputes.

Despite its remoteness, Bulawayo Jewry has been notable for its active communal and cultural life, and especially for its strong Zionist affiliation. In 1958 a primary Jewish day

Figure 3. The synagogue in Bulawayo, Rhodesia. The foundation stone was laid in 1897. Photo Bulawayo Hebrew Congregation.

school was established, which in 1968 had 158 pupils (57% of the total Jewish school attendance). There is also a Progressive congregation (established in 1956) with its own rabbi. In addition to local communal institutions, two national organizations have their headquarters in Bulawayo, both formed in 1943—the Rhodesian Zionist Council and the Rhodesian Jewish Board of Deputies.

Jews established many of the light industries, and predominate in the furniture and clothing sectors. Many are prominent in commerce and are well represented in medicine, dentistry, law, and accountancy. They have also taken an active part in civic affairs. The first mayor of Bulawayo was a Jew, I. Hirschler (1897–98); later Jewish mayors have been E. Basch (1907–11), H. B. Ellenbogen (1927–29), C. M. Harris (1934–36), A. Menashe (1965–67), and J. Goldwasser (1968–). Cecil Isidore Jacobs (1896–1967), prominent in communal and legal circles, was president of the Rhodesian Jewish Board of Deputies for seven years.

Bibliography: G. Saron and L. Hotz (eds.), *Jews in South Africa* (1955), 264–5; 272–3.

[M. WAG.]

BULGARIA, East Balkan republic located along the Black Sea.

Ancient Period. A Jewish settlement is known to have existed in Macedonia in the time of Caligula (37–41 C.E.; Philo, *Embassy to Gaius,* par. 281). A late-second century Latin inscription found at the village of Gigen on the shore of the Danube (near Nikopol, the site of the ancient Roman settlement Oescus) bearing a *menorah* testifies to the existence of a Jewish community. The Latin inscription mentions the *archisynagogos Joseph. Theodosius I's decree to the governors of Thrace and Illyria in 379 shows that Jews were persecuted in these areas and synagogues destroyed.

Byzantine and Bulgar Rule. When the Byzantine emperor Leo III (718–41) persecuted the Jews, a number of them may have fled to Bulgaria. There, during the reign of the Bulgar czar Boris I (852–89), the Jews are said to have tried to exploit the religious unrest among the Bulgars, then heathens, by converting them to Judaism, but Christian emissaries were more successful. The faith of the early Bulgarian Christians was, however, a syncretistic mixture of Christian, Jewish, and pagan beliefs. A curious insight of the contemporary religious situation is afforded by the 106 questions submitted by Bulgarian representatives to Pope Nicholas I (858–67). Among the questions on which guidance was requested were the proper regulations for offering the first fruits; the law concerning amulets; which day is the day of rest—Saturday or Sunday; which animals and poultry may be eaten; whether it is wrong to eat the flesh of an animal that has not been slaughtered; should burial rituals be performed for suicides; how many days must a husband abstain from intercourse with his wife after she has given birth; should a fast be observed during a drought; should women cover their heads in houses of prayer; and so on. The names of the Bulgarian princes at this time—David, Moses, Aaron, and Samuel—may also show Jewish influence.

The monks Cyril (Constantine) and Methodius from Salonika, who were sent to Greater Moravia in 863 by the Byzantine emperor Michael III (840–67) to convert the Moravians, had mixed with Jews in their native town and studied with Jewish teachers. Cyril invented a new script called Glagolitic (later Cyrillic) in which to write Slavonic. The script was based on the Greek alphabet, but used the Hebrew alphabet as well in order to represent sounds which did not exist in the Greek alphabet, e.g., *Sh* and *Ts.* It is believed that Cyril made his translations of parts of the Bible from the Hebrew original.

There is evidence of Jewish settlement in Nikopol in 967. In the early 12th century Leo Mung, born a Jew and later a pupil of the 11th-century Bulgarian talmudist Tobiah b. Eliezer, became archbishop of the diocese of *Ochrida and Primate of Bulgaria. The Bogomil movement, a Christian sect that spread through Bulgaria in the 11th century, rejected most books of the Old Testament, but awakened interest in Judaism as the source of certain Christian theological doctrines. The Bulgarian attitude to Jews at the time was generally favorable; Jewish merchants from Italy and Ragusa (*Dubrovnik) who settled in Bulgaria received royal privileges. Also during the Crusades many Jews may have found refuge in Bulgaria. Jacob b. Elijah in his polemical letter to the apostate Pablo *Christiani mentions two Jews who were thrown from a mountaintop for refusing to obey the order of Czar John Asen II (1218–41) to put out the eyes of Theodore I Angelus, Greek ruler of Salonika in 1230. Czar Ivan Alexander (1331–71) married a Jewish woman named Sarah, who took the name Theodora on her baptism; her influence on state affairs was considerable. The church's struggle with heresy in Bulgaria also affected the Jews. The Church Council of 1352 excommunicated Jews and heretics. Three Jews were condemned to death on a false charge of blaspheming saints. Although the verdict was repealed by the czar, the mob took vengeance on the accused.

The largest part of the Bulgarian Jewish community before the 15th century belonged to the Byzantine (Romaniot) Jewish rite. Only a minority spoke Bulgarian. The *Romaniots had their own special prayer book, which eventually was replaced by the Sephardi prayer book. They regarded the sending of gifts from the groom to the bride as

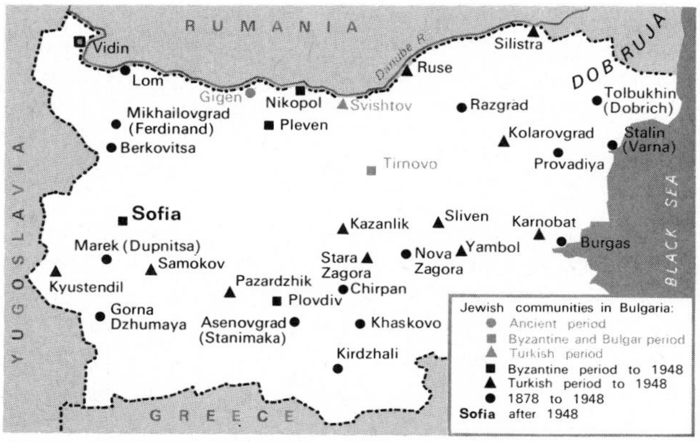

Jewish population of Bulgaria, 1878–1967.

part of the marriage ceremony, and if the bride did not later marry the sender of the gifts, she had, in their opinion, to receive a divorce *(get)* before she could marry another man (see Kid. 3:2). The bride's dowry was guarded and the husband was forbidden to negotiate with it. Furthermore, according to their custom a husband could not inherit from his wife. The Romaniots did not accept the decree of R. *Gershom b. Judah in the 11th century forbidding bigamy. Among the rabbis of the Romaniot synagogue was Abraham Semo (15th century) who befriended the new Ashkenazi community that settled in Sofia (1470). Another famous rabbi of the Romaniots was Joseph b. Isaac ibn Ezra (late 16th–early 17th centuries), who wrote the book *Massa Melekh* (1601).

Many Jews went to Bulgaria from Hungary after the expulsion of 1376. These Hungarian Jews kept their own particular customs, but later adopted the customs of the other Ashkenazim, and eventually all of them adopted Sephardi customs and spoke *Ladino. A famous contemporary sage was Rabbi Shalom Ashkenazi of Neustadt, who founded a yeshivah at *Vidin. His pupil Rabbi Dosa the Greek wrote in 1430 *Perush ve-Tosafot,* a supercommentary to Rashi on the Pentateuch.

Turkish Rule. At the time of the final Turkish conquest of Bulgaria (1396), Jews were living in Vidin, *Nikopol, Silistra, *Pleven, *Sofia, Yambol, Philippopolis (now *Plovdiv), and *Stara Zagora. Jewish refugees came to Bulgaria from Bavaria, which had banished them in 1470, and, according to various travelers, Judeo-German was heard for a long time in the streets of Sofia. Despite their adoption of Sephardi customs, language, and names, the Ashkenazi Jews maintained separate synagogues for a long time and followed the medieval German rite. The Ashkenazi prayer book was printed in 1548–50 in Salonika by R. Benjamin ha-Levi Ashkenazi of Nuremberg who was also the rabbi of the Sofia Ashkenazi community.

Spanish Jews reached Bulgaria apparently after 1494, settling in the trading towns in which Jews were then living. They came to Bulgaria from Salonika, through Macedonia, and from Italy, through Ragusa and Bosnia. Until 1640 Sofia had three separate Jewish communities—the Romaniots, the Ashkenazim, and the Sephardim. Then a single rabbi was appointed for all three communities. R. *Levi b. Ḥabib lived for a short time in Pleven and R. Joseph *Caro lived in Nikopol for 13 years (1523–36). Caro founded a yeshivah there and continued to write his great work *Beit Yosef.* In the 17th century Bulgarian Jewry was caught up in the whirlwind of the pseudo-messianic movement of Shabbetai Ẓevi; Samuel *Primo and *Nathan of Gaza, proponents of Shabbateanism, were active in Sofia in 1673.

Jews conducted trade with Turkey, Walachia, Moldavia, Ragusa, and Venice. Jewish traders were granted firmans giving them various privileges. One of the most important trading towns in the 16th century was Tatar-Pazardzhik, to which the Jewish merchants of Salonika turned after the wars with Venice (1571–73). They established commercial relations with Sofia merchants and some of them settled there as well. Merchants from *Skoplje (Turkish Üsküb) bought clothing in Salonika and sold it in Sofia and neighboring towns. In 1593 Sinan Pasha founded an annual fair at Ozundzhovo in the district of Khaskovo, southern Bulgaria. It was attended by Jews from European Turkey and Western Europe. Some Jews also farmed the taxes on European merchandise. The Jewish merchants were able to extend their commercial activities when the Ragusa merchants, who had taken part in the Bulgarian rising of 1688 against the Ottoman rule, had to give up their businesses. In Samokov some Jews owned

Figure 1. The Central Synagogue, Sofia, built in 1878. New York, YIVO.

quarries and leather tanneries. Jewish government officials of that period are also known. In the early 19th century a Jew, Bakish, of Tatar-Pazardzhik, held an important position in the court of the sultan, and proposed the introduction of a uniform system of Turkish coinage.

Independent Bulgaria. General rioting, robbery, and arson broke out in Sofia in 1878 when the Turks retreated from the town; the Jews formed their own militia and a fire brigade to prevent the Turks from setting fire to the town; the fire brigade was retained after independence. Among those who welcomed Russian General Gurko were the rabbi of Sofia. Gabriel Mercado Almosnino, and three other Jews. During the war Jewish property was looted and in Vidin, Kazanlik, and Svishtov, where the local population regarded them as supporters of the Turks, Jewish property was plundered, and Jews were expelled in atrocious circumstances; most of them fled to Adrianople and Constantinople. Before the Congress of Berlin in 1878 the major Jewish organizations of Western Europe had tried to secure equal rights for Bulgarian (as well as Serbian and Rumanian) Jewry; the Berlin Treaty included a clause obliging the Balkan countries to give equal rights to Jews. Rabbi Gabriel Almosnino attended the Bulgarian Constituent Assembly *(Sobranie)* in 1879 as the Jewish delegate *ex officio* as the chief rabbi and cosigned the constitution. In 1880 an official code to regulate the organization of the Jewish communities was formulated. Jews also participated as advisers in town councils. However, the Bulgarian population displayed signs of resentment against the Jews. Most Bulgarian political parties were steeped in anti-Semitism. The Bulgarian peasantry did all in their power to prevent Jews from acquiring land, and from time to time there were blood libels.

In 1885, during the war between Serbia and Bulgaria, Jews were drafted into the Bulgarian Army for the first time. The principle of equality concerning the defense of minority groups was emphasized after World War I in the Treaty of Neuilly (1919). However, despite all declarations, the principle of equal rights had no genuine value for Jews; in practice the various Bulgarian governments discriminated against Jews. Anti-Jewish legislation was introduced indirectly in internal clauses and in secret memoranda. Jews were not accepted at the military academy, the state bank, or in government or municipal service. The national uprising in 1923 prepared the ground for the spread of anti-Semitism and its intensification. In the difficult years that followed the Bulgarian people's wrath was channeled toward the minority groups, especially the Jews, whom they held responsible for their hardships. Anti-Semitic nationalist associations sprang up. In 1936 the Ratnik ("Warrior") anti-Semitic association was founded; it was structured on the lines of Hitlerite organizations, accepting their theory of race and adapting it to its own ideological concepts.

Pre-World War II. In the decades preceding World War II, the relative percentage of Jews within the Bulgarian population declined steadily, indicating a lower birth rate than the national average. The 1934 census showed 48,565 Jews, constituting 0.8% of the total population. (The respective percentages for the years 1920 and 1926 were 0.9 and 0.85.) In the mid-1930s more than half of Bulgaria's Jews resided in Sofia. Most Jews were engaged in commerce, and the majority were self-employed. In the prewar years, the number of wage earners showed a certain upward trend. A growing identification with Jewish national ideals characterized the intellectual development of the Bulgarian Jewish community. In the interwar period the Zionist movement completely dominated all Jewish communal organization, including the highest elected body, the Jewish Consistory. The younger generation spoke Bulgarian rather than the Ladino of their fathers.

The Zionist Movement. Bulgarian Jewry joined the movement for national revival as early as the days of Ḥovevei Zion (founded in 1882). Three Bulgarian delegates attended the First Zionist Congress in 1897 at Basle—Ẓvi *Belkovsky, Karl *Herbst, and Yehoshu'a (Joshua) *Kalef. Before the congress, in 1895, Bulgarian Jews had founded the settlement *Har-Tuv in Ereẓ Israel. However, there was also considerable emigration to other countries. In 1900 several Jews settled on the land at Kefken in Turkey, on the shores of the Black Sea. Other Bulgarian Jews took up farming in Adarpazari (in the Kocaeli district near Istanbul). Among the pioneers of Zionism in Bulgaria, the most noteworthy was Joseph Marco *Baruch. Between 1919 and 1948, during the British Mandate, 7,057 Bulgarian Jews emigrated to Palestine.

Organization of the Jewish Community. After 1878 a chief rabbinate was created, headed by a chief rabbi. In 1900 a conference of Jewish communities assembled and passed a new constitution, which, however, was not recognized by the Bulgarian government. The constitution dealt with elections to synagogue or community and school committees. The community committees chose a central council (Consistory) of Bulgarian Jewry from among their members. The council functioned independently of the chief rabbi, who was also head of the central rabbinical court. The central rabbinical court exercised authority over the rabbinical courts of Sofia, Plovdiv, and Rushchuk (now Ruse).

Education. Bulgarian Jewish education passed through three periods: (1) the period of the *meldar,* the Sephardi religious school, equivalent to the Ashkenazi *ḥeder,* which flourished in Bulgaria before national independence; (2) the period after independence during which the Alliance Israélite Universelle maintained many schools; and (3) the period of modern, national education. Jewish schools were maintained at the expense of the community. Many Jewish children, especially in large cities, attended schools of other denominations.

Rabbis and Scholars of Bulgaria. Rabbi Isaac b. Moses of Beja (16th century), who lived in Nikopol after the Turko-Walachian war (1598), wrote the book *Bayit Ne'eman* (1621). Rabbi Isaiah Morenzi (d. after 1593), who also lived in Nikopol, introduced new customs into the yeshivah founded by Joseph Caro. Another rabbi of Nikopol was Abraham b. Aziz *Borgil, author of the book *Leḥem Abbirim* (1605). Moses Alfalas of Sofia, a famous preacher, published *Va-Yakhel Moshe* (Venice, 1597). In the 18th century Solomon Shalem of Adrianopolis and Issachar Abulafia were among the famous rabbis. Chief rabbis after Bulgarian independence (1878) were Gabriel Almosnino, Moses Tadjer, Simon Dankowitz from Czechoslovakia, Mordecai Gruenwald, and Marcus *Ehrenpreis. Ẓemaḥ Rabbiner was chief preacher to the Bulgarian communities. David Pipano, author of *Ḥagor ha-Efod* (1925) and other books, was head of the rabbinical court. Other scholars of Bulgaria include Solomon *Rosanes, author of *Divrei Yemei Yisrael be-Togarmah*, the standard history of Turkish Jewry. Mention may be made also of Saul Mézan, author of *Les Juifs espagnols en Bulgarie*.

Journalism. In 1899 the Bulgarian-language newspaper *Chelovecheski prava* ("Human Rights") was published to repudiate the libels of anti-Semitic newspapers. The first Ladino newspaper, *La Alborada* ("The Dawn"), was launched in 1884. Later, Ladino publications ceased publication and were replaced by Bulgarian-language periodicals. [S.Mar.]

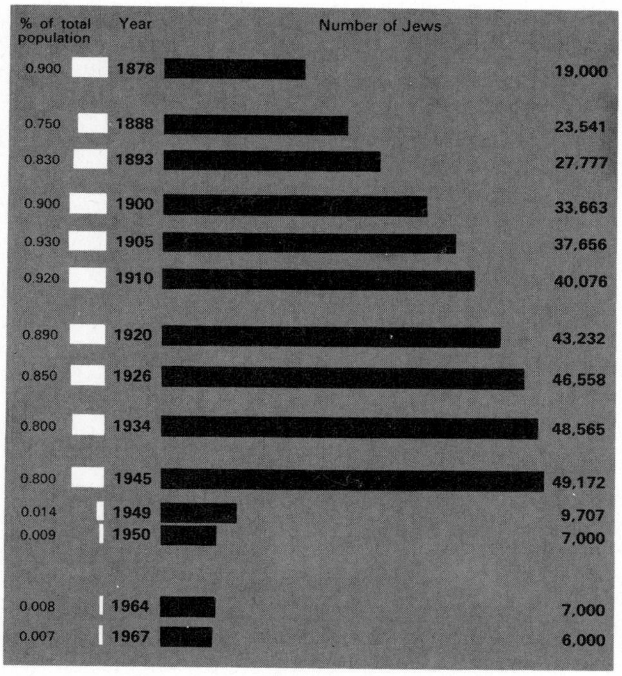

Demography of Jewish Population (within the boundaries of historical Bulgaria).

In World War II. Comprehensive anti-Jewish legislation in Bulgaria was introduced after the outbreak of World War II. The regime's main motivation in its anti-Semitic pursuits could be explained by its determination to conform to the orientation of Nazi Germany, with which Bulgaria was allied. The turning point in events came on Feb. 15, 1940, with the appointment of Bogdan Filov, a noted scientist and a determined Germanophile, to the premiership. In July 1940 the government announced its decision to curb the freedom of the Jewish minority. In August of the same year the cabinet approved the anti-Jewish "Law for the Protection of the Nation," patterned after Nazi regulations. On Dec. 24, 1940, Parliament approved the proposed legislation, which was officially promulgated on Jan. 23, 1941. On March 1, Bulgaria joined the Tripartite Pact and the German Army entered the country. A declaration of war on the western Allies followed; yet Bulgaria did not enter the war against the Soviet Union, mainly because of Slavophile sentiments. In June 1942 Minister of Interior Gabrovski, the architect of the anti-Jewish legislation, demanded and received from Parliament a blank authorization empowering the government with absolute prerogatives on all questions pertaining to the Jews. Protests against this measure, coming from such well-known democrats as Nikola Mushanov, were of no avail. At the end of August the government promulgated new restrictive regulations and provided for the establishment of a Commissariat for Jewish Affairs. On Sept. 3, 1942, the lawyer Alexander *Belev, a German-trained anti-Semite, became the head of this Commissariat.

The Deportations Program. In January 1943 Adolf Beckerle, the German minister to Sofia, was joined by SS-Obergruppenfuehrer Theodor Dannecker, an associate of *Eichmann, who came to Bulgaria in order to arrange for the deportation of Bulgarian Jews to the eastern territories. By the summer of 1942, the Bulgarian government had already surrendered into German hands Bulgarian Jews residing in countries occupied by Germany. On Feb. 2, 1943, Gabrovski and Dannecker agreed that all Jews living in Greek and Yugoslav Macedonia and in Thrace, administered by Bulgaria since the spring of 1941, would also be surrendered to the Germans for deportation. On Feb. 22, Belev and Dannecker signed a formal agreement to deport 20,000 Jews. As the total number of Jews living in Bulgarian-held Thrace and Macedonia was only slightly over 10,000, Dannecker informed Eichmann that Jews from Bulgaria proper, mainly from the capital and other large towns, would also be deported. On March 2, the government approved the surrender of 20,000 Jews into German hands, but the fiction that only Jews from Macedonia and Thrace were to be deported continued to be maintained. The collection of Macedonian and Thracian Jews into special transit camps began immediately. Preparations were also begun for the concentration of those Jews from Bulgaria proper who were to make up the agreed figure of 20,000.

Opposition to the Deportations. Rumors of the forthcoming deportations aroused unexpected opposition. An action group headed by the vice-president of the Bulgarian Parliament, Dimiter Peshev, was organized in the town of Kustendil. Peshev appeared before the minister of interior on March 9, and insisted that the deportation orders be altered forthwith. Both humanitarian and political considerations motivated the protest movement. In the aftermath of the German debacle at Stalingrad, it was thought that Bulgaria should not endanger her chances of an eventual disengagement from the German alliance by giving her hand to so monstrous an act. The initiative of Dimiter Peshev developed into a minor revolt within the government's own majority in Parliament. On March 17 Peshev presented the prime minister with a petition against the deportations signed by 42 deputies. Political figures outside Parliament and prominent figures from the Greek Orthodox Church hierarchy joined in the effort. Under the pressure, the government of Bogdan Filov decided on a compromise. It ordered all deportations of Bulgarian Jews to be stopped. The surrender of Macedonian and Thracian Jews, however, was carried out. Transported in part by

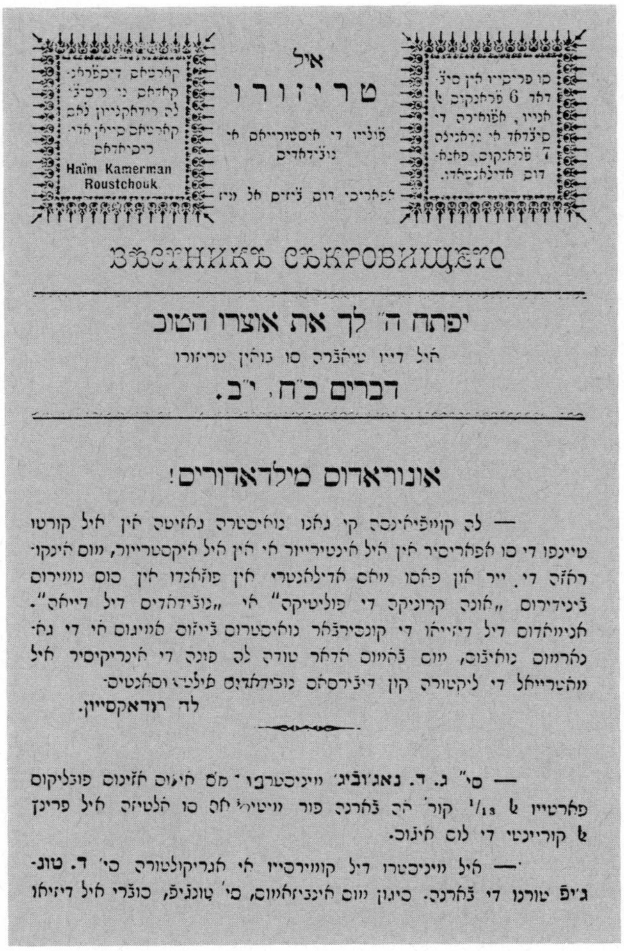

Figure 2. Front page of the Ladino newspaper *el Tresoro* ("The Treasure"), Rushchuk, Bulgaria, 1894. Jerusalem, Ben Zvi Institute.

railroad and in part by river boats on the Danube, a total of 11,384 Jews from the "new territories" were taken to the death camps in the east (Poland), where the overwhelming majority perished. Unlike the Italians, the Bulgarians treated the Jews with exceptional cruelty and strictly applied the racial restrictions: the Jews were prohibited the free use of the main thoroughfares, were not allowed to move from one town to another or to engage in commerce, had to wear the yellow badge, and were issued special yellow identity cards. Jewish houses were identified as such by a special sign. In the summer of 1942, several hundred young Jews were sent to forced labor, and in January 1943 young conscripts were sent to Bulgaria to work on road construction. Every town with a Jewish population had its commissioner for Jewish affairs, whose task it was to ensure that the anti-Jewish orders were properly carried out. Any jewelry and gold currency in the possession of Jews was confiscated and handed over to the Bulgarian national bank. Later, the government justified its action by contending that since Macedonia and Thrace were never formally annexed to Bulgaria, and since Thracian and Macedonian Jews were not given Bulgarian citizenship, the regime could not effectively withstand German pressures. On March 26, Dimiter Peshev was reprimanded by Parliament and removed from the vice-presidency. His bold intervention on behalf of the Jews of Bulgaria later helped save his life at the People's Trials held in the winter of 1945. The Nazi representatives in Sofia continued to press for the deportation of the Bulgarian Jewish community during April and May of 1943. In the light of the parliamentary upheavals of March, the government showed signs of vacillation. At the end of May it ordered the resettlement of the Jews of Sofia in the provinces as a first step toward their eventual dispatch to the death camps in the east. Neither an abortive mass demonstration attempted by the Jews of Sofia on May 24, nor several protestations by pro-Jewish public figures prevented the execution of the order. Furthermore, several hundred prominent Jewish families were sent to the Somovit concentration camp established on the banks of the Danube. Throughout the war male Jews continued to work in forced labor camps, employed in various public construction projects. With these programs, the summit of anti-Jewish persecution was reached, and the gravest danger of deportation to the German-occupied eastern territories passed. On Aug. 28, 1943, King Boris III died under somewhat mysterious circumstances. According to N. Oren, Boris showed no special affection for the Jews of his country, nor did he exhibit any particular humanitarian inclinations. The contention that Boris' own act of benevolence had prevented the deportation of the Jews from Bulgaria proper is without firm foundation, but, in common with his government, Boris responded to the pressures from below generated by Peshev and his friends. According to Nuremberg Document No. NG-062, although Boris had agreed to the deportation of Jews from Macedonia and Thrace, he was unwilling to deport Jews from Bulgaria proper, with the exception of "Bolshevist-Communist elements." The other Bulgarian Jews were to be sent to forced-labor camps to work on road construction.

Abolishment of Anti-Jewish Policies. In September a Regency Council and a new government headed by Dobri Bozhilov were established. Minister of Interior Gabrovski was not included in the new cabinet. Belev, the head of the Commissariat for Jewish Affairs, was also dropped and replaced by the more moderate Khristo Stomaniakov. In December the resettled Jews of Sofia were allowed to return to the capital for brief periods in order to attend to private affairs. Early in 1944 a small number of Jewish families were permitted to leave the country for Palestine. These and other signs of relaxation were aimed at establishing Bulgaria's greater independence in foreign affairs, and the Bozhilov regime's effort to appear more reasonable in the eyes of the western Allies. Representations on behalf of the Bulgarian Jewish community by Jewish organizations to both Washington and London produced a number of Allied protests, communicated to the Bulgarian government throughout 1943 and 1944. At the end of May 1944 the cabinet of Bozhilov was replaced by a new cabinet headed by Ivan Bagrianov. Determined to extricate Bulgaria from her war involvement, the Bagrianov regime opened truce negotiations with the western Allies. Earlier, secret talks were held between Nikola Balabanov, Bulgaria's minister to Turkey, and Ira Hirschmann, representative of the United States War Refugee Board. In August Hirschmann was informed of the decision of the Sofia government to abolish all anti-Jewish measures. On Aug. 24 the minister of interior told representatives of the Bulgarian Jewish community that the Commissariat for Jewish Affairs had been abolished. All anti-Jewish legislation was officially abrogated on Aug. 29. The decrees of abolition were published on Sept. 5, 1944, by which time a new government, headed by the democratically oriented agrarian leader Kosta Muraviev, had come to power.

On Sept. 5, 1944, while truce talks were being held between Bulgarian and Anglo-American representatives in Cairo, the Soviet Union declared war on Bulgaria. On Sept. 8, the Soviet Army entered the country, and on the following day the Muraviev government was overthrown and replaced by a coalition government of the Fatherland Front, which was dominated by the Bulgarian Communist

Party. Following an armistice agreement, signed in Moscow on Oct. 28, 1944, Bulgaria was placed under the surveillance of a Soviet-controlled Allied Control Commission, which governed the country until the ratification of a peace treaty in 1947. With the institution of the Fatherland Front regime, organized Jewish life was reestablished. After September 1944 there existed 34 Jewish communities headed by a Central Jewish Consistory as well as a Jewish weekly, *Yevreyski vesti* ("Jewish News"), and an anti-Fascist Jewish society named "Ilya Ehrenburg." According to Consistory figures, there were a total of 49,172 Jews in the country in the autumn of 1945. More than three-quarters of them lived in seven urban communities: Sofia, 27,700; Plovdiv, 5,800; Ruse, 1,927; Varna, 1,223; Kustendil, 1,100; Yambol, 1,076; Dupnitsa, 1,050.

The Postwar Period. Revival of Jewish Life. From the beginning of the Fatherland Front's rule, Jewish communal life fell under the control of the Communists and their sympathizers. Jewish communities were controlled by the Central Jewish Committee of the Fatherland Front, which was in turn subordinate to the Front's Commission for National Minorities. The Communists supervised the Central Jewish Consistory, and, as a rule, policy statements were signed jointly by the Central Jewish Committee and the Consistory. In January 1945 the official Jewish Communist leaders announced Bulgarian Jewry's severance from all international Jewish organizations, Zionist or otherwise. Bulgarian Jews were to be considered Bulgarians of Jewish origin, having nothing in common with other communities around the world. The Zionist organization was called bourgeois and chauvinist. The majority of Bulgarian Jews, however, continued to support the Zionist organization. In 1946 its president, Vitali Haimov, claimed 13,000 active members. Zionist organizations continued to function in the face of continuous harassment. Independent weeklies were published until 1948 by the General Zionists and Po'alei Zion. The majority of Jewish youth were organized by He-Ḥalutz ha-Ẓa'ir and *Ha-shomer Ha-Ẓa'ir.

Figure 3. Maran Beth Joseph synagogue, Nikopol, Bulgaria, destroyed by the Nazis in 1943. Sofia, Jewish Scientific Institute.

Since political power resided with the Jewish Communists, whereas rank-and-file support was given to the Zionist groups, the Communists, under the leadership of Zhak Natan, undertook to absorb the Zionists by way of "unification" in the common "struggle against anti-Semitism and Fascism." In May 1946 the Zionist groups joined the Communists in a formal agreement providing equal representation in the Consistory, the Central Jewish Committee of the Fatherland Front, and all other Jewish communal organizations. An effective Communist majority was assured, however, since the balance of power was in favor of pro-Communist Jewish Social Democrats and pro-Communist "non-partisans."

Economic Restitution. The economic condition of Bulgarian Jews was desperate. Immediate restitution of property lost during the war was essential if the Jewish population was to recover from the deep poverty to which it had been reduced. In March 1945 the government passed the Law of Restitution, providing for the return of all Jewish rights and property, but many months passed before the law began to be enforced. Determined to achieve the eventual socialization of all property, the Fatherland Front regime actually prevented the execution of its own laws. Throughout the existence of the Front, there continued to be a huge discrepancy between the letter of the Law of Restitution and its implementation. Only a small part of Jewish losses were actually recovered, and these were further reduced by the postwar inflation. Thanks to relief measures from international Jewish organizations, a large number of Bulgarian Jews were able to carry on until their eventual emigration. The regime exhibited greater interest in punishing those guilty of anti-Jewish persecutions during the war. A special section of the People's Court, set up at the end of 1944, dealt with crimes against the Jews, and the sentences it issued were among the most severe in postwar Europe.

Exodus to Israel. During the first two years of its tenure, the Fatherland Front regime expressed open hostility to Jewish emigration, particularly to Palestine. The first signs of change in this attitude came in 1946. The reversal of Soviet policy on Palestine was reflected in Bulgaria and reinforced by local conditions that showed the Zionist movement to be much more influential in the Jewish population than expected. Upon assuming the premiership in December 1946, the veteran Communist leader Georgi Dimitrov told a group of Jewish leaders that, in principle, resettlement in Palestine would be allowed. The real turn in events came with Gromyko's U.N. speech in favor of the partition of Palestine and the establishment of an independent Jewish state. Although they supported the Jewish efforts in Palestine, the Communist Jewish leaders continued their assault on all Zionist manifestations at home. Ironically, the campaign against local Zionists was intensified alongside growing Jewish Communist support for the Haganah and Israel's War of Independence. Throughout the postwar period "illegal" movement from Bulgaria to Palestine was considered a crime. On several occasions frontier guards shot and killed Jewish youth attempting to leave the country clandestinely, though groups of children whose *aliyah* certificates had been issued within the framework of the Youth Aliyah movement during the wartime regime were allowed to leave legally. Only after the United Nations' Partition Plan was voted upon did the regime permit the emigration of able-bodied young men and women, who were to join in the "fight against imperialism."

Between September 1944 and October 1948, 7,000 Bulgarian Jews left for Palestine. The exodus was due to deep-rooted Zionist sentiments, a relative alienation from

Bulgarian intellectual and political life, and depressed economic conditions. Humanitarian considerations and a general feeling of goodwill on the part of the Bulgarian people helped to ease the process of resettlement. The Bulgarian Communist Party was not weakened by the exodus because few Communist Jews held central positions of power. Bulgarian policies toward national minorities were also a factor that motivated emigration. In the late 1940s Bulgaria was anxious to rid itself of national minority groups, such as Armenians and Turks, and thus make its population more homogeneous. Further numbers were allowed to depart in the winter of 1948 and the spring of 1949. The mass exodus continued (between 1949 and 1951, 44,267 Jews emigrated to Israel) until only a few thousand Jews remained in the country. Their estimated number in the late 1960s was 7,000, half of whom reside in Sofia, 1,000 in Plovdiv, and the remainder in other cities.

CONTEMPORARY LIFE. The organized religious life of the community has steadily declined, and there are no recognized rabbis to provide leadership or religious schools to perpetuate Jewish education. The rate of intermarriage is on the increase. Religious affairs are directed by the Jewish Religious Council, which is affiliated with the Cultural and Educational Society of Jews in Bulgaria, a non-religious, Communist-dominated organization that replaced the Consistory in 1957 and is responsible for conducting Jewish affairs and officially representing the Jewish community. It conducts lectures, supports a theater group, and has presented programs and exhibitions honoring Jewish anti-Nazi resistance. The Bulgarian Academy of Sciences published a number of works on Jewish subjects, among them an authoritative collection of responsa pertinent to the economic history of the Balkan Jews (A. Hananel and E. Eškenazi, *Fontes Hebraici* . . . , 2 vols., 1958–60, Heb., Bul., Fr.). The Hebrew Scientific Institute was founded in 1947; since 1952 it was a part of the Bulgarian Academy of Sciences. The Jewish Religious Council also continues to publish *Yevreyski vesti,* which incorporates news from the Jewish press in other countries—including news on Israel. The Bulgarian government looks with disfavor on ties with other Jewish communities, but the remnant of Bulgarian Jews lives free from persecution. [NI.O.]

Relations with Israel. Bulgaria recognized the State of Israel upon its establishment, and formed diplomatic ties with her. The two states also developed trade relations. Over the years, however, Bulgaria grew closer and closer to the official Soviet line on relations with Israel. In the process of deteriorating relations, a Bulgarian Air Force plane shot down an El Al passenger plane that had crossed the Bulgarian border in error in August 1955, killing all the passengers aboard. In 1967, after the *Six-Day War, Bulgaria severed diplomatic relations and discontinued trade relations with Israel (the expected turnover for 1967 was to have been about $10 million). In addition, Bulgarian representatives in the U.N. were conspicuous in the sharpness of their attacks against Israel. In the beginning of 1968, however, Bulgaria resumed trade relations with Israel. [E.P.]

Bibliography: Rosanes, Togarmah, passim; idem, in: *El mondo sefardi* (Ladino, 1923), 33–38; P. Meyer, *Jews in the Soviet Satellites* (1953), 559–629; Belkovsky, in: *Ha-Perotokol shel ha-Congress ha-Ẓiyyoni ha-Rishon: Maẓẓav ha-Yehudim be-Vulgaryah* (1947); Marcus, in: *Sinai,* 26 (1950), 236–46; idem, in: *Mirah u-Ma'arav,* 4 (1930), 152–8; idem, in: *Maḥberet,* I (1952), 30–31; 3 (1954), 61–62; 10 (1961), 19–23; S. Mézan, *Juifs espagnols en Bulgarie* (1925); N. M. Gelber, in: JSOS, 8 (1946), 103–26; N. Greenberg (ed.), *Dokumenti* (Bul., 1945); N. Oren, in: *Yad Vashem Studies,* 7 (1968), 83–106; *Bulgarian Atrocities in Greek Macedonia and Thrace* (Athens, 1945); R. Kashani, *Sekirat Sefarim al ha-Yahadut be-*. . . *Bulgaryah* (1962); B. Arditi, *Yehudei Bulgaryah bi-Shenot ha-Mishtar ha-Nazi* (1962); BJPES, 2 (1935), 19–25; *Godishnik* ("Yearbook"), 1 (1966), 63–79 (Eng. summ. 178); 2 (1967), 21–40 (Eng. 232–3), 65–110 (Eng. 236–7); 3 (1968), 31–58 (Eng. 201–2); J. Caleb, *La situation des Juifs en Bulgarie* (1919); A. Hananel and E. Eškenazi, *Fontes hebraici ad res œconomicas socialesque terrarum balcanicarum,* 2 vols. (1958–60); S. Levy, in: *Cahiers Sefardis,* 1 (1947), 142–6; F. B. Chary, in: *East European Quarterly,* 4 (1970), 88–93.

BULGARIAN LITERATURE. The early history of Bulgarian literature is closely linked with that of the Bulgarian language, and with both there are interesting Jewish associations. During the 9th century C.E., as part of his proselytizing campaign in the Balkans, the missionary monk Cyril of Salonika (also called Constantine the Philosopher) created Glagolitic, the basic Slav alphabet, later modified by Clement of Ohrid to form the Cyrillic alphabet. Since the Greek symbols on which this was based could not convey all the phonemes of the old Slav tongue, several consonantal symbols had to be drawn from other sources, including the Hebrew alphabet which yielded Б (ב), Ц (צ), Ч (ץ), Ш (ש), and Щ(ש)—the phonetic equivalents of *b, ts, ch, sh,* and *shch.* This new alphabet facilitated the translation of Greek liturgical works into the new literary language—Old Church Slavonic (or Bulgarian)—to which Cyril, his brother Methodius, and perhaps such of their pupils as Clement, added a version of the Bible, reputedly translated from the original Hebrew. According to some authorities, they had learned Hebrew from the Jews of Salonika and Kherson; Cyril and Methodius also translated part of a Hebrew grammar. The influence of a Hebrew textual source (as well as of Greek or Latin translations) has been detected in an Old Church Slavonic version of the Psalms—the 12th-century *Psalterium Sinaiticum*—now in the possession of the St. Catherine's Monastery in the Sinai Peninsula. Other medieval Bulgarian works translated or drawn from Jewish sources include *Shestodnev* ("The Six Days"), an account of the creation of the world in the biblical tradition, composed by Ioan (John) the Exarch (b. 860). During the 11th and 12th centuries the Bogomils—a heretical Christian sect, the Western counterparts of which were known as the Cathars or Albigensians—produced a literature rich in biblical themes.

The Figure of the Jew in Bulgarian Literature. From the beginning of the Bulgarian national revival in the early 19th century, most Bulgarian writers instinctively sympathized with their Jewish fellow-victims of oppression. While protesting against anti-Semitism, some of these non-Jewish writers portrayed Jewish suffering as a tragic destiny, while others advocated a solution to the problem, either through total emancipation or Zionism. Authors in the first category were Peyo (Kracholov) Yavorov (1877–1914), a leading symbolist poet who wrote *Yevrei* ("Jews," 1901) on Jewish martyrdom; Petko Yordanov Todorov (1879–1916), whose *Kamuni* ("Stones") published in *Idilii* (1908) describes the Jewish tragedy; and the versatile Petko Rachev Slaveykov (1827–1895), who portrayed Jewish suffering with an elegiac pathos reminiscent of the Psalms in his poem *"Plachete za oniez"* ("Weep for These," 1852). The poet and playwright Emanuil Pop Dimitrov (1885–1943) used his knowledge of Bulgarian Jewry in two biblical works, *Deshcherite na Yeftaya* ("Jephthah's Daughter") and *Rut* ("Ruth"), which appeared between the world wars. On the other hand, there were writers like Konstantin Konstantinov (1890–) who, after World War I, regarded the Jew as a comrade in the struggle for social justice. Jewish participation in the Bulgarian national movement is a prominent theme of the novel *Robi* ("Slaves," 1930) by the social writer Anton Strashimirov (1872–1937); Aleko Konstantinov (1863–1897), outraged by the police brutality against Joseph Marcou *Baruch, the founder of the Bulgarian Zionist movement, wrote a pro-Jewish pamphlet entitled *I sega biyat, brate moy* ("We Fight On, My Brother," 1921). Other works in this genre were E.P. Dimitrov's *Yevrei* ("Jews"), and *Poslednata kal* ("The Last Mud," 1929), a story by Yordan Kovachev (1875–1934). Hostile treatment of the Jew is rare in Bulgarian literature, the one outstanding example being the classic drama *Kem propast* ("Toward the Abyss," 1910) by the prolific Ivan Vazov (1850–1921). In this play, which has a medieval setting, the central character, Queen Theodora, is shown to have been responsible for the defeat of her realm. The figure of Theodora is directly inspired by the converted Jewess, originally named Sarah, whom the Bulgarian czar Ivan Alexander married in 1335. Periodically from the late-19th century and especially during the decade of Fascist rule (1934–1944), some pamphleteers and journalists encouraged anti-Semitic tendencies, but their activities gained little popular support.

After World War II Bulgarian writers generally saw the Jew as an anti-fascist hero. In his novel *Na zhivot ili smert* ("Life or Death," 1953) Dimitur Anghelov (1904–) portrays the Jewish democrat Sami Mevorakh executed by the Fascists; Dimitur Dimov (1909–1966) brings several Jewish characters into his novel *Tyutyun* ("Tobacco," 1953), sympathetically describing the Communist Max Eshkenazi and the partisan Varvara, and including some dialogue in Judeo-Spanish (Ladino); while Dimitur Talev (1898–1966) introduces into his novel *Glasovete vi chuyam* ("I Hear Your Voices," 1954) several Jewish heroes, including a young Macedonian revolutionary. Similar figures also appear in the novel *Krayat na delnite* ("The End of the Brigands," 1955) by Emil Manov (1918–); in the play *Borbata produlzhava* ("The Fight Continues," 1945) by Krum Kulyavkov (1893–1955), and in a number of other works. In the tragedy *Ivan Shishman* (1962) by Kamen Zidarov (1902–), Queen Theodora (whom Ivan Vazov had earlier treated rather unsympathetically) is presented in a positive light.

The Jewish Contribution to Bulgarian Literature. It was only after World War I that Jews began to write literary works in Bulgarian, Ladino having previously served as their principal vehicle of cultural expression. The pioneer in this field was a gifted poet Dora Gabe (1886–), the daughter of a Russian-Jewish immigrant; she later became president of the Bulgarian branch of the PEN Club. Haim Benadov (1908–), an exponent of the short satirical novel, wrote several works depicting the life of poor Jews in a suburb of Sofia. Three Jewish poets who dedicated their writing to the Zionist ideal were Oram ben Ner (pseudonym of Saul Mezan, 1893–1944), who wrote *Pesni za Erusalim* ("Songs for Jerusalem," 1924); Simcho Isakov (1919–1949), author of *Stikhove* ("Poems," 1953); and Leo Kohen, who published *Moyat narod* ("My People," 1930) and *Poeziya i zhivot* ("Poetry and Life," 1938). Another Jewish writer, Bucha Bekhar, wrote popular stories of country life. Jews who distinguished themselves as literary critics include Moise Benaroya; Albert Mikhael wrote plays and was a prolific contributor to the Jewish press; and political writers and journalists of note include Benjamin and Eliezer Arditti, Joseph Israël, Isak Naimovich, and Joseph Herbst, who was murdered by the Fascists. This short, but important Jewish contribution to Bulgarian literary life undoubtedly inspired the petition which the leading Bulgarian writers addressed to the Bulgarian parliament in 1940, protesting against the proposed law aimed at depriving Bulgarian Jews of their citizenship. Many more Jewish authors gained eminence after World War II and especially during the 1960s, when the Bulgarian Writers' Union included ten Jewish members, headed by Dora Gabe. Armand Barukh (1908–) was mainly known for his novel *Ralevi* (1955), while Viktor Barukh (1921–) was the author of the novella *Yaponskata kukla* ("The Japanese Doll," 1965). Three important Jewish poets were Valeri Petrov (1920–), son of the jurist, Professor Nissim Mevorakh, whose best-known work was *V mekata esen* ("In the Sweet Autumn," 1961); David d'Ovadia (1923–), whose works salute wartime resistance heroes; and Salis Tadjer (1924–), a novelist as well as a poet, whose verse collections include *Kopnezh v pustinyata* ("The Dream in the Desert," 1960), *Bulgariya v mene* ("Bulgaria Within Me," 1964), and *Ako zabravya* ("If I Forget," 1966). The outstanding Bulgarian Jewish playwright of the 1960s was Dragomir Asenov (pseudonym of Jacques Melamed, 1926–), who wrote such highly successful plays as *Rozhden den* ("Birthday," 1965), and *Rozi za Doktor Shomov* ("Roses for Dr. Shomov," 1967). Other noted postwar writers were Haim Oliver (1918–), Albert Dekalo (1920–), and Angel Wagenstein (1922–). The two leading Jewish literary critics were Yako Molkhov (1915–), author of *Problemi na dneshniya bulgarski roman* ("Problems of the Contemporary Bulgarian Novel," 1956); and Maxim Naimovich (1921–), who also wrote fiction. A few Jewish writers in Bulgaria have also dealt with specifically Jewish themes, particularly the events of the recent past. The fate of one Jew provides the *leitmotiv* of a trilogy of novels by Dragomir Asenov: *Kafyavi khorizonti* ("Brown Horizons," 1961), *Golyamnyat kamenen dom* ("The Big Stone House," 1963), and *Plodut na vetrovete* ("The Fruit of the Winds," 1966). Viktor Barukh sets his novels *Otrecheni ot zakona* ("Outlaws," 1960) and *Svatbeni sveshchi* ("Wedding Candles," 1968) in the Bulgarian Fascist era; but in the latter work courageously implied that anti-Semitism had become a problem under the Communist regime. For this Barukh received praise from party critics. There is a similar background in Salis Tadjer's story *Zhakito* ("Jacquito," 1967), in *Zheltata zvezda* ("The Yellow Star," 1964), and in a biographical sketch of the anti-fascist heroine Anna Ventura, *Nashata Ana* ("Our Anna," 1963). Two works on Jewish themes by the novelist Haim Benadov, a committed Jew, the first written on the eve of World War I and the second a quarter-century later, are *Khora ot nizinite* ("The People of the Abyss," 1939) and *Sreshchu praznika* ("On the Eve of the Holiday," 1965).

Bibliography: L. Kohen, in: *Biblioteka Probuda*, 2 no. 6 (1939); G. Konstantinov, et al., *Bŭlgarski pisateli: biografii i bibliografii* (1961); Ts. Minkov (ed.); *Bŭlgarska literatura*, 1 (1962); *Evrei, zaginali v antifashistkata borba* (1958).

[S.M.I.]

BULLS, PAPAL, generally official statements by the head of the Roman Catholic Church. Although the term "Bull" (from the Latin *bullum*, "seal") was sometimes applied to imperial documents as well, its use has been limited as defined above. Bulls bearing the seal of the reigning pope and dealing with matters of Jewish interest were fairly numerous in the Middle Ages, though they constituted a small fraction of the vast papal correspondence; in recent centuries their number has decreased. Earlier they took the form of letters addressed to prelates, to secular rulers, to the Christian faithful in general, and in rare instances directly to Jews. Later, they increasingly took the form of memoranda (briefs outlining policy), headed by the phrase *Ad futuram rei memoriam* ("A reminder for the future"). Either type of document usually began with a statement of

Title page of papal bull by Gregory XIII, 1581, forbidding Jewish and infidel (Muslim) doctors to treat Christian patients. Jerusalem, Medical Association of Israel.

general attitude, proceeded to a discussion of the specific problem involved, continued with the pope's decision on the resolution of the problem, and concluded with a statement of the penalties for disobedience. The statement of attitude frequently cited scriptural verses or referred back to the authority of the incumbent's predecessors. The following are examples of some of the more significant papal bulls concerning the Jews, illustrative of Church policy. They are identified, as usual, by their initial words.

Sicut Judaeis, first issued by *Calixtus II around 1120, was a general Bull of Protection for the Jews, who had suffered at the hands of participants in the First Crusade (1095–96) and were being maltreated by their Christian neighbors. It forbade killing them, using force to convert them, and otherwise molesting them, their synagogues, and cemeteries. The bull was modeled on a letter, which began with the same phrase, sent to the bishop of Palermo by Pope *Gregory I in 598, objecting to the use of force as a conversionary method. Calixtus' formulation was repeated by most of the popes from the 12th to the 15th centuries. They often added references to problems current in their day. Several of them condemned the accusation of ritual murder (see *blood libel).

Post miserabile, by *Innocent III in 1198, was addressed to the prelates of Europe and dealt at length with the need for another crusading effort in the Holy Land. Among the privileges granted to those who took the cross was the protection of their property while they were away, including the suspension of payment of principal and interest on their debts to Jews. The formula in which this suspension was expressed became standard in calls to Crusades which followed in the next few centuries.

Etsi non displiceat, by Innocent III in 1205, addressed to the king of France, is a list of accusations against the Jews: usury, blasphemy, arrogance, employing Christian slaves, and even murder. The king is urged to put a stop to the evils. Yet the same "evils" continue to be mentioned by various popes for centuries and to be completely disregarded by others.

In generali concilio, by *Honorius III in 1218, addressed to the archbishop of Toledo, demanded the enforcement of the decision of the Fourth *Lateran Council that Jews wear clothing to distinguish them from Christians; also that Jews be made to pay the tithe to local churches. Both items were frequently repeated by later popes.

Etsi Judaeorum, by *Gregory IX in 1233, addressed to the prelates of France, urged the prevention of attacks on the Jews, usually motivated by greed. The sentiment, if not the exact words, was repeated by a number of popes in the 14th and 15th centuries.

Si vera sunt, also by Gregory IX, in 1239, addressed to the kings and prelates of France and Spain, ordered the seizure and examination of the Talmud and all other Jewish books suspected of blasphemies against Jesus and Christianity. The burning of such Jewish books was ordered several times from the 13th to the 16th centuries.

Lachrymabilem Judaeorum, by *Innocent IV in 1247, addressed to the prelates of Germany in response to Jewish complaints, urged an end to murder and persecution on the baseless blood libel. Several other popes made the same plea, but neither consistently nor forcefully.

Turbato corde, by *Clement IV in 1267, addressed to the inquisitors of heresy, expressed dismay over the rumor that Jews were trying to induce Christians (possibly converts from Judaism) to turn to their religion. Charges of such Judaizing activity were raised frequently by later popes.

Vineam Soreth, by *Nicholas III in 1278, addressed to Franciscans in Austria and Lombardy, ordered the selection of trained men to preach Christianity to the Jews. Secular rulers were requested not to interfere with the preachers. Henceforward, frequent reference is made to this method of missionizing among Jews.

Quamvis perfidiam, by *Clement VI in 1348, addressed to various prelates, urged the protection of Jews against the accusation that they had brought on the *Black Death by poisoning the wells. It was an instance of specific application of protection in the face of a threat to Jewish life.

Etsi doctoribus gentium, by antipope *Benedict XIII (Peter of Luna) in 1415, a brief for the guidance of Church policy, was one of the most complete collections of anti-Jewish laws. Though not by a recognized pope, it served as a precedent for several later popes.

Numquam dubitavimus, by *Sixtus IV in 1482, empowered Ferdinand of Aragon to appoint inquisitors to extirpate heresy and to prevent Jewish practices among those who had been converted to Christianity.

Cum nimis absurdum, by *Paul IV in 1555, was a brief in the spirit of antipope Benedict XIII. It established the ghetto in Rome, limited Jewish economic activities, prohibited more than one synagogue in a town, and forbade contact between Jews and Christians.

Hebraeorum gens, by Pius V in 1569, a brief, accused the Jews of many evils, including the practice of magic. It ordered the expulsion of the Jews from all papal territory, excepting Rome and Ancona.

Sancta mater ecclesia, by *Gregory XIII in 1584, confirming his *Vices eius nos* of 1577, ordered the Jews of Rome to send 100 men and 50 women every Saturday afternoon to listen to conversionist sermons which were delivered in a church near the ghetto.

Christiana pietas, by *Sixtus V in 1586, relieved the Jews of many oppressive social and economic restrictions which had been imposed upon them by Paul IV and Pius V. They enjoyed this relief for only a few years, for in 1593 *Clement VIII issued a number of edicts restoring the previous situation which remained in force till the 19th century.

Bibliography: *Dictionnaire de droit canonique,* 2 (1937), s.v. *Bulle;* M. Stern, *Urkundliche Beitraege ueber die Stellung der Paepste zu den Juden* (1893–95), passim. SICUT JUDAEIS. S. Grayzel, in: HJ, 2 (1940), 1–12; idem, in: *Studies and Essays . . . A. A. Neuman* (1962), 243ff.; cf. Baron, Social[2], 4 (1957), 7ff., and 235 nn. 3, 4. POST MISERABILE: S. Grayzel, *The Church and the Jews in the XIIIth Century* (1933), 86–87. ETSI NON DISPLICEAT and IN GENERALI CONCILIO: *ibid.,* 144–7. ETSI JUDAEORUM: *ibid.,* 200–3. SI VERA SUNT: *ibid.,* 240–3. LACHRYMABILEM JUDAEORUM: *ibid.,* 286–7. TURBATO CORDE: P. Browe, *Die Judenmission im Mittelatter* (1942), 258, n.216. VINEAM SORETH: *ibid.,* 30, n.57. QUAMVIS PERFIDIAM: A. Lang, *Acta salzburgo-aquilejensia,* 1 (1906), 302; cf. Baer, Spain, 2 (1966), 27f. ETSI DOCTORIBUS GENTIUM: J. Amador de los Ríos, *Historia social, política y religiosa de los Judíos,* 2 (1875–76), 626–53. NUMQUAM DUBITAVIMUS: F. Fita y Colomer, *La España hebrea,* 1 (1889–98), 83ff. CUM NIMIS ABSURDUM: Vogelstein-Rieger, 2 (1895), 152; E. Rodoconachi, *Le-Saint-Siège et les Juifs* (1891), 173. HEBRAEORUM GENS: Vogelstein-Rieger, 2 (1895), 167ff. SANCTA MATER ECCLESIA: *ibid.,* 173; A. Milano, *Il ghetto di Roma* (1964), 269–81. CHRISTIANA PIETAS: *ibid.,* 269–81; Vogelstein-Rieger, 2 (1895), 173, 183–6.

[S.G.]

BULOFF, JOSEPH (1899–), U.S. Yiddish actor. At the age of 20 Buloff played with the Vilna Troupe, performing in Russian, German, Yiddish, and Polish. In 1926 he was invited by Maurice *Schwartz to join the Yiddish Art Theater in New York. After he worked with him for about a year he became director of the Jewish Literary and Dramatic Society in Chicago (1927–29). In the thirties Buloff began to act in English. In 1951 he directed *Mrs. McThing* on Broadway, which he staged in Hebrew in Israel. He appeared in the Broadway version of John Hersey's *The Wall* and on television. In 1968 he toured with *The Kibbitzer* in Israel where he later settled.

[R.SH.]

BUND (abbr. of **Algemeyner Yidisher Arbeter Bund in Lite, Poyln un Rusland;** "General Jewish Workers' Union in Lithuania, Poland and Russia"), Jewish socialist party founded in Russia in 1897; after a certain ideological development it came to be associated with devotion to Yiddish, autonomism, and secular Jewish nationalism, envisaging Jewish life as lived out in Eastern Europe (*"Doykeyt";* "Hereness," in Bund ideology), sharply opposed to Zionism and other conceptions of a world-embracing Jewish national identity.

Beginnings (Pre-Bund). The structure and ideology of the Bund, while stemming from the social patterns and needs, from the problems and tensions within Jewish society in the *Pale of Settlement in the second half of the 19th century, were also an outcome of the aims, tendencies within, divisions in, and methods of the Russian socialist movement in the multinational empire of the czars.

The first stirrings of the Jewish labor movement in general, and the formation of the Bund subsequently, occurred in "Jewish Lithuania," i.e., the six northwestern Lithuanian-Belorussian provinces with some adjoining districts, headed by Vilna. From here came the earliest leaders and pioneers of the Bund. In this region the working element was relatively important in Jewish society and its proportion among the proletariat (occupied in crafts and industry) in the cities and towns was higher than elsewhere. The trend to *assimilation was less strong in a region where sociocultural and political conflict among the Russian, Polish, Lithuanian, and Belorussian elements was rife, none of whose aims appealed to the Jewish population which had attained independently a high cultural standard, exemplified in its celebrated yeshivot. From the Lithuanian-Belorussian provinces the Jewish labor movement spread only gradually to Poland and the Ukraine.

The Jewish labor movement, in particular "pre-Bund" and Bund socialism, drew its support from three sectors in Jewish society. The first, the hired-worker class, was just then assuming corporate consciousness and cohesion as an outcome of the capitalization of the crafts and the breakup of the traditional craft associations *(*ḥevrot),* which brought about the separate organization of apprentices (from the mid-19th century especially in the garment industry). Sporadic strikes had taken place in the 1870s among the textile and tobacco workers. Secondly, there were the circles of the radical intelligentsia who in this region combined revolutionary ideas and Marxist ideology with feelings of involvement with their Jewish identity and of responsibility toward the Jewish proletariat. Finally there was the semi-intelligentsia, who, though lacking a formal general education, were deeply rooted in Jewish culture.

In the 1870s Aaron Samuel *Liebermann and his circle made the first attempts to spread socialist ideas among the Jewish people in their own language and to start a revolutionary movement. From the 1880s this became a continuous development creating the Jewish labor movement.

Study circles for Jewish intellectuals to promote culture and socialism among Jewish working men were formed in Vilna during 1886 and 1887, and all their activities were conducted in Russian. Workers' mutual assistance funds were founded and attempts were also made to found artels. Gradually, however, the ideology of these circles changed, and, from following the traditional populist position taken by Russian socialists, turned to Marxism as advocated by Plekhanov. The circles of intelligentsia also gradually changed their attitude toward the Jewish artisan and abandoned their former "cosmopolitan" stand, which in practice had meant the "Russification" of the Jewish elements in Russia.

The change matured through several stages during the years 1890 to 1895, in which a leading part was taken by A. I. *Kremer, S. *Gozhanski, J. *Mill, I. Eisenstadt, Z. *Kopelsohn, V. *Kossovski, and A. *Mutnik(ovich), among others. The number of circles and their membership increased, while efforts to obtain an amelioration of working conditions were intensified, in particular to shorten the working day in the sock-knitting, tobacco, and tailoring trades where conditions were notoriously disgraceful.

In addition to the general revolutionary tension in Russia at this time, unrest among Jews was enhanced by the widespread anti-Semitism in general society and government circles, which, combined with the social and economic constriction in the overcrowded *shtetl,* also led to massive emigration, and revived Ḥovevei Zion activity (see *Zionism). Eventually the leaders of these circles reached the conclusion that Jewish workers could and must form their own socialist labor movement, since their specific circumstances necessitated demands which were largely peculiar to the Jewish worker. They also considered that the Jewish environment in general was more objectively receptive to the idea of opposition to and revolt against the authoritarian czarist regime. A new line of action was formulated by Kremer in his "On Agitation" that was to influence the whole Russian Social Democratic movement. Elaborated by Gozhanski ("Letter to Agitators," 1893) and Julius *Martov (May Day lecture, 1895), it called for a change from activity in closed propaganda "circles" to mass "agitation" in order to rally workers to struggle for better conditions as a "phase" toward revolutionary political consciousness and activity. To enable the "agitation" to reach the Jewish masses, both orally and in writing, it was decided to replace Russian by Yiddish as the medium for propaganda, and "Jargon committees" were formed (in Vilna in 1895) for this purpose. Thus the movement was integrated into the concomitant process of revival of the Yiddish language and literature. The radical Jewish intelligentsia was called upon to abandon its "mistrust of the Jewish masses" and "national passivism," to work for the establishment of an organization of Jewish workers aimed at obtaining their rights, and to carry on a "political national struggle" in order to obtain civic emancipation for all Jews. This organization should associate itself with the non-Jewish proletariat and the all-Russian labor movement in an "indissoluble bond," but

Figure 1. The Bund's delegates to the first convention of the Russian Social Democratic Labor Party in Minsk, 1898. Left to right: A. Mutnik, A. I. Kremer, S. Katz. New York, Bund Archives of the Jewish Labor Movement.

only on the basis of equal partnership and not of integration of the Jewish within the general labor movement. This dualism was to be the cause of ideological oscillation throughout the whole of the Bund's existence.

The "Workers' Opposition" to the "new program" led by A. *Gordon failed, and from 1894 the new trend gained support in many industrial centers. Funds *("Kases")* hitherto established for mutual assistance were converted into workers' struggle funds (trade unions). At the beginning of 1896, 32 such funds existed in Vilna alone. A wave of successful strikes ensued. The Jewish labor groups were represented at the congress of the Socialist International in London in 1896. A central "Group of Jewish Social Democrats" was formed, and published the periodical *Yidisher Arbayter* (1896–1905), as well as *Arbayter Shtime* (1897–1905), both of which later became the organs of the Bund.

The Bund. The Bund was founded at a secret convention held in Vilna on Oct. 7–9, 1897, with the participation of 13 delegates (eight of them working men). At the founding convention of the Russian Social Democratic Labor Party in March 1898, three of the nine delegates were Bundists. The Bund entered the Russian party as an autonomous body, and Kremer was elected a member of its central committee. The sovereign institution of the underground Bund was its periodic convention. In addition to the founding meeting, the following conventions were held: the second convention, October 1898, in Kovno; the third, December 1899, in Kovno; the fourth, May 1901, in Bialystok; the fifth, June 1903, in Zurich; the sixth, October–November 1905, in Zurich; the seventh, August–September 1906, in Lemkeny; the eighth, December 1917, in Petrograd (Leningrad). The convention elected a central committee which was the chief political administrative and representative body of the Bund. Between the conventions, conferences, whose authority was more limited, also met. Larger branches were headed by committees, mostly comprising members nominated by the central committee. The "strike funds," including the national unions of bristlemakers and tanners, were integrally incorporated within the Bund. There were also groups of intellectuals. The number of Bund members from 1903 to 1905 varied between 25,000 and 35,000. The "Committee Abroad," which was founded in December 1898 by students and workers who had left Russia, its members including at various periods the most important Bund leaders, served as the Bund representative vis-à-vis the international socialist movement, raised funds, printed literature, and organized its transportation. Considerable assistance was given to the Bund by its "*Landsmanschaften" and branches of sympathizers in the United States, headed by the "Central Farband," which in 1906 comprised 58 organizations with 3,000 members. Although the Bund opposed cooperation with the Jewish labor movement in other countries, it had a significant influence on the formation of the *Jewish Social Democratic Party in Galicia in 1905. Bundist principles contributed to the establishment of the Jewish Socialist Federation of America in 1912. Some prominent activists of the American Jewish Labor Movement came from the ranks of the Bund, including S. *Hillman, B. Hoffmann (*Ẓivion), B. *Vladeck, Y. B. Salutzki-Hardman, M. *Olgin, N. Chanin, and D. *Dubinsky. The activity and ideas of the Bund also had influence on Jewish socialism in Argentina, Bulgaria, and Salonika (Greece).

From the beginning of the 20th century, the Bund concentrated its activities on the political sphere, and the party became an important factor in Jewish public life. The fourth convention of the Bund (1901) already recommended discretion in the proclamation of strikes—for the government was suppressing them severely and they brought little amelioration of the workers' conditions—and called for struggle through purely political agitation, May Day demonstrations and strikes, accompanied by political demands. This trend gained in strength as a result of various economic, social, and political factors (see also *Independent Jewish Workers' Party).

Feelings became inflamed when Jewish workers were flogged during the May Day demonstrations in 1902 on the order of the governor of Vilna who was subsequently shot by a Bundist youth, Hirsh *Lekert. However, the tendency to advocate violent measures—"organized vengeance"—which evolved in the Bund after this assault was short-lived. The pogroms at the beginning of the 20th century intensified political alertness among the Jews as a whole, and efforts were made toward active *self-defense. These bloody attacks dissipated the reservations of many who had formerly held aloof from the revolutionary activity of the Bund. The Bund then became one of the principal promoters, and in some places the main organizer, of the self-defense movement to combat the perpetrators of the pogroms. It began to find support among the Jewish middle classes, and gained adherents in the provincial towns of Poland and southern Russia. From mid-1903 to mid-1904 the Bund held 429 political meetings, 45 demonstrations, and 41 political strikes, and issued 305 pamphlets, of which 23 dealt with the pogroms and self-defense. The number of Bundist political prisoners in 1904 reached 4,500. A children's organization, Der Klayner Bund, was formed. The Bund reached its peak influence during the revolution of 1905. It then acquired semilegal status, played an important role in general revolutionary and political activities, and began to publish a daily newspaper under various names *(Veker, Folkstsaytung).*

About this time (at the fourth convention in 1901) the Bund advanced beyond its former demand for equal political and civic rights for Jews. Various internal and external factors pressured this change, such as the solutions advocated by S. *Dubnow, the views of H. *Zhitovsky, and the growth of Zionism. The Bund now drew a Marxist legitimation for its nationalist tendencies from the Austrian Social Democratic Party which had changed its structure to a federal-nationalist one, approximate to the concepts of *autonomism, as the basis for a constitution of a multinational state. The third convention of the Bund (1899) still rejected Mill's suggestion that the demand for Jewish "national rights" be included in its program. However, at the fourth convention, promoted by M. *Liber, a representative of the second generation of Bund leaders, with the support of the older leaders, Kremer, Mill, and Kossovski who were absent at the convention, the proposition was advanced that Russia should be converted into a federation of nations without reference to region of domicile, with the provision that the concept of nationality should be applied to the Jews. However, as a compromise with opponents of this proposal, it was decided not to campaign for Jewish autonomy as a concrete demand for fear of "inflating the national feeling" which was liable "to blur the class consciousness of the proletariat and lead to chauvinism." This limitation was not observed in practice even in 1904, and was officially removed at the sixth convention in 1905. A further resolution of the fourth convention sought to reconstruct the Russian Social Democratic Labor Party on a national-federal basis. This proposal was rejected by the second convention of the Russian Social Democratic Party. In consequence the Bund seceded from it and constituted itself as an independent party.

Even after its fourth convention, the Bund did not consider the Jews a worldwide national entity, and was opposed to a global Jewish policy, limiting its demands for rights and autonomy with reference to Russian Jewry. The Bund rejected, in the name of class-war principles, any collaboration with other Jewish parties, even in the organization of self-defense against pogroms. While assimilationist Russian Social Democrats regarded Bundist ideology as "inconsistent Zionist," the Bund, for its part, defined Zionism as reactionary and bourgeois or petit-bourgeois, even including such parties as the *Po'alei Zion, the *Jewish Socialist Workers' Party (the Sejmists), and the *Zionist Socialist Workers Party (the Territorialists), in this category. From 1903 the struggle with other Jewish parties sharpened, as the Bund's Zionist and other rivals penetrated the proletarian camp. The Bund itself remained in a constant state of ideological vacillation and internal strife in its perpetual effort to square nationalism with internationalism, and the conception of the Jewish proletariat as part of the all-Russian proletariat with its position as part of Jewry. Opposing nationalist, cosmopolitan, and semi-assimilationist elements confronted each other within the Bund and prevented a clear-cut decision either for or against devotion of its efforts to seeking full Jewish political and cultural identity, while even its positive attitude toward the use of Yiddish was mainly governed by pragmatic considerations. Hence the Bund adopted the doctrine of neutralism developed by the party ideologist V. *Medem with the fundamental reservations of Kossovski. Neutralism assumed that no prognosis of the survival of the Jewish people could be advanced: they might equally be expected to subsist or assimilate. The task of the Bund was to fight for a political framework which would guarantee freedom of evolution for both trends, but not to regard as incumbent on it to assist intentionally national continuity. During 1905–06, the Bund sided on many questions with the Bolsheviks, whose support at the convention of the Social Democratic Party in Stockholm in 1906 enabled the Bund to return to the all-Russian organization. After a sharp cleavage of opinion, the "softliners," prominent among them Medem, Rosenthal, and B. *Mikhalevich, prevailed, and amalgamation with the Social Democrats was decided at the seventh convention of the Bund (1906). The question of the national program was left open, and in practice the Bund retained its independence.

1907 to 1917. With the failure of the 1905 revolution the Bund suffered a serious decline and succeeded in maintaining only the nucleus of its organization. Terrorization, frustration, and despair, together with the massive emigration, considerably reduced the ranks of the Bund. With the limitation of political and trade union activities, the semilegal activities of the Bund now concentrated on culture—the organization of literary and musical societies, evening courses, and drama circles. The Bund became an advocate of fundamental Yiddishism. The eighth conference of the Bund (October 1910) decided in favor of pressing for freedom of rest on the Sabbath and for state Yiddish schools. The Bund agreed to participate in several conferences and cultural institutions of a general Jewish nature, such as the *Society for the Promotion of Culture among the Jews of Russia and the meeting of Jewish communal leaders, where the Bundists demanded greater autonomy, and secularization, and democratization in Jewish communal life. The theory of Neutralism was rejected by some prominent Bundists. In 1910–11 the Bund made renewed efforts to strengthen its organization, both openly and by underground activity. It took part in the elections to the fourth *Duma (1912). In Warsaw the joint candidate of the Polish Socialist Party (P.P.S.) and the Bund, E. Jagello, was returned thanks to the support of the nonsocialist Jewish electorate. The Bund campaigned actively on several Jewish issues, including the Polish anti-Jewish *boycott, and the ousting of Jewish workers from their places of employment. It organized a protest strike (Oct. 8, 1913) in reaction to the *Beilis trial, which was observed by some 20,000 Jewish workers. The Bundist press was also revived *(Lebns-Fragen, Tsayt)*. In regard to the division in Russian social-democratic opinion between those who supported continued underground activity and those opposing it, the Bund in general adopted a mediatory stand. After the final split between the Bolsheviks and Mensheviks in 1912, the Bund remained within the Menshevik Social Democratic Party, which now tended to favor Jewish national-cultural autonomy, while the Bolsheviks hardened their position against it. The Bund belonged to the socialist wing that condemned all belligerents in World War I, and approved the manifestos of Zimmerwald, 1915, and Kienthal, 1916. The Bund at this time turned more expressly toward adopting a general Jewish stand. At a consultation held in Kharkov (spring 1916) the Bund decided, in contrast to its former position, to take part in activities of the communal Jewish relief organizations, such as *ORT, *OZE, and *Yekopo. It also recognized there, to a certain extent, that the Jewish question had assumed some international significance. The Bund publicized cases of persecution of Jews in Russia through its committee abroad. However, discussion on the question of constituting a World Jewish Congress was not resolved.

The 1917 Revolutions and their Aftermath. By the end of 1917 the Bund had approximately 40,000 members, in almost 400 branches, of whom 20% were outside the former Pale of Settlement, mostly refugees expelled from the Pale. On the general political scene, Bund leaders (M. Liber and R. *Abramowitz) were spokesmen for both the right and left wings of the Mensheviks, and the Bund discussed and took a stand on problems connected with the revolution. At the same time, it brought forward the claim for Jewish national-cultural autonomy. It participated in communal elections and was represented on the organizing committee for a general Jewish convention to be held in December 1917. However, it opposed the moving of Zionist formulations there as well as debate on the guarantee of rights to Jews living outside Russia. In the Ukraine, the Bund, led by M. *Rafes, was in favor of an autonomous Ukraine as part of federal Russia. At the elections for the Jewish National Assembly of the Ukraine (November 1918), the Bund received 18% of the votes.

From fall 1918, Bundist sympathies, especially in the Ukraine, the scene of frightful pogroms, began to incline toward the Communists. In March 1919, the "Communist Bund" (Kombund) was established in the Ukraine led by

Figure 2. Secret meeting of a Bundist self-defense group in the woods at Pinsk, 1905. New York, Bund Archives of the Jewish Labor Movement.

Rafes. In May it joined the United Jewish Communist Party to form the Komfarband, which in August amalgamated with the Communist Party of the Ukraine. At the all-Russian (12th) conference of the Bund held in Moscow (April 1920), a split occurred. The majority, led by A. *Weinstein and *Esther (Lifschitz), favored affiliation with the Communists, but on an autonomous basis. Although this condition was rejected by the Communist International, the conference at Minsk (March 1921) nevertheless decided to join the Russian Communist Party. In January 1925 there were only 2,795 former Bundists in the Communist Party, forming 9% of its Jewish members. These included some leaders of the *Yevsektsiya (Jewish section of the Russian Communist Party). A minority at the 12th conference (which included Abramowitz, Eisenstadt, and G. *Aronson) broke away and established the short-lived Social Democratic Bund. Sooner or later the activists in both factions became victims of Communist government persecution.

The Polish Bund. In November 1914, when the threat of German invasion became apparent, a Committee of the Bundist Organizations in Poland was formed in Warsaw by the central committee of the Bund (including J. *Portnoy and V. *Shulman). The forced dissociation from the all-Russian movement, and the resurrection of Poland led the Polish Bund to constitute itself as an independent body. The more moderate regime of the German occupation authorities enabled the Bund in Poland, though still functioning clandestinely, to stress Jewish demands, and to set up Jewish trade unions, workers' kitchens, cooperative shops, and a network of cultural institutions. It began to publish a weekly organ (from the end of 1918, a daily), *Lebns-Fragen.* The Bund also participated in elections to the municipal councils. At the first conference of the Polish Bund at Lublin (end of December 1917) an independent central committee for Poland was elected. At the first all-Polish convention in Cracow (April 1920), the Bund organization became united with the Jewish Social Democratic Party of Galicia.

Subsequently the following conventions were held: the second, in December 1921, in Danzig; the third, December 1924, in Warsaw; the fourth, January 1929, in Warsaw; the fifth, June 1930, in Lodz; the sixth, February 1935, in Warsaw; the seventh, November 1937, in Warsaw. The most prominent leaders of the Polish Bund were H. *Ehrlich and V. *Alter. It published a daily organ *Naye Folkstsaytung* between 1921 and 1939. The Polish Bund functioned as a legal, independent political party from the outset, unlike the Russian parent body. It maintained a youth organization, Zukunft, which numbered 15,000 members on the eve of World War II; a children's organization, S.K.I.F., from 1926; a women's organization, Y.A.F.; and a sports organization, Morgnshtern. During the first years of its existence the Polish Bund was severely persecuted because of its opposition to the war against Soviet Russia. During the 1930s some of its activists were incarcerated in the *Bereza Kartuska concentration camp. The party was split into permanent factions, which were proportionately represented in its central institutions, the centrist or rightist faction (Einser) and the leftist (Tsvayer). The split originally occurred over affiliation to the International. Parallel to development of the Kombund in Russia, the Bund in Poland also shifted its allegiance to the "dictatorship of the proletariat" and "government of the Soviets." The Cracow convention in 1920 decided in principle on affiliation with the Comintern, which demanded that the Bund accept its full program as a condition to affiliation. The intended affiliation did not materialize but caused some older prominent Bundists to feel out of place within the movement and they finally emigrated (V. Medem, A. *Litwak); others (notably P. *Rosenthal) formed the short-lived Social Democratic Bund. One group, however, established the Kombund which later joined the Communist Party. The question of affiliation with the Comintern continued to disturb and divide the Bund for a long time, the majority shifting first one way and then the other. Even the leftist faction, whose chief spokesman was Joseph *Lesteminsky ("Chmuzner"), had reservations in regard to affiliation if this was likely to impair the unity of the Bund. The fifth convention (1930) decided, by a small majority, on affiliation to the Socialist International, where the Bund formed part of the left wing. Another cause of division was its relationship with the Polish Socialist Party (P.P.S.), which left-wing Bundists regarded as anathema because of its "nationalism and reformism" and its policy to form a center-left front with the nonsocialist peasant parties. A convergence between the two parties occurred, mainly as a result of the Bund's affiliation to the Socialist International and radicalization within the P.P.S. during the 1930s.

Among the Jewish public, the Bund pursued its relentless campaign against Zionism and religious Orthodoxy, but in contrast to its former policy, collaborated in various fields with other Jewish labor parties. On more than one occasion it aligned with the left Po'alei Zion in municipal elections. In 1930, a common list was drawn up with the right Po'alei Zion for the elections to the Sejm (parliament). The Bund held the overwhelming majority in the national council of Jewish Trade Unions, which, at the end of 1921, comprised seven unions with 205 branches and 46,000 members, and, in 1939, 14 unions with 498 branches and approximately 99,000 members. The Polish Bund, not without opposition, approved initiatives and institutions to work with and organize small-scale artisans' and contractors' cooperatives (1927) in conjunction with the *American Jewish Joint Distribution Committee and ORT.

In 1921 the Central Yiddish Schools Organization (CYShO) was established, with large participation of the Bund. The Bund was adamant in its extreme opposition to instruction in Hebrew but slightly modified its attitude toward the traditional Jewish holidays and the teaching of Jewish history. In the 1930s the Bund was active in the party lists for Jewish representation on municipal councils and for the communal leadership. It maintained a bureau to deal with emigration—but its fixed attachment to the principle of "Doykeyt" ("hereness") prevented the Polish Bund from appreciating the importance of Jewish emigration.

The Polish Bund achieved its greatest political influence between 1936 and 1939, on the eve of the Holocaust. It scored a substantial success in the municipal elections. This was due less to its socialist appeal than to the role it played in campaigning against the rabid anti-Semitism within the Polish government and general public after Hitler's rise to power. The Bund displayed initiative and energy in organizing self-defense groups, a protest strike after the pogrom of *Przytyk, a Workers' Congress against anti-Semitism (1936), which was banned by the authorities, as also a proposed Congress for the Struggle of the Jewish Population in Poland (1938).

During the Nazi occupation of Poland, the Bund took an active part in the Jewish resistance movement (prominently A. Blum, L. Feiner, B. Goldstein, M. Edelman). S. *Zygelbojm left the Bund underground in order to represent it on the National Council of the Polish Government-in-Exile in London. His suicide in 1943 was a heroic symbolic act of identification with the Jewish martyrs and a protest against the silence and apathy of the general public in face of the annihilation. The Bund was also active among the refugees from Poland in the Soviet Union. Two of its prominent leaders—V. *Alter and H. Ehrlich—were executed in 1941 by the Stalinist regime on false espionage accusations.

After World War II the Bund renewed its activities among the survivors of Polish Jewry but it was liquidated in 1948 with the Communists' liquidation of the general political life of the country.

The International Jewish Labor Bund. At the beginning of World War II, some of the Polish Bundists succeeded in reaching the United States, mainly with the assistance of the Jewish Labor Committee. An American Representation of the Bund was formed and for some time continued activity under the leadership of Portnoy. Beginning with 1941 the monthly *Unzer Zeit* has been published in New York. The first world conference of the Bund was held in Brussels (1947). It established a World Coordinating Committee of Bundist and Affiliated Socialist Jewish Organizations, with headquarters in New York. Its secretary until 1961 was Emmanuel Novogrodski, formerly the secretary of the Bund in Poland and later of the Representation in the United States. The World Bund affiliates include the Bund organization of Israel, as well as the older Bundist organizations of various countries, most of which had already existed before World War II, and later absorbed the refugee members of the former Polish Bund. The fourth conference of the World Bund was held in April 1965. The International Jewish Labor Bund is affiliated to the Socialist International. Its present transfiguration embodies the previously rejected idea of Jewish world nationality. The Bund differs from other sections of Jewish labor opinion in the United States in that it does not recognize the special importance of the State of Israel in the life of the Jewish people or necessity for a Jewish international policy. At the same time the Bund demands that the Jewish population in Israel recognize the supremacy of world Jewry. It claims a "neutralist" position on the Israel-Arab conflict. A minority in the Bund, as represented by Liebmann, *Hersh and J. *Pat, have attempted to argue for a certain re-evaluation toward a more positive attitude of the Bund toward the State of Israel.

Figure 3. Henryk Erlich speaking in front of the Warsaw Bund club at the close of the May Day demonstration, 1933. New York, Bund Archives of the Jewish Labor Movement.

Bibliography: J. S. Hertz (ed.), *Doyres Bundistn,* 3 vols. (1956–69); idem, *Di Yidishe Sotsialistishe Bavegung in Amerike* (1954), 99–138; idem, *Der Bund in Bilder 1897–1957* (1958); *Di Geshikhte fun Bund,* 3 vols. (1960–66); *Royter Pinkes,* 2 vols. (1921–24); *Der Bund in der Revolutsie fun 1905–1906* (1930); J. Shein, *Bibliografie fun Oysgabes . . . in di Yorn 1918–1939* (1963), 29–56; A. Kirzhnitz (ed.), *Der Yiddisher Arbeter, Khrestomatie,* 4 vols. (1925–28); A. Menes, R. Abramowitz, and V. Medem, in: B. Dinur et al., *Kelal Yisrael* (1954), 535–41; A. Menes, in: *The Jewish People, Past and Present,* 2 (1948), 355–68; R. Abramowitz, *ibid.,* 369–98; E. Tcherikower (ed.), *Historishe Shriftn,* 3 (1939); S. Eisenstadt, *Perakim be-Toledot Tenu'at ha-Po'alim ha-Yehudit,* 2 vols. (1944); M. V. Bernstein, in: Velt-Federatsie fun Paylishe Yidn, *Yorbukh,* 1 (1964), 161–222 (incl. bibl.); Velt Konferents fun Bundishe Organizatsie un Grupes, *Tezn un Materialn* (1947); N. A. Buchbinder, *Geshikhte fun der Yidisher Arbeter Bavegung in Rusland* (1931); A. S. Stein, *Ḥaver Artur, Demuyyot u-Ferakim me-Ḥayyei ha-"Bund"* (1953); idem, in: *Gesher,* 3 no. 4 (1957), 94–110; *Bolshaya Sovetskaya Entsiklopediya,* 8 (1927), 102–20, 120–3; S. Erlich, *Garber-Bund un Bershter-Bund* (1937); B.

Goldstein, *The Stars Bear Witness* (1949); J. L. H. Keep, *The Rise of Social Democracy in Russia* (1963), index; K. S. Pinson, in: JSOS, 7 (1945), 233–64; A. L. Patkin, *The Origins of the Russian-Jewish Labour Movement* (1947), 101–214; E. Scherer, in: B. J. Vlavianos (ed.), *Struggle for Tomorrow* (1954), 131–96; *Jewish Labor Bund Bulletin* (1947–53); M. Mishkinsky, in: *Cahiers d'Histoire Mondiale (Journal of World History)*, 11 no. 1–2 (1968), 284–96 (Eng.); idem, in: *YIVO Annual of Jewish Social Science*, 14 (1969), 27–52; idem, in: *Ba-Sha'ar*, 9 (1966), 527–36; idem, in: *Zion*, 31 (1966), 87–115; E. Mendelsohn, *The Formative Years of the Jewish Workers' Movement in Tsarist Russia* (1970); K. Wildman, *The Making of a Workers' Revolution: Russian Social Democracy, 1891–1903* (1967), index; H. J. Tobias, in: *The Russian Review*, 20 (1961), 344–57; 24 (1965), 393–406; L. Schapiro, in: *Slavonic and East European Review*, 40 (1961–62), 156–67; B. K. Johnpoll, *The Politics of Futility: The General Jewish Workers' Bund of Poland, 1917–1943* (1967). [M.M.]

BUNIN, ḤAYYIM ISAAC (1875–1943), author and teacher. Bunin was born in Gomel, Belorussia. He spent most of his life as a wandering teacher in Russia, Lithuania, and Poland, settling in Warsaw in 1929. Bunin devoted himself in particular to research on *Ḥabad Ḥasidism, on which he first published a series of essays and studies in *Ha-Shilo'aḥ* (1913–15, 1928, 1929, 1931). His monumental work, *Mishneh Ḥabad*, mainly a compilation from the sources and sayings of its leaders, appeared in installments from 1932 to 1936. His publicist writings and literary compositions were published in the Hebrew and Yiddish press after World War I in the journals *Ha-Ẓefirah*, *Ha-Mizraḥi*, and *Ha-Toren*, among others. In 1922 in Lodz he published and edited a journal entitled *She'ar Yashuv*. He also published *Limmudei ha-Yahadut* ("Instruction in Judaism," 1917) and his *Ketavim* (1936). He perished in *Treblinka during the Holocaust. [E.Z.]

BUNSHAFT, GORDON (1909–), U.S. architect. Born in Buffalo, New York, in 1946 he became partner in the architectural firm of Skidmore, Owens, and Merrill for whom he designed the Lever Building, New York (1952). This building, which was widely imitated, established his reputation as a leading designer for large-scale commercial structures. It was the first block to be covered on three sides by a glass curtain wall. Bunshaft designed industrial and other office buildings, the Albright-Knox Art Gallery, Buffalo, and the Library for Manuscripts and Rare Books at Yale University. [ED.]

Lever House, New York City, designed by Gordon Bunshaft and completed in 1952. Photo Ezra Stoller, Mamaroneck, N.Y.

BUNZEL, RUTH LEAH (1898–), U.S. anthropologist. Born in New York City, Bunzel was an art student before she studied anthropology under Franz *Boas. She obtained an intimate knowledge of primitive art and artists by her research on the potters of the Pueblo Indians of the American Southwest. In 1960 she became professor of anthropology at Columbia University. Her field research on American Indians was done in New Mexico, Arizona, Guatemala, and Mexico; she also undertook social and anthropological studies of the Chinese community of New York City. Her later research interests were in problems of a national character, American and Chinese, and in the interrelations of personality and culture.

Among her publications are *The Pueblo Potter* (1929) and *The Golden Age of American Anthropology* (1960), which she edited with Margaret Mead. She contributed to F. Boas' *General Anthropology* (1938), and to the journal *Psychiatry*. [E.F.]

BUNZL, Austrian and British industrialists. HUGO (1883–1960) was born in Bratislava. He joined his family's textile firm which was established by his grandfather, Moritz, in 1852. Under the leadership of Bunzl and his brothers, MARTIN, ROBERT, EMIL, FELIX, and GEORGE, the business expanded into Austria, Hungary, and Yugoslavia. In 1904 the management left Bratislava and moved to Vienna, where, during World War I, Hugo entered into papermaking and soon became Austria's leading paper manufacturer. His mills were famous for their social welfare provisions. This earned for their owner the name of "The Red Industry Baron." In 1938 the Nazi occupation forced Bunzl to leave Austria and abandon his interests there. He moved to England where he rebuilt his company and developed it into an international enterprise with mills in 17 countries.

GEORGE (1915–), industrialist, joined the firm in 1936 and in 1960 became chairman of the board. He was prominent as an art collector and was active in Jewish communal work. [J.O.R.]

°**BURCHARD OF WORMS** (c. 965–1025), bishop of Worms from 1000. The publication of the *Decretum*, a canonical collection compiled by Burchard or under his direction between 1008 and 1012, was an important event in the history of canon law. The canons concerning Jews appear in Book IV, which deals with questions of baptism and confirmation. As the theological basis for behavior toward the Jews, Burchard refers to a passage from the *Moralia* of *Gregory the Great which recalls the prophecy of their final conversion. Extensive use of Burchard's *Decretum* was made in the canonical collection of *Ivo of Chartres toward the end of the 11th century but a much more hostile attitude to the Jews was evident by then.

Bibliography: J. Petrau-Gay, in: *Dictionnaire de droit canonique*, 2 (1935), 1141–57; B. Blumenkranz, *Juifs et chrétiens . . .* (1960), passim. [B.BL.]

BURCHARDT, HERMANN (1857–1909), German explorer. The son of a wealthy merchant family in Berlin, Burchardt worked for many years in his father's business but was never happy there. Following his father's death he set out in 1890 on a series of travels to remote corners of

Asia, North Africa, the Middle East and Australia. Following a brief return to Berlin in 1892, during which he studied oriental languages, he renewed his expeditions with a sharpened ethnological interest and greater linguistic equipment. In the course of his journeys he amassed a large collection of photographs of places never previously visited by Europeans, which was later presented to the Berlin University Library, and also collected legends and folklore of the areas he visited. While on an extended trip in Yemen he took an interest in the all-but-forgotten Jews of that country and later brought them to the attention of world Jewry. He met his death at the hands of marauders in the Arabian desert between Mecca and Sanʿa.

During his lifetime Burchardt contributed articles to various journals of ethnography. His photographs of South Arabian inscriptions were edited and published by Martin Hartman in his *Orientalische Literaturzeitung* (1907–09) and portions of his travel diaries were published posthumously by Eugen *Mittwoch in 1926, together with a detailed report written by Burchardt's traveling companion and Arabic tutor Ahmad al-Jarādi. He wrote an essay on the Jews of Persia in *Ost und West* (1906).

Bibliography: A. Jarādi, *Aus dem Jemen; Herman Burchardts letzte Reise durch Suedarabien,* ed. by E. Mittwoch (Ar. and Ger., 1926).

[E.Fi.]

°**BURCHARDUS DE MONTE SION** (13th century), German Dominican. Born at Strasbourg or Magdeburg, Burchardus traveled to the East in 1232, visiting Egypt, Syria, and Cilicia. From 1275 to 1285 he resided in Jerusalem where sometime before 1283 he wrote his *Descriptio Terrae Sanctae* (Eng. by A. Steward, 1896). Burchardus arranged his book by "divisions" radiating from Acre. For a pious medieval author he was tolerant, and an accurate observer. [M.A.-Y.]

°**BURCKHARDT, JOHANN LUDWIG** (1784–1817), Swiss orientalist and explorer. Burckhardt specialized in oriental studies in Leipzig and in Goettingen. In 1809, he set out on behalf of the British Society for African Exploration for Aleppo (Syria), where he mastered the Muslim way of life so well that he was able to travel through Arab lands under the name of Ibrahim ibn Abdullah, without arousing any suspicion. Burckhardt visited Palmyra, Damascus, the Lebanon, and afterward the Hauran. From there he proceeded to Safed, Tiberias, Nazareth, Beth-Shean, and by way of the Sinai peninsula, to Cairo. Reports on his journey based on his personal notes were published between 1819 and 1830. One of these monographs (London, 1822) is a description of his travels in Syria and the Holy Land. Burckhardt paid special attention to the layout of the ancient cities which he visited, and to the Greek and Latin inscriptions. From Burckhardt the Europeans first learned of the antiquities of Petra (see also *Seetzen). Burckhardt also was the first to draw an accurate map of the Gulf of Elath. He died in Cairo, possibly by poison.

Bibliography: *Beitraege zu Burckhardts Leben und Charakter . . .* (1828); A. Crichton, *Memoir of Burckhardt* (1843). [M.A.-Y.]

BURDUJENI, small town in Moldavia, Rumania. Jews began to settle there from 1792 when the urban settlement was founded, and there were 183 Jewish taxpaying heads of families in 1820. During the 19th century the number of Jews grew to constitute the majority of the population, numbering 1,140 (two-thirds of the total) in 1859, and 2,038 in 1899. A Jewish school for boys was founded in 1898 with the help of the Jewish Colonization Association (ICA). In 1907 anti-Jewish riots broke out in Burdujeni. After World War I the Jewish population decreased, numbering 1,244 (25.7% of the total population) in 1930. A Jewish elementary school for boys was functioning then in the town. [El.F.]

Holocaust Period. The Jewish population in Burdujeni was 1,261 in 1941, comprising about one-fifth of the total population. In January 1941, after the annexation of Bessarabia and northern Bukovina by the U.S.S.R., the Soviets closed their new border with Rumania. The 110 Jews who were waiting in Burdujeni to cross to the Soviet Union were imprisoned by the Rumanians, while the non-Jews waiting there were left unharmed and allowed to remain. A few weeks later the Jews were driven across the border and many were killed by the Soviet border guards or by mines. Those who tried to make their way back to Rumania were shot by the Rumanians. Only 58 had remained in Burdujeni, and these were sent to Târgu-Jiu concentration camp. On Oct. 9, 1941, all the Jews of Burdujeni were deported to Transnistria and their property confiscated. About half of them died there, and only after the war did the survivors return. Most of them emigrated to Israel. About 20 Jewish families were living there in 1970. [Th.L.]

Bibliography: PK Romanyah, 76–77; M. Carp, *Cartea neagră,* 3 (1947), index.

BURG, YOSEF (1909–), Israel politician; one of the leaders of the *National Religious Party. Burg was born in Dresden, Germany. His father, Abraham, who came from East Galicia, was active in the *Mizrachi and in the

Yosef Burg, a leader of Israel's National Religious Party. Photo Government Press Office, Tel Aviv.

establishment of religious institutions in Dresden, and Burg attended the *talmud torah* founded by his father. He received his doctorate from the University of Berlin, and was ordained a rabbi by the Hildesheimer Rabbinical Seminary in Berlin. During his student days he was active in Berit Ḥalutzim Datiyyim ("Union of Religious Ḥalutzim") in Berlin, and during the Nazi regime worked for *Youth Aliyah. He settled in Ereẓ Israel in 1939, but three months later he was sent to Germany and was a delegate to the 21st Zionist Congress in Geneva. Burg was elected to the Zionist General Council and remained in Geneva as one of the directors of Youth Aliyah until 1940, when he returned to Ereẓ Israel. From 1942 to 1946 he was a teacher and lecturer and directed a school for youth and adults in Tel Aviv. From 1946–49 he was director of the Central European section of Mizrachi and Ha-Po'el ha-Mizrachi in Paris which aided the survivors of the Holocaust and established institutions for displaced children.

Burg was a member of the central bodies of the National

Religious Party and was a member of the Knesset from 1949. He was deputy speaker of the Knesset (1949–51), minister of health (1951–52), minister of posts (1952–58), minister of social welfare (1959–70), and became minister of the interior in 1970. He was a member of the board of directors of *Bar-Ilan University and chairman of the Social Welfare Council in Israel. [Y.Go.]

BURGENLAND, one of the federal states of Austria, on the Hungarian border. Located in Burgenland were the "seven communities" *(sheva kehillot),* noted for their outstanding yeshivot and eminent rabbis: *Eisenstadt (Heb. ש״א), *Mattersburg, *Deutschkreutz, *Frauenkirchen, Kittsee (Hung. Kőpcsény; Heb. קיצע), Kobersdorf (Hung. Kabold; Heb. ק״ד), and Lackenbach (Hung. Lakompak; Heb. ל״ב). Other communities in the region were those of Gattendorf (in Jewish sources, Kottendorf), Guessing, Neufeld (for some time included in the "seven communities"), Rechnitz, and Schlaining. Under Hungarian administration, the community of *Sopron was closely connected with the seven. According to legend there was a Jewish settlement in the region in the eighth century, but the first documentary record is from 1373 in the Eisenstadt city book. From 1491, when the region was included in Lower Austria, the communities of Burgenland were ruled by local lords, who treated them well. In 1496 *Maximilian I resettled in the area Jews expelled from *Styria. In 1529 *Ferdinand I renewed the Jewish privileges. The Burgenland communities began to flourish when between 1622 and 1626 they came under the protection of the counts Esterházy. From 1647 the region was administratively a part of Hungary within the framework of the Austrian empire. At the time of the expulsion of the Jews from Lower Austria in 1670, the communities of Eisenstadt, Kobersdorf, and Mattersdorf (Mattersburg) were also forced to leave, but these communities were transferred by the Esterházys to other localities in their territories. The charter granted by the Esterházys in 1690 to the Eisenstadt community, which also guaranteed them protection in time of war, was extended later to all the communities in the region, and formed the basis of their considerable measure of self-administration. The representatives of the seven communities met periodically in Eisenstadt, mainly to apportion among themselves the heavy taxes and "gifts" *(mezigot)* which they had to make to all the staff of the count, including the coachman, and to defend their legal position. The minutes of these meetings were recorded in the "black ledger" of the seven communities. When in 1749 the Hungarian government fixed the "tolerance-tax" to be paid by Jewish residents according to counties, five of the communities (excluding Frauenkirchen and Kittsee) were included in the county of Sopron, thus terminating their special status. They organized themselves as the "five communities" and were joined by a sixth community formed by the Jews scattered throughout Sopron county. As a result of changes following the 1848 revolution in Austria-Hungary, all the communities except those of Eisenstadt and Mattersdorf lost their autonomy. Many Jews left Burgenland, mainly for Vienna.

In the late 19th century the Burgenland communities became the mainstay of separatist *Orthodoxy in Hungary. The rabbi of Deutschkreutz, Menahem Katz-Wannfried, invited the rabbis of Hungary to decide on secession (1869). At the end of the 19th century the communities diminished in importance. After World War I and the collapse of Austria-Hungary Burgenland became part of the new Austrian republic. In 1920 the combined communal organization was renewed as the Burgenlaendische Orthodoxe Landeskanzlei, and included additionally the communities of Guessing, Rechnitz, and Schlaining. The Austrian school law of 1936 gave the Jewish schools in Burgenland equal status with Catholic and Protestant schools. The Jewish population in Burgenland numbered 3,800 in 1938.

Immediately after the Anschluss, the Jews were driven out; 1,900 had been expelled or had emigrated by February 1938, and 1,510 were removed, entirely destitute, to Vienna. Ten places, including Eisenstadt, were declared "free of Jews" *(*Judenrein).* A notorious incident was the fate of 51 Burgenland Jews, who were placed on a narrow land-strip in the middle of the Danube, because neither Czechoslovakia nor Hungary would let them enter their territory. Nearly all the synagogues in Burgenland were destroyed on November 10, 1938, the others at a later date.

There were no organized Jewish communities in Burgenland in the early 1970s; the cemeteries were cared for by the Vienna community. Many of the relics of the communities were preserved in the special department (developed out of the museum established by Sandor *Wolf) of the Burgenlaendisches Landesmuseum in Eisenstadt, and the Zentralarchiv der ehemaligen Judengemeinden des Burgenlandes contained nearly 100,000 items.

Bibliography: B. Wachstein, *Urkunden und Akten zur Geschichte der Juden in Eisenstadt und der Siebengemeinden* (1926); idem, *Die Grabinschriften des alten Judenfriedhofs in Eisenstadt* (1922); M. Markbreiter, *Beitraege zur Geschichte der juedischen Gemeinde Eisenstadt* (1908); A. Fuerst, *Sitten und Gebraeuche in der Eisenstaedter Judengasse* (1908); idem, in: *Mult és Jövő,* 2 (1912), 158–62, 199–201, 257–8; S. Wolf, *ibid.,* 261–76; Taglicht, in: YIVO, *Landau Bukh* (1926), 337–46; Moses, in: JJLG 18 (1926), 305–26; 19 (1928), 195–221; S. Tamir (Lipsky), *Pirkei Sheliḥut* (1967), 63–65; MHJ, 10 (1967), index s.v. *Kabold, Kismarton, Kőpcsény, Lakompak, Nagymarton;* H. Gold (ed.) *Gedenkbuch der untergegangenen Judengemeinden des Burgenlandes* (1970).

[A.Fu./Ed.]

BURGOS, city in Spain, formerly capital of Old Castile. Information about Jewish settlement in the neighborhood of Burgos dates from 974, and in Burgos itself from the 11th century. The Jews then resided close to the citadel of Burgos, while in the 12th century they moved to the fortified enclosure of the castle. It was here that the emissaries of the Cid raised a loan from certain Jews to finance his campaigns. In 1200 a Burgos Jew was acting as *almoxarife* (collector of revenues) and Todros b. Meir *Abulafia, also connected with the court, lived there too.

During the 13th century the Burgos community became the largest Jewish center in north Castile. Some 120–150 families lived there at the end of the century, occupied as merchants, tax farmers, and physicians, and owning real estate and vineyards. During the reign of Ferdinand III (1217–1252) they paid a regular tax of 30 denarii to Burgos cathedral, and from 1282 also a tithe to the Church. The rabbis of Burgos appointed the administrative officers (muqaddimin) of the Sahagun community, a day's journey distant, and the *bet din* of Burgos also served Sahagun. The non-Jewish authorities assisted in enforcing adherence to Jewish observances by the community when necessary, and sometimes imposed fines on offenders. In the second half of the 13th century the kabbalist R. Moses b. Solomon b. Simeon, a disciple of R. Jacob ha-Kohen, was living in Burgos, while many kabbalists were to be found in the small towns of the vicinity. In 1325 Alfonso XI bestowed an annual grant of 4,000 maravedis on the convent of Santa Maria la Real, out of the yearly tax paid by Burgos Jewry; the grant was subsequently increased by a further 1,000 maravedis from the same source.

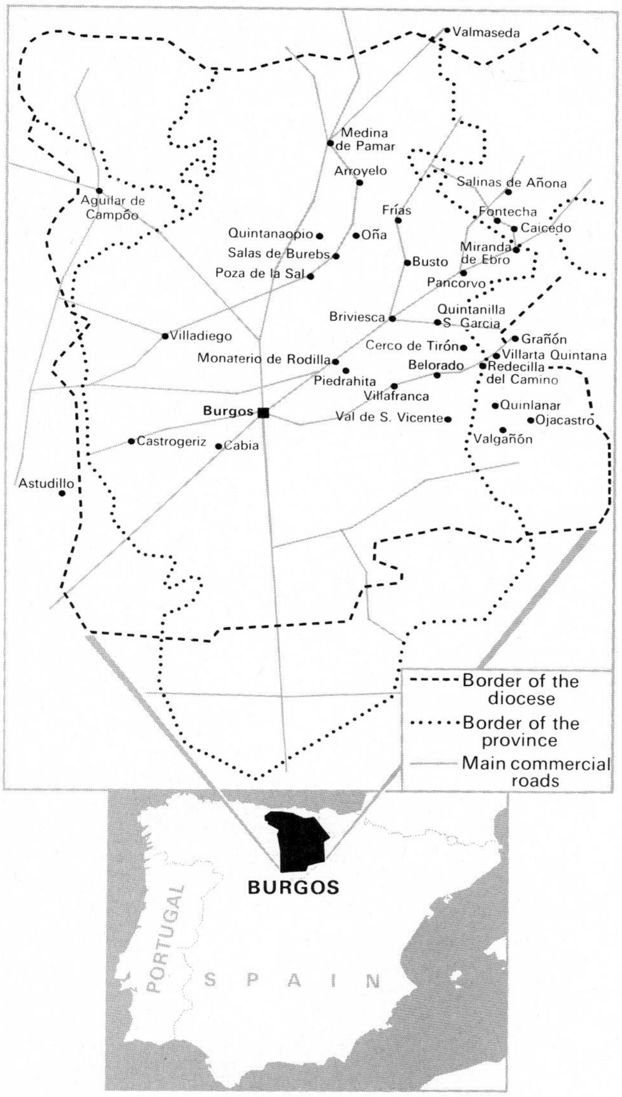

Jewish centers of population in the diocese and province of Burgos at the period of maximum settlement, before 1492. *Sefarad*, Vol. 8, 1948.

During the civil war for the crown of Castile (1366–68) the city supported Pedro. When Henry captured Burgos he exacted a sum of one million gold maravedis from the Jews; to meet this demand the community was forced to sell the crowns and ornaments on all the Torah scrolls, except the celebrated "scroll of Ezra the Scribe." In addition Henry declared a moratorium on Jewish loans to Christians, ruining the Jewish creditors. When Henry was forced to leave Castile, Burgos again passed to Pedro, and on Henry's second entry he was attacked from the Jewish quarter and the fortress, which only surrendered after the walls had been destroyed. In 1379 new restrictions were enforced and Jewish trading outside the *Judería* was prohibited.

During the persecutions of 1391, the Jews of Burgos took refuge in the houses of the Christian merchants. A small number were martyred. Some were baptized and later settled in a special quarter for Conversos. In 1414 many Jews became converted through the activities of Vicente *Ferrer. During the 1440s only 23 heads of families are recorded as liable to pay tax. Several Jews are known to have practiced as physicians in the 1450s and 1460s. In 1485 the Jews of Burgos and district paid $56\frac{1}{2}$ castellanos toward the cost of the war with the Moors in Granada, and both Jews and Moors were forbidden to engage in commerce, ostensibly in order to keep prices low. Toward the end of the 1480s even more severe restrictions were imposed on the Jewish residents, until the municipality was directed by the crown to alleviate their condition. The majority of the Jews of Burgos adopted Christianity after the Edict of Expulsion of 1492; those who remained in the faith left, presumably for Portugal. The Conversos in Burgos adapted themselves to Christianity, and few were tried by the *Inquisition.

Bibliography: Baer, Urkunden, 2 (1936), index; Baer, Spain, 2 (1966), index; P. Luciano Serrano, *Los Reyes Católicos y la ciudad de Burgos* (1943), 187ff., 209, 255; F. Cantera, *Alvar Garcia de Santa Maria* (1952); idem, in: *Sefarad,* 6 (1946), 135ff.; 18 (1958), 99–108; N. González, *Burgos la ciudad marginal de Castilla* (1958), 116–21; Suárez-Fernández, Documentos, index; P. León Tello, in: *Instituto Tello Téllez de Meneses,* 25 (1966), index; Roth, Dark Ages, 364, 368, 374.

[Z.Av./Ed.]

BURGUNDY, former French duchy (to be distinguished from the county of Burgundy, for which see *Franche-Comté). Jews were living in Burgundy at least from the first half of the ninth century, primarily in *Chalon-sur-Saône and *Macon. From the tenth century, Jews cultivated fields and vineyards in the neighborhood of these two towns. The Jewish population of Burgundy reached its maximum in the 13th century. The presence of Jews is attested in about 50 additional towns in the duchy, including *Auxerre, Auxonne, *Avallon, *Baigneux-les-Juifs, Beaune, *Bourg, and *Dijon. The Jews of the duchy were under the jurisdiction of the duke, except in Dijon where both the municipality and the duke claimed them. In addition to the regular *taille,* or poll tax, the Jews were required to pay extraordinary taxes, known as the *"rançon"* (ransom). The amounts paid in taxes increased constantly. For the fiscal year 1277, the Jews in the duchy paid a total of almost 1,500 livres, while between 1297 and 1302 those in the bailiwick of Auxerre alone paid almost the same amount. The position of the Jews deteriorated at the beginning of the 14th century. Although ducal protection was specifically recommended by Duke Robert II who declared in his testament in 1302, "I desire that the Jews shall live on my land," in 1306 they received the same treatment as the Jews in the kingdom of France and were expelled. Most of them took refuge in the county of Burgundy. The debts and securities seized in Chalon and Buxy alone amounted to 33,295 livres. A few Jews apparently returned to Burgundy from 1311, and a general permission to return was given in 1315, when they mainly settled in the same localities as previously. The Jews in Burgundy continued to share the fate of the Jews in the kingdom of France, both expulsion in 1322 and readmission in 1359. In 1374 Duke Philip the Bold granted privileges to the Jews in Burgundy, but limited the number of families with authorized residence to 12, increased in 1380 to 20. Despite popular requests for their expulsion, the duke made them a new grant of privileges in 1384; he also increased the number of families to 52, although in fact fewer were willing to take advantage of this. In this period, Jews were only living in Dijon, Chalon, and Beaune. In 1394, before the end of their 12-year term, they were all expelled. Numerous medieval Jewish scholars were natives of Burgundy. The liturgy used by the Burgundian communities had some special features.

Bibliography: G. Duby, in: *Société . . . maconnaise* (1953), 28–30, 119–21; B. Blumenkranz, *Juifs et chrétiens . . .* (1960), 27–30; J. Richard, *Ducs de Bourgogne* (1954), 342, 360f., 379f.; Gauthier, in: *Mémoires . . . de la société d'émulation du Jura* (1914), 57ff.; Gross, Gal Jud, 108ff.; Schwab, in: REJ, 53 (1907), 114ff.

[B.Bl.]

BURIAL.

In the Bible. Decent burial was regarded to be of great importance in ancient Israel, as in the rest of the ancient Near East. Not only the Egyptians, whose extravagant provision for the dead is well known, but also the peoples of Mesopotamia dreaded above all else the thought of lying unburied. One of the most frequently employed curses found in Mesopotamian texts is: "May the earth not receive your corpses," or the equivalent. In the same way one can measure the importance that Israelites attached to burial by the frequency with which the Bible refers to the fear of being left unburied. Thus, one of the curses for breach of the covenant is: "Thy carcasses shall be food unto all fowls of the air, and unto the beasts of the earth" (Deut. 28:26). Again and again the prophets use this threat, especially Jeremiah. He says, in judgment on King Jehoiakim, "He shall be buried with the burial of an ass, drawn and cast forth beyond the gates of Jerusalem" (22:19).

There is also abundant positive evidence for the importance of burial. Abraham's purchase of the cave at Machpelah as a family tomb (Gen. 23) and the subsequent measures taken by later patriarchs to ensure that they would be buried there (Gen. 49:29–33; 50:25–26) occupy a prominent place in the patriarchal narratives. Biblical biographies ordinarily end with the statement that a man died, and an account of his burial (e.g., Josh. 24:30), especially if this was in some way unusual (e.g., that of Uzziah, the leprous king, II Chron. 26:23); this is not only a literary convention, but reflects the value assigned to proper interment. To give a decent burial to a stranger ranks with giving bread to the hungry and garments to the naked (Tob. 1:17–18). Tombs of the Israelite period in Palestine show that considerable, though not lavish, care was given by those who could afford it, to the hewing out of tombs and the provision of grave goods.

Nevertheless, this assessment of the importance of decent burial must be qualified. Archaeology reveals no distinctively Israelite burial practices during almost the whole of the biblical period. The Israelites continued to use modes of burial employed in Palestine long before the conquest. It follows that it is risky to draw firm conclusions about Israelite religious beliefs on the basis of specific burial practices, e.g., the provision of grave goods or lack of them, communal or individual burial, and so on, since any or all of these may have been dictated by immemorial custom rather than by consciously held conviction. The law says relatively little about burial, and where it treats the subject, the concern is to avoid defilement by the dead (Num. 19:16; Deut. 21:22–23). The dead do not praise God, they are forgotten and cut off from His hand (Ps. 88:6, 10–12), and in consequence mourning and the burial of the dead are at most peripheral matters in Israelite religion.

Figure 1. Catacomb in the necropolis at Bet She'arim, showing a burial recess hewn out of rock on the left. Second–fourth century C.E. Israel Department of Antiquities and Museums.

The one thing expressed most clearly by Israelite burial practices is the common human desire to maintain some contact with the community even after death, through burial in one's native land at least, and if possible with one's ancestors. "Bury me with my fathers," Jacob's request (Gen. 49:29), was the wish of every ancient Israelite. Thus, the aged Barzillai did not wish to go with David, "that I may die in mine own city, [and be buried] by the grave of my father and of my mother" (II Sam. 19:38); and Jerusalem was beloved to Nehemiah, in exile, as "the city of my fathers' sepulchers" (Neh. 2:5). In harmony with this desire, the tomb most typical of the Israelite period is a natural cave or a chamber cut into soft rock, near the city. Bodies would be laid on rock shelves provided on three sides of the chamber, or on the floor, and as generations of the same family used the tomb, skeletons and grave goods might be heaped up along the sides or put into a side chamber to make room for new burials. This practice of family burial, though not universal if only because not all could afford it (see references to the graves of the common people in II Kings 23:6; Jer. 26:23), was common enough to give rise to the Hebrew expressions "to sleep with one's fathers" (e.g., I Kings 11:23) and "to be gathered to one's kin" (Gen. 25:8; et al.) as synonyms for "to die."

There is no explicit biblical evidence as to how soon after death burial took place (Deut. 21:23 refers to hanged criminals only), but it is likely that it was ordinarily within a day after death. This was dictated by the climate and by the fact that the Israelites did not embalm the dead (Jacob and Joseph were embalmed following Egyptian custom, Gen. 50:2, 26). *Cremation was not practiced by the ancient Israelites. There is no archaeological evidence that this was their practice, and the references to "burnings" at the funeral of certain kings (Jer. 34:5; II Chron. 16:14; 21:19) presumably refer to the burning of incense or some of the king's possessions, not the body. On the other hand, it may be going too far to say, as is often done, that cremation was regarded as an outrage. That the men of Jabesh-Gilead burned the mutilated bodies of Saul and his sons is not spoken of as a desecration, but as part of their loyalty *(ḥesed)* to their overlord (I Sam. 31:9–13; II Sam. 2:5). The references to burning of certain criminals, often cited in this connection, refer to a mode of execution, not to a mode of burial (Gen. 38:24; Lev. 20:14; 21:9), and note the remarkable way in which the Mishnah (Sanh. 7:2) prescribes that this be carried out—burning of the corpse is not involved. Bodies were buried clothed and carried to the tomb on a bier (II Sam. 3:31), but not in a coffin. Joseph's coffin is to be understood as Egyptian custom (Gen. 50:26).

The New Testament sheds some light on Jewish burial practices of the first century C.E. Jesus' disciples took his body, bought a great quantity of myrrh and aloes, "and wound it in linen clothes with the spices, as the manner of the Jews is to bury" (John 19:40). There was a delay in completing the preparation of the body for burial because of the Sabbath (Mark 16:1; Luke 23:56). Luke (7:11–17) gives a vivid picture of the simple funeral of the poor; the body of a young man of Nain is borne out of the city on a pallet, clothed but without coffin, followed by the weeping mother and "much people of the city." [D.R.H.]

In Post-Biblical Times. Rabbinic legend stressed the antiquity of inhumation by relating that Adam and Eve learned the art of burial from a raven which showed them how to dispose of the body of their dead son Abel by

Figure 2. Stone ossuary found near Jerusalem second–third century C.E. Jerusalem, Israel Department of Antiquities and Museums. Photo Prisma, Jerusalem.

scratching away at a spot in the earth where it had interred one of its own kin (PdRE 21). Maimonides ruled that even a testamentary direction not to be buried is to be overruled by the scriptural injunction of burial (Maim. Yad, Evel, 12:1 and *Sefer ha-Mitzvot,* Positive Commandments no. 231). The Talmud (Git. 61a) rules that the burial of gentiles is also a religious duty (cf. Tosef., Git. 5:5 and TJ, Git. 5:9, 47c).

In talmudic times, burial took place in caves, hewn tombs, sarcophagi, and catacombs; and a secondary burial, i.e., a re-interment *(*likkut aẓamot)* of the remains sometimes took place about one year after the original burial in *ossuaries (Maim. Yad, Evel, 12:8). The rabbinic injunction (Sanh. 47a) that neither the righteous and the sinners, nor two enemies (Jeroham b. Meshullam, *Sefer Adam ve-Ḥavvah* (Venice, 1553), 231d, *netiv* 28) should be buried side by side is the origin of the custom of reserving special rows in the cemetery for rabbis, scholars, and prominent persons.

Jewish custom insists on prompt burial as a matter of respect for the dead, a consideration of particular relevance in hot climates. According to one kabbalistic source, burial refreshes the soul of the deceased, and only after burial will it be admitted to God's presence (*Midrash ha-Ne'lam* to Ruth; cf. Zohar, Ex. 151a). The precedents set by the prompt burials of Sarah (Gen. 23) and of Rachel (Gen. 35:19) are reinforced by the Torah's express command that even the body of a man who had been hanged shall not remain upon the tree all night, but "thou shalt surely bury him the same day" (Deut. 21:23). The Talmud (BK 81a) states that speedy burial of a corpse found unattended *(met mitzvah)* was one of the ten enactments ordained by Joshua at the conquest of Canaan and is incumbent even on the high priest who was otherwise forbidden to become unclean through contact with the dead (Nazir 7:1). Josephus records that it is forbidden to let a corpse lie unburied (Apion, 2:211), and consideration for the dead is one of the central features of Tobit (2:8). Some delays in burial are, however, justified: "Honor of the dead" demands that the proper preparation for a coffin and shrouds be made, and that relatives and friends pay their last respects (Sanh. 47a; Sh. Ar., YD 357: 1). Even then, however, only a few hours should elapse (David b. Solomon ibn Abi Zimra, Responsa, Warsaw ed., 1 (1882), no. 311). In talmudic times, while the burial was not delayed, graves were "watched" for a period of three days to avoid all possibility of pseudo-death (Sem. 8:1). Later, however, it became customary to bury as soon after death as possible and in 1772, when the duke of Mecklenburg-Schwerin (with Moses Mendelssohn's approval) decreed an interval of three days before the burial, the leading rabbinic authorities protested vigorously (*Ḥatam Sofer,* YD 338). Certain delays are unavoidable. Funerals may not take place on the Sabbath or on the Day of Atonement; and although the rabbis at one time permitted funerals on the first day of a festival, provided that certain functions were performed by gentiles, and regarded the second day of *yom tov* "as a weekday as far as the dead are concerned" (Beẓah 6a), some modern communities prefer postponement. Where there are two interments at the same time, respect demands that the burial of a scholar precedes that of an *am ha-areẓ* ("average citizen"), and that of a woman always precedes that of a man.

The duty of burial, although primarily an obligation incumbent on the heirs (Gen. 23:3 and 25:9; Ket 48a), ultimately rests with the whole community. In talmudic times, the communal fraternal societies *(*ḥevra kaddisha)* for the burial of the dead evolved out of an appreciation of this duty (MK 27b).

Similarly, escorting the dead (especially a deceased scholar) to his last resting place is considered a great *mitzvah* "the fruit of which a man enjoys in this world while the stock remains for him in the world to come" (Pe'ah 1:1 as adapted in the morning service). It justifies even an interruption in the study of the Torah (Ket. 17a and Sh. Ar., YD 361:1) and is called "the true kindness" *(ḥesed shel emet)* since one can expect no reciprocation of any sort (Rashi to Gen. 47:29; cf. Gen. R., ad loc.). Josephus states that "All who pass by when a corpse is buried must accompany the funeral and join in the lamentations" (Apion, 2:205); the minimum duty is to rise as the funeral cortege passes (TJ, Bik. 3:3, 65c; Sh. Ar., YD 361:4), and accompany it for four cubits ("four paces"). "One who sees a funeral procession and does not escort it," states the Talmud (Ber. 18a), "transgresses thereby 'whoso mocketh the poor (i.e., the dead) blasphemeth his Maker' (Prov. 17:5), and should be placed under a ban" (YD 361:3). Only if the hearse passes a bridal cortege is the bride given preference: to honor the living is considered greater than to honor the dead (Ket. 17a, Sem. 11:6, although cf. Maimonides' conflicting opinion, Yad, Evel 14:8). A custom instituted by kabbalists, and still largely observed in Jerusalem, forbids children to follow the bier of their father and attend his funeral.

Figure 3. The restored Jason's Tomb in Jerusalem, first century B.C.E. Israel Department of Antiquities and Museums.

Figure 4a. Chased and beaten silver lid for a *ḥevra kaddisha* jug, Nikolsburg, Moravia, c. 1725. The four men are pallbearers. Prague, State Jewish Museum, Inv. No. 3941.

The more elaborate ancient rituals have either disappeared or been modernized. The recital of psalms in the home still precedes the burial act; however, the custom of having musicians (Ket. 46b), torchbearers, and barefooted professional mourners in the funeral procession has been discontinued. In Great Britain, the custom of reciting the *meḥillah* (asking pardon of the corpse on the arrival at the cemetery) was discontinued by Chief Rabbi Marcus Adler in 1887. The dressing *(halbashah)* of the dead (even princes) in costly garments of gold or silver is forbidden (Maim., Yad, Evel 4:2), despite the rabbis' view that anyone who dresses the dead in comely shrouds (*takhrikhim,* from the Hebrew verb "to wrap up") testifies to a belief in the resurrection (*Nimmukei Yosef* to Alfasi, MK 17a). R. Judah ha-Nasi expressly ordered that he be buried in a simple linen shirt (MK 27b). Since talmudic times, it has been customary to bury a male in the *tallit* which he had used during his lifetime, after its fringes have been deliberately rendered ritually unfit. The victim of an unnatural death is buried in his blood-soaked garments over which the white shrouds are placed in order that all parts of the body should be interred (Naḥmanides, *Torat ha-Adam; Inyan ha-Hoẓa'ah*).

Coffins were unknown to the early Israelites (as they are to contemporary Oriental Jewry). The corpse was laid horizontally and face upward on a bier (II Sam. 3:31); the custom of burying important personages in coffins evolved only later. R. Judah ha-Nasi, however, ordered that holes be drilled in the base of his coffin so that his body might touch the soil (TJ, Kil. 9:4, 32b) and Maimonides mentions the custom of burial in wooden coffins (Yad, Evel 4:4). In Ereẓ Israel, coffins are not usually used. In the Diaspora, it is still customary to spread earth from Ereẓ Israel on the head and face of the corpse, but the customs of placing ink and pen beside a deceased bridegroom (Sem. 8:7) and a key and book of accounts beside a childless man *(ibid.)* have been discontinued (*Baḥ,* YD 350). The older practice of food offerings to the dead (Deut. 26:14; Tob. 4:17; Ecclus. 30:18), of placing lamps in graves, and of burying the personal effects of princes and notables with the corpse (as was done for Gamaliel I by Onkelos (Av. Zar. 11a)), have completely disappeared. The more recent custom of placing flowers on the grave is discouraged by Orthodox rabbis because of **ḥukkat ha-goi.* Before the funeral, the mourners tear their upper garment as a symbol of mourning *(*Ḳeri'ah).*

The funeral service, now often conducted in the vernacular, varies according to the age of the deceased. A male child who died before he was seven days old is circumcised and given a Hebrew name at the cemetery *(Haggahot Maimoniyyot,* Milah 1:15). Only two men and one woman participate at the funeral of children who die before they reach the age of 30 days, although children who have learned to walk and thus are already known to many people are escorted as adults. In such and normal cases, the coffin is carried on the shoulders of the pallbearers into the cemetery prayer hall (*ohel;* Maim., Yad, Evel 4:2) where the **Ẓidduk ha-Din* ("acknowledgment of the Divine judgment") beginning with the affirmation "The Rock, His work is perfect, for all His ways are judgment" is recited. In some communities, this prayer is recited after the coffin has been lowered into the grave, and on those days on which the **Taḥanun* is not said, Psalm 16 is substituted for *Ẓidduk ha-Din.* In the cemetery while the coffin is being borne to the grave, it is customary (except on those days when the *Taḥanun* is not recited) to halt at least three times and recite Psalm 91. In talmudic times, seven stops were made for lamentations (see Ket. 2:10; BB 6:7), symbolizing the seven times that the word *hevel* ("vanity") occurs in Ecclesiastes 1:2 (BB 100b); corresponding to the days of the creation of the world and also to the seven stages which man experiences during his lifetime (Eccles. R. 1:2). Some Sephardi rites have the custom of seven *hakkafot* ("circumambulations") at the grave.

When the coffin is lowered into the grave, those present say, "May he (or she) come to his (or her) place in peace"; they then fill in the grave. As they leave, they throw grass and earth behind them in the direction of the grave, while saying, "Remember (God) that we are of dust." Prior to leaving the cemetery they wash their hands (in Jerusalem, it

Figure 4b. Stoneware *ḥevra kaddisha* jug, Nikolsburg, Moravia, 1936. Made to fit the lid shown in Figure 4a, it is probably a copy of the broken original container. The corpse here is covered, and is followed by members of the community, the first one holding an alms box. Prague, State Jewish Museum, Inv. No. 8048.

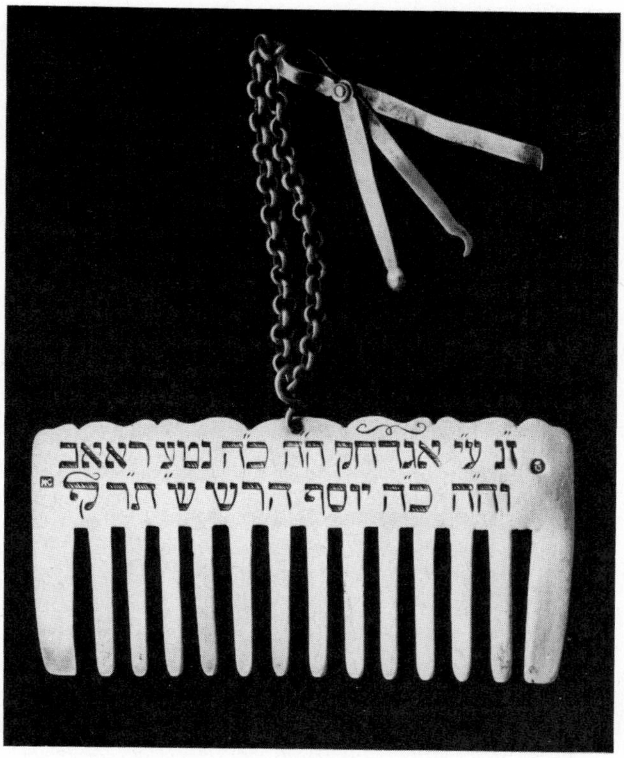

Figure 5. Silver comb and other implements used in the preparation of a corpse for burial, Hungary, mid-19th century. Jerusalem, Israel Museum, IM 191/16. Photo, David Harris, Jerusalem.

is customary not to dry them afterward). In the *ohel,* Psalm 91 and the **Kaddish* are recited by the mourners. The participants at the funeral then recite "May the Almighty comfort you among the other mourners for Zion and Jerusalem" as they stand in two rows between which the mourners pass. The precise order of the funeral varies from place to place and from community to community. Many of the customs among the Sephardi Jews are closer to those of talmudic times than Ashkenazi customs.

Reform Jewish Practice. Certain burial practices are unique to Reform Jews (mainly in the U.S.). Embalming and delay of burial for a day or two are permitted if necessary to wait for the arrival of relatives from a distant city (sometimes funerals are delayed even without this reason). Reform Jews are usually buried in ordinary clothes, without dirt in the coffin. Reform rabbis generally permit cremation, although it is still rare among Jews. Suicides are buried in their family plots. [Ed.]

Sephardi Practice. In the Sephardi communities in Ereẓ Israel, it is customary to carry the bier of a rabbi or scholar by hand, whereas for an ordinary person it is carried on the shoulders. When the men of the burial society leave the house they break an earthenware jar in front of it, symbolic of man as a "broken sherd" and in order to frighten away the evil spirits.

In Safed it was customary to immerse the corpse in the *mikveh* of R. Isaac Luria which is close by the cemetery whereas in Tiberias, Lake Kinneret was used for this purpose.

In most communities it is usual to walk in a ceremonial circle seven times around the bier reciting appropriate verses and in some, coins are thrown to the four directions and the verse "And to the children of Abraham's concubines he gave gifts" (Gen. 25:6) is recited. The "children of the concubines" are the evil spirits and the money is in order to satisfy them so that they should not make claims on the deceased.

It was also customary for old men to buy a grave and actually go into it, after which they would give a festive banquet.

In Egypt the funeral service usually was held in the synagogue. Occasionally the deceased's *tefillin* were buried with him and he was buried with his head toward Jerusalem. In Yemen, however, the body was buried with the feet toward Jerusalem so that when the dead will be revived he will stand and immediately bow toward the Holy City.

In Libya if a man died and left a wife in the early stages of pregnancy, those carrying the bier would lift it high when they left the house and the widow would pass under it in order to demonstrate that the deceased is the father and prevent malicious gossip later. Sons did not go near the bier and did not enter the cemetery but stayed at the entrance where they recited the *Kaddish* at the end of the burial service. The burial society supplied the mourners' meal and buried the remains of it in the ground so that mourning should not return to that family.

If the deceased was an old scholar a small meal was eaten before the bier was removed from the house. Participation in the meal was meant to ensure long life. At such a funeral no dirges or lamentations were recited. **Yigdal* and **Adon Olam* and a special *piyyut* in honor of Simeon b. Yoḥai were recited instead.

In Yemen the mourners followed the bier in black *tallitot* (prayer shawls) and the sons of the deceased uncovered their right arms and shoulders (cf. BK 17a). The participants walk around the bier seven times and a formal declaration releasing the deceased from all penalties that may have been put on him is made.

In Kurdistan the sons of the deceased do not follow the bier but remain in the courtyard of their house.

Figure 6. Three stages of burial, from Johann Bodenschatz' *Kirchliche Verfassung der heutigen Juden.* Germany, 1740. Top: the body is taken to the purification hall. Lower left: the corpse is put into the coffin for burial. Lower right: mourners throw grass and earth behind them as they leave the graveside. Cecil Roth Collection. Photo David Harris, Jerusalem.

See also *Cemetery; *Cremation; *Death; *Hakkafot; *Keri'ah; *Likkut Aẓamot; *Mourning; *Tohorah.

[R.KA.]

Bibliography: De Vaux, Anc Isr, 56–61 (incl bibl. p. 523); Callaway, in: BA, 26 (1963), 74–91; Bender, in: JQR, 6 (1894), 317–47, 664–71; 7 (1895), 101–18, 259–69; J. J. Greenwald, *Kol Bo al Avelut* (1947); H. Rabinowicz, *Guide to Life* (1964); J. M. Tykocinski, *Gesher ha-Ḥayyim* (1944); S. Freehof, *Current Reform Response* (1969), index.

BURLA, family of Jerusalem rabbis from the 18th century onward; members of the Burla family are also found in Greece and Turkey.

ISRAEL JACOB BURLA (d. 1798). He is mentioned in 1770 as one of the seven leading scholars who headed the Jerusalem community. He was a member of the *bet din* of Yom Tov Algazi, and later *av bet din.* In 1774, a year after the invasion of Ereẓ Israel by the armies of Ali Bey, ruler of Egypt, he and Yakar b. Abraham Gershon Kitover traveled to Europe as emissaries, to acquaint the communities there with the misfortunes of the Jerusalem community and to enlist their aid. His letter of appointment, printed in Portuguese in Amsterdam, 1776, contains an account of important historical events. His plan for a system of taxation, written at the request of the communal leaders of Siena, during his stay there in 1777, was published in Italian in a pamphlet entitled *Legge del Ẓorkhei Ẓibbur* (Florence, 1778). In 1782 Israel was back in Jerusalem, where he remained for the rest of his life. His responsa, *Mekor Yisrael* (1882), were published by his great-grandson, Joseph Nissim Burla, together with the responsa, *Naḥalat Ye'udah,* of his son, Judah Burla.

His son JUDAH BEKHOR BEN ISRAEL JACOB (d. 1803) was also a Jerusalem scholar. His signature appears on approbations beginning with 1789, and in 1795, while still a young man, he was the third member of the *bet din* of Raphael Joseph b. Rabbi. After Napoleon's invasion of Ereẓ Israel in 1799, and the consequent suffering of the Jerusalem community, he went as an emissary to Arab countries, and in 1800 was in Baghdad. His responsa, *Naḥalat Ye'udah,* were published together with those of his father.

SAMUEL BURLA (d. 1876) was a wealthy Jew of Janina, who settled in Jerusalem and was appointed Greek consul. MENAHEM BEN JACOB BURLA (possibly Israel Jacob's son), Hebron scholar, traveled abroad in 1835 as an emissary for the Hebron community.

JOSEPH NISSIM BEN ḤAYYIM JACOB BURLA (1828–1903) was a rabbinical emissary, and preacher. In 1859 he was sent to Morocco together with Baruch Pinto. Joseph Nissim was one of those who built and settled in the Mishkenot Sha'ananim quarter, the first settlement outside the walls of Jerusalem. The sermon he preached at its consecration in 1863 was published under the name *Divrei Yosef* (1863). That same year he was sent as an emissary to North Africa and Western Europe on behalf of the Battei Maḥaseh community in Jerusalem and in 1871 he was sent to Turkey. In 1878–81 he and his son Ḥayyim Jacob were emissaries to North Africa and Tripoli. In 1882 he helped Nissim *Behar found the Torah u-Melakhah school. Joseph Nissim was the author of: (1) *Leket Yosef* (1900), a collection of laws arranged in alphabetical order; (2) *Va-Yeshev Yosef* (1905), responsa, published together with *Shuvu Banim,* sermons; (3) *Yosef Ḥai* (Jerusalem, National Library, Mss. Heb. 8° 716, 715), the first part a collection of his sermons for the years 1848 and 1852, and the second part a talmudic methodology; (4) *Olat Shabbat* (*ibid.* 4° 153), sermons; (5) *Petaḥ ha-Ohel* (ibid. 8° 719), a talmudic methodology; (6) a responsum on the Mishkenot Sha'ananim development, in manuscript in the Benayahu collection. He also composed prayers and *piyyutim,* some of the latter being included in *Yagel Ya'akov* by his nephew Jacob Ḥai Burla.

His son, ḤAYYIM JACOB (1847–1929), accompanied his father as an emissary to Turkey and Morocco. Twelve volumes of his sermons, along with a register of promissory notes, accounts, etc., are in the National Library of Jerusalem (443, 8°).

JACOB ḤAI BEN JUDAH BURLA (d. 1892) was a Jerusalem cantor. He founded the Ḥemed Baḥurim society for evening and Sabbath study, and published a number of *tikkunim* ("orders of study for special occasions"): *Marpe la-Nefesh* (1873), studies for the Sabbath in accordance with *Ḥemdat Yamim; Tikkun ha-Berit* (1881); and *Oraḥ Ḥayyim* (1890), a *tikkun karet* ("an order of expiation"). He also published *Yismaḥ Yisrael* (1875), a small collection of poems, a Ladino edition of *Shivḥei ha-Ari* (1876), and *Yagel Ya'akov* (1885), poems by himself and other authors.

JOSHUA BEN BEKHOR JUDAH BURLA (1852–1939), bookbinder by trade, was in charge of the graves of Rachel in Bethlehem and Simeon ha-Ẓaddik in Jerusalem. He was the father of the writer, Yehuda *Burla.

Bibliography: Tragan, in: *Hashkafah,* 4 (1902/3), 264; Frumkin-Rivlin, 3 (1929), 133–4, 209, 301; M. Molcho, *Be-Veit ha-Almin shel Yehudei Saloniki,* 2 (1932), 11–12; M. D. Gaon, *Yehudei ha-Mizraḥ be-Ereẓ Yisrael,* 2 (1938), 134–40; Yaari, Sheluḥei, index; Benayahu, in: *Aresheth,* 3 (1961), 160–1; S. Halevy, *Ha-Sefarim ha-Ivriyyim she-Nidpesu bi-Yrushalayim* (1963), 46–47.

[ED.]

BURLA (Bourla), YEHUDA (1886–1969), Hebrew novelist, one of the first modern Hebrew writers of Sephardi Middle Eastern background. Born in Jerusalem, Burla was a descendant of a family of rabbis and scholars (originally from Izmir, Turkey) that had settled in Ereẓ Israel some three centuries previously. He studied in yeshivot and the Jerusalem Teachers' Seminary (1908–11). During World War I he served in the Turkish army as an interpreter. After the war he was director of Hebrew schools in Damascus for five years. He taught in Haifa and Tel Aviv. From 1930 he spent several years as head of the Arab Department of the Histadrut, was an envoy of Keren Hayesod to the Latin American countries (1946) and director of Arab Affairs in the Ministry of Minorities (1948). Burla served several terms as president of the Hebrew Authors' Association and as chairman of the Bio-Bibliographical foundation, Genazim.

When he was 18, Burla read the classical modern Hebrew authors (*Mendele Mokher Seforim, Ḥ. N. *Bialik, J. Ḥ. *Brenner, I. L. *Peretz) for the first time, and discovered that they portrayed only the life of the Ashkenazim of Eastern Europe, while neglecting the world of the Middle Eastern Sephardim. He determined to correct this imbalance by depicting the milieu, language, customs, and thinking of this hitherto neglected community. When he completed his final year in the Teachers' Seminary, he wrote his first story *Lunah,* which he sent to the noted writer Joseph Ḥayyim Brenner. A week later came the decision, a turning point in Burla's life: "You are talented," said Brenner, "Write!"

Beginning with *Lunah,* a love story set in the Sephardi communities of old Jerusalem, and continuing with his many other works, Burla became the first modern Hebrew writer to deal extensively with the life of Middle Eastern Sephardim. He may be termed the epic writer of this Jewry, encompassing Jewish life in Arab and Balkan lands as well as in Ereẓ Israel—Jerusalem, Safed, Hebron—from its Turkish period to the State of Israel. Just as an entire Eastern European Ashkenazi society could be

Yehuda Burla, Hebrew novelist. Photo Talpiot, Haifa.

reconstructed from the works of *Shalom Aleichem and S.Y. *Agnon, so the Sephardi Jewish world can be recreated from Burla's writings. His novels and stories depict a way of life that is fast disappearing as a result of immigration and acculturation to Israel life. His fiction recorded the garb, diet, language, and folklore of that community.

Lunah set the tone in subject matter (Sephardi Jewry), theme (characters overwhelmed by the power of love and the forces of destiny), and narrative mode (a blend of realism and romanticism) of his ensuing works. His second story *Beli Kokhav* ("Without a Star," 1937) continues this method. Here the setting changes to Bedouins instead of Jews, but the same tragic fate in love befalls the protagonists. Burla's first novel *Ishto ha-Senu'ah* ("His Hated Wife," 1928) centers on a Sephardi Jew in Ereẓ Israel who does not love his wife, but, afraid of the financial ruin that a divorce might bring, remains married to her. The same theme of emptiness in marriage is seen in *Naftulei Adam* (1929, *In Darkness Striving,* 1968), the story of a man who is continually unfaithful to his wife and falls in love with a selfless Arab divorcee. In this series of infidelities as a traveling merchant in the Arab villages on the outskirts of Damascus, he expresses his soul's longing for beauty and his gratitude to God who blessed him with such good fortune. Tragedy in love and the eventual insanity of the beloved are themes developed in *Alilot Akavyah* ("The Adventures of Akavyah," 1939). This two-part novel portrays a romantic and primitive child of nature with a sense of prophetic mission. He falls in love with an Armenian woman in the Anatolian mountains, is later rejected by her, then goes to Ereẓ Israel where he meets her reincarnation. Burla's two major historical novels deal with Sephardi Jews who had visions of Zion restored. *Elleh Masei Yehudah Halevi* ("The Journeys of Judah Halevi," 1959) depicts the life of the great poet of the Golden Age who 800 years ago called for a return to Ereẓ Israel, and *Ba-Ofek* ("On the Horizon" (three parts), 1943) portrays R. Judah Ḥai *Alkalai, the early 19th century Sephardi rabbi who urged immediate resettlement of Zion without waiting for miracles.

Although Burla's subject matter is mainly the Jews of the Middle Eastern communities, his aesthetics and literary discipline are Western, shaped both by his education and his readings in modern Hebrew literature. His writing has no educational or didactic purpose, as did the works of the first Hebrew authors of Ashkenazi Jewry. Burla is primarily a storyteller. He is not a revolutionary in form or style, but a traditional, somewhat romantic, narrator of the realistic school. Other works by Burla include: (1.) story collections: *Im Shaḥar* (1946), *Nashim* (1949), *Tom va-Meri* (1951), *Be-Ma'gelei Ahavah* (1953), *Reshafim* (1961); (2.) novels: *Meranenet* (1930), *Bat Ẓiyyon* (1930–1), *Na'amah* (1934), *Bi-Kedushah o-Ahavah* (1935), *Senunit Rishonah* (1954), *Ba'al be-Amav* (1962); (3.) collected works (8 volumes) were published in 1962. For English translations of Burla's works see Goell, Bibliography, 19, 64f., 102.

Bibliography: Kressel, Leksikon (1965), 192–3; Y. Lichtenbaum, *Soferei Yisrael* (1959), 142–5; D. Kimḥi, *Soferim* (1953), 121–7; A. Ben-Or, *Toledot ha-Sifrut ha-Ivrit be-Dorenu,* 2 (1955), 74–93; A. Barash, Y. Burla, and S. Yizhar, *Sheloshah Sippurim* (1964), 41–43 (with some autobiographical notes of Burla); *Yehuda Burla, Storyteller of the Jewish Orient,* pamphlet (Jewish Agency, Department of Education and Culture), New York (1963; mimeographed); Waxman, Literature, 4 (1960), 189–94.

[C.L.]

BURMA, republic in southeast Asia. Jews from Calcutta, Cochin, and Persia may have settled in various towns of Burma in the first half of the 19th century. A Jewish merchant Goldenberg from Rumania engaged in trade of teakwood and accumulated great wealth. Solomon Reineman of Galicia arrived in Rangoon, the capital of Burma, in 1851 as a supplier for the British army and opened stores in various places. His *Masot Shelomo* ("Solomon's Travels," 1884) contains a long chapter on Burma, and is the first Hebrew account of the country and its towns. In 1857 the synagogue Maẓmi'aḥ Yeshu'ah was built in Rangoon, and in the early decades of the present century a prayerhall was founded in Mandalay with the help of Ezra Shaul. The Jewish community, scattered in several places in the country, included members of the *Bene Israel group from Bombay, Arabic-speaking Jews from Calcutta, and Jews from Cochin and other parts of the Oriental Diaspora. The number of Jews in Rangoon and other places once reached several hundred. With World War II and the Japanese invasion of Burma, community life was disrupted and many Jews fled to India or Ereẓ Israel. In 1968 the number of Jewish inhabitants was negligible.

[W.J.F.]

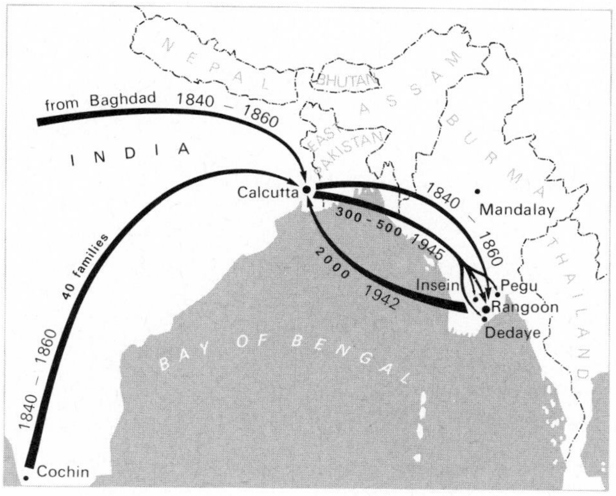

Movement of Jews to and from Burma in the 19th and 20th centuries.

Burma-Israel Relations. Burma became independent in January 1948 and therefore did not participate in the deliberations of the UN on the partition of Palestine. The specific Jewish aspect of the problem was completely alien to her and, like many Asian countries, she regarded the Jewish settlement in Palestine as a manifestation of "Western Colonialism." Thus, in the spring of 1949, when Israel applied for membership in the UN, Burma cast a negative vote. However, following a seeming stabilization of the situation in the Middle East, in December 1949 Burma accorded full recognition to Israel. The first contacts between the two countries were created in the framework of the international labor movement. In 1952 a Burmese socialist mission visited Israel and additional contacts were developed when an Israel delegation, headed by the then foreign minister, Moshe *Sharett, took part in the first Asian Socialist Congress in Rangoon in 1953. Shortly after, full diplomatic relations were established and Israel's first minister to Burma, David Hacohen, opened a legation in Rangoon. The Burmese opened theirs in Israel in 1955. Until 1963 the relations between the two countries developed swiftly. Prime Minister U Nu paid the first state visit to Israel in 1955, shortly after the Bandung Conference, at which Burma unsuccessfully fought for Israel's admittance to the caucus of Asian-African countries. A special agreement concluded in 1956 served as a framework for the constantly growing cooperation. Israel sent a large number of professional and agricultural experts to further Burmese projects. A model agricultural settlement was set up by Israel experts in the northern dry zone (the "Namsang" project); a joint shipping line was built (the "Burma Five Star Line"); irrigation schemes were set in motion; nurses were trained; the Burma Pharmaceutical Industry (B.P.I.) was provided with Israel technological assistance; a joint construction and contracting firm was established; and expert counselors co-managed important Burmese projects. This cooperation also extended to the Burmese army, the nucleus of whose parachute corps was Israel trained. Under a commercial contract, Israel imported substantial quantities of rice from Burma. A constant exchange of visits was made by leaders of both countries: the chiefs-of-staff paid almost annual visits; Israel's president Ben-Zvi went to Burma in 1958, Prime Minister Ben-Gurion in 1961, Golda Meir, then foreign minister, in 1962. General Ne Win, who succeeded U Nu, also visited Israel. Both countries' missions were raised to ambassadorial level in 1957.

This wide-ranged cooperation came to a rather abrupt end in 1963, when Burma, under General Ne Win, embarked on a new policy of nationalization, self-reliance, and reemphasis on strict neutrality and uninvolvement with non-Burmese factors. Since then, the Israel-Burma joint ventures have been brought to a conclusion, although some Burmese students and professionals have gone to Israel to study, and a number of Israel experts have gone to Burma. Mutual trade also continued. [M.PR.]

Bibliography: J. Saphir, *Even Sappir,* 2 (1874), 114; S. Reineman, *Masot Shelomo,* ed. by W. Schorr (1885), 192–204; D. S. Sassoon, *History of the Jews in Baghdad* (1949); D. Hacohen, *Yoman Burmah* (1963); M. Sharett, *Masot be-Asyah* (1957).

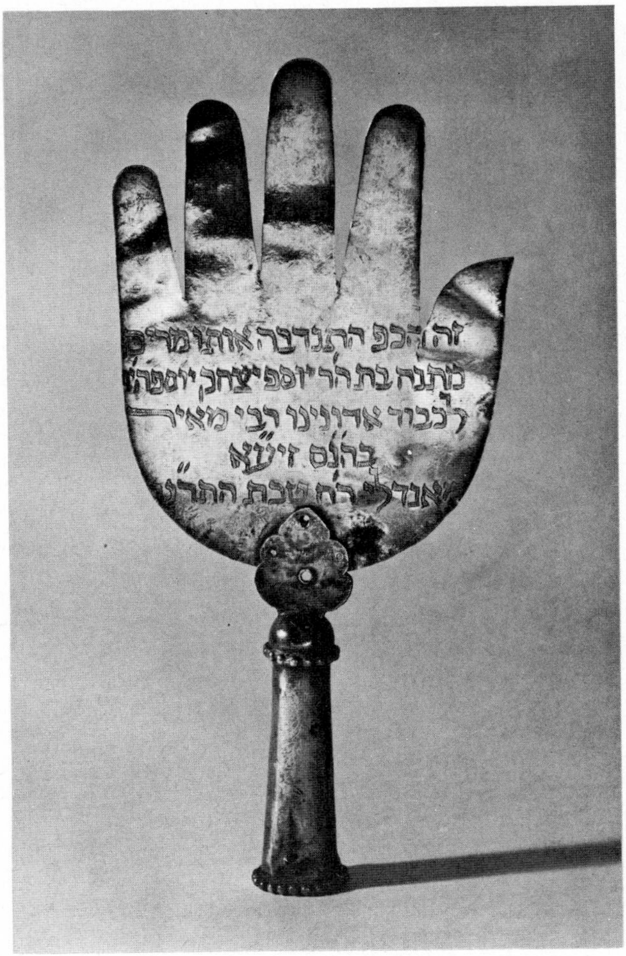

Silver finial for a *Sefer Torah,* Mandalay, Burma, 1849. The inscription states that it is the gift of Miriam bat Joseph Isaac in honor of R. Meir Baal ha-Nes. $9\frac{3}{4} \times 4\frac{1}{4}$ in. (24.7×11 cm.). Jerusalem, Sir Isaac and Lady Wolfson Museum in Hechal Shlomo.

BURNING BUSH, the *seneh,* which is connected with God's revelation to Moses and of which it is stated that "The bush burned with fire, and the bush was not consumed" (Ex. 3:1–4). Various identifications have been proposed for the plant. One suggestion is that it is a variety of thorn-bush which grows extensively in desert wadis, namely, the wild jujube *(Zizyphus spina-Christi)* known in Arabic as in Egyptian as *nabs.* An ancient inscription found in the Sinai Desert reads: "The god Safdu who dwells in the *nabs,*" an expression analogous to the biblical Divine epithet "Dweller in the bush" (Deut. 33:16). Others identify the *seneh* with a variety of acacia widely found in Sinai or with a parasite plant that lives on it; the climber, *Loranthus acaciae,* is covered by red flowers and fruit, and from a distance creates the illusion of being on fire. Others see a similarity between the biblical word and the plant known in Arabic as *sana,* the desert plant *Cassia obovata,* which grows very low and might appear too humble a vehicle for the revelation. However, the opening of an incantation prescribed in the Talmud suggests that the *seneh* is a rather low tree. It reads: "O *seneh,* it is not because you are the tallest of the trees that the Holy One, blessed by He, caused His Divine Presence to rest upon you, but because you are the lowliest of all the trees" (Shab. 67a). Yet others, on the basis of the traditions of the monastery of St. Catherine in Sinai, identify it with the shrub *Colutea istria* which has bright yellow flowers and distended pods, or with the bramble, or blackberry *(Rubus sanguineus (sanctus)).* The latter identification is supported by rabbinic literature in which the bramble is referred to as *seneh* and its fruit, first red and later black, as *innevei seneh* ("the berries of the *seneh*"; TJ, Ma'as. 1:3, 48d). In their many homilies in *Midrash Rabbah* on the revelation of God in the *seneh,* the sages had the bramble in mind, and sought to explain why God had chosen to reveal Himself to Moses in this particular plant. The homilies cited here are those that contain some description of it. The bramble grows on wadi banks (also in Sinai) and in moist fields, hence the

Figure 1. Moses and the burning bush. Marginal illustration in an Armenian Bible, Constantinople, 1653. Jerusalem, Library of the Armenian Patriarchate, Ms. 1927, fol. 49.

homiletical interpretation: "Even as the *seneh* grows both in a garden and by a river, so Israel has a share in this world and in the world to come." "Even as this *seneh* flourishes wherever there is water, so Israel flourishes only by virtue of the Torah which is called water." The bramble has no central stem but instead produces long, thin branches with spiked thorns and is therefore used as a hedge: "Even as this *seneh* is used as a hedge for gardens, so is Israel [a hedge] for the world." The thorns of the bramble are unusual in that "they all bend downward" so that whoever picks the sweet black fruit "puts his hand into it and feels nothing but when he withdraws his hand it gets scratched. Even so when Israel went down to Egypt no one knew them, but when they went out, they went out with signs and wonders." Similarly a bird "gets into it and feels nothing but when it goes out, its wings are scratched." The bramble has pink flowers that resemble small roses and hence "the *seneh* produces thorns and produces roses." Its leaves consist of between three to five leaflets and the fact that "the *seneh* has five leaves" was used in an allusion to Abraham, Isaac, Jacob, Moses, and Aaron. (The sources of the above Midrashim are Ex. R. 2:5 and Song R. 1:6.) These descriptions confirm the sages' identification of the *seneh* associated with God's revelation to Moses with the bramble. This is the earliest and most authentic tradition.

Figure 2. The "burning bush" *(Colutea istria)* at St. Catherine's Monastery in the Sinai Desert. Photo Zev Radovan, Jerusalem.

Bibliography: Dalman, in: ZDPV, 27 (1904), 169; Haupt, in: ZDMG, 63 (1909), 508f.; Loew, Flora, 3 (1924), 175–88; J. Feliks, *Olam ha-Ẓome'aḥ ha-Mikra'i* (1957), 110–2, 317. [J.F.]

BURNS, ARTHUR FRANK (1904–), U.S. economist. Born in Stanislau, Austria, Burns studied at Columbia University, New York, and then taught at Rutgers and Columbia. In 1930 he began a long association with the National Bureau of Economic Research, whose president he became in 1957. Burns served as a presidential adviser and was a member of numerous government bodies concerned with economic matters. From 1953 to 1956 (during the Eisenhower administration) he was chairman of the President's Council of Economic Advisers, and, in 1969, was appointed by President Nixon as chairman of the U.S. National Reserve Board. His publications include *Economic Research and the Keynesian Thinking of Our Times* (1946); *Measuring Business Cycles* (with W. C. Mitchell; 1946); *Frontiers of Economic Knowledge* (1954); and *Prosperity without Inflation* (1957). [J.O.R.]

Arthur F. Burns, U.S. economist.

BURRIANA, city in the medieval kingdom of Aragon, eastern Spain. Shortly after the Christian reconquest of the area in 1233, Jews settled in the citadel and the unwalled area nearby, as well as in the neighboring village of Villareal. The history of the communities in the two places were closely connected. During the 13th century, Jewish landowners were granted various privileges. The cities of Burriana, Murviedro (Sagunto), Onda, and Segorbe formed a single tax administrative unit *(collecta),* assessed to pay an annual tax of 2,000 sólidos. Astruc Jacob Siso served as bailiff of Burriana until 1273. Documents give a picture of his varied commercial activities, including loans to royalty, administration of the salt tax, and supervision of works on the fortress of Peñiscola. Another local notable was Solomon Vidal who received from James I land for orchards, vineyards, and gardens, and for building a residence, and was appointed bailiff of Villareal in 1276. In 1326 James II gave instructions that land for a cemetery should be made available to the community. When the bailiff appointed an unacceptable candidate as *ḥazzan* in 1369, the community appealed to Pedro IV who ordered the bailiff to appoint someone with more suitable qualifications. The physician Vidal Garcian practiced here in 1390; his son Lobell was physician to the royal family. During the massacres of 1391 the Jewish quarter was destroyed. The king empowered Francisco Desplugues, governor of Valencia, to restore looted property to its rightful owners. The municipality and city elders *(jurados)* were fined 13,000 sólidos of the Barcelona mint, and the optimates and council of Villareal, 7,000 sólidos. Subsequently the Burriana community recovered to some extent. Martin I freed a number of reputed Conversos who had come to Burriana from Castile and whose extradition had been demanded. At the time of the expulsion in 1492 the Burriana Jews left Spain from the nearby port of Valencia.

Bibliography: Baer, Urkunden, 1 pt. 1 (1929), index; Piles Ros, in: *Sefarad,* 12 (1952), 105–24; 15 (1955), 98, 101; 20 (1960), 367ff.

[H.B.]

BURSA (**Brusa,** formerly **Prusa**), city in northwestern Anatolia, capital of the Ottomans in 14th century; afterward a provincial capital. According to Hebrew inscriptions of 820 C.E., Jews lived in Bursa in the Byzantine period. When Bursa was captured by the Ottomans (1326), the city was vacated by its inhabitants but the Jews returned shortly after. Spanish exiles settled in the city in the first half of the 16th century and the existing community of *Romaniot (Byzantine) Jews assimilated among them. The Jews in Bursa lived in a special quarter where they continued to reside until the 1960s. The Ez̦ Ḥayyim synagogue, which resembles a mosque, is the oldest of the town's three synagogues, the others (Gerush and Mayor) having been established later by Spanish exiles. In 1592 several Jews were accused of luring a man named Mirza b. Ḥusain into their home and tying him to a pillar where they drew blood from him though he ultimately escaped. The sultan ordered the eight Jews involved to be exiled to Rhodes. Before Passover 1865, another blood libel accusation occurred, but the authorities took immediate measures to punish Greeks who began riots in the Jewish quarter. The Jews of Bursa were chiefly occupied in trade. The merchants were mainly connected with the town's famous silk industry and there were also many craftsment. More recently the majority imported and exported skins, grain, and silk. In the second half of the 17th century, 1,200 Jews lived in Bursa, and before World War I the community numbered 3,500. In 1927 this fell to 1,865, due to a considerable emigration to South America. In 1939 there were 2,400 Jews, but in 1969 only 350–400 remained.

Bibliography: Rosanes, Togarmah, 1 (1930²), 2–3; 2 (1938), 47; A Galanté, *Histoire des Juifs d'Anatolie,* 2 (1939), 94ff.; idem, *Appendice à l'Histoire des Juifs d'Anatolie* (1948), 18–21; Heyd, in: *Sefunot,* 5 (1961), 137–44; Nathan, in: JJSO, 6 (1964). 180–1.

[A.SH.]

BURSTEIN, family of actors. PESACH (1900–), born in Warsaw, joined a wandering Yiddish troupe as a boy. In 1924 he was engaged by Thomashefsky's Broadway company and appeared in many productions. In 1940 he married the Yiddish actress Lilian Lux and with her formed a company which had its own theater, the Hopkinson, in Brooklyn, N.Y. They played there in summer and toured abroad in winter. In 1954, they settled in Israel. The family enjoyed its biggest success in the musical *The Megilla,* based on poems by Itzik *Manger, and featuring their son MICHAEL (Mordecai; 1945–), a popular singer and performer in plays and films in Israel.

[D.L.S.]

The Israel Yiddish actors, Pesach Burstein, his wife, Lilian Lux, and their son, Michael, in Itzik Manger's *The Megilla,* 1968. Photo Nahum Guttman, Tel Aviv.

BURSTEIN, ABRAHAM (1893–1966), U.S. rabbi, author, and editor. Born in Cleveland, Burstein was ordained at the Jewish Theological Seminary in 1917. After serving in graves registration for the Jewish Welfare Board in France, he held pulpits in New England and New York. He was chaplain for the New York Department of Correction from 1934 until his death, chaplain of the Jewish Theatrical Guild from 1924, and executive secretary of the Jewish Academy of Arts and Sciences. Burstein was editor of the *Jewish Outlook,* editor and researcher of many Jewish scholarly works, and a leading book reviewer for the Anglo-Jewish press for many years. Author of books for children, he wrote *Boy of Cordova* (1934) about Moses ben Maimon, *Adventure on Manhattan Island* (1957) about Peter Stuyvesant and the Jews, and *A Jewish Child's Garden of Verses* (1940). He also wrote *Religious Parties in Israel* (1936) and *Laws Concerning Religion in the United States* (1950).

[A.J.K.]

BURSTEIN, ISRAEL (1891–1951), Hebraist. Born in Nadvornaya, Galicia, he studied at the University of Vienna, specializing in research on Hebrew language, the results of which he published in his book *Vollstaendige Grammatik der neuhebraeischen Sprache* (1929). After the *anschluss* of Austria by the Nazis, Burstein immigrated to Palestine in 1939 where he became an associate of the Va'ad ha-Lashon (see *Academy of the Hebrew Language). His main work *Torat ha-Hegeh ba-Lashon ha-Ivrit* (1941) deals with Hebrew phonology. He elaborated a new method of Hebrew shorthand and a system for the fusion of Hebrew numbers (based on the Hebrew alphabet) with the commonly used (Arabic) numerals.

Bibliography: Kressel, Leksikon, 1 (1965), 197–8.

[ED.]

BURSZTYN, MICHAL (1897–1945), Polish-Yiddish novelist. Bursztyn, who was born in Warsaw, taught history and literature there. He was one of the younger generation of writers that rose to prominence after Poland became independent in 1918, when increasing anti-Semitism made the lot of Jewish intellectuals particularly unbearable. His first novel, *Iber di Khurves fun Ployne* ("On Ployne's Ruins," 1931), won him immediate recognition. This work and his three later novels, *Goyrl* ("Destiny," 1936), *Bay di Taykhen fun Mazovie* ("By the Rivers of Mazovia," 1937), and *Broyt mit Zalts* ("Bread and Salt," 1939), are, in common with his first work, peopled with tragic characters, representatives of a despairing generation on the verge of an abyss. His style is simple, his characters clearly delineated, his landscapes vivid. Trapped in the Kovno ghetto in 1941, Bursztyn suffered in several concentration camps and died in Dachau.

Bibliography: M. Ravitch, *Mayn Leksikon,* 1 (1945), 40–42; M. Yellin, in: *Kiddush ha-Shem,* ed. by S. Niger (1948), 407–9; LNYL, 1 (1956), 273–5. [M.RAV.]

BURTON, SIR MONTAGUE (1885–1952), British industrialist and philanthropist. Born in Russia, Burton went to Leeds, England, as a young man and, after working as a tailor, founded a clothing factory in 1910. He soon became known as a pioneer of cheap, well-made men's clothes and established a chain of shops which was the largest of its kind in Europe, employing over 20,000 people. Burton held radical views on the relations between employer and employee, and his factories were known for their good working conditions and generous welfare schemes. He endowed chairs of industrial relations in the universities of Cambridge, Leeds, and Cardiff, and of international relations at Oxford, London, Nottingham, and the Hebrew University of Jerusalem. An enthusiastic traveler, Burton wrote a two-volume diary of his journeys, *Globe Girdling* (1936–38). [ED.]

BURY ST. EDMUNDS, English country town. A Jewish community grew up in the 12th century, under the aegis of its famous monastery, where Jews were allowed to deposit their deeds and money and send their families for refuge in time of danger. During the slack rule of Abbot Hugh (1173–80) the monastery fell deeply into debt to a group of Norwich Jews. His successor, Abbot Samson, set about freeing it from its debts. In 1181 the Jews were accused of ritual murder and on Palm Sunday 1190, 57 Jews were killed in a massacre. Shortly afterward, Samson procured a royal writ to expel the survivors on the grounds that all inhabitants ought to be vassals of St. Edmund—the first occurrence of its kind in England. The whole episode became famous through Carlyle's account in *Past and Present* (1843). No basis exists for the suggestion that Moyse's Hall was the medieval synagogue.

Bibliography: J. Jacobs, *Jews of Angevin England* (1893), 59–61 passim; Gollancz, in: JHSET, 2 (1894–95), 116–22; Haes, *ibid.,* 3 (1896–98), 18–35; Roth, England; H. G. Richardson, *English Jewry under Angevin Kings* (1960), 43–44; 80–81. [C.R.]

BUSAL, ḤAYYIM BEN JACOB OBADIAH DE (d.c. 1565), rabbi and kabbalist in Salonika. Busal, a Spanish exile, studied under Elijah Mizraḥi in Constantinople and was a disciple of Isaac Amarillo in Salonika. After the death of Eliezer Hashimoni (1530), Busal was elected to succeed him as rabbi of the Catalan community in Salonika. His tenure was marked by conflicts in the Salonika communities, particularly between the rabbi and lay leaders over the extent of their respective authorities. A major dispute occurred between Busal and the community before 1540. Busal was required to issue a certain document (of an unknown nature) and was warned that his refusal to comply with the requirement would disqualify him and any of his sons from being rabbi of the community. Busal refused to submit the document. Another dispute took place between him and one of the great rabbis of Salonika, Joseph Taitaẓak. Tam b. Yaḥya of Constantinople endorsed the legal decisions of Busal; however, after Taitaẓak wrote to Tam, the latter changed his mind and withdrew his support from Busal (responsa *Oholei Tam* no. 162 in *Tummat Yesharim,* Venice, 1620). Shortly after 1550, Busal went to Constantinople (Joseph Caro, *Avkat Rokhel,* no. 209). Nevertheless he continued to serve as rabbi of the Catalan community until his death. The poet Saadiah Longo wrote an elegy on him and considered him one of the important scholars of his generation. The manuscripts of most of the numerous responsa he issued have been lost. However, several of his responsa, as well as his endorsements *(haskamot),* have been printed or mentioned in the works of his contemporaries (e.g., *Mabit,* resp. no. 218; *Divrei Rivot,* nos. 130, 186; *Maharashdam,* YD, resp. nos. 61 and 89 and EH nos. 2, 21, 129; *Mishpetei Shemu'el,* resp. no. 100). Ḥayyim Benveniste mentions some of his responsa (*Ba'ei Ḥayyei,* YD no. 215; EH nos. 7, 11, 12). Busal was engaged for many years in the composition of his code of law following the order of the talmudic tractates. In 1546 he had completed his work on the order of *Zera'im,* as well as 13 additional tractates. He was one of the few Salonika scholars—who were mostly also kabbalists—whose kabbalistic works were published. His kabbalistic works include *Be'er Mayim Ḥayyim,* the first two parts of which were published (Salonika, 1546). The other parts exist only in manuscript (Munich, Ms. 46). There are also some passages on eschatology (Oxford, Ms. Opp. Add. 4° 105 and 181).

Bibliography: Michael, Or, no. 891; M. Benayahu, in: *Sinai,* 28 (1951), 186–88; I. Molho and A. Amarijlio, in: *Sefunot,* 2 (1958), 32, 35. [ED.]

BUSEL, JOSEPH (1891–1919), Zionist-Socialist pioneer; one of the originators of the idea of the *kevuẓah* (see *kibbutz movement) and among its founders in Ereẓ Israel. Busel was born in Lachowicze, Minsk Region (Belorussia). Before he went to Ereẓ Irael in 1908 he worked in an agricultural settlement established by *PICA in the Kherson province in the Ukraine. In Ereẓ Israel he joined the group cultivating land at the settlement of Kinneret, where he evolved the idea of the independent agricultural collective group. In 1910 Busel, together with members of his "commune of Ḥaderah," settled at Um-Juni (*Deganyah), which became the first *kevuẓah.* He played a major role in formulating and implementing the principles on which the *kevuẓah* was founded, e.g., equal burden of work for men and women, and communal child care. Busel was a leader of *Ha-Poel ha-Ẓair, and during World War I was active in the general institutions of the *yishuv* in Ereẓ Israel. He drowned while crossing Lake Kinneret from Tiberias to Deganyah. His wife, HAYYUTA BUSEL (1890–), was an educator and agriculturalist. She was born in Lachowicze, settled in Ereẓ Israel and married Joseph in 1917. She was a leading member of the *Histadrut and women's labor movement, and of *Iḥud ha-Kevuẓot ve-ha-Kibbutzim. She settled in Deganyah.

Bibliography: G. Hanoch (Rotfeld) (ed.), *J. Busel-Esrim Shanah le-Moto* (1939); M. Braslavski, *Tenu'at ha-Po'alim ha-Ereẓ Yisre'elit,* 4 (1963[2]), index; Y. Shalom (ed.), *Sefer Busel* (1960), 233–300. [S.K.]

BUSH (Busch), ISIDOR (1822–1898), journalist, political liberal, and viticulturist. Bush was born in Prague, the son of Jacob Busch, partner of the Hebrew printer Anton von Schmid. He entered the printing profession at the age of 15 under the influence of M. H. Letteris, who worked for his father as a proofreader, and became interested in Hebrew literature. For a number of years he published yearbooks in German to which well-known Jewish writers contributed. In 1842 he initiated the *Jahrbuch fuer Israeliten,* the first almanac by Jewish authors for a Jewish public. Together with I. S. Reggio he published the Hebrew-German *Bikkurei ha-Ittim ha-Ḥadashim* (one issue, Vienna, 1845), and edited its German section, stressing in his preface the need to disseminate the Hebrew language. In 1848 he and Letteris published the weekly *Oesterreichisches Centralorgan fuer Glaubensfreiheit, Kultur, Geschichte und Literatur der Juden* and he also issued *Mikhtevei Ivrit,* a compilation of Hebrew letters (1847).

He participated in the revolutionary movements of 1848 and, after their failure, fled to America. In New York City in 1849, he became a bookseller and publisher-editor of the liberal German weekly *Israels Herold,* which soon failed. He then moved to St. Louis, where his wife's relatives, the well-known Taussig family, had already settled. Bush engaged in a number of business ventures, only one of which, the introduction of viticulture, seems to have been genuinely successful. At various times he was also a grocer, real estate promoter, banker, actuary, hardware dealer, and railroad executive. However, his major interests were cultural, political, and communal. He was a founder of Congregation Beth El, a leader in B'nai B'rith, and a popularizer of Jewish learning. He served as a St. Louis alderman in 1866 and as a member of the Board of Education from 1881 to 1884. In 1865 Bush was secretary of the Missouri State Board of Immigration, for which he had been prepared by his presidency for 12 years of the St. Louis German Immigrant Aid Society. His most notable political activity was as a Republican member of the Missouri state constitutional conventions during the Civil War, in which he warmly supported the Union cause and abolitionism in an area where large numbers of Confederate sympathizers lived.

Bibliography: Kisch, in: HJ, 2 (1940), 65–84; Wax, *ibid.,* 5 (1943), 182–203; B.W.Korn, *Eventful Years and Experiences* (1954), 240; Ruzicka, in: *Juedisches Archiv,* 1 no. 1–2 (1928), 16–21.

[B.W.K.]

BUSH, SOLOMON (1753–1795), U.S. patriot and Revolutionary War soldier. Bush was born in Philadelphia, Pa., the son of a merchant, Mathias Bush. He was seriously wounded during a skirmish against the British in September 1777, and taken prisoner. Freed, Bush was made a lieutenant colonel in the Continental army (1779), the highest rank held by a Jewish officer in the Revolutionary army. In 1782 Bush contributed toward a new building for the Mikveh Israel Congregation in Philadelphia. A prominent Mason, Bush also joined the Quaker Abolitionist Society. At his own request he was buried in the Friends Burial Ground in Philadelphia. [L.He.]

BUSHIRE (Abu Shehr), port on the Persian Gulf. As a trading post of the English East India Company, Bushire was also a center for Jewish merchants engaged in export of silk and woolen cloth for European markets. A Jewish settler on the island of Kharg opposite Bushire, established as a Dutch trading post in 1761, had a monopoly on the sugar and spice trade for the Basra market. Jewish merchants participated in the trade along the Persian Gulf and also in the Indian trade to Surat, Bombay, and Madras. It was to Bushire that Sheikh *Sassoon ibn Ṣāliḥ (d. 1830), the chief banker of Baghdad, father of David Sassoon, fled to escape the persecution of the pasha. Letters exchanged between the religious leaders of Baghdad and the Jewish merchants of Bushire indicate a close connection between the two communities. The Jewish traveler *David d'Beth Hillel estimated Bushire's Jewish population around 1828 at "about 200 poor families." A considerable Jewish colony persisted into the late 19th century.

Bibliography: D.S.Sassoon, *History of the Jews in Baghdad* (1946), index; A. Ben Jacob, *Yehudei Bavel* (1965), 116, 212, 362.

[W.J.F.]

BUSK, small town in Ukrainian S.S.R. (E. Galicia); in Poland until 1772 and from 1918 to 1939. Jews were known there before the 16th century. In 1518 the king exempted them from taxes for one year as they had suffered from Tatar raids. In the first half of the 18th century Busk was known as a Shabbatean center (see *Shabbetai Ẓevi), and later King Augustus III assigned the town as a residence for Frankists. Naḥman b. Samuel of Busk represented the Frankists in the disputation at Kamenets-Podolski in 1756. Jacob *Frank himself stayed for a while in Busk, leaving there in 1759 to take part in the disputation at Lvov. There were about 481 Jews living in Busk in 1765, about 2,000 in 1909, and 1,460 in 1921. [Ed.]

Holocaust Period. About 1,900 Jews lived in Busk when German forces entered in July 1941. Jews were immediately kidnapped for slave labor; the free movement in public of Jews was restricted, and Jews were physically attacked. A *Judenrat was set up, headed by Isaac Margalit. It attempted to organize the Jews for the emergency, in particular by ensuring work for the entire community, in the belief that thereby deportation could be avoided. The Germans carried out the first *Aktion* on the Day of Atonement 1942. In November a ghetto was set up for all the Jews in the area. A resistance movement, headed by Jacob Eisenberg, collected arms inside the ghetto and made plans for a breakthrough to the forests, but these could not be carried out, because on May 19–21, 1943, the ghetto was liquidated. There is a society of former residents of Busk in Israel and a B'nai B'rith branch in New York comprising former residents of the town. [A.W.]

Bibliography: *Russko-Yevreyskiy Arkhiv,* 3 (1908), 96, 103–4, 126; I. Schipper, *Di Kulturgeshikhte fun di Yidn in Poyln beys Mitlalter* (1926), index; T. Brustin-Bernstein, in: *Bleter far Geshikhte,* 6 no. 3 (1953), 45–153; *Sefer Busk* (Heb., Yid., Eng., and Pol., 1965).

BUSNACH (Heb. בוג'נאח), Algerian family of shipowners and merchants. In the 17th century the Busnach family emigrated to Leghorn, Italy, but was reestablished in Algeria in the 18th century. In 1721 Naphtali left Italy and after two years in Minorca (then under English rule), settled in Algiers. Together with his relatives the *Delmar and Bacri families, he established here a powerful commercial firm. His grandson Naphtali ben Moses played a significant political role in Algeria in the latter part of the 18th century. Enjoying an unprecedented degree of trust by the bey and in direct contact with European governments whose representatives had to rely on his intervention, he dominated foreign policy, made beys and overthrew them, controlled the administration of the treasury, and with the help of his uncle Joseph Bacri and his many agents in Europe, monopolized trade. Nicknamed the "viceroy of Algiers," he was jealous and dominating. However, he had remarkable courage. His coreligionists described him as pious, educated, generous, and upright; in February 1800 he was appointed "head of the Jewish nation." Busnach's power displeased the Turkish garrison, which on occasion revolted against excessive shortages of grain; they blamed the shortages on Busnach's export of large quantities of wheat to France. In 1805, Naphtali b. Moses was assassinated by a janissary. Subsequently, when Algiers was pillaged, the Busnach family took refuge in Leghorn, settling there for the second time.

Bibliography: A. Devoulx (J. M. Haddey), *Le Livre d'or des israélites algériens* (1871), 41–43, 47, 74–77; I. Bloch, *Inscriptions tumulaires* (1888), 70–72, 82–83, 93–105; *Revue Africaine,* 86 (1952), 272–383; Hirschberg, Afrikah, 2 (1965), index.

[D.Co.]

BUSTANAI BEN ḤANINAI (c. 618–670), the first exilarch in Babylonia after the Arab conquest. According to legend, toward the end of the Persian rule in Babylonia the king decreed that all the descendants of the house of David be exterminated, including the exilarch Ḥaninai, whose wife was pregnant at the time. Later the king had a dream in which he saw himself hewing fruit trees in a grove *(bustan)*. Before the last tree was felled a venerable old man appeared before him and struck him on the forehead. On the advice of his courtiers the king consulted a Jewish sage concerning the meaning of this dream. The sage, who was Ḥaninai's father-in-law, interpreted that the old man represented King David trying to prevent the extermination of his descendants. The king then summoned Ḥaninai's widow to court and supplied her with all her needs. When she bore a son, she named him Bustanai in memory of the king's dream. When Bustanai grew up, he appeared in court before the king and the wisdom he displayed on that occasion amazed all who were present. Thereafter the king honored him and appointed him exilarch, to the great satisfaction of the Jews. After the Arabs conquered Babylonia, Caliph Omar confirmed Bustanai as exilarch; he gave Izdundad, one of the captive daughters of Chosroes II, king of Persia, to Bustanai in marriage, while the caliph himself married her sister, thereby giving de facto recognition to Bustanai as one of the successors of the kings of Persia. (According to the *Sefer ha-Kabbalah* of Abraham ibn Daud, it was the daughter of Yezdegerd III, the son of Chosroes, and the caliph was ʿAli.) This legendary story throws light upon the course of events after the death of Bustanai. The Persian princess bore Bustanai three sons. When Bustanai died, however, his other sons by his Jewish wives sought to treat their brothers by the Persian princess as slaves, because their mother had not been converted to Judaism. The scholars of the *yeshivot,* however, decided in favor of Izdundad, and her relatives, who held high offices in the government, also decided in her favor; her eldest son even married a daughter of a chief *dayyan.* Nevertheless the question of the legitimacy of her sons remained a subject of controversy in the halakhic literature of the geonic period and thereafter. Sherira Gaon in the tenth century made a point of stressing that he was of the house of David but not a descendant of Bustanai. Bustanai was the progenitor of the Babylonian exilarchs of the period of the Arab rule. His first successors were the offspring of his son born by one of his Jewish wives. Among the offspring of his Persian wife who attained the office of exilarch was Zakkai, a fourth-generation descendant of Bustanai.

Bibliography: *Ma'aseh Bustanai* (on the various editions see Benjacob, Oẓar, 353, no. 1814; *Devir,* 1 (1923), 159n; *Seder Olam Zuta* (1865); B. M. Lewin (ed.), *Iggeret R. Sherira Gaon* (1944), appendix, xiv–xv; Tykocinski, in: *Devir,* 1 (1923), 145–79; Bruell, Jahrbuecher, 2 (1876), 102–12; Lazarus, *ibid.,* 10 (1890), 24ff.; Graetz, Gesch, 5 (1895³), 113ff.; Graetz, Hist, 6 (1949), index s.v. *Bostanaï;* Margoliouth, in: JQR, 14 (1902), 303–7; M. J. bin Gorion, *Der Born Judas,* 5 (Ger., 1921), 90–102, 300; Marx, in: *Livre d'hommage S. Poznański* (1927), 76–81.

[Si.A./Ed.]

BUSTENAI (Heb. בּוּסְתְּנַאי; "Owner of Orchard"), a Hebrew weekly of the *Farmers' Union and the *General Zionists, published in Palestine (1929–39). The journal supported the views of Chaim Weizmann, advocated Arab-Jewish cooperation, and the employment of Arabs by Jews under certain circumstances. This last point was a perpetual matter of controversy between the paper and the labor circles which demanded that the Jewish economy, especially agriculture, employ Jewish labor exclusively. The editors were Moshe *Smilansky, T. Z. Miller, who edited the agricultural column and coined many Hebrew agricultural technical terms, S. Perlman, and the journalist P. Ginsburg (1894–1947). *Bustenai* also published a magazine for youth, *Bustenai la-No'ar* (1935–37), and the monthly (later bi-monthly) *Mi-Yamim Rishonim* (1934–35) which published material on the history of the *yishuv* and the new agricultural settlements in Palestine. [G.K.]

BUTENSKY, JULES LEON (1871–1947), U.S. sculptor. Butensky was born at Novogrudok in Russia. The son of a poor carpenter, he was given a talmudic education, but was advised by Boris *Schatz to study sculpture. He consequently went to Vienna, where he studied at the Academy of Arts. In 1893 he moved to Paris to avoid military service, and settled in New York in 1904.

"Universal Peace" by Jules Leon Butensky. Bronze, showing swords being beaten into plowshares (Isa. 2:4). New York, Metropolitan Museum of Art.

Most of Butensky's sculpture was of biblical or Jewish inspiration. It was characterized by spiritual depth and power. Among his works are "Universal Peace," in the Metropolitan Museum, New York; "Exile," in the White House, Washington; and studies of "Goliath," "Hillel and Shammai," and "Yehuda Halevi." [Ed.]

BUTNAH (Heb. בּוּטְנָה), the site of a fair in Ereẓ Israel, famous in mishnaic and talmudic times. The fair was apparently established by Hadrian and is mentioned together with those of Acre and Gaza (TJ, Av. Zar. 1:4, 39d; Gen. R. 47–end). Josephus refers to Butnah as "a huge terebinth tree" (Wars, 4:533). After the collapse of the Bar Kokhba war (132–35 C.E.), large numbers of Jews were sold into slavery there. It was identified with *Mamre in the Second Temple period. In later times Jews, Christians, and pagans worshiped there. The emperor Constantine erected a church at Butnah and abolished the pagan cult, but as late as the sixth century Butnah attracted both Jewish and Christian pilgrims. It has been identified with Rāmat al-Khalil, about $1\frac{1}{4}$ mi. (2 km.) north of Hebron, and east of the Jerusalem–Hebron highway. The site was excavated in 1926–28 by E. Mader, who discovered remains of a Herodian enclosure surrounded by a strong wall (enclosing an area of 213×164 ft. (65×50 m.), as well as a Constantinian church, an altar, and a sacred well filled with the offerings (money, figurines, etc.) of worshipers. Butnah is apparently also to be identified with Ayelet mentioned in the Mishnah (Ma'as. Sh. 5:2), a locality one day's journey south of Jerusalem, and with the Bet Ilnis mentioned in *Sifrei Deuteronomy* (306). In the Roman period it was one of the forts of the Palestinian frontier fortifications *(limes)*. It is represented on the *Madaba Map by a church and the inscription *[Ter]ebinthos*.

Bibliography: S. Klein, *Ereẓ Yehudah* (1939), 166ff.; A. E. Mader, in: *Rivista di archeologia cristiana*, 6 (1929), 249–312; idem, in: RB, 39 (1930), 84–117, 199–225; idem, *Altchristliche Basiliken . . .* (1918), 47–103; idem, *Mambre*, 2 vols. (Ger., 1957).

[M.A.-Y.]

°**BUTRYMOWICZ, MATEUSZ** (1745–1814), Polish noble, officer and politician, proponent of a liberal plan to ameliorate the status of the Jews. His interests in landed property in Belorussia convinced Butrymowicz that it was necessary to solve the problem of the status of the large Jewish population there. In 1789 he reprinted a tract, published in 1782 under the title "The Jews, or on the Urgent Necessity for Reform of the Jews in the Lands of the Polish Crown, by an Anonymous Citizen," entitling it "A Way of Transforming the Jews into Useful Citizens of the Country" and adding his own comments. He opposed limiting Jewish rights and advocated assimilation by liberal methods. While against state interference with the principles of Judaism, he suggested introducing certain changes in the Jewish way of life and limiting the number of Jewish holidays. Butrymowicz considered that Jews should be granted the same rights as were accorded to burghers, and that Jewish communal authority should be limited to religious matters. He did not consider the question of Jewish military service relevant. As a deputy to the Sejm (diet) of 1788–92, he worked for the passing of reform legislation on these principles. He elaborated his ideas in a speech made in the Sejm on Jan. 31, 1789, suggesting that changes be introduced into the occupational structure of the Jewish population by excluding Jews from innkeeping and directing them to agriculture, crafts, and commerce. On Dec. 4, 1789, he submitted his suggestions in a memorandum entitled "Jewish Reform" to King Stanislas Poniatowski. In May 1790 Butrymowicz was appointed to the Commission for Jewish Reform, becoming its most active member. At the same time he and two other deputies, Jacek Jezierski and Tomasz Wawrzecki, denounced in the Sejm the anti-Jewish riot that had taken place in Warsaw.

Bibliography: W. Smoleński, *Stan i sprawa Żydów polskich w 18. w.* (1876), 52–95; Gelber, in: *Miesięcznik Żydowski*, 2 (1931), 429–40; Dubnow, Hist Russ, index; Dubnow, Weltgesch, 8 (1928), 42, 316–28; Waniczkówna, in: *Polski słownik biograficzny*, 3 (1937), 153–4; Ringelblum, in: I. Schipper (ed.), *Żydzi w Polsce odrodzonej*, 1 (1932), 69–71; R. Mahler, *Divrei Yemei Yisrael*, 1 pt. 2 (1954), 315–22.

[J.Go.]

BUTTENWIESER, U.S. family. JOSEPH LEON (1865–1938), lawyer, realtor, and community leader. Buttenwieser was born in Philadelphia, Pa., the son of German immigrants. A successful lawyer and real estate operator, Buttenwieser influenced New York State real property legislation. He belonged to the American Jewish elite, and participated actively in communal and philanthropic activities in New York. He was prominent in the establishment of the Federation for the Support of Jewish Philanthropic Societies and served as its president during 1924–26. He served on the board of directors of the Hebrew Technical Institute for 28 years, and played a major role in the Hebrew Sheltering Guardian Society, United Hebrew Charities, and United Palestine Appeal, as well as the Associated Alumni of City College. BENJAMIN JOSEPH (1900–), son of Joseph, banker, civic leader, and philanthropist. Born in New York City, he graduated from Columbia College (1919), intending to devote himself to an academic career. However, he joined the investment banking firm of Kuhn, Loeb and Company as a clerk, and by 1932 had become a partner. After service as an officer in the navy during World War II, Buttenwieser decided to go into public service. He was named assistant high commissioner for Germany by John J. McCloy in 1949, serving there as his adviser on economic matters and de-Nazification. He resigned in 1951, sensing a revival of German anti-Semitism and "arrogant nationalism." Buttenwieser was active in American politics from the 1930s. He became a leading backer of the Republican Wendell Wilkie in 1940. He was active in New York City and State civic affairs, serving as chairman of the State-City Fiscal Relations Committee in 1956, and participating in labor mediation panels.

Buttenwieser's philanthropic commitments, both Jewish and nonsectarian, were manifold. In 1959 he became a trustee of Columbia University, to which his family contributed substantially. Prominent in the work of the Federation of Jewish Philanthropies from his youth, Buttenwieser served as its president in the 1940s. His wife HELEN LEHMAN (1905–), lawyer and civic leader, a niece of Herbert H. *Lehman, started her career as a social worker. She practiced law in New York City for many years, in addition to numerous civic activities.

Bibliography: *New York Times* (Aug. 18, 1938), on Joseph Leon; *Current Biography Yearbook* (1950), 78–80 (on Benjamin Joseph); *New York Times* (June 29, 1962), on Helen Lehman.

[Mo.Ro.]

BUTTENWIESER, MOSES (1862–1939), Bible scholar. Buttenwieser studied at German universities and then went to the United States, and was appointed professor of biblical exegesis at the Hebrew Union College, Cincinnati, in 1897. He accepted the general approach of the K. H. Graf-J. Wellhausen school, but did not follow it

Moses Buttenwieser, biblical scholar. Photo American Jewish Archives, Hebrew Union College, Cincinnati.

slavishly. He drastically reconstructed the text of Job. He denied that apocalyptic developed out of prophecy: Ezekiel and his successors, he held, were genuine prophets, though not of the highest rank, whereas apocalyptic was altogether contrived, and borrowed its characteristic features from

Iranian tradition. According to Buttenwieser, Isaiah held consistently to his conviction that Jerusalem was doomed to fall; and the narrative of Isaiah 37 (= II Kings 19) is legendary. Taking up a view first advanced by Seineke in the 1880s, he argued that Deutero-Isaiah lived in Ereẓ Israel rather than Babylonia.

He effectively stressed the precative use of the Hebrew perfect tense; in the light of this phenomenon, many Psalms previously understood as acknowledgement of past favors prove to be pleas for Divine help in the present. His English translations of the Bible are exceptionally vigorous and poetic. His earliest publications dealt with the medieval Hebrew apocalypses, *Die hebraeische Elias-Apokalypse* (1897), and *Outline of the Neo-Hebraic Apocalyptic Literature* (1901). Thereafter he concentrated on biblical studies, his principal works being *The Prophets of Israel* (1914), *The Book of Job* (1922), and *The Psalms, Chronologically Treated with a New Translation* (1938; 1969[2], with introd. by N. M. Sarna).

Bibliography: Oko, in: *Hebrew Union College Monthly*, 8 (May 1922), 185–209 (incl. bibl.); 26 (Apr. 1939), 1–4, 12 (incl. bibl.); idem, in: AJYB, 6 (1904/05), 72; *Dictionary Catalog of the Klau Library*, 5 (1964), 314, col. 1, 316, col. 1. [B.J.B.]

BUTZEL, family in Detroit, Michigan. Martin Butzel (1828–1906), born in Burgellern, Bavaria, immigrated to the U.S. in 1845. In 1851 he opened a dry goods store in Peekskill, New York, then moved to Detroit, and became associated with his brother-in-law, Emil S. Heineman, in the wholesale clothing business. In 1862 Martin, his brother Magnus, and Heineman opened the firm of Heineman, Butzel and Company, supplying uniforms for the Union Army, and later manufacturing ready-made clothing and men's furnishings. Martin was a member of the first Detroit Public Lighting Commission and a charter member of the Merchants and Manufacturers Exchange and the Board of Charities. He was president of Detroit's Temple Beth El (1874–78) and of the Beth El Hebrew Relief Society. He took an active interest in the Palestine Colony in Bad Axe, Michigan, an unsuccessful venture in colonization by Russian Jewish refugees in the 1890s. Magnus (1830–1900), brother of Martin, born in Burgellern, Bavaria, left Bavaria in 1852 and joined his brother Martin in Peekskill, in the dry goods business. He moved to Detroit in 1861 as a partner in the clothing business. Magnus was a member of the Detroit Board of Education, president of the Detroit Public Library Commission, one of the first directors of the Detroit Board of Commerce, and a leader in the Michigan Republican Party. He was a leader in B'nai B'rith and congregational life. Leo M. (1874–1961), son of Martin Butzel, was born in Detroit. In 1919 he became the first president of the First National Company, an investment affiliate of the First National Bank of Detroit, and in 1925 he became a director of the bank. A recognized authority on corporation law, Leo was considered the city's outstanding lawyer for many years. His role was particularly important in developing the corporate structure of the automobile industry. Butzel was active in Temple Beth El and the American Jewish Committee. His three children included Martin L. (1906–), prominent Detroit attorney, and president of Temple Beth El and the Detroit chapter of the American Jewish Committee. Henry M. (1871–1963), son of Magnus, was born in Detroit. He graduated from the University of Michigan (1891), where he was a founder of the student newspaper *Michigan Daily*. He was admitted to the Michigan Bar (1892) and, with his brother Fred, established the law firm of Butzel and Butzel in 1897. The firm specialized in corporation law and was general counsel for major companies and banks. In 1929 Henry was appointed to the Michigan Supreme Court. He was subsequently elected for a short term in 1930, then reelected in 1931, 1939, and 1949. He served as chief justice three times, in accordance with the rotation system. With his brother Fred, Henry founded the Detroit Legal Aid Bureau of the Bar Association. He was chairman of the Legal Aid Committee during World War I. Henry served as president of Temple Beth El, and also was president of the

Fred M. Butzel, U.S. lawyer and philanthropist. Photo Jewish Welfare Federation, Detroit, Mich.

United Jewish Charities and of other Jewish organizations, receiving many public honors. Fred M. Butzel (1877–1948), brother of Henry, was born in Detroit and joined his brother Henry in law practice. However, Fred devoted most of his time to public service and became one of the nation's distinguished Jewish leaders. A main philanthropic interest was youth work. Fred was active during World War I in the Detroit Patriotic Fund, predecessor of the Community Chest (later the United Foundation), which he also helped to organize. He was president of the Servicemen's Bureau, Detroit Community Union, and Legal Aid Bureau, which he and his brother Henry founded. He served as commissioner of the House of Correction. Deeply concerned with the problems of the Negro, Fred served for 30 years on the board of the Detroit Urban League, was president of Parkside Hospital, a Negro institution, and helped finance the college education of many Negro boys. He took a deep interest in immigrants and aided hundreds of newcomers to the United States. Fred Butzel was one of the few American-born Jews who actively espoused Zionism in its early years. He was president of the United Jewish Charities, one of the original directors of the Detroit Motor Bus Company, vice-president of the Detroit Board of Commerce, and a director of the Detroit Federal Savings and Loan Association. In 1952 the Detroit headquarters of the Jewish Welfare Federation and many of its agencies were named after him. [I.I.K.]

BUXBAUM, NATHAN (1890–1943), Polish leader of the *Po'alei Zion movement, and later of left-wing Po'alei Zion. Buxbaum was born in Lemberg (Lvov) and while at school, he was first secretary-general and from 1912 chairman of the high-school students' Po'alei Zion movement. After serving in the Austrian army during World War I, he became a leader of Po'alei Zion and edited the movement's newspaper, *Der Yidisher Arbayter*. When the party split in 1920, Buxbaum joined left-wing Po'alei Zion and edited its journal, *Folksblat*. In 1924 he moved to Warsaw where he was active in the administration of the party and contributed to its publications in Yiddish. From 1927 Buxbaum was a member of the Warsaw City Council. He visited Ereẓ Israel in 1937 and published a series of enthusiastic articles about the labor settlements. When World War II broke out, he lived in Lvov until he was brought to Warsaw by the National Jewish Council (the Jewish underground engaged in the rescue of Jews). He lived on the "Aryan side," but in early 1943 was deported to *Bergen-Belsen, from where he was taken in October 1943 to an unknown destination.

Bibliography: N. Neustadt (ed.), *Ḥurban u-Mered shel Yehudei Varsha* (1947²), 263–4. [G.K.]

°BUXTORF, JOHANNES (I) (1564–1629), Hebraist, professor of Hebrew at the University of Basle. He was also called "the elder," or "the father" (to distinguish him from his son Johannes Buxtorf II). Buxtorf devoted himself to compiling an edition of the Hebrew Bible with the Aramaic Targum, Masoretic Text, and the most important Jewish commentaries. He employed two Jewish scholars for this work. Buxtorf secured the right of residence for the scholars from the Basle authorities, since, at that time, no Jews were allowed to live there. Buxtorf contended that the masoretic vocalization and cantillation marks are of very ancient origin. He also accepted Elijah *Levita's conception that the Hebrew canon was the product of Ezra and the men of the great assembly. His Bible research brought him into the field of rabbinical literature, of which he possessed a rich collection. He maintained a correspondence with Jewish scholars in Germany, Holland, and Constantinople, as well as with non-Jewish Hebrew scholars. Many of his letters are preserved at the library of the University of Basle and are an important source for the study of the spiritual conditions of his time. His famous Hebraic library, which was supplemented by his son and grandsons, became part of the Basle Public Library (1705). Among his most important works are: (1) a textbook of Hebrew (*Praeceptiones Grammaticae Hebraicae,* 1605), which ran into 16 editions, one of them in English translation (London, 1656); (2) several Hebrew vocabularies and lexicons: *Lexicon Hebraicum et Chaldaicum* (1607), *Concordantiae Bibliorum Hebraicae* (1632); *Lexicon Chaldaicum Talmudicum* completed by his son (1640) which, although unreliable, served for generations as a guide for Christian scholars in their Jewish studies; (3) a catalog of his Hebrew books (with 324 entries); (4) a treatise on Hebrew abbreviations, and (5) a collection of over 100 Hebrew letters of medieval scholars (*Institutio Epistolaris Hebraica,* 1610). Buxtorf's attitude toward the Jews, as voiced in his work *Juden Schuel* (1603), was negative. This book enjoyed several editions and was known in its Latin version by the name *Synagoga Judaica.* [Z.Av./Ed.]

°BUXTORF, JOHANNES (II) (1599–1664), Hebraist, the son of Johannes Buxtorf I, succeeded his father in the chair of Bible and Hebrew studies at the University of Basle and edited some of his unpublished works. In common with his father, he held the view that the Masoretic Text is the genuine version of the Bible (*De Literarum Hebraicarum Genuina antiquitate,* 1643) and that the Hebrew square script preceded the Samaritan. The vocalization of Hebrew, he maintained, originated at least as early as the time of Ezra. These issues were the subject of his fierce controversies with another Hebraist, Ludovicus Capelus, with each defending his viewpoint in a series of scholarly studies. Buxtorf's view was formally adopted by the Swiss Church in 1675. Buxtorf translated *Maimonides' *Guide of the Perplexed* (1629), *Judah Halevi's *Kuzari* (1666), and part of Isaac *Abrabanel's commentaries to the Bible into Latin. The numerous Jewish scholars in many lands with whom he was in contact included *Manasseh Ben Israel. His collection of letters is preserved at the university libraries of Basle and Zurich. [H.R.]

Bibliography: **(I):** E. F. Kautzsch, *Johannes Buxtorf der Aeltere* (1879); Steinschneider, Handbuch, 28ff.; idem, in: ZHB, 2 (1897), 94; Fuerst, Bibliotheca, 1 pt. 1 (1863), 138; Herzog-Hauck, 3 (1897), 612–4. **(II):** Kayserling, in: REJ, 8 (1884), 74–95; 13 (1886), 260–76; Steinschneider, in: ZHB, 2 (1897), 94.

BUZAGLO, Anglo-Moroccan family, sons of Moses Buzaglo, rabbi in Mogador. Abraham Buzaglo (1710–1782), after an adventurous career, settled about 1762 in England, and in 1765 was granted a patent for a new type of stove, known after him as "buzaglo." Making use of this invention, he introduced a new method of physical therapy whereby muscular exercise is undertaken after the body has been thrown into a profuse sweat; he recommended this method especially for gout. For a time it had great success, and is widely referred to in the literature of that period. He also invented a carriage warmer. Joseph Buzaglo (d. 1767), who called himself De Paz, had a lively

Caricature of Abraham Buzaglo's treatment for gout. Aquatint engraved by Paul Sandby, 1783. London, Alfred Rubens Collection.

career in France, during which he was condemned to the galleys, invented an incendiary bullet, and was imprisoned in the Bastille on a charge of spying for England. On his release from the Bastille he negotiated a commercial treaty between Denmark and Morocco, but when difficulties ensued, the sultan condemned him to death by burning and he again spent a long time in prison. Released through the intercession of the Danish authorities he followed his brothers to England, and died in St. Eustatius (West Indies) on a fruitless journey to trace his son, who had become a soldier. Joseph's brother was Shalom *Buzaglo.

Bibliography: A. Rubens, *Anglo-Jewish Portraits* (1935), 19–20; Loewe, in: JHSET, 16 (1945–51), 35–45; Zimmels, *ibid.,* 117 (1953), 290–2; ESN, 107–8; Castries, in: *Hespéris* 6 (1926), 330–9; Hartog, in: AJA, 19 (1967), 74. [C.R.]

BUZAGLO (Buzaglio, Buzagli, Busaglo), SHALOM BEN MOSES (c. 1700–1780), Moroccan kabbalist. Buzaglo was born in Marrakesh. Among his teachers in Kabbalah were Abraham b. Israel *Azulai, one of the rabbis of Marrakesh (d. 1741), Jacob Pinto, and Isaiah ha-Kohen. In his native land Buzaglo was persecuted by the sultan and was subjected to torture by fire. As a result of this experience he signed himself, "brand plucked out of the fire" (Zech. 3:2). In about 1745 he left Morocco and settled in London and there wrote his books on esoteric and exoteric matters. His major work was his commentary on the *Zohar. In the controversy between Jacob *Emden and Jonathan *Eybeschuetz both sides attempted to influence Buzaglo to endorse their particular points of view but he tried to remain neutral. He acknowledged, however, that Eybeschuetz' amulets were Shabbatean in character, but he also accepted the argument that they had been falsified. Buzaglo's commentaries on the Zohar were first published in 1750–1755 in Amsterdam and London. These are *Mikdash Melekh*, a commentary on the whole Zohar, book by book, in four volumes (to which he also added Moses *Zacuto's commentary from a manuscript); *Hadrat Melekh*, on difficult passages in the Zohar; *Penei Melekh, Hod Melekh*, and *Kevod Melekh*, all on the *Idras* in the Zohar and on *Sifra di-Ẓeni'uta Kisse Melekh* on *Tikkunei ha-Zohar*. *Mikdash Melekh* was the first systematic commentary on the whole Zohar to be published. It was very popular and was printed several times. Subsequently the text of the Zohar together with Buzaglo's commentaries were printed in Leghorn (1858) and in Zolkiew (1862). These were based mainly on Lurianic Kabbalah, including all the scattered work of Isaac *Luria's disciples, which Buzaglo usually copied word for word, occasionally quoting other opinions. Although this book does not convey the literal meaning of the Zohar, it has had a continuing value for scholars. In several books he added his own novellae on the Talmud. He spent his last years in London where he seems to have served for a time as a member of an Ashkenazi *bet din*. A number of his pamphlets referring to an halakhic dispute which broke out in London in 1774 were also published. He died in London. Several of his manuscripts were preserved in the *bet ha-midrash* of the Great Synagogue in London.

Bibliography: J.Emden, *Sefat Emet* (1752), 30–31; J. Ben-Naim, *Malkhei Rabbanan* (1931), 112; G. Scholem, *Bibliographia Kabbalistica* (1933), 188–91; Roth, Mag Bibl, s.v.; E. Duschinsky, in: JHSET, 7 (1915), 272–90.

[G.Sch.]

BUZAU (Rum. **Buzău**), town in Walachia (Muntenia), central Rumania. The Jewish community there grew in the 19th century from three families in 1831 to 1,660 persons (7.6% of the total population) in 1899. An organized community was formed in the 1830s, but the communal organization in the second half of the 19th century was unstable. A Jewish school was founded in 1873. According to the official census, the Jewish population numbered 1,604 (4.5% of the total population) in 1930. Communal institutions before World War II included an elementary school for boys and for girls, a kindergarten, and a bathhouse. [El.F.]

Holocaust Period. In 1941 there were 1,193 Jews living in Buzau. When war with the Soviet Union broke out (June 1941), all Jewish men between the ages of 18 and 60 were arrested and held as hostages until the end of 1941. Jews from the neighboring towns and villages were evacuated to Buzau. The community extended aid to many persons whom the racial laws had deprived of their livelihood. It also took care of 900 orphans who arrived in Buzau from Transnistria in April 1944. After World War II, the number of Jews in Buzau diminished considerably as a result of emigration to Israel. The Jewish population numbered 274 in 1956. In 1970, there were about 30 families with a rabbi and *shoḥet*.

[Th.L.]

Bibliography: E. Schwarzfeld, in: *Anuar pentru Israeliti*, 7 (1884/85), 73; M. Schwarzfeld, in: *Fraternitatea*, 4 (1882), 262; Reicher, in: *Sinai* (Bucharest), 2 (1929), xxviii (Heb. part); *Almanahul Ziarului Tribuna Evreiască*, 1 (1937/38), 263; Filderman, in: *Sliha*, 1 no. 4 (1956), 3; M. Carp, *Cartea Neagră*, 3 vols. (1946–48), index; *Pe marginea prăpastiei*, 1 (1942), 224, 227; PK Romanyah, 24–28.

BUZZARD (Heb. אַיָּה, *ayyah*), bird of prey of which different species are found in Israel. The long-legged buzzard *(Buteo ferox)* feeds on birds, mammals, and insects. It can see very far and is apparently the *ayyah* referred to in Job 28:7 (AV: "vulture"), where the desert is described as a place which "even the eye of the *ayyah* has not seen." It is

Buzzard *(Buteo vulgaris)*. J. Feliks, Jerusalem.

enumerated among the unclean animals (Lev. 11:14; Deut. 14:13). According to Abbahu, it is identical with the *ra'ah* mentioned in the same verse "and why is it called *ra'ah*—because of its remarkable sight" (*ra'ah*, it saw), adding "it can be in Babylon and see a carcass in the land of Israel!" (Ḥul. 63b).

Bibliography: Lewysohn, Zool, 167ff.; Tristram, Nat Hist, 187ff.; J. Feliks, *Animal World of the Bible* (1962), 67. [J.F.]

BYADULYA-YASAKAR, ZMITROK (pen name of **Samuil Yefimovich Plavnik**; 1886–1941), Soviet Belorussian writer, who was one of the founders of Belorussian literature. The son of a coachman, Byadulya-Yasakar studied in a yeshivah, and began writing Hebrew verse at the age of 13. Only glimpses of this early phase of his career appear in his autobiographical novel *V dremuchikh lesakh* ("In the Depths of the Forest," 1939). Byadulya-Yasakar began publishing his works in 1910, under the pseudonyms "Byadulya" for prose works and "Yasakar" for verse. His prerevolutionary books portrayed downtrodden Belorussian peasants. An impassioned Belorussian nationalist, Byadulya-Yasakar was at first hostile to the Communist regime, to which he only gradually became reconciled. Except for the tales and poems rooted in Belorussian folklore—*Paleskiya bayki* ("Fairy Tales of Polesie," 1922) and *Yaryla* (1922)—his later work was conventional. Byadulya-Yasakar's more important achievements include two historical novels, *Salavey* ("Nightingale," 1927) and *Yazep Krushinski* (1929–1932); the background to the latter is the Russian Civil War.

Bibliography: A. Adamovich, *Opposition to Sovietization in Belorussian Literature, 1917–1957* (1958). [M.F.]

BYDGOSZCZ (Ger. **Bromberg**), capital of Bydgoszcz province, north central Poland. There were Jews living in the fortress of Bydgoszcz *(castrum Bydgoscense)* in the 11th and 12th centuries. Later a considerable number of Jews, engaged in trading provisions with Gdańsk, were found in the city adjoining the fortress, which was built by the order of Casimir the Great in 1346. In 1555 the city was authorized to expel the Jews, who moved to the nearby city of Fordon. The authorization was annulled by Frederick the Great after Bydgoszcz was annexed by Prussia in 1772. By 1788 there were 41 Jews living in Bydgoszcz, chiefly occupied in the silk trade, but a community was not officially established in Bydgoszcz until 1809. Jewish settlement in Bydgoszcz was subject to the agreement of the municipality until this restriction was revoked by the "Jewish Law" of July 23, 1847; subsequently the number of Jewish residents increased. The status of the Jewish community was enhanced through the efforts of the banker Louis Aronsohn, a member of the Prussian Landtag (Diet). In 1884 a magnificent synagogue was established, as well as a school and benevolent institutions. The 27 communities of the district formed a federation, presided over by Aronsohn in 1897. In 1905 the Jews numbered 2,600 out of a total population of 54,231. When the city was incorporated into Poland in 1918, most of the Bydgoszcz Jews moved to Germany; the community archives were transferred to the general archives of the German Jews in Berlin. In 1924 there were only 1,000 Jews living in Bydgoszcz, but by 1931 their number had increased to 3,000. [N.M.G.]

Holocaust Period. In the period of World War II Bydgoszcz was the second main town (after Danzig) of "Reichsgau Danzig-Westpreussen," a district created and incorporated into the Nazi Reich by a decree of Oct. 26, 1939, several weeks after the outbreak of World War II. Most of the Jewish families living in Bydgoszcz fled before the entry of the German Army. Those who stayed behind were murdered. The Nazis diligently searched the entire vicinity and left no Jews alive. After World War II the community was not rebuilt. [De.D.]

Bibliography: J. Herzberg, *Geschichte der Juden in Bromberg* (1903); G. Sonnenschein, in: *Polski Almanach gmin żydowskich* (1939), 99–108.

BYK, EMIL (1845–1906), lawyer, politician, and assimilationist leader in Austrian *Galicia. Byk was among the founders in 1869 of *Shomer Israel, the first Jewish political organization in Galicia, which adopted at first the policy of liberalism within the Austrian centralist framework. On Byk's initiative the Jewish communities in Galicia held a convention in Lemberg (Lvov) in July 1878 in order to establish their national framework. During the elections for the Austrian parliament in 1873, Shomer Israel, under Byk's leadership, adopted a special list of candidates in alignment with the Ruthenians, which was directed against the Poles. Later, however, the changed political situation caused Byk to alter his views. In 1879 he began to support the Polish national platform in Galicia, and joined the Polish faction in the Austrian parliament. In internal Jewish affairs Byk also took up a pro-Polish assimilationist stand. He was one of the most determined opponents of the Zionist movement, and also opposed in the Austrian parliament, to which he was first elected as deputy for Brody in 1891, the proposed establishment of a special Jewish *curia* (electoral constituency). He was president of the Lemberg Jewish community (1903–06), and led it in an assimilationist pro-Polish spirit. Byk considered the central government in Vienna and not the Poles responsible for anti-Semitism in Galicia. Before his death in 1906, he convened the representatives of the communities in Galicia to rally opposition to the claims put forward by the anti-assimilationist Jews. The Zionists demonstrated against the convention.

Bibliography: S. R. Landau, *Der Polenklub und seine Hausjuden* (1907), 6,8,13,33,40–42; J. Tenenbaum, *Galitsye, Mayn Alte Haym* (1952), index; Gelber, in: EG, 4 pt. 1 (1956), 310–32; idem, *Toledot ha-Tenu'ah ha-Ẓiyyonit be-Galiẓyah, 1875–1918,* 2 vols. (1958), index.
[N.M.G.]

BYKHOV (or **Stary Bykhov**), city on the River Dnieper, Mogilev oblast, Belorussian S.S.R. It was one of the most important fortified cities in Belorussia. The Jewish community is mentioned in the reports of the period of the *Chmielnicki massacres 1648–49. The minutebook of the *ḥevra kaddisha* of Bykhov contains entries from 1673. Three hundred Jews in Bykhov were massacred when it was captured by the Russians in 1659. After its reversion to Poland in 1669, the Jews received a grant of privilege from the king relieving them of taxes for 20 years to ease conditions after the destruction of the city. A conference of the communities of the "Lands of Russia" (a part of Belorussia; see *Councils of the Lands) met in Bykhov in 1670. In 1758 the community was given a special privilege by the lord of the city. The Jewish population numbered 887 in 1766; 3,046 in 1847; 3,037 in 1897 (47.6% of the total); and 2,575 in 1926 (32.5%). The Jews were massacred by the Germans during World War II. Subsequently two monuments were erected in Bykhov to their memory. One bears the Russian inscription "Here lie buried the Jews of Bykhov murdered by German Fascists" above which is a *magen david.* In 1970, about 800 Jews lived in Bykhov; there was no synagogue.

Bibliography: Dubnow, Divrei, 7 (1940), 18, 52, 82; P. Marek, in: *Voshkod,* 23 no. 5 (1903), 71–91; Kogan, in: *Yevreyskaya starina,* 4 (1911), 114–6.
[S.K.]

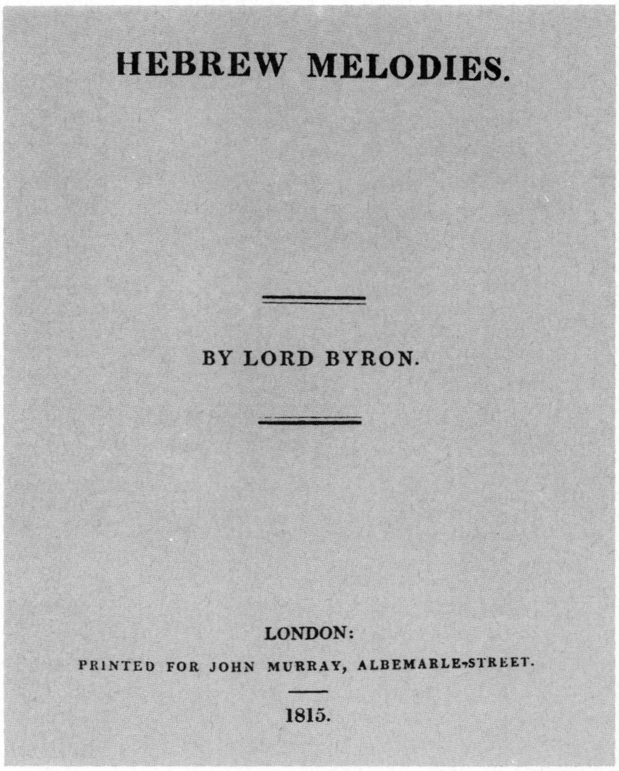
HEBREW MELODIES.

BY LORD BYRON.

LONDON:
PRINTED FOR JOHN MURRAY, ALBEMARLE-STREET.
1815.

Title page of the first edition of Byron's *Hebrew Melodies,* 1815. Cecil Roth Collection.

°**BYRON, GEORGE GORDON, LORD** (1788–1824), English poet. Byron's affection for the Old Testament and romantic interest in oppressed peoples led him to collaborate with Isaac *Nathan in publishing the *Hebrew Melodies* for which Nathan composed or adapted the music. Though not all are specifically Jewish in theme, some express sympathy for the plight of the Jews. They were published in 1815 as *A Selection of Hebrew Melodies, Ancient and Modern; with appropriate symphonies and accompaniments; the poetry written expressly for the work by the Right Hon. Lord Byron.* One of the best known of these poems is "The Destruction of Sennacherib." " Weep for those that wept by Babel's Stream" contains the familiar lines: "The wild dove hath her nest/the fox his cave/ Mankind their Country/Israel but the grave!"

These poems were translated into Hebrew by J. L. Gordon as *Zemirot Yisrael* (1884) and into Yiddish by Nathan Horowitz (1926). There are musical settings by Balakirev, *Hiller, Loewe, *Mendelssohn, Moussorgski, Schumann, *Joachim, Hugo Wolf and others.

In a later work, the satirical *Age of Bronze* (1823), Byron adopted a hostile attitude toward the Jews, whose emancipation he opposed and whose alleged support for foreign tyranny (Turks against Greeks) he denounced with many unpleasant allusions. More controversy was aroused in Christian circles by Byron's biblical verse play, *Cain* (1821), which reflected the radical poet's religious skepticism.

Bibliography: JHSET, 2 (1894–95), 5, 8–10; E. W. Marjarum, *Byron as Skeptic and Believer* (1938); M. F. Modder, *Jew in the Literature of England* (1939), 113–7; O. S. Phillips, *Isaac Nathan, Friend of Byron* (1940); Sendrey, Music (1951); H. Fisch, *Dual Image* (1959), 53–54.

[Ed.]

BYTOM (Ger. **Beuthen**), town in *Silesia, Poland; in Germany till 1945. There were probably Jews living in Bytom before the *Black Death (1349), but the community disappeared; it was reestablished in 1655–59 by Polish Jews. In 1708 Jews without right of domicile in Bytom were expelled, those who remained being mainly taxfarmers. A cemetery was established in 1732, the first synagogue built in 1810, and a larger one in 1869. The Jewish population numbered seven persons in 1784; 131 in 1792; 255 in 1810; 2,549 in 1900; 3,500 in 1932 (3.77% of the total population), and 1,362 in 1939. A number of Polish Jews settled there after World War I. Attacks on Jews and Jewish shops occurred as early as 1923. In 1932 the community maintained a synagogue, an elementary and a religious school, and benevolent and cultural organizations. During World War II, 1,078 Jews were deported from Bytom (1942), most of them to *Auschwitz. After the war a new community was established by Polish Jews, which maintained a Hebrew school and a producers' cooperative. In 1962 there were 248 Jews living in Bytom.

Bibliography: Germ Jud, 1 (1963), 26; 2 (1968), 79; FJW, 102; M. Kopfstein, *Geschichte der Synagogen-Gemeinde Beuthen* (1891); *Juedisches Gemeindeblatt fuer Beuthen, Gleiwitz, Hindenburg* (1936); AJYB (1962/63), 366–7.

[Ed.]

BYZANTINE EMPIRE. Jewish communities existed in the Byzantine Empire throughout its history, from the foundation of *Constantinople in 330 to the Ottoman conquest of the city in 1453. The centers of Jewish population and the status of the Jews there underwent drastic changes throughout this long period and shifted under the impact of events within and outside the empire. The history of the Jews in the Byzantine Empire can therefore be divided into three major sections.

From Constantine to the Iconoclastic Period (c. 720). Legal and Social Status. Numerous Jewish communities were located in the eastern Mediterranean region, including the Balkans, present-day Greece, Asia Minor, Constantinople, Syria, Ereẓ Israel (which alone had 43 communities), and Egypt. The legal status accorded to the Jewish faith within the Roman Empire as a *religio licita* (a religion permitted by law) was not changed explicitly. However, the attitude of the Byzantine rulers and society in practice, the methods employed by the Church, the language of official documents and legislation on details, combined to humiliate the Jews and narrow the confines of Jewish society and religion and the opportunities open to Jews. Almost at the beginning of his legislative activity *Constantine described the Jewish religion as "baleful," and warned Jews, under threat of capital punishment, not to molest converts to Christianity. The second part of the law containing this injunction made it a crime to become a Jew: a Jew who circumcised his slave forfeited ownership of the slave (Cod. Theod. 16:8(4, 1, 5)). Constantine and his mother Helena inspired a movement to Christianize Ereẓ Israel. His son *Constantius added to his father's legislation a prohibition on marriage between Jews and Christians. An abortive revolt by the Jews in Ereẓ Israel against the provincial commander Gallus during his reign was suppressed in 351. The benign interlude of the reign of Emperor *Julian the Apostate only resulted in increased enmity on the Christian side and disappointment to the Jews.

The failure of Julian's plans to revive the pagan empire and its tolerance of the Jewish religion contributed to the breakdown of the old concepts and existent attitudes between religions and people. The consistent fanaticism prevailing in Byzantine Christendom covers the long span from Julian's death until the fall of Constantinople in 1453. Emperor *Theodosius I revived missionary activity and prohibited Jewish parents from disinheriting children who had apostatized to Christianity. However, the burning of the synagogue in Callinicum (Mesopotamia) in 388 led to a clash between the imperial traditions and the aims of the Church. The emperor still tried to uphold the imperial tradition of law and order for all, including the Jews. He therefore ordered that the perpetrators of the outrage in Callinicum should be punished and the synagogue reconstructed at their expense. *Ambrose, the bishop of Milan, viewed the emperor's order as sacrilegious and succeeded in compelling him to annul it. Thus toward the end of the fourth century the humiliation of the Jews and ascendancy of ecclesiastical ideas in regulating their affairs became established in the Byzantine Empire in both theory and practice. The temporary expulsion of the Jews from *Alexandria by the patriarch Cyril in 415 also marked a victory for the hatred stirred up by the Church among the populace with assistance from the authorities. The code of *Theodosius II (438) summed up the former anti-Jewish legislation, and included a prohibition on building new synagogues, permitting structural repairs only if absolutely necessary. Certain Purim celebrations were forbidden. In spirit and language this fifth-century codification crystallizes the atmosphere prevailing in the Byzantine Empire in the fourth century. A Church rent by internal struggles, bent on heresy hunting with the help of the imperial authority, and using increasingly violent and uncouth language toward its Christian adversaries, developed over the fourth century a vitriolic anti-Jewish polemic literature. Both writers and preachers seemingly vied with one another in their acrimony toward, and vilification of, the Jews and Judaism. In the eight sermons delivered by John Chrysostom from his pulpit in Antioch in 387, every imaginable evil is ascribed to the Jews. The

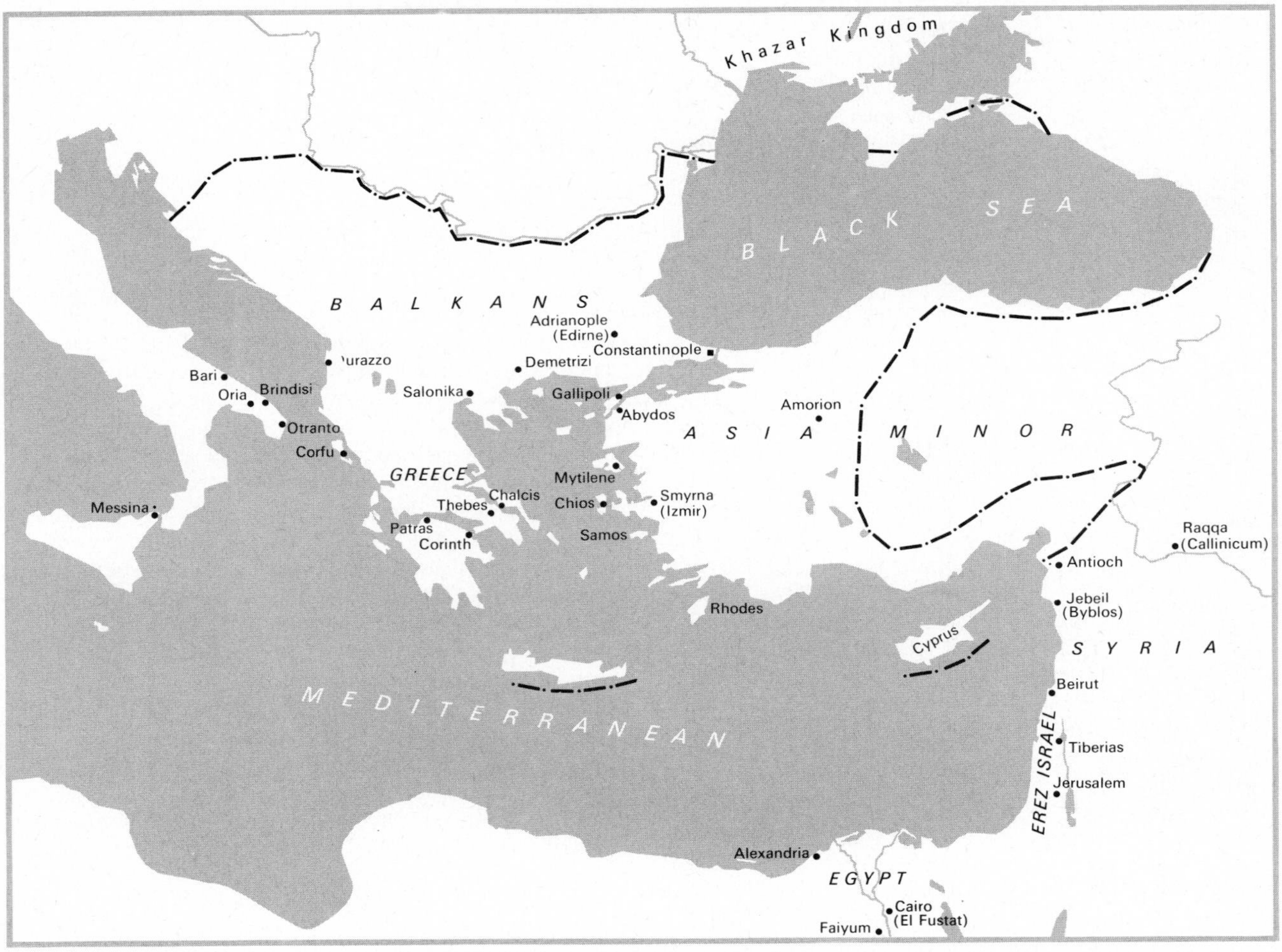

Byzantine Empire end of 12th century, showing the major centers of Jewish settlement.

venom embodied in these writings and sermons to a large degree lies at the root of medieval Jew hatred, spreading beyond the boundaries of the Byzantine Empire and its culture.

In the sixth century the reign of *Justinian I inaugurated a hardening of attitudes toward the Jews and a departure for the worse in their treatment. The Jewish-Arab kingdom of *Ḥimyar in southern Arabia was destroyed on Byzantine instigation. Justinian attempted to regulate internal Jewish life and modes of worship in accordance with what he considered necessary and right from a Christian point of view through a number of laws and practical actions. In his famous *novella* 146, of the year 553, he even attempted to dictate to the Jews concerning their Divine worship and forbade the use of the *deuterosis* (Mishnah) for understanding the Torah; he also took it upon himself to lay down which biblical translation (*Targum) they might use. This gross interference in Jewish religious practice is justified in the *novella* by hints that there was a division within Jewish society on these matters. However, while it is known that Greek was then beginning to be used in the Byzantine communities, which developed the "Romaniot" rite of prayer, it is also certain that no professing Jews would have asked for an imperial order to use translations which were mainly Christological. Justinian's tendency to resort to coercion found its severest expression in his *novella* 37, of 535, prohibiting the practice of Judaism in the reconquered territories in North Africa. All these measures were included in his *Corpus juris civilis,* with other anti-Jewish legislation. The first half of the sixth century saw a severely enforced but short-lived attempt by the emperor to abolish formally the last shreds left to Judaism of its status as a *religio licita.* Under assault from enemies from both within and without, the emperors of the weak empire of the second half of the sixth and first half of the seventh centuries permitted anti-Jewish riots and forced conversions of the Jews, such as ordered by Emperor Phocas in 608. The Jews reacted by revolts in self-defense. In the uprising near Antioch in 608 the patriarch was killed. The clashes of opposing forces and violence came to a head under Emperor *Heraclius, when the Jews, notable among them *Benjamin of Tiberias, allied themselves with the invading Persians during their capture of Jerusalem. On its recapture in 629, Heraclius avenged himself on the Jewish population by a series of massacres.

The appearance of Islam and the the Muslim conquests deprived the Byzantine Empire of Ereẓ Israel and Egypt among other territories and awakened messianic expectations among the Jews (see *Messianic movements). In the remnant left to the Byzantine Empire the prevailing attitude toward the Jews was not relaxed. A council presided over by Emperor Justinian II in 692 prohibited Jews and Christians from bathing together in public places, and Christians from consulting Jewish physicians.

Social and Cultural Life. At the beginning of this period, the Jews formed part and parcel of civic life in the towns. Like others, they refused to serve in the decurionate and Constantine's enforcement of their obligation to do so expressed the general reluctance of the citizenry to undertake this onerous municipal function and a specifically anti-Jewish bias on the part of the emperor. The Jews gradually withdrew from, or were forced out of, civic life, although they still continued to be active in the *circus parties for a long time. The abolition of the Jewish patriarchate (see *Nasi*) in Ereẓ Israel in 425 threw back Jewish communal life onto the local leadership, already well established before this troubled time. The community's elders *(presbyteroi)*, *archipherecites, and leaders with other titles led Jewish society in the various localities in all aspects of life. Apparently birth and wealth, in addition to scholarship, were major factors in attaining these leading positions. In the economic sphere, the Jews were only gradually ousted from their professions and positions of wealth, and from their places of residence in the cities (see *Constantinople). Many of them engaged in overland and maritime commerce. In a number of areas, such as Ereẓ Israel and Egypt, there was still a solid Jewish peasant population. In the sixth century *dyeing is mentioned as a major Jewish industry, remaining so down to the end of the Byzantine Empire.

In the cultural sphere, the center in Ereẓ Israel and its institutions led creative endeavor within the Byzantine communities in every field, even after the Arab incursions. Ereẓ Israel was the main source of Hebrew liturgical poetry, its leading poets including *Yose b. Yose, *Yannai, and Eleazar *Kallir. The monk Romanos, an apostate from Judaism, had a formative influence on Byzantine hymnology, transposing the mode of religious expression and worship used by the *paytanim* to the Byzantine liturgy and cultural expression. The violent changes at the end of the seventh and beginning of the eighth centuries aroused visions of an apocalyptic nature (see *Apocalypse) among Byzantine Jewry.

From the Iconoclastic period to the Fourth Crusade (1204). LEGAL AND SOCIAL STATUS. Throughout this period Jews were living in the major cities in the territories still remaining under Byzantine rule. The situation of the Jews in the Byzantine domains of southern Italy is well documented through the contacts they had with Ereẓ Israel as well as with countries under Christian rule, and by information given in the chronicle of *Ahimaaz. Main centers were *Bari, *Oria, and *Otranto. *Benjamin of Tudela in the mid-12th century describes many communities in the Balkans and Asia Minor, and in Constantinople, with their varied economy. The very nature of the Iconoclastic movement made its adherents suspicious of possible Jewish influences. The actual degree of such influence, if any, on the emperors and priests who rejected icon worship is still very much in dispute. Their opponents, the icon worshipers, regarded this influence as a certainty, and the iconoclasts were branded in sermons and tales circulating at the time as "Jews." The final restoration of icon worship in 843 was accompanied by renewed violent anti-Jewish manifestations. *Basil I issued a decree ordering the forcible conversion of his Jewish subjects in 873–74, and in the Ahimaaz chronicle he is depicted as the arch-enemy of Judaism and the Jews. The decree was rescinded by Leo VI. In 943 *Romanus I Lecapenus made another attempt at forcible conversion. There are reports of Jews who fled to *Khazaria from these persecutions. Byzantine Jewry in the 11th and 12th centuries apparently lived under a regime of absolute humiliation although assured of relative safety for their lives and property.

SOCIAL AND CULTURAL LIFE. The economic structure of the Jews in the Byzantine Empire remained substantially the same in this period. Benjamin of Tudela found Jews in the Balkans engaged in agriculture, besides being occupied in the silk weaving and cloth dyeing industries which were widespread Jewish occupations throughout the Byzantine communities. According to his descriptions of the communal leadership, the smaller communities were headed by two elders and the larger by five. He seems to indicate that the *Karaites had a separate communal organization and leadership. The most flourishing area of Byzantine Jewish cultural life at the time was to be found in southern Italy. The stories in the Ahimaaz chronicle describe the strong ties of the Jews there with the center of learning in Ereẓ Israel and denote that a good knowledge of Hebrew was widespread, as well as showing the imprint of mystical and even magical elements on Jewish society in this area. Members of the upper circles of Jewish society are pictured as living a warm and diversified family life. The *Josippon chronicle, which was compiled in southern Italy in this period, reflects in many places the influence of Byzantine views and chronographical techniques. Southern Italy in the 9th to 11th centuries produced a considerable number of *paytanim*. Through its contacts with the north, it became the fountainhead of the Jewish culture of *Ashkenaz and the matrix of the Ashkenazi prayer rite. The Karaite communities also had a rich and variegated cultural life from the second half of the 11th century, centering around Constantinople. Prominent Karaite scholars of Byzantium were *Jacob b. Reuben, Judah *Hadassi, and *Tobias b. Moses. In some of the writings of this period apocalyptic ideas continue to find expression, as in the Vision of *Daniel. The First Crusade of 1096 gave rise to a messianic movement in Salonika.

From the Fourth Crusade to the Capture of Constantinople by the Turks in 1453. LEGAL AND SOCIAL STATUS. The Fourth Crusade (1204) disrupted the Byzantine Empire and placed its Jewish communities under the various administrations set up by the Latin (i.e., Western European) countries which had taken part in the crusade. The Jewish quarter in Constantinople, Pera, was burned down and pillaged during the sack of the city by the Latins. After the Latin rule ended in 1261 Jews lived both in Pera and outside the area, including parts of the city where the Venetians had been given special rights and commercial privileges. The existence of a Jewish quarter outside Pera elicited a complaint from the patriarch Athanasius to Emperor Andronicus II (1282–1328), who before 1319 assigned the Jews a quarter near that of the Venetians, although they were not restricted to that area. Many engaged in tanning, and the majority apparently were wealthy. Neither the native dynasty nor the Latin rulers made basic changes in the status of the Jews. In the parts of Greece and the Balkans, however, which fell to various Greek rulers and minor royalty (often referred to as "despots"), proscriptions of Judaism were issued at times, as in Epirus and Salonika under Theodore I Angelus (1214–1230), and in Nicea under John III Vatatzes (1222–1254). Other former imperial lands, such as Chalcis, Rhodes, Patras, and Cyprus, were ruled by the Genoese, the Venetians, the Knights of Malta, the Veronese, and the Turks. The Jews continued to pursue their previous occupations, particularly the silk trade and commerce.

SOCIAL AND CULTURAL LIFE. Jews in all these areas continued to follow the Romaniot rite which developed specific features. Among the Karaites there was extensive cultural activity, represented by such scholars as *Aaron b. Joseph ha-Rofe, the *Bashyazi family, and Caleb b. Elijah *Afendopolo. The year 1453 marked the end of the Byzantine Empire. For the Jews its downfall, after a short period of disruption, brought a renewed lease on life in the *Ottoman Empire in much improved conditions. Less than half a century later, the Jews exiled from Spain and Portugal found communities in the former Byzantine Empire ready and able to shoulder the burden of absorbing the refugees economically, and capable of integrating their social and cultural life. Although little information is available about conditions in the communities in this period, scholars and leaders of the stature of Elijah b. Abraham *Mizraḥi and Moses b. Elijah *Capsali, with their diversified scholarship, creative abilities, and well-developed methods of leadership, could not have arisen out of a void. That the conditions existed in which they were able to flourish shows that in the period before the Ottoman conquest, Byzantine Romaniot Jewry had large reserves of intellectual ability and social cohesion, continuing a situation which still prevailed after the troubles of 1204.

For pre-Byzantine period, see *Asia Minor.

Bibliography: J. Starr, *The Jews in the Byzantine Empire 641–1204* (1939, repr. 1969); idem, *Romania: The Jewries of the Levant after the Fourth Crusade* (1949); idem, in: *Speculum* 8 (1933), 500–3; idem, in: JPOS, 15 (1935), 280–93; idem, in: HTR, 29 (1936), 93–107; idem, in: REJ, 102 (1937), 81–92; idem, in: *Byzantinisch-neugriechische Jahrbuecher*, 16 (1940), 192–6; A. Scharf, *Jews in Byzantium* (1970); H. Lewy, *Olamot Nifgashim* (1962), 221f.; Baron, Social², index; Hirschberg, Afrikah, 1 (1965), 30–39; K. Hilkowitz, in: *Zion*, 4 (1939), 307–16; Y. Even-Shemuel (Kaufmann), *Midreshei Ge'ullah* (1957), 16–252; Juster, Juifs, index; Z. Ankori, *Karaites in Byzantium* (1959); S. Assaf, in: *Sefer ha-Yovel... S. Krauss* (1937), 169–77; A. Galanté, *Les Juifs de Constantinople sous Byzance* (1940); R. S. Lopez, in: *Speculum*, 20 (1945), 22ff.; M. N. Adler (ed.), *Itinerary of Benjamin of Tudela* (1907); B. Klar (ed.), *Megillat Aḥima'aẓ* (1944); M. Salzman (ed. and tr.), *Chronicle of Ahimaaz* (1924); D. Flusser, in: *Zion*, 18 (1953), 109–26; Alon, Toledot², 1 (1958), 19–24; S. Simonsohn, in: *Dat ve-Ḥevrah*, ed. by Ha-Ḥevrah ha-Historit ha-Yisre'elit (1964), 81–92.

[AN.SH.]

BZENEC (Ger. **Bisenz**), town in Moravia, Czechoslovakia. The synagogue demolished in 1859 had probably stood for 500 years. Its community was one of the oldest in Moravia. It is referred to by a Bzenec medieval chronicler as *nidus judaeorum* ("nest of Jews"). The Jewish quarter was destroyed in 1458. In 1604 there were 400 Jewish residents, living in 49 buildings, and a Jewish hospital. The Jewish quarter was again destroyed in 1605. The community suffered extreme hardship during the Prussian invasion of 1742; in 1777 the 93 houses in Jewish ownership were burnt down. It became a political community (see *Politische Gemeinden) in 1852. A new synagogue was built in 1863. There was a *mazzah* factory in Bzenec and a sugar refinery owned by Rudolph *Auspitz. Rabbis of Bzenec include Nehemiah *Bruell (1866–70) and Moses Rosenmann (1894–97). The community numbered 137 families in 1753; 965 persons in 1857; 416 in 1900; and 138 (3.4% of the total population) in 1930. In 1942 the Jews in Bzenec were deported via *Kyjov to Nazi death camps and the synagogue equipment sent to the Jewish Central Museum in Prague. A small congregation administered by the Kyjov community was reestablished after World War II. In 1956 a monument in memory of the Nazi victims was dedicated in the cemetery.

Bibliography: J. Hoff, in: H. Gold (ed.), *Die Juden und Judengemeinden Maehrens* (1929), 119–22; M. Stein (ed.), *Jahrbuch des traditionstreuen Rabbiner-Verbandes in der Slovakei* (1925/26), 15–21.

[ED.]

Come ye and let us go up to the mountain of the Lord
of His ways and we will walk in His paths for out of Z
Jerusa